U.S. Master Tax Guide®

KEY FIGURES FOR THE 2012 TAX YEAR

To stay current with legislation that may affect these rates and amounts, visit the CCH website at CCHGroup.com/TaxUpdates.

STANDARD DEDUCTIONS		
Married, Filing Joint Return	$	11,900
Surviving Spouse	$	11,900
Head of Household	$	8,700
Unmarried (Not S.S. or H.H.)	$	5,950
Married, Filing Separate Return	$	5,950
Dependent Standard Deduction (Minimum)	$	950
Additional Amount for Blindness or Age	$	1,150
Additional Amount as Above if Unmarried and Not S.S.	$	1,450
ITEMIZED DEDUCTIONS		
Nonbusiness Casualty Loss (AGI Threshold)		10%
Medical Deduction (AGI Threshold)		7.5%
Miscellaneous Itemized Deduction (AGI Threshold)		2%
Phaseout of Itemized Deductions		N/A
EXEMPTIONS		
Personal and Dependent Amount	$	3,800
Estate Amount	$	600
Simple Trust Amount	$	300
Complex Trust Amount	$	100
Qualified Disability Trust Amount	$	3,800
Phaseout of Exemptions		N/A
EDUCATION PROVISIONS		
American Opportunity (Modified Hope) Credit	$	2,500
Lifetime Learning Credit	$	2,000
Coverdell Education Savings Account Contribution	$	2,000
Student Loan Interest Deduction	$	2,500
U.S. Savings Bond Interest Exclusion (Phaseout Starts)		
Married, Filing Joint Return	$	109,250
Single, S.S. or H.H.	$	72,850
AMT EXEMPTION AMOUNT		
Married, Filing Joint Return and Surviving Spouses	$	45,000*
Unmarried (Not S.S.) and Head of Household	$	33,750*
Married, Filing Separate Return	$	22,500*
Estates and Trusts	$	22,500*
CAPITAL GAINS AND QUALIFIED DIVIDENDS		
(Tax Rates on Assets Held More Than 12 Months)		
Taxpayers in 10% or 15% Income Tax Bracket		0%
Other Income Tax Brackets		15%
Unrecaptured Gain on Real Estate (Section 1250 gain)		25%
Collectibles and Qualified Small Business Stock		28%

* Visit CCHGroup.com/TaxUpdates for legislative developments that may affect the 2012 AMT exemption amounts.

QUICK TAX FACTS

CCH

QUICK TAX FACTS

CCH

ESTATE AND GIFT TAXES

Estate & Gift Applicable Exclusion Amount	$	5,120,000
Annual Gift Tax Exclusion		
Per Donee	$	13,000
Splits Gifts by Spouses	$	26,000
Gifts to Noncitizen Spouse	$	139,000
Maximum Estate & Gift Tax Rate		35%

CODE SEC. 179 EXPENSE ALLOWANCE

Maximum Deduction	$	139,000
Investment Limitation	$	560,000

PAYROLL TAXES

FICA or Self-Employed Rate (OASDI + Medicare)		13.3%
FICA (Employer) Rate (OASDI + Medicare)		7.65%
FICA (Employee) Rate (OASDI + Medicare)		5.65%
OASDI (Employer) Rate		6.2%
OASDI (Employee) Rate		4.2%
OASDI Maximum Base	$	110,100
Medicare (Employer and Employee) Rate		1.45%
FUTA Rate		6.0%
FUTA Wage Base	$	7,000
Nanny Tax Threshold	$	1,800

RETIREMENT/PENSION PLANS

Maximum Annual Benefit for Defined Benefit Plan	$	200,000
Maximum Annual Contribution for Defined Contribution Plan	$	50,000
Highly Compensated Employee Definition	$	115,000
SEP Minimum Compensation Amount	$	550
SEP Compensation Limit	$	250,000
401(k) Maximum Compensation Amount	$	250,000
401(k) Maximum Elective Deferral	$	17,000
IRA Maximum Contribution Limit	$	5,000
SIMPLE Elective Deferral Limit	$	11,500
Catch-up Contributions (For Individuals Age 50 and Over):		
Traditional and Roth IRAs	$	1,000
SIMPLEs	$	2,500
401(k), 403(b) and 457 Plans	$	5,500
Retirement Savings Contributions Credit (Maximum Contribution)	$	2,000

HEALTH SAVINGS ACCOUNTS (HSAs)

Maximum Contribution Amount		
Self-Only Coverage	$	3,100
Family Coverage	$	6,250

TRANSPORTATION

Business Mileage Rate		55.5¢
Medical and Moving Mileage Rate		23¢
Charitable Mileage Rate		14¢
Depreciation Component of Standard Mileage Rate		23¢
High Cost Locality Per Diem Travel Rate (after 9/30/11)	$	242
Low Cost Locality Per Diem Travel Rate (after 9/30/11)	$	163
High Cost Locality Per Diem Travel Rate (after 9/30/12)	$	242
Low Cost Locality Per Diem Travel Rate (after 9/30/12)	$	163

90094730

2013 U.S. Master Tax Guide®

CCH Editorial Staff Publication

Access the Latest Tax Legislation Developments and your free CPE Course

A special webpage created by CCH for the *U.S. Master Tax Guide*® will keep you up-to-date with late-breaking tax legislative developments occurring after publication of the 2013 edition. Visit CCHGroup.com/TaxUpdates to find the information you'll need to keep U.S. Master Tax Guide your first source for practical tax guidance. You will also find a link to your free *Top Federal Tax Issues for 2013* course – a great and easy way to earn valuable CPE credit!

CCH
a Wolters Kluwer business

This publication is designed to provide accurate and authoritative information in regard to the subject matter covered. It is sold with the understanding that the publisher is not engaged in rendering legal, accounting, or other professional service. If legal advice or other expert assistance is required, the services of a competent professional person should be sought.

ISBN: 978-0-8080-2980-9 (paperback edition)
ISBN: 978-0-8080-3245-8 (hardbound edition)

©2012 CCH. All Rights Reserved.

4025 W. Peterson Ave.
Chicago, IL 60646-6085
800 248 3248
CCHGroup.com

No claim is made to original government works; however, within this Product or Publication, the following are subject to CCH's copyright: (1) the gathering, compilation, and arrangement of such government materials; (2) the magnetic translation and digital conversion of data, if applicable; (3) the historical, statutory and other notes and references; and (4) the commentary and other materials.

Printed in the United States of America

FSC www.fsc.org MIX Paper from responsible sources FSC® C101537

Preface

Income taxation in the United States has been around for more than 95 years. From the very beginning, CCH was there and is still setting the standard as the number one quick reference resource for tax professionals. CCH is proud to serve the tax professional community with this new edition of the *U.S. Master Tax Guide* ®. The 96th Edition of this industry standard explains the complex set of tax rules and is designed to provide fast and reliable answers to tax questions affecting individuals and businesses. In all, 29 chapters contain comprehensive, timely, and precise explanation of the ever-changing federal income tax rules for individuals, businesses, estates, and trusts.

The 2013 Edition reflects the *Middle Class Tax Relief and Job Creation Act of 2012* (P.L. 112-96), signed by President Obama on February 22, 2012, which extends the two percent reduction on the employee's half of the Old Age, Survivors and Disability Insurance (OASDI) tax through the end of 2012. It also included an equal reduction for self-employed individuals and workers under the Railroad Retirement System. The payroll tax reduction was initially provided in 2011, and was extended through the end of February, 2012, by the *Temporary Payroll Tax Cut Continuation Act of 2011* (P.L. 112-78) signed by President Obama on December 23, 2011.

As this edition of the *Guide* goes to press, there are several legislative proposals pending either dealing with either a total extension of the sunset of the 2001 and 2003 Bush era tax cuts, a modified extension of the 2001 and 2003 Bush era tax cuts, or fundamental tax reform, including patching the alternative minimum tax (AMT) exemption amount. In an effort to keep users of the *Guide* current on events taking place after the date of publication, CCH has established a website at *CCHGroup.com/TaxUpdates* for any late-breaking 2012 year-end tax legislation or for other significant tax developments that might affect the *Guide's* coverage.

As in previous editions, major legislative provisions are highlighted at ¶ 1 and reflected throughout the *Guide*, while important nonlegislative tax developments are conveniently highlighted at ¶ 2 and concisely explained for quick reference and understanding. In addition, the *Guide* comes complete with many time-saving features that help practitioners quickly and easily determine how particular tax items and situations should be treated (see the following page for a listing and description of these "Key Features"). The *Guide* also contains a handy Quick Tax Facts card that can be detached for an at-a-glance reference to key tax figures and other often-referenced amounts.

Not only does the *U.S. Master Tax Guide* ® assist in the preparation of 2012 tax returns, it also serves as a reference tool for more comprehensive tax research and tax planning via extensive footnotes and other references to the Internal Revenue Code, Income Tax Regulations, and CCH's STANDARD FEDERAL TAX REPORTS ®, FEDERAL ESTATE AND GIFT TAX REPORTER, TAX RESEARCH CONSULTANT, and Practical Tax Explanations series.

For additional analysis of new and complex tax issues, and as a way to earn valuable continuing education credits, *Top Federal Tax Issues for 2013* is provided along with the *Guide*. This course provides helpful insights for the practitioner to keep abreast of the most significant new rules and changes by explaining the most important new provisions and developments in 2013 specifically applicable to 2013 and the IRS rules and regulations that go into effect in 2013. It also examines current audit and litigation issues that have developed over the past year to create a new environment for tax strategies initiated in 2012.

We also point you to other CCH resources that complement the *Guide* and support your tax season work. *1040 Express Answers* is designed to help you and your staff prepare 1040 tax returns quickly, easily, and accurately with line-by-line guidance to common tax preparation questions. *1065 Express Answers* is the ideal quick-answer tool for busy practitioners who prepare partnership returns and the partners' Schedule K-1s. The compliance-oriented *1120S Express Answers* will help you in preparing S corporation tax returns with concise and reliable answers right at your fingertips. The *1041 Express Answers* provides practical, plain-English guidance for practitioners who prepare fiduciary income tax returns. *Business Express Answers* provides concise compliance-oriented guidance on C and S corporations, partnerships, limited liability companies (LLCs), and tax-exempt organizations. See *CCHGroup.com/TaxUpdates* for more details.

Finally, for treatment of state tax topics, please refer to CCH's *State Tax Guidebooks* (13 states available–CA, CT, FL, IL, MD, MA, MI, NJ, NY, NC, OH, PA and TX) and CCH's *State Tax Handbook* covering all 50 states and the District of Columbia.

November 2012

Key Features

In addition to 29 chapters of tax law explanations, the *U.S. Master Tax Guide*® provides a wealth of information in the pages that lead up to Chapter 1. Some of these time-saving tools and features are described below, listed by paragraph location.

OVERVIEW (¶ 1-7): The Overview division contains informative features available to facilitate research and dealing with clients, including the following.

- "Tax Legislation," a highlight of provisions from this year's enacted tax legislation.
- "Looking Ahead — Potential Tax Developments for 2013," a look ahead by CCH's Principal Analyst Mark Luscombe, J.D., LL.M., C.P.A.
- "AGI Phaseout Thresholds," includes a number of tax items subject to phaseout restrictions.
- "Where to File Returns," a listing of income tax return mailing addresses.
- "2013 Tax Calendar," shows the filing dates for 2012 tax returns and tax payments throughout 2013.

TAX RATES (¶ 11-53): This section contains the 2012 and projected 2013 tax rate schedules for individuals and estates and trusts, the corporate tax rate schedule and related rates, and the estate and gift tax rate schedule, as well as a listing of key excise tax rates.

CHECKLISTS (¶ 55-65): A collection of checklists designed to provide tax return preparers with quick answers (and references) to common questions regarding the inclusion of items in income, the deductibility of certain expenses, the treatment of various medical expenses, the availability of tax credits, and a forms list.

SPECIAL TAX TABLES (¶ 83-88): This is a collection of often-used interest rates and percentages including:

- Applicable Federal Rates (AFRs)
- Adjusted Applicable Federal Rates
- Federal Long-term Tax-Exempt Rates
- Low-Income housing Credit percentages

ADDITIONAL FORMATS: To provide flexibility for users, the *Guide* is available in a loose-leaf edition with quarterly updates, either a softbound or hardbound print edition, and an e-Book version. The *Guide* is also available on *IntelliConnect*, CCH's industry-leading research platform that combines the quick-reference ease and reliability of the *Guide* with current primary sources including the Internal Revenue Code, Income Tax Regulations, cases, IRS rulings and more.

TAX UPDATE RESOURCE: CCH has established a website at *CCHGroup.com/Tax-Updates* for users of the *Guide* to visit periodically in order to stay current with post-publication tax legislation and key tax developments affecting 2012 returns.

CCH Tax and Accounting Publishing

EDITORIAL STAFF

Paul Gazzolo, *Vice President, Publishing*

Elizabeth Albers, *Director, Books and Production*

Mark L. Friedlich, J.D., *Director, International and Accounting*

Jennifer M. Lowe, J.D., *Director, State Tax*

Tracy Gaspardo Mortenson, J.D., C.P.A., *Director, Electronic Publishing Development*

Sarah Stevens, J.D., LL.M., M.B.A., *Director, Federal Tax*

Explanation and Analysis

Louis W. Baker, J.D., M.B.A.

David Becker, J.D.

Glenn L. Borst, J.D., LL.M.

Anne E. Bowker, J.D., LL.M.

John Buchanan, J.D., LL.M.

Mildred Carter, J.D.

James A. Chapman, J.D., LL.M.

Tom Cody, J.D., LL.M., M.B.A.

Casie Cooper

Donna J. Dhein, C.P.A.

Kurt Diefenbach, J.D.,
Managing Editor

Liliana Dimitrova, LL.B., LL.M.

Karen Elsner, C.P.A.

Alicia C. Ernst, J.D.

Elena Eyber, J.D.

Shannon Jett Fischer, J.D.

Donna M. Flanagan, J.D.

Mary Jo Gagnon, C.P.A.

Brant Goldwyn, J.D.

Irene Goodman, J.D.

Bruno L. Graziano, J.D., M.S.A.

Joy A. Hail, J.D.

Carmela Harnett,
Senior Manager

Kay L. Harris, J.D.

Michael Henaghan, J.D., LL.M.

Karen Heslop, J.D.,
Senior Managing Editor

Kathleen M. Higgins

Dem A. Hopkins, J.D.

Caroline L. Hosman, J.D., LL.M.

David M. Jaffe, J.D.

George G. Jones, J.D., LL.M.,
Managing Editor

Lynn S. Kopon, J.D., LL.M.

Mary W. Krackenberger, J.D.

Kristina Kulle, J.D., LL.M.

Thomas K. Lauletta, J.D.

Adam R. Levine, J.D., LL.M.

Laura M. Lowe, J.D.,
Managing Editor

Mark A. Luscombe, J.D., LL.M, C.P.A.,
Principal Analyst

Jerome A. Maes, J.D.

Michael Menzhuber, J.D., LL.M.

Sheri Wattles Miller, J.D.

Ellen Mitchell, EA

Robert A. Morse, J.D., LL.M.

John J. Mueller, J.D., LL.M.,
Managing Editor

Kieran Murray, J.D., LL.M.

Jean T. Nakamoto, J.D.

Jerome Nestor, J.D., M.B.A., C.P.A.,
Managing Editor

Karen A. Notaro, J.D., LL.M.,
Portfolio Managing Editor

Lawrence A. Perlman, J.D., LL.M., C.P.A.

Deborah M. Petro, J.D., LL.M.

Robert Recchia, J.D., M.B.A., C.P.A.

Jennifer J. Rodibaugh, J.D.

Leo Roinila, J.D., LL.M.

John W. Roth, J.D., LL.M.

Linda Scharf, J.D.

Carolyn M. Schiess, J.D.

Michael G. Sem, J.D.

Lisa Simioni, J.D., LL.M.

James Solheim, J.D., LL.M.

Raymond G. Suelzer, J.D., LL.M.

Kenneth L. Swanson, J.D., LL.M.

Mary P. Taylor, J.D.

Laura A. Tierney, J.D.

James C. Walschlager, M.A.

Kelley Wolf, J.D.

George L. Yaksick, Jr., J.D.

Ken Zaleski, J.D.

Susan M. Zengerle, J.D., LL.M.,
Managing Editor

Washington News Staff

Jeff Carlson, M.A.

Stephen K. Cooper

Kathryn Hough

Rosalyn Johns-Thomas

Joyce Mutcherson-Ridley

William Pegler

Electronic and Print Production

IzyanSuhaila AbdulHali

Linda Barnich

Curt Berkowitz

Angela D. Bretschneider

Douglas Bretschneider

Nancy Chapman

Aris Cheong,
Production Manager

Lou Dagostino

Amelia Eslava

Tara K. Farley

Mary Ellen Guth

Christine Hansen

Linda Kalteux

Chantal M. Mahler

Andrejs Makwitz

Haffiz Mansor

Tina Medina

Helen Miller

Samantha Munson

Jennifer Nelson

Elaine Ogawa,
Managing Editor

Jennifer K. Schencker

David Schuster

Farahiah Senin

Siva Shanmugam

Monika Stefan

Zuhriati Tahir

Jim F. Walschlager

Jennifer Youngless

Christopher Zwirek

CONTENTS

DETAILED TABLE OF CONTENTS

Paragraph

Filing 2012 Returns

OVERVIEW

¶ 1 Tax Legislation

2012 Tax Legislation. *Middle Class Tax Relief and Job Creation Act of 2012.* On February 22, 2012, President Obama signed into law the *Middle Class Tax Relief and Job Creation Act of 2012* (P.L. 112-96), which extended the two percent reduction on the employee's half of the Old Age, Survivors and Disability Insurance (OASDI) tax through the end of 2012. It also included equal reductions for self-employed individuals and workers under the Railroad Retirement System. Under the law, the employee's portion of the OASDI tax remains at 4.2 percent throughout 2012 (with the employer's portion remaining at 6.2 percent), and self-employed individuals are subject to a 10.4 percent payroll tax rate.

In addition to the extension of the payroll tax holiday, the new law:

(1) repealed the time shift in due dates for corporate estimated tax payments imposed under prior acts;

(2) extended unemployment benefits; and

(3) extended the Medicare "doc fix."

Congress passed only three other tax-related bills during 2012 but none of them made any changes to the Internal Revenue Code. The first bill was the *FAA Modernization and Reform Act of 2012* (P.L. 112-95), which extended the excise taxes that fund the capital improvements of the U.S. airport and airway system, as well as the Federal Aviation Administration (FAA), through the end of the 2015 fiscal year. In addition to extending the expenditure authority of the Airport and Airway Trust Fund, as well as the excise taxes that fund it, the new law:

(1) alters the treatment of fractional aircraft ownership programs, including the addition of a new excise tax on fuel used in such programs;

(2) provides for increased transparency by providing consumers with full disclosure of transportation fees and taxes in advertised prices; and

(3) allows rollovers to IRAs of amounts received by qualified airline employees as a result of carrier bankruptcies.

The second bill was the *Highway Investment, Job Creation, and Economic Growth Act of 2012* (P.L. 112-141), which extended Highway Trust Fund expenditure authority through September 30, 2014, and highway-related excise taxes through September 30, 2016. The bill also provides for pension funding stabilization, as well as transfers of excess pension assets to retiree health accounts and retiree group term life insurance accounts.

Finally, there was the *Leahy-Smith America Invents Act* (P.L. 112-29) which bans the issuing of patents for tax strategies. No new patents may be issued after September 16, 2011, the day the Act was signed into law.

There is still pending before Congress at the time of publication several bills with key tax provisions. In particular, legislation that would extend some or all of the 2001 and 2003 Bush-era tax cuts, the patch for the alternative minimum tax (AMT), and several different bills that would extend for anywhere from six months to one year some or all of the expiring tax credits and deductions. In addition, there are several bills pending to ameliorate the impact of the mandatory reduction in the budgets of U.S. Armed Forces and social welfare organizations, which were instituted by the legislation enacted in 2011 that raised the deficit limitation on Congressional spending.

For information on further legislative and other key tax-related developments after 2012, visit the *U.S. Master Tax Guide* website at *CCHGroup.com/TaxUpdates*.

¶ 2 What's New on 2012 Returns

The *U.S. Master Tax Guide* reflects all of the important administrative and judicial developments of 2012, including final regulations, major court decisions, and important rulings of the Internal Revenue Service. Legislative highlights are at ¶ 1. Below are additional highlights of the changes in 2012 with the greatest impact on individuals and businesses.

Individuals

Income levels at which individuals must file income tax returns have increased for 2012 . . . . . . ¶ 101
Basic standard deduction amounts have increased for 2012 . . . . . . ¶ 126
The deduction for each personal exemption is $3,800 for 2012 . . . . . . ¶ 133
Inflation-adjusted income amounts that trigger the reduction of allowable itemized deductions and personal exemptions for high-income taxpayers are repealed for 2012 . . . . . . ¶ 133, ¶ 1014
"Kiddie" tax amount is $1,900 for 2012 . . . . . . ¶ 706
The standard mileage rate for all business use of a car is 55.5 cents per mile for 2012 . . . . . . ¶ 947
Per diem rates under the high-low method of substantiating travel expenses are $242 for high-cost localities and $163 for low-cost localities for travel after September 30, 2012 . . . . . . ¶ 954A
Student loan interest, up to $2,500 in 2012, may be deducted from gross income by qualifying taxpayers . . . . . . ¶ 1082
The transportation fringe benefit exclusion amount for employer-provided parking is $240 per month for 2012, and the exclusion amount for employer-provided transit passes and commuter highway vehicles is $125 per month for 2012 . . . . . . ¶ 2188E

Depreciation, Amortization and Depletion

The maximum Code Sec. 179 deduction for 2012 is $139,000 . . . . . . ¶ 1208
The Code Sec. 179 investment limitation for 2012 is $560,000 . . . . . . ¶ 1208
Updated discussion of the new capitalization regulations (the "repair regs") . . . . . . ¶ 903, ¶ 1238, ¶ 1240

Tax Credits

For 2012, the maximum earned income credit for eligible taxpayers with no qualifying children is $475, with one qualifying child is $3,169, with two qualifying children is $5,236, and with three or more qualifying children is $5,891 . . . . . . ¶ 87, ¶ 1322
The child tax credit is $1,000 for 2012 . . . . . . ¶ 1305
The education tax credits (American Opportunity (modified Hope) and lifetime learning) are $2,500 and $2,000, respectively, for 2012 . . . . . . ¶ 1303

Securities Transactions

Updated discussion of the effective date for the basis reporting requirements for debt instruments and options . . . . ¶ 1980

Retirement and Benefits

Updated discussion of the health insurance reporting requirements by employers . . . . ¶ 2190A

Withholding

The 2012 OASDI wage base for FICA and self-employment tax purposes is $110,100 . . . . ¶ 47, ¶ 49, ¶ 2648, ¶ 2670

The 2012 wage threshold for "Nanny Tax" reporting is $1,800 . . . . ¶ 2650

Estate, Gifts and Generation-Skipping Transfer Tax

Updated discussion of making the portability election . . . . ¶ 2934, ¶ 2938

¶ 3 Looking Ahead—Potential Tax Developments for 2013

The year 2012 has so far been a year without significant tax legislation. Congress did manage to enact legislation providing for long-term transportation excise taxes after several years of short-term extensions, but other significant tax issues have not yet been addressed.

The nearly seventy regularly expiring tax provisions that expired at the end of 2011 have not yet been extended for 2012, creating uncertainty for taxpayers as to whether those provisions will apply for 2012. The tax breaks from the 2001 and 2003 tax acts generally expire at the end of 2012 and have not been extended. Most taxpayers could therefore face higher tax rates in 2013. The possible fate of these tax cuts is a factor that should be considered in 2012 year-end tax planning. The tax provisions of the 2010 health care reform legislation continue to phase in, having survived a Supreme Court challenge in 2012. New Medicare contribution taxes take effect in 2013. The payroll tax deduction that has been around for a couple of years and is scheduled to expire at the end of 2012 has not yet been extended, and there seems to be little movement toward extending it.

For these and other reasons, such as a mandated across-the-board reduction in federal spending in 2013 if other spending cuts are not agreed upon by Congress, words such as "taxmageddon" and "fiscal cliff" have been applied to what is facing taxpayers and the country in 2013 if Congress does not act. Many economists feel that a lack of Congressional action on these issues before 2013 could damage the economy and the current slow economic recovery.

Getting the November 2012 elections behind us, the anticipation of which has probably contributed to the Congressional paralysis, may permit action on some of these outstanding issues in the lame duck session of Congress. Even that is not a certainty, however. Republican success in the elections may encourage Congressional Republicans to wait for the new Congress in 2013 to try to craft tax legislation more to their liking. Democratic success in the elections may encourage some Republicans to compromise with Democratic proposals, but compromise might be easier in 2013 after tax increases have already automatically taken place. Republicans could then support legislation that involves a roll back of some of the tax increases without appearing to violate their "no tax increase" pledges. Still, due these predictions that allowing all of the year-end tax increases and spending cuts to take effect could severely damage the economy, there will be considerable pressure on Congress to act in the lame duck session.

The Expired Provisions

The longer Congress delays action on the nearly seventy provisions that expired at the end of 2011, the more 2012 year-end tax planning must be delayed. Delay also impacts the timeliness of tax forms and software, which could delay or add confusion to the tax filing season for 2012 tax returns in 2013.

Congress has been working on some proposals to extend expired provisions. In contrast to extensions in prior years, Congress seems to be taking a closer look at the merits of each provision up for extension. Legislative proposals have left off the table a larger than normal number of these expired provisions. Most of the better known and more popular provisions have been proposed to be extended. These include, for individuals, alternative minimum tax (AMT) relief, the sales tax deduction, the above-the-line deduction for tuition and fees, the option for taxpayers over age 70½ to make IRA distributions directly to charity, and the credit for energy-efficient home improvements. For business, they include the research credit among many others. A number of provisions have been added to or dropped from the list for extension during the course of committee negotiations.

2001 and 2003 Tax Cuts

The main point of contention over extending the tax cuts from the 2001 and 2003 tax acts is the Republican insistence on extending the tax cuts for all taxpayers and the Democratic insistence on only extending them for taxpayers with incomes under $200,000 ($250,000 for joint filers). The result of the impasse is that the tax cuts may expire for all taxpayers. This could mean higher ordinary income tax rates, higher capital gain rates, and higher dividend rates for all taxpayers in 2013. Other effects of the sunset of the tax cuts include higher estate and gift tax rates and lower exclusions, a return of the phase-out of itemized deductions and exemptions, a return of the marriage penalty in the standard deduction and 15 percent tax bracket, and a smaller child tax credit. Taxpayers who believe these higher rates will become effective in 2013 may want to take action in 2012 to accelerate income into 2012, postpone deductions into 2013, or undertake year-end gifting strategies.

Medicare Contribution Taxes

The Medicare contribution taxes enacted in 2010 as part of health care reform become effective in 2013. These taxes apply to taxpayers with modified adjusted gross income in excess of $200,000 ($250,000 for joint filers). An additional 0.9 percent tax is imposed on the earned income of an employee or self-employed person in excess of those thresholds. A new 3.8 percent tax is imposed on the lower of a taxpayer's net investment income or adjusted gross income in excess of those thresholds.

Taxpayers planning for the new Medicare taxes may want to focus on reducing net investment income and/or lowering adjusted gross income. These strategies could include shifting to investments that produce tax-free income, maximizing qualified retirement plan contributions, and accelerating income into 2012 before these taxes take effect.

Other tax provisions of health care reform coming into effect in 2013 include an increase in the AGI threshold for medical expenses from 7.5 percent to 10 percent and a $2,500 limit on annual contributions to health flexible spending accounts. The future of all of these tax provisions from health care reform is clouded by Republican promises to try to repeal the legislation should they be successful in the November elections.

Tax Reform

Fundamental tax reform remains on the agenda for 2013. Both the Republicans and Democrats have promulgated outlines of some of the elements that they would like to see included in tax reform. One common theme involves rate reductions combined with base broadening by eliminating various deductions and credits. There remains a lot of debate about whose rates to cut, by how much, and whose current tax breaks to reduce or eliminate. It is not clear that sufficient bipartisan consensus has yet emerged to achieve significant tax reform in the coming year.

The year 2013 presents taxpayers with some of the most significant tax changes to face taxpayers in several years, combined with considerable uncertainty as to whether Congress will act to prevent some or all of these changes from taking place.

¶ 4 AGI Phaseout Thresholds

Adjusted gross income (AGI) levels in excess of certain phaseout thresholds limit the following deductions, credits and other tax benefits. This chart provides the beginning point for the 2012 thresholds and the ending point of the phaseout (where applicable).

Tax Item	*Taxpayers Affected*	*Phaseout—Begin*	*Phaseout—End*
Itemized Deductions (Overall Limit)	single, head of household, joint filers	repealed	N/A
	married filing separately	repealed	N/A
7.5% Floor on Medical Deductions	those itemizing medical expenses	7.5% of AGI	N/A
2% Floor on Misc. Itemized Deductions	those itemizing misc. expenses	2% of AGI	N/A
10% Floor on Casualty Loss	those itemizing casualty loss	10% of AGI	N/A
Personal Exemption	single	repealed	N/A
	head of household	repealed	N/A
	joint filers	repealed	N/A
	married filing separately	repealed	N/A
Child Tax Credit*	single, head of household	$75,000	phaseout varies by taxpayer
	married filing separately	$55,000	phaseout varies by taxpayer
	joint filers	$110,000	phaseout varies by taxpayer
Dependent Care Credit	single, head of household, joint filers	35% credit if AGI not over $15,000	20% credit if AGI over $43,000
Elderly and Disabled Credit	single, head of household	$7,500	$17,500
	joint filers	$10,000	$20,000 if one qualifying spouse; $25,000 if two qualifying spouses
	married filing separately	$5,000	$12,500
Adoption Credit*	all filers	$189,710	$229,710
Adoption Assistance Programs*	all filers	$189,710	$229,710
Earned Income Credit	single, head of household, no child	$7,770	$13,980
	single, head of household, one child	$17,090	$36,920
	single, head of household, two children	$17,090	$41,952
	single, head of household, three or more children	$17,090	$45,060
	joint filers, no child	$12,980	$19,190
	joint filers, one child	$22,300	$42,130
	joint filers, two children	$22,300	$47,162
	joint filers, three or more children	$22,300	$50,270
American Opportunity (modified Hope) Credit*	single, head of household	$80,000	$90,000
	joint filers	$160,000	$180,000

Tax Item	*Taxpayers Affected*	*Phaseout—Begin*	*Phaseout—End*
Lifetime Learning Credit*	single, head of household	$52,000	$62,000
	joint filers	$104,000	$124,000
Student Loan Interest Deduction*	single, head of household	$60,000	$75,000
	joint filers	$125,000	$155,000
Savings Bonds Interest Exclusion*	single, head of household	$72,850	$87,850
	joint filers	$109,250	$139,250
Coverdell Education Accounts (formerly Education IRAs)*	single, head of household, married filing separately	$95,000	$110,000
	joint filers	$190,000	$220,000
IRA Deduction* (for taxpayers covered by retirement plan at work)	single, head of household	$58,000	$68,000
	joint filers	$92,000	$112,000
	married filing separately	$0	$10,000
Roth IRA Eligibility*	single, head of household	$110,000	$125,000
	joint filers	$173,000	$183,000
	married filing separately	$0	$10,000
Rental Real Estate Passive Losses	single, head of household, joint filers	$100,000	$150,000
	married filing separately	$50,000	$75,000
Mortgage Bond Subsidy Recapture*	all filers	AGI relative to area median income	N/A

* Modified AGI, as defined by the relevant Code sections, is used instead of AGI.

¶ 5 Where to File Returns

Individuals. Listed below are the mailing addresses to use for filing self-prepared individual income tax return and for tax professionals when filing individual tax returns on behalf of their clients (¶ 111). Individual taxpayers and tax professionals may also consult the IRS website at http://www.irs.gov/uac/Where-To-File-Addresses-for-Tax-Professionals for the most current mailing addresses. See ¶ 2701 for a discussion of service centers.

Note: The IRS has reorganized its processing of tax returns. As a result of these efforts, many taxpayers *may* have different filing service centers than those used previously.

☐ Per the IRS, if an addressed envelope came with the return, it should be used. If you do not receive one, or if you moved during the year, mail your return to the Internal Revenue Service Center for the place where you reside. The first line of the address should be Internal Revenue Service, but no street address is needed. To facilitate processing for all taxpayers of the 50 states and the District of Columbia who do not need to enclose a payment with the return, each form (1040, 1040A, 1040EZ) uses a different ZIP+4 ZIP Code extension. If you are filing a client's Form 1040A and are not enclosing a payment, use the address in the middle column with the ZIP Code extension, -0015. If you are filing a client's Form 1040EZ and are not enclosing a payment, use the address in the middle column with the ZIP Code extension, -0014. If a payment is enclosed with the form, each form (1040, 1040A, 1040EZ) uses the same mailing address shown in the last column below.

If you are filing **Form 1040** *and are located in:*	*And are not enclosing a payment, mail your return to:*	*And are enclosing a payment, mail your return to:*
Alabama, Georgia, North Carolina, South Carolina	Kansas City, MO 64999-0002	P.O. Box 105017 Atlanta, GA 30348-5017
Florida, Louisiana, Mississippi, Texas	Austin, TX 73301-0002	P.O. Box 1214 Charlotte, NC 28201-1214
Alaska, Arizona, California, Colorado, Hawaii, Nevada, Oregon, Washington	Fresno, CA 93888-0002	P.O. Box 7704 San Francisco, CA 94120-7704
Arkansas, Idaho, Illinois, Indiana, Iowa, Kansas, Michigan, Minnesota, Montana, Nebraska, New Mexico, North Dakota, Ohio, Oklahoma, South Dakota, Utah, Wisconsin, Wyoming	Fresno, CA 93888-0002	P.O. Box 802501 Cincinnati, OH 45280-2501
Kentucky, Missouri, New Jersey, Tennessee, Virginia, West Virginia	Kansas City, MO 64999-0002	P.O. Box 970011 St. Louis, MO 63197-0011

Connecticut, Delaware, District of Columbia, Maine, Maryland, Massachusetts, New Hampshire, New York, Pennsylvania, Rhode Island, Vermont	Kansas City, MO 64999-0002	P.O. Box 37008 Hartford, CT 06176-0008
A foreign country, American Samoa, or Puerto Rico (or are excluding income under Code Sec. 933), or use an APO or FPO address, or files Form 2555, 2555-EZ, or 4563, or is a dual-status alien or nonpermanent resident of Guam or the Virgin Islands	Austin, TX 73301-0215	P.O. Box 1303 Charlotte, NC 28201-1303
Guam: permanent residents	Department of Revenue and Taxation, Government of Guam, P.O. Box 23607, GMF, GU 96921	
Virgin Islands: permanent residents	V.I. Bureau of Internal Revenue, 9601 Estate Thomas, Charlotte Amalie, St. Thomas, VI 00802	

Corporations and Partnerships. A corporation or partnership should file Form 1120 or Form 1065 in accordance with the "Where to File" addresses listed in the instructions to the forms. A corporation or partnership is "located in" the place where it has its principal place of business or principal office or agency. If a corporation or partnership is without a principal office or agency or principal place of business in the United States, returns are to be filed with the Internal Revenue Service Center in Ogden, Utah.

Estates and Trusts. Generally, a fiduciary of an estate or trust, including the fiduciary of a charitable or split interest trust (described in Code Sec. 4947(a)) or of a pooled income fund (described in Code Sec. 642(c)(5), should file Form 1041 in accordance with the instructions to Form 1041. A fiduciary is "located in" the place where he (it) resides or has his (its) principal place of business.

Private Delivery Services. Certain private delivery services designated by the IRS are available to meet the "timely mailed as timely filing/paying" rule for tax returns and payments. The designated private delivery services are:

• DHL Express (DHL) and DHL Same Day Service.

• Federal Express (FedEx): FedEx Priority Overnight, FedEx Standard Overnight, FedEx 2Day, FedEx International Priority, and FedEx International First.

• United Parcel Service (UPS): UPS Next Day Air, UPS Next Day Air Saver, UPS 2nd Day Air, UPS 2nd Day Air A.M., UPS Worldwide Express Plus, and UPS Worldwide Express.

The private delivery service will provide information for getting written proof of the mailing date.

¶ 6 2013 Tax Calendar

Each date shown below is the statutorily prescribed last day for filing the return or making the payment of tax indicated. For income tax returns, the due dates apply to calendar-year taxpayers only. Employment tax due dates are determined on a calendar-year basis for all taxpayers. **If any due date falls on a Saturday, Sunday, or legal holiday, the due date is the next succeeding day that is not a Saturday, Sunday, or legal holiday (national, District of Columbia, or statewide in the state where the return is to be filed).**

This day 2013 — **Tax Return Due Dates**

Jan. 15th—

Estimated Taxes. Final installment of 2012 estimated tax (Form 1041-ES) by individuals unless income tax return is filed with final payment by January 31, 2013. Payment in full of estimated tax by farmers and fishermen unless income tax returns are filed by March 1, 2013.

Final installment of 2012 estimated tax (Form 1041-ES) by trusts, and by calendar-year estates and certain residuary trusts in existence more than two years, unless Form 1041 is filed and taxes are paid in full by January 31, 2013.

Jan. 31st—

Employers' Taxes. Employers of nonagricultural and nonhousehold employees file return on Form 941 for withheld income and FICA taxes in last quarter of 2012.[1]

Employers of agricultural workers must file the annual Form 943 to report income and FICA taxes withheld on 2012 wages.[1]

Employers must file Form 940, annual return of federal unemployment (FUTA) taxes for 2012.[1]

Withholding. Employees' statements (Form W-2 and Form 1099-R) for amounts withheld in 2012 to be furnished by employer to employees. Statements for amounts withheld on certain gambling winnings (Form W-2G) to be furnished by payer to recipients.

Individuals. Individuals (other than farmers and fishermen) who owed, but did not pay, estimated tax on January 15th must file final 2012 income tax return and pay tax in full to avoid late payment penalty.

Trusts and Estates. Trusts, as well as estates and certain residuary trusts in existence more than two years, that owed but did not pay estimated tax on January 15th must file final 2012 income tax return and pay tax in full to avoid late payment penalty.

Information Returns. Annual statements must be furnished to recipients of: dividends and liquidating distributions (Form 1099-DIV); interest, including interest on bearer certificates of deposit (Form 1099-INT); patronage dividends (Form 1099-PATR); original issue discount (Form 1099-OID); certain government payments, including unemployment compensation and state and local tax refunds of $10 or more (Form 1099-G); royalty payments of $10 or more, rent or other business payments of $600 or more, prizes and awards of $600 or more, crop insurance proceeds of $600 or more, fishing boat proceeds, and medical and health care payments of $600 or more (Form 1099-MISC); debt canceled by certain financial entities including financial institutions, credit unions, and Federal Government agencies of $600 or more (Form 1099-C); distributions from retirement or profit-sharing plans, IRAs, SEPs, or insurance contracts (Form 1099-R); payments received from a third party settlement entity (1099-K).

Business recipients of $600 or more of interest on any mortgage must furnish Form 1098 to payer.

This day 2013	Tax Return Due Dates
	Information called for on Form 8300 must be provided to each payer in a transaction of more than $10,000 in cash at any time during 2012. (Form 8300 must have been filed with the IRS by the 15th day after the date of the transaction.)
	Partnerships must provide Form 8308 to the transferor and transferee in any exchange of a partnership interest that involved unrealized receivables or substantially appreciated inventory items.
	Trustees or issuers of IRAs or SEPs must provide participants with a statement of the account's value.
Feb. 15th—	**Individuals.** Last day for filing Form W-4 by employees who wish to claim exemption from withholding of income tax for 2013.
	Information Returns. Annual statements must be furnished to recipients of proceeds from broker and barter exchange transactions (Form 1099-B); proceeds from real estate transactions (Form 1099-S); broker payments in lieu of dividends or tax-exempt interest, and gross proceeds paid to an attorney (Form 1099-MISC).
Feb. 28th—	**Information Returns.** Annual 1099 series returns (together with transmittal Form 1096 for paper filings or, if filing electronically, by April 1st, must be filed with the IRS to report payments to recipients who received Form 1099 on January 31st, as indicated above.
	Business recipients of $600 or more of interest from an individual on any mortgage must file Form 1098 with the IRS (together with transmittal Form 1096 for paper filings or, if filing electronically, by April 1st.
	Withholding. Form W-2 "A" copies for 2012 (together with transmittal Form W-3) must be filed with the Social Security Administration. If filing electronically, the due date is extended to April 1st.
	Form W-2G and Form 1099-R for 2012 "A" copies (together with transmittal Form 1096 for paper filings or, if filing electronically, by April 1st, must be filed with the IRS.
Mar. 1st—	**Individuals.** Last day for farmers and fishermen who owed, but did not pay, estimated tax on January 15th to file 2012 calendar-year income tax return and pay tax in full to avoid late payment penalty.
Mar. 15th—	**Corporations.** Due date of 2012 income tax returns (Form 1120) for calendar-year U.S. corporations or calendar-year foreign corporations with offices in the U.S. Fiscal-year U.S. corporations and foreign corporations with a U.S. office must file by the 15th day of the 3rd month following the close of the tax year.
	Last date for filing application (Form 7004) by calendar-year corporations for automatic six-month extension to file 2012 income tax return.
	Form 5452 for reporting nontaxable corporate distributions made to shareholders during calendar year 2012 should be filed by calendar-year corporations with income tax return. Fiscal-year corporations file Form 5452 with income tax return for first fiscal year ending after calendar year in which distributions were made.
	Calendar-year corporations' 2012 information return (Form 5471) with respect to foreign corporations. (Fiscal-year corporations file form with income tax return.)
	Last date for a calendar-year corporation to file an amended income tax return (Form 1120X) for the calendar year 2009.[2]
	S Corporations. Due date of 2012 income tax returns for calendar-year S corporations (Form 1120S) and to provide each shareholder with a copy of Schedule K-1.
	Last date for filing application (Form 7004) by S corporations for automatic six-month extension to file 2012 income tax return.

This day 2013	Tax Return Due Dates
	Last date for filing Form 2553 to elect to be treated as an S corporation beginning with calendar year 2013. The penalty for filing the election late is to postpone treatment as an S corporation until calendar year 2014.
	Withholding. File returns on Form 1042 and Form 1042-S to report tax withheld at the source from nonresident aliens, foreign corporations, foreign partnerships and foreign fiduciaries of a trust or estate.
Apr. 1st—	**Information Returns—Electronic Filing.** Due date for filing Form 1098 (for reporting receipt of mortgage interest) or Form 1099 (for reporting certain payments) with the IRS electronically (not by magnetic media).
	Withholding—Electronic Filing. Last day for filing Form W-2 with the SSA or Form W-2G with the IRS if filing electronically (not by magnetic media).
Apr. 15th—	**Individuals.** Income tax and self-employment tax returns of individuals for calendar year 2012 and income tax returns of calendar-year decedents who died in 2012 (Form 1040, Form 1040A, or Form 1040EZ). Fiscal-year individuals must file returns or requests for extension by the 15th day of the 4th month after the close of the tax year.
	Last day for calendar-year individuals to file application (Form 4868) for automatic six-month extension to file 2012 income tax return.
	Individuals' information returns (Form 5471) with respect to foreign corporations to be filed with Form 1040.
	Last day for individuals to file amended income tax returns (Form 1040X) for the calendar year 2009.
	Estimated Tax. Calendar-year corporations pay first installment of 2013 estimated income taxes. Fiscal-year corporations are to make payments on the 15th day of the 4th, 6th, 9th, and 12th months of the tax year.
	Payment of first installment of 2013 estimated income taxes by calendar-year individuals (other than farmers and fishermen) (Form 1040-ES). Estimated tax payments for fiscal-year individuals are due on the 15th day of the 4th, 6th, and 9th months of the tax year and the 1st month of the following tax year.
	Trusts (and calendar-year estates and certain residuary trusts in existence more than two years) must make first payment of estimated taxes for 2013 (Form 1041-ES). Fiscal-year estates must make payments on the 15th day of the 4th, 6th, and 9th months of the fiscal year and the 1st month of the following fiscal year.
	Trusts and Estates. Fiduciary income tax return (Form 1041) for calendar year 2012. (Fiscal-year estates must file by the 15th day of the 4th month following close of the tax year.)
	Last day for calendar year estates and trusts to file application (Form 7004) for automatic five-month extension of time to file 2012 income tax return.
	Last day for estates and trusts to file amended tax returns for calendar year 2009.
	Partnerships. Last day for filing income tax return (Form 1065) for calendar year 2012. Returns for fiscal-year partnerships are due on the 15th day of the 4th month after the close of the tax year.
	Last day for calendar-year U.S. partnerships to file application (Form 7004) for automatic five-month extension to file 2012 income tax return.
	Last day for calendar-year partnerships to file an amended return for 2009.

This day 2013 — **Tax Return Due Dates**

Information Returns. Annual information return (Form 1041-A) for split-interest trusts and complex trusts claiming charitable deductions under Code Sec. 642(c) and annual information return (Form 5227) for Code Sec. 4947(a)(2) trusts must be filed.

Apr. 30th— **Employers' Taxes.** Employers of nonagricultural and nonhousehold employees must file return on Form 941 to report income tax withholding and FICA taxes for the first quarter of 2013.[3]

May 15th— **Exempt Organizations.** Annual information return (Form 990) for 2012 by calendar-year organizations exempt or claiming exemption from tax under Code Sec. 501 or Code Sec. 4947(a)(1). Fiscal-year organizations must file by 15th day of 5th month after close of the tax year.

Calendar-year private foundations and Code Sec. 4947(a) trusts treated as private foundations must file Form 990-PF, and private foundations must pay the first quarter installment of estimated excise tax on net investment or tax on unrelated business income. Fiscal-year organizations must file by 15th day of 5th month after close of tax year, for both Form 990-PF and estimated taxes referred to above.

Calendar-year Code Sec. 501(a) organizations with unrelated business income must file income tax return on Form 990-T. Fiscal-year organizations must file by 15th day of 5th month following close of tax year.

Exempt organizations requesting an extension of time to file Form 990 may file Form 8868.

May 31st— **Information Returns.** Annual statement to IRS regarding 2012 account balances for an IRA or SEP (Form 5498). Participants and IRS must be provided with IRA plan contribution information.

June 17th— **Individuals.** Last day for nonresident alien individuals not subject to withholding to file income tax return for calendar year 2012.

Estimated Tax. Calendar-year corporations must pay second installment of 2013 estimated tax.

Payment of second installment of 2013 estimated tax by individuals (other than farmers and fishermen), by trusts and by estates and certain residuary trusts in existence more than two years. Nonresident aliens who have no wages subject to U.S. withholding must make first payment (Form 1040-ES (NR)).

Corporations. Last day for foreign corporations that do not maintain an office or place of business in U.S. to file income tax return (Form 1120F) for calendar year 2012.

July 31st— **Employers' Taxes.** Employers of nonagricultural and nonhousehold employees must file return on Form 941 to report income tax withholding and FICA taxes for the second quarter of 2013.[4]

Sept. 16th— **Estimated Tax.** Payment of third installment of 2013 estimated tax by calendar-year corporations.

Payment of third installment of 2013 estimated tax by individuals (other than farmers and fishermen), by trusts and by estates and certain residuary trusts in existence more than two years.

Corporations. Last day for filing 2012 income tax return by calendar-year corporations that obtained automatic six-month filing extension.

Exempt Organizations. Last day for exempt calendar-year farmers' cooperatives to file 2012 income tax returns (Form 1120-C). Fiscal-year cooperatives must file by the 15th day of the 9th month following the close of the tax year. An automatic six-month extension of the filing date may be obtained by filing Form 7004.

This day 2013	Tax Return Due Dates
	Estates and Trusts. Last day for filing 2012 Form 1041 for calendar-year estates and trusts that obtained an automatic five-month filing extension.
	Partnerships. Last day for filing 2012 Form 1065 for calendar-year partnerships that obtained an automatic five-month filing extension.
October 15th—	**Individuals.** Last day for filing 2012 income tax return by calendar-year individuals who obtained automatic six-month filing extension.
Oct. 31st—	**Employers' Taxes.** Employers of nonagricultural and nonhousehold employees must file return on Form 941 to report income tax withholding and FICA taxes for the third quarter of 2013.[5]
Dec. 16th—	**Estimated Tax.** Payment of last installment of 2013 estimated tax by calendar-year corporations.
This day 2014	
Jan. 15th—	**Estimated Tax.** Final installment of 2013 estimated tax by individuals, trusts and estates and certain residuary trusts in existence more than two years. (Payment of estimated tax in full by individuals, trusts and estates that are first required to pay estimated tax for calendar year 2013.) Payment not necessary if returns filed and tax paid in full by January 31, 2014. Payment of estimated tax in full by farmers and fishermen who are not filing final returns by March 3, 2014.
Jan. 31st—	**Individuals.** Final income tax return for 2013 by calendar-year individuals and by trusts and estates in existence more than two years who owed but did not pay 2013 estimated tax otherwise due January 15th.

[1] If timely deposits in full payment of tax due were made, the due date for Forms 940, 941, and 943 is February 11.

[2] In general, fiscal-year corporations must file within three years of the date the original return was due.

[3] If timely deposits in full payment of taxes due were made, the due date for Form 941 is May 10.

[4] If timely deposits in full payment of taxes due were made, the due date for Form 941 is August 12.

[5] If timely deposits in full payment of taxes due were made, the due date for Form 941 is November 11.

EMPLOYMENT TAX DEPOSITS

Income Tax Withholding, FICA Taxes, Backup Withholding. Employment taxes are withheld income tax, FICA contributions, and backup withholding on reportable payments. Generally, an employer must make either MONTHLY or SEMI-WEEKLY deposits during a calendar year based upon the aggregate amount of employment taxes paid during the "lookback" period. The lookback period for each calendar year is the 12-month period that ended the preceding June 30. Thus, an employer's obligation to make deposits in 2013 will be based upon the aggregate employment taxes paid during the period July 1, 2011, through June 30, 2012 (¶ 2651). New employers are considered to have an aggregate tax liability of zero for any calendar quarter in which the employer did not exist.

Monthly Deposits. Monthly deposits are required if the aggregate amount of employment taxes reported by the employer for the lookback period is $50,000 or less. Monthly deposits are due on the 15th day of the following month in which the payments were made.

Semi-Weekly Deposits. An employer is a semi-weekly depositor for the entire calendar year if the aggregate amount of employment taxes during the lookback period exceeds $50,000. Further, a monthly depositor will become a semi-weekly depositor on the first day after the employer becomes subject to the One-Day Rule, discussed below. Semi-weekly deposits are generally due on either Wednesday or Friday—depending upon the timing of the employer's pay period. Employers with payment dates (paydays) that fall on Wednesday, Thursday, or Friday must deposit the employment taxes on or before the following Wednesday. Employers with payment dates that fall on Saturday, Sunday, Monday, or Tuesday must make their deposit on or before the following Friday. However, an employer will always have three business days in which to make the deposit. Thus, if any of the three weekdays following the close of a semi-weekly period is a holiday, then the employer will have an additional business day in which to make the deposit.

One-Day Rule. If an employer has accumulated $100,000 or more of undeposited employment taxes, then the taxes must be deposited by the close of the next banking day.

Federal Unemployment (FUTA) Taxes. The calendar year is divided into four quarters for purposes of determining when deposits of federal unemployment tax (FUTA) are necessary. The periods end on March 31, June 30, September 30, and December 31. If the employer's FUTA tax liability is $500 or less, then the employer does not have to deposit the tax, instead the amount may be carried forward and added to the liability for the next quarter to determine if a deposit is required. If the employer owes more than $500 in undeposited federal unemployment tax at the end of a quarter (including any FUTA tax carried forward from an earlier quarter), then the tax owed must be deposited by the end of the next month by either a electronic funds transfer (EFTPS) direct or a EFTPS financial institution.

Schedules and Tables

TAX RATES

TAX RATE SCHEDULES FOR 2012 AND 2013 (PROJECTED)

NOTE. The 2012 Tax Rate Schedules reproduced below are based on the rate changes and inflation adjustments to the tax brackets released by the Internal Revenue Service in Rev. Proc. 2011-52, I.R.B. 2011-45.

> **Comment:** Absent further legislation, the lower income tax rates applicable to individuals, estates and trusts under Code Sec. 1 are scheduled to expire for tax years beginning after December 31, 2012, under the sunset provisions of the Economic Growth and Tax Relief Reconciliation Act of 2001 (EGTRRA) (P.L. 107-16) as amended by the Tax Relief, Unemployment Insurance Reauthorization, and Job Creation Act of 2010 (Tax Relief Act of 2010) (P.L. 111-312). The projected 2013 Tax Rate Schedules produced below were prepared by CCH based on the EGTRRA sunset provision. The projected 2013 tax rate schedules for married individuals filing jointly and surviving spouses, and married individuals filing separately also reflect the sunset of the marriage penalty relief. The official 2013 Tax Rate Schedules and Tables had not been released by the Internal Revenue Service at the time of publication.

The 2012 and projected 2013 tax rate schedules for single individuals are at ¶ 11; for married individuals filing jointly and surviving spouses, see ¶ 13; for married individuals filing separately, see ¶ 15; for heads of households, see ¶ 17; and for estates and nongrantor trusts, see ¶ 19.

¶ 11 SCHEDULE X: Single Individuals

2012

Taxable Income Over	But Not Over	Pay	+	% on Excess	of the amount over—
$0—	$8,700	$0		10%	$0
8,700—	35,350	870.00		15	8,700
35,350—	85,650	4,867.50		25	35,350
85,650—	178,650	17,442.50		28	85,650
178,650—	388,350	43,482.50		33	178,650
388,350—	......	112,683.50		35	388,350

2013 (Projected)

Taxable Income Over	But Not Over	Pay	+	% on Excess	of the amount over—
$0—	$36,250	$0		15%	$0
36,250—	87,850	5,437.50		28	36,250
87,850—	183,250	19,885.50		31	87,850
183,250—	398,350	49,459.50		36	183,250
398,350—	......	126,895.50		39.6	398,350

¶ 13 SCHEDULE Y-1: Married Filing Jointly and Surviving Spouses

2012

Taxable Income Over	But Not Over	Pay	+	% on Excess	of the amount over—
$0—	$17,400	$0		10%	$0
17,400—	70,700	1,740.00		15	17,400
70,700—	142,700	9,735.00		25	70,700
142,700—	217,450	27,735.00		28	142,700
217,450—	388,350	48,665.00		33	217,450
388,350—	......	105,062.00		35	388,350

2013 (Projected)

Taxable Income Over	But Not Over	Pay	+	% on Excess	of the amount over—
$0—	$60,550	$0		15%	$0
60,550—	146,400	9,082.50		28	60,550
146,400—	223,050	33,120.50		31	146,400
223,050—	398,350	56,882.00		36	223,050
398,350—	......	119,990.00		39.6	398,350

¶ 15 SCHEDULE Y-2: Married Individuals Filing Separately

2012

Taxable Income Over	But Not Over	Pay	+	% on Excess	of the amount over—
$0—	$8,700	$0		10%	$0
8,700—	35,350	870.00		15	8,700
35,350—	71,350	4,867.50		25	35,350
71,350—	108,725	13,867.50		28	71,350
108,725—	194,175	24,332.50		33	108,725
194,175—	. . . . . .	52,531.00		35	194,175

2013 (Projected)

Taxable Income Over	But Not Over	Pay	+	% on Excess	of the amount over—
$0—	$30,275	$0		15%	$0
30,275—	73,200	4,541.25		28	30,275
73,200—	111,525	16,560.25		31	73,200
111,525—	199,175	28,441.00		36	111,525
199,175—	. . . . . .	59,995.00		39.6	199,175

¶ 17 SCHEDULE Z: Heads of Households

2012

Taxable Income Over	But Not Over	Pay	+	% on Excess	of the amount over—
$0—	$12,400	$0		10%	$0
12,400—	47,350	1,240.00		15	12,400
47,350—	122,300	6,482.50		25	47,350
122,300—	198,050	25,220.00		28	122,300
198,050—	388,350	46,430.00		33	198,050
388,350—	. . . . . .	109,229.00		35	388,350

2013 (Projected)

Taxable Income Over	But Not Over	Pay	+	% on Excess	of the amount over—
$0—	$48,600	$0		15%	$0
48,600—	125,450	7,290.00		28	48,600
125,450—	203,150	28,808.00		31	125,450
203,150—	398,350	52,895.00		36	203,150
398,350—	. . . . . .	123,167.00		39.6	398,350

¶ 19 INCOME TAX RATE SCHEDULES FOR USE BY ESTATES AND NONGRANTOR TRUSTS

2012

Taxable Income Over	But Not Over	Pay	+	% on Excess	of the amount over—
$0—	$2,400	$0		15%	$0
2,400—	5,600	360.00		25	2,400
5,600—	8,500	1,160.00		28	5,600
8,500—	11,650	1,972.00		33	8,500
11,650—	. . . . . .	3,011.50		35	11,650

2013 (Projected)

Taxable Income Over	But Not Over	Pay	+	% on Excess	of the amount over—
$0—	$2,450	$0		15%	$0
2,450—	5,700	367.50		28	2,450
5,700—	8,750	1,277.50		31	5,700
8,750—	11,950	2,223.00		36	8,750
11,950—	. . . . .	3,375.00		39.6	11,950

TAX RATES

¶ 20 2012 Tax Computation Worksheet

Note: At the time of publication, the Internal Revenue Service had not yet released either a draft or final version of the Tax Computation Worksheet for use in preparing 2012 income tax returns. As always, for the latest information, see CCHGroup.com/TaxUpdates.

Scan this code with your mobile device to see
CCHGroup.com/TaxUpdates

CCH Comment: *U.S. Master Tax Guide* customers may also request a copy of the *2012 Tax Tables Booklet*, which will publish once the final Tax Computation Worksheet is available, by contacting CCH Customer Support. Please visit the CCH Customer Support Site at support.cch.com (first-time visitors will need to register). You can also chat with us online at support.cch.com/chat/booksupport/ or email us at CCHCustomerService@wolterskluwer.com.

Caution: This is a draft 2012 Tax Table. At the time of publication, the IRS had not yet released the 2012 Tax Table. For the latest information, see CCHGroup.com/TaxUpdates.

2012 TAX TABLE—INDIVIDUALS

¶ 25 2012 Tax Table for Use with Form 1040

Note: At the time of publication, the Internal Revenue Service had not yet released a final version of the 2012 Tax Table for use in preparing 2012 income tax returns. For the latest information, see CCHGroup.com/TaxUpdates.

Scan this code with your mobile device to see CCHGroup.com/TaxUpdates

CCH Comment: U.S. Master Tax Guide customers may also request a copy of the *2012 Tax Tables Booklet*, which will publish once the final 2012 Tax Table is available, by contacting CCH Customer Support. Please visit the CCH Customer Support Site at support.cch.com (first-time visitors will need to register). You can also chat with us online at support.cch.com/chat/booksupport/ or email us at CCHCustomerService@wolterskluwer.com.

☐ The Tax Table that follows is for use with Form 1040. A similar Tax Table applies to Forms 1040A and 1040EZ.

2012 TAX TABLE Based on Taxable Income. For persons with taxable incomes of less than $100,000.

Read down the income columns of the tax table until you find the line covering the taxable income shown on line 43 of Form 1040 (line 27 of Form 1040A or line 6 of Form 1040EZ). Then read across that income line until you find the column heading that describes your filing status. Enter the tax found there on line 44, Form 1040 (line 28, Form 1040A or line 10, Form 1040EZ).

⋙→ Caution: This is a draft 2012 Tax Table. At the time of publication, the IRS had not yet released the 2012 Tax Table. For the latest information, see CCHGroup.com/TaxUpdates.

2012 Tax Table

CAUTION

See the instructions for line 44 to see if you must use the Tax Table below to figure your tax.

Example. Mr. and Mrs. Brown are filing a joint return. Their taxable income on Form 1040, line 43, is $25,300. First, they find the $25,300–25,350 taxable income line. Next, they find the column for married filing jointly and read down the column. The amount shown where the taxable income line and filing status column meet is $2,929. This is the tax amount they should enter on Form 1040, line 44.

Sample Table

At Least	But Less Than	Single	Married filing jointly *	Married filing sepa-rately	He of ho ho
			Your tax is—		
25,200	**25,250**	3,349	2,914	3,349	3,
25,250	**25,300**	3,356	2,921	3,356	3,
25,300	**25,350**	3,364	(2,929)	3,364	3,
25,350	**25,400**	3,371	2,936	3,371	3,

If line 43 (taxable income) is—		And you are—			
At least	But less than	Single	Married filing jointly *	Married filing sepa-rately	Head of a house-hold
0	**5**	0	0	0	0
5	**15**	1	1	1	1
15	**25**	2	2	2	2
25	**50**	4	4	4	4
50	**75**	6	6	6	6
75	**100**	9	9	9	9
100	**125**	11	11	11	11
125	**150**	14	14	14	14
150	**175**	16	16	16	16
175	**200**	19	19	19	19
200	**225**	21	21	21	21
225	**250**	24	24	24	24
250	**275**	26	26	26	26
275	**300**	29	29	29	29
300	**325**	31	31	31	31
325	**350**	34	34	34	34
350	**375**	36	36	36	36
375	**400**	39	39	39	39
400	**425**	41	41	41	41
425	**450**	44	44	44	44
450	**475**	46	46	46	46
475	**500**	49	49	49	49
500	**525**	51	51	51	51
525	**550**	54	54	54	54
550	**575**	56	56	56	56
575	**600**	59	59	59	59
600	**625**	61	61	61	61
625	**650**	64	64	64	64
650	**675**	66	66	66	66
675	**700**	69	69	69	69
700	**725**	71	71	71	71
725	**750**	74	74	74	74
750	**775**	76	76	76	76
775	**800**	79	79	79	79
800	**825**	81	81	81	81
825	**850**	84	84	84	84
850	**875**	86	86	86	86
875	**900**	89	89	89	89
900	**925**	91	91	91	91
925	**950**	94	94	94	94
950	**975**	96	96	96	96
975	**1,000**	99	99	99	99

If line 43 (taxable income) is—		And you are—			
At least	But less than	Single	Married filing jointly *	Married filing sepa-rately	Head of a house-hold
1,000					
1,000	**1,025**	101	101	101	101
1,025	**1,050**	104	104	104	104
1,050	**1,075**	106	106	106	106
1,075	**1,100**	109	109	109	109
1,100	**1,125**	111	111	111	111
1,125	**1,150**	114	114	114	114
1,150	**1,175**	116	116	116	116
1,175	**1,200**	119	119	119	119
1,200	**1,225**	121	121	121	121
1,225	**1,250**	124	124	124	124
1,250	**1,275**	126	126	126	126
1,275	**1,300**	129	129	129	129
1,300	**1,325**	131	131	131	131
1,325	**1,350**	134	134	134	134
1,350	**1,375**	136	136	136	136
1,375	**1,400**	139	139	139	139
1,400	**1,425**	141	141	141	141
1,425	**1,450**	144	144	144	144
1,450	**1,475**	146	146	146	146
1,475	**1,500**	149	149	149	149
1,500	**1,525**	151	151	151	151
1,525	**1,550**	154	154	154	154
1,550	**1,575**	156	156	156	156
1,575	**1,600**	159	159	159	159
1,600	**1,625**	161	161	161	161
1,625	**1,650**	164	164	164	164
1,650	**1,675**	166	166	166	166
1,675	**1,700**	169	169	169	169
1,700	**1,725**	171	171	171	171
1,725	**1,750**	174	174	174	174
1,750	**1,775**	176	176	176	176
1,775	**1,800**	179	179	179	179
1,800	**1,825**	181	181	181	181
1,825	**1,850**	184	184	184	184
1,850	**1,875**	186	186	186	186
1,875	**1,900**	189	189	189	189
1,900	**1,925**	191	191	191	191
1,925	**1,950**	194	194	194	194
1,950	**1,975**	196	196	196	196
1,975	**2,000**	199	199	199	199

If line 43 (taxable income) is—		And you are—			
At least	But less than	Single	Married filing jointly *	Married filing sepa-rately	Head of a house-hold
2,000					
2,000	**2,025**	201	201	201	201
2,025	**2,050**	204	204	204	204
2,050	**2,075**	206	206	206	206
2,075	**2,100**	209	209	209	209
2,100	**2,125**	211	211	211	211
2,125	**2,150**	214	214	214	214
2,150	**2,175**	216	216	216	216
2,175	**2,200**	219	219	219	219
2,200	**2,225**	221	221	221	221
2,225	**2,250**	224	224	224	224
2,250	**2,275**	226	226	226	226
2,275	**2,300**	229	229	229	229
2,300	**2,325**	231	231	231	231
2,325	**2,350**	234	234	234	234
2,350	**2,375**	236	236	236	236
2,375	**2,400**	239	239	239	239
2,400	**2,425**	241	241	241	241
2,425	**2,450**	244	244	244	244
2,450	**2,475**	246	246	246	246
2,475	**2,500**	249	249	249	249
2,500	**2,525**	251	251	251	251
2,525	**2,550**	254	254	254	254
2,550	**2,575**	256	256	256	256
2,575	**2,600**	259	259	259	259
2,600	**2,625**	261	261	261	261
2,625	**2,650**	264	264	264	264
2,650	**2,675**	266	266	266	266
2,675	**2,700**	269	269	269	269
2,700	**2,725**	271	271	271	271
2,725	**2,750**	274	274	274	274
2,750	**2,775**	276	276	276	276
2,775	**2,800**	279	279	279	279
2,800	**2,825**	281	281	281	281
2,825	**2,850**	284	284	284	284
2,850	**2,875**	286	286	286	286
2,875	**2,900**	289	289	289	289
2,900	**2,925**	291	291	291	291
2,925	**2,950**	294	294	294	294
2,950	**2,975**	296	296	296	296
2,975	**3,000**	299	299	299	299

(Continued)

*This column must also be used by a qualifying widow(er).

Need more information or forms? Visit IRS.gov.

Caution: This is a draft 2012 Tax Table. At the time of publication, the IRS had not yet released the 2012 Tax Table. For the latest information, see CCHGroup.com/TaxUpdates.

2012 Tax Table—*Continued*

If line 43 (taxable income) is— At least	But less than	And you are— Single	Married filing jointly *	Married filing separately	Head of a household
		Your tax is—			
3,000					
3,000	3,050	303	303	303	303
3,050	3,100	308	308	308	308
3,100	3,150	313	313	313	313
3,150	3,200	318	318	318	318
3,200	3,250	323	323	323	323
3,250	3,300	328	328	328	328
3,300	3,350	333	333	333	333
3,350	3,400	338	338	338	338
3,400	3,450	343	343	343	343
3,450	3,500	348	348	348	348
3,500	3,550	353	353	353	353
3,550	3,600	358	358	358	358
3,600	3,650	363	363	363	363
3,650	3,700	368	368	368	368
3,700	3,750	373	373	373	373
3,750	3,800	378	378	378	378
3,800	3,850	383	383	383	383
3,850	3,900	388	388	388	388
3,900	3,950	393	393	393	393
3,950	4,000	398	398	398	398
4,000					
4,000	4,050	403	403	403	403
4,050	4,100	408	408	408	408
4,100	4,150	413	413	413	413
4,150	4,200	418	418	418	418
4,200	4,250	423	423	423	423
4,250	4,300	428	428	428	428
4,300	4,350	433	433	433	433
4,350	4,400	438	438	438	438
4,400	4,450	443	443	443	443
4,450	4,500	448	448	448	448
4,500	4,550	453	453	453	453
4,550	4,600	458	458	458	458
4,600	4,650	463	463	463	463
4,650	4,700	468	468	468	468
4,700	4,750	473	473	473	473
4,750	4,800	478	478	478	478
4,800	4,850	483	483	483	483
4,850	4,900	488	488	488	488
4,900	4,950	493	493	493	493
4,950	5,000	498	498	498	498
5,000					
5,000	5,050	503	503	503	503
5,050	5,100	508	508	508	508
5,100	5,150	513	513	513	513
5,150	5,200	518	518	518	518
5,200	5,250	523	523	523	523
5,250	5,300	528	528	528	528
5,300	5,350	533	533	533	533
5,350	5,400	538	538	538	538
5,400	5,450	543	543	543	543
5,450	5,500	548	548	548	548
5,500	5,550	553	553	553	553
5,550	5,600	558	558	558	558
5,600	5,650	563	563	563	563
5,650	5,700	568	568	568	568
5,700	5,750	573	573	573	573
5,750	5,800	578	578	578	578
5,800	5,850	583	583	583	583
5,850	5,900	588	588	588	588
5,900	5,950	593	593	593	593
5,950	6,000	598	598	598	598
6,000					
6,000	6,050	603	603	603	603
6,050	6,100	608	608	608	608
6,100	6,150	613	613	613	613
6,150	6,200	618	618	618	618
6,200	6,250	623	623	623	623
6,250	6,300	628	628	628	628
6,300	6,350	633	633	633	633
6,350	6,400	638	638	638	638
6,400	6,450	643	643	643	643
6,450	6,500	648	648	648	648
6,500	6,550	653	653	653	653
6,550	6,600	658	658	658	658
6,600	6,650	663	663	663	663
6,650	6,700	668	668	668	668
6,700	6,750	673	673	673	673
6,750	6,800	678	678	678	678
6,800	6,850	683	683	683	683
6,850	6,900	688	688	688	688
6,900	6,950	693	693	693	693
6,950	7,000	698	698	698	698
7,000					
7,000	7,050	703	703	703	703
7,050	7,100	708	708	708	708
7,100	7,150	713	713	713	713
7,150	7,200	718	718	718	718
7,200	7,250	723	723	723	723
7,250	7,300	728	728	728	728
7,300	7,350	733	733	733	733
7,350	7,400	738	738	738	738
7,400	7,450	743	743	743	743
7,450	7,500	748	748	748	748
7,500	7,550	753	753	753	753
7,550	7,600	758	758	758	758
7,600	7,650	763	763	763	763
7,650	7,700	768	768	768	768
7,700	7,750	773	773	773	773
7,750	7,800	778	778	778	778
7,800	7,850	783	783	783	783
7,850	7,900	788	788	788	788
7,900	7,950	793	793	793	793
7,950	8,000	798	798	798	798
8,000					
8,000	8,050	803	803	803	803
8,050	8,100	808	808	808	808
8,100	8,150	813	813	813	813
8,150	8,200	818	818	818	818
8,200	8,250	823	823	823	823
8,250	8,300	828	828	828	828
8,300	8,350	833	833	833	833
8,350	8,400	838	838	838	838
8,400	8,450	843	843	843	843
8,450	8,500	848	848	848	848
8,500	8,550	853	853	853	853
8,550	8,600	858	858	858	858
8,600	8,650	863	863	863	863
8,650	8,700	868	868	868	868
8,700	8,750	874	873	874	873
8,750	8,800	881	878	881	878
8,800	8,850	889	883	889	883
8,850	8,900	896	888	896	888
8,900	8,950	904	893	904	893
8,950	9,000	911	898	911	898

(Continued)

*This column must also be used by a qualifying widow(er).

TAX RATES

»»→ Caution: This is a draft 2012 Tax Table. At the time of publication, the IRS had not yet released the 2012 Tax Table. For the latest information, see CCHGroup.com/TaxUpdates.

2012 Tax Table—*Continued*

If line 43 (taxable income) is— At least	But less than	And you are— Single	Married filing jointly *	Married filing sepa-rately	Head of a house-hold
		Your tax is—			
9,000					
9,000	9,050	919	903	919	903
9,050	9,100	926	908	926	908
9,100	9,150	934	913	934	913
9,150	9,200	941	918	941	918
9,200	9,250	949	923	949	923
9,250	9,300	956	928	956	928
9,300	9,350	964	933	964	933
9,350	9,400	971	938	971	938
9,400	9,450	979	943	979	943
9,450	9,500	986	948	986	948
9,500	9,550	994	953	994	953
9,550	9,600	1,001	958	1,001	958
9,600	9,650	1,009	963	1,009	963
9,650	9,700	1,016	968	1,016	968
9,700	9,750	1,024	973	1,024	973
9,750	9,800	1,031	978	1,031	978
9,800	9,850	1,039	983	1,039	983
9,850	9,900	1,046	988	1,046	988
9,900	9,950	1,054	993	1,054	993
9,950	10,000	1,061	998	1,061	998
10,000					
10,000	10,050	1,069	1,003	1,069	1,003
10,050	10,100	1,076	1,008	1,076	1,008
10,100	10,150	1,084	1,013	1,084	1,013
10,150	10,200	1,091	1,018	1,091	1,018
10,200	10,250	1,099	1,023	1,099	1,023
10,250	10,300	1,106	1,028	1,106	1,028
10,300	10,350	1,114	1,033	1,114	1,033
10,350	10,400	1,121	1,038	1,121	1,038
10,400	10,450	1,129	1,043	1,129	1,043
10,450	10,500	1,136	1,048	1,136	1,048
10,500	10,550	1,144	1,053	1,144	1,053
10,550	10,600	1,151	1,058	1,151	1,058
10,600	10,650	1,159	1,063	1,159	1,063
10,650	10,700	1,166	1,068	1,166	1,068
10,700	10,750	1,174	1,073	1,174	1,073
10,750	10,800	1,181	1,078	1,181	1,078
10,800	10,850	1,189	1,083	1,189	1,083
10,850	10,900	1,196	1,088	1,196	1,088
10,900	10,950	1,204	1,093	1,204	1,093
10,950	11,000	1,211	1,098	1,211	1,098
11,000					
11,000	11,050	1,219	1,103	1,219	1,103
11,050	11,100	1,226	1,108	1,226	1,108
11,100	11,150	1,234	1,113	1,234	1,113
11,150	11,200	1,241	1,118	1,241	1,118
11,200	11,250	1,249	1,123	1,249	1,123
11,250	11,300	1,256	1,128	1,256	1,128
11,300	11,350	1,264	1,133	1,264	1,133
11,350	11,400	1,271	1,138	1,271	1,138
11,400	11,450	1,279	1,143	1,279	1,143
11,450	11,500	1,286	1,148	1,286	1,148
11,500	11,550	1,294	1,153	1,294	1,153
11,550	11,600	1,301	1,158	1,301	1,158
11,600	11,650	1,309	1,163	1,309	1,163
11,650	11,700	1,316	1,168	1,316	1,168
11,700	11,750	1,324	1,173	1,324	1,173
11,750	11,800	1,331	1,178	1,331	1,178
11,800	11,850	1,339	1,183	1,339	1,183
11,850	11,900	1,346	1,188	1,346	1,188
11,900	11,950	1,354	1,193	1,354	1,193
11,950	12,000	1,361	1,198	1,361	1,198
12,000					
12,000	12,050	1,369	1,203	1,369	1,203
12,050	12,100	1,376	1,208	1,376	1,208
12,100	12,150	1,384	1,213	1,384	1,213
12,150	12,200	1,391	1,218	1,391	1,218
12,200	12,250	1,399	1,223	1,399	1,223
12,250	12,300	1,406	1,228	1,406	1,228
12,300	12,350	1,414	1,233	1,414	1,233
12,350	12,400	1,421	1,238	1,421	1,238
12,400	12,450	1,429	1,243	1,429	1,244
12,450	12,500	1,436	1,248	1,436	1,251
12,500	12,550	1,444	1,253	1,444	1,259
12,550	12,600	1,451	1,258	1,451	1,266
12,600	12,650	1,459	1,263	1,459	1,274
12,650	12,700	1,466	1,268	1,466	1,281
12,700	12,750	1,474	1,273	1,474	1,289
12,750	12,800	1,481	1,278	1,481	1,296
12,800	12,850	1,489	1,283	1,489	1,304
12,850	12,900	1,496	1,288	1,496	1,311
12,900	12,950	1,504	1,293	1,504	1,319
12,950	13,000	1,511	1,298	1,511	1,326
13,000					
13,000	13,050	1,519	1,303	1,519	1,334
13,050	13,100	1,526	1,308	1,526	1,341
13,100	13,150	1,534	1,313	1,534	1,349
13,150	13,200	1,541	1,318	1,541	1,356
13,200	13,250	1,549	1,323	1,549	1,364
13,250	13,300	1,556	1,328	1,556	1,371
13,300	13,350	1,564	1,333	1,564	1,379
13,350	13,400	1,571	1,338	1,571	1,386
13,400	13,450	1,579	1,343	1,579	1,394
13,450	13,500	1,586	1,348	1,586	1,401
13,500	13,550	1,594	1,353	1,594	1,409
13,550	13,600	1,601	1,358	1,601	1,416
13,600	13,650	1,609	1,363	1,609	1,424
13,650	13,700	1,616	1,368	1,616	1,431
13,700	13,750	1,624	1,373	1,624	1,439
13,750	13,800	1,631	1,378	1,631	1,446
13,800	13,850	1,639	1,383	1,639	1,454
13,850	13,900	1,646	1,388	1,646	1,461
13,900	13,950	1,654	1,393	1,654	1,469
13,950	14,000	1,661	1,398	1,661	1,476
14,000					
14,000	14,050	1,669	1,403	1,669	1,484
14,050	14,100	1,676	1,408	1,676	1,491
14,100	14,150	1,684	1,413	1,684	1,499
14,150	14,200	1,691	1,418	1,691	1,506
14,200	14,250	1,699	1,423	1,699	1,514
14,250	14,300	1,706	1,428	1,706	1,521
14,300	14,350	1,714	1,433	1,714	1,529
14,350	14,400	1,721	1,438	1,721	1,536
14,400	14,450	1,729	1,443	1,729	1,544
14,450	14,500	1,736	1,448	1,736	1,551
14,500	14,550	1,744	1,453	1,744	1,559
14,550	14,600	1,751	1,458	1,751	1,566
14,600	14,650	1,759	1,463	1,759	1,574
14,650	14,700	1,766	1,468	1,766	1,581
14,700	14,750	1,774	1,473	1,774	1,589
14,750	14,800	1,781	1,478	1,781	1,596
14,800	14,850	1,789	1,483	1,789	1,604
14,850	14,900	1,796	1,488	1,796	1,611
14,900	14,950	1,804	1,493	1,804	1,619
14,950	15,000	1,811	1,498	1,811	1,626

(Continued)

*This column must also be used by a qualifying widow(er).

»»→ Caution: This is a draft 2012 Tax Table. At the time of publication, the IRS had not yet released the 2012 Tax Table. For the latest information, see CCHGroup.com/TaxUpdates.

2012 Tax Table—*Continued*

If line 43 (taxable income) is—		And you are—			
At least	But less than	Single	Married filing jointly *	Married filing sepa-rately	Head of a house-hold
		Your tax is—			
15,000					
15,000	**15,050**	1,819	1,503	1,819	1,634
15,050	**15,100**	1,826	1,508	1,826	1,641
15,100	**15,150**	1,834	1,513	1,834	1,649
15,150	**15,200**	1,841	1,518	1,841	1,656
15,200	**15,250**	1,849	1,523	1,849	1,664
15,250	**15,300**	1,856	1,528	1,856	1,671
15,300	**15,350**	1,864	1,533	1,864	1,679
15,350	**15,400**	1,871	1,538	1,871	1,686
15,400	**15,450**	1,879	1,543	1,879	1,694
15,450	**15,500**	1,886	1,548	1,886	1,701
15,500	**15,550**	1,894	1,553	1,894	1,709
15,550	**15,600**	1,901	1,558	1,901	1,716
15,600	**15,650**	1,909	1,563	1,909	1,724
15,650	**15,700**	1,916	1,568	1,916	1,731
15,700	**15,750**	1,924	1,573	1,924	1,739
15,750	**15,800**	1,931	1,578	1,931	1,746
15,800	**15,850**	1,939	1,583	1,939	1,754
15,850	**15,900**	1,946	1,588	1,946	1,761
15,900	**15,950**	1,954	1,593	1,954	1,769
15,950	**16,000**	1,961	1,598	1,961	1,776
16,000					
16,000	**16,050**	1,969	1,603	1,969	1,784
16,050	**16,100**	1,976	1,608	1,976	1,791
16,100	**16,150**	1,984	1,613	1,984	1,799
16,150	**16,200**	1,991	1,618	1,991	1,806
16,200	**16,250**	1,999	1,623	1,999	1,814
16,250	**16,300**	2,006	1,628	2,006	1,821
16,300	**16,350**	2,014	1,633	2,014	1,829
16,350	**16,400**	2,021	1,638	2,021	1,836
16,400	**16,450**	2,029	1,643	2,029	1,844
16,450	**16,500**	2,036	1,648	2,036	1,851
16,500	**16,550**	2,044	1,653	2,044	1,859
16,550	**16,600**	2,051	1,658	2,051	1,866
16,600	**16,650**	2,059	1,663	2,059	1,874
16,650	**16,700**	2,066	1,668	2,066	1,881
16,700	**16,750**	2,074	1,673	2,074	1,889
16,750	**16,800**	2,081	1,678	2,081	1,896
16,800	**16,850**	2,089	1,683	2,089	1,904
16,850	**16,900**	2,096	1,688	2,096	1,911
16,900	**16,950**	2,104	1,693	2,104	1,919
16,950	**17,000**	2,111	1,698	2,111	1,926

If line 43 (taxable income) is—		And you are—			
At least	But less than	Single	Married filing jointly *	Married filing sepa-rately	Head of a house-hold
		Your tax is—			
17,000					
17,000	**17,050**	2,119	1,703	2,119	1,934
17,050	**17,100**	2,126	1,708	2,126	1,941
17,100	**17,150**	2,134	1,713	2,134	1,949
17,150	**17,200**	2,141	1,718	2,141	1,956
17,200	**17,250**	2,149	1,723	2,149	1,964
17,250	**17,300**	2,156	1,728	2,156	1,971
17,300	**17,350**	2,164	1,733	2,164	1,979
17,350	**17,400**	2,171	1,738	2,171	1,986
17,400	**17,450**	2,179	1,744	2,179	1,994
17,450	**17,500**	2,186	1,751	2,186	2,001
17,500	**17,550**	2,194	1,759	2,194	2,009
17,550	**17,600**	2,201	1,766	2,201	2,016
17,600	**17,650**	2,209	1,774	2,209	2,024
17,650	**17,700**	2,216	1,781	2,216	2,031
17,700	**17,750**	2,224	1,789	2,224	2,039
17,750	**17,800**	2,231	1,796	2,231	2,046
17,800	**17,850**	2,239	1,804	2,239	2,054
17,850	**17,900**	2,246	1,811	2,246	2,061
17,900	**17,950**	2,254	1,819	2,254	2,069
17,950	**18,000**	2,261	1,826	2,261	2,076
18,000					
18,000	**18,050**	2,269	1,834	2,269	2,084
18,050	**18,100**	2,276	1,841	2,276	2,091
18,100	**18,150**	2,284	1,849	2,284	2,099
18,150	**18,200**	2,291	1,856	2,291	2,106
18,200	**18,250**	2,299	1,864	2,299	2,114
18,250	**18,300**	2,306	1,871	2,306	2,121
18,300	**18,350**	2,314	1,879	2,314	2,129
18,350	**18,400**	2,321	1,886	2,321	2,136
18,400	**18,450**	2,329	1,894	2,329	2,144
18,450	**18,500**	2,336	1,901	2,336	2,151
18,500	**18,550**	2,344	1,909	2,344	2,159
18,550	**18,600**	2,351	1,916	2,351	2,166
18,600	**18,650**	2,359	1,924	2,359	2,174
18,650	**18,700**	2,366	1,931	2,366	2,181
18,700	**18,750**	2,374	1,939	2,374	2,189
18,750	**18,800**	2,381	1,946	2,381	2,196
18,800	**18,850**	2,389	1,954	2,389	2,204
18,850	**18,900**	2,396	1,961	2,396	2,211
18,900	**18,950**	2,404	1,969	2,404	2,219
18,950	**19,000**	2,411	1,976	2,411	2,226

If line 43 (taxable income) is—		And you are—			
At least	But less than	Single	Married filing jointly *	Married filing sepa-rately	Head of a house-hold
		Your tax is—			
19,000					
19,000	**19,050**	2,419	1,984	2,419	2,234
19,050	**19,100**	2,426	1,991	2,426	2,241
19,100	**19,150**	2,434	1,999	2,434	2,249
19,150	**19,200**	2,441	2,006	2,441	2,256
19,200	**19,250**	2,449	2,014	2,449	2,264
19,250	**19,300**	2,456	2,021	2,456	2,271
19,300	**19,350**	2,464	2,029	2,464	2,279
19,350	**19,400**	2,471	2,036	2,471	2,286
19,400	**19,450**	2,479	2,044	2,479	2,294
19,450	**19,500**	2,486	2,051	2,486	2,301
19,500	**19,550**	2,494	2,059	2,494	2,309
19,550	**19,600**	2,501	2,066	2,501	2,316
19,600	**19,650**	2,509	2,074	2,509	2,324
19,650	**19,700**	2,516	2,081	2,516	2,331
19,700	**19,750**	2,524	2,089	2,524	2,339
19,750	**19,800**	2,531	2,096	2,531	2,346
19,800	**19,850**	2,539	2,104	2,539	2,354
19,850	**19,900**	2,546	2,111	2,546	2,361
19,900	**19,950**	2,554	2,119	2,554	2,369
19,950	**20,000**	2,561	2,126	2,561	2,376
20,000					
20,000	**20,050**	2,569	2,134	2,569	2,384
20,050	**20,100**	2,576	2,141	2,576	2,391
20,100	**20,150**	2,584	2,149	2,584	2,399
20,150	**20,200**	2,591	2,156	2,591	2,406
20,200	**20,250**	2,599	2,164	2,599	2,414
20,250	**20,300**	2,606	2,171	2,606	2,421
20,300	**20,350**	2,614	2,179	2,614	2,429
20,350	**20,400**	2,621	2,186	2,621	2,436
20,400	**20,450**	2,629	2,194	2,629	2,444
20,450	**20,500**	2,636	2,201	2,636	2,451
20,500	**20,550**	2,644	2,209	2,644	2,459
20,550	**20,600**	2,651	2,216	2,651	2,466
20,600	**20,650**	2,659	2,224	2,659	2,474
20,650	**20,700**	2,666	2,231	2,666	2,481
20,700	**20,750**	2,674	2,239	2,674	2,489
20,750	**20,800**	2,681	2,246	2,681	2,496
20,800	**20,850**	2,689	2,254	2,689	2,504
20,850	**20,900**	2,696	2,261	2,696	2,511
20,900	**20,950**	2,704	2,269	2,704	2,519
20,950	**21,000**	2,711	2,276	2,711	2,526

(Continued)

* This column must also be used by a qualifying widow(er).

Caution: This is a draft 2012 Tax Table. At the time of publication, the IRS had not yet released the 2012 Tax Table. For the latest information, see CCHGroup.com/TaxUpdates.

2012 Tax Table—*Continued*

If line 43 (taxable income) is— At least	But less than	And you are— Single	Married filing jointly *	Married filing sepa-rately	Head of a house-hold
		Your tax is—			
21,000					
21,000	**21,050**	2,719	2,284	2,719	2,534
21,050	**21,100**	2,726	2,291	2,726	2,541
21,100	**21,150**	2,734	2,299	2,734	2,549
21,150	**21,200**	2,741	2,306	2,741	2,556
21,200	**21,250**	2,749	2,314	2,749	2,564
21,250	**21,300**	2,756	2,321	2,756	2,571
21,300	**21,350**	2,764	2,329	2,764	2,579
21,350	**21,400**	2,771	2,336	2,771	2,586
21,400	**21,450**	2,779	2,344	2,779	2,594
21,450	**21,500**	2,786	2,351	2,786	2,601
21,500	**21,550**	2,794	2,359	2,794	2,609
21,550	**21,600**	2,801	2,366	2,801	2,616
21,600	**21,650**	2,809	2,374	2,809	2,624
21,650	**21,700**	2,816	2,381	2,816	2,631
21,700	**21,750**	2,824	2,389	2,824	2,639
21,750	**21,800**	2,831	2,396	2,831	2,646
21,800	**21,850**	2,839	2,404	2,839	2,654
21,850	**21,900**	2,846	2,411	2,846	2,661
21,900	**21,950**	2,854	2,419	2,854	2,669
21,950	**22,000**	2,861	2,426	2,861	2,676
22,000					
22,000	**22,050**	2,869	2,434	2,869	2,684
22,050	**22,100**	2,876	2,441	2,876	2,691
22,100	**22,150**	2,884	2,449	2,884	2,699
22,150	**22,200**	2,891	2,456	2,891	2,706
22,200	**22,250**	2,899	2,464	2,899	2,714
22,250	**22,300**	2,906	2,471	2,906	2,721
22,300	**22,350**	2,914	2,479	2,914	2,729
22,350	**22,400**	2,921	2,486	2,921	2,736
22,400	**22,450**	2,929	2,494	2,929	2,744
22,450	**22,500**	2,936	2,501	2,936	2,751
22,500	**22,550**	2,944	2,509	2,944	2,759
22,550	**22,600**	2,951	2,516	2,951	2,766
22,600	**22,650**	2,959	2,524	2,959	2,774
22,650	**22,700**	2,966	2,531	2,966	2,781
22,700	**22,750**	2,974	2,539	2,974	2,789
22,750	**22,800**	2,981	2,546	2,981	2,796
22,800	**22,850**	2,989	2,554	2,989	2,804
22,850	**22,900**	2,996	2,561	2,996	2,811
22,900	**22,950**	3,004	2,569	3,004	2,819
22,950	**23,000**	3,011	2,576	3,011	2,826

If line 43 (taxable income) is— At least	But less than	And you are— Single	Married filing jointly *	Married filing sepa-rately	Head of a house-hold
		Your tax is—			
23,000					
23,000	**23,050**	3,019	2,584	3,019	2,834
23,050	**23,100**	3,026	2,591	3,026	2,841
23,100	**23,150**	3,034	2,599	3,034	2,849
23,150	**23,200**	3,041	2,606	3,041	2,856
23,200	**23,250**	3,049	2,614	3,049	2,864
23,250	**23,300**	3,056	2,621	3,056	2,871
23,300	**23,350**	3,064	2,629	3,064	2,879
23,350	**23,400**	3,071	2,636	3,071	2,886
23,400	**23,450**	3,079	2,644	3,079	2,894
23,450	**23,500**	3,086	2,651	3,086	2,901
23,500	**23,550**	3,094	2,659	3,094	2,909
23,550	**23,600**	3,101	2,666	3,101	2,916
23,600	**23,650**	3,109	2,674	3,109	2,924
23,650	**23,700**	3,116	2,681	3,116	2,931
23,700	**23,750**	3,124	2,689	3,124	2,939
23,750	**23,800**	3,131	2,696	3,131	2,946
23,800	**23,850**	3,139	2,704	3,139	2,954
23,850	**23,900**	3,146	2,711	3,146	2,961
23,900	**23,950**	3,154	2,719	3,154	2,969
23,950	**24,000**	3,161	2,726	3,161	2,976
24,000					
24,000	**24,050**	3,169	2,734	3,169	2,984
24,050	**24,100**	3,176	2,741	3,176	2,991
24,100	**24,150**	3,184	2,749	3,184	2,999
24,150	**24,200**	3,191	2,756	3,191	3,006
24,200	**24,250**	3,199	2,764	3,199	3,014
24,250	**24,300**	3,206	2,771	3,206	3,021
24,300	**24,350**	3,214	2,779	3,214	3,029
24,350	**24,400**	3,221	2,786	3,221	3,036
24,400	**24,450**	3,229	2,794	3,229	3,044
24,450	**24,500**	3,236	2,801	3,236	3,051
24,500	**24,550**	3,244	2,809	3,244	3,059
24,550	**24,600**	3,251	2,816	3,251	3,066
24,600	**24,650**	3,259	2,824	3,259	3,074
24,650	**24,700**	3,266	2,831	3,266	3,081
24,700	**24,750**	3,274	2,839	3,274	3,089
24,750	**24,800**	3,281	2,846	3,281	3,096
24,800	**24,850**	3,289	2,854	3,289	3,104
24,850	**24,900**	3,296	2,861	3,296	3,111
24,900	**24,950**	3,304	2,869	3,304	3,119
24,950	**25,000**	3,311	2,876	3,311	3,126

If line 43 (taxable income) is— At least	But less than	And you are— Single	Married filing jointly *	Married filing sepa-rately	Head of a house-hold
		Your tax is—			
25,000					
25,000	**25,050**	3,319	2,884	3,319	3,134
25,050	**25,100**	3,326	2,891	3,326	3,141
25,100	**25,150**	3,334	2,899	3,334	3,149
25,150	**25,200**	3,341	2,906	3,341	3,156
25,200	**25,250**	3,349	2,914	3,349	3,164
25,250	**25,300**	3,356	2,921	3,356	3,171
25,300	**25,350**	3,364	2,929	3,364	3,179
25,350	**25,400**	3,371	2,936	3,371	3,186
25,400	**25,450**	3,379	2,944	3,379	3,194
25,450	**25,500**	3,386	2,951	3,386	3,201
25,500	**25,550**	3,394	2,959	3,394	3,209
25,550	**25,600**	3,401	2,966	3,401	3,216
25,600	**25,650**	3,409	2,974	3,409	3,224
25,650	**25,700**	3,416	2,981	3,416	3,231
25,700	**25,750**	3,424	2,989	3,424	3,239
25,750	**25,800**	3,431	2,996	3,431	3,246
25,800	**25,850**	3,439	3,004	3,439	3,254
25,850	**25,900**	3,446	3,011	3,446	3,261
25,900	**25,950**	3,454	3,019	3,454	3,269
25,950	**26,000**	3,461	3,026	3,461	3,276
26,000					
26,000	**26,050**	3,469	3,034	3,469	3,284
26,050	**26,100**	3,476	3,041	3,476	3,291
26,100	**26,150**	3,484	3,049	3,484	3,299
26,150	**26,200**	3,491	3,056	3,491	3,306
26,200	**26,250**	3,499	3,064	3,499	3,314
26,250	**26,300**	3,506	3,071	3,506	3,321
26,300	**26,350**	3,514	3,079	3,514	3,329
26,350	**26,400**	3,521	3,086	3,521	3,336
26,400	**26,450**	3,529	3,094	3,529	3,344
26,450	**26,500**	3,536	3,101	3,536	3,351
26,500	**26,550**	3,544	3,109	3,544	3,359
26,550	**26,600**	3,551	3,116	3,551	3,366
26,600	**26,650**	3,559	3,124	3,559	3,374
26,650	**26,700**	3,566	3,131	3,566	3,381
26,700	**26,750**	3,574	3,139	3,574	3,389
26,750	**26,800**	3,581	3,146	3,581	3,396
26,800	**26,850**	3,589	3,154	3,589	3,404
26,850	**26,900**	3,596	3,161	3,596	3,411
26,900	**26,950**	3,604	3,169	3,604	3,419
26,950	**27,000**	3,611	3,176	3,611	3,426

(Continued)

*This column must also be used by a qualifying widow(er).

Caution: This is a draft 2012 Tax Table. At the time of publication, the IRS had not yet released the 2012 Tax Table. For the latest information, see CCHGroup.com/TaxUpdates.

2012 Tax Table—*Continued*

If line 43 (taxable income) is— At least	But less than	And you are— Single	Married filing jointly *	Married filing separately	Head of a household
		Your tax is—			
27,000					
27,000	**27,050**	3,619	3,184	3,619	3,434
27,050	**27,100**	3,626	3,191	3,626	3,441
27,100	**27,150**	3,634	3,199	3,634	3,449
27,150	**27,200**	3,641	3,206	3,641	3,456
27,200	**27,250**	3,649	3,214	3,649	3,464
27,250	**27,300**	3,656	3,221	3,656	3,471
27,300	**27,350**	3,664	3,229	3,664	3,479
27,350	**27,400**	3,671	3,236	3,671	3,486
27,400	**27,450**	3,679	3,244	3,679	3,494
27,450	**27,500**	3,686	3,251	3,686	3,501
27,500	**27,550**	3,694	3,259	3,694	3,509
27,550	**27,600**	3,701	3,266	3,701	3,516
27,600	**27,650**	3,709	3,274	3,709	3,524
27,650	**27,700**	3,716	3,281	3,716	3,531
27,700	**27,750**	3,724	3,289	3,724	3,539
27,750	**27,800**	3,731	3,296	3,731	3,546
27,800	**27,850**	3,739	3,304	3,739	3,554
27,850	**27,900**	3,746	3,311	3,746	3,561
27,900	**27,950**	3,754	3,319	3,754	3,569
27,950	**28,000**	3,761	3,326	3,761	3,576
28,000					
28,000	**28,050**	3,769	3,334	3,769	3,584
28,050	**28,100**	3,776	3,341	3,776	3,591
28,100	**28,150**	3,784	3,349	3,784	3,599
28,150	**28,200**	3,791	3,356	3,791	3,606
28,200	**28,250**	3,799	3,364	3,799	3,614
28,250	**28,300**	3,806	3,371	3,806	3,621
28,300	**28,350**	3,814	3,379	3,814	3,629
28,350	**28,400**	3,821	3,386	3,821	3,636
28,400	**28,450**	3,829	3,394	3,829	3,644
28,450	**28,500**	3,836	3,401	3,836	3,651
28,500	**28,550**	3,844	3,409	3,844	3,659
28,550	**28,600**	3,851	3,416	3,851	3,666
28,600	**28,650**	3,859	3,424	3,859	3,674
28,650	**28,700**	3,866	3,431	3,866	3,681
28,700	**28,750**	3,874	3,439	3,874	3,689
28,750	**28,800**	3,881	3,446	3,881	3,696
28,800	**28,850**	3,889	3,454	3,889	3,704
28,850	**28,900**	3,896	3,461	3,896	3,711
28,900	**28,950**	3,904	3,469	3,904	3,719
28,950	**29,000**	3,911	3,476	3,911	3,726

If line 43 (taxable income) is— At least	But less than	And you are— Single	Married filing jointly *	Married filing separately	Head of a household
		Your tax is—			
29,000					
29,000	**29,050**	3,919	3,484	3,919	3,734
29,050	**29,100**	3,926	3,491	3,926	3,741
29,100	**29,150**	3,934	3,499	3,934	3,749
29,150	**29,200**	3,941	3,506	3,941	3,756
29,200	**29,250**	3,949	3,514	3,949	3,764
29,250	**29,300**	3,956	3,521	3,956	3,771
29,300	**29,350**	3,964	3,529	3,964	3,779
29,350	**29,400**	3,971	3,536	3,971	3,786
29,400	**29,450**	3,979	3,544	3,979	3,794
29,450	**29,500**	3,986	3,551	3,986	3,801
29,500	**29,550**	3,994	3,559	3,994	3,809
29,550	**29,600**	4,001	3,566	4,001	3,816
29,600	**29,650**	4,009	3,574	4,009	3,824
29,650	**29,700**	4,016	3,581	4,016	3,831
29,700	**29,750**	4,024	3,589	4,024	3,839
29,750	**29,800**	4,031	3,596	4,031	3,846
29,800	**29,850**	4,039	3,604	4,039	3,854
29,850	**29,900**	4,046	3,611	4,046	3,861
29,900	**29,950**	4,054	3,619	4,054	3,869
29,950	**30,000**	4,061	3,626	4,061	3,876
30,000					
30,000	**30,050**	4,069	3,634	4,069	3,884
30,050	**30,100**	4,076	3,641	4,076	3,891
30,100	**30,150**	4,084	3,649	4,084	3,899
30,150	**30,200**	4,091	3,656	4,091	3,906
30,200	**30,250**	4,099	3,664	4,099	3,914
30,250	**30,300**	4,106	3,671	4,106	3,921
30,300	**30,350**	4,114	3,679	4,114	3,929
30,350	**30,400**	4,121	3,686	4,121	3,936
30,400	**30,450**	4,129	3,694	4,129	3,944
30,450	**30,500**	4,136	3,701	4,136	3,951
30,500	**30,550**	4,144	3,709	4,144	3,959
30,550	**30,600**	4,151	3,716	4,151	3,966
30,600	**30,650**	4,159	3,724	4,159	3,974
30,650	**30,700**	4,166	3,731	4,166	3,981
30,700	**30,750**	4,174	3,739	4,174	3,989
30,750	**30,800**	4,181	3,746	4,181	3,996
30,800	**30,850**	4,189	3,754	4,189	4,004
30,850	**30,900**	4,196	3,761	4,196	4,011
30,900	**30,950**	4,204	3,769	4,204	4,019
30,950	**31,000**	4,211	3,776	4,211	4,026

If line 43 (taxable income) is— At least	But less than	And you are— Single	Married filing jointly *	Married filing separately	Head of a household
		Your tax is—			
31,000					
31,000	**31,050**	4,219	3,784	4,219	4,034
31,050	**31,100**	4,226	3,791	4,226	4,041
31,100	**31,150**	4,234	3,799	4,234	4,049
31,150	**31,200**	4,241	3,806	4,241	4,056
31,200	**31,250**	4,249	3,814	4,249	4,064
31,250	**31,300**	4,256	3,821	4,256	4,071
31,300	**31,350**	4,264	3,829	4,264	4,079
31,350	**31,400**	4,271	3,836	4,271	4,086
31,400	**31,450**	4,279	3,844	4,279	4,094
31,450	**31,500**	4,286	3,851	4,286	4,101
31,500	**31,550**	4,294	3,859	4,294	4,109
31,550	**31,600**	4,301	3,866	4,301	4,116
31,600	**31,650**	4,309	3,874	4,309	4,124
31,650	**31,700**	4,316	3,881	4,316	4,131
31,700	**31,750**	4,324	3,889	4,324	4,139
31,750	**31,800**	4,331	3,896	4,331	4,146
31,800	**31,850**	4,339	3,904	4,339	4,154
31,850	**31,900**	4,346	3,911	4,346	4,161
31,900	**31,950**	4,354	3,919	4,354	4,169
31,950	**32,000**	4,361	3,926	4,361	4,176
32,000					
32,000	**32,050**	4,369	3,934	4,369	4,184
32,050	**32,100**	4,376	3,941	4,376	4,191
32,100	**32,150**	4,384	3,949	4,384	4,199
32,150	**32,200**	4,391	3,956	4,391	4,206
32,200	**32,250**	4,399	3,964	4,399	4,214
32,250	**32,300**	4,406	3,971	4,406	4,221
32,300	**32,350**	4,414	3,979	4,414	4,229
32,350	**32,400**	4,421	3,986	4,421	4,236
32,400	**32,450**	4,429	3,994	4,429	4,244
32,450	**32,500**	4,436	4,001	4,436	4,251
32,500	**32,550**	4,444	4,009	4,444	4,259
32,550	**32,600**	4,451	4,016	4,451	4,266
32,600	**32,650**	4,459	4,024	4,459	4,274
32,650	**32,700**	4,466	4,031	4,466	4,281
32,700	**32,750**	4,474	4,039	4,474	4,289
32,750	**32,800**	4,481	4,046	4,481	4,296
32,800	**32,850**	4,489	4,054	4,489	4,304
32,850	**32,900**	4,496	4,061	4,496	4,311
32,900	**32,950**	4,504	4,069	4,504	4,319
32,950	**33,000**	4,511	4,076	4,511	4,326

(Continued)

TAX RATES

*This column must also be used by a qualifying widow(er).

»»→ Caution: This is a draft 2012 Tax Table. At the time of publication, the IRS had not yet released the 2012 Tax Table. For the latest information, see CCHGroup.com/TaxUpdates.

2012 Tax Table—*Continued*

If line 43 (taxable income) is—		And you are—			
At least	But less than	Single	Married filing jointly *	Married filing separately	Head of a household
		Your tax is—			
33,000					
33,000	**33,050**	4,519	4,084	4,519	4,334
33,050	**33,100**	4,526	4,091	4,526	4,341
33,100	**33,150**	4,534	4,099	4,534	4,349
33,150	**33,200**	4,541	4,106	4,541	4,356
33,200	**33,250**	4,549	4,114	4,549	4,364
33,250	**33,300**	4,556	4,121	4,556	4,371
33,300	**33,350**	4,564	4,129	4,564	4,379
33,350	**33,400**	4,571	4,136	4,571	4,386
33,400	**33,450**	4,579	4,144	4,579	4,394
33,450	**33,500**	4,586	4,151	4,586	4,401
33,500	**33,550**	4,594	4,159	4,594	4,409
33,550	**33,600**	4,601	4,166	4,601	4,416
33,600	**33,650**	4,609	4,174	4,609	4,424
33,650	**33,700**	4,616	4,181	4,616	4,431
33,700	**33,750**	4,624	4,189	4,624	4,439
33,750	**33,800**	4,631	4,196	4,631	4,446
33,800	**33,850**	4,639	4,204	4,639	4,454
33,850	**33,900**	4,646	4,211	4,646	4,461
33,900	**33,950**	4,654	4,219	4,654	4,469
33,950	**34,000**	4,661	4,226	4,661	4,476
34,000					
34,000	**34,050**	4,669	4,234	4,669	4,484
34,050	**34,100**	4,676	4,241	4,676	4,491
34,100	**34,150**	4,684	4,249	4,684	4,499
34,150	**34,200**	4,691	4,256	4,691	4,506
34,200	**34,250**	4,699	4,264	4,699	4,514
34,250	**34,300**	4,706	4,271	4,706	4,521
34,300	**34,350**	4,714	4,279	4,714	4,529
34,350	**34,400**	4,721	4,286	4,721	4,536
34,400	**34,450**	4,729	4,294	4,729	4,544
34,450	**34,500**	4,736	4,301	4,736	4,551
34,500	**34,550**	4,744	4,309	4,744	4,559
34,550	**34,600**	4,751	4,316	4,751	4,566
34,600	**34,650**	4,759	4,324	4,759	4,574
34,650	**34,700**	4,766	4,331	4,766	4,581
34,700	**34,750**	4,774	4,339	4,774	4,589
34,750	**34,800**	4,781	4,346	4,781	4,596
34,800	**34,850**	4,789	4,354	4,789	4,604
34,850	**34,900**	4,796	4,361	4,796	4,611
34,900	**34,950**	4,804	4,369	4,804	4,619
34,950	**35,000**	4,811	4,376	4,811	4,626
35,000					
35,000	**35,050**	4,819	4,384	4,819	4,634
35,050	**35,100**	4,826	4,391	4,826	4,641
35,100	**35,150**	4,834	4,399	4,834	4,649
35,150	**35,200**	4,841	4,406	4,841	4,656
35,200	**35,250**	4,849	4,414	4,849	4,664
35,250	**35,300**	4,856	4,421	4,856	4,671
35,300	**35,350**	4,864	4,429	4,864	4,679
35,350	**35,400**	4,874	4,436	4,874	4,686
35,400	**35,450**	4,886	4,444	4,886	4,694
35,450	**35,500**	4,899	4,451	4,899	4,701
35,500	**35,550**	4,911	4,459	4,911	4,709
35,550	**35,600**	4,924	4,466	4,924	4,716
35,600	**35,650**	4,936	4,474	4,936	4,724
35,650	**35,700**	4,949	4,481	4,949	4,731
35,700	**35,750**	4,961	4,489	4,961	4,739
35,750	**35,800**	4,974	4,496	4,974	4,746
35,800	**35,850**	4,986	4,504	4,986	4,754
35,850	**35,900**	4,999	4,511	4,999	4,761
35,900	**35,950**	5,011	4,519	5,011	4,769
35,950	**36,000**	5,024	4,526	5,024	4,776
36,000					
36,000	**36,050**	5,036	4,534	5,036	4,784
36,050	**36,100**	5,049	4,541	5,049	4,791
36,100	**36,150**	5,061	4,549	5,061	4,799
36,150	**36,200**	5,074	4,556	5,074	4,806
36,200	**36,250**	5,086	4,564	5,086	4,814
36,250	**36,300**	5,099	4,571	5,099	4,821
36,300	**36,350**	5,111	4,579	5,111	4,829
36,350	**36,400**	5,124	4,586	5,124	4,836
36,400	**36,450**	5,136	4,594	5,136	4,844
36,450	**36,500**	5,149	4,601	5,149	4,851
36,500	**36,550**	5,161	4,609	5,161	4,859
36,550	**36,600**	5,174	4,616	5,174	4,866
36,600	**36,650**	5,186	4,624	5,186	4,874
36,650	**36,700**	5,199	4,631	5,199	4,881
36,700	**36,750**	5,211	4,639	5,211	4,889
36,750	**36,800**	5,224	4,646	5,224	4,896
36,800	**36,850**	5,236	4,654	5,236	4,904
36,850	**36,900**	5,249	4,661	5,249	4,911
36,900	**36,950**	5,261	4,669	5,261	4,919
36,950	**37,000**	5,274	4,676	5,274	4,926
37,000					
37,000	**37,050**	5,286	4,684	5,286	4,934
37,050	**37,100**	5,299	4,691	5,299	4,941
37,100	**37,150**	5,311	4,699	5,311	4,949
37,150	**37,200**	5,324	4,706	5,324	4,956
37,200	**37,250**	5,336	4,714	5,336	4,964
37,250	**37,300**	5,349	4,721	5,349	4,971
37,300	**37,350**	5,361	4,729	5,361	4,979
37,350	**37,400**	5,374	4,736	5,374	4,986
37,400	**37,450**	5,386	4,744	5,386	4,994
37,450	**37,500**	5,399	4,751	5,399	5,001
37,500	**37,550**	5,411	4,759	5,411	5,009
37,550	**37,600**	5,424	4,766	5,424	5,016
37,600	**37,650**	5,436	4,774	5,436	5,024
37,650	**37,700**	5,449	4,781	5,449	5,031
37,700	**37,750**	5,461	4,789	5,461	5,039
37,750	**37,800**	5,474	4,796	5,474	5,046
37,800	**37,850**	5,486	4,804	5,486	5,054
37,850	**37,900**	5,499	4,811	5,499	5,061
37,900	**37,950**	5,511	4,819	5,511	5,069
37,950	**38,000**	5,524	4,826	5,524	5,076
38,000					
38,000	**38,050**	5,536	4,834	5,536	5,084
38,050	**38,100**	5,549	4,841	5,549	5,091
38,100	**38,150**	5,561	4,849	5,561	5,099
38,150	**38,200**	5,574	4,856	5,574	5,106
38,200	**38,250**	5,586	4,864	5,586	5,114
38,250	**38,300**	5,599	4,871	5,599	5,121
38,300	**38,350**	5,611	4,879	5,611	5,129
38,350	**38,400**	5,624	4,886	5,624	5,136
38,400	**38,450**	5,636	4,894	5,636	5,144
38,450	**38,500**	5,649	4,901	5,649	5,151
38,500	**38,550**	5,661	4,909	5,661	5,159
38,550	**38,600**	5,674	4,916	5,674	5,166
38,600	**38,650**	5,686	4,924	5,686	5,174
38,650	**38,700**	5,699	4,931	5,699	5,181
38,700	**38,750**	5,711	4,939	5,711	5,189
38,750	**38,800**	5,724	4,946	5,724	5,196
38,800	**38,850**	5,736	4,954	5,736	5,204
38,850	**38,900**	5,749	4,961	5,749	5,211
38,900	**38,950**	5,761	4,969	5,761	5,219
38,950	**39,000**	5,774	4,976	5,774	5,226

(Continued)

*This column must also be used by a qualifying widow(er).

Need more information or forms? Visit IRS.gov.

Caution: This is a draft 2012 Tax Table. At the time of publication, the IRS had not yet released the 2012 Tax Table. For the latest information, see CCHGroup.com/TaxUpdates.

2012 Tax Table—*Continued*

If line 43 (taxable income) is— At least	But less than	Single	Married filing jointly *	Married filing sepa-rately	Head of a house-hold
		Your tax is—			
39,000					
39,000	39,050	5,786	4,984	5,786	5,234
39,050	39,100	5,799	4,991	5,799	5,241
39,100	39,150	5,811	4,999	5,811	5,249
39,150	39,200	5,824	5,006	5,824	5,256
39,200	39,250	5,836	5,014	5,836	5,264
39,250	39,300	5,849	5,021	5,849	5,271
39,300	39,350	5,861	5,029	5,861	5,279
39,350	39,400	5,874	5,036	5,874	5,286
39,400	39,450	5,886	5,044	5,886	5,294
39,450	39,500	5,899	5,051	5,899	5,301
39,500	39,550	5,911	5,059	5,911	5,309
39,550	39,600	5,924	5,066	5,924	5,316
39,600	39,650	5,936	5,074	5,936	5,324
39,650	39,700	5,949	5,081	5,949	5,331
39,700	39,750	5,961	5,089	5,961	5,339
39,750	39,800	5,974	5,096	5,974	5,346
39,800	39,850	5,986	5,104	5,986	5,354
39,850	39,900	5,999	5,111	5,999	5,361
39,900	39,950	6,011	5,119	6,011	5,369
39,950	40,000	6,024	5,126	6,024	5,376
40,000					
40,000	40,050	6,036	5,134	6,036	5,384
40,050	40,100	6,049	5,141	6,049	5,391
40,100	40,150	6,061	5,149	6,061	5,399
40,150	40,200	6,074	5,156	6,074	5,406
40,200	40,250	6,086	5,164	6,086	5,414
40,250	40,300	6,099	5,171	6,099	5,421
40,300	40,350	6,111	5,179	6,111	5,429
40,350	40,400	6,124	5,186	6,124	5,436
40,400	40,450	6,136	5,194	6,136	5,444
40,450	40,500	6,149	5,201	6,149	5,451
40,500	40,550	6,161	5,209	6,161	5,459
40,550	40,600	6,174	5,216	6,174	5,466
40,600	40,650	6,186	5,224	6,186	5,474
40,650	40,700	6,199	5,231	6,199	5,481
40,700	40,750	6,211	5,239	6,211	5,489
40,750	40,800	6,224	5,246	6,224	5,496
40,800	40,850	6,236	5,254	6,236	5,504
40,850	40,900	6,249	5,261	6,249	5,511
40,900	40,950	6,261	5,269	6,261	5,519
40,950	41,000	6,274	5,276	6,274	5,526

If line 43 (taxable income) is— At least	But less than	Single	Married filing jointly *	Married filing sepa-rately	Head of a house-hold
		Your tax is—			
41,000					
41,000	41,050	6,286	5,284	6,286	5,534
41,050	41,100	6,299	5,291	6,299	5,541
41,100	41,150	6,311	5,299	6,311	5,549
41,150	41,200	6,324	5,306	6,324	5,556
41,200	41,250	6,336	5,314	6,336	5,564
41,250	41,300	6,349	5,321	6,349	5,571
41,300	41,350	6,361	5,329	6,361	5,579
41,350	41,400	6,374	5,336	6,374	5,586
41,400	41,450	6,386	5,344	6,386	5,594
41,450	41,500	6,399	5,351	6,399	5,601
41,500	41,550	6,411	5,359	6,411	5,609
41,550	41,600	6,424	5,366	6,424	5,616
41,600	41,650	6,436	5,374	6,436	5,624
41,650	41,700	6,449	5,381	6,449	5,631
41,700	41,750	6,461	5,389	6,461	5,639
41,750	41,800	6,474	5,396	6,474	5,646
41,800	41,850	6,486	5,404	6,486	5,654
41,850	41,900	6,499	5,411	6,499	5,661
41,900	41,950	6,511	5,419	6,511	5,669
41,950	42,000	6,524	5,426	6,524	5,676
42,000					
42,000	42,050	6,536	5,434	6,536	5,684
42,050	42,100	6,549	5,441	6,549	5,691
42,100	42,150	6,561	5,449	6,561	5,699
42,150	42,200	6,574	5,456	6,574	5,706
42,200	42,250	6,586	5,464	6,586	5,714
42,250	42,300	6,599	5,471	6,599	5,721
42,300	42,350	6,611	5,479	6,611	5,729
42,350	42,400	6,624	5,486	6,624	5,736
42,400	42,450	6,636	5,494	6,636	5,744
42,450	42,500	6,649	5,501	6,649	5,751
42,500	42,550	6,661	5,509	6,661	5,759
42,550	42,600	6,674	5,516	6,674	5,766
42,600	42,650	6,686	5,524	6,686	5,774
42,650	42,700	6,699	5,531	6,699	5,781
42,700	42,750	6,711	5,539	6,711	5,789
42,750	42,800	6,724	5,546	6,724	5,796
42,800	42,850	6,736	5,554	6,736	5,804
42,850	42,900	6,749	5,561	6,749	5,811
42,900	42,950	6,761	5,569	6,761	5,819
42,950	43,000	6,774	5,576	6,774	5,826

If line 43 (taxable income) is— At least	But less than	Single	Married filing jointly *	Married filing sepa-rately	Head of a house-hold
		Your tax is—			
43,000					
43,000	43,050	6,786	5,584	6,786	5,834
43,050	43,100	6,799	5,591	6,799	5,841
43,100	43,150	6,811	5,599	6,811	5,849
43,150	43,200	6,824	5,606	6,824	5,856
43,200	43,250	6,836	5,614	6,836	5,864
43,250	43,300	6,849	5,621	6,849	5,871
43,300	43,350	6,861	5,629	6,861	5,879
43,350	43,400	6,874	5,636	6,874	5,886
43,400	43,450	6,886	5,644	6,886	5,894
43,450	43,500	6,899	5,651	6,899	5,901
43,500	43,550	6,911	5,659	6,911	5,909
43,550	43,600	6,924	5,666	6,924	5,916
43,600	43,650	6,936	5,674	6,936	5,924
43,650	43,700	6,949	5,681	6,949	5,931
43,700	43,750	6,961	5,689	6,961	5,939
43,750	43,800	6,974	5,696	6,974	5,946
43,800	43,850	6,986	5,704	6,986	5,954
43,850	43,900	6,999	5,711	6,999	5,961
43,900	43,950	7,011	5,719	7,011	5,969
43,950	44,000	7,024	5,726	7,024	5,976
44,000					
44,000	44,050	7,036	5,734	7,036	5,984
44,050	44,100	7,049	5,741	7,049	5,991
44,100	44,150	7,061	5,749	7,061	5,999
44,150	44,200	7,074	5,756	7,074	6,006
44,200	44,250	7,086	5,764	7,086	6,014
44,250	44,300	7,099	5,771	7,099	6,021
44,300	44,350	7,111	5,779	7,111	6,029
44,350	44,400	7,124	5,786	7,124	6,036
44,400	44,450	7,136	5,794	7,136	6,044
44,450	44,500	7,149	5,801	7,149	6,051
44,500	44,550	7,161	5,809	7,161	6,059
44,550	44,600	7,174	5,816	7,174	6,066
44,600	44,650	7,186	5,824	7,186	6,074
44,650	44,700	7,199	5,831	7,199	6,081
44,700	44,750	7,211	5,839	7,211	6,089
44,750	44,800	7,224	5,846	7,224	6,096
44,800	44,850	7,236	5,854	7,236	6,104
44,850	44,900	7,249	5,861	7,249	6,111
44,900	44,950	7,261	5,869	7,261	6,119
44,950	45,000	7,274	5,876	7,274	6,126

(Continued)

*This column must also be used by a qualifying widow(er).

»»→ Caution: This is a draft 2012 Tax Table. At the time of publication, the IRS had not yet released the 2012 Tax Table. For the latest information, see CCHGroup.com/TaxUpdates.

2012 Tax Table—*Continued*

If line 43 (taxable income) is—		And you are—			
At least	But less than	Single	Married filing jointly *	Married filing separately	Head of a household
		Your tax is—			
45,000					
45,000	45,050	7,286	5,884	7,286	6,134
45,050	45,100	7,299	5,891	7,299	6,141
45,100	45,150	7,311	5,899	7,311	6,149
45,150	45,200	7,324	5,906	7,324	6,156
45,200	45,250	7,336	5,914	7,336	6,164
45,250	45,300	7,349	5,921	7,349	6,171
45,300	45,350	7,361	5,929	7,361	6,179
45,350	45,400	7,374	5,936	7,374	6,186
45,400	45,450	7,386	5,944	7,386	6,194
45,450	45,500	7,399	5,951	7,399	6,201
45,500	45,550	7,411	5,959	7,411	6,209
45,550	45,600	7,424	5,966	7,424	6,216
45,600	45,650	7,436	5,974	7,436	6,224
45,650	45,700	7,449	5,981	7,449	6,231
45,700	45,750	7,461	5,989	7,461	6,239
45,750	45,800	7,474	5,996	7,474	6,246
45,800	45,850	7,486	6,004	7,486	6,254
45,850	45,900	7,499	6,011	7,499	6,261
45,900	45,950	7,511	6,019	7,511	6,269
45,950	46,000	7,524	6,026	7,524	6,276
46,000					
46,000	46,050	7,536	6,034	7,536	6,284
46,050	46,100	7,549	6,041	7,549	6,291
46,100	46,150	7,561	6,049	7,561	6,299
46,150	46,200	7,574	6,056	7,574	6,306
46,200	46,250	7,586	6,064	7,586	6,314
46,250	46,300	7,599	6,071	7,599	6,321
46,300	46,350	7,611	6,079	7,611	6,329
46,350	46,400	7,624	6,086	7,624	6,336
46,400	46,450	7,636	6,094	7,636	6,344
46,450	46,500	7,649	6,101	7,649	6,351
46,500	46,550	7,661	6,109	7,661	6,359
46,550	46,600	7,674	6,116	7,674	6,366
46,600	46,650	7,686	6,124	7,686	6,374
46,650	46,700	7,699	6,131	7,699	6,381
46,700	46,750	7,711	6,139	7,711	6,389
46,750	46,800	7,724	6,146	7,724	6,396
46,800	46,850	7,736	6,154	7,736	6,404
46,850	46,900	7,749	6,161	7,749	6,411
46,900	46,950	7,761	6,169	7,761	6,419
46,950	47,000	7,774	6,176	7,774	6,426

If line 43 (taxable income) is—		And you are—			
At least	But less than	Single	Married filing jointly *	Married filing separately	Head of a household
		Your tax is—			
47,000					
47,000	47,050	7,786	6,184	7,786	6,434
47,050	47,100	7,799	6,191	7,799	6,441
47,100	47,150	7,811	6,199	7,811	6,449
47,150	47,200	7,824	6,206	7,824	6,456
47,200	47,250	7,836	6,214	7,836	6,464
47,250	47,300	7,849	6,221	7,849	6,471
47,300	47,350	7,861	6,229	7,861	6,479
47,350	47,400	7,874	6,236	7,874	6,489
47,400	47,450	7,886	6,244	7,886	6,501
47,450	47,500	7,899	6,251	7,899	6,514
47,500	47,550	7,911	6,259	7,911	6,526
47,550	47,600	7,924	6,266	7,924	6,539
47,600	47,650	7,936	6,274	7,936	6,551
47,650	47,700	7,949	6,281	7,949	6,564
47,700	47,750	7,961	6,289	7,961	6,576
47,750	47,800	7,974	6,296	7,974	6,589
47,800	47,850	7,986	6,304	7,986	6,601
47,850	47,900	7,999	6,311	7,999	6,614
47,900	47,950	8,011	6,319	8,011	6,626
47,950	48,000	8,024	6,326	8,024	6,639
48,000					
48,000	48,050	8,036	6,334	8,036	6,651
48,050	48,100	8,049	6,341	8,049	6,664
48,100	48,150	8,061	6,349	8,061	6,676
48,150	48,200	8,074	6,356	8,074	6,689
48,200	48,250	8,086	6,364	8,086	6,701
48,250	48,300	8,099	6,371	8,099	6,714
48,300	48,350	8,111	6,379	8,111	6,726
48,350	48,400	8,124	6,386	8,124	6,739
48,400	48,450	8,136	6,394	8,136	6,751
48,450	48,500	8,149	6,401	8,149	6,764
48,500	48,550	8,161	6,409	8,161	6,776
48,550	48,600	8,174	6,416	8,174	6,789
48,600	48,650	8,186	6,424	8,186	6,801
48,650	48,700	8,199	6,431	8,199	6,814
48,700	48,750	8,211	6,439	8,211	6,826
48,750	48,800	8,224	6,446	8,224	6,839
48,800	48,850	8,236	6,454	8,236	6,851
48,850	48,900	8,249	6,461	8,249	6,864
48,900	48,950	8,261	6,469	8,261	6,876
48,950	49,000	8,274	6,476	8,274	6,889

If line 43 (taxable income) is—		And you are—			
At least	But less than	Single	Married filing jointly *	Married filing separately	Head of a household
		Your tax is—			
49,000					
49,000	49,050	8,286	6,484	8,286	6,901
49,050	49,100	8,299	6,491	8,299	6,914
49,100	49,150	8,311	6,499	8,311	6,926
49,150	49,200	8,324	6,506	8,324	6,939
49,200	49,250	8,336	6,514	8,336	6,951
49,250	49,300	8,349	6,521	8,349	6,964
49,300	49,350	8,361	6,529	8,361	6,976
49,350	49,400	8,374	6,536	8,374	6,989
49,400	49,450	8,386	6,544	8,386	7,001
49,450	49,500	8,399	6,551	8,399	7,014
49,500	49,550	8,411	6,559	8,411	7,026
49,550	49,600	8,424	6,566	8,424	7,039
49,600	49,650	8,436	6,574	8,436	7,051
49,650	49,700	8,449	6,581	8,449	7,064
49,700	49,750	8,461	6,589	8,461	7,076
49,750	49,800	8,474	6,596	8,474	7,089
49,800	49,850	8,486	6,604	8,486	7,101
49,850	49,900	8,499	6,611	8,499	7,114
49,900	49,950	8,511	6,619	8,511	7,126
49,950	50,000	8,524	6,626	8,524	7,139
50,000					
50,000	50,050	8,536	6,634	8,536	7,151
50,050	50,100	8,549	6,641	8,549	7,164
50,100	50,150	8,561	6,649	8,561	7,176
50,150	50,200	8,574	6,656	8,574	7,189
50,200	50,250	8,586	6,664	8,586	7,201
50,250	50,300	8,599	6,671	8,599	7,214
50,300	50,350	8,611	6,679	8,611	7,226
50,350	50,400	8,624	6,686	8,624	7,239
50,400	50,450	8,636	6,694	8,636	7,251
50,450	50,500	8,649	6,701	8,649	7,264
50,500	50,550	8,661	6,709	8,661	7,276
50,550	50,600	8,674	6,716	8,674	7,289
50,600	50,650	8,686	6,724	8,686	7,301
50,650	50,700	8,699	6,731	8,699	7,314
50,700	50,750	8,711	6,739	8,711	7,326
50,750	50,800	8,724	6,746	8,724	7,339
50,800	50,850	8,736	6,754	8,736	7,351
50,850	50,900	8,749	6,761	8,749	7,364
50,900	50,950	8,761	6,769	8,761	7,376
50,950	51,000	8,774	6,776	8,774	7,389

(Continued)

*This column must also be used by a qualifying widow(er).

Need more information or forms? Visit IRS.gov.

Caution: This is a draft 2012 Tax Table. At the time of publication, the IRS had not yet released the 2012 Tax Table. For the latest information, see CCHGroup.com/TaxUpdates.

2012 Tax Table—*Continued*

If line 43 (taxable income) is—		And you are—			
At least	But less than	Single	Married filing jointly *	Married filing separately	Head of a household
		Your tax is—			
51,000					
51,000	**51,050**	8,786	6,784	8,786	7,401
51,050	**51,100**	8,799	6,791	8,799	7,414
51,100	**51,150**	8,811	6,799	8,811	7,426
51,150	**51,200**	8,824	6,806	8,824	7,439
51,200	**51,250**	8,836	6,814	8,836	7,451
51,250	**51,300**	8,849	6,821	8,849	7,464
51,300	**51,350**	8,861	6,829	8,861	7,476
51,350	**51,400**	8,874	6,836	8,874	7,489
51,400	**51,450**	8,886	6,844	8,886	7,501
51,450	**51,500**	8,899	6,851	8,899	7,514
51,500	**51,550**	8,911	6,859	8,911	7,526
51,550	**51,600**	8,924	6,866	8,924	7,539
51,600	**51,650**	8,936	6,874	8,936	7,551
51,650	**51,700**	8,949	6,881	8,949	7,564
51,700	**51,750**	8,961	6,889	8,961	7,576
51,750	**51,800**	8,974	6,896	8,974	7,589
51,800	**51,850**	8,986	6,904	8,986	7,601
51,850	**51,900**	8,999	6,911	8,999	7,614
51,900	**51,950**	9,011	6,919	9,011	7,626
51,950	**52,000**	9,024	6,926	9,024	7,639
52,000					
52,000	**52,050**	9,036	6,934	9,036	7,651
52,050	**52,100**	9,049	6,941	9,049	7,664
52,100	**52,150**	9,061	6,949	9,061	7,676
52,150	**52,200**	9,074	6,956	9,074	7,689
52,200	**52,250**	9,086	6,964	9,086	7,701
52,250	**52,300**	9,099	6,971	9,099	7,714
52,300	**52,350**	9,111	6,979	9,111	7,726
52,350	**52,400**	9,124	6,986	9,124	7,739
52,400	**52,450**	9,136	6,994	9,136	7,751
52,450	**52,500**	9,149	7,001	9,149	7,764
52,500	**52,550**	9,161	7,009	9,161	7,776
52,550	**52,600**	9,174	7,016	9,174	7,789
52,600	**52,650**	9,186	7,024	9,186	7,801
52,650	**52,700**	9,199	7,031	9,199	7,814
52,700	**52,750**	9,211	7,039	9,211	7,826
52,750	**52,800**	9,224	7,046	9,224	7,839
52,800	**52,850**	9,236	7,054	9,236	7,851
52,850	**52,900**	9,249	7,061	9,249	7,864
52,900	**52,950**	9,261	7,069	9,261	7,876
52,950	**53,000**	9,274	7,076	9,274	7,889

If line 43 (taxable income) is—		And you are—			
At least	But less than	Single	Married filing jointly *	Married filing separately	Head of a household
		Your tax is—			
53,000					
53,000	**53,050**	9,286	7,084	9,286	7,901
53,050	**53,100**	9,299	7,091	9,299	7,914
53,100	**53,150**	9,311	7,099	9,311	7,926
53,150	**53,200**	9,324	7,106	9,324	7,939
53,200	**53,250**	9,336	7,114	9,336	7,951
53,250	**53,300**	9,349	7,121	9,349	7,964
53,300	**53,350**	9,361	7,129	9,361	7,976
53,350	**53,400**	9,374	7,136	9,374	7,989
53,400	**53,450**	9,386	7,144	9,386	8,001
53,450	**53,500**	9,399	7,151	9,399	8,014
53,500	**53,550**	9,411	7,159	9,411	8,026
53,550	**53,600**	9,424	7,166	9,424	8,039
53,600	**53,650**	9,436	7,174	9,436	8,051
53,650	**53,700**	9,449	7,181	9,449	8,064
53,700	**53,750**	9,461	7,189	9,461	8,076
53,750	**53,800**	9,474	7,196	9,474	8,089
53,800	**53,850**	9,486	7,204	9,486	8,101
53,850	**53,900**	9,499	7,211	9,499	8,114
53,900	**53,950**	9,511	7,219	9,511	8,126
53,950	**54,000**	9,524	7,226	9,524	8,139
54,000					
54,000	**54,050**	9,536	7,234	9,536	8,151
54,050	**54,100**	9,549	7,241	9,549	8,164
54,100	**54,150**	9,561	7,249	9,561	8,176
54,150	**54,200**	9,574	7,256	9,574	8,189
54,200	**54,250**	9,586	7,264	9,586	8,201
54,250	**54,300**	9,599	7,271	9,599	8,214
54,300	**54,350**	9,611	7,279	9,611	8,226
54,350	**54,400**	9,624	7,286	9,624	8,239
54,400	**54,450**	9,636	7,294	9,636	8,251
54,450	**54,500**	9,649	7,301	9,649	8,264
54,500	**54,550**	9,661	7,309	9,661	8,276
54,550	**54,600**	9,674	7,316	9,674	8,289
54,600	**54,650**	9,686	7,324	9,686	8,301
54,650	**54,700**	9,699	7,331	9,699	8,314
54,700	**54,750**	9,711	7,339	9,711	8,326
54,750	**54,800**	9,724	7,346	9,724	8,339
54,800	**54,850**	9,736	7,354	9,736	8,351
54,850	**54,900**	9,749	7,361	9,749	8,364
54,900	**54,950**	9,761	7,369	9,761	8,376
54,950	**55,000**	9,774	7,376	9,774	8,389

If line 43 (taxable income) is—		And you are—			
At least	But less than	Single	Married filing jointly *	Married filing separately	Head of a household
		Your tax is—			
55,000					
55,000	**55,050**	9,786	7,384	9,786	8,401
55,050	**55,100**	9,799	7,391	9,799	8,414
55,100	**55,150**	9,811	7,399	9,811	8,426
55,150	**55,200**	9,824	7,406	9,824	8,439
55,200	**55,250**	9,836	7,414	9,836	8,451
55,250	**55,300**	9,849	7,421	9,849	8,464
55,300	**55,350**	9,861	7,429	9,861	8,476
55,350	**55,400**	9,874	7,436	9,874	8,489
55,400	**55,450**	9,886	7,444	9,886	8,501
55,450	**55,500**	9,899	7,451	9,899	8,514
55,500	**55,550**	9,911	7,459	9,911	8,526
55,550	**55,600**	9,924	7,466	9,924	8,539
55,600	**55,650**	9,936	7,474	9,936	8,551
55,650	**55,700**	9,949	7,481	9,949	8,564
55,700	**55,750**	9,961	7,489	9,961	8,576
55,750	**55,800**	9,974	7,496	9,974	8,589
55,800	**55,850**	9,986	7,504	9,986	8,601
55,850	**55,900**	9,999	7,511	9,999	8,614
55,900	**55,950**	10,011	7,519	10,011	8,626
55,950	**56,000**	10,024	7,526	10,024	8,639
56,000					
56,000	**56,050**	10,036	7,534	10,036	8,651
56,050	**56,100**	10,049	7,541	10,049	8,664
56,100	**56,150**	10,061	7,549	10,061	8,676
56,150	**56,200**	10,074	7,556	10,074	8,689
56,200	**56,250**	10,086	7,564	10,086	8,701
56,250	**56,300**	10,099	7,571	10,099	8,714
56,300	**56,350**	10,111	7,579	10,111	8,726
56,350	**56,400**	10,124	7,586	10,124	8,739
56,400	**56,450**	10,136	7,594	10,136	8,751
56,450	**56,500**	10,149	7,601	10,149	8,764
56,500	**56,550**	10,161	7,609	10,161	8,776
56,550	**56,600**	10,174	7,616	10,174	8,789
56,600	**56,650**	10,186	7,624	10,186	8,801
56,650	**56,700**	10,199	7,631	10,199	8,814
56,700	**56,750**	10,211	7,639	10,211	8,826
56,750	**56,800**	10,224	7,646	10,224	8,839
56,800	**56,850**	10,236	7,654	10,236	8,851
56,850	**56,900**	10,249	7,661	10,249	8,864
56,900	**56,950**	10,261	7,669	10,261	8,876
56,950	**57,000**	10,274	7,676	10,274	8,889

(Continued)

*This column must also be used by a qualifying widow(er).

Caution: This is a draft 2012 Tax Table. At the time of publication, the IRS had not yet released the 2012 Tax Table. For the latest information, see CCHGroup.com/TaxUpdates.

2012 Tax Table—*Continued*

If line 43 (taxable income) is— At least	But less than	And you are— Single	Married filing jointly *	Married filing separately	Head of a household
		Your tax is—			
57,000					
57,000	**57,050**	10,286	7,684	10,286	8,901
57,050	**57,100**	10,299	7,691	10,299	8,914
57,100	**57,150**	10,311	7,699	10,311	8,926
57,150	**57,200**	10,324	7,706	10,324	8,939
57,200	**57,250**	10,336	7,714	10,336	8,951
57,250	**57,300**	10,349	7,721	10,349	8,964
57,300	**57,350**	10,361	7,729	10,361	8,976
57,350	**57,400**	10,374	7,736	10,374	8,989
57,400	**57,450**	10,386	7,744	10,386	9,001
57,450	**57,500**	10,399	7,751	10,399	9,014
57,500	**57,550**	10,411	7,759	10,411	9,026
57,550	**57,600**	10,424	7,766	10,424	9,039
57,600	**57,650**	10,436	7,774	10,436	9,051
57,650	**57,700**	10,449	7,781	10,449	9,064
57,700	**57,750**	10,461	7,789	10,461	9,076
57,750	**57,800**	10,474	7,796	10,474	9,089
57,800	**57,850**	10,486	7,804	10,486	9,101
57,850	**57,900**	10,499	7,811	10,499	9,114
57,900	**57,950**	10,511	7,819	10,511	9,126
57,950	**58,000**	10,524	7,826	10,524	9,139
58,000					
58,000	**58,050**	10,536	7,834	10,536	9,151
58,050	**58,100**	10,549	7,841	10,549	9,164
58,100	**58,150**	10,561	7,849	10,561	9,176
58,150	**58,200**	10,574	7,856	10,574	9,189
58,200	**58,250**	10,586	7,864	10,586	9,201
58,250	**58,300**	10,599	7,871	10,599	9,214
58,300	**58,350**	10,611	7,879	10,611	9,226
58,350	**58,400**	10,624	7,886	10,624	9,239
58,400	**58,450**	10,636	7,894	10,636	9,251
58,450	**58,500**	10,649	7,901	10,649	9,264
58,500	**58,550**	10,661	7,909	10,661	9,276
58,550	**58,600**	10,674	7,916	10,674	9,289
58,600	**58,650**	10,686	7,924	10,686	9,301
58,650	**58,700**	10,699	7,931	10,699	9,314
58,700	**58,750**	10,711	7,939	10,711	9,326
58,750	**58,800**	10,724	7,946	10,724	9,339
58,800	**58,850**	10,736	7,954	10,736	9,351
58,850	**58,900**	10,749	7,961	10,749	9,364
58,900	**58,950**	10,761	7,969	10,761	9,376
58,950	**59,000**	10,774	7,976	10,774	9,389

If line 43 (taxable income) is— At least	But less than	And you are— Single	Married filing jointly *	Married filing separately	Head of a household
		Your tax is—			
59,000					
59,000	**59,050**	10,786	7,984	10,786	9,401
59,050	**59,100**	10,799	7,991	10,799	9,414
59,100	**59,150**	10,811	7,999	10,811	9,426
59,150	**59,200**	10,824	8,006	10,824	9,439
59,200	**59,250**	10,836	8,014	10,836	9,451
59,250	**59,300**	10,849	8,021	10,849	9,464
59,300	**59,350**	10,861	8,029	10,861	9,476
59,350	**59,400**	10,874	8,036	10,874	9,489
59,400	**59,450**	10,886	8,044	10,886	9,501
59,450	**59,500**	10,899	8,051	10,899	9,514
59,500	**59,550**	10,911	8,059	10,911	9,526
59,550	**59,600**	10,924	8,066	10,924	9,539
59,600	**59,650**	10,936	8,074	10,936	9,551
59,650	**59,700**	10,949	8,081	10,949	9,564
59,700	**59,750**	10,961	8,089	10,961	9,576
59,750	**59,800**	10,974	8,096	10,974	9,589
59,800	**59,850**	10,986	8,104	10,986	9,601
59,850	**59,900**	10,999	8,111	10,999	9,614
59,900	**59,950**	11,011	8,119	11,011	9,626
59,950	**60,000**	11,024	8,126	11,024	9,639
60,000					
60,000	**60,050**	11,036	8,134	11,036	9,651
60,050	**60,100**	11,049	8,141	11,049	9,664
60,100	**60,150**	11,061	8,149	11,061	9,676
60,150	**60,200**	11,074	8,156	11,074	9,689
60,200	**60,250**	11,086	8,164	11,086	9,701
60,250	**60,300**	11,099	8,171	11,099	9,714
60,300	**60,350**	11,111	8,179	11,111	9,726
60,350	**60,400**	11,124	8,186	11,124	9,739
60,400	**60,450**	11,136	8,194	11,136	9,751
60,450	**60,500**	11,149	8,201	11,149	9,764
60,500	**60,550**	11,161	8,209	11,161	9,776
60,550	**60,600**	11,174	8,216	11,174	9,789
60,600	**60,650**	11,186	8,224	11,186	9,801
60,650	**60,700**	11,199	8,231	11,199	9,814
60,700	**60,750**	11,211	8,239	11,211	9,826
60,750	**60,800**	11,224	8,246	11,224	9,839
60,800	**60,850**	11,236	8,254	11,236	9,851
60,850	**60,900**	11,249	8,261	11,249	9,864
60,900	**60,950**	11,261	8,269	11,261	9,876
60,950	**61,000**	11,274	8,276	11,274	9,889

If line 43 (taxable income) is— At least	But less than	And you are— Single	Married filing jointly *	Married filing separately	Head of a household
		Your tax is—			
61,000					
61,000	**61,050**	11,286	8,284	11,286	9,901
61,050	**61,100**	11,299	8,291	11,299	9,914
61,100	**61,150**	11,311	8,299	11,311	9,926
61,150	**61,200**	11,324	8,306	11,324	9,939
61,200	**61,250**	11,336	8,314	11,336	9,951
61,250	**61,300**	11,349	8,321	11,349	9,964
61,300	**61,350**	11,361	8,329	11,361	9,976
61,350	**61,400**	11,374	8,336	11,374	9,989
61,400	**61,450**	11,386	8,344	11,386	10,001
61,450	**61,500**	11,399	8,351	11,399	10,014
61,500	**61,550**	11,411	8,359	11,411	10,026
61,550	**61,600**	11,424	8,366	11,424	10,039
61,600	**61,650**	11,436	8,374	11,436	10,051
61,650	**61,700**	11,449	8,381	11,449	10,064
61,700	**61,750**	11,461	8,389	11,461	10,076
61,750	**61,800**	11,474	8,396	11,474	10,089
61,800	**61,850**	11,486	8,404	11,486	10,101
61,850	**61,900**	11,499	8,411	11,499	10,114
61,900	**61,950**	11,511	8,419	11,511	10,126
61,950	**62,000**	11,524	8,426	11,524	10,139
62,000					
62,000	**62,050**	11,536	8,434	11,536	10,151
62,050	**62,100**	11,549	8,441	11,549	10,164
62,100	**62,150**	11,561	8,449	11,561	10,176
62,150	**62,200**	11,574	8,456	11,574	10,189
62,200	**62,250**	11,586	8,464	11,586	10,201
62,250	**62,300**	11,599	8,471	11,599	10,214
62,300	**62,350**	11,611	8,479	11,611	10,226
62,350	**62,400**	11,624	8,486	11,624	10,239
62,400	**62,450**	11,636	8,494	11,636	10,251
62,450	**62,500**	11,649	8,501	11,649	10,264
62,500	**62,550**	11,661	8,509	11,661	10,276
62,550	**62,600**	11,674	8,516	11,674	10,289
62,600	**62,650**	11,686	8,524	11,686	10,301
62,650	**62,700**	11,699	8,531	11,699	10,314
62,700	**62,750**	11,711	8,539	11,711	10,326
62,750	**62,800**	11,724	8,546	11,724	10,339
62,800	**62,850**	11,736	8,554	11,736	10,351
62,850	**62,900**	11,749	8,561	11,749	10,364
62,900	**62,950**	11,761	8,569	11,761	10,376
62,950	**63,000**	11,774	8,576	11,774	10,389

(Continued)

*This column must also be used by a qualifying widow(er).

Need more information or forms? Visit IRS.gov.

Caution: This is a draft 2012 Tax Table. At the time of publication, the IRS had not yet released the 2012 Tax Table. For the latest information, see CCHGroup.com/TaxUpdates.

2012 Tax Table—*Continued*

If line 43 (taxable income) is—		And you are—			
At least	But less than	Single	Married filing jointly *	Married filing separately	Head of a household
		Your tax is—			
63,000					
63,000	**63,050**	11,786	8,584	11,786	10,401
63,050	**63,100**	11,799	8,591	11,799	10,414
63,100	**63,150**	11,811	8,599	11,811	10,426
63,150	**63,200**	11,824	8,606	11,824	10,439
63,200	**63,250**	11,836	8,614	11,836	10,451
63,250	**63,300**	11,849	8,621	11,849	10,464
63,300	**63,350**	11,861	8,629	11,861	10,476
63,350	**63,400**	11,874	8,636	11,874	10,489
63,400	**63,450**	11,886	8,644	11,886	10,501
63,450	**63,500**	11,899	8,651	11,899	10,514
63,500	**63,550**	11,911	8,659	11,911	10,526
63,550	**63,600**	11,924	8,666	11,924	10,539
63,600	**63,650**	11,936	8,674	11,936	10,551
63,650	**63,700**	11,949	8,681	11,949	10,564
63,700	**63,750**	11,961	8,689	11,961	10,576
63,750	**63,800**	11,974	8,696	11,974	10,589
63,800	**63,850**	11,986	8,704	11,986	10,601
63,850	**63,900**	11,999	8,711	11,999	10,614
63,900	**63,950**	12,011	8,719	12,011	10,626
63,950	**64,000**	12,024	8,726	12,024	10,639
64,000					
64,000	**64,050**	12,036	8,734	12,036	10,651
64,050	**64,100**	12,049	8,741	12,049	10,664
64,100	**64,150**	12,061	8,749	12,061	10,676
64,150	**64,200**	12,074	8,756	12,074	10,689
64,200	**64,250**	12,086	8,764	12,086	10,701
64,250	**64,300**	12,099	8,771	12,099	10,714
64,300	**64,350**	12,111	8,779	12,111	10,726
64,350	**64,400**	12,124	8,786	12,124	10,739
64,400	**64,450**	12,136	8,794	12,136	10,751
64,450	**64,500**	12,149	8,801	12,149	10,764
64,500	**64,550**	12,161	8,809	12,161	10,776
64,550	**64,600**	12,174	8,816	12,174	10,789
64,600	**64,650**	12,186	8,824	12,186	10,801
64,650	**64,700**	12,199	8,831	12,199	10,814
64,700	**64,750**	12,211	8,839	12,211	10,826
64,750	**64,800**	12,224	8,846	12,224	10,839
64,800	**64,850**	12,236	8,854	12,236	10,851
64,850	**64,900**	12,249	8,861	12,249	10,864
64,900	**64,950**	12,261	8,869	12,261	10,876
64,950	**65,000**	12,274	8,876	12,274	10,889
65,000					
65,000	**65,050**	12,286	8,884	12,286	10,901
65,050	**65,100**	12,299	8,891	12,299	10,914
65,100	**65,150**	12,311	8,899	12,311	10,926
65,150	**65,200**	12,324	8,906	12,324	10,939
65,200	**65,250**	12,336	8,914	12,336	10,951
65,250	**65,300**	12,349	8,921	12,349	10,964
65,300	**65,350**	12,361	8,929	12,361	10,976
65,350	**65,400**	12,374	8,936	12,374	10,989
65,400	**65,450**	12,386	8,944	12,386	11,001
65,450	**65,500**	12,399	8,951	12,399	11,014
65,500	**65,550**	12,411	8,959	12,411	11,026
65,550	**65,600**	12,424	8,966	12,424	11,039
65,600	**65,650**	12,436	8,974	12,436	11,051
65,650	**65,700**	12,449	8,981	12,449	11,064
65,700	**65,750**	12,461	8,989	12,461	11,076
65,750	**65,800**	12,474	8,996	12,474	11,089
65,800	**65,850**	12,486	9,004	12,486	11,101
65,850	**65,900**	12,499	9,011	12,499	11,114
65,900	**65,950**	12,511	9,019	12,511	11,126
65,950	**66,000**	12,524	9,026	12,524	11,139
66,000					
66,000	**66,050**	12,536	9,034	12,536	11,151
66,050	**66,100**	12,549	9,041	12,549	11,164
66,100	**66,150**	12,561	9,049	12,561	11,176
66,150	**66,200**	12,574	9,056	12,574	11,189
66,200	**66,250**	12,586	9,064	12,586	11,201
66,250	**66,300**	12,599	9,071	12,599	11,214
66,300	**66,350**	12,611	9,079	12,611	11,226
66,350	**66,400**	12,624	9,086	12,624	11,239
66,400	**66,450**	12,636	9,094	12,636	11,251
66,450	**66,500**	12,649	9,101	12,649	11,264
66,500	**66,550**	12,661	9,109	12,661	11,276
66,550	**66,600**	12,674	9,116	12,674	11,289
66,600	**66,650**	12,686	9,124	12,686	11,301
66,650	**66,700**	12,699	9,131	12,699	11,314
66,700	**66,750**	12,711	9,139	12,711	11,326
66,750	**66,800**	12,724	9,146	12,724	11,339
66,800	**66,850**	12,736	9,154	12,736	11,351
66,850	**66,900**	12,749	9,161	12,749	11,364
66,900	**66,950**	12,761	9,169	12,761	11,376
66,950	**67,000**	12,774	9,176	12,774	11,389
67,000					
67,000	**67,050**	12,786	9,184	12,786	11,401
67,050	**67,100**	12,799	9,191	12,799	11,414
67,100	**67,150**	12,811	9,199	12,811	11,426
67,150	**67,200**	12,824	9,206	12,824	11,439
67,200	**67,250**	12,836	9,214	12,836	11,451
67,250	**67,300**	12,849	9,221	12,849	11,464
67,300	**67,350**	12,861	9,229	12,861	11,476
67,350	**67,400**	12,874	9,236	12,874	11,489
67,400	**67,450**	12,886	9,244	12,886	11,501
67,450	**67,500**	12,899	9,251	12,899	11,514
67,500	**67,550**	12,911	9,259	12,911	11,526
67,550	**67,600**	12,924	9,266	12,924	11,539
67,600	**67,650**	12,936	9,274	12,936	11,551
67,650	**67,700**	12,949	9,281	12,949	11,564
67,700	**67,750**	12,961	9,289	12,961	11,576
67,750	**67,800**	12,974	9,296	12,974	11,589
67,800	**67,850**	12,986	9,304	12,986	11,601
67,850	**67,900**	12,999	9,311	12,999	11,614
67,900	**67,950**	13,011	9,319	13,011	11,626
67,950	**68,000**	13,024	9,326	13,024	11,639
68,000					
68,000	**68,050**	13,036	9,334	13,036	11,651
68,050	**68,100**	13,049	9,341	13,049	11,664
68,100	**68,150**	13,061	9,349	13,061	11,676
68,150	**68,200**	13,074	9,356	13,074	11,689
68,200	**68,250**	13,086	9,364	13,086	11,701
68,250	**68,300**	13,099	9,371	13,099	11,714
68,300	**68,350**	13,111	9,379	13,111	11,726
68,350	**68,400**	13,124	9,386	13,124	11,739
68,400	**68,450**	13,136	9,394	13,136	11,751
68,450	**68,500**	13,149	9,401	13,149	11,764
68,500	**68,550**	13,161	9,409	13,161	11,776
68,550	**68,600**	13,174	9,416	13,174	11,789
68,600	**68,650**	13,186	9,424	13,186	11,801
68,650	**68,700**	13,199	9,431	13,199	11,814
68,700	**68,750**	13,211	9,439	13,211	11,826
68,750	**68,800**	13,224	9,446	13,224	11,839
68,800	**68,850**	13,236	9,454	13,236	11,851
68,850	**68,900**	13,249	9,461	13,249	11,864
68,900	**68,950**	13,261	9,469	13,261	11,876
68,950	**69,000**	13,274	9,476	13,274	11,889

(Continued)

TAX RATES

*This column must also be used by a qualifying widow(er).

Caution:* *This is a draft 2012 Tax Table. At the time of publication, the IRS had not yet released the 2012 Tax Table. For the latest information, see CCHGroup.com/TaxUpdates.

2012 Tax Table—*Continued*

If line 43 (taxable income) is—		And you are—			
At least	But less than	Single	Married filing jointly *	Married filing separately	Head of a household
		Your tax is—			
69,000					
69,000	**69,050**	13,286	9,484	13,286	11,901
69,050	**69,100**	13,299	9,491	13,299	11,914
69,100	**69,150**	13,311	9,499	13,311	11,926
69,150	**69,200**	13,324	9,506	13,324	11,939
69,200	**69,250**	13,336	9,514	13,336	11,951
69,250	**69,300**	13,349	9,521	13,349	11,964
69,300	**69,350**	13,361	9,529	13,361	11,976
69,350	**69,400**	13,374	9,536	13,374	11,989
69,400	**69,450**	13,386	9,544	13,386	12,001
69,450	**69,500**	13,399	9,551	13,399	12,014
69,500	**69,550**	13,411	9,559	13,411	12,026
69,550	**69,600**	13,424	9,566	13,424	12,039
69,600	**69,650**	13,436	9,574	13,436	12,051
69,650	**69,700**	13,449	9,581	13,449	12,064
69,700	**69,750**	13,461	9,589	13,461	12,076
69,750	**69,800**	13,474	9,596	13,474	12,089
69,800	**69,850**	13,486	9,604	13,486	12,101
69,850	**69,900**	13,499	9,611	13,499	12,114
69,900	**69,950**	13,511	9,619	13,511	12,126
69,950	**70,000**	13,524	9,626	13,524	12,139
70,000					
70,000	**70,050**	13,536	9,634	13,536	12,151
70,050	**70,100**	13,549	9,641	13,549	12,164
70,100	**70,150**	13,561	9,649	13,561	12,176
70,150	**70,200**	13,574	9,656	13,574	12,189
70,200	**70,250**	13,586	9,664	13,586	12,201
70,250	**70,300**	13,599	9,671	13,599	12,214
70,300	**70,350**	13,611	9,679	13,611	12,226
70,350	**70,400**	13,624	9,686	13,624	12,239
70,400	**70,450**	13,636	9,694	13,636	12,251
70,450	**70,500**	13,649	9,701	13,649	12,264
70,500	**70,550**	13,661	9,709	13,661	12,276
70,550	**70,600**	13,674	9,716	13,674	12,289
70,600	**70,650**	13,686	9,724	13,686	12,301
70,650	**70,700**	13,699	9,731	13,699	12,314
70,700	**70,750**	13,711	9,741	13,711	12,326
70,750	**70,800**	13,724	9,754	13,724	12,339
70,800	**70,850**	13,736	9,766	13,736	12,351
70,850	**70,900**	13,749	9,779	13,749	12,364
70,900	**70,950**	13,761	9,791	13,761	12,376
70,950	**71,000**	13,774	9,804	13,774	12,389
71,000					
71,000	**71,050**	13,786	9,816	13,786	12,401
71,050	**71,100**	13,799	9,829	13,799	12,414
71,100	**71,150**	13,811	9,841	13,811	12,426
71,150	**71,200**	13,824	9,854	13,824	12,439
71,200	**71,250**	13,836	9,866	13,836	12,451
71,250	**71,300**	13,849	9,879	13,849	12,464
71,300	**71,350**	13,861	9,891	13,861	12,476
71,350	**71,400**	13,874	9,904	13,875	12,489
71,400	**71,450**	13,886	9,916	13,889	12,501
71,450	**71,500**	13,899	9,929	13,903	12,514
71,500	**71,550**	13,911	9,941	13,917	12,526
71,550	**71,600**	13,924	9,954	13,931	12,539
71,600	**71,650**	13,936	9,966	13,945	12,551
71,650	**71,700**	13,949	9,979	13,959	12,564
71,700	**71,750**	13,961	9,991	13,973	12,576
71,750	**71,800**	13,974	10,004	13,987	12,589
71,800	**71,850**	13,986	10,016	14,001	12,601
71,850	**71,900**	13,999	10,029	14,015	12,614
71,900	**71,950**	14,011	10,041	14,029	12,626
71,950	**72,000**	14,024	10,054	14,043	12,639
72,000					
72,000	**72,050**	14,036	10,066	14,057	12,651
72,050	**72,100**	14,049	10,079	14,071	12,664
72,100	**72,150**	14,061	10,091	14,085	12,676
72,150	**72,200**	14,074	10,104	14,099	12,689
72,200	**72,250**	14,086	10,116	14,113	12,701
72,250	**72,300**	14,099	10,129	14,127	12,714
72,300	**72,350**	14,111	10,141	14,141	12,726
72,350	**72,400**	14,124	10,154	14,155	12,739
72,400	**72,450**	14,136	10,166	14,169	12,751
72,450	**72,500**	14,149	10,179	14,183	12,764
72,500	**72,550**	14,161	10,191	14,197	12,776
72,550	**72,600**	14,174	10,204	14,211	12,789
72,600	**72,650**	14,186	10,216	14,225	12,801
72,650	**72,700**	14,199	10,229	14,239	12,814
72,700	**72,750**	14,211	10,241	14,253	12,826
72,750	**72,800**	14,224	10,254	14,267	12,839
72,800	**72,850**	14,236	10,266	14,281	12,851
72,850	**72,900**	14,249	10,279	14,295	12,864
72,900	**72,950**	14,261	10,291	14,309	12,876
72,950	**73,000**	14,274	10,304	14,323	12,889
73,000					
73,000	**73,050**	14,286	10,316	14,337	12,901
73,050	**73,100**	14,299	10,329	14,351	12,914
73,100	**73,150**	14,311	10,341	14,365	12,926
73,150	**73,200**	14,324	10,354	14,379	12,939
73,200	**73,250**	14,336	10,366	14,393	12,951
73,250	**73,300**	14,349	10,379	14,407	12,964
73,300	**73,350**	14,361	10,391	14,421	12,976
73,350	**73,400**	14,374	10,404	14,435	12,989
73,400	**73,450**	14,386	10,416	14,449	13,001
73,450	**73,500**	14,399	10,429	14,463	13,014
73,500	**73,550**	14,411	10,441	14,477	13,026
73,550	**73,600**	14,424	10,454	14,491	13,039
73,600	**73,650**	14,436	10,466	14,505	13,051
73,650	**73,700**	14,449	10,479	14,519	13,064
73,700	**73,750**	14,461	10,491	14,533	13,076
73,750	**73,800**	14,474	10,504	14,547	13,089
73,800	**73,850**	14,486	10,516	14,561	13,101
73,850	**73,900**	14,499	10,529	14,575	13,114
73,900	**73,950**	14,511	10,541	14,589	13,126
73,950	**74,000**	14,524	10,554	14,603	13,139
74,000					
74,000	**74,050**	14,536	10,566	14,617	13,151
74,050	**74,100**	14,549	10,579	14,631	13,164
74,100	**74,150**	14,561	10,591	14,645	13,176
74,150	**74,200**	14,574	10,604	14,659	13,189
74,200	**74,250**	14,586	10,616	14,673	13,201
74,250	**74,300**	14,599	10,629	14,687	13,214
74,300	**74,350**	14,611	10,641	14,701	13,226
74,350	**74,400**	14,624	10,654	14,715	13,239
74,400	**74,450**	14,636	10,666	14,729	13,251
74,450	**74,500**	14,649	10,679	14,743	13,264
74,500	**74,550**	14,661	10,691	14,757	13,276
74,550	**74,600**	14,674	10,704	14,771	13,289
74,600	**74,650**	14,686	10,716	14,785	13,301
74,650	**74,700**	14,699	10,729	14,799	13,314
74,700	**74,750**	14,711	10,741	14,813	13,326
74,750	**74,800**	14,724	10,754	14,827	13,339
74,800	**74,850**	14,736	10,766	14,841	13,351
74,850	**74,900**	14,749	10,779	14,855	13,364
74,900	**74,950**	14,761	10,791	14,869	13,376
74,950	**75,000**	14,774	10,804	14,883	13,389

(Continued)

*This column must also be used by a qualifying widow(er).

»»→ Caution: This is a draft 2012 Tax Table. At the time of publication, the IRS had not yet released the 2012 Tax Table. For the latest information, see CCHGroup.com/TaxUpdates.

2012 Tax Table—*Continued*

If line 43 (taxable income) is—		And you are—			
At least	But less than	Single	Married filing jointly *	Married filing separately	Head of a household
		Your tax is—			
75,000					
75,000	**75,050**	14,786	10,816	14,897	13,401
75,050	**75,100**	14,799	10,829	14,911	13,414
75,100	**75,150**	14,811	10,841	14,925	13,426
75,150	**75,200**	14,824	10,854	14,939	13,439
75,200	**75,250**	14,836	10,866	14,953	13,451
75,250	**75,300**	14,849	10,879	14,967	13,464
75,300	**75,350**	14,861	10,891	14,981	13,476
75,350	**75,400**	14,874	10,904	14,995	13,489
75,400	**75,450**	14,886	10,916	15,009	13,501
75,450	**75,500**	14,899	10,929	15,023	13,514
75,500	**75,550**	14,911	10,941	15,037	13,526
75,550	**75,600**	14,924	10,954	15,051	13,539
75,600	**75,650**	14,936	10,966	15,065	13,551
75,650	**75,700**	14,949	10,979	15,079	13,564
75,700	**75,750**	14,961	10,991	15,093	13,576
75,750	**75,800**	14,974	11,004	15,107	13,589
75,800	**75,850**	14,986	11,016	15,121	13,601
75,850	**75,900**	14,999	11,029	15,135	13,614
75,900	**75,950**	15,011	11,041	15,149	13,626
75,950	**76,000**	15,024	11,054	15,163	13,639
76,000					
76,000	**76,050**	15,036	11,066	15,177	13,651
76,050	**76,100**	15,049	11,079	15,191	13,664
76,100	**76,150**	15,061	11,091	15,205	13,676
76,150	**76,200**	15,074	11,104	15,219	13,689
76,200	**76,250**	15,086	11,116	15,233	13,701
76,250	**76,300**	15,099	11,129	15,247	13,714
76,300	**76,350**	15,111	11,141	15,261	13,726
76,350	**76,400**	15,124	11,154	15,275	13,739
76,400	**76,450**	15,136	11,166	15,289	13,751
76,450	**76,500**	15,149	11,179	15,303	13,764
76,500	**76,550**	15,161	11,191	15,317	13,776
76,550	**76,600**	15,174	11,204	15,331	13,789
76,600	**76,650**	15,186	11,216	15,345	13,801
76,650	**76,700**	15,199	11,229	15,359	13,814
76,700	**76,750**	15,211	11,241	15,373	13,826
76,750	**76,800**	15,224	11,254	15,387	13,839
76,800	**76,850**	15,236	11,266	15,401	13,851
76,850	**76,900**	15,249	11,279	15,415	13,864
76,900	**76,950**	15,261	11,291	15,429	13,876
76,950	**77,000**	15,274	11,304	15,443	13,889

If line 43 (taxable income) is—		And you are—			
At least	But less than	Single	Married filing jointly *	Married filing separately	Head of a household
		Your tax is—			
77,000					
77,000	**77,050**	15,286	11,316	15,457	13,901
77,050	**77,100**	15,299	11,329	15,471	13,914
77,100	**77,150**	15,311	11,341	15,485	13,926
77,150	**77,200**	15,324	11,354	15,499	13,939
77,200	**77,250**	15,336	11,366	15,513	13,951
77,250	**77,300**	15,349	11,379	15,527	13,964
77,300	**77,350**	15,361	11,391	15,541	13,976
77,350	**77,400**	15,374	11,404	15,555	13,989
77,400	**77,450**	15,386	11,416	15,569	14,001
77,450	**77,500**	15,399	11,429	15,583	14,014
77,500	**77,550**	15,411	11,441	15,597	14,026
77,550	**77,600**	15,424	11,454	15,611	14,039
77,600	**77,650**	15,436	11,466	15,625	14,051
77,650	**77,700**	15,449	11,479	15,639	14,064
77,700	**77,750**	15,461	11,491	15,653	14,076
77,750	**77,800**	15,474	11,504	15,667	14,089
77,800	**77,850**	15,486	11,516	15,681	14,101
77,850	**77,900**	15,499	11,529	15,695	14,114
77,900	**77,950**	15,511	11,541	15,709	14,126
77,950	**78,000**	15,524	11,554	15,723	14,139
78,000					
78,000	**78,050**	15,536	11,566	15,737	14,151
78,050	**78,100**	15,549	11,579	15,751	14,164
78,100	**78,150**	15,561	11,591	15,765	14,176
78,150	**78,200**	15,574	11,604	15,779	14,189
78,200	**78,250**	15,586	11,616	15,793	14,201
78,250	**78,300**	15,599	11,629	15,807	14,214
78,300	**78,350**	15,611	11,641	15,821	14,226
78,350	**78,400**	15,624	11,654	15,835	14,239
78,400	**78,450**	15,636	11,666	15,849	14,251
78,450	**78,500**	15,649	11,679	15,863	14,264
78,500	**78,550**	15,661	11,691	15,877	14,276
78,550	**78,600**	15,674	11,704	15,891	14,289
78,600	**78,650**	15,686	11,716	15,905	14,301
78,650	**78,700**	15,699	11,729	15,919	14,314
78,700	**78,750**	15,711	11,741	15,933	14,326
78,750	**78,800**	15,724	11,754	15,947	14,339
78,800	**78,850**	15,736	11,766	15,961	14,351
78,850	**78,900**	15,749	11,779	15,975	14,364
78,900	**78,950**	15,761	11,791	15,989	14,376
78,950	**79,000**	15,774	11,804	16,003	14,389

If line 43 (taxable income) is—		And you are—			
At least	But less than	Single	Married filing jointly *	Married filing separately	Head of a household
		Your tax is—			
79,000					
79,000	**79,050**	15,786	11,816	16,017	14,401
79,050	**79,100**	15,799	11,829	16,031	14,414
79,100	**79,150**	15,811	11,841	16,045	14,426
79,150	**79,200**	15,824	11,854	16,059	14,439
79,200	**79,250**	15,836	11,866	16,073	14,451
79,250	**79,300**	15,849	11,879	16,087	14,464
79,300	**79,350**	15,861	11,891	16,101	14,476
79,350	**79,400**	15,874	11,904	16,115	14,489
79,400	**79,450**	15,886	11,916	16,129	14,501
79,450	**79,500**	15,899	11,929	16,143	14,514
79,500	**79,550**	15,911	11,941	16,157	14,526
79,550	**79,600**	15,924	11,954	16,171	14,539
79,600	**79,650**	15,936	11,966	16,185	14,551
79,650	**79,700**	15,949	11,979	16,199	14,564
79,700	**79,750**	15,961	11,991	16,213	14,576
79,750	**79,800**	15,974	12,004	16,227	14,589
79,800	**79,850**	15,986	12,016	16,241	14,601
79,850	**79,900**	15,999	12,029	16,255	14,614
79,900	**79,950**	16,011	12,041	16,269	14,626
79,950	**80,000**	16,024	12,054	16,283	14,639
80,000					
80,000	**80,050**	16,036	12,066	16,297	14,651
80,050	**80,100**	16,049	12,079	16,311	14,664
80,100	**80,150**	16,061	12,091	16,325	14,676
80,150	**80,200**	16,074	12,104	16,339	14,689
80,200	**80,250**	16,086	12,116	16,353	14,701
80,250	**80,300**	16,099	12,129	16,367	14,714
80,300	**80,350**	16,111	12,141	16,381	14,726
80,350	**80,400**	16,124	12,154	16,395	14,739
80,400	**80,450**	16,136	12,166	16,409	14,751
80,450	**80,500**	16,149	12,179	16,423	14,764
80,500	**80,550**	16,161	12,191	16,437	14,776
80,550	**80,600**	16,174	12,204	16,451	14,789
80,600	**80,650**	16,186	12,216	16,465	14,801
80,650	**80,700**	16,199	12,229	16,479	14,814
80,700	**80,750**	16,211	12,241	16,493	14,826
80,750	**80,800**	16,224	12,254	16,507	14,839
80,800	**80,850**	16,236	12,266	16,521	14,851
80,850	**80,900**	16,249	12,279	16,535	14,864
80,900	**80,950**	16,261	12,291	16,549	14,876
80,950	**81,000**	16,274	12,304	16,563	14,889

(Continued)

TAX RATES

*This column must also be used by a qualifying widow(er).

⋙→ Caution: This is a draft 2012 Tax Table. At the time of publication, the IRS had not yet released the 2012 Tax Table. For the latest information, see CCHGroup.com/TaxUpdates.

2012 Tax Table—*Continued*

If line 43 (taxable income) is— At least	But less than	And you are— Single	Married filing jointly *	Married filing separately	Head of a household
		Your tax is—			
81,000					
81,000	**81,050**	16,286	12,316	16,577	14,901
81,050	**81,100**	16,299	12,329	16,591	14,914
81,100	**81,150**	16,311	12,341	16,605	14,926
81,150	**81,200**	16,324	12,354	16,619	14,939
81,200	**81,250**	16,336	12,366	16,633	14,951
81,250	**81,300**	16,349	12,379	16,647	14,964
81,300	**81,350**	16,361	12,391	16,661	14,976
81,350	**81,400**	16,374	12,404	16,675	14,989
81,400	**81,450**	16,386	12,416	16,689	15,001
81,450	**81,500**	16,399	12,429	16,703	15,014
81,500	**81,550**	16,411	12,441	16,717	15,026
81,550	**81,600**	16,424	12,454	16,731	15,039
81,600	**81,650**	16,436	12,466	16,745	15,051
81,650	**81,700**	16,449	12,479	16,759	15,064
81,700	**81,750**	16,461	12,491	16,773	15,076
81,750	**81,800**	16,474	12,504	16,787	15,089
81,800	**81,850**	16,486	12,516	16,801	15,101
81,850	**81,900**	16,499	12,529	16,815	15,114
81,900	**81,950**	16,511	12,541	16,829	15,126
81,950	**82,000**	16,524	12,554	16,843	15,139
82,000					
82,000	**82,050**	16,536	12,566	16,857	15,151
82,050	**82,100**	16,549	12,579	16,871	15,164
82,100	**82,150**	16,561	12,591	16,885	15,176
82,150	**82,200**	16,574	12,604	16,899	15,189
82,200	**82,250**	16,586	12,616	16,913	15,201
82,250	**82,300**	16,599	12,629	16,927	15,214
82,300	**82,350**	16,611	12,641	16,941	15,226
82,350	**82,400**	16,624	12,654	16,955	15,239
82,400	**82,450**	16,636	12,666	16,969	15,251
82,450	**82,500**	16,649	12,679	16,983	15,264
82,500	**82,550**	16,661	12,691	16,997	15,276
82,550	**82,600**	16,674	12,704	17,011	15,289
82,600	**82,650**	16,686	12,716	17,025	15,301
82,650	**82,700**	16,699	12,729	17,039	15,314
82,700	**82,750**	16,711	12,741	17,053	15,326
82,750	**82,800**	16,724	12,754	17,067	15,339
82,800	**82,850**	16,736	12,766	17,081	15,351
82,850	**82,900**	16,749	12,779	17,095	15,364
82,900	**82,950**	16,761	12,791	17,109	15,376
82,950	**83,000**	16,774	12,804	17,123	15,389
83,000					
83,000	**83,050**	16,786	12,816	17,137	15,401
83,050	**83,100**	16,799	12,829	17,151	15,414
83,100	**83,150**	16,811	12,841	17,165	15,426
83,150	**83,200**	16,824	12,854	17,179	15,439
83,200	**83,250**	16,836	12,866	17,193	15,451
83,250	**83,300**	16,849	12,879	17,207	15,464
83,300	**83,350**	16,861	12,891	17,221	15,476
83,350	**83,400**	16,874	12,904	17,235	15,489
83,400	**83,450**	16,886	12,916	17,249	15,501
83,450	**83,500**	16,899	12,929	17,263	15,514
83,500	**83,550**	16,911	12,941	17,277	15,526
83,550	**83,600**	16,924	12,954	17,291	15,539
83,600	**83,650**	16,936	12,966	17,305	15,551
83,650	**83,700**	16,949	12,979	17,319	15,564
83,700	**83,750**	16,961	12,991	17,333	15,576
83,750	**83,800**	16,974	13,004	17,347	15,589
83,800	**83,850**	16,986	13,016	17,361	15,601
83,850	**83,900**	16,999	13,029	17,375	15,614
83,900	**83,950**	17,011	13,041	17,389	15,626
83,950	**84,000**	17,024	13,054	17,403	15,639
84,000					
84,000	**84,050**	17,036	13,066	17,417	15,651
84,050	**84,100**	17,049	13,079	17,431	15,664
84,100	**84,150**	17,061	13,091	17,445	15,676
84,150	**84,200**	17,074	13,104	17,459	15,689
84,200	**84,250**	17,086	13,116	17,473	15,701
84,250	**84,300**	17,099	13,129	17,487	15,714
84,300	**84,350**	17,111	13,141	17,501	15,726
84,350	**84,400**	17,124	13,154	17,515	15,739
84,400	**84,450**	17,136	13,166	17,529	15,751
84,450	**84,500**	17,149	13,179	17,543	15,764
84,500	**84,550**	17,161	13,191	17,557	15,776
84,550	**84,600**	17,174	13,204	17,571	15,789
84,600	**84,650**	17,186	13,216	17,585	15,801
84,650	**84,700**	17,199	13,229	17,599	15,814
84,700	**84,750**	17,211	13,241	17,613	15,826
84,750	**84,800**	17,224	13,254	17,627	15,839
84,800	**84,850**	17,236	13,266	17,641	15,851
84,850	**84,900**	17,249	13,279	17,655	15,864
84,900	**84,950**	17,261	13,291	17,669	15,876
84,950	**85,000**	17,274	13,304	17,683	15,889
85,000					
85,000	**85,050**	17,286	13,316	17,697	15,901
85,050	**85,100**	17,299	13,329	17,711	15,914
85,100	**85,150**	17,311	13,341	17,725	15,926
85,150	**85,200**	17,324	13,354	17,739	15,939
85,200	**85,250**	17,336	13,366	17,753	15,951
85,250	**85,300**	17,349	13,379	17,767	15,964
85,300	**85,350**	17,361	13,391	17,781	15,976
85,350	**85,400**	17,374	13,404	17,795	15,989
85,400	**85,450**	17,386	13,416	17,809	16,001
85,450	**85,500**	17,399	13,429	17,823	16,014
85,500	**85,550**	17,411	13,441	17,837	16,026
85,550	**85,600**	17,424	13,454	17,851	16,039
85,600	**85,650**	17,436	13,466	17,865	16,051
85,650	**85,700**	17,450	13,479	17,879	16,064
85,700	**85,750**	17,464	13,491	17,893	16,076
85,750	**85,800**	17,478	13,504	17,907	16,089
85,800	**85,850**	17,492	13,516	17,921	16,101
85,850	**85,900**	17,506	13,529	17,935	16,114
85,900	**85,950**	17,520	13,541	17,949	16,126
85,950	**86,000**	17,534	13,554	17,963	16,139
86,000					
86,000	**86,050**	17,548	13,566	17,977	16,151
86,050	**86,100**	17,562	13,579	17,991	16,164
86,100	**86,150**	17,576	13,591	18,005	16,176
86,150	**86,200**	17,590	13,604	18,019	16,189
86,200	**86,250**	17,604	13,616	18,033	16,201
86,250	**86,300**	17,618	13,629	18,047	16,214
86,300	**86,350**	17,632	13,641	18,061	16,226
86,350	**86,400**	17,646	13,654	18,075	16,239
86,400	**86,450**	17,660	13,666	18,089	16,251
86,450	**86,500**	17,674	13,679	18,103	16,264
86,500	**86,550**	17,688	13,691	18,117	16,276
86,550	**86,600**	17,702	13,704	18,131	16,289
86,600	**86,650**	17,716	13,716	18,145	16,301
86,650	**86,700**	17,730	13,729	18,159	16,314
86,700	**86,750**	17,744	13,741	18,173	16,326
86,750	**86,800**	17,758	13,754	18,187	16,339
86,800	**86,850**	17,772	13,766	18,201	16,351
86,850	**86,900**	17,786	13,779	18,215	16,364
86,900	**86,950**	17,800	13,791	18,229	16,376
86,950	**87,000**	17,814	13,804	18,243	16,389

(Continued)

*This column must also be used by a qualifying widow(er).

»»→ Caution: This is a draft 2012 Tax Table. At the time of publication, the IRS had not yet released the 2012 Tax Table. For the latest information, see CCHGroup.com/TaxUpdates.

2012 Tax Table—*Continued*

If line 43 (taxable income) is—		And you are—			
At least	But less than	Single	Married filing jointly *	Married filing separately	Head of a household
		Your tax is—			
87,000					
87,000	**87,050**	17,828	13,816	18,257	16,401
87,050	**87,100**	17,842	13,829	18,271	16,414
87,100	**87,150**	17,856	13,841	18,285	16,426
87,150	**87,200**	17,870	13,854	18,299	16,439
87,200	**87,250**	17,884	13,866	18,313	16,451
87,250	**87,300**	17,898	13,879	18,327	16,464
87,300	**87,350**	17,912	13,891	18,341	16,476
87,350	**87,400**	17,926	13,904	18,355	16,489
87,400	**87,450**	17,940	13,916	18,369	16,501
87,450	**87,500**	17,954	13,929	18,383	16,514
87,500	**87,550**	17,968	13,941	18,397	16,526
87,550	**87,600**	17,982	13,954	18,411	16,539
87,600	**87,650**	17,996	13,966	18,425	16,551
87,650	**87,700**	18,010	13,979	18,439	16,564
87,700	**87,750**	18,024	13,991	18,453	16,576
87,750	**87,800**	18,038	14,004	18,467	16,589
87,800	**87,850**	18,052	14,016	18,481	16,601
87,850	**87,900**	18,066	14,029	18,495	16,614
87,900	**87,950**	18,080	14,041	18,509	16,626
87,950	**88,000**	18,094	14,054	18,523	16,639
88,000					
88,000	**88,050**	18,108	14,066	18,537	16,651
88,050	**88,100**	18,122	14,079	18,551	16,664
88,100	**88,150**	18,136	14,091	18,565	16,676
88,150	**88,200**	18,150	14,104	18,579	16,689
88,200	**88,250**	18,164	14,116	18,593	16,701
88,250	**88,300**	18,178	14,129	18,607	16,714
88,300	**88,350**	18,192	14,141	18,621	16,726
88,350	**88,400**	18,206	14,154	18,635	16,739
88,400	**88,450**	18,220	14,166	18,649	16,751
88,450	**88,500**	18,234	14,179	18,663	16,764
88,500	**88,550**	18,248	14,191	18,677	16,776
88,550	**88,600**	18,262	14,204	18,691	16,789
88,600	**88,650**	18,276	14,216	18,705	16,801
88,650	**88,700**	18,290	14,229	18,719	16,814
88,700	**88,750**	18,304	14,241	18,733	16,826
88,750	**88,800**	18,318	14,254	18,747	16,839
88,800	**88,850**	18,332	14,266	18,761	16,851
88,850	**88,900**	18,346	14,279	18,775	16,864
88,900	**88,950**	18,360	14,291	18,789	16,876
88,950	**89,000**	18,374	14,304	18,803	16,889
89,000					
89,000	**89,050**	18,388	14,316	18,817	16,901
89,050	**89,100**	18,402	14,329	18,831	16,914
89,100	**89,150**	18,416	14,341	18,845	16,926
89,150	**89,200**	18,430	14,354	18,859	16,939
89,200	**89,250**	18,444	14,366	18,873	16,951
89,250	**89,300**	18,458	14,379	18,887	16,964
89,300	**89,350**	18,472	14,391	18,901	16,976
89,350	**89,400**	18,486	14,404	18,915	16,989
89,400	**89,450**	18,500	14,416	18,929	17,001
89,450	**89,500**	18,514	14,429	18,943	17,014
89,500	**89,550**	18,528	14,441	18,957	17,026
89,550	**89,600**	18,542	14,454	18,971	17,039
89,600	**89,650**	18,556	14,466	18,985	17,051
89,650	**89,700**	18,570	14,479	18,999	17,064
89,700	**89,750**	18,584	14,491	19,013	17,076
89,750	**89,800**	18,598	14,504	19,027	17,089
89,800	**89,850**	18,612	14,516	19,041	17,101
89,850	**89,900**	18,626	14,529	19,055	17,114
89,900	**89,950**	18,640	14,541	19,069	17,126
89,950	**90,000**	18,654	14,554	19,083	17,139
90,000					
90,000	**90,050**	18,668	14,566	19,097	17,151
90,050	**90,100**	18,682	14,579	19,111	17,164
90,100	**90,150**	18,696	14,591	19,125	17,176
90,150	**90,200**	18,710	14,604	19,139	17,189
90,200	**90,250**	18,724	14,616	19,153	17,201
90,250	**90,300**	18,738	14,629	19,167	17,214
90,300	**90,350**	18,752	14,641	19,181	17,226
90,350	**90,400**	18,766	14,654	19,195	17,239
90,400	**90,450**	18,780	14,666	19,209	17,251
90,450	**90,500**	18,794	14,679	19,223	17,264
90,500	**90,550**	18,808	14,691	19,237	17,276
90,550	**90,600**	18,822	14,704	19,251	17,289
90,600	**90,650**	18,836	14,716	19,265	17,301
90,650	**90,700**	18,850	14,729	19,279	17,314
90,700	**90,750**	18,864	14,741	19,293	17,326
90,750	**90,800**	18,878	14,754	19,307	17,339
90,800	**90,850**	18,892	14,766	19,321	17,351
90,850	**90,900**	18,906	14,779	19,335	17,364
90,900	**90,950**	18,920	14,791	19,349	17,376
90,950	**91,000**	18,934	14,804	19,363	17,389
91,000					
91,000	**91,050**	18,948	14,816	19,377	17,401
91,050	**91,100**	18,962	14,829	19,391	17,414
91,100	**91,150**	18,976	14,841	19,405	17,426
91,150	**91,200**	18,990	14,854	19,419	17,439
91,200	**91,250**	19,004	14,866	19,433	17,451
91,250	**91,300**	19,018	14,879	19,447	17,464
91,300	**91,350**	19,032	14,891	19,461	17,476
91,350	**91,400**	19,046	14,904	19,475	17,489
91,400	**91,450**	19,060	14,916	19,489	17,501
91,450	**91,500**	19,074	14,929	19,503	17,514
91,500	**91,550**	19,088	14,941	19,517	17,526
91,550	**91,600**	19,102	14,954	19,531	17,539
91,600	**91,650**	19,116	14,966	19,545	17,551
91,650	**91,700**	19,130	14,979	19,559	17,564
91,700	**91,750**	19,144	14,991	19,573	17,576
91,750	**91,800**	19,158	15,004	19,587	17,589
91,800	**91,850**	19,172	15,016	19,601	17,601
91,850	**91,900**	19,186	15,029	19,615	17,614
91,900	**91,950**	19,200	15,041	19,629	17,626
91,950	**92,000**	19,214	15,054	19,643	17,639
92,000					
92,000	**92,050**	19,228	15,066	19,657	17,651
92,050	**92,100**	19,242	15,079	19,671	17,664
92,100	**92,150**	19,256	15,091	19,685	17,676
92,150	**92,200**	19,270	15,104	19,699	17,689
92,200	**92,250**	19,284	15,116	19,713	17,701
92,250	**92,300**	19,298	15,129	19,727	17,714
92,300	**92,350**	19,312	15,141	19,741	17,726
92,350	**92,400**	19,326	15,154	19,755	17,739
92,400	**92,450**	19,340	15,166	19,769	17,751
92,450	**92,500**	19,354	15,179	19,783	17,764
92,500	**92,550**	19,368	15,191	19,797	17,776
92,550	**92,600**	19,382	15,204	19,811	17,789
92,600	**92,650**	19,396	15,216	19,825	17,801
92,650	**92,700**	19,410	15,229	19,839	17,814
92,700	**92,750**	19,424	15,241	19,853	17,826
92,750	**92,800**	19,438	15,254	19,867	17,839
92,800	**92,850**	19,452	15,266	19,881	17,851
92,850	**92,900**	19,466	15,279	19,895	17,864
92,900	**92,950**	19,480	15,291	19,909	17,876
92,950	**93,000**	19,494	15,304	19,923	17,889

(Continued)

*This column must also be used by a qualifying widow(er).

»»→ Caution: This is a draft 2012 Tax Table. At the time of publication, the IRS had not yet released the 2012 Tax Table. For the latest information, see CCHGroup.com/TaxUpdates.

2012 Tax Table—*Continued*

If line 43 (taxable income) is— At least	But less than	And you are— Single	Married filing jointly *	Married filing separately	Head of a household
		Your tax is—			
93,000					
93,000	93,050	19,508	15,316	19,937	17,901
93,050	93,100	19,522	15,329	19,951	17,914
93,100	93,150	19,536	15,341	19,965	17,926
93,150	93,200	19,550	15,354	19,979	17,939
93,200	93,250	19,564	15,366	19,993	17,951
93,250	93,300	19,578	15,379	20,007	17,964
93,300	93,350	19,592	15,391	20,021	17,976
93,350	93,400	19,606	15,404	20,035	17,989
93,400	93,450	19,620	15,416	20,049	18,001
93,450	93,500	19,634	15,429	20,063	18,014
93,500	93,550	19,648	15,441	20,077	18,026
93,550	93,600	19,662	15,454	20,091	18,039
93,600	93,650	19,676	15,466	20,105	18,051
93,650	93,700	19,690	15,479	20,119	18,064
93,700	93,750	19,704	15,491	20,133	18,076
93,750	93,800	19,718	15,504	20,147	18,089
93,800	93,850	19,732	15,516	20,161	18,101
93,850	93,900	19,746	15,529	20,175	18,114
93,900	93,950	19,760	15,541	20,189	18,126
93,950	94,000	19,774	15,554	20,203	18,139
94,000					
94,000	94,050	19,788	15,566	20,217	18,151
94,050	94,100	19,802	15,579	20,231	18,164
94,100	94,150	19,816	15,591	20,245	18,176
94,150	94,200	19,830	15,604	20,259	18,189
94,200	94,250	19,844	15,616	20,273	18,201
94,250	94,300	19,858	15,629	20,287	18,214
94,300	94,350	19,872	15,641	20,301	18,226
94,350	94,400	19,886	15,654	20,315	18,239
94,400	94,450	19,900	15,666	20,329	18,251
94,450	94,500	19,914	15,679	20,343	18,264
94,500	94,550	19,928	15,691	20,357	18,276
94,550	94,600	19,942	15,704	20,371	18,289
94,600	94,650	19,956	15,716	20,385	18,301
94,650	94,700	19,970	15,729	20,399	18,314
94,700	94,750	19,984	15,741	20,413	18,326
94,750	94,800	19,998	15,754	20,427	18,339
94,800	94,850	20,012	15,766	20,441	18,351
94,850	94,900	20,026	15,779	20,455	18,364
94,900	94,950	20,040	15,791	20,469	18,376
94,950	95,000	20,054	15,804	20,483	18,389

If line 43 (taxable income) is— At least	But less than	And you are— Single	Married filing jointly *	Married filing separately	Head of a household
		Your tax is—			
95,000					
95,000	95,050	20,068	15,816	20,497	18,401
95,050	95,100	20,082	15,829	20,511	18,414
95,100	95,150	20,096	15,841	20,525	18,426
95,150	95,200	20,110	15,854	20,539	18,439
95,200	95,250	20,124	15,866	20,553	18,451
95,250	95,300	20,138	15,879	20,567	18,464
95,300	95,350	20,152	15,891	20,581	18,476
95,350	95,400	20,166	15,904	20,595	18,489
95,400	95,450	20,180	15,916	20,609	18,501
95,450	95,500	20,194	15,929	20,623	18,514
95,500	95,550	20,208	15,941	20,637	18,526
95,550	95,600	20,222	15,954	20,651	18,539
95,600	95,650	20,236	15,966	20,665	18,551
95,650	95,700	20,250	15,979	20,679	18,564
95,700	95,750	20,264	15,991	20,693	18,576
95,750	95,800	20,278	16,004	20,707	18,589
95,800	95,850	20,292	16,016	20,721	18,601
95,850	95,900	20,306	16,029	20,735	18,614
95,900	95,950	20,320	16,041	20,749	18,626
95,950	96,000	20,334	16,054	20,763	18,639
96,000					
96,000	96,050	20,348	16,066	20,777	18,651
96,050	96,100	20,362	16,079	20,791	18,664
96,100	96,150	20,376	16,091	20,805	18,676
96,150	96,200	20,390	16,104	20,819	18,689
96,200	96,250	20,404	16,116	20,833	18,701
96,250	96,300	20,418	16,129	20,847	18,714
96,300	96,350	20,432	16,141	20,861	18,726
96,350	96,400	20,446	16,154	20,875	18,739
96,400	96,450	20,460	16,166	20,889	18,751
96,450	96,500	20,474	16,179	20,903	18,764
96,500	96,550	20,488	16,191	20,917	18,776
96,550	96,600	20,502	16,204	20,931	18,789
96,600	96,650	20,516	16,216	20,945	18,801
96,650	96,700	20,530	16,229	20,959	18,814
96,700	96,750	20,544	16,241	20,973	18,826
96,750	96,800	20,558	16,254	20,987	18,839
96,800	96,850	20,572	16,266	21,001	18,851
96,850	96,900	20,586	16,279	21,015	18,864
96,900	96,950	20,600	16,291	21,029	18,876
96,950	97,000	20,614	16,304	21,043	18,889

If line 43 (taxable income) is— At least	But less than	And you are— Single	Married filing jointly *	Married filing separately	Head of a household
		Your tax is—			
97,000					
97,000	97,050	20,628	16,316	21,057	18,901
97,050	97,100	20,642	16,329	21,071	18,914
97,100	97,150	20,656	16,341	21,085	18,926
97,150	97,200	20,670	16,354	21,099	18,939
97,200	97,250	20,684	16,366	21,113	18,951
97,250	97,300	20,698	16,379	21,127	18,964
97,300	97,350	20,712	16,391	21,141	18,976
97,350	97,400	20,726	16,404	21,155	18,989
97,400	97,450	20,740	16,416	21,169	19,001
97,450	97,500	20,754	16,429	21,183	19,014
97,500	97,550	20,768	16,441	21,197	19,026
97,550	97,600	20,782	16,454	21,211	19,039
97,600	97,650	20,796	16,466	21,225	19,051
97,650	97,700	20,810	16,479	21,239	19,064
97,700	97,750	20,824	16,491	21,253	19,076
97,750	97,800	20,838	16,504	21,267	19,089
97,800	97,850	20,852	16,516	21,281	19,101
97,850	97,900	20,866	16,529	21,295	19,114
97,900	97,950	20,880	16,541	21,309	19,126
97,950	98,000	20,894	16,554	21,323	19,139
98,000					
98,000	98,050	20,908	16,566	21,337	19,151
98,050	98,100	20,922	16,579	21,351	19,164
98,100	98,150	20,936	16,591	21,365	19,176
98,150	98,200	20,950	16,604	21,379	19,189
98,200	98,250	20,964	16,616	21,393	19,201
98,250	98,300	20,978	16,629	21,407	19,214
98,300	98,350	20,992	16,641	21,421	19,226
98,350	98,400	21,006	16,654	21,435	19,239
98,400	98,450	21,020	16,666	21,449	19,251
98,450	98,500	21,034	16,679	21,463	19,264
98,500	98,550	21,048	16,691	21,477	19,276
98,550	98,600	21,062	16,704	21,491	19,289
98,600	98,650	21,076	16,716	21,505	19,301
98,650	98,700	21,090	16,729	21,519	19,314
98,700	98,750	21,104	16,741	21,533	19,326
98,750	98,800	21,118	16,754	21,547	19,339
98,800	98,850	21,132	16,766	21,561	19,351
98,850	98,900	21,146	16,779	21,575	19,364
98,900	98,950	21,160	16,791	21,589	19,376
98,950	99,000	21,174	16,804	21,603	19,389

(Continued)

*This column must also be used by a qualifying widow(er).

Need more information or forms? Visit IRS.gov.

»»→ Caution: This is a draft 2012 Tax Table. At the time of publication, the IRS had not yet released the 2012 Tax Table. For the latest information, see CCHGroup.com/TaxUpdates.

DRAFT AS OF October 26, 2012

TAX RATES

2012 Tax Table—*Continued*

If line 43 (taxable income) is—		And you are—			
At least	But less than	Single	Married filing jointly *	Married filing separately	Head of a household
		Your tax is—			
99,000					
99,000	**99,050**	21,188	16,816	21,617	19,401
99,050	**99,100**	21,202	16,829	21,631	19,414
99,100	**99,150**	21,216	16,841	21,645	19,426
99,150	**99,200**	21,230	16,854	21,659	19,439
99,200	**99,250**	21,244	16,866	21,673	19,451
99,250	**99,300**	21,258	16,879	21,687	19,464
99,300	**99,350**	21,272	16,891	21,701	19,476
99,350	**99,400**	21,286	16,904	21,715	19,489
99,400	**99,450**	21,300	16,916	21,729	19,501
99,450	**99,500**	21,314	16,929	21,743	19,514
99,500	**99,550**	21,328	16,941	21,757	19,526
99,550	**99,600**	21,342	16,954	21,771	19,539
99,600	**99,650**	21,356	16,966	21,785	19,551
99,650	**99,700**	21,370	16,979	21,799	19,564
99,700	**99,750**	21,384	16,991	21,813	19,576
99,750	**99,800**	21,398	17,004	21,827	19,589
99,800	**99,850**	21,412	17,016	21,841	19,601
99,850	**99,900**	21,426	17,029	21,855	19,614
99,900	**99,950**	21,440	17,041	21,869	19,626
99,950	**100,000**	21,454	17,054	21,883	19,639
		$100,000 or over — use the Tax Computation Worksheet			

*This column must also be used by a qualifying widow(er).

Need more information or forms? Visit IRS.gov. -96-

CORPORATION INCOME TAX RATES FOR 2012

¶ 33 Corporations

The corporate tax rates are as follows:

Taxable Income Over	But Not Over	Pay	+	% on Excess	of the amount over—
$0—	$50,000	$0		15%	$0
50,000—	75,000	7,500		25	50,000
75,000—	100,000	13,750		34	75,000
100,000—	335,000	22,250		39	100,000
335,000—	10,000,000	113,900		34	335,000
10,000,000—	15,000,000	3,400,000		35	10,000,000
15,000,000—	18,333,333	5,150,000		38	15,000,000
18,333,333—				35	0

Taxable income of certain personal service corporations is taxed at a flat rate of 35% (¶ 219).

¶ 34 Controlled Group of Corporations

A controlled group of corporations is subject to the regular corporate income tax rates (¶ 33) as though the group is one corporation (¶ 289).

¶ 35 Personal Holding Companies

In addition to regular corporate income taxes (¶ 33), a special tax is imposed on any corporation which is a personal holding company. For 2012, the additional tax is 15 percent of the corporation's undistributed personal holding company income (¶ 275).

¶ 36 Insurance Companies and Regulated Investment Companies

The regular corporate tax rates (¶ 33) apply to an insurance company's taxable income (¶ 2370 and ¶ 2378). In the case of regulated investment companies, the corporate tax rates apply to investment company taxable income (¶ 2303).

¶ 37 Accumulated Earnings Tax

In addition to regular corporate income taxes (¶ 33), a corporation may be subject to a special tax on its accumulated taxable income. For 2012, the tax is 15 percent of the corporation's accumulated taxable income. A corporation is entitled to a $250,000 accumulated earnings credit ($150,000 for personal service corporations) against the tax (¶ 251).

¶ 38 Foreign Corporations

The income of a foreign corporation that is not effectively connected with a U.S. trade or business is taxed at a rate of 30 percent. Domestic corporate rates (¶ 33) apply to the income of a foreign corporation that is effectively connected with a U.S. trade or business (¶ 2425).

¶ 39 Real Estate Investment Trusts

A real estate investment trust will be subject to regular corporate income tax rates (¶ 33) on its "real estate investment trust taxable income" (¶ 2329).

ESTATE AND GIFT TAXES

¶ 40 Unified Transfer Tax Rate Schedules

Unified Transfer Tax Rate Schedule, 2010*—2012

Column A *Taxable amount over*	Column B *Taxable amount not over*	Column C *Tax on amount in column A*	Column D *Rate of tax on excess over amount in column A Percent*
$0	$10,000	$0	18
10,000	20,000	1,800	20
20,000	40,000	3,800	22
40,000	60,000	8,200	24
60,000	80,000	13,000	26
80,000	100,000	18,200	28
100,000	150,000	23,800	30
150,000	250,000	38,800	32
250,000	500,000	70,800	34
500,000	....	155,800	35

*The estates of decedents dying in 2010 were allowed to elect out of the estate tax regime, effectively reducing their estate tax rate to zero (¶ 2901) (Act Sec. 301(c) of P.L. 111-312).

Unified Transfer Tax Rate Schedule, 2002—2009*

Column A *Taxable amount over*	Column B *Taxable amount not over*	Column C *Tax on amount in column A*	Column D *Rate of tax on excess over amount in column A Percent*
$0	$10,000	$0	18
10,000	20,000	1,800	20
20,000	40,000	3,800	22
40,000	60,000	8,200	24
60,000	80,000	13,000	26
80,000	100,000	18,200	28
100,000	150,000	23,800	30
150,000	250,000	38,800	32
250,000	500,000	70,800	34
500,000	750,000	155,800	37
750,000	1,000,000	248,300	39
1,000,000	1,250,000	345,800	41
1,250,000	1,500,000	448,300	43
1,500,000	2,000,000	555,800	45
2,000,000	2,500,000	780,800	49
2,500,000	....	1,025,800	50 *

* The top marginal rate was 49 percent for decedents dying and gifts made in 2003; 48 percent in 2004; 47 percent in 2005; 46 percent in 2006; and 45 percent in 2007, 2008 and 2009.

Generation-Skipping Transfer (GST) Tax. All GSTs are subject to tax at a flat rate equal to the product of the maximum federal estate tax rate under the unified rate schedule (35 percent for 2012) and the "inclusion ratio" (¶ 2943). However, the tax rate applicable to GSTs made in 2010 is zero percent (Act Sec. 302(c) of P.L. 111-312).

Nonresident Aliens. The transfer tax rates that apply to U.S. citizens and resident aliens also apply to nonresident aliens, for certain property situated within the United States (¶ 2903 and ¶ 2940).

After 2012. Absent further legislative action:

- A unified transfer tax rate schedule similar to the schedule for 2002-2009 shown above will apply to the estates of decedents dying, and gifts made, after 2012, but the tax rate will be 53 percent on taxable amounts in excess of $2.5 million but not more than $3 million, and 55 percent on taxable amounts in excess of $3 million.
- The maximum rate will be 55 percent for GSTs made after 2012.
- A five-percent surtax will apply to taxable estate and gift transfers above $10 million (up to $17.184 million), for taxable transfers made after 2012.

¶ 41 Transfer Tax Credits, Exclusions, and Exemptions

Estate Tax Applicable Credit and Exclusion Amounts, 2002—2012

Year	*Applicable Credit Amount*	*Applicable Exclusion Amount*
2002 and 2003	$345,800	$1,000,000
2004 and 2005	555,800	1,500,000
2006 through 2008	780,800	2,000,000
2009	1,455,800	3,500,000
2010* and 2011	1,730,800	5,000,000
2012	1,772,800	5,120,000 (adjusted)

* The estates of decedents dying in 2010 were given the option of electing out of the estate tax regime in exchange for allowing assets acquired from a decedent to receive a modified carryover basis (¶ 2901) (Act Sec. 301(c) of P.L. 111-312).

Gift Tax Applicable Credit and Exclusion Amounts, 2002—2012

Year	*Applicable Credit Amount*	*Applicable (Lifetime) Exclusion Amount*
2002 through 2009	$345,800	$1,000,000
2010	330,800	1,000,000
2011	1,730,800	5,000,000
2012	1,772,800	5,120,000 (adjusted)

Gift Tax Annual Exclusion. There is an annual exclusion of $13,000 per donee for gifts made in 2012, with an annual maximum of $26,000 per donee for spouses who use gift-splitting (¶ 2905).

Generation Skipping Transfer (GST) Exemption Amounts, 2002—2012

Year	*Exemption Amount*
2002	$1,100,000 (adjusted)
2003	1,120,000 (adjusted)
2004 and 2005	1,500,000
2006 through 2008	2,000,000
2009	3,500,000
2010* and 2011	5,000,000
2012	5,120,000 (adjusted)

* For GSTs occurring in 2010 only, the applicable rate for GST purposes was zero (Act Sec. 302(c) of P.L. 111-312).

Nonresident Aliens. The annual gift tax exclusion is available to nonresident alien donors (¶ 2905). Where permitted by treaty, the estate of a nonresident alien is allowed a credit equal to the unified credit available to a U.S. citizen multiplied by the proportion of the decedent's entire gross estate situated in the United States (¶ 2940). In computing the credit, property is not treated as situated in the United States if such property is exempt from tax under any treaty. In other cases, a unified credit of $13,000 is allowed.

The estate of a resident of a U.S. possession is entitled to a unified credit equal to the greater of (1) $13,000; or (2) $46,800 multiplied by the percentage of the decedent's gross estate situated in the United States (Code Sec. 2102).

With respect to the gift tax, no portion of the unified credit may be used as a credit against gift taxes payable on a lifetime transfers by a nonresident alien.

After 2012. Absent further legislative action:

- The estate tax applicable exclusion amount (¶ 2901) will be $1 million for the estates of decedents dying after 2012.
- The gift tax applicable (lifetime) exclusion (¶ 2910) will be $1 million for gifts made after 2012.
- The GST exemption amount (¶ 2943) will be $1 million, adjusted for inflation, for GSTs occurring after 2012.

¶ 43 Credit for State Death Taxes

The table below is used to calculate the amount of the credit available for state death taxes paid with respect to property included in a decedent's gross estate for decedents dying before 2005 and after 2012. For the estates of decedents dying after 2004 and before 2013, the state death tax credit was replaced with a deduction from the gross estate for state death taxes actually paid.

State Death Tax Credit Table

Adjusted Taxable Estate* At least	But less than	Credit =	+ %	Of Excess Over
$0	$40,000	$0	0.0	$0
40,000	90,000	0	.8	40,000
90,000	140,000	400	1.6	90,000
140,000	240,000	1,200	2.4	140,000
240,000	440,000	3,600	3.2	240,000
440,000	640,000	10,000	4.0	440,000
640,000	840,000	18,000	4.8	640,000
840,000	1,040,000	27,600	5.6	840,000
1,040,000	1,540,000	38,800	6.4	1,040,000
1,540,000	2,040,000	70,800	7.2	1,540,000
2,040,000	2,540,000	106,800	8.0	2,040,000
2,540,000	3,040,000	146,800	8.8	2,540,000
3,040,000	3,540,000	190,800	9.6	3,040,000
3,540,000	4,040,000	238,800	10.4	3,540,000
4,040,000	5,040,000	290,800	11.2	4,040,000
5,040,000	6,040,000	402,800	12.0	5,040,000
6,040,000	7,040,000	522,800	12.8	6,040,000
7,040,000	8,040,000	650,800	13.6	7,040,000
8,040,000	9,040,000	786,800	14.4	8,040,000
9,040,000	10,040,000	930,800	15.2	9,040,000
10,040,000	....	1,082,800	16.0	10,040,000

* The adjusted taxable estate is the taxable estate reduced by $60,000.

OTHER TAXES

¶ 47 Self-Employment Taxes

For calendar year 2012, a tax rate of 13.3% is imposed on net earnings from self-employment. The rate consists of a 10.4% component for Social Security (old-age, survivors, and disability insurance (OASDI)) and a 2.9% component for Medicare hospital insurance (HI). The OASDI rate applies only to net earnings from self-employment up to the OASDI wage base of $110,100 in 2012. The Medicare rate applies to all net earnings in 2012. A tax rate of 15.3% is imposed on net earnings for calendar year 2013. The rate consists of a 12.4% component for Social Security (old-age, survivors, and disability insurance (OASDI) and a 2.9% component for Medicare hospital insurance (HI) (¶ 2664). The rate for Medicare is increased by 0.9% to 3.8% for 2013 for net earnings from self-employment in excess of $200,000 ($250,000 in the case of a joint return, $125,000 in the case of a married individual filing separately). In the case of a joint return, the additional 0.9% tax for Medicare is imposed on the combined income of both spouses. The OASDI rate for 2013 applies to net earnings from self-employment up to the OASDI earnings base of $ 113,700. The Medicare rate applies to all net earnings in 2013.

¶ 49 Employment Taxes

FICA Taxes. Under the Federal Insurance Contributions Act (FICA), taxes are imposed on both employers and employees on wages paid to the employee for Social Security old-age, survivors, and disability insurance (OASDI), and Medicare hospital insurance (HI) (¶ 2648). For calendar year 2012, the tax rate on the employee's portion of wages is 5.65%, consisting of a 4.2% rate for OASDI and a 1.45% rate for Medicare. The tax rate on the employer is 7.65%, consisting of a 6.2% rate for OASDI and a 1.45% rate for Medicare. The OASDI rate for employees and employers only applies to wages up to the OASDI wage base, which is $110,100 in 2012.

For calendar year 2013, the tax rate on the employee's portion of wages is 7.65%, consisting of a 6.2% rate for OASDI and a 1.45% rate for Medicare. The Medicare rate on the employee's portion of wages is increased to 2.35% for 2013 for wages in excess of $200,000 ($250,000 in the case of a joint return, $125,000 in the case of a married individual filing separately). In the case of a joint return, the additional 0.9% tax for Medicare is imposed on the combined income of both spouses. The tax rate on the employer for 2013 is 7.65%, consisting of a 6.2% rate for OASDI and a 1.45% rate for Medicare. The OASDI rate for employees and employers only applies to wages up to the OASDI wage base, which is $113,700 in 2013. The Medicare rate applies to all wages in 2013.

Medicare Payments. Medicare Part B premiums ($99.90 per month in 2012) qualify as deductible medical expenses (¶ 1019).

Unemployment Compensation. Under the Federal Unemployment Tax Act (FUTA), a tax is imposed on the first $7,000 of wages paid to a covered employee by an employer who employs one or more persons in covered employment in each of 20 days in a year, each day being in a different week, or who has a payroll for covered employment of at least $1,500 in a calendar quarter in the current or preceding calendar year (¶ 2649). The FUTA tax rate is 6.0% for wages paid in 2012. Since employers are allowed credits against the FUTA rate through participation in state unemployment insurance laws, the net FUTA rate actually paid by most employers is 0.6% in 2012, except when credit reductions are in effect in a state. The unemployment tax also applies to any person who paid total cash wages of $1,000 or more to a household employee during any calendar quarter in the current or preceding calendar year.

Railroad Retirement Tax. The Railroad Retirement and Survivors' Improvement Act provides benefits similar to those as under Social Security and Medicare. Tier I benefits are financed by taxes on employers and employees equal to those under FICA. Thus, for calendar year 2012, the tax rate on the employee's portion of wages is 5.65%, consisting of a 4.2% rate for OASDI and a 1.45% rate for Medicare. The tax rate on the employer is 7.65%, consisting of a 6.2% rate for OASDI and a 1.45% rate for Medicare. The OASDI rate for employees and employers only applies to wages up to the OASDI wage base, which is $110,100 in 2012. The tax rate on the employee's portion of wages for calendar year 2013 is 7.65%, consisting of a 6.2% rate for OASDI and a 1.45% rate for Medicare. The Medicare rate on the employee's portion of wages is increased to 2.35% for 2013 for wages in excess of $200,000 ($250,000 in the case of a joint return, $125,000 in the case of a married individual filing separately). In the case of a joint return, the additional 0.9% tax for Medicare is imposed on the combined income of both spouses. The tax rate on the employer is 7.65%, consisting of a 6.2% rate for OASDI and a 1.45% rate for Medicare. The OASDI rate for employees and employers only applies to wages up to the OASDI wage base, which is $ 113,700 in 2013. The Medicare rate applies to all wages in 2013.

Tier II benefits are also available equivalent to a private pension plan and financed with employers and employees contributing a certain percentage of pay toward to system to finance benefits. For calendar year 2012, a tier II tax rate of 12.1% for employers and 3.9% for employees is imposed on annual compensation within a compensation base of $81,900. The tier II annual compensation base for 2013 is $84,300.

¶ 53 Excise Taxes

Identified below are various excise taxes.

FUELS

Gasoline	
Gasoline (per gallon)	18.4¢
Diesel fuel, biodiesel, and kerosene	
Diesel fuel (except if used on a farm for farming purposes) (per gallon)	24.4¢
Diesel fuel for use in trains (per gallon)	0.1¢
Diesel-water fuel emulsions (per gallon)	19.8¢
Kerosene (except if used in a farm for farming purposes) (per gallon)	24.4¢
B-100 (100 percent biodiesel) (per gallon)	24.4¢
Special fuels	
Special motor fuel (per gallon)	18.4¢
Liquefied petroleum gas (LPG)	18.3¢
"P Series" fuels	18.4¢
Compressed natural gas (CNG) (per energy equivalent of a gallon of gasoline)	18.3¢
Liquefied hydrogen	18.4¢
Any liquid fuel derived from coal (including peat) through the Fischer-Tropsch process (per gallon)	24.4¢
Liquid fuel derived from biomass (per gallon)	24.4¢
Liquefied natural gas (LNG) (per gallon)	24.3¢
Liquefied gas derived from biomass (per gallon)	18.4¢
Qualified ethanol produced from coal (per gallon)	18.4¢
Qualified methanol produced from coal (per gallon)	18.4¢
Partially exempt ethanol produced from natural gas (per gallon)	11.4¢
Partially exempt methanol produced from natural gas (per gallon)	9.25¢
Fuel used on inland waterways	
Inland waterways fuel use tax (per gallon)	20.1¢
Aviation fuels	
Kerosene used in commercial aviation (when removed from a refinery or terminal directly into the fuel tank of an aircraft) (per gallon)	4.4¢
Kerosene used in noncommercial aviation (when removed from a refinery or terminal directly into the fuel tank of an aircraft) (per gallon)	21.9¢
Noncommercial aviation gasoline (per gallon)	19.4¢
Fuel used in fractional aircraft ownership program flights (per gallon)	14.1¢ surtax after 3/31/2012
Fuel credits	
Alcohol or alcohol in fuel mixtures if 190 proof or greater (per gallon) (ethanol)	45¢ credit until 2012
Alcohol of 190 proof or greater if benefited from the small ethanol producers credit (per gallon)	55¢ credit until 2012
Alcohol and alcohol in fuel mixtures if less than 190, but at least 150 proof (per gallon) (ethanol)	33.33¢ credit until 2012
Alcohol if less than 190, but at least 150 proof if benefited from the small ethanol producers credit (per gallon)	43.33¢ credit until 2012
Alcohol if 190 proof or greater (per gallon) (methanol)	60¢ credit until 2012
Alcohol if at least 150, but less than 190 proof (per gallon) (methanol)	45¢ credit until 2012
Cellulosic biofuel that is not alcohol (per gallon)	$1.01 credit until 2013
Cellulosic biofuel that is alcohol (other than ethanol) (per gallon)	41¢ credit until 2013
Biodiesel and biodiesel mixtures (per gallon)	$1.00 credit until 2012
Agri-biodiesel (per gallon)	$1.00 credit until 2012
Agri-biodiesel if benefited from the small agri-biodiesel producer credit (per gallon)	$1.10 credit until 2012
Renewable diesel and renewable diesel mixtures (per gallon)	$1.00 credit until 2012

Alternative fuel (as defined in Code Sec. 6426(d)(2)) (per gallon) . . 50¢ credit until 2012 (but until 9/30/2014 for liquefied hydrogen)

Crude oil

Crude oil (per barrel) . . . . 8¢

HEAVY TRUCKS, TRAILERS

Truck chassis or body (that is suitable for use with a vehicle in excess of 33,000 lbs. gross vehicle weight) . . . . 12% of retail price

Trailer and semitrailer chassis or body (that is suitable for use with a trailer or semitrailer in excess of 26,000 lbs. gross vehicle weight) . . . . 12% of retail price

Parts and accessories installed on taxable vehicles within 6 months after being placed in service (when cost of parts or accessories exceeds $1,000) . . . 12% of retail price

HIGHWAY-TYPE TIRES

Tires with load capacity of 3,500 lbs. or less . . . . No tax

Tires with load capacity over 3,500 lbs. . . . . . . 9.45¢ for each 10 lbs. of tire load capacity over 3,500 lbs.

Super single tires designed for steering . . . . 9.45¢ for each 10 lbs. of tire load capacity over 3,500 lbs.

Super single tires not designed for steering . . 4.725¢ for each 10 lbs. of tire load capacity over 3,500 lbs.

Biasply tires . . . . 4.725¢ for each 10 lbs. of tire load capacity over 3,500 lbs.

GAS GUZZLER TAX

Mileage ratings per gallon of at least 22.5 . . . . $ 0

Mileage ratings per gallon of at least 21.5 but less than 22.5 1,000

Mileage ratings per gallon of at least 20.5 but less than 21.5 1,300

Mileage ratings per gallon of at least 19.5 but less than 20.5 1,700

Mileage ratings per gallon of at least 18.5 but less than 19.5 2,100

Mileage ratings per gallon of at least 17.5 but less than 18.5 2,600

Mileage ratings per gallon of at least 16.5 but less than 17.5 3,000

Mileage ratings per gallon of at least 15.5 but less than 16.5 3,700

Mileage ratings per gallon of at least 14.5 but less than 15.5 4,500

Mileage ratings per gallon of at least 13.5 but less than 14.5 5,400

Mileage ratings per gallon of at least 12.5 but less than 13.5 6,400

Mileage ratings per gallon of less than 12.5 7,700

FACILITIES AND SERVICES

Communications

Local telephone service and teletypewriter service 3%

Transportation by air

Domestic passenger tickets: 7.5% plus $3.80 (from 1/1/12-12/31/12) for each flight segment (excepting segments to or from rural airports)

Alaska and Hawaii passenger tickets (amount per person per departure) (from 1/1/12-12/31/12) $8.40

International passenger tickets (amount per person for each arrival and for each departure) (from 1/1/12-12/31/12) $16.70

Air freight waybill 6.25%

Transportation by water

Persons $3.00

Port use tax on imports (harbor maintenance tax) . . . . 0.125% of cargo value

ALCOHOL TAXES

Distilled spirits (per gallon) $13.50

Beer (per barrel—31 gallons or less) $18.00

First 60,000 barrels removed during calendar year by U.S. brewer producing not more than 2 million barrels during year (per barrel) $7.00

Wines	
Not more than 14% alcohol (per gallon)	$1.07
More than 14 to 21% alcohol (per gallon)	$1.57
More than 21 to 24% alcohol (per gallon)	$3.15
More than 24% alcohol (per gallon)	$13.50
Artificially carbonated wines (per gallon)	$3.30
Champagne and other sparkling wines (per gallon)	$3.40
Hard cider derived from apples containing at least ½ of 1% and less than 7% alcohol (per gallon)	$0.226
TOBACCO TAXES	
Cigars weighing not more than 3 lbs. (per 1,000)	$50.33
Cigars weighing more than 3 lbs.	52.75% of sales price, not to exceed 40.26 cents per cigar
Cigarettes weighing not more than 3 lbs. (per 1,000)	$50.33
Cigarettes weighing more than 3 lbs. (per 1,000)	$105.69
Cigarette papers (per 50 papers)	3.15¢
Cigarette tubes (per 50 tubes)	6.30¢
Snuff (per pound)	$1.51
Chewing tobacco (per pound)	50.33¢
Pipe tobacco (per pound)	$2.8311 cents
Roll-your-own tobacco (per pound)	$24.78
WAGERING TAXES	
State authorized wagers placed with bookmakers and lottery operators	0.25% of wager amt.
Unauthorized wagers placed with bookmakers and lottery operators	2% of wager amt.
License fee on state authorized persons accepting wagers (per year, per person)	$50
License fee on unauthorized persons accepting wagers (per year, per person)	$500
HIGHWAY MOTOR VEHICLE USE TAX	
Vehicles of less than 55,000 lbs.	No tax
Vehicles of 55,000 lbs.—75,000 lbs. (per year)	$100 per year + $22 for each 1,000 lbs. (or fraction thereof) over 55,000 lbs.
Vehicles over 75,000 lbs. (per year)	$550
FIREARMS	
Transfer taxes (per firearm)	$5 (concealable weapons) or $200
Occupational taxes (per year)	$1,000 (importers or manufacturers), or $500 (dealers, small importers and manufacturers)
Pistols and revolvers	10% of sales price
Firearms other than pistols and revolvers	11% of sales price
Ammunition (shells and cartridges)	11% of sales price
OTHER TAXES	
Electric outboard motors	3% of sales price
Sport fishing equipment	10% of sales price
Bows with a peak draw weight of at least 30 pounds	11% of sales price
Quivers, broadheads, points	11% of sales price
Arrow shafts	46¢ per shaft
Coal—underground mines	lower of $1.10 per ton or 4.4% of sales price
Coal—surface mines	lower of 55¢ per ton or 4.4% of sales price
Vaccines	75¢ per dose on taxable vaccines
Indoor tanning services	10% of amount paid, starting July 1, 2010
Casualty insurance and indemnity, fidelity and surety bonds (per dollar of premium paid)	4¢
Life insurance, sickness and accident policies, and annuity contracts (per dollar of premium paid)	1¢
Reinsurance of taxable contracts above (per dollar of premium paid)	1¢

Preparing Income Tax Returns

CHECKLISTS

¶ 55 Checklist for Items of Income

The determination of whether an item of income is includible in income and, thus, taxable, or whether it is excludable from income is crucial to the determination of tax liability. An item that is includible increases tax liability, depending on the amount, whereas an excludable item decreases tax liability. The following chart, which is arranged alphabetically by income item, indicates whether the item is includible or excludable from income. A reference to further details in the 2013 *U.S. Master Tax Guide* is also provided.

Income Item	*Includible in Income*	*Paragraph Reference*
Accident and health insurance premiums, employer-paid (except for long-term care benefits provided through flexible spending accounts and subject to limitation as to medical savings accounts)	No	¶ 859
Accident and health plans proceeds (under insurance purchased by taxpayer or under employee supported plans) where premiums did not give taxpayer a previous medical expense deduction	No	¶ 853
Agreement not to compete, payments received for	Yes	¶ 713
Airline deregulation benefits, special rule, unemployment compensation	Yes	¶ 722
Alaska Permanent Fund dividends	Yes	¶ 105
Alimony, support and separate maintenance payments, receipt of	Yes	¶ 772
Allowances received by dependents of members of the Armed Forces	No	¶ 896
Annuities (amounts in excess of cost)	Yes	¶ 819
Annuities, interest on advance premiums	Yes	¶ 724
Annuity contract, death benefit	Yes	¶ 817
Antitrust action, punitive damages recovered	Yes	¶ 852
Armed Forces pay (except "combat zone" or "missing" status pay)	Yes	¶ 891
Athletic facilities on employer's premises, value of use	No	¶ 863
Attorney's contingent fee, includible in plaintiff's gross income	Yes	¶ 852
Awards, generally	Yes	¶ 852
Back pay	Yes	¶ 852
Bad debts, prior taxes and interest on taxes, recovery of, provided no tax benefit in prior year	No	¶ 799
Bargain purchases from employer to extent discount exceeds gross profit percentage	Yes	¶ 789

CHECKLISTS

Income Item	Includible in Income	Paragraph Reference
Barter income	Yes	¶ 785
Beauty contest winners, receipt of scholarships and amounts for personal appearances	Yes	¶ 785
Bequests and devises, generally	No	¶ 847
Bonds, state, city, etc., interest on, generally	No	¶ 724
Bonuses	Yes	¶ 713
Buried treasure	Yes	¶ 701
Business interruption insurance proceeds:		
. based on income experience	Yes	¶ 980B
. based on per diem idleness	No	¶ 980B
Business profits	Yes	¶ 759
Business relocation payments	Yes	¶ 863
Business subsidies for construction or contributions by customer or potential customer	Yes	¶ 759
Cancellation of debt	Yes	¶ 885
Capital contributions to corporation	No	¶ 1660
Car pool receipts by car owner for transportation of other employees	No	¶ 945
Car used for business purposes by full-time car salesperson, value of use	No	¶ 947
Cell phones, substantiated business use	No	¶ 943
Checks, uncashed by payee, for previously deducted items	Yes	¶ 1543
Child or dependent care plan benefits, employer-subsidized, limited	No	¶ 869
Child support payments	No	¶ 776
Christmas bonuses from employer, based on percentage of salary (aside from token gifts such as hams, turkeys, etc., given for goodwill)	Yes	¶ 713
Civil Rights Act violation, back pay recovery	Yes	¶ 852
Clergy fees and contributions received unless earned as agent of religious order	Yes	¶ 713
COBRA premium assistance, for years ending after February 17, 2009	No	¶ 896B
"Combat zone" pay, military	No	¶ 895
Commissions	Yes	¶ 701
Commodity credit loans, receipt of (optional)	Yes	¶ 769
Compensated Work Therapy program payments	No	¶ 891
Compensation, property received, value of	Yes	¶ 1681
Contract cancellation, payments received for	Yes	¶ 1563
Contribution in aid of construction	Yes	¶ 1660
Damages:		
. back pay	Yes	¶ 852
. loss of anticipatory benefits (business)	Yes	¶ 863
. personal physical injuries or sickness	No	¶ 852
. slander or libel of personal reputation	Yes	¶ 852
Death benefits, employer-paid	Yes	¶ 813
Debts:		
. cancellation of, related to principal residence, from 2007 to 2012, up to $2,000,000	No	¶ 885
. nongratuitous cancellation of	Yes	¶ 885
Defamation damage award, compensating injury to business and professional reputation	Yes	¶ 852
Deferred income under certain nonqualified deferred compensation plans	Yes	¶ 2176
Dependent care assistance program payments, limited	No	¶ 869

Income Item	*Includible in Income*	*Paragraph Reference*
Disability payments, other than for loss of wages, all taxpayers, including veterans	No	¶ 891
Disability pensions, Veterans' Administration	No	¶ 891
Disaster unemployment payments	Yes	¶ 722
Discharge of indebtedness:		
. debt on a principal residence, from 2007 to 2012, up to $2,000,000	No	¶ 885
. nongratuitous	Yes	¶ 885
Dividends, stock distributed in lieu of money	Yes	¶ 733
Drawing account, excess cancelled by employer	Yes	¶ 713
Educational assistance, employer-provided under a nondiscriminatory plan, up to $5,250 per year (including educational assistance for graduate-level courses beginning in 2002 to 2012)	No	¶ 871
Embezzlement proceeds	Yes	¶ 785
Employee achievement awards, qualified	No	¶ 919
Employee discount, qualified	No	¶ 863
Employment contract, amounts received by employee for cancellation	Yes	¶ 713
Endowment policies, generally as to non-annuity payments until cost is recovered	No	¶ 841
Farm income	Yes	¶ 767
Farmers, government payments to offset operating losses or lack of profits	Yes	¶ 767
Fellowships and scholarships, degree programs	No	¶ 879
Financial counseling:		
. fees, employer-paid	Yes	¶ 713
. services, employer-provided, related to a qualified retirement plan	No	¶ 863
Foreign earned income, limited election	No	¶ 2402
Foster parents, reimbursements for care of a qualified foster child	No	¶ 883
Fringe benefits, if no additional cost service, qualified employee discount, working condition fringe, *de minimis* fringe, qualified transportation fringe, qualified moving expense reimbursement	No	¶ 863
Future services, prepayment for	Yes	¶ 1537
Gain on sale of personal residence:		
. up to $250,000 ($500,000 for joint filers)	No	¶ 1705
Gains:		
. condemnation of nonresidential property unless award is used for replacement	Yes	¶ 1716
. discount on later sale or redemption of bonds purchased with excess number of interest coupons detached (stripped bonds)	Yes	¶ 1952
. obligations purchased or satisfied for less than face value	Yes	¶ 1958
. partner's sale of asset to partnership	Yes	¶ 443
. sales of depreciable property	Yes	¶ 1780
. sales of goodwill	Yes	¶ 1743
. sales of patents	Yes	¶ 1767
. sales of property, generally	Yes	¶ 1701
. sales of stock in foreign corporations	Yes	¶ 2487
. sales of stock of foreign investment company	Yes	¶ 2490
. swap-fund transfers	Yes	¶ 1731

CHECKLISTS

Income Item	Includible in Income	Paragraph Reference
Gambling winnings:		
. illegal	Yes	¶ 2497
. legal	Yes	¶ 2642
Gifts	No	¶ 849
Government employees, additional compensation as inducement to accept foreign service employment ("post differentials")	Yes	¶ 714
Health insurance proceeds, not paid by the insured's employer or financed by the insured's employer through contributions that were not included in the employee's gross income	No	¶ 851
Health Savings Accounts partner's/shareholder's contributions made by partnership/S corporation	Yes	¶ 1020A
Hedging transactions, commodity futures transactions	Yes	¶ 1949
Hobby income (nonprofit activities, deductions limited)	Yes	¶ 1195
Illegal transactions, gains from: gambling, betting, lotteries, illegal businesses, embezzlement, protection money, etc.	Yes	¶ 2497
Illness, employee's compensation during, except to extent qualifying as insurance benefits	Yes	¶ 851
Incentive stock options	No	¶ 1923
Income tax refunds:		
. state, to extent of tax benefit from prior deduction	Yes	¶ 799
Inheritances	No	¶ 847
Insider's profits	Yes	¶ 1760
Insurance policy dividends:		
. distributed, up to total of all net premiums paid	No	¶ 2373
. retained by insurer and applied against premium	No	¶ 2373
Insurance proceeds:		
. business interruption insurance, based on lost income	Yes	¶ 1713
. use or occupancy, actual loss of net profits	Yes	¶ 1713
Interest-free loans:		
. loans in excess of *de minimis* amount, deemed interest	Yes	¶ 795
. loans within *de minimis* amount	No	¶ 795
Interest on:		
. bank deposits or accounts	Yes	¶ 724
. bonds, debentures, or notes	Yes	¶ 724
. claim awarded by judgment	Yes	¶ 852
. condemnation awards	Yes	¶ 1716
. deferred legacies	Yes	¶ 847
. federal obligations	Yes	¶ 2838
. insurance contracts	Yes	¶ 724
. refund of federal taxes	Yes	¶ 2765
Involuntary conversions, gain from, if reinvested	No	¶ 1748
Juror's mileage allowance	No	¶ 713
Jury fees	Yes	¶ 1010
Layoff pay benefits:		
. supplemental unemployment benefit plan, company-financed	Yes	¶ 722
Lease cancellation, payments received for	Yes	¶ 762
Leased retail space, cash or rent reductions received for construction or improvements	No	¶ 676
Legal services plan, employer contributions and value of benefits received	Yes	¶ 713

Income Item	*Includible in Income*	*Paragraph Reference*
Lessee's improvements, value of to lessor upon termination of lease	No	¶ 1234
Libel or slander of personal reputation, exemplary damages	Yes	¶ 852
Life insurance contract, distributed from retirement plan	Yes	¶ 721
Life insurance dividends:		
. distributed, up to total of all net premiums paid	No	¶ 2373
. retained by insurer and applied against premium	No	¶ 2373
Life insurance dividends, veterans	No	¶ 891
Life insurance, group-term premiums paid by employer, to extent of employer's cost of $50,000 or less of insurance	No	¶ 909
Life insurance proceeds, paid on death of the insured	No	¶ 803
Living expenses paid by insurance while damaged home being repaired	No	¶ 877
Lodging and meals:		
. furnished for employer's convenience and the employee must accept lodging as a condition of employment	No	¶ 873
. furnished for an employee affected by Hurricane Katrina or by the 2008 Midwestern storms	No	¶ 873
Losses, previously deducted, reimbursement for or expense items	Yes	¶ 1131
Meals, cost of, furnished on employer's premises for employer's convenience	No	¶ 873
Medicaid rebates to drug manufacturers	No	¶ 799
Medical care reimbursements, employer-financed accident and health plan	No	¶ 853
Mileage allowance	Yes	¶ 893
Military personnel, basic pay	Yes	¶ 895
Military service, employer-payments to employees	Yes	¶ 896
Mortgage indebtedness, prepayment at a discount to the extent of the discount	Yes	¶ 885
Moving expenses, qualified, employer-reimbursement	No	¶ 863
Mustering-out pay, military personnel	Yes	¶ 896
National Labor Relations Board, back-pay award	Yes	¶ 2604
National Service Life Insurance dividends	No	¶ 891
Nobel prize and similar awards if donated by recipient to qualified entity	No	¶ 785
Nonqualified deferred compensation plan, assets set aside to fund	Yes	¶ 2176
Obligations, federal interest on	Yes	¶ 724
Old age, disability, survivors' benefit payments, Social Security or Railroad Retirement Acts, below base amount	No	¶ 716
Parsonage, rental value of, furnished to a minister or rabbi as part of compensation; rental allowances if used to rent or provide a home	No	¶ 875
Partnership, distributive share of taxable income	Yes	¶ 431
Patents, sale to controlled foreign corporation	Yes	¶ 2491
Peace Corps volunteers, basic living and travel allowances	No	¶ 873

Income Item	Includible in Income	Paragraph Reference
Pensions:		
. annuities, etc., for personal injuries or sickness resulting from active service in armed forces of any country, National Oceanic and Atmospheric Administration, or U.S. Public Health Service	No	¶ 852
. distributions attributable to employer contributions	Yes	¶ 2124B
Personal physical injuries, damages	No	¶ 852
Political campaign contributions, with exceptions	No	¶ 696
Prizes	Yes	¶ 785
Professional fees	Yes	¶ 713
Pulitzer prize and similar awards if donated by recipient to qualified entity	No	¶ 785
Punitive damages	Yes	¶ 852
Purchases, nondiscriminatory employee-discounts	No	¶ 863
Railroad Retirement Act benefits, below base amount	No	¶ 716
Rebates, credits, price reductions received by customers	No	¶ 759
Rent reductions received by retail tenants for construction or improvements	No	¶ 764
Rents	Yes	¶ 762
Retired public safety officer's government pension plan distributions, up to $3,000 used for health insurance premiums	No	¶ 2124C
Retirement pay attributable to employer contributions other than veterans' disability retirement pay	Yes	¶ 716
Reward, informer's	Yes	¶ 701
Royalties	Yes	¶ 763
Salaries, including those of state and federal employees and amounts employer withholds for income, Social Security, and Railroad Retirement taxes	Yes	¶ 714
Scholarships and fellowships, degree programs, qualified	No	¶ 879
Security deposits, when retained by lessor	Yes	¶ 986
Sickness and injury benefits:		
. employer's plan, subject to limitations	No	¶ 851
. workers' compensation equivalent	No	¶ 851
Social Security old age, disability and survivor's benefits, below base amount	No	¶ 716
State contracts, profits on	Yes	¶ 759
Stock distributions in general	No	¶ 733A
. convertible preferred stock or debentures	Yes	¶ 1738
. disproportionate distributions	Yes	¶ 1738
. distributions of common and preferred stock	Yes	¶ 1738
. dividends on preferred stock	Yes	¶ 733
. increasing shareholder's proportionate interest	Yes	¶ 1738
. in lieu of money	Yes	¶ 1738
Stock options incentive	No	¶ 1923
Strike benefits, generally	Yes	¶ 702
Strike benefits, union and non-union employees in need, paid in form of food, clothes, etc.	No	¶ 702
Supper money, employer-paid, occasional due to overtime work	No	¶ 873
Supplemental security income (SSI) payments	No	¶ 716
Support payment, received from former spouse	Yes	¶ 772
Surviving spouse, decedent's salary continued, limited depending on intent	No	¶ 863
Survivor annuities, paid to family of public safety officer	No	¶ 813

Income Item	*Includible in Income*	*Paragraph Reference*
Taxes:		
. employees', employer-paid	Yes	¶ 713
. refunds of, not previously deducted or deducted without tax benefit	No	¶ 799
Tenancy, payments for surrender of	Yes	¶ 676
Tips	Yes	¶ 717
Treasure trove	Yes	¶ 701
Treaty-exempt income	No	¶ 2450
Tuition, employer-paid under qualified plans, up to $5,250 per year (including tuition paid for graduate-level courses beginning in 2002 to 2012)	No	¶ 871
Unemployment benefit plans, supplemental payments	Yes	¶ 722
Unemployment benefits	Yes	¶ 722
Unemployment benefits, up to $2,400 per year beginning in 2009	No	¶ 722
Universal service support program payments	Yes	¶ 1537
U.S. Savings Bonds, earned increase during year, if cash-method taxpayer elects	Yes	¶ 730
Use and occupancy insurance proceeds, income experience	Yes	¶ 877
Vacation fund allowance, union agreement	Yes	¶ 713
Veterans Administration payments	No	¶ 893
Veterans' benefits, generally	No	¶ 891
Veterans' bonuses, state	No	¶ 896
Wages	Yes	¶ 713
Workers' Compensation Acts, payments under	No	¶ 851
"Wrap-around" annuity contracts sold by life insurance companies, interest on	Yes	¶ 817

¶ 57 Checklist for Deductions

The Internal Revenue Code permits a number of wide-ranging deductions that may be taken into account in arriving at taxable income. However, the Code contains a number of rules and restrictions concerning the expenses that qualify as deductions and the taxpayers who may claim them. Although deductions generally reduce taxable income, deductions from gross income, available to all qualifying taxpayers, must be distinguished from deductions from adjusted gross income, available only to those taxpayers who itemize. Certain miscellaneous itemized deductions, including unreimbursed employee business expenses and investment expenses, are deductible by an individual only if the aggregate amount of such deductions exceeds two percent of adjusted gross income (¶ 1011). In addition, deductions that can be taken currently must be distinguished from those that can be taken over a number of tax years through depreciation or amortization.

The chart below lists a number of expenses that a taxpayer might incur. The chart indicates for each expense a symbol(s) representing the possible availability of a deduction, its timing, and whether it is deductible from gross income or adjusted gross income. Many deductions have special rules. The chart also provides the 2013 *U.S. Master Tax Guide* paragraph number where further information on the deduction may be found.

The following symbols are used:

D/GI = Deductible from gross income

D/AGI = Deductible from adjusted gross income

D/Am = Deductible over a period of time

ND = Nondeductible

Abandonment of business real property	D/GI, ¶ 1118
Accident and health plans	
. employer contributions	D/GI, ¶ 908
Accounting fees	
. business	D/GI, ¶ 901
. capital transactions	D/Am, ¶ 903
. connected with trade or business	D/GI, ¶ 901
. investors	D/AGI, ¶ 1086
. organization of business ($5,000 deduction and excess amortizable over 15 years)	D/GI, D/Am, ¶ 904
. reorganization of business	ND, ¶ 904
Accounting system, installation	D/GI, ¶ 991
Administrative expenses of estate	D/AGI, ¶ 2925
Admissions to political dinners, programs, inaugural balls, etc.	ND, ¶ 976
Advertising expenses	
. business cards	D/GI, ¶ 969
. catalogs	
. . long term	D/Am, ¶ 969
. generally	D/GI, ¶ 969
. home demonstrations	D/GI, ¶ 969
. package design costs	D/GI, ¶ 969
. political convention programs and other political publications	ND, ¶ 969
. prizes and contests	D/GI, ¶ 969
. product launch costs	D/GI, ¶ 969
. promotional activities	D/GI, ¶ 918
Airline pilot, special clothing	D/AGI, ¶ 1083
Airplane, heavy maintenance expenses	D/GI, ¶ 902
Alcohol fuels credit, unused	D/Am, ¶ 1365I
Alimony payments	D/GI, ¶ 1008
Amortization of premium on taxable bonds (optional)	D/AGI, ¶ 1012
Appraisal fees	
. acquisition of capital asset	ND, ¶ 990
. connection with trade or business	D/AGI, ¶ 1092
Architect's fees (capital expenditure)	D/Am, ¶ 903
Architectural services	
. domestic production activities	D/GI, ¶ 980F
Attorney's and accountant's fees in contesting tax claims (nonbusiness)	D/AGI, ¶ 1092
Attorney's fees	
. accounting suit by former partner, defense of	D/GI, ¶ 1010A
. acquisition of corporate control	ND, ¶ 237

. business debts, collection of	D/GI, ¶ 1093
. civil rights suits	D/GI, ¶ 1010A
. condemnation proceeding, defense of	ND, ¶ 1010A
. disbarment proceedings	D/GI, ¶ 981
. divorce	
. . obtaining alimony	D/GI, ¶ 1093
. . proceedings	ND, ¶ 1093
. . property settlement	ND, ¶ 1093
. personal affairs	ND, ¶ 1093
. slander prosecution (personal)	ND, ¶ 1010A
. tax advice on investments	D/AGI, ¶ 1983;¶ 1086
. title clearance	
. . land	ND, ¶ 1093
. . stock	ND, ¶ 1093
. will preparation	ND, ¶ 973
Automobile expenses	
. business use by employee	
. . unreimbursed	D/AGI, ¶ 947
. business use by self-employed person	
. . chauffeur's salary	D/GI, ¶ 906
. . cost of car	D/GI, D/Am, ¶ 1214
. . garage rentals	D/GI, ¶ 946
. . gas	D/GI, ¶ 946
. . insurance	D/GI, ¶ 946
. . license fees	D/GI, ¶ 946
. . loss on sale	D/GI, ¶ 946
. . oil and lubrication	D/GI, ¶ 946
. . parking	D/GI, ¶ 946
. . repairs	D/GI, ¶ 946
. . tires	D/GI, ¶ 946
. . washing	D/GI, ¶ 946
. nonbusiness casualty loss (limited)	D/AGI, ¶ 1124
. pleasure use	ND, ¶ 1211
. rural mail carriers (limited)	D/AGI, ¶ 947
Bad debts	
. business	D/GI, ¶ 1145
. nonbusiness	D/GI, ¶ 1169
Bar admission and examination fees	ND, ¶ 981
Baseball player's uniforms	D/AGI, ¶ 1083
Baseball team equipment for business publicity	D/GI, ¶ 969
Black lung benefits trust, employer contributions	D/GI, ¶ 692
Bookmakers, business expenses	D/GI, ¶ 785
Building property, energy efficient property for commercial buildings (2006-2013)	D/GI, ¶ 977D

Building replacements (capital expenditure)	D/Am, ¶ 991
Burglar alarm system, cost of installing (business capital expenditure)	D/Am, ¶ 991
Burial expenses	ND, ¶ 2925
Business bad debts	D/GI, ¶ 1145
Business conventions	
. cruise ship (limited)	D/GI, ¶ 959
. foreign conventions (limited)	D/GI, ¶ 960
. political conventions (must be related to trade or business)	D/GI, ¶ 959; ¶ 976
. travel expenses	D/GI, ¶ 949
Business expenses	D/GI, ¶ 901
Business meals	50% D/GI, ¶ 914
Business startup expenses ($5,000 deduction and excess amortizable over 15 years)	D/GI, D/Am, ¶ 904
Campaign contributions	ND, ¶ 976
Capital expenditures	ND, D/Am, ¶ 991
Capital loss individual (limited)	D/GI, ¶ 1754
Car expenses (see "Automobile expenses")	
Career counseling costs	D/AGI, ¶ 1081
Caribbean convention expenses (business)	D/GI, ¶ 955
Carrying charges deductible as interest where installment sales contract states carrying charge separately	D/AGI, ¶ 1614
Casualty losses, personal, deduction limited to amount of each loss in excess of $100 and then only to the extent losses exceed 10% of adjusted gross income	D/AGI, ¶ 1124
Charitable contributions	
. corporations (limited)	D/GI, ¶ 927
. . computer technology equipment to schools and public libraries (through 2011)	D/GI, ¶ 930
. individuals (limited)	D/AGI, ¶ 1058; ¶ 1059
. . appreciated property	D/AGI, ¶ 1062
. where organization carries on lobbying activities	ND, ¶ 974
Child support payments	ND, ¶ 776
Circulation expenditures, newspapers, magazine periodicals	D/GI, ¶ 971

Classroom expenses, teachers (2002-2011) . . . D/GI, ¶ 1084
Clinical testing deduction if credit is elected . . . . . ND, ¶ 1365S
Club dues (limited) . . . . . D/AGI, ¶ 913A
Coal royalty contracts
. expenses related to . . . ND, ¶ 1289
. if there is no production, or no income, under contracts . . . . D/AGI, ¶ 1289
Commissions
. paid as compensation . D/GI, ¶ 906
. sale of real estate or securities
. . dealers . . . . D/GI, ¶ 1983
. . other taxpayers . . . . ND, ¶ 906
Commissions on sale of real estate and securities, dealer only (other than taxpayers deduct from selling price) D/GI, ¶ 1983
Commuting expenses . . . . ND, ¶ 945
Compensation, reasonable . D/GI, ¶ 906
Computer software (business use)
. development costs . . . D/GI, D/Am, ¶ 980
. leased software . . . . D/GI, ¶ 980
. purchased software . . D/Am, ¶ 980
Construction
. domestic production activities . . . . D/GI, ¶ 980F
Contributions by employer to employer-financed accident and health plans for benefit of employees . . . . D/GI, ¶ 908
Contributions by employer to state unemployment insurance and state disability funds . . . . D/GI, ¶ 922
Contributions by members to a labor union (voluntary) ND, ¶ 1080
Contributions paid (within certain limits) during year to charitable, etc., organizations . . . . D/AGI, ¶ 1058
Convention (political) programs, cost of advertising in . . . . . . ND, ¶ 976
Conventions (see "Business conventions")
Cooperative housing corporation, share of taxes or interest paid by . . . . . D/AGI, ¶ 1040
Copyright costs . . . . D/Am, ¶ 1089
Cost recovery, business property or property held for the production of income . . . . D/Am, ¶ 1747
Credit and debit card convenience fees for paying taxes . . . . D/AGI, ¶ 1092
Cruise ship business conventions (limited) . . . D/GI, ¶ 959
Custodian fees . . . . D/AGI, ¶ 1086
Day care providers
. standard meal deduction . . . . D/GI, ¶ 964
Defending title to property (capital expenditure) . . . ND, ¶ 1611
Demolition of structure . . . ND, ¶ 1112
Dependents . . . . D/AGI, ¶ 103
Depletion . . . . D/Am, ¶ 1289
Depreciation, business property or property held for production of income . D/Am, ¶ 1747
. election to expense (limited) . . . . D/GI, ¶ 1747
Diaper service . . . . ND, ¶ 1015
Disbarment proceedings, attorneys' fees and expenses in defending . . D/GI, ¶ 981
Doctor's staff privilege fees at hospital (capital expenditures) . . . . D/Am, ¶ 981
Domestic production activities . . . . D/GI, ¶ 980A
Dues
. chamber of commerce . D/GI, ¶ 913A
. charitable, religious, educational organizations . . . . . . D/AGI, ¶ 1059
. clubs organized for business, pleasure, recreation, or any other social purpose . . . . . ND, ¶ 913
. professional associations . . . . D/GI, ¶ 981
. union dues . . . . D/AGI, ¶ 1080
Education expenses
. higher education expenses (2002-2011) D/GI, ¶ 1082
Education expenses (employee)
. maintaining or improving required skills . . . . . D/AGI, ¶ 1082
. minimum requirements for job . . . . ND, ¶ 1082
. new trade or business . ND, ¶ 1082
Educational assistance plan payments . . . . D/GI, ¶ 2192D
Efficiency engineers' fees . . D/GI, ¶ 901
Electricity
. domestic production activities . . . . D/GI, ¶ 980
Embezzlement loss . . . . . D/GI, ¶ 1125
Employee's expenses
. entertaining customers
. . reimbursed expenses D/GI, ¶ 915
. . unreimbursed expenses . . . . 50% D/AGI, ¶ 910

Item	Treatment
. meals and lodging away from home	
. . reimbursed	D/GI, ¶ 954
. . unreimbursed lodging	D/AGI, ¶ 949
. . unreimbursed meals	50% D/AGI, ¶ 910
. move to a new work location	D/GI, ¶ 1076
. transportation expenses	
. . unreimbursed (limited)	D/AGI, ¶ 916
Employees' life insurance, paid by employer	
. employee beneficiary	D/GI, ¶ 909
. employer beneficiary	ND, ¶ 909
Employees, payments for injuries to, not compensated by insurance; disability benefits	D/GI, ¶ 2190B
Employees, severance payments to	D/GI, ¶ 2190F
Employees, training expenses for	D/GI, ¶ 1082
Employment, fees for obtaining	D/AGI, ¶ 1081
Employment taxes	
. employer's payment under Federal Unemployment Tax Act	
. . employer (but not deductible if paid on wages of domestics)	D/GI, ¶ 2650
. employer's taxes under Federal Insurance Contributions Act	
. . employer (deductible only as business expense)	D/GI, ¶ 923
. employer's taxes under Railroad Retirement Act	
. . employer (deductible only as business expense)	D/GI, ¶ 716
. Federal Unemployment Tax Act	D/GI, ¶ 2649
. Railroad Retirement Act	D/GI, ¶ 716
. Social Security Act	D/GI, ¶ 923
Energy efficient property, commercial building property (2006-2013)	D/GI, ¶ 977D
Engineering services	
. domestic production activities	D/GI, ¶ 980F
Entertainment expenses (business, nonemployee)	
. athletic club dues	ND, ¶ 913A
. facilities owned and used by the taxpayer	ND, ¶ 913
. food	
. . furnished to employees on premises	D/GI, ¶ 915
. . meals directly related to business	50% D/GI, ¶ 911
. . provided for customers	50% D/GI, ¶ 914
Environmental cleanup costs (brownfields) (through 2011)	D/GI, ¶ 977
Environmental cleanup costs, construction groundwater treatment facilities	ND, ¶ 977
Environmental cleanup costs, hazardous waste from taxpayer's business	D/GI, ¶ 977
Environmental cleanup costs, hazardous waste from taxpayer's manufacturing business	ND, ¶ 977
Environmental impact statement, preparation of	D/Am, D/GI, ¶ 977
Environmental protection agency, sulfur regulation compliance (limited)	D/GI, ¶ 1285
Estate tax	ND, ¶ 2912
Excess deductions on termination of estate or trust	D/AGI, ¶ 507
Excise taxes on personal goods	ND, ¶ 1611
Expenditures violating public policy	ND, ¶ 973
Farmers	
. domestic production activities	D/GI, ¶ 980G
. fertilizers, lime, etc.	D/GI, ¶ 985
. soil and water conservation	D/GI, ¶ 982
Federal income tax	ND, ¶ 924
Federal National Mortgage Association	
. first buyers, excess of issue price over market value on date of issuance	D/GI, ¶ 975
Fiduciaries' fees	D/AGI, ¶ 528
Film and television	
. domestic production activities	D/GI, ¶ 980D
. small film and television production (limited)	D/GI, ¶ 901
Finance charges other than carrying charges or loan fees (limited)	D/AGI, ¶ 1045
Fines and penalties	
. child labor violations	ND, ¶ 972
. Fair Labor Standards Act awards	D/GI, ¶ 972
. federal income tax penalties	ND, ¶ 972

CHECKLISTS

. . key employees	D/GI, ¶ 804
. personal residence	ND, ¶ 1047
. required for credit	
. . premiums paid by creditor	D/GI, ¶ 1048A
. . premiums paid by debtor	ND, ¶ 1048A
Intangible assets (as defined in Code Sec. 197)	D/Am, ¶ 1288
Interest and carrying charges related to a commodity straddle position in excess of income generated by straddle position	ND, ¶ 1949
Interest (with exceptions and limitations, see below)	D/AGI, ¶ 937
. education loans (limited)	D/GI, ¶ 1005
. interest related to tax-exempt income	ND, ¶ 970
. interest related to life insurance contracts (limited)	D/AGI, ¶ 721
. personal obligations (limited)	ND, ¶ 1052
. points, purchase of residence	D/AGI, ¶ 1055
. prepaid	D/Am, D/GI, ¶ 1055
. property held for production of rent or royalties	D/GI, ¶ 1089
. trade or business debts	D/GI, ¶ 937
Interest forfeiture	
. premature withdrawal from time savings account	D/GI, ¶ 1120
Interest on tax deficiencies	
. corporation	D/GI, ¶ 937A
. individual, generally	ND, ¶ 937A
. . related to trade or business	D/GI, ND, ¶ 937A
. underpayment attributable to nondisclosed reportable transaction	ND, ¶ 2838
Investigatory costs	
. acquisition of specific business	ND, ¶ 904
. . business search	D/GI, D/Am, ¶ 904
Investor's expenses (except incurred in earning tax-exempt interest)	D/AGI, ¶ 1086
ISO 9000 costs	D/GI, ¶ 901
Job hunting expenses	
. new trade or business	ND, ¶ 1081
. resume preparation costs	D/AGI, ¶ 1081
. same trade or business	D/AGI, ¶ 1081
. travel and transportation to new area	D/AGI, ¶ 1081
Jockey's riding apparel	D/AGI, ¶ 1083
Labor union dues	D/AGI, ¶ 1080
Laundry, dry cleaning, pressing charges (business travel)	D/AGI, ¶ 902
Legal expenses and fees	
. business	D/GI, ¶ 973
. investors	D/AGI, ¶ 1086
. production of income	D/AGI, ¶ 1093
. tax determination	D/AGI, ¶ 1092
Legislators	
. congressional living expenses, away from home	
. . expenses of moving to capital	D/AGI, ¶ 956
. state	
. . local transportation	D/AGI, ¶ 956
. . meals and lodging	D/AGI, ¶ 956
. . travel expenses	D/AGI, ¶ 956
License fees	
. treated as personal property tax	D/AGI, ¶ 1021
Life insurance premiums, debts incurred to purchase, paid by employer	D/GI, ¶ 909
. employee or other beneficiary	D/GI, ¶ 909
. employer beneficiary	ND, ¶ 804
Loan cost—stock reacquisition	ND, ¶ 1044
Lobbying expense	
. appearances before legislative bodies	ND, ¶ 974
. expenditures to influence voters	ND, ¶ 974
. professional lobbyist's expenses	D/GI, ¶ 974
Losses	
. gambling (trade or business)	D/AGI, ¶ 1121
. net operating loss	D/GI, ¶ 1173
. sale or exchange of property	
. . business property	D/GI, ¶ 1007
. . related parties	ND, ¶ 905
. . capital assets (business motive)	D/GI, ¶ 1007
. theft or casualty	
. . individual property	D/AGI, ¶ 1124; ¶ 1125
. . rent-or royalty-generating property	D/GI, ¶ 1089
. worthless stock and securities	D/GI, ¶ 1916
Lump sum distribution-ordinary income portion	D/GI, ¶ 2124A
Machinery	
. incidental repairs	D/GI, ¶ 991

Materials and supplies, business (incidentals) . . D/GI, ¶ 901
Maternity clothes . . . . ND, ¶ 1016
Meals provided for employees
. employer's cost of providing meals on premises . . . D/GI, ¶ 873
. meals directly related to business . . . . 50% D/GI, ¶ 911
Medical, dental and hospital expenses (to the extent exceeding 7.5% of adjusted gross income) (for a detailed list of such expenses, see ¶ 59) . . . . D/AGI, ¶ 1015
Medical, dental and hospital expenses less than 7.5% of adjusted gross income . . ND, ¶ 1015
Medical insurance premiums (see ¶ 59)
Medical savings account . . D/GI, ¶ 2197C
Mine development expenditures . . . . D/GI, ¶ 988
Mine exploration expenditures . . . . D/GI, ¶ 987
Mortgages
. insurance premiums (2007-2011) . . . . D/AGI, ¶ 1048A
. interest . . . . D/AGI, ¶ 1047
Moving expenses
. meals . . . . ND, ¶ 1073
. other expenses
. . employee, reimbursed . . . . D/GI, ¶ 1076
. . employee, unreimbursed . . . . D/GI ¶ 1073
. . self employed . . . . . D/GI, ¶ 1073
Moving machinery . . . . . . D/GI, ¶ 902
Musician's clothing, used exclusively in business . . D/AGI, ¶ 1083
National Labor Relations Board award to employees, payment by employer . . . D/GI, ¶ 2604
Net operating loss deduction . . . . D/GI, ¶ 1430
New business, cost of starting up ($5,000 deduction and excess amortizable over 15 years) . . . . D/GI, D/Am, ¶ 904
Nonbusiness bad debts (limited) . . . . D/GI, ¶ 1007
Nontrade or nonbusiness expenses incurred in preserving income-producing property . . . . D/AGI, ¶ 1085
Nurse's uniform . . . . D/AGI, ¶ 1083
Office in home (limited)
. employee . . . . D/AGI, ¶ 965,
. principal place of business . . . . D/GI, ¶ 945
Office supplies . . . . D/GI, ¶ 963
Operating loss in prior or subsequent year . . . . . . D/GI, ¶ 1173
Organization expenses of corporation ($5,000 deduction and excess amortizable over 15 years) . . . . D/GI, D/Am, ¶ 904
Original construction of greens on a golf course . ND, ¶ 991
Outside salesperson
. meals—see Meals, employees' business
. moving expenses—see Moving expenses
. travel expenses . . . . . D/AGI, ¶ 941B; ¶ 1073
Package design costs . . . . D/GI, ¶ 969
Partners' fixed or guaranteed payments for services or for use of capital (allowed as business deduction to partnership) . . . . D/GI, ¶ 421
Partnership organization expenses, unless election to amortize . . . . ND, ¶ 477
Passport fee, business trip . D/GI, ¶ 955
Passport fee (except for business purposes) . . . . ND, ¶ 955
Penalties . . . . generally ND, ¶ 972
. Environmental Protection Agency:
. . Clean Air Act violation . . . . ND, ¶ 972
. . nonconformance penalty . . . . D/GI, ¶ 972
. penalty on early withdrawal of time deposit . . . . D/GI, ¶ 1120
Performing artists (limitation on gross income)
. employee business expenses . . . . D/GI, ¶ 941A
Permanent improvements
. business property . . . D/Am, ¶ 1201
. tenants . . . . D/Am, ¶ 764
"Points" on home mortgage (if customarily required in geographic area in which indebtedness was incurred) . . . . D/AGI, ¶ 1055
Police officer's uniform and cost of cleaning . . . . . . D/AGI, ¶ 1083
Political contributions
. corporations, businesses, etc. . . . . ND, ¶ 976
. individuals . . . . ND, ¶ 976

Political publications, cost of advertising in . . . . ND (generally), ¶ 976
Postage costs, business . . . D/GI, ¶ 901
Premiums paid on a business insurance "professional overhead expense disability policy" . . . . D/GI, ¶ 908A
Prepaid interest or finance charges . . . . D/Am, ¶ 1055
Prizes and contests—see "Promotional activities"
Professional associations, dues
. unreimbursed employee expense . . . . D/AGI, ¶ 981
Professional books and journals and information services
. unreimbursed employee expense . . . . D/AGI, ¶ 981
Promotional activities
. coupons . . . . D/GI, ¶ 918
. prizes and contests . . . D/GI, ¶ 969
Protective clothing . . . . . . D/AGI, ¶ 1083
Raffle tickets, cost of . . . . . ND, ¶ 1061
Railroad retirement tax paid by employers . . . . D/GI, ¶ 716
Railway trainman's uniform D/AGI, ¶ 1083
Real estate impact fees . . . ND, ¶ 1288A
Reconditioning and health-restoring expenses of employees paid by employers . . . . D/GI, ¶ 1016
Refinery property (limited) . D/GI, ¶ 977C
Reforestation costs . . . . . . D/GI, D/Am, ¶ 530
Reimbursed expenses (otherwise deductible) . . D/GI, ¶ 942
Removal of architectural and transportation barriers to the handicapped and elderly (limited) . . . . . . D/AGI, ¶ 1365M
Rent, business property . . . D/GI, ¶ 986
Reorganization expenditures . . . . ND, ¶ 904
Repairs to business property . . . . D/GI, D/Am, ¶ 977E
Repairs to personal residence . . . . ND, ¶ 966
Research and experimental expenditures connected with a trade or business . D/GI, D/Am, ¶ 979
Restaurant smallwares (limited) . . . . D/GI, ¶ 1825
Retirement plans, contributions to
. employer . . . . D/GI, ¶ 2102
. individuals (limited) . . D/GI, ¶ 2102
. self-employed individuals . . . . D/GI, ¶ 2163
. simplified employee pension contributions D/GI, ¶ 2153A
Return, federal or state income tax, gift tax, etc., cost of having prepared (including investor) . . . . D/AGI, ¶ 973
Safe deposit boxes, rental for protection of income producing property
. investor . . . . D/AGI, ¶ 1085
Salaries
. bonuses . . . . D/GI, ¶ 906
. commissions . . . . . . D/GI, ¶ 906
. related parties . . . . . . D/GI, ¶ 915
Salespersons' expenses
. reimbursed . . . . D/GI, ¶ 942
. unreimbursed . . . . . . D/AGI ¶ 942
. . automobile expenses D/AGI, ¶ 946
. . entertaining customers, reimbursed . . . . D/GI, ¶ 915
. . entertaining customers, unreimbursed . . . . . . 50% D/AGI, ¶ 910
. . gifts to customers (up to $25) . . . . D/AGI, ¶ 918
. . membership dues in business or social clubs . . . . ND, ¶ 981
. . subscriptions to business, professional or trade publications, if for business reasons . D/AGI, ¶ 981
. . transportation expenses, unreimbursed . . . . . D/AGI, ¶ 916
. . travel expenses . . . . D/AGI, ¶ 949
Sales tax on purchase of new motor vehicles . . . . D/AGI, ¶ 1021
Self-employment tax (limited to 50%) . . . . D/GI, ¶ 2664
Servants, social security taxes paid for . . . . ND, ¶ 923
Severance payments . . . . . D/GI, ¶ 2190F
Shareholder's proxy fight expenses . . . . D/AGI, ¶ 309
Smallwares, restaurant (limited) . . . . D/GI, ¶ 1825
Social security taxes
. employees . . . . ND, ¶ 923
. employers . . . . D/GI (only as business expense), ¶ 923
Soil and water conservation expenditures, farmers . . D/GI, D/Am, ¶ 982
Stamp taxes
. dealers/investors . . . . D/GI, ¶ 1611
. trade or business . . . . D/GI, ¶ 1611

CHECKLISTS

Truck tires
. replacement tires (limited) . . . . D/GI, ¶ 946
. with life less than a year . . . . D/GI, ¶ 946
Truck use tax (unless as business expense) . . . . ND, ¶ 1021
Uncollectible notes (see "Bad debts")
Uniform and special clothing costs
. baseball uniforms . . . . D/AGI, ¶ 1083
. clothing required for business . . . . D/AGI, ¶ 1083
. employer-reimbursed costs . . . . D/GI, ¶ 1083
. jockey's riding apparel . D/AGI, ¶ 1083
. nurses' uniforms . . . . D/AGI, ¶ 1083
. protective clothing . . . D/AGI, ¶ 1083
. work shoes, metal tipped . . . . D/AGI, ¶ 1083
Union payments
. dues . . . . D/AGI, ¶ 1080
. fines . . . . D/AGI, ¶ 972
Utilities, personal . . . . ND, ¶ 963
Wages and salaries . . . . . . D/GI, ¶ 906
Waiters, waitresses
. special uniforms . . . . D/AGI, ¶ 1083
Water, potable
. domesitc production activities . . . . D/GI, ¶ 980D
Work shoes, metal tipped for protection of worker . . . D/AGI, ¶ 1083

CHECKLISTS

¶ 59 Checklist for Medical Expenses

Generally, a medical expense deduction is allowed for expenses incurred in the diagnosis, cure, mitigation, treatment or prevention of disease, or for the purpose of affecting any structure or function of the body for the individual or for the individual's spouse or dependents. The deduction covers expenses that have not been reimbursed by medical insurance or other sources.

Despite the broad scope of medical expenses, not every expense incurred for medical care is deductible. Also, there is a 7.5-percent floor on the medical expense deduction. The chart, below, lists specific types of expenses and whether or not a deduction for the expense is permitted. The user can easily check whether an official determination has been made as to the deductibility of a particular type of expense.

Medical Expense	*Deductible*	*Authority*
Abortion		
. legal	Yes	Rev. Rul. 73-201, 1973-1 CB 140, as clarified by Rev. Rul. 73-603, 1973-2 CB 76, and Rev. Rul. 97-9, 1997-1 CB 77
Accident and health insurance		
. medical care portion separately stated and reasonable in amount	Yes	Code Sec. 213(d)(1)(D) and (d)(6) and Reg. § 1.213-1(e)(4)
. medical care portion not separately stated or, if separately stated, not reasonable in amount	No	Code Sec. 213(d)(6)(A) and Reg. § 1.213-1(e)(4)
Acupuncture	Yes	Rev. Rul. 72-593, 1972-2 CB 180
Adoption		
. medical costs of adopted child	Yes	Rev. Rul. 60-255, 1960-2 CB 105
. medical costs of natural mother	No	*B.L. Kilpatrick,* 68 TC 469, Dec. 34,493
Air conditioner		
. allergy relief	Yes	Rev. Rul. 55-261, 1955-1 CB 307
. cystic fibrosis relief	Yes	*R. Gerard,* 37 TC 826, Dec. 25,331 (Acq.)
. permanent improvement to property	No	*G.W. Wade,* 61-2 USTC ¶ 9709
Alcoholism, treatment of	Yes	Rev. Rul. 73-325, 1973-2 CB 75
Ambulance hire	Yes	Reg. § 1.213-1(e)(1)(ii)
Anticipated medical expenses	No	*W.B. Andrews,* 37 TCM 744, Dec. 35,144(M), TC Memo. 1978-174
Attendant to accompany blind or deaf student	Yes	Rev. Rul. 64-173, 1964-1 CB (Part 1) 121; *R.A. Baer Est.,* 26 TCM 170, Dec. 28,352(M), TC Memo. 1967-34
Automobile (see Car)		
Baby sitting expenses to enable parent to see doctor	No	Rev. Rul. 78-266, 1978-2 CB 123
Birth control pills	Yes	Rev. Rul. 73-200, 1973-1 CB 140
Blind persons		
. attendant to accompany student	Yes	Rev. Rul. 64-173, 1964-1 (Part I) CB 121
. braille books and magazines, excess cost of regular editions	Yes	Rev. Rul. 75-318, 1975-2 CB 88
. seeing-eye dog	Yes	Rev. Rul. 55-261, 1955-1 CB 307
. special education (see Schools, special)		
. special educational aids to mitigate condition	Yes	Rev. Rul. 58-223, 1958-1 CB 156
Breast pumps and supplies	Yes	Announcement 2011-14, 2011-9 I.R.B. 532

Medical Expense	*Deductible*	*Authority*
Capital expenditures		
. home modifications for handicapped individual	Yes	Rev. Rul. 87-106, 1987-2 CB 67
. permanent improvement to property	No	Reg. § 1.213-1(e)(1)(iii)
. primary purpose medical care	Yes	Reg. § 1.213-1(e)(1)(iii)
Car		
. depreciation on	No	*M.S. Gordon,* 37 TC 986, CCH Dec. 25,364; *R.K. Weary,* CA-10, 75-1 USTC ¶ 9173, 510 F.2d 435, *cert. denied,* 423 U.S. 838
. equipped to accommodate wheelchair passengers	Yes	Rev. Rul. 70-606, 1970-2 CB 66
. insurance, medical coverage for persons other than taxpayer, spouse and children	No	Rev. Rul. 73-483, 1973-2 CB 75
. special controls for a person with a disability	Yes	*S.H. Weinzimer,* 17 TCM 712, Dec. 23,100(M), TC Memo. 1958-137
Chauffeur, salary of	No	*W.E. Buck,* 47 TC 113, CCH Dec. 28,175
Chemical dependency treatment (see Alcoholism, treatment of, and Drug addiction, recovery from)		
Childbirth preparation classes		
. "coach"	No	IRS Letter Ruling 8919009, 2-6-89, CCH IRS LETTER RULINGS REPORTS
. mother	Yes	IRS Letter Ruling 8919009, 2-6-89, CCH IRS LETTER RULINGS REPORTS
Chiropractors	Yes	Rev. Rul. 63-91, 1963-1 CB 54
Christian Science treatment	Yes	Rev. Rul. 55-261, 1955-1 CB 307, as modified by Rev. Rul. 63-91, 1963-1 CB 54
Clarinet and lessons, alleviation of severe teeth malocclusion	Yes	Rev. Rul. 62-210, 1962-2 CB 89
Clothing, suitable for use other than therapy	No	*M.C. Montgomery,* 51 TC 410, Dec. 29,270, aff'd on other issues, CA-6, 70-2 USTC ¶ 9466, 428 F2d 243
Computer data bank, storage and retrieval of medical records	Yes	Rev. Rul. 71-282, 1971-2 CB 166
Contact lenses	Yes	Reg. § 1.213-1(e)(1)(iii)
. replacement insurance	Yes	Rev. Rul. 74-429, 1974-2 CB 83
Contraceptives, prescription	Yes	Rev. Rul. 73-200, 1973-1 CB 140
Cosmetic surgery		
. necessary to ameliorate a deformity arising from a congenital abnormality, personal injury, or disfiguring disease	Yes	Code Sec. 213(d)(9); Senate Finance Committee Report to P.L. 101-508
. unnecessary	No	Code Sec. 213(d)(9); Senate Finance Committee Report to P.L. 101-508
Crime victims, compensated medical expenses of	No	Rev. Rul. 74-74, 1974-1 CB 18
Crutches	Yes	Reg. § 1.213-1(e)(1)(iii)
Dancing lessons	No	*R.C. France,* CA-6, 82-1 USTC ¶ 9225

CHECKLISTS

Medical Expense	*Deductible*	*Authority*
Deaf persons		
. hearing aid	Yes	Rev. Rul. 55-261, 1955-1 CB 307
. hearing-aid animal	Yes	Rev. Rul. 68-295, 1968-1 CB 92
. lip reading expenses for the deaf	Yes	Rev. Rul. 55-261, 1955-1 CB 307
. notetaker, deaf student	Yes	*R.A. Baer Est.*, 26 TCM 170, Dec. 28,352(M), TC Memo. 1967-34
. special education (see Schools, special)		
. telephone, specially equipped, including repairs	Yes	Rev. Rul. 71-48, 1971-1 CB 99, as amplified by Rev. Rul. 73-53, 1973-1 CB 139
. television, closed-caption decoder	Yes	Rev. Rul. 80-340, 1980-2 CB 81
. visual alert system	Yes	IRS Letter Ruling 8250040, 9-13-82, CCH IRS LETTER RULINGS REPORTS
Dental fees	Yes	Reg. § 1.213-1(e)(1)(ii)
Dentures (artificial teeth)	Yes	Reg. § 1.213-1(e)(1)(ii)
Deprogramming services	No	IRS Letter Ruling 8021004, February 26, 1980 (estimated), CCH IRS LETTER RULINGS REPORTS
Diagnostic fees	Yes	Reg. § 1.213-1(e)(1)(ii)
Diaper service	No	Rev. Rul. 55-261, 1955-1 CB 307
Diapers, disposable, used due to severe neurological disease	Yes	IRS Letter Ruling 8137085, 6-17-81, CCH IRS LETTER RULINGS REPORTS
Doctors' fees	Yes	Reg. § 1.213-1(e)(1)(i)
Domestic aid, type that would be rendered by nurse	Yes	Rev. Rul. 58-339, 1958-2 CB 106
Drug addiction, recovery from	Yes	Rev. Rul. 72-226, 1972-1 CB 96
Drugs, illegal/controlled substances, even when prescribed	No	Rev. Rul. 97-9, 1997-1 CB 77
Drugs, prescription	Yes	Code Sec. 213(b)
Dust elimination system	No	*F.S. Delp,* 30 TC 1230, Dec. 23,167
Dyslexia, language training	Yes	Rev. Rul. 69-607, 1969-2 CB 40
Ear piercing	No	Rev. Rul. 82-111, 1982-1 CB 48
Electrolysis	No	Code Sec. 213(d)(9); Senate Finance Committee Report to P.L. 101-508
Elevator, alleviation of cardiac condition	Yes	*J.E. Berry,* DC Okla., 58-2 USTC ¶ 9870, 174 FSupp 748; Rev. Rul. 59-411, 1959-2 CB 100, as modified by Rev. Rul. 83-33, 1983-1 CB 70
Eye examinations and glasses	Yes	Reg. § 1.213-1(e)(1)(ii), (iii)
Fallout shelter, prevention of disease	No	*F.H. Daniels,* 41 TC 324, Dec. 26,414
Fertility enhancement	Yes	IRS Publication No. 502, "Medical and Dental Expenses"
Fluoride device; on advice of dentist	Yes	Rev. Rul. 64-267, 1964-2 CB 69
Funeral expenses	No	*K.P. Carr,* 39 TCM 253, Dec. 36,352(M), TC Memo. 1979-400
Furnace	No	*J.L. Seymour,* 14 TC 1111, Dec. 17,675
Glasses	Yes	Reg. § 1.213-1(e)(1)(ii)
Gravestone	No	*C.W. Libby Est.,* 14 TCM 699, Dec. 21,110(M), TC Memo. 1955-180
Guide animals (see Service animals)		
Hair transplants, surgical	No	Code Sec. 213(d)(9); Senate Finance Committee Report to P.L. 101-508

Medical Expense	*Deductible*	*Authority*
Halfway house, adjustment to mental hospital	Yes	IRS Letter Ruling 7714016, January 10, 1977, CCH IRS LETTER RULINGS REPORTS
Handicapped persons (see, also, specific handicap or equipment)		
. home modification (see Capital expenses)		
. special training or education (see Schools, special)		
Health club dues		
. not related to a particular medical condition	No	Rev. Rul. 55-261, 1955-1 CB 307
. prescribed by physician for medical condition	Yes	Rev. Rul. 55-261, 1955-1 CB 307
Health Maintenance Organization (HMO)	Yes	IRS Publication No. 502, "Medical and Dental Expenses"
Hearing aids (see Deaf persons)		
Hospital care, in-patient	Yes	Reg. § 1.213-1(e)(1)(v)
Hospital services	Yes	Reg. § 1.213-1(e)(1)(ii)
Hygienic supplies	No	Reg. § 1.213-1(e)(2); *O.G. Russell*, 12 TCM 1276, Dec. 19,973(M)
Indian medicine man	Yes	*R.H. Tso*, 40 TCM 1277, Dec. 37,260(M), TC Memo. 1980-339
Insulin	Yes	Code Sec. 213(b)
Insurance		
. accident and health insurance (see Accident and health insurance)		
. long term care insurance (within limits)	Yes	Code Sec. 213(d)(1)(D); Code Sec. 7702B
. Medicare A coverage	Yes	Rev. Rul. 79-175, 1979-1 CB 117
. premiums for loss of income	No	Reg. § 1.213-1(e)(4)
. premiums for loss of life, limb or sight	No	Reg. § 1.213-1(e)(4)
. premiums for medical care	Yes	Reg. § 1.213-1(e)(4)
. self-employed	Yes	Code Sec. 162(l)
Iron lung	Yes	Rev. Rul. 55-261, 1955-1 CB 307
Laboratory fees	Yes	Reg. § 1.213-1(e)(1)(ii)
Lactation expenses	Yes	Announcement 2011-14, 2011-9 I.R.B. 532
Laetrile, prescribed	No	Rev. Rul. 97-9, 1997-1 CB 77
Lamaze classes (see Childbirth preparation classes)		
Laser eye surgery	Yes	Rev. Rul. 2003-57, 2003-1 CB 959
Lead paint, removal	Yes	Rev. Rul. 79-66, 1979-1 CB 114
Legal expenses		
. authorization of treatment for mental illness	Yes	Rev. Rul. 71-281, 1971-2 CB 165
. divorce upon medical advice	No	*J.H. Jacobs*, 62 TC 813, Dec. 32,773
Lifetime medical care, prepaid; retirement home	Yes	Rev. Rul. 75-302, 1975-2 CB 86, Rev. Rul. 75-303, 1975-2 CB 87, as clarified by Rev. Rul. 93-72, 1993-2 CB 77
Limbs, artificial	Yes	Reg. § 1.213-1(e)(1)(ii)
Lodging		
. care not provided in hospital or equivalent outpatient facility	No	*A.L. Polyak*, 94 TC 337, CCH Dec. ¶ 46,443
. limited to $50 per night	Yes	Code Sec. 213(d)(2)

CHECKLISTS

Medical Expense	*Deductible*	*Authority*
Long term care expenses	Yes	Code Sec. 213(d)(1)(C); Code Sec. 7702B
Marriage counseling	No	Rev. Rul. 75-319, 1975-2 CB 88
Maternity clothes	No	Rev. Rul. 55-261, 1955-1 CB 307
Mattress, prescribed for alleviation of arthritis	Yes	Rev. Rul. 55-261, 1955-1 CB 307
Nursing home, medical reasons	Yes	*W.B. Counts,* 42 TC 755, Dec. 26,893 (Acq.)
Nursing services (including board and social security tax if paid by taxpayer)	Yes	Rev. Rul. 57-489, 1957-2 CB 207
Obstetrical expenses	Yes	Reg. § 1.213-1(e)(1)(ii)
Operations		
. illegal	No	Reg. § 1.213-1(e)(1)(ii)
. legal	Yes	Reg. § 1.213-1(e)(1)(ii)
Optometrists	Yes	Rev. Rul. 55-261, 1955-1 CB 307
Orthodontia	Yes	Reg. § 1.213-1(e)(1)(ii)
Orthopedic shoes, excess cost	Yes	IRS Letter Ruling 8221118, 2-26-82, CCH IRS LETTER RULINGS REPORTS
Osteopaths	Yes	Rev. Rul. 63-91, 1963-1 CB 54
Oxygen equipment, breathing difficulty	Yes	Rev. Rul. 55-261, 1955-1 CB 307
Patterning exercises, handicapped child	Yes	Rev. Rul. 70-170, 1970-1 CB 51
Plumbing, special fixtures for handicapped	Yes	Rev. Rul. 70-395, 1970-2 CB 65
Prosthesis	Yes	Reg. § 1.213-1(e)(1)(ii)
Psychiatric care	Yes	Rev. Rul. 55-261, 1955-1 CB 307
Psychologists	Yes	Rev. Rul. 63-91, 1963-1 CB 54
Psychotherapists	Yes	Rev. Rul. 63-91, 1963-1 CB 54
Reclining chair for cardiac patient	Yes	Rev. Rul. 58-155, 1958-1 CB 156
Reconstructive surgery, breast	Yes	Rev. Rul. 2003-57, 2003-1 CB 959
Remedial reading for dyslexic child	Yes	Rev. Rul. 69-607, 1969-2 CB 40
Residence, loss on sale, move medically recommended	No	Rev. Rul. 68-319, 1968-1 CB 92
Retirement home, cost of medical care	Yes	*H.W. Smith Est.,* 79 TC 313, Dec. 39,273 (Acq.)
Sanitarium rest home, cost of, medical, educational, or rehabilitative reasons	Yes	Reg. § 1.213-1(e)(1)(v)
Schools, special, relief of handicap	Yes	Rev. Rul. 58-533, 1958-2 CB 108; Rev. Rul. 69-499, 1969-2 CB 39; Rev. Rul. 70-285, 1970-1 CB 52
Scientology "audits" and "processing"	No	*D.H. Brown,* CA-8, 75-2 USTC ¶ 9718, 523 F2d 365, *aff'g* 62 TC 551, Dec. 32,701; Rev. Rul. 78-190, 1978-1 CB 74
Self-help, medical	No	*B. Doody,* 32 TCM 547, Dec. 32,006(M), TC Memo. 1973-126
Service animals		
. hearing-aid animal	Yes	Rev. Rul. 68-295, 1968-1 CB 92
. other	Yes	Senate Finance Committee Report to P.L. 100-647
. seeing-eye dog	Yes	Rev. Rul. 55-261, 1955-1 CB 307
Sexual dysfunction, treatment for	Yes	Rev. Rul. 75-187, 1975-1 CB 92
Smoking, program to stop	Yes	Rev. Rul. 99-28, 1999-1 CB 1269
Spiritual guidance	No	*M. Miller,* 40 TCM 243, Dec. 36,911(M), TC Memo. 1980-136

Medical Expense	*Deductible*	*Authority*
Sterilization operation, legal	Yes	Rev. Rul. 73-603, 1973-2 CB 76, clarifying Rev. Rul. 73-201, 1973-1 CB 140
Swimming pool, treatment of polio or arthritis	Yes	*C.B. Mason,* DC Hawaii, 57-2 USTC ¶ 10,012; Rev. Rul. 83-33, 1983-1 CB 70
Tattoos	No	Rev. Rul. 82-111, 1982-1 CB 48
Taxicab to doctor's office	Yes	Rev. Rul. 55-261, 1955-1 CB 307
Teeth, artificial	Yes	Reg. § 1.213-1(e)(1)(ii)
Teeth, whitening	No	Rev. Rul. 2003-57, I.R.B. 2003-22
Telephone, specially equipped		
. deaf persons	Yes	Rev. Rul. 71-48, 1971-1 CB 99, amplified by Rev. Rul. 73-53, 1973-1 CB 139
. modified for person in an iron lung	Yes	Rev. Rul. 55-261, 1955-1 CB 307
Television, closed caption decoder	Yes	Rev. Rul. 80-340, 1980-2 CB 81
Toilet articles	No	*O.G. Russell,* 12 TCM 1276, Dec. 19,973(M)
Transplant, donor's costs of	Yes	Rev. Rul. 68-452, 1968-2 CB 111; Rev. Rul. 73-189, 1973-1 CB 139
Transportation, cost incurred essentially and primarily for medical care	Yes	Code Sec. 213(d)(1)(B) and Reg. § 1.213-1(e)(1)(iv)
Trips, general health improvement	No	Reg. § 1.213-1(e)(1)(iv)
Vacations, health restorative	No	Reg. § 1.213-1(e)(1)(iv) and Rev. Rul. 57-130, 1957-1 CB 108
Vacuum cleaner, alleviation of dust allergy	No	Rev. Rul. 76-80, 1976-1 CB 71
Vasectomy, legal	Yes	Rev. Rul. 73-201, 1973-1 CB 140, clarified by Rev. Rul. 73-603, 1973-2 CB 76, and Rev. Rul. 97-9, 1997-1 CB 77
Visual alert system for hearing impaired	Yes	IRS Letter Ruling 8250040, 9-13-82, CCH IRS LETTER RULINGS REPORTS
Weight loss program for treatment of specific disease	Yes	Rev. Rul. 2002-19, 2002-1 CB 778
Weight loss programs to improve appearance, prescribed	No	Rev. Rul. 79-151, 1979-1 CB 116; IRS Publication 502, "Medical and Dental Expenses"
Wheelchair	Yes	Reg. § 1.213-1(e)(1)(iii)
Wig, alleviation of mental discomfort resulting from disease	Yes	Rev. Rul. 62-189, 1962-2 CB 88
X-rays	Yes	Reg. § 1.213-1(e)(1)(ii)

CHECKLISTS

¶ 61 Checklist for Credits

The Internal Revenue Code provides for a number of credits that may be taken into account when arriving at a tax liability. A tax credit directly reduces a taxpayer's tax liability dollar for dollar, rather than reducing the taxpayer's taxable income as a deduction does. Both individual and business taxpayers are eligible for tax credits, and certain credits are available to both types of taxpayers.

The two charts below show the availability of the nonbusiness and business credits. All paragraph references are to the 2013 *U.S. Master Tax Guide*. The date ranges are time periods for which the credits are available for calendar-year taxpayers. Fiscal-year taxpayers should consult the referenced paragraph to determine if any special requirements are applicable.

Nonbusiness Credits

Nonbusiness Credits	*Years Available*	*Paragraph Reference*
Adoption credit:		
. nonrefundable	Until 12/31/2009; after 12/31/2011	¶ 1307
. refundable	1/1/2010—12/31/2011	¶ 1326A
Alternative fuel vehicle refueling property credit:		
. non-hydrogen property	1/1/2006—12/31/2011	¶ 1355
. hydrogen property	1/1/2006—12/31/2014	¶ 1355
Alternative motor vehicle credit:		
. advanced lean burn technology vehicle credit	1/1/2006—12/31/2010	¶ 1347
. alternative fuel motor vehicle credit	1/1/2006—12/31/2010	¶ 1349
. fuel cell motor vehicle credit	1/1/2006—12/31/2014	¶ 1346
. hybrid motor vehicle credit	1/1/2006—12/31/2009	¶ 1348
. plug-in electric motor vehicle conversion credit	2/18/2009—12/31/2011	¶ 1352
Child and dependent care credit	Permanent	¶ 1301
Child tax credit	Permanent	¶ 1305
COBRA premium credit	9/1/2008—8/31/2011	¶ 1391
Earned income credit	Permanent	¶ 1322
Educational credits:		
. American Opportunity credit	1/1/2009—12/31/2012	¶ 1303
. Hope scholarship credit	Until 12/31/2008; after 12/31/2012	¶ 1303
. lifetime learning credit	Permanent	¶ 1303
Elderly and permanently and totally disabled credit	Permanent	¶ 1302
First-time homebuyer credit:		
. generally	4/9/2008—4/30/2010	¶ 1324
. certain military personnel	1/1/2009—4/30/2011	¶ 1324
. long-term resident	11/7/2009—4/30/2010	¶ 1324
First-time homebuyer credit for the District of Columbia	Until 12/31/2011	¶ 1308
Foreign tax credit	Permanent	¶ 1361
Health insurance costs credit for certain individuals:		
. for TAA and/or alternative TAA eligible individuals	1/1/2002—12/31/2013	¶ 1332
. for PBGC eligible individuals	Permanent	¶ 1332
Health insurance premium assistance credit	After 12/31/2013	¶ 1331
Making Work Pay credit	1/1/2009—12/31/2010	¶ 1325
Minimum tax credit:		
. nonrefundable	Permanent	¶ 1309
. refundable	12/20/2006—12/31/2012	¶ 1327
Mortgage interest credit	Permanent	¶ 1306

Nonbusiness Credits	*Years Available*	*Paragraph Reference*
Mutual fund capital gains credit	Permanent	¶ 1330
Nonbusiness energy property credit:		
. lifetime limit of $500	1/1/2006—12/31/2007; 1/1/2011—12/31/2011	¶ 1341
. lifetime limit of $1,500	1/1/2009—12/31/2010	¶ 1341
Plug-in electric drive motor vehicle credit:		
	1/1/2009—12/31/2009	¶ 1350
	1/1/2010—until phased out	¶ 1351
Plug-in electric vehicle credit for small vehicles	2/18/2009—12/31/2011	¶ 1354
Residential energy efficient property credit	1/1/2006—12/31/2016	¶ 1342
Retirement savings contributions credit	Permanent	¶ 1304
Tax credit bonds:		
. build America bond credit	Bonds issued between 2/18/2009—12/31/2010	¶ 1378
. clean renewable energy bond credit	Bonds issued between 1/1/2006—12/31/2009	¶ 1372
. Midwestern bond credit	Bonds issued between 1/1/2009—12/31/2009	¶ 1380
. new clean renewable energy bond credit	Bonds issued after 10/3/2008	¶ 1374
. qualified energy conservation bond credit	Bonds issued after 10/3/2008	¶ 1375
. qualified forestry conservation bond credit	Bonds issued between 5/23/2008—5/22/2010	¶ 1373
. school construction bond credit .	Bonds issued between 2/18/2009—12/31/2010	¶ 1377
. zone academy bond credit	Bonds issued between 10/4/2008—12/31/2011	¶ 1376
Withheld tax on wages credit	Permanent	¶ 1321

Business Credits

Business Credits	*Years Available*	*Paragraph Reference*
Agricultural chemicals security credit .	5/23/2008—12/31/2012	¶ 1365HH
Alcohol fuels credit:		
. cellulosic biofuel	1/1/2009—12/31/2012	¶ 1365I
. other alcohol fuels	Until 12/31/2011	¶ 1365I
Alternative fuel vehicle refueling property credit:		
. non-hydrogen property	1/1/2006—12/31/2011	¶ 1355
. hydrogen property	1/1/2006—12/31/2014	¶ 1355
Alternative motor vehicle credit:		
. advanced lean burn technology vehicle credit	1/1/2006—12/31/2010	¶ 1347
. alternative fuel motor vehicle credit	1/1/2006—12/31/2010	¶ 1349
. fuel cell motor vehicle credit . . .	1/1/2006—12/31/2014	¶ 1346
. hybrid motor vehicle credit	1/1/2006—12/31/2009	¶ 1348
. plug-in electric motor vehicle conversion credit	2/18/2009—12/31/2011	¶ 1352

CHECKLISTS

Business Credits	*Years Available*	*Paragraph Reference*
Biodiesel and renewable diesel fuels credit:		
. small agri-biodiesel producer credit	8/9/2005—12/31/2011	¶ 1365X
. renewable biodiesel	1/1/2006—12/31/2011	¶ 1365X
. other biodiesel	1/1/2005—12/31/2011	¶ 1365X
Carbon dioxide sequestration credit . . .	10/3/2008—until phased out	¶ 1365JJ
Community development corporation (CDC) contribution credit	Permanent	¶ 1365KK
Coal production credit	After 8/8/2005	¶ 1365D
Disabled access credit	Permanent	¶ 1365M
Disaster area housing credit	11/1/2008—5/1/2009	¶ 1365EE
Distilled spirits excise tax carrying credit	After 9/30/2005	¶ 1365Z
Electricity produced from renewable resources credit (available 5 to 10 years after facilities are placed into service):		
. Indian coal production facilities . .	Placed in service before 1/1/2009	¶ 1365N
. refined coal facilities	Placed in service before 12/31/2011	¶ 1365N
. small irrigation power facilities . .	Placed in service before 10/3/2008	¶ 1365N
. wind facilities	Placed in service before 12/31/2012	¶ 1365N
. all other facilities	Placed in service before 12/31/2013	¶ 1365N
Employee retention credit for 2010 hires:	After an employee hired 2/4/2010—12/31/2010 is retained 52 weeks	¶ 1365FF
Employer credit for differential wage payments to military personnel	6/18/2008—12/31/2011	¶ 1365II
Employer credit for providing child care	1/1/2002—12/31/2012	¶ 1365V
Empowerment zone credit	Until 12/31/2011	¶ 1365O
Energy credit	Permanent[1]	¶ 1365C
Energy efficient appliance credit	1/1/2006—12/31/2011	¶ 1365DD
Energy efficient home credit	1/1/2006—12/31/2011	¶ 1365CC
Energy project credit	After 2/17/2009	¶ 1365F
Federal excise fuel tax credit	Permanent	¶ 1329
FICA tip credit	Permanent	¶ 1365R
Foreign tax credit	Permanent	¶ 1361
Gasification project credit	After 8/8/2005	¶ 1365E
General business credit	See specific credit component	¶ 1365
Health insurance credit for small employers	After 12/31/2009	¶ 1333
Indian employment credit	Until 12/31/2011	¶ 1365Q
Investment credit	See specific credit component	¶ 1365A
Low-income housing credit	Permanent	¶ 1365K
Low sulfur diesel fuel production credit	After 13/31/2002	¶ 1365Y
Mine rescue team training credit	1/1/2006—12/31/2011	¶ 1365GG
Minimum tax credit	Permanent	¶ 1309
New markets tax credit	Until 12/31/2011; carryover amounts useable until 12/31/2016	¶ 1365T

Business Credits	*Years Available*	*Paragraph Reference*
Nonconventional source fuel production credit	For coke or coke gas produced before 1/1/2010 that is sold no later than four years after the coke or coke gas is first sold	¶ 1365BB
Nuclear power facilities production credit	8/9/2005—12/31/2020	¶ 1365AA
Orphan drug credit	Permanent	¶ 1365S
Pension plan startup costs credit for small employers	Permanent	¶ 1365U
Plug-in electric drive motor vehicle credit:		
	1/1/2009—12/31/2009	¶ 1350
	1/1/2010—until phased out	¶ 1351
Plug-in electric vehicle credit for small vehicles	2/18/2009—12/31/2011	¶ 1354
Puerto Rico and U.S. possessions credit (available only to existent claimants from American Samoan companies) .	Until 12/31/2011	¶ 1362
Railroad track maintenance credit	1/1/2005—12/31/2011	¶ 1365W
Rehabilitation credit	Permanent	¶ 1365B
Renewal community employment credit	Until 12/31/2009	¶ 1365P
Research credit	Until 12/31/2011	¶ 1365J
Therapeutic discovery project credit . .	1/1/2009—12/31/2010	¶ 1365LL
Work opportunity credit:		
. generally	Until 12/31/2011	¶ 1365G
. disconnected youth	1/1/2009—12/31/2010	¶ 1365G
. unemployed veteran	1/1/2009—12/31/2010	¶ 1365G
. qualified veteran	11/22/2011—12/31/2012	¶ 1365G

[1] Exceptions apply.

CHECKLISTS

¶ 63 Checklist for Forms

The following chart lists many of the forms in use by the IRS and provides paragraph references to the main discussions of those forms in the 2013 *U.S. Master Tax Guide*.

Form	*Paragraph reference*
56	¶ 2747
433-A	¶ 2723
433-B	¶ 2723
656	¶ 2723
656-A	¶ 2723
706	¶ 2938; ¶ 2944
706, Schedule A	¶ 2912
706, Schedule A-1	¶ 2922
706, Schedule B	¶ 2912
706, Schedule C	¶ 2912
706, Schedule D	¶ 2915
706, Schedule E	¶ 2919
706, Schedule F	¶ 2912
706, Schedule G	¶ 2913; ¶ 2914
706, Schedule H	¶ 2918
706, Schedule I	¶ 2917
706, Schedule J	¶ 2925
706, Schedule K	¶ 2925
706, Schedule L	¶ 2925
706, Schedule M	¶ 2926
706, Schedule O	¶ 2932
706, Schedule Q	¶ 2934
706, Schedule R	¶ 2944
706, Schedule R-1	¶ 2944
706-A	¶ 2922
706-CE	¶ 2934
706-D	¶ 2933
706-GS(D)	¶ 2944
706-GS(T)	¶ 2944
706-NA	¶ 2940
709	¶ 2910
712	¶ 2915
843	¶ 2813
851	¶ 295
866	¶ 2721
870	¶ 2712
906	¶ 2721
911	¶ 2707
940	¶ 2650
941	¶ 2650
943	¶ 2650
944	¶ 2650
945	¶ 2650
966	¶ 211
970	¶ 1565
972	¶ 259
973	¶ 259
976	¶ 2317
982	¶ 885
990	¶ 625
990, Schedule C	¶ 613
990-BL	¶ 625
990-PF	¶ 625
990-T	¶ 658
990-W	¶ 633
1023	¶ 623
1024	¶ 692
1028	¶ 698
1040	¶ 105
1040, Schedule A	¶ 1011
1040, Schedule B	¶ 105
1040, Schedule C	¶ 105
1040, Schedule D	¶ 128
1040, Schedule E	¶ 105
1040, Schedule EIC	¶ 1322
1040, Schedule F	¶ 767
1040, Schedule H	¶ 2652
1040, Schedule J	¶ 767
1040, Schedule R	¶ 1302
1040, Schedule SE	¶ 2664
1040A	¶ 105
1040A, Schedule EIC	¶ 1322
1040-C	¶ 2411
1040-ES	¶ 2679
1040-EZ	¶ 105
1040NR	¶ 2425
1040-SS	¶ 2501
1040-V	¶ 2525
1040X	¶ 2505
1041	¶ 510
1041, Schedule I	¶ 1401
1041, Schedule J	¶ 567
1041, Schedule K-1	¶ 510
1041-A	¶ 537
1041-ES	¶ 511
1041-QFT	¶ 575
1041-T	¶ 511
1042	¶ 2455
1042-S	¶ 2455
1042-T	¶ 2455
1045	¶ 1173
1065	¶ 406
1065, Schedule D	¶ 431
1065, Schedule K-1	¶ 706
1066	¶ 2343
1066, Schedule Q	¶ 2344
1098	¶ 2565
1098-C	¶ 1070A
1098-E	¶ 2565
1098-T	¶ 2565
1099-A	¶ 2565
1099-B	¶ 2565
1099-C	¶ 2565
1099-DIV	¶ 2565
1099-G	¶ 2565
1099-H	¶ 2565
1099-INT	¶ 2565
1099-K	¶ 2565
1099-MISC	¶ 2565
1099-OID	¶ 1952
1099-PATR	¶ 2565
1099-R	¶ 2565
1099-S	¶ 2565
1116	¶ 2476
1118	¶ 2476
1120	¶ 211
1120, Schedule PH	¶ 275
1120, Schedule UTP	¶ 2501

Form	*Paragraph reference*
1120-C	¶ 698
1120-F	¶ 2425
1120-FSC	¶ 2501
1120-H	¶ 699
1120-IC-DISC	¶ 2501
1120-L	¶ 2370
1120-ND	¶ 2501
1120-PC	¶ 2501
1120-POL	¶ 696
1120-REIT	¶ 2326
1120-RIC	¶ 2301
1120S	¶ 351
1120-SF	¶ 2501
1120X	¶ 2759
1122	¶ 295
1127	¶ 2537
1127-A	¶ 2537
1128	¶ 1513
1138	¶ 1173
1139	¶ 2773
1310	¶ 178
2063	¶ 2411
2106	¶ 942; ¶ 1215
2120	¶ 147
2210	¶ 2889
2210-F	¶ 2889
2220	¶ 241
2350	¶ 2509
2438	¶ 2305; ¶ 2329
2439	¶ 1330; ¶ 2305; ¶ 2329
2441	¶ 1301
2553	¶ 306
2555	¶ 2408
2848	¶ 504; ¶ 2708A
3115	¶ 1529
3468	¶ 1365A
3520	¶ 588
3520-A	¶ 588
3800	¶ 1365
3903	¶ 1073
3921	¶ 2565
3922	¶ 2565
4070	¶ 2604
4136	¶ 1329
4137	¶ 717
4255	¶ 1365A
4361	¶ 2667
4466	¶ 247
4562	¶ 1201; ¶ 1208; ¶ 1214
4563	¶ 2414
4626	¶ 1401
4684	¶ 1124; ¶ 1125
4720	¶ 590A; ¶ 610; ¶ 614; ¶ 617; ¶ 635; ¶ 637
4768	¶ 2938
4797	¶ 1208; ¶ 1211; ¶ 1713; ¶ 1747; ¶ 1779
4868	¶ 2509
4876-A	¶ 2498
4952	¶ 1094
4970	¶ 567
4972	¶ 2124A
5213	¶ 1195
5227	¶ 537
5304-SIMPLE	¶ 2155
5305-SEP	¶ 2156
5305-SIMPLE	¶ 2155
5329	¶ 2124B; ¶ 2124C; ¶ 2153E; ¶ 2153H; ¶ 2154C
5405	¶ 1324
5471	¶ 2487
5498	¶ 2565
5500	¶ 2130
5500-SF	¶ 2130
5558	¶ 2130
5695	¶ 1341; ¶ 1342
5713	¶ 2496
5735	¶ 162
5768	¶ 613
5884	¶ 1365G
6166	¶ 2450
6198	¶ 2045
6251	¶ 1401
6252	¶ 1801
6478	¶ 1365I
6765	¶ 1365J
6781	¶ 1948
7004	¶ 2509
8027	¶ 2604
8082	¶ 415
8275	¶ 2856; ¶ 2858; ¶ 2863
8275-R	¶ 2856; ¶ 2858; ¶ 2863
8282	¶ 627
8283	¶ 1070A
8288	¶ 2442
8288-A	¶ 2442
8300	¶ 2565
8332	¶ 139A
8379	¶ 163
8396	¶ 1306
8582	¶ 2053
8582-CR	¶ 2053
8586	¶ 1365K
8594	¶ 1620
8596	¶ 2565
8596-A	¶ 2565
8606	¶ 2153D; ¶ 2153G; ¶ 2154C; ¶ 2154F
8611	¶ 1365K
8615	¶ 103
8621	¶ 2490
8689	¶ 2416
8716	¶ 1501
8801	¶ 1309; ¶ 1327
8802	¶ 2450
8804	¶ 2503
8809	¶ 2455
8810	¶ 2053
8811	¶ 2343
8812	¶ 1305
8814	¶ 103
8815	¶ 730A
8818	¶ 730A
8820	¶ 1365S
8822	¶ 2711
8822-B	¶ 2711
8824	¶ 1721; ¶ 1732

Form	*Paragraph reference*
8825	¶ 2053
8826	¶ 1365M
8827	¶ 1309
8828	¶ 105
8829	¶ 961
8832	¶ 201
8833	¶ 2450
8834	¶ 1354
8835	¶ 1365N
8839	¶ 1307; ¶ 1326A
8840	¶ 2409
8843	¶ 2409
8844	¶ 1365P; ¶ 1365O
8845	¶ 1365Q
8846	¶ 1365R
8849	¶ 1329
8850	¶ 1365G
8853	¶ 2197C
8854	¶ 2412
8855	¶ 516
8857	¶ 162
8859	¶ 1308
8863	¶ 1303
8864	¶ 1365X
8865	¶ 2487
8866	¶ 1219
8867	¶ 2518
8868	¶ 2509
8869	¶ 304
8871	¶ 696
8872	¶ 696
8874	¶ 1365T
8875	¶ 2340
8879	¶ 2517
8880	¶ 1304
8881	¶ 1365U
8882	¶ 1365V
8885	¶ 1332
8886	¶ 2004
8886-T	¶ 619
8888	¶ 2153
8889	¶ 1020A
8896	¶ 1365Y
8898	¶ 2414
8899	¶ 627
8900	¶ 1365W
8903	¶ 980A
8906	¶ 1365Z
8907	¶ 1365BB
8908	¶ 1365CC
8909	¶ 1365DD
8910	¶ 1345
8911	¶ 1355
8912	¶ 1372
8918	¶ 2005
8919	¶ 105
8923	¶ 1365GG
8925	¶ 804
8927	¶ 2317
8928	¶ 2190A
8930	¶ 2124
8931	¶ 1365HH
8932	¶ 1365II
8933	¶ 1365JJ
8936	¶ 1351
8938	¶ 2570
8940	¶ 623
8941	¶ 1333
8944	¶ 2503
8948	¶ 2503
8949	¶ 1741
8955-SSA	¶ 2130
9465	¶ 2529
FBAR	¶ 2570
HUD-1	¶ 1055
SS-4	¶ 2652
SS-5	¶ 116
SS-8	¶ 2604
T	¶ 1772
TD F 90-22.1	¶ 2570
W-2	¶ 2565
W-2G	¶ 2642
W-3	¶ 2650
W-4	¶ 2634
W-4P	¶ 2643
W-4S	¶ 2604
W-4V	¶ 2629
W-7	¶ 2579
W-7A	¶ 2579
W-8BEN	¶ 2455
W-8ECI	¶ 2455
W-8EXP	¶ 2455
W-8IMY	¶ 2455
W-9	¶ 2579

¶ 64 Guide to Information Returns

The following chart lists information returns in use by the IRS. It provides reportable payment types and amounts, as well as the due dates for filing the returns with the IRS and for providing statements to a payee or other person.

(If any date shown falls on a Saturday, Sunday, or legal holiday, the due date is the next business day.)

				Due Date	
Form	**Title**	**What To Report**	**Amounts To Report**	**To IRS**	**To Recipient (unless indicated otherwise)**
1042-S	Foreign Person's U.S. Source Income Subject to Withholding	Income such as interest, dividends, royalties, pensions and annuities, etc., and amounts withheld under Chapter 3. Also, distributions of effectively connected income by publicly traded partnerships or nominees.	See form instructions	March 15	March 15
1097-BTC	Bond Tax Credit	Tax credit bond credits to shareholders.	All amounts	February 28*	On or before the 15th day of the 2nd calendar month after the close of the calendar month in which the credit is allowed
1098	Mortgage Interest Statement	Mortgage interest (including points) and certain mortgage insurance premiums you received in the course of your trade or business from individuals and reimbursements of overpaid interest.	$600 or more	February 28*	(To Payer/ Borrower) January 31
1098-C	Contributions of Motor Vehicles, Boats, and Airplanes	Information regarding a donated motor vehicle, boat, or airplane.	Gross proceeds of more than $500	February 28*	(To Donor) 30 days from date of sale or contribution
1098-E	Student Loan Interest Statement	Student loan interest received in the course of your trade or business.	$600 or more	February 28*	January 31
1098-T	Tuition Statement	Qualified tuition and related expenses, reimbursements or refunds, and scholarships or grants (optional).	See instructions	February 28*	January 31
1099-A	Acquisition or Abandonment of Secured Property	Information about the acquisition or abandonment of property that is security for a debt for which you are the lender.	All amounts	February 28*	(To Borrower) January 31
1099-B	Proceeds From Broker and Barter Exchange Transactions	Sales or redemptions of securities, futures transactions, commodities, and barter exchange transactions.	All amounts	February 28*	February 15**

				Due Date	
Form	Title	What To Report	Amounts To Report	To IRS	To Recipient (unless indicated otherwise)
1099-C	Cancellation of Debt	Cancellation of a debt owed to a financial institution, the Federal Government, a credit union, RTC, FDIC, NCUA, a military department, the U.S. Postal Service, the Postal Rate Commission, or any organization having a significant trade or business of lending money.	$600 or more	February 28*	January 31
1099-CAP	Changes in Corporate Control and Capital Structure	Information about cash, stock, or other property from an acquisition of control or the substantial change in capital structure of a corporation.	Over $1000	February 28*	(To Shareholders) January 31
1099-DIV	Dividends and Distributions	Distributions, such as dividends, capital gain distributions, or nontaxable distributions, that were paid on stock and liquidation distributions.	$10 or more, except $600 or more for liquidations	February 28*	January 31**
1099-G	Certain Government Payments	Unemployment compensation, state and local income tax refunds, agricultural payments, and taxable grants.	$10 or more for refunds and unemployment	February 28*	January 31
1099-H	Health Coverage Tax Credit (HCTC) Advance Payments	Health insurance premiums paid on behalf of certain individuals.	All amounts	February 28*	January 31
1099-INT	Interest Income	Interest income.	$10 or more ($600 or more in some cases)	February 28*	January 31**
1099-K	Merchant Card and Third-Party Network Payments	Merchant card	All amounts		
		Third-party network payments.	$20,000 or more **and** 200 or more transactions	February 28*	January 31
1099-LTC	Long-Term Care and Accelerated Death Benefits	Payments under a long-term care insurance contract and accelerated death benefits paid under a life insurance contract or by a viatical settlement provider.	All amounts	February 28*	January 31
1099-MISC	Miscellaneous Income	Rent or royalty payments; prizes and awards that are not for services, such as winnings on TV or radio shows.	$600 or more, except $10 or more for royalties		
	(Also, use to report direct sales of $5,000 or more of consumer goods for resale.)	Payments to crew members by owners or operators of fishing boats including payments of proceeds from sale of catch.	All amounts		

Form	Title	What To Report	Amounts To Report	Due Date: To IRS	Due Date: To Recipient (unless indicated otherwise)
		Section 409A income from nonqualified deferred compensation plans (NQDCs).	All amounts		
		Payments to a physician, physicians' corporation, or other supplier of health and medical services. Issued mainly by medical assistance programs or health and accident insurance plans.	$600 or more	February 28*	January 31**
		Payments for services performed for a trade or business by people not treated as its employees. Examples: fees to subcontractors or directors and golden parachute payments.	$600 or more		
		Fish purchases paid in cash for resale.	$600 or more		
		Crop insurance proceeds.	$600 or more		
		Substitute dividends and tax-exempt interest payments reportable by brokers.	$10 or more		February 15**
		Gross proceeds paid to attorneys.	$600 or more		February 15**
1099-OID	Original Issue Discount	Original issue discount.	$10 or more	February 28*	January 31**
1099-PATR	Taxable Distributions Received From Cooperatives	Distributions from cooperatives passed through to their patrons including any domestic production activities deduction and certain pass-through credits.	$10 or more	February 28*	January 31
1099-Q	Payments From Qualified Education Programs (Under Sections 529 and 530)	Earnings from qualified tuition programs and Coverdell ESAs.	All amounts	February 28*	January 31
1099-R	Distributions From Pensions, Annuities, Retirement or Profit-Sharing Plans, IRAs, Insurance Contracts, etc.	Distributions from retirement or profit-sharing plans, any IRA, insurance contracts, and IRA recharacterizations.	$10 or more	February 28*	January 31
1099-S	Proceeds From Real Estate Transactions	Gross proceeds from the sale or exchange of real estate and certain royalty payments.	Generally, $600 or more	February 28*	February 15
1099-SA	Distributions From an HSA, Archer MSA, or Medicare Advantage MSA	Distributions from an HSA, Archer MSA, or Medicare Advantage MSA.	All amounts	February 28*	January 31

Form	Title	What To Report	Amounts To Report	Due Date: To IRS	Due Date: To Recipient (unless indicated otherwise)
3921	Exercise of an Incentive Stock Option Under Section 422(b)	Transfer of stock pursuant to the exercise of an incentive stock option under section 422(b).	All amounts	February 28*	January 31
3922	Transfer of Stock Acquired Through an Employee Stock Purchase Plan Under Section 423(c)	Transfer of stock acquired through an employee stock purchase plan under section 423(c).	All amounts	February 28*	January 31
5498	IRA Contribution Information	Contributions (including rollover contributions) to any individual retirement arrangement (IRA) including a SEP, SIMPLE, and Roth IRA; Roth conversions; IRA recharacterizations; and the fair market value (FMV) of the account.	All amounts	May 31	(To Participant) For FMV/RMD Jan 31; For contributions, May 31
5498-ESA	Coverdell ESA Contribution Information	Contributions (including rollover contributions) to a Coverdell ESA.	All amounts	May 31	April 30
5498-SA	HSA, Archer MSA, or Medicare Advantage MSA Information	Contributions to an HSA (including transfers and rollovers) or Archer MSA and the FMV of an HSA, Archer MSA, or Medicare Advantage MSA.	All amounts	May 31	(To Participant) May 31
W-2G	Certain Gambling Winnings	Gambling winnings from horse racing, dog racing, jai alai, lotteries, keno, bingo, slot machines, sweepstakes, wagering pools, poker tournaments, etc.	Generally, $600 or more; $1,200 or more from bingo or slot machines; $1,500 or more from keno	February 28*	January 31
W-2	Wage and Tax Statement	Wages, tips, other compensation; social security, Medicare, and withheld income taxes. Include bonuses, vacation allowances, severance pay, certain moving expense payments, some kinds of travel allowances, and third-party payments of sick pay.	See instructions	**To SSA**	**To Recipient**
				Last day of February*	January 31

* The due date is March 31 if filed electronically.
** The due date is March 15 for reporting by trustees and middlemen of WHFITs.

¶ 65 Checklist for Types of Payments

The following chart lists common payments and the forms used to file and report them. It is not a complete list of all payments, and the absence of a payment from the list does not indicate that the payment is not reportable.

Type of Payment	Report on Form
Abandonment	1099-A
Accelerated death benefits	1099-LTC
Acquisition of control	1099-CAP
Advance health insurance payments	1099-H
Agriculture payments	1099-G
Allocated tips	W-2
Alternate TAA payments	1099-G
Annuities	1099-R
Archer MSAs:	
Contributions	5498-SA
Distributions	1099-SA
Attorney, fees and gross proceeds	1099-MISC
Auto reimbursements, employee	W-2
Auto reimbursements, nonemployee	1099-MISC
Awards, employee	W-2
Awards, nonemployee	1099-MISC
Barter exchange income	1099-B
Bond tax credit	1097-BTC
Bonuses, employee	W-2
Bonuses, nonemployee	1099-MISC
Broker transactions	1099-B
Cancellation of debt	1099-C
Capital gain distributions	1099-DIV
Car expense, employee	W-2
Car expense, nonemployee	1099-MISC
Changes in capital structure	1099-CAP
Charitable gift annuities	1099-R
Commissions, employee	W-2
Commissions, nonemployee	1099-MISC
Commodities transactions	1099-B
Compensation, employee	W-2
Compensation, nonemployee	1099-MISC
Contributions of motor vehicles, boats, and airplanes	1098-C
Cost of current life insurance protection	1099-R
Coverdell ESA contributions	5498-ESA
Coverdell ESA distributions	1099-Q
Crop insurance proceeds	1099-MISC
Damages	1099-MISC
Death benefits	1099-R
Accelerated	1099-LTC
Debt cancellation	1099-C
Dependent care payments	W-2
Direct rollovers	1099-Q, 1099-R, 5498
Direct sales of consumer products for resale	1099-MISC
Directors' fees	1099-MISC
Discharge of indebtedness	1099-C
Dividends	1099-DIV
Donation of motor vehicle	1098-C
Education loan interest	1098-E
Employee business expense reimbursement	W-2
Employee compensation	W-2
Excess deferrals, excess contributions, distributions of	1099-R
Exercise of incentive stock option under section 422(b)	3921
Fees, employee	W-2

Type of Payment	Report on Form
Fees, nonemployee	1099-MISC
Fishing boat crew members proceeds	1099-MISC
Fish purchases for cash	1099-MISC
Foreclosures	1099-A
Foreign persons' income	1042-S
401(k) contributions	W-2
404(k) dividend	1099-DIV
Gambling winnings	W-2G
Golden parachute, employee	W-2
Golden parachute, nonemployee	1099-MISC
Grants, taxable	1099-G
Health care services	1099-MISC
Health insurance advance payments	1099-H
Health savings accounts:	
Contributions	5498-SA
Distributions	1099-SA
Income attributable to domestic production activities, deduction for	1099-PATR
Income tax refunds, state and local	1099-G
Indian gaming profits paid to tribal members	1099-MISC
Interest income	1099-INT
Tax-exempt	1099-INT
Interest, mortgage	1098
IRA contributions	5498
IRA distributions	1099-R
Life insurance contract distributions	1099-R, 1099-LTC
Liquidation, distributions in	1099-DIV
Loans, distribution from pension plan	1099-R
Long-term care benefits	1099-LTC
Medicare Advantage MSAs:	
Contributions	5498-SA
Distributions	1099-SA
Medical services	1099-MISC
Merchant card payments	1099-K
Mileage, employee	W-2
Mileage, nonemployee	1099-MISC
Military retirement	1099-R
Mortgage insurance premiums	1098
Mortgage interest	1098
Moving expense	W-2
Nonemployee compensation	1099-MISC
Nonqualified deferred compensation:	
Beneficiary	1099-R
Employee	W-2
Nonemployee	1099-MISC
Original issue discount (OID)	1099-OID
Patronage dividends	1099-PATR
Pensions	1099-R
Points	1098
Prizes, employee	W-2
Prizes, nonemployee	1099-MISC
Profit-sharing plan	1099-R
Punitive damages	1099-MISC
Qualified plan distributions	1099-R
Qualified tuition program payments	1099-Q
Real estate transactions	1099-S
Recharacterized IRA contributions	1099-R, 5498
Refund, state and local tax	1099-G

Type of Payment	Report on Form
Rents	1099-MISC
Retirement	1099-R
Roth conversion IRA contributions	5498
Roth conversion IRA distributions	1099-R
Roth IRA contributions	5498
Roth IRA distributions	1099-R
Royalties	1099-MISC
Timber, pay-as-cut contract	1099-S
Sales:	
Real estate	1099-S
Securities	1099-B
Section 1035 exchange	1099-R
SEP contributions	W-2, 5498
SEP distributions	1099-R
Severance pay	W-2
Sick pay	W-2
SIMPLE contributions	W-2, 5498
SIMPLE distributions	1099-R
Student loan interest	1098-E
Substitute payments in lieu of dividends or tax-exempt interest	1099-MISC
Supplemental unemployment	W-2
Tax refunds, state and local	1099-G
Third-party network payments	1099-K
Tips	W-2
Transfer of stock acquired through an employee stock purchase plan under section 423(c)	3922
Tuition	1098-T
Unemployment benefits	1099-G
Vacation allowance, employee	W-2
Vacation allowance, nonemployee	1099-MISC
Wages	W-2

SPECIAL TAX TABLES

¶ 83 Applicable Federal Rates

Following are the monthly applicable federal interest rates for January 2012 through November 2012 published by the IRS for purposes of testing imputed interest in below-market interest loans (¶ 795) and debt-for-property transactions (¶ 1954). The rates are also relevant under the golden parachute rules (¶ 907) and for testing interest in connection with deferred payments for the use of property (¶ 1859).

In the case of below-market interest loans that are demand or gift loans, an amount deemed the "foregone" interest is treated as transferred from the lender to the borrower and retransferred by the borrower to the lender as interest. In order to simplify the computation of such foregone interest, the IRS prescribes a "blended annual rate," which is 0.22% on loans for the calendar year 2012.

	Period for Compounding			
	Annual	*Semiannual*	*Quarterly*	*Monthly*
January 2012				
Short-Term				
AFR	.19	.19	.19	.19
110% AFR	.21	.21	.21	.21
120% AFR	.23	.23	.23	.23
130% AFR	.25	.25	.25	.25
Mid-Term				
AFR	1.17	1.17	1.17	1.17
110% AFR	1.29	1.29	1.29	1.29
120% AFR	1.40	1.40	1.40	1.40
130% AFR	1.53	1.52	1.52	1.52
150% AFR	1.77	1.76	1.76	1.75
175% AFR	2.06	2.05	2.04	2.04
Long-Term				
AFR	2.63	2.61	2.60	2.60
110% AFR	2.89	2.87	2.86	2.85
120% AFR	3.15	3.13	3.12	3.11
130% AFR	3.42	3.39	3.38	3.37

SPECIAL TABLES

	Period for Compounding			
	Annual	Semiannual	Quarterly	Monthly
February 2012				
Short-Term				
AFR	.19	.19	.19	.19
110% AFR	.21	.21	.21	.21
120% AFR	.23	.23	.23	.23
130% AFR	.25	.25	.25	.25
Mid-Term				
AFR	1.12	1.12	1.12	1.12
110% AFR	1.23	1.23	1.23	1.23
120% AFR	1.34	1.34	1.34	1.34
130% AFR	1.47	1.46	1.46	1.46
150% AFR	1.69	1.68	1.68	1.67
175% AFR	1.97	1.96	1.96	1.95
Long-Term				
AFR	2.58	2.56	2.55	2.55
110% AFR	2.84	2.82	2.81	2.80
120% AFR	3.09	3.07	3.06	3.05
130% AFR	3.36	3.33	3.32	3.31
March 2012				
Short-Term				
AFR	.19	.19	.19	.19
110% AFR	.21	.21	.21	.21
120% AFR	.23	.23	.23	.23
130% AFR	.25	.25	.25	.25
Mid-Term				
AFR	1.08	1.08	1.08	1.08
110% AFR	1.19	1.19	1.19	1.19
120% AFR	1.30	1.30	1.30	1.30
130% AFR	1.40	1.40	1.40	1.40
150% AFR	1.63	1.62	1.62	1.61
175% AFR	1.90	1.89	1.89	1.88
Long-Term				
AFR	2.65	2.63	2.62	2.62
110% AFR	2.91	2.89	2.88	2.87
120% AFR	3.18	3.16	3.15	3.14
130% AFR	3.45	3.42	3.41	3.40
April 2012				
Short-Term				
AFR	.25	.25	.25	.25
110% AFR	.28	.28	.28	.28
120% AFR	.30	.30	.30	.30
130% AFR	.33	.33	.33	.33
Mid-Term				
AFR	1.15	1.15	1.15	1.15
110% AFR	1.27	1.27	1.27	1.27
120% AFR	1.38	1.38	1.38	1.38
130% AFR	1.51	1.50	1.50	1.50
150% AFR	1.74	1.73	1.73	1.72
175% AFR	2.02	2.01	2.00	2.00
Long-Term				
AFR	2.72	2.70	2.69	2.68
110% AFR	2.99	2.97	2.96	2.95
120% AFR	3.27	3.24	3.23	3.22
130% AFR	3.54	3.51	3.49	3.48

	Annual	Semiannual	Quarterly	Monthly
May 2012				
Short-Term				
AFR	.28	.28	.28	.28
110% AFR	.31	.31	.31	.31
120% AFR	.34	.34	.34	.34
130% AFR	.36	.36	.36	.36
Mid-Term				
AFR	1.30	1.30	1.30	1.30
110% AFR	1.44	1.43	1.43	1.43
120% AFR	1.57	1.56	1.56	1.55
130% AFR	1.70	1.69	1.69	1.68
150% AFR	1.96	1.95	1.95	1.94
175% AFR	2.29	2.28	2.27	2.27
Long-Term				
AFR	2.89	2.87	2.86	2.85
110% AFR	3.18	3.16	3.15	3.14
120% AFR	3.47	3.44	3.43	3.42
130% AFR	3.76	3.73	3.71	3.70
June 2012				
Short-Term				
AFR	.23	.23	.23	.23
110% AFR	.25	.25	.25	.25
120% AFR	.28	.28	.28	.28
130% AFR	.30	.30	.30	.30
Mid-Term				
AFR	1.07	1.07	1.07	1.07
110% AFR	1.18	1.18	1.18	1.18
120% AFR	1.28	1.28	1.28	1.28
130% AFR	1.39	1.39	1.39	1.39
150% AFR	1.62	1.61	1.61	1.60
175% AFR	1.88	1.87	1.87	1.86
Long-Term				
AFR	2.64	2.62	2.61	2.61
110% AFR	2.90	2.88	2.87	2.86
120% AFR	3.16	3.14	3.13	3.12
130% AFR	3.44	3.41	3.40	3.39
July 2012				
Short-Term				
AFR	.24	.24	.24	.24
110% AFR	.26	.26	.26	.26
120% AFR	.29	.29	.29	.29
130% AFR	.31	.31	.31	.31
Mid-Term				
AFR	.92	.92	.92	.92
110% AFR	1.01	1.01	1.01	1.01
120% AFR	1.10	1.10	1.10	1.10
130% AFR	1.20	1.20	1.20	1.20
150% AFR	1.38	1.38	1.38	1.38
175% AFR	1.62	1.61	1.61	1.60
Long-Term				
AFR	2.30	2.29	2.28	2.28
110% AFR	2.54	2.52	2.51	2.51
120% AFR	2.77	2.75	2.74	2.73
130% AFR	3.00	2.98	2.97	2.96

Period for Compounding applies to the Annual, Semiannual, Quarterly and Monthly columns.

SPECIAL TABLES

	Period for Compounding			
	Annual	Semiannual	Quarterly	Monthly
August 2012				
Short-Term				
AFR	.25	.25	.25	.25
110% AFR	.28	.28	.28	.28
120% AFR	.30	.30	.30	.30
130% AFR	.33	.33	.33	.33
Mid-Term				
AFR	.88	.88	.88	.88
110% AFR	.97	.97	.97	.97
120% AFR	1.06	1.06	1.06	1.06
130% AFR	1.14	1.14	1.14	1.14
150% AFR	1.32	1.32	1.32	1.32
175% AFR	1.55	1.54	1.54	1.54
Long-Term				
AFR	2.23	2.22	2.21	2.21
110% AFR	2.45	2.44	2.43	2.43
120% AFR	2.68	2.66	2.65	2.65
130% AFR	2.91	2.89	2.88	2.87
September 2012				
Short-Term				
AFR	.21	.21	.21	.21
110% AFR	.23	.23	.23	.23
120% AFR	.25	.25	.25	.25
130% AFR	.27	.27	.27	.27
Mid-Term				
AFR	.84	.84	.84	.84
110% AFR	.92	.92	.92	.92
120% AFR	1.01	1.01	1.01	1.01
130% AFR	1.09	1.09	1.09	1.09
150% AFR	1.26	1.26	1.26	1.26
175% AFR	1.48	1.47	1.47	1.47
Long-Term				
AFR	2.18	2.17	2.16	2.16
110% AFR	2.40	2.39	2.38	2.38
120% AFR	2.62	2.60	2.59	2.59
130% AFR	2.84	2.82	2.81	2.80
October 2012				
Short-Term				
AFR	.23	.23	.23	.23
110% AFR	.25	.25	.25	.25
120% AFR	.28	.28	.28	.28
130% AFR	.30	.30	.30	.30
Mid-Term				
AFR	.93	.93	.93	.93
110% AFR	1.02	1.02	1.02	1.02
120% AFR	1.12	1.12	1.12	1.12
130% AFR	1.21	1.21	1.21	1.21
150% AFR	1.40	1.40	1.40	1.40
175% AFR	1.64	1.63	1.63	1.62
Long-Term				
AFR	2.36	2.35	2.34	2.34
110% AFR	2.61	2.59	2.58	2.58
120% AFR	2.84	2.82	2.81	2.80
130% AFR	3.08	3.06	3.05	3.04

	Period for Compounding			
	Annual	Semiannual	Quarterly	Monthly
November 2012				
Short-Term				
AFR	.22	.22	.22	.22
110% AFR	.24	.24	.24	.24
120% AFR	.26	.26	.26	.26
130% AFR	.29	.29	.29	.29
Mid-Term				
AFR	.89	.89	.89	.89
110% AFR	.98	.98	.98	.98
120% AFR	1.07	1.07	1.07	1.07
130% AFR	1.16	1.16	1.16	1.16
150% AFR	1.34	1.34	1.34	1.34
175% AFR	1.57	1.56	1.56	1.55
Long-Term				
AFR	2.40	2.39	2.38	2.38
110% AFR	2.65	2.63	2.62	2.62
120% AFR	2.89	2.87	2.86	2.85
130% AFR	3.13	3.11	3.10	3.09

¶ 84 Adjusted Applicable Federal Rates

Code Sec. 1288 provides that, in determining original issue discount on tax-exempt obligations, an adjustment must be made to the applicable federal rates (¶ 83) to take into account the tax exemption for interest on the obligations.

Adjusted Applicable Federal Rates

	Annual Compounding	SemiAnnual Compounding	Quarterly Compounding	Monthly Compounding
January 2012				
Short-term rate	.38%	.38%	.38%	.38%
Mid-term rate	1.50%	1.49%	1.49%	1.49%
Long-term rate	3.47%	3.44%	3.43%	3.42%
February 2012				
Short-term rate	.35%	.35%	.35%	.35%
Mid-term rate	1.24%	1.24%	1.24%	1.24%
Long-term rate	3.26%	3.23%	3.22%	3.21%
March 2012				
Short-term rate	.26%	.26%	.26%	.26%
Mid-term rate	1.05%	1.05%	1.05%	1.05%
Long-term rate	2.97%	2.95%	2.94%	2.93%
April 2012				
Short-term rate	.22%	.22%	.22%	.22%
Mid-term rate	.95%	.95%	.95%	.95%
Long-term rate	3.04%	3.02%	3.01%	3.00%
May 2012				
Short-term rate	.27%	.27%	.27%	.27%
Mid-term rate	1.30%	1.30%	1.30%	1.30%
Long-term rate	3.26%	3.23%	3.22%	3.21%
June 2012				
Short-term rate	.26%	.26%	.26%	.26%
Mid-term rate	1.16%	1.16%	1.16%	1.16%
Long-term rate	3.06%	3.04%	3.03%	3.02%

SPECIAL TABLES

July 2012

	Annual Compounding	SemiAnnual Compounding	Quarterly Compounding	Monthly Compounding
Short-term rate	.27%	.27%	.27%	.27%
Mid-term rate	1.05%	1.05%	1.05%	1.05%
Long-term rate	3.02%	3.00%	2.99%	2.98%

August 2012

	Annual Compounding	SemiAnnual Compounding	Quarterly Compounding	Monthly Compounding
Short-term rate	.25%	.25%	.25%	.25%
Mid-term rate	1.07%	1.07%	1.07%	1.07%
Long-term rate	3.01%	2.99%	2.98%	2.97%

September 2012

	Annual Compounding	SemiAnnual Compounding	Quarterly Compounding	Monthly Compounding
Short-term rate	.23%	.23%	.23%	.23%
Mid-term rate	.95%	.95%	.95%	.95%
Long-term rate	2.80%	2.78%	2.77%	2.76%

October 2012

	Annual Compounding	SemiAnnual Compounding	Quarterly Compounding	Monthly Compounding
Short-term rate	.23%	.23%	.23%	.23%
Mid-term rate	1.04%	1.04%	1.04%	1.04%
Long-term rate	2.87%	2.85%	2.84%	2.83%

November 2012

	Annual Compounding	SemiAnnual Compounding	Quarterly Compounding	Monthly Compounding
Short-term rate	.24%	.24%	.24%	.24%
Mid-term rate	.98%	.98%	.98%	.98%
Long-term rate	2.84%	2.82%	2.81%	2.80%

¶ 85 Federal Long-Term Tax-Exempt Rates

Code Sec. 382 provides that the long-term tax-exempt rate for purposes of net operating loss carryforwards shall be the highest of the adjusted federal long-term rates (¶ 84) for the three months ending with the month in which the particular ownership change occurs. Each rate below is the highest for the 3-month period.

Long-Term Tax-Exempt Rates

Month	*Rate*
January 2012	3.55%
February 2012	3.55%
March 2012	3.47%
April 2012	3.26%
May 2012	3.26%
June 2012	3.26%
July 2012	3.26%
August 2012	3.06%
September 2012	3.02%
October 2012	3.01%
November 2012	2.87%

¶ 86 Applicable Credit Percentages for Low-Income Housing

Code Sec. 42 provides that applicable credit percentages for low-income housing are to be computed so that the present value of the 10 annual credit amounts at the beginning of the 10-year credit period equals either 70% or 30% of the qualified basis of the low-income units in a project. The discount rate for determining the present value in these computations is a rate equal to 72% of the average of the month's AFR for mid-term and long-term obligations. The applicable credit percentage for new construction or rehabilitation expenditures not federally subsidized is indicated under the 70% rate column. The applicable credit percentage for subsidized construction or rehabilitation expenditures and the acquisition of existing housing is indicated under the 30% rate column. See ¶ 1365K.

Applicable Credit Percentages for Low-Income Housing

Month	*70% Rate*	*30% Rate*
January 2012	7.44%	3.19%
February 2012	7.42%	3.18%
March 2012	7.43%	3.18%
April 2012	7.44%	3.19%
May 2012	7.48%	3.21%
June 2012	7.43%	3.18%
July 2012	7.37%	3.16%
August 2012	7.36%	3.15%
September 2012	7.35%	3.15%
October 2012	7.38%	3.16%
November 2012	7.38%	3.16%

Caution: This is a draft 2012 Earned Income Credit (EIC) Table. At the time of publication, the IRS had not yet released the 2012 Earned Income Credit (EIC) Table. For the latest information, see CCHGroup.com/TaxUpdates.

¶ 87 Earned Income Credit

The earned income credit tables are used in conjunction with the Form 1040 or Form 1040A, and Schedule EIC. The Schedule EIC must be filed with the taxpayer's tax return in order to claim the earned income credit. The credit, as computed on the EIC Worksheet found in the Form 1040 instructions, is entered on the appropriate line of Form 1040 or Form 1040A. Form 1040EZ may be used to claim the earned income credit in limited circumstances.

Note: At the time of publication, the Internal Revenue Service had not yet released a final version of the 2012 Earned Income Credit (EIC) Table for use in preparing 2012 income tax returns. As always, for the latest information, see CCHGroup.com/TaxUpdates.

Scan this code with your mobile device to see CCHGroup.com/TaxUpdates

CCH Comment: U.S. Master Tax Guide customers may also request a copy of the *2012 Tax Tables Booklet*, which will publish once the final 2012 Earned Income Credit (EIC) Table is available, by contacting CCH Customer Support. Please visit the CCH Customer Support Site at support.cch.com (first-time visitors will need to register). You can also chat with us online at support.cch.com/chat/booksupport/ or email us at CCHCustomerService@wolterskluwer.com.

»»→ Caution: This is a draft 2012 Earned Income Credit (EIC) Table. At the time of publication, the IRS had not yet released the 2012 Earned Income Credit (EIC) Table. For the latest information, see CCHGroup.com/TaxUpdates.

2012 Earned Income Credit (EIC) Table

Caution. This is **not** a tax table.

1. To find your credit, read down the "At least - But less than" columns and find the line that includes the amount you were told to look up from your EIC Worksheet.

2. Then, go to the column that includes your filing status and the number of qualifying children you have. Enter the credit from that column on your EIC Worksheet.

Example. If your filing status is single, you have one qualifying child, and the amount you are looking up from your EIC Worksheet is $2,455, you would enter $842.

If the amount you are looking up from the worksheet is—		And your filing status is— Single, head of household, or qualifying widow(er) and you have—			
		No children	One child	Two children	Three children
At least	But less than	Your credit is—			
2,400	2,450	186	825	970	1,091
2,450	2,500	189	842	990	1,114

If the amount you are looking up from the worksheet is–		And your filing status is– Single, head of household, or qualifying widow(er) and you have–				Married filing jointly and you have–			
		No Children	One Child	Two Children	Three Children	No Children	One Child	Two Children	Three Children
At least	But less than	Your credit is–				Your credit is–			
$0	$50	$2	$9	$10	$11	$2	$9	$10	$11
50	100	6	26	30	34	6	26	30	34
100	150	10	43	50	56	10	43	50	56
150	200	13	60	70	79	13	60	70	79
200	250	17	77	90	101	17	77	90	101
250	300	21	94	110	124	21	94	110	124
300	350	25	111	130	146	25	111	130	146
350	400	29	128	150	169	29	128	150	169
400	450	33	145	170	191	33	145	170	191
450	500	36	162	190	214	36	162	190	214
500	550	40	179	210	236	40	179	210	236
550	600	44	196	230	259	44	196	230	259
600	650	48	213	250	281	48	213	250	281
650	700	52	230	270	304	52	230	270	304
700	750	55	247	290	326	55	247	290	326
750	800	59	264	310	349	59	264	310	349
800	850	63	281	330	371	63	281	330	371
850	900	67	298	350	394	67	298	350	394
900	950	71	315	370	416	71	315	370	416
950	1,000	75	332	390	439	75	332	390	439
1,000	1,050	78	349	410	461	78	349	410	461
1,050	1,100	82	366	430	484	82	366	430	484
1,100	1,150	86	383	450	506	86	383	450	506
1,150	1,200	90	400	470	529	90	400	470	529
1,200	1,250	94	417	490	551	94	417	490	551
1,250	1,300	98	434	510	574	98	434	510	574
1,300	1,350	101	451	530	596	101	451	530	596
1,350	1,400	105	468	550	619	105	468	550	619
1,400	1,450	109	485	570	641	109	485	570	641
1,450	1,500	113	502	590	664	113	502	590	664
1,500	1,550	117	519	610	686	117	519	610	686
1,550	1,600	120	536	630	709	120	536	630	709
1,600	1,650	124	553	650	731	124	553	650	731
1,650	1,700	128	570	670	754	128	570	670	754
1,700	1,750	132	587	690	776	132	587	690	776
1,750	1,800	136	604	710	799	136	604	710	799
1,800	1,850	140	621	730	821	140	621	730	821
1,850	1,900	143	638	750	844	143	638	750	844
1,900	1,950	147	655	770	866	147	655	770	866
1,950	2,000	151	672	790	889	151	672	790	889
2,000	2,050	155	689	810	911	155	689	810	911
2,050	2,100	159	706	830	934	159	706	830	934
2,100	2,150	163	723	850	956	163	723	850	956
2,150	2,200	166	740	870	979	166	740	870	979
2,200	2,250	170	757	890	1,001	170	757	890	1,001
2,250	2,300	174	774	910	1,024	174	774	910	1,024
2,300	2,350	178	791	930	1,046	178	791	930	1,046
2,350	2,400	182	808	950	1,069	182	808	950	1,069
2,400	2,450	186	825	970	1,091	186	825	970	1,091
2,450	2,500	189	842	990	1,114	189	842	990	1,114

(Continued)

SPECIAL TABLES

Need more information or forms? Visit IRS.gov. **-56-**

Caution: This is a draft 2012 Earned Income Credit (EIC) Table. At the time of publication, the IRS had not yet released the 2012 Earned Income Credit (EIC) Table. For the latest information, see CCHGroup.com/TaxUpdates.

Earned Income Credit (EIC) Table - *Continued* **(Caution. This is not a tax table.)**

If the amount you are looking up from the worksheet is–		And your filing status is– Single, head of household, or qualifying widow(er) and you have–				Married filing jointly and you have–			
At least	But less than	No Children	One Child	Two Children	Three Children	No Children	One Child	Two Children	Three Children
		Your credit is–				Your credit is–			
2,500	2,550	193	859	1,010	1,136	193	859	1,010	1,136
2,550	2,600	197	876	1,030	1,159	197	876	1,030	1,159
2,600	2,650	201	893	1,050	1,181	201	893	1,050	1,181
2,650	2,700	205	910	1,070	1,204	205	910	1,070	1,204
2,700	2,750	208	927	1,090	1,226	208	927	1,090	1,226
2,750	2,800	212	944	1,110	1,249	212	944	1,110	1,249
2,800	2,850	216	961	1,130	1,271	216	961	1,130	1,271
2,850	2,900	220	978	1,150	1,294	220	978	1,150	1,294
2,900	2,950	224	995	1,170	1,316	224	995	1,170	1,316
2,950	3,000	228	1,012	1,190	1,339	228	1,012	1,190	1,339
3,000	3,050	231	1,029	1,210	1,361	231	1,029	1,210	1,361
3,050	3,100	235	1,046	1,230	1,384	235	1,046	1,230	1,384
3,100	3,150	239	1,063	1,250	1,406	239	1,063	1,250	1,406
3,150	3,200	243	1,080	1,270	1,429	243	1,080	1,270	1,429
3,200	3,250	247	1,097	1,290	1,451	247	1,097	1,290	1,451
3,250	3,300	251	1,114	1,310	1,474	251	1,114	1,310	1,474
3,300	3,350	254	1,131	1,330	1,496	254	1,131	1,330	1,496
3,350	3,400	258	1,148	1,350	1,519	258	1,148	1,350	1,519
3,400	3,450	262	1,165	1,370	1,541	262	1,165	1,370	1,541
3,450	3,500	266	1,182	1,390	1,564	266	1,182	1,390	1,564
3,500	3,550	270	1,199	1,410	1,586	270	1,199	1,410	1,586
3,550	3,600	273	1,216	1,430	1,609	273	1,216	1,430	1,609
3,600	3,650	277	1,233	1,450	1,631	277	1,233	1,450	1,631
3,650	3,700	281	1,250	1,470	1,654	281	1,250	1,470	1,654
3,700	3,750	285	1,267	1,490	1,676	285	1,267	1,490	1,676
3,750	3,800	289	1,284	1,510	1,699	289	1,284	1,510	1,699
3,800	3,850	293	1,301	1,530	1,721	293	1,301	1,530	1,721
3,850	3,900	296	1,318	1,550	1,744	296	1,318	1,550	1,744
3,900	3,950	300	1,335	1,570	1,766	300	1,335	1,570	1,766
3,950	4,000	304	1,352	1,590	1,789	304	1,352	1,590	1,789
4,000	4,050	308	1,369	1,610	1,811	308	1,369	1,610	1,811
4,050	4,100	312	1,386	1,630	1,834	312	1,386	1,630	1,834
4,100	4,150	316	1,403	1,650	1,856	316	1,403	1,650	1,856
4,150	4,200	319	1,420	1,670	1,879	319	1,420	1,670	1,879
4,200	4,250	323	1,437	1,690	1,901	323	1,437	1,690	1,901
4,250	4,300	327	1,454	1,710	1,924	327	1,454	1,710	1,924
4,300	4,350	331	1,471	1,730	1,946	331	1,471	1,730	1,946
4,350	4,400	335	1,488	1,750	1,969	335	1,488	1,750	1,969
4,400	4,450	339	1,505	1,770	1,991	339	1,505	1,770	1,991
4,450	4,500	342	1,522	1,790	2,014	342	1,522	1,790	2,014
4,500	4,550	346	1,539	1,810	2,036	346	1,539	1,810	2,036
4,550	4,600	350	1,556	1,830	2,059	350	1,556	1,830	2,059
4,600	4,650	354	1,573	1,850	2,081	354	1,573	1,850	2,081
4,650	4,700	358	1,590	1,870	2,104	358	1,590	1,870	2,104
4,700	4,750	361	1,607	1,890	2,126	361	1,607	1,890	2,126
4,750	4,800	365	1,624	1,910	2,149	365	1,624	1,910	2,149
4,800	4,850	369	1,641	1,930	2,171	369	1,641	1,930	2,171
4,850	4,900	373	1,658	1,950	2,194	373	1,658	1,950	2,194
4,900	4,950	377	1,675	1,970	2,216	377	1,675	1,970	2,216
4,950	5,000	381	1,692	1,990	2,239	381	1,692	1,990	2,239
5,000	5,050	384	1,709	2,010	2,261	384	1,709	2,010	2,261
5,050	5,100	388	1,726	2,030	2,284	388	1,726	2,030	2,284
5,100	5,150	392	1,743	2,050	2,306	392	1,743	2,050	2,306
5,150	5,200	396	1,760	2,070	2,329	396	1,760	2,070	2,329
5,200	5,250	400	1,777	2,090	2,351	400	1,777	2,090	2,351
5,250	5,300	404	1,794	2,110	2,374	404	1,794	2,110	2,374
5,300	5,350	407	1,811	2,130	2,396	407	1,811	2,130	2,396
5,350	5,400	411	1,828	2,150	2,419	411	1,828	2,150	2,419
5,400	5,450	415	1,845	2,170	2,441	415	1,845	2,170	2,441
5,450	5,500	419	1,862	2,190	2,464	419	1,862	2,190	2,464

(Continued)

 Need more information or forms? Visit IRS.gov.

Caution: This is a draft 2012 Earned Income Credit (EIC) Table. At the time of publication, the IRS had not yet released the 2012 Earned Income Credit (EIC) Table. For the latest information, see CCHGroup.com/TaxUpdates.

Earned Income Credit (EIC) Table - *Continued* **(Caution. This is not a tax table.)**

If the amount you are looking up from the worksheet is–		And your filing status is– Single, head of household, or qualifying widow(er) and you have–				Married filing jointly and you have–			
At least	But less than	No Children	One Child	Two Children	Three Children	No Children	One Child	Two Children	Three Children
		Your credit is–				Your credit is–			
5,500	5,550	423	1,879	2,210	2,486	423	1,879	2,210	2,486
5,550	5,600	426	1,896	2,230	2,509	426	1,896	2,230	2,509
5,600	5,650	430	1,913	2,250	2,531	430	1,913	2,250	2,531
5,650	5,700	434	1,930	2,270	2,554	434	1,930	2,270	2,554
5,700	5,750	438	1,947	2,290	2,576	438	1,947	2,290	2,576
5,750	5,800	442	1,964	2,310	2,599	442	1,964	2,310	2,599
5,800	5,850	446	1,981	2,330	2,621	446	1,981	2,330	2,621
5,850	5,900	449	1,998	2,350	2,644	449	1,998	2,350	2,644
5,900	5,950	453	2,015	2,370	2,666	453	2,015	2,370	2,666
5,950	6,000	457	2,032	2,390	2,689	457	2,032	2,390	2,689
6,000	6,050	461	2,049	2,410	2,711	461	2,049	2,410	2,711
6,050	6,100	465	2,066	2,430	2,734	465	2,066	2,430	2,734
6,100	6,150	469	2,083	2,450	2,756	469	2,083	2,450	2,756
6,150	6,200	472	2,100	2,470	2,779	472	2,100	2,470	2,779
6,200	6,250	475	2,117	2,490	2,801	475	2,117	2,490	2,801
6,250	6,300	475	2,134	2,510	2,824	475	2,134	2,510	2,824
6,300	6,350	475	2,151	2,530	2,846	475	2,151	2,530	2,846
6,350	6,400	475	2,168	2,550	2,869	475	2,168	2,550	2,869
6,400	6,450	475	2,185	2,570	2,891	475	2,185	2,570	2,891
6,450	6,500	475	2,202	2,590	2,914	475	2,202	2,590	2,914
6,500	6,550	475	2,219	2,610	2,936	475	2,219	2,610	2,936
6,550	6,600	475	2,236	2,630	2,959	475	2,236	2,630	2,959
6,600	6,650	475	2,253	2,650	2,981	475	2,253	2,650	2,981
6,650	6,700	475	2,270	2,670	3,004	475	2,270	2,670	3,004
6,700	6,750	475	2,287	2,690	3,026	475	2,287	2,690	3,026
6,750	6,800	475	2,304	2,710	3,049	475	2,304	2,710	3,049
6,800	6,850	475	2,321	2,730	3,071	475	2,321	2,730	3,071
6,850	6,900	475	2,338	2,750	3,094	475	2,338	2,750	3,094
6,900	6,950	475	2,355	2,770	3,116	475	2,355	2,770	3,116
6,950	7,000	475	2,372	2,790	3,139	475	2,372	2,790	3,139
7,000	7,050	475	2,389	2,810	3,161	475	2,389	2,810	3,161
7,050	7,100	475	2,406	2,830	3,184	475	2,406	2,830	3,184
7,100	7,150	475	2,423	2,850	3,206	475	2,423	2,850	3,206
7,150	7,200	475	2,440	2,870	3,229	475	2,440	2,870	3,229
7,200	7,250	475	2,457	2,890	3,251	475	2,457	2,890	3,251
7,250	7,300	475	2,474	2,910	3,274	475	2,474	2,910	3,274
7,300	7,350	475	2,491	2,930	3,296	475	2,491	2,930	3,296
7,350	7,400	475	2,508	2,950	3,319	475	2,508	2,950	3,319
7,400	7,450	475	2,525	2,970	3,341	475	2,525	2,970	3,341
7,450	7,500	475	2,542	2,990	3,364	475	2,542	2,990	3,364
7,500	7,550	475	2,559	3,010	3,386	475	2,559	3,010	3,386
7,550	7,600	475	2,576	3,030	3,409	475	2,576	3,030	3,409
7,600	7,650	475	2,593	3,050	3,431	475	2,593	3,050	3,431
7,650	7,700	475	2,610	3,070	3,454	475	2,610	3,070	3,454
7,700	7,750	475	2,627	3,090	3,476	475	2,627	3,090	3,476
7,750	7,800	475	2,644	3,110	3,499	475	2,644	3,110	3,499
7,800	7,850	471	2,661	3,130	3,521	475	2,661	3,130	3,521
7,850	7,900	467	2,678	3,150	3,544	475	2,678	3,150	3,544
7,900	7,950	463	2,695	3,170	3,566	475	2,695	3,170	3,566
7,950	8,000	459	2,712	3,190	3,589	475	2,712	3,190	3,589
8,000	8,050	456	2,729	3,210	3,611	475	2,729	3,210	3,611
8,050	8,100	452	2,746	3,230	3,634	475	2,746	3,230	3,634
8,100	8,150	448	2,763	3,250	3,656	475	2,763	3,250	3,656
8,150	8,200	444	2,780	3,270	3,679	475	2,780	3,270	3,679
8,200	8,250	440	2,797	3,290	3,701	475	2,797	3,290	3,701
8,250	8,300	436	2,814	3,310	3,724	475	2,814	3,310	3,724
8,300	8,350	433	2,831	3,330	3,746	475	2,831	3,330	3,746
8,350	8,400	429	2,848	3,350	3,769	475	2,848	3,350	3,769
8,400	8,450	425	2,865	3,370	3,791	475	2,865	3,370	3,791
8,450	8,500	421	2,882	3,390	3,814	475	2,882	3,390	3,814

(Continued)

Caution: This is a draft 2012 Earned Income Credit (EIC) Table. At the time of publication, the IRS had not yet released the 2012 Earned Income Credit (EIC) Table. For the latest information, see CCHGroup.com/TaxUpdates.

Earned Income Credit (EIC) Table - *Continued* **(Caution.** This is **not** a tax table.)

If the amount you are looking up from the worksheet is–		And your filing status is– Single, head of household, or qualifying widow(er) and you have–				Married filing jointly and you have–			
At least	But less than	No Children	One Child	Two Children	Three Children	No Children	One Child	Two Children	Three Children
		Your credit is–				Your credit is–			
8,500	8,550	417	2,899	3,410	3,836	475	2,899	3,410	3,836
8,550	8,600	413	2,916	3,430	3,859	475	2,916	3,430	3,859
8,600	8,650	410	2,933	3,450	3,881	475	2,933	3,450	3,881
8,650	8,700	406	2,950	3,470	3,904	475	2,950	3,470	3,904
8,700	8,750	402	2,967	3,490	3,926	475	2,967	3,490	3,926
8,750	8,800	398	2,984	3,510	3,949	475	2,984	3,510	3,949
8,800	8,850	394	3,001	3,530	3,971	475	3,001	3,530	3,971
8,850	8,900	391	3,018	3,550	3,994	475	3,018	3,550	3,994
8,900	8,950	387	3,035	3,570	4,016	475	3,035	3,570	4,016
8,950	9,000	383	3,052	3,590	4,039	475	3,052	3,590	4,039
9,000	9,050	379	3,069	3,610	4,061	475	3,069	3,610	4,061
9,050	9,100	375	3,086	3,630	4,084	475	3,086	3,630	4,084
9,100	9,150	371	3,103	3,650	4,106	475	3,103	3,650	4,106
9,150	9,200	368	3,120	3,670	4,129	475	3,120	3,670	4,129
9,200	9,250	364	3,137	3,690	4,151	475	3,137	3,690	4,151
9,250	9,300	360	3,154	3,710	4,174	475	3,154	3,710	4,174
9,300	9,350	356	3,169	3,730	4,196	475	3,169	3,730	4,196
9,350	9,400	352	3,169	3,750	4,219	475	3,169	3,750	4,219
9,400	9,450	348	3,169	3,770	4,241	475	3,169	3,770	4,241
9,450	9,500	345	3,169	3,790	4,264	475	3,169	3,790	4,264
9,500	9,550	341	3,169	3,810	4,286	475	3,169	3,810	4,286
9,550	9,600	337	3,169	3,830	4,309	475	3,169	3,830	4,309
9,600	9,650	333	3,169	3,850	4,331	475	3,169	3,850	4,331
9,650	9,700	329	3,169	3,870	4,354	475	3,169	3,870	4,354
9,700	9,750	326	3,169	3,890	4,376	475	3,169	3,890	4,376
9,750	9,800	322	3,169	3,910	4,399	475	3,169	3,910	4,399
9,800	9,850	318	3,169	3,930	4,421	475	3,169	3,930	4,421
9,850	9,900	314	3,169	3,950	4,444	475	3,169	3,950	4,444
9,900	9,950	310	3,169	3,970	4,466	475	3,169	3,970	4,466
9,950	10,000	306	3,169	3,990	4,489	475	3,169	3,990	4,489
10,000	10,050	303	3,169	4,010	4,511	475	3,169	4,010	4,511
10,050	10,100	299	3,169	4,030	4,534	475	3,169	4,030	4,534
10,100	10,150	295	3,169	4,050	4,556	475	3,169	4,050	4,556
10,150	10,200	291	3,169	4,070	4,579	475	3,169	4,070	4,579
10,200	10,250	287	3,169	4,090	4,601	475	3,169	4,090	4,601
10,250	10,300	283	3,169	4,110	4,624	475	3,169	4,110	4,624
10,300	10,350	280	3,169	4,130	4,646	475	3,169	4,130	4,646
10,350	10,400	276	3,169	4,150	4,669	475	3,169	4,150	4,669
10,400	10,450	272	3,169	4,170	4,691	475	3,169	4,170	4,691
10,450	10,500	268	3,169	4,190	4,714	475	3,169	4,190	4,714
10,500	10,550	264	3,169	4,210	4,736	475	3,169	4,210	4,736
10,550	10,600	260	3,169	4,230	4,759	475	3,169	4,230	4,759
10,600	10,650	257	3,169	4,250	4,781	475	3,169	4,250	4,781
10,650	10,700	253	3,169	4,270	4,804	475	3,169	4,270	4,804
10,700	10,750	249	3,169	4,290	4,826	475	3,169	4,290	4,826
10,750	10,800	245	3,169	4,310	4,849	475	3,169	4,310	4,849
10,800	10,850	241	3,169	4,330	4,871	475	3,169	4,330	4,871
10,850	10,900	238	3,169	4,350	4,894	475	3,169	4,350	4,894
10,900	10,950	234	3,169	4,370	4,916	475	3,169	4,370	4,916
10,950	11,000	230	3,169	4,390	4,939	475	3,169	4,390	4,939
11,000	11,050	226	3,169	4,410	4,961	475	3,169	4,410	4,961
11,050	11,100	222	3,169	4,430	4,984	475	3,169	4,430	4,984
11,100	11,150	218	3,169	4,450	5,006	475	3,169	4,450	5,006
11,150	11,200	215	3,169	4,470	5,029	475	3,169	4,470	5,029
11,200	11,250	211	3,169	4,490	5,051	475	3,169	4,490	5,051
11,250	11,300	207	3,169	4,510	5,074	475	3,169	4,510	5,074
11,300	11,350	203	3,169	4,530	5,096	475	3,169	4,530	5,096
11,350	11,400	199	3,169	4,550	5,119	475	3,169	4,550	5,119
11,400	11,450	195	3,169	4,570	5,141	475	3,169	4,570	5,141
11,450	11,500	192	3,169	4,590	5,164	475	3,169	4,590	5,164

(Continued)

 Need more information or forms? Visit IRS.gov.

Caution: This is a draft 2012 Earned Income Credit (EIC) Table. At the time of publication, the IRS had not yet released the 2012 Earned Income Credit (EIC) Table. For the latest information, see CCHGroup.com/TaxUpdates.

Earned Income Credit (EIC) Table - *Continued* **(Caution.** This is **not** a tax table.)

If the amount you are looking up from the worksheet is–		And your filing status is– Single, head of household, or qualifying widow(er) and you have–				Married filing jointly and you have–			
		No Children	One Child	Two Children	Three Children	No Children	One Child	Two Children	Three Children
At least	But less than	Your credit is–				Your credit is–			
11,500	11,550	188	3,169	4,610	5,186	475	3,169	4,610	5,186
11,550	11,600	184	3,169	4,630	5,209	475	3,169	4,630	5,209
11,600	11,650	180	3,169	4,650	5,231	475	3,169	4,650	5,231
11,650	11,700	176	3,169	4,670	5,254	475	3,169	4,670	5,254
11,700	11,750	173	3,169	4,690	5,276	475	3,169	4,690	5,276
11,750	11,800	169	3,169	4,710	5,299	475	3,169	4,710	5,299
11,800	11,850	165	3,169	4,730	5,321	475	3,169	4,730	5,321
11,850	11,900	161	3,169	4,750	5,344	475	3,169	4,750	5,344
11,900	11,950	157	3,169	4,770	5,366	475	3,169	4,770	5,366
11,950	12,000	153	3,169	4,790	5,389	475	3,169	4,790	5,389
12,000	12,050	150	3,169	4,810	5,411	475	3,169	4,810	5,411
12,050	12,100	146	3,169	4,830	5,434	475	3,169	4,830	5,434
12,100	12,150	142	3,169	4,850	5,456	475	3,169	4,850	5,456
12,150	12,200	138	3,169	4,870	5,479	475	3,169	4,870	5,479
12,200	12,250	134	3,169	4,890	5,501	475	3,169	4,890	5,501
12,250	12,300	130	3,169	4,910	5,524	475	3,169	4,910	5,524
12,300	12,350	127	3,169	4,930	5,546	475	3,169	4,930	5,546
12,350	12,400	123	3,169	4,950	5,569	475	3,169	4,950	5,569
12,400	12,450	119	3,169	4,970	5,591	475	3,169	4,970	5,591
12,450	12,500	115	3,169	4,990	5,614	475	3,169	4,990	5,614
12,500	12,550	111	3,169	5,010	5,636	475	3,169	5,010	5,636
12,550	12,600	107	3,169	5,030	5,659	475	3,169	5,030	5,659
12,600	12,650	104	3,169	5,050	5,681	475	3,169	5,050	5,681
12,650	12,700	100	3,169	5,070	5,704	475	3,169	5,070	5,704
12,700	12,750	96	3,169	5,090	5,726	475	3,169	5,090	5,726
12,750	12,800	92	3,169	5,110	5,749	475	3,169	5,110	5,749
12,800	12,850	88	3,169	5,130	5,771	475	3,169	5,130	5,771
12,850	12,900	85	3,169	5,150	5,794	475	3,169	5,150	5,794
12,900	12,950	81	3,169	5,170	5,816	475	3,169	5,170	5,816
12,950	13,000	77	3,169	5,190	5,839	475	3,169	5,190	5,839
13,000	13,050	73	3,169	5,210	5,861	472	3,169	5,210	5,861
13,050	13,100	69	3,169	5,236	5,891	468	3,169	5,236	5,891
13,100	13,150	65	3,169	5,236	5,891	464	3,169	5,236	5,891
13,150	13,200	62	3,169	5,236	5,891	460	3,169	5,236	5,891
13,200	13,250	58	3,169	5,236	5,891	456	3,169	5,236	5,891
13,250	13,300	54	3,169	5,236	5,891	452	3,169	5,236	5,891
13,300	13,350	50	3,169	5,236	5,891	449	3,169	5,236	5,891
13,350	13,400	46	3,169	5,236	5,891	445	3,169	5,236	5,891
13,400	13,450	42	3,169	5,236	5,891	441	3,169	5,236	5,891
13,450	13,500	39	3,169	5,236	5,891	437	3,169	5,236	5,891
13,500	13,550	35	3,169	5,236	5,891	433	3,169	5,236	5,891
13,550	13,600	31	3,169	5,236	5,891	430	3,169	5,236	5,891
13,600	13,650	27	3,169	5,236	5,891	426	3,169	5,236	5,891
13,650	13,700	23	3,169	5,236	5,891	422	3,169	5,236	5,891
13,700	13,750	20	3,169	5,236	5,891	418	3,169	5,236	5,891
13,750	13,800	16	3,169	5,236	5,891	414	3,169	5,236	5,891
13,800	13,850	12	3,169	5,236	5,891	410	3,169	5,236	5,891
13,850	13,900	8	3,169	5,236	5,891	407	3,169	5,236	5,891
13,900	13,950	4	3,169	5,236	5,891	403	3,169	5,236	5,891
13,950	14,000	*	3,169	5,236	5,891	399	3,169	5,236	5,891
14,000	14,050	0	3,169	5,236	5,891	395	3,169	5,236	5,891
14,050	14,100	0	3,169	5,236	5,891	391	3,169	5,236	5,891
14,100	14,150	0	3,169	5,236	5,891	387	3,169	5,236	5,891
14,150	14,200	0	3,169	5,236	5,891	384	3,169	5,236	5,891
14,200	14,250	0	3,169	5,236	5,891	380	3,169	5,236	5,891
14,250	14,300	0	3,169	5,236	5,891	376	3,169	5,236	5,891
14,300	14,350	0	3,169	5,236	5,891	372	3,169	5,236	5,891
14,350	14,400	0	3,169	5,236	5,891	368	3,169	5,236	5,891
14,400	14,450	0	3,169	5,236	5,891	365	3,169	5,236	5,891
14,450	14,500	0	3,169	5,236	5,891	361	3,169	5,236	5,891

(Continued)

* If the amount you are looking up from the worksheet is at least $13,950 but less than $13,980, and you have no qualifying children, your credit is $1. Otherwise, you cannot take the credit.

»»→ Caution: This is a draft 2012 Earned Income Credit (EIC) Table. At the time of publication, the IRS had not yet released the 2012 Earned Income Credit (EIC) Table. For the latest information, see CCHGroup.com/TaxUpdates.

Earned Income Credit (EIC) Table - *Continued* **(Caution.** This is **not** a tax table.)

If the amount you are looking up from the worksheet is–		And your filing status is–							
		Single, head of household, or qualifying widow(er) and you have–				Married filing jointly and you have–			
		No Children	One Child	Two Children	Three Children	No Children	One Child	Two Children	Three Children
At least	But less than	Your credit is–				Your credit is–			
14,500	14,550	0	3,169	5,236	5,891	357	3,169	5,236	5,891
14,550	14,600	0	3,169	5,236	5,891	353	3,169	5,236	5,891
14,600	14,650	0	3,169	5,236	5,891	349	3,169	5,236	5,891
14,650	14,700	0	3,169	5,236	5,891	345	3,169	5,236	5,891
14,700	14,750	0	3,169	5,236	5,891	342	3,169	5,236	5,891
14,750	14,800	0	3,169	5,236	5,891	338	3,169	5,236	5,891
14,800	14,850	0	3,169	5,236	5,891	334	3,169	5,236	5,891
14,850	14,900	0	3,169	5,236	5,891	330	3,169	5,236	5,891
14,900	14,950	0	3,169	5,236	5,891	326	3,169	5,236	5,891
14,950	15,000	0	3,169	5,236	5,891	322	3,169	5,236	5,891
15,000	15,050	0	3,169	5,236	5,891	319	3,169	5,236	5,891
15,050	15,100	0	3,169	5,236	5,891	315	3,169	5,236	5,891
15,100	15,150	0	3,169	5,236	5,891	311	3,169	5,236	5,891
15,150	15,200	0	3,169	5,236	5,891	307	3,169	5,236	5,891
15,200	15,250	0	3,169	5,236	5,891	303	3,169	5,236	5,891
15,250	15,300	0	3,169	5,236	5,891	299	3,169	5,236	5,891
15,300	15,350	0	3,169	5,236	5,891	296	3,169	5,236	5,891
15,350	15,400	0	3,169	5,236	5,891	292	3,169	5,236	5,891
15,400	15,450	0	3,169	5,236	5,891	288	3,169	5,236	5,891
15,450	15,500	0	3,169	5,236	5,891	284	3,169	5,236	5,891
15,500	15,550	0	3,169	5,236	5,891	280	3,169	5,236	5,891
15,550	15,600	0	3,169	5,236	5,891	277	3,169	5,236	5,891
15,600	15,650	0	3,169	5,236	5,891	273	3,169	5,236	5,891
15,650	15,700	0	3,169	5,236	5,891	269	3,169	5,236	5,891
15,700	15,750	0	3,169	5,236	5,891	265	3,169	5,236	5,891
15,750	15,800	0	3,169	5,236	5,891	261	3,169	5,236	5,891
15,800	15,850	0	3,169	5,236	5,891	257	3,169	5,236	5,891
15,850	15,900	0	3,169	5,236	5,891	254	3,169	5,236	5,891
15,900	15,950	0	3,169	5,236	5,891	250	3,169	5,236	5,891
15,950	16,000	0	3,169	5,236	5,891	246	3,169	5,236	5,891
16,000	16,050	0	3,169	5,236	5,891	242	3,169	5,236	5,891
16,050	16,100	0	3,169	5,236	5,891	238	3,169	5,236	5,891
16,100	16,150	0	3,169	5,236	5,891	234	3,169	5,236	5,891
16,150	16,200	0	3,169	5,236	5,891	231	3,169	5,236	5,891
16,200	16,250	0	3,169	5,236	5,891	227	3,169	5,236	5,891
16,250	16,300	0	3,169	5,236	5,891	223	3,169	5,236	5,891
16,300	16,350	0	3,169	5,236	5,891	219	3,169	5,236	5,891
16,350	16,400	0	3,169	5,236	5,891	215	3,169	5,236	5,891
16,400	16,450	0	3,169	5,236	5,891	212	3,169	5,236	5,891
16,450	16,500	0	3,169	5,236	5,891	208	3,169	5,236	5,891
16,500	16,550	0	3,169	5,236	5,891	204	3,169	5,236	5,891
16,550	16,600	0	3,169	5,236	5,891	200	3,169	5,236	5,891
16,600	16,650	0	3,169	5,236	5,891	196	3,169	5,236	5,891
16,650	16,700	0	3,169	5,236	5,891	192	3,169	5,236	5,891
16,700	16,750	0	3,169	5,236	5,891	189	3,169	5,236	5,891
16,750	16,800	0	3,169	5,236	5,891	185	3,169	5,236	5,891
16,800	16,850	0	3,169	5,236	5,891	181	3,169	5,236	5,891
16,850	16,900	0	3,169	5,236	5,891	177	3,169	5,236	5,891
16,900	16,950	0	3,169	5,236	5,891	173	3,169	5,236	5,891
16,950	17,000	0	3,169	5,236	5,891	169	3,169	5,236	5,891
17,000	17,050	0	3,169	5,236	5,891	166	3,169	5,236	5,891
17,050	17,100	0	3,169	5,236	5,891	162	3,169	5,236	5,891
17,100	17,150	0	3,163	5,229	5,883	158	3,169	5,236	5,891
17,150	17,200	0	3,155	5,218	5,873	154	3,169	5,236	5,891
17,200	17,250	0	3,147	5,208	5,862	150	3,169	5,236	5,891
17,250	17,300	0	3,139	5,197	5,852	146	3,169	5,236	5,891
17,300	17,350	0	3,131	5,187	5,841	143	3,169	5,236	5,891
17,350	17,400	0	3,123	5,176	5,830	139	3,169	5,236	5,891
17,400	17,450	0	3,115	5,165	5,820	135	3,169	5,236	5,891
17,450	17,500	0	3,107	5,155	5,809	131	3,169	5,236	5,891

(Continued)

Need more information or forms? Visit IRS.gov.

Caution: This is a draft 2012 Earned Income Credit (EIC) Table. At the time of publication, the IRS had not yet released the 2012 Earned Income Credit (EIC) Table. For the latest information, see CCHGroup.com/TaxUpdates.

Earned Income Credit (EIC) Table - *Continued* **(Caution. This is not a tax table.)**

If the amount you are looking up from the worksheet is–		And your filing status is– Single, head of household, or qualifying widow(er) and you have–				Married filing jointly and you have–			
At least	But less than	No Children	One Child	Two Children	Three Children	No Children	One Child	Two Children	Three Children
		Your credit is–				Your credit is–			
17,500	17,550	0	3,099	5,144	5,799	127	3,169	5,236	5,891
17,550	17,600	0	3,091	5,134	5,788	124	3,169	5,236	5,891
17,600	17,650	0	3,083	5,123	5,778	120	3,169	5,236	5,891
17,650	17,700	0	3,075	5,113	5,767	116	3,169	5,236	5,891
17,700	17,750	0	3,067	5,102	5,757	112	3,169	5,236	5,891
17,750	17,800	0	3,059	5,092	5,746	108	3,169	5,236	5,891
17,800	17,850	0	3,051	5,081	5,736	104	3,169	5,236	5,891
17,850	17,900	0	3,043	5,071	5,725	101	3,169	5,236	5,891
17,900	17,950	0	3,035	5,060	5,715	97	3,169	5,236	5,891
17,950	18,000	0	3,027	5,050	5,704	93	3,169	5,236	5,891
18,000	18,050	0	3,019	5,039	5,694	89	3,169	5,236	5,891
18,050	18,100	0	3,011	5,029	5,683	85	3,169	5,236	5,891
18,100	18,150	0	3,003	5,018	5,673	81	3,169	5,236	5,891
18,150	18,200	0	2,995	5,007	5,662	78	3,169	5,236	5,891
18,200	18,250	0	2,987	4,997	5,651	74	3,169	5,236	5,891
18,250	18,300	0	2,979	4,986	5,641	70	3,169	5,236	5,891
18,300	18,350	0	2,971	4,976	5,630	66	3,169	5,236	5,891
18,350	18,400	0	2,963	4,965	5,620	62	3,169	5,236	5,891
18,400	18,450	0	2,955	4,955	5,609	59	3,169	5,236	5,891
18,450	18,500	0	2,947	4,944	5,599	55	3,169	5,236	5,891
18,500	18,550	0	2,939	4,934	5,588	51	3,169	5,236	5,891
18,550	18,600	0	2,931	4,923	5,578	47	3,169	5,236	5,891
18,600	18,650	0	2,924	4,913	5,567	43	3,169	5,236	5,891
18,650	18,700	0	2,916	4,902	5,557	39	3,169	5,236	5,891
18,700	18,750	0	2,908	4,892	5,546	36	3,169	5,236	5,891
18,750	18,800	0	2,900	4,881	5,536	32	3,169	5,236	5,891
18,800	18,850	0	2,892	4,871	5,525	28	3,169	5,236	5,891
18,850	18,900	0	2,884	4,860	5,515	24	3,169	5,236	5,891
18,900	18,950	0	2,876	4,850	5,504	20	3,169	5,236	5,891
18,950	19,000	0	2,868	4,839	5,494	16	3,169	5,236	5,891
19,000	19,050	0	2,860	4,828	5,483	13	3,169	5,236	5,891
19,050	19,100	0	2,852	4,818	5,472	9	3,169	5,236	5,891
19,100	19,150	0	2,844	4,807	5,462	5	3,169	5,236	5,891
19,150	19,200	0	2,836	4,797	5,451	*	3,169	5,236	5,891
19,200	19,250	0	2,828	4,786	5,441	0	3,169	5,236	5,891
19,250	19,300	0	2,820	4,776	5,430	0	3,169	5,236	5,891
19,300	19,350	0	2,812	4,765	5,420	0	3,169	5,236	5,891
19,350	19,400	0	2,804	4,755	5,409	0	3,169	5,236	5,891
19,400	19,450	0	2,796	4,744	5,399	0	3,169	5,236	5,891
19,450	19,500	0	2,788	4,734	5,388	0	3,169	5,236	5,891
19,500	19,550	0	2,780	4,723	5,378	0	3,169	5,236	5,891
19,550	19,600	0	2,772	4,713	5,367	0	3,169	5,236	5,891
19,600	19,650	0	2,764	4,702	5,357	0	3,169	5,236	5,891
19,650	19,700	0	2,756	4,692	5,346	0	3,169	5,236	5,891
19,700	19,750	0	2,748	4,681	5,336	0	3,169	5,236	5,891
19,750	19,800	0	2,740	4,671	5,325	0	3,169	5,236	5,891
19,800	19,850	0	2,732	4,660	5,315	0	3,169	5,236	5,891
19,850	19,900	0	2,724	4,649	5,304	0	3,169	5,236	5,891
19,900	19,950	0	2,716	4,639	5,293	0	3,169	5,236	5,891
19,950	20,000	0	2,708	4,628	5,283	0	3,169	5,236	5,891
20,000	20,050	0	2,700	4,618	5,272	0	3,169	5,236	5,891
20,050	20,100	0	2,692	4,607	5,262	0	3,169	5,236	5,891
20,100	20,150	0	2,684	4,597	5,251	0	3,169	5,236	5,891
20,150	20,200	0	2,676	4,586	5,241	0	3,169	5,236	5,891
20,200	20,250	0	2,668	4,576	5,230	0	3,169	5,236	5,891
20,250	20,300	0	2,660	4,565	5,220	0	3,169	5,236	5,891
20,300	20,350	0	2,652	4,555	5,209	0	3,169	5,236	5,891
20,350	20,400	0	2,644	4,544	5,199	0	3,169	5,236	5,891
20,400	20,450	0	2,636	4,534	5,188	0	3,169	5,236	5,891
20,450	20,500	0	2,628	4,523	5,178	0	3,169	5,236	5,891

(Continued)

* If the amount you are looking up from the worksheet is at least $19,150 but less than $19,190, and you have no qualifying children, your credit is $2. Otherwise, you cannot take the credit.

Need more information or forms? Visit IRS.gov. -62-

SPECIAL TABLES

»»→ Caution: This is a draft 2012 Earned Income Credit (EIC) Table. At the time of publication, the IRS had not yet released the 2012 Earned Income Credit (EIC) Table. For the latest information, see CCHGroup.com/TaxUpdates.

Earned Income Credit (EIC) Table - *Continued* (Caution. This is not a tax table.)

If the amount you are looking up from the worksheet is–		And your filing status is– Single, head of household, or qualifying widow(er) and you have–				Married filing jointly and you have–			
		No Children	One Child	Two Children	Three Children	No Children	One Child	Two Children	Three Children
At least	But less than	Your credit is–				Your credit is–			
20,500	**20,550**	0	2,620	4,513	5,167	0	3,169	5,236	5,891
20,550	**20,600**	0	2,612	4,502	5,157	0	3,169	5,236	5,891
20,600	**20,650**	0	2,604	4,492	5,146	0	3,169	5,236	5,891
20,650	**20,700**	0	2,596	4,481	5,135	0	3,169	5,236	5,891
20,700	**20,750**	0	2,588	4,470	5,125	0	3,169	5,236	5,891
20,750	**20,800**	0	2,580	4,460	5,114	0	3,169	5,236	5,891
20,800	**20,850**	0	2,572	4,449	5,104	0	3,169	5,236	5,891
20,850	**20,900**	0	2,564	4,439	5,093	0	3,169	5,236	5,891
20,900	**20,950**	0	2,556	4,428	5,083	0	3,169	5,236	5,891
20,950	**21,000**	0	2,548	4,418	5,072	0	3,169	5,236	5,891
21,000	**21,050**	0	2,540	4,407	5,062	0	3,169	5,236	5,891
21,050	**21,100**	0	2,532	4,397	5,051	0	3,169	5,236	5,891
21,100	**21,150**	0	2,524	4,386	5,041	0	3,169	5,236	5,891
21,150	**21,200**	0	2,516	4,376	5,030	0	3,169	5,236	5,891
21,200	**21,250**	0	2,508	4,365	5,020	0	3,169	5,236	5,891
21,250	**21,300**	0	2,500	4,355	5,009	0	3,169	5,236	5,891
21,300	**21,350**	0	2,492	4,344	4,999	0	3,169	5,236	5,891
21,350	**21,400**	0	2,484	4,334	4,988	0	3,169	5,236	5,891
21,400	**21,450**	0	2,476	4,323	4,978	0	3,169	5,236	5,891
21,450	**21,500**	0	2,468	4,313	4,967	0	3,169	5,236	5,891
21,500	**21,550**	0	2,460	4,302	4,956	0	3,169	5,236	5,891
21,550	**21,600**	0	2,452	4,291	4,946	0	3,169	5,236	5,891
21,600	**21,650**	0	2,444	4,281	4,935	0	3,169	5,236	5,891
21,650	**21,700**	0	2,436	4,270	4,925	0	3,169	5,236	5,891
21,700	**21,750**	0	2,428	4,260	4,914	0	3,169	5,236	5,891
21,750	**21,800**	0	2,420	4,249	4,904	0	3,169	5,236	5,891
21,800	**21,850**	0	2,412	4,239	4,893	0	3,169	5,236	5,891
21,850	**21,900**	0	2,404	4,228	4,883	0	3,169	5,236	5,891
21,900	**21,950**	0	2,396	4,218	4,872	0	3,169	5,236	5,891
21,950	**22,000**	0	2,388	4,207	4,862	0	3,169	5,236	5,891
22,000	**22,050**	0	2,380	4,197	4,851	0	3,169	5,236	5,891
22,050	**22,100**	0	2,372	4,186	4,841	0	3,169	5,236	5,891
22,100	**22,150**	0	2,364	4,176	4,830	0	3,169	5,236	5,891
22,150	**22,200**	0	2,356	4,165	4,820	0	3,169	5,236	5,891
22,200	**22,250**	0	2,348	4,155	4,809	0	3,169	5,236	5,891
22,250	**22,300**	0	2,340	4,144	4,799	0	3,169	5,236	5,891
22,300	**22,350**	0	2,332	4,134	4,788	0	3,165	5,231	5,885
22,350	**22,400**	0	2,324	4,123	4,777	0	3,157	5,220	5,875
22,400	**22,450**	0	2,316	4,112	4,767	0	3,149	5,210	5,864
22,450	**22,500**	0	2,308	4,102	4,756	0	3,141	5,199	5,854
22,500	**22,550**	0	2,300	4,091	4,746	0	3,133	5,189	5,843
22,550	**22,600**	0	2,292	4,081	4,735	0	3,125	5,178	5,833
22,600	**22,650**	0	2,284	4,070	4,725	0	3,117	5,168	5,822
22,650	**22,700**	0	2,276	4,060	4,714	0	3,109	5,157	5,812
22,700	**22,750**	0	2,268	4,049	4,704	0	3,101	5,146	5,801
22,750	**22,800**	0	2,260	4,039	4,693	0	3,093	5,136	5,790
22,800	**22,850**	0	2,252	4,028	4,683	0	3,085	5,125	5,780
22,850	**22,900**	0	2,244	4,018	4,672	0	3,077	5,115	5,769
22,900	**22,950**	0	2,236	4,007	4,662	0	3,069	5,104	5,759
22,950	**23,000**	0	2,228	3,997	4,651	0	3,061	5,094	5,748
23,000	**23,050**	0	2,220	3,986	4,641	0	3,053	5,083	5,738
23,050	**23,100**	0	2,212	3,976	4,630	0	3,045	5,073	5,727
23,100	**23,150**	0	2,204	3,965	4,620	0	3,037	5,062	5,717
23,150	**23,200**	0	2,196	3,954	4,609	0	3,029	5,052	5,706
23,200	**23,250**	0	2,188	3,944	4,598	0	3,021	5,041	5,696
23,250	**23,300**	0	2,180	3,933	4,588	0	3,013	5,031	5,685
23,300	**23,350**	0	2,172	3,923	4,577	0	3,005	5,020	5,675
23,350	**23,400**	0	2,164	3,912	4,567	0	2,997	5,010	5,664
23,400	**23,450**	0	2,156	3,902	4,556	0	2,989	4,999	5,654
23,450	**23,500**	0	2,148	3,891	4,546	0	2,981	4,989	5,643

(Continued)

»»→ Caution: This is a draft 2012 Earned Income Credit (EIC) Table. At the time of publication, the IRS had not yet released the 2012 Earned Income Credit (EIC) Table. For the latest information, see CCHGroup.com/TaxUpdates.

Earned Income Credit (EIC) Table - *Continued* **(Caution.** This is **not** a tax table.)

If the amount you are looking up from the worksheet is–		And your filing status is– Single, head of household, or qualifying widow(er) and you have–				Married filing jointly and you have–			
At least	But less than	No Children	One Child	Two Children	Three Children	No Children	One Child	Two Children	Three Children
		Your credit is–				Your credit is–			
23,500	23,550	0	2,140	3,881	4,535	0	2,973	4,978	5,633
23,550	23,600	0	2,132	3,870	4,525	0	2,965	4,967	5,622
23,600	23,650	0	2,125	3,860	4,514	0	2,957	4,957	5,611
23,650	23,700	0	2,117	3,849	4,504	0	2,949	4,946	5,601
23,700	23,750	0	2,109	3,839	4,493	0	2,941	4,936	5,590
23,750	23,800	0	2,101	3,828	4,483	0	2,933	4,925	5,580
23,800	23,850	0	2,093	3,818	4,472	0	2,925	4,915	5,569
23,850	23,900	0	2,085	3,807	4,462	0	2,917	4,904	5,559
23,900	23,950	0	2,077	3,797	4,451	0	2,909	4,894	5,548
23,950	24,000	0	2,069	3,786	4,441	0	2,901	4,883	5,538
24,000	24,050	0	2,061	3,775	4,430	0	2,893	4,873	5,527
24,050	24,100	0	2,053	3,765	4,419	0	2,885	4,862	5,517
24,100	24,150	0	2,045	3,754	4,409	0	2,877	4,852	5,506
24,150	24,200	0	2,037	3,744	4,398	0	2,869	4,841	5,496
24,200	24,250	0	2,029	3,733	4,388	0	2,861	4,831	5,485
24,250	24,300	0	2,021	3,723	4,377	0	2,853	4,820	5,475
24,300	24,350	0	2,013	3,712	4,367	0	2,845	4,810	5,464
24,350	24,400	0	2,005	3,702	4,356	0	2,837	4,799	5,454
24,400	24,450	0	1,997	3,691	4,346	0	2,829	4,788	5,443
24,450	24,500	0	1,989	3,681	4,335	0	2,821	4,778	5,432
24,500	24,550	0	1,981	3,670	4,325	0	2,813	4,767	5,422
24,550	24,600	0	1,973	3,660	4,314	0	2,805	4,757	5,411
24,600	24,650	0	1,965	3,649	4,304	0	2,797	4,746	5,401
24,650	24,700	0	1,957	3,639	4,293	0	2,789	4,736	5,390
24,700	24,750	0	1,949	3,628	4,283	0	2,781	4,725	5,380
24,750	24,800	0	1,941	3,618	4,272	0	2,773	4,715	5,369
24,800	24,850	0	1,933	3,607	4,262	0	2,765	4,704	5,359
24,850	24,900	0	1,925	3,596	4,251	0	2,757	4,694	5,348
24,900	24,950	0	1,917	3,586	4,240	0	2,749	4,683	5,338
24,950	25,000	0	1,909	3,575	4,230	0	2,741	4,673	5,327
25,000	25,050	0	1,901	3,565	4,219	0	2,733	4,662	5,317
25,050	25,100	0	1,893	3,554	4,209	0	2,725	4,652	5,306
25,100	25,150	0	1,885	3,544	4,198	0	2,717	4,641	5,296
25,150	25,200	0	1,877	3,533	4,188	0	2,709	4,631	5,285
25,200	25,250	0	1,869	3,523	4,177	0	2,701	4,620	5,274
25,250	25,300	0	1,861	3,512	4,167	0	2,693	4,609	5,264
25,300	25,350	0	1,853	3,502	4,156	0	2,685	4,599	5,253
25,350	25,400	0	1,845	3,491	4,146	0	2,677	4,588	5,243
25,400	25,450	0	1,837	3,481	4,135	0	2,669	4,578	5,232
25,450	25,500	0	1,829	3,470	4,125	0	2,661	4,567	5,222
25,500	25,550	0	1,821	3,460	4,114	0	2,653	4,557	5,211
25,550	25,600	0	1,813	3,449	4,104	0	2,645	4,546	5,201
25,600	25,650	0	1,805	3,439	4,093	0	2,637	4,536	5,190
25,650	25,700	0	1,797	3,428	4,082	0	2,629	4,525	5,180
25,700	25,750	0	1,789	3,417	4,072	0	2,621	4,515	5,169
25,750	25,800	0	1,781	3,407	4,061	0	2,613	4,504	5,159
25,800	25,850	0	1,773	3,396	4,051	0	2,606	4,494	5,148
25,850	25,900	0	1,765	3,386	4,040	0	2,598	4,483	5,138
25,900	25,950	0	1,757	3,375	4,030	0	2,590	4,473	5,127
25,950	26,000	0	1,749	3,365	4,019	0	2,582	4,462	5,117
26,000	26,050	0	1,741	3,354	4,009	0	2,574	4,452	5,106
26,050	26,100	0	1,733	3,344	3,998	0	2,566	4,441	5,095
26,100	26,150	0	1,725	3,333	3,988	0	2,558	4,430	5,085
26,150	26,200	0	1,717	3,323	3,977	0	2,550	4,420	5,074
26,200	26,250	0	1,709	3,312	3,967	0	2,542	4,409	5,064
26,250	26,300	0	1,701	3,302	3,956	0	2,534	4,399	5,053
26,300	26,350	0	1,693	3,291	3,946	0	2,526	4,388	5,043
26,350	26,400	0	1,685	3,281	3,935	0	2,518	4,378	5,032
26,400	26,450	0	1,677	3,270	3,925	0	2,510	4,367	5,022
26,450	26,500	0	1,669	3,260	3,914	0	2,502	4,357	5,011

(Continued)

SPECIAL TABLES

Caution: This is a draft 2012 Earned Income Credit (EIC) Table. At the time of publication, the IRS had not yet released the 2012 Earned Income Credit (EIC) Table. For the latest information, see CCHGroup.com/TaxUpdates.

Earned Income Credit (EIC) Table - *Continued* (**Caution.** This is **not** a tax table.)

If the amount you are looking up from the worksheet is–		And your filing status is– Single, head of household, or qualifying widow(er) and you have–				Married filing jointly and you have–			
At least	But less than	No Children	One Child	Two Children	Three Children	No Children	One Child	Two Children	Three Children
		Your credit is–				Your credit is–			
26,500	26,550	0	1,661	3,249	3,903	0	2,494	4,346	5,001
26,550	26,600	0	1,653	3,238	3,893	0	2,486	4,336	4,990
26,600	26,650	0	1,645	3,228	3,882	0	2,478	4,325	4,980
26,650	26,700	0	1,637	3,217	3,872	0	2,470	4,315	4,969
26,700	26,750	0	1,629	3,207	3,861	0	2,462	4,304	4,959
26,750	26,800	0	1,621	3,196	3,851	0	2,454	4,294	4,948
26,800	26,850	0	1,613	3,186	3,840	0	2,446	4,283	4,938
26,850	26,900	0	1,605	3,175	3,830	0	2,438	4,273	4,927
26,900	26,950	0	1,597	3,165	3,819	0	2,430	4,262	4,916
26,950	27,000	0	1,589	3,154	3,809	0	2,422	4,251	4,906
27,000	27,050	0	1,581	3,144	3,798	0	2,414	4,241	4,895
27,050	27,100	0	1,573	3,133	3,788	0	2,406	4,230	4,885
27,100	27,150	0	1,565	3,123	3,777	0	2,398	4,220	4,874
27,150	27,200	0	1,557	3,112	3,767	0	2,390	4,209	4,864
27,200	27,250	0	1,549	3,102	3,756	0	2,382	4,199	4,853
27,250	27,300	0	1,541	3,091	3,746	0	2,374	4,188	4,843
27,300	27,350	0	1,533	3,081	3,735	0	2,366	4,178	4,832
27,350	27,400	0	1,525	3,070	3,724	0	2,358	4,167	4,822
27,400	27,450	0	1,517	3,059	3,714	0	2,350	4,157	4,811
27,450	27,500	0	1,509	3,049	3,703	0	2,342	4,146	4,801
27,500	27,550	0	1,501	3,038	3,693	0	2,334	4,136	4,790
27,550	27,600	0	1,493	3,028	3,682	0	2,326	4,125	4,780
27,600	27,650	0	1,485	3,017	3,672	0	2,318	4,115	4,769
27,650	27,700	0	1,477	3,007	3,661	0	2,310	4,104	4,759
27,700	27,750	0	1,469	2,996	3,651	0	2,302	4,093	4,748
27,750	27,800	0	1,461	2,986	3,640	0	2,294	4,083	4,737
27,800	27,850	0	1,453	2,975	3,630	0	2,286	4,072	4,727
27,850	27,900	0	1,445	2,965	3,619	0	2,278	4,062	4,716
27,900	27,950	0	1,437	2,954	3,609	0	2,270	4,051	4,706
27,950	28,000	0	1,429	2,944	3,598	0	2,262	4,041	4,695
28,000	28,050	0	1,421	2,933	3,588	0	2,254	4,030	4,685
28,050	28,100	0	1,413	2,923	3,577	0	2,246	4,020	4,674
28,100	28,150	0	1,405	2,912	3,567	0	2,238	4,009	4,664
28,150	28,200	0	1,397	2,901	3,556	0	2,230	3,999	4,653
28,200	28,250	0	1,389	2,891	3,545	0	2,222	3,988	4,643
28,250	28,300	0	1,381	2,880	3,535	0	2,214	3,978	4,632
28,300	28,350	0	1,373	2,870	3,524	0	2,206	3,967	4,622
28,350	28,400	0	1,365	2,859	3,514	0	2,198	3,957	4,611
28,400	28,450	0	1,357	2,849	3,503	0	2,190	3,946	4,601
28,450	28,500	0	1,349	2,838	3,493	0	2,182	3,936	4,590
28,500	28,550	0	1,341	2,828	3,482	0	2,174	3,925	4,580
28,550	28,600	0	1,333	2,817	3,472	0	2,166	3,914	4,569
28,600	28,650	0	1,326	2,807	3,461	0	2,158	3,904	4,558
28,650	28,700	0	1,318	2,796	3,451	0	2,150	3,893	4,548
28,700	28,750	0	1,310	2,786	3,440	0	2,142	3,883	4,537
28,750	28,800	0	1,302	2,775	3,430	0	2,134	3,872	4,527
28,800	28,850	0	1,294	2,765	3,419	0	2,126	3,862	4,516
28,850	28,900	0	1,286	2,754	3,409	0	2,118	3,851	4,506
28,900	28,950	0	1,278	2,744	3,398	0	2,110	3,841	4,495
28,950	29,000	0	1,270	2,733	3,388	0	2,102	3,830	4,485
29,000	29,050	0	1,262	2,722	3,377	0	2,094	3,820	4,474
29,050	29,100	0	1,254	2,712	3,366	0	2,086	3,809	4,464
29,100	29,150	0	1,246	2,701	3,356	0	2,078	3,799	4,453
29,150	29,200	0	1,238	2,691	3,345	0	2,070	3,788	4,443
29,200	29,250	0	1,230	2,680	3,335	0	2,062	3,778	4,432
29,250	29,300	0	1,222	2,670	3,324	0	2,054	3,767	4,422
29,300	29,350	0	1,214	2,659	3,314	0	2,046	3,757	4,411
29,350	29,400	0	1,206	2,649	3,303	0	2,038	3,746	4,401
29,400	29,450	0	1,198	2,638	3,293	0	2,030	3,735	4,390
29,450	29,500	0	1,190	2,628	3,282	0	2,022	3,725	4,379

(Continued)

 Need more information or forms? Visit IRS.gov.

Caution: This is a draft 2012 Earned Income Credit (EIC) Table. At the time of publication, the IRS had not yet released the 2012 Earned Income Credit (EIC) Table. For the latest information, see CCHGroup.com/TaxUpdates.

Earned Income Credit (EIC) Table - *Continued* **(Caution.** This is **not** a tax table.)

If the amount you are looking up from the worksheet is–		And your filing status is– Single, head of household, or qualifying widow(er) and you have–				Married filing jointly and you have–			
At least	But less than	No Children	One Child	Two Children	Three Children	No Children	One Child	Two Children	Three Children
		Your credit is–				Your credit is–			
29,500	29,550	0	1,182	2,617	3,272	0	2,014	3,714	4,369
29,550	29,600	0	1,174	2,607	3,261	0	2,006	3,704	4,358
29,600	29,650	0	1,166	2,596	3,251	0	1,998	3,693	4,348
29,650	29,700	0	1,158	2,586	3,240	0	1,990	3,683	4,337
29,700	29,750	0	1,150	2,575	3,230	0	1,982	3,672	4,327
29,750	29,800	0	1,142	2,565	3,219	0	1,974	3,662	4,316
29,800	29,850	0	1,134	2,554	3,209	0	1,966	3,651	4,306
29,850	29,900	0	1,126	2,543	3,198	0	1,958	3,641	4,295
29,900	29,950	0	1,118	2,533	3,187	0	1,950	3,630	4,285
29,950	30,000	0	1,110	2,522	3,177	0	1,942	3,620	4,274
30,000	30,050	0	1,102	2,512	3,166	0	1,934	3,609	4,264
30,050	30,100	0	1,094	2,501	3,156	0	1,926	3,599	4,253
30,100	30,150	0	1,086	2,491	3,145	0	1,918	3,588	4,243
30,150	30,200	0	1,078	2,480	3,135	0	1,910	3,578	4,232
30,200	30,250	0	1,070	2,470	3,124	0	1,902	3,567	4,221
30,250	30,300	0	1,062	2,459	3,114	0	1,894	3,556	4,211
30,300	30,350	0	1,054	2,449	3,103	0	1,886	3,546	4,200
30,350	30,400	0	1,046	2,438	3,093	0	1,878	3,535	4,190
30,400	30,450	0	1,038	2,428	3,082	0	1,870	3,525	4,179
30,450	30,500	0	1,030	2,417	3,072	0	1,862	3,514	4,169
30,500	30,550	0	1,022	2,407	3,061	0	1,854	3,504	4,158
30,550	30,600	0	1,014	2,396	3,051	0	1,846	3,493	4,148
30,600	30,650	0	1,006	2,386	3,040	0	1,838	3,483	4,137
30,650	30,700	0	998	2,375	3,029	0	1,830	3,472	4,127
30,700	30,750	0	990	2,364	3,019	0	1,822	3,462	4,116
30,750	30,800	0	982	2,354	3,008	0	1,814	3,451	4,106
30,800	30,850	0	974	2,343	2,998	0	1,807	3,441	4,095
30,850	30,900	0	966	2,333	2,987	0	1,799	3,430	4,085
30,900	30,950	0	958	2,322	2,977	0	1,791	3,420	4,074
30,950	31,000	0	950	2,312	2,966	0	1,783	3,409	4,064
31,000	31,050	0	942	2,301	2,956	0	1,775	3,399	4,053
31,050	31,100	0	934	2,291	2,945	0	1,767	3,388	4,042
31,100	31,150	0	926	2,280	2,935	0	1,759	3,377	4,032
31,150	31,200	0	918	2,270	2,924	0	1,751	3,367	4,021
31,200	31,250	0	910	2,259	2,914	0	1,743	3,356	4,011
31,250	31,300	0	902	2,249	2,903	0	1,735	3,346	4,000
31,300	31,350	0	894	2,238	2,893	0	1,727	3,335	3,990
31,350	31,400	0	886	2,228	2,882	0	1,719	3,325	3,979
31,400	31,450	0	878	2,217	2,872	0	1,711	3,314	3,969
31,450	31,500	0	870	2,207	2,861	0	1,703	3,304	3,958
31,500	31,550	0	862	2,196	2,850	0	1,695	3,293	3,948
31,550	31,600	0	854	2,185	2,840	0	1,687	3,283	3,937
31,600	31,650	0	846	2,175	2,829	0	1,679	3,272	3,927
31,650	31,700	0	838	2,164	2,819	0	1,671	3,262	3,916
31,700	31,750	0	830	2,154	2,808	0	1,663	3,251	3,906
31,750	31,800	0	822	2,143	2,798	0	1,655	3,241	3,895
31,800	31,850	0	814	2,133	2,787	0	1,647	3,230	3,885
31,850	31,900	0	806	2,122	2,777	0	1,639	3,220	3,874
31,900	31,950	0	798	2,112	2,766	0	1,631	3,209	3,863
31,950	32,000	0	790	2,101	2,756	0	1,623	3,198	3,853
32,000	32,050	0	782	2,091	2,745	0	1,615	3,188	3,842
32,050	32,100	0	774	2,080	2,735	0	1,607	3,177	3,832
32,100	32,150	0	766	2,070	2,724	0	1,599	3,167	3,821
32,150	32,200	0	758	2,059	2,714	0	1,591	3,156	3,811
32,200	32,250	0	750	2,049	2,703	0	1,583	3,146	3,800
32,250	32,300	0	742	2,038	2,693	0	1,575	3,135	3,790
32,300	32,350	0	734	2,028	2,682	0	1,567	3,125	3,779
32,350	32,400	0	726	2,017	2,671	0	1,559	3,114	3,769
32,400	32,450	0	718	2,006	2,661	0	1,551	3,104	3,758
32,450	32,500	0	710	1,996	2,650	0	1,543	3,093	3,748

(Continued)

Caution: This is a draft 2012 Earned Income Credit (EIC) Table. At the time of publication, the IRS had not yet released the 2012 Earned Income Credit (EIC) Table. For the latest information, see CCHGroup.com/TaxUpdates.

DRAFT AS OF October 26, 2012

Earned Income Credit (EIC) Table - *Continued* (**Caution.** This is **not** a tax table.)

If the amount you are looking up from the worksheet is–		And your filing status is– Single, head of household, or qualifying widow(er) and you have–				Married filing jointly and you have–			
		No Children	One Child	Two Children	Three Children	No Children	One Child	Two Children	Three Children
At least	But less than	Your credit is–				Your credit is–			
32,500	32,550	0	702	1,985	2,640	0	1,535	3,083	3,737
32,550	32,600	0	694	1,975	2,629	0	1,527	3,072	3,727
32,600	32,650	0	686	1,964	2,619	0	1,519	3,062	3,716
32,650	32,700	0	678	1,954	2,608	0	1,511	3,051	3,706
32,700	32,750	0	670	1,943	2,598	0	1,503	3,040	3,695
32,750	32,800	0	662	1,933	2,587	0	1,495	3,030	3,684
32,800	32,850	0	654	1,922	2,577	0	1,487	3,019	3,674
32,850	32,900	0	646	1,912	2,566	0	1,479	3,009	3,663
32,900	32,950	0	638	1,901	2,556	0	1,471	2,998	3,653
32,950	33,000	0	630	1,891	2,545	0	1,463	2,988	3,642
33,000	33,050	0	622	1,880	2,535	0	1,455	2,977	3,632
33,050	33,100	0	614	1,870	2,524	0	1,447	2,967	3,621
33,100	33,150	0	606	1,859	2,514	0	1,439	2,956	3,611
33,150	33,200	0	598	1,848	2,503	0	1,431	2,946	3,600
33,200	33,250	0	590	1,838	2,492	0	1,423	2,935	3,590
33,250	33,300	0	582	1,827	2,482	0	1,415	2,925	3,579
33,300	33,350	0	574	1,817	2,471	0	1,407	2,914	3,569
33,350	33,400	0	566	1,806	2,461	0	1,399	2,904	3,558
33,400	33,450	0	558	1,796	2,450	0	1,391	2,893	3,548
33,450	33,500	0	550	1,785	2,440	0	1,383	2,883	3,537
33,500	33,550	0	542	1,775	2,429	0	1,375	2,872	3,527
33,550	33,600	0	534	1,764	2,419	0	1,367	2,861	3,516
33,600	33,650	0	527	1,754	2,408	0	1,359	2,851	3,505
33,650	33,700	0	519	1,743	2,398	0	1,351	2,840	3,495
33,700	33,750	0	511	1,733	2,387	0	1,343	2,830	3,484
33,750	33,800	0	503	1,722	2,377	0	1,335	2,819	3,474
33,800	33,850	0	495	1,712	2,366	0	1,327	2,809	3,463
33,850	33,900	0	487	1,701	2,356	0	1,319	2,798	3,453
33,900	33,950	0	479	1,691	2,345	0	1,311	2,788	3,442
33,950	34,000	0	471	1,680	2,335	0	1,303	2,777	3,432
34,000	34,050	0	463	1,669	2,324	0	1,295	2,767	3,421
34,050	34,100	0	455	1,659	2,313	0	1,287	2,756	3,411
34,100	34,150	0	447	1,648	2,303	0	1,279	2,746	3,400
34,150	34,200	0	439	1,638	2,292	0	1,271	2,735	3,390
34,200	34,250	0	431	1,627	2,282	0	1,263	2,725	3,379
34,250	34,300	0	423	1,617	2,271	0	1,255	2,714	3,369
34,300	34,350	0	415	1,606	2,261	0	1,247	2,704	3,358
34,350	34,400	0	407	1,596	2,250	0	1,239	2,693	3,348
34,400	34,450	0	399	1,585	2,240	0	1,231	2,682	3,337
34,450	34,500	0	391	1,575	2,229	0	1,223	2,672	3,326
34,500	34,550	0	383	1,564	2,219	0	1,215	2,661	3,316
34,550	34,600	0	375	1,554	2,208	0	1,207	2,651	3,305
34,600	34,650	0	367	1,543	2,198	0	1,199	2,640	3,295
34,650	34,700	0	359	1,533	2,187	0	1,191	2,630	3,284
34,700	34,750	0	351	1,522	2,177	0	1,183	2,619	3,274
34,750	34,800	0	343	1,512	2,166	0	1,175	2,609	3,263
34,800	34,850	0	335	1,501	2,156	0	1,167	2,598	3,253
34,850	34,900	0	327	1,490	2,145	0	1,159	2,588	3,242
34,900	34,950	0	319	1,480	2,134	0	1,151	2,577	3,232
34,950	35,000	0	311	1,469	2,124	0	1,143	2,567	3,221
35,000	35,050	0	303	1,459	2,113	0	1,135	2,556	3,211
35,050	35,100	0	295	1,448	2,103	0	1,127	2,546	3,200
35,100	35,150	0	287	1,438	2,092	0	1,119	2,535	3,190
35,150	35,200	0	279	1,427	2,082	0	1,111	2,525	3,179
35,200	35,250	0	271	1,417	2,071	0	1,103	2,514	3,168
35,250	35,300	0	263	1,406	2,061	0	1,095	2,503	3,158
35,300	35,350	0	255	1,396	2,050	0	1,087	2,493	3,147
35,350	35,400	0	247	1,385	2,040	0	1,079	2,482	3,137
35,400	35,450	0	239	1,375	2,029	0	1,071	2,472	3,126
35,450	35,500	0	231	1,364	2,019	0	1,063	2,461	3,116

(Continued)

Need more information or forms? Visit IRS.gov.

»»→ Caution: This is a draft 2012 Earned Income Credit (EIC) Table. At the time of publication, the IRS had not yet released the 2012 Earned Income Credit (EIC) Table. For the latest information, see CCHGroup.com/TaxUpdates.

Earned Income Credit (EIC) Table - *Continued* **(Caution.** This is **not** a tax table.)

If the amount you are looking up from the worksheet is–		And your filing status is– Single, head of household, or qualifying widow(er) and you have–				Married filing jointly and you have–			
		No Children	One Child	Two Children	Three Children	No Children	One Child	Two Children	Three Children
At least	But less than	Your credit is–				Your credit is–			
35,500	35,550	0	223	1,354	2,008	0	1,055	2,451	3,105
35,550	35,600	0	215	1,343	1,998	0	1,047	2,440	3,095
35,600	35,650	0	207	1,333	1,987	0	1,039	2,430	3,084
35,650	35,700	0	199	1,322	1,976	0	1,031	2,419	3,074
35,700	35,750	0	191	1,311	1,966	0	1,023	2,409	3,063
35,750	35,800	0	183	1,301	1,955	0	1,015	2,398	3,053
35,800	35,850	0	175	1,290	1,945	0	1,008	2,388	3,042
35,850	35,900	0	167	1,280	1,934	0	1,000	2,377	3,032
35,900	35,950	0	159	1,269	1,924	0	992	2,367	3,021
35,950	36,000	0	151	1,259	1,913	0	984	2,356	3,011
36,000	36,050	0	143	1,248	1,903	0	976	2,346	3,000
36,050	36,100	0	135	1,238	1,892	0	968	2,335	2,989
36,100	36,150	0	127	1,227	1,882	0	960	2,324	2,979
36,150	36,200	0	119	1,217	1,871	0	952	2,314	2,968
36,200	36,250	0	111	1,206	1,861	0	944	2,303	2,958
36,250	36,300	0	103	1,196	1,850	0	936	2,293	2,947
36,300	36,350	0	95	1,185	1,840	0	928	2,282	2,937
36,350	36,400	0	87	1,175	1,829	0	920	2,272	2,926
36,400	36,450	0	79	1,164	1,819	0	912	2,261	2,916
36,450	36,500	0	71	1,154	1,808	0	904	2,251	2,905
36,500	36,550	0	63	1,143	1,797	0	896	2,240	2,895
36,550	36,600	0	55	1,132	1,787	0	888	2,230	2,884
36,600	36,650	0	47	1,122	1,776	0	880	2,219	2,874
36,650	36,700	0	39	1,111	1,766	0	872	2,209	2,863
36,700	36,750	0	31	1,101	1,755	0	864	2,198	2,853
36,750	36,800	0	23	1,090	1,745	0	856	2,188	2,842
36,800	36,850	0	15	1,080	1,734	0	848	2,177	2,832
36,850	36,900	0	7	1,069	1,724	0	840	2,167	2,821
36,900	36,950	0	*	1,059	1,713	0	832	2,156	2,810
36,950	37,000	0	0	1,048	1,703	0	824	2,145	2,800
37,000	37,050	0	0	1,038	1,692	0	816	2,135	2,789
37,050	37,100	0	0	1,027	1,682	0	808	2,124	2,779
37,100	37,150	0	0	1,017	1,671	0	800	2,114	2,768
37,150	37,200	0	0	1,006	1,661	0	792	2,103	2,758
37,200	37,250	0	0	996	1,650	0	784	2,093	2,747
37,250	37,300	0	0	985	1,640	0	776	2,082	2,737
37,300	37,350	0	0	975	1,629	0	768	2,072	2,726
37,350	37,400	0	0	964	1,618	0	760	2,061	2,716
37,400	37,450	0	0	953	1,608	0	752	2,051	2,705
37,450	37,500	0	0	943	1,597	0	744	2,040	2,695
37,500	37,550	0	0	932	1,587	0	736	2,030	2,684
37,550	37,600	0	0	922	1,576	0	728	2,019	2,674
37,600	37,650	0	0	911	1,566	0	720	2,009	2,663
37,650	37,700	0	0	901	1,555	0	712	1,998	2,653
37,700	37,750	0	0	890	1,545	0	704	1,987	2,642
37,750	37,800	0	0	880	1,534	0	696	1,977	2,631
37,800	37,850	0	0	869	1,524	0	688	1,966	2,621
37,850	37,900	0	0	859	1,513	0	680	1,956	2,610
37,900	37,950	0	0	848	1,503	0	672	1,945	2,600
37,950	38,000	0	0	838	1,492	0	664	1,935	2,589
38,000	38,050	0	0	827	1,482	0	656	1,924	2,579
38,050	38,100	0	0	817	1,471	0	648	1,914	2,568
38,100	38,150	0	0	806	1,461	0	640	1,903	2,558
38,150	38,200	0	0	795	1,450	0	632	1,893	2,547
38,200	38,250	0	0	785	1,439	0	624	1,882	2,537
38,250	38,300	0	0	774	1,429	0	616	1,872	2,526
38,300	38,350	0	0	764	1,418	0	608	1,861	2,516
38,350	38,400	0	0	753	1,408	0	600	1,851	2,505
38,400	38,450	0	0	743	1,397	0	592	1,840	2,495
38,450	38,500	0	0	732	1,387	0	584	1,830	2,484

(Continued)

SPECIAL TABLES

* If the amount you are looking up from the worksheet is at least $36,900 but less than $36,920, and you have one qualifying child, your credit is $2. Otherwise, you cannot take the credit.

»»→ Caution: This is a draft 2012 Earned Income Credit (EIC) Table. At the time of publication, the IRS had not yet released the 2012 Earned Income Credit (EIC) Table. For the latest information, see CCHGroup.com/TaxUpdates.

Earned Income Credit (EIC) Table - *Continued* **(Caution.** This is **not** a tax table.)

If the amount you are looking up from the worksheet is–		And your filing status is– Single, head of household, or qualifying widow(er) and you have–				Married filing jointly and you have–			
		No Children	One Child	Two Children	Three Children	No Children	One Child	Two Children	Three Children
At least	But less than	Your credit is–				Your credit is–			
38,500	38,550	0	0	722	1,376	0	576	1,819	2,474
38,550	38,600	0	0	711	1,366	0	568	1,808	2,463
38,600	38,650	0	0	701	1,355	0	560	1,798	2,452
38,650	38,700	0	0	690	1,345	0	552	1,787	2,442
38,700	38,750	0	0	680	1,334	0	544	1,777	2,431
38,750	38,800	0	0	669	1,324	0	536	1,766	2,421
38,800	38,850	0	0	659	1,313	0	528	1,756	2,410
38,850	38,900	0	0	648	1,303	0	520	1,745	2,400
38,900	38,950	0	0	638	1,292	0	512	1,735	2,389
38,950	39,000	0	0	627	1,282	0	504	1,724	2,379
39,000	39,050	0	0	616	1,271	0	496	1,714	2,368
39,050	39,100	0	0	606	1,260	0	488	1,703	2,358
39,100	39,150	0	0	595	1,250	0	480	1,693	2,347
39,150	39,200	0	0	585	1,239	0	472	1,682	2,337
39,200	39,250	0	0	574	1,229	0	464	1,672	2,326
39,250	39,300	0	0	564	1,218	0	456	1,661	2,316
39,300	39,350	0	0	553	1,208	0	448	1,651	2,305
39,350	39,400	0	0	543	1,197	0	440	1,640	2,295
39,400	39,450	0	0	532	1,187	0	432	1,629	2,284
39,450	39,500	0	0	522	1,176	0	424	1,619	2,273
39,500	39,550	0	0	511	1,166	0	416	1,608	2,263
39,550	39,600	0	0	501	1,155	0	408	1,598	2,252
39,600	39,650	0	0	490	1,145	0	400	1,587	2,242
39,650	39,700	0	0	480	1,134	0	392	1,577	2,231
39,700	39,750	0	0	469	1,124	0	384	1,566	2,221
39,750	39,800	0	0	459	1,113	0	376	1,556	2,210
39,800	39,850	0	0	448	1,103	0	368	1,545	2,200
39,850	39,900	0	0	437	1,092	0	360	1,535	2,189
39,900	39,950	0	0	427	1,081	0	352	1,524	2,179
39,950	40,000	0	0	416	1,071	0	344	1,514	2,168
40,000	40,050	0	0	406	1,060	0	336	1,503	2,158
40,050	40,100	0	0	395	1,050	0	328	1,493	2,147
40,100	40,150	0	0	385	1,039	0	320	1,482	2,137
40,150	40,200	0	0	374	1,029	0	312	1,472	2,126
40,200	40,250	0	0	364	1,018	0	304	1,461	2,115
40,250	40,300	0	0	353	1,008	0	296	1,450	2,105
40,300	40,350	0	0	343	997	0	288	1,440	2,094
40,350	40,400	0	0	332	987	0	280	1,429	2,084
40,400	40,450	0	0	322	976	0	272	1,419	2,073
40,450	40,500	0	0	311	966	0	264	1,408	2,063
40,500	40,550	0	0	301	955	0	256	1,398	2,052
40,550	40,600	0	0	290	945	0	248	1,387	2,042
40,600	40,650	0	0	280	934	0	240	1,377	2,031
40,650	40,700	0	0	269	923	0	232	1,366	2,021
40,700	40,750	0	0	258	913	0	224	1,356	2,010
40,750	40,800	0	0	248	902	0	216	1,345	2,000
40,800	40,850	0	0	237	892	0	209	1,335	1,989
40,850	40,900	0	0	227	881	0	201	1,324	1,979
40,900	40,950	0	0	216	871	0	193	1,314	1,968
40,950	41,000	0	0	206	860	0	185	1,303	1,958
41,000	41,050	0	0	195	850	0	177	1,293	1,947
41,050	41,100	0	0	185	839	0	169	1,282	1,936
41,100	41,150	0	0	174	829	0	161	1,271	1,926
41,150	41,200	0	0	164	818	0	153	1,261	1,915
41,200	41,250	0	0	153	808	0	145	1,250	1,905
41,250	41,300	0	0	143	797	0	137	1,240	1,894
41,300	41,350	0	0	132	787	0	129	1,229	1,884
41,350	41,400	0	0	122	776	0	121	1,219	1,873
41,400	41,450	0	0	111	766	0	113	1,208	1,863
41,450	41,500	0	0	101	755	0	105	1,198	1,852

(Continued)

-69- *Need more information or forms? Visit IRS.gov.*

Caution: This is a draft 2012 Earned Income Credit (EIC) Table. At the time of publication, the IRS had not yet released the 2012 Earned Income Credit (EIC) Table. For the latest information, see CCHGroup.com/TaxUpdates.

Earned Income Credit (EIC) Table - *Continued* **(Caution.** This is **not** a tax table.)

If the amount you are looking up from the worksheet is–		And your filing status is–							
		Single, head of household, or qualifying widow(er) and you have–				Married filing jointly and you have–			
		No Children	One Child	Two Children	Three Children	No Children	One Child	Two Children	Three Children
At least	But less than	Your credit is–				Your credit is–			
41,500	41,550	0	0	90	744	0	97	1,187	1,842
41,550	41,600	0	0	79	734	0	89	1,177	1,831
41,600	41,650	0	0	69	723	0	81	1,166	1,821
41,650	41,700	0	0	58	713	0	73	1,156	1,810
41,700	41,750	0	0	48	702	0	65	1,145	1,800
41,750	41,800	0	0	37	692	0	57	1,135	1,789
41,800	41,850	0	0	27	681	0	49	1,124	1,779
41,850	41,900	0	0	16	671	0	41	1,114	1,768
41,900	41,950	0	0	6	660	0	33	1,103	1,757
41,950	42,000	0	0	0	650	0	25	1,092	1,747
42,000	42,050	0	0	0	639	0	17	1,082	1,736
42,050	42,100	0	0	0	629	0	9	1,071	1,726
42,100	42,150	0	0	0	618	0	*	1,061	1,715
42,150	42,200	0	0	0	608	0	0	1,050	1,705
42,200	42,250	0	0	0	597	0	0	1,040	1,694
42,250	42,300	0	0	0	587	0	0	1,029	1,684
42,300	42,350	0	0	0	576	0	0	1,019	1,673
42,350	42,400	0	0	0	565	0	0	1,008	1,663
42,400	42,450	0	0	0	555	0	0	998	1,652
42,450	42,500	0	0	0	544	0	0	987	1,642
42,500	42,550	0	0	0	534	0	0	977	1,631
42,550	42,600	0	0	0	523	0	0	966	1,621
42,600	42,650	0	0	0	513	0	0	956	1,610
42,650	42,700	0	0	0	502	0	0	945	1,600
42,700	42,750	0	0	0	492	0	0	934	1,589
42,750	42,800	0	0	0	481	0	0	924	1,578
42,800	42,850	0	0	0	471	0	0	913	1,568
42,850	42,900	0	0	0	460	0	0	903	1,557
42,900	42,950	0	0	0	450	0	0	892	1,547
42,950	43,000	0	0	0	439	0	0	882	1,536
43,000	43,050	0	0	0	429	0	0	871	1,526
43,050	43,100	0	0	0	418	0	0	861	1,515
43,100	43,150	0	0	0	408	0	0	850	1,505
43,150	43,200	0	0	0	397	0	0	840	1,494
43,200	43,250	0	0	0	386	0	0	829	1,484
43,250	43,300	0	0	0	376	0	0	819	1,473
43,300	43,350	0	0	0	365	0	0	808	1,463
43,350	43,400	0	0	0	355	0	0	798	1,452
43,400	43,450	0	0	0	344	0	0	787	1,442
43,450	43,500	0	0	0	334	0	0	777	1,431
43,500	43,550	0	0	0	323	0	0	766	1,421
43,550	43,600	0	0	0	313	0	0	755	1,410
43,600	43,650	0	0	0	302	0	0	745	1,399
43,650	43,700	0	0	0	292	0	0	734	1,389
43,700	43,750	0	0	0	281	0	0	724	1,378
43,750	43,800	0	0	0	271	0	0	713	1,368
43,800	43,850	0	0	0	260	0	0	703	1,357
43,850	43,900	0	0	0	250	0	0	692	1,347
43,900	43,950	0	0	0	239	0	0	682	1,336
43,950	44,000	0	0	0	229	0	0	671	1,326
44,000	44,050	0	0	0	218	0	0	661	1,315
44,050	44,100	0	0	0	207	0	0	650	1,305
44,100	44,150	0	0	0	197	0	0	640	1,294
44,150	44,200	0	0	0	186	0	0	629	1,284
44,200	44,250	0	0	0	176	0	0	619	1,273
44,250	44,300	0	0	0	165	0	0	608	1,263
44,300	44,350	0	0	0	155	0	0	598	1,252
44,350	44,400	0	0	0	144	0	0	587	1,242
44,400	44,450	0	0	0	134	0	0	576	1,231
44,450	44,500	0	0	0	123	0	0	566	1,220

(Continued)

* If the amount you are looking up from the worksheet is at least $42,100 but less than $42,130, and you have one qualifying child, your credit is $2. Otherwise, you cannot take the credit.

»»→ Caution: This is a draft 2012 Earned Income Credit (EIC) Table. At the time of publication, the IRS had not yet released the 2012 Earned Income Credit (EIC) Table. For the latest information, see CCHGroup.com/TaxUpdates.

Earned Income Credit (EIC) Table - *Continued* **(Caution.** This is **not** a tax table.)

If the amount you are looking up from the worksheet is–		And your filing status is– Single, head of household, or qualifying widow(er) and you have–				Married filing jointly and you have–			
At least	But less than	No Children	One Child	Two Children	Three Children	No Children	One Child	Two Children	Three Children
		Your credit is–				Your credit is–			
44,500	44,550	0	0	0	113	0	0	555	1,210
44,550	44,600	0	0	0	102	0	0	545	1,199
44,600	44,650	0	0	0	92	0	0	534	1,189
44,650	44,700	0	0	0	81	0	0	524	1,178
44,700	44,750	0	0	0	71	0	0	513	1,168
44,750	44,800	0	0	0	60	0	0	503	1,157
44,800	44,850	0	0	0	50	0	0	492	1,147
44,850	44,900	0	0	0	39	0	0	482	1,136
44,900	44,950	0	0	0	28	0	0	471	1,126
44,950	45,000	0	0	0	18	0	0	461	1,115
45,000	45,050	0	0	0	7	0	0	450	1,105
45,050	45,100	0	0	0	*	0	0	440	1,094
45,100	45,150	0	0	0	0	0	0	429	1,084
45,150	45,200	0	0	0	0	0	0	419	1,073
45,200	45,250	0	0	0	0	0	0	408	1,062
45,250	45,300	0	0	0	0	0	0	397	1,052
45,300	45,350	0	0	0	0	0	0	387	1,041
45,350	45,400	0	0	0	0	0	0	376	1,031
45,400	45,450	0	0	0	0	0	0	366	1,020
45,450	45,500	0	0	0	0	0	0	355	1,010
45,500	45,550	0	0	0	0	0	0	345	999
45,550	45,600	0	0	0	0	0	0	334	989
45,600	45,650	0	0	0	0	0	0	324	978
45,650	45,700	0	0	0	0	0	0	313	968
45,700	45,750	0	0	0	0	0	0	303	957
45,750	45,800	0	0	0	0	0	0	292	947
45,800	45,850	0	0	0	0	0	0	282	936
45,850	45,900	0	0	0	0	0	0	271	926
45,900	45,950	0	0	0	0	0	0	261	915
45,950	46,000	0	0	0	0	0	0	250	905
46,000	46,050	0	0	0	0	0	0	240	894
46,050	46,100	0	0	0	0	0	0	229	883
46,100	46,150	0	0	0	0	0	0	218	873
46,150	46,200	0	0	0	0	0	0	208	862
46,200	46,250	0	0	0	0	0	0	197	852
46,250	46,300	0	0	0	0	0	0	187	841
46,300	46,350	0	0	0	0	0	0	176	831
46,350	46,400	0	0	0	0	0	0	166	820
46,400	46,450	0	0	0	0	0	0	155	810
46,450	46,500	0	0	0	0	0	0	145	799
46,500	46,550	0	0	0	0	0	0	134	789
46,550	46,600	0	0	0	0	0	0	124	778
46,600	46,650	0	0	0	0	0	0	113	768
46,650	46,700	0	0	0	0	0	0	103	757
46,700	46,750	0	0	0	0	0	0	92	747
46,750	46,800	0	0	0	0	0	0	82	736
46,800	46,850	0	0	0	0	0	0	71	726
46,850	46,900	0	0	0	0	0	0	61	715
46,900	46,950	0	0	0	0	0	0	50	704
46,950	47,000	0	0	0	0	0	0	39	694
47,000	47,050	0	0	0	0	0	0	29	683
47,050	47,100	0	0	0	0	0	0	18	673
47,100	47,150	0	0	0	0	0	0	8	662
47,150	47,200	0	0	0	0	0	0	**	652
47,200	47,250	0	0	0	0	0	0	0	641
47,250	47,300	0	0	0	0	0	0	0	631
47,300	47,350	0	0	0	0	0	0	0	620
47,350	47,400	0	0	0	0	0	0	0	610
47,400	47,450	0	0	0	0	0	0	0	599
47,450	47,500	0	0	0	0	0	0	0	589

(Continued)

* If the amount you are looking up from the worksheet is at least $45,050 but less than $45,060, and you have three qualifying children, your credit is $1. Otherwise, you cannot take the credit.
** If the amount you are looking up from the worksheet is at least $47,150 but less than $47,162, and you have two qualifying children, your credit is $1. Otherwise, you cannot take the credit.

»»→ Caution: This is a draft 2012 Earned Income Credit (EIC) Table. At the time of publication, the IRS had not yet released the 2012 Earned Income Credit (EIC) Table. For the latest information, see CCHGroup.com/TaxUpdates.

Earned Income Credit (EIC) Table - *Continued* **(Caution. This is not a tax table.)**

If the amount you are looking up from the worksheet is–		And your filing status is– Single, head of household, or qualifying widow(er) and you have–				Married filing jointly and you have–			
At least	But less than	No Children	One Child	Two Children	Three Children	No Children	One Child	Two Children	Three Children
		Your credit is–				Your credit is–			
47,500	47,550	0	0	0	0	0	0	0	578
47,550	47,600	0	0	0	0	0	0	0	568
47,600	47,650	0	0	0	0	0	0	0	557
47,650	47,700	0	0	0	0	0	0	0	547
47,700	47,750	0	0	0	0	0	0	0	536
47,750	47,800	0	0	0	0	0	0	0	525
47,800	47,850	0	0	0	0	0	0	0	515
47,850	47,900	0	0	0	0	0	0	0	504
47,900	47,950	0	0	0	0	0	0	0	494
47,950	48,000	0	0	0	0	0	0	0	483
48,000	48,050	0	0	0	0	0	0	0	473
48,050	48,100	0	0	0	0	0	0	0	462
48,100	48,150	0	0	0	0	0	0	0	452
48,150	48,200	0	0	0	0	0	0	0	441
48,200	48,250	0	0	0	0	0	0	0	431
48,250	48,300	0	0	0	0	0	0	0	420
48,300	48,350	0	0	0	0	0	0	0	410
48,350	48,400	0	0	0	0	0	0	0	399
48,400	48,450	0	0	0	0	0	0	0	389
48,450	48,500	0	0	0	0	0	0	0	378
48,500	48,550	0	0	0	0	0	0	0	368
48,550	48,600	0	0	0	0	0	0	0	357
48,600	48,650	0	0	0	0	0	0	0	346
48,650	48,700	0	0	0	0	0	0	0	336
48,700	48,750	0	0	0	0	0	0	0	325
48,750	48,800	0	0	0	0	0	0	0	315
48,800	48,850	0	0	0	0	0	0	0	304
48,850	48,900	0	0	0	0	0	0	0	294
48,900	48,950	0	0	0	0	0	0	0	283
48,950	49,000	0	0	0	0	0	0	0	273
49,000	49,050	0	0	0	0	0	0	0	262
49,050	49,100	0	0	0	0	0	0	0	252
49,100	49,150	0	0	0	0	0	0	0	241
49,150	49,200	0	0	0	0	0	0	0	231
49,200	49,250	0	0	0	0	0	0	0	220
49,250	49,300	0	0	0	0	0	0	0	210
49,300	49,350	0	0	0	0	0	0	0	199
49,350	49,400	0	0	0	0	0	0	0	189
49,400	49,450	0	0	0	0	0	0	0	178
49,450	49,500	0	0	0	0	0	0	0	167
49,500	49,550	0	0	0	0	0	0	0	157
49,550	49,600	0	0	0	0	0	0	0	146
49,600	49,650	0	0	0	0	0	0	0	136
49,650	49,700	0	0	0	0	0	0	0	125
49,700	49,750	0	0	0	0	0	0	0	115
49,750	49,800	0	0	0	0	0	0	0	104
49,800	49,850	0	0	0	0	0	0	0	94
49,850	49,900	0	0	0	0	0	0	0	83
49,900	49,950	0	0	0	0	0	0	0	73
49,950	50,000	0	0	0	0	0	0	0	62
50,000	50,050	0	0	0	0	0	0	0	52
50,050	50,100	0	0	0	0	0	0	0	41
50,100	50,150	0	0	0	0	0	0	0	31
50,150	50,200	0	0	0	0	0	0	0	20
50,200	50,250	0	0	0	0	0	0	0	9
50,250	50,270	0	0	0	0	0	0	0	2

¶ 88 Average Itemized Deductions

For those taxpayers who itemize their deductions on Schedule A of Form 1040, the following chart should be of special interest. This chart (based on preliminary statistics for 2010 returns) shows the average deductions of taxpayers for tax year 2010 for interest (¶ 1043), taxes (¶ 1021), medical and dental expenses (¶ 1015), and charitable contributions (¶ 1058). While it may be interesting for those who itemize their deductions to compare them with these average figures, the chart should *not* be considered as indicating amounts that would be allowed by the IRS. In any case, taxpayers must be able to substantiate claimed itemized deductions.

Individual Income Tax Returns, Preliminary Data, 2010, Table 1 (Source: *Winter 2012 Statistics of Income (SOI) Bulletin*).

PRELIMINARY AVERAGE ITEMIZED DEDUCTIONS FOR TAX YEAR 2010 BY ADJUSTED GROSS INCOME RANGES

Adjusted Gross Income Ranges	*Medical Expenses*	*Taxes*	*Interest*	*Charitable Contributions*
Under $ 15,000	$9,083	$3,124	$7,911	$1,472
$ 15,000 to $ 30,000	7,590	3,271	7,609	2,058
$ 30,000 to $ 50,000	7,192	3,950	7,976	2,285
$ 50,000 to $ 100,000	7,312	6,111	9,320	2,815
$ 100,000 to $ 200,000	9,932	10,860	12,093	3,857
$ 200,000 to $ 250,000	19,850	18,078	16,450	5,824
$ 250,000 or more	30,408	47,178	23,194	19,651

Chapter 1

INDIVIDUALS

Filing of Tax Returns

101. Who Must File an Individual Tax Return. All U.S. citizens and resident aliens (¶ 2409) are liable for federal income tax on their world wide income, without regard to whether the income arose from sources within or outside of the United States (Code Sec. 1; Reg. § 1.1-1(b)).[1] For each tax year, a return (¶ 105) must be filed by a U.S. citizen or a resident alien who has at least a specified minimum amount of gross income.

The filing threshold for most individuals is the sum of the applicable exemption amount (¶ 133) and the applicable standard deduction amount (¶ 126) for the tax year. However, only the additional standard deduction for taxpayers age 65 or older at the end of the tax year is taken into account for purposes of the income thresholds; the additional standard deduction for taxpayers who are blind at the end of the tax year is *not* considered. A taxpayer's gross income for this purpose is computed without regard to the exclusion of gain from the sale of a personal residence (¶ 1705) and the exclusion of foreign earned income and housing expenses for U.S. citizens and residents living abroad (¶ 2402).

Generally, the income levels at which individuals must file income tax returns for 2012 are (Code Sec. 6012):[2]

Single individual (including individuals treated as unmarried for tax purposes; see ¶ 173)	$9,750
Single individual, 65 or older	11,200
Married individual, separate return	3,800
Married couple, joint return	19,500
Married couple, joint return, one spouse 65 or older	20,650
Married couple, joint return, both spouses 65 or older	21,800
Head of household	12,500
Head of household, 65 or older	13,950
Qualifying widow(er) (surviving spouse)	15,700
Qualifying widow(er) (surviving spouse), 65 or older	16,850

The above income levels for a married couple filing a joint return are not applicable if, at the close of their tax year, the couple does not share the same household or if some other taxpayer is entitled to a dependency exemption for either spouse, e.g., a married student who is supported by a parent. In this case, a return for 2012 must be filed if gross income equals $3,800 or more.

Dependents. A child or other individual who can be claimed as a dependent on another person's tax return must file a return if that individual's income exceeds certain threshold amounts for earned or unearned income (Code Sec. 6012(a)(1)(C)).[3] Earned income includes salaries, wages, tips, professional fees, and taxable scholarship and fellowship grants. Unearned income includes investment-type income such as taxable interest, ordinary dividends, capital gain distributions, unemployment compensation, Social Security benefits, pensions, annuities, cancellation of debt income, and distribu-

References are to Standard Federal Tax Reports; Tax Research Consultant; and Practical Tax Explanations.

[1] ¶ 3260, ¶ 3265; INDIV: 100; § 1,001

[2] ¶ 35,142; FILEIND: 15,152; § 1,305.05

[3] ¶ 35,142; FILEIND: 15,152; § 1,305.05

tions of unearned income from a trust. The parent of a child who is subject to the kiddie tax and who has income only from interest or dividends may elect to report the child's income on the parent's return (¶ 103). The child will then *not* have to file a return.

With respect to a dependent child or other individual who is *neither* age 65 or older, or blind, at the end of 2012 and for whom a dependency exemption is allowable to another taxpayer (¶ 137), a return must be filed for the 2012 tax year if the individual has:

- over $950 of unearned income;
- over $5,950 of earned income; or
- a total of unearned and earned income which exceeds the larger of $950 or earned income (up to $5,650) plus $300.

All married dependents under age 65 with gross income of at least $5 whose spouse files a separate return on Form 1040 and itemizes deductions on Schedule A must file a return.

With respect to a dependent child or other individual who is *either* age 65 or older, or blind, at the end of 2012, and for whom a dependency exemption is allowed to another taxpayer (¶ 137), a return must be filed if the individual's:

- earned income exceeds his or her maximum standard deduction amount;
- unearned income is in excess of the sum of $950 plus additional standard deduction amounts to which he or she is entitled; or
- gross income exceeds the total of earned income up to the regular standard deduction amount or $950, whichever is larger, plus the applicable additional standard deduction amounts (¶ 126).

If a guardian or other person is charged with the care of a minor individual or the minor individual's property, or a person under a disability, the return for the individual should be filed by the responsible person, unless already filed by the individual or some other person (¶ 504).

Return Requirement. If the applicable gross income test is met, then a return must still be filed even though the individual's exemptions and deductions are such that no tax would be due. If the gross income test is *not* met, then a return should be filed whenever a refund of tax or any refundable credit, such as the earned income credit, is available. A return is also required if:

- net earnings from self-employment in 2012 are at least $400 (¶ 2664);
- Social Security or Medicare (FICA) taxes are due on tip income not reported to an employer (¶ 717);
- Social Security or Medicare (FICA) taxes are due on wages received from an employer who did not withhold the taxes;
- uncollected Social Security, Medicare, or Railroad Retirement Tax Act (RRTA) taxes are due on tips reported to an employer or on group-term life insurance;
- liability for alternative minimum tax is incurred (¶ 1401);
- additional tax on a qualified retirement plan or individual retirement account (IRA) is due as calculated on Form 5329 (¶ 2153G, ¶ 2153H, and ¶ 2153I);
- additional tax on a health savings account (HSA) or Archer medical savings accounts are due as calculated on Form 5329 (¶ 859A and ¶ 2197B);
- household employment taxes (¶ 2652);
- tax is due from the recapture of any of the following: the first-time homebuyer credit (¶ 1324); the investment credit (¶ 1365A); the low-income housing credit (¶ 1365K); the new markets credit (¶ 1365T); the qualified plug-in electric drive motor vehicle credit (¶ 1351); the Indian employment credit (¶ 1365Q); the alternative motor vehicle credit (¶ 1345); the employer-provided child care credit (¶ 1365V); the alternative fuel vehicle refueling property credit (¶ 1355); the qualified plug-in electric and electric drive motor vehicle credit

(¶ 1354); education credits (¶ 1303); household employment taxes (¶ 2652); COBRA premium assistance credit (¶ 1391); or on the disposition of a home purchased with a federally subsidized mortgage; or

- wages of $108.28 or more were earned from a church or qualified church-controlled organization that is exempt from employer FICA and Medicare taxes (¶ 2601).

Any person who is required to file an income tax return must report on that return the amount of tax-exempt interest received or accrued during the tax year (¶ 724) (Code Sec. 6012(d)).

103. Returns of Children or Dependents. A child or dependent is generally taxed in the same manner as any other taxpayer on income, including wages, income from property, and trust income (¶ 554). However, special rules apply to children in calculating their tax liability if they are required to file a return (¶ 101). First, no personal exemption is allowed to an individual eligible to be claimed as a dependent on another taxpayer's return (¶ 135) (Code Sec. 151(d)(2)).[4] Second, the basic standard deduction for dependents in 2012 is limited to the greater of $950 or the sum of $300 plus earned income but not in excess of the standard deduction amount for unmarried individuals (¶ 126) (Code Sec. 63(c)(5); Rev. Proc. 2011-52).[5] Finally, if a child's income tax is not paid, an assessment made against the child will be treated as if it were made against the child's parent to the extent that the tax is attributable to amounts received for the child's services (Code Sec. 6201(c)).[6]

Kiddie Tax. Ordinarily, a child's tax liability is computed in the same manner as any other taxpayer after taking into account the limits on the personal exemption and standard deduction, if applicable (¶ 123). Certain children with investment income, however, may be subject to tax on that income at the parent's top marginal rate if this results in a higher tax than would apply at the child's rate (Code Sec. 1(g)).[7] This is commonly called the "kiddie tax" and it applies if:

- the child is required to file a tax return;
- the child does not file a joint return for the tax year;
- the child's investment income is more than $1,900 for 2012;
- either parent of the child is alive at the end of the year; and
- the child is:
  - — under the age of 18 at the end of the tax year;
  - — under the age of 19 at the end of the tax year and does not provide more than half of his or her own support with earned income; or
  - — under the age of 24 at the end of the tax year, a full-time student, and does not provide more than half of his or her own support with earned income.

The kiddie tax applies to the child's net unearned income which is the portion of the child's adjusted gross income (AGI) for the tax year that is not attributable to earned income. This amount is further reduced in 2012 by $950 ($1,000 in 2013) and by the greater of either the dependent standard deduction ($950 for 2012) or the child's itemized deductions relating to the production of the unearned income (Code Sec. 1(g)(4)). Even though, under state law, compensation for a child's personal services may be treated as belonging to the parent, and even though the money is not retained by the child, for federal income tax purposes, it is considered gross income of the child (Reg. § 1.73-1).[8]

The marginal tax rate of the parent with the greater amount of taxable income applies in the case of married individuals filing separately. If the child's parents are divorced or legally separated and the custodial parent has not remarried, the return of

References are to Standard Federal Tax Reports; Tax Research Consultant; and Practical Tax Explanations.

[4] ¶ 8000; FILEIND: 15,152.25; § 1,505

[5] ¶ 6020; FILEIND: 15,152.25; § 1,505

[6] ¶ 37,502; INDIV: 18,156.10; § 3,005.30

[7] ¶ 3260; INDIV: 18,154; § 1,510.05

[8] ¶ 6150; INDIV: 18,152; § 3,005.30

the custodial parent should be used. If the custodial parent has remarried, the stepparent is treated as the child's parent for purposes of determining the marginal tax rate. Form 8615 is used to figure the kiddie tax.

Parent's Election. The parents of a child may elect to include on their return the unearned income of a child to avoid the kiddie tax (Code Sec. 1(g)(7); Rev. Proc. 2011-52; Rev. Proc. 2012-41). The election, however, can only be made if all of the following requirements are met:

- the child is required to file a tax return and would otherwise be subject to the kiddie tax;
- the child's only income for the tax year is from interest and dividends, including Alaska Permanent Fund dividends;
- the income was more than $950 but less than $9,500 for 2012 ($1,000 and $10,000 in 2013, respectively);
- no estimated tax payments were made for the year in the child's name and Social Security number, including any overpayment of tax from the previous tax year; and
- the child is not subject to backup withholding.

The election is made by filing Form 8814. Electing parents are then taxed on their child's income in excess of $1,900 for the 2012 tax year. They must also report an additional tax liability of either $95 if the child's taxable income is more than $950 or 10 percent of the child's income if it is less than $950.

Comment: Absent further legislation, the 10 percent tax bracket will be terminated for tax years beginning in 2013. Thus, the tax rate on a child's first $950 of taxable income, adjusted for inflation, will be 15 percent.

105. Forms in Use for 2012. Three principal forms are available for use by the majority of individuals for filing income tax returns. These forms include Form 1040, a shorter return form, Form 1040A, and for certain taxpayers with no dependents, Form 1040EZ. If the applicable filing conditions are met, any of the forms in the 1040 series may serve as a separate return or as a joint return. If a married person's filing status, however, is married filing separately and the taxpayer uses Form 1040 and itemizes deductions, his or her spouse can file Form 1040 and either itemize deductions or claim a standard deduction of zero. If the individual decides to claim a standard deduction of zero, he or she may choose to file Form 1040A. These rules do not apply to a spouse who is eligible to file as unmarried or as head of household (¶ 173).

Comment: At the time of publication, the Internal Revenue Service had not yet released in either draft or final version the 2012 Form 1040 and its instructions, including many of the supporting forms and schedules. For the latest information, please consult CCHGroup.com/TaxUpdates.

Form 1040EZ. For the 2012 tax year, the simplified income tax return, Form 1040EZ, may be used by a taxpayer who:

- is filing single or married filing jointly (a nonresident alien at any time during the year may *only* file Form 1040EZ if married filing jointly);
- does not claim any dependents (¶ 137);
- does not claim any adjustments to income (¶ 1005);
- does not claim any tax credits other than the earned income tax credit (¶ 1322);
- is under age 65 and not blind (including spouse if filing a joint return) at the end of 2012;
- has taxable income of less than $100,000 (¶ 123);
- has income from *only* wages, salaries, tips, unemployment compensation, taxable scholarships and/or fellowship grants, Alaska Permanent Fund dividends, and taxable interest income not exceeding $1,500;

• does not owe household employment taxes on wages paid to a household employee; and

• is not a debtor in a chapter 11 bankruptcy case filed after October 16, 2005.

If the taxpayer does *not* meet *all* the requirements, then he or she must use either Form 1040 or Form 1040A.

Form 1040A. For the 2012 tax year, Form 1040A may be used by an unmarried individual filing single, a married couple filing jointly or separately, an individual filing as head of household (¶ 173), or a qualifying widow(er) with a dependent child (a surviving spouse) (¶ 175) if the taxpayer:

• has gross income only from: wages, salaries, and tips; interest and ordinary dividends (including Alaska Permanent Fund dividends); capital gains distributions; taxable scholarship and fellowship grants; taxable distributions from IRAs, pensions and annuities; unemployment compensation; and taxable Social Security or railroad retirement benefits;

• has only adjustments to gross income for the deduction of educator expenses (¶ 1084), IRA contributions (¶ 2153A), student loan interest paid (¶ 1082), or tuition and fees paid (¶ 1082);

Comment: Absent further legislation, the deduction for educator expenses terminated on December 31, 2011.

• does not itemize deductions (¶ 1011);

• has taxable income of less than $100,000;

• does not claim any tax credits other than the child tax credit (¶ 1305), the additional child tax credit, the educational credits (¶ 1303), the earned income credit (¶ 1322), the child and dependent care credit (¶ 1301), the elderly and disabled credit (¶ 1302), or the retirement savings contributions credit (¶ 1304); and

• does not have an alternative minimum tax (AMT) adjustment on stock acquired from the exercise of an incentive stock option (¶ 1435).

Form 1040. For the 2012 tax year, Form 1040 must be used by a taxpayer if he or she:

• has taxable income of $100,000 or more;

• itemizes deductions;

• has income that cannot be reported on Form 1040EZ or Form 1040A including self-employment (net earnings of at least $400) (¶ 2667), rents and royalties (¶ 762 and ¶ 763), taxable state and local income tax refunds (¶ 799), alimony received (¶ 771), capital gains (¶ 1735), business income (¶ 759), or farm income (¶ 767);

• claims any credit against tax other than those credits which may be claimed on Form 1040A;

• claims any adjustments to income other than the adjustments listed for Form 1040A;

• receives in any month tips of $20 or more that are not reported fully to the employer, has a Form W-2 that shows allocated tips that must be reported in income, owes Social Security or Medicare tax on tips not reported to the employer, or has a Form W-2 that shows any uncollected Social Security, Medicare, or Railroad Retirement Tax Act (RRTA) taxes on tips or on group-term life insurance;

• owes or claims any of the items set out as *Other Taxes* in the discussion following, with the exception of the alternative minimum tax;

• is the grantor of, or transferor to, a foreign trust (¶ 588);

• can exclude foreign earned income received as a U.S. citizen (¶ 2402) or resident alien, certain income received from sources in Puerto Rico due to being a bona fide resident of Puerto Rico, or certain income received from sources in a U.S. possession while a resident of American Samoa (¶ 2414);

• receives or pays accrued interest on securities transferred between interest payment dates (¶ 728);

• earns wages of $108.28 or more from a church or church-controlled organization that is exempt from employer social security taxes;

• receives any nontaxable dividends or capital gain distributions;

• is reporting original issue discount in an amount more or less than that shown on Form 1099-OID;

• receives income as a partner (¶ 415 and ¶ 431), an S corporation shareholder (¶ 309), or a beneficiary of an estate or trust (¶ 554);

• has financial accounts in foreign countries (exceptions apply if the combined value of the accounts was $10,000 or less or if the accounts were with a U.S. military banking facility operated by a U.S. financial institution);

• is reporting household employment taxes (¶ 2652);

• receives a health savings account (HSA) funding distribution from their individual retirement account (IRA) (¶ 2197B);

• is a debtor in a bankruptcy case filed after October 16, 2005; or

• must repay the first-time homebuyer credit (¶ 1324).

Calculating Tax. The basic Form 1040 is a single-sheet, two-page form. To it are added any necessary supporting schedules, depending upon the particular circumstances of the individual taxpayer. Adjustments to gross income on the bottom of page 1 of Form 1040 are principally those deductions that may be taken whether or not the standard deduction is employed. They include the deductions for:

• educator expenses (¶ 1084);

Comment: Absent further legislation, the deduction for qualified educator expenses terminated on December 31, 2011.

• employee business expenses of certain fee-basis state or local government officials (¶ 941), performing artists (¶ 941A), and reservist's business expenses (¶ 941E);

• health savings accounts, including Archer Medical Saving Accounts (MSAs) and Health Savings Accounts (HSAs) (¶ 1020, ¶ 1020A, and ¶ 2197C);

• moving expenses (¶ 1073);

• one-half of self-employment tax (¶ 2664);

• contributions to self-employed retirement plans (¶ 2163);

• health insurance premiums paid by self-employed individuals (¶ 908);

• the forfeited interest penalty for premature withdrawals from a time savings account (¶ 1120);

• alimony paid (¶ 771);

• contributions to individual retirement arrangements (IRAs) (¶ 2168);

• student loan interest (¶ 1082);

• qualified tuition and fees (¶ 1082);

Comment: Absent further legislation, the deduction for payment of qualified tuition and fees terminated on December 31, 2011.

• the domestic production activities deduction (¶ 980A);

• jury duty pay given to an employer (¶ 941 and ¶ 1010);

• amortization of forestation or reforestation expenses (¶ 1287);

• repayment of supplemental unemployment benefits (¶ 1009);

• contributions to Code Sec. 501(c)(18) pension plans (¶ 602);

• contributions by certain chaplains to Code Sec. 403(b) plans (¶ 2160);

• expenses incurred with respect to the rental of personal property (¶ 1085);

• attorney's fees and court costs for certain federal claims (¶ 1093); and

- attorney fees and court costs you paid in connection with an award from the IRS for information that significantly contributed to the detection of tax law violations (¶ 1010A).

Credits. A number of credits whose excess over tax liability is not refundable in the current year are subtracted from the resulting tax in the following order:

- foreign tax credit (¶ 2475);
- credit for child and dependent care expenses (¶ 1301);
- education credits (¶ 1303);
- retirement savings contributions credit (¶ 1304);
- child tax credit (¶ 1305);
- residential energy credit (¶ 1341);
- credit for the elderly or for the permanently and totally disabled (¶ 1302);
- mortgage interest credit (¶ 1306);
- first-time homebuyer credit for District of Columbia (¶ 1308);

Comment: Absent further legislation, the first-time homebuyers credit for District of Columbia terminated on December 31, 2011.

- alternative motor vehicle credit (personal use) (¶ 1345 and following);
- alternative fuel vehicle refueling property credit (personal use) (¶ 1355);
- general business credit (¶ 1365);
- empowerment zone and renewal community employment credit (¶ 1365O);
- credit for prior year alternative minimum tax (¶ 1309);
- the clean renewable energy bond credit (¶ 1372);
- the qualified plug-in electric drive motor vehicle credit (personal use) (¶ 1351); and
- the qualified plug-in electric and electric motor vehicle credit (personal use) (¶ 1354).

Other Taxes. The following taxes are then added:

- alternative minimum tax (¶ 1401);
- self-employment tax (¶ 2664);
- FICA, Medicare, and/or RRTA tax owing on tip income not reported to the employer, computed on Form 4137 and employee FICA, Medicare, and/or RRTA tax on tips where the employer did not withhold proper amounts, computed on Form 8919 (¶ 2606);
- excess contribution, excess distribution, and premature distribution taxes for IRAs and qualified pension or annuity plans, excess accumulations in qualified pension plans (including IRAs), Archer MSAs and HSAs, or early distribution tax for a modified endowment contract entered into after June 20, 1988, computed on Form 5329 (¶ 1020, ¶ 1020A, ¶ 2124C, ¶ 2153E, and ¶ 2179);
- household employment taxes (¶ 2652);
- recapture of any of the following: the first-time homebuyer credit (¶ 1324); the investment credit (¶ 1365A); the low-income housing credit (¶ 1365K); the new markets credit (¶ 1365T); the qualified plug-in electric drive motor vehicle credit (¶ 1351); the Indian employment credit (¶ 1365Q); the alternative motor vehicle credit (¶ 1345); the employer-provided child care credit (¶ 1365V); the alternative fuel vehicle refueling property credit (¶ 1355); the qualified plug-in electric and electric motor vehicle credit (¶ 1354); education credits (¶ 1303); household employment taxes (¶ 2650); COBRA premium assistance credit (¶ 1391); or on the disposition of a home purchased with a federally subsidized mortgage; or
- the "Section 72(m)(5) excess benefits tax" imposed on a five-percent owner of a business who receives a distribution of excess benefits from a qualified pension or annuity plan;

- uncollected FICA, Medicare, and/or RRTA tax on tips with respect to employees who received wages that were insufficient to cover the FICA, Medicare, and RRTA tax due on tips reported to their employers;
- uncollected FICA, Medicare, and/or RRTA tax on group-term life insurance (¶ 721);
- any excise tax due on "golden parachute" payments (¶ 907); and
- tax on accumulated distribution of trusts.

Payments. To arrive at final tax due or refund owed, the taxpayer subtracts from the above balance the following:

- federal income tax withheld (¶ 2601);
- 2012 estimated tax payments and amounts applied from 2011 return;
- earned income credit (¶ 1322);
- amounts paid with the application for automatic filing extension (¶ 2509);
- additional child tax credit (¶ 1305);
- refundable portion of the American opportunity (modified Hope) credit (¶ 1303)
- excess Social Security tax and/or Tier I railroad retirement (RRTA) tax withheld from individuals paid more than a total of $110,100 in wages by two or more employers and/or excess Tier II RRTA tax withheld from individuals paid more than a total of $81,900 by two or more employers (¶ 2648);
- health insurance costs credit (¶ 1333);
- credit for excise tax on gasoline and special fuels used in business and credit on certain diesel-powered vehicles (¶ 1329);
- a shareholder's share of capital gains tax paid by a regulated investment company (mutual fund) (¶ 2305); and
- the refundable portion of long-term unused prior year minimum tax credit (¶ 1327).

The following schedules and forms are filed with the basic Form 1040 as needed:

- Schedule A for itemizing deductions;
- Schedule B for reporting (a) more than $1,500 of ordinary dividend income and/or other stock distributions, (b) more than $1,500 of taxable interest income or claiming the exclusion of interest from series EE U.S. savings bonds issued after 1989 used for higher educational expenses, and (c) declaring any interests in foreign accounts and trusts;
- Schedule C or Schedule C-EZ for claiming profit or loss from a sole proprietorship;
- Schedule D for reporting a summary of capital gains and losses;
- Schedule E for reporting income or loss from (a) rents and royalties, (b) partnerships and S corporations, (c) estates and trusts, and (d) real estate mortgage investment conduits (REMICs);
- Schedule EIC for providing information regarding the earned income credit;
- Schedule F for computing income and expenses from farming;
- Schedule H for reporting employment taxes for domestic workers paid $1,800 or more during 2012;
- Schedule J for reporting farm income averaging;
- Schedule R for claiming the tax credit for the elderly or the disabled;
- Schedule SE for computing the tax due on income from self-employment;
- Form 2106 or 2106-EZ for computing employee business expenses;
- Form 3903 for calculating moving expenses;

- Form 4562 for reporting depreciation and amortization;
- Form 4684 for reporting personal casualty or theft losses;
- Form 4797 for reporting gains and losses from sales of business assets or from involuntary conversions other than casualty or theft losses (business casualty and theft losses are reported on Form 4684, Section B);
- Form 6251 for computing the alternative minimum tax;
- Form 8283 for claiming a deduction for a noncash charitable contribution where the total claimed value of the contributed property exceeds $500;
- Form 8582 for computing the amount of passive activity loss;
- Form 8606 for reporting nondeductible IRA contributions, for figuring the basis of an IRA, and for calculating nontaxable distributions;
- Form 8615 for computing the tax for certain children who have investment income in excess of $1,900 in 2012;
- Form 8814 for electing to report a child's unearned income on the parents' income tax return;
- Form 8829 for figuring allowable expenses for business use of a home;
- Form 8834 for figuring the personal credit amount for the purchase of a qualified plug-in electric or electric vehicle credit;
- Form 8853 for figuring the allowable deduction for contributions to an Archer Medical Savings Account (Archer MSA);
- Form 8888 for direct deposit of income tax refunds into more than one account including, but not limited to, individual retirement accounts;
- Form 8889 for figuring the allowable deduction for contributions to a Health Savings Account (HSA);
- Form 8919, for reporting uncollected Social Security and Medicare taxes on wages; and
- Form 8949 for reporting sales and exchanges of capital assets.

The following forms are for computing and claiming credits:

- Form 1116 to compute the foreign tax credit for individuals, estates or trusts;
- Form 2441 to figure the child and dependent care credit;
- Form 3800 if more than one of the components of the general business credit are claimed;
- Form 5405 for calculating the amount of the credit recapture for first-time homebuyer claims made on 2008 returns (¶ 1324);
- Form 5884 to calculate the work opportunity credit;
- Form 8396 to figure the mortgage interest credit and any carryforwards;
- Form 8801 to compute the credit for prior year alternative minimum tax including the refundable portion;
- Form 8812 to claim the additional child tax credit;
- Form 8828 to compute the recapture of a federal mortgage subsidy;
- Form 8834 to determine the amount of qualified electric vehicle passive activity credits from prior years;
- Form 8839 to claim the adoption credit;
- Form 8863 to claim the education credits;
- Form 8880 to claim the credit for qualified retirement savings contributions;
- Form 8882 to claim the credit for employer-provided child care facilities and services;
- Form 8885 to claim the health insurance costs credit;
- Form 8903 to claim the deduction for domestic production activity;

- Form 8910 to claim the alternative motor vehicle credit;
- Form 8911 to claim the alternative fuel vehicle refueling property credit; and
- Form 8912 to claim the credit for holders of tax credit bonds;

IRS Computation of Tax. Any taxpayer who files an individual tax return by the due date, April 15, 2013, can have the IRS compute the tax under certain conditions on Form 1040, Form 1040A, and Form 1040EZ. The IRS may also figure the credit for the elderly or the disabled, and the earned income credit. See IRS Pub. 967 for the requirements for a taxpayer to have the IRS compute his or her tax liability or these credits. These returns must have all applicable lines completed, be signed (by both spouses if filing jointly) and dated. If taxpayers want to designate a friend, family member or any other person to be allowed to discuss their 2012 tax return with the IRS, they must check the Yes box in the Third Party Designee area and provide the necessary information. Inclusion of a daytime telephone number of the taxpayer will speed the process should any questions arise. Form W-2 and any other required forms necessary to complete the return should be attached. If the taxpayer overpaid their taxes for the year, the IRS will refund that amount. If an amount is due, the taxpayer must pay the amount no later than 30 days from the billing date or due date of the return; failure to do so may result in penalties and interest.

Rounding Off Amounts. Dollar amounts on the return and accompanying schedules and forms may be rounded off to the nearest whole dollar.

107. Due Date for Individual Returns. Individual income tax returns are generally due on or before the 15th day of the 4th month following the close of the tax year (April 15 in the case of a calendar-year taxpayer) (¶ 2505) (Code Sec. 6072; Reg. § 1.6072-1).[9] U.S. citizens and resident aliens living outside the country have an additional two months to file their returns (June 15 in the case of a calendar-year taxpayer). Similarly, a nonresident alien who has wages *not* subject to withholding generally may also file a return as late as the 15th day of the 6th month after the close of the tax year. A nonresident alien who has wages subject to withholding, however, must file a return by the 15th day of the 4th month following the close of the tax year. If any due date falls on a Saturday, Sunday, or legal holiday, the return may be filed on the next succeeding day that is not a Saturday, Sunday, or legal holiday (Code Sec. 7503; Reg. § 301.7503-1).[10] An individual taxpayer can obtain—without seeking IRS approval—an automatic six-month extension of time to file his or her tax return (¶ 109).

109. Extension for Filing. An individual may obtain an automatic six month extension for filing Forms 1040, 1040A or 1040EZ by filing Form 4868 before the due date of the return accompanied by a reasonable estimate of tax due for the year (¶ 2509) (Reg. § 1.6081-4).[11] A U.S. citizen or resident who lives and has a main place of business or post of duty outside the U.S. and Puerto Rico, or who is in military or naval service on duty outside the U.S. and Puerto Rico, generally must file his or her return by the 15th of the six month after the close of the tax year (June 15 in the case of a calendar-year taxpayer). Such individuals are given an automatic additional four-month extension for filing their income tax return, which may be obtained by filing Form 4868 (Reg. § 1.6081-5).[12] An automatic extension of time for filing a return will not extend the time for payment of any tax due, and interest and penalties may apply. Finally, interest will be charged on any unpaid tax from the original due date of the return.

111. Where to File Returns. The IRS strongly encourages all taxpayers to file their returns electronically through their e-file system. For those individuals that prefer to mail their income tax returns, the returns are filed with the Internal Revenue Service Center for the region in which the individual's residence or principal place of business is located (Code Sec. 6091; Reg. § 1.6091-2).[13] Taxpayers must be aware that income tax

References are to Standard Federal Tax Reports; Tax Research Consultant; and Practical Tax Explanations.

[9] ¶ 36,720, ¶ 36,721; FILEIND: 18,052.20; § 1,325.05

[10] ¶ 42,630, ¶ 42,631; FILEBUS: 15,056; § 1,325.05

[11] ¶ 36,793; FILEBUS: 15,104; § 1,325.10

[12] ¶ 36,795; FILEBUS: 15,104.15; § 1,325.10

[13] ¶ 36,800, ¶ 36,808; FILEBUS: 12,150; § 1,325.20

returns which include a tax payment are mailed to a different address than returns showing a refund or no tax liability. U.S. citizens living abroad, nonresident aliens, and certain other taxpayers are to file their income tax returns if no payment of tax is required at the IRS Service Center located in Austin, Texas. If a payment is required, the return should be filed at the IRS Service Center in Charlotte, North Carolina. For a list of addresses of filing locations, see ¶ 5 or the IRS website at http://www.irs.gov/uac/Where-To-File-Addresses-for-Tax-Professionals.

116. Identifying Number. Every taxpayer must record his or her taxpayer identification number (TIN) on their return (Code Sec. 6109(a); Reg. § 301.6109-1).[14] This is either the taxpayer's Social Security number, Individual Taxpayer Identification Number (ITIN) (for use by resident or nonresident aliens who do not qualify for a Social Security number), or Adoption Taxpayer Identification Number (ATIN) (a temporary taxpayer identification number for use by adoptive parents adopting a child for whom they are unable to obtain either a social security number or an ITIN). If a taxpayer does not have a TIN, he or she should apply for either a Social Security number using Form SS-5, an ITIN using Form W-7, or an ATIN using Form W-7A. Taxpayers must provide TINs for dependents and qualifying children for the purpose of claiming a dependency exemption (¶ 133), the earned income tax credit (¶ 1322), the child care credit (¶ 1301), the adoption credit (¶ 1307), and the child tax credit (¶ 1305). An ATIN, however, cannot be used for purposes of claiming the earned income tax credit. Individuals claiming the earned income tax credit must also include TINs for themselves and their spouses, if married. Failure to include a correct TIN will be treated as a mathematical or clerical error, as will instances when the information provided differs from the information on file with the IRS that is obtained from the Social Security Administration (Code Sec. 6213(g)(2)(F)).[15] The parent of any child to whom the rules governing taxation of unearned income of minor children apply must provide his or her TIN to the child for inclusion on the child's tax return (¶ 103).

117. Estimated Taxes. Individuals are required to make estimated tax payments if the amount of tax they pay through withholding on wages and other payments will not adequately cover their tax liability for the year (¶ 2875). As 2012 ends, the first responsibility of the calendar-year taxpayer is to review payments of estimated tax for 2012 to make sure that these tax payments and the income tax withheld from wages during the year are sufficient to avoid penalties on the last installment, which is due January 15, 2013. The 2012 estimated tax payments (plus income tax withheld from wages) are credited against tax due for 2012. Any underpayment of tax must be made up by a payment with the final return, and any overpayment is either refunded or credited against the estimated tax for the next year, whichever the taxpayer elects on the return (¶ 2679). For the special rules related to estimated tax payments for farmers and fishermen, see ¶ 2691.

Overpayment. An individual who has been making payments of estimated tax for 2012, and who finds that by paying the installment scheduled for January 15, 2013, he or she will overpay the 2012 tax, may:

- make the payment as scheduled on or before January 15, 2013, file the return on or before April 15, 2013, and direct whether the overpayment should be refunded or credited toward the 2013 estimated tax;
- reduce the payment due on or before January 15, 2013, so that the estimated tax payments plus withholding will meet the tax liability that will be shown on the return to be filed on or before April 15, 2013;
- pay enough estimated tax to cover the minimum requirement as described at ¶ 2875 in order to avoid a penalty on the January 15, 2013, payment and then pay any difference on the final return, filed on or before April 15, 2013; or

References are to Standard Federal Tax Reports; Tax Research Consultant; and Practical Tax Explanations.

[14] ¶ 36,960, ¶ 36,961; FILEBUS: 12,106; § 1,335

[15] ¶ 37,545; FILEBUS: 12,106; § 1,335

• file the final return on or before January 31, 2013, add up all payments of estimated tax plus any withholding, and use this return for a final accounting of 2012 tax liability.

Underpayment. The law provides a penalty for underpayment of estimated tax. A taxpayer can, however, avoid this penalty by paying the minimum installment authorized under one of the exceptions described at ¶ 2682. The taxpayer may file the tax return for calendar year 2012 on or before January 31, 2013, and pay any balance of tax that may still be due for 2012. Under this method, no penalty will apply for failure to make the last quarterly installment and any penalty for underpayment of any of the three earlier installments will not be increased (¶ 2688).

Computation of Tax Liability

123. Taxable Income of Individuals. An individual computes his or her tax liability for a tax year by multiplying taxable income by the applicable tax rate, subtracting allowable credits, and adding other taxes. The computation of taxable income starts with gross income (¶ 701), from which certain deductions (commonly referred to as either adjustments to gross income or the above-the-line deductions) are subtracted to determine the taxpayer's adjusted gross income (AGI) (¶ 1005). After AGI is determined, certain other deductions are subtracted from a taxpayer's AGI to determine his or her taxable income. This includes the deduction for personal and dependency exemptions (¶ 133), the standard deduction (¶ 126), or, in lieu of the standard deduction, the taxpayer's itemized deductions (¶ 1011). Once taxable income is determined, the taxpayer's tax liability is generally computed by applying the appropriate tax rates based on the taxpayer's filing status (single, married filing jointly, head of household, surviving spouse, or married filing separately). Subject to certain exceptions, taxpayers *must* use either the tax rate tables or tax schedules issued by the IRS to compute their income tax. See ¶ 128 for a discussion of the tax rate tables and tax schedules.

126. Standard Deduction. An individual taxpayer who does not elect to itemized deductions (¶ 1014) computes taxable income by subtracting from adjusted gross income (AGI) the standard deduction and the deduction for personal exemptions (¶ 133). Taxpayers have a choice of itemizing deductions or claiming the standard deduction, whichever will result in a higher deduction. The standard deduction amount is the sum of the basic standard deduction, plus the additional standard deduction amounts for aged and blind taxpayers.[16]

Basic Standard Deduction. The basic standard deduction amount varies according to the taxpayer's filing status and is adjusted annually for inflation. The basic standard deduction amounts available to individuals in 2012 are (Code Sec. 63(c)(7); Rev. Proc. 2011-52):

Filing status	*2012 standard deduction amount*
Married filing jointly and surviving spouses	$11,900
Married filing separately	5,950
Head of household filers	8,700
Single filers	5,950

Comment: Absent further legislation, the marriage penalty relief for the standard deduction, whereby the standard deduction amount for taxpayers using a filing status of married filing jointly or surviving spouse is 200 percent of the amount for taxpayers using a filing status of single or married filing separately, will sunset on December 31, 2012.

A taxpayer who can be claimed as a dependent on another taxpayer's return is limited to a smaller standard deduction (regardless of whether the individual actually is claimed as a dependent). The dependent's basic standard deduction may not exceed the greater of $950 or the sum of $300 and the individual's earned income, up to the applicable standard deduction amount ($5,950 for single taxpayers for 2012) (Code Sec.

References are to Standard Federal Tax Reports; Tax Research Consultant; and Practical Tax Explanations.

[16] ¶ 6020; FILEIND: 12,100; § 1,010.15

63(c)(5); Rev. Proc. 2011-52).[17] The limit applies to the basic standard deduction and not to any additional amount such as for elderly or blind taxpayers. A scholarship or fellowship grant that is *not* excludable from the dependent's gross income (¶ 879) is considered earned income for this purpose (IRS Pub. 501).

Elderly and/or Blind Taxpayers. Taxpayers who are age 65 or older, or blind, or both, at the end of the tax year receive an additional standard deduction amount that is added to the basic standard deduction shown in the table above. The additional amount is $1,150 for tax years beginning in 2012 for married individuals, whether filing jointly or separately, and surviving spouses. The additional amount is $1,450 for tax years beginning in 2012 for unmarried individuals, whether filing as single or as head of household (Code Sec. 63(f); Rev. Proc. 2011-52).[18] Two additional standard deduction amounts are allowed to an individual who is both over 65 and blind at the end of the tax year. Thus, married taxpayers filing jointly, both of whom are over 65 and blind, would claim four of the additional standard deduction amounts.

A taxpayer claiming the additional standard deduction for age must be either age 65 or blind, or both, before the close of the tax year. An individual who reaches age 65 on January 1st of any year is deemed to have reached that age on the preceding December 31st. A taxpayer claiming the additional amount for blindness must obtain a certified statement from a doctor or registered optometrist. The statement, which should be kept with the taxpayer's records, must state either that: (1) the individual cannot see better than 20/200 in the better eye with glasses or contact lenses; or (2) the individual's field of vision is 20 degrees or less.

A married taxpayer filing separately may claim the additional amounts for a spouse who had no gross income and was not claimed as a dependent by another taxpayer. A taxpayer who claims a dependency exemption for an individual who is either age 65 or older, blind, or both may *not* claim the additional standard deduction amounts for that individual.

Taxpayers Ineligible for Standard Deduction. When married taxpayers file separate returns, both spouses should either itemize their deductions or claim the standard deduction. This is because if one spouse itemizes and the other does not, the non-itemizing spouse's standard deduction amount will be zero, even if such spouse is age 65 or older, or blind, or both. This rule does not apply if one spouse qualifies to file as head-of-household. A zero standard deduction amount also applies to nonresident aliens, estates or trusts, common trust funds, or partnerships, and to individuals with short tax years due to a change in their annual accounting period (Code Sec. 63(c)(6)).[19] Taxpayers who itemize even though their itemized deductions are less than the standard deduction must check the box on the last line of Schedule A of Form 1040 to make this election.

128. Tax Rates and Tables for Individuals. Most individuals determine their income tax liability by applying the appropriate tax rate to their taxable income (¶ 123) based on their filing status (¶ 152 and ¶ 173). For tax years beginning before January 1, 2013, there are six tax rates applicable to individuals including: 10, 15, 25, 28, 33, and 35 percent (Code Sec. 1).[20]

For 2012, the 10-percent bracket is to apply to the first $8,700 of taxable income for single filers and married taxpayers filing separately, the first $12,400 of taxable income for head-of-household filers, and the first $17,400 of taxable income for married taxpayers filing jointly and surviving spouses (Rev. Proc. 2011-52). For 2012, the upper limit of the 15-percent tax bracket for joint filers remains at 200 percent of the upper limit of the 15-percent tax bracket for single filers (Code Sec. 1(f)(8)).

> **Comment:** Absent further legislation, for tax years beginning after December 31, 2012, the 10-percent bracket will be eliminated and the remaining brackets will

References are to Standard Federal Tax Reports; Tax Research Consultant; and Practical Tax Explanations.

[17] ¶ 6020; FILEIND: 12,106; § 1,010.15

[18] ¶ 6020; FILEIND: 12,104; § 1,010.15

[19] ¶ 6020; FILEIND: 12,108; § 1,010.15

[20] ¶ 3260; FILEIND: 15,054; § 1,015

revert to 15, 28, 31, 36, and 39.6 percent. Additionally, the marriage penalty relief afforded by the upper limit of the 15-percent tax bracket for joint filers equalling 200 percent of the upper limit of the 15-percent tax bracket for single filers will no longer be available.

Subject to certain exceptions listed below, individuals *must* use either the tax rate tables or tax schedules issued by the IRS to compute their income tax. Taxpayers whose taxable income is less than $100,000 must use the tax tables reproduced at ¶ 25. Taxpayers whose taxable income is $100,000 or more will use the tax rate schedules at ¶ 11 for single taxpayers, ¶ 13 for married individuals filing jointly and surviving spouses, ¶ 15 for married individuals filing separately, ¶ 17 for heads of households, and ¶ 19 for estates and trusts. A taxpayer with taxable income of $100,000 or more must use the Tax Computation Worksheet in the Form 1040 Instructions (reproduced at ¶ 20) in order to compute his or her tax. Also, taxpayers may *not* use the table if they file short-period returns because of a change in their annual accounting periods (¶ 1507).

Tax Calculation on Form 8615. Form 8615 must be used to figure the tax of a child subject to the "kiddie tax" rules (¶ 103). Taxpayers required to calculate their tax on Form 8615 may compute taxable income using Form 1040 or Form 1040A. Form 8615 is not filed if the child's parent elects to include the child's unearned income on the parent's return.

Capital Gain Tax Calculation. Taxpayers who had a net capital gain from a sale or exchange use Form 1040, Schedule D, Part III, to determine which of the capital gains tax worksheets to use to calculate the amount of tax on the capital gains. For taxpayers with sales or exchanges of assets taxed at the 28-percent rate or with unrecaptured Code Sec. 1250 gains or both complete the "Schedule D Tax Worksheet" in the Instructions to Schedule D of Form 1040. All other taxpayers, including those with only qualified dividends and net capital gains from a distribution of a regulated investment company (RIC), complete the "Qualified Dividends and Capital Gains Tax Worksheet" in the Form 1040 or 1040A instructions.

129. Unearned Income Medicare Contribution Tax. An individual, estate, or trust is subject to a tax for tax years beginning after December 31, 2012, on the lesser of net investment income for the tax year or the excess modified adjusted gross income (MAGI) for the tax year over a threshold amount (Code Sec. 1411).[21] Although the tax is an addition to regular income tax liability, it is taken into account for purposes of calculating estimated tax penalties of the individual, estate, or trust (Code Sec. 6654(a) and (f)).

The tax in the case of an individual is 3.8 percent of the lesser of (1) the taxpayer's net investment income for the tax year, or (2) the excess of MAGI for the tax year over the threshold amount of $200,000 ($250,000 in the case of joint filers and surviving spouses, and $125,000 in the case of a married taxpayer filing separately). MAGI is the taxpayer's AGI increased by any foreign earned income excluded from gross income for the year, less any properly allocable deductions, exclusions, or credits. The tax applies to all individuals subject to U.S. taxation other than nonresident aliens.

The tax in the case of an estate or trust is 3.8 percent of the lesser of the estate or trust's undistributed net investment income for the tax year, or any excess of its MAGI over the dollar amount at which the highest tax bracket for estates and trusts begins for the tax year (¶ 19). The tax does not apply to any trust whose unexpired interests are devoted to religious, charitable, scientific, literary, or educational purposes, to foster national or international amateur sports competition provided no part of its activities involve the provision of athletic facilities or equipment, or to the prevention of cruelty to children or animals.

Net investment income is the excess of the following items less any otherwise allowable deductions properly allocable to such income or gain:

References are to Standard Federal Tax Reports; Tax Research Consultant; and Practical Tax Explanations.

[21] ¶ 32,602; FILEIND: 15,052.35; § 1,022.10

• gross income from interest, dividends, annuities, royalties and rents unless this income is derived in the ordinary course of a trade or business other than a passive trade or business;

• other gross income from a passive trade or business; and

• net gain which is included in computing taxable income of the taxpayer that is attributable to the disposition of property unless such property is held in a trade or business other than a passive trade or business.

A passive trade or business for this purpose includes any trade or business of the taxpayer that is either a passive activity or consists of trading financial instruments or commodities. Income from other trades or businesses conducted by a sole proprietor, partnership, or S corporation is not considered net investment income. In the case of the disposition of an interest in a partnership or S corporation, net gain or loss is considered net investment income only to the extent it would be taken into account by the partner or shareholder if all of the property of the partnership or S corporation were sold at fair market value immediately before the disposition of the interest. Net investment does not include any distribution from qualified employee benefit plans or arrangements including: a qualified pension, profit sharing, and stock-bonus plan; qualified annuity plan under Code Sec. 403(a) or (b); traditional and Roth IRA; or Code Sec. 457 plan of a government or tax-exempt organization.

131. Individual Health Care Coverage Requirement. A penalty is imposed for tax years beginning after December 31, 2013, on an "applicable individual" for each month he or she fails to maintain minimum essential health care coverage (Code Sec. 5000A).[22] If the taxpayer claims a dependent on his or her return who is an applicable individual, then the taxpayer, rather than the dependent, is liable for any penalty that would otherwise be imposed on the dependent during the taxpayer's tax year. Married taxpayers who file a joint return are jointly liable for the penalty that is imposed on either one of them for any month during the tax year.

The penalty is included on the taxpayer's income tax return for the tax year that includes the month for which the penalty is imposed. It must be paid upon notice and demand by the IRS, and is assessed and collected in the same manner as other civil penalties. A taxpayer, however, will not be subject to any criminal prosecution or criminal penalty for failing to timely pay the penalty. In addition, the IRS *cannot* use liens or levies to collect any of the unpaid penalty. The penalty can be used as an offset for any refund of taxes.

Applicable Individuals. Every individual is an applicable individual subject to the penalty for failure to maintain minimum health care coverage (Code Sec. 5000A(d)). Prisoners, undocumented aliens, certain health care sharing ministry members, and individuals certified as being opposed to having coverage on religious grounds, however, are not considered applicable individuals subject to the penalty. An individual who is otherwise an applicable individual may be exempt from the penalty if he or she:

• has household income below his or her income thresholds for filing an income tax return for the year;

• cannot afford health care coverage (the required contribution for coverage through employer-sponsored plan or bronze level plan through Health Benefit Exchange exceeds eight percent of the individual's household income);

• experiences a short lapse of minimum essential coverage for a period of less than three months (this exemption, however, only applies to the first underinsured period during the calendar year);

• experiences a hardship with respect to the capability to obtain coverage under a qualified health plan;

References are to Standard Federal Tax Reports; Tax Research Consultant; and Practical Tax Explanations.

[22] ¶ 34,962; INDIV: 42,550; § 42,001

- is a dependent of another taxpayer for which a dependency exemption can be claimed;
- either resides in a U.S. territory in which he or she is a bona fide resident or resides outside the United States during a period that qualifies him or her for the foreign earned income exclusion; or
- is a member of an Indian tribe as used for purposes of the Indian employment credit.

A taxpayer's household income for this purpose is generally the sum of his or her modified adjusted gross income (MAGI), plus the MAGI of all other individuals in the taxpayer's family, i.e., the number of exemptions claimed on his or her tax return (Code Sec. 5000A(c)(4)). However, for purposes of the unaffordable coverage exemption, household income is the amount for the most recent tax year and must be increased by any required contribution made through a salary reduction agreement and excluded from the individual's gross income, e.g., health insurance premiums paid through a cafeteria plan.

Amount of Penalty. The penalty for failing to maintain minimum essential health care coverage for any month is the lesser of: (1) the national average premium for bronze-level coverage plan offered through a Health Benefit Exchange for the tax year for a family the size of the taxpayer's family; or (2) the sum of a "monthly penalty" for the tax year, which is the greater of 1/12 of (i) a flat dollar amount equal to the applicable dollar amount for each individual not properly insured by the taxpayer, but not exceeding 300 percent of the applicable dollar amount, or (ii) an applicable percentage of the excess of the taxpayer's household income that exceeds his or her filing threshold for the year (Code Sec. 5000A(c)(1)).

The applicable dollar amount and the applicable percentage to determine the monthly penalty in 2014 will be $95 for each uninsured applicable individual and one percent of the household income in excess of the taxpayer's filing threshold. Both the applicable dollar amount and the applicable percentage for determining the monthly penalty increases for 2015 to $325 for each applicable individual and to two percent of household income in excess of the taxpayer's filing threshold. The applicable dollar amount and the applicable percentage for determining the monthly penalty increases further for 2016 to $695 for each applicable individual and to 2.5 percent of household income in excess of the taxpayer's filing threshold. For calendar years beginning after 2016, the $695 applicable dollar amount will be adjusted for inflation but the applicable percent will remain at 2.5 percent..

Minimum Essential Coverage. For purposes of the penalty, minimum essential coverage is coverage under a government sponsored program, i.e., Medicare, Medicaid, CHIP, etc., employer-sponsored plan, individual health care plan, a group health plan in effect on March 23, 2010, or any other coverage recognized by the IRS. Minimum essential coverage does not include health insurance coverage that consists of excepted benefits such as accident or disability benefits, liability insurance, workers compensation, credit-only insurance, automobile medical payments, or coverage for on-site medical clinics.

If benefits are provided under a separate policy, certificate, or insurance contract, then excepted benefits also include: limited scope dental or vision benefits, benefits for long-term care, nursing home care, home health care, community-based care, or any combination thereof, and other similar, limited benefits; coverage only for a specified disease or illness; hospital indemnity or other fixed indemnity insurance; and Medicare supplemental health insurance, coverage supplemental to the medical and dental coverage provided to military personnel, and similar supplemental coverage provided to coverage under a group health plan.

Personal and Dependency Exemptions

133. Exemption Amount. An individual may claim a personal exemption deduction (¶ 135) and an exemption deduction for each person he or she claims as a dependent (¶ 137) on his or her tax return. The amount of a personal exemption (for the taxpayer and spouse) and of a dependency exemption (for each of the taxpayer's dependents) is adjusted annually for inflation. The exemption amount is $3,800 for 2012 (Code Sec. 151(d); Rev. Proc. 2011-52).[23] The dependency exemption is denied to claimants who fail to provide the dependent's correct taxpayer identification number on the return claiming the dependency exemption (Code Sec. 151(e)).

For tax years beginning in 2010 through 2012, the deduction for personal and dependency exemptions is *not* reduced or eliminated for higher-income taxpayers and they may claim the full amount of the deduction (Code Sec. 151(d)).[24]

> **Comment:** Absent further legislation, the reduction of the phase out of the personal and dependency exemptions will sunset on December 31, 2012. High-income taxpayers will be required to reduce their exemptions by two percent for each $2,500 or fraction thereof that their adjusted gross income (AGI) exceeds an inflation-adjusted threshold amount for 2013.

135. Personal Exemptions. An individual may generally claim a personal exemption deduction for himself or herself equal to the exemption amount for the year ($3,800 for 2012) (¶ 133) on their tax return, plus any exemptions for dependents (¶ 137) (Code Sec. 151(b); Reg. § 1.151-1; Rev. Proc. 2011-52).[25] *No* exemption, however, is allowed to an individual who is eligible to be claimed as a dependent on another taxpayer's return. Thus, students who work part-time during the year or for the summer may *not* claim a personal exemption on their own return if their parents, or any other taxpayers, are *entitled* to claim them on their return. If dependents who are not allowed their own exemptions have gross income in an amount not exceeding $950 in 2012, they will *not* be taxed on that amount and need *not* file income tax returns (¶ 101).

A husband and wife are allowed at least two personal exemptions when filing a joint return, even if one spouse has no income. If a husband and wife file a joint return, neither can be claimed as a dependent on the return of any other person. If a husband and wife file separate returns, each must take his or her own exemption on their respective return. If a husband or wife file separate returns and one of the spouses has no gross income and is *not* the dependent of another taxpayer, then the spouse with gross income may claim the personal exemption for the other spouse on his or her separate return. A married taxpayer who files a separate return may *not* claim two exemptions for his spouse, one as a spouse and one as a dependent.

A resident alien may claim his or her own personal exemption and, if he or she files a joint return, may claim a similar exemption for his or her spouse. However, unless one of the elections noted at ¶ 2410 applies, the filing of a joint return is *not* permissible if either spouse was a nonresident alien at any time during the tax year (Code Sec. 6013(a)(1); Reg. § 1.6013-1(b)).[26]

137. Exemption for Dependent. A taxpayer may claim an exemption deduction ($3,800 for 2012) for each person he or she claims as a dependent that is a qualifying child (¶ 137A) or qualifying relative (¶ 137B), in addition to his or her personal exemption deduction (¶ 135) (Code Secs. 151(c) and 152; Rev. Proc. 2011-52).[27] Anyone claimed as a dependent, or the taxpayer's spouse if filing a joint return, by another taxpayer, however, is barred from claiming another individual as a dependent (Code Sec. 152(b)(1)). Thus, an individual cannot be claimed as a dependent if he or she files a joint return with his or her spouse for the same tax year, unless filed as a claim for refund (¶ 138). The individual to be claimed as a dependent must also be a U.S. citizen, national, or resident of the United States or a contiguous country.

137A. Qualifying Child Definition. A individual taxpayer is allowed to claim a dependency exemption (¶ 137) for each person who is a qualifying child (Code Sec. 152(c)).[28] The following five requirements must all be met for an individual to be considered a qualifying child.

References are to Standard Federal Tax Reports; Tax Research Consultant; and Practical Tax Explanations.

[23] ¶ 8000, ¶ 8005.12; FILEIND: 6,050; § 1,205

[24] ¶ 8000; FILEIND: 6,052; § 1,205

[25] ¶ 8000, ¶ 8001; FILEIND: 6,104; § 1,210.05

[26] ¶ 35,160, ¶ 35,161; FILEIND: 3,250; § 37,125.15

[27] ¶ 8000, ¶ 8007; FILEIND: 6,150; § 1,201

[28] ¶ 8007; FILEIND: 6,168.10; § 1,215.05

• *Relationship.* The individual must bear one of the following relationships to the taxpayer:

— a son, daughter, stepson, stepdaughter, or a descendant of such child; or

— a brother, sister, stepbrother, stepsister, or a descendant of such person (Code Sec. 152(c)(2) and (f)(1)).

The relationship test includes foster and adopted children. An eligible foster child is a child who is placed with the taxpayer by an authorized placement agency or by a decree issued by the courts. An eligible adopted child includes both a legally adopted child and a child legally placed for adoption.

• *Age.* The individual must be under the age of 19 at the end of the calendar year, under the age of 24 at the end of the calendar year and a full-time student, or totally and permanently disabled (¶ 1302) at any time during the year, regardless of age, and must be younger than the taxpayer (Code Sec. 152(c)(3)). An individual is a full-time student if enrolled or registered for at least part of five calendar months in a year at a qualified educational institution or a qualified on-farm training program (Code Sec. 152(f)(2); Reg. § 1.151-3(b)).

• *Principal Place of Abode.* The individual must have the same principal place of abode as the taxpayer for more than one-half of the year (Code Sec. 152(c)(1)(B)). Temporary absences for illness, school, vacation, or military service may count as time living with the taxpayer. Special rules apply in the case of children of divorced or separated parents (¶ 139A). A child who is born or dies during the tax year is considered as living with the taxpayer for the entire year if the taxpayer's home was the child's home for the entire time he or she was alive (Rev. Rul. 73-156).

• *Support.* The individual must *not* provide more than one-half of their own support for the year (Code Sec. 152(c)(1)(D) and (f)(5)). For this purpose, if the child is the taxpayer's child and is a full-time student, amounts received as scholarships are not considered support.

• *Joint Return.* The individual cannot have filed a joint return with their spouse except as a claim for refund (¶ 138) (Code Sec. 152(c)(1)(E)).

In the event that an individual may be claimed as the qualifying child by two or more taxpayers, the taxpayers may decide between themselves who will claim the individual as a qualifying child. If the taxpayers cannot agree and more than one taxpayer is entitled to claim the individual as a qualifying child, regardless of whether they file a return and actually claim the qualifying child, the IRS will disallow all but one of the claims based on the tie-breaking rules discussed at ¶ 139.

If the child or individual fails to meet all the requirements to be considered a qualifying child, the individual may still be claimed as a dependent if he or she meets all the requirements for a qualifying relative (¶ 137B).

137B. Qualifying Relative Definition. An individual taxpayer is allowed to claim a dependency exemption (¶ 137) for each person who is a qualifying relative and who fails to meet the requirements to be considered a qualifying child (¶ 137A). The following four requirements must all be met for an individual to be considered a qualifying relative (Code Sec. 152(d)).[29]

• *Relationship.* The individual must fall within one of the following relationships (once established, a relationship does not terminate due to divorce or death of a spouse):

— a child, stepchild, adopted child, eligible foster child, or a descendant of such child (see ¶ 137A for the definition of adopted and foster child);

— a brother, sister, stepbrother, stepsister, half brother, or half sister;

References are to Standard Federal Tax Reports; Tax Research Consultant; and Practical Tax Explanations.

[29] ¶ 8007; FILEIND: 6,168.15; § 1,220.05

— a parent, grandparent, or other direct ancestor (other than foster parent), as well as any stepparent;

— a brother or sister of the taxpayer's parent (aunt or uncle), and any son or daughter of the taxpayer's brother or sister (niece or nephew);

— a son-in-law, daughter-in-law, father-in-law, mother-in-law, brother-in-law or sister-in-law; or

— an individual that for the entire year has the same principal place of abode as the taxpayer and is a member of the taxpayer's household (temporary absences for illness, school, vacation, or military service are permitted) (Code Sec. 152(d)(2)).

• *Gross Income.* The individual's gross income for the calendar year (¶ 143) in which the taxpayer's tax year begins must be less than the exemption amount for the year (¶ 133) ($3,800 for 2012) (Code Sec. 152(d)(1)(B); Rev. Proc. 2011-52).

• *Support.* Over half of the individual's total support for that calendar year must have been furnished by the taxpayer (¶ 147) (Code Sec. 152(d)(1)(C)).

• *Not A Qualifying Child.* The individual must *not* be the qualifying child of the taxpayer or of any other taxpayer for the tax year (¶ 137A) (Code Sec. 152(d)(1)(D)).

For purposes of the requirement that an individual not be the qualifying child of another taxpayer, an unrelated child that lives with and is supported by a taxpayer may be claimed as a qualifying relative if the other individual for whom the child is a qualifying child does not file a return or files a return solely to claim a refund of withheld taxes (Notice 2008-5). For example, a boyfriend would be allowed to claim a dependency exemption for his girlfriend's unrelated child provided she is not required to file a return under Code Sec. 6012 or, if she files a return, it is only for the purpose of claiming a refund. If she files a return to claim the earned income credit, then she is considered to have filed a return and the boyfriend is denied the dependency exemption.

In the event that an individual can be claimed as the qualifying relative by two or more taxpayers, the taxpayers may decide between themselves who will claim the individual as a qualifying relative. If the taxpayers cannot agree and more than one taxpayer is entitled to claim the individual as a qualifying relative, regardless of whether they file a return and actually claim the qualifying relative, the IRS will disallow all but one of the claims based on the tie-breaking rules discussed at ¶ 139.

138. Married Dependents. A married individual cannot be claimed as a dependent (¶ 133) if he or she joins with his or her spouse to file a joint return (¶ 154) (Code Sec. 152(b)(2)).[30] Thus, a parent cannot claim a married child as a dependent if the child joins his or her spouse in filing a joint return. The only exception to this rule is if the sole purpose for filing the joint return was to obtain a refund and neither the dependent nor the spouse would have a tax liability if they had filed separately (Rev. Rul. 65-34, affirming Rev. Rul. 54-567). In this situation, the IRS views the return as simply a claim for refund.

139. Two or More Taxpayers Claiming the Same Qualifying Child. An individual may meet the requirements to be a qualifying child or qualifying relative of more than one taxpayer. However, only one taxpayer can claim the individual for purposes of claiming the dependency exemption (¶ 137). Generally, if an individual may be claimed as a qualifying child by two or more taxpayers, the taxpayers may decide between themselves who will treat the child as a qualifying child. If the taxpayers cannot agree and more than one taxpayer is entitled to claim the individual as a qualifying child, regardless of whether a return is filed and the qualifying child claimed, the IRS will disallow all but one of the claims based on the following tie-breaking rules (Code Sec. 152(c)(4)).[31] For a discussion of the separate tie-breaker rules for divorced and separated parents, see ¶ 139A.

References are to Standard Federal Tax Reports; Tax Research Consultant; and Practical Tax Explanations.

[30] ¶ 8005.56, ¶ 8007; FILEIND: 6,162; § 1,210.05

[31] ¶ 8007; FILEIND: 6,168.10; § 1,215.35

- If only one of the taxpayers is the child's parent, then the child is the qualifying child for that parent.

- If the child's parents do not file a joint return, then the child is the qualifying child of the parent with whom the child lived with the longest during the year. The period of residence will be determined by counting the number of nights spent with each taxpayer (Reg. § 1.152-4).

- If the child resided with both parents equally during the year and the parents do not file a joint return, then the child is the qualifying child of the parent with the highest adjusted gross income (AGI).

- If none of the taxpayers claiming the child are the child's parent, then the child is the qualifying child of the person with the highest AGI.

- If the parents may claim the child as a qualifying child, but do not actually do so, then the child may be the qualifying child of any other taxpayer but only if his or her AGI is higher than the AGI of either parent.

When applying the tie-breaking rules above, the taxpayer is allowed to claim the child as a qualifying child for purposes of the dependency exemption (¶ 137), head-of-household filing status (¶ 173), the child tax credit (¶ 1305), the dependent care credit (¶ 1301), the exclusion for dependent care benefits (¶ 2192A), and the earned income credit (¶ 1322) (Notice 2006-86).

139A. Exemptions for Children of Divorced Parents. The dependency exemption for a child who is a qualifying child or qualifying relative of divorced or separated parents usually will go to the parent who has primary custody of the child for the calendar year. The custodial parent is determined by the number of nights in which the child resided with the parent (Code Sec. 152(e); Reg. § 1.152-4).[32] When the child spends an equal amount of time with each parent, the parent with the higher adjusted gross income (AGI) is allowed to claim the dependency exemption.

The custodial parent, however, can waive the dependency exemption and the child may be treated as the qualifying child or qualifying relative of the noncustodial parent if all of the following requirements are met:

- the parents are divorced or legally separated under a decree of divorce or separate maintenance, separated under a written separation agreement, or live apart at all times during the last six months of the calendar year including parents who were never married and who do not live together;

- one or both parents provide more than half of the child's total support for the calendar year determined without regard to any multiple support agreement (¶ 147); however, when a parent has remarried, support received from the parent's spouse is treated as received from the parent (Code Sec. 152(d)(5)(B));

- one or both parents have legal custody of the child for more than half of the calendar year; and

- the custodial parent makes a written declaration on Form 8332 that he or she will not claim the exemption and the noncustodial parent attaches the declaration to his or her tax return for each year the exemption is claimed.

If all of the above requirements are met, the noncustodial parent may claim the child as a qualifying child for purposes of the dependency exemption (¶ 137), the child tax credit (¶ 1305), and any education credits attributable to education expenses made for the child by the noncustodial parent (¶ 1303). Even if the dependency exemption is released, the custodial parent may still claim the child as a qualifying child for purposes of the head of household filing status (¶ 173), dependent care credit (¶ 1301), exclusion of dependent care benefits (¶ 2192A), and earned income tax credit (¶ 1322) (Notice 2006-86).

References are to Standard Federal Tax Reports; Tax Research Consultant; and Practical Tax Explanations.

[32] ¶ 8007, ¶ 8150; FILEIND: 6,168.20; § 1,215.40

Moreover, so long as the first three conditions listed above are met, regardless of whether the custodial parent releases the claim to an exemption, if the child is the qualifying child or qualifying relative of one of the parents, he or she can be treated as a dependent of both parents for purposes of: (1) the child's receipt of benefits under a parent's employer-provided health care plan (¶ 2190A); (2) contributions to an accident or health plan by a parent's employer on behalf of the child (¶ 2190A); (3) the child's use of a fringe benefit that qualifies as a no-additional-cost service or qualified employee discount (¶ 2188A and ¶ 2188B, respectively); (4) the child's deductible medical expense (¶ 1015); and (5) the child's qualified medical expenses paid from distributions from a health savings account (HSA) or Archer medical savings account (MSA) that are excludable from gross income (¶ 2197B and ¶ 2197C, respectively) (Rev. Proc. 2008-48).

141. Claiming the Dependency Exemption. Personal exemptions are claimed on Form 1040 or Form 1040A. The taxpayer, spouse, and dependents are listed in the "Exemptions" section on page 1 of either form. The total number of exemptions is then multiplied by the exemption amount ($3,800 for 2012) and used to figure taxable income (¶ 133). On a joint return, the dependency exemption is allowed if the dependent is the qualifying child or qualifying relative of one of the spouses (¶ 137) (Reg. § 1.152-2(d); Rev. Proc. 2011-52).[33]

If a parent is barred from claiming an exemption for a child because that child fails to meet either the qualifying child (¶ 137A) or qualifying relative (¶ 137B) requirements, the child may claim a personal exemption on his or her own return. Also a dependent, whether a qualifying child or a qualifying relative, who has earned income on which tax has been withheld should file a return even though claimed as a dependent by another. The return will serve as a claim for refund of the tax withheld where the dependent incurs no tax liability. If a dependent child of the taxpayer has only earned income in excess of the standard deduction amount for the year (¶ 126), $1 or more of unearned income and gross income in excess of $950, or self-employment income of $400 or more, a return must be filed whether or not the child is claimed as a dependent (¶ 101 and ¶ 2670).

In a community property state (¶ 710), if a child's support is derived from community income, some or all of the exemptions may, by agreement, be taken by either the husband or wife on a separate return. A single exemption amount, however, may *not* be divided between them.[34]

143. Gross Income of a Qualifying Relative Dependent. To be a qualifying relative for purposes of the dependency exemption (¶ 137B), a qualifying relative's gross income for the calendar year in which the taxpayer's tax year begins must be less than the exemption amount for that year ($3,800 for 2012) (Rev. Proc. 2011-52) (¶ 133). In determining whether a dependent has gross income in excess of the exemption amount, it is statutory gross income, not gross sales, adjusted gross, net or any other amount of income, that is counted. Thus, gross income is taken into account without deductions. For example, gross rents are counted, without reduction for rental expenses or depreciation. A partner's share of partnership gross income, rather than net income, is counted. Any income excludable from the claimed dependent's gross income, i.e., exempt interest, disability, or Social Security, however, is disregarded, as well as income received by a permanently and totally disabled individual at a sheltered workshop school (IRS Pub. 17; Code Sec. 152(d)(4)).[35] Excludable income is counted in determining whether the taxpayer has furnished over half of the dependent's support (¶ 147).

Example: Paul's mother, who lived in his home, earned $500 in 2012 from baby-sitting. She was injured in an accident and received $2,650 in compensatory damages. Paul contributed $2,000 for her support in 2012. The damage award is not taxable income and is not counted for purposes of the $3,800 gross income test, but if Paul's mother spent at least $1,500 of this amount (plus the $500 she received for baby-sitting) in 2012 for her own support, Paul could *not* claim her as a

References are to Standard Federal Tax Reports; Tax Research Consultant; and Practical Tax Explanations.

[33] ¶ 8050; FILEIND: 6,168.05; § 1,201

[34] ¶ 8005.23; INDIV: 24,160; § 1,201

[35] ¶ 8007; FILEIND: 6,168.15; § 1,220.15

1 INDIVIDUALS

dependent because he would not have furnished *more* than one-half of her support. If less than $2,000 was spent by Paul's mother for her own support, Paul would be entitled to the dependency exemption.

147. Support of a Qualifying Relative Dependent. To be a qualifying relative for purposes of the dependency exemption (¶ 137B), a taxpayer must furnish more than one-half of the *total* support for the individual for the tax year. See, however, the special rule for children of divorced parents at ¶ 139 (Code Sec. 152(d)(1); Reg. § 1.152-1).[36] Thus, if an individual provides more than one-half of his or her own support for the tax year, then generally no other taxpayer can meet the support test and no one can claim that individual as a qualifying relative. If any other individual provides more than one-half of a person's support, only that other person can meet the support test, except in the case of certain divorced parents (¶ 139A).

Multiple Support Agreement. If no one taxpayer provides more than one-half of the support for an individual, any taxpayer who actually provides more than 10 percent of the individual's support can be treated as having met the support test if a multiple support agreement is filed (Code Sec. 152(d)(3); Reg. § 1.152-3).[37] To be eligible to use a multiple support agreement, more than one-half of the individual's support must be received from a group of persons including the taxpayer, each of whom would otherwise have been entitled to claim the individual as a dependent if they each had furnished more than one-half of the individual's support, and no one taxpayer furnished more than one-half of that support. The person claiming the dependency exemption completes Form 2120 verifying that each person who contributed more than 10 percent of the support signed a written declaration stating that they will not claim the exemption. The statement must include the calendar year for which the waiver for claiming the dependency exemption applies, the name of the qualifying relative, and their name, address and Social Security number. These statements must be retained with the taxpayer's records in the event the taxpayer is called upon to justify claiming the dependency exemption.

Support Defined. The support test is applied by comparing the amount of support provided by the taxpayer with the total amount of support received by the dependent from all sources during the calendar year in which the taxpayer's tax year begins. "Total" support is the sum of:

- the fair rental value of lodging furnished to a qualifying relative dependent;
- the costs of all items of expense paid out directly by or for the benefit of the qualifying relative dependent, such as clothing, education, medical and dental care, gifts, transportation, church contributions, and entertainment and recreation; and
- a proportionate share of the expenses incurred in supporting the whole household that cannot be directly attributed to each individual, such as food.[38]

The proportionate share of household expenses does not include items that represent the cost of maintaining a house, such as heat, electricity, repairs, taxes, etc., because these costs are accounted for in the fair rental value of the lodging furnished to the dependent. Medical care includes the premiums paid on a medical care policy, but not the benefits provided by the policy. Medicare benefits, both basic and supplementary, as well as Medicaid, are also disregarded in determining support.

Some capital expenditures qualify as items of support, such as the cost of an automobile purchased for a qualifying relative dependent and the cost of furniture and appliances. However, the following have been held not to be items of support: (1) income and Social Security taxes paid by a dependent child from his own income; (2) funeral expenses of a qualifying relative dependent; (3) costs incurred by a parent in exercising visitation rights, and (4) life insurance premium costs.[39]

References are to Standard Federal Tax Reports; Tax Research Consultant; and Practical Tax Explanations.

[36] ¶ 8007, ¶ 8008; FILEIND: 6,168.15; § 1,220.20

[37] ¶ 8007, ¶ 8100; FILEIND: 6,168.15; § 1,220.20

[38] ¶ 8005.54, ¶ 8005.80; FILEIND: 6,168.15; § 1,220.20

[39] ¶ 8005.38, ¶ 8005.80; FILEIND: 6,152.05; § 1,220.20

In determining whether a taxpayer furnished more than one-half of a qualifying relative dependent's total support, the support provided by the taxpayer, by the dependent, and by third parties must be taken into account. In addition, only the amount of the cash actually expended for items of support is taken into account. The source and tax status of money used to provide support is, generally, not controlling. It may come from taxable income, tax-exempt receipts, and loans. Furthermore, the year in which the support is received, and not the year of payment of the indebtedness incurred, is controlling in determining whether over one-half of the support is furnished by the taxpayer, regardless of his or her method of tax accounting.[40]

In the case of the taxpayer's child (¶ 137), or stepchild who is a student, any amounts received as scholarships do not have to be taken into account (Reg. § 1.152-1(c)).[41] Educational benefits received under the U.S. Navy's educational assistance program are *not* considered to be scholarships.[42]

Survivor and old-age insurance benefits received under the Social Security Act and used for support are considered as having been contributed by the recipient to his own support.[43] Benefit payments made to an individual under state public assistance laws and measured solely by the needs of the recipient are considered as having been used entirely by that individual for his own support unless it is shown otherwise.[44] Amounts expended by a state for the training and education of handicapped children, including mentally retarded children who qualify as "students" and are in a state institution that qualifies as an "educational institution," are not considered to constitute support, except where the state assumes custody of the child involved.[45] Aid to Families with Dependent Children (AFDC) payments are considered support by the state and not by the parent.[46]

149. Effect of Death on Exemption. The personal or dependency exemption amount claimed by a taxpayer (¶ 133) is not reduced because of the death of a taxpayer, his spouse, or a dependent during the tax year (Reg. § 1.152-1(b)).[47]

> **Example 1:** A child is born on December 31, 2012, and dies in January 2013. A full exemption is allowed for the child in both years.

The death of one spouse will also *not* deprive the survivor of the right to claim the exemptions of the deceased. The crucial date for determining marital status is the last day of the tax year; however, where a spouse dies during the tax year, this determination is made as of the date of death (Code Sec. 7703(a)).[48]

On the final separate return of a decedent, in addition to the deceased's own personal exemption, the exemptions for the surviving spouse may be taken if the survivor had no gross income and was not a dependent of anyone else (¶ 135). Further, since the dependency exemption is based upon furnishing over half the support during the calendar year in which the tax year of the taxpayer begins, a decedent who furnished over half the support to a person otherwise qualifying as a dependent would be entitled to the full exemption for such dependent, without proration.

> **Example 2:** Allen furnishes the full support for his aged father up to the date of Allen's death on September 1, 2012, and over one-half of the total support for the year. A $3,800 exemption is allowed for the father on Allen's final return. But if Allen died on April 1 and his brother, Bob, supported their father for the balance of the year, incurring a larger expense than Allen did during the first part of the year, Bob would be entitled to the exemption. If the support in the latter case was furnished equally by Bob and another brother, Carl, from April 1 on, and if none of the three brothers furnished over half of the father's support for the calendar year, any one of them, including the executor of Allen's estate, on Allen's final return, could take the exemption if the other two brothers renounced their right to the

References are to Standard Federal Tax Reports; Tax Research Consultant; and Practical Tax Explanations.

[40] ¶ 8005.81; FILEIND: 6,168.15; § 1,220.20

[41] ¶ 8008; FILEIND: 6,168.15; § 1,220.20

[42] ¶ 8005.62; FILEIND: 6,168.15; § 1,220.20

[43] ¶ 8005.71; FILEIND: 6,168.15; § 1,220.20

[44] ¶ 8005.60; FILEIND: 6,168.15; § 1,220.20

[45] ¶ 8005.72; FILEIND: 6,168.15; § 1,220.20

[46] ¶ 8005.60; FILEIND: 6,168.15; § 1,220.20

[47] ¶ 8008; FILEIND: 6,164; § 1,220.10

[48] ¶ 43,170; FILEIND: 3,202; § 1,210.10

exemption for that year (¶ 147). Regardless of the amount of support, no exemption is allowed to any of the three brothers for their father if the father had gross income of $3,800 or more during calendar year 2012 (¶ 137B).

150. Missing and/or Kidnapped Children. A dependency exemption may be claimed for any child of the taxpayer, regardless of whether they qualify as a qualifying child or qualifying relative, if the child is presumed by a law enforcement agency to have been kidnapped by someone other than a member of the family and had resided at the taxpayer's principal place of abode for more than one-half of the year before the kidnapping (Code Sec. 152(f)(6)).[49]

Filing Status

152. Joint Return—Who May File. Married taxpayers may elect to file a joint return or file as married persons filing separately. In most cases, it is more beneficial for married taxpayers to file a joint return (¶ 156). A husband and wife may file a joint return even though one spouse has no income or deductions (Code Sec. 6013; Reg. § 1.6013-1),[50] but only if:

- their tax years begin on the same date;
- they are not legally separated under a decree of divorce or separate maintenance on the last day of the tax year; and
- neither is a nonresident alien at any time during the year.

A U.S. citizen or resident and his or her nonresident alien spouse, however, can elect to file a joint return if they agree to be taxed on their worldwide income and supply all necessary books and records and other information pertinent to the determination of tax liability (¶ 2410) (Code Sec. 6013(g)). Further, a one-time election to file a joint return is available in the year in which a nonresident alien spouse becomes a resident (Code Sec. 6013(h)).

If a husband and wife are on a calendar-year basis or have fiscal years that begin on the same date, then they can file a joint return. However, if they have different tax years for some reason other than the intervention of death (¶ 164), then they cannot file a joint return. If newly married spouses with different tax years want to change the year of one spouse to coincide with that of the other so as to be able to file jointly, then they may do so by following the rules described at ¶ 1513. A husband and wife may file a joint return even though they have different accounting methods, e.g., one is on the cash basis and the other is on the accrual basis, if such methods clearly reflect their income.

Even though a husband and wife are not living together on the last day of the tax year, they may still file a joint return if they are *not* legally separated under a decree of divorce or separate maintenance on that date (Reg. § 1.6013-4).[51] Spouses who are separated under an interlocutory decree of divorce are considered husband and wife and are entitled to file a joint return until the decree becomes final. However, certain married individuals living apart may file separate returns as heads of households (¶ 173).

Spouses of military personnel serving in a combat zone and missing in action may file a joint return for any tax year until the tax year beginning two years after the termination of combat activities in that zone (Code Sec. 6013(f)).[52]

154. Joint Return—Election to File. When married individuals file separate returns for a tax year, they can elect to make a joint return for that year after the period for timely filing has expired. This change of election is usually achieved by the filing of an amended return on Form 1040X within three years of the last date prescribed by law for the filing of the separate return or returns, without taking into account any extension of time granted to either spouse (Code Sec. 6013(b)(2)).[53] However, the change to a joint return cannot be made:

References are to Standard Federal Tax Reports; Tax Research Consultant; and Practical Tax Explanations.

[49] ¶ 8007; FILEIND: 6,166; § 1,215.10

[50] ¶ 35,160, ¶ 35,161; FILEIND: 18,056; § 1,320.05

[51] ¶ 35,165; FILEIND: 18,056.10; § 1,320.10

[52] ¶ 35,160; FILEIND: 18,056.30; § 1,320.10

[53] ¶ 35,160; FILEIND: 18,056.05; § 1,320.25

- after either spouse timely files a petition with the Tax Court pursuant to a notice of deficiency which was mailed to either spouse for the tax year;
- after either spouse commences a suit in any court for the recovery of any part of the tax for such tax year;
- after either spouse enters into a closing agreement with respect to such tax year; or
- after either spouse has compromised any civil or criminal case arising with respect to such tax year.

Once a joint return has been filed for a tax year, the spouses may *not* thereafter file separate returns after the time for filing the return of either spouse has expired (Reg. § 1.6013-1(a)).[54] The exception being if either spouse dies during the tax year, then only the executor or administrator of the estate of the deceased spouse may elect to change from a joint to a separate return (¶ 168).

The Tax Court has ruled that a couple could elect to file a joint return even though the IRS had previously prepared and filed returns for the husband with a status of married filing separately (*J.V. Millsap*, 91 TC 926 (1988)). The IRS's filing of substitute returns did not bar the taxpayer from contesting either the deficiency or the IRS's choice of his filing status. The former standard that the IRS's choice precludes taxpayers from selecting a different filing status will be applied only when the issue is appealable to the U.S. Court of Appeals for the Tenth Circuit (*R.E. Smalldridge*, 86-2 USTC ¶ 9764 (1986)).

156. Joint Return v. Separate Return. Generally, it is more beneficial for married taxpayers to file a joint return (¶ 152). The filing of a joint return will result in a savings of tax in those instances in which differences in the tax rate brackets for joint and separate returns result in higher tax rates for married individuals filing separately. Unlike with separate returns, taxable income (¶ 123) on a joint return is the entire taxable income of the couple. Although there are two taxpayers on the joint return, there is only one taxable income and only one adjusted gross income (AGI) amount (Reg. § 1.6013-4).[55] In addition, the total exemptions (¶ 135) of a husband and wife are subtracted in determining taxable income.

> **Example:** For 2012, Joe has taxable income in the amount of $14,500, and his wife, Trisha, has taxable income in the amount of $36,000. If they elect to file a joint return, they will not be subject to the 25-percent tax rate because their combined taxable income of $50,500 does not exceed the $70,700 threshold amount for 2012 (¶ 13). If they elect to file separate returns, however, $650, which represents the portion of Trisha's income that exceeds the $35,350 threshold, falls within the 25-percent tax bracket for the year (¶ 15).

Also, if only one spouse has income, it would be impractical for the income earner to use married filing separately status. This filing status carries a basic standard deduction of $5,950 for 2012, whereas joint filers have a basic standard deduction of $11,900 for 2012 (¶ 126). It should be noted that a married individual generally may also *not* claim the credit for the elderly or permanently disabled (¶ 1302), the child and dependent care credit (¶ 1301), the earned income credit (¶ 1322), or the educational credits (¶ 1303) unless he or she files a joint return with his or her spouse.

There are circumstances under which married taxpayers might reduce their tax liability by filing separate returns. For example, a spouse whose medical expenses are high, but not high enough to exceed 7.5 percent of the AGI reported on a joint return (10 percent of AGI for tax years beginning after 2012), may exceed the AGI threshold on a separate return (¶ 1015). In light of the two-percent-of-AGI floor on miscellaneous itemized deductions (¶ 1011), a spouse who incurs substantial unreimbursed employee business or investment expenses might be better off filing separately. The same rationale holds true for casualty and disaster loss deductions, which are subject to a 10-percent-of-AGI floor (¶ 1137).

References are to Standard Federal Tax Reports; Tax Research Consultant; and Practical Tax Explanations.

[54] ¶ 35,161; FILEIND: 18,056.05; § 1,320.25

[55] ¶ 35,165; FILEIND: 18,056.35; § 1,320.05

Actual tax comparisons should be made using both joint and separate returns if there is doubt as to which method produces a more favorable result. Considerations other than tax savings might enter into the decision to file a separate, rather than a joint return. For example, one spouse may wish to avoid a deficiency liability assessed against the other spouse (¶ 162).

> **Comment:** Absent further legislation, the marriage penalty relief afforded by setting the standard deduction for joint filers and surviving spouses to equal 200 percent of the standard deduction of single and married filing separate filers will sunset on December 31, 2012.

162. Joint Return—Liability for Taxes. A husband and wife are liable jointly and individually for the entire tax, penalties, and interest arising out of a joint return. Relief is available under certain circumstances, commonly referred to as "innocent spouse relief" (Code Sec. 6015).[56] Three types of innocent spouse relief are available to the electing spouse: liability relief (commonly referred to as innocent spouse relief) (Code Sec. 6015(b)), separation of liability (Code Sec. 6015(c)), or equitable relief (Code Sec. 6015(f)). A spouse must generally request one of these types of relief on Form 8857 within two years of the IRS beginning collection of a tax deficiency or assessment. Equitable relief requests after July 25, 2011, however, may be requested within the limitations period for filing any claim for refund (¶ 2763) or for the collection of tax (¶ 2735) (Notice 2011-70). Transitional rules also apply for individuals in various stages of seeking, or having been denied, equitable innocent spouse relief.

Any determination by the IRS regarding any type of innocent spouse relief is reviewable in Tax Court.[57] Notice of the election for relief is required to be given to the non-electing spouse who may participate in any hearings on the relief requested (Code Sec. 6015(h)(2); Reg. § 1.6015-6(a)(1)).[58] The Tax Court has held that the non-electing spouse has the right to a "stand-alone" hearing regarding the appropriateness of granting relief to the electing spouse (*T. Corson*, 114 TC 354 (2000) and *K.A. King*, 115 TC 118 (2000)). However, the appellate courts have limited the jurisdiction of the Tax Court with regard to spousal relief. The Tax Court has no jurisdiction to make any spousal relief determination unless the IRS has issued a deficiency notice to the taxpayer (*G.A. Ewing*, CA-9, 2006-1 USTC ¶ 50,191; *T.E. Bartman*, CA-8, 2006-1 USTC ¶ 50,298). There are additional requirements for jurisdictions located in community property states (IRS Pub. 555).

Liability Relief (Innocent Spouse Relief). To qualify for liability relief (commonly referred to as innocent spouse relief), the taxpayer must meet *all* the following requirements:

- have filed a joint return which has an *understatement of tax* due to *erroneous items* of the other spouse;
- establish that at the time of signing the tax return the taxpayer did not know, or have reason to know, there was an understatement of tax; and
- taking into account all the facts and circumstances, show that it would be unfair to hold the innocent spouse liable for the understatement of tax (Code Sec. 6015(b)).[59]

A key element for the IRS will be whether the electing spouse received any substantial benefits, or later was divorced, separated from or deserted by, the other spouse.

Separation of Liability. Alternatively, the taxpayer may elect to obtain relief by separation of liabilities (Code Sec. 6015(c)).[60] To qualify, an individual must have filed a joint return, and either:

- be no longer married to, or be legally separated from, the spouse with whom the joint return was filed, or

References are to Standard Federal Tax Reports; Tax Research Consultant; and Practical Tax Explanations.

[56] ¶ 35,185; INDIV: 18,050; § 39,040.05

[57] ¶ 35,192.815; INDIV: 18,052.20; § 39,040.05

[58] ¶ 35,185, ¶ 35,187E; INDIV: 18,052.15; § 39,040.25

[59] ¶ 35,185; INDIV: 18,054; § 39,040.10

[60] ¶ 35,185; INDIV: 18,056; § 39,040.15

- must *not* have been a member of the same household with the spouse for a 12-month period ending on the date of the filing of Form 8857.

The burden of proof on income and deductions is on the taxpayer who elects relief under separation of liability.

Equitable Relief. Should an individual fail to qualify for either of the first two types of relief, one may still obtain relief from the tax liabilities, interest and penalties by electing equitable relief (Code Sec. 6015(f)).[61] The taxpayer must show that, under *all* facts and circumstances, it would be unfair to be held liable for the understatement or underpayment of taxes. One should note that under equitable relief, the innocent spouse can receive relief from tax liabilities caused by underpayment of taxes (IRS Pub. 971).

163. Joint Return—Injured Spouse Claim. When married taxpayers file a joint return and one spouse has not paid child or spousal support or certain federal debts, e.g., student loans, all or part of the tax overpayment shown on the joint return may be used to satisfy the past-due debt of the delinquent spouse. However, the nonobligated spouse may be entitled to a refund of his or her part of the overpayment if that individual:

- is not required to pay the past-due amount;
- received and reported income, such as wages, taxable interest, etc., on the joint return; and
- made and reported payments, such as withheld federal income taxes or estimated taxes, on the joint return (Financial Management Service Reg. § 285.3).[62]

To make this type of claim, the nonobligated spouse must write "Injured Spouse" in the upper left corner of Form 1040 and attach Form 8379. If the joint return has already been filed for 2012 or prior years, the nonobligated spouse should file Form 8379 by itself to claim the refund.

164. Joint Return—Effect of Death. A joint return may be filed when one or both spouses died during the year, and the tax year of both began on the same day, whether this year is a fiscal or calendar year. When a joint return is filed, it is treated as if the tax years of both spouses ended on the closing date of the surviving spouse's tax year (Reg. § 1.6013-3).[63]

166. Joint Return—Surviving Spouse. A surviving spouse who is a widow or widower with dependent children may continue to use the tax rates for married taxpayers jointly for two tax years immediately following the year of death of his or her spouse (¶ 175). A joint return may *not* be filed in the year a spouse dies if the surviving spouse has remarried before the close of the tax year. The survivor, however, may file a joint return with the new spouse if all other requirements are met. The survivor may not file a joint return with the deceased spouse if the tax year of either spouse is a fractional part of a year resulting from a change of accounting period (Reg. § 1.6013-1(d)).[64]

> **Example:** Stan and Tracy file joint returns on a calendar-year basis. Tracy dies on March 1, 2012. Thereafter, Stan receives permission to change his accounting period to a fiscal year beginning July 1, 2012. A joint return cannot be filed for the short tax year ending June 30, 2012.

168. Joint Return—Return with a Deceased Spouse. Generally, where one spouse dies, a joint return can be filed only by the executor or administrator and the survivor (¶ 178). The surviving spouse, alone, however, may file a joint return if:

- no return was filed by the decedent for the tax year at issue;
- no executor or administrator was appointed; and

References are to Standard Federal Tax Reports; Tax Research Consultant; and Practical Tax Explanations.

[61] ¶ 35,185; INDIV: 18,054.20; § 39,040.20

[62] ¶ 38,527; IRS: 33,102; § 40,015.15

[63] ¶ 35,164; FILEIND: 18,056.25; § 1,320.05

[64] ¶ 35,161; FILEIND: 18,056.20, FILEIND: 18,056.25; § 38,145.05

- no executor or administrator was appointed before the last day for filing the return of the surviving spouse, including any extensions of time for filing.

Even if all of the above tests are met, an administrator or executor, subsequently appointed, may disaffirm a joint return made by the surviving spouse by filing a separate return for the decedent. This disaffirmance must be made within one year after the last day allowed for filing the return of the surviving spouse including extensions. If a disaffirmance is made, then the already filed joint return will be considered the survivor's separate return. The survivor's tax will be figured on the basis of this joint return, with all of the items properly includible in the return of the deceased spouse deleted from the joint return (Reg. § 1.6013-1(d)).[65]

173. Head of Household Filing Status. Individuals who qualify to file as head of household are generally entitled to a higher standard deduction (¶ 126) and lower tax rates than single individuals. See Tax Rate Schedule Z (¶ 17) or the Tax Computation Worksheet (¶ 20) and the "Head of a Household" column in the Tax Table (¶ 25). In order to qualify for head of household status, an individual must be unmarried, considered unmarried, or a surviving spouse (¶ 175) at the close of the tax year (Code Sec. 2(b)).[66] In addition, the taxpayer must maintain a household which, for more than one-half of the tax year, is the principal place of abode of a qualifying individual who is a member of the household.

A qualifying individual includes a qualifying child of the taxpayer (¶ 137A) determined without regard to the rules for divorced parents (¶ 139A). If, however, the child (i) is married at the close of the taxpayer's tax year, (ii) files a joint return with his or her spouse, or (iii) is not a citizen, national, or a resident of the United States, Canada, or Mexico, then the taxpayer is barred from claiming head of household filing status. For purposes of this requirement, an adopted child or a foster child, as defined under the qualifying child rules, is treated as the taxpayer's child by blood.

A qualifying individual also includes any other person who is a dependent of the taxpayer if they are entitled to claim that person as a dependency deduction (¶ 137). A taxpayer, however, cannot claim head-of-household if the only reason for being able to claim an individual as a dependent is based on either the individual living as a member of the taxpayer's household for the full year as a qualifying relative (¶ 137B), or claiming the dependency exemption under a multiple support agreement (¶ 147).

An individual qualifies for head of household status if a *separate* household is maintained for the tax year for a parent. The separate household must be the parent's principal place of abode, and the parent must qualify as the child's dependent (¶ 137). A parent's principal place of abode can include residence in a rest home or home for the aged. An institutionalized or hospitalized dependent, other than a parent, may also qualify a taxpayer as head of a household if the taxpayer can prove that the taxpayer's home was the "principal" place of abode of the dependent, even though the dependent may never return home because of the nature of the infirmity (Code Sec. 2(b)(1)(B); Reg. § 1.2-2(b)(4)).[67]

Marital Status. The marital status of an individual for the purpose of applying the head of household rates is determined at the end of a tax year. A taxpayer is considered to be unmarried at the end of a tax year if his or her spouse was a nonresident alien at any time during the tax year, or if he or she is legally separated from his or her spouse under a decree of divorce or separate maintenance at the close of the tax year. A taxpayer under an interlocutory decree of divorce is not legally separated. A widow or widower may not use the head of household rates in those tax years in which he or she is eligible to use the joint tax rates under the surviving spouse rules discussed at ¶ 175.

A married taxpayer will be considered unmarried and eligible for head of household status if the taxpayer's spouse was not a member of the household for the last six months of the year and if the household is the principal place of abode of a child for whom the taxpayer is entitled to a dependency exemption (¶ 137) (Code Secs. 2(c) and

References are to Standard Federal Tax Reports; Tax Research Consultant; and Practical Tax Explanations.

[65] ¶ 35,161; FILEIND: 18,056.25; § 1,320.20

[66] ¶ 3310; FILEIND: 3,150; § 1,115.05

[67] ¶ 3310, ¶ 3325; FILEIND: 3,154; § 1,115.30

7703(b)).[68] The taxpayer, however, will still be eligible for head-of-household status even if no dependency exemption is available for a child because the taxpayer waived the exemption (¶ 139A). A nonresident alien who is considered unmarried may not use the head of household tax rate but must use the tax rate schedule for single individuals (Reg. § 1.2-2(b)(6)).[69]

Maintains Household. An individual "maintains a household" if (1) the individual furnishes with funds attributable to the taxpayer more than one-half the cost of maintaining the home during the tax year and (2) at least one of the qualifying individuals described previously lives there for more than one-half of the year except for temporary absence. An exemption is made for institutionalized or hospitalized dependents. Birth or death of a qualifying individual during the year will not disqualify the taxpayer as the head of a household if the individual lived in the household during the part of the year when he or she was alive (Code Sec. 2(b)(1); Reg. § 1.2-2(c)).[70]

The cost of maintaining a household includes the expenses incurred for the mutual benefit of the occupants by reason of its use as the principal place of abode. These expenses include property taxes, mortgage interest, rent, utility charges, upkeep and repairs, property insurance, food consumed on the premises, and other household expenses. They do *not* include the cost of clothing, education, medical treatment, vacations, life insurance, transportation, food consumed off the premises, or the value of services rendered by the taxpayer or by any person who qualifies the taxpayer as head of a household (Reg. § 1.2-2(d)).[71]

175. Surviving Spouse Filing Status. A surviving spouse (qualifying widow(er)) may use the joint return tax rates for two tax years following the year of death of the husband or wife, but *only* if the survivor remains unmarried and maintains a household (¶ 173) that, for the entire tax year, is the principal place of abode of a child, adopted child, foster child, or stepchild for whom the taxpayer is entitled to the dependency exemption (¶ 137) (Code Sec. 2(a)).[72] See ¶ 164 for a discussion of filing a joint return for the year of death of one spouse.

A widow or widower who qualifies as a surviving spouse uses the joint return rate schedule (Schedule Y-1) at ¶ 13, the Tax Computation Worksheet at ¶ 20 or the Tax Table at ¶ 25 and must use either Form 1040 or Form 1040A. This benefit is afforded a surviving spouse only if he or she was entitled to file a joint return with the deceased spouse during the latter's lifetime.

It should be emphasized that the benefit entitles the survivor only to the joint return tax rates; it does not authorize him or her to file a joint return or claim any personal exemptions other than his or her own and those of the dependent or dependents for whom the household is maintained. For 2012, a qualifying widow(er) (surviving spouse) with dependent children is generally entitled to joint return rate benefits if the spouse died at any time during 2010 or 2011 (Code Sec. 2(a)(1)(A)).

In determining eligibility for filing as a surviving spouse, the date of death of a person serving in a combat zone and missing in action is considered to be two years after the termination of combat activities in that zone, unless death has been established at an earlier time (Code Sec. 2(a)(3)).

176. Single Filing Status. Unmarried individuals who do not qualify to file their returns as a married individual (¶ 152), as a surviving spouse (¶ 175) or as a head of household (¶ 173) must file their return as a single taxpayer (Code Sec. 1(c)).[73] See ¶ 103 for a discussion on the filing requirements for a child with earned and unearned income.

References are to Standard Federal Tax Reports; Tax Research Consultant; and Practical Tax Explanations.

[68] ¶ 3310, ¶ 43,170; FILEIND: 3,204; § 1,115.10

[69] ¶ 3325; FILEIND: 3,250; § 1,115.10

[70] ¶ 3310, ¶ 3325; FILEIND: 3,154.05; § 1,115.15

[71] ¶ 3325; FILEIND: 3,154.10; § 1,115.15

[72] ¶ 3310; FILEIND: 3,100; § 1,120

[73] ¶ 3,260; FILEIND: 3,050; § 1,110

Tax Treatment of Decedent's Final Return

178. Who Must File for a Decedent. An income tax return must be filed for a deceased person who would have been required to file a return if he or she were still alive during the tax year (¶ 101) (Code Sec. 6012). This final return covers a short year, including the part of the year up to the date of death. A decedent's final return is due at the same time his or her return would have been due had he or she lived (¶ 107).[74] The final return is filed on Form 1040, Form 1040A, or Form 1040EZ if the decedent met the gross income filing test for the short period, or otherwise would have been required to file a return, e.g., the decedent had more than $400 of self-employment earnings. The word "DECEASED," the decedent's name, and the date of death should be written across the top of page 1 of the return.

The return for the decedent must be filed by his administrator, executor, or any other person charged with responsibility for the decedent's affairs. The surviving spouse should, however, file the decedent's final return if there is no executor or administrator. A surviving spouse may also file a joint return for the decedent's final year (¶ 168). Whoever files the return for the decedent may file a separate return or a joint return (¶ 164). All personal exemptions to which the decedent was entitled while he was alive may be claimed. If a refund is due, Form 1310 must be attached to the return to allow the personal representative to claim and receive the refund.

180. Due Date. The final return of a decedent is due by the date on which the return would have been due had death not occurred (¶ 107). Thus, for a calendar-year taxpayer who died in 2012, the final return is due by April 15, 2013 (Reg. § 1.6072-1(a)).[75]

182. How Income Is Treated. When a cash-basis taxpayer dies, only income actually or constructively received up to the date of death is included in the final return. If the decedent was on the accrual basis of accounting, income accrued up to the date of death is included in the final return. Income that accrues *only because of death*, however, is not included (Code Sec. 451; Reg. § 1.451-1(b)).[76] These rules also apply to successive decedents as rights to receive "income in respect of a prior decedent" (Reg. § 1.691(a)-1(c)).[77]

Any amount of gross income *not* reported on the return of the decedent is, when received, includible in the income of the person receiving such amounts by inheritance or survivorship as "income in respect of a decedent." The person receiving the income may be the decedent's estate or, if the estate does not collect an item of income but distributes the right to receive it to a testamentary trust or to the heir, next of kin, legatee, or devisee, it is included in the income of such trust, heir, next of kin, legatee, or devisee (Code Sec. 691(a); Reg. § 1.691(a)-2).[78]

The depreciation recapture rules under Code Sec. 1245 and Code Sec. 1250 apply to sales or other dispositions of property subject to those rules where the income therefrom is treated as income on the decedent's final return or as income in respect of a decedent under Code Sec. 691. See ¶ 1779 and following for a complete discussion. These rules, however, do not apply to transfers of depreciable property at death (Code Secs. 1245(b)(2) and 1250(d)(2)).[79]

184. Installment Obligation. Collections on an installment obligation acquired from a decedent are treated as items of income in respect of a decedent (¶ 182) if the decedent had been reporting the profit on the installment basis (Code Sec. 691(a)(4); Reg. § 1.691(a)-5).[80] If, however, the obligor of the installment obligation acquires the uncollected obligation, then the decedent's estate is considered to have made a taxable disposition of the installment obligation. Thus, any previously unreported gain will be

References are to Standard Federal Tax Reports; Tax Research Consultant; and Practical Tax Explanations.

[74] ¶ 35,142; ACCTNG: 24,256; § 1,305.10

[75] ¶ 36,721; ACCTNG: 24,256.05; § 1,305.10

[76] ¶ 21,002, ¶ 21,003; ACCTNG: 9,408; § 38,145.05

[77] ¶ 24,901; ESTTRST: 6,060; § 38,145.05

[78] ¶ 24,900, ¶ 24,902; ESTTRST: 6,054; § 38,145.05

[79] ¶ 30,902, ¶ 31,000; DEPR: 18,104; § 38,145.05

[80] ¶ 24,900, ¶ 24,905; ESTTRST: 6,056, ESTTRST: 6,116; § 18,370

recognized by the estate. This rule also applies if the obligation is canceled because of the death of the payee or if the estate allows the obligation to become unenforceable because it is canceled by the executor.

187. Deductions for Decedents. Deductible expenses and other items are not accrued on the final return of a decedent unless his or her accounting method requires it, but are deductible instead by the estate or person who pays them or is liable for their payment (Code Sec. 461; Reg. § 1.461-1(b)).[81] Similar treatment is given to the foreign tax credit (Code Sec. 691(b); Reg. § 1.691(b)-1).[82]

Expenses for medical care of the decedent, paid out of his estate within one year from the date of his death, are deductible on the decedent's final income tax return (Reg. § 1.213-1(d)).[83] However, the estate must attach a statement (in duplicate) to the decedent's return waiving the right to claim the deduction on the estate tax return.

Business expenses, income-producing expenses, interest, and taxes for which the decedent was liable but which were not properly allowable as a deduction on his last return will be allowed when paid as a deduction by the estate or, if the estate was not liable, then as a deduction by the person who by reason of the decedent's death acquires—subject to such obligation—an interest in property of the decedent (Reg. § 1.691(b)-1(a)).[84] The percentage depletion deduction is allowed only to the person who receives the income in respect of the decedent to which the deduction relates (Reg. § 1.691(b)-1(b)).

189. How Recipient Treats Decedent's Income. A decedent's income that is to be accounted for by the recipient retains the same character it would have had in the hands of the decedent (Code Sec. 691(a)(3); Reg. § 1.691(a)-3).[85] Thus, if the income would have been earned income, exempt income, or interest to the decedent, it is the same kind of income to the recipient.

191. Deduction of Estate Taxes. If a person includes in gross income an item of income that had accrued as of the date of death of a decedent or prior successive decedents, so that it was included in the valuation of the estate for estate tax purposes, that person may take a corresponding deduction based on the estate tax attributable to the net value of the income item (Code Sec. 691(c); Reg. § 1.691(c)-1).[86] This deduction is taken by individuals on Form 1040 and by estates and trusts on Form 1041. In the case of individuals, it may be taken only if deductions are itemized on Schedule A. For individuals, as well as for estates and trusts, the deduction is not subject to the two-percent-of-adjusted-gross-income floor on miscellaneous deductions (Code Sec. 67(b)(7)).[87] In the case of any generation-skipping transfer tax imposed on a taxable termination or a direct skip as a result of the death of the transferor, a deduction is available for the portion of this tax attributable to items of gross income that were not properly includible in the gross income of the trust before the date of such termination (Code Sec. 691(c)(3)).[88]

1 INDIVIDUALS

References are to Standard Federal Tax Reports; Tax Research Consultant; and Practical Tax Explanations.

[81] ¶ 21,802, ¶ 21,805; ESTTRST: 6,206, ESTTRST: 6,208; § 38,145.05

[82] ¶ 24,900, ¶ 24,907; ESTTRST: 6,206.30; § 3,050

[83] ¶ 12,541; ESTTRST: 6,208.05; § 7,220

[84] ¶ 24,907; ESTTRST: 6,206.05; § 32,925.05

[85] ¶ 24,900, ¶ 24,901; ESTTRST: 6,056; § 32,910

[86] ¶ 24,900, ¶ 24,909; ESTTRST: 6,156; § 32,925.10

[87] ¶ 6060; FILEIND: 12,054; § 7,110.10

[88] ¶ 24,900; ESTTRST: 6,158; § 32,925.10

Chapter 2

CORPORATIONS

Corporate Formation

201. How Organizations Are Taxed. A corporation, like any business entity, is formed by one or more persons to conduct a business venture and divide profits among investors (Reg. §§301.7701-2, 301.7701-3).[1] A corporation files a charter or articles of incorporation in a state, in a U.S. possession, with a foreign government (¶ 2425), or (in certain cases) with the U.S. government. It prepares by-laws, has its business affairs overseen by a board of directors, and issues stock. Under the check-the-box regulations, entities formed under a corporation statute are automatically classified as corporations and may not elect to be treated as any other kind of entity; other entities are allowed to elect corporate status on Form 8832. Thus, an entity that is a partnership or limited liability company (¶ 402B) under the laws of the state in which it is formed may elect to be taxed as a C corporation or an S corporation under the Code. However, partnerships that are publicly traded are taxed as corporations unless 90 percent or more of the gross income consists of qualifying passive-type income (Code Sec. 7704; Reg. §§1.7704-1 and 1.7704-3).[2]

For tax purposes, the predominant forms of business enterprises are C corporations, S corporations (¶ 301), partnerships (¶ 401), and sole proprietorships. These different forms are treated differently under federal tax law and care should be taken in choosing the appropriate entity for the business. Although many of the Code's provisions apply to all of these entities, some areas of the law are specially tailored for each type. The classification of an entity will have a lingering tax impact throughout the entity's existence.

Of the types of business organization, C corporations are subject to the toughest tax bite. Their earnings are taxed twice. First, a *corporate* income tax is imposed on its net earnings (¶ 219). Then after the earnings are distributed to shareholders as dividends, each shareholder must pay taxes separately on his or her share of the dividends (¶ 733–¶ 740). A corporation can reduce, or even eliminate, its federal income tax liability by distributing its income as salary to shareholder-employees who actually perform valuable services for the corporation (¶ 713). Although this can reduce taxation at the corporate level, employees who receive payments from a corporation in exchange for services must still pay tax on the amount received, which is treated as salary.

This scheme of taxation differs radically from that applied to partnerships, limited liability companies, S corporations, and sole proprietorships. These entities do not pay

References are to Standard Federal Tax Reports; Tax Research Consultant; and Practical Tax Explanations.

[1] ¶ 43,082, ¶ 43,083; CCORP: 100, PART: 3,102; § 30,015.05, § 30,015.10

[2] ¶ 43,180, ¶ 43,180B, ¶ 43,181D; PART: 3,250

an entity-level tax on their earnings. There is no income tax on partnerships (¶ 404), or on limited liability companies (¶ 402B) treated as partnerships for federal tax purposes. Nor (in most cases) is there an S corporation income tax (¶ 319) or sole proprietorship income tax. Rather, the owners or members of these entities are taxed on their share of the entity's earnings.

203. Tax-Free Contributions in Exchange for Stock. A corporation is formed by the transfer of money or property from shareholders to the corporate entity in return for corporate stock. If one or more shareholders transfer money or property to a corporation solely in exchange for stock of that corporation, and if the shareholders control the corporation immediately after the exchange, neither the shareholders nor the corporation recognizes any gain or loss (Code Secs. 351(a) and 1032).[3] To be considered in "control," the shareholders as a group must own, immediately after the exchange (1) at least 80 percent of the total combined voting power of all classes of stock entitled to vote, and (2) at least 80 percent of the total number of shares of all other classes of stock (Code Sec. 368(c)).[4] The exchanges need not actually be simultaneous to avoid the imputation of gain (Reg. § 1.351-1(a)(1)).[5] Rather, all that is required is a situation where the rights of the parties have been previously defined and the execution of the agreement proceeds in an orderly manner.

Money or property transferred to a controlled corporation generally includes all property, tangible or intangible, with certain limitations (Code Sec. 351(d)).[6] Stock issued for services, indebtedness of the corporation which is not evidenced by a security, or interest on indebtedness of the corporation that accrued on or after the beginning of the transferor's holding period for the debt are not considered as issued in return for property.

Corporate shareholders can be individuals, estates, trusts, partnerships, or other corporations (Reg. § 1.351-1(a)(1)).[7] However, the rules permitting tax-free transfers to a corporation in exchange for corporate stock do not apply if the transferee corporation is an investment company (Code Sec. 351(e)(1)).[8]

If the transferor owners receive additional property along with the stock when they transfer property to the corporation, the transfer can still qualify as a contribution to a controlled corporation described in Code Sec. 351 (Code Sec. 351(b); Reg. § 1.351-2(a)).[9] However, the owners are taxed on any additional property received ("boot"). Thus, gain is recognized, but only to the extent of the cash received, plus the fair market value of the other property received. No loss is recognized on the transfer.

Assumption of Liabilities. If property transferred in what would otherwise be a Code Sec. 351 tax-free transaction is subject to liabilities, the acceptance of the transfer or the assumption of the liabilities does not prevent the transaction from being tax free (Code Sec. 357).[10] This rule does not apply if the principal purpose of the transfer is tax avoidance or if liabilities assumed by the transferee exceed the transferor's basis in the property.

Bankruptcy. A debtor must recognize gain or loss upon its transfer of assets to a controlled corporation pursuant to a plan approved by a bankruptcy court (other than a reorganization plan) in which the stock is exchanged (Code Sec. 351(e)(2)).[11] Essentially, the transaction is treated as if the property had first been transferred to the creditors and then transferred by them to the controlled corporation. If less than all the stock is transferred to creditors, only a proportionate share of the gain or loss must be recognized. Both the basis of the stock and of the assets are adjusted for the gain or loss recognized on the transfer to the corporation. Note that this rule does not apply to a

References are to Standard Federal Tax Reports; Tax Research Consultant; and Practical Tax Explanations.

[3] ¶ 16,402, ¶ 29,622; CCORP: 3,050; § 26,105.05

[4] ¶ 16,750; CCORP: 3,054; § 26,105.05

[5] ¶ 16,403; CCORP: 3,054; § 26,105.05

[6] ¶ 16,402; CCORP: 3,052; § 26,110.05

[7] ¶ 16,403; CCORP: 3,050; § 26,101

[8] ¶ 16,402; CCORP: 3,062; § 26,160.05

[9] ¶ 16,402, ¶ 16,404B; CCORP: 3,102.10; § 26,120

[10] ¶ 16,520; CCORP: 3,106; § 26,125.05

[11] ¶ 16,402; CCORP: 3,114

transfer by one corporation to another corporation in a bankruptcy case. Instead, such a transfer is considered a Code Sec. 368(a)(1)(G) reorganization and its tax consequences are determined accordingly (¶ 2247).

Reporting Requirements. If a person receives stock of a corporation in exchange for property and no gain or loss is recognized, the person and the corporation must each attach to their tax returns a complete statement of all the facts pertinent to the exchange, including (Reg. § 1.351-3):[12]

(1) The name and employer identification number (if any) of the transferee corporation, or of every significant transferor, as applicable;

(2) The date(s) of the transfer(s) of assets;

(3) The aggregate fair market value and basis, determined immediately before the exchange, of the property transferred by such transferor, or received by the transferee, in the exchange; and

(4) The date and control number of any private letter ruling(s) issued by the Internal Revenue Service in connection with the section 351 exchange.

Return and Payment of Tax

211. Annual and Short-Period Corporate Returns. A corporation must file an income tax return, even if it has no income or if no tax is due (Code Sec. 6012(a)(2); Reg. § 1.6012-2).[13] Form 1120 must be filed on or before the 15th day of the third month that follows the close of its tax year (Code Sec. 6072(b); Reg. § 1.6072-2).[14] If the last day of a corporation's tax year does not end on the last day of a month (as in the case of a dissolved corporation whose tax year ends on the date of dissolution), the return is due on or before the 15th day of the third full month following the date of dissolution. If the due date for filing a return falls on a Saturday, Sunday, or legal holiday, the return must be filed by the first following business day (¶ 2549). Timely mailing generally is regarded as timely filing (¶ 2553).

A corporation's tax year generally may be a calendar year or a fiscal year (¶ 1501). Restrictions apply, however, to the choice of tax years by S corporations, personal service corporations, and REITs or REMICs. A corporation's return may not cover a period of more than a year. In a slight exception to this rule, a corporation may elect to use an annual filing period that fluctuates between 52 and 53 weeks (¶ 1505). A return may cover less than a year if a corporation was formed during the year or dissolved during the year (¶ 1505). For example, if a corporation elects the calendar year method but starts operations on August 1, it must report income from August 1 to December 31. If it dissolves on June 30, it must file a short-period return covering the period from January 1 to June 30. In addition to filing its regular income tax return, a corporation that has adopted a resolution to dissolve itself or liquidate all or part of its stock must file Form 966 (Code Sec. 6043; Reg. § 1.6043-1).[15]

215. Due Date for Corporate Taxes. The due date for the payment of a corporation's taxes is generally the same as the due date for the filing of a return, without regard to filing extensions—the 15th day of the third month that follows the close of its tax year (Code Sec. 6151).[16] A corporation that anticipates a tax liability of $500 or more must estimate its taxes and make quarterly estimated tax payments (including estimated payments of the alternative minimum tax) using electronic fund transfers. If the liability exceeds the total estimated payments, the corporation must pay the remaining amount by the due date of its return. Failure to pay estimated taxes may be penalized (¶ 241). Corporations may file for an extension of time to file returns or to pay taxes (¶ 2509 and ¶ 2537).

References are to Standard Federal Tax Reports; Tax Research Consultant; and Practical Tax Explanations.

[12] ¶ 16,404C; CCORP: 3,404; § 26,165

[13] ¶ 35,142, ¶ 35,145; FILEBUS: 3,052.05; § 39,025

[14] ¶ 36,720, ¶ 36,724; FILEBUS: 3,052.05; § 26,030.05

[15] ¶ 35,880, ¶ 35,881; FILEBUS: 9,352, CCORP: 27,054; § 38,145.10

[16] ¶ 37,080; FILEBUS: 6,102.05; § 39,305.05

Computation of Tax Liability

219. Corporate Tax Rates. Corporations are subject to the following tax rates on their taxable income (Code Secs. 11 and 1201):[17]

If taxable income is: Over—	*But not over—*	*Tax is—*			*Of the amt. over—*
$0	$50,000			15%	$0
50,000	75,000	$7,500	+	25%	50,000
75,000	100,000	13,750	+	34%	75,000
100,000	335,000	22,250	+	39%	100,000
335,000	10,000,000	113,900	+	34%	335,000
10,000,000	15,000,000	3,400,000	+	35%	10,000,000
15,000,000	18,333,333	5,150,000	+	38%	15,000,000
18,333,333	—			35%	0

Qualified Personal Service Corporations. The corporate graduated rates do not apply to qualified personal service corporations. Such corporations are instead taxed at a flat rate of 35 percent of taxable income (¶ 273). Qualified personal service corporations perform services in the fields of health, law, engineering, architecture, accounting (including the preparation of tax returns), actuarial science, the performing arts, or consulting. Substantially all of the stock of a personal service corporation is held by employees, retired employees, or their estates (¶ 1575) (Code Secs. 11(b)(2) and 448(d)(2)).[18]

Foreign Corporations. Foreign corporations are taxed at regular U.S. corporate rates on most income that is effectively connected with a U.S. trade or business (¶ 2429) and are subject to a flat 30-percent withholding tax on U.S.-source fixed or determinable income that is not effectively connected (¶ 2431). Tax treaties between the U.S. and foreign countries may provide for lower rates or exemptions from taxation.

Additional Taxes. In addition to the regular corporate income tax, the alternative minimum tax (AMT) may be imposed on a corporation having tax preference items (¶ 1401). A corporation is exempt from the AMT if it is the corporation's first year or it is a small corporation with average annual gross receipts for the three-tax-year period (or portion thereof) ending before the current tax year not in excess of $7.5 million (¶ 1415). The $7.5-million amount is reduced to $5 million for the corporation's first three-tax-year period. Certain corporations used by their shareholders for the purpose of avoiding taxes might also be subject to the accumulated earnings tax (¶ 251) or the personal holding company tax (¶ 275–¶ 287).

221. Corporate Taxable Income. The corporate tax rates (¶ 219) are applied to a corporation's "taxable income" (Code Sec. 11).[19] Taxable income is the corporation's gross income for the year minus allowable deductions. The principal items of corporation income include gross sales receipts, dividends and interest received, rent and royalty income, and capital gains. The common deductions for a corporation in computing its taxable income include compensation paid to officers and workers, expenses for repairs and maintenance of property, taxes, licenses, interest paid, depreciation and depletion, advertising, and deductible amounts paid to pension and profit-sharing plans and employee benefit programs. In addition, a corporation may be entitled to special deductions for dividends received from other corporations (¶ 223), affiliates (¶ 229), and foreign corporations (¶ 247), as well as deductions for organizational expenses (¶ 223) and domestic production activities (¶ 239).

A corporation generally must use the accrual method of accounting to determine when income and expenses are reported (¶ 1515). The cash basis of accounting may be used, however, by a personal service corporation, if the corporation is engaged in a

References are to Standard Federal Tax Reports; Tax Research Consultant; and Practical Tax Explanations.

[17] ¶ 3365, ¶ 30,352; CCORP: 100, SALES: 15,210; § 16,527.10, § 26,010

[18] ¶ 3365, ¶ 20,800; CCORP: 100; § 27,110

[19] ¶ 3365; CCORP: 100; § 26,001

farming business (¶ 2028), or if its average annual gross receipts exceed an average of $5 million for the three tax years preceding the current tax year (Code Sec. 448).[20] Securities dealers must use the mark-to-market method of accounting (Code Sec. 475).[21]

223. Dividends Received from Other Corporations. A corporation is entitled to a special deduction from gross income for dividends received from a domestic corporation that is subject to income tax (Code Sec. 243).[22] The deduction is: (1) 70 percent of dividends received from corporations owned less than 20 percent (by stock vote and value) by the recipient corporation; (2) 80 percent of dividends received from a 20-percent-owned corporation—a corporation having at least 20 percent (but generally less than 80 percent) of its stock owned by the recipient corporation; (3) 100 percent of qualifying dividends received from members of the same affiliated group (generally, 80-percent-or-more common ownership) to which the recipient corporation belongs (¶ 223B); and (4) 100 percent of dividends received by a small business investment company (¶ 1916). These rules also apply to dividends received from a foreign corporation that are paid out of the earnings and profits of a taxable domestic predecessor corporation (¶ 223C).

The aggregate amount of dividends-received deductions that may be taken by a corporation is limited to 70 percent (80 percent in the case of 20-percent-owned corporations) of its taxable income, computed without regard to any net operating loss deduction, the domestic production activities deduction, dividends-received deduction, dividends-paid deduction in the case of public utilities, the deduction for the U.S.-source portion of dividends from 10-percent-owned foreign corporations, the deduction for certain dividends received from wholly owned foreign subsidiaries, capital loss carryback, or adjustment for nontaxed portions of extraordinary dividends received. This limitation is applied first with respect to any 80-percent-deductible dividends and then separately for 80-percent-deductible dividends (after reducing taxable income by the 80-percent-deductible dividends), but it does not apply for the year if the full deduction results in a net operating loss (Code Sec. 246(b)).[23] Further, it does not apply in the case of dividends received by a small business investment company.

The dividends-received deduction is not allowed in computing the accumulated earnings tax (¶ 251) or the tax on personal holding companies (¶ 275). The deduction is allowed to a resident foreign corporation, as well as to a domestic corporation. No deduction is allowed for dividends received from a corporation exempt from income tax (including an exempt farmers' cooperative) during the tax year or the preceding year (Code Sec. 246(a)).[24]

Holding Period. The dividends-received deduction is only allowed if the underlying stock is held for at least 46 days during the 91-day period beginning on the date 45 days before the ex-dividend date of the stock (Code Sec. 246(c)).[25] If the stock is cumulative preferred stock with an arrearage of dividends, it must be held at least 91 days during the 181-day period beginning on the date 90 days before the ex-dividend date. The ex-dividend date is the first day the stock trades without a buyer having a right to an announced dividend and, to account for the delay needed to accommodate settlement, is normally two business days before the record date (the day when the company determines who is the record owner of the stock). A person who buys stock on the trading day before the ex-dividend date will receive a dividend, while a person who buys the stock on the ex-dividend date will not.

The holding period is reduced for any period during which the taxpayer's risk of loss with respect to the stock is diminished because the taxpayer has (1) an option to sell, is under an obligation to sell, or has made (and not closed) a short sale of substantially identical stock or securities; (2) granted an option to purchase substantially

References are to Standard Federal Tax Reports; Tax Research Consultant; and Practical Tax Explanations.

[20] ¶ 20,800; ACCTNG: 6,050; § 38,215.05

[21] ¶ 22,265; SALES: 45,350; § 38,235.05

[22] ¶ 13,051; CCORP: 9,050; § 26,501

[23] ¶ 13,200; CCORP: 9,212; § 26,510.15

[24] ¶ 13,200; CCORP: 9,200; § 26,510.10

[25] ¶ 13,200; CCORP: 9,204; § 26,510.20

identical stock or securities; or (3) reduced the risk by virtue of holding one or more other positions with respect to substantially similar or related property.

Debt-Financed Portfolio Stock. The dividends-received deduction is reduced for dividends received from debt-financed portfolio stock by a percentage related to the amount of debt incurred to purchase such stock. The deduction is calculated by multiplying the difference between 100 percent and the average portfolio indebtedness by 70 percent (80 percent in the case of 20-percent-owned corporations) (Code Sec. 246A).[26] However, any required reduction is limited to the amount of the interest deduction allocable to the related dividend. This deduction does not apply to dividends that are eligible for 100-percent dividends-received deduction for (1) qualifying dividends received from a member of an affiliated group and (2) dividends received from a small business investment company.

Other Limitations. Capital gain dividends from a regulated investment company (mutual fund) or a real estate investment trust, and distributions that are a return of capital, do not qualify for the dividends-received deduction (Code Sec. 243(d)).[27] Additionally, the deduction is not allowed to the extent that the taxpayer is under an obligation (pursuant to a short sale or otherwise) to make related payments with respect to positions in substantially similar or related property (Code Sec. 246(c)(1)(B)).[28]

The deduction for dividends received on certain preferred stock of a public utility is reduced to the extent the public utility was allowed a dividends paid deduction (Code Secs. 244 and 247).[29]

227. Debt-Equity Rule. For instruments issued by corporations and advances made to corporations, a question can arise as to whether such instruments and advances are treated as bona fide debt of the corporation or as an equity interest in the corporation. If they are treated as a bona fide debt of the corporation, the corporation can deduct interest payments as a business expense, and the shareholders can receive principal payments as a tax-free return of capital. However, if they are treated as stock, the corporation cannot deduct distributions of the corporation's earnings and profits made with respect to such instruments (Code Sec. 385).[30]

The Code lists five factors that may be considered in making the debt-equity determination:

(1) whether there is a written, unconditional promise to pay on demand or on a specified date a sum certain in money in return for an adequate consideration in money or money's worth, and to pay a fixed rate of interest,

(2) whether there is subordination to or preference over any indebtedness of the corporation,

(3) the ratio of debt to equity of the corporation,

(4) whether there is convertibility into the stock of the corporation, and

(5) the relationship between holdings of stock in the corporation and holdings of the interest in question.

The courts have developed other guidelines to be used in making a debt-equity determination.[31]

229. 100-Percent Dividends-Received Deduction for Affiliates. Affiliated corporations are allowed a 100-percent dividends-received deduction for qualifying dividends received from members of the affiliated group (Code Sec. 243).[32] A qualifying dividend is any dividend received by a corporation that is a member of the same affiliated group as the corporation distributing it.

If the affiliated group includes at least one life insurance company, no dividend by any member of the group will be treated as qualified unless a special election is in effect

References are to Standard Federal Tax Reports; Tax Research Consultant; and Practical Tax Explanations.

[26] ¶ 13,250; CCORP: 9,208; § 26,510.20

[27] ¶ 13,051; CCORP: 9,062; § 26,510.10

[28] ¶ 13,200; CCORP: 9,206; § 26,510.10

[29] ¶ 13,053, ¶ 13,300; CCORP: 9,210, CCORP: 9,250; § 26,510.10

[30] ¶ 17,340; CCORP: 9,410.05

[31] ¶ 15,704.264; CCORP: 3,304

[32] ¶ 13,051; CCORP: 9,100; § 26,505

for the tax year in which the dividend is received. If any member of an affiliated group elects the foreign tax credit, then all members of the group that pay or accrue foreign taxes must elect the credit in order for any dividend paid by a member of the group to qualify for the 100-percent dividends-received deduction.

231. Dividends from Foreign Corporations. A domestic corporation is entitled to a 70-percent (80-percent in the case of 20-percent-owned corporations (¶ 223)) deduction of the U.S.-source portion of dividends received from a foreign corporation that is at least 10 percent owned, by vote and value, by the domestic corporation (Code Sec. 245(a)).[33] The U.S.-source portion of a dividend is the amount that bears the same ratio to the dividend as undistributed U.S. earnings bear to total undistributed earnings.

A 100-percent dividends-received deduction is allowed to a domestic corporation for dividends paid by a wholly owned foreign subsidiary out of its earnings and profits for the tax year (Code Sec. 245(b)).[34] All of the foreign subsidiary's gross income must be effectively connected with a U.S. trade or business.

Debt-Financed Portfolio Stock. Any reduction in the dividends-received deduction resulting from the rules concerning debt-financed portfolio stock (¶ 223) must be computed before applying the above ratios.

237. Organizational Expenditures. A corporation may elect to deduct up to $5,000 of any organizational expenses it incurs in the tax year in which it begins business (Code Sec. 248; Reg. § 1.248-1).[35] A taxpayer is deemed to have made an election to deduct and amortize organizational expenses in the taxable year in which the active trade or business to which the expenditures relate begins. A taxpayer may choose to forego the deemed election by clearly electing to capitalize its organizational expenditures on a timely filed federal income tax return, including extensions, for the taxable year in which the active trade or business to which the expenditures relate begins. The $5,000 deducted for organizational expenses must be reduced by the amount by which the expenses exceed $50,000. Any remaining balance of organizational expenditures which are not immediately deductible must be amortized over a 180-month period.

Organizational expenditures are those which are (1) connected directly with the creation of the corporation, (2) chargeable to capital account, and (3) of a character that would be amortizable over the life of the corporation if its life were limited by its charter. They include expenses of temporary directors and organizational meetings, state fees for incorporation privileges, accounting service costs incident to organization, and legal service expenditures, such as for drafting of documents, minutes of organizational meetings, and terms of the original stock certificates.

Expenditures connected with issuing or selling stock or with the transfer of assets to a corporation are not amortizable. Instead, such costs must be netted against the proceeds of the stock sale. Pre-opening or start-up expenses, such as employee training, advertising, and expenses of lining up suppliers or potential customers, are not organizational expenses, but may be amortizable as start-up expenditures (¶ 904). Likewise, corporate expenditures that are incurred in investigating the creation or acquisition of an active trade or business or in creating such a trade or business do not qualify for amortization as organizational expenses, but may qualify as start-up expenses (Rev. Rul. 99-23).[36]

239. Domestic Production Activities. A corporation may claim a deduction against gross income equal to the applicable percentage of its qualified production activities income (QPAI) or its taxable income (whichever is less) (i.e., manufacturer's deduction (¶ 980A)) (Code Sec. 199).[37] The amount of the deduction for any tax year, however, may not exceed 50 percent of the W-2 wages the taxpayer deducts in calculating its QPAI.

References are to Standard Federal Tax Reports; Tax Research Consultant; and Practical Tax Explanations.

[33] ¶ 13,150; CCORP: 9,152; § 26,510.10

[34] ¶ 13,150; CCORP: 9,154; § 26,510.10

[35] ¶ 13,350, ¶ 13,351C; BUSEXP: 9,452.05; § 9,210.05

[36] ¶ 12,371.25; DEPR: 21,404.10; § 9,205.10

[37] ¶ 12,468; BUSEXP: 6,000; § 6,001

Estimated Tax

241. Penalty for Underpayment of Corporate Estimated Tax. A corporation that anticipates a tax bill of $500 or more must estimate its income tax liability for the current tax year and pay four quarterly estimated tax installments (using electronic funds transfers) during that year (Code Sec. 6655).[38] Any underpayment of a required installment results in an addition to tax on the amount of the underpayment for the period of underpayment. The addition to tax is based on current interest rates (¶ 2838).

The period of underpayment begins with the due date of the underpaid installment and ends with the earlier of (1) the date that the underpayment is satisfied or (2) the 15th day of the third month after the close of the tax year. Each estimated tax payment is credited against unpaid installments in the order in which they are required to be paid.

No addition to tax applies if the tax shown on the return (or the actual tax if no return is filed) is less than $500. If there is an underpayment, Form 2220 should be attached to the return to show whether the addition to tax applies and, if so, the amount of the penalty.

What is the Tax? The tax liabilities to which corporate estimated tax applies are: (1) the corporate income tax (¶ 219), the alternative tax on corporate capital gains (¶ 1738), or the income tax imposed on insurance companies (¶ 2370), whichever applies; (2) the alternative minimum tax (¶ 1401), and (3) the tax on gross transportation income of foreign corporations (Code Sec. 887).[39] For this purpose, the 30-percent tax on foreign corporations not connected with a U.S. business is considered a corporate income tax. The total expected tax liability is reduced by the sum of the credits against tax. Special rules apply for estimating the book income adjustment by corporations that use the annualization method to calculate estimated tax liability.

243. Time and Amount of Corporate Estimated Tax Payments. For calendar-year corporations, estimated tax installments are due on April 15, June 15, September 15, and December 15. Installments of fiscal-year corporations are due on the 15th day of the fourth, sixth, ninth, and twelfth months of the tax year (Code Sec. 6655).[40] If any due date falls on a Saturday, Sunday, or legal holiday, the payment is due on the first following business day. Corporations required to deposit taxes must transfer their tax deposits electronically from their accounts to the IRS's general account (Reg. § 31.6302-1(h)).[41]

To avoid a penalty for underpayment of estimated taxes (¶ 241), each installment must equal at least 25 percent of the lesser of:

(1) 100 percent of the tax shown on the current year's tax return (or of the actual tax if no return is filed), or

(2) 100 percent of the tax shown on the corporation's return for the preceding tax year, provided a positive tax liability was shown and the preceding tax year consisted of 12 months (Code Sec. 6655(d))[42] (but see special limitation on "*Large Corporations,*" below).

A lower installment amount may be paid if it is shown that use of an annualized income method or, for corporations with seasonal incomes, an adjusted seasonal method would result in a lower required installment (¶ 245).

Example: The X Corporation, a calendar-year taxpayer, estimates at the end of March that its federal income tax for the current tax year would be $800,000. Accordingly, it pays $200,000 [25% of ($800,000 × 100%)] of estimated tax by April

References are to Standard Federal Tax Reports; Tax Research Consultant; and Practical Tax Explanations.

[38] ¶ 39,565; FILEBUS: 6,050, FILEBUS: 6,056, FILEBUS: 6,058; § 26,015.05, § 26,015.10

[39] ¶ 27,580; INTL: 3,602

[40] ¶ 39,565; FILEBUS: 6,054.05; § 26,015.10

[41] ¶ 38,055B; FILEBUS: 6,106.10; § 39,320.20

[42] ¶ 39,565; FILEBUS: 6,052.05; § 26,015.05

15, and another $200,000 by June 15. At the end of August, a recalculation shows that its tax for the year is expected to be $1 million. Assuming that there is no later change in the estimated tax, the estimated tax installments for September and December are computed as follows:

Estimated tax required to be paid by 9/15 [75% of ($1 million × 100%)]	$750,000
Less payments made in April and June	$400,000
Payment due in September	$350,000
Payment due in December [25% of ($1 million × 100%)]	$250,000
Total estimated tax payments	$1,000,000

Large Corporations. A "large corporation"—one with taxable income of at least $1 million in any one of the three immediately preceding tax years—is prohibited from using its prior year's tax liability (method (2), above), *except* in determining the first installment of its tax year (Code Sec. 6655(d)(2) and (g)(2)).[43] Any reduction in a large corporation's first installment as a result of using the prior year's tax must be recaptured in the corporation's second installment. In applying the $1-million test, taxable income is computed without regard to net operating loss carryovers or capital loss carrybacks. Also, a controlled group of corporations (¶ 291) must divide a single $1-million amount among its members.

Corporations with $1 Billion in Assets. Corporations with more than $1 billion in assets are required to make larger and smaller estimated tax payments in certain months in 2017. Specifically, for a payment due in July, August, or September of 2017, the amount due is 100.25 percent of the estimated tax the taxpayer would otherwise be required to pay. For a payment in October, November, or December of 2017, the amount due is 99.75 percent of the amount that would otherwise be due (Act Sec. 4 of Amendment to Africa Growth and Opportunity Act (P.L. 112-163)).

245. Annualization and Seasonal Income Methods. A corporation may make a lower required installment (¶ 243) where its annualized income installment or adjusted seasonal installment is less than the regular amount of the required installment. The annualized income installment is the product of the tax on the corporation's taxable income (including alternative minimum taxable income and modified alternative minimum taxable income) for the corresponding portion of the tax year on an annualized basis, and reduced by all prior required installments for the tax year (Code Sec. 6655(e); Reg. § 1.6655-2).[44] A corporation can choose between using the standard monthly periods or either of two optional monthly periods. An election to use either of the two optional monthly periods is effective only for the year of election. The election must be made on or before the date required for the first installment payment.

Installment	*Standard Monthly Periods*	*Optional Monthly Periods #1*	*Optional Monthly Periods #2*
1st	first 3 months	first 2 months	first 3 months
2nd	first 3 months	first 4 months	first 5 months
3rd	first 6 months	first 7 months	first 8 months
4th	first 9 months	first 10 months	first 11 months

To annualize income, multiply the income for the applicable period by 12 and divide by the number of months in the period. A corporation that uses the annualization method and switches to another method during the same tax year must, in its first installment under the new method, recapture 100 percent of any reduction achieved in the earlier installments.

Adjusted Seasonal Installments. Adjusted seasonal installments may be used only if the average of the corporation's taxable income for the same six-month period in the three preceding years was 70 percent or more of annual taxable income. An adjusted

References are to Standard Federal Tax Reports; Tax Research Consultant; and Practical Tax Explanations.

[43] ¶ 39,565; FILEBUS: 6,052.05; § 26,015.05

[44] ¶ 39,565, ¶ 39,568; FILEBUS: 6,052.10; § 26,015.10

seasonal installment is the excess (if any) of (a) 100 percent of the amount determined by following the four steps set forth below over (b) the aggregate amount of all prior required installments for the tax year. The steps are as follows:

(1) take the taxable income for the portion of the tax year up to the month in which the installment is due (filing month);

(2) divide this amount by the "base period percentage" for such months;

(3) determine the tax on the result; and

(4) multiply the tax by the base period percentage for the filing month and all preceding months during the tax year.

For any period of months, the "base period percentage" is the average percentage that the taxable income for the corresponding months in each of the three preceding tax years bears to the taxable income for those years (Code Sec. 6655(e)(3); Reg. § 1.6655-3).[45]

247. Quick Refund for Estimated Tax Overpayment. A corporation may apply for a refund of an overpayment of estimated tax immediately after the close of its tax year if its overpayment is at least 10 percent of the expected tax liability and amounts to at least $500. Overpayment, for this purpose, is the excess of the estimated tax paid over what the corporation expects its final income tax liability to be at the time the application is filed. The application must be filed by the 15th day of the 3rd month after the close of the tax year and before the day on which the corporation files its income tax return for the tax year for which a quick refund is requested (Code Sec. 6425; Reg. §§ 1.6425-1—1.6425-3).[46] The taxpayer should file Form 4466. An extension of time to file Form 1120 will not extend the time for filing Form 4466.

Accumulated Earnings Tax

251. Accumulated Earnings Tax. In addition to being liable for regular income taxes, every corporation (other than personal holding companies (¶ 277), tax-exempt organizations (¶ 601), or passive foreign investment companies (¶ 2490)) may be liable for the accumulated earnings tax. The tax is in the form of a penalty and applies if a corporation is formed or used for the purpose of avoiding the imposition of income tax upon its shareholders by permitting its earnings or profits to accumulate instead of being distributed (Code Secs. 531 and 532).[47] A corporation is presumed to be availed of for a tax avoidance purpose if its earnings are accumulated beyond the reasonable needs of its business (¶ 265). The tax may be imposed on a corporation without regard to the number of shareholders, meaning it applies to both closely held and publicly held corporations.

For tax years beginning before January 1, 2013, the accumulated earnings tax is 15 percent of the corporation's accumulated taxable income (¶ 253). There is no particular form which a corporation files to compute the tax. Instead, the IRS enforces the tax by reaching a conclusion whether enough dividends were paid during the tax year based on the corporation's filed income tax return. Interest on any underpayment is computed from the date the corporation's tax return is due without regard to extensions (Code Sec. 6601(b)(4)).[48]

Caution: For tax years beginning after 2012, absent further Congressional action, the accumulated earnings tax rate increases to 39.6 percent, the highest rate of tax for individuals that would be applicable in those years.

253. Accumulated Taxable Income. The accumulated earnings tax is imposed on a corporation's accumulated taxable income for the tax year. Accumulated taxable income is the corporation's taxable income with certain adjustments, and minus the sum of the

References are to Standard Federal Tax Reports; Tax Research Consultant; and Practical Tax Explanations.

[45] ¶ 39,565, ¶ 39,570; FILEBUS: 6,052.10; § 26,015.10

[46] ¶ 38,840–¶ 38,843; IRS: 33,358; § 26,015.20

[47] ¶ 23,001, ¶ 23,010; CCORP: 18,250; § 26,901

[48] ¶ 39,410; PENALTY: 9,054.05

dividends-paid deduction (¶ 259) and the accumulated earnings credit (¶ 261). The adjustments to taxable income include the following (Code Sec. 535; Reg. § 1.535-2):[49]

(1) A deduction is allowed for federal income taxes, as well as for income, war, and excess profits taxes of foreign countries and U.S. possessions (to the extent not allowed as deductions in computing taxable income) accrued during the tax year, regardless of the accounting method used. The deduction will not include any accumulated earnings tax or personal holding company tax paid.

(2) Charitable contributions for the tax year are deductible without regard to the 10-percent-of-taxable-income limitation.

(3) No deduction is allowed for dividends received or for dividends paid by public utilities on certain preferred stock.

(4) The net operating loss deduction is not allowed.

(5) A corporation (other than a mere holding company or investment company) is allowed a deduction for net capital losses incurred for the tax year determined without regard to capital loss carryovers. The deduction, however, is reduced by the lesser of the (1) capital gains deducted in earlier years that have not already been used in a previous year to reduce the capital loss reduction or (2) the corporation's accumulated earnings and profits at the close of the preceding year.

(6) A deduction is allowed for net capital gains for the year taking into account capital loss carryovers, reduced by the taxes attributable to them. In the case of a foreign corporation, only net capital gains that are effectively connected with the conduct of a trade or business within the United States that are not exempt under treaty are taken into account.

(7) No capital loss carryback or carryover is allowed.

(8) A controlled foreign corporation (CFC) is allowed to deduct the amount of its subpart F income which is required to be included in the income of its U.S. shareholders (¶ 2488). However, if the corporation would otherwise calculate its accumulated taxable income on a gross basis, then the corporation's deduction must be reduced by any deduction which may have reduced a U.S. shareholder's income inclusion.

Although exempt interest income is excludable from accumulated taxable income for purposes of determining the accumulated earnings tax base, it is considered for purposes of determining whether earnings and profits have been accumulated beyond the reasonable needs of the business (¶ 265).[50]

Holding or Investment Companies. If a corporation is a mere holding or investment company, then in determining its accumulated taxable income: (1) net capital losses may not be deducted, (2) net short-term capital gains are deductible only to the extent of any capital loss carryovers, and (3) accumulated earnings and profits cannot be less than they would have been had the rules in (1) and (2) been applied in computing earnings and profits (Code Sec. 535(b)(8)).[51]

Foreign Corporations. A foreign corporation is subject to U.S. income tax on U.S. source income, including the accumulated earnings tax (¶ 2425). Thus, foreign source income is generally excluded in accumulated taxable income. However, if 10 percent or more of the earnings and profits of any foreign corporation is derived from U.S. sources, then any distribution out of such earnings and profits (and any interest payment) retains its character as U.S.-source income upon receipt by a U.S.-owned foreign corporation (Code Sec. 535(d)).[52] A U.S.-owned foreign corporation is any foreign corporation in which 50 percent or more of voting power or total value is held directly or indirectly by U.S. persons.

References are to Standard Federal Tax Reports; Tax Research Consultant; and Practical Tax Explanations.

[49] ¶ 23,040, ¶ 23,042; CCORP: 18,252; § 26,905.10

[50] ¶ 23,018.897; CCORP: 18,150; § 26,910.10

[51] ¶ 23,040; CCORP: 18,104

[52] ¶ 23,040; CCORP: 18,052

259. Dividends-Paid Deduction. Dividends paid by regulated investment companies (mutual), real estate investment trusts (REITs), personal holding companies and corporations subject to the accumulated earnings tax are deductible in determining taxable income (Code Sec. 561).[53] The deduction is the sum of dividends paid during the tax year, consent dividends, and, in the case of a personal holding company, dividends carried over from the two preceding tax years (¶ 275). The deduction is unaffected by the taxpayer's accounting method, but rather is based upon the amount of dividends actually paid by the corporation and received by the shareholder. A personal holding company may elect, and a corporation subject to the accumulated earnings tax is required, to include dividends paid within 2 ½ months of the end of the tax year in the deduction (Code Sec. 563).[54]

The dividends-paid deduction may be claimed for any payment which is a distribution of property to shareholders with respect to their stock and paid out of earnings and profits (¶ 747) (Code Sec. 562).[55] For a personal holding company, however, the deduction is up to the amount of undistributed personal holding company income, regardless of its earnings and profits (Code Sec. 316(b) (2) (A)). No deduction is allowed for preferential dividends. On the other hand, distributions in complete liquidation of a corporation other than a personal holding company are included as part of the deduction. Distributions in complete liquidation of a personal holding company can be included depending on whether the distributee is a noncorporate or corporate shareholder. For a regulated investment company, the deduction is computed without regard to capital gain dividends and exempt-interest dividends (¶ 2303). For a REIT, the deduction is computed without regard to excluded net income from foreclosure property (¶ 2329). For a personal holding company, the deduction includes dividends carried over from the two preceding tax years (¶ 275).

Consent Dividend. A consent dividend is any dividend which a shareholder agrees to include in taxable income, even though the corporation does not make an actual distribution (Code Sec. 565).[56] The consent dividend is treated as paid by the corporation on the last day of its tax year and immediately contributed as paid-in capital by the shareholder. Consent dividends may be paid only with respect to consent stock, which is either common stock or preferred stock with unlimited participation; thus, the consent dividend must not be a preferential dividend. Shareholders consent on Form 972, which the corporation includes with Form 973 when filing its return to claim the deduction for dividends-paid deduction for consent dividends.

261. Accumulated Earnings Credit. For a corporation other than a mere holding or investment company, the accumulated earnings credit allowed in computing accumulated taxable income (¶ 253) is an amount equal to the part of the earnings and profits of the tax year retained for the reasonable needs of the business, reduced by the net capital gain (which is itself reduced by the amount of income tax attributable to it). A minimum amount of $250,000 ($150,000 for personal service corporations (¶ 219)) may be accumulated from past and present earnings combined by all corporations, including holding or investment companies. This minimum amount is the only credit allowable to a holding or investment company (Code Sec. 535(c)).[57] Only one $250,000 accumulated earnings credit is allowed to a controlled group of corporations (¶ 291) (Code Sec. 1561(a) (2)).[58] The single credit is to be divided equally among the corporations.

263. Basis of Liability for Accumulated Earnings Tax. Although the accumulated earnings tax is computed as a percentage of the corporation's accumulated taxable income (¶ 251), liability for the tax hinges on whether the corporation was formed or availed of to avoid the income tax on income otherwise receivable by its shareholders. A corporation can be subject to the accumulated earnings tax for a year in which it has accumulated taxable income on hand even though, because of a stock redemption, no

References are to Standard Federal Tax Reports; Tax Research Consultant; and Practical Tax Explanations.

[53] ¶ 23,450; CCORP: 9,300; §26,905.15

[54] ¶ 23,490; CCORP: 9,308; §26,905.15

[55] ¶ 23,470; CCORP: 9,304; §26,905.15

[56] ¶ 23,530; CCORP: 9,316; §26,905.15

[57] ¶ 23,040; CCORP: 18,254; §26,905.20

[58] ¶ 33,340; CCORP: 18,254

earnings and profits were accumulated for the tax year (*GPD, Inc.*, CA-6, 75-1 USTC ¶ 9142).[59]

The courts have shifted the focus of attention from earnings and profits to liquidity.[60] The reason for this change in emphasis is that the earnings-and-profits figure often is no indication of the funds available to the corporation to meet its business needs and pay dividends to its shareholders. Whether a corporation can be subjected to the accumulated earnings tax is therefore determined by comparing the reasonable needs of its business (¶ 265) to its total liquid assets at the end of the year. Liquid assets include the corporation's cash and marketable securities.

265. Reasonable Needs of the Business. In order to justify an accumulation of income, there must be a reasonable business need for it and a definite plan for its use. Since a corporation is given a credit (¶ 261) for its reasonable business needs (including reasonably anticipated needs) in figuring the accumulated earnings tax, the resolution of most disputes hinges on this issue.

The Code does not contain a comprehensive definition of reasonable business needs. However, a number of acceptable and unacceptable grounds for accumulating income are listed in the regulations (Reg. § 1.537-2).[61] Acceptable grounds include: (1) business expansion and plant replacement; (2) acquisition of a business through purchase of stock or assets; (3) debt retirement; (4) working capital; and (5) investments or loans to suppliers or customers necessary to the maintenance of the corporation's business. The self-insurance of product liability risks is also a business need for which earnings and profits may be accumulated to a reasonable extent (Code Sec. 537(b)(4); Reg. § 1.537-2(b)(6)).[62]

Unacceptable grounds include: (1) loans to shareholders and expenditures for their personal benefit; (2) loans to relatives or friends of shareholders or to others who have no reasonable connection with the business; (3) loans to a sister (commonly controlled) corporation; (4) investments that are not related to the business; and (5) accumulations to provide against unrealistic hazards (Reg. § 1.537-2(c)).[63]

Courts have used an operating-cycle approach to determine the amount of working capital a corporation needs. An operating cycle consists of (1) an inventory cycle (conversion of cash and raw materials into inventory), (2) a receivables cycle (conversion of inventory into accounts receivable and cash), and, possibly, (3) a credit cycle (accounts payable turnover).[64]

A stock redemption under Code Sec. 303 to pay death taxes and expenses (¶ 745) and a redemption of stock in order to bring a private foundation within the 20-percent excess business holdings limit (¶ 640) are good cause for an accumulation of income (Code Sec. 537(a)).[65] Although other types of stock redemptions are not accorded this certainty, accumulations to redeem a minority interest (or the interest of one of two 50-percent stockholders) have been approved where they would eliminate dissent, would prevent the minority interest from falling into hostile hands, or were an essential ingredient of an employee incentive plan. Court decisions in this area show that except in rare circumstances, the redemption of a majority interest is not good cause for accumulating income.[66]

267. Burden of Proof of Reasonable Business Needs. On the issue of whether a corporation has accumulated income in excess of the reasonable needs of its business, the burden of proof in the Tax Court is on the government in two instances (Code Sec. 534; Reg. § 1.534-2).[67] First, the burden is on the government if, in advance of a formal deficiency notice, it does not notify the corporation by certified or registered mail of its

References are to Standard Federal Tax Reports; Tax Research Consultant; and Practical Tax Explanations.

[59] ¶ 23,045.37; CCORP: 18,100

[60] ¶ 23,045.65, ¶ 23,074.36; CCORP: 18,170; § 26,910.10

[61] ¶ 23,072; CCORP: 18,150; § 26,910.10

[62] ¶ 23,070, ¶ 23,072; CCORP: 18,166

[63] ¶ 23,072; CCORP: 18,150

[64] ¶ 23,074.625; CCORP: 18,158

[65] ¶ 23,070; CCORP: 18,168; § 26,910.10

[66] ¶ 23,018.895; CCORP: 18,168

[67] ¶ 23,020, ¶ 23,022, ¶ 23,025; CCORP: 18,200; § 26,915

intention to assess a deficiency based in whole or in part on the accumulated earnings tax or fails to state the tax years at issue. Second, in the event of such notification, the burden falls on the government if the corporation responds within 60 days with a statement of the grounds on which it relies to establish the reasonableness of all or any part of its accumulation of income. In other courts, the burden of proof is wholly on the corporation.

269. Tax Avoidance Intent for Accumulated Earnings Tax. One of the conditions that must exist before a corporation can be subject to the accumulated earnings tax is an intent to avoid the income tax on its shareholders (Code Sec. 533).[68] If the corporation accumulates income beyond the reasonable needs of its business (or if it is a mere holding or investment company), a presumption of tax avoidance intent arises. This presumption can be overcome by showing that tax avoidance was not one of the purposes of the accumulation of income (*Donruss Co.*, 69-1 USTC ¶ 9167, and *Shaw-Walker*, 69-1 USTC ¶ 9198).[69]

Personal Service Corporations

273. Personal Service Corporations. A personal service corporation is one that furnishes personal services performed by employee-owners (Code Secs. 269A and 280H).[70] An "employee-owner" is an employee who owns, directly or indirectly, more than 10 percent of the outstanding stock of the corporation on any day during the company's tax year. If a corporation meets these requirements and also has as its principal purpose the avoidance or evasion of federal income tax by reducing the income of any employee-owner or securing tax benefits for any employee-owner that would not otherwise be available, the IRS may reallocate income, deductions, and other tax attributes between the personal service corporation and the employee-owner. The purpose of evading or avoiding income tax can be shown by a reduction in the tax liability of, or the increase of tax benefits to, an employee-owner or by any other increase in tax benefits. Code Sec. 280H restricts the amount that can be deducted by a personal service corporation for amounts paid to owners if the corporation has elected a non-calendar tax year.

Personal Holding Companies

275. Tax on Personal Holding Companies. In addition to being liable for regular income taxes, a corporation that is classified as a personal holding company (¶ 277) will be liable for a separate tax on its "undistributed personal holding company income." The personal holding company tax was enacted when the highest corporate income tax rate was well below the highest individual income tax rate. It was designed to prevent individuals from establishing a corporation to receive and hold investment income or compensation so that it would be taxed at a lower rate (i.e., "incorporated pocket-books"). Even though the corporate and individual income tax rates have somewhat equalized, the personal holding company tax still applies.

Effective for tax years beginning before January 1, 2013, the personal holding company tax is 15 percent of a corporation's undistributed personal holding company income (Code Sec. 541; Reg. § 1.541-1).[71]

> **Caution:** For tax years beginning after 2012, absent further Congressional action, the accumulated earnings tax rate increases to 39.6 percent, the highest rate of tax for individuals that would be applicable in those years.

Undistributed personal holding company income is computed by making the following adjustments to the corporation's taxable income, not just its personal holding company income (Code Sec. 545).[72]

References are to Standard Federal Tax Reports; Tax Research Consultant; and Practical Tax Explanations.

[68] ¶ 23,015; CCORP: 18,100; § 26,910.05

[69] ¶ 23,018.26; CCORP: 18,102; § 26,910.05

[70] ¶ 14,300, ¶ 15,160; CCORP: 100; § 27,101

[71] ¶ 23,152, ¶ 23,153; CCORP: 36,250; § 27,001

[72] ¶ 23,250; CCORP: 36,250; § 27,010.20

(1) A deduction is allowed for federal income taxes, as well as for income, war, and excess profits taxes of foreign countries and U.S. possessions (to the extent not allowed as deductions in computing taxable income) accrued during the tax year, regardless of the accounting method used.

(2) Charitable contributions for the tax year are deductible but the 20-to-50-percent contribution base for individuals must be used, rather than the 10-percent base normally allowed to corporations.

(3) No deduction is allowed for dividends received or for dividends paid by public utilities on certain preferred stock.

(4) The net operating loss deduction is not allowed.

(5) A deduction is allowed for net capital gains for the year, reduced by the taxes attributable to them. In the case of a foreign corporation, only net capital gains that are effectively connected with the conduct of a trade or business within the United States that are not exempt under treaty are taken into account.

(6) Any deduction for ordinary and necessary business expenses, as well as depreciation, attributable to the operation and maintenance of property owned or operated by the corporation is limited only to the extent of derived from the property.

After these adjustments are made, the dividends-paid deduction is deducted from the adjusted taxable income (¶ 259). The amount of deduction for a personal holding company includes a dividend carryover from the two preceding tax years (Code Sec. 564).[73] The carryover is the excess of the dividends paid in the two preceding years over the income for such years. Any remaining balance is the corporation's undistributed personal holding company income.

Personal holding company taxes are computed and reported on Schedule PH, which is attached to the corporation's Form 1120.

277. Personal Holding Company Defined. A "personal holding company" (Code Sec. 542; Reg. §§1.542-1—1.542-3)[74] is any corporation in which at least 60 percent of adjusted ordinary gross income for the tax year is personal holding company income (¶ 281) and at any time during the last half of the tax year more than 50 percent in value of its outstanding stock is owned, directly or indirectly, by or for not more than five individuals (¶ 285). For this purpose, individuals include: a qualified pension, profit-sharing, or stock bonus plan (¶ 2101); a supplemental unemployment benefit (SUB) trust (¶ 692); a private foundation (¶ 631); or part of a trust permanently set aside or used exclusively for charitable purposes (¶ 537).

A number of specified corporations are exempt from the personal holding company tax even though they meet the income and stock ownership qualifications (Code Sec. 542(c)). These include tax-exempt corporations (¶ 601); banks or domestic building and loan associations (¶ 2383); certain lending and finance companies that meet gross income, deduction and loan tests; life insurance companies (¶ 2370); surety companies, corporations in bankruptcy or similar proceedings (unless the purpose of the case is to avoid the personal holding company tax), and foreign corporations. A small business investment company is exempt from personal holding company tax if it is licensed by the Small Business Administration, but only if any shareholder of the company owns directly or indirectly a 5-percent-or-more proprietary interest in a small business concern to which the investment company provides funds or 5 percent or more in value of outstanding stock of such a concern.

281. Personal Holding Company Income. The term "personal holding company income" for purposes of the personal holding company tax (¶ 275) means the portion of the adjusted ordinary gross income that consists of (Code Sec. 543):[75]

References are to Standard Federal Tax Reports; Tax Research Consultant; and Practical Tax Explanations.

[73] ¶ 23,510; CCORP: 9,314; §26,905.15

[74] ¶ 23,190–¶ 23,193; CCORP: 36,000; §27,001

[75] ¶ 23,210; CCORP: 36,150; §27,010.15

(1) dividends, interest, royalties (other than mineral, oil and gas, copyright, or computer software royalties), and annuities; however, such income does not include interest received by a broker or dealer in connection with any securities or money market instruments held as property held primarily for sale to customers, margin accounts, or any financing for a customer secured by securities or money market instruments;

(2) rents, unless they constitute 50 percent or more of the adjusted ordinary gross income and unless the sum of dividends paid during the tax year, dividends paid after the close of the tax year but considered paid on the last day of the year, and consent dividends (¶ 259), equals or exceeds the amount by which personal holding company income exceeds 10 percent of the ordinary gross income;

(3) mineral, oil, and gas royalties, unless (a) they constitute 50 percent or more of the adjusted ordinary gross income, (b) the other personal holding company income for the tax year is not more than 10 percent of the ordinary gross income, and (c) the ordinary and necessary business expense deductions, other than compensation for personal services rendered by shareholders, are 15 percent or more of adjusted ordinary gross income;

(4) copyright royalties, unless (a) apart from royalties derived from the works of shareholders, they make up 50 percent or more of the ordinary gross income, (b) personal holding company income for the tax year (not taking into account copyright royalties and dividends in any corporation in which the taxpayer owns at least 50 percent of all classes of voting stock and at least 50 percent of the value of all classes of stock) is 10 percent or less of the ordinary gross income, and (c) ordinary and necessary business expense deductions, other than compensation for personal services rendered by shareholders and deductions for royalties, equal or exceed 25 percent of the amount by which the ordinary gross income exceeds the sum of royalties paid or accrued and depreciation allowed;

(5) rents from the distribution and exhibition of produced films (that is, rents from a film interest acquired before the film production was substantially complete) unless such rents are 50 percent or more of the ordinary gross income;

(6) amounts received as compensation for the use of, or right to use, tangible property of the corporation where, at any time during the tax year, 25 percent or more in value of the outstanding stock of the corporation is owned, directly or indirectly, by or for an individual entitled to the use of the property, whether such right is obtained directly from the corporation or by means of a sublease or other arrangement. This paragraph applies only if the corporation's other personal holding company income (computed with certain adjustments) for the tax year is more than 10 percent of its ordinary gross income;

(7) amounts received by a corporation from contracts for personal services, including gain from the sale or other disposition thereof, if (a) some person other than the corporation has the right to designate (by name or by description) the individual who is to perform the services or if the individual who is to perform the services is designated (by name or by description) in the contract and (b) at some time during the tax year 25 percent or more in value of the outstanding stock of the corporation is owned, directly or indirectly, by or for the individual who has performed, is to perform, or may be designated (by name or by description) as the one to perform such services; and

(8) income required to be reported by a corporate beneficiary under the income tax provisions relating to estates and trusts.

Active Business Computer Software Royalties. "Active business computer software royalties" received in connection with the licensing of computer software are excluded from personal holding company income (Code Sec. 543(d)).[76] To qualify for the exclusion: (1) the royalties must be derived by a corporation actively engaged in the trade or

[76] ¶ 23,210; CCORP: 36,156.15

business of developing, manufacturing, or producing computer software; (2) the royalties must make up at least 50 percent of the corporation's gross income; (3) business and research expenses relating to the royalties must equal or exceed 25 percent of ordinary gross income; and (4) dividends must equal or exceed the excess of personal holding company income over 10 percent of ordinary gross income. If one member of an affiliated group receives software royalties, it will be treated as having met the above requirements if another member meets the requirements.

283. Adjusted Ordinary Gross Income. In determining whether 60 percent or more of a corporation's "adjusted ordinary gross income" is personal holding company income (¶ 281), the following adjustments must be made (Code Sec. 543(b)(2)):[77]

(1) Rental income must be reduced by deductions for depreciation and amortization, property taxes, interest, and rents paid that are attributable to such income.

(2) Income from mineral, oil, and gas royalties and from working interests in oil and gas wells must be reduced by deductions for depreciation, amortization and depletion, property and severance taxes, interest, and rents paid which are attributable to such income.

(3) Interest on U.S. bonds held for sale by a dealer who is making a primary market for these obligations and interest on condemnation awards, judgments, and tax refunds must be excluded.

(4) Rent received from the lease of tangible personal property manufactured by a taxpayer engaged in substantial manufacturing or production of property of the same type must be reduced by deductions for depreciation and amortization, taxes, rent, and interest paid that are attributable to such income.

All capital gains are excluded in determining whether the 60-percent test has been met because it is based on adjusted ordinary gross income.

285. Constructive Ownership of Personal Holding Company. Constructive ownership rules apply in determining whether (1) a corporation is a personal holding company (¶ 277), (2) amounts received under a personal service contract are personal holding company income (¶ 281), (3) copyright royalties are personal holding company income, or (4) compensation for the use of property is personal holding company income (Code Sec. 544; Reg. § 1.544-1).[78] Under the constructive ownership rules:

(1) Stock owned, directly or indirectly, by or for a corporation, partnership, estate, or trust is considered as being owned proportionately by its shareholders, partners, or beneficiaries.

(2) An individual is considered as owning the stock owned, directly or indirectly, by or for his family (brothers and sisters (whole or half blood), spouse, ancestors, and lineal descendants), or by or for his partner.

(3) If any person has an option to acquire stock, such stock is considered as owned by such person. An option to acquire an option, and each one of a series of such options, is regarded as an option to acquire stock. This rule is applied in preference to rule (2), above, when both rules apply.

(4) Stock constructively owned by a corporation, partnership, estate, or trust will be reattributed to its owners or beneficiaries so that they are treated as constructive owners of the stock. However, stock constructively and not actually owned by an individual will not be reattributed.

(5) Outstanding securities convertible into stock (whether or not during the tax year) are considered as outstanding stock, but only if the effect of the inclusion of all such securities is to make the corporation a personal holding company.

References are to Standard Federal Tax Reports; Tax Research Consultant; and Practical Tax Explanations.

[77] ¶ 23,210; CCORP: 36,106; § 27,010.10

[78] ¶ 23,230; CCORP: 36,058; § 27,005

287. Deficiency Dividend Deduction. If a deficiency is determined in the personal holding company tax (¶ 275), the corporation may then distribute dividends and, in redetermining the undistributed personal holding company income, reduce or eliminate the deficiency by means of a deduction for "deficiency dividends" in the amount of the dividends so paid (Code Sec. 547; Reg. §§ 1.547-1—1.547-7).[79] The distribution must be made within 90 days after the deficiency determination. Claim for the deduction must be filed within 120 days of the determination.

Controlled Corporate Groups

289. Allocation of Tax Benefits. A controlled group of corporations (¶ 291) is allowed only one set of graduated income tax brackets (¶ 219) and one $250,000 accumulated earnings credit (¶ 261). Controlled groups are also allowed one $40,000 exemption amount for alternative minimum tax purposes (¶ 1470). Each of these items is to be allocated equally among the members of the group unless they all consent to a different apportionment (Code Sec. 1561).[80]

Dividends-Received Deduction. Since a parent-subsidiary controlled group is also an affiliated group, a 100-percent dividends-received deduction may be taken with respect to dividends paid from one member to another (¶ 223B). A 70-percent deduction is allowed for distributions between members of a brother-sister controlled group (¶ 291).

291. What Is a Controlled Group. There are two types of controlled corporate groups—parent-subsidiary and brother-sister (Code Sec. 1563(a)).[81] A parent-subsidiary controlled group exists if: (1) one or more chains of corporations are connected through stock ownership with a common parent corporation; (2) 80 percent or more of the voting power or value of the stock of each corporation in the group other than the parent is owned by one or more corporations in the group; and (3) the common parent owns at least 80 percent of the voting power or value of the stock of one of the other corporations in the group (not counting stock owned directly by other members).

A brother-sister controlled group exists if five or fewer persons (individuals, estates, or trusts) own stock possessing more than 50 percent of the total combined voting power of all classes of stock entitled to vote, or more than 50 percent of the total value of all stock, taking into account the stock ownership of each person only to the extent the person owns stock in each corporation.

293. Controlled Corporations—Expenses, Interest, and Losses. Controlled groups of corporations are subject to the related-party transaction rules of Code Sec. 267 (¶ 1717), under which controlled members must use a matching rule that defers the deductibility of an expense or interest by a payor until the payment is included in the payee's income (Code Sec. 267(a)(2)).[82] Also, losses on sales between members of a controlled group must be deferred until the property is sold to an unrelated person (Code Sec. 267(f)).[83] The loss-deferral rule does not apply, however, to sales to a domestic international sales corporation (DISC) (see ¶ 2498), to sales of inventory in the ordinary course of business if one of the parties is a foreign corporation, or to loan repayment losses attributable to foreign currency value reductions.

Consolidated Returns

295. Consolidated Returns. The privilege of filing a consolidated return is extended to an affiliated group of corporations under Code Secs. 1501 and 1504(b).[84] An "affiliated group" is defined as one or more chains of includible corporations connected through stock ownership with a common parent that is an includible corporation if (1) the common parent directly owns stock possessing at least 80 percent of the total voting power of at least one of the other includible corporations and has a value equal to at least

References are to Standard Federal Tax Reports; Tax Research Consultant; and Practical Tax Explanations.

[79] ¶ 23,290–¶ 23,297; CCORP: 36,300; § 27,015

[80] ¶ 33,340; CCORP: 42,050

[81] ¶ 33,360; CCORP: 42,102, CCORP: 42,104

[82] ¶ 14,150; BUSEXP: 21,160; § 17,605

[83] ¶ 14,150; CCORP: 42,260, SALES: 39,112; § 17,605

[84] ¶ 33,121, ¶ 33,260; CCORP: 45,050

80 percent of the total value of the stock of the corporation, and (2) stock meeting the 80-percent test in each includible corporation other than the common parent is owned directly by one or more of the other includible corporations (Code Sec. 1504(a)).[85]

A consolidated return may be filed only if all corporations that were members of the affiliated group *at any time* during the tax year consent to all the consolidated return regulations prior to the last day for filing the return. The making of a consolidated return is such consent. The common parent corporation, when filing a consolidated return, must attach Form 851. In addition, for the first year a consolidated return is filed, each subsidiary must attach a Form 1122 (consent to be included in the consolidated return).

The following corporations may not file consolidated returns (Code Sec. 1504(b)):[86]

(1) tax-exempt corporations (¶ 601), except that such organizations may be affiliated with other such organizations at least one of which is organized only to hold title for exempt organizations and from which the others derive income;

(2) life insurance companies (¶ 2370), except for those included in the group at the election of the common parent (Code Sec. 1504(c));[87]

(3) foreign corporations;

(4) corporations electing the Sec. 936 possessions tax credit (¶ 2419);

(5) regulated investment companies and real estate investment trusts (but see ¶ 2340 for circumstances in which a REIT may treat income and deductions of a qualified subsidiary as its own);

(6) domestic international sales corporations (DISCs); and

(7) S corporations.

297. Advantages and Disadvantages. The advantages in filing consolidated returns include: (1) offsetting operating losses of one company against the profits of another (see the rule for dual resident companies below); (2) offsetting capital losses of one company against the capital gains of another (see ¶ 2285 on newly acquired corporations); (3) avoidance of tax on intercompany distributions; (4) deferral of income on intercompany transactions; (5) use by the corporate group of the excess of one member's foreign tax credit over its limitation; and (6) designation of the parent corporation as agent of the group for all tax purposes.

The disadvantages include: (1) the effect on later years' returns; (2) deferral of losses on intercompany transactions; (3) additional bookkeeping required to keep track of deferred intercompany transactions; (4) intercompany profit in inventories still within the group must be reflected in annual inventory adjustments; (5) possible elimination of foreign tax credits when the limiting fraction is diminished because of lack of foreign income on the part of some members; and (6) possible accumulated earnings tax liability when the consolidated accumulated earnings and profits of the group exceed the minimum credit amount.

Dual Resident Companies. If a U.S. corporation is subject to foreign tax on its worldwide income, or on a residence basis as opposed to a source basis, any net operating loss it incurs in a year cannot reduce the taxable income of any other member of a U.S. affiliated group for any tax year (Reg. § 1.1503-2(c)).[88] The IRS has issued regulations addressing the losses of dual resident companies filing consolidated returns (Reg. § § 1.1503(d)-1—1.1503(d)-8).[89]

Preferred Dividends. Income out of which a member of an affiliated group, other than a common parent, distributes preferred dividends to a nonmember may not be offset by the group's net operating losses or capital losses (Code Sec. 1503(f)).[90] Taxes on that income may not be offset by most group tax credits.

Golden Parachutes. All members of an affiliated group are treated as a single corporation when determining excessive payments that are contingent on a change in corporate control (¶ 907) (Code Sec. 280G(d)(5)).[91]

References are to Standard Federal Tax Reports; Tax Research Consultant; and Practical Tax Explanations.

[85] ¶ 33,260; CCORP: 45,052
[86] ¶ 33,260; CCORP: 45,050
[87] ¶ 33,260; CCORP: 45,054.10
[88] ¶ 33,242; CCORP: 45,264
[89] ¶ 33,245–¶ 33,252; CCORP: 45,264
[90] ¶ 33,240; CCORP: 45,318
[91] ¶ 15,150; COMPEN: 30,050; § 45,020

Chapter 3
S CORPORATIONS

S Corporation Status

301. Introduction—S Corporation Status. An S corporation is a corporation that elects and is eligible to choose S corporation status (¶ 303–¶ 305) and whose shareholders at the time consent to the corporation's choice (¶ 306). In general, an S corporation does not pay any income tax (with exceptions discussed in ¶ 335 and following). Instead, the corporation's income and deductions are passed through to its shareholders. The shareholders then must report the income and deductions on their own income tax returns.

To the extent the special S corporation rules (found in Code Sec. 1361 and following) do not apply, S corporations are governed by the "regular" (C corporation) corporate tax rules. Thus, while the taxation of income earned by, and the allocation of losses incurred by, S corporations closely parallel the taxation of partnerships with respect to items of partnership income and loss, S corporations generally are treated as regular corporations for purposes of the rules relating to corporate distributions, redemptions, liquidations, and reorganizations, as well as contributions of capital by S corporation shareholders (Code Sec. 1371).[1]

303. Corporations Eligible to Elect S Corporation Status. To become an S corporation, an organization must be a "small business corporation" (Code Sec. 1361; Reg. § 1.1361-1(b)).[2] All the following requirements must be met:

(1) The entity must be a domestic corporation that is organized under the laws of any state or U.S. territory or a domestic eligible entity (like a partnership or limited liability company) that elects to be taxed as a corporation under the check-the-box rules (Reg. §§ 1.1361-1(c), 301.7701-3).[3]

(2) The corporation may have as shareholders only individuals, estates, certain trusts, and certain exempt organizations. Partnerships and corporations cannot be shareholders.

(3) Only U.S. citizens or residents can be shareholders.

(4) The corporation can have only one class of stock.

A few limited types of corporations are ineligible to be small business corporations (Code Sec. 1361(b)(2)):[4]

- a financial institution that uses the reserve method of accounting;
- an insurance company taxed under subchapter L of the Code (¶ 2370);
- a corporation that has elected to take the Puerto Rico and possessions tax credit (¶ 2419); or
- a DISC or former DISC.

References are to Standard Federal Tax Reports; Tax Research Consultant; and Practical Tax Explanations.

[1] ¶ 32,140; SCORP: 368; § 28,901

[2] ¶ 32,021, ¶ 32,024A; SCORP: 150; § 28,001

[3] ¶ 32,024A, ¶ 43,080; PART: 3,102, SCORP: 152

[4] ¶ 32,021; SCORP: 154; § 28,001

An existing domestic eligible entity that is treated as a partnership for tax purposes is allowed to change its tax status and elect to be taxed as an S corporation. In other words, provided requirements applicable to check-the-box elections and S corporations are met, the entity may elect to change its tax status from partnership to corporation and also file an S election. There will be no intervening C year between the partnership tax year and the S tax year, so long as the check-the-box and S elections are effective on the same date and both sets of deadlines are met (Rev. Rul. 2009-15).[5]

100-Shareholder Limitation. A qualifying S corporation can have no more than 100 shareholders (Code Sec. 1361(b)(1)(A) and (c)).[6] In certain cases, two or more shareholders can be counted as only one shareholder for this purpose if they have one of several relationships to one another. For example, a husband and wife (and their estates) are counted as a single shareholder. In addition, all qualifying members of a family who hold corporation stock are treated as one shareholder of the S corporation. A family is defined as a common ancestor, the lineal descendants of the common ancestor, and the spouses (or former spouses) of the common ancestor and the descendants. The common ancestor can be no more than six generations removed from the youngest shareholder who is treated as a member of the family on the latest of: (1) the date the S corporation election is made (¶ 306); (2) the earliest date that a family member first holds stock in the corporation; or (3) October 22, 2004. Additionally, in determining whether certain children are lineal descendants and members of a family, any legally adopted child, any child lawfully placed with the individual for legal adoption, and any eligible foster child are treated as a child by blood. The estate of a family member is treated as a member of the family for purposes of determining the number of shareholders.

304. Eligible S Corporation Shareholders. All shareholders of an S corporation must be individuals, estates, certain specified trusts, or certain tax-exempt organizations (Code Sec. 1361(b)(1)(B)).[7] Partnerships and C corporations are not eligible to hold stock in an S corporation. The prohibition on a partnership holding S corporation stock does not extend to an LLC with a single, individual member that is taxed as a disregarded entity. The owner of the single-member LLC is treated as the owner of the S corporation stock. Single-member LLCs that "check the box" to be taxed as C corporations may not hold stock in an S corporation. Taxpayers who only hold restricted bank director stock are not considered shareholders for determining whether an S corporation has an ineligible shareholder (Code Sec. 1361(f)).

Trusts. Trusts eligible to hold S corporation shares include grantor trusts (where the grantor is regarded as the shareholder) and voting trusts (where each beneficiary is treated as a shareholder) (Code Sec. 1361(c)(2); Reg. § 1.1361-1(h)).[8]

With one exception, an individual retirement arrangement (IRA) trust is not an eligible S corporation shareholder (*Taproot Administrative Services, Inc.*, 133 TC 202 (2009), aff'd, CA-9, 2012-1 USTC ¶ 50,256; Rev. Rul. 92-73).[9] An IRA or a Roth IRA may hold stock in a bank S corporation if the IRA held the stock on October 22, 2004 (Code Sec. 1361(c)(6)).[10] If the IRA decides to sell bank stock held on October 22, 2004, it can sell the stock to the IRA beneficiary within 120 days after the corporation made the S corporation election without violating the prohibited transaction rules.

Any testamentary trust that receives S corporation stock is an eligible S corporation shareholder unless the trust is treated as an eligible shareholder only for two years after the deemed owner's death. The IRS may extend the two-year limit under an extension for estate tax payments. A charitable remainder trust is not an eligible S corporation shareholder (Rev. Rul. 92-48).[11]

References are to Standard Federal Tax Reports; Tax Research Consultant; and Practical Tax Explanations.

[5] ¶ 32,026.809, ¶ 32,053.58; LLC: 18,200; § 28,010.05

[6] ¶ 32,021; SCORP: 156; § 28,005.05

[7] ¶ 32,021; SCORP: 158; § 28,010.05

[8] ¶ 32,021, ¶ 32,024A; SCORP: 158.20; § 28,010.10, § 28,010.20

[9] ¶ 32,026.815; SCORP: 158.35; § 28,010.40

[10] ¶ 32,021; SCORP: 158.35; § 28,010.40

[11] ¶ 24,468.22; SCORP: 160.05; § 28,715.05

ESBTs. An electing small business trust (ESBT) can be an S corporation shareholder (Code Sec. 1361(c)(2)(A)(v), Code Sec. 1361(c)(2)(B)(v), and (e)).[12] An ESBT is a trust that does not have as a beneficiary any person other than an individual, estate, or organization eligible to accept charitable contributions under Code Sec. 170 (other than a political entity). Any portion of an ESBT that consists of S corporation stock is treated as a separate trust and will be taxed at the highest rate of tax for estates and trusts with limited deductions and credits, and no exemption amount for alternative minimum tax purposes.

Also, an ESBT cannot have any interest acquired by purchase, and a specific election to be treated as an electing trust must have been filed by the trustee. This election is irrevocable without the consent of the IRS. This type of trust does not include a qualified subchapter S trust (see below) or a trust that is exempt from income tax.

In the case of an ESBT, each potential current beneficiary of the trust is treated as a shareholder, except that for any period if there is no potential current beneficiary of the trust, the trust itself is treated as the shareholder. A potential current beneficiary is a person who is entitled to a distribution from the trust or who may receive a distribution at the discretion of any person. Any person who may benefit from a power of appointment is not a potential current beneficiary if the power has not been exercised. If the potential current beneficiaries of an ESBT would disqualify an S corporation, the ESBT has a grace period of one year to dispose of its stock in the S corporation, thereby avoiding disqualification.

QSSTs. A qualified subchapter S trust (QSST) whose beneficiary chooses to be treated as owner of the S corporation stock held by the trust also may hold stock in an S corporation (Code Sec. 1361(d); Reg. § 1.1361-1(j)).[13] A QSST must own stock in at least one S corporation and must distribute all of its income to one individual who is a U.S. citizen or resident. The QSST beneficiary is taxed on all items of income, loss, deduction, and credit attributable to the S corporation stock held by the QSST. However, the QSST, not the beneficiary, is treated as the owner of the S corporation stock for purposes of determining the tax consequences of the trust's disposition of the S corporation stock. In addition, the terms of the QSST must provide:

(1) there may be only one income beneficiary at any time;

(2) trust corpus may be distributed only to the income beneficiary;

(3) each income interest must end no later than the death of the income beneficiary; and

(4) if the trust ends at any time during the life of the income beneficiary, it must distribute all of its assets to the beneficiary.

Successive income beneficiaries are permitted. The income beneficiary's election to treat the trust as a QSST may be revoked only with the consent of the IRS. The election is effective for up to two months and 15 days before the election date. A separate election must be made with respect to each corporation the stock of which is held by the trust and must be made by each successive income beneficiary.

Exempt Organizations as Shareholders. Certain tax-exempt organizations can be S corporation shareholders. These are qualified pension, profit-sharing, and stock bonus plans; charitable organizations; and Code Sec. 501(c)(3) organizations.

QSSS. Even though a corporation generally cannot be an S corporation shareholder, an S corporation is permitted to own a qualified subchapter S subsidiary (QSSS or QSub) (Code Sec. 1361(b)(3)).[14] This includes any domestic corporation that qualifies as an S corporation and is 100 percent owned by an S corporation parent that elects to treat it as a QSSS. A QSSS is not taxed as a separate corporation, and all its tax items are treated as belonging to the parent. Form 8869 should be used by all S corporations to elect QSub treatment for wholly owned corporate subsidiaries.

References are to Standard Federal Tax Reports; Tax Research Consultant; and Practical Tax Explanations.

[12] ¶ 32,021; SCORP: 158.30; § 28,010.30

[13] ¶ 32,021, ¶ 32,024; SCORP: 160; § 28,010.25

[14] ¶ 32,021; SCORP: 550; § 28,020.05

305. Single Class of Stock Requirement.

A qualifying S corporation may have only one class of stock outstanding. These shares must confer identical rights to distribution and liquidation proceeds (Code Sec. 1361(b)(1)(D) and (c)(5); Reg. § 1.1361-1(l)).[15] Differences in voting rights, however, are permitted. A corporate obligation that qualifies as "straight debt" is not considered a second class of stock. Buy-sell and redemption agreements restricting transferability of the stock are generally disregarded in determining whether the corporation has a single class of stock.

Stock of an S corporation does not include stock received for the performance of services that is substantially nonvested, unless the holder has made a Code Sec. 83(b) election to include the value of the stock in income (Reg. § 1.1361-1(b)(3)).[16] However, stock warrants, call options, or other similar stock rights to purchase stock (collectively, "options") generally are treated as stock of the corporation if the options are substantially certain to be exercised at a strike price substantially below fair market value. This rule does not apply if the option was issued:

(1) to a commercial lender;

(2) in connection with the performance of services, provided the option is nontransferable and does not have a readily ascertainable fair market value when issued; or

(3) at a strike price that is at least 90 percent of the stock's fair market value (Reg. § 1.1361-1(l)(4)(iii)).[17]

In addition, restricted bank director stock is not taken into account as outstanding stock in applying the provisions of subchapter S (Code Sec. 1361(f)(1)).[18] Accordingly, it is not treated as a second class of stock in the S corporation.

306. How to Make an S Election. The election of S corporation status must be made by a qualified corporation (¶ 303–¶ 305), with the unanimous consent of the shareholders, on or before the 15th day of the 3rd month of its tax year in order for the election to be effective beginning with the year when made (Code Sec. 1362(a), (b), and (c); Reg. § 1.1362-6).[19] The election is made on Form 2553. The corporation must meet all of the eligibility requirements for the pre-election portion of the tax year, and all persons who were shareholders during the pre-election portion also must consent to the election. If these requirements are not met during the pre-election period, the election becomes effective the following year.

A "domestic eligible entity" (¶ 402A) may file both its check-the-box and S elections simply by filing Form 2553. It does not need to file Form 8832. The two elections will apply as of the same effective date (Reg. § 301.7701-3(c)(1)(v)(C)).[20]

Late Elections. Two simplified methods for shareholders to request relief for late filing of S corporation elections, electing small business trust elections, qualified subchapter S trust (QSST) elections, and qualified subchapter S subsidiary (QSub) elections are available (Rev. Procs. 2003-43 and 2007-62).[21] Under Rev. Proc. 2003-43, certain eligible entities may be granted relief for failing to timely file these elections if the request for relief is filed within 24 months of the due date of the election. Relief may be granted under Rev. Proc. 2007-62 where the application for relief is filed no later than six months after the due date (with extensions) of the S corporation's tax return for such year. These procedures are to be followed in lieu of the letter ruling process. Therefore, user fees do not apply to corrective actions under these procedures.

If a domestic eligible entity has failed to timely file both its S corporation election and its election to be treated as a corporation, different relief procedures apply (Rev. Procs. 2004-48 and 2007-62).[22] An entity seeking to obtain this relief must file Form 2553

References are to Standard Federal Tax Reports; Tax Research Consultant; and Practical Tax Explanations.

[15] ¶ 32,021, ¶ 32,024A; SCORP: 162; § 28,015.05, § 28,015.10

[16] ¶ 32,024A; SCORP: 162.05

[17] ¶ 32,024A; SCORP: 162.15; § 28,015.10

[18] ¶ 32,021; SCORP: 162.05

[19] ¶ 32,040, ¶ 32,047; SCORP: 200; § 28,105.05

[20] ¶ 43,083; STAGES: 6,154.10; § 28,125

[21] ¶ 32,053.41; SCORP: 206; § 28,140.05

[22] ¶ 32,053.41; SCORP: 206; § 28,140.20

within six months after the due date of the tax return for the first year of the intended S corporation election, excluding extensions. The entity must explain (on the bottom of the first page of Form 2553) the entity's failure to timely file the S corporation and entity classification elections; among the eligibility requirements is reasonable cause for that failure. An entity that obtains relief under the revenue procedure is treated as having made both an election to be classified as an association taxable as a corporation under Reg. § 301.7701-3(c) and an S corporation election as of the same date.

Shareholders in community property states are also eligible for automatic relief for late S elections if their spouses did not file timely shareholder consents (Rev. Proc. 2004-35).[23] To qualify for relief, the S corporation election must be invalid solely because the spouse's signature is missing from the election form. Shareholders must alert the IRS that they are seeking relief under Rev. Proc. 2004-35 and identify the number of shares they own as of the date of the election. Each spouse must sign a separate statement indicating his or her consent to the election.

307. Termination of S Election. S corporation status is automatically terminated if any event occurs that would prohibit the corporation from making the election in the first place (Code Sec. 1362(d)(2); Reg. § 1.1362-2(b)).[24] The election is ended as of the date on which the disqualifying event occurs. Also, if a corporation has accumulated earnings and profits as of the end of three consecutive years, and the corporation's passive investment income exceeds 25 percent of its gross receipts in each of those three years, its election is ended beginning with the following tax year. (Code Sec. 1362(d)(3); Reg. § 1.1362-2(c)).[25] For this purpose, dividends received by an S corporation from a C corporation subsidiary of which the S corporation owns 80 percent or more of stock are not treated as passive investment income to the extent the dividends are attributable to the earnings and profits derived from the active conduct of a trade or business.

An S corporation election may be revoked with the consent of shareholders holding more than 50 percent of the outstanding shares of stock (voting and nonvoting) on the day the revocation is made. A revocation may designate a prospective effective date (Code Sec. 1362(d)(1); Reg. § 1.1362-2(a)).[26] If no date is specified, a revocation made on or before the 15th day of the 3rd month of a corporation's tax year is effective on the first day of the tax year. A revocation made after this date is effective on the first day of the following tax year.

If an election is ended or revoked, the corporation may not reelect S corporation status without IRS consent until the 5th year after the year in which the termination or revocation became effective (Code Sec. 1362(g); Reg. § 1.1362-5).[27] An S corporation whose status as a qualified subchapter S subsidiary (QSub or QSSS) has ended also cannot elect to be treated as a qualified subchapter S subsidiary until the 5th year after the year in which the termination was effective (Code Sec. 1361(b)(3)(D)).[28]

In addition to formally filing an election to end S corporation status, an S corporation can simply create a situation that bars it from being an S corporation. For example, an election to revoke S corporation status relates back to the beginning of the tax year only if the election is made before the 16th day of the third month of the corporation's tax year. Elections made after that date apply to the next tax year. However, if an S corporation wants to end S status immediately, an S corporation can create a situation where S status will immediately be ended. For example, the S corporation's shareholders can create another corporation and transfer one share of S corporation stock to the new corporation. Because corporations cannot be S corporation shareholders, the S corporation status ends on the date the share of stock is transferred to a disqualified shareholder and it is not necessary to wait until the next tax year for the revocation of the S corporation election to become effective.

References are to Standard Federal Tax Reports; Tax Research Consultant; and Practical Tax Explanations.

[23] ¶ 32,053.41; SCORP: 206; § 28,115.10

[24] ¶ 32,040, ¶ 32,043; SCORP: 304; § 28,210

[25] ¶ 32,040, ¶ 32,043; SCORP: 306; § 28,215.05

[26] ¶ 32,040, ¶ 32,043; SCORP: 302; § 28,205.05

[27] ¶ 32,040, ¶ 32,046; SCORP: 312; § 28,130

[28] ¶ 32,021; SCORP: 558; § 28,020.10

Reorganizations. A corporation's Subchapter S election does not terminate merely because it is a party to a reorganization if it continues to meet the S corporation eligibility requirements.[29] Typically, the issue arises because the reorganization results in an ineligible shareholder owning stock of the S corporation. For example, the IRS ruled that S election of an S corporation that was acquired by another corporation in a stock-for-stock "B" reorganization terminated on the date of acquisition. The IRS has similarly ruled that "A", "C", and "F" reorganizations did not cause the S elections of the respective corporations to terminate where all owners of the corporations after the transaction were eligible S corporation shareholders.

Frequently, reorganizations can involve transfers of the same corporate stock several different times to different parties as part of the transaction. The intermediate parties may be deemed to hold the stock only for an instant before transferring it to its ultimate holder. There is a question as to whether a corporation's Subchapter S election terminates where one or more of these intermediate parties is not an eligible S corporation shareholder. This issue is not addressed by the Code or regulations; however, the IRS has privately ruled that having such shareholders, who acquire a corporation's stock only to immediately transfer it to another party, does not cause the corporation's S election to terminate (IRS Letter Rulings 200453007 and 9010042).

Correction of Inadvertent Terminations. If a corporation's S election is inadvertently terminated or invalid when made, and the corporation makes a timely correction, the IRS can waive the termination or can permit the election (Code Sec. 1362(f); Reg. § 1.1362-4).[30] The IRS is also authorized to provide a waiver where an election to treat family members as one shareholder or to treat a corporation as a qualified subchapter S subsidiary is invalid when made or inadvertently terminated. To obtain a waiver, the corporation must correct any condition that barred it from qualifying as an S corporation, or otherwise made an election invalid, and must obtain any required shareholder consents. All shareholders must agree to make such adjustments as may be required by the IRS.

Election to End Tax Year. If a shareholder disposes of his interest in an S corporation and all "affected" shareholders consent to the termination, the tax year can be treated as two tax years, the first of which ends on the date of termination (Code Sec. 1377(a)(2)).[31] For this purpose, affected shareholders include the shareholder whose interest is terminated and all shareholders to whom such shareholder has transferred shares during the tax year.

Taxation of Shareholders

309. Taxation of S Corporation Shareholders. Each shareholder of an S corporation separately accounts for his pro rata share of corporate items of income, deduction, loss, and credit in his tax year in which the corporation's tax year ends (Code Sec. 1366(a); Reg. §§ 1.1366-1(a) and 1.1377-1).[32] Certain items must be separately stated whenever they could affect the shareholder's individual tax liability (¶ 320). A shareholder's share of each item generally is computed based on the number of shares he held on each day of the corporation's tax year.

The character of an item included in a shareholder's pro rata share of S corporation income is generally determined as if the item was realized directly from the source from which the corporation realized it or was incurred in the same manner in which the corporation incurred it, subject to exceptions (Code Sec. 1366(b); Reg. § 1.1366-1(b)).[33] Thus, when income passes through from the S corporation to the shareholder, the character of that income passes through as well. For example, if an S corporation makes a charitable contribution to a qualifying organization, a shareholder's pro rata share of the S corporation's charitable contribution is characterized as made to a qualifying organization.

Similarly, if an S corporation has capital gain on the sale or exchange of a capital asset, a shareholder's pro rata share of that gain is also characterized as a capital gain

References are to Standard Federal Tax Reports; Tax Research Consultant; and Practical Tax Explanations.

[29] ¶ 32,053.69; SCORP: 304.10; § 28,920

[30] ¶ 32,040, ¶ 32,045; SCORP: 308; § 28,220

[31] ¶ 32,240; SCORP: 402.15; § 28,445.10

[32] ¶ 32,080, ¶ 32,081, ¶ 32,240C; SCORP: 402; § 28,405

[33] ¶ 32,080, ¶ 32,081; SCORP: 402.05; § 28,420

regardless of whether the shareholder is otherwise a dealer in that type of property. However, this general rule does not apply when the S corporation is formed or availed of for a principal purpose of selling or exchanging contributed property that, in the hands of the shareholder, would not have produced capital gain if sold or exchanged by the shareholder. The same exception applies when the S corporation is formed or availed of for a principal purpose of selling or exchanging contributed property that, in the hands of a shareholder, would have produced capital loss if sold or exchanged by the shareholder. Any loss recognized by the corporation is treated as a capital loss to the extent that, immediately before the contribution, the adjusted basis of the property in the hands of the shareholder exceeded the fair market value of the property.

Duty of Consistency. A shareholder of an S corporation must treat a Subchapter S item in a manner consistent with the treatment of that item on the corporate return (Code Sec. 6037).[34] Any shareholder who does not treat the item consistently must file a statement identifying the inconsistency.

At-Risk and Passive Activity Rules. The at-risk rules disallow losses that exceed an investor's amount at risk (¶ 2045). Generally, the amount at risk is the amount of investment that an investor could lose. The at-risk rules apply to all individuals, including S corporation shareholders and are applied at the shareholder level (Code Sec. 465).[35] The at-risk amount is determined at the close of the S corporation's tax year. Thus, an S corporation shareholder who realizes that his or her at-risk amount is low, and wishes to deduct an anticipated S corporation net loss, can make additional contributions to the entity.

Likewise, passive activity loss (PAL) rules generally are applied at the shareholder level (¶ 2053) (Code Sec. 469).[36] However, several determinations that affect the application of the PAL rules must be made at the corporate level. For example, the determination of whether an activity constitutes a trade or business, as opposed to a rental activity, is made at the corporate level. The distinction between portfolio and nonportfolio income is also made at the corporate level. This information is conveyed via the Schedule K-1 that is provided to the shareholder by the corporation. The shareholder then uses the information to apply the PAL and at-risk limitations when preparing his individual tax return.

Since a QSST (¶ 304) is treated as the shareholder when it disposes of S corporation stock, the application of the at-risk and PAL rules would normally be determined at the trust level, not the beneficiary level. To ensure that the beneficiary can take disallowed losses on the QSST's disposition of the stock, the at-risk and passive activity loss rules apply as if the beneficiary disposed of the stock (Code Sec. 1361(d)(1)).

Small Business Stock. Because S corporations are not entitled to ordinary loss treatment from the sale of qualified small business stock under Code Sec. 1244 (¶ 1911), and because the character of loss items passes through to shareholders, S corporation shareholders cannot claim ordinary losses incurred by the S corporation from the sale of qualified small business stock (*V.D. Rath*, 101 TC 196 (1993)). However, when the S corporation stock itself is qualified small business stock, shareholders may get an ordinary loss deduction if all the requirements are met.

312. Domestic Production Activities of S Corporation Shareholders. An S corporation cannot claim the domestic production activities deduction (DPAD) (¶ 980A and following). Instead, the deduction is determined at the shareholder level (Code Sec. 199(d)(1); Reg. § 1.199-5(c)).[37] Generally, each shareholder computes its deduction separately on Form 8903 by aggregating its pro rata share of qualified production activity (QPA) items of the S corporation (i.e., income, expenses) with its share of QPA items from other sources. The shareholder does not have to be directly engaged in the S corporation's trade or business to claim the deduction on the basis of its share of QPA items.

References are to Standard Federal Tax Reports; Tax Research Consultant; and Practical Tax Explanations.

[34] ¶ 35,520; PART: 60,402; § 28,425

[35] ¶ 21,850; SCORP: 406; § 28,430.30

[36] ¶ 21,960; BUSEXP: 33,000; § 28,430.35

[37] ¶ 12,468, ¶ 12,472D; BUSEXP: 6,214; § 6,020.05

For purposes of determining the deduction, the activities of an S corporation are not attributed to its shareholders (or vice-versa) (Reg. § 1.199-5(g)). For example, if the S corporation manufactures qualified production property within the United States and then distributes the property to the shareholder who subsequently sells, licenses, leases or otherwise disposes of the property, then the income derived by the shareholder will not qualify as domestic production gross receipts (DPGR). A limited exception is provided for expanded affiliated groups.

Allocation of Items. A shareholder's pro rata share of expenses allocable to the S corporation's QPA is taken into account even if the corporation has no taxable income. If the shareholder is unable to claim a loss or deduction of the corporation for regular tax purposes (i.e., at-risk, passive loss, or basis limitations), then such loss or deduction cannot be used when computing the DPAD. The amount of any loss or deduction is subject to proportionate reduction if it is only partially allowed for regular tax purposes. Also, a loss or deduction that is temporarily disallowed for regular tax purposes may be taken into account in computing the DPAD in the tax year that it is allowed for regular tax purposes.

Instead of taking into account its pro rata share of each QPA item of the S corporation, a shareholder may compute its deduction by combining its pro rata share of the S corporation's qualified productions activities income (QPAI) and W-2 wages with its QPAI and W-2 wages from other sources. This option only applies if the S corporation has elected to use the small business overall method for allocating costs, expenses, and other deductions to its DPGR. Special rules apply to 20-percent shareholders of S corporations engaged in film or television production.

Sale of Stock. Gain or loss recognized on the sale of S corporation stock will not be taken into account by a shareholder in computing its QPAI (Reg. § 1.199-5(f)). This is because the sale of an interest in the corporation does not reflect the realization of DPGR by the entity.

W-2 Wage Limitation. A shareholder of an S corporation computes the W-2 wage limitation for the DPAD by aggregating its share of W-2 wages from the S corporation allocable to DPGR with W-2 wages allocable to DPGR from other sources.

315. Basis in S Corporation Stock. An S corporation shareholder's basis in his stock is determined under the same rules as apply to C corporation shareholders. Thus, the original basis of the shareholder's stock is the purchase price for the stock (money or the fair market value of any property given in exchange for the stock) (Code Sec. 1012).[38] Stock acquired by gift normally carries over the donor's basis (¶ 1630). The basis of stock acquired from a decedent is its fair market value on the date of the decedent's death or on the alternate valuation date, if elected (¶ 1633). During the time the corporation is an S corporation, each shareholder must make adjustment to his stock (¶ 317).

Similarly, the rules providing for contributions to controlled corporations under Code Sec. 351 (¶ 203) and tax-free corporate reorganizations under Code Sec. 368 (¶ 2209) are generally applicable to S corporations (Code Sec. 1371).[39] Thus, the basis of stock received under a tax-free reorganization is equal to the transferor's basis in the property transferred plus any gain, minus the fair market value of the boot received and minus any loss recognized in the transaction.

Stock for Services. An S corporation may grant stock to an employee or other service provider as part of a compensation package. Typically, in a stock-for-services arrangement, S corporation stock may be transferred to an employee at a particular price or for nothing, with the rights to the stock becoming vested only after a number of years of employment. The value of the S stock at that vesting point has usually appreciated from its value at the time of transfer. The difference between the amount that the employee

References are to Standard Federal Tax Reports; Tax Research Consultant; and Practical Tax Explanations.

[38] ¶ 29,330; SALES: 6,050; § 28,605.10

[39] ¶ 32,140; CCORP: 3,200, REORG: 6,104; § 26,130

pays for the S stock and the fair market value of the stock at the time the employee's rights to the stock are vested must be included in the employee's ordinary gross income (¶ 713). The S corporation gets a compensation deduction for the amount the employee includes in income in the year the employee includes it in income.

317. Adjustments to Basis in S Corporation Stock. The stock basis of each S corporation shareholder (¶ 315) is *increased* by the shareholder's portion of:

(1) all income items of the corporation (including tax-exempt income) that are separately computed and passed through to shareholders;

(2) the income of the corporation that is not separately computed; and

(3) the excess of the corporation's deductions for depletion over the basis of the property subject to depletion (Code Sec. 1367(a)(1); Reg. § 1.1367-1(b)).[40]

A shareholder's basis is *decreased* by the portion of:

(1) distributions that are not includible in the shareholder's income (¶ 309);

(2) all loss and deduction items of the corporation that are separately stated and passed through to shareholders (but see the discussion below with respect to charitable contributions of appreciated property);

(3) the nonseparately computed loss of the corporation;

(4) any expense of the corporation not deductible in computing its taxable income and not properly chargeable to capital account; and

(5) the amount of the shareholder's deduction for depletion with respect to oil and gas wells to the extent that it does not exceed his proportionate share of the adjusted basis of such property (Code Sec. 1367(a)(2); Reg. § 1.1367-2).[41]

If a shareholder's stock basis is reduced to zero, the remaining net decrease attributable to losses and deductions is applied to reduce any basis in debt owed to the shareholder by the corporation (¶ 318). Distributions may not be applied against basis in debt. Any net increase in basis in a subsequent year is applied to restore the basis of indebtedness before it may be applied to increase the shareholder's stock basis.

Generally, stock basis adjustments are determined as of the close of the corporation's tax year, and the adjustments are effective as of that date. However, if a shareholder disposes of stock during the corporation's tax year, the adjustments with respect to that stock are effective immediately before the disposition (Reg. § 1.1367-1(d)).[42] An adjustment for a nontaxable item is determined for the tax year in which the item would have been includible or deductible under the corporation's method of accounting for federal income tax purposes if the item had been subject to federal income taxation.

Charitable Deductions. For tax years beginning before 2012, the amount of a shareholder's basis reduction in the stock of an S corporation by reason of a charitable contribution made by the corporation equals the shareholder's pro rata share of the adjusted basis of the contributed property (Code Sec. 1367(a)(2)).

Cancellation of Indebtedness. Discharge of indebtedness income of an S corporation that is excluded from the corporation's income (¶ 885) is not taken into account as an item of income that flows through to any shareholder (¶ 309) and so does not increase a shareholder's basis in S corporation stock (Code Sec. 108(d)(7)(A); Reg. § 1.108-7(d)).[43]

318. Basis in S Corporation Debt. For purposes of deducting S corporation losses, a shareholder has basis in certain debts of the S corporation to the shareholder (Code Sec. 1366(d)(1)(B)).[44] However, unlike a partner in a partnership, an S corporation shareholder does not receive basis or an increase in basis for debt of the S corporation to an outside lender. Thus, if an S corporation borrows money from a bank or other unrelated lender, the shareholders cannot claim basis attributable to this corporate-level

References are to Standard Federal Tax Reports; Tax Research Consultant; and Practical Tax Explanations.

[40] ¶ 32,100, ¶ 32,100B; SCORP: 410.05; § 28,610.05

[41] ¶ 32,100, ¶ 32,100C; SCORP: 410.05; § 28,615

[42] ¶ 32,100B; SCORP: 410; § 28,620

[43] ¶ 7002, ¶ 7006; SALES: 12,212.10, SCORP: 404.10; § 28,610.10

[44] ¶ 32,080; SCORP: 410.10; § 28,630.05

debt. A mere guaranty by the shareholder of the S corporation's debt to a third party generally does not qualify for an increase in the shareholder's basis.

The courts have held that, in order for a shareholder to have basis in debt owed to that shareholder by an S corporation, there must be an actual economic outlay by the shareholder to the corporation (*M.G. Underwood*, 63 TC 468 (1975), aff'd, CA-5, 76-2 USTC ¶ 9557).[45] In other words, only the kind of debt that proves an actual investment by the shareholder, not merely one given in return for a promise by the shareholder for some future outlay, gives rise to or increases basis.

The IRS rejects the "actual economic outlay" test and would substitute in its place a requirement that the debt in question must represent a bona fide indebtedness of the S corporation to the shareholder (Prop. Reg. § 1.1366-2(a)(2)(i)).[46] Proposed regulations provide that, in order for a loan to increase the shareholder's basis in S corporation debt, the loan must represent a bona fide indebtedness from the S corporation to the shareholder. General federal tax principles determine whether indebtedness is bona fide, based on the facts and circumstances.

Both the courts and the IRS agree that the S corporation's indebtedness must run directly to the shareholder, not merely to an entity in which he is an owner. Thus, indebtedness running from the S corporation to a passthrough entity in which the shareholder has an interest will not be attributed to the shareholder for this purpose.

The basis that a shareholder has in debt owed to that shareholder by the S corporation must be adjusted like the shareholder's basis in stock. Adjustments are calculated before the basis in indebtedness is affected (Code Sec. 1367(b)(2); Reg. § 1.1367-2).[47] When decreases relating to losses, deductions, noncapital, nondeductible expenses, and certain oil and gas depletion deductions have reduced stock basis to zero, any excess is applied to reduce debt basis. Any indebtedness by the corporation to the shareholder that has been satisfied by the corporation or disposed of or forgiven by the shareholder during the tax year is not held by the shareholder at the close of that year and is not subject to basis reduction. Generally, the adjustments to debt basis are made as of the close of the tax year. If the shareholder terminates his interest in the corporation during the tax year, however, the adjustments in basis to debt are applied with respect to any S corporation debt held by the shareholder immediately before the termination of the shareholder's interest in the corporation. If there is a reduction in the shareholder's basis in S corporation debt, any net increase in any subsequent tax year is applied first to the restoration of that reduction before any increase is applied to S stock basis.

319. S Corporation's Taxable Income. Income and loss realized by an S corporation are passed through to the shareholders (¶ 309). Computation of an S corporation's taxable income parallels the computation of the taxable income of an individual, except that organizational expenditures may be amortized (¶ 237) and the reduction in certain corporate tax benefits (¶ 289) must be made if the S corporation was a C corporation for any of the three immediately preceding tax years. Certain deductions, such as those for personal exemptions, charitable contributions, medical expenses, alimony, and net operating losses, are not allowed to the S corporation when calculating taxable income (Code Sec. 1363(b)).[48] Certain items must be separately stated when passed through to shareholders (¶ 320).

An S corporation cannot carry over or carry back any item from a year that the corporation is not an S corporation to a year that the corporation is an S corporation (Code Sec. 1371).[49] Thus, no carryforward or carryback, such as a net operating loss, arising from a tax year for which a corporation is a C corporation may be carried to a tax year for which the corporation is an S corporation. No carryforward or carryback arises at the corporate level in a tax year for which a corporation is an S corporation. However, a tax year for which a corporation is an S corporation is treated as a tax year for

References are to Standard Federal Tax Reports; Tax Research Consultant; and Practical Tax Explanations.

[45] ¶ 32,084.325; SCORP: 410.05; § 28,630.10

[46] ¶ 32,082A; SCORP: 404.05; § 28,630.10.

[47] ¶ 32,100, ¶ 32,100C; SCORP: 410.10; § 28,630.15

[48] ¶ 32,060; SCORP: 352; § 28,405

[49] ¶ 32,140; SCORP: 354; § 28,415

purposes of determining the number of tax years to which an item may be carried back or carried forward. Thus, while the item remains intact during the time the corporation is an S corporation, those years count for any carryforward period applicable to the item.

320. Separately Stated Items of S Corporation Income. Certain items of the taxable income of an S corporation (¶ 319) must be separately stated (Code Sec. 1363(b)).[50] These items must be reported and computed separately from items that can be combined. Items that must be separately stated include, but are not limited to:

(1) net income or loss from rental activities, including rental real estate activities;

(2) portfolio income or loss and expenses related to portfolio income or loss;

(3) Code Sec. 1231 net gain or loss;

(4) charitable contributions, grouped by the percentage limitations of Code Sec. 170(b);

(5) Code Sec. 179 expense deductions;

(6) the low-income housing credit;

(7) investment interest expense;

(8) tax preference and adjustment items needed to compute shareholders' alternative minimum tax;

(9) gains and losses from wagering transactions;

(10) medical, dental, etc., expenses;

(11) itemized deductions;

(12) capital gain or loss grouped by applicable holding periods;

(13) foreign taxes paid or accrued;

(14) tax-exempt income; and

(15) passive activity items for each of the corporation's activities (Code Sec. 1366(a)(1)(A); Reg. § 1.1366-1(a)).[51]

Each shareholder must take also into account the shareholder's pro rata share of the nonseparately computed income or loss of the S corporation. Nonseparately computed income or loss is the corporation's gross income less the deductions allowed to the corporation, determined by excluding any item requiring separate computation.

Nonbusiness Bad Debts. An S corporation may claim a nonbusiness bad debt deduction (¶ 1169) in the same manner as an individual when computing an S corporation's taxable income. Accordingly, an S corporation that incurs a nonbusiness bad debt must separately state the debt as a short-term capital loss (Rev. Rul. 93-36). Partially or wholly worthless business debts, on the other hand, are included in nonseparately stated S corporation income or loss (¶ 1145).

321. Limits on S Corporation Deductions. A shareholder's currently deductible share of the corporation's losses and deductions is limited to the total of his adjusted basis in the corporation's stock and any debt the corporation may owe him (Code Sec. 1366(d)).[52] The debt must be bona fide. Where purported loans from the shareholder to an S corporation involve no actual economic outlay, courts have found that they were not bona fide debt and did not increase the adjusted basis against which deductions allocated to the shareholder may be taken (¶ 318).[53]

An S corporation's itemized deductions are separately stated items (¶ 320). Thus, the 2-percent floor on miscellaneous itemized deductions (¶ 1011) is applied at the shareholder level rather than at the S corporation level (Temp. Reg. § 1.67-2T(b)(1)).[54] Shareholders of an S corporation take into account separately their pro rata share of the

References are to Standard Federal Tax Reports; Tax Research Consultant; and Practical Tax Explanations.

[50] ¶ 32,060; SCORP: 352; § 28,405

[51] ¶ 32,080, ¶ 32,081; SCORP: 352; § 28,405

[52] ¶ 32,080; SCORP: 404; § 28,430.15

[53] ¶ 32,084.32; SCORP: 410.10; § 28,630.10

[54] ¶ 6062; INDIV: 39,102.05; § 28,440.45

corporation's miscellaneous itemized deductions, add them to their other individual miscellaneous deductions, and can deduct them to the extent they exceed 2 percent of their individual adjusted gross incomes.

The election to expense the cost of Code Sec. 179 property (¶ 1208) is made at the S corporation level (Reg. § 1.179-1(h)).[55] The dollar, investment, and taxable income limitations apply at both the S corporation and shareholder levels (Code Sec. 179(d)(8); Reg. § 1.179-2).[56]

Charitable Deductions. The basis limitation does not apply to a charitable contribution of appreciated property to the extent the shareholder's pro rata share of the contribution exceeds the shareholder's pro rata share of the adjusted basis of the property (Code Sec. 1366(d)(4)).[57] Thus, the basis limitation does not apply to the amount of deductible appreciation in the contributed property. The IRS has provided guidance for contributions of appreciated property by S corporations (Rev. Rul. 2008-16).

Suspended Losses and Deductions. If the amount of the loss or deduction of a shareholder is limited for a tax year, the excess is treated as incurred by the corporation in the next tax year for that individual shareholder and may be carried forward until used by that shareholder (Code Sec. 1366(d)(2)).[58] Disallowed losses and deductions may be transferred only to a current or former spouse of the shareholder when the S corporation stock is transferred between spouses or incident to divorce in a nontaxable transaction (¶ 1734).

If the shareholder's losses or deductions are limited for the last tax year in which the corporation is an S corporation, the excess is treated as incurred by the shareholder on the last day of the corporation's post-termination transition period (¶ 329) (Code Sec. 1366(d)(3)). The excess amount cannot exceed the shareholder's adjusted basis of the stock in the corporation, determined at the close of the last day of the post-termination transition period. The losses or deductions taken into account during this period reduce the shareholder's basis in the stock of the corporation. Losses of an S corporation that are suspended under the at-risk rules (¶ 2045) are carried forward to the post-termination period.

322. Employee Benefits Provided to S Corporation Shareholders. The tax treatment of fringe benefits (¶ 863) paid to employees of an S corporation is different for owner-employees than for other employees (Code Sec. 1372).[59] Fringe benefits paid to S corporation employees who are not shareholders, or who own 2 percent or less of the outstanding S corporation stock, are tax free. They can be excluded from the employees' taxable wages and are deductible as fringe benefits by the corporation. Employee-owners owning more than 2 percent of the S corporation stock, on the other hand, are not treated as employees for fringe benefit purposes, and their fringe benefits may not be tax free. More-than-2-percent owners are treated in the same manner as partners in a partnership (¶ 421).

Health Insurance Expenses. An owner-employee who owns more than 2 percent of the S corporation stock can deduct 100 percent of the amount paid for medical insurance for himself, his spouse and dependents under a plan established by the S corporation (Code Sec. 162(l)(1) and (5); Notice 2008-1).[60] The S corporation must either pay the plan's premium payments itself or must reimburse the shareholder for the payments.

For purposes of the deduction, a more-than-2-percent shareholder's wages from the S corporation are treated as the shareholder's earned income. No deduction is allowed in excess of an individual's earned income within the meaning of Code Sec. 401(c) derived from the trade or business with respect to which the plan providing the health insurance is established.

References are to Standard Federal Tax Reports; Tax Research Consultant; and Practical Tax Explanations.

[55] ¶ 12,121; DEPR: 12,156; § 28,440.15

[56] ¶ 12,120, ¶ 12,122; DEPR: 12,112; § 9,815.15

[57] ¶ 32,080; SCORP: 402.10; § 28,440.10

[58] ¶ 32,080, ¶ 32,240; SCORP: 404; § 28,430.25

[59] ¶ 32,160; SCORP: 352.20; § 28,801

[60] ¶ 8500, ¶ 32,161.50; SCORP: 352.20; § 28,815

Tax Treatment of Distributions

323. S Corporation Distributions. Distributions of cash or property received by a shareholder from an S corporation are taxed accordingly depending on whether the corporation has earnings and profits. An S corporation generally has no earnings and profits unless attributable to tax years when the corporation was not an S corporation. An S corporation may also succeed to the earnings and profits of an acquired or merged corporation.

For an S corporation without earnings and profits, distributions are treated first as a nontaxable return of capital to the extent of the shareholder's basis in stock and then as a gain from the sale or exchange of property (Code Sec. 1368(b); Reg. § 1.1368-1(c)).[61] For an S corporation with earnings and profits, unless an election is made to distributed the earnings and profits as dividends (¶ 333), distributions are treated as:

(1) a nontaxable return of capital, to the extent of the corporation's "accumulated adjustments account" (AAA) (¶ 325),

(2) dividends, to the extent of the S corporation's accumulated earnings and profits,

(3) a nontaxable return of capital, to the extent of the shareholder's remaining stock basis, and

(4) gain from the sale or exchange of property (Code Sec. 1368(c); Reg. § 1.1368-1(d)).[62]

Before applying these rules, the shareholder's stock basis and the AAA are adjusted for the corporate items passed through from the corporate tax year during which the distribution is made.

If an employee stock ownership plan (ESOP) holds S corporation shares that are employer securities, and the ESOP took out a loan to purchase the employer securities, the prohibited transaction rules will not apply to distributions by the S corporation that are used to repay the loan, and the plan's status as an ESOP will not be jeopardized (Code Sec. 4975(f)(7)).[63]

325. Accumulated Adjustments Account. The accumulated adjustments account (AAA) is used to compute the tax effect of distributions made by an S corporation with accumulated earnings and profits (¶ 323) (Code Sec. 1368(e); Reg. § 1.1368-2).[64] The AAA is generally a measure of the corporation's accumulated gross income, less expenses, that has not been distributed. The AAA is zero on the first day of a corporation's first S corporation tax year. It is *increased* by:

(1) all corporate income items (excluding tax-exempt income items) that are separately stated and passed through to shareholders (¶ 320);

(2) nonseparately computed corporate income; and

(3) the excess of deductions for depletion over the basis of the property subject to depletion.

The AAA is *decreased* by:

(1) certain nontaxable corporate distributions;

(2) all loss and deduction items of the corporation that are separately stated and passed through (other than items that are not deductible in computing taxable income and not properly chargeable to capital account);

(3) the nonseparately computed loss of the corporation;

(4) the nondeductible amounts that are unrelated to the production of tax-exempt income; and

(5) the amount of the shareholder's deduction for oil and gas depletion.

References are to Standard Federal Tax Reports; Tax Research Consultant; and Practical Tax Explanations.

[61] ¶ 32,120, ¶ 32,120B; SCORP: 452; § 28,505

[62] ¶ 32,120, ¶ 32,120B; SCORP: 454; § 28,510

[63] ¶ 34,400; RETIRE: 75,302

[64] ¶ 32,120, ¶ 32,120C; SCORP: 458; § 28,510.10

As indicated, an S corporation's AAA is not increased by tax-exempt income and it is not decreased by an expense related to the tax-exempt income. For example, premiums paid by an S corporation on an employer-owned life insurance contract (COLI), of which the S corporation is a beneficiary, do not reduce the S corporation's AAA. Nor is the AAA increased by death benefits received by the corporation under the policy that meets one of the exceptions for COLI (¶ 804) (Rev. Rul. 2008-42).[65]

No adjustment is made for federal taxes arising when the corporation was a C corporation. Because the AAA may become negative, the account becomes positive only after the negative balance is restored by later income (Code Sec. 1368(e)(1)(A); Reg. § 1.1368-2).[66] The amount in the AAA as of the close of a tax year is determined without regard to any net negative adjustment for the tax year. A negative adjustment occurs in any tax year in which negative adjustments to the account exceed increases to the account.

Distributions received by an S corporation shareholder in a stock redemption that is treated as a Code Sec. 301 distribution are treated as distributions that reduce the S corporation's AAA (Rev. Rul. 95-14).[67] For a distribution in redemption of an S corporation's stock, if the redemption is treated as an exchange under Code Sec. 302 or Code Sec. 303, the AAA is decreased by an amount determined by multiplying the account balance by the number of shares redeemed and dividing the product by the total number of shares outstanding. This adjustment is made before the distribution rules are applied (Code Sec. 1368(e)(1)(B)).

The AAA relates only to the most recent continuous period in which the corporation has been an S corporation. However, the period does not include tax years beginning before January 1, 1983 (Code Sec. 1368(e)(2); Reg. § 1.1368-2(a)).[68] If corporate distributions during a tax year exceed the amount in the AAA at the end of that year, the balance of the account is allocated among distributions in proportion to their respective sizes (¶ 329) (Code Sec. 1368(c)).[69]

329. Post-Termination Distributions by S Corporations. If an S corporation ends its election, the corporation has the opportunity for a limited period of time to unfreeze the income that was previously taxed to shareholders under the pass-through rules but that was not actually distributed by the corporation. Specifically, any cash distribution by the corporation with respect to its stock during the post-termination transition period is applied against and reduces stock basis to the extent that the amount of the distribution does not exceed the AAA (Code Sec. 1371(e)).[70]

The term "post-termination transition period" is (Code Sec. 1377(b)):

(1) the period beginning on the day after the last day of the corporation's last tax year as an S corporation and ending on the later of: (a) the day which is one year after such last day or (b) the due date for filing the return for the last tax year as an S corporation (including extensions);

(2) the 120-day period beginning on the date of any determination pursuant to an audit of the taxpayer which follows the termination of the corporation's election and which adjusts a subchapter S item of income, loss, or deduction of the corporation arising during the S period (Code Sec. 1368(e)(2));[71] or

(3) the 120-day period beginning on the date of a determination that the corporation's election had ended for a previous tax year.

If the AAA is not exhausted by the end of the post-termination transition period, it disappears. Any distributions made thereafter are taxed under the usual subchapter C rules—as a distribution of current earnings and profits, as a distribution of accumulated earnings and profits as a return of capital to the extent of the shareholder's basis, and,

References are to Standard Federal Tax Reports; Tax Research Consultant; and Practical Tax Explanations.

[65] ¶ 32,121.20; SCORP: 458.05; § 28,510.10

[66] ¶ 32,120, ¶ 32,120C; SCORP: 458.05, SCORP: 458.10; § 28,510.10

[67] ¶ 32,121.20; SCORP: 458.15; § 28,510.10

[68] ¶ 32,120, ¶ 32,120C; SCORP: 458; § 28,510.10

[69] ¶ 32,120; SCORP: 454; § 28,510.10

[70] ¶ 32,140; SCORP: 462; § 28,515

[71] ¶ 32,120; SCORP: 462; § 28,515

finally, as a capital gain. Because the AAA is always reflected in the basis of the shareholder's stock, failure to exhaust it during the transition period moves it, in effect, below current and accumulated earnings and profits in the priority system for distributions. The grace period for post-termination distributions applies only to cash distributions. It does not apply to noncash distributions. A noncash distribution is taxed under the usual subchapter C rules.

333. S Corporation Election to Distribute Earnings. An S corporation can avoid the priority system (¶ 323) for treatment of distributions by electing to treat distributions as dividends. An S corporation might elect to treat a distribution as taxable dividends if it wants to avoid S-status termination for excess passive investment income (Code Sec. 1368(e)(3); Reg. § 1.1368-1(f)(2)).[72] However, all shareholders who receive a distribution during the tax year must consent to such treatment. If such an election is made, the corporation is not required to distribute its entire AAA (¶ 325) at the end of its tax year before it can pay a dividend.

Taxation of Corporation

335. Taxation of S Corporation. Since an S corporation is a pass-through entity, it is generally not subject to federal income taxes. However, an S corporation may be liable for, and is required to make estimated tax payments attributable to the following corporate-level tax liabilities:

(1) the tax imposed on built-in gains or capital gains (¶ 337);

(2) the tax on excess net passive income (¶ 341);

(3) the recapture of the investment credit on the disposition of property placed in service before 1985;[73] and

(4) the recapture of LIFO benefits upon conversion to an S corporation (¶ 339) (Code Sec. 6655(g)(4)).[74]

If the S corporation was incorporated after 1982, immediately became an S corporation, and has no earnings or profits, only the capital gains tax applies. If the S corporation was incorporated and elected S corporation status before 1987, the tax on built-in gains does not apply.

337. Tax on Built-In Gains of S Corporation. The tax on built-in gains is a corporate-level tax on S corporations that dispose of assets that appreciated in value during years when the corporation was a C corporation (Code Sec. 1374).[75] The tax applies only to corporations that made S corporation elections after 1986. A tax imposed on certain capital gains of S corporations continues to apply to corporations that made S elections before 1987.

An S corporation may be liable for tax on its built-in gains if:

(1) it was a C corporation prior to making its S corporation election;

(2) the S corporation election was made after 1986;

(3) it has a net recognized built-in gain within the recognition period; and

(4) the net recognized built-in gain for the tax year does not exceed the net unrealized built-in gain minus the net recognized built-in gain for prior years in the recognition period, to the extent that such gains were subject to tax.

A recognized built-in loss is any loss recognized during the recognition period on the disposition of any asset to the extent that the S corporation establishes that: (1) the asset was held by the S corporation at the beginning of its first tax year as an S corporation, and (2) the loss is not greater than the excess of (a) the adjusted basis of the asset at the beginning of the corporation's first tax year as an S corporation, over (b) the fair market value of the asset at that time.

References are to Standard Federal Tax Reports; Tax Research Consultant; and Practical Tax Explanations.

[72] ¶ 32,120, ¶ 32,120B; SCORP: 456; § 28,515

[73] ¶ 32,140.80; SCORP: 362; § 28,410.05

[74] ¶ 39,565; SCORP: 370; § 29,020.15

[75] ¶ 32,201; SCORP: 356; § 28,305.05

Recognition Period. For assets disposed of during an S corporation's tax year beginning in 2012, the recognition period for net built-in gain is the ten-year period beginning on the first day on which the corporation is an S corporation or acquires C corporation assets in a carryover basis transaction (Code Sec. 1374(d)(7); Reg. § 1.1374-1(d)).[76] For example, if the first day of the recognition period is July 12, 2012, the last day of the recognition period will be July 11, 2022. For tax years beginning in 2011, the recognition period is five years; for tax years beginning in 2009 or 2010, the recognition period is seven years. The reduction in the recognition period for 2009, 2010, and 2011 applies separately with respect to any asset acquired in a carryover basis transaction.

Amount of Tax. The tax is computed by applying the highest corporate income tax rate to the S corporation's net recognized built-in gain for the tax year. The amount of the net recognized built-in gain is taxable income. However, any net operating loss carryforward arising in a tax year in which the corporation was a C corporation is allowed as a deduction against the net recognized built-in gain of the S corporation. Capital loss carryforwards may also be used to offset recognized built-in gains (Code Sec. 1374(b) and (d); Reg. § 1.1374-5).[77] Furthermore, business tax credit carryovers of an S corporation, arising in a tax year in which the corporation was a C corporation, can offset the built-in gains tax of the S corporation (Code Sec. 1374(b)(3)(B); Reg. § 1.1374-6).[78]

The term "net recognized built-in gain" means the lesser of (1) the amount that would be the taxable income of the S corporation if only recognized built-in gains and recognized built-in losses were taken into account, or (2) the corporation's taxable income (Code Sec. 1374(d)(2); Reg. § 1.1374-2).[79] In the case of a corporation that made its S corporation election on or after March 31, 1988, any net recognized built-in gain that is not subject to the built-in gains tax due to the net income limitation is carried forward. The amount of recognized built-in gain passed through and taxed to shareholders is reduced by the tax imposed on the built-in gain and paid by the S corporation (Code Sec. 1366(f)(2)).[80]

339. LIFO Recapture by S Corporation. A C corporation that maintains its inventory using the last-in, first-out (LIFO) method for its last tax year before an S corporation election becomes effective must include in gross income a LIFO recapture amount when it converts to S corporation status. LIFO recapture is also required for transfers of inventory from a C corporation to an S corporation in a tax-free reorganization (Code Sec. 1363(d); Reg. § 1.1363-2).[81] The LIFO recapture amount is the amount, if any, by which the amount of the inventory assets using the first-in, first-out (FIFO) method exceeds the inventory amount of such assets under the LIFO method (¶ 1559).

The tax attributable to the inclusion in income of any LIFO recapture amount is payable by the corporation in four equal installments. The first payment is due on or before the due date of the corporate tax return for the electing corporation's last tax year as a C corporation. The three subsequent installments are due on or before the respective due dates of the S corporation's returns for the three succeeding tax years. No interest is payable on these installments if they are paid by the respective due dates.

341. Passive Investment Income of S Corporation. S corporations with Subchapter C earnings and profits and with total passive investment income totaling more than 25 percent of gross receipts are subject to an income tax computed by multiplying the corporation's excess net passive income by the highest corporate income tax rate (Code Sec. 1375; Reg. § 1.1375-1).[82] Passive investment income is gross receipts derived from royalties, rents, dividends, interest (excluding interest on installment sales of inventory to customers and income of certain lending and financing businesses), and

References are to Standard Federal Tax Reports; Tax Research Consultant; and Practical Tax Explanations.

[76] ¶ 32,201, ¶ 32,201C; SCORP: 356.05; § 28,305.15

[77] ¶ 32,201, ¶ 32,202H; SCORP: 356.10, SCORP: 356.25; § 28,305.40

[78] ¶ 32,201, ¶ 32,202J; SCORP: 356.30; § 28,305.45

[79] ¶ 32,201, ¶ 32,202B; SCORP: 356.05; § 28,305.20

[80] ¶ 32,080; SCORP: 356; § 28,305.65

[81] ¶ 32,060, ¶ 32,061B; SCORP: 352.35; § 28,315.05

[82] ¶ 32,220, ¶ 32,221; SCORP: 360; § 28,310.05

annuities (Code Sec. 1362(d)(3)(C); Reg. §1.1362-2(c)(5)).[83] However, such income derived by an S corporation in the ordinary course of its trade or business is generally excluded from the definition of passive investment income. In the case of an S corporation bank (including a bank holding company and a depository institution holding company), passive investment income does not include interest earned by the bank and any dividends received on assets that the bank is required to hold. The exception for assets applies to stock in the Federal Reserve Bank, Federal Home Loan Bank, or Federal Agriculture Mortgage Bank, and participation certificates issued by a Federal Intermediate Credit Bank.

Excess net passive income is the amount that bears the same ratio to net passive income as the amount of passive investment income that exceeds 25 percent of gross receipts bears to passive investment income (Code Sec. 1375(b); Reg. §1.1375-1(b)).[84] Net passive income is passive investment income reduced by any allowable deduction directly connected with the production of such income except for the net operating loss deduction (¶ 1173) and the special deductions allowed to corporations in computing taxable income (¶ 221—¶ 237). Excess net passive income cannot exceed the corporation's taxable income for the year computed without regard to any net operating loss deduction and without regard to the special deductions allowed to corporations, other than the deduction for organizational expenditures (¶ 237). Passive investment income is determined without taking into account any recognized built-in gain or loss during the recognition period (¶ 337). This means that S corporations without earnings and profits cannot be taxed on excess net passive income if they have no taxable income. This can happen if the corporation has net operating losses and income from passive investments. The tax is not merely carried over; there is no tax due if during the year the corporation did not have taxable income.

The tax on excess net passive income reduces each item of passive income by the amount of tax attributable to it and thereby reduces the amount of passive investment income that each shareholder must take into account in computing gross income (Code Sec. 1366(f)(3)).[85]

The only credits allowable against the passive investment income tax are those for certain uses of gasoline and special fuels (¶ 1329) (Code Sec. 1375(c); Reg. §1.1375-1(c)).[86]

The IRS may waive the tax on excess net passive income if the S corporation establishes that it made a good-faith determination at the close of the tax year that it had no C corporation earnings and profits and that it distributed such earnings and profits within a reasonable time after determining that they existed (Code Sec. 1375(d); Reg. §1.1375-1(d)).[87]

349. Foreign Income of S Corporation. Foreign taxes paid by an S corporation pass through to shareholders who can elect to treat them as deductions or credits on their individual returns (Code Sec. 1373).[88] Since an S corporation is treated as a partnership (rather than a corporation) for purposes of the foreign tax credit provisions of the Code, neither it nor its shareholders may claim the indirect foreign tax credit (¶ 2475) for taxes paid by a foreign corporation in which the S corporation is a shareholder. The foreign loss recapture rules apply to an S corporation that previously passed foreign losses through to the shareholders and subsequently terminates its S corporation status. For the purpose of computing the amount of foreign losses that must be recaptured, the making or termination of an S corporation election is treated as a disposition of the business.

Returns and Tax Year

351. S Corporation Returns. An S corporation is required to file Form 1120S for each of the corporation's tax years, regardless of whether the corporation has taxable

References are to Standard Federal Tax Reports; Tax Research Consultant; and Practical Tax Explanations.

[83] ¶ 32,040, ¶ 32,043; SCORP: 360; §28,310.20

[84] ¶ 32,220, ¶ 32,221; SCORP: 358; §28,310.10

[85] ¶ 32,080; SCORP: 402.05; §28,310.05

[86] ¶ 32,220, ¶ 32,221; SCORP: 360; §28,310.05

[87] ¶ 32,220, ¶ 32,221; SCORP: 360; §28,310.25

[88] ¶ 32,180; SCORP: 364; §13,405.20

income for that year (Reg. § 1.6012-2(h)).[89] An S corporation's return is due on or before the 15th day of the third month following the close of the tax year (Reg. § 1.6037-1(b)).[90] An automatic six-month extension of time to file the S corporation's return may be obtained by filing Form 7004 on or before the due date of its Form 1120S (Reg. § 1.6081-3(a)).[91]

An S corporation is required to provide to each shareholder a copy of the information shown on Schedule K-1 that is attached to Form 1120S. The information must be provided on or before the day the corporation files Form 1120S (Code Sec. 6037(b)).[92]

353. Failure to File Penalties for S Corporations. For returns required to be filed for tax years that begin after December 31, 2009, an S corporation that fails to timely file Form 1120S (or files an incomplete return) is liable for a penalty of $195 per shareholder, per month for a maximum of twelve months, unless reasonable cause is shown (Code Sec. 6699).[93] An S corporation may not contest the penalty assessment in the Tax Court, but can pay the entire penalty and then sue for a refund.

An S corporation may also be subject to penalties for failure to furnish Schedules K-1 to its shareholders (Code Sec. 6722).[94] For each failure to furnish Schedule K-1 to a shareholder when due and each failure to include on Schedule K-1 all the information required to be shown (or the inclusion of incorrect information), a $100 penalty may be imposed with regard to each Schedule K-1 for which a failure occurs. If the requirement to report correct information is intentionally disregarded, each penalty is increased to $250 or, if greater, 10 percent of the aggregate amount of items required to be reported.

355. Tax Year of S Corporation. The tax year of an S corporation must be a permitted year. Permitted years include the calendar year, a tax year elected under Code Sec. 444, a 52-53 week tax year ending with reference to the calendar year or a tax year elected under Code Sec. 444, or any other tax year for which the corporation establishes a business purpose to the satisfaction of the IRS under Code Sec. 442 (Reg. § 1.1378-1(a)).[95] The procedures for an S corporation to establish a business purpose are contained in Rev. Proc. 2006-46.[96]

An S corporation may elect to have a tax year other than its required tax year. Generally, this election may be made only if the deferral period of the tax year elected is not longer than three months. The S corporation makes this election by filing Form 8716 (¶ 1501). If such an election is made, the S corporation may be required to make certain tax payments.

References are to Standard Federal Tax Reports; Tax Research Consultant; and Practical Tax Explanations.

[89] ¶ 35,145; SCORP: 500; § 29,010.10

[90] ¶ 35,481; SCORP: 500; § 29,010.10

[91] ¶ 36,790; FILEBUS: 15,104.10; § 29,010.10

[92] ¶ 35,520; SCORP: 500; § 29,010.10

[93] ¶ 40,023; PENALTY: 3,208.45; § 29,010.20

[94] ¶ 40,230; PENALTY: 3,204.05; § 28,425

[95] ¶ 32,261; SCORP: 252, SCORP: 258; § 28,410.15

[96] ¶ 32,262.10; SCORP: 256; § 28,410.15

Chapter 4
PARTNERSHIPS

Choice of Entity

401. Partnership Distinguished. A "partnership" includes a syndicate, group, pool, joint venture, or other unincorporated organization that carries on any business, financial operation, or venture, and that is not, within the meaning of the Code, a trust, estate, or corporation (Code Sec. 761).[1] A noncorporate entity with at least two members can be classified under the "check-the-box" rules (¶ 402A) either as a partnership or as an association taxable as a corporation. A noncorporate entity with one member can be taxed either as a corporation or as a sole proprietorship (Reg. § 301.7701-3).[2]

401A. Limited Partnerships. A limited partnership has one or more general partners and one or more limited partners. Limited partnerships are formed under the limited partnership laws of each state. Unlike general partnerships in which all the partners are responsible for partnership liabilities, limited partners are not responsible for partnership liabilities beyond the amount of their investments. In addition, under state law, limited partners cannot participate in partnership management.

401B. Limited Liability Partnerships. Limited liability partnerships (LLPs) are generally used by professionals such as accountants or attorneys. An LLP is a general partnership in which each individual partner remains liable for his own malpractice as well as the liabilities arising out of the wrongful acts or omissions of those over whom the partner has supervisory duties. The increasing use of LLPs reflects changed perceptions as to the traditional concepts of joint and several liability for large professional partnerships with hundreds of partners scattered over the country or even on different continents.

Each state and the District of Columbia have LLP-enabling legislation. Some states offer members of LLPs limited protection from partnership liabilities, such as limiting the protection to malpractice claims against other partners. Other states offer full protection from liabilities, including the partnership's contractual liabilities. These are called "full shield" states.

As a practical matter, LLPs are most likely to be used to give liability protection to partners in an existing partnership. This conversion does not create a new partnership, as the IRS has ruled that the registration of a general partnership as a registered limited liability partnership does not cause a termination of the partnership for purposes of Code Sec. 708(b) (Rev. Rul. 95-55).[3] In such a case, the partnership is required to continue to use the same method of accounting used before its registration. Each partner's total

References are to Standard Federal Tax Reports; Tax Research Consultant; and Practical Tax Explanations.

[1] ¶ 25,600; PART: 3,100; § 30,015.05

[2] ¶ 43,082; PART: 3,102; § 30,015.10

[3] ¶ 25,202.27; PART: 3,108; § 30,005.15

percentage interest in the partnership's profits, losses, and capital remains the same after the registration as an LLP.

Limited Liability Limited Partnerships. Some states have passed legislation allowing limited liability limited partnerships (LLLPs). These entities operate like a traditional limited partnership, but the "general partner" also has the limitations on personal liability of a partner in a limited liability partnership.

402. Exclusion from Partnership Provisions. In two different sets of circumstances, entities that would otherwise be considered partnerships may elect to not have all or part of Subchapter K apply or to not be treated as partnerships for federal income tax purposes. Application of the partnership tax rules can be avoided in certain cases where the income of the partners can be adequately determined without partnership-level computation and in the case of certain husband-wife partnerships.

Unincorporated organizations may elect not to be taxed as partnerships if they are used either for investment purposes only or for the joint production, extraction, or use—but not the sale—of property under an operating agreement (Code Sec. 761(a)).[4] The exclusion also can be used by securities dealers for a short period for the purpose of underwriting, selling, or distributing a particular issue of securities. The exclusion can be elected only if the partners' incomes can be determined without computing the entity's income first.

An unincorporated organization may choose to be completely or only partially excluded from the partnership provisions. However, the IRS does not allow an organization making the partial election to be excluded from the tax-year conformity rules of Code Sec. 706 or from the limitations on the allowance of losses (¶ 416 and ¶ 425) (Rev. Rul. 57-215).[5] This election removes the entity from all or a portion of the subchapter K partnership provisions.

Qualified Joint Ventures. A business co-owned by a husband and wife who file a joint return may elect not to be treated as a partnership for federal tax purposes Code Sec. 761(f)).[6] Code Sec. 761(f) provides that a "qualified joint venture" will not be treated as a partnership for federal tax purposes. A qualified joint venture is a joint venture involving the conduct of a trade or business if (1) the only members of the joint venture are a husband and wife, (2) both spouses materially participate in the trade or business, and (3) both spouses elect to have the provision apply. The IRS takes the position that qualified joint ventures include only businesses that are owned and operated by spouses as co-owners, and do not include businesses that are run as a state law entity, such as a limited liability company (IRS Pub. 1635).

All items of income, gain, loss, deduction, and credit from a qualified joint venture are divided between the spouses in accordance with their respective interests in the venture. Each spouse takes into account his or her respective share of these items as a sole proprietor. Each spouse should account for his or her respective share on the appropriate form, such as Schedule C (Code Sec. 761(f)).

402A. Check-the-Box Regulations. Most entities that qualify for partnership treatment also qualify for electing out of partnership treatment under the check-the-box regulations. Any business entity not required to be treated as a corporation for federal tax purposes may choose its own classification (Reg. § 301.7701-3).[7] An entity with two or more members can be classified either as a partnership or as an association taxed as a corporation. An entity with only one member can choose to be taxed as a corporation or can be disregarded as an entity separate from its owner. A single-member limited liability company (SMLLC) cannot elect partnership status because a partnership, by definition, has two or more partners.

The default classification for entities existing before January 1, 1997, is the classification the entity claimed immediately prior to that date. For new domestic entities that

References are to Standard Federal Tax Reports; Tax Research Consultant; and Practical Tax Explanations.

[4] ¶ 25,600; PART: 3,350; § 30,015.20

[5] ¶ 25,602.11; PART: 3,356.15; § 30,015.20

[6] ¶ 25,600; PART: 3,358; § 30,015.20

[7] ¶ 43,083; PART: 3,102; § 30,015.10

do not file an election, an entity with two or more members is classified as a partnership. A domestic entity with one member is ignored and the taxpayer is treated as a sole proprietorship. Thus, a domestic LLC will be taxed as a partnership or disregarded entity unless it files an election to be taxed as a corporation.

The check-the-box rules apply somewhat differently to foreign business organizations. Entities listed in Reg. § 301.7701-2(b)(8) are considered corporations and are not eligible to be partnerships under the check-the-box rules. Any other foreign entity may be taxed as either a corporation or partnership (or a disregarded entity if it has one owner). A foreign business entity where all owners have limited liability will generally be treated as a corporation unless it elects to be taxed as a partnership. A foreign business entity where one or more owners has unlimited liability will generally be taxed as a partnership unless it elects to be taxed as a corporation. Thus, the foreign equivalent of an LLC (such as a German GmbH), where all members have limited liability, will be taxed as a corporation unless it elects to be taxed as a partnership.

Note that the term "limited liability" is not precisely defined by the regulations, and it may be uncertain whether the IRS would consider a given foreign law to provide for limited liability for all members of an entity. It will usually be easier and safer for practitioners to file an election under the check-the-box rules for a foreign entity rather than to determine what its default classification would be.

An election not to be taxed as a partnership under the check-the-box regulations is filed on Form 8832 and applies to all Code provisions. This is different from an election under Code Sec. 761 (¶ 402), which removes a partnership only from the provisions of subchapter K (Code Sec. 701—Code Sec. 777).

402B. Limited Liability Companies. A state-registered limited liability company (LLC) can be taxed as a partnership for federal income tax purposes. However, its members, like corporate shareholders, are not personally liable for the entity's debts or liabilities. Under the check-the-box rules, an LLC can choose partnership status to avoid taxation at the entity level as an "association taxed as a corporation."

Unlike limited partners, LLC members may participate in management without risking personal liability for company debts. No limitations are placed on the number of owners (compared to a maximum of 100 shareholders for S corporations) or different types of owners of an LLC (S corporations may generally only have U.S. resident individuals or certain types of trusts as shareholders). Additional advantages over S corporations include the ability to make disproportionate allocations and distributions (Code Sec. 704)[8] and to distribute appreciated property to members without the recognition of gain (Code Sec. 731(b)).[9] Members may also exchange appreciated property for membership interests without the recognition of gain or loss (Code Sec. 721).[10]

Conversion from Partnership to LLC. A conversion of a partnership into an LLC that is taxed as a partnership for federal income tax purposes is treated as a nontaxable partnership-to-partnership conversion (Rev. Rul. 95-37).[11] The conversion is treated as a contribution of assets to the new partnership under Code Sec. 721 and does not result in gain or loss to the partners. The tax results are the same whether the LLC is formed in the same state as the former partnership or in a different state. Upon such a conversion, the tax year of the converting partnership does not close with respect to any of the partners, and the resulting LLC does not need to obtain a new taxpayer identification number.

Conversion from C Corporation to LLC. The conversion of an existing C corporation into an LLC taxed as a partnership is generally treated as a liquidation of the corporation and thus a taxable event for both the corporation and the shareholders (Code Sec. 7701; LTR 9701029).[12] Obviously, the possible tax hit diminishes the attractiveness of existing corporate entities converting to LLCs. This is especially true if the corporation holds

References are to Standard Federal Tax Reports; Tax Research Consultant; and Practical Tax Explanations.

[8] ¶ 25,120; PART: 30,000; § 30,501

[9] ¶ 25,320; PART: 33,152; § 30,530.05

[10] ¶ 25,240; PART: 9,050; § 30,105.10

[11] ¶ 25,243.13; PART: 3,106.10; § 30,930.20

[12] ¶ 43,080; LLC: 18,150

appreciated property. Only a corporation with little or no net worth and shareholders with bases exceeding the amount of any distribution can escape this tax result. This conversion can be accomplished in one of two ways: the assets of the corporation can be contributed to the LLC in return for membership interests which are then distributed to the shareholders in liquidation of the corporation; or the corporation can distribute its assets in complete liquidation, and the shareholders can then contribute their undivided interests in the assets to the LLC in exchange for the membership interests.

Conversion from S Corporation to LLC. For an S corporation to convert to an LLC taxed as a partnership, it must undergo the same process (explained above) as a C corporation. However, unlike a C corporation, when an S corporation distributes appreciated assets to its shareholders in exchange for their stock, there is no double tax. Because the S corporation is a flowthrough entity, the gain incurred at the corporate level passes through to the shareholders and is generally included in income on the shareholder's individual tax return. Any gain recognized by the shareholder as a result of the gain attributable to the liquidating distribution increases the shareholder's stock basis. The shareholder's increased basis then reduces the amount of gain recognized or increases the amount of loss recognized.

Thus, with one exception relating to the built-in gains tax (Code Sec. 1374), there is a single level of taxation to contend with here. Although, with an S corporation, there is usually only this one level of taxation, rather than the two levels of taxation inherent with the C corporation, this single level of taxation may still be enough to dissuade an S corporation from converting to an LLC.

Series LLCs. Several states, including Delaware, permit the creation of separate series within an LLC. The debts and other liabilities of each series are only enforceable against that series. Each series is recognized as a distinct entity for state law purposes and each series can have its own separate business purposes. A series can be terminated without affecting the other series of the LLC. Under proposed regulations, effective on or after they are published as final, each series of a series organization (such as a series LLC) would be treated for federal tax purposes as an entity formed under local law, regardless of whether local law actually treats the series as a separate entity (Prop. Reg. § 301.7701-1(a)(5)).[13]

Publicly Traded Partnerships

403. Special Tax Rules. A publicly traded partnership (PTP) is taxed as a corporation unless 90 percent or more of its gross income is derived from qualifying passive income sources (such as interest, dividends, real property rents, gain from the disposition of real property, mining and natural resource income, and gain from the disposition of capital assets or Code Sec. 1231(b) property held for the production of such income) (Code Sec. 7704).[14] A PTP is a partnership with interests traded on an established securities market or readily tradable on a secondary market (or its substantial equivalent), including master limited partnerships. A partnership that was publicly traded on December 17, 1987, continues to be treated as a partnership rather than a corporation if it meets certain conditions (Code Sec. 7704(g); Reg. § 1.7704-2(a)(1)).[15]

A grandfather rule exempts "electing 1987 partnerships" from corporate treatment if the partnership existed as a PTP or was treated as having existed as a PTP on December 17, 1987, elected to continue its partnership status, and does not add a substantial new line of business. A grandfathered electing 1987 partnership must pay an annual 3.5-percent tax on any income from the conduct of an active business.

Partnership-Level Issues

404. Partners, Not Partnership, Subject to Tax. A partnership does not pay federal income tax; rather, income or loss "flows through" to the partners who are taxed in their individual capacities on their distributive shares of partnership taxable income. However, a partnership is a tax-reporting entity that must file an annual partnership return (¶ 406). In determining federal income tax, a partner must take into account his

References are to Standard Federal Tax Reports; Tax Research Consultant; and Practical Tax Explanations.

[13] ¶ 43,084.08; LLC: 100 [14] ¶ 43,180; PART: 3,254 [15] ¶ 43,181; PART: 3,256

distributive share of partnership income or loss for the year, as well as his distributive share of certain separately stated items (¶ 431) of partnership income, gain, loss, deduction, or credit. A partner's distributive share of partnership items is includible on his individual income tax return (or corporate income tax return for corporate partners) for his tax year in which the partnership tax year ends (Code Sec. 706(a)).[16]

A partner is generally not taxed on distributions of cash (including marketable securities) or property received from the partnership, except to the extent that any money (including marketable securities) distributed exceeds the partner's adjusted basis in his partnership interest immediately before the distribution (¶ 453). Taxable gain can also result from distributions of property that was contributed to a partnership with a "built-in gain" (if property has a fair market value in excess of its adjusted basis) and from property distributions that are characterized as sales and exchanges (¶ 432).

406. Return Used by Partnership. Annual information reporting on Form 1065 is required regardless of whether the partnership has taxable income for the tax year. Although Code Sec. 6063[17] states that the return may be signed by any one of the partners, the instructions to Form 1065 indicate that the form must be signed by one of the partnership's general partners or, in the case of an LLC, by one of the member managers (¶ 415). A U.S. partnership's return on Form 1065 is due on or before the 15th day of the fourth month following the close of the tax year. A foreign partnership that does not have U.S.-source income is not required to file a partnership return if the partnership has no effectively connected income and no U.S. partners at any time during the partnership's tax year (Reg. § 1.6031(a)-1(b)(3)(ii)).[18]

Form 7004 should be used to apply for an automatic five-month filing extension (Reg. § 1.6081-2).[19]

If a partnership that is required to file a return for any tax year fails to file a return on time or fails to include all the information required to be shown on the return, the partnership is subject to a penalty for each month or fraction of a month the failure continues, up to a maximum of twelve months, unless the partnership shows that the failure is due to reasonable cause. For returns required to be filed for tax years that begin after December 31, 2009, the penalty generally is $195, multiplied by the number of persons who were partners in the partnership during any part of the tax year. Reasonable cause exists only if significant mitigating factors are present, or the failure to file arose from factors beyond the filer's control, and the filer establishes that it acted in a responsible manner both before and after the failure. A partnership may not contest the penalty assessment in the Tax Court but must pay the entire penalty and then sue for a refund (Code Sec. 6698).[20] Certain domestic partnerships with 10 or fewer partners do not have to pay the penalty if all partners have fully reported their distributive shares on timely filed income tax returns (Rev. Proc. 84-35).[21]

Generally, a partnership that is required to file a Form 1065 must furnish each partner with a Schedule K-1 that provides the partner's distributive share of partnership income, gain, loss, deduction, or credit and any additional information that is necessary to enable the partner to determine the correct income tax treatment of a partnership item (Temp. Reg. § 1.6031(b)-1T(a)(3); Rev. Proc. 2012-17).[22] Effective February 13, 2012, in order to provide Schedule K-1 to partners in an electronic format, a partnership must obtain their consent. IRS approval to use a substitute K-1 is not required if the electronic copy furnished is an exact copy of the official Schedule K-1.

410. Reorganization, Dissolution, or Changes in Membership. The tax year of a partnership closes with respect to a partner whose entire interest in the partnership ends, whether by a sale of the entire interest or otherwise (Code Sec. 706(c)(2)(A)).[23]

References are to Standard Federal Tax Reports; Tax Research Consultant; and Practical Tax Explanations.

[16] ¶ 25,160; PART: 6,052; § 30,125

[17] ¶ 36,640; PART: 18,160.05; § 30,435

[18] ¶ 35,383; PART: 18,160.15; § 39,205.15

[19] ¶ 36,788; PART: 18,160.05; § 39,215.20

[20] ¶ 39,995; PART: 18,162.10; § 30,435

[21] ¶ 40,000.10; PART: 18,160.10; § 30,435

[22] ¶ 35,385, ¶ 35,389.24; PART: 18,162.15; § 30,435

[23] ¶ 25,160; PART: 6,154; § 38,145.15

The sale of a portion of a partnership interest does not result in the closing of the partnership's tax year with respect to the selling partner.

In the case of a sale, exchange, gift, or liquidation of a partner's entire interest in a partnership, the partnership "closes the books" as to that partner (Code Sec. 706(c)(2)(A); Reg. § 1.706-1(c)(2)).[24] In this case, the date of the disposition of the partnership interest is treated *as to the withdrawing partner* as if it is the close of the tax year. That partner's share of the partnership tax items is then determined as of that date, and the partner must include his share of partnership tax items in his income for the tax year in which his partnership interest ends. However, a partnership does not have to make an interim closing of the books. Instead, a retiring partner's share of income may, by agreement among the partners, be estimated by taking a pro rata portion of the amount of such items the partner would have included in his income had he remained a partner until the end of the partnership tax year. The prorated amount may be based on the portion of the tax year that has elapsed prior to the sale, exchange, or liquidation, or may be determined under any other method that is reasonable.

Changes in Partnership Interests During Tax Year. If there is a change in any partner's interest in the partnership (for instance, because of the retirement of a partner, entry of a new partner or simply a change in the allocations of partnership items), each remaining partner's distributive share must take into account the varying interests during the partnership tax year (Code Sec. 706(d); Reg. § 1.706-1).[25] Generally, this rule may be satisfied either by using an interim closing of the books or by prorating income, losses, etc., for the entire year. However, special rules apply with respect to cash-basis items and tiered partnerships.

If there is a change in any partner's interest in the partnership, the distributive shares of certain cash-method items are determined by assigning the appropriate portion of each item to each day to which it is attributable and then by allocating the daily portions among the partners in proportion to their interests in the partnership at the close of each day. For this purpose, cash-method items are (1) interest, (2) taxes, (3) payments for services or for the use of property, and (4) any other item specified in the regulations. Cash-method items deductible or includible within the tax year but attributable to a time period before the beginning of the tax year (for example, payment during the tax year for services performed in the prior tax year) are assigned by Code Sec. 706(d)(2)(C) to the first day of the tax year. If persons to whom such items are allocable are no longer partners on the first day of the tax year, then their portion of the items must be capitalized by the partnership and allocated to the basis of partnership assets pursuant to Code Sec. 755. Cash-method items attributable to periods following the close of the tax year (for example, properly deductible prepaid expenses) are assigned to the last day of the tax year.

In the case of changes in a partner's interest in an upper-tier partnership that has an ownership interest in a lower-tier partnership, each partner's distributive share of any items of the upper-tier partnership attributable to the lower-tier partnership is determined by (1) assigning the appropriate portion of each such item to the appropriate days of the upper-tier partnership's tax year on which the upper-tier partnership is a partner in the lower-tier partnership and (2) allocating the assigned portion among the partners in proportion to their interests in the upper-tier partnership as of the close of each day (Code Sec. 706(d)(3)).[26]

415. Administrative and Judicial Proceedings at Partnership Level. The determination of the tax treatment of partnership items is generally made at the partnership level in a single administrative partnership proceeding rather than in separate proceedings with each partner. Rules from the Tax Equity and Fiscal Responsibility Act of 1982 (P.L. 97-248) (or "TEFRA audit rules") govern proceedings that must be conducted at the partnership level for the assessment and collection of tax deficiencies or for tax refunds arising out of the partners' distributive shares of income, deductions, credits,

References are to Standard Federal Tax Reports; Tax Research Consultant; and Practical Tax Explanations.

[24] ¶ 25,160, ¶ 25,161; PART: 24,112; § 30,910.05

[25] ¶ 25,160, ¶ 25,161; PART: 24,112.20, PART: 24,114; § 30,425.10, § 30,910.05

[26] ¶ 25,160; PART: 24,114; § 30,910.05

and other partnership items. (Code Secs. 6221–6233).[27] (See also ¶ 482 for special rules applying to electing large partnerships.)

Notice of the beginning of administrative proceedings and the resulting final partnership administrative adjustment (FPAA) must be given to all partners whose names and addresses are furnished to the IRS, except those with less than a 1-percent interest in partnerships that have more than 100 partners (Code Sec. 6223).[28] However, a group of partners having an aggregate profits interest of 5 percent or more may request notice to be mailed to a designated partner. Each partnership should have a "tax matters partner" who is to receive notice on behalf of small partners not entitled to notice and to keep all of the partners informed of all administrative and judicial proceedings at the partnership level (Code Sec. 6231).[29] The tax matters partner is either the general partner designated as such by the partnership or, in the absence of a designation, the general partner with the largest interest in partnership profits for the relevant tax year. Settlement agreements may be entered into between the tax matters partner and the IRS that bind the parties to the agreement and may extend to other partners who request to enter into consistent settlement agreements (Code Sec. 6224).[30]

Consistency Requirement. Each partner is required to treat partnership items on his return in a manner consistent with the treatment of such items on the partnership return (Code Sec. 6222).[31] A partner may be penalized for intentional disregard of this requirement. The consistency requirement may be waived if the partner files a statement (Form 8082) identifying the inconsistency or shows that it resulted from an incorrect schedule furnished by the partnership.

The IRS may apply entity-level audit procedures when it appears from the return that such procedures should apply. The IRS's determination will stand even if it later proves to be erroneous (Code Sec. 6231(g)).[32]

Innocent Spouse Relief. Innocent spouse relief is available with respect to partnership-level proceedings (Code Sec. 6230).[33]

If the spouse of a partner in a partnership subject to the TEFRA audit rules asserts that the innocent spouse rules apply with respect to a liability attributable to any adjustment to a partnership item, the spouse may file a request for an abatement of the assessment with the IRS. The spouse must file the request within 60 days after the notice of a computational adjustment has been mailed by the IRS. Upon receipt of the request, the IRS must abate the assessment. If the IRS chooses to reassess the abated tax, it then has 60 days after the date of the abatement in which to make any reassessment. In such a scenario, the regular deficiency procedures apply.

If the taxpayer claiming innocent spouse relief files a Tax Court petition under Code Sec. 6213 with respect to the request for abatement, the Tax Court can determine only whether the innocent spouse requirements have in fact been satisfied. For purposes of this determination, the treatment of the TEFRA partnership items under the settlement, the final partnership administrative adjustment (FPAA) or the court decision that gave rise to the liability in question is conclusive.

Small Partnership Exception. The TEFRA audit rules do not apply to partnerships with 10 or fewer partners if each partner is an individual U.S. resident, a C corporation or an estate, and each partner's share of any partnership item is the same as his distributive share of every other partnership item. However, these small partnerships may elect to have the TEFRA audit rules apply (Code Sec. 6231(a)(1)(B)).[34] The partnership also can specially allocate items without jeopardizing its exception from the TEFRA audit rules. Once a small partnership elects to have the TEFRA rules apply, the election cannot be revoked without IRS consent.

References are to Standard Federal Tax Reports; Tax Research Consultant; and Practical Tax Explanations.

[27] ¶ 37,565; PART: 60,050; § 31,105

[28] ¶ 37,590; PART: 60,150; § 31,110.15

[29] ¶ 37,770; PART: 60,100; § 31,110.10

[30] ¶ 37,640; PART: 60,200; § 31,110.10

[31] ¶ 37,570; PART: 60,058; § 31,130.10

[32] ¶ 37,770; IRS: 27,104; § 31,105

[33] ¶ 37,750; PART: 60,312; § 39,040.05

[34] ¶ 37,770; PART: 60,054; § 31,105

416. Required Tax Year. Generally, a partnership cannot have a tax year other than its "majority-interest taxable year" (Code Sec. 706(b)).[35] This is the tax year that, on each "testing day," constitutes the tax year of one or more partners having an aggregate interest in partnership profits and capital of more than 50 percent. The testing day is the first day of the partnership's tax year (determined without regard to the majority interest rule). In general, a partnership that changes to a majority-interest tax year is not required to change to another tax year for the two tax years following the year of change.

If the partnership has no majority-interest tax year, then its tax year must be the same as the tax year of all of the partnership's principal partners (partners who individually own 5 percent or more of the partnership's profits or capital).[36] Partnerships that are unable to determine a tax year under either of the foregoing methods must adopt a tax year that results in the least aggregate deferral of income to the partners (Reg. § 1.706-1).[37] A partnership may avoid the tax year rules set out above if it can establish a business purpose for selecting a different tax year (Code Sec. 706(b)(1)(C); Reg. § 1.706-1(b)(2)).[38]

Code Sec. 444 Election. Certain partnerships are permitted to make an election to have a tax year other than the normally required tax year (Code Sec. 444).[39] For any tax year for which an election is made, a partnership generally must make a "required payment" that is intended to represent the tax on the income deferred through the use of a tax year other than a required year. The payment is due on May 15 of the calendar year following the calendar year in which the Code Sec. 444 election year begins (Code Sec. 7519; Temp. Reg. § 1.7519-2T(a)(4)(ii)) (¶ 1501).[40]

417. Partnership as Pass-Through Entity. While a partnership is not subject to tax, its "taxable income" is the key feature by which the partnership passes through its income or loss to its partners (Code Sec. 701).[41] Each partner generally must account for his distributive share of partnership taxable income in computing his income tax. The partner's share of partnership tax items is reported to him by the partnership on Schedule K-1 of Form 1065. A partner's basis in his partnership interest is increased by his distributive share of partnership taxable income, while the partner's basis generally decreases by the amount distributed to him by the partnership. Thus, if a partnership distributes all of its taxable income by the end of the partnership tax year, the basis of each partner's interest in the partnership does not change (Code Secs. 705 and 731(a)).[42]

The taxable income of a partnership is computed in the same manner as that of an individual except that the following deductions and carryovers are not allowed to a partnership:

(1) the deduction for personal exemptions,

(2) the deduction for foreign taxes (note that the taxes are allocated to the partners as separately stated items),

(3) the net operating loss deduction (which is determined at the partner level, not the partnership level),

(4) the deduction for charitable contributions (which is allocated to the partners as a separately stated item),

(5) individuals' itemized deductions (medical expenses, etc.) set out in Code Secs. 211–223,

(6) the capital loss carryover (which is determined at the partner level, not the partnership level),

References are to Standard Federal Tax Reports; Tax Research Consultant; and Practical Tax Explanations.

[35] ¶ 25,160; PART: 6,102; § 30,120.10

[36] ¶ 25,160; PART: 6,104; § 30,120.15

[37] ¶ 25,161; PART: 6,106; § 30,120.20

[38] ¶ 25,160, ¶ 25,161; PART: 6,108

[39] ¶ 20,600; PART: 6,110; § 30,120.30

[40] ¶ 42,770, ¶ 42,773; PART: 6,110; § 31,120.05

[41] ¶ 25,060; PART: 18,050; § 30,401

[42] ¶ 25,140, ¶ 25,320; PART: 15,056, PART: 18,050; § 30,210.10

(7) the domestic production activities deduction (which is determined at the partner level, not the partnership level), and

(8) depletion deductions under Code Sec. 611 with respect to oil and gas wells (which are allocated to the partners as separately stated items) (Code Sec. 703(a); Reg. § 1.703-1).[43]

In addition, certain items of gain, loss, etc. must be separately stated (¶ 431).

418. Anti-Abuse Regulations. Regulations give the IRS the power to recast transactions that attempt to use the partnership provisions for tax-avoidance purposes (Reg. § 1.701-2).[44] Under the rules, a partnership must be *bona fide* and each partnership transaction must be entered into for a substantial business purpose. The form of each transaction must be respected under substance-over-form rules. Finally, the tax consequences to each partner of partnership operations and transactions must accurately reflect the partners' economic agreement and clearly reflect each partner's income.

Whether there is a "principal purpose" of "substantially" reducing the present value of the partners' aggregate tax liability is determined at the partnership level.

In abusive situations, the IRS can treat a partnership as the aggregate of its partners, in whole or in part, as appropriate to carry out the purpose of any Code or regulation provision. However, to the extent that a Code or regulation provision prescribes treatment of the partnership as an entity and the treatment and ultimate tax results are clearly contemplated by the provision, the IRS will not recast a transaction.

419. Elections by Partnerships. Most elections affecting the computation of income derived from a partnership must be made by the partnership. Thus, elections as to methods of accounting, methods of computing depreciation, the Code Sec. 179 expensing election, the election not to use the installment sales provision, the option to expense intangible drilling and development costs, and similar elections must be made by the partnership and must apply to all partners, insofar as the partnership transactions are concerned (Reg. § 1.703-1(b)).[45] In the case of an involuntary conversion of partnership property, the partnership also must purchase replacement property and elect nonrecognition of gain treatment (Rev. Rul. 66-191).[46]

Individual partners must make the elections to (1) use as a credit or as a deduction their distributive shares of foreign taxes of the partnership, (2) deduct or capitalize their shares of the partnership's mining exploration expenditures, and (3) reduce basis in connection with discharge of indebtedness under Code Sec. 108 (Code Sec. 703(b)).[47]

Regulations provide for an automatic six-month extension for making elections if the time for making the election also is the due date of the return for which the election is made (Reg. §§ 301.9100-1, 301.9100-2, and 301.9100-3).

421. Guaranteed Payments to Partners. Any fixed payments to partners for services or for the use of capital made without regard to partnership income are treated as though paid to a nonpartner for purposes of computing partnership gross income and business expense deductions (¶ 432). Thus, guaranteed payments are regarded as ordinary income to the recipient and are deductible by the partnership as ordinary and necessary business expenses (assuming they are, in fact, "ordinary and necessary") (¶ 901) (Code Sec. 707(c); Reg. § 1.707-1(c)).[48] This rule applies only to the extent that the amounts paid are in fact "guaranteed payments" determined without regard to the income of the partnership (Code Sec. 707(c); Reg. § 1.707-4).[49] The partner must report the payments on his return for the tax year within or with which ends the partnership year in which the partnership deducted the payments as paid or accrued under its method of accounting.

References are to Standard Federal Tax Reports; Tax Research Consultant; and Practical Tax Explanations.

[43] ¶ 25,100, ¶ 25,101; PART: 18,052; § 30,405

[44] ¶ 25,061B; PART: 3,110; § 30,130

[45] ¶ 23,950.218, ¶ 25,101; PART: 18,150; § 30,301

[46] ¶ 29,650.704; SALES: 27,000; § 18,101

[47] ¶ 25,100; PART: 18,154; § 30,301

[48] ¶ 25,180, ¶ 25,181; PART: 27,100; § 30,735.05

[49] ¶ 25,180, ¶ 25,181C; PART: 27,102; § 30,735.10

Example 1: In the AB partnership, Ann is the managing partner and is entitled to receive a fixed annual payment of $100,000 for her services, without regard to the income of the partnership. Her distributive share of partnership profit and loss is 10%. After deducting her guaranteed payment, the partnership has $300,000 ordinary income. Ann must include $130,000 ($100,000 guaranteed payment plus $30,000 distributive share) as ordinary income for her tax year within or with which the partnership tax year ends. If the partnership had shown a $100,000 loss after deduction of Ann's guaranteed payment, her guaranteed payment ($100,000) would be reported as income and her $10,000 distributive share of the loss, subject to the loss limitations of Code Sec. 704(d) (¶ 425), would be taken into account on her individual tax return.

If a partner is entitled to a minimum payment and the percentage of profits is less than the minimum payment, the guaranteed payment is the difference between the minimum payment and the distributive share of the profits determined before the deduction of the minimum payment (Reg. § 1.707-1(c)).[50] Only the amount of the guaranteed payment may qualify as a deductible business expense of the partnership.

Example 2: The AB partnership agreement provides that Ann is to receive 30% of partnership income before taking into account any guaranteed payments, but not less than $100,000. The income of the partnership is $600,000, and Ann is entitled to $180,000 (30% of $600,000) as her distributive share. Because her distributive share exceeds the minimum amount that was guaranteed, no part of the $180,000 is a guaranteed payment. If the partnership had income of only $200,000, Ann's distributive share would have been $60,000 (30% of $200,000), and the remaining $40,000 payable to Ann would have been a guaranteed payment.

A partner who receives a guaranteed salary payment is not regarded as an employee of the partnership for the purpose of withholding of income or Social Security taxes or for pension plans. The guaranteed salary is includible in self-employment income for the purpose of the self-employment tax along with the partner's share of ordinary income or loss of the partnership (Reg. § 1.707-1(c); Rev. Rul. 56-675).[51]

Fringe Benefits. The value of fringe benefits provided to a partner for services rendered in the capacity as a partner is generally treated as a guaranteed payment (Code Sec. 162(l); Rev. Rul. 91-26).[52] As such, the value of the benefit is generally deductible by the partnership as an ordinary and necessary business expense; the value of the benefit is included in the partner's gross income, unless a Code provision allowing exclusion of the benefit specifically provides that the exclusion applies to partners.

Thus, a payment of premiums by a partnership for a partner's health or accident insurance is generally deductible by the partnership and included in the partner's gross income. As an alternative, a partnership may choose to account for premiums paid for a partner's insurance by reducing that partner's distributions; in this case the premiums are not deductible by the partnership and all partners' distributive shares are unaffected by payment of the premiums. A partner can deduct 100 percent of the cost of the health insurance premiums paid on his behalf.

Partner Loss Deductions

425. Loss Limited to Partner's Basis. The amount of partnership loss (including capital loss) that may be recognized by a partner is limited to the amount of the adjusted basis (before reduction by the current year's loss) of his interest in the partnership at the end of the partnership tax year in which the loss occurred. Any disallowed loss is carried forward to and may be deducted by the partner in subsequent partnership tax years (to the extent that his basis exceeds zero before deducting the loss) (Reg. § 1.704-1(d)).[53] Techniques that have been used to increase a partner's basis so that he can deduct losses that otherwise would be unavailable are making additional contributions to the capital of the partnership (¶ 443) and increasing the partner's share of partnership liabilities, if this is permitted under the "substantial economic effect" rules (¶ 428).

References are to Standard Federal Tax Reports; Tax Research Consultant; and Practical Tax Explanations.

[50] ¶ 25,181; PART: 27,112; § 30,735.15

[51] ¶ 25,181, ¶ 25,183.30; PART: 27,112; § 30,735.20

[52] ¶ 8500, ¶ 25,183.16; PART: 27,100, PART: 27,104; § 21,225, § 30,735.10, § 30,735.20

[53] ¶ 25,121; PART: 15,202; § 30,430.10

426. Partners and the At-Risk Rules. The rules limiting a partner's deduction for any tax year to the amount he is at risk in the partnership for that year (¶ 2045) apply at the partner level, not the partnership level (Temp. Reg. § 1.469-2T(d)(6); Code Sec. 465).[54] A partner is not at risk for any portion of a partnership liability for which he has no personal liability. The at-risk loss limitation rules are applied after taking into account the basis limitation for partners' losses but before the limitations applicable to computing any passive activity loss for the year.

Real Estate Exception. The at-risk rules generally apply to the holding of property in the same manner as they apply to other activities (Code Sec. 465(b)(6)).[55] However, an exception applies to the holding of real estate. A taxpayer is "at risk" with respect to qualified nonrecourse financing that is secured by the real property used in the activity of holding real estate. Thus, lending provided by any person actively and regularly engaged in the business of lending money is qualified nonrecourse financing. Such lenders generally include banks, savings and loan associations, credit unions, insurance companies regulated under federal, state, or local law, or pension trusts. Further, qualified nonrecourse financing includes a loan made by any federal, state, or local government or a governmental entity or a loan that is guaranteed by any federal, state, or local government. Convertible debt cannot be treated as qualified nonrecourse financing.

In addition, qualified nonrecourse financing can be provided by a related person (generally, family members, fiduciaries, and corporations, or partnerships in which a person has at least a 10-percent interest) if the financing from the related person is commercially reasonable and on substantially the same terms as loans involving unrelated persons.

427. Partnerships and the Passive Activity Loss Rules. The passive activity loss limitations (¶ 2053) apply at the partner level to each partner's share of any loss or credit attributable to a passive activity of the partnership (Code Sec. 469).[56] A partnership may engage in both passive and nonpassive activities. For example, a partnership may engage in business that is a passive activity of its limited partners (who normally do not participate in the management of a limited partnership), and it may also have investment assets that produce portfolio income (not a passive activity). Thus, a partner who disposes of his interest in a partnership must allocate any gain or loss among the various activities of the partnership in order to determine the amount that is passive gain or loss and the amount that is nonpassive gain or loss. In general, the allocation is made in accordance with the relative value of the partnership's assets.

To allow a partner to make these calculations, a partnership must report separately a partner's share of income or losses and credits from each of its: (1) trade or business activity, (2) rental real estate activity, and (3) rental activity other than rental real estate. A partnership's portfolio income, which is excluded from passive income, must also be separately reported (Code Sec. 703).[57]

Generally, a passive activity of a partner is: (1) a trade or business activity in which the partner does not materially participate or (2) any rental activity. Except as otherwise provided (Temp. Reg. § 1.469-5T(e)(2)),[58] an interest in an activity as a limited partner in a limited partnership is not one in which the partner materially participates. If a partnership reports amounts from more than one activity on a partner's Schedule K-1 and one or more of the activities is passive to the partner, the partnership must attach a statement detailing the income, losses, deductions, and credits from each passive activity and the line of Schedule K-1 on which that amount is included.

References are to Standard Federal Tax Reports; Tax Research Consultant; and Practical Tax Explanations.

[54] ¶ 21,850, ¶ 21,963; PART: 15,204; § 17,301

[55] ¶ 21,850; BUSEXP: 42,160; § 17,305.10

[56] ¶ 21,960; PART: 15,206; § 30,430.05

[57] ¶ 25,100; PART: 15,206; § 30,410

[58] ¶ 21,965; PART: 15,206; § 17,435.20

427A. Net Operating Loss Deduction of Partners. The benefit of the net operating loss deduction (¶ 1173) is not allowed to the partnership but instead to its partners. For purposes of determining his individual net operating loss, each partner takes into account his distributive share of income, gain, loss, deduction, or credit of the partnership as if each item were realized directly from the source from which it was realized by the partnership or incurred in the same manner as it was incurred by the partnership (Reg. § 1.702-2).[59]

Partner's Distributive Share of Partnership Items

428. Allocations Under Partnership Agreement Must Have Substantial Economic Effect. A partner's distributive share of income, gain, loss, deduction, or credit is generally determined by the partnership agreement. Allocations of any partnership item under the partnership agreement must have substantial economic effect if they are to be recognized for Code purposes. If a partnership agreement does not provide for the allocation of partnership items or if partnership allocations lack substantial economic effect, the partner's distributive share is determined according to his interest in the partnership (Code Sec. 704; Reg. § 1.704-1(b)).[60]

Economic Effect. Allocations have economic effect if they are consistent with the underlying economic arrangement of the partners (Reg. § 1.704-1(b)(2)(ii)).[61] For instance, a limited partner who has no risk under the partnership agreement other than his initial capital contribution ordinarily may not be allocated losses attributable to a partnership recourse liability to the extent such losses exceed his capital contribution. These "recourse" losses ordinarily must be allocated to the partners (usually the general partners) who bear the ultimate burden of discharging the partnership's liability. A partnership's "nonrecourse deductions"—those attributable to those liabilities of the partnership for which no partner bears personal liability (for example, a mortgage secured only by a building and the land on which it is located)—are deemed to lack economic effect and, consequently, must be allocated according to the partners' interests in the partnership (¶ 448).

Partnership allocations may be deemed to have substantial economic effect if a set of complicated *optional* safe harbor provisions are met (Reg. § 1.704-1(b)(2).[62] Generally, to satisfy the safe harbor, a partnership must maintain its "book" capital accounts as set out by Reg. § 1.704-1 and make tax allocations consistent with the capital accounts. A second safe harbor in Reg. § 1.704-2 applies to the allocation of nonrecourse deductions.

Substantiality. The economic effect of an allocation is generally considered substantial if there is a reasonable possibility that the allocation will substantially affect the dollar amounts to be received by the partners from the partnership, independent of tax consequences (Reg. § 1.704-1(b)(2)(iii)).[63]

Contributed Property. Income, gain, loss, and deductions attributable to property contributed to a partnership by a partner must be allocated among the partners to take into account the variation between the property's fair market value and its basis to the partnership at the time of contribution (Code Sec. 704(c)).[64] (The partnership's basis in the contributed property at the time of contribution in exchange for a partnership interest is the basis of the property in the hands of the contributing partner.) The potential gain or loss (built-in gain or loss) with respect to the contributed property must be allocated to the contributing partner. A similar rule applies to contributions by cash-method partners of accounts payable and other accrued but unpaid items.

Special rules prevent use of allocations to improperly shift the tax consequences associated with contributed property among partners in a partnership (Reg. § 1.704-3(a)(10)).[65] Under the Code Sec. 704(c) anti-abuse rule, an allocation method is

References are to Standard Federal Tax Reports; Tax Research Consultant; and Practical Tax Explanations.

[59] ¶ 25,084; PART: 18,306; § 30,405

[60] ¶ 25,120, ¶ 25,121; PART: 21,100; § 30,610.05

[61] ¶ 25,121; PART: 21,150; § 30,610.05

[62] ¶ 25,121; PART: 21,358; § 30,610.10

[63] ¶ 25,121; PART: 21,100; § 30,615.05

[64] ¶ 25,120; PART: 9,150; § 30,625.05

[65] ¶ 25,134; PART: 9,152.05; § 30,625.05

not reasonable if the property contribution and the corresponding allocation of tax items regarding the property are made with a view to shifting the tax consequences of built-in gain or loss among the partners in a manner that substantially reduced the present value of the partners' aggregate tax liability. Also, the distribution of built-in gain or loss property to partners other than the contributing partner within seven years of its contribution to the partnership may result in the recognition of gain or loss to the contributing partner if distributed to the other partners (¶ 453).

430. Disproportionate Distributions. The disproportionate distribution rules apply if an actual or constructive distribution to a partner changes his proportionate interest in the partnership's unrealized receivables or inventory. The purpose of these rules is to prevent conversion of ordinary income to capital gain on the distribution or a change in share of unrealized receivables or substantially appreciated inventory.

A disproportionate distribution is treated as a sale or exchange of the receivables or inventory items from the partnership to the partner (Code Sec. 751(b)).[66] This results in ordinary income rather than capital gain. Under Code Sec. 751(f), these rules cannot be avoided through the use of tiered partnerships. Sale or exchange treatment does not apply to a distribution of property that the distributee contributed to the partnership or to payments to a retiring partner or a successor in interest of a deceased partner.

Although the "substantially appreciated inventory" test was dropped for most appreciated inventory in the case of a sale or exchange of a partnership interest (¶ 434), it remains in effect for disproportionate distributions from a partnership to its partners. Inventory is considered to be "substantially appreciated" if its fair market value exceeds the partnership's basis in the property by 120 percent or more. The inventory need not appreciate in value after the partnership acquired it to satisfy the 120-percent test.

431. Separate Reporting of Partnership Items. In determining tax, each partner must account separately for his distributive share of the following partnership items (Code Sec. 702):[67]

(1) short-term capital gains and losses,

(2) long-term capital gains and losses,

(3) gains and losses from sales or exchanges of property used in a trade or business or subject toinvoluntary conversion (¶ 1747),

(4) charitable contributions (¶ 1061),

(5) dividends for which there is a dividends-received deduction (¶ 223),

(6) taxes paid or accrued to foreign countries and to U.S. possessions (¶ 2475),

(7) taxable income or loss, exclusive of items requiring separate computation, and

(8) other items required to be stated separately either by Reg. § 1.702-1[68] or because separate statement could affect the income tax liability of any partner, including:

- recovery of bad debts, prior taxes, and delinquency amounts,
- gains and losses from wagering transactions (¶ 785),
- soil and water conservation expenditures (¶ 982),
- deductible investment expenses (¶ 1085),
- medical and dental expenses (¶ 1015),
- alimony payments (¶ 771),
- amounts paid to cooperative housing corporations (¶ 1040),
- intangible drilling and development costs (¶ 989),

References are to Standard Federal Tax Reports; Tax Research Consultant; and Practical Tax Explanations.

[66] ¶ 25,500; PART: 30,100; § 30,540.10

[67] ¶ 25,080; PART: 18,054; § 30,410

[68] ¶ 25,081; PART: 18,054; § 30,410

- alternative minimum tax adjustments and tax preference items (¶ 1425, ¶ 1430),
- investment tax credit recapture (¶ 1365A),
- recapture of mining exploration expenditures (¶ 987),
- information necessary for partners to compute oil and gas depletion allowances (¶ 1289),
- cost of recovery property being currently expensed (¶ 1208),
- work opportunity tax credit (¶ 1365G),
- alcohol fuels credit (¶ 1365I),
- net earnings from self-employment (¶ 2670),
- investment interest (¶ 1094),
- income or loss to the partnership on certain distributions of unrealized receivables and inventory items to a partner (¶ 453),
- any items subject to a special allocation under the partnership agreement (¶ 428),
- contributions (and the deductions for contributions) made on a partner's behalf to qualified retirement plans (¶ 2156), and
- domestic production activities income and expenses (¶ 431A).

In general, the need for a separate statement of various partnership items gives rise to the separate reporting of these items on Form 1065 and Schedules K and K-1.

Partnerships that regularly carry on a trade or business are required to furnish to tax-exempt partners a separate statement of items of unrelated business taxable income (Code Sec. 6031(d)).[69]

431A. Domestic Production Activities by Partnerships. A partnership cannot claim the deduction for qualified production activities (i.e., manufacturer's deduction) (¶ 980A and following). Instead, the deduction is determined at the partner level (Code Sec. 199(d)(1); Reg. § 1.199-5(b)(1); Notice 2005-14).[70] Generally, each partner computes its deduction separately on Form 8903 by aggregating its proportionate share of qualified production activity (QPA) items of the partnership (i.e., income, expenses) with its share of QPA items from other sources. The partner does not have to be directly engaged in the partnership's trade or business to claim the deduction on the basis of its share of QPA items.

However, a partner will not be treated as directly conducting the QPA of the partnership (and vice versa) with respect to property transferred between the parties (Reg. § 1.199-5(g)).[71] For example, if a partner manufactures qualified production property within the United States and then contributes the property to the partnership which subsequently sells, licenses, leases, or otherwise disposes of the property, then the income derived by the partnership will not qualify as domestic production gross receipts (DPGR). A limited exception is provided for certain qualifying oil and gas partnerships and expanded affiliated groups.

Allocation of Items. QPA items of a partnership are allocated to each partner as any other tax item (¶ 428). This includes special allocations of QPA items, subject to the rules of Reg. § 1.704-1(b), including the rules for determining substantial economic effect. A partner's distributive share of expenses allocable to the partnership's QPA must be taken into account even if the partnership has no taxable income. If a partner is unable to claim a loss or deduction for regular tax purposes (i.e., at-risk, passive loss, or basis limitations), then such loss or deduction cannot be taken into account in computing the Code Sec. 199 deduction. The amount of any loss or deduction is subject to proportionate reduction if it is only partially allowed for regular tax purposes. Also, a loss

References are to Standard Federal Tax Reports; Tax Research Consultant; and Practical Tax Explanations.

[69] ¶ 35,381; PART: 18,162.15; § 30,410

[70] ¶ 12,468, ¶ 12,472, ¶ 12,476.15; BUSEXP: 6,206, BUSEXP: 6,212.10; § 30,415.05

[71] ¶ 12,472D; BUSEXP: 6,212.10; § 30,415.05

or deduction that is temporarily disallowed for regular tax purposes may be used in computing the Code Sec. 199 deduction in the tax year that it is allowed for regular tax purposes.

Instead of taking into account its distributive share of each QPA item of the partnership, a partner may compute its deduction by combining its distributive share of the partnership's qualified production activities income (QPAI) and W-2 wages with its QPAI and W-2 wages from other sources. However, this option only applies if the partnership has elected to use the small business overall method for allocating costs, expenses, and other deductions to its DPGR (¶ 980A and following). A partner's share of QPAI from a partnership may be less than zero under this method.

Special rules apply to 20-percent partners of partnerships engaged in film or television production (Code Sec. 199(d)(1)(A)(iv)).

Sale of Partnership Interest. Gain or loss recognized on the sale of a partnership interest will not be taken into account by a partner in computing its QPAI (Reg. § 1.199-5(f)). This is because the sale of the partnership interest does not reflect the realization of DPGR by the entity. However, if the taxpayer receives a distribution of unrealized receivables or partnership inventory for its entire partnership interest (Code Sec. 751 property (¶ 434 and ¶ 436)), then any gain or loss which would be attributable to the sale or other disposition of such assets which would give rise to QPAI may be taken into account by the partner.

W-2 Wage Limitation. A partner computes the W-2 wage limitation for the Code Sec. 199 deduction by aggregating its share of W-2 wages from the partnership allocable to DPGR with its W-2 wages allocable to DPGR from other sources.

432. Members' Dealings with Own Partnership. Transactions may be deemed to be between the partnership and a nonpartner if direct or indirect allocations and distributions to a partner are related to the partner's performance of services for, or to the transfer of property to, the partnership and, when viewed together, are properly characterized as a payment to the partner acting other than in his capacity as a member of the partnership (Code Sec. 707(a)).[72] This rule prevents the use of disguised payments to circumvent the requirement that a partnership capitalize certain expenses (such as syndication and organization expenses).

Disguised Sales. While recognizing the fact that a taxpayer may enter into transactions with a partnership both as a partner and as a nonpartner, the Code also recognizes that such transactions are sometimes structured to bypass the requirement that certain partnership payments be capitalized. In order to prevent such manipulation, the Code provides that if:

(1) a partner performs services for a partnership or transfers property to a partnership,

(2) there is a related direct or indirect allocation and distribution to the partner, and

(3) the performance of the partner's service (or the partner's transfer of property) and the allocation and distribution, when viewed together, are properly characterized as a transaction that occurred between the partnership and the partner acting as a nonpartner,

then the transaction is treated as if it occurred between the partnership and a nonpartner for income tax purposes.[73]

If this provision applies to a transaction, then the "allocation and distribution" made by the partnership to the partner is recharacterized as a payment for services or property and, where required, the payment must be capitalized or otherwise treated in a manner consistent with its recharacterization, and the partners' shares of taxable income or loss must be redetermined.

References are to Standard Federal Tax Reports; Tax Research Consultant; and Practical Tax Explanations.

[72] ¶ 25,180; PART: 27,050; § 30,701

[73] ¶ 25,180; PART: 27,058; § 30,715.05

Whether a transfer constitutes a disguised sale is based on facts and circumstances. However, contributions and distributions made within a two-year period are presumed to be a sale, while such transactions occurring more than two years apart are presumed not to be a sale (Reg. § 1.707-3(c) and (d)).[74] Certain key exceptions to these presumptions are listed for guaranteed payments for capital, reasonable preferred returns, and operating cash flow distributions (Reg. § 1.707-4).[75]

Transactions Between Controlled Partnerships. Special rules also apply to controlled partnerships. Loss is not allowed from a sale or exchange of property (other than an interest in the partnership) between a partnership and a person whose interest in the partnership's capital *or* profits is more than 50 percent. Loss is also not allowed if the sale or exchange is between two partnerships in which the same persons own more than 50 percent of the capital or profits interests (Code Sec. 707(b)(1)).[76] In either case, if one of the purchasers or transferees realizes gain on a later sale, the gain is taxable only to the extent it exceeds the amount of the disallowed loss attributable to the property sold. Gain recognized on transactions involving controlled partnerships are treated as ordinary income if the property sold or exchanged is not a capital asset in the hands of the transferee (Code Sec. 707(b)(2)).[77]

Code Sec. 267(a)(1) disallows deductions for losses from the sale or exchange of property between persons who are in 1 of the 12 relationships ("related taxpayers") described in Code Sec. 267(b), including a partnership and a corporation controlled by the same persons (¶ 1717). Although this loss-denial rule does not apply to a transaction between a partnership and a partner, it does apply to a transaction between a partnership and a person who has a relationship with a partner that is otherwise specified in Code Sec. 267(b) (Reg. § 1.267(b)-1(b)).[78] Under Code Sec. 267(a)(2), accrued interest and expense deductions are not deductible until paid if the amount giving rise to the deduction is owed to a related cash-method taxpayer. For purposes of this rule, a partnership and persons holding interests in the partnership (actually or constructively) or persons related (under Code Sec. 267(b) or 707(b)(1)) to actual or constructive partners are treated as related persons (¶ 905 and ¶ 1527) (Code Sec. 267(e)(1)).[79]

Sale and Liquidation of Partner's Interest

434. Purchase or Sale of a Partnership Interest. The sale or exchange of a partnership interest generally is treated as the sale of a single capital asset rather than a sale of each of the underlying partnership properties (Code Sec. 741).[80] The amount of gain or loss is based on the partner's basis in his partnership interest and the amount realized on the sale (Code Sec. 721).[81] (The sale of a partnership interest to a partner or to a nonpartner should be distinguished from the redemption of a partner's interest by the partnership. Redemptions are discussed at ¶ 435.)

Despite the general rule that the gain or loss on the sale of a partnership interest is a capital gain or loss, a partner may recognize ordinary income or loss under the constructive sale rules if he receives a disproportionate distribution of partnership unrealized receivables or inventory (¶ 430).

If a partner abandons or forfeits his partnership interest, he recognizes a loss equal to his basis in his partnership interest. Thus, a partner with a zero basis in its partnership interest is not allowed an abandonment loss (*E.J. LeBlanc*, FedCl, 2010-1 USTC ¶ 50,104). If the partnership has liabilities, the abandoning partner is deemed to have received a distribution from the partnership when he is relieved of the liabilities. In such a case, the partner's loss is his basis in his interest less any liabilities of which he is relieved. An abandonment of a partnership interest, if there are no partnership liabilities from which the partner is relieved, results in an ordinary loss because no sale or

References are to Standard Federal Tax Reports; Tax Research Consultant; and Practical Tax Explanations.

[74] ¶ 25,181B; PART: 27,058; § 30,715.15, § 30,715.20

[75] ¶ 25,181C; PART: 27,058; § 30,715.25

[76] ¶ 25,180; PART: 27,152; § 30,720.05

[77] ¶ 25,180; PART: 27,154; § 30,720.15

[78] ¶ 14,153; PART: 27,152; § 30,720.10

[79] ¶ 14,150; PART: 27,160; § 30,725.05

[80] ¶ 25,440; PART: 39,050; § 30,905.05

[81] ¶ 25,240; PART: 39,050; § 30,905.05

exchange has taken place (*P.B. Citron*, 97 TC 200 (1991); *G.G. Gannon*, 16 TC 1134 (1951)).[82] If there are partnership liabilities of which the abandoning partner is relieved, the resulting gain or loss is a capital gain or loss (*A.O. Stilwell*, 46 TC 247 (1966)).[83] Even a *de minimis* actual or deemed distribution generally results in a capital loss treatment to the partner. Capital loss is also mandated if the transaction is, in substance, a sale or exchange (Rev. Rul. 93-80).[84]

Unrealized Receivables and Inventory. A partner recognizes ordinary income or loss on any portion of a sale of a partnership interest that is attributable to his share of the partnership's unrealized receivables and inventory (Code Sec. 751(a)).[85] The gain is measured by the portion of the selling price attributable to unrealized receivables and inventory and the partner's basis in these assets. The partner's basis is the basis the partner's share of partnership unrealized receivables and inventory would have if these assets were distributed to him in a current distribution (Reg. § 1.751-1(a)(2)).[86] Capital gain or loss is determined by subtracting his remaining basis from the rest of the amount realized (Reg. § 1.741-1(a)).[87]

435. Partnership Interest Redeemed by Partnership. If a partner's interest is liquidated solely through a distribution of partnership property other than money (including marketable securities), no gain is recognized. The partner's basis in his partnership interest is transferred to the distributed assets, and any gain is recognized when the assets are disposed of (Code Sec. 731(a)).[88]

If a partner receives money or marketable securities as all or part of his liquidating distribution, he recognizes gain to the extent that the value of the cash or marketable securities exceeds his basis in the partnership interest (Code Secs. 731(c) and 732(b)).[89] A partner recognizes loss if no property other than money, unrealized receivables and inventory items is distributed to him, and his basis in his partnership interest exceeds the amount of money plus the basis of the distributed receivables and inventory (Code Sec. 731(a)).[90] However, if the partner is relieved of any or all of his share of partnership liabilities, the relief from liability is treated the same as a cash distribution (Reg. § 1.731-1(a)(1)).[91]

If a partner receives cash and unrealized receivables and inventory for his partnership interest, loss can be recognized in the amount by which the basis in the partnership interest exceeds the amount of money, plus the basis of the distributed receivables and inventory (Code Sec. 731(a)(2)).[92]

> **Example:** Martin has an adjusted basis in his partnership interest of $100,000. He retires from the partnership and receives as a distribution in liquidation of his interest his share of partnership property. This share is $50,000 cash and inventory with a basis to him of $30,000. Martin can recognize a loss of $20,000, his basis minus the money received and his basis in the inventory distributed to him ($100,000 - ($50,000 + $30,000) = $20,000).

If a partner receives money or property in exchange for any part of his partnership interest, the amount attributable to the partner's share of the partnership's unrealized receivables or inventory items results in ordinary income or loss. This treatment applies to the unrealized receivables portion of the payments to a retiring partner or successor in interest of a deceased partner only if that part is not treated as paid in exchange for partnership property. The rationale behind this rule is that the inventory or the accounts receivable would give rise to ordinary income had the partnership interest not been sold. However, if the partner does not sell the distributed inventory items within five years

References are to Standard Federal Tax Reports; Tax Research Consultant; and Practical Tax Explanations.

[82] ¶ 25,442.12, ¶ 25,422.545, PART: 39,058; § 30,905.45, § 30,905.50

[83] ¶ 25,422.545; PART: 39,058; § 30,905.10

[84] ¶ 25,442.12; PART: 39,058; § 30,905.10

[85] ¶ 25,500; PART: 42,050; § 30,905.25

[86] ¶ 25,501; PART: 42,050; § 30,905.25

[87] ¶ 25,441; PART: 39,050, PART: 42,050; § 30,905.25

[88] ¶ 25,320; PART: 36,100; § 30,910.05

[89] ¶ 25,340, ¶ 25,320; PART: 36,102, PART: 51,256.15; § 30,510.10, § 30,805.20

[90] ¶ 25,320; PART: 36,102; § 30,910.05

[91] ¶ 25,321; PART: 36,102; § 30,220.05

[92] ¶ 25,320; PART: 36,104; § 30,210, § 30,910.05

from the date of distribution, the gain can be recognized as a capital gain (Code Sec. 735(a)(2)).[93] For purposes of this rule, the term "inventory" does not include real estate or depreciable trade or business property (Code Sec. 735(c)(1)).[94] (Compare the general definition of "inventory" at ¶436, below.)

For exchanges of partnership interests involving unrealized receivables or inventory, the partnership must file an information return describing the exchange and furnish statements to each party (Reg. § 1.6050K-1).[95]

436. "Unrealized Receivables" and "Inventory Items" Defined. The term "unrealized receivables" includes any rights to income for services or goods that are not capital assets that have not been included in gross income under the method of accounting employed by the partnership (Code Sec. 751(c); Reg. § 1.751-1(c)).[96] For the most part, this classification relates to cash-method partnerships that have acquired a contractual or legal right to income for goods or services. In the usual case, the term does not apply to an accrual-method partnership because it has already included unrealized receivables in gross income.

The term "unrealized receivables" also includes certain property to the extent of the amount of gain that would have been realized and recharacterized or recaptured as ordinary income by the partnership if it had sold the property at its fair market value at the time of the sale or exchange of the partnership interest being considered. The types of property covered, which include depreciable personal property and real property, are listed in the flush language of Code Sec. 751(c). This property is not treated as an unrealized receivable for purposes of Code Sec. 736, relating to payments in liquidation of a retiring or deceased partner's interest.

The term "inventory items" is broader than the term itself might suggest (Code Sec. 751(d); Reg. § 1.751-1(d)(2)).[97] It includes not only inventory, but also any other assets that would not be treated either as capital assets or section 1231 assets (generally, depreciable property and land used in a trade or business) if they were sold by the partnership (or by the partner, if he had held them). Thus, the term might include a copyright or artistic work, accounts receivable for services and inventory, or any unrealized receivables.

Distributions of inventory made in exchange for all or a part of a partner's interest in other partnership property, including money, are governed by the "substantially appreciated" rule (Code Sec. 751(b); Reg. § 1.751-1(d)).[98] Thus, gain from such distributions is taxed as ordinary income if the fair market value of the partnership's inventory exceeds 120 percent of its adjusted basis.

438. Retiring Partner's or Successor's Shares. Payments made in liquidation of the interest of a retiring or deceased partner are considered distributions by the partnership to the extent that the payments are in exchange for the partner's interest in partnership property; otherwise they are considered a distributive share of partnership income or guaranteed payment (Code Secs. 736 and 761(d)).[99] This provision does not apply if the estate or other successor in interest of a deceased partner continues as a partner in its own right under local law. In addition, it applies only to payments made by the partnership and not to transactions, such as the sale of a partnership interest, between the partners (Reg. § 1.736-1(a)(1)).[100]

Under Code Sec. 731, distributions are generally nontaxable except to the extent that money distributed exceeds the partner's adjusted basis for his partnership interest (¶453); the excess is treated as capital gain. However, all gain relating to inventory is treated as being from the sale of a noncapital asset (Code Sec. 751(b)).[101] The partners' valuation in an arm's-length agreement of a retiring or deceased partner's interest in

References are to Standard Federal Tax Reports; Tax Research Consultant; and Practical Tax Explanations.

[93] ¶25,400; PART: 33,154, PART: 36,202; § 30,915.10

[94] ¶25,400; PART: 36,202; § 30,915.05

[95] ¶36,241; PART: 42,058; § 30,915.20

[96] ¶25,500, ¶25,501; PART: 42,100; § 30,540.15

[97] ¶25,500, ¶25,501; PART: 42,152; § 30,540.20

[98] ¶25,500, ¶25,501; PART: 30,050; § 30,915.05

[99] ¶25,420, ¶25,600; PART: 48,050; § 30,560

[100] ¶25,421; PART: 48,050; § 30,560.05

[101] ¶25,500; PART: 48,050; § 30,575

partnership property is presumptively correct, but that presumption may be rebutted (Reg. § 1.736-1(b)(1)).[102]

Payments for unrealized receivables and goodwill are treated as distributive shares of partnership income or as guaranteed payments if capital is not a material income-producing factor and the retiring or deceased partner was a general partner.[103] Such payments are deductible by the partnership. If these two requirements are not met, payments for goodwill are treated as payments for partnership property and do not create a deduction for the partnership. However, payments for goodwill can be treated as payments for property if: goodwill was originally purchased by the partnership or otherwise acquired in a transaction resulting in a cash basis to the partnership, *or* the partnership agreement calls for a reasonable payment for goodwill.[104]

Such payments result in capital gain or loss to the extent of the partnership's basis in the goodwill. In fixing the amount attributable to goodwill, an amount arrived at under an arm's-length agreement generally is accepted by the IRS. A formula approach involving the capitalization of earnings in excess of a fair market rate of return on the partnership's net tangible assets may be used, but only where there is no better basis for making such a determination (Rev. Rul. 68-609).[105]

These excluded amounts and other payments made for an interest in the partnership property are treated as either distributive shares of partnership income or as guaranteed payments (Code Sec. 736(a)). If the payments are determined by reference to partnership income, they are taxed as a distributive share to the recipient; if not, they are treated as "guaranteed payments" (¶ 421). Accordingly, if the payments consist of a percentage of partnership profits, they reduce the distributive shares of income of the remaining partners. If they are guaranteed payments, the effect is the same because they are deductible as business expenses in determining partnership taxable income. In either event, the payments are treated as ordinary income in the hands of the recipient partner.

Example 1: Partnership ABC is a personal service partnership and its balance sheet is as follows:

Assets			Liabilities and Capital		
	Adjusted basis	Market value		Adjusted basis	Market value
Cash	$130,000	$130,000	Liabilities .	$30,000	$30,000
Accounts receivable . .	0	300,000	Capital: A	100,000	210,000
			B	100,000	210,000
Capital and Sec. 1231 assets .	200,000	230,000	C	100,000	210,000
Total	$330,000	$660,000	Total .	$330,000	$660,000

General Partner A retires from the partnership in accordance with an agreement whereby his share of liabilities (⅓ of $30,000) is assumed. In addition, he is to receive $90,000 in the year of retirement plus $100,000 in each of the two succeeding years, a total of $300,000 (including his $10,000 share of liabilities), for his partnership interest. The value of A's interest in the partnership's section 736(b) property is $120,000 (⅓ of $360,000, the sum of $130,000 cash and $230,000, the fair market value of Code Sec. 1231 assets). The accounts receivable are not included in A's interest in partnership property because A is a general partner in a partnership in which capital is not a material income-producing factor. Assuming that the basis of A's interest is $110,000 ($100,000, the basis of his capital investment, plus $10,000, his share of partnership liabilities), he realizes a capital gain of $10,000 on the sale of his interest in partnership property. The $180,000 balance to be received by him is treated as guaranteed payments taxable to A as ordinary income.

References are to Standard Federal Tax Reports; Tax Research Consultant; and Practical Tax Explanations.

[102] ¶ 25,421; PART: 48,050; § 30,565.10

[103] ¶ 25,420; PART: 48,150; § 30,565.05, § 30,575

[104] ¶ 25,420; PART: 48,154, PART: 48,156; § 30,565.05, § 30,575

[105] ¶ 25,422.51; PART: 48,308, VALUE: 12,050; § 30,565.05, § 30,575

The $100,000 that A receives in each of the three years would ordinarily be allocated as follows: $40,000 as payments for A's interest in section 736(b) property ($120,000/$300,000 × $100,000) and the balance of $60,000 as guaranteed payments. While the $10,000 capital gain is normally recognized in the first year, A may elect to prorate the gain over the three-year period.

Example 2: Assume the same facts as in Example 1, above, except that the agreement provides for payments to A for three years of a percentage of annual income instead of a fixed amount. In such case, all payments received by A are treated as payments for A's interest in partnership property until he has received $120,000. Thereafter, the payments are treated as a distributive share of partnership income to A (Reg. § 1.736-1(b)(7)).

For income tax purposes, a retired partner or a deceased partner's successor is treated as a partner until his interest has been completely liquidated (Reg. § 1.736-1(a)(6)).[106]

440. Partner Receiving Income "In Respect of a Decedent". All payments to the successor of a deceased partner under Code Sec. 736(a), relating to payments made in liquidation of a deceased partner's interest and considered as a distributive share or guaranteed payment (¶ 438), are income in respect of a decedent (Code Sec. 753).[107] Under Code Sec. 691, the payments are taxed to the recipient when received to the extent that they are not properly includible in the short tax year ending with the decedent's death.

The estate or heir of a deceased partner is also treated as receiving income in respect of a decedent to the extent that amounts are received from an outsider in exchange for rights to future payments by the partnership representing distributive shares or guaranteed payments (Reg. § 1.753-1(a)).[108]

Partnership Contributions, Distributions, and Basis

443. Contribution to Partnership. No gain or loss is recognized, either by the partnership or by any of its partners, upon a contribution of property to the partnership in exchange for a partnership interest (Code Sec. 721(a)).[109] This is true whether the contribution is made to an existing partnership or to a newly formed partnership (Reg. § 1.721-1).[110] However, a partner must recognize any gain realized on the transfer of appreciated property to a partnership that would be treated as an investment company if the partnership were incorporated (Code Secs. 707(c) and 721(b)).[111] Further, the value of a capital interest in a partnership that is transferred to a partner in exchange for his services is taxable to him as ordinary income, provided that the interest is not subject to a substantial risk of forfeiture (¶ 731) (Reg. § 1.721-1(b)).[112]

The receipt of a profits interest (as opposed to a capital interest) in exchange for services rendered is not taxable as ordinary income (Rev. Proc. 93-27).[113]

The basis of a partner's interest acquired in exchange for his contribution to the partnership is the amount of the money contributed plus the adjusted basis to the contributing partner of any property contributed (Code Sec. 722).[114] If a partner receives a partnership interest as compensation for services rendered or to be rendered, resulting in taxable income to the incoming partner, that income is added to the basis of his interest (Reg. § 1.722-1).[115] If the contributed property is subject to debt or if liabilities of the partner are assumed by the partnership, the basis of the contributing partner's interest is reduced by the portion of the indebtedness assumed by the other partners. Such assumption of the partner's debt by others is treated as a distribution of money to

References are to Standard Federal Tax Reports; Tax Research Consultant; and Practical Tax Explanations.

[106] ¶ 25,421; PART: 48,200; § 30,565.05

[107] ¶ 25,540; PART: 48,304; § 30,205.05, § 32,901

[108] ¶ 25,541; PART: 48,304; § 32,901

[109] ¶ 25,240; PART: 9,050; § 30,105.05

[110] ¶ 25,241; PART: 9,050; § 30,105.05

[111] ¶ 25,180, ¶ 25,240; PART: 9,050; § 30,595.05

[112] ¶ 25,241; PART: 9,050; § 30,205.15

[113] ¶ 25,243.12; PART: 12,100; § 30,115.05

[114] ¶ 25,260; PART: 15,050; § 30,205.05

[115] ¶ 25,261; PART: 12,152; § 30,205.15

him and as a contribution of money by those assuming the debt (¶ 447) (Code Sec. 752).[116]

The basis to the partnership of property contributed by a partner is the adjusted basis of such property in the hands of the contributing partner at the time of the contribution and any gain he recognized on the transfer to the partnership under Code Sec. 721(b) (Code Sec. 723).[117] However, it has been held that the basis of a nonbusiness asset (for example, a personal automobile) converted to a business asset upon contribution to a partnership was its fair market value at the time of contribution (*L.Y.S. Au*, CA-9, 64-1 USTC ¶ 9447).[118] The holding period of a contributed asset includes the period during which it was held by the contributing partner (Reg. § 1.723-1).[119]

Only the contributing partner may take into account any built-in loss. In determining items allocated to the other (noncontributing) partners, the basis of the contributed property is the property's fair market value at the time of contribution (Code Sec. 704(c)(1)(C)).[120]

Under Code Sec. 724,[121] unrealized receivables and inventory items contributed by the partner to the partnership retain their ordinary income character in the hands of the partnership. That is, unrealized receivables remain ordinary income property up to the time of disposal by the partnership and inventory items remain ordinary income property for the five-year period beginning on the date of contribution (Code Sec. 735(a)).[122] In addition, a partner's contribution of property with a built-in capital loss (when the fair market value of the property is less than its adjusted basis) results in retention of the property's capital loss status in the hands of the partnership to the extent of built-in loss for the five-year period beginning on the date of contribution.

To prevent avoidance of these rules through the partnership's exchange of contributed unrealized receivables, inventory items, or capital loss property in a nonrecognition transaction (or series of transactions), the rule applies to any substituted basis property resulting from the exchange. It does not apply, however, to any stock in a C corporation received in an exchange of property for stock if the contributor is in control following the exchange (Code Secs. 351 and 735(c)(2)).[123] For this purpose, control is at least 80 percent of the total combined voting power of all classes of stock entitled to vote and at least 80 percent of the total number of shares of all other classes of stock of the corporation (Code Sec. 368(c)).[124]

445. Increases and Decreases in Basis of Partner's Interest. The basis of a partner's interest is *increased* by his distributive share of partnership taxable income, the partnership's tax-exempt income, and the excess of the partnership deductions for depletion over the basis to the partnership of the depletable property. The basis of the partner's interest is *decreased* (but not below zero) by distributions to him from the partnership (applying the rules at ¶ 453) and by the sum of his share of partnership losses, his share of partnership expenditures not deductible in computing its taxable income and not chargeable to capital account, and his depletion deduction for oil and gas wells (Code Sec. 705(a)).[125] Distributions are to be taken into account before losses in adjusting the partner's interest basis (Rev. Rul. 66-94).[126]

Example: Partner A of ABC partnership has an $80,000 basis for her partnership interest. During the tax year, she receives cash distributions of $50,000, and her share of the partnership's losses is $40,000. Her interest is adjusted as follows:

References are to Standard Federal Tax Reports; Tax Research Consultant; and Practical Tax Explanations.

[116] ¶ 25,520; PART: 9,100; § 30,220.10

[117] ¶ 25,280; PART: 9,056; § 30,105.10

[118] ¶ 25,282.02; PART: 9,056; § 30,105.10

[119] ¶ 25,281; PART: 9,056; § 30,105.10

[120] ¶ 25,120; PART: 45,112; § 30,625.05

[121] ¶ 25,300; PART: 9,250; § 30,105.20

[122] ¶ 25,400; PART: 9,252; § 30,105.20

[123] ¶ 16,402, ¶ 25,400; CCORP: 3,050; § 26,101, § 30,105.20

[124] ¶ 16,750; CCORP: 3,054; § 26,101, § 30,105.20

[125] ¶ 25,140; PART: 15,050; § 30,210.10, § 30,210.15

[126] ¶ 25,144.12; PART: 15,058.10; § 30,210.20

Basis at beginning of year	$80,000	
Less cash distributions	50,000	$30,000
Less share of losses ($40,000) but only to the extent that the basis is not reduced below zero		30,000
Adjusted basis for interest		0

Because basis is decreased by distributions received before reduction by A's share of partnership losses, no gain is recognized under Code Sec. 731 on the cash distribution. However, $10,000 of A's share of partnership loss is disallowed and carried forward to subsequent tax years (¶ 425).[127]

Bases of partnership interests may also be determined by reference to proportionate shares of the adjusted basis of partnership property that would be distributable if the partnership were to be ended. This alternative rule is available only in limited circumstances if a partner cannot practicably apply the general rule or when the IRS approves (Code Sec. 705(b); Reg. § 1.705-1(b)).[128]

For purposes of determining a partner's basis in his partnership interest or for figuring gain or loss on a distribution, advances or drawings of money or property against a partner's distributive share of income are treated as current distributions made on the last day of the partnership's tax year (Reg. § 1.731-1(a)(1)(ii)).[129] Money received by a partner under an obligation to repay the partnership is not a distribution but is a loan that is treated as a transaction between the partnership and a nonpartner (Reg. §§ 1.707-1(a) and 1.731-1(c)(2)).[130]

447. Liabilities Treated as Distributions or Contributions. Any increase in a partner's share of partnership liabilities, including a partner's assumption of partnership liabilities or receipt of partnership property subject to a liability (limited to the fair market value of the encumbered property), is treated as a contribution of money that increases a partner's basis in his interest (Code Secs. 722 and 752(a)).[131] A decrease in a partner's share of partnership liabilities is treated as a distribution of money by the partnership, which decreases the distributee partner's basis in his partnership interest (but not below zero) (Code Secs. 733 and 752(b)).[132] When a partner's basis has been reduced to zero, such "deemed distributions" can result in a taxable gain (¶ 453).

448. Allocation of Liabilities Among Partners. Partners' shares of partnership liabilities (and corresponding allocations of basis) depend upon whether the liability is "recourse" or "nonrecourse." In addition, separate rules apply in the case of nonrecourse debts of the partnership if a partner is the lender or has guaranteed repayment of the debt.

Recourse Liabilities. Liabilities are recourse to the extent that a partner bears the economic risk of loss if the liability is not satisfied by the partnership. Recourse liabilities are allocated in accordance with the partners' economic risk of loss (Reg. § 1.752-2(a)).[133] As a general matter, economic risk of loss is borne by a partner to the extent that he must make a contribution to the partnership (including the obligation to restore a deficit capital account) or pay a creditor if all partnership assets, including money, were deemed worthless and all partnership liabilities were due and payable (Reg. § 1.752-2(b)(1)).[134] Accordingly, a limited partner cannot be allocated recourse liabilities in excess of his capital contribution and future contribution obligations unless he has agreed to restore any deficit in his capital account or to indemnify other partners for their debts with respect to a liability. A partner does not bear the economic risk of loss if he is entitled to reimbursement (for example, through an indemnification agreement or a state law right to subrogation) from other partners or the partnership (Reg.

References are to Standard Federal Tax Reports; Tax Research Consultant; and Practical Tax Explanations.

[127] ¶ 25,320; PART: 15,202.05; § 30,210.15

[128] ¶ 25,140, ¶ 25,141; PART: 15,100; § 30,210.25

[129] ¶ 25,321; PART: 33,052.10; § 30,210.20

[130] ¶ 25,181, ¶ 25,321; PART: 33,052.05; § 30,210.20

[131] ¶ 25,260, ¶ 25,520; PART: 9,100; § 30,215.05

[132] ¶ 25,360, ¶ 25,520; PART: 9,100; § 30,215.05

[133] ¶ 25,523; PART: 15,254; § 30,215.15

[134] ¶ 25,523; PART: 15,254.10; § 30,215.15

§ 1.752-2(b)(5)).[135] Recourse liabilities must be allocated to a partner if a related person bears the risk of loss for the liability (Reg. § 1.752-4(b)).[136]

Nonrecourse Liabilities. Nonrecourse liabilities are those for which no partner bears the economic risk of loss—for example, a mortgage on an office building that is secured only by a lien on the building and on the rents, but with no personal obligation to repay the loan on the part of any of the owners. Such liabilities are generally shared by the partners in a manner that correlates with their allocations of deductions attributable to these liabilities under Code Sec. 704(b).[137] See ¶ 428. A partner's share of nonrecourse liabilities of a partnership equals the sum of: (1) the partner's share of partnership minimum gain, (2) the amount of any taxable gain under Code Sec. 704(c) that would be allocated to the partner if the partnership disposed of all partnership property subject to one or more nonrecourse liabilities of the partnership in full satisfaction of the liabilities and no other consideration, and (3) the partner's share of the excess nonrecourse liabilities as determined in accordance with the partner's share of partnership profits (Reg. § 1.752-3(a)).[138]

Although excess nonrecourse liabilities are allocated in accordance with the partners' respective profits interests, the partnership agreement may state their profits interests for purposes of sharing nonrecourse liabilities, provided that the stated sharing ratios are reasonably consistent with the allocation of some significant item of partnership income or gain among the partners. Because no partner bears the economic risk of loss for nonrecourse liabilities, limited partners may be allocated shares of such liabilities (and the basis in such liabilities) in amounts exceeding their total capital contribution obligations.

Partner Nonrecourse Loans and Guarantees. A partner who lends money to the partnership on a nonrecourse basis bears the economic risk of loss for the liability. Likewise, a partner who guarantees an otherwise nonrecourse liability bears the risk of loss to the extent of his guarantee (Reg. § 1.752-2(d)(2)).[139]

A loss incurred on the abandonment or worthlessness of a partnership interest is an ordinary loss if sale or exchange treatment does not apply. If there is an actual or deemed distribution to the partner, or if the transaction is otherwise in substance a sale or exchange, the partner's loss is capital except as provided in Code Sec. 751(b).[140] A "deemed distribution" includes the relief from partnership debts in which the abandoning partner shares. As with other losses, the partners must establish the finality and uncollectability of the loss (Reg. § 1.165-1(d)).[141]

453. Gain or Loss on Distribution. The income of a partnership is taxable to the partners in accordance with their distributive shares (¶ 428). It does not matter when or if the income is actually distributed to the partners. However, distributions to partners decrease the partners' bases for their partnership interests (¶ 445).

> **Example 1:** A partner contributes $100,000 to the capital of a partnership. During the first year, his share of the partnership taxable income is $25,000, but only $10,000 of this amount is actually distributed to him. The $25,000 taxable income increases his basis to $125,000, and the $10,000 distribution decreases it to $115,000.

No gain or loss is recognized by a partnership on a distribution of property to a partner, including money, except to the extent that any money distributed exceeds the adjusted basis of the partner's interest in the partnership immediately before the distribution (Code Sec. 731(b)).[142] Loss is not recognized by the partner, except upon a distribution in liquidation of a partner's interest in a partnership. If no property other than money and certain securities is distributed to such partner, loss is recognized to

References are to Standard Federal Tax Reports; Tax Research Consultant; and Practical Tax Explanations.

[135] ¶ 25,523; PART: 15,254.25; § 30,215.15

[136] ¶ 25,525; PART: 15,254.20; § 30,215.35

[137] ¶ 25,120; PART: 15,254.05; § 30,215.20

[138] ¶ 25,524; PART: 21,358; § 30,215.20

[139] ¶ 25,523; PART: 15,254.20; § 30,215.25

[140] ¶ 25,500; PART: 39,050; § 30,905.45

[141] ¶ 9804.33; INDIV: 54,256; § 16,905.20

[142] ¶ 25,320; PART: 33,000, PART: 36,000; § 30,530.05

the extent of the excess of the adjusted basis of the partner's interest in the partnership over the sum of any money distributed and the basis to the partner of any unrealized receivables (Code Sec. 751(c)) and inventory (Code Sec. 751(d)).[143]

If a distribution of money exceeds a partner's basis for his interest, gain is recognized by the partner as though he had sold or exchanged his partnership interest (Code Sec. 731(a)).[144] This applies both to current distributions (that is, those not in liquidation of an entire interest) and to distributions in liquidation of a partner's entire interest in a partnership (Reg. § 1.731-1(a)).[145]

> **Example 2:** A purchases a partnership interest for $100,000. During the first year, A receives a cash distribution of $100,000 and a distribution of property with a fair market value of $30,000. He recognizes no gain on the distributions since the amount of money distributed does not exceed A's basis for his partnership interest ($100,000). If he had received a cash distribution of $130,000, a $30,000 gain would have been recognized.

Distribution of marketable securities generally is treated the same as a distribution of money. The securities are valued at their fair market value on the date of the distribution (Code Sec. 731(c); Reg. § 1.731-2).[146]

Gain is determined only by reference to ***money*** (including marketable securities) distributed. Generally, a partner recognizes no gain on a distribution of property until he sells or otherwise disposes of the distributed property. Thus, if the taxpayer in Example 2 had received property in kind rather than cash or marketable securities, no gain would have been realized (Reg. § 1.731-1(a)).[147]

However, a distribution of property encumbered by a liability may cause a partner's share of partnership liabilities to decrease, resulting in a "deemed distribution" of money to that partner (¶ 447). For instance, if a partner receives a distribution of property subject to a secured liability, the liability becomes a personal liability of the distributee partner, and there is a decrease in the liabilities of all other partners who had been allocated a share of the liability (Code Sec. 752(b)).[148] These partners must decrease the bases in their partnership interests in the amount of their "deemed distributions" (but not below zero), and any amounts deemed distributed in excess of their respective bases are taxable as capital gain.

The nonrecognition rules of Code Sec. 731 may not apply if, within "a short period" before or after property is contributed to a partnership, there is a distribution of either (1) other partnership property to the contributing partner or (2) the contributed property to another partner (Code Sec. 707(a)(2)(B); Reg. § 1.731-1(c)(3)).[149] If the distribution is made in order to effect an exchange of property between the partnership and a partner or between two or more partners, then the transaction is treated as an exchange, and the "disguised sale" rules (¶ 432) may apply. There is a presumption that distributions made within two years of a contribution are made as part of a sale arrangement (Reg. § 1.707-3(c)).[150] However, the presumption can be rebutted if the facts and circumstances clearly establish that there is no sale (Reg. § 1.707-4).[151]

Loss is recognized only if the distribution terminates the partner's interest—and then only if the distribution is limited to money, unrealized receivables, or inventory items (¶ 436). The amount of the recognized loss is the excess of the adjusted basis of the partner's interest over the sum of any money distributed and the basis to him, which is ordinarily the same as the basis to the partnership (¶ 456) of any unrealized receivables or inventory items (Code Sec. 731(a)(2)).[152]

References are to Standard Federal Tax Reports; Tax Research Consultant; and Practical Tax Explanations.

[143] ¶ 25,321; PART: 36,104; § 30,515.15

[144] ¶ 25,320; PART: 36,102; § 30,515.10

[145] ¶ 25,321; PART: 33,050, PART: 36,050; § 30,515.05

[146] ¶ 25,320, ¶ 25,321B; PART: 33,104; § 30,515.10

[147] ¶ 25,321; PART: 33,150; § 30,515.10

[148] ¶ 25,520; PART: 33,204; § 30,515.05

[149] ¶ 25,180, ¶ 25,321; PART: 27,058; § 30,595.05

[150] ¶ 25,181B; PART: 27,058.05; § 30,7150.15

[151] ¶ 25,181C; PART: 27,058.10; § 30,715.30.

[152] ¶ 25,320; PART: 36,100; § 30,510.20

Example 3: A partner whose basis for his partnership interest is $100,000 retires from the partnership, receiving $50,000 in cash and inventory items having a basis to the partnership of $30,000. The taxpayer has a capital loss of $20,000.

These provisions do not apply to the extent that payments are made in liquidation to a retiring or deceased partner and are treated as a distributive share or guaranteed payment (¶ 438), to a distribution for unrealized receivables or appreciated inventory items (¶ 436) (Code Sec. 731(d)),[153] or if the rules governing precontribution gain (¶ 454) are called into play.

454. Property Distribution Within Certain Periods of Contribution. A partner who contributes property may have to recognize gain or loss if the contributed property is distributed to another partner within seven years (Code Sec. 704(c)).[154] The gain or loss recognized under this rule is limited to the difference between the property's tax basis and its fair market value at the time of contribution. Upon distribution of the property within the seven-year period, the "precontribution" gain or loss recognized is equal to the amount that would have been allocated to the contributing partner had the partnership sold, rather than distributed, the property. Appropriate adjustments must be made to the basis of the contributing partner's partnership interest and to the basis of the distributed property to reflect any gain or loss recognized (¶ 445 and ¶ 456).

The recognition rule does not apply if the property is distributed to the contributing partner (or its successor). Also, the rule does not apply with respect to certain distributions made as part of an exchange of like-kind property.

A similar rule may cause a partner contributing appreciated property to recognize precontribution gain if he receives a distribution of other partnership property (except money or marketable securities) within a seven-year period (Code Sec. 737(b)).[155] Precontribution gain must be recognized to the extent that it exceeds the partner's basis for his partnership interest at the time the distribution is received.

456. Basis of Property Distributed to Partner. The basis of property received in a distribution, other than in liquidation of a partner's interest, is ordinarily the same as the basis in the hands of the partnership immediately prior to distribution. In no case may the basis of property in the hands of the distributee exceed the basis of his partnership interest reduced by the amount of money distributed to him in the same transaction (Code Sec. 732(a)).[156]

Example 1: Taxpayer has a basis of $100,000 for his partnership interest. He receives a nonliquidating distribution of $40,000 in cash and property with a basis to the partnership of $80,000. The basis to the partner of the distributed property is $60,000 ($100,000 minus $40,000). (The partnership can "recover" the $20,000 difference by making the election described at ¶ 459.)

The basis of property distributed *in liquidation* of a partner's interest is the basis of the distributee's partnership interest less any money received in the same transaction (Code Sec. 732(b)).[157]

A distributee partner's basis adjustment is allocated among distributed assets, first to unrealized receivables and inventory items in an amount equal to the partnership's basis in each such property (Code Sec. 732(c)).[158] Under these rules, the term "unrealized receivables" includes any property the sale of which would create ordinary income. This would include, for example, depreciation-recapture property. However, the amount of unrealized receivables is limited to that amount that would be treated as ordinary income if the property were sold at fair market value (Code Sec. 751(c)).[159]

Basis is allocated first to the extent of each distributed property's adjusted basis to the partnership. Any remaining basis adjustment that is an increase is allocated among

References are to Standard Federal Tax Reports; Tax Research Consultant; and Practical Tax Explanations.

[153] ¶ 25,320; PART: 45,060; § 30,515.05

[154] ¶ 25,120; PART: 33,156; § 30,595.05

[155] ¶ 25,425; PART: 33,154; § 30,590.05

[156] ¶ 25,340; PART: 33,202; § 30,510.30

[157] ¶ 25,340; PART: 36,150; § 30,510.30

[158] ¶ 25,340; PART: 33,162.15; § 30,510.30

[159] ¶ 25,500; PART: 30,106, PART: 33,250, PART: 36,102; § 30,510.35

properties with unrealized appreciation in proportion to their respective amounts of unrealized appreciation (to the extent of each property's appreciation) and then in proportion to their respective fair market values.

Example 2: A partnership has two assets, a tractor and a steam shovel. Both assets are distributed to a partner whose adjusted basis in his partnership interest is $550,000. The tractor has a basis to the partnership of $50,000 and a fair market value of $400,000. The steam shovel has a basis to the partnership of $100,000 and a fair market value of $100,000. Basis is first allocated to the tractor in the amount of $50,000 and to the steam shovel in the amount of $100,000 (their adjusted bases to the partnership). The remaining basis adjustment is an increase of $400,000 (the partner's $550,000 basis minus the partnership's total basis of $150,000 in the distributed assets). Basis is then allocated to the tractor in the amount of $350,000, its unrealized appreciation, with no allocation to the steam shovel attributable to unrealized appreciation because its fair market value equals the partnership's adjusted basis. The remaining basis adjustment of $50,000 is allocated in the ratio of the assets' fair market values, which are $40,000 to the tractor (for a total basis of $440,000) and $10,000 to the steam shovel (for a total basis of $110,000).

If the remaining basis adjustment is a decrease, it is allocated among properties with unrealized depreciation in proportion to their respective amounts of unrealized depreciation (to the extent of each property's depreciation), and then in proportion to their respective adjusted bases, taking into account the adjustments already made.

The result of these changes is that a partner's substituted basis in distributed partnership property is allocated among multiple properties based on the fair market value of the distributed properties. Under the prior rules, allocations were based on the partnership's proportionate basis in the distributed properties.

Optional Basis Adjustments. If a partner has acquired his partnership interest (1) by purchase from a former partner or another partner or (2) from a deceased partner, he can elect to have a special basis adjustment for property other than money received in a distribution from the partnership within two years after the partnership interest was acquired. This can be done if the partnership has not made an election to have the special basis adjustment apply to its assets. The partner's election accomplishes substantially the same result as if the partnership had made the election (Code Sec. 732(d)).[160] This special basis adjustment is the difference between the amount paid for his interest, that is, his basis for his partnership interest and his share of the adjusted basis of the partnership assets.

The special basis adjustment applies to property received in current distributions as well as to distributions in complete liquidation of the partner's interest. Reg. § 1.732-1(d)(1)(iv) provides that if the partner makes the election when a distribution of depreciable or depletable property is received, the special basis adjustment is not diminished by any depletion or depreciation on that portion of the basis of partnership property that arises from the special basis adjustment. Depletion or depreciation on that portion for the period before distribution is allowed or allowable only if the partnership made the election.

If a transferee-partner wishes to make the election, it must be made on his tax return for the year of the distribution if the distribution includes any property subject to depreciation, depletion, or amortization. If it does not include any such property, the election may be made with the return for any tax year not later than the first tax year in which the basis of the distributed property is pertinent in determining income tax.

459. Optional Adjustment to Basis of Partnership Assets. If the basis of distributed assets in the hands of the distributee partner is less than the basis of the assets in the hands of the partnership, there may be an "unused" basis. The partnership may elect to adjust the basis of its remaining assets to take up this unused basis (¶ 470) (Code Secs. 734, 754 and 755).[161]

References are to Standard Federal Tax Reports; Tax Research Consultant; and Practical Tax Explanations.

[160] ¶ 25,340; PART: 45,100; § 30,520.05

[161] ¶ 25,380, ¶ 25,560, ¶ 25,580; PART: 45,250; § 30,520.05

If gain is recognized by a partner because of a distribution of money (¶ 453), a similar increase in the partnership's basis of its remaining assets may be made. If an election is made, the partnership may have to decrease the basis of its remaining assets. The decrease would be required for the excess of the basis of distributed assets to the partner over the basis that the partnership had for those assets, in the event of a distribution in liquidation of a partner's interest. Decrease would also be required to the extent that any distribution to a partner resulted in loss to the partner (Code Sec. 734(b)).[162] Loss results to the partner only if the distribution terminates the partner's interest and generally consists only of money, unrealized receivables, and inventories (¶ 453).

Example: An equal three-person partnership has the following assets:

	Partnership's Basis	*Fair Market Value*
Cash	$120,000	$120,000
Land	60,000	120,000
Securities	90,000	120,000
Total	$270,000	$360,000

If a partner retires and the partnership pays him $120,000 for the fair market value of his partnership interest, the partnership is really distributing $40,000 as his pro rata share of the partnership's cash and paying him $80,000 for his ⅓ interest in the land and in the securities. However, the retiring partner's share of the partnership's basis for these properties totals only $50,000. Therefore, the partnership, if it wishes to reflect the $30,000 excess cost, may elect to adjust the basis of the land and securities.

A partnership is barred from increasing the adjusted basis of remaining property following a distribution of an interest in another partnership if such other partnership has not made a consistent Code Sec. 754 election. In other words, tiered partnerships must make consistent elections.

The allocation of any increase or decrease in basis is made among the various partnership assets or categories of assets. These rules contemplate generally that the allocation will be made first to "like-kind" assets and will reduce the difference between fair market value and basis of each asset adjusted (Code Sec. 755).[163]

No allocation of basis decrease may be made to stock of a corporate partner. Such basis decrease must be allocated to other partnership property. The partnership recognizes gain to the extent the decrease in basis exceeds the basis of the other partnership assets.

462. Character of Gain or Loss on Disposition of Distributed Property. A partner recognizes ordinary gain or loss on the disposition of unrealized receivables or inventory items distributed by the partnership (¶ 436), regardless of whether the inventory has substantially appreciated in value (Code Sec. 735; Reg. § 1.735-1).[164] In the case of inventory items, this rule applies only if the sale takes place within five years of the date of distribution. If the sale takes place after this period, gain may be treated as capital gain if the assets are capital assets in the hands of the partner at that time.

If a partner disposes of distributed unrealized receivables or inventory items in a nonrecognition transaction (or series of transactions), these rules apply to treat gain or loss on the substituted basis property as ordinary income or loss, except in the case of stock in a C corporation received in a Code Sec. 351 exchange.[165] The House Committee Report to the Deficit Reduction Act of 1984 (P.L. 98-369) states that it is intended that the basis tainting rules regarding distributed property apply only for the period during which the underlying rules as to character of gain or loss under Code Sec. 735 would apply if the property were not disposed of in a nonrecognition transaction. For example, if an inventory item was distributed by the partnership, and the partner subsequently

References are to Standard Federal Tax Reports; Tax Research Consultant; and Practical Tax Explanations.

[162] ¶ 25,380; PART: 45,050; § 30,520.05

[163] ¶ 25,580; PART: 45,150; § 30,520.05

[164] ¶ 25,400, ¶ 25,401; PART: 33,166.05; § 30,535.05

[165] ¶ 25,400; PART: 36,202; § 30,535.05

disposed of it in a nonrecognition transaction, ordinary income treatment would apply to any substitute basis property only for the duration of the five-year period beginning on the date of the original distribution.

467. Adjustment of Basis on Sale of Partnership Interest. Generally, the transfer of a partnership interest does not affect the basis of partnership assets. However, the partnership may elect to adjust the basis of partnership assets to reflect the difference between the transferee's basis for his partnership interest (generally, the purchase price) and his proportionate share of the adjusted basis of all partnership property (his share of the partnership's adjusted basis in the partnership property). This election applies only to the transferee partner and applies where there is a "transfer of an interest in a partnership by sale or exchange or upon the death of a partner" and not upon the contribution of property (including money) to the partnership (Code Sec. 743; Reg. § 1.743-1(a)).[166]

Basis adjustments must be made to undistributed partnership property any time there is a distribution of property to a partner with respect to which there is a substantial basis reduction (more than $250,000), whether or not the partnership has a Code Sec. 754 election in effect (Code Sec. 734(b)).[167]

The amount of the increase or decrease is an adjustment affecting the transferee partner only. In addition, a partner's proportionate share of the adjusted basis of partnership property is determined in accordance with his interest in partnership capital. Where, however, an agreement on contributed property is in effect, the agreement must be taken into account in determining a partner's proportionate share (Reg. § 1.743-1(b)).[168]

A Code Sec. 743 basis adjustment is mandatory in the case of a transferred partnership interest with a substantial built-in loss. A substantial built-in loss exists if the partnership's adjusted basis in the property is more than $250,000 of the fair market value. An electing investment partnership is excepted from this rule. It will not be treated as having a substantial built-in loss and therefore it is not required to make basis adjustments to partnership property (Code Sec. 743(e)(1)).[169]

The basis adjustment must be allocated among the partnership assets in accordance with the rules set out in Code Sec. 755 (¶ 459).[170]

470. Election for Basis Adjustment. An election to make the basis adjustments described at ¶ 459 and ¶ 467 is made in a written statement filed with the partnership return for the first year to be covered by the election. The election applies to all property distributions and transfers of partnership interests taking place in the year of the election and in all later partnership tax years until revoked (Reg. § 1.754-1(a)).[171]

Family Partnerships

474. Income-Splitting Device. The family partnership is a common device for splitting income among family members and having more income taxed in the lower tax brackets. A family member is recognized as a partner for income tax purposes if he owns a capital interest in a partnership in which capital is a material income-producing factor, whether or not he purchased the interest. If capital is *not* a material income-producing factor, a partnership resulting from a gift of an interest might be disregarded as an invalid attempt to assign income. In any event, if all the income is attributable to the personal efforts of the donor, the donor is taxed on the entire income. In addition, the donee's distributive share of income must be proportionate to his capital interest, and his control over the partnership must be consistent with his status as partner (Code Sec. 704(e); Reg. § 1.704-1(e)).[172]

Family limited partnerships are also used for estate planning purposes (¶ 2903.)

References are to Standard Federal Tax Reports; Tax Research Consultant; and Practical Tax Explanations.

[166] ¶ 25,480, ¶ 25,481; PART: 45,100; § 30,810

[167] ¶ 25,380; PART: 21,264.10; § 30,810

[168] ¶ 25,481; PART: 45,100; § 30,810

[169] ¶ 25,480; PART: 45,112; § 30,810

[170] ¶ 25,580; PART: 45,150; § 30,810

[171] ¶ 25,561; PART: 45,250; § 30,825

[172] ¶ 25,120, ¶ 25,121; PART: 54,100; § 31,301

Organization, Syndication, Start-Up Costs

477. Syndication and Organization Fees. Except as provided in Code Sec. 709(b), no deduction is allowed a partnership or a partner for the costs of organizing a partnership (organization fees) or of selling partnership interests (syndication fees) ¶ 481) (Code Sec. 709; (Reg. § 1.709-1).[173] Guaranteed payments (¶ 421) made to partners for their services in organizing a partnership are capital expenditures and are not deductible by the partnership.

Code Sec. 709(b) provides that the partnership may elect to deduct up to $5,000 in organizational expenses in the same manner as start-up expenditures. The $5,000 amount is reduced (but not below zero) by the amount by which the organizational expenditures exceed $50,000. The remainder of the organizational expenditures may be amortized ratably over a 180-month period, beginning with the month the active trade or business begins. The partnership is deemed to have made an election to deduct and amortize such expenses for the taxable year in which the active trade or business to which the expenditures relate begins. For expenditures paid or incurred after August 16, 2011, a taxpayer may choose to forego the deemed election by affirmatively electing to capitalize its start-up and/or organizational expenditures on a timely filed federal income tax return, including extensions, for the tax year in which the active trade or business to which the expenditures relate begins (Reg. § 1.195-1).

481. Start-Up Expenditures. Start-up expenditures generally cannot be deducted (Code Sec. 195).[174] However, a taxpayer may elect to deduct a limited amount of start-up expenditures in the tax year in which the trade or business begins. The amount of start-up expenditures paid or incurred that may be deducted is the lesser of: the start-up expenditures with respect to the active trade or business; or $5,000, reduced by the amount by which the start-up expenditures with respect to the active trade or business exceed $50,000.

The remainder of the start-up expenditures may be amortized ratably over a 180-month period, beginning with the month the active trade or business begins. The partnership is deemed to have made an election to deduct and amortize such expenses for the taxable year in which the active trade or business to which the expenditures relate begins.

In the case of start-up expenses incurred by the partnership itself and for which an election is made, the amortization deduction is taken into account in computing partnership income. In the case of qualifying investigatory expenses incurred in connection with acquiring a partnership interest, the deduction is taken by the partner who has incurred the expenses (¶ 904).

Electing Large Partnerships

482. Simplified Reporting for Electing Large Partnerships. Partnerships with 100 or more members in the preceding tax year may elect "large partnership" status (Code Sec. 771—777).[175] An electing large partnership combines most items of partnership income, deduction, credit, and loss at the partnership level and passes through net amounts to the partners. Special rules apply to partnerships engaging in oil and gas activities and to partnerships with residual interests in real estate mortgage investment conduits (REMICs). Service partnerships and commodity pools generally are unable to elect large partnership treatment.

A partnership may lose its large partnership status if the number of partners falls below 100 during any partnership tax year. Rules for determining the treatment of a partnership whose membership falls below 100 have not been provided by the IRS.

An electing large partnership does not terminate for tax purposes solely because 50 percent or more of its interests are sold or exchanged within a 12-month period.

References are to Standard Federal Tax Reports; Tax Research Consultant; and Practical Tax Explanations.

[173] ¶ 25,220; ¶ 25,221C; PART: 18,200; § 9,210.15

[174] ¶ 12,370; PART: 18,104.10; § 9,205.05

[175] ¶ 25,604—¶ 25,628; PART: 3,450; § 30,435

484. Deductions and Credits Generally Combined at Partnership Level. Miscellaneous itemized deductions are not separately reported to the partners (Code Sec. 773(b)(3)).[176] In place of applying the 2-percent floor for itemized deductions, 70 percent of the itemized deductions are disallowed at the partnership level. The 70-percent cut is designed to approximate the amount of the deduction that would be lost to the individual partners under the 2-percent floor. The remaining 30 percent is allowed at the partnership level in determining the large partnership's taxable income and is not subject to the 2-percent floor at the partner level.

Tax credits other than the low-income housing credit, the rehabilitation credit and the credit for producing fuel from nonconventional sources are reported as a single item. Credit recapture also is recognized at the partnership level.

485. Gains and Losses of Electing Large Partnerships. For electing large partnerships, the netting of capital gains and losses occurs at the partnership level (Code Sec. 773)[177] Passive activity items are separated from capital gains stemming from partnership portfolio income. Each partner separately takes into account the partner's distributive shares of net capital gain or net capital loss for passive activity and portfolio items.

Any partnership gains and losses under Code Sec. 1231 (¶ 1747) are netted at the partnership level. Net gain is treated as long-term capital gain and is subject to the rules described above, and any net loss is treated as ordinary loss and consolidated with the partnership's other taxable income.

488. Audit Procedures for Electing Large Partnerships. The TEFRA partnership audit rules normally applicable to partnerships do not apply to electing large partnerships. An electing large partnership, like other partnerships, appoints a representative to handle IRS matters. Unlike under the TEFRA rules, the representative does not have to be a partner (Code Sec. 6255(b)).[178] Only the partnership, and not the individual partners, receive notice of partnership adjustments (Code Sec. 6245(b)).[179] Only the partnership has the right to appeal the adjustment (Code Sec. 6247(a)).[180] After a partnership-level adjustment, prior-year partners and prior tax years generally are not affected. However, prior years can be affected if there has been a partnership dissolution or a finding that the shares of a distribution to partners were erroneous. Instead, the adjustments generally are passed through to current partners.

References are to Standard Federal Tax Reports; Tax Research Consultant; and Practical Tax Explanations.

[176] ¶ 25,612; PART: 18,452, PART: 18,454

[177] ¶ 25,612; PART: 18,452, PART: 18,454

[178] ¶ 37,949Q; PART: 60,652

[179] ¶ 37,937; PART: 60,660

[180] ¶ 37,949D; PART: 60,662

Chapter 5

TRUSTS ☐ ESTATES

Estates and Trusts as Taxable Entities

501. Trust, Estate, and Fiduciary Defined. A trust is a separate taxable entity for federal income tax purposes. A "trust" usually involves an arrangement created either by a will upon the creator's death or by a trust instrument that may take effect during the creator's life (Reg. § 301.7701-4(a)).[1] Under either arrangement, a trustee takes title to the property in order to protect or conserve it for beneficiaries. Usually, the beneficiaries merely accept the trust's benefits. However, even if the beneficiaries are the persons who planned or created it, the trust will still be recognized as a separate taxable entity if its purpose is to vest the trustee with the responsibility to protect and preserve property on behalf of beneficiaries who cannot share in the discharge of this responsibility. Federal tax law provides specific guidelines for what constitutes a business trust or investment trust (¶ 502) and a liquidating trust (¶ 503). Some types of trusts are governed by special tax rules, such as grantor trusts (¶ 571), charitable trusts (¶ 590), and common trust funds (¶ 595).

Decedents' estates are also considered separate taxable entities for income tax purposes during the period of administration (¶ 507). Other types of "estates" are discussed at ¶ 504—¶ 506.

Trustees, executors, and certain receivers are considered fiduciaries. A "fiduciary" is a person who occupies a position of special confidence toward another, who holds in trust property in which another person has the beneficial title or interest, or who receives and controls income of another (Reg. § 301.7701-6).[2] However, a person who is an "agent" of another person is not necessarily a "fiduciary" for federal income tax purposes, even though a "fiduciary relationship" may be said to exist for state law purposes. For example, when a person receives income as an agent, intermediary debtor, or conduit, and the income is paid over to another, the agent is not considered a fiduciary for tax purposes. The fiduciary is responsible for computing the entity's income tax liability and paying the resulting tax (¶ 510), and may be personally liable for any tax delinquencies if others are paid in preference to the IRS (¶ 512).

Small Business Trusts. An electing small business trust (ESBT) is a special kind of trust permitted to be a shareholder in an S corporation. An ESBT has no beneficiaries other than individuals or estates eligible to be S corporation shareholders, except that charitable organizations may hold contingent remainder interests. The portion of any ESBT that consists of stock in one or more S corporations is treated as a separate trust (¶ 304 and ¶ 516).

Qualified Domestic Trusts. A qualified domestic trust (QDOT) is a trust that meets certain requirements and is subject to a special estate tax. Property that is transferred from a citizen decedent to a nonresident alien spouse will not qualify for the usual estate tax marital deduction unless it is transferred from the decedent to a QDOT (¶ 2926).

References are to Standard Federal Tax Reports; Tax Research Consultant; and Practical Tax Explanations.

[1] ¶ 43,090; ESTTRST: 3,050; § 32,005.05

[2] ¶ 43,094; ESTTRST: 100; § 32,030.05

502. Business and Investment Trusts. A "business" or commercial trust is a trust created as a means of carrying on a profit-making business, usually using capital or property supplied by the beneficiaries (Reg. § 301.7701-4(b)).[3] The trustees or other designated persons are, in effect, managers of the undertaking, whether appointed or controlled by the beneficiaries. This arrangement is treated for federal tax purposes as an association, which may be taxed as a corporation, or as a partnership, and is distinguishable from the type of trust discussed at ¶ 501. The fact that the trust property is not supplied by beneficiaries is not sufficient in itself to avoid the trust being classified and taxed as a business entity.

An "investment" trust may also be taxed as an association, rather than a trust, if there is a power under the trust agreement to vary the investment of the certificate holders (Reg. § 301.7701-4(c)).[4] However, if this power is lacking, the arrangement is taxed as a trust. Unit investment trusts, as defined in the Investment Company Act of 1940, that are set up to hold mutual fund shares for investors are also not taxed as trusts. Instead, their income is taxed directly to the investors (Reg. § 1.851-7).[5]

503. Liquidating Trusts. A liquidating trust formed for the primary purpose of liquidating and distributing the assets transferred to it is taxed as a trust, and not as an association, despite the possibility of profit (Reg. § 301.7701-4(d)).[6] All activities of the trust must be reasonably necessary to, and consistent with, accomplishing the primary purpose of liquidation and distribution. If the liquidation is unreasonably prolonged, or if the liquidation purpose becomes so obscured by business activities that the declared purpose of liquidation can be said to have been lost or abandoned, the arrangement is no longer a liquidating trust.

504. Estate of Minor, Incompetent, or Person Under a Disability. The estate of an infant, incompetent person, or other person under a disability is not a taxable entity separate from the person for whom the fiduciary (¶ 501) is acting (Reg. § 1.641(b)-2(b)).[7] Therefore, the estate of such a person is not required to file a fiduciary return on Form 1041.

Generally, a guardian is required to file a tax return as an agent for a minor or legally disabled person if the individual would otherwise be required to file a return (Code Sec. 6012(b)(2); Reg. § 1.6012-3(b)(3)).[8] However, a minor can file a return for himself or herself or have someone else file it, relieving the guardian of this obligation. For the tax year during which an incompetent person is declared competent and the fiduciary is discharged, the former incompetent person must file the tax return. An agent filing a return for another person should file Form 2848, granting power of attorney, with the taxpayer's return (Reg. § 1.6012-1(a)(5)).[9] If an agent is used, both the agent and the taxpayer for whom the return is made may be liable for penalties for erroneous, false, or fraudulent returns. One spouse may execute a valid return on behalf of his or her mentally incompetent or disabled spouse prior to appointment of a legal guardian without a formal power of attorney (Rev. Rul. 56-22).[10]

505. Bankruptcy Estate of Individual Debtor. Property held by a trustee in bankruptcy for an individual under Chapter 7 (liquidation) or Chapter 11 (business reorganization) of the Bankruptcy Code is considered the estate of the debtor (Code Sec. 1398).[11] The estate is treated as a separate taxable entity unless the bankruptcy case is dismissed. The fiduciary of a Chapter 7 or Chapter 11 bankruptcy estate is obligated to file the estate's return. If the bankruptcy plan creates a liquidating trust, the fiduciary must file the trust's return (Code Sec. 6012(b)(4)).[12] The bankruptcy trustee must file a Form 1041 for the bankruptcy estate for any tax year in which the estate in bankruptcy has gross income that equals or exceeds the sum of the personal exemption amount

References are to Standard Federal Tax Reports; Tax Research Consultant; and Practical Tax Explanations.

[3] ¶ 43,090; ESTTRST: 3,102; § 30,005.35
[4] ¶ 43,090; ESTTRST: 3,154; § 30,005.35
[5] ¶ 26,407; RIC: 3,150; § 45,430.05
[6] ¶ 43,090; ESTTRST: 3,158; § 32,125
[7] ¶ 24,265; FILEIND: 18,064; § 39,030.25
[8] ¶ 35,142, ¶ 35,146; FILEIND: 18,064; § 1,305.25, § 39,020.05
[9] ¶ 35,143; FILEBUS: 12,102; § 41,205.05
[10] ¶ 35,150.734; FILEIND: 18,064; § 39,020.05
[11] ¶ 32,410; INDIV: 66,050, INDIV: 66,066
[12] ¶ 35,142; INDIV: 66,066.05; § 32,030.05

(¶ 133) plus the basic standard deduction for married persons filing separately (¶ 126) for the year ($9,750 for 2012) (Code Sec. 6012(a)(8)). The tax year for which the fiduciary files a return begins on the date of the bankruptcy petition filing. The return may be for a calendar year or a fiscal year. A trustee in bankruptcy has no authority to file a return on Form 1040 for a bankrupt individual; the individual must file an individual return.

Taxable income for bankruptcy estates is computed in the same manner as for individuals, including the right to a personal exemption, but the tax rates for married persons filing separately apply (¶ 15) (Code Sec. 1398(c); Instructions to Form 1041). If a bankruptcy estate does not itemize deductions, it can claim the standard deduction available for a married person filing separately (¶ 126).

A separate taxable entity is not created when a case is brought under Chapter 13 of the Bankruptcy Code, which involves adjustment of debts of an individual with regular income. A separate taxable entity also is not created when an individual is in receivership (Reg. § 1.641(b)-2(b)).[13]

506. Bankruptcy Estate of Partnership or Corporate Debtor. The commencement of bankruptcy proceedings for a partnership or corporation does not create a separate taxable entity (Code Sec. 1399).[14] Thus, there is no obligation imposed upon the bankruptcy trustee to file a Form 1041 on behalf of the estate. However, a receiver, trustee in dissolution, trustee in bankruptcy, or assignee who, by order of a court, has possession of or holds title to all or substantially all the property or business of a corporation must file the income tax return for such corporation on Form 1120 (Reg. § 1.6012-3(b)(4)).[15] The receiver, trustee, or assignee must file the return whether or not it is operating the property or business of the corporation. A receiver in charge of only *a small part* of the property of a corporation, such as a receiver in mortgage foreclosure proceedings, need not file the return. Bankrupt partnerships must file their returns on Form 1065.

507. Termination of Estates and Trusts. An estate is recognized as a taxable entity only during the period of administration or settlement (i.e., the period actually required by the executor or administrator to perform the ordinary duties of administration, such as collection of assets, payment of debts and legacies, etc.) (Reg. § 1.641(b)-3(a)).[16] This is true whether the period is longer or shorter than that specified under local law for estate settlement. However, estate administration may not be unduly prolonged. For federal tax purposes, the estate is considered terminated after the expiration of a reasonable period for the performance of administration duties, or when all estate assets have been distributed except for a reasonable amount set aside in good faith for the payment of contingent liabilities and expenses. If the estate has joined in making a valid election to treat a qualified revocable trust as part of the estate (¶ 516), then it does not terminate prior to the end of the election period.

A trust is recognized as a taxable entity until the trust property has been distributed to successors, plus a reasonable time after this event as is necessary for the trustee to complete trust administration (Reg. § 1.641(b)-3(b)).[17] Further, like an estate, a trust is considered terminated when all the assets have been distributed except for a reasonable amount set aside in good faith to pay contingent liabilities and expenses (other than a claim by a beneficiary in that capacity).

Once an estate or trust is considered terminated for tax purposes, its gross income, deductions, and credits subsequent to termination are considered to be the gross income, deductions, and credits of the persons who succeed to the property (Reg. § 1.641(b)-3(d)).

Fiduciary Return and Payment of Tax

510. Return of Estate or Trust by Fiduciary. A fiduciary must file a return on Form 1041 for an estate or trust if: (1) the estate has gross income of $600 or more for the tax

References are to Standard Federal Tax Reports; Tax Research Consultant; and Practical Tax Explanations.

[13] ¶ 24,265; INDIV: 66,052.10
[14] ¶ 32,420; INDIV: 66,150
[15] ¶ 35,146; FILEBUS: 3,068
[16] ¶ 24,266; ESTTRST: 9,054, ACCTNG: 24,256.10; § 32,005.10, § 38,145.20
[17] ¶ 24,266; ESTTRST: 9,054, ACCTNG: 24,256.10; § 32,005.15, § 38,145.20

year; (2) the trust (other than a trust exempt under Code Sec. 501(a)) has for the tax year any taxable income, or gross income of $600 or more regardless of the amount of taxable income; (3) any beneficiary of the estate or trust is a nonresident alien (unless the trust is exempt under Code Sec. 501(a)); or (4) an individual's bankruptcy estate under Chapter 7 or Chapter 11 of the Bankruptcy Code has gross income equal to or greater than the sum of the personal exemption amount plus the basic standard deduction amount for married individuals filing separately (¶ 505) (Code Sec. 6012(a); Reg. § 1.6012-3).[18] A foreign estate or trust generally must file Form 1040NR (Instructions to Form 1041).

When there is more than one fiduciary, the return can be filed by any one of them. However, when an estate has both domiciliary and ancillary representatives, each representative must file a return (Reg. § 1.6012-3(a)(1) and (3)). A trustee of two or more trusts must file a separate return for each trust, even though the trusts were created by the same grantor for the same beneficiaries (Reg. § 1.6012-3(a)(4)). Two or more trusts may be treated as one trust under certain circumstances (¶ 515).

The return must be filed on or before the 15th day of the fourth month following the close of the tax year (Code Sec. 6072(a)).[19] An estate or trust can apply for an automatic five-month extension of time for filing the fiduciary return by filing Form 7004 on or before the due date for filing Form 1041, and making a proper estimate of the amount of tax due for the tax year (Reg. § 1.6081-6; Instructions to Form 7004).[20] The automatic extension period is six months for an individual's Chapter 7 or 11 bankruptcy estate (¶ 505) or for a qualified funeral trust (¶ 575). The automatic extension does not extend the time for payment of any tax due on the return. In addition, the extension to file does not extend the time for a beneficiary of the estate or trust to file its income tax return or to pay any tax on the beneficiary's return.

The fiduciary of an estate or trust need not file a copy of the will or trust instrument with the estate or trust income tax return unless requested by the IRS (Reg. § 1.6012-3(a)(2)).[21] If requested, the fiduciary should file a copy (including any amendments), accompanied by a written declaration of truth and completeness and a statement indicating the provisions of the will or trust instrument that determine the extent to which estate or trust income is taxable to the estate or trust, the beneficiaries, or the grantor.

An estate or trust that is obligated to file an income tax return must furnish a copy of Schedule K-1 of Form 1041 to each beneficiary (1) who receives a distribution from the estate or trust for the year, or (2) to whom any item with respect to the tax year is allocated (Code Sec. 6034A).[22] This statement must contain the information required to be shown on the return and be furnished on or before the date on which the return is to be filed. In addition, a copy must be attached to Form 1041. A penalty may be assessed for each failure to file or furnish a correct information return (¶ 2816) or payee statement (¶ 2823).

Accounting Period. When filing its first return, an estate may choose the same accounting period as the decedent, or it may choose a calendar tax year or any fiscal tax year. If it chooses the decedent's accounting period, its first return will be for a short period to cover the unexpired term of the decedent's regular tax year (Code Secs. 441 and 443).[23] An exemption of $600 is allowed on a short-period return, without proration (¶ 534) (Reg. § 1.443-1(a)(2)).[24] However, if the estate gets approval from the IRS to change the accounting period, the exemption on the short-period return may be prorated (Reg. § 1.443-1(b)(1)(v)).

Trusts (other than trusts exempt from tax under Code Sec. 501 and wholly charitable trusts under Code Sec. 4947(a)) must adopt a calendar tax year (Code Sec.

References are to Standard Federal Tax Reports; Tax Research Consultant; and Practical Tax Explanations.

[18] ¶ 35,142, ¶ 35,146; IRS: 30,256.10, IRS: 66,152.05; § 32,610.05, § 39,030.10

[19] ¶ 36,720; FILEIND: 18,052.20; § 32,610.15, § 39,205.25

[20] ¶ 36,797; FILEBUS: 15,104.20; § 32,610.15, § 39,215.20

[21] ¶ 35,146; IRS: 30,256.10, IRS: 66,152.05; § 32,610.15

[22] ¶ 35,460; ESTTRST: 100; § 32,610.20, § 39,155.35

[23] ¶ 20,302, ¶ 20,500; ACCTNG: 24,252; § 32,025, § 38,140.05, § 38,145.20

[24] ¶ 20,501; ESTTRST: 12,052; § 32,350, § 38,140.05

644).[25] Thus, a trust must generally file Form 1041 on or before April 15 following the close of the tax year. An existing trust that is required to change its tax year must annualize any income earned in the short year. A trust must obtain IRS approval to change its annual accounting period to its required (calendar) tax year (¶ 1513).

Payment of Tax and Estimated Tax. The entire income tax liability of an estate or trust must be paid on or before the due date for its return (Code Sec. 6151).[26] In addition, estates that have been in existence for more than two years and both new and existing trusts must pay estimated tax in the same manner as individuals (¶ 511).

511. Payment of Estimated Tax. In general, estates and trusts are required to make quarterly estimated tax payments in the same manner as individuals (¶ 2682). However, estates and grantor trusts that receive the residue of a probate estate under the grantor's will are only required to make estimated tax payments for tax years that end two or more years after the decedent's death (Code Sec. 6654(l)).[27]

Estates or trusts with a short tax year must pay installments of tax on or before the 15th day of the fourth, sixth and ninth months of the tax year and the 15th day of the first month of the following tax year (¶ 2685). The amount of each installment in a short tax year is determined by dividing the required annual payment by the number of payments required for that year (Notice 87-32).[28]

Estates and trusts generally have 45 days (rather than the 15 days allowed individuals) to compute the payments under the estimated tax annualization rules. The payment due dates are unchanged (Code Sec. 6654(l)).[29] First-time filers must file Form 1041-ES which includes vouchers to be included with quarterly payments. After the first payment, the IRS should provide pre-printed vouchers. A fiduciary paying estimated tax for more than one trust should submit a separate Form 1041-ES and a separate check for each trust. However, a fiduciary may submit a single check for multiple trusts provided that a separate estimated tax voucher is submitted for each trust (Announcement 87-32).[30]

The trustee of a trust, or the fiduciary of an estate whose tax year is reasonably expected to be its last tax year, may elect to treat any or all of an estimated tax payment as a payment made by the beneficiary and credited toward the beneficiary's tax liability (Code Sec. 643(g)).[31] If elected, the payment is not treated as an estimated tax payment made by the estate or trust. The election is made on Form 1041-T and must be filed on or before the 65th day after the close of the tax year (March 6, 2013, for calendar tax year 2012).

512. Personal Liability of Fiduciary. Any fiduciary (other than a trustee acting under the Bankruptcy Code) who pays any debt due by the decedent or the estate, in whole or in part, before federal tax obligations are satisfied becomes personally liable for the tax of the estate to the extent of such payments (Reg. § 1.641(b)-2; 31 U.S.C. § 3713).[32] However, the fiduciary is not liable for amounts paid out for debts that have priority over the federal taxes due and owing on the estate, such as a decedent's funeral expenses or probate administration costs. Further, an executor or administrator who pays other debts is not personally liable unless the executor or administrator has either personal knowledge of a tax due the United States or knowledge that would put a reasonably prudent person on notice that such tax debts exist.[33] Discharge of the fiduciary does not terminate the fiduciary's personal liability for the payment of other debts of the estate without satisfying prior tax claims.

Taxation of Estates and Trusts

514. Taxation of Estates and Trusts—Introduction. An estate or trust is a separate taxable entity (¶ 501). In general, its entire income for its tax year must be reported on

References are to Standard Federal Tax Reports; Tax Research Consultant; and Practical Tax Explanations.

[25] ¶ 24,350; ACCTNG: 24,104, ACCTNG: 24,252.25; § 32,025, § 32,610.15

[26] ¶ 37,080; ESTTRST: 100, FILEBUS: 6,102; § 39,305.05

[27] ¶ 39,550; FILEIND: 21,058; § 32,615.05

[28] ¶ 39,560.82; FILEIND: 21,058; § 32,615.05

[29] ¶ 39,550; FILEIND: 21,050; § 1,410, § 32,615.05, § 40,225.10

[30] ¶ 39,560.82; FILEIND: 21,058; § 32,615.05

[31] ¶ 24,320; ESTTRST: 27,054, FILEIND: 21,054.10; § 1,410, § 32,615.10

[32] ¶ 24,265, ¶ 40,730; IRS: 60,202; § 32,030.10, § 39,545

[33] ¶ 40,735.25; IRS: 60,206; § 32,030.10, § 39,545

Form 1041, which must be filed by the fiduciary (¶ 510). If income is required to be distributed currently or is properly distributed to a beneficiary, the estate or trust is regarded as a conduit with respect to that income. It is allowed a deduction for the portion of gross income that is currently distributable to the beneficiaries or is properly paid or credited to them (¶ 542—¶ 545). Generally, the beneficiaries are taxed on the part of the income currently distributed, and the estate or trust is taxed on the portion that it has accumulated. The income allocated to a beneficiary retains the same character in the beneficiary's hands that it had in the hands of the estate or trust (Reg. §§ 1.652(b)-1 and 1.662(b)-1).[34]

For purposes of the income taxation of estates and nongrantor trusts, the term "income" (without specifying "gross income," "taxable income," "undistributed net income," or "distributable net income") refers to income of the estate or trust for the tax year determined under the terms of its governing instrument and applicable local law—that is, income as it would be computed in an accounting to the court having jurisdiction over the estate or trust (Code Sec. 643(b); Reg. § 1.643(b)-1).[35] Trust provisions that depart fundamentally from concepts of income and principal are not recognized for tax purposes. However, an allocation of amounts between income and principal pursuant to applicable local law will be respected if local law provides for a reasonable apportionment between the income and remainder beneficiaries of the trust's total return for the year, including ordinary and tax-exempt income, capital gains, and appreciation.

Income items of an estate or trust are discussed at ¶ 520–¶ 527. Ordinary deductions of an estate or trust are discussed at ¶ 528–¶ 536. The charitable contribution deduction is discussed at ¶ 537–¶ 538. The deduction for distributions to beneficiaries and the concept of distributable net income (DNI) are discussed at ¶ 542–¶ 549. The treatment of tax credits of an estate or trust is discussed at ¶ 540.

515. Multiple Trusts. One grantor may create several trusts, and the income may be taxed separately for each trust. When there is intent to create separate trusts for multiple beneficiaries, the fact that the corpus of each trust is kept in one fund will not necessarily defeat the grantor's intent. Although it is not necessary to divide the corpus physically in order to carry out the intent of the parties, it is necessary to comply literally with the terms of the trust instrument in other respects.[36]

However, two or more trusts will be treated as one trust if (1) the trusts have substantially the same grantor or grantors and substantially the same primary beneficiary or beneficiaries, and (2) a principal purpose of the trusts is the avoidance of income tax (Code Sec. 643(f)).[37] A special safe-harbor provision applies to any trust that was irrevocable on March 1, 1984, except to the extent that corpus is contributed to the trust after that date.

516. Computation of Tax. An estate or trust computes its tax liability by using the separate estate and trust income tax rate schedule at ¶ 19. The taxable income of an estate or trust for purposes of the regular income tax is determined by subtracting from its gross income (¶ 520) allowable deductions (¶ 528), amounts distributable to beneficiaries (to the extent of distributable net income (DNI)) (¶ 543), and the proper exemption (¶ 534) (Code Sec. 641; Reg. §§ 1.641(a)-1 and 1.641(b)-1).[38]

The alternative minimum tax (AMT) of an estate or trust is computed by determining DNI under the general rules (¶ 543), subject to further adjustments under the minimum tax rules. The AMT is computed on Part III of Schedule I, Form 1041 (¶ 1401).

Grantor trusts and employees' trusts are subject to special tax treatment (¶ 571 and ¶ 2101).

Qualified Revocable Trusts. A trustee of a qualified revocable trust (QRT) and the executor, if any, of a decedent's estate may join in an election to treat the revocable trust

References are to Standard Federal Tax Reports; Tax Research Consultant; and Practical Tax Explanations.

[34] ¶ 24,383, ¶ 24,425; ESTTRST: 24,154, ESTTRST: 30,106; § 32,005.05, § 32,501, § 32,701

[35] ¶ 24,320, ¶ 24,329; ESTTRST: 18,050; § 32,010.10

[36] ¶ 24,267.67; ESTTRST: 3,202; § 32,185

[37] ¶ 24,320; ESTTRST: 3,204; § 32,185

[38] ¶ 24,260, ¶ 24,262, ¶ 24,264; ESTTRST: 100; § 32,005.05, § 32,010, § 32,015, § 32,020

as part of the estate (Code Sec. 645; Reg. § 1.645-1).[39] The election allows the revocable trust to enjoy certain income tax treatment that would otherwise be accorded only to the decedent's estate, such as claiming the unlimited deduction for amounts permanently set aside for charity without first actually paying the amount (¶ 537), waiving the active participation requirement under the passive loss rules for two years after the decedent's death (¶ 2063), and qualifying for amortization of reforestation expenditures (¶ 530). A QRT is any trust or portion of a trust that, on the date of the decedent's death, is treated as owned by the decedent as grantor by reason of a power to revoke the trust (¶ 582), but without regard to powers held by the decedent's spouse (¶ 578). The election is made on Form 8855 which must be filed by the due date (including extensions) of the Form 1041 for the first tax year of the related estate or filing trust. The election period begins on the date of the decedent's death, and ends on the earlier of the day on which both the trust and related estate have distributed all of their assets, or the day before the applicable date, which is either (1) two years after the date of death, if no federal estate tax return is required, or (2) six months after the final determination of estate tax liability, if a federal estate tax return must be filed.

Electing Small Business Trust. An electing small business trust (ESBT) (¶ 501) is taxed in a different manner than other trusts (Code Sec. 641(c); Reg. § 1.641(c)-1).[40] First, the portion of the ESBT that consists of stock in one or more S corporations is treated as a separate trust for purposes of computing the income tax attributable to the S corporation stock held by the trust. This portion of the trust's income is taxed at the highest rate imposed on estates and trusts, and includes:

(1) the items of income, loss, deduction or credit allocated to the trust as an S corporation shareholder;

(2) gain or loss from the sale of the S corporation stock;

(3) any state or local income taxes and administrative expenses of the trust properly allocable to the S corporation stock; and

(4) any interest expense paid or accrued on debt incurred to acquire S corporation stock.

Capital losses are allowed in computing an ESBT's income only to the extent of capital gains. Moreover, no deduction is allowed for amounts distributed to beneficiaries and, except as described above, no additional deductions or credits are allowed. Also, the ESBT's income is not included in the DNI of the trust and, therefore, is not included in the beneficiaries' income. Furthermore, no item relating to the S corporation stock is apportioned to any beneficiary. The trust's AMT exemption amount is zero. Special rules apply upon termination of all or a part of the ESBT (¶ 304).

Gifts from Expatriates. A domestic trust that receives property, directly or indirectly, by gift, devise, bequest, or inheritance from a "covered expatriate" (¶ 2412) after the date of expatriation must pay a tax equal to the value of such "covered gift or bequest" multiplied by the greater of the highest federal estate tax rate or the highest federal gift tax rate in effect. Similarly, a covered gift or bequest made to a foreign trust is subject to the tax, but only at the time a distribution of income or principal is made to a U.S. citizen or resident from the trust that is attributable to the covered gift or bequest. A foreign trust can elect to be treated as a domestic trust for these purposes; the election can be revoked with IRS consent (¶ 2948).

517. Medicare Contribution Tax. Effective for tax years beginning after December 31, 2012, an estate or trust must pay a 3.8 percent unearned income Medicare contribution tax on the lesser of: (1) its undistributed net investment income for the tax year (¶ 129), or (2) any excess of its adjusted gross income determined under Code Sec. 67(e) (¶ 528) over the dollar amount at which the highest tax bracket for estates and trusts begins for the tax year (¶ 19) (Code Sec. 1411(a)(2)).[41] The tax does not apply to any trust whose unexpired interests are devoted to the charitable purposes described in Code Sec. 170(c)(2)(B) (Code Sec. 1411(e)(2)).

References are to Standard Federal Tax Reports; Tax Research Consultant; and Practical Tax Explanations.

[39] ¶ 24,355, ¶ 24,356; EST-TRST: 39,300; § 32,105.10

[40] ¶ 24,260, ¶ 24,266F; SCORP: 166.35; § 32,165

[41] ¶ 32,602; FILEIND: 15,052.35; § 32,022

520. Gross Income of Estate or Trust. The gross income of an estate or trust is generally determined in the same manner as that of an individual (Code Sec. 641(b); Reg. § 1.641(a)-2).[42] It includes all items of income received during the tax year, including:

(1) income accumulated in trust for the benefit of unborn or unascertained persons or persons with contingent interests;

(2) income accumulated or held for future distribution under the terms of the will or trust;

(3) income that is to be distributed currently by the fiduciary to the beneficiaries, and income collected by the guardian of an infant that is to be held or distributed as the court may direct;

(4) income received by the estate of a deceased person during the period of administration or settlement of the estate; and

(5) income that, at the discretion of the fiduciary, may be either distributed to the beneficiaries or accumulated.

Although all the items above are includible in gross income, the tax liability may rest on either the estate or trust as a separate entity or on the beneficiary (¶ 542).

The allocation of income and deductions between a decedent's estate and the surviving spouse in community property states depends on state community property laws. In most states, the surviving spouse is taxed on one-half of the income flowing from the community property of the estate.[43]

522. Income from Real Estate. State law determines whether income from real estate during the period of administration is taxable to the decedent's estate or to the heirs or devisees. The IRS has ruled that if state law provides that real property is subject to administration, income derived from the property is taxable to the estate even though legal title may pass directly to the heirs or devisees. However, if the administrator is not entitled to possession or control of real property, income from the property is taxable to the heirs or devisees and not to the estate. Even if the property is not subject to the administrator's control, all or a part of the gain from a sale of property is taxable to the estate to the extent that the property was sold, under state law, to raise funds for its administration (Rev. Rul. 57-133; Rev. Rul. 59-375).[44]

523. Income from Personal Property. Income from personal property, including a gain from the sale or exchange of such property, is taxable to the estate. This is because title to personal property vests in the administrator or executor immediately upon appointment and does not pass to the heirs or legatees until the estate is fully administered and distribution is ordered or approved by the courts, and notwithstanding the fact that the basis of the property distributed relates back to the date of the decedent's death.[45]

524. Sale of Property by Estate or Trust. The gain or loss realized on the sale of property acquired by an estate, trust or beneficiary is determined under special basis rules, the applicability of which depends on how the property was acquired and the nature of the property sold (¶ 1601 and ¶ 1701).

For estates of decedents dying in 2010, if the executor elected *not* to have the federal estate tax apply to the estate (¶ 2901), then the decedent's estate, a qualified revocable trust (¶ 516), or an heir may be able to exclude from gross income the gain on the sale of the decedent's personal residence (Code Sec. 121(d)(11); Act Sec. 301 of the Tax Relief, Unemployment Insurance Reauthorization, and Job Creation Act of 2010 (P.L. 111-312)).[46] The general rules for the personal residence gain exclusion are discussed at ¶ 1705. This exclusion is not available for estates of 2010 decedents whose executors did not make the special election, or for estates of decedents dying after 2010.

References are to Standard Federal Tax Reports; Tax Research Consultant; and Practical Tax Explanations.

42 ¶ 24,260, ¶ 24,263; ESTTRST: 9,052, ESTTRST: 24,100; § 32,201

43 ¶ 2350.2473; INDIV: 24,200, ESTTRST: 9,108; § 32,205.25

44 ¶ 24,267.5204; ESTTRST: 9,102; § 32,205.30

45 ¶ 24,267.515; ESTTRST: 9,052; § 32,210.05

46 ¶ 7260; REAL: 15,150; § 1,610.30, § 34,920

526. Gain on Transfer to Beneficiary. Generally, gain or loss is realized by an estate or trust, or by the other beneficiaries, on the distribution of property in kind that satisfies a beneficiary's right to receive a specific dollar amount, specific property other than the property distributed, or other income if income is required to be distributed currently (Reg. § 1.661(a)-2(f)).[47] A special rule generally limits gain on transfers to qualified heirs of property for which a special use valuation election under Code Sec. 2032A was made (¶ 2922). However, for estates of decedents dying in 2010 for which the executor elected *not* to have the federal estate tax apply (¶ 2901), this rule limits gain on exchanges that satisfy pecuniary bequests with appreciated property (Code Sec. 1040; Act Sec. 301 of the Tax Relief, Unemployment Insurance Reauthorization, and Job Creation Act of 2010 (P.L. 111-312)).[48]

For purposes of the rule limiting gain on transfers to qualified heirs of special use valuation property, a marital deduction trust (¶ 2926) comprising a portion of the residuary estate and measured by a percentage of the value of the adjusted gross estate is considered as being provided for in a fixed dollar amount (Rev. Rul. 60-87).[49] Upon a distribution of property to such a trust, the estate realizes gain or loss equal to the difference between the property's fair market value at the distribution date and its federal estate tax value.

Distribution of a stated percentage of trust corpus to the beneficiary before termination of the trust is not considered a satisfaction of a trust obligation for a definite amount of cash or equivalent value in property. Instead, it is treated as a partial distribution of a share of the trust principal. Thus, there is no sale or exchange, and neither the trustee nor the beneficiary realizes taxable income (Rev. Rul. 55-117).[50] However, a trustee or executor may elect to recognize gain or loss on the distribution of noncash property to a beneficiary as if the property had been sold to the beneficiary at its fair market value (Code Sec. 643(e)(3)).[51] The election is made on the return for the year of distribution and applies to all distributions made by the estate or trust during its entire tax year. Thus, an election to recognize gain or loss cannot be made separately for each distribution.

In the event the election is made, the beneficiary's basis in the distributed property is the estate's or trust's adjusted basis just prior to the distribution, adjusted by the gain or loss recognized by the estate or trust. If the election is not made, the beneficiary's basis is the same as the trust's or estate's, and any gain or loss is recognized by the beneficiary when the beneficiary disposes of the property. Gain recognition on certain property distributions to expatriates is discussed at ¶ 566.

527. Income of Foreign Estates or Trusts. For purposes of computing the taxable income of a foreign estate or foreign trust, the estate or trust is treated as a nonresident alien individual who is not present in the United States at any time (¶ 2409 and ¶ 2425) (Code Sec. 641(b)).[52]

The estate of a nonresident alien is taxed on its income received from U.S. sources, including capital gains and dividends (Rev. Rul. 68-621).[53] However, the estate is allowed a deduction for distributions to both nonresident aliens and U.S. beneficiaries to the extent that these distributions are not in excess of its distributable net income (¶ 545). The portion of the distribution allocated to capital gains is not includible in the gross income of nonresident alien beneficiaries if they have not resided in the United States for a period of at least 183 days (¶ 2435). The portion of a distribution that represents dividends is, however, includible in the gross income of nonresident alien beneficiaries. The fiduciary must withhold U.S. taxes from these dividend distributions at the statutory rate or the applicable treaty rate.

References are to Standard Federal Tax Reports; Tax Research Consultant; and Practical Tax Explanations.

[47] ¶ 24,402; ESTTRST: 21,150; § 32,215, § 32,520

[48] ¶ 29,779, ¶ 29,780; ESTTRST: 21,252; § 18,225

[49] ¶ 24,267.5281; ESTTRST: 21,158; § 32,520

[50] ¶ 24,267.5281; ESTTRST: 21,158; § 32,505.15, § 32,520

[51] ¶ 24,320; ESTTRST: 21,102; § 32,505.15, § 32,520

[52] ¶ 24,260; ESTTRST:100; § 32,005.05

[53] ¶ 24,267.4985; ESTTRST: 30,106; § 32,005.05, § 37,005

528. Deductions Generally. In general, estates and trusts are allowed the same deductions as individuals (Code Sec. 641(b); Reg. § 1.641(b)-1).[54] However, the standard deduction available to estates and trusts is zero (Code Sec. 63(c)(6)(D)).[55] In addition, special rules govern the computation of certain deductions and the allocation of deductions between the beneficiaries and the estate or trust (¶ 529). Further, the estate or trust is permitted to claim a deduction for certain distributions to beneficiaries (¶ 544 and ¶ 545).

Two-Percent Floor on Itemized Deductions. In general, an estate or trust is subject to the two-percent-of-adjusted-gross-income (AGI) floor on miscellaneous itemized deductions (¶ 1011) (Code Sec. 67(e)).[56] The AGI of an estate or trust is computed in the same manner as it is for an individual (¶ 1005), except that the following deductions are allowed from gross income: (1) deductions for expenses paid or incurred in connection with the administration of the estate or trust that would not have been incurred had the property not been so held; (2) the personal exemption deduction allowed to estates and trusts (¶ 534); and (3) the deduction for distribution to beneficiaries (¶ 544 and ¶ 545). The IRS has regulatory authority to apply the two-percent floor at the beneficiary level, rather than the entity level, with respect to simple trusts.

The U.S. Supreme Court has ruled that only estate or trust expenses that would be uncommon, unusual, or unlikely for a hypothetical individual to incur are not subject to the two-percent floor (*M.J. Knight, Trustee,* SCt, 2008-1 USTC ¶ 50,132).[57] These types of costs would not "commonly" or "customarily" be incurred by individuals. Hence, investment advisory fees incurred by an estate or trust are generally subject to the two-percent floor. Expenses incurred in administering a bankruptcy estate are fully deductible from gross income (CCA 200630016).

Proposed regulations likewise provide that the two-percent floor applies to administration expenses incurred by an estate or nongrantor trust if they commonly or customarily would be incurred by a hypothetical individual holding the same property (Prop. Reg. § 1.67-4).[58] If the estate or trust pays a single fee or commission both for costs that are subject to the two-percent floor and costs that are not, it must allocate the bundled fee between the two types of costs using any reasonable method. However, for tax years beginning before the date that final regulations are published in the Federal Register, taxpayers are not required to determine the portion of a bundled fiduciary fee that is subject to the two-percent floor. Instead, taxpayers may deduct 100 percent of the bundled fiduciary fee without regard to the two-percent floor (Notice 2011-37).[59]

529. Expense Deduction. In general, an estate or trust is allowed deductions for any ordinary and necessary expenses incurred in carrying on a trade or business (¶ 901), in the production of income or the management or conservation of income-producing property (¶ 1085), or in connection with the determination, collection, or refund of any tax (¶ 1092). Reasonable amounts paid or incurred by a fiduciary on account of administration, including fiduciary fees and litigation expenses, are deductible as well. Such expenses are deductible even if the estate or trust is not engaged in a trade or business, unless the expenses were for the production or collection of tax-exempt income (Reg. § 1.212-1(i)).[60]

Deductions are not allowed for: (1) expenses that are allocable to one or more classes of income exempt from tax (other than interest income) or (2) any amount relating to expenses for the production of income that is allocable to tax-exempt interest income (¶ 970). The IRS allows a deduction for an executor's or administrator's commissions, as paid or accrued, except the portion allocable to tax-exempt income.[61]

Alimony Payments. An estate can deduct the value of periodic alimony payments it makes under the rules regarding deductions for distributions to beneficiaries.[62]

References are to Standard Federal Tax Reports; Tax Research Consultant; and Practical Tax Explanations.

[54] ¶ 24,260, ¶ 24,264; ESTTRST: 12,000; § 32,301

[55] ¶ 6020; ESTTRST: 12,050; § 32,301

[56] ¶ 6060; ESTTRST: 12,054; § 32,345

[57] ¶ 6064.75; ESTTRST: 12,054; § 32,345

[58] ¶ 6063AG; ESTTRST: 12,054; § 32,345

[59] ¶ 6064.75; ESTTRST: 12,054; § 32,345

[60] ¶ 12,521; ESTTRST: 12,054, ESTTRST: 12,056; § 32,315.05

[61] ¶ 12,523.51, ¶ 24,686.80; ESTTRST: 12,058; § 32,315.15

[62] ¶ 6094.31, ¶ 24,267.403, ¶ 24,407.56; ESTTRST: 27,052.10; § 1,905.20, § 32,310

Double Deductions Prohibited. Amounts deductible as administration expenses or losses for estate tax (¶ 2925) or generation-skipping transfer tax purposes may not also be deducted, or offset against the sales price of property in determining gain or loss (i.e., selling expenses), for income tax purposes by the estate or any other person (Code Sec. 642(g); Reg. § 1.642(g)-1).[63] However, the estate can deduct such items for income tax purposes if it files a statement (in duplicate) that the items have not been claimed as deductions for estate tax purposes and that all rights to deduct them for such purposes are waived.

Note that one deduction or portion of a deduction may be allowed for income tax purposes if the appropriate statement is filed, while another deduction or portion is allowed for estate tax purposes (Reg. § 1.642(g)-2).[64] Deductions for taxes, interest, business expenses, and other items accrued *at the decedent's date of death* are allowed as a deduction for estate tax purposes as claims against the estate, and are also allowed as a deduction in respect of a decedent for income tax purposes. However, the estate cannot take an income tax deduction for the decedent's medical and dental expenses that it has paid. These expenses can only be claimed on the estate tax return or the decedent's final income tax return (¶ 1018).

530. Depreciation and Depletion Deductions. Depreciation and depletion deductions must be apportioned between an estate or trust and its beneficiaries (Code Secs. 167(d), 611(b), and 642(e); Reg. §§ 1.167(h)-1, 1.611-1(c), and 1.642(e)-1).[65] Different rules govern estates and trusts.

In the case of a trust, the allowable deduction for depreciation or depletion is apportioned between the income beneficiaries and the trustee on the basis of the trust income allocable to each. However, if the trust instrument or local law requires or permits the trustee to maintain a reserve for depreciation or depletion, the deduction is first allocated to the trustee to the extent that income is set aside for such a reserve. Any part of the deduction in excess of the income set aside for the reserve is then apportioned between the income beneficiaries and the trust on the basis of the trust income (in excess of the income set aside for the reserve) allocable to each. No effect is given to any allocation that gives any beneficiary or the trustee a share of the deduction greater than a pro rata share of the trust income. The allocation is disregarded despite any provisions in the trust instrument, unless the trust instrument or local law requires or permits the trustee to maintain a reserve for depreciation or depletion.

In the case of an estate, the depreciation or depletion allowance is apportioned between the estate and the heirs, legatees, and devisees on the basis of the income from the property allocable to each.

Section 179 Election. Although an estate or trust is entitled to take MACRS depreciation on qualified assets, neither can make a Section 179 election to expense depreciable business assets (¶ 1208) (Code Sec. 179(d)(4)).[66]

Reforestation Expenditures. Estates can elect to expense reforestation expenditures and amortize any excess expenditures (¶ 1287) (Code Sec. 194).[67] Trusts cannot elect the expense deduction but can elect to amortize such expenditures. Total reforestation expenditures incurred must be apportioned between the income beneficiaries and the fiduciary. Amounts apportioned to a beneficiary must be taken into account in determining the dollar limit on the reforestation expenditures that the beneficiary can expense.

531. Losses and Bad Debt Deductions. An estate or trust can deduct losses from a trade or business or from transactions entered into for profit (¶ 1101). Similarly, the rules governing nonbusiness casualty and theft losses (¶ 1124) apply to an estate or trust. Thus, after the $100-per-occurrence floor has been satisfied, losses in excess of nonbusiness casualty and theft gains are deductible to the extent that they exceed 10 percent of the adjusted gross income (AGI) of the estate or trust. For this purpose, an

References are to Standard Federal Tax Reports; Tax Research Consultant; and Practical Tax Explanations.

[63] ¶ 24,280, ¶ 24,299; EST-TRST: 9,200, ESTTRST: 9,202; § 32,310

[64] ¶ 24,300; ESTTRST: 9,202; § 32,310

[65] ¶ 11,002, ¶ 11,048, ¶ 23,920, ¶ 23,922, ¶ 24,280, ¶ 24,297; ESTTRST: 12,102; § 32,335.05

[66] ¶ 12,120; DEPR: 12,050; § 32,335.05

[67] ¶ 12,330; FARM: 24,112; § 32,335.15

estate's or trust's administration expenses are allowable as a deduction in computing its AGI (Code Sec. 165(h)(5)(C)).[68]

A nonbusiness casualty or theft loss sustained or discovered during the settlement of an estate is deductible on the estate's income tax return only if it has not been allowed for estate tax purposes (Code Sec. 165(h)(5)(D); Reg. §§1.165-7(c) and 1.165-8(b)).[69] A statement to this effect should be filed with the return for the year for which the deduction is claimed.

Net Operating Losses. An estate or trust is allowed a deduction for net operating losses (NOLs) (¶1173) (Reg. §1.642(d)-1).[70] However, an estate cannot deduct an NOL (or a capital loss (¶1752)) sustained by a decedent during the decedent's last tax year. These losses must be deducted on the decedent's final return.[71] In addition, in computing gross income and deductions for the NOL calculation, a trust must not take into account income and deductions attributable to the grantor or any substantial owner under the grantor trusts rules (¶571). Also, in calculating NOLs, an estate or trust cannot claim the deductions for charitable contributions (¶537) and distributions to beneficiaries (¶544 and ¶545).

Bad Debts. An estate or trust is entitled to claim bad debt deductions under the rules governing individuals (¶1145).

Passive Losses. The passive activity loss rules (¶2053) apply to estates and trusts, but not grantor trusts (¶2056).

532. Taxes Paid Deduction. An estate or trust is entitled to the same deductions for taxes as individuals (¶1021). In addition, an estate or trust is permitted an offset of the allocable federal estate tax against income in respect of a decedent (¶191). The portion of state income taxes allocable to exempt income, other than exempt interest income, is not deductible (¶970). The portion of state income taxes attributable to exempt interest income and to income subject to federal income tax is deductible (Rev. Rul. 61-86).[72]

533. Interest Paid Deduction. Interest paid or accrued during the tax year is deductible by an estate or trust under the same rules that apply to individuals (¶1043) (Code Sec. 163).[73] However, there are a number of important differences. For example, interest owed and accrued at the death of the decedent can be deducted on the estate's income tax return as a deduction in respect of the decedent for the tax year in which the interest is paid. If the interest accrues after the decedent's death, it may be claimed as either an estate tax deduction or an income tax deduction (¶529). In addition, interest is not deductible by an estate or trust on a debt incurred, or continued, to purchase or carry obligations the interest on which is wholly exempt from federal income taxes (¶970). Personal interest of an estate or trust is also nondeductible (¶1045). Further, the deduction for investment interest may not exceed net investment income for the tax year (Code Sec. 163(d)).[74] Net capital gain attributable to the disposition of property held for investment is generally excluded from investment income for purposes of computing this limitation. However, a special election is available to increase net capital gain includible in investment income by reducing the amount eligible capital gain treatment (¶1094).

534. Exemption Amount. An estate can claim a personal exemption of $600 in determining its taxable income (Code Sec. 642(b); Reg. §1.642(b)-1).[75] A "simple" trust (¶542)—one that is required to distribute all of its income currently—is allowed an exemption of $300. A "complex" trust is entitled to a $100 exemption. A qualified disability trust, whether taxed as a simple or complex trust, can claim an exemption in the amount available to an unmarried individual who is not a surviving spouse or head of

References are to Standard Federal Tax Reports; Tax Research Consultant; and Practical Tax Explanations.

[68] ¶9802; ESTTRST: 12,060.10; §7,705.10, §32,401

[69] ¶9802, ¶10,004, ¶10,100; ESTTRST: 12,060.10; §7,705.15, §32,401

[70] ¶24,296; ESTTRST: 12,062; §32,401, §32,410

[71] ¶24,267.451; ESTTRST: 6,208.15, ESTTRST: 12,062; §32,401

[72] ¶9502.453; ESTTRST: 12,064; §32,325

[73] ¶9102; ESTTRST: 12,064; §32,320

[74] ¶9102; ESTTRST: 12,064; §7,414, §7,420.05, §32,320

[75] ¶24,280, ¶24,286; ESTTRST: 12,052; §32,350

a household (¶ 133). If a final distribution of assets has been made during the year, all income of the estate or trust must be reported as distributed to the beneficiaries, without reduction for the amount claimed for the exemption (¶ 535).

Comment: Absent further legislation, the exemption for a qualified disability trust will be subject to phase-out for tax years beginning after December 31, 2012 (¶ 133).

535. Unused Loss Carryovers and Excess Deductions on Termination. A beneficiary succeeding to the property of an estate or trust can deduct a net operating loss (NOL) carryover (¶ 1179 and ¶ 1185), a capital loss carryover (¶ 562 and ¶ 1754), and deductions in excess of gross income for the year in which the estate or trust terminates (Code Sec. 642(h); Reg. §§1.642(h)-1—1.642(h)-5).[76] Excess deductions on termination of an estate or trust are allowed only in computing taxable income and must be taken into account in computing the beneficiary's tax preference items. Such deductions may not be used in computing adjusted gross income. In computing excess deductions, the deductions for personal exemptions and amounts set aside for charitable purposes are disregarded. The deduction is claimed as an itemized deduction or capital loss (depending on its nature) on the beneficiary's tax return filed for the year in which the estate or trust terminates.

An individual debtor's bankruptcy estate (¶ 505) succeeds to certain tax attributes of the debtor, including any NOL carryover (Code Sec. 1398(g)).[77] The tax attributes that become part of the estate are determined as of the first day of the debtor's tax year in which the bankruptcy case commences. If any carryback year of the estate is a tax year before the estate's first tax year, the carryback is taken into account in the tax year of the debtor that corresponds to such carryback year and, accordingly, may offset the pre-bankruptcy income of the debtor (Code Sec. 1398(j)(2)(A)). When the estate closes upon the issuance of a final decree, the debtor succeeds to the same attributes as the estate, including any unused NOL carryover (Code Sec. 1398(i)). The debtor, however, cannot carry an unused NOL carryback from a tax year that ended after commencement of the bankruptcy case to a tax year that precedes the tax year in which the bankruptcy case was commenced (Code Sec. 1398(j)(2)(B)).

536. Domestic Production Activities Deduction. An estate or a nongrantor trust, and the beneficiaries of the estate or trust, may claim the deduction for domestic production activities (i.e., manufacturer's deduction) (¶ 980A) (Code Sec. 199(d)(1)(B); Reg. §1.199-5(e)).[78] In computing the deduction, an estate or trust apportions W-2 wages, domestic production gross receipts (DPGR), cost of goods sold allocable to DPGR, and expenses, losses and deductions properly allocable to DPGR between the beneficiaries and the fiduciary, and among the beneficiaries. The nine-percent applicable percentage limitation on the deduction is applied to the lesser of the estate's or trust's qualified production activities income (QPAI) or its adjusted gross income (AGI), as determined under the AGI computation rules for estates and trusts (¶ 528).

The estate or trust calculates each beneficiary's share (as well as the estate's or trust's own share, if any) of the estate's or trust's QPAI and W-2 wages at the estate or trust level. The QPAI and W-2 wages are allocated to each beneficiary and to the estate or trust based on the relative proportion of the estate's or trust's distributable net income (DNI) for the tax year that is distributed or required to be distributed to the beneficiary or is retained by the estate or trust (¶ 542 and ¶ 543). If the estate or trust has no DNI for the tax year, QPAI and W-2 wages are allocated entirely to the estate or trust.

Each beneficiary computes its Code Sec. 199 deduction by combining its share of QPAI and W-2 wages from the estate or trust with its share of QPAI and W-2 wages from other sources. When determining its total QPAI and W-2 wages from such other sources, the beneficiary does not take into account the items allocated from the estate or trust. The beneficiary's share of W-2 wages from the estate or trust is determined under

References are to Standard Federal Tax Reports; Tax Research Consultant; and Practical Tax Explanations.

[76] ¶ 24,280, ¶ 24,301–¶ 24,305; ESTTRST: 12,150; §32,415

[77] ¶ 32,410; INDIV: 66,106, INDIV: 66,108; §3,420.10, §17,010.05

[78] ¶ 12,468, ¶ 12,472D; BUSEXP: 6,216; §6,020.20, §32,355

the law applicable to pass-thru entities based on the beginning date of the estate's or trust's tax year, not the beneficiary's tax year (Reg. § 1.199-5(e)(3)).

Grantor Trust. For a grantor trust (¶ 571), the owner computes its QPAI with respect to the owned portion of the trust as if that QPAI had been generated by activities performed directly by the owner (Reg. § 1.199-5(d)). Similarly, for purposes of the wage limitation (¶ 980C), the owner takes into account its share of the trust's W-2 wages that are attributable to the owned portion of the trust. The nongrantor trust provisions (discussed above) do not apply to the owned portion of the trust.

537. Charitable Deduction. Estates and complex trusts are allowed an unlimited charitable deduction for amounts paid to recognized charities (¶ 1061) out of gross income (other than unrelated business income of a trust) under the terms of the governing instrument during the tax year (Code Sec. 642(c)).[79] For example, amounts bequeathed to charity that are paid out of corpus under state law are not deductible from income as charitable contributions or as distributions to beneficiaries.[80] However, payments in compromise of bequests to charity are deductible.[81] Limitations on the charitable deduction for estates and trusts are discussed at ¶ 538.

The trustee or administrator may elect to treat charitable payments made during the year following the close of a tax year as having been paid in the earlier year for deduction purposes (Code Sec. 642(c)(1); Reg. § 1.642(c)-1(b)).[82] The election must be made no later than the time, including extensions, prescribed by law for filing the income tax return for the tax year in which payment is made. The election is binding for the tax year for which it is made and may not be revoked after the time for making the election has expired.

Estates may also claim an unlimited deduction for amounts of gross income permanently set aside for charitable purposes (Reg. § 1.642(c)-2).[83] The income must be permanently set aside for a purpose specified in Code Sec. 170(c) or it must be used exclusively for: (i) religious, charitable, scientific, literary, or educational purposes; (ii) the prevention of cruelty to children or animals; or (iii) the establishment, acquisition, maintenance, or operation of a nonprofit public cemetery. For most complex trusts, the unlimited deduction for gross income that is permanently set aside for charitable purposes does not apply.

A provision in a governing instrument or local law that specifically identifies the source out of which amounts are to be paid, permanently set aside, or used for charitable purposes must have economic effect independent of income tax consequences in order to be respected for federal tax purposes (Reg. § 1.642(c)-3(b)(2)).[84]

Pooled income funds (¶ 593) may claim a set-aside deduction only for gross income attributable to gain from the sale of a long-term capital asset that is permanently set aside for the benefit of the charity (Reg. § 1.642(c)-2(c)).[85] No deduction is allowed with respect to gross income of the fund that is (1) attributable to income other than net long-term capital gains; or (2) earned with respect to amounts transferred to the fund before August 1, 1969. The investment and accounting requirements applicable to trusts also apply to pooled income funds.

The charitable deduction is normally computed on Schedule A of Form 1041. However, pooled income funds claiming the set-aside deduction for long-term capital gain and nonexempt charitable trusts under Code Sec. 4947(a)(1) treated as private foundations must compute their deduction on a separate schedule, rather than Schedule A. Also, a nonexempt charitable trust not treated as a private foundation must file Form 990 in addition to Schedule A if its gross receipts are normally more than $50,000. However, the trust may file Form 990 or Form 990-EZ to satisfy its Form 1041 filing requirement if it has zero taxable income (¶ 625).

References are to Standard Federal Tax Reports; Tax Research Consultant; and Practical Tax Explanations.

[79] ¶ 24,280, ¶ 24,308.1135; ESTTRST: 15,050; § 32,340.05

[80] ¶ 24,308.115; ESTTRST: 15,050; § 32,340.05, § 32,340.20

[81] ¶ 24,308.105; ESTTRST: 15,260; § 32,340.20

[82] ¶ 24,280, ¶ 24,288; ESTTRST: 15,200; § 32,340.05

[83] ¶ 24,290; ESTTRST: 15,250, ESTTRST: 15,252; § 32,340.15

[84] ¶ 24,291; ESTTRST: 15,064; § 32,340.20

[85] ¶ 24,290; ESTGIFT: 45,252.45; § 32,340.30

Every trust claiming a charitable deduction for amounts permanently set aside (other than nonexempt charitable trusts under Code Sec. 4947(a)(1), and split-interest trusts under Code Sec. 4947(a)(2)) is required to file an information return on Form 1041-A generally by April 15 following the close of the trust's calendar year (Code Sec. 6034).[86] However, Form 1041-A does not have to be filed if the trust must distribute all of its income for the tax year (i.e., a simple trust). Split-interest trusts (i.e., pooled income funds (¶ 593), charitable remainder trusts (¶ 590), and charitable lead trusts (¶ 2932)) file their information return on Form 5227.

Both the trust and the trustee can be liable for a penalty of $10 per day up to a maximum of $5,000 for failure to timely file Form 1041-A (Code Sec. 6652(c)(2)(A) and (C)).[87] A split-interest trust that fails to file or to provide the required information on Form 5227 can be liable for a penalty of $20 per day, up to a maximum of $10,000. If the split-interest trust's gross income exceeds $250,000, the penalty is $100 per day, up to a $50,000 maximum. An additional penalty may be assessed against the person required to file the return if he or she knowingly fails to file or provide the information. Criminal penalties also apply for willful failure to file a return and filing a false or fraudulent return (Reg. § 1.6034-1(d)).[88]

538. Charitable Deduction Disallowance and Limitations. A trust is not entitled to an unlimited charitable deduction (¶ 537) for income that is allocable to its unrelated business income for the tax year (Code Secs. 642(c)(4) and 681(a); Reg. §§ 1.642(c)-3(d), 1.681(a)-1, and 1.681(a)-2).[89] The "unrelated business income" of a trust is computed in much the same manner as the unrelated business taxable income (UBTI) of a tax-exempt organization (¶ 655 and ¶ 687). However, in computing its UBTI, a trust can claim deductions for payments to charities, subject to the percentage limitations applicable to individuals' charitable deductions (¶ 1058).

Charitable deductions are not allowed for otherwise deductible gifts to an organization upon which a tax has been imposed for termination of private foundation status, unless the IRS has abated the tax (¶ 649) (Code Sec. 508(d)(1) and (3)).[90] General contributors will be denied deductions after the organization is notified of the loss of its private foundation status. Substantial contributors (¶ 635) will be denied deductions in the year in which action is taken to terminate the organization's private foundation status.

If a charitable contribution consists of gain from the sale of qualified small business stock (section 1202 stock) held for more than five years (¶ 1905), the charitable deduction amount must be adjusted for any gain excluded from gross income (Code Sec. 642(c)(4)).[91]

Deductions are also denied for contributions to any private foundation, nonexempt charitable trust, or split-interest trust, as defined in Code Sec. 4947, that fails to meet the governing instrument requirements for private foundations (Code Sec. 508(d)(2)).[92] Deductions for gifts and bequests to any organization are disallowed during the period that the organization fails to notify the IRS that it is claiming exempt status as a charitable organization (¶ 623). Churches, organizations with gross receipts of $5,000 or less, and certain other organizations designated by the IRS are exempt from the notification requirements. Charitable deductions are also disallowed for bequests and gifts to a foreign private foundation after the IRS notifies it that it has engaged in a prohibited transaction, or for a year in which such an organization loses its exempt status for engaging in such a transaction (Code Sec. 4948(c)(4)).[93]

540. Tax Credits. Generally, the tax credits allowed to individuals (¶ 1301–¶ 1391) are allowed to estates and trusts (Reg. § 1.641(b)-1).[94] The credits typically must be

References are to Standard Federal Tax Reports; Tax Research Consultant; and Practical Tax Explanations.

[86] ¶ 35,440; ESTTRST: 15,360; § 39,155.30

[87] ¶ 39,480; PENALTY: 3,208; § 33,605.05, § 39,155.30

[88] ¶ 35,441; IRS: 66,150, IRS: 66,200; § 40,245.05, § 41,625.25

[89] ¶ 24,280, ¶ 24,291, ¶ 24,840, ¶ 24,841, ¶ 24,842; ESTTRST: 15,352; § 32,340.05, § 33,901

[90] ¶ 22,790; EXEMPT: 21,502; § 33,240.05

[91] ¶ 24,280; ESTTRST: 15,304; § 16,605.05

[92] ¶ 22,790; EXEMPT: 21,504; § 33,205.20

[93] ¶ 34,160; EXEMPT: 21,352; § 33,205.10, § 33,240.15

[94] ¶ 24,264; ESTTRST: 12,200, ESTTRST: 12,204; § 32,305

5 TRUSTS/ESTATES

apportioned between the estate or trust and the beneficiaries on the basis of the income allocable to each. However, the foreign tax credit (¶ 1361) is allocated according to the proportionate share of the foreign taxes (Code Sec. 642(a); Reg. § 1.642(a)(2)-1).[95]

The general business tax credit is a limited nonrefundable credit against income tax that is claimed after all other nonrefundable credits are claimed (¶ 1365). The amount of the general business tax credit may not exceed the "net income tax" minus the greater of the tentative minimum tax or 25 percent of the net regular tax liability over $25,000. For estates and trusts, the $25,000 amount must be reduced to an amount that bears the same ratio to $25,000 as the portion of the income of the estate or trust that is not allocated to the beneficiaries bears to the total income of the estate or trust (Code Sec. 38(c)(6)(D)).[96] Any unused credit can be carried back one year and forward 20 years (carryback is three years and carryforward is 15 years for credits that arose in tax years before 1998) (Code Sec. 39).[97]

Estates and trusts are also entitled to claim various refundable tax credits, including the credit for federal income tax withheld on wages and backup withholding (¶ 1321 and ¶ 2645), the regulated investment company credit (¶ 1330), and the credit for federal excise taxes paid on fuels (¶ 1329).

Income Distribution Deduction

542. Simple v. Complex Trust. The deduction allowed to simple trusts (¶ 544) and to estates and complex trusts (¶ 545) for distributions to beneficiaries is determined by reference to distributable net income (¶ 543).

A "simple" trust is a trust that (1) is required to distribute all of its income currently whether or not distributions of current income are in fact made; and (2) does not allow any amount to be paid or set aside for charitable contributions (Code Sec. 651; Reg. § 1.651(a)-1).[98] A trust may be a simple trust even though, under local law or the governing trust instrument, capital gains must be allocated to corpus. The "income" required to be distributed in order for the trust to qualify as a simple trust is the income determined under local law and the governing instrument (Code Sec. 643(b); Reg. § 1.643(b)-1).[99] Generally, this will include only ordinary income, because capital gains, under most trust instruments and state laws, are considered corpus. A trust will lose its classification as a simple trust (but not its $300 exemption) for any year during which it distributes corpus (¶ 544). Thus, a trust can never be a simple trust during the year of termination or in a year of partial liquidation (Reg. § 1.651(a)-3).[100]

"Complex trust" applies to all trusts other than simple trusts described above (Reg. § 1.661(a)-1).[101] Generally, the same rules that apply to complex trusts also apply to estates.

Loans by Foreign Trusts. A foreign trust will not be treated as a simple trust if it makes a loan of cash, cash equivalents, or marketable securities to, or permits the uncompensated use of any other trust property by, a grantor or beneficiary who is a U.S. person, or a party related to the grantor or beneficiary (Code Sec. 643(i)).[102] The amount of the loan or the fair market value of the property's use is treated as a distribution by the trust for purposes of the distribution deduction (¶ 545), the gross income of trust beneficiaries (¶ 556), and the treatment of excess trust distributions (¶ 567). For trust property other than a loan of cash or marketable securities, distribution treatment does not apply if the trust is paid the fair market value for the property's use within a reasonable time period. Any subsequent transaction between the trust and the original borrower regarding the loan principal—such as the complete or partial repayment, satisfaction, cancellation, or discharge of the loan—or the return of the property used is disregarded.

References are to Standard Federal Tax Reports; Tax Research Consultant; and Practical Tax Explanations.

[95] ¶ 24,280, ¶ 24,282; ESTTRST: 12,202; § 13,405.20, § 32,305

[96] ¶ 4250; ESTTRST: 12,204, BUSEXP: 54,056; § 13,605.10

[97] ¶ 4300; BUSEXP: 54,056, BUSEXP: 54,058; § 13,605.15

[98] ¶ 24,360, ¶ 24,361; ESTTRST: 24,050; § 32,501, § 32,510

[99] ¶ 24,320, ¶ 24,329; ESTTRST: 24,052; § 32,010.10

[100] ¶ 24,363; ESTTRST: 24,056; § 32,501

[101] ¶ 24,401; ESTTRST: 24,050; § 32,501, § 32,515.05

[102] ¶ 24,320; ESTTRST: 18,200; § 32,501

543. Distributable Net Income. The deductions allowable to an estate or trust for amounts paid or credited to beneficiaries (¶ 544 and ¶ 545) are limited to the entity's "distributable net income" (DNI). The entity's DNI may also limit the amount of the distribution taxable to the beneficiary (¶ 554), and it is a factor in applying the conduit rule (¶ 559).

The DNI of an estate or trust generally consists of the same items of gross income and deductions that make up the taxable income of the estate or trust. However, there are important modifications: (1) no deduction is allowed for distributions to beneficiaries; (2) the deduction for the personal exemption is disallowed; (3) tax-exempt interest on state and local bonds is included, reduced by amounts which would be deductible but for the disallowance of deductions on expenses and interest related to tax-exempt income; (4) for a foreign trust, gross income from outside the United States (reduced by amounts which would be deductible but for the disallowance of deductions on expenses related to tax-exempt income) and within the United States is included; (5) capital gains are excluded if they are allocable to corpus and are not (a) paid, credited, or required to be distributed to any beneficiary during the tax year, or (b) paid, permanently set aside, or to be used for a charitable purpose (¶ 537); (6) capital losses are excluded except to the extent of their use in determining the amount of capital gains paid, credited, or required to be distributed to any beneficiary during the tax year; and (7) in the case of a simple trust, extraordinary dividends or taxable stock dividends that the fiduciary, acting in good faith, allocates to corpus are excluded (Code Sec. 643(a); Reg. §§ 1.643(a)-0—1.643(a)-7).[103] The DNI of the estate or trust is determined by taking into account a net operating loss (NOL) deduction (¶ 531 and ¶ 556).[104] However, the exclusion of gain from the sale or exchange of qualified small business stock (section 1202 stock) held for more than five years (¶ 1905) is not taken into account in determining DNI (Code Sec. 643(a)(3)).[105]

544. Deduction for Distributions to Beneficiaries of a Simple Trust. A simple trust (¶ 542) may deduct the amount of income that the trustee is under a duty to distribute currently to beneficiaries, even if the trustee makes the actual distribution after the close of the tax year (Code Sec. 651; Reg. §§ 1.651(a)-2, 1.651(b)-1).[106] If other amounts are distributed—such as a payment from corpus to meet the terms of an annuity payable from income or corpus—the complex trust rules apply for that year, except that the $300 exemption (¶ 534) is still allowed (Reg. § 1.642(b)-1).[107] If the income required to be distributed exceeds the distributable net income (DNI), the distribution deduction is limited to the DNI (¶ 543), computed without including exempt income (and related deductions).

545. Deduction for Distributions to Beneficiaries of Estate or Complex Trust. An estate or a complex trust (¶ 542) may deduct any amount of income for the tax year that is required to be distributed currently to beneficiaries (Code Sec. 661(a); Reg. § 1.661(a)-2).[108] This includes any amount required to be distributed that may be paid out of income or corpus, to the extent that it is in fact paid out of income. An estate or complex trust may also deduct any other amounts properly paid or credited or required to be distributed in the tax year, including amounts distributable at the discretion of the fiduciary and a distribution in kind. The amount to be taken into account in determining the deduction depends on whether the estate or trust elected to recognize gain on a noncash distribution of property in kind (¶ 526). In no case may the deduction exceed the distributable net income (DNI) of the estate or trust (¶ 543).

Special provisions exclude from the estate or trust's distribution deduction any "unlimited" charitable contribution (¶ 537), and certain gifts or bequests of a specific sum of money or specific property if paid or distributed all at once or in not more than three installments (¶ 556 and ¶ 564) (Code Sec. 663(a); Reg. §§ 1.663(a)-1 and

References are to Standard Federal Tax Reports; Tax Research Consultant; and Practical Tax Explanations.

[103] ¶ 24,320, ¶ 24,321–¶ 24,328; ESTTRST: 18,050; § 32,505.05

[104] ¶ 24,296, ¶ 24,431.493; ESTTRST: 12,062; § 32,410, § 32,505.05

[105] ¶ 24,320; ESTTRST: 18,056; § 16,605, § 32,505.05

[106] ¶ 24,360, ¶ 24,362, ¶ 24,366; ESTTRST: 24,102; § 32,510

[107] ¶ 24,286; ESTTRST: 24,100; § 32,510

[108] ¶ 24,400, ¶ 24,402; ESTTRST: 27,056; § 32,515.05

1.663(a)-2).[109] Also, an estate or trust cannot include in the distribution deduction for the current tax year an amount deemed distributed to a beneficiary in a prior tax year (Reg. § 1.663(a)-3).[110]

Where a will is silent, state law determines whether income or gain during the period of estate administration is "properly paid or credited" to a legatee (Rev. Rul. 71-335).[111] Also, a testamentary trustee can be a legatee or beneficiary for the purpose of a taxable distribution.[112]

When estate or trust income is of varying types, the distribution deduction is treated as consisting of the same proportion of each class of items entering into the DNI calculation as the total of each class bears to total DNI (Code Sec. 661(b); Reg. § 1.661(b)-1).[113] However, items will be allocated in accordance with a trust instrument or local law providing for a different method of allocation. No deduction is allowed to the estate or trust for the part of a beneficiary's distribution that consists of DNI that is not included in the gross income of the estate or trust, such as tax-exempt interest income (Code Sec. 661(c); Reg. § 1.661(c)-1).[114]

In applying the above rule, all deductions entering into the computation of DNI (including charitable contributions) are allocated among the different types of income that make up the DNI in the following manner (Reg. § § 1.652(b)-3 and 1.661(b)-2):[115]

(1) The deductions *directly* attributable to an income class are allocated to that income. (Thus, real estate taxes, repairs, the trustee's share of depreciation, fire insurance premiums, etc., would be allocated to rental income.)

(2) The deductions *not directly* attributable to a specific income class (such as trustee's commissions, safe deposit box rental, and state income and personal property taxes) may be allocated to any income item (including capital gains) included in computing DNI. However, a trust with nontaxable income must allocate a portion of these deductions to nontaxable income.

(3) Any excess deductions from step (1) may be assigned to any other class of income (including capital gains) in the manner described in step (2). However, excess deductions attributable to tax-exempt income may not be offset against any other class of income. Also, excess deductions from a passive activity (¶ 2053) cannot be allocated to income from a nonpassive activity, or to portfolio income earned by the estate or trust (Instructions to Form 1041).

For purposes of the computation, the "unlimited" charitable deduction (¶ 537) is first allocated ratably among all classes of income entering into DNI before any other expenses, unless a different allocation is specified by the governing instrument or local law (Reg. § § 1.643(a)-5 and 1.661(b)-2).[116] The charitable deduction is allocated by multiplying it by a ratio: the numerator is the amount of each single class of income, and the denominator is the total of all income classes.

Examples illustrating the allocations are provided at ¶ 559.

546. 65-Day Election. The fiduciary of an estate or a complex trust can elect annually to treat any distribution or any portion of a distribution to a beneficiary made within the first 65 days following the end of a tax year as having been distributed in the prior year (Code Sec. 663(b); Reg. § § 1.663(b)-1 and 1.663(b)-2).[117] The election is made on Form 1041, is irrevocable for the year involved, and is binding for that year only. The amount to which the election can apply is the greater of (1) the estate or trust's income (¶ 514); or (2) distributable net income (¶ 543) for the tax year, reduced by any amounts paid, credited, or required to be distributed during the tax year other than those

References are to Standard Federal Tax Reports; Tax Research Consultant; and Practical Tax Explanations.

[109] ¶ 24,440, ¶ 24,441, ¶ 24,442; ESTTRST: 27,102, ESTTRST: 27,104; § 32,515.05

[110] ¶ 24,443; ESTTRST: 27,106; § 32,515.05

[111] ¶ 24,407.78; ESTTRST: 27,054; § 32,515.05

[112] ¶ 24,407.7951; ESTTRST: 30,050

[113] ¶ 24,400, ¶ 24,403; ESTTRST: 27,056; § 32,515.05, § 32,515.10

[114] ¶ 24,400, ¶ 24,405; ESTTRST: 27,056; § 32,515.05

[115] ¶ 24,386, ¶ 24,404; ESTTRST: 27,056, ESTTRST: 30,250; § 32,515.10

[116] ¶ 24,326, ¶ 24,404; ESTTRST: 27,056, ESTTRST: 30,256; § 32,515.05, § 32,515.10

[117] ¶ 24,440, ¶ 24,444, ¶ 24,445; ESTTRST: 30,304; § 32,515.30

amounts that are subject to the 65-day election. There is no 65-day election for distributions of accumulated income (¶ 567).

548. Annuities Distributable from Income or Corpus. In the case of recurring distributions, payments by an estate or trust (where the amounts to be distributed, paid, or credited are a charge upon the corpus *or* the income) are usually taxable to the beneficiary and deductible by the estate or trust, to the extent that they are made from income (Code Sec. 661(a)(1); Reg. § 1.661(a)-2(b)).[118]

549. Widow(er)'s Allowance. A widow(er)'s or dependent's statutory allowance or award for support during administration of the estate is deductible by an estate if it is paid pursuant to a court order or decree or under local law (Reg. § 1.661(a)-2(e)).[119] The allowance can be paid from either income or principal, but the deduction is limited to the estate's distributable net income (DNI) for the year. Such payments are includible in the recipient's income to the extent of his or her share of the estate's DNI (Reg. §§ 1.662(a)-2(c) and 1.662(a)-3(b)).[120] The allowance is treated as a distribution to a beneficiary, even if it is considered to be a debt of the estate rather than a payment to a beneficiary under local law (Rev. Rul. 75-124).[121]

Taxation of Beneficiaries

554. Taxation of Simple Trust Beneficiary. The income (as defined at ¶ 514) required to be distributed currently to a beneficiary of a simple trust (¶ 542) is taxable to the beneficiary, whether or not distributed during the tax year, up to the amount of distributable net income (DNI) (¶ 543) (Code Sec. 652; Reg. §§ 1.652(a)-1—1.652(b)-3).[122] If the income required to be distributed exceeds DNI, only a proportionate share of each item is includible in the beneficiary's income. In making this apportionment, each item retains the same character (such as rent, dividends, etc.) that it had in the hands of the trust, and is treated as consisting of the same proportion of each class of items entering into the DNI calculation as the total of each class bears to total DNI, unless the trust instrument specifically allocates a particular type of income to a particular beneficiary. Deductions reflected in the computation of DNI are allocated among the various types of income (¶ 545). On termination of a trust, unused loss carryovers and excess deductions of the trust are allowed to certain beneficiaries (¶ 535). The amounts reported on the beneficiary's return must be consistent with the amounts reported on the trust return (¶ 2823) (Code Sec. 6034A(c)).[123]

556. Taxation of Beneficiary of Estate or Complex Trust. A beneficiary of a complex trust (¶ 542) or a decedent's estate must include in taxable income the income (as defined at ¶ 514) that is required to be distributed currently to the beneficiary, whether or not it is actually distributed during the tax year, plus any other amounts that are properly paid, credited, or required to be distributed to the beneficiary for the year (Code Sec. 662; Reg. § 1.662(a)-1).[124] For example, income of a trust is taxable to the beneficiaries even where there is no direction as to distribution or accumulation and state law requires distribution.[125] If a fiduciary elects to treat a distribution to a beneficiary made in the year as an amount paid in a prior year (¶ 546), the amount covered by the election is included in the beneficiary's income for the year for which the trust takes the deduction. Special rules also apply to distributions by certain trusts out of accumulated income (¶ 567).

If the amount of income required to be distributed currently to all beneficiaries exceeds distributable net income (DNI) (¶ 543) (computed without the "unlimited" charitable deduction (¶ 537)), then each beneficiary includes in income an amount that bears the same ratio to DNI as the amount of income required to be distributed currently to the beneficiary bears to the amount required to be distributed currently to all beneficiaries (Reg. § 1.662(a)-2(b)).[126]

References are to Standard Federal Tax Reports; Tax Research Consultant; and Practical Tax Explanations.

[118] ¶ 24,400, ¶ 24,402; ESTTRST: 27,052; § 32,515.05

[119] ¶ 24,402; ESTTRST: 27,052.10; § 32,525.10

[120] ¶ 24,422, ¶ 24,423; ESTTRST: 27,052.10; § 32,710.05

[121] ¶ 24,431.84; ESTTRST: 27,052.10; § 32,525.10

[122] ¶ 24,380–¶ 24,386; ESTTRST: 24,150; § 32,705.05

[123] ¶ 35,460; ESTTRST: 100; § 32,701

[124] ¶ 24,420, ¶ 24,421; ESTTRST: 30,000; § 32,710.05

[125] ¶ 24,431.65; ESTTRST: 24,052.05; § 32,710.05

[126] ¶ 24,422; ESTTRST: 30,108; § 32,710.05

If the sum of income required to be distributed currently, plus other amounts properly paid, credited, or required to be distributed, exceeds DNI, then the beneficiary includes such other amounts in gross income only to the extent that DNI exceeds income required to be distributed currently (Reg. § 1.662(a)-3(c)).[127] If the other amounts are paid, credited, or required to be distributed to more than one beneficiary, each beneficiary includes in gross income his or her proportionate share of such other amounts includible in gross income. The beneficiary's proportionate share is the amount which bears the same ratio to DNI (after subtracting income required to be distributed currently) as such other amounts distributed to the beneficiary bear to the other amounts distributed to all beneficiaries. The amount to be used in determining the beneficiary's share of estate or trust income depends on whether the estate or trust elected to recognize gain on the distribution (¶ 526).

Any amount which, under a will or trust instrument, is used in full or partial discharge or satisfaction of a legal obligation of any person is included in that person's gross income as though the amount was directly distributed to him or her as a beneficiary (Reg. § 1.662(a)-4).[128] "Legal obligation" includes a legal obligation to support another person only if the obligation is not affected by the adequacy of the dependent's own resources. The amount of trust income included in the gross income of a person obligated to support a dependent is limited by the extent of the person's legal obligation under local law. For example, in the case of a parent's obligation to support his or her child, to the extent that the support obligation (including education) is determined under local law by the family's station in life and the means of the parent, it is determined without consideration of the trust income in question. This rule does not pertain to alimony payments or income of an alimony trust (¶ 771).

If a net operating loss (NOL) carryback of the estate or trust (¶ 531) reduces the DNI of the estate or trust for the prior tax year to which the NOL is carried, the beneficiary's tax liability for such prior year may be recomputed based upon the revised DNI of the estate or trust (Rev. Rul. 61-20).[129]

In allocating the various types of income to the beneficiaries so as to give effect to these tax rules, the amount reflected in the trust's or estate's DNI is determined first. It is charged with directly related expenses and a proportionate part of other expenses, including the "unlimited" charitable deduction (¶ 537) to the extent it is chargeable to income of the current year (Reg. §§ 1.662(b)-1 and 1.662(b)-2).[130] Then, each beneficiary's share of income paid, credited, or required to be distributed to the beneficiary is multiplied by fractions, for each class of income, in which the numerator is the amount of such income included in DNI (whether the aggregate is more or less than the DNI) and the denominator is the total DNI (¶ 545). However, if the governing instrument specifies or local law requires a different allocation, such allocation is to be followed. These computations are illustrated at ¶ 559.

Special provisions exclude certain amounts from the beneficiary's gross income (and from the estate or trust's distribution deduction) (Code Sec. 663(a); Reg. §§ 1.663(a)-1, 1.663(a)-2, and 1.663(a)-3).[131] Any amount paid, permanently set aside, or to be used for charitable purposes and allowable for the unlimited charitable deduction (¶ 537) cannot be part of the distribution deduction or treated as an amount distributed for purposes of determining the beneficiary's gross income. Additionally, amounts deemed to be distributed to a beneficiary in a *prior* tax year cannot be deducted by the estate or trust, and are not included in the beneficiary's gross income for the current tax year. Certain gifts or bequests of a specific sum of money or specific property if paid or distributed all at once or in not more than three installments are also excluded (¶ 564).

On termination of an estate or trust, unused loss carryovers and excess deductions of the estate or trust are allowed to certain beneficiaries (¶ 535).

References are to Standard Federal Tax Reports; Tax Research Consultant; and Practical Tax Explanations.

[127] ¶ 24,423; ESTTRST: 30,154; § 32,710.05

[128] ¶ 24,424; ESTTRST: 30,052; § 32,710.05

[129] ¶ 24,431.493; ESTTRST: 12,062; § 32,410

[130] ¶ 24,425, ¶ 24,426; ESTTRST: 30,106; § 32,710.05

[131] ¶ 24,440–¶ 24,443; ESTTRST: 27,100; § 32,710.05, § 32,710.15

The amounts reported on the beneficiary's return must be consistent with the amounts reported on the estate or trust return (¶ 2823) (Code Sec. 6034A(c)).[132]

557. Separate Shares as Separate Estates or Trusts. Where a trust or an estate has two or more beneficiaries and is to be administered in well-defined and separate shares, these shares must be treated as separate estates or trusts in determining the amount of distributable net income (DNI) allocable to the beneficiaries (¶ 554 and ¶ 556) (Code Sec. 663(c); Reg. §§1.663(c)-1—1.663(c)-5).[133] This rule limits the tax liability of a beneficiary on a distribution of income and corpus where the income is being accumulated for the benefit of another beneficiary. The separate-share treatment is mandatory, not elective. A trustee or an executor must apply it even if separate and independent accounts are not maintained for each share, or if assets are not physically segregated.

The separate-share rule does not affect situations in which a single trust instrument creates not one but several separate trusts, as opposed to separate shares in the same trust. It also does not apply to trusts that provide for successive interests (e.g., a trust that provides a life estate to A and a remainder to B).

The treatment of separate shares as separate estates or trusts applies *only* for determining DNI in computing the distribution deduction allowable to the estate or trust and the amount includible in the income of the beneficiary. It cannot be applied to obtain more than one deduction for the personal exemption or to split the income of the estate or trust into several shares so as to be taxed at a lower-bracket rate.

559. How the Complex Trust Rules Operate. The examples below illustrate computations of distributable net income (DNI), the distributive share of a beneficiary, and the taxable income of a complex trust. No "throwback" distributions (¶ 567) are involved.

Example 1: Trust income: A complex trust has the following items of income in 2012:

Dividends	$16,000
Taxable interest	10,000
Exempt interest	10,000
Rent	4,000
Long-term capital gain allocable to corpus	6,000
The trust has expenses as follows:	
Expenses directly allocable to rent	$2,000
Commissions allocable to income	3,000
Commissions allocable to corpus	1,500

On these facts, the trust would have "income" of $40,000 (¶ 514). The income items consist of dividends, taxable interest, exempt interest and rent. No expenses or charges against income or corpus are subtracted; only "receipts" treated as income under local law and the governing instrument are counted (e.g., rent). Also, the long-term capital gain is excluded from this income in order to apply the conduit rule (as illustrated in Example 3) because it is not income under local law. It is, however, included in the taxable income computation.

Example 2: Distributable net income: In computing the trust's DNI, the "net" amount of tax-exempt interest is added to the net income of the trust (after subtracting any charitable contribution). The "net" amount of tax-exempt interest is the full amount of such interest minus any expenses directly allocable to it and a proportionate part of all "general" expenses such as commissions. As noted in Example 1, there are $4,500 in general expenses (i.e., expenses not directly allocable to rental income), so 25 percent ($10,000/$40,000) of $4,500, or $1,125, is allocated to the exempt interest ($10,000), leaving a net of $8,875. This $1,125 must also be excluded from the deductions claimed by the trust as an expense "indirectly" related to the production of exempt interest income and therefore disallowed by Code Sec. 265 (¶ 970). Accordingly, DNI is $33,500, computed as follows:

References are to Standard Federal Tax Reports; Tax Research Consultant; and Practical Tax Explanations.

[132] ¶ 35,460; ESTTRST: 100; §32,701

[133] ¶ 24,440, ¶ 24,446–¶ 24,449; ESTTRST: 27,200; §32,515.20

Dividends		$16,000
Taxable interest		10,000
Exempt interest ($10,000 less $1,125 allocable to exempt interest)		8,875
Rent		4,000
Total		$38,875
Deductions:		
Rent expense	$2,000	
Commissions ($4,500 less $1,125 allocable to exempt interest)	3,375	5,375
Distributable net income		$33,500

Example 3: Taxable income of beneficiary: There is one beneficiary to whom the trustee must distribute $20,000 under the terms of the trust instrument. The first step in computing the amount taxable to the beneficiary is to determine the extent to which each income item is reflected in DNI, allocating expenses to the various items. Those allocable to exempt interest have already been reflected in the $8,875 figure carried into DNI in Example 2, so no further allocation of that item is needed. Allocation is needed for dividends, rent, and taxable interest income, but this allocation does not have to be proportionate. Expenses directly related to any source or type of income must be allocated directly to that income, but *general* expenses can be allocated to any taxable income the taxpayer wishes when computing DNI as long as no deficit is created for any item. In this example, it is assumed the trustee allocates all general expenses to taxable interest. Accordingly, the trustee charges the entire $3,375 of general expenses to the taxable interest ($10,000) so that the $33,500 DNI, for the purpose of applying the "conduit" rule, is deemed to have been derived from:

Rent	$2,000
Taxable interest	6,625
Dividends	16,000
Tax-exempt interest	8,875
	$33,500

The total corresponds to the DNI and is only an intermediate or "identification" step. Because the amounts actually distributable are less than the amount of DNI, the next step is to multiply each of the above amounts by $20,000/$33,500 to determine what part of each is taxable to the beneficiary and deductible by the trust. Using these figures (the same result could be obtained by determining $2,000/$33,500 of $20,000, $6,625/$33,500 of $20,000, and so on), the apportionment is as follows:

Rent	$1,194.03
Taxable interest	3,955.22
Dividends	9,552.24
Tax-exempt interest	5,298.51
	$20,000.00

The beneficiary's share of income and deductions is reported on Schedule K-1 of Form 1041. The beneficiary will omit the $5,298.51 tax-exempt interest in reporting income from the trust. The $1,194.03 rent, $9,552.24 dividend and $3,955.22 taxable interest income should be reported on the beneficiary's Form 1040.

Example 4: Taxable income of the trust: The trust is allowed a deduction for the amount required to be distributed currently up to the amount of its DNI, but not for any portion that consists of tax-exempt income. The deduction for distributions, therefore, is $14,701.49 ($20,000 minus $5,298.51). Taxable income of the trust is then computed as follows:

Dividends	$16,000.00	
Taxable Interest	10,000.00	
Rent	4,000.00	
Long-term capital gain	6,000.00	$36,000.00

Less:		
Expenses allocable to rent	$2,000.00	
Commissions allocable to income ($3,000 minus the 25% [$750] allocable to exempt interest)	2,250.00	
Commissions allocable to corpus ($1,500 minus the 25% [$375] allocable to exempt interest)	1,125.00	
Distribution to beneficiary	14,701.49	
Exemption	100.00	20,176.49
Taxable income		$15,823.51

562. Capital Gain or Loss of Estate or Trust. Capital gains, whether long or short term, are generally excluded from distributable net income (DNI) (i.e., are taxed to an estate or trust) to the extent allocated to corpus and not (1) paid, credited, or required to be distributed to any beneficiary during the tax year, or (2) paid, permanently set aside, or to be used for a charitable purpose (Code Sec. 643(a)(3); Reg. § 1.643(a)-3).[134] Capital gains are included in DNI, however, to the extent they are: (1) allocated to income; (2) allocated to corpus but consistently treated by the fiduciary as part of a distribution to a beneficiary; or (3) allocated to corpus but actually distributed to a beneficiary or used by the fiduciary in determining the amount that is distributed or required to be distributed to a beneficiary (¶ 543).

A net capital loss of an estate or trust will reduce the taxable income of the estate or trust, but no part of the loss is deductible by the beneficiaries. If the estate or trust distributes all of its income, the capital loss will not result in a tax benefit for the year of the loss. Losses from the sale or exchange of capital assets are first netted at the trust level against any capital gains, except for capital gains utilized by the fiduciary in determining the amount to be distributed to a particular beneficiary (Reg. § 1.643(a)-3(d)).[135] On termination of an estate or trust, any unused capital loss carry-over of the estate or trust is available to the beneficiaries (¶ 535).

564. Gift or Bequest. An estate or trust may not deduct as a distribution to a beneficiary, and a beneficiary does not include in income, a gift or bequest of a specific sum of money or of specific property that is paid or credited in three installments or less (Code Sec. 663(a)(1); Reg. § 1.663(a)-1).[136] However, an amount will *not* be treated as an excluded gift or bequest if the governing instrument provides that the specific sum is payable only from the income of the estate or trust. The following are also *not* treated as an excluded gift or bequest of a sum of money or of specific property: (i) an annuity, or periodic gifts of specific property in lieu of or having the effect of an annuity; (ii) a residuary estate or the corpus of a trust; or (iii) a gift or bequest paid in a lump sum or in three installments or less, if required by the governing instrument to be paid in more than three installments. In determining the number of installments, gifts or bequests of articles of personal use (e.g., personal and household effects, cars, etc.) are disregarded. Also disregarded are transfers of specific real estate, title to which passes directly from the decedent to the devisee under local law.

565. Different Tax Year. If a beneficiary has a different tax year from that of an estate or complex trust, the amount to be included in the beneficiary's gross income must be based on the distributable net income of the estate or trust and the amounts paid, credited, or required to be distributed to the beneficiary for any tax year or years of the estate or trust ending with or within his or her tax year (Code Sec. 662(c); Reg. § 1.662(c)-1).[137] Similarly, if a beneficiary of a simple trust has a tax year different from that of the trust, the amount that the beneficiary includes in gross income must be based on the amount of the trust's income for any tax year or years ending with or within his or her tax year (Code Sec. 652(c); Reg. § 1.652(c)-1).[138]

References are to Standard Federal Tax Reports; Tax Research Consultant; and Practical Tax Explanations.

[134] ¶ 24,320, ¶ 24,324; EST-TRST: 18,056; § 32,505.10

[135] ¶ 24,324; ESTTRST: 18,058; § 32,505.10

[136] ¶ 24,440, ¶ 24,441; EST-TRST: 27,102; § 32,710.15

[137] ¶ 24,420, ¶ 24,427; EST-TRST: 30,306; § 32,710.10

[138] ¶ 24,380, ¶ 24,387; EST-TRST: 24,158; § 32,705.15

566. Withholding on Distributions to Expatriates. If a "covered expatriate" (¶ 2412) is a beneficiary of a nongrantor trust on the day before the individual's expatriation date, and receives a direct or indirect distribution of any property from the trust, then the trustee must deduct and withhold 30 percent of the taxable portion of the distribution (Code Sec. 877A(f)).[139] Additionally, if the fair market value of the property distributed exceeds the adjusted basis in the hands of the trust, the trust must recognize gain as if the property were sold to the expatriate at its fair market value.

The taxable portion of the distribution is that portion which would be includible in the covered expatriate's gross income had the expatriate continued to be subject to tax as a U.S. citizen or resident. A "nongrantor trust" is the portion of any trust of which the individual is not considered the owner under the grantor trust rules (¶ 571) as determined immediately before the expatriation date.

The withholding rules apply in a manner similar to those that apply to nonresident aliens (¶ 2455), but the distribution item is not subject to the nonresident alien withholding tax itself or the withholding tax on wages (¶ 2601). Further, the covered expatriate is treated as having waived any claim to a withholding reduction under any treaty with the United States, unless the expatriate agrees to other treatment that the IRS deems appropriate. Items subject to withholding are taxed according to the rules that apply to nonresident aliens (¶ 2429 and ¶ 2431).

567. "Throwback" of Accumulated Income. Special "throwback rules" generally apply to trust distributions made in tax years beginning before August 6, 1997 (Code Secs. 665—668).[140] Although the throwback rules have been repealed for most trusts, they continue to apply to trusts created before March 1, 1984, that would be treated as multiple trusts under Code Sec. 643(f) and to foreign trusts and domestic trusts that were once treated as foreign trusts.

The throwback rules are designed to prevent the accumulation of trust income by a complex or accumulation trust over a period of years with a distribution to a beneficiary only in low-income years. The rules have the effect of carrying back to preceding years any distributions in excess of distributable net income for the distribution year and taxing them to the beneficiaries as if they were distributed in the year the income was accumulated by the trust. This additional income is taxed to the beneficiary in the year that the beneficiary receives the accumulation distribution, but the beneficiary's tax liability is computed on Form 4970 under special rules. Beneficiaries who receive the accumulation distribution from a foreign trust report it and the partial tax on Form 3520. Schedule J of Form 1041 is used to determine the amount, the year, and the character of the additional distributions taxable to beneficiaries under the throwback rules; the trustee must give a copy of Part IV of Schedule J to each beneficiary. The beneficiary is allowed an offset or credit against the partial tax for the proportionate part of the trust's tax for the prior year, thus eliminating any double tax on the income. Beneficiaries of estates are not subject to the throwback rules.

Grantor Trusts

571. Overview of Grantor Trust Rules. Under the grantor trust rules, a person (i.e., the grantor) who transfers property to a trust and retains certain powers or interests (¶ 576–¶ 584) is treated as the owner of the trust property for income tax purposes (Code Sec. 671).[141] As a result, the income, deductions, and credits attributable to the trust are included in determining the grantor's taxable income to the extent of the owned portion of the trust. For income tax purposes, conversion of a nongrantor trust to a grantor trust is not a "transfer" of the property held by the nongrantor trust to the owner of the grantor trust, so the owner is not required to recognize gain (CCA 200923024).

Family Trusts. Income-producing property is often conveyed in trust for the benefit of a family member in an effort to split any income generated by the property or to otherwise lessen the original owner's tax liability. However, there must be an actual transfer of property to accomplish the desired tax savings; it is not enough to transfer income generated by the property.

References are to Standard Federal Tax Reports; Tax Research Consultant; and Practical Tax Explanations.

[139] ¶ 27,430; EXPAT: 3,320; § 37,135

[140] ¶ 24,480, ¶ 24,500, ¶ 24,520, ¶ 24,540; ESTTRST: 33,000; § 32,715.05

[141] ¶ 24,680; ESTTRST: 36,000; § 32,801

In addition, the limitations of the grantor trust rules prevent a taxpayer from escaping tax on the income from property where the taxpayer in effect remains the property owner by retaining control over the trust. For example, a "family estate trust" (i.e., a trust to which an individual transfers personal assets and the right to income in exchange for the beneficial enjoyment of such assets and compensation) is taxed as a grantor trust (Rev. Rul. 75-257).[142] The grantor's assignment of lifetime services or salary to the trust is not recognized for income tax purposes. Such trusts are deemed a "nullity" for income tax purposes and their income is taxable to the persons who created them. Acceptance of this broad economic principle deprives a grantor of any possible refuge in the technicalities of the grantor trust provisions. Expenses incurred in setting up family estate trusts are not deductible under Code Sec. 212.[143] Intra-family transfers of income-producing property cannot also be used to reduce income tax liability by shifting income from the parents' higher tax bracket to their child's generally lower tax bracket. Under the "kiddie tax" rules, if the net unearned income of the child exceeds an annual inflation-adjusted amount, it is taxed at the parents' top marginal rate (¶ 706).

575. Funeral Trusts. A qualified funeral trust (QFT) is a nonforeign funeral trust that elects not to be treated as a grantor trust, so that the income tax on the annual earnings of the trust is payable by the trustee (Code Sec. 685).[144] Generally, a QFT is an arrangement that would otherwise be treated as a grantor trust, under which an individual purchases funeral services or necessary property for himself or for another individual from a funeral home prior to death and funds the purchase via contributions. There are no dollar limitations on contributions to a QFT. The contributions must be held, invested, and reinvested by the trust solely to make payments for funeral services or property upon the individual's or the other trust beneficiaries' death. If the election is made, the income tax rate schedule generally applicable to estates and trusts (¶ 19) is applied to the trust by treating each beneficiary's interest as a separate trust. However, the trust is not entitled to a personal exemption (¶ 534). The trustee's election must be made separately for each such "separate" trust. No gain or loss is recognized to a purchaser of a funeral trust contract as a result of any payment from the trust to the purchaser due to the cancellation of the contract.

The trustee elects QFT status by filing Form 1041-QFT. The election must be filed no later than the due date (with extensions) for filing the trust income tax return for the year of election. The election applies to each trust reported in the QFT return. The trustee can use the form to file for a single QFT or multiple QFTs having the same trustee. The election may be made for the trust's first eligible year or for any subsequent year. Once made, the election cannot be revoked without IRS consent.

576. Reversionary Interest in Grantor. A grantor is considered to be the owner of any portion of a trust in which the grantor or the grantor's spouse (¶ 578) has a reversionary interest in either the trust corpus or income if the value of the interest exceeds five percent of the value of that portion of the trust (Code Sec. 673).[145] The value of the interest is measured as of the inception of the portion of the trust in which the grantor holds an interest. In determining whether the grantor's reversionary interest exceeds the five-percent threshold, the maximum exercise of discretion in the grantor's favor is assumed. Any postponement of the reacquisition or enjoyment of the interest is considered to be a new transfer in trust. However, no trust income is included in the grantor's income that would not have been included absent postponement. In addition, a grantor is exempt from the reversionary interest rule if the interest takes effect only upon the death of a beneficiary who is a minor lineal descendant of the grantor (under age 21) and if the beneficiary has the entire present interest in all or part of the trust.

578. Powers Held by Grantor's Spouse. A grantor is treated as holding any power or interest in a trust that is held by a person who was the grantor's spouse at the time the power or interest was created, or who became the grantor's spouse after creation of the power or interest (but only with respect to periods that the individual was the

References are to Standard Federal Tax Reports; Tax Research Consultant; and Practical Tax Explanations.

[142] ¶ 24,783.1973; ESTTRST: 3,116; § 46,530.10

[143] ¶ 12,523.50; BUSEXP: 12,064.40; § 46,530.10

[144] ¶ 24,895; ESTTRST: 39,350; § 32,175

[145] ¶ 24,710; ESTTRST: 39,050; § 32,810

grantor's spouse) (Code Sec. 672(e)).[146] Thus, the grantor trust provisions cannot be avoided by having the spouse of the grantor possess prohibited powers or interests (e.g., spousal remainder trusts). Individuals who are legally separated under a decree of divorce or separate maintenance are not considered to be married for this purpose.

579. Power to Control Beneficial Enjoyment. A grantor is taxed on trust income if the grantor or the grantor's spouse (¶ 578) retains the power to control the beneficial enjoyment of trust property or income (Code Sec. 674; Reg. § 1.674(a)-1).[147] However, there are a number of exceptions including, but not limited to, (1) an unexercised power to apply income to support a dependent; (2) power to allocate income among charitable beneficiaries; (3) power to distribute corpus limited by a reasonably definite standard; and (4) power to withhold income temporarily (Reg. § § 1.674(b)-1—1.674(d)-2).[148]

581. Retention of Administrative Powers. The grantor is taxed on trust income if the grantor or the grantor's spouse (¶ 578) retains administrative powers enabling the grantor to obtain, by dealings with the trust, financial benefits that would not be available in an arm's-length transaction (Code Sec. 675; Reg. § 1.675-1).[149] For example, if the grantor or his or her spouse borrows trust corpus or income at any time during a tax year, the grantor is taxed on the trust income for that entire year, even if the grantor repays the loan with interest during the same year (Rev. Rul. 86-82).[150]

582. Power to Revoke Trust. If a grantor creates a trust and reserves a right to revoke it, the income of the trust is treated as the grantor's income (Code Sec. 676; Reg. § § 1.676(a)-1 and 1.676(b)-1).[151] The trust income is not taxed to the grantor if the power can only affect the beneficial enjoyment of the income after the occurrence of an event such that the grantor would not be treated as the owner if the power were a reversionary interest (¶ 576). However, the grantor may be treated as the owner after the event occurs unless the power to revoke is then relinquished.

584. Income for Grantor's Benefit. The grantor is taxed on trust income that is or may be accumulated for or distributed to the grantor or the grantor's spouse, or used to pay life insurance premiums on either the grantor's or the spouse's life (except for policies irrevocably payable to charities) (Code Sec. 677; Reg. § § 1.677(a)-1 and 1.677(b)-1).[152] To the extent that trust income may be used in satisfaction of the grantor's legal obligation to support a beneficiary (such as a child, but not a spouse), it is regarded as distributable to the grantor. But if the discretion to so use the income is not in the grantor, acting as such, but in another person (for example, the trustee or the grantor acting as trustee or co-trustee), then that income is includible in the grantor's gross income only to the extent that it is actually used for the beneficiary's support or maintenance. In addition, any capital gain that, under state law, is added to trust corpus is taxable to the grantor if the corpus reverts to the grantor upon termination of the trust (Reg. § § 1.671-3(b)(2) and 1.677(a)-1(f); Rev. Rul. 58-242; Rev. Rul. 75-267).[153]

585. Income Taxable to Person Other Than Grantor. A person other than the grantor of a trust, including a beneficiary, may be taxed on the trust's income if that person has a power, exercisable alone, to vest trust corpus or income in himself or herself (Code Sec. 678; Reg. § § 1.678(a)-1–1.678(d)-1).[154] For example, if a father establishes a trust for the benefit of his children, but the trust provides that the grantor's brother may take trust property at any time, the brother is treated as the owner and trust income is taxed to him. This rule does not apply if the power is renounced or disclaimed within a reasonable period.

References are to Standard Federal Tax Reports; Tax Research Consultant; and Practical Tax Explanations.

[146] ¶ 24,700; ESTTRST: 36,054; § 32,805.20

[147] ¶ 24,720, ¶ 24,721; ESTTRST: 45,050; § 32,815.05

[148] ¶ 24,722–¶ 24,725; ESTTRST: 45,050, ESTTRST: 45,052; § 32,815.10

[149] ¶ 24,740, ¶ 24,741; ESTTRST: 45,100; § 32,820.05

[150] ¶ 24,742.10; ESTTRST: 45,106; § 32,820.10

[151] ¶ 24,760, ¶ 24,761, ¶ 24,762; ESTTRST: 39,250; § 32,825

[152] ¶ 24,780–¶ 24,782; ESTTRST: 42,000; § 32,830.05, § 32,830.10, § 32,830.15

[153] ¶ 24,684, ¶ 24,781, ¶ 24,783.101, ¶ 24,783.34; ESTTRST: 39,150, ESTTRST: 42,054; § 32,830.40

[154] ¶ 24,800–¶ 24,804; ESTTRST: 36,200; § 32,805.10

A U.S. person who is a beneficiary of a trust is treated as the grantor to the extent that the beneficiary transferred property, directly or indirectly and for less than adequate consideration, to a foreign person who otherwise would have been treated as the owner under the grantor trust rules (Code Sec. 672(f)(5)).[155]

586. Return for Grantor Trust. Generally, items of income, deduction, or credit that are treated as belonging to a trust grantor or another person are not reported by the trust on Form 1041 (Reg. § 1.671-4).[156] Instead, these items are reflected on the income tax return of the grantor (or other person who is taxable on the trust income). A separate statement should be attached to Form 1041 stating the name, taxpayer identification number, and address of the person to whom the income is taxable, and setting forth the income, deductions, and credits; however, there are other optional reporting methods available to certain types of grantor trusts. Widely held fixed investment trusts have specific information reporting requirements (Reg. § 1.671-5).[157]

588. Foreign Grantor Trust Rules. Any U.S. person transferring property to a foreign trust (other than an employee benefits plan or a tax-exempt organization) that has a U.S. beneficiary will be treated as the owner of that portion of the trust attributable to the property transferred (Code Secs. 678(b) and 679).[158] The IRS can presume that the trust has a U.S. beneficiary unless the transferor submits to the IRS any information that the IRS requires regarding the transfer, and demonstrates to the IRS's satisfaction that (1) under the terms of the trust, no part of the trust's income or corpus may be paid or accumulated during the tax year to or for the benefit of a U.S. person, even if that person's interest is contingent on a future event; and (2) no part of the trust's income or corpus could be paid to or for the benefit of a U.S. person if the trust were terminated at any time during the tax year. The transferor must ensure that the trust satisfies certain reporting requirements, and submit any information the IRS may require regarding the foreign trust (Code Secs. 6048(b) and 6677(a)).[159] A foreign trust with at least one U.S. owner must file Form 3520-A in order for the U.S. owner to satisfy its annual information reporting requirements. Generally, the U.S. grantor trust rules do not apply to any portion of a trust that would otherwise be deemed to be owned by a foreign person (Code Sec. 672(f)).[160]

U.S. persons who are treated as owners of foreign trusts under the grantor rules (¶ 571) must file Form 3520.

Other Special Trusts

590. Charitable Remainder Trusts. Whenever there is a noncharitable income beneficiary of a trust, gifts of remainder interests qualify for a charitable contribution deduction only if the trust is a charitable remainder annuity trust (CRAT) or a charitable remainder unitrust (CRUT) (Code Sec. 664; Reg. §§ 1.664-1, 1.664-2 and 1.664-3).[161] Charitable contribution deductions are denied for gifts of remainder interests in all other types of trusts. However, if the donor gives *all* the interests in a trust to charity, the above rules do not apply, and a deduction is allowable (¶ 1070).

Qualification. An *annuity trust* is a trust from which a sum certain or a specified amount is to be paid to the income beneficiary (Code Sec. 664(d)(1); Reg. §§ 1.664-1 and 1.664-2). The specified amount cannot be less than five percent or more than 50 percent of the initial net fair market value of all property placed in trust, and it must be paid at least annually to the income beneficiary. Furthermore, the value of the charitable remainder interest must be at least 10 percent of the initial net fair market value of all of the property placed in trust. There are several provisions designed to provide relief to trusts that do not meet the "10-percent" test. No contributions can be made to a CRAT after the initial contribution, and the governing instrument must contain a prohibition against future contributions.

References are to Standard Federal Tax Reports; Tax Research Consultant; and Practical Tax Explanations.

[155] ¶ 24,700; ESTTRST: 36,056.05; § 32,801
[156] ¶ 24,685; ESTTRST: 36,104; § 32,610.25
[157] ¶ 24,685K; ESTTRST: 36,300; § 32,610.25
[158] ¶ 24,800, ¶ 24,820; ESTTRST: 36,250; § 32,801, § 32,805.10
[159] ¶ 36,000, ¶ 39,815; ESTTRST: 36,258; § 39,135.15
[160] ¶ 24,700; ESTTRST: 36,056.05; § 32,801
[161] ¶ 24,460, ¶ 24,461, ¶ 24,464, ¶ 24,465; ESTGIFT: 45,200; § 32,150

A *unitrust* is a trust that specifies that the income beneficiary is to receive annual payments based on a fixed percentage of the net fair market value of the trust's assets as determined each year (Code Sec. 664(d)(2); Reg. §§1.664-1 and 1.664-3). The fixed percentage cannot be less than five percent or more than 50 percent of the net fair market value of the trust's assets for the year. However, a qualified CRUT may provide for the distribution each year of five percent of the net fair market value of its assets or the amount of the trust income, whichever is lower. For this purpose, trust income excludes capital gains, and trust assets must be valued annually. This payment requirement may not be discretionary with the trustee. Additional contributions can be made to a unitrust. For most transfers in trust, the value of the charitable remainder interest with respect to each contribution to the unitrust must be at least 10 percent of the net fair market value of such contributed property as of the date the property is contributed to the trust. If an additional contribution would cause the trust to fail the "10-percent" remainder test, then the contribution will be treated as a transfer to a separate trust under regulations. Other provisions may provide relief to trusts that fail to meet the "10-percent" test.

CRATs and CRUTs cannot have noncharitable remainder interests. Generally, the remainder interests must pass to a charity upon the termination of the last income interest, and the trust instrument must contain a provision that determines how the final payment of a specified distribution is to be made. However, a charitable trust may make certain limited "qualified gratuitous" transfers of qualified employer securities to an employee stock ownership plan (ESOP) without adversely affecting the status of the charitable remainder trust.

To avoid the possible disqualification of a charitable remainder trust due to a surviving spouse's right of election against the grantor spouse's estate under state law, the IRS created a safe harbor requiring the surviving spouse to irrevocably waive the right (Rev. Proc. 2005-24). However, until further guidance is published, the IRS will disregard the existence of a right of election *without* requiring a waiver, but only if the surviving spouse does not exercise the right (Notice 2006-15).[162]

There may be more than one noncharitable income beneficiary, either concurrently or successively, and the income interest may be a life estate or for a term of years not in excess of 20 years. However, a contingency clause may be placed in the trust instrument providing that the noncharitable interest is to terminate and the charitable remainder interest is to be accelerated upon the happening of an event, such as the remarriage of the noncharitable beneficiary (Code Sec. 664(f)).[163] The income beneficiary can receive only a specified or fixed amount from the trust, and the trustee cannot have additional power to invade corpus or to alter, amend, or revoke the trust for the benefit of the noncharitable income beneficiary. The trustee cannot be restricted from investing in income-producing assets (Reg. §1.664-1(a)(3)).[164]

Division of Trust. The IRS has provided guidelines for dividing a CRAT or a CRUT into two or more separate and equal trusts without violating the charitable remainder trust requirements (Rev. Rul. 2008-41).[165]

Reporting. A CRAT or CRUT does not file Form 1041, but instead is required to file Form 5227. In addition, the fiduciary of a CRAT or CRUT may be required to file other returns regarding the excise tax on unrelated business taxable income (¶590A), and the excise taxes on private foundations that apply to charitable remainder trusts (¶591). Form 5227 must generally be filed on or before the 15th day of the fourth month following the close of the tax year of the trust (Rev. Proc. 83-32).[166]

590A. Taxation of Charitable Remainder Trust. A charitable remainder annuity trust (CRAT) or a charitable remainder unitrust (CRUT) (¶590) is generally exempt from income tax (Code Sec. 664(c); Reg. §1.664-1).[167] However, if a CRAT or CRUT has

References are to Standard Federal Tax Reports; Tax Research Consultant; and Practical Tax Explanations.

[162] ¶24,468.18; ESTGIFT: 45,202.15, ESTGIFT: 45,204.05; §32,150.25

[163] ¶24,460; ESTGIFT: 45,202.20, ESTGIFT: 45,204.20; §32,150.25

[164] ¶24,461; ESTGIFT: 45,200; §32,150.25

[165] ¶24,468.12; ESTTRST: 15,354; §32,150.25

[166] ¶24,468.20; ESTTRST: 15,360; §32,150.25

[167] ¶24,460, ¶24,461; ESTTRST: 15,354, ESTGIFT: 45,200; §32,150, §32,601, §33,901

unrelated business taxable income (UBTI) (¶ 670), it is subject to a 100-percent excise tax on its UBTI, but will retain its tax-exempt status. The excise tax is treated as paid from corpus, and trust income that is UBTI is income of the trust for purposes of determining the character of distributions made to beneficiaries (¶ 590B). The tax is reported on Form 4720, which must be filed by the due date for Form 5227 (¶ 590). The rule preventing the IRS from filing an additional deficiency notice once a taxpayer files a Tax Court petition challenging the deficiency also applies to this tax. In addition to the tax on UBTI, a charitable remainder trust may be subject to the income and excise taxes imposed on private foundations (¶ 591).

590B. Treatment of Charitable Remainder Trust Beneficiaries. Under either a charitable remainder annuity trust or a charitable remainder unitrust (¶ 590), the amount paid to a beneficiary is considered as having the following characteristics in the beneficiary's hands: (1) ordinary income to the extent of the trust's ordinary income for the tax year and its undistributed ordinary income from prior years; (2) capital gains to the extent of the trust's capital gains for the tax year and its undistributed capital gains, determined on a cumulative net basis, for prior years; (3) other income (including tax-exempt interest) to the extent of the trust's other income for the tax year and its undistributed other income from prior years; and (4) a distribution of trust corpus (Code Sec. 664(b); Reg. § § 1.664-1—1.664-4).[168] Items within the ordinary income and capital gains categories are assigned to different subcategories based on the federal income tax rate applicable to each type of income within the category. Categories of income that are taxed at the same rate can be combined into a single class if the tax rate will not change in the future. If the tax rate is temporary, then the categories must be maintained as separate groups (Reg. § 1.664-1(d)(1)(i)).[169]

The characterizations of income items distributed or deemed distributed at any time during the tax year of the charitable remainder trust are determined as of the end of the tax year. Distributions are subject to the tax rate applicable to the income class from which the distribution is derived, not the tax rate applicable when the income was received by the trust (Reg. § 1.664-1(d)(1)(ii)(a)). Gains and losses of long-term capital gain classes are netted prior to netting short-term capital loss against any class of long-term capital gain (Reg. § 1.664-1(d)(1)(iv)). Special transition rules also apply for classifying long-term capital gains and losses (Reg. § 1.664-1(d)(1)(vi)).[170]

591. Private Foundation Rules Applicable to Charitable Trusts. The income and excise taxes imposed on private exempt foundations extend to all nonexempt charitable trusts with certain modifications (Code Sec. 4947).[171] First, a nonexempt trust that devotes all of its unexpired interests to charitable, religious, educational, and other purposes that enable contributors to obtain a charitable deduction is treated as a private foundation (¶ 631). Thus, it may be subject to the excise taxes on: investment income (¶ 633), self-dealing (¶ 635), failure to distribute income (¶ 637), excess business holdings (¶ 640), investments that jeopardize charitable purposes (¶ 642), and certain taxable expenditures (lobbying, electioneering, etc., ¶ 644). For this purpose, "unexpired interests" include life or term income interests, interests in trust corpus, and remainder interests.

Second, a nonexempt trust that does not devote all of its unexpired interests to charitable purposes (split-interest trust) is subject to the excise taxes on self-dealing, excess business holdings, investments that jeopardize charitable purposes, and certain taxable expenditures (lobbying, electioneering, etc.) as if it were a private foundation. However, the taxes apply to income to be paid to trust beneficiaries under the terms of the trust instrument only if the trust was a charitable remainder annuity trust or a charitable remainder unitrust (¶ 590). The taxes do not, in any event, apply to amounts in trust for which a deduction is not allowable if segregated from deductible amounts.

In addition, the taxes on excess business holdings and investments that jeopardize charitable purposes do not apply to a split-interest trust if (1) the charity is only an

References are to Standard Federal Tax Reports; Tax Research Consultant; and Practical Tax Explanations.

[168] ¶ 24,460–¶ 24,466; ESTGIFT: 45,210; § 32,150

[169] ¶ 24,461; ESTGIFT: 45,210; § 32,150

[170] ¶ 24,461; ESTGIFT: 45,210.05; § 32,601

[171] ¶ 34,140; EXEMPT: 21,300; § 33,201

income beneficiary and its beneficial interest is no more than 60 percent of the value of the trust property; or (2) the charity's only interest in the trust is as a remainderman. Split-interest trusts are treated like private foundations with regard to the rules on governing instruments and the tax on involuntary termination of status for repeated or willful violations (¶ 631 and ¶ 649).

The excise tax on investment income and failure to distribute income do not apply to split-interest trusts under any circumstances.

593. Pooled Fund Arrangements. Generally, a pooled income fund is a trust to which a person transfers an irrevocable remainder interest in property for the benefit of a public charity while retaining an income interest in the property for the life of one or more beneficiaries living at the time of the transfer (Code Sec. 642(c)(5); Reg. § 1.642(c)-5).[172] Income, estate, and gift tax charitable contribution deductions are allowed for the value of remainder interests in property transferred to a pooled income fund (Code Sec. 642(c)(3)). To protect the value of depreciable property that will pass to the charitable remainderman, the governing instrument of the pooled income fund must provide for the creation of a depreciation reserve.[173] In addition, the fund: (1) must commingle all property contributed to it; (2) cannot invest in tax-exempt securities; and (3) must be maintained by the recipient charity with no donor or income beneficiary acting as a trustee. However, the charity does not have to act as trustee of the fund.

Each person who has an income interest resulting from a transfer of property to the fund must be paid an annual income based on the fund's yearly rate of return (i.e., the trust cannot accumulate income for any beneficiary). A pooled income fund's method of calculating its yearly rate of return must be supported by a full statement attached to the fund's annual income tax return. The fund and its beneficiaries are taxable under the rules applicable to trusts, except that the grantor trust rules (¶ 571) do not apply. In addition to its income tax return, a pooled income fund must file an annual information return on Form 5227 regarding its charitable deductions (¶ 537).

595. Common Trust Fund. Each participant in a common trust fund (¶ 2389) must report its share of the taxable income of the fund, whether or not distributed or distributable. The taxable income of a common trust fund is computed in much the same manner as an individual's taxable income, except for the exclusion of capital gains and losses and the deduction for charitable contributions (Code Sec. 584).[174]

References are to Standard Federal Tax Reports; Tax Research Consultant; and Practical Tax Explanations.

[172] ¶ 24,280, ¶ 24,293; ESTGIFT: 45,252; § 32,340.30

[173] ¶ 24,308.1877, ¶ 24,308.1880; ESTGIFT: 45,252; § 32,340.30

[174] ¶ 23,630; RIC: 12,300

Chapter 6
EXEMPT ORGANIZATIONS

Overview

601. Overview. A variety of organizations may qualify for exemption from federal income taxation. The most common basis for exempt status is as a charitable organization under Code Sec. 501(c)(3) (¶ 602). Generally, charitable organizations can be either publicly supported or private foundations. While all charitable organizations are subject to limitations on how they operate, private foundations may be subject to excise taxes for engaging in prohibited activities (¶ 631). In addition to charitable organizations under Code Sec. 501(c)(3), there are also a number of organizations that may qualify for exempt status if they have a socially beneficial purpose (¶ 692). Regardless of how an entity qualifies as a tax-exempt organization, it may still be subject to federal income tax on any business income not related to its exempt purpose (¶ 655) and any income arising from debt-financed property (¶ 687). All tax-exempt organizations are also subject to various reporting requirements, such as annual information reporting (¶ 625), involvement in tax shelter transactions (¶ 619), and other disclosure requirements (¶ 627).

Code Sec. 501(c)(3) Organizations

602. Charitable Organizations Under Code Sec. 501(c)(3). Code Sec. 501 provides that various classes of nonprofit organizations may be exempt from federal income tax unless they are deemed to be feeder organizations (¶ 694)[1] or they engage in certain prohibited transactions.[2] The most common basis for invoking tax-exempt status falls under Code Sec. 501(c)(3)'s broad exemption for religious, charitable, scientific, literary, and educational organizations (collectively referred to as charitable organizations).[3] Charitable organizations are generally either public charities or private foundations (¶ 631). Among other benefits, exempt status conferred by Code Sec. 501(c)(3) allows a public charity to receive tax-deductible contributions from its donors (¶ 627 and ¶ 1061). Any corporation, community chest, fund, trust, or foundation may qualify for the exemption. Application for recognition of Code Sec. 501(c)(3) federal tax-exempt status is made on Form 1023 (¶ 623).

To qualify for tax-exempt status under Code Sec. 501(c)(3), the entity must be organized and operated exclusively for religious (¶ 604), charitable, scientific, educational, or literary purposes, the prevention of cruelty to children or animals, the promotion of amateur sports competition, or the testing for public safety. A charitable purpose is interpreted broadly and may include purposes beyond those stated in Code Sec. 501(c)(3). For example, a charitable purpose can include: providing relief to the poor or disadvantaged; the advancement of education, religion, or science; or lessening the burdens of government through the promotion of social welfare or other community

References are to Standard Federal Tax Reports; Tax Research Consultant; and Practical Tax Explanations.

[1] ¶ 22,670; EXEMPT: 15,350; § 33,005.05

[2] ¶ 22,680; EXEMPT: 12,208; § 33,105

[3] ¶ 22,602; EXEMPT: 3,000, EXEMPT: 9,000; § 33,005.05

development (Reg. § 1.501(c)(3)-1(d)).[4] An educational organization can include a child-care center whose services are available to the general public and whose purpose is to enable individuals to be gainfully employed (Code Sec. 501(k)).[5] Regardless of an entity's charitable purpose, it must meet certain organizational, operational and private benefit tests to qualify as a tax-exempt charitable organization (Reg. § 1.501(c)(3)-1).[6]

Organizational Test. The organizational test requires that the entity's articles of organization specifically limit its purpose to one or more exempt purposes, including that its assets are dedicated to an exempt purpose (Reg. § 1.501(c)(3)-1(b)).[7] The articles of organization also must not expressly permit the organization to carry on activities which do not further the organization's exempt purpose, except where the nonexempt activities are an insubstantial part of the organization's activities. For example, the articles of organization must not allow more than an insubstantial part of the organization's activities to influence legislation by propaganda or otherwise (¶ 613); or authorize the organization to directly or indirectly participate or intervene in any political campaign on behalf of or in opposition to any candidate for public office (¶ 614). Whether an organization meets the organizational requirement is determined exclusively from the language of the articles of organization and not from the activities conducted by the organization. For this purpose, "articles of organization" include trust instruments, corporate charters, articles of association or any other written instrument by which an organization is created.

Operational Test. The operational test requires that an entity must be operated exclusively for one or more exempt purposes. This means the organization engages primarily in activities that accomplish one or more of its exempt purposes (Reg. § 1.501(c)(3)-1(c)).[8] Only an insubstantial part of the entity's activities may be in the furtherance of nonexempt purposes. Whether an organization has a substantial nonexempt purpose is determined by taking into account all facts and circumstances, including the size and extent of all of the organization's activities. If the entity is an action organization, then it will *not* be considered as operated exclusively for an exempt purpose. An entity is an action organization if it devotes a substantial part of its activities to attempting to influence legislation or if it participates in political campaigns. However, if an organization fails the operational test because it is an action organization, it may still qualify for tax-exempt status as a social welfare organization under Code Sec. 501(c)(4) (¶ 692). If a charitable organization provides commercial-type insurance as an insubstantial part of its activities, then the insurance activity will be treated as an unrelated trade or business (¶ 655) (Code Sec. 501(m) and (n)).[9]

An entity will not be considered as operating exclusively for exempt purposes if any of its net earnings inure in whole or in part to the benefit of private shareholders or individuals. A "private shareholder or individual" is any person having a personal and private interest in the activities of the organization, such as founders of the organization, employees, board members, or family members of officers, employees, etc. The inurement prohibition does not prohibit all payments to a private shareholder or individual, but instead is directed at payments that are made for purposes other than as reasonable compensation for goods or services (¶ 617).

Private Benefit Test. An organization is not organized or operated exclusively for charitable purposes unless it serves a public rather than a private interest (outside interests, as opposed to inside interests addressed by the inurement prohibition under the operation test). The question of private benefit often arises in situations in which a charitable organization enters into partnerships and other joint ventures with for-profit entities. The charitable organization can form such ventures and still satisfy the operational test only if it is permitted to act exclusively in furtherance of its exempt purpose

References are to Standard Federal Tax Reports; Tax Research Consultant; and Practical Tax Explanations.

[4] ¶ 22,608; EXEMPT: 3,150; § 33,101

[5] ¶ 22,602; EXEMPT: 3,300; § 33,101

[6] ¶ 22,608; EXEMPT: 3,050, EXEMPT: 3,100; § 33,101

[7] ¶ 22,608; EXEMPT: 3,050; § 33,115

[8] ¶ 22,608; EXEMPT: 3,100; § 33,120

[9] ¶ 22,602; EXEMPT: 15,160.10, EXEMPT: 15,160.15; § 33,101

and only incidentally for the benefit of the for-profit partners (Rev. Rul. 98-15).[10] In addition, the for-profit party cannot be allowed to control or use the charitable organization's activities or assets for its own benefit unless the control or use is incidental.

Charitable Hospitals. In addition to the requirements that apply to all Code Sec. 501(c)(3) organizations, each hospital facility operated by a charitable organization is subject to four additional requirements (Code Sec. 501(r)), as follows: (1) each facility must conduct and implement a community health needs assessment, failure to do so may result in an excise tax of $50,000 (Code Sec. 4959; (2) each facility must adopt, implement, and widely publicize a written financial assistance policy; (3) each facility may not bill patients who qualify for financial assistance more than the amount generally billed to insured patients; (4) the facility (or affiliates) may not undertake extraordinary collection actions against patients (Code Sec. 501(r)).

604. Churches and Religious Organizations. A church or religious organization is exempt from federal income tax and eligible to receive tax-deductible contributions if it meets the Code Sec. 501(c)(3) requirements (¶ 602). The term "church" is not specifically defined in the Code but generally is used in its generic sense as a place of worship including, for example, mosques and synagogues. It also includes conventions or associations of churches, as well as integrated auxiliaries of a church. For this purpose, a convention or association of churches is a cooperative undertaking by churches of the same or differing denominations (Rev. Rul. 74-224).[11] The fact that the convention or association may extend membership to individuals and those individuals have voting rights will not cause it to lose exempt status (Code Sec. 7701(n)).[12]

It is important to distinguish churches from other religious organizations. To balance the need for the IRS to combat efforts on the part of some individuals and organizations to use churches to avoid taxes, and the equally important need to protect legitimate churches from undue IRS interference in their activities, the Code and regulations contain detailed rules governing when the IRS may inquire into or examine the activities of a "church" (Code Sec. 7611; Reg. § 301.7611-1; Prop. Reg. § 301.7611-1).[13] Religious organizations that are not churches may still be eligible for tax-exempt status, including nondenominational ministries, interdenominational and ecumenical organizations, and other entities whose principal purpose is the study or advancement of religion (IRS Pub. 1828). Unlike churches, however, religious organizations that want to be tax exempt must apply to the IRS for tax-exempt status by filing Form 1023 (¶ 623).

A religious or apostolic association that does not meet the requirements to be a Code Sec. 501(c)(3) organization may nonetheless qualify as exempt from federal income taxation if it has a common or community treasury. The exemption applies even if the association engages in business for the common good of its members, provided that the members include in their gross income their pro rata share of the association's taxable income as dividends received, whether distributed or not (Code Sec. 501(d); Reg. § 1.501(d)-1).[14] There is no official exemption application form for this purpose. However, the association must file Form 1065 each tax year for information purposes (Reg. § 1.6033-2(e)).[15]

607. Supporting Organizations. A charitable organization under Code Sec. 501(c)(3) that carries out its exempt purpose by providing support to other exempt organizations (usually public charities) is considered a public charity rather than a private foundation (¶ 631). To qualify as a supporting organization, an organization must not only meet the requirements to be a charitable organization under Code Sec. 501(c)(3) but must also be:

References are to Standard Federal Tax Reports; Tax Research Consultant; and Practical Tax Explanations.

[10] ¶ 22,609.411; EXEMPT: 15,452, EXEMPT: 15,458; § 33,125

[11] ¶ 11,620.205; EXEMPT: 21,052; § 33,101

[12] ¶ 43,080; EXEMPT: 21,052; § 33,101

[13] ¶ 42,910, ¶ 42,912, ¶ 42,912C; IRS: 18,406; § 33,101

[14] ¶ 22,602, ¶ 22,659; EXEMPT: 3,202; § 33,005.05

[15] ¶ 35,422; EXEMPT: 12,054.20; § 33,005.05

- organized and operated exclusively for the benefit of, to perform the functions of, or to carry out the purposes of a public charity (organizational and operational test, ¶ 602);

- operated or controlled by a public charity (relationship test); and

- not controlled either directly or indirectly by a disqualified person (¶ 635), other than a foundation manager or publicly supported charity (lack of control test) (Code Sec. 509(a)(3)).[16]

To satisfy the relationship test, a supporting organization must hold one of three close relationships with the supported organization (Reg. § 1.509(a)-4; Prop. Reg. § 1.509(a)-4).[17] In a Type I relationship, the supported organization must exercise a substantial degree of control over the programs, activities, and policies of the supporting organization (comparable to a parent-subsidiary relationship). In a Type II relationship, there must be common control or supervision by persons controlling or supervising both the supporting organization and the supported organization (comparable to brother-sister corporations). In a Type III relationship, the supporting organization must be operated in connection with the supported organization by being responsive to its needs and demands, and by being significantly involved in its operations to the point that the supported organization is dependent upon the supporting organization for the type of support it provides. Regardless of whether these relationship requirements are met, if a Type I or Type III organization supports an organization that is controlled by a donor, then the supporting organization will be treated as a private foundation rather than as a public charity (Code Sec. 509(f)(2)).

A number of special rules also apply to Type III supporting organizations. For example, each tax year, a Type III organization must provide each supported organization with any information that may be required by the IRS to ensure that the relationship requirements of being a Type III organization are met (Code Sec. 509(f)(1)). This may include the Type III organization's annual information return (Form 990), any tax return filed (Form 990-T), and any annual report. In addition, a Type III organization may not be operated in connection with any public charity that is organized outside the United States. Similarly, a trust will not be considered to be a Type III organization *solely* based on the facts that it is a charitable trust under state law, the public charity is a beneficiary of the trust, and the public charity has the power to enforce the trust terms (Act Sec. 1241(c) of P.L. 109-280).

Tax-exempt organizations use Form 8940 to request determinations about a change in type of supporting organization.

610. Donor Advised Funds. A Code Sec. 501(c)(3) charitable organization (other than a private foundation) may establish a donor advised fund which is a separate account identified by reference to contributions made by a donor to the organization under which the donor (or person appointed by the donor) reasonably expects to provide nonbinding advice regarding distributions or investments (Code Sec. 4966(d)(2)).[18] The donor may be entitled to a charitable deduction for contributions to a donor advised fund (¶ 1061), but only if the sponsoring organization legally owns and controls the contributions. For this purpose, a donor advised fund does not include any fund that only makes distributions to a single identified organization or governmental entity, or a fund that allows the donor to provide advice as to which individuals receive grants for travel, study, or similar purposes through a committee that is appointed by the sponsoring organization and is not controlled by a donor or group of donors with advisory privileges, and under which all grants are made on an objective and nondiscriminatory basis. The IRS has discretionary authority to exempt a fund or account from treatment as a donor advised fund. The charitable organization must provide information to the IRS when it applies for tax-exempt status (¶ 623) whether it maintains or intends

References are to Standard Federal Tax Reports; Tax Research Consultant; and Practical Tax Explanations.

[16] ¶ 22,800; EXEMPT: 21,200; § 33,020.05

[17] ¶ 22,804, ¶ 22,804C; EXEMPT: 21,200; § 33,020.10

[18] ¶ 34,317; EXEMPT: 33,000; § 33,720.05

to maintain the donor advised fund, and the manner in which it plans to operate those funds (Code Sec. 508(f)).[19]

An excise tax is imposed on any "taxable distribution" from a donor advised fund which is any distribution to a natural person or to any other person if the distribution is for any purpose other than an exempt purpose under Code Sec. 501(c)(3) (¶ 602) (Code Sec. 4966).[20] It also includes any distribution to a disqualified supporting organization (¶ 607), unless the sponsoring organization exercises responsibility for the distribution (Notice 2006-109). A taxable distribution does not include any distribution to a 50-percent organization (¶ 1059), to the sponsoring organization, or to another donor advised fund. The excise tax is 20 percent of the distribution and is imposed on the sponsoring organization. A separate five-percent excise tax is imposed on any fund manager who knowingly agrees to the distribution (up to $10,000 per distribution). A fund manager includes any officer, director, or trustee of the sponsoring organization, as well as an employee having authority with respect to the distribution. If more than one fund manager knowingly participates in the transaction, then all those managers will be jointly and severally liable. Both the tax on the sponsoring organization and fund manager are reported on Form 4720. The IRS has discretionary authority to abate both taxes (¶ 647).

An excise tax is also imposed if a donor advised fund makes a distribution to any person that results in (directly or indirectly) a more-than-incidental benefit to the donor, donor advisor, member of the donor's family, or any entity in which the donor holds more than a 35-percent ownership interest (Code Sec. 4967).[21] The tax is 125 percent of the benefit received and is imposed on the donor, donor advisor, and related persons who recommended the distribution or received the prohibited benefit. A tax of 10 percent of the benefit (up to $10,000) is also imposed on fund managers who agreed to the making of a distribution knowing it would confer a more-than-incidental benefit. All persons liable for the taxes are jointly and severally liable. If the taxes are imposed, the IRS has discretionary authority to abate them (¶ 647). However, neither tax will be imposed if the distribution is subject to tax as an excess benefit transaction (¶ 617). Also, a donor advised fund will be treated as a private foundation for purposes of the excise tax on excess business holdings (¶ 640).

613. Limitations on Lobbying Activities. An organization that otherwise qualifies as a Code Sec. 501(c)(3) charitable organization will be denied tax-exempt status if: (1) a *substantial* part of its activities consists of carrying on propaganda or attempting to influence legislation, or (2) it participates or intervenes in any political campaign on behalf of, or in opposition to, any candidate for public office (Code Sec. 501(h); Reg. § 1.501(h)-1).[22] If a charitable organization engages in substantial legislative activity or participates in any political campaign, then it is an action organization (¶ 602) and not operated exclusively for one or more exempt purposes (Reg. § 1.501(c)(3)-1(c)(3)).[23] There are no specific guidelines as to what constitutes *substantial* legislative activities for this purpose. Instead, the substantial part test is determined on the facts and circumstances of each case. However, the IRS has issued guidance for the facts and circumstances to be evaluated in determining whether or not a Code Sec. 501(c)(3) organization has participated or intervened in a political campaign for public office (Rev. Rul. 2007-41).[24] If the organization has made a political expenditure, it will be subject to an excise tax (¶ 614).

As an alternative to the substantial part test, many charitable organizations may elect on Form 5768 a sliding scale limitation on expenditures to objectively determine their permissible level of lobbying activities (Code Sec. 501(h); Reg. § 1.501(h)-2).[25] The

References are to Standard Federal Tax Reports; Tax Research Consultant; and Practical Tax Explanations.

[19] ¶ 22,790; EXEMPT: 33,056; § 33,505

[20] ¶ 34,317; EXEMPT: 33,150; § 33,720.10

[21] ¶ 34,319; EXEMPT: 33,200; § 33,720.05

[22] ¶ 22,602, ¶ 22,663; EXEMPT: 6,100; § 33,710.05

[23] ¶ 22,608; EXEMPT: 6,102; § 33,710.05

[24] ¶ 22,609.103; EXEMPT: 6,104; § 33,710.05

[25] ¶ 22,602, ¶ 22,664; EXEMPT: 6,150; § 33,710.05

election can be made at any time during the organization's tax year. It is effective for the entire tax year and all succeeding years until revoked. Organizations that may not make this election include: churches or a convention or association of churches (¶ 604), private foundations (¶ 631), and supporting organizations (¶ 607) for social welfare organizations, labor unions, trade associations and organizations that test for public safety (¶ 692).

The basic permitted level for lobbying expenditures (but not grassroots lobbying) is 20 percent of the first $500,000 of the electing organization's exempt-purpose expenditures for the year, 15 percent of the second $500,000, 10 percent of the third $500,000, and five percent of any additional expenditures with a maximum annual limitation of $1 million (Code Sec. 4911).[26] In the case of so-called grassroots lobbying—attempts to influence the general public on legislative matters—the basic permitted level is limited to 25 percent of the general lobbying level described above. An excise tax of 25 percent is imposed on any excess lobbying expenditures above these limits. In addition, if an organization's lobbying expenditures normally—on an average over a four-year period—exceed 150 percent of these limits (computed on Schedule C of Form 990), the organization will lose its tax-exempt status (Reg. § 1.501(h)-3).[27]

614. Excise Tax on Political Expenditures. A 10-percent excise tax is imposed on a Code Sec. 501(c)(3) organization for each political expenditure made during the tax year (Code Sec. 4955).[28] For this purpose, a political expenditure is generally defined as any amount paid or incurred by the organization in connection with any participation or intervention in any political campaign on behalf of (or in opposition to) any candidate for public office (¶ 613). A separate 2.5-percent excise tax (up to $5,000) is imposed on any organization manager who agrees to the making of the expenditure if the manager knows that it is a political expenditure, unless the agreement is not willful and due to reasonable cause. An organization manager includes a director, officer, trustee, or any individual with comparable responsibilities.

If the political expenditure is not corrected within a "taxable period," then a second-tier excise tax is imposed on the organization equal to 100 percent of the amount of the expenditure. Organization managers who refuse to agree to all or part of the correction are also subject to a second-tier tax of 50 percent of the amount of the expenditure (up to $10,000). If more than one manager is liable for either the first- or second-tier taxes, then each manager will be jointly and severally liable. The "taxable period" is the period beginning on the date on which the taxable expenditure is made and ending on the earlier of the date on which a deficiency notice for the first-tier tax is mailed or the date it is assessed. A correction of a political expenditure means the foundation takes all reasonable means to recover the expenditure to the extent possible and establishes safeguards to prevent future political expenditures. If full recovery is not possible, then the foundation must take whatever corrective action is prescribed by the IRS. Both the first and second levels of taxes may be abated under certain circumstances (¶ 647). The organization's taxes are reported on Form 4720.

617. Excess Benefit Transactions. An excise tax is imposed on any "excess benefit transaction" involving a charitable organization under Code Sec. 501(c)(3) (other than a private foundation), a social welfare organization under Code Sec. 501(c)(4), or a qualified nonprofit health insurance issuer under Code Sec. 501(c)(29) (Code Sec. 4958).[29] The tax may be applied instead of, or in addition to, the organization being disqualified as an exempt organization due to the prohibition on private inurement (¶ 602). An excess benefit transaction is any transaction in which an economic benefit is provided to a "disqualified person" by the organization that exceeds any consideration given. It also includes any grant, loan, or other payment from a donor advised fund (¶ 610) or a qualified supporting organization (¶ 607) to a disqualified person.

References are to Standard Federal Tax Reports; Tax Research Consultant; and Practical Tax Explanations.

[26] ¶ 33,960; EXEMPT: 6,156.05; § 33,710.05

[27] ¶ 22,665; EXEMPT: 6,160; § 33,710.05

[28] ¶ 34,240; EXEMPT: 6,106; § 33,710.10

[29] ¶ 34,250; EXEMPT: 6,056; § 33,130

The tax is imposed on the disqualified person and is 25 percent of the amount of the excess benefit or the amount of the grant, loan, or other compensation received from a donor advised fund or qualified supporting organization. A manager of the exempt organization who knowingly participates in the transaction is subject to a separate excise tax of 10 percent, up to $20,000 per act. If more than one manager knowingly participates in the transaction, then all those managers will be jointly and severally liable. However, a manager will not be liable if participation is not willful and due to reasonable cause. For this purpose, a manager includes a director, officer, trustee, and any other individual of the exempt organization with comparable responsibilities.

If the excess benefit is not corrected within the "taxable period" (¶ 614), then a second-tier excise tax is imposed on the disqualified person equal to 200 percent of the amount of the excess benefit, grant, loan, or other payment. If more than one person is liable for either the first- or second-tier taxes on disqualified persons, then such persons will be jointly and severally liable. The taxes on disqualified persons and organization managers are reported on Form 4720. However, both levels of taxes may be abated under certain circumstances (¶ 647). In addition, private foundations are subject to different sanctions (¶ 635).

Disqualified Persons. For this purpose, a disqualified person is generally a person who is in a position to exercise substantial influence over the affairs of the exempt organization (including a qualified supporting organization), regardless of the individual's title. Certain family members and entities in which a disqualified person holds at least a 35-percent ownership interest are also treated as disqualified persons (Code Sec. 4958(f)). In the case of any donor advised fund, a disqualified person includes any donor, donor advisor and investment advisor to the fund, as well as any family member or any entity controlled by such persons. A disqualified person with respect to a qualified supporting organization includes any substantial contributor (¶ 635), family member of a substantial contributor, or a 35-percent controlled entity.

619. Involvement in Tax Shelter Transactions. Generally, a tax-exempt entity that is a party to a prohibited tax shelter transaction (¶ 2001), or which becomes a party to a subsequently listed transaction at any time during the tax year, is subject to an excise tax on a percentage of the entity's net income or proceeds attributable to the prohibited transaction. The rate of tax depends on whether the exempt entity ***knew or had reason to know*** that the transaction was a prohibited tax shelter transaction at the time it became a party to the transaction (Code Sec. 4965).[30] In addition, any manager of a tax-exempt entity who approves or otherwise causes the exempt entity to be a party to a prohibited tax shelter transaction at any time during the tax year, and knew or had reason to know that the transaction was a prohibited tax shelter transaction, must pay a separate excise tax for each approval. For this purpose, a tax-exempt entity includes any tax-exempt organization under Code Sec. 501(c) or religious organization under Code Sec. 501(d), including any charitable organization and any qualified retirement plan, as well as individual retirement accounts (IRA), health savings accounts (HSA), Archer medical savings accounts (MSA), and qualified tuition plans. The tax-exempt entity must file a disclosure of its being a party to a prohibited tax shelter transaction on Form 8886-T and the identity of any other party (including both taxable and tax-exempt parties) to the transaction which is known by the entity (Code Sec. 6033(a)(2); Reg. § 1.6033-5).[31]

623. Application and Modification of Exempt Status. Charitable organizations seeking exempt status under Code Sec. 501(c)(3) must file an application for exemption on Form 1023 within 15 months (or 27 months with an automatic 12-month extension) from the end of the month in which they are organized (Code Sec. 508; Reg. § 1.508-1).[32] An organization that fails to file a timely notice will not qualify for exempt status for any period prior to the date actual notice is given. A second notification is required to be included on the application if the organization wants to claim public charity status. An organization that fails to notify the IRS of public charity status will be presumed to be a

References are to Standard Federal Tax Reports; Tax Research Consultant; and Practical Tax Explanations.

[30] ¶ 34,305; EXEMPT: 6,252; § 33,715

[31] ¶ 35,420, ¶ 35,424E; EXEMPT: 6,254; § 33,715

[32] ¶ 22,790, ¶ 22,791; EXEMPT: 12,054; § 33,505

private foundation (¶ 631). An organization will be a publicly supported organization qualifying for public charity status in its first five years if it can show, on its Form 1023, that it is reasonably expected to receive the requisite public support during the period (Reg. § 1.170A-9(f)(4)(v)).

Organizations that are not required to file an application for exempt status or notification of public charity status include: (1) any organization (other than a private foundation) whose annual gross receipts normally do not exceed $5,000; (2) churches and their affiliates; (3) any subordinate organization (other than a private foundation) covered by a group exemption of a parent; and (4) certain nonexempt charitable trusts (¶ 591) (Reg. § 1.508-1(a)(3)). However, for such an organization to establish its exemption with the IRS and receive a determination letter, it should file the appropriate information return as proof of its exemption (¶ 625) (Reg. § 1.508-1(a)(4)).

The IRS will issue a favorable determination letter or exemption ruling if the organization's application and supporting documents establish that it meets the particular requirements under which it is claiming tax-exempt status (Rev. Proc. 2012-9).[33] A ruling may also be modified or revoked by the IRS at any time (Reg. § 601.201(n)(6)).[34] Generally, revocations occur prospectively, however, a retroactive revocation may occur where: (1) the IRS was not fully or correctly informed as to the material facts on which the exemption ruling was based, or (2) there have been material changes in law or fact after the original ruling was issued.

If an organization receives an unfavorable exemption ruling, or its exempt status is revoked, it may seek judicial review only after it has exhausted all administrative remedies with the IRS. If an adverse ruling is issued (or if the IRS fails to issue a ruling), the organization can seek a declaratory judgment that it qualifies for exempt status (Code Sec. 7428).[35] If the organization has actually begun operations before it receives an adverse ruling (or its exempt status is revoked retroactively), it may either pay the taxes on its activities it thought were exempt and file for a refund or it can protest the assessment of any taxes in the Tax Court.

Tax-exempt organizations use Form 8940 to request determinations (other than initial exemption applications) about their tax-exempt status. These determinations include advance approval for foundation set-asides and scholarship approvals, change in type of supporting organization, and termination of foundation status.

625. Annual Information Return. Generally, all tax-exempt organizations are required to file an annual information return with the IRS, including organizations whose application for exemption is pending, as well as nonexempt charitable trusts (¶ 591) (Code Sec. 6033; Reg. § 1.6033-2).[36] For most organizations, the return is filed on or before the 15th day of the fifth month following the close of the organization's tax year on Form 990, Form 990-EZ, or Form 990-N, depending on its gross receipts and total assets. However, other forms may be required for certain organizations. For example, private foundations file Form 990-PF (¶ 631), farmers' cooperatives file Form 1120-C (¶ 698), religious and apostolic organizations file Form 1065 (¶ 604), and black lung benefits trusts file Form 990-BL. Organizations that exclude exempt function income from their gross income may be required to file a variation of Form 1120 in lieu of, or in addition to, Form 990 or Form 990-EZ, such as political organizations which file Form 1120-POL (¶ 696) and certain homeowner associations which file Form 1120-H (¶ 699).

Exempt organizations that are not required to file Form 990 or Form 990-EZ, regardless of gross receipts and total assets, include: any organization (other than a private foundation or supporting organization (¶ 607)) that has annual gross receipts of $50,000 or less; any church (including its integrated auxiliary) and convention or association of churches (¶ 604); an exclusively religious activity of a religious order;

References are to Standard Federal Tax Reports; Tax Research Consultant; and Practical Tax Explanations.

[33] ¶ 22,604.10; EXEMPT: 12,054; § 33,535

[34] ¶ 22,609.4825, ¶ 43,356; EXEMPT: 12,104; § 33,801

[35] ¶ 41,720; EXEMPT: 12,150; § 33,801

[36] ¶ 35,420, ¶ 35,422; EXEMPT: 12,252; § 33,605.05

church-sponsored mission societies; governmental units exempt from taxation; corporations organized under an act of Congress; certain schools affiliated with a church or religious order; and certain foreign or U.S. possession organizations (Code Sec. 6033(a)(3); Reg. § 1.6033-2(g)(1); Rev. Proc. 2011-15).[37] An exempt organization that is not required to file Form 990 or Form 990-EZ because its annual gross receipts normally do not exceed $50,000 is still required to file an annual information return electronically on Form 990-N (Code Sec. 6033(i); Reg. § 1.6033-6; Rev. Proc. 2011-15). If a small tax-exempt organization does not file for three consecutive years, its exempt status will be revoked (Code Sec. 6033(j)).

Information Required. Form 990 and Form 990-EZ require an exempt organization to provide information on its finances, governance, compliance with certain federal tax filings and requirements, compensation paid to certain persons, exempt and nonexempt activities, and, in the case of a charitable hospital, the needs identified in its community health needs assessments and a copy of its audited financial statements (Code Sec. 6033(b)). Additional schedules and information are required to be completed depending upon the activities and type of the organization. For example, a charitable organization under Code Sec. 501(c)(3) must include information on its lobbying activities (¶ 613) and any donor advised funds (¶ 610) it sponsors (Code Sec. 6033(e) and (k)). A qualified nonprofit health insurance issuer under Code Sec. 501(c)(29) must include information on the amount of reserves on hand, and the amount of reserves required by each state in which the issuer is licensed to issue qualified health plans (Code Sec. 6033(m)). If an organization was tax-exempt for any of its last five tax years preceding its dissolution, liquidation, termination, or substantial contraction, then it must also include on Form 990 or Form 990-EZ information relating to that event (Code Sec. 6043(b)).[38] Organizations exempt from reporting information on its dissolution or termination include churches, organizations other than private foundations with $5,000 or less in annual gross receipts, and other organizations specified in Reg. § 1.6043-3(b).[39]

Disclosure. Tax-exempt organizations, including private foundations, must make available for public inspection, at the organization's principal, regional, and district offices (having three or more employees) during regular business hours, its three most recent annual information returns, as well as a copy of its application for exemption. Charitable organizations must also make available for public inspection any returns related to the organization's unrelated business taxable income (UBTI) filed in the previous three tax years (Code Sec. 6104).[40] Organizations do not have to honor requests if they reasonably believe that the request is part of a harassment campaign (Reg. § 301.6104(d)-3).[41] Requests may be made either in person or in writing. Copies of an organization's Form 990 must be furnished immediately for requests made in person and within 30 days for written requests. Organizations are permitted to charge a reasonable fee for reproduction and mailing costs. An exempt organization can comply with these disclosure requirements by posting information on its website.

Penalties. A penalty of $20 per day (up to a maximum for any return of $10,000 or five percent of the organization's gross receipts, whichever is less) is imposed on each tax-exempt organization that fails to file an annual information return, files a late return without reasonable cause, or fails to file the information return on dissolution or substantial contraction (Code Sec. 6652(c)).[42] For organizations with gross receipts in excess of $1 million for any year, the penalty increases to $100 per day (up to a maximum for any return of $50,000 or five percent of gross receipts). An additional penalty of $10 a day (up to a maximum $5,000 on any return) is imposed on any officer, trustee, employee, etc., who fails to file the return without reasonable cause after requested by the IRS. There is no monetary penalty on an organization that is required to file Form 990-N but fails to do so. However, if an organization fails to file an annual

References are to Standard Federal Tax Reports; Tax Research Consultant; and Practical Tax Explanations.

[37] ¶ 35,420, ¶ 35,422, ¶ 35,425.24; EXEMPT: 12,252.05; § 33,605.05

[38] ¶ 35,880; EXEMPT: 12,252.30; § 33,605.05

[39] ¶ 35,885; EXEMPT: 12,252.30; § 33,605.05

[40] ¶ 36,900; EXEMPT: 12,258; § 33,615

[41] ¶ 36,910E; EXEMPT: 12,258; § 33,615

[42] ¶ 39,480; PENALTY: 3,208.15; § 33,615

return for three consecutive years, its exempt status is considered revoked (Code Sec. 6033(j)).[43]

Failure to comply with the public disclosure requirements results in a penalty of $20 per day, with a maximum of $10,000 for any annual return. The penalty for a willful failure to comply with the public disclosure requirements is increased to $5,000 for each return or application (Code Sec. 6685).[44] There is no maximum penalty for failure to disclose the organization's exemption application.

627. Other Reporting and Disclosure Requirements. In addition to filing an application for exempt status (¶ 623) and annual information returns (¶ 625), exempt organizations (other than private foundations) have a number of other filing requirements.

Nondeductible Contributions. All tax-exempt organizations that are not eligible to receive deductible charitable contributions (such as lobbying groups, political action committees, labor unions, trade associations, social clubs and political organizations (¶ 692 and ¶ 1061)) must disclose this fact in a conspicuous and easily recognizable format in their fundraising solicitations (Code Sec. 6113).[45] Violation of this requirement without reasonable cause will subject an organization to a penalty of $1,000 per day of solicitation (up to $10,000 for any calendar year); a higher penalty will apply if the failure was intentional (Code Sec. 6710).[46]

Quid Pro Quo Contributions. Charitable organizations are required to inform donors in a written statement that quid pro quo contributions in excess of $75 are deductible only to the extent that the contributions exceed the value of goods or services provided by the organization (Code Sec. 6115).[47] Failure to make the required disclosure subjects the organization to a penalty of $10 per contribution unless due to reasonable cause (Code Sec. 6714).[48] A quid pro quo contribution is any payment made partly as a contribution to the organization and partly in consideration for goods or services provided by the organization (fundraising dinners, benefit auctions).

Donated Vehicles. A charitable organization is required to provide a donor of a motor vehicle, boat, or airplane with a contemporaneous written acknowledgment of the donation using Form 1098-C, including a certification of the organization's use or sale of the vehicle (¶ 1070A). A donee organization that fails to provide the acknowledgment or that provides a fraudulent acknowledgment will be subject to a penalty (Code Sec. 6720).[49]

Donated Intellectual Property. A charitable organization that receives or accrues net income during a tax year from a qualified intellectual property contribution must file an information return on Form 8899 and provide a copy to the donor (¶ 1062A) (Code Sec. 6050L(b)).[50] The return is required for any tax year that occurs during the 10-year period beginning on the date of the contribution and if the legal life of the donated property has not expired. The organization will be subject to a penalty for failure to file the return (¶ 2816).

Dispositions of Donated Property. A charitable organization is required to file a donee information return on Form 8282 if it sells or otherwise disposes of any charitable deduction property within three years after donated to the organization (Code Sec. 6050L(a)).[51] Charitable donation property is any property (other than cash or public securities) for which the donor claims a charitable contribution deduction of at least $5,000 and for which the organization signed an acknowledgment on Form 8283. The organization will be subject to a penalty for failure to file the return (¶ 2816).

References are to Standard Federal Tax Reports; Tax Research Consultant; and Practical Tax Explanations.

[43] ¶ 35,420; EXEMPT: 12,252.05; § 33,605.05

[44] ¶ 39,871; EXEMPT: 12,258; § 33,615

[45] ¶ 37,040; EXEMPT: 12,302; § 33,620.15

[46] ¶ 40,115; EXEMPT: 12,302.25; § 33,620.15

[47] ¶ 37,065; EXEMPT: 12,306; § 33,620.05

[48] ¶ 40,180; EXEMPT: 12,306.20; § 33,620.05

[49] ¶ 40,207; INDIV: 51,462; § 33,610.35

[50] ¶ 36,260; INDIV: 51,168; § 33,610.10

[51] ¶ 36,260; EXEMPT: 12,262; § 33,610.10

Split-dollar Insurance. A charitable organization engaging in a split-dollar life insurance arrangement is subject to an excise tax equal to the premiums paid by the organization (Code Sec. 170(f)(10)(F)).[52]

Private Foundations

631. Private Foundation Defined. Charitable organizations under Code Sec. 501(c)(3) are either public charities or private foundations (¶ 602). Public charities generally are organizations that have broad public support or that actively function in a supporting relationship to such organizations. On the other hand, a private foundation typically is funded by one individual, family, or corporation. Thus, a private foundation is any Code Sec. 501(c)(3) organization *other than*:

- a charitable deduction donee listed in Code Sec. 170(b)(1)(A) (¶ 1059);
- a publicly supported organization receiving more than ⅓ of its annual support from members and the public, and not more than ⅓ of its support from investment income and unrelated business income (¶ 655);
- a qualified supporting organization (¶ 607); and
- an organization operated for public safety testing (Code Sec. 509).[53]

An organization that fails a public support test for two consecutive years will be treated as a private foundation as of the beginning of the second year of failure for certain purposes. The organization will be treated as a private foundation for all purposes beginning the first day of the third consecutive year (Reg. § 1.509(a)-3(c)(1)(i)).

Like all Code Sec. 501(c)(3) organizations, a private foundation must provide notice to the IRS for it to be exempt from taxation (¶ 623). However, even if notice is provided, a private foundation will be denied tax-exempt status unless its governing instrument specifically prohibits it from accumulating income (¶ 637), engaging in certain prohibited activities including acts of self-dealing (¶ 635), retaining excess business holdings (¶ 640), making investments which jeopardize its charitable purpose (¶ 642), or making certain taxable expenditures (¶ 644) (Code Sec. 508(e))[54] (¶ 1068). All private foundations must also file an annual information return on Form 990-PF reporting gross income, receipts, disbursements, etc. (¶ 625). If at any time during the tax year the foundation has at least $5,000 of assets, it must also include information on its assets, managers, and grants or contributions made during the year (Code Sec. 6033(c); Reg. § 1.6033-3).[55]

633. Taxation of Investment Income. A two-percent excise tax is imposed on the "net investment income" of a private foundation for each tax year (Code Sec. 4940).[56] The tax is reduced to one percent if the foundation satisfies certain requirements as to the amount of charitable distributions it made during the year and if it was not liable for the excise tax on undistributed income (¶ 637) in any of the preceding five tax years. The excise tax is reported on the foundation's annual return, Form 990-PF. Estimated payments of the foundation's liability for the tax (as well as its unrelated business taxable income (UBTI) (¶ 670)) are computed on Form 990-W and the first-quarter installment is due by the 15th day of the fifth month following the foundation's tax year (May 15 for calendar year foundations) (Code Sec. 6655(g)(3)).[57] For this purpose, the net investment income of a private foundation generally includes the foundation's gross investment income and net capital gain, less the ordinary and necessary business expenses incurred for the production or collection of gross investment income. Gross investment income includes interest, dividends, rents, royalties, and payments with respect to securities loans, as well as any similar source of income such as income from annuities and notional principal contracts. It does not include income to the extent it is

References are to Standard Federal Tax Reports; Tax Research Consultant; and Practical Tax Explanations.

[52] ¶ 11,600; FILEBUS: 9,300; § 7,580

[53] ¶ 22,800; EXEMPT: 21,000; § 33,205.10

[54] ¶ 22,790; EXEMPT: 21,450; § 33,205.20

[55] ¶ 35,420, ¶ 35,423; EXEMPT: 21,552; § 33,205.15

[56] ¶ 34,000; EXEMPT: 24,050; § 33,210.05

[57] ¶ 39,565; EXEMPT: 15,204; § 33,210.10

taken into account as UBTI including any gain or loss from the sale or disposition of property (no capital loss carryovers or carrybacks are allowed).

The tax on investment income will not apply to an exempt "operating foundation," which is any operating foundation that has been publicly supported for at least 10 years, at all times during the tax year it is governed by representatives at least 75 percent of whom represent the general public, and at no time during the tax year does it have an officer who is a disqualified individual. For this purpose, a disqualified individual is a substantial contributor to the foundation, an owner of more than 20 percent of a business or trust which is a substantial contributor, or a member of the family of any of the preceding. An operating foundation is a foundation that spends at least 85 percent of the lesser of its adjusted net income or its minimum investment return in carrying on its exempt activities (Code Sec. 4942(j)(3); Reg. §53.4942(b)-1).[58] A nonoperating private foundation is generally a grant-making organization that does not operate its own charitable program.

635. Prohibitions on Self-Dealing. Certain acts of self-dealing are prohibited between a disqualified person and a private foundation (Code Sec. 4941).[59] This includes the sale or exchange of property, loans or other extensions of credit, the furnishing of goods or services, payments of compensation, or the transfer of income or assets to the disqualified person. It does not include the pro rata division of a trust that qualifies as a charitable remainder trust (¶ 590) into two separate trusts (Rev. Rul. 2008-41).[60] For this purpose, a disqualified person includes:

- a substantial contributor (any person who contributes more than $5,000 if that amount is more than two percent of the total contributions received by the foundation before the end of its tax year);
- a foundation manager, including an officer, director, or trustee;
- the owner of more than 20 percent of a corporation, partnership, trust or other enterprise which is a substantial contributor;
- a member of the family of any of the preceding (including spouse, ancestor, child, grandchild, great grandchild, or spouse of any of these descendants);
- a corporation, trust, estate, or partnership more than 35 percent of which is owned or held by any of the preceding; or
- a government official (Code Sec. 4946).[61]

The disqualified person is subject to a 10-percent excise tax on the amount involved in any act of self-dealing for each year in the taxable period. Any foundation manager who knowingly participates in the self-dealing act is subject to a five-percent excise tax on the amount involved but only if participation was willful and not due to reasonable cause. A second-level tax of 200 percent (50 percent on the manager) applies if the prohibited act is not corrected within the taxable period. For this purpose, the taxable period begins on the date on which the self-dealing act occurs and ends on the earliest of: (1) the date on which the deficiency notice for the first-level tax is mailed; (2) the date on which the first-level tax is assessed; or (3) the date on which the act of self-dealing is completely corrected (Code Sec. 4941(e)).[62] The maximum tax imposed on a foundation manager is $20,000 per act for each level of tax. The IRS has discretionary authority to abate both levels of tax for the manager and the disqualified person (¶ 647). However, the IRS also has the authority to impose a third-level tax or terminate the foundation's status (¶ 649) if there are repeated or flagrant acts of self-dealing (Code Sec. 6684).[63] The initial excise tax on an act of self-dealing is reported on Form 4720.

637. Failure to Distribute Income. A private foundation (other than an operating foundation (¶ 633)) is required to distribute annually its minimum investment return for

References are to Standard Federal Tax Reports; Tax Research Consultant; and Practical Tax Explanations.

[58] ¶ 34,040, ¶ 34,044; EXEMPT: 24,450; § 33,210.05

[59] ¶ 34,020; EXEMPT: 24,150; § 33,215.05

[60] ¶ 34,031.65; EXEMPT: 24,200; § 33,215.05

[61] ¶ 34,120; EXEMPT: 24,700; § 33,215.05

[62] ¶ 34,020; EXEMPT: 24,150; § 33,215.05

[63] ¶ 39,865; EXEMPT: 24,162; § 33,215.05

the tax year, which generally equals five percent of the foundation's net investment assets (adjusted for certain taxes and loan repayments). Failure to do so will cause the foundation to be subject to an excise tax of 30 percent of any undistributed income (Code Sec. 4942).[64] Undistributed income is the amount by which the minimum investment return of the foundation exceeds the amount of qualifying distributions made during the tax year. Qualifying distributions include distributions to public charities and private operating foundations, and payments for expenses and assets used for charitable purposes. It does not generally include payments made by the nonoperating private foundation to a supporting organization (¶ 607) (Code Sec. 4942(g)(1)).

If the foundation fails to make the necessary distributions within the taxable period, then a second-level tax will be imposed equal to 100 percent of the undistributed income. For this purpose, the "taxable period" is the period that begins on the first day of the tax year, and ends on the earlier of the date on which the deficiency notice for the initial tax is mailed or the date on which it is assessed. The IRS has discretionary authority to abate both levels of tax (¶ 647). However, a third-level tax may be imposed if there are repeated or flagrant acts of failure to distribute income (Code Sec. 6684).[65] The initial excise tax on undistributed income is reported on Form 4720.

640. Involvement in Unrelated Businesses. A private foundation is allowed to own a certain amount of business enterprises jointly with disqualified persons (¶ 635). However, to curb any abuses, the foundation is subject to an excise tax of 10 percent of any "excess business holdings" during the tax year (Code Sec. 4943).[66] If such excess business holdings are not divested within the taxable period (¶ 637), then a second-level tax of 200 percent is imposed. In general, the permitted amount of business ownership that a private foundation and disqualified person may have in any enterprise that is not substantially related to the exempt purposes of the foundation is 20 percent. If third parties have effective control of the business enterprise, then the limit is 35 percent. Special rules apply to certain grandfathered holdings. The IRS has discretionary authority to abate both levels of tax (¶ 647). However, a third-level tax may be imposed if there are repeated or flagrant acts of excess business holdings (Code Sec. 6684).[67]

The excise tax on excess business holdings will apply to donor advised funds (¶ 610) and certain qualified supporting organizations (¶ 607). In applying the tax to donor advised funds, a disqualified person is defined as any donor, a member of the donor's family, or a 35-percent controlled entity (Code Sec. 4943(e)). A qualified supporting organization will be subject to the excess business holdings tax only if it is a Type III supporting organization, or a Code Sec. 501(c)(3) organization that meets the organizational and operational test of a qualified supporting organization and it is not controlled by a disqualified person (Code Sec. 4943(f)). For this purpose, a disqualified person with respect to the supporting organization is any person with substantial influence over the organization (or any family member of such a person), as well as any substantial contributor, family member of a substantial contributor, or 35-percent controlled entity.

642. Investments Jeopardizing Exempt Purpose. A 10-percent excise tax is imposed on any investment of a private foundation that jeopardizes the foundation's exempt status (Code Sec. 4944; Reg. §53.4944-1).[68] A "jeopardizing" investment is generally one that shows a lack of reasonable business care and prudence in providing for the foundation's short- and long-term financial needs. Examples of investments that will be closely scrutinized include trading in securities on margin, trading in commodity futures, investing in working interests in oil and gas wells, buying puts, calls, straddles or warrants, and selling short. A 10-percent excise tax is also imposed on any foundation manager who knowingly participates in such an investment (up to $10,000 per investment), unless such participation is not willful but due to a reasonable cause. A second-

References are to Standard Federal Tax Reports; Tax Research Consultant; and Practical Tax Explanations.

[64] ¶ 34,040; EXEMPT: 24,300; § 33,220.05

[65] ¶ 39,865; EXEMPT: 24,304; § 33,220.05

[66] ¶ 34,060; EXEMPT: 24,500; § 33,225.05

[67] ¶ 39,865; EXEMPT: 24,502; § 33,225.05

[68] ¶ 34,080, ¶ 34,081; EXEMPT: 24,600; § 33,230.05

level tax of 25 percent is imposed on the foundation if the jeopardy situation is not corrected within the taxable period (¶ 637). Any foundation manager who refuses to agree to part or all of the correction will be subject to a second-level tax of five percent of the investment (up to $20,000). If more than one foundation manager is liable for either level of tax, then all such managers will be jointly and severally liable. The IRS has discretionary authority to abate both levels of tax (¶ 647). However, a third-level tax may be imposed on either the foundation or a manager if there are repeated or flagrant acts of jeopardizing investments (Code Sec. 6684).[69]

644. Lobbying and Other Prohibited Expenditures. A private foundation is subject to a 20-percent excise tax on the amount of any "taxable expenditure" made during the tax year. Any foundation manager who, without reasonable cause, willfully agrees to the expenditure knowing it is improper, is subject to a five-percent excise tax on the expenditure (up to $10,000) (Code Sec. 4945).[70] A taxable expenditure generally includes any amount paid by the foundation for legislative or political purposes, or any grant to an individual for travel, study, or other similar purpose (unless made under objective standards). It also includes any grant to any organization unless the grantee organization is a public charity, qualified supporting organization (¶ 607), exempt operating foundation (¶ 633), or the nonoperating private foundation exercises responsibility for the expenditure of the grant (Code Sec. 4945(d)). A taxable expenditure does not include the pro rata division of a trust that qualifies as a charitable remainder trust (¶ 590) into two separate trusts (Rev. Rul. 2008-41).[71] A second-level tax of 100 percent is imposed on the foundation if the taxable expenditure is not corrected within the taxable period (¶ 637). Any foundation manager who refuses to agree to part or all of the correction will be subject to a second-level tax of 50 percent of the investment (up to $20,000). If more than one foundation manager is liable for either level of tax, then all such managers will be jointly and severally liable. The IRS has discretionary authority to abate both levels of tax for the foundation or the manager (¶ 647). However, a third-level tax may be imposed if there are repeated or flagrant acts of taxable expenditures (Code Sec. 6684).[72]

647. Abatement of Taxes. The IRS has discretionary authority not to assess certain first-tier excise taxes, or to abate such taxes if already assessed, or to provide a credit or refund if the tax is already collected. The IRS will exercise this authority only if the violation giving rise to the imposition of the excise tax in question was due to reasonable cause and not willful neglect, and is corrected within the "correction period" (Code Sec. 4962).[73] First-tier excise taxes to which this relief may apply include: all of the excise taxes imposed on private foundations and disqualified persons (¶ 631), *except for:* the tax on acts of self-dealing (¶ 635); the excise tax on the lobbying and political activities of public charities (¶ 614); the excise tax on excess benefit transactions (¶ 617); and the excise taxes on taxable distributions and prohibited benefits from donor advised funds (¶ 610). The IRS may withhold or abate an assessment of any second-tier excise taxes if the taxable event in question is corrected voluntarily during the correction period (Code Sec. 4961).[74] For this purpose, the correction period is the period beginning on the date of the taxable event and ending 90 days after the deficiency notice for the second-tier tax is mailed (Code Sec. 4963).[75]

649. Termination of Private Foundation Status. The status of any organization as a private foundation may be terminated voluntarily or involuntarily (Code Sec. 507).[76] A voluntary termination requires the foundation to notify the IRS of its plan to terminate. An involuntary termination occurs when the IRS notifies the foundation of the intent to terminate its status because of willful repeated violations or a willful and flagrant

References are to Standard Federal Tax Reports; Tax Research Consultant; and Practical Tax Explanations.

[69] ¶ 39,865; EXEMPT: 24,600; § 33,230.05

[70] ¶ 34,100; EXEMPT: 24,650; § 33,235.05

[71] ¶ 34,031.65; EXEMPT: 24,200; § 33,215.05

[72] ¶ 39,865; EXEMPT: 24,650; § 33,235.05

[73] ¶ 34,280; EXEMPT: 24,750; § 33,220.10

[74] ¶ 34,260; EXEMPT: 24,750; § 33,220.10

[75] ¶ 34,300; EXEMPT: 24,756; § 33,220.10

[76] ¶ 22,771; EXEMPT: 27,000; § 33,240.05

violation giving rise to excise taxes on the foundation (¶ 631). In either case, the private foundation must pay a termination tax equal to the lesser of: the aggregate amount of tax benefits received by the foundation and any of its substantial contributors (¶ 635) since its inception resulting from its exempt status under Code Sec. 501(c)(3); or the value of its net assets. The pro rata division of a trust that qualifies as a charitable remainder trust (¶ 590) into two separate trusts does not terminate private foundation status or cause the termination tax to apply (Rev. Rul. 2008-41).[77]

The IRS may abate a portion or all of the termination tax. The tax may be abated if, prior to providing notice to the IRS of its voluntary termination, the foundation distributes all of its net assets to another private foundation or public charity described in Code Sec. 170(b)(1)(A) (¶ 1059) that has been in existence for at least five years immediately before the distribution. Under these circumstances, the transfer of assets is not a termination of the foundation's status. Instead, the foundation retains its status until it gives actual notice of its termination to the IRS. When notice is provided after all net assets are transferred, then the termination tax will be zero (but the distributions may give rise to excise taxes). The termination tax may also be abated if the foundation becomes a public charity within 12 months or it actually operates as a public charity for at least five years. However, notice of termination must be provided to the IRS prior to the beginning of the 12-month or five-year termination period.

Tax-exempt organizations use Form 8940 to request determinations about termination of foundation status.

Unrelated Business Taxable Income

655. Organizations Subject to Tax. Although a variety of nonprofit organizations with charitable or socially beneficial purposes may be granted tax-exempt status under Code Sec. 501, they are still subject to an unrelated business income tax (UBIT) (¶ 658) (Code Sec. 511).[78] Unrelated business income is income from a trade or business regularly carried on by the exempt organization (¶ 664) that is not substantially related (¶ 667) to the organization's exempt purposes (Code Sec. 512).[79] All types of exempt organizations are subject to UBIT except government instrumentalities (other than colleges or universities) and federally licensed businesses or educational institutions sponsored by a religious order (Reg. § 1.511-2).[80] Additionally, title-holding companies may be exempt from UBIT if the holding corporation and the payee organization file a consolidated return.

658. Rates and Payment. Tax-exempt organizations are taxed on their unrelated business taxable income (UBTI) (¶ 670) at ordinary corporate income tax rates (¶ 219 and ¶ 1401) or, if the organization is not incorporated, at trust income tax rates (¶ 19) (Code Sec. 511(a)).[81] Returns are made on Form 990-T, to be filed at the same time as the organization's annual information return (¶ 625) (Reg. § 1.6012-2(e)).[82] Estimated payments of the exempt organization's liability for UBTI are computed on Form 990-W. The first-quarter installment is due by the 15th day of the fifth month following the organization's tax year (May 15 for calendar year organizations) (Code Sec. 6655(g)(3)).[83]

664. Business Must Be "Regularly" Carried On. The unrelated business taxable income (UBTI) of a tax-exempt organization is its gross income from any unrelated trade or business *regularly* carried on by the organization, minus any deductions for expenses related to the trade or business (¶ 682) (Code Sec. 512(a); Reg. §§ 1.512(a)-1 and 1.513-1(c)).[84] In determining whether a trade or business is regularly carried on, the frequency and continuity with which an activity is pursued is judged with comparable

References are to Standard Federal Tax Reports; Tax Research Consultant; and Practical Tax Explanations.

[77] ¶ 34,031.65; EXEMPT: 24,200; § 33,215.05

[78] ¶ 22,820; EXEMPT: 15,000; § 33,905

[79] ¶ 22,830; EXEMPT: 15,050; § 33,910

[80] ¶ 22,822; EXEMPT: 15,058; § 33,905

[81] ¶ 22,820; EXEMPT: 15,202; § 33,901

[82] ¶ 35,145; EXEMPT: 15,204; § 33,901

[83] ¶ 39,565; EXEMPT: 15,204; § 33,901

[84] ¶ 22,830, ¶ 22,831, ¶ 22,841; EXEMPT: 15,054, EXEMPT: 15,252; § 33,910, § 33,915

6 EXEMPT ORGS

commercial activities of nonexempt organizations. In the case of a social club, voluntary employees' beneficiary association (VEBA), or an organization for the payment of supplemental unemployment benefits (SUB) (¶ 692), UBTI is subject to tax only to the extent that it is not set aside for the purposes that constitute the basis for the organization's exemption (Code Sec. 512(a)(3); Temp. Reg. § 1.512(a)-5T).[85]

667. Business Must Be Unrelated to Exempt Functions. The unrelated business taxable income (UBTI) of a tax-exempt organization includes any income from a business *not substantially related* to the organization's exempt purpose (Code Sec. 513; Reg. § 1.513-1).[86] A business activity is not substantially related to an organization's exempt purpose if it does not contribute importantly to accomplishing that purpose (other than through the production of funds). Whether an activity contributes importantly depends on the facts, including the size and extent of the activities involved in relation to the exempt function they serve. However, a number of activities will *not* be considered an unrelated trade or business, including any trade or business which:

- has substantially all the work in carrying on the business performed for the organization without compensation;
- is carried on by a Code Sec. 501(c)(3) organization or governmental college or university primarily for the convenience of its members, students, etc.;
- consists of selling merchandise, substantially all of which has been received by the organization as gifts or contributions;
- is a qualified entertainment activity or a qualified convention and trade show activity (Code Sec. 513(d)) (¶ 685);
- in the case of a public charity hospital, performs services that a tax-exempt cooperative hospital organization may perform (¶ 699) (Code Sec. 513(e));
- consists of conducting any bingo games if the games are conducted in accordance with local law and do not compete with profit-making businesses (Code Sec. 513(f));
- in the case of a mutual or cooperative telephone or electric company, engages in qualified pole rentals (Code Sec. 513(g));
- includes the exchanging or renting of member donor lists between exempt organizations or the distribution of low-cost articles ($9.90 for 2012; $10.20 for 2013) incidental to the solicitation of charitable contributions (Code Sec. 513(h); Rev. Proc. 2012-41; Rev. Proc. 2011-52); or
- involves the soliciting and receiving of qualified sponsorship payment (Code Sec. 513(i)) (¶ 685).

670. Unrelated Business Taxable Income Defined. The unrelated business taxable income (UBTI) of an exempt organization is its gross income derived from any unrelated trade or business regularly carried on (¶ 664 and ¶ 667), less the deductions directly connected with such trade or business (¶ 682) (Code Sec. 512).[87] The following income items (and any related deductions) are generally excluded from the calculation of UBTI: dividends, interest, annuities and royalties (¶ 673); rents from real property or incidental rents from personal property leased with real property (¶ 676); gains or losses from the disposition of property other than stock in trade (¶ 679); certain research income; certain amounts received from controlled entities and foreign corporations; income of a mutual or cooperative electric company derived from the sale of electricity from its members; and gains or losses on the disposition of qualified brownfield sites. Annual dues not exceeding $151 for 2012 ($155 for 2013) that are paid to an exempt agricultural or horticultural organization will also be excluded from UBTI (Code Sec. 512(d); Rev. Proc. 2011-52; Rev. Proc. 2012-41).

References are to Standard Federal Tax Reports; Tax Research Consultant; and Practical Tax Explanations.

[85] ¶ 22,830, ¶ 22,834; EXEMPT: 15,206, EXEMPT: 15,208; § 33,910, § 33,915

[86] ¶ 22,840, ¶ 22,841; EXEMPT: 15,056; § 33,920

[87] ¶ 22,830; EXEMPT: 15,200, EXEMPT: 15,300; § 33,935.05

An exempt organization's calculation of UBTI must include its share of income and deductions from an unrelated trade or business conducted by a partnership (including a publicly traded partnership) or S corporation in which it is a partner or shareholder (Code Sec. 512(c) and (e)). However, if the tax year of the organization differs from the partnership's, then the amounts used to calculate UBTI will be based on the income and deductions of the partnership in the tax year that ends within the tax year of the exempt organization. In addition, the organization's share of S corporation income and deductions must be included regardless of whether they would normally be excluded from UBTI (dividends, interest, royalties, etc.).

673. Dividends, Interest, Annuities and Royalties (Investment Income). Generally, the unrelated business taxable income (UBTI) of an exempt organization (¶ 670) will *not* include investment income such as dividends, interest, annuities, royalties, payments with respect to securities loans, amounts received or accrued as consideration for entering into agreements to make loans, and income derived from notional principal contracts (as well as income from ordinary investments that are substantially similar) (Code Sec. 512(b); Reg. § 1.512(b)-1(a)).[88] Royalties for this purpose include amounts paid to an exempt organization for use of its name, trademarks, and other intellectual property rights in connection with the sale of merchandise or services.[89] However, where an exempt organization provides active services in relation to the marketing of products or services associated with its name or other rights, the income may not be excluded as royalty income. The exclusion for investment income also does not apply to income derived from debt-financed property (¶ 687).

Membership Organizations. Special rules apply to certain membership organizations including a social and recreational club, voluntary employees' beneficiary association (VEBA), or a supplemental unemployment compensation benefit trust (SUB) (¶ 692). Unlike other exempt organizations, these organizations cannot exclude investment income from UBTI and losses from nonexempt activities cannot generally be used to offset investment income. However, gross income does not include exempt function income, which is income from dues, fees, and charges for providing facilities and services for members, dependents, and guests, as well as income set aside for charitable purposes or by a VEBA to provide insurance benefits (Code Sec. 512(a)(3)).[90] A special exclusion also applies for gain such organizations realize on the sale of assets used in pursuing their exempt function to the extent the proceeds are reinvested (within a four-year period) in other assets for such purposes. For this purpose, a title-holding corporation whose income is payable to a membership organization will be treated as the exempt organization. To prevent bypassing these limitations through termination of tax-exempt status, a ***nonexempt*** social club or other membership organization operated primarily to furnish goods or services to members may deduct the cost of furnishing these goods, services, insurance, etc., only to the extent of membership-related income (Code Sec. 277).[91] A nonexempt social club or VEBA is also not allowed to claim the corporate dividends-received deduction (¶ 221).

Look-Through Rules. If an exempt organization receives or accrues a payment of interest, annuity, royalty or rent (but not a dividend) from an entity that it controls, then the payment is includible in the organization's UBTI to the extent it either reduces the net unrelated business income of the controlled entity or increases its net unrelated losses (Code Sec. 512(b)(13)).[92] However, any payment received or accrued after 2005 and before 2012 under a binding written contract in effect on August 17, 2006, is included in the exempt organization's UBTI only to the extent it exceeds the amount that would have been paid if the payment met the requirements for related parties under the transfer pricing rules of Code Sec. 482. A valuation misstatement penalty applies to excess payments that are included in UBTI. In addition, the exempt organization must

References are to Standard Federal Tax Reports; Tax Research Consultant; and Practical Tax Explanations.

[88] ¶ 22,830, ¶ 22,835; EXEMPT: 15,302; § 33,935.05

[89] ¶ 22,837.83; EXEMPT: 15,310; § 33,935.05

[90] ¶ 22,830; COMPEN: 54,350, EXEMPT: 15,206, EXEMPT: 15,208; § 33,935.05

[91] ¶ 14,600; ACCTNG: 12,216; § 33,935.05

[92] ¶ 22,830; EXEMPT: 15,304; § 33,935.05

report the payments from a controlled entity on its annual return (Code Sec. 6033(h)).[93] For this purpose, the threshold of control of a subsidiary which triggers UBTI is having more than 50-percent ownership (more than 50 percent of stock by vote or value in a corporation, or more than 50 percent of a profits, capital, or beneficial interest of a partnership or other entity). The constructive ownership rules of Code Sec. 318 apply in these circumstances (¶ 743).

676. Rents. Excludable from the unrelated business taxable income (UBTI) of an exempt organization (¶ 670) are amounts received from the rental of real property, including those rents from personal property leased with real property so long as they are incidental in relation to the total amount of rents under the lease (10 percent or less of total rents from all leased property) (Code Sec. 512(b)(3); Reg. § 1.512(b)-1(c)).[94] However, payments for the use or occupancy of rooms and other space (for example, in a hotel, boarding house, storage facility) where services are also provided primarily for the occupant's convenience and are not those customarily rendered in rental for occupancy only (such as maid service) do not constitute rent from real property. Rents are taxable if they are: (1) rents from real property leased with personal property where more than 50 percent of the rent is attributable to the personal property; (2) rents from both the real and the personal property where the amount of such rents depends on the income or profits derived by any person from the leased property (other than an amount based on a fixed percentage of gross receipts or sales); and (3) unrelated income from debt-financed property (¶ 687).

679. Gains and Losses from Sales or Exchanges. Excluded from the unrelated business taxable income (UBTI) of an exempt organization (¶ 670) are all gains or losses from the sale, exchange or other disposition (including involuntary conversions and casualties) of property *other than*: (1) stock in trade or other property of a kind properly includible in inventory; (2) property held primarily for sale to customers in the ordinary course of a trade or business; or (3) timber cutting that the organization has elected to consider as a sale or exchange (Code Sec. 512(b)(5); Reg. § 1.512(b)-1(d)).[95] The exclusion also applies to all gains or losses recognized in connection with the organization's investment activities from the lapse or termination of options to buy and sell securities (whether or not written by the organization), as well as options to buy or sell real property. The exclusion does not apply to gains from the sale or other disposition of debt-financed property (¶ 687). Gains from certain pension plan investments in property of troubled financial institutions acquired after 1993 are also excluded (Code Sec. 512(b)(16)).

682. Deductions. In computing unrelated business taxable income (UBTI) (¶ 670), an exempt organization is entitled to deduct all ordinary and necessary business *directly connected* with carrying on the unrelated trade or business (¶ 667). To be directly connected with the conduct of an unrelated business, deductions must have a proximate and primary relationship to carrying on the business. Expenses attributable to an exempt activity are generally not deductible unless: (1) the unrelated business exploits the exempt activity; (2) the business is of a type normally carried on for profit by a taxable organization; and (3) the exempt activity is of a type normally carried on by a taxable organization in carrying on its business. When facilities or personnel are used for both exempt functions and the conduct of an unrelated business, it is necessary to allocate expenses on a reasonable basis (Code Sec. 512(a) and (b)(12); Reg. § 1.512(a)-1).[96]

In addition to deduction of ordinary and necessary business expenses, an exempt organization is allowed a specific deduction of $1,000, as well as the deduction for charitable contributions allowed to corporations (¶ 927), net operating losses (NOLs)

References are to Standard Federal Tax Reports; Tax Research Consultant; and Practical Tax Explanations.

[93] ¶ 35,420; EXEMPT: 15,304; § 33,935.05

[94] ¶ 22,830, ¶ 22,835; EXEMPT: 15,306; § 33,935.05

[95] ¶ 22,830, ¶ 22,835; EXEMPT: 15,302; § 33,935.05

[96] ¶ 22,830, ¶ 22,831; EXEMPT: 15,250; § 33,930

(¶ 1173), and domestic production activities (equal to the appropriate percentage of the lesser of qualified production activities income or unrelated business taxable income, rather than taxable income; ¶ 980A). The charitable contribution deduction is allowed whether or not directly connected with the carrying on of the trade or business, but is limited to 10 percent of the organization's UBTI, computed without regard to the contributions deduction (Code Sec. 512(b)(10)). An exempt trust that is subject to the unrelated business income tax at trust rates generally is allowed a deduction for charitable contributions in the same amounts as allowed for individuals (¶ 1058). With respect to the NOL deduction, the deduction must only reflect taxable "business income" and carryovers and items attributable to exempt income and expenses are disregarded (Code Sec. 512(b)(6)).

685. Advertising, Sponsorships, and Trade Shows. The sale of advertising in a periodical, journal, or magazine of an exempt organization is considered an unrelated business of the organization that exploits an exempt activity when the advertising activity is regularly carried on (¶ 664) (Reg. § 1.512(a)-1(d) and (f)).[97] An activity such as advertising does not lose its identity as a trade or business merely because it is carried on within a larger complex of other activities which may or may not be related to the organization's exempt purpose (Reg. § 1.513-1(b)).[98] As a result, advertising revenue is used in computing the organization's unrelated business taxable income (UBTI) (¶ 670) but may be offset by the expenses directly related to the advertising business activity. If facilities and personnel are both used to carry on exempt activities and unrelated advertising, the expenses must be allocated on a reasonable basis.

For this purpose, income realized by an exempt organization from the sponsorship of a public event will generally constitute advertising services. However, the solicitation and receipt of qualified sponsorship payments by an exempt organization is not an unrelated business, and the payments are excluded from computing UBTI (Code Sec. 513(i); Reg. § 1.513-4).[99] A qualified sponsorship payment is any payment by a payor engaged in a trade or business that does not expect any substantial return from the exempt organization other than the use or acknowledgment of the payor's name, logo, or product lines in connection with the activities of the tax-exempt organization. A qualified sponsorship payment does *not* include any payment:

- for advertising of the payor's product or services, including messages that contain qualitative or comparative language, price information, an endorsement, or an inducement to purchase, sell or use the payor's products and services;
- contingent upon factors indicating the degree of public exposure at one or more events (attendance, broadcast ratings);
- entitles the payor to the use or acknowledgment of the business name, logo, or product lines in the exempt organization's publication; or
- made in connection with a qualified convention or trade show activity (a convention or trade show conducted by a charitable organization (¶ 602), social welfare program, labor organization or business league (¶ 692) that has as one of its purposes the promotion of interest in the products and services of the industry in general, or to educate the attendees regarding new developments or products and services related to the exempt activities of the organizations (Reg. § 1.513-3)).[100]

Taxable Income from Debt-Financed Property

687. Unrelated Debt-Financed Income. A percentage of income from debt-financed property must be included in an exempt organization's unrelated business taxable income (UBTI) (¶ 670) regardless of whether the organization is engaged in a

References are to Standard Federal Tax Reports; Tax Research Consultant; and Practical Tax Explanations.

[97] ¶ 22,831; EXEMPT: 15,158; § 33,925.05

[98] ¶ 22,841; EXEMPT:15,158; § 33,925.05

[99] ¶ 22,840, ¶ 22,843G; EXEMPT: 15,122; § 33,925.05

[100] ¶ 22,843; EXEMPT: 15,112; § 33,925.05

trade or business (Code Sec. 514(a); Reg. § 1.514(a)-1).[101] The percentage included in UBTI is the same percentage (not to exceed 100 percent) as the "average acquisition indebtedness" on the property (¶ 689) for the tax year divided by the "average amount of the adjusted basis" of the property. Deductions with respect to each debt-financed property are allowed by applying the same percentage to expenses related to the property, except for any deduction resulting from the carryback or carryover of net capital losses. For this purpose, debt-financed property generally means any property held to produce income, including gain from its disposition (for example, rental real estate, corporate stock, etc.) on which there is an acquisition indebtedness at any time during the tax year (or preceding 12 months if the property is disposed of during the tax year) (Code Sec. 514(b); Reg. § 1.514(b)-1(a)).[102] Certain property, however, is not debt-financed property even if it is held to produce income (¶ 691).

689. Acquisition Indebtedness. For any debt-financed property of an exempt organization (¶ 687), "acquisition indebtedness" is the outstanding amount of principal debt: (1) incurred to acquire or improve property; (2) incurred before the acquisition or improvement if it would not have been incurred but for the acquisition or improvement; and (3) incurred after acquisition or improvement if it would not have been incurred but for the acquisition or improvement and was reasonably foreseeable at the time (Code Sec. 514(c); Reg. § 1.514(c)-1).[103]

If property is acquired subject to a mortgage, the amount of the mortgage (or similar lien) is considered acquisition indebtedness, even if the organization does not assume or agree to pay the debt (Code Sec. 514(c)(2)). However, when mortgaged property is received by bequest or devise (or by gift under certain circumstances), the debt will not be treated as an acquisition indebtedness for 10 years from the date of acquisition. A lien for taxes or assessments under state law will be treated similar to a mortgage to the extent the amount becomes due and the organization has an opportunity to pay it.

Acquisition indebtedness does not include a debt which was incurred by an exempt organization in the exercise of its exempt purpose. Generally, it also does not include debt incurred by certain qualified organizations (qualified employee benefits trust; an exempt school; exempt title-holding company; retirement income account of church plan) in acquiring or improving real property. Annuities may be excluded from the definition of acquisition indebtedness, as well as certain obligations insured by the Federal Housing Administration or incurred by a small business investment company (¶ 1916) (Code Sec. 514(c)(5) and (c)(6)).

691. Exempt Properties. The following types of property are excluded from the definition of debt-financed property (¶ 687):

(1) property substantially all the use of which (85 percent or more) is related to the exercise or performance of an organization's tax-exempt function (special rules apply to real property used as a medical clinic);

(2) property to the extent that its income is subject to tax as income from the carrying on of an unrelated trade or business (however, if any gain on disposition of the property is not included in unrelated business taxable income, it may be income from debt-financed property (¶ 655 and ¶ 679));

(3) property to the extent that its income is derived from certain research activities and is excluded from gross income of an unrelated trade or business;

(4) property to the extent it is used in a business where substantially all of the work of carrying on the business is performed without compensation, the Code Sec. 501(c)(3) organization carrying on the business does so primarily for the convenience of members, students, patients, etc., or the business consists of selling merchandise substantially all of which has been received as contributions; and

References are to Standard Federal Tax Reports; Tax Research Consultant; and Practical Tax Explanations.

[101] ¶ 22,850, ¶ 22,851; EXEMPT: 18,050; § 33,940.05

[102] ¶ 22,850, ¶ 22,853; EXEMPT: 18,100; § 33,940.05

[103] ¶ 22,850, ¶ 22,854; EXEMPT: 18,200; § 33,940.15

(5) certain brownfield site property to the extent the gain or loss from its sale or exchange would be excluded from gross income of an unrelated trade or business (Code Sec. 514(b); Reg. § 1.514(b)-1).[104]

For purposes of (1), (3) and (4) above, use of property by a related organization is taken into account in determining use of an exempt organization. In addition, special rules apply to life income contracts and real property located in the neighborhood of other property owned and used for exempt purposes by the exempt organization.

Other Tax-Exempt Organizations

692. Other Tax-Exempt Organizations under Code Sec. 501(c). In addition to charitable organizations (¶ 602), Code Sec. 501 exempts other types of nonprofit organizations from federal income tax unless they are deemed to be feeder organizations (¶ 694). Among the most common are civic leagues and social welfare organizations, business leagues, social and recreation clubs, and fraternal beneficiary societies. Contributions to these organizations are generally *not* deductible as charitable contributions. An organization described in this section generally files an application for exemption on Form 1024 and an annual information return on Form 990 (¶ 625).

Civic Leagues. A civic league or organization is exempt from federal income taxes if it is not organized for profit and is operated exclusively for the promotion of social welfare (Code Sec. 501(c)(4)).[105] This includes a local association of employees the membership of which is limited to the employees of a designated employer in a particular municipality and whose net earnings are devoted exclusively to charitable, educational, or recreational purposes. An exemption is not allowed if any part of the net earnings of the civic league or organization inures to the benefit of any private shareholder or individual (¶ 602). If the organization provides an excess benefit to certain persons, an excise tax may be imposed (¶ 617).

A civic league or organization will be considered to be operated exclusively for the promotion of social welfare if it primarily engages in promoting the common good and general welfare of the community (for example, volunteer fire departments or community association) (¶ 699). Promoting social welfare does not include participation or intervention in the political campaign of any candidate for office. In addition, the promotion of social welfare does not include the operation of a social club for the benefit of its members or carrying on a business similar to for-profit organizations (Reg. § 1.501(c)(4)-1).[106] This includes providing commercial-type insurance unless it is an insubstantial part of the organization's activities, in which case the activity will be treated as an unrelated trade or business (¶ 655) (Code Sec. 501(m) and (n)).[107]

Labor, Agricultural, and Horticultural Organizations. A qualifying labor, agricultural or horticultural organization is tax-exempt if: (1) no net earnings of the organization inure to the benefit of any member, and (2) it has as its objective the betterment of the conditions of those engaged in such pursuits, the improvement of the grade of their products, and the development of a higher degree of efficiency in their respective occupations (Code Sec. 501(c)(5); Reg. § 1.501(c)(5)-1).[108] This does not include administration of any type of retirement plan. Generally, a qualifying labor organization is an association of workers such as a labor union. An agricultural and horticultural organization is involved with raising livestock, forestry, harvesting crops or aquatic resources, the cultivation of useful or ornamental plants, and similar pursuits (Code Sec. 501(g); IRS Pub. 557).

References are to Standard Federal Tax Reports; Tax Research Consultant; and Practical Tax Explanations.

[104] ¶ 22,850, ¶ 22,853; EXEMPT: 18,100; § 33,940.10

[105] ¶ 22,602; EXEMPT: 9,300; § 33,405.05

[106] ¶ 22,610; EXEMPT: 9,300; § 33,405.05

[107] ¶ 22,602; EXEMPT: 15,160.10, EXEMPT: 15,160.15; § 33,405.05

[108] ¶ 22,602, ¶ 22,612; EXEMPT: 9,050; § 33,410.05

Business Leagues. A business league, chamber of commerce, real estate board, board of trade or professional football league is tax-exempt if it is not organized for profit and no part of its net earnings inures to the benefit of any private shareholder or individual (Code Sec. 501(c)(6); Reg. §1.501(c)(6)-1).[109] A business league is an association of persons having some common business interest, a purpose to promote such common interest and not engaging in a regular business of a kind ordinarily carried on for profit. For example, an association engaged in furnishing information to prospective investors is not a business league, since its activities do not further any common business interest.

Social Clubs. A social club or similar organization is exempt from federal income taxes if it is organized and operated exclusively for pleasure, recreation, and other nonprofitable purposes and no part of its net earnings inures to the benefit of any person having an interest in the activities of the organization (Code Sec. 501(c)(7); Reg. §1.501(c)(7)-1; IRS Pub. 557).[110] Membership in the club must be limited, but personal contact, commingling and fellowship must exist between the members. In addition, the club's charter, bylaws, or other governing instrument, or any written policy statement must not provide for discrimination against any person on the basis of race, color, or religion (Code Sec. 501(i)). However, a club that in good faith limits its membership to the members of a particular religion to further the teachings or principles of that religion will not be considered as discriminating on the basis of religion. Also, the restriction on religious discrimination does not apply to a club that is an auxiliary of a fraternal beneficiary society if that society limits its membership to the members of a particular religion.

A social club is generally only exempt if it is supported solely by membership fees, dues, and assessments. Thus, the club cannot be engaged in any business activities, such as making its facilities available to the public or by selling real estate, timber, or other products. However, a club may receive up to 35 percent of its gross income, including investment income, from sources outside of its membership without losing tax-exempt status. Up to 15 percent of the gross receipts may be derived from the use of the club's facilities or services by the public or from other activities not furthering social or recreational purposes for members. If an organization has outside income that is more than these limits, all the facts and circumstances will be taken into account in determining whether the organization qualifies for exempt status (IRS Pub. 557).

Fraternal Beneficiary Societies. A fraternal beneficiary society, order, or association is exempt from federal income taxes if: (1) it operates under the lodge system for the exclusive benefit of the members of a fraternity itself operating under the lodge system; and (2) it provides for the payment of life, sickness, accident, or other benefits to the members of such society, order, or association or their dependents (Code Sec. 501(c)(8)).[111] Contributions by an individual to such societies are deductible as charitable contributions if the gift is to be used exclusively for religious, charitable, scientific, literary, or educational purposes, or for the prevention of cruelty to children or animals (¶1061). A domestic fraternal society, order, or association that operates under the lodge system but does not provide for the payment of life, sickness, accident, or other benefits may nonetheless qualify for exemption if its net earnings are devoted exclusively to religious, charitable, scientific, literary, educational, and fraternal purposes (Code Sec. 501(c)(10)).

Other Nonprofit Organizations. Other nonprofit organizations that may be exempt from federal income taxes include:

- corporations organized under an Act of Congress (Code Sec. 501(c)(1));
- title holding corporations for exempt organizations (Code Sec. 501(c)(2) and (25));

References are to Standard Federal Tax Reports; Tax Research Consultant; and Practical Tax Explanations.

[109] ¶22,602, ¶22,614; EXEMPT: 9,100; §33,415.05

[110] ¶22,602, ¶22,616; EXEMPT: 9,400; §33,415.05

[111] ¶22,602; EXEMPT: 9,150; §33,425.05

- voluntary employees' beneficiary associations (VEBAs) providing life, sickness, accident and other benefits to members or their dependents or beneficiaries (Code Secs. 501(c)(9) and 505);
- local teachers' retirement fund associations (Code Sec. 501(c)(11));
- local benevolent life insurance associations (Code Sec. 501(c)(12));
- cemetery companies (Code Sec. 501(c)(13));
- state-chartered credit unions and mutual reserve funds (Code Sec. 501(c)(14));
- mutual insurance companies or associations (other than life insurance) (Code Sec. 501(c)(15));
- corporations used to finance crop operations (¶ 698) (Code Sec. 501(c)(16));
- supplemental unemployment benefit (SUB) trusts (Code Sec. 501(c)(17));
- employee funded pension trusts created before June 25, 1959 (Code Sec. 501(c)(18));
- posts or organizations for veterans, members of the armed services, and their families (Code Sec. 501(c)(19));
- black lung benefit trusts (Code Sec. 501(c)(21));
- domestic trusts set up to pay for withdrawal liability from multiemployer pension plans under ERISA (Code Sec. 501(c)(22));
- veterans organizations created before 1880 (Code Sec. 501(c)(23));
- trusts set up by a corporation in connection with the termination of its pension, profit sharing, or stock bonus plan (Code Sec. 501(c)(24));
- state-sponsored high-risk health coverage organizations (Code Sec. 501(c)(26));
- state-sponsored workers' compensation reinsurance organizations (Code Sec. 501(c)(27));
- national railroad retirement investment trust (Code Sec. 501(c)(28));
- a qualified nonprofit health insurance issuer under the Consumer Operated and Oriented Plan (CO-OP) program established by the Secretary of Health and Human Services (Code Sec. 501(c)(29)); and
- a reinsurance entity established or entered into a contract with by a state government to collect payments and make payments to the health insurance issuers that cover high risk individuals in the individual market during the three-year period beginning January 1, 2014 (Act Sec. 1341(a) of Patient Protection and Affordable Care Act of 2010 (P.L. 111-148)).

694. Feeder Organizations. An organization whose primary purpose is to operate a trade or business, with all the profits paid to one or more tax-exempt entities, is known as a feeder organization (Code Sec. 502; Reg. § 1.502-1).[112] The fact that the income is turned over to a tax-exempt organization does not entitle the feeder organization to tax-exempt status. A feeder organization is subject to tax unless its activities are an integral part of the exempt activities of the parent organization. For this purpose, a trade or business of a feeder organization does *not* include: (1) the deriving of rents if the rents received would not be subject to the unrelated business income tax (¶ 655); (2) any trade or business in which substantially all the work of carrying on the trade or business is performed by unpaid individuals or volunteers; or (3) any trade or business that sells merchandise, substantially all of which has been donated or contributed.

References are to Standard Federal Tax Reports; Tax Research Consultant; and Practical Tax Explanations.

[112] ¶ 22,670, ¶ 22,671; EXEMPT: 15,350; § 33,301

6 EXEMPT ORGS

696. Political Organizations. A political organization is generally considered tax exempt to the extent that it is organized and operated to accept contributions and make expenditures for influencing the selection, nomination, election or appointment of any individual to public office (Code Sec. 527).[113] Examples of political organizations include political parties, federal, state or local candidate committees, other political action committees (PACs), as well as certain newsletters and segregated funds. The exempt function income of a political organization consists solely of: (1) contributions of money or property; (2) membership dues or fees; or (3) proceeds from a political fundraising event or the sale of political campaign materials. Any other income received (less deductions not related to exempt functions) is taxed at the highest income tax rate for corporations and capital gains. In calculating its taxable income, a political organization is permitted a $100 deduction, but it will not be allowed a net operating loss deduction, the dividends received deduction, and other special deductions allowed to corporations (¶ 221).

Political organizations with any taxable income must figure and report their tax on Form 1120-POL. Political organizations with $25,000 or more of gross receipts ($100,000 for certain state or local organizations) must also file an annual information return on Form 990 or 990-EZ (Code Sec. 6033(g)).[114] All political organizations must notify the IRS (electronically on Form 8871) of their existence within 24 hours of establishment (Code Sec. 527(i)). They must also provide periodic reports on Form 8872 of the contributions they receive and their expenditures (Code Sec. 527(j)). Organizations do not have to meet these two requirements if they have gross receipts of less than $25,000, are already required to file similar reports with the Federal Election Commission, or are certain state or local political organizations. Failure to provide notification will result in all income (including exempt function income) being taxed. In addition, failure to provide periodic reports will result in all undisclosed contributions and expenditures being taxed. The IRS has a safe harbor that waives the amounts due for failing to comply with the reporting requirements due to reasonable cause but not willful neglect (Rev. Proc. 2007-27).[115] The public disclosure of all returns and forms filed by a political organization is required (Code Sec. 6104).[116]

698. Farmers' Cooperatives. A cooperative (or federation of cooperatives) of farmers, fruit growers, and persons engaged in similar pursuits may qualify for tax-exempt status if the cooperative is organized and operated for the purpose of marketing the products of members and returning to them net proceeds, or purchasing supplies and equipment for the use of members at cost plus expenses (Code Sec. 521; Reg. § 1.521-1).[117] The cooperative can deal with nonmembers, so long as the business does not account for more than 15 percent of all of its business. Application for exemption is filed on Form 1028. A farmers' association which has capital stock will not be denied exemption so long as: (1) the dividend rate is fixed at the legal rate of interest for the state of incorporation or eight percent (whichever is greater), and (2) substantially all of the stock is owned by producers who market their products or purchase their supplies through the association. A farmers' cooperative will also not be denied exemption if it computes its net earnings by offsetting certain earnings and losses in determining any amount available for distribution to patrons (Code Sec. 1388(j)(1)).[118]

Exempt farmers' cooperatives, and nonexempt corporations operating on a cooperative basis, are subject to regular corporate income and capital gain taxes and must file Form 1120-C to report taxable income (Code Secs. 1381 and 1382; Reg. § 1.1382-3).[119] However, in computing taxable income, all cooperatives are allowed certain deductions from gross income in addition to other deductions allowed to corporations (¶ 221). For

References are to Standard Federal Tax Reports; Tax Research Consultant; and Practical Tax Explanations.

[113] ¶ 22,900; EXEMPT: 9,850; § 33,428.05

[114] ¶ 35,420; EXEMPT: 9,864; § 33,428.30

[115] ¶ 22,911.70; EXEMPT: 9,864; § 33,428.30

[116] ¶ 36,900; EXEMPT: 9,864; § 33,428.30

[117] ¶ 22,880, ¶ 22,881; FARM: 12,200

[118] ¶ 32,380; FARM: 12,250

[119] ¶ 32,300, ¶ 32,320, ¶ 32,323; FARM: 12,100, FARM: 12,150, FARM: 12,200; § 36,040

example, an exempt farmers' cooperative is permitted a deduction for any dividends paid on capital stock, for amounts paid on a patronage basis arising from certain nonpatronage earnings, and for amounts paid in redemption of certain nonqualified written notices of allocation. In addition, all cooperatives are allowed a deduction for any "patronage dividend" paid or allocated to its members during the tax year. A patronage dividend is an amount paid to a member:

- on the basis of quantity or value of business done with the cooperative;
- under an obligation of the cooperative to pay such amount, where the obligation existed before the cooperative received the amount paid; and
- which is determined by reference to the net earnings of the cooperative from business done with or for its members. However, net earnings will not be reduced by amounts paid as dividends on capital stock to the extent that the dividends are in addition to amounts otherwise payable to patrons (Code Sec. 1388(a)).[120]

699. Additional Exempt Organizations. There are a number of organizations other than charitable (¶ 602) and social (¶ 692) that may be exempt from federal income taxes, including homeowners' associations, credit counseling organizations, and cooperative service organizations.

Homeowners' Association. A homeowners' association formed to own and maintain common areas and enforce covenants to preserve the appearance of a development may qualify as a tax-exempt social welfare organization under Code Sec. 501(c)(4) (¶ 692). A homeowners' association that is not exempt as a social welfare organization and that is either a condominium management, real estate management, or timeshare association, may nonetheless elect to exclude certain exempt function income from its gross income, including membership dues, fees, and assessments from member-owners. Electing associations are taxed at a flat rate of 30 percent (32 percent for timeshare associations) on both ordinary income and capital gains which are nonexempt. Form 1120-H is used by the association to make the election for each tax year and to report annual taxable income (Code Sec. 528).[121]

Credit Counseling Organizations. An organization that provides credit counseling services as a substantial purpose may not qualify as a tax-exempt organization unless it qualifies as a Code Sec. 501(c)(3) charitable or educational organization (¶ 602), or as a Code Sec. 501(c)(4) social welfare organization (¶ 692) (Code Sec. 501(q)).[122] In addition, the organization: (1) must provide services tailored to customers' specific needs; (2) must not refuse to provide services to customers due to inability to pay or ineligibility for debt management plan enrollment; (3) make no loans to customers; (4) have a reasonable fee policy and must not pay or receive referral fees; (5) have limited ownership of related service providers; and (6) have independent board members with public interests.

Cooperative Service Organizations. A cooperative hospital service organization is exempt from federal income taxation if it performs specifically listed services for two or more patron hospitals that are tax exempt under Code Sec. 501(c)(3) or if it is owned and operated by the federal government or by a state or local government (Code Sec. 501(e)).[123] Services that may be performed include data processing, purchasing (which includes purchasing insurance on a group basis, such as malpractice and general liability insurance), laboratory, billing and collection (including the purchase of patron accounts receivable on a recourse basis), food, personnel, and clinical services. It does not include laundry services.[124] A cooperative arrangement formed and controlled by a group of exempt educational organizations for the collective investment of their funds may also qualify for tax-exempt status (Code Sec. 501(f)).[125] Such organizations qualify for exemption only if all of the relevant requirements of Code Sec. 501(c)(3) are also satisfied.

References are to Standard Federal Tax Reports; Tax Research Consultant; and Practical Tax Explanations.

[120] ¶ 32,380; FARM: 12,104; § 36,040

[121] ¶ 22,920; EXEMPT: 9,500; § 33,429.05

[122] ¶ 22,602; EXEMPT: 10,050; § 33,105

[123] ¶ 22,602; EXEMPT: 3,154; § 33,105

[124] ¶ 22,662.30; EXEMPT: 3,154

[125] ¶ 22,602; EXEMPT: 3,300

6 EXEMPT ORGS

Chapter 7
INCOME

What Is "Income"

701. Gross Income Defined. Gross income for federal income tax purposes means all income from whatever source, except for those items specifically excluded by the Code (Code Sec. 61).[1]

Fifteen of the more common types of gross income are enumerated by Code Sec. 61. They are: (1) compensation for services, including fees, commissions, fringe benefits, and similar items; (2) gross income from business; (3) gains from dealings in property; (4) interest; (5) rents; (6) royalties; (7) dividends; (8) alimony and separate maintenance payments; (9) annuities; (10) income from life insurance and endowment contracts; (11) pensions; (12) income from the discharge of indebtedness; (13) a partner's share of partnership income; (14) income in respect of a decedent; and (15) income from an interest in an estate or trust.

Although nearly every type of accession to wealth appears to fall within this comprehensive definition, income items should be checked against the specific exclusions in Code Secs. 101–140 (¶ 801). For special rules relating to foreign income, see ¶ 2401. For a detailed list of income items and exclusions, see the Checklist for Items of Income at ¶ 55. For a discussion of gifts and inheritances, see ¶ 847 and ¶ 849.

702. Determining Income. Court decisions have developed a concept of the term "income" that is quite different from the layman's concept. The Supreme Court has defined income as an undeniable accession to wealth, clearly realized, and over which the taxpayer has complete dominion (*Glenshaw Glass Co.*, SCt, 55-1 USTC ¶ 9308). Further, the Supreme Court has repeatedly held that Congress's broad definition of what constitutes gross income was intended to tax all gain unless specifically exempted.[2] In addition to those items specifically excludable from gross income by law (¶ 801), certain other items are not considered income.

Return of Capital. A return of capital, such as repayment of a loan, is not income unless the loan has been previously deducted as a bad debt, resulting in a tax benefit.[3]

References are to Standard Federal Tax Reports; Tax Research Consultant; and Practical Tax Explanations.

[1] ¶ 5502; INDIV: 6,050; § 3,001

[2] ¶ 8636.363; INDIV: 6,052; § 3,001

[3] ¶ 5504.103; INDIV: 6,058; § 17,101

Similarly, car pool reimbursements are not income even if only one person provides the car and does the driving.[4]

Damages. Damages, other than punitive damages, that compensate an injured person for personal physical injuries or physical sickness are excludable from gross income (Code Sec. 104(a)(2)). Damages received for personal nonphysical injuries, such as employment discrimination or injury to reputation, are generally taxable (¶ 852).

Interest on a judgment, including mandatory prejudgment interest, is generally includible in income.[5]

See ¶ 759 for treatment of damages awarded for business claims.

Attorney Fees and Court Costs. Court costs and attorney fees paid in connection with an action based on unlawful discrimination under federal law, as well as certain other claims, i.e., whistleblower actions, are deductible from the determination of adjusted gross income (¶ 1010A) (Code Sec. 62(a)(20)).[6]

Housing Assistance. Rental assistance payments made by the Department of Housing and Urban Development under the National Housing Act and relocation payments made under the Housing and Community Development Act of 1974 are nontaxable. However, payments made by individuals or other nongovernmental entities are not considered payments for the general welfare and are taxable.[7]

Gift v. Income. The characterization of a payment or transfer as either a gift or as taxable income must be made on a case-by-case basis.[8] The Supreme Court has held that the value of a "gift" transferred to a business friend for furnishing the names of potential customers is taxable compensation (¶ 849).[9]

Strike and Lockout Benefits. Strike benefits received from a labor union may be treated as nontaxable gifts when the benefits paid in the form of food, clothing, and rent are: (1) given to both member and nonmember strikers, (2) dependent upon individual need, (3) dependent on the unavailability of unemployment compensation or local public assistance, and (4) given without condition. The fact that benefits are paid only to union members is not, of itself, determinative as to taxability.[10]

Unrealized Appreciation. Unrealized appreciation in the value of property is not income.[11]

Ownership of Income

704. Tax Liability. In the vast majority of cases, the identity of the taxpayer is clear. The taxpayer is simply the person who is legally entitled to receive income. Thus, an individual who receives wages for services is obviously the person who must pay income tax on the wages. However, under some circumstances (¶ 705), a person may be taxed on income even though, at the time of payment, another receives it because of an anticipatory assignment of income.

705. Assignment of Income. Generally, an individual can escape tax on income from property only if the individual makes a valid gift or assignment of the income-producing property itself, as distinguished from an assignment of the income. The U.S. Supreme Court has held that an individual who gave his wife the legally enforceable right to receive the future income generated by his law practice was still taxable on that income (*G.C. Earl*, SCt, 2 USTC ¶ 496).[12] In another case, the Court ruled that an individual who gave his son interest coupons, which were detached from bonds that he owned, was liable for the tax on the interest accrued before the gift and later paid to his

References are to Standard Federal Tax Reports; Tax Research Consultant; and Practical Tax Explanations.

[4] ¶ 5504.144; INDIV: 33,554; § 4,015

[5] ¶ 6662.513; INDIV: 12,112; § 3,805.35

[6] ¶ 6002; FILEIND: 9,088; § 3,810.30

[7] ¶ 5504.184; INDIV: 33,354; § 4,050

[8] ¶ 6553.115; INDIV: 33,100; § 3,615

[9] ¶ 5507.294; INDIV: 33,102

[10] ¶ 6553.46; COMPEN: 6,068; § 22,410.10

[11] ¶ 5504.119; INDIV: 6,052; § 3,001

[12] ¶ 6553.74; INDIV: 27,052; § 4,110

son (*P.R.G. Horst*, SCt, 40-2 USTC ¶ 9787).[13] See ¶ 706 for the taxation of the unearned income of minor and/or dependent children.

706. Unearned Income of Minor Child. The amount of net unearned income of a child meeting certain statutory requirements that exceeds an annual inflation-adjusted amount generally is taxed at the parents' highest marginal rate. This is referred to as the "kiddie tax." It is designed to lessen the effectiveness of intra-family transfers of income-producing property that would shift income from the parents' high marginal tax rate to the child's generally lower tax rate, to reduce a family's overall income tax liability. The kiddie tax applies to a child's unearned income regardless of source and requires a calculation of the parents' allocable tax, which is the increase in the parents' tax liability that results from adding the net unearned income of all of the parents' children meeting the kiddie tax age requirements to the parents' taxable income (Code Sec. 1(g)).[14]

See ¶ 103 for additional discussion of the kiddie tax and ¶ 143 for dependents with earned income.

709. Joint Tenancy and Tenancy in Common. When property is held in joint tenancy with a right of survivorship, income from the property, including gain or loss upon its sale, is divided between the owners to the extent that each is entitled, under state law, to share in the income. There must be evidence that the joint ownership was bona fide and not used merely as a tax-avoidance scheme. These rules also apply to tenants in common.[15]

710. Community Property Income. In community property states (Arizona, California, Idaho, Louisiana, Nevada, New Mexico, Texas, Washington, and Wisconsin), property acquired by a husband and wife during their marriage is generally regarded as owned by them together, each owning an undivided interest in the whole property. Similarly, income from the property is divided equally between them. Although each state has exceptions in classifying income as separate or community property, the general rule is that salaries, wages, and other compensation for the services of either or both the husband and wife are community income; but it does not follow in every state that income from separate property is separate income. The states also differ in their treatment of property acquired by inheritance or intestate succession. However, the IRS can disallow the benefits of any community property law to a spouse for any income that the spouse treats as his or hers alone if that spouse fails to notify the other spouse of the nature and amount of income (Code Sec. 66).[16]

Registered Domestic Partners and Same Sex Married Couples. The IRS extended recognition of community property laws to registered domestic partners domiciled in Nevada, Washington, or California, as well as same sex married couples in California, beginning in 2010 (CCA 201021050; IRS Pub. 555). Thus, each partner or spouse must report one-half of the combined community income on their federal income tax return. Amended returns may be filed to report one-half of community property income for years prior to 2010. Community property laws were updated to include allocation of one-half of the income earned by one partner to the other for California on January 1, 2007, Nevada on October 1, 2009, and Washington on June 12, 2008. Under the Defense of Marriage Act (P.L. 104-199), these individuals are still considered not married for federal income tax purposes.

711. Joint v. Separate Return in Community Property States. If separate returns are filed by a married couple residing in a community property state, one-half of the community income (¶ 710) must be reported by each spouse. In Idaho, Louisiana, Texas, and Wisconsin, income from the separate property of a spouse is community income, with one-half being allocable to each spouse. In the other community property states, income from separate property is separate income.[17]

References are to Standard Federal Tax Reports; Tax Research Consultant; and Practical Tax Explanations.

[13] ¶ 2150.64; INDIV: 27,052; § 4,135.05

[14] ¶ 3260; INDIV: 18,154; § 1,510.05

[15] ¶ 2250.35; INDIV: 18,100; § 3,001

[16] ¶ 6050; INDIV: 24,050, INDIV: 24,152; § 34,601

[17] ¶ 2350.2475; INDIV: 24,050; § 45,915.20

Regardless of which rule is applied, it is usually more beneficial to file a joint return. For those taxpayers living in states where income from separate property remains separate income, separate returns may be beneficial if one spouse has: (1) a nonbusiness casualty loss attributable to separate property that is not deductible on a joint return because it must be reduced by the $100 floor plus 10 percent of the taxpayer's adjusted gross income or (2) medical expenses that are not deductible on a joint return because of the 7.5 percent (10 percent generally for tax years beginning after December 31, 2012 (¶ 1015)) of adjusted gross income floor on medical expense deductions (Code Sec. 165(h)(1); Code Sec. 213(a)).

A U.S. citizen or resident who is married to a nonresident alien may elect to file a joint return if both agree to be taxed on their worldwide income (Code Sec. 6013(g); Reg. § 1.6013-6(a)).[18] If the couple does not make this election and has community property income, any community property income is generally treated as if the spouses have been living apart all year (Code Sec. 879).[19] Further, there is a special one-time election that permits a nonresident alien spouse to file a joint return with his or her resident spouse for the year in which the alien becomes a U.S. resident (Code Sec. 6013(g) and (h)).[20] Moreover, if both spouses are nonresident aliens, one spouse's income that is connected with a U.S. trade or business is treated as income of that spouse only, regardless of foreign community property laws (Code Sec. 879(a)).[21]

Separated Spouses and Innocent Spouse Relief in Community Property States. The usual community property rules do not apply to spouses living apart from each other if: (1) they are separated for the entire year, (2) they file separate returns, and (3) they do not transfer to each other more than a *de minimis* amount of earned income (Code Sec. 66(a)).[22] Also, a spouse who files a separate return may be relieved of liability for tax on his or her share of community income earned by the other spouse if he or she did not know, or have reason to know, of community income items attributable to the other spouse. Further, the IRS may provide relief from a tax liability or deficiency arising from community property where failure to do so would be inequitable (Code Secs. 66(c) and 6015(f); Reg. § 1.6015-1(h); Notice 2012-8).[23]

Salaries, Wages, and Benefits

713. Compensation for Personal Services. All compensation for personal services, no matter what the form of payment, must be included in gross income (Reg. § 1.61-2).[24] Wages, salaries, commissions, bonuses, fringe benefits that do not qualify for statutory exclusions, tips, payments based on a percentage of profits, directors' fees, jury fees, election officials' fees, retirement pay and pensions, and other forms of compensation are income in the year received, and not in the year earned, unless the taxpayer reports income on an accrual basis (¶ 1515).

> **Example:** A cash-method salesperson who receives commissions in January 2013 for sales made in 2012 must include those amounts in the 2013 return.

Under the claim-of-right doctrine (¶ 1543), a taxpayer receiving income under a claim of right and without restrictions on its use or disposition is taxed on that income in the year received even though the right to retain the income is not yet fixed or the taxpayer may later be required to return it.[25]

Compensation is income even though the amount is not fixed in advance, as in the case of marriage fees, baptismal offerings, and similar sums received by a member of the clergy.[26] A year-end bonus is usually taxable, particularly if based on salary or length of service. Severance pay and vacation pay are also taxable as compensation. The value of a turkey, ham, or other nominally valued item distributed to an employee on holidays is not reportable income even though the employer is entitled to deduct the cost as a

7 INCOME

References are to Standard Federal Tax Reports; Tax Research Consultant; and Practical Tax Explanations.

[18] ¶ 35,160, ¶ 35,167; FILEIND: 3,250; § 1,320.15
[19] ¶ 27,460; INDIV: 24,156; § 39,035.55
[20] ¶ 35,160; FILEIND: 3,250; § 1,320.15
[21] ¶ 27,460; INDIV: 24,156
[22] ¶ 6050; INDIV: 24,150; § 45,920.10
[23] ¶ 6050, ¶ 35,185, ¶ 35,186C, ¶ 35,192.25; INDIV: 24,154; § 45,920.10
[24] ¶ 5506; COMPEN: 6,050; § 3,005.05
[25] ¶ 21,005.122; ACCTNG: 27,050; § 4,225.05
[26] ¶ 5507.141; COMPEN: 6,050; § 3,005.05

business expense. However, a distribution of cash, a gift certificate or gift card, or a similar item of value readily convertible to cash, must be included in the employee's income.[27]

The amount of compensation reported on the return is the gross amount before any reductions for withheld income tax or social security taxes, union dues, insurance, or other deductions by the employer.

Restricted Property Transfers. If stock or other property is given as compensation for services instead of cash, the fair market value (FMV) of the property is income unless the property is subject to a substantial risk of forfeiture. The FMV of the property included in income becomes its basis to the employee (Code Sec. 83).[28] If the property is sold to the employee for less than its market value, the difference between the amount paid and the value of the property is also income.[29]

If the stock or other property is subject to a substantial risk of forfeiture, no amount is included in income until the year that the property becomes substantially vested as the result of the removal of the risk of forfeiture (Code Sec. 83(a); Reg. § 1.83-1(a)(1)).[30] However, any income (such as a dividend) from the property, or right to use the property, that is subject to a substantial risk of forfeiture is included in income as compensation when received (Rev. Proc. 80-11; Rev. Proc. 83-38). Property is considered substantially vested when it is either (1) transferable to another person who is not required to give up the property or its value if the substantial risk of forfeiture occurs or (2) no longer subject to a substantial risk of forfeiture (Code Sec. 83(c)(1); Reg. § 1.83-3).[31]

A substantial risk of forfeiture exists if the right to the property depends on (1) the future performance (or refraining from performance) of substantial services by any person, or (2) the occurrence of a condition related to the transfer (Code Sec. 83(c)(1); Reg. § 1.83-3). For property transferred on or after January 1, 2013, proposed regulations clarify that a substantial risk of forfeiture may be established only by these two principles; no other conditions should be considered. In order to determine if a condition related to the purpose of the transfer exists the proposed regulations would also clarify that it is necessary to determine (1) the likelihood that the forfeiture event will occur, and (2) the likelihood that the forfeiture event will be enforced (Prop. Reg. § 1.83-3(c)(1)). The proposed regulations may be relied upon for property transferred after May 30, 2012 (NPRM REG-141075-09, published in the Federal Register on May 30, 2012).

A taxpayer who receives property subject to a substantial risk of forfeiture may elect to include the FMV of the property (less any amount paid for the property) in income in the year that the property is received (Code Sec. 83(b); Reg. § 1.83-2; Rev. Proc. 2012-29).[32] Once the value of the property is included in income, any subsequent appreciation is taxed as capital gain when the property is disposed of, rather than as ordinary income.

Nonstatutory stock options, incentive stock options, and employee stock purchase plans are discussed further at ¶ 1923 and ¶ 1929. Capital gains rates are discussed at ¶ 1736.

Fringe Benefits, Generally. Certain fringe benefits may be excludable from an employee's gross income (¶ 863). Benefits such as air flights, cars, computers, educational benefits, entertainment (¶ 910), or travel (¶ 949) may be excludable as working condition fringe benefits (¶ 2188D). However, these benefits may be includible in income to the extent the employee uses them for personal purposes. An employee is generally required to include in income the amount by which the FMV of a fringe benefit exceeds the sum of: (1) the amount, if any, paid for the benefit, and (2) the

References are to Standard Federal Tax Reports; Tax Research Consultant; and Practical Tax Explanations.

[27] ¶ 5507.2942; COMPEN: 6,350; § 21,120

[28] ¶ 6380; SALES: 6,062; § 21,435.05

[29] ¶ 6384; SALES: 6,062; § 21,435.10

[30] ¶ 6380, ¶ 6381; COMPEN: 6,104; § 21,435.05

[31] ¶ 6380, ¶ 6383; COMPEN: 18,202; § 21,415.05

[32] ¶ 6380, ¶ 6382; COMPEN: 18,300; § 21,490.05

amount, if any, specifically excludable by some other provision of the law (Reg. § 1.61-21(b)(1)).

Employer-Provided Vehicle. The value of the personal use of an employer-provided car may be computed under annual lease value tables. The annual lease value of an automobile is computed by first determining the FMV of the automobile on the first date it was made available to any employee for personal use. Under a safe-harbor provision, the employer's cost can be substituted for FMV, provided certain conditions are met. Once the FMV is established, the Annual Lease Value Table, prepared by the IRS and reproduced below, must be consulted to determine the annual lease value that corresponds to the FMV (Reg. § 1.61-21(d)(2)(iii)). The annual lease values include the FMV of maintenance and insurance for the automobile but do not include the cost of gasoline provided by the employer. The fuel provided can be valued either at its FMV or at 5.5 cents per mile for all miles driven within the United States, Canada, or Mexico by the employee (Reg. § 1.61-21(d)(3)).

Automobile fair market value (1)	*Annual Lease Value (2)*
$ 0 to 999	$600
1,000 to 1,999	850
2,000 to 2,999	1,100
3,000 to 3,999	1,350
4,000 to 4,999	1,600
5,000 to 5,999	1,850
6,000 to 6,999	2,100
7,000 to 7,999	2,350
8,000 to 8,999	2,600
9,000 to 9,999	2,850
10,000 to 10,999	3,100
11,000 to 11,999	3,350
12,000 to 12,999	3,600
13,000 to 13,999	3,850
14,000 to 14,999	4,100
15,000 to 15,999	4,350
16,000 to 16,999	4,600
17,000 to 17,999	4,850
18,000 to 18,999	5,100
19,000 to 19,999	5,350
20,000 to 20,999	5,600
21,000 to 21,999	5,850
22,000 to 22,999	6,100
23,000 to 23,999	6,350
24,000 to 24,999	6,600
25,000 to 25,999	6,850
26,000 to 27,999	7,250
28,000 to 29,999	7,750
30,000 to 31,999	8,250
32,000 to 33,999	8,750
34,000 to 35,999	9,250
36,000 to 37,999	9,750
38,000 to 39,999	10,250
40,000 to 41,999	10,750
42,000 to 43,999	11,250
44,000 to 45,999	11,750
48,000 to 49,999	12,750
50,000 to 51,999	13,250
52,000 to 53,999	13,750
54,000 to 55,999	14,250
56,000 to 57,999	14,750
58,000 to 59,999	15,250

For vehicles having a fair market value in excess of $59,999, the Annual Lease Value is equal to: (0.25 × the fair market value of the automobile) + $500.

Cents-Per-Mile Valuation. The value of the personal use of an employer-provided vehicle may be determined by multiplying personal use mileage, provided it is at least 10,000 miles, by the standard mileage rate (55.5 cents per mile for 2012) if certain requirements are satisfied (Reg. § 1.61-21(e); Rev. Proc. 2010-51; Notice 2012-1). For a passenger automobile first made available to an employee in calendar year 2012, the FMV of the vehicle cannot exceed $15,900 and for a truck or van the fair market value cannot exceed $16,700 (Rev. Proc. 2012-13). Fuel provided by the employer must be valued separately, at either its FMV or at 5.5 cents per mile for miles driven in North America (Reg. § 1.61-21(d)(3)(ii)(B)).

Employer-Provided Commuting Vehicle. If certain requirements are met, the use of an employer-provided commuting vehicle is valued at $1.50 each way, i.e., to and from work, per employee (Reg. § 1.61-21(f)). Even if two or more employees commute in the vehicle, e.g., a car pool, each employee includes $1.50 each way in income. To qualify, personal use of the vehicle must be *de minimis* and the employer must require the employee or employees to commute to and/or from work in the vehicle for bona-fide noncompensatory business reasons.

Employer-Provided Transportation Due to Unsafe Conditions. If it is unsafe for an employee, who would normally do so, to walk or use public transportation to get to work and certain other requirements are met, the employee includes only $1.50 per one-way commute in income with respect to cab fare or an employer-provided vehicle (Reg. § 1.61-21(k)).[33]

Frequent Flyer Miles. The IRS will not try to tax the personal use of airline frequent flyer miles or other in-kind promotional benefits attributable to the taxpayer's business or official travel. Any future guidance on the taxability of these benefits will be applied prospectively. This relief does not apply to travel or other promotional benefits that are converted to cash, to compensation that is paid in the form of travel or other promotional benefits, or to other circumstances where these benefits are used for tax-avoidance purposes (Announcement 2002-18).[34]

Noncommercial Aircraft Flights. The value of personal flights, domestic or international, on employer-provided noncommercial aircraft is determined under an IRS formula (Reg. § 1.61-21(g)) that is based on Standard Industry Fare Level (SIFL) flight mileage rates, a terminal charge and the weight of the aircraft.[35] If a trip made primarily for business purposes includes business and personal flights, the excess of the value of all the actual flights over the value of the flights that would have been taken if there had been no personal flights is includible in gross income. If the trip is primarily personal, the value of the personal flights that would have been taken if there had been no business flights is includible in gross income (Reg. § 1.61-21(g)(4)).

No amount is included in income if the employee takes a personal trip on a noncommercial aircraft and at least one-half of the aircraft's seating capacity is occupied by employees whose flights are primarily business related and excludable from income (Reg. § 1.61-21(g)(12)).

Moving Expense Reimbursement. Moving expense reimbursements are generally excludable as a qualified fringe benefit (¶ 1076).

Vacation and Club Expenses. The portion of an employee's vacation, athletic club, or health resort expenses that is paid by the employer is taxable to the employee.[36]

Cafeteria Plans. Employer contributions under written cafeteria plans are excludable from the gross income of participants to the extent that they choose qualified benefits (¶ 861).

Occupational Disability or Insurance Benefit. Compensation received under a workers' compensation act for personal injuries or sickness and amounts received by a taxpayer under a policy of accident and health insurance are excludable from gross income (Code Sec. 104(a)(1); Reg. § 1.104-1) (¶ 851).

References are to Standard Federal Tax Reports; Tax Research Consultant; and Practical Tax Explanations.

[33] ¶ 5906; COMPEN: 33,152.20, COMPEN: 33,156, COMPEN: 33,160; § 21,130.10, § 21,130.15

[34] ¶ 5907.35; BUSEXP: 24,906.15; § 3,085

[35] ¶ 5906; COMPEN: 33,202; § 21,105.10

[36] ¶ 5507.47; COMPEN: 6,254; § 3,005.05

714. Compensation of Federal or State Employee. The salaries of all employees or officials of the United States government are taxed the same as those of other individuals (Code Sec. 3401(c)). This is also true for state and local government employees.[37]

715. Treatment of Excessive Salaries. Although an employer is denied a deduction for compensation paid to the extent that the payment is unreasonable, the full amount of the payment is includible in the recipient's income. In the case of an employee-shareholder, excessive compensation may be treated as dividend income. Excessive salaries are taxed only to the extent of the gain if the excess amounts are determined to be payments to the recipient for property rather than compensation (Reg. § 1.162-8).[38]

716. Social Security and Equivalent Railroad Retirement Benefits. A portion of a taxpayer's social security benefits or an equivalent portion of tier 1 railroad retirement benefits may be taxable (Code Sec. 86). The includible amount is the lesser of one-half of the annual benefits received or one-half of the excess of the taxpayer's provisional income over a specified base amount, at lower provisional income levels. However, at higher provisional income levels, up to 85 percent of the social security benefits may be included (see *85-Percent Inclusion*, following). The Form 1040 instructions contain a worksheet for computing the taxable amount.

Provisional income is the taxpayer's modified adjusted gross income plus one-half of the social security or tier 1 railroad retirement benefits. Modified adjusted gross income is the taxpayer's adjusted gross income plus any tax-exempt interest received. Adjusted gross income is determined without including any social security benefits or equivalent railroad retirement benefits and without subtracting certain items from gross income, including the interest exclusion that applies to savings bonds used to finance higher education (¶ 730A), the amounts excluded under an employer's adoption assistance program (¶ 2192A), the deduction for qualified U.S. production activities income (¶ 980A), the deduction for interest on education loans (¶ 1082), the amounts excluded under the foreign income exclusion (¶ 2402), and the amounts excluded for income from sources within Puerto Rico and the U.S. possessions (¶ 2414—¶ 2415). The base amount is: (1) $32,000 for joint filers, (2) $0 if married filing separately and the taxpayer lived with his or her spouse at any time during the year, and (3) $25,000 for married individuals filing separately who live apart from their spouse for the entire year and individuals filing as single or head-of-household (Code Sec. 86(c)).[39]

Comment: Absent further legislation, the tuition and fees deduction terminated for years beginning after December 31, 2011, and, therefore, will not impact modified adjusted gross income.

Example 1: John and Jane Mapes have an adjusted gross income of $24,000 for 2012. John, who is retired, receives social security benefits of $7,200 per year. The couple also receives $6,000 a year from a mutual fund that invests solely in tax-exempt municipal bonds. On their joint return for 2012, the Mapeses would make the following computation to determine how much, if any, of John's social security benefits must be included in their gross income:

(1) Adjusted gross income	$24,000
(2) Plus: All tax-exempt interest	6,000
(3) Modified adjusted gross income	30,000
(4) Plus: One-half of social security benefits	3,600
(5) Provisional income	33,600
(6) Less: Base amount	32,000
(7) Excess above base amount	1,600
(8) One-half of excess above base amount	800
(9) One-half of social security benefits	3,600
(10) Amount includible in gross income (lesser of (8) or (9))	800

References are to Standard Federal Tax Reports; Tax Research Consultant; and Practical Tax Explanations.

[37] ¶ 33,502; COMPEN: 6,650; § 3,005.05

[38] ¶ 8639; COMPEN: 6,400; § 9,305

[39] ¶ 6420; INDIV: 6,200; § 3,310

Although tier 2 railroad retirement benefits are not taken into account under the above rules, these benefits are taxed in the same manner as benefits paid under private employer retirement plans (Code Sec. 72(r)).[40]

85-Percent Inclusion. Up to 85 percent of an individual's social security benefits may be includible in gross income. The rules affect married taxpayers filing jointly with provisional income in excess of $44,000, married taxpayers filing separately and not living apart the entire year with provisional income of $0, and all other taxpayers with provisional income in excess of $34,000 (Code Sec. 86(c)(2)).[41]

Those who exceed the higher threshold adjusted base amounts must include in income the lesser of: (1) 85 percent of social security benefits or (2) 85 percent of the excess of provisional income over the threshold amount, plus the smaller of: (a) the amount that would otherwise be includible if the second threshold did not apply, i.e., the amount calculated under the 50-percent rules discussed previously, or (b) $4,500 ($6,000 for joint filers; $0 for filers who are married, not living apart from their spouse, and filing separately).

Example 2: Assume the same facts as in Example 1 above, except that the Mapes' provisional income is increased from $33,600 to $53,600. The includible amount is determined as follows:

(1) Provisional income	$53,600
(2) Adjusted base amount	44,000
(3) Excess of (1) over (2)	9,600
(4) 85% of amount in (3)	8,160
(5) Amount otherwise includible (½ of benefits in the Mapes' case)	3,600
(6) Base amount for joint filers	6,000
(7) Lesser of (5) or (6)	3,600
(8) Sum of amounts in (4) and (7)	11,760
(9) 85% of social security benefits	6,120
(10) Amount includible in gross income (lesser of (8) or (9))	6,120

Supplemental security income (SSI) payments are *not* treated as social security benefits that may be partially includible in gross income (Code Sec. 86)[42]

Individual Retirement Account (IRA) Contributions. Employed individuals who are covered by a retirement plan and who are receiving social security benefits must make a special computation to determine the amount of an allowable IRA deduction (¶ 2153A).

717. Tips. Tips received by cab drivers, waiters, barbers, hotel, railroad and cruise ship employees, etc., are taxable (Reg. § 1.61-2(a)(1)).[43] In the absence of proof of the actual amount of tips received, tip income may be reconstructed on the basis of average tips in a given locality for a given type of service.[44]

Tipped employees may use Form 4070A, which should be retained with the individual's tax records, to maintain a daily record of their tips. Cash, check, and credit card tips in excess of $20 per month are reported to the employer on Form 4070 or a similar statement by the 10th day of the following month (¶ 2605) (Code Sec. 6053) (IRS Pub. 531). An employer may also allow tips to be reported electronically (Reg. § 31.6053-1(b)(2)).

Form 4137 is used to compute an employee's liability for social security and Medicare taxes on monthly tips in excess of $20 that were not reported to the employer or on tips allocated by a large food and beverage establishment (¶ 2605). If an employer was unable to withhold social security and Medicare taxes on reported tip income, the uncollected taxes are shown on Form W-2 and reported as an additional tax on the

References are to Standard Federal Tax Reports; Tax Research Consultant; and Practical Tax Explanations.

[40] ¶ 6102; INDIV: 6,204; § 24,101

[41] ¶ 6420; INDIV: 6,200, INDIV: 6,202; § 3,310

[42] ¶ 6420; INDIV: 6,204; § 46,410.05

[43] ¶ 5506; COMPEN: 6,058; § 21,301

[44] ¶ 5507.4651; ACCTNG: 3,168; § 21,325.05

tipped employee's income tax return. Noncash tips and tips of less than $20 per month are not subject to social security and Medicare tax. These amounts, however, are subject to income tax and must be reported on the employee's return.

See ¶ 2605 regarding duty to report tips monthly to employer on Form 4070, ¶ 2606 regarding employer's withholding requirements, and ¶ 1341 regarding an employer credit for social security taxes on employee cash tips.

718. Pension. A pension paid to a retired employee is usually taxable compensation (¶ 2101) (Reg. § 1.61-11).[45]

719. Salary Payments to Employee's Survivor. The IRS and the Tax Court have generally taken the position that salary payments made to the surviving spouse of a deceased employee are taxable income, while several U.S. Courts of Appeal have viewed the payments as tax-free gifts.[46]

720. Compensation Other Than in Cash. When services are paid for in property, the fair market value at the time of receipt must be included in gross income (Reg. § 1.61-2(d)).[47] A note received in payment for services, and not merely as security for the payment, comes within this rule and its fair market value must be included in income. A portion of each payment received under the note is excludable from gross income as a recovery of capital.[48]

721. Group-Term and Split-Dollar Life Insurance. An employee must include in income the cost, based on the IRS uniform premium cost tables, reproduced below, of more than $50,000 of group-term life insurance provided by the employer (Code Sec. 79; Reg. §§ 1.79-1—1.79-3).[49] An employee's age is determined as of the last day of the employee's tax year.

> **Example 1:** X Corp. pays the premiums on a $70,000 group-term insurance policy on the life of its president, Fox, who is 51 years old at the end of 2012. The IRS-established uniform cost for $1,000 of group-term coverage for twelve months is $2.76 ($0.23 × 12) (Reg. § 1.79-3(d)(2)). The cost of the policy includible in Fox's gross income is computed as follows:

Total insurance coverage	$70,000.00
Tax-free insurance	50,000.00
Insurance coverage subject to tax	$20,000.00
Taxable cost of policy includible in Fox's gross income ($2.76 × 20)	$55.20

The $50,000 limit relates to the group-term life insurance coverage which the employee receives during any part of the tax year.

> **Example 2:** An employee's group-term life insurance noncontributory coverage for the first six months of the tax year is $50,000 and for the remainder of the tax year is $95,000. The cost of $45,000 of such insurance for the second six months of the tax year is includible in his or her gross income.

Any amount paid by the employee toward the purchase of group-term life insurance coverage on the employee's life during the tax year reduces the amount includible in gross income. If a discriminatory group-term insurance plan exists, the cost of the life insurance paid by the employer for the tax year is includible in the gross income of key employees and certain former key employees (Code Sec. 79(d); Reg. § 1.79-3(d)(2)).[50]

References are to Standard Federal Tax Reports; Tax Research Consultant; and Practical Tax Explanations.

[45] ¶ 5710; RETIRE: 42,050; § 3,040

[46] ¶ 6507.83; COMP: 48,206

[47] ¶ 5506, ¶ 5508; SALES: 6,062; § 3,005.10

[48] ¶ 5508.35; COMPEN: 6,106; § 16,505.25

[49] ¶ 6360, ¶ 6362, ¶ 6364, ¶ 6367; COMPEN: 48,106; § 21,005.10, § 21,005.15

[50] ¶ 6360; COMPEN: 48,110; § 21,005.20

Table 1—For Post-June 30, 1999 Coverage

Cost Per $1,000 of Protection for One-Month Period

Age	*Cost*
Under 25	5 cents
25 through 29	6 cents
30 through 34	8 cents
35 through 39	9 cents
40 through 44	10 cents
45 through 49	15 cents
50 through 54	23 cents
55 through 59	43 cents
60 through 64	66 cents
65 through 69	$1.27
70 and above	$2.06

Split-Dollar Life Insurance Plans Entered into After September 17, 2003. Regulations provide two different mutually exclusive regimes for taxing split-dollar life insurance arrangements: an economic benefit regime and a loan regime (Reg. §§1.61-22 and 1.7872-15). Ownership of the life insurance contract determines which regime applies. If the executive is the owner, the employer's premium payments are treated as loans to the executive. If the employer is the owner, the employer's premium payments are treated as providing taxable economic benefits to the executive. These benefits include the executive's interest in the policy cash value and current life insurance protection. The regulations also provide similar rules for split-dollar arrangements between family members, and other parties such as corporations and their shareholders.

Split-Dollar Life Insurance Policies Entered into Before September 18, 2003. Under a split-dollar plan, the employer and employee join in purchasing an insurance contract on the employee's life in which there is a substantial investment element (Code Sec. 61(a)(10)).[51] The employer pays that part of the annual premium that represents the increase in the cash surrender value each year, and the employee pays the balance of the annual premium. The employer is entitled to receive, out of the proceeds of the policy, an amount equal to the cash surrender value, or at least a sufficient part of the cash surrender value equal to the funds it has provided for premium payments. The employee's beneficiary as named by the employee is entitled to the rest of the proceeds.

The practical effect of this type of arrangement is that although the employee must pay a substantial part of the first premium, after the first year his share of the premium decreases rapidly, and the employee obtains valuable insurance protection with a relatively small outlay for premiums in the early years and at little or no cost in later years.

Prior to the release of regulations in September 2003, split-dollar arrangements were classified into two groups. Under the "endorsement system," the employer owns the policy and is responsible for the payment of the annual premiums. The employee is required to reimburse the employer for the employee's share of the premiums.

Under the "collateral assignment system," the employee owns the policy in form and pays the entire premium. The employer makes annual loans without interest, or below the fair rate of interest, to the employee of amounts equal to the yearly increases in the cash surrender value, but not exceeding the annual premiums. Under this system, the employee assigns the policy to the employer as collateral security for the loans, which generally are payable at the termination of employment or at the employee's death.

Valuation of current life insurance protection must be computed under Table 2001, reproduced below, or the insurer's lower published premium rates, but only for the purpose of valuing current life insurance protection for Code purposes.

References are to Standard Federal Tax Reports; Tax Research Consultant; and Practical Tax Explanations.

[51] ¶ 5502; COMPEN: 48,150; §21,005.20

Valuing Term Insurance Benefit. In the past, the IRS allowed the value of the insurance component to be determined using either the P.S. 58 rate table contained in Rev. Rul. 55-747[52] *or* the insurance company's *lower* published term rates if certain conditions were satisfied. The P.S. 58 rates were generally revoked, effective for tax years ending after December 31, 2001, or, at the taxpayer's option, for tax years ending after January 9, 2001, and replaced with Table 2001 rates that reflected the lower cost of term insurance protection (Notice 2001-10, revoked by Notice 2002-8). However, for split-dollar arrangements entered into before January 28, 2002, the P.S. 58 rates may be used to determine the value of current life insurance protection that is provided to an employee if the arrangement requires use of the P.S. 58 rates.

Taxpayers also may continue to determine the value of current life insurance protection by using the insurer's lower published premium rates that are available for all standard risks for initial-issue one-year term insurance. However, for arrangements entered into after January 28, 2002, and before the effective date of future guidance, for periods after 2003, the IRS will not consider an insurer's lower published premium rates to be available to all standard risks who apply for term insurance unless:

- the insurer generally makes the availability of such rates known to persons who apply for term insurance coverage from the insurer, and
- the insurer regularly sells term insurance at such rates to individuals who apply for term insurance coverage through the insurer's normal distribution channels.

Neither lower published premium rates nor Table 2001 rates may be relied upon to value current life insurance protection for the purpose of establishing the value of any policy benefits to which another party may be entitled (Notice 2002-59).

Arrangements Entered into Before Publication of Regulations. For split-dollar arrangements entered into prior to the 2003 regulations, the IRS will not tax the growth of the cash value during the term of the arrangement solely because the growth component is not payable to the employer (Notice 2002-8). Further, the IRS will not treat such an arrangement as having been terminated, thus resulting in a taxable transfer of property for so long as the economic benefit of the term insurance is being properly reported as income by the employee.

The IRS will also allow employer premium payments under a split-dollar arrangement entered into before the effective date of the regulations to be treated as loans to the employee. Loan treatment can be chosen even for an existing arrangement. However, if this is done, all previous employer premium payments must be treated as loans entered into at the beginning of the first tax year in which loan recharacterization is chosen.

Finally, for arrangements entered into before January 28, 2002, in which an employer has or is entitled to recoup all of its payments, the IRS will not assert that there has been a taxable transfer of property upon termination of the arrangement if (1) the arrangement is terminated before January 1, 2004, or (2) for all periods beginning after December 31, 2003, employer payments are treated as loans. All prior payments are recharacterized as loans entered into at the beginning of the year that option (2) is chosen.

Table 2001
Interim Table of One-Year Term Premiums for $1,000
Life Insurance Protection

Age	*Premium*	*Age*	*Premium*
0	$0.70	4	0.13
1	0.41	5	0.13
2	0.27	6	0.14
3	0.19	7	0.15

References are to Standard Federal Tax Reports; Tax Research Consultant; and Practical Tax Explanations.

52 ¶ 5508.24; COMPEN: 48,150; § 21,005.20

Age	Premium	Age	Premium
8	0.16	54	3.65
9	0.16	55	4.15
10	0.16	56	4.68
11	0.19	57	5.20
12	0.24	58	5.66
13	0.28	59	6.06
14	0.33	60	6.51
15	0.38	61	7.11
16	0.52	62	7.96
17	0.57	63	9.08
18	0.59	64	10.41
19	0.61	65	11.90
20	0.62	66	13.51
21	0.62	67	15.20
22	0.64	68	16.92
23	0.66	69	18.70
24	0.68	70	20.62
25	0.71	71	22.72
26	0.73	72	25.07
27	0.76	73	27.57
28	0.80	74	30.18
29	0.83	75	33.05
30	0.87	76	36.33
31	0.90	77	40.17
32	0.93	78	44.33
33	0.96	79	49.23
34	0.98	80	54.56
35	0.99	81	60.51
36	1.01	82	66.74
37	1.04	83	73.07
38	1.06	84	80.35
39	1.07	85	88.76
40	1.10	86	99.16
41	1.13	87	110.40
42	1.20	88	121.85
43	1.29	89	133.40
44	1.40	90	144.30
45	1.53	91	155.80
46	1.67	92	168.75
47	1.83	93	186.44
48	1.98	94	206.70
49	2.13	95	228.35
50	2.30	96	250.01
51	2.52	97	265.09
52	2.81	98	270.11
53	3.20	99	281.05

PS-58 Uniform One-Year Term Premiums for $1,000 Life Insurance Protection

Age	Premium	Age	Premium
15	$1.27	25	1.93
16	1.38	26	2.02
17	1.48	27	2.11
18	1.52	28	2.20
19	1.56	29	2.31
20	1.61	30	2.43
21	1.67	31	2.57
22	1.73	32	2.70
23	1.79	33	2.86
24	1.86	34	3.02

Age	Premium	Age	Premium
35	3.21	58	17.56
36	3.41	59	19.08
37	3.63	60	20.73
38	3.87	61	22.53
39	4.14	62	24.50
40	4.42	63	26.63
41	4.73	64	28.98
42	5.07	65	31.51
43	5.44	66	34.28
44	5.85	67	37.31
45	6.30	68	40.59
46	6.78	69	44.17
47	7.32	70	48.06
48	7.89	71	52.29
49	8.53	72	56.89
50	9.22	73	61.89
51	9.97	74	67.33
52	10.79	75	73.23
53	11.69	76	79.63
54	12.67	77	86.57
55	13.74	78	94.09
56	14.91	79	102.23
57	16.18	80	111.04
		81	120.57

722. Unemployment Compensation. Recipients of unemployment compensation benefits must include in income the entire annual amount of benefits received (Code Sec. 85).[53] Payments to laid-off employees from company-financed supplemental unemployment benefit plans (also referred to as "guaranteed annual wage" plans) constitute taxable income to the employees in the year received.[54] Payors report unemployment compensation on Form 1099-G.

723. Deferred Compensation. Not all compensation is paid in the year when services are rendered. Some may be deferred to a later year. There are two types of deferred compensation arrangements—funded and unfunded.

Funded Arrangements. If deferred compensation is contributed to a trust or is used to purchase an annuity or other insurance contract, the arrangement is funded and a participant may be subject to tax on the trust's income (¶ 2176).

Unfunded Arrangements. If the deferral takes the form of an employer's unsecured promise (not represented by a note) to pay compensation for current services at some time in the future, and if the employee uses the cash method of accounting, the amount promised is not includible in the employee's gross income until it is received or made available (¶ 906) (Rev. Rul. 64-279 and Rev. Rul. 70-435, modifying Rev. Rul. 60-31).[55] This rule is not altered merely because the employee agrees with the employer in advance to receive compensation on a deferred basis, so long as the agreement is made before the taxpayer obtains an unqualified and unconditional right to the compensation (*J.F. Oates*, CA-7, 53-2 USTC ¶ 9596).[56]

Unfunded Plans of State and Local Governments and Other Tax-Exempt Organizations. The above-described treatment of unfunded deferred compensation plans is modified for participants in plans maintained by state and local governments and other tax-exempt organizations, except for churches and qualified church-controlled organizations (Code Sec. 457).[57] If the rules discussed below are satisfied by such plans or arrangements, the deferred compensation is includible in income only when received

7 INCOME

References are to Standard Federal Tax Reports; Tax Research Consultant; and Practical Tax Explanations.

[53] ¶ 6410, ¶ 6412; INDIV: 6,208; § 3,075

[54] ¶ 5507.60; COMPEN: 6,064; § 5,035

[55] ¶ 21,009.1967; COMPEN: 15,050; § 25,610.15

[56] ¶ 21,009.135; COMPEN: 15,050; § 25,610.15

[57] ¶ 21,531; COMPEN: 15,150; § 25,310.10, § 25,610.15

by, or unconditionally made available to, a participant. For distributions from a government plan, the deferred compensation is included in income only when actually paid (Code Sec. 457(a)). If the rules are not satisfied, the present value of the deferred compensation is includible in gross income for the first tax year in which there is no substantial risk of forfeiture. Any interest or other earnings credited to the deferred compensation are taxable (under the annuity rules) only when made available. These plans are discussed further in ¶ 2161.

Unfunded Plans of Taxable Employers. An unfunded plan of a taxable employer is not subject to limitations similar to those that apply to a tax-exempt employer. As a practical matter, however, such a plan is limited to providing benefits in excess of those permitted under qualified plans or benefits for highly compensated and managerial employees. This is because any other unfunded deferred compensation plan of a taxable employer would be subject to ERISA participation, vesting, funding, and fiduciary standards (ERISA Secs. 4(b)(5), 201(2), 301(a)(3), and 401(a)(1)). For discussion of nonqualified deferred compensation plans, see ¶ 2175 and following.

Interest

724. Interest Generally. All interest received or accrued is fully taxable (Reg. § 1.61-7),[58] except interest on: (1) tax-exempt state or municipal bonds (¶ 729), (2) certain ESOP loans (¶ 2111), and (3) interest on U.S. savings bonds used to pay qualified educational expenses (¶ 730A). A cash-basis taxpayer is taxed on interest when received. Interest on bank deposits, coupons payable on bonds, etc., is considered available and taxed to a cash-basis taxpayer under the doctrine of constructive receipt and is taxed when credited or due (¶ 1533).

Interest earned on corporate obligations is generally taxed when actually received by, or credited to, a cash-basis taxpayer (Reg. § 1.61-7(a)). The same rule applies to interest on certificates of deposit, time obligations, and similar deposit arrangements on which interest is credited periodically and can be withdrawn without penalty even though the principal cannot be withdrawn without penalty prior to maturity. However, interest on a six-month certificate that is not credited or made available to the holder without penalty before maturity is not includible in the holder's income until the certificate is redeemed or matures (Rev. Rul. 82-42, amplifying Rev. Rul. 80-157).[59]

Increments in value on growth savings certificates are taxable in the year that the increase occurs because the certificate holder has a present right to redeem the certificate (Rev. Rul. 66-44).[60] Any increment in the value of life insurance or annuity prepaid premiums or premium deposits is income when made available to the policyholder for withdrawal or when credited against premiums payable.[61] Interest on a judgment is taxable even if the underlying award is nontaxable.[62]

When a bond with defaulted interest coupons is bought "flat," i.e., the price covers both principal and unpaid interest, any interest received that was in default on the date of purchase is not taxable but is a return of capital. If the bond is sold, this amount must be applied to reduce the basis, in turn increasing the gain or reducing the loss. If interest is received for a period which *follows* the date of purchase, it is taxable in full.[63]

Under the accrual method, interest is taxable as it accrues even though it is payable later. An exception to this rule is where it is discovered before the close of the tax year that the interest owed to the taxpayer will not be collected.[64]

State and Local Bonds; Tax-Credit Bonds. The federal government provides financial assistance to state and local governmental agencies by excluding from the gross income of the recipient the interest on certain tax-exempt state and local bonds (Code Sec.

References are to Standard Federal Tax Reports; Tax Research Consultant; and Practical Tax Explanations.

[58] ¶ 5702; INDIV: 12,052; § 3,101

[59] ¶ 21,009.3247; INDIV: 12,102; § 3,101

[60] ¶ 21,009.1142; INDIV: 12,102; § 38,315.15

[61] ¶ 5504.2665; INDIV: 12,118; § 3,101

[62] ¶ 30,575.166; INDIV: 12,112; § 3,805.35

[63] ¶ 5704.3062; INDIV: 12,252; § 19,315.20

[64] ¶ 5704.32; INDIV: 12,254; § 3,101

103).[65] The federal government also authorizes the issuers of such bonds to issue tax-credit bonds. A tax-credit bond essentially provides the issuer with a tax-free loan. The bond holders receive a tax credit on their federal income tax at the specified credit rate, instead of interest payments, and the issuer only has to repay the principal. The bond holders must include the credit amount in income, then claim the credit against tax on their return. In effect, the holders will usually receive the same net amount from the credit as they would receive in interest from a conventional state or local bond. See ¶ 1371 for discussion of tax credit bonds.

726. Mortgage Interest. The Supreme Court held that when a taxpayer forecloses on a mortgage and purchases the property at a foreclosure sale by bidding in property for the full amount of the mortgage plus accrued unpaid interest, taxable income is realized in the amount of the accrued interest even if the fair market value of the property bid in is less than the principal due on the mortgage (*Midland Mutual Life Ins. Co.*, SCt, 37-1 USTC ¶ 9114). Other courts have applied the same rule to *voluntary* conveyances by the mortgagor in consideration for the cancellation of the principal and interest of the mortgage. There is no interest income, however, in the case of such a conveyance if the property is worth less than the principal of the loan.[66] Nor is any income realized if only the principal of the mortgage is bid. For repossessions of real property, see ¶ 1841.

If a creditor bids in property for a debt, a loss may be deductible if the property is worth less than the debt.[67] Any such loss must take into account the basis and fair market value of the property bid in, and therefore a loss may exist even though the creditor bid in the property for more than the debt (*Hadley Falls Trust Co.*, CA-1, 40-1 USTC ¶ 9352).[68] The fair market value of the mortgaged property is presumed to be the bid in the absence of clear and convincing proof to the contrary (Reg. § 1.166-6). See ¶ 1145 for a discussion of the bad debt deduction.

Seller-Provided Financing. A taxpayer who receives or accrues interest from seller-provided financing must include on his or her income tax return the name, address and taxpayer identification number of the person from whom the interest was received or accrued (Code Sec. 6109(h)).[69] Failure to provide this required information will expose the taxpayer to information reporting penalties (¶ 2833).

727. Imputed Interest. Holders of bonds or other obligations issued at a discount may be required to include in income a portion of the discount as imputed interest in each year the obligation is held even though no interest corresponding to this amount is paid or accrued during the period (¶ 1952). Holders of notes or other debt instruments that were issued in exchange for property or services may be required to include in income imputed interest where no interest is provided in the debt instrument or the rate of interest is less than the applicable federal rate (¶ 1954). Other loans bearing interest at less than the applicable federal rate may also result in imputed interest income to the lender (¶ 795).

728. Bond Transaction Between Interest Dates. When a bond is sold between interest dates and an amount representing the interest earned up to the date of sale is added to the selling price, the buyer, upon later receiving the full interest payment, reports as income only the portion representing interest that accrued from the date of sale (Reg. § 1.61-7(d)).[70] Because the buyer has paid for the accrued interest as part of the sales price, it is a return of capital rather than interest income, except to the extent it exceeds the amount paid the seller (Reg. § 1.61-7(c)). The seller must include in income in the year of the sale the portion of the selling price representing interest accrued to the date of sale. This interest adjustment has no effect on the cost of the bond and apparently has no connection with the adjustment for amortizable bond premium (¶ 1967).

References are to Standard Federal Tax Reports; Tax Research Consultant; and Practical Tax Explanations.

[65] ¶ 6600; SALES: 51,050; § 3,105

[66] ¶ 5704.043, ¶ 5704.338; REAL: 6,202

[67] ¶ 10,750.10; BUSEXP: 48,204

[68] ¶ 10,670.123; BUSEXP: 48,204

[69] ¶ 36,960; FILEBUS: 12,106; § 18,515.05

[70] ¶ 5702; INDIV: 12,252.20; § 3,101

729. Private Activity Bonds. Although interest on obligations of a state or local government is generally excludable from gross income (Code Sec. 103(a)),[71] bond interest is not tax free when it is derived from nonexempt private activity bonds, state or local bonds that have not been issued in registered form, or arbitrage bonds (Code Sec. 103(b)).[72] Private activity bonds that qualify for tax exemption include exempt facility bonds (a category which includes enterprise zone facility bonds (Code Sec. 1394)), qualified veterans' mortgage bonds, qualified student loan bonds, qualified redevelopment bonds, qualified Code Sec. 501(c)(3) bonds, and qualified mortgage and small-issue bonds.[73] Qualified private activity bonds must meet the applicable volume cap requirements of Code Sec. 146[74] and the applicable requirements of Code Sec. 147[75] (Code Sec. 141(e)).[76]

Capital expenditures of public schools, except schools owned or operated by private, for-profit businesses, may be financed with private activity bonds. However, bonds issued after 2001 that are used to provide qualified public educational facilities can be treated as exempt facility bonds (Code Sec. 142(a)(13)). A qualified public educational facility is defined as a public school facility owned by a private, for-profit corporation pursuant to a public-private partnership agreement with a state or local educational agency (Code Sec. 142(k)(1)). In addition, facilities that can be financed with exempt facility bonds include qualified green building and sustainable design projects with bonds issued after December 31, 2004, but before October 1, 2012, and qualified highway or surface freight transfer facilities with bonds issued after August 10, 2005 (Code Sec. 142(a)(14), (a)(15), (l)(8), and (l)(9)).[77]

> **Comment:** Absent further legislation, the treatment of bonds used to provide qualified educational facilities under Code Sec. 142(a)(13) as exempt facility bonds is scheduled to expire for tax years beginning after December 31, 2012.

A special exception allows qualified scholarship funding bonds to be treated as state and local bonds (Code Sec. 150(d)).[78] Such bonds must be issued by a not-for-profit corporation that is established and operated exclusively for the purpose of acquiring student loan notes incurred under the Higher Education Act of 1965 and is organized at the request of a state or political subdivision. Also, a qualified volunteer fire department may issue bonds that will be treated as issued by a political subdivision if it is operated under a written agreement with a political subdivision to provide fire-fighting or emergency medical services (Code Sec. 150(e)).

Bonds issued by a governmental unit to fund the acquisition of existing electric and gas generating and transmission systems are generally treated as private activity bonds (Code Sec. 141(d)).[79]

Generally, income of state and local governments that is derived from the exercise of an essential governmental function is tax exempt. However, arbitrage restrictions limit the ability of governmental units to profit from the investment of tax-exempt bond proceeds (Code Sec. 148).

Specific tax-exempt private activity bonds, called Gulf Opportunity Zone bonds or GO Zone bonds, may be authorized after December 31, 2005 through December 31, 2011, for the purpose of financing construction or repair of real estate and infrastructure in the Gulf Opportunity Zone (Code Sec. 1400N(a)).[80] These bonds can be issued by Alabama, Louisiana, Mississippi, or any political subdivision of those states, and must meet the relevant state law bond issue requirements. GO Zone bonds can be treated as exempt facility bonds or as qualified mortgage bonds. A GO Zone repair or reconstruc-

References are to Standard Federal Tax Reports; Tax Research Consultant; and Practical Tax Explanations.

[71] ¶ 6600; SALES: 51,100; § 3,105.05

[72] ¶ 6600; SALES: 51,050; § 3,105.05

[73] ¶ 7702, ¶ 7740, ¶ 7780, ¶ 7810; SALES: 51,100; § 3,105.10

[74] ¶ 7850; SALES: 51,154; § 3,105.10

[75] ¶ 7860; SALES: 51,166; § 3,105.10

[76] ¶ 7702; SALES: 51,150; § 3,105.10

[77] ¶ 7740; SALES: 51,200; § 3,105.10

[78] ¶ 7930; SALES: 51,058; § 3,105.05

[79] ¶ 7702; SALES: 51,114; § 3,105.10

[80] ¶ 32,483; SALES: 51,222, SALES: 51,222.05; § 9,001

tion loan will be treated as a qualified rehabilitation loan for purposes of the qualified mortgage bond rules (Code Sec. 1400N(a)(7)). In addition, bonds of this type may be issued for any Midwestern disaster area, meaning parts of Arkansas, Illinois, Indiana, Iowa, Kansas, Michigan, Minnesota, Missouri, Nebraska, and Wisconsin in which storms, tornadoes, or flooding resulted in a federal declaration of major disaster. These bonds are known as qualified Midwestern disaster area bonds, and may be issued prior to January 1, 2013 (Heartland Disaster Tax Relief Act of 2008 (P.L 110-343), § 702, Division C).

Tax-exempt interest on private activity bonds is ordinarily considered a tax preference for purposes of the alternative minimum tax (AMT). Thus, the amount of interest received is taken into account in computing alternative minimum taxable income (AMTI) for AMT purposes. However, interest on bonds issued in 2009 or 2010, that would otherwise be considered private activity bonds for AMT purposes, is *not* treated as a tax preference item (¶ 1425) (Code Sec. 57(a)(5)(C)(vi)).

730. United States Savings Bonds. A taxpayer on the accrual basis must include each year the increase in value of a United States savings bond, issued at a discount and payable at par on maturity, in an amount equal to the increase in redemption value as indicated in the table of redemption values shown on the bond, even if the interest will not be received until the bond is surrendered (IRS Pub. 550).[81]

Using the cash method, none of the increase in value of the bonds issued at a discount (Series E and EE) or interest on Series I bonds is taxable until the earlier of (1) the year the bonds are cashed in or disposed of, or (2) the year in which they mature (IRS Pub. 550). A taxpayer on the cash basis *may,* however, elect to treat the annual increase in value of Series EE (former Series E) and Series I bonds as income in each year (Code Sec. 454; Reg. § 1.454-1(a)).

Taxable income is not recognized when Series EE or E bonds on which interest reporting was postponed are traded for Series HH or H bonds unless cash is received in the trade. Any cash received is taxed to the extent of interest earned on the Series EE or E bonds. When the Series HH or H bonds mature, or, if earlier, when they are disposed of, the difference between their redemption value and cost is reported as interest income. Cost is the amount paid for the Series EE or E bonds plus any additional amount paid for the Series HH or H bonds. A taxpayer may elect to treat all previously unreported accrued interest on Series EE or E bonds traded for Series HH bonds as income in the year of the trade.

Interest income from U.S. savings bonds is generally reported on Schedule B of the taxpayer's Form 1040 or Form 1040A.

730A. Exclusion for U.S. Savings Bond Income Used for Higher Education. An individual who redeems any qualified U.S. savings bond during the year in order to pay qualified higher education expenses may exclude from income amounts received, provided certain requirements are met (Code Sec. 135).[82] A qualified U.S. savings bond is any such bond issued after 1989 to an individual who has reached age 24 before the date of issuance and which was issued at a discount under 31 U.S.C. § 3105 (Series I or EE bonds). Qualified higher education expenses include tuition and fees required for enrollment or attendance at an eligible educational institution of either a taxpayer, the taxpayer's spouse, or any dependent of the taxpayer for whom the taxpayer is allowed a deduction under Code Sec. 151 (Code Sec. 135(c)(2)). Also, taxpayers are entitled to the exclusion if the redemption proceeds are contributed to a qualified tuition program.

A taxpayer must be able to verify the amount of interest excluded. Therefore, the following records should be kept:

- A written record of each post-1989 Series EE U.S. savings bond that is cashed in. It must include the serial number, issue date, face value, and total

References are to Standard Federal Tax Reports; Tax Research Consultant; and Practical Tax Explanations.

[81] ¶ 6602.585; INDIV: 12,150; § 3,115.10

[82] ¶ 7550; INDIV: 12,162; § 3,120.05

redemption proceeds (principal and interest) of each bond. Form 8818 may be used for this purpose.

- Some form of documentation to show that qualified higher education expenses were paid during the year. This could include canceled checks, credit card receipts or bills from the educational institution.

The amount that may be excludable is limited when the aggregate proceeds of qualified U.S. savings bonds redeemed by a taxpayer during a tax year exceed the qualified higher education expenses paid during that year (Code Sec. 135(b)(1)). Qualified higher education expenses must be reduced by the sum of the amounts received with respect to an individual for a tax year as a qualified scholarship that is not includible in gross income under Code Sec. 117, as an educational assistance allowance under certain chapters of title 38 of the United States Code, as a payment, other than a gift or inheritance, that is exempt from tax (such as employer-provided educational assistance), or as a payment, waiver, or reimbursement under a qualified tuition program (Code Sec. 135(d)(1)). The amount must be further reduced by expenses taken into account for the American Opportunity (or Hope; ¶ 1303) or Lifetime Learning credits (¶ 1303) as well as amounts taken into account in determining the exclusion for distributions from a qualified tuition program or the exclusion for distributions from an education savings account (Code Sec. 135(d)(2)).

The exclusion is subject to a phaseout in the years in which the bonds are cashed and the tuition is paid (Code Sec. 135(b)(2)(B)).[83] For 2012, the phaseout range is $109,250–$139,250 for joint filers and $72,850–$87,850 for all other filers (Rev. Proc. 2011-52).

Below the phaseout threshold, taxpayers may exclude bond interest up to the amount of qualified higher education expenses. Above the upper phaseout limit, no exclusion is allowed. For those falling within the ranges, the amount of interest excludable from income is reduced, depending on the taxpayer's modified adjusted gross income (AGI). Modified AGI (MAGI) is adjusted gross income *after* applying (1) the partial exclusion for social security and tier 1 railroad retirement benefits (Code Sec. 86), (2) amounts deducted for contributions to individual retirement arrangements (Code Sec. 219), and (3) adjustments for limitations on passive activity losses and credits (Code Sec. 469), and *before* taking into account (1) the interest exclusion under discussion, (2) the exclusion for qualified adoption expenses (Code Sec. 137; ¶ 2192A), (3) the domestic production activities deduction (Code Sec. 199; ¶ 980A), (4) the deduction for interest paid on qualified education loans (Code Sec. 221; ¶ 1082), (5) the foreign income exclusion (Code Sec. 911; ¶ 980A), and (6) the exclusion for income from sources within Puerto Rico and the U.S. possessions (Code Secs. 931 and 933; ¶ 2414—¶ 2415) (Code Sec. 135(c)(4)). This exclusion is not available to married individuals who file separate returns. The amount of excludable savings bond interest is determined using Form 8815, which is then filed with the taxpayer's Form 1040 or Form 1040A.

Comment: Absent further legislation, the tuition and fees deduction terminated for years beginning after December 31, 2011, and, therefore, will not impact modified adjusted gross income.

731. Issues of U.S. Obligations. With one minor exception, interest on all obligations of the United States and its agencies and instrumentalities issued after February 28, 1941, is subject to federal taxes to the same extent as private obligations (Reg. § 1.103-4).[84]

Dividends

733. Dividends. Ordinary dividends are fully includible in gross income. The term "dividend" or "ordinary dividend" for income tax purposes means any distribution made by a corporation to its shareholders, whether in money or other property, out of its earnings and profits accumulated after February 28, 1913, or out of earnings and profits

References are to Standard Federal Tax Reports; Tax Research Consultant; and Practical Tax Explanations.

[83] ¶ 7550; INDIV: 12,162; § 3,120.15

[84] ¶ 6606; SALES: 51,052; § 3,115.05

of the tax year (¶ 747) (Code Sec. 316(a); Reg. § 1.316-1).[85] If a dividend is in cash, the amount of the dividend is the amount of the cash. If the dividend is in both cash and noncash property, the amount of the dividend is the amount of the cash plus the fair market value of the property distributed (¶ 735). Special rules apply to distributions received by 20 percent corporate shareholders (Code Sec. 301(e)).[86]

Dividends are generally taxed as ordinary income. However, qualified dividend income received by an individual between January 1, 2003, and December 31, 2012, is taxed at capital gains rates, which are lower than those applicable to ordinary income (Code Sec. 1(h)(11)). Qualified dividend income is defined as dividends received during the tax year from a domestic corporation or a qualified foreign corporation (Code Sec. 1(h)(11)).[87] For 2008 through 2012, capital gains rates are zero percent for taxpayers in the 10- or 15-percent brackets and 15 percent for those in the higher tax brackets. See ¶ 1736 for discussion of capital gains rates.

> **Comment:** Absent further legislation, the taxation of qualified dividends at capital gains rates will not apply to tax years beginning after December 31, 2012. Therefore, for tax years beginning after December 31, 2012, dividends received by individuals, trusts, and estates from domestic or foreign corporations will be taxed at the applicable ordinary income tax rates.

Corporate stock dividends passed through to investors by a mutual fund or other regulated investment company, partnership, real estate investment trust, or held by a common trust fund are also eligible for the reduced rate assuming the distribution would otherwise be classified as qualified dividend income.

> **Comment:** Absent further legislation, for tax years beginning after December 31, 2012, the treatment of qualified dividend income passed through a regulated investment company (mutual fund), real estate investment trust, or other pass-through entity as qualified dividend income in the hands of recipients will expire.

Investments in tax-deferred retirement vehicles such as regular IRAs, 401(k)s and deferred annuities receive no benefit from the rate reduction. Distributions from these accounts are taxed at ordinary income tax rates even if the funds represent dividends paid on the stocks held in the account.

The reduced tax rates also do not apply to dividends paid by corporations such as credit unions, mutual insurance companies, farmers' cooperatives, nonprofit voluntary employee benefit associations (VEBAs), mutual savings banks, building and loan associations, and certain stock owned for short terms (Code Sec. 1(h)(11)(B)(ii)).[88] Special rules apply to Code Sec. 306 stock, which includes: (1) stock other than common stock received as a tax-free stock dividend, (2) stock other than common stock received in certain tax-free divisions or reorganizations, and (3) stock, including common stock, with a substituted or carryover basis determined by reference to other Code Sec. 306 stock.[89] Special rules also apply to dividends received from foreign corporations (Code Sec. 1(h)(11)(C)).[90]

> **Comment:** Absent further legislation, for tax years beginning in 2013, the capital gain tax regime will not apply to proceeds received by individuals upon the disposition of Code Sec. 306 stock (¶ 739).

Holding Period. To qualify for the lower rates, investors are required to hold the stock from which the dividend is paid for more than 60 days in the 121-day period beginning 60 days before the ex-dividend date. The ex-dividend date is the date following the record date on which the corporation finalizes the list of shareholders who will receive the dividend (Code Sec. 1(h)(11)(B)(iii)).[91]

References are to Standard Federal Tax Reports; Tax Research Consultant; and Practical Tax Explanations.

[85] ¶ 15,702, ¶ 15,703; CCORP: 6,050; § 26,201

[86] ¶ 15,302; CCORP: 12,160; § 26,601

[87] ¶ 3260; CCORP: 6,062, SALES: 15,202.55; § 26,101, § 26,205

[88] ¶ 3260; SALES: 15,202.55; § 26,101

[89] ¶ 15,450; CCORP: 24,152; § 26,101

[90] ¶ 3260; SALES: 15,202.55; § 26,101

[91] ¶ 3260; CCORP: 6,062; § 26,101

733A. Stock Dividends and Stock Rights. Generally, a stockholder need not include in gross income the value of stock received as a stock dividend (Code Sec. 305(a); Reg. § 1.305-1—Reg. § 1.305-8).[92] However, the following distributions by a corporation of its stock or stock rights are taxed as a dividend under the rules discussed at ¶ 733. These exceptions include: (1) distributions in lieu of money (Reg. § 1.305-2), (2) disproportionate distributions (Reg. § 1.305-3), (3) convertible preferred stock and debentures (Reg. § 1.305-6), (4) distributions of common and preferred stock (Reg. § 1.305-4), (5) certain transactions increasing a shareholder's proportionate interest (Code Sec. 305(c); Reg. § 1.305-7), and (6) dividends on preferred stock, unless the limited exception applies (Reg. § 1.305-5). An increase in the conversion ratio of convertible preferred stock made solely to take account of stock dividends or stock splits on the stock into which the convertible stock can be converted is tax free.

The basis of the stock, stock rights, or fractional shares acquired in a nontaxable distribution is an allocable portion of the basis of the stock on which the distribution was made. To determine the basis of the stock received in a tax-free distribution, the shareholder allocates a part of the basis of the stock previously held to the new stock or stock rights (Code Sec. 307(a)). The basis allocation is made in the proportion of the fair market value of the old stock to the fair market value of the new stock or stock rights on the date of the distribution (not the record date) (Reg. § 1.307-1).[93] If the fair market value of rights received in the distribution are less than 15 percent of the fair market value of the old stock, the shareholder takes a basis of zero in the stock rights unless the shareholder elects to allocate a portion of the basis of the old stock in a timely filed return for the year in which the rights were received. An election, once made, is irrevocable (Reg. § 1.307-2).[94]

Any corporation that receives an extraordinary dividend with respect to any share of stock that the corporation has not held for more than two years before the dividend announcement date must reduce its basis in such stock, but not below zero, by the untaxed portion of the extraordinary dividend received. A dividend is extraordinary under the two-year rule if it equals or exceeds 10 percent (5 percent in the case of stock preferred as to dividends) of the shareholder's adjusted basis in the stock (Code Sec. 1059).[95]

733B. Corporate Debt v. Equity. The determination of whether an instrument issued by a corporation is to be treated as stock or as evidence of indebtedness for federal income tax purposes (including whether a distribution is a dividend) is resolved by weighing various factors, such as the source of the payments made to the holder and whether there is an unconditional promise to pay a sum certain together with a fixed rate of interest. For instruments issued after October 24, 1992, the corporate issuer's characterization of the nature of the instrument, made at the time of issuance, is binding upon the corporation and all the holders, but not the IRS. However, interest holders are not bound by the issuer's characterization if they disclose any inconsistent treatment on their tax returns (Code Sec. 385(c)).[96]

The IRS closely scrutinizes instruments containing a combination of debt and equity characteristics which are designed to be treated as debt for federal income tax purposes (Notice 94-47). Of particular interest are instruments that contain such equity features as an unreasonably long maturity or an ability to repay principal with the issuer's stock. No deduction is allowed for any interest paid or accrued on a disqualified debt instrument issued after June 8, 1997 (Code Sec. 163(l)). The term means any debt that is payable in equity of the issuer or a related party or equity held by the issuer, or any related party, in any other person, specifically if: (1) a substantial portion of the principal or interest is required to be paid or converted, or at the issuer's or related party's option is payable in, or convertible into, equity of the issuer or a related party; (2) a substantial portion of the principal or interest is required to be determined, or may be determined at the option of

References are to Standard Federal Tax Reports; Tax Research Consultant; and Practical Tax Explanations.

[92] ¶ 15,400, ¶ 15,401–¶ 15,401H, ¶ 15,402; CCORP: 6,252; § 26,235.05

[93] ¶ 15,501; SALES: 6,302, CCORP: 6,250; § 26,235.10

[94] ¶ 15,501B; SALES: 6,302; § 26,235.10

[95] ¶ 30,020, ¶ 30,021; SALES: 6,358; § 26,201, § 26,245

[96] ¶ 17,340, ¶ 17,351.01; CCORP: 3,300; § 26,201

the issuer or related party, by reference to the value of equity of the issuer or related party; or (3) the debt is part of an arrangement designed to result in payment of the instrument with or by reference to the equity. An exception to the no deduction rule applies for certain instruments issued by dealers in securities (Code Sec. 165(l)(5)).

In addition, the IRS examines corporate transactions designed to produce interest deductions with respect to a related issuance of stock and to provide companies with significant tax advantages in satisfying their equity capital requirements (Notice 94-48). The overall substance of an arrangement whereby a corporation creates a partnership that issues notes to investors and uses most of its capital to buy stock of the corporation is viewed by the IRS as merely an issuance of preferred stock by the corporation. Thus, such a corporation could not deduct an allocable portion of interest expense on the note without an offsetting inclusion of dividend income.

734. When Is a Dividend Received. A dividend on corporate stock is taxable when, in an unqualified manner, it is made subject to the demand of the shareholder (Code Sec. 301; Reg. § 1.301-1(b)).[97] For cash-method shareholders, this generally occurs when payment is actually received. For accrual-method shareholders, this generally occurs when the dividend is constructively received or at the time of declaration. However, as an exception to the constructive receipt rule, a dividend is taxable when the check is actually received, even though it may be dated and mailed in an earlier tax year, unless the recipient requested delivery by mail in order to delay recognition of income. Therefore, both accrual and cash basis taxpayers essentially may use the cash method for including dividends in income and must report the income as received.[98]

Voluntary repayment of a dividend legally declared and distributed does not negate the receipt of dividend income by a shareholder.[99]

Dividends paid by regulated investment companies, i.e., a mutual fund, are not always taxable when received (¶ 2303).

Dividends and interest in excess of $1,500 must be reported on Schedule B of the taxpayer's Form 1040 or Form 1040A.

735. Dividend Paid in Property. If any part of a dividend is paid in a form other than cash, the property received must be included in gross income at its fair market value at the date of distribution, regardless of whether this date is the same as that on which the distribution is includible in gross income (Code Sec. 301(b)(1) and (3)).[100] When property is distributed to a corporate shareholder, the adjusted basis of the property in the hands of the distributing corporation at the time of the distribution, plus any gain recognized by the distributing corporation, is substituted for the fair market value of the property if the adjusted basis is less than the fair market value.

The amount of income realized on a distribution is reduced, but not below zero, by the amount of any liability to which property is subject or which is assumed (Code Sec. 301(b)(2); Reg. § 1.301-1).[101] The basis of property received in a distribution is the fair market value of such property (Code Sec. 301(d)).

If a distribution is paid in property having a fair market value in excess of the corporation's earnings and profits (¶ 747), the dividend is limited to earnings and profits, accumulated and current. The portion of the distribution that is not a dividend is applied to reduce the basis of the stock. If the amount of the nondividend distribution exceeds the basis of the stock, the excess is treated as a gain from the sale or exchange of the stock (Code Sec. 301(c)).

736. Gain or Loss to Corporation on Nonliquidating Distributions. A corporation does not recognize a gain or loss on the distribution of its stock, or rights to its stock, to shareholders. Similarly, a corporation generally does not recognize gain or loss on the distribution to its shareholders of corporate property (Code Sec. 311(a)).[102] A corpora-

References are to Standard Federal Tax Reports; Tax Research Consultant; and Practical Tax Explanations.

[97] ¶ 15,302, ¶ 15,303; CCORP: 6,060; § 3,030.05

[98] ¶ 21,009.1235; CCORP: 6,060; § 3,030.05

[99] ¶ 15,704.46, ¶ 15,704.473; CCORP: 6,058; § 3,030.05

[100] ¶ 15,302; CCORP: 6,150; § 26,205

[101] ¶ 15,302, ¶ 15,303; CCORP: 6,154; § 26,205

[102] ¶ 15,550; CCORP: 6,100; § 26,235.10

tion generally must recognize gain, however, when it distributes appreciated property to its shareholders in any ordinary, nonliquidating distribution to the extent that the fair market value of the property exceeds its adjusted basis (Code Sec. 311(b)).[103] Gain or loss rules applicable to corporations on liquidating distributions are discussed at ¶ 2257.

739. Disposition of Section 306 Stock. Code Sec. 306 is designed to prevent a stockholder from receiving a nontaxable stock dividend, other than common on common, or from receiving a stock distribution, other than common stock, in connection with a reorganization and disposing of it to avoid reporting dividend income.[104]

If Code Sec. 306 stock (¶ 733) is redeemed by a corporation, the amount realized is treated as a distribution of property to which Code Sec. 301 applies and, therefore, will be treated as ordinary income or as a taxable distribution to the extent that it is made out of earnings and profits (¶ 733, ¶ 742, and ¶ 747). If the stock is disposed of otherwise than by a redemption, the amount realized is treated as ordinary income to the extent that the amount realized is not more than the amount that would have been realized as a dividend if, instead of the stock, the corporation had distributed cash in an amount equal to the fair market value of the stock. Therefore, it would be ordinary income up to the stockholder's share of the amount of earnings and profits of the corporation available for distribution.

> **Comment:** Absent further legislation, for tax years beginning in 2013, the capital gain tax regime will not apply to proceeds received by individuals upon the disposition of Code Sec. 306 stock (¶ 733).

A shareholder who received a preferred stock dividend on common stock and who donated the dividend to a tax-exempt charitable foundation realized no income on the stock transfer. In addition, the donor would not realize any income from the later sale of the Code Sec. 306 stock by the foundation.[105]

740. Special Rules and Exceptions for Code Sec. 306 Stock. A holder of Code Sec. 306 stock (¶ 733) is not subject to the ordinary income recognition rule for a transfer of Code Sec. 306 stock if the disposition occurs as part of a transaction that cannot be used to bail out earnings and profits. The rules governing gain realized on Code Sec. 306 stock do not apply to a disposition:[106] (1) if it is not a redemption, (a) is not made, directly or indirectly, to a related person under the constructive ownership rules, and (b) terminates the entire stock interest of the shareholder in the corporation, including stock constructively owned; (2) if it is a complete redemption of all the stock held in the corporation by the shareholder or in redemption of stock held by a shareholder who is not a corporation and in partial liquidation of the distributing corporation; (3) if it is redeemed in a complete liquidation of the corporation; (4) to the extent that gain or loss is not recognized with respect to the disposition; or (5) if the IRS is satisfied that the distribution of the stock and the disposition or redemption, simultaneously or previously, of the stock on which the distribution was made were not in pursuance of a plan having as one of its principal purposes the avoidance of income tax. The sale of new preferred stock to an employees' trust was held not to be within the scope of Code Sec. 306(a).[107]

Dividends: Distribution in Redemption of Stock

742. Redemption of Stock as a Dividend. If a corporation cancels or redeems its stock in such a manner as to make the distribution equivalent to a dividend distribution, the amount received by the shareholder, to the extent that it is paid out of earnings and profits, is a taxable dividend (Reg. § 1.302-1).[108]

Whether a distribution in connection with a cancellation or redemption of stock is equivalent to a taxable dividend depends on the facts in each case. A cancellation or redemption of a part of the stock, pro rata among all the shareholders, will generally be

References are to Standard Federal Tax Reports; Tax Research Consultant; and Practical Tax Explanations.

[103] ¶ 15,550; CCORP: 6,152; § 26,210

[104] ¶ 15,450, ¶ 15,452; CCORP: 24,050; § 26,235.25

[105] ¶ 15,452.19; CCORP: 24,150; § 26,235.25

[106] ¶ 15,450; CCORP: 24,200; § 26,235.25

[107] ¶ 15,452.21; CCORP: 24,200; § 26,235.25

[108] ¶ 15,326, ¶ 15,330; CCORP: 21,102; § 26,305.05

considered as resulting in a dividend distribution (Reg. § 1.302-2).[109] A redemption can be treated as an exchange of stock, rather than as a dividend, if one of the following four tests is met (Code Sec. 302(b)):[110] (1) the redemption is substantially disproportionate with respect to the shareholder; (2) the redemption terminates the shareholder's entire interest in the corporation; (3) the redemption is not substantially equivalent to a dividend; or (4) the redemption is of stock held by a noncorporate shareholder and is made in partial liquidation of the redeeming corporation. Amounts received by a shareholder in a distribution in complete liquidation of a corporation are not equivalent to the distribution of a taxable dividend (Code Sec. 331).[111]

A distribution is substantially disproportionate as to a shareholder if, after the redemption, the shareholder owns less than 50 percent of the combined voting power of all classes of voting stock and there is an exchange of stock but not of a dividend. Further, the ratio of the shareholder's holdings of voting stock after the redemption to all the voting stock must be less than 80 percent of the ratio of the voting stock the shareholder owned immediately before the redemption to the entire voting stock in the corporation. In addition, a distribution is not substantially disproportionate unless the stockholder's ownership of common stock (whether voting or nonvoting) after and before redemption also meets the 80-percent test (Reg. § 1.302-3).[112]

If a shareholder is entirely bought out, the transaction is treated as an exchange of the stock, and no part of the distribution is taxed as a dividend (Reg. § 1.302-4).[113]

A distribution that is in redemption of stock held by a noncorporate shareholder in partial liquidation of the distributing corporation is a distribution in exchange for the stock and is not taxed as a dividend (Code Sec. 302(b)(4)).[114]

Stock Redemption Expenses. A corporation is not allowed a deduction for any amount paid or incurred in connection with any redemption of its stock or the stock of any related person. This restriction does not apply to deductions for interest paid or accrued within the tax year on indebtedness, deductions for dividends paid in connection with the redemption of stock in a regulated investment company, or deductions for amounts properly allocable to indebtedness and amortized over the term of the debt (Code Sec. 162(k)).[115]

743. Constructive Ownership of Stock. Certain provisions relating to corporate distributions and adjustments, such as distributions in redemption of stock noted at ¶ 742, treat an individual as constructively owning stock held by a related person. Under these constructive ownership rules an individual is treated as owning stock owned, directly or indirectly, by a spouse (if not legally separated under a decree of divorce or separate maintenance), children (including adopted children), grandchildren, and parents (Code Sec. 318(a)(1)).

Stock constructively owned by an individual under the family attribution rule is not treated as owned by that individual for the purpose of applying the constructive stock ownership rule to make another the owner of such stock (Reg. § 1.318-4).[116]

Stock owned, directly or indirectly, by or for a partnership, S corporation, or estate is considered as being owned proportionately by the partners, S corporation shareholders, or beneficiaries. Stock owned, directly or indirectly, by or for a partner, S corporation shareholder, or beneficiary is treated as being owned by the partnership, S corporation, or estate.

Stock owned, directly or indirectly, by or for a trust is considered as being owned by its beneficiaries in proportion to their actuarial interests in the trust. Stock owned, directly or indirectly, by or for a beneficiary of a trust is considered as being owned by the trust. However, a contingent beneficial interest of not more than 5 percent of the

References are to Standard Federal Tax Reports; Tax Research Consultant; and Practical Tax Explanations.

[109] ¶ 15,327; CCORP: 21,250; § 26,305.05

[110] ¶ 15,325; CCORP: 21,150; § 26,301

[111] ¶ 16,002; CCORP: 27,050; § 26,320.05

[112] ¶ 15,328; CCORP: 21,150; § 26,315.05

[113] ¶ 15,329; CCORP: 21,204; § 26,320.05

[114] ¶ 15,325; CCORP: 21,700; § 26,330

[115] ¶ 8500; CCORP: 21,450; § 26,365

[116] ¶ 15,905; CCORP: 21,502; § 26,310.30

value of the trust property is not to be taken into account (Code Sec. 318(a)(2) and (3); Reg. § 1.318-2).[117]

If 50 percent or more in value of the stock in a corporation is owned, directly or indirectly, by or for any person, that person is considered as owning the stock owned, directly or indirectly, by or for the corporation in the proportion that the value of the stock the person owns bears to the value of all the stock in the corporation. The corporation, on the other hand, is considered as owning the stock owned, directly or indirectly, by or for any person holding 50 percent or more in value of its stock, directly or indirectly (Code Sec. 318(a)(2)(C) and (a)(3)(C)).[118]

744. Redemption of Stock Through Use of Related Corporations. If stock of an issuing corporation is acquired by a corporation that is controlled by the issuing corporation, the amount paid for the stock will be a dividend by the issuing corporation, provided that, under the rules outlined at ¶ 742, this amount would be considered a taxable dividend. Also, when the stock of one corporation is sold to a related corporation, i.e., brother-sister corporations, the sale proceeds are considered as distributed in redemption of the stock of the corporation which bought it, governed by the rules at ¶ 742. If the sales are related, it is immaterial whether they are made simultaneously (Reg. § 1.304-2).[119] Whether the sales are related is determined upon the facts and circumstances surrounding all the sales. To the extent that a redemption involving related corporations is treated as a distribution under Code Sec. 301, the transferor and the acquiring corporation are treated as if the transferor had transferred the stock involved to the acquiring corporation in exchange for stock of the acquiring corporation, in a Code Sec. 351(a) nontaxable contribution of capital, and then the acquiring corporation had redeemed the stock it was deemed to have issued (Code Sec. 304(a)(1)).

745. Redemption of Stock to Pay Estate Taxes and Expenses. A distribution of property by a corporation in redemption of its stock that has been included in the gross estate of a decedent for estate tax purposes can qualify as an exchange to the extent that the amount of the distribution does not exceed the sum of the estate, generation-skipping transfer, inheritance, legacy, and succession taxes, including interest, on the estate, plus the funeral and administration expenses allowable as deductions from the gross estate for federal estate tax purposes (Code Sec. 303(a) and (d)).[120] For discussion of the estate tax, see ¶ 2901 and following.

To qualify for this treatment, the redemption must have been made not later than 90 days after the period of limitations on assessment of the federal estate tax, which is three years after the return is filed (Code Sec. 303(b)(1)(A)). When a petition for redetermination of an estate tax deficiency has been filed with the Tax Court, the redemption period is extended to any time before the expiration of 60 days after the decision of the Tax Court becomes final. A distribution made more than 60 days after the decision of the Tax Court becomes final can be timely, providing it is made within 90 days after expiration of the three-year period.[121]

In order for the redemption not to be treated as a taxable dividend, the value of the decedent's stock in a closely held company must exceed 35 percent of the gross estate, after the deductions for allowable funeral and administration expenses and losses (Code Sec. 302(b)(2)). The shares must be redeemed from a person whose interest in the estate is reduced by payment of estate, generation-skipping transfer, inheritance, and succession taxes or funeral and administration expenses. The value of these redeemed shares is limited to the sum of these deductible expenses.[122]

If stock in a corporation is the subject of a generation-skipping transfer occurring at the same time and as a result of the death of an individual, the tax imposed is treated as an estate tax for purposes of the redemption rules. The period of distribution is

References are to Standard Federal Tax Reports; Tax Research Consultant; and Practical Tax Explanations.

[117] ¶ 15,900, ¶ 15,902; CCORP: 21,508; § 26,310.20

[118] ¶ 15,900; CCORP: 21,510; § 26,310.15

[119] ¶ 15,377; CCORP: 21,450; § 26,340

[120] ¶ 15,350; CCORP: 21,650; § 26,340.05

[121] ¶ 15,353.80; CCORP: 21,650; § 26,340.25

[122] ¶ 15,353.30; CCORP: 21,650; § 26,340.15

measured from the date of the generation-skipping transfer, and the relationship of stock to the decedent's estate is measured with reference solely to the amount of the generation-skipping transfer (Code Sec. 303(d)).[123]

Dividends: Earnings and Profits

747. Sources of Distributions. To be subject to income tax as a dividend (¶ 733), a distribution received by a shareholder must be paid out of earnings and profits of the distributing corporation. A dividend is any distribution made by a corporation to its shareholders out of its earnings and profits accumulated after February 28, 1913, or out of the earnings and profits of the tax year, computed as of the close of the tax year without diminution by reason of any distributions made during the tax year, without regard to the amount of the earnings and profits at the time the distribution was made (Code Sec. 316; Reg. § 1.316-1).[124]

In order to determine the source of a distribution, consideration should be given first, to the earnings and profits of the tax year; second, to the earnings and profits accumulated since February 28, 1913, but only in the case when, and to the extent that, the distributions made during the tax year are not regarded as out of the earnings and profits of that year; third, to the earnings and profits accumulated before March 1, 1913, only after all of the earnings and profits of the tax year and all the earnings and profits accumulated since February 28, 1913, have been distributed; and fourth, to sources other than earnings and profits only after the earnings and profits have been distributed (Reg. § 1.316-2).[125]

If the current year's earnings and profits are sufficient to cover all distributions made during the year, each distribution is a taxable dividend. If the year's cash distributions, however, exceed current earnings and profits, a part of the earnings and profits must be allocated proportionately to each distribution, on the basis of the following formula: distribution × (current earnings and profits ÷ total distributions). The remaining portion of each distribution not covered by current earnings and profits is then treated as a taxable dividend to the extent of accumulated earnings and profits. If these are not sufficient to cover the remaining portion of any distribution, they are to be applied against each distribution in chronological order until exhausted.

748. Computation of Earnings and Profits. In computing earnings and profits, all income that is exempt from tax must be included, as well as all items includible in gross income under Code Sec. 61 (Reg. § 1.312-6).[126] Thus, exempt income such as life insurance proceeds and fully tax-exempt interest on state or municipal obligations is included. Similarly, cancellation of indebtedness income and intercorporate dividends are included. The starting point for the computation of earnings and profits is the corporation's taxable income, which is then adjusted to more accurately reflect true economic income available for distribution. This involves the different treatment of certain items from their treatment for tax purposes, including depreciation, depletion, certain reserves, and other items. In many cases, gain or loss from a sale or other disposition will be included in earnings and profits at the time and to the extent that it is recognized for tax purposes (Reg. § 1.312-6).[127] However, there are exceptions to this general rule, and the corporation's earnings and profits are very unlikely to be the same as the corporation's taxable income. As one example, income from installment sales is treated differently than earnings and profits (¶ 756). As another example, some items that are required to be capitalized for income tax purposes are deducted in the computation of earnings and profits (Rev. Rul. 60-123).

The general rule on the distribution of property, including cash, by a corporation is that the earnings and profits for future distributions are reduced by the amount of money distributed, the principal amount of any obligations of the corporation distributed, and the adjusted basis of any other property distributed (Reg. § 1.312-1).[128] If

7 INCOME

References are to Standard Federal Tax Reports; Tax Research Consultant; and Practical Tax Explanations.

[123] ¶ 15,350; CCORP: 21,662; § 26,340.05

[124] ¶ 15,702, ¶ 15,703; CCORP: 12,050; § 26,215

[125] ¶ 15,703B; CCORP: 12,050; § 26,215

[126] ¶ 15,611; CCORP: 12,102; § 26,601

[127] ¶ 15,611; CCORP: 12,100; § 26,610

[128] ¶ 15,601; CCORP: 12,152; § 26,615.05

appreciated property is distributed with respect to stock, earnings and profits must be increased by the amount of the gain realized upon the distribution even if the gain is not recognized for purposes of computing taxable income. There are special rules for distributions to 20-percent corporate shareholders.

749. Effect of Deficit on Earnings and Profits. Even if there is an operating deficit at the beginning of the year, total dividends paid are taxable to the extent of profits for the *entire* year (¶ 747) (Reg. § 1.316-1(e)).[129]

750. Effect of Loss on Earnings and Profits. A loss for a preceding year cannot be used to decrease the earnings and profits of the tax year (Reg. § 1.312-6(d)).[130]

751. Redemptions and Earnings and Profits. A corporation that distributes amounts in redemption of its stock can reduce its post-February 28, 1913, accumulated earnings and profits only by the ratable share of those earnings and profits attributable to the redeemed stock (Code Sec. 312(n)(7)).[131]

752. Effect of Reorganization on Earnings and Profits. When a corporate reorganization results in no recognized gain or loss, the company's life as a continuing venture does not stop, so that what were earnings and profits of the original company remain, for purposes of distribution, earnings and profits of the continuing corporation.[132]

753. Effect of Nontaxable Distribution on Earnings and Profits. Nontaxable stock dividends or stock rights do not reduce earnings and profits. The same rule applies to distributions of the stock or securities, or rights to acquire stock or securities, of other corporations and distributions of property or money when they were nontaxable to the recipient when made (Code Sec. 312(d)).[133]

754. Distribution Other Than a Dividend. Any distribution that is a dividend is included in gross income. The portion of a distribution that is not a dividend reduces the adjusted basis of the stock. Any excess of distributions over the basis is treated as a gain from the sale or exchange of property (Code Sec. 301(c)).[134]

755. Effect of Depreciation on Earnings and Profits. Depreciation claimed on the corporation's income tax return that is in excess of the straight-line method increases the corporation's current earnings and profits (Code Sec. 312(k)).[135] For tangible property placed in service in tax years beginning after 1986, the alternative MACRS method is used to compute depreciation in order to determine the corporation's earnings and profits (¶ 1247). For depreciable assets first placed in service after 1980, but before 1987, the adjustment to earnings and profits for depreciation is determined under the straight-line ACRS, using extended recovery periods (¶ 1252).[136] For assets placed in service before 1981, the amount of the depreciation deduction for the purpose of computing earnings and profits is generally the amount allowable under the traditional straight-line method, although a corporation that uses the permissible non-accelerated depreciation method, e.g., the machine-hour method, can use that method for earnings and profits purposes.

Also, in computing the earnings and profits of a corporation, any amount that can be deducted under certain provisions (listed below) can be deducted ratably over a period of five years, beginning with the year the amount is deductible under Code Sec. 179 or one of the other relevant sections (Code Sec. 312(k)(3)(B)).[137] This includes property that can be deducted under Code Sec. 179, or Code Sec. 179A for certain clean-fuel vehicles and refueling property placed in service before December 31, 2005, or Code Sec. 179B for certain environmental expenses paid or incurred after December 31, 2002, but not later than December 31, 2009, or Code Sec. 179C for certain refinery property

References are to Standard Federal Tax Reports; Tax Research Consultant; and Practical Tax Explanations.

[129] ¶ 15,703; CCORP: 12,050; § 26,605.05

[130] ¶ 15,611, ¶ 15,612.45; CCORP: 12,050; § 26,605.10

[131] ¶ 15,600; CCORP: 12,210; § 26,305.05

[132] ¶ 17,031.21; CCORP: 12,200; § 26,601

[133] ¶ 15,600; CCORP: 12,156; § 26,235.10

[134] ¶ 15,302; CCORP: 12,050; § 26,215

[135] ¶ 15,600; CCORP: 12,108; § 26,625.15

[136] ¶ 15,612.31; CCORP: 12,108; § 11,001, § 26,625.15

[137] ¶ 15,600; DEPR: 3,452; § 26,625.10

placed in service after August 8, 2005, or Code Sec. 179D for certain energy-efficient property placed into service after December 31, 2005, but before January 1, 2014, or Code Sec. 179E for 50 percent of the cost of advanced mine safety equipment placed in service after December 20, 2006, and before January 1, 2010.[138]

756. Effect of Installment Sales on Earnings and Profits. A corporation that sells property on the installment basis is treated for earnings and profits purposes as if it had not used the installment method (Code Sec. 312(n)(5)).[139]

757. Effect of LIFO Reserve Changes on Earnings and Profits. A corporation's earnings and profits generally must be increased or decreased by the amount of any change in the corporation's "LIFO recapture amount" at the end of each tax year (Code Sec. 312(n)(4)).[140] The term "LIFO recapture amount" means the amount, if any, by which the inventory amount of the inventory assets under the first-in, first-out (FIFO) method exceeds the inventory amount of the assets under the last-in, first-out (LIFO) method.

Business Income

759. Business Profit. The definition of gross income in Code Sec. 61[141] includes "gross income derived from business." Gross income derived from business is usually the same as gross profit, *not* gross receipts (Reg. § 1.61-3(a)). Gross profit is the total receipts from sales minus the cost of the goods sold. In the case of most mercantile businesses, cost of goods sold includes the purchase price of the article sold plus delivery costs, warehousing, etc. In a manufacturing firm it includes the entire factory cost—materials, direct labor, and factory overhead, including depreciation attributable to manufacturing processes—applicable to goods manufactured and sold. Cost of goods sold should be distinguished from deductions allowed by law. Thus, salaries, rent, etc., are deductions and *not* cost of goods sold.[142]

Damages for Lost Profit or Capital. Damage awards and amounts received in settlement of claims for business injuries that represent compensation for lost profits are taxable as ordinary income. This rule applies to proceeds from business interruption insurance, liquidated damages, and awards for breach of contract. Damages for injury to goodwill are a nontaxable return of capital to the extent that the amounts received do not exceed the taxpayer's basis in goodwill. Similarly, injury to or loss of capital is treated as a nontaxable return of capital to the extent of basis; any excess is treated as a capital gain if received for damage to a capital asset.[143] Punitive damages, such as treble damages under antitrust laws, constitute taxable ordinary income (Reg. § 1.61-14(a)).[144]

See ¶ 852 for damages arising out of employment discrimination claims.

760. Credits Included in Income. If the taxpayer claims a credit for gasoline and special fuels on Form 4136 (¶ 1329), the amount of the credit must be included in gross income to the extent that a business deduction for the products was taken.[145] A cash-basis taxpayer must claim the credit and include the amount in gross income in the same tax year. An accrual-basis taxpayer should include the credit in the gross income for the tax year in which the fuel was actually used.

A taxpayer who is eligible for the alcohol fuels credit (¶ 1365I) must include the allowable credit in gross income for the tax year in which the credit is earned (Code Sec. 87).[146] The total credit allowable is included even though the taxpayer cannot use the credit currently because of the credit limitation based on tax liability.

References are to Standard Federal Tax Reports; Tax Research Consultant; and Practical Tax Explanations.

[138] ¶ 12,120, ¶ 12,130; DEPR: 12,050; § 26,625.10

[139] ¶ 15,600; CCORP: 12,106; § 26,625.25

[140] ¶ 15,600; CCORP: 12,106; § 26,625.45

[141] ¶ 5502; INDIV: 6,050; § 3,010

[142] ¶ 5511; INDIV: 6,050; § 3,010

[143] ¶ 5900.14, ¶ 5900.15, ¶ 5900.26; INDIV: 6,354; § 3,810.20

[144] ¶ 5815; INDIV: 6,356; § 3,820

[145] ¶ 4150, ¶ 5602.35; INDIV: 6,376; § 13,540

[146] ¶ 6430; INDIV: 6,376

Rents and Royalties

762. Rents. Amounts received or accrued as rents in payment for the use of property must be included in gross income. The payment by a lessee of any expenses of a lessor is generally considered additional rental income to the lessor (Reg. § 1.61-8(c)).[147] Consideration received by the lessor for cancellation of a lease is in substitution for rental payments and, thus, not a return of capital. Any reduction in the value of property due to cancellation of a lease is a deductible loss only when fixed by a closed transaction.[148]

Expenses attributable to property held for the production of rents or royalties are deductible in computing adjusted gross income (¶ 1089).

Rental real estate expenses and income are generally reported on Part I of Schedule E of Form 1040.

763. Royalties. Royalties from copyrights on literary, musical, or artistic works and similar property or from a patent on an invention are includible in gross income (Code Sec. 61).[149] Royalties received from oil, gas, or other mineral properties are also includible in gross income.[150] For the treatment of timber, coal and iron ore royalties, see ¶ 1772. For the depletion allowance for royalties, see ¶ 1289.

Royalties are generally reported on Part I of Schedule E (Form 1040). However, Schedule C or Schedule C-EZ (Form 1040) is used to report royalties received by the holder of an operating oil, gas, or mineral interest and self-employed writers, inventors, artists, etc.

764. Improvements by Lessee. Ordinarily, no income is derived by a lessor by reason of acquisition of improvements made by the lessee upon termination of a lease (Reg. § 1.109-1).[151] This exclusion applies to improvements that revert to the lessor upon expiration of a lease as well as to those acquired by the lessor upon forfeiture of a lease prior to the end of the full term. When improvements are made in lieu of rent, however, the lessor has gross income to the extent of the fair market value of the improvements in the year they were made.[152]

Construction Allowances. A retail tenant that receives cash or rent reductions from the retail lessor with respect to a lease of 15 years or less entered into after August 5, 1997, does not include that amount in gross income (Code Sec. 110(a)). This exclusion applies only if the amounts are used for qualified construction or improvement to the retail space. The lessor must depreciate the improvement as MACRS nonresidential real property (¶ 1234 and ¶ 1240). If the improvement is disposed of or abandoned at the termination of the lease, the lessor must continue to depreciate after the improvement was disposed of or abandoned and may claim a gain or loss by reference to the remaining adjusted basis of the improvement (¶ 1118).

765. Lessor's Obligations Paid by Lessee. Property taxes paid by a tenant on behalf of a landlord are additional rent (Reg. § 1.61-8(c)).[153] When the taxes paid are income to the lessor, they may be treated as if paid by the lessor in determining their deductibility. If a lessee agrees to pay, in lieu of rent, a dividend on the lessor's stock or interest on its mortgages, the payments will result in rental income to the lessor.[154]

Farming Income

767. Farming As a Business. Income from farming is treated in the same way as income from any other business. Every individual, partnership or corporation which cultivates, operates, or manages a farm for gain or profit, either as owner or tenant, is designated as a farmer. A person who cultivates or operates a farm for recreation or

References are to Standard Federal Tax Reports; Tax Research Consultant; and Practical Tax Explanations.

[147] ¶ 5705, REAL: 12,050; § 3,020

[148] ¶ 5706.5162; REAL: 12,252; § 18,630

[149] ¶ 5502; SALES: 24,250; § 3,025

[150] ¶ 5502; FARM: 18,150; § 11,625.10

[151] ¶ 7021; SALES: 42,252; § 18,625

[152] ¶ 7020; REAL: 12,304; § 18,625

[153] ¶ 5705; REAL: 12,070; § 18,610.20

[154] ¶ 5706.564; REAL: 12,070; § 18,610.05

pleasure, and who experiences a continual net loss from year to year, generally lacks a profit motive and may not deduct the losses (¶ 1195).

In addition to filing Form 1040, an individual engaged in farming must file a Schedule F (Form 1040). Partnerships engaged in farming must file Form 1065, and corporations engaged in farming must file the appropriate Form 1120. The general rules for all cash-basis taxpayers also apply to a farmer on the cash basis (¶ 1515). An individual farmer must also file Schedule SE (Form 1040) for computing earnings from self-employment (¶ 2676).

Cash Basis. A farmer on the cash basis does not use inventories and must include in gross income all cash or the value of merchandise or other property received from the sale of livestock and produce that have been raised, profits from the sale of livestock or other items that have been bought, and gross income received from all other sources (Reg. § 1.61-4).[155] A cash-basis farmer may defer recognition of gain from the sale of a crop delivered in one year until the following year if a valid contract with the purchaser or the purchaser's agent prohibits payment until the following year, but not if the payment is deferred merely at the seller's request. If the sales contract states that the farmer has the right to the proceeds of the sale from the purchaser at any time after delivery of the item, the farmer must include the sales price in income in the year of the sale, regardless of when payment is received.[156]

Profit from the sale of livestock or other items bought by a farmer is computed by deducting the cost from the sales price. For the sale of animals that originally were bought as draft or work animals, or for breeding or dairy purposes and not for resale, the profit is the difference between the sale price and the depreciated basis of the animal sold.

A cash-basis farmer who receives insurance proceeds as a result of destruction or damage to crops may elect to include the proceeds in income in the year after the year of damage if the farmer can show that the income from the crops would normally have been reported in the following year. This includes payments received under the Agricultural Act of 1949, Title II of the Disaster Assistance Act or Title I of the Disaster Assistance Act of 1989 as a result of damage to crops caused by drought, flood, or other natural disaster, or the inability to plant crops because of such a natural disaster (Code Sec. 451(d); Reg. § 1.451-6; Rev. Rul. 91-55).[157]

A cash-method farmer who is forced to sell livestock due to drought, flood, or other weather-related conditions in an area designated as eligible for assistance by the federal government may elect to be taxed on the forced sale income (gain that normally would not have been realized in the year of the forced sale) in the following year if the farmer can show that the income from the sale of livestock would normally have been reported in such following year (Code Sec. 451(e)).[158]

Accrual Method. A farmer on the accrual method must use inventories taken at the start and the end of the tax year (Reg. § 1.61-4(b)).[159]

Although most farmers may use the cash method, the accrual method of accounting is required for certain farming corporations and partnerships and for all farming tax shelters including farming syndicates (¶ 2028 and ¶ 2032) (Code Sec. 447).[160]

Gross profit of a farmer on the accrual basis is calculated by: (1) adding the inventory value of livestock and products on hand at the end of the year with the amount received from the sale of livestock and products during the year, including miscellaneous receipts such as for the hire of machinery, all subsidy or conservation payments, and gross income from all other sources, and then (2) deducting from that total the sum of the inventory value of livestock and products on hand at the beginning of the year and the cost of livestock and products bought during the year (Reg. § 1.61-4(b)).

References are to Standard Federal Tax Reports; Tax Research Consultant; and Practical Tax Explanations.

[155] ¶ 5601; FARM: 3,056; § 36,001

[156] ¶ 21,009.453; FARM: 3,056; § 36,035

[157] ¶ 21,002, ¶ 21,018, ¶ 21,021.28; FARM: 3,202; § 36,020

[158] ¶ 21,002; FARM: 3,204; § 36,035

[159] ¶ 5601; FARM: 3,058, FARM: 3,100; § 36,315

[160] ¶ 20,700; FARM: 100, FARM: 3,060; § 36,315.10

Livestock raised or bought for sale must be inventoried (¶ 1569). Livestock bought for draft, breeding or dairy purposes and not for sale may be inventoried or, instead, be treated as capital assets subject to depreciation, if the method used is consistently followed from year to year. If inventoried livestock is sold, its cost must not be taken as an additional deduction in the return of income since the cost is reflected in the inventory. Sales of this livestock are generally reported on Form 4797.

Other Methods. Two other inventory methods are available to farmers—the farm-price method and the unit-livestock-price method (¶ 1569).

Income Averaging. An individual engaged in a farming business or fishing business may elect to average farm income over three years (Code Sec. 1301).[161] The tax imposed in any tax year equals the sum of the tax computed on taxable income reduced by the amount of farm income elected for averaging plus the increase in tax that would result if taxable income for each of the three prior tax years were increased by an amount equal to one-third of the elected farm income. Schedule J (Form 1040) is used to report the income averaging.

For income from the sale of farm property other than inventory, see the material beginning at ¶ 1701. For tax shelter farming operations, see ¶ 2032.

For expenses of a farmer, see ¶ 982–¶ 985. For the application of the uniform capitalization rules, see ¶ 999.

768. Patronage Dividend. A cooperative and its patrons are taxed in a way that the business earnings of the cooperative are taxable currently either to the cooperative or, through patronage dividends, to the patrons (¶ 698) (Code Secs. 1382 and 1385).[162]

769. Commodity Credit Corporation Loan. Income from the sale of a crop is normally reported in the year of the sale. If the farmer has pledged all or part of the crop production to secure a Commodity Credit Corporation (CCC) loan, however, the farmer may elect to report the loan proceeds as income in the year received rather than reporting the income in the year of the sale. IRS permission is not required to begin reporting CCC loans in this manner, but once a loan has been reported in income in the year received, all succeeding loans must be reported in the same way unless the IRS grants permission to change the method of reporting. The election is made on Schedule F (1040). The amount reported as income becomes the farmer's basis in the commodity and is used to determine gain or loss upon the ultimate disposition of the commodity (Code Sec. 77; Reg. §§1.77-1 and 1.77-2).[163] The IRS has adopted procedures for automatic approval in changing accounting methods for reporting CCC loans as loans rather than income (Rev. Proc. 2011-14).[164]

The repayment amount for a loan secured by an eligible commodity is generally based on the lower of the original loan rate or the alternative repayment rate, as determined by the CCC, for the commodity as of the repayment date. On repayment, therefore, a market gain may be realized if the loan is repaid when the alternative rate is lower than the original rate. When a CCC loan is repaid, regardless of the manner of repayment, the CCC is required to file an information return reporting market gain associated with the repayment (Code Sec. 6039J(a)). The CCC is to report market gain from the repayment of a CCC loan on Form 1099-G.

Alimony Payments

771. Classification. Alimony and separate maintenance payments are income to the recipient and are deductible by the payor if certain requirements are met (¶ 772) (Code Secs. 62(a)(10), 71 and 215).[165]

References are to Standard Federal Tax Reports; Tax Research Consultant; and Practical Tax Explanations.

[161] ¶ 31,787; FARM: 3,300; § 36,001

[162] ¶ 32,320, ¶ 32,360; FARM: 12,102; § 36,040

[163] ¶ 6300, ¶ 6301, ¶ 6302, ¶ 6304; FARM: 3,170; § 36,005.05

[164] ¶ 20,620.285; ACCTNG: 21,302.10; § 36,005.15, § 38,610.15

[165] ¶ 6002, ¶ 6090, ¶ 6094, ¶ 12,570; INDIV: 21,150; § 1,901

Alimony payments are taken as a deduction from gross income in arriving at adjusted gross income and therefore may be claimed by taxpayers regardless of whether they itemize.

772. Divorce and Separation Instruments. Payments made under a divorce or separation instrument are includible in the gross income of the recipient and deductible by the payor if the following requirements are met: (1) the payment is in cash or its equivalent, (2) the payment is received by or on behalf of a spouse under a divorce or separation instrument, (3) the instrument does not designate the payment as not includible in gross income and not allowable as a deduction under Code Sec. 215, (4) spouses who are legally separated under a decree of divorce or separate maintenance cannot be members of the same household at the time the payment is made, (5) there is no liability to make any payment for any period after the death of the payee spouse or to make any payment, either in cash or property, as a substitute for such payments after the death of the payee spouse, (6) the spouses must not file joint returns with each other, and (7) the payment is not fixed as child support (Code Sec. 71(a), (b), and (e)).[166]

A divorce or separation instrument is defined as: (1) a divorce or separate maintenance decree or a written instrument incident to such a decree, (2) a written separation agreement, or (3) a decree that is not a divorce decree or separate maintenance decree but that requires a spouse to make payments for the support or maintenance of the other spouse (Code Sec. 71(b)(2)).[167]

773. Year of Taxability or Deductibility. Alimony payments are generally includible in income in the year received (Code Sec. 71(a); Reg. § 1.71-1)[168] and are deductible in the year paid (Code Sec. 215; Reg. § 1.215-1),[169] regardless of whether the taxpayer employs the cash method or the accrual method of accounting. A recapture rule prevents front-loading of alimony payments (¶ 774).

774. Three-Year Recapture of Excess Alimony Payments. A special recapture rule applies to *excess* alimony payments (Code Sec. 71(f)).[170] Its purpose is to prevent property settlement payments from qualifying for alimony treatment. The rule requires the recapture of excess amounts that have been treated as alimony either during the calendar year in which payments began (the first post-separation year) or in the next succeeding calendar year (the second post-separation year). Excess alimony payments are recaptured in the payor-spouse's tax year beginning in the third post-separation year by requiring the payor-spouse to include the excess in income that year. The payee, who previously included the payments in income as alimony, is entitled to deduct the amount recaptured from gross income in his or her tax year beginning in the third post-separation year.

Excess alimony, the amount that must be recaptured in the third post-separation year, is the sum of the excess payments made in the first post-separation year plus the excess payments made in the second post-separation year.

The amount of excess payments in the first and second post-separation years is determined under a statutory formula. For the first recapture year, the excess payment amount is the excess, if any, of the total alimony paid in the first post-separation year over the sum of $15,000 and the average of the amount of alimony paid in the second post-separation year minus excess payments for that year and the amount of alimony paid in the third post-separation year. Thus, for the first post-separation year, the following formula would be used:

7 INCOME

References are to Standard Federal Tax Reports; Tax Research Consultant; and Practical Tax Explanations.

166 ¶ 6090, ¶ 6094; INDIV: 21,200; § 1,905.05

167 ¶ 6090; INDIV: 21,204, INDIV: 21,300; § 1,905.15

168 ¶ 6090, ¶ 6091; INDIV: 21,156; § 1,901

169 ¶ 12,570, ¶ 12,571; INDIV: 21,156; § 1,901

170 ¶ 6090; INDIV: 21,350; § 1,910.05

$$\text{excess payments} = \text{alimony paid in 1st year} - \left(\$15{,}000 + \frac{\left[\left(\text{alimony paid in 2nd year} - \text{excess payments in 2nd year} \right) + \text{alimony paid in 3rd year} \right]}{2} \right)$$

To determine the excess payments in the first year it is necessary to determine the excess payments in the second year. The amount of excess payments in the second year is the excess, if any, of the amount of alimony paid during the second year over the sum of the amount of alimony paid in the third year plus $15,000.

$$\text{excess payments} = \text{alimony paid in 2nd year} - \left(\text{alimony paid in 3rd year} + \$15{,}000 \right)$$

Once the excess payments for both the first and second post-separation years have been determined, the results are added together to determine the amount that must be recaptured in the third post-separation year.

Example 1: In 2011, Mr. Black makes payments totalling $50,000 to his ex-wife. He makes no payments in either 2012 or 2013. Assuming none of the exceptions set forth below apply, $35,000 will be recaptured in 2013. Mr. Black will have to report an additional $35,000 in income, while his ex-wife will be entitled to a $35,000 reduction in income.

Example 2: In 2011, Ms. Gold makes payments totalling $50,000 to her ex-husband. In 2012, she makes $20,000 in payments, but in 2013 she makes no payments. Assuming that none of the exceptions set forth below apply, the total amount that must be recaptured in the third year is $32,500. This represents $5,000 from the second year ($20,000 minus $15,000) and $27,500 from the first year. The amount recaptured from the first year equals the excess of $50,000 over the sum of $15,000 plus $7,500. The $7,500 is the average of the payments for years two and three after reducing the payments by the $5,000 recaptured for year two ($20,000 payment in year two plus $0 payment in year three minus the $5,000 that was required to be recaptured equals $15,000; divided by two equals $7,500).

IRS Pub. 504 contains a worksheet for computing alimony recapture.

Exceptions to Recapture Rule. The recapture of excess payments is not required if the alimony payments terminate because either party dies or the payee-spouse remarries before the end of the third post-separation year. The rules also do not apply to temporary support payments received under an instrument described in Code Sec. 71(b)(2)(C). In addition, they do not apply where the payments fluctuate because of a continuing liability to pay—for at least three years—a fixed portion of income from the earnings of a business or property or from compensation from employment or self-employment (Code Sec. 71(f)(5)(C)).[171] The rules also does not apply if alimony or payments decline by $15,000 or less over the three-year period.

775. Indirect Alimony Payments. Only one type of trust, the Code Sec. 682 trust, is contemplated in connection with divorce or separate maintenance under instruments executed or modified after 1984. When a beneficial interest in a trust is transferred or created incident to a divorce or separation, the beneficiary-spouse is entitled to the same treatment as the beneficiary of a regular trust, notwithstanding that the payments by the trust qualify as alimony or otherwise discharge a support obligation (Code Sec. 682).[172]

776. Child Support. Payments made that fix an amount or a portion of the payment as child support qualify as child support for tax purposes and are not deductible by the payor or taxable to the payee (Code Sec. 71(c)).[173] If any amount specified in the instrument is to be reduced based on a contingency set out in the instrument relating to a child—such as attaining a specified age, dying, leaving school, or marrying—the

References are to Standard Federal Tax Reports; Tax Research Consultant; and Practical Tax Explanations.

171 ¶ 6090; INDIV: 21,356; § 1,910.10

172 ¶ 24,860, ¶ 24,864; INDIV: 21,214; § 2,210.10

173 ¶ 6090; INDIV: 21,450; § 2,001

amount of the specified reduction is treated as child support from the outset. The same rule applies if the reduction called for by the instrument is to occur at a time that can clearly be associated with such contingency. Thus, payments that vary with the status of a child are not deductible.

Example: A divorce instrument provides that alimony payments will be reduced by $500 per month when a child reaches age 18. Under these circumstances, $500 of each payment is treated as child support.

778. Property Transfers Between Spouses or Former Spouses Incident to Divorce. No gain or loss is recognized to the transferor on a transfer of property, either outright or in trust, between spouses or between former spouses incident to divorce (Code Sec. 1041(a)),[174] nor is the value of the property includible in the gross income of the transferee (Code Sec. 1041(b)(1)). The transferee's basis is equal to the transferor's adjusted basis (Code Sec. 1041(b)(2)).[175] A transfer between former spouses is incident to divorce if it occurs within one year after the marriage ceases or is related to the cessation of the marriage (Code Sec. 1041(c)).[176]

Nonrecognition is not available to the transferor if the transferee is a nonresident alien (Code Sec. 1041(d))[177] or if there is a transfer in trust to the extent that liabilities assumed by the transferee, including liabilities to which the property is subject, exceed the transferor's adjusted basis in the property (Code Sec. 1041(e)). The transferee's basis is increased for any such gain recognized by the transferor.

Other Income

785. Taxation of Miscellaneous or Other Income. Several income items are considered miscellaneous or other income (IRS Pub. 525; Instructions for Form 1040).

Prizes and Awards. Prizes and awards, other than certain types of fellowship grants and scholarships (¶ 879) and limited employee achievement awards, are includible in gross income (Code Sec. 74(a)). Awards for religious, charitable, scientific, educational, artistic, literary, or civic achievement are excludable from the recipient's income only if the award is transferred unused by the payor to a governmental unit or a tax-exempt charitable, religious, or educational organization designated by the recipient. In addition, the recipient must be selected without any action on his or her part to enter the contest or proceeding and cannot be required to render substantial future services as a condition to receiving the prize or award (Code Sec. 74).[178] Thus, Nobel and Pulitzer prize recipients may not exclude from income the value of their awards unless these conditions are met.

Employee achievement awards, i.e., items of tangible personal property, are excludable from gross income only to the extent that the cost of the award is deductible by the employer. The awards cannot represent disguised compensation, and the excludable amount can total no more than $400 for nonqualified awards or $1,600 for qualified awards (¶ 919) (Code Secs. 74(c) and 274(j)(2)).[179]

Gambling Income and Illegal Gains. Gain arising from gambling, betting and lotteries is includible in gross income. A gain from an illegal transaction, such as bootlegging, extortion, embezzlement or fraud, is also includible.[180]

Gambling losses are discussed at ¶ 1121.

Bartering. The value of bartered services must be included in gross income, usually on Schedule C (Form 1040) or C-EZ (Form 1040). For example, if the owner of an apartment building permitted an artist to use an apartment in exchange for works of art, the building owner's income included the value of the art, and the artist's income included the fair rental value of the apartment.[181]

References are to Standard Federal Tax Reports; Tax Research Consultant; and Practical Tax Explanations.

174 ¶ 29,800; INDIV: 21,050; § 21,105.05
175 ¶ 29,800; INDIV: 21,062; § 21,105.05
176 ¶ 29,800; INDIV: 21,054; § 21,105.05
177 ¶ 29,800; INDIV: 21,050; § 21,105.05
178 ¶ 6200; INDIV: 33,150; § 3,060
179 ¶ 6200, ¶ 14,402; INDIV: 33,154; § 3,060.15
180 ¶ 5815; INDIV: 6,250; § 3,085
181 ¶ 5508.15; COMPEN: 6,110; § 3,085

If two individuals are members of a barter club and each agrees to exchange services, the value of the services received by each must be included in gross income. Barter clubs must report exchanges on Form 1099-B in accordance with the rules under Code Sec. 6045.[182] Trade or credit units used by a barter club to account for transactions are also includible in gross income when credited to the taxpayer's account.[183]

Cancelled Debt. In general, if a debt is canceled or forgiven, other than as a gift or bequest, the canceled amount must be included in income. Cancelled nonbusiness debt income is generally reported on Form 1040. Whether or not the interest portion of the canceled debt must be included in income depends on whether the interest would be deductible if paid. Exclusions are discussed in ¶ 885.

Insurance. Life insurance proceeds are generally excludable (¶ 803—¶ 809). However, if dividends received exceed the total net premiums paid for the contract, this is reportable income.

Recoveries. With the exception of state or local income tax refunds that are reported separately as income on Form 1040, the balance of all other recoveries (i.e. reimbursements for amounts received for items deducted in an earlier year) are reported as other income on Form 1040. Recoveries are discussed further in ¶ 799.

Jury Duty Pay. Jury pay is reportable other income on Form 1040 and may be deductible (¶ 1010).

Certain Taxable Distributions. Distributions from a Coverdell Education savings account (¶ 898) or a qualified tuition program (¶ 899) that exceed the amount used to pay for qualified education expenses and are not part of a qualified rollover are includible in income. A similar rule applies to distributions from health savings account (¶ 2197B) and Archer MSA(s) (¶ 2197C). Amounts from a health savings account because an individual failed to remain eligible during the testing period is also reportable income.

Below-Market Loans. If a below-market gift or demand loan is made, the forgone interest (at the federal rate) is interest income (¶ 795).

Income From the Rental of Real Estate. If property is rented for the purpose of generating income (i.e. renting a room in one's home), but the taxpayer is not in the business of renting, any rental income is considered other income. Expenses up to the amount of income are deductible.

Hobbies. Income from an activity not engaged for profit is considered other income. Losses and expenses are generally deductible (¶ 1195).

Recapture of Charitable Tax Benefits. The recapture of the charitable contribution deduction for property disposed of within three years of contribution (¶ 1062) or the recapture of a charitable contribution deduction relating to the contribution of a partial interest (¶ 1063) is considered other income.

Shareholder's or Employee's Bargain Purchase

789. Bargain Purchase. If a corporation transfers property to a shareholder, or an employer transfers property to an employee at less than its fair market value, whether or not the transfer is in the form of a sale or exchange, the difference may be income to the purchaser—as dividends in the case of the shareholder and as compensation for personal services in the case of the employee (Reg. § 1.61-2).[184] However, qualified employee discounts are excludable from income (¶ 863).

In the case of a purchase at less than fair market value by a stockholder, the shareholder is treated as having received a distribution from the transferor-corporation and is subject to the general tax rules for including it in income (Reg. § 1.301-1).[185] If there is a later sale of the property, the gain or loss is measured by starting with a basis

References are to Standard Federal Tax Reports; Tax Research Consultant; and Practical Tax Explanations.

[182] ¶ 35,920; FILEBUS: 9,260; § 3,085

[183] ¶ 5508.15; INDIV: 6,378; § 3,085

[184] ¶ 5506; COMPEN: 6,150; § 3,005.05

[185] ¶ 15,303; CCORP: 6,060; § 3,005.05

that is the amount paid for the property, increased by the amount previously included in income.

For treatment of securities transactions as potential income, see ¶ 1901.

Creditor's Financial Income

793. Creditor's Financial Income. A cash-basis creditor reports interest on loans or obligations as it is received. An accrual-basis creditor reports this type of interest as it is earned, i.e., over the term of the loan, as installment payments are due, etc., or when it is received if payment is received earlier than when due.

Rule of 78s. The IRS will *not* give any tax effect to a provision in a loan agreement that provides interest must be allocated in accordance with the Rule of 78s, because that method of allocating interest does not accurately reflect the true cost of borrowing. A limited exception permits the Rule of 78s method, however.[186]

Loan Commission. A loan commission is taxed to an accrual-basis lender in the year the loan is made. A commission deducted from the face amount of the loan is taxed to a cash-basis lender only when received upon payment of the loan or sale of the obligation.[187]

Below-Market Interest Loans

795. Imputed Interest on Below-Market Interest Loans. Under Code Sec. 7872,[188] loans that carry little or no interest are generally recharacterized as arm's-length transactions in which the lender is treated as having made a loan to the borrower bearing the statutory federal rate of interest. Concurrently, there is deemed to be a transfer in the form of gift, dividend, contribution to capital, compensation, or other manner of payment, depending upon the nature of the loan, from the lender to the borrower which, in turn, is retransferred by the borrower to the lender to satisfy the accruing interest (Code Sec. 7872(a)(1)). This rule applies to: (1) gift loans, (2) corporation-shareholder loans, (3) compensation loans between employer and employee or between independent contractor and client, (4) tax-avoidance loans, (5) any below-market interest loans in which the interest arrangement has a significant effect on either the lender's or borrower's tax liability, and (6) loans to any qualified continuing care facility not exempt under Code Sec. 7872(g).

In the case of a demand loan or a gift loan, the imputed interest amount is deemed to be transferred from the lender to the borrower on the last day of the calendar year of the loan. As for a term loan, other than a gift loan, there is an imputed transfer from the lender to the borrower, in an amount equal to the excess of the amount loaned over the present value of all payments required under the loan, which is deemed to have taken place on the date the loan was made.

Exceptions. A *de minimis* exception applies to gift loans totalling $10,000 or less between individuals if the loan is not directly attributable to the purchase or carrying of income-producing assets (Code Sec. 7872(c)(2)). There is also a $10,000 *de minimis* exception for compensation-related or corporation-shareholder loans that do not have tax avoidance as a principal purpose (Code Sec. 7872(c)(1)). Further, in the case of gift loans between individuals where the total amount outstanding does not exceed $100,000, the amount deemed transferred from the borrower to the lender at the end of the year will be imputed to the lender only to the extent of the borrower's annual net investment income (Code Sec. 7872(d)). If such income is less than $1,000, no imputed interest is deemed transferred to the lender.

The rule also does not apply to below-market loans owed by a facility which, on the last day of the year in which the loan is made, is a qualified continuing care facility, if the loan was made pursuant to a continuing care contract, and if the lender or the lender's spouse reaches the age of 62 before the close of the tax year (Code Sec. 7872(h)).

References are to Standard Federal Tax Reports; Tax Research Consultant; and Practical Tax Explanations.

[186] ¶ 9104.62; INDIV: 12,250; § 7,405.20

[187] ¶ 20,620.214; COMPEN: 6,302; § 18,510

[188] ¶ 43,956, ¶ 43,960; INDIV: 12,200; § 19,401

Rules exempt certain below-market interest loans by individuals to continuing care facilities made pursuant to a continuing care contract (Code Sec. 7872(g)).[189] Also, in the case of an employer loan to an employee made in connection with the purchase of a principal residence at a new place of work, the applicable statutory federal rate for testing the loan is the rate as of the date the written contract to purchase the residence was entered into (Code Sec. 7872(f)(11)).[190]

Recoveries

799. Tax Treatment of Recoveries. The receipt of an amount that was part of an earlier deduction or credit is considered a recovery and generally must be included, partially or totally, in income in the year of receipt (Code Sec. 111).[191] Common types of recoveries are refunds, reimbursements, and rebates. Interest on amounts recovered is income in the year of the recovery.

When the refund or other recovery is for amounts that were paid in separate years, the recovery must be allocated between these years.

> **Example 1:** Marcia VanNauker paid her 2012 estimated state income tax liability of $4,000 in four equal installments in April, June, and September of 2012 and in January of 2013. In May of 2013, she received a $400 refund based on her 2012 state income tax return. Because the tax liability was paid in two years, the amount recovered must be allocated pro rata between the years in which the liability was paid. Because 75 percent of the liability was paid in 2012, 75 percent of the $400 refund ($300) is for amounts paid in 2012 and is a recovery item in 2013 when received. The remaining $100 is offset against the otherwise deductible state tax payments made in 2013. Refunds of federal income taxes are not included in income because the taxes are not allowed as a deduction from income.

Itemized Deduction Recoveries. Recoveries of amounts claimed only as itemized deductions are not includible if the taxpayer did not itemize in the year for which the recovery was received. If a deduction is taken, the includible amount is limited to the amount of the deduction. Thus, the amount included is the lesser of the amount deducted or the amount recovered.

> **Example 2:** Brent Martin receives a $1,500 medical expense reimbursement in 2012 for expenses incurred in 2011. However, due to the threshold on medical expenses, he was able to claim only a $450 deduction in 2011. The amount that he must include in income in 2012 is $450.

For situations in which a high-income individual's itemized deductions are reduced by the smaller of three percent of adjusted gross income in excess of the threshold phaseout amount or 80 percent of allowable deductions (no phaseout applies in 2010, 2011, or 2012 (¶ 1014)), and, later, all or a portion of the previously deducted amount is recovered, the amount includible in income in the year of receipt is the difference between (1) the amount of the prior year's itemized deductions after reduction and (2) the deductions that would have been claimed (the greater of (a) itemized deductions after reduction or (b) the standard deduction) had the individual paid the proper amount in the prior year and not received a recovery or refund in a subsequent year (Rev. Rul. 93-75).

The total amount of all recoveries in a tax year must be included in the taxpayer's income if they are equal to, or less than, the amount by which the taxpayer's itemized deductions exceeded the standard deduction for his or her filing status in the prior year, and the taxpayer had any taxable income in the prior year. Recoveries of state or local income taxes are reported on a different line of Form 1040 than other recoveries; therefore, after the total amount that must be included has been determined, a further allocation may be necessary for reporting purposes.

IRS Pub. 525 contains a worksheet for computing the amount of a taxable itemized deduction recovery.

References are to Standard Federal Tax Reports; Tax Research Consultant; and Practical Tax Explanations.

189 ¶ 43,956; INDIV: 12,204; § 19,430.15

190 ¶ 43,956; COMPEN: 6,200; § 19,401

191 ¶ 7060, ¶ 7061; INDIV: 6,300; § 4,210

Special Rules for Recovery of State Tax Refunds. Taxpayers may elect, for tax years beginning after December 31, 2003, but before January 1, 2012, to deduct state and local sales taxes instead of state and local income taxes (¶ 1021) (Code Sec. 164). If the taxpayer pays state taxes and deducts those taxes on his federal income tax return in Year 1, and then in Year 2 receives a refund of the state taxes that were paid, the refund is not taxable if, in Year 1, the taxpayer (a) did not itemize his deductions, or (b) elected to deduct state and local general sales taxes instead of state and local income taxes.

If the taxpayer takes state and local income taxes paid in Year 1 as an itemized deduction on the federal income tax return for that year, and receives a refund in Year 2 of those state and local income taxes, the instructions to Form 1040 provide a worksheet to determine whether any of that refund is taxable.

If the amount of the Year 1 state and local income tax refund is more than the Year 1 state and local income taxes deducted minus the amount that could have been deducted as state and local sales taxes, then the taxpayer is directed to IRS Pub. 525 under "Itemized Deduction Recoveries." The publication provides that the maximum refund that must be included in income is limited to the excess of the tax that the taxpayer chose to deduct over the tax that the taxpayer did not choose to deduct.

Nonitemized Deductions and Amounts Recovered for Credits. Recoveries of amounts for which a nonitemized deduction or a tax credit, other than the foreign tax credit (¶ 2475) or investment tax credit (¶ 1365A), was claimed in prior tax years must be included in income to the extent that the deduction or credit reduced the taxpayer's tax liability in the year of the deduction (Code Sec. 111(b)). Special rules apply when a deduction reduced taxable income but the taxpayer's actual tax liability was not reduced because of the application of the alternative minimum tax (AMT) rules or because tax credits were claimed that reduced the tax liability to zero. If the taxpayer has both itemized and nonitemized recoveries, the amount includible in income is determined by first figuring the nonitemized recoveries, then adding the nonitemized recoveries to taxable income, and, finally, figuring the itemized recoveries.

Chapter 8
EXCLUSIONS FROM INCOME

Nontaxable Income

801. What the Law Excludes. Gross income includes all income that is not specifically excludable by statute or administrative and judicial decisions. In addition to the items listed in Code Secs. 101—140, the following are excludable from gross income:

(1) items of income that, under the Constitution, are not taxable by the federal government;

(2) items of income that are exempt from tax under the provisions of any act of Congress not inconsistent with, or repealed by, the revenue acts; and

(3) items that are nontaxable under the provisions of foreign tax treaties designed to prevent double taxation.

These exclusions and exemptions should not be confused with *deductions* from gross income, i.e., losses, expenses, bad debts, etc., which must be shown on a tax return. An exclusion generally does *not* have to be shown on a return.

Life Insurance

803. General Rule. Life insurance contract proceeds paid by reason of the death of the insured are generally excluded from gross income regardless of whether they represent the return of premiums paid, the increased value of the policy due to investment, or the death benefit feature, i.e., the policy proceeds exceeding the value of the contract immediately prior to the death of the insured.

It is immaterial whether the proceeds are received in a single sum or otherwise. However, if the proceeds are left with the insurer under an agreement to pay interest, any interest earned and paid is income to the recipient (Code Sec. 101; Reg. §§1.101-1(a) and 1.101-3).[1]

A contract must qualify as a life insurance contract under applicable state or foreign law and meet either a cash value accumulation test or a guideline premium/cash value corridor test (Code Sec. 7702).[2] If a contract does not satisfy at least one of these tests, it will be treated as a combination of term insurance and a currently taxable deposit fund, and the policyholder must treat income on the contract as ordinary income in any year paid or accrued (Code Sec. 7702(g)).[3]

Amounts received before the insured's death under a life insurance contract on the life of a terminally or chronically ill individual are also excludable from gross income. For chronically, but not terminally, ill individuals, the exclusion is subject to a maximum amount, adjusted for inflation, per day under policies that pay a set amount each day known as per diem policies. If a portion of a life insurance contract benefit is assigned or sold to a viatical settlement provider, any amount received from the sale or assignment is generally excludable (Code Sec. 101(g)).[4]

804. Company-Owned Life Insurance (COLI). In the case of a company-owned life insurance (COLI) contract issued after August 17, 2006, there is a limit on the amount of proceeds paid by reason of the death of the employee that may be excludable from gross income (Code Sec. 101(j)).[5] The applicable policyholder, the employer, or a related person generally may only exclude an amount not exceeding the total of the premiums and other amounts paid by the policyholder with any excess death benefits being includible in gross income.

Exceptions. The income inclusion rule does not apply to an amount received by reason of the death of certain insured individuals if notice and consent requirements are satisfied. This exception applies if the insured:

(1) was an employee of the applicable policyholder at any time during the 12-month period before the insured's death; or

(2) at the time the contract was issued with respect to the policyholder, was (a) a director, (b) a highly compensated employee under Code Sec. 414(q), determined without regard to the election regarding the top-paid 20 percent of the employees (¶2117), or (c) a highly compensated individual under Code Sec. 105(h)(5), who is in the group of the highest paid 35 percent of employees (¶2190A).

The inclusion rule also does not apply if certain notice and consent requirements are satisfied with respect: to proceeds that are paid to a member of the insured's family, as defined in Code Sec. 267(c)(4); to any individual who is the designated beneficiary of the insured under the contract, other than the applicable policyholder; to a trust established for the benefit of the insured's family or a designated beneficiary; or to the estate of the insured. In addition, the rule does not apply to proceeds that are used to buy an equity, capital or profits interest in the policyholder from the insured's heir.

An officer, director, or highly compensated employee within the meaning of Code Sec. 414(q) is an employee for these purposes. The exceptions to the inclusion rule apply only if the insured is a U.S. citizen or resident.

Notice and consent. To keep excess benefits from being included in income, the policyholder must satisfy the following notice and consent requirements before the issuance of the insurance contract:

(1) the employee must be notified in writing that the policyholder intends to insure the life of the employee and of the maximum face amount for which the employee can be insured;

References are to Standard Federal Tax Reports; Tax Research Consultant; and Practical Tax Explanations.

[1] ¶6502, ¶6503, ¶6508; INDIV: 30,302, INDIV: 30,306; §3,515.05

[2] ¶43,150; INDIV: 30,402, INDIV: 30,404; §3,505

[3] ¶43,150; INDIV: 30,412; §3,505

[4] ¶6502; INDIV: 30,350; §3,515.10

[5] ¶6502; INDIV: 30,304; §3,515.15

(2) the employee must provide written consent to being insured under the contract and acknowledge that such coverage may continue after the insured terminates employment; and

(3) the employee must be informed in writing that an applicable policyholder will be a beneficiary of any proceeds payable upon death of the employee.

Annual reporting. The policyholder of the contract must also satisfy annual reporting and record retention requirements (Code Sec. 6039I).[6] A policyholder satisfies the reporting requirements by attaching Form 8925 to the policyholder's tax return (Reg. § 1.6039I-1(b)).

805. Installment Options. If the beneficiary of a life insurance policy receives the proceeds in installments, any interest element in the life insurance proceeds accruing after the date of the insured's death is included in the income of the beneficiary (Code Sec. 101(d); Reg. § 1.101-4).[7]

807. Transfer of Policy Ownership. If a life insurance policy is transferred for valuable consideration, payments on account of the death of the insured are income to the transferee to the extent that they exceed the premiums and other consideration given for the life insurance policy (¶ 845). If the policy was transferred as a tax-free exchange or gift, however, the donor's investment basis in the contract is carried over to the donee, and the death benefits are excludable from gross income. The benefits are also excludable if such a transfer of the contract was to the insured, a partner of the insured, a partnership including the insured, or a corporation of which the insured was a shareholder or officer (Code Sec. 101(a)(2); Reg. § 1.101-1(b)).[8]

809. Dividends. Amounts received from an annuity policy prior to the annuity starting date in the nature of dividends, or return of premiums or other consideration, are not taxable until the amounts received exceed the aggregate of premiums or other consideration paid or deemed to have been paid for the annuity. However, amounts received in the nature of dividends after the start date of the annuity may be fully taxable (¶ 823) (Code Sec. 72(e); Reg. § 1.72-11(b)).[9]

Certain Death Benefits

813. Certain Death Benefits. The amount paid as a survivor annuity to the spouse, former spouse, or child of a public safety officer killed in the line of duty is excludable from the recipient's gross income if the annuity is provided under a governmental plan (Code Sec. 101(h)).[10]

Gross income also does not include amounts paid by an employer by reason of the death of an employee who is a specified terrorist victim or an astronaut killed in the line of duty. The exclusion applies to death benefits from a qualified plan that satisfy the incidental death benefit rule (Code Sec. 101(i)).[11]

Annuity

817. Exclusion Ratio. Amounts received as an annuity under any annuity, endowment, or life insurance contract, and paid out for reasons other than death of the insured, are excludable from income to the extent of the taxpayer's basis in the contract. The tax-free portion of the income is spread evenly over the annuitant's life expectancy. However, for contracts with an annuity starting date before 1987, the exclusion remains the same no matter how long the annuitant lives. These annuity rules also apply to contracts whose payments are made over a prescribed number of years (Code Sec. 72; Reg. §§ 1.72-1—1.72-11).[12] For Armed Forces personnel annuities, see ¶ 891.

References are to Standard Federal Tax Reports; Tax Research Consultant; and Practical Tax Explanations.

[6] ¶ 35,699C; FILEBUS: 9,376; § 3,515.15

[7] ¶ 6502, ¶ 6510; INDIV: 30,308; § 3,515.05b

[8] ¶ 6502, ¶ 6503; INDIV: 30,310; § 3,515.05

[9] ¶ 6102, ¶ 6113; COMPEN: 48,058; § 3,515.05

[10] ¶ 6502; INDIV: 33,560; § 3,530.05

[11] ¶ 6502; INDIV: 33,562; § 3,530.10

[12] ¶ 6102; ¶ 6102B–¶ 6113; INDIV: 30,056; § 3,210

A contract, with certain exceptions, will not be treated as an annuity contract unless it provides that: (1) if the contract holder dies on or after the annuity starting date, but before the entire interest in the contract is distributed, the remainder must be distributed at least as rapidly as under the method used as of the day the holder died, and (2) the entire interest in the contract must be distributed within five years of the holder's death (Code Sec. 72(s)).[13]

To determine the portion of the annuity that is excludable from the recipient's gross income, an "exclusion ratio" is to be determined for each contract (¶ 819). In general, this ratio is determined by dividing the "investment in the contract" by the "expected return" (Reg. § 1.72-2). The exclusion ratio is then applied to the total amount received as an annuity during the tax year. Any excess amount over the portion determined by the application of the exclusion ratio is includible in the recipient's gross income (Reg. § 1.72-4). In the case of distributions from an individual retirement arrangement (IRA), the exclusion ratio is determined by dividing the employee's total nondeductible contributions by the balance of the account. All of an individual's IRAs and distributions during a year must be aggregated (¶ 2153G). A nontaxable distribution of IRA assets is reported on Form 8606 (Instructions to Form 8606; IRS Pub. 590).

For annuities with a starting date after 1986, the exclusion of a portion of each annuity payment cannot be continued indefinitely. Once the total of all exclusions taken for payments under the annuity contract equals the investment in the contract, all subsequent payments are included in income in full (Code Sec. 72(b)(2)).[14] On the other hand, if the annuitant dies before the investment in the contract is fully recovered tax free through the annuity exclusion, a deduction is provided for the annuitant's last year in an amount equal to the unrecovered portion of the investment (Code Sec. 72(b)(3)).[15]

Partial Annuitization of Annuity Contracts. For amounts received in tax years beginning after 2010, if any amount is received as an annuity for a period of 10 years or more, or for the lives of one or more individuals, under any portion of an annuity, endowment, or life insurance contract, then that portion of the contract is treated as a separate contract (Code Sec. 72(a)(2)). Thus, a portion of the contract may be annuitized, while the balance is not annuitized. In such cases, the investment in the contract is allocated on a pro rata basis between each portion of the contract from which amounts received as an annuity and the portion of the contract from which amounts are not received as an annuity. The allocation is made for purposes of applying:

(1) the rules relating to the exclusion ratio;

(2) the definitions of the investment in the contract, the expected return, and the annuity starting date; and

(3) the rules for amounts not received as an annuity.

In addition, a separate annuity starting date is determined with respect to each portion of the contract from which amounts are received as an annuity.

819. The "Exclusion Ratio" Formula. The excludable portion of an annuity payment is the annuity payment multiplied by the "exclusion ratio" (¶ 817). The remainder is taxable to the recipient, whether it is the primary annuitant or a secondary annuitant under a joint or joint and survivor annuity. The exclusion ratio is the "investment in the contract" (¶ 821) divided by the "expected return" (¶ 825) under the contract as of the "annuity starting date" (¶ 823). For example, if, as of the annuity starting date, a taxpayer's investment in an annuity contract is $6,000 and his expected return is $10,000, his exclusion ratio is $6,000/$10,000, or 60 percent. If the taxpayer receives a monthly annuity payment of $200, the monthly exclusion is $120 ($200 × 60 percent).

821. "Investment in the Contract" Defined. In determining the exclusion ratio for an annuity (¶ 819), the "investment in the contract" generally is the total amount of premiums or other consideration paid for the contract, less amounts, if any, received

References are to Standard Federal Tax Reports; Tax Research Consultant; and Practical Tax Explanations.

[13] ¶ 6102; INDIV: 30,206; § 3,260.05

[14] ¶ 6102; INDIV: 30,056; § 3,210

[15] ¶ 6102; INDIV: 30,054; § 3,260.15

before the "annuity starting date" and not included in gross income (Code Sec. 72(c)(1); Reg. §1.72-6).[16] However, owner-employees may not include the deductible costs of purchasing insurance as part of their investment in the contract (Code Sec. 72(m)(2); Reg. §1.72-17A(c)). A special adjustment is provided for a refund annuity (¶837). For special rules for computing an employee's investment in an annuity received through an employer, see ¶2124A.

Nonresident Aliens. Certain employer or employee contributions made by or on behalf of nonresident aliens are not considered part of the individual's investment in the contract. The excluded contributions are those:

(1) made with respect to compensation for labor or services by an employee who was a nonresident alien at the time the labor or services were performed and treated as from sources outside the United States; and

(2) that were not subject to tax by the United States or a foreign country but would have been subject to tax if paid in cash.

Thus, contributions to a foreign pension plan are included in the calculation of the participant's basis only if the participant has been subject to tax on the contribution by the United States or a foreign country (Code Sec. 72(w)).[17]

823. "Annuity Starting Date" Defined. In determining the exclusion ratio for an annuity (¶819), the "annuity starting date" is the first day of the first period for which an amount is received as an annuity under the contract. This is the later of:

(1) the date upon which the obligations of the contract become fixed; or

(2) the first day of the period (year, half-year, quarter, or month, depending on whether the payments are made annually, semi-annually, quarterly, or monthly) that ends on the date of the first annuity payment (Code Sec. 72(c)(4); Reg. §1.72-4(b)).[18]

825. "Expected Return" Computation. In determining the exclusion ratio for an annuity (¶819), the "expected return" under the contract is limited to amounts receivable as an annuity or as annuities. If no life expectancy is involved, as in the case of installment payments for a fixed number of years, the expected return is found by totaling the amounts to be received (Code Sec. 72(c)(3); Reg. §1.72-5(a) and (c)).[19] To determine the expected return under contracts involving life expectancy, actuarial tables prescribed by the IRS must be used. The tables provide a multiplier, based on life expectancy, that is applied to the annual payment to obtain the expected return under the contract (Reg. §1.72-9).

The expected return will vary, depending on when contributions were made and when amounts were received as an annuity. Gender-neutral tables must be used if the total investment in the contract is made after June 30, 1986. If there was an investment in the contract as of June 30, 1986, and there has been a further investment in the contract after that date, an individual may, instead of using the gender-neutral tables, elect to calculate the exclusion under a special rule. Under this rule, an exclusion amount is calculated using the gender-based tables—as if the investment in the contract as of June 30, 1986, were the only investment in the contract. Then a second exclusion is calculated, using the gender-neutral tables, as if the post-June 30, 1986, investment were the only investment. The two exclusion amounts are then added together to produce the final exclusion. Although, generally, the gender-based annuity tables formerly in effect must still be used if all contributions were made prior to June 30, 1986, an election may be made to use the updated tables if the annuity payments are received after June 30, 1986 (Reg. §§1.72-5 and 1.72-6).[20]

For use in the following examples, a portion of Table V (gender-neutral for post-June 30, 1986, investment in the contract (Reg. §1.72-9))[21] for ordinary life annuities for one life is reproduced below:

References are to Standard Federal Tax Reports; Tax Research Consultant; and Practical Tax Explanations.

[16] ¶6102, ¶6107; INDIV: 30,060; §3,220.05

[17] ¶6102; RETIRE: 42,304.05; §3,220.05

[18] ¶6102, ¶6104; INDIV: 30,054.15; §3,205

[19] ¶6102, ¶6106; INDIV: 30,058; §3,215.05

[20] ¶6106, ¶6107; INDIV: 30,058; §3,215.05

[21] ¶165; INDIV: 30,058.05; §910

TABLE V.—ORDINARY LIFE ANNUITIES—ONE LIFE—EXPECTED RETURN MULTIPLES

Age	*Multiple*	*Age*	*Multiple*
55	28.6	64	20.8
56	27.7	65	20.0
57	26.8	66	19.2
58	25.9	67	18.4
59	25.0	68	17.6
60	24.2	69	16.8
61	23.3	70	16.0
62	22.5	71	15.3
63	21.6	72	14.6

Example 1: In 2012, X purchases for $8,000 an annuity that provides for payments to him of $50 per month for life. At the annuity starting date, his age at his nearest birthday is 64 years. Table V (gender-neutral) must be used since all investment in the contract is post-June 1986 and it shows that for an individual of X's age, the multiple to be used in computing the expected return is 20.8. X's expected return and annual exclusion, therefore, are computed as follows:

Annual payment ($50 per month × 12 months)		$600
Table V multiple		20.8
Expected return ($600 × 20.8)		$12,480
Exclusion ratio	$\frac{8,000}{12,480}$, or 64.10%	
Annual exclusion (64.10% of $600)		$385

If payments under the contract are made quarterly, semiannually, or annually, or if the interval between the annuity starting date and the date of the first payment is less than the interval between future payments, an adjustment of the multiple found in the actuarial tables may be required (Reg. § 1.72-5).[22] The amount of the adjustment is found in the following table:

If the number of whole months from the annuity starting date to the first payment date is	0-1	2	3	4	5	6	7	8	9	10	11	12
And payments under the contract are to be made:												
Annually	+.5	+.4	+.3	+.2	+.1	0	0	−.1	−.2	−.3	−.4	−.5
Semiannually	+.2	+.1	0	0	−.1	−.2	..	..	..	..	..	..
Quarterly	+.1	0	−.1	..	..	..	..	..	..	..	..	..

Example 2: Assume the same facts as in Example 1 above except that the payments under the contract are to be made semiannually in the amount of $300, the first payment being made six full months from the annuity starting date. The table shows the adjustment to be "−.2". Therefore, X's multiple from Table V, 20.8, is adjusted by subtracting .2. His adjusted multiple then is 20.6, and his expected return and semiannual exclusion are computed as follows:

Annual payment ($300 × 2)		$600
Table V adjusted multiple		20.6
Expected return ($600 × 20.6)		$12,360
Exclusion ratio	$\frac{8,000}{12,360}$, or 64.72%	
Semiannual exclusion (64.72% of $300)		$194.16

References are to Standard Federal Tax Reports; Tax Research Consultant; and Practical Tax Explanations.

[22] ¶ 6106; INDIV: 30,058.10; § 3,215.10

There is a simpler computation, illustrated in Example 3, but it may be used only if the annuity amount does not vary from year to year. This computation determines the annual exclusion by dividing the taxpayer's investment in the contract, i.e., the taxpayer's cost, by the appropriate multiple from the actuarial tables.

Example 3: Assume the same facts as in Example 1. X's annual exclusion is computed as follows:

Cost of annuity	$8,000
Annual payment ($50 per month × 12 months) . . .	$600
Table V multiple	20.8
Annual exclusion $\frac{8,000}{20.8}$	$385
Annual taxable income ($600 less $385)	$215

827. Joint and Survivor Annuities and Joint Annuities. In the case of a joint and survivor annuity contract that provides the first annuitant with a fixed monthly income for life and, after his or her death, provides an identical monthly income for life to the second annuitant, the multiple used in computing expected return is found in Table II (gender-based) or Table VI (gender-neutral) under the ages of the living annuitants as of the annuity starting date (Reg. § 1.72-5(b)).[23] For use in the following example, a portion of Table VI (gender-neutral for post-June 30, 1986, investment in the contract) providing expected return multiples for ordinary joint life and last survivor annuities for two lives is reproduced below.

TABLE VI.—ORDINARY JOINT LIFE AND LAST SURVIVOR ANNUITIES—TWO LIVES— EXPECTED RETURN MULTIPLES

Ages	65	66	67	68	69	70	71	72
65	25.0	24.6	24.2	23.8	23.4	23.1	22.8	22.5
66	24.6	24.1	23.7	23.3	22.9	22.5	22.2	21.9
67	24.2	23.7	23.2	22.8	22.4	22.0	21.7	21.3
68	23.8	23.3	22.8	22.3	21.9	21.5	21.2	20.8
69	23.4	22.9	22.4	21.9	21.5	21.1	20.7	20.3
70	23.1	22.5	22.0	21.5	21.1	20.6	20.2	19.8
71	22.8	22.2	21.7	21.2	20.7	20.2	19.8	19.4
72	22.5	21.9	21.3	20.8	20.3	19.8	19.4	18.9

Example: In 2012, Y purchased a joint and survivor annuity providing for payments of $200 a month to be made to Y for life and, upon his death, to his wife, Z, during her lifetime. At the annuity starting date Y's age at his nearest birthday is 68 and Z's is 66. The annuity cost is $44,710. The expected return is as follows:

Annual payment ($200 × 12)	$2,400
Table VI multiple (age 68; age 66)	23.3
Expected return ($2,400 × 23.3)	$55,920

The annual exclusion for both Y and Z is computed as follows:

Exclusion ratio	$\frac{44,710}{55,920}$, or 79.95%
Annual exclusion (79.95% of $2,400)	$1,918.80

If a joint and survivor annuity provides for a different monthly income, rather than an identical monthly income, payable to the second annuitant, there is a special computation of expected return that involves the use of both Table I and Table II or

References are to Standard Federal Tax Reports; Tax Research Consultant; and Practical Tax Explanations.

[23] ¶ 6106; INDIV: 30,066; § 3,215.15

Table V and Table VI, whichever are applicable. If a contract involving two annuitants provides for fixed monthly payments to be made as a joint life annuity until the death of the first annuitant (in other words, only as long as both remain alive), the expected return for such a contract is determined under Table IIA or VIA. Adjustment of the multiple obtained from the annuity tables, as explained at ¶ 825 for single life annuities, may also be necessary for joint and survivor annuities and joint annuities if payments are made less often than monthly or if the first payment is accelerated.

829. Special Types of Annuities. To compute the exclusion ratio (¶ 819) for a contract that is acquired for a single consideration and that provides for the payment of two or more annuity obligations or elements, the investment in the contract is divided by the aggregate of the expected returns under all the annuity elements (Reg. § § 1.72-4(e), 1.72-5(e), and 1.72-6(b)).[24] In the case of variable annuities, a special rule is provided for determining the portion of each payment to be "an amount received as an annuity" and excludable from gross income each year (Reg. § 1.72-2(b)(3)).[25] The computation of the expected return for temporary life annuities is determined by multiplying the total of the annuity payments to be received annually by the multiple shown in Table I or V, whichever is applicable, under the age as of the annuity starting date and, if applicable, the gender of the annuitant's life (Reg. § 1.72-5(a)(3)—(5)).[26]

835. Exclusion for Year Annuity Begins. If the first payment an annuitant receives is for a fractional part of a year, the annuitant need only determine the exclusion ratio (¶ 819) as a percentage and apply it to the payment received for the fractional part of the payment period, resulting in the amount of the annuitant's exclusion for the tax year (Reg. § 1.72-4(a)).[27]

> **Example:** John purchased an annuity that provides for semiannual payments of $3,000. The annuity starting date is November 1, and on December 31, John received $1,000 as his first payment under the contract. John's exclusion percentage is 70 percent. He may exclude 70 percent of $1,000, or $700, from his calendar-year income.

837. Refund Annuity. If an annuity contract has a refund feature, including a contract for a life annuity with a minimum period of payments certain, an adjustment must be made to the original investment in the contract when determining the exclusion ratio (¶ 819). The original investment in the contract must be reduced by the value of the refund payment or payment certain as of the annuity starting date (Code Sec. 72(b)(4) and (c); Reg. § 1.72-7).[28] The computation of the adjustment is detailed and involves the use of Table III (gender-based) or Table VII (gender-neutral) of Reg. § 1.72-9.[29]

Generally, an annuity contract contains a refund feature if:

(1) the annuity payments depend, in whole or in part, upon the continuing life of one or more persons;

(2) there are payments on or after the death of the annuitant if a specified amount or a stated number of payments has not been made prior to death; and

(3) the payments are in the nature of a refund of the consideration paid (Code Sec. 72(c)(2); Reg. § 1.72-7).[30]

839. Employee's Annuity. Amounts received as an annuity from qualified employee plans under Code Sec. 401(a), employee annuities under Code Sec. 403(a), and annuity contracts under Code Sec. 403(b) must generally use a simplified method to

References are to Standard Federal Tax Reports; Tax Research Consultant; and Practical Tax Explanations.

[24] ¶ 6104, ¶ 6106, ¶ 6107; INDIV: 30,070; § 3,205

[25] ¶ 6102D; INDIV: 30,068; § 3,235

[26] ¶ 6106; INDIV: 30,058.15; § 3,215.05

[27] ¶ 6104; INDIV: 30,056; § 3,210

[28] ¶ 6102, ¶ 6108; INDIV: 30,068; § 3,220.05

[29] ¶ 165; INDIV: 30,062; § 3,220.10

[30] ¶ 6102, ¶ 6108; INDIV: 30,062, RETIRE: 42,304; § 3,220.10

compute the taxable and tax-free portion of the distributions (Code Sec. 72(d); Notice 98-2).[31]

Post-November 18, 1996, Annuities. Under the simplified method for annuity starting dates beginning after November 18, 1996, but before January 1, 1998, the total number of monthly annuity payments expected to be received is based on the primary annuitant's age at the annuity starting date. The same expected number of payments applies to a single life annuity or a joint and survivor annuity. The expected number of payments is set forth in the following table:

Age of Primary Annuitant on the Annuity Starting Date	*Number of Anticipated Payments*
55 and under	360
56-60	310
61-65	260
66-70	210
71 and over	160

For annuity starting dates after December 31, 1997, annuities paid over the life of a single individual have anticipated payments as listed in the table above. If, however, the annuity is payable over the lives of more than one individual, the number of anticipated payments is listed in the table below:

Combined Age of Annuitants	*Number of Anticipated Payments*
110 and under	410
More than 110 but not more than 120	360
More than 120 but not more than 130	310
More than 130 but not more than 140	260
More than 140	210

The number of anticipated payments listed in the table above is based on the employee's age on the annuity starting date. If the number of payments is fixed under the terms of the annuity, that number is to be used rather than the number of anticipated payments listed in the table.

Example 1: At retirement, Jeff Anderson, age 65, begins receiving retirement benefits in the form of a joint and 50 percent survivor annuity to be paid for the joint lives of Jeff and his wife, Jan, age 59. Jeff's annuity starting date is January 1, 2012. Jeff contributed $24,000 to the plan and has received no distributions prior to the annuity starting date. He will receive a monthly retirement benefit of $1,000, and his wife Jan will receive a monthly survivor benefit of $500 upon his death. Jeff's investment in the contract is $24,000 (the after-tax contributions to the plan). The set number of monthly payments will be 310 (Jeff's age, 65, plus Jan's age, 59, at the starting date of the annuity equals 124). The tax-free portion of each $1,000 monthly annuity payment to Jeff is now $77.42, determined by dividing Jeff's investment ($24,000) by the number of monthly payments (310). If Jeff has not recovered the full $24,000 investment at his death, Jan will exclude $77.42 from each $500 monthly annuity payment. Any annuity payments received after 310 payments have been made will be includible in gross income. If Jeff and his wife die before 310 payments have been made, a deduction is allowed on the survivor's last income tax return in the amount of the unrecovered investment.

The simplified method does not apply if the primary annuitant has attained age 75 on the annuity starting date unless there are fewer than five years of guaranteed payments under the annuity (Code Sec. 72(d)(1)(E)). Also, if in connection with commencement of annuity payments, the recipient receives a lump-sum payment that is not part of the annuity stream, then the payment is taxed under the annuity rules of Code Sec. 72(e) as if received before the annuity starting date and the investment in the

References are to Standard Federal Tax Reports; Tax Research Consultant; and Practical Tax Explanations.

[31] ¶ 17,502, ¶ 18,270, ¶ 7102, ¶ 6140.82; RETIRE: 42,304.10; § 24,405.10

contract used to calculate the simplified exclusion ratio for the annuity payments is reduced by the amount of the payment (Code Sec. 72(d) (1) (D)).

Pre-November 19, 1996, Annuities. The IRS provided an elective alternative to application of the usual annuity rules for distributions from qualified plans when the annuity starting date was before November 19, 1996. This is a simplified safe-harbor method for determining the tax-free and taxable portions of certain annuity payments made from qualified employee plans, employee annuities, and annuity contracts (Notice 88-118).[32] Distributees who elected to use this method are considered to have complied with Code Sec. 72(b). Payors may also use this method to report the taxable portion of the annuity payments on Form 1099-R. The safe-harbor method may be used *only* if the following three conditions are met:

(1) the annuity payments depend upon the life of the distributee or the joint lives of the distributee and beneficiary;

(2) the annuity payments are made from an employee plan qualified under Code Sec. 401(a), an employee annuity under Code Sec. 403(a), or an annuity contract under Code Sec. 403(b); and

(3) the distributee is less than age 75 when annuity payments commence or, if the distributee is age 75 or older, there are fewer than five years of guaranteed payments.

Under the safe-harbor method, the total number of monthly annuity payments expected to be received is based on the distributee's age at the annuity starting date rather than on the life expectancy tables in Reg. § 1.72-9. The same expected number of payments applies to a distributee whether the individual is receiving a single life annuity or a joint and survivor annuity. These payments are set forth in the following table:

Age of Distributee	*Number of Payments*
55 and under	300
56-60	260
61-65	240
66-70	170
71 and over	120

Under the safe-harbor method, the distributee recovers the investment in the contract in level amounts over the number of monthly payments determined from the above table. The portion of each monthly annuity payment that is excluded from gross income by a distributee who uses the safe-harbor method for income tax purposes is a level dollar amount determined by dividing the investment in the contract, including any applicable death benefit exclusion, by the set number of annuity payments from the above table as follows:

$$\frac{\text{Investment}}{\text{Number of monthly payments}} = \text{Tax-free portion of monthly annuity}$$

For distributees with annuity starting dates after 1986, annuity payments received after the investment is recovered, usually after the set number of payments has been received, are fully includible in gross income.

Example 2: Assume the same facts as in Example 1 above, except Jeff's annuity start date was January 1, 1996. Under the safe-harbor method, Jeff's investment in the contract is $24,000 (the after-tax contributions to the plan). The set number of monthly payments for a distributee who is age 65 is 240. The tax-free portion of each $1,000 monthly annuity payment to Jeff is $100, determined by dividing Jeff's investment ($24,000) by the number of monthly payments (240). If Jeff has not recovered the full $24,000 investment at his death, Jan will also exclude $100 from each $500 monthly annuity payment. Any annuity payments received after 240 payments have been made will be fully includible in gross income. If Jeff

References are to Standard Federal Tax Reports; Tax Research Consultant; and Practical Tax Explanations.

[32] ¶ 6798; RETIRE: 42,304.10; § 24,405.10

and his wife die before 240 payments have been made, a deduction is allowed on the survivor's last income tax return in the amount of the unrecovered investment.

The dollar amount is excluded from each monthly payment even if the annuity payment amount changes. If the amount excluded is greater than the amount of the monthly annuity, because of decreased survivor payments, each monthly annuity payment is excluded completely until the entire investment is recovered. If annuity payments cease before the set number of payments has been made, a deduction for the unrecovered investment is allowed on the distributee's last tax return. Where payments are made to multiple beneficiaries, the excludable amount is based on the oldest beneficiary's age. A pro rata portion is excluded by each beneficiary.

General Rules. For purposes of these rules, the investment in the contract (¶ 821) is determined without regard to the adjustment made for a refund feature (Code Sec. 72(d)(1)(C)).

In any case where the annuity payments are not made on a monthly basis, appropriate adjustments must be made to take into account the basis on which the payments are actually made (Code Sec. 72(d)(1)(F)).

Employee contributions under a defined contribution plan may be treated as a separate contract (Code Sec. 72(d)(2)).

Railroad Retirement Act Tier 2 benefits received by retired railroad workers and their survivors are subject to federal income tax in the same manner as pension plan benefits paid by private employers (Code Sec. 72(r)).[33]

841. Discharge of Annuity Obligation. Any amount received, whether in a single sum or otherwise, under an annuity, endowment, or life insurance contract in full discharge of the obligation under the contract as a refund of the consideration paid for the contract or any amount received under such contract on its complete surrender, redemption or maturity is includible in gross income to the extent the amounts exceed the investment in the contract (Code Sec. 72(e); Reg. § 1.72-11).[34] The remainder is taxable to the recipient, whether the recipient is the primary annuitant or a secondary annuitant under a joint or joint and survivor annuity. A penalty is imposed on a policyholder who receives a premature distribution, e.g., before age 59½, unless one of a number of exceptions, such as death or disability, applies (Code Sec. 72(q)).[35]

843. Installment Option. If an insured elects under an option in an insurance contract to receive the proceeds as an annuity, instead of a lump sum, and the election is made within 60 days after the day on which the lump sum first became payable, no part of it is taxable under the doctrine of constructive receipt (Code Sec. 72(h); Reg. § 1.72-12).[36] The installment payments are taxed in accordance with the annuity rules.

845. Transfer for Value. If a life insurance, endowment, or annuity contract is transferred for a valuable consideration, and the proceeds of the contract are paid to the transferee for reasons other than the death of the insured, e.g., on surrender, redemption, or maturity of the contract, the transferee, including a beneficiary of, or the estate of, a transferee, is taxed as follows:

(1) if the proceeds are received as an annuity or in installments for a fixed period, the transferee computes the tax under the exclusion ratio formula (¶ 819); or

(2) if the proceeds are received in a lump sum, the transferee includes in income only that portion of the proceeds in excess of the consideration paid.

Regardless of how the proceeds are received and taxed, the transferee's consideration paid consists of the actual value of the consideration paid for the transfer, plus the amount of premiums or other consideration paid after the transfer. This transferee rule,

References are to Standard Federal Tax Reports; Tax Research Consultant; and Practical Tax Explanations.

[33] ¶ 6102; INDIV: 33,358

[34] ¶ 6102, ¶ 6113; INDIV: 30,102.10; § 3,230.10

[35] ¶ 6102; INDIV: 30,204; § 3,255

[36] ¶ 6102, ¶ 6117; INDIV: 30,208; § 3,265.35

however, does not apply if the transferred contract has a basis for gain or loss in the hands of the transferee determined by reference to the transferor's basis, as in the case of a gift or tax-free exchange (Code Sec. 72(g); Reg. § 1.72-10).[37]

A loss realized upon the surrender or forfeiture of an annuity contract by the original purchaser is deductible as an ordinary loss under Code Sec. 165, the basis of the contract being its cost less the amounts previously excluded from gross income (Rev. Rul. 61-201).[38] The IRS maintains the loss is deducted on Form 1040, Schedule A as a miscellaneous itemized deduction subject to the two-percent-of-adjusted-gross-income floor (IRS Pub. 575).

Bequest or Gift

847. Bequest. The value of property acquired by bequest, devise, or inheritance is excludable from gross income (Code Sec. 102; Reg. § 1.102-1).[39] The *income* flowing from the property, however, is *not* exempt, as, for example, amounts received as investment income from the property or as profit from a sale of the property. The exclusion also does not apply if the bequest consists of income from property. Thus, a bequest of annual rent from the testator's property for 10 years is taxable income to the beneficiary. The beneficiary is required to include in gross income each year the amount of the annual rent. For the basis of inherited property, see ¶ 1633—¶ 1639.

A bequest of a specific sum or of specific property from an estate or trust may be exempt from tax if it is paid or credited all at once or in not more than three installments (Code Sec. 663(a)(1); Reg. § 1.663(a)-1).[40] An amount which is paid from the estate or trust income may qualify as a bequest for this purpose if the amount could have been paid from either income or principal. However, an amount that can only be paid from the estate or trust income will not be treated as a bequest and, thus, will *not* be exempt even when paid in less than four installments.

849. Gift. The value of a gift is excludable from gross income, but *any income* from the gift, including profit upon sale, is taxable (Code Sec. 102(b)). A gift of income from the property of an estate or trust is not exempt except in the case of a gift of a specific sum or of specific property paid or credited all at once or in not more than three installments (¶ 847). For a donee's basis for gift property, see ¶ 1630.

Tips are not gifts and are therefore taxable (¶ 717).[41] Food, clothing, and rent payments furnished as strike benefits by a labor union to a needy worker participating in a strike may be considered gifts. In determining whether a gift was made, the fact that benefits were paid only to union members is not controlling.[42]

The exclusion from gross income applicable to the value of property acquired by gift does not apply to any amount transferred by or for an employer to, or for the benefit of, an employee (Code Sec. 102(c)).[43] However, certain employee achievement awards (¶ 785) and certain fringe benefits provided by employers are excludable (¶ 863).

Certain Benefits and Awards

851. Occupational Disability or Insurance Benefit. Compensation received under a workers' compensation act for personal injuries or sickness and amounts received by a taxpayer under a policy of accident and health insurance are excludable from gross income (Code Sec. 104(a)(1); Reg. § 1.104-1).[44] The exclusion also applies to benefits having the characteristics of life insurance proceeds paid under a workers' compensation act to the survivor or survivors of a deceased employee (Reg. § 1.101-1(a)).[45] For a discussion of disability income plans, see ¶ 2190B.

References are to Standard Federal Tax Reports; Tax Research Consultant; and Practical Tax Explanations.

[37] ¶ 6102, ¶ 6112; INDIV: 30,064; § 3,220.05

[38] ¶ 9900.111; INDIV: 30,216; § 3,245.10

[39] ¶ 6550, ¶ 6551; INDIV: 33,102, INDIV: 33,104; § 3,601

[40] ¶ 24,440, ¶ 24,441; INDIV: 33,104; § 32,710.05g

[41] ¶ 5507.4651; COMPEN: 6,058; § 21,301

[42] ¶ 6553.46; COMPEN: 6,068

[43] ¶ 6550; INDIV: 33,102.05; § 3,605.10

[44] ¶ 6660, ¶ 6661; INDIV: 33,406, COMPEN: 45,300; § 3,705.10

[45] ¶ 6503; INDIV: 33,406

Amounts received as a pension, annuity, or similar allowance for personal injuries or sickness resulting from active service in the armed forces of any country or in the Coast and Geodetic Survey or the Public Health Service, or as a disability annuity payable under section 808 of the Foreign Service Act of 1980, are also excludable from gross income (Code Sec. 104(a)(4); Reg. § 1.104-1).[46] The exclusion generally is limited to amounts received for combat-related injury or illness. However, the exclusion will not be less than the maximum amount of disability compensation from the Veterans Administration to which the individual is, or would be, entitled upon application (Code Sec. 104(b)).[47]

Benefits that are payable under state law for occupational injury or illness arising out of employment are nontaxable if the benefits are in the nature of workers' compensation payments (Reg. § 1.104-1(b)).[48] No fault insurance disability benefits received by a passenger injured in an automobile accident under the automobile owner's policy as compensation for loss of income or earning capacity are also excludable from gross income.[49]

If an otherwise excludable amount is for reimbursement of medical expenses previously deducted for tax purposes, the amount must be included in gross income to the extent of the prior deduction. If a portion of an award is specifically allocated to future injury-related medical expenses, the future expenses must be offset by the awarded portion and are not deductible to that extent.[50]

Terrorist Attacks. Disability income received by an individual for injuries received in a terrorist attack while the individual was performing services as a U.S. employee outside the United States is also excludable from gross income (Code Sec. 104(a)(5)).[51]

852. Personal Injuries or Sickness. Amounts received as damages, other than punitive damages, on account of ***personal physical injuries or sickness*** are excludable from income (Code Sec. 104(a)(2)).[52] Damages for emotional distress, including the physical symptoms of emotional distress, may not be treated as damages on account of a personal physical injury or sickness, except to the extent of amounts paid for medical care attributable to emotional distress. Accordingly, back pay received in satisfaction of a claim for denial of a promotion due to employment discrimination is not excludable because it is "completely independent of," and thus is *not* "damages received on account of," personal physical injuries or sickness (Rev. Rul. 96-65).

Interest and Punitive Damage Awards. Interest included in an award of damages for personal injury is includible in gross income.[53] Also, punitive damages arising out of personal physical injury action are includible in gross income (Code Sec. 104(a)(2)).[54] However, punitive damages may be excludable from income if received in a civil action for wrongful death and the applicable state law provides that only punitive damages may be awarded (Code Sec. 104(c)).

Attorney's Fees. The full amount of a litigant's award, including the attorney's contingent fee, regardless of whether paid directly to the attorney or to the individual, is includible in the litigant's gross income under the anticipatory assignment of income theory (*J.W. Banks II* and *S.J. Banaitis*, SCt, 2005-1 USTC ¶ 50,155). For a discussion of the deduction of legal fees and court costs as a miscellaneous deduction, see ¶ 1093. However, attorneys fees and court costs paid in prosecuting claims based on unlawful discrimination and certain other federal claims, including but not limited to whistleblower actions, are deductible from gross income as an above-the-line deduction (¶ 1010A) (Code Sec. 62(a)).

References are to Standard Federal Tax Reports; Tax Research Consultant; and Practical Tax Explanations.

[46] ¶ 6660, ¶ 6661; INDIV: 33,410; § 42,210

[47] ¶ 6660; INDIV: 33,410; § 42,210

[48] ¶ 6661; INDIV: 33,406; § 3,705

[49] ¶ 6662.26; INDIV: 33,408; § 42,205

[50] ¶ 6662.41; INDIV: 33,402.10; § 7,210.05

[51] ¶ 6660; COMPEN: 45,406; § 3,710

[52] ¶ 6660; INDIV: 33,402; § 3,805.05

[53] ¶ 6662.513; INDIV: 12,112; § 3,805.35

[54] ¶ 6660; INDIV: 33,402.05; § 3,805.30

853. Accident and Health Plans. Amounts received by employees under employer-financed accident and health plans may qualify for exclusion from income (Code Sec. 105; Reg. §§1.105-1 and 1.105-5).[55] A self-employed person is not an employee for purposes of this exclusion. The exclusion applies to a state government plan including the District of Columbia, as well as to a plan of a private employer. See ¶2190A for further discussion of accident and health plans.

857. Application of Annuity Rules to Accident or Health Benefits. Amounts received as accident or health benefits are not taxable under the annuity rules at ¶817 (Reg. §1.72-15).[56] However, some employer-established plans pay participants both amounts taxable under the annuity rules (¶817—¶845) and amounts excludable from gross income as payments under an accident or health plan. Specific rules are provided for determining which amounts are excludable in these cases. Benefits attributable to the employee's contributions are excludable from gross income under the rules at ¶851. Benefits attributable to the employer's contributions are taxable except to the extent that they are excludable under the rules at ¶2190A.

859. Employer Contribution to Accident or Health Plans. Contributions by an employer to provide through insurance or otherwise the accident and health benefits described in ¶853 are not taxable to the employees (Code Sec. 106; Reg. §1.106-1).[57] This rule also covers contributions made by a church to purchase health and accident insurance for its minister.[58] The employer's contributions are deductible business expenses (Reg. §1.162-10; Temp. Reg. §1.162-10T).[59]

See ¶2190A for further discussion of accident and health plans. See ¶322 and ¶421 for treatment of an S corporation shareholder or partner whose accident or health insurance premiums are paid by the S corporation or partnership.

859A. Health Savings Accounts. A health savings account (HSA) is a trust established for the exclusive purpose of paying for qualified medical expenses of the account beneficiary (Code Sec. 223).[60] HSAs can be established by employees through an employer's cafeteria plan (¶2195). Contributions to the account generally are either deductible or excluded from gross income, and the amount that may be contributed each year is limited. Excess contributions are subject to an excise tax. Distributions made from the account are not includible in gross income as long as they are used exclusively for qualified medical expenses. Distributions that are not used for such expenses are includible in income and are subject to a 20 percent additional tax as well. See ¶1020A and ¶2197B for a further discussion of HSAs.

860. Medical Savings Accounts. An Archer Medical Savings Account (MSA) is a trust established for the exclusive purpose of paying for qualified medical expenses of the account holder (Code Sec. 220).[61] Contributions to the account generally are either deductible or excluded from income, and the amount of contributions that may be made each year is limited. Excess contributions are subject to an excise tax. Distributions made from the account are not included in gross income as long as they are used exclusively for qualified medical expenses. Distributions that are not used for such expenses not only are includible in income but are subject to a 20 percent penalty tax as well. See ¶2197B for a further discussion of MSAs.

861. Cafeteria Plans. Cafeteria plans, also referred to as flexible benefit plans, are employer-sponsored benefit plans that allow employees to choose either receiving compensation as cash or receiving nontaxable benefits from a menu of qualified benefits (Code Sec. 125).[62] With a few exceptions, benefits are qualified benefits if they are excludable from an employee's gross income when offered outside of a cafeteria plan

References are to Standard Federal Tax Reports; Tax Research Consultant; and Practical Tax Explanations.

[55] ¶6700, ¶6701, ¶6708; COMPEN: 45,154; §42,205

[56] ¶6124; INDIV: 30,152.05; §42,220

[57] ¶6800, ¶6801; COMPEN: 45,152; §42,220

[58] ¶6803.20; COMPEN: 45,152; §42,220

[59] ¶8750, ¶8751; COMPEN: 45,202; §42,220

[60] ¶12,776; INDIV: 42,450; §42,501

[61] ¶12,670; INDIV: 42,500; §42,601

[62] ¶7,320; COMPEN: 51,000; §45,025.10

and do not defer the receipt of compensation (Code Sec. 125(f)). A cafeteria plan may include: accident and health insurance (¶ 2192A); dependent care assistance program (¶ 2192B); disability coverage (¶ 2190B); group-term life insurance (¶ 2190C); health savings account (HSAs) (¶ 2197B); and 401(k) plans (¶ 2106).

Employees participating in cafeteria plans can develop individualized benefit packages without the additional tax burdens arising from benefits they do not select. An employee who chooses to receive cash instead of nontaxable benefits must include the amount of cash received in the employee's gross income in the year in which it was actually received. If a benefit is excludable from gross income under another Code section, it continues to be excludable from gross income when an employee selects it as a benefit under a cafeteria plan (*American Family Mutual Ins. Co. v. United States*, DC Wis, 93-1 USTC 50,158). See ¶ 2195 for a further discussion of cafeteria plans.

Flexible Spending Arrangements. A flexible spending arrangement (FSA) is an employer-sponsored benefit program that is offered as part of a cafeteria plan and designed to provide covered employees with a method of paying for certain covered expenses, e.g., medical or dependent care, with pre-tax dollars. Basically, a covered employee makes contributions, through payroll deductions, to a health or a dependent care FSA. Since contributions to an FSA reduce an employee's gross income, these amounts, though compensatory in nature, are not subject to federal income tax, social security tax, or Medicare tax. The FSA, in effect, allows the employee, through income and FICA tax savings, to reduce the out-of-pocket costs of covered expenses. See ¶ 2196 for further information on FSAs.

863. Fringe Benefits. The following noncash benefits qualify for exclusion from an employee's gross income:

(1) no-additional-cost services (e.g., free standby flights by airlines to their employees);

(2) qualified employee discounts (e.g., reduced sales prices of products and services sold by the employer);

(3) working condition fringe benefits (e.g., use of company car for business purposes);

(4) *de minimis* fringe benefits (e.g., use of copying machine for personal purposes);

(5) qualified transportation fringe benefits (e.g., transportation in a "commuter highway vehicle," transit passes, and qualified parking);

(6) qualified moving expense reimbursements;

(7) qualified retirement planning services; and

(8) qualified military base realignment and closure fringe benefits (Code Sec. 132; Reg. § 1.132-1).[63]

The above benefits can also be excluded from the income of retired and disabled former employees, widows and widowers of deceased employees, and spouses and dependent children of employees. Applicable nondiscrimination conditions must be met (Code Sec. 132(h)).[64] See ¶ 2188 for further discussion of fringe benefits under Code Sec. 132.

869. Employer-Provided Child or Dependent Care Services. Up to $5,000 of child or dependent care assistance services that are paid by an employer and furnished pursuant to a written plan generally are excludable from an employee's gross income (Code Sec. 129).[65] See ¶ 2192B for further discussion of child and dependent care benefits.

References are to Standard Federal Tax Reports; Tax Research Consultant; and Practical Tax Explanations.

[63] ¶ 7420, ¶ 7422; COMPEN: 36,000; § 21,101

[64] ¶ 7420; COMPEN: 36,200; § 20,815.05

[65] ¶ 7380; COMPEN: 36,600; § 20,001

871. Employer Payment of Employee's Educational Expenses. Up to $5,250 of payments received by an employee for tuition, fees, books, supplies, etc., under an employer's educational assistance program may be excluded from gross income (Code Sec. 127; Reg. § 1.127-1).[66] See ¶ 2192D for further discussion of employer-provided educational assistance.

Comment: Absent further legislation, for tax years beginning after 2012, an employee can no longer exclude from gross income amounts paid or expenses incurred by an employer for educational assistance furnished under a qualified educational assistance program. Thus, employer provided educational assistance may be excluded from an employee's gross income and wages beginning in 2013 only if it qualifies as a working condition fringe benefit (¶ 2188D).

873. Employer-Provided Food and Lodging. Meals that are excludable from an employee's income under Code Sec. 119 are also considered a *de minimis* fringe benefit under Code Sec. 132.[67] See ¶ 2188C for further discussion of employer-provided food and lodging benefits.

875. Minister's Home or Rental Allowance. Ministers of the gospel may exclude from gross income the rental value of homes furnished by churches as part of their compensation (Code Sec. 107; Reg. § 1.107-1).[68] This includes the portion of a retired minister's pension designated as a rental allowance by the national governing body of a religious denomination having complete control over the retirement fund.[69] The exemption also applies to the rental value of a residence furnished to a retired minister but not a widow.[70]

A minister is entitled to deduct mortgage interest and real property taxes paid on a personal residence even if the amounts expended are derived from a rental allowance that is excludable from the minister's gross income (Code Sec. 265(a)(6)).[71]

Reimbursed Living Expenses

877. Exclusion for Reimbursement. A taxpayer whose principal residence is damaged or destroyed by fire, storm, or other casualty and who must temporarily occupy another residence during the repair can exclude from gross income any insurance payments received as reimbursement for *increased* living expenses during such period. This also applies to a person who is denied access to his principal residence by governmental authorities because of the occurrence or threat of occurrence of a casualty (Code Sec. 123; Reg. § 1.123-1).[72]

The exclusion is limited to the excess of actual living expenses incurred by the taxpayer and members of the household over the normal living expenses they would have incurred during the period. The exclusion covers additional costs incurred in renting suitable housing and any extraordinary expenses for transportation, food, utilities, and miscellaneous items.

Scholarship or Fellowship Grant

879. Scholarship or Fellowship Grant Is Not Income. Any amount received as a qualified scholarship by an individual who is a candidate for a degree at a qualified educational organization, which normally maintains a regular faculty and curriculum and normally has a regularly enrolled body of students in attendance where its educational activities are regularly carried on, is excluded from that individual's gross income (Code Sec. 117; Reg. § 1.117-1).[73] A qualified scholarship includes any amount received by an individual as a scholarship or fellowship grant so long as the amount was used for

References are to Standard Federal Tax Reports; Tax Research Consultant; and Practical Tax Explanations.

[66] ¶ 7350, ¶ 7351; COMPEN: 36,554; § 20,101

[67] ¶ 7420; COMPEN: 36,500; § 21,201

[68] ¶ 6850, ¶ 6851; COMPEN: 6,554; § 3,005.20

[69] ¶ 6852.12; COMPEN: 6,556; § 3,005.20

[70] ¶ 6852.31; COMPEN: 6,556; § 3,005.20

[71] ¶ 14,050; COMPEN: 6,554; § 46,110.10

[72] ¶ 7300, ¶ 7301; INDIV: 33,450; § 4,005.10

[73] ¶ 7170, ¶ 7172; INDIV: 60,060; § 3,905.05

qualified tuition and related expenses such as fees, books, supplies, and equipment required for courses of instruction at a qualified educational organization. A qualified scholarship does not include amounts used for incidental expenses, e.g., room and board, travel, research, clerical help, and equipment and other expenses that are *not* required for either enrollment or attendance at an educational organization (Proposed Reg. § 1.117-6(c)(2)).

Tuition Reduction. The amount of any qualified tuition reduction to employees of educational institutions is similarly excludable from gross income (Code Sec. 117(d)).[74] The tuition reduction must be provided to an employee of a qualified educational organization as defined under Code Sec. 170(b)(1)(A)(ii). The reduction can be for education provided by the employer or by another qualified educational organization. Moreover, it can be for education provided to the employee, the employee's spouse, dependent child, or other person treated as an employee under Code Sec. 132(h). However, it can only be used for education below the graduate level unless it is for the education of an employee who is a graduate student and who is engaged in teaching or research activities for the employer. Benefits under a qualified tuition reduction program may be excludable only if the program does not discriminate in favor of highly compensated employees.

Employer-Related Grants. Employer-related grants are *not* excludable from gross income, if they are considered to be compensation or an incentive to employees (Rev. Proc. 76-47).[75] When educational scholarships are made available to or for the benefit of employees on a preferential basis, such preferential grants suggest an intent to provide additional compensation or an employment incentive and are included in gross income unless they are shown to fall outside the pattern of employment. This is true even if the grants are made by an independent third party, such as a private foundation or a voluntary employees' beneficiary association (VEBA). Educational grants are considered to fall outside the pattern of employment only if seven conditions and at least one of two percentage tests are satisfied. The seven conditions are:

(1) The programs must not be used by the employer, the private foundation, or the organizer to recruit or to induce employees to continue their employment or otherwise follow a course of action sought by the employer.

(2) Selection of grant recipients must be made by a committee consisting wholly of individuals totally independent, except for participation on this committee, and separate from the private foundation, its organizer, and the employer concerned.

(3) The program must impose identifiable minimum requirements for grant eligibility, and these requirements must be related to the purpose of the program.

(4) Selection of grant recipients must be based solely upon substantial objective standards that are completely unrelated to the employment of the recipients or their parents and to the employer's line of business.

(5) A grant may not be terminated because the recipient or the recipient's parent terminates employment with the employer subsequent to the awarding of the grant regardless of the reason for the termination of employment. If a grant is awarded for one academic year and the recipient must reapply for a grant for a subsequent year, the recipient may *not* be considered ineligible for a further grant simply because that individual or the individual's parent is no longer employed by the employer.

(6) The courses of study for which grants are available must not be limited to those that would be of particular benefit to the employer or to the foundation.

(7) The terms of the grant and the courses of study for which grants are available must meet all other requirements for the exclusion and must be consis-

References are to Standard Federal Tax Reports; Tax Research Consultant; and Practical Tax Explanations.

[74] ¶ 7170; INDIV: 60,060.10; § 3,910

[75] ¶ 7183.29; INDIV: 60,060.10; § 3,905.15, § 3,910

tent with a disinterested purpose of enabling the recipients to obtain an education in their individual capacities solely for their personal benefit and must not include any commitments, understandings or obligations, conditional or unconditional, suggesting that the studies are undertaken by the recipients for the benefit of the employer or the foundation, or have as their objective the accomplishment of any purpose of the employer or the foundation, even though consistent with its exempt status, other than enabling the recipients to obtain an education in their individual capacities and solely for their personal benefit.

Under the percentage tests, the number of grants awarded under the program to children of employees must not exceed either (1) 25 percent of the children who were eligible for such grants, were applicants for the grants, and were considered by the selection committee making such grants; or (2) 10 percent of the number of employees' children who can be shown to be eligible for grants in that year, whether or not they submitted an application.

Compensation for Teaching, Research, or Other Services Performed. The exclusions for qualified scholarships and qualified tuition reductions do not apply to amounts representing payments for teaching, research, or other services performed by the student that are required as a condition for receiving the qualified scholarship or qualified tuition reduction (Code Sec. 117(c)).[76] Athletic scholarships awarded to students who are expected, but not required, to participate in sports qualify for exclusion.[77] Under an exception, amounts received by degree candidates from the National Health Service Corps (NHSC) Scholarship Program or the Armed Forces Scholarship Program for tuition, fees, books, supplies, and required equipment are excluded from the recipient's gross income even though there is a future service obligation connected to these qualified scholarships (Code Sec. 117(c)(2)). Amounts received by health care professionals under the NHSC Loan Repayment Program are excludable from gross income and employment taxes (Code Sec. 108(f)(4)). This provision also extends to loan repayments received under similar state programs qualified for funding under the Public Health Service Act and repayments under other state loan repayment or forgiveness programs that are intended to provide for increased availability of health care services in under-served or health professional shortage areas.

Comment: Absent further legislation, for tax years after December 31, 2012, amounts an individual receives under the NHSC Program or the Armed Forces Scholarship Program will not be eligible for tax-free treatment as qualified scholarships without regard to any service obligation.

Government Cost-Sharing Payments

881. Certain Agricultural Cost-Sharing Payments Are Excludable. Agricultural and forestry cost-sharing payments made by state or federal governments may be excluded from gross income if:

(1) the Secretary of Agriculture determines that the payments were made primarily for soil and water conservation, environmental protection or restoration, wildlife habitat development, or forest improvement, and

(2) the Treasury Department determines that the payments do not result in a substantial increase in the annual income derived from the property with respect to which the payments were made.

No adjustment to the basis of the property involved is made for the payments and, therefore, no income tax deduction or credit may be taken with respect to them (Code Sec. 126).[78] Further, if the property or improvement purchased with the payments is disposed of within 20 years, the payment amounts are recaptured as ordinary income. A 100-percent recapture rate applies if disposition occurs within the first 10 years, with an

References are to Standard Federal Tax Reports; Tax Research Consultant; and Practical Tax Explanations.

[76] ¶ 7170; INDIV: 60,060.15; § 3,905.10

[77] ¶ 7183.22; INDIV: 60,060.05, INDIV: 60,060.10; § 3,905.05

[78] ¶ 7330; FARM: 3,168; § 4,060

8 | EXCLUSIONS

annual decrease of 10 percent thereafter (Code Sec. 1255; Temp. Reg. § § 16A.1255-1 and 16A.1255-2).[79]

Small Business Stock

882. Exclusion for Gain from Small Business Stock. Noncorporate taxpayers may exclude from gross income a certain percentage of capital gain from the sale or exchange of qualified small business stock held for more than five years and issued after August 10, 1993 (¶ 1905). Capital gain which is excluded is not used in computing a taxpayer's long-term capital gain or loss and it is not investment income for purposes of the investment interest limitation. However, the capital gain *not* excluded is taxed at the maximum 28 percent capital gains rate (Code Sec. 1(h)(4)(A)(ii)).[80] Generally, the exclusion is 50 percent of any gain from the sale or exchange of qualified small business stock held for more than five years (60 percent in the case of qualified stock of an enterprise zone business (¶ 999B)). The exclusion increases to 75 percent for stock acquired after February 17, 2009, and before September 28, 2010, and held for more than five years, and up to 100 percent for qualified small business stock acquired after September 27, 2010, and before January 1, 2012, and held for more than five years.

Comment: Absent further legislation, beginning January 1, 2012, the increased exclusion rates applicable to any gain from the sale or exchange of qualified small business stock held for more than five years will no longer apply.

Foster Care Payments

883. Income Received for Foster Care. Payments made by a state or qualified foster care placement agency as difficulty of care payments or to reimburse a foster home provider for the expenses of caring for individuals placed in the home by a state agency or a qualified foster care placement agency are excludable from gross income (Code Sec. 131).[81] A qualified foster care placement agency is a placement agency that is licensed or certified by a state or local government or an entity designated by such a government to make foster care payments. Foster care payments are excludable only for foster care individuals who live in the foster care provider's home. Regular foster care payments are not excludable to the extent they are made for more than five individuals who have attained age 19. In the case of difficulty of care payments, i.e., payments for additional care required by a physically, mentally, or emotionally handicapped person, payments are *not* excludable to the extent they are made for more than 10 individuals under age 19 and more than five individuals who have attained 19 years of age.

Cancellation of Debt

885. Discharge of Debt. Income from the discharge of indebtedness is includible in gross income unless it is excludable under Code Sec. 108 or other applicable legislative provision. Five types of exclusions are provided: (1) a debt discharge in a bankruptcy action under Title 11 of the U.S. Code in which the taxpayer is under the jurisdiction of the court and the discharge is either granted by or is under a plan approved by the court; (2) a discharge when the taxpayer is insolvent outside bankruptcy; (3) a discharge of qualified farm indebtedness; (4) a discharge of qualified real property business indebtedness, and (5) a discharge of qualified principal residence indebtedness occurring before January 1, 2013. Under certain circumstances, income from the cancelation of student loans is also excludable (see *Student Loans*, following). Form 982 is filed with a debtor's income tax return to report excludable income from the discharge of indebtedness.[82]

Comment: Absent further legislation, beginning January 1, 2013, the exclusion from gross income applicable to qualified principal residence indebtedness will no longer apply.

References are to Standard Federal Tax Reports; Tax Research Consultant; and Practical Tax Explanations.

[79] ¶ 31,080, ¶ 31,081, ¶ 31,082; FARM: 3,168.15; § 16,715.05

[80] ¶ 3260; SALES: 15,300; § 16,605.05

[81] ¶ 7400; INDIV: 33,250, INDIV: 33,252; § 4,010.05

[82] ¶ 7002; SALES: 12,152, SALES: 12,202; § 3,420.05

A corporation that satisfies a debt by transferring corporate stock to its creditor, or a partnership that transfers a capital or profits interest in the partnership to a creditor, is treated as if it has paid the creditor with money equal to the fair market value of the stock or interest. The corporation or partnership will thus have income from discharge of indebtedness to the extent that the principal of the debt exceeds the value of the stock or partnership interest (and any other property transferred) (Code Sec. 108(e)(8)).[83] A similar rule applies to debtors, corporate or noncorporate, issuing debt instruments in satisfaction of indebtedness (Code Sec. 108(e)(10)).

Discharge of indebtedness income can result even if the canceled debt is nonrecourse, i.e., no individual is personally liable for repayment of the debt. Thus, where property securing a nonrecourse debt is transferred in exchange for cancellation of the debt, such as a foreclosure sale, the amount realized from the sale or exchange includes the principal amount of the debt discharged. The IRS has ruled that the writedown of the principal amount of a nonrecourse note by a holder who was not the seller of the property results in the realization of discharge of indebtedness income, even if there is no disposition of the property (Rev. Rul. 91-31).[84]

Effect of Exclusion on Tax Attributes. When an amount is excluded from gross income as the result of a discharge of indebtedness in a Title 11 case, a discharge of indebtedness during insolvency, or a discharge of qualified farm indebtedness, a taxpayer is required to reduce its tax attributes. The reduction in the foreign tax credit, minimum tax credit, passive activity credit, and general business credit carryovers is to be made at a rate of 33⅓ cents per dollar of excluded income (Code Sec. 108(b)(3)(B)).[85]

Insolvency. The term "insolvent" refers to an excess of liabilities over the fair market value of assets immediately prior to discharge. This exclusion is limited to the amount by which the taxpayer is insolvent. The taxpayer's insolvent amount includes the amount by which a nonrecourse debt exceeds the fair market value of the property securing the debt, but only to the extent that the excess nonrecourse debt is discharged.[86]

Nonrecourse debt in excess of the property's fair market value is separated into two components for purposes of the insolvency exception. First, the excess nonrecourse debt that is forgiven is treated as a liability for purposes of the insolvency exception. Otherwise, the debt discharge could result in a tax when the debtor lacks the ability to pay it. Second, the excess of nonrecourse debt that is not forgiven is not treated as a liability for purposes of the insolvency exception. The IRS's reasoning is that nondischarged debt does not directly impede the taxpayer's ability to pay tax on discharge of recourse or nonrecourse debt, and thus, is not relevant in determining the extent of his insolvency (Rev. Rul. 92-53). The IRS has extended the principles of Rev. Rul. 92-53 to determine the extent a partner may be insolvent under Code Sec. 108(d)(3). In the ruling, equal partners borrowed funds to purchase real estate, using the real estate to secure a note. The real estate's value subsequently fell below the principal amount due under the note and the bank reduced the principal amount on the note (forgiving a portion of the debt). The IRS ruled that each partner could treat its portion of the cancelled nonrecourse debt as its own liability in order to determine if, and to what extent, each partner was considered insolvent under Code Sec. 108(d)(3). Each partner's portion of cancelled nonrecourse debt is determined under the rules of Code Sec. 704(b). Accordingly, a partnership's discharged excess nonrecourse debt should be associated with the partner who, in the absence of the insolvency or other Code Sec. 108 exclusion, would be required to pay the tax liability arising from the discharge of that debt (Rev. Rul. 2012-14, amplifying Rev. Rul. 92-53).

Farmers. Income arising from the discharge of qualified farm indebtedness owed to an unrelated lender, including a federal, state, or local government or agency, or

References are to Standard Federal Tax Reports; Tax Research Consultant; and Practical Tax Explanations.

[83] ¶ 7002; SALES: 12,254; § 3,401

[84] ¶ 5802.34; SALES: 12,154; § 3,415

[85] ¶ 7002; SALES: 12,206; § 3,420.05

[86] ¶ 7010.38; SALES: 12,200; § 3,415

instrumentality of such an agency, may be excluded from a taxpayer's income if certain requirements are met. The debt must be incurred directly in connection with the operation by the taxpayer of the trade or business of farming. Also, at least 50 percent of the taxpayer's aggregate gross receipts for the three tax years preceding the tax year in which the discharge of indebtedness occurs must be attributable to the trade or business of farming. The discharge of indebtedness income is excludable only to the extent absorbed by tax attributes (credits are reduced at a rate of 33⅓ cents per dollar of excluded income) and the adjusted bases of qualified property (any property held or used in a trade or business or for the production of income) (Code Sec. 108(g)). Basis reduction occurs first with respect to depreciable property, then with respect to land used in the business of farming, and finally with respect to other qualified property (Code Sec. 1017(b)(4)).[87]

Qualified Real Property Business Indebtedness. A taxpayer other than a C corporation may elect to exclude from gross income amounts realized from the discharge of debt incurred or assumed in connection with real property used in a trade or business and secured by that property (Code Sec. 108(a)(1)(D) and (c)).[88] If the debt is incurred or assumed after 1992, it must be incurred or assumed to acquire, construct, reconstruct, or substantially improve the real property. The excludable amount is limited to the excess of the outstanding principal amount of the debt over the fair market value of the business real property reduced by the outstanding principal amount of any other qualified business indebtedness secured by the property. Also, the exclusion may not exceed the aggregate adjusted bases of depreciable real property held by the taxpayer immediately before discharge. The excluded amount reduces the basis of depreciable real property.

The election to treat debt as qualified real property business indebtedness must be filed with the taxpayer's timely income tax return, including extensions, for the tax year in which the discharge occurs (Reg. § 1.108-5(b)). The election, which is revocable with the consent of the IRS Commissioner, is made on Form 982. A taxpayer who fails to make a timely election must request consent to file a late election under Reg. § 301.9100-3.

Qualified Principal Residence Indebtedness. Excludable from gross income is any amount of income from the discharge, in whole or in part, of "qualified principal residence indebtedness" which occurs on or after January 1, 2007, through December 31, 2012. The debt referred to is acquisition indebtedness, as defined in the home mortgage interest deduction provisions of Code Sec. 163(h), but with a $2 million limit ($1 million for a married taxpayer filing a separate return) (Code Sec. 108(a)(1)(E) and (h)(2)).

> **Comment:** Absent further legislation, beginning January 1, 2013, the exclusion from gross income applicable to qualified principal residence indebtedness will no longer apply.

An individual's acquisition indebtedness is indebtedness with respect to his or her principal residence if it is incurred in the acquisition, construction, or substantial improvement of that residence, and the debt is secured by the residence. Qualified principal residence interest also includes refinancing of the indebtedness, but only to the extent of the amount of the refinanced indebtedness. Principal residence has the same meaning for purposes of the exclusion as it does for purposes of Code Sec. 121 (Code Sec. 108(h)(5)).

Several provisions are included to prevent the abuse of the exclusion of income from the discharge of qualified principal indebtedness. The discharge of a loan will not be excludable from gross income if it is as a result of (1) services performed for the lender, or (2) other factors unrelated to either the financial condition of the taxpayer or a decline in value of the residence. In addition, if only a portion of discharged indebted-

References are to Standard Federal Tax Reports; Tax Research Consultant; and Practical Tax Explanations.

[87] ¶ 7002; SALES: 12,152; § 3,420.20

[88] ¶ 7002; SALES: 12,152; § 3,420.30

ness is qualified principal residence indebtedness, the exclusion applies only to the amount of discharged debt that exceeds the portion of the debt that is not qualified principal residence indebtedness. The basis of the taxpayer's principal residence is reduced, but not below zero, by the amount of qualified principal residence interest that is excluded from income (Code Sec. 108(h)(1)).[89]

Student Loans. A special income exclusion applies to the discharge of all or part of a student loan if, pursuant to the loan agreement, the discharge is made because the individual works for a specified period of time in certain professions for any of a broad class of employers, e.g., as a doctor or nurse in an under served rural area (Code Sec. 108(f)).[90] The loan must be made by: (1) a federal, state, or local government or instrumentality, agency, or subdivision of that government; (2) a tax-exempt public benefit corporation that has assumed control of a public hospital with public employees; or (3) an educational institution if (a) it received funds to loan from an entity described in (1) or (2), above, or (b) the student serves, pursuant to a program of the institution, in an occupation or area with unmet needs under the direction of a governmental unit or a tax-exempt Code Sec. 501(c)(3) organization, e.g., charitable, religious, educational, or scientific organization. Loans refinanced through such a program by the institution or certain tax-exempt organizations also qualify for the exclusion.

Deferral of Discharge of Indebtedness Income Resulting from Reacquisition of Business Indebtedness. A taxpayer could elect to include income arising from the discharge through reacquisition of certain indebtedness in gross income ratably over a five-tax-year period (Code Sec. 108(i)).[91] This applied to indebtedness discharged in connection with the reacquisition in 2009 or 2010 of a corporate or business debt instrument. The discharge of indebtedness income is included in the taxpayer's income ratably over a five-year period beginning with the fifth tax year after the year of reacquisition if the reacquisition occurred in 2009, or the fourth tax year after reacquisition if the reacquisition occurred in 2010.

If the taxpayer issued a new debt instrument for the debt instrument being reacquired, and there was original issue discount (OID) with respect to the original instrument, the taxpayer can deduct the OID ratably over the same period as that for which the discharge of indebtedness income is deferred. If a debt instrument was issued by the taxpayer and the proceeds were used to reacquire a debt instrument also issued by the taxpayer, the new instrument is treated as being issued for the instrument being reacquired. The election to defer OID income is made on an instrument-by-instrument basis, and is irrevocable once made.

Military Exemptions

891. Armed Forces Benefits. Amounts received from a pension, annuity, or similar payment for *personal injuries* or *sickness* that resulted from combat-related service in the armed forces of *any* country, the National Oceanic and Atmospheric Administration, or the Public Health Service of the U.S., or from a disability annuity under the provisions of section 808 of the Foreign Service Act of 1980, are excludable from gross income (¶ 851) (Code Sec. 104(a)(4); Reg. § 1.104-1(e)).[92]

Retirement pay received from the government by Armed Service members is *not* excludable from gross income (Code Sec. 61(a)(11)).[93] Disability retirement pay that is computed on the basis of the percentage of disability is fully excludable from gross income, but disability retirement pay that is computed by reference to years of service is excludable only to the extent allowed under the percentage-of-disability method (Code Sec. 104).[94]

Dividends and proceeds from maturing government endowment insurance contracts under the National Service Life Insurance Act of 1940 and all other acts relating to

References are to Standard Federal Tax Reports; Tax Research Consultant; and Practical Tax Explanations.

[89] ¶ 7010.01; SALES: 12,200; § 3,420.05

[90] ¶ 7002; SALES: 12,152.10; § 3,420.25

[91] ¶ 7010.01, ¶ 7010.05; SALES: 12,252; § 3,420.05

[92] ¶ 6660, ¶ 6661; INDIV: 33,410; § 42,210

[93] ¶ 5502, ¶ 5507.121; COMPEN: 45,404; § 45,805.40

[94] ¶ 6660, ¶ 6662.79; COMPEN: 45,402; § 45,805.35

veterans are excludable from gross income.[95] Interest on dividends left on deposit with the Department of Veterans Affairs is also excludable. If an individual uses accumulated dividends to buy additional paid-up National Service Life Insurance, neither the dividends nor the paid-up insurance is taxable (Rev. Rul. 91-14).

Veterans' benefits under any law administered by the Department of Veterans Affairs are excludable from gross income.[96] This includes amounts paid to veterans or their families in the form of economic recovery payments under the American Recovery and Reinvestment Act of 2009, educational, training, or subsistence allowances, disability compensation and pension payments for disabilities, compensation for participation in a work therapy program, grants for homes designed for wheelchair living, grants for motor vehicles for veterans who lost their sight or the use of their limbs, and veterans' pensions (38 USC § 5301 and following).

893. Armed Forces Allowances. Allowances for subsistence, quarters, travel, and moving furnished to a commissioned officer, chief warrant officer, warrant officer, or enlisted personnel of the Armed Forces, National Oceanic and Atmospheric Administration, or Public Health Service are excludable from gross income (Reg. § 1.61-2(b)).[97]

Housing and cost-of-living allowances received by Armed Forces members to cover the excess cost of quarters and subsistence while on permanent duty at a post outside the U.S. are also excludable from gross income (Rev. Rul. 61-5).[98] The same rule applies to family separation allowances received on account of overseas assignment.[99] The fact that a member of the military service, National Oceanic and Atmospheric Administration, or Public Health Service receives a tax-free housing allowance will not bar a deduction for mortgage interest or real property taxes on the member's home (Code Sec. 265(a)(6)).[100]

895. Combat Zone Compensation. Enlisted members of the Armed Forces and warrant officers, both commissioned and noncommissioned, may exclude from gross income all pay received for any month during any part of which they served in a combat zone or were hospitalized as a result of wounds, disease, or injury incurred while serving in a combat zone. The exclusion for months of hospitalization does not apply for any month beginning more than two years after the termination of combatant activities in the zone. The same exclusion applies to commissioned officers, but it is limited to the maximum enlisted amount. This amount is the highest rate of basic pay at the highest pay grade that enlisted personnel may receive plus the amount of hostile fire/imminent danger pay that the officer receives (Code Sec. 112; Reg. § 1.112-1).[101]

The following areas, among others, have been designated combat zones qualifying American military personnel serving in these areas for special tax benefits:

(1) the Persian Gulf, the Red Sea, the Gulf of Oman, part of the Arabian Sea, the Gulf of Aden and the geographic areas of Iraq, Kuwait, Saudi Arabia, Oman, Bahrain, Qatar, and the United Arab Emirates, including the airspace above, effective on January 17, 1991 (Executive Order No. 12744; Notice 2003-21),

(2) Bosnia, Herzegovina, Croatia, and Macedonia, effective on November 21, 1995 (P.L. 104-117; Notice 96-34),

(3) the Federal Republic of Yugoslavia (Serbia/Montenegro), Albania, the Adriatic Sea, and the Ionian Sea above the 39th parallel, effective on March 24, 1999 (Executive Order 13119; Notice 99-30, supplementing Notice 96-34),

(4) Afghanistan and its airspace, including Jordan, Pakistan, and Tajikistan, effective on September 19, 2001 (Executive Order No. 13239; Notice 2002-17),

References are to Standard Federal Tax Reports; Tax Research Consultant; and Practical Tax Explanations.

[95] ¶ 5504.74; ESTGIFT: 21,164
[96] ¶ 5504.785; COMPEN: 45,404
[97] ¶ 5506, ¶ 7222.79; COMPEN: 6,606; § 45,805.25
[98] ¶ 5507.111; COMPEN: 33,110
[99] ¶ 5507.110; COMPEN: 33,110
[100] ¶ 14,050; INDIV: 48,554; § 7,420.05
[101] ¶ 7080, ¶ 7081; COMPEN: 6,604; § 3,005.15a

(5) Kyrgyzstan and Uzbekistan, effective on October 1, 2001 (Notice 2002-17), and

(6) areas supporting Operation Iraqi Freedom, effective on April 10, 2003.

Combat pay excludable from gross income may nevertheless be included in earned income for purposes of the earned income tax credit (¶ 1322) and calculating the refundable portion of the child tax credit (¶ 1305). Similarly, combat pay may be treated as compensation in determining the amount military personnel can contribute to their individual retirement accounts (IRAs) (¶ 2153).

896. Qualified Military Benefits. A variety of benefits for military personnel were excludable from gross income under a variety of statutes, regulations, and long-standing administrative practices prior to enactment of the Tax Reform Act of 1986. In the 1986 Act, it was determined that, in the future, no such exclusions would be permitted except under some provision of the Internal Revenue Code. However, the Act added to the Code a provision that, in effect, grandfathered all of the previous non-Code exclusions (Code Sec. 134).[102] Under this provision, all such exclusions that were in effect on September 9, 1986, continue to be in effect. If a benefit in effect on September 9, 1986, is thereafter modified or adjusted for increases in the cost of living or the like under authority existing on that date, the adjustments are also excludable. Benefits not otherwise categorized as qualified military benefits but provided in connection with an individual's status or service as a member of the uniformed services may be excluded from gross income under other Code sections if their requirements for exclusion are met.

Death Gratuity Payments. Section 1478, Title 10, of the U.S. Code provides that upon notification of the death of military personnel on active duty or combat-related activities (such as duty training), a death gratuity will be paid to or for the survivor of the service member. The death gratuity payment effective for death occurring on or after October 7, 2001, is $100,000 (National Defense Authorization Act for Fiscal Year 2006, P.L. 109-163, § 664). The exclusion from gross income is also allowed for any adjustment in the amount of the death gratuity payments. The limitation on post-September 9, 1986, modifications does not apply to this benefit. Thus, cost-of-living adjustments or other increases in the gratuity amount will not be subject to tax.

Dependent Care Assistance Program. Qualified military benefits include dependent care assistance provided under a dependent care assistance program (¶ 2192B) for a current or former uniformed forces service member or for a dependent (Code Sec. 134(b)(4)).

Veterans' Bonuses and Payments. The definition of qualified military benefit includes bonus payments by a state or local government entity to a member or former member of the military, or to any dependents of such a member. The payment must be made "only by reason of" the member's service in a combat zone. Thus, the state or local program under which the bonus is paid must specify that the bonus is *only* available with respect to members who served in a combat zone (Code Sec. 134(b)(6)).

Benefits for Volunteer Emergency Responders

896A. Benefits for Volunteer Emergency Responders. For tax years beginning after 2007 and before 2011, members of qualified volunteer emergency response organizations may generally exclude from gross income certain qualified state and local tax benefits (Code Sec. 139B).[103] The exclusion is subject to an annual limitation of $30 multiplied by the number of months during the tax year in which the volunteer performs such services.

A qualified volunteer emergency response organization is any volunteer organization that provides firefighting or emergency medical services and is required by the state or political subdivision, under a written agreement, to provide such services. A

References are to Standard Federal Tax Reports; Tax Research Consultant; and Practical Tax Explanations.

[102] ¶ 7500; COMPEN: 6,606, COMPEN: 6,608; § 4,065.20

[103] ¶ 7649J; INDIV: 33,312; § 4,080

qualified state and local tax benefit is any reduction or rebate of state or local real property taxes, state or local personal property taxes, or state or local income taxes. Any deduction under Code Sec. 164 for state and local taxes is determined with regard to the reduction or rebate (Code Sec. 139B(b)(1)). Expenses paid or incurred by the taxpayer in connection with the performance of services are taken into account as a charitable deduction under Code Sec. 170 only to the extent the expenses exceed the amount excluded from income (as calculated under the annual limitation) (Code Sec. 139B(b)(2)).

Employment Tax Treatment. The excluded benefits and payments under Code Sec. 139B are *not* wages for purposes of federal income tax withholding, FICA, and FUTA (Code Secs. 3121(a)(23), 3306(b)(20), and 3401(a)(23)).

COBRA Premium Assistance

896B. COBRA Premium Assistance. Assistance eligible individuals who became eligible to elect COBRA continuation health care coverage under their employer's plan as a result of an involuntary termination of their employment during the period beginning September 1, 2008, and ending May 31, 2010, were required to pay only 35 percent of the premiums for the coverage. The individual's gross income did *not* include the amount of the premium reduction (Code Sec. 139C).[104] See ¶ 2653 for further discussion of COBRA premium assistance.

Premium assistance for eligible unemployed individuals ended on August 31, 2011.

Disaster Relief Payments

897. Disaster Relief Payments. Individuals who are the victims of a disaster are provided an exclusion from gross income for qualified disaster relief payments, as well as for payments received under Section 406 of the Air Transportation Safety and System Stabilization Act (Code Sec. 139).[105] This exclusion also applies to self-employment and employment taxes, and thus, no withholding is required for qualified disaster relief payments. However, the exclusion does not apply to any individual, or a representative, identified by the Attorney General to have been a participant or conspirator in a terrorist action.

Disaster Relief Payments Defined. Qualified disaster relief payments include payments, from any source, to or for the benefit of an individual to reimburse or pay reasonable and necessary:

(1) personal, family, living or funeral expenses incurred as a result of a qualified disaster,

(2) expenses incurred for the repair or rehabilitation of a personal residence or for the repair or replacement of its contents to the extent attributable to a qualified disaster,

(3) payments made by a commercial airlines to families of passengers killed as a result of a qualified disaster, and

(4) payments made by a federal, state or local government in connection with a qualified disaster (Code Sec. 139(b)).

Taxpayers in a federally declared disaster (formerly known as a presidentially declared disaster) area who receive grants from state programs, charitable organizations or employers to cover medical, transportation, or temporary housing expenses do not include these grants in gross income (Rev. Rul. 2003-12). However, qualified disaster relief payments do not include payments for any expense compensated for by insurance or otherwise, or payments in the nature of income replacement, such as payments to individuals of lost wages, unemployment compensation, or payments in the nature of business income replacement.

References are to Standard Federal Tax Reports; Tax Research Consultant; and Practical Tax Explanations.

[104] ¶ 7649L; COMPEN: 45,206.45; § 4,085

[105] ¶ 7646; INDIV: 33,310.05; § 4,055.10

A qualified disaster is:

(1) a disaster that results from a terroristic or military action as defined under Code Sec. 692(c)(2);

(2) a federally declared disaster as defined under Code Sec. 165(h)(3)(c)(i);

(3) a disaster that results from an accident involving a common carrier, or from any other event, which is determined by the IRS to be of a catastrophic nature; or

(4) a disaster determined by an applicable federal, state or local authority, as determined by the IRS, to warrant assistance.

Air Transportation Safety Act. Taxpayers who are eligible to receive payments under Section 406 of the Air Transportation Safety and System Stabilization Act as a result of physical harm or death incurred from the terrorist-related aircraft crashes on or after September 11, 2001, can exclude these amounts (Code Sec. 139(f)).

Coverdell Education Savings Accounts

898. Coverdell Education Savings Accounts. Individuals may open a Coverdell Education Savings Account (Coverdell ESA), formerly called an education IRA, to help pay for the qualified education expenses of a designated beneficiary (Code Sec. 530).[106] A Coverdell ESA is a tax-exempt trust or custodial account organized exclusively in the United States. At the time it is organized the trust must be designated as a Coverdell ESA and the designated beneficiary must be under age 18 or a special needs individual. Contributions to a Coverdell ESA must be made in cash and are *not* deductible. In addition, the maximum annual contribution that can be made is limited to $2,000 a year excluding rollovers. For tax years beginning before 2013, the annual contribution is phased out for joint filers with modified adjusted gross income (AGI) at or above $190,000 and less than $220,000 (at or above $95,000 and less than $110,000 for single filers). The reduction in permitted contributions based on modified AGI applies only to individual contributors. Thus, contributions made by entities, such as a corporation or tax-exempt organization are not subject to the phase-out rules. Amounts remaining in the account must be distributed within: (1) 30 days after the beneficiary reaches age 30 or (2) 30 days after the death of the beneficiary (see "*Rollovers*," following).

> **Comment:** Absent further legislation, for tax years beginning after December 31, 2012, the maximum annual contribution that can be made to a Coverdell ESA will be reduced from $2,000 to $500. In addition, the modified AGI limits used for determining the phase-out of contributions for married taxpayers filing jointly will no longer be twice the modified AGI limits for single taxpayers.

Coordination with Other Educational Benefits. Qualified expenses will first be reduced for tax-exempt scholarships or fellowship grants (¶ 879) and any other tax-free educational benefits. Expenses will then be reduced for amounts taken into account in determining the Hope and Lifetime Learning credits (¶ 1303). Where a student receives distributions from both a Coverdell ESA and a qualified tuition program (¶ 899) that together exceed these remaining expenses, the expenses must be allocated between the distributions (Code Sec. 530(d)(2)(C)).

> **Comment:** Absent further legislation, for tax years beginning after December 31, 2012, the coordination rules that allow a student to take advantage of the Coverdell ESA provisions, the education credits, and the qualified tuition program in the same tax year will not apply. Thus, beginning in 2013, if a beneficiary claims an exclusion under the Coverdell ESA provisions, that beneficiary may not claim either of the education credits for the same tax year.

Distributions. Generally, contributions to Coverdell ESAs are treated as gifts to the beneficiaries. Distributions from Coverdell ESAs are excludable from gross income to the extent that the distribution does not exceed the qualified higher education expenses

References are to Standard Federal Tax Reports; Tax Research Consultant; and Practical Tax Explanations.

106 ¶ 22,950; INDIV: 60,202;
§ 1,810.05

incurred by the designated beneficiary during the year in which the distribution is made (Code Sec. 530(d)(2)(A)). Qualified distributions are tax exempt regardless of whether the designated beneficiary attends an eligible educational institution on a full-time, half-time, or less than half-time basis. However, room and board expenses constitute qualified higher education expenses only if the student is enrolled at an eligible institution on at least a half-time basis (see *Qualifying Education Expenses*, following).

Distributions are deemed paid from both contributions, which are always tax free, and earnings, which may be excludable. The amount of contributions distributed is determined by multiplying the distribution by the ratio that the aggregate amount of contributions bears to the total balance of the account at the time the distribution is made (Code Sec. 530(d)(1)).

If aggregate distributions exceed expenses during the tax year, qualified education expenses are deemed to be paid from a pro rata share of both principal and interest. Thus, the portion of earnings excludable from gross income is based on the ratio that the qualified higher education expenses bear to the total amount of the distribution. The remaining portion of earnings are included in the income of the distributee.

> **Comment:** Absent further legislation, in tax years beginning after December 31, 2012, the distribution of excess contribution amounts must be made (returned) by the due date (not including extensions) for filing the beneficiary's tax return for the tax year in which the contribution was made and be accompanied by the amount of income attributable to the excess contribution.

Distributions Not Used for Education. The tax imposed on any taxpayer who receives a payment or distribution from a Coverdell ESA that is includible in gross income will be increased by an additional 10 percent (Code Sec. 530(d)(4)(A)). The additional 10-percent penalty does not apply to distributions: (1) made to a designated beneficiary or the estate of a designated beneficiary after the designated beneficiary's death; (2) attributable to the designated beneficiary being disabled as defined under Code Sec. 72(m)(7); (3) made on account of a scholarship or allowance, as defined under Code Sec. 25A(g)(2), received by the account holder to the extent the amount of the distribution does not exceed the amount of the scholarship or allowance; or (4) that constitute the return of excess contributions and earnings thereon (although earnings are includible in income) (Code Sec. 530(d)(2)(A)).

Military Academy Attendance. Generally, since recipients of appointments to military academies are required to fulfill service obligations, the appointments are not considered scholarships and the 10-percent penalty applies. Withdrawals from Coverdell ESAs made on account of the beneficiary's attendance at a service academy are not subject to the penalty to the extent the distribution is used for the costs of advanced education (Code Sec. 530(d)(4)). The penalty waiver covers appointments to the United States Military, Navy, Air Force, Coast Guard, and Merchant Marine Academies.

Rollovers. Amounts held in a Coverdell ESA may be distributed and put into a Coverdell ESA for a member of the designated beneficiary's family. These distributions will not be included in the distributee's gross income provided the rollover occurs within 60 days of the distribution. Similarly, any change in the beneficiary of a Coverdell ESA does not constitute a distribution for gross income purposes if the new beneficiary is a member of the family of the original beneficiary and of the same or higher generation (Code Sec. 529(c)(5)(B)). A person's family members are determined under Code Sec. 529(e)(2) (Code Sec. 530(d)(2)(A)). Amounts held in a Coverdell ESA may also be rolled over into another Coverdell ESA for the benefit of the same beneficiary.

Qualified Education Expenses. Qualified education expenses include expenses for elementary, secondary, undergraduate, and graduate level education. Tuition, fees, books, supplies, equipment, and special needs services, if required, fall under the definition of education expenses for the designated beneficiary to attend undergraduate or graduate level courses at an eligible education institution. The term also includes room and board provided that the student incurring the expense is enrolled at an eligible education institution on at least a halftime basis. In 2009 and 2010 only, expenses incurred for computer technology or equipment, including Internet access charges, were also qualified expenses for post-secondary students.

Qualified elementary and secondary expenses also include expenses for academic tutoring, the purchase of computer technology or equipment, or Internet access or related services, room and board, uniforms, transportation, and supplementary items and services such as extended day programs as required or provided by the school (Code Secs. 529(e)(3)(A) and 530(b)(3)).[107] Computer expenses do *not* include software designed for sports, games, or hobbies unless the nature of the software is predominately educational.

> **Comment:** Absent further legislation, for tax years beginning after December 31, 2012, qualified education expenses will no longer include expenses incurred while the beneficiary is in attendance or enrolled at an elementary or secondary school (i.e., kindergarten through grade 12, as defined by state law).

Eligible Educational Institution. An eligible educational institution is generally an accredited post-secondary educational institution offering credit toward a bachelor's degree, an associate's degree, a graduate-level or professional degree, or other recognized post-secondary credential. Generally, proprietary and post-secondary vocational institutions are eligible educational institutions (Code Sec. 530(b)(3)). Elementary and secondary schools, i.e., kindergarten through grade 12, are also eligible institutions. Schools may be public, private or religious.

Prohibited Uses of Accounts. A Coverdell ESA will lose its tax-exempt status if it engages in a prohibited transaction or is pledged as security for a loan. Prohibited transactions include loans and use of account assets by the beneficiary or a fiduciary (Code Sec. 4975(c)).[108]

Transfers Upon Death or Divorce. Death or divorce of the designated beneficiary need not cause a taxable distribution to the spouse or ex-spouse. The transfer of a beneficiary's interest in a Coverdell ESA to a spouse or ex-spouse under a divorce or separation agreement is not a taxable transfer, and after the transfer the interest in the account is treated as belonging to the spouse or ex-spouse (Code Sec. 530(d)(7)).[109]

Estate and Gift Tax Treatment. Any contribution to a Coverdell ESA is treated as a completed gift of a present interest from the contributor to the beneficiary at the time of the contribution. Contributions are eligible for the annual gift tax exclusion (¶ 2905) and are excludable for purposes of the generation-skipping transfer tax (Code Sec. 530(d)(3)).[110]

Military Death Benefits as Contributions. An individual who receives a military death gratuity or Servicemembers' Group Life Insurance payment may contribute up to the full amount of such gratuity or payment into a Coverdell ESA, without regard to the annual contribution limit and the income phase-out of the limit that would otherwise apply. A military death benefit contribution to a Coverdell ESA will be considered a tax-free rollover contribution if it is made within one year of the date on which the amount is received, and does not exceed the total amount of gratuity and life insurance payments received, less the amount of such payments contributed to a Roth IRA or to another Coverdell ESA. Such rollovers will be disregarded for purposes of the limit on the number of tax-free rollovers per year (Code Sec. 530(d)(9)).

Qualified Tuition Programs

899. Qualified Tuition Programs. Generally, distributions from a qualified tuition program (QTP, also known as a qualified tuition plan or Code Sec. 529 plan) are not included in the income of the donor or the designated beneficiary, as long as the distributions do not exceed the beneficiary's qualified higher education expenses (Code

References are to Standard Federal Tax Reports; Tax Research Consultant; and Practical Tax Explanations.

107 ¶ 22,950; INDIV: 60,206; § 1,810.25

108 ¶ 34,400; INDIV: 60,202.35; § 25,465

109 ¶ 22,950; INDIV: 60,202.30; § 1,810.40

110 ¶ 22,950; INDIV: 60,202.10; § 1,810.15

Sec. 529(c)(3)(B)). A QTP is a program under which an individual may prepay tuition credits or make cash contributions to an account on behalf of a beneficiary for payment of qualified higher education expenses. The program must be established and maintained by a state, state agency, or by an eligible educational institution, i.e., private college or university. Eligible schools generally include any accredited post-secondary educational institution, so long as contributions made to the program are held in a qualified trust, i.e., one which meets the requirements under Code Sec. 408(a)(2) and (5).[111] A QTP is exempt from all federal income taxation, except for the tax imposed on unrelated business income (¶ 655 and following) (Code Sec. 529).[112]

Form 990-T. Colleges and universities of states and other governmental units, as well as subsidiary corporations wholly owned by such colleges and universities, are subject to the Form 990-T filing requirements, unless otherwise exempted as a Code Sec. 501(c)(1) corporation.

Contributions. Contributions to a QTP on behalf of any beneficiary cannot exceed the necessary amount of qualified higher education expenses (QHEEs) for the beneficiary. There are no adjusted gross income phaseout limits. In addition, a taxpayer can contribute to both a QTP and a Coverdell account (¶ 898) in the same year for the same beneficiary.

Qualified Higher Education Expenses (QHEEs). For this purpose, QHEEs include tuition, fees, books, supplies, and equipment required by an educational institution for enrollment or attendance. They also include the reasonable cost of room and board if the beneficiary is enrolled at least halftime. In 2009 and 2010 only, QHEEs included computer equipment, software and Internet access to be used by the beneficiary and the beneficiary's family during any of the years when the beneficiary was enrolled at an eligible school (Code Sec. 529(e)(3)).[113] Certain expenses of special needs beneficiaries may also be considered QHEEs. The amount of QHEEs must be reduced by the amount of any other tax free benefits, i.e., scholarship or fellowship grants excluded from gross income (¶ 879), or the Hope and Lifetime Learning credits (¶ 1303).

Distributions. Distributions from a QTP, including cash, earnings, and in-kind distributions, may be excluded from a designated beneficiary's gross income to the extent that the distribution is used to pay for qualified higher education expenses (QHEEs). Distributions in excess of QHEEs are included in gross income and are subject to an additional 10-percent tax if the reason is other than the death or disability of the beneficiary, or to the extent that the distribution exceeds amounts not covered by scholarships (Code Sec. 529(c)(6)).[114]

Rollovers and Tranfers. Generally, amounts can be rolled over from one qualified tuition program to another for the benefit of the same designated beneficiary, or another beneficiary who is a member of the same family, without tax consequences. In order to qualify for rollover treatment, a distribution from the first QTP must be paid into the second QTP no later than the 60th day after the payment or distribution is made. If the rollover is made to another QTP of the same beneficiary, then only one such transfer is permitted within 12 months of the previous transfer to any QTP for that designated beneficiary (Code Sec. 529(c)(3)).[115]

Estate and Gift Tax Treatment. A contribution to a QTP is treated as a completed gift of a present interest for gift tax purposes (Code Sec. 529(c)(2)). Thus, the contribution qualifies for the annual gift-tax exclusion (¶ 2905). If a donor's contribution exceeds the annual exclusion amount, then he or she may elect to take the excess into account ratably over five years. A QTP contribution does not qualify for the unlimited gift tax exclusion for money used to pay educational expenses (¶ 2907). No portion of a contribution is generally includible in the estate of a donor who dies after June 8, 1997,

References are to Standard Federal Tax Reports; Tax Research Consultant; and Practical Tax Explanations.

[111] ¶ 18,902; INDIV: 60,204, RETIRE: 66,100; § 1,805.10

[112] ¶ 22,940; INDIV: 60,204, EXEMPT: 9,950; § 1,805.05

[113] ¶ 22,940; INDIV: 60,206; § 1,805.20

[114] ¶ 22,940; INDIV: 60,204.15; § 1,805.35

[115] ¶ 22,940; INDIV: 60,204.20; § 1,805.45

unless the donor dies during the five-year period in which excess contributions to a QTP are being ratably taken into account.

Other Income

899A. Other Excluded Income. Several other items of income are excluded from gross income.

Holocaust Reparation Payments. Restitution or reparation payments received by persons who suffered Nazi persecution and survived the Holocaust are excludable from gross income (Act Sec. 2 of the Holocaust Restitution Tax Fairness Act of 2002 (P.L. 107-358)).[116] The exclusion extends to any interest earned on these payments. These excludable payments are also *not* included when applying any tax provision that takes into account excluded income in computing modified adjusted gross income, such as the taxation of Social Security benefits.

Native American Health Care Benefits. The amount of qualified health care benefits provided after March 23, 2010, by Indian tribal governments to a member of an Indian tribe, the member's spouse or dependents are excludable from the beneficiary's gross income (Code Sec. 139D).[117] See ¶ 2190A for further discussion of Indian health care benefits.

Energy Conservation Subsidies. The value of any subsidy provided, directly or indirectly, by a public utility to a customer for the purchase or installation of energy conservation measures for a dwelling unit is excluded from the customer's gross income (Code Sec. 136).[118] Energy conservation measures are any installations or modifications designed to reduce the consumption of electricity or natural gas or to improve management of energy demand.

Exclusions are also available to human trafficking victims (Notice 2012-12) and certain settlements received by Native Americans (Notice 2012-60).

8 EXCLUSIONS

References are to Standard Federal Tax Reports; Tax Research Consultant; and Practical Tax Explanations.

[116] ¶ 5504.0285; INDIV: 33,308; § 3,835

[117] ¶ 7649N; INDIV: 33,512; § 3,715

[118] ¶ 7560; INDIV: 33,552; § 4,001

Chapter 9

BUSINESS EXPENSES

Trade or Business Expenses

901. Deductibility of Business Expenses—Generally. A taxpayer, whether a corporation, an individual, a partnership, a trust, or an estate, generally may deduct from gross income the ordinary and necessary expenses of carrying on a trade or business that are paid or incurred in the tax year (Code Sec. 162; Reg. § 1.162-1).[1] Business expenses incurred by a cash-basis taxpayer while conducting a business but paid in a year after terminating the business are deductible as business expenses in the year paid (Rev. Rul. 67-12).[2] However, a deduction is not permitted for any expenditure that is a capital expense (¶ 903). Expenses for property used for both business and personal activities must be allocated between the different activities. The origin and character of a claim control whether an expense is a deductible business expense or a nondeductible personal expense.

Ordinary and Necessary. Whether business expense is ordinary and necessary is based upon the facts surrounding the expense. An expense is necessary if it is appropriate and helpful to the taxpayer's business (*S.B. Heininger*, SCt, 44-1 USTC ¶ 9109).[3] An expense is ordinary if it is one that is common and accepted in the particular business activity.

Trade or Business. A "trade or business," although not defined in the tax law, has been characterized as an activity carried on for a livelihood or for profit. A profit motive must be present and some type of economic activity must be conducted. In determining whether an activity is engaged in for profit, all facts and circumstances with respect to the activity are to be taken into account (Reg. § 1.183-2(b)).[4] No one factor is determinative in making this determination. In addition, it is not intended that only the factors described below are to be taken into account in making the determination, or that a

References are to Standard Federal Tax Reports; Tax Research Consultant; and Practical Tax Explanations.

[1] ¶ 8500, ¶ 8501; BUSEXP: 3,100; § 9,001

[2] ¶ 8520.1546; BUSEXP: 3,058.20; § 9,001

[3] ¶ 8520.517; BUSEXP: 3,100; § 9,010.05

[4] ¶ 12,173; BUSEXP: 15,150; § 17,210.05

determination is to be made on the basis that the number of factors (whether or not listed in the regulations) indicating a lack of profit objective exceeds the number of factors indicating a profit objective, or vice versa. Among the factors which should normally be taken into account are the following: the manner in which the taxpayer carries on the activity; the expertise of the taxpayer or his advisors; the time and effort expended by the taxpayer in carrying on the activity; the expectation that assets used in the activity may appreciate in value; the success of the taxpayer in carrying on other similar or dissimilar activities; the taxpayer's history of income or losses with respect to the activity; the amount of occasional profits, if any, which are earned; the financial status of the taxpayer; and elements of personal pleasure or recreation.

903. Capital Expenditures. An expense is considered a capital expense if it is paid for permanent improvements or betterments made to increase the value of a property or estate or for restoring property or making good its exhaustion for which an allowance has been made (Temp. Reg. § 1.263(a)-1T).[5] Generally, capital expenses must be deducted by means of depreciation, amortization or depletion (¶ 1201). Capital expenses include amounts paid to produce or acquire tangible or intangible property, to improve tangible property, to facilitate the acquisition of a trade or business or a change in a business entity's capital structure, or to acquire or create an interest in land. They also include amounts paid in corporate financings and restructurings, such as amounts paid by bondholders and shareholders to be used in corporate reorganizations, voluntary contributions by shareholders to a corporation, and amounts paid by a holding company to carry out a guaranty of dividends on the stock of a subsidiary corporation in certain circumstances. See Checklist at ¶ 57.

Acquire or Produce Property. Taxpayers are required to capitalize amounts paid or incurred to produce or acquire tangible and intangible property, both real or personal, including leasehold improvement property, land and land improvements, buildings, machinery and equipment, and furniture and fixtures (Temp. Reg. § 1.263(a)-2T).[6] However, a *de minimis* expensing rule allows a qualifying taxpayer to deduct during the tax year qualifying amounts not in excess of the greater of: (1) 0.1 percent of the taxpayer's gross receipts for the tax year as determined for federal income tax purposes, or (2) 2 percent of the taxpayer's total depreciation and amortization expense for the tax year as determined on its applicable financial statement. A qualifying taxpayer is a taxpayer with an applicable financial statement who has at the beginning of the tax year written accounting procedures treating as an expense for non-tax purposes amounts paid or incurred for property costing less than a certain dollar amount and who treats such amounts paid or incurred during the tax year as an expense on its applicable financial statement.

The *de minimis* rule applies to amounts paid or incurred for the acquisition or production (including amounts paid to facilitate the acquisition or production) of a unit of property that would otherwise be capitalized or for the acquisition or production of any material or supply. A qualifying taxpayer may elect to capitalize amounts that otherwise qualify for the *de minimis* rule. An applicable financial statement is: (1) a financial statement required to be filed with the Securities and Exchange Commission (SEC) (the 10-K or the Annual Statement to Shareholders); (2) a certified audited financial statement that is accompanied by the report of an independent CPA that is used for (i) credit purposes, (ii) reporting to shareholders, partners, or similar persons, or (iii) any other substantial non-tax purpose; or (3) a financial statement (other than a tax return) required to be provided to the federal or a state government or any federal or state agencies (other than the SEC or the IRS).

Improvements. Expenses for permanent improvements to increase the value of property or to restore property must generally be capitalized (Temp. Reg. § 1.263(a)-3T).[7] For this purpose, a unit of property is improved if the amounts paid for activities performed after the property is placed in service by the taxpayer either result in a betterment to the unit of property, restore the unit of property, or adapt the unit of

References are to Standard Federal Tax Reports; Tax Research Consultant; and Practical Tax Explanations.

[5] ¶ 13,702BC; BUSEXP: 9,100; § 10,201

[6] ¶ 13,703L; BUSEXP: 9,080; § 10,215.15

[7] ¶ 13,704BC; BUSEXP: 9,092; § 10,215.12

property to a new or different use. Generally, a taxpayer must capitalize all the direct costs of an improvement, as well as all the indirect costs (such as otherwise deductible repair or removal costs) that directly benefit or are incurred by reason of an improvement. Indirect costs that do not directly benefit and are not incurred by reason of an improvement generally are not capital improvements, regardless of whether they are paid or incurred at the same time as a capital improvement. Whether amounts are related to the same improvement depends on the facts and circumstances of the activities being performed, and whether the costs are incurred by reason of a single improvement or directly benefit a single improvement.

Intangible Property. Amounts also must be capitalized if they are paid or incurred for specific categories of expenditures that are incurred in acquiring, creating, or enhancing, or that facilitate the acquisition or creation of an intangible that is acquired from another person in a purchase or similar transaction, certain rights, privileges, or benefits that are created or originated by the taxpayer; a separate and distinct intangible asset, or a future benefit that the IRS identifies in published guidance (Reg. § 1.263(a)-4).[8]

Repairs. Expenses that keep property in an ordinarily efficient operating condition and do not add to its value or appreciably prolong its useful life are generally deductible as repairs (Temp. Reg. § 1.162-4T).[9]

904. Business Start-Up Costs. Taxpayers who pay or incur business start-up costs and who subsequently enter the trade or business can elect to expense up to $5,000 of the costs. The $5,000 deduction amount is reduced dollar for dollar when the start-up expenses exceed $50,000. The balance of start-up expenses (if any) are amortized over a period of not less than 180 months, starting with the month in which the business begins (Code Sec. 195).[10] The election must be made no later than the date (including extensions) for filing the return for the tax year in which the business begins or is acquired). The election is made by completing Part VI of Form 4562. A taxpayer who does not make the election must capitalize the expenses.

A taxpayer is deemed to have made an election to deduct and amortize start-up expenses for the tax year in which the active trade or business to which the expenses relate begins. A taxpayer may choose to forego the deemed election by affirmatively electing to capitalize its start-up costs on a timely filed federal income tax return, including extensions, for the tax year in which the active trade or business to which the expenses relate begins. The election either to deduct and amortize start-up costs, or capitalize them, applies to all start-up expenses that are related to the active trade or business (Reg. § 1.195-1).[11]

To qualify for deduction and amortization, the start-up expense must be paid or incurred in connection with:

- investigating the creation or acquisition of an active trade or business;
- creating an active trade or business; or
- any activity engaged in for profit or for the production of income before the day on which the active trade or business begins, in anticipation of that activity becoming an active trade or business.

In addition, the start-up expense must be a cost that would be allowable as a deduction if it were paid or incurred in connection with an existing active business in the same field as that entered into by the taxpayer (Code Sec. 195(c)).[12]

The term "start-up costs" does not include any amount with respect to which a deduction is allowed for interest on indebtedness (¶ 1043), taxes (¶ 1021), or research and experimental expenses (¶ 979). If the trade or business is disposed of completely by the taxpayer before the end of the 180-month (or longer) period, any remaining deferred expenses may be deductible as a loss (¶ 1101) (Code Sec. 195(b)(2)).[13]

References are to Standard Federal Tax Reports; Tax Research Consultant; and Practical Tax Explanations.

[8] ¶ 13,704C; BUSEXP: 9,104.20; § 10,210.05.

[9] ¶ 8620; BUSEXP: 9,150; § 9,930.05

[10] ¶ 12,370; DEPR: 21,400; § 9,201

[11] ¶ 12,370F; BUSEXP: 12,252; § 9,215

[12] ¶ 12,370; DEPR: 21,400; § 9,205.10

[13] ¶ 12,370; DEPR: 21,450; § 9,205.05

The organizational costs of business entities are a separate class of expense from start-up expenses, though subject to similar rules. Corporate organization fees are discussed at ¶ 237. Costs of organizing a partnership are discussed at ¶ 477 and ¶ 481.

905. Expenses, Interest Deductions, and Losses—Related Taxpayers. When the payor and payee are related taxpayers (¶ 1717), and the payor is on the accrual method of accounting and the payee is on the cash method, no deduction will be allowed for any trade or business expense or interest payable to the payee until the payee includes the payment in income (Code Sec. 267(a)(2)).[14] A similar rule denies a deduction for a loss (except for a loss from a distribution in corporate liquidation) for property sold or exchanged between related taxpayers (Code Sec. 267(a) and (d)).[15] However, upon later sale or exchange of the property by the transferee at a gain, the gain is recognized only to the extent that it exceeds the previously disallowed loss.

Compensation Paid

906. Compensation for Personal Service. A taxpayer carrying on a trade or business is entitled to deduct a reasonable allowance for salaries or other compensation for personal services. The deduction is allowable for the year in which the salary is paid or incurred (Reg. § 1.162-7).[16]

Publicly held corporations are generally not able to deduct compensation paid to certain covered employees to the extent that the compensation exceeds $1 million per tax year (Code Sec. 162(m)(1); Reg. § 1.162-27).[17] The $1-million limit also does not apply to certain "performance-based compensation" (Code Sec. 162(m)(4)(C)).[18] A "covered employee," is any employee of the taxpayer who, as of the close of the tax year, is:

- the principal executive officer of the taxpayer;
- an individual acting in a capacity as principal executive officer; or
- required to have his compensation reported to shareholders under SEC rules by reason of the individual's being among the three highest compensated officers for the tax year (Notice 2007-49).[19]

Performance-based compensation is compensation issued in the form of stock rights and options exercised when the plan specifies the maximum number of shares that may be granted to all employees in the aggregate. Under proposed regulations applicable to tax years ending on or after the date of their publication as final regulations, it also includes a specific per-employee limitation on the amount granted (Prop. Reg. § 1.162-27(e)(2)(vi)(A)).[20]

A bonus is deductible if paid for services performed, and if, when added to other salaries, it does not exceed reasonable compensation (Reg. § 1.162-9).[21] Awards paid under a corporate bonus plan are not qualified performance-based compensation if the plan allows payments to be made, even if the specified performance goals have not been met, upon the employee's retirement, termination without cause, or voluntary termination of employment for good reason (Rev. Rul. 2008-13).[22] If the bonus was paid solely for attaining a performance goal, the goal must be determined by a compensation committee consisting solely of two or more outside directors. An outside director cannot be a current employee, a former employee who receives compensation during the year, or a current or former officer (Rev. Rul. 2008-32).[23]

Compensation paid to a relative is deductible if the relative performs needed services that would otherwise be performed by an unrelated party. The deduction is

References are to Standard Federal Tax Reports; Tax Research Consultant; and Practical Tax Explanations.

[14] ¶ 14,150; ACCTNG: 12,150; § 17,601

[15] ¶ 14,150; SALES: 39,100; § 17,615

[16] ¶ 8635; COMPEN: 9,050; § 9,305.05

[17] ¶ 8500, ¶ 9051B; COMPEN: 12,350; § 9,310

[18] ¶ 8500; COMPEN: 12,356; § 9,310

[19] ¶ 8636.2763; COMPEN: 12,354

[20] ¶ 49,485; COMPEN: 12,356.15; § 9,310.15

[21] ¶ 8641; COMPEN: 9,054; § 9,335

[22] ¶ 8636.2768; COMPEN: 12,356.10

[23] ¶ 8636.2764; COMPEN: 12,356.10; § 9,310.15.

limited to the amount that would have been paid to a third party (*Transport Mfg. & Equip. Co.*, CA-8, 70-2 USTC ¶ 9627).[24]

Reasonable compensation is the amount that would ordinarily be paid for like services by like enterprises in like circumstances (Reg. § 1.162-7(b)(3)).[25] Thus, whether compensation is reasonable in a given situation depends on the relevant facts and circumstances. Some factors considered include personal ability, responsibility of the position, and economic conditions in the locality. The U.S. Court of Appeals for the Seventh Circuit has used an independent-investor test. This test presumes that compensation is reasonable if the company's investors earn their expected rate of return (*Exacto Spring Corporation*, CA-7, 99-2 USTC ¶ 50,964).[26]

Officer-Stockholders of Closely Held Corporations. Officer-stockholders of closely held corporations may deduct repayments of salary to their corporation that are made pursuant to an agreement requiring such repayments in the event that the IRS determines the salaries to be excessive (Rev. Rul. 69-115).[27] However, the officer-stockholders may claim the deduction only if the agreement is legally enforceable and was in existence *before* the payment of the amounts.

Deferred Compensation Plans. For unfunded deferred compensation plans, the employer's deduction for compensation is claimed when the compensation (or amount attributable to it) is included in the gross income of the recipient (Code Sec. 404(a)(5) and (b)(1)).[28] For the time of inclusion, see ¶ 723. Other benefits that are excluded from the recipient's gross income are deductible when they otherwise would have been includible in the recipient's gross income but for the exclusion (Code Sec. 404(b)(2)).[29] This rule also applies to compensation paid to independent contractors (Code Sec. 404(d)).[30]

A plan is unfunded if it consists of an unsecured promise to pay compensation at some time in the future. If the employer sets aside a reserve for the future obligation, the plan is unfunded if the employee has no rights in the reserve or its earnings and if the reserve remains solely the property of the employer or other payor, subject to the claims of creditors (Rev. Rul. 55-525).[31]

A plan is presumed to defer compensation if the compensation is received after the 15th day of the third calendar month after the end of the employer's tax year in which the related services are rendered. This presumption may be overcome if the employer establishes that it was administratively or economically impractical to avoid the deferral of compensation beyond the 2½-month period. Payments within the 2½-month period are not treated as deferred compensation and may be accrued by an accrual-method employer in the year earned by the employee (Temp. Reg. § 1.404(b)-1T, Q&A-2).[32]

For a discussion of rules governing the employer's deduction for compensation for deferred compensation plans, see ¶ 2122, ¶ 2122A, ¶ 2178, and ¶ 2197.

Deduction Limit for TARP Recipients. Under the Troubled Asset Relief Program (TARP) established pursuant to the Emergency Economic Stabilization Act of 2008 (P.L. 110-343), the federal government is authorized to purchase troubled assets from financial institutions, either through a public auction or directly from the institution. During the period in which financial assistance under TARP remains outstanding, each TARP recipient will be subject to the $500,000 compensation deduction limit (Code Sec. 162(m)(5)).[33] The deduction limit applies during the period that the TARP obligation remains outstanding. There is no threshold amount of assistance an entity must receive to qualify for TARP recipient treatment for these purposes.

References are to Standard Federal Tax Reports; Tax Research Consultant; and Practical Tax Explanations.

[24] ¶ 8637.752; COMPEN: 9,202; § 9,305.20

[25] ¶ 8635; COMPEN: 9,100; § 9,305.10

[26] ¶ 8637.227, ¶ 8637.57; COMPEN: 9,114; § 9,305.10

[27] ¶ 8640.165; COMPEN: 9,456; § 7,101

[28] ¶ 18,330; COMPEN: 15,250; § 25,605

[29] ¶ 18,330; COMPEN: 12,108.10; § 25,605

[30] ¶ 18,330; COMPEN: 15,252; § 25,605

[31] ¶ 18,352.48; COMPEN: 15,050; § 25,610.15

[32] ¶ 18,354; COMPEN: 15,254; § 24,005

[33] ¶ 8500; COMPEN: 12,358; § 9,310.05

907. Golden Parachutes. A corporation that enters into a contract agreeing to pay an employee additional compensation in the event that control or ownership of the corporation changes is barred from taking a deduction for an "excess parachute payment" made to a "disqualified individual" (Code Sec. 280G).[34] A disqualified individual is an employee or independent contractor who performs personal services for any corporation and is an officer, shareholder, or highly compensated person. A personal service corporation is treated as an individual. The disqualified individual is subject to an excise tax of 20 percent of the excess parachute payment in addition to the income tax due (Code Sec. 4999(a)).[35]

Parachute Payment Defined. A parachute payment is any payment in the nature of compensation to a disqualified individual if:

- the payment is contingent on a change in the ownership or effective control of the corporation or a substantial portion of the assets of the corporation; and
- the aggregate present value of such contingent payments equals or exceeds three times an individual's base amount.

Any payment in the nature of compensation to a disqualified individual that violates any securities law or regulations is also considered a parachute payment. Reasonable compensation for personal services to be rendered on or after the date of change or for personal services actually rendered before the date of change are not treated as parachute payments. Additionally, parachute payments do not include payments to or from certain qualified plans (Code Sec. 280G(b)).[36]

Base Amount. The base amount is the individual's annualized includible compensation for the base period (the most recent five tax years ending before the date on which the ownership of control changed, or that portion of the period during which the disqualified individual performed personal services for the corporation) (Code Sec. 280G(b)(3)(A); Code Sec. 280G(d)(2)).[37]

Exceptions. Generally, a parachute payment does not include any payment made to a disqualified individual by a small business corporation or other corporations, if, immediately before the change, none of their stock was readily tradable on an established securities market and shareholder approval requirements are met (Code Sec. 280G(b)(5)).[38]

Excess Parachute Payment. An excess parachute payment is an amount equal to the excess of any parachute payment over the portion of the base amount allocated to the payment. The allocable base amount is subtracted from the parachute payment, and the remainder is the excess parachute payment (Code Sec. 280G(b)).[39]

Limitation on Payment. Under the Troubled Asset Relief Program (TARP) established pursuant to the Emergency Economic Stabilization Act of 2008 (P.L. 110-343), the federal government is authorized to purchase troubled assets from financial institutions, either through a public auction or directly from the institution. If a firm sells troubled assets directly to the Treasury under the TARP, the firm is required to follow certain standards that limit executive compensation, including prohibiting any golden parachute payment to "senior executive officers." A senior executive officer is an individual who is one of the top five highly paid executives of a public company whose compensation is required to be disclosed pursuant to the Securities Exchange Act of 1934, and non-public company counterparts (Act Sec. 111 of the American Recovery and Reinvestment Act of 2009 (P.L. 111-5)).

908. Contributions for Employee Benefits and Health Insurance. An employer's deduction for contributions to a funded welfare benefit plan for sickness, accident, hospitalization, or medical benefits is governed by Code Sec. 419 (¶ 2190) (Temp. Reg.

References are to Standard Federal Tax Reports; Tax Research Consultant; and Practical Tax Explanations.

[34] ¶ 15,150; COMPEN: 30,050; § 21,805.15

[35] ¶ 34,940; COMPEN: 30,250; § 21,820

[36] ¶ 15,150; COMPEN: 30,100; § 21,815.05

[37] ¶ 15,150; COMPEN: 30,150; § 21,805.25

[38] ¶ 15,150; COMPEN: 30,110; § 21,815.20

[39] ¶ 15,150; COMPEN: 30,150; § 21,805.25

§ 1.162-10T).[40] Although amounts that are added to a self-insurance reserve account are not currently deductible, actual claims charged to the account are deductible (*General Dynamics Corp.*, SCt, 87-1 USTC ¶ 9280).[41] Group health plans that fail to provide continuing coverage to qualified beneficiaries may subject employers to an excise tax (Code Sec. 4980B).[42]

Self-Employed Persons. Self-employed persons may deduct from gross income 100 percent of amounts paid during the year for health insurance for themselves, spouses, and dependents (Code Sec. 162(l)).[43] The deduction cannot exceed the taxpayer's net earned income derived from the trade or business for which the insurance plan was established, minus the deductions for 50 percent of the self-employment tax and/or the deduction for contributions to qualified retirement plans, self-employed pensions (SEPs), or SIMPLE plans. Amounts eligible for the deduction do not include amounts paid during any month, or part of a month, that the self-employed individual was able to participate in a subsidized health plan maintained by his or her employer or spouses' employer.

Children Under the Age of 27. Children under the age of 27 are considered dependents of a taxpayer for purposes of the deduction for the health insurance costs of a self-employed person, spouse, and dependents. A child includes: a son, daughter, stepson, or stepdaughter of the taxpayer; a foster child placed with the taxpayer by an authorized placement agency or by judgment, decree, or other order of any court of competent jurisdiction; and a legally adopted child of the taxpayer or a child who has been lawfully placed with the taxpayer for legal adoption (Code Sec. 152(f)(1)).[44]

Excise Tax on High-Cost Employer-Provided Insurance. A 40-percent excise tax will be imposed on health coverage providers starting in 2018 to the extent that the aggregate value of employer-sponsored health coverage for an employee exceeds a threshold amount (Code Sec. 4980I).[45]

908A. Disability Payments. A premium on a personal disability insurance policy is deductible if it is paid by a business or professional person (¶ 2190B). A business or professional person may deduct premiums on a policy that pays overhead expenses during a period of disability, but the proceeds under such a policy are includible in gross income (Rev. Rul. 55-264).[46] When an insurance premium is paid in advance for more than one year, only a pro rata portion of the premium is deductible for each year, regardless of the taxpayer's method of accounting (Reg. § 1.461-1; Rev. Rul. 70-413).[47]

908B. Employer-Provided Daycare. Payments to a daycare center are a deductible business expense where the purpose of providing the availability of the day care center is:

- to provide an employee with a place to send his or her child while at work knowing that the child is receiving proper care;
- to reduce absenteeism, increase productivity, and reduce company training costs; and
- to reduce employee turnover (Rev. Rul. 73-348).[48]

However, an S corporation was not allowed to deduct amounts it paid for daycare for its sole shareholder's preschool children where there was no direct relationship to the taxpayer's business, and, despite the S corporation employing over 20 individuals, the S corporation only paid daycare expenses for the taxpayer's children (*F.M. Settimo*, 92 TCM 473 (2006)).[49]

References are to Standard Federal Tax Reports; Tax Research Consultant; and Practical Tax Explanations.

[40] ¶ 8751; COMPEN: 42,100; § 9,345

[41] ¶ 8522.3947; BUSEXP: 18,210; § 9405.30, § 9,345

[42] ¶ 34,600; COMPEN: 45,206; § 42,850.05

[43] ¶ 8500; COMPEN: 45,250; § 5,401

[44] ¶ 8007; FILEIND: 6,154.05; § 1,215.10

[45] ¶ 34,619ZE; COMPEN: 45,208; § 42,245.15

[46] ¶ 8522.385; BUSEXP: 18,220; § 9,415.05

[47] ¶ 21,805, ¶ 21,817.21; BUSEXP: 18,216; § 9,420.05

[48] ¶ 8752.21; BUSEXP: 3,104; § 9,010.15

[49] ¶ 8520.517; BUSEXP: 3,104; § 9,010.15

909. Life Insurance Premiums. Premiums paid by an employer for insurance on the life of an officer or employee are deductible only if it can be shown that:

- premium payments are in the nature of additional compensation;
- total compensation, including premiums, is not unreasonable; and
- the employer is not directly or indirectly a beneficiary under the policy (*L. Hyman & Co.*, 21 BTA 159 (1930); *Brown Agency, Inc.*, 21 BTA 1111 (1931)).[50]

However, no deduction is allowed an employer for premiums paid under a split dollar arrangement (¶ 721).

Premiums on group-term life insurance covering the lives of employees are deductible by the employer if the employer is not a direct or indirect beneficiary (Code Sec. 264(a)(1); Reg. § 1.264-1).[51] The payment of such premiums generally represents income to the employee to the extent that the coverage provided exceeds $50,000 (¶ 721).

Generally, no deduction is allowed for interest paid or accrued on a debt incurred or continued to purchase or carry any single premium life insurance, endowment or annuity contract. If substantially all the premiums on a life insurance or endowment contract are paid within four years from date of purchase, or if an amount is deposited with the insurer for payment of a substantial number of future premiums on the contract, it is regarded as a single premium contract (Code Sec. 264(a)(2) and (c)).[52]

Interest on a debt incurred to purchase or continue a life insurance, endowment, or annuity contract pursuant to a plan of purchase contemplating the systematic borrowing of part or all of the increases in cash value is not deductible (Code Sec. 264(a)(3)).[53] However, Code Sec. 264(d) allows an interest deduction in limited situations. Special rules may permit the deduction of interest incurred for key person policies owned by corporations (Code Sec. 264(e)).[54]

Entertainment, Meal, and Gift Expenses

910. Entertainment Expenses. Special limits are imposed by Code Sec. 274 on the deduction of business-related entertainment, meals, and gift expenses. These limits are in addition to those imposed by other Code sections. For example, no deduction is allowed for the cost of entertainment, amusement, or recreation unless that cost is either (1) *directly related* to the active conduct of a trade or business or (2) for entertainment directly before or after a substantial and bona fide business discussion *associated with* the conduct of that trade or business.

Specific exceptions to these general requirements are discussed at ¶ 915. Entertainment includes entertaining guests at nightclubs, sporting events, theaters, etc. A taxpayer's trade or business is considered in applying an objective test as to what constitutes entertainment. For example, if an appliance distributor conducts a fashion show for the spouses of retailers, the show would generally be considered entertainment (Code Sec. 274(a)(1)(A); Reg. § 1.274-2(b)(1)(ii)).[55] There are numerous exceptions to the 50-percent limitation rule, which are discussed at ¶ 917.

Two-Percent-of-AGI Floor. In most situations, an employee's unreimbursed business expenses must be claimed as a miscellaneous itemized deduction, subject to the two-percent-of-adjusted-gross-income (AGI) floor, on Schedule A (Form 1040) (¶ 1011). The percentage limit (e.g., 50 percent) on meal and entertainment expenses must be taken into account prior to application of the two-percent-of-AGI floor (¶ 916) (Code Sec. 67; Temp. Reg. § 1.67-1T(a)).[56] Certain employees defined by the Code may deduct their unreimbursed expenses directly from gross income (¶ 941B).

911. Directly Related Test. For an entertainment expense to meet the directly related test in order to be deducted as a business expense (¶ 910), the taxpayer must

References are to Standard Federal Tax Reports; Tax Research Consultant; and Practical Tax Explanations.

[50] ¶ 8522.386, ¶ 14,002, ¶ 14,008.12; BUSEXP: 18,154.05; § 9405.05.

[51] ¶ 14,002, ¶ 14,003; COMPEN: 48,100; § 21,005.05

[52] ¶ 14,002; INDIV: 48,556; § 9405.05

[53] ¶ 14,002; INDIV: 48,556; § 9,405.15

[54] ¶ 14,002; COMPEN: 48,062; § 9,405.15

[55] ¶ 14,402, ¶ 14,405; BUSEXP: 24,550; § 9,610.05, § 9,635.05

[56] ¶ 6060, ¶ 6061; BUSEXP: 12,102, FILEIND: 12,054; § 9,635.05

have had more than a general expectation of deriving income, or some other specific business benefit, at some indefinite future time. The taxpayer must engage in the active conduct of business with the person being entertained. In addition, the active conduct of business must be the principal aspect of the combined business and entertainment (Reg. § 1.274-2(c)).[57]

912. Associated Entertainment. Entertainment expenses associated with the active conduct of the taxpayer's business are deductible if they directly precede or follow a bona fide and substantial business discussion (¶ 910). This includes goodwill expenditures to obtain new business or encourage continuation of existing business relationships. The business discussion must be the principal aspect of the combined entertainment and business and must represent an active effort by the taxpayer to obtain income or other specific business benefit (Reg. § 1.274-2(d)).[58]

913. Entertainment Facility. No business deduction is generally allowed for any expense for entertainment facilities, such as yachts, hunting lodges, swimming pools, tennis courts, or bowling alleys (¶ 910) (Code Sec. 274(a)(1)(B)).[59] However, expenses for recreational facilities primarily for the benefit of employees generally are deductible (Reg. § 1.274-2(f)(2)(v)).[60]

913A. Club Dues. As a general rule, no business deduction is permitted for club dues. This rule extends to business, social, athletic, luncheon, sporting, airline, and hotel clubs (Code Sec. 274(a)(3); Reg. § 1.274-2(a)(2)(iii)).[61] However, dues paid to professional or public service organizations (e.g., accounting associations, or Kiwanis and Rotary clubs) are deductible if they are paid for business reasons and the organization's principal purpose is *not* to conduct entertainment activities for members or their guests or to provide those parties with access to entertainment facilities.

914. Entertainment-Related Meals. Generally, an entertainment-related meal expense is *not* deductible unless the taxpayer establishes that the expense is directly related to the active conduct of a trade or business. However, if a meal expense directly precedes or follows a substantial and bona fide business discussion (including a business meeting at a convention), then it is deductible if it is established that the expense was associated with the active conduct of a trade or business. The taxpayer must be able to substantiate the expense (¶ 953) (Code Sec. 274(d); Temp. Reg. § 1.274-5T(c), (f)).[62]

There are two additional restrictions placed on the deduction of meal expenses: (1) meal expenses generally are not deductible if neither the taxpayer nor the taxpayer's employee is present at the meal, and (2) a deduction will not be allowed for food and beverages to the extent that such expense is lavish or extravagant under the circumstances. These restrictions do not apply to the expenses described in exceptions (2), (3), (4), (7), (8), and (9) at ¶ 915 (Code Sec. 274(k)).[63]

915. Exceptions to Entertainment Rules. The following entertainment expenses are not subject to the special rules for the deduction of entertainment expenses (¶ 912, ¶ 913, and ¶ 914). They are deductible provided that they meet the ordinary and necessary requirements and are properly substantiated (Code Sec. 274(e); Reg. § 1.274-2(f)(2)).[64] However, they may be subject to the 50-percent limit rule (¶ 916 and ¶ 917). The exceptions are:

(1) food and beverages for employees furnished on the business premises;

(2) expenses for services, goods, and facilities that are treated as compensation and as wages for withholding tax purposes (note that if the recipient is a specified individual (generally, an officer, director, or 10-percent shareholder or a

References are to Standard Federal Tax Reports; Tax Research Consultant; and Practical Tax Explanations.

[57] ¶ 14,405; BUSEXP: 24,558; § 9,615

[58] ¶ 14,405; BUSEXP: 24,560; § 9,615

[59] ¶ 14,402; BUSEXP: 24,650; § 9,625.10

[60] ¶ 14,405; BUSEXP: 24,562.20; § 9,630.25

[61] ¶ 14,402, ¶ 14,405; BUSEXP: 24,658; § 9,625.15

[62] ¶ 14,402, ¶ 14,410; BUSEXP: 24,810; § 10,105

[63] ¶ 14,402; BUSEXP: 24,562; § 9,601

[64] ¶ 14,402, ¶ 14,405; BUSEXP: 24,562; § 9,630.10

related person), the employer's deduction cannot exceed the amount of compensation reported);

(3) reimbursed expenses, but only:

(a) if the services relating to the expenses for which reimbursement is made are performed for an employer and the employer has not treated the expenses as wages subject to withholding; or

(b) if the services are performed for a person other than an employer and the taxpayer incurring the reimbursed expenses accounts to that person;

(4) recreational expenses primarily for employees who are not highly compensated (¶ 2117) (for example, a company picnic);

(5) expenses of employees', stockholders', agents', or directors' *business* meetings;

(6) expenses directly related and necessary to attendance at a *business* meeting of a tax-exempt business league, including a real estate board, chamber of commerce or board of trade;

(7) expenses for goods, services, and facilities made available to the public;

(8) expenses for entertainment sold to customers in a bona fide transaction for adequate consideration; and

(9) goods, services, and facilities that are furnished to nonemployees as entertainment, amusement or recreation expenses and that are includible in the recipients' incomes and reported on a Form 1099-MISC by the taxpayer.

916. 50-Percent Limit for Meal and Entertainment Expenses. The amount allowable as a business deduction for meal and entertainment expenses is generally limited to 50 percent of such expenses. Food and beverage costs incurred in the course of travel away from home fall within the scope of this rule (Code Sec. 274(n)).[65] The 50-percent limit is applied only after determining the amount of the otherwise allowable deductions. For instance, the portion of a travel meal that is lavish and extravagant must first be subtracted from the meal cost before the 50-percent limit is applied. Related expenses, such as taxes and tips in the case of meals and other charges, and room rental and parking fees in the case of entertainment expenses, must be included in the total expense before applying the 50-percent limit. Allowable deductions for transportation costs to and from a business meal are not reduced.

Transportation Workers. The deductible percentage of the cost of meals consumed while away from home by individuals subject to Department of Transportation hours of service rules (e.g., interstate truck and bus drivers and certain railroad, airline, and merchant marine employees) is 80 percent.

Leased Employees. If an employee or independent contractor incurs meal and incidental expenses (M&IE) in connection with the performance of services for another person and is not reimbursed, then the 50-percent limit applies to any deduction claimed by the employee or independent contractor (Prop. Reg. § 1.274-2(f)(2)(iv); Rev. Rul. 2008-23; *Transport Labor Contract/Leasing, Inc.*, CA-8, 2006-2 USTC ¶ 50,478).[66] However, if an employee or independent contractor accounts for the expenses to a leasing company and is reimbursed under an allowance arrangement, and the payment is treated as compensation, then he is not subject to the 50-percent limit. Instead, the leasing company bears the expense and is subject to the 50-percent limit.

On the other hand, a leasing company will not be subject to the 50-percent limit if, in connection with its performance of services for a third party, it is reimbursed under an allowance arrangement with the third party, and it accounts to the third party in the same manner that the employee accounted for the expenses. In such circumstances, the third party bears the expenses and is subject to the 50-percent limit for the deduction that it claims.

References are to Standard Federal Tax Reports; Tax Research Consultant; and Practical Tax Explanations.

[65] ¶ 14,402; BUSEXP: 24,600; § 9,635

[66] ¶ 49,544, ¶ 14,408A.37; BUSEXP: 24,604; § 9,635.05

917. Exceptions to 50-Percent Limit for Meal and Entertainment Expenses. The following expenses are *not* subject to the 50-percent limit on meal and entertainment expense deductions (80-percent limit for certain transportations workers) (¶ 916):

(1) expenses described in categories (2), (3), (4), (7), (8), and (9) at ¶ 915;

(2) food and beverage expenses associated with benefits that are excludable from the recipient's gross income as a *de minimis* fringe benefit;

(3) the cost of a ticket package to a sporting event and related expenses if the event is organized to benefit a tax-exempt organization, all net proceeds of the event are contributed to such organization, and volunteers perform substantially all of the work in carrying out the event; in other situations, a deduction for a ticket may not exceed the ticket's face value;

(4) an employee's meal expenses incurred while moving that are reimbursed by the employer and includible in the employee's gross income (¶ 1073); and

(5) expenses for food and beverages provided to employees on certain (a) vessels and (b) oil or gas platforms and drilling rigs and their support camps (Code Sec. 274(l)(1) and (n)).[67]

Skyboxes. When a skybox is rented for more than one event, the deduction may not exceed the price of non-luxury box seats (subject to the usual 50-percent limit) (Code Sec. 274(l)(2)).[68]

Tickets to Collegiate Sporting Events. For any payment to or for an institution of higher education that would be allowable as a charitable deduction but for the fact that the taxpayer thereby receives (directly or indirectly) the right to purchase tickets for seating at an athletic event in an athletic stadium of the institution, 80 percent of that payment is treated as a charitable contribution (Code Sec. 170(l)).[69]

918. Business Gifts. Deductions for business gifts, whether made directly or indirectly, are limited to $25 per recipient per year (Code Sec. 274(b)(1); Reg. § 1.274-3).[70] Items clearly of an advertising nature that cost $4 or less and signs, display racks, or other promotional materials given for use on business premises are not gifts.

919. Employee Achievement Awards. An employer may deduct up to $400 of the cost of an employee achievement award for all nonqualified plan awards to each employee (Code Sec. 274(j)).[71] The employer's deduction for the cost of qualified plan award made to a particular employee is limited to $1,600 per year, taking into account all other qualified and nonqualified awards made to that employee during the tax year.

An employee achievement award is an item of tangible personal property awarded to an employee as part of a meaningful presentation for length-of-service or safety achievements and under circumstances that do not create a significant likelihood of disguised compensation.

A qualified plan award is an employee achievement award provided under an established written plan or program that does not discriminate in favor of highly compensated employees (¶ 2117) as to eligibility or benefits. An employee achievement award is not a qualified plan award if the average cost of all employee achievement awards under the plan exceeds $400. This average cost calculation includes the entire cost of all qualified plan awards, ignoring employee achievement awards of nominal value.

A length of service award will not qualify if it is received during the employee's first five years of service or if the employee has received another length of service award (other than an award excludable as a *de minimis* fringe benefit (¶ 2188C) during the year or within the last four years. An award will not be considered a safety achievement award if made to a manager, administrator, clerical employee, or other professional employee, or if, during the tax year, awards for safety achievement previously have been

References are to Standard Federal Tax Reports; Tax Research Consultant; and Practical Tax Explanations.

[67] ¶ 14,402; BUSEXP: 24,604; § 9,640.05

[68] ¶ 14,402; BUSEXP: 24,662; § 9,650

[69] ¶ 11,600; INDIV: 51,052.40; § 7,510.75

[70] ¶ 14,402, ¶ 14,406; BUSEXP: 24,706; § 9,945.05

[71] ¶ 14,402; BUSEXP: 24,714, BUSEXP: 24,716; § 9,340.10

made to more than 10 percent of the employees, excluding managers, administrators, clerical employees, or other professional employees.

Taxes

920. Taxes Directly Attributable to Business. Business taxpayers can deduct the taxes listed at ¶ 1021 and any other state, local, and foreign taxes paid or accrued within the tax year to the extent that they are directly attributable to a trade or business or to property held for the production of rents or royalties (Code Sec. 164(a)).[72] Any tax not listed at ¶ 1021 that is paid or accrued by the taxpayer in connection with the acquisition of property is treated as part of the cost of the acquired property or, if in connection with the disposition of property, as a reduction in the amount realized.

The uniform capitalization rules require some taxpayers to capitalize certain taxes that would otherwise be deductible (¶ 990–¶ 999).

921. Business Deduction for Federal Unemployment Insurance Tax. The federal unemployment insurance tax (FUTA) is deductible as a business expense by the employer after application of state credits (*A. Trujillo*, 68 TC 670 (1977)).[73] On the accrual basis, the deduction may be accrued for the calendar year in which the wages were paid even though payment of the tax is not due until the following year. On the cash basis, the tax is deductible when paid.

922. Business Deduction for State Unemployment Insurance and Disability Fund Contributions. An employer covered by state unemployment insurance laws is entitled to deduct as taxes only those contributions that are classified as taxes under state law and are incurred in carrying on a trade or business or the production of income (Rev. Rul. 71-59).[74] In states that require employees to contribute to state unemployment compensation funds, such contributions may be claimed as itemized deductions (as state income taxes).[75] Also, compulsory employee contributions to state disability funds are deductible as itemized deductions (as state income taxes). However, employee contributions to private disability benefit plans are not deductible by employees. See also the checklist at ¶ 57.

923. Business Deduction for Social Security Taxes. The federal Social Security tax on an employer is deductible by the employer as a business expense (¶ 2601). The contribution of an employer on wages paid to a domestic worker is not deductible unless it is classified as a business expense (*R.A. Biggs*, CA-6, 71-1 USTC ¶ 9306).[76]

The tax imposed on employees by the Social Security Act is not deductible by the employee (*B.A. Gasparutti*, 76 TCM 726 (1998)).[77] If the employer pays the tax without deduction from the employee's wages under an agreement with the employee, the amount is deductible by the employer and is income to the employee (Rev. Rul. 86-14).[78]

A self-employed individual may deduct from gross income 50 percent of the self-employment tax, other than the additional 0.9-percent Medicare tax on incomes over a certain threshold, imposed for the same tax year (¶ 2670) (Code Sec. 164(f)).[79] However, for any tax year that begins in 2011 or 2012, the self-employment tax liability deduction equals the sum of 59.6 percent of the applicable Social Security taxes and 50 percent of the applicable Medicare taxes (Act Sec. 601 of the Tax Relief, Unemployment Insurance Reauthorization, and Job Creation Act of 2010 (P.L. 111-312), amended by Act Sec. 1001 of the Middle Class Tax Relief and Job Creation Act of 2012 (P.L. 112-96)).

Qualified employers do not have to pay their share of Social Security or Railroad Retirement Act taxes on wages or compensation paid after March 18, 2010, and prior to January 1, 2011, to newly hired qualified individuals who were formerly unemployed (¶ 2648).

References are to Standard Federal Tax Reports; Tax Research Consultant; and Practical Tax Explanations.

[72] ¶ 9500; BUSEXP: 21,454; § 16,415, § 16,425

[73] ¶ 9502.31; PAYROLL: 9,100; § 22,205.10

[74] ¶ 8752.692; BUSEXP: 21,506; § 9,365

[75] ¶ 9502.31; INDIV: 45,112.20; § 22,301

[76] ¶ 9502.30; PAYROLL: 9,050; § 22,210.60

[77] ¶ 9502.29; INDIV: 45,152.10; § 7,345

[78] ¶ 5508.96; PAYROLL: 9,050; § 7,345

[79] ¶ 9500; BUSEXP: 21,504; § 7,340

924. Deduction for Federal and State Income Tax. Federal income taxes are not deductible in determining taxable income (Code Sec. 275).[80] However, they are deductible in determining the amount of a corporation's income subject to the accumulated earnings tax (¶ 251) and the personal holding company tax (¶ 275) (Reg. §§ 1.535-2; 1.545-2).[81] Corporations and partnerships may deduct their state income taxes as business expenses. State income taxes that are based on net business income may only be deducted by self-employed individuals on Schedule A (Form 1040) as an itemized deduction. However, if the state income tax is based on gross business income, the tax may be deducted as a business expense (Temp. Reg. § 1.62-1T(d)).[82]

Charitable Contributions

927. Corporate Limits. The deduction of a corporation for charitable contributions is limited to 10 percent of its taxable income for the year, computed without regard to:

- the deduction for charitable contributions;
- the deductions for dividends received and for dividends paid on certain preferred stock of public utilities;
- any net operating loss carryback to the tax year;
- the deduction for domestic production activities; and
- any capital loss carryback to the tax year (Code Sec. 170(b)(2); Reg. § 1.170A-11).[83]

Individuals can take an immediate deduction for the donation of conservation property up to 50 percent of their contributions base. For tax years beginning on or before December 31, 2011, corporate donors that qualify as farmers or ranchers are permitted to deduct up to 100 percent of their contribution base (adjusted gross income computed without regard to any net operating loss carryback) for qualified conservation contributions of capital gain real estate.

A corporation is permitted to carry over to the five succeeding tax years charitable contributions that exceed the 10-percent limit, but deductions in those years are also subject to the maximum limitation (Code Sec. 170(d)(2)). Except for the carryover rule, a deduction is allowed only for a charitable contribution paid during the tax year. An accrual-basis corporation, however, may elect to treat as paid during the tax year all or a portion of a contribution that is actually paid within two-and-one-half months after the close of the tax year if it was authorized by the board of directors during the year (Code Sec. 170(a)(2)).

930. Contributions of Inventory or Scientific Property. Generally, the deduction for a charitable contribution of ordinary income property is the fair market value of that property less the amount that would have been ordinary income if the property had been sold at its fair market value on the date of the contribution (¶ 1062). There are, however, three exceptions to this rule in the case of contributions by corporations.

Inventory-Type Property. If a corporation (other than an S corporation) makes a gift of inventory, property held for sale to customers in the ordinary course of business, or depreciable or real property used in the trade or business, it may, if certain conditions are met, deduct its basis for the property, plus one-half of the property's unrealized appreciation. The claimed deduction, however, may not exceed twice the basis of the property (Code Sec. 170(e)(3)).[84] Moreover, no deduction is allowed for any part of the appreciation that would be ordinary income resulting from recapture. To qualify, the gift must be made to a qualified public charity or a private operating foundation, and the donee's use of the property must be for the care of infants or the ill or needy.

C corporations can claim a similar enhanced deduction for donations of book inventories to public schools made through December 31, 2011 (Code Sec.

References are to Standard Federal Tax Reports; Tax Research Consultant; and Practical Tax Explanations.

[80] ¶ 14,500; BUSEXP: 21,350; § 7,345

[81] ¶ 23,042, ¶ 23,252; CCORP: 18,252, CCORP: 36,254; § 26,905.05

[82] ¶ 6003; INDIV: 45,100; § 9,940.10

[83] ¶ 11,600, ¶ 11,672; CCORP: 9,350; § 7,575.15

[84] ¶ 11,600; CCORP: 9,354; § 7,575.25

170(e)(3)(D)). The enhanced deduction generally increases the deductible amount from the donated inventory item's basis to the lesser of (1) the donated inventory item's basis plus one-half of the item's appreciation, or (2) two times the donated inventory item's basis.

Caution: The enhanced deduction for book inventories does not apply for contributions after December 31, 2012, and will not be extended absent further legislation.

Scientific Research Property. A corporation (other than an S corporation, a personal holding company, or a service organization) is entitled to the same deduction for a qualified research contribution of certain ordinary income property to an institution of higher education or to an exempt scientific research organization for research purposes as that for inventory-type property (Code Sec. 170(e)(4)).[85] To qualify as a research contribution:

- the contributed property must have been constructed or assembled by the donor;
- the contribution must be made within two years of construction or assembly; and
- the original use of the property must be by the donee.

Several additional requirements that must also be satisfied.

Computer Equipment (Expired). A C corporation is entitled to an enhanced deduction for a charitable contribution of computer technology or equipment to an elementary or secondary school or public library (Code Sec. 170(e)(6)).[86] The amount of the deduction is equal to the taxpayer's basis in the donated property plus one-half of the amount of ordinary income that would have been realized if the property had been sold. The deduction can not exceed twice the taxpayer's basis in the donated property. The contribution must be made within three years of the property's acquisition or substantial completion of its construction or assembly, and the original use of the property must have been by the donor or the donee. The enhanced charitable deduction for contributions of computer technology and/or equipment to schools or public libraries does not apply to contributions made during any tax year beginning after December 31, 2011.

Caution: The enhanced deduction for computer technology or equipment does not apply for contributions made in any tax year beginning after December 31, 2012, and will not be extended absent further legislation.

930A. Contributions of Food (Expired). Corporate and noncorporate taxpayers are entitled to an enhanced deduction for charitable donations of food inventory through December 31, 2011 (Code Sec. 170(e)(3)(C)(iv)).[87] The food inventory has to consist of items fit for human consumption and has to be contributed to a qualified charity or private operating foundation for use in the care of the ill, the needy, or infants. The enhanced deduction does not apply to contributions after December 31, 2011, and charitable donations of food after that date are subject to the 10 percent of taxable income limitation (¶ 927).

931. Contribution Rules. The rules concerning a deduction for the following charitable contributions are the same regardless of whether the contribution is made by a corporate or a noncorporate taxpayer:

- gifts of appreciated property (¶ 1062),
- use of property—partial interests (¶ 1063),
- reduction for interest (¶ 1065),
- gift of future interest in tangible personal property (¶ 1069),
- transfers in trust (¶ 1070),
- appraisals (¶ 1071), and
- denial of deduction (¶ 1068).

References are to Standard Federal Tax Reports; Tax Research Consultant; and Practical Tax Explanations.

[85] ¶ 11,600; CCORP: 9,354; § 7,575.25

[86] ¶ 11,600; CCORP: 9,358; § 7,575.25

[87] ¶ 11,600; INDIV: 51,152.15; § 7,525.20

Interest

937. Business Deduction for Interest. Interest expense or other borrowing costs incurred in a trade or business or in the production of rental or royalty income is deductible from gross income (Code Sec. 163).[88] See ¶ 1055 and ¶ 1056 for the rules on prepaid interest and ¶ 1094 for the rules on investment interest paid by noncorporate taxpayers. There are, however, a number of limits on claiming interest deduction on certain types of debt (¶ 940). For example, interest paid on debt that is allocable to the production of certain property must be capitalized rather than deducted in the year paid (¶ 993).

937A. Interest on Income Tax Liability. Interest paid or accrued on income tax assessed on an individual's federal, state or local income tax liability is not a business deduction even though the tax due is related to income from a trade or business (Temp. Reg. § 1.163-9T(b)(2)(i)(A)).[89] This rule also applies to an individual's partnership and S corporation activities. See ¶ 2723 and ¶ 2724 for interest allocations pursuant to compromise and partial payments. Penalties on deficiencies and underestimated tax cannot be deducted.

938. Interest Paid by Bank. A bank or trust company may deduct interest paid during the year on deposits and certificates of indebtedness (Reg. § 1.163-1(c)).[90]

939. Interest on Margin Account. Interest on a margin account is deductible by a cash-basis investor when it is paid to the broker or when the interest becomes available to the broker through the investor's account (Rev. Rul. 70-221).[91] See ¶ 1094 for investment interest.

940. Exceptions and Limitations to Deduction of Interest. There are a number of Code sections which limit or preclude a taxpayer from claiming an interest deduction on certain types of indebtedness (¶ 937). See also ¶ 1045 for limits on personal interest.

Uniform Capitalization Rules. Interest paid or incurred during the production period and allocable to real property or tangible personal property may be required to be capitalized (¶ 993) (Code Sec. 263A(f)).[92]

Original Issue Discount Bonds. The interest deduction is generally limited (¶ 1952) (Code Sec. 163(e)).[93]

Bonds Not in Registered Form. Failure to meet the registration requirement generally results in a denial of an interest deduction (¶ 1963) (Code Sec. 163(f)).[94]

Commodity Straddles. Interest on debt incurred to purchase or carry commodity investments that are part of a straddle is not currently deductible. The interest must be added to the basis of the commodity. Hedging transactions, however, are exempted from this capitalization rule (¶ 1948 and ¶ 1949) (Code Sec. 263(g)).[95]

Earnings Stripping. A corporation is not allowed a deduction for excessive interest paid if the interest will not be taxed as income to the recipient (Code Sec. 163(j)).[96] A corporate partner's share of interest paid or accrued to or by the partnership is treated as paid or accrued by or to the corporation directly.

Corporate Indebtedness Incurred to Acquire Another Corporation's Stock. Generally, there is a $5-million annual limit on the interest deductible by a corporation on a debt incurred to acquire stock or two-thirds of the operating assets of another corporation (Code Sec. 279).[97]

References are to Standard Federal Tax Reports; Tax Research Consultant; and Practical Tax Explanations.

[88] ¶ 9102; BUSEXP: 21,000; § 9,915

[89] ¶ 9400; INDIV: 48,350; § 7,345

[90] ¶ 9103; RIC: 12,204; § 7,405.05

[91] ¶ 9104.568; INDIV: 48,450; § 45,405.25c

[92] ¶ 13,800; BUSEXP: 9,050; § 10,330.05

[93] ¶ 9102; ACCTNG: 36,224.05; § 7,405.20

[94] ¶ 9102; BUSEXP: 21,206; § 7,405.05

[95] ¶ 13,700; SALES: 48,160; § 16,505.40

[96] ¶ 9102; BUSEXP: 21,210; § 26,201

[97] ¶ 14,700; CCORP: 9,400; § 7,405.10

Employee's Expenses

941. Employee Business Expenses. The performance of services as an employee is considered to be a trade or business. Thus, employee business expenses are generally deductible. *Reimbursed* employee business expenses are deductible from gross income (Code Sec. 62(a)(2)(A)).[98] However, reimbursements that are paid under an accountable plan are excluded from the employee's gross income, and employees may not claim a deduction on their return as a business expense (¶ 942). *Unreimbursed* employee business expenses are deductible as miscellaneous itemized deductions, subject to the two-percent-of-adjusted-gross-income (AGI) floor (¶ 1011) and the 50-percent limit for meal and entertainment expenses (80 percent for employees subject to the Department of Transportation's hours of service limitations) (¶ 916). Schedule A (Form 1040) is used. Special rules apply to qualified performing artists (¶ 941A), statutory employees (¶ 941B), impairment-related work expenses (¶ 1013), fee-based government employees (¶ 941D), schoolteachers (¶ 941C), and members of the National Guard and Reserves (¶ 941E). An employee is also allowed a deduction from gross income for jury duty pay surrendered to an employer in exchange for regular salary (¶ 1010) (Code Sec. 62(a)(13)).[99]

941A. Performing Artist. A qualified performing artist may deduct business expenses in arriving at adjusted gross income on Form 2106 or Form 2106-EZ. Generally, to qualify for this deduction an individual must:

- render services in the performing arts during the tax year for at least two employers;
- have total business deductions attributable to the performance of such services that exceed 10 percent of the income received from such services; and
- have adjusted gross income of $16,000 or less (Code Sec. 62(b)).[100]

941B. Statutory Employees. Individuals who are considered to be statutory employees may deduct their allowable business expenses from gross income (Code Sec. 3121(d); Rev. Rul. 90-93).[101] The term "statutory employees" includes:

- a full-time traveling or city salesperson who solicits orders from wholesalers, restaurants, or similar establishments on behalf of a principal; the merchandise sold must be for resale (e.g., food sold to a restaurant) or for supplies used in the buyer's business;
- a full-time life insurance agent whose principal business activity is selling life insurance and/or annuity contracts for one life insurance company;
- an agent-driver or commission-driver engaged in distributing meat, vegetables, bakery goods, beverages (other than milk), or laundry or dry cleaning services; and
- a home worker performing work on material or goods furnished by the employer.

An employer should indicate on the worker's Form W-2 whether the worker is classified as a statutory employee. Statutory employees report their wages, income, and allowable expenses on Schedule C (Form 1040) or Schedule C-EZ (Form 1040). Statutory employees are not liable for self-employment tax because their employers are obligated to treat such individuals as employees for social security tax purposes.

941C. School Teachers. For tax years beginning after 2011, school teachers may deduct expenses paid or incurred for the purchase of school supplies only as miscellaneous itemized deductions subject to the two-percent-of-adjusted-gross-income floor. For tax years beginning before 2012, eligible educators can deduct up to $250 of the expenses paid or incurred as an above-the-line adjustment to gross income (¶ 1084) (Code Sec. 62(a)(2)(D)).[102]

References are to Standard Federal Tax Reports; Tax Research Consultant; and Practical Tax Explanations.

[98] ¶ 6002; INDIV: 36,050; § 5,310

[99] ¶ 6002; FILEIND: 9,076; § 5,040

[100] ¶ 6002; INDIV: 36,058; § 5,315

[101] ¶ 8524.2547; INDIV: 63,154; § 5,305

[102] ¶ 6002; INDIV: 36,364; § 5,325

941D. Fee-Based Government Officials. Expenses paid or incurred with respect to services performed by an official as an employee of a state or local government are deductible in computing adjusted gross income (Code Sec. 62(a)(2)(C)).[103] The employee must be compensated in whole or in part on a fee basis.

941E. National Guard and Reserve Members. Members of the National Guard and the Reserves are allowed to deduct travel expenses while away from home to attend meetings and training sessions as an above-the-line deduction (Code Secs. 62(a)(2)(E) and 162(p)).[104] This type of travel has been deemed to be travel away from home in the pursuit of a trade or business when an individual is away from home overnight in connection with their service as a member of the guard or reserves. Expenses incurred in connection with the performance of such service are deductible as an above-the-line deduction only when the taxpayer is more than 100 miles away from home. The amount of deductible expenses is limited to the federal per diem rate for the locality of the meeting or training session.

942. Reimbursed and Unreimbursed Employee Business Expenses. The tax treatment of an employee's reimbursed business expenses depends on whether the employer's reimbursement or expense allowance arrangement is an accountable or nonaccountable plan (¶ 952A) (Code Sec. 62; Reg. § 1.62-2).[105] If expenses are reimbursed under an *accountable* plan, the reimbursement is not reported as income on the employee's Form W-2 and, therefore, the expense may not be claimed as a deduction on the employee's tax return. In this situation, the 50-percent limit on deductions for meals and entertainment applies to the employer (¶ 916). If the employee's deductible business expenses exceed the amounts paid by the accountable plan, and these expenses are adequately substantiated (¶ 943), then the excess expenses are deductible as miscellaneous itemized deductions, subject to the two-percent-of-adjusted-gross-income (AGI) floor (¶ 1011) and the 50-percent limit for meals and entertainment (¶ 916). If expenses are reimbursed under a *nonaccountable* plan, the reimbursements are included in the employee's income. Business expenses that are reimbursed under a nonaccountable plan or not reimbursed at all can be deducted, to the extent they can be adequately substantiated, as miscellaneous itemized deductions, subject to the two-percent-of-adjusted-gross-income (AGI) floor (¶ 1011), and the 50-percent limit for meals and entertainment (¶ 916). The employee reports the expenses on Form 2106 or Form 2106-EZ.

943. Substantiation for Employees' Returns. Business expenses which exceed the reimbursements received under an accountable plan, which are reimbursed under a nonaccountable plan, or which are not reimbursed at all may be deducted by the employee (¶ 942). As with any other deductible expense, an employee must adequately substantiate business expenses in order to deduct them.

More specific substantiation requirements apply with respect to the following expenses, which are deemed particularly susceptible to abuse: expenses with respect to travel away from home (including meals and lodging), entertainment expenses, business gifts, and expenses in connection with the use of "listed property" (¶ 1211). These expenses must generally be substantiated by adequate records or other sufficient evidence corroborating the taxpayer's own statement (Code Sec. 274(d); Temp. Reg. § 1.274-5T).[106] The expenses must be substantiated as to amount, time, place, and business purpose. For entertainment and gift expenses, the business relationship of the person being entertained or receiving the gift must also be substantiated.

Substantiation by Adequate Records. A contemporaneous log is not required, but a record of the elements of the expense or use of the listed property made at or near the time of the expenditure or use, supported by sufficient documentary evidence, has a high degree of credibility. Adequate accounting generally requires the submission of an account book, expense diary or log, or similar record maintained by the employee and

References are to Standard Federal Tax Reports; Tax Research Consultant; and Practical Tax Explanations.

[103] ¶ 6002; INDIV: 36,050; § 5,320

[104] ¶ 6002, ¶ 8500; FILEIND: 9,054.25; § 5,330

[105] ¶ 6002, ¶ 6004; INDIV: 36,054; § 10,120.05

[106] ¶ 14,402, ¶ 14,410; BUSEXP: 24,800; § 10,105.05, § 10,110.05

recorded at or near the time of incurrence of the expense. Documentary evidence, such as receipts or paid bills, is not generally required for expenses that are less than $75. Documentary evidence for lodging expenses is required (Reg. § 1.274-5(c)(2)(iii)).[107] The employee should also maintain a record of any amounts charged to the employer.

Substantiation of Amount of Meal and Incidental Expenses. The amount of meal and/or incidental expenses (M&IE) deducted by an employee can be substantiated either by retaining evidence of the actual expenses or by use of the standard meal allowance (¶ 954B). The amount of the standard meal allowance varies by location, and for some locations, by the time of year. An individual using the standard meal allowance must still keep records, such as a daily planner or log, to prove the time, place, and business purpose of the expenses. There is no standard lodging amount similar to the standard meal allowance. Employees must be able to substantiate the actual cost of their lodging in order to deduct it.

Transportation and Car Expenses

945. Local Transportation Expenses. Businesses (including self-employed persons and statutory employees) may deduct ordinary and necessary local transportation expenses from gross income (Reg. § 1.162-1(a)).[108] The manner of an employee's deduction for transportation expenses generally depends on whether the employee is reimbursed under an accountable plan (¶ 942). Local transportation expenses are generally those incurred for the business use of a car. However, they also include the cost of travel by rail, bus, or taxi.

Commuting Expenses. Commuting expenses between a taxpayer's residence and a business location within the area of the taxpayer's tax home generally are not deductible (Rev. Rul. 75-432).[109] However, a deduction is allowed for expenses incurred in excess of ordinary commuting expenses for transporting job-related tools and materials (*D. Fausner*, CA-5, SCt, 73-2 USTC ¶ 9515).[110] An individual who works at two or more different places in a day may deduct the costs of getting from one place to the other (Rev. Rul. 55-109, modified by Rev. Rul. 90-23).[111]

There is an exception to the general rule that commuting expenses are not deductible. If a taxpayer has at least one regular place of business away from home, then daily transportation expenses for commuting between the taxpayer's residence and a temporary work location in the same trade or business can be deducted (¶ 951) (Rev. Rul. 99-7).[112] For this purpose, a temporary work location is defined using a one-year standard. If employment at a work location is realistically expected to last (and does in fact last) for one year or less, the employment is temporary, absent facts and circumstances to the contrary. Employment at a work location is not temporary, regardless of whether or not it lasts for more than one year, if it is realistically expected to last more than one year or there is no realistic expectation that employment will last for one year or less. A taxpayer may at first realistically expect that employment at a work location will last one year or less, but, at a later date, realistically expect that the work will last for more than one year. In this situation, the employment will be treated as temporary until the date that the taxpayer's realistic expectation changes and will be treated as not temporary after that date (unless facts and circumstances indicate otherwise).

For the rules concerning deductions while on a temporary assignment away from home, see ¶ 951.

Travel from a Home Office. An individual who uses his home as his principal place of business (¶ 961) is permitted to deduct transportation expenses between the home and another work location in the same trade or business (Rev. Rul. 99-7).[113] This rule applies

References are to Standard Federal Tax Reports; Tax Research Consultant; and Practical Tax Explanations.

[107] ¶ 14,410; BUSEXP: 24,806.15; § 10,105.15

[108] ¶ 8501; BUSEXP: 24,450; § 8,005

[109] ¶ 8550.269; BUSEXP: 24,458; § 8,010.05

[110] ¶ 8590.25; BUSEXP: 24,460; § 8,010.05

[111] ¶ 8570.175; BUSEXP: 24,454; § 8,010.05

[112] ¶ 8570.146; BUSEXP: 24,458; § 8,010.05

[113] ¶ 8570.146; BUSEXP: 24,456; § 8,010.05

regardless of whether the work location is temporary or regular and regardless of the distance. See ¶ 961 for a discussion of home office expenses.

946. Car Expense. Expenses for gasoline, oil, tires, repairs, insurance, depreciation, parking fees and tolls, licenses, and garage rent incurred for cars used in a trade or business are deductible. The deduction is allowed only for that part of the expenses that is attributable to business (Code Sec. 162; § 1.162-1).[114] Generally, an employee's unreimbursed expenses can be deducted only as a miscellaneous itemized deduction subject to the two-percent-of-adjusted-gross-income (AGI) floor (¶ 941). See ¶ 1208–¶ 1215 concerning the expensing election and depreciation of a car.

947. Substantiation of Car Expenses. A taxpayer can substantiate car expenses by keeping an exact record of the amount paid for gasoline, insurance, and other costs. However, the standard mileage rate method is a simplified method available to both employees and self-employed persons in computing deductions for car expenses in lieu of calculating the operating and fixed costs allocable to business purposes (Code Sec. 274(d); Temp. Reg. § 1-274-5T).[115]

Standard Mileage Rate. Under the standard mileage method, the taxpayer determines the amount of the allowable deduction by multiplying all the business miles driven during the year by the standard mileage rate. The business portion of parking fees and tolls may be deducted in addition to the standard mileage rate. The standard mileage rate is 55.5 cents per mile for 2012. The standard mileage rate is 51 cents per mile for January 1 through June 30, 2011. The standard mileage rate increases to 55.5 cents per mile for July 1 through December 31, 2011 (Notice 2012-1; Announcement 2011-40; Rev. Proc. 2010-51; Notice 2010-88).[116]

Rural mail carriers receive a qualified reimbursement for expenses incurred for the use of their vehicles for performing the collection and delivery of mail in a rural route. They are allowed an miscellaneous itemized deduction, subject to the two-percent-of-adjusted-gross-income limitation, for their automobile expenses that exceed their qualified reimbursement (Code Sec. 162(o)).[117] Qualified reimbursements in excess of actual automobile expenses continue to be excluded from gross income (H.R. Conf. Rep. No. 108-755).

The standard mileage rate method may be used by businesses, self-employed individuals, or employees in computing the deductible costs of operating automobiles they own or lease for business purposes. The business standard mileage rate may not be used to compute the deductible expenses of five or more automobiles owned or leased by a taxpayer and used simultaneously (such as in fleet operations). Use of the standard mileage rate in the first year of business use is considered an election to exclude the car from MACRS depreciation (¶ 1236).

For automobiles owned by a taxpayer and used in a trade or business, and for which the business standard mileage rate is used, depreciation is considered to have been allowed at the rate of 23 cents per mile for 2012 and 22 cents per miles for 2011 (Notice 2012-1; Rev. Proc. 2010-51).[118] The depreciation reduces the basis of the automobile (but not below zero) in determining adjusted basis.

Fixed and Variable Rate (FAVR) Method. The maximum standard automobile cost for purposes of the alternative fixed and variable rate (FAVR) allowance is $28,000 for 2012 and $26,900 for 2011 (Notice 2012-1; Notice 2010-88; Rev. Proc. 2010-51).[119] Under the FAVR method, an employer reimburses its employee's expenses with a mileage allowance using a flat rate or a stated schedule that combines periodic fixed and variable payments. An employee's car expenses will be deemed substantiated if the payor (usually the employer) reimburses the employee's expenses with the FAVR mileage allowance using a flat rate or a stated schedule that combines periodic fixed and variable payments. At least five employees must be covered by such an arrangement at all times

References are to Standard Federal Tax Reports; Tax Research Consultant; and Practical Tax Explanations.

[114] ¶ 8500, ¶ 8501; BUSEXP: 24,500; § 9,005

[115] ¶ 14,402, ¶ 14,410; BUSEXP: 24,502; § 8,065

[116] ¶ 8590.55; BUSEXP: 24,502; § 8,065

[117] ¶ 8500; BUSEXP: 24,506.15; § 8,050

[118] ¶ 14,417.50; BUSEXP: 24,506.05; § 10,125.15.

[119] ¶ 8590.55; BUSEXP: 24,912.106; § 10,125.20

during the calendar year, but at no time can the majority of covered employees be management employees. Additional requirements that must be met.

948. Interest on Car Loans. Interest paid by an employee on a car loan is nondeductible personal interest (¶ 1045). A self-employed taxpayer may claim the interest paid on the business portion of a car as a business expense. The nonbusiness portion is nondeductible personal interest (Code Sec. 163(a)).[120]

Traveling Expenses Away from Home

949. Traveling Expenses Generally. A deduction is allowed for ordinary and necessary traveling expenses incurred by a taxpayer while away from home in the conduct of a trade or business (Code Sec. 162(a)(2); Reg. § 1.162-2).[121] An individual is not away from home unless his duties require him to be away from the general area of his tax home for a period substantially longer than an ordinary workday and it is reasonable for him to need to sleep or rest. In some cases, travel expenses may be deductible even though the taxpayer is away from home for a period of less than 24 hours.

Local Lodging. Under proposed regulations, expenses paid or incurred for local lodging may be deductible as ordinary and necessary expenses of a taxpayer's trade or business, including the trade or business of being an employee (Prop. Reg. § 1.162-31).[122] The proposed regulations provide a safe harbor for certain local lodging at a business meeting, conference, or other activity or function. Other local lodging expenses may be deductible as business expenses depending the relevant facts and circumstances. The rule applies to lodging provided by the employer or lodging that the employer requires the employee to obtain and must meet the following conditions.

(1) The lodging must be necessary for the individual to participate in a meeting or other business function.

(2) The lodging must not be provided for more than five calendar days and must not recur more frequently than once per calendar quarter.

(3) The employer must require the employee to remain at the meeting or function overnight.

(4) The lodging is not lavish or extravagant and does not provide any significant element of personal pleasure, recreation, or benefit.

The proposed regulations will apply to expenses paid or incurred on or after the date they are published as final regulations. Taxpayers may, however, rely on them.

950. Tax Home Defined. A individual's tax home for purposes of deducting travel expenses (¶ 949) is considered to be: (1) the taxpayer's regular or principal (if there is more than one regular) place of business, or (2) if the taxpayer has no regular or principal place of business because of the nature of the work, the taxpayer's regular place of abode in a real and substantial sense (Notice 93-29).[123] If a taxpayer fails to fall within either category, the taxpayer is an itinerant or someone who has a home wherever he happens to be working. Thus, the taxpayer is never away from home for purposes of deducting traveling expenses.

When there are multiple areas of business activity or places of regular employment, the principal place of business is treated as the tax home. In determining the principal place of business, the following factors are considered:

(1) the time spent on business activity in each area;

(2) the amount of business activity in each area; and

(3) the amount of the resulting financial return in each area.

Business travel expenses incurred while away from the principal place of business are deductible.[124]

References are to Standard Federal Tax Reports; Tax Research Consultant; and Practical Tax Explanations.

[120] ¶ 9102; INDIV: 48,350; § 8,205

[121] ¶ 8500, ¶ 8527; BUSEXP: 24,050; § 9,510.05

[122] ¶ 9051J; INDIV: 36,306; § 9,505

[123] ¶ 8570.1327; BUSEXP: 24,100; § 9,510.05

[124] ¶ 8570.1327; BUSEXP: 24,104; § 9,510

The tax home of a member of the U.S. Congress is the member's residence in the state or district that the member represents. However, deduction for meals and lodging while in Washington, DC, are limited to $3,000 per year, after applying the two-percent-of-adjusted-gross-income (AGI) floor for miscellaneous itemized deductions (Code Sec. 162(a)).[125]

The Supreme Court has held that a member of the Armed Forces is not away from home while at the individual's permanent duty station (*H.A. Stidger*, SCt, 67-1 USTC ¶ 9309).[126] However, members of the National Guard and Reserves can deduct qualifying expenses as an above-the-line deduction when attending meetings or training sessions (¶ 941E).

951. Temporary v. Indefinite Test. In determining when an individual is away from home for purposes of deducting travel expenses (¶ 949), the nature of the stay and the length of time away from the individual's principal place of business are of prime importance. If the assignment is temporary in nature, the taxpayer is considered away from home and a travel expense deduction is allowed. If the assignment is for an indefinite period of time, the location of the assignment becomes the individual's new tax home, and the individual may not deduct traveling expenses while there. When an individual works away from home at a single location for more than one year, the employment will be treated as indefinite, and related travel expenses will not be deductible (Code Sec. 162(a); Rev. Rul. 93-86; Rev. Rul. 99-7).[127] Employment expected to last more than one year is classified as indefinite, regardless of whether the work actually exceeds a year. Employment that is expected to, and does in fact, last for one year or less is temporary.

The one-year rule does not apply to federal employees certified by the Attorney General as traveling on behalf of the United States in temporary duty status to investigate or prosecute, or to provide support services for the investigation or prosecution of, a federal crime. Such employees may deduct their travel expenses even if their assignment is expected to last for more than one year.

952. Deductible Travel Expenses. The costs of the following items are ordinarily deductible, if paid or incurred while a business owner or employee is traveling away from home on business (¶ 949): meals and lodging; transportation, including a reasonable amount for baggage; necessary samples and display materials; hotel rooms, sample rooms, telephone and fax services, and public stenographers; and the costs (including depreciation (¶ 1211)) of maintaining and operating a car for business purposes (Reg. § 1.162-2).[128]

No deduction is allowed for the travel expenses of a spouse, dependent, or other individual who accompanies the taxpayer or employee on a business trip unless such person is an employee of the person who is paying or reimbursing the expenses, the travel of such person serves a bona fide business purpose, and the expenses of such person are otherwise deductible (Code Sec. 274(m)(3)).[129]

A taxpayer may deduct traveling expenses between the principal place of business and place of business at a temporary or minor post of duty. When the taxpayer's family lives at the temporary or minor post of duty, the taxpayer may still claim travel expenses. However, the deduction for meals and lodging is limited to the portion of the taxpayer's expenses that are allocable to the taxpayer's presence there in the actual performance of the taxpayer's duties (Rev. Rul. 55-604).[130]

References are to Standard Federal Tax Reports; Tax Research Consultant; and Practical Tax Explanations.

[125] ¶ 8500; BUSEXP: 24,120; § 9,510.10

[126] ¶ 8570.1236; BUSEXP: 24,120.20; § 9,505

[127] ¶ 8500, ¶ 8570.1327, ¶ 8570.143; BUSEXP: 24,110; § 9,510.25

[128] ¶ 8527; BUSEXP: 24,052; § 9,501

[129] ¶ 14,402; BUSEXP: 24,200; § 9,530

[130] ¶ 8570.175; BUSEXP: 24,104; § 9,505

The deduction for the cost of meals and lodging while away from home on business is limited to amounts that are not lavish or extravagant under the circumstances (Code Sec. 162(a)(2)).[131] The deduction for meals is limited to 50 percent of the total expenses (¶ 916).

952A. Accountable v. Nonaccountable Plans. The arrangement under which an employer reimburses business expenses incurred by employees (or provides advances to cover such expenses) is either an accountable plan or a nonaccountable plan. Amounts paid under an accountable plan are deductible by the employer and not reported as income to the employee. Amounts paid under a nonaccountable plan are deductible by the employer as compensation reportable on the employee's Form W-2 and subject to withholding requirements. Withholding rules relating to employee expense reimbursements are explained at ¶ 2607 and ¶ 2608. The tax treatment of an employee's business expenses and reimbursements under each type of plan is explained at ¶ 942.

A plan is an accountable plan only if it satisfies the following three conditions:

(1) the expenses covered under the plan must have a business connection;

(2) the plan must require employees to substantiate the covered expenses; and

(3) the plan must require employees who receive advances to return any amounts in excess of their substantiated expenses (Reg. § 1.62-2(c)).[132]

If a plan satisfies these requirements, but an employee fails to return an excess advance to the employer within a reasonable period, only the amount of the substantiated expenses is treated as paid under an accountable plan. The retained excess is treated as paid under a nonaccountable plan. If a plan does not satisfy these requirements, an employee cannot force the employer to treat it as an accountable plan by substantiating the expenses and returning the excess.

Business Connection. The business connection requirement is satisfied if the expenses are deductible business expenses of the employer, paid or incurred in connection with the performance of services as an employee. If a plan also covers bona fide expenses that are related to the employer's business but not deductible, such as travel that is not away from home, the plan is treated as two separate arrangements, one accountable, the other nonaccountable (Reg. § 1.62-2(d)).[133]

Substantiation. The substantiation an accountable plan must require for the expenses it covers must be sufficient to substantiate the expense under the general substantiation rules, which vary depending on the type of expense (Reg. § 1.62-2(e)).[134] If the expense is for travel, meals, lodging, entertainment, gifts, or attributable to the use of listed property (¶ 1211), the substantiation requirement is satisfied if enough information is submitted to the employer to satisfy substantiation requirements (¶ 953), including travel and car expenses deemed substantiated.

If the expense is not in one of the categories stated above, such as expenses for printing a report, then the expense is considered substantiated if enough information is submitted to the employer to enable the employer to identify the specific nature of each expense and to conclude that the expense was attributable to the employer's business activities. The elements of each expense should be substantiated, including the amount, place, time, or date, and business purpose.

Deemed Substantiation of Employee's Reimbursed Expenses. An employee's expenses are deemed to be substantiated, for purposes of the accountable plan requirements, if the employee provides an adequate accounting of the expenses to the employer in the form of adequate records (Reg. § 1.274-5(f)(4)).[135] The adequate accounting requirement can be satisfied as to the amount of car expenses and lodging and/or meals and incidental expenses by using the per diem allowances discussed at ¶ 947 (car expenses)

References are to Standard Federal Tax Reports; Tax Research Consultant; and Practical Tax Explanations.

[131] ¶ 8500; BUSEXP: 24,556; § 9,635

[132] ¶ 6004; INDIV: 36,056; § 10,120.10

[133] ¶ 6004; INDIV: 36,056.05; § 10,120.10

[134] ¶ 6004; INDIV: 36,056.10; § 10,120.10

[135] ¶ 14,410; BUSEXP: 24,800; § 10,115.10

and ¶ 954–¶ 954B (meals and incidental expenses only). Note that in order to deduct unreimbursed expenses for lodging on their own return, an employee or self-employed individual must have evidence of the actual costs.

Return of Excess Advances. The return of excess advances requirement is satisfied if employees are required to return amounts received in excess of the expenses that are substantiated or deemed substantiated within a reasonable period of time (Reg. § 1.162-2(f)).[136] Advances must be provided within a reasonable period before the covered expenses are anticipated to be paid or incurred and must be reasonably calculated not to exceed the anticipated expenses. If an employee fails to return the excess within a reasonable period of time, only amounts paid that are not in excess of the amounts substantiated will be treated as paid under an accountable plan. Excess amounts retained will be treated as paid under a nonaccountable plan and must be included in income by the employee. An accountable plan that reimburses expenses pursuant to an IRS-approved mileage (¶ 947) or per diem allowance (¶ 954–¶ 954B) must require the return of the portion that relates to days or miles of travel not substantiated.

Reasonable Period of Time. The provision of advances, the substantiation of expenses, and the return of excess advances must each take place within a reasonable period of time. A reasonable period depends on facts and circumstances, but the IRS has provided two safe harbor methods: the fixed date method and the periodic statement method (Reg. § 1.62-2(g)).[137] Under the fixed date method, the following are treated as occurring within a reasonable period of time:

(1) advance payments made no more than 30 days before expenses are reasonably anticipated to be paid or incurred;

(2) substantiation provided no more than 60 days after expenses are paid or incurred; and

(3) return of excess amounts made no more than 120 days after expenses are paid or incurred.

The periodic statement method is a safe harbor for determining reasonable time for the provision of substantiation and the return of excess advances. Under this method, the employer must:

(1) give each employee periodic statements (no less than quarterly) that set forth the amounts paid under the reimbursement arrangement in excess of the substantiated amount and

(2) request that the employee either substantiate or return the excess amounts within 120 days of the statement date. An expense substantiated or amount returned within that period will satisfy the reasonable period requirement.

953. Substantiation Requirements. In order to claim any deduction, a taxpayer must be able to prove, if the return is audited, that the expenses were in fact paid or incurred. Small expenses and those that are clearly related to the business may be substantiated by the taxpayer's statement or by keeping receipts, sales slips, invoices, cancelled checks, or other evidence of payments. The following expenses, which are deemed particularly susceptible to abuse, must generally be substantiated by adequate records or sufficient evidence corroborating the taxpayer's own statement: expenses with respect to travel away from home (including meals and lodging), entertainment expenses, business gifts, and expenses in connection with the use of listed property such as cars and computers (¶ 1211) (Code Sec. 274(d)).[138] The expenses must be substantiated as to amount, time, place, and business purpose. For entertainment and gift expenses, the business relationship of the person being entertained or receiving the gift must also be substantiated (Temp. Reg. § 1.274-5T(a)–(c)).[139] An employer's reim-

References are to Standard Federal Tax Reports; Tax Research Consultant; and Practical Tax Explanations.

[136] ¶ 6004; INDIV: 36,056.15; § 8,065

[137] ¶ 6004; INDIV: 36,056.10; § 10,120.10

[138] ¶ 14,402; BUSEXP: 24,810; § 10,105

[139] ¶ 14,410; BUSEXP: 24,800; § 10,105.10b

bursement arrangement must require employees to satisfy these substantiation requirements in order to be treated as an accountable plan (¶ 952A).

Substantiation by Adequate Records. A contemporaneous log is not required, but a record of the elements of the expense or use of the listed property made at or near the time of the expenditure or use, supported by sufficient documentary evidence, has a high degree of credibility. Adequate accounting generally requires the submission of an account book, expense diary or log, or similar record maintained by the employee and recorded at or near the time of incurrence of the expense. Documentary evidence, such as receipts or paid bills, is not generally required for expenses that are less than $75. However, documentary evidence is required for all lodging expenses (Reg. § 1.274-5(c)(2)(iii)).[140] The employee should also maintain a record of any amounts charged to the employer.

The *Cohan* rule, which allows the courts to estimate the amount of a taxpayer's expenses when adequate records do not exist, does not apply for the expenses covered by the substantiation rules of Code Sec. 274(d) (Temp. Reg. § 1.274-5T(a)(1)).[141] However, if a taxpayer has established that the records have been lost due to circumstances beyond the taxpayer's control, such as destruction by fire or flood, then the taxpayer has a right to substantiate claimed deductions by a reasonable construction of the expenditures or use (Temp. Reg. § 1.274-5T(c)(5)).[142]

Employees of the executive and judicial branches and certain employees of the legislative branch of the federal government may substantiate their requests for reimbursement of ordinary and necessary business expenses with an account book or expense log instead of submitting documentary evidence (e.g., receipts or bills) (Rev. Proc. 97-45).[143]

954. Per Diem Methods for Substantiating Employers' Meals and Lodging Expenses. A taxpayer must substantiate the amount, time, place, and business purpose of expenses paid or incurred in traveling away from home. Although the taxpayer has the option of keeping the actual records of travel expenses, the IRS has provided per diem allowances under which the amount of away-from-home meals and incidental expenses (M&IE) may be deemed to be substantiated. These per diem allowances eliminate the need for substantiating actual costs (Rev. Proc. 2011-47).[144] If per diem allowances are used to calculate the deductible amount, the time, place, and business purpose of the travel must still be substantiated by adequate records or other evidence.

Although most frequently used in the employer-employee relationship, per diem allowances may be used in connection with arrangements between any payor and payee, such as between independent contractors and those contracting with them. However, employees related to the payor within the related party rules of Code Sec. 267(b) (using a 10-percent common ownership standard, ¶ 432) cannot use per diem substantiation methods.

Employees. The per diem method can be used to substantiate an employee's reimbursed expenses (for purposes of the employer's return) only if the arrangement is considered an accountable plan and the allowance:

(1) is paid with respect to ordinary and necessary expenses incurred or which the employer reasonably expects to be incurred by an employee for lodging, meals and/or incidental expenses while traveling away from home in connection with the performance of services as an employee;

(2) is reasonably calculated not to exceed the amount of the expense or the anticipated expenses; and

(3) is paid at the applicable federal per diem rate, a flat rate or stated schedule.

References are to Standard Federal Tax Reports; Tax Research Consultant; and Practical Tax Explanations.

[140] ¶ 14,410; BUSEXP: 24,806.15; § 10,105.15

[141] ¶ 14,410; BUSEXP: 24,802; § 10,105.05

[142] ¶ 14,410; BUSEXP: 24,806; § 10,105.25

[143] ¶ 14,417.38; BUSEXP: 24,906.106; § 10,105.05

[144] ¶ 14,417.421; BUSEXP: 24,808; § 10,125.10

Types of Per Diem Allowances. There are three types of per diem allowances:

(1) M&IE only, which provides a per diem allowance for meals and incidental expenses only (¶ 954A);

(2) lodging plus M&IE, which provides a per diem allowance to cover lodging as well as meals and incidental expenses (¶ 954B); and

(3) incidental expenses only, to be used when no meal or lodging expenses are incurred (¶ 954B).

Incidental expenses include tips given to bellhops, hotel maids, and other service providers; taxis or other transportation; and the mailing costs associated with filing travel vouchers and payment of employer-sponsored charge card billings.

Expenses of laundry, lodging taxes, and telephone calls are not incidental expenses (IRS Pub. 463). Lodging taxes for travel within the continental United States and for nonforeign travel outside the continental United States are not considered incidental expenses but rather reimbursable miscellaneous expenses. However, lodging taxes are considered incidental expenses for foreign travel (41 C.F.R. 301-11.27 (2004)). Finally, under 41 C.F.R. 301-12.1, energy surcharges are to be considered reimbursable miscellaneous expenses.

Allowances Exceeding Federal Rates. If expenses are substantiated using a per diem amount, regardless of whether it covers lodging plus M&IE or only M&IE, and the reimbursement exceeds the relevant federal per diem rates for that type of allowance, then the employee (or independent contractor) is required to include the excess in gross income. The excess portion is treated as paid under a nonaccountable plan; thus, it must be reported on the employee's W-2 and is subject to withholding.

954A. Lodging Plus Meals and Incidental Expenses Per Diem. Under the lodging plus meals and incidental expenses (M&IE) per diem method (¶ 954A), the amount of an employee's (or other payee's) reimbursed expenses that is deemed substantiated (for purposes of the employer's return) is equal to the lesser of the employer's per diem allowance or the federal per diem amount for the locality of travel for the period in which the employee is away from home (Rev. Proc. 2011-47).[145] The employer is not required to produce lodging receipts if per diem allowances are used to substantiate such expenses. The locality of travel is the place where the employee stops for sleep or rest. Employees and self-employed individuals may determine their allowable deductions for unreimbursed M&IE while away from home by using the applicable federal M&IE rate (¶ 954B). However, unreimbursed lodging costs must be substantiated by required records (e.g., hotel receipts).

Per Diem Rates. The federal per diem rate for lodging plus M&IE depends upon the locality of travel. For various geographic areas within the continental United States (the 48 contiguous states plus the District of Columbia) (CONUS), the federal per diem rate for a given locality is equal to the sum of a maximum lodging amount and the M&IE rate for that locality. Federal per diem rates have also been established for nonforeign localities outside of the continental United States (OCONUS). These areas include Alaska, Hawaii, Puerto Rico, and possessions of the United States. Rates are also established for foreign travel (foreign OCONUS).

Rates for CONUS, OCONUS, and foreign travel are published under the Federal Travel Regulations for government travel and are updated periodically (Notice 2012-63).[146] The travel rates are issued to coincide with the government's fiscal year of October to September.

High-Low Method. In lieu of using the maximum per diem rates from the CONUS table, the high-low method, which is a simplified method for determining a lodging plus M&IE per diem, can be used to compute per diem allowances for travel within the continental United States. This method divides all CONUS localities into two categories: low-cost or high-cost localities (Rev. Proc. 2011-47).[147]

References are to Standard Federal Tax Reports; Tax Research Consultant; and Practical Tax Explanations.

[145] ¶ 14,417.421; BUSEXP: 24,912.05; § 10,125.10

[146] ¶ 14,417.421; BUSEXP: 24,912; § 660, § 670, § 680, § 690

[147] ¶ 14,417.421; BUSEXP: 24,912.05; § 10,125.10

For travel on or after October 1, 2012, through September 30, 2013, the following per diem rates for lodging expenses and M&IE were set by the IRS for high-cost and low-cost localities (Notice 2012-63):[148]

	Lodging expense rate	*M&IE rate*	*Maximum per diem rate*
High-cost locality	$177	$65	$242
Low-cost locality	111	52	163

For travel on or after October 1, 2011, through September 30, 2012, the following per diem rates for lodging expenses and M&IE were set by the IRS for high-cost and low-cost localities (Notice 2011-81):

	Lodging expense rate	*M&IE rate*	*Maximum per diem rate*
High-cost locality	$177	$65	$242
Low-cost locality	111	52	163

Certain areas are treated as high-cost only during periods of the year (e.g., peak tourist season) and as low-cost during other periods of time. Thus, employers who use the high-low method must determine whether the employee traveled in a high-cost area and if the area was classified as high-cost during the actual period of travel.

If the high-low method is used for an employee, then the payor may not use the actual federal maximum per diem rates for that employee during the calendar year for travel within the continental United States. However, the applicable federal rates for travel outside the continental United States (OCONUS rates) may be used, and the M&IE only rate may be used or the reimbursement of actual expenses may be made.

Proration of M&IE Allowance. If an individual is traveling away from home for only a portion of the day, there are two alternative methods that may be used to prorate the per diem rate or the M&IE rate. Under the first method, 75 percent of the M&IE rate (or the M&IE portion of the per diem rate) is allowed for each partial day during which an employee or self-employed individual is traveling on business. Under the second method referred to as the reasonable business practice method, the M&IE rate may be prorated using any method that is consistently applied and in accordance with reasonable business practice. For example, if an employee travels from 9 a.m. one day until 5 p.m. the next day, a proration method that gives an amount equal to two times the M&IE rate will be treated as in accordance with reasonable business practice (Rev. Proc. 2011-47).[149]

Transition Rules. Taxpayers are allowed to continue to use the per diem rates effective prior to October 1, 2012, for the remainder of 2012 or they may begin to use the new per diem rates for reimbursement for travel as long as the rates and method used are consistent for all employees and from year to year. Taxpayers who used the high-low substantiation method for reimbursement of an individual's travel expenses during the first nine months of calendar year 2012 must continue to use that method for the remainder of calendar-year 2012. However, taxpayers who use the high-low method of substantiation during the first nine months of calendar-year 2012 to reimburse an individual's travel expenses have the option of either continuing to use the rates and localities in effect for travel on or after January 1, 2012, or to use the rates and localities in effect for travel on or after October 1, 2012. The rates and localities that the taxpayer elects to use for reimbursement of an individual's travel expense must be used consistently during this October–December period.

954B. Meals-and-Incidental-Expense-Only Per Diem Allowances. An meals-and-incidental-expenses-(M&IE)-only per diem allowance may be used to substantiate an employee's or other payee's meal and incidental expenses for purposes of the employer's return (Rev. Proc. 2011-47).[150] The amount that is deemed substantiated is equal to the lesser of the per diem allowance or the amount computed at the federal M&IE rate for the locality of travel for the period that the employee is away from home.

References are to Standard Federal Tax Reports; Tax Research Consultant; and Practical Tax Explanations.

[148] ¶ 14,417.421; BUSEXP: 24,912; § 10,125.10

[149] ¶ 14,417.28; BUSEXP: 24,808; § 10,125.10

[150] ¶ 14,417.421; BUSEXP: 24,808; § 10,125.10

If meal and incidental expenses are substantiated using a per diem allowance, the entire amount is treated as a food and beverage expense subject to the 50-percent limitation on meal and entertainment expenses (¶ 916).

The M&IE rate must be prorated for partial days of travel away from home (¶ 954A). If an employee's meals are provided to him by his employer, even though the employee may be working from home, he is only entitled to deduct the incidental expense portion of the applicable federal per diem meal and incidental expense (M&IE) rates (*R.J. Zbylut*, 95 TCM 1172 (2008)).

Self-Employed Persons and Employees. Self-employed individuals and employees whose expenses are not reimbursed may also use the M&IE-only rate to substantiate meal and incidental expenses while traveling away from home. The taxpayer must actually prove (through adequate records or sufficient corroborative evidence (¶ 953)) the time, place, and business purpose of the travel. While the M&IE rate may be used by an employee or self-employed person to substantiate meal and incidental expenses, the amount of lodging costs must be proven by documentary evidence (e.g., a receipt).

Optional Method for Incidental Expenses Only Deduction. Taxpayers have available an optional method for claiming the deduction for only incidental expenses in lieu of using actual expenses. Taxpayers who do not incur any meal expenses may deduct $5 per calendar day (or partial day) as ordinary and necessary incidental expenses, paid or incurred, while traveling to any CONUS or OCONUS localities. The $5 daily rate applies to incidental expenses incurred during travel on or after October 1, 2010, and before October 1, 2013 (Notice 2012-63; Notice 2011-81; Rev. Proc. 2010-39).[151] The optional method is subject to the proration rules for partial days and substantiation requirements for taxpayers who use the per diem method for substantiation (Rev. Proc. 2011-47).[152] The optional method for incidental expenses only cannot also be used by taxpayers already using the following per diem methods:

(1) the lodging plus M&IE per diem method;

(2) the M&IE-only method; or

(3) the high-low method and the optional M&IE-only method (¶ 954A).

Transportation Workers. The M&IE rates for travel away from home on or after October 1, 2010, and before October 1, 2013, for both self-employed persons and employees in the transportation industry are $59 for CONUS localities and $65 for OCONUS localities (Notice 2012-63; Notice 2011-81; Rev. Proc. 2010-39).[153] An individual is in the transportation industry only if the individual's work: (1) directly involves moving people or goods by airplane, barge, bus, ship, train, or truck and (2) regularly requires travel away from home that involves travel to localities with differing federal M&IE rates during a single trip.

Transition Rules. Taxpayers under the calendar-year convention for the transportation industry, who used the federal M&IE rates during the first nine months of calendar year 2012 to substantiate the amount of an individual's travel expense, may not use the special transportation industry rates until January 1, 2013 (Rev. Proc. 2011-47).[154] Likewise, taxpayers who used the special transportation industry rates for the first nine months of calendar year 2012 to substantiate the amount of an individual's travel expenses may not use the federal M&IE rates until January 1, 2013.

955. Foreign Travel. Generally, traveling expenses (including meals and lodging) of a taxpayer who travels outside of the United States away from home must be allocated between time spent on the trip for business and time spent for pleasure (¶ 949) (Code Sec. 274(c); § 1.274-4).[155] When the trip is for not more than one week or when the time spent on personal activities on the trip is less than 25 percent of the total time away from home, no allocation is required and all expenses are deductible. Travel outside the United States does not include any travel within the United States. However, travel that

References are to Standard Federal Tax Reports; Tax Research Consultant; and Practical Tax Explanations.

[151] ¶ 14,417.421; BUSEXP: 24,912; § 10,125.10

[152] ¶ 14,417.421; BUSEXP: 24,808; § 10,125.10

[153] ¶ 14,417.421; BUSEXP: 24,912; § 10,125.10

[154] ¶ 14,417.28; BUSEXP: 24,808; § 10,125.10

[155] ¶ 14,402, ¶ 14,408; BUSEXP: 24,300; § 9,535.05

is not from one point in the United States to another point in the United States is considered travel outside the United States.

When the foreign trip is longer than a week (seven consecutive days counting the day of return but not the day of departure) or 25 percent or more of the time away from home is spent for personal reasons, a deduction for travel expenses will be denied to the extent that they are not allocable to the taxpayer's business (or the taxpayer's management of income-producing property).

No allocation is required on a foreign trip when (1) the individual traveling had no substantial control over the arranging of the business trip or (2) a personal vacation was not a major consideration in making the trip. An employee traveling under a reimbursement or expense account allowance arrangement is not considered as having substantial control over the arranging of a business trip unless the employee is a managing executive (an employee who can, without being vetoed, decide on whether and when to make the trip) or is a 10-percent-or-more owner of the employer.

For special rules governing expenses of attending foreign conventions, seminars, and other similar meetings, see ¶ 959 and ¶ 960.

956. Travel Expenses of State Legislators. A state legislator whose residence is further than 50 miles from the state capitol building may elect to be deemed to be away from home in the pursuit of a trade or business on any day that the legislature is in session (including periods of up to four consecutive days when the legislature is not in session) or on any day when the legislature is not in session but the legislator's presence is formally recorded at a committee meeting (Code Sec. 162(h)).[156]

957. Luxury Water Travel. A deduction for transportation by ocean liner, cruise ship, or other form of water transportation is limited to a daily amount equal to twice the highest per diem travel amount allowable to employees of the federal government while on official business away from home but within the United States. The limitation does not apply to any expense allocable to a convention, seminar, or other meeting that is held on a cruise ship (¶ 959). Separately stated meal and entertainment expenses are subject to the 50-percent limitation rule (¶ 916), prior to the application of the per diem limitation. Statutory exceptions to the 50-percent limit apply (¶ 917) (Code Sec. 274(m)).[157]

958. Travel as a Form of Education. A deduction for travel expenses is not allowed if the expense would be deductible only on the basis that the travel itself constitutes a form of education (Code Sec. 274(m)).[158] See also ¶ 1082.

959. Convention Expenses. Deductible travel expenses include those incurred in attending a convention related to the taxpayer's business, even though the taxpayer is an employee (Code Sec. 274(h); Reg. § 1.162-2(d)).[159] The fact that an employee uses vacation or leave time or that attendance at the convention is voluntary will not necessarily negate the deduction. See also ¶ 960. Expenses for a convention or meeting in connection with investments, financial planning, or other income-producing property are not deductible.

Cruise Ships. A limited deduction is available for expenses incurred for conventions on U.S. cruise ships. This deduction (limited to $2,000 with respect to all cruises beginning in any calendar year) applies only if:

(1) all ports of such cruise ship are located in the United States or in U.S. possessions;

(2) the taxpayer establishes that the convention is directly related to the active conduct of his trade or business; and

(3) the taxpayer includes certain specified information in the return on which the deduction is claimed.

References are to Standard Federal Tax Reports; Tax Research Consultant; and Practical Tax Explanations.

[156] ¶ 8500; BUSEXP: 24,120; § 9,510

[157] ¶ 14,402; BUSEXP: 24,400; § 9,550.10

[158] ¶ 14,402; INDIV: 60,122.20; § 9,501

[159] ¶ 8527, ¶ 14,402; BUSEXP: 24,160; § 9,515

960. Foreign Conventions. No deduction is allowed for expenses allocable to a convention, seminar, or meeting held outside the North American area unless the taxpayer establishes that the meeting is directly related to the active conduct of his trade or business and that it is as reasonable for the meeting to be held outside the North American area (Code Sec. 274(h)).[160] The factors to be taken into account are:

(1) the purpose of the meeting and the activities taking place at such meeting;

(2) the purposes and activities of the sponsoring organization or group;

(3) the places of residence of the active members of the sponsoring organization or group and the places at which other meetings of the organization or group have been held or will be held; and

(4) such other relevant factors as the taxpayer may present.

The North American area means the 50 states of the United States and the District of Columbia, the possessions of the United States, Canada, Mexico, the Republic of the Marshall Islands, the Federated States of Micronesia, and the Republic of Palau. Costs incurred in attending conventions held in the Caribbean or on certain Pacific Islands may also be deductible if the host country is a designated beneficiary country, there is a bilateral or multilateral agreement in effect providing for the exchange of tax information with the United States, and the country has not been found to discriminate in its tax laws against conventions held in the United States. A list of qualifying countries is provided in Rev. Rul. 2011-26. Expenses for foreign conventions on cruise ships are not deductible.

Home Office and Vacation Home Expenses

961. Business Use of Home. Taxpayers are not entitled to deduct any expenses for using their homes for business purposes unless the expenses are attributable to a portion of the home (or separate structure) used exclusively on a regular basis

(1) as the principal place of any business carried on by the taxpayer;

(2) as a place of business that is used by patients, clients, or customers in meeting or dealing with the taxpayer in the normal course of business; or

(3) in connection with the taxpayer's business if the taxpayer is using a separate structure that is appurtenant to, but not attached to, the home (Code Sec. 280A(c)).[161]

If the taxpayer is an employee, the business use of the home must also be for the convenience of the employer (¶ 965). The allowable deduction is computed on Form 8829.

Generally, a specific portion of the taxpayer's home must be used solely for the purpose of carrying on a trade or business in order to satisfy the exclusive use test. This requirement is not met if the portion is used for both business and personal purposes. However, an exception is provided for a wholesale or retail seller whose dwelling unit is the sole fixed location of the trade or business. In this situation, the ordinary and necessary expenses allocable to space within the dwelling unit that is used as a storage unit for inventory or product samples are deductible provided that the space is used on a regular basis and is a separately identifiable space suitable for storage. Another special exception applies to licensed day care operators (¶ 964).

A taxpayer's principal place of business for this purpose includes a place of business that is used by the taxpayer for the administrative or management activities of any trade or business of the taxpayer if there is no other fixed location where the taxpayer conducts substantial administrative or management activities. Taxpayers who perform administrative or management activities for their trade or business at places other than the home office are not automatically prohibited from taking the deduction based on failure to meet the principal place of business requirement. According to the House Committee Report to P.L. 105-34,[162] the following taxpayers are *not* prevented from taking a home office deduction:

References are to Standard Federal Tax Reports; Tax Research Consultant; and Practical Tax Explanations.

[160] ¶ 14,402; BUSEXP: 24,350; § 9,540

[161] ¶ 14,850; BUSEXP: 27,150; § 8,101

[162] ¶ 14,850.017; BUSEXP: 27,152.05; § 8,120.05

(1) taxpayers who do not conduct substantial administrative or management activities at a fixed location other than the home office, even if administrative or management activities (e.g., billing activities) are performed by other people at other locations;

(2) taxpayers who carry out administrative and management activities at sites that are not fixed locations of the business (e.g., cars or hotel rooms) in addition to performing the activities at the home office;

(3) taxpayers who conduct an insubstantial amount of administrative and management activities at a fixed location other than the home office (e.g., occasionally doing minimal paperwork at another fixed location); and

(4) taxpayers who conduct substantial nonadministrative and nonmanagement business activities at a fixed location other than the home office (e.g., meeting with, or providing services to customers, clients, or patients at a fixed location other than the home office).

Auction and Consignment Sellers. Auction and consignment sellers may compute their deduction to the extent of expenses allocable to space in the residence used on a regular basis to store inventory and/or product samples if the residence is the sole fixed location of the auction or consignment business (IRS Fact Sheet FS-2007-23).[163]

Residential Telephone. Basic local telephone service charges on the first line in a residence are not deductible as business expenses. Additional charges for long-distance calls, equipment, optional services (e.g., call waiting), or additional telephone lines may be deductible (Code Sec. 262(b)).[164]

963. Limitation on Home Office Deductions. The home office deduction (¶ 961) cannot exceed the gross income from the activity, reduced by the home expenses that would be deductible in the absence of any business use (mortgage interest, property taxes, etc.) and the business expenses not related to the use of the home (Code Sec. 280A(c)(5)).[165] The business related expenses are deducted in a specific order, as follows:

(1) expenses that are required by the business but not allocable to the use of the home (such as office supplies);

(2) expenses that would be deductible even if the home was not used as a place of business (such as mortgage interest and real estate taxes);

(3) expenses related to the household that are allocable to the business use (such as utilities and insurance); and

(4) the allocable depreciation expenses.

The deduction of the expenses under items (3) and (4) above cannot create a loss. Unused expenses under items (3) and (4) are carried over to the next year but are still subject to the same limitation rules.

Example: A teacher operates a retail sales business in which she makes a qualified business use of a home office. Assume that 25 percent of the general expenses for the dwelling unit are allocable to the home office. The taxpayer's gross income and expenses from the retail sales business are:

Gross income			$25,000
Home Office Expenses	Total	Allocable to Office	
Interest and property taxes	$8,000	$2,000	
Insurance, maintenance, utilities . .	2,000	500	
Depreciation	6,000	1,500	
Total home office expenses			$4,000
Expenses allocable to retail sales business, but not allocable to home office use (e.g., supplies, wages paid)			$24,000
Total expenses			$28,000

References are to Standard Federal Tax Reports; Tax Research Consultant; and Practical Tax Explanations.

[163] ¶ 8521.112; BUSEXP: 27,158; § 8,125

[164] ¶ 13,600; BUSEXP: 27,056.15; § 8,205

[165] ¶ 14,850; BUSEXP: 27,300; § 8,140

For the teacher to determine the amount of the home office deduction, the business related expenses must be applied against the gross income in the prescribed order. The teacher must first reduce her gross income by the expenses directly related to the retail sales business but not allocable to the business use of the home ($24,000). Next, the teacher applies those expenses allocable to the business use of the home but that are deductible even if there was no retail sales business ($2,000). Since the gross income from the activity is reduced less than zero, the allocable expenses of insurance, maintenance, utilities, and depreciation are carried over to the next tax year. The carryover amounts ($500 and $1,500) will be subject to the same limitation rules for the determining the amount of the home office deduction. Thus, the school teacher has a business loss of $1,000 from the retail sales business for the current tax year and a carryforward amount of $2,000 of unused home office expenses to the next tax year.

964. Home Office Deduction for Day Care Services. Taxpayers who use their personal residences on a regular basis in the trade or business of providing qualifying day care services (for the care of children, handicapped persons, or the elderly) do not have to meet the exclusive use test under the home office deduction rules (¶ 961) in order to deduct business-related expenses (Code Sec. 280A(c)(4)).[166] However, the deduction is available only if the taxpayer has applied for, has been granted, or is exempt from having a license, certification, or approval as a day care center or as a family or group day care home under the provisions of applicable state law. The deduction of expenses allocable to day care use is limited as described at ¶ 963. Form 8829 must be filed.

965. Home Office Deduction by Employees. In order for employees to qualify for the home office deduction (¶ 961), they must not only meet the exclusive use requirement, but the exclusive use of the home office must be for the convenience of their employers (Code Sec. 280A(c)(1) and (6)).[167] However, regardless of whether or not an employee meets the exclusive use requirements, an employee is denied a home office deduction for any portion of the home rented to the employer (except for expenses such as home mortgage interest and real property taxes that are deductible absent business use). Generally, an employee's home office expenses must be taken as a miscellaneous itemized deduction, subject to the two-percent-of-adjusted-gross-income floor on Schedule A (Form 1040) (¶ 1011). Statutory employees (¶ 941B) claim home office deductions on Schedule C (Form 1040).

966. Deductions on Rental Residence or Vacation Home. Special rules limit the amount of deductions that may be taken by an individual or an S corporation in connection with the rental of a residence or vacation home, or a portion thereof, that is also used as the taxpayer's residence (Code Sec. 280A).[168] A vacation home includes a dwelling unit, including a house, apartment, condominium, house trailer, boat, or similar property. Deductions that may be claimed without regard to whether or not the home is used for trade or business or for the production of income (e.g., mortgage interest, property taxes, or a casualty loss) are not limited.

Personal Usage Defined. A vacation home is deemed to have been used by the taxpayer for personal purposes on a particular day if, for any part of the day, the home is used:

(1) for personal purposes by the taxpayer, any other person who owns an interest in the home, or the relatives (spouses, brothers, sisters, ancestors, lineal descendants, and spouses of lineal descendants) of either;

References are to Standard Federal Tax Reports; Tax Research Consultant; and Practical Tax Explanations.

[166] ¶ 14,850; BUSEXP: 27,160; § 46,710.15

[167] ¶ 14,850; BUSEXP: 27,166; § 8,130.05, § 8,130.10

[168] ¶ 14,850; BUSEXP: 27,100, BUSEXP: 27,200; § 1,701, § 1,720.05

(2) by any individual who uses the home under a reciprocal arrangement, whether or not a rental is charged; and

(3) by any other individual who uses the home unless a fair rental is charged.

If the taxpayer rents the home at a fair rental value to any person (including a relative listed above) for use as that person's principal residence, the use by that person is not considered personal use by the taxpayer. This exception applies to a person who owns an interest in the home only if the rental is under a shared equity financing agreement.

Rental Use of Fewer Than 15 Days. If the property is rented for fewer than 15 days during the year, no deductions attributable to such rental are allowable and no rental income is includible in gross income.

Rental Use Exceeding 14 Days. If the property is rented for more than 14 days during the year, deductions are available. If the home is used as a personal residence, that is, used by the taxpayer for personal purposes for more than the greater of 14 days or 10 percent of the number of days during the year for which the home is rented at a fair market rental, the amount of rental deductions is limited to the gross rental income. If the home is not used as a personal residence by the taxpayer, the deduction is not limited to the rental income. The deduction may also be reduced or eliminated under the passive activity loss rules (¶ 2053) or the hobby loss rules if the rental of the residence is not engaged in for profit (¶ 1195).

Ordering of Deduction. Rental expenses are deducted in a specific order from gross rental income. Mortgage interest, real property taxes, and casualty losses attributable to the rental use are deducted first. Next, operating expenses other than depreciation attributable to the rental use are deducted. Last, depreciation and other basis adjustments attributable to rental income are deducted. To determine the amount of these expenses attributable to rental use, the expenses are allocated based on a ratio that the total number of rental days bears to the total days used for all purposes during the year. When the personal usage exceeds the greater of either 14 days or 10 percent of the rental days, according to the IRS, expenses attributable to the use of the rental unit are limited in the same manner as that prescribed under the hobby loss rules at ¶ 1195 (i.e., the total deductions may not exceed the gross rental income, as well as the expenses being limited to a percentage that represents the total days rented divided by the total days used).

The Tax Court, however, has rejected this formula (*D.D. Bolton*, 77 TC 104 (1981); *E.G. McKinney*, 42 TCM 467 (1981)).[169] Its position is that mortgage interest and real estate taxes are not subject to the same percentage limitations as are other expenses because they are assessed on an annual basis without regard to the number of days that the property is used. As a result, the percentage limitation for interest and taxes is computed by dividing the total days rented by the total days in the year. This creates the potential of leaving more gross rental income to offset allocated rental expenses.

> **Example:** During the year an individual rents out his vacation home for 91 days and uses the home for personal purposes for 30 days. The gross rental income from the unit is $2,700 for the year. He pays $621 of real property taxes and $2,854 of mortgage interest on the property for the year. The additional expenses for maintenance, repair, and utilities total $2,693.
>
> The IRS allocation of all expenses would be based on 75 percent (91 days rented ÷ 121 days used). In contrast, the Tax Court would allocate taxes and interest based on 25 percent (91 days rented ÷ 365 days) and use the 75-percent limitation for the additional expenses for maintenance, repair, etc.

References are to Standard Federal Tax Reports; Tax Research Consultant; and Practical Tax Explanations.

[169] ¶ 14,858.15; BUSEXP: 27,100; § 1,720.10

	IRS	Tax Court
1. Gross rental income	$2,700	$2,700
2. Less: Interest ($2,854)	- 2,141	- 714
Property tax ($621)	- 466	- 155
3. Remaining available income	$93	$1,831
4. Utilities, maintenance, etc.	- 93	- 1,831
5. Net income	$0	$0
6. Unused expense allowable as itemized deductions:		
Interest	$713	$2,140
Property tax	155	466
7. Total allowable deductions	$3,568	$5,306

Bed and Breakfast Inns. The special restrictions on deductions related to a residence used for business and personal purposes do not apply to the portion of the residence used exclusively as a bed and breakfast inn. Expenses related to that portion of a residence may be limited under the hobby loss rules (¶ 1195) (Code Sec. 280A(f)).[170]

967. Conversion of Property. Individuals who convert their principal residences into rental units (or vice versa) will not be considered to have used the unit for personal purposes for any day during the tax year which occurs before (or after) a qualified rental period for purposes of applying the deduction limitation (¶ 966) allocable to the qualified rental period (Code Sec. 280A(d)(4)).[171] The expenses, however, must be allocated between the periods of rental and personal use. A qualified rental period is a consecutive period of 12 or more months, beginning (or ending) during the tax year, during which the unit is rented or held for rental at its fair market value. The 12-month rental requirement does not apply if the residence is sold or exchanged before it has been rented or held for rental for the full 12 months.

> **Example:** A taxpayer moved out of his principal residence on February 28, 2012, to accept employment in another town. The house was rented at its fair market value from March 15, 2012, through May 14, 2013. The use of the house as a principal residence from January 1 through February 28, 2012, is not counted as personal use. If the taxpayer moved back and reoccupied the home on June 1, 2013, the use of the house as a principal residence from June 1 through December 31, 2013, is not counted as personal use.

Other Business Expenses

968. Fire and Casualty Insurance Premiums. A premium paid for insurance against losses from fire, accident, storm, theft, or other casualty is deductible if it is an ordinary and necessary expense of a business (Reg. § 1.162-1).[172] However, the uniform capitalization rules may require that insurance costs on real or tangible personal property produced or acquired for resale be included in inventory or capitalized, rather than being deducted (¶ 990–¶ 999).

An arrangement between a business and an insurance company that provides for the reimbursement of future remediation costs the business is certain to incur does not constitute an insurance contract for federal income tax purposes, the IRS has determined. The arrangement does not involve the requisite risk shifting to constitute insurance and, therefore, payments made by the business are not deductible as insurance premiums (Rev. Rul. 2007-47, amplifying Rev. Rul. 89-96).[173]

969. Advertising Expenses. Advertising expenses are deductible if they are reasonable in amount and bear a reasonable relation to the business. Deductible expenses may be for the purpose of developing goodwill as well as gaining immediate sales. The cost of advertising is deductible when paid or incurred, even though the advertising program extends over several years or is expected to result in benefits extending over a

References are to Standard Federal Tax Reports; Tax Research Consultant; and Practical Tax Explanations.

170 ¶ 14,850, ¶ 14,858.21; BUSEXP: 27,054.15; § 1,705

171 ¶ 14,850; BUSEXP: 27,208; § 1,715.20

172 ¶ 8501; BUSEXP: 18,202; § 9,415.05

173 ¶ 8522.3915; BUSEXP: 18,200; § 9,415.05

period of years (Rev. Rul. 92-80).[174] The Tax Court and the IRS require that the cost of printing a catalog that is not replaced annually be amortized over the expected life of the catalog. However, some courts have held to the contrary, taking the view that catalog costs are in the nature of an advertising expense (*Sheldon & Co.*, CA-6, 54-2 USTC ¶ 9526).[175] The cost of public service or other impartial advertising, such as advertising designed to encourage the public to register and to vote, are deductible (Rev. Rul. 62-156).[176]

No deduction may be claimed for expenses of advertising in political programs or for admission to political fund-raising or inaugural functions and similar events (Code Sec. 276).[177] This includes admission to any dinner or program if any part of the proceeds of the event directly or indirectly inures to or for the use of a political party or a political candidate.

Package Design Costs. Package design costs include the graphic arrangement or design of shapes, colors, words, pictures, lettering, and other elements on a given product package, or the design of a container with respect to its shape or function (Reg. § 1.263(a)-4(b)(3)(v)).[178] The Tax Court has held that packaging design costs were a deductible advertising expense even though the design provided the company with significant future benefits (*RJR Nabisco*, 76 TCM 71 (1998) (Nonacq.)).[179]

970. Expenses of Earning Tax-Exempt Income. No deduction is allowed for any expense allocable to the earning of tax-exempt income (Code Sec. 265).[180] No deduction is allowed for interest paid on a debt incurred or continued in order to purchase or carry tax-exempt bonds or other obligations, regardless of whether the interest expense was incurred in business, in a profit-inspired transaction, or in any other connection.

Generally, banks, thrift institutions, and all other financial institutions may not deduct any portion of their interest expenses allocable to tax-exempt interest on obligations acquired after August 7, 1986. This includes amounts paid in respect of deposits, investment certificates, or withdrawable or repurchasable shares. For bonds issued in 2009 and 2010, there is a *de minimis* safe harbor exception to the 100-percent disallowance rule.

Qualified tax-exempt obligations that are issued by a qualifier small issuer are not taken into account as investments in tax-exempt bonds and, therefore, not subject to the 100-percent disallowance rule. Instead, only 20 percent of the interest expense allocable to qualified tax-exempt obligations is disallowed. A qualified small issuer is an issuer that reasonably anticipates that the amount of its tax-exempt obligations (other than certain private activity bonds) will not exceed $10 million during the calendar year. A qualified tax-exempt obligation is a tax-exempt obligation that (1) is issued after August 7, 1986, by a qualified small issuer, (2) is not a private activity bond, and (3) is designated by the issuer as qualifying for the exception from the general rule.

971. Circulation Expenses. Any expenditure to establish, maintain, or increase the circulation of a newspaper, magazine, or other periodical may be deducted in the year paid or incurred even though the taxpayer reports only an allocable portion of the subscription income for each year of the subscription period (¶ 1537) (Code Sec. 173; Reg. § 1.173-1).[181] Taxpayers may also elect to capitalize circulation expenses and amortize them over a three-year period (¶ 1450).

972. Fines, Penalties, Kickbacks, Drug Trafficking. A fine or a penalty paid to a government for the violation of any law is not a deductible business expense (Code Sec. 162(f)).[182] Any illegal bribe or kickback paid directly or indirectly to a domestic government official or employee is not deductible. Bribes and kickbacks paid directly or indirectly to an employee or official of a foreign government are not deductible if they are unlawful under the federal Foreign Corrupt Practices Act of 1977. No deduction is

References are to Standard Federal Tax Reports; Tax Research Consultant; and Practical Tax Explanations.

[174] ¶ 8851.152; BUSEXP: 18,252; § 9,901

[175] ¶ 21,817.2075; BUSEXP: 18,260; § 9,901

[176] ¶ 8952.40; BUSEXP: 18,252; § 9,901

[177] ¶ 14,550; BUSEXP: 18,310; § 9,120.05

[178] ¶ 13,704C; BUSEXP: 9,104.10; § 9,970

[179] ¶ 8851.1338; BUSEXP: 18,252.10; § 9,970

[180] ¶ 14,050, ¶ 14,051; BUSEXP: 18,600; § 7,420.05, § 9,001

[181] ¶ 12,030, ¶ 12,031; DEPR: 21,252; § 11,520

[182] ¶ 8500; BUSEXP: 18,800; § 9,105, § 9,115

allowed for any payment made directly or indirectly to any person if the payment is a bribe, kickback, or other illegal payment under any U.S. law or under any generally enforced state law that subjects the payor to a criminal penalty or to the loss of license or privilege to engage in a trade or business (Code Sec. 162(c)(2) and (3); Reg. § 1.162-18).[183] A deduction is also denied for any kickback, rebate, or bribe made by any provider of services, supplier, physician, or other person who furnished items or services for which payment is or may be made under the Social Security Act, or in whole or in part out of federal funds under a state plan approved under the Act, if the kickback, rebate, or bribe is made in connection with the furnishing of such items or services or the making or receiving of such payments. For all the above purposes, a kickback includes a payment in consideration of the referral of a client, patient, or customer.

If a taxpayer is convicted of a criminal violation of the antitrust laws, which contain a treble damage provision, or enters a plea of guilty or no contest to a charged violation, no deduction is allowed for two-thirds of the amount paid to satisfy the judgment or in settlement of a suit brought under section 4 of the Clayton Act (Code Sec. 162(g); Reg. § 1.162-22).[184]

No deduction is allowed for a federal tax penalty (Reg. § 1.162-21(b)(1)(ii)).[185] No deduction or credit is allowed for amounts paid or incurred in the illegal trafficking in drugs listed in the federal Controlled Substances Act. However, a deduction for the cost of goods sold is permitted (Code Sec. 280E).[186] Damage awards paid in connection with the violation of a federal civil statute and similar penalties may be deductible if they are compensatory, rather than punitive, in nature (Reg. § 1.162-21(b)(2)).[187]

973. Legal Expenses. Legal expenses paid or incurred in connection with a business transaction or primarily for the purpose of preserving existing business reputation and goodwill are ordinarily deductible (*F.W. Staudt*, 12 TCM 1417 (1953)).[188] The deductibility tests are substantially the same as those for other business expenses and preclude a current deduction for a legal expense incurred in the acquisition of capital assets. It is not necessary that litigation be involved for legal fees to be deductible. In addition to attorney fees, legal expenses include fees or expenses of accountants and expert witnesses, as well as court stenographic and printing charges.

A taxpayer may deduct, as a business expense, that part of the cost of tax return preparation that is properly allocable to the business, as well as expenses incurred in resolving asserted tax deficiencies relating to the business (*D. Pistoresi*, 77 TCM 1368 (1999); *C. Wood*, 37 TC 70 (1961) (Acq.).[189]

For the deductibility of legal expenses arising from the determination of nonbusiness taxes or income-producing property, see ¶ 1092 and ¶ 1093. Litigation costs have to be capitalized when, under the origin of the claim test (or the nature of the claim leading to the payments), they are considered to be incurred to acquire a capital asset.

974. Lobbying Expenses. Lobbying expenses directed towards influencing federal or state legislation are generally not deductible (Code Sec. 162(e); Reg. § 1.162-20(c)).[190] The prohibition does not generally apply to in-house expenses that do not exceed $2,000 for a tax year. Lobbying expenses pertaining to local legislation are deductible.

975. Federal National Mortgage Association Stock. Initial holders of stock issued by the Federal National Mortgage Association may deduct, as a business expense, the excess of the price paid over the market price of the stock on the date of issuance (Code Sec. 162(d); Reg. § 1.162-19(a)).[191] The basis in the stock is reduced to reflect the deduction.

References are to Standard Federal Tax Reports; Tax Research Consultant; and Practical Tax Explanations.

[183] ¶ 8500, ¶ 8857; BUSEXP: 18,800; § 9,105

[184] ¶ 8500, ¶ 8955; BUSEXP: 18,800; § 9,125

[185] ¶ 8953; INDIV: 45,060; § 9,115

[186] ¶ 15,050; BUSEXP: 18,800; § 9,110

[187] ¶ 8953; BUSEXP: 18,650; § 9,115

[188] ¶ 8526.4503; BUSEXP: 18,050; § 9,920.05

[189] ¶ 8520.73; BUSEXP: 18,050; § 9,920.05

[190] ¶ 8500, ¶ 8951, ¶ 8952; BUSEXP: 18,302; § 9,120.05, § 9,120.10

[191] ¶ 8500, ¶ 8859; SALES: 6,372.35; § 7,405

976. Political Contributions. Contributions made to a political candidate or party are not deductible as a business expense (Code Sec. 162(e)(2)(A)).[192]

977. Environmental Clean-Up Costs (Expired). For expenses paid or incurred before January 1, 2012, a taxpayer can elect to deduct certain environmental cleanup costs in the year in which they occurred, rather than to treat them as a capital expense (Code Sec. 198).[193] The deduction only pertains to the cleanup of hazardous substances located on sites within areas that meet specific requirements. The IRS has provided guidance for taxpayers to make this election (Rev. Proc. 98-47).[194]

> **Caution:** The deduction allowed by Code Sec. 198 is not available, absent further legislation, for expenses paid or incurred after December 31, 2011.

977A. Small Refiners' Deduction for Upgrades to Produce Low Sulfur Fuels. Small refiners that invest in upgrading their facilities to produce low-sulfur fuels are allowed to elect to deduct a portion of the costs (Code Sec. 179B).[195] Qualified small refiners may deduct up to 75 percent of the capital costs paid or incurred for the purposes of complying with the Highway Diesel Fuel Sulfur Control Requirements of the Environmental Protection Agency (¶ 1285).

977B. Domestic Film and Television Productions Deduction. A taxpayer may elect to deduct the cost of any qualified film or television production commenced before January 1, 2012 (Code Sec. 181).[196] The maximum deduction is $15 million ($20 million for films produced in certain low-income or distressed communities). For a production commencing before 2008, the deduction is not available if the aggregate production cost exceeds $15 million ($20 million for films produced in certain low-income or distressed communities). See ¶ 1229 for general discussion of the amortization of film and television production costs.

977C. New Refinery Property Deduction. The builders of new liquid fuel refineries may elect to deduct up to 50 percent of the cost of building a qualified refinery property in the year it is placed in service (Code Sec. 179C).[197] The deduction is available to taxpayers who place a qualified refinery property in service after August 8, 2005, and before January 1, 2014. The expensing deduction is also available with respect to refineries processing liquid fuel directly from shale or tar sands (¶ 1285A).

977D. Energy-Efficient Commercial Buildings Deduction. Taxpayers may deduct a portion of the costs of installation of energy-efficient systems into commercial buildings (Code Sec. 179D).[198] The maximum deduction is generally $1.80 per square foot of a qualified commercial property, less the total amount of deductions under this provision taken in prior tax years. Qualified systems include interior lighting, heating, cooling, ventilation, hot water systems, and the building envelope. The deduction is available for qualified commercial property placed in service after December 31, 2005, but before January 1, 2014 (¶ 1286).

977E. Qualified Disaster Costs (Expired). In general, taxpayers may not deduct expenses paid or incurred in connection with a disaster except for qualified disaster expenses paid or incurred after December 31, 2007, in connection with a disaster declared after that date and occurring before January 1, 2010 (Code Sec. 198A).[199]

Qualified disaster expenses include any expenditure that is:

(1) paid or incurred in connection with a trade, business, or business-related property;

(2) otherwise chargeable to a capital account; and

References are to Standard Federal Tax Reports; Tax Research Consultant; and Practical Tax Explanations.

[192] ¶ 8500; BUSEXP: 18,310; § 9,120.05

[193] ¶ 12,460; BUSEXP: 18,750, BUSEXP: 18,756; § 10,230

[194] ¶ 12,465.30; BUSEXP: 18,756; § 10,230

[195] ¶ 12,134; BUSEXP: 18,908; § 10,220

[196] ¶ 12,144; DEPR: 12,300; § 10,220

[197] ¶ 12,137; BUSEXP: 18,900; § 10,220

[198] ¶ 12,138; BUSEXP: 18,950; § 10,250

[199] ¶ 12,466; BUSEXP: 19,050; § 10,045.10

(3) made for (a) the abatement or control of hazardous substances that were released on account of a federally declared disaster; (b) the removal of debris from, or the demolition of structures on, business-related real property that is damaged or destroyed as a result of a federally declared disaster; or (c) the repair of business-related property damaged as a result of a federally declared disaster.

978. Expenses of Mercantile and Manufacturing Businesses. Merchants and manufacturers generally are subject to the uniform capitalization rules. See the discussion at ¶ 990–¶ 999. However, ordinary and necessary business expenses not covered by such rules may be currently deducted (Reg. § 1.162-1).[200]

979. Research and Experiment Expenses. A taxpayer may elect to deduct certain research and experimental expenses by claiming the deduction on the income tax return for the first tax year in which the costs are paid or incurred in connection with its business (Code Sec. 174).[201] Only costs of research in the laboratory or for experimental purposes, whether carried on by the taxpayer or on behalf of the taxpayer by a third party, are deductible. Market research and normal product testing costs are not considered research expenditures. Once made, the election is applicable to all research costs incurred in the project for the current and all subsequent years.

The costs of obtaining a patent, including attorneys' fees paid or incurred in making and perfecting a patent application, qualify as research or experimental expenditures, but the costs of acquiring another's patent, model, production, or process do not qualify (Reg. § 1.174-2(a)(1)).[202] When the election to defer expenses has been made, the right to amortize ceases when the patent issues. Unrecovered expenditures are recovered through depreciation over the life of the patent (Reg. § 1.174-4(a)(4)).[203] There is a credit for increased research and experimental expenses (¶ 1365J). A purchased patent may qualify as a section 197 intangible to be amortized over 15 years (¶ 1288).

980. Computer Software Costs. The tax treatment of computer software used in a trade or business depends on whether the taxpayer has leased the software, developed it internally, or purchased it (Code Sec. 162; Reg. § 1.162-11; Rev. Proc. 2000-50).[204]

Generally, rental payments for leased software are deductible as business expenses over the term of the lease in the same manner as any other rental payments (Rev. Proc. 2000-50, § 7).[205] However, acquired computer software is amortizable over 15 years if it is a section 197 intangible (¶ 1288) (Code Secs. 167(f)(1) and 197; Reg. § 1.167(a)-14(b)(1); Rev. Proc. 2000-50, § 6).[206] Software that is not subject a section 197 intangible is amortized using the straight-line method over a period of 36 months beginning on the first day of the month that the software is placed in service.

Costs incurred by a taxpayer to develop software for sale to others or for internal use may be treated like research and experimental expenses (¶ 979) and may be deducted currently, amortized over either a 60-month period (or shorter if established as appropriate), or amortized over a 36-month period, so long as such costs are treated consistently (Rev. Proc. 2000-50, § 5).[207]

Computer software is any program designed to cause a computer to perform a desired function (Code Secs. 167(f)(1)(B) and 197(e)(3)(B); Rev. Proc. 2000-50, § 2).[208] It does not include any data base or similar item unless the data base or item is in the public domain and is incidental to the operation of otherwise qualifying computer software.

Software Bundled with Hardware. Software costs that are included, but not separately stated, in the cost of computer hardware are capitalized and depreciated as part of

References are to Standard Federal Tax Reports; Tax Research Consultant; and Practical Tax Explanations.

[200] ¶ 8501; BUSEXP: 3,050; § 10,310.05

[201] ¶ 12,040; BUSEXP: 9,102.10; § 9,705.05

[202] ¶ 12,043; DEPR: 21,300; § 9,705.10

[203] ¶ 12,046; DEPR: 21,300; § 9,710

[204] ¶ 8500, ¶ 8753, ¶ 8754.1695; DEPR: 15,162.85; § 11,535.05

[205] ¶ 8754.1695; BUSEXP: 18,856.106; § 11,525.15

[206] ¶ 8500, ¶ 12,450, ¶ 11,030D, ¶ 8754.1695; DEPR: 15,162.85; § 11,535.05

[207] ¶ 8754.1695; DEPR: 21,308.20; § 11,535.25

[208] ¶ 8500, ¶ 11,030D, ¶ 8754.1695; DEPR: 21,054.15; § 11,410.25

the hardware (Reg. § 1.167(a)-14(b)(2)).[209] In other words, the entire amount is treated as the cost of hardware (tangible property) and is depreciable under MACRS over a five-year recovery period.

Web Site Development Costs. The IRS has yet to issue formal guidance on the treatment of web site development costs.

Domestic Production Activities

980A. Deduction for Domestic Production Activities. A taxpayer may claim a deduction against gross income equal to nine percent of its qualified production activities income (QPAI) (¶ 980B) or its taxable income without regard to the deduction (whichever is less) (Code Sec. 199).[210] In the case of an individual, estate, or trust, QPAI or adjusted gross income (rather than taxable income), figured without regard to the deduction, is used to calculate the deduction. Form 8903 is used to calculate the deduction. In the case of corporate taxpayers, the deduction against gross income is equal to the applicable percentage of its QPAI or its alternative minimum taxable income.

The amount of the domestic production activities deduction for any tax year, however, may not exceed 50 percent of the W-2 wages paid by the taxpayer (¶ 980C) that are allocable to the taxpayer's domestic production gross receipts (¶ 980D).

980B. Qualified Production Activities Income. A taxpayer's qualified production activities income (QPAI) is its domestic production gross receipts (DPGR) attributable to the actual conduct of a trade or business during the tax year, reduced by: (1) the cost of goods sold allocable to DPGR; (2) other deductions, expenses, and losses that are directly allocable to DPGR; and (3) a ratable share of other deductions, expenses, and losses that are not directly allocable to DPGR or another class of income (Code Sec. 199(c)(1)).[211]

QPAI must be determined on an item-by-item basis and is the sum of QPAI from each item (whether positive or negative) (Reg. §§ 1.199-1(c) and 1.199-3(d)).[212] Thus, a taxpayer cannot determine QPAI on a division-by-division, product-line-by-product-line, or transaction-by-transaction basis. This prevents a taxpayer from isolating loss activities from other activities in order to maximize their deduction. An "item" is defined as property, or any portion of property, that is offered to sale to customers that meets all of the requirements of the manufacturer's deduction.

Limited Deduction for Oil-Related Qualified Production Activity Income. A taxpayer having oil-related qualified production activities income must reduce the domestic production activities deduction by three percent of the least of:

(1) the taxpayer's oil-related qualified production activities income for the tax year;

(2) the taxpayer's qualified production activities income for the tax year; or

(3) taxable income (determined without regard to the domestic production activities deduction) (Code Sec. 199(d)(9)(A)).[213]

If the taxpayer entitled to the deduction is an individual, then modified adjusted gross income (AGI) is substituted for taxable income (Code Sec. 199(d)(2)).

980C. W-2 Wage Limitation. The deduction for domestic production activities may not exceed 50 percent of the W-2 wages paid by the taxpayer to its employees for the calendar year ending during the tax year which are properly allocable to the taxpayer's domestic gross production receipts (the wages that the taxpayer deducts in calculating its qualified production activities income) (Code Sec. 199(b)(2); Reg. § 1.199-2(a)).[214]

W-2 wages are defined as amounts required to be reported for wages and compensation on Form W-2, plus compensation deferred under Code Sec. 457 plans and elective

References are to Standard Federal Tax Reports; Tax Research Consultant; and Practical Tax Explanations.

[209] ¶ 11,030D; DEPR: 15,162.85; § 11,535.20

[210] ¶ 12,468; BUSEXP: 6,000; § 6,001

[211] ¶ 12,468; BUSEXP: 6,000; § 6,015.05

[212] ¶ 12,472, ¶ 12,472B; BUSEXP: 6,100; § 6,015.05

[213] ¶ 12,468; BUSEXP: 6,052.10; § 6,010

[214] ¶ 12,468, ¶ 12,472A; BUSEXP: 6,054; § 6,010

deferrals under other employer plans (i.e., 401(k)s, 403(b)s, SIMPLEs, and SEPs, as well as designated Roth contributions) (Reg. § 1.199-2(e)).[215] While all of these payments are reported on Form W-2, no single box includes all types of payments. Thus, taxpayers may use one of three safe harbors for computing W-2 wages (Rev. Proc. 2006-47):[216]

(1) *Unmodified box method:* Under the unmodified box method, W-2 wages are the *lesser of*: (a) the total amount entered for all employees in Box 1 (wages, tips, other compensation) or (b) the total amount entered for all employees in Box 5 (Medicare wages and tips).

(2) *Modified Box 1 method:* Under the modified Box 1 method, the total amount reported in Box 1 for all employees is reduced by the total amount included in Box 1 for all employees that are: (a) not wages subject to federal income tax withholding and (b) amounts that are not wages but the taxpayer has elected to withhold income on (e.g., supplemental unemployment compensation benefits and certain sick pay). The result is then increased by the total amount reported in Box 12 for all employees which are coded D, E, F, G, or S to arrive at the taxpayer's W-2 wages.

(3) *Tracking wages method:* Under the tracking wages method, the taxpayer actually tracks total wages paid to its employees that are subject to federal income tax withholding and that are reported on Form W-2 (not including supplemental unemployment benefits). The result is then increased by the amount reported in Box 12 and coded D, E, F, G, or S to arrive at the taxpayer's W-2 wages.

Amounts that are treated by a taxpayer as W-2 wages in one tax year (e.g., nonqualified deferred compensation) may not be treated as W-2 wages in another tax year or as W-2 wages of another taxpayer. In addition, an employer with a short-tax year must use a modified version of the tracking wages method. A taxpayer that acquires a major portion of a trade or business may not take into account wages paid to common law employees of the predecessor employer for services rendered to the predecessor employer, even if those wages are reported on Forms W-2 furnished by the taxpayer.

980D. Domestic Production Gross Receipts. Domestic production gross receipts (DPGR) are the gross receipts of the taxpayer that are derived from:

(1) the lease, rental, license, sale, exchange, or other disposition of:

(a) qualifying production property (generally, tangible personal property, computer software, and sound recordings) manufactured, produced, grown, or extracted by the taxpayer in whole or in significant part within the United States,

(b) any qualified film produced by the taxpayer in the United States, or

(c) electricity, natural gas, or potable water produced by the taxpayer in the United States;

(2) construction performed within the United States; and

(3) engineering or architectural services performed in the United States for construction projects located in the United States (Code Sec. 199(c)(4)).[217]

DPGR does not include gross receipts from:

(1) the sale of food and beverages prepared by the taxpayer at a retail establishment;

(2) transmission or distribution of electricity; or

(3) distribution of electricity, natural gas, or potable water.

For this purpose, the United States is defined as including all 50 states and the District of Columbia, as well as the territorial waters of the United States, and the seabed and subsoil of those submarine areas that are adjacent to the territorial waters of the United States and over which the U.S. has exclusive rights, in accordance with interna-

References are to Standard Federal Tax Reports; Tax Research Consultant; and Practical Tax Explanations.

[215] ¶ 12,472A; BUSEXP: 6,054; § 6,010

[216] ¶ 12,476.75; BUSEXP: 6,054.05; § 6,010

[217] ¶ 12,468; BUSEXP: 6,100; § 6,015.10

tional law, with respect to the exploration and exploitation of natural resources (Reg. § 1.199-3(h)).[218] The United States generally does not include possessions and territories of the United States or the airspace or space over the United States and these areas. However, for tax years beginning after December 31, 2005, and before January 1, 2012, a taxpayer can take into account its Puerto Rico business activity for its first six tax years in calculating its DPGR and qualified production activities income (QPAI), if all of the taxpayer's gross receipts from Puerto Rican sources were subject to U.S. income taxation (Code Sec. 199(d)(8)).[219] For purposes of the 50-percent-of-W-2-wages limitation, those taxpayers can take into account wages paid to U.S. citizens who were bona fide residents of Puerto Rico.

Generally, a taxpayer may allocate which of its gross receipts are DPGR and non-DPGR using any reasonable method. A specific identification method must be used if the information is readily available and it can be used without undue burden or expense (Reg. § 1.199-1(d)).[220] If a taxpayer has a *de minimis* amount of non-DPGR (less than five percent of total gross receipts), then all of the taxpayer's gross receipts may be treated as DPGR.

Generally, gross receipts derived from the performance of a service other than construction, engineering, and architectural activities do not qualify as DPGR (Reg. § 1.199-3(i)).[221] There are five exceptions to this rule. A taxpayer may include in DPGR the gross receipts derived from a qualified warranty, delivery, distribution, installation, and provision of an operating manual, as well as a *de minimis* amount of embedded services (less than five percent of the gross receipts) with respect to an underlying item of qualifying property. A service is considered embedded if its price is not separately stated from the amount charged for the qualified property.

If a taxpayer exchanges qualified production property it manufactured, produced, etc., for other property in a taxable or nontaxable exchange, the value of the property received may be treated as DPGR. However, unless the taxpayer further manufactures, produces, etc., the property received, any gross receipts from the subsequent sale will not be DPGR even if the property was qualified property in the hands of the other person. Generally, DPGR will also not include any gross receipts derived by the taxpayer from the lease, rental, or license of qualified production property for use by any related person (Code Sec. 199(c)(7)).[222]

980E. Qualified Production Property. Generally, only one taxpayer may claim the domestic production activities deduction with respect to the manufacture, production, growth, or extraction (MPGE) of qualifying production property (QPP) (i.e., tangible personal property, computer software, and sound recordings) (Reg. § 1.199-3(f)(1)).[223] The deduction is claimed by the taxpayer who has the benefits and burdens of ownership of the property (i.e., bears the risk of loss) under federal income tax principles during the period that the qualifying MPGE activity occurs.

The QPP must be MPGE by the taxpayer in whole or in significant part within the United States. QPP will be treated as having been MPGE in significant part in the United States if the MPGE activity performed within the United States is substantial in nature. This is determined on a facts and circumstances basis taking into account the nature and relative value added by the taxpayer's U.S. activity (Reg. § 1.199-3(e) and (g)).[224] A safe harbor provides that the significant part requirement will be satisfied if conversion costs (i.e., direct labor and related factory expenses) to MPGE the property are incurred by the taxpayer within the United States and such costs account for 20 percent or more of the total cost of goods sold of the property. For this purpose, packaging, repackaging, labeling, and minor assembly operations are not considered so substantial in nature as to qualify as the MPGE of QPP. In addition, research and experimental activities and the

References are to Standard Federal Tax Reports; Tax Research Consultant; and Practical Tax Explanations.

[218] ¶ 12,472B; BUSEXP: 6,150; § 6,015.10

[219] ¶ 12,468; BUSEXP: 6,104.05; § 6,015.10

[220] ¶ 12,472; BUSEXP: 6,102.05; § 6,015.20

[221] ¶ 12,472B; BUSEXP: 6,160; § 6,015.10

[222] ¶ 12,468; BUSEXP: 6,104; § 6,015.15

[223] ¶ 12,472B; BUSEXP: 6,160.25; § 6,015.10

[224] ¶ 12,472B; BUSEXP: 6,160.25; § 6,015.10

creation of intangibles (other than computer software and sound recordings) do not qualify as substantial activities and may be excluded in calculating the safe harbor.

980F. Construction, Engineering, or Architectural Activities. The domestic production gross receipts (DPGR) of a taxpayer includes the proceeds from the sale, exchange, or other disposition of real property constructed by the taxpayer in the United States (whether or not sold or completed), including compensation for the performance of construction services by the taxpayer and any qualified construction warranty (Reg. § 1.199-3(m)).[225] It also includes proceeds derived from engineering or architectural services performed in the United States for real property construction projects. DPGR does not include proceeds from the lease or rental of real property constructed by the taxpayer. Nor does it include gross receipts attributable to the sale or other disposition of land (though the taxpayer may reduce its cost related to DPGR by the cost of the land).

980G. Allocation of Costs and Deductions. If a taxpayer can specifically identify from its books and records the cost of goods sold (CGS) allocable to its domestic production gross receipts (DPGR) (without undue burden or expense), then CGS allocable to DPGR is that amount regardless of whether the taxpayer uses another allocation method to allocate gross receipts (Reg. § 1.199-4(b)).[226] If a taxpayer cannot specifically identify CGS allocable to DPGR (e.g., inventory accounted for under the LIFO method), the taxpayer may use any reasonable method. This includes allocation based on gross receipts, number of units produced, or total production costs. An allocation of CGS between DPGR and non-DPGR that is different from the taxpayer's method for allocating gross receipts will ordinarily *not* be considered reasonable unless the method used for allocating CGS is demonstrably more accurate. However, a qualifying small taxpayer may use the small business simplified overall method to allocate CGS and other deductions (see below).

Three methods are provided for apportioning deductions directly allocable to DPGR and a ratable portion of deductions not directly allocable to DPGR or another class of income. For purposes of all three methods, net operating losses (NOLs) and deductions not attributable to the actual conduct of a trade or business (i.e., standard deduction, exemptions) may not be allocated or apportioned to DPGR.

(1) The *Section 861* method is required to be used by a taxpayer unless it is eligible and chooses to use one of the other methods. Under the Section 861 method, a taxpayer must allocate a deduction to the relevant class of gross income to which the deduction relates and then apportion the deduction within each class between DPGR and non-DPGR (Reg. § 1.199-4(d)).[227] If non-DPGR is treated as DPGR by reason of a safe harbor or *de minimis* rule, then deductions related to such non-DPGR may be apportioned to DPGR.

(2) Under the *simplified deduction method*, deductions other than CGS may be ratably apportioned between DPGR and non-DPGR based on relative gross receipts (Reg. § 1.199-4(e)).[228] A taxpayer is eligible to use this method at any time if: (a) its average annual gross receipts during the three-year period prior to the tax year is $100 million or less or (b) its total assets at the end of the tax year attributable to its trade or business are $10 million or less. In the case of a pass-through entity, eligibility to use this method is determined at the owner level. The method is also applied at the owner level, except for trusts and estates.

(3) Under the *small business simplified overall method*, a qualifying small taxpayer may ratably apportion its total costs for the tax year (including CGS and other deductions) between DPGR and non-DPGR based on relative gross receipts (Reg. § 1.199-4(f)).[229] A taxpayer is eligible to use this method if: (a) its average annual gross receipts during the three-year period prior to the tax year is $5 million

References are to Standard Federal Tax Reports; Tax Research Consultant; and Practical Tax Explanations.

[225] ¶ 12,472B; BUSEXP: 6,156; § 6,015.10

[226] ¶ 12,472C; BUSEXP: 6,102.10; § 6,015.20

[227] ¶ 12,472C; BUSEXP: 6,108.10; § 6,015.20

[228] ¶ 12,472C; BUSEXP: 6,108.15; § 6,015.20

[229] ¶ 12,472C; BUSEXP: 6,108.20; § 6,015.20

or less, and its total costs for the tax year are less than $5 million; (b) it is engaged in the business of farming and is not required to use the accrual method of accounting; or (c) it is eligible to use the cash method of accounting under Rev. Proc. 2002-28 (¶ 1515). In the case of a pass-through entity, eligibility to use the method is determined (and application is made) at the entity level.

Wage Expense Safe Harbor. A taxpayer using either the Section 861 method of cost allocation or the simplified deduction method may determine the amount of W-2 wages that is properly allocable to DPGR for a tax year by multiplying the amount of W-2 wages for the tax year by the ratio of the taxpayer's wage expense included in calculating qualified production activities income (QPAI) for the tax year to the taxpayer's total wage expense used in calculating the taxpayer's taxable income (or adjusted gross income, if applicable) for the tax year, without regard to any wage expense disallowed by Code Secs. 465, 469, 704(d), or 1366(d) (Reg. § 1.199-2(e)(2)).[230] A taxpayer that uses the Code Sec. 861 method of cost allocation or the simplified deduction method to determine QPAI must use the same expense allocation and apportionment methods that it uses to determine QPAI to allocate and apportion wage expense for purposes of this safe harbor. A taxpayer that uses the small business simplified overall method may use the small business simplified overall method safe harbor for determining the amount of W-2 wages that is properly allocable to DPGR. Under this safe harbor, the amount of W-2 wages that is properly allocable to DPGR is equal to the same proportion of W-2 wages that the amount of DPGR bears to the taxpayer's total gross receipts.

980H. Application to Pass-Through Entities. The deduction for domestic production activities is generally applied at the shareholder, partner, or similar level of a pass-through entity (Code Sec. 199(d)(1)).[231] The entity allocates to each partner or shareholder its share of QPAI and W-2 wages from the entity. Only an eligible entity may calculate QPAI and W-2 wages at the entity level. An eligible entity is:

(1) an eligible Code Sec. 861 partnership,

(2) an eligible widely-held pass-thru entity, or

(3) an eligible small pass-thru entity.

Entities that are ineligible to calculate QPAI and W-2 wages at the entity level include qualifying in-kind partnerships (under Reg. § 1.199-3(i)(7)) and EAG partnerships (as described in Reg. § 1.199-3(i)(8)).

If a taxpayer must combine QPAI and W-2 wages from a partnership, S corporation, trust, or estate with the taxpayer's total QPAI and W-2 wages from other sources, then for purposes of apportioning the taxpayer's interest expense, the taxpayer's interest in such partnership (and, where relevant in apportioning the taxpayer's interest expense, the partnership's assets), the taxpayer's shares in such S corporation, or the taxpayer's interest in such trust shall be disregarded (Reg. § 1.199-4(d)).[232]

In addition, special rules permit patrons of agricultural or horticultural cooperatives to claim the deduction for their portion of any patronage dividend or per-unit allocation received that is allocable to the QPAI of the cooperative (Code Sec. 199(d)(3); Reg. § 1.199-6).[233] For a discussion of the application of the deduction to S corporations, see ¶ 312; for partnerships, see ¶ 431A; and for nongrantor trusts and estates, see ¶ 536.

Expenses of Professional Persons

981. Professional Persons. Expenses incurred for operating a car used in making professional calls, dues to professional organizations, rent paid for office space, and other ordinary and necessary business expenses are deductible by a professional person. Amounts for books and equipment may be deducted if the useful life of the item is not more than one year (Reg. § 1.162-6).[234]

References are to Standard Federal Tax Reports; Tax Research Consultant; and Practical Tax Explanations.

[230] ¶ 12,472A; BUSEXP: 6,054.20; § 6,010

[231] ¶ 12,468; BUSEXP: 6,206; § 6,020.10

[232] ¶ 12,472C; BUSEXP: 6,108.10; § 6,015.20

[233] ¶ 12,468, ¶ 12,472E; BUSEXP: 6,102.10; § 6,015.10e

[234] ¶ 8633; BUSEXP: 3,050; § 9,005.25

No deduction is allowed for dues paid to any club organized for business, pleasure, recreation, or other social purposes (Code Sec. 274(a)(3); Reg. § 1.274-2(a)(2)(iii)(b)).[235] However, this disallowance does not extend to professional organizations (e.g., bar and accounting associations) or public service organizations (e.g., Kiwanis and Rotary clubs) (¶ 913A).

A professional who performs services as an employee and who incurs unreimbursed related expenses may deduct such expenses only as itemized deductions subject to the two-percent-of-adjusted-gross-income floor (¶ 941 and ¶ 1011).

Information Services. Amounts paid for subscriptions to professional journals, and the cost of information services such as Federal or State Tax Reporters, Unemployment Reporters, Labor Law or Trade Regulation Reporters, Estate Tax Reporters, and other law reporters, or their online equivalents, that have a useful life of one year or less, are deductible by a lawyer, accountant or other taxpayer who buys a service in connection with the performance of his or her duties (*J.I. Peyser*, 1 TCM 807 (1943); *G. Nehus*, 68 TCM 1503 (1994)).[236] The cost of a professional library having a more permanent value should be capitalized.

Other Expenses. A deduction is allowed to members of the clergy, lawyers, merchants, professors, and physicians for expenses incurred in attending business conventions (¶ 959) (Reg. § 1.162-2).[237] For foreign conventions, see ¶ 960. A member of the medical profession is allowed a deduction for business entertainment, subject to the rules discussed at ¶ 910, so long as there is a direct relationship between the expense and the development or expansion of a medical practice (*R.A. Sutter*, 21 TC 170 (1953) (Acq.)).[238] A doctor's staff privilege fee paid to a hospital is a capital expenditure (*G.L. Heigerick*, 45 TC 475 (1966)).[239] For other deductions, see the Checklist at ¶ 57.

Farmer's Expenses

982. Farming Expenses. Deductions are permitted for expenses incurred in carrying on the business of farming, including a horticultural nursery business (Reg. § 1.162-12).[240] Among allowable deductions are the following: cost of tools; cost of feeding and raising livestock (excluding produce grown on the farm and labor of the taxpayer); and cost of gasoline, repairs, and upkeep of a car or truck used wholly in the business of farming, or a portion of the cost, if used for both farming and personal use. Special rules, however, apply to certain property produced in a farming business (¶ 999) and to farm tax shelters (¶ 2028). See ¶ 767 for income averaging rules.

Expenses for the purchase of farm machinery or equipment, breeding, dairy or work animals, a car, and drilling water wells for irrigation purposes are capital items usually subject to depreciation (Reg. § 1.162-12).[241] Any machinery or equipment (other than a grain bin, cotton ginning asset, fence, or land improvement), the original use of which began with the taxpayer after December 31, 2008, and was placed in service by the taxpayer in a farming business in 2009, has a recovery period of five years under the general depreciation system (GDS) (10 years under the alternative depreciation system (ADS)) (Code Sec. 168(e)(3)(B)(vii) and (g)(3)(B)).[242]

Conservation Expenses. A farmer may generally deduct soil and water conservation expenditures that do not give rise to a deduction for depreciation, that are not otherwise deductible and that would increase the basis of the property absent the election to deduct them (Code Sec. 175; Reg. § 1.175-1–1.175-6).[243] However, current deductions for soil and water conservation expenses are limited to those that are consistent with a conservation plan approved by the Soil Conservation Service of the U.S.D.A. or, in the absence of a federally approved plan, a soil conservation plan of a comparable state

References are to Standard Federal Tax Reports; Tax Research Consultant; and Practical Tax Explanations.

[235] ¶ 14,402, ¶ 14,405; BUSEXP: 24,658; § 9,625

[236] ¶ 8634.1206; BUSEXP: 3,050; § 9,935.05

[237] ¶ 8527; BUSEXP: 24,160; § 9,515

[238] ¶ 8523.2717; BUSEXP: 24,160; § 9,610.05

[239] ¶ 8634.1154; BUSEXP: 9,100; § 10,201

[240] ¶ 8755; FARM: 9,050; § 36,101

[241] ¶ 8755; FARM: 9,078.05; § 36,110.10

[242] ¶ 11,250; DEPR: 3,156.15, DEPR: 3,458; § 36,130

[243] ¶ 12,060, ¶ 12,061–¶ 12,066; FARM: 9,162; § 36,110.05

agency. Expenses related to the draining or filling of wetlands or to land preparation for the installation or operation of center pivot irrigation systems may not be deducted under this provision (Code Sec. 175(c)(3)).[244] The deduction is limited annually to 25 percent of the taxpayer's gross income from farming. Excess expenses can be carried over to succeeding tax years, without time limitation, but in each year the total deduction is limited to 25 percent of that year's gross income from farming.

Deductible soil and water conservation expenses include such costs as: leveling; grading; construction; control and protection of diversion channels, drainage ditches, outlets, and ponds; planting of windbreaks; and other treatment or moving of earth. Also deductible are endangered species recovery expenditures paid or incurred by a taxpayer engaged in the business of farming for the purpose of achieving site-specific management actions recommended in recovery plans approved pursuant to the Endangered Species Act of 1973 (P.L. 93-205). No current deduction is allowed for the purchase, construction, installation, or improvement of depreciable masonry, tile, metal, or wood structures, appliances, and facilities, such as tanks, reservoirs, pipes, canals, and pumps. Assessments levied by a soil or water conservation or drainage district in order to defray expenses made by the district may also be deductible.

Schedule F Loss Limitation. The amount of net farm losses that can be claimed for any tax year in which a taxpayer, other than a C corporation, has received applicable subsidies is limited to the excess farm loss (Code Sec. 461(j)(1)).[245] Farm losses that can be claimed by such taxpayers are limited for the tax year the subsidies are received to the greater of $300,000 ($150,000 for a married taxpayer filing separately) or the taxpayer's aggregate net farm income for the five preceding tax years.

983. Land Clearing Expenses. Land clearing expenditures must be capitalized and added to the farmer's basis in the land (*AMFAC, Inc.*, CA-9, 80-2 USTC ¶ 9630).[246] However, business expenses for ordinary maintenance activities related to property already used in farming (e.g., brush clearing) are currently deductible (*E.G. Barham*, DC Ga., 69-1 USTC ¶ 9356).[247]

984. Development Costs. Generally, farmers have the option of deducting or capitalizing developmental expenses that are ordinary and necessary business expenses (Reg. § 1.162-12).[248] However, plants produced by farms that have a preproductive period of more than two years must be capitalized. For certain farms (corporations, partnerships, and tax shelters) that are required to use the accrual method, the expenses must be capitalized regardless of the length of the preproductive period (¶ 999). Special rules apply to farming syndicates (¶ 2032).

985. Expensing Fertilizer Costs. A farmer, other than a farm syndicate, may elect to deduct current expenses otherwise chargeable to capital account made for fertilizer, lime, ground limestone, marl, or other materials for enriching, neutralizing, or conditioning land used in farming. If no election is made, expenditures producing benefits extending over more than one year are capitalized and recovered by amortization (Reg. § 1.180-1 and 1.180-2).[249] The election, which is effective only for the tax year claimed, is made by claiming the deduction on the return. For farm syndicates and prepayments by cash-basis farmers, see ¶ 1539, ¶ 2028 and ¶ 2032.

Landlord or Tenant Expenses

986. Landlord or Tenant. A tenant may deduct rent paid for business property as well as any amounts, such as property taxes and interest, that the lease requires the tenant to pay on behalf of the landlord (Reg. § 1.162-11).[250] An amount paid by a *lessee* for cancellation of a lease on business property is generally deductible (*A.J. Cassatt*, CA-3, 43-2 USTC ¶ 9579).[251] However, payments by the *lessor* for the cancellation of a lease have

References are to Standard Federal Tax Reports; Tax Research Consultant; and Practical Tax Explanations.

[244] ¶ 12,060; FARM: 9,150; § 36,110.05

[245] ¶ 21,802; FARM: 9,208; § 36,215

[246] ¶ 12,068.27; FARM: 9,102; § 36,101

[247] ¶ 8520.7455; FARM: 9,168; § 36,320.10

[248] ¶ 8755; FARM: 9,102, FARM: 9,104; § 36,315.05

[249] ¶ 12,141, ¶ 12,142; FARM: 9,064; § 36,115, § 36,320.20

[250] ¶ 8753; REAL: 12,066; § 7,305

[251] ¶ 8754.16; REAL: 12,252.10; § 18,605.15

generally been regarded as capital expenditures, amortizable over the unexpired term of the canceled lease (*Peerless Weighing & Vending Machine Corp*, 52 TC 850 (1969)).[252]

Under the one-year rule, a cash-basis taxpayer can deduct otherwise allowable rent attributable to the current or a previous year in the year in which the taxpayer actually pays the rent (Reg. § 1.461-1(a)).[253] This is true even though most of the lease term is in the following year if the lease expires within a year of payment. Prepaid rent for a lease extending more than one year from the date of payment must be capitalized and amortized over the term of the lease. Some rental payments are subject to the uniform capitalization rules (¶ 990). For an improvement made by the lessee on leased premises, see ¶ 1234.

If an owner of property occupies part of the property as a personal residence and rents part of it, expenses and depreciation allocable to the rented space may be deductible (¶ 966).

Payments made under a conditional sales contract are not deductible as rent. A conditional sales contract generally exists when at least a portion of the rental payments is applied to the purchase of the property under advantageous terms (IRS Fact Sheet FS-2007-14, 2-23-07).

Under certain conditions, taxpayers who are in the business of producing real property or tangible personal property for resale, or who purchase property for resale, may not claim rental or lease expenses as a current deduction. Instead, they must include some or all of these costs in the basis of the property they produce or acquire for resale under the uniform capitalization rules. These costs are recovered when the property is sold (IRS Fact Sheet FS-2007-14, 2-23-07).

Mining Company's Expenses

987. Mine Exploration. Mining companies may elect to deduct domestic exploration expenses (except for oil or gas), provided that the amount deducted is recaptured once the mine reaches production stage or is sold (Code Sec. 617).[254] Recapture is accomplished by a company's electing either to (1) include in income for that year the previously deducted exploration expenditures chargeable to the mine, increase the basis of the property by the amount included in income, and subsequently recover this amount through depletion or (2) forgo depletion from the property which includes or comprises the mine until deductions forgone equal exploration expenditures previously deducted.

Expenses not recaptured by one of these methods are recaptured on the sale or other disposition of the mining property with the amount recaptured treated as ordinary income. Certain transfers are not subject to these recapture rules (Code Sec. 617(b) and (d)(3)).[255]

Deductions allowed a corporation (other than an S corporation) for mineral exploration and development costs under Code Secs. 616(a) and 617(a) must be reduced by 30 percent (Code Sec. 291(b)).[256] The 30 percent of expenses that cannot be deducted must be capitalized and amortized over a 60-month period on Form 4562. Taxpayers may also elect to capitalize mine exploration expenses and amortize them over a 10-year period (¶ 1450).

Geological and geophysical (G&G) expenditures paid or incurred in connection with oil and gas exploration or development in the United States must be amortized ratably over a 24-month period beginning on the mid-point of the tax year that the expenses were paid or incurred. If a property or project is abandoned or retired during the 24-month amortization period, any remaining basis must continue to be amortized (Code Sec. 167(h)).[257] Major integrated oil companies must ratably amortize any G&G costs incurred over seven years.

References are to Standard Federal Tax Reports; Tax Research Consultant; and Practical Tax Explanations.

[252] ¶ 13,709.417; REAL: 12,252.20; § 18,605.15

[253] ¶ 21,805; ACCTNG: 6,316; § 38,405

[254] ¶ 24,110; FARM: 21,052; § 11,635

[255] ¶ 24,110; FARM: 21,058.20; § 11,635

[256] ¶ 15,190; FARM: 21,102; § 11,635

[257] ¶ 11,001; FARM: 21,176; § 11,501

988. Mine Development. Expenses paid or incurred with respect to a domestic mine or other natural deposit (other than oil or gas) after the existence of ores or minerals in commercially marketable quantities has been discovered can be deducted currently unless the taxpayer elects to treat them as deferred expenses and deduct them ratably as the ore or mineral is sold (Code Sec. 616; Reg. § 1.616-1).[258] Such expenses do not include those made for the acquisition or improvement of depreciable property. However, depreciation allowances are considered as development costs.

The 30-percent reduction in the allowable deduction and the election to amortize over a 10-year period (discussed at ¶ 987 in the case of exploration expenses) applies also to mine development expenses (Code Sec. 291(b)).[259]

988A. Foreign Mine Exploration and Development. Foreign mining exploration and development expenses (other than oil, gas, or geothermal wells) are to be recovered over a 10-year, straight-line amortization schedule beginning with the tax year in which the costs were paid or incurred (Code Secs. 616(d) and 617(h)).[260] However, the taxpayer may elect to add such expenses to the adjusted basis of the property for purposes of computing cost depletion.

989. Oil, Gas, or Geothermal Well Drilling Expense. Operators of a domestic oil, gas, or geothermal well may elect to currently deduct intangible drilling and development costs (IDCs) rather than charge such costs to capital, recoverable through depletion or depreciation (Code Sec. 263(c); Reg. § 1.612-4).[261] The election is binding upon future years. IDCs generally include all expenses made by the operator incident to and necessary for the drilling of wells and the preparation of wells for the production of oil, gas, or geothermal energy that are neither for the purchase of tangible property nor part of the acquisition price of an interest in the property. IDCs include labor, fuel, materials and supplies, truck rent, repairs to drilling equipment, and depreciation for drilling equipment.

An integrated oil company (generally, a producer that is not an independent producer) must reduce the deduction for IDCs otherwise allowable by 30 percent (Code Sec. 291(b)).[262] The amount disallowed as a current expense deduction must be amortized over a 60-month period. Taxpayers may elect to capitalize, rather than currently deduct, IDCs and amortize these expenditures over a 60-month period (¶ 1450).

If the operator has elected to capitalize intangible drilling and development costs, and the well later proves to be nonproductive (a dry hole), the operator may elect to deduct those costs as an ordinary loss (Reg. § 1.612-4(b)(4)).[263] The election, once made, is binding for all years. As to the recapture of intangible drilling expenses upon sale of oil, gas, or geothermal property, see ¶ 2025.

Foreign Wells. Operators may not opt to currently deduct IDCs for wells located outside the U.S. (Code Sec. 263(i)).[264] Such costs must be recovered over a 10-year straight-line amortization schedule or, at the operator's election, added to the adjusted basis of the property for cost depletion. Dry hole expenses incurred outside the U.S. are currently deductible.

989A. Advanced Mine Safety Equipment Expensing (Expired). A taxpayer may make an election to expense 50 percent of the cost of advanced mine safety equipment paid or incurred before January 1, 2012 (Code Sec. 179E).[265] The cost of any eligible equipment that is expensed under Code Sec. 179 cannot be taken into account in calculating this special deduction for mine safety equipment. The deduction is subject to recapture as ordinary income under the Code Sec. 1245 depreciation recapture rules.

Caution: Absent further legislation, the election allowed by Code Sec. 179E is not available for costs paid or incurred after December 31, 2011.

References are to Standard Federal Tax Reports; Tax Research Consultant; and Practical Tax Explanations.

[258] ¶ 24,090, ¶ 24,091; FARM: 21,110; § 11,630

[259] ¶ 15,190; FARM: 21,118; § 11,630

[260] ¶ 24,090, ¶ 24,110; FARM: 21,052; § 11,630

[261] ¶ 13,700, ¶ 23,949; FARM: 21,150; § 11,615

[262] ¶ 15,190; FARM: 21,154.10; § 11,630

[263] ¶ 23,949; FARM: 21,152.10; § 15,320

[264] ¶ 13,700; FARM: 21,152.20; § 45,525.15

[265] ¶ 12,139; BUSEXP: 19,000; § 10,255

Uniform Capitalization Rules

990. Uniform Capitalization Rules. Taxpayers subject to the uniform capitalization rules are required to capitalize all direct costs and an allocable portion of most indirect costs that are associated with production or resale activities. The uniform capitalization rules apply to the following:

(1) real or tangible personal property produced by the taxpayer for use in a trade or business or in an activity engaged in for profit;

(2) real or tangible personal property produced by the taxpayer for sale to customers; or

(3) real or personal property (both tangible and intangible) acquired by the taxpayer for resale. However, the uniform capitalization rules do not apply to intangible or intangible personal property acquired for resale if the taxpayer's annual gross receipts for the preceding three tax years do not exceed $10 million (Code Sec. 263A):[266]

Costs attributable to producing or acquiring property generally are capitalized by charging them to capital accounts or basis, and costs attributable to property that is inventory in the hands of the taxpayer generally are capitalized by including them in inventory.

Property Excepted from Rules. Among the classes of property excepted from the rules are:

(1) property produced by the taxpayer for its own use other than in a trade or business or in an activity conducted for profit;

(2) research and experimental expenditures (¶ 979);

(3) capital costs incurred in complying with EPA sulfur regulations under Code Sec. 179B, intangible drilling and development costs under Code Secs. 263(c), (i), and 291(b)(2), and mine development and exploration costs pursuant to Code Secs. 616 and 617;

(4) any property produced by the taxpayer pursuant to a long-term contract;

(5) any costs incurred in raising, growing or harvesting trees (including the costs associated with the real property underlying such trees) other than trees bearing fruit, nuts, or other crops and ornamental trees (those which are six years old or less when severed from the roots); and

(6) costs (other than circulation expenditures) subject to amortization (¶ 1450).

990A. Writers, Photographers, and Artists. Expenses paid or incurred by a self-employed individual (including expenses of a corporation owned by a free-lancer and directly related to the activities of a qualified employee-owner) in the business of being a writer, photographer, or artist whose personal efforts create or may reasonably be expected to create the product are exempt from uniform capitalization rules (Code Sec. 263A(h)).[267] Generally, expenses for producing jewelry, silverware, pottery, furniture, and similar household items are not exempt.

991. Costs Required To Be Capitalized. Generally, direct material and labor costs and indirect costs must be capitalized with respect to property that is produced or acquired for resale (Code Sec. 263A(a)(2); Reg. § 1.263A-1(e)).[268] Direct material costs include the costs of those materials that become an integral part of the subject matter and of those materials that are consumed in the ordinary course of the activity. Direct labor costs include the cost of labor that can be identified or associated with a particular activity such as basic compensation, overtime pay, vacation pay, and payroll taxes.

Indirect costs include all costs other than direct material and labor costs. Indirect costs require a reasonable allocation to determine the portion of such costs that are attributable to each activity of the taxpayer. Indirect costs include: repair and mainte-

References are to Standard Federal Tax Reports; Tax Research Consultant; and Practical Tax Explanations.

[266] ¶ 13,800; BUSEXP: 9,052; § 10,305.05

[267] ¶ 13,800; BUSEXP: 9,062; § 10,305.10

[268] ¶ 13,800, ¶ 13,811; BUSEXP: 9,056; § 10,310.15

nance of equipment or facilities; utilities; rental of equipment, facilities, or land; indirect labor and contract supervisory wages; indirect materials and supplies; depreciation, amortization and cost recovery allowance on equipment and facilities (to the extent allowable as deductions); certain administrative costs; insurance; contributions paid to or under a stock bonus, pension, profit-sharing, annuity, or other deferred compensation plan; rework labor, scrap and spoilage; and certain engineering and design expenses.

992. Costs Not Required To Be Capitalized. Costs that are not required to be capitalized with respect to property produced or acquired for resale include marketing, selling, advertising and distribution expenses (Reg. § 1.263A-1(e)(4)(iv)).[269] The IRS has established procedures that allow for the capitalization or amortization of package design costs (Rev. Proc. 98-39).[270] Other costs that need not be capitalized include bidding expenses incurred in the solicitation of contracts not awarded the taxpayer; certain general and administrative expenses; and compensation paid to officers attributable to the performance of services that do not directly benefit or are not incurred by reason of a particular production activity.

993. Interest Capitalization Rules. Interest costs paid or incurred during the production period and allocable to real property or tangible personal property produced by the taxpayer that has a class life of at least 20 years, an estimated production period exceeding two years, or an estimated production period exceeding one year and a cost exceeding $1 million must be capitalized (Code Sec. 263A(f)).[271]

994. Property Acquired for Resale. Unless an election is made to use the simplified resale method at ¶ 995, the rules applicable to the production of property apply to costs incurred with respect to property acquired for resale in a trade or business or in an activity conducted for profit (Code Sec. 263A(b)).[272] Property held for resale may include literary, musical, or artistic compositions; stocks; certificates, notes, bonds, debentures, or other evidence of indebtedness; or an interest in, right to subscribe to, or purchase of any of the foregoing, and other intangible properties. However, in the case of personal property acquired for resale, a taxpayer is not subject to the uniform capitalization rules if its average annual gross receipts for the three preceding tax years (or, if less, the number of preceding tax years the taxpayer (and any predecessor) has been in existence) do not exceed $10 million. The uniform capitalization rules apply in the case of real property acquired for resale, regardless of the taxpayer's gross receipts.

995. Simplified Methods of Accounting for Resale Costs. Generally, taxpayers may elect to use one of the simplified resale methods for allocating costs to property acquired for resale (Reg. § 1.263A-3(c)).[273] However, in the case of a single trade or business that consists of both production and resale activities, only the simplified production method (¶ 996) is available. Under the simplified resale methods, preliminary inventory balances are calculated without the inclusion of the additional costs (listed below) required to be capitalized. The amount of additional costs attributable to prior periods and the amount of additional costs determined to be capitalized for the current period are then taken into account with the inventory balances as initially calculated in order to arrive at an ending inventory balance.

The following categories of costs are required to be capitalized with respect to property acquired for resale, regardless of whether a taxpayer elects one of the simplified resale methods: (1) off-site storage or warehousing; (2) purchasing; (3) handling, processing, assembly, and repackaging; and (4) certain general and administrative expenses).

996. Simplified Method of Accounting for Production Costs. An election to use the simplified production method may be made to account for the additional costs required to be capitalized with respect to property produced by the taxpayer that is: (1) stock in trade or other property properly includible in inventory or (2) property held

References are to Standard Federal Tax Reports; Tax Research Consultant; and Practical Tax Explanations.

[269] ¶ 13,811; BUSEXP: 9,052; § 10,310.30

[270] ¶ 13,709.469; BUSEXP: 9,350; § 9,970

[271] ¶ 13,800; BUSEXP: 9,060; § 10,330.05

[272] ¶ 13,800; BUSEXP: 9,052.25; § 10,305.15

[273] ¶ 13,824; BUSEXP: 9,056.35; § 10,325.05

primarily for sale to customers in the ordinary course of business (Reg. § 1.263A-2(b)(2)(i)).[274]

Categories of property eligible for the simplified production method also include properties constructed by a taxpayer for use in its trade or business if the taxpayer: (1) is also producing inventory property and the constructed property is substantially identical in nature and is produced in the same manner as the inventory property or (2) produces such property on a routine and repetitive basis.

997. Simplified Service Cost Method. A simplified method is available for determining capitalizable mixed service costs for eligible property (Reg. § 1.263A-1).[275] The election to use the simplified method must be made independently from other allowable simplified methods.

999. Capitalization of Farming Business Expenses. The uniform capitalization rules apply to plants and animals produced by certain farming businesses (corporations, partnerships, and tax shelters) that are required to use the accrual method. For other farming businesses, the uniform capitalization rules apply only to plants produced in the farming business that have a preproductive period of more than two years (Code Sec. 263A(d)(1)).[276]

Generally, the rules do not apply to costs that are attributable to the replanting, cultivation, maintenance, and development of any plants (of the same type of crop) bearing an edible crop for human consumption (normally eaten or drunk by humans) that were lost or damaged as the result of freezing temperatures, disease, drought, pests, or casualty (Code Sec. 263A(d)(2)).[277] Replanting or maintenance costs may be incurred on property other than the damaged property if the acreage is not in excess of the acreage of the damaged property.

A farming business is a trade or business involving the cultivation of land or the raising or harvesting of any agricultural or horticultural commodity (Code Sec. 263A(e)(4)).[278] Examples include a nursery or sod farm, the raising of ornamental trees (including evergreen trees six years old or less when severed from their roots), the raising or harvesting of trees bearing fruit, nuts, or other crops, and the raising, shearing, feeding, caring for, training, and managing of animals.

Any farmer (other than a corporation, partnership, or tax shelter required to use the accrual method) may elect not to have the uniform capitalization rules made applicable to any plant produced in his business (Code Sec. 263A(d)(3) and (e); Reg. § 1.263A-1(b)(3)).[279] However, such election may not be made for any costs incurred within the first four years in which any almond or citrus trees were planted.

Unless IRS consent is obtained, farmers may only make the election not to have the uniform capitalization rules apply for the first tax year during which the farmer produces property to which the uniform capitalization rules apply (Code Sec. 263A(d)(3)).[280] Once the election is made, it is revocable only with the consent of the IRS.

Incentives for Economically Distressed Communities

999A. Tax Incentives for Distressed Communities. Special tax incentives have encouraged the development of economically distressed areas by businesses located in empowerment zones (¶ 999B), renewal communities (¶ 999C), the District of Columbia Enterprise Community Zone (¶ 999D), hurricane-related GO Zones (¶ 999F), and the National disaster area (¶ 999G). The locations of qualifying empowerment zones and renewal communities are listed in the instructions to Form 8844. Also, they can be found in IRS Pub. 954 (Tax Incentives for Empowerment Zones and Other Distressed Communities).

References are to Standard Federal Tax Reports; Tax Research Consultant; and Practical Tax Explanations.

[274] ¶ 13,817; ACCTNG: 15,210.05; § 10,320.20

[275] ¶ 13,811; ACCTNG: 15,212; § 10,315.15

[276] ¶ 13,800; FARM: 9,104; § 10,305.20

[277] ¶ 13,800; FARM: 9,104; § 36,320.15

[278] ¶ 13,800; FARM: 9,104; § 36,320.25

[279] ¶ 13,800, ¶ 13,811; FARM: 9,104; § 36,320.20

[280] ¶ 13,800; FARM: 9,104; § 36,320.20

Designation as an empowerment zone (¶ 999B) (including the status of the District of Columbia Enterprise Community Zone (¶ 999D) as an empowerment zone) generally terminated after December 31, 2011. Designation as a renewal community (¶ 999C) generally terminated December 31, 2009.

999B. Empowerment Zones. Prior to December 31, 2011, certain areas were desginated as empowerment zones (Code Sec. 1391).[281]

Work Opportunity Credit. The work opportunity credit may be claimed for "designated community residents" and "qualified summer youth employees" living within an empowerment zone or enterprise community hired through December 31, 2011 (¶ 1365G) (Code Sec. 51(c)(4)(B),(d)).[282]

60-Percent Gain Exclusion for Small Business Stock. Taxpayers other than corporations may exclude 50 percent of the gain on the sale or exchange of qualified small business stock (¶ 1905) (Code Sec. 1202(a)(1)).[283] For gain attributable to periods before January 1, 2017, the amount that can be excluded is increased to 60 percent if the small business stock is stock in a corporation that qualifies as an empowerment zone business that was acquired after December 21, 2001. In general, the corporation must qualify as an enterprise zone during substantially all of the time the stock is held). In applying this rule, the end of the empowerment zone designation on December 31, 2011, is ignored in determining whether the corporation qualified as an enterprise zone during substantially all of the time the stock was held. Gain from the sale of small business stock of a qualified business entity in the District of Columbia enterprise zone is not eligible for the increased exclusion).

999C. Renewal Communities. Even though renewal community status terminates after December 31, 2009, the work opportunity credit, the commercial revitalization deduction and the capital gain exclusion continue to be available in 2011.

Work Opportunity Credit. The work opportunity credit may be claimed for high-risk youth and qualified summer youth employees living within a renewal community (see also ¶ 1342) (Code Sec. 51(d)).[284] Claiming either the work opportunity credit or the welfare-to-work credit may reduce or eliminate the employment credit, as discussed at ¶ 999B.

Revitalization Deduction for Commercial Buildings. A taxpayer who receives a revitalization allocation from a state agency may elect to either (Code Sec. 1400I):[285]

(1) deduct one-half of any qualified revitalization expenditures otherwise chargeable to the capital account with respect to any qualified revitalization building in the tax year that the building is placed in service; or

(2) amortize all such expenditures ratably over 120 months beginning in the month that the building is placed in service.

The deduction does not apply to buildings placed in service after December 31, 2009.

A taxpayer who claims a deduction for one-half of its expenditures may only claim depreciation deductions on the remaining half. No depreciation deductions are allowed for expenditures amortized over five years. The deduction is treated as depreciation for purposes of the Code Sec. 1250 depreciation recapture rules and is allowed in full for alternative minimum tax (AMT) purposes.

Expenditures taken into account in computing any tax credit (for example, the rehabilitation credit) cannot be taken into account in computing the deduction and special passive activity loss rules apply (Code Sec. 469(i)(3)(C) and (i)(6)(B)(iii)).[286]

Renewal Community Capital Gain Exclusion. Gross income does not include capital gain (or section 1231 gain) from the sale or exchange of a qualified community asset held for more than five years and acquired after December 31, 2001, and before January

References are to Standard Federal Tax Reports; Tax Research Consultant; and Practical Tax Explanations.

[281] ¶ 32,386; BUSEXP: 57,000; § 10,001

[282] ¶ 4800; BUSEXP: 54,250; § 13,805.05

[283] ¶ 30,372; BUSEXP: 57,056.10; § 9,001

[284] ¶ 4800; BUSEXP: 54,250; § 13,805.05.

[285] ¶ 32,465.01; BUSEXP: 57,204.25; § 9,001

[286] ¶ 21,960; BUSEXP: 33,708; § 9,001

1, 2010 (Code Sec. 1400F).[287] Gain attributable to periods before 2002 and after 2014 does not qualify for the exclusion.

If a qualified community asset is sold (or otherwise transferred) to a subsequent purchaser, it will qualify for the capital gain exclusion for the purchaser provided that the stock or partnership interest continues to represent an interest in a renewal community business or the tangible property continues to be used in a renewal community business (Code Secs. 1400B(b)(4)(B)(ii) and 1400F(b)(4)(B)).

Gain on tangible property which is substantially improved by a taxpayer before January 1, 2012, and any land on which such property is located qualifies for the exclusion if during any 24-month period beginning after December 31, 2001, additions to the basis of the property exceed the greater of the adjusted basis of the property at the start of the 24-month period or $5,000.

Special rules apply that limit the exclusion in the same way as with DC Zone assets (¶ 999D) (Code Secs. 1400B(e) and 1400F(c)(3)).[288]

999D. District of Columbia. Gross income does not include qualified capital gain from the sale or exchange of any DC Zone asset held for more than five years (Code Sec. 1400B).[289] In general, a DC Zone asset includes only (Code Sec. 1400B(b)):

(1) DC Zone business stock—stock acquired for cash at original issue after 1997 and before 2016 from a domestic corporation that is a DC Zone business;

(2) a DC Zone partnership interest—a capital or profits interest in a domestic partnership interest originally issued after 1997 and acquired before 2016 for cash from a partnership that is a DC Zone business; and

(3) DC Zone business property—tangible property acquired by purchase (as defined in Code Sec. 179(d)(2)) after December 31, 1997, and before January 1, 2017, the original use of which commences with the taxpayer in the taxpayer's DC Zone business. The property may not be acquired from a related person or another member of a controlled group.

A taxpayer who acquires stock, a partnership interest, or tangible property from another person in whose hands the asset was a DC Zone asset may also qualify for the exclusion.

Qualified capital gain is gain recognized on the sale or exchange of a DC Zone asset that is a capital asset or that is a Section 1231 asset (i.e., depreciable personal property and real property). It does not include gain attributable to periods before January 1, 1998, or after December 31, 2014, gain which would be recaptured as ordinary income under the Code Sec. 1245 depreciation recapture rules, gain which would be recaptured as ordinary income under the Code Sec. 1250 recapture rules if all depreciation on real property (rather than depreciation in excess of straight-line) was subject to recapture, and gain attributable to a transaction with a related person within the meaning of Code Sec. 267(b) or Code Sec. 707(b)(1).

District of Columbia Enterprise Zone. Prior to January 1, 2012, the District of Columbia Enterprise Zone (DC Zone) was treated as an empowerment zone, and qualifying taxpayers were entitled to the same wage credit, work opportunity credit, and increased expense allowance (¶ 999B) applicable to other empowerment zones (Code Sec. 1400).[290] In addition, the capital gain exclusion described below is available. The $5,000 credit that was available to certain first-time homebuyers within the District of Columbia is no longer available after December 31, 2011 (¶ 1308).

999F. Hurricane-Related GO Zones. The Gulf Opportunity Zone Act of 2005 (P.L. 109-135) and the Katrina Emergency Tax Relief Act of 2005 (P.L. 109-73) amended the Code to provide special tax benefits to assist taxpayers affected by Hurricanes Katrina, Rita, and Wilma (Code Sec. 1400M).[291] The IRS has also provided relief for certain

References are to Standard Federal Tax Reports; Tax Research Consultant; and Practical Tax Explanations.

[287] ¶ 32,437; BUSEXP: 57,204.05; § 9,001

[288] ¶ 32,426, ¶ 32,437; SALES: 15,354.15; § 16,525.05

[289] ¶ 32,426; SALES: 15,352.15; § 16,525.05

[290] ¶ 32,422; BUSEXP: 57,056.30; § 13,810

[291] ¶ 32,478; BUSEXP: 57,300; § 10,001

taxpayers affected by the storms under its own authority. Benefits for victims of Gulf Storms are extended through December 31, 2011. For each storm there is, from largest to smallest, a disaster area, a covered disaster area, and a Gulf Opportunity Zone. A variety of benefits and relief were available depending on the geographic area involved including: casualty and theft losses (¶ 1131); involuntary conversions (¶ 1715); net operating losses; extended carrybacks of net operating losses to the extent they are applicable to certain GO Zone expenses (¶ 1141); early distributions from retirement plans without penalty (¶ 2124); special rules for calculating the earned income and additional child tax credits (¶ 1305); increased Hope and lifetime learning credits for students attending a school located in the GO Zone (¶ 1303); Code Sec. 179 expense (¶ 1208); expanded definition of "targeted employee" for purposes of Work Opportunity Credit (¶ 1365G); increased deduction for reforestation costs (¶ 1287); deduction of demolition and cleanup costs (¶ 1112); rehabilitation tax credit (¶ 1365B); and the issuance of GO Zone Bonds (¶ 729).

The Hurricane Katrina disaster area covered the entire states of Alabama, Florida, Louisiana, and Mississippi. The Katrina covered disaster area covers all of Louisiana and Mississippi, plus certain counties in Alabama and Florida.

The Gulf Opportunity Zone (GO Zone), also known as the core disaster area, covered the portion of the Hurricane Katrina disaster area determined by the Federal Emergency Management Agency (FEMA) to be eligible for either individual or individual and public assistance from the federal government. The GO Zone includes certain counties in Alabama, Louisiana, and Mississippi.

The Hurricane Rita disaster area covered the entire states of Texas and Louisiana. The Rita covered disaster area is the same. The Rita GO Zone covers the portion of the Hurricane Rita disaster area determined by FEMA to be eligible for either individual or individual and public assistance from the federal government. The Rita GO Zone includes certain counties in Louisiana and Texas.

The Hurricane Wilma disaster area covered the entire state of Florida. The Wilma covered disaster area includes certain counties in Florida counties. The Wilma GO Zone covers the portion of the Hurricane Wilma disaster area determined by FEMA to be eligible for either individual or individual and public assistance from the federal government and includes certain counties in Florida.

999G. National Disaster Area (Expired). The National disaster area relief provisions include any areas affected by any federally declared disaster during 2009. The special tax benefits for these disaster areas included: (1) expensing of qualified disaster expenses (Code Sec. 198A);[292] (2) special rules for treatment of NOLs (¶ 1179); (3) first-year bonus depreciation (¶ 1237); and (4) an increased Code Sec. 179 deduction (¶ 1208).

References are to Standard Federal Tax Reports; Tax Research Consultant; and Practical Tax Explanations.

[292] ¶ 12,466; BUSEXP: 19,050; § 10,001

Chapter 10

NONBUSINESS EXPENSES

Deductions, Generally

1001. Major Classifications. Deductions for individuals fall into two basic categories: those taken from adjusted gross income if an eligible taxpayer elects to itemize deductions, and those taken from gross income regardless of whether the taxpayer itemizes. Itemized deductions should be claimed only if they exceed the taxpayer's standard deduction (¶ 126). The standard deduction amount varies according to filing status. This amount, along with the taxpayer's personal and dependency exemptions, reduces adjusted gross income to arrive at taxable income.[1]

1003. Personal Expenses. A personal, living or family expense is *not* deductible unless the Code specifically provides otherwise (Reg. § 1.262-1).[2] Nondeductible expenses include, but are not limited to, rent and insurance premiums paid for the taxpayer's own dwelling, life insurance premiums paid by the insured, and payments for food, clothing, domestic help, and upkeep of an automobile.

Adjusted Gross Income

1005. Deductions Allowed. Adjusted gross income (AGI) is an intermediate figure between gross income and taxable income that is the starting point for computing certain deductions, credits and other tax benefits that are based on or limited by income (Code Sec. 62; Reg. § 1.62-1T).[3] See the chart at ¶ 4 for a listing of the 2012 AGI phaseout thresholds.

AGI is gross income minus deductions:

(1) on account of a trade or business carried on by the taxpayer, except for services as an employee (¶ 1006);

(2) for trade or business expenses paid or incurred by a qualified performing artist for services in the performing arts as an employee (¶ 941A);

(3) for allowed losses from the sale or exchange of property (¶ 1007);

(4) attributable to rental or royalty property (¶ 1089);

(5) for depreciation or depletion allowed to a life tenant of property, or to an income beneficiary of property held in trust, or to an heir, legatee, or devisee of an estate (¶ 1090);

References are to Standard Federal Tax Reports; Tax Research Consultant; and Practical Tax Explanations.

[1] ¶ 6020; FILEIND: 12,100; § 1,010.15

[2] ¶ 13,601; INDIV: 39,052; § 8,201, § 8,205

[3] ¶ 6002, ¶ 6003; FILEIND: 9,000; § 5,001

(6) for contributions by self-employed persons to pension, profit-sharing, and annuity plans (¶ 2163);

(7) for cash payments to individual retirement accounts (IRAs), and to retirement savings plans of certain married individuals to cover a nonworking spouse (¶ 2153A);

(8) for interest forfeited to a bank, savings association, etc., on premature withdrawals from time savings accounts or deposits (¶ 1120);

(9) for alimony payments (¶ 1008);

(10) for the amortization of reforestation expenses (¶ 1287);

(11) for certain repayments of supplemental unemployment compensation benefits to a trust described in Code Sec. 501(c)(9) or (17), required because of receipt of trade readjustment allowances (¶ 1009);

(12) for jury duty pay remitted to employer (¶ 1010);

(13) for moving expenses (¶ 1073);

(14) for interest on education loans (¶ 1082);

(15) for contributions to an Archer medical savings account (¶ 1020);

(16) for expenses paid or incurred by a fee-basis state or local government official for services performed (¶ 941D);

(17) for unreimbursed classroom expenses incurred by eligible educators (¶ 1084);

Comment: Absent further legislation, the deduction from gross income by eligible educators for unreimbursed classroom expenses is not available for tax years beginning after December 31, 2011.

(18) for post-secondary tuition and related expenses (¶ 1082);

Comment: Absent further legislation, the deduction of post-secondary tuition and related expenses from gross income is not available for tax years beginning after December 31, 2011.

(19) for contributions to a health savings account (HSA) (¶ 1020A);

(20) for attorney fees and court costs paid in connection with an unlawful federal discrimination claim, or a whistleblower award for providing information on tax law violations (¶ 1010A);

(21) for travel expenses of National Guard and Reserve members while away from home to attend meetings and training sessions (¶ 941E); and

(22) for domestic production activities (also referred to as manufacturer's deduction or DPAD) (¶ 980A).

The Code specifically allows a deduction from gross income for expenses paid or incurred in connection with the performance of services as an employee under a reimbursement or expense allowance arrangement with the employer or third party (Code Sec. 62(a)(2)(A)). In practice, employee expenses that are reimbursed under an accountable plan are *not* reported on the taxpayer's return. Generally, employee expenses that are not reimbursed or reimbursed under a nonaccountable plan are deductible, if adequately substantiated, only as miscellaneous itemized deductions subject to the two-percent-of-adjusted-gross-income floor and the 50-percent limit for meals and entertainment (¶ 942 and ¶ 943).

1006. Trade or Business Deductions. Expenses directly attributable to a trade or business carried on by a taxpayer are deducted from gross income. For this purpose, the performance of services as an employee is *not* considered to be a trade or business. However, the practice of a profession, not as an employee, is considered the conduct of a trade or business (Code Sec. 62(a)(1); Reg. § 1.62-1T(d)).[4] See ¶ 941 and following for business deductions that are available to employees.

References are to Standard Federal Tax Reports; Tax Research Consultant; and Practical Tax Explanations.

[4] ¶ 6002, ¶ 6003; FILEIND: 9,052; § 5,005, § 9,101

1007. Losses from Sales or Exchanges. Any allowable loss from the sale or exchange of property may be claimed as a deduction in arriving at adjusted gross income (AGI) (Code Sec. 62(a)(3); Reg. § 1.62-1T(c)(4)).[5] This includes allowable losses from sales or exchanges of capital assets; losses that are treated as losses from sales or exchanges of capital assets, i.e., losses on worthless stocks and bonds or nonbusiness bad debts; and any allowable losses from sales or exchanges of noncapital assets (¶ 1701). These deductions are allowed in addition to any losses attributable to a trade or business, or to losses incurred in connection with property held for the production of rents or royalties. An individual's capital loss deduction is generally limited to the individual's capital gains plus $3,000 of ordinary income (¶ 1752).

A loss on an involuntary conversion is deductible in computing AGI only if it is attributable to property used in a trade or business or to property held for the production of rents or royalties. A taxpayer may be entitled, however, to an itemized deduction for the involuntary conversion of property used for personal purposes if the loss arises from a casualty (¶ 1713) (Code Sec. 165(c)).[6]

1008. Deduction for Alimony Paid. Alimony payments are deductible from gross income in the year paid whether the taxpayer uses the cash or accrual method of accounting (Code Secs. 62(a)(10) and 215).[7] Back alimony is deductible in the year paid if it would have been deductible if paid on time.[8] See ¶ 771 and following for more details.

1009. Repayment of Supplemental Unemployment Compensation Benefits. Repayments of supplemental unemployment compensation benefits to trusts or voluntary employees' beneficiary associations (VEBAs) required because of subsequent receipt of trade readjustment allowances under the Trade Act of 1974 are deductible from gross income (Code Sec. 62(a)(12)).[9] Repayment of most other unemployment compensation benefits in a year following the year of receipt are deductible as an itemized deduction on Schedule A of Form 1040 (IRS Pub. 525). If the repayment of either type of unemployment compensation exceeds $3,000, the taxpayer may compute the tax for the tax year of the repayment by using the claim-of-right doctrine calculation as provided by Code Sec. 1341 (¶ 1543).[10]

1010. Jury Pay. An employee can deduct jury pay surrendered to an employer who continued to pay the employee's normal salary while the employee was on jury duty (Code Sec. 62(a)(13)).[11]

1010A. Legal Fees and Costs. An individual can deduct from gross income attorney's fees and court costs incurred in connection with an action involving: (1) a claim of unlawful discrimination; (2) certain claims against the federal government; or (3) a private cause of action under the Medicare Secondary Payer statute (Code Sec. 62(a)(20)).[12] The deduction is limited to the amount includible in gross income on account of a judgment or settlement, whether as a lump sum or in periodic payments. The deduction is claimed by entering the amount and "UDC" on the dotted line next to the appropriate line of Form 1040 and including the amount in the total for that line.

An "above-the-line" deduction (also referred to as an adjustment to gross income) is also allowed for court costs and attorney's fees paid by or on behalf of the taxpayer in connection with any whistleblower award under Code Sec. 7623(b) for providing information regarding tax law violations. The deduction cannot exceed the amount includible in gross income as a result of the award (Code Sec. 62(a)(21)).[13] The taxpayer claims this deduction by entering the amount and "WBF" on the dotted line next to the appropriate line of Form 1040 and including the amount in the total for that line.

For deductibility of legal fees associated with the production of income, see ¶ 1093.

References are to Standard Federal Tax Reports; Tax Research Consultant; and Practical Tax Explanations.

[5] ¶ 6002, ¶ 6003; FILEIND: 9,056; § 5,010

[6] ¶ 9802; SALES: 27,050; § 18,101

[7] ¶ 6002, ¶ 12,570; INDIV: 21,154; § 1,945

[8] ¶ 6094.80; INDIV: 21,154; § 1,945

[9] ¶ 6002; FILEIND: 9,074; § 5,035

[10] ¶ 31,880; FILEIND: 9,074; § 4,230.05

[11] ¶ 6002; FILEIND: 9,076; § 5,040

[12] ¶ 6002; FILEIND: 9,088; § 5,805

[13] ¶ 6002; FILEIND: 9,088

Floor on Miscellaneous Itemized Deductions

1011. Two-Percent Floor on Miscellaneous Itemized Deductions. Many expenses that are not deductible from gross income (¶ 1005) may be deductible from adjusted gross income (AGI) as itemized deductions, which are reported on Schedule A of Form 1040. A taxpayer should elect to itemize deductions, with certain exceptions, if they exceed the applicable standard deduction (¶ 126) (Code Sec. 63(d)).[14] Certain itemized deductions are treated as miscellaneous itemized deductions, which are allowed only to the extent that their total exceeds two percent of the individual's AGI (Code Sec. 67(a)).[15] See ¶ 1012 for a list of the itemized deductions *not* subject to the two-percent floor. Any limitation or restriction placed upon an itemized deduction, i.e., the 50-percent reduction for meals (¶ 916), generally applies prior to the two-percent-of-adjusted-gross-income floor (Reg. § 1.67-1T(a)(2)).[16]

Indirect deductions from pass-through entities are subject to the miscellaneous itemized limitation because they are treated as if they were incurred by the individual taxpayer. This rule applies to nonpublicly offered mutual funds, but does not apply to estates, certain trusts, cooperatives, certain publicly offered mutual funds (RICs), and real estate investment trusts (REITs) (Code Sec. 67(c); Temp. Reg. § 1.67-2T).[17] Estates and trusts are generally treated as individuals (¶ 528).

Statutory employees, e.g., full-time life insurance salespersons, are not treated as employees for purposes of deducting expenses incurred in their business. Thus, these expenses may be claimed as trade or business expenses on Schedule C of Form 1040, and are not treated as miscellaneous itemized deductions (¶ 941B).

1012. Itemized Deductions Not Subject to the Two-Percent Floor. The following itemized deductions, reported on Schedule A of Form 1040, are *not* subject to the two-percent-of-adjusted-gross-income (AGI) floor discussed at ¶ 1011 (Code Sec. 67(b)):[18]

(1) interest (¶ 1043);

(2) taxes (¶ 1021 and ¶ 1028);

(3) personal casualty and theft losses (¶ 1101);

(4) charitable contributions (¶ 1058);

(5) medical and dental expenses (¶ 1015);

(6) impairment-related work expenses (¶ 1013);

(7) estate tax in the case of income in respect of a decedent (¶ 191);

(8) deductions allowable in connection with personal property used in a short sale (¶ 1944);

(9) deductions relating to computation of tax when the taxpayer restores an amount in excess of $3,000 held under claim of right (¶ 1543);

(10) deductions where annuity payments cease before an investment is recovered pursuant to Code Sec. 72(b)(3) (¶ 817);

(11) amortizable bond premiums (¶ 1967);

(12) deductions of taxes, interest, and business depreciation by a cooperative housing corporation tenant-stockholder (¶ 1040); and

(13) gambling losses (¶ 785 and ¶ 1121).

1013. Impairment-Related Work Expenses. Ordinary and necessary business expenses incurred by a handicapped worker for attendant care services at the worker's place of employment, or for other expenses in connection with the worker's place of employment that are necessary for the individual to be able to work, are not subject to the two-percent-of-adjusted-gross-income floor (¶ 1011). Handicapped persons include individuals who have a physical or mental disability, including blindness or deafness that

References are to Standard Federal Tax Reports; Tax Research Consultant; and Practical Tax Explanations.

[14] ¶ 6020; FILEIND: 12,050; § 7,005

[15] ¶ 6060; FILEIND: 12,054; § 7,105.05

[16] ¶ 6061; INDIV: 39,100; § 7,105.05

[17] ¶ 6060, ¶ 6062; INDIV: 39,102; § 7,105.40

[18] ¶ 6060; FILEIND: 12,054; § 7,110.05

limits employment, or a physical or mental impairment, including sight or hearing impairment, that substantially limits one or more major life activities (Code Sec. 67(d)).[19]

Phaseout of Itemized Deductions

1014. When AGI Exceeds Inflation-Adjusted Dollar Amount. No reduction of itemized deductions is required, since the reduction of itemized deduction for high-income taxpayers has been repealed through December 31, 2012. For tax years beginning after December 31, 2012, however, an individual whose adjusted gross income (AGI) exceeds a threshold amount must reduce the amount of allowable itemized deductions by the *lesser* of: (1) three percent of the excess over the threshold amount, adjusted annually for inflation; or (2) 80 percent of allowable deductions (Code Sec. 68).[20] No reduction is required in the case of deductions for medical expenses, investment interest, and casualty, theft or wagering losses.

> **Comment:** Absent further legislation, for tax years beginning after December 31, 2012, individuals with an AGI exceeding the inflation-adjusted threshold amount will have to reduce their itemized deductions per the above rule.

The reduction was applied after any disallowance of miscellaneous itemized deductions subject to the two-percent-of-adjusted-gross-income floor (¶ 1011) had been taken into account (Code Sec. 68(d)).[21] The reduced amount was reported on Schedule A of Form 1040.

Medical Expenses

1015. Medical and Dental Expenses. An itemized deduction is allowed for expenses paid during the tax year for the medical care of the taxpayer, the taxpayer's spouse, or a dependent to the extent that these expenses exceed 7.5 percent of adjusted gross income (AGI) (Code Sec. 213).[22] The expenses are reported on Schedule A of Form 1040. On a joint return, the percentage limitation is based on the total AGI of both spouses. The deduction may be taken for any person who was the taxpayer's dependent or spouse when the services were rendered or the expenses were paid (Reg. § 1.213-1(e)(3)).[23] For purposes of this deduction, dependent is defined at Code Sec. 152 (¶ 137), except that (1) dependent status is determined without regard to whether the dependent claims any dependency exemptions, files a joint return, or has gross income in excess of the exemption amount (Code Sec. 213(a); Reg. § 1.213-1(a)(3)) and (2) a child of divorced parents is treated as the dependent of both parents, even without a declaration by the custodial parent releasing the claim to the dependency exemption (¶ 139A) (Code Sec. 213(d)(5); Rev. Proc. 2008-48).

The deduction is limited to unreimbursed medical expenses (Code Sec. 213(a); Reg. § 1.213-1(g)). Reimbursement received for expenses deducted in a previous tax year is includible in gross income in the year received to the extent the expenses were previously deducted. Reimbursement for an earlier tax year in which no deduction was claimed is excludable from gross income.

Although medical expenses are generally deductible in the year paid, advance payments generally are *not* deductible until services are rendered (Reg. § 1.213-1(a)).[24] Prepayments for lifetime care in a retirement home, nursing center or similar institution are, however, deductible in the year paid if the obligation to pay was incurred at the time the payment was made, and the promise to provide lifetime care was conditioned on the payment (Rev. Rul. 93-72). Charges to credit cards qualify as payment of medical expenses in the year the expenses are charged, regardless of when the credit card company is paid (Rev. Rul. 78-39).

Threshold Increase in 2013. The threshold to claim an itemized deduction for unreimbursed medical expenses is increased to 10 percent of AGI for tax years begin-

References are to Standard Federal Tax Reports; Tax Research Consultant; and Practical Tax Explanations.

[19] ¶ 6060; INDIV: 36,400; § 7,110.35

[20] ¶ 6080; FILEIND: 12,056; § 7,015

[21] ¶ 6080; FILEIND: 12,056; § 1,010.20

[22] ¶ 12,540; INDIV: 42,000, INDIV: 42,300; § 7,201

[23] ¶ 12,541; INDIV: 42,356; § 7,205

[24] ¶ 12,541; INDIV: 42,250; § 7,215.05

ning after December 31, 2012 (Code Sec. 213(a)). During tax years 2013 through 2016, however, the lower 7.5-percent-of-AGI threshold continues to apply for taxpayers or their spouses who are age 65 and older before the close of the tax year (Code Sec. 213(f)).

See ¶ 1016 for the definition of medical expenses, ¶ 1017 for the treatment of drugs and supplies, ¶ 1018 for the treatment of medical expenses paid after death, ¶ 1019 for health insurance premiums, ¶ 1020 for deductible contributions to Archer medical savings accounts (MSAs), and ¶ 1020A for deductible contributions to health savings accounts (HSAs).

1016. Medical Expenses Defined. Medical expenses eligible to be deducted as itemized deductions (¶ 1015) include amounts paid for the diagnosis, cure, mitigation, treatment or prevention of disease, or for the purpose of affecting any structure or function of the body. Medical expenses also include: transportation and lodging costs incurred on trips primarily for and essential to medical care; qualified long-term care services; and medical insurance, including premiums paid under the Social Security Act relating to supplementary medical insurance for the aged or for any qualified long-term care insurance contracts that do not exceed certain limits (Code Sec. 213).[25] The lodging deduction is limited to amounts that are not lavish or extravagant and cannot exceed $50 per night for each individual (Code Sec. 213(d)(2)). The lodging deduction may also be claimed for a person who must accompany the individual seeking medical care. Meals, however, are not deductible. Medical expenses do not include amounts allowable as child or dependent care credit (¶ 1301) (Code Sec. 213(e)) or funeral expenses.[26]

The deduction is not limited to amounts paid for the least expensive form of medical care applicable. A physician's recommendation is unnecessary when the expenditures are for items that are wholly medical in nature and serve no other function. Thus, amounts paid by a healthy individual for self-initiated diagnostic tests and similar procedures, e.g., an annual physical, a full body scan or a self-administered pregnancy test kit, are deductible (Rev. Rul. 2007-72).

The costs of birth control pills prescribed by a physician, a legal abortion or a vasectomy are deductible (Rev. Rul. 73-200; Rev. Rul. 73-201; Rev. Rul. 73-603). Payments for psychiatric treatment of sexual inadequacy are medical expenditures, but marriage counseling fees are not (Rev. Rul. 75-319). The cost of fertility enhancement procedures are deductible if incurred in connection with *in vitro* fertilization or surgery (IRS Pub. 502). Costs incurred to obtain donated eggs, including donor, agency, testing and legal expenses, are also deductible (IRS Letter Ruling 200318017).

Expenses for elective cosmetic surgery are *not* deductible unless the surgery or procedure is necessary to ameliorate a deformity arising from, or directly related to, a congenital abnormality, a personal injury resulting from accident or trauma, or a disfiguring disease. Cosmetic surgery includes any procedure directed at improving the patient's appearance that does not meaningfully promote the proper function of the body or prevent or treat illness or disease (Code Sec. 213(d)(9)). Thus, costs to whiten teeth discolored by age are not deductible, but costs for breast reconstruction after a mastectomy and for vision correction by laser surgery are deductible (Rev. Rul. 2003-57). A weight-loss program is a medical expense if undertaken to relieve a disease or defect, such as obesity or hypertension (Rev. Rul. 2002-19). Smoking-cessation programs, whether or not prescribed, and prescription drugs to alleviate symptoms of nicotine withdrawal are also medical expenses, but over-the-counter gums or patches are not (Rev. Rul. 99-28).

When transportation expenses are deductible as a medical expense, the cost of operating a car for 2012 may be calculated at a standard rate of 23 cents per mile plus parking fees and tolls (Rev. Proc. 2010-51; Notice 2012-1).

Special schooling for a physically or mentally handicapped child or one needing psychiatric treatment is deductible (Rev. Rul. 78-340). Amounts paid for inpatient treatment of alcoholism or drug addiction at a therapeutic center and for meals and

References are to Standard Federal Tax Reports; Tax Research Consultant; and Practical Tax Explanations.

[25] ¶ 12,540; INDIV: 42,052; § 7,225

[26] ¶ 12,543.452; INDIV: 42,082.10; § 7,230

lodging furnished as a necessary incident to the treatment are deductible (Rev. Rul. 73-325). Amounts paid to acquire, train, and maintain a dog or other service animal for assisting a blind, deaf or physically disabled individual are deductible (Rev. Rul. 68-295; Rev. Rul. 57-461; Rev. Rul. 55-261).

The entire cost of maintenance in a nursing home or home for the aged, including meals and lodging, is a medical expense if an individual is there because of a physical condition and the availability of medical care is a principal reason for the individual's residence. If an individual is in such an institution primarily for personal or family reasons, then only that portion of the cost attributable to medical or nursing care, excluding meals and lodging, is deductible. Payments to perform both nursing care and housework may be deducted only to the extent of the nursing cost.[27]

Capital expenditures for home improvements and additions that are primarily for medical care qualify as a medical expense only to the extent that the cost of the improvement exceeds any increase in the value of the affected property (Reg. § 1.213-1(e)(1)).[28] The entire cost of any improvement that does not increase the value of the property is deductible. Deductions have been allowed for the installation of an elevator, a swimming pool, and a central air-conditioning system. Capital expenditures incurred to remove structural barriers to accommodate the condition of a physically handicapped person generally do not improve the value of the residence and, therefore, are fully deductible (Rev. Rul. 87-106). The entire cost of special equipment used to mitigate the effects of a physical impairment is also deductible.

See ¶ 59 for a checklist of medical expenses.

1017. Medicines and Drugs. In computing the deduction for medicine and drugs, only amounts paid for insulin and prescription medications may be taken into account (Code Sec. 213(b)).[29] Although amounts paid for over-the-counter (OTC) medicines or drugs are not taken into account in calculating the deduction, amounts paid for OTC equipment, supplies, or diagnostic devices may be deductible medical expenses (Rev. Rul. 2003-58).

Example: In 2012, a taxpayer with an adjusted gross income of $38,000 paid $1,750 to a doctor for medical services, $1,325 to a hospital, $340 for prescription drugs, and $250 for OTC cold remedies and vitamins. His medical expense deduction is computed as follows:

Doctor	$1,750
Hospital	1,325
Medicine and drugs	340
OTC remedies and vitamins	0
2012 medical expenses	$3,415
Less: 7.5% of $38,000 (adjusted gross income)	2,850
Allowable deduction for 2012	$565

1018. Medical Expenses Paid After Death. A decedent's medical expenses that are paid by the decedent's estate within one year of the day after the decedent's death are treated as paid when incurred and may be deducted on the decedent's income tax return for the year incurred if the estate waives an estate tax deduction for the expenses (Reg. § 1.213-1(d)).[30] Alternatively, the estate may deduct the medical expenses as a claim against the estate for federal estate tax purposes (¶ 2925). Medical expenses disallowed for income tax purposes because of the 7.5-percent limitation (¶ 1015) may *not* be claimed on the estate tax return when the estate allocates medical expenses between a decedent's final income tax and estate tax returns (Rev. Rul. 77-357).

1019. Health and Accident Insurance Premiums. A medical expense deduction is allowed for premiums paid for medical care insurance, including contact lens insurance,

References are to Standard Federal Tax Reports; Tax Research Consultant; and Practical Tax Explanations.

[27] ¶ 12,543.726, ¶ 12,543.727; INDIV: 42,066; § 7,245, § 7,250

[28] ¶ 12,541; INDIV: 42,064; § 7,285.05

[29] ¶ 12,540; INDIV: 42,056; § 7,235

[30] ¶ 12,541; INDIV: 42,256; § 7,220

subject to the 7.5-percent limitation (¶ 1015) (Code Sec. 213(d)(1)(D); Reg. § 1.213-1(e)(4)).[31] If the insurance contract provides payments for more than medical care, e.g., indemnity for loss of income or life, limb or sight, premiums are deductible only to the extent a reasonable charge for the medical care is stated separately in the contract or in a separate statement from the insurer. Premiums paid by a taxpayer under age 65 for insurance covering medical care expenses of the taxpayer, the taxpayer's spouse, or a dependent after the taxpayer turns 65 are considered to be medical expenses in the year paid if the premiums are payable on a level payment basis under the contract: (1) for a period of 10 years or more or (2) until the year the taxpayer reaches age 65, but in no case for a period of less than five years.

Premiums paid for a qualified long-term care insurance contract are a medical expense, but the deductible amount of the premium is limited by the age of the individual at the close of the tax year. The inflation-adjusted maximum deductible amount for 2012 is (Rev. Proc. 2011-52):

- age 40 or less, $350;
- more than age 40 but not more than 50, $660
- more than age 50 but not more than 60, $1,310;
- more than age 60 but not more than 70, $3,500; and
- more than age 70, $4,370.

The inflation-adjusted maximum deductible amount for 2013 is (Rev. Proc. 2012-41):

- age 40 or less, $360;
- more than age 40 but not more than 50, $680
- more than age 50 but not more than 60, $1,360;
- more than age 60 but not more than 70, $3,640; and
- more than age 70, $4,550.

Amounts paid as self-employment tax (¶ 2664) or as employment tax (¶ 2648) for hospital insurance under the Medicare program are *not* medical expenses. Similarly, the basic cost of Medicare insurance (Medicare A) is not deductible unless voluntarily paid by the taxpayer for coverage (Rev. Rul. 79-175). However, the cost of extra Medicare (Medicare B) is deductible (Rev. Rul. 66-216).

Self-employed persons can deduct from gross income 100 percent of amounts paid for health insurance coverage (¶ 908).

1020. Archer Medical Savings Accounts. Eligible individuals may claim an above the line deduction (an adjustment to gross income) for contributions they make during the tax year to their Archer medical savings account (Archer MSA). Individuals who are self-employed or work for small employers may be able to maintain Archer MSAs to pay medical expenses, provided that the accounts are used in conjunction with a high deductible health insurance plan (HDHP) (Code Sec. 220; Notice 96-53).[32] The 2012 HDHP annual deductible amounts and limitations are: (1) a minimum deductible of $2,100 and a maximum deductible of $3,150 with a maximum out-of-pocket limitation of $4,200 for individual coverage, and (2) a minimum deductible of $4,200 and a maximum deductible of $6,300 with a maximum out-of-pocket limitation of $7,650 for family coverage (Rev. Proc. 2011-52). For 2013, HDHP has the following annual deductible amounts and limitations: (1) a minimum deductible of $2,150 and a maximum deductible of $3,200, and maximum out-of-pocket limitation of $4,300 for individual coverage, and (2) a minimum deductible of $4,300, maximum deductible of $6,450, and maximum out-of-pocket limitation is $7,850 for family coverage (Rev. Proc. 2012-41). For a complete discussion of Archer MSAs, see ¶ 2197C.

1020A. Health Savings Accounts. Eligible individuals with high-deductible health insurance plans (HDHP) may claim an adjustment to gross income (an above the line deduction) for contributions they make during the tax year to their health savings

References are to Standard Federal Tax Reports; Tax Research Consultant; and Practical Tax Explanations.

[31] ¶ 12,540, ¶ 12,541; INDIV: 42,100; § 7,240.05

[32] ¶ 12,670; INDIV: 42,500; § 42,601

account (HSA). Individuals—and employees, through an employer's cafeteria plan—can establish HSAs to reimburse them for qualified medical expenses paid during the year (Code Sec. 223).[33] The maximum annual contribution for 2012 is limited to $3,100 for individuals with self-only coverage, and $6,250 for individuals with family coverage. The maximum annual contribution for 2013 is limited to $3,250 for individuals with self-only coverage, and $6,450 for individuals with family coverage. (Code Sec. 223(b); Rev. Proc. 2011-32; Rev. Proc. 2012-26).[34] Individuals who reach age 55 by the end of the tax year and are not enrolled in Medicare can increase their annual contributions by $1,000. Contributions, including catch-up contributions, cannot be made to a HSA after the participant is enrolled in Medicare. Excess contributions are subject to a six-percent excise tax and included in gross income. For a complete discussion on contributions, eligible individuals, the definition of high-deductible health plans, and taxation of distributions, see ¶ 2197B.

Taxes, Generally

1021. Deductible Taxes. Taxes not directly connected with a trade or business or with property held for production of rents or royalties may be deducted only as an itemized deduction on Schedule A of Form 1040. These include the following (Code Sec. 164):[35]

(1) State, local or foreign real property tax (¶ 1026 and ¶ 1028).

(2) State or local personal property tax (Reg. § 1.164-3(c)).

(3) State, local or foreign income, war profits, or excess profits tax (¶ 1023 and ¶ 2475).

(4) Generation-skipping transfer tax imposed on income distributions (¶ 2942).

(5) State and local general sales tax (at the taxpayer's election and in lieu of state and local income taxes) (Code Sec. 164(b)(5)).

State and local taxes imposed on personal property are deductible if three conditions are met: the tax must be (1) *ad valorem*, i.e., substantially in proportion to the value of the property, (2) imposed on an annual basis, and (3) imposed with respect to personal property (Reg. § 1.164-3(c)).[36] Payment for car registration and licensing or a motor vehicle tax may be deductible as a personal property tax if it is imposed annually and assessed in proportion to the value of the car.

In tax years before 2012, taxpayers could elect to deduct *either* state and local income tax paid or general state and local sales taxes paid on Schedule A. If they elected to deduct the general state and local sales taxes paid, they could claim either the total amount paid by substantiation with receipts, or the amount from IRS tables plus the amounts of general state and local sales taxes paid on the purchase a motor vehicle, boat or other items to be determined by the IRS (Notice 2005-31).

> **Comment:** Absent further legislation, the election to deduct either state and local income tax paid or the general state and local sales tax paid is not available for tax years beginning after December 31, 2011.

If a foreign trust receives a gift or bequest from a covered expatriate (¶ 2412), a tax is imposed on the gift or bequest, and is payable by a U.S. citizen or resident beneficiary who receives from the trust a distribution attributable to the gift or bequest (¶ 516). The distribution recipient is allowed an income tax deduction under Code Sec. 164 for the amount of this tax paid or accrued, but only to the extent the tax is imposed on the portion of the distribution included in the recipient's gross income (¶ 2948) (Code Sec. 2801(a) and (e)(4)(B)).

See ¶ 1022 for when a tax is deductible, ¶ 1023 for the deductibility of foreign income and profits taxes, ¶ 1024 for the deductibility of advance payments of state

References are to Standard Federal Tax Reports; Tax Research Consultant; and Practical Tax Explanations.

[33] ¶ 12,776; INDIV: 42,450; § 42,501

[34] ¶ 12,776; INDIV: 42,452.05, INDIV: 42,454.05; § 42,515.10, § 42,515.15, § 42,515.30

[35] ¶ 9500; INDIV: 45,000; § 7,301

[36] ¶ 9506; INDIV: 45,104; § 7,320

income taxes, ¶ 1025 for nondeductible taxes, ¶ 1026 for the deductibility of taxes used to pay for local improvements, and ¶ 1027 for the deductibility of self-employment taxes. For discussion of real property taxes, see ¶ 1028.

1022. Taxes Deductible When Paid or Accrued. The deduction for taxes is allowed only for the year in which the taxes are paid or accrued (Code Sec. 164).[37] Cash-basis taxpayers deduct taxes in the year paid, including amounts withheld from wages, payments of estimated tax, and payments applicable to other tax years. Accrual-basis taxpayers may generally deduct taxes in the year they accrue (¶ 1515). A failure to deduct taxes in the proper year does not allow the taxpayer to deduct the taxes in a later year. Instead, the taxpayer must file an amended return for the year the taxes were paid or accrued.

The date when a tax becomes due and payable is not necessarily its accrual date. State income taxes accrue during the year in which the income is earned.[38] Uncontested additional assessments accrue at the same time they would have accrued upon a correct original assessment.[39] For accrual of real estate taxes, see ¶ 1031 and ¶ 1036.

A contested tax accrues when the taxpayer transfers cash or property to satisfy the tax, if the contest exists after the transfer and a deduction would have otherwise been allowed for the year of transfer. This rule does not apply to taxes imposed by a foreign country or U.S. possession (Code Sec. 461(f)).[40]

1023. Deduction of Foreign Income and Profits Taxes. Foreign income and profits taxes are deductible only if no credit is claimed for them on the taxpayer's U.S. income tax return. The taxpayer must choose either the credit or the deduction; the taxes cannot be divided to support both a credit and a deduction. Foreign taxes accrue in the period for which they are imposed (¶ 2475 and ¶ 2485).

1024. Deduction of Advance Payments of State Income Taxes. Advance payments of estimated state income taxes made by a cash-basis taxpayer pursuant to state law are deductible in the year paid unless, on the date of payment, the taxpayer cannot reasonably determine that there is an additional amount owed (Rev. Rul. 82-208).

1025. Nondeductible Taxes. The taxes that cannot be deducted either as taxes or as business expenses are (Code Sec. 275):[41]

(1) federal income taxes, including Social Security and railroad retirement taxes paid by employees and one-half of the self-employment taxes (¶ 2664);

(2) federal war profits and excess profits taxes;

(3) estate, inheritance, legacy, succession, and gift taxes (¶ 2901);

(4) income, war profits, and excess profits taxes imposed by a foreign country or a U.S. possession, if the taxpayer chooses to take a foreign tax credit for these taxes (¶ 2475);

(5) taxes on real property that must be treated as imposed on another taxpayer because of apportionment between buyer and seller (¶ 1032); and

(6) certain additions to taxes imposed on public charities, private foundations, qualified pension plans, real estate investment trusts, stock compensation of insiders in expatriated corporations, golden parachute payments and greenmail.

Drug Sale and Health Insurance Provider Fees; Medical Devices Tax. Nondeductible taxes also include the annual fee imposed on drug manufacturers and importers for U.S. branded prescription drug sales after 2010, the 2.3-percent excise tax imposed on manufacturers, producers and importers of certain medical devices after 2012, and the annual fee imposed on certain health insurance providers after 2013 (Act Secs. 9008(f), 9009(e) and 9010(f) of the Patient Protection and Affordable Care Act (P.L. 111-148)).

References are to Standard Federal Tax Reports; Tax Research Consultant; and Practical Tax Explanations.

[37] ¶ 9500; INDIV: 45,200; § 7,310

[38] ¶ 9502.445, ¶ 21,817.115; INDIV: 45,202; § 7,310, § 7,325

[39] ¶ 9502.10; INDIV: 45,200; § 7,310

[40] ¶ 21,802; INDIV: 45,208; § 38,430.15

[41] ¶ 14,500; INDIV: 45,150; § 7,345

1026. Deduction of Improvement Taxes. Any tax that is in reality an assessment for local benefits such as streets, sidewalks, and similar improvements is *not* deductible by a property owner, except where it is levied for the purpose of maintenance and repair or of meeting interest charges on local benefits. It is the taxpayer's burden to show the allocation of amounts assessed to the different purposes (Code Sec. 164(c)(1); Reg. § 1.164-4).[42]

1027. Deduction of Self-Employment Tax. A taxpayer can deduct one-half of the self-employment tax paid in the computation of the taxpayer's adjusted gross income for income tax purposes (¶ 1025). High-income taxpayers, however, will not be able to deduct the additional 0.9 percent Medicare tax imposed on their self-employment income received after December 31, 2012 (Code Sec. 164(f)) (¶ 2664).

Real Property Taxes

1028. Deductibility of Real Property Taxes. Local, state, and foreign real property taxes are generally deductible only by the person upon whom they are imposed in the year in which they were paid or accrued (Code Sec. 164(a)(1); Reg. § 1.164-1(a)).[43] Real property taxes are taxes imposed on interests in real property and levied for the general public welfare. These taxes do not include taxes assessed for local benefits (¶ 1026) (Reg. § 1.164-3).[44] State or local tax includes only taxes imposed by a state, the District of Columbia, possessions of the U.S., or a political subdivision thereof. Foreign tax includes taxes imposed by the authority of a foreign country or its political subdivisions.

Stockholder-owners in a cooperative housing corporation may deduct their proportionate shares of the taxes paid by the corporation (¶ 1040). Condominium unit owners may also deduct real property taxes paid on their personal interests in the property (Rev. Rul. 64-31). Their homeowner association assessments, however, are not deductible as real property taxes because the assessments are not paid to the state or a political subdivision (Rev. Rul. 76-495).[45]

Ministers and military personnel are allowed to deduct taxes paid on their homes even if they receive a parsonage or military allowance excludable from gross income (¶ 1050). Cash-basis mortgagors that pay taxes directly to the mortgagee are entitled to deduct the taxes in the year when the mortgagee pays the taxing authority.

1029. Real Property Construction Period Interest and Taxes. Interest and taxes on real property paid or incurred during the construction period generally must be capitalized (¶ 991 and ¶ 993) (Code Sec. 263A).[46]

1030. Carrying Charges on Real Property. If a taxpayer elects to capitalize taxes on unimproved and unproductive real property, no deduction is allowed for such taxes (¶ 1614) (Code Sec. 266).[47]

1031. Alternative Elections to Accrue Real Property Taxes for Accrual-Method Taxpayers. The economic performance rule generally delays an accrual-method taxpayer's deduction for real property taxes until they are paid (¶ 1540). An accrual basis seller or buyer, however, may elect to accrue real property taxes that are related to a definite period of time ratably over that period (Code Sec. 461(c); Reg. § 1.461-1(c)).[48] Alternatively, if the real estate taxes are a "recurring item," a taxpayer may elect to accrue the taxes and claim the deduction on the date the tax is assessed or becomes a lien against the property (Code Sec. 461(h)(3); Reg. § 1.461-5).[49] Either election may be made without IRS consent for the first tax year in which a taxpayer accrues real property taxes. For later years, the IRS has provided automatic consent procedures for taxpayers to make the elections (Rev. Proc. 2011-14).

References are to Standard Federal Tax Reports; Tax Research Consultant; and Practical Tax Explanations.

[42] ¶ 9500, ¶ 9508; INDIV: 45,156; § 7,315.05

[43] ¶ 9500, ¶ 9501; INDIV: 45,102; § 7,315.05

[44] ¶ 9506; INDIV: 45,100, INDIV: 45,156; § 7,315.05

[45] ¶ 9502.422, ¶ 9502.515; INDIV: 45,052; § 7,315.05

[46] ¶ 13,800; REAL: 3,054; § 10,320.05, § 10,330.05

[47] ¶ 14,100; REAL: 3,112; § 10,220

[48] ¶ 21,802, ¶ 21,805; INDIV: 45,206.10; § 7,315.15, § 38,440

[49] ¶ 21,802, ¶ 21,811; ACCTNG: 12,104.10; § 38,435.10

Making the Election. Whether a taxpayer should make the election to ratably accrue property taxes or adopt the recurring item exception to the economic performance rule depends on the taxpayer's tax year and lien date of the jurisdiction in which the real property is located. Except where taxes are prepaid, either option is more favorable than the payment rule.

Example 1: X is a calendar-year, accrual-method taxpayer who owns Blackacre in Cook County, Illinois, where the real property tax year is the calendar year and 2012 real property taxes were assessed and became a lien on the property on January 1, 2012. One-half of the taxes are due on March 1, 2013, and the other half on August 1, 2013. Under its three options for accruing real property taxes, X would allocate its deduction between 2012 and 2013 as follows:

- *Payment rule.* 2012: none. 2013: 12/12.
- *Ratable accrual.* 2012: 12/12. 2013: none.
- *Recurring item exception.* 2012: 12/12 (provided that X adopted the recurring item exception on either a timely filed original return or on an amended return filed after paying the second installment but before September 15, 2013). 2013: none.

10 NONBUSINESS

Example 2: Assume X owns Greenacre in Alabama, where taxes for the fiscal year from October 1, 2012, to September 30, 2013, were assessed and became a lien on the property on October 1, 2012. Taxes are due on October 1, 2013. Under its three options for accruing real property taxes, X would allocate its deduction between 2012 and 2013 as follows:

- *Payment rule.* 2012: none. 2013: 12/12.
- *Ratable accrual.* 2012: 3/12. 2013: 9/12.
- *Recurring item exception.* 2012: none (because taxes are not due until more than 8½ months after end of 2012). 2013: 12/12. However, X could advance its entire deduction into 2012 by prepaying its real property taxes on or before September 15, 2013.

1032. Apportionment of Real Property Tax Upon Sale. The real property tax deduction must be apportioned between the seller and the buyer according to the number of days in the real property tax year that each holds the property (¶ 1033). When property is sold during any real property tax year, the taxes are imposed upon the seller up to, but not including, the date of sale. The taxes are imposed on the buyer beginning with the date of sale. Proration is required whether or not the seller and purchaser actually apportion the tax (Reg. § 1.164-6(a) and (b)(1)).[50] However, when property is sold before or after the real property tax year, see ¶ 1038.

Example 1: A sells his farm to B on August 1, 2012. Both use the cash- and calendar-year basis of accounting. Taxes for the real property tax year, April 1, 2012, to March 31, 2013, become due and payable on May 15, 2013. B pays the real estate taxes when they fall due. Regardless of any agreement between the parties, for federal income tax purposes 122/366 of the real estate taxes are treated as imposed upon A and are deductible by him.

Example 2: Assume the same facts as in Example 1 above, except that A uses the accrual basis of accounting. If A has not elected to accrue the real property taxes ratably, he will be treated as having accrued 122/366 of the taxes on the date of sale. The balance is deductible by B when she pays the taxes, if she is on the cash basis, unless the rule at ¶ 1035 applies because the seller (A) is personally liable for the taxes. If B is on the accrual basis, she follows the rules explained at ¶ 1031.

1033. Real Property Tax Year Defined. The real property tax year is the period to which the tax relates under state law, local law or the law imposing the tax. If a state and one or more local governmental units each imposes a tax, the real property tax year for each tax must be determined (Reg. § 1.164-6(c)).[51]

References are to Standard Federal Tax Reports; Tax Research Consultant; and Practical Tax Explanations.

[50] ¶ 9603; INDIV: 45,300; § 7,315.10

[51] ¶ 9603; INDIV: 45,312; § 7,315.10b

1034. Cash-Basis Sellers. The portion of the real estate tax imposed on a cash-basis seller under the rules described at ¶ 1032 may be deducted by the seller in the tax year of the sale, whether or not actually paid in that tax year, if: (1) the buyer is liable for the real estate tax for the real property tax year; or (2) the seller is liable for the real estate tax for the real property tax year and the tax is not payable until after the date of sale. When the tax is not a liability of any person, the person who holds the property at the time the tax becomes a lien on the property is considered liable for the tax (Reg. § 1.164-6(d)(1) and (3)).[52]

1035. Cash-Basis Buyers. The portion of the real estate tax imposed on a cash-basis buyer under the rules described at ¶ 1032 may be deducted by the buyer in the tax year of the sale, whether or not the tax is actually paid by the buyer in the tax year of the sale, if the seller is liable for the real estate tax. When the tax is not a liability of any person, the person who holds the property at the time the tax becomes a lien on the property is considered liable for the tax (Reg. § 1.164-6(d)(2) and (3)).[53]

1036. Accrual-Basis Buyers and Sellers. For accrual-basis buyers or sellers who do not elect ratable accrual for property taxes (¶ 1031), the portion of their tax liability (¶ 1032) that may not be deducted for any tax year by reason of their accounting method is treated as if accrued on the date of sale (Reg. § 1.164-6(d)(6)).[54]

1037. Excess Deduction. If a taxpayer deducted real estate taxes in excess of the portion of such tax treated as imposed upon the taxpayer under the rules discussed at ¶ 1032 in a tax year before the year of sale, the excess amount is included in the taxpayer's gross income in the year of sale, subject to the tax benefit rule (¶ 799) (Reg. § 1.164-6(d)(5)).[55]

> **Example:** A is a cash-basis taxpayer whose real property tax is due and payable on November 30 for the next calendar year, which is also the real property tax year. A paid the 2012 real property taxes on November 30, 2011, and deducted them on his 2011 income tax return. On June 30, 2012, A sold the real property. Only the taxes from January 1 through June 29, 2012, i.e., the 180⁄366 portion, are treated as imposed on A. The excess amount deducted by A on his 2011 income tax return is includible in his gross income in 2012.

1038. Property Sold Before or After Real Property Tax Year. If property is sold after the real property tax becomes a personal liability or a lien but before the beginning of the related real property tax year (¶ 1033), the seller may not deduct any amount for real property taxes for the related real property tax year. To the extent that the buyer holds the property for that real property tax year, the buyer may deduct the amount of the taxes for the tax year in which they are paid or accrued. Conversely, where the property is sold before the tax becomes a personal liability or a lien but after the end of the related real property tax year, the buyer cannot deduct any amount for taxes for the related real property tax year. To the extent that the seller holds the property for that real property tax year, the seller may deduct the amount of the taxes for the tax year they are paid or accrued (Reg. § 1.164-6(b)(1)(ii) and (iii)).[56]

1040. Cooperative Housing Corporation. A tenant-stockholder may deduct amounts paid or accrued to the cooperative housing corporation (CHC) to the extent that they represent the tenant's proportionate share of: (1) real estate taxes on the apartment building or houses and the land on which they are situated; or (2) interest on debt contracted in the acquisition, construction, alteration, rehabilitation, or maintenance of such building, houses or land (Code Sec. 216; Reg. § 1.216-1).[57] The limitations on deductible residential interest apply (¶ 1047).

For purposes of the deduction, a corporation is a CHC if:

- the corporation has only one class of outstanding stock;
- solely by reason of owning the stock, each stockholder is entitled to occupy a house or apartment in a building owned or leased by the corporation;

References are to Standard Federal Tax Reports; Tax Research Consultant; and Practical Tax Explanations.

52 ¶ 9603; INDIV: 45,316; § 7,315.10

53 ¶ 9603; INDIV: 45,316; § 7,315.10

54 ¶ 9603; INDIV: 45,318; § 7,315.10

55 ¶ 9603; INDIV: 45,318; § 4,210, § 7,315.10

56 ¶ 9603; INDIV: 45,308, INDIV: 45,310; § 7,315.10c

57 ¶ 12,600, ¶ 12,601; REAL: 9,200; § 7,445

- no stockholder is entitled to receive any distribution which is not out of the corporation's earnings and profits, except on a partial or complete liquidation; and

- 80 percent or more of the corporation's gross income is derived from tenant-stockholders, 80 percent or more of the total square footage of its property is at all times used or available for use by the tenant-stockholders for residential purposes or purposes ancillary to residential use, or 90 percent or more of the corporation's expenses paid or incurred are for the acquisition, construction, management, maintenance, or care of the property for the tenant-stockholders' benefit.

Under the 80-percent-of-gross-income test, amounts received from tenant-stockholders to defray expenses for items like secretarial services, parking, utilities, recreation facilities, cleaning and related services are included in gross income derived from tenants, while amounts received from commercial leases and the operation of a business other than housing are excluded (Rev. Rul. 55-556). Income attributable to a unit that a governmental entity is entitled to occupy under a lease or stock ownership is also excluded (Code Sec. 216(b)(4); Reg. § 1.216-1(e)(4)).[58]

Interest

1043. Deduction of Interest Paid or Accrued. A taxpayer may generally deduct interest paid or accrued during the tax year on Schedule A of Form 1040 (Code Sec. 163).[59] Deductible interest must pertain to a debt of the taxpayer and result from a debtor-creditor relationship based upon a valid and enforceable obligation to pay a fixed or determinable sum of money. For example, interest paid by children on their parent's mortgage was not deductible.[60] There are numerous exceptions to and limitations on the deductibility of interest (¶ 940, ¶ 1044, and ¶ 1056).

1044. Limitations on Interest Deduction. Interest deductions are limited or precluded for certain types of indebtedness (¶ 940).

Investment Indebtedness Interest. The deduction by noncorporate taxpayers is limited to net investment income (¶ 1094) (Code Sec. 163(d)).[61]

Life Insurance. Interest on loans incurred or continued to pay premiums on certain insurance contracts is nondeductible (¶ 909) (Code Sec. 264(a)).[62]

Mortgage Credit Certificates. The deduction for interest paid or accrued on indebtedness with respect to which a mortgage credit certificate has been issued is reduced by the amount of credit allowable (¶ 1306) (Code Sec. 163(g)).[63]

Personal Interest. Personal interest is *not* deductible (¶ 1045) (Code Sec. 163(h)).[64]

Prepaid Interest. Cash-basis taxpayers generally must capitalize prepaid interest and deduct it as if on the accrual basis (¶ 1055) (Code Sec. 461(g)).[65]

Loan to Purchase and Carry Tax-Exempt Securities. A deduction for interest paid on a debt incurred or continued to purchase or carry tax-exempt bonds or other tax-exempt obligations is generally denied (¶ 970) (Code Sec. 265(a)).[66]

Related Taxpayers. Accrual-basis taxpayers are placed on the cash basis for interest owed to related cash-basis taxpayers (Code Sec. 267(a)).[67] A corporation is not allowed a deduction for excessive interest paid to a tax-exempt related person or on a loan guaranteed by certain tax-exempt or foreign related persons. For purposes of the

References are to Standard Federal Tax Reports; Tax Research Consultant; and Practical Tax Explanations.

[58] ¶ 12,600, ¶ 12,601; REAL: 9,108
[59] ¶ 9102; INDIV: 48,150; § 7,401
[60] ¶ 9104.264, ¶ 9104.344, ¶ 9104.728; INDIV: 48,200, INDIV: 48,200; § 7,405.10, § 7,405.15
[61] ¶ 9102; INDIV: 48,450; § 7,414.05
[62] ¶ 14,002; INDIV: 48,556; § 7,420.10
[63] ¶ 9102; INDIV: 48,050; § 13,020, § 18,515.05
[64] ¶ 9102; INDIV: 48,350; § 7,410
[65] ¶ 21,802; INDIV: 48,252; § 7,405.20d
[66] ¶ 14,050; INDIV: 48,552; § 7,420.05
[67] ¶ 14,150; INDIV: 48,254; § 7,405.10, § 9,140

disallowance, a corporate partner's distributive share of a partnership's interest income or expense is treated as the partner's interest income or expense, and its share of the partnership's liabilities is treated as the partner's liabilities (Code Sec. 163(j)).[68]

Judicial Exceptions. The courts have denied a deduction for the interest charged upon conversion of a life insurance policy to a higher-premium policy,[69] and for interest paid on loans to buy U.S. Treasury notes where there was nothing to be realized from the transaction beyond a tax deduction.[70]

1045. Nondeductible Personal Interest. Personal interest is *not* deductible (Code Sec. 163(h)).[71] Personal interest is any interest incurred by an individual other than:

- interest paid or accrued on indebtedness properly allocable to a trade or business, other than services as an employee (¶ 937);
- investment interest (¶ 1094);
- interest taken into account in computing income or loss from a passive activity of the taxpayer (¶ 2053);
- qualified residence interest (¶ 1047);
- interest on the unpaid portion of the estate tax for the period during which there is an extension of time for payment of the tax on the value of a reversionary or remainder interest in property (¶ 1051); and
- interest on qualified education loans (¶ 1082).

1047. Qualified Residence Interest (Home Mortgage Interest) Deduction. Although personal interest generally is not deductible (¶ 1045), interest payments attributable to purchase of a qualified residence (home mortgage interest) are deductible in the year paid or accrued. Qualified residence interest is interest that is paid or accrued during the tax year on acquisition and/or home equity indebtedness with respect to any qualified residence (¶ 1048) (Code Sec. 163(h)(3)).[72] Qualified residence interest also can include interest on a loan secured by a qualified residence in a state where the security instrument is otherwise restricted by a debtor protection law. Interest paid or accrued by a trust or estate is deductible if the debt is secured by a beneficiary's qualified residence. A qualified residence includes the taxpayer's principal residence, and one other residence, e.g., vacation home, that is not rented out at any time during the tax year, or that is used by the taxpayer for a number of days exceeding the greater of 14 days or 10 percent of the number of days that it is rented out at a fair rental value (Code Sec. 163(h)(4)).[73] Married taxpayers who file separate returns are treated as one taxpayer, with each entitled to take into account one residence unless both consent in writing to having only one taxpayer take into account both residences. For seller-provided financing, taxpayers deducting qualified residence interest must include on their Schedule A of Form 1040, the name, address and taxpayer identification number (TIN) of the person to whom interest is paid or accrued (Code Sec. 6109(h)).[74]

See ¶ 1048A for treatment of certain mortgage insurance premiums as qualified residence interest.

1048. Acquisition and Home Equity Indebtedness Defined. Acquisition indebtedness is debt incurred in acquiring, constructing, or substantially improving a qualified residence and is secured by the residence for purposes of the qualified residence mortgage interest deduction (¶ 1047). Refinanced debt remains acquisition debt to the extent that it does not exceed the principal amount of acquisition debt immediately before refinancing (Code Sec. 163(h)(3)(B)).[75] Home equity indebtedness is any nonacquisition debt that is secured by a qualified residence to the extent it does not exceed the fair market value of the residence reduced by any acquisition indebtedness (Code

References are to Standard Federal Tax Reports; Tax Research Consultant; and Practical Tax Explanations.

[68] ¶ 9102; BUSEXP: 21,210; § 7,405.10
[69] ¶ 9104.45; INDIV: 48,556; § 7,405.10
[70] ¶ 9104.364; INDIV: 48,552; § 7,405.10
[71] ¶ 9102; INDIV: 48,350; § 7,410
[72] ¶ 9102; INDIV: 48,400; § 18,515.05
[73] ¶ 9102; INDIV: 48,400; § 18,515.10
[74] ¶ 36,960; REAL: 6,050; § 18,515.05
[75] ¶ 9102; INDIV: 48,400; § 18,515.15, § 18,515.20

Sec. 163(h)(3)(C)). Interest on such debt is deductible even if the proceeds are used for personal expenditures (IRS Pub. 936).

Limitations. The amount of qualified mortgage interest (¶ 1047) that may be deducted is limited to interest on the aggregate amount of acquisition indebtedness that is not in excess of $1 million ($500,000 for married filing separate). The aggregate amount of home equity indebtedness may not exceed $100,000 ($50,000 for married filing separate). Interest attributable to debt over these limits is nondeductible personal interest (¶ 1045) (Code Sec. 163(h)(3)).[76]

The $1 million limit on acquisition indebtedness applies to the entire amount of acquisition debt incurred in acquiring the home, not to each co-owner's portion of the debt (CCA 200911007). The IRS has also ruled that home acquisition indebtedness may also constitute home equity indebtedness to the extent the debt *exceeds* $1 million, but subject to the $100,000 and fair market value limitations (Rev. Rul. 2010-25). The IRS will *not* follow Tax Court decisions which have disallowed such treatment for the portion of debt in excess of the $1 million.

Example 1: A buys a home to be used as a principal residence for $375,000 that is secured by a mortgage in the amount of $350,000. The mortgage qualifies as home acquisition debt because the loan amount does not exceed the home's cost. Thus, since the acquisition indebtedness is less than $1 million, the entire amount of the interest payments is deductible.

Example 2: The fair market value of B's home is $310,000, and the balance of the mortgage (home acquisition debt) is $295,000. B takes out a home equity loan in the amount of $42,500. B's home equity debt, on which interest payments will be deductible as qualified home equity indebtedness, is limited to $15,000: the smaller of (1) the $100,000 maximum limit or (2) the excess of the home's fair market value ($310,000) over the home acquisition debt ($295,000).

Pre-October 13, 1987, Indebtedness. Interest on acquisition indebtedness incurred on or before October 13, 1987, is fully deductible, and is not subject to the $1 million limitation. The amount of this grandfathered debt reduces the amount of the $1 million limitation available for new acquisition debt, e.g., for improvements.

Grandfathered debt is any debt incurred on or before October 13, 1987, that is secured by a qualified residence on that date and at all times thereafter before the interest is paid or accrued. It also includes debt secured by a qualified residence to refinance existing pre-October 13 debt, to the extent that the refinancing does not increase the principal amount or extend the term of the debt beyond the existing term of the acquisition debt immediately before the refinancing. If acquisition debt is not amortized over its term, as in the case of a balloon note, interest on any otherwise qualified refinancing is deductible for the term of the first refinancing for up to 30 years (Code Sec. 163(h)(3)(D)).[77]

1048A. Deduction of Mortgage Insurance Premiums. Certain premiums paid for qualified mortgage insurance in connection with acquisition indebtedness (¶ 1048) incurred after December 31, 2007, and before January 1, 2012, are deductible as qualified residence interest (¶ 1047) (Code Sec. 163(h)(3)(E) and (4)(E)).[78] For every $1,000 by which the taxpayer's adjusted gross income (AGI) exceeds $100,000, however, the amount of premiums treated as interest is reduced by 10 percent. For married taxpayers filing separately, the amount of premiums treated as interest is reduced by 10 percent for every $500 that AGI exceeds $50,000. The deduction does not apply to premiums paid, accrued, or properly allocable to any period after December 31, 2011. Qualified mortgage insurance is that provided by the Department of Veterans Affairs (VA), the Federal Housing Administration (FHA), or the Rural Housing Administration (RHA), as well as private mortgage insurance.

Comment: Absent further legislation, the mortgage insurance premium deduction expired on December 31, 2011.

References are to Standard Federal Tax Reports; Tax Research Consultant; and Practical Tax Explanations.

[76] ¶ 9102; REAL: 6,056.15; § 18,515.15, § 18,515.20

[77] ¶ 9102; REAL: 6,056

[78] ¶ 9102; REAL: 6,060; § 18,520

For prepaid mortgage insurance, except VA or RHA contracts, amounts paid that are allocable to periods after the payment year are capitalized and treated as paid in the allocable periods. Prepaid premiums must be allocated ratably over the shorter of the stated term of the mortgage or 84 months, beginning with the month in which the insurance was obtained. If the mortgage is satisfied before the end of its term, no deduction is allowed for any premium allocable to periods after the mortgage is satisfied (Code Sec. 163(h)(4)(F); Reg. § 1.163-11).[79]

1049. Deduction of Redeemable Ground Rents. Annual or periodic payments of redeemable ground rent, except amounts paid in redemption of this rent, are treated as interest paid on mortgage indebtedness (Code Sec. 163(c)).[80] Therefore, such ground rents are subject to the rules pertaining to qualified residences (¶ 1047). A redeemable ground rent is a ground rent payable under a freely assignable lease that, including possible renewal periods, is for a term in excess of 15 years, where the lessee has a right to terminate the lease and buy the lessor's interest in the land by paying a set amount, and the lessor's interest is primarily a security interest to protect the rental payments (Code Sec. 1055(c)(1); Reg. § 1.1055-1).[81]

1050. Deduction of Mortgage Interest of Ministers and Military Personnel. Ministers and military personnel are allowed to deduct mortgage interest on their qualified residences (¶ 1047) even though they receive a parsonage or military housing allowance that is excludable from gross income (Code Sec. 265(a)(6)).[82] Military personnel includes members of the Army, Navy, Air Force, Marine Corps, Coast Guard, National Oceanic and Atmospheric Administration, and Public Health Service (Rev. Rul. 87-32).

1051. Interest Paid on Delinquent or Deferred Taxes. Interest imposed on delinquent federal, state or local income taxes is generally nondeductible personal interest, regardless of the source of the income generating the tax liability (¶ 1045) (Temp. Reg. § 1.163-9T(b)(2)(i)(A)).[83] Interest on federal and state income tax deficiencies accruing after death is generally deductible by the estate as an administration expense (Rev. Rul. 69-402).

For estates of decedents dying after 1997, interest payable on any unpaid portion of federal estate tax during an extension period for payment of the tax where the estate consists largely of a closely-held business under Code Sec. 6166 (¶ 2939) is *not* deductible for federal income tax purposes (Code Sec. 163(k)).[84] However, any interest expense accrued for federal estate taxes during an extension for payment of tax under Code Sec. 6163 on the value of a reversionary or remainder interest in property, or under Code Sec. 6166 for estates of decedents who died before 1998, may be claimed as an administrative expense deduction from federal estate tax, or as an income tax deduction under Code Sec. 163(h)(2)(E)[85] if the right to an estate tax deduction for the interest has been waived (Code Sec. 642(g)).[86]

Interest paid on sales and excise taxes incurred in connection with a trade or business or investment activity, and interest paid by a transferee for a C corporation's delinquent taxes, is not personal interest (Temp. Reg. § 1.163-9T(b)(2)(iii)).[87]

Prepaid Interest

1055. Deductibility of Prepaid Interest by Cash-Basis Taxpayers. A cash-basis taxpayer generally cannot take a current deduction for prepaid interest. Instead, the taxpayer must deduct prepaid interest over the period of the loan to the extent that the interest represents the cost of using the borrowed funds during each tax year in the period. Points paid on loans, other than certain home mortgage loans, are deducted

References are to Standard Federal Tax Reports; Tax Research Consultant; and Practical Tax Explanations.

[79] ¶ 9102, ¶ 9401D; REAL: 6,060; § 18,520

[80] ¶ 9102; REAL: 6,052.45; § 18,515.05

[81] ¶ 29,940, ¶ 29,941; REAL: 6,052.45; § 18,515.05

[82] ¶ 14,050; INDIV: 48,554; § 18,515.05

[83] ¶ 9400; INDIV: 48,352; § 28,440.30

[84] ¶ 9102; INDIV: 48,354; § 34,410.20

[85] ¶ 9102; INDIV: 48,350; § 7,410, § 32,310

[86] ¶ 24,280; ESTTRST: 9,200; § 32,310, § 32,320

[87] ¶ 9400; INDIV: 48,350; § 7,410

ratably over the term of the loan (Code Sec. 461(g)).[88] Penalty payments made for the privilege of prepaying mortgage indebtedness are currently deductible as interest (Rev. Rul. 57-198).

The prepaid interest rule does not contemplate that interest will be treated as paid in equal payments over the term of the loan. Thus, interest paid on an amortizing loan as part of an equal constant payment, including principal and interest, is not subject to the prepaid interest rule merely because the payments consist of a larger interest portion in the earlier years of the loan than in later years.

Points on a home mortgage loan for the purchase or improvement of, and secured by, a principal residence are deductible in the year paid to the extent that the payment of points is an established practice in the area, and the amount paid does not exceed the points generally charged in the area for a home loan (Code Sec. 461(g)(2)).[89] Taxpayers may also choose to amortize points over the life of their loan if, for instance, the standard deduction in the year the points were paid exceeds the taxpayer's itemized deductions, including the points (IRS Letter Ruling 199905033).[90]

As a matter of administrative practice, the IRS treats as deductible in the year paid any points paid by a cash-basis taxpayer that:

- are designated as points on the RESPA settlement statement (Form HUD-1), for example, as "loan origination fees," including amounts so designated on VA and FHA loans, "loan discount," "discount points," or "points";
- are calculated as a percentage of the principal loan amount;
- are paid to acquire the taxpayer's principal residence in connection with a loan secured by that residence;
- are paid directly by the taxpayer, which may include earnest money, an escrow deposit, or down payment applied at closing, and not derived from loan proceeds; points paid by a seller, including points charged to the seller, are considered directly paid by the taxpayer from funds not derived from loan proceeds if they are subtracted by the taxpayer from the purchase price of the residence in computing its basis; and
- conform to an established business practice of charging points for loans for the acquisition of personal residences in the area. No part of the points may be in lieu of appraisal, inspection, title, and attorney fees, property taxes, or other amounts that are ordinarily stated separately on the settlement statement (Rev. Proc. 94-27).

This safe harbor does not apply to points paid for a loan to acquire a principal residence to the extent the principal amount exceeds the limit on acquisition indebtedness (¶ 1048). Nor does it apply to points paid on home improvement loans, second or vacation home loans, refinancing or home equity loans, or lines of credit. The fact that a taxpayer cannot satisfy the requirements of the safe harbor does not necessarily mean that points are not currently deductible. It does mean that the IRS will not automatically consider them to be currently deductible.

Points paid to refinance a home mortgage are not deductible in full in the year paid, but must be deducted ratably over the period of the loan because they are incurred for the repayment of the taxpayer's existing indebtedness and are not paid in connection with the purchase or improvement of the home. The U.S. Court of Appeals for the Eighth Circuit, however, allowed a full deduction in the year paid for points on a long-term home mortgage loan refinancing a short-term balloon loan used to acquire the home (*J.R. Huntsman*, CA-8, 90-2 USTC ¶ 50,340, nonacq. except in the Eighth Circuit).[91] Also, the portion of the points allocable to the proceeds of a refinancing that are used for improvements may be deducted in the year paid. The portion allocable to the repayment

References are to Standard Federal Tax Reports; Tax Research Consultant; and Practical Tax Explanations.

[88] ¶ 21,802; INDIV: 48,256; § 7,405.20d, § 18,515.35, § 38,410.40

[89] ¶ 21,802; INDIV: 48,256; § 18,515.35

[90] ¶ 9402.55; INDIV: 48,256; § 38,410.40

[91] ¶ 9402.62; INDIV: 48,256; § 18,515.35, § 38,410.40

of existing indebtedness or other purposes is deducted ratably over the period of the loan (Rev. Rul. 87-22).[92]

A loan discount, i.e., where a lender delivers to an individual borrower an amount smaller than the face amount of the loan and the difference is the agreed charge for the use of borrowed money, is interest (Rev. Rul. 75-12).

1056. Deductibility of Prepaid Interest by Accrual-Basis Taxpayers. Taxpayers who use the accrual method accrue and deduct interest ratably over the loan period, regardless of whether the interest is prepaid (Rev. Rul. 68-643).

Charitable Contributions

1058. Contributions by Individuals. Individuals who itemize their deductions are entitled to deduct contributions to a qualified charitable organization on Schedule A of Form 1040 (Code Sec. 170).[93] The charitable deduction for any one tax year is limited to a percentage of the individual taxpayer's contribution base determined by the type of organization receiving the donation and the type of property donated (¶ 1059). Any amount in excess of the percentage limitation for the tax year may be carried forward for a period of five years (¶ 1060). When spouses file a joint return, the percentage limitation depends on their aggregate contribution base. A limit also applies to the amount of a charitable deduction allowed for gifts of appreciated property (¶ 1062), and is imposed before applying the percentage limitation.

A charitable contribution is a contribution or gift to a qualifying organization (¶ 1061). Except in the case of a carryover of a deduction, a taxpayer may deduct the fair market value of property contributed to charity, subject to the percentage limitation, only in the year of payment (Reg. § 1.170A-1(a)).[94] Contributions charged to a bank credit card, however, are deductible in the year charged even though paid in a later year (Rev. Rul. 78-38). Taxpayers who are recognized by the Alaska Eskimo Whaling Commission as whaling captains can claim a charitable contribution deduction of up to $10,000 per tax year for reasonable and necessary expenses paid in carrying out sanctioned Alaskan subsistence whale hunting activities (Code Sec. 170(n)).[95]

IRA Distributions. For tax years before 2012, individuals age 70½ or older could distribute up to $100,000 tax-free from their individual retirement accounts (IRAs) to certain charitable organizations without including the distribution in gross income (¶ 2153G). The distribution had to be made directly by the trustee to a 50-percent organization (¶ 1059), but *not* to a supporting organization or a donor advised fund (¶ 1061), and the entire distribution must otherwise be deductible as a charitable donation, disregarding the percentage limitations, even though the individual cannot claim a charitable deduction for the donation.

> **Comment:** Absent further legislation, the exclusion from income and the nondeductibility of a charitable contribution withdrawal made from an IRA is unavailable to taxpayers after December 31, 2011.

See ¶ 2153G for a special rule that permits a qualified charitable distribution made in January 2011 to be treated as having been made on December 31, 2010.

1059. Percentage Limits on Individuals' Contributions. An individual's charitable deduction for any one tax year is limited to a percentage of the individual's contribution base determined by the type of organization receiving the donation and the type of property donated (Code Sec. 170(b)(1)).[96] The deduction limit also depends, in part, on whether the donation of property is made to the charitable organization or for its use (¶ 1063). A donation of an income interest in property is made for the use of the charity, whether or not it is transferred in trust. A donation of a remainder interest in property is made for the use of the organization if it is transferred in trust to be held and administered for the organization (Reg. § 1.170A-8(a)(2)).[97]

References are to Standard Federal Tax Reports; Tax Research Consultant; and Practical Tax Explanations.

[92] ¶ 9402.60; INDIV: 48,256; § 18,515.35

[93] ¶ 11,600; INDIV: 51,000; § 7,501

[94] ¶ 11,615; INDIV: 51,402; § 7,505.10

[95] ¶ 11,600; INDIV: 51,052.55

[96] ¶ 11,600; INDIV: 51,250; § 7,565.05

[97] ¶ 11,661; INDIV: 51,250; § 7,505.05

An individual's contribution base is the taxpayer's adjusted gross income (AGI), computed without regard to the charitable deduction and any net operating loss carryback (Code Sec. 170(b)(1)(G); Reg. § 1.170A-8(a)).[98] When a married couple files a joint return, the percentage limitations are applied against the couple's aggregate income.

Contributions of ordinary income property (¶ 1062) to tax-exempt organizations is limited to a maximum deduction of 50 percent of a taxpayer's contribution base (¶ 1058) for the tax year (Code Sec. 170(b)(1)(A); Reg. § 1.170A-9).[99] Contributions of capital gain property to tax-exempt organizations is limited to a maximum deduction of 30 percent of the taxpayer's contribution base for the tax year (¶ 1062) (Code Sec. 170(b)(1)(C)).[100] Tax-exempt organizations for this purpose include:

(1) churches or conventions or associations of churches (¶ 604);

(2) educational institutions;

(3) hospitals or medical research organizations, not including home health care organizations, convalescent homes, homes for children or the aged, or vocational institutions that train handicapped individuals;

(4) endowment foundations in connection with a state college or university;

(5) state, federal or local government units, if the contribution is made for exclusively public purposes;

(6) organizations referred to in Code Sec. 170(c)(2) (¶ 1061) normally receiving a substantial part of their support from the public or a governmental unit;

(7) private operating foundations (¶ 633);

(8) private nonoperating foundations (¶ 631 and ¶ 633) that distribute all contributions received to public charities and private operating foundations, or make certain other qualifying distributions, within 2½ months after the end of the tax year;

(9) private foundations (¶ 631) that pool all contributions into a common fund and allow a substantial contributor to designate a recipient charity, where income from the pool is distributed within 2½ months after the tax year in which it was realized and corpus attributable to any donor's contribution is distributed to a charity not later than one year after the death of the donor or surviving spouse with the right to designate the recipients of the corpus;

(10) publicly supported organizations normally receiving (a) more than ⅓ of their support in each tax year from the public and organizations listed at (1)—(6), above, in the form of grants, gifts, contributions, or membership fees, and gross receipts from an activity that is not an unrelated trade or business (less certain receipts), and (b) not more than ⅓ of their support from gross investment income and unrelated business taxable income (less taxes); and

(11) certain supporting organizations (¶ 607).

The deduction limitation on contributions of ordinary income property to "other," non-50-percent, charitable organization donees—nonoperating foundations and organizations such as war veterans' and fraternal organizations, and public cemeteries—and on gifts *for the use of* 50-percent organization donees, is the lesser of: (1) 30 percent of the taxpayer's contribution base, or (2) the excess of 50 percent of the taxpayer's contribution base for the tax year over the amount of charitable contributions qualifying for the 50-percent deduction ceiling, including carryovers (Code Sec. 170(b)(1)(B)).[101] Contributions of capital gain property to these organizations are subject to a 20-percent contribution base limitation (Code Sec. 170(b)(1)(D)).[102]

References are to Standard Federal Tax Reports; Tax Research Consultant; and Practical Tax Explanations.

[98] ¶ 11,600, ¶ 11,662; INDIV: 51,252; § 7,565.05

[99] ¶ 11,600; INDIV: 51,254; § 7,565.05, § 7,565.10

[100] ¶ 11,600; INDIV: 51,256; § 7,565.20

[101] ¶ 11,600; INDIV: 51,258; § 7,565.15

[102] ¶ 11,600; INDIV: 51,256; § 7,565.25

Charitable contributions made by bona fide residents of U.S. possessions (¶ 2414) or Puerto Rico (¶ 2415) are deductible only to the extent allocable to income that is *not* excluded possession-source or Puerto Rico-source income (Reg. § 1.170A-1(j)(9)).[103]

For deduction limitations on charitable contributions by corporations, see ¶ 927.

Qualified Conservation Contributions. Individual donors who made a qualified conservation contribution (QCC) of real property (¶ 1063) were allowed to claim their deduction against the 50-percent contribution base, and any excess over this base amount could be carried forward for 15 years. These rules are applied separately from the rules that apply to other donations (Code Sec. 170(b)(1)(E)).[104]

> **Comment:** Absent further legislation, the 50-percent of contribution base limitation on deduction for a QCC made by individual donors expired on December 31, 2011. Donors who make a QCC in tax years beginning after December 31, 2011, will have their charitable donation limited by the rules for contribution appreciated property (¶ 1062), and any excess over the contribution base can only be carried forward for five years (¶ 1060).

Qualified Farmers and Ranchers. Qualified farmers and ranchers, i.e., individual taxpayers with more than 50 percent of gross income from farming or ranching, making a QCC had their deduction limited to 100 percent of the contribution base for tax years before 2012. The 100-percent limit only applied if the contribution included a restriction that the property must remain generally available for agriculture or livestock production (Code Sec. 170(b)(1)(E)).

> **Comment:** Absent further legislation, the 100-percent deduction limitation for restricted QCCs by qualified farmers and ranchers expired for donations completed after December 31, 2011.

1060. Individuals' Five-Year Carryover. Individuals may carry forward for five years their charitable contributions that exceed the deductible ceiling for the year of the contribution (¶ 1059) (Code Sec. 170(b)(1)(D)(ii) and (d); Reg. § 1.170A-10).[105] The amount of the excess that may be deducted in any carryover year is limited to the lesser of: (1) the remaining portion of any excess contribution not already deducted or (2) an amount equal to 50 percent (or 30 percent for capital gain carryover) of the taxpayer's contribution base (¶ 1058) after first deducting the sum of the charitable contributions (to which the 50-percent or 30-percent limitation applies) paid in the carryover year and any excess contributions that have precedence in order of time over the present carryover. The excess must be reduced to the extent that it reduces taxable income as computed for net operating loss (NOL) carrybacks and carryovers (¶ 1179) and increases the NOL deduction for a tax year succeeding the contribution year.

If the value of a taxpayer's qualified conservation contribution (QCC) made in a tax year before 2012 (¶ 1059) exceeded the special 50-percent contribution base for such a donation, the excess can be carried forward for 15 years (Code Sec. 170(b)(1)(E)(ii)).

1061. Contributions That Are Deductible. A charitable contribution is deductible only if it is a contribution or gift to, or for the use of, the following qualified organizations:

- the United States, a state, a local government, the District of Columbia, or a U.S. possession, for exclusively public purposes;
- a corporation, trust, or community chest, fund, or foundation, created or organized in the United States or a possession or under the law of the United States, a possession, a state, or the District of Columbia, organized and operated exclusively for religious, charitable, scientific, literary or educational purposes, or to foster national or international amateur sports competition, or for the prevention of cruelty to children or animals; no part of the charity's net earnings may inure to the benefit of any private shareholder or individual. Also, the organization must not be disqualified for tax exemption under Code Sec. 501(c)(3) by attempting to influence legislation;

References are to Standard Federal Tax Reports; Tax Research Consultant; and Practical Tax Explanations.

[103] ¶ 11,615; INDIV: 51,150; § 7,501

[104] ¶ 11,600; INDIV: 51,256, INDIV: 51,364; § 7,565.30

[105] ¶ 11,600, ¶ 11,663; INDIV: 51,262; § 7,570.05

• a cemetery company owned and operated exclusively for the benefit of its members or any corporation chartered solely for burial purposes as a cemetery corporation and not operated for profit or for the benefit of any private shareholder or individual;

• a post or organization of war veterans, or its auxiliary society or unit, organized in the United States or its possessions, if no part of the net earnings inures to the benefit of any private shareholder or individual; or

• a domestic fraternal society, order, or association, operating under the lodge system, by only individual donors if the contributions are used exclusively for religious, charitable, scientific, literary or educational purposes, or for the prevention of cruelty to children or animals (Code Sec. 170(c)).[106]

Pew rents, building fund assessments, and periodic church dues are deductible (Rev. Rul. 70-47).

Clothing and Household Items. A deduction for a donation of clothing and household items is allowed only if the donated property is in good used condition or better. Household items do not include food, paintings, antiques, other objects of art, jewelry, gems or collections. The IRS can deny a deduction for such donated property that is of minimal value. These restrictions do not apply if: (1) a deduction of more than $500 is claimed for the single clothing or household item, and (2) a qualified appraisal for that item is attached to the return (¶ 1071). For partnerships and S corporations, the restrictions are applied at the entity level, and denial of the deduction is at the partner or shareholder level (Code Sec. 170(f)(16)).[107]

Services. The value of service rendered to a charitable organization is *not* deductible as a contribution, e.g. the value of a blood donation (Reg. § 1.170A-1(g); Rev. Rul. 162).[108] An out-of-pocket, unreimbursed expense, e.g., uniforms, telephone or equipment, incurred in rendering such service, however, is a deductible contribution (Rev. Rul. 84-61, modifying Rev. Rul. 58-279). No deduction is allowed for an out-of-pocket expenditure made by any person on behalf of a charitable organization other than an organization described in Code Sec. 501(h)(5), i.e., churches, if the expenditure is made for the purpose of influencing legislation (Code Sec. 170(f)(6)). No charitable or business deduction is allowed for contributions made to organizations that conduct lobbying activities relating to matters of direct financial interest to the donor, unless the donor's direct conduct of the activities would have given rise to a business expense deduction (¶ 974) (Code Sec. 170(f)(9)).[109]

Certain payments made under leave-based donation programs, in which an employer makes charitable donations in exchange for an employee's election to forgo paid leave, have been deductible by the employer as compensation (¶ 906) but were neither includible in the employee's income nor deductible by the employee as a charitable contribution.[110]

Travel Expenses. Deductions are allowed for transportation or other travel expenses, including meals and lodging, incurred in the performance of services away from home on behalf of a charitable organization if there is no significant element of personal pleasure, recreation or vacation. If there is such an element, deductions are denied even though the expenses are paid directly by the individual, indirectly through a contribution to the organization, or by reimbursement by the organization. This rule does not apply to the extent that an individual pays for travel for third parties who are participants in the charitable activity. However, deductions are disallowed where two unrelated taxpayers pay each other's travel expenses or members of a group contribute to a fund that pays for all travel expenses (Code Sec. 170(j)).[111] Individuals who qualify for a deduction for the use of an automobile in 2012 may use the statutory standard mileage rate of 14 cents per mile, plus parking fees and tolls, in lieu of a deduction based on the

References are to Standard Federal Tax Reports; Tax Research Consultant; and Practical Tax Explanations.

[106] ¶ 11,600; INDIV: 51,100; § 7,520.05, § 7,520.35

[107] ¶ 11,600; INDIV: 51,152; § 7,595

[108] ¶ 11,615, ¶ 11,620.65; INDIV: 51,056; § 7,540

[109] ¶ 11,600; INDIV: 51,118; § 7,540

[110] ¶ 11,620.522; INDIV: 51,056; § 4,110, § 7,540

[111] ¶ 11,600, ¶ 11,620.029; INDIV: 51,056; § 7,545

actual expenses incurred. Depreciation and insurance are not includible in the deductible contribution (Code Sec. 170(i)).[112]

Fund-Raising Activities. An amount paid for a ticket to a charity event—e.g., a ball, bazaar, show, or athletic event—is presumed to represent the purchase price for an item of value. The burden is on the taxpayer to show either that the payment is not a purchase or that the payment exceeds the fair market value of the admission or other privileges associated with the event. The purchase price of a raffle ticket is not deductible (Rev. Rul. 83-130; Rev. Rul. 67-246, distinguished by Rev. Rul. 74-348, and amplified by Rev. Proc. 90-12).

> **Example:** A pays $20 to see a special showing of a motion picture, the net proceeds of which go to a qualified charitable organization. Printed on the ticket is "Contribution—$20." If the regular price for the movie is $9, A made a contribution of $11 to a qualified charitable organization.

A fund-raising organization that provides token benefits to contributors can advise them that their donations are fully deductible only if the token benefits have an insubstantial value. If items are mailed to potential donors, the organization can advise that a contribution is fully deductible only if the items are low cost, provided for free, and not distributed at the donor's request or consent (Rev. Proc. 92-49; Rev. Proc. 90-12). A charity that receives a ***quid pro quo contribution*** in excess of $75 must provide a statement to the donor describing what portion of the donation represents consideration for goods or services (¶ 627) (Code Sec. 6115).[113]

Eighty percent of an otherwise deductible payment made to a college or university for the right to purchase tickets to an athletic event, including tickets to skyboxes, is treated as a charitable contribution regardless of whether the tickets would have been available if the payment had not been made (Code Sec. 170(l); IRS Letter Ruling 200004001).[114]

Transfers of property to a charitable organization that are directly related to the donor's business and made with a reasonable expectation of financial return equivalent to the value of the transfers do not qualify for a charitable deduction but may qualify as a trade or business expense (Reg. § 1.170A-1(c)(5)).[115]

Donor Advised Funds. The deduction for a contribution made to a donor advised fund (¶ 610) is allowed only if: (1) the fund's sponsoring organization is not a cemetery, a war veterans' organization, a lodge, or a "Type III supporting organization" that is not a "functionally integrated Type III supporting organization" (¶ 607 and ¶ 640), and (2) the donor obtains a contemporaneous written acknowledgment from the sponsoring organization that the organization has exclusive legal control over the assets contributed (Code Sec. 170(f)(18)).[116] Distributions from donor advised funds that are for noncharitable purposes are taxable, as are certain transactions between a donor advised fund and its donors, donor advisors, or related persons (Code Secs. 4966 and 4967).[117] The IRS has discretion to abate such taxes (¶ 647).

1062. Gifts of Appreciated Property. The amount of a noncash charitable contribution is generally the property's fair market value at the time of the contribution, reduced by limitations that apply to certain appreciated property (Code Sec. 170(e); Reg. §§ 1.170A-1(c) and 1.170A-4).[118] The deductible amount for appreciated property depends on whether it is ordinary income property, capital gain property, or a combination of both. The reduction rules described below do not apply if, due to the transfer of the contributed property, the donor recognizes income or gain in the same tax year in which the contribution is made.

Ordinary Income Property. Ordinary income property is property that, if sold at its fair market value on the date of contribution, would give rise to ordinary income or

References are to Standard Federal Tax Reports; Tax Research Consultant; and Practical Tax Explanations.

[112] ¶ 11,600; INDIV: 51,056; § 7,545

[113] ¶ 37,065; INDIV: 51,052; § 7,600.20

[114] ¶ 11,600, ¶ 11,680.10; INDIV: 51,052; § 7,510.75

[115] ¶ 11,615; INDIV: 51,150

[116] ¶ 11,600; INDIV: 51,100; § 7,520.40

[117] ¶ 34,317, ¶ 34,319; EXEMPT: 24,000; § 33,720.05

[118] ¶ 11,600, ¶ 11,615, ¶ 11,632; INDIV: 51,200; § 7,525.05

short-term capital gain. The deduction for such property is limited to the fair market value of the property less the amount that would be ordinary income. Such property includes inventory and stock in trade, artworks and manuscripts created by the donor, letters and memoranda, capital assets held for less than the required holding period for long-term capital gain treatment, and Code Sec. 306 stock (¶ 739 and ¶ 740) (Code Sec. 170(e)(1)(A); Reg. § 1.170A-4).[119]

Capital Gain Property. Capital gain property includes any asset on which a long-term capital gain would be realized if the taxpayer sold the asset for its fair market value on the date of contribution. As a general rule, gifts of capital gain property are deductible at their fair market value on the date of contribution. However, the individual's contribution must be reduced by the potential long-term gain (appreciation) if:

- the property is contributed to certain private nonoperating (grant-making) foundations (Code Sec. 170(e)(1)(B)(ii)) (However, a deduction is allowed for the fair market value of qualified appreciated stock, which is publicly traded stock that would produce long-term capital gain if sold (Code Sec. 170(e)(5)));
- the gift is tangible personal property put to a use that is unrelated to the purpose or function upon which the organization's exemption is based (Code Sec. 170(e)(1)(B)(i)(I));
- the gift is tangible personal property which is "applicable property" (but without regard to whether a deduction greater than the donor's basis has been allowed) that the organization sells, exchanges, or disposes of in the tax year when the contribution was made, and the organization has not made a certification regarding the property (see "*Recapture of Charitable Tax Benefits*," following) (Code Sec. 170(e)(1)(B)(i)(II));
- the donation consists of patents, certain copyrights, trademarks, trade names, trade secrets, know-how, certain software, or similar intellectual property or applications or registrations of such property (Code Sec. 170(e)(1)(B)(iii));
- the donation consists of taxidermy property contributed by the person who prepared, stuffed or mounted the property, or who paid or incurred the cost of preparation, stuffing or mounting (Code Sec. 170(e)(1)(B)(iv)); or
- the taxpayer elects to disregard the special 30-percent capital gains limitation in favor of the 50-percent limitation (Reg. § 1.170A-4(b)(2)).[120]

Combination Property. The charitable contribution deduction is specially computed if the donor's sale of the property at fair market value would have produced both ordinary income and capital gain (Code Sec. 170(e)). The fair market value is reduced by the ordinary income that would have resulted from the sale, and the remainder of the fair market value is treated as capital gain property, subject to the above rules. The types of property to which this special computation applies include property subject to depreciation recapture (¶ 1779 and ¶ 1788) and to recapture of farmland expenditures (¶ 1797), as well as interests in oil, gas, or geothermal property.

Recapture of Charitable Tax Benefits. If a donee organization disposes of applicable property within three years of the contribution and does not provide certification regarding the property, the donor taxpayer will be required to include as ordinary income for the year of the disposition the difference between the amount of the charitable deduction allowed for the donated capital gains property and the donor's basis. "Applicable property" is appreciated tangible personal property with a claimed value over $5,000, the use of which the donee certifies as related to its exempt function or purpose, and for which a deduction greater than the donor's basis is allowed. The certification is a written statement, signed under penalty of perjury by an officer of the donee, which either: (1) certifies that the property's use was *substantial and related* to the donee's exempt purpose, and describes how the property was used and how such use furthered the exempt purpose or (2) states the donee's intended use of the property

References are to Standard Federal Tax Reports; Tax Research Consultant; and Practical Tax Explanations.

[119] ¶ 11,600, ¶ 11,632; INDIV: 51,204; § 7,525.10

[120] ¶ 11,600, ¶ 11,632; INDIV: 51,200, INDIV: 51,206, INDIV: 51,254; § 7,525.15

at the time of the contribution and certifies that such use became impossible or infeasible to implement (Code Sec. 170(e)(7)).[121]

Food Inventories. Noncorporate and corporate taxpayers were allowed to claim an enhanced deduction for certain donations of food inventories for tax years beginning before 2012 (¶ 930A). For a taxpayer other than a C corporation, the total deduction for food inventory donations during the tax year was limited to a maximum of 10 percent of the taxpayer's net income from those trades or businesses making such donations (Code Sec. 170(e)(3)(C)).[122]

Comment: Absent further legislation, the enhanced deduction for certain donations of food inventory expired for tax years beginning after December 31, 2011.

1062A. Donee Income from Intellectual Property. A donor is allowed an additional charitable deduction based on a sliding-scale percentage of net income received by, or accrued to, the donee that is allocable to donated qualified intellectual property over a 10-year period. Qualified intellectual property includes patents and other intellectual property (¶ 1062) but does not include property donated to certain private nonoperating (grant-making) foundations. This additional deduction is allowed only to the extent that the total amount calculated using the sliding scale exceeds the deduction amount claimed on the property contribution without regard to the additional amount. The donor must inform the donee at the time of the contribution of its intent to treat the donation as a qualified intellectual property contribution. A donee, other than certain private foundations, that receives or accrues net income during a tax year from any qualified intellectual property contribution must make an information return and provide a copy to the donor (Code Secs. 170(m) and 6050L(b); Notice 2005-41).[123]

1063. Use of Property—Partial Interests. No charitable deduction is generally allowed for gifts to charity of the rent-free use of property and other nontrust gifts where less than the taxpayer's entire interest in the property is contributed, except in the following cases: (1) a contribution of an undivided portion of a taxpayer's entire interest in property, e.g., a one-fourth interest in property; (2) a contribution of a remainder interest in a personal residence or farm; (3) a qualified conservation contribution (QCC); and (4) where a charitable deduction would have been allowed had the interest been transferred in trust (¶ 538 and ¶ 1070) (Code Sec. 170(f)(3); Reg. § 1.170A-7).[124]

Additional Fractional Interest Charitable Contributions. The charitable deduction for additional contributions of tangible personal property in which the donor has previously contributed an undivided fractional interest is equal to the lesser of the fair market value of (1) the property used to determine the deduction for the initial fractional contribution, or (2) the property at the time of the additional contribution. The deduction will be recaptured if, on or before the earlier of the 10th anniversary of the initial fractional contribution or the donor's date of death, either (1) the donor fails to contribute the remaining interests to the donee, or (2) the donee fails to take substantial physical possession of the property and use it in a manner related to its exempt purpose. The recaptured amount will be subject to interest and an additional 10-percent tax (Code Sec. 170(o)).[125]

Qualified Conservation Contributions (QCC). A QCC is a contribution of a qualified real property interest to a qualified organization exclusively for conservation purposes that are protected in perpetuity. Qualified real property includes a donor's entire interest in real property other than an interest in subsurface oil, gas or other minerals, and the right to access to such minerals, a remainder interest, and a restriction granted in perpetuity on the property's use (i.e., an easement). A qualified organization includes certain governmental units, public charities that meet certain public support tests, and certain supporting organizations. A qualified conservation purpose includes: (1) preserving land for public outdoor recreation or education; (2) protecting a relatively natural

References are to Standard Federal Tax Reports; Tax Research Consultant; and Practical Tax Explanations.

[121] ¶ 11,600; INDIV: 51,200; § 7,525.15c

[122] ¶ 11,600; CCORP: 9,354; § 7,525.20

[123] ¶ 11,600, ¶ 36,260, ¶ 11,660.32; INDIV: 51,168; § 7,585

[124] ¶ 11,600, ¶ 11,651; INDIV: 51,350; § 7,550.05—§ 7,550.20

[125] ¶ 11,600; INDIV: 51,354; § 7,550.15b

habitat of fish, wildlife, or plants; (3) preserving open space for the public's scenic enjoyment or under a governmental conservation policy that will yield significant public benefit; and (4) preserving an historically important land area or certified historic structure (Code Sec. 170(h)).[126]

For any QCC, the deduction is reduced by an amount equal to the contribution's fair market value multiplied by a fraction: the sum of the rehabilitation credits (¶ 1365B) allowed to the taxpayer for the five preceding tax years on any building that is part of the donation, over the building's fair market value on the contribution date (Code Sec. 170(f)(14)).

Facade Easements. A facade easement may qualify as a QCC. There are several requirements for contributions of facade easements regarding buildings located in registered historic districts and certified as being of historic significance. The easement must preserve the building's entire exterior and prohibit any change that is inconsistent with the exterior's historical character. Both the donor and donee must certify in writing that the donee: (1) is a qualified organization whose purpose is environmental protection, land conservation, or open space or historic preservation and (2) has the resources and a commitment to manage and enforce the restriction. The donor's return must include: (1) a qualified appraisal of the property interest (¶ 1071); (2) photographs of the building's entire exterior; and (3) a description of all restrictions on the building's development (Code Sec. 170(h)(4)(B)). Taxpayers who seek deductions over $10,000 for such contributions must submit a statutory $500 filing fee with their return (Code Sec. 170(f)(13)).

1064. Care of Unrelated Student in the Home. Charitable contributions include unreimbursed amounts spent to maintain a full-time elementary or high school student, who is *not* a dependent or relative, in the taxpayer's home under a written agreement with a program sponsored by a charitable organization providing educational opportunities for students. The deduction is limited to actual expenditures, up to $50 per month, while the student is a member of the taxpayer's household. Dependent is defined at Code Sec. 152 (¶ 137), but without regard to whether the dependent claims dependency exemptions, files a joint return or has gross income in excess of the exemption amount (Code Sec. 170(g); Reg. § 1.170A-2).[127]

1065. Reduction for Interest. If a liability is assumed by the recipient or by any other person, or if the contributed property is subject to a liability, the contribution must be reduced by the interest paid by the taxpayer-donor, whether prepaid or to be paid in the future, attributable to any period after the contribution. If the gift is a bond, note or other evidence of indebtedness, the amount of the contribution is further reduced by the interest that is paid or to be paid by the taxpayer-donor on indebtedness incurred or continued to purchase or carry such bond that is attributable to any period prior to the contribution (Code Sec. 170(f)(5); Reg. § 1.170A-3).[128]

1066. Contribution by Partnership. Although a partnership cannot claim a charitable deduction in figuring its taxable income, each partner is allowed a deduction for the partner's distributive share of the partnership's charitable contribution (¶ 417) (Code Secs. 702(a) and 703(a); Reg. § 1.702-1(a)).[129] See ¶ 1061 for special rules regarding partnership donations of clothing and household items.

1068. Denial of Deduction. A contribution is *not* deductible unless it is made to, or for the use of, an organization that qualifies as one of the types described at ¶ 1061. Contributions made directly to an individual or to groups of individuals are not deductible, including those made directly to individuals in the military.[130] Gifts to private schools and organizations, including churches, that practice racial discrimination in their admissions policies are not deductible (Rev. Rul. 75-231).

References are to Standard Federal Tax Reports; Tax Research Consultant; and Practical Tax Explanations.

[126] ¶ 11,600; INDIV: 51,364; § 7,550.20

[127] ¶ 11,600, ¶ 11,621; INDIV: 51,120; § 7,535

[128] ¶ 11,600, ¶ 11,631; INDIV: 51,160

[129] ¶ 25,080, ¶ 25,081, ¶ 25,100; PART: 18,054; § 30,405

[130] ¶ 11,620.111; INDIV: 51,120; § 7,520.05

If a taxpayer makes a gift to a private foundation or a nonexempt trust, i.e., an annuity trust or unitrust, a deduction will be allowed only if the governing instrument specifically prohibits income accumulations and certain conflict-of-interest activities (¶ 635 and ¶ 644) (Code Sec. 508(d)).[131] The IRS has issued sample acceptable governing instrument clauses (Rev. Rul. 70-270). Many states have enacted statutes that accomplish the required governing instrument adjustments, and the IRS has published a list of those that satisfy the Code requirements (¶ 538 and ¶ 631) (Rev. Rul. 75-38).

An organization formed after October 9, 1969, and claiming exemption under Code Sec. 501(c)(3) (¶ 1061) must file notice of intent to be exempt (¶ 623), the exemption being retroactive to the date of organization only if the notice was timely. Contributions to such an organization are deductible only if the notice is filed. Contributions made to a late-filing organization are not deductible if made before the date of filing (Code Secs. 170(f)(1) and 508(d); Reg. § 1.508-1 and 1.508-2).[132] The IRS periodically updates and publishes a cumulative list of eligible organizations which may be searched on the IRS website, at http://www.irs.gov/Charities-&-Non-Profits/Exempt-Organizations-Select-Check (Rev. Proc. 2011-33).

Deductions are disallowed for contributions by a "substantial contributor" (¶ 635) to a foundation in a tax year in which there is an action resulting in a termination tax (¶ 649) (Code Secs. 170(f)(1) and 508(d); Reg. §§ 1.508-1 and 1.508-2).[133] Deductions are also denied for contributions made in connection with church-related tax avoidance schemes, i.e., the "donation" of assets to a personal "church" that effectively redistributes them to the donor. Deficiencies arising from the denial of deduction based on these schemes usually result in assessment of interest and penalties.[134]

1069. Gift of Future Interest in Tangible Personal Property. When a taxpayer transfers to a charitable organization a future interest in tangible personal property, such as a painting, manuscript, sculpture, or other art object, a charitable contribution deduction is *not* allowed until all intervening interests in, and rights to, the actual possession or enjoyment of the property have expired or are held by persons other than the taxpayer, related taxpayers and controlled partnerships (Code Sec. 170(a)(3); Reg. § 1.170A-5).[135]

1070. Transfer in Trust. No deduction is allowed for the value of a contribution of a remainder interest that the donor transfers in trust unless the trust is a pooled income fund (¶ 593), a charitable remainder annuity trust, or a charitable remainder unitrust (¶ 590). If the donor gives *all* the interests in a trust to charity, however, a deduction is allowable (Code Sec. 170(f)(2); Reg. § 1.170A-6).[136]

1070A. Reporting, Recordkeeping and Substantiation. Taxpayers report their charitable contributions by entering the total amount contributed on Schedule A of Form 1040, but written records are required to substantiate the deductions.

Cash Donations. No deduction will be allowed for contributions of cash, checks or other monetary gifts, *regardless of the amount,* unless the donor maintains either: (1) a bank record, including a cancelled check, a bank or credit union statement, or a credit card statement; or (2) a receipt, letter, or other written communication from the donee, indicating the donee's name and the contribution date and amount (Code Sec. 170(f)(17); IRS Pub. 526).[137]

Payroll Deductions. For charitable contributions made by payroll deduction, the taxpayer must retain: (1) a pay stub, Form W-2 or other employer-furnished document indicating the amount withheld for payment to the donee organization; and (2) a pledge card or other document prepared by the donee organization, or at its direction, showing the donee's name. For contributions of $250 or more, the pledge card or other document

References are to Standard Federal Tax Reports; Tax Research Consultant; and Practical Tax Explanations.

[131] ¶ 22,790; INDIV: 51,118
[132] ¶ 11,600, ¶ 22,790, ¶ 22,791, ¶ 22,792; INDIV: 51,100
[133] ¶ 11,600, ¶ 22,790, ¶ 22,791, ¶ 22,792; INDIV: 51,118
[134] ¶ 39,651G.225; INDIV: 51,118
[135] ¶ 11,600, ¶ 11,634; INDIV: 51,350; § 7,560
[136] ¶ 11,600, ¶ 11,635; INDIV: 51,350; § 7,555.05, § 7,555.20
[137] ¶ 11,600; INDIV: 51,454; § 7,600.10a

must also include a statement that the donee does not provide goods or services in whole or partial consideration for any contributions made to it by payroll deduction; these requirements are in addition to those for contributions of $250 or more (see *Contributions of $250 or More,* following) (Notice 2006-110).

Lump-Sum Donations Through CFC. To substantiate a lump-sum charitable contribution made through the Combined Federal Campaign (CFC) or similar programs, e.g., the United Way campaigns, which distribute the amounts received to one or more qualified organizations (¶ 1061), the CFC organization must provide the donor with a written communication that includes the name of the donee organization that is the ultimate recipient of the contribution. This requirement is in addition to those for contributions of $250 or more (see *Contributions of $250 or More,* following) (Notice 2008-16).

Noncash Donations of Less than $250. For each noncash donation for which a deduction of less than $250 is claimed, the taxpayer generally must maintain a receipt from the donee, e.g., a letter or other written communication, indicating the donee's name, the date and location of the donation, and a detailed description, but not the value, of the donated property. If it would be impracticable to obtain a receipt, the donor must maintain reliable written records regarding each item contributed (Reg. § 1.170A-13(b)).[138]

Contributions of $250 or More. Charitable contributions of $250 or more must be substantiated by a contemporaneous written acknowledgment from the donee organization unless the donee files a return with the IRS reporting the information that would be included in the written acknowledgment. Generally, the acknowledgment must include: (1) the amount of cash contributed, and a description of any property contributed; (2) a description and good-faith estimate of the value of any goods or services with more than insubstantial value received in exchange for the contributions; and (3) if the donee provides any intangible religious benefits, a statement to that effect (Code Sec. 170(f)(8); Reg. § 1.170A-13(f)).[139]

Noncash Donations of more Than $500. For property contributions for which a deduction of more than $500 is claimed, the taxpayer, other than a C corporation that is not a personal service corporation or closely-held C corporation, must include with its return for the tax year of the contribution a written description of the donated property and any other required information as the IRS may prescribe by regulation. If the documentation requirement is not met, the deduction will be denied unless the failure is due to reasonable cause and not to willful neglect. To determine the $500 threshold, all similar items of property donated to one or more donees are treated as a single item of property (Code Sec. 170(f)(11)).[140] Noncash contributions over $500 (over $5,000 for C corporations other than closely-held or personal service corporations) must be described in Section A of Form 8283, which is attached to the taxpayer's return. A noncash contribution that exceeds $5,000 must also be appraised and described in Section B of Form 8283 (¶ 1071) (Reg. § 1.170A-13(c)).[141]

Donations of Clothing or Household Items. Donations of clothing or household items that are *not* in good used condition or better are allowed only if a deduction of more than $500 is claimed for a single item and a qualified appraisal (¶ 1071) for that item is attached to the return (¶ 1061).

Vehicle Donations. Taxpayers donating to a charity a qualified vehicle, e.g., car, truck, boat, or aircraft, valued at over $500 must obtain from the charity and attach to his or her return either a Form 1098-C or a similar contemporaneous written acknowledgment of the contribution. The acknowledgment must identify the donor taxpayer, list the taxpayer's and the vehicle's identification numbers, and include a description and good faith estimate of the value of any goods or services provided by the charity in exchange for the vehicle. If the goods or services consist solely of intangible religious benefits, the

References are to Standard Federal Tax Reports; Tax Research Consultant; and Practical Tax Explanations.

[138] ¶ 11,685; INDIV: 51,454, INDIV: 51,456; § 7,600.05, § 7,600.10

[139] ¶ 11,600, ¶ 11,685; INDIV: 51,454; § 7,600.15

[140] ¶ 11,600; INDIV: 51,456.15; § 7,600.10b

[141] ¶ 11,685; INDIV: 51,456.20; § 7,600.10b, § 7,600.25

acknowledgment must say so. If the charity sells the vehicle without significant intervening use or material improvement, the acknowledgment must also certify that the vehicle was sold in an arm's length transaction between unrelated parties, list the gross proceeds, and state that the deduction may not exceed the gross proceeds. If the charity retains the vehicle for its significant use or makes a material improvement, the acknowledgment must certify the use or improvement, the time frame the charity will use the vehicle, and that the vehicle will not be transferred before the use or improvement is completed. The taxpayer is then allowed to claim the fair market value of the vehicle as a charitable donation (Code Sec. 170(f)(12); Notice 2005-44; Notice 2006-1).[142]

If the charity sells the vehicle to a needy individual at a price significantly below fair market value, or gratuitously transfers the vehicle, the taxpayer can claim the donated vehicle's fair market value only if the sale or transfer directly furthers the charity's purpose. However, if a charity sells the vehicle at auction, the IRS will not accept as substantiation an acknowledgment stating that the vehicle is to be transferred to a needy individual for significantly below fair market value. In that case, the donor taxpayer may claim a deduction greater than $500, but only to the extent that the gross sale proceeds exceed that amount and the donor substantiates the contribution with an acknowledgment listing the gross proceeds (Notice 2007-70, modifying Notice 2006-1).

Qualified Conservation Contributions (QCCs). Documentation and certification requirements must be met for certain QCCs of facade easements (¶ 1063).

1071. Appraisals for Noncash Contributions. A charitable deduction will be denied to any taxpayer for certain noncash contributions that fails to meet specific appraisal requirements. See ¶ 1070A for documentation requirements. An exception exists if the failure is due to reasonable cause and not to willful neglect. For purposes of determining the threshold dollar amounts for the reporting requirements (as described following), all similar items of noncash property, whether donated to a single donee or multiple donees, are aggregated and treated as a single property donation. For partnerships and S corporations, the requirements are applied at the entity level, but if the entities fail to meet the requirements, denial of the deduction will be made at the partner or shareholder level (Code Sec. 170(f)(11)).[143]

If a deduction of more than $5,000 is being claimed for a noncash donation, the taxpayer, including a C corporation, must—

- obtain a qualified appraisal of the property, and
- attach Form 8283 to its return for the tax year in which the donation is made; if a deduction of $500,000 or more is being claimed, the qualified appraisal itself must be attached to the return when filed.

These substantiation requirements do *not* apply to donations of:

- cash;
- patents and other intellectual property (¶ 1062);
- publicly-traded securities for which market quotations are readily available on an established securities market;
- inventory or property held by the taxpayer primarily for sale to customers in the ordinary course of his trade or business (¶ 1741); or
- a qualified vehicle sold by the donee organization without any significant intervening use or material improvement and for which an acknowledgment is provided (¶ 1070A).

A qualified appraisal is an appraisal prepared according to regulations or other IRS guidance, and conducted by a qualified appraiser under generally-accepted appraisal standards and other IRS guidance. A qualified appraiser must have either earned an appraisal designation from a recognized professional organization or otherwise meet minimum requirements, must regularly perform appraisals for pay, and must meet any

References are to Standard Federal Tax Reports; Tax Research Consultant; and Practical Tax Explanations.

[142] 11,600; INDIV: 51,152, INDIV: 51,460; § 7,590.05, § 7,590.15

[143] ¶ 11,600; INDIV: 51,456.20, INDIV: 51,458; § 7,600.25

other requirements prescribed by the IRS. A qualified appraiser must also demonstrate verifiable education and experience in valuing the type of property being appraised, and must not have been prohibited from practicing before the IRS during the three-year period ending on the appraisal date (Code Sec. 170(f)(11)(E); Reg. § 1.170A-13(c); Notice 2006-96).[144]

An appraisal summary, made on Section B of Form 8283, must be attached to the tax return on which the deduction of more than $5,000 is first claimed. Appraisals are also required if a taxpayer donates a number of similar items, whether or not to the same donee, such as stamps or coins, with a total value in excess of $5,000. For donations of publicly traded securities for which market quotations are *not* readily available on an established securities market, a partially completed appraisal summary is required if the claimed value exceeds $5,000. The appraisal summary only needs to be partially completed for nonpublicly traded stock with a claimed value between $5,000 and $10,000 (Reg. § 1.170A-13(c)).[145] The qualified appraisal requirement is waived for closely held and personal service corporations that contribute inventory, stock in trade, or other property normally held for sale in its business for the ill, needy, or infants (Notice 89-56).

Appraisal fees incurred by an individual in determining the fair market value of donated property are not treated as part of the charitable contribution, but they may be claimed as a miscellaneous deduction on Schedule A of Form 1040 (Rev. Rul. 67-461).

Accuracy-Related Penalties. Appraisers are subject to civil penalties for certain appraisals that result in substantial or gross valuation misstatements (Code Sec. 6695A).[146]

Moving Expense

1073. Moving Expense Deduction. Employees and self-employed individuals may deduct as an adjustment to gross income (an above-the-line deduction) the reasonable expenses of moving themselves and their families if the move is related to starting work in a new location (Code Sec. 217).[147] The deduction is computed on Form 3903 and reported on Form 1040.

Deductible moving expenses are limited to the cost of (1) transportation of household goods and personal effects and (2) travel (including lodging but not meals) to the new residence (Code Sec. 217(b)).[148] Where an automobile is used in making the move, a taxpayer may deduct either: (1) the actual out-of-pocket expenses incurred, i.e., gasoline and oil, but not repairs, depreciation, etc., or (2) a standard mileage allowance of 23 cents per mile plus parking fees and tolls for 2012 (Rev. Proc. 2010-51; Notice 2012-1).[149]

1075. Eligibility for Deduction. To deduct moving expenses (¶ 1073), a taxpayer must meet a distance test, a length-of-employment test and a commencement-of-work test. The new principal place of work must be at least 50 miles farther from the taxpayer's old residence than the old residence was from the taxpayer's old place of work. If there was no old place of work, the new place of work must be at least 50 miles from the old residence (Code Sec. 217(c)).[150]

During the 12-month period immediately following the move, the taxpayer must be employed full time for at least 39 weeks. A self-employed taxpayer must be employed or performing services full time for at least 78 weeks of the 24-month period immediately following the move and at least 39 weeks during the first 12 months. The full-time work requirement is waived, however, due to death, disability, involuntary separation from work, other than for willful misconduct, or transfer to another location for the benefit of the employer (Code Secs. 217(c) and (d)).

References are to Standard Federal Tax Reports; Tax Research Consultant; and Practical Tax Explanations.

[144] ¶ 11,600, ¶ 11,685; INDIV: 51,458.05, INDIV: 51,458.15; § 7,600.25

[145] ¶ 11,685; INDIV: 51,458.10; § 7,600.25b

[146] ¶ 39,971; PENALTY: 3,334; § 7,600.25

[147] ¶ 12,620; INDIV: 39,104; § 5,101

[148] ¶ 12,620; INDIV: 39,106.05; § 5,105.05

[149] ¶ 12,623.11; INDIV: 39,106.10; § 5,105.15

[150] ¶ 12,620; INDIV: 39,120; § 5,120.10

In general, the move must be in connection with the commencement of work at the new location and the moving expenses must be incurred within one year from the time the taxpayer first reports to the new job or business. If the move is not made within one year, the expenses ordinarily will not be deductible unless it can be shown that circumstances prevented the taxpayer from incurring the expenses within that period (Reg. § 1.217-2(a)(3)).[151]

An eligible taxpayer is permitted to deduct moving expenses even though the 39- or 78-week employment requirement has not been satisfied by the due date for the return including extensions for the tax year in which the moving expenses were incurred and paid. A taxpayer who fails to meet the requirements, however, must either file an amended return or include as gross income on the next year's return the amount previously claimed as expenses (Code Sec. 217(d); Reg. § 1.217-2(d)(3)).[152]

An individual who retires from an overseas job may deduct moving expenses incurred in returning to the United States. A surviving spouse or dependent who shared the residence of a decedent who worked outside the U.S. at the time of death may also deduct moving expenses incurred in returning to the U.S. within six months after the death (Code Sec. 217(i)).[153]

1076. Reimbursement by Employer. Gross income does not include qualified moving expense reimbursements, which are amounts received directly or indirectly by an individual employee from an employer as a payment for or reimbursement of expenses that would be deductible as a moving expense if directly paid or incurred by the employee (¶ 863) (Code Sec. 132(a)(6) and (g)).[154] Any amount, other than a qualified reimbursement, received or accrued, directly or indirectly, from the employer as a payment for or reimbursement of moving expenses must be included in the employee's gross income as compensation for services (Code Sec. 82)[155] and is considered wages subject to withholding (Code Sec. 3401(a)(15); Reg. § 31.3401(a)(15)-1).[156]

1077. Foreign Moves. The rules governing moving expenses incurred in connection with the commencement of work outside the U.S. and its possessions are similar to those discussed in ¶ 1073 and ¶ 1075. However, a deduction is also allowed for reasonable expenses of moving household goods and personal effects to and from storage, and of storing them while the new place of work abroad is the taxpayer's principal place of work (Code Sec. 217(h)).[157]

1078. Moves of Armed Forces Members. Gross income does not include moving and storage expenses that are furnished in kind by the military or cash reimbursements or allowances to the extent of expenses actually paid or incurred incident to a permanent change of station for a member of the U.S. Armed Forces on active duty. These expenses need not be reported and such moves are exempt from the time and mileage requirements (¶ 1075). An income exclusion is also provided for moving and storage expenses incurred by the spouse or dependents of such an Armed Forces member, even if they do not reside with the member either before or after the move (Code Sec. 217(g)). Reimbursements in excess of actual expenses are includible in the member's income as wages, while expenses in excess of reimbursements are deductible (Reg. § 1.217-2(g)(2)(ii)).[158]

Dues, Education, and Other Expenses

1080. Union Dues. Union dues, initiation fees and out-of-work-benefit assessments are deductible as an itemized deduction on Schedule A of Form 1040, subject to the two-percent-of-adjusted-gross-income (AGI) floor (¶ 1011) (Reg. § 1.162-15(c)).[159] The self-employed may deduct union dues as a business expense (¶ 1005).

References are to Standard Federal Tax Reports; Tax Research Consultant; and Practical Tax Explanations.

151 ¶ 12,622; INDIV: 39,108; § 5,115

152 ¶ 12,620, ¶ 12,622; INDIV: 39,122; § 5,120.15, § 5,125

153 ¶ 12,620; INDIV: 39,128; § 5,101

154 ¶ 7420; INDIV: 39,130; § 5,130

155 ¶ 6374; INDIV: 39,130; § 5,130

156 ¶ 33,502, ¶ 33,528; COMPEN: 33,116; § 5,130, § 22,110.10p

157 ¶ 12,620; INDIV: 39,126; § 5,101

158 ¶ 12,620, ¶ 12,622; INDIV: 39,124; § 5,135

159 ¶ 8852, ¶ 8853.20; INDIV: 36,302; § 7,105.35

1081. Job-Hunting Expenses. Individuals may deduct all expenses incurred in seeking employment in the *same* trade or business regardless of whether or not the search is successful. Such expenses include the typing, printing, and mailing of resumes, and travel and transportation expenses. Travel and transportation expenses to and from an area are deductible only if the trip relates primarily to seeking new employment. If the travel is primarily personal in nature, only the actual expenses of the search at the destination are deductible.[160]

Expenses are not deductible if an individual is seeking employment in a *new* trade or business even where employment is secured. Individuals cannot deduct job-hunting expenses if they are seeking their first job, entering a new trade or business, or if there is a substantial lack of continuity between the time of their past employment and the seeking of new employment.

Job-hunting expenses are deductible only as an itemized deduction on Schedule A of Form 1040, subject to the two-percent-of-adjusted-gross-income (AGI) floor (¶ 1011).

1082. Education and Related Expenses. There are several types of deductions for education expenses. One of these tax benefits is that interest paid during the tax year on any qualified education loan is deductible as an adjustment to gross income, i.e., an above-the-line deduction, on Form 1040 or 1040A (Code Sec. 221).[161] The debt must be incurred by the taxpayer solely to pay qualified higher education expenses. The maximum deductible amount of interest is $2,500, but the amount of any deduction is reduced by an amount, but not below zero, that equals the otherwise allowable deduction times a fraction, the numerator being the excess of modified adjusted gross income (MAGI) over $50,000 ($100,000 for joint filers), which is annually adjusted for inflation, and the denominator being $15,000 ($30,000 for joint filers). For 2012, the maximum deduction is reduced when MAGI exceeds $60,000 ($125,000 for joint returns) and is completely eliminated when MAGI is $75,000 ($155,000 for joint returns) (Rev. Proc. 2011-52).

> **Comment:** Absent further legislation, the qualified educational loan interest deduction may only be claimed for the first 60 months of required payments and the expanded phaseout range will be eliminated for tax years beginning after December 31, 2012. The phaseout range will revert to $40,000 to $55,000 ($60,000 to $75,000 for joint filers), which will not be adjusted for inflation.

Another educational tax benefit was the ability to take an adjustment to income (or an above-the-line deduction) for qualifying tuition and related expenses for enrollment or attendance by the taxpayer, the taxpayer's spouse or dependent at any accredited post-secondary institution. The deductible amount was based on the taxpayer's adjusted gross income (AGI). The maximum deductible amount for tax years 2004 through 2011 was $4,000 for taxpayers with AGI of $65,000 or less ($130,000 for joint filers) and $2,000 for taxpayers with AGI above $65,000 but less than or equal to $80,000 ($130,000 and $160,000, respectively, for joint filers). No deduction is available to taxpayers with AGI above $80,000 ($160,000 for joint filers) (Code Sec. 222).[162]

> **Comment:** Absent further legislation, the tuition and fees deduction is no longer available to taxpayers for tax years beginning after December 31, 2011.

The taxpayer's own education expenses may qualify to be deducted as a business expense, even if they lead to a degree, if the education either: (1) maintains or improves skills *required* in the taxpayer's employment or other trade or business, including refresher courses, current developments courses, or academic or vocational courses, or (2) meets the express *requirements* of the taxpayer's employer, or of laws or regulations, *imposed* for a bona fide business purpose of the employer and as a condition to the taxpayer's retention of an established employment relationship, status, or rate of compensation (Reg. § 1.162-5).[163] Education in excess of the minimum requirement may qualify as education undertaken to maintain or improve the required skills.

References are to Standard Federal Tax Reports; Tax Research Consultant; and Practical Tax Explanations.

[160] ¶ 8524.25; INDIV: 36,250; § 7,105.15

[161] ¶ 12,692; INDIV: 60,054; § 5,901

[162] ¶ 12,770; INDIV: 60,064; § 5,201, § 5,210

[163] ¶ 8631; INDIV: 60,102; § 7,901

Educational expenses that are personal or constitute an inseparable aggregate of personal and capital expenditures are not deductible, even though they may maintain or improve a skill or meet the express requirements of the employer or under law. Nondeductible capital or personal education expenses are those that: (1) are required of the taxpayer in order to meet the minimum educational requirements for qualification in the taxpayer's present employment, trade, or business or (2) qualify the taxpayer for a new trade or business.

The minimum education necessary to qualify for a position or other trade or business is determined from a consideration of such factors as requirements of the employer, laws or regulations, and the standards of the profession, trade, or business involved. The fact that an individual is already performing service in an employment status does not mean he or she has met the minimum educational requirements. However, once an individual has met the minimum requirements in effect when he or she enters the employment, profession, or trade or business, the individual is treated as continuing to meet those requirements even though they have changed. For these individuals, expenses for meeting the new requirements would be deductible.

A change of duties is not a new trade or business if the new duties and the taxpayer's present employment involve the same general work. Thus, there is no new trade or business when a teacher moves from an elementary to a secondary school, from one subject to another, or from a teaching position to a principal's position (Reg. § 1.162-5(b)(3)).[164]

Unreimbursed expenditures for such items as tuition, books, laboratory fees, dues paid to professional societies, fees paid for professional journals, etc., are deducted by an employee as an itemized deduction, subject to the two-percent of AGI floor (¶ 1011) (Reg. § 1.162-6; IRS Pub. 970).[165] The cost of technical books of relatively permanent value used in connection with professional work is a capital expenditure and must be depreciated (IRS Pub. 946) (¶ 1240).[166]

Travel as a Form of Education. No deduction is allowed for travel as a form of education, such as when a French teacher spends summers in Paris to maintain familiarity with the language (Code Sec. 274(m)(2)).[167] Travel in pursuit of an education, however, may be deductible if the educational expense itself is deductible as a business expense; for example, a French teacher travels to Paris to take otherwise deductible classes that are offered only at the Sorbonne.[168]

1083. Uniforms and Special Clothing. The cost and upkeep of a uniform, including laundering and cleaning, are deductible only if the uniform is required as a condition of employment and is not adaptable to general wear. Uniform expense reimbursements paid under an accountable plan (¶ 943) are not reported on the employee's Form W-2 or included in the employee's income (Reg. § 1.62-2(c)(4)).[169] Costs that exceed the reimbursement are deductible as an itemized deduction, subject to the two-percent-of-adjusted-gross-income (AGI) floor (¶ 1011). Reimbursement made under a nonaccountable plan (¶ 943) must be included in income but may be deducted as an itemized deduction on Schedule A of Form 1040, subject to the two-percent of AGI floor and other limitations (Reg. § 1.62-2(c)(5)). Armed Forces reservists may deduct the unreimbursed cost, less nontaxable uniform allowance, of a uniform required at drills or other functions if they are prohibited from wearing it for regular use (Rev. Rul. 76-453, modifying Rev. Rul. 55-109).

A deduction is allowed for special items required in the employee's work that do not replace items of ordinary clothing, such as special work shoes and gloves, shop caps, and protective clothing.[170]

References are to Standard Federal Tax Reports; Tax Research Consultant; and Practical Tax Explanations.

[164] ¶ 8631; INDIV: 60,118.15; § 7,915.05

[165] ¶ 8633; INDIV: 60,100; § 7,105.10

[166] ¶ 8634.01; INDIV: 60,100; § 45,710.15

[167] ¶ 14,402; INDIV: 60,122; § 7,920.10

[168] ¶ 14,402.018; INDIV: 60,122; § 7,920.10

[169] ¶ 6004; INDIV: 36,200; § 5,310, § 7,105.10, § 7,105.20

[170] ¶ 8524.2658; INDIV: 36,202; § 7,105.20

1084. Teachers' Classroom Expenses. Eligible educators were allowed an above-the-line deduction (an adjustment to gross income) of up to $250 for unreimbursed expenses incurred in connection with books, supplies (other than nonathletic supplies for courses in health or physical education), computer equipment and supplementary materials used in the classroom for tax years before 2012 (Code Sec. 62(a)(2)(D)).[171] An eligible educator is an individual who, for at least 900 hours during a school year, is a kindergarten through grade 12 teacher, instructor, counselor, principal or aide in a school that provided elementary or secondary education as determined under state law (Code Sec. 62(d)(1)).

Comment: Absent further legislation, the teacher's classroom expenses deduction expired for tax years beginning after December 31, 2011.

Production of Income

1085. Nontrade or Nonbusiness Expenses. An individual may deduct ordinary and necessary expenses paid or incurred for the production or collection of income, or for the management, conservation, or maintenance of property held for the production of income, as long as the expenses are proximately related to these purposes and reasonable in amount (Code Sec. 212; Reg. § 1.212-1(d)).[172] The expenses are claimed as an itemized deduction on Schedule A of Form 1040, subject to the two-percent-of-adjusted-gross-income (AGI) floor (¶ 1011). Expenses attributable to property held for rents or royalties are deductible from gross income and are not subject to the two-percent of AGI floor (¶ 1089). No deduction is allowed for interest on indebtedness incurred or continued to purchase or carry obligations earning fully tax-exempt interest or other exempt income (¶ 1970) (Code Sec. 265(a)).[173]

1086. Investor's Expenses. Investment counsel fees, custodian fees, fees for clerical help, office rent, state and local transfer taxes, and similar expenses paid or incurred by individuals in connection with their investments are deductible as itemized deductions on Schedule A of Form 1040, subject to the two-percent-of-adjusted-gross-income (AGI) floor (¶ 1011) (Reg. § 1.212-1(g)),[174] except where they relate to rents and royalties (¶ 1089). A dealer or trader in securities is *not* an investor and may deduct these items as business expenses, subject to the uniform capitalization rules (¶ 990).[175]

1089. Expenses Attributable to Rental or Royalty Property. Ordinary and necessary expenses attributable to property held for the production of rents or royalties may be deducted in determining adjusted gross income (AGI) (Code Sec. 62(a)(4); Reg. § 1.62-1T(c))[176] even if the property is not actually producing income. These deductions include interest, taxes, depreciation, depletion, losses, etc. (Reg. § 1.212-1).[177]

Property held for the production of royalties includes intangible as well as tangible property. Therefore, depreciation on a patent or copyright may be deducted. Similarly, operating owners, lessees, sublessors or sublessees, or purchasers of royalty interests can deduct their shares of a depletion allowance on natural resources (¶ 1201 and ¶ 1289).

Expenses must be prorated if a property is devoted to rental purposes for part of a year and to personal use for the other part. See the example on proration at ¶ 963. See also ¶ 966 for special rules governing the deduction of expenses of rental vacation homes. For the applicability of the at-risk and passive activity rules, see ¶ 2045 and ¶ 2053.

1090. Expenses of Life Tenant or Income Beneficiary. When property is held by one person for life, with the remainder to another person, the deduction for depreciation or depletion is allowed to the life tenant and is computed as if the life tenant were the

References are to Standard Federal Tax Reports; Tax Research Consultant; and Practical Tax Explanations.

[171] ¶ 6002; INDIV: 36,364; § 5,325

[172] ¶ 12,520, ¶ 12,521; BUSEXP: 12,050; § 7,801, § 7,805, § 7,825

[173] ¶ 14,050; INDIV: 48,552; § 7,845.05

[174] ¶ 12,521; BUSEXP: 12,150; § 7,105.40, § 7,840.05, § 7,840.15

[175] ¶ 8521.1475, ¶ 8521.148; BUSEXP: 12,150; § 7,840.10

[176] ¶ 6002, ¶ 6003; FILEIND: 9,058; § 5,045, § 7,801, § 7,875.05

[177] ¶ 12,521; BUSEXP: 12,158.05; § 7,875.10

absolute owner of the property (Reg. §§1.167(h)-1 and 1.611-1(c)).[178] After the life tenant's death, the deduction, if any, is allowed to the remainderman. For property held in trust or by an estate, the deduction is apportioned as explained at ¶ 530.

1091. Guardianship Expenses. A deduction is permitted for a reasonable amount paid or incurred for the services of a guardian or committee for a ward or minor and for other ordinary and necessary expenses incurred in connection with the production or collection of income inuring to the ward or minor, or in connection with the management, conservation, or maintenance of income-producing property belonging to the ward or minor (Reg. §1.212-1(j)).[179] Expenses of a competency proceeding are deductible if the purpose of the proceeding is the management and conservation of income-producing property owned by the taxpayer.[180]

1092. Expenses Connected with the Determination of Tax. Any ordinary and necessary expense incurred in connection with the determination, collection, or refund of any tax is deductible as an itemized deduction on Schedule A of Form 1040, subject to the two-percent-of-adjusted-income (AGI) floor (¶ 1011) (Code Sec. 212(3)).[181] This includes tax return preparation fees allocable to an individual's Form 1040 and supporting schedules and forms. Form 1040 expenses attributable to a trade or business, including Schedules C, C-EZ, E and F, however, are deductible from gross income and are *not* itemized deductions (Rev. Rul. 92-29, modifying Rev. Rul. 70-40).

This provision applies to income, estate, gift, property and other taxes imposed at the federal, state or local level (Reg. §1.212-1(l)).[182] Legal expenses incurred in determining tax liability include legal fees paid for obtaining a ruling on a tax question (Rev. Rul. 89-68) and defending against a criminal indictment for tax evasion (Rev. Rul. 68-662). Expenses that pertain to both tax and nontax matters must be allocated and substantiated because only the tax element of the expense is deductible (Rev. Rul. 72-545).

Appraisal fees may be deductible as an expense paid in connection with the determination of income tax liability. Appraisal fees incurred in determining the fair market value of property donated to a charity or to establish the amount of loss are two examples of deductible expenses (Rev. Rul. 58-180; Rev. Rul. 67-461).

Credit or debit card convenience fees charged for electronic payment of federal individual income taxes, including estimated taxes, are deductible as miscellaneous itemized deductions (IRS News Release IR-2009-37).

1093. Legal Expenses. Legal expenses are deductible as miscellaneous itemized deductions on Schedule A of Form 1040, subject to the two-percent-of-adjusted-income (AGI) floor (¶ 1011), if they are paid or incurred for the production of income or for the management, conservation, or maintenance of income-producing property (Reg. §1.212-1).[183] Legal expenses incurred in defending or perfecting title to property, in the acquisition or disposition of property, or in developing or improving property are *not* deductible and must be capitalized. Legal expenses paid or incurred in recovering investment property and amounts of income includible in gross income are generally deductible. The U.S. Court of Appeals for the Sixth Circuit has ruled, however, that legal expenses incurred in recovering stock were deductible only to the extent that they were allocable to the recovery of interest and dividends (*J.K. Nickell*, CA-6, 87-2 USTC ¶ 9585).

Divorce and Separation. Legal expenses paid by one spouse in resisting the other's monetary demands in connection with a divorce, separation or support decree are generally nondeductible personal expenses (¶ 1003). Legal expenses properly attributable to producing or collecting alimony under a divorce decree, separation agreement or

References are to Standard Federal Tax Reports; Tax Research Consultant; and Practical Tax Explanations.

[178] ¶ 11,048, ¶ 23,922; DEPR: 15,258; §5,015, §11,015.30, §11,605.15

[179] ¶ 12,521; BUSEXP: 12,210; §7,801

[180] ¶ 12,523.13, ¶ 12,523.33; BUSEXP: 12,210; §7,801

[181] ¶ 12,520; FILEIND: 12,050, BUSEXP: 12,064; §7,835

[182] ¶ 12,521; INDIV: 45,112; §7,835

[183] ¶ 12,521; BUSEXP: 18,050; §7,105.45, §7,855

support decree, however, may be deductible as a miscellaneous itemized deduction, subject to the two-percent of AGI floor (¶ 1011) (Reg. § 1.262-1(b)(7)).[184]

1094. Limitation on Investment Interest Deduction. A noncorporate taxpayer may deduct on Form 4952 interest paid on investment indebtedness to the extent of the taxpayer's net investment income (Code Sec. 163(d)).[185] Net investment income is the excess of investment income over investment expenses. The disallowed investment interest can be carried over to a succeeding tax year (Rev. Rul. 95-16).

Interest subject to the investment interest limitation is interest on debt properly allocable to property held for investment, which is generally defined as:

(1) property that produces interest, dividends, annuities, or royalties that are not derived in the ordinary course of a trade or business;

(2) property that produces gain or loss not derived in the ordinary course of a trade or business from the sale or exchange of property that either produces item (1) types of income or that is held for investment (but which is not an interest in a passive activity); and

(3) an interest in a trade or business activity that is not a passive activity and in which the taxpayer did not materially participate (Code Sec. 163(d)(5)(A); IRS Pub. 550).

It does not include qualified residence interest (¶ 1047), interest properly allocable to a rental real estate activity in which the taxpayer actively participates, within the meaning of the passive loss rule (¶ 2062), or interest that is taken into account in computing income or loss from a passive activity (¶ 2053).

Net capital gain from the disposition of investment property is not considered investment income. However, individuals may elect to treat all or any portion of such net capital gain as investment income by paying tax on the elected amounts at their ordinary income rates. The taxpayer may elect similar treatment for qualified dividend income (Code Sec. 163(d)(4)(B); Reg. § 1.163(d)-1).[186] Thus, the taxpayer loses the benefit of the otherwise applicable maximum capital gains tax rate with respect to the elected amount. The election must be made on Form 4952 on or before the due date of the return for the tax year in which the net capital gain or the qualified dividend income is recognized. Once made, the election is revocable with the consent of the IRS.

Comment: Absent further legislation, the general exclusion of qualified dividends received by a noncorporate taxpayer from investment income, and the election allowing the taxpayer to include them as investment income, are not available for tax years beginning after December 31, 2012.

A noncorporate limited partner's distributive share of partnership interest expense incurred in the business of the partnership is subject to the limitation on the deduction of investment interest (Rev. Rul. 2008-12; Rev. Rul. 2008-38).

References are to Standard Federal Tax Reports; Tax Research Consultant; and Practical Tax Explanations.

[184] ¶ 12,523.3273, ¶ 13,601, ¶ 13,603.223; BUSEXP: 12,302; § 7,105.45

[185] ¶ 9102; INDIV: 48,450; § 7,414.05

[186] ¶ 9102; INDIV: 48,450; § 7,414.15

Chapter 11
LOSSES

Overview of Losses

1101. Losses, Generally. A taxpayer may generally deduct losses that occur during the tax year and have not been compensated for by insurance or otherwise (Code Sec. 165(a)).[1] Tax treatment of a loss depends upon the nature of the activity in which the loss was incurred. To be deductible, a loss must be evidenced by closed and completed transactions and fixed by identifiable events. Only a bona fide loss is allowable, and substance governs over mere form in the determination (Reg. § 1.165-1(b)).[2]

In computing adjusted gross income (AGI) (¶ 1005), a taxpayer can deduct *allowable* losses that are incurred in a trade or business, resulting from a sale or exchange of property (¶ 1701), are attributable to property held for the production of rents or royalties, or are penalties for premature withdrawals of funds (¶ 1120). An individual's allowable losses, however, are specifically limited to:

(1) losses incurred in a trade or business;

(2) losses incurred in a transaction entered into for profit; or

(3) losses of property that arise from fire, storm, shipwreck or other casualty, or from theft (Code Sec. 165(c)).[3]

Thus, barring a casualty or theft (¶ 1124), an individual's personal losses that are not related to business or profit-making activities are not deductible. Gambling losses can be used only to offset gambling winnings (¶ 1121). Similarly, hobby losses can only be used to offset income from the hobby activity, not any other income (¶ 1195).

The basis (¶ 1601) for determining the amount of the loss deduction is the taxpayer's adjusted basis (¶ 1604) as calculated under Code Sec. 1011 (Code Sec. 165(b)).[4] The deduction for a loss cannot exceed the taxpayer's adjusted basis in the property. In addition, the deduction must be reduced by any salvage value and any amount recovered from insurance or another source (Reg. § 1.165-1(c)).[5]

Capital losses are permitted only to the extent allowed under the rules governing the capital loss limitation, carrybacks and carryovers (Code Sec. 165(f)). See ¶ 1752 for the treatment of capital losses.

For the treatment of a loss on stock in a small business company, see ¶ 1911. For losses on worthless securities, see ¶ 1916. For losses on wash sales of securities, see ¶ 1916. For the disallowance of losses on the sale, exchange, or worthlessness of bonds not issued in registered form, see ¶ 1963. For losses limited by the "at-risk" rules, see ¶ 2045. For losses from passive activities, see ¶ 2053.

References are to Standard Federal Tax Reports; Tax Research Consultant; and Practical Tax Explanations.

[1] ¶ 9802; BUSEXP: 30,000; § 16,901

[2] ¶ 9803; BUSEXP: 30,100; § 16,905.05

[3] ¶ 9802; BUSEXP: 30,150; § 16,901

[4] ¶ 9802; BUSEXP: 30,202; § 16,905.15

[5] ¶ 9803; BUSEXP: 30,202; § 16,905.15

1104. When Is a Loss Sustained. A loss is generally deductible only for the tax year in which it is sustained, i.e., the tax year in which its occurrence is evidenced by closed and completed transactions and it is fixed by identifiable events occurring in the year (Reg. § 1.165-1(b) and (d)(1)).[6] No deduction may be claimed in the year of loss for any portion of a loss for which there remains a reasonable prospect of recovery. A deduction may be taken only in the year in which it becomes reasonably certain that there will be no recovery (Reg. § 1.165-1(d)(2)).[7] A special election exists for determining when to deduct disaster losses (¶ 1141).

No deduction is available for a *partial* loss resulting from a decline in value of property, except as reflected in inventory (Reg. § 1.165-1(b)).[8] An exception to this rule is the charge-off of the worthless part of a business debt (¶ 1145). See ¶ 1148 regarding bad debt reserves.

1107. Loss on Sale of Residence. A loss realized from a sale or exchange of residential property acquired and held as a personal residence is not deductible by an individual. A loss on the sale or exchange of residential property realized at the time it is being rented or otherwise used for income-producing purposes, however, is deductible (Reg. § 1.165-9).[9] If the property is used as the taxpayer's personal residence after having been acquired as income-producing property, then a loss realized on its sale or exchange at the time it is being used as a residence is not deductible. For the basis of residential or converted property, see ¶ 1626.

1112. Capitalization of Demolition Costs and Losses. A taxpayer may not deduct losses sustained in demolition of buildings and their structural components, including certified historic structures. Any amount expended or loss sustained by an owner or lessee on account of the demolition of any structure must be capitalized as part of the basis of the land on which the structure was located (Code Sec. 280B).[10]

A 50-percent deduction is allowed, however, for qualified disaster recovery assistance clean-up costs paid or incurred from the date in 2008 on which severe storms, tornados or flooding occurred in the Midwestern disaster area through December 31, 2010, attributable to the violent weather in Midwestern disaster areas.[11] Consult IRS Pub. 4492-B for more details, including a list of affected states and counties, the relevant dates, and qualified disaster recovery clean-up costs.

1115. Foreclosure Loss or Tax Sale. Where the owner of an equity interest receives less than his or her basis in real estate when it is sold upon foreclosure of a mortgage, his or her investment may represent a deductible loss only if the property foreclosed upon is business or investment property.[12] The nature of the loss—capital loss or ordinary loss—depends in each case upon the nature of the property foreclosed upon and whether or not it is a capital asset (¶ 1741) or required to be treated as a capital asset under Code Sec. 1231 (¶ 1747). The loss occurs when the redemption period expires or in the year the property became worthless. If there is no equity of redemption, however, the loss is fixed by the foreclosure sale and not by the decree of foreclosure that ordered the sale.[13] These principles also apply to a sale for delinquent taxes.[14]

If real property is disposed of by reason of foreclosure or similar proceedings, the amount of depreciation subject to recapture (¶ 1779) is determined as if the taxpayer ceased to hold the property on the date on which such proceedings were begun (Code Sec. 1250(d)(7)).[15]

References are to Standard Federal Tax Reports; Tax Research Consultant; and Practical Tax Explanations.

[6] ¶ 9803; BUSEXP: 30,104; § 16,905.20

[7] ¶ 9803; BUSEXP: 30,110; § 16,905.20

[8] ¶ 9803; BUSEXP: 30,104; § 16,905.05

[9] ¶ 10,102; BUSEXP: 30,158; § 16,930

[10] ¶ 14,900; BUSEXP: 39,150; § 16,915

[11] ¶ 32,483; BUSEXP: 57,304.15; § 10,001

[12] ¶ 9805.155, ¶ 10,103.54; BUSEXP: 30,268; § 18,205.20

[13] ¶ 21,817.45, ¶ 21,817.451; BUSEXP: 30,268; § 18,205.20

[14] ¶ 9808.453; BUSEXP: 30,268; § 18,205.20

[15] ¶ 31,000; DEPR: 18,260.15; § 11,710

1118. Abandonment and Obsolescence Losses. A loss may be allowed for the abandonment of a depreciable asset in the amount of its adjusted basis if the owner manifests an irrevocable intent to abandon (discard) the asset so that it will neither be used again by the taxpayer nor retrieved for sale, exchange, or other disposition (Reg. § 1.167(a)-8(a)).[16] An abandonment loss is an ordinary loss regardless of whether or not the abandoned asset is a capital asset and is reported on Form 4797 (IRS Pub. 544).

A taxpayer cannot deduct the costs of acquiring and developing creative property (screenplays, scripts, story outlines, and similar property for film development or production) as an abandonment loss unless the taxpayer establishes either: (1) an intent to abandon the property and an affirmative act of abandonment, or (2) identifiable events which show a closed and completed transaction establishing the property's worthlessness (Rev. Rul. 2004-58). This is so even though, for financial accounting purposes, a taxpayer changes his or her income statement to recognize loss when it is determined the creative property will not be used. To minimize accounting disputes, the IRS has provided a safe harbor allowing taxpayers to amortize ratably over a 15-year period any creative property costs that have been properly written off by the taxpayer under generally accepted accounting principles for financial reporting purposes (¶ 1229) (Rev. Proc. 2004-36).

If a nondepreciable asset is abandoned following a sudden termination of its usefulness, an obsolescence loss is allowed in an amount equal to its adjusted basis. An obsolescence loss, in the case of nondepreciable property, is deductible in the tax year in which it is sustained, even though the overt act of abandonment or the loss of title to the property may not occur in that year (Reg. § 1.165-2).[17]

1120. Interest Forfeited on Premature Withdrawals. Interest that was previously earned on a time savings account or deposit with a savings institution and that is later forfeited because of premature withdrawals is deductible from gross income in the year when the interest is forfeited (Code Sec. 62(a)(9)).[18]

> **Example:** Tom Smith opened a four-year time savings account in January 2011. He was credited with $400 in interest earned for 2011 and reported this income on his 2011 return. He withdrew the funds in October 2012. This premature withdrawal triggered a penalty provision so that he received only $230 of interest for 2011, plus $195 in interest earned on the account for 2012. Thus, he has incurred a loss of $170 ($400 of interest reported for 2011 less $230 actually received with respect to that year). This $170 loss should be claimed on his 2012 return. He should also report the $195 in interest earned for 2012 on his 2012 return.

The necessary information is provided on Form 1099-INT. The deduction must be claimed on either Form 1040 or 1040A; no deduction is available on Form 1040EZ.

1121. Wagering Loss. Losses from wagering are deductible to the extent of the gains from wagering, regardless of the legality of the activity under local law (Code Sec. 165(d)).[19] A professional gambler may deduct losses directly from gambling income. A nonprofessional gambler must include all gambling income in gross income but can claim the losses only as an itemized deduction on Schedule A of Form 1040 (¶ 1012). Spouses who file a joint return can combine their gambling winnings and losses (Reg. § 1.165-10).[20]

Casualty and Theft Losses

1124. Casualty Loss. An individual may deduct a loss from nonbusiness property only if it arises from fire, storm, shipwreck, or other casualty, or from theft (Code Sec. 165(c)(3)).[21] Each loss is subject to a $100 floor (¶ 1134), and total losses are deductible

References are to Standard Federal Tax Reports; Tax Research Consultant; and Practical Tax Explanations.

[16] ¶ 11,020; BUSEXP: 39,104; § 16,910.05, § 16,910.10

[17] ¶ 9901; BUSEXP: 39,102; § 16,910.15

[18] ¶ 6002; FILEIND: 9,068; § 5,020

[19] ¶ 9802; BUSEXP: 30,256; § 7,110.20, § 16,940.05

[20] ¶ 10,104; BUSEXP: 30,256; § 7,110.20, § 16,940.05

[21] ¶ 9802; INDIV: 54,050; § 7,701

only to the extent that the total loss amount for the year exceeds 10 percent of adjusted gross income (AGI) (¶ 1137). An individual cannot claim a casualty loss deduction for damage to insured property unless a timely insurance claim is filed (Code Sec. 165(h)(5)(E)).[22] For determining the amount of the deduction for a casualty loss, see ¶ 1131. Casualty and theft losses are reported on Form 4684. Theft losses are discussed at ¶ 1125.

A casualty loss is generally deductible only for the tax year in which the loss is sustained (¶ 1104) (Reg. § 1.165-7(a)(1)).[23] When the extent of the damage cannot reasonably be ascertained in the year of occurrence, however, the deduction can be taken in a later year when the extent of the damage is known.

A loss from a casualty arises from an event due to some sudden, unexpected, or unusual cause.[24] Damage to nonbusiness property caused by hurricane,[25] flood,[26] quarry blast,[27] vandalism,[28] sonic boom,[29] earthquake,[30] or earthslide[31] is deductible. Loss to shoreline buildings and structures from battering by waves and winds or flooding of buildings, but not damage from gradual erosion or inundation, is a casualty loss.[32] Damage or loss to property caused by an unusual and unprecedented drought can be treated as a casualty loss.[33] Although cash or property received as compensation for, or to repair or replace, damaged property reduces the amount of the loss, the deduction will not be reduced by excludable gifts received by a disaster victim, even if such gifts are used to rehabilitate the property.[34] If, as the result of insurance or other reimbursement, a taxpayer realizes a gain from a casualty or theft loss, recognition of the gain can be deferred under the involuntary conversion rules by making an election and purchasing qualifying replacement property within the applicable replacement period (¶ 1713).

A casualty includes damage to an automobile resulting from a collision, whether due to the faulty driving of another or the taxpayer, unless caused by the taxpayer's willful act (Reg. § 1.165-7(a)(3)).[35] The IRS takes the position that a casualty loss deduction for termite damage is not permitted because the "suddenness" test is not met, but some courts have allowed the deduction.[36] Storm damage to ornamental trees, as well as to orchards, is deductible as a casualty loss; however, loss of ornamental trees from Dutch elm or other diseases or insects lacks the "sudden force" requirement for classification as a casualty.[37] A loss sustained as a result of negligent workmanship in repairing a leaky roof is a casualty loss.[38]

A casualty loss of nonbusiness property, as well as of business property, can result in a net operating loss (NOL) (¶ 1176). The $100 floor and the 10-percent-of-AGI limitation are applied in the nonbusiness situation in determining an NOL.

Corrosive Drywall Damage. The IRS has issued safe harbor guidance for homeowners who have incurred property losses resulting from the effects of corrosive drywall installed in homes between 2001 and 2009 (Rev. Proc. 2010-36; IRS News Release IR-2010-102). Individuals who pay to repair the damages to their personal residences or household appliances resulting from the corrosive drywall may be able to treat certain unreimbursed amounts paid as a casualty loss in the year of payment.

References are to Standard Federal Tax Reports; Tax Research Consultant; and Practical Tax Explanations.

[22] ¶ 9802; INDIV: 54,168; § 7,701
[23] ¶ 10,004; INDIV: 54,250; § 7,705.30
[24] ¶ 10,005.157; INDIV: 54,058, INDIV: 54,060; § 7,705.05
[25] ¶ 10,005.42; INDIV: 54,084; § 7,705.05
[26] ¶ 10,005.33; INDIV: 54,084; § 7,705.05
[27] ¶ 10,005.56; INDIV: 54,084; § 7,705.05
[28] ¶ 10,005.85; INDIV: 54,084; § 7,705.05
[29] ¶ 10,005.4645; INDIV: 54,084; § 7,705.05
[30] ¶ 10,005.18; INDIV: 54,084; § 7,705.05
[31] ¶ 10,005.63; INDIV: 54,084; § 7,705.05
[32] ¶ 10,005.466; INDIV: 54,058; § 7,705.05
[33] ¶ 10,005.17; INDIV: 54,064; § 7,705.05
[34] ¶ 10,005.117; INDIV: 54,168; § 7,705.25
[35] ¶ 10,004; INDIV: 54,068; § 7,705.05
[36] ¶ 10,005.671; INDIV: 54,062; § 7,705.05
[37] ¶ 10,005.68, ¶ 10,005.80–¶ 10,005.818; INDIV: 54,062; § 7,705.05
[38] ¶ 10,005.904; INDIV: 54,158; § 7,705.05

1125. Theft Loss. A loss from theft is generally deductible for the tax year in which the taxpayer discovers the loss (Code Sec. 165(e); Reg. § 1.165-8(a)).[39] No deduction may be claimed in the year of discovery, however, if a reimbursement claim exists with respect to which there is a reasonable prospect of recovery (Reg. § 1.165-1(d)(3)).[40] As with casualty losses, an individual cannot claim a deduction for theft of insured property unless a timely insurance claim is filed (Code Sec. 165(h)(5)(E)).[41] Theft includes, but is not limited to, larceny, embezzlement and robbery. No deduction is available for lost or mislaid articles.[42] The deduction for theft losses is determined in the same way as for other casualty losses (¶ 1131). Casualty and theft losses are reported on Form 4684. Casualty losses are discussed at ¶ 1124.

Losses from Ponzi-Type Schemes. Investors who incur losses from criminally fraudulent investment arrangements such as "Ponzi" schemes are entitled to claim a theft loss, rather than a capital loss (Rev. Rul. 2009-9). The loss is deductible as a loss on a transaction entered into for profit, and it is not subject to the $100 floor (¶ 1134) or the 10-percent-of-adjusted-gross-income (AGI) limitation (¶ 1137) for personal theft losses, or the limitations on itemized deductions (¶ 1011 and ¶ 1014). The theft loss is deductible in the year it is discovered. If the theft loss deduction creates or increases a net operating loss (NOL) in the year the loss is deducted, the taxpayer may carry back up to three years and forward up to 20 years the portion of the NOL attributable to the theft loss (¶ 1179).

The IRS has also provided an optional safe harbor under which a qualified investor may deduct as a theft loss up to 95 percent of a qualified investment if the investor does not pursue any potential third-party recovery, or 75 percent of a qualified investment if the investor is pursuing or intends to pursue any potential third-party recovery. The deduction is reduced by the amount of any actual recovery and any recovery from insurance or the Securities Investor Protection Corporation (Rev. Proc. 2009-20, as modified by Rev. Proc. 2011-58).

1128. Loss on Bank Deposits. An individual may elect to treat the loss on a nonbusiness account in an insolvent or bankrupt financial institution as a personal casualty loss in the year in which the loss can reasonably be estimated (Code Sec. 165(l)).[43] If elected, the casualty loss deduction is subject to a $100 floor (¶ 1134) and the 10-percent-of-adjusted-gross-income (AGI) limitation (¶ 1137). The election is made on Form 4684.

In lieu of the above election, an individual can elect to treat the loss as an ordinary loss arising from a transaction entered into for profit in the year the loss can be reasonably estimated, provided that no portion of the deposit is federally insured. The aggregate amount of such losses for any tax year with respect to which the ordinary loss election may be made is limited to $20,000 ($10,000 in the case of a married individual filing separately) for each financial institution and must be reduced by the amount of insurance proceeds that the taxpayer can reasonably expect to receive under state law (Code Sec. 165(l)(5)). The loss is deducted on Schedule A of Form 1040 as a miscellaneous itemized deduction subject to the two-percent-of-adjusted-gross-income (AGI) floor (¶ 1011). The name of the financial institution and "Insolvent Financial Institution" should be written on the appropriate line of Schedule A. The calculation of the deducted loss should be included with the return (IRS Pub. 529).

Once made, both elections apply to all losses on deposits in the financial institution during the tax year and are revocable only with IRS consent. Taxpayers making the elections are prohibited from deducting such losses as bad debts (Code Sec. 165(l)(6) and (7)). The elections cannot be made by an individual who is an owner of one percent or more of the value of the institution's stock, an officer of the institution, or a relative of an owner or officer (Code Sec. 165(l)(2)). If neither election is made, then the loss is

References are to Standard Federal Tax Reports; Tax Research Consultant; and Practical Tax Explanations.

[39] ¶ 9802, ¶ 10,100; INDIV: 54,100; § 7,710.05, § 7,710.15

[40] ¶ 9803; BUSEXP: 30,110; § 7,710.25

[41] ¶ 9802; INDIV: 54,168; § 7,701

[42] ¶ 10,101.237; INDIV: 54,102; § 7,710.10

[43] ¶ 9802; INDIV: 54,082; § 7,105.55, § 7,705.10

treated as a nonbusiness bad debt in the year of final determination of the actual loss and is reported as a short-term capital loss on Form 8949 (Schedule D of Form 1040 for tax years before 2011) (¶ 1145 and ¶ 1752).

1131. Amount of Casualty or Theft Loss. The deduction amount of a casualty loss for business and income-producing property or nonbusiness property is the *lesser* of:

(1) the difference between the fair market value (FMV) of the property immediately before the casualty and its FMV immediately after, or

(2) the adjusted basis of the property immediately before the casualty (Reg. § 1.165-7(b)).[44]

If business or income-producing property is totally destroyed, however, and if the property's FMV immediately before the casualty is less than its adjusted basis, then the casualty loss is the adjusted basis of the property. A personal casualty loss is subject to a $100 floor (¶ 1134) and to a 10-percent-of-adjusted-gross-income (AGI) limitation (¶ 1137) in determining the allowable deduction. The $100 floor and AGI limitation do not apply to a business or income-producing property casualty or theft loss.

When money is stolen, the theft loss is the amount stolen. The amount of a theft loss in the case of nonbusiness property other than money is the lesser of the value of the property or its adjusted basis. In the case of stolen business or income-producing property, the theft loss is the adjusted basis of the property stolen (Reg. §§ 1.165-7(b) and 1.165-8(c)).[45]

A casualty loss is reduced by any salvage received. A casualty or theft loss is also reduced by any insurance or other compensation received (Code Sec. 165(a)). An individual cannot claim a personal casualty or theft loss to the extent the loss is covered by insurance unless a timely insurance claim is filed with respect to the loss (Code Sec. 165(h)(5)(E); Reg. § 1.165-1(c)(4)).[46]

When there is damage to different kinds of *business* property, losses must be computed separately for each single, identifiable property damaged or destroyed. This rule does not apply to *nonbusiness* property. Thus, if a tree is blown down in the front yard of a taxpayer's residence, the loss is the difference in the FMV of the taxpayer's whole property before and after damage to the tree (Reg. § 1.165-7(b)).[47]

The taxpayer's basis for property damaged or destroyed by casualty or theft is reduced by the amount allowable as a casualty or theft loss deduction, as well as by the amount of any insurance or other recovery for the loss (Rev. Rul. 71-161).[48]

1134. $100 Floor for Personal Casualty or Theft Loss. The deduction for a personal casualty or theft loss is limited to the amount that the loss from each casualty or theft exceeds $100 (Code Sec. 165(h)(1); Reg. § 1.165-7(b)(4)).[49] The $100 floor applies separately to the loss from each single casualty or theft. If several items of nonbusiness property are damaged or stolen in the course of a single casualty or theft, the $100 floor is applied only once against the sum of the allowable losses established for each item. In the case of married taxpayers filing a joint return, *only one* $100 floor applies to each casualty or theft loss; if married taxpayers file separate returns, each spouse is subject to the $100 limitation for each casualty or theft loss. When property is used for both business and personal purposes, the $100 floor applies only to the net loss attributable to that portion of the property used for personal purposes.

1137. 10-Percent-of-Adjusted-Gross-Income Limitation. Gains and losses from personal casualties and thefts are separately netted without regard to holding periods for the initial determination of whether there was a gain or loss (Code Sec. 165(h)(2)).[50]

References are to Standard Federal Tax Reports; Tax Research Consultant; and Practical Tax Explanations.

[44] ¶ 10,004; BUSEXP: 30,212, INDIV: 54,152; § 7,705.10, § 7,705.15

[45] ¶ 10,004, ¶ 10,100; BUSEXP: 30,212, INDIV: 54,152; § 7,705.10, § 7,710.20

[46] ¶ 9802, ¶ 9803; INDIV: 54,168; § 7,701, § 7,705.10, § 7,705.15

[47] ¶ 10,004; INDIV: 54,152, BUSEXP: 30,212; § 7,705.10, § 7,705.15

[48] ¶ 10,005.16; SALES: 6,360.05; § 16,110.25

[49] ¶ 9802, ¶ 10,004; INDIV: 54,202, INDIV: 54,354; § 7,705.15

[50] ¶ 9802; INDIV: 54,204, INDIV: 54,206; § 7,705.15

The $100 floor (¶ 1134) is applied before this netting occurs. If the recognized gains exceed the recognized losses, all such gains and losses are treated as capital gains and losses; the gains must be recalculated by combining short-term gains with short-term losses and long-term gains with long-term losses. If the recognized losses exceed the recognized gains after netting, all gains and losses will be treated as ordinary gains and losses. Net personal casualty and theft losses are deductible for the tax year to the extent that they exceed the sum of personal casualty or theft gains plus 10 percent of adjusted gross income (AGI).

Form 4684 is used to calculate gain or loss from a casualty or theft of nonbusiness property. Allowable gains are reported on Schedule D of Form 1040. Allowable losses are reported as an itemized deduction on Schedule A of Form 1040.

Example 1: A taxpayer who has AGI of $50,000 (without regard to casualty gains or losses), a $25,000 casualty gain, and a $15,000 casualty loss (after the $100 floor) will report a $10,000 capital gain on Schedule D.

Example 2: A taxpayer who has AGI of $40,000, a $25,000 casualty loss (after the $100 floor), and a $15,000 casualty gain is allowed a $6,000 itemized deduction. The $10,000 loss resulting from netting the casualty gains against the casualty losses is deductible only to the extent that it exceeds 10 percent of AGI ($10,000 – $4,000 = $6,000).

Limitation for Estates and Trusts. The 10-percent-of-AGI limitation on personal casualty and theft losses applies to estates and trusts. AGI is computed in the same manner as it is for individuals, except that estates and trusts are allowed to deduct their administration expenses in arriving at AGI (Code Sec. 165(h)(5)(C)).[51] No deduction for a personal casualty or theft loss may be taken if, at the time of filing a decedent's return, the loss has been claimed for estate tax purposes (¶ 531) (Code Sec. 165(h)(5)(D)).

1141. Disaster Loss. A taxpayer that sustains a loss occurring in a disaster area and attributable to a federally declared disaster can either (1) deduct the loss on the tax return for the year in which the loss occurred, or (2) elect to deduct the loss on the return for the preceding tax year (Code Sec. 165(i)).[52] This special disaster loss treatment is also available for a personal residence rendered unsafe by a disaster in an area determined by the President of the United States to warrant federal government assistance if the taxpayer has been ordered to demolish or relocate the residence by the state or local government (Code Sec. 165(k)).[53]

The election to deduct a 2012 disaster loss in 2011 must be made on or before the due date (without extensions) of the taxpayer's 2012 return (April 15, 2013, for calendar-year individuals; March 15, 2013, for calendar-year corporations). The loss may be claimed by filing an amended 2011 return (¶ 2759). Although Reg. § 1.165-11(e) states that revocation must be made within 90 days after election, the Tax Court has held that revocation of such an election may be made any time before expiration of the time for filing the return for the year of the loss.[54]

The disaster loss deduction is calculated using the same rules as those for any other personal casualty loss. If, however, the taxpayer elects to claim a disaster loss on the return for the year immediately preceding the loss year, the 10-percent-of-adjusted-gross-income (AGI) limitation is determined with respect to the preceding year's AGI.

The IRS is authorized to issue guidance or other rules allowing the use of an appraisal used to secure a federal loan or loan guarantee as a result of federally declared disaster to establish the disaster loss amount (Code Sec. 165(i)(4)).

References are to Standard Federal Tax Reports; Tax Research Consultant; and Practical Tax Explanations.

[51] ¶ 9802; ESTTRST: 12,060.10; § 32,401

[52] ¶ 9802, ¶ 10,201.25; INDIV: 54,302; § 7,715.05

[53] ¶ 9802, INDIV: 54,306; § 7,715.20

[54] ¶ 10,200, ¶ 10,201.13; INDIV: 54,304; § 7,715.10

Bad Debts

1145. Business Bad Debts. Debts from a trade or business, i.e., business bad debts, can be deducted from gross income as an ordinary loss when and to the extent that they become partly or totally worthless (Code Sec. 166).[55] A business debt is a debt: (1) created or acquired in connection with the trade or business of the taxpayer who is claiming the deduction, or (2) the worthlessness of which has been incurred in the taxpayer's trade or business (Reg. § 1.166-5(b)).[56] A business bad debt deduction, however, is not available to (1) shareholders who have advanced money to a corporation as a contribution to capital[57] or (2) creditors who hold a debt that is evidenced by a bond, debenture, note, or other evidence of indebtedness that is issued by a corporation or by a governmental unit, with interest coupons or in registered form (Code Secs. 165(g)(2)(C) and 166(e)).[58] See ¶ 1916 for a discussion of loss from worthless securities.

Dominant Motivation Test. Nonbusiness bad debts are treated as short-term capital losses, subject to a $3,000 per year deduction limitation ($1,500 per year for married individuals filing separate returns) (¶ 1752) and are deductible only when totally worthless (¶ 1169). Since the tax treatment accorded business bad debts and nonbusiness bad debts differs, the taxpayer must show that his or her dominant motivation was business related in order to obtain the more favorable tax treatment (Reg. § 1.166-5(b)).[59]

Guarantors. A noncorporate taxpayer who incurs a loss arising from his or her guaranty of a loan is entitled to deduct the loss only if the guaranty arose out of his or her trade or business, or in a transaction entered into for profit. If the guaranty was connected with a trade or business, the resulting loss is an ordinary loss (business bad debt). If the guaranty was not connected with a true trade or business but was profit inspired, the resulting loss is a short-term capital loss (nonbusiness bad debt). No deduction is available if the guaranty payment does not fall within the above categories, if there is no legal obligation on the taxpayer to make the guaranty payment, or if the guaranty was entered into after the debt became worthless (Reg. § 1.166-9).[60]

Employee Loans. An employee's rendering of services for pay is a trade or business for purposes of the bad debt provisions. Therefore, a loan to an employer to protect a job can give rise to a business bad debt deduction if the employer defaults. If a loan by a shareholder-employee is intended to protect the shareholder's job rather than to protect the shareholder's investment in the company, then the failure to repay the loan results in a business bad debt deduction. The larger the shareholder's investment, the smaller his or her salary, and the larger his or her other sources of income, the more likely that a dominant nonbusiness motive existed for making the loan.[61]

1148. Accounting for Bad Debt Deduction. Bad debts are generally deductible in the tax year in which they become worthless (Code Sec. 166(a); Reg. § 1.166-3).[62] For both a business or nonbusiness debt, the deduction is available when the debt becomes wholly worthless. A deduction is allowed for a business debt that becomes partially worthless, but only to the extent the debt is charged off during the tax year. A worthless debt arising from unpaid wages, rent, interest, or a similar item is not deductible unless the income that such item represents has been reported for income tax purposes by a taxpayer (Reg. §§ 1.166-1(e) and 1.166-6(a)(2)).[63] A cash-basis taxpayer can deduct a bad debt only if an actual cash loss has been sustained or if the amount deducted was included in income. Nearly all accrual-basis taxpayers must use the specific charge-off method for receivables and cannot use the reserve method of accounting. Small banks

References are to Standard Federal Tax Reports; Tax Research Consultant; and Practical Tax Explanations.

[55] ¶ 10,602; BUSEXP: 48,000; § 17,120.05

[56] ¶ 10,691; BUSEXP: 48,156; § 17,120.05

[57] ¶ 10,650.7301; BUSEXP: 48,108; § 17,120.10

[58] ¶ 9802, ¶ 10,602; BUSEXP: 30,262, BUSEXP: 48,154; § 16,555, § 16,935

[59] ¶ 10,691; BUSEXP: 48,156; § 17,120

[60] ¶ 10,753; BUSEXP: 48,400, BUSEXP: 48,402; § 17,125

[61] ¶ 10,700.241; BUSEXP: 48,160.40; § 17,120.10

[62] ¶ 10,602, ¶ 10,605; BUSEXP: 48,250; § 17,110.05

[63] ¶ 10,603, ¶ 10,701; BUSEXP: 48,062, BUSEXP: 48,204; § 17,115

and thrift institutions, however, can use the experience method of accounting to deduct bad debts (Code Secs. 585 and 593(f), (g)).[64]

1151. Secured Bad Debt. When secured or mortgaged property is sold either to the secured party or to a third party for less than the amount of the debt, the creditor is entitled to a bad debt deduction in an amount equal to the difference between the sale price and the amount of the debt, to the extent that the creditor can show that such difference is wholly or partially uncollectible. No bad debt deduction is allowed if a mortgage is foreclosed and the creditor buys the mortgaged property at a price equal to the unpaid indebtedness. However, loss or gain is realized on the transaction and is measured by the difference between the amount of the obligations of the debtor that are applied to the purchase or bid price of the property and the fair market value of the property, to the extent that the obligations are capital or represent items the income from which has been returned by the creditor (Reg. § 1.166-6).[65] See ¶ 1838 and ¶ 1841 for a discussion on repossession of property sold on the installment plan.

1166. Debts Owed by Political Parties. No deduction is generally allowable for a worthless debt owed by a political party. However, banks and accrual-basis taxpayers who are in the business of providing goods and services (e.g., polling, media, or organizational services) to political campaigns and candidates may be allowed to deduct such bad debts (Code Sec. 271).[66]

1169. Nonbusiness Bad Debts. If a nonbusiness bad debt held by a taxpayer other than a corporation becomes *entirely* worthless during the tax year, then the loss may be deducted as a short-term capital loss regardless of how old the debt (Code Sec. 166(d); Reg. § 1.166-5).[67] Unlike business bad debts (¶ 1145), however, no deduction is permitted unless and until the debt becomes totally worthless. A nonbusiness bad debt is any debt other than one created or acquired in connection with the taxpayer's trade or business, or one that, when worthless, creates a loss that is incurred in the taxpayer's trade or business. For limitations on deduction of a capital loss, see ¶ 1752. For worthlessness of a debt evidenced by a bond or other security of a corporation or a government, see ¶ 1916.

A nonbusiness bad debt deduction is allowable for unrecoverable deposits made for the construction of a residence when the construction company becomes insolvent and fails to perform under the contract (Rev. Rul. 69-457).[68]

Net Operating Losses

1173. Application of Net Operating Loss. A net operating loss (NOL) from a trade or business may be claimed as a deduction in the current tax year equal to the aggregate amount of NOL carryovers and carrybacks to the year (¶ 1179) (Code Sec. 172(a); Reg. § 1.172-1).[69] The NOL deduction, however, may not exceed the amount of taxable income for the year of the deduction. An NOL arises in any tax year when the taxpayer's deductible expenses for the year exceed its gross income, subject to certain adjustments (¶ 1176). The NOL deduction is available to most taxpayers, including corporations, individuals, estates and trusts, and common trust fund participants. An NOL deduction may not be claimed by a partnership or S corporation, but partners and S corporation shareholders may use their distributive shares to calculate their individual NOLs (¶ 319 and ¶ 417). Other entities which may not claim the NOL deduction include regulated investment companies and life insurance companies (Code Secs. 805(b)(4) and 852(b)(2)(B)).[70]

References are to Standard Federal Tax Reports; Tax Research Consultant; and Practical Tax Explanations.

[64] ¶ 23,650, ¶ 23,710; RIC: 12,202

[65] ¶ 10,701; BUSEXP: 48,274, SALES: 6,064.10; § 17,110.10, § 17,115

[66] ¶ 14,306; BUSEXP: 48,068

[67] ¶ 10,602, ¶ 10,691; BUSEXP: 48,152, BUSEXP: 48,250; § 17,120.05

[68] ¶ 10,700.38; BUSEXP: 48,064; § 17,120.05

[69] ¶ 12,002, ¶ 12,003; BUSEXP: 45,000, BUSEXP: 45,050; § 17,001

[70] ¶ 25,770, ¶ 26,420; BUSEXP: 45,050

Forms. Individuals, estates, and trusts compute the NOL for the loss year and the carrybacks and carryforwards on Form 1045 (Code Sec. 6411; Reg. § 1.6411-1).[71] Form 1045 is filed to claim a quick refund for the excess taxes paid in the carryback years that are attributable to the NOL. Form 1045, however, may be used only if filed within one year after the close of the NOL year (but not before Form 1040 or Form 1041 for the NOL year is filed). Form 1045 is processed within the later of 90 days after being filed or 90 days after the last day of the month that includes the due date (including extensions) for filing Form 1040 or Form 1041 for the loss year.

As an alternative to Form 1045, an individual may file an amended return on Form 1040X for each carryback year to claim a refund. Form 1040X must generally be filed within three years after the due date of the return for the NOL year. Estates and trusts file an amended Form 1041 as issued for the carryback year and check the "amended return" box. If an amended return is filed the taxpayer must still attach the NOL computations using the Form 1045 computation schedules. The IRS generally processes an amended return within six months after filing.

Corporations may file for a quick refund using Form 1139, which also needs to be filed within one year after the close of the NOL year (but not before the return for the NOL year is filed). A corporation may file an amended return on Form 1120X in place of Form 1139 for each carryback year, generally within three years after the due date of the return for the NOL year.

A corporation that expects an NOL in the current tax year may file Form 1138 to extend the time for payment of the tax for the immediately preceding tax year (Code Sec. 6164; Reg. § 1.6164-1).[72] The extension applies only to payments of tax that are required to be paid after Form 1138 is filed. The extension expires at the end of the month in which the return for the tax year of the expected NOL is required to be filed (including extensions). However, if the corporation files Form 1139 before the extension period ends, the time for payments is further extended until the date that the IRS mails notice that it has allowed or disallowed the application (Reg. § 1.6164-5).[73]

Forms 1045 and 1139 may also be used to claim a quick refund of taxes from the carryback of a net *capital* loss (corporations only), an unused general business credit, a net Code Sec. 1256 contracts loss (individuals only), or a claim of right adjustment under Code Sec. 1341(b)(1).

For additional information on Forms 1045 and 1139, see ¶ 2773.

1176. Net Operating Loss Defined. A net operating loss (NOL) is the excess of allowable deductions over gross income, computed under the law in effect for the loss year, with the required adjustments (Code Sec. 172(c)).[74]

Noncorporate Taxpayers. The following adjustments are made in computing the NOL of a noncorporate taxpayer (Code Sec. 172(d); Reg. § 1.172-3):[75]

(1) No deduction for NOL carryovers or carrybacks from other years is allowed.

(2) An individual may not take any personal or dependency exemptions into account, and an estate or a trust cannot take the deduction available to it in lieu of the deduction for personal exemptions.

(3) Nonbusiness capital losses are deductible only to the extent of nonbusiness capital gains. Business capital losses are deductible only to the extent of the sum of (a) business capital gains and (b) any nonbusiness capital gains that remain after deducting nonbusiness capital losses and other nonbusiness deductions (item (4), below). The exclusion for gain from qualified small business stock under Code Sec. 1202 (¶ 1905) is not allowed.

References are to Standard Federal Tax Reports; Tax Research Consultant; and Practical Tax Explanations.

[71] ¶ 38,720, ¶ 38,722; BUSEXP: 45,256.05; § 17,025

[72] ¶ 37,240, ¶ 37,241; BUSEXP: 45,260; § 39,315.10

[73] ¶ 37,247; BUSEXP: 45,260.10; § 39,315.25

[74] ¶ 12,002; BUSEXP: 45,100; § 17,005.05

[75] ¶ 12,002, ¶ 12,005; BUSEXP: 45,106; § 17,005.10

(4) Nonbusiness deductions are allowed only to the extent of nonbusiness income (including net nonbusiness capital gains). Further, any excess may not be allowed against business capital gains (and thereby increase the NOL). Generally, nonbusiness income includes income from passive investments, such as interest, dividends, annuities, endowment income, etc. Salary is considered business income. A loss on a rental property is considered a business loss. The nonbusiness deduction for a taxpayer who itemizes is the total of his or her itemized deductions other than the personal or business-related casualty loss deduction (¶ 1124), which is treated as attributable to the taxpayer's trade or business for NOL purposes. For one who does not itemize, the standard deduction is a nonbusiness deduction. Deductible contributions to a retirement plan by a self-employed individual on his or her own behalf are considered nonbusiness deductions.

(5) The domestic production activities deduction (i.e., the manufacturer's deduction) (¶ 980A) is not allowed.

Corporations. The following adjustments are made in computing the NOL of a corporation (Code Sec. 172(d); Reg. § 1.172-2):[76]

(1) No deduction for NOL carryovers or carrybacks from other years is allowed.

(2) A corporation is entitled to deductions for dividends received from a domestic corporation, those received on certain preferred stock of public utilities, those received from certain foreign corporations, and those paid on certain preferred stock of public utilities, without regard to the limitations (based on taxable income) imposed on such deductions in computing taxable income (¶ 237 and ¶ 241).

(3) The domestic production activities deduction (i.e., the manufacturer's deduction) (¶ 980A) is not allowed.

1179. Carryover and Carryback of Net Operating Losses. If the taxpayer has a net operating loss (NOL) for the current tax year (¶ 1176), then the loss may be carried back to prior tax years or carried forward to future years as a deduction against taxable income (¶ 1173). If a NOL carryover is not fully absorbed in a carryover year, then the following adjustments must be made to taxable income in the carryback or carryover year to determine the portion of the current year NOL still available to carry to another tax year (Code Sec. 172(b)(2); Reg. § 1.172-5).[77]

(1) The NOL deduction for the intervening year is computed by taking into account only carryback and carryovers from tax years *preceding* the loss year.

(2) For taxpayers other than corporations, capital losses are deductible only to the extent of capital gains.

(3) Personal and dependency exemptions are not allowed.

(4) The domestic production activities deduction (i.e., the manufacturer's deduction) (¶ 980A) is not allowed.

NOLs can generally be carried back to the two years preceding the loss year and then forward up to 20 years following the loss year. Further, for NOLs that arose in tax years beginning before August 6, 1997, taxpayers could have carried back an NOL to the three years preceding the loss year and then forward to 15 years following the loss year. No deduction is allowed in the year the loss is incurred (Code Sec. 172(b); Reg. § 1.172-4).[78]

Election to Forgo Carryback. A taxpayer may elect to waive the entire carryback period (Code Sec. 172(b)(3)).[79] If this election is made, the loss may be carried forward

References are to Standard Federal Tax Reports; Tax Research Consultant; and Practical Tax Explanations.

[76] ¶ 12,002, ¶ 12,004; BUSEXP: 45,104; § 17,005.15

[77] ¶ 12,002, ¶ 12,007; BUSEXP: 45,150, BUSEXP: 45,202; § 17,010.05, § 17,015.15

[78] ¶ 12,002, ¶ 12,006; BUSEXP: 45,150; § 17,010.05, § 17,010.20

[79] ¶ 12,002; BUSEXP: 45,152; § 17,010.15

only. The election must be made by the return due date (including extensions) for the tax year of the NOL. The election may also be made on an amended return filed within six months of the due date of an original timely return (excluding extensions). Refer to the instructions for Form 1139 or Form 1045 for specific statement requirements. Once made, the election is irrevocable.

Casualties and Disasters. A three-year carryback period is available for: (1) a NOL of an individual arising from a fire, storm, shipwreck, other casualty, or theft, and (2) a NOL of a small business or taxpayer engaged in farming if the loss is attributable to a federally declared disaster (Code Sec. 172(b)(1)(F)). A small business is one with an average annual gross receipts of $5 million or less. An eligible loss does not include a farming loss or qualified disaster loss (see *Farming Loss* and *Federally Declared Disasters,* following).

2008 and 2009 NOLs. A taxpayer can elect a three-, four- or five-year carryback period for a NOL for any tax year that ended after December 31, 2007, and began before January 1, 2010 (Code Sec. 172(b)(1)(H)).[80] The NOL amount that can be carried back to the fifth preceding tax year is limited to 50 percent of the taxpayer's taxable income for that preceding tax year. Most taxpayers can make the election for only one tax year (2008 *or* 2009); an eligible small business (one that met a $15 million or less gross receipts test for the year of the loss) may be able to elect an extended carryback period for 2008 *and* 2009 NOLs. If a taxpayer has elected this extended carryback period for 2008 or 2009 NOLs, then the three-year carryback period for casualty or theft losses of individuals, and NOLs of farmers or small businesses from federally declared disasters does not apply. A similar carryback election is allowed for operations losses of life insurance companies (¶ 2377). The IRS has issued detailed guidance on the election procedures (Notice 2010-58; Rev. Procs. 2009-26 and 2009-52).

2008 Midwestern Disaster Area Losses. A five-year NOL carryback period is available for certain "qualified Disaster Recovery Assistance losses" due to the severe storms, tornados and flooding in the summer of 2008 in the Midwestern disaster area (Code Sec. 1400N(k); Division C, Act Sec. 702(a)(1)(A) and (d)(6) of the Emergency Economic Stabilization Act of 2008 (P.L. 110-343)).[81] See IRS Pub. 4492-B for more details, including a list of affected states and counties.

Federally Declared Disasters. A five-year NOL carryback period applies for qualified disaster losses (Code Sec. 172(b)(1)(J) and (j)).[82] A "qualified disaster loss" is the *lesser* of: (1) the sum of (a) losses occurring in a disaster area and attributable to a federally declared disaster occurring after 2007 and before 2010, plus (b) the qualified disaster expenses deduction (¶ 977E) allowable for the tax year (or which would be allowable if not otherwise treated as an expense), or (2) the NOL for the tax year. Remaining NOLs, if any, are subject to the general two-year carryback period. The qualified disaster loss is treated as a separate NOL to be taken into account *after* the remaining portion of the NOL for the tax year and may not include loss regarding property used in connection with golf courses, country clubs, massage parlors, hot tub or suntan facilities, liquor stores, or gambling or animal racing property. A taxpayer can elect to waive the five-year carryback period.

Farming Loss. A farming loss may be carried back for five years (Code Sec. 172(b)(1)(G) and (i)). A farming loss is the *smaller* of (1) the amount that would be the NOL for the tax year if only income and deductions attributable to farming businesses (¶ 999) were taken into account, or (2) the NOL for the tax year. A taxpayer may elect to waive the five-year carryback for a farming loss. In this case, the two-year carryback period generally applies (Code Sec. 172(i)(3)).[83] For ordering purposes, the farming loss is treated as a separate NOL to be taken into account *after* the remaining portion of the

References are to Standard Federal Tax Reports; Tax Research Consultant; and Practical Tax Explanations.

[80] ¶ 12,002; BUSEXP: 45,154.55, BUSEXP: 45,154.60; § 17,010.17

[81] ¶ 32,483, ¶ 32,487.056; BUSEXP: 57,304.45; § 10,001, § 17,010.05

[82] ¶ 12,002; BUSEXP: 45,154.05; § 17,010.20

[83] ¶ 12,002; BUSEXP: 45,154.40; § 36,210

11 LOSSES

NOL for the tax year (Code Sec. 172(i)(2)). A farming loss does not include a qualified disaster loss (see *Federally Declared Disasters,* previously).

Short Tax Years. If the IRS approves a request for a change in accounting period when the short period required to effect the change is a tax year in which the taxpayer has a NOL, the taxpayer can carry back the short-period NOL only if it is either (1) $50,000 or less, or (2) less than the full 12-month period NOL beginning with the first day of the short period as determined when the 12-month period has expired (Rev. Proc. 2003-34, modifying Rev. Procs. 2002-37 and 2002-39; Rev. Proc. 2006-45).[84]

Specified Liability Losses. A 10-year carryback period applies to specified liability losses (Code Sec. 172(b)(1)(C) and (f); Notice 2005-20).[85] A specified liability loss is the portion of a NOL that (1) is attributable to product liability or (2) arises out of satisfaction of a liability under federal or state law requiring land reclamation, nuclear power plant decommissioning, drilling platform dismantling, environmental remediation, or a payment under any workers' compensation act. For ordering purposes, the specified liability loss is treated as a separate NOL to be taken into account *after* the remaining portion of the NOL for the tax year.

Real Estate Investment Trusts (REITs). A NOL from a REIT year—a tax year in which an entity operated as a real estate investment trust (¶ 2326)—cannot be carried back to any preceding tax year. A NOL from a non-REIT year cannot be carried back to a REIT year. A REIT NOL can be carried forward 20 years (Code Sec. 172(b)(1)(B); Reg. § 1.172-10).[86]

Corporate Equity Reduction Transactions (CERTs). A C corporation may not carry back a portion of its NOL if $1 million or more of interest expense is incurred in a "major stock acquisition" of another corporation or in an "excess distribution" by the corporation (Code Sec. 172(b)(1)(E) and (h)).[87] The amount subject to the limitation is the lesser of: (1) the corporation's deductible interest expense allocable to the CERT or (2) the amount by which the corporation's interest expense for the current tax year exceeds the average interest expense for the three tax years preceding the tax year in which the CERT occurs.

Electric Utilities. For any tax year ending after 2005 and before 2009, an electric utility could elect a five-year carryback period for a portion of NOLs that arose in tax years 2003, 2004 and 2005. The carried-back NOL amount was limited to 20 percent of the sum of the taxpayer's electric transmission property capital expenditures and pollution control facility capital expenditures for the tax year preceding the tax year for which the election was made. Only one election could be made with respect to any NOL for a tax year, and an election could not be made for more than one tax year beginning in any calendar year (Code Sec. 172(b)(1)(I)).[88]

1185. NOL Carryovers Between Predecessors and Successors. A net operating loss (NOL) may generally be carried back or carried forward only by the taxpayer who sustained the loss. A beneficiary of an estate or trust, however, is entitled to any carryover amount remaining unused after the last tax year of the estate or trust (¶ 535) (Code Secs. 642(h), 1398(g) and (j); Reg. § 1.642(h)-1).[89] A successor corporation is allowed to carry over the NOL and certain other items of its predecessor under specified conditions (¶ 2277). A divorced taxpayer who suffered an NOL in a year when he or she was single can carry it back to his or her portion of income in previous years when a joint return was filed (Rev. Rul. 60-216, amplified by Rev. Rul. 65-140).[90]

1188. Recomputation After Carryback. In a year in which a net operating loss (NOL) is carried back, any income, deductions, or credits that are based on or limited to a percentage of adjusted gross income (AGI) must be recomputed based on AGI after

References are to Standard Federal Tax Reports; Tax Research Consultant; and Practical Tax Explanations.

[84] ¶ 12,014.30; BUSEXP: 45,150, NOL: 12,202; § 38,130.20

[85] ¶ 12,002; BUSEXP: 45,154; § 17,010.25

[86] ¶ 12,002, ¶ 12,012; BUSEXP: 45,154

[87] ¶ 12,002; NOL: 15,202

[88] ¶ 12,002; BUSEXP: 45,154.50

[89] ¶ 24,280, ¶ 24,301, ¶ 32,410; BUSEXP: 30,060, BUSEXP: 45,054; § 32,415

[90] ¶ 12,014.443; BUSEXP: 45,208.20; § 17,020

applying the NOL deduction for the carryback year. The charitable contribution deduction, however, is not recomputed. Taxable income is recomputed taking into account the NOL and the preceding adjustments. Income tax, alternative minimum tax, and any credits that are based on or limited to the amount of tax are then recomputed (Reg. § 1.172-5).[91]

Hobby Losses

1195. Hobby Expenses and Losses. Losses incurred by individuals, S corporations, partnerships, and estates and trusts that are attributable to an activity not engaged in for profit—so-called "hobby losses"—are generally deductible only to the extent of income produced by the activity (Code Sec. 183; Reg. § 1.183-1).[92] Some expenses that are deductible whether or not they are incurred in connection with a hobby (e.g., taxes, interest, and casualty losses) are deductible even if they exceed hobby income. These expenses, however, reduce the amount of hobby income against which hobby expenses can be offset (Code Sec. 183(b)). The hobby expenses then offset the reduced income, in the following order: (1) operating expenses other than amounts resulting in a basis adjustment and (2) depreciation and other basis adjustment items (Reg. § 1.183-1). The itemized deduction for hobby expenses to the extent of income derived from the activity is subject to the two-percent-of-adjusted-gross-income floor on miscellaneous itemized deductions (¶ 1011).

An activity is presumed not to be a hobby if profits result in any three of five consecutive tax years ending with the tax year in question, unless the IRS proves otherwise (Code Sec. 183(d)). An activity involving the breeding, training, showing, or racing of horses is presumed not to be a hobby if profits result in two out of seven consecutive years. A special election on Form 5213 permits suspension of the presumption until after the fourth (or sixth, for horse breeding, training, showing or racing) after which the taxpayer first engages in the activity. A taxpayer need not waive the statute of limitations for unrelated items on the return in order to take advantage of the presumption (Code Sec. 183(e)).

References are to Standard Federal Tax Reports; Tax Research Consultant; and Practical Tax Explanations.

[91] ¶ 12,007; BUSEXP: 45,202; § 17,015.10, § 17,015.15

[92] ¶ 12,170, ¶ 12,171; BUSEXP:15,000; § 17,201

Chapter 12

DEPRECIATION, AMORTIZATION AND DEPLETION

Allowance for Depreciation

1201. Property Subject to Depreciation. Taxpayers may deduct a reasonable allowance for the exhaustion, wear and tear of property used in a trade or business, or of property held for the production of income (Reg. § 1.167(a)-1).[1] Depreciation is not allowable for property used solely for personal purposes, such as a residence.

Depreciation begins in the tax year that an asset is placed in service and ends in the tax year that it is retired from service or is fully depreciated (Reg. § 1.167(a)-10).[2] Generally, an asset is considered placed in service when it is in a condition or state of readiness and availability for a specifically assigned function.

Methods. The Modified Accelerated Cost Recovery System (MACRS) (¶ 1236) applies to tangible property generally placed in service after 1986 and the Accelerated Cost Recovery System (ACRS) applies to property placed in service after 1980 and before 1987 (¶ 1252). Under MACRS and ACRS, the cost or other basis of an asset is generally recovered over a specific recovery period. Post-1980 depreciation on tangible assets first placed in service before 1981 is computed under the method elected for the years they were placed in service. For assets placed in service after 1970 and before 1981, the taxpayer had a choice of the Asset Depreciation Range (ADR) System[3] (¶ 1282) or the general depreciation rules (¶ 1216). For tangible assets first placed in service before 1971, the taxpayer could have elected the Class Life System (CLS)[4] for

References are to Standard Federal Tax Reports; Tax Research Consultant; and Practical Tax Explanations.

[1] ¶ 11,003; DEPR: 15,050; § 11,005

[2] ¶ 11,279.0595; DEPR: 15,652, DEPR: 3,054.104; § 11,020

[3] ¶ 11,029.021; DEPR: 15,800; § 15,301

[4] ¶ 11,031.021; DEPR: 15,750; § 11,101

pre-1971 assets or the general depreciation rules. In no event may an asset that is not subject to MACRS or ACRS be depreciated below a reasonable salvage value (Reg. § 1.167(a)-1(a)).[5]

Depreciation based on a useful life is calculated over the estimated useful life of the asset while actually used by the taxpayer and not over the longer period of the asset's physical life (Reg. § 1.167(a)-1(b)).[6] For rules governing the depreciation of self-constructed assets, see the uniform capitalization rules at ¶ 990–¶ 999.

Converted Residence. When an individual vacates a principal residence and offers it for sale, it may be depreciable for the period before the sale if the individual is seeking a profit based on the post-conversion appreciation in value.[7] MACRS must be used to depreciate a residence converted to business use after 1986. For computation of depreciation when a home is used partly for business or rental purposes, see ¶ 961 and following. For depreciable basis, see ¶ 1203.

Estates and Trusts. For depreciation by an estate or trust, see ¶ 530.

Inventory. Depreciation is allowed for tangible property, but not for inventories, stock in trade, land apart from its improvements, or a depletable natural resource (Reg. § 1.167(a)-2).[8]

Farmers. Farm buildings and other physical farm property (except land) are depreciable. Livestock acquired for work, breeding, or dairy purposes may be depreciated unless included in inventory (Reg. § 1.167(a)-6(b)).[9]

Intangibles. An intangible business asset that is not amortizable over 15 years under Code Sec. 197 (¶ 1288) may be amortized under Code Sec. 167, generally using the straight-line method, provided that it has an ascertainable value and useful life that can be measured with reasonable accuracy.[10] Certain intangibles with no ascertainable useful life that are created by a taxpayer may be amortized over 15 years (Reg. § 1.167(a)-3(b)). See ¶ 1288A.

Software. Computer software that is not an amortizable Code Sec. 197 intangible (¶ 1288) may be depreciated using the straight-line method over 36 months beginning on the first day of the month the software is placed in service (Code Sec. 167(f)(1); Reg. § 1.167(a)-14(b)).[11] See ¶ 980. However, the cost of software developed for internal use or sale may be currently deducted as a research and development expense, amortized using the straight-line method over 5 years beginning on the date of completion of development, or amortized over 36 months under Code Sec. 167(f) from the date the software is placed in service (Rev. Proc. 2000-50). Off-the-shelf computer software may be expensed under Code Sec. 179 if placed in service in a tax year beginning before 2013 (Code Sec. 179(d)(1)). See ¶ 1208. Software included as part of the purchase price of a computer that has no separately stated cost is depreciated as part of the cost of the computer over a 5-year recovery period (Reg. § 1.167(a)-14(b); Rev. Proc. 2000-50).

Web Site Development Costs. The IRS has not issued formal guidance on the treatment of web site development costs. However, informal internal IRS guidance suggests that one appropriate approach is to treat these costs like an item of software and depreciate them over three years. It is clear, however, that taxpayers who pay large amounts to develop sophisticated sites have been allocating their costs to items such as software development (currently deductible like research and development costs under Code Sec. 174) and currently deductible advertising expense.[12]

Residential Mortgage Servicing Rights. Depreciable residential mortgage servicing rights that are not Code Sec. 197 intangibles may be depreciated under the straight-line method over 108 months (Code Sec. 167(f)(3)).[13]

References are to Standard Federal Tax Reports; Tax Research Consultant; and Practical Tax Explanations.

[5] ¶ 11,003, ¶ 11,009.04; DEPR: 15,050; § 11,101

[6] ¶ 11,003, ¶ 11,005.021; DEPR: 15,700; § 11,110

[7] ¶ 11,007.512; DEPR: 15,154; § 11,010.05

[8] ¶ 11,006; DEPR: 15,150; § 11,005

[9] ¶ 11,015; DEPR: 15,158, FARM: 9,078; § 36,320

[10] ¶ 11,009.015; DEPR: 15,162; § 11,005

[11] ¶ 11,002, ¶ 11,009.027; DEPR: 15,162.85; § 11,535

[12] ¶ 11,009.027, ¶ 13,709; BUSEXP: 18,852; § 11,005

[13] ¶ 11,002, ¶ 11,009.03; DEPR: 15,162.90; § 11,540

Term Interests. The purchaser of a term interest in property held for business or investment is generally entitled to recover its cost over its expected life. However, no depreciation or amortization deduction is allowed for certain term interests in property for any period during which the remainder interest is held directly (or indirectly) by a related person (Code Sec. 167(e)).[14]

Form. Form 4562 is generally used to claim the depreciation or amortization deduction and is attached to the taxpayer's tax return. However, individuals and other noncorporate taxpayers (including S corporations) need not complete Form 4562 if their only depreciation (or amortization) deduction is for property (other than listed property (¶ 1211)) placed in service before the current tax year. Form 4562 must be filed if a section 179 deduction (including a carryover) is claimed in the current tax year.

Basis for Depreciation

1203. Cost or Other Basis Recoverable Through Depreciation Allowance. Generally, the cost of a depreciable asset reduced by any amount claimed as an expense deduction under Code Sec. 179 or as first-year bonus depreciation may be recovered through depreciation. Other downward adjustments to cost to prevent a duplication of benefits received from credits and deductions claimed with respect to the property in the tax year of purchase may also be necessary. For example, for the effect of the investment credit on depreciable basis, see ¶ 1365A. When property held for personal use, such as a residence, is converted to business or income-producing use, the basis for depreciation is the lesser of the property's fair market value or adjusted basis on the date of conversion (Reg. § 1.167(g)-1; Reg. § 1.168(i)-4(b)).[15] In the case of a residence converted to business use after 1986, MACRS must be used.

When a building and land have been acquired for a lump sum, only the building is depreciated. The basis for depreciation cannot exceed the same proportion of the lump sum as the value of the building bore to the value of the entire property at the time of acquisition (Reg. § 1.167(a)-5).

If property is subject to both depreciation and amortization, depreciation is allowable only for the portion that is not subject to the allowance for amortization and may be taken concurrently with amortization (Reg. § 1.167(a)-5).[16]

Section 179 Expense Election

1208. Election to Expense Certain Depreciable Business Assets. An expense deduction is provided for taxpayers (other than estates, trusts or certain noncorporate lessors) who elect to treat the cost of qualifying property, called section 179 property, as an expense rather than a capital expenditure (Code Sec. 179).[17] The election, which is made on Form 4562, is generally attached to the taxpayer's original return (including a late-filed original return). However, for tax years beginning in 2003 through 2012, a taxpayer may make, revoke, or change an election without IRS consent on an amended return filed during the period prescribed for filing an amended return (i.e., generally, three years from the filing of the original return) (Code Sec. 179(c)(2); Reg. § 1.179-5).[18]

> **CCH Comment:** Absent further legislation, for tax years beginning after 2012, an election not made on an original return must be made on an amended return filed by the due date of the original return (including extensions) unless permission is obtained. Permission to revoke or change an election will also be also required.

Dollar Limitation. The maximum Code Sec. 179 deduction is $250,000 for tax years beginning in 2008 and 2009. For tax years beginning in 2010 and 2011, the limitation is increased to $500,000. For tax years beginning in 2012 the maximum deduction is $139,000 (Code Sec. 179(b)(1); Rev. Proc. 2011-52).

References are to Standard Federal Tax Reports; Tax Research Consultant; and Practical Tax Explanations.

[14] ¶ 11,002, ¶ 11,049.035; DEPR: 15,262; § 11,005

[15] ¶ 11,046, ¶ 11,007.045; DEPR: 15,154; § 16,101

[16] ¶ 11,012, ¶ 11,014.021; SALES: 6,202; § 11,001

[17] ¶ 12,120, ¶ 12,126; DEPR: 12,000; § 9,801

[18] ¶ 12,120, ¶ 12,126.073; DEPR: 12,050, DEPR: 12,150; § 9,830

CCH Comment: Absent further legislation, for tax years beginning in 2013 and thereafter, the section 179 dollar limitation is $25,000 (Code Sec. 179(b)(1)).

For tax years beginning in 2010 and 2011, up to $250,000 of the $500,000 annual dollar limit may be used to expense qualified real property, which generally consists of qualified leasehold improvements, qualified restaurant property, and qualified retail improvement property (Code Sec. 179(f)). See "*Qualified Real Property,*" below.

See ¶ 1214 for a $25,000 Code Sec. 179 expensing limitation on sport utility vehicles, short-bed trucks, and vans that are exempt from the luxury car depreciation caps.

De minimis expensing policy rule. Taxpayers with an applicable financial statement may claim a current deduction for amounts paid or incurred to acquire or produce relatively low-cost units of property, including materials and supplies, if specific requirements are met. The aggregate cost which may be expensed annually is subject to a ceiling equal to the greater of .1 (one-tenth) percent of gross receipts or 2 percent of total depreciation and amortization reported on the financial statement (Temporary Reg. § 1.263(a)-2T(g)). See ¶ 903.

Investment Limitation. The maximum Code Sec. 179 dollar limitation is reduced dollar for dollar by the cost of qualified property placed in service during the tax over an investment limitation. The investment limitation is $800,000 for tax years beginning in 2008 and 2009, and $2,000,000 for tax years beginning in 2010 and 2011. For tax years beginning in 2012 the investment limitation is $560,000 per year (Rev. Proc. 2011-52).

CCH Comment: Absent further legislation, for tax years beginning in 2013 and thereafter the investment limitation is $200,000 (Code Sec. 179(b)(2)).

Taxable Income Limitation. The total cost of property that may be expensed for any tax year cannot exceed the total amount of taxable income derived from the active conduct of any trade or business during the tax year, including employee salaries and wages (Code Sec. 179(b)(3)). An amount disallowed as the result of the taxable income limitation is carried forward. The deduction for carryforwards and the amounts expensed for qualifying property placed in service in a carryforward year, however, may not exceed the maximum annual dollar cost ceiling, investment limitation, or taxable income limitation. No amount attributable to qualified real property (discussed below) may be carried over to a tax year beginning after 2011 (Code Sec. 179(f)(4)(A)).

Qualifying Section 179 Property. To qualify as section 179 property, the property must be tangible section 1245 property (new or used), depreciable under MACRS, and acquired by purchase for use in the active conduct of a trade or business (Code Sec. 179(d)).[19] Code Sec. 50(b) property and air conditioning and heating units do not qualify as section 179 property (Code Sec. 179(d), last sentence). Code Sec. 50(b) property includes property used predominantly outside of the United States, property used with respect to lodging, such as apartment buildings but not hotels and motels, and property used by tax-exempt organizations (unless the property is used predominantly in connection with an unrelated business income activity). A taxpayer may also make an election to treat qualified real property (discussed below) placed in service in a tax year that begins in 2010 or 2011 as section 179 property (Code Sec. 179(f)(1)).

Depreciable off-the-shelf computer software placed in service in tax years beginning in 2003 through 2012 may be expensed under Code Sec. 179 (Code Sec. 179(d)(1)(A)). This is software described in Code Sec. 197(e)(3)(A)(i) (i.e., software that is readily available for purchase by the general public, is subject to a nonexclusive license, and has not been substantially modified) which is depreciable over three years under Code Sec. 167(f)(1)(A).[20]

Qualified Real Property. A taxpayer may elect to treat the cost of qualified real property placed in service in a tax year that begins in 2010 or 2011 as section 179 property (Code Sec. 179(f)). The maximum amount of qualified real property that may

References are to Standard Federal Tax Reports; Tax Research Consultant; and Practical Tax Explanations.

[19] ¶ 12,120, ¶ 12,126.021; DEPR: 12,200; § 9,810

[20] ¶ 12,126.021; DEPR: 12,200; § 9,810

12 DEPRECIATION

be expensed is limited to $250,000. The expensed amount is counted toward the overall $500,000 annual expensing limit for 2010 and 2011 discussed above.

Example 1: A calendar-year taxpayer places $600,000 of qualified real property in service in 2011 and elects to treat the property as section 179 property. Assume that the taxpayer also places $400,000 of other section 179 property in service in 2011. The annual dollar limit for 2011 ($500,000) is not subject to reduction under the investment limitation because the taxpayer did not place more than $2,000,000 of section 179 property in service in 2011 (only $1,000,000 of section 179 property was placed in service). The taxpayer may elect to expense up to $250,000 of the cost of its qualified real property. If it elects to expense $250,000 of the qualified real property, then it may only elect to expense up to $250,000 of its other section 179 property.

Qualified real property is:

(1) qualified leasehold improvement property described in Code Sec. 168(e)(6) (¶ 1234),

(2) qualified restaurant property (i.e., a restaurant building or improvement described in Code Sec. 168(e)(7)) (¶ 1240), and

(3) qualified retail improvement property described in Code Sec. 168(e)(8) (¶ 1240).

The property must be depreciable, acquired by purchase for use in the active conduct of a trade or business, and does not include property described in the last sentence of Code Sec. 179(d)(1) (i.e., property described in Code Sec. 50(b) and air conditioning or heating units as discussed in *"Qualifying Section 179 Property,"* above).

No amount of a section 179 deduction attributable to qualified real property which is disallowed under the taxable income limitation may be carried over to a tax year beginning after 2011 (Code Sec. 179(f)(4)(A)). To the extent that any amount attributable to qualified real property is not allowed to be carried over to a tax year beginning after 2011, the taxpayer is treated as if no section 179 election had been made (Code Sec. 179(f)(4)(B)). The amount of a disallowed carryover attributable to qualified real property placed in service in any tax year other than the taxpayer's last tax year beginning in 2011 is treated as property that was placed in service on the first day of the taxpayer's last tax year beginning in 2011 (Code Sec. 179(f)(4)(C)).

Example 2: A calendar-year taxpayer places $50,000 of qualified real property in service in 2010 and elects to treat the property as section 179 property. No other section 179 property is placed in service. The taxpayer further elects to expense the entire $50,000. However, assume that the taxpayer has no taxable income in 2010. The $50,000 is carried forward to 2011. If the taxpayer has no taxable income in 2011, the $50,000 may not be carried forward to 2012 and the taxpayer is treated as if the $50,000 of qualified real property was placed in service on January 1, 2011. Depreciation is computed as if the property was placed in service on that date.

If a taxpayer places both qualified real property that is treated as section 179 property and other types of section 179 property in service in a tax year in which there is a carryforward due to application of the taxable income limitation, the amount of the carryforward is allocated pro rata between the qualified real property and the other types of section 179 property placed in service during the tax year that the taxpayer elected to expense (Code Sec. 179(f)(4)(D)).

Purchase Defined. Property is acquired by purchase unless it (1) is acquired from certain related persons, (2) is transferred between members of a controlled group, (3) has a substituted basis in whole or in part, or (4) is acquired from a decedent and has a basis determined under Code Sec. 1014(a) (i.e., a fair-market value basis) (Code Sec. 179(d)(2)).

Recapture. The Code Sec. 179 expense deduction is treated as depreciation for recapture purposes. Thus, gain on a disposition of section 179 property that is section 1245 property is treated as ordinary income to the extent of the Code Sec. 179 expense allowance claimed plus any depreciation claimed. Qualified real property is section 1250 property. The section 179 expense deduction claimed on qualified real property is subject to recapture as ordinary income under the rules that apply to section 1245 property (Code Sec. 1245(a)(3)(C)).

If business use of section 179 property fails to exceed 50 percent during any year of the property's depreciation period, a portion of the amount expensed is recaptured as ordinary income (Code Sec. 179(d)(10); Reg. § 1.179-1(e)). The recapture amount is the difference between the expense claimed and the depreciation that would have been allowed on the expensed amount for prior tax years and the tax year of recapture. Recapture is reported on Form 4797.

In the case of a listed property, such as a passenger automobile, the recapture rules described at ¶ 1211 for property used 50 percent or less for business apply in place of the preceding recapture rule.

Empowerment Zones, Renewal Communities, and District of Columbia. The section 179 dollar limit ($500,000 for 2010 and 2011) is increased an additional $35,000 for qualifying assets placed in service in certain distressed communities (Code Sec. 1397A; Code Sec. 1400J; Code Sec. 1400). The $35,000 increase is subject to recapture if the property is removed from the distressed community. In general, in the case of an empowerment zone (including an enterprise zone located in the District of Columbia) the qualifying property must be placed in service before January 1, 2012 (Code Sec. 1391(d)(1); Code Sec. 1400). The additional expense allowance for renewal communities only applies to qualifying property acquired before January 1, 2010 (Code Sec. 1400J(b)(1)(A)).[21] See ¶ 999A.

Qualified Disaster Assistance Property. The section 179 dollar limit ($500,000 for tax years beginning in 2010 and 2011) is increased by the lesser of $100,000 or the cost of qualified Disaster Assistance property placed in service during the tax year that is also section 179 property. The investment limitation ($2,000,000 for tax years beginning in 2010 and 2011) is increased by the lesser of $600,000 or the cost of qualified section 179 Disaster Assistance property placed in service during the tax year. Qualified Disaster Assistance property must rehabilitate property damaged, or replace property destroyed or condemned, as a result of a federally declared disaster. This provision applies to property placed in service after December 31, 2007, with respect to federally declared disasters declared after such date and occurring before January 1, 2010 (Code Sec. 179(e)).

Limitations on Automobiles and Other Listed Property

1211. Business Usage Requirement for Listed Property. Depreciation deductions for "listed property" are subject to special rules (Code Sec. 280F).[22] Listed property includes passenger automobiles (as defined at ¶ 1214), other forms of transportation if the property's nature lends itself to personal use (e.g., airplanes, boats, vehicles excluded from the definition of a passenger automobile, etc.), entertainment, recreational and amusement property, computers and peripheral equipment, and any other property specified by regulation. Unless used more than 50 percent for business, MACRS deductions on listed property must be determined under the MACRS alternative depreciation system (ADS) (Code Sec. 280F(b)(1)) (¶ 1247).

If the listed property satisfies the more-than-50 percent business use requirement in the tax year it is placed in service but fails to meet that test in a later tax year that occurs during any year of the property's ADS recovery period, depreciation deductions (including bonus depreciation) previously taken are subject to recapture in such later year (Code Sec. 280F(b)(2)). MACRS depreciation for years preceding the year in which the business use fell to 50 percent or less is recaptured to the extent that the MACRS depreciation (including any depreciation) for such years exceeds the depreciation that would have been allowed under ADS. Depreciation thereafter must be computed using ADS.

References are to Standard Federal Tax Reports; Tax Research Consultant; and Practical Tax Explanations.

[21] ¶ 12,126.03; DEPR: 12,116; § 9,815.05

[22] ¶ 15,100, ¶ 15,108; DEPR: 3,500; § 11,301

If the more-than-50 percent business use test is not satisfied in the tax year the property is placed in service, the property does not qualify for the Code Sec. 179 expensing election (¶ 1208). If the more-than-50 percent business use test is initially satisfied but is not met in a later tax year, the deduction taken under the Code Sec. 179 election is treated as a depreciation deduction for purposes of the listed property depreciation recapture rule above. For example, if a taxpayer expenses the entire cost of a listed property, the difference between the amount expensed and the ADS deductions that would have been allowed on that amount prior to the recapture year is recaptured as ordinary income.

See ¶ 1214 for additional limits on passenger automobiles.

Reporting. Part IV of Form 4797 is used to calculate any recapture amount.

1214. Limitations on Passenger Automobiles, Including Trucks, SUVs, and Vans. The maximum MACRS deductions (including the Section 179 expensing deduction (¶ 1208) and first-year bonus depreciation allowance (¶ 1237)) that may be claimed for a passenger automobile other than a truck, including an SUV treated as a truck, or van placed in service in calendar year 2004 or later are shown in the chart below (Code Sec. 280F).[23] For earlier years, see IRS Publication 463.

For Cars Placed in Service		*Depreciation Allowable in—*				
After	*Before*	*Year 1*	*Year 2*	*Year 3*	*Year 4, etc.*	*Authority*
12/31/03	1/01/05	10,610 * 2,960	4,800	2,850	1,675	Rev. Proc. 2004-20
12/31/04	1/01/06	2,960	4,700	2,850	1,675	Rev. Proc. 2005-13
12/31/05	1/01/07	2,960	4,800	2,850	1,775	Rev. Proc. 2006-18
12/31/06	1/01/08	3,060	4,900	2,850	1,775	Rev. Proc. 2007-30
12/31/07	1/01/10	10,960 * 2,960	4,800	2,850	1,775	Rev. Proc. 2008-22 Rev. Proc. 2009-24
12/31/09	1/01/12	11,060 * 3,060	4,900	2,950	1,775	Rev. Proc. 2010-18 Rev. Proc. 2011-21
12/31/11	1/01/13	11,160 * 3,160	5,100	3,050	1,875	Rev. Proc. 2012-23

* The higher first-year limit applies if the vehicle qualifies for bonus depreciation under the general provision of Code Sec. 168(k) and no election out is made. The higher limit does not apply if bonus depreciation is claimed under the authority of any other bonus depreciation provision, such as the provision for Gulf Opportunity Zone Property or Disaster Assistance Property. See ¶ 1237.

Assuming that the 200 percent declining balance method and half-year convention apply, a car placed in service in 2012 is subject to the first-year cap if the cost of the vehicle exceeds $15,800 ($15,800 × 20% = $3,160). If 50 percent bonus depreciation is claimed, a car placed in service in 2012 must cost more than $18,600 before the first-year cap limits the depreciation deduction (($18,600 × 50%) + ($9,300 × 20%) = $11,160).

Trucks (including SUVs treated as trucks) and vans are subject to their own set of depreciation caps if placed in service after 2002. These caps (reproduced in the table below) reflect the higher costs associated with such vehicles. Keep in mind, however, that trucks and vans that have a loaded gross vehicle weight rating greater than 6,000 pounds are not subject to any caps (see below). *Also, certain trucks and vans placed in service after July 6, 2003 are not subject to the caps if, because of their design, they are not likely to be used for personal purposes (see below).* The following chart shows the depreciation caps for trucks and vans placed in service in calendar year 2003 and later.

[23] ¶ 15,100, ¶ 15,108; DEPR: 3,504; § 11,330.05

For Trucks and Vans Placed in Service		*Depreciation Allowable in—*				
After	*Before*	*Year 1*	*Year 2*	*Year 3*	*Year 4, etc.*	*Authority*
12/31/02	5/06/03	7,960 * 3,360	5,400	3,250	1,975	Rev. Proc. 2003-75
5/05/03	1/01/04	11,010 * 3,360	5,400	3,250	1,975	Rev. Proc. 2003-75
12/31/03	1/01/05	10,910 * 3,260	5,300	3,150	1,875	Rev. Proc. 2004-20
12/31/04	1/01/06	3,260	5,200	3,150	1,875	Rev. Proc. 2005-13
12/31/05	1/01/07	3,260	5,200	3,150	1,875	Rev. Proc. 2006-18
12/31/06	1/01/08	3,260	5,200	3,050	1,875	Rev. Proc. 2007-30
12/31/07	1/01/09	11,160 * 3,160	5,100	3,050	1,875	Rev. Proc. 2008-22
12/31/08	1/01/10	11,060 * 3,060	4,900	2,950	1,775	Rev. Proc. 2009-24
12/31/09	1/01/11	11,160 * 3,160	5,100	3,050	1,875	Rev. Proc. 2010-18
12/31/10	1/01/12	11,260 * 3,260	5,200	3,150	1,875	Rev. Proc. 2011-21
12/31/11	1/01/13	11,360 * 3,360	5,300	3,150	1,875	Rev. Proc. 2012-23

* The higher first-year limit applies if the vehicle qualifies for bonus depreciation under the general provision of Code Sec. 168(k) and no election out is made. The higher limit does not apply if bonus depreciation is claimed under the authority of any other bonus depreciation provision, such as the provision for Gulf Opportunity Zone Property or Disaster Assistance Property. See ¶ 1237.

12 DEPRECIATION

Assuming that the 200 percent declining balance method and half-year convention apply and that no bonus is claimed, a truck or van placed in service in 2012 is subject to the first-year cap if the cost of the vehicle exceeds $16,800 ($16,800 × 20% = $3,360). If 50 percent bonus depreciation is claimed, a truck or van placed in service in 2012 must cost more than $18,933.33 (($18,933.33 × 50%) + ($9,466.67 × 20%) = $11,360)).

The above maximum annual limits (often referred to as the luxury car limits) are based on 100 percent business use. If business use is less than 100 percent, the limits must be reduced to reflect the actual business use percentage.

For electric passenger automobiles built by an original equipment manufacturer and placed in service after August 5, 1997 and before 2007, the yearly statutory limits that apply to depreciation for luxury cars are tripled and then adjusted for inflation (Code Sec. 280F(a)(1)(C)(ii)). The annual limits above apply to electric vehicles placed in service after 2006. The limits for electric vehicles placed in service before 2007 are located in the Revenue Procedures cited in the "Authority" column in the charts above.[24]

For passenger vehicles that initially used nonclean-burning fuel, but were modified to allow them to be propelled by clean-burning fuel, the Code Sec. 280F limits do not apply to the cost of the installed device that equips the car to use clean-burning fuel. The balance of the car's cost remains subject to the Code Sec. 280F limits (Code Sec. 280F(a)(1)(C)).[25]

Passenger Automobile Defined. For purposes of the depreciation caps, a passenger automobile includes any four-wheeled vehicle manufactured primarily for use on public streets, roads, and highways that has an *unloaded* gross vehicle weight rating (GVWR) (i.e., curb weight fully equipped for service but without passengers or cargo) of 6,000

References are to Standard Federal Tax Reports; Tax Research Consultant; and Practical Tax Explanations.

[24] ¶ 15,100, ¶ 15,108.025; DEPR: 3,504, BUSEXP: 18,704; § 11,330.05

[25] ¶ 15,100, ¶ 12,133.029; DEPR: 3,504; § 11,330.05

pounds or less (Code Sec. 280F(d)(5)(A)). However, a truck or van is only treated as a passenger automobile subject to the caps if it has a *gross* vehicle weight rating (i.e., maximum total weight of a loaded vehicle as specified by the manufacturer) of 6,000 pounds or less (Code Sec. 280F(d)(5)(B)). A truck or van, therefore, is not subject to the depreciation caps if its GVWR exceeds 6,000 pounds. A sport utility vehicle is generally treated as a truck (even if built on a unibody (i.e., car chassis)) and, therefore, if its GVWR is in excess of 6,000 pounds it is also exempt from the caps.[26] See footnoted material for further discussion of the definition of a "truck" as well as a list of SUVs, trucks, and vans with a GVWR in excess of 6,000 pounds. Ambulances or hearses and vehicles used directly in the trade or business of transporting persons or property for hire (e.g., taxis and limousines) are not considered passenger automobiles subject to the caps regardless of their weight.

Luxury Car Depreciation Examples. The depreciation deduction that is claimed on the return for any tax year during a vehicle's recovery (depreciation) period is the lesser of the depreciation deduction for the tax year (computed as if there were no depreciation caps) or the cap that applies for the tax year.[27]

If, after the recovery period for a passenger automobile ends, the taxpayer continues to use the car in its trade or business, the unrecovered basis (referred to as "Sec. 280F unrecovered basis") may be deducted at the maximum annual rate provided in the chart above for the fourth and succeeding years. This rule permits depreciation deductions beyond the recovery period. Unrecovered basis is the difference between the cost of the vehicle and the amount of depreciation claimed on the return during the recovery period (or that would have been claimed on the return if business use had been 100 percent). The MACRS recovery period for a passenger automobile is five full years from the date the vehicle is deemed placed in service under the applicable half-year or mid-quarter convention (¶ 1245). Due to operation of the applicable convention, depreciation deductions are claimed over the six tax years that the five-year recovery period falls within.

The following example illustrates how depreciation is computed if the 50 percent bonus depreciation allowance is not claimed.

Example 1: On April 5, 2012, a calendar-year taxpayer purchased a car for $30,000. Business use of the car each year is 100 percent. Depreciation is computed under the general MACRS 200 percent declining-balance method over a five-year recovery period using a half-year convention subject to the luxury car limitations. Bonus depreciation does not apply because the car is used or an election out for 5-year property was made. Allowable depreciation during the regular recovery period (2012 through 2017) is computed as follows:

Year	*100% Business-Use MACRS Depreciation*	*Luxury Car Limit*	*Deduction: Lesser of Col. 2 or 3*	*Sec. 280F Unrecovered Basis*
2012	$6,000	$3,160	$3,160	$26,840
2013	9,600	5,100	5,100	21,740
2014	5,760	3,050	3,050	18,690
2015	3,456	1,875	1,875	16,815
2016	3,456	1,875	1,875	14,940
2017	1,728	1,875	1,728	13,212

Note that the unrecovered basis is computed by subtracting the depreciation that would have been allowed (taking the applicable cap into consideration) if business use was 100%. Thus, for example, the unrecovered basis at the close of 2012 is $26,840 ($30,000 - $3,160). The $13,212 unrecovered basis at the close of the regular recovery period is deducted in the post recovery period years at the rate of $1,875 per year (assuming 100 percent business use).

The following example shows how luxury car depreciation is computed if the 50 percent bonus deduction is claimed.

References are to Standard Federal Tax Reports; Tax Research Consultant; and Practical Tax Explanations.

[26] ¶ 15,108.022; BUSEXP: 24,852.05, DEPR: 12,150; § 840

[27] ¶ 15,108.40; DEPR: 3,600, DEPR: 3,504.15; § 11,330.10

Example 2: On April 5, 2012, a calendar-year taxpayer purchased a new car for $30,000. Business use of the car each year is 100 percent. Depreciation is computed under the general MACRS 200 percent declining-balance method over a five-year recovery period using a half-year convention subject to the luxury car limitations. Allowable depreciation during the regular recovery period (2012 through 2017) is computed as follows:

Year	*100% Business-Use MACRS Depreciation*	*Luxury Car Limit*	*Deduction: Lesser of Col. 2 or 3*	*Sec. 280F Unrecovered Basis*
2012.	$18,000	$11,160	$11,160	$18,840
2013.	4,800	5,100	4,800	14,040
2014.	2,880	3,050	2,880	11,160
2015.	1,728	1,875	1,728	9,432
2016.	1,728	1,875	1,728	7,704
2017.	864	1,875	864	6,840

Beginning in 2018, the unrecovered basis is the $6,840 difference between the $30,000 cost and the sum of the return deductions claimed in 2012 through 2017. The unrecovered basis is deducted at the rate of $1,875 per year assuming that 100 percent business use continues. However, the unrecovered basis is reduced by $1,875 each year regardless of the percentage of business use.

Special rules for vehicles subject to 100 percent bonus rate in 2010 or 2011. If the 100 percent bonus deduction was claimed in 2010 or 2011 on a new car that is subject to the caps and a safe-harbor election was not made, a taxpayer claimed the amount of the first-year cap since this was less than the bonus allowance. No depreciation may be claimed in any succeeding years of the vehicle's recovery period because the depreciation deduction for each of those years computed as if there were no depreciation caps is $0 (the full cost is deemed deducted as a bonus allowance) and $0 is less than the cap amount for each of those years. To address this "anomaly" a safe harbor election allowed a taxpayer to claim a 100 percent bonus deduction in the amount of the first-year cap in the year that the vehicle was placed in service and then determine its depreciation deductions for the remaining years in the recovery period by computing those deductions as if a 50 percent bonus allowance was claimed in the year the vehicle was placed in service. A taxpayer made this election by computing its depreciation deductions in accordance with the election (Rev. Proc. 2011-26).

$25,000 Section 179 Expensing Cap on Sport Utility Vehicles, Certain Trucks, and Certain Vans That Are Exempt from Luxury Car Depreciation Caps. The maximum amount of the cost of an SUV that may be expensed under Code Sec. 179 if the SUV is exempt from the luxury car caps (e.g., has a GVWR in excess of 6,000 pounds) is limited to $25,000, effective for SUVs placed in service after October 22, 2004. The $25,000 limitation also applies to exempt trucks with an interior cargo bed length of less than six feet and exempt passenger vans that seat fewer than ten persons behind the driver's seat. Exempt cargo vans are generally not subject to the $25,000 limitation (Code Sec. 179(b)(5)).

Exclusion from Depreciation Caps for Certain Trucks and Vans Not Likely To Be Used for Personal Purposes. Effective for trucks and vans placed in service after July 6, 2003, a truck or van that is a qualified nonpersonal use vehicle as defined in Reg. § 1.274-5(k) is excluded from the definition of a passenger automobile and is not subject to the annual depreciation limits (Reg. § 1.280F-6(c)(3)(iii)). In general, a qualified nonpersonal use vehicle is one that has been specially modified in such a way that it is not likely to be used more than a *de minimis* amount for personal purposes.[28]

Reporting. The allowable depreciation deduction for any listed property, including automobiles, is reported on Form 4562 (Part V).

References are to Standard Federal Tax Reports; Tax Research Consultant; and Practical Tax Explanations.

[28] ¶ 15,108.042; DEPR: 3,502.05; § 11,305

12 DEPRECIATION

1215. Leased Listed Property Inclusion Amounts. The lessee of a passenger automobile (as defined for depreciation cap purposes at ¶ 1214) used for business is required to include an additional amount in income to offset rental deductions for each tax year during which the vehicle is leased (Code Sec. 280F(c)(2); Reg. § 1.280F-7).[29] The inclusion amount is based on the cost of the vehicle and generally applies to a vehicle with a fair market value exceeding an inflation-adjusted dollar amount. The inclusion amount is not required on trucks, vans, and SUVs that would be exempt from the depreciation caps if owned by the lessee (e.g., an SUV treated as a truck with a GVWR in excess of 6,000 pounds).

Lease inclusion tables are issued annually by the IRS in the same revenue procedure in which the annual depreciation caps are issued (see list of these revenue procedures at ¶ 1214). The appropriate table is based on the calendar year that the vehicle was first leased. The same table is used for each year of the lease term.

Each revenue procedure includes a lease inclusion table for passenger automobiles and a lease inclusion table for trucks and vans (including SUVs treated as a truck). Prior to 2003 trucks and vans used the same table that applied to other passenger automobiles. Prior to 2007 electric vehicles had a separate lease inclusion table. Electric vehicles first leased in 2007 are now subject to the table that applies to passenger automobiles or trucks and vans, as appropriate. The inclusion tables for vehicles first leased in 2012 are reproduced below. For tables for vehicles first leased in earlier calendar years, see the STANDARD FEDERAL TAX REPORTER ¶ 15,108.048, Practical Tax Explanations § 850, or IRS Publication 463.

A lessee's inclusion amount for each tax year that the vehicle is leased is computed as follows: (1) use the fair market value of the vehicle on the first day of the lease term to find the appropriate dollar (inclusion) amounts on the IRS table (see below); (2) prorate the dollar amount from the table for the number of days of the lease term included in the tax year; and (3) multiply the prorated amount by the percentage of business and investment use for the tax year. For the last tax year during any lease that does not begin and end in the same tax year, the dollar amount for the preceding tax year should be used.

> **Example:** A car costing $25,500 is leased for four years by a calendar-year taxpayer beginning on April 1, 2012 and is used 100 percent for business. The annual dollar amounts from the table for leases beginning in 2012 are: $6 for the first tax year during the lease, $12 for the second tax year, $19 for the third tax year, $21 for the fourth tax year, and $26 for the fifth and following tax years. In 2012, the inclusion amount is $4.52 (275/365 × $6). The inclusion amounts for 2013, 2014, and 2015 are $12, $19, and $21 respectively since the vehicle is leased for the entire year during these tax years. In 2016, the inclusion amount is $5.18 (90/365 × $21 (the dollar amount for 2015, the preceding tax year, is used in the last year of the lease)).

Listed Property Other Than Passenger Automobiles. Lessees of listed property (other than passenger automobiles) are required to include in income a usage-based inclusion amount in the first tax year that the business use percentage of such property is 50 percent or less (Code Sec. 280F(c); Reg. § 1.280F-7(b)).[30]

Reporting. The inclusion amount is reported on Form 2106 by employees, Schedule C (Form 1040) by the self-employed, and Schedule F by farmers.

References are to Standard Federal Tax Reports; Tax Research Consultant; and Practical Tax Explanations.

[29] ¶ 15,100, ¶ 15,107; DEPR: 3,512; § 11,330.05

[30] ¶ 15,108.054; DEPR: 3,512.10; § 11,330.05

Dollar Amounts for Passenger Automobiles
(That are not Trucks or Vans)
With a Lease Term Beginning in Calendar Year 2012
[Rev. Proc. 2012-23, I.R.B. 2012-14]

Fair Market Value of Passenger Automobile		*Tax Year During Lease*				
Over	*Not Over*	*1st*	*2nd*	*3rd*	*4th*	*5th and Later*
$18,500	$19,000	2	4	5	6	8
19,000	19,500	2	4	7	7	9
19,500	20,000	2	5	8	8	10
20,000	20,500	3	5	9	10	11
20,500	21,000	3	6	9	12	12
21,000	21,500	3	7	10	12	14
21,500	22,000	3	8	11	13	16
22,000	23,000	4	8	13	15	17
23,000	24,000	4	10	15	17	20
24,000	25,000	5	11	17	19	23
25,000	26,000	6	12	19	21	26
26,000	27,000	6	14	20	24	28
27,000	28,000	7	15	22	26	31
28,000	29,000	7	16	25	28	33
29,000	30,000	8	18	25	32	35
30,000	31,000	9	19	27	34	38
31,000	32,000	9	20	30	36	41
32,000	33,000	10	21	32	38	43
33,000	34,000	10	23	33	41	46
34,000	35,000	11	24	35	43	49
35,000	36,000	12	25	37	45	52
36,000	37,000	12	27	39	47	54
37,000	38,000	13	28	41	49	57
38,000	39,000	13	29	43	52	59
39,000	40,000	14	30	45	54	62
40,000	41,000	14	32	47	56	65
41,000	42,000	15	33	49	58	68
42,000	43,000	16	34	51	61	70
43,000	44,000	16	36	52	63	73
44,000	45,000	17	37	54	66	75
45,000	46,000	17	38	57	67	78
46,000	47,000	18	39	59	70	80
47,000	48,000	19	40	61	72	83
48,000	49,000	19	42	62	75	86
49,000	50,000	20	43	64	77	89
50,000	51,000	20	45	66	79	91
51,000	52,000	21	46	68	81	94
52,000	53,000	21	47	70	84	96
53,000	54,000	22	48	72	86	99
54,000	55,000	23	49	74	88	102
55,000	56,000	23	51	76	90	104
56,000	57,000	24	52	78	92	107
57,000	58,000	24	54	79	95	110
58,000	59,000	25	55	81	97	113
59,000	60,000	26	56	83	100	115
60,000	62,000	26	58	86	103	119
62,000	64,000	28	60	90	108	124
64,000	66,000	29	63	94	112	129
66,000	68,000	30	66	97	117	135
68,000	70,000	31	68	102	121	140
70,000	72,000	32	71	105	126	145
72,000	74,000	33	74	109	130	151
74,000	76,000	35	76	113	135	156
76,000	78,000	36	78	117	140	161
78,000	80,000	37	81	120	145	166
80,000	85,000	39	86	127	152	176
85,000	90,000	42	92	137	163	189
90,000	95,000	45	98	147	175	202
95,000	100,000	48	105	155	187	215
100,000	110,000	52	115	170	203	235
110,000	120,000	58	127	189	227	262

Dollar Amounts for Passenger Automobiles
(That are not Trucks or Vans)
With a Lease Term Beginning in Calendar Year 2012
[Rev. Proc. 2012-23, I.R.B. 2012-14]

Fair Market Value of Passenger Automobile		*Tax Year During Lease*				
Over	*Not Over*	*1st*	*2nd*	*3rd*	*4th*	*5th and Later*
120,000	130,000	64	140	208	250	288
130,000	140,000	70	153	227	272	315
140,000	150,000	75	166	246	296	340
150,000	160,000	81	179	265	318	368
160,000	170,000	87	192	284	341	394
170,000	180,000	93	204	304	364	420
180,000	190,000	99	217	323	387	446
190,000	200,000	105	230	342	409	473
200,000	210,000	111	243	361	432	499
210,000	220,000	116	256	380	455	526
220,000	230,000	122	269	399	478	552
230,000	240,000	128	282	418	501	578
240,000	And up	134	294	437	524	605

Dollar Amounts for Trucks and Vans
With a Lease Term Beginning in Calendar Year 2012
[Rev. Proc. 2012-23, I.R.B. 2012-14]

Fair Market Value of Truck or Van		*Tax Year During Lease*				
Over	Not Over	1st	2nd	3rd	4th	5th and later
19,000	19,500	1	4	5	6	7
19,500	20,000	2	4	6	7	9
20,000	20,500	2	5	7	8	10
20,500	21,000	2	5	8	10	11
21,000	21,500	3	6	9	10	13
21,500	22,000	3	6	10	12	14
22,000	23,000	3	8	11	14	15
23,000	24,000	4	9	13	16	18
24,000	25,000	4	10	15	19	21
25,000	26,000	5	11	17	21	24
26,000	27,000	6	12	19	23	26
27,000	28,000	6	14	21	25	29
28,000	29,000	7	15	23	27	32
29,000	30,000	7	17	24	30	34
30,000	31,000	8	18	26	32	37
31,000	32,000	9	19	28	34	40
32,000	33,000	9	20	31	36	42
33,000	34,000	10	21	33	39	44
34,000	35,000	10	23	34	41	48
35,000	36,000	11	24	36	44	50
36,000	37,000	12	25	38	46	53
37,000	38,000	12	27	40	48	55
38,000	39,000	13	28	42	50	58
39,000	40,000	13	29	44	53	60
40,000	41,000	14	31	45	55	63
41,000	42,000	14	32	48	57	66
42,000	43,000	15	33	50	59	69
43,000	44,000	16	34	52	61	72
44,000	45,000	16	36	53	64	74
45,000	46,000	17	37	55	66	77
46,000	47,000	17	38	58	68	79
47,000	48,000	18	40	59	70	82
48,000	49,000	19	41	61	73	84
49,000	50,000	19	42	63	75	87
50,000	51,000	20	43	65	78	89
51,000	52,000	20	45	66	80	93
52,000	53,000	21	46	68	83	95
53,000	54,000	21	48	70	84	98
54,000	55,000	22	49	72	87	100
55,000	56,000	23	50	74	89	103
56,000	57,000	23	51	76	92	105

Dollar Amounts for Trucks and Vans
With a Lease Term Beginning in Calendar Year 2012
[Rev. Proc. 2012-23, I.R.B. 2012-14]

Fair Market Value of Truck or Van		*Tax Year During Lease*				
Over	Not Over	1st	2nd	3rd	4th	5th and later
57,000	58,000	24	52	78	94	108
58,000	59,000	24	54	80	96	111
59,000	60,000	25	55	82	98	114
60,000	62,000	26	57	85	101	118
62,000	64,000	27	60	88	106	123
64,000	66,000	28	62	93	110	128
66,000	68,000	29	65	96	115	134
68,000	70,000	30	67	100	120	139
70,000	72,000	32	70	103	125	144
72,000	74,000	33	72	108	129	149
74,000	76,000	34	75	111	134	155
76,000	78,000	35	78	115	138	160
78,000	80,000	36	80	119	143	165
80,000	85,000	38	85	125	151	175
85,000	90,000	41	91	135	163	187
90,000	95,000	44	98	144	174	201
95,000	100,000	47	104	154	185	214
100,000	110,000	52	113	169	202	234
110,000	120,000	57	127	187	225	261
120,000	130,000	63	139	207	248	287
130,000	140,000	69	152	226	271	313
140,000	150,000	75	165	245	294	339
150,000	160,000	81	178	264	316	366
160,000	170,000	87	190	283	340	392
170,000	180,000	92	204	302	362	419
180,000	190,000	98	216	322	385	445
190,000	200,000	104	229	340	409	471
200,000	210,000	110	242	359	431	498
210,000	220,000	116	255	378	454	524
220,000	230,000	122	267	398	477	551
230,000	240,000	127	281	416	500	577
240,000	And up	133	294	435	523	603

Depreciation Methods

1216. Methods of Computing Depreciation. Most tangible property placed in service after 1986 must be depreciated using MACRS (¶ 1243). Depreciation for tangible property placed in service after 1980 and before 1987 is computed under ACRS (¶ 1252).

For tangible property placed in service before 1981, depreciation may be computed under the straight-line method (¶ 1224), the double declining-balance method (¶ 1226), the sum-of-the-years-digits method (¶ 1228), and other "consistent methods" (¶ 1231) (former Code Sec. 167(b)), depending on the taxpayer's election in the year the property was placed in service.[31] However, accelerated depreciation for pre-1981 realty is limited (former Code Sec. 167(j)).[32]

For an asset purchased before 1981, only a part of a full year's depreciation was allowed in the year it was placed in service. The allowable deduction was computed by multiplying the first full year's depreciation allowance by the months the property was owned and dividing by 12. The same rule applies in the year of sale.[33]

1218. Methods for Depreciating Real Estate. Real property placed in service after 1986 is depreciated under MACRS (¶ 1236). Real property placed in service after 1980 and before 1987 is depreciated under ACRS (¶ 1252). Additions and improvements to a building, including structural components of a building, placed in service after 1986 are depreciated under MACRS (see ¶ 1240). Post-1986 rehabilitation expenditures are also

References are to Standard Federal Tax Reports; Tax Research Consultant; and Practical Tax Explanations.

[31] ¶ 11,037.021; DEPR: 15,306; § 10,301

[32] ¶ 11,059.01; DEPR: 15,356; § 10,301

[33] ¶ 11,025.03; DEPR: 15,654.05; § 11,001

depreciated using MACRS (¶ 1236). Elements of a building which qualify as personal property may be separately depreciated under the cost segregation rules using shortened MACRS recovery periods (¶ 1240). Real property which is converted from personal use to residential rental property or nonresidential real property is depreciated as MACRS 27.5-year residential rental property or MACRS 39-year nonresidential real property even if the property was acquired for personal use prior to 1987.

1221. Change in Depreciation Method. A change in the method of computing depreciation is generally a change in accounting method that requires the consent of the IRS and the filing of Form 3115 (Reg. § 1.167(e)-1).[34] If the change from an impermissible accounting method to a permissible accounting method results in a negative (taxpayer favorable) Code Sec. 481(a) adjustment, the adjustment is taken into account in a single tax year. A positive adjustment is taken into account over four tax years (one-year if the positive adjustment is less than $25,000 and the taxpayer makes an election to include it in income in one year). No Code Sec. 481(a) adjustment is allowed when a taxpayer changes from one permissible method to another permissible method. These changes are applied on a "cut-off" basis.[35] Reg. § 1.446-1(e)(2)(ii)(*d*)(*2*) and (*3*) list changes in depreciation or amortization that are or are not considered a change in accounting method.[36]

Although a taxpayer has not adopted an accounting method unless two or more returns have been filed, the IRS will allow a taxpayer who has only filed one return on which incorrect depreciation has been claimed to either file Form 3115 and claim a Code Sec. 481(a) adjustment on the current-year return or file an amended return. The asset must have been placed in service in the tax year immediately preceding the tax year of the change (Rev. Proc. 2007-16).

For changes that are not a change in accounting method, such as mathematical or posting errors, a taxpayer may only file amended returns for open years. Changes in accounting method are generally made by filing Form 3115. Procedures for changing from an impermissible method (e.g., where incorrect or no depreciation has been claimed) to a permissible method and from permissible to permissible methods with respect to pre-1986 (i.e., pre-ACRS) property are generally governed by the automatic consent procedures of Rev. Proc. 2011-14 (Appendix Section 6). Otherwise, the advance consent procedures of Rev. Proc. 97-27 are followed.[37]

A taxpayer who has sold depreciable property without claiming any depreciation or all of the depreciation allowable may claim the depreciation by filing Form 3115 by the expiration of the period of limitations for filing an amended return for the year of the sale. The Form 3115 may be filed with the original federal tax return for the tax year in which the depreciable property is disposed of (Rev. Proc. 2007-16).[38]

For depreciable property placed in service in a tax year ending before December 30, 2003, the IRS will not assert that a change in computing depreciation is a change in accounting method (IRS Chief Counsel Notice CC-2004-007, January 28, 2004, as clarified by Chief Counsel Notice 2004-24, July 14, 2004).[39]

1224. "Straight-Line" or "Fixed-Percentage" Method of Depreciation. The "straight-line" method of computing the depreciation deduction assumes that the depreciation sustained is uniform during the useful life of the property. The cost or other basis, less estimated salvage value, is deductible in equal annual amounts over the estimated useful life (Reg. § 1.167(b)-1).[40] An asset may not be depreciated below its salvage value. Straight-line depreciation under MACRS and ACRS is generally computed

References are to Standard Federal Tax Reports; Tax Research Consultant; and Practical Tax Explanations.

[34] ¶ 11,043.01; DEPR: 15,304; § 11,025

[35] ¶ 11,043.021; DEPR: 15,304.15; § 11,025,

[36] ¶ 11,043.015; DEPR: 15,304.15, DEPR: 15,304.20; § 11,025

[37] ¶ 11,043.021; DEPR: 15,304; § 11,025

[38] ¶ 11,043.021; DEPR: 15,304; § 11,025

[39] ¶ 11,043.015; DEPR: 15,304.22

[40] ¶ 11,033, ¶ 11,037.022; DEPR: 15,400; § 11,130

in this manner, except that a recovery period is used instead of the useful life and salvage value is not considered (Code Sec. 168(b)(4))[41] (¶ 1243 and ¶ 1252).

1226. Declining-Balance Method of Depreciation. Under this method, depreciation is greatest in the first year and smaller in each succeeding year (Reg. § 1.167(b)-2).[42] The depreciable basis (e.g., cost) is reduced each year by the amount of the depreciation deduction, and a uniform rate of 200 percent of the straight-line rate ("double-declining balance" or "200 percent declining balance" method) or 150 percent of the straight-line rate ("150 percent declining balance" method) is applied to the resulting balances (Reg. § 1.167(b)-2).[43] Under the MACRS rules, the double-declining-balance method is used to depreciate 3-, 5-, 7-, and 10-year property and the 150 percent declining balance method is used to depreciate 15- and 20-year property (¶ 1243).

1228. Sum-of-the-Years-Digits Method. Under the sum-of-the-years-digits method, changing fractions are applied each year to the original cost or other basis, less salvage. The numerator of the fraction each year represents the remaining useful life of the asset and the denominator, which remains constant, is the sum of the numerals representing each of the years of the estimated useful life (the sum-of-the-years digits). This method, if elected, may be used for group, classified, or composite accounts (Reg. § 1.167(b)-3).[44]

1229. Income Forecast Method. The use of the income forecast method only applies to film, videotape, sound recordings, copyrights, books, patents, and other property that may be specified by IRS regulations. (The IRS has issued proposed regulations that would apply to property placed in service on or after the date final regulations are published (Prop. Reg. § 1.167(n)-1)). The income forecast method may not be used to depreciate intangible property that is amortizable under Code Sec. 197 (¶ 1288) or consumer durables subject to rent-to-own contracts (¶ 1240) (Code Sec. 167(g)(6); Rev. Rul. 60-358).[45]

Under the income forecast method, the cost of an asset (less any salvage value) placed in service after September 13, 1995, is multiplied by a fraction, the numerator of which is the net income from the asset for the tax year and the denominator of which is the total net income forecast to be derived from the asset before the close of the 10th tax year following the tax year in which the asset is placed in service. The unrecovered adjusted basis of the property as of the beginning of the 10th tax year is claimed as a depreciation deduction in the 10th tax year following the tax year in which the asset was placed in service.

If the income forecast changes during the 10-year period, the formula is as follows: the unrecovered depreciable cost of the asset at the beginning of the tax year of revision multiplied by a fraction, the numerator of which is the net income from the asset for the tax year of revision and the denominator of which is the revised forecasted total net income from the asset for the year of revision and the remaining years before the close of the 10th tax year following the tax year in which the asset was placed in service.

Generally, during the 3rd and 10th tax years after the asset is placed in service, a taxpayer is required to pay or may receive interest based on the recalculation of depreciation using actual income figures. This look-back rule does not apply to property that has a cost basis of $100,000 or less or if the taxpayer's income projections were within 10 percent of the income actually earned.

Effective for property placed in service after October 22, 2004, residuals and participations may be included in the adjusted basis of a property in the tax year that it is placed in service or excluded from adjusted basis and deducted in the year of payment (Code Sec. 167(g)(7)). Election guidance is provided in Notice 2006-47.

Reporting. Form 8866 is used to compute the look-back interest due or owed.

References are to Standard Federal Tax Reports; Tax Research Consultant; and Practical Tax Explanations.

[41] ¶ 11,250; DEPR: 3,202; § 11,130

[42] ¶ 11,034, ¶ 11,037.023; DEPR: 15,450; § 11,130

[43] ¶ 11,034; DEPR: 15,450; § 11,130

[44] ¶ 11,035, ¶ 11,037.025; DEPR: 15,500; § 11,025

[45] ¶ 11,002, ¶ 11,037.036; DEPR: 3,156.60, DEPR: 15,556; § 11,205

Creative Property Costs of Film Makers. A taxpayer may choose to amortize creative property costs ratably over 15 years beginning on the first day of the second half of the tax year in which the cost is written off for financial accounting purposes in accordance with Statement of Position 00-2 (SOP 00-2), as issued by the American Institute of Certified Public Accountants (AICPA) on June 12, 2000 (Rev. Proc. 2004-36).[46] Creative property costs are costs to acquire and develop for purposes of potential future film development, production, and exploitation: (1) screenplays; (2) scripts; (3) story outlines; (4) motion picture production rights to books and plays; and (5) similar properties. If the election is not made, these costs are generally recovered under the income forecast method only if a film is actually produced. If a film is not made, deduction of the costs as a loss is usually denied (Rev. Rul. 2004-58).

Election to Expense First $15 Million of Film Costs. Effective for qualified film and television productions commencing after December 31, 2007, and before January 1, 2012, a taxpayer may elect to expense the first $15 million of production costs ($20 million for productions in low income communities or distressed areas) (Code Sec. 181). In the case of qualified film and television productions that commence after October 22, 2004, and before January 1, 2008, a taxpayer may only elect to expense productions with an aggregate cost that does not exceed $15,000,000 ($20 million in low-income communities or distressed areas). Election guidance is provided in Reg. § 1.181-2.

1231. Other Consistent Methods. In addition to the depreciation methods explained at ¶ 1224–¶ 1228, a taxpayer may use any other consistent method, such as the sinking fund method, if the total deductions during the first two-thirds of the useful life are not more than the total allowable under the declining-balance method (Reg. § 1.167(b)-4).[47]

Leased Property

1234. Lessee/Lessor Improvements, Lease Acquisition Costs. Unless a leasehold improvement placed in service before January 1, 2012, qualifies as "15-year leasehold improvement property" under the rule described below or is a qualified improvement placed in service before January 1, 2012, to a retail building or a restaurant (see ¶ 1240), the cost of an addition or improvement made by the lessee or lessor to real property that is a structural component is depreciated under MACRS in the same manner as the depreciation deduction for the real property would be calculated if the real property had been placed in service at the same time as the addition or improvement (Code Sec. 168(i)(6) and (8)(A); Temporary Reg. § 1.167(a)-4T).[48] For example, permanent walls installed in a commercial building (structural components) are separately depreciated as 39-year real property beginning in the month that the walls are placed in service using the mid-month convention. If, upon termination of the lease, a lessee does not retain an improvement (made by the lessee), loss is computed by reference to the improvement's adjusted basis at the time of the lease termination. A lessor that disposes of or abandons a leasehold improvement (made by the lessor) upon termination of the lease may use the adjusted basis of the improvement at such time to determine gain or loss (Code Sec. 168(i)(8)(B); Temporary Reg. § 1.168(i)-8T(c)(3)).

Leasehold additions and improvements that are not structural components are generally depreciated as MACRS personal property. See *Cost Segregation,* at ¶ 1240.

15-Year Qualified Leasehold Improvement Property. Qualified leasehold improvement property placed in service after October 22, 2004, and before January 1, 2012, is depreciated under MACRS over 15 years (39 years if ADS applies) using the straight-line method and the half-year or mid-quarter convention, as applicable (Code Sec. 168(e)(3)(E)(iv)), Code Secs. 168(b)(3)(G) and (g)(3)(B)). Qualified leasehold improvement property is defined the same way as the term is defined in Code Sec. 168(k)(3) for purposes of the bonus depreciation deduction (see *Qualified Leasehold Improvement Property* at ¶ 1237) subject to an exception that generally prohibits an individual who

References are to Standard Federal Tax Reports; Tax Research Consultant; and Practical Tax Explanations.

[46] ¶ 11,009.046; DEPR: 21,500; § 11,555

[47] ¶ 11,036, ¶ 11,037.031; DEPR: 15,306; § 11,025

[48] ¶ 11,250, ¶ 11,011.021; DEPR: 3,052; § 11,105

acquires qualified leasehold improvement property from a lessor from treating the property as qualified leasehold improvement property (Code Sec. 168(e)(6)). Thus, the improvements must be made to the interior portion of nonresidential real property that is more than three years old by the lessor or lessee under or pursuant to the terms of a lease. Elevators and escalators, internal structural framework of the building, structural components that benefit a common area, and improvements relating to the enlargement of a building do not qualify (Code Sec. 168(k)(3)).

Lease Acquisition Costs. In amortizing the cost of acquiring a lease over the lease term, a renewal period is counted as part of the lease term if less than 75 percent of the acquisition cost is attributable to the unexpired lease period (not counting the renewal period) (Code Sec. 178).[49]

Construction Allowances. A lessor must depreciate improvements made by the lessee with a qualified construction allowance (Code Sec. 110) as nonresidential real property. See ¶ 764.

1235. Sale v. Lease of Property. Whether a transaction is treated as a lease or as a purchase for tax purposes is important in determining who is entitled to claim depreciation and other deductions for related business expenses.[50] In most situations, the rules for determining whether a transaction is a lease or a purchase evolved from a series of court decisions and IRS rulings. Basically, the rules look to the economic substance of a transaction, not its form, to determine who is the owner of the property for tax purposes when the parties characterize it as a lease (Rev. Proc. 2001-28, Rev. Proc. 2001-29).

Motor Vehicle Leases. A qualified motor vehicle lease agreement that contains a terminal rental adjustment clause (a provision permitting or requiring the rental price to be adjusted upward or downward by reference to the amount realized by the lessor upon the sale of the vehicle) is treated as a lease if, but for the clause, it would have been treated as a lease for tax purposes (Code Sec. 7701(h)). This provision applies only to qualified agreements with respect to a motor vehicle (including a trailer).[51]

Modified Accelerated Cost Recovery System (MACRS)

1236. MACRS in General. MACRS is mandatory for most tangible depreciable property placed in service after December 31, 1986, unless transitional rules apply (Code Sec. 168).[52] Under MACRS, the cost of eligible property is recovered over a 3-, 5-, 7-, 10-, 15-, 20-, 27.5-, 31.5-, or 39-year period, depending upon the type of property (¶ 1240) by using statutory recovery methods (¶ 1243) and conventions (¶ 1245). Special transferee rules apply to property received in specified nonrecognition transactions (see Code Sec. 168(i)(7)) (¶ 1248).[53]

1237. MACRS Bonus Depreciation. A bonus depreciation deduction is allowed for qualifying MACRS property acquired after December 31, 2007, and before January 1, 2013, if it is placed in service before January 1, 2013. The original use of the qualifying property must begin with the taxpayer after December 31, 2007. Property that is acquired pursuant to a written binding contract entered into after December 31, 2007, and before January 1, 2013, is deemed acquired before January 1, 2013 (Code Sec. 168(k)).[54]

The placed-in-service-deadline is extended one year (before January 1, 2014) for "long production property" which otherwise qualifies for bonus depreciation. Long production property is defined as property that (a) is subject to the Code Sec. 263A uniform capitalization rules, (b) has a production period greater than one year and a cost exceeding $1 million, and (c) has a MACRS recovery period of at least 10 years or is used in the trade or business of transporting persons or property for hire, such as commercial aircraft. However, only pre-January 1, 2013, progress expenditures are taken

References are to Standard Federal Tax Reports; Tax Research Consultant; and Practical Tax Explanations.

[49] ¶ 12,100, ¶ 12,105.021; SALES: 42,204; § 11,515

[50] ¶ 8754.022; SALES: 42,000; § 11,015

[51] ¶ 11,274.023; SALES: 42,104; § 11,015

[52] ¶ 11,250, ¶ 11,279; DEPR: 3,052; § 11,101

[53] ¶ 11,250, ¶ 11,279.054; DEPR: 3,056; § 11,120

[54] ¶ 11,250, ¶ 11,277E, ¶ 11,279.058; DEPR: 3,600; § 11,225

into account if the extended placed-in-service deadline applies (Code Sec. 168(k)(2)(B)). The extended placed-in-service deadline also applies to certain noncommercial aircraft acquired by purchase. In contrast, 2013 progress expenditures on noncommercial aircraft placed in service before January 1, 2014, are eligible for bonus depreciation (Code Sec. 168(k)(2)(C)).

The bonus depreciation rate is generally 50 percent. However, if qualifying MACRS property is acquired after September 8, 2010, and before January 1, 2012, and is placed in service before January 1, 2012, the rate is increased to 100 percent (Code Sec. 168(k)(5)). The original use of the property must begin with the taxpayer after September 8, 2010. In the case of long-production property and certain noncommercial aircraft, the 100 percent rate will apply if the long-production property or noncommercial aircraft is acquired after September 8, 2010, and before January 1, 2013, and placed in service before January 1, 2013. The entire basis of the long-production property or noncommercial aircraft is eligible for the 100 percent rate if these deadlines are met. If long-production property or a noncommercial aircraft is acquired (or constructed, manufactured, or produced) pursuant to a written binding contract entered into after September 8, 2010, and before January 1, 2013, the 100 percent rate acquisition deadline is deemed satisfied (Rev. Proc. 2011-26, Section 3).

For purposes of the 50 percent bonus rate, property is generally deemed acquired when possession or control is taken (i.e., taxpayer has risk of loss) (Reg. §§1.48-2(b)(6) and 1.167(c)-1(a)(2)). For purposes of the 100 percent bonus rate, property is considered acquired when its cost is paid for by a cash-basis taxpayer or when its cost is incurred by an accrual-basis taxpayer (Rev. Proc. 2006-11, Section 3.02(1)(a)). Property constructed, manufactured, or produced by or for a taxpayer is deemed acquired for purposes of the 50 percent and 100 percent rates when work of a significant physical nature begins. Under an elective safe-harbor method, work of a significant physical nature begins when more than 10 percent of the total cost of a project has been paid for by a cash basis taxpayer or incurred by an accrual basis taxpayer (Reg. §1.168(k)-1(b)(4)(iii); Rev. Proc. 2011-26, Section 3.02(1)(c)(2)).

If a larger self-constructed property does not qualify for bonus depreciation because its construction began before January 1, 2008, then individual components of the larger property, whether acquired or self-constructed, do not qualify for bonus depreciation (Reg. §1.168(k)-1(b)(4)(iii)(C)(1) and (2)). However, if a larger constructed property does not qualify for the 100 percent rate solely because its construction began after December 31, 2007, and before September 9, 2010, a taxpayer may elect to claim the 100 percent rate on individual components of the property, whether acquired or self-constructed, that separately meet the requirements for the 100 percent rate (Rev. Proc. 2011-26, Section 3.02(1)(c)(2)).

Property purchased by a taxpayer in a sale-leaseback transaction within three months after the original purchaser placed the property in service may qualify for the allowance if the original purchaser placed the property in service after December 31, 2007 (after September 8, 2010, for the 100 percent rate to apply). The last purchaser in a syndicated leasing transaction may also qualify if certain requirements are satisfied (Code Sec. 168(k)(2)(E)).

Property acquired pursuant to a written binding contract entered into before January 1, 2008, by the taxpayer or a related party does not qualify for bonus depreciation (Code Sec. 168(k)(2)(A)(iii) and (k)(2)(E)(iv)).

Bonus depreciation is treated as depreciation for recapture purposes upon the sale of the property (Reg. §1.168(k)-1(f)(3)). Unlike the Section 179 expensing allowance (¶1208), there is no taxable income or investment limitation on the bonus allowance. There is no limit on the overall amount of bonus depreciation that may be claimed on qualifying property. The length of the tax year or date during the tax year that the qualifying property was placed in service does not affect the amount of the bonus deduction, except that a 100 percent rate applies to property acquired after September 8, 2010, and placed in service before January 1, 2012.

Qualifying Property. The bonus allowance is only available for new property ("original use" must begin with the taxpayer) which is depreciable under MACRS and has a recovery period of 20 years or less, is MACRS water utility property, is computer software depreciable over three years under Code Sec. 167(f) (¶ 980), or is qualified leasehold improvement property (defined below). Property which must be depreciated using the MACRS alternative depreciation system (ADS) (¶ 1247) does not qualify. If ADS is elected, however, the property may qualify. A listed property (¶ 1211), such as a passenger automobile (¶ 1214), which is used 50 percent or less for business, does not qualify. If business use of such a property falls to 50 percent or less, bonus depreciation and any amount expensed under Code Sec. 179 (¶ 1208) must be recaptured. Property amortized under Code Sec. 197 (¶ 1288) does not qualify.

AMT. Bonus depreciation is allowed in full for alternative minimum tax purposes (¶ 1430). If bonus depreciation is claimed, no AMT adjustment is required on the regular MACRS deductions (i.e., the deductions are allowed in full for AMT purposes) (Code Sec. 168(k)(2)(F); Reg. § 1.168(k)-1(d)(iii)).

Election Out. A taxpayer may elect out of bonus depreciation with respect to any class of property (Code Sec. 168(k)(2)(D)(iii)). The election out applies to all property in the class or classes of property for which the election is made. A taxpayer was allowed to elect a 50 percent bonus rate in place of the 100 percent bonus rate for any property class but only for a tax year that included September 8, 2010 (Rev. Proc. 2011-26, Section 4).

Qualified Leasehold Improvement Property. An improvement to an interior portion of nonresidential real property (whether or not depreciated under MACRS) by a lessor or lessee under or pursuant to a lease may qualify for bonus depreciation. The improvement must be placed in service more than three years after the building was first placed in service (i.e., the building must be more than three years old). The lessor and lessee may not be related persons. Expenditures for (1) the enlargement of a building, (2) any elevator or escalator, (3) any structural component that benefits a common area, or (4) the internal structural framework of the building do not qualify (Code Sec. 168(k)(3)). Retail improvement property (¶ 1240) and restaurant improvements (¶ 1240) that also meet the requirements of leasehold improvement property qualify for bonus depreciation (Rev. Proc. 2011-26, Section 3.03(1)(b)(3)).

Computation. The bonus deduction is claimed on the cost of the property after reduction by any Code Sec. 179 allowance (¶ 1208) claimed. Regular MACRS deductions are computed on the cost as reduced by any Code Sec. 179 allowance and bonus depreciation.

> **Example 1:** Taxpayer purchases qualifying 5-year MACRS property subject to the half-year convention for $1,500 and claims a $600 Code Sec. 179 allowance. Using the 50-percent rate, bonus depreciation is $450 (($1,500 - $600) × 50%). Regular MACRS depreciation deductions are computed on a depreciable basis of $450 ($1,500 - $600 - $450). The regular first-year MACRS allowance is $90 ($450 × 20% (first-year table percentage)).

Election by Corporation to Forgo Bonus Depreciation and Claim Accelerated Research and/or AMT Credit Carryforward from Tax Years Beginning Before 2006. A corporation may make an election in its first tax year ending after March 31, 2008, pursuant to which it will forgo the bonus depreciation deduction on eligible qualified property and in return claim a refundable credit (in each tax year that eligible qualified property is placed in service) for a portion of:

(1) its unused general business credit carryforward that is attributable to research credits from tax years that began before January 1, 2006 (determined by using the ordering rules of Code Sec. 38(d)); and/or

(2) its unused alternative minimum tax liability credit attributable to tax years that began before January 1, 2006 (Code Sec. 168(k)(4); Rev. Proc. 2009-33, modifying Rev. Proc. 2009-16 and Rev. Proc. 2008-65).[55]

References are to Standard Federal Tax Reports; Tax Research Consultant; and Practical Tax Explanations.

[55] ¶ 11,279.0583; DEPR: 3,606; § 11,115.25c

Foregone bonus depreciation not claimed on eligible qualified property that is "round 2 extension property" (generally, property placed in service in 2011 and 2012) may only be used to free up pre-January 1, 2006, AMT credits (Code Sec. 168(k)(4)(I)(i)).

The computation for the refundable AMT credit for round 2 extension property (and extension property) is made on a worksheet provided with Form 8827 (Credit for Prior Year Minimum Tax—Corporations). The computation of the refundable research credit for extension property is made on a worksheet found in Form 3800 (General Business Credit).

Effective for property placed in service after December 31, 2010, eligible qualified property is property that is acquired after March 31, 2008, and before January 1, 2013, and placed in service before January 1, 2013 (before January 1, 2014, for longer-period production property and certain noncommercial aircraft) and that is eligible for the bonus depreciation deduction. No binding written purchase contract may be in effect before April 1, 2008 (Code Sec. 168(k)(2)(A) and (4)(D)).

Effective for property placed in service before January 1, 2011, eligible qualified property is property that is acquired after March 31, 2008, and before January 1, 2010, and placed in service before January 1, 2010 (before January 1, 2011, for longer-period production property and certain noncommercial aircraft) and that is eligible for the bonus depreciation deduction. No binding written purchase contract may be in effect before April 1, 2008 (Code Sec. 168(k)(2)(A) and (4)(D), prior to amendment by the Tax Relief, Unemployment Insurance Reauthorization, and Job Creation Act of 2010 (P.L. 111-312)).

The Small Business Jobs Act of 2010 (P.L. 111-240) extended bonus depreciation an additional year to include qualifying assets acquired after December 31, 2007, and before January 1, 2011, and placed in service after December 31, 2009, and before January 1, 2011 (before January 1, 2012, for property with a long production period and certain noncommercial aircraft). Property that qualifies for bonus depreciation only on account of this one-year extension is not treated as eligible qualified property (former Code Sec. 168(k)(4)(D)(iv) and (v), effective for property placed in service after December 31, 2010).

A corporation that makes the accelerated credit election in its first tax year ending after March 31, 2008, may also make an election to exclude "extension property" (Code Sec. 168(k)(4)(H)(i)). Extension property is property that qualifies for bonus depreciation only by reason of the one-year extension of the bonus depreciation (i.e., under the provision that makes bonus depreciation available to qualifying property placed in service in 2009 (in 2010 for property with a long production period and certain noncommercial aircraft)) (Code Sec. 168(k)(4)(H)(iii)). Thus, if this election is made, the corporation may claim bonus depreciation on the extension property and the extension property is not taken into account in determining the accelerated AMT and/or research credit.

A corporation that did not make the accelerated credit election for its first tax year ending after March 31, 2008, may make the election to apply the provision to its first tax year ending after December 31, 2008, and all subsequent tax years. The election applies to eligible qualified property that is extension property (Code Sec. 168(k)(4)(H)(ii)).

If a corporation previously made an election to forgo bonus depreciation for its first tax year beginning after March 31, 2008, or made an election to forgo bonus depreciation with respect to extension property for its first tax year ending after December 31, 2008, the election to forgo bonus depreciation will apply to "round 2 extension property," unless the corporation makes an election not to forgo bonus depreciation on round 2 extension property (Code Sec. 168(k)(4)(I)(ii)).

If a corporation did not previously make an election to forgo bonus depreciation in its first tax year beginning after March 31, 2008, and did not make an election to forgo bonus depreciation with respect to extension property for its first tax year ending after December 31, 2008, the corporation may make an election to forgo bonus depreciation in its first tax year ending after December 31, 2010, and each subsequent tax year.

However, if the election is made, it only applies to round 2 extension property (Code Sec. 168(k)(4)(I)(iii)).

Round 2 extension property is property that is eligible qualified property (as defined above in Code Sec. 168(k)(4)(D)) solely by reason of the two-year extension of the bonus depreciation allowance for property acquired after December 31, 2007, and placed in service in 2011 or 2012, and, in the case of longer-period production property and certain noncommercial aircraft, to property placed in service in 2013 (Code Sec. 168(k)(4)(I)(iv)).

The total amount of the unused research and AMT credits that may be claimed for any tax year is generally equal to the bonus depreciation amount for that tax year. The bonus depreciation amount is 20 percent of the difference between (1) the aggregate bonus depreciation and regular depreciation that would be allowed on eligible qualified property placed in service during the tax year if bonus depreciation was claimed and (2) the aggregate depreciation that would be allowed on the eligible qualified property placed in service during the tax year if no bonus depreciation was claimed (Code Sec. 168(k)(4)(C)(i)).

The bonus depreciation amount for any tax year, however, may not exceed the "maximum increase amount" reduced (but not below zero) by the sum of the bonus depreciation amounts for all preceding tax years (Code Sec. 168(k)(4)(C)(ii)). The bonus depreciation amount, as limited by this rule, is referred to as the "maximum amount." The maximum increase amount is the lesser of: (1) $30 million, or (2) 6 percent of the sum of the "business credit increase amount" (i.e., unused research credits from tax years beginning before 2006) and the "AMT credit increase amount" (i.e., unused AMT credits from tax years beginning before 2006) (Code Sec. 168(k)(4)(C)(ii) and (iii); Rev. Proc. 2008-65, Section 5.03). When computing the maximum increase amount with respect to round 2 extension property, the business credit increase amount is disregarded (Code Sec. 168(k)(4)(I)(i)(II)) because the bonus depreciation amount may not be used to offset unused pre-2006 research credits.

A separate bonus depreciation amount, maximum amount, and maximum increase amount are computed and applied to eligible qualified property which is extension property, eligible qualified property which is round 2 extension property, and eligible qualified property which is not extension property or round 2 extension property (Code Sec. 168(k)(4)(H)(i)(II); Code Sec. 168(k)(4)(I)(ii) and (iii); Rev. Proc. 2009-33, Section 5.02). This separate computation means that a corporation may claim a maximum $30 million of credits with respect to property that is not extension property or round 2 extension property, a maximum $30 million of credits with respect to property that is extension property, and a maximum $30 million of credits with respect to property that is round 2 extension property.

To claim a tax credit for an unused research credit from a tax year beginning before January 1, 2006, a corporation increases the Code Sec. 38(c) tax liability limitation for the tax year by the bonus depreciation amount for the tax year as computed above (Code Sec. 168(k)(4)(A)(iii) and (B)). The bonus depreciation amount allocated to the Code Sec. 38(c) tax liability limitation, however, may not exceed the corporation's pre-2006 research credit carryforwards reduced by any amount allocated to the Code Sec. 38(c) tax liability limitation under this provision in earlier tax years. The bonus depreciation amount may be allocated between the Code Sec. 38(c) tax liability limitation for the general business credit and the Code Sec. 53(c) tax liability limitation for the AMT tax credit. The amount allocated to the AMT tax liability limitation may not exceed the pre-2006 AMT credits reduced by any bonus depreciation amount allocated to the Code Sec. 53(c) tax liability limitation in previous tax years (Code Sec. 168(k)(4)(E)(ii)).

If this election is made depreciation is computed without claiming bonus depreciation and by using the MACRS straight-line method (Code Sec. 168(k)(4)(A)). Thus, the amount of bonus depreciation that would otherwise be deducted in a single year is recovered through straight-line depreciation deductions over the applicable MACRS recovery period for the property.

> **Example 2:** QPEX is a calendar-year corporation that places round 2 extension property that is 10-year MACRS property costing $100,000 in service in June 2012.

QPEX made the election for its first tax year ending after March 31, 2008, and does not make the election to exclude round 2 extension property. It first computes the bonus depreciation and regular depreciation on the MACRS round 2 extension property. Bonus depreciation is $50,000 ($100,000 × 50%). Regular depreciation is $5,000 (($100,000 – $50,000 × 10% first- year percentage for 10-year property = $5,000). The $55,000 sum of the bonus depreciation and regular depreciation is reduced to $45,000 by the $10,000 depreciation that could be claimed in 2012 on the property if the bonus deduction was not claimed ($100,000 × 10% first- year percentage for 10-year property = $10,000). Assume that QPEX has $200,000 in unused pre-2006 AMT credits and claimed no AMT credit with respect to round 2 extension property placed in service in 2011. The bonus depreciation amount is equal to the lesser of: (1) $9,000 ($45,000 × 20%); (2) $12,000 ((6 percent of QPEX's unused pre-2006 AMT credits ($200,000 × 6% = $12,000)); or (3) $30 million. Since $9,000 is less than the amounts in items (2) and (3), the bonus depreciation amount is $9,000. In this situation QPEX could increase its AMT tax liability limitation by $9,000 and claim a refundable $9,000 AMT credit.

50 Percent Bonus Allowance for Gulf Opportunity Zone Property. Taxpayers were allowed to claim a bonus depreciation allowance equal to 50 percent of the adjusted basis of qualified Gulf Opportunity Zone property acquired after August 27, 2005, and placed in service on or before December 31, 2007 (Code Sec. 1400N(d); Notice 2006-77, providing extensive regulatory type guidance).[56]

The placed-in-service deadline for nonresidential and residential property is December 31, 2008. The deadline is extended to December 31, 2011, if the building is located in the Louisiana parishes of Calcasieu, Cameron, Orleans, Plaquemines, St. Bernard, St. Tammany, or Washington or the Mississippi counties of Hancock, Harrison, Jackson, Pearl River, or Stone. Bonus depreciation may be claimed on portions of buildings (e.g., floors of multi-story buildings) that are placed in service by the December 31, 2011, deadline.

If the Gulf Zone bonus allowance is claimed, the bonus allowance and regular depreciation deductions on the property are allowed in full for AMT purposes. If business use drops to less than 80 percent, the deduction is subject to recapture under rules similar to those that apply to the Code Sec. 179 allowance (¶ 1208).

50 Percent Bonus Allowance for Qualified Disaster Assistance Property. Effective for property placed in service after December 31, 2007, a taxpayer who has suffered an economic loss attributable to a federally declared disaster declared after that date and which occurred before January 1, 2010, may claim an additional first-year depreciation deduction equal to 50 percent of the adjusted basis of qualified Disaster Assistance property (QDAP) (Code Sec. 168(n)).[57]

50 Percent Bonus Allowance for Mine Safety Equipment. A taxpayer may elect to deduct 50 percent of the cost of qualified advanced mine safety equipment paid or incurred after December 20, 2006, if the equipment is placed in service before January 1, 2012 (Code Sec. 179E).[58]

50 Percent Bonus Allowance for Qualified Reuse and Recycling Property. A 50-percent additional depreciation allowance may be claimed on the adjusted basis of qualified reuse and recycling property acquired and placed in service after August 31, 2008. The property must be acquired by purchase, its original use must begin with the taxpayer, it must have a useful life of a least five years, and no pre-September 1, 2008, binding acquisition contract may be in effect. Reuse and recycling property is machinery and equipment (not including buildings, real estate, rolling stock or equipment used to transport reuse and recyclable materials) that is used exclusively to collect, distribute, or recycle qualified reuse and recyclable materials. Machinery and equipment include appurtenances such as software necessary to operate the equipment. Qualified reuse and recyclable materials are scrap plastic, glass, textiles, rubber, packaging, and metal,

References are to Standard Federal Tax Reports; Tax Research Consultant; and Practical Tax Explanations.

[56] ¶ 32,487.031; DEPR: 3,650; § 11,225

[57] ¶ 11,279.0586; SALES: 42,104; § 11,225.05

[58] ¶ 12,139D.01; BUSEXP: 19,000; § 10,255

as well as recovered fiber and electronic scrap. A taxpayer may elect out for any class of property (Code Sec. 168(m)).[59]

50 Percent Bonus Allowance for Cellulosic Biofuel Plant Property. A 50-percent additional depreciation allowance may be claimed on the adjusted basis of qualified cellulosic biofuel plant property placed in service after October 3, 2008, and before January 1, 2013 (Code Sec. 168(l)).[60]

1238. Property Subject to MACRS. Generally, most tangible depreciable property placed in service after 1986 is depreciated using the Modified Accelerated Cost Recovery System (MACRS). MACRS property is depreciable if it wears out, has a useful life that exceeds one year, and is used in a trade or business or for the production of income. Such property does not include property for which an election was made to use a depreciation method not expressed in terms of years, such as the unit of production or income forecast method; public utility property (unless a normalization method of accounting is used); motion picture films and videotapes; sound recordings; intangible property; and property placed in service before 1987 that is excluded from MACRS under the anti-churning rules (Code Sec. 168(f)).[61] Public utility property that does not qualify under MACRS (Code Sec. 168(f)(2))[62] is depreciated under Code Sec. 167(a)[63] using the same depreciation method and useful life as is used to compute the ratemaking depreciation allowance for the property.[64]

Accounting for MACRS property in item, pool, and general asset accounts. MACRS property may be accounted for (a) individually in an item account, (b) by placing a group of identically depreciated assets (i.e., assets with the same recovery period, depreciation method, convention, and placed-in-service tax year) in a multiple asset (pool) account, or (c) by electing to include a single asset or a group of identically depreciated assets in a general asset account (GAA) (Temporary Reg. § 1.168(i)-1T; Temporary Reg. § 1.168(i)-7T).[65] Generally, no loss is realized upon the disposition of an asset from a GAA and the entire amount realized is recognized as gain unless the taxpayer makes an election to treat the disposition as a qualifying disposition and recognize gain or loss by reference to the disposed of asset's adjusted depreciable basis. For a taxpayer's first or second tax year beginning after December 31, 2011, a taxpayer may make a late GAA account election and/or a late election to treat the disposition of an asset from a GAA as a qualifying disposition. During this two-year period, a taxpayer may also make a late election to recognize gain or loss on the disposition of all of or the last asset from a GAA by taking into account the adjusted depreciable basis of the GAA (Rev. Proc. 2012-20, adding Section 6.32 to the Appendix of Rev. Proc. 2011-14). Effective for tax years beginning on or after January 1, 2012, the retirement of a structural component of a building is treated as a disposition which triggers the recognition of a loss which in turn requires reduction of the basis of the building by the amount of the loss (Temporary Reg. § 1.168(i)-8T). For this reason it may be desirable to elect to place new and existing buildings in a GAA thereby allowing taxpayers the opportunity to decide on a case-by-case basis whether to follow the default no loss realization rule when a structural component is retired (thereby making a building basis reduction unnecessary) or to make an election to treat the retirement as a qualifying disposition that triggers recognition of the loss. See "*Structural Components*" at ¶ 1240.

1240. MACRS Depreciation Periods. The Modified Accelerated Cost Recovery System (MACRS) depreciation (recovery) period for an asset is based on its class life as of January 1, 1986, or is specifically prescribed by Code Sec. 168.[66] The recovery periods for MACRS assets can be found in a table that appears in IRS Publication 946. This table

References are to Standard Federal Tax Reports; Tax Research Consultant; and Practical Tax Explanations.

[59] ¶ 11,279.0587; DEPR: 3,800; § 11,235

[60] ¶ 11,279.0585; DEPR: 3,850; § 11,220

[61] ¶ 11,250, ¶ 11,279.021; DEPR: 15,150; § 11,105

[62] ¶ 11,250; DEPR: 6,150; § 11,110

[63] ¶ 11,002; DEPR: 15,700; § 11,110

[64] ¶ 11,070.01; DEPR: 6,150; § 11,110

[65] ¶ 11,279.0372, ¶ 11,279.038; DEPR: 3,559, DEPR: 15,210; § 11,105.07 § 11,140

[66] ¶ 163.01, ¶ 11,279.021; DEPR: 15,150; § 11,110

is an updated version of the table that appears in Rev. Proc. 87-56. Under MACRS, assets are classified according to their class life as follows:

Three-Year Property. Three-year property includes property with a class life of four years or less. Any race horse placed in service after December 31, 2008, and before January 1, 2014, or any other horse over 12 years old at the time it is placed in service is classified as three-year property (Code Sec. 168(e)(1) and (3)). A race horse more than two years old at the time placed in service is three-year property if placed in service on or before December 31, 2008, or on or after January 1, 2014.[67] Certain "rent-to-own" consumer durable property (e.g., televisions and furniture) is three-year property (Code Sec. 168(e)(3)(iii)).[68] Breeding hogs (Rev. Proc. 87-56 Asset Class 01.236) and tractor units for use over the road (Rev. Proc. 87-56 Asset Class 00.26) are three-year property. A tractor unit is a highway truck designed to tow a trailer or semitrailer and which does not carry cargo on the same chassis as the engine (Reg. § 145.4051-1(e)(1)).

Five-Year Property. Five-year property generally includes property with a class life of more than four years and less than 10 years. This property includes: (1) cars, (2) light and heavy general-purpose trucks, (3) qualified technological equipment, (4) computer-based telephone central office switching equipment, (5) research and experimentation property that is Sec. 1245 property, (6) semi-conductor manufacturing equipment, (7) geothermal, solar and wind energy properties, (8) certain biomass properties that are small power production facilities, (9) computers and peripheral equipment, and (10) office machinery (typewriters, calculators, etc.) (Code Sec. 168(e)(1) and (3)).[69]

Furniture, appliances, window treatments, and carpeting used in residential rental property are five-year property (Announcement 99-82). Personal property used in wholesale or retail trade or in the provision of personal and professional services for which a specific recovery period is not otherwise provided is five-year property (Asset Class 57.0 of Rev. Proc. 87-56). For example, a professional library used by an accountant or attorney is five-year property. Examples of *personal* service businesses include hotels and motels, laundry and dry cleaning establishments, beauty and barber shops, photographic studios and mortuaries (Rev. Proc. 77-10). Examples of *professional* service businesses include services offered by doctors, dentists, lawyers, accountants, architects, engineers, and veterinarians (Rev. Proc. 77-10).

Five-year property also includes taxis (Rev. Proc. 87-56 Asset Class 00.22), buses (Rev. Proc. 87-56 Asset Class 00.23), airplanes not used in commercial or contract carrying of passengers or freight and all helicopters (Rev. Proc. 87-56 Asset Class 00.21), trailers and trailer-mounted containers (Rev. Proc. 87-56 Asset Class 00.27), breeding cattle and dairy cattle (Rev. Proc. 87-56 Asset Class 01.21), breeding sheep and breeding goats (Rev. Proc. 87-56 Asset Class 01.21), and assets used in construction by certain contractors, builders, and real estate subdividers and developers (Rev. Proc. 87-56 Asset Class 15.0).

Seven-Year Property. Seven-year property includes property with a class life of 10 years or more but less than 16 years (Code Sec. 168(e)(1)). This property includes office furniture, equipment and fixtures that are not structural components (Rev. Proc. 87-56 Asset Class 00.11). Desks, files, safes, overhead projectors, cell phones, fax machines and other communication equipment not included in any other class fall within this category. Seven-year property also includes: assets (except helicopters) used in commercial and contract carrying of passengers and freight by air (Rev. Proc. 87-56 Asset Class 45.0); certain livestock (Rev. Proc. 87-56 Asset Class 01.1); breeding or work horses 12 years old or less when placed in service (Rev. Proc. 87-56 Asset Class 01.221); other horses that are not three-year property (Rev. Proc. 87-56 Asset Class 01.225); assets used in recreation businesses (Rev. Proc. 87-56 Asset Class 80.0); and assets used in theme and amusement parks (Rev. Proc. 87-56 Asset Class 80.0). Railroad track and

References are to Standard Federal Tax Reports; Tax Research Consultant; and Practical Tax Explanations.

[67] ¶ 11,250, ¶ 11,279.023; DEPR: 3,156.05; § 11,110

[68] ¶ 11,250, ¶ 11,279.023; DEPR: 3,156.60; § 11,110

[69] ¶ 11,250, ¶ 11,279.023; DEPR: 3,156.10; § 11,110

property (such as a fishing vessel) that does not have a class life and is not otherwise classified is seven-year property (Code Sec. 168(e)(3)(C)).[70]

10-Year Property. Ten-year property is property with a class life of 16 years or more and less than 20 years (Code Sec. 168(e)(1)).[71] Ten-year property includes vessels, barges, tugs, and similar means of water transportation not used in marine construction or as a fishing vessel (Rev. Proc. 87-56 Asset Class 00.28) and, effective for property placed in service after October 3, 2008, smart electric meters and qualified smart electric grid systems (Code Sec. 168(e)(3)(D)). MACRS deductions for trees or vines bearing fruit or nuts that are placed in service after 1988 are determined under the straight-line method over a 10-year recovery period (Code Sec. 168(b)(1)).[72] Single purpose agricultural or horticultural structures placed in service after 1988 are ten-year property (Code Sec. 168(e)(3)(D)(i)).

15-Year Property. Property with a class life of 20 years or more but less than 25 years is generally considered 15-year property (Code Sec. 168(e)(1)). It includes municipal wastewater treatment plants and telephone distribution plants and other comparable equipment used for the two-way exchange of voice, data communications, and retail motor fuels outlets (Code Sec. 168(e)(3)(E)).[73] A property qualifies as a retail motor fuels outlet (as opposed, for example, to a convenience store which is 39-year real property) if (1) 50 percent or more of gross revenues are derived from petroleum sales, or (2) 50 percent or more of the floor space is devoted to petroleum marketing sales, or (3) the property is 1,400 square feet or less (Rev. Proc. 97-10).[74]

15-year property includes car wash buildings (and related land improvements), billboards, and section 1250 real property (including service station buildings) and depreciable land improvements used in marketing petroleum and petroleum products (Rev. Proc. 87-56 Asset Class 57.1). Water transportation assets (other than vessels) used in the commercial and contract carrying of freight and passengers by water are 15-year property (Rev. Proc. 87-56 Asset Class 44.0).

Land improvements not specifically included in any other asset class and otherwise depreciable are 15-year property (Rev. Proc. 87-56 Asset Class 00.3). Examples of land improvements include sidewalks, driveways, curbs, roads, parking lots, canals, waterways, drainage facilities, sewers (but not municipal sewers), wharves and docks, bridges, and nonagricultural fences. Landscaping and shrubbery is a depreciable land improvement if it is located near a building and would be destroyed if the building were replaced (Rev. Rul. 74-265; IRS Publication 946). Playground equipment is a land improvement (IRS Letter Ruling 8848039).[75]

Depreciable gas utility clearing and grading costs incurred after October 22, 2004, to place pipelines into service are 15-year property (Code Sec. 168(e)(3)(E)(vi)).

15-Year Restaurant Improvements and Buildings. Qualified restaurant property placed in service after October 22, 2004, and before January 1, 2012, is 15-year MACRS property, depreciable using the straight-line method using the half-year or mid-quarter convention, as applicable.[76] The ADS recovery period is 39 years. Qualified restaurant property is section 1250 property which is an improvement to a building. The improvement must be placed in service more than three years after the date the building was first placed in service. More than 50 percent of the building's square footage must be devoted to preparation of and seating for on-premises consumption of prepared meals. For improvements placed in service after 2008, it is not necessary that the restaurant building be more than three years old (Code Sec. 168(e)(3)(E)(v) and (e)(7)).

A restaurant building placed in service after December 31, 2008, and before January 1, 2012, is also included in the definition of qualified restaurant property and is

References are to Standard Federal Tax Reports; Tax Research Consultant; and Practical Tax Explanations.

[70] ¶ 11,250, ¶ 11,279.023; DEPR: 3,156.15; § 11,110

[71] ¶ 11,250, ¶ 11,279.023; DEPR: 3,156.20; § 11,110

[72] ¶ 11,250, ¶ 11,279.023; DEPR: 3,156.20; § 11,110

[73] ¶ 11,250, ¶ 11,279.023; DEPR: 3,156.25; § 11,110

[74] ¶ 11,279.023; DEPR: 3,156.25; § 11,110

[75] ¶ 11,279.0518; DEPR: 6,062.10; § 11,110

[76] ¶ 11,279.0311; DEPR: 3,156.256; § 11,215

depreciated as 15-year property using the straight-line method and half-year or mid-quarter convention if more than 50 percent of the building's square footage is devoted to preparation of, and seating for on-premises consumption of, prepared meals. A 39-year ADS recovery period applies (Code Sec. 168(e)(7)(A); Code Sec. 168(b)(3)(I)).

The Code Sec. 168(k) bonus depreciation deduction may not be claimed on qualified restaurant property placed in service after December 31, 2008, unless it meets the definition of qualified leasehold improvement property (¶ 1237) (Code Sec. 168(e)(7)(B); Rev. Proc. 2011-26).

15-Year Qualified Retail Improvement Property. Qualified retail improvement property placed in service after December 31, 2008, and before January 1, 2012, is depreciated under MACRS using a 15-year recovery period, the straight-line method, and the half-year or mid-quarter convention.[77] The ADS recovery period is 39 years. Qualified retail improvement property is an improvement to the interior portion of a building that is nonresidential real property. The improvement must be placed in service more than three years after the building was first placed in service. The improved interior portion must be open to the general public and used in the retail trade or business of selling tangible personal property to the general public. Elevators and escalators, internal structural framework of the building, structural components that benefit a common area, and improvements relating to the enlargement of a building do not qualify. Qualified retail improvement property is ineligible for bonus depreciation under Code Sec. 168(k) unless it also meets the definition of qualified leasehold improvement property (¶ 1237) (Code Sec. 168(e)(8); Rev. Proc. 2011-26).

20-Year Property. Twenty-year property includes property with a class life of 25 years and more, other than Code Sec. 1250 real property with a class life of 27.5 years or more. Water utility property and municipal sewers placed in service before June 13, 1996, and farm buildings (e.g., barns and machine sheds) are included within this class (Code Sec. 168(e)(1) and (3)).[78]

Depreciable electric utility clearing and grading costs incurred after October 22, 2004, to place transmission and distribution lines into service are 20-year property (Code Sec. 168(e)(3)(F)).

25-Year Property. Water utility property and municipal sewers placed in service after June 12, 1996 are included in this class (Code Sec. 168(c) and (e)(5)). The straight-line depreciation method is mandatory for 25-year property (Code Sec. 168(b)(3)(F)).

27.5-Year Residential Rental Property. Residential rental property (Code Sec. 168(e)(2)(A))[79] includes buildings or structures with respect to which 80 percent or more of the gross rental income is from dwelling units. It also includes manufactured homes that are residential rental property and elevators and escalators.

Nonresidential Real Property. Nonresidential real property is Code Sec. 1250 real property (¶ 1786) that is not (1) residential rental property or (2) property with a class life (as provided in Rev. Proc. 87-56) of less than 27.5 years (Code Sec. 168(e)(2)(B)).[80] The cost of nonresidential real property generally placed in service after May 12, 1993, is recovered over 39 years. For property placed in service after 1986 and before May 13, 1993, cost is recovered over 31.5 years.

Farm Machinery and Equipment. Machinery and equipment, grain bins, and fences (but no other land improvements) used in specified agricultural activities are classified as MACRS 7-year property and have a 10-year ADS recovery period (Rev. Proc. 87-56 Asset Class 01.1). However, any machinery or equipment (other than any grain bin, cotton ginning asset, fence, or other land improvement) which is used in a farming business (as defined in Code Sec. 263A(e)(4)), the original use of which commences with the taxpayer after December 31, 2008, and which is placed in service before January

References are to Standard Federal Tax Reports; Tax Research Consultant; and Practical Tax Explanations.

[77] ¶ 11,279.0313; DEPR: 3,156.255; § 11,230

[78] ¶ 11,250, ¶ 11,279.023; DEPR: 3,156.30; § 11,110

[79] ¶ 11,250, ¶ 11,279.023; DEPR: 3,156.35; § 11,110

[80] ¶ 11,250, ¶ 11,279.023; DEPR: 3,156.40; § 11,110

1, 2010, is classified as MACRS 5-year property (Code Sec. 168(e)(3)(B)(vii)) and has a 10-year ADS recovery period (Code Sec. 168(g)(3)(B)).

Property used in a farming business is depreciated using the 150 percent declining balance method as explained at ¶ 1243 (Code Sec. 168(b)(2)(B)).

Indian Reservation Property. For qualified Indian reservation property that is placed in service after 1993 and before January 1, 2012, special MACRS recovery periods are provided for both regular tax and alternative minimum tax purposes that permit faster write-offs (Code Sec. 168(j)).[81]

Additions and Improvements. Additions and improvements made to an existing property are depreciated under MACRS in the same way that the existing property would be depreciated if it were placed in service at the same time as the addition or improvement (Code Sec. 168(i)(6)). For example, a new floor added to a commercial building in 2012 is treated as 39-year MACRS nonresidential real property even if the building is depreciated under a pre-MACRS method.[82] However, any elements of an addition or improvement to a building that qualify as personal property may be depreciated as personal rather than real property by reason of the cost segregation rule described below. Special rules apply to leasehold improvement property (¶ 1234) and improvements to restaurants and buildings used in a retail business, as explained above.

Structural components. Effective for tax years beginning on or after January 1, 2012, the retirement of a structural component of a building is treated as a disposition and, therefore, triggers the recognition of a loss in an amount equal to the undepreciated portion of the basis of the retired structural component. Previously, the retirement of a structural component of a building was not considered a disposition. Instead, a taxpayer was required to continue depreciating the replaced/retired structural component and no adjustment to the basis of the building was made (Proposed Reg. § 1.168-2(l)(1); Field Service Advice 199937022, June 17, 1999; Field Service Advice 200141026, July 11, 2001). The term structural component is defined in Reg. § 1.48-1(e)(2). Taxpayers currently depreciating a previously retired structural component are required to cease depreciating the component, file a change in accounting method to claim a loss deduction in the form of a Code Sec. 481(a) adjustment, and reduce the basis of the building by the amount of the allowable loss deduction (Rev. Proc. 2012-20 adding Section 6.29 to the Appendix Rev. Proc. 2011-14). Alternatively, a taxpayer may make a retroactive GAA election and either (a) continue to depreciate the retired component by following the default "no loss realization" rule for GAAs or (b) make a retroactive election to treat the prior retirement as a qualifying disposition from the GAA and claim a loss deduction in the form of a Code Sec. 481(a) adjustment (Rev. Proc. 2012-20, adding Section 6.32 to the Appendix of Rev. Proc. 2011-14).[83] See ¶ 1238. For buildings placed in service in a tax year ending before December 30, 2003, a taxpayer may instead file amended returns for open tax years that remove depreciation claimed in the open years on the retired structural component (Rev. Proc. 2012-20, Section. 5.01). The basis of the building is reduced by the otherwise allowable loss deduction on the retired component and going forward depreciation may not be claimed on the retired component.

Roofs. The IRS maintains that the replacement of all of the shingles on a roof or the asphalt and gravel on a flat roof is a capital expenditure. Although the IRS position is supported by many court decisions, the Tax Court has held that the cost of removing and replacing the entire perlite and asphalt and gravel covering on a leaky roof (as well as replacing an expansion joint to prevent further leaking) was a deductible repair (*Oberman Manufacturing Co.*, 47 TC 471, Dec. 28,334). The IRS has attempted to clarify the treatment of roofs in temporary regulations that are effective for tax years beginning on or after January 1, 2012 (Temporary Reg. § 1.263(a)-3T; Rev. Proc. 2012-19). Under the temporary regulations, the replacement of an entire roof (including the sheathing and rafters) or a significant portion of a roof that has deteriorated over time is a

References are to Standard Federal Tax Reports; Tax Research Consultant; and Practical Tax Explanations.

[81] ¶ 11,250, ¶ 11,279.031; DEPR: 3,156.55; § 11,120

[82] ¶ 11,279.05; DEPR: 6,052; § 11,110

[83] ¶ 11,279.0373; ¶ 11,279.038; DEPR: 3,559; DEPR: 15,210; § 11,140

restoration that is capitalized as an improvement (Temporary Reg. § 1.263(a)-3T(i)(5), Examples 12 and 13). The replacement of a worn and leaking waterproof membrane on a roof comprised of structural elements, insulation, and a waterproof membrane with a similar but new membrane is not required to be capitalized (Temporary Reg. § 1.263(a)-3T(i)(5), Example 14). Also, a taxpayer is not required to treat the amount paid to replace all of the asphalt shingles on a roof that is damaged by a storm with comparable wooden or asphalt shingles as a capitalized "betterment" because it does not result in a material addition, or material increase in the capacity, productivity, efficiency, strength, or quality of the building structure or the output of the building structure compared to the condition of the building structure prior to the storm (Temporary Reg. § 1.263(a)-3T(h)(3)(iii)(C)(4), Examples (13), (14), and (15)).[84]

Cost Segregation. The Tax Court has ruled that elements of a building that are treated as personal property under the former investment tax credit rules (Reg. § 1.48-1(c)) may be separately depreciated under MACRS and ACRS as personal property (*Hospital Corp. of America*, 109 TC 21, Dec. 52,163). The IRS has acquiesced to the court's holding that the former investment tax credit rules apply in determining whether an item is a structural component (i.e., real property) or personal property but nonacquiesced to its finding that various disputed items were in fact personal property under these rules (Notice of Acquiescence, 1999-35 I.R.B. 314). The separate depreciation of personal property elements of a building is referred to as cost segregation.[85]

The determination of whether an item is personal property or a structural component will often depend upon the specific facts. However, the following items, if related to the operation and maintenance of a building, are examples of structural components: bathtubs, boilers, ceilings (including acoustical ceilings), central air conditioning and heating systems, chimneys, doors, electrical and wiring, fire escapes, floors, hot water heaters, HVAC units, lighting fixtures, paneling, partitions (if not readily removable), plumbing, roofs, sinks, sprinkler systems, stairs, tiling, walls, and windows (Reg. § 1.48-1(e)(2)).

1243. MACRS Recovery Methods. Under the Modified Accelerated Cost Recovery System (MACRS), the cost of depreciable property is recovered using (1) the applicable depreciation method, (2) the applicable recovery period, and (3) the applicable convention (Code Sec. 168(a)).[86]

The cost of property in the 3-, 5-, 7-, and 10-year classes is recovered using the 200 percent declining-balance method (i.e., the applicable depreciation method) over three, five, seven, and ten years, respectively (i.e., the applicable recovery period), and the half-year convention (unless the mid-quarter convention applies), with a switch to the straight-line method in the year that maximizes the deduction (Code Sec. 168(b)(1)).[87] The cost of 15- and 20-year property is recovered using the 150 percent declining-balance method over 15 and 20 years, respectively, and the half-year convention (unless the mid-quarter convention applies), with a switch to the straight-line method to maximize the deduction (Code Sec. 168(b)(2)).[88] The cost of residential rental and nonresidential real property is recovered using the straight-line method and the mid-month convention over 27.5- and 39-year recovery periods, respectively (Code Sec. 168(b)(3)).[89]

Instead of the applicable depreciation method (200 percent declining balance method for 3-, 5-, 7-, and 10-year property and 150 percent declining balance method for 10- and 15-year property), taxpayers may irrevocably elect to claim straight-line MACRS deductions over the regular recovery period. The election applies to all property in the MACRS class for which the election is made that is placed in service during the tax year and is made on the return for the year the property is first placed in service (Code Sec.

References are to Standard Federal Tax Reports; Tax Research Consultant; and Practical Tax Explanations.

[84] ¶ 13,709.0575; BUSEXP: 9,152.05; § 11,110

[85] ¶ 11,279.051; DEPR: 6,058; § 11,110

[86] ¶ 11,279.03; DEPR: 3,200; § 11,115

[87] ¶ 11,250, ¶ 11,279.03; DEPR: 3,202; § 11,115

[88] ¶ 11,250, ¶ 11,279.03; DEPR: 3,202; § 11,115

[89] ¶ 11,250, ¶ 11,279.03; DEPR: 3,202; § 11,115

168(b)(5)). For example, if the election is made for 3-year property, it applies to all 3-year property placed in service in the tax year of the election.

An election may be made to recover the cost of 3-, 5-, 7-, and 10-year property using the 150 percent declining-balance method over the regular recovery periods (the ADS recovery period for property placed in service before 1999) (¶ 1247) (Code Sec. 168(b)(2)(C)). This election, like the straight-line election above, is made separately for each property class placed in service during the tax year of the election.[90] A taxpayer may also elect the MACRS alternative depreciation system (ADS) with respect to any class of property. ADS uses the straight-line method over recovery periods that are usually longer than those that normally apply under MACRS. See ¶ 1247.

3-, 5-, 7-, and 10-year property used in the trade or business of farming must be depreciated under the 150 percent declining balance method unless an election was made to deduct preproductive period expenditures, in which case the ADS must be used (Code Sec. 168(b)(2)(B)). Consequently, Tables 1-8, below, may not be used for such property.

Computation of Deduction Without Tables. The MACRS deduction on personal property is computed by first determining the rate of depreciation (dividing the number one by the recovery period).[91] This basic rate is multiplied by 1.5 or 2 for the 150 percent or 200 percent declining-balance method, as applicable, to determine the declining balance rate. The adjusted basis of the property is multiplied by the declining-balance rate and the half-year or mid-quarter convention (whichever is applicable) is applied in computing depreciation for the first year. The depreciation claimed in the first year is subtracted from the adjusted basis before applying the declining-balance rate in determining the depreciation deduction for the second year.

Under the MACRS straight-line method (used, for example, on real property or if ADS applies), a new applicable depreciation rate is determined for each tax year in the applicable recovery period. For any tax year, the applicable depreciation rate (in percentage terms) is determined by dividing one by the length of the applicable recovery period remaining as of the beginning of such tax year. The rate is applied to the unrecovered basis of such property in conjunction with the appropriate convention. If as of the beginning of any tax year the remaining recovery period is less than one year, the applicable depreciation rate under the straight-line method for that year is 100 percent.

> **Example 1:** An item of 5-year property is purchased by a calendar-year taxpayer in January ("Year 1") at a cost of $10,000. No Code Sec. 179 expense allowance or bonus depreciation is claimed. The 200 percent declining-balance method and half-year convention apply. Depreciation computed without the use of the IRS tables is determined as follows: the declining-balance depreciation rate is determined and compared with the straight-line rate. A switch is made to the straight-line rate in the year depreciation equals or exceeds that determined under the declining-balance method. The applicable rate is applied to the unrecovered basis. The 200 percent declining-balance depreciation rate is 40 percent (1 divided by 5 (recovery period) times 2). The straight-line rate (which changes each year) is 1 divided by the length of the applicable recovery period remaining as of the beginning of each tax year (after considering the applicable convention for purposes of determining how much of the applicable recovery period remains as of the beginning of the year). For year four, the straight-line rate is .40 (1 divided by 2.5), which is the same as the declining balance rate. For year five, the straight-line rate is .6667 (1 divided by 1.5). For year six, the straight-line rate is 100 percent because the remaining recovery period is less than one year.

References are to Standard Federal Tax Reports; Tax Research Consultant; and Practical Tax Explanations.

[90] ¶ 11,279.035; DEPR: 3,202.05; § 11,115

[91] ¶ 11,279.027; DEPR: 3,204.05; § 11,130

Year	*Method*	*Rate*		*Unrecovered Basis*					*Depreciation*
1	DB	.40	×	$ 10,000 × .5 (half-yr. conv.)			. . . .	=	$ 2,000
2	DB	.40	×	(10,000 – 2,000)	=	$8,000	. .	=	3,200
3	DB	.40	×	(8,000 – 3,200)	=	4,800	. .	=	1,920
4	DB	.40	×	(4,800 – 1,920)	=	2,880	. .	=	1,152
5	SL	.6667	×	(2,880 – 1,152)	=	1,728	. .	=	1,152
6	SL	1.000	×	(1,728 – 1,152)	=	576	. .	=	576
						0			
						Total	. .		$10,000

The computation of MACRS without tables is discussed in detail by the IRS in Rev. Proc. 87-57.

Computation of Deduction Using Tables. MACRS depreciation tables, which contain the annual percentage depreciation rates to be applied to the unadjusted basis of property in each tax year, may be used to compute depreciation instead of the above rules.[92] The tables incorporate the appropriate convention and a switch from the declining-balance method to the straight-line method in the year that the latter provides a depreciation allowance equal to, or larger than, the former. The tables may be used for any item of property (that otherwise qualifies for MACRS) placed in service in a tax year.

Selected MACRS depreciation tables are reproduced below. A complete set of tables is at ¶ 164 of the STANDARD FEDERAL TAX REPORTER and at § 820 of the Practical Tax Explanations. Tables for the TAX RESEARCH CONSULTANT are located in the "Tax Rates and Tables" publication.

If a table is used to compute the annual depreciation allowance for any item of property, it must be used throughout the entire recovery period of such property. However, a taxpayer may not continue to use a table if there are any adjustments to the basis of the property for reasons other than (1) depreciation allowances or (2) an addition or improvement to such property that is subject to depreciation as a separate item of property.

The IRS MACRS depreciation tables may not be used in situations involving short tax years (¶ 1244).

Example 2: Depreciation on 5-year property purchased by a calendar-year taxpayer in January of the current tax year at a cost of $10,000 is computed under the general MACRS 200 percent declining-balance method over a five-year recovery period using the half-year convention. No amount is expensed under Code Sec. 179 or claimed as a bonus deduction.

If the depreciation tables provided by the IRS are used, depreciation is computed as follows: the applicable depreciation rate in Table 1 under the column for a 5-year recovery period for the applicable recovery year is applied to the cost of the property.

Year	*Rate*	*Unadj. Basis*	*Depreciation*		*Basis*		
1	.20 ×	$ 10,000 =	$ 2,000	($10,000 –	$2,000)	=	$8,000
2	.32 ×	10,000 =	3,200	(8,000 –	3,200)	=	4,800
3	.192 ×	10,000 =	1,920	(4,800 –	1,920)	=	2,880
4	.1152 ×	10,000 =	1,152	(2,880 –	1,152)	=	1,728
5	.1152 ×	10,000 =	1,152	(1,728 –	1,152)	=	576
6	.0576 ×	10,000 =	576	(576 –	576)	=	0
		Total	$10,000				

References are to Standard Federal Tax Reports; Tax Research Consultant; and Practical Tax Explanations.

[92] ¶ 164.01; DEPR: 3,204; § 11,130

Table 1. General Depreciation System
Applicable Depreciation Method: 200 or 150 Percent
Declining Balance Switching to Straight Line
Applicable Recovery Periods: 3, 5, 7, 10, 15, 20 years
Applicable Convention: Half-year

If the Recovery Year is:	3-year	5-year	7-year	10-year	15-year	20-year
	and the Recovery Period is:					
	the Depreciation Rate is:					
1	33.33	20.00	14.29	10.00	5.00	3.750
2	44.45	32.00	24.49	18.00	9.50	7.219
3	14.81	19.20	17.49	14.40	8.55	6.677
4	7.41	11.52	12.49	11.52	7.70	6.177
5		11.52	8.93	9.22	6.93	5.713
6		5.76	8.92	7.37	6.23	5.285
7			8.93	6.55	5.90	4.888
8			4.46	6.55	5.90	4.522
9				6.56	5.91	4.462
10				6.55	5.90	4.461
11				3.28	5.91	4.462
12					5.90	4.461
13					5.91	4.462
14					5.90	4.461
15					5.91	4.462
16					2.95	4.461
17						4.462
18						4.461
19						4.462
20						4.461
21						2.231

Table 2. General Depreciation System
Applicable Depreciation Method: 200 or 150 Percent
Declining Balance Switching to Straight Line
Applicable Recovery Periods: 3, 5, 7, 10, 15, 20 years
Applicable Convention: Mid-quarter (property placed in service in first quarter)

If the Recovery Year is:	3-year	5-year	7-year	10-year	15-year	20-year
	and the Recovery Period is:					
	the Depreciation Rate is:					
1	58.33	35.00	25.00	17.50	8.75	6.563
2	27.78	26.00	21.43	16.50	9.13	7.000
3	12.35	15.60	15.31	13.20	8.21	6.482
4	1.54	11.01	10.93	10.56	7.39	5.996
5		11.01	8.75	8.45	6.65	5.546
6		1.38	8.74	6.76	5.99	5.130
7			8.75	6.55	5.90	4.746
8			1.09	6.55	5.91	4.459
9				6.56	5.90	4.459
10				6.55	5.91	4.459
11				0.82	5.90	4.459
12					5.91	4.460
13					5.90	4.459
14					5.91	4.460
15					5.90	4.459
16					0.74	4.460
17						4.459
18						4.460
19						4.459
20						4.460
21						0.565

Table 3. General Depreciation System
Applicable Depreciation Method: 200 or 150 Percent
Declining Balance Switching to Straight Line
Applicable Recovery Periods: 3, 5, 7, 10, 15, 20 years
Applicable Convention: Mid-quarter (property placed in service in second quarter)

If the Recovery Year is:	and the Recovery Period is: 3-year	5-year	7-year	10-year	15-year	20-year
	the Depreciation Rate is:					
1	41.67	25.00	17.85	12.50	6.25	4.688
2	38.89	30.00	23.47	17.50	9.38	7.148
3	14.14	18.00	16.76	14.00	8.44	6.612
4	5.30	11.37	11.97	11.20	7.59	6.116
5		11.37	8.87	8.96	6.83	5.658
6		4.26	8.87	7.17	6.15	5.233
7			8.87	6.55	5.91	4.841
8			3.33	6.55	5.90	4.478
9				6.56	5.91	4.463
10				6.55	5.90	4.463
11				2.46	5.91	4.463
12					5.90	4.463
13					5.91	4.463
14					5.90	4.463
15					5.91	4.462
16					2.21	4.463
17						4.462
18						4.463
19						4.462
20						4.463
21						1.673

Table 4. General Depreciation System
Applicable Depreciation Method: 200 or 150 Percent
Declining Balance Switching to Straight Line
Applicable Recovery Periods: 3, 5, 7, 10, 15, 20 years
Applicable Convention: Mid-quarter (property placed in service in third quarter)

If the Recovery Year is:	and the Recovery Period is: 3-year	5-year	7-year	10-year	15-year	20-year
	the Depreciation Rate is:					
1	25.00	15.00	10.71	7.50	3.75	2.813
2	50.00	34.00	25.51	18.50	9.63	7.289
3	16.67	20.40	18.22	14.80	8.66	6.742
4	8.33	12.24	13.02	11.84	7.80	6.237
5		11.30	9.30	9.47	7.02	5.769
6		7.06	8.85	7.58	6.31	5.336
7			8.86	6.55	5.90	4.936
8			5.53	6.55	5.90	4.566
9				6.56	5.91	4.460
10				6.55	5.90	4.460
11				4.10	5.91	4.460
12					5.90	4.460
13					5.91	4.461
14					5.90	4.460
15					5.91	4.461
16					3.69	4.460
17						4.461
18						4.460
19						4.461
20						4.460
21						2.788

Table 5. General Depreciation System
Applicable Depreciation Method: 200 or 150 Percent Declining Balance Switching to Straight Line
Applicable Recovery Periods: 3, 5, 7, 10, 15, 20 years
Applicable Convention: Mid-quarter (property placed in service in fourth quarter)

If the Recovery Year is:	and the Recovery Period is: 3-year	5-year	7-year	10-year	15-year	20-year
	the Depreciation Rate is:					
1	8.33	5.00	3.57	2.50	1.25	0.938
2	61.11	38.00	27.55	19.50	9.88	7.430
3	20.37	22.80	19.68	15.60	8.89	6.872
4	10.19	13.68	14.06	12.48	8.00	6.357
5		10.94	10.04	9.98	7.20	5.880
6		9.58	8.73	7.99	6.48	5.439
7			8.73	6.55	5.90	5.031
8			7.64	6.55	5.90	4.654
9				6.56	5.90	4.458
10				6.55	5.91	4.458
11				5.74	5.90	4.458
12					5.91	4.458
13					5.90	4.458
14					5.91	4.458
15					5.90	4.458
16					5.17	4.458
17						4.458
18						4.459
19						4.458
20						4.459
21						3.901

Table 6. General Depreciation System
Applicable Depreciation Method: Straight Line
Applicable Recovery Period: 27.5 years
Applicable Convention: Mid-month

If the Recovery Year is:	And the Month in the First Recovery Year the Property is Placed in Service is: 1	2	3	4	5	6	7	8	9	10	11	12
	the Depreciation Rate is:											
1	3.485	3.182	2.879	2.576	2.273	1.970	1.667	1.364	1.061	0.758	0.455	0.152
2	3.636	3.636	3.636	3.636	3.636	3.636	3.636	3.636	3.636	3.636	3.636	3.636
3	3.636	3.636	3.636	3.636	3.636	3.636	3.636	3.636	3.636	3.636	3.636	3.636
4	3.636	3.636	3.636	3.636	3.636	3.636	3.636	3.636	3.636	3.636	3.636	3.636
5	3.636	3.636	3.636	3.636	3.636	3.636	3.636	3.636	3.636	3.636	3.636	3.636
6	3.636	3.636	3.636	3.636	3.636	3.636	3.636	3.636	3.636	3.636	3.636	3.636
7	3.636	3.636	3.636	3.636	3.636	3.636	3.636	3.636	3.636	3.636	3.636	3.636
8	3.636	3.636	3.636	3.636	3.636	3.636	3.636	3.636	3.636	3.636	3.636	3.636
9	3.636	3.636	3.636	3.636	3.636	3.636	3.636	3.636	3.636	3.636	3.636	3.636
10	3.637	3.637	3.637	3.637	3.637	3.637	3.636	3.636	3.636	3.636	3.636	3.636
11	3.636	3.636	3.636	3.636	3.636	3.636	3.637	3.637	3.637	3.637	3.637	3.637
12	3.637	3.637	3.637	3.637	3.637	3.637	3.636	3.636	3.636	3.636	3.636	3.636
13	3.636	3.636	3.636	3.636	3.636	3.636	3.637	3.637	3.637	3.637	3.637	3.637
14	3.637	3.637	3.637	3.637	3.637	3.637	3.636	3.636	3.636	3.636	3.636	3.636
15	3.636	3.636	3.636	3.636	3.636	3.636	3.637	3.637	3.637	3.637	3.637	3.637
16	3.637	3.637	3.637	3.637	3.637	3.637	3.636	3.636	3.636	3.636	3.636	3.636
17	3.636	3.636	3.636	3.636	3.636	3.636	3.637	3.637	3.637	3.637	3.637	3.637
18	3.637	3.637	3.637	3.637	3.637	3.637	3.636	3.636	3.636	3.636	3.636	3.636
19	3.636	3.636	3.636	3.636	3.636	3.636	3.637	3.637	3.637	3.637	3.637	3.637
20	3.637	3.637	3.637	3.637	3.637	3.637	3.636	3.636	3.636	3.636	3.636	3.636
21	3.636	3.636	3.636	3.636	3.636	3.636	3.637	3.637	3.637	3.637	3.637	3.637
22	3.637	3.637	3.637	3.637	3.637	3.637	3.636	3.636	3.636	3.636	3.636	3.636
23	3.636	3.636	3.636	3.636	3.636	3.636	3.637	3.637	3.637	3.637	3.637	3.637
24	3.637	3.637	3.637	3.637	3.637	3.637	3.636	3.636	3.636	3.636	3.636	3.636
25	3.636	3.636	3.636	3.636	3.636	3.636	3.637	3.637	3.637	3.637	3.637	3.637
26	3.637	3.637	3.637	3.637	3.637	3.637	3.636	3.636	3.636	3.636	3.636	3.636
27	3.636	3.636	3.636	3.636	3.636	3.636	3.637	3.637	3.637	3.637	3.637	3.637
28	1.970	2.273	2.576	2.879	3.182	3.485	3.636	3.636	3.636	3.636	3.636	3.636
29	0.000	0.000	0.000	0.000	0.000	0.000	0.152	0.455	0.758	1.061	1.364	1.667

Table 7. General Depreciation System
Applicable Depreciation Method: Straight Line
Applicable Recovery Period: 31.5 years
Applicable Convention: Mid-month

If the Recovery Year is:	And the Month in the First Recovery Year the Property is Placed in Service is:											
	1	2	3	4	5	6	7	8	9	10	11	12
	the Depreciation Rate is:											
1	3.042	2.778	2.513	2.249	1.984	1.720	1.455	1.190	0.926	0.661	0.397	0.132
2	3.175	3.175	3.175	3.175	3.175	3.175	3.175	3.175	3.175	3.175	3.175	3.175
3	3.175	3.175	3.175	3.175	3.175	3.175	3.175	3.175	3.175	3.175	3.175	3.175
4	3.175	3.175	3.175	3.175	3.175	3.175	3.175	3.175	3.175	3.175	3.175	3.175
5	3.175	3.175	3.175	3.175	3.175	3.175	3.175	3.175	3.175	3.175	3.175	3.175
6	3.175	3.175	3.175	3.175	3.175	3.175	3.175	3.175	3.175	3.175	3.175	3.175
7	3.175	3.175	3.175	3.175	3.175	3.175	3.175	3.175	3.175	3.175	3.175	3.175
8	3.175	3.174	3.175	3.174	3.175	3.174	3.175	3.175	3.175	3.175	3.175	3.175
9	3.174	3.175	3.174	3.175	3.174	3.175	3.174	3.175	3.174	3.175	3.174	3.175
10	3.175	3.174	3.175	3.174	3.175	3.174	3.175	3.174	3.175	3.174	3.175	3.174
11	3.174	3.175	3.174	3.175	3.174	3.175	3.174	3.175	3.174	3.175	3.174	3.175
12	3.175	3.174	3.175	3.174	3.175	3.174	3.175	3.174	3.175	3.174	3.175	3.174
13	3.174	3.175	3.174	3.175	3.174	3.175	3.174	3.175	3.174	3.175	3.174	3.175
14	3.175	3.174	3.175	3.174	3.175	3.174	3.175	3.174	3.175	3.174	3.175	3.174
15	3.174	3.175	3.174	3.175	3.174	3.175	3.174	3.175	3.174	3.175	3.174	3.175
16	3.175	3.174	3.175	3.174	3.175	3.174	3.175	3.174	3.175	3.174	3.175	3.174
17	3.174	3.175	3.174	3.175	3.174	3.175	3.174	3.175	3.174	3.175	3.174	3.175
18	3.175	3.174	3.175	3.174	3.175	3.174	3.175	3.174	3.175	3.174	3.175	3.174
19	3.174	3.175	3.174	3.175	3.174	3.175	3.174	3.175	3.174	3.175	3.174	3.175
20	3.175	3.174	3.175	3.174	3.175	3.174	3.175	3.174	3.175	3.174	3.175	3.174
21	3.174	3.175	3.174	3.175	3.174	3.175	3.174	3.175	3.174	3.175	3.174	3.175
22	3.175	3.174	3.175	3.174	3.175	3.174	3.175	3.174	3.175	3.174	3.175	3.174
23	3.174	3.175	3.174	3.175	3.174	3.175	3.174	3.175	3.174	3.175	3.174	3.175
24	3.175	3.174	3.175	3.174	3.175	3.174	3.175	3.174	3.175	3.174	3.175	3.174
25	3.174	3.175	3.174	3.175	3.174	3.175	3.174	3.175	3.174	3.175	3.174	3.175
26	3.175	3.174	3.175	3.174	3.175	3.174	3.175	3.174	3.175	3.174	3.175	3.174
27	3.174	3.175	3.174	3.175	3.174	3.175	3.174	3.175	3.174	3.175	3.174	3.175
28	3.175	3.174	3.175	3.174	3.175	3.174	3.175	3.174	3.175	3.174	3.175	3.174
29	3.174	3.175	3.174	3.175	3.174	3.175	3.174	3.175	3.174	3.175	3.174	3.175
30	3.175	3.174	3.175	3.174	3.175	3.174	3.175	3.174	3.175	3.174	3.175	3.174
31	3.174	3.175	3.174	3.175	3.174	3.175	3.174	3.175	3.174	3.175	3.174	3.175
32	1.720	1.984	2.249	2.513	2.778	3.042	3.175	3.174	3.175	3.174	3.175	3.174
33	0.000	0.000	0.000	0.000	0.000	0.000	0.132	0.397	0.661	0.926	1.190	1.455

Table 7A. General Depreciation System
Applicable Depreciation Method: Straight-Line
Applicable Recovery Period: 39 years
Applicable Convention: Mid-month—taken from the IRS Pub. 946—CCH.

If the Recovery Year is:	And the Month in the First Recovery Year the Property is Placed in Service is:											
	1	2	3	4	5	6	7	8	9	10	11	12
	the Depreciation Rate is:											
1	2.461	2.247	2.033	1.819	1.605	1.391	1.177	0.963	0.749	0.535	0.321	0.107
2—39	2.564	2.564	2.564	2.564	2.564	2.564	2.564	2.564	2.564	2.564	2.564	2.564
40	0.107	0.321	0.535	0.749	0.963	1.177	1.391	1.605	1.819	2.033	2.247	2.461

Table 7B. Alternative Depreciation System
Applicable Depreciation Method: Straight-Line
Applicable Recovery Period: 40 years
Applicable Convention: Mid-month

If the Recovery Year is:	and the Month in the First Recovery Year the Property is Placed in Service is:											
	1	2	3	4	5	6	7	8	9	10	11	12
	the Depreciation Rate is:											
1	2.396	2.188	1.979	1.771	1.563	1.354	1.146	0.938	0.729	0.521	0.313	0.104
2—40	2.500	2.500	2.500	2.500	2.500	2.500	2.500	2.500	2.500	2.500	2.500	2.500
41	0.104	0.312	0.521	0.729	0.937	1.146	1.354	1.562	1.771	1.979	2.187	2.396

Table 8. General and Alternative Depreciation Systems
Applicable Depreciation Method: Straight Line
Applicable Recovery Periods: 2.5 — 50 years
Applicable Convention: Half-year

If the Recovery Year is:	and the Recovery Period is: 2.5	3.0	3.5	4.0	4.5	5.0	5.5	6.0	6.5	7.0	7.5	8.0	8.5	9.0	9.5
	the Depreciation Rate is:														
1	20.00	16.67	14.29	12.50	11.11	10.00	9.09	8.33	7.69	7.14	6.67	6.25	5.88	5.56	5.26
2	40.00	33.33	28.57	25.00	22.22	20.00	18.18	16.67	15.39	14.29	13.33	12.50	11.77	11.11	10.53
3	40.00	33.33	28.57	25.00	22.22	20.00	18.18	16.67	15.38	14.29	13.33	12.50	11.76	11.11	10.53
4		16.67	28.57	25.00	22.23	20.00	18.18	16.67	15.39	14.28	13.33	12.50	11.77	11.11	10.53
5				12.50	22.22	20.00	18.19	16.66	15.38	14.29	13.34	12.50	11.76	11.11	10.52
6						10.00	18.18	16.67	15.39	14.28	13.33	12.50	11.77	11.11	10.53
7								8.33	15.38	14.29	13.34	12.50	11.76	11.11	10.52
8										7.14	13.33	12.50	11.77	11.11	10.53
9												6.25	11.76	11.11	10.52
10														5.56	10.53

If the Recovery Year is:	and the Recovery Period is: 10.0	10.5	11.0	11.5	12.0	12.5	13.0	13.5	14.0	14.5	15.0	15.5	16.0	16.5	17.0
	the Depreciation Rate is:														
1	5.00	4.76	4.55	4.35	4.17	4.00	3.85	3.70	3.57	3.45	3.33	3.23	3.13	3.03	2.94
2	10.00	9.52	9.09	8.70	8.33	8.00	7.69	7.41	7.14	6.90	6.67	6.45	6.25	6.06	5.88
3	10.00	9.52	9.09	8.70	8.33	8.00	7.69	7.41	7.14	6.90	6.67	6.45	6.25	6.06	5.88
4	10.00	9.53	9.09	8.69	8.33	8.00	7.69	7.41	7.14	6.90	6.67	6.45	6.25	6.06	5.88
5	10.00	9.52	9.09	8.70	8.33	8.00	7.69	7.41	7.14	6.90	6.67	6.45	6.25	6.06	5.88
6	10.00	9.53	9.09	8.69	8.33	8.00	7.69	7.41	7.14	6.89	6.67	6.45	6.25	6.06	5.88
7	10.00	9.52	9.09	8.70	8.34	8.00	7.69	7.41	7.14	6.90	6.67	6.45	6.25	6.06	5.88
8	10.00	9.53	9.09	8.69	8.33	8.00	7.69	7.41	7.15	6.89	6.66	6.45	6.25	6.06	5.88
9	10.00	9.52	9.09	8.70	8.34	8.00	7.69	7.41	7.14	6.90	6.67	6.45	6.25	6.06	5.88
10	10.00	9.53	9.09	8.69	8.33	8.00	7.70	7.40	7.15	6.89	6.66	6.45	6.25	6.06	5.88
11	5.00	9.52	9.09	8.70	8.34	8.00	7.69	7.41	7.14	6.90	6.67	6.45	6.25	6.06	5.89
12			4.55	8.69	8.33	8.00	7.70	7.40	7.15	6.89	6.66	6.45	6.25	6.06	5.88
13					4.17	8.00	7.69	7.41	7.14	6.90	6.67	6.45	6.25	6.06	5.89
14							3.85	7.40	7.15	6.89	6.66	6.46	6.25	6.06	5.88
15									3.57	6.90	6.67	6.45	6.25	6.06	5.89
16											3.33	6.46	6.25	6.06	5.88
17													3.12	6.07	5.89
18															2.94

If the Recovery Year is:	and the Recovery Period is: 17.5	18.0	18.5	19.0	19.5	20.0	20.5	21.0	21.5	22.0	22.5	23.0	23.5	24.0	24.5
	the Depreciation Rate is:														
1	2.86	2.78	2.70	2.63	2.56	2.500	2.439	2.381	2.326	2.273	2.222	2.174	2.128	2.083	2.041
2	5.71	5.56	5.41	5.26	5.13	5.000	4.878	4.762	4.651	4.545	4.444	4.348	4.255	4.167	4.082
3	5.71	5.56	5.41	5.26	5.13	5.000	4.878	4.762	4.651	4.545	4.444	4.348	4.255	4.167	4.082
4	5.71	5.55	5.41	5.26	5.13	5.000	4.878	4.762	4.651	4.545	4.445	4.348	4.255	4.167	4.082
5	5.72	5.56	5.40	5.26	5.13	5.000	4.878	4.762	4.651	4.546	4.444	4.348	4.255	4.167	4.082
6	5.71	5.55	5.41	5.26	5.13	5.000	4.878	4.762	4.651	4.545	4.445	4.348	4.255	4.167	4.082
7	5.72	5.56	5.40	5.26	5.13	5.000	4.878	4.762	4.651	4.546	4.444	4.348	4.255	4.167	4.082
8	5.71	5.55	5.41	5.26	5.13	5.000	4.878	4.762	4.651	4.545	4.445	4.318	4.255	4.167	4.082
9	5.72	5.56	5.40	5.27	5.13	5.000	4.878	4.762	4.651	4.546	4.444	4.348	4.255	4.167	4.081
10	5.71	5.55	5.41	5.26	5.13	5.000	4.878	4.762	4.651	4.545	4.445	4.348	4.255	4.167	4.082
11	5.72	5.56	5.40	5.27	5.13	5.000	4.878	4.762	4.651	4.546	4.444	4.348	4.256	4.166	4.081
12	5.71	5.55	5.41	5.26	5.13	5.000	4.878	4.762	4.651	4.545	4.445	4.348	4.255	4.167	4.082
13	5.72	5.56	5.40	5.27	5.13	5.000	4.878	4.762	4.651	4.546	4.444	4.348	4.256	4.166	4.081
14	5.71	5.55	5.41	5.26	5.13	5.000	4.878	4.762	4.651	4.545	4.445	4.348	4.255	4.167	4.082
15	5.72	5.56	5.40	5.27	5.13	5.000	4.878	4.762	4.651	4.546	4.444	4.348	4.256	4.166	4.081
16	5.71	5.55	5.41	5.26	5.12	5.000	4.878	4.762	4.651	4.545	4.445	4.348	4.255	4.167	4.082
17	5.72	5.56	5.40	5.27	5.13	5.000	4.878	4.762	4.652	4.546	4.444	4.347	4.256	4.166	4.081
18	5.71	5.55	5.41	5.26	5.12	5.000	4.878	4.762	4.651	4.545	4.445	4.348	4.255	4.167	4.082
19		2.78	5.40	5.27	5.13	5.000	4.878	4.761	4.652	4.546	4.444	4.347	4.256	4.166	4.081
20				2.63	5.12	5.000	4.879	4.762	4.651	4.545	4.445	4.348	4.255	4.167	4.082
21						2.500	4.878	4.761	4.652	4.546	4.444	4.347	4.256	4.166	4.081
22								2.381	4.651	4.545	4.445	4.348	4.255	4.167	4.082
23										2.273	4.444	4.347	4.256	4.166	4.081
24												2.174	4.255	4.167	4.082
25														2.083	4.081

12 DEPRECIATION

If the Recovery Year is:	and the Recovery Period is:														
	25.0	25.5	26.0	26.5	27.0	27.5	28.0	28.5	29.0	29.5	30.0	30.5	31.0	31.5	32.0
	the Depreciation Rate is:														
1	2.000	1.961	1.923	1.887	1.852	1.818	1.786	1.754	1.724	1.695	1.667	1.639	1.613	1.587	1.563
2	4.000	3.922	3.846	3.774	3.704	3.636	3.571	3.509	3.448	3.390	3.333	3.279	3.226	3.175	3.125
3	4.000	3.922	3.846	3.774	3.704	3.636	3.571	3.509	3.448	3.390	3.333	3.279	3.226	3.175	3.125
4	4.000	3.922	3.846	3.774	3.704	3.636	3.571	3.509	3.448	3.390	3.333	3.279	3.226	3.175	3.125
5	4.000	3.922	3.846	3.774	3.704	3.636	3.571	3.509	3.448	3.390	3.333	3.279	3.226	3.175	3.125
6	4.000	3.921	3.846	3.774	3.704	3.636	3.571	3.509	3.448	3.390	3.333	3.279	3.226	3.175	3.125
7	4.000	3.922	3.846	3.773	3.704	3.636	3.572	3.509	3.448	3.390	3.333	3.279	3.226	3.175	3.125
8	4.000	3.921	3.846	3.774	3.704	3.636	3.571	3.509	3.448	3.390	3.333	3.279	3.226	3.175	3.125
9	4.000	3.922	3.846	3.773	3.704	3.637	3.572	3.509	3.448	3.390	3.333	3.279	3.226	3.175	3.125
10	4.000	3.921	3.846	3.774	3.704	3.636	3.571	3.509	3.448	3.390	3.333	3.279	3.226	3.174	3.125
11	4.000	3.922	3.846	3.773	3.704	3.637	3.572	3.509	3.448	3.390	3.333	3.279	3.226	3.175	3.125
12	4.000	3.921	3.846	3.774	3.704	3.636	3.571	3.509	3.448	3.390	3.333	3.279	3.226	3.174	3.125
13	4.000	3.922	3.846	3.773	3.703	3.637	3.572	3.509	3.448	3.390	3.334	3.279	3.226	3.175	3.125
14	4.000	3.921	3.846	3.773	3.704	3.636	3.571	3.509	3.448	3.390	3.333	3.279	3.226	3.174	3.125
15	4.000	3.922	3.846	3.774	3.703	3.637	3.572	3.509	3.449	3.390	3.334	3.278	3.226	3.175	3.125
16	4.000	3.921	3.846	3.773	3.704	3.636	3.571	3.509	3.448	3.390	3.333	3.279	3.226	3.174	3.125
17	4.000	3.922	3.846	3.774	3.703	3.637	3.572	3.509	3.449	3.390	3.334	3.278	3.226	3.175	3.125
18	4.000	3.921	3.846	3.773	3.704	3.636	3.571	3.508	3.448	3.390	3.333	3.279	3.226	3.174	3.125
19	4.000	3.922	3.846	3.774	3.703	3.637	3.572	3.509	3.449	3.390	3.334	3.278	3.226	3.175	3.125
20	4.000	3.921	3.847	3.773	3.704	3.636	3.571	3.508	3.448	3.390	3.333	3.279	3.226	3.174	3.125
21	4.000	3.922	3.846	3.774	3.703	3.637	3.572	3.509	3.449	3.389	3.334	3.278	3.225	3.175	3.125
22	4.000	3.921	3.847	3.773	3.704	3.636	3.571	3.508	3.448	3.390	3.333	3.279	3.226	3.174	3.125
23	4.000	3.922	3.846	3.774	3.703	3.637	3.572	3.509	3.449	3.389	3.334	3.278	3.225	3.175	3.125
24	4.000	3.921	3.847	3.773	3.704	3.636	3.571	3.508	3.448	3.390	3.333	3.279	3.226	3.174	3.125
25	4.000	3.922	3.846	3.774	3.703	3.637	3.572	3.509	3.449	3.389	3.334	3.278	3.225	3.175	3.125
26	2.000	3.921	3.847	3.773	3.704	3.636	3.571	3.508	3.448	3.390	3.333	3.279	3.226	3.174	3.125
27			1.923	3.774	3.703	3.637	3.572	3.509	3.449	3.389	3.334	3.278	3.225	3.175	3.125
28					1.852	3.636	3.571	3.508	3.448	3.390	3.333	3.279	3.226	3.174	3.125
29							1.786	3.509	3.449	3.389	3.334	3.278	3.225	3.175	3.125
30									1.724	3.390	3.333	3.279	3.226	3.174	3.125
31											1.667	3.278	3.225	3.175	3.125
32													1.613	3.174	3.125
33															1.562

If the Recovery Year is:	and the Recovery Period is:														
	32.5	33.0	33.5	34.0	34.5	35.0	35.5	36.0	36.5	37.0	37.5	38.0	38.5	39.0	39.5
	the Depreciation Rate is:														
1	1.538	1.515	1.493	1.471	1.449	1.429	1.408	1.389	1.370	1.351	1.333	1.316	1.299	1.282	1.266
2	3.077	3.030	2.985	2.941	2.899	2.857	2.817	2.778	2.740	2.703	2.667	2.632	2.597	2.564	2.532
3	3.077	3.030	2.985	2.941	2.899	2.857	2.817	2.778	2.740	2.703	2.667	2.632	2.597	2.564	2.532
4	3.077	3.030	2.985	2.941	2.899	2.857	2.817	2.778	2.740	2.703	2.667	2.632	2.597	2.564	2.532
5	3.077	3.030	2.985	2.941	2.899	2.857	2.817	2.778	2.740	2.703	2.667	2.632	2.597	2.564	2.532
6	3.077	3.030	2.985	2.941	2.899	2.857	2.817	2.778	2.740	2.703	2.667	2.632	2.597	2.564	2.532
7	3.077	3.030	2.985	2.941	2.898	2.857	2.817	2.778	2.740	2.703	2.667	2.632	2.597	2.564	2.532
8	3.077	3.030	2.985	2.941	2.899	2.857	2.817	2.778	2.740	2.703	2.667	2.631	2.597	2.564	2.532
9	3.077	3.030	2.985	2.941	2.898	2.857	2.817	2.778	2.740	2.703	2.667	2.632	2.597	2.564	2.532
10	3.077	3.030	2.985	2.941	2.899	2.857	2.817	2.778	2.740	2.703	2.667	2.631	2.598	2.564	2.532
11	3.077	3.030	2.985	2.941	2.898	2.857	2.817	2.778	2.740	2.703	2.667	2.632	2.597	2.564	2.532
12	3.077	3.030	2.985	2.941	2.899	2.857	2.817	2.778	2.740	2.703	2.667	2.631	2.598	2.564	2.532
13	3.077	3.030	2.985	2.941	2.898	2.857	2.817	2.778	2.740	2.703	2.667	2.632	2.597	2.564	2.532
14	3.077	3.030	2.985	2.941	2.899	2.857	2.817	2.778	2.740	2.703	2.667	2.631	2.598	2.564	2.531
15	3.077	3.031	2.985	2.941	2.898	2.857	2.817	2.778	2.740	2.703	2.666	2.632	2.597	2.564	2.532
16	3.077	3.030	2.985	2.941	2.899	2.857	2.817	2.778	2.740	2.703	2.667	2.631	2.598	2.564	2.531
17	3.077	3.031	2.985	2.941	2.898	2.857	2.817	2.778	2.740	2.703	2.666	2.632	2.597	2.564	2.532
18	3.077	3.030	2.985	2.841	2.899	2.857	2.817	2.778	2.740	2.702	2.667	2.631	2.598	2.564	2.531
19	3.077	3.031	2.985	2.941	2.898	2.857	2.817	2.778	2.739	2.703	2.666	2.632	2.597	2.564	2.532
20	3.077	3.030	2.985	2.941	2.898	2.857	2.817	2.778	2.740	2.702	2.667	2.631	2.598	2.564	2.531
21	3.077	3.031	2.985	2.941	2.899	2.857	2.817	2.778	2.739	2.703	2.666	2.632	2.597	2.564	2.532
22	3.077	3.030	2.985	2.941	2.898	2.857	2.817	2.777	2.740	2.702	2.667	2.631	2.598	2.564	2.531
23	3.077	3.031	2.985	2.941	2.899	2.857	2.817	2.778	2.739	2.703	2.666	2.632	2.597	2.564	2.532
24	3.077	3.030	2.985	2.941	2.898	2.857	2.817	2.777	2.740	2.702	2.667	2.631	2.598	2.564	2.531
25	3.077	3.031	2.985	2.942	2.899	2.857	2.817	2.778	2.739	2.703	2.666	2.632	2.597	2.564	2.532
26	3.077	3.030	2.985	2.941	2.898	2.857	2.817	2.777	2.740	2.702	2.667	2.631	2.598	2.564	2.531
27	3.077	3.031	2.985	2.942	2.899	2.857	2.817	2.778	2.739	2.703	2.666	2.632	2.597	2.564	2.532
28	3.077	3.030	2.985	2.941	2.898	2.858	2.817	2.777	2.740	2.702	2.667	2.631	2.598	2.564	2.531
29	3.077	3.031	2.985	2.942	2.899	2.857	2.817	2.778	2.739	2.703	2.666	2.632	2.597	2.564	2.532
30	3.077	3.030	2.985	2.941	2.898	2.858	2.817	2.777	2.740	2.702	2.667	2.631	2.598	2.564	2.531
31	3.076	3.031	2.986	2.942	2.899	2.857	2.817	2.778	2.739	2.703	2.666	2.632	2.597	2.564	2.532
32	3.077	3.030	2.985	2.941	2.898	2.858	2.816	2.777	2.740	2.702	2.667	2.631	2.598	2.564	2.531
33	3.076	3.031	2.986	2.942	2.899	2.857	2.817	2.778	2.739	2.703	2.666	2.632	2.597	2.565	2.532
34		1.515	2.985	2.941	2.898	2.858	2.816	2.777	2.740	2.702	2.667	2.631	2.598	2.564	2.531
35				1.471	2.899	2.857	2.817	2.778	2.739	2.703	2.666	2.632	2.597	2.565	2.532
36						1.429	2.816	2.777	2.740	2.702	2.667	2.631	2.598	2.564	2.531
37								1.389	2.739	2.703	2.666	2.632	2.597	2.565	2.532
38										1.351	2.667	2.631	2.598	2.564	2.531
39												1.316	2.597	2.565	2.532
40														1.282	2.531

12 DEPRECIATION

and the Recovery Period is:

the Depreciation Rate is:

If the Recovery Year is:	40.0	40.5	41.0	41.5	42.0	42.5	43.0	43.5	44.0	44.5	45.0	45.5	46.0	46.5	47.0
1	1.250	1.235	1.220	1.205	1.190	1.176	1.163	1.149	1.136	1.124	1.111	1.099	1.087	1.075	1.064
2	2.500	2.469	2.439	2.410	2.381	2.353	2.326	2.299	2.273	2.247	2.222	2.198	2.174	2.151	2.128
3	2.500	2.469	2.439	2.410	2.381	2.353	2.326	2.299	2.273	2.247	2.222	2.198	2.174	2.151	2.128
4	2.500	2.469	2.439	2.410	2.381	2.353	2.326	2.299	2.273	2.247	2.222	2.198	2.174	2.151	2.128
5	2.500	2.469	2.439	2.410	2.381	2.353	2.326	2.299	2.273	2.247	2.222	2.198	2.174	2.151	2.128
6	2.500	2.469	2.439	2.410	2.381	2.353	2.326	2.299	2.273	2.247	2.222	2.198	2.174	2.151	2.128
7	2.500	2.469	2.439	2.410	2.381	2.353	2.326	2.299	2.273	2.247	2.222	2.198	2.174	2.150	2.128
8	2.500	2.469	2.439	2.410	2.381	2.353	2.326	2.299	2.273	2.247	2.222	2.198	2.174	2.151	2.128
9	2.500	2.469	2.439	2.410	2.381	2.353	2.325	2.299	2.273	2.247	2.222	2.198	2.174	2.150	2.128
10	2.500	2.469	2.439	2.410	2.381	2.353	2.326	2.299	2.273	2.247	2.222	2.198	2.174	2.151	2.128
11	2.500	2.469	2.439	2.410	2.381	2.353	2.325	2.299	2.273	2.247	2.222	2.198	2.174	2.150	2.128
12	2.500	2.469	2.439	2.410	2.381	2.353	2.326	2.299	2.273	2.247	2.222	2.198	2.174	2.151	2.128
13	2.500	2.469	2.439	2.410	2.381	2.353	2.325	2.299	2.273	2.247	2.222	2.198	2.174	2.150	2.128
14	2.500	2.469	2.439	2.409	2.381	2.353	2.326	2.299	2.273	2.247	2.222	2.198	2.174	2.151	2.128
15	2.500	2.469	2.439	2.410	2.381	2.353	2.325	2.299	2.273	2.247	2.222	2.198	2.174	2.150	2.128
16	2.500	2.469	2.439	2.409	2.381	2.353	2.326	2.299	2.273	2.247	2.222	2.198	2.174	2.151	2.128
17	2.500	2.469	2.439	2.410	2.381	2.353	2.325	2.299	2.273	2.247	2.222	2.198	2.174	2.150	2.127
18	2.500	2.469	2.439	2.409	2.381	2.353	2.326	2.299	2.273	2.247	2.222	2.198	2.174	2.151	2.128
19	2.500	2.469	2.439	2.410	2.381	2.353	2.325	2.299	2.273	2.247	2.222	2.198	2.174	2.150	2.127
20	2.500	2.469	2.439	2.409	2.381	2.353	2.326	2.299	2.273	2.247	2.222	2.198	2.174	2.151	2.128
21	2.500	2.469	2.439	2.410	2.381	2.353	2.325	2.299	2.273	2.247	2.222	2.198	2.174	2.150	2.127
22	2.500	2.469	2.439	2.409	2.381	2.353	2.326	2.299	2.273	2.247	2.222	2.198	2.174	2.151	2.128
23	2.500	2.469	2.439	2.410	2.381	2.353	2.325	2.299	2.272	2.247	2.222	2.198	2.174	2.150	2.127
24	2.500	2.469	2.439	2.409	2.381	2.353	2.326	2.299	2.273	2.247	2.222	2.198	2.174	2.151	2.128
25	2.500	2.469	2.439	2.410	2.381	2.353	2.325	2.299	2.272	2.247	2.222	2.198	2.174	2.150	2.127
26	2.500	2.469	2.439	2.409	2.381	2.353	2.326	2.299	2.273	2.247	2.222	2.198	2.174	2.151	2.128
27	2.500	2.469	2.439	2.410	2.381	2.353	2.325	2.299	2.272	2.247	2.223	2.198	2.174	2.150	2.127
28	2.500	2.469	2.439	2.409	2.381	2.353	2.326	2.299	2.273	2.247	2.222	2.198	2.174	2.151	2.128
29	2.500	2.469	2.439	2.410	2.381	2.353	2.325	2.299	2.272	2.247	2.223	2.198	2.174	2.150	2.127
30	2.500	2.469	2.439	2.409	2.381	2.353	2.326	2.299	2.273	2.248	2.222	2.197	2.174	2.151	2.128
31	2.500	2.469	2.439	2.410	2.381	2.353	2.325	2.299	2.272	2.247	2.223	2.198	2.174	2.150	2.127
32	2.500	2.470	2.439	2.409	2.381	2.353	2.326	2.299	2.273	2.248	2.222	2.197	2.174	2.151	2.128
33	2.500	2.469	2.439	2.410	2.381	2.353	2.325	2.298	2.272	2.247	2.223	2.198	2.174	2.150	2.127
34	2.500	2.470	2.439	2.409	2.381	2.353	2.326	2.299	2.273	2.248	2.222	2.197	2.174	2.151	2.128
35	2.500	2.469	2.439	2.410	2.381	2.353	2.325	2.298	2.272	2.247	2.223	2.198	2.174	2.150	2.127
36	2.500	2.470	2.139	2.409	2.381	2.353	2.326	2.299	2.273	2.248	2.222	2.197	2.174	2.151	2.128
37	2.500	2.469	2.439	2.410	2.381	2.353	2.325	2.298	2.272	2.247	2.223	2.198	2.174	2.150	2.127
38	2.500	2.470	2.439	2.409	2.381	2.353	2.326	2.299	2.273	2.248	2.222	2.197	2.174	2.151	2.128
39	2.500	2.469	2.439	2.410	2.381	2.353	2.325	2.298	2.272	2.247	2.223	2.198	2.174	2.150	2.127
40	2.500	2.470	2.439	2.409	2.381	2.353	2.326	2.299	2.273	2.248	2.222	2.197	2.173	2.151	2.128
41	1.250	2.469	2.439	2.410	2.380	2.352	2.325	2.298	2.272	2.247	2.223	2.198	2.174	2.150	2.127
42			1.220	2.409	2.381	2.353	2.326	2.299	2.273	2.248	2.222	2.197	2.173	2.151	2.128
43					1.190	2.352	2.325	2.298	2.272	2.247	2.223	2.198	2.174	2.150	2.127
44							1.163	2.299	2.273	2.248	2.222	2.197	2.173	2.151	2.128
45									1.136	2.247	2.223	2.198	2.174	2.150	2.127
46											1.111	2.197	2.173	2.151	2.128
47													1.087	2.150	2.127
48															1.064

If the Recovery Year is:	and the Recovery Period is: 47.5	48.0	48.5	49.0	49.5	50.0
	the Depreciation Rate is:					
1	1.053	1.042	1.031	1.020	1.010	1.000
2	2.105	2.083	2.062	2.041	2.020	2.000
3	2.105	2.083	2.062	2.041	2.020	2.000
4	2.105	2.083	2.062	2.041	2.020	2.000
5	2.105	2.083	2.062	2.041	2.020	2.000
6	2.105	2.083	2.062	2.041	2.020	2.000
7	2.105	2.083	2.062	2.041	2.020	2.000
8	2.105	2.083	2.062	2.041	2.020	2.000
9	2.105	2.083	2.062	2.041	2.020	2.000
10	2.105	2.083	2.062	2.041	2.020	2.000
11	2.105	2.083	2.062	2.041	2.020	2.000
12	2.105	2.083	2.062	2.041	2.020	2.000
13	2.105	2.083	2.062	2.041	2.020	2.000
14	2.105	2.083	2.062	2.041	2.020	2.000
15	2.105	2.083	2.062	2.041	2.020	2.000
16	2.105	2.083	2.062	2.041	2.020	2.000
17	2.105	2.083	2.062	2.041	2.020	2.000
18	2.105	2.083	2.062	2.041	2.020	2.000
19	2.105	2.084	2.062	2.041	2.020	2.000
20	2.105	2.083	2.062	2.041	2.020	2.000
21	2.105	2.084	2.062	2.041	2.020	2.000
22	2.105	2.083	2.062	2.041	2.020	2.000
23	2.105	2.084	2.062	2.041	2.020	2.000
24	2.105	2.083	2.062	2.041	2.020	2.000
25	2.105	2.084	2.062	2.041	2.020	2.000
26	2.106	2.083	2.062	2.041	2.020	2.000
27	2.105	2.084	2.062	2.041	2.020	2.000
28	2.106	2.083	2.062	2.041	2.020	2.000
29	2.105	2.084	2.062	2.041	2.020	2.000
30	2.106	2.083	2.062	2.041	2.020	2.000
31	2.105	2.084	2.062	2.041	2.021	2.000
32	2.106	2.083	2.062	2.041	2.020	2.000
33	2.105	2.084	2.062	2.041	2.021	2.000
34	2.106	2.083	2.062	2.040	2.020	2.000
35	2.105	2.084	2.062	2.041	2.021	2.000
36	2.106	2.083	2.062	2.040	2.020	2.000
37	2.105	2.084	2.061	2.041	2.021	2.000
38	2.106	2.083	2.062	2.040	2.020	2.000
39	2.105	2.084	2.061	2.041	2.021	2.000
40	2.106	2.083	2.062	2.040	2.020	2.000
41	2.105	2.084	2.061	2.041	2.021	2.000
42	2.106	2.083	2.062	2.040	2.020	2.000
43	2.105	2.084	2.061	2.041	2.021	2.000
44	2.106	2.083	2.062	2.040	2.020	2.000
45	2.105	2.084	2.061	2.041	2.021	2.000
46	2.106	2.083	2.062	2.040	2.020	2.000
47	2.105	2.084	2.061	2.041	2.021	2.000
48	2.106	2.083	2.062	2.040	2.020	2.000
49		1.042	2.061	2.041	2.021	2.000
50				1.020	2.020	2.000
51						1.000

1244. MACRS Short Tax Years. A short tax year is any tax year with less than 12 months. Special rules are provided for determining MACRS deductions when: (1) property is placed in service in a short tax year, (2) a short tax year occurs during the recovery period of property, or (3) a disposition of property occurs before the end of the recovery period (Rev. Proc. 89-15). If any of the above situations exist, refinements are made to the use of the applicable conventions and the IRS MACRS depreciation tables at ¶ 1243 may *not* be used.[93]

The mid-month convention is applied without regard to the length of the tax year. For example if residential rental property is placed in service in the first month of a six-month tax year, 5 ½ months depreciation is claimed.

Under the half-year convention, property placed in service or disposed of in a short tax year is deemed placed in service or disposed of on the midpoint of the short tax year, which always falls on either the first day or the midpoint of the month.

Under the mid-quarter convention, property is deemed placed in service or disposed of on the midpoint of the quarter, which always falls on either the first day or the midpoint of a month, in the short tax year that it is placed in service or disposed of.

Depreciation for the first recovery year in the recovery period is computed by multiplying the basis in the property by the applicable depreciation rate. The depreciation allowance allocable to the first tax year that includes a portion of the first recovery year is derived by multiplying the depreciation for the first recovery year by a fraction, the numerator of which is the number of months (including fractions of months) the property is deemed to be in service during the tax year under the applicable convention and the denominator of which is 12.

The correlation of a depreciation allowance between recovery years and tax years after the first tax year in the recovery period may be made under either an allocation or a simplified method.

1245. Applicable MACRS Conventions. Specified averaging conventions apply to depreciation computations made under MACRS (Code Sec. 168(d)).[94] The recovery period begins on the date on which the property is placed in service under the applicable convention. The depreciation table percentages take into account the applicable convention in the first and last year of the regular recovery period. However, if property is disposed of prior to the end of the regular recovery period, the result obtained by using the table percentage for the year of disposition must be adjusted to take into account the applicable convention.

Half-Year Convention. Under the half-year convention, which can apply to any property other than residential rental and nonresidential real property, an asset is treated as placed in service or disposed of in the middle of the tax year. Thus, one-half of a full year's depreciation is allowed in the tax year in which the asset is placed in service regardless of the date that the asset is placed in service during the tax year.

A half-year of depreciation is allowed in the tax year of disposition if there is a disposition of property before the end of the recovery period.[95] The table percentage for the year of disposition does not take this into account; therefore, only one-half of the depreciation as computed using the applicable table percentage is allowed.

> **Example 1:** Five-year property with a depreciable basis of $1,000 (after reduction by any amount expensed under Code Sec. 179 and claimed as bonus depreciation) and subject to the half-year convention is placed in service in 2010 and sold in 2012. Using Table 1 at ¶ 1243, 2010 depreciation is $200 ($1,000 × 20%); 2011 depreciation is $320 ($1,000 × 32%); and 2012 depreciation is $96 ($1,000 × 19.20% × 50% to reflect half-year convention in year of disposition).

Mid-Month Convention. A mid-month convention applies to residential rental property, including low-income housing, and nonresidential real property. Property is

References are to Standard Federal Tax Reports; Tax Research Consultant; and Practical Tax Explanations.

[93] ¶ 11,279.053; DEPR: 3,202, DEPR: 3,350, DEPR: 3,252; § 11,130

[94] ¶ 11,250, ¶ 11,279.037; DEPR: 3,252; § 11,125

[95] ¶ 11,279.037; DEPR: 3,252; § 11,125

deemed placed in service or disposed of during the middle of the month. The deduction is based on the number of months the property was in service. Thus, one-half month's depreciation is allowed for the month the property is placed in service and for the month of disposition if there is a disposition of property before the end of the recovery period.

> **Example 2:** A commercial building costing $100,000 is purchased by a calendar-year taxpayer in February 2011 and sold in August 2012. Using Table 7A at ¶ 1243, 2011 depreciation is $2,247 ($100,000 × 2.247% (first-year percentage for property placed in service in second month of tax year)) and 2012 depreciation is $1,603 ($100,000 × 2.564% (second-year percentage for property placed in service in second month) × 7.5/12 to reflect 7.5 months in service in 2012 (January through mid-August) under the mid-month convention).

Mid-Quarter Convention. Under the mid-quarter convention, all property placed in service, or disposed of, during any quarter of a tax year is treated as placed in service at the midpoint of the quarter (Code Sec. 168(d)(3); Reg. § 1.168(d)-1).[96] Depreciation under the mid-quarter convention may be determined using Tables 2-5, above.

The mid-quarter convention applies to all property, other than nonresidential real property and residential rental property, if more than 40 percent of the aggregate bases of such property is placed in service during the last three months of the tax year. Property placed in service and disposed of within the same tax year is disregarded for purposes of the 40 percent test.

In determining whether the mid-quarter convention is applicable, the aggregate basis of property placed in service in the last three months of the tax year must be computed regardless of the length of the tax year. Thus, if a short tax year consists of three months or less, the mid-quarter convention applies regardless of when the depreciable property is placed in service during the tax year.

The bonus deduction (¶ 1237) does not reduce the aggregate basis of property taken into account for purposes of determining whether the mid-quarter convention applies. However, any amount properly expensed under Code Sec. 179 (¶ 1208) does reduce aggregate basis. Thus, a taxpayer may be able to avoid the mid-quarter convention (if this is desirable) by allocating the Code Sec. 179 deduction to property placed in service in the last quarter. No similar reduction is made for the amount of bonus depreciation. Also, the mid-quarter convention does not operate to reduce the deduction otherwise allowable under Code Sec. 179 or for bonus depreciation.

> **Example 3:** A calendar-year taxpayer places $100 of used 5-year property in service in the first quarter of 2012 and $100 of new 10-year property in service in the fourth quarter. The taxpayer claims a 50% bonus allowance on the 10-year property. The mid-quarter convention applies to the 5-year property and to the 10-year property because 50% of the aggregate adjusted basis of the property placed in service in 2012 (without regard to the bonus allowance) was placed in service in the fourth quarter. If the bonus allowance was not claimed on the 10-year property and the entire basis of the 10-year property was expensed under section 179, the half-year convention would apply to the 5-year property placed in service in the first quarter.

For purposes of the 40 percent test, depreciable basis does not include adjustments resulting from transfers of property between members of the same affiliated group filing a consolidated return.

If the MACRS deduction for property subject to the mid-quarter convention is computed without tables, depreciation for the first year is determined by computing the depreciation for the full tax year and then multiplying it by the following percentages for the quarter of the tax year the property is placed in service: first quarter, 87.5%; second quarter, 62.5%; third quarter, 37.5%; and fourth quarter, 12.5%.

1247. MACRS Alternative Depreciation System (ADS). The Modified Accelerated Cost Recovery System (MACRS) alternative depreciation system (ADS) must be used

References are to Standard Federal Tax Reports; Tax Research Consultant; and Practical Tax Explanations.

[96] ¶ 11,250, ¶ 11,279.037;
DEPR: 3,252.15; § 11,125

12 DEPRECIATION

for (1) tangible property used outside the U.S., (2) tax-exempt use property, (3) tax-exempt bond-financed property, (4) property imported from a foreign country for which an Executive Order is in effect because the country maintains trade restrictions or engages in other discriminatory acts, and (5) property for which an ADS election has been made (Code Sec. 168(g)).[97] Mandatory ADS property does not qualify for bonus depreciation (¶ 1237).

Under ADS, the deduction is computed by applying the straight-line method, the applicable convention and the applicable longer recovery period (12 years for personal property with no class life, 40 years for real property, 50 years for railroad grading and tunnel bores, and the class life for all other property) for the respective class of property (Code Sec. 168(g)(2)(C)).[98] ADS is also used to compute the earnings and profits of a foreign or domestic corporation. The allowable depreciation deductions for luxury cars and other types of listed property used 50 percent or less in business are also determined under this method (¶ 1211 and ¶ 1214).

Electing ADS. In lieu of the regular MACRS deduction, taxpayers may irrevocably elect to apply the MACRS alternative depreciation system to any class of property for any tax year (Code Sec. 168(g)(7)).[99] If elected, ADS applies to all property in the MACRS class placed in service during the tax year. For example, if the election is made for five-year property, it applies to all five-year property placed in service in the tax year of the election. For residential rental property and nonresidential real property, the election is made on a property-by-property basis. Property for which ADS is elected may qualify for bonus depreciation (¶ 1237).

1248. Special Transferee Rules. A transferee in certain corporate and partnership transactions is treated as the transferor and must use the latter's recovery period and method in computing the MACRS deduction for the portion of the transferee's basis that does not exceed the transferor's adjusted basis in the property (Code Sec. 168(i)(7)).[100] This rule applies to nonrecognition transfers under Code Sec. 332 (subsidiary liquidations) (¶ 2261); transfers to a controlled corporation (¶ 1731); transfers related to certain reorganizations (¶ 2209); contributions to a partnership (¶ 443); certain partnership distributions (¶ 453); and transactions between members of the same affiliated group during any tax year for which a consolidated return is made by such group. It does not apply to transactions relating to the sale or exchange of 50 percent or more of the total interest in a partnership's capital and profits within a 12-month period (Code Sec. 708(b)(1)(B)).

1249. Recapture Upon Disposition of Depreciable Property. See ¶ 1779.

1250. Like-Kind Exchanges and Involuntary Conversions. The exchanged basis (i.e., carryover basis) of MACRS property acquired in a like-kind exchange or involuntary conversion for other MACRS property is depreciated by applying the following rules (Reg. § 1.168(i)-6):[101]

(1) If the replacement MACRS property has the same or a shorter recovery period and the same or a more accelerated depreciation method than the relinquished MACRS property, the exchanged (carryover) basis is depreciated over the remaining recovery period of, and using the depreciation method and convention of, the relinquished MACRS property.

(2) If the recovery period of the replacement MACRS property is longer than that of the relinquished MACRS property, the exchanged basis is depreciated over the remainder of the recovery period that would have applied to the replacement MACRS property if the replacement MACRS property had originally been placed in

References are to Standard Federal Tax Reports; Tax Research Consultant; and Practical Tax Explanations.

[97] ¶ 11,250, ¶ 11,279.04; DEPR: 3,456; § 11,135

[98] ¶ 11,250, ¶ 11,279.04; DEPR: 3,450, DEPR: 3,458; § 11,135

[99] ¶ 11,250, ¶ 11,279.04; DEPR: 3,460; § 11,135

[100] ¶ 11,279.054; DEPR: 3,306.05; § 11,150

[101] ¶ 11,279.0545; DEPR: 3,306.30; § 18,055

service when the relinquished MACRS property was placed in service by the acquiring taxpayer.

(3) If the depreciation method of the replacement MACRS property is less accelerated than that of the relinquished MACRS property, the exchanged basis is depreciated beginning in the year of replacement using the less accelerated depreciation method of the replacement MACRS property that would have applied to the replacement MACRS property if the replacement MACRS property had originally been placed in service when the relinquished MACRS property was placed in service by the acquiring taxpayer.

The excess basis of the replacement property (i.e., the noncarryover basis usually attributable to additional cash paid for the replacement property) is separately depreciated as if originally acquired in the year of replacement.

These rules are effective for like-kind exchanges and involuntary conversions in which the time of disposition and replacement both occur after February 27, 2004. A taxpayer, however, may apply the regulations retroactively (Reg. § 1.168(i)-6(k)). A taxpayer may also elect not to apply the regulations to a post-effective date exchange or conversion and depreciate the entire basis of the acquired property as a single depreciable asset beginning in the tax year of replacement (Reg. § 1.168(i)-6(i) and (j)).

Bonus depreciation may be claimed on the entire basis of qualifying acquired property (¶ 1237) (Reg. § 1.168(k)-1(f)(5)). However, only the excess basis (noncarryover basis) may qualify for expensing under Code Sec. 179 even if an election not to apply the temporary regulations is made (Reg. § 1.168(i)-6(g) and (i)).

Accelerated Cost Recovery System (ACRS)

1252. Pre-1987 ACRS in General. The Accelerated Cost Recovery System (ACRS) must be used to compute the depreciation deduction for most tangible depreciable property placed in service after 1980 and before 1987 (pre-1987 Code Sec. 168).[102] Cost recovery methods and periods are the same for both new and used property, and salvage value is disregarded in computing ACRS allowances. Post-1980 depreciation on tangible assets first placed in service before 1981 is computed using the method elected by the taxpayer when the property was placed in service (including the Class Life ADR depreciation system (¶ 1284) and other methods of depreciation discussed at ¶ 1216).

Under ACRS, the cost of eligible property is recovered over a 3-year, 5-year, 10-year, 15-year, 18-year, or 19-year period, depending on the type of property. ACRS applies to recovery property, as defined at ¶ 1255. The deduction is determined by applying the statutory table percentage for the appropriate class of property to its unadjusted basis. The unadjusted basis of property under ACRS is the basis of the property (as determined for purposes of computing gain or loss), unadjusted for depreciation, amortization or depletion. It does not include that portion of the basis for which there is an election to amortize (¶ 1287) or to expense the cost of Code Sec. 179 property (¶ 1208) (pre-1987 Code Sec. 168(d)(1)).[103]

For personal ACRS recovery property placed in service after 1980 and before 1987, one-half year's depreciation is allowed, regardless of how long it is held in the year that it is placed in service. No deduction is allowed in the year of disposition of personal recovery property. Special prorations by month (using a mid-month convention) are provided for real recovery property (¶ 1261).

Straight-Line Election. An election to recover costs by using a straight-line method over the regular recovery period or a longer recovery period was also available under ACRS and was made on the taxpayer's return for the year in which the property was placed in service (pre-1987 Code Sec. 168(f)(4)).[104]

1255. ACRS Recovery Property. For ACRS purposes, recovery property is tangible depreciable property that is placed in service after 1980 and before 1987. It does not

References are to Standard Federal Tax Reports; Tax Research Consultant; and Practical Tax Explanations.

[102] ¶ 11,258.01; DEPR: 3,054; § 11,001

[103] ¶ 11,258.041; DEPR: 3,104; § 11,001

[104] ¶ 11,258.031; DEPR: 3,404.15; § 11,001

include property for which an election is made to compute depreciation on a method not based on a depreciation period (unit-of-production method, income forecast method, etc.), public utility property for which the normalization method of accounting is not used, intangible assets such as patents and copyrights (¶ 1201), property for which an election to amortize was made, or motion picture films and videotapes (pre-1987 Code Sec. 168(c) and (e)).[105] For purposes of determining the class of recovery property into which an asset falls, recovery property is defined as either Code Sec. 1245 class property or Code Sec. 1250 class property.

Code Sec. 1245 class property includes tangible Code Sec. 1245 property, as defined at ¶ 1785, other than (1) elevators and escalators and (2) certain rapidly amortized realty. *Code Sec. 1250 class property* includes tangible Section 1250 property, as defined at ¶ 1786, and elevators and escalators.

1258. ACRS Personal Property. The ACRS statutory percentage for personal property placed in service after 1980 and before 1987 is determined using prescribed percentage tables based on the type of property (3-year, 5-year, 10-year or 15-year). These table percentages are not reproduced because such property should generally be fully depreciated at this time. The tables, however, are contained in ACRS Prop. Reg. § 1.168-2.

Generally, no recovery deduction is allowed in the year of disposition of ACRS personal property.

1261. ACRS Real Property. Under ACRS, the unadjusted basis of real property is recovered over a period of 19 years for real property placed in service after May 8, 1985, and before 1987. For real property placed in service after March 15, 1984, and before May 9, 1985, unadjusted basis is recovered over a period of 18 years. A 15-year recovery period applies to real property placed in service after 1980 and before March 16, 1984, and to low-income housing.[106]

In computing the ACRS deduction, a full-month convention is used for real recovery property placed in service before March 16, 1984, and for low-income housing, and a mid-month convention is used for real recovery property (other than low-income housing) placed in service after March 15, 1984. Under the full-month convention, real property placed in service at any time during a particular month is treated as placed in service on the first day of such month, thereby permitting a full month's cost recovery for the month the property is placed in service. For a disposition at any time during a particular month before the end of a recovery period, no cost recovery is permitted for such month of disposition. Under the mid-month convention, real property placed in service at any time during a particular month is treated as placed in service in the middle of such month, thereby permitting one-half month's cost recovery for the month the property is placed in service. For a disposition of real property during a month before the end of a recovery period, one-half month's cost recovery is allowed for the month of disposition.

In using the following tables, there are separate rate schedules depending upon the month in the first tax year that the property is placed in service. Further, where real property is sold before the end of the recovery period, the ACRS deduction for the year of disposition is to reflect only the months of the year during which the property was in service. For a short tax year, appropriate adjustments must also be made to the table amounts (¶ 1270). A complete set of ACRS depreciation tables is provided in IRS Publication 534 (Depreciating Property Placed In Service Before 1987).

References are to Standard Federal Tax Reports; Tax Research Consultant; and Practical Tax Explanations.

[105] ¶ 11,258.01, ¶ 11,258.045; DEPR: 3,058.20; § 11,001

[106] ¶ 11,258.025; DEPR: 3,158; § 11,001

Table I *18-Year Real Property (placed in service after June 22, 1984) for Which Alternate ACRS Method Over a 35-Year Period Is Elected*

	Month Placed in Service				
Year	1-2	3-6	7-10	11	12
1st	3%	2%	1%	0.4%	0.1%
2-30th	3%	3%	3%	3%	3%
31st	2%	2%	2%	2.6%	2.9%
32-35th	2%	2%	2%	2%	2%
36th		1%	2%	2%	2%

Table II *18-Year Real Property (placed in service after March 15 and before June 23, 1984) 15-Year Real Property and Low-Income Housing (placed in service before May 9, 1985) for Which Alternate ACRS Method Over a 35-Year Period Is Elected*

	Month Placed in Service		
Year	1-2	3-6	7-12
1st	3%	2%	1%
2-30th	3%	3%	3%
31-35th	2%	2%	2%
36th		1%	2%

Table III *Low-Income Housing (placed in service after May 8, 1985) for Which Alternate ACRS Method Over a 35-Year Period Is Elected*

	Month Placed in Service											
Year	1	2	3	4	5	6	7	8	9	10	11	12
1st	2.9%	2.6%	2.4%	2.1%	1.9%	1.7%	1.4%	1.2%	1.0%	0.7%	0.5%	0.2%
2-20th	2.9%	2.9%	2.9%	2.9%	2.9%	2.9%	2.9%	2.9%	2.9%	2.9%	2.9%	2.9%
21-35th	2.8%	2.8%	2.8%	2.8%	2.8%	2.8%	2.8%	2.8%	2.8%	2.8%	2.8%	2.8%
36th		0.3%	0.5%	0.8%	1.0%	1.2%	1.5%	1.7%	1.9%	2.2%	2.4%	2.7%

Table IV *19-Year Real Property for Which Alternate ACRS Method Over a 35-Year Period Is Elected*

	Month Placed in Service											
Year	1	2	3	4	5	6	7	8	9	10	11	12
1st	2.7%	2.5%	2.3%	2.0%	1.8%	1.5%	1.3%	1.1%	0.8%	0.6%	0.4%	0.1%
2-20th	2.9%	2.9%	2.9%	2.9%	2.9%	2.9%	2.9%	2.9%	2.9%	2.9%	2.9%	2.9%
21-35th	2.8%	2.8%	2.8%	2.8%	2.8%	2.8%	2.8%	2.8%	2.8%	2.8%	2.8%	2.8%
36th	0.2%	0.4%	0.6%	0.9%	1.1%	1.4%	1.6%	1.8%	2.1%	2.3%	2.5%	2.8%

Table V *18-Year Real Property (placed in service after June 22, 1984) 19-Year Real Property for Which Alternate ACRS Method Over a 45-Year Period Is Elected*

	Month Placed in Service											
Year	1	2	3	4	5	6	7	8	9	10	11	12
1st	2.1%	1.9%	1.8%	1.6%	1.4%	1.2%	1%	0.8%	0.6%	0.5%	0.3%	0.1%
2-11th	2.3%	2.3%	2.3%	2.3%	2.3%	2.3%	2.3%	2.3%	2.3%	2.3%	2.3%	2.3%
12-45th	2.2%	2.2%	2.2%	2.2%	2.2%	2.2%	2.2%	2.2%	2.2%	2.2%	2.2%	2.2%
46th	0.1%	0.3%	0.4%	0.6%	0.8%	1%	1.2%	1.4%	1.6%	1.7%	1.9%	2.1%

Table VI *18-Year Real Property (placed in service after March 15 and before June 23, 1984) 15-Year Real Property and Low-Income Housing (placed in service after December 31, 1980) for Which Alternate ACRS Method Over a 45-Year Period Is Elected*

	Month Placed in Service											
Year	1	2	3	4	5	6	7	8	9	10	11	12
1st	2.3%	2%	1.9%	1.7%	1.5%	1.3%	1.2%	0.9%	0.7%	0.6%	0.4%	0.2%
2-10th	2.3%	2.3%	2.3%	2.3%	2.3%	2.3%	2.3%	2.3%	2.3%	2.3%	2.3%	2.3%
11-45th	2.2%	2.2%	2.2%	2.2%	2.2%	2.2%	2.2%	2.2%	2.2%	2.2%	2.2%	2.2%
46th		0.3%	0.4%	0.6%	0.8%	1%	1.1%	1.4%	1.6%	1.7%	1.9%	2.1%

1264. ACRS: Predominant Use Outside the U.S. Under ACRS, the unadjusted basis of personal property used outside the U.S. is recovered over a period equal to the ADR class life for that property as of January 1, 1981.[107] Generally, no recovery deduction is allowed in the year of disposition of personal recovery property used predominantly outside the U.S. The unadjusted basis of real property and low income housing used predominantly outside the U.S. is to be recovered over a period of 35 years. For real recovery property (other than low-income housing) placed in service after March 15, 1984, a mid-month convention is used. There are separate rate schedules depending on the month in the first tax year that the property is placed in service.

1267. ACRS: Components of Sec. 1250 Class Property. Under ACRS, structural components of Sec. 1250 class property may not be depreciated separately. Composite depreciation is required on the entire building, unless the components qualify for amortization elections (pre-1987 Code Sec. 168(f)(1)).[108] Components which are considered personal property can be separately depreciated under the cost segregation rules. See ¶ 1240.

Substantial Improvements. If a taxpayer made a substantial improvement to a building, it was treated as a separate building rather than as one or more components. The taxpayer could use the regular ACRS deduction or may elect the straight-line ACRS deduction for the improvement over the regular or a longer recovery period regardless of the ACRS method that is used for the rest of the building.

Components and improvements placed in service after 1986 are depreciated using MACRS even if the building is not MACRS property. See "*Additions and Improvements*" at ¶ 1240.

1270. ACRS: Short Tax Years. For a tax year of less than 12 months, the amount of the ACRS deduction is the amount that bears the same relationship to the amount of the deduction as the number of months and partial months in the short year bears to 12 (pre-1987 Code Sec. 168(f)(5)).[109] Generally, for real property and low-income housing placed in service or disposed of in a short tax year, the above rule does not apply and the deduction is based on the number of months the property is in service during the year, regardless of the length of the tax year and regardless of the recovery period and method used.

Any unrecovered allowance (the difference between the recovery allowance properly allowable for the short tax year and the recovery allowance that would have been allowable if such year were not a short tax year) is claimed in the tax year following the last year in the recovery period (Prop. Reg. § 1.168-2(f)(3)).[110] However, there is a maximum limitation on the amount of an unrecovered allowance that may be claimed as a recovery allowance in a tax year. The unrecovered allowance claimed as a recovery allowance in the tax year following the last year of the recovery period may not exceed the amount of the recovery allowance permitted for the last year of the recovery period, assuming that such year consists of 12 months. Any remainder is carried forward until exhausted.

References are to Standard Federal Tax Reports; Tax Research Consultant; and Practical Tax Explanations.

[107] ¶ 162.01; DEPR: 6,106; § 11,001

[108] ¶ 11,258.05; DEPR: 3,206.45; § 11,001

[109] ¶ 11,258.055; DEPR: 3,354; § 11,001

[110] ¶ 11,252, ¶ 11,258.055; DEPR: 3,354; § 11,001

Class Life ADR System

1282. Post-1980 Depreciation Under ADR. If the Asset Depreciation Range (ADR) System was elected for tangible assets first placed in service after 1970 and before 1981, post-1980 depreciation on such assets must be computed under the ADR System.[111]

1284. ADR in General. Under ADR, all tangible assets were placed in specific classes. A class life (called "asset guideline period" in the regulations[112]) was given for each class of assets. In addition, each class of assets other than land improvements and buildings was given a range of years (called "asset depreciation range") that was about 20 percent above and below the class life. For details on the ADR system, see ¶ 11,029.01 and following of the STANDARD FEDERAL TAX REPORTER, DEPR: 15,800 of the Tax Research Consultant and § 11,025.10 and § 11,025.15 of Practical Tax Explanations.

Deductions for Refiners

1285. Deduction for EPA Sulfur Regulation Compliance Costs of Small Refiners. Small business refiners may elect to immediately deduct as an expense up to 75 percent of the qualified capital costs paid or incurred during the tax year for the purpose of complying with the Highway Diesel Fuel Sulfur Control Requirements of the Environmental Protection Agency (EPA) (Code Sec. 179B). Costs paid or incurred with respect to any facility of a small business refiner during the period beginning on January 1, 2003, and ending on the earlier of the date that is one year after the date on which the taxpayer must comply with the applicable EPA regulations or December 31, 2009, qualify for the deduction (Code Sec. 179B(a); Code Sec. 45H(c)(2)–(5)). Election guidance is provided in Temporary Reg. § 1.179B-1T(d).

1285A. Expensing Election for New or Expanded Refineries. A taxpayer may elect to expense 50 percent of the cost of qualified refinery property placed in service after August 8, 2005, and before January 1, 2014. The property must be placed in service before January 1, 2010, if its construction is not subject to a written binding contract entered into after June 14, 2005, and before January 1, 2010, or, in the case of self constructed property, construction did not begin after June 14, 2005, and before January 1, 2010. The original use of the refinery property must commence with the taxpayer. An improvement to an existing refinery can qualify if the improvement increases production capacity by specified levels (Code Sec. 179C; Reg. § 1.179C-1).

Deduction for Energy Efficiency Improvements

1286. Deduction for Energy Efficiency Improvements to Depreciable Buildings. A taxpayer may deduct the cost of certain energy efficiency improvements installed on or in a depreciable building located in the U.S., effective for improvements placed in service after December 31, 2005, and before January 1, 2014 (Code Sec. 179D; Notice 2006-52, as clarified by Notice 2008-40; Notice 2012-26, modifying Notice 2008-40). The deduction applies to "energy efficient commercial building property," which is defined as depreciable property installed as part of a building's (1) interior lighting systems, (2) heating, cooling, ventilation, and hot water systems, or (3) envelope as part of a certified plan to reduce the total annual energy and power costs of these systems by at least 50 percent in comparison to a reference building that meets specified minimum standards. The deduction is limited to the lesser of the cost of the qualifying property reduced by the aggregate amount deducted in any prior tax year or the product of $1.80 and the total square footage of the building reduced by the aggregate amount deducted in any prior tax year.

References are to Standard Federal Tax Reports; Tax Research Consultant; and Practical Tax Explanations.

[111] ¶ 11,029.01; DEPR: 15,800; § 11,001

[112] ¶ 11,026, ¶ 11,029.01; DEPR: 15,812; § 11,001

A taxpayer may also claim a partial deduction for the costs of property that meet energy savings targets set by the IRS in Notice 2006-52, as modified by Notice 2012-26. The deduction is determined by substituting $.60 for $1.80.

For property placed in service on or after March 12, 2012, the taxpayer may use the following energy savings percentages to determine if a partial deduction is available: (1) building envelope—10 percent; heating, cooling, ventilation, and hot water systems—15 percent; and interior lighting systems—25 percent; or (2) building envelope—10 percent; heating, cooling, ventilation, and hot water systems—20 percent; and interior lighting systems—20 percent.

For property placed in service on or after January 1, 2009 and before March 12, 2012, the taxpayer may use the following energy savings percentages: building envelope—10 percent; heating, cooling, ventilation, and hot water systems—20 percent; and interior lighting systems—20 percent.

Generally, the deduction is claimed by the building's owner. However, in the case of a public building, the person primarily responsible for designing the property may claim the deduction. The deduction reduces the depreciable basis of the building and is treated as a depreciation deduction for section 1245 recapture purposes (Code Sec. 1245(a)(3)(C)).

The Department of Energy maintains a list of the software that must be used to calculate power consumption and energy costs for purposes of certifying the required energy savings necessary to claim the deduction (Notice 2008-40). The certification is not attached to the taxpayer's return but must be retained as part of the taxpayer's books and records. The deduction is claimed on the "Other deductions" line of the taxpayer's return. There is no special form for computing the deduction.

Taxpayers who failed to claim a Code Sec. 179D deduction may file an automatic accounting method change to do so (Rev. Proc. 2011-14, Appendix Section 8.04, as amended by Rev. Proc. 2012-39).

Allowance for Amortization

1287. Property Subject to Amortization. Amortization is the recovery of certain capital expenditures, that are not ordinarily deductible, in a manner that is similar to straight-line depreciation. That portion of the basis of property that is recovered through amortization deductions may not also be depreciated.

Pollution Control Facilities. Taxpayers may elect to amortize over a 60-month period the cost of certified pollution control facilities added to or used in connection with a plant in operation before 1976. The amortization deduction is available only for the portion of the facility's basis attributable to the first 15 years of its recovery period if it has a MACRS recovery period in excess of 15 years. The remaining basis is depreciable. An air pollution control facility placed in service after April 11, 2005 in connection with a coal-fired plant placed in operation after 1975 qualifies for an 84-month amortization period (Code Sec. 169). The 60-month amortization period continues to apply to an air pollution facility placed in service after April 11, 2005 in connection with a coal-fired plant placed in operation before 1976 (Code Sec. 169).[113]

Architectural and Transportation Barriers. Business taxpayers can elect to deduct up to $15,000 of the costs of removing certain architectural and transportation barriers for handicapped or elderly persons in the year paid or incurred instead of capitalizing and depreciating such costs (Code Sec. 190).[114]

Reforestation Expenditures. A taxpayer (other than a trust) may elect to expense up to $10,000 of qualified reforestation expenditures each tax year for each qualified timber property. A taxpayer may elect to amortize over 84 months amounts for which a current deduction is not elected (Code Sec. 194).[115] The expense election may be made by

References are to Standard Federal Tax Reports; Tax Research Consultant; and Practical Tax Explanations.

[113] ¶ 11,502, ¶ 11,517; DEPR: 21,150; § 11,501

[114] ¶ 12,260, ¶ 12,264; BUSEXP: 9,102.35; § 10,220

[115] ¶ 12,330, ¶ 12,335; FARM: 24,100; § 11,505

estates. Trusts and estates may make the amortization election. Election guidance is provided in Notice 2006-47.

Start-Up and Organizational Costs. See ¶ 904.

Oil and Gas Geological and Geophysical Expenditures. Geological and geophysical (G&G) expenditures paid or incurred in connection with oil and gas exploration or development in the United States must be amortized ratably over a 24-month period beginning on the mid-point of the tax-year that the expenses were paid or incurred. If a property or project is abandoned or retired during the 24-month amortization period, any remaining basis must continue to be amortized (Code Sec. 167(h)). Major integrated oil companies, however, must ratably amortize any G&G costs over five years (Code Sec. 167(h)(5)).[116]

Musical Compositions and Copyrights. For tax years beginning before January 1, 2011, a taxpayer could elect five-year ratable amortization of capitalized expenses paid or incurred in creating or acquiring a musical composition (including the accompanying words) or a copyright to a musical composition if the expenses are not exempt from capitalization as the qualified creative expenses of an individual (¶ 990A), the expenses are not amortizable under Code Sec. 197 because acquired as part of the acquisition of a trade or business, or the taxpayer uses a simplified UNICAP method for property acquired for resale (¶ 995) (Code Sec. 167(g)(8)). The provision is effective for expenses paid or incurred with respect to property placed in service in tax years beginning after December 31, 2005.

1288. Amortization of Section 197 Intangibles. The capitalized cost of goodwill and most other intangibles used in a trade or business or for the production of income are ratably amortized over a 15-year period generally beginning in the month of acquisition (Code Sec. 197).[117] Intangibles amortizable under this provision are referred to as "section 197 intangibles."

The following intangibles are section 197 intangibles: (1) goodwill, going concern value, and covenants not to compete entered into in connection with the acquisition of a trade or business (¶ 1743); (2) workforce in place; (3) information base; (4) a patent, copyright, formula, design, or similar item; (5) any customer-based intangible; (6) any supplier-based intangible; (7) any license, permit, or other right granted by a governmental unit or agency; and (8) any franchise, trademark, or trade name (Code Sec. 197(d)).[118]

Generally, self-created intangibles are not amortized under Code Sec. 197 unless created in connection with the acquisition of a trade or business. Exceptions are provided for government-granted licenses, permits, and rights, covenants not to compete entered into in connection with the purchase of a business, and franchises, trademarks, and trade names (Code Sec. 197(c)(2)).[119] However, certain self-created intangibles without an ascertainable useful life may be amortized over 15-years under Reg. § 1.167(a)-3(b). See ¶ 1288A.

The following intangibles are specifically excluded from the definition of a section 197 intangible: (1) interests in a corporation, partnership, trust, or estate; (2) interests under certain financial contracts; (3) interests in land; (4) computer software not acquired in connection with the purchase of a business, or which is readily available for purchase by the general public, is subject to a nonexclusive license, and has not been substantially modified (¶ 980); (5) certain separately acquired rights and interests, including an interest in a patent or copyright or an interest in a film, sound recording, videotape, book, or similar property; (6) interests under existing leases of tangible property; (7) interests under existing indebtedness; (8) sports franchises acquired on or before October 22, 2004; (9) residential mortgage servicing rights not acquired in

References are to Standard Federal Tax Reports; Tax Research Consultant; and Practical Tax Explanations.

[116] ¶ 11,009.047; FARM: 21,134; § 11,550

[117] ¶ 12,450, ¶ 12,455; DEPR: 21,050; § 11,401

[118] ¶ 12,450, ¶ 12,455.023; DEPR: 21,052; § 11,405

[119] ¶ 12,450, ¶ 12,455.033; DEPR: 21,052.60; § 11,415

12 DEPRECIATION

connection with the acquisition of a business; and (10) professional fees and transaction costs incurred in a corporate organization or reorganization (Code Sec. 197(e)).[120]

No loss may be claimed when an amortizable section 197 intangible is disposed of if any other section 197 intangibles acquired in the same transaction are retained. The bases of the retained section 197 intangibles are increased by the amount of the unrecognized loss (Code Sec. 197(f)).[121]

1288A. 15-Year Safe-Harbor Amortization for Certain Self-Created Intangibles. A taxpayer is permitted to amortize certain created intangibles that do not have readily ascertainable useful lives over a 15-year period using the straight-line method and no salvage value (Reg. § 1.167(a)-3(b); Rev. Proc. 2006-12, as modified by Rev. Proc. 2006-37, providing change of accounting method procedures).[122] For example, amounts paid to acquire memberships or privileges of indefinite duration, such as a trade association membership, are covered by this safe harbor.

A taxpayer may use the 15-year amortization period on any intangible other than (1) any intangible acquired from another person; (2) created financial interests; (3) any intangible that has a useful life that can be estimated with reasonable accuracy; or (4) an intangible asset for which an amortization period or useful life is specifically prescribed or proscribed by the Code, regulations, or other published IRS guidance. In addition, amounts paid to facilitate an acquisition of a trade or business, a change in the capital structure of a business entity, and certain other similar transactions described in Reg. § 1.263(a)-5 do not qualify. The 15-year amortization period is extended to 25 years for an intangible benefit described in Reg. § 1.263(a)-4(d)(8). These are intangibles created by transferring ownership of real property to another person or by making a monetary contribution for the acquisition or improvement of real property owned by another person. However, for the treatment of impact fees, see Rev. Rul. 2002-9, which requires developers to allocate the cost of impact fees to the basis of the buildings constructed.

What Is Depletion?

1289. Deduction for Depletion. A deduction for depletion is allowed in determining the taxable income from natural resources. The deduction is similar to depreciation in that it allows the taxpayer to recover the cost of an asset over the resources' productive life. "Depletion" is the exhaustion of natural resources, such as mines, wells, and timberlands, as a result of production. The right to a depletion allowance is based upon the taxpayer's economic interest in the property (Reg. § 1.611-1(b)(i)).[123] An economic interest exists if the taxpayer (1) has acquired by investment any interest in minerals in place or in standing timber and (2) looks to the income from the extraction of the minerals or severance of the timber for a return on investment.[124]

The basic method of computing depletion is "cost depletion" (Code Sec. 612).[125] The basis upon which the deduction is allowed is the adjusted basis of the property (Reg. § 1.612-1).[126] Determination of cost depletion first requires an estimate of the number of units (tons, barrels, etc.) that make up the deposit. Then that part of the cost or other adjusted basis of the property that is allocable to the depletable reserves is divided by the number of units. The quotient is the cost depletion per unit. This amount, multiplied by the number of units extracted and sold during the year, determines the cost depletion deductible for the year. Each year the "cost basis" of the property is reduced, but not below zero, by the amount of depletion deducted for that year, whether cost or percentage depletion was used. The remaining basis is used in computing cost depletion for the next year.

References are to Standard Federal Tax Reports; Tax Research Consultant; and Practical Tax Explanations.

[120] ¶ 12,450, ¶ 12,455.034; DEPR: 21,054; § 11,410

[121] ¶ 12,450, ¶ 12,455.035; DEPR: 21,056.05; § 11,425

[122] ¶ 11,009.045; BUSEXP: 9,104.20; § 11,415

[123] ¶ 23,922; FARM: 15,052; § 11,610

[124] ¶ 23,924.027; FARM: 15,054; § 11,610

[125] ¶ 23,940, ¶ 23,942; FARM: 15,100; § 11,615

[126] ¶ 23,941, ¶ 23,942.021; FARM: 15,106; § 11,615

An alternative method of computing depletion, known as percentage depletion, may be used for almost all depletable property. However, timber is excluded from this method (Reg. § 1.611-1(a)(1)).[127] Under this method, a flat percentage of *gross income* from the property is taken as the depletion deduction. The percentage depletion deduction may not exceed 50 percent (100 percent in the case of oil or gas properties) of the *taxable income* from the property (see ¶ 1294 for special rules concerning independent producers and royalty owners) computed without regard to the depletion allowance or the manufacturing deduction under Code Sec. 199. In computing taxable income, the deductible mining expenses must be decreased by the amount of Sec. 1245 gains allocable to the property (Code Sec. 613(a)).[128] If cost depletion results in a greater deduction, cost depletion must be used (Reg. § 1.613-1).[129]

Ordinarily, the lease of a mineral property requires the lessee to make an advance payment, known as a bonus or advance royalty. In such a case, the lessor's cost depletion allowance must be allocated between the advance lump-sum payment and the royalties received during the period of extraction (Reg. § 1.612-3).[130] Unlike bonuses or advance royalties, "shut-in" oil payments and delay rentals are not depletable.[131]

Coal and iron ore royalties retained upon the disposition of coal and iron ore generally held for more than one year before mining are eligible for percentage depletion for any tax year in which the maximum rate of tax imposed on net capital gain equals or exceeds the maximum rate for ordinary income (Code Sec. 631(c)).[132]

Depletion is subject to recapture as ordinary income upon the sale or other disposition of an oil, gas, geothermal, or other mineral property at a gain (Code Sec. 1254).[133] Recapture is limited to the amount by which the depletion deduction reduced the adjusted basis of the disposed property.

Mineral Production Payments

1291. Mineral Production Payments. A mineral production payment is treated as a loan by the owner of the production payment to the owner of the mineral property (Code Sec. 636).[134] Thus, a carved-out mineral production payment—created when the owner of a mineral property sells or carves out a portion of the future production with payment secured by an interest in the minerals—is treated as a mortgage loan on the mineral property rather than as an economic interest in the property. All the income from the property is taxed to the seller (owner of the working interest) and is subject to depletion by him. The owner of the production payment does not get depletion.

When the owner of a mineral interest sells the working interest, a retained production payment is treated as a purchase money mortgage loan and not as an economic interest in the mineral property. Accordingly, all the income from the property is taxed to the purchaser and is subject to depletion by him. The seller who retains the production payment is not entitled to depletion.

Percentage Depletion

1294. Oil and Gas Production. A 22 percent depletion rate is allowed for oil and gas production in the case of regulated natural gas and natural gas sold under a fixed contract (but not certain casinghead gas contracts[135]); a 10 percent rate applies to geopressurized methane gas wells (Code Sec. 613A(b)).[136]

A 15 percent depletion rate applies to independent producers and royalty owners with limitations based on average daily production (Code Sec. 613A(c)).[137] The rate

References are to Standard Federal Tax Reports; Tax Research Consultant; and Practical Tax Explanations.

[127] ¶ 23,922, ¶ 29,960, ¶ 23,963; FARM: 24,054; § 11,620

[128] ¶ 23,960, ¶ 23,963; FARM: 15,308; § 11,620

[129] ¶ 23,961, ¶ 23,963.01; FARM: 15,100; § 11,620

[130] ¶ 23,946, ¶ 23,948.01; FARM: 15,116; § 11,615

[131] ¶ 23,963.60; FARM: 18,260; § 11,615

[132] ¶ 24,150, ¶ 24,156.021; FARM: 18,350; § 11,625

[133] ¶ 31,060, ¶ 31,066; FARM: 21,200; § 16,710.05

[134] ¶ 24,170, ¶ 24,176; FARM: 18,208; § 11,610

[135] ¶ 23,924.039, ¶ 23,988.01; FARM: 15,204; § 11,625

[136] ¶ 23,980, ¶ 23,988.021; FARM: 15,202; § 11,625

[137] ¶ 23,980, ¶ 23,988.024; FARM: 15,206; § 11,625

applies to an average daily production of 1,000 barrels of oil and six million cubic feet of gas. The percentage depletion deduction is generally limited to the lesser of 65 percent of the *taxable income* before the depletion allowance (Code Sec. 613A(d)(1))[138] or 100 percent of the *taxable income from the property* before the depletion allowance (see ¶ 1289). For purposes of the 65 percent limit, taxable income is computed without regard to any net operating loss carryback, capital loss carryback, or manufacturing deduction under Code Sec. 199. Any portion of a depletion allowance disallowed under the 65 percent limit may be carried over. Percentage depletion is also denied for lease bonuses, advance royalty payments, or other amounts payable without regard to actual production from an oil, gas or geothermal property (see ¶ 1296) (Code Sec. 613(e)(3) and Code Sec. 613A(d)(5)).[139]

For tax years (1) beginning after December 31, 1997, and before January 1, 2008, or (2) beginning after December 31, 2008, and before January 1, 2012, the 100-percent taxable income limit on percentage depletion deductions for oil and gas properties is suspended for marginal properties (Code Sec. 613A(c)(6)(H)).[140] Thus, the limitation is not suspended for tax years beginning in 2012 but is suspended for tax years beginning in 2009, 2010, and 2011.

The 15 percent depletion rate for marginal oil or gas production properties held by independent producers or royalty owners increases by one percent (up to a maximum 25 percent rate) for each whole dollar that the reference price for crude oil for the preceding calendar year is less than $20 per barrel (Code Sec. 613A(c)(6)).[141] The allowance for depletion is computed using the increased rate with respect to the portion of the taxpayer's average daily marginal production of domestic crude oil and natural gas that does not exceed the taxpayer's depletable quantities of those products. An election may be made to have this rule apply to the pro rata portion of marginal production. The applicable percentage for marginal production for tax years beginning in 2001 through 2012 is 15 percent (Notice 2012-50).

1296. Geothermal Deposits. Geothermal deposits (geothermal reservoirs consisting of natural heat that is stored in rocks or in an aqueous liquid or vapor (whether or not under pressure)) are eligible for a 15 percent depletion allowance (Code Sec. 613(e)).[142]

1298. Coal or Other Minerals. Percentage depletion is allowed, under Code Sec. 613(b),[143] at the following percentages of "gross income from the property":

(a) 22%—sulphur and uranium; and, if from deposits in the United States, anorthosite, clay, laterite, and nephelite syenite (to the extent that alumina and aluminum compounds are extracted therefrom), asbestos, bauxite, celestite, chromite, corundum, fluorspar, graphite, ilmenite, kyanite, mica, olivine, quartz crystals (radio grade), rutile, block steatite talc, and zircon, and ores of the following metals: antimony, beryllium, bismuth, cadmium, cobalt, columbium, lead lithium, manganese, mercury, molybdenum, nickel, platinum and platinum group metals, tantalum, thorium, tin, titanium, tungsten, vanadium and zinc.

(b) 15%—if from deposits in the United States, gold, silver, copper, iron ore, and oil shale (except shale described in (e) below).

(c) 14%—metal mines (other than metals from deposits in the United States to which the 22 percent rate in (a) applies), rock asphalt, and vermiculite; if (a) above and (e) and (f) below do not apply, ball clay, bentonite, china clay, sagger clay, and clay used or sold for use for purposes dependent on its refractory properties.

References are to Standard Federal Tax Reports; Tax Research Consultant; and Practical Tax Explanations.

[138] ¶ 23,980, ¶ 23,988.024; FARM: 15,218; § 11,625

[139] ¶ 23,960, ¶ 23,980, ¶ 23,988.036; FARM: 15,206; § 11,625

[140] ¶ 23,980, ¶ 23,988.044; FARM: 15,150; § 11,625

[141] ¶ 23,980, ¶ 23,988.044; FARM: 15,216; § 11,625

[142] ¶ 23,960, ¶ 23,965.03; FARM: 15,158; § 11,625

[143] ¶ 23,960, ¶ 23,965.01; FARM: 15,154; § 11,625

(d) 10%—asbestos from deposits outside the United States, brucite, coal, lignite, perlite, sodium chloride, and wollastonite.

(e) 7½%—clay and shale used or sold for use in the manufacture of sewer pipe or brick, and clay, shale, and slate used or sold for use as sintered or burned lightweight aggregates.

(f) 5%—gravel, peat, pumice, sand, scoria, shale (except shale described in (b) and (e) above) and stone (except stone falling within the general 14 percent group described in (g)); clay used, or sold for use, in the manufacture of drainage and roofing tile, flower pots, and kindred products; also, if from brine wells, bromite, calcium chloride, and magnesium chloride.

(g) 14%—all other minerals not included in any of the categories listed above. For purposes of this paragraph, the term "all other minerals" does not include (A) soil, sod, dirt, turf, water, or mosses; (B) minerals from sea water, the air, or similar inexhaustible sources; or (C) oil and gas wells.

"Gross income from the property," on which percentage depletion is based, is that amount of income which comes from the extraction of the ores or minerals from the ground and the application of mining processes, including mining transportation (Code Sec. 613(c)).[144] Mining processes include certain specified treatment processes. In general, it can be said that the percentage depletion allowance is based on the mined product after application of those treatment processes applied by "ordinary" miners. Hence, an integrated miner-manufacturer computes gross income from mining at the point when the non-integrated miner disposes of the product. Gross income is computed by use of the representative market or field price. However, when it is impossible to determine such a field price, and where the IRS does not determine that a more appropriate method should be used, the proportionate profits method must be used (Reg. § 1.613-4(d)).[145]

12 DEPRECIATION

References are to Standard Federal Tax Reports; Tax Research Consultant; and Practical Tax Explanations.

[144] ¶ 23,960, ¶ 23,968.04; FARM: 15,258; § 11,620

[145] ¶ 23,967, ¶ 23,968.04; FARM: 15,264; § 11,620

Chapter 13

TAX CREDITS

Nonrefundable Credits

1301. Child and Dependent Care Credit. A nonrefundable credit is allowed for a portion of qualifying child or dependent care expenses paid for the purpose of allowing the taxpayer (and the taxpayer's spouse, if married filing a joint return) to be gainfully employed (Code Sec. 21).[1] The credit is computed on Form 2441 for filers of Form 1040 and 1040A. The credit cannot be claimed on Form 1040EZ. To be eligible for the credit, the taxpayer must incur employment-related expenses in providing care for one of the following qualified individuals:

- a dependent of the taxpayer who is a qualifying child of the taxpayer and has not attained the age of 13 (¶ 137A);
- a dependent of the taxpayer who is a qualifying child or qualifying relative of the taxpayer (¶ 137) (determined without regards to whether the individual may be claimed as a dependent by another taxpayer, has income in excess of the dependency exemption amount, or files a joint return with his or her spouse) and is physically or mentally incapable of caring for himself or herself and who has the same principal place of abode as the taxpayer for more than half of the year; or
- the taxpayer's spouse, if the spouse is physically or mentally incapable of caring for himself or herself and has the same principal place of abode as the taxpayer for more than half of the year.

Amount of Credit. The maximum amount of employment-related expenses to which the credit may be applied is $3,000 if one qualifying individual is involved or $6,000 if two or more qualifying individuals are involved (less excludable employer dependent care assistance program payments) (Code Sec. 21(c)). The credit amount is equal to the amount of qualified expenses times the applicable percentage, as determined by the taxpayer's adjusted gross income (AGI). Taxpayers with an AGI of $15,000 or less use the highest applicable percentage of 35 percent. For taxpayers with an AGI over $15,000, the credit is reduced by one percentage point for each $2,000 of AGI (or fraction thereof) over $15,000 (Code Sec. 21(a)(2)). The minimum applicable percentage of 20 percent is used by taxpayers with an AGI greater than $43,000. Thus, the maximum dependent care credit amount is $1,050 for one qualifying dependent and $2,100 for two or more qualifying dependents.

Example: A widower paid a housekeeper $5,000 during the year to take care of his home and 10-year-old daughter while he is working. His adjusted gross income

References are to Standard Federal Tax Reports; Tax Research Consultant; and Practical Tax Explanations.

[1] ¶ 3502; INDIV: 57,050; § 12,201

was $25,000. Since there is only one qualifying child, the maximum credit he can claim is $900 (30 percent of $3,000).

Comment: Absent further legislation, for tax years beginning after 2012, the maximum amount of employment-related expenses to which the credit may be applied will be $2,400 if one qualifying individual is involved or $4,800 if two or more qualifying individuals are involved (less excludable employer dependent care assistance program payments). Further, the applicable percentage against which the taxpayer's employment-related expenses are multiplied will begin at 30 percent and will be reduced (but not below 20 percent) by one percentage point for each $2,000 (or fraction thereof) by which the taxpayer's AGI exceeds $10,000.

Qualifying Expenses. Qualifying expenses include expenses paid for household services and for the care of a qualifying individual that allow the taxpayer (and the taxpayer's spouse if filing a joint return) to work or look for work. Services outside the home qualify if they involve the care of a qualified individual who regularly spends at least eight hours a day in the taxpayer's home. However, no expenses incurred to send a child or other dependent to an overnight camp are considered qualifying expenses for credit purposes. Payments to a relative may be qualifying expenses unless the taxpayer claims a dependency exemption for the relative or if the relative is the taxpayer's child and is under age 19.

Qualifying employment-related expenses are considered in determining the credit only to the extent of earned income—wages, salary, remuneration for personal services, net self-employment income, etc. For married taxpayers, expenses are limited to the earned income of the lower-earning spouse. Generally, if one spouse is not working, no credit is allowed. However, if the nonworking spouse is physically or mentally incapable of caring for himself or herself or is a full-time student at an educational institution for at least five calendar months during the year, the law assumes an earned income amount—for each month of disability or school attendance—of $250 if there is one qualifying individual or of $500 if there are two or more qualifying individuals (Code Sec. 21(d)(2)).

Claiming the Credit. Generally, a married taxpayer *must* file a joint return to claim the credit. For this purpose, a married person living apart from his or her spouse under the circumstances described at ¶ 173 is considered unmarried. Also, a divorced or legally separated taxpayer having custody of a child who is disabled or under the age 13 is entitled to the credit even though he or she has released the right to a dependency exemption for the child (¶ 139A) (Code Sec. 21(e)(5)). Taxpayers must provide each qualifying individual's taxpayer identification number (generally a Social Security number) in order to claim the credit as well as an identifying number of the dependent care service provider (either their Social Security number or their employer identification number (EIN)) (Code Sec. 21(e)(9) and (10)).

1302. Credit for the Elderly or the Permanently and Totally Disabled. A tax credit is available to individuals who are: (1) 65 years of age before the close of the tax year or (2) under age 65 but are retired and were permanently and totally disabled when they retired (Code Sec. 22).[2] Married taxpayers must file a joint return to claim the credit unless the spouses live apart throughout the tax year. The credit is computed on Schedule R of Form 1040 and 1040A.

The credit is 15 percent of an applicable initial amount based on an individual's filing status and reduced by certain income. For individuals age 65 or older, the applicable initial amount is as follows:

Single individual	$5,000
Married individuals, joint return, one spouse is a qualified individual	5,000
Married individuals, joint return, both spouses are qualified individuals	7,500
Married individual, separate return	3,750

This initial amount is then reduced by amounts received as pension, annuity, or disability benefits that are excludable from gross income and are payable under the

References are to Standard Federal Tax Reports; Tax Research Consultant; and Practical Tax Explanations.

[2] ¶ 3550; INDIV: 57,100; § 12,501

Social Security Act (Title II), the Railroad Retirement Act of 1974, a Veterans Affairs program, or that are otherwise excluded under a non-Code provision. However, no reduction is made for pension, annuity or disability benefits for personal injuries or sickness payable from a Veterans Affairs program.

The maximum amount determined above is further reduced by one-half of the excess of the taxpayer's adjusted gross income (AGI) over the following levels, based on filing status (Code Sec. 22(d)):

Single taxpayer	$7,500
Married taxpayers, combined AGI on joint return	10,000
Married individual filing separately	5,000

For permanently and totally disabled individuals under age 65, the applicable initial amount noted above may not exceed the amount of disability income for the tax year. In determining their initial amounts, special rules apply to a married couple filing a joint return where both spouses qualify for the credit and at least one of them is under age 65. Disability income means the total amount that is included in an individual's gross income for the tax year under Code Secs. 72 (¶ 817) or 105(a) (¶ 2190A) to the extent the amount constitutes wages (or payments in lieu of wages) for periods during which the individual is absent from work due to permanent and total disability (Code Sec. 22(c)(2)(B)).

An individual is considered permanently and totally disabled for this purpose if he or she is unable to engage in any substantial gainful activity by reason of any medically determinable physical or mental impairment that can be expected to result in death or to last for a continuous period of not less than 12 months. This impairment should be substantiated by a letter from a certified physician kept in the taxpayer's records (Code Sec. 22(e)(3)).

Example: Alex, age 66 and single, has AGI of $9,000 for the year and receives $4,000 of nontaxable Social Security benefits for the year. To determine his credit, he would make the following computation:

Initial amount	$5,000
Less: Social security benefits	4,000
Reduced initial amount	$1,000
Less: One-half of AGI above $7,500	750
Amount eligible for credit	$250
Credit: $250 × 15%	$38

1303. Credits for Higher Education Tuition. There are three education-related credits: the Hope scholarship credit (unavailable for 2012), the American Opportunity (modified Hope) credit and the lifetime learning credit. These credits may be claimed on Form 8863 by individuals for qualified tuition expenses incurred by students pursuing college or graduate degrees, or vocational training (Code Sec. 25A).[3] The credits are elective, generally nonrefundable (except for the American Opportunity credit, which is 40-percent refundable), and cannot be claimed using the same expenses for which another tax benefit is also received. The credits are also not permitted to be claimed by more than one taxpayer in the same year (i.e., either the parents or the dependent child (¶ 137)). Higher income parents whose adjusted gross income (AGI) would result in the phaseout of the dependency exemption may waive claiming the dependency exemption to allow their student dependent to claim an educational credit, assuming the student child has a sufficient tax liability to be offset by an educational credit (Reg. § 1.25A-1(f)(1)). However, this does not entitle the student dependent to claim a personal exemption on his or her tax return (¶ 135).

American Opportunity Credit. The American Opportunity credit is a modification of the Hope scholarship credit for tax years beginning after December 31, 2008, but before

References are to Standard Federal Tax Reports; Tax Research Consultant; and Practical Tax Explanations.

[3] ¶ 3820; INDIV: 60,150; § 12,401

January 1, 2013 (Code Sec. 25A(i)).[4] The credit amount is the sum of 100 percent of the first $2,000 of qualified tuition and related expenses plus 25 percent of the next $2,000 of qualified tuition and related expenses, for a total maximum credit of $2,500 per eligible student per year. The credit is available for the first four years of a student's post-secondary education. Up to 40 percent of the credit amount is refundable should the taxpayer's tax liability be insufficient to offset the nonrefundable credit amount. The credit amount phases out ratably for taxpayers with modified AGI between $80,000 and $90,000 ($160,000 and $180,000 for joint filers) (Code Sec. 25A(i)(4)). Modified AGI is the taxpayer's AGI with any amounts excluded under the provisions for foreign or U.S. possessions earned income and foreign housing expenses (¶ 2402). The American opportunity credit may not be taken by married taxpayers who file separate returns (Code Sec. 25A(g)).

Comment: Absent further legislation, the American Opportunity credit modification to the Hope scholarship credit (the Hope credit) terminates on December 31, 2012. Taxpayers in only their first two years of post-secondary education will be able to claim the more generous Hope credit for qualifying educational expenses rather than the more limited lifetime learning credit. See the discussions of the Hope and lifetime learning credit following.

Hope Scholarship Credit. For tax years beginning after December 31, 2012, the Hope scholarship credit amount per eligible student is equal to 100 percent of the first $1,000 of qualified tuition expenses and 50 percent of the second $1,000 of qualified tuition paid during the year, indexed for inflation. An eligible student for the Hope credit is any individual who:

- has not elected to claim the Hope credit in any two earlier years;
- has not completed the first two years of post-secondary education before the beginning of the current tax year;
- is enrolled at least half-time in a program that leads to a degree, certificate, or other recognized educational credentials; and
- has not been convicted of any Federal or State felony class drug offense for possession or distribution.

Lifetime Learning Credit. The lifetime learning credit is equal to 20 percent of the amount of qualified tuition expenses paid on the first $10,000 of tuition, an amount which is not inflation adjusted. In contrast to the American Opportunity credit and the Hope credit, the lifetime learning credit maximum is calculated per taxpayer and does not vary based on the number of eligible students in the taxpayer's family. A student is eligible for the lifetime learning credit if the student is enrolled in one or more courses at a qualified educational institution. The allowable amount of the lifetime learning credit is reduced for taxpayers who have modified AGI above certain amounts. The phaseout of the credits begins for single taxpayers in 2012 when modified AGI reaches $52,000 and completely phases out when modified AGI reaches $62,000. For joint filers, the phaseout range is $104,000 to $124,000 in 2012 (Code Sec. 25A(d); Rev. Proc. 2011-52). The lifetime learning credit may not be taken by married taxpayers who file separate returns (Code Sec. 25A(g)).

Qualified Expenses. The credits are available for qualified tuition and related expenses incurred for the taxpayer, the taxpayer's spouse, or the taxpayer's dependent who is an eligible student at a qualified educational institution (Code Sec. 25A(f) and (i)(3)). In general, qualified expenses do not include room and board, books (unless required for enrollment), student health fees, or transportation. However, for purposes of claiming the American Opportunity credit, qualifying expenses include course materials. The amount of qualified tuition and related expenses paid with any tax-free funds (i.e., scholarships or Pell grants) reduces the amount available for claiming the credits. A qualified educational institution is defined as any post-secondary educational institu-

References are to Standard Federal Tax Reports; Tax Research Consultant; and Practical Tax Explanations.

[4] ¶ 3820; INDIV: 60,152; § 12,417

tion eligible to participate in a student aid program administered by the Department of Education (Code Sec. 25A(f)(2)).

Coordination with Other Provisions. To coordinate the education credits with other provisions of the Code, educational expenses eligible for the credits must first be reduced by tax-free educational assistance such as scholarships or fellowships, veterans' educational assistance allowances, employer-provided educational assistance, or any other educational assistance excluded from gross income, other than gifts, bequests, devises, or inheritances (Reg. § 1.25A-5(c)). Taxpayers are then permitted to elect to claim either the Hope credit (or American Opportunity credit) or the lifetime learning credit for a student in any tax year. The expenses used to claim an educational credit also reduce the amount of eligible expenses available for purposes of determining the exclusion of distributions from Coverdell educational savings accounts (ESAs) (¶ 898) or qualified tuition programs (QTPs) (¶ 899). Since any excess distributions from an ESA or a QTP over the eligible educational expenses are includible in gross income and subject to a 10-percent additional tax, not claiming an educational credit may result in a lower tax liability. However, taxpayers should be aware that the 10-percent additional tax for excess distributions from ESAs or QTPs is waived if the excess is caused by claiming an educational credit. Taxpayers who receive distributions in excess of eligible expense from both an ESA and a QTP in the same year must allocate the expenses between the two distributions. Finally, only after eligible expenses are reduced by an educational credit and distributions from ESAs or QTPs, the remaining expenses may be used to determine the exclusion amount for Series EE United States Savings Bonds (Code Secs. 25A(g)(2), 135(d)(2), 529(c)(3)(B), and 530(d)(2)(C)).[5]

1304. Retirement Savings Contributions Credit. Eligible low-income taxpayers may claim a nonrefundable credit for contributions to elective deferral plans or individual retirement accounts (IRAs) (Code Sec. 25B).[6] The credit is referred to as the retirement savings contributions credit and has also been referred to as the savers credit. The credit amount equals the eligible taxpayer's applicable percentage, determined by filing status and adjusted gross income (AGI), multiplied by the total qualified retirement savings contributions (not to exceed $2,000) for the tax year. The maximum credit amount is $1,000. The credit is in addition to the exclusion or deduction from gross income for making elective deferrals and IRA contributions that are otherwise allowed.

Eligibility. To be eligible for the credit, a taxpayer making a contribution to a qualified retirement savings plan must be at least 18 years of age at the close of the tax year, must not be claimed as a dependent by someone else (¶ 137), and must not be a full-time student (¶ 137A). A qualified retirement savings plan contribution is the sum of:

- contributions to a traditional or Roth IRA (other than rollover contributions) (Code Sec. 219(e));
- any elective deferrals of compensation to a 401(k), 403(b) tax-sheltered annuity, or SIMPLE or SEP plan (Code Sec. 402(g)(3));
- any elective deferrals of compensation to a Code Sec. 457(b) plan of a state or local government or tax-exempt organization; and
- any voluntary employee contributions to any qualified retirement plan (Code Sec. 4974(c)).

The amount of contributions to be taken into account in determining the credit, however, must be reduced by any distributions from such qualified retirement plans over a test period (Code Sec. 25B(d)(2)). The test period is defined as the current tax year, the two preceding tax years, and the following tax year up to the due date of the return including extensions. However, distribution amounts that qualify as a trustee-to-

References are to Standard Federal Tax Reports; Tax Research Consultant; and Practical Tax Explanations.

[5] ¶ 3820, ¶ 7550, ¶ 22,940, ¶ 22,950; INDIV: 60,150; § 1,810, § 12,420

[6] ¶ 3835; INDIV: 57,550; § 12,701

trustee transfer or as a rollover distribution to another qualified retirement account are not included in the reduction calculation.

Claiming the Credit. Form 8880 is used to calculate the amount of the credit, which is then reported on Form 1040. For 2012, the credit is phased out when AGI exceeds $57,500 for joint return filers, $43,125 for heads of households, and $28,750 for single and married filing separately (Notice 2011-90). For 2013, the credit is phased out when AGI exceeds $59,000 for joint return filers, $44,250 for heads of households, and $29,500 for single and married filing separately (IRS News Release IR-2012-77). The applicable percentage is the percentage as determined by the inflation adjusted income ranges for 2012 in the following table:

Adjusted Gross Income						
Joint return		*Head of a household*		*All other cases*		*Applicable percentage*
Over	*Not over*	*Over*	*Not over*	*Over*	*Not over*	
$0	$34,500	$0	$25,875	$0	$17,250	50
34,500	37,500	25,875	28,125	17,250	18,750	20
37,500	57,500	28,125	43,125	18,750	28,750	10
57,500	—	43,125	—	28,750	—	0

The applicable percentage is the percentage as determined by the inflation adjusted income ranges for 2013 in the following table:

Adjusted Gross Income						
Joint return		*Head of a household*		*All other cases*		*Applicable percentage*
Over	*Not over*	*Over*	*Not over*	*Over*	*Not over*	
$0	$35,500	$0	$26,625	$0	$17,750	50
35,500	38,500	26,625	28,875	17,750	19,250	20
38,500	59,000	28,875	44,250	19,250	29,500	10
59,000	—	44,250	—	29,500	—	0

Tax Liability Limitation. For tax years beginning after 2011, the total amount of the credit claimed by a taxpayer cannot exceed the excess of the sum of the taxpayer's regular tax liability and alternative minimum tax liability, over the sum of the nonrefundable personal credits allowed to the taxpayer other than the adoption expenses credit, the American opportunity tax credit, the residential energy property credit, the plug-in electric vehicle credit, the alternative motor vehicle credit, and the qualified plug-in electric drive motor vehicle credit and the foreign tax credit. (Code Sec. 25B(g)).[7]

Comment: Absent further legislation, the tax liability limitation on the retirement savings contribution credit (saver's credit) will revert to the general credit limitation rule under Code Sec. 26(a)(1).

1305. Child Tax Credit. Taxpayers who have one or more qualifying children that they may claim as dependents (¶ 137) may be entitled to a child tax credit of $1,000 per child through 2012 (Code Sec. 24).[8] The credit is allowed only for tax years consisting of 12 months. The credit is calculated using a worksheet in the Form 1040 Instructions.

Comment: Absent further legislation, for tax years beginning after December 31, 2012, the credit amount will decrease to $500 per qualifying child and a some or all of the credit will be refundable for families of three or more children.

Qualifying Child. The definition of qualifying child for purposes of the child tax credit is the same as that for claiming a dependency exemption (¶ 137A) except that the child must not have attained the age of 17 by the end of the year. In addition, the qualifying child must be either a U.S. citizen, national, or resident of the United States (Code Sec. 24(c)).

References are to Standard Federal Tax Reports; Tax Research Consultant; and Practical Tax Explanations.

[7] ¶ 3835; INDIV: 57,554; § 12,701

[8] ¶ 3760; INDIV: 57,450; § 12,101

Limitation of Child Tax Credit Based on Modified AGI. The child tax credit begins to phase out when the taxpayer's modified adjusted gross income (AGI) reaches $110,000 for joint filers, $55,000 for married taxpayers filing separately, and $75,000 for single taxpayers. The credit is reduced by $50 for each $1,000, or fraction thereof, of modified AGI above the threshold amount (Code Sec. 24(b)). Modified AGI is defined as AGI determined without regard to the exclusions for foreign or U.S. possessions earned income and foreign housing expenses (¶ 2402).

Nonrefundable Portion of Child Tax Credit. In general, the child tax credit is a nonrefundable personal credit. In tax year 2012, the nonrefundable child tax credit is limited to the excess of the sum of the taxpayer's regular tax plus alternative minimum tax liability over the sum of the taxpayer's other nonrefundable personal credits (other than the child tax credit, the American opportunity credit, the retirement savings contributions credit, the residential alternative energy credit, the credit for certain plug-in electric vehicles, the alternative motor vehicle credit, and the new qualified plug-in electric drive motor vehicle credit) and the foreign tax credit. Code Sec. 24(b)(3).[9]

Refundable Amount of Child Tax Credit. For tax years beginning in 2009 through 2012, a portion of the child tax credit is refundable for all taxpayers (referred to as the additional child tax credit), regardless of the amount of the taxpayer's regular tax or AMT liability. The credit is refundable in an amount equal to the lesser of the unclaimed portion of the nonrefundable credit amount or 15 percent of the taxpayer's earned income in excess of $3,000 (Code Sec. 24(d)).[10] Military families may elect to include otherwise excludable combat zone pay in their earned income when calculating the refundable portion of the credit. Taxpayers with three or more children may use an alternative method to calculate their refundable child tax credit. Under this method, the refundable credit is the excess of the taxpayer's share of Social Security taxes (including one-half of any self-employment taxes) over his or her earned income credit for the tax year. The additional child tax credit is claimed on Form 8812.

1306. Mortgage Interest Credit. Low-income homeowners who obtain qualified mortgage credit certificates (MCCs) from state or local governments may claim a tax credit on Form 8396 during any tax year for which the certificate is in effect for a portion of the interest paid or incurred (Code Sec. 25).[11] An MCC is in effect for interest attributable to the period beginning on the date the certificate is issued and ending when either: (1) it is revoked by the issuing authority, or (2) the taxpayer sells the residence or ceases to use it as a personal residence. Any mortgage interest claimed as an itemized deduction must be reduced by any credit claimed under this provision (Code Sec. 163(g)).

Amount of Credit. The credit is an amount equal to the product of: (1) the certificate credit rate (which may not be less than 10 percent or more than 50 percent) and (2) the interest paid or accrued by the taxpayer for the year on the remaining principal of the certified indebtedness (plus, a limited carryforward, if any). If the credit rate exceeds 20 percent, the tax credit for any year may not exceed $2,000 (Code Sec. 25(a)(2)(A)).

Tax Liability Limitation. In 2012, the mortgage interest credit may not exceed the taxpayer's regular tax liability reduced by her tentative minimum tax (determined without regard to the foreign tax credit), and reduced further by the sum of all nonrefundable personal credits other than the child tax credit, retirement savings contributions credit, American opportunity tax credit, credit for residential energy efficient property, credit for new plug-in electric drive motor vehicles, credit for small plug-in electric vehicles, alternative motor vehicle credit, and the credit for first-time homebuyers in the District of Columbia. Any unclaimed credit amount may be carried over to each of three succeeding tax years. The carryover amount is added to the

References are to Standard Federal Tax Reports; Tax Research Consultant; and Practical Tax Explanations.

[9] ¶ 3760; INDIV: 57,456; § 12,120.10

[10] ¶ 3760; INDIV: 57,454.05; § 12,120.15

[11] ¶ 3800; INDIV: 57,150, INDIV: 57,156; § 13,020.05

current year credit amount and subject to the same tax liability limitation (Code Sec. 25(e)(1)).[12]

Recapture of Tax Benefit. A recapture of the tax benefit received from MCCs is triggered if the home is disposed of, or ceases to be the taxpayer's principal place of residence, during the first nine years after the testing date under Code Sec. 143(m) (Code Sec. 25(i)). The test date is defined as the date the taxpayer becomes liable either in whole or part of the federal-subsidized debt on the principal residence (Code Sec. 143(m)(4)(D)). The recapture amount equals the product of the federally-subsidized amount of indebtedness times the holding period percentage times the income percentage (Code Sec. 143 (m)(4)(A), (B), and (C)). This recapture amount is treated as an addition to tax for the disposition tax year.

1307. Adoption Credit. For tax years beginning after 2011 (and prior to 2010), taxpayers may claim a nonrefundable credit for qualified adoption expenses for each eligible child (Code Sec. 23).[13] The maximum credit amount for the 2012 tax year is $12,650. The credit is phased out ratably in 2012 for taxpayers with a modified adjusted gross income (MAGI) over $189,710, and no credit is allowed to taxpayers with a MAGI of $229,710 or more (Rev. Proc. 2011-52). MAGI is defined as the taxpayer's adjusted gross income (AGI) plus any amounts excluded by reasons of the foreign housing, foreign earned income, or U.S. possession income exclusions (¶ 2402 and ¶ 2414). The credit amount and the phase out range are adjusted annually for inflation.

> **Comment:** Absent further legislation, the nonrefundable adoption credit is effective for tax years beginning after December 31, 2011, replacing the refundable adoption credit under Code Sec. 36C, which was in effect for tax years 2010 and 2011. Additionally, absent further legislation for tax years beginning after December 31, 2012, the adoption credit may only be claimed for expenses incurred to adopt a child with special needs. The amount of credit also is reduced to $6,000 with a narrower phase out range of $75,000 to $115,000.

Qualified Adoption Expenses. Qualified adoption expenses include reasonable and necessary adoption fees, court costs, attorney fees, and other expenses which are directly related to the legal adoption of an eligible child. Expenses incurred in violation of state or federal law or in connection with the adoption of a child of the taxpayer's spouse are not eligible for the credit. Costs associated with a surrogate-parenting arrangement are also ineligible for use in claiming the credit (Code Sec. 23(d)(1)).

Expenses used to claim any other deduction or credit may not be used to claim the adoption credit (Code Sec. 23(b)(3)). This includes amounts excluded from gross income that are paid or incurred by an employer for the employee's qualified adoption expenses pursuant to an adoption assistance program (¶ 2192A). The dollar limitation for the exclusion is identical to the dollar limitation for the credit ($12,650 for 2012). However, any qualified adoption expenses incurred in excess of the amount provided under an employer's adoption assistance program may be used to claim the adoption credit.

Eligible Child and Special Needs Child. For purposes of the adoption credit, an eligible child is an individual who has not attained the age of 18 as of the time of the adoption or who is physically or mentally incapable of caring for himself or herself. This definition also includes a child with special needs. A special needs child is any child who, as determined by the state, should not or cannot be returned to the home of his or her parents, is a citizen or resident of the United States, and a specific factor or condition makes it reasonable to conclude that the child cannot be placed with adoptive parents unless assistance is provided (Code Sec. 23(d)(2) and (d)(3)).

Claiming the Credit. Generally, adoption expenses incurred or paid during a tax year prior to the year in which the adoption is finalized may be claimed as a credit in the tax year following the year the expense were incurred. Adoption expenses incurred during the year the adoption becomes final or in the year following the finalization of the

References are to Standard Federal Tax Reports; Tax Research Consultant; and Practical Tax Explanations.

[12] ¶ 3800; INDIV: 57,456; § 13,020.10

[13] ¶ 3700; INDIV: 57,350; § 12,301

adoption are claimed in the year they were incurred (Code Sec. 23(a)(2)). Adoption expenses for any qualified child who is not a U.S. citizen or resident cannot be claimed as a credit until the adoption is finalized (Code Sec. 23(e)). Taxpayers who adopt a child with special needs are allowed to claim the full amount of the credit regardless of actual expenses paid or incurred in the year the adoption becomes final (Code Sec. 23(a)(3)). Married couples must file a joint return in order to claim the credit unless the special rules for married individuals who are separated or living apart apply (¶ 173). The credit must be claimed on Form 8839 with proper documentation attached.

Carryovers. As noted above, for tax years beginning after 2011, the adoption credit is nonrefundable. However, the unused portions of the adoption credit may be carried forward for five years (Code Sec. 23(c)). Credits that are carried over are treated as used on a first-in, first-out (FIFO) basis. For tax years beginning in 2012, the excess adoption credit that can be carried over to the next tax year is the amount that exceeds:

- the sum of the taxpayer's regular tax liability, plus the taxpayer's alternative minimum tax (AMT) liability, over

- the sum of the taxpayer's nonrefundable personal credits for the year (other than the adoption credit itself and the residential alternative energy credit), plus the foreign tax credit (Code Sec. 23(c)(2) and (b)(4)).

1308. Credit for First-Time Homebuyer in the District of Columbia. For purchases before January 1, 2012, first-time homebuyers who purchased a principal residence in the District of Columbia from an unrelated person could claim a nonrefundable personal credit of up to $5,000 of the purchase price ($2,500 in the case of a married person filing separately) (Code Sec. 1400C).[14] The credit was claimed on Form 8859. Although the credit was nonrefundable, any unused credit can be carried over to the next succeeding year (or years) (Code Sec. 1400C(d)).

1309. Alternative Minimum Tax Credit. Taxpayers are permitted a tax credit against their regular income tax liability for some or all of alternative minimum tax (AMT) paid in previous years. The minimum tax credit is allowed for the amount of adjusted net minimum tax for all tax years reduced by the minimum tax credit for all prior tax years (Code Sec. 53).[15] Any unused credit may be carried forward indefinitely as a credit against regular tax liability. However, it is limited to the extent that the regular tax liability reduced by other nonrefundable credits exceeds the tentative minimum tax for the tax year. The credit may not be used to offset any future AMT liability. However, special rules allow individuals with long-term unused minimum tax credit to claim an additional refundable minimum tax in 2007 through 2012 (¶ 1327). The credit is claimed by individuals, trusts, and estates on Form 8801 and by corporations on Form 8827.

For noncorporate taxpayers, the "adjusted net minimum tax" is the taxpayer's AMT liability reduced by the amount that would have been the AMT if only certain specified adjustments and preferences had been taken into account (Code Sec. 53(d)(1)). The adjustments are those described in Code Sec. 56(b)(1)[16] (¶ 1435), including the standard deduction, personal exemptions, medical and dental expenses, miscellaneous itemized deductions, taxes, and interest expenses. The exclusion-type preference items include certain items described in Code Sec. 57 (¶ 1425): certain depletion deductions exceeding adjusted basis, tax-exempt interest on specified private activity bonds, and one-half of the exclusion for gains on the sale of certain small business stock issued after August 10, 1993 (Code Sec. 53(d)). In determining corporate credits for prior year minimum tax liability, adjusted net minimum tax is the taxpayer's AMT for the year.

Limitation on Nonrefundable Credits

1315. Limitation on Nonrefundable Credits. For tax years beginning after December 31, 2011, the total amount of the nonrefundable personal credits that may be claimed

References are to Standard Federal Tax Reports; Tax Research Consultant; and Practical Tax Explanations.

[14] ¶ 32,428; INDIV: 57,500; § 13,005

[15] ¶ 5002; FILEIND: 30,452; § 15,510.05

[16] ¶ 5200; FILEIND: 30,452; § 15,510.10

may not exceed the excess, if any, of the regular tax liability for the tax year over the tentative minimum tax liability determined without regard to the alternative minimum foreign tax credit (Code Sec. 26(a)(1)). Certain specified nonrefundable credits are excluded from application of this rule and are subject to special limitations and claiming order. These specified credits are; the child tax credit (¶ 1305), the adoption credit (¶ 1307), the American Opportunity tax credit (¶ 1303), the retirement savings contributions (saver's) credit (¶ 1304), the residential energy efficient property credit (¶ 1342), the small plug-in electric vehicles credit (¶ 1354), the alternative motor vehicle credit (¶ 1345), and the new plug-in electric drive motor vehicle credit (¶ 1351).

> **Comment:** Absent further legislation, Code Sec. 26(a)(2), which allowed for all nonrefundable personal credits to be claimed against the sum of the regular and minimum tax liabilities, is no longer in effect for tax years beginning after December 31, 2011.

Refundable Credits

1321. Credit for Taxes Withheld on Wages. A taxpayer is allowed a credit against income tax liability for income taxes withheld from his or her salary or wages (Code Sec. 31).[17] A taxpayer is also allowed a "special refund" of any Social Security taxes which were over-withheld from his or her wages. Excess Social Security taxes may be withheld where an individual works for more than one employer during the year and, in total, earns more than the Social Security wage base of $110,100 in 2012 ($113,700 in 2013). The maximum amount of Social Security taxes that may be withheld is 4.2 percent (6.2 percent in years other than 2011 and 2012) of the wage base (¶ 2648). The same rule applies to excess withheld railroad retirement taxes. However, since there is no wage base for calculating Medicare taxes, there can be no over-withholding of such taxes. The "special refund" for over-withheld Social Security taxes may be claimed as a credit on Form 1040. However, if the individual is not required to file an income tax return, he or she may file a "special refund" claim (Reg. § 31.6413(c)-1).[18] A nonresident alien (or foreign corporation) is allowed a credit against income tax liability for taxes withheld on U.S. source income that is not effectively connected with a U.S. trade or business (Code Sec. 33).[19] For a discussion on the withholding of tax on payments other than wages to nonresident aliens, see ¶ 2455.

1322. Earned Income Credit. A refundable earned income credit (EIC) is available to certain low-income individuals (Code Sec. 32).[20] To be eligible to claim the credit, a taxpayer must have earned income with an adjusted gross income (AGI) below a certain level, have a valid Social Security number, use a filing status other than married filing separately, be a U.S. citizen or resident alien, have no foreign income, and not have investment income above a certain amount. The amount of credit varies depending on the number of the taxpayer's qualifying children and their AGI level.

> **Comment:** Absent further legislation, for tax years beginning after December 31, 2012, taxpayers use the same procedure to compute the credit but, instead of subtracting the specified phaseout amount from AGI, it is subtracted from modified AGI. In addition, for tax years beginning after December 31, 2012, the amount of the earned income credit is reduced by the alternative minimum tax for the year.

Amount of Credit. The credit amount is determined by multiplying an applicable credit percentage by the individual's earned income that does not exceed a maximum amount (called the earned income amount). In 2012, the maximum earned income amount for taxpayers with one qualifying child is $9,320, with two or more qualifying children is $13,090, and with no qualifying child is $6,210 (Rev. Proc. 2011-52). The credit amount is then reduced by a limitation amount determined by multiplying the applicable phaseout percentage by the excess of the amount of the individual's AGI (or earned income, if greater) over a phaseout amount (discussed below). The earned

References are to Standard Federal Tax Reports; Tax Research Consultant; and Practical Tax Explanations.

[17] ¶ 4060; INDIV: 57,302, INDIV: 57,308; § 12,801, § 12,805

[18] ¶ 38,754; IRS: 33,108; § 12,801, § 12,805

[19] ¶ 4100; INTL: 3,554.05, INDIV: 57,308; § 12,801, § 12,805

[20] ¶ 4080; INDIV: 57,250; § 12,601

income amount and the phaseout amount are adjusted yearly for inflation. The amount of allowable credit is determined through the use of the tables that appear at ¶ 87.

The credit percentages and phaseout percentages limit the maximum amount of credit that may be claimed (Code Sec. 32(b)(1)). For 2012, the maximum earned income credit for taxpayers with one qualifying child is $3,169, with two qualifying children is $5,236, with three or more qualifying children is $5,891, and with no qualifying children is $475 (Rev. Proc. 2011-52).

Credit Limitations. In 2012, the credit begins to phase out when taxpayers with a filing status of single, surviving spouse, or head of household and with one or more qualifying children have an AGI of $17,090, and with no qualifying children have an AGI of $7,770. Phaseout of the credit is complete when taxpayers with a filing status of single, surviving spouse, or head of household with one qualifying child have an AGI of $36,920; with two qualifying children have an AGI of $41,952; with three or more qualifying children have an AGI of $45,060; and with no qualifying children have an AGI of $13,980. The credit amount begins to phase out when taxpayers with a filing status of married filing jointly and with one or more qualifying children have an AGI of $22,300, and with no qualifying children have an AGI of $12,980. Phaseout of the credit is complete when taxpayers with a filing status of married filing jointly with one qualifying child have an AGI of $42,130; with two qualifying children have an AGI of $47,162; with three or more qualifying children have an AGI of $50,270; and with no qualifying children have an AGI of $19,190 (Rev. Proc. 2011-52).

Earned Income. The credit is based on earned income, which includes all wages, salaries, tips, and other employee compensation (including union strike benefits), plus the amount of the taxpayer's net earnings from self-employment (determined with regard to the deduction for one-half of self-employment taxes (¶ 923)). Earned income is determined without regard to community property laws (Code Sec. 32(c)(2)). Earned income does not include: (1) interest and dividends; (2) welfare benefits (including AFDC payments); (3) veterans' benefits; (4) pensions or annuities; (5) alimony; (6) Social Security benefits; (7) workers' compensation; (8) unemployment compensation; (9) taxable scholarships or fellowships that are not reported on Form W-2; (10) fixed or determinable periodic income of a nonresident alien not connected with a U.S. business (¶ 2431); (11) amounts received for services performed by prison inmates while in prison; or (12) payments received from work activities (including work associated with the refurbishing of public housing) if sufficient private sector employment is not available and from community service programs (Sections 407(d)(4) and (7) of the Social Security Act). The earned income credit calculation is based on the taxpayer's adjusted gross income (Code Sec. 2(a)(2)(B) and (c)(2)).

Members of the Armed Forces. Taxpayers that are members of the Armed Forces are allowed to elect to treat combat pay that is otherwise excluded from gross income (¶ 895) as earned income for purposes of claiming the earned income credit (Code Sec. 32(c)(2)(B)(vi)). The election applies to all excludable combat pay received by the taxpayer.

Qualifying Child. A qualifying child for purposes of claiming the earned income credit is generally the same as for claiming the dependency exemption without regard to the support test (¶ 137A) (Code Sec. 32(c)(3)). In addition, the relationship, residency, and age tests must be met with the following modifications. For the residency test, the child must have the same principal place of abode as the taxpayer for more than half of the tax year and the abode must be located within the United States. A qualifying child for the earned income credit does not include a child who is married unless the taxpayer is entitled to claim him or her as a dependent. The taxpayer claiming the qualifying child must include the name, age and taxpayer identification number of the qualifying child on the return. Finally, the rules for determining among several taxpayers who may claim a child as a qualifying child for purposes of the earned income credit are the same as for determining who may claim a qualifying child for the dependency exemption (¶ 139).

No Qualifying Child. An individual who does not have a qualifying child may be eligible for the credit if: (1) the principal residence of such individual is in the United States for more than half of the tax year, (2) the individual (or the spouse of the individual) is at least age 25 and under age 65 before the close of the tax year, and (3) the individual is not claimed as a dependent by another (Code Sec. 32(c)(1)(A)(ii)).

Disqualifying Income. The earned income credit may not be claimed by taxpayers whose investment income exceeds $3,200 for 2012 (Code Sec. 32(i); Rev. Proc. 2011-52). Disqualified income includes an individual's capital gain net income and net passive income in addition to interest, dividends, tax-exempt interest, and non-business rents or royalties. The credit may also not be claimed by taxpayers who are not eligible to work in the United States. For example, a nonresident alien usually cannot claim an earned income credit (Code Sec. 32(c)(1)(E)). Also, a person who claims a foreign earned income exclusion cannot claim an earned income credit (Code Sec. 32(c)(1)(D)).

Claiming the Credit. Taxpayers claiming the credit must provide their Social Security (or taxpayer identification) number and the Social Security (or taxpayer identification) numbers of their spouse and dependents, if any. Failure to provide all required Social Security numbers is treated as a mathematical error (Code Sec. 6213(g)(2)).[21] Married persons must file a joint return in order to claim the credit. However, a married person living apart from a spouse under circumstances described at ¶ 173 need not file a joint return to claim the credit. Taxpayers with one or more qualifying children should complete Schedule EIC for Forms 1040 or 1040A. Taxpayers with no qualifying children may use Form 1040EZ to determine whether they are eligible to claim the earned income credit. Credit amounts are determined by using the tables at ¶ 87. Finally, the credit may be claimed only for a full 12-month tax year, except in the case of death.

1324. First-Time Homebuyer Credit. A refundable first-time homebuyer credit was available to qualified individuals who purchased a home before May 1, 2010, to be used as their principal residence (Code Sec. 36).[22] The credit may be recaptured in years after the purchase. The credit could be claimed by first-time homebuyers and also by existing homeowners who met certain conditions. The amounts, rules, restrictions, and eligibility applicable to the credit have changed several times since the initial enactment. The credit and any recapture of the credit are reported on Form 5405.

First-Time Homebuyers. The first-time homebuyer credit was available to individuals who had no ownership interest in a principal residence during the three-year period ending on the date of the purchase of a home to be used as a principal residence. In the case of joint filers, neither spouse could have such an ownership interest during that period. For residences purchased on or after January 1, 2009, and before May 1, 2010, the maximum amount of credit that could be claimed was equal to the lesser of: 10 percent of the purchase price or $8,000 ($4,000, if married, filing separate).

The maximum credit amount was available for purchases which were under a written binding contract before May 1, 2010, to close before July 1, 2010, and which were completed before October 1, 2010 (Code Sec. 36(h)). The credit could be allocated in any reasonable manner among unrelated purchasers provide that no credit amount was allocated to unqualified individual (Notice 2009-12). Generally, no recapture of the $8,000 credit is required unless the taxpayer disposes of the home within 36 months of the date of purchase (see *Recapture*, following).

For residences purchased after April 8, 2008, and before January 1, 2009, the amount of the credit that could be claimed was equal to the lesser of: 10 percent of the purchase price or $7,500 ($3,750, if married, filing separate). The $7,500 credit amount must be recaptured over a 15-year period. The recapture amount is treated as an addition to tax for each year of the recapture period and is equal to 6.67 percent of the credit amount claimed (or 1⁄15 of the credit amount). The recapture period begins with the second tax year following the tax year in which the credit was claimed. If the taxpayer disposes of or ceases to use the home as a principal residence within the 15-year recapture period, any remaining amount of the credit must be recaptured in the year of disposition.

References are to Standard Federal Tax Reports; Tax Research Consultant; and Practical Tax Explanations.

[21] ¶ 37,545; IRS: 27,206.50; § 39,515.10

[22] ¶ 4186; INDIV: 57,950; § 13,010

Long-Term Residents. For individuals who were long-term residents of a principal residence and who purchased a new principal residence after November 6, 2009, and before May 1, 2010, a reduced version of the first-time homebuyer credit was allowed. The amount of the credit was equal to: 10 percent of the purchase price, or $6,500 ($3,250, if married, filing separate). The credit was available to purchasers who enter into a written binding contract prior to May 1, 2010, to close before July 1, 2010, and completed the purchase before October 1, 2010 (Code Sec. 36(h)). A long-term resident was an individual and, if married, their spouse, who has owned and used the same home as a principal residence in any five consecutive years during the last eight years ending on the date of purchase (Code Sec. 36(c)(6)). Generally, no recapture of the credit is required unless the taxpayer disposes of the home within 36 months of the date of purchase (see *Recapture*, following).

Principal Residence. The term "principal residence" for purposes of the first-time homebuyer's credit has the same definition as in Code Sec. 121 (the principal residence gain exclusion provision) (¶ 1705).

Self-Constructed New Homes. Taxpayer-constructed residences were treated as purchased on the date the home was first occupied.

Election to Treat Purchase as Occurring in the Previous Year. Taxpayers were allowed to elect to claim the first-time homebuyer credit either in the year of purchase or in the year previous to the year of purchase. If the election was made, the home purchase was treated as having occurred on December 31 of the previous year. The rules pertaining to eligibility and amount of the credit generally applied as of the date of the purchase, not as of the December 31 election date.

Extension for Certain Governmental and Military Personnel. Certain government officials and Armed Forces personnel serving on qualified official extended duty for at least 90 days during the period beginning after December 31, 2008, but before May 1, 2010, could claim the first-time homebuyer credit on any purchase made before May 1, 2011. The same one-year time extension also applied to purchases that were under written binding contract before May 1, 2011, and the purchase was completed before July 1, 2011.

Recapture of the credit amount is waived in the case of disposition or cessation of the use of the home as a principal residence in the event the individual (if married, their spouse) receives orders for qualified official extended duty service. Qualified official extended duty service is defined as service on qualified official extended duty as a member of the Armed Forces, the Foreign Service, or an employee of the intelligence community (Code Sec. 36(f) and (h)).

Phaseout. For residences purchased after November 6, 2009, the phaseout of the first-time homebuyer credit began when a taxpayer's modified adjusted gross income (MAGI) exceeded $125,000 ($225,000 for joint filers). MAGI is defined as adjusted gross income increased by the exclusions for foreign earned income, U.S. possession earned income and foreign housing costs (¶ 2402 and ¶ 2414). The phaseout range was $20,000, and no credit was available to taxpayers with a MAGI of $145,000 or more ($245,000 for joint filers). For purchases before November 7, 2009, the MAGI phaseout threshold began at $75,000 ($150,000 for joint filers), and the credit completely phased out at $95,000 ($170,000 for joint filers).

Restrictions. The first-time homebuyer credit was subject to different sets of restrictions based on date the home is purchased. The following restrictions applied from the initial date of enactment of the credit (April 8, 2008):

- Nonresident aliens cannot claim the first-time homebuyer credit.
- No credit is available to taxpayers that dispose of, or cease to use, the home as a principal residence before the close of the tax year.
- No credit is allowed if the basis of the home for the purchaser is determined in any way by reference to the basis in the seller or if the property is acquired from a decedent.

For houses purchased after November 6, 2009:

• The credit is not allowed if the purchase price of the residence exceeds $800,000.

• The credit is not allowed if the taxpayer can be claimed by another taxpayer as a dependent.

• The credit is not allowed unless either the taxpayer or the taxpayer's spouse is 18 years old or older on the date the residence is purchased.

• The credit is not allowed if the taxpayer acquires property from a person related to the taxpayer (or the taxpayer's spouse).

The first-time homebuyer credit could also not be claimed for purchases prior to January 1, 2009, if tax-exempt mortgage revenue bond proceeds were used to finance the purchase. However, this prohibition was repealed for purchases after December 31, 2008.

Interaction with the D.C. Homebuyer Credit. For houses purchased after 2008, if the taxpayer (or the taxpayer's spouse) is eligible for the Code Sec. 36 first-time homebuyer credit, the D.C. first-time homebuyer credit cannot be claimed (¶ 1308). For homes purchased in 2008, the first-time homebuyer credit allowed under Code Sec. 36 cannot be claimed if the taxpayer (or the taxpayer's spouse) was eligible for the District of Columbia first-time homebuyer credit.

Recapture. The amount of the first-time homebuyer credit claimed must be recaptured if the home, purchased after December 31, 2008, ceases to be the principal residence of the taxpayer at any time within the 36-month period from the date of purchase. The recapture amount is claimed as an addition to tax in the year the property is disposed of or ceases to be the taxpayer's principal residence. The recapture amount cannot exceed the amount of gain from the sale of the home to an unrelated third party. The exceptions to the required recapture are:

• Death of the taxpayers.

• Involuntary conversion if the taxpayer acquires a new principal residence within two years. However, the accelerated recapture rule will apply to the new principal residence during the remainder of the recapture period.

• Transfer between spouses or incident to a divorce. However, the transferee steps into the shoes of the transferor in respect to the recapture and accelerated recapture rules.

Reporting. When claiming the credit in tax years ending after November 6, 2009, a copy of the signed settlement statement (HUD-1) for the purchase was required to be attached to the return. Any errors in claiming the credit are treated as mathematical errors, allowing the IRS to issue a summary assessment for any additional tax without going through the deficiency procedures.

1325. Making Work Pay Credit (Expired). The Making Work Pay Credit was effective for tax years beginning after December 31, 2008, and before January 1, 2011, and was applied against an individual's income tax liability (Code Sec. 36A). The credit amount was equal to the lesser of: (1) 6.2 percent of the taxpayer's earned income or (2) $400 ($800 for joint filers). The credit was phased out for single taxpayers with a modified adjusted gross income (MAGI) that exceeded $75,000 ($150,000 for joint filers) at the rate of two percent of the excess MAGI over the threshold amount. MAGI is adjusted gross income increased by excluded foreign or U.S. possessions earned income and foreign housing expenses. All taxpayers were eligible for the credit except for nonresident aliens, taxpayers who could be claimed as a dependent on another taxpayer's return, estates or trusts, or taxpayers who failed to include their Social Security numbers on their returns. Taxpayers received the credit generally through a reduction of income taxes withheld from wages.

1326A. Refundable Adoption Credit (Expired). For tax years beginning after December 31, 2009, but before January 1, 2012, taxpayers could claim a refundable credit for a set amount of qualified adoption expenses incurred for adopting an eligible child (Code Sec. 36C).[23] The credit was phased out ratably for taxpayers with a modified adjusted gross income (AGI) over a threshold amount.

Comment: Absent further legislation, the refundable adoption credit available in tax years beginning 2010 and 2011, terminated on December 31, 2011. The adoption credit reverts to being a nonrefundable personal credit under Code Sec. 23 (¶ 1307). The definitions for qualifying expenses and eligible children remain the same.

1327. Refundable Long-Term Unused Minimum Tax Credit. For individuals with a "long-term unused minimum tax credit" for tax years before January 1, 2013, the minimum tax credit allowable for that year (¶ 1309) is not less than the "AMT refundable credit amount," regardless of the minimum tax credit otherwise allowed to the taxpayer (Code Sec. 53(e)(2)).[24] The credit is calculated on Form 8801.

A "long-term unused minimum tax credit" for a tax year is the portion of the minimum tax credit attributable to the adjusted net minimum tax (¶ 1309) for tax years before the third tax year immediately preceding such tax year (Code Sec. 53(e)(3)). For this purpose, the credits are treated as allowed on a first-in, first-out (FIFO) basis.

The "AMT refundable credit amount" is, with respect to any tax year, the amount (not in excess of the long-term unused minimum tax credit for such tax year) equal to the greater of: (1) 50 percent of the long-term unused minimum tax credit for such tax year or (2) the amount (if any) of the AMT refundable credit amount determined for the taxpayer's preceding tax year (Code Sec. 53(e)(2)).

1329. Credit for Federal Tax on Gasoline, Special Fuels. A credit for federal excise taxes on gasoline and special fuels may be taken where the fuel item is used for: (1) farming purposes, (2) nonhighway purposes of a trade or business, (3) operation of intercity, local, or school buses, or (4) certain nontaxable purposes (Code Sec. 34).[25] The credit is computed on Form 4136, which must be attached to Form 1040, or the taxpayer can file a claim for refund on Form 8849 or a credit against fuel tax liability on Form 720.

1330. Credit for Capital Gain Tax. Undistributed capital gain of a mutual fund (regulated investment company) must be included proportionately in the gross income of its shareholders. The capital gain tax that the company pays on this gain is treated as having been paid by the shareholders and is allowed as a credit against the tax (Code Sec. 852(b)(3)(D)(ii)).[26] In order to claim the credit, Copy B of Form 2439 must be attached to the taxpayer's return (¶ 2305).

Health Care Credits

1331. Health Insurance Premium Assistance Refundable Credit. Effective for tax years ending after December 31, 2013, certain individuals who purchase qualified health care coverage through an American Health Benefit Exchange are entitled to a refundable income tax credit equal to the premium assistance credit amount (Code Sec. 36B(a)).[27]

Eligibility for Premium Credit. A qualified individual is defined as a person who:

- is seeking to enroll in a qualified health plan in the individual market offered through an Exchange and residing in the state that established the Exchange,
- has a household income of at least 100 percent, but no more than 400 percent, of the federal poverty line (FPL) for a family of that size,
- if married, must file a joint return, and
- cannot be claimed as a dependent on another taxpayer's return (¶ 137) (Code Sec. 36B(c)(1)).

References are to Standard Federal Tax Reports; Tax Research Consultant; and Practical Tax Explanations.

[23] ¶ 4198; INDIV: 57,350; § 12,301

[24] ¶ 4870; FILEIND: 30,452; § 15,510.15

[25] ¶ 4150; BUSEXP: 54,800; § 13,501

[26] ¶ 26,420; RIC: 3,260; § 19,205.05

[27] ¶ 4196; INDIV: 58,150; § 42,015.05

Lawful resident aliens, who are ineligible for Medicaid, with household income below 100 percent of the FPL for a family of that size are imputed to have a household income equal to 100 percent of the FPL and eligible for the credit. An individual who is not a U.S. citizen, national, or alien lawfully present in the United States is not eligible (Code Sec. 36B(e)). Qualified individuals do not include individuals who are incarcerated unless the incarceration is pending the disposition of charges (Code Sec. 5000A). However, the individual may be allowed a tax credit if a family member is enrolled in a qualified plan (Reg. § 1.36B-2(b)(4)).

Family size is equal to the number individuals that are allowed as personal exemptions for the tax year. Family size may include individuals who are not subject to or are exempt from the Code Sec. 5000A penalty (Reg. § 1.36B-1(d)). Household income equals the taxpayer's modified adjusted gross income (AGI) and includes all income of individuals who are the taxpayer's dependents if a tax return is required to be filed. Household income does not include the modified AGI of a family member who files a tax return solely to report tax under a different Code section (i.e. other than Code Sec. 5000A), such as a Code Sec. 72(t) early distribution penalty (Reg. § 1.36B-1(e)(1)(ii)). Modified AGI is AGI increased by any amount of excluded foreign income, foreign housing allowance expenses, tax-exempt interest, and Social Security and tier 1 Railroad Retirement benefits (Code Sec. 36B(d)(2)(B)).

Credit Amount. The premium assistance credit amount for any tax year is the sum of the premium assistance amounts for all of the taxpayer's coverage months during the tax year (Code Sec. 36B(b)(1)). The premium assistance amount for any coverage month is the lesser of:

- the monthly premium for one or more qualified health plans offered in the individual market Exchange within a state covering the taxpayer, the taxpayer's spouse, or any dependent of the taxpayer who is enrolled through an Exchange established by the state, or

- the excess, if any, of the adjusted monthly premium for the applicable second lowest cost silver plan with respect to the taxpayer over an amount equal to 1/12th of the product of the applicable percentage and the taxpayer's household income for the tax year (Code Sec. 36B(b)(2)).

A coverage month is any month in which the taxpayer, the taxpayer's spouse, or any dependent is covered by a qualified health plan enrolled in through an Exchange and the premium is paid by the taxpayer or through advance payment of the premium assistance credit. A coverage month does not include any month that the individual is eligible for minimum essential coverage outside the individual market. A month also is not a coverage month if the taxpayer's share of premiums is not paid in full by the unextended due date for filing the taxpayer's income tax return for the tax year (Reg. § 1.36B-3(c)(1)). The applicable second lowest cost silver plan is the second lowest cost silver plan of the individual market Exchange in the rating area where the taxpayer resides that is offered through the same Exchange offering the qualified health plan providing (1) self-only coverage for single taxpayers with no dependents or those who purchase self-only coverage and (2) family coverage for all other taxpayers (Code Sec. 36B(b)(3)(B)).

The adjusted monthly premium for an applicable second lowest cost silver plan is the monthly premium that would be charged for the plan if each individual covered under a qualified health plan were covered by that silver plan, and the premium was adjusted only for the age of each individual pursuant to section 2701 of the Public Health Service Act. The applicable percentage is between 2.0 and 9.5 percent of a taxpayer's household income for any tax year with respect to a taxpayer whose household income is between 100 and 400 percent of the FPL for that tax year (Code Sec. 36B(b)(3)). If there is at least one silver level plan offered on an Exchange that does not cover all members of a taxpayer's coverage family under one policy and premium, the premium for the applicable plan is the single premium or the combination of premiums that is the second lowest cost silver option for covering the entire family (Reg. § 1.36B-3(f)(3)).

Advance Payment of Credit. The premium assistance credit must be reduced, but not below zero, by the amount of any advance payment of the credit (Code Sec. 36B(f)(1)). If the advance payments for a tax year exceed the premium assistance credit allowed, the excess is an increase to the tax imposed for the tax year (Code Sec. 36B(f)(2)(A)). For taxpayers with household incomes less than 400 percent of the FPL for the tax year, the increase is limited to between $600 and $2,500 ($300 and $1,250 for unmarried taxpayers other than surviving spouses and heads of household) (Code Sec. 36B(f)(2)(B)).

1332. Health Insurance Costs Credit. Eligible individuals may claim a refundable tax credit for the cost of qualified health insurance for themselves and qualified family members during each eligible coverage month. The credit amount is 72.5 percent of the costs during coverage months beginning after February 12, 2011, and ending before January 1, 2014; 80 percent during coverage months beginning after April 30, 2009, and ending on or before February 12, 2011; and 65 percent during coverage months beginning on or before April 30, 2009 (Code Sec. 35).[28] An eligible coverage month occurs when, on the first day of the month during the taxpayer's tax year, the taxpayer: (1) is an eligible individual; (2) is covered by a qualified health insurance plan on which the taxpayer paid the premiums; (3) has no "other specified coverage" (including under Medicare or COBRA); and (4) is not imprisoned by any federal, state, or local authority (Code Sec. 35(b)). Taxpayers determine their eligibility on, and claim the credit by filing, Form 8885 along with Form 1040 and attaching copies of the required documentation. See also IRS Pub. 502.

Eligible Individuals. The credit is available only to individuals receiving or who are eligible to receive trade adjustment assistance (TAA) (or TAA-alternative payments) and retirees age 55 or older receiving benefits from the Pension and Benefit Guarantee Corporation (PBGC) (Code Sec. 35(c)). A qualifying family member of an eligible individual includes the taxpayer's spouse and any dependents to which the taxpayer is entitled to a dependency exemption (¶ 137) (Code Sec. 35(d)). A spouse is not considered a qualifying family member if the taxpayers are married at the end of the year, both are considered eligible individuals, and each files a separate income tax return (Code Sec. 35(g)(5)). However, the rules for head of household relating to separated parents and individuals living apart for six months apply (¶ 173) (Code Sec. 35(g)(6)). In the case of separated or divorced parents, dependents are considered qualifying family members only for the custodial parent (¶ 139A) (Code Sec. 35(d)(2)).

Qualifying Premiums. Premiums paid by taxpayers for coverage in a qualified health insurance plan as defined in Code Sec. 35(e)(1) are to be taken into account in determining the health insurance costs credit. Qualified health insurance does *not* include either a flexible spending or similar arrangement (¶ 861) or any insurance whose coverage is substantially for "excepted benefits" under Code Sec. 9832(c) (Code Sec. 35(e)(3)).

Insurance coverage that qualifies as "other specified coverage" under Code Sec. 35(f) includes: (1) any insurance which is considered to be for medical care under a health plan maintained by the employer of the taxpayer or the taxpayer's spouse where at least 50 percent of the cost is paid or incurred by the employer; (2) any insurance coverage under a cafeteria plan in which the premiums are paid or incurred by the employer in lieu of a right to receive cash benefits or other qualified benefits under a cafeteria plan; (3) participation in Medicare, Medicaid, or State Child Health Insurance Program (SCHIP); and (4) participation in a health benefits plan for federal employees and military personnel (Code Sec. 35(f)). The credit is also coordinated with the COBRA premium assistance provision (¶ 1391) to prevent double benefits (Code Sec. 139C).

Coordination with Other Provisions. Amounts taken into account for the determination of the health insurance costs credit may not be used in computing either the health insurance costs for the self-employed deduction (¶ 908) or the itemized deduction for

References are to Standard Federal Tax Reports; Tax Research Consultant; and Practical Tax Explanations.

[28] ¶ 4170; INDIV: 57,602; § 42,315

medical/dental costs (¶ 1015–¶ 1019). Amounts received from Archer medical saving accounts (¶ 1020) or health saving accounts (¶ 1020A) may not be used to compute the health insurance costs credit. Payment made for the benefit of a third party who is not a qualifying family member cannot be included in the amount of premiums paid for qualified health insurance in determining the credit (Code Sec. 35(g)(1), (2) and (3)).

Advance Payment. The advance payment program makes monthly payments on behalf of eligible individuals directly to providers of qualified health insurance. The advance payments cannot equal more than the credit percentage (72.5, 80, or 65 percent) of the anticipated health insurance costs of the eligible taxpayer. The aggregate amount of all advance payments during the tax year reduces the health insurance costs credit amount dollar for dollar but not below zero (Code Secs. 35(g)(8)(A) and 7527). The Secretary of the Treasury is allowed to refund to the taxpayer amounts paid prior to the advance payment program making premiums payments (Code Sec. 7527(e)).

Additional Requirements for State Plans. State health plans must make an election to be considered a qualified health insurance plan for the health insurance costs credit. In addition to the election, several additional requirements must be satisfied (Code Sec. 35(e)(2)).

1333. Small Employer Health Insurance Credit. An eligible small employer may claim a tax credit in tax years beginning after 2009 if it makes nonelective contributions that pay for at least one-half of the cost of health insurance premiums for the coverage of its participating employees (Code Sec. 45R).[29] The credit is computed on Form 8941 and is claimed as a component of the general business credit (¶ 1365).

The amount of the credit for employee health insurance expenses of an eligible small employer in tax years through 2013 is equal to 35 percent of the lesser of:

(1) the total amount of nonelective contributions the employer makes on behalf of its employees during the tax year under a contribution arrangement for the payment of premiums for qualified health insurance coverage (as defined in Code Sec. 9832(b)(1)) of its employees, or

(2) the total amount of nonelective contributions that would have been made during the tax year if each employee taken into account in item (1) had enrolled in a qualified health plan that had a premium equal to the amount that the Secretary of Health and Human Services determines is the average premium for the small group market in the state in which the employer is offering health insurance coverage or the area within the state that is specified by the Secretary of Health and Human Services (Code Sec. 45R(a), (b) and (g)).

Contribution Arrangements. The employer must make nonelective contributions through an "arrangement." In the case of a tax year beginning in 2010 through 2013, the arrangement must require an employer to make a nonelective contribution on behalf of each employee who enrolls in a qualified health plan offered by the employer in an amount equal to a uniform percentage, but not less than 50 percent, of the premium cost of the plan (Code Sec. 45R(d)(4) and (g)(3)). An employer contribution is considered a nonelective contribution so long as it is not made through a salary reduction arrangement (Code Sec. 45R(e)(3)).

Credit Phaseout. The credit is reduced (but not below zero) by the sum of:

- the credit amount multiplied by the number of the employer's full-time equivalent employees for the tax year in excess of 10, divided by 15; and

- the credit amount multiplied by the employer's average annual wages in excess of the applicable dollar amount for the tax year ($25,000 in tax years beginning in 2010-2013), divided by the applicable dollar amount (Code Sec. 45R(c)).

References are to Standard Federal Tax Reports; Tax Research Consultant; and Practical Tax Explanations.

[29] ¶ 4500ZN; BUSEXP: 55,850; § 42,115.05

Eligible Small Employer Defined. An employer determines its status as an eligible small employer each tax year. An employer is an eligible small employer if, during the tax year:

- the employer has 25 or fewer full-time equivalent employees;
- the average annual wages of these employees is not greater than twice the applicable dollar amount for the tax year ($25,000 in tax years beginning in 2010 through 2013); and
- the employer has a qualified health care arrangement in effect (Code Sec. 45R(d)(1)).

Full-Time Equivalent Employee Defined. The number of full-time equivalent employees during a tax year is equal to the total number of hours for which employees were paid wages by the employer divided by 2,080. The result, if not a whole number, is rounded to the next lowest whole number. In making this computation, only the first 2,080 hours of each employee's wages are taken into account. Hours in excess of this amount are not counted (Code Sec. 45R(d)(2)). For purposes of determining average annual wages and the number of full-time equivalent employees, hours of service worked by, and wages paid to, a seasonal worker are not taken into account unless the worker works for the employer on more than 120 days during the tax year (Code Sec. 45R(d)(5)(A)).

Employee Defined. For purposes of the credit, the following individuals are not considered employees (Code Sec. 45R(e)(1)):

(1) any self-employed individual (as defined in Code Sec. 401(c)(1));

(2) any two-percent shareholder (as defined in Code Sec. 1372(b)) of an eligible small business which is an S corporation;

(3) any five-percent owner (as defined in Code Sec. 416(i)(1)(B)(i)) of an eligible small business; or

(4) any individual who bears any of the relationships of a qualifying relative described in Code Sec. 152(d)(2)(A)-(G) (¶137B) to an individual described in items (1), (2), or (3), above, or is a dependent with the same principal abode as the individual and is a member of the individual's household, as described in Code Sec. 152(d)(2)(H).

Leased employees as defined in Code Sec. 414(a) are considered employees (Code Sec. 45R(e)(1)).

Wages Defined. Wages for purposes of the credit are defined by reference to Code Sec. 3121(a), relating to the definition of wages for purposes of the Federal Insurance Contributions Act (FICA) but without regard to any dollar limitation (Code Sec. 45R(e)(4)) (¶2648).

Additional Rules. The following special rules described in Code Sec. 52 relating to the work opportunity credit (Code Sec. 51) apply to the small employer health insurance credit (Code Sec. 45R(e)(5)(B)):

- an estate or trust must apportion the credit between itself and its beneficiaries based on income allocable to each (Code Sec. 52(d));
- in computing the credit, a regulated investment company (RIC), real estate investment trust (REIT), and cooperative organization (Code Sec. 1381(a)) must apply rules similar to the rules provided in Code Sec. 46(e) and (h), as in effect prior to the date of enactment of the Revenue Reconciliation Act of 1990 (P.L. 101-508) (Code Sec. 52(e)).

A third special rule seems to suggest that the small employer health insurance credit is not available to a tax-exempt organization, other than a tax-exempt cooperative described in Code Sec. 521 (Code Secs. 45R(e)(5)(B) and Code Sec. 52(c)). This reference appears to be erroneous, however. In fact, Code Sec. 45R provides special computation rules applicable to certain tax-exempt organizations. See below, under *Special Computation Rules for Tax-Exempt Eligible Small Employers.*

Certain Persons Treated as Single Employer. All controlled groups, partnerships, and affiliated service groups treated as a single employer under Code Sec. 414(b), (c), (m), or (o) are treated as one employer (Code Sec. 45R(e)(5)(A)).

General Business Credit. The small employer health insurance credit is a component of the general business credit (Code Sec. 38(b)(36)) (¶ 1365). The general business credit may be carried back one tax year and forward 20 tax years. For alternative minimum tax (AMT) purposes, the small employer health insurance credit is treated as a specified credit that may be claimed in full against both regular and AMT liabilities (Code Sec. 38(c)(4)(B)(vi)). This rule is effective for credits determined in tax years beginning after December 31, 2009, and to carrybacks of such credits. Any portion of the credit that is not claimed by the expiration of the 20-year carryforward period may be claimed as a deduction in the first tax year after expiration of the carryforward period (Code Sec. 196(c)(14)).

Deduction for Premiums Is Reduced by Credit Amount. The deduction for employer-paid premiums for qualified health plans or, in the case of tax years through 2013, for health insurance coverage is reduced by the amount of the small employer health insurance credit determined with respect to those premiums (Code Sec. 280C(h)).

Credit Amount After 2013. The credit amount for a tax year beginning after 2013 is equal to 50 percent of the lesser of:

> (1) the total amount of nonelective contributions the employer makes on behalf of its employees during the tax year under a contribution arrangement for premiums for qualified health plans offered to its employees through an Exchange, or
>
> (2) the total amount of nonelective contributions that would have been made during the tax year if each employee taken into account in item (1) had enrolled in a qualified health plan that had a premium equal to the average premium for the small group market in the rating area in which the employee enrolls for coverage (Code Sec. 45R(b)).

For tax years beginning after 2013, the arrangement must offer the insurance through an Exchange. For earlier tax years, the arrangement may, but is not required to, offer the insurance through an Exchange (Code Sec. 45R(d)(4) and (g)(3)).

Special Computation Rules for Tax-Exempt Eligible Small Employers. The credit percentage for a tax-exempt eligible small employer is 25 percent for a tax year that begins in 2010 through 2013 and increase to 35 percent for a tax year that begins after 2013 (Code Sec. 45R(b) and (g)(2)(A)). A tax-exempt eligible small employer is an eligible small employer that is a Code Sec. 501(c) organization that is exempt from tax (Code Sec. 45R(f)(2)). Other tax-exempt organizations generally are not eligible to claim the credit. However, a farmers' cooperative is eligible to claim the credit as a taxable employer if it otherwise meets the requirements (Notice 2010-82). If the credit exceeds the amount of payroll taxes of the organization during the calendar year in which the tax year begins, then the credit amount is limited to the amount of the payroll taxes (Code Sec. 45R(f)(1)).

Payroll taxes are defined as amounts required to be withheld from the tax-exempt organization's employees for Medicare under Code Sec. 3101(b) and income tax withholding under Code Sec. 3401(a), and amounts of the taxes imposed on the tax-exempt organization for Medicare under Code Sec. 3111(b) (Code Sec. 45R(f)(3)(A)). The special rule contained in Code Sec. 24(d)(2)(C), which treats amounts paid pursuant to an agreement entered into by American employers with respect to foreign affiliates that are the equivalent of social security taxes imposed by Code Sec. 3101 or railroad retirement taxes (Code Sec. 3201(a)), applies (Code Sec. 45R(f)(3)(B)).

Energy Credits

1341. Nonbusiness Energy Property Credit. A nonrefundable tax credit is available to individuals for the installation of nonbusiness energy property, such as residential exterior doors and windows, insulation, heat pumps, furnaces, central air conditioners, and water heaters (Code Sec. 25C).[30] The credit applies to qualified energy efficiency improvements and qualified energy property installed before January 1, 2008, or after December 31, 2008, but before January 1, 2012. The property must be installed in, or on, a dwelling unit in the United States that is owned and used by the taxpayer as the taxpayer's principal residence. Original use of the property must commence with the taxpayer. The credit is claimed on Form 5695.

Credit Amount. For property placed in service in 2011, the credit amount is equal to 10 percent of the amount paid or incurred for qualified energy efficiency improvements during the tax year, and 100 percent of the amount paid or incurred for qualified energy property during the tax year, up to a set amount depending on the type of property (Code Sec. 25C(b)). The maximum credit amount for qualified energy property is $200 for exterior windows and skylights, reduced by the aggregate credit allowed for exterior windows and skylights in prior years; $50 for any advanced main air circulating fan; $150 for any qualified furnace or boiler; and $300 for any other item. For all nonbusiness energy property, there is a $500 maximum lifetime credit.

For property placed in service in 2009 or 2010, the credit amount is equal to 30 percent of the amount paid or incurred for both qualified energy efficiency improvements and qualified energy property during the tax year. The amount of credit a taxpayer may claim is limited to a maximum of $1,500 for both 2009 and 2010 (Code Sec. 25C(b), prior to amendment by the Tax Relief, Unemployment Insurance Reauthorization, and Jobs Creation Act of 2010 (P.L. 111-312)).

Qualified Energy Efficiency Improvements. Qualified energy improvements include any energy efficient building envelope component that meets certain energy conservation criteria (Code Sec. 25C(c)). A building envelope component is defined as any insulation material or system which is designed to prevent heat loss or gain, exterior windows (including skylights), exterior doors, and any metal roof with either pigmented coating or cooling granules designed to reduce heat gain.

Qualified Energy Property. Qualified energy property is defined as energy-efficient building property, qualified natural gas, propane, or oil furnace or hot water boiler, or an advance main air circulating fan that meet specific performance and quality standards (Code Sec. 25C(d)). Qualified energy-efficient building property includes electric heat pump water heaters, qualified electric heat pumps, qualified central air conditioners, and qualified stove which use biomass fuels.

1342. Residential Energy Efficient Property Credit. A nonrefundable tax credit is available to help individual taxpayers pay for residential alternative energy equipment installed on or in connection with a dwelling unit located in the United States and used as a residence by the taxpayer (Code Sec. 25D).[31] The credit is available for the cost of eligible solar water heaters, solar electricity equipment, fuel cell plants, qualified small wind energy property, and qualified geothermal heat pump property placed in service before January 1, 2017 (Code Sec. 25D(g)). Cooperative and condominium dwellers can claim the credit by splitting the cost of installing equipment with other unit owners. The credit is claimed on Form 5695.

Credit Amount. The credit amount is equal to 30 percent of the cost of eligible property, but the maximum amount of credit for the installation of qualified fuel cell property for any tax year is $500 per half kilowatt hour (Code Sec. 25D(b)(1)). The amount of the residential energy efficient property credit cannot exceed the excess of the sum of the taxpayer's regular tax and alternative minimum tax minus the sum of the taxpayer's other personal nonrefundable credits (plus the foreign tax credit) (Code Sec. 25D(c)(1)). Any excess amount is carried over and added to the credit amount for the next tax year.

Qualifying Property. Qualifying solar heating property is any property used to heat water for use in a dwelling unit that receives at least half of its energy from the sun.

References are to Standard Federal Tax Reports; Tax Research Consultant; and Practical Tax Explanations.

[30] ¶ 3839; INDIV: 57,800; § 13,201

[31] ¶ 3844; INDIV: 57,850; § 13,301

None of the cost allocated to heat a swimming pool or hot tub may be considered a qualified expenditure. Qualifying solar electric property is any property that generates electricity from solar energy to be used in a dwelling unit. Qualified fuel cell property is any fuel cell property with a nameplate capacity of least 0.5 kilowatt hours of electricity generated by using an electrochemical process with an electricity-generating efficiency greater that 30 percent. Qualified small wind energy property is any wind turbine that generates electricity for use in the residence of the taxpayer. It does not include any wind facility for which a credit can be claimed for electricity produced from renewable resources (¶ 1365N). Qualified geothermal heat pump property is any property that uses the ground or ground water as a thermal source to heat a dwelling unit (Code Sec. 25D(d)).

Alternative Motor Vehicle Credit

1345. Alternative Motor Vehicle Credit. Taxpayers who buy a motor vehicle may be eligible for the alternative motor vehicle credit (Code Sec. 30B).[32] The credit amount is equal to the sum of the following component credits: (1) a qualified fuel cell motor vehicle credit (¶ 1346); (2) an advanced lean burn technology motor vehicle credit (¶ 1347); (3) a qualified hybrid motor vehicle credit (¶ 1348); (4) a qualified alternative motor vehicle credit (¶ 1349); and (5) a plug-in conversion credit (¶ 1352). The individual components comprising the alternative motor vehicle credit are calculated based on various factors such as vehicle weight, vehicle fuel efficiency, lifetime fuel savings, etc. Each has a different phaseout or termination rule. The credit amount claimed is the sum of the components applicable to a particular vehicle, whether used for personal or business purposes. The credit is claimed on Form 8910.

Common Requirements. There are distinct requirements for each of the four components of the credit. However, three requirements are common to each of the components: (1) the original use of the vehicle must commence with the taxpayer; (2) the vehicle must be acquired for use or lease by the taxpayer and not for resale; (3) the vehicle must be made by a manufacturer; and (4) the vehicle must be primarily used in the United States.

Any credit amount claimed under the alternative motor vehicle credit for personal use is treated as a nonrefundable personal credit subject to the credit limitation under Code Sec. 26 (¶ 1315) (Code Sec. 30B(g)(2)(A)). Taxpayers with qualified motor vehicles that are used in a trade or business and subject to depreciation claim the alternative motor vehicle credit as a part of, and subject to, the rules of the general business credit (¶ 1365) (Code Sec. 38). Thus, any unused credit in a tax year is eligible to be carried back three years and forward 20 years. A seller claiming the alternative motor vehicle credit for a vehicle sold to a tax-exempt entity can only claim the credit as a part of the general business credit (Code Sec. 30B(h)(6)).

1346. Fuel Cell Motor Vehicle Credit. The first component of the alternative motor vehicle credit is a qualified fuel cell motor vehicle credit for qualifying vehicles placed in service during 2006 through 2014 (Code Sec. 30B(b)).[33] In addition to the common requirements for qualifying vehicles (¶ 1345), there are specific requirements for a vehicle to be classified as a qualified fuel cell motor vehicle. The vehicle must be propelled by power derived from one or more cells which convert chemical energy directly into electricity by combining oxygen with hydrogen fuel. In addition, if the vehicle is a passenger vehicle or light truck, it must be certified to meet specific environmental emission standards.

The amount of the credit is calculated based on the gross vehicle weight rating (GVWR) of the vehicle, supplemented by the fuel efficiency of the vehicle relative to the 2002 model-year city fuel economy. The credit can range from $8,000 for vehicles under 8,500 pounds GVWR and up to $40,000 for vehicles over 26,000 pounds GVWR. Qualified fuel cell vehicles that meet the definition of either a "passenger automobile" or "light

References are to Standard Federal Tax Reports; Tax Research Consultant; and Practical Tax Explanations.

[32] ¶ 4059A; INDIV: 57,702; § 12,905.05

[33] ¶ 4059A; INDIV: 57,704; § 12,905.10

truck" and meet certain standards for increased fuel efficiency may increase their credit amount based on the increase in fuel efficiency over the 2002 city fuel economy standards. The increase in the credit amount ranges from $1,000 up to $4,000. A list of qualified fuel cell vehicles eligible for the credit, and their credit amount is available on the IRS website at http://www.irs.gov/Businesses/Corporations/Qualified-Fuel-Cell-Vehicles.

1347. Advanced Lean Burn Technology Vehicle Credit. The second component of the alternative motor vehicle credit is the advanced lean burn technology motor vehicle credit for qualifying vehicles placed in service during 2006 through 2010 (Code Sec. 30B(c)).[34] In addition to the common requirements for qualifying vehicles (¶ 1345), there are specific requirements for classification as an advanced lean burn technology motor vehicle. An advanced lean burn technology motor vehicle is a passenger vehicle or light truck with an internal combustion engine that: (1) is designed to operate primarily using more air than is necessary for complete combustion of the fuel, (2) incorporates direct injection, and (3) achieves at least 125 percent of the 2002 model year city fuel economy. Additionally, 2004-and-later model vehicles must meet specified environmental emission standards based on gross vehicle weight rating (GVWR).

The credit amount is calculated based on the fuel efficiency of the vehicle relative to the 2002 model year city fuel economy supplemented by a conservation credit based on the vehicle's lifetime fuel savings. The range of the credit amount is from $400 to $2,400. The credit amount for new advanced lean burn technology motor vehicles may be increased by a conservation credit, which ranges from $250 to $1,000. The advanced lean burn technology motor vehicle credit begins to phase out after a manufacturer sells a specific quantity of qualifying vehicles. A list of advanced lean-burn technology vehicles eligible for the credit, and their credit amount is available on the IRS website at http://www.irs.gov/Businesses/Corporations/Qualified-Advanced-Lean-Burn-Technology-Vehicles.

1348. Hybrid Motor Vehicle Credit. The third component of the alternative motor vehicle credit is the qualified hybrid motor vehicle credit for qualifying vehicles placed in service after December 31, 2005, and before either December 31, 2009, or December 31, 2010, depending on the size of the vehicle (Code Sec. 30B(d)).[35] The qualified hybrid motor vehicle credit for passenger automobiles or light trucks with a gross vehicle weight rating (GVWR) of no more than 8,500 pounds terminated for vehicles purchased after December 31, 2010. The credit for heavy vehicles terminated after December 31, 2009. In addition to the common requirements for qualifying vehicles (¶ 1345), there are requirements specific to the qualified hybrid motor vehicle credit. The vehicle must draw propulsion energy from both an internal combustion or heat engine and a rechargeable energy storage system. In addition, the vehicle must have received a certificate of conformity that it meets or exceeds specific environmental emission standards. The vehicle must also meet the maximum available power standards required for the vehicle's GVWR.

The amount of the credit allowed for a qualified vehicle with a GVWR of 8,500 pounds or less is the sum of the amounts determined for fuel economy and the conservation credit. The credit amount ranges from $400 up to $2,400. The credit amount for qualified hybrid motor vehicles that are passenger automobiles or light trucks with a GVWR of no more than 8,500 pounds may be increased by a conservation credit, which ranges from $250 up to $1,000. Thus, the credit ranges from $400 to $3,400. The hybrid motor vehicle credit begins to phase out after a manufacturer sells a specific quantity of qualifying vehicles. A list of qualified hybrid vehicle eligible for the credit, and their credit amount is available on the IRS website at http://www.irs.gov/uac/Summary-of-the-Credit-for-Qualified-Hybrid-Vehicles.

1349. Alternative Fuel Motor Vehicle Credit. The fourth component of the alternative motor vehicle credit is the qualified alternative fuel motor vehicle credit for

References are to Standard Federal Tax Reports; Tax Research Consultant; and Practical Tax Explanations.

[34] ¶ 4059A; INDIV: 57,706; § 12,905.15

[35] ¶ 4059A; INDIV: 57,708; § 12,905.20

qualifying vehicles placed in service during 2006 through 2010 (Code Sec. 30B(e)).[36] In addition to the common requirements of qualifying vehicles (¶ 1345), the vehicle must be capable of operating on an alternative fuel (e.g., compressed natural gas, liquefied natural gas, liquefied petroleum gas, hydrogen or any liquid consisting of at least 85-percent methanol).

The amount of the credit allowed for a qualifying vehicle is calculated as the applicable percentage of the incremental cost of any new vehicle placed into service during the tax year. The applicable percentage is 50 percent, plus 30 percent if the vehicle has received a certificate of conformity that it meets or exceeds specific environmental emission standards. The incremental cost of a new qualified alternative motor vehicle is the amount by which the manufacturer's suggested retail price (MSRP) of the vehicle exceeds the MSRP of a gasoline-or diesel-powered version of the same model. However, the incremental cost is limited with respect to the vehicle's gross vehicle weight rating (GVWR) (Code Sec. 30B(E)(3)). A list of qualified alternative fuel motor vehicles eligible for the credit, and their credit amount is available on the IRS website at http://www.irs.gov/Businesses/Qualified-Alternative-Fuel-Motor-Vehicles-(QAFMV)-and–Heavy-Hybrid-Vehicles.

Credit for Mixed-Fuel Vehicles. The credit for qualified alternative fuel motor vehicles also applies to vehicles that qualify as mixed-fuel vehicles, but at a fraction of the credit amount. In addition to the common requirements of qualifying vehicles (¶ 1345), there are two additional requirements for qualification as a mixed-fuel vehicle. The vehicle must be certified by the manufacturer as being able to efficiently operate on a mixture of an alternative fuel and a petroleum-based fuel. The vehicle must also have received either a certificate of conformity that it meets or exceeds specific environmental emission standards.

The credit amount allowed for a mixed fuel vehicle is 70 percent of the credit that would be allowed as if the vehicle qualified for the alternative fuel motor vehicle credit and is a 75/25 mixed-fuel vehicle or 90 percent of the credit allowed as if the vehicle qualified for the alternative fuel motor vehicle credit and is a 90/10 mixed-fuel vehicle. A 75/25 mixed-fuel vehicle operates using at least 75-percent alternative fuel and no more than 25-percent petroleum-based fuel, while a 90/10 mixed-fuel vehicle operates using at least 90-percent alternative fuel and no more than 10-percent petroleum-based fuel.

1350. Qualified Plug-In Electric Drive Motor Vehicle Credit (In 2009). A tax credit was available for the purchase of a qualified plug-in electric drive motor vehicles placed in service after December 31, 2008, and before January 1, 2010. To qualify for the credit, the vehicle had to meet certain requirements (Code Sec. 30D, prior to amendment by the American Recovery and Reinvestment Act of 2010 (P.L. 111-5)).[37] Taxpayers could elect not to claim the credit. The basis of a qualified vehicle is reduced by the amount of any credit claimed. If the vehicle was to be used by a tax-exempt organization or governmental unit, the seller of the vehicle could claim the credit, but only if they clearly disclosed in writing to the entity the amount of any credit allowable with respect to the vehicle.

Credit Amount. The amount of the credit was $2,500, plus $417 for each kilowatt hour of traction battery capacity in excess of four kilowatt hours. The credit amount was limited based on the weight of the vehicle and the number of vehicles sold. The maximum credit amount that could be claimed for a vehicle was: $7,500 for a vehicle with a gross vehicle weight rating (GVWR) of not more than 10,000 pounds; $10,000 for a vehicle with a GVWR of more than 10,000 pounds but not more than 14,000 pounds; $12,500 for a vehicle with a GVWR of more than 14,000 pounds but not more than 26,000 pounds; and $15,000 for a vehicle with a GVWR of more than 26,000 pounds.

Business Versus Personal Use. If the plug-in electric drive motor vehicle was used in a trade or business and was therefore subject to depreciation, the credit allowed for the business use portion was treated as part of the general business credit subject to the tax

References are to Standard Federal Tax Reports; Tax Research Consultant; and Practical Tax Explanations.

[36] ¶ 4059A; INDIV: 57,710; § 12,905.25

[37] ¶ 4059L; INDIV: 58,000; § 12,915.10

liability limitation and carryover rules (¶ 1365). If the plug-in electric drive motor vehicle was considered personal property, the credit was treated as a nonrefundable personal credit subject to the limitation on such credits (¶ 1315).

1351. Qualified Plug-In Electric Drive Motor Vehicle Credit (After 2009). A tax credit is allowed for the purchase price of a qualified plug-in electric drive motor vehicle placed in service after December 31, 2009 (Code Sec. 30D).[38] The credit amount is $2,500 plus $417 for each kilowatt hour of battery capacity in excess of five kilowatt hours up to $5,000. Thus, the maximum credit amount per vehicle is $7,500 (Code Sec. 30D(b)). For qualified vehicles used in a trade or business, the credit is claimed as a portion of the general business credit (¶ 1365). For qualified vehicles used for personal use, the credit is treated as a nonrefundable personal credit use subject to the limitation on such credits (¶ 1315). The credit is claimed using Form 8936.

Qualified Vehicles. To qualify as a plug-in electric drive vehicle, the vehicle must: (1) be made by a manufacturer, (2) be acquired for use or lease but not resale, (3) have its original use commencing with the taxpayer, (4) be treated as a motor vehicle for purposes of Title II of the Clean Air Act, (5) have a gross vehicle weight rating of not more than 14,000 pounds, and (6) be propelled to a significant degree by an electric motor that draws electricity from a battery with a capacity of not less than four kilowatt hours and that is capable of being recharged from an external source of electricity (Code Sec. 30D(d)(1)). The term "motor vehicle" means any vehicle that has at least four wheels and is manufactured primarily for use on public streets, roads, and highways (Code Sec. 30D(d)(2)).

Phaseout. The qualified plug-in electric motor vehicle credit begins to phaseout after 200,000 vehicles have been sold for use in the United States. The phaseout period begins with the second calendar quarter following the calendar quarter in which the 200,000th unit is sold. For the first two quarters of the phaseout period, the credit is cut to 50 percent of the full credit amount. The credit is cut to 25 percent for the third and fourth quarters of the phaseout period. Thereafter, no credit is allowed (Code Sec. 30D(e)).

Special Rules. No qualified plug-in electric drive motor vehicle credit is allowed for property used predominantly outside of the United States. This credit amount is reduced by the amount of any other or credit amount allowed for the qualified plug-in electric drive vehicle. The individual's basis in the vehicle is reduced by the amount of credit claimed. In the event the vehicle no longer qualifies for the credit, the Secretary of the Treasury is authorized to issue regulations providing for the recapture of the credit. Taxpayers have the option to elect out of claiming this credit for a qualified vehicle. Finally, a vehicle is not eligible to be a qualified vehicle unless it is in compliance with the Clean Air Act for applicable makes and models of the vehicle and satisfies the motor vehicle standards under Title 49 of the United States Code (Code Sec. 30D(f)).

1352. Plug-In Electric Drive Motor Vehicle Conversion Credit. The fifth component of the alternative motor vehicle credit is the plug-in electric drive motor vehicle conversion credit for qualifying vehicles placed in service after February 17, 2009, and converted before January 1, 2012 (Code Sec. 30B(i)).[39] The credit is available for converting an existing vehicle into a vehicle that, in addition to the common requirements of qualifying vehicles (¶ 1345), is a qualified plug-in electric drive motor vehicle under Code Sec. 30D (¶ 1351).

The plug-in conversion credit is equal to 10 percent of the cost of converting the vehicle, up to $40,000, for a maximum credit of $4,000. The credit is treated as part of the alternative motor vehicle credit and may be claimed even if another alternative motor vehicle credit under Code Sec. 30B was claimed for the same motor vehicle in any preceding tax year (¶ 1345).

1354. Certain Plug-In Electric Vehicle Credit. A credit is allowed for the cost of acquiring certain electrically powered two-wheeled, three-wheeled, and low-speed vehi-

References are to Standard Federal Tax Reports; Tax Research Consultant; and Practical Tax Explanations.

[38] ¶ 4059L; INDIV: 58,000; § 12,915.15

[39] ¶ 4059A; INDIV: 57,712; § 12,905.30

cles acquired after February 17, 2009, and before January 1, 2012 (Code Sec. 30).[40] The credit is equal to 10 percent of the cost of each qualified plug-in electric vehicle the taxpayer places in service during the tax year with a maximum credit of $2,500 per vehicle. A vehicle qualifies for the credit if it is a qualified plug-in electric vehicle (¶ 1351), except that the battery for a 2- or 3-wheel vehicle must have a capacity of not less than 2.5 kilowatt hours and the vehicle must be low-speed as defined under section 571.3 of title 49 of the Code of Federal Regulations. The credit is claimed using Form 8834.

Any credit amount claimed will reduce the taxpayer's basis. The taxpayer may not claim a deduction or another credit for expenses used to claim this credit. The seller of a qualified vehicle to a tax-exempt entity may claim the credit after full disclosure of the available credit amount to the tax-exempt buyer. The vehicle cannot be used outside the United States. The credit amount is to be recaptured if the vehicle ceases to be a qualifying vehicle. Taxpayers also have the option to elect not to claim this credit for a qualifying vehicle.

1355. Alternative Fuel Vehicle Refueling Property Credit. Taxpayers are permitted a credit for the installation of qualified alternative fuel refueling property placed in service before 2012 (before 2015 for refueling property related to hydrogen) (Code Sec. 30C).[41] The credit is claimed on Form 8911 regardless of whether the property is personal or used in a trade or business. Taxpayers may elect not to have the credit to apply to otherwise qualifying property.

Credit Amount. The credit amount is 30 percent of the cost of alternative fuel vehicle refueling property placed in service by the taxpayer during the tax year, with a per-location limit of $30,000 for property subject to depreciation (such as a commercial or retail refueling stations) and $1,000 for personal use property (such as residential property). In 2009 and 2010, the credit amount is 50 percent of the cost of non-hydrogen-related property and 30 percent of the cost of hydrogen-related property, with a per-location limit of $50,000 for non-hydrogen-related property subject to depreciation, $2,000 for non-hydrogen-related personal use property, $200,000 for hydrogen-related property subject to depreciation, and $1,000 for hydrogen-related personal use property.

If the credit is attributable to property that is subject to the rules of depreciation, then it is considered to be part of the general business credit under Code Sec. 38 (¶ 1365). The amount of the credit that is not attributable to depreciable property cannot exceed the excess of the taxpayer's regular income tax liability (as defined in Code Sec. 26(b)) reduced by the sum of nonrefundable personal credits and the foreign tax credit over the taxpayer's tentative minimum tax (Code Sec. 30C(d)).

Credits for property sold to a tax-exempt entity may be claimed by the seller but only if they disclose in a written document the amount of credit allowable. For purposes of claiming this credit for property sold to a tax-exempt entity, the property is treated as if it is depreciable property, and thus is subject to the business tax credit limitation rule. Qualifying property used outside the United States cannot be used to claim the credit. The qualifying property's basis must be reduced by the amount of the credit claimed. However, should the property cease to be qualifying property, the credit may be recaptured. Taxpayers also have the option to elect not to claim this credit (Code Sec. 30(e)).

Qualifying Property. Qualifying alternative fuel vehicle refueling property is property used for storing a clean-burning fuel or for dispensing clean-burning fuel into the fuel tank of a motor vehicle, but only if the property is located at the point where the fuel is delivered into the tank of the vehicle. It also includes any equipment that is used to recharge a motor vehicle that is propelled by electricity, but only if the property is located at the point where the vehicles are recharged. Only the following fuels shall be considered clean burning:

References are to Standard Federal Tax Reports; Tax Research Consultant; and Practical Tax Explanations.

[40] ¶ 4053; INDIV: 58,010; § 12,920

[41] ¶ 4059F; INDIV: 57,750; § 12,910

• any fuel that is least 85 percent by volume consisting of ethanol, natural gas, compressed natural gas, liquefied natural gas, liquefied petroleum gas, or hydrogen;

• any fuel mixture that consists of a combination of at least two fuels which include biodiesel, diesel fuel, or kerosene with at least 20 percent of the volume being biodiesel without regard to any kerosene in the mixture; and

• electricity (Code Sec. 30C(c)).

Foreign Tax Credit

1361. Foreign Tax Credit. An individual taxpayer may either deduct foreign income taxes paid or accrued as an itemized deduction on Schedule A of Form 1040 or may apply them as a credit against his or her U.S. income tax liability (¶ 2475) (Code Sec. 27).[42] The credit is claimed by individuals on Form 1116 unless the total foreign taxes paid are less than $300 for single filers ($600 for joint filers). For these taxpayers, the credit may be claimed directly on Form 1040 if all filing requirements are satisfied (¶ 2476). A corporate taxpayer may also either deduct foreign income taxes paid or accrued or elect to claim such payments as a credit against its U.S. income tax liability. Form 1118 is used to calculate the amount of credit in a single tax year.

1362. Puerto Rico and U.S. Possessions Credit. The Puerto Rico and possessions tax credit under Code Secs. 30A and 936 has terminated for corporate taxpayers conducting a trade or business in Puerto Rico for tax years after 1995. However, in the case of existing claimants, the possessions tax credit continued to apply to Guam, American Samoa, and the Commonwealth of the Northern Mariana Islands without change for tax years beginning after 1995 and ending for tax years after 2006. A modified version of the credit for certain existing claimants continued to apply to American Samoa for tax years beginning after 2006 and ending before 2012 (Act Sec. 756(a), of the Tax Relief, Unemployment Insurance Reauthorization, and Job Creation Act of 2010 (P.L. 111-312)). A corporation claiming the credit for economic activity in American Samoa must file Form 5735. The amount of the credit equals the sum of:

• 60 percent of the qualified American Samoa wages and allocable employee fringe benefit expenses, plus

• the sum of the following depreciation allowances:

— 15 percent of the corporation's depreciation allowances with respect to short-life qualified American Samoa tangible property,

— 40 percent of the corporation's depreciation allowances with respect to medium-life qualified American Samoa tangible property, and

— 65 percent of the corporation's depreciation allowances with respect to long-life qualified American Samoa tangible property.

The rule that denies a credit or for any possessions or foreign tax paid with respect to taxable income taken into account in computing the Code Sec. 936 credit amount does not apply.[43]

General Business Credits

1365. General Business Credit. The general business credit (Code Sec. 38)[44] is a limited, nonrefundable credit that is claimed after all other nonrefundable credits (¶ 1315), other than the minimum tax credit, are claimed. The general business credit for a tax year is the sum of: (1) the business credit carried forward to the current year, (2) the amount of the current year business credit, and (3) the business credit carried back to the year.

Generally, the current year general business credit is the sum of:

• the investment credit (¶ 1365A);

• the work opportunity credit (¶ 1365G);

References are to Standard Federal Tax Reports; Tax Research Consultant; and Practical Tax Explanations.

[42] ¶ 4002; INTLOUT: 3,000; § 13,401

[43] ¶ 4058, ¶ 28,380; INTL: 24,154.20; § 13,435

[44] ¶ 4250; BUSEXP: 54,000; § 13,601

- the alcohol fuels credit (¶ 1365I);
- the research activities credit (¶ 1365J);
- the low-income housing credit (¶ 1365K);
- the disabled access credit (¶ 1365M);
- the renewable electricity production credit (¶ 1365N);
- the empowerment zone employment credit (¶ 1365O);
- the Indian employment credit (¶ 1365Q);
- the employer social security credit (FICA tip credit) (¶ 1365R);
- the orphan drug credit (¶ 1365S);
- the new markets credit (¶ 1365T);
- the small employer pension plan startup costs credit (¶ 1365U);
- the employer-provided child care facilities and services credit (¶ 1365V);
- the qualified railroad track maintenance credit (¶ 1365W);
- the biodiesel and renewable diesel fuels credit (¶ 1365X);
- the low sulfur diesel fuel production credit (¶ 1365Y);
- the distilled spirits credit (¶ 1365Z);
- the advanced nuclear power facility production credit (¶ 1365AA);
- the nonconventional source fuels credit (¶ 1365BB);
- the energy efficient home credit (¶ 1365CC);
- the energy efficient appliance credit (¶ 1365DD);
- the alternative motor vehicle credit (portion allocable to a trade or business) (¶ 1345);
- the alternative fuel vehicle refueling property credit (portion allocable to a trade or business) (¶ 1355);
- the mine rescue team training credit (¶ 1365GG);
- the agricultural chemical security credit (¶ 1365HH);
- the differential wage payment credit (¶ 1365II);
- the carbon dioxide sequestration credit (¶ 1365JJ);
- the qualified plug-in electric drive motor vehicle credit (portion allocable to a trade or business) (¶ 1351);
- the credit for certain plug-in electric vehicles (¶ 1354);
- the small employer health insurance credit (¶ 1333);
- the new hire retention credit (¶ 1365FF);
- the credit for contributions to selected community development corporations (CDC) (¶ 1365KK); and
- general credits from an electing large partnership (¶ 482–¶ 488).

Each of these credits is computed separately. If more than one of these components is claimed, or if there is a general business credit carryback or carryforward, Form 3800 along with the appropriate form must be filed with the return. For this purpose, components of the general business credit arising in a single year are deemed used in the same order in which they are listed above, with the following exceptions: the empowerment zone employment credit, the work opportunity credit, the alcohol fuels credit, the low-income housing credit (for buildings placed in service after 2007), the renewable electricity credit, the FICA tip credit, the qualified railroad track maintenance credit, and the credit for small employer health insurance premiums. Each of these credits has a special tax liability limitation rule and, while a part of the general business credit, are not reported on Form 3800 (Code Sec. 38).

Tax Liability Limitations. The general business credit may not exceed a limitation based on the amount of tax liability (Code Sec. 38(c)). Generally, the general business credit may not exceed net income tax less the greater of the taxpayer's tentative minimum tax liability or 25 percent of net regular tax liability above $25,000. However, the limitation is determined separately for the portion of the credit attributable to the empowerment zone employment credit, the work opportunity credit, the alcohol fuels credit, the low-income housing credit, the renewable electricity credit, the FICA tip credit, the qualified railroad track maintenance credit, the credit for small employer health insurance premiums, and, for 2010, eligible small business credits (see *Carrybacks and Carryforwards of Unused Credits*, following). When calculating the limitation as it applies to these specified credits, the tentative minimum tax is to be treated as zero, which results in these credits being fully allowable against both the regular and alternative minimum tax (AMT) liabilities of the taxpayer.

For the empowerment zone employment credit, the credit amount may not exceed the excess of the net income tax over the greater of 75 percent of the taxpayer's tentative minimum tax liability or 25 percent of net regular tax liability above $25,000. This result is then reduced by the general business credit allowed for the tax year other than the work opportunity credit, the alcohol fuels credit, the low-income housing credit, the renewable electricity credit, the FICA tip credit, the qualified railroad track maintenance credit, the credit for small employer health insurance premiums, and, for 2010, eligible small business credits (Code Sec. 38(c)(2)).

For purposes of calculating these limitations, net regular income tax liability is the sum of the taxpayer's regular tax liability as defined in Code Sec. 38(b) (¶ 1420) and AMT liability as defined in Code Sec. 55, less all other nonrefundable credits (Code Secs. 21—30D, and 1400C except the credit for prior year minimum tax). Net regular tax liability is the regular tax liability reduced by these credits.

For a married couple filing separate returns, the $25,000 figure above is limited to $12,500 for each spouse. If, however, one spouse has no current credit or unused credit, the spouse having current credit or unused credit may use the full $25,000 figure in determining his or her credit for the year. For a controlled group of corporations, the group may divide the $25,000 figure among its members in any way the members choose. For an estate or trust, the $25,000 figure is reduced to an amount that bears the same ratio to $25,000 as the portion of the estate's or trust's income that is not allocated to the beneficiaries bears to the total income of the estate or trust (Code Sec. 38(c)(6)).

Carrybacks and Carryforwards of Unused Credits. When the credit exceeds the tax liability limitation in any year, the excess or unused amount may be carried back one year and forward 20 years (15-year carryforward for credits that arise in tax years beginning before 1998) (Code Sec. 39).[45] The order in which these credits are claimed in any carryback or carryforward year is as follows: (1) carryforwards to that year on a first-in, first-out (FIFO) basis, (2) the business credit earned in that year, and (3) the carrybacks to that year on a FIFO basis.

A special carryback period of five years applies for the 2010 tax year of small businesses (Code Sec. 39(a)(4)). Eligible small business credits of an eligible small business determined for its first tax year beginning in 2010 may be carried back five years and forward 20 years. Eligible small business credits are the credits described in Code Sec. 38(b), which comprise the current year business credit component of the general business credit. An eligible small business is a sole proprietorship, partnership, or non-publicly traded corporation with $50 million or less in average annual gross receipts during the three tax years preceding the first tax year beginning in 2010. The eligible small business credits determined for 2010 may be claimed against the eligible small business's regular and AMT liabilities.

Separate carryback and carryforward records must be maintained for the amount of the general business credit attributable to the empowerment zone employment credit,

References are to Standard Federal Tax Reports; Tax Research Consultant; and Practical Tax Explanations.

[45] ¶ 4300; BUSEXP: 54,058; § 13,605.15

and to each of the other components of the general business credit. Separate record-keeping is necessary because the empowerment zone employment credit may offset up to 25 percent of the taxpayer's AMT (Code Sec. 38(c)(2)(A)). Several of the credits that remain unused at the end of the carryforward period, or when the taxpayer ceases to exist, may be claimed as a deduction in the following year (Code Sec. 196).[46]

1365A. Investment Credit–Generally. Taxpayers may claim an investment credit which is the sum of the rehabilitation credit (¶ 1365B), the energy credit (¶ 1365C), the qualified advanced coal project credit (¶ 1365D), the qualified gasification project credit (¶ 1365E), the qualifying advanced energy project credit (¶ 1365F), and the qualifying therapeutic discovery project credit (¶ 1365LL) (Code Sec. 46).[47] The investment credit is claimed on Form 3468 and is one of the components of the general business credit, subject to the tax liability limitation and the carryover rules (¶ 1365).

The amount of investment credit allowed on investment credit property of a partnership for a tax year is generally apportioned among partners according to the ratio in which the partners divide the general profits of the partnership. The investment credit amount on an S corporation's investment credit property for a tax year is apportioned among the shareholders on a daily basis according to each shareholder's proportion of ownership. The investment credit amount allowed on investment credit property of an estate or trust is apportioned between the estate or trust and the beneficiaries on the basis of the income allocable to each.

At-Risk Limitation. No investment credit is allowed for investment credit property to the extent that the property is financed with nonqualified nonrecourse borrowing (Code Sec. 49).[48] Thus, the credit base of investment credit property is reduced by the amount of nonqualified nonrecourse financing regarding the property, as determined at the close of the tax year in which the property is placed in service.

Nonqualified nonrecourse financing is any nonrecourse financing which is not qualified commercial financing. Qualified commercial financing is any financing of property if: (1) the property is acquired from an unrelated person; (2) the amount of the nonrecourse financing does not exceed 80 percent of the property's credit base; and (3) the financing is borrowed from a qualified person, or represents a loan from any Federal, state or local government or instrumentality, or which is guaranteed by any Federal, state or local government or instrumentality. The credit base is equal to the sum of the portion of the basis of a qualified rehabilitation building attributable to qualified rehabilitation expenditures, the basis of energy property, and the basis of any property that is part of a qualifying advanced coal project, a qualifying gasification project or a qualified advanced energy project. A qualified person is any person who actively and regularly engages in the business of lending money and is not the person from whom the property was acquired, a person who receives a fee with respect to the taxpayer's investment in the property, or a person who is related to the taxpayer (Code Sec. 49(a)(1)(D)).

Decreases in nonqualified recourse financing on the property in tax years following the year in which the property was placed in service increase the credit base of the property. This rule does not apply if the decrease occurs through the surrender or other use of property financed by nonqualified nonrecourse financing. Similarly, increases in nonqualified nonrecourse financing on the property in tax years following the year in which the property was placed in service decrease the credit base of the property and trigger recapture (Code Sec. 49(a)(2) and (b)).

The limitation applies to investment credit property placed in service by individuals and by certain closely held corporations engaged in business activities that are subject to the loss limitation rules of the at-risk rules (¶ 2045). For a partnership or S corporation, the investment credit at-risk limitation applies at the partner or shareholder level (Code Sec. 49(a)(1)(E)).

References are to Standard Federal Tax Reports; Tax Research Consultant; and Practical Tax Explanations.

[46] ¶ 12,400; BUSEXP: 54,058.10; § 13,605.20

[47] ¶ 4502; BUSEXP: 51,050; § 13,701

[48] ¶ 4750; BUSEXP: 51,400; § 13,730.05

The investment credit at-risk limitation does not apply to certain energy property. To come within this exception, nonqualified nonrecourse financing may not exceed 75 percent of the basis of energy property at the close of the tax year in which the property is placed in service. In addition, any nonqualified nonrecourse financing for such property must be a level payment loan (a loan repaid in substantially equal installments, including both principal and interest).

An increase in the amount at risk is treated as if it occurred in the year that the property was first placed in service for purposes of computing the investment credit and for computing any recapture of such credit. However, the investment credit attributable to the increase in the amount at risk is claimed by the taxpayer during the tax year in which the decrease in the amount of nonqualified nonrecourse financing occurs.

If at the close of a tax year there is a net increase in the amount of nonqualified nonrecourse financing regarding such property, thereby causing a decrease in the taxpayer's amount at risk, the investment credit must be recomputed and the decrease in investment credits for previous tax years is recaptured as additional tax in the year that the net increase in nonqualified nonrecourse financing occurs.

Ineligible Property. No investment credit is allowed for the following types of property: (1) property used predominantly outside the United States (however, limited exceptions apply); (2) property used predominantly to furnish lodging (or in connection with the furnishing of lodging), except in the case of nonlodging commercial facilities, a hotel or motel furnishing accommodations predominantly to transients, certified historic structures to the extent of that portion of the basis attributable to qualified rehabilitation expenditures, and energy property; and (3) property used by a tax-exempt organization (other than a farmers' cooperative) unless it is used predominantly in an unrelated trade or business (Code Sec. 50(b)).[49] Generally, property used by, or leased to, a governmental unit, foreign person, or foreign entity is not eligible for the investment credit. However, the portion of the property attributable to qualified rehabilitation expenditures or held under a short-term lease (generally under six months) does qualify for the investment credit.

Basis Reduction. The basis of property for which an investment credit is claimed is reduced by the full amount of the credit except for the energy credit property whose basis is reduced by 50 percent of the credit amount (¶ 1365B) (Code Sec. 50(c)).[50] The reduced basis is used to compute depreciation and any gain or loss on the disposition of property.

If the investment credit is recaptured on property for which an investment credit downward basis adjustment was made, the basis of the property immediately before the event resulting in recapture must be increased by the recapture amount and by 50 percent of the recapture amount for an energy credit. In determining the amount of gain that is recaptured as ordinary income on a sale or disposition of depreciable personal property (Code Sec. 1245) or depreciable realty (Code Sec. 1250), the amount of the investment credit downward basis adjustment is treated as a allowed for depreciation. Thus, the basis adjustment is treated as depreciation subject to ordinary income recapture. For section 1250 property, the recapture applies only to the excess of depreciation claimed over depreciation computed under the straight-line method, with the latter computed on the basis without reduction for the applicable investment credit downward basis adjustment.

If an investment credit for which a downward basis adjustment was made does not result in a tax benefit because it remains unused at the end of the 20-year credit carryover period for tax years after December 31, 1997 (15-year general business credit carryforward period for tax years prior to January 1, 1998), a deduction is allowed under Code Sec. 196 to the taxpayer for 50 percent of the unused energy and 100 percent of any other unused investment credit attributable to the basis reduction.

References are to Standard Federal Tax Reports; Tax Research Consultant; and Practical Tax Explanations.

[49] ¶ 4752; BUSEXP: 51,250; § 13,701

[50] ¶ 4752; BUSEXP: 51,056; § 13,740

Special Investment Credit Rules. Special limitations apply to the amount of investment credit that may be claimed by mutual funds (regulated investment companies), real estate investment trusts, noncorporate lessors, and certain other regulated companies (Code Sec. 50(d)).[51]

Early Disposition. When investment credit property is disposed of (including dispositions due to casualties or thefts), or ceases to be investment credit property before the end of its recapture period, the tax for the year of disposal or cessation is increased by the amount of the credit that is recaptured (Code Sec. 50(a)).[52] A taxpayer subject to recapture must file Form 4255.

The amount of the recapture is a percentage of the original credit claimed, depending on how long the property is held before recapture is required. The recapture percentages are 100 percent within the first full year after placement in service, 80 percent within the second full year, 60 percent within the third full year, 40 percent within the fourth full year, 20 percent within the fifth full year, and zero thereafter. Advance rehabilitation or energy credits on progress expenditures are also subject to recapture. Special recapture rules apply to certain energy property.

The recapture rules do not apply to the following transfers: (1) a transfer between spouses or incident to divorce (¶ 778) (but a later disposition by the transferee will result in recapture to the same extent as if the disposition had been made by the transferor at that later date), (2) a transfer because of death, and (3) a transfer to which Code Sec. 381(a) (concerning carryovers after corporate acquisitions) applies. Similarly, the recapture rules do not apply where there is a mere change in the form of operating a business, provided that the property is retained in the business and the taxpayer retains a substantial interest in the business.

1365B. Rehabilitation Credit. A part of the investment credit (¶ 1365A), the rehabilitation investment credit is 20 percent of qualified rehabilitation expenses (QRE) for certified historic structures and 10 percent of QRE for qualified rehabilitated buildings (QRB) first placed in service before 1936 (other than certified historic structures) (Code Sec. 47).[53] An election may also be made to claim an advance rehabilitation investment credit. No energy credit (¶ 1365C) is allowed on that portion of the basis of property that is attributable to QRE (Code Sec. 48(a)(2)(B)). Certain restrictions apply to property which is used as lodging (Code Sec. 50(b)).

Eligibility. A building and its structural components constitute a QRB if they are substantially rehabilitated for the tax year and placed in service by any person before the beginning of the rehabilitation. Property other than a certified historic structure must also satisfy: (1) the applicable wall retention test, (2) an age requirement, and (3) a location-of-rehabilitation requirement (Code Sec. 47(c)(1); Reg. § 1.48-12(b)).[54] Property is considered substantially rehabilitated only if the expenditures during an elected 24-month measurement period (60-month period for phased rehabilitations) ending with or within the tax year are greater then the adjusted basis of the property or $5,000.

QRE does not include: (1) an enlargement or new construction; (2) the cost of acquisition; (3) noncertified rehabilitation of a certified historic structure; (4) rehabilitation of tax-exempt use property; (5) expenditures, generally, that are not depreciated under the MACRS straight-line method over specified recovery periods; or (6) a lessee-incurred expenditure if, on the date the rehabilitation of the building is completed, the remaining term of the lease (determined without regard to renewal periods) is less than the applicable recovery period (Reg. § 1.48-12(c)).

Generally, the rehabilitation investment credit for QRE must be claimed in the tax year in which the property attributable to the expenditures is placed in service, provided that the building is a QRB for such tax year (Code Sec. 47(b)). However, the credit may

References are to Standard Federal Tax Reports; Tax Research Consultant; and Practical Tax Explanations.

[51] ¶ 4752; BUSEXP: 51,650, BUSEXP: 51,606; § 13,701

[52] ¶ 4752; BUSEXP: 51,450, BUSEXP: 51,500; § 13,735

[53] ¶ 4600; BUSEXP: 51,152; § 13,705

[54] ¶ 4600, ¶ 4609; BUSEXP: 51,154; § 13,705

be claimed before the date the property is placed in service under the rules for qualified progress expenditures (Code Sec. 47(d)).

Buildings in Disaster Areas. The rehabilitation tax credit percentage is increased for certified historic structures or QRBs in the Gulf Opportunity (GO) Zone and the Midwest disaster area (¶ 1179). The tax credit percentage is increased from 20 to 26 percent for any certified historic structure and from 10 to 13 percent for qualified rehabilitated buildings provided the structure or building is located in either disaster area. For the GO Zone, the increase applies to QRE that are paid or incurred on or after August 28, 2005, and before January 1, 2012 (Code Sec. 1400N(h)). For the Midwest disaster area, the increase applies to QRE made on building or structures damaged or destroyed by the Midwestern storms and that are paid or incurred on or after the applicable disaster date, and before January 1, 2012.

Advance Credits for Progress Expenditures. An election may be made to claim an advance rehabilitation investment credit for progress expenditures on certain rehabilitated buildings before such property is placed in service (Code Sec. 47(d)).[55] Property qualifying for an advance rehabilitation investment credit on progress expenditures includes a building that is being rehabilitated by, or for, the taxpayer, if the normal rehabilitation period for the building is two or more years and it is reasonable to expect that the building will be a qualified rehabilitated building when it is placed in service.

The amount of QREs that are considered progress expenditures for which an advance rehabilitation investment credit may be claimed is the amount of QRE properly chargeable to the capital account for self-rehabilitated buildings. For non-self-rehabilitated buildings, the amount is the lesser of: (a) the QRE paid to another person for the rehabilitation of the building during the tax year or (b) the portion of the overall cost of the rehabilitation completed during the tax year.

1365C. Energy Credit. A part of the investment credit (¶ 1365A), the business energy investment credit is generally equal to 10 percent of the taxpayer's basis in qualified energy property placed in service during the tax year. However, effective for property placed in service before 2017, the credit percentage is increased to 30 percent for (1) qualified fuel cell property, (2) equipment that uses solar energy to generate electricity, to heat or cool a structure, or provide solar process heat (except used to heat a swimming pool), (3) equipment that uses solar energy to illuminate the inside of a structure using fiber-optic distributed sunlight, and (4) qualified small wind energy property (Code Sec. 48).[56] However, the credit for qualified fuel cell property may not exceed $1,500 for each 0.5 kilowatt of capacity. Qualified energy property eligible for the 10-percent credit generally includes microturbine property and other energy property, including combined heat and power system property, geothermal heat pump systems, and public utility property.

To qualify for the credit, the energy property must be depreciable (or amortizable) and must meet performance and quality standards prescribed by IRS regulations. In addition, the taxpayer must complete the construction, reconstruction, or erection of the property or, if the property is acquired, the taxpayer must be the first person to use it. The basis of all energy property prior to the credit determination is reduced by any tax-exempt or subsidized financing. No energy credit is allowed for that portion of the basis of property for which a rehabilitation investment credit (¶ 1365B) is claimed. An advance energy investment credit may be claimed under special rules for progress expenditures. The energy credit may be claimed against the alternative minimum tax.

Investment Credit Election. A taxpayer may make an irrevocable election to treat certain qualified property that is part of a qualified investment credit facility as energy property eligible for a 30-percent investment credit under Code Sec. 48(a)(5). If the election is made, no renewable electricity production credit is allowed under Code Sec. 45 (¶ 1365N) for any tax year with respect to any qualified investment credit facility. For purposes of the election, qualified investment credit facilities are facilities otherwise

References are to Standard Federal Tax Reports; Tax Research Consultant; and Practical Tax Explanations.

[55] ¶ 4600; BUSEXP: 51,160; § 13,705

[56] ¶ 4651; BUSEXP: 51,102; § 13,710

eligible for the renewable electricity production credit with respect to which no credit under renewable electricity production has been allowed. Qualified facilities (within the meaning of Code Sec. 45) include those producing electricity using wind, closed-loop biomass, open-loop biomass, geothermal energy, landfill gas, municipal solid waste (trash), hydropower, or marine and hydrokinetic renewable energy. In order to qualify for the election, wind facilities must be placed in service after December 31, 2008, and before January 1, 2013. All other facilities must be placed in service after December 31, 2008, and before January 1, 2014, in order to qualify.

Coordination With Grants Authorized for 2009, 2010, or 2011. The Secretary of Treasury is authorized to provide a grant to each person who places into service specified energy property that is either: (1) an electricity production facility otherwise eligible for the renewable electricity production credit under Code Sec. 45 or (2) qualifying property otherwise eligible for the energy investment credit under Code Sec. 48 (Act Sec. 1603(a) of the American Recovery and Reinvestment Act of 2009 (P.L. 111-5), as amended by the Tax Relief, Unemployment Insurance Reauthorization, and Job Creation Act of 2010 (P.L. 111-312)). In order to be eligible for the grant, the specified energy property must be:

- placed in service during 2009, 2010, or 2011, or
- placed in service after 2011 and before the credit termination date for such property, if construction of the property began during 2009, 2010, or 2011.

However, no energy credit (Code Sec. 48) or electricity from renewable resources credit (Code Sec. 45) is allowed for the year of the grant or any subsequent year (Code Sec. 48(d)(1)). In the event that a credit amount was claimed for the facility prior to the grant being made, the credit amount is recaptured by adding the prior claimed credit amounts to the tax liability of the grant year. The taxpayer must adjust any carryovers of general business credits to reflect the amount of the recaptured credit (Code Sec. 48(d)(2)).

1365D. Qualified Advanced Coal Project Credit. A qualifying advanced coal project credit may be claimed as a component of the investment credit (¶ 1365A) (Code Sec. 48A).[57] The credit is available only to taxpayers who have applied for and received certification that their project satisfies the relevant requirements outlined by the IRS, in consultation with the Secretary of Energy. The credit is equal to 20 percent of qualified investments in integrated combined cycle projects, 15 percent of qualified investments in other advanced coal-based projects, and 30 percent of qualified investments in advanced coal-based generation technology projects. The IRS is required to recapture any tax benefits should the project fail to maintain carbon dioxide separation and sequestration.

1365E. Qualified Gasification Project Credit. A qualifying gasification project credit may be claimed as a component of the investment credit (¶ 1365A) (Code Sec. 48B).[58] The credit is available only to taxpayers who have applied for and received certification that their project satisfies the relevant requirements outlined by the IRS, in consultation with the Secretary of Energy. The credit is equal to 20 percent of qualified investments in qualifying gasification projects, increased to 30 percent for qualifying gasification projects that include equipment that separates and sequesters at least 75 percent of the project's total carbon dioxide emissions. A qualifying gasification facility is one that combines coal, petroleum residue, biomass, or other materials with steam under high pressure to create a synthetic gas, or "syngas." The IRS is authorized to recapture any tax benefits if the project fails to attain or maintain the 75-percent separation and sequestration requirement.

1365F. Advanced Energy Project Credit. A tax credit is allowed equal to 30 percent of a taxpayer's qualified investment for the tax year with respect to any qualifying advanced energy project (Code Sec. 48C).[59] The credit is part of the investment credit (¶ 1365A) and the basis of any property that is part of a qualifying advanced energy project is included in the credit base for purposes of applying the investment

References are to Standard Federal Tax Reports; Tax Research Consultant; and Practical Tax Explanations.

[57] ¶ 4672; BUSEXP: 51,700; § 13,715

[58] ¶ 4676; BUSEXP: 51,750; § 13,720

[59] ¶ 4685; BUSEXP: 51,800; § 13,725

credit at-risk limitation rules under Code Sec. 49. The credit is not allowed for any qualified investment for which a credit is also allowed for the energy credit, the qualifying advanced coal project credit, or the qualifying gasification project credit.

The amount of the taxpayer's "qualified investment" for any tax year includes the basis of eligible property placed in service during that tax year that is part of a qualifying advanced energy project (Code Sec. 48C(b)). For this purpose, a taxpayer can elect to increase the amount of its qualified investment for the tax year by its qualified progress expenditures made during the year. Qualified progress expenditures are amounts paid (paid or incurred in the case of self-constructed property) during the year for the construction of eligible property which has a normal construction period of at least two years and a useful life of seven years or more. However, no qualified progress expenditures may be taken into account in the tax year the property is placed in service. In addition, the credit amount with respect to any qualifying advanced energy project for all tax years cannot exceed the amount designated by the Secretary of Treasury as eligible for the credit.

A qualifying advanced energy project is a project that re-equips, expands, or establishes a manufacturing facility for the production of: (1) property designed to be used to produce energy from the sun, wind, or geothermal deposits (within the meaning of Code Sec. 613(e)(2)) or other renewable resources; (2) fuel cells, microturbines, or an energy storage system for use with electric or hybrid-electric motor vehicles; (3) electric grids to support the transmission of intermittent sources of renewable energy, including storage of such energy; (4) property designed to capture and sequester carbon dioxide emissions; (5) property designed to refine or blend renewable fuels or to produce energy conservation technologies (including energy-conserving lighting technologies and smart grid technologies); (6) new qualified plug-in electric drive motor vehicles, qualified plug-in electric vehicles, or components which are designed specifically for use with such vehicles, including electric motors, generators, and power control units; or (7) other advanced energy property designed to reduce greenhouse gas emissions as may be determined by the Secretary of Treasury (Code Sec. 48C(c)(1)). Any portion of the qualified investment in the qualifying project must be certified by the Secretary of Treasury as eligible for the credit. A qualifying project does not include any portion of a project for the production of any property used in the refining or blending of any transportation fuel (other than renewable fuels).

For purposes of the credit, eligible property is any property: (1) that is necessary for the production of property described above; (2) that is tangible personal property or other tangible property (not including a building or its structural components), but only if such property is used as an integral part of the qualified investment credit facility; and (3) with respect to which depreciation (or amortization in lieu of depreciation) is allowable (Code Sec. 48C(c)(2)).

In determining which qualifying advanced energy projects to certify, the Treasury Secretary will take into consideration only those projects where there is a reasonable expectation of commercial viability. In addition, the Treasury Secretary will consider which projects: (1) will provide the greatest domestic job creation (both direct and indirect) during the credit period; (2) will provide the greatest net impact in avoiding or reducing air pollutants or anthropogenic emissions of greenhouse gases; (3) have the greatest potential for technological innovation and commercial deployment; (4) have the lowest levelized cost of generated or stored energy, or of measured reduction in energy consumption or greenhouse gas emission (based on costs of the full supply chain); and (5) have the shortest project time from certification to completion (Code Sec. 48C(d)). Upon making certification, the Secretary of Treasury will publicly disclose the identity of the applicant and the amount of the credit with respect to that applicant.

1365G. Work Opportunity Tax Credit. A credit is available for wages paid by employers who hire individuals from certain targeted groups of hard-to-employ individuals—the work opportunity credit (Code Sec. 51).[60] Generally, the credit is 40 percent of the first $6,000 of qualified wages ($3,000 for qualified summer youth employees) paid to each member of a targeted group during the first year of employment and 25 percent in the case of wages attributable to individuals meeting only minimum employment levels. The credit is taken for first-year wages paid to eligible individuals who begin work before January 1, 2012 (before January 1, 2013, for qualified veterans) (Code Sec. 51(c)(4), as amended by the VOW to Hire Heroes Act of 2011 (P.L. 112-56)), unless an election is made to not claim the credit. Any business for such wages must be reduced by the amount of the credit, as computed on Form 5884.

> **Comment:** Absent further legislation, the work opportunity credit, with the exception of certain qualified veterans, terminated on December 31, 2011. The credit terminates on December 31, 2012, for certain qualified veteran.

Tax Liability Limitations. Although the work opportunity credit is a component of the general business credit (¶ 1365), credit amounts are not subject to the general business credit tax liability limitation rule but are to be calculated separately. The credit limitation formula is changed to treat the tentative minimum tax as zero, resulting in allowing taxpayers to fully utilize the credit against both the regular tax and the minimum tax liabilities (Code Sec. 38(c)(4)). The credit limitation calculation applies to any carrybacks of such credit amounts to any previous year. For credit amounts generated by individuals beginning work in tax years beginning prior to January 1, 2007, the amount of credit to claim is subject to the tax liability limitation and the carry over rules governing the general business credit (¶ 1365). No credit is allowed for wages paid to an individual for services rendered at the employer's plant or facility that are substantially similar to services performed by employees who are participants in a strike or who are affected by a lockout.

Minimum Employment Period. An employee must have completed a minimum of 120 hours of service for the wages to be taken into account for calculation of the work opportunity credit. The hours-of-service test is the only way the minimum employment period is measured for purposes of the credit. If the 120-hour test is met but the employee fails to perform at least 400 hours of service, the employer is entitled to a credit of 25 percent. For 400 or more hours of service, the percentage is 40 percent of the employee's wages (Code Sec. 51(i)(3)).

Target Groups. Wages paid to individuals who are certified members of one of the following groups qualify for the work opportunity credit (Code Sec. 51(d)):

- a qualified IV-A recipient (the individual must be a member of a family that received Temporary Assistance for Needy Families (TANF) assistance for any 9 of the 18 months before the hire date);
- a qualified ex-felon (the individual must have a hire date within one year of being released from prison);
- a designated community resident (the individual must be at least 18 years of age but less than 40 years of age on the hiring date and live in an empowerment zone, an enterprise or renewal community, or a rural renewal county;
- a vocational rehabilitation referral (the individual must have a physical or mental handicap resulting in a substantial handicap to employment and be referred to the employer upon completion of rehabilitative services);
- a qualified summer youth employee (the individual must be a new hire who performs services between May 1 and September 15, be 16 or 17 years of age on the later of the hire date or May 1, and must live in an empowerment zone or an enterprise or renewal community) (the maximum qualified wages is $3,000 with the maximum credit amount being $1,200);
- a qualified food stamps recipient (the individual must be at least 18 of age but younger than 40 years of age and be a member of a family that either received

References are to Standard Federal Tax Reports; Tax Research Consultant; and Practical Tax Explanations.

[60] ¶ 4800; BUSEXP: 54,250; § 13,805.05

food stamp benefits for the six months before the hire date or received food stamp benefits for three of the five months before the hire date but lost the benefits for failure to comply with the program's work requirements);

• a qualified supplemental security income (SSI) recipient (the individual must have received SSI within 60 days before the hire date); or

• a long-term family assistance recipient (the individual must be a member of a family that received the maximum amount of IV-A (TANF) assistance over an 18-month period ending within two years of the hire date) (up to $10,000 are considered qualified first year wages, up to $10,000 are considered qualified second year wages, and the credit percentage equals 50 percent for the second year (maximum credit amount of $5,000)).

An employer of an individual who is a member of one of these groups must either have the individual certified by an authorized local agency prior to the individual's first day of work or file an application for certification of the individual within 28 days of the first day of work (Code Sec. 51(d)(12)). Employers use Form 8850 to pre-screen employees and to make a written request that the local agency certify an employee as being a member of a targeted group. Employers are permitted to submit Form 8850 electronically. Two alternative methods of certification using electronic signatures are permitted, in addition to the electronic submission of the form (Notice 2012-13).

Special rules apply to qualified veterans, who comprise another targeted group. For qualified disabled veterans hired after May 25, 2007, and before November 22, 2011, the credit may be claimed for up to $12,000 in qualified first-year wages if the veteran is hired no more than one year after having been discharged or released from active duty in the U.S. Armed Forces (for a maximum credit of $4,800) (Code Sec. 51(b)(3) and (d)(3), as amended by P.L. 112-56). For qualified veterans who are hired after November 21, 2011, and before January 1, 2013, the limit on qualified wages used in calculating the credit is $6,000 for a certified short-term, i.e., unemployment of least four weeks but less than six months during the one-year period ending on the hiring date, unemployed veteran (for a maximum credit of $2,400). The limit on qualified wages is $14,000 for a certified long-term, i.e., unemployment of least six months during the one-year period ending on the hiring date, unemployed veteran (for a maximum credit of $5,600). In addition, the limit on qualified wages used in calculating the credit for a veteran with a service-connected disability is increased to $24,000 (for a maximum credit of $9,600) if the veteran is certified as having been unemployed for an aggregate of six months or more during the one-year period ending on the hiring date.

Employers of veterans hired on or after November 22, 2011, and before May 22, 2012, have until June 19, 2012, to complete and submit Form 8850 to the local agency (Notice 2012-13). The rule requiring filing within 28 days of hiring will apply to veterans hired after May 21, 2012.

Targeted Groups for 2009 and 2010 Only. Unemployed veterans or disconnected youth who begin work for an employer after December 31, 2008, and before January 1, 2011, are treated as members of a targeted group for whom the employer may claim the work opportunity tax credit (Code Sec. 51(d)(14)(A)). An unemployed veteran includes any individual who is certified by the designated local agency as: (1) having served on active duty in the Armed Forces for more than 180 days or having been discharged or released from active duty in the Armed Forces for a service-connected disability, (2) having been discharged or released from active duty in the Armed Forces at any time during the five-year period ending on the hiring date, and (3) having received unemployment compensation under state or federal law for at least four weeks during the one-year period ending on the hiring date. Disconnected youth group includes any individual certified by the designated local agency as: (1) having attained age 16, but not age 25, on the hiring date, (2) not regularly attending any secondary, technical, or post-secondary school during the six-month period preceding the hiring date, (3) not being regularly employed during the six-month preceding the hiring date, and (4) not being readily employable due to the lack of a sufficient number of basic skills.

Tax-Exempt Organizations and Qualified Veterans. Tax-exempt organizations (other than exempt farmers' cooperatives (¶ 698)), in general, cannot claim the work opportunity credit (Code Sec. 52(c)). However, Code Sec. 501(c) exempt organizations (¶ 602 and ¶ 692) that employ veterans who are members of a targeted group may take advantage of the credit. These organizations must use Form 5884-C to claim the credit. This form is filed separately and should not be attached to any other return filed by the exempt organization. In the case of exempt organizations, the credit is allowed against the employer's Federal Insurance Contribution Act (FICA) tax obligation on wages paid to the veteran within one year of hiring (Code Sec. 3111(e)). However, the liability on the organization's employment tax return is not reduced by the credit; rather, the credit is processed separately and the amount properly claimed is refunded to the exempt organization. This is likely to occur after the filing of the return, so organizations are cautioned not to reduce their FICA obligation on their returns in anticipation of the refund (Notice 2012-13).

1365I. Alcohol Fuels Credit. The alcohol fuels credit is the sum of the alcohol mixture credit, the alcohol credit, the small ethanol producer credit, and the cellulosic biofuel producer credit (Code Sec. 40).[61] The credit, as computed on Form 6478, is a component of the general business credit (¶ 1365), but the credit limitation is calculated separately from the general business credit limitation. The alcohol fuels credit amount may be claimed against both the regular and the alternative minimum tax liability (Code Sec. 38(c)(4)).

> **Comment:** Absent further legislation, the alcohol fuels credit terminated on December 31, 2011.

Alcohol Mixture Credit. The credit amount is equal to 60 cents per gallon of nonethanol alcohol of at least 190 proof (45 cents per gallon of nonethanol alcohol of at least 150 proof but less than 190 proof) utilized in the production of a qualified mixture fuel (alcohol mixed with gasoline or a special fuel) that is used by the producer or that is sold in the producer's trade or business in the United States prior to January 1, 2012. The alcohol mixture credit is 45 cents per gallon of ethanol alcohol of at least 190 proof (33.33 cents per gallon of ethanol alcohol of at least 150 proof but less than 190 proof) (Code Sec. 40(b)(1), (d)(7), and (h)(1)).

Alcohol Credit. The credit amount is equal to 60 cents per gallon of nonethanol alcohol of at least 190 proof (45 cents per gallon of nonethanol alcohol of at least 150 proof but less than 190 proof) not mixed with gasoline or a special fuel (other than any denaturant) that is used by a person as a fuel in a trade or business or that is sold at retail and placed in the fuel tank of the purchaser's vehicle in the United States prior to January 1, 2012. The alcohol credit is 45 cents per gallon of ethanol alcohol of at least 190 proof (33.33 cents per gallon of ethanol alcohol of at least 150 proof but less than 190 proof) not mixed with gasoline or a special fuel (other than any denaturant) (Code Sec. 40(b)(2), (d)(7), and (h)(1)).

Small Ethanol Producer Credit. An eligible small ethanol producer (a producer with a production capacity of up to 60 million gallons of alcohol per year) may claim the small ethanol producer credit of 10 cents per gallon on production of up to 15 million gallons per year of ethanol sold or used for purposes of fuel or added to a fuel mixture in the user's trade or business in the United States prior to January 1, 2012. The 15 million annual limitation of the production of ethanol is determined without regard to any qualified cellulosic biofuel production (see following) (Code Sec. 40(b)(4)(C)). The ethanol must be used by the producer for specific purposes or sold to another person who will use the ethanol for those purposes. Those purposes are: (1) to use in a trade or business to produce an alcohol mixture (other than casual off-farm production), (2) to use as a fuel in a trade or business, or (3) to sell to another person at retail and putting the ethanol in the buyer's fuel tank.

Cellulosic Biofuel Production Credit. The credit amount is equal to $1.01 per gallon of qualified cellulosic biofuel produced by a qualified cellulosic biofuel producer before January 1, 2013 (Code Sec. 40(b)(6)). Cellulosic biofuel is defined as any liquid fuel

References are to Standard Federal Tax Reports; Tax Research Consultant; and Practical Tax Explanations.

[61] ¶ 4302; BUSEXP: 54,100; § 14,205

produced from lignocellulosic or hemicellulosic matter that is available on a renewable or recurring basis and that meets the Environmental Protection Agency registration requirements for fuel and fuel additives established under section 211 of the Clear Air Act. The fuel called "black liquor," as well as crude tall oil (made by reacting acid with black liquor soap), does not qualify for the credit (Code Sec. 40(b)(6)). Renewable sources of lignocellulosic and hemicellulosic matter include energy crops and trees, wood and wood residues, plants, grasses, agricultural residues, fibers, and animal wastes and other waste material, including municipal solid waste. The cellulosic biofuel must be used by the producer for specific purposes or sold to another person who will use the cellulosic biofuel for those purposes. Those purposes are: (1) to use in a trade or business to produce an alcohol mixture (other than casual off-farm production), (2) to use as a fuel in a trade or business, or (3) to sell to another person at retail and putting the ethanol in the buyer's fuel tank. A qualified cellulosic biofuel producer is one that is registered with the IRS as a cellulosic biofuel producer whose production is produced and used in its entirety within the United States. The cellulosic biofuel claimed under Code Sec. 40 cannot also be claimed under Code Sec. 40A as renewable diesel or biodiesel.

Special Rules. Special rules apply for S corporations, partnerships, and other pass-thru entities which include allocation to patrons of farm cooperatives. All taxpayers have the option of electing to not claim the alcohol fuels credit. Any excise tax exemption claimed with respect to alcohol produced for alcohol fuels reduces the amount of the income tax credit. The carryforward period for the alcohol fuels credit is limited to three tax years after the relevant fuel's termination year. An alcohol fuels credit carryforward that is unused at the end of the carryforward period is deductible in the following tax year (Code Sec. 196).

Recapture of Credit. If the alcohol fuels credit is claimed, the producer must pay a tax on each gallon at the original credit rate if the producer separates alcohol from the mixture, uses the alcohol mixture other than as fuel, mixes alcohol on which the credit was allowed for retail sale, uses the alcohol other than as fuel, or, for ethanol fuel or cellulosic biofuel, does not use the fuel for the required purpose (Code Sec. 40(d)(3)). The tax must be reported on Form 720.

1365J. Credit for Increased Research Expenditures. A credit for incremental research expenses (computed on Form 6765) is claimed as one of the components of the general business credit (¶ 1365) (Code Sec. 41).[62] The credit is available for amounts paid or incurred through December 31, 2011 (Code Sec. 41(h)(1)(B)).

> **Comment:** Absent further legislation, the credit for increasing research activities (i.e., the research credit) terminates on December 31, 2011.

The credit is subject to the general business credit's tax liability limitation and carryover rules (¶ 1365). The research credit that remains unused at the end of the carryforward period is allowed as a deduction in the year following the expiration of such period (Code Sec. 196). The does not apply to unused amounts claimed under the reduced research credit election.

Amount of Credit. Unless an election is made to use the alternative simplified credit computation, the research credit is the sum of: (1) 20 percent of the excess of qualified research expenses for the current tax year over a base period amount, (2) 20 percent of the basic research payments made to a qualified organization, and (3) 20 percent of the amounts paid or incurred by a taxpayer in carrying on any trade or business to an energy research consortium for qualified energy research (Code Sec. 41(a)). Special base period adjustments are required where there is an acquisition or disposition of the major portion of a business that paid or incurred research expenses.

Base Amount. For purposes of calculating the credit, the base period amount is the product of the taxpayer's fixed-base percentage and average annual gross receipts for

References are to Standard Federal Tax Reports; Tax Research Consultant; and Practical Tax Explanations.

[62] ¶ 4350; BUSEXP: 54,150; § 13,901

the four tax years preceding the credit period (Code Sec. 41(c)). The base amount may not be less than 50 percent of the qualified research expenses for the credit year. The fixed-base percentage (aggregate qualified research expenses compared to aggregate gross receipts for 1984 through 1988 tax years) may not exceed 16 percent.

Start-Up Company. A start-up company's fixed-base percentage is three percent for each of the first five tax years for which it has qualified research expenses. However, the fixed-base percentage for the sixth through tenth tax years in which qualified research expenses were incurred is a portion of the percentage which qualified research expenses bear to gross receipts for specified preceding years. For subsequent tax years, the fixed-base percentage is the whole percentage that qualified research expenses bear to gross receipts for any five years selected by the taxpayer from the fifth through tenth tax years. The definition of a start-up company includes a taxpayer who has both gross receipts and qualified research expenses for the first time in a tax year that begins after 1983 (Code Sec. 41(c)(3)(B)).

Alternative Simplified Credit. Taxpayers may elect an alternative method to calculate the increased research activities credit amount using an alternative simplified credit (Code Sec. 41(c)(5)). Under the alternative simplified credit method, a taxpayer can claim an amount equal to 14 percent of the amount by which the qualified research expenses exceed 50 percent of the average qualified research expenses for the three preceding tax years (Code Sec. 41(c)(5)). If the taxpayer has no qualified research expenses for any of the preceding three years, then the credit is equal to six percent of the qualified research expenses for the current tax year. If the taxpayer makes the election to use the alternative simplified credit method, the election is effective for succeeding tax years unless revoked with the consent of the IRS.

Deduction for Research and Experimental Expenditures. A taxpayer claiming the credit must reduce the business deduction for research and experimental expenditures (¶ 979) by the amount of the research credit (Code Sec. 280C(c)). Capitalized expenses must also be reduced by the amount of the research credit that exceeds the amount otherwise allowable as a deduction for such expenses. An annual irrevocable election is available to claim a reduced research credit and thereby avoid reducing the research expense deduction (or capital expenditures). Under the election, the research credit must be reduced by the product of the research credit computed in the regular manner and the maximum corporate tax rate.

Qualified Research Expenses. Qualified research expenses for purposes of calculating the credit are the same as those for the business deduction (¶ 979) other than expenses for foreign research, research in the social sciences, arts or humanities, or subsidized research. However, research eligible for the credit is limited to research undertaken to discover information that is technological in nature and intended to be useful in the development of a new or improved business component. Further, the research must relate to elements of a process of experimentation for a functional purpose (i.e., it must relate to a new or improved function, performance, reliability, or quality). Qualified research expenses cover in-house expenses for the taxpayer's own research (i.e., wages, including income from employees' exercise of stock options, for substantially engaging in or directly supervising or supporting research activities, supplies, and computer use charges) and 65 percent of amounts paid or incurred for qualified research done by a person other than an employee of the taxpayer. The percentage is increased to 75 percent of amounts paid or incurred for qualified research performed by a qualified research consortium. A qualified research consortium is a tax-exempt organization under either Code Sec. 501(c)(3) or (c)(6). The consortium must be operating primarily to conduct energy research and it must have at least five unrelated customers, with no single person accounting for more than 50 percent of the revenues of the organization.

Qualified Energy Research Expenditures. The 20-percent credit amount applies to expenditures to an energy research consortium for qualified energy research only. The percent limitation placed on outside research has been repealed for purposes of energy research. Amounts paid or incurred for any energy research conducted outside of the United States, Puerto Rico, or any possession of the United States cannot be taken into account in determining the 20 percent of amounts paid or incurred by a taxpayer in carrying on any trade or business during the tax year to an energy research consortium under Code Sec. 41(a)(3) (Code Sec. 41(f)(6)(C)).

Special Rule for Pass-Thru Entities. For individuals with interests in unincorporated businesses, partners, trust or estate beneficiaries, or S corporation shareholders, any allowable pass-through of the credit cannot exceed the amount of tax attributable to the individual's taxable income allocable to that individual's interest in the entity (Code Sec. 41(g)).

1365K. Low-Income Housing Credit. A nonrefundable income tax credit is available on a per-unit basis for low-income units in qualified low-income buildings in qualified low-income housing projects (Code Sec. 42).[63] The owner of a qualified low-income housing project that is constructed, rehabilitated, or acquired may claim the credit in each of 10 tax years in an amount equal to the applicable credit percentage appropriate to the type of project, multiplied by the qualified basis allocable to the low-income units in each qualified low-income building.

The credit is claimed over a 10-year period that begins with the tax year in which the project is placed in service or, at the taxpayer's election, the next tax year (but only if the building is a qualified low-income building as of the close of the first year of such period). The first-year credit is reduced to reflect the time during the year that any low-income units are unoccupied. If the reduction is made, a credit is allowed in the eleventh year in an amount equal to the reduction. The credit is calculated on Form 8586 and, as a component of the general business credit, is subject to the general business credit's tax liability limitation and carryover rules (¶ 1365).[64] The credit is denied to otherwise qualified buildings unless the owner of the building is subject to an enforceable 30-year low-income use agreement with the housing agency (Code Sec. 42(h)(6)). However, the credit is not limited or disallowed by the rules applicable to activities not entered into for profit (¶ 1195) (Reg. § 1.42-4).[65]

Usually, the applicable credit rates are the appropriate percentages issued by the IRS for the month in which the building is placed in service. Different percentages are provided for new construction or rehabilitation, subsidized construction or rehabilitation, and the acquisition of existing housing (¶ 86). An irrevocable election is available to determine the credit percentage applicable to a building in advance of the date that it is placed in service.

Generally, rehabilitation expenditures are treated as expenditures for a separate new building provided that the expenditures are allocable to, or substantially benefit, low-income units and that they are incurred during any 24-month period and the greater of $6,000 per low-income unit or 20 percent of the adjusted basis of the building; the limits are $3,000 and 10 percent of adjusted basis for buildings that are allocated a credit dollar amount on or before July 30, 2008. A qualified low-income housing project is any project for residential rental property that meets requirements for low-income tenant occupancy, gross rent restrictions, state credit authority, and IRS certification. The project must continue to meet these requirements for 15 years or recapture of a portion of the credit may be required using Form 8611. A qualified low-income building must be subject to MACRS depreciation.

State Allocations. The low-income housing credit can be claimed for any tax year, but generally only to the extent that the owner of a qualified low-income building receives a housing credit allocation from a state or local housing credit agency (Code Sec. 42(h)).

1365M. Disabled Access Credit. An eligible small business is entitled to a nonrefundable income tax credit for expenditures incurred to make a business accessi-

References are to Standard Federal Tax Reports; Tax Research Consultant; and Practical Tax Explanations.

[63] ¶ 4380; BUSEXP: 54,200; § 14,420

[64] ¶ 4380; BUSEXP: 54,224; § 14,420

[65] ¶ 4384A; BUSEXP: 54,218; § 14,420

ble to disabled individuals (Code Sec. 44).[66] The amount of the credit is 50 percent of the amount of eligible access expenditures for a year that exceed $250 but that do not exceed $10,250. The credit is computed on Form 8826 and, as a component of the general business credit, is subject to the tax liability limitation and the carryover rules (¶ 1365). Any unused credit remaining at the end of the carryforward period is lost. No other deduction or credit is permitted for any amount for which a disabled access credit is allowed.

Eligibility. An eligible small business is any person that elects to claim the disabled access credit that had gross receipts (less returns and allowances) for the preceding tax year that did not exceed $1 million or that employed no more than 30 full-time employees during the preceding tax year. Eligible access expenditures include reasonable and necessary amounts paid or incurred by an eligible small business for the purpose of enabling the business to comply with the requirements of the Americans with Disabilities Act of 1990.

Eligible expenditures also include expenditures: (1) for the purpose of removing architectural, communication, physical, or transportation barriers that prevent a business from being accessible to, or usable by, disabled individuals (other than amounts for new construction); (2) to provide qualified interpreters or other effective methods of making aurally delivered materials available to hearing-impaired individuals; (3) to provide qualified readers, taped texts, and other effective methods of making visually delivered materials available to visually impaired individuals; (4) to acquire or modify equipment or devices for disabled individuals; or (5) to provide other similar services, modifications, materials, or equipment.

1365N. Credit for Electricity Produced from Renewable Sources. A credit is available for the domestic production of electricity from qualified energy resources at a qualified facility, if the electricity is sold to an unrelated third party (Code Sec. 45).[67] In addition, the credit is also allowed for the sale of certain refined coal produced within the United States at a qualified refined coal production facility, but only if sold to an unrelated person. The credit for refined coal production, however, may not be claimed if production from the facility was eligible for the nonconventional fuel source credit for any tax year (¶ 1365BB).

Credit Amounts and Limitations. The credit amount for electricity produced in a qualified wind, closed-loop biomass, geothermal energy, or solar facility is 2.2 cents per kilowatt hour in 2012. Electricity produced in qualified open-loop biomass, small irrigation power, landfill gas, trash combustion, or qualified hydroelectric facilities generate a credit amount of 1.1 cents per kilowatt-hour in 2012. The credit amount for production of refined coal in 2012 is $6.475 per ton and for Indian coal it is $2.267 per ton (Notice 2012-35).

The credit is reduced in the same ratio as the excess of the reference price for the calendar year in which the sale occurs over eight cents bears to three cents. The reference price and the eight-cent threshold amount are each adjusted annually by multiplying them by an inflation adjustment factor for the calendar year in which the sale occurs. For 2012, the inflation adjustment factor for qualified energy resources and refined coal is 1.4799 and for Indian coal is 1.1336. The reference price for electricity produced from wind is 5.31 cents per kilowatt-hour; for refined coal production the reference price for 2002 is 31.90 and for 2012 is $58.49 per ton; the reference prices for electricity produced from closed-loop biomass, open-looped biomass, geothermal energy, solar energy, small irrigation power, municipal solid waste, and qualified hydropower production facilities have not been determined for calendar year 2012. The renewable electricity production credit is not subject to a phaseout in 2012 (Notice 2012-35).

The credit is claimed on Form 8835 and is one of the components of the general business credit (¶ 1365). The credit limitation for the renewable energy source credit is

References are to Standard Federal Tax Reports; Tax Research Consultant; and Practical Tax Explanations.

[66] ¶ 4400; BUSEXP: 54,350; § 14,101

[67] ¶ 4410; BUSEXP: 54,550; § 14,215

determined separately from the other general business credits and, in the calculation of the tax liability limitation, the tentative minimum tax is to be treated as zero. The result of this treatment is that the renewable energy source credit amounts are available to be used against both the regular and the alternative minimum tax liabilities for the current year (Code Sec. 38(c)(4)).

Qualified Energy Facilities. The credit for electricity from renewable energy sources can be claimed over a five-or 10-year period depending on the facility. The following facilities qualify for the five-year period: (1) open-loop biomass facilities that use agricultural livestock waste nutrients originally placed in service after October 22, 2004, and on or before August 8, 2005; (2) open-loop biomass facilities that do not use agricultural livestock waste nutrients originally placed in service before January 1, 2005; (3) geothermal facilities originally placed in service after October 22, 2004, and on or before August 8, 2005; (4) solar facilities originally placed in service after October 22, 2004, and on or before August 8, 2005; (5) small irrigation power facilities originally placed in service after October 22, 2004, and on or before August 8, 2005; (6) landfill gas facilities originally placed in service after October 22, 2004, and on or before August 8, 2005; and (7) trash combustion facilities (or certain new units placed in service in connection with an existing trash combustion facility) originally placed in service after October 22, 2004, and on or before August 8, 2005.

The following facilities qualify to claim the credit for the 10-year period for electricity from a renewable energy source: (1) wind facilities originally placed in service after December 31, 1993, and before January 1, 2013; (2) open-loop biomass facilities that use agricultural livestock waste nutrients originally placed in service after August 8, 2005, and before January 1, 2014; (3) open-loop biomass facilities that do not use agricultural livestock waste nutrients if placed in service on or after January 1, 2005, and before January 1, 2014; (4) closed-loop biomass facilities modified to use closed-loop biomass to co-fire with coal, other biomass, or both originally placed in service before January 1, 2014; (5) any other closed-loop biomass facilities originally placed in service after December 31, 1992, and before January 1, 2014; (6) geothermal facilities originally placed in service after August 8, 2005, and before January 1, 2014; (7) solar facilities originally placed in service after August 8, 2005, and before January 1, 2014; (8) small irrigation power facilities originally placed in service after August 8, 2005, and before October 3, 2008; (9) landfill gas facilities originally placed in service after August 8, 2005, and before January 1, 2014; (10) trash combustion facilities (or new units placed in service in connection with an existing trash combustion facility) originally placed in service after August 8, 2005, and before January 1, 2014; (11) refined coal production facilities placed in service after October 22, 2004, and before January 1, 2012; (12) certain hydroelectric and nonhydroelectric dams placed in service on or before August 8, 2005 (credit is determined by reference to electricity attributable to improvements placed in service after August 8, 2005, and before January 1, 2014); and (13) marine and hydrokinetic renewable energy facility placed in service after October 2, 2008, and before January 1, 2014 (Code Sec. 45(d)). In the case of Indian coal, the credit may be claimed over a seven-year period from an Indian coal production facility placed in service after January 1, 2006, and before January 1, 2009.

1365O. Empowerment Zone Credit (Expired). Employers located in empowerment zones are entitled to a 20-percent wage credit on the first $15,000 of annual wages paid to residents of the empowerment zone (¶ 999) (Code Sec. 1396). The empowerment zone credit is available for wages paid to eligible employees through the end of calendar year 2011 (Code Sec. 1391(d)(1)(A)(i)).[68] A similar credit is allowed to employers doing business in renewal communities (¶ 1365P). These credits are claimed on Form 8844 and, although part of the general business credit (¶ 1365), they are not a part of the general business credit tax liability limitation computation. The credit amounts are calculated separately, as are the yearly limitations on the amount of each credit that may be claimed against a taxpayer's tax liability.

References are to Standard Federal Tax Reports; Tax Research Consultant; and Practical Tax Explanations.

[68] ¶ 32,393; BUSEXP: 54,650; § 13,810

1365P. Renewal Community Employment Credit (Expired). The same type of employment credit as offered to employers in empowerment zones (¶ 1365O) was extended to employers doing business in renewal communities before December 31, 2009. The employers were entitled to a 15-percent wage credit on the first $10,000 of annual wages paid to residents of the renewal community (¶ 999C) (Code Sec. 1400H).[69] These credits were claimed on Form 8844 and, although part of the general business credit (¶ 1365), they were not a part of the general business credit tax liability limitation computation.

1365Q. Indian Employment Credit (Expired). A nonrefundable credit is available to employers for certain wages and health insurance costs paid or incurred in a tax year that begins on or before December 31, 2011, for qualified full- or part-time employees who are enrolled members of an Indian tribe or their spouses (Code Sec. 45A).[70] The credit is equal to 20 percent of the excess of eligible employee qualified wages and health insurance costs paid or incurred during a tax year over the amount of these costs paid or incurred during 1993. However, the credit is available only for the first $20,000 of qualified wages and health insurance costs paid for each qualified employee. Also, no wage is allowed for the portion of wages equal to the amount of the credit. Qualified wages are wages paid or incurred by an employer for services performed by a qualified employee excluding wages for which a work opportunity credit (¶ 1365G) is allowed. Qualified health insurance costs are costs paid or incurred by an employer for a qualified employee, except for costs paid under a salary reduction agreement.

> **Comment:** Absent further legislation, the Indian employment credit terminated on December 31, 2011.

Eligibility. An individual who receives more than 50 percent of wages from services performed in the trade or business of the employer is a qualified employee for any period *only* if: (1) the individual was an enrolled member of an Indian tribe or the spouse thereof; (2) substantially all of the services performed during the period by the employee for the employer were performed within an Indian reservation; and (3) the principal place of abode of the employee while performing the services was on or near the reservation on which the services are performed. Ineligible employees include employees who receive wages exceeding $30,000 as adjusted for inflation ($45,000 in 2011) (Code Sec. 45A(c)(3)).

The credit is calculated on Form 8845 and is claimed as one of the components of the general business credit (¶ 1365). Thus, it was subject to the tax liability limitation and carryover rules. Any unused credit at the end of the carryforward period is allowed as a deduction in the year following the expiration of the period (Code Sec. 196).

1365R. Credit for Employer-Paid Social Security Taxes on Employee Cash Tips (FICA Tip Credit). An employer in the food and beverage industry may claim a nonrefundable income tax credit for a portion of the employer's social security and Medicare taxes (FICA taxes) paid or incurred on employee tips (Code Sec. 45B).[71] Employee tip income is treated as employer-provided wages for purposes of Federal Insurance Contributions Act (FICA) taxes (Code Sec. 3121(q)). The credit is equal to the employer's FICA obligation of an employee attributable to tips in excess of those tips treated as wages for purposes of satisfying the minimum wage provisions of the Fair Labor Standards Act. No credit may be claimed for the employer's portion of FICA taxes on the tips used to meet the Federal minimum wage rate. For purposes of calculating the credit, the minimum wage rate has been permanently established at the amount in effect on January 1, 2007, or $5.15 per hour.

The credit is allowed for tips received from customers in connection with the providing, delivering, or serving of food or beverages for consumption if the tipping of employees delivering or serving food or beverages by customers is customary. The credit is available whether or not the employee reported the tips and regardless of where the services were performed. The employer may not deduct any amount consid-

References are to Standard Federal Tax Reports; Tax Research Consultant; and Practical Tax Explanations.

[69] ¶ 32,453; BUSEXP: 57,204.10; § 13,810

[70] ¶ 4430; BUSEXP: 54,700; § 13,815

[71] ¶ 4450; BUSEXP: 54,400; § 14,005

ered in determining this credit to claim any other tax benefit. An election may be made to have this credit not apply.

The credit is claimed on Form 8846. The FICA tip credit is a component of the general business credit (¶ 1365). For purposes of determining the amount of the FICA tip credit that may be claimed in the current tax year and any credit carrybacks from the current tax year, the tentative minimum tax is considered zero and the credit amounts is not subject to the general business credit tax liability limitation rule but is calculated separately (Code Sec. 38(c)(4)(A)). The result of setting the minimum tax at zero and reducing the net tax liability allows taxpayers to claim the maximum amount of the FICA tip credit against both their regular and the alternative minimum tax liabilities. Any credit that remains unused at the end of the carryover period is lost.

1365S. Credit for Clinical Testing Expenses for Certain Drugs for Rare Diseases and Conditions (Orphan Drug Credit). A credit, commonly known as the orphan drug credit, is allowed for an amount equal to 50 percent, subject to limitations, of the clinical testing expenses to develop drugs to treat rare diseases and conditions (Code Sec. 45C).[72] The credit is claimed on Form 8820 and, as a component of the general business credit, is subject to the general business credit's tax liability limitation and the carryover rules (¶ 1365).

1365T. New Markets Tax Credit. The new markets tax credit was created to increase investments in low-income communities. The credit is available for investments made in a qualified community development entity (CDE) before 2012, and is equal to five percent of the investment for the first three allowance dates and six percent of the investment for the next four allowance dates (Code Sec. 45D(a)).[73] The total credit available is equal to 39 percent of the investment over seven years. Active involvement of the low-income communities is required with strict penalties if the investment is terminated before seven years.

The new markets tax credit is a component of the general business credit, subject to its tax liability limitation and carryover rules (¶ 1365). The credit is calculated on Form 8874. Any unused credit at the end of the carryforward period is allowed as a deduction in the following tax year under Code Sec. 196. Any termination event requires recapture of the credit amount claimed, treated as an addition to tax in the termination year. Any amount carried forward or carried back will need to be adjusted accordingly. Finally, the claiming the new markets tax credit necessitates an adjustment in the basis of the investment in the CDE.

1365U. Small Employer Pension Plan Startup Costs Credit. Eligible small businesses may claim a credit for qualified startup costs incurred in establishing and administering an eligible employer benefit plan for their employees (Code Sec. 45E).[74] The credit amount equals 50 percent of the qualified startup costs incurred to create or maintain a new employee retirement plan. The credit is limited to $500 in any tax year and it may be claimed for qualified costs incurred in each of the three years beginning with the tax year in which the plan becomes effective. The credit is part of, and subject to, the tax liability limitation and carryover rules of the general business credit (¶ 1365). Form 8881 is used to calculate and claim the credit.

Eligibility. An eligible small business is one that has not employed more than 100 employees who received at least $5,000 of compensation from that employer in the preceding year. However, a business is not eligible if during the preceding three tax years it established or maintained a qualified employer plan with respect to which contributions were made, or benefits were accrued, for substantially the same employees as are in the new qualified employer plan. An eligible plan includes a new qualified defined benefit plan, defined contribution plan (including a 401(k) plan), savings incentive match plan for employees (SIMPLE), or simplified employee pension (SEP) plan. Qualified startup costs are any ordinary and necessary expenses incurred to establish or

References are to Standard Federal Tax Reports; Tax Research Consultant; and Practical Tax Explanations.

[72] ¶ 4470; BUSEXP: 54,450; § 14,405

[73] ¶ 4480; BUSEXP: 54,900; § 14,430

[74] ¶ 4491; BUSEXP: 54,950; § 14,010

administer an eligible plan or to educate employees about retirement planning. Qualified costs are not deductible to the extent that they are effectively offset by the tax credit. The credit is limited to the first $1,000 of qualified costs incurred in the first year the new plan is effective and in each of the following two years. The employer may elect to take the credit in the year immediately preceding the first year the new plan is effective or elect not to claim the credit for a tax year.

1365V. Employer-Provided Child Care Credit. Businesses may claim a tax credit for qualified expenses related to either an employer-provided child care center or a service related to locating qualified child care for tax years beginning before January 1, 2013 (Code Sec. 45F).[75] The amount of the credit for a given tax year is the sum of 25 percent of the qualified child care expenditures and 10 percent of the qualified resource and referral expenditures. The maximum amount of credit allowed in any given year is $150,000. Form 8882 is used to calculate and claim the credit. The credit is part of the general business credit and is subject to its tax liability limitation and carryover rules (¶ 1365). No double benefit is allowed for expenditures used to claim the employer-provided child care credit and the basis of the qualified child care facility must be reduced by the amount of the credit taken. In addition, there is no deduction allowed in the year following the final year of any carryforward of unused employer-provided child care credit. If a qualified child care facility ceases to operate as a qualified child care facility (or there is a change in ownership), the business may have to recapture part or all of the credit claimed. In the event of recapture, the tax liability of that tax year must be increased by an amount equal to the applicable percentage times the aggregate decrease in the general business credit as if all previously allowed employer-provided child care credits with respect to the employer's child care facility had been zero (Code Sec. 45F(d)(2)(A)). Any carryforward or carryback amounts of the employer-provided child care credit must also be adjusted.

Qualifying Facility. A qualified child care facility is a facility whose "principal use" is to provide child care assistance and that meets the requirements of all applicable laws and regulations of the state and local government in which it is located, including the licensing requirements applicable to a child care facility. The principal use requirement is waived for facilities located in the principal residence of the operator of the facility. Additional requirements include that: (1) enrollment must be open to the employees of the taxpayer during the tax year; (2) at least 30 percent of the enrollees at the facility are the dependents of the taxpayer's employees, in the event the facility is the principal trade or business of the taxpayer; and (3) the use of the child care facility cannot discriminate in favor of highly compensated employees (¶ 2190A).

Qualifying Expenditures. Qualified child care expenditures are any amounts paid or incurred: (1) to acquire, construct, rehabilitate, or expand property which is to used as a qualified child care facility of the taxpayer; (2) for the operating costs of a qualified child care facility, including the costs related to the training of employees, scholarship programs, and providing increased compensation for employees with high levels of child care training; or (3) under a contract with a qualified child care facility to provide child care services to the taxpayer's employees. Costs associated with item (1) must qualify for depreciation or amortization and must not be the principal residence of the taxpayer. Expenses for items (2) and (3) cannot exceed the fair market value of such care. Further, qualified child care resources and referral expenditures are expenses paid or incurred by the taxpayer under a contract to provide child care services to the taxpayer's employees. These expenditures cannot discriminate in favor of highly compensated employees.

1365W. Railroad Track Maintenance Credit (Expired). An income tax credit is available to small- and mid-sized railroad companies for qualified railroad track maintenance expenses (Code Sec. 45G).[76] The credit is equal to 50 percent of the qualified expenses paid or incurred by an eligible taxpayer before January 1, 2012. The credit

[75] ¶ 4493; BUSEXP: 55,000; § 14,015

[76] ¶ 4495; BUSEXP: 55,050; § 14,415

cannot exceed $3,500 multiplied by the number of miles of railroad track owned or leased by the eligible taxpayer as of the close of the tax year. Eligible taxpayers are Class II and Class III railroad companies and persons who operate over their rail lines or provide related rail services. The credit is a part of the general business credit but is not subject to the tax liability limitation rule. The railroad track maintenance credit is instead allowed against the sum of the regular income tax and alternative minimum tax liabilities (Code Sec. 38(c)). The credit is subject to the general business credit's carryover rules (¶ 1365). No provision is made for deduction of unused credits at the end of the carryforward period or if the taxpayer ceases to exist. The credit is claimed on Form 8900.

1365X. Biodiesel Fuels Credit (Expired). The biodiesel fuels credit was created to encourage the production and use of biodiesel fuels (Code Sec. 40A).[77] The credit is the sum of the biodiesel mixture credit, the biodiesel credit, and the small agri-biodiesel producers credit. The biodiesel mixture and the biodiesel credit amounts are increased to $1.00 for each gallon of biodiesel used in the production of a qualified biodiesel fuel that is sold or used in the course of a trade or business in the United States. This increase matches the credit amount of $1.00 per gallon should either the biodiesel or the biodiesel mixture fuel meet the definition of an agri-biodiesel fuel.

> **Comment:** Absent further legislation, the biodiesel fuels credit expires on December 31, 2011.

Biodiesel fuels are defined as monoalkyl esters of long chain fatty acids derived from plant or animal matter that meet the requirements for fuels or fuel additives imposed by the Environmental Protection Agency. Biodiesel fuel mixture is defined as biodiesel mixed with diesel fuel, determined without regard to any use of kerosene. Agri-biodiesel is biodiesel derived solely from virgin oils, including esters derived from virgin vegetable oils from corn, soybeans, sunflower seeds, cottonseeds, canola, crambe, rapeseeds, safflowers, flaxseeds, rice bran, and mustard seeds, camelina, and animal fats. Tax penalties are imposed if the credit for biodiesel mixture is claimed and the fuels are later separated. The credit is part of the general business credit and is subject to its tax liability limitation and carryover rules (¶ 1365). Any unused credit at the end of the carryforward period, or if the taxpayer ceases to exist, may be claimed as a deduction (Code Sec. 196). The credit may be claimed for the fuels produced and sold in the United States before January 1, 2012, on Form 8864 (Code Sec. 40A(g)).

Small Agri-Biodiesel Producers. An additional amount is added to the biodiesel fuels credit for qualified small agri-biodiesel producers (Code Sec. 40A(b)(4)). The credit amount is 10 cents per gallon of qualified agri-biodiesel fuel produced by a qualified agri-biodiesel fuel producer in the United States. A qualified agri-biodiesel fuel producer's production of qualified agri-biodiesel cannot exceed 15 million gallon per year. This credit parallels the credit requirements for small alcohol fuel producers under Code Sec. 40 (¶ 1365I).

1365Y. Low Sulfur Diesel Fuel Production Credit (Expired). Qualified small business refiners could claim a credit for qualified expenditures to produce low sulfur diesel fuel (Code Sec. 45H).[78] The credit was equal to five cents per gallon of qualified low sulfur diesel fuel produced during the tax year at a qualified facility. The maximum credit amount could not exceed 25 percent of the qualifying costs incurred for such facility less the aggregate credit amounts determined in prior years with respect to such facility. The low sulfur diesel fuel credit is a component of the general business credit and is subject to its tax liability limitation and carryover rules (¶ 1365). Qualified taxpayers that elect to claim this credit use Form 8896. No provision under Code Sec. 196 is made to deduct this credit if there remains any unused credit amount at the end of the carryforward period or the taxpayer ceases to exist.

Eligibility. A small business refiner was defined as a refiner of crude oil that did not employ more than 1,500 individuals on any day during the tax year and its average daily

References are to Standard Federal Tax Reports; Tax Research Consultant; and Practical Tax Explanations.

[77] ¶ 4310; BUSEXP: 55,100; § 14,220

[78] ¶ 4497; BUSEXP: 55,150; § 14,225

refinery production of the one-year period ending on December 31, 2002, did not exceed 205,000 barrels. Qualifying costs are those costs paid or incurred at the facility during the applicable period for purposes of compliance with the applicable Environmental Protection Agency (EPA) regulations. Qualifying costs included but were not limited to: (1) expenditures for the construction of new process operation units, (2) expenditures for the dismantling and reconstruction of existing process units to be used in the production of low sulfur diesel fuel, (3) costs of associated adjacent or offsite equipment, and (4) engineering, construction period interest, and sitework expenses. The applicable period for paying of incurring such qualifying costs for such facility began on January 1, 2003, and ended on the earlier of one year after the date the taxpayer must comply with EPA regulations or December 31, 2009. The qualifying low sulfur diesel fuel must have contained no more sulfur than 15 parts per million and comply with the EPA's Highway Diesel Fuel Sulfur Control Requirements.

Phaseout and Limitations. The credit amount was phased out for qualified refiners whose production exceeds 155,000 barrels, and the credit amount was completely phased out when production equaled 205,000 barrels. Deductions otherwise available to qualified refiners during the tax year were reduced by the amount of credit determined for that tax year (Code Sec. 280C(d)). Finally, cooperatives that owned a qualified small business refinery could elect to apportion the credit to its patrons, but the election, if made, was irrevocable.

1365Z. Distilled Spirits Excise Tax Carrying Credit. An income tax credit is available for wholesalers, qualified distillers and importers that carry distilled spirits subject to excise taxes in inventory (Code Sec. 5011).[79] The credit amount is calculated to generally equal the approximate interest charges that the eligible taxpayer would incur while holding the distilled spirits in inventory. The credit is a component of the general business credit and is subject to its tax liability limitation and carryover rules (¶ 1365). The credit is claimed on Form 8906.

1365AA. Advanced Nuclear Power Facilities Production Credit. A business tax credit is available to taxpayers that produce electricity from an advanced nuclear power facility (Code Sec. 45J).[80] The credit is equal to 1.8 cents times the number of kilowatt hours of electricity produced at a qualifying advanced nuclear power facility and sold to an unrelated person during the tax year. It may only be claimed during the eight-year period beginning on the date the facility was originally placed in service. A qualifying advanced nuclear power facility is any advanced nuclear facility owned by the taxpayer that uses nuclear energy to produce electricity and was placed in service after August 8, 2005, and before January 1, 2021. Any nuclear facility with a reactor design (or a substantially similar design of comparable capacity) approved before 1994 by the Nuclear Regulatory Commission is not a qualifying advanced nuclear power facility. Certain limitations restrict the amount of credit that may be claimed in any tax year, including that the credit is part of the general business credit and as such is subject to the tax liability limitation and carryover rules (¶ 1365).

1365BB. Nonconventional Source Fuel Production Credit. A tax credit is allowed for the domestic production of qualified fuels derived from nonconventional sources produced by the taxpayer within the United States or U.S. possession and sold to unrelated persons (Code Sec. 45K).[81] The credit is available for coke or coke gas produced in facilities placed in service before January 1, 1993, or after June 30, 1998, and before January 1, 2010, that is sold during the period beginning after the later of January 1, 2006, or the year the facility is placed in service but no later than four years after the start of such period. The credit is no longer available for fuel produced from biomass and liquid, gaseous, or solid synthetic fuels.

The credit is a component of the general business credit and is subject to the ordering, tax liability limitation, and carryover rules of the general business credit (¶ 1365). The credit amount is reduced pro rata by any grants, tax-exempt bonds and

References are to Standard Federal Tax Reports; Tax Research Consultant; and Practical Tax Explanations.

[79] ¶ 34,965; BUSEXP: 55,250

[80] ¶ 4500A; BUSEXP: 55,300; § 14,235

[81] ¶ 4050; BUSEXP: 54,500; § 14,240

subsidized energy financing the project receives. No double benefits are allowed as the credit amount is reduced by any credit amount claimed as an energy credit and/or enhanced oil recovery credit. The credit is claimed on Form 8907.

Credit Amount. The credit amount is equal to $3 multiplied by the barrel-of-oil equivalent of qualified fuels produced and sold by the taxpayer to an unrelated third party. The $3 amount is annually inflation adjusted (Code Sec. 45K(a) and (b)(2)). The inflation adjustment factor for calendar year 2011 is 1.1712, and thus the inflation-adjusted credit amount per barrel-of-oil equivalent sold in 2011 is $3.51 (Notice 2012-30). The inflation factor is determined and published no later than April 1st for the preceding calendar year. For fuel other than coke or coke gas, the credit amount was reduced by an amount which bears the same ratio to the credit amount as the reference price for the calendar year exceeding $23.50 bears to $6, adjusted for inflation.

1365CC. Energy Efficient Home Credit. Eligible contractors who build an energy-efficient home acquired by a person for use as a residence before 2012 can claim an income tax credit of up to $2,000 (Code Sec. 45L).[82] Eligible contractors also include manufacturers of energy-efficient manufactured homes. A residence qualifies as an energy-efficient home if it is located in the United States and is certified to have an annual heating and/or cooling consumption at least 50-percent less than a comparable house with at least 10 percent of the 50 percent saving coming from the building envelope. A reduced credit of $1,000 is available for homes with a heating or cooling consumption at least 30-percent less than a comparable house and for homes with the Energy Star label. This credit is a component of and subject to the tax liability limitation and carryover rules of the general business credit (¶ 1365). The credit is claimed on Form 8908.

1365DD. Energy Efficient Appliance Credit. An income tax credit is available to manufacturers of energy-efficient home appliances for tax years after 2005 and before 2012 (Code Sec. 45M).[83] The total amount of credit available for a tax year is equal to the sum of the credit amount separately calculated for each type of qualified energy-efficient appliance (dishwashers, clothes washers, and refrigerators) produced by the taxpayer during the calendar year ending with or within that tax year. The credit amount for each type of qualified appliance is determined by multiplying the eligible production for that type of appliance by the type's applicable amount. The maximum credit amount is reduced each subsequent year by the amount of credit, if any, claimed in the prior year. In addition, there are sublimits for each type of home appliance. This credit is a component of and subject to the tax liability limitation and carryover rules of the general business credit (¶ 1365). The credit is claimed on Form 8909.

1365FF. Employee Retention Credit. An employee retention credit is available for qualified individuals hired after February 3, 2010, and before January 1, 2011 (Act Sec. 102 of the Hiring Incentives to Restore Employment Act (P.L. 111-147)).[84] Qualified employers who retain qualified individuals as employees for 52 consecutive weeks can increase any current year general business credit by up to $1,000 per retained worker. Thus, the additional general business credit amount cannot be claimed until after the retained worker remains employed for 52 consecutive weeks. Qualified employees are individuals who:

- certified that he or she has not been employed for more than 40 hours during the 60-day period ending on the date that he or she was hired,
- was not hired to replace another employee unless that employee separated from the employer voluntarily or for cause, and
- is not a related individual as defined in Code Sec. 51(i)(1).

1365GG. Mine Rescue Team Training Credit (Expired). Eligible employers are entitled to a credit for mine rescue team training expenses incurred in tax years beginning after December 21, 2005, but before January 1, 2012. The credit amount is

References are to Standard Federal Tax Reports; Tax Research Consultant; and Practical Tax Explanations.

[82] ¶ 4500I; BUSEXP: 55,350; § 14,315

[83] ¶ 4500N; BUSEXP: 55,400; § 14,320.05

[84] ¶ 4250; BUSEXP: 54,070; § 13,835

equal to the lesser of: (1) 20 percent of the training program costs paid or incurred during the tax year for each qualified mine rescue team employee, including wages paid while attending the training program, or (2) $10,000 (Code Sec. 45N).[85] An eligible employer is any taxpayer that employs individuals as miners in underground mines located in the United States. A qualified mine rescue team employee is a full-time miner employee who is eligible for more than six months of the tax year to serve as a mine rescue team member because he or she has met certain training requirements. To prevent any double benefits that may arise from the claiming of this credit, eligible mine employers cannot claim as a wage the amount of any mine rescue team training credit determined for the tax year (Code Sec. 280C). The mine rescue team training credit is claimed on Form 8923 and is a component of the general business credit subject to its tax liability limitation and carryover rules (¶ 1365).

1365HH. Agricultural Chemicals Security Credit. For qualified chemical security expenditures paid or incurred after May 22, 2008, and before 2013, eligible agricultural businesses may claim the agricultural chemical security credit (Code Sec. 45O).[86] The credit amount is equal to 30 percent of the qualified chemical security expenditures. The credit limit is $100,000 per facility reduced by the aggregate of amount of this credit claimed in the previous five years. In addition, each taxpayer has an annual limit of $2 million. The taxpayer is defined to include controlled groups under rules set out in Code Sec. 41(f). The taxpayer's deductible expenses are reduced by the amount of credit claimed. In addition, the credit is a component of the general business credit subject to its tax liability limitation and carryover rules (¶ 1365). The credit is claimed on Form 8931.

Eligibility. Eligible agricultural businesses are businesses that: (1) sell agricultural products, including certain specified agricultural chemicals, at retail predominantly to farmers and ranchers or (2) manufacture, formulate, distribute, or aerially apply specified agricultural chemicals. Qualified chemical expenditures are amounts paid or incurred for: (1) employee security training and background checks, (2) limitations and prevention of access to controls of specified agricultural chemicals stored at a facility, (3) tagging, locking tax valves, and chemical additives to prevent the theft of specified agricultural chemicals or to render such chemicals unfit for illegal use, (4) protection of the perimeter of specified agricultural chemicals, (5) installation of security lighting, cameras, recording equipment and intrusion detection sensors, (6) implementation of measures to increase computer or computer network securities, (7) conducting security vulnerability assessments, (8) implementing a site security plan, and (9) other measures provided for by regulation.

1365II. Employer Credit for Differential Wage Payments to Military Personnel (Expired). Eligible employers making differential wage payments after June 17, 2008, but before January 1, 2012, can claim a credit equal to 20 percent of eligible payments for each employee (Code Sec. 45P).[87] An eligible differential wage payment is a payment that: (1) must be made by an employer to an individual with respect to any period during which the individual is performing services in the uniformed armed forces on active duty for a period of more than 30 days and (2) must represent all or a portion of the wages that the individual would have received from the employer if the individual were performing services for the employer (Code Sec. 3401) (¶ 895 and ¶ 2609). The differential wage payment is limited to $20,000 per employee paid during the tax year. A qualified employee is an individual who has been employed by the employer for a period of 91 days immediately preceding the period for which any differential wage payments were made. A qualified employer is a small business employer that: (1) employs an average of fewer than 50 individuals on any day during the tax year and (2) provides differential wage payments to every qualified employee under a written plan. The deduction for wages is reduced by the amount of differential wage payment credit claimed as well as reducing any other credit related to compensation paid to eligible

References are to Standard Federal Tax Reports; Tax Research Consultant; and Practical Tax Explanations.

[85] ¶ 4500S; BUSEXP: 55,450; § 14,435

[86] ¶ 4500W; BUSEXP: 55,550; § 14,445

[87] ¶ 4500Z; BUSEXP: 55,500; § 14,020

employees. The differential wage payment credit is a component of the general business credit subject to its tax liability limitation and carryover rules (¶ 1365). The credit is claimed on Form 8932.

Comment: Absent further legislation; the employer credit for differential wage payments to military personnel terminates on December 31, 2011.

1365JJ. Carbon Dioxide Capture Credit. Taxpayers may claim a credit for the capture and transport of carbon dioxide from an industrial source after October 3, 2008, for use in enhanced oil recovery or for permanent storage in a geologic formation (Code Sec. 45Q).[88] The credit is $20 per metric ton of qualified carbon dioxide that is captured by the taxpayer at a qualified facility and disposed of in secure geological storage, and $10 per metric ton of qualified carbon dioxide that is captured by the taxpayer at a qualified facility, used as a tertiary injectant in a qualified enhanced oil or natural gas recovery project, and disposed of in secure geologic storage. The $10 and $20 credit amounts are adjusted for inflation. The inflation adjusted amounts for calendar year 2012 are $20.88 per metric ton of qualified CO2 under Code Sec. 45Q(a)(1) and $10.44 per metric ton of qualified CO2 under Code Sec. 45Q(a)(2) (Notice 2012-42).

The credit is recaptured with respect to any qualified carbon dioxide that ceases to be captured, disposed of, or used as a tertiary injectant in accordance with the credit requirements (Code Sec. 45Q(d)(6)). The credit is attributable to the person that captures and physically or contractually ensures the disposal, or the use as a tertiary injectant, of the qualified carbon dioxide, except to the extent provided by regulations (Code Sec. 45Q(d)(5)). The credit applies with respect to qualified carbon dioxide before the end of the calendar year in which the IRS, in consultation with the Environmental Protection Agency, certifies that 75-million metric tons of qualified carbon dioxide have been captured or disposed of or used as a tertiary injectant (Code Sec. 45Q(e)). The credit is a component of the general business credit subject to its tax liability limitation and carryover rules (¶ 1365). The credit is claimed on Form 8933.

Eligibility. Qualified carbon dioxide is carbon dioxide captured from an industrial source that would otherwise be released into the atmosphere as an industrial emission of greenhouse gas and that is measured at the source of capture and verified at the point of disposal or injection. Qualified carbon dioxide includes the initial deposit of captured carbon dioxide used as a tertiary injectant, but does not include carbon dioxide that is recaptured, recycled, and reinjected as part of the enhanced oil and natural gas recovery process (Code Sec. 45Q(b)). Only carbon dioxide captured and disposed of or used within the United States or its possessions (including the continental shelf areas as defined in Code Sec. 638) is taken into account in computing the credit (Code Sec. 45Q(d)(1)).

1365KK. Credit for Contributions to CDCs (Expired). A credit could be claimed for qualified cash contributions (including loans or investments) made to qualified community development corporations (CDCs) (Act Sec. 13311 of the Omnibus Budget Reconciliation Act of 1993 (P.L. 103-66)).[89] Five percent of the amount contributed could be claimed as a credit for each tax year during a 10-year credit period beginning with the tax year in which the contribution was made. Contributions must have been made before June 30, 1999. This credit was claimed as one of the components of the general business credit (¶ 1365).

1365LL. Therapeutic Discovery Project Credit (Expired). A tax credit was allowed for 50 percent of an eligible taxpayer's qualified investment for tax year beginning in 2009 and 2010 with respect to any qualifying therapeutic discovery project (Code Sec. 48D).[90] The credit was part of the investment credit (¶ 1365A) and the basis of any property that is part of a qualifying therapeutic discovery project was included in the credit base for purposes of applying the investment credit at-risk limitation rules under Code Sec. 49 (Code Secs. 46(6) and 49(a)(1)(C)(vi)).

References are to Standard Federal Tax Reports; Tax Research Consultant; and Practical Tax Explanations.

[88] ¶ 4500ZH; BUSEXP: 55,600; § 14,450

[89] ¶ 4250; BUSEXP: 54,750; § 14,425

[90] ¶ 4700; BUSEXP: 51,850; § 13,728

Tax Credit Bonds

1371. Tax Credit Bonds. As an alternative to traditional tax-exempt bonds, states and local governments may issue tax credit bonds for certain purposes. Unlike tax-exempt bonds, tax credit bonds are not interest-bearing obligations. Rather, the taxpayer holding a tax credit bond on a credit-allowance date is entitled to a tax credit. The credit can be claimed against both the regular income tax and alternative minimum tax liabilities. To standardize the tax treatment of these bonds, they must meet certain requirements regarding the determination of the amount of the credit bond holders are entitled to receive. In addition, in order for a bondholder to qualify for the tax credit, the bond must meet certain requirements with respect to proceeds expenditures, arbitrage, maturity limitations, and conflicts of interest (Code Sec. 54A)).[91]

Credit Amount. A taxpayer holding a tax credit bond on a credit-allowance date is entitled to a tax credit calculated on Form 8912. If the bond is held by a partnership or S corporation, the allocation of the credit to the shareholders or partners is treated as a distribution (Code Sec. 54A(g)). If the bond is held by a mutual fund (regulated investment company (RIC) or real estate investment trust (REIT)), the credit is allocated and any interest treated as gross income is distributed to the shareholders or beneficiaries under procedures to be prescribed by the Secretary of the Treasury (Code Sec. 54A(h)).

The amount of the credit with respect to any allowance date is 25 percent of the annual credit amount determined on that allowance date (Code Sec. 54A(b)). The allowance dates are: March 15, June 15, September 15, and December 15. The annual credit amount is determined by multiplying the bond's applicable credit rate by the face amount on the holder's bond. The applicable credit rate is set by the Secretary of the Treasury at a rate that would permit issuance of a tax credit bond without discount and interest cost to the issuer. The taxpayer holding a tax credit bond on a quarterly credit-allowance date is entitled to a tax credit (Code Sec. 54A(a) and (e)(1)). The credit accrues quarterly and is includible in gross income as if it were an interest payment on the bond (Code Sec. 54A(f)).

The credit in a tax year cannot be larger than the sum of the taxpayer's regular tax liability plus minimum tax liability, minus the total of the taxpayer's credits against tax. The subtracted credits do not include refundable credits or the qualified tax bond credit itself (Code Sec. 54A(c)). Unused qualified tax credit bond amounts may be carried over to succeeding tax years. Special rules apply to S corporation, partnership, regulated investment companies, and real estate investment trust bond holders.

Reporting Requirements. The qualified issuer must submit reports similar to reports required under Code Sec. 149(e), which applies to tax-exempt bonds (Code Sec. 54A(d)(3)). For other return purposes, the credit is reported as an interest payment (Code Sec. 6049(d)(9)). Holders of tax credit bonds receiving a credit amount of $10 or more are issued a Form 1099-INT.

Refundable Credit Election. To stimulate the rebuilding and improvement of local and state infrastructure, issuers of certain tax credit bonds to elect to claim a refundable credit generally equal to the amount of interest that would be payable to the holders of the bonds (Code Sec. 6431(f)). This election may be made only for bonds issued after March 18, 2010. The election can be made by issuers of new clean renewable energy bonds (¶ 1374), qualified energy conservation bonds (¶ 1375), qualified zone academy bonds other than those issued under the 2011 bond limitation or any carryforward of such allocation (¶ 1376), and qualified school construction bonds (¶ 1377). This election is similar to the alternative election available to issuers of Build America bonds (¶ 1378).

1372. Clean Renewable Energy Bond Credit. Clean renewable energy bonds (CREBs) were authorized be issued in 2006 through 2009 to finance a limited amount of capital expenditures incurred by certain tax-exempt electricity providers to increase

References are to Standard Federal Tax Reports; Tax Research Consultant; and Practical Tax Explanations.

[91] ¶ 4882; BUSEXP: 55,800; § 14,501

their capacity to produce electricity from clean renewable sources (Code Sec. 54).[92] The CREBs are tax credit bonds and are subject to rules similar to those that apply to qualified tax credit bonds (¶ 1371).

1373. Qualified Forestry Conservation Bonds. After May 22, 2008, state and local governments, or qualified non-profit organizations, may generally issue up to $500 million in qualified forestry conservation credit bonds (QFCB) for the acquisition of forest and forest lands that are subject to conservation restrictions (Code Sec. 54B).[93] The qualified purpose of the bonds is the acquisition of forest and forest lands from an unrelated third person that meets the following requirements: (1) some portion of the land acquired must be adjacent to United States Forest Service Land; (2) at least half of the land acquired must be transferred to the United States Forest Service at no net cost, and not more than half of the land acquired may either remain with or be donated to a state; (3) all of the land must be subject to a habitat conservation plan for native fish approved by the United States Fish and Wildlife Service; and (4) the amount of acreage acquired must be at least 40,000 acres. QFCB are tax credit bonds subject to rules similar to those that apply to qualified tax credit bonds (¶ 1371).

1374. New Clean Renewable Energy Bonds (NCREBs). "New clean renewable energy bonds" (NCREBs) provide a federal subsidy to allow nonprofit electricity producers, including cooperatives and government-owned utilities, to compete more evenly with for-profit companies that can take advantage of the production tax credit under Code Sec. 45 (Code Sec. 54C).[94] New clean renewable energy bonds are tax credit bonds subject to rules similar to those that apply to qualified tax credit bonds (¶ 1371).

An NCREB is a bond issued as part of an issue if: (1) 100 percent of the available project proceeds of the issue are to be used for capital expenditures incurred by governmental bodies, public power providers, or cooperative electric companies for one or more qualified renewable energy facilities; (2) the bond is issued by a qualified issuer; and (3) the issuer designates the bond as an NCREB (Code Sec. 54C(a)). The proceeds from these bonds are to be use at qualified renewable energy facilities that are producing electrical power and are owned by a public power provider, a governmental body or a cooperative electric company and that qualify under the renewable electricity production credit (Code Sec. 45). These facilities include wind facilities, closed-loop biomass facilities, open-loop biomass facilities, geothermal or solar energy facilities, small irrigation power facilities, landfill gas facilities, trash combustion facilities, or qualified hydropower facilities (Code Sec. 54C(d)(1)).

1375. Qualified Energy Conservation Bonds. State and local governments, or qualified non-profit organizations, are authorized to issue qualified energy conservation bonds (QECBs) to finance energy conservation projects, including capital expenditures, research expenditures, expenses for mass commuting facilities, demonstration projects, and public education campaigns (Code Sec. 54D).[95] These bonds are subject to the requirements for tax credit bonds (¶ 1371) with the annual tax credit limited to 70 percent of the face amount times the applicable credit rate.

1376. Qualified Zone Academy Bond Credit. State and local governments were authorized to issue qualified zone academy bonds (QZAB) through 2011 to be used to improve certain eligible public schools (Code Sec. 1397E and Code Sec. 54E).[96] QZABs issued after October 3, 2008, are subject to the requirements for qualified tax credit bonds (¶ 1371). QZABs issued prior to October 3, 2008, are instead subject to the provisions under Code Sec. 1397E.

Comment: Absent further legislation, the authority for state and local governments to issue qualified zone academy bonds expired on December 31, 2011.

References are to Standard Federal Tax Reports; Tax Research Consultant; and Practical Tax Explanations.

[92] ¶ 4874; BUSEXP: 55,750

[93] ¶ 4890; BUSEXP: 55,804; § 14,510.10

[94] ¶ 4897; BUSEXP: 55,806; § 14,510.15

[95] ¶ 4902; BUSEXP: 55,808; § 14,510.20

[96] ¶ 32,405, ¶ 4910; BUSEXP: 57,150; § 14,510.25

1377. Qualified School Construction Tax Credit Bonds. Tax credit bonds known as "qualified school construction bonds" could be issued through December 31, 2010 (Code Sec. 54F).[97] These bonds must satisfy the requirements for qualified tax credit bonds (¶ 1371) (Code Sec. 54A(d)(1)(E)). A bond is a qualified school construction bond if: (1) 100 percent of the available project proceeds of the issue of which it is a part are to be used for the construction, rehabilitation, or repair of a public school facility or to acquire land on which a facility funded by the same issue is to be built; (2) the bond is issued by a state or local government within the jurisdiction of which the school is located; and (3) the issuer designates the bond as a qualified school construction bond (Code Sec. 54F(a)).

1378. Build America Bonds. State and local governments could issue taxable build America bonds through January 1, 2011, which provide the bondholder with both taxable interest and a tax credit (Code Sec. 54AA).[98] A build America bond is any obligation, other than a private activity bond, that meets these three requirements: (1) the bond must be issued before January 1, 2011; (2) the issuer must make an irrevocable election to have Code Sec. 54AA apply to the bond; and (3) but for that election, the interest on the bond would have been excludable under Code Sec. 103 (Code Sec. 54AA(d)(1)).

> **Comment:** Absent further legislation, the authority for state and local governments to issue build America bonds that would allow bondholders to claim a tax credit expired on December 31, 2010.

For purposes of the rules under Code Sec. 149(b) that exclude federally guaranteed bonds from the category of tax-exempt bonds, build America bonds are not treated as federally guaranteed by virtue of their cash payment or credit features. Also, for purposes of the rules under Code Sec. 148 that exclude arbitrage bonds from the category of tax-exempt bonds, the yield on build America bonds must be determined without regard to the credit. Finally, build America bonds cannot have an issue price that has more than a *de minimis* amount of premium over the stated principal amount of the bond (a *de minimis* amount is generally ¼ of one percent of the stated redemption price at maturity, multiplied by the number of years to maturity) (Code Sec. 54AA(d)(2)).

Unlike tax credit bonds, which provide a tax credit in lieu of interest payments, build America bonds pay interest to the bondholders and also provide a tax credit. The bondholder must include the interest in gross income but is allowed a credit against federal income tax liability for a portion of the interest payments received (Code Sec. 54AA(a) and (f)(1)). The credit is itself treated as interest that is includible in gross income (Code Sec. 54AA(f)(2)). The tax credit is equal to 35 percent of the interest payable on the interest payment date of the bond (Code Sec. 54AA(b)). The interest payment date is any date on which the bondholder of record is entitled to a payment of interest under the bond (Code Sec. 54AA(e)).

Tax Liability Limitations. The amount of the credit cannot exceed the excess of the sum of the bondholder's regular tax liability and alternative minimum tax liability over the sum of the credits allowed under Code Secs. 21 through 54E, not including Code Secs. 31 through 37 and the build America bond credit itself. Any unused credit may be carried forward to succeeding tax years (Code Sec. 54AA(c)).

Rules similar to Code Sec. 54(g), (h) and (i) apply for purposes of the credit (Code Sec. 54AA(f)(2)). Thus, in the case of a build America bond held by an S corporation or partnership, the allocation of the credit to the shareholders or partners is treated as a distribution. For build America bonds held by a real estate investment trust (REIT), the credit is allowed to the respective beneficiaries (and any gross income included in income with respect to the credit is treated as distributed to them) under procedures to be prescribed by the Treasury Secretary.

References are to Standard Federal Tax Reports; Tax Research Consultant; and Practical Tax Explanations.

[97] ¶ 4918; BUSEXP: 55,812; § 14,510.30

[98] ¶ 4932; BUSEXP: 55,814; § 14,515

Qualified Bonds Issued Before 2011. State and local governments may elect to issue certain build America bonds as "qualified bonds" before January 1, 2011. These qualified bonds are issued in exchange for a payment credit, determined in accordance with Code Sec. 6431. This credit to the issuer is in lieu of the credit that would otherwise be allowed to the bondholder and is generally equal to 35 percent of the interest paid on the bond (Code Sec. 54AA(g)(1)).

1380. Midwestern Tax Credit Bonds (Expired). States located in the Midwestern disaster area (¶ 1179) were authorized to issue Midwestern tax credit bonds during 2009, which could be used, in effect, to extend the maturity of existing obligations by two years at lower interest costs (Code Sec. 1400N(l)).[99] These bonds are subject to the requirements of tax credit bonds as discussed in ¶ 1371.

1385. Mutual Fund Election to Pass-Through Tax Credit Bond Credits. Regulated investment companies (RICs) may elect to pass through to their shareholders credits attributable to tax credit bonds held by the RIC, replacing the required pass-through of the credits (Code Sec. 853A).[100] If the election is made, the RIC is not allowed any credits attributable to the tax credit bonds and includes in gross income, as interest, the amount of income that the RIC would have included if the election did not apply, increasing the amount of the dividends paid by the same amount.

In order to qualify for the election, a RIC must hold, directly or indirectly, one or more tax credit bonds on one or more applicable dates during the tax year and must also meet the 90 percent distribution requirements of a RIC under Code Sec. 852(a)(1). The RIC must also have been taxed as a RIC under Code Sec. 852 for all tax years ending on or after November 8, 1983, or have no accumulated earnings and profits from a tax year to which the RIC provisions did not apply.

Where the election is made, shareholders of the RIC are to include in income the shareholder's proportionate share of the interest income attributable to the credits and are simultaneously allowed the proportionate share of credits (Code Sec. 853A(b)(3)). A RIC must report to shareholders in a written notice the shareholder's proportionate share of credits and gross income in respect of the credits. The shareholder's proportionate share of credits and gross income in respect of the credits cannot exceed the amounts so designated by the RIC in the notice.

Miscellaneous Credits

1391. COBRA Premium Credit. A temporary reduction in premiums for COBRA coverage is provided to assistance eligible individuals who are involuntarily terminated from their employment (Code Sec. 6432).[101] An assistance eligible individual is treated for purposes of COBRA continuation coverage as having paid the premium required for coverage if the individual pays 35 percent of the premium. In effect, the individual is provided with a 65-percent reduction in premiums. An "assistance eligible individual" is defined as any qualified beneficiary if: (1) at any time during the period beginning on September 1, 2008, and ending on May 31, 2010, the qualified beneficiary is eligible for COBRA continuation coverage; (2) the beneficiary elects such coverage; and (3) the qualifying event for which the beneficiary would otherwise lose health plan coverage is the involuntary termination of the covered employee's employment during such period (Act Sec. 3001(a)(3) and (a)(17) of the American Recovery and Reinvestment Act of 2009 (P.L. 111-5), as amended and added by the Department of Defense Appropriations Act, 2010 (P.L. 111-118), the Temporary Extension Act of 2010 (P.L. 111-144), and the Continuing Extension Act of 2010 (P.L. 111-157)).

The 65-percent premium reduction or subsidy terminates with the first month beginning on or after the earlier of: (1) the date that is 15 months after the first day of the first month for which the subsidy applies, (2) the end of the maximum required period of continuation coverage for the beneficiary under the Code's COBRA rules or the applicable state or federal law, or (3) the date the assistance eligible individual is

References are to Standard Federal Tax Reports; Tax Research Consultant; and Practical Tax Explanations.

[99] ¶ 32,483; BUSEXP: 57,302.15; § 10,001

[100] ¶ 26,448; RIC: 3,366; § 14,505

[101] ¶ 38,935; COMPEN: 45,206.45; § 42,845.05

eligible for coverage under Medicare or any other employer-sponsored health plan. Employees who were terminated between September 1, 2008, and February 17, 2009, but who failed to initially elect COBRA continuation coverage, are given an additional 60 days to elect coverage and receive the subsidy.

A person to whom premiums for COBRA continuation coverage are payable will be reimbursed for the amount of premiums not paid by plan beneficiaries because of the temporary subsidy. The reimbursement is made in the form of a credit against the person's liability for payroll taxes. If the reimbursement due exceeds the amount of such taxes, the IRS pays the person the amount of the excess. No payment will be made with respect to any assistance eligible individual until after the person has received the reduced premium from the individual (Code Sec. 6432(a)).

Elimination of Premium Subsidy for High-Income Individuals. If premium assistance is provided for any COBRA continuation coverage that covers a taxpayer, the taxpayer's spouse, or any dependents of the taxpayer during any portion of the tax year, and the taxpayer's modified adjusted gross income (AGI) for the tax year exceeds $125,000 ($250,000 for joint returns), then the income tax liability imposed on the taxpayer is increased by the amount of the assistance received. This recapture is phased-in ratably and becomes complete when modified AGI reaches $145,000 ($290,000 for joint returns). An option is provided, in a form and manner to be prescribed by the Secretary of the Treasury, for high-income individuals to make a permanent election to waive assistance and avoid recapture. Any increase in tax as a result of this recapture is not treated as a part of regular tax liability and, therefore, may not be offset by tax credits.

Income Exclusion for Plan Beneficiaries. A plan beneficiary who qualifies as an "assistance eligible individual" may exclude from gross income the 65-percent premium reduction for COBRA continuation coverage (Code Sec. 139C).

Coordination Between HCTC and COBRA Premium Assistance. If an assistance eligible individual receives a premium reduction for COBRA continuation coverage for any month during the tax year, the individual cannot be treated as an eligible individual, a certified individual, or a qualifying family member for purposes of the health insurance costs credit under Code Sec. 35 or the advance payment program for the credit under Code Sec. 7527 with respect to that month (¶ 1332) (Code Sec. 35(g)(9)).

Chapter 14

ALTERNATIVE MINIMUM TAX

Calculating Alternative Minimum Tax

1401. Alternative Minimum Tax (AMT) Liability. The alternative minimum tax (AMT) is a separate method of determining income tax designed to ensure that taxpayers do not completely avoid income tax through the use of deductions, exemptions, losses, and credits. Generally, all taxpayers subject to regular income tax are subject to the AMT, including individuals, estates, trusts, and corporations (Code Secs. 55(a) and 59(c)).[1] Partnerships and S corporations are not subject to the AMT. Instead, partners and shareholders compute their AMT liability separately by taking into account their share of partnership or S corporation items. Special rules apply to partners of an electing large partnership using a simplified pass-through system (¶ 1455).

A taxpayer's AMT for a tax year is the excess of their tentative minimum tax over regular tax liability. AMT must be paid in addition to the regular tax liability and other federal taxes owed (¶ 1420). Thus, if a taxpayer's tentative minimum tax for a tax year is $75,000 while their regular tax liability is $50,000, the taxpayer must pay an AMT of $25,000 in addition to the $50,000 regular tax for a total tax liability of $75,000.

For noncorporate taxpayers, tentative minimum tax is equal to: (1) 26 percent of the first $175,000 ($87,500 for a married individuals filing separately) of alternative minimum taxable income (AMTI), plus (2) 28 percent of any AMTI in excess of the threshold. For corporations, tentative minimum tax is 20 percent of AMTI, but certain small corporations and corporations in their first year of existence are exempt (¶ 1415). A taxpayer's AMTI is their regular taxable income increased by AMT preferences and modified by AMT adjustments (¶ 1405). A certain amount of AMTI is exempt from tax (¶ 1410). After applying the AMT rates, both noncorporate and corporate taxpayers reduce the computed amount by the AMT foreign tax credit (¶ 1470), with the result being their tentative minimum tax. Subject to limits, any AMT liability of taxpayer may be reduced by nonrefundable personal credits and general business credits (¶ 1475). Form 6251 is used by individuals to compute AMT. Estates and trusts use Schedule I of Form 1041. Corporations use Form 4626.

Net Capital Gain and Qualified Dividends. The taxation of net capital gain and qualified dividends for AMT purposes is the same as for regular income tax purposes, including the netting of capital gains and losses into separate tax-rate groups (¶ 1736 and ¶ 1739). (Code Sec. 55(b)(3)). The capital gain or loss amounts, however, may differ from the regular tax amounts because of AMT tax preferences and adjustments affecting the basis of capital assets in computing AMTI.

Minimum Tax on a Minor Child. A child who is subject to the "kiddie tax" (¶ 103) is subject to the AMT. The child computes tentative minimum tax in the same manner as any individual taxpayer. Thus, all adjustments and preferences apply, and AMT liability on the child's net unearned income is computed under the rules that apply to other taxpayers except that the child's exemption amount is limited (¶ 1410). The child's

References are to Standard Federal Tax Reports; Tax Research Consultant; and Practical Tax Explanations.

[1] ¶ 5100, ¶ 5400; FILEIND: 30,000; § 15,005

exemption amount and his or her ultimate AMT liability are not dependent on the computation of the parent's AMTI or AMT exemption amount.

1405. Alternative Minimum Taxable Income (AMTI). A taxpayer's alternative minimum taxable income (AMTI) for purposes of determining alternative minimum tax (AMT) liability (¶ 1401) is the taxpayer's regular taxable income modified by AMT tax preference items and various AMT adjustments (Code Sec. 55(b)(2); Reg. § 1.55-1).[2] All provisions of the Code and regulations that apply in determining regular taxable income also generally apply in determining AMTI. If, however the taxpayer's regular income tax is determined by reference to an amount other than regular taxable income, then that amount is treated as taxable income for AMT purposes (e.g., unrelated business taxable income (¶ 655), real estate investment trust (REIT) taxable income (¶ 2329), and life insurance company taxable income (¶ 2370)). Nonresident aliens and foreign corporations only include income effectively connected with a U.S. trade or business in their AMTI (¶ 2429). AMTI does not include fixed or determinable annual or periodic (FDAP) income (¶ 2431).

AMT tax preference items and adjustments both involve alterations to various deductions or exclusions allowed in computing regular income tax. Tax preference items are deductions or exclusions that are allowed in computing regular taxable income but that are not allowed in computing AMTI. This includes the exclusion of gain from qualified small business stock, percentage depletion, and interest earned on tax-exempt private activity bonds (¶ 1425). Thus, tax preferences items can only increase an individual's AMTI; they cannot decrease it. Taxpayers may avoid having some of these deductions classified as tax preference items if, instead of claiming the deductions entirely in one tax year, they elect to claim the deductions ratably over a three-year, five-year, or ten-year period (¶ 1450).

AMT adjustments on the other hand are items of income or deduction that are computed differently in determining AMTI than they are for regular taxable income. The result is that adjustments may increase or decrease AMTI. For example, all taxpayers must recompute depreciation, the expensing of mining exploration and development costs, income from long-term contracts, and net operating losses (NOLs) in computing AMTI (¶ 1430).

Individuals, estates, and trusts must also make adjustments specific to them including adjustments for itemized deductions, the standard deduction, personal exemptions, and incentive stock options (¶ 1435). In determining the AMTI of an individual, estate, or trust, however, any reference to the taxpayer's adjusted gross income (AGI) or modified AGI is treated as a reference to the taxpayer's AGI or modified AGI as determined for regular tax purposes (Reg. § 1.55-1(b)). Corporations must make a number of adjustments to various items in calculating AMTI that only pertain to them, including adjusted current earnings (¶ 1440). The reduction or cutback of certain corporate preference items for regular tax purposes must generally be applied before a corporation applies the AMT rules (¶ 1445).

Taxpayers subject to the passive activity loss rules may not claim passive activity losses that are disallowed for regular tax purposes (¶ 1460). In addition, certain farm losses of individuals, estates, and trusts may not be claimed. The limitations on the deductibility of other losses, including the at-risk rules (¶ 2045), the partnership losses by partners (¶ 425), and S corporation losses by shareholders (¶ 321), do apply in determining a taxpayer's AMTI (Code Sec. 59(h)).[3] These limitations are applied separately taking into account all AMT tax preferences and adjustments. Thus, the amount of losses suspended and carried over may differ for AMT and regular tax purposes.

1410. AMT Exemption Amounts. A certain amount of the alternative minimum taxable income (AMTI) (¶ 1405) of a taxpayer is exempt from the alternative minimum

References are to Standard Federal Tax Reports; Tax Research Consultant; and Practical Tax Explanations.

[2] ¶ 5100; FILEIND: 30,000; § 15,005, § 15,110.05

[3] ¶ 5400; FILEIND: 30,150; § 15,401

tax (AMT) depending on the type of taxpayer and, for individuals, the taxpayer's filing status and tax year (Code Sec. 55(d)).[4]

> **Comment:** Absent further legislation, the exemption amounts for individuals for tax years beginning in 2012 are: $45,000 for married individuals filing a joint return and surviving spouses, $33,750 for a single individual who is not a surviving spouse, and $22,500 for a married individual filing a separate return.

The AMT exemption amount of a corporation is $40,000. In the case of a controlled group of corporations (¶ 291), the single $40,000 exemption is shared by all members of the group (Code Sec. 1561(a)(3)). The AMT exemption amount of an estate or trust (other than an electing small business trust (¶ 304) is $22,500. The AMTI exemption amount is zero in the case of the portion of an electing small business trust that is treated as a separate trust (Code Sec. 641(c)(2)(B)).

The exemption amounts are phased out for taxpayers with high AMTI. Specifically, the exemption amounts are reduced 25 percent for each $1 of the excess of AMTI over: (1) $150,000 for married individuals filing a joint return, surviving spouses, and corporations; (2) $112,500 for single individuals other than surviving spouses; and (3) $75,000 for married individuals filing a separate return and estates and trusts (Code Sec. 55(d)(3)). The threshold at which the AMT exemption begins to phase out is not adjusted for inflation.

For married individuals filing joint returns and surviving spouses, the AMT exemption amount of $45,000 for 2012 is completely phased out when AMTI reaches $330,000. For single individuals who are not surviving spouses, the exemption amount of $33,750 for 2012 is completely phased out when AMTI reaches $247,500. For married taxpayers filing a separate return, the exemption amount of $22,500 for 2012 is completely phased out when AMTI reaches $165,000. Similarly, for an estate or trust, the exemption amount of $22,500 is completely phased out when AMTI reaches $165,000. The $40,000 exemption amount of a corporation is not completely phased out until AMTI reaches $310,000.

> **Comment:** Absent further legislation, the amount of AMTI at which the AMT exemption is phased out for individuals is decreased for tax years beginning in 2012 because the phaseout calculation is tied to the exemption amount.

AMT Exemption Amount for a Child. A child who is subject to the "kiddie tax" (¶ 103) is subject to AMT and computes his or her tentative minimum tax in the same manner as any individual taxpayer. The AMTI exemption amount of a child subject to the kiddie tax, however, is limited to the sum of the child's earned income plus $6,950 in 2012 and $7,150 in 2013 (Code Sec. 59(j); Rev. Proc. 2011-52: Rev. Proc. 2012-41).

1415. AMT Exemption for Small Corporations. A corporation is generally subject to the alternative minimum tax (AMT) at a flat rate of 20 percent (¶ 1401) on alternative minimum taxable income (AMTI) (¶ 1405). A small corporation that meets a gross receipts tests, however, will not be liable for the AMT so long as it remains a small corporation—its tentative minimum tax will be treated as zero (Code Sec. 55(e)).[5]

For a corporation to qualify as an exempt small corporation, its average gross receipts must not exceed $7.5 million for all three-tax-year periods prior to the year for which qualification is sought. The threshold is reduced to $5 million for the first three-year-period (or portion of that period if the corporation has not been in existence for that long). Once a corporation qualifies as a small corporation, it will continue to be exempt from the AMT for so long as its average annual gross receipts for the prior three-year period does not exceed $7.5 million.

If the corporation is in existence for less than three years at the time it seeks to qualify for the exemption, then the gross receipts test is applied based on the period during which it has existed. If a corporation ceases to be a small corporation, it cannot

References are to Standard Federal Tax Reports; Tax Research Consultant; and Practical Tax Explanations.

[4] ¶ 5100; FILEIND: 30,400; § 15,015, § 15,115

[5] ¶ 5100; STAGES: 9,120.15; § 15,105.15

qualify as such for any subsequent tax year. The AMT in such circumstances will only apply prospectively. If a corporation's first tax year is the first year of the corporation's existence, then the corporation is generally treated as an exempt small corporation regardless of its gross receipts for the year—its tentative minimum tax will be zero. In applying the small corporation exemption, any reference to the corporation includes its predecessors.

Taxpayers generally may be eligible to claim a tax credit based upon their AMT liability for the prior tax year (¶ 1309). The credit allowed against the regular tax of a small corporation is limited to the amount by which the corporation's regular tax liability (reduced by other credits) exceeds 25 percent of the excess (if any) of the corporation's regular tax (reduced by other credits) over $25,000.

Example: XYZ is a calendar-year corporation that is first incorporated in 2011. It is neither aggregated with an existing corporation nor treated as having a predecessor. It will qualify as a small corporation for 2011, regardless of its gross receipts for the year. In order to qualify as a small corporation for 2012, XYZ's gross receipts for 2011 must be $5 million or less. If XYZ qualifies for 2012, it will also qualify for 2013 if its average gross receipts for the two-taxable-year period including 2011 and 2012 is $7.5 million or less. If XYZ does not qualify for 2012, it cannot qualify for 2013 or any subsequent year. If XYZ qualifies for 2013, it will qualify for 2014 if its average gross receipts for the three-taxable-year period including 2011, 2012, and 2012 is $7.5 million or less.

1420. Regular Tax Compared with Tentative Minimum Tax. A taxpayer is subject to the alternative minimum tax (AMT) to the extent that tentative minimum tax exceeds regular tax liability (¶ 1401). A taxpayer's regular tax liability for this purpose is income tax liability under the Code reduced by the AMT foreign tax credit (¶ 1470) and the U.S. possession or Puerto Rico tax credit (¶ 2419) (Code Sec. 55(c)).[6] The income averaging rules for farmers and fishermen do not apply when determining the taxpayer's regular tax liability for AMT purposes (¶ 767). Taxes not included in regular tax liability include the following (Code Sec. 26(b)):

- accumulated earnings tax (Code Sec. 531);
- tax on personal holding companies (Code Sec. 541);
- alternative minimum tax (AMT);
- 30-percent withholding tax on the fixed or determinable annual of periodical (FDAP) income of nonresident aliens and foreign corporations (Code Secs. 871(a) and 881);
- foreign corporations' branch profits taxes (Code Sec. 884);
- tax on the built-in gains of an S corporation (Code Sec. 1374);
- tax on an S corporation's passive investment income (Code Sec. 1375);
- additional tax on early distributions from retirement plans (Code Sec. 72(m)(5)(B), (q), (t), and (v));
- excise tax on the transfer of a residual interest in real estate mortgage investment company (REMIC) to a "disqualified organization" (Code Sec. 860E(e));
- tax on foreign expropriation loss recoveries (Code Sec. 1351(d));
- tax on nonqualified withdrawals from certain Merchant Marine capital construction funds (Code Sec. 7518(g)(6));
- tax imposed on a corporation for environmental purposes (Code Sec. 59A);
- tax that arises out of the recapture of mortgage bond federal subsidies (Code Sec. 143(m));

References are to Standard Federal Tax Reports; Tax Research Consultant; and Practical Tax Explanations.

[6] ¶ 5100; FILEIND: 30,400; § 15,005, § 15,110.05

• interest on tax liabilities deferred under the installment method (Code Secs. 453(l)(3) and 453A(c));

• the additional tax on Archer medical savings accounts (MSAs) distributions not used for qualified medical expenses (Code Sec. 220(f)(4));

• the additional tax on certain distributions from Coverdell education savings accounts (Code Sec. 530(d)(4));

• the "tax" on certain transfers of high-yield interests to disqualified holders (Code Sec. 860K);

• the penalty imposed for distributions from Medicare Advantage medical savings accounts that were not used for qualified medical expenses (Code Sec. 138(c)(2));

• the additional tax on health savings account (HSAs) distributions not used for qualified medical expenses (Code Sec. 223(f));

• the additional tax under Code Sec. 409A(a)(1)(B) on income from nonqualified deferred compensation plans;

• the recapture of the first-time homebuyer credit under Code Sec. 36(f);

• the tax (including interest and an additional tax) imposed on certain compensation that is deferred under a nonqualified deferred compensation plan (Code Sec. 457A(c)(1)(B));

• taxes relating to certain failures to maintain high deductible health plan coverage (Code Secs. 106(e)(3)(A)(ii), 223(b)(8)(B)(i)(II), and 408(d)(9)(D)(i)(II)); and

• tax relating to recapture of certain deductions for fractional gifts (Code Sec. 170(o)(3)(B)).

AMT Tax Preference Items and Adjustments

1425. AMT Tax Preference Items. For alternative minimum tax (AMT) purposes, a taxpayer's regular taxable income is increased by tax preferences in computing alternative minimum taxable income (AMTI) (¶ 1405) (Code Sec. 57).[7] Because tax preference items are instrumental in generating tax savings by reducing a taxpayer's taxable income, they must be added back to the taxable income of corporate and noncorporate taxpayers in computing AMTI so that unreasonably high tax breaks may be recaptured. Tax preference items include the following:

• Seven percent of any gain realized on the sale of qualified small business stock and excluded from gross income under Code Sec. 1202 is generally treated as a tax preference item (¶ 1905). For dispositions occurring after September 27, 2010, and before January 1, 2012, however, the excluded gain is not a tax preference item (Code Sec. 1202(a)(4)). Since the exclusion generally equals 50 percent of the realized gain, only 3.5 percent of the gain recognized is treated as a tax preference item. For stock acquired after February 17, 2009, and before September 28, 2010, the exclusion amount is 75 percent, so 5.25 percent of the recognized gain is treated as a tax preference item.

> **Comment:** Absent further legislation, 42 percent of any gain realized on the sale of qualified small business stock after December 31, 2012, and excluded from gross income is treated as a tax preference item.

• Tax-exempt interest (less any related expenses) on specified private activity bonds which are issued after August 7, 1986, is a tax preference item (except for bonds issued in 2009 and 2010).

• The amount by which the depletion deduction (¶ 1289) claimed by a taxpayer (other than an independent oil and gas producer) for an interest in a

References are to Standard Federal Tax Reports; Tax Research Consultant, and Practical Tax Explanations.

[7] ¶ 5300; FILEIND: 30,100, FILEIND: 30,250; § 15,301

property exceeds the adjusted basis of the interest at the end of a tax year is a tax preference item.

• If a taxpayer deducts intangible drilling costs (IDCs) (¶ 989), the difference between that deduction and the amount that would have been deductible if the costs had been capitalized and ratably amortized over a 120-month period is a tax preference item to the extent it exceeds 65 percent of the taxpayer's net income from oil, gas, and geothermal properties. Independent producers are not subject to this preference. Their AMTI, however, may not be reduced by more than 40 percent of the AMTI that would otherwise be determined if the taxpayer took the IDC tax preference into account and did not compute an alternative tax net operating loss deduction (¶ 1430).

• The accelerated depreciation of property placed in service before 1987 is treated as a tax preference item to the extent that it was a preference item under prior law, unless the taxpayer elected to apply the MACRS system to the property for regular tax purposes. Accelerated depreciation claimed on real property and leased personal property placed in service before 1987 is an item of tax preference to the extent it exceeds the amount allowable under the straight-line method. For pollution control facilities placed in service prior to 1987, the excess of rapid amortization under Code Sec. 169 over the depreciation that would be allowed under Code Sec. 167 is a tax preference item.

For ACRS leased recovery property (except 19-year real property and low-income housing), the preference amount is the excess of the ACRS deduction claimed over the amount that would have been allowed if the deduction had been calculated using the modified half-year convention and the straight-line method over an extended recovery period. For 19-year real property and low-income housing, the preference amount is the excess of the ACRS deduction over the deduction that would have been allowed if straight-line depreciation (with a 19-year recovery period for real property and a 15-year recovery period for low-income housing) had been used and computed without regard to salvage value.

1430. AMT Adjustments for All Taxpayers. In addition to adding back certain tax preference items (¶ 1425), the alternative minimum tax (AMT) is aimed at recovering some tax savings generated by other deductions and methods for computing tax liability. This is achieved by requiring taxpayers to recompute certain regular tax deductions in a less preferential manner when computing alternative minimum taxable income (AMTI) (¶ 1405). Adjustments are usually required in order to eliminate "time value" tax savings that result from allowing the acceleration of deductions (e.g., the MACRS depreciation) or the deferral of income (e.g., the completed-contract method of determining income from long-term contracts). Thus, the recomputation for AMT purposes usually results in an increase to AMTI. Some adjustments have to be made solely by noncorporate taxpayers (¶ 1435), while others have to be made solely by corporate taxpayers (¶ 1440). All taxpayers, whether corporate or noncorporate, must make certain adjustments when determining AMTI, as discussed below.

Depreciation. For property placed in service after 1998, if the 200-percent declining balance method is used for regular tax purposes for 3-, 5-, 7-, or 10-year property, then the 150-percent declining balance method and regular tax depreciation period must be used for AMT purposes (Code Sec. 56(a)(1)).[8] For all other property placed in service after 1998, no AMT adjustment is required, as AMT and regular tax depreciation are identical.

For property placed in service after 1986 and before 1999, if the 200-percent declining balance method is used for regular tax purposes for 3-, 5-, 7-, or 10-year property, then the 150-percent declining balance method and the alternative depreciation system (ADS) recovery period must be used for AMT purposes. If the 150-percent

References are to Standard Federal Tax Reports; Tax Research Consultant; and Practical Tax Explanations.

[8] ¶ 5200; FILEIND: 30,102; § 15,230

declining balance method is used for 15- or 20-year property, then the 150-percent declining balance method and the ADS recovery period are used for AMT purposes. If the 150-percent declining balance method election is in effect for regular tax purposes for 3-, 5-, 7-, 10-, 15-, or 20-year property, then no adjustment is required for AMT purposes, as the AMT and regular tax depreciation are computed the same way (i.e., using the 150-percent declining balance method over the ADS recovery period). In the case of 27.5-year residential real property, or in the case of 31.5- or 39-year real property, AMT depreciation is computed using the straight-line method and ADS recovery period (40 years). If the straight-line election is in effect for regular tax purposes for 3-, 5-, 7-, 10-, 15-, or 20-year property, then for AMT purposes the straight-line method and ADS recovery period must be used. If the ADS method (elective or nonelective) is used for regular tax purposes, then no adjustment is required for AMT purposes, as AMT and regular tax depreciation are computed the same way on real and personal property subject to such method.

Adjusting MACRS depreciation deductions, rather than treating them as tax preference items, may provide taxpayers with some major benefits as they compute AMTI in the later years of a property's use. Although MACRS deductions will exceed AMT deductions in the early years of a property's use (assuming that AMT and MACRS deductions are not computed in the same manner), the reverse will be true in the later years. Thus, the higher deductions produced under the applicable AMT method in later years may be used to reduce AMTI and, therefore, reduce the potential for AMT liability. Another benefit from the adjustment approach to depreciation is that depreciation for all property is combined in calculating AMTI, allowing for the netting of excess MACRS deductions with excess alternative deductions. Consequently, a taxpayer who has excess MACRS deductions on a new piece of property may be able to avoid paying an AMT on the excess deductions by offsetting them with excess alternative deductions generated by an older piece of property.

No AMT adjustments have to be made for: (1) the amount expensed under Code Sec. 179; (2) motion pictures, video tapes, and public utility property for which the normalization method of accounting is not used; (3) property which is depreciated under the units of production method or under a depreciation method which is not based on a term of years (other than the retirement-replacement-betterment method or similar method); or (4) natural gas gathering lines placed in service after April 11, 2005 (Code Sec. 56(a)(1)(B)).

When property that generated depreciation deductions is sold, its adjusted basis must be computed under the AMT rules in order to determine the gain or loss from the sale for AMT purposes (Code Sec. 56(a)(6)).[9] The difference between the regular tax gain or loss and the recomputed AMT gain or loss is a tax preference adjustment in the year of sale.

> **Example 1:** A taxpayer has purchased a piece of property for $100,000 and, over several tax years, has claimed a total of $25,000 of depreciation deductions for regular tax purposes. In AMTI calculations made during the same tax years, he has claimed adjusted depreciation deductions totaling $10,000. He sells the property in the current tax year for $150,000. The adjusted basis of the property in regular tax calculations is $75,000 ($100,000 – $25,000), leaving him with a regular tax gain of $75,000 ($150,000 – $75,000). The AMT adjusted basis is $90,000 ($100,000 – $10,000). The amount of gain that must be included in his AMTI calculations is only $60,000 ($150,000 – $90,000).

Mining Exploration and Development Costs. Taxpayers who have expensed mining exploration and development expenses (or amortized these costs in computing their regular tax (¶ 987 and ¶ 988) must capitalize and amortize these costs over a 10-year period in calculating AMTI, beginning with the tax year in which the expenses were incurred (Code Sec. 56(a)(2)).[10] If a tax loss is incurred from a mine, all expenses which

References are to Standard Federal Tax Reports; Tax Research Consultant; and Practical Tax Explanations.

[9] ¶ 5200; FILEIND: 30,102; § 15,230

[10] ¶ 5200; FILEIND: 30,106; § 15,255

have been capitalized but not yet amortized may be deducted from AMTI. When property that generated mining exploration and development deductions is sold, its adjusted basis must be computed under the AMT rules in order to determine the gain or loss from the sale for AMT purposes.

Long-Term Contracts. The percentage-of-completion method of accounting for gain or loss from long-term contracts (other than home construction contracts) (¶ 1551) must be substituted for any other accounting method, such as the completed contract method or the cash basis method, to determine AMTI for long-term contracts (Code Sec. 56(a)(3)).[11] The percentage-of-completion is determined using simplified cost allocation procedures in the case of construction contracts of certain small contractors if the contract has an estimated duration of less than two years.

Alternative Tax Net Operating Losses. Net operating loss (NOL) deductions must be recomputed in calculating AMTI (Code Sec. 56(a)(4) and (d)).[12] The alternative tax NOL (ATNOL) is computed in the same manner as an ordinary NOL (¶ 1173) after taking into account all AMT adjustments, and is reduced by any tax preference items (¶ 1425) to the extent they increased the amount of the NOL for the tax year. The ATNOL may not offset more than 90 percent of AMTI, determined without regard to the ATNOL deduction and the domestic production activities deduction. Unused ATNOLs are carried forward or back to the earliest year in which they can be used, according to the same rules as NOLs. The amount of ATNOLs carried forward or back is reduced by 90 percent of the AMTI for any year to which they are carried, whether or not the taxpayer is liable for the AMT in that year.

> **Example 2:** A taxpayer's income for a tax year is $75,000, while her losses total $100,000, of which $20,000 is from tax preference items. Her NOL for regular taxation is $25,000. In computing AMTI, tax preference items cannot be used. Consequently, only $80,000 of the losses may offset income, leaving the taxpayer with an ATNOL of $5,000.

Pollution Control Facilities. For property placed in service after 1986 and before 1999, the five-year amortization method for depreciating pollution control facilities (¶ 1287) must be replaced by the alternative depreciation system (ADS) (¶ 1247) (Code Sec. 56(a)(5)).[13] The pollution control facility adjustment is computed under MACRS using the straight-line method for property placed in service after 1998. When the pollution control facility is sold, its adjusted basis must be computed under the AMT rules in order to determine the gain or loss from the sale for AMT purposes.

Domestic Production Activities Deduction. The domestic production activities deduction is allowed for both individuals and corporations against the AMT (¶ 980A). The deduction is equal to nine percent of the lesser of (1) the taxpayer's qualified production activities income determined without regard to available AMT adjustments, or (2) the taxpayer's taxable income (or in the case of a corporation its AMTI), determined without regard to the deduction (Code Sec. 199(a) and (d)(6)).

1435. AMT Adjustments for Noncorporate Taxpayers. In addition to alternative minimum tax (AMT) adjustments that affect all taxpayers (¶ 1430), individuals and other noncorporate taxpayers must make a number of adjustments to various tax items in calculating alternative minimum taxable income (AMTI) that only pertain to them (¶ 1405).

Itemized Deductions. Individuals are entitled to claim itemized deductions in calculating AMTI with certain adjustments (Code Sec. 56(b)).[14] Further, the limit on itemized deductions that applies for regular tax purposes does not apply for AMT purposes (¶ 1014).

An individual may not claim state, local, and other taxes paid and claimed as itemized deductions on Schedule A (including state and local sales taxes paid in lieu of

References are to Standard Federal Tax Reports; Tax Research Consultant; and Practical Tax Explanations.

[11] ¶ 5200; FILEIND: 30,202; § 15,240

[12] ¶ 5200; FILEIND: 30,156; § 15,415

[13] ¶ 5200; FILEIND: 30,110

[14] ¶ 5200; FILEIND: 30,300; § 15,205

income taxes) (¶ 1021) in calculating AMTI. If such taxes are later refunded and included in taxable income for regular tax purposes, they are not included in AMTI. State and local taxes arising from the operation of a trade or business that are taken into account in computing the individual's adjusted gross income (AGI) may be claimed as a deduction to AMTI.

Itemized deductions may be claimed for medical expenses in computing AMTI, but the expenses must exceed 10 percent of the taxpayer's AGI, rather than the 7.5-percent-of-AGI floor that applies in 2012 for regular tax liability purposes (¶ 1015). An itemized deduction may also be claimed for qualified housing interest which is similar to the qualified residence interest deduction that may be claimed against regular tax (¶ 1047) (Code Sec. 56(e)).[15] Qualified housing interest is interest paid on a loan used to purchase, build, or substantially improve a taxpayer's (1) principal residence, or (2) other dwelling unit personally used by the taxpayer during the tax year for the greater of 14 days or 10 percent of the number of days during which the dwelling is leased. Interest on a refinanced loan is also deductible if the loan does not exceed the balance remaining on the original loan.

Investment interest expenses are deductible in computing AMTI to the same extent as regular tax liability—that is limited to the taxpayer's net investment income (¶ 1094) (Code Sec. 56(b)(1)(C)). Investment interest does not include qualified housing interest, even if it is otherwise allocable to property held for investment. Tax-exempt interest on private activity bonds is included in investment income for this purpose, and interest expended to carry the bonds is included in investment interest expenses.

A noncorporate taxpayer cannot claim any miscellaneous itemized deductions subject to the two-percent adjusted gross income (AGI) floor (¶ 1011). This means that while these deductions can be claimed in computing regular tax liability, they must be added back to AMTI. For example, legal expenses are generally deductible as a miscellaneous itemized deduction and therefore cannot be deducted for AMTI. Attorney fees and court costs paid in connection with an unlawful federal discrimination claim or whistleblower award for providing information on tax law violations, however, are deductions taken into account as an above-the-line deduction in computing the individual's AGI and can therefore be claimed as a deduction to AMTI (¶ 1010A).

Personal Exemptions and the Standard Deduction. No deduction for, or in lieu of, personal exemptions may be claimed against AMTI. The basic and additional standard deduction may also not be claimed for AMTI purposes (Code Sec. 56(b)(1)(E)).[16]

Incentive Stock Options. An individual does not recognize gain or loss when an incentive stock option (ISO) is granted or exercised for regular tax purposes (¶ 1925). Instead, gain or loss is recognized when the stock is sold. The individual, however, must make an adjustment for AMT purposes by increasing AMTI by the amount the option price exceeds the stock's fair market value at the time the individual's rights to the stock are freely transferable or not subject to a substantial risk of forfeiture (Code Sec. 56(b)(3)).[17] This generally occurs when the option is exercised. The basis of stock acquired through the exercise of the ISO is increased for AMT purposes by the amount of the AMT adjustment. There is no AMT adjustment of basis increase if the stock is nontransferable and subject to a substantial risk of forfeiture. The individual in such circumstances may make a Code Sec. 83(b) election to take the AMT adjustment into account in the tax year (¶ 713). There is no AMT adjustment, however, if the option is exercised and the stock is disposed of in the same tax year. Although the exercise of an ISO can trigger an AMT liability, a taxpayer may be able to recover the liability through the alternative minimum tax credit in future years (¶ 1309).

> **Comment:** The price of stock acquired through an ISO may substantially decrease in value after the option is exercised. As a result, the taxpayer may not realize any actual income or a loss when the stock is sold. If the stock is sold at a

References are to Standard Federal Tax Reports; Tax Research Consultant; and Practical Tax Explanations.

[15] ¶ 5200; FILEIND: 30,310.05; § 15,220.05

[16] ¶ 5200; FILEIND: 30,302; § 15,205

[17] ¶ 5200; FILEIND: 30,204; § 15,245

loss, the taxpayer would be subject to $3,000 limit on deducting capital losses for regular tax purposes. Thus, even though the individual could have a significant AMT liability from exercising the ISO, he or she could have a loss for regular tax purposes from selling the stock which cannot be used against the AMT liability. To alleviate this problem, if a taxpayer has any long-term unused AMT credit, then a portion of the credit may be used to offset regular tax liability as a result of any excess losses (¶ 1327).

Circulation and Research Expenses. Circulation expenses which are expensed for regular tax calculations (¶ 971), must be capitalized for AMTI calculations and ratably amortized over a three-year period starting with the tax year in which the expenses are incurred. Similarly, research and experiment expenses (¶ 979) must be ratably amortized over a 10-year period (Code Sec. 56(b)(2)).[18] These adjustments, in effect, treat the excess of expense deductions over amortization deductions as a tax preference. Besides noncorporate taxpayers, personal holding companies must also recompute circulation expenses for AMTI. No recomputation of research and experiment expenses is required if a taxpayer has materially participated (i.e, regular, continuous, and substantial involvement) in the activity that generated the costs. If a loss is sustained on property that generated the research and experiment or circulation expenses, a deduction is allowed equal to the lesser of (1) the unamortized expenses or (2) the amount that would be allowed as a loss had the expenses remained capitalized. The adjusted basis of such property must be computed under the AMT rules in order to determine the gain or loss from the sale for AMT purposes (Code Sec. 56(a)(6)). The difference between the regular tax gain or loss and the recomputed AMT gain or loss is a tax preference adjustment in the year of sale.

1440. AMT Adjustments for Corporate Taxpayers. In addition to alternative minimum tax (AMT) adjustments that affect all taxpayers (¶ 1430), corporations must make a number of adjustments to various tax items in calculating alternative minimum taxable income (AMTI) that only pertain to them.

Adjusted Current Earnings. A portion of the difference between the AMTI and the adjusted current earnings (ACE) of corporations—other than S corporations, regulated investment companies, real estate investment trusts, or real estate mortgage investment conduits—is treated as an adjustment to AMTI (Code Secs. 56(c)(1) and (g)).[19] This adjustment does not attempt to recapture the tax benefit derived by a corporation from the use of a particular tax deduction or exclusion. Instead, it is aimed at recapturing some of the overall tax savings enjoyed by corporations that report large earnings to their shareholders and creditors but, due to a variety of tax benefits, pay little or no tax. To achieve recapture, a corporation's AMTI must be increased by 75 percent of the amount by which its ACE exceeds its AMTI, computed without the adjustments for ACE or alternative tax net operating losses (ATNOLs) (¶ 1430).

> **Example 1:** A corporation has AMTI of $100,000 before it makes adjustments for ATNOLs or ACE. The current tax year's ACE amounts to $200,000, leaving the corporation with an ACE adjustment of $75,000 (.75 × ($200,000 – $100,000)), which increases AMTI to $175,000 ($100,000 + $75,000).

In some years, AMTI may be decreased, rather than increased, by the ACE adjustment. If a corporation's ACE is less than its AMTI, ACE may reduce AMTI by 75 percent of the amount by which AMTI exceeds ACE (.75 × (AMTI – ACE)). The overall amount by which the ACE adjustment may decrease AMTI over a period of years may not be greater than the overall amount by which the ACE adjustment has increased AMTI over that period. In a given tax year, this ceiling is determined by limiting the amount of AMTI available for reduction to the excess of prior year increases in AMTI caused by the ACE adjustment over prior year reductions caused by an ACE shortfall.

> **Example 2:** In a corporation's current tax year, it calculates ACE of $50,000 and AMTI of $70,000. Multiplying the difference between AMTI and ACE by 0.75

References are to Standard Federal Tax Reports; Tax Research Consultant; and Practical Tax Explanations.

[18] ¶ 5200; FILEIND: 30,112; § 15,250, § 15,252

[19] ¶ 5200; STAGES: 9,120.05; § 15,125.05

leaves the corporation with $15,000, an amount that may possibly be used to reduce AMTI and thereby reduce the amount of minimum tax to which AMTI may be subjected for other tax preferences. In its prior tax years, the corporation calculated an overall positive ACE adjustment of $10,000. This amount serves as a limit on the amount by which ACE may reduce AMTI in the current year, leaving the corporation with only a $10,000 reduction of AMTI rather than a $15,000 reduction. The possible reduction of $5,000 that remains may not be carried over to later tax years.

A quick look at the rather simple ACE adjustment formula makes it clear that the most important factor in establishing the size of the preference is determining what makes up a corporation's ACE. In a broad view, ACE is made up of a corporation's earnings and profits, adjusted so that it takes on some of the principles used to calculate income for tax returns, including some of the principles for calculating the earnings and profits figure used to determine the taxation of dividend distributions to shareholders. Thus, the computation of ACE starts with AMTI as a base, which carries with it the built-in income, deductions, and exclusions used to determine regular as well as AMTI.

For depreciable property placed into service before 1994, AMTI must be adjusted using the applicable ACE depreciation method, a method that may differ from that used for regular tax reporting or even for the portion of AMTI that does not include the ACE preference. No ACE depreciation adjustment is made for property placed in service after 1993. The alternative (straight-line) MACRS method is used to determine allowable ACE depreciation for property placed in service after 1989 and before 1994.

Income, other than exempt discharge of indebtedness income, that is exempt from regular tax and AMT liability but that is included in the computation of earnings and profits must be included in the computation of ACE. This includes items such as interest payments on state and local bonds that are excluded from regular taxation but typically are included in the earnings and profits corporations report in financial sheets disclosed to the public. Expenses incurred in earning this kind of income, while not deductible in determining regular tax or AMT, are deductible in determining ACE.

Other adjustments include (but are not limited to) the following.

- If a corporation does not claim a deduction against earnings and profits, it may not claim the deduction in the computation of ACE (except for certain dividends).

- Intangible drilling costs (IDC) (¶ 989), the costs of organizing a corporation (¶ 237), and the costs of circulating periodicals (¶ 971) which may be expensed or amortized for regular tax purposes must be capitalized in computing ACE.

- ACE must be increased or decreased by an increase or decrease in a corporation's LIFO recapture amount, which is the amount by which the value of the corporation's inventory under the FIFO method of inventory valuation exceeds the value under the LIFO method.

- The installment method of accounting (¶ 1801) may not be used in most cases, in the computation of ACE.

- Income that has built up on a life insurance contract must be included in a corporation's ACE.

- The cost depletion method (¶ 1289) must be used to determine depletion deductions of corporations other than independent oil and gas producers and royalty owners.

- A corporation that has undergone an ownership change in which new shareholders have acquired more than half of the value of the corporation's stock must undertake a wholesale recomputation of the basis of its assets so that the basis of each asset takes on the value of the asset at the time of the corporation's acquisition by the new shareholders.

- ACE may not include loss from the exchange of one pool of debt obligations for another pool that consists of obligations with the same effective interest rates and maturities as obligations in the first pool.

• The adjusted basis of assets for purposes of making ACE adjustments is determined under these ACE adjustment rules.

• No adjustment related to the earnings and profits effect of charitable contributions is made to ACE.

• A property and casualty insurance company that elects to be taxed only on taxable investment income for regular tax purposes determines its ACE without regard to underwriting income or underwriting expense in tax years beginning after 1997.

Merchant Marine Capital Construction Funds. Contributions made by shipping companies to capital construction funds (established under § 607 of the Merchant Marine Act of 1936, 46 U.S.C. 1177) may not be deducted from AMTI, and a fund's earnings (including gains or losses) may not be excluded from AMTI (Code Sec. 56(c)(2)).[20] No reduction in the basis of a vessel, barge, or container need be made to reflect amounts withdrawn from a fund if the amounts have been included in AMTI.

Blue Cross and Blue Shield Organizations. The special deduction from regular tax allowed to Blue Cross and Blue Shield organizations under Code Sec. 833 for one-fourth of their annual claims and administrative expenses (less the prior tax year's adjusted surplus) may not be claimed against AMTI (Code Sec. 56(c)(3)).[21]

1445. AMT Interaction with Corporate Preference Cutbacks. Several tax benefits that may be claimed by corporations must be reduced by 20 or 30 percent (Code Secs. 59(f) and 291).[22] Like tax preferences that are subject to alternative minimum tax (AMT) (¶ 1425), these tax items have been selected for reduction in order to prevent excessive tax benefits. However, the approach adopted under the preference cutback rules differs from other AMT principles. Rather than being subject to the AMT after they have been claimed against regular taxable income, these items are reduced in size before the AMT rules are applied.

The following reductions must first be made to these tax preferences:

• Corporations that have sold or otherwise disposed of section 1250 property (¶ 1786) must provide ordinary income treatment to 20 percent of the portion of the gain on the disposition that has not been treated as ordinary income. The 20-percent treatment does not have to be applied if section 1250 property was part of a certified pollution control facility (¶ 1287). Also, if a real estate investment trust (REIT) (¶ 2326) disposes of section 1250 property, section 1250 gain which is treated as not coming from ordinary income and is distributed to shareholders as a capital gain dividend is excluded from ordinary income treatment. Corporate shareholders of a REIT must treat capital gain dividends as subject to the 20-percent ordinary income treatment.

• The percentage depletion deduction (¶ 1298) for iron ore and coal (including lignite) must be reduced by 20 percent of the excess of (a) the percentage depletion deduction (determined before the 20-percent reduction is made), over (b) the adjusted basis (determined without including the depletion deduction claimed in a tax year) of the minerals at the close of the tax year.

• There must be a 20-percent reduction in the amount of deductions claimed by a financial institution (subject to Code Sec. 585 or Code Sec. 593) for certain interest expenses on debts incurred to purchase tax-exempt obligations acquired after December 31, 1982, and before August 8, 1986.

• The basis of certified pollution control facilities that is used for computing rapid amortization deductions must be reduced by 20 percent. ACRS depreciation must be used to depreciate the reduced basis.

References are to Standard Federal Tax Reports; Tax Research Consultant; and Practical Tax Explanations.

[20] ¶ 5200; INDIV: 33,558

[21] ¶ 5200; EXEMPT: 15,160.10

[22] ¶ 5,400, ¶ 15,190; CCORP: 100; § 26,020.05

- A corporation's (including an integrated oil company's) deductions for intangible drilling costs and mineral exploration and development costs (¶ 987, ¶ 988, and ¶ 989) must be reduced by 30 percent. Reduced deductions may be deducted ratably over a 60-month period that starts with the month in which costs are paid or incurred. If the related property is disposed, the deductions may be recaptured (¶ 2025).

1450. Election to Avoid Tax Preference Status. A taxpayer can avoid having alternative minimum tax (AMT) preference or adjustment for certain expenses if the taxpayer elects to capitalize the expenses and deduct them ratably over specified periods for regular tax purposes beginning with the tax year (or month) in which the expenses were made (Code Sec. 59(e)).[23] Taxpayers may limit their elections to only a portion of their deductions, leaving the remaining deductions subject to AMT. A three-year period may be claimed for circulation expenses (¶ 971), a 60-month period may be claimed for intangible drilling costs (IDC) (¶ 989), and a 10-year period may be claimed for research and experiment expenses (¶ 979), and mineral exploration and development expenses (¶ 987 and ¶ 988). Partners and S corporation shareholders must make elections separately.

1455. Net AMT Adjustment of Electing Large Partnerships. A partnership is not subject to the alternative minimum tax (AMT) and its partners generally compute their AMT liability separately by taking into account their share of partnership items (¶ 1401). However, in the case of an electing large partnership using a simplified reporting system of partnership items (¶ 482), AMT tax preference items and adjustments are computed at the partnership level with the partnership reporting to its partners a net AMT adjustment for passive loss limitation activities and other activities (Code Sec. 722).[24] The net AMT adjustment is determined by using the adjustments applicable to individuals in the case of noncorporate partners (¶ 1435) and the adjustments applicable to corporations in the case of corporate partners (¶ 1440). Except as provided in regulations, the applicable net AMT adjustment is treated as a deferral tax preference for purposes of computing the minimum tax credit (¶ 1309).

1460. Losses Not Allowed for AMT. In computing alternative minimum taxable income (AMTI), a noncorporate taxpayer may not claim certain farm losses. In addition, taxpayers subject to the passive activity loss rules may not claim passive activity losses when computing AMTI when the losses are disallowed for regular tax purposes.

Passive Farm Tax Shelter Losses. Noncorporate taxpayers, including personal service corporations, who are not material participants in a farming business but use a farming tax shelter to avoid regular tax liability may not deduct passive farming losses in computing AMTI (Code Sec. 58(a)).[25] Farm tax shelters are farm syndicates (¶ 2032) or passive farm activities in which the taxpayer (or the taxpayer's spouse) is not a material participant (¶ 2059). The amount of denied losses must be reduced by the amount of a taxpayer's insolvency during a tax year (Code Sec. 58(c)). Insolvency is the excess of a taxpayer's liabilities over the fair market value of the taxpayer's assets. Taxpayers may not net income and losses from various farming tax shelters to determine an overall loss or gain. Each tax shelter must be regarded separately. Thus, a taxpayer who suffers a $1,000 loss from one tax shelter, but has a $1,000 gain from another, must include a $1,000 gain in AMTI calculations. Also, tax preferences included in losses must be adjusted so that their preference is eliminated. Farm losses that have been disallowed as deductions from AMTI in one tax year may be claimed as deductions from farm income from that activity in the succeeding tax year. Taxpayers who dispose of their interest in a farm tax shelter are allowed to claim their losses against AMTI.

References are to Standard Federal Tax Reports; Tax Research Consultant; and Practical Tax Explanations.

[23] ¶ 5400; FILEIND: 30,114; § 15,250, § 15,252, § 15,255, § 15,320

[24] ¶ 25,060, ¶ 32,060; SCORP: 352.15, STAGES: 9,214; § 15,025

[25] ¶ 5350; FILEIND: 30,154; § 15,410

Other Passive Business Activity Losses. With some modifications, the regular tax rules limiting the deductibility of losses from passive, nonfarm business activities must be followed in finding the alternative minimum tax (AMT) of individuals, trusts, estates, closely held C corporations, and personal service corporations (Code Sec. 58(b)).[26] Thus, deductions for passive losses may be claimed only against passive income. One modification requires a taxpayer to reduce the amount of denied losses by the amount of his insolvency during a tax year. Furthermore, the passive activity loss is determined without regard to any qualified housing interest. Finally, passive losses must be adjusted, as they would be under other AMT rules, to eliminate tax preferences.

> **Example:** In calculating his regular tax, Doug Pratt has a passive loss deduction of $15,000 for net losses from real estate rentals. The losses are partially based on MACRS deductions, an AMT adjustment (¶ 1430). His AMT liability must be determined by computing depreciation deductions under the alternative depreciation system (ADS). This leaves him with a passive loss deduction of only $5,000 against AMTI. Since he already has adjusted his depreciation deductions in determining whether there is a passive loss, he does not have to include them as part of any adjustment for depreciation in calculating AMTI.

1465. AMT Liability of REITs, RICs, and Common Trust Funds. Tax preference items and adjustments which are treated differently for alternative minimum tax (AMT) and regular tax purposes must be apportioned between real estate investment trusts (REITs) or regulated investment companies (RICs), and their shareholders and holders of beneficial interests. Participants in common trust funds must apportion these items among themselves on a pro rata basis (Code Sec. 59(d)).[27]

Credits Against Minimum Tax

1470. Alternative Minimum Tax Foreign Tax Credit. The alternative minimum tax (AMT) foreign tax credit may be claimed by taxpayer's in computing their tentative minimum tax (¶ 1401). The AMT foreign tax credit is similar to the foreign tax credit for regular income tax purposes (¶ 2475), except that it is limited to the foreign tax on foreign source alternative minimum taxable income (AMTI) instead of foreign tax on regular taxable income (Code Sec. 59(a)).[28] Thus, the AMT foreign tax credit cannot exceed the taxpayer's tentative minimum tax multiplied by the ratio of the taxpayer's foreign source AMTI to worldwide AMTI. Alternatively, the taxpayer may elect to compute the AMT foreign tax credit limit by multiplying the tentative minimum tax by the ratio of the taxpayer's foreign source regular taxable income to worldwide AMTI. Amounts disallowed by the foreign tax credit limitation may be carried back two years and forward five years, subject to the same limitation in those years for both regular tax and AMT purposes.

1475. Other Tax Credits Under AMT. For tax years beginning in 2012, the aggregate amount of nonrefundable personal credits allowed to an individual (other than certain specified credits) is limited to the excess of the individual's regular tax liability over tentative minimum tax for the year (determined without regard to the alternative minimum tax (AMT) foreign tax credit) (Code Sec. 26(a)).[29] Thus, the only credits that are fully allowed against the taxpayer's combined regular tax and AMT liability are the adoption credit (¶ 1307), the child tax credit (¶ 1305), the American Opportunity tax credit(¶ 1303), the retirement savings contributions credit (¶ 1304), the residential energy efficient property credit (¶ 1342), the small plug-in vehicle credit (¶ 1354), the alternative motor vehicle credit (¶ 1345), and the plug-in electric drive motor vehicle credit (¶ 1351). Special calculation or carryover rules also apply to the mortgage

References are to Standard Federal Tax Reports; Tax Research Consultant; and Practical Tax Explanations.

[26] ¶ 5350; FILEIND: 30,152; § 15,405

[27] ¶ 5400; FILEIND: 30,404.25; § 15,025

[28] ¶ 5400; FILEIND: 30,352; § 15,505

[29] ¶ 3850; INDIV: 57,200; § 12,005

certificate credit for low-income homeowners (¶ 1306), the foreign tax credit for regular income tax (¶ 2475), and the District of Columbia first-time homebuyer credit (¶ 1308).

The amount of general business credit that a taxpayer can claim during a tax year may not exceed the sum of the taxpayer's combined regular tax liability and AMT liability, less the above nonrefundable personal tax credits, and less the greater of (1) the taxpayer's tentative minimum tax, or (2) 25 percent of the taxpayer's net regular tax liability over $25,000 (¶ 1365) (Code Sec. 38(c)).[30] However, several specified credits are allowed to the full extent of the taxpayer's combined regular tax and AMT liability, although they may be subject to particular limitations specific to the individual credit. These credits include the alcohol fuels credit (¶ 1365I), the low-income housing credit (¶ 1365K), the renewable electricity production credit (¶ 1365N), the FICA employer tip credit (¶ 1365R), the railroad track maintenance credit (¶ 1365W), the small employer health insurance credit (¶ 1333), the rehabilitation credit (¶ 1365B), the business energy credit (¶ 1365C), the work opportunity credit (¶ 1365G), and certain eligible small business credits (¶ 1365). The limitation is made separately for the empowerment zone employment credit, substituting 75 percent of tentative AMT for 100 percent of AMT.

1480. AMT and Possessions Tax Credit. Corporate income for which the Puerto Rican economic activity credit or the possessions tax credit may be claimed (¶ 1362) is not includible in AMTI and therefore is not subject to the minimum tax (Code Sec. 59(b)).[31]

References are to Standard Federal Tax Reports; Tax Research Consultant; and Practical Tax Explanations.

[30] ¶ 4250; BUSEXP: 54,056; § 15,515.15

[31] ¶ 5400; INTL: 27,066

Chapter 15
TAX ACCOUNTING

Accounting Period

1501. Tax Year. Taxable income is computed on the basis of a period called a tax year. A tax year is the annual accounting period regularly used by a taxpayer in keeping its books and records to compute income. This period is usually a calendar year or a fiscal year. A calendar year is a period of 12 months ending on December 31. A fiscal year is a period of 12 months ending on the last day of any month other than December; a 52-53 week fiscal year, however, may end on a different day of the month (¶ 1503). Special rules exist when a taxpayer must file a return for a period that is less than 12 months (short-period return) (¶ 1505) (Code Sec. 441).[1]

> **Example 1:** A corporation began doing business on August 15, 2012. The end of its first tax year cannot be later than July 31, 2013, because a tax year may not cover more than a 12-month period and must end on the last day of a month, unless it is a 52-53-week tax year.

A new taxpayer may adopt either a calendar or a fiscal year on their first tax return, but certain taxpayers are required to adopt a specific tax year (Reg. § 1.441-1).[2] An existing taxpayer that wants to change its tax year must follow IRS procedures (¶ 1513). If a taxpayer adopts an improper tax year, such as a fiscal year (other than a 52-53 week tax year) that does not end with a calendar month, the IRS may require the taxpayer to adopt a proper tax year or to request IRS approval to change tax years (¶ 1513) (Rev. Rul. 85-22).[3]

> **Example 2:** Assume that the new corporation in Example 1 determines there is no advantage in keeping its books on the basis of any year other than the calendar year. Therefore, it adopts the calendar-year basis. It should close its books as of December 31, 2012, and file its first return for the short period from August 15, 2012, through December 31, 2012. This is its first tax year. All its later tax years will be full calendar years until its dissolution or until it changes to a fiscal year.

A fiscal year will be recognized only if it is established as the taxpayer's annual accounting period and only if the taxpayer keeps his or her books accordingly. A taxpayer who has no annual accounting period, does not keep adequate records, or whose present tax year does not qualify as a fiscal year must compute taxable income on a calendar-year basis (Reg. § 1.441-1).[4]

A partnership generally must use the same tax year as that of its owners unless the partnership can establish a business purpose for having a different tax year (Code Sec. 706(b); Reg. § 1.706-1).[5] The tax year of the owners for this purpose is the tax year of the

References are to Standard Federal Tax Reports; Tax Research Consultant; and Practical Tax Explanations.

[1] ¶ 20,302; ACCTNG: 24,050; § 38,101

[2] ¶ 20,303; ACCTNG: 24,052; § 38,105

[3] ¶ 20,307.70; ACCTNG: 24,058; § 38,135.20

[4] ¶ 20,303; ACCTNG: 24,056; § 38,110

[5] ¶ 25,160, ¶ 25,161; ACCTNG: 24,352; § 30,120.05

partner(s) owning the majority interest in the partnership—the tax year of the partner(s) owning in total more than a 50-percent interest in partnership profits and capital (¶ 416). If there is no majority interest tax year, the partnership must adopt the same tax year as that of its principal partners, each of whom must have at least a 5-percent interest in partnership profits or capital. When neither condition is met, the partnership must use the tax year that produces the least aggregate deferral of income to the partners.

An S corporation or a personal service corporation (PSC) (¶ 273) must generally use the calendar year unless the entity can establish a business purpose for having a different tax year (Code Secs. 441(i) and 1378(b)).[6] For this purpose, a corporation is not considered a PSC unless more than 10 percent of its stock (by value) is held by employee-owners. If a corporation is a member of an affiliated group filing a consolidated return, all members of that group must be considered in determining whether the corporation is a PSC.

Certain partnerships, S corporations, and PSCs may elect on Form 8716 to use a tax year other than a required tax year (Code Sec. 444).[7] To neutralize tax benefits resulting from such a tax year, electing partnerships and S corporations must compute and make any required payments (i.e., the amount of tax that would otherwise be due from partners and stockholders had those entities used the required tax year) exceeding $500 (Code Sec. 7519).[8] The required payment is due on or before May 15 of the calendar year following the calendar year in which the election year begins (Temp. Reg. § 1.7519-2T(a)(4)).[9] Electing PSCs must make minimum distributions to their employee-owners by the end of a calendar year falling within a tax year to avoid certain deduction deferrals for amounts paid to employee-owners (Code Sec. 280H).[10]

Generally, the Section 444 election must be made by the earlier of: (1) the 15th day of the fifth month following the month that includes the first day of the tax year for which the election is first effective or (2) the due date (without extensions) of the return that results from the election (Temp. Reg. § 1.444-3T(b)(1)).[11] The election remains in effect until an entity changes its tax year or otherwise terminates such an election (Code Sec. 444(d)).[12] The election may not be made by an entity that is a member of a tiered structure unless the tiered structure consists only of partnerships or S corporations (or both), all of which have the same tax year.

Common trust funds (certain investment funds maintained by a bank; ¶ 2389) are required to adopt the calendar year as their tax year (Code Sec. 584(i)).[13]

The tax year of a domestic international sales corporation (DISC) (¶ 2498) must be the same as that of the shareholder or group of shareholders with the same tax year who have the highest percentage of voting power. Voting power is determined on the basis of total combined voting power of all classes of stock of the corporation entitled to vote. If two or more shareholders or groups are tied for the highest percentage, the tax year used is that of any such shareholder or group (Code Sec. 441(h)).[14]

1503. 52- or 53-Week Accounting Period. A taxpayer may elect to use a fiscal tax year that varies from 52 to 53 weeks if that period always ends on the same day of the week (Monday, Tuesday, etc.) and that day is either the last such day in a calendar month or the closest such day to the last day of a calendar month (Code Sec. 441(f); Reg. § 1.441-2).[15]

> **Example:** A new taxpayer wishes to have its accounting period end on the last Saturday in August. In 2012, its tax year ends on August 25, completing a 52-week year (August 28, 2011, through August 25, 2012). In 2013, its tax year ends on August 31, completing a 52-week year (August 26, 2012, through August 31, 2013).

References are to Standard Federal Tax Reports; Tax Research Consultant; and Practical Tax Explanations.

[6] ¶ 20,302, ¶ 32,260; ACCTNG: 24,354, ACCTNG: 24,356; § 27,120, § 28,410.15

[7] ¶ 20,600; ACCTNG: 24,450; § 38,115.05

[8] ¶ 42,770; ACCTNG: 24,500; § 38,115.10

[9] ¶ 42,773; ACCTNG: 24,504.05; § 38,115.10

[10] ¶ 15,160; ACCTNG: 24,550; § 38,115.15

[11] ¶ 20,604; ACCTNG: 24,454; § 38,115.05

[12] ¶ 20,600; ACCTNG: 24,458; § 38,115.05

[13] ¶ 23,630; RIC: 12,304.15

[14] ¶ 20,302; ACCTNG: 24,110.10

[15] ¶ 20,302, ¶ 20,304; ACCTNG: 24,302; § 38,105

With this type of tax year, most of the taxpayer's tax years are 52 weeks long. As an alternative, the taxpayer could select a tax year that ends on the Saturday that is nearest to the end of August. In 2012, therefore, the tax year ends on September 1 (the Saturday nearest the end of August). In 2013, the tax year will end on August 31.

If a pass-through entity or an owner of a pass-through entity, or both, use a 52-53-week tax year and the tax year of the entity and owner end with reference to the same calendar month, then for purposes of determining the tax year in which items of income, gain, loss, deductions, or credits from the entity are taken into account by the owner, the owner's tax year will be deemed to end on the last day of the entity's tax year. Under this rule, a pass-through entity is a partnership, S corporation, trust, estate, closely held real estate investment trust, common trust fund, controlled foreign corporation, foreign personal holding company, or passive foreign investment company that is a qualified electing fund (Reg. § 1.441-2(e)).[16]

1505. Short-Period Return. A return for a period of less than 12 months may need to be filed by a taxpayer who changes its annual accounting period (¶ 1513) or is in existence during only part of what would otherwise be the tax year (Code Sec. 443; Reg. § 1.443-1).[17]

Taxpayers who are not in existence for a full 12-month period include:

(1) a corporation that begins business or goes out of business at any time other than the beginning or end of its accounting period,

(2) an individual taxpayer who dies prior to the end of the accounting period, and

(3) a decedent's estate that comes into existence on the date of the decedent's death and adopts an accounting period ending less than 12 months from that date.

If the taxpayer is not in existence for a full tax year, the tax is computed as if the return had actually covered a full tax year. When a short period occurs as a result of a change in accounting period, the tax is computed on an annualized basis (¶ 1507). An alternative relief method is also available for taxpayers that change their accounting period (¶ 1509). Short-period returns of decedents and dissolving corporations, and the first return of a new corporation, however, are not required to be annualized.

If a change to or from a 52-53 week tax year results in a short period of 359 days or more, the tax is computed as if the return had actually covered a full tax year. If the short period is less than seven days, the short period becomes a part of the following tax year. If the short period is more than six days but less than 359 days, the tax is computed under the annualized method (Code Sec. 441(f)(2)).[18] Special annualization rules apply to taxpayers that make such a change (¶ 1507).

1507. Method for Annualizing Income for Short Periods. When there has been a change in an accounting period that necessitates the filing of a short-period return (¶ 1505), income for the period must be converted to an annual basis. This conversion is accomplished by: (1) multiplying the taxpayer's modified taxable income for the short period by 12 and (2) dividing the result by the number of months in the short period. Then the tax is computed on the resulting taxable income by using the tax rate schedules and not the tax tables for individuals. The tax so computed is divided by 12 and multiplied by the number of months in the short period (Code Sec. 443).[19]

The modified taxable income for the short period is the gross income for the period less any allowable deductions (other than the standard deduction) and an adjusted personal exemption amount. Actual itemized deductions for the short period are allowed in lieu of the standard deduction amount. The adjusted personal exemption amount is

References are to Standard Federal Tax Reports; Tax Research Consultant; and Practical Tax Explanations.

[16] ¶ 20,304; ACCTNG: 24,308; § 38,105

[17] ¶ 20,500, ¶ 20,501; ACCTNG: 24,250; § 38,140.05

[18] ¶ 20,302; ACCTNG: 24,306; § 38,140.15

[19] ¶ 20,500; ACCTNG: 24,260; § 38,140.10, § 38,140.15

the total of an individual taxpayer's personal exemptions times the ratio of the number of months in the short period to 12.

Example: Tom has been making his returns on the basis of a fiscal year ending April 30. He changes to a year ending June 30 in 2012. He must file his return for the year ending April 30, 2012, on or before August 15, 2012. On or before October 15, 2012, he must file his return for the short period of two months beginning May 1, 2012, and ending June 30, 2012. His gross income for the short period is $9,600, and his itemized deductions total $600. He is married, age 60, and has no dependents. His wife has no income or deductions. The tax before credits on their joint return is computed as follows:

Gross income	$9,600
Itemized deductions*	600
Net income	9,000
Less 2/12 of $7,600 (2 × $3,800) exemptions	1,267
Modified taxable income for short period	7,733
Annualized taxable income—$7,733 × 12/2	46,398
Tax on $46,398	6,090
Tax for short period, 2/12 of $6,090	1,015

* Assume that the itemized deductions are not miscellaneous itemized deductions and that amounts are rounded up to the nearest dollar. An individual making a short-period return because of a change in annual accounting period is not eligible for the standard deduction (Code Sec. 63(c)(6)(C)).

When a short-period return is filed, the taxpayer's self-employment tax (¶ 2664) should be computed on the actual self-employment income for the short period and not prorated for a portion of a 12-month period.[20] A net operating loss deduction should be applied against actual income for the short period before annualizing (Rev. Proc. 2002-39, modified by Rev. Proc. 2003-34 and Rev. Proc. 2003-79).[21]

A taxpayer that is changing to or from a 52-53-week fiscal tax year and that must annualize income will apply the same rules as other taxpayers in determining the income of the short period, but will calculate income on an annual basis by multiplying the income of the short period by 365 and dividing the result by the number of days in the short period (Code Sec. 441(f)(2)(B)(iii)). Tax is computed on that annualized income and, as computed, is multiplied by the ratio of the number of days in the short period to 365; the resulting figure is the tax for the short year.

1509. Alternative Method for Annualizing Income for Short Periods. An alternative method is provided for annualizing income when computing tax for a short-period return (¶ 1505) (Code Sec. 443(b)(2); Reg. § 1.443-1(b)(2)).[22] Under this method, the tax for the short period is the greater of:

(1) a tax on the actual taxable income for the 12-month period beginning with the start of the short period (using the law in effect for that 12-month period) multiplied by the modified taxable income (¶ 1507) for the short period and divided by the modified taxable income for the 12-month period, or

(2) a tax on the modified taxable income for the short period.

If a taxpayer does not exist at the end of the 12-month period described in (1), above, or if a corporate taxpayer has distributed substantially all its assets before the end of that period, the tax is computed by using a 12-month period ending with the last day of the short period. In such cases, in order to claim the benefits of the alternative method, the taxpayer must attach a return covering the 12-month period ending on the last day of the short year to the return initially computed for the short period.

References are to Standard Federal Tax Reports; Tax Research Consultant; and Practical Tax Explanations.

[20] ¶ 35,203.30; INDIV: 63,058; § 38,140.15

[21] ¶ 20,406; ACCTNG: 24,260; § 38,140.15

[22] ¶ 20,500, ¶ 20,501; ACCTNG: 24,260.15; § 38,140.25

If there was a change in accounting period resulting in a short period, the taxpayer must first compute the tax using the general annualization method and file the return. If the alternate method would result in lower taxes, a claim for credit or refund must be filed no later than the due date by which a return would have been required to be filed if the 12-month period beginning with the short period were considered a tax year. The application of the taxpayer for use of the alternate method is considered as a claim for credit or refund.

1513. Change of Accounting Period. The change from one accounting period to another generally requires prior permission of the IRS and requires the filing of a return for the short period (¶ 1505). To request IRS approval to change, Form 1128 generally must be filed by the due date of the taxpayer's return (not including extensions) for the first effective year. A change in the accounting period will be approved where it is established that a substantial business purpose exists for making the change but generally will not be approved where the sole purpose of the change is to maintain or obtain a preferential tax status (Reg. § 1.442-1(b)).[23] The IRS will consider all the facts and circumstances relating to the change, including the tax consequences. Among the non-tax factors is the effect of the change on the taxpayer's annual cycle of business activity. The agreement between the taxpayer and the IRS under which the change is carried out will, in appropriate cases, provide terms, conditions, and adjustments necessary to prevent a substantial distortion of income that would otherwise result from the change. For example, effects that would constitute substantial distortions of income include:

(1) deferring a substantial portion of the taxpayer's income or shifting a substantial portion of deductions from one year to another so as to reduce substantially the taxpayer's tax liability;

(2) causing a similar deferral or shift in the case of any other person, such as a partner, a beneficiary, or an S corporation shareholder; or

(3) creating a short period in which there is either: (a) a substantial net operating loss, capital loss or credit (including a general business credit); or (b) a substantial amount of income to offset an expiring net operating loss, capital loss, or credit (Reg. § 1.442-1(b)(3)).[24]

Non-individual Taxpayers. Automatic approval procedures are provided for certain corporations that have not requested a tax year change within the most recent 48-month period ending with the last month of the requested tax year (Rev. Proc. 2006-45, modified by Rev. Proc. 2007-64). Automatic approval procedures are also provided for trusts and certain partnerships, S corporations, electing S corporations, and personal service corporations that have not requested a tax year change within the most recent 48-month period ending with the last month of the requested tax year, that meet certain conditions (Rev. Proc. 2006-46). If the automatic approval procedures do not apply, the IRS has provided other procedures for taxpayers to follow in order to obtain the IRS's prior approval of an adoption, change, or retention in an annual accounting period through application to the IRS national office (Reg. § 1.442-1(b)(3); Rev. Proc. 2002-39, modified by Rev. Proc. 2003-34 and Rev. Proc. 2003-79).[25]

Individuals. Certain individuals may also follow automatic approval procedures (Reg. § 1.442-1(b)(3); Rev. Proc. 2003-62). The only individual who may change his or her tax year without IRS consent is a newly married individual who is adopting the annual accounting period of his or her spouse to file a joint return (Reg. § 1.442-1(d)).[26]

Improper Tax Year. As an alternative to the above procedures, any taxpayer may correct a prior adoption of an improper tax year by filing Form 1128 with an amended return on a calendar year basis (Rev. Proc. 85-15).[27]

References are to Standard Federal Tax Reports; Tax Research Consultant; and Practical Tax Explanations.

[23] ¶ 20,401, ¶ 20,406.41; ACCTNG: 24,200; § 38,101

[24] ¶ 20,401; ACCTNG: 24,200; § 38,120.20, § 38,125.10, § 38,130.25

[25] ¶ 20,401; ACCTNG: 24,200; § 38,120.05, § 38,125.05, § 38,130.05

[26] ¶ 20,401; ACCTNG: 24,152; § 38,110

[27] ¶ 20,406.15; ACCTNG: 24,166; § 38,110

Accounting Method

1515. Cash v. Accrual Basis. Taxable income must be computed not only on the basis of a fixed accounting *period* (¶ 1501) but also in accordance with a *method* of accounting regularly employed in keeping the taxpayer's books. A "method of accounting" includes the overall method of accounting for income and expenses, as well as the method of accounting for special items such as depreciation (Reg. § 1.446-1(a)).[28] There are two common overall methods of accounting for income: the cash basis and the accrual basis.

The cash basis (cash receipts and disbursements) is the method of accounting used by most individuals. Income is generally reported in the year that it is actually or constructively received in the form of cash or its equivalent or other property. The constructive receipt of income is income not actually received but within the taxpayer's control (¶ 1533). However, there is no constructive receipt if there are substantial limits or restrictions on the right to receive it. Deductions or credits are generally taken for the year in which the related expenditures were actually paid, unless they should be taken in a different period to more clearly reflect income (such as depreciation allowances and prepaid expenses) (Reg. § 1.446-1(c)(1)(i)).[29]

Under the accrual method, income is accounted for when the taxpayer has the right to receive it—when all the events that determine that right have occurred. It is not the actual receipt but the *right to receive* that governs. Expenses are deductible on the accrual basis in the year incurred—when all the events have occurred that fix the amount of the item and determine the liability of the taxpayer to pay it (Reg. § 1.446-1(c)(1)(ii)).[30] See ¶ 1540 for a discussion of this "all-events test" as it relates to economic performance.

The accounting method used must clearly reflect income (¶ 1525). An approved standard method of accounting (such as the cash basis or the accrual basis) ordinarily is regarded as clearly reflecting income. A taxpayer may use one accounting method to keep his or her personal books and another for the books of his or her trade or business. A taxpayer may use different accounting methods if the taxpayer has two or more separate businesses as long as separate and distinct sets of records are maintained. However, the use of multiple accounting methods is not permitted if there is a creation or shifting of profits or losses between the taxpayer's various trades or businesses (Reg. § 1.446-1).[31] Generally, and except as otherwise required, a hybrid method of accounting combining two or more methods of accounting—such as a combination of the cash method as the taxpayer's overall method of accounting and the accrual method for inventories—may be used so long as the combination clearly reflects income and is consistently used (Reg. § 1.446-1(c)(1)(iv)).[32]

Taxpayers that are required to use inventories (¶ 1553) must use the accrual method to account for purchases and sales (Reg. § 1.446-1(c)(2)).[33] Furthermore, the following taxpayers must generally use the accrual method of accounting as their overall method of accounting for tax purposes:

(1) C corporations,

(2) partnerships that have a C corporation as a partner,

(3) trusts that are subject to the tax on unrelated trade or business income (charitable trusts), but only for that income, and

(4) tax shelters (Code Sec. 448(a) and (d)(6)).[34]

Qualified personal service corporations (¶ 219) are treated as individuals rather than as corporations for purposes of category (2), above.

References are to Standard Federal Tax Reports; Tax Research Consultant; and Practical Tax Explanations.

[28] ¶ 20,607; ACCTNG: 200; § 38,201

[29] ¶ 20,607; ACCTNG: 208; § 38,210, § 38,215.05

[30] ¶ 20,607; ACCTNG: 210; § 38,220.05

[31] ¶ 20,607; ACCTNG: 208.05; § 38,205.05

[32] ¶ 20,607; ACCTNG: 6,400; § 38,225

[33] ¶ 20,607; ACCTNG: 15,060; § 38,215.05

[34] ¶ 20,800; ACCTNG: 6,050; § 38,215.05

Notwithstanding the general requirement that these taxpayers use the accrual method, the cash method of accounting may be used instead if the entity is not a tax shelter and:

(1) is engaged in a farming or tree-raising business (unless the taxpayer is a corporation or has a corporation as a partner; ¶ 2028),

(2) is a qualified personal service corporation, or

(3) is an eligible small business (Code Sec. 448(b)).

A small business is exempt from using the accrual method if it has met the $5 million or less gross receipts test for all prior tax years beginning after 1985. An entity meets the $5 million gross receipts test if the average annual gross receipts for the three tax years ending with the prior tax year does not exceed $5 million (Temp. Reg. § 1.448-1T(f)).[35] Furthermore, most businesses that are required to account for inventories may use the cash method if average annual gross receipts do not exceed $1 million (Rev. Proc. 2001-10). Certain other small businesses required to account for inventories may also use the cash method if average annual gross receipts do not exceed $10 million (Rev. Proc. 2002-28).[36]

1516. Prorating Income of Accrual-Method Taxpayers. When the effective date of a tax rate change occurs within a tax year, an accrual-method taxpayer must compute the tax for the entire tax year by using both the old and the new rates (Code Sec. 15).[37] The final tax is the sum of (1) the tax calculated at the old rates that is proportionate to the portion of the tax year before the effective date of the new tax and (2) the tax calculated at the new rates that is proportionate to the portion of the tax year beginning with the effective date.

When the tax rate change involves the highest rate of income tax, the taxpayer must compute the tax for the year by using a weighted average of the highest rates before and after the change determined on the basis of the respective portions of the tax year before the date of change and on or after the date of change.

1517. Accruing Income Doubtful of Collection. On the accrual basis of accounting, income such as interest is taxable as it accrues even though it is received at a later date. However, if there is a real doubt that the interest is collectible when it becomes due, it need not be accrued.[38] But where the uncollectible item arises from a sale of property, the proper procedure is to report the sale and then take a bad debt deduction as appropriate.

Generally, an accrual-basis taxpayer is not required to accrue as income any amount to be received for the performance of services that, based on experience, will not be collected (Code Sec. 448(d)(5); Reg. § 1.448-2(a)).[39] This treatment with respect to those amounts is a method of accounting that must be elected by the taxpayer. The nonaccrual experience method of accounting is limited to amounts to be received for the performance of qualified services (health, law, engineering, architecture, accounting, actuarial science, performing arts, or consulting) and for services provided by certain small businesses.

1519. Accruing Uncertain and Contingent Liabilities. On the accrual basis of accounting, expenses are deductible in the tax year when all events have occurred that fix the amount of the item and determine the liability of the taxpayer to pay it (¶ 1540). Thus, there can be no accrual of an expense until any contingency disappears and the liability becomes fixed and certain.[40] Similarly, an accrual-method taxpayer generally cannot accrue a liability that the taxpayer is contesting, as the liability is not fixed and certain. However, if the taxpayer is contesting an asserted liability and transfers money or property to provide for the satisfaction of the liability, the taxpayer can take a deduction in the year of the transfer if the contest continues to exist after the transfer

References are to Standard Federal Tax Reports; Tax Research Consultant; and Practical Tax Explanations.

[35] ¶ 20,801B; ACCTNG: 208.15; § 38,215.10

[36] ¶ 20,803.75; ACCTNG: 6,050, ACCTNG: 15,058; § 38,215.10

[37] ¶ 3385; ACCTNG: 24,310.10, FILEIND: 15,054.25; § 38,140.10

[38] ¶ 21,005.20; ACCTNG: 9,058; § 38,220.10

[39] ¶ 20,800, ¶ 20,802; ACCTNG: 9,058.10; § 38,320.25

[40] ¶ 21,805; ACCTNG: 12,056; § 38,430.10

and the liability would otherwise be allowed as a deduction in the year of transfer (or an earlier tax year) (Code Sec. 461(f)).[41]

See ¶ 1547 for a discussion of reserves for contingent or estimated expenses.

1525. Method Prescribed by IRS. The IRS can prescribe a method of accounting that will clearly reflect income if, in the IRS's opinion, the method used by the taxpayer fails to do so (Code Sec. 446(b)).[42] If the IRS requires a change in accounting methods, the taxpayer must compute an income adjustment due to the change (¶ 1531) (Code Sec. 481(a)).[43]

1527. Accruing Interest and Expenses Owed to Related Taxpayers. When different methods of accounting are used by related taxpayers, accrued interest and expenses owed to a related taxpayer may not be deducted until the time that the interest or expense payment is includible in the gross income of the cash-basis payee (Code Sec. 267(a)(2)).[44] Thus, an accrual-basis payor is placed on the cash basis for the purpose of deducting business expenses and interest owed to a related cash-basis taxpayer. The deduction is deferred until the cash-basis payee takes the item into income.

Related taxpayers include certain family members, members of a controlled group of corporations, controlling shareholders and controlled corporations, and owners of pass-through entities, such as a partnership and its partners and an S corporation and its shareholders (Code Sec. 267(b) and (e)). A personal service corporation (PSC) and any of its employee-owners are also considered related parties for this purpose, regardless of the amount of the corporation's stock owned, directly or indirectly, by the employee-owner. Thus, the PSC may not deduct payments made to owner-employees before the tax year in which such persons must include the payment in gross income.

1529. Change of Accounting Method. As a general rule, a taxpayer may not change his or her method of accounting without obtaining advance permission from the IRS (Code Sec. 446(e); Reg. § 1.446-1(e)).[45] A change of accounting method includes a change in the overall plan of accounting as well as a change in the treatment of any material item. In most cases, a method of accounting is not established for an item unless there is a pattern of consistent treatment. A change in the treatment of a material item is one involving the timing of its inclusion in income or deduction (not the traditional accounting meaning dealing with the relationship of amounts).

Consent is required whether the change is made from an acceptable or an unacceptable method. If the taxpayer fails to file a request to change his or her method of accounting, the absence of IRS consent to the change will not prevent the imposition of penalties (or additions to tax) or diminish the penalties (or additions to tax) (Code Sec. 446(f)).[46] A taxpayer that changes its method of accounting for a tax year generally must make certain adjustments to its income, referred to as Code Sec. 481 adjustments (¶ 1531).

Changes in accounting method include, but are not limited to:

(1) a change from the cash to the accrual basis;

(2) any change in the method of valuing inventories (¶ 1571);

(3) a change in depreciation or amortization method (¶ 1221);

(4) a change from the cash or accrual basis to one of the long-term contract methods (percentage-of-completion capitalized-cost and percentage-of-completion), or vice versa, or from one long-term contract method to the other (¶ 1551);

(5) a change involving the adoption, use, or discontinuance of any other specialized basis, such as the crop method (¶ 1569); and

(6) a change where the Code and regulations specifically require that IRS consent be obtained.

References are to Standard Federal Tax Reports; Tax Research Consultant; and Practical Tax Explanations.

[41] ¶ 21,802; ACCTNG: 12,058; § 38,430.15

[42] ¶ 20,606; ACCTNG: 21,110; § 38,620

[43] ¶ 22,270; ACCTNG: 21,152; § 38,625.05

[44] ¶ 14,150; ACCTNG: 12,150, ACCTNG: 12,152.10; § 9,140, § 27,125.25

[45] ¶ 20,606, ¶ 20,607; ACCTNG: 21,102; § 38,610.05

[46] ¶ 20,606; ACCTNG: 21,050; § 38,610.05

The IRS will automatically approve certain taxpayers' changes of accounting method. This approval is granted for the tax year for which the taxpayer requests the change if the taxpayer complies with the automatic change procedures. The automatic change procedures are included in Rev. Proc. 2011-14, modified by Rev. Proc. 2011-22, Rev. Proc. 2011-27, Rev. Proc. 2011-28, Rev. Proc. 2011-43, Rev. Rul. 2012-1, Rev. Proc. 2012-19, Rev. Proc. 2012-20, and Rev. Proc. 2012-39.[47] For changes of accounting method which are *not* granted automatic approval by the IRS, taxpayers must comply with a separate set of request procedures included in Rev. Proc. 97-27, modified by Rev. Proc. 2002-19, Rev. Proc. 2007-67, Rev. Proc. 2009-39, Rev. Proc. 2011-14, and Rev. Proc. 2012-39.[48]

Application for permission to change the method of accounting must generally be filed on Form 3115 during the tax year in which the taxpayer desires to make the proposed change (Reg. § 1.446-1(e)(3)(i)).[49]

1531. Adjustments Required by Changes in Method of Accounting. Taxpayers who voluntarily change their method of accounting with the IRS's permission, or who are compelled by the IRS to make a change because the method used does not clearly reflect income, must make certain adjustments to income in the year of the change (Code Sec. 481(a); Reg. § 1.481-1).[50] The adjustments are those determined to be necessary to prevent duplication or omission of items.

Since the adjustments for the year of change might result in the bunching of income, two statutory methods of limiting the tax in the changeover year may be applied if the adjustments for the changeover year increase taxable income by more than $3,000 (Reg. § 1.481-2).[51] If both limitations apply, the one resulting in the lower tax should be used. Under the first method, the old method of accounting must have been used in the two preceding years; if so, the tax increase in the changeover year is limited to the tax increases that would result if the adjustments were spread ratably over that year and the two preceding years. Under the second method, the taxpayer must be able to reconstruct his or her income under the new method of accounting for one or more consecutive years immediately preceding the changeover year. The increase in the changeover year's tax because of the adjustments may not be more than the net tax increases that would result if the adjustments were allocated back to those preceding years under the new method. Any amounts that cannot be allocated back must be included in the changeover year's income for purposes of computing the limitation.

In addition to the statutorily prescribed methods of allocation limiting the tax in the changeover year, IRS guidance provides that the adjustment period for a voluntary accounting method change is one tax year (the year of change) for a net negative Code Sec. 481(a) adjustment and four tax years (the year of change and next three tax years) for a net positive Code Sec. 481(a) adjustment. A net positive Code Sec. 481(a) adjustment is taken into account ratably over the adjustment period for taxpayers that agree to the IRS conditions. A taxpayer may elect to use a one-year adjustment period (the year of change) in lieu of the four-year adjustment period otherwise provided for a positive adjustment if the net adjustment is less than $25,000 (Rev. Proc. 2011-14; Rev. Proc. 97-27).[52] Moreover, a taxpayer may request approval of an alternative method of allocating the amount of the adjustments (Reg. § 1.481-4).[53]

A change in accounting method resulting from limitations placed on the use of the cash method of accounting (¶ 1501) is treated as a change initiated by the taxpayer with the consent of the IRS. The related Code Sec. 481 adjustment is includible in income over a period not generally exceeding four years (Code Sec. 448(d)(7)).[54]

References are to Standard Federal Tax Reports; Tax Research Consultant; and Practical Tax Explanations.

[47] ¶ 20,620.285; ACCTNG: 21,102.05; § 38,610.10

[48] ¶ 20,620.284; ACCTNG: 21,102; § 38,610.20

[49] ¶ 20,607; ACCTNG: 21,104; § 38,615

[50] ¶ 22,270, ¶ 22,271; ACCTNG: 21,150; § 38,625.05

[51] ¶ 22,272; ACCTNG: 21,152; § 38,625.10

[52] ¶ 22,277.40; ACCTNG: 21,158, ACCTNG: 21,162; § 38,625.05

[53] ¶ 22,275; ACCTNG: 21,156; § 38,625.05

[54] ¶ 20,800; ACCTNG: 21,164.15; § 38,625.05

Timing of Income and Expenses

1533. Constructive Receipt of Income for Cash Basis Taxpayers. It is not always necessary that a taxpayer take possession of money or property representing income before it is considered received. Income that is constructively received is taxed to a cash-basis taxpayer as though it had been actually received. There is constructive receipt when income is credited without restriction and made available to the taxpayer. There must be no substantial limitation or condition on the taxpayer's right to bring the funds within his or her control. An insubstantial forfeiture provision, a notice requirement, or the loss of bonus interest for deposits or accounts in certain financial institutions is not a substantial limitation (Reg. § 1.451-2(a)).[55]

Common examples of constructive receipt include matured and payable interest coupons, interest credited on savings bank deposits, and dividends unqualifiedly made subject to a stockholder's demand. However, if a dividend is declared payable on December 31 and the corporation follows a practice of paying the dividend by checks mailed so that the shareholders will not receive them until January of the following year, the dividend is not considered to be constructively received by the stockholders in December (Reg. § 1.451-2(b)).[56] For the time of receipt by shareholders of certain mutual fund dividends, see ¶ 2309. Accrued interest on an unwithdrawn insurance policy dividend is gross income to the taxpayer for the first tax year during which the interest may be withdrawn.

Salaries credited on corporate books are taxable to an officer in the year when the officer may withdraw the compensation at will if the corporation has funds available to pay the salaries without causing financial difficulties. Bonuses that are based on yearly sales and that are otherwise not available to an officer are taxable in the year of receipt.[57]

Accrued interest on a deposit that may not be withdrawn at the close of an individual's tax year because of an institution's actual or threatened bankruptcy or insolvency is not includible in the depositor's income until the year in which that interest is withdrawable (Code Sec. 451(g)).[58]

Constructive receipt does not give rise to constructive payment. Thus, for example, the fact that the negotiable note of a responsible and solvent maker, received in payment of salary, interest, rent, etc., must be reported by a recipient on the cash basis as income to the extent of its fair market value when received does not mean that the maker (on a cash basis) may also deduct the same amount at that time. Delivery of a note is not a payment on the cash basis, and the deduction may be taken only in the year when the note is paid. Giving collateral to secure the note does not change the promise to pay into an actual payment.[59]

1537. Prepaid Income. Payments received in advance are usually income to an accrual-basis or cash-basis taxpayer in the year of receipt, provided that there is no restriction on the use of those payments. This is true even though the payments are returnable on the happening of some specified event. A distinction must be made, however, between prepayments that may be refunded for services or goods and deposits over which the taxpayer does not have complete dominion and control on receipt.[60] For example, a utility company was not required to include deposits from uncreditworthy customers in income on receipt because it was required to return the deposit on request by a customer who established creditworthiness.

References are to Standard Federal Tax Reports; Tax Research Consultant; and Practical Tax Explanations.

[55] ¶ 21,007; ACCTNG: 6,150; § 38,315.05

[56] ¶ 21,007, ¶ 21,009.1235; ACCTNG: 6,210, ACCTNG: 6,218; § 3,101, § 38,315.15

[57] ¶ 21,009.17; ACCTNG: 6,152.10; § 38,315.05

[58] ¶ 21,002; ACCTNG: 6,218; § 38,315.15

[59] ¶ 21,817.185; ACCTNG: 6,262; § 38,315.05

[60] ¶ 21,005.7039; ACCTNG: 6,152, ACCTNG: 9,104; § 38,310.05

Prepaid Merchandise. Inclusion in the year of receipt is also required for advance payments received on the sale of merchandise. However, under certain circumstances the IRS permits accrual-basis sellers to include certain advance payments in income in the tax year in which those payments are properly accruable under the method of accounting used for tax purposes if they are reported at that time or later for financial reporting purposes (Reg. § 1.451-5).[61] If the method used for financial reporting results in an earlier accrual, then the advance payments are taxed according to the financial reporting method. When a long-term contract method of accounting (¶ 1551) is used, advances are included in income under that method without regard to how the income from these payments is accounted for in the seller's financial reports.

An advance payment for this purpose is any amount received by an accrual-basis taxpayer under an agreement (1) for the sale or other disposition in a future tax year of goods held by the taxpayer primarily for sale to customers in the ordinary course of his or her trade or business or (2) for the building, installation, construction or manufacture of items by the taxpayer where the agreement is not completed within that tax year. An exception exists where substantial advance payments for inventoriable goods have been received and goods are on hand or available to satisfy the agreement in the year of receipt. Payments for gift certificates are substantial when received, but in other cases, advance payments are not substantial until they exceed the cost of goods to be sold. In such cases, all advance payments received by the last day of the second tax year following the year in which the substantial advance payments are received and not previously included in income under the taxpayer's method of accounting must be included in income in the second tax year (Reg. § 1.451-5(c)).[62]

Certain manufacturers, wholesalers and retailers that receive advance payments for multi-year service warranty contracts may elect to recognize income from advance payments as a series of equal payments over the life of the contracts. This election is permitted only if an eligible taxpayer purchases insurance to cover its obligations under a service warranty contract within 60 days after the sale of the contract (Rev. Proc. 97-38).[63]

Prepaid Services and Mixed Prepayments. Taxpayers who receive advance payments for services and advance payments for the transfer of both goods and services are allowed a limited deferral beyond the tax year of receipt for certain advance payments (Rev. Proc. 2004-34, modified by Rev. Proc. 2011-18).[64] Generally, excludible payments include the payment for services; the sale of goods other than those for which the taxpayer uses a method of deferral allowed for advance payments of goods discussed above; the use of intellectual property (including license or lease); the use of property ancillary to the provision of services (for example, hotel rooms, booths at trade shows, campsites, banquet facilities); the sale, lease, or license of computer software; guaranty or warranty contracts ancillary to any of the above; subscriptions; memberships in an organization; a gift card sale in which the taxpayer is primarily liable to the customer and the gift card is redeemable by the taxpayer or an entity legally obligated to the taxpayer; or any combination of the above.

The term "advance payment" does not include: rent, other than that paid for the use of intellectual property, computer software, and property ancillary to the provision of services; insurance premiums to the extent governed by the taxation of insurance companies; payments with respect to financial instruments such as debt instruments, deposits, letters of credit, notional principal contracts, options, forward contracts, futures contracts, foreign currency contracts, credit card agreements, financial derivatives, and including purported prepayments of interest; payments with respect to service warranty contracts; payments with respect to warranty and guaranty contracts under which a third party is the primary obligor; certain payments with respect to nonresident aliens and

References are to Standard Federal Tax Reports; Tax Research Consultant; and Practical Tax Explanations.

[61] ¶ 21,016; ACCTNG: 9,200; § 38,310.10

[62] ¶ 21,016; ACCTNG: 9,206; § 38,310.10

[63] ¶ 20,620.20; ACCTNG: 9,484.25; § 38,310.05

[64] ¶ 21,005.7043; ACCTNG: 27,154; § 38,310.10

foreign corporations; and payments in property transferred in connection with the performance of services to which the restricted property rules of Code Sec. 83 apply.

Qualifying taxpayers generally may defer to the next succeeding tax year the inclusion in gross income for federal income tax purposes of advance payments to the extent the advance payments are not recognized in revenues for financial statement purposes (or, in certain cases, are not earned) in the tax year of receipt. Except in the case of certain short tax years, the IRS does not permit deferral to a tax year later than the next succeeding tax year. These rules neither restrict a taxpayer's ability to use the methods of deferral for the advance payment of merchandise (see "*Prepaid Merchandise,*" above) nor limit the period of deferral available under that regulation.

> **Example 1:** Advance payment for 48 dancing lessons under a one-year contract is received on November 1, 2012, by a calendar-year taxpayer. Eight lessons are given in 2012. The remaining lessons are provided in 2013. In its applicable financial statement, the dance studio recognizes 1/6 of the payment in revenues for 2012 and 5/6 of the payment in revenues for 2013. If the dance studio, an accrual-basis taxpayer, elects the above deferral method, 1/6 of the payment is includible in 2012 income and 5/6 of it is taxable as 2013 income, even if not all of the remaining 40 lessons are given in 2013.

> **Example 2:** Assume the same facts as in the previous example, except that the advance payment is received for a 2-year contract under which up to 96 lessons are provided. The dance studio provides eight lessons in 2012, 48 lessons in 2013, and 40 lessons in 2014. In its applicable financial statement, the studio recognizes 1/12 of the payment in revenues for 2012, 6/12 of the payment in revenues for 2013, and 5/12 of the payment in gross revenues for 2014. For federal income tax purposes, the studio must include 1/12 of the payment in gross income for 2012 and the remaining 11/12 of the payment in gross income for 2013.

Certain accrual-basis membership organizations and publishers can defer prepaid dues and subscription income (Code Secs. 455 and 456).[65]

Accrued Income. A number of Code provisions may require cash-basis taxpayers to report income that has not yet been received. The computation of that income often uses present value concepts. In addition, those Code provisions may require accrual-basis taxpayers to compute income for tax purposes in a manner that differs from generally accepted accounting methods. For a discussion of accruals of rental payments (Code Sec. 467), see ¶ 1541. For a discussion of original issue discount (Code Sec. 1272), see ¶ 1952. For a discussion of certain debt instruments issued for property (Code Sec. 1274), see ¶ 1954. An accrual-method publisher of magazines, paperbacks, or records may elect to exclude from gross income the income attributable to the qualified sale of magazines, paperbacks, or records that are returned before the close of the merchandise return period (Code Sec. 458).[66]

1539. Prepaid Expenses of Cash-Basis Taxpayers. Cash-basis taxpayers may deduct certain prepaid *expenses* in the year paid under certain conditions (Code Sec. 461; Reg. § 1.461-1).[67] A distinction is made between expenditures that are more in the nature of expenses and those that are capital in nature. If the payment creates an asset having a useful life extending substantially beyond the end of the tax year in which paid, the expenditure may not be deductible, or may be deductible only in part, in that year. If payment is made for a capital asset or is capital in nature, a deferment and charge-off for depreciation, amortization, or other comparable allowance are proper. See ¶ 1201. Taxpayers are generally not required to capitalize amounts paid for a right or benefit, such as rent or insurance, that does not extend beyond the earlier of 12 months after the first date on which the taxpayer realizes the right or benefit or the end of the tax year following the tax year in which the payment is made (Reg. § 1.263(a)-4(f)(1)).[68] Special rules apply to certain rental agreements (¶ 1541).

References are to Standard Federal Tax Reports; Tax Research Consultant; and Practical Tax Explanations.

65 ¶ 21,510, ¶ 21,520; ACCTNG: 9,250, ACCTNG: 9,300; § 38,320.45

66 ¶ 21,540; ACCTNG: 12,206; § 38,320.20

67 ¶ 21,802, ¶ 21,805; ACCTNG: 6,266; § 38,410.05

68 ¶ 13,704C; BUSEXP: 9,104.20; § 10,210.40

Example: Jonathan Mathis, a calendar-year taxpayer who uses the cash basis of accounting, signs a three-year business property lease on December 1 of the tax year and agrees to pay $18,000 upfront plus a monthly rental of $1,000 for 36 months. He can deduct only $1,500 for the tax year ($1,000 rent plus 1⁄36 of $18,000). The $18,000 is an amount paid for securing the lease and must be amortized over the lease term.

Cash-basis farmers and ranchers can deduct prepaid feed costs in the year of payment if:

(1) the advance feed expenditure is a payment and not a deposit;

(2) the payment is for a business purpose; and

(3) the deduction does not cause a material distortion of income.[69]

However, generally, no deduction is allowed to a cash-basis farmer (other than farming syndicates) in the year of prepayment for advance payments for feed, seed, fertilizer, or other supplies to the extent those prepayments exceed 50 percent of total deductible farming expenses (excluding prepaid supplies) (Code Sec. 464(f)).[70] (For rules applicable to farming syndicates, see ¶ 2032.) The limitation does not apply to a "farm-related taxpayer" if:

(1) the aggregate prepaid farm supplies for the preceding three tax years are less than 50 percent of the aggregate deductible farming expenses (other than prepaid farm supplies) for that period, or

(2) the taxpayer has excess prepaid farm supplies for the tax year by reason of any change in business operation directly attributable to extraordinary circumstances.

A farm-related taxpayer is one whose principal residence is on a farm, who has a principal occupation of farming, or who is a family member of such a taxpayer. The family of an individual includes brothers and sisters, whether by whole or half blood, spouse, ancestors, and lineal descendants (Code Sec. 464(c)(2)(E)). It may also include a corporation that is engaged full-time in farming activities.

Estimated state income taxes paid in advance are deductible by a cash-basis taxpayer in the year paid (Rev. Rul. 56-124).[71]

See ¶ 1055 for a discussion of the allowance of deductions for prepaid interest payments.

1540. Expenses of Accrual-Basis Taxpayers. Under the "all-events" test, an accrual-basis taxpayer is generally entitled to deduct the face amount of an accrued expense in the tax year in which (1) all of the events have occurred that determine the fact of liability and (2) the amount of the liability can be determined with reasonable accuracy (Code Sec. 461(h)).[72]

The all-events test is not treated as met before economic performance occurs with respect to the particular item of expense or obligation that underlies the taxpayer's liability. For a liability of a taxpayer that requires a payment for property or services, economic performance is deemed to occur as the property or services are provided to the taxpayer. If the liability arises out of the taxpayer's use of property, economic performance occurs as the taxpayer uses the property (Reg. § 1.461-4(d)).[73]

Example 1: A partnership on the accrual basis contractually obligates itself in October 2012 to pay Techno Inc. $10,000 for research and development to be performed in 2013. No amount is deductible before performance is rendered in 2013.

References are to Standard Federal Tax Reports; Tax Research Consultant; and Practical Tax Explanations.

[69] ¶ 21,817.205; FARM: 9,054; § 38,410.20

[70] ¶ 21,840; FARM: 9,054; § 38,410.20

[71] ¶ 21,817.1875; ACCTNG: 6,318; § 38,410.25

[72] ¶ 21,802; ACCTNG: 12,050, ACCTNG: 12,100; § 38,430.05

[73] ¶ 21,810; ACCTNG: 12,102; § 38,435.05

Taxpayers are permitted to accrue payments before services are rendered or property is received if the taxpayer can reasonably expect the services or property to be provided within 3½ months after payment.

> **Example 2:** An accrual-method, calendar-year taxpayer makes payment on December 1, 2012, for goods it expects to receive by March 12, 2013. It may deduct the payment or otherwise take it into account for its 2012 tax year.

If the liability of the taxpayer requires him to provide services or property, then economic performance occurs as the taxpayer incurs costs.

> **Example 3:** Zop Corp., a calendar-year, accrual-method taxpayer, sells lawn mowers under a three-year warranty that obligates it to make reasonable repairs to each mower it sells. In 2012, Zop repairs 12 mowers sold in 2011 at a cost of $2,500. Economic performance with respect to Zop's liability to perform services under the warranty occurs as Zop incurs costs in connection with the liability. Consequently, the $2,500 expense incurred by Zop is a deduction for the 2012 tax year.

However, certain manufacturers, wholesalers and retailers that make advance payments to purchase insurance policies that cover their obligations under multi-year service warranty contracts must capitalize the cost of the policies and deduct that cost ratably over the life of the policies. This rule applies regardless of whether the taxpayer uses the cash or accrual method (Rev. Proc. 97-38).[74]

Economic performance generally occurs only when payment is made to the person to whom the liability is owed. However, payment is considered to be economic performance for the following:

(1) liabilities to another person arising out of any workers' compensation, tort, or breach of contract claims against the taxpayer or any violation of law by the taxpayer;

(2) rebates and refunds;

(3) awards, prizes, and jackpots;

(4) insurance, warranty and service contracts; and

(5) taxes other than creditable foreign taxes (Reg. § 1.461-4(g)).[75]

Under certain limited circumstances, an irrevocable payment to a court-ordered settlement fund that completely extinguishes specified tort liabilities will also constitute economic performance (Code Sec. 468B).[76]

Recurring Items. Certain recurring items are treated as incurred in advance of economic performance by taxpayers other than tax shelters. Under this exception, an item is treated as incurred during a tax year if:

(1) the all-events test, without regard to economic performance, is satisfied during that year;

(2) the economic performance test is met within the shorter of 8½ months or a reasonable time after the close of the year;

(3) the item is recurring in nature and the taxpayer consistently treats similar items as incurred in the tax year in which the all-events test is met; and

(4) either the item is not material or accrual of the item in the year that the all-events test is met results in a better matching against the income to which it relates than accrual of the item in the tax year of economic performance.(Code Sec. 461(h)(3); Reg. § 1.461-5).[77]

In determining whether an item is material or whether a more proper matching against income results from deduction of an expense prior to economic performance, the

References are to Standard Federal Tax Reports; Tax Research Consultant; and Practical Tax Explanations.

[74] ¶ 20,620.20; ACCTNG: 9,484.25

[75] ¶ 21,810; ACCTNG: 12,102.20; § 38,435.05

[76] ¶ 21,950; ACCTNG: 12,214; § 38,435.20

[77] ¶ 21,802, ¶ 21,811; ACCTNG: 12,104.10; § 38,435.10

treatment of the expense on financial statements is to be taken into account but will not necessarily govern the tax treatment of the expense.

A taxpayer may adopt the recurring item exception as part of its method of accounting for any type of expense for the first tax year in which that type of expense is incurred. Generally, any change to or from the recurring item exception is a change in the taxpayer's method of accounting (¶ 1529) (Reg. § 1.461-5(d)).

An item is recurring if it can generally be expected to be incurred from one tax year to the next (Reg. § 1.461-5(b)(3)). However, a taxpayer may treat a liability as recurring even if it is not incurred in each tax year. Also, a liability that has never previously been incurred may be treated as recurring if it is reasonable to expect that it will be incurred on a recurring basis in the future.

1541. Deferred Payments Under Certain Rental Agreements. Lessors and lessees of certain leaseback and long-term rental agreements that involve the use of property must report income and expenses arising out of those agreements by applying statutory accrual-basis and present-value principles (Code Sec. 467; Reg. § 1.467-1).[78] This treatment, in effect, is an extension of the principles embodied in the rules on taxation of original issue discount. Although the rules under Code Sec. 467 apply to the use of property, the IRS is given authority to extend similar rules to agreements for services.

Section 467 rental agreements cover tangible property with respect to which either (1) at least one amount, allocable to the use of property in the calendar year, is to be paid after the close of the following calendar year (deferred payments), or (2) there are increases in the amount to be paid as rent under the agreement (stepped rents). A Section 467 rental agreement does not encompass a rental agreement in which the sum of the amounts to be paid is $250,000 or less.

The lessor or lessee of any such agreement must report for any tax year (regardless of the accounting method used) the sum of (1) the accrued rental payments and (2) any interest for the year (calculated at the rate of 110 percent of the applicable federal rate compounded semiannually) on unpaid rents (amounts that were attributed to a prior tax year but are still unpaid as of the current tax year).

The accrued rental payments—except in tax-avoidance transactions and agreements that do not allocate rents—are calculated by (1) allocating rents in accordance with the agreement and (2) including the present value of rents allocable to the period but paid after the close of the period. In tax-avoidance transactions and agreements that do not allocate rents, the rent that accrues during the tax year is equal to the allocable portion of the "constant rental amount." The constant rental amount is equal to the amount which, if paid as of the close of each lease period, would result in an aggregate present value equal to the present value of the aggregate payments required under the lease.

1543. Claim-of-Right Doctrine. Under the claim-of-right doctrine, payments must be included in gross income if the taxpayer receives them without restriction under a claim of right.[79] This is true even though the taxpayer may discover in a later year that he or she had no right to the payments in the earlier year and is required to repay the same amount. The taxpayer may deduct the repayments in the year in which they are made.

When the repayments exceed income for the year of repayment, or when the income (after subtraction of those repayments) is taxed at a rate lower than that at which the income in the year of inclusion was taxed, the deduction does not compensate the taxpayer adequately for the tax paid in the earlier year. The law eliminates this inequity if the amount repaid exceeds $3,000. In that case, the taxpayer is to reduce his or her tax for the year of repayment by the amount of tax for the previous year which was attributable to inclusion of this amount; any excess is to be claimed as a refund. However, if a smaller tax liability results from simply deducting the repaid amount in the

References are to Standard Federal Tax Reports; Tax Research Consultant; and Practical Tax Explanations.

[78] ¶ 21,910, ¶ 21,910D; REAL: 12,356; § 38,410.35

[79] ¶ 21,005.1251; ACCTNG: 27,000; § 38,310.05

year of repayment, the taxpayer is to claim the deduction instead (Code Sec. 1341; Reg. § 1.1341-1).[80]

In either case, the adjustment is made for the year of repayment. The return for the prior year—the year in which the item was received—is not reopened; in no case will there be an allowance for interest on the tax paid for the earlier year.

Example: In 2011, a single taxpayer reported taxable income of $55,000 (adjusted gross income of $64,500 minus $3,700 personal exemption minus $5,800 standard deduction), consisting entirely of sales commissions, on which he paid a tax of $9,881. In 2012, it is determined that the commissions were erroneously computed for 2011. Accordingly, the taxpayer pays back $6,000 of the commissions. His taxable income for 2012, without regard to the $6,000 repayment, is $13,200.

The tax for 2012 will be computed as follows:

(a) Tax on $7,200 ($13,200 less $6,000)		$720
(b) Tax on $13,200		1545
Less: Difference between—		
Tax paid for 2011 on $55,000	9,881	
Tax payable in 2011 on $49,000 ($55,000 – $6,000)	8,381	1,500
		45

The tax for 2012 is the lesser of the amount computed under (a) or (b). In this case, the amount computed under (b) is less than the amount computed under (a). Thus, the tax for 2012 is $45, the amount computed under (b).

When the tax for the year of restoration under a claim of right is reduced by the amount of the tax already paid on the item in a previous year, the amount restored is not considered for any purpose. For example, taxpayers cannot use that amount in computing a net operating loss for the year of restoration (Reg. § 1.1341-1(b)(2)).[81] The reduction of tax in the year of repayment does not apply where the taxpayer did, in fact, have an unrestricted right to receive the amount in the prior year and the obligation to repay arose as the result of subsequent events.

1545. Dealer's Reserve for Income. Dealers who discount customers' installment paper with financial institutions that withhold a small percentage of the price and credit it to a reserve account as security for the dealer's guaranty of payment of the installment paper must accrue those credits as income in the year when the installment paper is transferred to the financial institution.[82] This has been applied to accrual-basis home sellers who guarantee buyers' loans by requiring them to accrue as income in the year of sale the proceeds pledged as loan security to the lender. As to a cash-basis taxpayer, however, the pledged amounts are taxable to him only as they become available for withdrawal (the pledged amount was in a restricted savings account and could be withdrawn in specified amounts only as the buyer reduced the loan principal by certain amounts).

1547. Reserve for Estimated Expense. Although reserves for contingent liabilities are often set up in business practice, amounts credited to them are generally not deductible for income tax purposes because the fact of liability is not fixed.[83] For example, advance deductions have been denied for additions to a reserve for expected cash discounts on outstanding receivables, amounts credited by a manufacturer to a reserve for possible future warranty service, and additions to a reserve covering estimated liability of a carrier for tort claims.[84] However, to the extent that the Code specifically provides for a deduction for a reserve for estimated expenses, the economic performance rules (¶ 1540) do not apply (Code Sec. 461(h)(5)).[85]

References are to Standard Federal Tax Reports; Tax Research Consultant; and Practical Tax Explanations.

[80] ¶ 31,880, ¶ 31,881; ACCTNG: 27,500; § 4,230.05

[81] ¶ 31,881; ACCTNG: 27,558; § 38,310.05

[82] ¶ 31,882.25; ACCTNG: 9,406; § 38,320.05

[83] ¶ 21,817.688; ACCTNG: 12,200; § 38,430.10

[84] ¶ 21,817.688; ACCTNG: 12,202; § 38,430.10

[85] ¶ 21,802; ACCTNG: 12,104; § 38,430.10

1549. Accrual of Vacation and Sick Leave Pay. A vacation or sick leave pay deduction is generally limited to the amount of pay earned during the year to the extent (1) the amount is paid to employees during the year or (2) the amount is vested as of the last day of the tax year and is paid to employees within 2.5 months after the end of the year. If the vacation or sick leave pay is not paid until after the expiration of that period, the employer may deduct vacation pay when paid and sick leave pay in its tax year that includes the last day of the employee's tax year for which the payment is reported as income by the employee (Code Sec. 404(a)(5); Temp. Reg. § 1.404(b)-1T).[86] However, vacation and sick leave pay incurred with respect to the production of real and tangible personal property or with respect to property acquired for resale is considered a direct labor cost that must be capitalized by taxpayers subject to the uniform capitalization rules (Reg. § 1.263A-1(e)(2)(i)(B)).[87] See ¶ 991.

Regardless of whether or not vested vacation pay is considered deferred compensation, FICA and FUTA taxes may be deducted by an accrual basis taxpayer prior to the tax year that the FICA and FUTA taxes are actually paid if: (1) all events have occurred to establish the fact of the taxpayer's liability for the FICA and FUTA taxes, (2) the amount of the payroll tax liability can be determined with reasonable accuracy, and (3) the taxpayer properly adopts the recurring item exception (¶ 1540) as a method of accounting with respect to the payroll taxes (Rev. Rul. 2007-12).[88]

Long-Term Contracts

1551. Long-Term Contract Method of Accounting. Taxable income from a long-term contract generally must be accounted for under the percentage-of-completion method of accounting (Code Sec. 460).[89] A taxpayer who has entered into a small construction contract or home construction contract, however, may use an exempt contract method of accounting (¶ 1552).

A long-term contract is a building, installation, construction, or manufacturing contract that is not completed within the tax year in which it is entered into. A manufacturing contract is not be considered long term unless the contract involves the manufacture of (1) unique items not normally carried in the finished goods inventory or (2) items normally requiring more than 12 calendar months to complete (regardless of the duration of the actual contract).

Percentage-of-Completion Method. Under the percentage-of-completion method, gross income is reported annually according to the percentage of the contract completed in that year. The completion percentage must be determined by comparing costs allocated and incurred before the end of the tax year with the estimated total contract costs (cost-to-cost method or simplified cost-to-cost method). Thus, for a particular tax year, the taxpayer includes a portion of the total contract price in gross income as the taxpayer incurs allocable contract costs for the year. Any contract income that has not been included in the taxpayer's gross income by the end of the tax year in which the contract is completed is included in gross income for the following tax year (Code Sec. 460(b); Reg. § 1.460-4(b)).[90]

Modified Percentage-of-Completion Method (10 Percent Method). A taxpayer may elect to defer the recognition of income and accounting for costs until the first tax year in which at least 10 percent of the estimated total costs of the contract have been incurred.

Look-Back Rule. To the extent that the percentage-of-completion method applies to a long-term contract, a taxpayer who errs in his or her estimate of the contract price or costs must recompute his or her tax liability on the basis of the actual contract price and costs for the years for which that method was used. The taxpayer may elect not to apply or reapply the look-back method if, for each prior contract year, the cumulative taxable

References are to Standard Federal Tax Reports; Tax Research Consultant; and Practical Tax Explanations.

[86] ¶ 18,330, ¶ 18,354; ACCTNG: 12,300; § 38,435.15

[87] ¶ 13,811; ACCTNG: 15,208.10; § 10,310.10

[88] ¶ 21,817.128; ACCTNG: 12,052.15; § 9,365

[89] ¶ 21,550; ACCTNG: 33,000; § 38,230.05

[90] ¶ 21,550, ¶ 21,555; ACCTNG: 33,100; § 38,230.20

income or loss under the contract, as determined using estimated contract price or costs, is within 10 percent of the cumulative taxable income or loss as determined using actual contract price and costs. A taxpayer will either pay or receive interest (at the rate for overpayment of tax provided by Code Sec. 6621, compounded daily) on the amount by which the recomputed tax liability for a year exceeds or is less than the previously reported tax liability (Code Sec. 460(b)(2)).[91] Only one rate of interest will apply for each "accrual period," the period which begins on the date after the original return due date for the tax year and which ends on the original return due date for the following tax year. The applicable adjusted overpayment rate of interest is the overpayment rate in effect for the calendar quarter in which the accrual period begins.

Pass-through entities (partnerships, S corporations, and trusts) that are not closely held must use a simplified look-back method if substantially all of the income under a long-term contract is from sources in the United States (Code Sec. 460(b)(4)). A closely held entity is an entity where 50 percent or more of the value of the beneficial interests are owned by five or fewer persons. The amount of taxes deemed overpaid or underpaid under a contract in any year is determined at the entity level and is the product of the amount of contract income overreported or underreported for the year times the top marginal tax rate applicable for the year (the top corporate tax rate, or the top individual tax rate if more than 50 percent of the beneficial interests in the entity are held by individuals).

Allocation and Capitalization of Costs. In general, all costs (including research and experimental costs) that directly benefit or are incurred because of a long-term contract are to be allocated to the contract under Code Sec. 451 and the regulations thereunder that apply to extended period long-term contracts. However, independent research and development costs, expenses incurred in making unsuccessful bids and proposals, and marketing, selling and advertising costs may be expensed. For a cost-plus or federal long-term contract, costs that are not allocated to the contract under the extended period long-term contract rules must be capitalized if identified by the taxpayer (or a related person) as attributable or allocable to the contract. Such an attribution or allocation can be created by the terms of the contract or by federal, state, or local laws and regulations. Allocation of production period interest is governed by rules (Code Sec. 263A(f)) (¶ 1561) that apply to property not produced under a long-term contract (Code Sec. 460(c)).

Pension expenses (including previously deducted pension expense that represents past service costs) are subject to the uniform capitalization rules (Code Sec. 263A) and the long-term contract cost allocation rules (Code Sec. 460). Thus, an allocable portion of all otherwise deductible pension costs, whether they relate to current or past services, is included in the basis of property that is produced or held for resale or is allocated to long-term contracts that are subject to the cost allocation rules.

1552. Exempt Contract Methods of Accounting. Although taxable income from a long-term contract generally must be accounted for under the percentage-of-completion method of accounting (¶ 1551), income from a small construction contract or a home construction contract may be taken into account using either the exempt-contract-percentage-of-completion method or the completed contract method. The look-back rule and the cost allocation rules (except for the allocation of production period interest) are not required for these contracts (Code Sec. 460(e); Reg. § 1.460-4).[92] A taxpayer may change his or her method of accounting to conform with either of these special methods only after he or she secures permission from the IRS (¶ 1529).

Small Construction Contracts. A small construction contract is a contract expected to be completed within two years that is performed by a taxpayer whose average annual gross receipts for the three prior tax years do not exceed $10 million.

References are to Standard Federal Tax Reports; Tax Research Consultant; and Practical Tax Explanations.

[91] ¶ 21,550; ACCTNG: 33,200; § 38,230.55

[92] ¶ 21,550, ¶ 21,555; ACCTNG: 33,066, ACCTNG: 33,152; § 38,230.15, § 38,230.30

Home and Residential Construction Contracts. A home construction contract is any construction contract where 80 percent or more of the estimated total contract costs are reasonably expected to be attributable to dwelling units contained in buildings with four or fewer dwelling units, and to improvements to real property related to such dwelling units. A home construction contract related to buildings with more than four dwelling units is a residential construction contract, for which the availability of the exempt contract methods is limited (see *Percentage-of-Completion/Capitalized Cost Method*).

Exempt-Contract-Percentage-of-Completion Method. Under the exempt-contract-percentage-of-completion method, the taxpayer includes in income the portion of the total contract price that corresponds to the percentage of the entire contract that the taxpayer has completed during the tax year (Reg. § 1.460-4(c)).

Completed Contract Method. Under the completed contract method, the taxpayer does not report income until the tax year in which the contract is completed and accepted (Reg. § 1.460-4(d)). Expenses allocable to the contract are deductible in the year in which the contract is completed. Expenses not allocated to the contract (i.e., period costs) are deductible in the year in which they are paid or incurred, depending on the method of accounting employed.

Percentage-of-Completion/Capitalized-Cost Method. For residential construction contracts, the taxpayer may report 70 percent of the income using the percentage-of-completion method and the remaining 30 percent using an exempt contract method (Reg. § 1.460-4(e)).

Inventories

1553. Requirement to Use Inventories. A taxpayer generally must use inventories to clearly reflect income where the production, purchase, or sale of merchandise is an income-producing factor (Code Sec. 471(a); Reg. § 1.471-1).[93] To figure taxable income, a taxpayer must value inventory at the beginning of each tax year depending on the items included in inventory (¶ 1557) and the method of valuation (¶ 1559). A taxpayer whose average annual gross receipts does not exceed $1 million and a taxpayer whose average annual gross receipts does not exceed $10 million are generally not required to use inventories or the accrual method of accounting (Rev. Proc. 2002-28; Rev. Proc. 2001-10). However, a taxpayer who does not otherwise use inventories must treat merchandise inventory in the same manner as a material or supply that is not incidental (see Reg. § 1.162-3T); the uniform capitalization rules (Code Sec. 263A) will not apply to that merchandise inventory. A farmer may also use the cash method of accounting for purchases and sales. See the accrual method requirement for certain farming corporations at ¶ 2028. However, any taxpayer, including a farmer, who uses inventories must use the accrual method of accounting for purchases and sales.

1557. Items Included in Inventory. An inventory is an itemized list, with valuations, of goods held for sale or consumption in a manufacturing or merchandising business. Taxpayers must usually verify the amount of items in inventory by a physical count of the items as of the last day of the tax year. Taxpayers may use estimates of inventory shrinkage that are confirmed by a physical count after year-end if the taxpayer normally does a physical inventory count at each location on a regular and consistent basis and the taxpayer makes proper adjustments to those inventories and to its estimating methods to the extent the estimates are greater than or less than the actual shrinkage.

Inventory should include all finished or partly finished goods and only those raw materials and supplies which have been acquired for sale or which will physically become a part of merchandise intended for sale. Merchandise should be included in inventory only if title to it is vested in the taxpayer. A seller should include in inventory goods under contract for sale but not yet segregated and applied to the contract and goods out on consignment. The seller should not include goods sold (including contain-

References are to Standard Federal Tax Reports; Tax Research Consultant; and Practical Tax Explanations.

[93] ¶ 22,202, ¶ 22,203;
ACCTNG: 15,052; § 38,501

ers) where title has passed to the buyer. A buyer should include in inventory merchandise purchased (including containers) where title has passed to him, even where the merchandise is in transit or has not been physically received (Reg. § 1.471-1).[94]

It is necessary to identify the particular goods in inventory so that proper costs can be applied to the quantities. Identification of inventories is ordinarily accomplished by the first-in, first-out (FIFO) rule, unless the items are specifically identified (¶ 1564). A taxpayer can also elect to identify inventory items by use of the last-in, first-out (LIFO) rule (¶ 1565).

Real property held for sale by a dealer may not be inventoried because each parcel of real estate is unique.[95] Likewise, capital assets, equipment, accounts, notes, investments, cash, or similar assets may not be included in inventories.

For inventories of farmers and dealers in securities, see ¶ 1569 and ¶ 1903.

1559. Valuation of Inventory. An inventory must conform to the best accounting practice in the particular trade or business and it must clearly reflect income. An inventory that, under the best accounting practice, can be used in a balance sheet showing the financial position of the taxpayer will generally be regarded as clearly reflecting income. In determining whether income is clearly reflected, great weight is given to consistency in inventory practice, but a legitimate accounting system will be disallowed where it distorts income (Reg. § 1.471-2).[96]

Two methods commonly used to value inventories are cost method (¶ 1561) or the lower of cost or market method (¶ 1563) (Reg. § 1.471-2).[97] Opening and closing inventories must be valued by the same method. If the "lower of cost or market" method is used, it must be consistently applied to each item in the inventory. Cost and market value are determined as to each item, and the lower amount is included in the inventory valuation. A taxpayer is not permitted to inventory the entire stock at cost and also at market and use the lower of the two results (Reg. § 1.471-4).[98] Deviations are permitted, however, as to goods inventoried under the last-in, first-out identification method (¶ 1565) and as to animals inventoried under the "unit-livestock-price" method (¶ 1569).

The IRS will also, in general, accept the rolling-average inventory valuation method used to value inventories for financial accounting purposes as clearly reflecting income for federal income tax purposes (Rev. Proc. 2008-43, modified by Rev. Proc. 2008-52). However, if inventory is held for several years or costs fluctuate substantially, the rolling-average cost method may not clearly reflect income, depending on the particular facts and circumstances. Moreover, if the taxpayer does not use the rolling-average method for financial accounting purposes, then that method may not accurately determine costs or clearly reflect income for tax purposes.

Special rules apply to a dealer in securities (¶ 1903).

Whether the "cost" or the "lower of cost or market" method is used, inventoried goods that are unsalable, or unusable in normal transactions because of wear and tear, obsolescence, or broken lots, should be valued at bona fide selling price, less cost of selling; that is, at the actual offering of goods during a period ending not later than 30 days after inventory date. Adjustment of the valuation on a reasonable basis, not less than scrap value, is permitted in the case of unsalable or unusable raw material or partly finished goods (Reg. § 1.471-2(c)).[99]

1561. Inventory at Cost: Uniform Capitalization Rules. Uniform capitalization rules govern the inclusion in inventory or capital accounts of all allocable costs that are incurred with respect to real and tangible personal property that is produced by the taxpayer or acquired for resale and would otherwise be considered in computing taxable

References are to Standard Federal Tax Reports; Tax Research Consultant; and Practical Tax Explanations.

[94] ¶ 22,203; ACCTNG: 15,056; § 38,505.05

[95] ¶ 22,204.36; ACCTNG: 15,058; § 38,505.05

[96] ¶ 22,205; ACCTNG: 15,152; § 38,501

[97] ¶ 22,205; ACCTNG: 15,250; § 35,535.05

[98] ¶ 22,209; ACCTNG: 15,254; § 38,535.15

[99] ¶ 22,205; ACCTNG: 15,256; § 38,515.20

income (Code Sec. 263A(a) and (b)).[100] For this purpose, tangible personal property includes a film, sound recording, videotape, book, or similar property. Except for the interest capitalization rules, the uniform capitalization rules also apply to costs incurred with respect to real or personal (whether tangible or intangible) property that is acquired for resale. Certain small businesses with average annual gross receipts not exceeding $10 million for the three previous years that acquire personal property for resale are exempt from these rules.

Costs attributable to inventory must be added to costs of producing or acquiring the inventory, and costs attributable to producing other property must be capitalized. Direct material and labor costs, as well as the portion of indirect costs allocable to that property, are subject to these rules (Reg. § 1.263A-1(a)(3)).

The uniform capitalization rules replace the inventory cost rules of Code Sec. 471 in the case of property to which they apply. The rules do not apply to inventories valued at market under either the market method or the lower of cost or market method (¶ 1563) if the market valuation used by the taxpayer generally equals the property's fair market value (i.e., price of sale to customers less direct disposition costs). However, the uniform capitalization rules do apply in determining the market value of any inventory for which market is determined with reference to replacement cost or reproduction cost.

Costs incurred with respect to property produced for personal use, timber (including certain ornamental trees), or property produced under long-term contracts, or costs deductible as Code Sec. 174 research and experimental expenditures or as certain oil, gas, and other mineral property, foreign drilling, amortizable or developmental expenditures, and costs (other than circulation expenditures) subject to the 10-year amortization rule for tax preferences are excluded from those rules (Code Sec. 263A(c)).[101]

Certain costs incurred by an individual (or personal service corporation, ¶ 219) engaged in the business of being a writer, photographer, or artist (¶ 990A) that are otherwise deductible are also exempt from those rules (Code Sec. 263A(h)). In addition, the following costs may be currently deducted under Reg. § 1.263A-1(e)(4): marketing and selling expenses and general and administrative expenses that do not directly benefit production or the acquisition of inventory.

Interest Capitalization Rules. Interest costs paid or incurred during the production period to finance the construction, building, installation, manufacture, development, or improvement of real or tangible personal property that is produced by the taxpayer must be capitalized (Code Sec. 263A(f); Reg. § 1.263A-8).[102] Property subject to the interest capitalization requirement includes property that is produced by the taxpayer for use in its trade or business or in an activity for profit and that has (1) a long useful life (real property or any other property with a class life of 20 years or more), (2) an estimated production period exceeding two years, or (3) an estimated production period exceeding one year and a cost exceeding $1 million. The production period begins on the date on which production of the property starts and ends on the date on which the property is ready to be placed in service or is ready to be held for sale.

The interest capitalization rules also apply to property that is produced for a taxpayer under a contract (Code Sec. 263A(g)(2)).[103] Thus, the portion of the taxpayer-customer's interest expense allocable to costs required to be capitalized (including progress payments, advances to the contractor, and an allocable portion of the general and administrative expenses of the taxpayer) must be capitalized.

Capitalization of interest is not required for property acquired for resale (inventory held by a dealer) (Code Sec. 263A(f)(1)(B)). Interest that constitutes qualified residence interest under Code Sec. 163(h) is also excluded from the capitalization rules (Code Sec. 263A(f)(2)(B)).

References are to Standard Federal Tax Reports; Tax Research Consultant; and Practical Tax Explanations.

100 ¶ 13,800; ACCTNG: 15,200; § 38,535.10

101 ¶ 13,800; BUSEXP: 9,050; § 38,535.10

102 ¶ 13,800, ¶ 13,852; BUSEXP: 9,060; § 10,330.05

103 ¶ 13,800; BUSEXP: 9,060; § 10,330.10

The determination of whether interest expense is allocable to the production of property is made under the following rules. Interest on a debt that financed production or construction costs of a particular asset is first allocated and capitalized as part of the cost of the item. If the production or construction costs for an asset exceed the amount of this direct debt, interest on other loans is also subject to capitalization under an avoided-cost rule to the extent of the excess. An assumed interest rate based on the average interest rates on the taxpayer's outstanding debt, excluding debt specifically traceable to production or construction, may be used for this purpose. For purposes of the interest allocation rule, production or construction expenditures include cumulative production costs (including previously capitalized interest) required to be capitalized (Reg. § § 1.263A-9 and 1.263A-11).[104]

Interest relating to property used to produce property subject to the interest capitalization rules is also subject to capitalization to the extent that interest is allocable to the produced property as determined under the above rules (Code Sec. 263A(f) (3)).[105]

For flow-through entities (partnerships, S corporations, estates and trusts), the interest capitalization rules are applied first at the entity level and then at the beneficiary level (Code Sec. 263A(f) (2) (C)).

Farming Businesses. For the uniform capitalization rules pertaining to farm businesses, see ¶ 999.

Inventory at Cost: Code Sec. 471 Rules. The rules below are to be used to value inventory at cost where the uniform capitalization rules do not apply. For merchandise on hand at the beginning of the year, "cost" is the amount at which it was included in the closing inventory of the preceding period. For merchandise *bought* after the beginning of the year, "cost" means the invoice price less trade or other discounts, except cash discounts approximating a fair interest rate, which may be deducted from cost, or reported as income, at the option of the taxpayer. Cost also includes transportation or other acquisition charges. For merchandise *produced* by the taxpayer, the costs attributed to inventoried goods must be determined under the uniform capitalization rules (see above).

1563. Inventory at "Cost or Market". If a "cost or market" inventory is used, the market value of each item is compared with the cost of the item, and the lower of the two values must be used for that item (¶ 1559).

Example: A lumber dealer has three grades of lumber at the end of his tax year. They are valued as follows:

Grade	*Cost*	*Market*	*Lower of Two*
A	$45,000	$60,000	$45,000
B	20,000	15,000	15,000
C	5,000	5,000	5,000
	$70,000	$80,000	$65,000

If the lumber dealer is using the cost method, his ending inventory is valued at $70,000. If the dealer is using the lower of cost or market method, the ending inventory is valued at $65,000.

Under normal conditions, market value is the prevailing current bid price at the inventory date in the volume in which the items are usually purchased by the taxpayer. If a current bid price is unobtainable, the best available evidence of fair market value must be used. Specific purchases or sales by the taxpayer or others, or compensation paid for cancellation of contracts for purchase commitments, may be used (Reg. § 1.471-4).[106]

The market value of goods in process and finished goods, for a manufacturer or processor, is reproduction cost. This is the total that materials, labor and factory burden or overhead would cost at current prices to bring the article to a comparable state of

References are to Standard Federal Tax Reports; Tax Research Consultant; and Practical Tax Explanations.

[104] ¶ 13,856, ¶ 13,864; ACCTNG: 15,208; § 10,330.15

[105] ¶ 13,800; BUSEXP: 9,060; § 10,330.15

[106] ¶ 22,209; ACCTNG: 15,254; § 38,535.15

completion. The market price basis does not apply to goods on hand or in the process of manufacture for delivery under firm sale contracts at fixed prices entered into before the inventory date where the taxpayer is protected against actual loss. Such goods must be inventoried at cost. A merchant may also use the "retail method" to approximate the lower of cost or market (Reg. § 1.471-8).[107]

If inventories are valued at cost under the lower of cost or market method, that valuation is subject to the uniform capitalization rules at ¶ 1561.

1564. "First-In, First-Out" (FIFO) Rule. The "first-in, first-out" (FIFO) method of identifying inventory assumes that items purchased or produced first are the first items sold, consumed or otherwise disposed of. Accordingly, items in inventory at the end of the year are matched with the costs of similar items that were most recently purchased or produced. The FIFO method of valuation is utilized for items taken in inventory that have been so commingled that they cannot be identified with specific invoices; thus, they are considered to be the items most recently purchased or produced. The cost is the actual cost of the items purchased and produced during the period in which the quantity of items in inventory was acquired. In the absence of an election to use the "last-in, first-out" method (¶ 1565), inventory is identified under the FIFO method (Code Sec. 471).[108]

1565. "Last-In, First-Out" (LIFO) Rule. The "last-in, first-out" (LIFO) method of identifying inventory is based on cost values (Code Sec. 472).[109] Under the LIFO method, inventory is taken at cost, but the items contained in the inventory are treated as being, first, those contained in opening inventory, to the extent of the opening inventory (whether or not they are physically on hand), and, second, those acquired during the tax year. The items treated as still in the opening inventory are taken in order of acquisition, except for the first year in which the method is used. For that year, the items in the opening inventory are taken at the average cost of those items. The closing inventory of the preceding year must also be adjusted and an amended return filed to reflect the changes. In the case of a retailer or certain manufacturers, items deemed to have been purchased during the year, that is, inventory increases, may be taken, at the taxpayer's election, on the basis of the most recent purchases, or at average cost for the year, or in order of acquisition.

A taxpayer need not obtain advance permission from the IRS to elect to use the LIFO method but must adopt it on the return for the year in which the method is first used. In addition, the taxpayer must file a Form 970 with the return and accept any modifications or adjustments required by the IRS. The election applies only to the class or classes of goods specified in the application. Although the election to adopt LIFO must generally cover the entire inventory of a business, manufacturers or processors may elect to have the method apply to raw materials only, including those in finished goods and work-in-process (Reg. § 1.472-1(h)).[110] Furthermore, if LIFO is used for tax purposes, it generally must also be used in preparing annual financial statements for credit purposes or for the purpose of reports to stockholders, partners, or proprietors. For purposes of this "report rule," all members of the same group of financially related corporations are treated as one taxpayer.

1567. Dollar-Value LIFO Method. Instead of determining quantity increases of each item in the inventory and then pricing them, as is required under regular LIFO (¶ 1565), the "dollar-value" LIFO method may be used (Reg. § 1.472-8).[111] The increase in LIFO value is determined by comparing the total dollar value of the beginning and ending inventories at base year (first LIFO year) prices and then converting any dollar-value increase to current prices by means of an index. Taxpayers are allowed, under the dollar-value LIFO method, to determine base year dollars through the use of government indexes (Code Sec. 472(f)).[112]

References are to Standard Federal Tax Reports; Tax Research Consultant; and Practical Tax Explanations.

[107] ¶ 22,217; ACCTNG: 15,256.35; § 38,535.20

[108] ¶ 22,202; ACCTNG: 15,154; § 38,520

[109] ¶ 22,230; ACCTNG: 18,050; § 38,525.05

[110] ¶ 22,231; ACCTNG: 18,100; § 38,525.07

[111] ¶ 22,239; ACCTNG: 18,200; § 38,525.10

[112] ¶ 22,230; ACCTNG: 18,204; § 38,525.10

Simplified Dollar-Value LIFO Method. Small businesses (those with average gross receipts for the three preceding years of $5 million or less) may elect to use a simplified dollar-value LIFO method to account for their inventories (Code Sec. 474(a) and (c)).[113] The method requires separate inventory pools for each major category in the applicable government price index. The election applies to all succeeding years unless the taxpayer obtains IRS permission to change to another method or becomes ineligible to use that method. If elected, it must be used to value all LIFO inventories.

1569. Special Accounting Methods for Farmers. In addition to the standard cost (¶ 1561) and the lower of cost or market (¶ 1563) methods for valuing inventory, a farmer on the accrual basis has a choice of two other systems. The "farm-price" method provides for the valuation of inventories at market price less the direct cost of disposition. If this method is used, it must be applied to the entire inventory except livestock which the taxpayer has elected to inventory under the "unit-livestock-price" method (Reg. § 1.471-6(d)).[114]

The "unit-livestock-price" method—adoptable when the farmer raises his or her own livestock or purchases young animals and raises them to maturity—provides for the valuation *of different classes* of animals at a standard unit price for each animal within a class. This method, once elected, must be applied to all livestock raised to maturity or purchased before maturity and raised to maturity, whether held for sale or for breeding, draft or dairy purposes. This includes unweaned calves. Unit prices assigned to classes must account for normal cost of production. For purchased livestock, the cost should be increased in accordance with unit prices only for animals acquired in the first six months of the tax year (Reg. § 1.471-6(g)).[115]

The "crop" basis of accounting may be used with IRS consent for crops which have not been gathered and disposed of during the tax year in which they are planted (Reg. § 1.61-4(c)).[116] The entire cost of producing the crop must be deducted no earlier than in the year in which the crop income is realized.

1571. Change in Inventory Accounting. A change in the method used to account for an inventory can be made only when authorized by the IRS. A change from a cash method to an inventory method is, in effect, a change to the accrual method of accounting for purchases and sales (Reg. § 1.446-1(c)(2); Rev. Proc. 2011-14). Permission to make such a change must generally be requested within the tax year that the change is to be effective (¶ 1529), with the exception of an election to change to the LIFO method. An election to use this method may be made by a statement on Form 970 attached to the first tax return in which it is used; however, adjustments will be required to prevent duplications and omissions of income and expenses (Reg. §§ 1.472-3 and 1.472-4).[117]

Allocation and Reconstruction of Income

1573. Allocation by IRS. When two or more organizations, trades, or businesses are owned or controlled by the same interests, the IRS may allocate gross income, deductions, or credits between them if it determines that this action is necessary to prevent evasion of taxes or to clearly reflect income (Code Sec. 482).[118] Moreover, the IRS is specifically authorized by statute to allocate any income, deduction, credit, exclusion, or other allowance between certain personal service corporations and their employee-owners when the principal purpose of forming or using such a corporation is to avoid or evade income tax (¶ 1575).

1575. Acquisitions to Avoid Tax. If a taxpayer acquires control of a corporation, directly or indirectly, to evade or avoid income tax by securing the benefit of a deduction, credit, or other allowance that would not otherwise be enjoyed, then that deduction, credit or other allowance will not be permitted. The same rules of disallow-

References are to Standard Federal Tax Reports; Tax Research Consultant; and Practical Tax Explanations.

[113] ¶ 22,260; ACCTNG: 18,250; § 38,525.15

[114] ¶ 22,213; FARM: 3,110; § 36,325

[115] ¶ 22,213; FARM: 3,112; § 36,325

[116] ¶ 5601; FARM: 3,064; § 36,315.15

[117] ¶ 22,234, ¶ 22,235; ACCTNG: 18,102; § 38,601

[118] ¶ 22,280; ACCTNG: 30,050; § 38,010.10

ance apply to a corporation that acquires property of another corporation that was not controlled by the acquiring corporation or its stockholders and that acquires a basis determined by reference to the basis in the hands of the transferor corporation (Code Sec. 269(a)).[119] The IRS is authorized to deny an acquiring corporation the carryover and other tax benefits of a subsidiary corporation, acquired in a qualified stock purchase for which an election of asset acquisition treatment is not made, if the subsidiary corporation is liquidated under a plan adopted within two years of the acquisition date and the principal purpose of the liquidation is tax avoidance or evasion (Code Sec. 269(b)).

If (1) substantially all of the services of a personal service corporation (PSC) are performed for, or on behalf of, one other corporation, partnership, or other entity and (2) the principal purpose for forming or using the PSC is the avoidance or evasion of income tax by reducing the income of or securing the benefit of any expense, deduction, credit, exclusion or other allowance for any employee-owner that would not otherwise be available, then the IRS can allocate all income, credits, exclusions, or other allowances between the PSC and its employee-owners in order to prevent tax evasion or avoidance or to clearly reflect the income of both (Code Sec. 269A).[120] A PSC is a corporation the principal activity of which is the performance of personal services that are substantially performed by the employee-owners. The term "employee-owner" is defined as any employee who owns, on any day during the tax year, more than 10 percent of the PSC's outstanding stock.

1577. Income Reconstruction. When a taxpayer has kept either inadequate or no books or records, the IRS has authority to compute income in order to clearly reflect the taxpayer's income (Code Sec. 446(b)).[121] The methods for reconstructing income vary depending on the facts and circumstances, and the records that are available. The IRS has developed several methods for reconstructing a taxpayer's income. The methods used most often are:

(1) *Bank deposits and expenditures method.* All bank deposits are assumed to represent income unless the taxpayer can establish otherwise. Although the taxpayer is given an opportunity to show that the deposits do not represent income, the IRS is not required to link the bank deposits with an identified income-producing activity (Reg. § 1.446-1).[122]

(2) *Net worth method.* An opening net worth or total value of assets at the beginning of a given year is established. The IRS then shows increases in the taxpayer's net worth for each subsequent year and calculates the difference between the adjusted net values of the assets at the beginning and end of each year under examination. Nondeductible expenses are added to the increases. If the resulting amount is greater than reported taxable income for that year, then the excess is treated as unreported taxable income.[123]

(3) *Percentage or unit mark-up method.* This method is used where inventories are a necessary income-producing factor but have not been kept or were incorrectly taken. Net income is determined by applying certain percentages, such as gross profits to sales, net income to gross income, or net income to sales, derived from other taxpayers in similar types of businesses.[124]

References are to Standard Federal Tax Reports; Tax Research Consultant; and Practical Tax Explanations.

[119] ¶ 14,250; CONSOL: 71,050; § 9,135

[120] ¶ 14,300; ACCTNG: 30,150; § 27,105

[121] ¶ 20,606; ACCTNG: 3,152; § 39,730.05

[122] ¶ 20,607; ACCTNG: 3,156; § 39,730.15

[123] ¶ 20,606; ACCTNG: 3,154; § 39,730.15

[124] ¶ 20,606; ACCTNG: 3,162; § 39,730.15

Chapter 16

BASIS FOR GAIN OR LOSS

Computing Gain or Loss

1601. Basis. The rules on determining the basis for computing gain or loss or depreciation on property acquired in most common transactions are outlined below, with references to the paragraphs where additional details appear. This basis, after adjustments described at ¶ 1611—¶ 1617, is subtracted from the amount realized to determine the amount of gain or loss from a sale or exchange (Code Sec. 1001).[1] Except where other rules are prescribed, the basis for gain or loss is determined under the law in effect when the property is sold.

Type of acquisition	Basis for gain or loss
Bargain purchases	
arm's-length	Cost (¶ 789)
corporation's, from nonstockholder	Cost (¶ 1660)
corporation's, from stockholder	Cost, unless saving is paid-in surplus (¶ 1660)
employee's	Cost plus amount taxable as compensation for services (¶ 789)
relative or friend	Cost, unless saving is a gift (¶ 1630)
stockholder's	Cost plus amount taxable as a dividend (¶ 789)
Bequests	For property acquired from a decedent, basis generally is fair market value at the date of the decedent's death (¶ 1633—¶ 1639)
Cash purchases	Cost (¶ 1604)
mortgage also assumed, or property taken subject to the mortgage	Full price, including mortgage amount (¶ 1725)
purchase money mortgage also given	Full purchase price (¶ 1725)
purchase notes also given	Full purchase price (¶ 1725)
redeemable ground rent assumed, or property taken subject to ground rent	Full purchase price (¶ 1725)
Community property	
survivor (death of spouse)	See "Bequests," above
Corporate property	
acquired for stock by controlled corporation	Transferor's basis (¶ 1660)
acquired for stock in taxable exchange	Fair market value of stock at time of exchange (¶ 1648)
contributions by nonstockholders	Zero (¶ 1660)
paid-in surplus	Transferor's basis (¶ 1660)
Dividend property	
corporate, stockholder of domestic corporation	Fair market value (¶ 735)
corporate, stockholder of foreign corporation	Fair market value (¶ 735)
noncorporate, stockholder	Fair market value (¶ 735)
Divorce or separation agreement	See ¶ 1734

References are to Standard Federal Tax Reports; Tax Research Consultant; and Practical Tax Explanations.

[1] ¶ 29,220; SALES: 9,050; § 16,015

Type of acquisition	Basis for gain or loss
Gift property	Donor's basis, increased by gift tax in some cases; basis for loss *limited* to lesser of donor's basis or fair market value at time of gift (¶ 1630)
Inventory goods	Last inventory value (¶ 1561)
Joint tenancy	
after death of one tenant	Basis depends on amount contributed by each joint tenant toward the original purchase price (¶ 1634, ¶ 1636)
Lessor's acquisitions of lessee's improvements	Zero, if excluded from income (¶ 764)
Life estate	Zero, if disposed of after October 9, 1969 (¶ 1633)
Livestock	
inventoried	Last inventory value (¶ 767)
purchased	Cost (¶ 767)
raised by accrual-basis farmer	Cost of raising (¶ 767)
raised by cash-basis farmer	Zero, if costs were charged to expense (¶ 767)
Mortgaged property (or property subject to redeemable ground rent)	Basis includes mortgage (or ground rent) (¶ 1725)
Partners' property	
partnership interest in exchange for contribution	Partners' adjusted basis of property contributed (¶ 443)
partnership interest purchased	Cost (¶ 434)
received in distribution other than liquidation	Partnership's adjusted basis at time of distribution (limited to partner's basis of his interest) (¶ 456)
received in partnership liquidation	Adjusted basis of partnership interest less cash received (¶ 456)
Partnership property	
after transfer of partnership interest or distributions to partners	Unaffected, unless election is made to adjust values (¶ 459, ¶ 467)
capital contribution	Partner's adjusted basis (¶ 443)
Purchase for more than value	Cost (¶ 1604), but excess may be a gift (¶ 1630)
Rehabilitated buildings, other than certified historic structures, for which investment credit on qualified expenditures available	Basis is reduced by allowable investment credit and the recaptured credit is added to basis (¶ 1365A)
Repossessed property after installment sale	
personal property	Fair market value (¶ 1838)
real property reacquired in satisfaction of purchaser's indebtedness secured by property	Adjusted basis of indebtedness plus gain resulting from reacquisition and reacquisition costs (¶ 1843)
Spousal transfers	See ¶ 1734
Stock	
acquired in wash sale	Basis of stock sold, adjusted for difference between selling price of sold stock and purchase price of acquired stock (¶ 1939)
bonus stock	Allocable portion of basis of old stock (¶ 1620, ¶ 1682)
nontaxable stock dividend	Allocable share of basis of stock on which declared (¶ 1620, ¶ 1682)
qualified small business stock rollover	See ¶ 1907
purchased	See ¶ 1975
received for services	Amount reported as income, plus cash paid (¶ 1681)
S corporation	See ¶ 317
specialized small business investment company stock rollover	See ¶ 1907
taxable stock dividend	Fair market value when issued (¶ 733A)
Stock rights	
nontaxable	Allocable share of basis of stock unless rights value is less than 15% of stock value (¶ 733A, ¶ 1682)
taxable	Fair market value when issued (¶ 733A)
Transfer in trust	Grantor's basis, plus gain or minus loss, upon transfer (¶ 1678)

1604. Adjusted Basis of Property. To determine the gain or loss from a sale or other disposition of property, the amount realized must be compared with the basis of the property to the taxpayer—generally measured by the original capital investment, adjusted to the date of sale (¶ 1611—¶ 1617) (Code Sec. 1011; Reg. § 1.1011-1).[2] In most situations, the basis of property is its cost to the taxpayer (Code Sec. 1012).[3] When property is acquired in a fully taxable exchange, the cost of the property acquired is the fair market value of the property given up.[4] Since, in an arm's-length transaction, both are presumed to be equal in value, the basis of the acquired property can be expressed as its fair market value.

1607. "Substituted" or Carryover Basis. A "substituted" basis is one that is continued or carried over from one taxpayer to another, or from one piece of property to another. The taxpayer has a substituted or carryover basis in property received as a gift (¶ 1630), in a transfer in trust (¶ 1678), in a tax-free exchange (¶ 1651), or acquired from a decedent dying in 2010 whose estate elects not to have federal estate tax apply (¶ 1633). The taxpayer also has a substituted basis in a personal residence purchased before May 7, 1997, if the recognition of gain realized on the sale of a prior residence was deferred under former Code Sec. 1034.[5]

Property Acquired by Purchase

1611. Additions to Basis of Property. In computing gain or loss on the sale of business or investment property, or gain on the sale of personal property, the cost or other basis must be *adjusted* for any expenditure, receipt, loss, or other item that is a capital expenditure (Code Sec. 1016(a)(1); Reg. §§ 1.1016-1—1.1016-10).[6] This necessitates an addition for improvements made to the property since its acquisition.[7] For example, the cost of capital improvements such as an addition, new roof, newly installed central air conditioning, or electrical rewiring is added to the owner's basis. Other components that add to the cost basis of property include: brokers' commissions and lawyers' fees incurred in buying real estate; expenditures incurred in defending or perfecting the title to property;[8] zoning costs;[9] the capitalized value of a redeemable ground rent (Code Sec. 1055); and sales tax, freight, installation and testing costs, excise taxes, and revenue stamps.[10]

Settlement Fees and Other Costs. The basis of real property includes settlement fees and closing costs such as abstract fees, charges for installing utility services, legal fees (including title search and preparation of the sales contract and deed), recording fees, surveys, transfer taxes, owner's title insurance, and amounts owed by the seller but paid by the buyer, such as back taxes or interest, recording or mortgage fees, charges for improvements or repairs, and sales commissions (Code Sec. 1012; Reg. § 1.1012-1(b); Rev. Rul. 68-528).[11] Amounts placed in escrow for future payments of items such as insurance and taxes do not increase basis. The creation of a mortgage does not diminish the owner's basis in a property. When a buyer assumes an existing mortgage and pays cash or other consideration, the buyer's basis in the property includes the outstanding portion of the mortgage and the value of the other consideration, and the seller realizes a benefit in the amount of the mortgage and the additional consideration (*B.B. Crane*, SCt, 47-1 USTC ¶ 9217).[12] Fees and costs related to getting a loan to purchase the property are not included in the basis of the property.

Assessments. Assessments for improvements or other items that increase the value of property are added to the basis of the property and not deducted as a tax. Such

References are to Standard Federal Tax Reports; Tax Research Consultant; and Practical Tax Explanations.

[2] ¶ 29,310, ¶ 29,311; SALES: 9,050, SALES: 6,350; § 16,005

[3] ¶ 29,330; SALES: 6,050; § 16,105.05

[4] ¶ 29,335.33; SALES: 6,060; § 16,105.15

[5] ¶ 29,426.01; SALES: 6,250; § 16,101

[6] ¶ 29,410, ¶ 29,411, ¶ 29,425; SALES: 6,352; § 16,110.10

[7] ¶ 29,412.84; SALES: 6,352.05; § 16,110.10

[8] ¶ 29,412.844; SALES: 6,352.20; § 16,105.30

[9] ¶ 13,709.659; SALES: 6,352.05; § 16,110.10

[10] ¶ 29,335.967, ¶ 29,335.577; SALES: 6,056.05; § 16,110.10

[11] ¶ 29,330, ¶ 29,331, ¶ 29,313.40; BUSEXP: 9,402.05; § 16,110.10

[12] ¶ 29,313.60; SALES: 6,054; § 18,505.05

improvements may include streets, sidewalks, water mains, sewers, and public parking facilities. The amount of such an assessment may be a depreciable asset. For example, the cost of a mall enclosure paid for by a business taxpayer through an assessment is depreciable. Assessments for maintenance or repairs, or for meeting interest charges on the improvements are currently deductible as a real property tax, although the burden is on the taxpayer to show the allocation of the amounts assessed to the different purposes (Code Sec. 164(c)(1); Reg. § 1.164-4).[13] Legal fees for obtaining a decrease in an assessment levied against property to pay for local improvements are added to the basis of the property and are not a deductible business expense (Rev. Rul. 70-62).

Taxes. Any tax paid in connection with the acquisition of a property is treated as part of the cost of the property. A tax paid in connection with the disposition of a property reduces the amount realized on the disposition (Code Sec. 164(a)).[14]

In computing the cost of real property, the buyer cannot take into account any amount paid to the seller as reimbursement for real property taxes which are treated as imposed upon the purchaser (¶ 1032). This rule applies whether or not the sales contract calls for the buyer to reimburse the seller for real estate taxes paid or to be paid by the seller. However, where the buyer pays or assumes liability for real estate taxes imposed upon the seller, the taxes are considered part of the cost of the property. It is immaterial whether or not the sales contract specifies that the sale price has been reduced by, or is in any way intended to reflect, real estate taxes allocable to the seller (Reg. § 1.1012-1(b)).[15]

Checklist. Common expenses and the corresponding deduction rules may be found at ¶ 57.

1614. Additions to Basis for Carrying Charges. A taxpayer may elect to treat taxes or other carrying charges (such as interest) on some property as capital charges rather than as an expense of the tax year (Code Sec. 266; Reg. § 1.266-1).[16] The items chargeable to the capital account are:

(1) in the case of unimproved and unproductive real property: annual taxes, interest on a mortgage, and other carrying charges;

(2) in the case of real property, whether improved or unimproved and whether productive or unproductive: interest on a loan, taxes of the owner of such property measured by compensation paid to the owner's employees, taxes of the owner on the purchase of materials or on the storage, use or other consumption of materials, and other necessary expenditures; these are items that are paid or incurred for the development or improvement of the property up to the time the development or construction work has been completed;

(3) in the case of personal property: taxes of an employer measured by compensation for services rendered in transporting machinery or other fixed assets to the plant or installing them, interest on a loan to buy such property or to pay for transporting or installing it, and taxes of the owner imposed on the purchase of such property or on the storage, use or other consumption, paid or incurred up to the date of installation or the date when the property is first put to use by the taxpayer, whichever is later; and

(4) any other taxes and carrying charges, otherwise deductible, which are chargeable to the capital account under sound accounting principles.

The election in (1) above is effective only for the year in which it is made. The election in (2) is effective until the development or construction work has been completed. The election in (3) is effective until the property is installed or first put to use, whichever date is later. The IRS determines whether the election in (4) is effective.

References are to Standard Federal Tax Reports; Tax Research Consultant; and Practical Tax Explanations.

[13] ¶ 9500, ¶ 9508; REAL: 3,104; § 7,315.05

[14] ¶ 9500; SALES: 6,354; § 16,110.25, § 16,430

[15] ¶ 29,331; REAL: 15,302; § 16,105.25

[16] ¶ 14,100, ¶ 14,101; SALES: 6,354, BUSEXP: 9,304; § 10,220

The election must be made by filing a statement with the taxpayer's original return indicating which items the taxpayer elects to treat as chargeable to the capital account (Reg. § 1.266-1(c)(3)).

1617. Reductions in Basis. In order to determine the amount of gain or loss on the sale or other disposition of property, the basis of property acquired in an exchange, and the basis for depreciation or depletion, the unadjusted basis (usually its cost, but in some cases the transferor's basis) of the property must be decreased by any items that represent a return of capital for the period during which the property has been held (Code Sec. 1016(a)).[17] These include:

- the Code Sec. 179 expense deduction for certain depreciable business assets (¶ 1208);
- the investment credit (except for 50 percent of the energy credits) (¶ 1365A) and other credits allowed based on the investment in a property;
- tax-free dividends (¶ 733A);
- recognized losses on involuntary exchanges (¶ 1687);
- casualty or theft loss deductions, as well as the amount of any insurance or other recovery for the loss (¶ 1131);
- deductions previously allowed or allowable for amortization, depreciation, obsolescence or depletion (¶ 1201 and following); and
- unrecognized gains on tax-free exchanges (¶ 1719).

Depreciation. The basis of property is reduced by the amount of depreciation claimed, or if greater, the depreciation which should have been claimed under the method chosen (Code Sec. 1016(a)(2); Reg. § 1.1016-3).[18] If no depreciation or insufficient depreciation was claimed, the basis is nonetheless reduced by the full amount of depreciation that should have been claimed. In order to mitigate the effect of this rule, the IRS has issued procedures that allow the taxpayer to change to a proper method of accounting for depreciation and claim a downward adjustment to income that reflects the additional amount of depreciation that should have been claimed (¶ 1221). If excess depreciation was claimed on an asset, the basis of the asset is reduced by the amount of depreciation that should have been claimed plus the part of the excess depreciation deducted that actually reduced the taxpayer's tax liability.

Motor Vehicles. The basis of a motor vehicle is reduced by any deduction or tax credit the taxpayer claimed with respect to the purchase. For example, the basis in a motor vehicle will be reduced for the credit for alternative motor vehicles (¶ 1345) (Code Secs. 30B(h)(4) and 1016(a)(35)); the credit for certain qualified plug-in electric vehicles purchased after February 17, 2009, and before 2012 (¶ 1354) (Code Secs. 30(e)(1) and 1016(a)(25)); and the credit for new qualified plug-in electric drive motor vehicles purchased in 2009 (¶ 1350) (former Code Sec. 30(D)(e)(4)) or after 2009 (¶ 1351) (Code Sec. 30D(f)(1)).

The basis of an automobile must also be reduced by the amount of any gas guzzler tax imposed by Code Sec. 4064 when use of the vehicle begins not more than one year after the first retail sale (Code Sec. 1016(d)).[19] The basis of alternative fuel vehicle refueling property used in a trade or business, or installed at the taxpayer's residence, and placed in service before 2012 (before 2015 for refueling property related to hydrogen) is reduced by the credit (¶ 1355), if the taxpayer elects to claim the credit (Code Secs. 30C(e)(1) and 1016(a)(36)).

Percentage Depletion. Even though a percentage depletion allowance is in excess of cost or other basis, it is not necessary to use a negative basis (less than zero) in computing gain on the sale of mineral property (¶ 1294–¶ 1298).[20]

References are to Standard Federal Tax Reports; Tax Research Consultant; and Practical Tax Explanations.

[17] ¶ 29,410; SALES: 6,350; § 16,110.25

[18] ¶ 29,410, ¶ 29,414; SALES: 6,364; § 16,110.20

[19] ¶ 29,410; SALES: 6,372.50

[20] ¶ 29,412.675; FARM: 18,068; § 11,610

Easements. Generally, the amount received for granting an easement for a limited use or for a limited period reduces the basis of the affected part of the property (Rev. Rul. 68-291). Gain is recognized to the extent that the amount received exceeds the basis of the affected part. The granting of a perpetual easement that denies the grantor any beneficial use of the property may be considered a sale of property even though the grantor retains legal title.[21]

Energy Efficiency and Conservation—Residential. The basis of a dwelling unit for which an excludable energy conservation subsidy was provided by a public utility (¶ 899A) must be reduced by the amount of the subsidy (Code Sec. 136(b)).[22]

The increase in basis of a personal residence that would result from certain expenditures that improve energy efficiency is reduced by credits allowed for those expenditures. An individual taxpayer's basis in nonbusiness energy property (i.e., the taxpayer's residence) must be reduced by the home improvement energy credit (¶ 1341) allowed for qualified energy efficiency improvements and residential energy property placed in service before January 1, 2008, and between January 1, 2009, and December 31, 2011 (Code Secs. 25C(f) and 1016(a)(33)). Similarly, the basis of an individual taxpayer's personal residence is reduced by the residential energy efficient property credit (¶ 1342) allowed for amounts spent on alternative energy equipment (such as solar or fuel cell equipment) placed in service prior to January 1, 2017 (Code Sec. 25D(f) and Code Sec. 1016(a)(34)). The basis of a qualified new energy-efficient home that a person acquires prior to January 1, 2012, for use as a residence, from a contractor eligible for a general business credit for building the home (¶ 1365CC) is reduced by the credit allowed (Code Secs. 45L(e) and 1016(a)(32)).

Energy Efficiency and Conservation—Business. The basis of an energy-efficient commercial building must be reduced by the deduction (¶ 1286) allowed for the costs of placing such property into service after December 31, 2005, and before January 1, 2014 (Code Secs. 179D(e) and 1016(a)(31)). Small business refiners must reduce the basis of property on which a deduction (¶ 1285) is allowed for qualified capital costs paid or incurred to comply with Environmental Protection Agency sulfur regulations (Code Secs. 179B(c) and 1016(a)(30)).

Homes Purchased Before May 7, 1997. The basis of a home purchased before May 7, 1997, must be reduced to reflect any gain realized on the sale of the prior home but deferred under former Code Sec. 1034.

Adoption Credit. The basis of a residence must be reduced by the amount of the adoption tax credit (¶ 1307) that was claimed with respect to improvements that increased that basis of the home (Code Secs. 23(g) and 1016(a)(26)).[23]

Child Care Credit. The basis of facilities acquired, constructed, rehabilitated, or expanded, and with respect to which an employer-provided child care credit (¶ 1365V) is allowed, must be reduced by the amount of the credit. If there is a recapture of the credit on the disposition of such property, the basis of the property is increased by the amount recaptured (Code Sec. 1016(a)(28)).

Canceled Debt. A taxpayer must reduce certain tax attributes by an amount excluded from gross income as the result of a discharge of indebtedness in a Title 11 bankruptcy case, a discharge of indebtedness during insolvency, or a discharge of qualified farm indebtedness (¶ 885).

Railroad Track. For tax years before January 1, 2012, eligible small and mid-sized railroad companies must reduce the basis of track on which they have been allowed a railroad track maintenance credit (Code Secs. 45G(e)(3) and 1016(a)(29)) (¶ 1365W).

Substituted Basis. Where the basis of the property is a substituted basis (¶ 1607), the same adjustments must be made for the period the property was held by the

References are to Standard Federal Tax Reports; Tax Research Consultant; and Practical Tax Explanations.

[21] ¶ 29,412.813; SALES: 6,356.05; § 16,110.25

[22] ¶ 7560; INDIV: 33,552; § 4,001

[23] ¶ 3700, ¶ 29,410; INDIV: 57,368; § 12,301

transferor, donor, or grantor, or during the period the property was held by the person for whom the basis is to be determined (Code Sec. 1016(b)).[24]

1620. Apportionment of Cost or Other Basis. When a sale is made of parts of property purchased as a unit, as in a subdivision of real estate, allocation of the total basis is required (Reg. § 1.61-6).[25] Other instances where allocation of the cost or other basis is necessary include stock of different classes received as a dividend or pursuant to a reorganization, a split-up, split-off, or spin-off; stock received as a bonus with the purchase of stock of a different character; stock purchase warrants attached to debenture bonds; and depreciable and nondepreciable property purchased for a lump sum.

Trade or Business Purchased. Applicable asset acquisition rules require the allocation of the purchase price of a trade or business among the assets in proportion to their fair market values in the following classes and the following order (Code Sec. 1060; Reg. §§ 1.338-6 and 1.1060-1):[26]

- Class I asset: Cash and general deposit accounts (including savings and checking accounts), other than certificates of deposits held in banks, savings and loan associations, and other depository institutions.
- Class II asset: Actively traded personal property, as well as certificates of deposit and foreign currency, even if they are not actively traded personal property.
- Class III asset: Assets that the taxpayer marks to market at least annually for federal income tax purposes.
- Class IV asset: Stock in trade of the taxpayer or other property of a kind that would properly be included in the inventory of the taxpayer if on hand at the close of the tax year, or property held by the taxpayer primarily for sale to customers in the ordinary course of its trade or business.
- Class V asset: All assets other than Class I, II, III, IV, VI, and VII assets.
- Class VI asset: Code Sec. 197 intangibles, except goodwill and going concern value.
- Class VII asset: Goodwill and going concern value whether or not they qualify as section 197 intangibles.

Before making the above allocation, the purchase price is first reduced by any cash and general deposit accounts (savings and checking) which the acquired business holds as assets. The buyer and seller of the assets of a trade or business are bound by any written agreements allocating consideration to the transferred assets. However, any allocation that is not found to be fair market value will be disregarded. The buyer and seller must attach Form 8594 to their income tax returns for the year of sale to report the allocation.

Land and Buildings. When a building and land are purchased for a lump sum, the purchase price must be allocated between the land and building on the basis of their fair market values. If the fair market values are uncertain, the allocation may be based on their assessed values for real estate tax purposes (Reg. §§ 1.61-6(a); 1.167(a)-5).[27]

Subdivided Lots. The basis of each lot of a subdivided property is equal to the purchase price of the entire property multiplied by a fraction, the numerator of which is the fair market value of the lot and the denominator of which is the fair market value of the entire property. The cost of common improvements is also allocated among the individual lots. A developer who sells subdivided lots before development work is completed may include, with IRS consent, an allocation of the estimated future cost for common improvements in the basis of the lots sold (Rev. Proc. 92-29).[28] There is a special rule relating to the recognition of capital gain on the sale of subdivided lots (¶ 1762).

References are to Standard Federal Tax Reports; Tax Research Consultant; and Practical Tax Explanations.

[24] ¶ 29,410; SALES: 6,374; § 16,101

[25] ¶ 5605; SALES: 6,200, SALES: 6,216; § 16,115

[26] ¶ 16,281, ¶ 30,060, ¶ 30,061; SALES: 33,052; § 18,401

[27] ¶ 5605, ¶ 11,012; SALES: 6,202.05; § 16,115

[28] ¶ 29,313.576; SALES: 6,216; § 38,430.10

1623. Allocation of Basis—Bargain Sale to Charity. If a charitable deduction is available, the basis of property sold to charity for less than its fair market value must be allocated between the portion of the property "sold" and the portion "given" to charity, based on the fair market value of each portion. Thus, the seller-donor realizes some taxable gain even if the selling price did not exceed the seller-donor's cost or other basis for the entire property (Code Sec. 1011(b); Reg. § 1.1011-2).[29] The adjusted basis of the portion of property sold to a charity is computed as:

$$\frac{\text{Amount realized (fair market value of part sold)}}{\text{Fair market value of entire property}} \times \text{Adjusted basis of entire property}$$

1626. Basis of Residential or Converted Property. Where property has been continually occupied by the taxpayer as a residence since its acquisition, no adjustment of the basis is made for depreciation since none is allowable. The cost of permanent improvements to the property is added to the basis, as are special assessments paid for local benefits that improve the property (¶ 1611). Recoveries against a builder for defective construction reduce the basis.[30]

If residential property is converted to rental property, an adjustment should be made for depreciation from the date of the conversion. Thus, the basis for gain in the case of rented residential property is the taxpayer's cost or other statutory basis, less depreciation allowable while the property was rented or held for rental.

The basis for loss may not exceed the value at the time the residence was converted to rental use, taking into account subsequent basis adjustments, including reduction for allowable depreciation. This is only a limitation; if a smaller loss results from the use of the adjusted cost basis, it must be used (Reg. § 1.165-9(b)).[31] The value of the property upon conversion to rental use has no effect on the basis for gain. If converted property is sold for a price that is greater than the basis for loss but less than the basis for gain, there is no gain or loss.

If rental property is converted to a personal residence, adjustments to basis for depreciation end on the date of the conversion. Any gain on the sale of the property will be recognized (subject to the exclusion rules at ¶ 1705) and may be subject to depreciation recapture (¶ 1779). Loss will not be recognized.

Property Acquired by Gift or Bequest

1630. Basis of Property Acquired by Gift. For property acquired by gift, the basis to the donee is generally the same as it would be in the hands of the donor or the last preceding owner by whom it was not acquired by gift (Code Sec. 1015(a); Reg. § 1.1015-1).[32] However, the basis for loss is the adjusted basis of the property prior to the date of the gift (¶ 1611—¶ 1617) or the fair market value of the property at the time of the gift, whichever is lower. In some cases, there is neither gain nor loss on the sale of property received by gift because the selling price is less than the basis for gain and more than the basis for loss.

If a gift tax was payable on a gift made on or after September 1, 1958, and before 1977, the basis of the property is increased by the amount of the gift tax, but not above the fair market value of the property at the time of the gift. As to gifts made before September 2, 1958, and held by the donee on that date, the basis is also increased by the amount of the gift tax, but not by more than any excess of the fair market value of the property at the time of the gift over the basis of the property in the hands of the donor at the time of the gift (Code Sec. 1015(d); Reg. § 1.1015-1).[33]

References are to Standard Federal Tax Reports; Tax Research Consultant; and Practical Tax Explanations.

[29] ¶ 29,310, ¶ 29,312; INDIV: 51,300, INDIV: 51,302; § 7,530

[30] ¶ 29,412.9968; SALES: 6,356.10; § 16,110.10

[31] ¶ 10,102; REAL: 15,054; § 16,930

[32] ¶ 29,390, ¶ 29,391; SALES: 6,102; § 16,205

[33] ¶ 29,390, ¶ 29,391; SALES: 6,104.10; § 16,210.05, § 28,605.25

In the case of a gift made after 1976 on which the gift tax is paid, the basis of the property is increased by the amount of gift tax attributable to the net appreciation in value of the gift. The net appreciation for this purpose is the amount by which the fair market value of the gift exceeds the donor's adjusted basis immediately before the gift (Code Sec. 1015(d)(6)).[34]

Zero basis generally applies to a life estate acquired by gift (¶ 1633).

1633. Basis of Property Acquired from a Decedent. The basis of any real or personal property acquired from a decedent is generally its fair market value on the date of the decedent's death or on the alternate valuation or special use valuation date (¶ 2922) (Code Sec. 1014).[35] If there is no federal estate tax liability, the basis of the property is its fair market value as of the date of the decedent's death for the purpose of state inheritance or transmission taxes (Reg. § 1.1014-3(a)).[36] Fair market value is presumptive, and may be rebutted by clear and convincing evidence (Rev. Rul. 54-97).[37] There are certain exceptions to the basis of property acquired from a decedent equaling fair market value (¶ 1636 and ¶ 1639), including income in respect of the decedent (¶ 182), and property subject to a qualified conservation easement.

Decedents Dying in 2010. Effective for decedents dying in 2010, the executor of the decedent's estate could have made an election not to have the estate be subject to the federal estate tax. If the election was made, a modified carryover basis rule applies to property acquired from the decedent. Specifically, the property recipient will receive a basis equal to the lesser of the property's adjusted basis in the hands of the decedent or its fair market value on the date of the decedent's death. Executors could have elected to increase the basis of estate property by up to $1.3 million (plus an increase for certain carryovers and unrealized losses of the decedent), with an additional basis increase of up to $3 million in the case of property passing to a surviving spouse. However, the basis of any property could not be increased above its fair market value in the decedent's hands on the date of the decedent's death (Code Sec. 1022).[38] The IRS has provided optional safe harbor procedures for determining modified carryover basis (Rev. Proc. 2011-41).[39]

Term Interests. In most instances, a zero basis is assigned to a life estate that was acquired by gift or bequest and sold or disposed of after October 9, 1969. Interests covered by this exception to the usual rules are: (1) life interests in property; (2) interests for a term of years in property; and (3) income interests in trusts. The zero basis requirement does not apply where the life tenant and remainderman sell their interests simultaneously so that the entire ownership of the property is transferred to another person or group of persons (Code Sec. 1001(e); Reg. § 1.1001-1; Reg. § 1.1014-5(b)).[40]

1634. Basis in Property Held in Joint Tenancy. A decedent's interest in property held in a joint tenancy (with a right of survivorship) or as tenants by the entirety that passes to the other owner by operation of law is considered property acquired from a decedent (Code Sec. 1014(b)(9); Reg. § 1.1014-2(b); Reg. § 1.1014-6(a)(1)).[41] Thus, the basis of the property in the hands of the survivor will generally depend upon the amount contributed by each joint tenant toward the original purchase price and, in the case of depreciable property, the manner in which income is divided under local (state) law.

References are to Standard Federal Tax Reports; Tax Research Consultant; and Practical Tax Explanations.

[34] ¶ 29,390; SALES: 6,104.05; § 16,210.15

[35] ¶ 29,370; ESTGIFT: 54,000; § 16,305.05

[36] ¶ 29,373; ESTGIFT: 54,058.05; § 16,305.15

[37] ¶ 29,380.38; ESTGIFT: 54,058.05; § 16,305.15

[38] ¶ 29,496; ESTGIFT: 51,060.10; § 16,310.05

[39] ¶ 29,498.10; ESTGIFT: 51,060.10; § 16,310.05

[40] ¶ 29,220, ¶ 29,221, ¶ 29,375; ESTGIFT: 54,056; § 2,115.30

[41] ¶ 29,370, ¶ 29,372, ¶ 29,376; ESTGIFT: 54,206; § 16,305.20

Example 1: Tom Smith and Susan Jones (unmarried) purchased a townhouse for $100,000, which they held as joint tenants with right of survivorship. Tom contributed $30,000 and Susan $70,000. Susan died when the property was worth $200,000; 70 percent of the fair market value ($140,000) is included in her estate. Tom's basis in the property is $170,000 ($30,000 + $140,000).

Example 2: Assume that Tom and Susan held the townhouse as a rental property and that $25,000 of depreciation was allowed prior to Susan's death. If Tom and Susan are entitled to one-half of the income from the property under local law, Tom's basis would be reduced by $12,500 to $157,500 ($170,000 - $12,500).

For purposes of the federal estate tax, the entire value of jointly held property with the right of survivorship is included in a decedent's gross estate except for the portion of the property for which the surviving joint tenant furnished consideration (¶ 2919). If the joint tenants are spouses, then it is a qualified joint interest and it does not matter who furnished the consideration for the property—one-half of the value is included in the gross estate of the first spouse to die. The surviving spouse's basis in the remaining portion of the qualified joint interest is one-half of the original cost (regardless of the amount that the survivor actually contributed) reduced by any depreciation deductions allocable to the surviving spouse (IRS Pub. 559).

Example 3: Assume the same facts as in Example 1, except that Tom and Susan are married. Tom's basis in the property is $150,000 ($50,000 (one-half of original cost) + $100,000 (one-half of fair market value included in Susan's estate).

1636. Carryover Basis Elections. Executors and administrators of estates of decedents dying after 1976 and before November 7, 1978, could elect to determine the basis under the otherwise repealed carryover basis rules.[42] The time for elections expired July 31, 1980, but valid elections will continue to affect computation of gain on dispositions of property to which such elections apply.

1639. Appreciated Property Reacquired by Donor from Decedent. For property acquired from a decedent who dies after December 31, 1981, the basis of the property when reacquired by the donor following the decedent's death is equal to the decedent's adjusted basis in the property immediately before the decedent's death if: (1) appreciated property was acquired by the decedent after August 13, 1981, as a gift; (2) the decedent received the gift within one year before his death; and (3) following the decedent's death, the donor of the gift, or the donor's spouse, reacquires the property (Code Sec. 1014(e)).[43]

Property Acquired by Exchange

1648. Basis of Property Transferred to Corporation in a Taxable Exchange. When a corporation acquires property for its stock in an exchange taxable to the transferor, its basis for the property is the fair market value of the stock on the date of the exchange. If the stock has no established market value at that time, it may be considered to be the equivalent of the fair market value of the property received.[44]

1651. Basis of Property Acquired in a Tax-Free Exchange. If property is acquired in an exchange on which no gain or loss is recognized, the basis of the property is the same as that for the property exchanged (Code Sec. 1031(d); Reg. § 1.1031(d)-1).[45] Substitute basis (¶ 1607) applies to:

- "like-kind" exchange of property held for productive use or investment (¶ 1721);
- some exchanges of stock for stock of the same corporation (¶ 1728);

References are to Standard Federal Tax Reports; Tax Research Consultant; and Practical Tax Explanations.

[42] ¶ 44,438.70; ESTGIFT: 54,060; § 16,101

[43] ¶ 29,370; ESTGIFT: 54,104; § 16,305.35

[44] ¶ 29,225.272; SALES: 6,060, SALES: 6,068; § 16,105.15

[45] ¶ 29,602, ¶ 29,612; SALES: 6,250; § 18,040

- exchanges of property solely for stock or securities of a "controlled" corporation (¶ 1731); and
- exchanges of stock or securities solely for stock or securities in a reorganization (¶ 2229).

Trade-in arrangements under which a taxpayer sells old equipment used in a trade or business to a dealer and purchases new equipment of like kind from the dealer are like-kind exchanges qualifying for nonrecognition treatment if the sale of the old equipment and the purchase of the new equipment are mutually dependent transactions, even if they are not simultaneous. The basis of the new equipment, for gain or loss or depreciation, is ordinarily the total of the adjusted basis of the trade-in plus whatever additional cash is needed. In effect, the basis of the new property is its purchase price, increased or decreased according to whether the trade-in value of the old equipment is greater or less than its depreciated cost. Special depreciation rules may apply to like-kind exchanges (¶ 1250).

1657. Basis of Boot Acquired in an Otherwise Tax-Free Exchange. In a like-kind exchange, money or other property, which is not permitted to be received without the recognition of gain or loss (¶ 1723), may be received together with securities or property that is permitted to be received without the recognition of gain or loss. In such exchanges, the cost or other applicable basis of the property acquired is the same as that of the property exchanged, decreased by the amount of any money received by the taxpayer in the transaction and increased by the amount of gain or decreased by the amount of loss recognized in the exchange. If such "other property" is received in an exchange that is tax free in part, the cost or other basis of the property disposed of must be allocated between the property received tax free and such "other property," assigning to the "other property" an amount equivalent to its fair market value (Code Sec. 1031(d)).[46]

1660. Basis of Property Transferred to a Corporation. The basis of property acquired by a corporation from a shareholder in exchange for stock in a Code Sec. 351 transaction in which the shareholder controls the corporation immediately after the exchange (¶ 203), as well as the basis of property from a shareholder as paid-in surplus or as a contribution to capital, is the same to the corporation as it was in the hands of the shareholder, increased by the amount of gain recognized by the shareholder on the transfer (Code Sec. 362(a); Reg. § 1.362-1).[47] If property is acquired by a corporation in a reorganization, the basis of the transferor (increased by any recognized gain) generally also follows through to the transferee corporation. However, carryover basis will not apply if the property acquired by the corporation consists of stock or securities in another corporation that is a party to the reorganization unless the stock or securities were acquired as consideration for the transfer (Code Sec. 362(b)). Rules for property acquired subject to a built-in loss (¶ 1667) and for property acquired upon liquidation of a subsidiary may apply (¶ 2261).

Property contributed to a corporation by nonstockholders on or after June 22, 1954, has a zero basis. Money contributed by an outsider on or after that date reduces the basis of corporate property acquired with it within 12 months after the contribution is received. To the extent that the contribution is not used to acquire property within this 12-month period, it reduces, as of the last day of the period, the basis of any other property held by the company (Code Sec. 362(c)).

1667. Limitations on Built-In Losses. If a corporation receives property in an exchange with an owner who is *not* subject to U.S. tax, and the property's fair market value (FMV) is less than the transferee's adjusted basis of all property received in the exchange (i.e., there is a built-in loss), the corporate transferee's basis in the property

References are to Standard Federal Tax Reports; Tax Research Consultant; and Practical Tax Explanations.

[46] ¶ 29,602; SALES: 6,252; § 18,040

[47] ¶ 16,610, ¶ 16,611; SALES: 6,272, SALES: 6,274, SALES: 6,276, CCORP: 3,204, CCORP: 39,302; § 26,135

received is its fair market value immediately after the transfer (Code Sec. 362(e)).[48] Thus, the foreign loss is not recognized for U.S. tax purposes. This treatment applies to property acquired by the corporation from a shareholder in exchange for stock in a Code Sec. 351 transaction in which the shareholder controls the corporation immediately after the exchange (¶ 203), as well as the basis of property from a shareholder as paid-in surplus or as a contribution to capital (¶ 1660).

Similarly, if a corporation acquires property in a section 351 exchange with an owner who *is* subject to U.S. tax, and the transferred property's adjusted basis exceeds its fair market value, the corporate transferee's basis in the property is generally limited to its fair market value immediately after the transaction. Any required basis reduction is allocated among the transferred properties in proportion to their built-in losses immediately before the transaction. For this type of exchange, the transferor owner and transferee controlled corporation can make an irrevocable election to limit the owner's basis in the stock received—rather than the corporation's basis in the property—to the aggregate fair market value of the transferred property. The IRS has provided guidance on the requirements of a valid election (Notice 2005-70). Proposed election procedures would revise and expand the election rules (Proposed Reg. § 1.362-4(c)(5)).

1669. Assumption of Liabilities. The assumption of liabilities by a shareholder in a Code Sec. 351 exchange with a controlled corporation (¶ 203) or in a reorganization (¶ 2229) is not treated as the equivalent of cash (¶ 2233). In a determination of basis after such transfers, the corporation whose liabilities were assumed (or whose property was taken subject to the liabilities) will treat the assumption or acquisition as money received, to the extent of the liabilities (Code Secs. 358(d) and 1031(d)).[49] This rule applies only to the corporation whose liabilities are assumed. It has no effect on the corporation that assumes the debts.

1672. Discharge of Debt. Under some conditions, a taxpayer realizes no income from a discharge of debt (¶ 885). Any amount of debt discharged and excluded from gross income reduces the basis of the property securing the debt (Code Sec. 1017).[50] Regulations prescribe the sequence of allocation where the debt is, or must be treated as, a general liability (Reg. §§ 1.108-4 and 1.1017-1).[51]

Other Acquired Property

1678. Basis of Property Transferred in Trust. If property is acquired by a transfer in trust, other than by a transfer in trust by gift, bequest or devise—for example, sale to the trust by the grantor)—after December 31, 1920, its basis is the same as it would be in the hands of the trust's grantor, increased by the gain, or decreased by the loss, recognized to the grantor under the law in effect as of the date of such transfer (Code Sec. 1015(b)).[52] When an existing charitable remainder trust is split pro rata into separate trusts, one for each beneficiary, the original trust's basis in the assets is split pro rata among the new trusts (Rev. Rul. 2008-41).

1681. Basis of Stock or Other Property Received for Services. If stock or other property is given as compensation for services instead of cash, the fair market value of the property is income unless the property is subject to a substantial risk of forfeiture (¶ 713). The fair market value of the property included in income becomes its basis to the employee (Code Sec. 83; Reg. § 1.83-4(b)).[53] If the property is sold to the employee for less than its market value, the difference between the amount paid and the value of the property is also income. In this case, the employee's basis for the property is the cash cost plus the amount reported as income.

References are to Standard Federal Tax Reports; Tax Research Consultant; and Practical Tax Explanations.

[48] ¶ 16,610; CCORP: 39,304.10; § 26,135

[49] ¶ 16,550, ¶ 29,602; SALES: 27,308, CCORP: 39,256.05; § 26,130

[50] ¶ 29,430; SALES: 6,368; § 3,420.15

[51] ¶ 7003E, ¶ 29,431; SALES: 6,368.10; § 3,420.10

[52] ¶ 29,390; SALES: 6,110; § 16,205

[53] ¶ 6380, ¶ 6384; SALES: 6,062; § 21,435.05

The basis for determining gain or loss when the property is sold is the amount included in income in the election year plus any amount paid for the property. If the property is forfeited after the election is made and before the property is substantially vested, there is a loss equal to the amount paid for the property minus the amount realized from the forfeiture. The Code Sec. 83(b) election is made by filing a written statement with the IRS (¶ 713).

Corporations may grant their employees the option to purchase stock in the corporation (¶ 1923—¶ 1931). For purposes of determining an individual's basis in property transferred in connection with the performance of services, rules similar to the annuity basis rules under Code Sec. 72(w) apply (Code Sec. 83(c)(4)) (¶ 821).

1682. Basis of Stock Received in Nontaxable Distributions. If a shareholder in a corporation receives stock or stock rights in a nontaxable distribution (¶ 733A), the basis of the old stock is allocated between the old stock and new stock in proportion to the fair market value of each on the date of the distribution (not the record date) (Code Sec. 307; Reg. § 1.307-1).[54] If only part of the stock dividend is nontaxable, the basis of the old stock is allocated between the old stock and the part of the new stock that is not taxable.

This rule applies with respect to stock rights only if such rights are exercised or sold. If exercised, the basis of the stock rights is added to the cost of the stock acquired. If sold, the basis allocable to the stock rights is used to determine the taxpayer's gain or loss. If the stock rights are allowed to expire, the basis of the shares with respect to which the rights were distributed remains intact.

In addition, if the fair market value of the stock rights on the date of distribution is less than 15 percent of the fair market value of the stock with respect to which the distribution is made, the basis of the stock rights is deemed to be zero unless the taxpayer elects to make a basis allocation (Code Sec. 307(b); Reg. § 1.307-2).[55] The election must be made in a statement attached to the shareholder's return for the year in which the rights are received. It is irrevocable with respect to the rights for which it is made. Also, the election must be made for all the rights received in a particular distribution by the shareholder on stock of the same class received by the shareholder at the time of the distribution.

Example: Bob bought 100 shares of Yeta Company common stock at $125 per share and later received 100 rights entitling him to purchase 20 shares of new common stock in Yeta Company at $100 per share. When the rights were distributed, the old shares had a fair market value of $120 per share, and the rights had a fair market value of $3 each. Three weeks later, Bob sold his rights for $4 each. He elects to apportion basis.

Cost of old stock on which rights were distributed	$12,500.00
Market value of old stock at date of distribution of rights .	12,000.00
Market value of rights at date of distribution	300.00
Cost apportioned to old stock after distribution of rights (12,000/12,300 of $12,500)	12,195.12
Cost apportioned to rights (300/12,300 of $12,500)	304.88
Selling price of rights	400.00
Gain ($400 – $304.88)	$95.12

In determining gain or loss from any later sale of the stock on which the rights were distributed, the adjusted cost of the old stock is $12,195.12, or $121.95 a share.

The holding period of nontaxable stock rights includes the holding period of the stock on which the rights are distributed. The holding period of the stock acquired by the exercise of the rights begins on the date that the rights are exercised (Code Sec. 1223(4); Reg. § 1.1223-1(e)).[56]

References are to Standard Federal Tax Reports; Tax Research Consultant; and Practical Tax Explanations.

[54] ¶ 15,500, ¶ 15,501; SALES: 6,302.10; § 26,235.10

[55] ¶ 15,501, ¶ 15,501B; SALES: 6,302.15; § 26,235.10

[56] ¶ 30,460, ¶ 30,461; SALES: 15,162.30; § 16,540.05

1684. Basis of Equipment for Which Medical Deduction Claimed. The basis of equipment whose cost qualifies as a medical expense (¶ 1016) does not include that portion of its cost that has been claimed as an itemized deduction since such amounts are not properly capitalized. However, the equipment's basis includes that portion of the cost that is nondeductible because of the 7.5-percent adjusted gross income (AGI) floor (10 percent beginning in 2013 unless the taxpayer or the taxpayer's spouse has attained age 65 before the close of the tax year) (¶ 1015).

To determine this portion, the total amount of the AGI limitation is multiplied by a fraction whose numerator is the cost of the equipment and whose denominator is the total amount of the taxpayer's medical expenses. Similarly, if a taxpayer's total allowable itemized deductions exceed the taxpayer's adjusted gross income, or are limited by the overall limitation on itemized deductions of high-income taxpayers (¶ 1014), that portion of the equipment's cost attributable to the nondeductible expenses may also be included in the equipment's basis.[57]

1687. Basis of Property Acquired Through Involuntary Conversion. The basis of property purchased as the result of an involuntary conversion (¶ 1713) on which gain is not recognized is the cost of the replacement property less the amount of gain not recognized on the conversion. If qualifying replacement property is received as the result of an involuntary conversion, the replacement property's basis is the same as the basis of the involuntarily converted property decreased by any loss recognized on the conversion and any money received and not spent on qualifying replacement property. The basis is increased by any gain recognized on the conversion and any cost of acquiring the replacement property (Code Sec. 1033(b); Reg. § 1.1033(b)-1).[58] Special depreciation rules may apply (¶ 1250).

1693. Basis of Property Transferred Between Spouses. No gain or loss is recognized on a transfer of property from an individual to, or in trust for the benefit of, a spouse or a former spouse if the transfer to the former spouse is incident to the divorce of the parties (¶ 1734). In such case, the basis of the transferred property in the hands of the transferee is the transferor's adjusted basis in the property. This nontaxable carryover basis provision does not apply to a spouse (or former spouse) who is a nonresident alien (Code Sec. 1041(d)). Nonrecognition of gain is not permitted with respect to the transfer of property in trust to the extent that the sum of the amount of any liabilities assumed, plus the amount of any liabilities to which the property is subject, exceeds the total of the adjusted basis of the property transferred (Code Sec. 1041(e)).[59] The transferee's basis is adjusted to take into account any gain recognized.

Valuation Rules

1695. Indeterminate Fair Market Value. Only in rare and extraordinary cases does property have no determinable fair market value (Reg. § 1.1001-1).[60] If the fair market value of an asset received in an exchange (such as a contract to receive royalties) cannot be determined with fair certainty, gain is not realized on the exchange until after the total payments received under the contract exceed the cost (or other basis) of the property surrendered in exchange.[61] The Tax Court has applied the *Cohan* rule (estimated or approximate value) to estimate the value of patents, patent applications, and stock rights, where the taxpayer could not prove their exact value.[62]

1697. Valuation of Securities and Real Estate. The fair market value of securities traded on the open market, or on a recognized exchange, is ordinarily the average of the high and low quoted prices on the valuation date. If only a minimal number of shares are

References are to Standard Federal Tax Reports; Tax Research Consultant; and Practical Tax Explanations.

[57] ¶ 29,413; SALES: 6,360.10; § 7,285.10

[58] ¶ 29,640, ¶ 29,644; SALES: 6,254; § 18,145.05

[59] ¶ 29,800; SALES: 6,262; § 18,230

[60] ¶ 29,221; VALUE: 1,000; § 16,405

[61] ¶ 29,225.153; ACCTNG: 6,114; § 16,405

[62] ¶ 8520.586, ¶ 16,612.175; SALES: 6052; § 26,410.15

traded on the valuation date, or if other abnormal market conditions exist, an alternative valuation method may be necessary.[63]

When corporate stock is not sold on the open market, its fair market value depends upon many factors, including the nature and history of the business, economic outlook and condition of the industry, book value of stock and financial condition of the business, earning capacity of the company, dividend-paying capacity, goodwill, prior sales, size of the block to be valued, and market price of similar but listed stock.[64] Isolated sales of small portions of the stock or forced sales are not considered evidence of fair market value.[65]

Restrictive sales agreements must be considered in the valuation of stock. If the stock is subject to a repurchase option, its value may not exceed the amount for which it may be repurchased. If there are restrictions making sale of stock impossible, and its value is highly speculative, it does not have a fair market value.[66]

There are three principal methods used in determining the fair market value of realty:[67]

(1) the comparable sales method, which involves gathering information on sales of property similar to the subject property and then making adjustments (both positive and negative) for various differences between the *comparables* and the property being appraised;

(2) the capitalization of income method, which estimates a property's fair market value based upon future benefits (cash-flow) to be derived from the ownership of the property; and

(3) the replacement cost method, which is based on the principle of substitution and estimates the fair market value of realty based on the assumption that a prudent person (in other words, a willing buyer) would not pay more for a property than it would cost to acquire a similar site and erect a comparable structure (less accrued depreciation).

Other factors that may be appropriate to consider with regard to a fair market value determination of realty include:

(1) the development potential of the realty with regard to its highest and best potential and realistic use;

(2) the possibility of zoning changes that may either enhance or diminish the marketability of the property;

(3) the taxpayer's ability to acquire adjacent parcels of realty allowing for expanded and, in many cases, enhanced uses;

(4) leases, debt, and other encumbrances on the property; and

(5) environmental concerns, restrictions, and hazards.

Appraisal affidavits of a retrospective nature, standing alone, are generally not accorded great weight.[68]

References are to Standard Federal Tax Reports; Tax Research Consultant; and Practical Tax Explanations.

[63] ¶ 29,225.187, ¶ 29,225.242; VALUE: 3,100; § 34,110.20

[64] ¶ 29,225.228; VALUE: 9,050; § 34,110.20

[65] ¶ 29,225.234; VALUE: 9,062.05; § 34,110.20

[66] ¶ 29,225.2563; VALUE: 9,200; § 34,110.20

[67] ¶ 11,660.555; VALUE: 15,100

[68] ¶ 29,225.1055; VALUE: 1,104; § 7,600.25

Chapter 17
SALES AND EXCHANGES
CAPITAL GAINS

Sales and Exchanges of Property

1701. Gain or Loss from Sale or Exchange of Property. A taxpayer's gain or loss from the sale or exchange of property generally must be recognized for income tax purposes (Code Sec. 1001(c)).[1] A taxpayer has gain if the amount realized from the sale or exchange is more than the taxpayer's adjusted basis in the property. A taxpayer has a loss when the adjusted basis of the property is more than the amount realized from the sale or exchange (Code Sec. 1001(a)).[2] However, not all gains and losses have to be recognized for income tax purposes.

In order to determine the tax consequences of a sale or exchange, the following questions must be answered:

(1) What is the amount realized in the transaction (¶ 1703)?

(2) What is the taxpayer's adjusted basis in the property (¶ 1601—¶ 1697)?

(3) Is the gain or loss on the transaction recognized (¶ 1719—¶ 1734)?

(4) Will the capital gain and loss provisions apply (¶ 1735—¶ 1744)?

(5) Is any part of the gain attributable to depreciation recapture (¶ 1779)?

Installment Payments. When real or personal property is sold by a nondealer and part or all of the selling price is to be paid after the year of sale, the recognized gain from the sale must be reported on the installment method, unless the taxpayer elects *not* to use it (¶ 1801).

Rollover into SSBIC Stock. Individuals and C corporations may elect to defer the recognition of capital gain from the sale of any publicly traded securities if the sale proceeds are invested in the stock or a partnership interest of a "specialized small

References are to Standard Federal Tax Reports; Tax Research Consultant; and Practical Tax Explanations.

[1] ¶ 29,220; SALES: 9,050; § 16,005, § 16,010

[2] ¶ 29,220; SALES: 9,052; § 16,015

business investment company" (SSBIC). These rollovers are subject to cumulative limits (¶ 1909).

Gain from Small Business Stock. Noncorporate taxpayers may generally exclude from gross income 50 percent of any gain (section 1202 gain) from the sale or exchange of qualified small business stock held for more than five years and issued after August 10, 1993. The exclusion amount is 75 percent for qualified stock acquired after February 17, 2009, and before September 28, 2010, and 100 percent for qualified stock acquired after September 27, 2010, and before January 1, 2012 (¶ 1905). Excluded section 1202 gain is given special treatment for alternative minimum tax (AMT) preference purposes (¶ 1425). A noncorporate taxpayer may also elect to roll over the realized gain from the sale of qualified small business stock held for more than six months if other small business stock is purchased during the 60-day period beginning on the date of sale (¶ 1907).

Demutualization of Life Insurance Company. A mutual insurance company can be converted into a stock company. As a result of this "demutualization" or conversion process, policyholders receive cash and/or shares of stock in exchange for their equity interest in the former mutual company. According to the IRS, if the conversion from a mutual company to a stock company qualifies as a tax-free reorganization (¶ 2205), any stock received by the policyholder has a zero basis. As a result, when the stock is sold, the taxpayer is generally required to recognize capital gain to the extent of the net sales price (¶ 1735). The taxpayer's holding period for the stock includes the time during which the taxpayer had an equity interest in the mutual insurance company. If the conversion did not qualify as a tax-free reorganization, capital gain or loss must be recognized in the year the stock is received. The taxpayer's holding period for the stock begins the day after it was received. If cash is received in exchange for the equity interest, the taxpayer must recognize a capital gain in the year the cash is received (IRS Pub. 550). However, some courts have found that a shareholder's basis in stock received from a demutualized insurance company is not zero (*E. Fisher*, CA-FC, 2010-1 USTC ¶ 50,289; *B. Dorrance*, DC-AZ, 2012-2 USTC ¶ 50,463).[3]

1703. Amount Realized. The amount realized on a sale or exchange of property is the total of monies received plus the fair market value of all other property or services received (Code Sec. 1001(b); *International Freighting Corp., Inc.*, CA-2, 43-1 USTC ¶ 9334).[4] If the property received in an exchange has no readily determinable fair market value, it is generally treated as being equal in value to the property disposed of in the exchange (*Philadelphia Park Amusement Co.*, CtCls, 54-2 USTC ¶ 9697).[5] If property disposed of was acquired as part of a larger transaction, the open transaction doctrine may apply, and no gain will be recognized until the taxpayer's basis in all the property acquired has been recovered (*E.A. Fisher*, CA-FC (unpub. op.), 2010-1 USTC ¶ 50,289, aff'g, FedCl, 2008-2 USTC ¶ 50,481).[6] Generally, the amount realized includes any liabilities from which the seller is relieved as a result of the sale or exchange (Reg. § 1.1001-2).[7]

The amount realized on the receipt of an annuity in exchange for property is the fair market value of the annuity contract at the time of the exchange. The entire amount of any gain or loss is recognized at the time of the exchange, regardless of the taxpayer's method of accounting (Prop. Reg. § 1.1001-1(j)).[8]

A taxpayer who makes a gift of property on condition that the donee pay the resulting gift taxes realizes gain to the extent that the gift taxes paid by the donee exceed the donor's basis in the property (*V.P. Diedrich*, SCt, 82-1 USTC ¶ 9419).[9]

References are to Standard Federal Tax Reports; Tax Research Consultant; and Practical Tax Explanations.

[3] ¶ 5700.225, ¶ 29,225.1726; SALES: 9,104.10, VALUE: 1,108, INDIV: 30,100, CCORP: 6,054; § 16,105.15

[4] ¶ 29,220, ¶ 29,225.1013; SALES: 9,100; § 16,401

[5] ¶ 29,225.1523; SALES: 9,104.10; § 16,405

[6] ¶ 5700.225; SALES: 36,404; § 16,401

[7] ¶ 29,223; SALES: 9,108; § 16,410

[8] ¶ 29,221D; SALES: 9,106; § 3,245.10

[9] ¶ 29,226.3062; SALES: 3,056.10; § 32,830.30

Gain or Loss from Sale of Residence

1705. Exclusion of Gain from Sale of Principal Residence. An individual may exclude from gross income up to $250,000 of gain ($500,000 on a joint return or return of a surviving spouse) realized on the sale or exchange of a principal residence (Code Sec. 121).[10] During the five-year period that ends on the sale or exchange date, the individual must meet an ownership test and a use test for at least two years to be eligible for the exclusion (¶ 1707). The exclusion may not be used more frequently than once every two years. A partial or reduced exclusion may be available even if a taxpayer does not meet the ownership and use requirements, or has already used the exclusion within the two years (¶ 1709).

Married Individuals. The maximum amount of gain that may be excluded is $500,000 for married individuals filing jointly in the tax year of the sale or exchange if:

(1) either spouse meets the ownership test with respect to the property,

(2) both spouses meet the use test with respect to the property, and

(3) neither spouse is ineligible for exclusion by virtue of a sale or exchange of a residence within the prior two years (Code Sec. 121(b)(2); Reg. § 1.121-2).[11]

The exclusion is determined on an individual basis. Thus, if a single individual who is otherwise eligible for an exclusion marries someone who has used the exclusion within the two years prior to the sale, the newly married individual is entitled to a maximum exclusion of $250,000. Once both spouses satisfy the eligibility rules and two years have passed since the exclusion was allowed to either of them, they may exclude up to $500,000 of gain on their joint return.

Surviving Spouse. A surviving spouse may use the full $500,000 exclusion if the sale is made not later than two years after the date of the other spouse's death and requirements (1)–(3) listed above are met immediately before the date of death (Code Sec. 121(b)(4); Reg. § 1.121-4(a)).[12] For this purpose, a surviving spouse is considered as owning and living in the home for the same period as the deceased spouse, so long as the surviving spouse does not remarry before the date of sale (Code Sec. 121(d)(2)).

> **Example 1:** Erik owned and lived in his home since 1991. On July 10, 2011, he marries Helen and they both live in Erik's home. Erik dies on March 3, 2012, and Helen inherits the home. On June 1, 2012, Helen sells the home; she had not remarried on or before the sales date. Helen satisfies the ownership and use tests because she is able to include the time that Erik owned and used the home.

Gain Allocable to Nonqualified Use. Gain that is allocable to periods of nonqualified use may not be excluded from gross income (Code Sec. 121(b)(4)[(5)]).[13] Nonqualified use is generally any use other than as a principal residence, which restricts the availability of the exclusion for second homes and vacation homes significantly. Several important exceptions apply. A period of nonqualified use does not include: (1) any period before January 1, 2009; (2) any portion of the five-year period ending on the sale or exchange date that is after the last date that the property is used as a principal residence; (3) any period of 10 years or less when the taxpayer or the taxpayer's spouse is serving on qualified official extended duty as an armed forces member, a Foreign Service member or an intelligence community employee; or (4) any period of two years or less for temporary absence due to a change of employment, health conditions, or other unforeseen circumstances.

> **Example 2:** On January 1, 2007, Eleanor buys a residence for $400,000 and uses it as rental property for two years, claiming $20,000 of depreciation deductions. On January 1, 2009, she converts the property to her principal residence. She moves out on January 13, 2011, and sells the property for $720,000 on January 1, 2012. The portion of the gain attributable to the depreciation deductions ($20,000)

References are to Standard Federal Tax Reports; Tax Research Consultant; and Practical Tax Explanations.

[10] ¶ 7260; REAL: 15,152; § 1,601

[11] ¶ 7260, ¶ 7262; REAL: 15,152.10; § 1,615.10

[12] ¶ 7260, ¶ 7264; REAL: 15,152.10; § 1,615.15

[13] ¶ 7260; REAL: 15,152.05; § 1,615.20

is included in income (see "*Gain Recognized to Extent of Depreciation*," following). Of the remaining $300,000 gain, 40 percent (two years divided by five years), or $120,000, is allocated to the nonqualified use and is not eligible for the exclusion. The period from January 14, 2011, to January 1, 2012, is after she last used it as her primary residence, so it is not a period of nonqualified use. Thus, the remaining gain of $180,000 is excluded from Eleanor's gross income in the tax year of the sale.

Like-Kind Exchanges. A taxpayer may qualify for both the exclusion of gain from the sale or exchange of a principal residence and nonrecognition of gain from a like-kind exchange (¶ 1721). If the residence was acquired in a like-kind exchange, the exclusion will not apply if the individual (or any person whose basis in the property is derived from the exchanging individual's basis) sells or exchanges the residence during the five-year period that begins on the date the residence was acquired (Code Sec. 121(d)(10)).[14]

Example 3: Wallace obtained a single family home in a like-kind exchange on September 1, 2007. After renting it out for 18 months, he decided to move in and used it as his principal residence, beginning March 1, 2009. If Wallace sells the home before September 1, 2012, the exclusion is not available.

Gain Recognized to Extent of Depreciation. The exclusion of gain on the sale or exchange of a principal residence does not apply to the extent of any depreciation allowable with respect to the rental or business use of a principal residence after May 6, 1997 (Code Sec. 121(d)(6); Reg. § 1.121-1(d)(1)).[15] If the amount of depreciation allowed is less than the depreciation allowable, the taxpayer may limit the amount of gain recognized to the amount of depreciation allowed if the taxpayer can establish the amount claimed by adequate records or other sufficient evidence (Code Sec. 1250(b)(3)).[16]

Remainder Interests. The exclusion applies to gain on the sale or exchange of a remainder interest in a principal residence, provided the buyer is not a member of the taxpayer's family or other related entity as defined by Code Sec. 267(b) or 707(b) (Code Sec. 121(d)(8)).[17] See ¶ 432 and ¶ 1717 for a discussion of related persons.

Expatriates. The exclusion is not available to a nonresident alien who has given up his or her U.S. citizenship or long-term resident status and is subject to the rules for individuals who expatriate from the United States (¶ 2412) (Code Sec. 121(e)).[18]

Involuntary Conversions. For purposes of determining the allowable exclusion of gain from the sale of a principal residence, the destruction, theft, seizure, requisition, or condemnation of property is treated as a sale or exchange of the residence (Code Sec. 121(d)(5)).[19] In addition, the ownership and use of property acquired in an involuntary conversion generally includes the ownership and use of the property treated as sold or exchanged. For purposes of the rules governing involuntary conversions (¶ 1713), the amount realized from the sale or exchange of property is equal to the amount of realized gain, reduced by the amount of gain that is permitted to be excluded from income under the $250,000/$500,000 exclusion.

Property Acquired from 2010 Decedent. The exclusion is available for the sale of a decedent's principal residence by the estate, heirs, or revocable trust established by the decedent prior to death if the decedent died in 2010, but only if the estate elects to have the modified carryover basis rules apply (¶ 1633) (Code Sec. 121(d)(11)).[20] For estates that do not make the election, and for estate of decedents who died before or after 2010, gain on the sale of the decedent's principal residence cannot be excluded from gross income.

References are to Standard Federal Tax Reports; Tax Research Consultant; and Practical Tax Explanations.

[14] ¶ 7260; REAL: 15,160; § 1,640

[15] ¶ 7260, ¶ 7261; DEPR: 18,112; § 1,615.25

[16] ¶ 31,000; DEPR: 18,262.10; § 11,710

[17] ¶ 7260; REAL: 15,152.05; § 1,625.10

[18] ¶ 7260; REAL: 15,152.05; § 1,610.25

[19] ¶ 7260; REAL: 15,158; § 1,625.15

[20] ¶ 7260; REAL: 15,150; § 1,610.30

Reporting Requirements. An individual who is qualified to exclude all of the realized gain from the sale of a home is not required to report the sale on the tax return for the year of sale. If, however, the individual can exclude only some of the gain or receives a Form 1099-S, then the sale or exchange is reported on Form 8949 (on Schedule D of Form 1040 for tax years before 2011). If the home was sold under the installment method and gain is recognized, then the sale is reported on Form 6252. Sale of the business or rental portion of the property (¶ 1707) may need to be reported on Form 4797.

1707. Ownership and Use Requirements. A taxpayer is eligible to exclude from gross income gain realized from the sale or exchange of a principal residence (¶ 1705) if, during the five-year period that ends on the date of the sale or exchange, the individual owned and used the property as a principal residence for periods aggregating two years or more (i.e., a total of 730 days (365 × 2)) (Code Sec. 121(a); Reg. § 1.121-1(c)).[21] The ownership and use tests may be met during nonconcurrent periods, provided that both tests are met during the five-year period that ends on the date of sale. If a taxpayer does not meet the ownership and use requirements, or has already used the exclusion within the two years, a reduced exclusion may be available (¶ 1709).

The home or dwelling unit that is sold does not have to be the principal residence at the time of purchase or sale, as long as the taxpayer's use of the home as a principal residence totals two years or more within the five-year period ending on the date of sale. Although a principal residence may include the surrounding land, the exclusion applies only if the taxpayer actually used the house or dwelling unit as his principal residence for the required period (*D.A Gates*, 135 TC 1, Dec. 58,259).[22] Short temporary absences for vacations or seasonal absences are counted as periods of use, even if the individual rents out the property during these periods of absence. However, an absence of an entire year is not considered a short temporary absence.

Divorced Individuals. If a residence is transferred to an individual incident to a divorce, the time the individual's spouse or former spouse owned the residence is added to the individual's period of ownership (Code Sec. 121(d)(3); Reg. § 1.121-4(b)).[23] An individual who owns a residence is deemed to use it as a principal residence during the time the individual's spouse or former spouse has use of the home under a divorce or separation agreement.

Incapacity. If an individual becomes physically or mentally incapable of self-care, the individual is deemed to use a residence as a principal residence during the time in which the individual owns the residence and resides in a licensed care facility (e.g., a nursing home) (Code Sec. 121(d)(7)).[24] In order for this rule to apply, the individual must have owned and used the residence as a principal residence for an aggregate period of at least one year during the five years preceding the sale or exchange.

Relief for Military, Foreign Service, Peace Corps, and Intelligence Personnel. A special exception to the two-out-of-five year rule exists for individuals (or their spouses) while they are serving on qualified official extended duty as U.S. uniformed services members, U.S. Foreign Service members, or intelligence community employees. The exception also applies for individuals (or their spouses) while serving outside the United States either as Peace Corps employees on qualified official extended duty or as Peace Corps enrolled volunteers or volunteer leaders (Code Sec. 121(d)(9) and (12); Reg. § 1.121-5).[25] These individuals may elect to suspend the five-year test period by not including the gain in the taxpayer's gross income on the tax return filed for the year of the sale. The suspension period cannot last more than 10 years, and the election may only be made with respect to one property. The individual may revoke the election at any time.

Qualified official extended duty means any extended duty while serving at a duty station that is at least 50 miles from the individual's principal residence or while residing

References are to Standard Federal Tax Reports; Tax Research Consultant; and Practical Tax Explanations.

[21] ¶ 7260, ¶ 7261; REAL: 15,156; § 1,610.05

[22] ¶ 7266.72; REAL: 15,156.10; § 1,610.05

[23] ¶ 7260, ¶ 7264; REAL: 15,152.10; § 1,610.10

[24] ¶ 7260; REAL: 15,156.10; § 1,610.15

[25] ¶ 7260, ¶ 7265; REAL: 15,156.15; § 1,610.20

in government quarters under government orders (Code Sec. 121(d)(9)(C)). Extended duty is any period of active duty due to a call or order to such duty for a period in excess of 90 days or for an indefinite time.

Allocation for Partial Use. An individual cannot claim the exclusion for any portion of the gain that is allocable to the portion of the property that is separate from the actual residence (i.e., the "dwelling unit") and not used as a residence (Reg. § 1.121-1(e)).[26] In determining the amount of gain allocable for mixed used property, the basis of the property and the amount realized must be allocated using the same method of allocation used to determine the depreciation adjustments. The IRS has provided a number of examples that illustrate how the allocation rules are used in various situations.

If part of the home was used for a business (e.g., home office) or to produce rental income, the individual does not need to allocate the basis of the property and the amount realized from the sale or exchange between the business portion of the home and the residential portion in determining excludible gain. However, gain must be recognized to the extent of claimed depreciation (¶ 1705). The rule is different when a separate part of the property was used for business purposes or rental income (e.g., the individual owned an apartment building and lived in one unit and rented out the other units). Generally, if the separate part of the property is used for business or rental purposes in the year of sale, the individual must treat the sale of the property as the sale of two properties (i.e., a dwelling unit and a business or rental property).

> **Example:** Bob Blaine sold his main home in 2012 at a $30,000 gain. He meets the ownership and use tests to exclude the gain from his income. However, he used part of the home as a business office in 2009 and claimed $500 depreciation. Because the business office was part of his home (not separate from it), he does not have to allocate the basis and amount realized between the business part of the property and the part used as a home. In addition, he does not have to report any part of the gain on Form 4797. Bob reports his gain, exclusion, and taxable gain of $500 on Form 8949.

Trusts and Single-Owner Entities. In certain instances, ownership of a principal residence by a grantor trust (¶ 571) or single-owner entity (¶ 402A), rather than by an individual, will satisfy the two-year ownership requirement for exclusion of gain (Reg. § 1.121-1(c)(3)).[27] If a residence is owned by a grantor trust, a taxpayer will be treated as owning the residence for the period that the taxpayer is treated as the owner of the trust or the portion of the trust that includes the residence. If a residence is owned by an eligible single-owner entity that is disregarded for federal tax purposes as an entity separate from its owner, the taxpayer-owner will be treated as owning the residence.

Co-ops. The ownership of stock in a cooperative housing corporation is the equivalent of ownership of a residence if the seller, during the five-year period ending on the date of sale, owned the stock for at least two years and lived in the house or apartment as a principal residence for at least two years (Code Sec. 121(d)(4); Reg. § 1.121-4(c)).[28]

1709. Reduced Exclusion of Gain from Sale of Principal Residence. An individual may be eligible for a partial or reduced exclusion of gain from the sale or exchange of a principal residence (¶ 1705) if the individual otherwise fails to meet the ownership and use requirements (¶ 1707) or has already used the exclusion within two years of the sale. The reduced exclusion is available if, based on the facts and circumstances, the primary reason for the sale of the home is due to a change in place of employment, health reasons, or unforeseen circumstances (Code Sec. 121(c); Reg. § 1.121-3).[29] If a qualified individual is able to satisfy one of the safe harbor tests discussed below, then the primary reason for the sale will be treated as having been due to a change in place of employment, health, or unforeseen circumstances. A qualified individual for this pur-

References are to Standard Federal Tax Reports; Tax Research Consultant; and Practical Tax Explanations.

[26] ¶ 7261; REAL: 15,156.20; § 1,610.35

[27] ¶ 7261; REAL: 15,156.05; § 1,610.25

[28] ¶ 7260, ¶ 7264; REAL: 9,304, REAL: 15,156.05; § 1,610.25

[29] ¶ 7260, ¶ 7263; REAL: 15,166; § 1,620.05

pose is the taxpayer, the taxpayer's spouse, a co-owner of the residence, or a person whose principal place of abode is in the same household as the taxpayer.

Change in Place of Employment. The primary reason test will be satisfied if the sale or exchange is due to a change in the location of a qualified individual's employment (Reg. § 1.121-3(c)). A safe harbor exists if the qualified individual's new place of employment is at least 50 miles farther from the residence sold or exchanged than was the former place of employment; if there was no former place of employment, the distance between the qualified individual's new place of employment and the residence sold or exchanged must be at least 50 miles. Employment includes beginning a job with a new employer, continuing a job with an existing employer, or beginning or continuing self-employment.

Health Reasons. The primary reason test will be satisfied if the reason for the sale is to obtain, provide, or facilitate the diagnosis, cure, mitigation, or treatment of disease, illness, or injury of a qualified individual, or to obtain or provide medical or personal care for a qualified individual suffering from a disease, illness, or injury (Reg. § 1.121-3(d)). A sale or exchange that is merely beneficial to the individual's general health does not qualify. A safe harbor exists if a physician recommends a change of homes for health reasons. For purposes of the reduced exclusion for health reasons, a qualified individual also includes any person who is related to a qualified individual, such as a child, sibling, parent, niece, nephew, or in-law, as well as a descendant of the taxpayer's grandparent (Reg. § 1.121-3(f)).

Unforeseen Circumstances. The primary reason test will be satisfied if the sale or exchange is due to the occurrence of an event that the taxpayer could not reasonably have anticipated before buying and occupying the residence (Reg. § 1.121-3(e)). A sale or exchange due to the individual's change in preference or improvement in financial position does not qualify. A safe harbor exists for the following situations:

- involuntary conversion of the home;
- damage to the home from natural or man-made disasters or acts of terrorism;
- a qualified individual's:
  - — death,
  - — loss of employment entitling the individual to unemployment compensation,
  - — change in employment status resulting in the taxpayer's inability to pay housing costs and basic living expenses,
  - — divorce or legal separation, or
  - — multiple births resulting from a single pregnancy; or
- other events that the IRS designates as unforeseen circumstances safe harbors.

Other Factors. If the individual does not satisfy one of the safe harbor tests described above, then the IRS will consider all the facts and circumstances when determining whether the primary reason for the sale or exchange is due to a change in place of employment, health, or unforeseen circumstances. Factors that will be considered include: (1) the circumstances giving rise to the sale; (2) the individual's financial ability to maintain the property; (3) material changes that would impact the suitability of the property as the individual's residence; and (4) the taxpayer's use of the property as the residence during the ownership period (Reg. § 1.121-3(b)).

Computing the Reduced Exclusion. The reduced exclusion is computed by multiplying the maximum allowable exclusion (i.e., $250,000 or $500,000) by a fraction (Reg. § 1.121-3(g)). The numerator is the shortest of (a) the period that the individual owned the property during the five-year period ending on the sale or exchange date; (b) the period that the individual used the property as a principal residence during the five-year period ending on the sale or exchange date; or (c) the period between the date of the most recent prior sale or exchange to which the exclusion applied and the current sale or exchange date. The numerator may be expressed in days or months. The denominator of the fraction is either 730 days or 24 months, depending on the time measurement used in the numerator.

Example 1: Al Jackson is an unmarried taxpayer who owned and used a principal residence for 12 months, sold it during the tax year and moved in with his sister. He sold the home because he was unable to care for himself after sustaining injuries in an accident. Jackson had not excluded gain from the sale of a residence within the prior two years. He may exclude up to $125,000 of any gain that he realizes from the sale ($250,000 maximum exclusion × 12/24 = $125,000).

Example 2: On September 1, 2011, Bill and Ruth Green purchased a townhouse in Boston for $450,000. A few months later, Ruth received an offer of employment in Atlanta, and on July 1, 2012, the Greens sold their townhouse and moved to Atlanta. Because they owned and resided in the townhouse for 10 months, they may exclude up to $208,333 of their realized gain ($500,000 maximum exclusion × 10/24 = $208,333).

Involuntary Conversion

1713. Gain or Loss from Involuntary Conversion. An involuntary conversion occurs when property is destroyed, stolen, condemned, or disposed of under the threat of condemnation and the taxpayer receives other property or money (usually insurance proceeds or a condemnation award) as compensation. To the extent the compensation exceeds the basis of the converted property, the taxpayer realizes gain (¶ 1701).

There are two specific sets of circumstances, however, under which gain from compulsory or involuntary conversion of property is not recognized for tax purposes (Code Sec. 1033; Reg. §§ 1.1033(a)-1, 1.1033(a)-2):[30]

- When property is converted involuntarily or by compulsion into other property that is similar or related in service or use, no gain is currently recognized. The basis of the old property is transferred to the new property (¶ 1687). This nonrecognition rule is mandatory.

- When property is involuntarily converted into money (e.g., insurance proceeds after fire destroys a building), or into property that is not similar or related in service or use, the owner may elect to postpone gain recognition if replacement property is purchased within a specified replacement period (¶ 1715). When the involuntary conversion results in a gain, the taxpayer may elect to recognize gain only to the extent that the amount realized from the converted property exceeds the cost of the replacement property. The election to defer all or part of the gain realized in the involuntary conversion is made by excluding the gain from gross income on the tax return for the tax year in which it is realized. A taxpayer who has realized gain from an involuntary conversion must provide details of the involuntary conversion on the tax return for the tax year in which the gain is realized (see discussion below).

Loss. Loss from an involuntary conversion is deductible only if the converted property was used in a business or for the production of income (¶ 1101). However, casualty or theft losses on personal property may be deductible (¶ 1124). For a discussion of the treatment of certain gains and losses from involuntary conversions as capital gains and losses, see ¶ 1748.

Residence. When an individual's principal residence has been involuntarily converted, the individual may exclude up to $250,000 of the realized gain ($500,000 in the case of a joint return or the return of a surviving spouse) as if the home had been sold (¶ 1705) (Code Sec. 121(d)(5)).[31] If the total realized gain is more than the maximum allowable exclusion, the individual may defer recognizing the excess if replacement property is purchased. The sale of land within a reasonable period of time following the destruction of a principal residence can qualify as part of the involuntary conversion of the residence (Rev. Rul. 96-32).[32]

References are to Standard Federal Tax Reports; Tax Research Consultant; and Practical Tax Explanations.

[30] ¶ 29,640, ¶ 29,641, ¶ 29,642; SALES: 27,050; § 18,101

[31] ¶ 7260; REAL: 15,158, SALES: 27,050; § 1,625.15

[32] ¶ 29,650.508; SALES: 27,104.10; § 18,140.10

Livestock. The destruction of livestock by disease, or the sale or exchange of livestock because of disease, is treated as an involuntary conversion (Code Sec. 1033(d); Reg. § 1.1033(d)-1).[33] Sales or exchanges of livestock (except poultry) in excess of the number that would normally be sold, made solely on account of drought, flood, or other weather-related conditions, may also be entitled to involuntary conversion treatment (Code Sec. 1033(e); Reg. § 1.1033(e)-1).[34] The generally applicable two-year period for purchasing replacement property is extended to four years when the weather-related condition (e.g., drought) results in the area being eligible for assistance from the federal government. The IRS will generally extend the replacement period due to persistent drought in the taxpayer's region until the end of the taxpayer's first tax year ending after the region's first drought-free year (Notice 2006-82). Each year, the IRS publishes a list of the counties that suffered droughts sufficient to extend the replacement period (Notice 2012-62).[35]

If, due to drought, flood, or other weather-related conditions, or soil or other environmental contamination, it is not feasible for a farmer to reinvest the proceeds from involuntarily converted livestock in property similar or related in service or use, the proceeds may be invested in other property used for farming, including real property. The replacement property will then be treated as property similar or related in service or use to the converted livestock (Code Sec. 1033(f)).[36] However, real property will qualify as replacement property only if the conversion was due to soil or other environmental contamination.

Reporting Requirements. Form 4797 is used to report the gain or loss from an involuntary conversion (other than from casualty or theft) of business property, capital assets used in a business, or capital assets used in connection with a transaction entered into for profit. Form 4684 is used to report involuntary conversions from casualties and thefts. Gains from involuntary conversions (other than from casualty or theft) of capital assets not held for business or profit are reported by individuals on Form 8949 (on Schedule D of Form 1040 for tax years before 2011).

A taxpayer in a separate statement must report all details connected to an involuntary conversion in the tax return for the year in which gain is realized (Reg. § 1.1033(a)-2(c)(2)).[37] The details should include a description of the property, the date and type of conversion, computation of the gain, the decision to replace, and expiration of the replacement period. After the nonrecognition election has been made, if the converted property is not replaced within the required period, or the replacement property costs less than anticipated at the election time, or a decision is made not to replace, then the taxpayer must recompute the tax liability in an amended return for the year(s) for which the election was made. If the taxpayer elects nonrecognition after filing the return and paying tax for the tax year(s) in which gain is realized but before the replacement period expires, the taxpayer should file a credit or refund claim for each year that gain was reported. The taxpayer must report all of the details of the replacement of converted property in the return for the year of replacement, even if no gain is realized in that year.

The IRS may assess a deficiency attributable to realized gain for a tax year within three years from the date the taxpayer notifies the IRS of the replacement of the converted property, an intention not to replace, or a failure to replace, within the required period (Code Sec. 1033(a)(2)(C); Reg. § 1.1033(a)-2(c)(5)).

1715. Replacement Property. A taxpayer does not recognize gain after an involuntary conversion (e.g., destruction, theft, or condemnation) to the extent that the converted property is replaced with property that is similar to, or related in use to, the property that was lost or taken (Code Sec. 1033(a)).[38] Generally, when money or dissimilar property is received, gain is recognized. However, if the taxpayer buys

References are to Standard Federal Tax Reports; Tax Research Consultant; and Practical Tax Explanations.

[33] ¶ 29,640, ¶ 29,646; SALES: 27,064.20; § 18,115

[34] ¶ 29,640, ¶ 29,647; SALES: 27,064.25; § 36,015.10

[35] ¶ 29,650.127; SALES: 27,064.25; § 36,015.10

[36] ¶ 29,640; SALES: 27,160; § 18,130

[37] ¶ 29,642; SALES: 27,202.05; § 18,160

[38] ¶ 29,640; SALES: 27,150; § 18,125, § 18,135.05

qualifying replacement property within the replacement period, the taxpayer can elect to postpone the recognition of gain. Even under this rule, gain must still be recognized to the extent that the net proceeds from the involuntary conversion are not invested in replacement property.

Replacement Property. "Replacement property" can be (1) other property similar or related in service or use to the property converted; or (2) 80 percent control of a corporation owning such other property. An actual purchase must take place (e.g., title must have passed); an enforceable contract to purchase is not sufficient.[39] If real property used in the taxpayer's trade or business (other than inventory or property held primarily for sale) or held for investment has been condemned or is under threat of condemnation, however, replacement property that is of a "like-kind" (¶ 1721) will be treated as similar or related in service or use if it is held either for productive use in trade or business or for investment (Code Sec. 1033(g); Reg. § 1.1033(g)-1).[40] The "like-kind" test does not apply to acquisitions of 80-percent control of a corporation owning such property or to involuntary conversions by fire, storm, or other casualty. A taxpayer may elect to treat an outdoor advertising display as real property except when the election to expense the property under Code Sec. 179 (¶ 1208) has been made.

Basis of Replacement Property. If property is compulsorily or involuntarily converted directly into property that is similar or related in service or use to the property converted, the basis of the acquired property is the same as the basis of the property converted (¶ 1687).

Property Acquired from Related Persons. Certain taxpayers cannot defer the recognition of gain on an involuntary conversion if the replacement property is acquired from a related person unless the related person obtained the property from an unrelated person during the replacement period (Code Sec. 1033(i)).[41] See ¶ 432 and ¶ 1717 for a discussion of related persons. The prohibition applies to a C corporation, a partnership in which one or more C corporations own more than a 50-percent interest, and any other taxpayer who realizes gain of more than $100,000 during the year from involuntary conversions. For partnerships or S corporations, the $100,000 limitation applies to both the partnership and each partner and to both the S corporation and each shareholder.

Replacement Period. Purchase of the replacement property, or of 80-percent control of a corporation that owns such property, must be completed within a period of time that begins on the actual date of the destruction, condemnation, etc., or the date on which the threat or imminence of condemnation or requisition begins, whichever is earlier (Code Sec. 1033(a)(2)(B)).[42] Generally, the replacement period ends two years after the close of the first tax year in which any part of the gain on the conversion is realized. The replacement period for condemned real property used in a trade or business or held for investment is three years. For a principal residence in a federally declared disaster area, the replacement period is four years. The replacement period for certain involuntarily converted livestock is also four years (¶ 1713). The replacement period is five years for property located in the Kansas disaster area that is converted on or after May 4, 2007, due to tornadoes and storms occurring on that date, and in the Midwestern disaster area that is converted on or after May 20, 2008, and before August 1, 2008, due to severe storms, tornados or flooding occurring during that period.[43] Taxpayers may also apply for an extension of the applicable time period (see "*Application for Extension*," following).

> **Example:** Laura has a basis in a commercial building, excluding the underlying land, of $100,000. The building is destroyed by fire, and Laura receives a $120,000 settlement from her insurance company, thus realizing a gain of $20,000. If she acquires a new building for the same use for $120,000 (or more) within the prescribed replacement period, she may elect not to recognize any gain on the involuntary conversion. If the replacement building costs only $110,000, Laura

References are to Standard Federal Tax Reports; Tax Research Consultant; and Practical Tax Explanations.

[39] ¶ 29,650.204; SALES: 27,152; § 18,125

[40] ¶ 29,640, ¶ 29,648; SALES: 27,158; § 18,135.20

[41] ¶ 29,640; SALES: 27,152.15; § 18,135.15

[42] ¶ 29,640; SALES: 27,164; § 18,135.05

[43] ¶ 29,650.048; SALES: 27,164; § 18,135.05

must recognize $10,000 of gain if she elects nonrecognition treatment. Without her election, she must recognize the entire $20,000 gain.

Real Property. If business or investment real property (other than inventory) is condemned, the replacement period ends three years, rather than two years, after the close of the first tax year in which only part of the gain is realized (Code Sec. 1033(g)(4)).[44] The three-year period does not apply to property involuntarily converted through destruction (e.g., casualty) or theft.

Principal Residences in Federal Disaster Area. Special rules apply to a principal residence located in a disaster area or the contents of such a principal residence that is involuntarily converted as the result of a federally declared disaster (Code Sec. 1033(h)(1)).[45] No gain is recognized by reason of the receipt of insurance proceeds for unscheduled personal property that was part of the contents of the residence. All other insurance proceeds (i.e., insurance reimbursement for scheduled items) for the residence or its contents are treated as a common pool of funds received for the conversion of a single item of property. The taxpayer must use insurance funds received for scheduled property to purchase property that is similar or related in service or use to the converted residence (or its contents) in order to avoid gain recognition (Rev. Rul. 95-22).[46] Gain is recognized only to the extent that the amount of the pool of funds exceeds the cost of any replacement property acquired. For unscheduled items, however, the taxpayer recognizes no gain upon receiving insurance funds, regardless of how he uses the funds.

The replacement period for a principal residence involuntarily converted as the result of a federally declared disaster is four years after the close of the first tax year in which any part of the gain upon the conversion is realized (Code Sec. 1033(h)(1)(B)). These rules also apply to the conversion of property in a rented residence that is the taxpayer's principal residence (Code Sec. 1033(h)(4)).

Business or Investment Property in Federal Disaster Area. Business or investment property that is located in a disaster area and is compulsorily or involuntarily converted as a result of a federally declared disaster need not be replaced with similar or related property (Code Sec. 1033(h)(2)).[47] The replacement property will be deemed to be similar or related in service or use provided it is tangible property held for productive use in a trade or business. The replacement property must generally be acquired within two years.

Application for Extension. The IRS may extend the replacement period if the taxpayer applies for an extension (Code Sec. 1033(a)(2)(B); Reg. § 1.1033(a)-2(c)(3)).[48] The taxpayer must submit a written explanation to the Internal Revenue Center where their tax return is filed, and show reasonable cause for being unable to replace the converted property within the required replacement period. The IRS does *not* provide a form that may be used to apply for the extension. The application should explain in detail the reasons for the extension request, and should be filed before the statutory replacement period expires. However, the IRS may accept a late request if it is made within a reasonable period of time after the replacement period expires and there is reasonable cause for the untimely filing. The IRS may grant an extension if the replacement property is being built and the replacement cannot be made within the replacement period, but it will not grant an extension based on the scarcity or high price of replacement property (Rev. Rul. 60-69).[49]

1716. Condemnation Award. If only a portion of a tract of land is appropriated by a government authority, the condemnation award may have two components: (1) compensation for the converted portion; and (2) severance damages for the retained portion. The entire award is considered compensation for the condemned property unless both

References are to Standard Federal Tax Reports; Tax Research Consultant; and Practical Tax Explanations.

[44] ¶ 29,640; SALES: 27,164; § 18,135.20

[45] ¶ 29,640; SALES: 27,066; § 18,140.10

[46] ¶ 29,650.317; SALES: 27,066; § 18,140.10

[47] ¶ 29,640; SALES: 27,066; § 18,140.15

[48] ¶ 29,640, ¶ 29,642; SALES: 27,164; § 18,135.05

[49] ¶ 29,650.202; SALES: 27,164; § 18,135.05

parties stipulate that a specific amount was paid for severance damages (Rev. Rul. 59-173).[50]

Severance damages may be paid, for example, when access to the owner's land has been impaired, or because the owner must replace fences and plant trees to restore the retained property to its former use. The owner's net severance damages (i.e., gross severance damages minus legal expenses and other costs) reduce the basis of the retained property. Any excess of the severance damages over the owner's basis is gain (Rev. Rul. 68-37). However, the owner may elect not to recognize the gain if it purchases replacement property (¶ 1715) (Rev. Rul. 83-49).

Transactions Between Related Persons

1717. Losses Not Allowed in Transactions Between Related Persons. Generally, a loss from the sale or exchange of property is not recognized when the parties to the transaction are related persons (Code Sec. 267(a); Reg. § 1.267(a)-1).[51] However, the buyer may be able to recognize the loss when he sells or exchanges the property at a gain.

Related Persons. The term "related persons" includes:

(1) Members of a family (brother, sister, spouse, ancestor, or lineal descendant);

(2) An individual and a corporation if the individual owns (directly or indirectly) more than 50 percent in value of the outstanding stock;

(3) Two corporations that are members of a controlled group of corporations (for this purpose, more than 50 percent ownership required);

(4) A grantor and a fiduciary of any trust;

(5) A fiduciary of one trust and a fiduciary of another trust, if the same person is grantor of both trusts;

(6) A fiduciary of a trust and any beneficiary of such trust;

(7) A fiduciary of a trust and a beneficiary of another trust, if the same person is a grantor of both trusts;

(8) A fiduciary of a trust and a corporation more than 50 percent in value of the outstanding stock of which is directly or indirectly owned by or for the trust or a grantor of the trust;

(9) A person and an exempt charitable or educational organization controlled by the person or, if the "person" is an individual, by the individual or his family;

(10) A corporation and a partnership if the same persons own (a) more than 50 percent in value of the outstanding stock of the corporation, and (b) more than 50 percent of the capital interest or profits interest in the partnership;

(11) An S corporation and another S corporation if the same persons own more than 50 percent in value of the outstanding stock of each corporation;

(12) An S corporation and a C corporation if the same persons own more than 50 percent in value of the outstanding stock of each corporation; or

(13) An executor and a beneficiary of an estate, except when the sale or exchange is made to satisfy a pecuniary bequest (Code Sec. 267(b); Reg. § 1.267(b)-1).[52]

Stock Ownership. In determining stock ownership: (1) stock held by a corporation, partnership, estate, or trust is considered owned proportionately by its shareholders, partners, or beneficiaries; (2) individuals are considered to own stock owned by their families, as defined above; and (3) stock owned by or for an individual's partner is

References are to Standard Federal Tax Reports; Tax Research Consultant; and Practical Tax Explanations.

[50] ¶ 29,650.504; SALES: 27,106, SALES: 27,106.20; § 18,105

[51] ¶ 14,150, ¶ 14,151; SALES: 39,100; § 17,601

[52] ¶ 14,150, ¶ 14,153; SALES: 39,150; § 17,605.10

considered owned by the individual if the individual also owns stock in the corporation (Code Sec. 267(c)).[53]

Previously Disallowed Loss. When the "related person" rule results in a denial of a loss deduction to the transferor of the property, the original transferee will be able to use the loss when he sells or exchanges the property. However, the loss can only be recognized to the extent of the gain realized by the seller/original transferee (Code Sec. 267(d); Reg. § 1.267(d)-1).[54]

> **Example:** A father sells business property with a $15,000 basis to his son for $5,000. The father's $10,000 realized loss is not deductible because he sold the property to a related person. Later, the son sells the property for $18,000 to an unrelated person. The son's realized gain is $13,000 (i.e., $18,000 minus $5,000). However, only $3,000 of this gain is recognized (i.e., $13,000 realized gain minus the father's $10,000 unrecognized loss).

Tax-Free Exchanges

1719. Gain or Loss from Exchange of Property. Gains from exchanges of property are generally recognized for tax purposes (Code Sec. 1001(c)).[55] Some types of exchanges, however, do not result in recognized gain or deductible loss. These include: like-kind exchanges (¶ 1721—¶ 1723), exchanges of insurance or annuity contracts (¶ 1724), mortgaged real estate (¶ 1725), government obligations (¶ 1726), stock exchanged for stock in the same corporation (¶ 1728) or for property (¶ 1729), transfers of property to a corporation controlled by the transferor (¶ 1731), exchanges by certain government employees to avoid conflicts of interest (¶ 1732), sales of stock to an employee stock ownership plan (¶ 1733), and transfers between spouses or former spouses (¶ 1734).

1721. Like-Kind Exchanges. No gain or loss is recognized upon the exchange of property held for productive use in a trade or business or for investment if the property received is of a like kind and is held either for productive use in a business or for investment (Code Sec. 1031(a)(1); Reg. § 1.1031(a)-1).[56] The nonrecognition rule generally does *not* apply to stock in trade or other property held primarily for sale, stocks, bonds, notes, certificates of trust, beneficial interests, partnership interests, securities, evidences of indebtedness or interest, or choses in action (Code Sec. 1031(a)(2)).[57] However, stock in certain mutual ditch, reservoir, or irrigation companies is not excluded from like-kind exchange treatment if the stock is treated as real property or an interest in real property under applicable state law (Code Sec. 1031(i)).

The like-kind exchange rules also do not apply to exchanges of property the taxpayer uses for personal purposes (e.g., home or family car) (IRS Pub. 544). A dwelling unit such as a vacation home, however, will generally be treated as held for business purposes if the taxpayer rented out the unit for at least two weeks in each of the two years before the exchange, and similarly rents out the property received for at least two weeks in the first two years after the exchange, and the taxpayer's personal use of the units in those years is minimal (Rev. Proc. 2008-16).[58] The disposition of a property used as a home and then converted to use as business property may be both a like-kind exchange and a sale of a principal residence qualifying for an exclusion of gain (¶ 1705) (Rev. Proc. 2005-14).

Trade-in Arrangements. If a taxpayer sells old equipment used in his trade or business to a dealer and purchases new equipment of like kind from the same dealer in reciprocal and mutually dependent transactions, a like-kind exchange has occurred even

References are to Standard Federal Tax Reports; Tax Research Consultant; and Practical Tax Explanations.

[53] ¶ 14,150; SALES: 39,154.25; § 17,605.15

[54] ¶ 14,150; ¶ 14,155; SALES: 39,110; § 17,605.20

[55] ¶ 29,220; SALES: 3,050; § 16,010

[56] ¶ 29,602, ¶ 29,603; SALES: 30,000; § 18,001,§ 18,005.05

[57] ¶ 29,602; SALES: 30,150; § 18,010.05

[58] ¶ 29,608.2495; SALES: 30,200, SALES: 30,202; § 18,005.10, § 18,060

though the parties execute separate contracts and treat the sale and purchase as unrelated transactions for recordkeeping purposes (Rev. Rul. 61-119).[59]

Related Persons. If property received in a like-kind exchange between certain controlled partnerships (¶ 432) or related persons (¶ 1717) is disposed of within two years after the date of the last transfer that was part of the like-kind exchange, the original exchange will not qualify for nonrecognition treatment (Code Sec. 1031(f)).[60] Any gain or loss that was not recognized by the taxpayer on the original exchange must be recognized as of the date that the like-kind property is disposed of by either the taxpayer or the related party. The use of a qualified intermediary does not prevent a like-kind exchange from being treated as a related party transaction. The running of the two-year period may be suspended when the holder of the exchanged property has substantially diminished the risk of loss by the use of a put, short sale, the holding by another person of a right to acquire such property,. or any other transaction (Code Sec. 1031(g)).[61] A disposition that would otherwise require recognition on the original exchange is not covered by the related-person rule if: (1) neither the original exchange nor the disposition had the avoidance of federal income tax as one of its principal purposes; (2) the disposition was due to the death of either related party; or (3) the disposition was due to the compulsory or involuntary conversion of the property (¶ 1713) (Code Sec. 1031(f)(2)).

Like-Kind Property Defined. Property is of like kind if it is of the same nature or character (Reg. § 1.1031(a)-1(b) and (c)).[62] All facts and circumstances should be considered in determining whether properties are of like kind, including state law and federal tax law classifications, but federal income tax law is controlling in determining whether the properties are of the same nature or character (CCA 201238027).[63]

Most exchanges of real property qualify as like-kind exchanges. However, real property located in the United States and real property located outside the United States are not like-kind property (Code Sec. 1031(h)(1)).[64]

Personal properties are of like kind if they are of a like kind or class. Depreciable tangible personal properties are of a like class if they fall within the same general asset class or the same product class (Reg. § 1.1031(a)-2(b)).[65] For depreciable tangible personal property, asset classes follow those used for depreciation purposes and that are set forth in Rev. Proc. 87-56. Product classes are determined by reference to the six-digit product codes of the North American Industrial Classification System (NAICS). Personal property predominantly used in the United States and personal property predominantly used outside of the United States are not like-kind property (Code Sec. 1031(h)(2)).[66]

Exchanges involving intangible personal property or nondepreciable tangible personal property may qualify for like-kind exchange treatment only if the properties are of like kind (Reg. § 1.1031(a)-2(c)).[67] For example, an exchange of a copyright on a novel for a copyright on another novel would generally be a like-kind exchange. However, an exchange of a copyright on a novel for a copyright on a song would not be a like-kind exchange. An exchange of goodwill or going concern value of one business for the goodwill or going concern value of another business is *not* a like-kind exchange. Intangibles such as trademarks, trade names, mastheads and other customer-based intangibles that can be separately described and valued apart from goodwill can qualify as like-kind property.[68]

References are to Standard Federal Tax Reports; Tax Research Consultant; and Practical Tax Explanations.

[59] ¶ 29,608.1178; SALES: 30,312; § 18,015.20

[60] ¶ 29,602, ¶ 29,608.2493; SALES: 30,206.10; § 18,020

[61] ¶ 29,602; SALES: 30,206.10; § 18,020

[62] ¶ 29,603; SALES: 30,100; § 18,005.15

[63] ¶ 29,608.1103; SALES: 30,100; § 18,005.15

[64] ¶ 29,602; SALES: 30,100, SALES: 30,160; § 18,010.20

[65] ¶ 29,606; SALES: 30,102; § 18,005.15

[66] ¶ 29,602; SALES: 30,162; § 18,010.20

[67] ¶ 29,606; SALES: 30,118; § 18,010.05

[68] ¶ 29,608.2654; SALES: 30,150; § 18,010.05

Substituted Basis. For the basis of property received in a like-kind exchange, see ¶ 1651.

Reporting. Form 8824 is used to report the like-kind exchange. If there is any recognized gain due to the receipt of boot (¶ 1723), Form 8949 is used by individuals to report gains of capital assets not held for business or profit, and Form 4797 is used to report gains of business property, capital assets used in a business, or capital assets used in connection with a transaction entered into for profit.

1722. Deferred Like-Kind Exchanges. An exchange of property may qualify for like-kind treatment even if the replacement property is received after the relinquished property has been transferred by the taxpayer, provided that specific identification and receipt requirements are satisfied (Code Sec. 1031(a)(3); Reg. § 1.1031(k)-1).[69] This type of transaction is known as a Starker exchange. After transferring the relinquished property, the taxpayer must identify replacement property within 45 days, and must receive the replacement property within 180 days or, if earlier, by the due date (including extensions) of the transferor's income tax return for the tax year in which the relinquished property was transferred. The deadlines may be extended where the parties are affected by a federally declared disaster (Rev. Proc. 2007-56). Property not in existence or still under construction may qualify as like-kind exchange property for this purpose (Reg. § 1.1031(k)-1(e)).[70]

Identifying Replacement Property. Replacement property must be identified before the end of the "identification period" that begins on the date that the relinquished property is transferred and ends at midnight on the 45th day thereafter (Code Sec. 1031(a)(3)(A); Reg. § 1.1031(k)-1(b)(2)).[71] Replacement property is treated as identified only if it is designated as replacement property in either: (1) a written agreement covering the exchange that is signed by all parties before the end of the identification period; or (2) a written document signed by the taxpayer and hand delivered, mailed, telecopied, or otherwise sent before the end of the identification period to a person involved in the exchange (such as an intermediary, escrow agent or title company) other than the taxpayer or a related party (Reg. § 1.1031(k)-1(c)).[72] In either situation, the replacement property must be unambiguously described. For transactions involving real property, a street address or legal description is generally an adequate identification of the property. A taxpayer may identify: (1) up to three replacement properties; or (2) any number of replacement properties provided their aggregate value does not exceed 200 percent of the aggregate value of all relinquished properties.

Safe Harbors. The taxpayer may not actually or constructively receive cash and then use the proceeds to buy the replacement property. The following four safe harbors protect nonrecognition treatment in a deferred like-kind exchange in which a property or security interest is received by the transferor. The transferor is not considered in receipt of money or other property if the transaction involves:

(1) qualifying security or guarantee arrangements;

(2) qualified escrow accounts or trusts;

(3) a qualified intermediary; or

(4) payment of interest or a growth factor (Reg. § 1.1031(k)-1(g)).[73]

Parking Transactions. An additional safe harbor is provided in situations involving a "reverse-Starker exchange" or "parking transaction"—an exchange in which replacement property is acquired before the relinquished property is transferred (Rev. Proc. 2000-37).[74] In the transaction, the taxpayer "parks" the desired replacement property with a third party (i.e., the accommodation party) until the taxpayer arranges for the transfer of the relinquished property to the ultimate transferee in a simultaneous or deferred exchange. If the rules for this safe harbor are complied with, the IRS will not challenge the qualification of property as either replacement property or relinquished

References are to Standard Federal Tax Reports; Tax Research Consultant; and Practical Tax Explanations.

[69] ¶ 29,602, ¶ 29,619; SALES: 30,600; § 18,015.05

[70] ¶ 29,619; SALES: 30,606; § 18,015.15

[71] ¶ 29,602, ¶ 29,619; SALES: 30,602.05; § 18,015.10

[72] ¶ 29,619; SALES: 30,602.10; § 18,015.10

[73] ¶ 29,619; SALES: 30,610; § 18,035.05

[74] ¶ 29,620.10; SALES: 30,614; § 18,015.25

property or the treatment of the exchange accommodation titleholder as the beneficial owner of the property. In order for this safe harbor to come into play, the property must be held in a qualified exchange accommodation arrangement (QEAA). Under a QEAA: (1) the title of the property must be held by a person other than the taxpayer or a disqualified person; and (2) the combined time period that the properties are held must not exceed 180 days. The safe harbor is not available if the replacement property held in a QEAA is owned by the taxpayer within the 180-day period ending on the date that title or other qualified indicia of ownership of the property is transferred to the exchange accommodation titleholder (Rev. Proc. 2004-51).

Interest on Funds Held by Intermediaries. Escrow accounts, trusts, and funds used to facilitate deferred exchanges (exchange funds) are generally treated as loaned by the taxpayer to an exchange facilitator (Reg. § 1.468B-6).[75] The exchange facilitator must take into account all items of income, deduction, and credit. Exchange funds are defined as relinquished property, cash, or cash equivalents that secure the transferee's obligation to transfer replacement property or proceeds from a transfer of relinquished property held in a qualified escrow account, qualified trust, or other escrow account, trust, or fund in a deferred exchange. An exchange facilitator is a qualified intermediary (QI), transferee, escrow holder, trustee or other party that holds exchange funds for a taxpayer in a deferred exchange pursuant to an escrow, trust or exchange agreement. Loan treatment will not apply if the escrow agreement, trust agreement, or exchange agreement specifies that the earnings attributable to the exchange funds are payable to the taxpayer. In this situation, the taxpayer must take into account all items of income, deduction, and credit attributable to the exchange funds. If the exchange funds are treated as loaned by the taxpayer to the exchange facilitator, interest is generally imputed to the taxpayer under Code Sec. 7872 (¶ 795), unless the exchange facilitator pays sufficient interest. The exchange facilitator has income from the imputed interest and offsetting deductions for the deemed paid interest.

Safe Harbor for Bankrupt Qualified Intermediaries. The IRS has provided a safe harbor method for reporting gain or loss for a taxpayer undertaking a deferred like-kind exchange if the qualified intermediary defaults on its obligations (Rev. Proc. 2010-14).[76] Generally, taxpayers are allowed to avoid recognition of gain until payment is received.

Direct Deeding of Property. In an exchange of real property involving three parties—the taxpayer, a qualified intermediary, and a third party that supplies the replacement property—the exchange may qualify as like kind even if the third party deeds the replacement property directly to the taxpayer (Rev. Rul. 90-34).[77] Therefore, it is not necessary for the transferee to take title to the replacement property and then transfer title to the taxpayer.

1723. Cash or Other Property Received in a Like-Kind Exchange. If money or property not of a like-kind (commonly referred as to boot) is received by a taxpayer as part of a like-kind exchange (¶ 1721), then the taxpayer recognizes gain from the transaction to the extent of the boot's fair market value (Code Sec. 1031(b); Reg. § 1.1031(b)-1).[78] A loss from a like-kind exchange in which the taxpayer receives boot may not be deducted (Code Sec. 1031(c); Reg. § 1.1031(c)-1).[79] Boot may consist of cash, relief from indebtedness (¶ 1725), property that is not like kind to the property being exchanged, or property excluded from like-kind treatment. Boot is often given to equalize the value of the like-kind properties being exchanged.

> **Example:** Bill exchanged real estate, with a basis of $10,000, for real estate with a fair market value of $12,000 and $4,000 in cash. His *realized* gain of $6,000 (i.e., $16,000 value received minus $10,000 basis) is *recognized* only to the extent of the $4,000 cash he received. His basis for the real estate he received is $10,000 (i.e., $10,000 basis in old property, minus $4,000 cash received, plus $4,000 *recognized* gain).

References are to Standard Federal Tax Reports; Tax Research Consultant; and Practical Tax Explanations.

[75] ¶ 21,950H; ACCTNG: 12,222; § 18,035.15

[76] ¶ 29,621.75; SALES: 30,610.15; § 18,035.20

[77] ¶ 29,621.30; SALES: 30,510

[78] ¶ 29,602, ¶ 29,609; SALES: 30,250; § 18,030

[79] ¶ 29,602, ¶ 29,611; SALES: 30,250; § 18,030

See ¶ 1728 for situations involving stock exchanged for stock in the same corporation, and ¶ 1731 for discussion of the tax-free transfer of property to a controlled corporation.

1724. Exchange of Insurance or Annuity Contracts. A life insurance, endowment, annuity, and qualified long-term care insurance policy are considered property for tax purposes so that any gain or loss realized on a sale or exchange of the policy is ordinarily taxable. However, no gain or loss results from an exchange of:

- a life insurance contract for another life insurance contract, or an endowment, annuity, or qualified long-term care insurance contract;
- an endowment contract for another endowment contract that provides for regular payment beginning at a date not later than the date payments would have begun under the contract exchanged, or for an annuity or long-term care insurance contract;
- an annuity contract for another annuity contract if both are payable over the life of the same annuitant, or for a qualified long-term care insurance contract; or
- a qualified long-term care insurance contract for another qualified long-term care insurance contract (Code Sec. 1035; Reg. § 1.1035-1).[80]

Gain or loss may be recognized if the exchange has the effect of transferring property to any person other than a United States person. Policyholders who surrender life insurance or annuity contracts of a financially troubled insurance company may qualify for nonrecognition of gain if, within 60 days, all cash received is reinvested in another policy or contract issued by another insurance company or in a single custodial account (Rev. Proc. 92-44; Rev. Proc. 92-44A).[81]

A partial exchange of the cash surrender value of an existing annuity contract for a second annuity contract will be treated as a tax-free exchange only if no amount, other than an amount received as an annuity for a period of 10 years or more or during one or more lives, is received during the 180 days beginning on the date of the transfer (Rev. Proc. 2011-38).[82] A subsequent direct transfer is not taken into account. These rules do not apply to partial annuitizations (¶ 817). Different rules applied to transfers completed before October 24, 2011 (Rev. Proc. 2008-24).

1725. Like-Kind Exchange of Mortgaged Real Estate. When taxpayers exchange mortgaged real estate for other real estate in an otherwise tax-free like-kind exchange (¶ 1721), the amount of the mortgage from which they are relieved is treated as other property or money (i.e., boot) (¶ 1723) (Code Sec. 1031(d); Reg. §§ 1.1031(b)-1(c), 1.1031(d)-2).[83] If mortgaged property is exchanged for mortgaged property, the net reduction of the mortgage indebtedness is treated as boot.

Example: Kathy owned real property, which had a fair market value of $100,000 and an adjusted basis of $75,000 and was subject to a $70,000 mortgage. She exchanged the property for like-kind property, which had a fair market value of $60,000 and was subject to a $30,000 mortgage. Her entire realized gain must be recognized:

Fair market value of property received	$60,000
Less mortgage on that property	30,000
	$30,000
Mortgage on property transferred by Kathy	70,000
Total consideration received	$100,000
Less basis of property transferred	75,000
Gain realized	$25,000

The total realized gain is recognized because it is less than the $40,000 net mortgage reduction.

References are to Standard Federal Tax Reports; Tax Research Consultant; and Practical Tax Explanations.

[80] ¶ 29,680, ¶ 29,681; INDIV: 30,502; § 3,250.10

[81] ¶ 29,682.30; INDIV: 30,502; § 3,250.10

[82] ¶ 29,682.108; INDIV: 30,502.10; § 3,250.10

[83] ¶ 29,602, ¶ 29,609, ¶ 29,614; SALES: 30,256, SALES: 30,258; § 18,030

It is immaterial whether a mortgage is assumed by the purchaser or whether the property is acquired subject to a mortgage (Reg. § 1.1031(d)-2).

1726. Exchange of Government Obligations. Obligations issued by the United States may be exchanged tax free for other such obligations (except to the extent that money is received in the exchange) (Code Sec. 1037; Reg. § 1.1037-1).[84] Municipal or state bonds may be exchanged pursuant to a refunding agreement without recognition of gain or loss, provided that there are no material differences in the terms of the exchanged bonds (Rev. Rul. 81-169).[85]

1728. Stock Exchanged for Stock of the Same Corporation. An exchange of common stock for common stock of the same corporation, or preferred stock for preferred stock of the same corporation, does not result in recognized gain or deductible loss (Code Sec. 1036; Reg. § 1.1036-1).[86] However, if money or other property is received in addition to the stock, gain (but not loss) may be recognized, but only to the extent of the money or fair market value of the other property received (¶ 1723). Nonqualified preferred stock is not treated as stock for these purposes.

1729. Stock Exchanged for Property. No gain or loss is recognized to a corporation upon the receipt of money or other property in exchange for its own stock, including treasury stock, regardless of the nature of the transaction or the facts and circumstances involved (Code Sec. 1032; Reg. § 1.1032-1).[87] Also, no gain or loss is recognized by a corporation upon the lapse or acquisition of an option, or with respect to a securities futures contract, to buy or sell its own stock, including treasury stock. This treatment does not apply if a corporation acquires shares of its own stock unless it acquires those shares in exchange for shares of its own stock, including treasury stock. See ¶ 736 for discussion of the nonrecognition of gain or loss when a corporation distributes its stock to shareholders.

1731. Tax-Free Transfer of Property to Controlled Corporation. No gain or loss is recognized if one or more persons (individuals, trusts or estates, partnerships or corporations) transfer property to a corporation solely in exchange for its stock and, immediately after the transfer, are in control of the transferee corporation (Code Sec. 351; Reg. § 1.351-1).[88] For further discussion of tax-free contributions of property to a corporation in exchange for stock, see ¶ 203. See ¶ 1660 for discussion of the basis of the property transferred to the controlled corporation.

1732. Property Exchanged to Avoid Conflicts of Interest. If an officer or employee of the executive branch or a judicial officer of the federal government sells any property in order to comply with conflict-of-interest requirements, the individual may elect to recognize gain only to the extent that the amount realized is more than the adjusted basis of any permitted property that the taxpayer purchased during the 60-day period beginning on the sale date (Code Sec. 1043).[89] Permitted property includes any U.S. obligation or diversified investment fund approved by the Office of Government Ethics. Any nonrecognized gain is applied to reduce (in the order acquired) the basis of any permitted property purchased by the taxpayer during the 60-day period. The deferral option is also available to any spouse, minor, or dependent child whose ownership of any property is attributable to the federal officer or employee under any applicable conflict-of-interest law. Sales made by a trustee are also subject to these rules if any person subject to the rules has a beneficial interest in the principal or income of the trust. Form 8824 is used to report conflict-of-interest sales.

References are to Standard Federal Tax Reports; Tax Research Consultant; and Practical Tax Explanations.

[84] ¶ 29,720, ¶ 29,721; SALES: 27,252; § 18,220

[85] ¶ 29,226.1117; SALES: 24,406, SALES: 24,510

[86] ¶ 29,700, ¶ 29,701; SALES: 27,300; § 18,215

[87] ¶ 29,622, ¶ 29,623; CCORP: 3,152; § 26,801

[88] ¶ 16,402, ¶ 16,403; CCORP: 3,050; § 26,110.05

[89] ¶ 29,840; SALES: 27,350; § 18,240

1733. Tax-Free Sale of Stock to ESOP. Taxpayers (other than C corporations) may elect to sell qualified securities to an employee stock ownership plan (ESOP) or worker-owned cooperative and replace the securities with other securities without recognition of gain (Code Sec. 1042; Temp. Reg. § 1.1042-1T).[90] The taxpayer makes the election by attaching a statement to its original or amended return for the tax year in which the sale occurs (IRS Pub. 550).

1734. Transfers of Property Between Spouses or Former Spouses. No gain or loss is recognized for transfers of property from an individual to a spouse or to a former spouse incident to a divorce (Code Sec. 1041; Temp. Reg. § 1.1041-1T).[91] The transferor's basis for the transferred property is carried over to the transferee. A transfer to a former spouse must occur within one year after the date on which the marriage ceased, or must be related to the cessation of the marriage. This nonrecognition treatment is not available for transfers to spouses or former spouses who are nonresident aliens.

Treatment of Capital Gain or Loss

1735. Characterization of Gain or Loss. Gain or loss realized on the disposition of property generally is recognized for federal income tax purposes (¶ 1701). The tax treatment of gain or loss is determined by its character. Gain or loss on the sale of property is ordinarily taken into account as part of ordinary income. However, individuals, estates, and trusts may be eligible for lower tax rates on their net long-term gain from the sale of a capital asset (¶ 1736). Whether a capital gain or loss is long-term or short-term depends on the period for which the taxpayer held the capital asset (¶ 1737). Corporate taxpayers are required to include both net long-term and short-term capital gains in gross income (¶ 1738). When capital losses exceed capital gains, then the deduction of the loss may be limited for all taxpayers (¶ 1752).

17 SALES

Capital gain or loss treatment requires a sale or exchange of property that is a capital asset (¶ 1741 and ¶ 1742). Taxpayers also have to follow specific procedures in calculating their recognized capital gain or loss (¶ 1739). In addition, special rules prevent taxpayers from converting all or a part of what would otherwise be capital gain into ordinary income (¶ 1740).

1736. Tax on Capital Gains—Individual, Estate, Trust. For individuals, estates, and trusts, up to three different tax rates can apply to net capital gains for regular income tax and alternative minimum tax purposes. Generally, gain from the sale of long-term capital assets and qualified dividend income (¶ 733) is subject to a capital gains rate of 15 percent (0 percent for taxpayers in the 10-percent or 15-percent income tax bracket) (Code Sec. 1(h)(1)).[92] For 2012, the zero-percent rate applies to married couples filing jointly with taxable income up to $70,700, and to single individuals with taxable income up to $35,350. The capital gains rate is 25 percent for unrecaptured Code Sec. 1250 gain (¶ 1779), and 28 percent for collectibles and gain on qualified small business stock (¶ 1905).

> **Comment:** Absent further legislation, in tax years beginning after December 31, 2012, the capital gains rate for individuals, estates, and trusts on long-term capital assets will be 20 percent (10 percent for taxpayers in the 15-percent income tax bracket). The capital gains rate on assets held more than five years will be 18 percent (eight percent for taxpayers in the 15-percent income tax bracket), and qualified dividend income will be taxed at ordinary income tax rates (¶ 733).

To calculate net capital gain (or loss) for the tax year, a noncorporate taxpayer must first net short and long-term capital gains and losses for each of the rate groups separately (¶ 1739). Capital gain or loss is short or long term depending on how long the taxpayer held the property prior to its sale or other disposition (¶ 1737). When a taxpayer elects to treat any amount of net capital gain as investment interest (¶ 1094), that amount is subtracted from the total net capital gain in order to determine the amount subject to the maximum capital gains rate (Code Sec. 1(h)(2)).

References are to Standard Federal Tax Reports; Tax Research Consultant; and Practical Tax Explanations.

[90] ¶ 29,820, ¶ 29,821; RETIRE: 75,354.05; § 24,825.15

[91] ¶ 29,800, ¶ 29,801; INDIV: 21,050; § 18,230

[92] ¶ 3260; SALES: 15,200; § 16,525.10

Depreciable Real Estate. A 25-percent tax rate is imposed on long-term capital gain attributable to certain prior depreciation that had been claimed on real property (Code Sec. 1(h)(1)(D) and (6)(A)).[93] This depreciation is referred to as "unrecaptured Section 1250 gain" and is the excess of:

(1) the amount of long-term capital gain (not otherwise treated as ordinary income) that would be treated as ordinary income if Code Sec. 1250(b)(1) included all depreciation and the applicable percentage that applied under Code Sec. 1250(a) was 100, over

(2) the excess of 28-percent rate loss over 28-percent rate gain.

Even under these capital gains rules, Code Sec. 1250 will continue to treat some prior claimed depreciation as ordinary income (¶ 1779) (i.e., usually the amount claimed in excess of the amount allowable under the straight-line method).

Example: During the tax year William Drake sold a building for $1 million. The building had originally cost $700,000 and, over the years, Drake had claimed $300,000 in depreciation. Upon the sale of the building, Drake recognizes a total gain of $600,000. Of the $300,000 in claimed depreciation, $100,000 was in excess of that allowed under the straight-line method. Under the capital gains rules, $200,000 of the total claimed depreciation is classified as unrecaptured Section 1250 gain. This is because if Code Sec. 1250 had applied to all depreciation, and not only additional depreciation, $300,000 of Drake's long-term capital gain would have been treated as ordinary income. Thus, the $100,000 in excess depreciation is taxed as ordinary income, the $200,000 in unrecaptured Section 1250 gain is subject to a maximum capital gains rate of 25 percent, and the remaining $300,000 of gain is subject to a maximum capital gains rate of 15 percent.

Under MACRS, all depreciation on real property must be computed under the straight-line method (¶ 1780). As a result, any gain on the sale of MACRS real property that was held more than 12 months and that is due to claimed deprecation will be classified as "unrecaptured Section 1250 gain" and subject to a maximum capital gains rate of 25 percent.

Collectibles. Generally, collectibles (e.g., stamps, antiques, gems, and most coins) are taxed at the tax rate of 28 percent even if held more than 12 months (Code Sec. 1(h)(4)(A)(i)).[94]

Small Business Stock. Noncorporate taxpayers may exclude from gross income a certain percentage of capital gain from the sale or exchange of qualified small business stock held for more than five years and issued after August 10, 1993 (¶ 1905). The percentage of excluded capital gain (section 1202 gain) is not used in computing a taxpayer's long-term capital gain or loss, and it is not investment income for purposes of the investment interest limitation. However, the percentage of capital gain *not* excluded is taxed at the maximum 28 percent capital gains rate (Code Sec. 1(h)(4)(A)(ii) and (7)).[95]

Pass-Through Entities. A pass-through entity—including an S corporation, partnership, estate, trust, regulated investment company (mutual fund), and real estate investment trust (REIT)—allocates capital gains to its shareholders or beneficiaries (Code Sec. 1(h)(10)).[96] Capital gain distributions from a mutual fund are taxed as long-term capital gains regardless of how long the shareholder has owned the fund shares (¶ 2311). If capital gain distributions are automatically reinvested in the fund, the reinvested amount is the basis of the additional shares (IRS Pub. 550).

1737. Holding Period for Capital Assets. The holding period for a capital asset (¶ 1741) is the length of time that the taxpayer owned the property before disposing of it through sale or exchange. Classifying the taxpayer's holding period as "short-term" or

References are to Standard Federal Tax Reports; Tax Research Consultant; and Practical Tax Explanations.

[93] ¶ 3260; SALES: 15,202.70; § 16,525.10

[94] ¶ 3260; SALES: 15,202.65; § 16,525.10

[95] ¶ 3260; SALES: 15,300; § 16,525.10

[96] ¶ 3260; SALES: 15,202.90; § 16,525.10

"long-term" determines the tax treatment of any recognized gain or loss (Code Secs. 1222 and 1223; Reg. § 1.1223-1).[97] The lowest long-term capital gain tax rate is generally available when a capital asset has been held more than 12 months (¶ 1736).

Comment: Absent further legislation, in tax years beginning after December 31, 2012, the 18-percent capital gains rate on assets held more than five years (¶ 1736) will be available if the capital asset is acquired after December 31, 2000. This requirement will not apply to the eight-percent capital gains rate on assets held more than five years for taxpayers in the 15-percent income tax bracket.

Calculating the Holding Period. In most situations when determining how long an asset was held, the taxpayer begins counting on the date after the day the property was acquired. The same date of each following month is the beginning of a new month regardless of the number of days in the preceding month (Rev. Rul. 66-7).[98] The date the asset is disposed of is part of the holding period. If an asset is acquired on the last day of a month, the first day on which it may be considered to have been held for more than one year is the first day of the *thirteenth* calendar month following the calendar month of acquisition. However, there are special rules that must be applied when determining the holding period of assets acquired by a tax-free exchange, gift, inheritance, and involuntary conversion.

Example: An asset acquired on March 31, 2011, must be held until April 1, 2012, in order to be considered held for more than one year.

Tax-Free Exchange. When property is received in a tax-free exchange (¶ 1719), the holding period of the property given up by the taxpayer is added ("tacked on") to the holding period of the property that the taxpayer received in the exchange (Code Sec. 1223).[99]

Gift. In most situations, the holding period of property acquired by gift or transfer in trust includes the time the property was held by both the donor and the donee. This rule applies when the donee is required to use the donor's basis as his or her own basis (Code Sec. 1223(2)).[100] However, when the fair market value at the time of the gift is used as the donee's basis (¶ 1630), the holding period starts the day after the gift was made (IRS Pub. 544).

Inherited. For property acquired from a decedent, the heir or beneficiary generally receives a step-up in basis in the property and the property is automatically deemed to have been held for more than one year (Code Sec. 1223(9)).[101] However, if the property is acquired from a decedent dying in 2010 whose executor made the election not to have the estate tax apply and to have the modified carryover basis rule apply (¶ 1633), then the taxpayer's holding period of the property is the same as the decedent's, whether or not the executor allocates any basis increase to the property (Rev. Proc. 2011-41).[102]

Involuntary Conversion. The holding period of property acquired in an involuntary conversion (¶ 1713) includes the holding period of the property converted if the basis of the new property is determined by reference to the basis of the old property (Code Sec. 1223(1)(A)).[103]

Stock. The holding period for stock and securities purchased on an exchange begins on the day following the day of purchase (i.e., the trade date), and ends on, and includes, the date of sale (rather than the day when payment is received and delivery is made (i.e., the settlement date)) (Rev. Rul. 66-97; Rev. Rul. 93-84).[104] The holding period for stock received in a nontaxable stock distribution or in a "spin-off" includes the holding period of the related stock on which the distribution is made (Code Sec. 1223(1) and (5)).[105]

References are to Standard Federal Tax Reports; Tax Research Consultant; and Practical Tax Explanations.

[97] ¶ 30,440, ¶ 30,460, ¶ 30,461; SALES: 15,150; § 16,540.05

[98] ¶ 30,463.3997, ¶ 30,463.4099; SALES: 15,152; § 16,540.05

[99] ¶ 30,460; SALES: 15,178; § 16,540.15

[100] ¶ 30,460; SALES: 15,178.05; § 16,540.25

[101] ¶ 30,460; SALES: 15,164; § 16,540.30

[102] ¶ 29,380.762; ESTGIFT: 51,060.10; § 16,310.05

[103] ¶ 30,460; SALES: 15,178.30; § 18,145.05

[104] ¶ 30,463.3746, ¶ 30,463.4383; SALES: 15,162; § 16,540.10

[105] ¶ 30,460; SALES: 15,178.25; § 16,540.10

Options. When assets are acquired by the exercise of a purchase option, the holding period starts the day after the option is exercised.[106]

Partnership Property. A partner's holding period for property received as a distribution from the partnership includes the period for which the partnership held the property (Code Sec. 735(b)).[107]

Treasury Obligations. In determining the holding period of U.S. Treasury Notes and Bonds sold at auction on the basis of yield, the acquisition date is the date the Secretary of Treasury, through news releases, gives notification of the successful bidders (Rev. Rul. 78-5).[108] The acquisition date of U.S. Treasury Notes sold through an offering on a subscription basis at a specified yield is the date the subscription is submitted.

1738. Corporate Capital Gains. A corporation must include both long-term and short-term capital gains in gross income to the extent the gains exceed capital losses for the year. As a result, capital gains of a corporation are generally taxed at ordinary corporate income tax rates (¶ 219). A corporation may pay an alternative tax of 35 percent on net capital gain instead of the regular income tax in any year in which the top corporate income tax rate exceeds 35 percent (determined without regard to the additional tax on a corporation with taxable income over $100,000 or over $15 million) (Code Sec. 1201(a)).[109] The net capital gain on which the alternative tax is imposed cannot exceed the corporation's taxable income. Net capital gain equals the excess of the net long-term capital gain for the tax year minus the net short-term capital loss for the tax year (Code Sec. 1222(11)).[110] As the maximum rate currently is 35 percent, the alternative tax has no immediate impact on corporations.

Timber Gains. Qualified timber gains of C corporations for the first and second tax years ending after May 22, 2008, are subject to a special reduced capital gains rate of 15 percent if the timber was held for more than 15 years (Code Sec. 1201(b)). Only the portion of the corporation's total timber gains properly allocable to the period after May 22, 2008, is eligible for the lower rate in the first tax year; only the portion allocable to the period of the year on or before May 22, 2009, is eligible for the lower rate in the second tax year. See ¶ 1772 for discussion of the election to treat timber cutting as a sale or exchange.

See ¶ 1752 and ¶ 1756 for treatment of corporate capital losses.

1739. Netting of Gains and Losses. Noncorporate taxpayers have to follow specific netting procedures in calculating their recognized capital gain or loss for the tax year (Code Sec. 1(h)(1); Notice 97-59).[111] The basic netting procedures provide that within each tax rate group for capital gains (15 percent, 25 percent, and 28-percent group), gains and losses are netted in order to arrive at a net gain or loss for the group. After this basic process has been completed, the following netting and ordering rules must be applied.

- *Short-term capital gains and losses.* Short-term capital losses (including short-term loss carryovers from a prior year) are applied first to reduce short-term capital gains, if any, that would otherwise be taxable at ordinary income tax rates. A net short-term loss is used first to reduce any net long-term capital gain from the 28-percent group. Any remaining short-term loss is then used to reduce gain from the 25-percent group and then groups taxed at the lower capital gains rates.

- *Long-term capital gains and losses.* A net loss from the 28-percent group (including long-term capital loss carryovers) is used first to reduce gain from the 25-percent group, then to reduce net gain from the 15-percent group. A net loss from the 15-percent group is used first to reduce net gain from the 28-percent group, and then to reduce gain from the 25-percent group.

  Comment: Absent further legislation, in tax years beginning after December 31, 2012, the "15-percent group" will instead be the "20 percent group."

References are to Standard Federal Tax Reports; Tax Research Consultant; and Practical Tax Explanations.

[106] ¶ 30,463.4013; SALES: 15,154.05; § 16,540.10

[107] ¶ 25,400; SALES: 15,178.15; § 30,535.10

[108] ¶ 30,463.67; SALES: 15,162.45

[109] ¶ 30,352; SALES: 15,210; § 16,527.10

[110] ¶ 30,440; SALES: 15,202.55; § 16,527.05

[111] ¶ 3260, ¶ 3285.55; SALES: 15,206.15; § 16,525.05

1740. Gain from Conversion Transactions. Capital gain from the disposition or termination of a position that is part of a financial "conversion transaction" is subject to recharacterization as ordinary income (Code Sec. 1258).[112] In general, the amount of capital gain treated as ordinary income is equal to the interest that would have accrued on the taxpayer's net investment at a yield equal to 120 percent of the applicable federal rate (AFR) compounded semiannually, or 120 percent of the federal short-term rates compounded daily if the term of the conversion transaction is indefinite. See ¶ 83 for AFRs.

A conversion transaction is generally one designed to convert ordinary income into capital gains. A transaction is a conversion transaction only if substantially all of the taxpayer's expected return is attributable to the time value of the taxpayer's net investment in the transaction (i.e., the taxpayer is in the economic position of a lender). In addition, the transaction must be:

- a transaction in which the taxpayer acquires property and on a substantially contemporaneous basis enters into a contract to sell the property (or substantially identical property) at a predetermined price;
- a straddle (¶ 1948);
- marketed or sold as producing capital gains from a transaction in which the taxpayer's return is substantially from the time value of the net investment; or
- specified by the IRS in regulations.

Example: Sam Jones purchases stock on January 2, 2010, for $100 and agrees on the same day to sell it to Wendell Johnson on January 2, 2012, for $115. A portion of the $15 gain from the sale of the stock equal to 120 percent of the AFR compounded semiannually for two years and applied to the $100 investment is recharacterized as ordinary income.

Transactions of options dealers and commodities traders in the normal course of their trade or business of dealing in options or trading Section 1256 contracts are *not* conversion transactions (Code Sec. 1258(d)(5)).[113] However, this exception does not apply to certain gains allocated to limited partners and limited entrepreneurs as defined in Code Sec. 464(e)(2).

Constructive Ownership Transactions. The amount of long-term capital gains that a taxpayer may recognize from certain constructive ownership transactions that arise from specified financial assets may be limited (Code Sec. 1260).[114] These "financial assets" include any equity interest in a pass-through entity (e.g., a partnership or REIT). The long-term gain is limited to the amount of gain that the taxpayer would have recognized if the financial asset had been held directly by the taxpayer during the term of the derivative contract. Any additional gain is recognized as ordinary income. Interest is imposed on the amount of ordinary income.

1741. Capital Asset. A capital gain or loss arises from the sale or exchange of a capital asset. Generally, a "capital asset" is any property, whether or not connected with a trade or business (Code Sec. 1221; Reg. § 1.1221-1).[115] The following items, however, are *not* capital assets:

- stock in trade, inventory, and property held primarily for sale to customers in the ordinary course of the taxpayer's trade or business;
- a note or account receivable acquired in the ordinary course of trade or business for services rendered or from the sale of stock in trade or property held primarily for sale in the ordinary course of business;
- depreciable business property;
- real property used in the taxpayer's trade or business;

References are to Standard Federal Tax Reports; Tax Research Consultant; and Practical Tax Explanations.

[112] ¶ 31,125; SALES: 15,250; § 16,701

[113] ¶ 31,125; SALES: 15,252.25; § 16,701

[114] ¶ 31,140; SALES: 45,500; § 16,701

[115] ¶ 30,420, ¶ 30,421; SALES: 15,100; § 16,505.05

17 SALES

- a copyright, a literary, musical or artistic composition, a letter or memorandum, or similar property (but not a patent or invention) held by the taxpayer who created it, or by one whose basis in the property is determined by reference to the basis of the one who created it, or in the case of a letter, memorandum or similar property, a taxpayer for whom such property was prepared or produced;
- a U.S. government publication (including the *Congressional Record*) held by a taxpayer who received it (or by another taxpayer in whose hands the publication would have a basis determined in whole or in part by reference to the original recipient's basis) other than by purchase at the price at which the publication is offered to the public;
- commodities derivative financial instruments held by commodities derivatives dealers;
- hedging transactions entered into in the normal course of the taxpayer's business; and
- supplies of a type regularly used or consumed by the taxpayer in the ordinary course of business.

Although creative works are generally not capital assets in the hands of their creators, a special rule allows taxpayers to elect to treat the sale or exchange of a musical composition or a copyright in a musical work created by the taxpayer's personal efforts (or having a basis determined by the reference to the creator's basis) as the sale or exchange of a capital asset (Code Sec. 1221(b)(3); Reg. § 1.1221-3).[116] The election is made separately for each composition or copyright sold by reporting the transaction as a sale of a capital asset on Form 8949 (on Schedule D of Form 1040 for tax years before 2011).

Gain from the sale of an individual's household furnishings, personal residence, or automobile is generally taxed under the capital gains rates. However, loss from the sale is not recognized unless the property was held for the production of income (¶ 1003 and ¶ 1101) (Reg. § 1.262-1(b)(4)).[117] For example, if an individual sells a residence that had been partially used as rental property, the individual has to allocate the original cost of the building, the selling price, depreciation (applicable to the rental portion only), and selling expenses between the personal and rental portions of the building as if there were two separate transactions (¶ 1707). The gain or loss associated with the sale of a personal residence is discussed at ¶ 1107, ¶ 1626, and ¶ 1705.

Stock and securities generally are considered to be held for production of income so that a loss on their sale is a capital loss, except in the hands of a dealer who holds them for sale to customers (¶ 1760).[118]

The sale or exchange of property results in ordinary income or loss if the property is classified as a "noncapital asset." The U.S. Supreme Court has ruled that the definition of a capital asset must be broadly interpreted, and an asset must come within one of the statutory categories of "noncapital" assets listed above in order for the property to be excluded from capital asset treatment (*Arkansas Best Corp.*, SCt, 88-1 USTC ¶ 9210).[119] The Court rejected the contention that ordinary income and loss treatment should apply to an asset that is otherwise capital simply because it is acquired for business purposes. Therefore, bank stock that was acquired by a holding company in order to prevent damage to the holding company's business reputation was held to be a capital asset even though it was acquired for a business purpose, because the stock did not fall within any of the exclusion categories. In an earlier decision, the Supreme Court ruled that assets held as part of hedging transactions that were an integral part of a business's inventory-purchase system were noncapital assets because they were inventory (*Corn Products Refining*, SCt, 55-2 USTC ¶ 9746).[120] Gains and losses from most business hedges entered into in order to reduce risk of price changes or currency fluctuations are treated as

References are to Standard Federal Tax Reports; Tax Research Consultant; and Practical Tax Explanations.

[116] ¶ 30,420, ¶ 30,425; SALES: 15,108.15; § 16,505.20

[117] ¶ 13,601; SALES: 15,206.05; § 8,201

[118] ¶ 30,422.684; SALES: 15,104.30; § 16,505.05

[119] ¶ 30,422.6865; SALES: 15,118.05

[120] ¶ 30,426.15; SALES: 15,118.10

ordinary gains and losses. The hedge must relate to ordinary income property held or to be held by the taxpayer who enters into the hedge. A taxpayer must make a same-day identification in its books and records of the hedges entered into (Reg. § 1.1221-2(f)).[121] Gain or loss from the sale, exchange or termination of a "securities futures contract" may be eligible for capital gain treatment (Code Sec. 1234B).[122]

Special Rules. Special rules apply when the sale involves Code Sec. 1231 assets (¶ 1747), patents (¶ 1767), depreciable property (¶ 1779), farm property (¶ 1797), or partnership interests (¶ 434).

1742. Sale or Exchange Requirement. The capital gain and loss provisions apply to the sale or exchange of a capital asset (Code Sec. 1222; Reg. § 1.1222-1).[123] In the case of real estate, a sale or exchange occurs on the earlier of the date of conveyance or the date when the burden and benefits of ownership pass to the purchaser.[124] A sale or exchange is considered to have occurred when there is a corporate liquidation (¶ 2253), when securities become worthless (¶ 1916), and upon any failure to exercise a privilege or option on property that would have been a capital asset if acquired (¶ 1919).

When bonds with past-due interest are purchased "flat" (i.e., the bonds were in default of interest payments), aggregate interest payments that are for the prepurchase period and are in excess of the purchase price but less than the face value of the bonds are properly characterized as capital gains because they are considered to be amounts received on retirement of the bonds (Rev. Rul. 60-284).[125] The sale of an endowment insurance policy before its maturity or of a paid-up annuity contract before the annuity starting date results in ordinary income (*E.J. Arnfeld*, CtCls, 58-2 USTC ¶ 9692).[126]

1743. Sale of a Trade or Business. When a trade or business is sold, generally each asset of the business is treated as being sold separately in determining the seller's income, gain or loss and the buyer's basis in each of the assets acquired (Rev. Rul. 55-79).[127] The seller must allocate the purchase price among the assets in order to determine the amount and character of any recognized gain or loss. The buyer must allocate the purchase price among the business assets to determine any allowable depreciation or amortization (Code Sec. 1060(a); Reg. § 1.1060-1(a)).[128] The buyer and seller may agree in writing to allocations of part or all of the consideration involved in the transaction and the fair market value of any assets transferred. The allocation generally is binding on both parties, unless the IRS determines that it is inappropriate (¶ 1620).

Reporting. Generally, the purchaser and the seller must both file Form 8594 to report the sale of assets used in a trade or business when the purchaser's basis in the assets is determined wholly by the amount paid. The form is attached to the tax return for the year in which the sale took place.

1744. Sale of Depreciable Assets Between Related Taxpayers. Capital gain treatment is denied when depreciable property (including patent applications) is sold or exchanged between related taxpayers (Code Sec. 1239; Reg. § 1.1239-1).[129] This rule applies to sales or exchanges between:

- a person and all entities that the person controls;
- a taxpayer and any trust in which the taxpayer or his spouse is a beneficiary, unless such beneficiary interest is a remote contingent interest; and
- an executor of an estate and a beneficiary of the estate, unless the sale or exchange is in satisfaction of a pecuniary bequest.

References are to Standard Federal Tax Reports; Tax Research Consultant; and Practical Tax Explanations.

[121] ¶ 30,424; SALES: 15,114.05; § 16,505.40

[122] ¶ 30,640; SALES: 45,550; § 18,845.10

[123] ¶ 30,440, ¶ 30,441; SALES: 15,050, SALES: 15,052; § 16,520.05

[124] ¶ 21,005.8838; SALES: 3,110; § 16,540.10

[125] ¶ 5704.3075; SALES: 24,508; § 45,415.15

[126] ¶ 30,422.58; INDIV: 30,212, INDIV: 30,356; § 45,450.10

[127] ¶ 30,422.125; SALES: 33,050; § 18,401

[128] ¶ 30,060, ¶ 30,061; SALES: 33,052; § 18,401

[129] ¶ 30,730, ¶ 30,731; SALES: 39,200; § 17,615

For purposes of this rule, entities that are controlled by a taxpayer include:

- a corporation if the taxpayer owns (directly or indirectly) more than 50 percent of the value of its stock;

- a partnership if the taxpayer owns (directly or indirectly) more than 50 percent of the capital or profits interest; and

- certain entities that are related persons with respect to the taxpayer, including two corporations that are members of the same controlled group, a corporation and a partnership if the same persons own more than 50 percent of each, and two S corporations, or an S corporation and a C corporation, if the same persons own more than 50 percent of the stock of each.

Section 1231

1747. Section 1231 Property Used in Trade or Business. Business real estate or any depreciable business property is generally excluded from the definition of capital assets (¶ 1741). However, if the business property qualifies as "section 1231 property," gain or loss realized from the sale, exchange, or involuntary conversion of the property may nonetheless qualify as capital gain or loss. Specifically, if a taxpayer's section 1231 gains exceed its section 1231 losses, then all of the taxpayer's section 1231 gains and losses are generally treated as long-term capital gains and losses (¶ 1736) (Code Sec. 1231(a)).[130] On the other hand, if the taxpayer's section 1231 losses exceed its section 1231 gains, then all of the taxpayer's section 1231 gains and losses are treated as ordinary income and losses. Taxpayers use Form 4797 to report the sale or exchange of section 1231 property.

Section 1231 Property. Section 1231 property includes:

- property used in the trade or business subject to depreciation and held more than one year, but excluding: property includible in inventory; property held primarily for sale to customers; a copyright, a literary, musical or artistic composition, or a letter, memorandum, or similar property; and certain federal government publications;

- real property used in the trade or business and held for more than one year but excluding property includible in inventory or held primarily for sale to customers;

- trade or business property held for more than one year and compulsory or involuntarily converted (¶ 1748);

- capital assets (¶ 1741) held for more than one year in connection with a trade or business or a transaction entered into for profit, and compulsory or involuntarily converted;

- an unharvested crop on land used in the trade or business and held for more than one year, if the crop and land are sold, exchanged, or involuntarily converted at the same time to the same person;

- livestock, but not poultry (¶ 1750); and

- timber, domestic iron ore, or coal (¶ 1772) (Code Sec. 1231(b); Reg. §§ 1.1231-1 and 1.1231-2).[131]

When section 1231 property is subject to depreciation recapture, the amount of the section 1231 gain is the amount by which the total gain exceeds the amounts recaptured and taxed at ordinary income rates (¶ 1779). Also, the recapture of certain farmland expenses may cause a reduction in section 1231 gain (¶ 1797). A gain or loss that is disallowed by other provisions of the law (e.g., a loss on a sale between family members) is not taken into account in determining section 1231 gains and losses (Code Sec. 1231(a)(4); Reg. § 1.1231-1(d)).

References are to Standard Federal Tax Reports; Tax Research Consultant; and Practical Tax Explanations.

[130] ¶ 30,572; SALES: 21,100; § 16,805

[131] ¶ 30,572, ¶ 30,573, ¶ 30,574; SALES: 21,100; § 16,805

Recapture of Net Section 1231 Losses. A taxpayer who has a net section 1231 gain for the tax year (i.e., excess of section 1231 gains over section 1231 losses) must review the five preceding tax years for possible recapture of net section 1231 losses for the prior years. If there were any net section 1231 losses during the period, the taxpayer must treat the current year's net section 1231 gain as ordinary income to the extent of the amount of unrecaptured net section 1231 losses for that past period (Code Sec. 1231(c)).[132] The losses are to be recaptured on a first-in, first-out (FIFO) basis.

> **Example:** Mary has a net section 1231 gain of $23,000 for 2012. She had a net section 1231 loss of $12,000 in 2010 and a net section 1231 loss of $15,000 in 2011. For 2012, under the recapture rules, Mary must include her $23,000 net section 1231 gain as ordinary income (i.e., she recaptures the $12,000 loss from 2010 and $11,000 of the $15,000 loss from 2011). The $4,000 balance of the loss from 2011 remains outstanding, and available for recapture if Mary realizes any net section 1231 gain during 2013-2016.

1748. Compulsory or Involuntary Conversion of Section 1231 Property. The capital gain and ordinary loss rules of Code Sec. 1231 apply to gains and losses realized from the compulsory or involuntary conversion of section 1231 property (¶ 1747), unless the nonrecognition rules for involuntary conversions apply (¶ 1713). (Code Sec. 1231(a)(3)(A)(ii); Reg. § 1.1231-1(d)(4) and (e)).[133] For this purpose, recognized gains and losses resulting from theft or seizure or an exercise of power of requisition or condemnation are treated as section 1231 gains or losses. When casualty or theft gains and losses result in a net loss, the transactions are not grouped with other section 1231 transactions. Instead, the net loss is treated as an ordinary loss.

Personal Assets—Casualty and Theft Losses. Casualty and theft losses on personal assets (i.e., those not used in a trade or business or for investment) are excluded from the operation of Code Sec. 1231. Instead, gains and losses if in excess of the $100 floor per loss (¶ 1134) from personal casualties and thefts are grouped separately. Any resulting net loss may be claimed as an itemized deduction to the extent it exceeds 10 percent of the taxpayer's adjusted gross income (AGI) (¶ 1124). If there is a net gain, it is classified as a capital gain. The period of time that the taxpayer owned the property determines whether the gain is long term or short term. Generally, taxpayers use Form 4684 to initially report a casualty loss and then report it as an itemized deduction on Schedule A of Form 1040.

1750. Livestock as Section 1231 Property. Capital gain and ordinary loss treatment under Code Sec. 1231 applies to the sale, exchange, or involuntary conversion of livestock (not including poultry) held for draft, breeding, dairy or sporting purposes (¶ 1747) (Code Sec. 1231(b)(3); Reg. § 1.1231-2).[134] To qualify for this treatment, horses and cattle must be held for at least 24 months and all other livestock must be held for at least 12 months. The holding period begins on the date of acquisition rather than on the date the animal is actually placed in one of the above uses. Livestock includes fur-bearing animals such as chinchillas, mink, and foxes.[135] For treatment of involuntary conversions of livestock due to disease or weather conditions, see ¶ 1713. For treatment of forced sales due to weather conditions (e.g., flood or drought), see ¶ 767.

1751. Lease or Distributor's Agreement Canceled. An amount received by a lessee for cancellation of a lease is treated as received in exchange for the lease. This rule applies also to amounts received by a distributor of goods for the cancellation of a distributor's agreement if the taxpayer has a substantial capital investment in the distributorship (Code Sec. 1241; Reg. § 1.1241-1).[136] If the lease or agreement is section 1231 property (¶ 1747), there will be a section 1231 gain or loss (Rev. Rul. 2007-37).[137]

References are to Standard Federal Tax Reports; Tax Research Consultant; and Practical Tax Explanations.

[132] ¶ 30,572; SALES: 21,250; § 16,830

[133] ¶ 30,572, ¶ 30,573; SALES: 21,052; § 16,820

[134] ¶ 30,572, ¶ 30,574; FARM: 3,252; § 16,805

[135] ¶ 30,575.154; FARM: 3,252; § 16,805

[136] ¶ 30,750, ¶ 30,751; SALES: 24,354.05; § 16,520.30

[137] ¶ 30,752.24; SALES: 24,354.05; § 16,520.30

Capital Loss Limitation, Carryover, Carryback

1752. Limitation on Capital Losses. To determine the deductibility of capital losses, all capital gains and losses (without distinction between long term and short term) incurred during the year must be totaled. Any capital losses are deductible only to the extent of any capital gains plus, in the case of noncorporate taxpayers, ordinary income of up to $3,000 (Code Sec. 1211(b); Reg. § 1.1211-1(b)).[138] Thus, both net long-term capital losses and net short-term capital losses may be used to offset up to $3,000 of an individual's ordinary income ($1,500 for married individuals filing separate returns). There are special rules for married persons, whether filing joint or separate returns (¶ 1757). Unused losses are carried forward (¶ 1754).

> **Example:** During a tax year, Janet Green, a single individual, had $30,000 of ordinary income, a net short-term capital loss of $3,500 and a net long-term capital loss of $300. Green's capital loss deduction is limited to $3,000 for the current tax year. The remaining $800 is carried forward.

Corporations. A corporation may use capital losses to offset only capital gains and not ordinary income (Code Sec. 1211(a); Reg. § 1.1211-1(a)).[139] However, its capital losses may be carried back or carried forward (¶ 1756).

1754. Capital Loss Carryover of Non-Corporate Taxpayers. Individuals and other noncorporate taxpayers may carry over a net capital loss to future tax years until the loss is used (Code Sec. 1212(b)).[140] A capital loss that is carried over to a later tax year retains its long term or short term character for the year to which it is carried. In determining the amount of the capital loss that can be carried over, short-term capital gain is increased by the lesser of:

- the ordinary income offset (whether $3,000 or the amount of the overall net loss), or
- taxable income increased by the sum of that offset and the deduction for personal exemptions (¶ 133) (any excess of allowable deductions over gross income for the loss year is treated as negative taxable income for this purpose).

A short-term capital loss carryover first offsets short-term gain in the carryover year. If a net short-term capital loss results, this loss first offsets net long-term capital gain, and then up to $3,000 of ordinary income ($1,500 for married individuals filing separate returns) (¶ 1752). A long-term capital loss carryover first reduces long-term capital gain in the carryover year, then net short-term capital gain, and finally up to $3,000 of ordinary income.

> **Example:** Jack Crowe had taxable income of $30,000 for the current tax year and filed a joint return. In computing taxable income, he reported a net short-term capital loss of $1,000 and a net long-term capital loss of $6,000. Crowe would use his $1,000 net short-term loss to offset $1,000 of ordinary income; he would then use $2,000 of his net long-term capital loss to offset $2,000 of ordinary income. The remaining $4,000 of his net long-term capital loss would be carried over to the following tax year ($4,000 is carried over because it is less than his taxable income of $30,000 increased by the ordinary income offset of $3,000 and the deduction for personal exemptions).

Code Sec. 1256 Contract Loss. An individual (but not an estate, trust, or corporation) who has a net Code Sec. 1256 contracts loss (i.e., net loss from futures contracts, foreign currency contracts, nonequity options, dealer options, or dealer securities futures contracts) in a given tax year may elect to carry the loss back to the three prior tax years (Code Sec. 1212(c)).[141]

References are to Standard Federal Tax Reports; Tax Research Consultant; and Practical Tax Explanations.

[138] ¶ 30,390, ¶ 30,391; SALES: 15,206.05; § 16,530

[139] ¶ 30,390, ¶ 30,391; SALES: 15,210, SALES: 15,212; § 16,535

[140] ¶ 30,400; SALES: 15,208; § 16,530

[141] ¶ 30,400; SALES: 48,108; § 18,801, § 45,420.10

1756. Corporate Capital Loss Carryover and Carryback. A corporation may carry back a capital loss to each of the three tax years preceding the loss year (Code Sec. 1212(a); Reg. § 1.1212-1(a)).[142] Any excess may be carried forward for five years following the loss year. However, the amount that can be carried back is limited to an amount that does not cause or increase a net operating loss in the carryback year. Any carryback or carryover is treated as short-term capital loss for the year to which it is carried. As such, it is grouped with any other capital losses for the year to which carried and is used to offset any capital gains. Any undeducted loss remaining after the three-year carryback and the five-year carryover is not deductible.

Foreign expropriation losses can be carried over for 10 years but are ineligible for three-year carryback. A foreign expropriation capital loss is the sum of the capital losses sustained (either directly or on securities that become worthless) by reason of the expropriation, intervention, seizure, or similar taking of property by the government of any foreign country, any political subdivision, or any agency or instrumentality of such a governmental unit.

For tax years beginning after December 22, 2010, a regulated investment company (mutual fund) can carry forward net capital losses indefinitely, and the treatment of the components of those losses as long-term or short-term is preserved (Code Sec. 1212(a)(3)). For tax years beginning before December 23, 2010, however, a mutual fund can carry net capital losses forward only for eight years, and any losses carried forward are treated as short-term capital losses in the year to which it is carried (Code Sec. 1212(a)(1)(C)(i), prior to amendment by the Regulated Investment Company Modernization Act of 2010 (P.L. 111-325)).

A quick refund procedure is available for corporate net operating loss carrybacks or capital loss carrybacks (¶ 2773).

1757. Capital Gain or Loss of Husband and Wife. All the capital gains and losses of a husband and wife are computed on a joint return as if they were the gains and losses of one person (Reg. § 1.1201-1(d)).[143] If a husband and wife file separate returns, the capital loss deduction (¶ 1752) for each is limited to $1,500 (one-half of the limit for a joint return) (Code Sec. 1211(b)(1)).[144] If separate returns are filed the year after a net capital loss was reported on a joint return, any carryover is allocated on the basis of the individual net capital loss of the spouses for the prior year's tax year (Reg. § 1.1212-1(c)).[145]

1758. Capital Gain or Loss of Partnerships and S Corporations. The capital gains and losses of a partnership or S corporation are generally segregated from its ordinary net income and carried separately into the income of the individual partners or shareholders. Partners (¶ 431) and shareholders (¶ 309) treat their distributive share of the capital gain or loss as if it were their own capital gain or loss. The same rule applies for Code Sec. 1231 transactions (¶ 1747) (Code Secs. 702(a) and 1366(a)).[146] S corporations may be taxed on capital gains in very limited situations (¶ 337).

Reporting. Generally, partnerships report capital gains and losses on Schedule D of Form 1065. The net gains and losses from Schedule D are entered on Schedule K, and each partner's share is entered on Schedule K-1 of Form 1065. S corporations generally report capital gains and losses on Schedule D of Form 1120S. The net gains and losses from Schedule D are entered on Schedule K, and each shareholder's share is entered on Schedule K-1 of Form 1120S.

1760. Gains or Losses of Investors, Dealers, and Traders. In order to determine whether a taxpayer's gains or losses are ordinary or capital in nature, it must be determined if the taxpayer entered into the transaction as an investor, dealer, or trader. The following is an overview of how these terms are defined.

References are to Standard Federal Tax Reports; Tax Research Consultant; and Practical Tax Explanations.

[142] ¶ 30,400, ¶ 30,401; SALES: 15,214; § 16,535

[143] ¶ 30,353; SALES: 15,206.10; § 16,530

[144] ¶ 30,390; SALES: 15,206.10; § 16,530

[145] ¶ 30,401; SALES: 15,208; § 16,530

[146] ¶ 25,080, ¶ 32,080; PART: 18,104, SCORP: 402; § 28,405, § 30,410

17 SALES

Investors. An investor is a taxpayer whose activities are limited to occasional transactions for his or her own account. The level of activity is less than that associated with a trade or business.[147] Gains and losses of an investor are subject to the capital gains and loss rules (¶ 1736).

Dealers. A dealer regularly purchases securities from, and sells securities to, customers in the ordinary course of a trade or business. Because they are in the business of buying and selling, the gains and losses of dealers are classified as ordinary gain or loss unless the securities are held primarily for personal investment (Code Sec. 1236).[148] Securities that are held by a dealer for personal investment purposes must be clearly identified in the dealer's records before the close of the day on which they were acquired and must never be held primarily for sale to the dealer's customers. Similarly, capital gain and loss treatment does not apply to real estate sales by a dealer in realty unless the property was held as an investment (¶ 1762).

Traders. A securities trader (including a "day trader") buys and sells securities for the trader's own account. A trader is one who seeks to profit from short-term changes in value rather than long-term holding of investments. The taxpayer's trading activity must be substantial, frequent, regular, and continuous.[149] Due to the fact that the securities that traders buy and sell are not held primarily for sale to customers (¶ 1741), their gains and losses are generally treated as capital in nature and are reported on Form 8949 (on Schedule D of Form 1040 for tax years before 2011). Traders that make a "mark-to-market" election, which allows them to treat gains and losses as ordinary (¶ 1901), report those gains and losses on Form 4797. Traders claim their business expenses on Schedule C of Form 1040 because they are in the business of trading. For the rules concerning the commissions paid by traders when buying and selling securities, see ¶ 1983.

Subdivision of Real Estate

1762. Subdivision and Sale of Real Estate. Noncorporate taxpayers and S corporations will not be treated as real estate dealers solely because they have subdivided a tract of land for sale (Code Sec. 1237(a)).[150] At least part of the gain on the sale of a lot or parcel is treated as capital gain when:

- the taxpayer has not previously held the tract or any lot or parcel thereof for sale in the ordinary course of business, and, in the same tax year as the sale occurs, does not hold any other real estate for sale in the ordinary course of business (this rule automatically disqualifies a real estate dealer);
- no substantial improvements are made while the tract is held by the taxpayer or pursuant to a contract of sale between the taxpayer and the buyer; and
- the taxpayer has held the particular lot sold for at least five years, unless it was acquired by inheritance or devise, in which case there is no minimum holding period requirement.

There is an exception to the substantial improvement rule above. Certain improvements, such as water, sewage, drainage, or road installation, are not considered substantial improvements if the property (including inherited property) is held for at least 10 years and would not have been marketable at the prevailing local price for similar building sites without such improvements (Code Sec. 1237(b)(3); Reg. § 1.1237-1(c)).[151] The taxpayer must also elect *not* to adjust the basis of the property (or other property) for the improvement costs or deduct them as expenses. The election is reported with the tax return for the year in which the lots covered by the election were sold. The election must include certain information including a plat of the subdivision and a list of all the improvements.

References are to Standard Federal Tax Reports; Tax Research Consultant; and Practical Tax Explanations.

[147] ¶ 8521.1475; SALES: 45,052; § 7,840.10

[148] ¶ 30,670; SALES: 45,054; § 18,805.05

[149] ¶ 30,422.6811; SALES: 45,058; § 18,805.15

[150] ¶ 30,690; REAL: 15,500; § 16,560.05

[151] ¶ 30,690, ¶ 30,691; REAL: 15,510; § 16,560.20

The profits realized on the sales of the first five lots or parcels from the same tract are classified as capital gains (Code Sec. 1237(b)(1); Reg. § 1.1237-1(e)(2)).[152] However, in the year in which the sixth sale or exchange is made, and thereafter, gain on each sale is taxed as ordinary income to the extent of five percent of the selling price. Selling expenses are deducted first from the five percent that would otherwise be considered ordinary income and then are used to reduce the capital gain on the sale or exchange (Code Sec. 1237(b)(2)). The selling expenses cannot be deducted from other income as ordinary business expenses.

Example 1: During the current tax year, Mark subdivides a tract of land that he bought approximately 10 years ago and sells three lots for $50,000 each. The adjusted basis for each lot is $30,000. Mark has a long-term capital gain of $20,000 from the sale of each lot.

Example 2: Assume the same facts as in Example 1, but in the current tax year, Mark also sells three additional lots, each having a basis of $30,000. The selling price of each lot is $50,000. Because he sold more than five lots, five percent of $50,000, or $2,500, of the gain on the sale of each of the six lots is ordinary income. The balance of the gain on each lot ($17,500) is treated as long-term capital gain.

If a taxpayer sells or exchanges any lots or parcels from a tract, and then does not sell or exchange any others for a period of five years from the last sale or exchange, the taxpayer can sell another five lots without having a portion of the gain taxed as ordinary income (Reg. § 1.1237-1(g)(2)).[153]

If a tract of land is bought with the purpose that it is to be subdivided and sold as separate lots or parcels, the seller must measure gain or loss on every lot or parcel sold on the basis of an equitable (not ratable) apportionment (such as their relative assessed valuations for real estate tax purposes) of the cost of the subdivision to each separate part (Reg. § 1.61-6(a)).[154]

Patents and Royalties

1767. Sale or Exchange of Patents. The transfer of a patent will be treated as the sale of a capital asset held for more than 12 months if the transfer is of all substantial rights to the patent or an undivided interest in such rights (Code Sec. 1235(a); Reg. §§ 1.1235-1 and 1.1235-2).[155] The payment for the patent may be a lump-sum, a periodic payment, or contingent upon the productivity or use of the property transferred. This treatment does not apply if the transfer was by gift or inheritance. The capital gains rule extends to a transfer by the original inventor and another individual who acquired the patent from the original inventor. However, the non-inventor must have acquired the patent before the invention was tested successfully under operating conditions. The inventor's employer and certain related persons are not eligible for long-term capital gain treatment if they acquire the patent from the inventor.

1772. Timber, Coal or Iron Ore. A taxpayer may elect to treat the cutting of timber (for sale or for use in a trade or business) as a sale or exchange of the timber during the year. The taxpayer must have owned the timber or held the contract right to cut the timber for more than one year (Code Sec. 631; Reg. §§ 1.631-1 and 1.631-2).[156] Under Code Sec. 1231, this timber is considered to be property used in the trade or business so that gain may be treated as long-term capital gain under certain conditions (¶ 1747). In order to make the election, a taxpayer must generally file Form T with the tax return for the year in which the election is to be effective.

Timber, coal, or domestic iron ore royalties are generally subject to Code Sec. 1231 treatment (¶ 1747) when the owner or a holder of an economic interest (including a

References are to Standard Federal Tax Reports; Tax Research Consultant; and Practical Tax Explanations.

[152] ¶ 30,690, ¶ 30,691; REAL: 15,504; § 16,560.10

[153] ¶ 30,691; REAL: 15,506; § 16,560.10

[154] ¶ 5605; REAL: 15,504; § 3,015, § 16,560.10

[155] ¶ 30,650, ¶ 30,651, ¶ 30,652; SALES: 24,050; § 18,705.05

[156] ¶ 24,150, ¶ 24,151, ¶ 24,153; FARM: 24,150; § 16,805

lessee) disposes of it under a contract with a retained economic interest (Code Sec. 631(b) and (c); Reg. §1.631-3).[157] An outright sale of timber will also qualify. This treatment is not available for iron ore mined outside the United States, or for coal or iron ore dispositions between related parties or persons owned and controlled by the same interests.

Franchise Grant and Sale

1774. Transfers of Franchises, Trademarks, or Trade Names. Amounts received from the transfer of a franchise, trademark, or trade name are generally treated as ordinary income by the transferor when the transferor retains any significant power, right, or continuing interest over the transferred asset (Code Sec. 1253).[158] Ordinary income treatment also applies to amounts received from the transfer, sale, or other disposition of a franchise, trademark, or trade name which are contingent on the transferred asset's productivity, use, or disposition. Amounts paid or incurred on account of the transfer of a franchise, trademark, or trade name are amortized over 15 years under Code Sec. 197 (¶ 1288). Amortization is claimed on Form 4562.

Contingent Serial Payments. A business deduction may be claimed for certain contingent serial payments paid or incurred on account of a transfer, sale, or other disposition of a trademark, trade name, or franchise. The deduction is allowed for payments that are contingent on the asset's productivity, use, or disposition if the contingent amounts are paid as part of a series of payments that are: (1) payable at least annually throughout the term of the transfer agreement; and (2) substantially equal in amount or payable under a fixed formula (Code Sec. 1253(d)(1)).

Disposition of Depreciable Property

1779. Depreciation Recapture Rules. A taxpayer that sells or disposes of depreciable or amortizable property is required to treat realized gain as ordinary income (rather than capital gain) to the extent of depreciation or amortization deductions previously allowed or allowable for the property. This recapture of depreciation or amortization applies to section 1245 property (¶ 1785) and section 1250 property (¶ 1786). The recapture rules apply notwithstanding any other Code provision (Reg. §§1.1245-6 and 1.1250-1(c)).[159]

Section 1245 Property. Gain realized from the disposition of section 1245 property (¶ 1785) is treated as ordinary income to the extent the adjusted basis of the property is exceeded by the lower of: (1) the recomputed basis of the property; (2) the amount realized upon a sale, exchange, or involuntary conversion of the property; or (3) the fair market value of the property in the case of any other disposition (Code Sec. 1245(a)).[160] For this purpose, recomputed basis is the property's adjusted basis plus previously allowed or allowable depreciation or amortization. Amounts expensed under the following provisions are considered amortization deductions: Code Sec. 179 (¶ 1208), Code Sec. 179A, Code Sec. 179B (¶ 1285), Code Sec. 179C (¶ 1285A), Code Sec. 179D (¶ 1286), Code Sec. 179E (¶ 989A), Code Sec. 181 (¶ 977B), Code Sec. 190 (¶ 1287), Code Sec. 193, and Code Sec. 194 (¶ 1287).

Section 1250 Property. Gain on the sale or other disposition of section 1250 property (¶ 1786) is treated as ordinary income to the extent of the excess of post-1969 depreciation allowances over the depreciation that would have been available under the straight-line method (¶ 1780) (Code Sec. 1250).[161] However, if section 1250 property is held for one year or less, all depreciation (and not just the excess over straight-line depreciation) is recaptured (Code Sec. 1250(b)(1)). See ¶ 1736 for capital gains treatment of "unrecaptured Section 1250 gain."

References are to Standard Federal Tax Reports; Tax Research Consultant; and Practical Tax Explanations.

[157] ¶ 24,150, ¶ 24,155; FARM: 18,250, FARM: 24,200; § 16,805

[158] ¶ 31,040; SALES: 24,300; § 18,745

[159] ¶ 30,908, ¶ 31,001; DEPR: 18,054; § 16,815

[160] ¶ 30,902; DEPR: 18,200; § 11,705.05

[161] ¶ 31,000; DEPR: 18,250; § 11,710

Special recapture rules phase out the depreciation recapture on section 1250 property by reducing it by one percent for each full month the property is held over a specified period in the case of residential rental property, for certain types of government assisted housing, subsidized housing, section 1250 property for which rapid depreciation of rehabilitation expenditures was claimed, and property mortgaged under the Housing Act of 1949 (Code Sec. 1250(a)(1)(B) and (2)(B)). In the case of a sale to a related party (¶ 1717), gain that is not recaptured may still be treated as ordinary income (¶ 1744). Different holding periods and recapture percentages may apply to substantial improvements made to section 1250 property that are considered separate property for recapture purposes, and also to property that consists of more than one element (Code Sec. 1250(f)).[162]

Dispositions. Depreciation recapture is triggered by the disposition of depreciable property, including sales, exchanges, and involuntary conversions. Special rules apply for transfers by gift or at death (¶ 1788), certain tax-free corporate or partnership transactions (¶ 1789), disposal in a like-kind exchange or involuntary conversion where gain is not recognized (¶ 1790), and property distributed by a partnership (¶ 1792). A disposition of section 1245 property includes a sale in a sale-and-leaseback transaction and a transfer upon the foreclosure of a security interest, but does not include a mere transfer of title to a creditor upon creation of a security interest or to a debtor upon termination of a security interest (Reg. § 1.1245-1).[163]

Installment Sale. In the case of disposal of section 1245 or section 1250 property in an installment sale, any income recaptured as ordinary income is to be recognized in the year of the disposition, and any gain in excess of the recapture income is to be reported under the installment method (¶ 1823).

Investment Credit Basis Reductions. For recapture purposes, the amount of an investment credit downward basis adjustment is treated as a deduction allowed for depreciation (¶ 1365A).

Additional Recapture for Corporations. For C corporations, the amount treated as ordinary income on the sale or other disposition of section 1250 property is increased by 20 percent of the additional amount that would be treated as ordinary income if the property were subject to recapture under the rules for section 1245 property (Code Sec. 291(a)(1)).[164]

Reporting Recapture. Form 4797 is used to calculate and report the amount of recaptured depreciation. A taxpayer subject to recapture of an investment credit downward basis adjustment must file Form 4255.

1780. Depreciation Subject to Recapture. In general, depreciation on tangible property placed in service after 1986 is determined under the Modified Accelerated Cost Recovery System (MACRS). Property placed in service after 1980 and before 1987 is covered under the Accelerated Cost Recovery System (ACRS). See ¶ 1216 and following for information concerning the methods of computing allowable depreciation deductions.

MACRS. Gain on the disposition of tangible personal property is treated as ordinary income to the extent of previously-allowed MACRS deductions (¶ 1779). If property from a general asset account is disposed of, the full amount of proceeds realized on the disposition is treated as ordinary income to the extent the unadjusted depreciable basis of the account (increased by amounts allowed as deductions under Code Secs. 179 and 190 for assets in the account) exceeds previously recognized ordinary income from prior dispositions (Code Sec. 168(i)(4); Reg. § 1.168(i)-1(e); Temp. Reg. § 1.168(i)-1T(e)(2)).[165]

References are to Standard Federal Tax Reports; Tax Research Consultant; and Practical Tax Explanations.

[162] ¶ 31,000; DEPR: 18,264

[163] ¶ 30,903; DEPR: 18,052; § 11,705.05

[164] ¶ 15,190; DEPR: 18,266; § 26,020.10

[165] ¶ 11,250, ¶ 11,275B, ¶ 11,275BF; DEPR: 3,554; § 11,145

Residential rental property and nonresidential real property that is placed in service after 1986 and is subject to the MACRS rules must be depreciated under the straight-line MACRS method (¶ 1243). Therefore, recapture of depreciation on such property is not required because no depreciation in excess of straight-line depreciation could have been taken.

ACRS. Gain on the disposition of personal recovery property and nonresidential real recovery property is treated as ordinary income to the extent of previously-allowed ACRS deductions (¶ 1779).[166] Gain on the disposition of residential rental real recovery property is treated as ordinary income to the extent that ACRS deductions exceed straight-line ACRS depreciation over the recovery period applicable to such property. Consequently, there would be no recapture if the straight-line ACRS method was elected for real property.

On the disposition of assets from mass asset accounts, taxpayers recognize the amount of the proceeds realized as ordinary income to the extent of the unadjusted basis in the account less any amounts previously included in income. Any excess proceeds realized are treated as capital gain, unless a nonrecognition provision applies. As far as the recovery of depreciation is concerned, the mass asset account is treated as though there was no disposition of the asset, and the unadjusted basis of the property is left in the capital account until fully recovered in future years (Code Sec. 168(d)(2), prior to amendment by P.L. 97-34).

Amounts Excluded from Depreciation Adjustments. In determining the amount of additional depreciation taken before the disposition of section 1250 property, a taxpayer's depreciation adjustments do *not* include amortization of emergency facilities, pollution control facilities, railroad grading and tunnel bores, child care facilities, expenditures to remove architectural and transportation barriers to the handicapped and elderly, or tertiary injectant expenses (Code Sec. 1250(b)(3)).[167]

1785. Code Sec. 1245 Property. Code Sec. 1245 property is property that is or has been depreciable (or subject to amortization under Code Sec. 197) and that is either:

- personal property (tangible and intangible); or
- other tangible property (not including a building or its structural components) used as an integral part of:
  - — manufacturing, production, or extraction; or
  - — the furnishing of transportation, communications, electrical energy, gas, water, or sewage disposal services (Code Sec. 1245(a)(3); Reg. § 1.1245-3).[168]

The term "other tangible property" includes research facilities or facilities for the bulk storage of fungible commodities used in connection with the activities listed. A leasehold of section 1245 property is also treated as Code Sec. 1245 property. Livestock is considered section 1245 property, and depreciation on purchased draft, breeding, dairy and sporting livestock is recaptured as ordinary income when sold. Raised livestock generally has no basis for depreciation, but to the extent that it does have a basis and is depreciated, it would be subject to recapture (IRS Pub. 225).

Section 1245 property also includes so much of any real property that has an adjusted basis reflecting adjustments for special amortization of pollution control facilities, clean-fuel vehicles and refueling property, capital costs of Environmental Protection Agency sulfur regulation compliance, refinery property, energy efficient commercial buildings, mine safety equipment, child care facilities, or railroad grading and tunnel bores; expenditures for removal of architectural and transportation barriers to the handicapped and elderly, reforestation, or tertiary injectants; and amounts expensed under Code Sec. 179. Section 1245 property also includes single purpose agricultural

References are to Standard Federal Tax Reports; Tax Research Consultant; and Practical Tax Explanations.

[166] ¶ 30,909.023; DEPR: 18,166; § 11,001

[167] ¶ 31,000; DEPR: 18,262; § 11,710

[168] ¶ 30,902, ¶ 30,905; DEPR: 18,150; § 11,705.10

and horticultural structures, and storage facilities used in connection with the distribution of petroleum products.

1786. Code Sec. 1250 Property. Code Sec. 1250 property is any real property that is or has been depreciable under Code Sec. 167 but is not subject to recapture under Code Sec. 1245. This includes all intangible real property (such as leases of land or section 1250 property), buildings and their structural components, and all tangible real property except section 1245 property (Code Sec. 1250(c); Reg. § 1.1250-1(e)).[169] For real property that is section 1245 property rather than section 1250 property, see ¶ 1785.

1788. Disposition of Depreciable Property by Gift or Death. The recapture of depreciation as ordinary income when a section 1245 or section 1250 property is sold or otherwise disposed (¶ 1779) does not apply to dispositions by gift or transfers at death (except a taxable transfer of section 1245 or section 1250 property in satisfaction of a specific bequest of money) (Code Secs. 1245(b) and 1250(d); Reg. §§ 1.1245-4 and 1.1250-3).[170] Upon a later sale, however, the donee will realize the same amount of ordinary income that the donor would have realized had the donor retained the property and sold it (except in the case of a tax-exempt donee). Also, if the taxpayer contributes section 1245 or section 1250 property to a charitable organization, the allowable charitable contribution deduction is reduced by the amount that would have been treated as ordinary income had the taxpayer sold the asset at its fair market value (¶ 1062).

1789. Disposition of Depreciable Property in Tax-Free Corporate or Partnership Transaction. When section 1245 or section 1250 property is disposed of in certain tax-free transactions (i.e., Code Secs. 332, 351, 361, 721, or 731), the transferor takes into account the depreciation recapture treated as ordinary income (¶ 1779) only to the extent that gain is recognized under those sections (Code Secs. 1245(b)(3) and 1250(d)(3); Reg. §§ 1.1245-4(c) and 1.1250-3(c)).[171] However, when there is an otherwise tax-free transfer to a tax-exempt organization (other than a cooperative described in Code Sec. 521), the gain is recognized in full to the transferor. On a later sale of section 1245 or section 1250 property received in one of these tax-free transactions, the transferee realizes depreciation recapture to the extent of the transferor's unrecognized unrecaptured section 1245 or section 1250 gain plus depreciation deducted by the transferee (not to exceed the actual gain).

1790. Disposition of Depreciable Property in Like-Kind Exchange or Involuntary Conversion. If section 1245 or section 1250 property is exchanged for like-kind property (¶ 1721) or is involuntarily converted (¶ 1713), depreciation recapture (¶ 1779) is recognized to the extent of any gain recognized on the exchange (if money or other property is received) or on the conversion (when the conversion proceeds are not all spent on replacement property), plus the fair market value of any property received in the exchange or acquired as replacement property that is not section 1245 or section 1250 property (Code Secs. 1245(b)(4) and 1250(d)(4); Reg. §§ 1.1245-4(d) and 1.1250-3(d)).[172] When this occurs, the basis of the acquired property is determined under the like-kind exchange or involuntary conversion rules (Reg. §§ 1.1245-5 and 1.1250-3(d)).[173]

> **Example:** Greg exchanges section 1245 property with an adjusted basis of $10,000 for like-kind property with a fair market value of $9,000 and unlike property with a fair market value of $3,500. Gain of $2,500 is recognized because unlike property was received. The basis of the property acquired by Greg is $12,500 ($10,000 adjusted basis of the transferred property plus $2,500 recognized gain), of which $3,500 (fair market value) is allocated to the unlike property and the remaining $9,000 is allocated to the acquired like-kind property.

References are to Standard Federal Tax Reports; Tax Research Consultant; and Practical Tax Explanations.

[169] ¶ 31,000, ¶ 31,001; DEPR: 18,252; § 11,710

[170] ¶ 30,902, ¶ 30,906, ¶ 31,000, ¶ 31,003; DEPR: 18,102, DEPR: 18,104; § 11,705.15, § 11,710

[171] ¶ 30,902, ¶ 30,906, ¶ 31,000, ¶ 31,003; DEPR: 18,106; § 11,705.15, § 11,710

[172] ¶ 30,902, ¶ 30,906, ¶ 31,000, ¶ 31,003; DEPR: 18,108; § 18,145.05

[173] ¶ 30,907, ¶ 31,003; SALES: 30,452; § 11,705.20, § 11,710

1792. Partnership Distribution of Depreciable Property. For purposes of the depreciation recapture rules (¶ 1779), the basis of section 1245 property (¶ 1785) or section 1250 property (¶ 1786) distributed by a partnership to a partner is determined by reference to the partnership's adjusted basis in the property (Code Secs. 1245(b)(5) and 1250(d)(5); Reg. §§1.1245-4(f) and 1.1250-3(f)).[174]

For determining the recomputed basis of the property in the hands of the partner, the amount of the depreciation or amortization adjustments for section 1245 property, or the additional depreciation for distributed section 1250 property, attributable to predistribution periods is equal to (1) the amount of gain that would have been treated as ordinary income under the recapture rules had the partnership sold the property at fair market value immediately before the distribution; minus (2) any gain treated as ordinary income under the partnership rules for distributions of receivables or inventory items (¶ 436).

1793. Corporate Distribution of Depreciable Property. A corporation that distributes a dividend consisting of section 1245 property (¶ 1785) or section 1250 property (¶ 1786) might be required to recognize ordinary income under the depreciation recapture rules (¶ 1779), even though it would not normally recognize gain under the corporate distribution rules (¶ 736) (Reg. §§1.1245-1(a), 1.1245-6(b), and 1.1250-1(c)).[175]

If a corporation transfers section 1245 property or section 1250 property to a shareholder in a sale or exchange for less than fair market value, the disposition will not be treated as a sale, exchange, or involuntary conversion for depreciation recapture purposes (Reg. §§1.1245-1(c) and 1.1250-1(a)). Accordingly, the corporation's gain for recapture purposes will be the amount by which the property's adjusted basis is exceeded by the lower of the property's fair market value on the disposition date or the property's recomputed basis (¶ 1779).

No depreciation adjustments (¶ 1779) are reflected in the adjusted basis of section 1245 property, and no additional depreciation is reflected in the adjusted basis of section 1250 property, on the date that the transferee acquires the property if the transferee's basis in the property is determined solely by the corporate distribution rules (¶ 735) (Reg. §§1.1245-2(c) and 1.1250-2(e)).[176]

Farmers' Recapture

1797. Recapture on Land Sale. If farm land is held for less than 10 years, a percentage of the total post-1969 deductions for soil and water conservation and land clearing expenses will be recaptured as ordinary income on Form 4797 (Code Sec. 1252).[177] If the land is held for five years or less, the recapture percentage is 100 percent. The recapture percentage is 80 percent if disposal is within the sixth year after acquisition. For the seventh, eighth and ninth years, the recapture percentages are 60 percent, 40 percent, and 20 percent, respectively. There is no recapture after the ninth year. See ¶ 982 concerning deductions for conservation expenses. Exceptions to this recapture rule exist for transfers by gift, transfers at death, and transfers in certain tax-free transactions (Reg. §1.1252-2).[178]

References are to Standard Federal Tax Reports; Tax Research Consultant; and Practical Tax Explanations.

[174] ¶ 30,902, ¶ 30,906, ¶ 31,000, ¶ 31,003; DEPR: 18,106.05; §30,535.20, §30,555

[175] ¶ 30,903, ¶ 30,908, ¶ 31,001; DEPR: 18,054

[176] ¶ 30,904, ¶ 31,002; DEPR: 18,204.05, DEPR: 18,262

[177] ¶ 31,020; FARM: 9,168; §36,030.10

[178] ¶ 31,022; FARM: 9,168.20; §36,030.10

Chapter 18

INSTALLMENT SALES
DEFERRED PAYMENTS

Installment Method

1801. Use of Installment Method. The installment method is a special way of reporting gains (not losses) from sales of property when at least one payment is received in a tax year after the year of sale (deferred payments). Under the installment method, gain from the sale is prorated and recognized over the years in which payments are received (Code Sec. 453).[1] As a result, each payment received usually consists of interest, return of basis, and gain on the sale.

The installment method must be used for installment sales unless the taxpayer elects not to use the installment method (¶ 1803) or it is otherwise prohibited. This rule applies to both cash and accrual basis taxpayers. The installment method generally is not available for most sales by dealers (¶ 1808), sales of property of a type that would be included in inventory, sales of personal property under a revolving credit plan (¶ 1805), sales of publicly traded property (¶ 1805), or sales of depreciable property between related taxpayers (¶ 1835). Thus, payments for such sales are treated as if they are received in the year of disposition, even if the taxpayer expects to receive some payments in future years.

Gain Calculation. The amount of gain from an installment sale that is taxable in a given year is calculated by multiplying the payments received in that year by the gross profit ratio for the sale (Code Sec. 453(c)).[2] The gross profit ratio is equal to the anticipated gross profit divided by the total contract price (¶ 1813). However, gain from installment sales of depreciable property subject to recapture under Code Sec. 1245 or Code Sec. 1250 is determined under a special rule (¶ 1823).

> **Example:** On December 1, 2012, Bob Smith sells vacant land that he has held for investment purposes for a number of years. His basis in the land is $12,000. The total contract price is $15,000. Bob receives a $5,000 down payment, with the $10,000 balance due in monthly installments of $500 each, plus interest at the applicable federal rate, beginning on January 1, 2013. His anticipated gross profit from the sale is $3,000. His gross profit percentage is 20% ($3,000 gross profit ÷ $15,000 contract price). Under the installment method, Bob must report $1,000

References are to Standard Federal Tax Reports; Tax Research Consultant; and Practical Tax Explanations.

[1] ¶ 21,402; SALES: 36,050; § 18,301

[2] ¶ 21,402; SALES: 36,100; § 18,320

18 INSTALLMENT SALE

($5,000 × 20%) as long-term capital gain in 2012, $1,200 ($6,000 × 20%) in 2013, and $800 ($4,000 × 20%) in 2014. The interest is reported as ordinary income.

Reporting Requirements for Gain. Gain from an installment sale is reported on Form 6252, which must be filed with the tax return in the year of sale and in each year payments are received. The gain calculated on Form 6252 is carried over and entered on Schedule D of the taxpayer's return or Form 4797, or both, as appropriate.

1802. Character of Gain on Installment Sale. Although use of the installment method determines when gain from an installment sale is reported, it does not affect the characterization of the gain as capital gain or ordinary income. The proper characterization depends on the nature of the asset sold (¶ 1735 and ¶ 1741).

1803. Election Not to Use Installment Method. If a taxpayer elects not to use the installment method (¶ 1801), the entire gain is reported in the year of the sale, even though not all of the sale proceeds are received in that year (Code Sec. 453(d); Temp. Reg. § 15A.453-1(d)).[3] For individuals, the election is made by reporting the gain on Form 8949 or Form 4797, whichever applies, instead of reporting the sale on Form 6252. For corporations, S corporations, partnerships, trusts, and estates, the election is made on Schedule D of the taxpayer's return. The election must be made by the due date, including extensions, of the tax return for the year in which the installment sale is made. If a taxpayer files a timely return without an election out, the taxpayer can elect out by filing an amended return within six months of the due date, excluding extensions (Reg. § 301.9100-2). The IRS will otherwise permit late elections only in rare circumstances if the taxpayer can show good cause for not making the election by the due date.

1805. Publicly Traded Property and Revolving Credit Plans. The installment method may *not* be used for: (1) sales of personal property under a revolving credit plan, (2) sales of stock or securities that are traded on an established securities market, or (3) to the extent provided by regulations, sales of other kinds of property that are regularly traded on an established market. All payments to be received from such sales are treated as received in the year of disposition (Code Sec. 453(k)).[4]

1808. Dealers May Not Use Installment Method. Dealers in real or personal property may not use the installment method to report the gain from "dealer dispositions." A "dealer disposition" includes:

(1) any disposition of personal property by a person who regularly sells or otherwise disposes of such property on an installment plan; and

(2) any disposition of real property that is held by the taxpayer for sale to customers in the ordinary course of the taxpayer's trade or business (Code Sec. 453(l)(1)).[5]

However, there are some exceptions to these general rules for dispositions of farm property, residential lots and timeshares (¶ 1811).

1811. Exceptions to "Dealer Disposition" Rule. Certain types of installment transactions by a dealer are not considered dealer dispositions (¶ 1808) and as a result the installment method of reporting may be used (Code Sec. 453(l)(2)).[6] These include:

(1) the disposition of any property used or produced in the trade or business of farming,

(2) the disposition of any residential lot, provided that the dealer or any related person is not obligated to make any improvements to the lot, and

(3) the disposition of timeshare rights to use or own residential real property for not more than six weeks per year, or a right to use specified campgrounds for recreational purposes.

References are to Standard Federal Tax Reports; Tax Research Consultant; and Practical Tax Explanations.

[3] ¶ 21,402, ¶ 21,404; SALES: 36,056; § 18,315

[4] ¶ 21,402; SALES: 36,052.05; § 18,310.20, § 18,310.25

[5] ¶ 21,402; SALES: 36,250; § 18,310.10

[6] ¶ 21,402; SALES: 36,054; § 18,310.10

Payment of Interest. To use the installment method for the sale of residential lots and timeshares, the taxpayer must pay interest on the amount of tax attributable to the installment payments received during the year. The interest is calculated for the period beginning on the date of sale and ending on the date the payment is received (Code Sec. 453(l)(3)).[7] The amount of interest is based upon the applicable federal rate in effect at the time of sale, compounded semiannually (¶ 1875).

Computation of Income

1813. Amount of Income for Installment Sales. For nondealer dispositions of property that are not subject to the depreciation recapture provisions of Code Sec. 1245 or Code Sec. 1250, the amount of income reported from an installment sale in any tax year (including the year of sale) is equal to the payments received during the year multiplied by the gross profit ratio for the sale (Code Sec. 453(c); Reg. § 15A.453-1(b)(2)).[8] Payments include all amounts actually or constructively received in the tax year under the installment obligation (¶ 1819).

The gross profit ratio is the gross profit on the installment sale divided by the total contract price. The gross profit is the selling price of the property minus its adjusted basis. The selling price of the property is not reduced by any existing mortgage or encumbrance, or by any selling expenses, but is reduced by any imputed interest (¶ 1859).

The total contract price (denominator of gross profit ratio) is the selling price minus that portion of qualifying indebtedness (¶ 1815) which the buyer assumes or takes the property subject to that does not exceed the seller's basis in the property (adjusted to reflect commissions and other selling expenses). In the case of an installment sale that is a partially nontaxable like-kind exchange (¶ 1723), the gross profit is reduced by that portion of the gain that is not recognized, and the total contract price is reduced by the value of the like-kind property received (Code Sec. 453(f)(6)).[9]

For certain nondealer sales of property over $150,000, a special interest charge may apply (¶ 1825).

1815. Qualifying Indebtedness for Installment Sales. For the purpose of determining the total contract price of an installment sale of property (¶ 1813), qualifying indebtedness includes:

(1) any mortgage or other indebtedness encumbering the property; and

(2) any indebtedness not secured by the property but incurred or assumed by the purchaser incident to the acquisition, holding or operation of the property in the ordinary course of business or investment (Temp. Reg. § 15A.453-1(b)(2)(iv)).[10]

Qualifying indebtedness does not include an obligation of the seller incurred incident to the *disposition* of the property, nor does it include an obligation functionally unrelated to the acquisition, holding or operation of the property. Any obligation incurred or assumed in contemplation of disposition of the property is not qualifying indebtedness if recovery of the seller's basis is accelerated.

Wrap-Around Mortgage. When property encumbered by an outstanding mortgage is sold in exchange for an installment obligation equal to the mortgage, the installment obligation is said to "wrap around" the mortgage. The seller generally uses the payments received from the installment obligation to pay the "wrapped" mortgage. In this situation, the IRS will follow the Tax Court's position and will not treat the buyer as having taken the property subject to, or as having assumed, the seller's mortgage (*Professional Equities, Inc.*, 89 TC 165, Dec. 44,064 (1987)).[11] As a result, the seller does not have to reduce the total contract price by the amount of the wrapped mortgage.

References are to Standard Federal Tax Reports; Tax Research Consultant; and Practical Tax Explanations.

[7] ¶ 21,402; SALES: 36,054.10; § 18,310.10

[8] ¶ 21,402, ¶ 21,404; SALES: 36,100; § 18,320

[9] ¶ 21,402; SALES: 36,114.05; § 18,350

[10] ¶ 21,404; SALES: 36,106; § 18,320

[11] ¶ 21,412.80; SALES: 36,106; § 18,320

1819. Installment Payments. When determining the amount of reportable income under the installment method (¶ 1813), a payment includes all amounts actually or constructively received in the tax year under an installment obligation, as well as the following debt instruments:

(1) evidence of indebtedness of a person other than the buyer;

(2) evidence of indebtedness of the buyer that is payable on demand, readily tradable, or issued with coupons or in registered form;

(3) a bank certificate or treasury note;

(4) qualifying indebtedness assumed (¶ 1815), or taken subject to, by the buyer, to the extent it exceeds the seller's basis for the sold property as adjusted for selling expenses;

(5) seller's indebtedness to the buyer that is canceled; and

(6) indebtedness on the sold property (for which the seller is not personally liable) when the buyer is the obligee of the indebtedness (Temp. Reg. § 15A.453-1(b)(3)).[12]

Debt instruments in registered form that the seller can establish are not readily tradable are not considered payments. In addition, like-kind property received in a partially tax-free exchange (¶ 1723) that is part of an installment sale transaction is not treated as a payment for purposes of determining the amount of income to be reported under the installment method (Code Sec. 453(f)(6)).[13]

1821. Contingent Payment Sales. A contingent payment sale must be reported on the installment method (¶ 1801) unless the seller elects not to use the installment method (Temp. Reg. § 15A.453-1(c)).[14] A contingent payment sale is a sale or other disposition of property in which the total selling price is not determinable by the close of the tax year in which the sale occurs. It does not include transactions with respect to which the installment obligation represents, under applicable principles of tax law: a retained interest in the property which is the subject of the transaction; an interest in a joint venture or partnership; an equity interest in a corporation; or similar transaction, regardless of the existence of a stated maximum selling price or a fixed payment term.

In a contingent payment sale, the basis of the property sold (including selling expenses) is allocated to payments received in each tax year and recovered as follows:

(1) for sales with a stated maximum selling price, basis is recovered according to a profit ratio based on the stated maximum selling price;

(2) for sales with a fixed payment period, basis is recovered ratably over the fixed period; and

(3) for sales with neither a maximum selling price nor a fixed payment period, basis is recovered ratably over a 15-year period.

Alternate methods of basis recovery may be required when the normal method would substantially accelerate or inappropriately defer the recovery of basis.

1823. Dispositions of Property Subject to Depreciation Recapture. For installment sales of real or personal property to which the depreciation recapture provisions of Code Sec. 1245 or 1250 apply (¶ 1779), any recapture income must be reported in the year of disposition, whether or not an installment payment is received in that year (Code Sec. 453(i)).[15] The ordinary income amount reported in the year of sale is added to the property's basis, and this adjusted basis is used in determining the remaining profit on the disposition. The remaining profit amount is used to compute the gross profit percentage to be applied to each installment payment.

References are to Standard Federal Tax Reports; Tax Research Consultant; and Practical Tax Explanations.

[12] ¶ 21,404; SALES: 36,102; § 18,325

[13] ¶ 21,402; SALES: 36,114.05; § 18,350

[14] ¶ 21,404; SALES: 36,112; § 18,330.05

[15] ¶ 21,402; SALES: 36,108; § 18,355.05

Example: On December 1, 2012, Bob sells a rental building for a total contract price of $100,000, plus interest at the applicable federal rate. He receives a note due in yearly installments of $20,000, plus interest, beginning January 1, 2013. Bob's adjusted basis in the building is $20,000. Assume that $10,000 of the total $80,000 gain is attributable to depreciation that must be recaptured as ordinary income under Code Sec. 1250 (¶ 1780). The $10,000 must be included in Bob's ordinary income for 2012 (the year of sale). The $10,000 is added to his $20,000 adjusted basis for purposes of determining the gross profit on the remaining gain. Therefore, gross profit is, $70,000 ($100,000 - $30,000). Of each $20,000 payment received in the following years, $14,000 is includible in income ($20,000 × ($70,000 ÷ $100,000)).

If a portion of the capital gain from an installment sale of depreciable real property consists of unrecaptured section 1250 gain, and another portion consists of other capital gains (¶ 1736), the taxpayer is required to take the unrecaptured section 1250 gain into account before the other capital gains are received (Reg. § 1.453-12).[16]

1825. Special Interest Rule for Nondealers of Property. A special interest charge may apply to an installment obligation that arises from a nondealer disposition of real or personal property (¶ 1813) under the installment method having a sales price over $150,000 (Code Sec. 453A).[17] The interest charge does not apply to nondealer dispositions of property used in the business of farming or personal use property. For this purpose, personal use property is property that is not substantially used in connection with the taxpayer's trade or business or in an investment activity (Code Sec. 1275(b)(3)). The interest charge also does not apply to dispositions of timeshares and residential lots (but the interest payment rule described in ¶ 1811 does apply).

Generally, the interest charge is imposed on the tax deferred under the installment method with respect to outstanding installment obligations. However, the interest charge will not apply unless the face amount of all obligations held by the taxpayer that arose during and remain outstanding at the close of the tax year exceeds $5 million (Code Sec. 453A(b)(2)(B)).[18]

If any indebtedness is secured by a nondealer installment obligation that arises from the disposition of any real or personal property having a sales price over $150,000, the net proceeds of the secured indebtedness will be treated as a payment received on the installment obligation on the later of the date that the indebtedness is secured or the date that the net proceeds are received (Code Sec. 453A(d)(1)).

The interest is not reported on Form 6252, but rather is entered as an additional tax on the tax return. For individuals, it is included in the amount to be entered on the line for "total taxes" on Form 1040. For corporations, it is entered on Schedule J of Form 1120.

Related-Party Sales

1833. Resale After Installment Sale to Related Persons. When a person makes an installment sale of property to a related person who sells the property before the installment payments are made in full, the amount realized by the related person from the second sale is treated as being received by the initial seller at the time of the second sale (Code Sec. 453(e)).[19] However, the resale rule does not generally apply when the second sale takes place more than two years after the first sale. A related person for this purpose includes the seller's spouse, child, grandchild and other lineal descendants, parent, grandparent and other ancestors, brother, sister, controlled corporation, partnerships, certain trusts, estate, or executors (Code Sec. 453(f)(1)).

In applying the resale rule, the amount treated as received by the initial seller is limited to the *lesser* of:

References are to Standard Federal Tax Reports; Tax Research Consultant; and Practical Tax Explanations.

16 ¶ 21,425; SALES: 36,100; § 18,355.05

17 ¶ 21,450; SALES: 36,150; § 18,375.05

18 ¶ 21,450; SALES: 36,150; § 18,375.10

19 ¶ 21,402; SALES: 36,200; § 18,360

(1) the total amount realized from the second disposition before the close of the tax year of disposition; or

(2) the total contract price for the first disposition, reduced by the sum of:

(a) the total amount received from the first disposition before the close of the year of the second disposition; and

(b) the total amount treated as received for prior years under the resale rule.

An exception to the resale applies for:

(1) any sale or exchange of stock to the issuing corporation is not treated as a first disposition;

(2) a compulsory or involuntary conversion, and any transfer thereafter, is not treated as a second disposition if the first disposition occurred before the threat or imminence of the conversion; and

(3) any transfer after the earlier of the death of the person making the first disposition or the death of the person acquiring the property in the first disposition, and any transfer thereafter, is not treated as a second disposition.

1835. Depreciable Property Sales to Related Persons. Generally, the installment method cannot be used for installment sales of depreciable property between related persons. As a result, all payments are deemed received in the year of sale. However, the installment method may be used if the IRS is satisfied that tax avoidance was not one of the principal purposes of the sale (Code Sec. 453(g)).[20] For this purpose, the term "related person" is defined in Code Sec. 1239(b) (¶ 1744) and includes corporations and partnerships that are more than 50 percent owned, either directly or indirectly, by the same person.

Repossessions of Property

1838. Repossession of Personal Property. When personal property that was sold in an installment sale is repossessed, the repossession is treated as a disposition of the installment obligation. Gain or loss is measured by the difference between the seller's basis in the obligation and the fair market value of the property on the date of repossession. The seller's basis in the obligation is equal to the face value of the obligation minus the deferred gross profit on the sale at the time of repossession (IRS Pub. 537).[21] The character of the gain or loss, if any, on the repossession is the same as on the original sale.

If the installment obligation is not completely satisfied by repossession of the property, and the seller is unable to collect the balance of the debt, the seller may be able to claim a bad debt deduction for the portion of the obligation that is not satisfied through repossession (¶ 1145 and ¶ 1169).

1841. Repossession of Real Property. When real property is sold on the installment method and the seller accepts an installment debt secured by the property, the seller will recognize only a limited amount of gain and no loss upon repossession of the property (Code Sec. 1038; Reg. § 1.1038-1).[22] Gain on the repossession is limited to the lesser of:

(1) the amount by which the amount of money and the fair market value of other property (other than obligations of the purchaser) received, prior to such reacquisition, with respect to the sale of such property, exceeds the amount of the gain on the sale of such property returned as income for periods prior to such reacquisition; or

(2) the amount by which the price at which the real property was sold exceeded its adjusted basis, reduced by the sum of (a) the amount of the gain on

References are to Standard Federal Tax Reports; Tax Research Consultant; and Practical Tax Explanations.

[20] ¶ 21,402; SALES: 36,204; § 18,310.30

[21] ¶ 21,406.048; SALES: 36,452; § 18,365.10

[22] ¶ 29,740, ¶ 29,741; SALES: 36,454; § 18,365.15

the sale of such property returned as income for periods prior to the reacquisition of such property, and (b) the amount of money and the fair market value of other property (other than obligations of the purchaser received with respect to the sale of such property) paid or transferred by the seller in connection with the reacquisition of such property.

The same rules apply when an estate or beneficiary repossesses real property that had been sold by a decedent on the installment method (Code Sec. 1038(g)).[23]

Repossession of Principal Residence. Special rules apply if a seller repossesses a principal residence that was sold under the installment method and realized gain from the sale was excluded under Code Sec. 121 (¶ 1705). If the seller resells the residence within one year of repossession, the original sale and the resale are treated as one transaction and realized gain is determined on the combined sale and resale (Code Sec. 1038(e)).[24] If the resale does not take place within one year, the general rules for repossessions of real property apply.

1843. Basis After Repossession of Real Property. Generally, the seller's basis in repossessed real property (¶ 1841) is the adjusted basis of the debt secured by the property (determined at the time of the repossession), increased by any gain recognized at the time of the repossession and by the seller's repossession costs (Code Sec. 1038(c)).[25] If the debt to the seller is not discharged as a result of the repossession, the basis of the debt is zero. If, before repossession, the seller has treated the secured debt as having become worthless or partially worthless, then, upon repossession, the seller is considered to have received an amount equal to the amount that was treated as worthless. However, the seller's adjusted basis in the debt is increased by the same amount (Code Sec. 1038(d)).

Dispositions of Installment Obligations

1846. Gain or Loss from Disposition of Installment Obligation. Gain or loss is generally recognized when an installment obligation is sold, disposed of, or satisfied other than at face value (Code Sec. 453B).[26] The amount of gain or loss is the difference between the basis of the obligation and either:

(1) the amount realized, if the obligation is satisfied other than at face value or is sold or exchanged; or

(2) the fair market value of the obligation, if the obligation is distributed or disposed of other than by sale or exchange.

For this purpose, the basis of the obligation to the transferor is the excess of the face value of the obligation over the income that would have been returnable had the obligation been satisfied in full. To determine the basis, the unpaid balance of the installment obligation is multiplied by the gross profit percentage, and the result is subtracted from the unpaid balance. The result is the basis in the installment obligation.

The cancellation or lapse of an installment obligation is treated as a disposition other than a sale or exchange. This includes a self-canceling installment note that is extinguished at the death of the holder (*R.E. Frane Est.*, 93-2 USTC ¶ 50,386).[27] Therefore, gain or loss is computed based on the fair market value of the obligation.

The character of any resulting gain or loss on the disposition of an installment obligation is determined by the character of the original asset that was sold (i.e., a capital or noncapital asset) (Code Sec. 453B(a)).[28] For a discussion of what constitutes a capital asset, see ¶ 1741.

1849. Transfers of Installment Obligations Between Spouses. The transfer of an installment obligation between spouses or incident to divorce (other than a transfer in

References are to Standard Federal Tax Reports; Tax Research Consultant; and Practical Tax Explanations.

[23] ¶ 29,740; ESTTRST: 9,166; § 18,365.15

[24] ¶ 29,740; REAL: 6,156.35; § 18,365.20

[25] ¶ 29,740; REAL: 6,156.25; § 18,365.15

[26] ¶ 21,470; SALES: 36,350; § 18,370

[27] ¶ 21,471.15; SALES: 36,352.15

[28] ¶ 21,470; SALES: 36,352; § 18,370

trust) will not trigger recognition of gain. Thus, the same tax treatment applies to the transferee spouse that would have applied to the transferor spouse (Code Sec. 453B(g)).[29]

1854. Effect of Death on Installment Obligations. The transfer of an installment obligation at the death of the obligee (other than to the buyer) is not a taxable disposition requiring the recognition of any gain or loss (¶ 1846) (Code Sec. 453B(c)).[30] Instead, the gain portion of any installment obligation acquired from a decedent is considered income in respect of a decedent (¶ 182). The taxpayer who receives such installment payments (estate, beneficiary, etc.) must report as income the same portion of the payments that would have been taxable income to the decedent. The amount considered to be an item of gross income in respect of the decedent is the excess of the face value of the obligation over its basis in the hands of the decedent.

While the transfer of an installment obligation upon a seller's death is generally not a taxable disposition, the seller's estate is deemed to have made a taxable disposition if the obligation is transferred by bequest, devise, or inheritance to the obligor or, if the estate allows, the obligation to become unenforceable. If the decedent and obligor-recipient of the obligation were related persons (¶ 1833), the fair market value of the obligation may not be determined at less than its face amount (Code Sec. 691(a)(5)).[31]

Corporate Liquidations

1856. Installment Obligations Received from Liquidating Corporations. Liquidating corporations, other than certain liquidating S corporations (¶ 1858), that distribute installment obligations to shareholders in exchange for their stock must currently recognize gain or loss from the distribution. However, a shareholder that receives a qualifying installment obligation may treat the exchange as though it were an ordinary sale of stock for an installment obligation. Thus, the shareholder may be able to use the installment method to report the gain from the exchange (Code Sec. 453(h)(1)(A); Reg. § 1.453-11(a)(1)).[32] If the liquidating corporation is traded on an established securities market, installment sale treatment is not available (Code Sec. 453(k)(2); Reg. § 1.453-11(a)(2)(i)). However, a shareholder *may* use the installment method if the stock of the liquidating corporation is not traded on an established market, even if the obligation arose from the sale by the liquidating corporation of securities that are traded on an established market (so that the liquidating corporation could not have used the installment method). For this rule to apply, the liquidating corporation must not have been formed or used to avoid the prohibition against using the installment method for publicly traded stock (Reg. § 1.453-11(c)(5)).

Gain on the transfer of a qualifying installment obligation to a shareholder during a liquidation is not immediately taxed to the shareholder. Instead, the payments received under the installment obligation are treated as payments for the stock, and any gain is included in the shareholder's income as payments are received. This rule applies when:

(1) stockholders exchange their stock in the corporation in a Code Sec. 331 liquidation (¶ 2253);

(2) the corporation, during the 12-month period beginning with the adoption of the plan of liquidation, had sold some or all of its assets in exchange for an installment note;

(3) the corporation, within that 12-month period, distributes the installment notes acquired in connection with those sales to the shareholders in exchange for their stock; and

(4) the liquidation is completed within that 12-month period.

References are to Standard Federal Tax Reports; Tax Research Consultant; and Practical Tax Explanations.

[29] ¶ 21,470; SALES: 36,354.40; § 18,370

[30] ¶ 21,470; SALES: 36,354.35; § 18,370

[31] ¶ 24,900; SALES: 36,352.15; § 18,370

[32] ¶ 21,402, ¶ 21,419; SALES: 36,354.20; § 26,710

This rule does not apply to obligations arising from a sale of inventory, stock in trade, or assets held for sale to customers in the ordinary course of business unless those assets are sold in a bulk sale (Code Sec. 453(h)(1)(B)).

Subsidiary Liquidations. In a complete liquidation of a subsidiary, in which gain or loss on distributions of property is generally not recognized by the parent or the subsidiary (¶ 2261), the distribution of installment obligations will not cause recognition of gain or loss (Code Sec. 453B(d)).[33]

1858. Installment Obligation Received in S Corporation Liquidations. If an installment obligation is distributed by an S corporation in a complete liquidation, and the receipt of the obligation is not treated as payment for stock in a complete 12-month liquidation (¶ 1856), then the corporation generally does not recognize gain or loss on the distribution. This is true even for accrual-basis S corporations (Code Sec. 453B(h)).[34]

Imputed Interest

1859. Inadequate or Unpaid Interest on Deferred Payments. Generally, when a sale or exchange of property involves the issuance of a debt instrument with deferred payments, as does an installment sale, the instrument should provide for the payment of adequate interest. If the instrument does not provide for the payment of adequate stated interest, interest income must be imputed to the seller or holder of the debt under the original issue discount (OID) rules of Code Sec. 1274 (¶ 1954) or the unstated interest rules of Code Sec. 483 (¶ 1868). The unstated interest rules will apply only if the transaction does not come within the scope of the OID rules (Code Sec. 483(d)(1)).[35]

If neither the unstated interest rules nor OID rules apply, interest may be imputed under other Code sections (Reg. § 1.483-1(a) and (c)(3); Reg. § 1.1274-1(b)). For example, interest is imputed to certain obligations given in exchange for services or for the use of property under Code Secs. 404 and 467 (¶ 1541), respectively (Reg. § 1.1274-1(a)). Further, the interest imputation rules of Code Sec. 7872 apply to certain below-market demand loans (Reg. § 1.1274-1(b)(3)).

In addition, the unstated interest rules and OID rules do not apply to transfers of property between spouses, or incident to divorce (Code Sec. 1041), to cash method debt instruments (Code Sec. 1274A(c)), and to the purchaser who gives debt when buying personal use property (Code Sec. 1275(b)).

The following steps should be taken with respect to deferred contracts:

(1) determine whether the transaction is covered by either the unstated interest rules or the OID rules (¶ 1868 and ¶ 1954);

(2) test for unstated interest or OID;

(3) compute the total unstated interest or OID under the contract; and

(4) apportion the unstated interest or OID over the payments.

1868. Scope of Code Sec. 483. The unstated interest rules of Code Sec. 483 impute interest income on any payments on the sale or exchange of property that are due more than six months after the sale or exchange if any payments are due more than one year after the sale or exchange (Code Sec. 483).[36]

Exceptions. The rules under Code Sec. 483 do not apply in the following situations:

(1) debt instruments for which an issue price is determined under Code Sec. 1273(b)(1), (2) or (3), or Code Sec. 1274;

(2) sales for $3,000 or less;

References are to Standard Federal Tax Reports; Tax Research Consultant; and Practical Tax Explanations.

[33] ¶ 21,470; SALES: 36,354.20; § 18,370

[34] ¶ 21,470; SCORP: 352.45; § 28,905.10

[35] ¶ 22,290; ACCTNG: 36,304; § 18,355.10

[36] ¶ 22,290; ACCTNG: 36,300; § 19,505.05

(3) with respect to the buyer, any purchase of personal property or educational services (under Code Sec. 163(b)) on an installment basis if the interest charge cannot be ascertained and is treated as six percent; and

(4) sales or exchanges of patents to the extent of any payments that are contingent on the productivity, use or disposition of the property transferred.

1872. Testing for and Imputing Unstated Interest. Code Sec. 483 applies when there is "unstated interest," which is the excess of the total payments (excluding any interest payments) due more than six months after the date of sale over the total of their present values (including the present values of any interest payments). Generally, present value is determined by using a discount rate equal to the applicable federal rate determined under Code Sec. 1274(d) (¶ 1875) (Code Sec. 483(b); Reg. § 1.483-3).[37] However, the discount rate will not exceed six percent, compounded semiannually, in the case of transfers of land between family members. This rule only applies if the aggregate sales price of all prior land sales between the family members does not exceed $500,000, and does not apply if any party to the sale is a nonresident alien (Code Sec. 483(e); Reg. § 1.483-3(b)).[38] In addition, a discount rate not in excess of nine percent (if less than the AFR) compounded semiannually, applies to most debt instruments given in consideration for the sale or exchange of property if the stated principal amount does not exceed a certain amount adjusted for inflation (Code Sec. 1274A) (¶ 1954).

1875. Adequate Stated Interest. A debt instrument with deferred payments is considered to have adequately stated interest for purposes of the unstated interest rules of Code Sec. 483 (¶ 1859) if the stated principal amount is at least equal to its imputed principal amount. The imputed principal amount is determined by totaling the present values of all principal and interest payments due on the instrument discounted at the applicable federal rate (AFR) (¶ 83). Payments within six months after the sale are taken into account.

The AFR is the lowest rate in effect for any month in the three-calendar-month period ending with the first calendar month in which there is a binding written contract. It is determined by reference to the term of the debt instrument, including renewal and extension options, as shown in the following table (Code Sec. 1274(d); Reg. §§ 1.483-3(a); 1.1274-4(a)).[39]

Term of Debt Instrument:	*Applicable Federal Rate:*
Not over 3 years	Federal short-term rate
Over 3 years but not over 9 years .	Federal mid-term rate
Over 9 years	Federal long-term rate

For sale and leaseback transactions, the discount rate is 110 percent of the AFR, compounded semiannually (Code Sec. 1274(e); Reg. § 1.1274-4(a)(2)).[40] For transactions in which a debt instrument is given in consideration for the sale or exchange of property (other than new Code Sec. 38 property) and the stated principal amount of the instrument does not exceed an inflation-adjusted amount ($5,339,300 for 2012) (Rev. Rul. 2011-27), a nine-percent rate may be substituted for the AFR (Code Sec. 1274A; Rev. Rul. 2011-27).[41] The discount rate will not exceed six percent, compounded semiannually, in the case of transfers of land between family members but only applies if the aggregate sales price of all prior land sales between the family members during the calendar year does not exceed $500,000. However, this limit on the discount rate does not apply if any party to the sale is a nonresident alien (Code Sec. 483(e); Reg. § 1.483-3(b)).[42]

1881. Assumptions of Debt. If any person in connection with the sale or exchange of property assumes any debt instrument or acquires any property subject to any debt instrument, in determining whether the unstated interest rules apply, the assumption or

References are to Standard Federal Tax Reports; Tax Research Consultant; and Practical Tax Explanations.

[37] ¶ 22,290, ¶ 22,294; ACCTNG: 36,308; § 19,510.10

[38] ¶ 22,290, ¶ 22,294; ACCTNG: 36,308.25; § 19,510.15

[39] ¶ 22,294, ¶ 31,300, ¶ 31,304; ACCTNG: 36,162; § 19,410.10

[40] ¶ 31,300, ¶ 31,304; ACCTNG: 36,308.20

[41] ¶ 31,320, ¶ 31,322.30; ACCTNG: 36,308; § 19,315.10

[42] ¶ 22,290, ¶ 22,294; ACCTNG: 36,308.25; § 19,510.15

acquisition is not generally taken into account. However, when the instrument's terms and conditions are modified in a manner that would constitute an exchange, the unstated interest rules may be applied (Reg. § 1.483-1(d)).[43]

Treatment of Interest

1883. Including Imputed Interest. The amount of unstated interest determined under Code Sec. 483 is classified as interest for tax purposes (Reg. § 1.483-1(a)(2)). As a result, it will be income to the seller. However, see the exceptions discussed at ¶ 1887.

Reporting Requirements. The reporting of unstated interest depends upon whether the seller is on the cash or accrual basis. Cash basis sellers include unstated interest as interest income in the year payments are received. Sellers on the accrual basis include unstated interest in income in the year payments are due (Reg. § 1.446-2(a)).[44]

1887. Deducting Imputed Interest. The amount of unstated interest determined under Code Sec. 483 is classified as interest for tax purposes (Reg. § 1.483-1(a)(2)). As a result, it may be deductible by the buyer.

Generally, the unstated interest rules do not apply to a debt instrument given in consideration for the sale or exchange of personal use property. Thus, unstated interest is not deductible by the issuer but must be accrued by the holder. Personal use property means any property substantially all the use of which by the taxpayer is not in connection with the taxpayer's trade or business or the for-profit and other activities described in Code Sec. 212.[45] If a cash-basis borrower incurs debt in connection with the acquisition or carrying of personal use property, any unstated interest is deductible only when paid.

References are to Standard Federal Tax Reports; Tax Research Consultant; and Practical Tax Explanations.

[43] ¶ 22,291; ACCTNG: 36,264; § 19,505.10

[44] ¶ 20,610; ACCTNG: 36,200; § 19,310.05

[45] ¶ 31,340; ACCTNG: 36,224; § 19,315.10, § 19,505.10

Chapter 19

SECURITIES TRANSACTIONS

Taxation of Securities Transactions

1901. Securities Transactions. Securities such as stocks and bonds held for investment are generally capital assets. Calculating gain or loss from the sale of securities follow the same rules that apply to other capital assets (¶ 1701). There are, however, a number of special rules that apply to the sale or exchange of certain securities including securities held by dealers (¶ 1903), worthless securities (¶ 1916), options to buy securities (¶ 1919), the wash sale rules (¶ 1935), short sales (¶ 1944), tax straddles (¶ 1948), and a corporation dealing in its own stocks or bonds (¶ 1729). In addition, gain on the sale of certain small business stock may be either excluded from gross income (¶ 1905) or rolled over to other small business stock (¶ 1907 and ¶ 1909), and certain losses may be treated as ordinary losses (¶ 1911 and ¶ 1913).

1903. Dealer in Securities. Securities held for sale by dealers to their customers in the ordinary course of a trade or business are not capital assets. Thus, gain or loss realized from the sale or disposition is treated as ordinary gain or loss unless the securities are held primarily for personal investment (Code Sec. 1236).[1] Securities that are held by a dealer for personal investment purposes must be clearly identified in the dealer's records before the close of the day on which they are acquired and must never be held primarily for sale to the dealer's customers. See ¶ 1760 for a discussion of the distinction between a dealer, trader, and investor.

Mark-to-Market Requirements. Dealers in securities must use the mark-to-market method of accounting for gain and loss on securities (Code Sec. 475(a)).[2] Under the mark-to-market rules, any security that is inventory in the hands of a dealer must be included in inventory at its fair market value. A securities dealer may use the fair market value as reported on the dealer's financial statements for this purpose (Reg. § 1.475(a)-4).[3]

Any security that is not classified as inventory in the dealer's hands and that is held at the close of the tax year is treated as if it were sold at its fair market value on the last business day of the year. The dealer must recognize any gain or loss that results from the deemed sale. Any gain or loss recognized is taken into account when calculating the dealer's gain or loss when the security is actually sold or exchanged.

The mark-to-market rules generally apply to all securities held by a dealer, other than those they hold as investments or not for sale (Code Sec. 475(b)).[4] The rules also

References are to Standard Federal Tax Reports; Tax Research Consultant; and Practical Tax Explanations.

[1] ¶ 30,670; SALES: 45,054; § 18,805.05

[2] ¶ 22,265; SALES: 45,350; § 38,235.05

[3] ¶ 22,265E; SALES: 45,362; § 38,235.05

[4] ¶ 22,265; SALES: 45,354; § 38,235.15

do not apply to debt instruments acquired in the ordinary course of a trade or business or securities that are hedges of certain positions. In order for a security to be exempt from the mark-to-market requirements, it must be clearly identified in the dealer's records before the close of the day on which it is acquired, originated, or entered into.

Commodity dealers, as well as traders in securities or commodities, may elect to have the mark-to-market requirements apply to their noninvestment positions (Code Sec. 475(e) and (f)).[5] For a commodities dealer, the election applies to commodities held by the dealer in the same manner as securities held by a dealer. A trader in securities or commodities that elects mark-to-market treatment must recognize gain or loss on any security or commodity held in connection with the trading business as if the security or commodity were sold at fair market value on the last business day of the tax year.

A commodities dealer may elect mark-to-market accounting without the consent of the IRS. Similarly, the mark-to-market election for traders of securities or commodities may be made without the consent of the IRS, and may be made separately for each trade or business of the taxpayer. In both cases, the election continues to apply until it is revoked with the IRS's consent. The election is made by attaching a statement to the tax return for the year prior to the year in which the election is to take effect—the timely-filed tax return for 2012 for the election to be effective for 2013. A new taxpayer makes the election by placing a statement in its books and records no later than 2 months and 15 days after the first day of the election year (Rev. Proc. 99-17). A commodities dealer or trader in securities or commodities that has elected to use the mark-to-mark method of accounting may obtain automatic consent for a change in accounting method for this purpose (Rev. Proc. 2011-14).

Gains and Losses on Small Business Stock

1905. Exclusion of Gain from Small Business Stock. A noncorporate taxpayer can exclude from gross income 50 percent of any gain from the sale or exchange of qualified small business stock held for more than five years (Code Sec. 1202).[6] The exclusion is 60 percent if the qualified small business stock is issued by a corporation in an empowerment zone. The exclusion is increased to 75 percent for all qualified small business stock acquired after February 17, 2009, and before September 28, 2010, and to 100 percent for stock acquired after September 27, 2010, and before January 1, 2012. Eligible gain from any single issuer is subject to a cumulative limit for any given tax year to the greater of: (1) $10 million reduced by the aggregate amount of eligible gain taken in prior years ($5 million for married taxpayers filing separately), or (2) 10 times the taxpayer's adjusted basis of all qualified stock of the issuer disposed of during the tax year.

For alternative minimum tax purposes, seven percent of the excluded gain is a tax preference item (¶ 1425) (Code Sec. 57(a)(7)).[7] However, none of the excluded gain is a preference item for the disposition of stock acquired after September 27, 2010, and before January 1, 2012 (Code Sec. 1202(a)(4)). The sale or exchange of the stock is reported on Form 8949 (Schedule D of Form 1040 for tax years before 2011).

> **Comment:** Absent further legislation, 42 percent of the excluded gain is generally a tax preference item for sales and exchanges in tax years beginning after December 31, 2012. For small business stock on which the holding period began after December 31, 2000, however, 28 percent of the excluded gain is a tax preference item for sales and exchanges in tax years beginning after December 31, 2012.

To be eligible as qualified small business stock, the stock must be issued after August 10, 1993, and acquired by the taxpayer at its original issue (directly or through an underwriter) in exchange for money, property, or as compensation for services provided to the corporation (Code Sec. 1202(c) and (d); Reg. § 1.1202-2).[8] Qualified

References are to Standard Federal Tax Reports; Tax Research Consultant; and Practical Tax Explanations.

[5] ¶ 22,265; SALES: 45,360; § 38,235.20

[6] ¶ 30,372; SALES: 15,300; § 16,605.05

[7] ¶ 5300; FILEIND: 30,256; § 15,305

[8] ¶ 30,372, ¶ 30,374; SALES: 15,304.05; § 16,605.10

stock that is converted to other stock of the corporation (such as preferred stock) is treated as qualified stock. Small business stock is not qualified if it has been the subject of certain redemptions that are more than *de minimis*. A taxpayer who acquires qualified stock by gift or inheritance is treated as having acquired such stock in the same manner as the transferor and adds the transferor's holding period to his or her own. A partnership may distribute qualified stock to its partners as long as the partner held his or her partnership interest when the stock was acquired, and only to the extent that his or her share of the partnership has not increased. Qualified stock acquired by exercising options or warrants, or converting debt, is deemed acquired at original issue.

The issuing corporation must be a domestic C corporation (other than a regulated investment company, cooperative, or other similar "pass-though" corporation). Both before and immediately after the qualified stock's issuance, the corporation must have aggregate gross assets that do not exceed $50 million. All corporations that are members of the same parent -subsidiary controlled group are treated as one corporation in applying this test. In addition, during substantially all of the taxpayer's holding period, at least 80 percent of the value of the corporation's assets must be used in the active conduct of one or more qualified trades or businesses. For this purpose, the performance of services in the fields of health, law, engineering, architecture, etc., will not be a qualified trade or business, nor are the hospitality, farming, insurance, finance or mineral extraction industries. However, a specialized small business investment company (SSBIC), licensed under section 301(d) of the Small Business Investment Act of 1958, will meet the active business test (¶ 1909).

1907. Rollover of Gain from Small Business Stock. A noncorporate taxpayer may elect to roll over capital gain from the sale of qualified small business stock (¶ 1905) held for more than six months if other qualified small business stock is purchased during the 60-day period beginning on the date of sale (Code Sec. 1045; Reg. § 1.1045-1).[9] The replacement stock must meet the active business requirement for the six-month period following its purchase. Except for purposes of determining the six-month active business test, the holding period of the stock purchased includes the holding period of the stock sold. Gain will only be recognized to the extent that the amount realized on the sale exceeds the cost of the replacement stock. The basis of the newly purchased stock must be reduced by the amount of gain rolled over. Special rules apply for partnerships or limited liability companies (LLCs) that want to roll over gain from a business that is held in the form of qualified small business stock. The sale of the stock is reported on Form 8949 (Schedule D of Form 1040 for tax years before 2011).

1909. Rollover of Gain from Publicly Traded Securities. Individuals and C corporations may elect to defer recognition of capital gain realized upon the sale of publicly traded securities if the sale proceeds are used within 60 days to purchase common stock or partnership interest in a specialized small business investment company (SSBIC) (Code Sec. 1044).[10] To the extent that the sale proceeds exceed the cost of the SSBIC common stock or partnership interest, gain must be recognized. For this purpose, an SSBIC is a partnership or corporation licensed under section 301(d) of the Small Business Investment Act of 1958 to finance small business concerns owned by disadvantaged persons.

An individual taxpayer (as well as married taxpayers filing a joint return) can roll over no more than $50,000 of gain in any given tax year or $500,000 during his or her lifetime ($25,000 or $250,000, respectively, for a married person filing separately). For C corporations, the annual and cumulative limits are $250,000 and $1 million, respectively. All corporations that are members of the same controlled group are treated as one taxpayer for this purpose, and any gain excluded by the predecessor of a C corporation is treated as gain excluded by the successor corporation. The deferred gain is reflected

References are to Standard Federal Tax Reports; Tax Research Consultant; and Practical Tax Explanations.

[9] ¶ 29,850, ¶ 29,852; SALES: 15,308, SALES: 27,450; § 16,610.05

[10] ¶ 29,845; SALES: 27,400; § 16,615, § 18,245

as a basis reduction. Basis is not reduced, however, when calculating gain eligible for the exclusion for qualified small business stock (¶ 1905).

The election to roll over gain into an SSBIC (which is revocable with IRS consent) must be made by the due date (including extensions) for the taxpayer's return for the year in which the publicly traded securities are sold. For individuals, the election is made by reporting the entire gain from the sale on Form 8949 (Schedule D of Form 1040 for tax years before 2011). A separate statement must also be attached showing: how the nonrecognized gain was calculated; the SSBIC in which the sale proceeds were invested; the date the SSBIC stock or partnership interest was purchased; and the basis of the SSBIC interest (Reg. § 1.1044(a)-1(b)).[11]

1911. Losses on Small Business Stock (Section 1244 Stock). A loss sustained on the sale, exchange, or worthlessness of small business stock (referred to as section 1244 stock) may be treated by an individual as an ordinary loss, even if the stock is a capital asset in the taxpayer's hands (Code Sec. 1244).[12] The maximum amount deductible as an ordinary loss in any tax year is $50,000 ($100,000 on a joint return). Any loss claimed as an ordinary loss is treated as a loss from a trade or business of the taxpayer in computing a net operating loss (NOL) for the tax year and reported on Form 4797. Any loss that the taxpayer has from section 1244 stock in excess of the dollar limits is treated as a capital loss and reported on Form 8949 (Schedule D of Form 1040 for tax years before 2011).

For stock to qualify as section 1244 stock, it must be stock of a domestic corporation (including preferred stock) issued after November 6, 1978, and meet the following requirements (additional requirements must be met for stock issued after June 30, 1958, and before November 7, 1978):

- the stock must have been issued to the taxpayer or a partnership in which the taxpayer was a partner at the time in exchange for money or property other than stock or securities;
- the issuing corporation must be a small business corporation, meaning that at the time the stock was issued the aggregate amount of money and other property (taken into account at its adjusted basis) received by the corporation as a contribution to capital and as a paid-in surplus (not only for the stock in question but any previously issued stock) did not exceed $1 million (qualification as a small business corporation under the S corporation rules does not automatically qualify its stock as section 1244 stock); and
- during the corporation's five most recent tax years ending before the date the stock is sold by the taxpayer, more than 50 percent of its gross receipts must have been derived from sources other than royalties, rents, dividends, interest, annuities, and gains from the sales of securities (the corporation must be largely an operating company, meaning that ordinary loss treatment is not available to corporations with little or no gross receipts) (Reg. §§ 1.1244(c)-1 and 1.1244(c)-2):[13]

1913. Losses on Small Business Investment Company Stock (SBIC). A loss sustained on the sale, exchange, or worthlessness of stock in a small business investment company (SBIC) (¶ 2392) may be treated by a taxpayer as an ordinary loss, even if the stock is a capital asset in the taxpayer's hands (Code Sec. 1242; Reg. § 1.1242-1(b)).[14] The SBIC must be licensed to operate as an SBIC at the time the loss is sustained by the taxpayer. In addition, the loss is not subject to the limitations on the allowance of nonbusiness deductions in computing net operating losses (NOLs). When a taxpayer has several transactions involving the stock of the SBIC, each transaction is considered separately to determine if the taxpayer's loss is an ordinary loss; transactions are not netted.

References are to Standard Federal Tax Reports; Tax Research Consultant; and Practical Tax Explanations.

[11] ¶ 29,845B; SALES: 27,402; § 16,615, § 18,245

[12] ¶ 30,790; SALES: 18,200; § 16,620.05

[13] ¶ 30,793, ¶ 30,794; SALES: 18,100; § 16,620.15

[14] ¶ 30,753, ¶ 30,754; SALES: 18,304; § 45,410.15

Worthless Securities

1916. Worthless Securities. A security that becomes completely worthless during the tax year is treated as sold or exchanged on the last day of the tax year at a loss (Code Sec. 165(g); Reg. § 1.165-5).[15] If the security is a capital asset, the loss is generally a capital loss subject to the limits on capital losses (¶ 1752). If the security is not a capital asset, the loss is an ordinary loss subject to the limits on ordinary losses (¶ 1101). The amount of the loss is the taxpayer's adjusted basis in the security, less any amount compensated for by insurance.

> **Example:** On December 10, 2011, Judy Green purchased shares of Xetco Corporation for $5,000. On May 1, 2012, she received formal notification that the shares of Xetco were worthless. In claiming a capital loss for the worthless shares on her 2012 tax return, Judy must treat the shares as becoming worthless on December 31, 2012. As a result, her $5,000 capital loss is recognized as long term even though she did not own the shares for more than 12 months before they became worthless.

A security becomes totally worthless when it has no value or potential value as the result of an identifiable event. The abandonment of a security establishes the worthlessness of the security to the taxpayer. To abandon a security, the taxpayer must permanently surrender and relinquish all rights in a security and receive no consideration for the exchange. Deductions for partial worthlessness are generally not allowed.

For this purpose, a security includes stock, the right to subscribe for or receive stock, and bonds, debentures, notes, certificates, or other evidence of indebtedness issued with interest coupons or in registered form by a corporation or government to pay a fixed or determinable sum of money. A worthless debt that does not meet the definition of a security (e.g., because it was not issued by a corporation or government) is treated as a bad debt (¶ 1145 and ¶ 1169).

Securities held by a securities dealer as inventory are not considered capital assets, and a loss from worthlessness is an ordinary loss (¶ 1903). An ordinary loss may also be claimed for losses from worthless securities that are section 1244 stock (¶ 1911), issued by a small business investment company (SBIC) (¶ 1913), held by a small business investment company (¶ 2392), securities in an affiliated corporation, or securities held by a bank (Code Sec. 582).[16]

Options

1919. Options to Buy or Sell Property. Gain or loss from the sale or exchange of an option to buy or sell property, including a cash settlement option and option on a section 1256 contract (¶ 1948), is considered gain or loss from the sale or exchange of the underlying property (Code Sec. 1234; Reg. § 1.1234-1).[17] Thus, a capital gain or loss results only if the option covers property which would be a capital asset in the hands of the taxpayer. The length of time the taxpayer held the option determines whether the capital gain or loss is short term or long term unless the sale or exchange is part of a hedging transaction (¶ 1949). If the underlying property is section 1231 property, then any gain or loss from the sale or exchange of the option may be section 1231 gain or loss (¶ 1747).

If the holder of an option incurs a loss from the failure to exercise the option, then the option is deemed to have been sold or exchanged on the date it expired. In the case of the grantor of an option for stock, securities, commodities, or commodity futures (including an option granted as part of a straddle (¶ 1948), gain or loss from any closing transaction and gain on the lapse of the option is treated as a short-term capital gain or loss. See ¶ 1921 for a discussion of holders and writers of options on securities (puts and calls).

The characterization rules above do not apply to gains or loss realized on the sale or exchange of an option by a dealer who holds options primarily for sale to customers

References are to Standard Federal Tax Reports; Tax Research Consultant; and Practical Tax Explanations.

[15] ¶ 9802, ¶ 10,000; BUSEXP: 30,262; § 16,935

[16] ¶ 23,608; BUSEXP: 48,154; § 16,935

[17] ¶ 30,610, ¶ 30,611; SALES: 45,202; § 19,110, § 19,115

(¶ 1903). They also do not apply to gain realized from the sale or exchange of an employee stock option (¶ 1925 and ¶ 1927), an option to lease property, an option to buy or sell inventory, an option equivalent to a dividend, an option involving section 306 stock (¶ 739), and an option included as part of a short sale (¶ 1944).

1921. Puts and Calls. Puts are options to sell, and calls are options to buy, stock, securities, or commodities at a set price on or before a specified date. Puts and calls are issued by writers (grantors) to holders for premiums. They end when the option is exercised by the holder, the option lapses, or due to a closing transaction (Rev. Rul. 78-182; IRS Pub. 550).[18]

Holders of Puts and Calls. The purchase of a put option or call option is not a taxable event. The cost of purchasing the put or call, however, is a nondeductible capital expenditure (Rev. Rul. 71-521).[19] If the holder sells a put or call without exercising it, the difference between its cost and the amount received is either a long-term or short-term capital gain or loss, depending on how long it was held (¶ 1919). If the option expires, its cost is either a long-term or short-term capital loss, depending on the taxpayer's holding period, which ends on the expiration date. If the holder exercises a call, its cost is added to the basis of the security purchased. If the holder exercises a put, the amount realized on the sale of the underlying security is reduced by the cost of the put when computing gain or loss on the sale of the stock. That gain or loss is long term or short term depending on the taxpayer's holding period for the underlying security (Rev. Rul. 78-182; IRS Pub. 550). The acquisition of a put is considered a short sale, and the exercise, sale, or lapse of the put is a closing of the short sale (¶ 1944).

Writers of Puts and Calls. If a taxpayer writes or grants a call or put, the premium received is not included in income at the time of receipt. Instead it is deferred until the option expires, the writer buys or sells the underlying security when the option is exercised, or the writer engages in a closed transaction. When the option expires, the premium can then be treated as a short-term capital gain. If a call is exercised and the writer sells the underlying security, then the premium is added to the amount realized on the sale and any gain or loss is long-term or short-term depending on the writer's holding period of the security. If a put is exercised and the writer buys the underlying security, then the premium reduces its basis in the security. The writer's holding period on the security begins on the date of the purchase, not on the date the put was written. The writer can also terminate a put or call through a closing transaction—such as repurchasing the option or substituting the original option by purchasing another option with identical terms. If the writer closes the transaction, the difference between the premium originally received and the amount paid in the closing transaction is short-term capital gain or loss.

> **Example 1:** Ten call options were issued on April 8 for $4,000. These equity options expired in December without being exercised. The holder (buyer) of the options recognizes a short-term capital loss of $4,000. The writer of the options recognizes a short-term capital gain of $4,000.

> **Example 2:** Assume the same facts as in Example 1, except that on May 10 the options were sold for $6,000. The holder (buyer) of the options who sold them recognizes a short-term capital gain of $2,000. If the writer of the options bought them back, he would recognize a short-term capital loss of $2,000.

> **Example 3:** Assume the facts as in Example 1, except that the options were exercised on May 27. The holder (buyer) adds the cost of the options to the basis of the stock bought through the exercise of the options. The writer adds the amount received from writing the options to the amount realized from selling the stock.

1923. Nonstatutory Stock Options. An employee or independent contractor granted a stock option as compensation for the performance of services is generally subject to the restricted property rules of Code Sec. 83 (¶ 713) when the option is

References are to Standard Federal Tax Reports; Tax Research Consultant; and Practical Tax Explanations.

[18] ¶ 30,614.14; SALES: 45,200; § 19,105

[19] ¶ 30,592.70; SALES: 45,202; § 19,120

granted or exercised, unless it is an incentive stock option (ISO) (¶ 1925) or option granted under an employee stock purchase plan (ESPP) (¶ 1929).[20]

An option with a readily ascertainable fair market value when granted is subject to the restricted property rules on the grant date. The taxpayer has ordinary income equal to the fair market value of the option on the grant date or when substantially vested, less any amount paid. An option without a readily ascertainable fair market value when granted is subject to the restricted property rules when it is exercised or disposed of by the taxpayer, even if the fair market value becomes ascertainable before the option is exercised or disposed. If the option is exercised, the taxpayer has ordinary income equal to the stock's fair market value at the exercise date or when substantially vested, less the exercise price.

If a stock option is sold or disposed in an arm's-length transaction, the taxpayer has income equal to the amount of money or property received, less the exercise price. If the sale or disposition is not an arm's-length transaction, the taxpayer also has income equal to the amount of money or property received. In addition, when the transferee exercises the option, the taxpayer (transferor) has income equal to the fair market value of stock acquired by the transferee, less the exercise price and any amount the taxpayer received from the sale. A sale or disposition of a nonstatutory stock option to a related person is not treated as an arm's-length transaction for this purpose. If the holder of an option incurs a loss on failure to exercise the option, then it is deemed to have been sold or exchanged on the date it expired (¶ 1919).

Readily Ascertainable Market Value. A stock option generally has a readily ascertainable fair market value if it is actively traded on an established securities market (Reg. § 1.83-7(b)).[21] Even if the option is not actively traded on an established securities market, it will be considered to have a readily ascertainable value if the taxpayer can demonstrate that the option is transferable, immediately exercisable, there is no condition or restriction on the underlying property that would have a significant effect on its fair market value, and the fair market value of the option privilege is readily ascertainable.

Sale of Stock. Stock acquired through the exercise of a nonstatutory stock option is treated as any other investment property when sold or exchanged. The taxpayer's basis in the stock is the amount paid for the stock, plus any amount included in income upon grant or exercise of the option. The taxpayer's holding period begins when the option was acquired if it had a readily ascertainable value, or the date the option was exercised if it did not.

Employer's Deduction. An employer may deduct the value of a nonqualified stock option as a business expense for the tax year in which the option is included in the gross income of the employee (Code Sec. 83(h); Reg. § 1.83-7(a)).[22] When the employer and the employee have different tax years, the employer generally claims the deduction in the tax year in which or with which the employee's tax year ends. If the option's market value, however, is not readily ascertainable at the time of grant, and the employee's rights in the stock are substantially vested upon exercise, the employer may take the deduction in accordance with its usual method of accounting (Reg. § 1.83-6(a)(3)).

Reporting Requirements. In most situations, when an employee exercises a nonqualified stock option, the employer is required to report the excess of the fair market value of the stock received over the amount that the employee paid for that stock (i.e., "the spread") on Form W-2.

References are to Standard Federal Tax Reports; Tax Research Consultant; and Practical Tax Explanations.

[20] ¶ 6380, ¶ 6388; COMPEN: 18,500; § 21,701

[21] ¶ 6388; COMPEN: 18,502, COMPEN: 18,504; § 21,710.05

[22] ¶ 6380, ¶ 6388; COMPEN: 18,508; § 21,720

1925. Incentive Stock Options. An incentive stock option (ISO) is an option granted by a corporation (or related corporation) to an employee giving him or her the right to purchase stock of the employer, often at a discount. Unlike a nonstatutory stock option (¶ 1923), if certain requirements are met, no gain or loss is generally realized by the employee when an ISO is granted or exercised (Code Sec. 421(a)).[23] Instead, the employee is not subject to income tax until shares acquired by the exercise of the option are sold. See ¶ 1927 for a discussion of ISO plan requirements.

Gain or loss from the sale of the stock received in an ISO is a capital gain or loss if: (1) the taxpayer does not dispose of the stock for at least two years from the date on which the option is granted, and (2) the stock is held for at least one year after the option is exercised (Code Sec. 422(a); Reg. § 1.422-1(a)).[24] The amount of gain or loss is the difference between the amount the optionee paid for the stock (the option price) and the amount the optionee received when he sold the stock. The employee must remain an employee of the corporation from the time the option is granted until three months before the option is exercised (one year if the employee ceased employment because of permanent and total disability). In the event the holder of an ISO dies, the deceased's executor, administrator, or representative may exercise the option but he or she does not have to exercise the option within three months after the death of the employee (Reg. § 1.421-2(c)).

If the employee sells the stock before the required holding period ends (a disqualifying disposition), gain on the sale is ordinary income equal to the fair market value of the stock when the option was exercised, less the exercise price (Code Sec. 421(b); Reg. § 1.421-2(b)).[25] Any excess gain is capital gain, and any loss is a capital loss. The gain is recognized for the tax year in which the sale occurs and any gain from a disqualifying disposition is excluded from wages for FICA and FUTA tax purposes and is not subject to income tax withholding.

Basis of ISO. An employee's basis in an ISO is the amount that the employee paid for the option. If the employee did not pay for the option and the option lapses, the employee does not have a deductible loss because he or she does not have a basis. An employee's basis in stock purchased through an ISO is the amount he paid for the stock when the option was exercised (plus any amount he paid for the option).

Annual Dollar Limit. The maximum value of stock with respect to which ISOs may first become exercisable in any one year is $100,000. Stock is valued when the option is granted. Options are ordered in the order in which they are granted, and options issued under ISO plans of any parent, subsidiaries, or predecessor corporations are taken into account (Code Sec. 422(d)).[26]

Alternative Minimum Tax (AMT). The favorable tax treatment of ISOs does not apply for purposes of the AMT. Instead, the *excess* of the (1) fair market value of the stock received upon the exercise of the option, over (2) the amount paid for the stock, plus any amount paid for the ISO, must generally be recognized as an AMT adjustment (Code Sec. 56(b)(3)).[27] As a result, individuals who have exercised ISOs to purchase stock with a high fair market value which declined before they could sell it are left with large AMT liabilities and no cash to pay them. See ¶ 1435 for information concerning the required AMT computations.

1927. Incentive Stock Options Plan Requirements. A stock option granted by an employer to an employee must satisfy several requirements to qualify for favorable tax treatment as an incentive stock option (ISO) (¶ 1925) (Code Sec. 422(b); Reg. § 1.422-2).[28] ISOs must be granted under a plan adopted by the granting corporation and approved by its shareholders that sets out the total number of shares that may be issued under options and the employees who may receive the options. The plan must be approved by the stockholders within 12 months before or after the date such plan is adopted.

References are to Standard Federal Tax Reports; Tax Research Consultant; and Practical Tax Explanations.

[23] ¶ 19,602; COMPEN: 24,050; § 21,510

[24] ¶ 19,800, ¶ 19,801A; COMPEN: 24,150; § 21,525.05

[25] ¶ 19,602, ¶ 19,609; COMPEN: 24,056, COMPEN: 24,154; § 21,530.10

[26] ¶ 19,800; COMPEN: 24,116; § 21,515.40

[27] ¶ 5200; COMPEN: 24,054; § 15,245

[28] ¶ 19,800, ¶ 19,801C; COMPEN: 24,100; § 21,515.05

The options must be granted within 10 years from the date the plan is adopted or approved, whichever is earlier. Further, the options must be exercisable within 10 years from the date of the grant. The option price may not be less than the fair market value of the stock at the time the option is granted, and the option may not be transferable other than at the grantee's death. The option may be exercised only by the employee. Finally, the employee, *at the time the option is granted*, may not own stock with more than 10 percent of the total combined voting power of all classes of stock of the employer corporation or its parent or any subsidiary.

1929. Employee Stock Purchase Plans. An employee stock purchase plan (ESPP) may grant employees the option to purchase stock in their employer or the employer's parent or subsidiary. Unlike a nonstatutory stock option (¶ 1923), if certain requirements are met, no gain or loss is generally realized by the employee when an option is granted or exercised under an ESPP (Code Sec. 421(a)).[29] Instead, the employee is not subject to income tax until shares acquired by the exercise of the option are sold. See ¶ 1931 for a discussion of ESPP plan requirements.

Gain or loss from the sale of the stock received in an ESPP is a capital gain or loss if: (1) the taxpayer does not dispose of the stock for at a least two years from the date on which the option is granted, and (2) the stock is held for at least one year after the option is exercised (Code Sec. 423(a)).[30] The amount of gain or loss is the difference between the amount the optionee paid for the stock (the option price) and the amount the optionee received when he sold the stock. The employee must remain an employee of the corporation from the time the option is granted until three months before the option is exercised (one year if the employee ceased employment because of permanent and total disability). In the event the holder of an ISO dies, the deceased's executor, administrator, or representative may exercise the option but he or she does not have to exercise the option within three months after the death of the employee (Reg. § 1.421-2(c)).

If the option price is less than the fair market value of the stock at the time the option is granted, then the favorable tax treatment does not apply when the taxpayer disposes of the stock. Instead, the employee recognizes ordinary income in the amount of the *lesser* of:

- the difference between the fair market value of the shares when sold (or the fair market value of the shares at the employee's death while owning the shares) and the option price for the shares, or

- the difference between the option price and the fair market value of the shares when the option was granted.

The balance of any gain is treated as capital gain. If the taxpayer realizes any loss from the sale, then it is a capital loss (Code Sec. 423(c)).[31] Withholding is not required with respect to amounts taxable under these rules.

An ESPP is different from an employee stock ownership plan (ESOP). While both plans involve employee ownership of company stock, an ESOP is a retirement plan that holds employer stock for the benefit of participating employees. For information on ESOPs, see ¶ 2111.

1931. Employee Stock Purchase Plan Requirements. An employee stock purchase plan (ESPP) must satisfy several requirements in order for options acquired under the plan to qualify for favorable tax treatment (¶ 1929) (Code Sec. 423).[32] ESPPs are written, shareholder-approved plans under which employees are granted options to purchase shares of their employer's stock or the stock of a parent or subsidiary corporation.

References are to Standard Federal Tax Reports; Tax Research Consultant; and Practical Tax Explanations.

[29] ¶ 19,602; COMPEN: 21,050; § 21,601

[30] ¶ 19,900; COMPEN: 21,054; § 21,625.10

[31] ¶ 19,900; COMPEN: 21,054.10; § 21,625.10

[32] ¶ 19,900; COMPEN: 21,052; § 21,610.05

An ESPP cannot grant options to any employee who has more than five percent of the voting power or value of the employer's stock, or that of any parent or subsidiary of the employer. All full-time employees must be included in the plan, except those with less than two years of employment, highly compensated employees (¶ 2117), part-time employees, and seasonal workers. The plan must be nondiscriminatory, though it may limit the amount of stock any employee can buy, and the amount of stock that each employee may become entitled to buy may be tied to compensation.

The option price may not be less than the *lesser* of 85 percent of: (1) the fair market value of the stock at the time the option is granted, or (2) the fair market value of the stock at the time the option is exercised. The option cannot be exercised later than 27 months from the date the option is granted (or five years from the date the option is granted, if the option price is based on the fair market value of the stock at the time the option is exercised). No employee can acquire the right to buy more than $25,000 of stock per year (valued at the time the option is granted).

Wash Sales

1935. Wash Sales of Stock or Securities. Under the wash sale rules, a taxpayer who realizes a loss upon a sale or other disposition of stock or securities may not claim a deduction for the loss unless the loss is incurred in the ordinary course of a trade or business as a securities dealer (¶ 1903) (Code Sec. 1091; Reg. § 1.1091-1).[33] A wash sale occurs if the taxpayer sells or disposes of the stock or securities, and within 30 days before or after that date (the 61-day period) the taxpayer acquires, or enters into a contract or option to acquire, substantially identical stock or securities (¶ 1937). The acquisition of substantially identical stock or securities through a traditional IRA or Roth IRA cannot be used to avoid the wash sale rule (Rev. Rul. 2008-5).

A loss realized on the closing of a short sale of stock or securities (¶ 1944) is similarly disallowed if within 30 days before or after the closing of the sale substantially identical stock or securities are sold or another short sale of substantially identical stock or securities is entered. The wash sale rules also apply to a loss realized on the sale, exchange, or termination of a securities futures contract to sell stock or securities. The disallowance of a loss under the wash sales rule does not apply to stock or securities acquired in nontaxable exchange. This includes stock or securities acquired by gift, bequest, or devise, or through gain nonrecognition transactions, including like-kind exchanges, exchanges of property for stock, exchanges of stock for stock, and spousal transfers incident to divorce. The wash sale rules also do not apply to any loss attributable to a section 1256 contract (Code Sec. 1256(f)(5)).

When a loss is disallowed because of the wash sales rules, the disallowed loss is added to the cost of the new stock or securities (unless the new stock or securities are acquired through an IRA). The result is the taxpayer's basis in the new stock or securities. This adjustment postpones the loss deduction until the disposition of the new stock or securities (Code Sec. 1091(d); Reg. § 1.1091-2).[34] The taxpayer's holding period of the new stock or securities includes the holding period of the stock or securities sold (Code Sec. 1223(3)).[35]

> **Example:** Betty buys 100 shares of Rapid Corporation stock for $1,000 on January 1, 2011. She sells these shares on January 2, 2012, for $750 and within 30 days from the sale Betty buys another 100 shares of Rapid Corporation for $800. Because Betty purchased substantially identical stock, she cannot deduct the $250 loss that she realized on the sale. Betty, however, adds the disallowed loss of $250 to the cost of her new shares. As a result, her basis in the new shares is $1,050 ($800 cost, plus the $250 loss she could not claim under the wash sale rules). If she sells the new shares on March 31, 2012, any gain is long-term capital gain.

References are to Standard Federal Tax Reports; Tax Research Consultant; and Practical Tax Explanations.

33 ¶ 30,180, ¶ 30,181; SALES: 45,150; § 18,905

34 ¶ 30,180, ¶ 30,182; SALES: 45,164; § 18,920

35 ¶ 30,460; SALES: 45,164; § 18,925

The wash sale rules apply without regard to the gain or loss realized on the sale of separate lots of the same stock or security. Thus, where the wash sale provisions apply to deny deductions for losses for one lot, any gain realized on a separate lot is not reduced by the losses (Rev. Rul. 70-231).[36] In addition, the wash sales rule does not specifically apply when stock is sold at a loss and a party related to the seller, such as his or her spouse, reacquires the stock within the prohibited 61-day period. The loss, however, may be disallowed under the related party rules of Code Sec. 267 (¶ 1717), on the ground that there is an indirect sale to the spouse (*J. P. McWilliams*, SCt, 47-1 USTC ¶ 9289).[37]

1937. Substantially Identical Stock or Securities. In determining whether stock or securities are substantially identical subject to the wash sales rule (¶ 1935), all facts and circumstances must be considered. Ordinarily, stocks or securities of one corporation are not considered substantially identical to stocks or securities of another corporation. They may, however, be substantially identical in some cases such as in a reorganization—the stocks and securities of the predecessor and successor corporations may be substantially identical (IRS Pub. 550).

Bonds or preferred stock of a corporation are not ordinarily considered substantially identical to the common stock of the same corporation. When the bonds or preferred stock are convertible into common stock of the same corporation, however, the relative values, price changes, and other circumstances may make these bonds or preferred stock and the common stock substantially identical (Rev. Rul. 77-201).[38]

1942. Share Lending Agreements. No gain or loss is recognized by a taxpayer on an exchange of securities if the exchange is made as part of a qualifying securities lending arrangement in which the taxpayer transfers the securities and later receives identical securities in return (Code Sec. 1058).[39] In effect, the taxpayer is merely lending securities to the other party to the transaction. This provision is designed to mitigate delays that a broker may face in obtaining securities by allowing the broker to borrow securities without creating tax consequences for the lender. However, the provision is available to any taxpayer that lends securities, not just those that lend to brokers. This treatment applies only if the securities lending agreement requires the borrower to return securities to the taxpayer that are identical to those which were lent. The taxpayer's basis in the securities received is the same as the taxpayer's basis in the securities that were loaned to the borrower.

Short Sales

1944. Short Sales. A short sale occurs when a taxpayer, expecting certain property to decline in value, enters into an agreement to sell that property, which he or she does not own (or owns but does not want to sell). In a short sale the taxpayer sells short by (1) borrowing property (e.g., shares of stock) and delivering it to the buyer, and (2) at a later date, purchasing similar property and delivering it to the original lender ("covering" or "closing" the transaction) (Code Sec. 1233(a); Reg. § 1.1233-1(a)).[40] Generally, the seller does not recognize gain or loss on the transaction until he or she delivers the property to the lender and the short sale is closed. If property that has been sold short becomes substantially worthless, however, the short seller must at that time recognize gain on the short sale, regardless of whether the short sale has been closed by the short seller's return of the borrowed property. In addition, entering a short sale may cause the taxpayer to be treated as making a constructive sale, in which case gain will have to be recognized (¶ 1945).

The gain or loss on a closed short sale is the difference between the amount realized on the sale of the borrowed property and the taxpayer's adjusted basis in the property used to close the transaction. Generally, the character of that gain or loss is

References are to Standard Federal Tax Reports; Tax Research Consultant; and Practical Tax Explanations.

[36] ¶ 30,183.11; SALES: 45,160; § 18,930

[37] ¶ 30,183.109; SALES: 45,166.10

[38] ¶ 30,183.14; SALES: 45,154; § 18,915

[39] ¶ 30,000; SALES: 3,302.35; § 18,855

[40] ¶ 30,590, ¶ 30,591; SALES: 45,100; § 19,001

determined by reference to the character of the property used to close the sale in the hands of the taxpayer. Thus, a taxpayer will have capital gain or loss if the property used to close the short sale is a capital asset. Hedging transactions, however, generally result in ordinary income or loss (¶ 1949). If a short seller has a gain on the transaction when the replacement property is purchased, the gain is recognized at that time. A loss is not recognized until the replacement property is delivered to the lender (Rev. Rul. 2002-44).

Holding Period. Generally, short sellers determine whether they have a short-term or long-term capital gain or loss by determining the amount of time they held the property that they deliver to the lender.

> **Example:** On January 2, Mary Edwards enters into an agreement to sell 100 shares of Niftexo Corporation for $10 a share to Susan Croft. Mary does not own any Niftexo shares, so she borrows the 100 shares from her broker and delivers these shares to Susan. On May 1, Mary purchases 100 shares of Niftexo at a price of $15 a share. The same day she delivers these shares to her broker in order to replace the shares she had borrowed. Her recognized loss of $500 is short term because her holding period of the Niftexo shares is determined by the amount of time she held the shares (i.e., less than one day).

Gain from short sale of a capital asset is short-term capital gain, however, if the taxpayer owned substantially identical property for one year or less on the date of the short sale, or if the taxpayer acquired substantially identical property after the short sale and by the date the sale is closed. The holding period of the substantially identical property begins on the closing of the short sale or on the date the property is sold, whichever happens first (Code Sec. 1233(b); Reg. § 1.1233-1(c)).[41]

In addition, any loss realized on the short sale of a capital asset is a long-term capital loss if the taxpayer owned substantially identical property for more than one year (Code Sec. 1233(d)). The loss is long term even when the property used to close the short sale is held by the seller for one year or less. A taxpayer can avoid the prohibition of losses from short sale if the position is part of a mixed straddle (¶ 1948). Special holding period rules apply to brokers' arbitrage transactions (Code Sec. 1233(f); Reg. § 1.1233-1(f)).[42] Losses on short sales of stock or securities are also subject to the wash sales rule (¶ 1935).

1945. Constructive Sale Treatment of Short Sales. In the past, certain hedging strategies such as short sales against the box, forward contracts, and notional principal contracts could be used to lock in gains on appreciated financial positions without immediate recognition of income. The rules under Code Sec. 1259, however, limit these strategies by treating certain hedging transactions as "constructive sales" (Code Sec. 1259(a)).[43]

If there is a constructive sale of an appreciated financial position, the taxpayer must recognize gain as if the position were sold, assigned, or otherwise terminated at its fair market value *as of the date of the constructive sale* and immediately repurchased. Any gain or loss subsequently realized on the position is adjusted to reflect gain recognized on the constructive sale. The taxpayer's holding period begins as if the taxpayer had first acquired the position on the date of the constructive sale.

An appreciated financial position is generally any position with respect to any stock, debt instrument, or partnership interest if there would be gain if the position were sold, assigned, or otherwise terminated at its fair market value (Code Sec. 1259(b)). It does not include any position that is subject to mark-to-market requirements, including section 1256 contracts (¶ 1948). It also does not include any position or hedge of a position with regard to straight debt if:

References are to Standard Federal Tax Reports; Tax Research Consultant; and Practical Tax Explanations.

[41] ¶ 30,590, ¶ 30,591; SALES: 45,104; § 19,010.10

[42] ¶ 30,590, ¶ 30,591; SALES: 45,112

[43] ¶ 31,130; SALES: 45,450; § 18,801

• the debt unconditionally entitles the holder to receive a specified principal amount;

• interest payments are payable based on a fixed rate or, to the extent provided in regulations, at a variable rate; and

• the debt is not convertible into stock of the issuer or any related person.

A constructive sale generally is one of four specified types of transactions offsetting an appreciated financial position that has the effect of substantially eliminating both the taxpayer's risk of loss and chance for further gain on the position: short sale, notional principal contracts, forward or futures contracts or, if the appreciated position is itself a short position, the purchase of property to cover the position (Code Sec. 1259(c)). Contracts for the sale of appreciated financial assets that are not publicly traded are excluded from the definition of a constructive sale if the contract settles within one year after the date it was entered. A safe harbor is also provided for certain short-term hedges that would otherwise be treated as constructive sales if three conditions are satisfied:

• the transaction is closed on or before the end of the 30th day after the end of the tax year in which the transaction was entered;

• the taxpayer holds the appreciated financial position throughout the 60-day period beginning on the date the transaction is closed; and

• at no time during that 60-day period is the taxpayer's risk of loss with respect to the position reduced by a circumstance that would be described in Code Sec. 246(c)(4) if references to stock included references to such position.

The "closed transaction" exception also applies to certain reestablished positions.

1946. Payments in Lieu of Dividends on Short Sales. A taxpayer who borrows stock to make a short sale (¶ 1944) may have to make payments to the lender in lieu of dividends distributed during the short position. The payments may be deductible as investment interest expense as an itemized deduction (¶ 1094) if the short sale is held open for at least 46 days (one year if extraordinary dividends are involved). If the short sale is closed by the 45th day after the date of the short sale (one year or less in the case of an extraordinary dividend), the short seller cannot claim the deduction and must instead increase the basis of the stock used to close the short sale by the amount of the payment (Code Sec. 263(h)).[44] The 45-day and one-year periods are suspended for any period in which the borrower holds options to buy substantially identical property or holds one or more positions in such property.

Straddles and Hedging Transactions

1948. Tax Straddles. A tax straddle is a combination of offsetting long and short positions in futures, options, or other actively traded personal property that substantially diminishes an investor's risk of loss on either of the positions in the straddle. For this purpose, personal property includes stock if it is actively traded or used by a corporation to offset positions taken by a shareholder. Taxpayers are generally prevented from using straddles to defer income or to convert short-term capital gain into long-term capital gain. Losses incurred on sales of actively traded personal property, including most stock, are deferred to the extent that the taxpayer had gains in offsetting positions that were not closed out by year-end (Code Sec. 1092).[45] The loss deferral rule does not apply if a straddle is identified on the taxpayer's books, in which case a loss realized on any position in the straddle is reflected by increasing the basis of offsetting positions in the straddle, starting with those that have unrecognized straddle period gain. The loss deferral rule also does not apply to hedging transactions (¶ 1949) or straddles consisting entirely of qualified covered call options. The reporting of straddle positions is done on Form 6781.

A taxpayer may elect out of these rules for mixed straddles, which are straddles in which at least one but not all of the positions are section 1256 contracts. A section 1256

References are to Standard Federal Tax Reports; Tax Research Consultant; and Practical Tax Explanations.

[44] ¶ 13,700; SALES: 45,118.05; § 19,015

[45] ¶ 30,200; SALES: 48,150; § 45,425.30

contract includes regulated futures contracts, foreign currency contracts, nonequity options, dealer equity options, and dealer securities futures contracts. Generally, section 1256 contracts are subject to a mark-to-market requirement and are treated as if they were sold on the last day of the year. Any capital gains or losses arising under this rule are treated as if they were 60 percent long-term and 40 percent short-term without regard to the actual holding period (Code Sec. 1256).[46] The mark-to-market rules do not apply to hedging transactions or equity options. Taxpayers are prohibited from converting ordinary income into capital gains through the use of straddle transactions if substantially all the taxpayer's expected return is attributable to the time value of net investment (¶ 1740). These rules generally do not apply to the normal trade of options dealers (¶ 1903).

1949. Hedging Transactions. A hedging transaction is one a taxpayer enters into in the normal course of business primarily to reduce the risk of changes in interest rates, price changes, or currency fluctuations (Code Sec. 1221(a)(7); Reg. § 1.1221-2).[47] Generally, the property involved in a hedging transaction is not classified as a capital asset. As a result, gain or loss on most hedging transactions is classified as ordinary income or loss. This rule also applies when a short sale or option is part of a hedging transaction. In order to be classified as a hedging transaction, the transaction must be entered into in the normal course of the taxpayer's business in order to manage risk. The determination of whether a transaction was entered into in order to manage the taxpayer's business risk is based upon all the facts and circumstances. A transaction that is not a hedging transaction may be a straddle (¶ 1948).

Identification. The hedging transaction must be identified before the close of the day on which the taxpayer entered into the transaction (Reg. § 1.1221-2(f)). The taxpayer must identify the property that is being hedged within 35 days after the transaction is entered into. The taxpayer's identification of the hedged property must be unambiguous and become part of the taxpayer's books and records.

Corporate Bonds and Other Debt Instruments

1950. Discounts, Premiums, and Issue Expenses of Corporate Bonds. The tax effects to a corporation from the issuance of bonds and from the reacquisition of such bonds depends upon whether the bonds are issued at face value, at a discount, or at a premium. A corporation generally does not realize gain or loss upon the issuance of bond or other debt instrument (Reg. § 1.61-12(c)).[48] If, however, a corporation repurchases a bond for less than its adjusted issue price, then it will realize income from the discharge of indebtedness (¶ 885). In the case of a bond repurchased at a discount during 2009 or 2010, the corporation can elect to defer the discharge of indebtedness income and recognize it ratably over a five-year period beginning in 2014 and through 2018 (Code Sec. 108(i)).[49]

In the case of bonds issued at a discount, the discount is amortized and deductible by the corporation over the life of the bond. If bonds are issued at a premium on or after March 2, 1998, the amount of the premium is amortized as an offset to the corporation's otherwise allowable interest deduction with the portion of bond premium allocable to the accrual period (Reg. § 1.163-13(a)).[50] The bond premium is allocable to an accrual period based on constant yield. Any amount allocable to a bond's conversion feature is not part of the bond premium (Code Sec. 171(b)(1)).[51] See ¶ 1967 for the tax treatment of a premium paid by the buyer of a bond. Any expenses related to issuing the bond (i.e., printing, advertising, legal fees) are amortized over the life of the bond and deducted as business expenses.[52]

References are to Standard Federal Tax Reports; Tax Research Consultant; and Practical Tax Explanations.

[46] ¶ 31,100; SALES: 48,100; § 18,830.05

[47] ¶ 30,420, ¶ 30,424; SALES: 15,114, SALES: 48,250; § 16,505.40

[48] ¶ 5,801; CCORP: 3,158; § 3,401

[49] ¶ 7002; SALES: 12,252; § 3,420.40

[50] ¶ 9,302D; BUSEXP: 21,214

[51] ¶ 11,850; CCORP: 3,154; § 11,530

[52] ¶ 5804.22; CCORP: 3,156; § 19,350

1952. Original Issue Discount. Any holder of any debt instrument that has an original issue discount (OID) must include in gross income an amount equal to the sum of the daily portions of the OID for each day during the tax year on which the holder held the debt instrument (Code Sec. 1272).[53] The basis of the debt instrument in the hands of the holder is increased by the amount required to be included in gross income. The OID requirement does not apply to short-term obligations with a fixed maturity of less than one year, tax-exempt obligations, U.S. savings bonds, and certain loans between natural persons. It also does not apply to any holder who has purchased the debt instrument at a premium or to any holder that is a life insurance company.

OID on a debt instrument is the excess of the stated redemption price at maturity over the issue price (Code Sec. 1273).[54] If the difference is less than 0.25 percent of the redemption price, multiplied by the number of full years from the date of issue to the date of maturity, the OID is zero. The determination of the issue price depends on whether the debt instrument is issued for property and whether the instrument or the property is publicly traded. See ¶ 1954 for a discussion of determining OID of certain debt instruments issued for the sale or exchange of property where payments are due more than six months after the date of the sale or exchange.

Interest Deduction. In the case of any debt instrument issued after July 1, 1982, the portion of OID allowable as a deduction to the issuer for any tax year is equal to the aggregate daily portions of the OID for days during that tax year (Code Sec. 163(e)).[55] The daily portions of OID for any day is determined by allocating to each day in any accrual period a ratable portion of the increase during the accrual period in the adjusted issue price of the debt instrument (Code Sec. 1272(a)(3)).[56]

Information Statement for Recipients. Any issuer with any bond outstanding or any other evidence of indebtedness in registered form issued at a discount must generally furnish the holder and the IRS with an information statement (Form 1099-OID) for the calendar year if there is OID of at least $10 (Code Sec. 6049).[57]

Stripped Bonds and Stripped Coupons. Special rules govern stripped bonds and stripped coupons purchased or sold after July 1, 1982 (Code Sec. 1286(a)).[58] Under this type of arrangement, one taxpayer strips an interest coupon from a bond and sells either the bond or the coupon. The bond and the coupon are treated as separate debt instruments issued with OID. The buyer of a stripped bond treats as OID the bond's value at maturity minus the price paid by the buyer. The buyer of a stripped coupon treats as OID the interest to be paid on the due date of the coupon minus the price paid by the buyer.

The seller of the stripped coupon or stripped bond must include in income the interest that accrued before the date of sale that was not previously included in income. Market discount must also be included in the seller's income. Both of these included items increase the seller's basis in the bond and coupons. The seller then allocates this adjusted basis between the item kept (e.g., the bond) and the item sold (e.g., the coupon) based on the fair market value of the items. The difference between the sales price of the item and its adjusted basis is the seller's gain or loss.

Stripped Stock. Preferred stock purchased after April 30, 1993, that has been stripped of some or all of its dividend rights is treated in the same manner as stripped bonds. OID is equal to the stated redemption price minus the amount paid for the stock (Code Sec. 305(e)).[59]

Tax-Exempt and Stripped Tax-Exempt Bonds. OID on a tax-exempt bond is generally treated as tax-exempt interest. However, when a tax-exempt bond is stripped, only a portion of the OID is treated as coming from a tax-exempt obligation. The balance is treated as OID on a taxable obligation. The Code contains the rules for determining the tax-exempt portion of the OID (Code Sec. 1286(d)).[60] See ¶ 1956 for related information.

References are to Standard Federal Tax Reports; Tax Research Consultant; and Practical Tax Explanations.

[53] ¶ 31,260; ACCTNG: 36,200; § 19,310.05
[54] ¶ 31,280; ACCTNG: 36,100; § 19,315.05
[55] ¶ 9102; BUSEXP: 21,102; § 7,405.20
[56] ¶ 31,260; ACCTNG: 36,214; § 19,310.10
[57] ¶ 36,020; ACCTNG: 36,550; § 19,320.10
[58] ¶ 31,480; ACCTNG: 36,350; § 19,335
[59] ¶ 15,400; ACCTNG: 36,356
[60] ¶ 31,480; ACCTNG: 36,500; § 19,335

1954. Original Issue Discount for Debt Instruments Issued for Property. In determining the original issue discount (OID) of certain debt instruments issued for property (¶ 1952), the issue price may be determined by the stated principal amount of the instrument when there is adequate stated interest, or the imputed principal amount if there is not adequately stated interest (Code Sec. 1274).[61] This rule applies to debt instruments given in consideration for the sale or exchange of property if: (1) the stated redemption price at maturity exceeds either the stated principal amount (when there is adequate stated interest) or the imputed principal amount; and (2) some or all of the payments due under the instrument are due more than six months after the date of the sale or exchange. The rule does not apply to:

- sales for $250,000 or less;
- sales of principal residences covered by Code Sec. 121 (¶ 1705);
- sales of farms by individuals, estates, testamentary trusts, or small business corporations or partnerships for $1 million or less;
- land transfers between related parties that are covered by Code Sec. 483(e);
- sales of patents for amounts that are contingent on the productivity, use, or disposition of the property transferred; or
- in the case of the borrower, sales or exchanges of personal use property (Code Sec. 1275(b)).[62]

If a debt-for-property transaction is not covered by these rules, the transaction may be subject to the imputed interest rules of Code Sec. 483 (¶ 1868). In addition, certain annuity contracts governed by Code Sec. 72 are excluded from the definition of "debt instrument" (Code Secs. 1274(c)(3) and 1275(a)(1)(B)).[63]

Adequately Stated Interest. A debt instrument generally provides for adequately stated interest if it's stated principal amount is at least equal to the sum of the present value of all principal and interest payments due on the instrument—referred to as the imputed principal amount (Code Sec. 1274(c)). The present value of all payments due on the instrument is determined based on the lowest applicable federal rate (AFR) in effect in the three-month period (1) ending with the first month in which there is a binding written contract, or (2) ending with the month in which the sale or exchange occurred (Code Sec. 1274(d)). The AFR is determined by reference to the term of the debt instrument, including renewal and extension options. See ¶ 83 for the applicable federal rates. In situations where the imputed interest rules of Code Sec. 483 apply to a debt instrument (¶ 1868), payments due within six months after the sale are taken into account at face value.

For a sale-leaseback transaction, a rate equal to 110 percent of the AFR applies in determining the present value of payments (Code Sec. 1274(e)). The AFR may not exceed nine percent, compounded semiannually, if the debt instrument is given in consideration for the sale or exchange of property (other than new Code Sec. 38 property) and the stated principal amount of the instrument does not exceed an inflation-adjusted amount ($5,339,300 for 2012) (Code Sec. 1274A; Rev. Rul. 2011-27).[64] The AFR may not exceed six percent, compounded semiannually, in the case of transfers of land between family members if the aggregate sales price of all prior land sales between the family members during the calendar year does not exceed $500,000. However, this limit does not apply if any party to the sale is a nonresident alien (Code Sec. 483(e); Reg. § 1.483-3(b)).[65]

Joint Election. For sales or exchanges of property (other than new Code Sec. 38 property), the lender and borrower may jointly elect out of the rules for OID on debt issued for property, and take the interest on the debt instrument into account under the cash method of accounting. The election can be made only if:

References are to Standard Federal Tax Reports; Tax Research Consultant; and Practical Tax Explanations.

[61] ¶ 31,300; ACCTNG: 36,150; § 19,315.10

[62] ¶ 31,340; ACCTNG: 36,154.45; § 19,315.10

[63] ¶ 31,340, ¶ 31,300; ACCTNG: 36,154; § 19,305.05, § 19,315.10

[64] ¶ 31,320, ¶ 31,322.30; ACCTNG: 36,162.20; § 19,315.10

[65] ¶ 22,290, ¶ 22,294; ACCTNG: 36,308.25; § 19,510.15

- the stated principal amount of the instrument does not exceed an inflation-adjusted amount ($3,813,800 for 2012) (Rev. Rul. 2011-27);
- the lender is on the cash-basis method of accounting and is not a dealer with respect to the property sold or exchanged; and
- these rules would otherwise have applied to the transaction (Code Sec. 1274A(c)).[66]

1956. Original Issue Discount on Tax-Exempt Bonds. Although original issue discount (OID) on tax-exempt obligations is generally treated as tax-exempt interest (¶ 1952), OID must be accrued for purposes of calculating the holder's tax basis in determining gain or loss if the bond is sold prior to maturity (Code Sec. 1288).[67] The holder is to accrue OID for various "accrual periods" using the constant-interest method, under which OID is allocated over the life of a bond by making adjustments to the issue price of the bond for each accrual period. The amount of OID allocated over an accrual period is determined by (1) multiplying the adjusted issue price of the bond by its yield to maturity and then (2) subtracting the interest payable as "qualified periodic interest" from the product. In determining OID on tax-exempt obligations, tax-exempt interest must be excluded. The tables at ¶ 84 present applicable federal interest rates that have been adjusted to account for tax-exempt interest.

1958. Market Discount Bonds. Gain from the sale of a market discount bond is treated as ordinary income to the extent of accrued market discount on the bond (Code Sec. 1276).[68] A market discount bond is a bond that was purchased at a discount. If the bond was originally issued at a discount, then the bond's revised issue price, or original issue price plus accrued original issue discount (OID), is substituted for the purchase price to determine if the bond is a market discount bond. Market discount bonds do not include obligations that mature within one year of issuance, U.S. savings bonds, installment bonds, and tax-exempt bonds purchased before May 1, 1993. The accrued market discount on a bond may be figured under either the ratable accrual method, or upon the irrevocable election of the taxpayer with respect to a particular bond, the constant interest method.

Instead of recognizing interest income upon the disposition of a market discount bond, a taxpayer may elect to include market discount in income currently using either the ratable accrual method or the constant interest method. This election, which is revocable only with the consent of the IRS, applies to all market discount bonds acquired during and after the tax year of the election. The election is made by filing a statement with the taxpayer's timely filed tax return that states that the market discount has been included in income. The statement should also indicate how the amount included in income was calculated (Rev. Proc. 92-67; Rev. Proc. 2011-14).

Any partial payment of principal on a market discount bond is ordinary income to the extent of accrued market discount on the bond for obligations acquired after October 22, 1986 (Code Sec. 1276(a)(3)).[69] The payment that is included in gross income reduces the amount of accrued market discount.

Net direct interest expenses on debt incurred to purchase or continue a market discount bond acquired after July 18, 1984, may be deducted currently only to the extent that the expenses exceed the market discount allocable to the number of days the bond is held by the taxpayer (Code Sec. 1277).[70] The taxpayer may elect to take any deferred interest deduction in a subsequent year to the extent of net interest income from the market discount bond. Any deferred interest expense that remains (whether or not the election is made) is deducted in the year of disposition.

1961. Discount on Short-Term Obligations. The holder of certain short-term obligations must include in gross income an amount equal to the sum of the daily

References are to Standard Federal Tax Reports; Tax Research Consultant; and Practical Tax Explanations.

[66] ¶ 31,320; ACCTNG: 36,154.65; § 19,315.10

[67] ¶ 31,520; ACCTNG: 36,502.10; § 3,105.05

[68] ¶ 31,360; ACCTNG: 36,400; § 19,325.05

[69] ¶ 31,360; ACCTNG: 36,408.15; § 19,325.05

[70] ¶ 31,380; ACCTNG: 36,410; § 19,325.10

portions of the acquisition discount for each day during the tax year that the holder held the bond (Code Sec. 1281).[71] Also required to be included in gross income as it accrues is any interest payable on the obligation, other than interest taken into account in determining the acquisition discount. An obligation for this purpose includes a bond, debenture, note, certificate, or other evidence of debt, but not a tax-exempt obligation (Code Sec. 1283(a)(1)).[72] Accrual of acquisition discount is required on short-term obligations:

- held by accrual method taxpayers, banks, regulated investment companies, or common trust funds, primarily for sale to customers in the ordinary course of trade or business;
- that have been identified by the taxpayer as part of a hedging transaction (¶ 1949); and
- that are stripped bonds or coupons while held by the person who stripped them or someone else whose basis in them is determined by reference to the basis in his hands.

In the case of short-term obligations other than government obligations, current inclusion under the original issue discount (OID) rules applies unless the holder elects to use the acquisition discount rules.

Net direct interest expense is deductible only to the extent that it exceeds the sum of: (1) the acquisition discount (excess of stated redemption price over basis) for each day during the year that the bond is held by the taxpayer, and (2) the amount of any interest payable on the obligation that accrues during the year but is not included in gross income for that year because of the taxpayer's accounting method. The daily portion of the acquisition discount is equal to the total discount divided by the number of days from the acquisition date to the maturity date (Code Secs. 1282(a) and 1283(b)(1)).[73]

1963. Unregistered Obligations. Most corporate and government debt obligations are required to be in registered form if the payor is to deduct interest (Code Sec. 163(f)(1)).[74] An excise tax is imposed on issues of registration-required obligations (other than tax-exempt bonds) that are not in registered form (Code Sec. 4701).[75] The excise tax is equal to one percent of the principal amount of the obligation multiplied by the number of calendar years (or portions thereof) during the term of the obligation. This is the period beginning on the date of issuance of the obligation and ending on the date of maturity.

If a registration-required obligation is not in registered form, any gain realized on its sale or other disposition is taxed as ordinary income (Code Sec. 1287)[76] and loss deductions are denied (Code Sec. 165(j))[77] unless the issuance of the obligation was subject to the excise tax under Code Sec. 4701 or certain other specified exceptions apply. Issuers of registration-required obligations face the loss of deductions for interest (including OID) on the bonds (Code Sec. 163(f))[78] and cannot reduce earnings and profits by the amount of any interest on the obligation (Code Sec. 312(m)).[79]

1965. Discounted U.S. Bonds Received in Tax-Free Exchange. Some types of U.S. savings bonds may be exchanged tax free for other types of U.S. savings bonds (¶ 730) (Code Sec. 1037).[80] When the original bond was issued at a discount, an amount equal to what would have been ordinary income from original issue discount (OID) (¶ 1952) if the exchange had been taxable is ordinary income when the bond received in exchange is disposed of or redeemed at a gain.

References are to Standard Federal Tax Reports; Tax Research Consultant; and Practical Tax Explanations.

[71] ¶ 31,420; ACCTNG: 36,452; § 19,330.05

[72] ¶ 31,460; ACCTNG: 36,452; § 19,330.05

[73] ¶ 31,440, ¶ 31,460; ACCTNG: 36,456; § 19,330.05

[74] ¶ 9102; BUSEXP: 21,206; § 19,340

[75] ¶ 33,941; BUSEXP: 30,252; § 19,340

[76] ¶ 31,500; SALES: 24,404.05; § 19,340

[77] ¶ 9802; SALES: 24,404.05; § 16,905.05

[78] ¶ 9102; BUSEXP: 21,206; § 7,401

[79] ¶ 15,600; CCORP: 12,104

[80] ¶ 29,720; SALES: 27,250; § 18,220

1967. Bond Premium Amortization by Bondholder. When a bond owner has paid a premium over the face amount of a taxable bond, he or she has the option of (1) amortizing the premium by deducting it over the life of the bond, or (2) not amortizing and treating the premium as part of basis (Code Sec. 171(a); Reg. § 1.171-4).[81] The amortization method must be elected by reporting the amortization on the tax return for the first year the election is to apply and attaching a statement to the tax return that the amortization election is being made. No amortization is allowed for tax-exempt bonds. However, a reduction in the basis of the bond by the amount of the bond premium is required (Code Sec. 1016(a)(5)).[82] For a dealer in municipal bonds, see ¶ 1970.

The amount of bond premium that can be amortized for the tax year (and deducted currently) is calculated under a constant yield method (Code Sec. 171(b); Reg. § 1.171-2).[83] Under this method, the amount of the amortizable bond premium and the amount attributable to a particular tax year must be determined on the basis of the taxpayer's yield to maturity, using the taxpayer's basis in the obligation (for purposes of determining loss on a sale or exchange) and compounding at the close of each accrual period.

If a bond is received in an exchange and the basis of the bond is determined at least in part from the basis of the property given up in the exchange, the basis of the bond cannot exceed its fair market value immediately after the exchange for purposes of determining bond premium. This rule generally does not apply to an exchange of securities in a reorganization.

Premium on Convertible Bond. Amortization is not allowed for any part of a premium that is paid for the conversion feature in a convertible bond. A corporation's deduction for the premium it is called upon to pay to repurchase its own convertible indebtedness is generally limited to the amount of the normal call premium (Code Sec. 249(a)).[84]

1970. Dealer in Tax-Exempt Bonds. A dealer in tax-exempt obligations must amortize any premiums just as if the interest on the bonds had been taxable. A dealer who does not inventory his securities or who inventories them at cost must reduce the adjusted basis of any municipal bonds he sells during the year by the total amortization for the period they were held. A dealer who values inventories other than at cost (for example, market value) must annually reduce his or her cost of securities sold by amortization on municipal bonds held during the year (Code Sec. 75; Reg. § 1.75-1).[85]

When a tax-exempt obligation is purchased and is sold or otherwise disposed of within 30 days after acquisition, or matures or is callable more than five years after it is acquired, an amortization adjustment must be made unless the bond is sold or disposed of at a gain. Thus, a dealer who inventories at other than cost and holds at the end of the year a bond maturing or callable more than five years after acquisition does not have to reflect amortization on it in cost of securities sold. If it is sold at a gain, no amortization adjustment is to be made. If it is not sold at a gain, the cost of securities sold is then reduced by the amortization for the entire period it was held.

Accounting Issues

1973. Reporting and Time of Sale for Publicly Traded Securities. A cash or accrual method taxpayer other than a dealer (¶ 1903) who sells stock or securities traded on an established securities market generally must recognize gains and losses on the trade date, rather than the settlement date (Rev. Rul. 93-84).[86] The holding period for such stock is also measured by using the trade date as the date sold and not the settlement date (¶ 1737). Gain or loss on short sale of securities, however, is recognized on the settlement date as set by exchange rules (¶ 1944). The installment method of reporting is not available for sales of stock or securities traded on an established securities market (Code Sec. 453(k)).

References are to Standard Federal Tax Reports; Tax Research Consultant; and Practical Tax Explanations.

[81] ¶ 11,850, ¶ 11,854; DEPR: 21,200; § 45,415.20

[82] ¶ 29,410; DEPR: 21,210; § 45,415.20

[83] ¶ 11,850, ¶ 11,852; DEPR: 21,200; § 45,415.20

[84] ¶ 13,400; DEPR: 21,202.20; § 45,415.20

[85] ¶ 6250, ¶ 6251; ACCTNG: 15,256.15

[86] ¶ 21,005.892, ¶ 21,402; SALES: 45,300; § 16,025

1975. Identification of Securities Sold. If a taxpayer can adequately identify the shares of securities sold or exchanged, his or her basis is the cost or other basis of the particular shares of stock or bond. An adequate identification is made if the taxpayer can show the certificates representing shares of stock from a lot which the taxpayer acquired on a certain date, or for a certain price, and which were delivered to the taxpayer's broker or other transferee. If a taxpayer buys and sells securities at various times in varying quantities and cannot adequately identify the shares that are sold, then the basis and holding period of the shares sold are generally determined on a first-in, first-out (FIFO) basis (Reg. § 1.1012-1(c)).[87] Most courts hold, however, that after a nontaxable reorganization in which the taxpayer receives shares of stock in another corporation in exchange for the original shares, the FIFO rule is not applicable.[88] In the case of the sale, exchange, or other disposition of a specified security on or after an applicable date (¶ 1980), the basis reported by the broker on Form 1099-B must be calculated on an account by account basis (Code Sec. 1012(c)).[89] Thus, the broker may be required to use different basis computation methods for different accounts.

A shareholder in a mutual fund may elect to figure gain or loss of identical shares using an average basis if the shareholder (1) acquired the shares at various times and prices, and (2) left the shares on deposit in an account handled by a custodian or agent who acquires or redeems shares of the mutual fund (Code Sec. 1012(d); Reg. § 1.1012-1(e)).[90] Shares are identical for this purpose if they have the same Committee on Uniform Security Identification Procedure (CUSIP) number or other security identifier number permitted by the IRS. The option to use an average basis is available only with respect to mutual fund shares and, beginning after 2010, dividend reinvestment plans. For periods on or after October 18, 2010, the average basis is determined by averaging the basis of all shares of identical stock in an account regardless of the holding period. For periods before October 18, 2010, a shareholder figures average basis using either the single-category method or a double-category method in which all shares in the mutual fund account at the time of each disposition are categorized as either short-term or long-term shares.

1980. Basis and Holding Period Reporting for Securities. If a broker is required to file a return on Form 1099-B with respect to the gross proceeds of the sale of a covered security on or after January 1, 2011 (¶ 2565), the broker must also report the customer's adjusted basis in the security and whether any gain or loss with respect to the security is long-term or short-term (Code Sec. 6045(g); Reg. § 1.6045-1).[91] A "covered security" is any specified security acquired on or after the applicable date if the security was acquired through a transaction in the account in which the security was held, or was transferred to that account from an account in which the security was a covered security, but only if the broker receiving custody of the security receives a statutory statement with respect to the transfer. A "specified security" includes any share of stock in a corporation; a note, bond, debenture or other evidence of indebtedness; a commodity, or a contract or a derivative with respect to a commodity; and other financial instruments as determined by the IRS. Special rules apply to broker reporting on sales by S corporations, short sales, and options transactions.

The "applicable date" is:

- January 1, 2011, for corporate stock, generally;
- January 1, 2012, for stock for which an average basis method is permissible, such as stock in a regulated investment company (mutual fund) or stock acquired in connection with a dividend reinvestment plan; and
- January 1, 2014, for other specified securities (in particular, debt instruments and options) (Notice 2012-34).

References are to Standard Federal Tax Reports; Tax Research Consultant; and Practical Tax Explanations.

[87] ¶ 29,331; SALES: 6,212; § 16,115

[88] ¶ 29,336.451; SALES: 6,212.25; § 16,115

[89] ¶ 29,330; SALES: 6,068; § 39,120.12

[90] ¶ 29,330, ¶ 29,331; SALES: 6,212.35, SALES: 6,212.45; § 19,220.05, § 19,220.20

[91] ¶ 35,920, ¶ 35,923; FILEBUS: 9,252, FILEBUS: 9,256; § 39,120.12

The broker must generally determine adjusted basis under the first-in, first-out (FIFO) method (¶ 1975) unless the taxpayer adequately identifies the stock sold. For any stock for which an average basis method is allowed, such as stock in a mutual fund acquired in connection with a dividend reinvestment plan, the customer's adjusted basis is determined according to the broker's default method, unless the customer notifies the broker that he or she elects another acceptable method regarding the account in which the stock is held. Basis is determined without regard to the wash sale rules (¶ 1935) unless the acquisition and sale transactions resulting in a wash sale occur in the same account and are in identical securities.

Securities Transfers Between Accounts. Every broker (and any other person specified in regulations) that transfers a covered security to another broker must furnish to the transferee broker a written statement that permits the transferee broker to satisfy the basis and holding-period reporting requirements (Code Sec. 6045A; Reg. § 1.6045A-1).[92] The written statement must be furnished no later than 15 days after the date of the transfer, except as provided otherwise by the IRS, or the transferor could be subject to a penalty (¶ 2823). The IRS will not assert penalties for a failure to furnish the transfer statement for any transfer of stock in 2011 that is not incidental to the stock's purchase or sale; the receiving broker can treat such stock as a noncovered security (Notice 2010-67).

Organizational Actions Affecting Basis. Issuers of specified securities must file Form 8937 describing any organizational action which affects the basis of the security, and the quantitative effect on the basis resulting from such action (Code Sec. 6045B; Reg. § 1.6045B-1).[93] A person required to file under this provision must also furnish a written statement to the holder of the specified security or their nominee, detailing the contents of the return. The return must be filed by the earlier of 45 days after the organizational action or January 15 of the year following the calendar year during which the organizational action took place. However, no return is required for organizational actions which occur before the applicable date with respect to that security.

The IRS may waive the return filing and information statement requirements if the person required to file the return makes publicly available, in the form and manner specified by the IRS, the name, address, phone number, and e-mail address of the information contact of that person, the description of the organizational action affecting the basis of the specified security, the quantitative effect of the organizational action on the basis, and any other information the IRS requires. Penalties may be imposed for failure to file correct information returns in connection with organizational actions, failure to furnish correct statements to holders or nominees, or failure to provide required publicly-available information in lieu of returns and written statements (¶ 2823).

1983. Commissions Paid on Securities. Commissions and other transaction costs paid to facilitate the sale of securities generally must be capitalized and cannot be deducted as business or nonbusiness expenses (Temp. Reg. § 1.263(a)-1T(d); Reg. § 1.263(a)-2(e)).[94] In the case of dealers in securities, however, commissions and other amounts paid to facilitate the sale of a security are treated as ordinary and necessary business expenses. Traders and investors treat the amounts capitalized as a reduction in the amount realized from the sale. They are taken into account either in the tax year in which the sale occurs or in the tax year in which the sale is abandoned if a loss deduction is permitted. The capitalized amount is not added to the basis of the property. See ¶ 1760 for information concerning the proper classification of a taxpayer as a trader, dealer, or investor. Ordinary and necessary expenses for investment advice, including a "wrap fee" on a brokerage account, paid by an investor in lieu of commissions on individual trades, are deductible investment expenses and are claimed as miscellaneous itemized deductions on the individual's Schedule A of Form 1040 in the year paid (Reg. § 1.212-1(g)).[95]

References are to Standard Federal Tax Reports; Tax Research Consultant; and Practical Tax Explanations.

[92] ¶ 35,931, ¶ 35,932; FILEBUS: 9,252, FILEBUS: 9,256; § 39,120.12

[93] ¶ 35,934, ¶ 35,935; FILEBUS: 9,380; § 39,120.12

[94] ¶ 13,702BC, ¶ 13,703; SALES: 9,152; § 7,105.40

[95] ¶ 12,521; BUSEXP: 12,154.05; § 7,840.05

Chapter 20

TAX SHELTERS □ AT-RISK RULES □ PASSIVE LOSSES

Reportable Transactions

2001. Reportable Transactions. Reporting and disclosure requirements apply to taxpayers (¶ 2004) and material advisors (¶ 2005) with respect to reportable transactions. A reportable transaction is any transaction with respect to which information is required to be included with a return or statement because, as determined under regulations prescribed under the general requirements for returns, statements or lists (Code Sec. 6011), that transaction is of a type which the IRS determines as having a potential for tax avoidance or evasion (Code Sec. 6707A(c)(1)).[1]

There are five categories of reportable transactions: listed transactions, confidential transactions, transactions with contractual protection, loss transactions, and transactions of interest (Reg. § 1.6011-4(b)).[2] A transaction will not be considered a reportable transaction, or will be excluded from any individual category of reportable transaction, if the IRS makes a determination by published guidance that the transaction is not subject to the reporting requirements. The IRS may make a determination by individual letter.

2004. Disclosure of Reportable Transactions by Taxpayers. Every taxpayer that has participated directly or indirectly in a reportable transaction (¶ 2001) and is required to file a tax return must attach a disclosure statement to its return (Reg. § 1.6011-4(a)).[3] The fact that a transaction is a reportable transaction will not affect the legal determination of whether the taxpayer's treatment of the transaction is proper.

Form 8886 must be used as the reportable transaction disclosure statement. The form must be attached to the taxpayer's tax return for each tax year for which a taxpayer participates in a reportable transaction. In addition, a copy of the disclosure statement must be sent to the Office of Tax Shelter Analysis (OTSA) at the same time that any disclosure statement is first filed with the taxpayer's tax return (Reg. § 1.6011-4(d) and (e)). If a reportable transaction results in a loss that is carried back to a prior year, the

References are to Standard Federal Tax Reports; Tax Research Consultant; and Practical Tax Explanations.

[1] ¶ 40,091; FILEBUS: 9,450; § 39,015.05

[2] ¶ 35,127; FILEBUS: 9,458; § 39,015.05

[3] ¶ 35,127; FILEBUS: 9,456; § 39,015.05

disclosure statement for the reportable transaction must be attached to the taxpayer's application for tentative refund or amended tax return for that prior year. In the case of a taxpayer that is a partnership, an S corporation, or a trust, the disclosure statement for a reportable transaction must be attached to the partnership's, S corporation's, or trust's tax return for each tax year in which the partnership, S corporation, or trust participates in the transaction. A taxpayer who is a partner, an S corporation shareholder, or beneficiary of a trust who receives a Schedule K-1 less than 10 calendar days before the due date of its return (including extensions) will have a 60 day extension to file Form 8886 with the OTSA if the taxpayer determines from the Schedule K-1 that it participated in a reportable transaction. Failure to file Form 8886 regarding a reportable transaction is subject to a penalty (¶ 2006).

Special reporting rules apply to listed transactions and transactions of interest. Also, in some cases, taxpayers must make multiple disclosures of a reportable transaction (Reg. § 1.6011-4(e)).

A taxpayer may submit a request to the IRS for a ruling as to whether a transaction is subject to the disclosure requirements. If a taxpayer requests a ruling on the merits of a specific transaction on or before the date that disclosure would otherwise be required and receives a favorable ruling, the disclosure rules will be deemed to have been satisfied. However, the ruling request must fully disclose all relevant facts relating to the transaction. If a taxpayer is uncertain whether a transaction must be disclosed, the taxpayer may make a protective disclosure. The taxpayer must disclose the transaction and indicate on the disclosure statement that the taxpayer is uncertain whether the transaction is required to be disclosed and that the disclosure statement is being filed on a protective basis. The taxpayer must retain a copy of all documents and other records related to a transaction subject to disclosure. The retained documents and records are those that are material to an understanding of the tax treatment or tax structure of the transaction (Reg. § 1.6011-4(f) and (g)).

2005. Disclosure of Reportable Transactions by Material Advisors. Each material advisor is required to timely file an information return with the IRS for any reportable transaction, including any listed transaction (Code Sec. 6111; Reg. § 301.6111-3).[4] The disclosure is made on Form 8918 and generally must be filed with the Office of Tax Shelter Analysis (OTSA) by the last day of the month that follows the calendar quarter in which the advisor became a material advisor with respect to the reportable transaction.

The material advisor's disclosure on Form 8918 must include: (1) information identifying and describing the transaction, (2) information describing any potential tax benefits expected to result from the transaction, and (3) whatever other information the IRS may prescribe. This includes enough information about the transaction to identify if any other person that the material advisor knows or has reason to know acted as a material advisor with respect to the transaction. A single Form 8918 may be filed for substantially similar transactions. An amended form must be filed if information previously provided is no longer accurate, if additional information becomes available, or if there are material changes to the transaction. If a potential material advisor is uncertain whether a transaction must be disclosed, a protective disclosure may be made. Any material advisor who fails to file Form 8918 when required or files a false or incomplete form is subject to a penalty (¶ 2008).

A material advisor means any person: (1) who provides material aid, assistance, or advice with respect to organizing, promoting, selling, implementing, or carrying out any reportable transaction, and (2) who directly or indirectly derives gross income in excess of $250,000 ($50,000 in the case of a reportable transaction substantially all of the tax benefits from which are provided to natural persons) for that aid, assistance, or advice. If more than one material advisor is required to disclose a reportable transaction, the material advisors may designate by written agreement a single material advisor to disclose the transaction.

References are to Standard Federal Tax Reports; Tax Research Consultant; and Practical Tax Explanations.

[4] ¶ 37,000, ¶ 37,001D; FILEBUS: 9,452, PENALTY: 3,254; § 39,015.05

Tax Shelter Penalties

2006. Penalty for Failure to Disclose Reportable Transaction. A penalty is imposed on any taxpayer who fails to file an information return regarding a reportable transaction (¶ 2001) (Code Sec. 6707A; Reg. § 301.6707A-1).[5] The penalty is equal to the lesser of $10,000 ($5,000 in the case of a natural person), or 75 percent of the decrease in tax shown on the return as a result of the transaction, or which would have resulted from the transaction if the transaction had been respected for federal tax purposes. The maximum penalty is $10,000 in the case of a natural person and $50,000 in any other case. However, in circumstances involving listed transactions, the maximum penalty is $100,000 for natural persons and $200,000 for other persons.

For reportable transactions other than listed transactions, the penalty can be rescinded (or abated) only in exceptional circumstances (i.e., abatement of the penalty would promote compliance with the tax laws and effective tax administration). Factors that will be taken into account in deciding whether to grant rescission include: (1) the taxpayer, on becoming aware of the failure to properly disclose a reportable transaction, filed a complete and proper (although untimely) Form 8886; (2) the failure to properly disclose was due to an unintentional mistake of fact (which existed despite the taxpayer's reasonable attempts to determine the correct facts); (3) the taxpayer has an established history of properly disclosing reportable transactions and complying with tax laws generally; (4) the failure to file was beyond the taxpayer's control; (5) the taxpayer cooperates with the IRS; and (6) assessment of the penalty weighs against good conscience and the taxpayer demonstrates there was good cause for and acted in good faith with respect to the failure. The penalty cannot be waived with respect to a listed transactions.

Any person seeking rescission of a penalty must make a written request within 30 days after the date that the IRS sends notice and demand for payment of the penalty. If the penalty is paid (not including interest) prior to the date that notice and demand is sent, the written request must be made within 30 days from the date of payment. In order to request rescission, the person must have either exhausted the administrative remedies available within the IRS Office of Appeals or agreed in writing to the assessment of the penalty and not to file or prosecute a claim for refund or credit of the penalty. IRS guidance sets forth information items required with the request, as well as factors considered in granting or denying the request. Collection efforts of the IRS will not be suspended because a rescission request has been made (Rev. Proc. 2007-21).

2007. Accuracy-Related Penalty on Reportable Transaction Understatement. An accuracy-related penalty applies if a taxpayer has a reportable transaction understatement for a tax year (Code Sec. 6662A). The penalty rate and defenses available to avoid the penalty vary depending on whether the transaction was adequately disclosed (¶ 2870).

2008. Material Advisor Penalty for Reportable Transactions. A penalty is imposed on any material advisor (¶ 2005) who fails to file an information return or who files a false or incomplete information return regarding a reportable transaction (¶ 2001) (Code Sec. 6707).[6] Generally, a $50,000 penalty is assessed for failure to furnish required information with respect to a reportable transaction. In the case of the failure to file an information return with respect to a listed transaction, the penalty assessed will be the greater of $200,000 or 50 percent of the gross income derived by the person required to file the return with respect to aid, assistance, or advice that is provided with respect to the listed transaction. The 50-percent limit is raised to 75 percent in cases involving an intentional failure to act. The penalty with respect to a listed transaction cannot be waived. The penalty with respect to reportable transactions other than listed transactions may be abated only in exceptional circumstances identical to those for abatement of the penalty for failure to disclose reportable transactions by taxpayers.

References are to Standard Federal Tax Reports; Tax Research Consultant; and Practical Tax Explanations.

[5] ¶ 40,091, ¶ 40,092; PENALTY: 3,252.10; § 39,015.05

[6] ¶ 40,085; PENALTY: 3,254; § 39,015.05

Each material advisor with respect to any reportable transaction (¶ 2001) is required to maintain a list identifying each person with respect to whom that advisor acted as a material advisor with respect to the transaction and containing any other information required by the IRS (Code Sec. 6112(a); Reg. § 301.6112-1).[7] Regulations set forth the requirements for the preparation and maintenance of advisee lists, including persons required to be included on lists, contents of the list, definitions, and requirements for retention and furnishing of the lists. All information that is required to be included in the advisee lists must be retained for seven years. Any person required to maintain advisee lists with respect to reportable transactions who receives a written request from the IRS, but who fails to make the lists available within 20 business days, may be assessed a $10,000 penalty for each day of failure after the 20th business day (Code Sec. 6708).[8]

2011. Abusive Tax Shelters Penalty. A penalty is imposed against the promoters of abusive tax shelters (Code Sec. 6700(a)).[9] The penalty is 50 percent of the gross income derived, or to be derived, from the abusive plan or arrangement activities engaged in, other than promotion activities involving gross valuation overstatements. The penalty for promotion of activities involving gross valuation overstatements is an amount equal to the lesser of $1,000 or 100 percent of the gross income derived, or to be derived, by the promoter from the activity. In applying the penalty, promotion of each entity or activity is a separate activity and each sale of an interest in the shelter is a separate activity. Assessment of the penalty is not barred by any statute of limitations (*J.A. Sage*, CA-5, 90-2 ustc ¶ 50,453).[10]

2012. Injunctions Related to Tax Shelters. An injunction may be obtained with respect to the following acts: (1) promoting an abusive tax shelter (¶ 2011); (2) aiding someone in understating a tax liability in a return or other document (¶ 2518); (3) failing to furnish information about a reportable transaction (¶ 2005); or (4) failing to maintain a list of advisees (¶ 2008) (Code Sec. 7408).[11] Once a court has enjoined a person from engaging in one or more of the above activities, the court may expand the injunction to include any other activity that is subject to a penalty under tax law.

Farming Operations

2028. Accrual Accounting for Farm Corporations. Certain corporations and partnerships having a corporation as a partner that are engaged in the business of farming must use the accrual method of accounting (Code Sec. 447).[12] In addition, these taxpayers are required to capitalize their preproductive period expenses (¶ 999). All farming corporations are subject to the accrual accounting rule except:

- S corporations,
- corporations or partnerships engaged in the trade or business of operating a nursery or sod farm, or raising or harvesting trees (other than fruit and nut trees), and
- corporations having annual gross receipts of $1 million or less for each prior tax year beginning after 1975 (including the receipts of predecessor corporations and members of a controlled group).

A family corporation meets the gross-receipts test if its gross receipts do not exceed $25 million for each prior tax year beginning after 1985. A family corporation is defined as:

- any corporation in which at least 50 percent of the total combined voting power of all classes of voting stock and at least 50 percent of all other classes of the corporation's stock are owned by members of the same family, or
- any of the closely held corporations described in Code Sec. 447(h).

References are to Standard Federal Tax Reports; Tax Research Consultant; and Practical Tax Explanations.

[7] ¶ 37,020, ¶ 37,021; FILEBUS: 9,410.05; § 39,015.05

[8] ¶ 40,095, ¶ 37,021; PENALTY: 3,254.10; § 39,015.05

[9] ¶ 40,025; PENALTY: 3,256

[10] ¶ 38,963.42; PENALTY: 3,256

[11] ¶ 41,670; PENALTY: 3,256.20; § 41,630.05

[12] ¶ 20,700; FARM: 3,060; § 36,315.10

If a corporation or qualified partnership (each of the partners of which is a corporation) has, for a 10-year period ending with its first tax year after 1975, and for all subsequent years, used an annual accrual method of accounting with respect to its trade or business of farming, and the entity raises crops which are harvested a year or more after planting, it may continue to use this method.

2032. Expenses of Farming Syndicates. A farming syndicate is a tax shelter and must use the accrual method of accounting (¶ 1515) (Code Sec. 461(i)(4)).[13] A farming syndicate is any farming partnership or enterprise (other than a corporation that is not an S corporation) if at any time (1) interests in the enterprise or partnership have been offered for sale in an offering required to be registered with any federal or state agency having authority to regulate such offering, or (2) more than 35 percent of the losses during any period are allocable to limited partners or limited entrepreneurs (Code Sec. 464(c)(1)).

A limited entrepreneur is a person who has an interest (other than a limited partnership interest) in an enterprise and who does not actively participate in the enterprise's management (Code Sec. 464(e)(2)(A)). An individual will not be treated as a limited partner or limited entrepreneur in a farming enterprise (other than one with respect to which securities have been registered) if the individual:

(1) has his or her principal residence on the farm on which the farming enterprise is being carried on,

(2) has an interest attributable to active participation in management of the farming enterprise for a period of not less than five years,

(3) as his or her principal business activity, actively participates in the management of a farming enterprise, regardless of whether he or she actively participates in the management of the enterprise in question, or

(4) actively participates in the management of another farming enterprise involving the raising of livestock (or is so treated under either (1) or (2)) and owns an interest in an enterprise involving the further processing of the livestock raised in the enterprise.

If an individual meets any of these conditions, any member of his or her family who owns an interest in a farming enterprise that is attributable to the individual's active participation will not be treated as a limited partner or limited entrepreneur (Code Sec. 464(c)(2)).[14]

Cash-method farmers who purchase feed, seed and similar supplies for use in a later tax year are limited in their ability to claim current deductions for these prepaid expenses. To the extent that prepaid farm expenses (including prepaid poultry expenses) exceed 50 percent of total deductible farming expenses, these expenses may be deducted only when used or consumed unless is a qualified farm-related taxpayer (Code Sec. 464(f)).[15] A taxpayer is a qualified farm-related taxpayer if the taxpayer satisfies the 50 percent test on the basis of the three preceding years or the taxpayer fails to satisfy the 50 percent test due to a change in business operations directly attributable to extraordinary circumstances. Qualified farm-related taxpayers may deduct the entire cost of prepaid farm supplies, regardless of when the supplies are used or consumed.

Accounting Rules

2040. Accounting Method. Tax shelters are generally required to use the accrual method of accounting (see ¶ 1515).

2042. Prepaid Expenses. Under Code Sec. 461(i), a tax shelter is prohibited from using the recurring-item exception to the economic performance rule (¶ 1540).[16] However, economic performance with respect to the drilling of an oil or gas well will be considered to have occurred within a tax year if drilling commences within 90 days of the close of the tax year. For purposes of these rules, a tax shelter is:

References are to Standard Federal Tax Reports; Tax Research Consultant; and Practical Tax Explanations.

[13] ¶ 21,802

[14] ¶ 21,840; FARM: 9,054.05

[15] ¶ 21,840; FARM: 9,054

[16] ¶ 21,802; ACCTNG: 12,354; § 38,410.40

• any enterprise (other than a C corporation) that is required to register its offering with a state or federal agency;

• any partnership, entity, plan, or arrangement, the significant purpose of which is tax evasion or avoidance; and

• any partnership or entity (other than a C corporation) if more than 35 percent of its losses are allocable to limited partners or limited entrepreneurs.

In the case of the trade or business of farming, a tax shelter includes a farming syndicate (¶ 2032).

At-Risk Limitation on Losses

2045. Limit of Losses to Amount at Risk. A taxpayer's deductible loss with respect to an activity is generally limited to the amount that the taxpayer has at risk with respect to the activity (Code Sec. 465).[17] The at-risk rules are designed to prevent taxpayers from offsetting trade, business, or professional income by losses from investments in activities that are largely financed by nonrecourse loans for which they are not personally liable (¶ 2049). Even if it has been determined that the loss is deductible under the at-risk rules, the loss may still be limited by the passive activity loss rules (¶ 2053).

Under the at-risk rules, loss deductions are limited to the amount of the taxpayer's cash contribution and the adjusted basis of other property the taxpayer contributes to the activity, plus any amounts borrowed for use in the activity if the taxpayer has personal liability for the borrowed amounts or has pledged assets not used in the activity as security for the borrowed amounts. The taxpayer will not be considered at risk with respect to amounts protected against loss through nonrecourse financing, guarantees, stop-loss agreements, or similar arrangements (Code Sec. 465(b)).[18] Also, amounts are not at risk if they are borrowed from (1) a creditor who has an interest other than as a creditor (which has been defined as a capital or net profits interest), or (2) a person related to a person with such an interest. Personal liability of the taxpayer for borrowed amounts generally hinges on whether the taxpayer is the ultimate obligor of the liability with no recourse against any other party.[19]

Any loss not allowed because of the at-risk limitation is carried over to the following tax year, to be deducted subject to the same limitation (Code Sec. 465(a)(2)). The amount allowed as a loss for any year reduces the amount at risk for later years. Conversely, if a taxpayer's amount at risk at the end of any tax year is less than zero, the loss equal to the difference is recaptured (Code Sec. 465(e)).[20] Unused amounts generally are allowed when the activity is transferred or otherwise disposed of (¶ 2051).

Form 6198 is used to compute the deductible loss, if any, under the at-risk rules. An activity subject to the passive loss rules must file Form 8582. If the activity is subject to both limitations, Form 6198 is completed first, and any allowable loss must be carried over to Form 8582.

For investment tax credit at-risk rules, see ¶ 1365A.

2047. Taxpayers Affected by At-Risk Rules. The at-risk rules (¶ 2045) apply to individuals, estates, and trusts (Code Sec. 465(a)(1)).[21] They apply to partners and S corporation shareholders at the partner or shareholder level, not at the entity level. Closely held corporations are generally subject to the at-risk rules if they meet the personal holding company stock ownership requirements. Thus, a C corporation is subject to the at-risk rule limitations if over 50 percent in value of its stock is owned, directly or indirectly, by five or fewer individuals at any time during the last half of its tax year. Closely held qualified C corporations that are deemed qualifying businesses, however, may be excluded from operation of the at-risk rules. Equipment leasing activities actively engaged in by certain closely held corporations are treated as a

References are to Standard Federal Tax Reports; Tax Research Consultant; and Practical Tax Explanations.

[17] ¶ 21,850; BUSEXP: 42,000; § 17,301

[18] ¶ 21,850; BUSEXP: 42,150; § 17,305.05

[19] ¶ 21,893.35; BUSEXP: 42,156.05; § 17,305.05

[20] ¶ 21,850; BUSEXP: 42,200; § 17,315

[21] ¶ 21,850; BUSEXP: 42,050; § 17,301

separate activity to which the loss limitation of the at-risk rules also do not apply (Code Sec. 465(c)).

2049. Activities Covered by At-Risk Limitations. The at-risk limitation of losses (¶ 2045) generally applies to all activities engaged in as a trade or business or for the production of income (Code Sec. 465(c)).[22] They also specifically apply to any taxpayer engaged in the activity of holding, producing, or distributing motion picture films or video tapes; farming; leasing of section 1245 property; and exploring for or exploiting oil and gas resources or geothermal deposits. The two activities not subject to the at-risk rules are: (1) the holding of real estate (other than mineral property) placed in service before January 1, 1987, and (2) the leasing of equipment by closely held corporations (i.e., those with five or fewer individuals owning more than 50 percent of the stock).

In the case of the specifically identified activities above, each film or tape, each piece of section 1245 property, each farm, and each oil, gas, or geothermal property is treated as a separate activity. However, for a partnership or an S corporation, all leased section 1245 properties that are placed in service in the same tax year are treated as a single activity.[23] Trade or business activities subject to the at-risk rules are to be aggregated and treated as a single activity if the taxpayer actively participates in the management of the trade or business or, where the trade or business is carried on by a partnership or S corporation, if 65 percent or more of the losses for the tax year are allocable to persons who actively participate in the management.

Application of At-Risk Rules on Taxpayer's Disposition of Activity

2051. Application of At-Risk Rules on Taxpayer's Disposition of Activity. Under proposed regulations, when a taxpayer transfers or otherwise disposes of an activity, any gain realized on the transfer or disposition of the activity is treated as gain from the activity, which generally permits the taxpayer to recognize any losses suspended under the at-risk rules (Prop. Reg. § 1.465-66).[24] The same rules apply if a partnership liquidates a partner's interest or an S corporation completely redeems a shareholder's interest.

Passive Activity Limitations on Losses and Credits

2053. Passive Activity Rules. Losses from passive activities may generally not be deducted from nonpassive income (for example, wages) (Code Sec. 469).[25] Similarly, tax credits from passive activities are generally limited to the tax allocable to those activities. In determining a taxpayer's allowable loss, the at-risk rules are applied before the passive activity loss rules (¶ 2045).

To the extent that the total deductions from passive activities exceed the total income from these activities for the tax year, the excess (the passive activity loss) is not allowed as a deduction for that year. A disallowed loss is suspended and carried forward as a deduction from the passive activity in the next succeeding tax year (Code Sec. 469(b)).[26] Any unused suspended losses are allowed in full when the taxpayer disposes of his or her entire interest in the activity in a fully taxable transaction (¶ 2076).

A passive activity is any activity that involves the conduct of a trade or business in which the taxpayer does not materially participate (¶ 2059). Special rules apply to rental real estate activities in which a taxpayer actively participates (¶ 2062). Losses and credits that are attributable to limited partnership interests are generally treated as arising from a passive activity (¶ 2059) (Code Sec. 469(h)(2)).[27] Losses from a working interest in oil and gas property are not subject to the passive activity limitations if the working interest is held directly or through an entity that does not limit liability, such as an interest as a general partner (Code Sec. 469(c)(3)).[28]

References are to Standard Federal Tax Reports; Tax Research Consultant; and Practical Tax Explanations.

[22] ¶ 21,850; BUSEXP: 42,100; § 17,310

[23] ¶ 21,850; BUSEXP: 42,106; § 17,310

[24] ¶ 21,883; BUSEXP: 42,210; § 17,320

[25] ¶ 21,960; BUSEXP: 33,000; § 17,401

[26] ¶ 21,960; BUSEXP: 33,200; § 17,470.05

[27] ¶ 21,960; BUSEXP: 33,160; § 17,435.20

[28] ¶ 21,960; BUSEXP: 33,108; § 17,420.10

Credits arising with respect to passive activities are generally treated in the same manner as losses, except that suspended credits are not allowed on disposition of the activity (Code Sec. 469(a)(1)(B)).[29] Thus, credits may be used to offset the tax attributable to net passive income (the difference between the tax that the taxpayer would have to pay (1) on all income and (2) on taxable income other than net passive income). In both cases, the effect of credits is disregarded.

In general, unused credits can be carried forward indefinitely. However, the character of a credit relating to a passive activity changes, in effect, when the credit becomes allowable under the passive loss rules (either there is sufficient passive income to allow its use, or it is within the scope of the $25,000 benefit for real estate activities). At this time, the credit is aggregated with credits relating to nonpassive activities of the taxpayer to determine whether all such credits are allowable considering the other limitations that apply to the use of credits (¶ 1365).

Forms. Most taxpayers use Forms 8582 and 8582-CR to calculate their allowable passive losses and credits. Form 8810 is used by personal service corporations and closely held C corporations. Form 8825 is used by partnerships and S corporations to report income and deductible expenses from rental real estate activities.

Form 8582 generally must also be filed by a taxpayer that has an overall gain from business or rental passive activities for the year (even after including suspended passive passive losses from earlier tax years). However, Form 8582 does not need to be filed if the taxpayer actively participated in rental real estate activities.

2054. Publicly Traded Partnerships. Special rules apply to passive activity losses from publicly traded partnerships (PTPs) (Code Sec. 469(k)).[30] A PTP is a partnership whose interests are traded on an established securities market or are readily tradable on a secondary market (or its substantial equivalent). A taxpayer's net income from a PTP may not be used to offset net losses from other PTPs or net losses from other passive activities. A disallowed loss from a PTP is carried forward and allowed as a deduction in a tax year when the PTP has net income or when the taxpayer disposes of his or her entire interest in the PTP.

Mutual funds, which are taxed under the regulated investment company (RIC) rules (¶ 2301), may invest in PTPs while retaining their RIC status. The income from the PTP is treated as passive activity income to the investing fund, and losses from the PTP are passive losses which cannot be used to offset any income other than from the same PTP (Code Sec. 469(k)(4)).

2056. Taxpayers Covered by Passive Activity Rules. The passive activity rules apply to individuals, estates, trusts (other than grantor trusts), and personal service corporations (Code Sec. 469(a)(2)).[31] Although the passive activity rules do not apply to partnerships, S corporations, and grantor trusts directly, they are applied at the partner, shareholder, and beneficiary or grantor level. See ¶ 2054 for discussion of special rules applicable to publicly traded partnerships.

Closely Held C Corporations. C corporations are generally not subject to the passive activity rules. However, the passive activity rules do apply to a closely held C corporation (other than a personal service corporation) to extent of its net active income. The corporation cannot use passive losses to offset portfolio income. A closely held C corporation's net active income is equal to its taxable income figured without any income or loss from a passive activity or any portfolio income or loss (Code Sec. 469(e)(2)).[32]

2058. Activity Defined. In applying the passive loss rules, taxpayers must determine which of their operations constitute an "activity." Identification of a taxpayer's activities is determined by the facts and circumstances (Reg. § 1.469-4).[33] One or more trade or business activities are treated as a single activity if they constitute an appropriate economic unit for the measurement of gain or loss for purposes of the passive

References are to Standard Federal Tax Reports; Tax Research Consultant; and Practical Tax Explanations.

[29] ¶ 21,960; BUSEXP: 33,250; § 17,495

[30] ¶ 21,960; BUSEXP: 33,458; § 17,415.05

[31] ¶ 21,960; BUSEXP: 33,050; § 17,405.05

[32] ¶ 21,960; BUSEXP: 33,054; § 17,405.15

[33] ¶ 21,964B; BUSEXP: 33,100; § 17,415.05

activity loss rules. Five factors are given the greatest weight in determining whether an activity or group of activities constitutes an appropriate economic unit:

- similarities or differences in types of business,
- extent of common control,
- extent of common ownership,
- geographical location, and
- business interdependencies among the activities.

Once activities are grouped together or kept separate, they may not be regrouped by the taxpayer in future years unless the original grouping was clearly inappropriate or became inappropriate due to a material change in facts and circumstances (Reg. § 1.469-4(e)).[34] When regrouping is appropriate, taxpayers must comply with disclosure requirements (Rev. Proc. 2010-13). The IRS may disallow and regroup a taxpayer's grouping of activities that does not reflect an appropriate economic unit and has circumvention of the passive activity loss rules as a primary purpose (Reg. § 1.469-4(f)(1)).[35]

Activities Held Through Partnerships or S Corporations. Activities are first grouped by partnerships or S corporations at the entity level (Reg. § 1.469-4(d)(5)).[36] If appropriate, a partner or shareholder should further combine these activities with other activities outside the entity.

Rental Activities. Rental activities are grouped according to the "appropriate economic unit" standard. However, a rental real estate activity may not be combined with an activity involving the rental of personal property (Reg. § 1.469-4(d)(2)).[37]

Combining Trade or Business and Rental Activities. A rental activity may not be grouped with a trade or business activity unless either the rental activity is insubstantial in relation to the trade or business activity or the trade or business activity is insubstantial in relation to the rental activity (Reg. § 1.469-4(d)(1)(i)).[38] There is a third alternative that each owner of the trade or business have the same proportionate ownership interest in the rental activity, in which case the portion of the rental activity that involves the rental of items of property to a trade or business activity may be grouped with the trade or business activity.

> **Example:** The Getaway Partnership owns a 10-story building in which it operates a travel agency on three floors and rents seven floors to tenants. The partnership is divided into two activities: a travel agency activity and a rental real estate activity. Deductions and credits attributable to the building are allocable to the travel agency activity only to the extent that they relate to the space occupied by the travel agency during the tax year.

Partial Disposition of Activity. If the taxpayer disposes of ***substantially all*** of an activity, he or she may treat the interest disposed of as a separate activity, provided that the taxpayer can establish the amount of gross income, deductions and credits allocable to that part of the activity for the tax year (Reg. § 1.469-4(g)).[39] Without this rule, taxpayers generally cannot claim suspended passive losses until they have disposed of their entire interest in an activity (¶ 2076).

2059. Passive Activity Defined. A passive activity is one that involves the conduct of any trade or business in which the taxpayer does not materially participate (Code Sec. 469(c); Temporary Reg. § 1.469-1T(e)).[40] Any rental activity is a passive activity whether or not the taxpayer materially participates (¶ 2062). However, there are special rules for real estate rental activities (¶ 2063) and real estate professionals (¶ 2064). Trading personal property that is actively traded, such as stocks and bonds, for the account of

References are to Standard Federal Tax Reports; Tax Research Consultant; and Practical Tax Explanations.

[34] ¶ 21,964B; BUSEXP: 33,102; § 17,415.10

[35] ¶ 21,964B; BUSEXP: 33,102.30; § 17,415.25

[36] ¶ 21,964B; BUSEXP: 33,102.20; § 17,415.17

[37] ¶ 21,964B; BUSEXP: 33,102.25; § 17,415.15

[38] ¶ 21,964B; BUSEXP: 33,102.25; § 17,415.15

[39] ¶ 21,964B; BUSEXP: 33,652; § 17,415.20

[40] ¶ 21,960, ¶ 21,962; BUSEXP: 33,100; § 17,420.05

owners of interests in the activity is not a passive activity. For example, the activity of a partnership that trades stock using money contributed by the partners is not a passive activity.

Material participation in an activity requires that a taxpayer is involved in the operations of the activity on a regular, continuous and substantial basis (Code Sec. 469(h); Temp. Reg. § 1.469-5T).[41] Generally, an individual is considered as materially participating in an activity during a tax year if he or she satisfies one of the following tests:

(1) the individual participates more than 500 hours;

(2) the individual's participation constitutes substantially all of the participation in the activity;

(3) the individual participates for more than 100 hours and this participation is not less than the participation of any other individual;

(4) the activity is a "significant participation activity" (see below) and the individual's participation in all significant participation activities exceeds 500 hours;

(5) the individual materially participated in the activity for any five years of the 10 years that preceded the year in question;

(6) the activity is a "personal service activity" (see below) and the individual materially participated in the activity for any three years preceding the tax year in question; or

(7) the individual satisfies a facts and circumstances test that requires the individual to show participation on a regular, continuous, and substantial basis for more than 100 hours during the tax year.

With respect to test (7), an individual's participation in managing the activity does not count toward the 100-hour requirement if any other person received compensation for managing the activity or any other person spent more time managing the activity.

Special rules are provided for determining the material participation of certain retired or disabled farmers and participation in the activity of a personal service or closely held corporation (Temp. Reg. § 1.469-5T(h)).[42]

Limited Partners. Losses and credits attributable to limited partnership interests are treated as arising from a passive activity unless the limited partner participated for more than 500 hours (test (1)), the limited partner materially participated in 5 of the 10 preceding tax years (test (5)), or the activity is a personal service activity in which the limited partner materially participated for any three preceding tax years (test (6)). A general partner who also holds a limited partnership interest is not treated as a limited partner (Code Sec. 469(h)(2); Temp. Reg. § 1.469-5T(e)).[43]

Significant Participation Activity. A significant participation activity is one in which the taxpayer participates more than 100 hours during the tax year but does not materially participate under any of the other six tests set forth above (Temp. Reg. § 1.469-5T(c)).[44]

Personal Service Activity. A personal service activity involves the performance of personal service in (1) the fields of health (including veterinary services), law, engineering, architecture, accounting, actuarial services, the performing arts, or consulting or (2) any other trade or business in which capital is not a material income-producing factor (Temp. Reg. § 1.469-5T(d)).[45]

References are to Standard Federal Tax Reports; Tax Research Consultant; and Practical Tax Explanations.

[41] ¶ 21,960, ¶ 21,965; BUSEXP: 33,150; § 17,435.05

[42] ¶ 21,965; BUSEXP: 33,158, BUSEXP: 33,164; § 17,435.25, § 17,435.35

[43] ¶ 21,960, ¶ 21,965; BUSEXP: 33,160; § 17,435.20

[44] ¶ 21,965; BUSEXP: 33,152.05; § 17,435.15

[45] ¶ 21,965; BUSEXP: 33,152; § 17,435.15

Definition of Participation. Generally, any work done by an individual with respect to an activity in which the individual owns an interest is treated as participation (Reg. § 1.469-5(f)(1); Temp. Reg. § 1.469-5T(f)).[46] However, participation does not include work that is not customarily done by an owner if one of the principal purposes for performing the work is to avoid the passive activity limitations. Work done in an individual's capacity as an investor in an activity is also not counted as participation, such as studying and reviewing the activity's financial statements and operational reports, preparing summaries or analyses of the activity's finances or operations for personal use, and monitoring the finances or operations of the activity in a nonmanagerial capacity.

An individual's participation does include participation of his or her spouse even if the spouse does not own an interest in the activity and separate returns are filed. Participation may be established by any reasonable means. It is not necessary to maintain contemporaneous daily records of participation. An approximate number of hours of participation may be based on appointment books, calendars, or narrative summaries.

2060. Portfolio Income. Portfolio income is not treated as income from a passive activity; it must be accounted for separately, and passive losses and credits generally may not be applied against it. Portfolio income includes interest, dividends, annuities and royalties, as well as gain or loss from the disposition of income-producing or investment property that is not derived in the ordinary course of a trade or business (Code Sec. 469(e)(1)).[47] No exception is provided for the treatment of portfolio income arising from working capital (amounts set aside for the reasonable needs of the business).

In the case of a lending transaction between a taxpayer and a pass-through entity in which the taxpayer owns a direct or indirect interest, a self-charged interest rule treats certain interest income as passive activity gross income and certain interest expense as passive activity deductions (Reg. § 1.469-7).[48] These rules also apply to lending transactions between identically owned pass-through entities.

Rental Activities

2062. Rental Activities Subject to Passive Activity Rules. A rental activity is generally treated as a passive activity regardless if the taxpayer materially participates in the activity (Code Sec. 469(c)(2); Temp. Reg. § 1.469-1T(e)(3)).[49] An activity is a "rental activity" if (1) during the tax year, tangible property held in connection with the activity is used by customers or is held for use by customers, and (2) the gross income of the activity represents amounts paid mainly for the use of the tangible property. A taxpayer's rental real estate activity is not considered passive activity if the taxpayer is a real estate professional (¶ 2064). In addition, if any one of the following tests is met, the activity is also not considered to be a rental activity for purposes of the passive loss rules:

- the average period of customer use of the property is seven days or less;
- the average period of customer use is 30 days or less and significant personal services are provided by or on behalf of the owner;
- without regard to the period of customer use, extraordinary personal services are provided by or on behalf of the owner;
- the rental of the property is incidental to a nonrental activity;
- the property is customarily made available during defined business hours for the nonexclusive use of customers; or
- the taxpayer provides property for use in an activity that is conducted by a partnership, S corporation, or joint venture in which the taxpayer owns an interest and the activity is not a rental activity.

References are to Standard Federal Tax Reports; Tax Research Consultant; and Practical Tax Explanations.

[46] ¶ 21,964C, ¶ 21,965; BUSEXP: 33,154; § 17,435.10

[47] ¶ 21,960; BUSEXP: 33,354; § 17,450.10

[48] ¶ 21,965B; BUSEXP: 33,462.20; § 17,450.15

[49] ¶ 21,960; BUSEXP: 33,106; § 17,430.05

If a taxpayer does not meet the requirements to be a real estate professional, but who own and actively participate in a rental real estate may nonetheless deduct up to $25,000 of losses from a passive rental real estate activity from non-passive income (¶ 2063).

2063. $25,000 Offset for Active Participation in Rental Real Estate Activity. Individuals who own and actively participate in a rental real estate activity may offset up to $25,000 of passive activity losses and credits ($12,500 for married filing separately) from the activity against active income (for example, wages) (Code Sec. 469(i)).[50] The exception is available only to individual taxpayers or their estates for tax years ending less than two years after the date of death. The estate qualifies during this period if the decedent actively participated before his or her death. To be eligible for this exception, the individual must own at least a 10-percent interest of all interests in the activity throughout the year. The interest of an individual's spouse is taken into account in determining 10-percent ownership whether or not a joint return is filed.

The active participation standard is less stringent than the material participation standard (¶ 2059). An individual may meet the active participation requirement if he or she participates in the making of management decisions (for example, approving new tenants, deciding on rental terms, approving expenditures) or arranges for others to provide services (for example, repairs) in a significant and bona fide sense. The requirement for active participation applies in the year in which the loss arose as well as the year in which the loss is allowed. However, real estate professionals may be able to treat rental property activities as nonpassive activities (¶ 2064).

The $25,000 maximum offset amount is reduced, but not below zero, by 50 percent of the amount by which adjusted gross income (AGI) exceeds $100,000. It is completely phased out when adjusted gross income reaches $150,000 (Code Sec. 469(i)(3)). For this purpose, AGI is computed without regard to: taxable Social Security and railroad retirement benefits, the exclusion for qualified U.S. savings bonds used to pay higher education expenses, the exclusion for employer adoption assistance payments, passive activity income or loss included on Form 8582, any overall loss from a publicly traded partnership, rental real estate losses allowed to real estate professionals, deductions attributable to domestic production activities, deductions for contributions to IRAs and pension plans, and the deductions for one-half of self-employment tax, interest on student loans, and higher education expenses.

Separate Returns. For married taxpayers who file separate returns and live apart, up to $12,500 of passive losses may be used to offset income. This amount is reduced by 50 percent of the amount by which the taxpayer's modified AGI exceeds $50,000. The special allowance is completely phased out when modified AGI reaches $75,000. Married taxpayers who file separately and live together at any time during the tax year are not eligible for the special allowance (Code Sec. 469(i)(5)).[51]

Offset of Credits. Passive activity credits attributable to rental real estate activities in which the taxpayer actively participates may be claimed under the $25,000 offset provision, but only after all eligible losses have been used. Special apply of the phaseout of the rehabilitation credit (¶ 1365B), low-income housing credit (¶ 1365K), and commercial revitalization deduction (¶ 999C).

2064. Real Estate Professionals. Certain real estate professionals may be able to treat rental real estate activities as nonpassive and thus not subject to the passive activity rules (Code Sec. 469(c)(7); Reg. § 1.469-9(g)).[52] To qualify: (1) more than one-half of the personal services performed in trades or businesses by the taxpayer during the tax year must involve real property trades or businesses in which the taxpayer (or the taxpayer's spouse) materially participates; and (2) the taxpayer must perform more than 750 hours of service during the tax year in real property trades or businesses in which the taxpayer (or the taxpayer's spouse) materially participates. These two requirements must be satisfied by one spouse if a joint return is filed. Personal services performed as an

References are to Standard Federal Tax Reports; Tax Research Consultant; and Practical Tax Explanations.

[50] ¶ 21,960; BUSEXP: 33,706; § 17,480.05

[51] ¶ 21,960; BUSEXP: 33,702; § 17,480.15

[52] ¶ 21,960, ¶ 21,965D; BUSEXP: 33,106.40; § 17,430.15

employee are not taken into account under either requirement unless the employee owns more than a 5-percent interest in the employer. A real property trade or business is a business with respect to which real property is developed or redeveloped, constructed or reconstructed, acquired, converted, rented or leased, operated or managed, or brokered.

The exception for real estate professionals is applied as if each interest of the taxpayer in rental real estate is a separate activity. However, a taxpayer may elect to treat all interests in rental real estate as a single activity for purposes of satisfying the material participation requirements (¶ 2059). To make the election, the taxpayer must file a statement with the taxpayer's original income tax return for the tax year declaring that he or she is a qualified taxpayer for the tax year and is making the election. Certain taxpayers may be permitted to make late elections (Rev. Proc. 2011-34).

A closely held corporation qualifies as a real estate professional if more than 50 percent of its annual gross receipts for the tax year are from real property trades or businesses in which it materially participates.

Disposition of Entire Interest in Passive Activity

2076. Disposition of Entire Interest in Passive Activity. When a taxpayer disposes of his or her entire interest in a passive activity in a taxable transaction, the taxpayer's suspended passive activity losses (¶ 2053) may be applied against his or her active income (Code Sec. 469(g)).[53] However, these losses must first be applied against the taxpayer's net income or gain from passive activities. Any remaining loss from the activity is then classified as nonpassive and may be used to offset income from nonpassive activities (for example, wages). Suspended credits are not allowed on the disposition of a passive activity.

Entire Interest. A disposition of a taxpayer's entire interest involves a disposition of the interest in all entities that are engaged in the activity and, to the extent the activity is held in the form of a sole proprietorship, of all of the assets used or created in the activity. If a partnership or S corporation conducts two or more separate activities and the entity disposes of all the assets used or created in one activity, the disposition constitutes a disposition of the entire interest. The same rule applies to grantor trusts.[54] In some instances, a taxpayer may claim a deduction for suspended losses even though he or she disposes of less than his or her entire interest (¶ 2058).

Taxable Transactions. To qualify as a fully taxable disposition, the disposition generally must be a sale of the interest to a third party in an arm's-length transaction and must not be a sham, a wash sale, or a transfer of repurchase rights (Code Sec. 469(g)(1)).[55] If a taxpayer disposes of an interest in a passive activity in a taxable transaction with a related party as defined by Code Sec. 267(b) (¶ 1717) or with a controlled partnership as defined by Code Sec. 707(b)(1) (¶ 432), the suspended losses will not be triggered. In these circumstances the taxpayer will be able to claim the loss only when the related person or controlled partnership disposes of the activity in a taxable transaction with an unrelated person. Abandonment is a fully taxable disposition.

Installment Sales. When a taxpayer sells his entire interest in a passive activity and reports the gain under the installment sale method, only a portion of the suspended loss may be deducted in the year of the sale. Suspended losses are allowed in the year of sale and thereafter in the ratio that the gain recognized in a tax year bears to the total gross profit from the sale to be realized when payment is completed (Code Sec. 469(g)(3)).[56]

Death. A transfer by reason of the taxpayer's death causes suspended losses to be allowed in the year of death to the extent that they exceed the amount by which the basis of the interest is stepped-up at death (¶ 1633).[57]

References are to Standard Federal Tax Reports; Tax Research Consultant; and Practical Tax Explanations.

[53] ¶ 21,960; BUSEXP: 33,652; § 17,490.05, § 17,490.10

[54] ¶ 21,966.0552; BUSEXP: 33,652; § 17,490.10

[55] ¶ 21,960; BUSEXP: 33,652, BUSEXP: 33,654; § 17,490.15, § 17,490.35

[56] ¶ 21,960; BUSEXP: 33,668; § 17,490.30

[57] ¶ 21,960; BUSEXP: 33,658; § 17,490.20

Gifts. Disposition of a passive activity by gift does *not* trigger the suspended losses. Instead, the basis of the transferred interest is increased by the amount of such losses (Code Sec. 469(j)(6)).[58]

Nontaxable Exchanges. An exchange of a taxpayer's interest in a passive activity in a nonrecognition transaction (e.g., a like-kind exchange (¶ 1721)) does not trigger suspended losses. However, to the extent that the taxpayer recognizes gain on the transaction (for example, to the extent of boot received), the gain is treated as passive activity income against which passive losses may be deducted.[59]

Casualty or Theft. A casualty or theft loss involving property used in a passive activity does not constitute a complete disposition of the taxpayer's interest in the activity unless loss of all property used or created in the activity results.[60]

Activity No Longer Passive. In the tax year that an activity ceases to be a passive activity, previously suspended losses from that activity are permitted to be claimed as deductions against the activity's net income. Similarly, prior year suspended passive activity credits may offset the current year's tax liability that is allocable to the current year's net income from the former passive activity. Tax liability for this purpose is figured on the net income as reduced by the prior year suspended losses (Code Sec. 469(f)(1)).[61]

Cessation of Closely Held C Corporation or PSC Status. If a closely held C corporation or a personal service corporation (PSC) changes its status, suspended losses from prior years will continue to be subject to the limitations that were imposed before the status changed (¶ 2056). Losses arising in years after the year in which the corporation's status changes are not subject to the passive loss rules (Code Sec. 469(f)(2)).

Tax-Exempt Use Property

2080. Limits on Tax-Exempt Use Losses. A taxpayer leasing property to a government or other tax-exempt entity (i.e., sale-in, lease-out (SILO) arrangement) is not allowed to claim deductions that are related to the property (known as tax-exempt use property) to the extent that they exceed the taxpayer's income from the lease payments (a tax-exempt use loss), subject to certain exceptions (Code Sec. 470).[62] Tax-exempt use property is generally defined in Code Sec. 168(h). It includes property owned by a partnership (or other pass-through entity) that has at least one tax-exempt partner and the allocations of partnership items attempt to inappropriately transfer the deductions from the tax-exempt partner to the taxable partners.

Tax-exempt losses disallowed may be carried over to the next tax year and can be deducted to the extent of the taxpayer's net income from the property for that year. If property ceases to be tax-exempt use property during the lease term, the carried over loss cannot be used to offset income from other property. If the property is disposed of, any disallowed loss is available under rules similar to passive activity losses (¶ 2076). However, the limitation on tax-exempt use property losses is applied before the passive activity rules.

References are to Standard Federal Tax Reports; Tax Research Consultant; and Practical Tax Explanations.

[58] ¶ 21,960; BUSEXP: 33,660; § 17,490.25

[59] ¶ 21,966.0553; BUSEXP: 33,662; § 17,490.15

[60] ¶ 21,966.0553; BUSEXP: 33,652.10; § 17,490.15

[61] ¶ 21,960; BUSEXP: 33,600; § 17,440

[62] ¶ 21,970; BUSEXP: 36,000

Chapter 21
RETIREMENT AND BENEFITS

Par.

Retirement Plans - Overview

2101. Introduction. An employer who wants to provide retirement benefits for employees may establish a pension, profit-sharing, or stock bonus plan that qualifies for certain tax benefits (Code Sec. 401).[1] Among the tax benefits offered by a qualified retirement plan are: (1) a tax exemption for the trust that is established to provide benefits (Code Sec. 501(a); Reg. § 1.401(f)-1(c)(1));[2] (2) a current deduction by the employer for contributions made to the trust (Code Sec. 404);[3] and (3) tax deferral for the employee on the employer's contributions and earnings (Code Secs. 402(a) and 403(a)(1)).[4] As an alternative to a qualified plan, an employer may establish and contribute to an IRA-based plan such as a SEP plan (Code Sec. 408(k)) or a SIMPLE IRA (Code Sec. 408(p)), or an employer may merely enable employees to choose to make direct contributions via payroll deductions to an IRA they have established.[5] An eligible small business with 100 or fewer employees may claim a credit for the start-up costs incurred in establishing certain benefit plans (¶ 1365U). Outside the employment relationship, individuals who have compensation during a year may establish and make contributions to traditional or Roth IRAs to save for their retirement (Code Secs. 408 and 408A).[6]

Qualified Retirement Plans. There are two broad categories of qualified retirement plans: defined contribution plans and defined benefit plans. Defined contribution plans include profit-sharing, stock bonus, and money purchase plans in which a separate

References are to Standard Federal Tax Reports; Tax Research Consultant; and Practical Tax Explanations.

[1] ¶ 17,502; RETIRE: 100; § 24,101
[2] ¶ 18,100, ¶ 22,602; RETIRE: 100; § 24,101
[3] ¶ 18,330; RETIRE: 100; § 24,101
[4] ¶ 18,202, ¶ 18,270; RETIRE: 100; § 24,101
[5] ¶ 18,902, ¶ 18,922.0245, ¶ 18,922.026; RETIRE: 63,000; § 25,001, § 25,101
[6] ¶ 18,902, ¶ 18,925; RETIRE: 66,000, RETIRE: 66,750; § 25,401, § 25,501

account is provided for each employee covered by the plan and the employee's retirement benefit is based on the contributions to the account, as well as any income, expenses, gains, losses, and forfeitures of other accounts that may be allocated to the account (Code Sec. 414(i)).[7] Defined benefit plans include pension and annuity plans that offer a specific retirement benefit to employees, usually in the form of a monthly retirement pension that is based on the employee's wages and years of service with the employer (Code Sec. 414(j)).[8] An employer's annual contributions to the plan are based on actuarial assumptions and are not allocated to individual accounts maintained for the employees (Reg. § 1.401-1(b)(1)(i)).[9]

2102. Plan Compliance Checklist. When setting up or reviewing a qualified retirement plan, does the plan comply with:

- nondiscrimination requirements (¶ 2117),
- coverage standards (¶ 2116),
- participation standards (¶ 2115),
- minimum vesting requirements (¶ 2119, ¶ 2143), and
- distribution rules (¶ 2124).

The plan should also be reviewed for compliance with limitations with respect to contributions and benefits (¶ 2104).

2103. Employment Tax Checklist. The following summarizes the employment tax treatment of various pension and retirement plans:

- Employer contributions to a qualified plan: income tax withholding (exempt); FICA (exempt); FUTA (exempt).
- Employer contributions to individual retirement account (IRA): income tax withholding (exempt, if it is reasonable to believe employee will be entitled to receive a deduction for the contribution); FICA (taxable); FUTA (taxable).
- Elective employee contributions and deferrals to qualified cash or deferred compensation plan (e.g., 401(k) plan): income tax withholding (exempt, subject to Code Sec. 402(g) limitations); FICA (taxable); FUTA (taxable).
- Employer contributions to certain nonqualified deferred compensation plans: income tax withholding (exempt); FICA (exempt); FUTA (exempt).
- Employer contributions to SEP IRA (exempt subject to Code Sec. 402(g) limitations); FICA (exempt, except for amounts contributed under a SARSEP) (¶ 2110); FUTA (exempt, except for amounts contributed under a SARSEP).
- Employer contributions to 403(b) annuity contracts: income tax withholding (exempt, subject to Code Sec. 402(g) limitations); FICA (taxable, if paid through a salary reduction agreement); FUTA (taxable, if paid through a salary reduction agreement).
- Distributions from qualified plans: income tax withholding (taxable, unless recipient elects exemption from withholding); FICA (exempt); FUTA (exempt).
- Employee salary reduction contributions to SIMPLE retirement account: income tax withholding (exempt); FICA (taxable); FUTA (taxable).
- Employer and elective employee contributions to a 457 plan: income tax withholding (exempt, subject to Code Sec. 457(b)(2) limitations); FICA (taxable); FUTA (taxable).

2104. Plan Adjustment Checklist. Have plan adjustments been made for the:

- maximum benefit limit for defined benefit plan of $200,000 for 2012 and $205,000 for 2013;

References are to Standard Federal Tax Reports; Tax Research Consultant; and Practical Tax Explanations.

[7] ¶ 19,150; RETIRE: 100; § 24,115

[8] ¶ 19,150; RETIRE: 100; § 24,120.05

[9] ¶ 17,504; RETIRE: 100; § 24,120.10

- annual defined contribution plan limit of $50,000 for 2012 and $51,000 for 2013;
- catch-up contribution limit to an applicable employer plan (other than a Code Sec. 401(k)(11) or Code Sec. 408(p) plan) for individuals aged 50 or over of $5,500 in 2012 and 2013;
- catch-up contribution limit to an applicable employer plan under Code Sec. 401(k)(11) or Code Sec. 408(p) for individuals aged 50 or over of $2,500 in 2012 and 2013;
- exclusion for elective deferrals of $17,000 for 2012 and $17,500 for 2013;
- annual compensation limit of $250,000 for 2012 and $255,000 for 2013;
- limitation used in the definition of highly compensated employee of $115,000 for 2012 and 2013;
- limitation regarding SIMPLE retirement accounts of $11,500 in 2012 and $12,000 in 2013; and
- limitation concerning the definition of a key employee in a top-heavy plan of $165,000 in 2012 and 2013.

If the plan is top heavy (more than 60 percent of the benefits accrued or contributions made to key employees), does plan:

- reflect current vesting schedules (Code Sec. 416(b));
- provide for minimum benefits (Code Sec. 416(c)); and
- meet requirements without integration with Social Security (Code Sec. 416(e)).

If plan is a SEP, have adjustments been made for:

- minimum compensation level for simplified employee pension (SEP) plans of $550 for 2012 and 2013;
- compensation limit for SEP plans of $250,000 for 2012 and $255,000 for 2013; and
- deferral amount for salary reduction SEPs (SARSEPs) (established prior to 1997) of $17,000 for 2012 and $17,500 for 2013.

If ESOP has been established, has adjustment been made for:

- the dollar amount for determining the maximum account in an ESOP subject to a five-year distribution period ($1,015,000 for 2012 and $1,035,000 for 2013); and
- the dollar amount used to determine the lengthening of the five-year distribution period ($200,000 for 2012 and $205,000 for 2013).

Defined Contribution Plans - Types

2105. Introduction. A defined contribution plan is a plan that provides an individual account for each participant and for benefits based solely on the amount contributed to the participant's account, along with any income, expenses, gains and losses, and any forfeitures by other participants that are allocated to the account (Code Sec. 414(i)). Defined contribution plans are sometimes referred to as individual account plans. A defined contribution plan can be: a 401(k) plan (¶ 2106), an employee stock ownership plan (¶ 2111), a money purchase plan (¶ 2107), a profit-sharing plan (¶ 2108), or a stock bonus plan (¶ 2111).

Defined contribution plans are subject to requirements regarding participation (¶ 2115) and coverage (¶ 2116), nondiscrimination (¶ 2117), and vesting (¶ 2119). There are also requirements regarding compensation limits (¶ 2120), contribution limits (¶ 2121), deduction limits (¶ 2122A), distributions (¶ 2124), rollovers (¶ 2125), anti-assignment (¶ 2127), prohibited transactions (¶ 2128), and plan loans (¶ 2129). Employers with at least two employees but not more than 500 employees may establish a combined defined benefit/401(k) plan (¶ 2150E).

2106. 401(k) Plans. A profit-sharing or stock-bonus plan can include a cash or deferred arrangement (CODA) under which each participating employee has the option of receiving an amount of their compensation in cash or having it contributed pre-tax to the plan (Code Secs. 401(k) and 402(e)(3); Reg. §§1.401(k)-1 and 1.402(a)-1(d).[10] The contribution is referred to as an elective contribution or elective deferral. A profit-sharing or stock-bonus plan with this type of arrangement is known as a 401(k) plan. If the plan meets certain requirements, the normal constructive receipt rule is preempted and the employees do not have to recognize the deferred amounts immediately in gross income. Certain eligible employers (¶2106G) may also adopt a Savings Incentive Match Plan for Employees (SIMPLE) option as part of a 401(k) plan (Code Sec. 401(k)(11)).[11] Generally, a SIMPLE 401(k) must meet the same requirements that apply to other 401(k) plans except for the nondiscrimination and top-heavy rules. It is also subject to special rules on contributions, deductions, and vesting (¶2106G).

A partnership may maintain a 401(k) plan and individual partners may make elective deferrals to the plan based on their compensation for the services they provide to the partnership (Reg. §1.401(k)-1(a)(6)(i)).[12] A sole proprietor is also permitted to maintain a 401(k) plan with elective deferrals based on net earnings from the business. In fact, most self-employed individuals will find that their tax deductible contributions to a 401(k) plan will be greater than those allowed to other types of self-employed retirement plans (¶2163). The Federal Thrift Savings Plan, which is often called the "Thrift Savings Plan," provides federal employees with the same savings and tax benefits that private employers offer their employees with 401(k) plans (Code Sec. 7701(j)).[13]

A 401(k) plan must meet the following specific requirements, in addition to the general requirements for all qualified plans (¶2105):

- the plan must not require as a condition of participation that an employee complete more than one year of service with the employer;
- the plan must not condition any other employee benefit (apart from matching contributions) upon an employee's election to make contributions to the 401(k) plan;
- the plan must provide that the participant's right to the value of their account that is attributable to elective contributions be fully vested at all times;
- the plan must not provide for distributions merely by reason of a stated period of participation or the lapse of a fixed number of years; and
- the plan must be prohibited from distributing amounts attributable to elective contributions *earlier* than one of the following events:
  - severance from employment, death or disability;
  - termination of the plan without establishment or maintenance of another defined contribution plan (Code Sec. 401(k)(10));
  - attainment of age 59½; or
  - employee hardship (¶2106E) (however, distributions at age 59½ or for hardship are not permitted in the case of a money purchase pension plan).

A 401(k) plan that includes a qualified Roth contribution program (¶2106F) may permit a qualified rollover contribution from a participant's non-Roth account to the participant's designated Roth account within the same plan (Code Sec. 402A(c)(4)(B)) (¶2125E).

2106A. Elective Deferrals. An employee's elective deferrals to a 401(k) plan are subject to an annual limit (Code Sec. 402(g)).[14] However, the limit does not just apply to each 401(k) plan to which the employee makes elective deferrals but instead applies to the aggregate amount of all the elective deferrals made by the employee for the year to

References are to Standard Federal Tax Reports; Tax Research Consultant; and Practical Tax Explanations.

[10] ¶17,502, ¶18,110, ¶18,202, ¶18,203; RETIRE: 3,200; §24,701

[11] ¶17,502; RETIRE: 3,350; §24,720

[12] ¶18,110B; RETIRE: 3,206; §24,705.10

[13] ¶43,080; RETIRE: 3,400; §24,701

[14] ¶18,202; RETIRE: 3,254; §24,710.10

all plans which permit such contributions, including other 401(k) plans, SEP IRAs, and 403(b) annuity plans (but not 457 plans, ¶ 2161). The annual limit is $17,000 for 2012 (Notice 2011-90) and $17,500 for 2013 (IRS News Release IR-2012-77).

Example: Tony, age 45, works for two employers. Each of the employers offers a 401(k) plan and Tony participates in both plans. During 2012, Tony deferred $11,500 of his wages into the 401(k) plan of Employer A and $6,000 of his wages into the 401(k) plan of Employer B. For 2012, Tony has made an excess deferral of $500 ($17,500 in aggregate deferrals - $17,000 maximum deferral allowable).

Nondiscrimination Requirement. A special nondiscrimination requirement applies to elective deferrals made to a 401(k) plan under which the plan will not be treated as qualified unless the actual deferral percentage (ADP) for eligible highly compensated employees (¶ 2117) for the plan year bears a relationship to the ADP for all other eligible employees for the preceding plan year that meets either of the following tests:

- the ADP for the group of eligible highly compensated employees (HCEs) is not more than the actual ADP of all other eligible employees multiplied by 1.25, or

- the excess of the ADP for the group of eligible highly compensated employees over that of all other eligible employees is not more than 2 percentage points, and the ADP for the group of eligible HCEs is not more than the ADP of all other eligible employees multiplied by 2 (Code Sec. 401(k)(3); Reg. § 1.401(k)-2).[15]

The employer may elect to calculate the ADP test for rank-and-file employees with reference to the current year rather than the preceding year. However, the election once made may not be revoked without IRS permission. In the case of a test year which is the first year of the plan (other than a successor plan), the ADP of rank-and-file employees for the preceding plan year will be deemed to be three percent or, if the employer elects, the ADP calculated on the basis of rank-and-file employees for the first plan year. If the 401(k) plan provides for matching employer contributions or allows employees contributions to be made on an after-tax basis, then a separate nondiscrimination test generally applies to those contributions (¶ 2117).

A plan can avoid failing to satisfy the ADP test by having the employer make qualified nonelective contributions or qualified matching contributions that are treated as elective contributions under the plan and that, in combination with the elective deferrals, satisfy the nondiscrimination requirements. The plan can also limit the elective deferrals by highly compensated employees to prevent any excess contributions or allow the highly compensated employees the option to have any excess contributions distributed back to them or recharacterized (Code Sec. 401(k)(8); Reg. § 1.401(k)-2(b)(1)). An employer may also adopt one of three designed-based safe harbors to satisfy the ADP test for its 401(k) plan. The ADP test will be deemed satisfied if:

- a prescribed level of matching or nonelective contributions are made under the plan on behalf of all eligible nonhighly compensated employees and if employees are provided a timely notice describing their rights and obligations under the plan (Code Sec. 401(k)(12) and (m)(11); Reg. § 1.401(k)-3);[16]

- the plan meets the requirements for a qualified automatic contribution arrangement (QACA) where eligible employees are uniformly treated as having elected to have the employer make elective contributions equal to a qualified percentage of compensation (no more than 10 percent, but at least three percent in the first year, four percent for the second year, five percent for the third year, and six percent for the fourth year) (Code Sec. 401(k)(13) and (m)(12)); or

- the plans meets the contribution and vesting requirements applicable to SIMPLE 401(k) plans (¶ 2106G).

References are to Standard Federal Tax Reports; Tax Research Consultant; and Practical Tax Explanations.

[15] ¶ 17,502, ¶ 18,110; RETIRE: 3,210; § 24,705.35

[16] ¶ 17,502; RETIRE: 3,210.60; § 24,705.35

2106B. Catch-Up Contributions. Individuals who will be at least age 50 by the end of the tax year may make an additional "catch-up" contribution to most types of retirement plans (e.g., 401(k), IRA, 403(b) and 457 plans). The maximum amount of the annual catch-up contribution depends upon the type of plan involved as well as the tax year for which the contribution is being made (Code Sec. 414(v)).[17] The maximum "catch-up" contribution to a 401(k) plan is $5,500 for 2012 and 2013 (Notice 2011-90; IRS News Release IR-2012-77). Catch-up contributions may only be made if the plan permits this type of contribution.

2106C. Excess Contributions. Elective deferrals that exceed the annual limit (¶ 2106A) are included in the employee's income and are subject to a 10-percent penalty (Code Secs. 402(g) and 4979).[18] The employee may generally withdraw the excess contribution from the plan before April 15 of the following tax year along with any attributable income. If the employee has made elective deferrals to more than one plan, then the employee can designate the amount of the excess that is to be withdrawn from each plan. If the excess contribution remains in the plan past the April 15 distribution date, it will be taxed a second time when distributed (Reg. § 1.402(g)-1(e)(8)(iii)).[19] The 10-percent penalty will not apply if the excess is distributed within 2½ months following the plan year in which the excess contribution was made.

2106D. Matching Contributions. As a general rule, matching contributions made to a 401(k) plan by the employer are not treated as an employee's elective contributions and are, therefore, not subject to the annual limit on deferrals. In addition, matching contributions made by a self-employed person to a 401(k) plan are not treated as part of the individual's elective contributions (Code Sec. 402(g)(8)).[20]

2106E. Hardship Distributions. A 401(k) plan may allow hardship distributions up to the amount of the participant's elective deferrals. A hardship distribution is one that (1) is made because of the employee's immediate and heavy financial need and (2) does not exceed the amount necessary to satisfy that need (Reg. § 1.401(k)-1(d)(3)).[21] Types of expenses that satisfy the requirement of immediate and heavy financial need include:

- medical expenses of the employee, spouse, and dependents;
- expenditures (excluding mortgage payments) to purchase a principal residence for the employee;
- post-secondary tuition for the employee, spouse, or dependents;
- expenditures to stave off eviction or foreclosure with respect to the employee's principal residence;
- burial or funeral expenses for the employee's deceased parent, spouse, or dependents; and
- expenses for the repair of casualty damage to the employee's principal residence.

An immediate and heavy financial need also includes any amounts necessary to pay any income taxes or penalties reasonably anticipated to result from the distribution. To the extent allowed under the plan, if medical, tuition, or funeral expenses incurred on behalf of the employee's spouse or dependent are deemed to be an immediate and heavy financial need, the incurring of the same expenses with regard to the employee'sbeneficiary under the plan can also be considered an immediate and heavy financial need (Notice 2007-7).

A distribution will be treated as necessary to satisfy the employee's immediate and heavy financial need if the following requirements are met:

References are to Standard Federal Tax Reports; Tax Research Consultant; and Practical Tax Explanations.

17 ¶ 19,150; RETIRE: 3,254; § 24,710.15

18 ¶ 18,202, ¶ 34,520; RETIRE: 3,254.05; § 24,710.10

19 ¶ 18,220, ¶ 34,520; RETIRE: 3,254; § 24,710.10

20 ¶ 18,202; RETIRE: 3,210.20, RETIRE: 3,254.05; § 24,710.25

21 ¶ 18,110; RETIRE: 3,302; § 24,715.15

- the distribution is not in excess of the amount needed to satisfy the financial need;
- the employee has obtained all distributions and nontaxable loans available under all plans of the employer; and
- the distribution triggers the suspension of elective contributions on behalf of the employee and other employee contributions to any deferred compensation plan of the employer for at least six months.

Example: Bill takes a hardship distribution from his 401(k) plan on April 1, 2013. In order to satisfy one of the safe harbor requirements, Bill will not be able to make any elective deferrals or after-tax contributions to the plan until October 1, 2013 (i.e., six-month suspension of contributions).

A hardship distribution is included in the employee's income and subject to the 10-percent additional tax on early distributions unless an exception applies (¶ 2124C). A hardship distribution generally may *not* be rolled over into an IRA or other type of retirement plan (Code Sec. 402(c)(4)(C)).[22] However, a hardship distribution that is a "qualified recovery assistance distribution" can be recontributed and treated as a rollover (¶ 2124).

2106F. Roth 401(k) Plans. Plans that allow employees to make pre-tax elective deferrals (such as 401(k) and 403(b) plans) may also allow participating employees to designate all or part of their elective deferrals to the plan to be treated as after-tax Roth contributions (Code Sec. 402A).[23] The designated Roth contributions are generally treated the same as pre-tax elective deferrals under the plan for purposes of limits on deferrals and nondiscrimination requirements, except that the plan must account for them separately. While the employee must include the Roth contributions in gross income, distributions are subject to rules similar to the rules applicable to distributions from a Roth IRA (¶ 2154C). However, unlike a Roth IRA (¶ 2154), amounts held in a Roth 401(k) account are subject to the required minimum distribution (RMD) rules (¶ 2124B). Beginning in 2011, Sec. 457 plans may include a designated Roth contribution program (¶ 2161).

2106G. SIMPLE 401(k) Plans. A SIMPLE 401(k) is a simplified cash or deferred arrangement (CODA) which generally must meet the same requirements that apply to other 401(k) plans (¶ 2106). However, in lieu of satisfying the nondiscrimination test for elective deferrals and matching contributions, a SIMPLE 401(k) plan is a qualified plan (and also will not be subject to the rules for "top-heavy plans" (¶ 2118)) by satisfying the following requirements.

Employee Contributions. Each employee eligible to participate in the SIMPLE 401(k) plan must have the right to make annual elective contributions, expressed as a percentage of compensation but not exceeding $11,500 for 2012 and $12,000 for 2013. An employee age 50 or over may make an additional catch-up contribution of $2,500 for 2012 and 2013 (Code Sec. 414(v)(2)(B)(ii); Notice 2011-90; IRS News Release IR-2012-77).[24] Nondeductible employee contributions and rollover contributions may not be made to a SIMPLE 401(k).

Employer Contributions. Generally, the employer must make matching contributions for each participant in a SIMPLE 401(k) in an amount not exceeding three percent of the employee's compensation (Code Sec. 401(k)(11)(B)).[25] However, instead of making matching contributions, an employer may elect to make nonelective contributions of two percent of compensation for each employee who is eligible to participate in the arrangement and who has at least $5,000 of compensation. Employees must be notified that the employer has chosen to make the two-percent contribution within a reasonable period of time before the 60th day before the beginning of the calendar year.

References are to Standard Federal Tax Reports; Tax Research Consultant; and Practical Tax Explanations.

[22] ¶ 18,202; RETIRE: 3,302; § 24,455.10

[23] 18,230; RETIRE: 3,258; § 24,725.05

[24] ¶ 19,150; RETIRE: 27,102.20; § 24,720.15

[25] ¶ 17,502; RETIRE: 3,350; § 24,720.15

Compensation. SIMPLE compensation means the sum of wages, tips, and other compensation from the eligible employer subject to federal income tax withholding and the employee's elective contributions made under any other plan, and if applicable, elective deferrals under a SIMPLE IRA plan, a SARSEP, or a 403(b) plan, and compensation deferred under a section 457 plan, required to be reported by the employer on Form W-2. For self-employed individuals, SIMPLE compensation means net earnings from self-employment determined prior to subtracting any contributions made under the SIMPLE 401(k) plan on behalf of the individual (Reg. § 1.401(k)-4(e)(5)).

Employer's Deduction. An employer's deduction for contributions to a defined contribution plan is generally limited to the *greater* of: (1) 25 percent of the compensation paid or accrued during the tax year to beneficiaries under a stock bonus or profit-sharing plan or (2) the amount that the employer is required to contribute to a SIMPLE 401(k) plan for the year (Code Sec. 404(a)(3)(A)(i)(I) and (II)).[26] Thus, an employer's deduction for its contributions to a SIMPLE 401(k) may be greater than the general limit of 25 percent of compensation paid (¶ 2122A).

Vesting. All contributions to a SIMPLE 401(k) must be fully vested when made, and the plan cannot impose any restrictions on withdrawals (Code Sec. 401(k)(11)).[27]

Establishing a SIMPLE 401(k). The IRS has issued a model amendment that may be used by employers that want to adopt a plan that contains a SIMPLE 401(k) plan (Rev. Proc. 97-9).[28] The model amendment includes provisions for employee contributions, employer options concerning its contributions, and notification to employees.

2107. Money Purchase Plans. A money purchase plan is a type of defined contribution plan (¶ 2105) in which, unlike a profit-sharing plan, the employer's annual contributions are fixed under the terms of the plan (Reg. § 1.401-1(b)(1)(i)).[29] For example, under a money purchase plan, the employer may be required to contribute five percent of each participating employee's wages, regardless of whether the employer shows a profit for the year.

2108. Profit-Sharing Plans. A profit-sharing plan is a type of defined contribution plan (¶ 2105) to which the employer makes discretionary contributions, so long as the plan provides a definite formula for allocating the contributions among participants and distributing accumulated funds (Reg. § 1.401-1(b)(1)(ii)).[30] The term "profit-sharing plan" is a misnomer because the employer does not have to make a profit for the year in order to make a contribution (other than a self-employed individual), and the plan may be maintained by a tax-exempt organization (Code Sec. 401(a)(27)).[31] In fact, the employer is not required to contribute every year or any particular percentage of profits or other particular amount, but contributions must be substantial and recurring. A profit-sharing plan can also be coordinated with the employer's paid time off plan so that the cash value of each employee's unused time off, either at the end of each year or at the termination of the employee's employment, is contributed to his account under the plan as a nonelective employer contribution or as an elective deferral by the employee such as with a 401(k) plan (¶ 2106A). In either case, the contributions are subject to the generally applicable nondiscrimination rules (¶ 2117) and limits on contributions and elective deferrals (¶ 2121).

2109. SIMPLE Plan. Eligible small employers (¶ 2155A) may adopt a simplified retirement plan called a "Savings Incentive Match Plan for Employees" or SIMPLE plan (Code Sec. 408(p)).[32] A SIMPLE plan can be either an IRA-based retirement plan (¶ 2155) or part of a 401(k) plan (¶ 2106G).

References are to Standard Federal Tax Reports; Tax Research Consultant; and Practical Tax Explanations.

[26] ¶ 18,330; RETIRE: 63,700; § 24,305.15

[27] ¶ 17,502; RETIRE: 3,350; § 24,720.25

[28] ¶ 18,112.80; RETIRE: 3,352; § 24,720.35

[29] ¶ 17,504; RETIRE: 33,206; § 24,115.20

[30] ¶ 17,504; RETIRE: 3,104.05; § 24,115.10

[31] ¶ 17,502; RETIRE: 3,102; § 24,115.10

[32] ¶ 18,902; RETIRE: 63,550; § 25,101

2110. Simplified Employee Pensions (SEPs). A simplified employee pension (SEP) is an IRA-based retirement plan, under which an employer makes contributions to IRAs established on behalf of each of its employees (¶ 2156) (Code Sec. 408(k)).[33]

2111. Stock Bonus Plans and ESOPs. A stock bonus plan is a defined contribution plan (¶ 2101) that must generally follow the same rules as a profit-sharing plan except that distributed benefits usually are in the form of employer stock (Reg. § 1.401-1(b)(1)(iii)).[34] An employee stock ownership plan (ESOP) is a special type of stock bonus plan that, if certain requirements are met, provides special tax advantages including the following (Code Secs. 409 and 4975(e)(7)):[35]

- An ESOP will qualify for an exemption from certain of the prohibited transaction rules that apply in the case of loans made by disqualified persons to qualified plans (¶ 2128) (Code Sec. 4975(d)(3)).[36]
- Under some circumstances, a shareholder, other than a C corporation, may elect not to recognize gain on the sale of qualified securities to an ESOP (Code Sec. 1042).[37] Nonrecognition depends upon the shareholder purchasing qualified replacement property within a specific period of time.
- A C corporation is entitled to a deduction for dividends on its stock held by an ESOP that are: (1) paid in cash directly to participants in the ESOP, (2) paid to the ESOP and subsequently distributed to the participants in cash no later than 90 days after the end of the plan year in which the dividends are paid to the ESOP, or (3) used to repay an ESOP loan (Code Sec. 404(k)).[38] In addition, C corporations may deduct dividends that are, at the election of plan participants or their beneficiaries, paid to an ESOP and reinvested in qualified employer securities.
- Contributions to an ESOP that are used to pay the principal on loans that were incurred to purchase employer securities may be deducted to the extent that they do not exceed 25 percent of the compensation paid to participants (Code Sec. 404(a)(9)).[39] This contribution rule does not apply to S corporations.

2112. Thrift or Savings Plans. A thrift or savings plan is a defined contribution plan for employees of the federal government in which employees are directly involved in contributing toward the ultimate benefits that will be provided. This type of plan resembles a 401(k) plan in the private sector. Certain employees are often eligible for a generous match under this type of plan.

Defined Contribution Plans - Requirements

2114. Introduction. A retirement plan must meet the qualification requirements of Code Sec. 401 to receive certain tax benefits.[40] The requirements are generally applied by reference to the employer maintaining the plan and all employees who perform services for the employer. The plan must be written, permanent, and for the exclusive benefit of employees. Thus, it must prohibit the assignment and alienation of benefits, restrict withdrawal rights and provide only incidental benefits other than retirement benefits. The plan must also not discriminate in terms of coverage or availability of contributions or benefits in favor of highly compensated employees or key employees. The annual accounting period adopted by the plan is called the plan year and it may or may not coincide with the employer's tax year. If there is a trust associated with plan, then it must be a valid written domestic trust established by the employer.

2115. Participation. Generally, a qualified plan may not condition an employee's participation in the plan on the completion of more than one year of service or the attainment of more than 21 years of age, whichever occurs later. Once these conditions are met, an employee must be eligible to participate within six months or, if earlier, by

References are to Standard Federal Tax Reports; Tax Research Consultant; and Practical Tax Explanations.

[33] ¶ 18,902; RETIRE: 63,050; § 25,005

[34] ¶ 17,504; RETIRE: 3,450; § 24,115.15

[35] ¶ 18,950, ¶ 34,400; RETIRE: 75,000; § 24,801

[36] ¶ 34,400; RETIRE: 75,302; § 24,825.10

[37] ¶ 29,820; RETIRE: 75,350; § 24,825.15

[38] ¶ 18,330; RETIRE: 75,204; § 24,815.15

[39] ¶ 18,330; RETIRE: 75,202.15; § 24,815.10

[40] ¶ 17,507; RETIRE: 100; § 24,201

the first day of the plan's next accounting year. However, participation may be conditioned on completion of two years of service if, after no more than two years of service, each participant has a vested right to their entire accrued benefit under the plan (Code Sec. 410(a)(1)).[41]

2116. Coverage. Generally, a plan may meet the minimum coverage requirement in one of two ways:

- under the "ratio percentage test," the percentage of rank-and-file employees who benefit from the plan divided by the percentage of highly compensated employees (¶ 2117) who benefit must equal at least 70 percent (Code Sec. 410(b)(1); Reg. § 1.410(b)-2(b)(2));[42]
- under the "average benefit test," (a) the plan must benefit employees under a classification set up by the employer and found by the IRS not to discriminate in favor of highly compensated employees, and (b) the average benefit percentage for nonhighly compensated employees must be at least 70 percent of the average benefit percentage for highly compensated employees (an employee's "benefit percentage" comprises the employer-provided contributions (including forfeitures) or benefits under all qualified plans of the employer, expressed as a percentage of the employee's compensation) (¶ 2120) (Code Sec. 410(b)(2); Reg. §§ 1.410(b)-2, 1.410(b)-4 and 1.410(b)-5).[43]

Additional Rule for Defined Benefit Plans. A defined benefit plan must also benefit at least the lesser of: (1) 50 employees or (2)(a) the greater of 40 percent of all employees or (b) two employees (one employee if there is only one employee) (Code Sec. 401(a)(26)).[44]

2117. Nondiscrimination. A qualified retirement plan must provide either contributions or benefits that do not discriminate in favor of highly compensated employees (Code Sec. 401(a)(4)).[45] This is satisfied if: either the contributions or benefits provided are nondiscriminatory in amount; the benefits, rights and features under the plan are available in a nondiscriminatory manner; and the plan is nondiscriminatory in effect, including plan amendments, terminations, and grants of past service credit. Generally, an employee is considered highly compensated for this purpose if he: (1) was a five-percent owner at any time during the current or preceding year or (2) had compensation (¶ 2120) from the employer for the preceding year in excess of $115,000 for 2012 and 2013 (Code Sec. 414(q)(1); Notice 2011-90; IRS News Release IR-2012-77).[46] The employer may elect to limit employees treated as highly compensated employees under (2) to those who are in the top 20 percent of employees when ranked on the basis of compensation paid during the year. Part-time employees, minors, union members, and any employee who works less than six months during the year may be excluded from the top-paid group.

Actual Contribution Percentage (ACP) Test. A special nondiscrimination test applies to elective contributions by plan participants and matching contributions by employers to a qualified plan (Code Sec. 401(m); Reg. § 1.401(m)-1).[47] Matching contributions are those made by the employer on account of a contribution by a participant or because of an elective contribution by a participant under a 401(k) plan (¶ 2106D). The test is satisfied if the actual contribution percentage (ACP) for the group of eligible highly compensated employees for the plan year does not exceed the greater of (1) 125 percent of such percentage for all other eligible employees for the preceding plan year or (2) the lesser of 200 percent of such percentage for all other eligible employees for the preceding plan year or such percentage for all other eligible employees for the preceding plan year plus two percentage points. The ACP test can be satisfied by the plan

References are to Standard Federal Tax Reports; Tax Research Consultant; and Practical Tax Explanations.

[41] ¶ 18,970; RETIRE: 12,200, RETIRE: 12,000; § 24,250.15

[42] ¶ 18,970, ¶ 18,988; RETIRE: 12,056; § 24,255.10

[43] ¶ 18,970, ¶ 18,988, ¶ 18,990, ¶ 18,991; RETIRE: 12,058; § 24,255

[44] ¶ 17,502; RETIRE: 12,100; § 24,120.25

[45] ¶ 19,050, ¶ 17,507, ¶ 17,717; RETIRE: 39,000; § 24,245.05

[46] ¶ 19,150; RETIRE: 3,210.30; § 24,140

[47] ¶ 17,502, ¶ 18,121; RETIRE: 27,150; § 24,705.30

adopting one of the alternative safe harbors for meeting the actual deferral percentage (ADP) test for 401(k) plans (¶ 2106A).[48]

Failure to satisfy the ACP test will not result in disqualification of the plan if the excess contributions (and the income allocable to them) are distributed within 12 months following the plan year in which they arose (Code Sec. 401(m)(6)(A)).[49] However, the employer is subject to a 10-percent tax based on the amount of the excess contributions unless the contributions (and the income allocable to them) are distributed to the highly compensated employees within 2½ months after the plan year in which they arose (Code Sec. 4979(f)(1)).[50] The amount of a corrective distribution (other than the portion representing the employee's contributions) is included in the employee's gross income. The 10-percent additional tax on early distributions (¶ 2124C) does not apply (Code Sec. 401(m)(7)).[51]

2118. Top-Heavy Plans. More stringent qualification requirements must be met for qualified plans or tax-sheltered annuity arrangements that primarily benefit an employer's key employees. These plans are referred to as "top-heavy plans" (Code Sec. 416(a)).[52] Most qualified plans must include language stating that they will comply with the top-heavy rules if they become top heavy. However, the top-heavy requirements do not apply to SIMPLE 401(k) (¶ 2106G) or SIMPLE IRA (¶ 2155) plans. A plan is top heavy if the accrued benefits or account balances of key employees are more than 60 percent of the total benefits or balances under the plan.

Accelerated Vesting. For any plan year in which a plan is top heavy, the benefits of each employee for that year must *either* be: (1) 100 percent vested if the employee has at least three years of service or (2) 20 percent vested after two years of service with a 20 percent increase for each later year of service (Code Sec. 416(b)).[53] See ¶ 2119 for the general vesting requirements.

Minimum Benefits and Contributions. In any plan year in which a defined benefit plan is top heavy, each participating non-key employee must be provided with a retirement benefit that is not less than two percent of average annual compensation (¶ 2120) for the employee's five consecutive years of highest compensation, multiplied by years of service (up to a maximum of ten years of service) (Code Sec. 416(c)(1)).[54] In any plan year in which a defined contribution plan is top heavy, each participating non-key employee must be provided with a contribution that is not less than three percent of such employee's compensation for that year. Employer matching contributions are taken into account when determining if this contribution requirement has been met. If the contribution rate for the key employee receiving the largest contribution is less than three percent, then the contribution rate for such key employee is used to determine the minimum contribution for non-key employees (Code Sec. 416(c)(2)).[55]

Key Employee Defined. A key employee is defined as an employee who, at any time during the plan year, is:

- an officer with compensation in excess of $165,000 for 2012 and 2013 (Code Sec. 416(i)(1); Notice 2011-90; IRS News Release IR-2012-77).[56]
- a more-than-five-percent owner, or
- a more-than-one-percent owner who received more than $150,000 (not subject to an inflation adjustment) in compensation.

In the case of a corporate employer, an employee is a five-percent owner when the employee owns more than five percent of the employer's outstanding stock or stock possessing more than five percent of the total combined voting power of all of the employer's stock. When the employer is not a corporation, a five-percent owner is any employee who owns more than five percent of the capital or profits interest in the

References are to Standard Federal Tax Reports; Tax Research Consultant; and Practical Tax Explanations.

[48] ¶ 17,502; RETIRE: 3,210.60; § 24,705.35

[49] ¶ 17,502; RETIRE: 27,154; § 24,705.35

[50] ¶ 34,520, ¶ 34,523; RETIRE: 27,154; § 24,705.35

[51] ¶ 17,502; RETIRE: 27,154; § 24,705.35

[52] ¶ 19,250; RETIRE: 21,050; § 24,280

[53] ¶ 19,250; RETIRE: 21,302; § 24,280.10

[54] ¶ 19,250; RETIRE: 21,354.05; § 24,280.15

[55] ¶ 19,250; RETIRE: 21,356; § 24,280.15

[56] ¶ 19,250; RETIRE: 21,102; § 24,280.20

employer. An employee is also treated as owning stock owned by certain members of the employee's family or, in the case of any employer that is not a corporation, by partnerships, estates, trusts or corporations in which the employee has an interest (Code Sec. 416(i)(1)(B)). The same rules apply to determine whether an individual owner is a one-percent owner.

2119. Vesting. A qualified plan must satisfy minimum vesting requirements (Code Sec. 411(a)).[57] Employee contributions must be vested (i.e., nonforfeitable) at all times, including those made through elective deferral of compensation. For defined contribution plans, employer contributions (including matching contributions) must be vested at least as quickly as they would be under either of the following methods.

Graded Vesting. Under this method, 20 percent of an employee's accrued benefit derived from employer contributions must vest after two years of service and an additional 20 percent must vest after each additional year of service.[58] After six years of service, the employee must be 100 percent vested.

Cliff Vesting. Under this method, an employee has no vested interest in the accrued benefit derived from employer contributions until the employee has completed three years of service but then must be 100 percent vested.[59]

Defined Benefit Plans and Pre-2007 Contributions to Defined Contribution Plans. For defined benefit plans and contributions to defined contribution plans made in plan years beginning before 2007, all employees' interests in their accrued benefits derived from employer contributions must vest at least as quickly as they would under either a three-to-seven-years graded vesting schedule or a five-year cliff vesting schedule. Plans may maintain separate vesting schedules for those contributions made before 2007 and those made after 2006 (Code Sec. 411(a)(2); Notice 2007-7).

2120. Compensation Limits. An employer-provided retirement plan will not qualify unless the annual compensation of each employee taken into account under the plan for any year does not exceed a specific dollar amount (Code Sec. 401(a)(17); Reg. § 1.401(a)(17)-1(a)).[60] The maximum amount of compensation that may be considered is $250,000 for 2012 and $255,000 for 2013 (Notice 2011-90; IRS News Release IR-2012-77). The compensation limit must be considered when determining an employee's maximum benefit or contribution (¶ 2121) and when applying the nondiscrimination rules (¶ 2117). For purposes of the limitation on contributions to a defined contribution plan, an employee's compensation includes any compensation received from the employer maintaining the plan included in gross income (net earnings from self-employment in the case of a self-employed individual), as well as any elective deferrals or other amounts contributed by the employer at the employee's election that may be excluded from an employee's gross income (e.g., cafeteria plan benefits, qualified transportation fringe benefits) (Code Sec. 415(c)(3)).[61]

2121. Contribution Limits. A qualified plan must limit the contributions and benefits that may be provided to each individual plan participant (Code Sec. 415).[62] For 2012, the maximum annual addition that may be made to a participant's account in a defined contribution plan may not exceed the *lesser* of $50,000 or 100 percent of the participant's compensation (¶ 2121) (Notice 2011-90). For 2013, the maximum annual addition that may be made to a participant's account in a defined contribution plan may not exceed the *lesser* of $51,000 or 100 percent of the participant's compensation (¶ 2121) (IRS News Release IR-2012-77).[63] The term "annual addition" includes employer and employee contributions, as well as forfeitures allocated to the account under the plan. See ¶ 2122A for the limits imposed on annual *deductions* of employer contributions.

References are to Standard Federal Tax Reports; Tax Research Consultant; and Practical Tax Explanations.

[57] ¶ 19,050, ¶ 19,076; RETIRE: 18,050; § 24,260

[58] ¶ 19,050, ¶ 19,076; RETIRE: 18,102; § 24,260

[59] ¶ 19,050, ¶ 19,076; RETIRE: 18,102; § 24,265

[60] ¶ 17,502, ¶ 17,902; RETIRE: 36,350; § 24,145

[61] ¶ 19,200; RETIRE: 75,104.05; § 24,145

[62] ¶ 19,200; RETIRE: 36,050; § 25,215.10

[63] ¶ 19,200; RETIRE: 36,200; § 24,275.15

2121A. Catch-Up Contributions. An individual who will be at least 50 years of age by the end of the tax year is permitted, if the plan allows, to make "catch-up" contributions to qualified plans allowing elective deferrals including 401(k), 403(b), 457, SARSEP, and SIMPLE plans. The maximum amount of the catch-up contribution depends upon the type of plan involved. For example, the maximum catch-up contribution to a 401(k), 403(b), 457, or SARSEP plan is $5,500 for 2012 and 2013. The maximum catch-up contribution to a SIMPLE 401(k) or SIMPLE IRA is $2,500 for 2012 and 2013 (Code Sec. 414(v); Notice 2011-90; IRS News Release IR-2012-77).[64]

2122. Deductions - General Rules. Subject to annual limits (¶ 2122A), employers are allowed to deduct their contributions to a qualified plan to the extent they are otherwise deductible under the Code as an ordinary and necessary expense or paid for the production of income. The deductions are allowed whether or not the rights of the employees to the contributions are forfeitable. However, contributions are generally deductible only for the tax year when paid regardless of whether the taxpayer uses the cash or accrual method of accounting, unless contributions in excess of the annual limits must be carried over to later years. A deductible contribution is deemed made on the last day of the tax year if it is paid no later than the due date (including extensions) of the taxpayer's return (Code Sec. 404(a)).[65] However, in the case of most defined benefit plans, the deadline for making the required contribution to the funding standard account is 8½ months after the close of the plan year (Code Sec. 412(c)(10)). As a result, the required funding date may actually come before the last day for making deductible contributions. Interest may be charged if the contribution to the standard account is not made by the due date (Code Sec. 412(m)). Elective and matching contributions under a 401(k) plan (¶ 2106A; ¶ 2106D) and other types of defined contribution plans (¶ 2105) are not deductible by the employer for a tax year if they are attributable to compensation earned by participants after the end of that tax year (Rev. Rul. 90-105 and Rev. Rul. 2002-46).[66]

S Corporations. A retirement plan established by an S corporation is generally governed by the same rules that apply to plans established by other corporations. As a result, S corporation shareholders are not entitled to claim retirement plan deductions based on their pro rata share of pass-through income from the S corporation. A court has ruled that this income could not be treated as earnings from self-employment for retirement plan purposes (*A.R. Durando*, CA-9, 95-2 USTC ¶ 50,615).

2122A. Deductions - Limits. There are limits on the annual deductions that may be claimed for an employer's contributions to a qualified plan. The limits are related to the contributions allowed to the plan (¶ 2121). In the case of a defined contribution plan, contributions that are in excess of the maximum amount allowed may not be deducted (Code Sec. 404(j)).[67]

The maximum deduction allowed for contributions to a defined contribution plan, including profit-sharing or stock bonus plans, as well as money purchase plans (except as provided otherwise in regulations), is 25 percent of the compensation of all the participants in the plan (Code Sec. 404(a)(3)).[68] For the deduction limits that apply to SIMPLE plans, see ¶ 2106G and ¶ 2155D.

Employer Maintaining More Than One Type of Plan. If an employer makes contributions to a defined contribution plan and also to a defined benefit plan, there is an overall limit on the deduction of these contributions. The deduction is limited to the *greater* of: (1) 25 percent of the compensation paid or accrued for that year to the participants in all such plans or (2) the amount necessary to satisfy the minimum funding standards of Code Sec. 412. The overall limitation does not apply when no individual is a participant in more than one plan maintained by the employer (Code Sec. 404(a)(7)).[69] Also, the overall deduction limit does not apply when only "elective contributions" (e.g., contribu-

References are to Standard Federal Tax Reports; Tax Research Consultant; and Practical Tax Explanations.

64 ¶ 19,150; RETIRE: 27,102.35; § 24,275.20

65 ¶ 18,330; RETIRE: 33,354; § 24,305.30

66 ¶ 18,347.27; RETIRE: 33,356; § 24,305.30

67 ¶ 18,330; RETIRE: 33,200; § 24,310

68 ¶ 18,330; RETIRE: 33,202, RETIRE: 60,202; § 24,305.15

69 ¶ 18,330; RETIRE: 33,306; § 24,305.20

tions made under 401(k) plans or SEP plans) are made to any of the employer's defined contribution plans during the tax year.

Elective Deferrals. Elective deferrals made by employees are not taken into account when determining deduction limits for stock bonus and profit-sharing plans, combination defined benefit and defined contribution plans, and ESOPs (Code Sec. 404(n)). The term "elective deferrals" includes amounts contributed to 401(k) plans, SEPs, SIMPLEs, and 403(b) tax-deferred annuities (Code Sec. 402(g)(3)).

Compensation. In applying the annual deduction limits, the amount of an employee's compensation that may be taken into account is limited in the same manner as for determining contributions and benefits (¶ 2120) (Code Sec. 404(l)).[70] However, "compensation," for purposes of the deduction limits, includes certain amounts that are generally excluded from gross income (e.g., elective deferrals and certain disability benefits and elective deferrals) (Code Sec. 404(a)(12)).

Carryovers. When an employer's contribution exceeds the maximum deductible amount for the year, the excess amount may be carried over and deducted in later tax years. However, the total of the carryovers and the regular contributions in the carryover year may not exceed the deductible limit for that year (Code Sec. 404(a)(1)(E) and (3)(A)(ii)).[71] Similarly, if the 25 percent overall limit for contributions to different types of plans is exceeded, the excess may be carried over. The combination of carryovers and regular deductions for any succeeding year may not exceed 25 percent of the compensation paid to participants in that year (Code Sec. 404(a)(7)(B)).[72]

2123. Payment of Benefits. An employer-provided retirement plan will not qualify unless it provides that the payment of benefits will begin (unless the participant elects otherwise) no later than the 60th day after the *latest* of the close of the plan year in which:

- the participant attains the earlier of age 65 or the normal retirement age specified in the plan;
- the participant marks the 10th anniversary of enrollment in the plan; or
- the participant terminates service with the employer (Code Sec. 401(a)(14)).[73]

Mandatory Cash-Outs. Generally, a qualified plan is restricted from distributing any portion of a participant's accrued benefits in any form without the participant's (or surviving spouse's) consent. However, the plan may pay out the balance of a participant's account without the participant's consent if the present value of the benefit does not exceed $5,000 (Code Sec. 411(a)(11)(A)).[74] If the present value of the benefit exceeds $1,000, and the participant does not elect otherwise, a mandatory distribution must be transferred directly to an IRA established by the plan for the benefit of the participant (Code Sec. 401(a)(31)(B); Notice 2005-5).

Phased Retirement Arrangements. A qualified plan is allowed to provide that a distribution may be made to an employee who has attained age 62 and who is not separated from employment at the time of the distribution but instead is in a phased retirement program (i.e., working retirement) (Code Sec. 401(a)(36)).

Death Benefits for Participants Serving in the Military. Survivors of a participant who has died while performing qualified military service are entitled to any benefits that would have been provided under the plan (other than benefit accruals relating to the period of military service) had the participant returned and then terminated employment on account of death (Code Sec. 401(a)(37)). Thus, survivor benefits such as accelerated vesting or ancillary life insurance benefits that are contingent upon a participant's termination of employment on account of death must be provided to the beneficiaries of a participant who has died during qualified military service. This requirement applies to

References are to Standard Federal Tax Reports; Tax Research Consultant; and Practical Tax Explanations.

[70] ¶ 18,330; RETIRE: 36,350; § 25,305.15

[71] ¶ 18,330; RETIRE: 33,300; § 25,305.15

[72] ¶ 18,330; RETIRE: 33,306; § 24,305.20

[73] ¶ 17,502; RETIRE: 42,106; § 24,425

[74] ¶ 19,050; RETIRE: 42,104; § 24,430

qualified plans, 403(b) tax-deferred annuities, and 457(b) eligible deferred compensation plans maintained by state and local governments.

2124. Distributions - General Rules. Generally, distributions from a qualified plan are taxed to the recipient unless the distribution is attributable to designated Roth contributions (¶ 2106F) or an eligible rollover distribution (¶ 2125A). The tax treatment of a distribution depends on the form of the distribution. If the plan distribution takes the form of an annuity (i.e., periodic pension payment), it is taxable under the annuity rules (¶ 817 and ¶ 839) (Code Secs. 402(a) and 403(a)(1)). For this purpose, the benefits derived from the employee's contributions to a defined contribution plan and the earnings on them may be treated as a separate contract from benefits derived from the employer's contributions (Code Sec. 72(d)(2)).[75] A participant's separate account in a defined benefit plan is treated as a defined contribution plan if the plan provides a benefit derived from employer contributions that is based partly on the balance of the separate account (Code Sec. 414(k)(2)).[76]

If a plan distribution is not in the form of an annuity, the following rules apply (Code Sec. 72(e); Reg. § 1.72-11):[77]

- If a distribution is made *before* the annuity starting date, it is treated in much the same way as an annuity distribution; that is, there is excluded from income that portion of the distribution that bears the same ratio to the distribution as the investment in the contract bears to the value of the contract (Code Sec. 72(e)(2)(B)). The total amount excluded cannot exceed the employee's investment in the contract.

- A nonannuity distribution made *on or after* the annuity starting date is generally included in full in gross income unless it reduces the dollar amount of subsequent annuity payments (Code Sec. 72(e)(2)(A)).

U.S. Civil Service Retirement Benefits. Retired federal employees generally receive annuity payments under the Civil Service Retirement System (CSRS) or the Federal Employee Retirement System (FERS). The portion of the payment that represents the employee's after-tax contributions to the retirement plan is not taxed. Form 1099-R will generally show the non-taxable portion of the CSRS or FERS payment as calculated under the simplified method (¶ 839) (IRS Pub. 721).

Death In Line of Duty. The amount paid as a survivor annuity to the spouse, former spouse, or child of a "public safety officer" killed in the line of duty is generally excludable from the recipient's gross income when the annuity is provided under a governmental retirement plan (Code Sec. 101(h)). The term "public safety officer" includes law enforcement officers, firefighters, and members of an ambulance crew, or public rescue squad (Act Sec. 1204 of the Omnibus Crime Control and Safe Streets Act of 1968 (P.L. 90-351). A chaplain killed in the line of duty may also be classified as a public safety officer for purposes of this exclusion.

Victims of Terrorism. If certain requirements are met, death benefits paid by an employer due to the death of an employee who was a victim of a terrorist act may be excluded from income (Code Sec. 101(i)). For this purpose, a self-employed individual may be considered an employee (Code Sec. 101(i)(3)).

Qualified Disaster Distributions. Unless the recipient elects otherwise, up to $100,000 in "qualified disaster recovery assistance distributions" received by a qualified individual from an eligible retirement plan (including an IRA) are included in the recipient's income ratably over three years, beginning with the year the distribution is received. If the distributee dies during the first or second year, the amount that has not been taxed is included in income in the year of the distributee's death (Code Sec. 1400Q(a)). An individual who received any qualified distribution may recontribute the amount of those distributions to an eligible retirement plan at any time during the three-year period beginning on the day after the distribution was received. To the extent that

References are to Standard Federal Tax Reports; Tax Research Consultant; and Practical Tax Explanations.

[75] ¶ 6102; RETIRE: 42,302; § 24,405.10

[76] ¶ 19,150; RETIRE: 42,302; § 24,405.10

[77] ¶ 6102, ¶ 6113; RETIRE: 42,550, INDIV: 30,100; § 24,405.10

such a recontribution is made, the original distribution will not be taxed (Code Sec. 1400Q(a)(3)). The individual can file an amended return or returns to claim a refund of the tax attributable to the amount recontributed.

A qualified disaster recovery assistance contribution is a distribution to a qualified individual by reason of the severe storms, tornadoes or flooding on or after May 20, 2008, and before August 1, 2008, in Arkansas, Illinois, Indiana, Iowa, Kansas, Michigan, Minnesota, Missouri, Nebraska and Wisconsin (IRS Publ. 4492-B). For residents in the Midwestern disaster area, the distribution must be made on or after the applicable disaster date, and before January 1, 2010. Distributions made after December 31, 2008, and before January 1, 2010, are included ratably in the recipient's income for 2009, 2010 and 2011.

Individuals use Form 8930 to determine the amount of a disaster recovery assistance distribution and report any recontribution. If the taxpayer elects to include the full amount in income in the year of the distribution, the taxpayer reports this amount on Form 8930.

Employer Securities. Distributions of an employer's securities under circumstances not involving a lump-sum distribution (¶ 2124A) are subject to the above rules except for unrealized appreciation attributable to shares that were purchased with the employee's own contributions (Code Sec. 402(e)(4)(A)).[78] That appreciation is not taxed until the securities are sold.

Loss. An employee may claim a loss on his return if he receives, entirely in cash or worthless securities, a distribution of his entire benefit from a qualified plan and the distribution is less than the employee's remaining basis in the plan (Rev. Rul. 72-305). The deductible loss is claimed on Schedule A (Form 1040) as a miscellaneous itemized deduction that is subject to the two-percent of adjusted gross income floor.

2124A. Lump-Sum Distributions. Special rules apply in determining the taxable portion of a lump-sum distribution from a qualified plan. A lump-sum distribution is a distribution of a participant's entire interest in a qualified plan within a single tax year of the recipient due to one of the following circumstances:

- the death of the employee,
- the employee has attained age 59½,
- on account of the employee's separation from service from the employer (as common-law employee), or
- after a participant who is a self-employed individual becomes totally and permanently disabled (Code Sec. 402(e)(4)(D)).[79]

The rules applicable to lump-sum distributions are applied without regard to community property laws. As a result, a lump-sum distribution is considered to belong entirely to the participant, rather than half to the participant and half to his or her spouse (*R.L. Karem*, TC, Dec. 49,091).[80] However, a spouse may acquire an interest in retirement plan assets by means of a qualified domestic relations order (QDRO) (¶ 2124D).

Determining Taxable Amount. The entire amount of the lump-sum distribution is not always subject to taxation. To determine the taxable portion of the lump-sum distribution, the following items must be subtracted from the total amount of the distribution:

- nondeductible amounts contributed to the plan by the participant (less any previous distributions the participant received that were not includible in gross income),
- any premiums paid by the plan to furnish a participant with life insurance protection that were included in gross income,

References are to Standard Federal Tax Reports; Tax Research Consultant; and Practical Tax Explanations.

[78] ¶ 18,202; RETIRE: 42,402; § 24,301

[79] ¶ 18,202; RETIRE: 42,350; § 24,405.20

[80] ¶ 18,207.11; RETIRE: 42,058.10; § 24,405.20

- any repayments of loans from the plan that were included in gross income (¶ 2129),
- the current actuarial value of any annuity contract that was included in the lump-sum distribution, and
- net unrealized appreciation in any employer securities that were distributed as part of the lump-sum distribution (unless the taxpayer elects to be taxed on this appreciation).

If the net unrealized appreciation is excluded from gross income upon distribution of the securities, tax is deferred until the securities are sold or exchanged. The cost or other basis of the employer securities is included in the taxable portion of the distribution (Code Sec. 402(e)(4)(B)).[81]

Born Before January 2, 1936. Employees born before January 2, 1936 (or their beneficiaries), may elect to have their lump-sum distributions from a qualified plan taxed under favorable rates. The election is also available to the employee's beneficiaries, including a spouse or former spouse who was named as an alternate payee under a QDRO. The recipient (employee, beneficiary, or alternate payee) must elect to use this special tax treatment for all such amounts received during the tax year (Code Sec. 402(d)(4)(B), prior to amendment by the Small Business Job Protection Act of 1996 (P.L. 104-188)). Also, this special treatment is *not* available if any portion of the lump-sum distribution is rolled over into another plan (Code Sec. 402(d)(4)(K), prior to amendment by P.L. 104-188).[82]

Taxation of Lump-Sum Distributions. If the participant was born before January 2, 1936, the distributee may choose among the following options for computing the tax on a lump-sum distribution of the participant's benefit. However, choices (2) and (3) may be selected only if the participant was a participant during at least five tax years preceding the year of distribution (Code Sec. 402(d)(4)(F), prior to amendment by P.L. 104-188).[83]

(1) A distributee may include the entire taxable amount in gross income. If this is done, it will be combined with all other gross income and, after deductions, taxed at the normal rates applying to income received in the tax year.

(2) A distributee may calculate a separate tax on the entire taxable amount by employing a 10-year averaging method (Act Sec. 1122(h)(5) of the Tax Reform Act of 1986 (P.L. 99-514)).[84]

(3) A distributee may (a) pay a separate 20 percent tax on the pre-1974 portion of the taxable amount and (b) calculate a separate tax under the 10-year averaging method for the post-1973 portion of the taxable amount (Act Sec. 1122(h)(3) of the Tax Reform Act of 1986 (P.L. 99-514)).[85] If the 20 percent flat tax is elected, the 20 percent rate is applied to the entire pre-1974 amount and not to that amount after it has been reduced by capital losses.

Making the Election. The distributee must make an election to use the averaging method (Code Sec. 402(d)(4)(B)(ii), prior to amendment by P.L. 104-188).[86] An election must also be made in order to use the flat 20-percent tax for the pre-1974 portion of a lump-sum distribution (Act Sec. 1122(h)(3) and (4) of the Tax Reform Act of 1986 (P.L. 99-514)). There are no special procedures for making an election. Form 4972 is used to compute the tax under the options that are available to the individual. In the event that a lump-sum distribution is shared by two or more distributees, the tax for each distributee is figured by using the method that is stipulated in the instructions to Form 4972.

An election to use 10-year averaging may be made only once for each plan participant (Code Sec. 402(d)(4)(B), prior to amendment by P.L. 104-188; Act Sec. 1122(h)(5) of the Tax Reform Act of 1986 (P.L. 99-514)). Therefore, a person is

References are to Standard Federal Tax Reports; Tax Research Consultant; and Practical Tax Explanations.

[81] ¶ 18,202; RETIRE: 42,356; § 24,410

[82] ¶ 18,202; RETIRE: 42,360.15; § 24,405.20; § 46,640.15

[83] ¶ 18,202, ¶ 18,217A.01; RETIRE: 42,360.15; § 24,405.20

[84] ¶ 18,217A.021; RETIRE: 42,360.15; § 24,405.20

[85] ¶ 18,217A.021; RETIRE: 42,360.15; § 24,405.20

[86] ¶ 18,202; RETIRE: 42,360.15; § 24,405.20

permitted to make an averaging election for a lump-sum distribution received from his own plan and another election for a lump-sum distribution received as a beneficiary of another plan.

An election to apply a flat 20-percent tax to the pre-1974 portion of such a distribution can be made only once with respect to the same participant. The election is treated as an election to use averaging, thus precluding any averaging for a subsequent lump-sum distribution with respect to the same participant (Act Sec. 1122(h) of the Tax Reform Act of 1986 (P.L. 99-514)).

10-Year Averaging Computation. Under 10-year averaging, the tax is computed (using the tax rates in the table below) on 1⁄10 of the excess of the portion of the distribution subject to averaging over the minimum distribution allowance. The result is then multiplied by 10. The minimum distribution allowance is: (1) the lesser of $10,000 or one-half of the portion subject to averaging, (2) reduced, but not below zero, by 20 percent of the amount by which the portion subject to averaging exceeds $20,000. If the amount subject to averaging is $70,000 or more, the minimum distribution is zero.

Ten-Year Averaging Rate Table

Over—	*But Not Over—*	*The Tax Is*	*of the Amount Over—*
$ -0-	$1,190	11%	$-0-
1,190	2,270	$130.90 + 12%	1,190
2,270	4,530	260.50 + 14%	2,270
4,530	6,690	576.90 + 15%	4,530
6,690	9,170	900.90 + 16%	6,690
9,170	11,440	1,297.70 + 18%	9,170
11,440	13,710	1,706.30 + 20%	11,440
13,710	17,160	2,160.30 + 23%	13,710
17,160	22,880	2,953.80 + 26%	17,160
22,880	28,600	4,441.00 + 30%	22,880
28,600	34,320	6,157.00 + 34%	28,600
34,320	42,300	8,101.80 + 38%	34,320
42,300	57,190	11,134.20 + 42%	42,300
57,190	85,790	17,388.00 + 48%	57,190
85,790	. . . .	31,116.00 + 50%	85,790

When calculating the tax under 10-year averaging on a distribution inherited from a decedent, the beneficiary may take a deduction for the federal estate tax (¶ 191) allocable to the lump-sum distribution (Code Sec. 691(c)(1)).[87]

Annuity Contract Distributed. A lump-sum distribution may include an annuity contract. If so, the contract is not taxed as a part of the lump-sum distribution. Rather, annuity payments are taxed under the annuity rules (¶ 817). However, the contract has an impact on the calculation of tax under 10-year averaging. Essentially, the actuarial value of the contract is included in the amount subject to averaging and the tax calculated on that amount. Then a separate tax is calculated on the actuarial value of the annuity alone. The latter is subtracted from the former, and the difference is the final tax (Code Sec. 402(d)(2), prior to amendment by P.L. 104-188).[88]

2124B. Required Minimum Distributions (RMDs). Generally, all types of qualified plans (as well as traditional IRAs, Code Sec. 403(a) or 403(b) annuity plans, and 457(b) government plans) must satisfy a minimum distribution requirement in which distribution of an employee's or IRA owner's interest in the plan or IRA must begin by the "required beginning date." For most employees, this is April 1 of the calendar year following *the later of*: (1) the calendar year in which the participant attains age 70½ or (2) the calendar year in which the employee retires (Code Sec. 401(a)(9); (Reg. § 1.401(a)(9)-1)).[89] In the case of a five-percent owner (¶ 2118) or IRA owner, the

References are to Standard Federal Tax Reports; Tax Research Consultant; and Practical Tax Explanations.

[87] ¶ 24,900; ESTTRST: 6,162.15; § 24,405.20

[88] ¶ 18,202, ¶ 18,217A.0565; RETIRE: 42,404; § 24,405.20

[89] ¶ 17,502, ¶ 17,723C; RETIRE: 42,150; § 24,440.10

required beginning date is April 1 of the year following the year in which the individual reaches age 70½.

If the employee's entire interest is not distributed by the required beginning date, then the employee's interest must generally be paid out over a period that does not exceed the life or life expectancy of the participant or the combined lives or life expectancies of the participant and his or her designated beneficiary (Code Sec. 401(a)(9)(A)).[90] The required minimum distribution (RMD) rules vary depending upon whether distributions begin before or after the employee's death. However, distributions made to a participant or the beneficiary of a participant must satisfy the RMD rules in each calendar year. The RMD for a particular year is generally equal to the participant's accrued benefit or account balance as of the end of the prior year, divided by the appropriate distribution period (Reg. §§1.401(a)(9)-5 and 1.401(a)(9)-6).

Waiver of Required Minimum Distributions for 2009. The minimum distribution rules were waived for calendar year 2009 for defined contributions plans (including any defined contribution Code Sec. 403(a) or 403(b) annuity plan or Code Sec. 457(b) government plan) and IRAs (Code Sec. 401(a)(9)(H)). As a result, plan participants or beneficiaries were not required to take any RMD for the 2009 calendar year, even if their required beginning date was April 1, 2010 (the temporary waiver is ignored in determining the required beginning date). The waiver did *not* apply to required distributions for the 2008 calendar that were taken during 2009 (by April 1, 2009). Plans should have been formally amended to eliminate or continue 2009 RMD(s) by the last day of the first plan year beginning on or after January 1, 2011 (January 1, 2012 for government plans).

Required Distributions Before Participant's Death. If RMDs begin while the participant is alive, the distribution period is derived from one of two tables. The *Uniform Lifetime Table* (reproduced below) is used to determine the distribution period for lifetime distributions to an unmarried individual or to a married individual if the individual's spouse is either: (1) not the sole designated beneficiary or (2) the sole designated beneficiary and not more than 10 years younger than the individual (Reg. §1.401(a)(9)-9). The *Joint and Last Survivor Table* is used to determine the distribution period for lifetime distributions to a married individual whose spouse is the sole beneficiary and is more than 10 years younger than the individual (Reg. §1.401(a)(9)-9).

Required Distributions After Participant's Death. If required distributions have been made to the participant before his or her death, then any remaining benefit payable to a beneficiary may be payable over the longer of the life expectancy of the beneficiary or of the participant (Code Sec. 401(a)(9)(B)(i); Reg. §1.401(a)(9)-5, Q & A-5(a)).[91] If required distributions have not been made to the participant before his or her death, then the participant's entire interest is to be distributed to the beneficiary within five years after the death (Code Sec. 401(a)(9)(B)(ii)).[92] The 2009 calendar year is ignored in counting the five-year period (Code Sec. 401(a)(9)(H)). However, most beneficiaries will be able to take advantage of one of two exceptions to the five-year distribution rule (Reg. §1.401(a)(9)-5, Q & A-5(b)). First, the five-year rule does not apply when:

- any portion of the participant's interest is payable to (or for the benefit of) a designated beneficiary;
- the portion of the participant's interest to which the beneficiary is entitled will be distributed over the life of the beneficiary or over a period not extending beyond the life expectancy of the beneficiary (for this purpose, the *Single Life Table* provided in the regulations and reproduced below is used to determine an individual beneficiary's life expectancy) (Reg. §1.401(a)(9)-9); and
- the distributions commence no later than one year after the date of the participant's death (Code Sec. 401(a)(9)(B)(iii)).[93]

Second, the five-year rule does not apply if:

References are to Standard Federal Tax Reports; Tax Research Consultant; and Practical Tax Explanations.

[90] ¶17,502; RETIRE: 42,158.10; §24,440.15

[91] ¶17,502; RETIRE: 42,160; §24,440.20

[92] ¶17,502; RETIRE: 42,162; §24,440

[93] ¶17,502; RETIRE: 42,162.10; §24,440.20

- the designated beneficiary is the participant's surviving spouse;
- the portion of the participant's interest to which the surviving spouse is entitled will be distributed over the life of that spouse (or over a period not exceeding his or her life expectancy); and
- the distributions commence no later than the date on which the participant would have attained age 70½ (Code Sec. 401(a)(9)(B)(iv)).[94]

If the surviving spouse dies before payments are required to begin, the five-year rule is to be applied as if the surviving spouse were the participant. Payments to a surviving spouse under a qualified joint and survivor annuity (¶ 2126) will satisfy this second exception.

Final Determination of Beneficiary. A beneficiary must be designated as of the date of the employee's death. However, the final determination of who is a beneficiary is not made until September 30 of the year following the calendar year of death (Reg. § 1.401(a)(9)-4, Q & A-4(a)). As a result, if an individual does not remain a beneficiary on the September 30 deadline, the individual is not taken into consideration when determining the RMDs that must be made from the retirement account. For example, individuals who are named beneficiaries as of the time of the participant's death may not be beneficiaries by the September 30 deadline because they have disclaimed their right to any portion of the retirement account.

Penalty for Failure to Receive RMDs. An excise tax is imposed on an employee or beneficiary who does not take an RMD. The tax is 50 percent of the amount by which the RMD exceeds the distribution actually made (Code Sec. 4974).[95] Part or all of the tax may be waived if any of the RMD shortfall is due to reasonable error and if steps are taken to correct it. The penalty is reported on Form 5329. If the individual believes that part or all of the tax should be waived due to reasonable error, a statement of explanation should be attached along with Form 5329. Any tax due must be paid at the time Form 5329, along with the statement of explanation, is filed.

Uniform Lifetime Table

Age of employee	*Distribution period*	*Age of employee*	*Distribution period*
70	27.4	92	10.2
71	26.5	93	9.6
72	25.6	94	9.1
73	24.7	95	8.6
74	23.8	96	8.1
75	22.9	97	7.6
76	22.0	98	7.1
77	21.2	99	6.7
78	20.3	100	6.3
79	19.5	101	5.9
80	18.7	102	5.5
81	17.9	103	5.2
82	17.1	104	4.9
83	16.3	105	4.5
84	15.5	106	4.2
85	14.8	107	3.9
86	14.1	108	3.7
87	13.4	109	3.4
88	12.7	110	3.1
89	12.0	111	2.9
90	11.4	112	2.6
91	10.8	113	2.4
		114	2.1
		115+	1.9

References are to Standard Federal Tax Reports; Tax Research Consultant; and Practical Tax Explanations.

[94] ¶ 17,502; RETIRE: 42,162.15; § 24,440.20

[95] ¶ 34,380; RETIRE: 42,652; § 24,450.15

Single Life Table (for use by beneficiaries)

Age	*Life Expectancy*	*Age*	*Life Expectancy*	*Age*	*Life Expectancy*	*Age*	*Life Expectancy*
		27 . . .	56.2	55 . . .	29.6	83 . . .	8.6
0 . . .	82.4	28 . . .	55.3	56 . . .	28.7	84 . . .	8.1
1 . . .	81.6	29 . . .	54.3	57 . . .	27.9	85 . . .	7.6
2 . . .	80.6	30 . . .	53.3	58 . . .	27.0	86 . . .	7.1
3 . . .	79.7	31 . . .	52.4	59 . . .	26.1	87 . . .	6.7
4 . . .	78.7	32 . . .	51.4	60 . . .	25.2	88 . . .	6.3
5 . . .	77.7	33 . . .	50.4	61 . . .	24.4	89 . . .	5.9
6 . . .	76.7	34 . . .	49.4	62 . . .	23.5	90 . . .	5.5
7 . . .	75.8	35 . . .	48.5	63 . . .	22.7	91 . . .	5.2
8 . . .	74.8	36 . . .	47.5	64 . . .	21.8	92 . . .	4.9
9 . . .	73.8	37 . . .	46.5	65 . . .	21.0	93 . . .	4.6
10 . . .	72.8	38 . . .	45.6	66 . . .	20.2	94 . . .	4.3
11 . . .	71.8	39 . . .	44.6	67 . . .	19.4	95 . . .	4.1
12 . . .	70.8	40 . . .	43.6	68 . . .	18.6	96 . . .	3.8
13 . . .	69.9	41 . . .	42.7	69 . . .	17.8	97 . . .	3.6
14 . . .	68.9	42 . . .	41.7	70 . . .	17.0	98 . . .	3.4
15 . . .	67.9	43 . . .	40.7	71 . . .	16.3	99 . . .	3.1
16 . . .	66.9	44 . . .	39.8	72 . . .	15.5	100 . . .	2.9
17 . . .	66.0	45 . . .	38.8	73 . . .	14.8	101 . . .	2.7
18 . . .	65.0	46 . . .	37.9	74 . . .	14.1	102 . . .	2.5
19 . . .	64.0	47 . . .	37.0	75 . . .	13.4	103 . . .	2.3
20 . . .	63.0	48 . . .	36.0	76 . . .	12.7	104 . . .	2.1
21 . . .	62.1	49 . . .	35.1	77 . . .	12.1	105 . . .	1.9
22 . . .	61.1	50 . . .	34.2	78 . . .	11.4	106 . . .	1.7
23 . . .	60.1	51 . . .	33.3	79 . . .	10.8	107 . . .	1.5
24 . . .	59.1	52 . . .	32.3	80 . . .	10.2	108 . . .	1.4
25 . . .	58.2	53 . . .	31.4	81 . . .	9.7	109 . . .	1.2
26 . . .	57.2	54 . . .	30.5	82 . . .	9.1	110 . . .	1.1
						111+. . .	1.0

2124C. Early Distribution Penalty. Generally, taxable distributions from a qualified retirement plan or IRA are subject to an 10-percent additional tax if they are made before the participant reaches age 59½ (Code Sec. 72(t)).[96] However, the 10-percent additional tax will *not* apply to (Code Sec. 72(t)):

- eligible distributions that are timely and properly rolled over into an IRA or other qualified plan (¶ 2125B);
- distributions upon death or disability of the participant;
- distributions after separation from service that are part of a series of substantially equal periodic payments (not less frequently than annually) over the life (or life expectancy) of the participant or the joint lives (or life expectancies) of the participant and the beneficiary;
- distributions (other than from SEPs or IRAs) after the participant's separation from service, provided the separation from service occurred during or after the calendar year in which the participant reached age 55 (Notice 87-13) (age 50, in the case of distributions from a government plan to a retired police officer, firefighter, or emergency medical services provider);
- distributions to a nonparticipant under a qualified domestic relations order (¶ 2124D);
- distributions not exceeding deductible medical expenses (determined without regard to whether deductions are itemized);
- certain distributions by ESOPs of dividends on employer securities;

References are to Standard Federal Tax Reports; Tax Research Consultant; and Practical Tax Explanations.

[96] ¶ 6102; RETIRE: 66,454; § 25,450.25

• distributions made on account of the IRS's levy against the participant's account;

• qualified recovery assistance distributions (¶ 2124) (Code Sec. 1400Q(a)(1));[97]

• qualified reservist distributions (¶ 2153D); and

• effective July 6, 2012, distributions from federal retirement plans that are made under a phased retirement program (Code Sec. 72(t)).

Additional Tax on IRA Distributions. The exceptions to the 10-percent additional tax described above generally apply to IRA distributions except for distributions to a participant who has reached age 55 and has separated from service. Also, though the transfer of an IRA interest under a divorce or separation agreement is not a taxable event, subsequent distributions from a transferred IRA are not excluded from the additional tax. Some additional exceptions to the tax apply for IRA distributions only (¶ 2153I).

SIMPLE Plan Penalty. For employees who withdraw any amount from a SIMPLE plan during the first two years of participation, the 10-percent additional tax is increased to 25 percent (Code Sec. 72(t)(6)).

Reporting Requirements. The 10-percent additional tax on early distributions is generally reported on Form 5329. If an exception to the tax exists, the individual should provide this information on Form 5329. However, if no exception exists and distribution "Code 1" (i.e., early distribution) is correctly shown in the Form 1099-R received by the individual, then Form 5329 does not need to be filed. Instead, the amount of the additional tax should be reported directly on the individual's Form 1040.

2124D. Distributions Incident to Divorce or Separation. A distribution made by a qualified plan to an "alternate payee" (e.g., spouse, ex-spouse, child or other dependent of the participant) under the terms of a qualified domestic relations order (QDRO) is taxable to the alternate payee and not to the participant (Code Sec. 402(e)(1)(A)).[98] The QDRO rules generally apply to distributions made from qualified plans (e.g., 401(k) plans, 403(b) tax-deferred annuities and 457 plans) (Code Sec. 414(p)(10) and Code Sec. 414(p)(12)).

QDRO Defined. A qualified domestic relations order (QDRO) is a judgment, decree, or order (including approval of a property settlement agreement) made under a state's domestic relations or community property law. The QDRO must relate to the provision of child support, alimony, or marital property rights to a spouse, former spouse, child, or other dependent of a plan participant. In order to be "qualified," the order must meet specified requirements as to content and generally may not require the plan to pay benefits that are not otherwise payable under the terms of the plan (Code Sec. 414(p)).[99]

Payment of the entire amount due the spouse or ex-spouse under a QDRO is eligible for special tax averaging treatment for lump-sum distributions if it would be eligible had it been paid to the participant (¶ 2124). All qualified plans must permit a participant (or a spouse or ex-spouse of a participant who is an alternate payee under a QDRO to elect to have any distribution that is eligible for rollover treatment transferred directly to an eligible transferee plan specified by the participant (Code Sec. 401(a)(31)). The participant's "investment in the contract" (¶ 2124A) is allocated between the participant and the spouse or ex-spouse, pro rata, on the basis of the present value of all benefits awarded to the spouse or ex-spouse and the present value of all benefits reserved to the participant (Code Sec. 72(m)(10)).[100]

Transfers of IRAs. Transfer of an individual's interest in an IRA by the terms of a divorce or separation agreement that meets the qualifications of Code Sec. 71(b)(2) is

References are to Standard Federal Tax Reports; Tax Research Consultant; and Practical Tax Explanations.

[97] ¶ 32,498; RETIRE: 42,554; § 25,450.25

[98] ¶ 18,202; RETIRE: 42,058.05; § 24,460.15

[99] ¶ 19,150; RETIRE: 42,250; § 24,460.05

[100] ¶ 6102; RETIRE: 42,304; § 24,460.15

not considered to be a taxable transfer. The transferred interest becomes the property of the spouse or ex-spouse and may be rolled over (Code Sec. 408(d)(6)).

2125. Rollovers - General Rules. In general, any distribution of all or any portion of the balance to the credit of an employee in a qualified plan can be rolled over to another qualified plan, except:

- a distribution that is one of a series of substantially equal periodic payments, made over the life (or life expectancy) of the participant or the joint lives (or joint life expectancies) of the participant and his or her beneficiary;
- a distribution that is one of a series of substantially equal periodic payments made over a specified period of 10 years or more;
- distributions required under the minimum distribution rules (¶ 2124B); and
- hardship distributions (¶ 2106E) (Code Sec. 402(c)(4)).[101]

Generally, the rollover must be made within 60 days. The IRS has the authority to grant a waiver of the 60-day rule in situations involving equity, good conscience, or situations beyond the control of the individual. For rollovers of distributions from traditional IRAs, see ¶ 2125A; for rollovers between qualified plans or to traditional IRAs, see ¶ 2125B; for rollovers by successor after death of participant, see ¶ 2125C; and for rollovers incident to divorce, see ¶ 2125D.

2125A. Rollover Distributions from IRAs. An individual may withdraw all or part of the assets of one traditional IRA and exclude the withdrawal from income if the individual either transfers it to another traditional IRA or returns it to the same IRA. However, the rollover or return must generally be accomplished within 60 days after the withdrawal. It is not necessary that the entire amount withdrawn be transferred, but only the amount that is transferred during the 60-day period will not be taxed. Any portion of the withdrawal that is not rolled over within the 60-day period will be taxed as ordinary income and may be subject to the 10-percent additional tax for early distributions (¶ 2153H). The IRS has the authority to grant a waiver of the 60-day rule in situations involving equity, good conscience, or situations beyond the control of the individual (Code Sec. 408(d)(3); Rev. Proc. 2003-16).[102]

Waiting Period. Once an individual has made a tax-free rollover, he or she must wait at least one year from the date of receipt of the amount withdrawn before becoming eligible to engage in another rollover. The one-year limitation applies separately to each IRA owned by the taxpayer (IRS Pub. 590). Thus, a distribution received from one IRA of the taxpayer may be rolled over even though a distribution from another IRA of the taxpayer was received less than a year before and was also rolled over. A mere change of trustee or custodian for an IRA is not considered a rollover (although it is also tax free), and; therefore, the one-year limitation does not apply.[103]

Required Distributions. A rollover distribution from one traditional IRA to another is *not* available for a required minimum distribution (¶ 2153F) (Code Sec. 408(d)(3)(E)).[104] See ¶ 2154E regarding a rollover from a traditional IRA into a Roth IRA. Rollovers from SIMPLE plans are discussed at ¶ 2155E.

Rollovers from IRAs to Employer Plans. Generally, an eligible rollover distribution from an IRA may be rolled over into a qualified plan, 403(b) plan, a tax-sheltered annuity, or 457 plan (Code Sec. 408(d)(3)(A)). A rollover of after-tax contributions can be made from one IRA to another IRA. However, after-tax contributions in an IRA cannot be rolled over into an employer's qualified plan (Code Sec. 408(d)(3)(A)(ii)).

2125B. Rollover Distributions Between Qualified Plans or to Traditional IRAs. In many situations, a distribution from an eligible retirement plan may be rolled over and thus excluded from current income (Code Sec. 402(c)).[105] Any part of the taxable

References are to Standard Federal Tax Reports; Tax Research Consultant; and Practical Tax Explanations.

[101] ¶ 18,202; RETIRE: 42,450; § 24,455.10

[102] ¶ 18,902; RETIRE: 42,450, RETIRE: 66,700; § 25,445.10

[103] ¶ 18,922.75; RETIRE: 66,704; § 25,445.10

[104] ¶ 18,902; RETIRE: 66,706; § 25,445.10

[105] ¶ 18,202; RETIRE: 42,450; § 25,445.05

portion of a distribution from an eligible retirement plan may be rolled over to a traditional IRA or to another qualified plan, unless the distribution is one of a series of substantially equal payments made:

- over the life (or life expectancy) of the participant or the joint lives (or joint life expectancies) of the participant and his or her beneficiary; or
- over a specified period of 10 years or more. In addition, a distribution may not be rolled over if it is required to be made under the required minimum distribution (RMD) rules (¶ 2124B).

A distribution may not be rolled over if it is required to be made as a required minimum distribution (RMD) (¶ 2124B). Waiver requests are discussed at ¶ 2125A.

Direct Transfers. A qualified plan must allow an employee to elect to have any distribution that is eligible to be rolled over transferred directly to a traditional IRA, a qualified defined contribution plan, a qualified retirement annuity plan, a tax-sheltered annuity (a 403(b) plan), or an eligible deferred compensation plan maintained by a government employer (a 457 plan), unless the plan reasonably believes that the employee will receive distributions eligible to be rolled over of less than $200 (Code Sec. 401(a)(31)(C), Code Sec. 402(c)(2), Reg. § 1.401(a)(31)-1).[106]

Plans that are eligible to receive direct rollovers generally are the same plans that can receive rollovers, except qualified plans are required to allow direct transfers to qualified plans only if they are defined contribution plans (Code Sec. 401(a)(31)(E)). The defined contribution plan that accepts the transfer must agree to separately account for the pre-tax and after-tax portions of the amount that is transferred (Code Sec. 401(a)(31)(C)(i)). After-tax contributions from qualified retirement plans can also be rolled over in a direct trustee-to-trustee transfer to a defined benefit plan or a Code Sec. 403(b) tax-sheltered annuity (Code Sec. 402(c)(2)(A)). The transferee plan must separately account for after-tax contributions and earnings. A traditional IRA to which the pre-tax and post-tax amounts are rolled over does not have to separately account for these amounts. A rollover that includes both pre-tax and post-tax amounts is considered as coming first from pre-tax amounts (Code Sec. 402(c)(2)).

Mandatory Rollovers. A qualified plan must provide for a direct rollover (i.e., a trustee to trustee transfer) from the plan into an IRA when the plan makes a mandatory distribution of the participant's benefit (an involuntary cash-out) (Code Sec. 401(a)(31)). The rule applies when a mandatory distribution from a qualified plan exceeds $1,000 and the plan specifies that nonforfeitable benefits that do not exceed $5,000 must be distributed immediately. However, the employee must have the right to elect to receive the distribution or have it rolled over into another IRA or qualified plan (Notice 2005-5).

Withholding. If a distributee does not elect a direct transfer, and receives the distribution and then transfers the funds to an eligible plan within 60 days, the payor of the distribution must withhold 20 percent of the distribution (Code Sec. 3405(c)).[107] If the distributee does elect a direct transfer, there is no withholding.

Written Explanation. The plan administrator must provide a written explanation to a recipient of the distribution options (including the direct trustee-to-trustee transfer option) within a reasonable period of time before making an eligible rollover distribution (Code Sec. 402(f)).[108]

2125C. Rollover Distributions By Successor After Death of Participant. When a distribution from a qualified plan that would be eligible for rollover treatment if made to the employee is received by the participant's surviving spouse, the spouse may roll that distribution into an account maintained in the survivor's name under the same terms and conditions that would have applied to the employee (¶ 2125B) (Code Sec. 402(c)(9)).[109] Successors other than a surviving spouse who receive a distribution from a qualified

References are to Standard Federal Tax Reports; Tax Research Consultant; and Practical Tax Explanations.

[106] ¶ 17,502, Code Sec. 18,202; RETIRE: 42,500; § 24,455.40

[107] ¶ 33,620; RETIRE: 42,700; § 24,445.20

[108] ¶ 18,202; RETIRE: 42,466; § 24,455.40

[109] ¶ 18,202; RETIRE: 42,460.05; § 24,455.30

plan are not entitled to roll over that distribution to an IRA or to another qualified plan account in their own name. Instead, a nonspouse beneficiary can roll a qualified plan distribution into an IRA established in the name of the decedent. The IRA is treated as an inherited IRA. This allows the beneficiary to take distributions from the IRA in accordance with the required minimum distribution rules (¶ 2124B) instead of taking the entire distribution into income in the year of the plan distribution (Code Sec. 402(c)(11)). The surviving spouse of the owner of an IRA is also eligible to roll over any amount received from that IRA to another IRA or qualified plan (¶ 2125A) (Code Sec. 408(d)(3)(C)).[110] However, this cannot be done by any other successor to the IRA.

2125D. Rollover Distributions Incident to Divorce. When a participant's spouse or former spouse is awarded all or part of the participant's interest in a qualified plan or 403(b) plan by a qualified domestic relations order (QDRO) (¶ 2124D), the distribution of any part of that interest to the spouse or former spouse may be rolled over on the same terms that would apply if the distribution were made to the participant (Code Sec. 414(p)(10)).[111] The QDRO provisions also apply to 457 plans (i.e., eligible deferred compensation plans of state and local governments and tax-exempt organizations) (¶ 2161).

The transfer of all or a portion of an IRA to a spouse or former spouse under a divorce or separation instrument that meets the definition established by Code Sec. 71(b)(2) is a nontaxable transaction as to both parties, and the IRA is thereafter treated as that of the spouse or former spouse (Code Sec. 408(d)(6)).[112] Accordingly, the spouse or former spouse may roll over to another IRA or IRAs all or any part of the interest transferred to him or her (¶ 2125A).

2125E. Rollover Distributions Between Certain Plans and Roth 401(k). Effective for distributions after September 27, 2010, a 401(k) plan (¶ 2106), a 403(b) plan (¶ 2160), or a governmental 457(b) plan (¶ 2161) that includes a qualified Roth contribution program may permit a qualified rollover of a distribution from a participant's non-Roth account to the participant's designated Roth account within the same plan (Code Sec. 402A(c)(4)(B)). The intra-plan non-Roth to Roth rollover rules mirror the eligible retirement plan to Roth IRA rollover rules (¶ 2154E). Both kinds of rollovers adopt the traditional IRA to Roth IRA conversion rules (¶ 2125A). The distribution to be rolled over must be otherwise allowed under the plan; thus, an employer may have to amend its non-Roth plan to allow in-service distributions or distributions prior to normal retirement age.

The converted amount is includible in gross income as a distribution for the tax year in which the amount is distributed or transferred. This amount is reduced by any after-tax contributions included in the amount rolled over. If the rollover was done in 2010, the amount the taxpayer would have included in gross income in 2010 is instead included in equal installments in 2011 and 2012, unless the taxpayer elected to include it all in 2010. Any election for any distribution during a tax year may not be changed after the due date for such tax year (Code Sec. 402A(c)(4)(A)).

2126. Joint and Survivor and Pre-Retirement Annuities. A qualified plan that pays benefits in the form of an annuity must generally provide for the payment in the form of a joint and survivor annuity for the participant and the surviving spouse (Code Secs. 401(a)(11)(A)(i) and 417).[113] The annuity must be the actuarial equivalent of an annuity for the single life of the employee, and the survivor portion may not be less than 50 percent of the annuity paid during the joint lives of the employee and spouse. A pre-retirement survivor annuity must be provided for the surviving spouse of a vested participant who dies prior to the earliest retirement age. An employee may "elect out" of either the joint and survivor or pre-retirement survivor annuity. However, the election may only be made with the written consent of the spouse and the consent must be

References are to Standard Federal Tax Reports; Tax Research Consultant; and Practical Tax Explanations.

[110] ¶ 18,902; RETIRE: 66,702.10; § 25,445.30

[111] ¶ 19,150; RETIRE: 9,308.05; § 24,460.15

[112] ¶ 18,902; RETIRE: 66,708; § 25,460

[113] ¶ 17,502, ¶ 19,260; RETIRE: 42,200; § 24,435.10

witnessed by a notary public or plan representative. The spouse's consent cannot be given in a prenuptial agreement (Reg. § 1.401(a)-20).[114]

2127. Anti-Assignment Provision. A qualified plan must provide that benefits under the plan may not be assigned or otherwise transferred (Code Secs. 401(a)(13) and 414(p)).[115] An exception is made for assignments ordered by a qualified domestic relations order (QDRO) issued under a state's domestic relations law (¶ 2124D). In addition, a participant's benefits may be reduced when the individual has committed a breach of fiduciary duty or committed a criminal act against the plan.

2128. Prohibited Transactions. Certain transactions between a qualified employees' trust and a plan fiduciary or other "disqualified person" are prohibited (Code Sec. 4975(c)).[116] The "disqualified person" who engages in the prohibited transaction is liable for excise taxes based upon the amount of the prohibited transaction. The basic excise tax rate is 15 percent. If the prohibited transaction is not corrected before the IRS assesses the tax or mails a notice of deficiency regarding it, the excise tax rate increases to 100 percent (Code Sec. 4975(b)).[117]

Plan Loans. Loans of plan assets to owners of the employer, including owner-employees, are generally prohibited transactions. Loans of IRA assets to the account owner are always prohibited, but a loan from an employer plan may qualify for an exception to the rule (Code Sec. 4975(f)(6)(B)(iii)). Loans from employer plans to disqualified persons are not prohibited if (Code Sec. 4975(d)(1)):

- loans are available to all participants on a reasonably equivalent basis;
- the plan must explicitly provide for such loans;
- the loan must have a reasonable rate of interest; and
- the loan must be adequately secured.

For this purpose, the term "owner-employee" is defined as: (1) a self-employed person who owns the entire interest in an unincorporated trade or business (i.e., a sole proprietor) or (2) an individual who owns more than a 10-percent capital or profits interest in a partnership (Code Sec. 401(c)(3)).[118]

2129. Plan Loans. Unless certain requirements are met, a loan to a participant from a qualified plan is treated as a distribution and included in the participant's gross income. A pledge or assignment of any part of a participant's interest in a plan is treated as a loan for this purpose (Code Sec. 72(p)(1); Reg. § 1.72(p)-1). The exceptions do not apply unless loan limitations and level amortization of the loan is required, with payments that occur not less frequently than quarterly (Code Sec. 72(p)(2)(C); Reg. § 1.72(p)-1, Q&A-4, -9, and -10). The loan must also be subject to an enforceable agreement.[119]

Allowable Loans. Subject to specific dollar limits, a loan will not be treated as a distribution if the loan must be repaid within five years or the loan proceeds must be used (within a reasonable time after the date of the loan) to acquire a dwelling unit that is to be used as the principal residence of the participant. When determining if a plan loan is allowable, all plans of the employer are treated as a single plan (Code Sec 72(p)(2)(D)(ii)). As a general rule, the *refinancing* of a home loan does not qualify under this exception (Reg. § 1.72(p)-1, Q&A-8(a)). However, the repayment of a loan from a third party that was used to acquire the principal residence may qualify under the exception.

> **Example 1:** On July 1, 2012, Betty purchased a home that she used as a principal residence. She paid a portion of the purchase price with a $50,000 loan from Global Bank. On August 1, 2012, Betty borrowed $50,000 from her 401(k)

References are to Standard Federal Tax Reports; Tax Research Consultant; and Practical Tax Explanations.

[114] ¶ 17,729; RETIRE: 42,212; § 24,435.25

[115] ¶ 17,502, ¶ 19,150; RETIRE: 9,300; § 24,230.20

[116] ¶ 34,400; RETIRE: 48,250; § 24,020.20

[117] ¶ 34,400; RETIRE: 48,250; § 51,201.25

[118] ¶ 17,502; RETIRE: 48,322; § 24,020.25

[119] ¶ 6102, ¶ 6133; RETIRE: 42,154, RETIRE: 42,802.05; § 24,465.15

plan. A few days later, Betty used the money from the plan loan to pay the $50,000 she owed Global Bank. Based on these facts, the plan loan would be treated as having been used to acquire Betty's principal residence. As a result, Betty's plan loan would *not* be treated as a taxable distribution.

Loan Limits. A loan from a qualified plan will be treated as a distribution only to the extent that, when added to the balances of all other loans to the participant (whenever made), the proceeds exceed the *lesser* of $50,000 or half the present value (but not less than $10,000) of the plan participant's vested benefits under the plan. The $50,000 amount must be reduced by the excess (if any) of: (1) the highest outstanding balance of loans from the plan during the one-year period ending on the day preceding the date of the loan over (2) the outstanding balance of those loans on the date of the loan (Code Sec. 72(p)(2)).[120]

Example 2: Jane Smith is a participant in her employer's qualified profit-sharing plan. She wishes to borrow the maximum amount subject to the five-year repayment rule on July 1, 2013. On that date, the value of her vested interest in the plan is $120,000. Her highest loan balance during the period July 1, 2012, through June 30, 2013, was $40,000, and her balance on July 1, 2013, is $35,000. The maximum amount that Jane may borrow on July 1, 2013, is $10,000. This is the amount that, when added to her $35,000 loan balance, does not exceed $45,000. The $45,000 amount is determined by reducing the $50,000 loan limit by the excess of her highest loan balance for the past year ($40,000) over the loan balance at the time of the new loan ($35,000).

Disaster Relief. The $50,000 and one-half of present value of vested benefits limits is increased to $100,000, or the greater of one-half of the present value of the employee's non-forfeitable accrued benefit under the plan, or $10,000 for loans to "qualified individuals" by reason of certain natural disasters that occurred within specified periods or on a specified date. Qualified individuals are those whose principal place of abode was in a disaster area on a specified date and who sustained an economic loss as a result of the storm (including Hurricanes Katrina, Rita, or the Wilma disaster areas, the Kansas disaster areas, and the Midwestern storms, tornados and flooding).

In addition to the increased limits, the loan repayment requirements are suspended for one year for qualified individuals (Code Sec. 1400Q(c)(2)). Loans may accrue additional interest during the suspension period, depending on the terms of the plan and the loan documents.[121]

2130. Returns. Generally, a qualified retirement plan must file Form 5500 (and accompanying schedules) each tax year to report detailed information concerning various aspects of employee benefit plans (e.g., accountant's report, information concerning the fiduciary and financial information) (Code Sec. 6058).[122] Small plans meeting certain eligibility requirements (generally plans with less than 100 participants) must file Form 5500-SF. However, some plans (one-participant plans) generally may file a simpler Form 5500-EZ if a plan's only participants are an individual and spouse who together own the business (whether or not incorporated) for which the plan is established. Form 5500-EZ may also be used by the plan of a partnership if the only participants are partners and their spouses. Form 5500-SF or 5500-EZ need not be filed if certain conditions are met (e.g., the plan, and any other plan of the employer, had total assets of $250,000 at the end of the plan year, unless it is the plan's final year).

If a Form 5500, Form 5500-SF, or Form 5500-EZ has to be filed, as a general rule, the form and its required schedules have to be filed no later than the last day of the seventh month after the plan year ends (e.g., July 31 for calendar year plans). A one-time extension of up to 2½ months may be obtained by filing Form 5558. An automatic extension for filing Form 5500, Form 5500-SF, or Form 5500-EZ will be granted if certain conditions are met (e.g., the plan year and the employer's tax year are the same and the employer has been granted an extension to file its tax return). Form 5500 and Form 5500-SF must be filed electronically with the Department of Labor. Form 5500-EZ must

References are to Standard Federal Tax Reports; Tax Research Consultant; and Practical Tax Explanations.

[120] ¶ 6102; RETIRE: 42,804.05; § 24,465.15

[121] ¶ 32,498; RETIRE: 42,804.05; § 24,475.05

[122] ¶ 36,500; RETIRE: 51,356; § 24,530.05

be filed on paper with the Internal Revenue Service. A one-participant plan that is eligible to file may elect to file Form 5500-SF electronically through the Department of Labor's system rather than filing a Form 5500-EZ on paper with the Internal Revenue Service.[123]

A plan may also be required to file the stand-alone Form 8955-SSA, the designated successor to Schedule SSA (Form 5500), to report certain information regarding separated participants with deferred vested benefits under the plan. Form 8955-SSA must be filed with the IRS by the last day of the seventh month following the last day of that plan year (plus extensions). It should not be filed with Form 5500 or Form 5500-SF. A one-time extension to file Form 8955-SSA (up to 2½ months) may be obtained by filing Form 5558 on or before the normal due date (not including any extensions).

Various penalties may be imposed for the failure to timely file the required Form 5500 series form, schedules, reports, or Form 8955-SSA (Code Sec. 6652; Code Sec. 6692).[124]

Defined Benefit Plans - Types

2135. Introduction. A defined benefit plan generally is a traditional pension plan which provides specific benefits to participants based on a formula reflecting compensation and years of service. Flat benefit plans are discussed at ¶ 2135A and unit benefit plans are discussed at ¶ 2135B. The employer (or other sponsor) must make sufficient contributions to the plan based on actuarial assumptions and calculations of the amount necessary to fund the promised benefits. Employee contributions are sometimes required or voluntary. Instead of funding the plan directly, an employer may buy an insurance policy or annuity contract to fund the plan (Code Secs. 403(a)(1) and 404(a)(2)).[125]

Employers with 500 or fewer employees may establish a combined defined benefit/401(k) plan (¶ 2150E).

2135A. Flat Benefit Plans. Under this type of defined benefit plan, the benefit for each participant is a fixed dollar amount, as long as a minimum number of years of service is reached. For instance, a formula for this type of plan could base a monthly retirement benefit upon a percentage of compensation multiplied by monthly compensation. For example, if the plan provided for 30 percent of monthly compensation upon 10 years of service or more, both a participant with 10 years of service and a participant with 30 years for service, who each had monthly compensation of $2,000, would each receive a monthly pension of $600.

2135B. Unit Benefit Plans. This type of defined benefit plan generally provides greater benefits for a long-service employee than for a short-term employee with the same average compensation. A formula for this type of plan would be a monthly retirement benefit based on a percentage of monthly compensation multiplied by years of service. For example, a participant who receives one percent with a monthly compensation for each year of service, who has $2,000 in monthly compensation, and 30 years of employment upon retirement would receive a monthly pension of $600. A participant with the same monthly compensation but only 10 years of employment would receive a monthly pension of $200.

Defined Benefit Plans - Requirements

2140. Introduction. Defined benefit plans must satisfy the general qualification requirements applicable to all qualified plans (beginning at ¶ 2114). They also must satisfy additional requirements relating to funding (¶ 2141), benefit limitations (¶ 2142), and vesting (¶ 2143). There are also deduction limits for contributions to defined benefit plans (¶ 2144).

2141. Minimum Funding Standards. Employers maintaining single-employer defined benefit plans are required to make minimum contributions to the plan each year

References are to Standard Federal Tax Reports; Tax Research Consultant; and Practical Tax Explanations.

[123] ¶ 39,480, ¶ 39,490.025; RETIRE: 51,356; § 24,530.05

[124] ¶ 39,480; RETIRE: 51,356; § 24,530.05

[125] ¶ 18,270, ¶ 18,330; RETIRE: 6,150, RETIRE: 33,254; § 24,120.15

based on the plan's assets (reduced by credit balances), funding target, and target normal cost. Under the rules, full funding of plans is required, with existing shortfalls generally required to be eliminated over seven years, unless a special funding schedule has been elected (Code Secs. 412, 430, and 436).[126] Failure to meet minimum funding requirements or correct shortfalls will generally subject the employer to an excise tax (Code Sec. 4971).[127] However, a temporary waiver of the minimum funding requirements may be provided to an employer that is unable to satisfy the minimum funding standard for a plan year without "substantial business hardship." The employer may be required to provide security to the plan as a condition for the waiver. In addition, no plan amendment that has the effect of increasing plan liabilities may generally be adopted during the waiver period.

2142. Benefit Limits. A qualified plan must limit the contributions and benefits that may be provided to each individual plan participant (Code Sec. 415).[128] See ¶ 2122A for the limits imposed on annual deductions. For 2012, the maximum annual retirement benefit for any participant of a defined benefit plan may not exceed the *lesser* of $200,000 or 100 percent of the participant's average compensation (¶ 2120) for the participant's three consecutive calendar years of highest compensation (Code Sec. 415(b); Notice 2011-90). For 2013, the maximum annual retirement benefit for any participant of a defined benefit plan may not exceed the *lesser* of $205,000 or 100 percent of the participant's average compensation (¶ 2120) for the participant's three consecutive calendar years of highest compensation (Code Sec. 415(b); IRS News Release IR-2012-77).[129] The maximum annual benefit is actuarially reduced when retirement benefits are paid before age 62 and increased when benefits are not paid until after age 65. If certain requirements are met, an annual benefit of up to $10,000 may be provided by the plan even if that exceeds the 100 percent of compensation limit. The benefit limit and the compensation limit are reduced in the case of individuals with less than 10 years of service with the employer.

2143. Vesting. For defined benefit plans, all employees' interests in their accrued benefits derived from employer contributions must vest at least as quickly as they would under either a three-to-seven-years graded vesting schedule or a five-year cliff vesting schedule. Plans may maintain separate vesting schedules for those contributions made before 2007 and those made after 2006 (Code Sec. 411(a)(2); Notice 2007-7).[130]

2144. Limits on Deductions for Contributions. The maximum deduction allowed for contributions to a defined benefit plan generally is determined actuarially based on the expected costs of the plan (Code Sec. 404(a)(1)(A)). However, deductions under these methods are subject to both a floor of the annual contributions necessary to satisfy the minimum funding standard (¶ 2141) and a ceiling of the full funding limitation for the plan. The amount that can be deducted for any year cannot exceed the greater of the following:

- *Level Funding Method*—The limit is an amount necessary to provide, for all participants under the plan, the remaining unfunded cost of their past and current service credits distributed as a level amount or level percentage of compensation over the remaining service of each participant. Under this method, the past service liability for each participant is deducted ratably over the employee's projected years of service until retirement.

- *Normal Cost Method*—The limit is an amount equal to the normal ("current") cost of the plan plus, if past service or other supplementary credits are provided, an amount not in excess of that necessary to amortize these credits in equal payments over 10 years. However, all defined benefit plans may deduct 100 percent of their unfunded current liability (Code Sec. 404(a)(1)(D)(i)).[131]

References are to Standard Federal Tax Reports; Tax Research Consultant; and Practical Tax Explanations.

[126] ¶ 19,100, ¶ 20,151, ¶ 20,211; RETIRE: 30,000; § 24,120.30

[127] ¶ 34,320; RETIRE: 30,502; § 24,120.30

[128] ¶ 19,200; RETIRE: 36,050; § 24,275.05

[129] ¶ 19,200; RETIRE: 36,150; § 24,275.10

[130] ¶ 19,050; RETIRE: 18,102; § 24,260

[131] ¶ 18,330; RETIRE: 33,252; § 24,305.10

Hybrid Plans

2150. Introduction. There are several types of hybrid plans that combine elements of traditional defined benefit plans with elements of defined contribution plans. For example, a "cash balance plan" is a hybrid defined benefit plan that provides benefits for each employee participant by reference to the amount of a hypothetical account balance based on hypothetical annual allocations and earnings determined under the terms of the plan (¶ 2150B). The hypothetical allocations and earnings are designed to mimic the allocations of actual contributions under a defined contribution plan (e.g., a money purchase pension plan). Another type of hybrid defined benefit plan is a pension equity plan (PEP) in which benefits of a plan participant are determined as a percentage of the individual's final average pay. The percentage is determined based on points received for years of service (¶ 2150D).

2150A. Floor Offset Plans. A floor offset plan is essentially a defined contribution plan with a defined benefit floor. Under such a plan, an employee who leaves employment before retirement age receives the amount in his individual account. However, an employee who continues to work until retirement receives the greater of the defined contribution accumulation or the promised defined benefit pension. The defined benefit and the defined contribution portions of the combined floor-offset plan must comply with statutory requirements applicable to both plans (i.e., the actuarial equivalence rule governing lump-sum distributions of accrued benefits).[132]

2150B. Cash Balance Plans. Cash balance plans are hybrid defined benefit plans that provide guaranteed benefits for employees that are insured by the Pension Benefit Guaranty Corporation. These plans establish a separate "hypothetical account" for each employee. The employer credits a specified percentage of compensation (i.e., pay credits) to each account and credits each account with interest earned (i.e., interest credits). The amounts to be contributed are actuarially determined to ensure sufficient funds to provide the promised benefit. If at retirement the balance in a participant's individual account is less than the amount promised by the employer, the participant will receive the promised amount. Participants may elect to receive their benefit in a lump-sum or as an annuity.

Since benefits are not based solely on actual contributions and forfeitures allocated to an employee's account and the actual investment experience and expenses of the plan allocated to the account, the arrangement is treated as a defined benefit plan rather than as a defined contribution plan. Accordingly, the plan is required to provide definitely determinable benefits, use a fixed interest rate, and adhere to the minimum funding standards.[133]

2150C. Target Benefit Plans. A target benefit plan is a plan under which an employer establishes a target benefit for his employees but where each employee's actual benefit is based on the amount in his individual account. The IRS defines a target benefit plan as a money purchase pension plan in which:

(1) the plan indicates a stated benefit commencing at the plan's normal retirement date;

(2) contributions necessary to fund the stated benefit with respect to a participant are determined under the individual level premium funding method using actuarial assumptions or factors stated in the plan;

(3) the contributions, and any forfeitures reducing those contributions, are allocated and separately accounted for with respect to each such participant; and

(4) the benefits provided under the plan are provided solely from the contribution amounts allocated in paragraph (3), employee contributions and any income, expenses and gains, reduced by any losses.

References are to Standard Federal Tax Reports; Tax Research Consultant; and Practical Tax Explanations.

[132] ¶ 17,710; RETIRE: 39,206; § 24,120.17

[133] ¶ 19,076.0345; RETIRE: 39,058; § 24,270.05

Because it is a money purchase pension plan, it is considered a defined contribution plan. However, the employer contributions are determined actuarially, as though the plan were a defined benefit plan. But the employer does not guarantee the targeted amount; its only obligation is to pay whatever benefit can be provided by the amount in the participant's account.[134]

2150D. Pension Equity Plans. Under a pension equity plan (PEP plan), benefits accrue on a level basis. Employees earn credits for each year they have worked. Upon termination, employees receive a lump-sum payment or an annuity that is based on accumulated credits and final average pay.[135]

2150E. Defined Benefit and 401(k) Plans (DB/K Plans). For plan years beginning after 2009, small employers will have the option to establish a combined defined benefit/401(k) plan (a "DB/K" plan). The relevant Code and Employee Retirement Income Security Act (P.L. 93-406), commonly referred to as ERISA, provisions are applied separately to the defined benefit and 401(k) plans that are part of a DB/K plan, subject to certain exceptions. The DB/K plan must be maintained by a small employer. A small employer is an employer who employed an average of at least two but not more than 500 employees on business days during the preceding calendar year and who employs at least two employees on the first day of the plan year (Code Sec. 414(x)(2)(A)).

The assets of the DB/K plan must be held in a single trust and must be clearly identified and allocated to the defined benefit plan and the applicable defined contribution plan to the extent necessary for the separate application of the Code and ERISA. Thus, for example, the Code Sec. 415 limitations apply separately to contributions under the 401(k) plan and to benefits under the defined benefit plan, both of which are part of the DB/K plan. Similarly, the spousal protection rules apply to the defined benefit plan but not to the 401(k) plan. In addition, the DB/K plan must also meet certain benefit, contribution, vesting, and nondiscrimination requirements.

Defined Benefit Plan Requirements. A defined benefit plan that is part of a DB/K plan must provide each participant with a benefit of not less than the applicable percentage of the participant's final average pay. For this purpose, final average pay is determined using the consecutive-year period (not exceeding five years) during which the participant has the greatest aggregate compensation. The applicable percentage is the lesser of (1) one percent multiplied by the participant's years of service or (2) 20 percent (Code Sec. 414(x)(2)(B)(i) and (ii)). Any benefits provided under a defined benefit plan that is part of a DB/K plan (including any benefits provided in addition to required benefits) must be fully vested after three years of service (Code Sec. 414(x)(2)(D)(i); Code Sec. 404(a)(1)(D)(i)).[136]

Cash Balance Plans. A special rule applies to a Code Sec. 411(a)(13)(B) applicable defined benefit plan, under which the accrued benefit is calculated as the balance of a hypothetical account or as an accumulated percentage of the participant's final average compensation, and which meets the interest credit requirements of Code Sec. 411(b)(5)(B)(i). Such a plan is treated as meeting the benefit requirement if each participant receives a pay credit for each plan year of not less than a certain percentage of compensation that is determined based on the participant's age. If the participant is age 30 or less, then the percentage is two percent; if the participant is over age 30 but less than age 40, then the percentage is four percent; if the participant is age 40 or over but less than age 50, then the percentage is six percent; and if the participant is age 50 or over, the percentage is eight percent. A defined benefit plan that is part of a DB/K plan must provide the required benefit to each participant, regardless of whether the participant makes elective deferrals to the applicable defined contribution plan that is part of the DB/K plan (Code Sec. 414(x)(2)(B)(iii) and (iv)).

Defined Contribution Plan Requirements. Certain automatic enrollment and matching contribution requirements must be met with respect to a 401(k) plan that is part of a

References are to Standard Federal Tax Reports; Tax Research Consultant; and Practical Tax Explanations.

[134] ¶ 19,200; RETIRE: 36,304; § 24,115.20

[135] ¶ 19,050; RETIRE: 39,058; § 24,001

[136] ¶ 19,150; RETIRE: 3,502; § 24,910

DB/K plan. First, the qualified cash or deferred arrangement under the plan must constitute an automatic contribution arrangement (Code Sec. 414(x)(2)(C)(i)(I)). An automatic contribution arrangement must generally provide that each employee eligible to participate in the arrangement is treated as having elected to make elective contributions in an amount of four percent of the employee's compensation. The employee, however, may elect not to make such contributions or to make contributions at a different rate. The automatic contribution arrangement must also meet certain notice requirements (Code Sec. 414(x)(5)(B)).[137]

Second, the employer must make matching contributions on behalf of each employee eligible to participate in the arrangement in an amount equal to 50 percent of the employee's elective deferrals, but no more than four percent of the compensation. The rate of matching contributions with respect to any elective deferrals for highly compensated employees must not be greater than the matching contribution rate for nonhighly compensated employees. Matching contributions in addition to the required matching contributions can also be made (Code Sec. 414(x)(2)(C)(i)(II)).

The employer can also make nonelective contributions under the 401(k) plan. These contributions, however, are not taken into account in determining whether the matching contribution requirement is met (Code Sec. 414(x)(2)(C)(ii)).

Matching contributions under the 401(k) plan (including contributions in excess of the required matching contributions) are fully vested when made, while nonelective contributions are fully vested after three years of service.

Other Requirements. All contributions, benefits, and other rights and features that are provided under a defined benefit plan or an applicable defined contribution plan that is part of a DB/K plan must be provided uniformly to all participants (Code Sec. 414(x)(2)(E)). This requirement applies regardless of whether nonuniform contributions, benefits, or other rights or features could be provided without violating the nondiscrimination rules. However, it is intended that a plan will not violate the uniformity requirement merely because benefits accrued for periods before a defined benefit or defined contribution plan became part of a DB/K plan are protected.

Reporting. A DB/K plan is treated as a single plan for purposes of the annual reporting rules (Code Sec. 414(x)(6)(B)). All the information required with respect to the defined benefit plan and the 401(k) plan that are part of the DB/K plan must be provided in a single Form 5500. In addition, only a single summary annual report must be provided to the participants.

Termination of the Plan. In the case of a termination of an eligible DB/K plan, the defined benefit and 401(k) components of the DB/K plan must be terminated separately (Code Sec. 414(x)(1)).

Individual Retirement Accounts (IRAs)

2152. Introduction. In addition to individuals being able to set up an individual retirement account (IRA) (¶ 2153), an employer may also establish and contribute to an IRA-based plan for providing retirement benefits to employees. In these arrangements, a separate IRA account is established and maintained on behalf of each participating employee. The employer's contributions to the accounts are deductible as compensation but generally are not recognized as income by the employee until distributed.

There are three types of IRA-based plans. Under a Simplified Employee Pension (SEP) plan the employer makes contributions directly to a traditional IRA (called a SEP-IRA) set up by or for each eligible employee (¶ 2156) (Code Sec. 408(k)). Certain eligible employers may also establish a Savings Incentive Match Plan for Employees (SIMPLE) plan in which employees are allowed salary reduction contributions to an IRA and the employer makes matching or nonelective contributions to the account (¶ 2155) (Code Sec. 408(p)(2)(C)).[138] Finally, under a payroll deduction IRA, an employer may

References are to Standard Federal Tax Reports; Tax Research Consultant; and Practical Tax Explanations.

[137] ¶ 19,150; RETIRE: 3,504; § 24,915

[138] ¶ 18,902; RETIRE: 63,000; § 25,001, § 25,101

establish a traditional or Roth IRA to which an employee authorizes a payroll deduction to be contributed to the account.

2153. Traditional Individual Retirement Accounts (IRAs). Individuals who receive compensation, including alimony, that is includible in gross income and who are under age 70½ throughout the tax year are entitled to make contributions to traditional individual retirement accounts (IRAs) (Code Sec. 219). Amounts earned in a traditional IRA are not taxed until distributions are made (Code Sec. 408(e)(1)).[139] Generally, contributions to a traditional IRA may be deducted. However, when the individual, or the individual's spouse, is an active participant in an employer-maintained retirement plan, the deduction may be reduced or eliminated (¶ 2153A) (Code Sec. 219(g)).[140] Nondeductible contributions may be made to a traditional IRA and/or Roth IRA (Code Sec. 408(o)).[141] Roth IRAs are discussed beginning at ¶ 2154.

IRA Contributions. The maximum combined contribution that can be made to all of an individual's traditional and Roth IRAs is $5,000 for 2012 and $5,500 for 2013 (Notice 2011-90; IRS News Release IR-2012-77). An individual who will be at least age 50 by the end of the tax year is allowed to make additional contributions to a traditional or Roth IRA. Under this catch-up rule, the maximum contribution amount for an individual who has attained age 50 before the end of the taxable year is generally $1,000 (Code Sec. 219(b)(5)(B)).

Individuals have until the due date of their tax returns to make contributions to their IRAs for the return year (generally April 15). Filing extensions are *not* taken into account. If the contribution is made by the due date, it will be treated as having been made on the last day of the tax year for which the return is filed (Code Sec. 219(f)(3)).[142] A deduction may be claimed for a contribution even though the contribution had not yet been made when the return is filed. However, the contribution must be made by the due date of the tax return (Rev. Rul. 84-18).[143]

If a contribution to a traditional IRA is *less* than the allowable maximum for that year, the individual cannot contribute more in a later year to make up the difference. If a contribution is *more* than the allowable maximum, the excess contribution may be withdrawn on or before April 15 or carried over and deducted in later years to the extent that the actual contributions in those later years are less than the allowable maximum (Code Sec. 219(f)(6)).[144] However, the excess contribution is subject to a six percent tax each year until it is corrected (Code Sec. 4973(a)).[145] The individual reports the six percent tax on Form 5329. Individuals with low to moderate incomes may be able to claim a nonrefundable credit based upon their contributions to IRAs (traditional and/or Roth) as well as other types of qualified retirement plans (¶ 1304).

Compensation. For purposes of determining an individual's eligibility to make contributions to an IRA, the term "compensation" includes earned income and alimony. It also includes differential wage payments received by a reservist from his or her civilian employer (Code Sec. 219(f)(1)). Compensation does *not* include pensions, annuities, or other forms of deferred compensation. However, under a safe-harbor rule, the IRS will accept as compensation the amount properly shown on the individual's Form W-2 as wages, tips, and other compensation, less any amount properly shown for nonqualified plans (Rev. Proc. 91-18).[146] The compensation of a self-employed person is the individual's "earned income," as defined at ¶ 2163. Combat pay earned by a member of the Armed Forces and excluded from gross income (¶ 895) may be treated as compensation for purposes of the limit on IRA contributions.

Tax Refunds. A taxpayer may choose to have a refund of federal income taxes directly deposited into up to three separate accounts, including an IRA. The IRA must be

References are to Standard Federal Tax Reports; Tax Research Consultant; and Practical Tax Explanations.

[139] ¶ 18,902; RETIRE: 66,500; § 25,401
[140] ¶ 12,650; RETIRE: 66,200; § 25,415.15
[141] ¶ 18,902; RETIRE: 66,250; § 25,420
[142] ¶ 12,650; RETIRE: 66,208; § 25,425.05, § 46,525.10
[143] ¶ 18,922.87; RETIRE: 66,208; § 25,425.05, § 46,525.10
[144] ¶ 12,650; RETIRE: 66,356.15; § 25,430.05
[145] ¶ 34,360; RETIRE: 66,354; § 25,430.05
[146] ¶ 18,922.1063; RETIRE: 66,206; § 25,415.10

established before the request for the direct deposit is made. The deposit counts against the taxpayer's annual contribution limit. Thus, the taxpayer should inform the IRA trustee which year the direct deposit contribution is for. The taxpayer must also verify that the direct deposit is made to the IRA by the due date of his or her return for that year without regard to extensions. A direct deposit request of an entire refund into an IRA should be made on a taxpayer's Form 1040. However, if a taxpayer chooses to have a refund split and deposited in up to three different accounts, then Form 8888 is used.

Allowable Investments. Although IRAs may hold almost any investment, they are generally prohibited from investing in "collectibles" (e.g., antiques and stamps). However, certain U.S. gold and silver bullion coins minted since October 1986 may be held by an IRA. An IRA may also hold certain platinum and state-issued coins, as well as gold, silver, platinum, and palladium bullion (Code Sec. 408(m)(3)).[147]

Deemed IRAs. Qualified plans may allow employees to make voluntary contributions to a separate account that will be deemed to be a traditional IRA or Roth IRA if the account meets all the requirements of the particular type of IRA (Code Sec. 408(q)). The employee must designate the contribution as a deemed IRA contribution. An employee's contributions to this account count against the annual limit on IRA contributions (Reg. § 1.408(q)-1(a)).

Modified Adjusted Gross Income. When determining the taxpayer's AGI for deduction limitation rules, the taxpayer's AGI is modified by taking into account Code Sec. 86 (the inclusion in income of Social Security and Railroad Retirement benefits) and Code Sec. 469 (the disallowance of passive activity losses) but not the Code Sec. 135 (exclusion of interest on educational U.S. Savings Bonds), Code Sec. 137 (exclusion of employer-paid adoption assistance), Code Sec. 221 (deduction for student loan interest), Code Sec. 199 (deduction for domestic production activities), Code Sec. 911 (foreign earned income and housing exclusion), and the deduction for contributions to IRAs (Code Sec. 219(g)(3)(A)).[148]

> **Comment:** Absent further legislation, the tuition and fees deduction terminated for years beginning after December 31, 2011, and, therefore, will not impact modified adjusted gross income.

2153A. Deductible Contribution Limits - In General. The maximum deduction that an individual may take for contributions to an IRA may be reduced when the individual or the spouse is an active participant and participates in any one of the following plans: a qualified plan (such as a defined contribution plan or defined benefit pension plan), simplified employee pensions (SEPs), SIMPLE accounts, a qualified annuity plan, a tax-sheltered annuity plan, a Code Sec. 501(c)(18) trust created before June 25, 1959, or a governmental retirement plan (Code Sec. 219(g)).[149] An eligible Code Sec. 457(b) deferred compensation plan is not treated as a plan for this purpose. When an individual is an active participant in an employer's plan, the amount of the deductible IRA contribution depends upon the individual's adjusted gross income and filing status. For details of the phaseout ranges for married individuals filing jointly, see ¶ 2153B. For single individuals and married individuals filing separate returns, see ¶ 2153C.

Active Participant Defined. The determination on active participant status is made without regard to whether an individual's rights under an employer-sponsored plan are nonforfeitable (Code Sec. 219(g)). In the case of a defined benefit plan, an individual who is not excluded under the eligibility provisions of the plan is considered to be an active participant if she is eligible to participate for any part of the plan year ending with or within the tax year, even though the individual has elected not to do so, has failed to make a mandatory contribution, or has failed to meet the minimum service requirements (Reg. § 1.219-2). In the case of a defined contribution plan, an individual is considered an active participant if contributions or forfeitures are allocated to the individual's account for the plan year that ends with or within that tax year. Finally, an individual is an active participant for any tax year in which the individual makes a

References are to Standard Federal Tax Reports; Tax Research Consultant; and Practical Tax Explanations.

[147] ¶ 18,902; RETIRE: 66,458.10; § 25,470

[148] ¶ 12,650; RETIRE: 66,202; § 25,415.15

[149] ¶ 12,650; RETIRE: 66,202; § 25,415.15

voluntary or mandatory employee contribution (Notice 87-16).[150] Social Security and Railroad Retirement (Tier I or Tier II) are not retirement arrangements for purposes of determining active participation. If an individual receives benefits from a previous employer's plan, the individual is not covered by the plan. An individual is also *not* considered an active participant in an employer-sponsored plan merely because the individual's spouse is an active participant (Code Sec. 219(g)(7)).[151]

An employer should have marked the box labeled "Retirement Plan" on the employee's Form W-2 if the employee participated in an employer plan for the year.

Social Security Recipients. An employed individual, either the taxpayer or the spouse, who is covered by a retirement plan, currently receiving Social Security benefits, and wants to determine the allowable deduction for contributions to a traditional IRA must compute taxable Social Security benefits twice. The first computation is for the purpose of determining the tentative amount of Social Security benefits that must be included in gross income if the individual did not make any IRA contribution. This computation determines the amount of hypothetical adjusted gross income for purposes of the IRA phaseout provision. The second computation determines the actual amount of taxable social security benefits by taking into account the deductible IRA contribution that was determined under the first computation. The necessary worksheets for these computations are contained in IRS Pub. 590 (¶ 716).

2153B. Deductible Contribution Limits - Married Persons Filing Joint Returns. For 2012, when a married couple files a joint return, usually each spouse may make contributions to his or her IRA up to the annual dollar limit of $5,000 or $6,000 if a catch-up contribution is allowable (Notice 2011-90). The deductible amount is $5,500 or $6,500 for 2013 respectively (IRS News Release IR-2012-77). If one spouse has little or no compensation, that spouse may "borrow" his or her spouse's compensation for purposes of enabling the maximum contribution (Code Sec. 219(c)).[152]

For 2012, the IRAs of the spouse with the greater amount of compensation ("higher-paid spouse") may receive deductible contributions of up to the lesser of: (1) $5,000 or $6,000 if catch-up contributions are allowable, as reduced for active participation, or (2) his or her compensation. For 2012, the IRAs of the spouse with the lesser amount of compensation ("lower-paid spouse") may receive deductible contributions equal to the lesser of:

- $5,000, or $6,000 if catch-up contributions are allowable, as reduced for active participation, or
- the sum of:
  - the compensation of the lower-paid spouse and
  - the compensation of the higher-paid spouse, reduced by: (i) the deduction allowed to the higher-paid spouse for IRA contributions, (ii) the amount of any designated nondeductible IRA contribution on behalf of the higher-paid spouse, and (iii) the amount of any contribution on behalf of the higher-paid spouse to a Roth IRA.

AGI Limits for Married Individuals. If both individuals are active participants in an employer's qualified retirement plan, their ability to claim a deduction for contributions made to traditional IRAs depends upon the amount of their modified AGI (¶ 2153). For 2012, the allowable IRA deduction will be reduced when modified AGI is between $92,000 and $112,000 (Notice 2011-90). For 2013, the allowable IRA deduction will be reduced when modified AGI is between $95,000 and $115,000 (IRS News Release IR-2012-77).

Example 1: Ralph and Alice file a joint return for 2012. They are both employed and both are covered by their employers' qualified plans. Their modified AGI for 2012 is $113,000. Since they are both active participants in qualified plans sponsored by their employers and their modified AGI exceeds the high end of the

References are to Standard Federal Tax Reports; Tax Research Consultant; and Practical Tax Explanations.

[150] ¶ 18,922.865; RETIRE: 66,202; § 25,415.15

[151] ¶ 12,650; RETIRE: 66,202; § 25,415.15

[152] ¶ 12,650; RETIRE: 66,302; § 25,415.15

phaseout range for 2012 (i.e., $112,000), they are not allowed to make deductible IRA contributions for 2012. They may make nondeductible contributions to traditional IRAs. As an alternative, they should consider the tax advantages of making their contributions to Roth IRAs (¶ 2180).

An individual will *not* be considered an active participant in an employer-sponsored plan merely because the individual's spouse is treated as an active participant (Code Sec. 219(g)(7)).[153] However, the maximum deductible IRA contribution for an individual who is not an active participant, but whose spouse is, will be phased out in 2012 at a modified AGI between $173,000 to $183,000 (jointly computed) (for 2013, the phaseout range will be $178,000 and $188,000).

Example 2: Bob is covered by a 401(k) plan sponsored by his employer. His wife, Betty, is not employed. The couple files a joint income tax return for 2012, with a modified AGI of $120,000. Betty may make a deductible contribution to a traditional IRA for the year because she is not an active participant in an employer-sponsored retirement plan and their combined modified AGI is below $173,000. However, Bob may not make a deductible IRA contribution because their combined modified AGI is above the phaseout range for active participants who are married and filing jointly ($92,000 to $112,000 for 2012).

Example 3: Assume the same facts as in Example 2, except that the couple's modified AGI was $200,000 for 2012. Neither Bob nor Betty would be able to make a deductible contribution to a traditional IRA.

2153C. Deductible Contribution Limits - Unmarried Persons and Married Persons Filing Separate Returns. For a single individual, head of household, or a married individual who files a separate return, contributions to traditional IRAs are generally deductible to the extent that they do not exceed the lesser of the "deductible amount," which is: (1) the individual's compensation for that year that is includible in gross income ("includible compensation") or (2) for 2012, $5,000 ($5,500 for 2013) or $6,000 ($6,500 for 2013) if catch-up contributions are allowable (Code Sec. 219(b)(1); Notice 2011-90; IRS News Release IR-2012-77). However, the maximum allowable deduction may be reduced when the individual is an active participant in an employer-maintained retirement plan (¶ 2153A). For information regarding the IRA deduction limits for married persons filing joint returns, see ¶ 2153B.

Single Individuals or Head of Household. For 2012, when a single individual or head of household is an active participant in an employer's retirement plan, the IRA deduction begins to phase out when modified adjusted gross income (AGI) (¶ 2153) reaches $58,000 and is completely phased out when modified AGI reaches $68,000. For 2013, the phaseout range is $59,000 to $69,000 (Code Sec. 219(g); Notice 2011-90; IRS News Release IR-2012-77).

Married Filing Separately. When an individual files as "married filing separately" and the individual, or the spouse, is an active participant in an employer's retirement plan, the IRA deduction begins to phase out when the individual's modified AGI exceeds $0. The deduction is completely phased out when modified AGI is $10,000 or more. This phaseout range is not adjusted for inflation. When determining if an individual is married or single for the purpose of determining which IRA deduction limit applies, spouses who file separate returns and live apart at all times during a tax year are *not* considered to be married during that tax year (Code Sec. 219(g)(4)).[154]

2153D. Nondeductible Contributions. An individual may make nondeductible contributions to a traditional IRA. These contributions may not exceed the *excess* of: (1) the maximum allowable contribution for the year (¶ 2153) over (2) the amount actually allowed as a deduction for the year (Code Sec. 408(o)(2)(B)).[155] In applying this rule, an individual may elect to treat otherwise deductible contributions as nondeductible contributions. However, the tax advantages of funding a Roth IRA should be considered before making nondeductible contributions to a traditional IRA (¶ 2154B).

References are to Standard Federal Tax Reports; Tax Research Consultant; and Practical Tax Explanations.

[153] ¶ 12,650; RETIRE: 66,202; § 25,415.15

[154] ¶ 12,650; RETIRE: 66,200, RETIRE: 66,202; § 25,415.15

[155] ¶ 18,902; RETIRE: 66,250; § 25,420

Example: In 2012, Bill Webb, age 48 and single, had earned income of $53,000 and a modified AGI of $59,000. He is an active participant in his employer's 401(k) plan. Because his modified AGI exceeds $58,000, a maximum contribution to a traditional IRA would not be fully deductible. Bill determines that his maximum deductible contribution would be $4,500. As a result, he could make an additional $500 nondeductible IRA contribution.

Nondeductible contributions may be made up to and including the due date of the return for the tax year. A filing extension does *not* extend the due date for making the contribution (Code Sec. 219(f)(3)). The same deadline applies to deductible IRA contributions and Roth IRA contributions. Nondeductible contributions to a traditional IRA must be reported on Form 8606, which is attached to Form 1040 or Form 1040A.

Reservist Contributions. Certain "qualified reservist distributions" are not subject to the tax on early distributions and may be recontributed to an IRA as a nondeductible contribution without counting against the dollar limits applicable to IRA contributions (Code Sec. 72(t)(2)(G)). A qualified reservist distribution is a distribution that is made:

- from an IRA or from an individual's elective deferrals under an employer plan (for example, a 401(k) or 403(b) plan);
- to an individual who is a reservist who was called to active duty for a period of more than 179 days or for an indefinite period; and
- during the period beginning on the date the reservist was called to active duty and ending on the date the active duty ended.

The distribution may be recontributed at any time within the two years after the end of the active duty period. A reservist who took a distribution after being called up and paid the early distribution penalty may file a claim for refund of the penalty.

2153E. Excess Contributions. Annual contributions to a traditional IRA and/or Roth IRA in excess of the allowable amount (¶ 2153) are subject to a cumulative six percent tax, which is reported on Form 5329 (Code Sec. 4973).[156] See ¶ 2153G for a discussion on the taxation of distributions.

2153F. Distribution - Requirements. Traditional IRAs are subject to the same required minimum distribution (RMD) rules that apply to qualified employer-provided retirement plans (¶ 2124B) (Code Sec. 408(a)(6) and (b)(3)).[157] This means that distributions to the owner or beneficiary of a traditional IRA must begin no later than April 1 following the calendar year in which the owner reaches age 70½ (Reg. § 1.408-8, Q&A-3). However, no minimum required distributions are required for the 2009 calendar year. A few special rules affecting RMDs from IRAs are discussed below.

Inherited Traditional IRA: Spouse. A surviving spouse may elect to treat an inherited traditional IRA as his or her own by having the account redesignated as an account belonging to the surviving spouse as owner rather than beneficiary. Alternatively, the surviving spouse will be treated as having made this election if: (1) any amounts in the IRA are not distributed within the time period that applied to the decedent or (2) the surviving spouse makes contributions (including rollover contributions) to the inherited IRA that are subject, or are deemed subject, to the lifetime distribution requirements. In order to make the election, the surviving spouse must be the sole beneficiary of the IRA and have an unlimited right to withdraw amounts from it (Reg. § 1.408-8, Q&A-5).[158] When a trust is named as the beneficiary of the IRA, this requirement has not been satisfied even if the spouse is the sole beneficiary of the trust. When the surviving spouse makes the election, he or she is treated as the owner of the IRA for all purposes. If the election is not made, then the RMDs are determined as though the spouse was the beneficiary of the IRA.

Inherited Traditional IRA: Nonspouse. A nonspouse beneficiary who inherits an IRA cannot treat it as his or her own account but must take RMDs determined under the rules applicable to beneficiaries receiving distributions from a qualified plan. When an

References are to Standard Federal Tax Reports; Tax Research Consultant; and Practical Tax Explanations.

[156] ¶ 34,360; RETIRE: 66,350; § 25,430.05

[157] ¶ 18,902; RETIRE: 66,400, RETIRE: 66,450; § 25,475.05

[158] ¶ 18,917A; RETIRE: 42,160.20; § 25,445.30

individual other than the decedent's spouse receives a lump sum distribution from an IRA, in general, the individual may not roll over that distribution into another IRA; it must be distributed within a certain period (Code Sec. 408(d)(3)(C)). The distribution, minus the aggregate amount of the owner's nondeductible IRA contributions, is taxed as ordinary income in the year the distribution is received (Rev. Rul. 92-47).[159]

Trust Named as Beneficiary. When a trust is named as the beneficiary of the IRA, the beneficiaries of the trust will be treated as the deceased individual's beneficiaries if certain requirements are met (Reg. § 1.401(a)(9)-4, Q&A-5). The requirements include: (1) validity of the trust, (2) identification of the trust's beneficiaries, and (3) the delivery of proper documentation to the plan administrator (Reg. § 1.401(a)(9)-4, Q&A-6).

More Than One IRA. If an individual is required to receive an RMD from more than one traditional IRA in a calendar year, the amount of the minimum distribution from each IRA must be calculated separately and the separate amounts totalled. However, the total may be withdrawn from one or more of the IRAs in whatever amounts the individual chooses (Reg. § 1.408-8, Q&A-9).[160]

2153G. Distributions - Taxation. If an individual never made nondeductible contributions to a traditional IRA, then any distributions from the IRA are fully taxable to the owner or beneficiary as ordinary income (Code Sec. 408(d)(1); Reg. § 1.408-4(a)). However, if nondeductible contributions were made, the owner has a *cost basis* in the IRA. An individual's cost basis in distributions made from a traditional IRA is the sum of the nondeductible contributions made to the IRA minus any prior withdrawals or distributions of nondeductible contributions (Notice 87-16). The recovery of this basis is not recognized as taxable income. As a result, the individual must determine how much of the IRA distribution is nontaxable. The taxable and nontaxable portions of the distribution are generally determined under the same rules that apply to annuity payments (¶ 817) (Code Secs. 72 and 408(d)(1) and (2)).[161] When applying these rules:

- all traditional IRAs of an individual (including SEPs described at ¶ 2156 and SIMPLE accounts described at ¶ 2155) are treated as a single contract;

- all distributions during the individual's tax year are treated as one distribution;

- the value of the contract, the income on the contract, and the investment in the contract are calculated (after adding back distributions made during the year) as of the close of the calendar year in which the tax year of the distribution begins; and

- total withdrawals excludable from income in all tax years cannot exceed the taxpayer's investment in the contract in all tax years.

Charitable Distributions. An individual could have distributed up to $100,000 of their IRA balance in 2010 and 2011 to a charitable organization without recognizing income on the distribution (Code Sec. 408(d)(8)). The exclusion from income only applied to a distribution otherwise includible in income that was made directly to a charitable organization on or after the date the account owner reached age 70½. The account owner could not deduct the contribution (¶ 1058).

For the 2010 tax year only, a special rule permitted a taxpayer to elect to have a qualified charitable distribution made in January 2011 treated as having been made on December 31, 2010 (Act Sec. 725(b)(2) of the Tax Relief Act of 2010 (P.L. 111-312)). If a taxpayer made the election as prescribed by the IRS, then the distribution made in January 2011 counted toward: (1) the taxpayer's $100,000 exclusion limitation for the 2010 calendar year; and (2) the taxpayer's required minimum distribution (RMD) for the 2010 calendar year.

References are to Standard Federal Tax Reports; Tax Research Consultant; and Practical Tax Explanations.

[159] ¶ 18,922.26; RETIRE: 66,502.05, RETIRE: 66,800; § 25,475.05, § 25,445.30

[160] ¶ 18,917A; RETIRE: 66,456; § 25,475.05

[161] ¶ 18,902, ¶ 6102; RETIRE: 66,500; § 25,450.15

Comment: Absent further legislation, the exclusion from gross income for qualified charitable distributions of up to $100,000 received from traditional or Roth IRAs will not apply in tax year beginning 2012.

HSA Funding Distributions. An individual may make a one-time transfer of funds from his or her IRA distribution directly to the IRA owner's health savings account (HSA) without recognizing income on the distribution (Code Sec. 408(d)(9); Notice 2008-51).[162] The transfer can only be made, however, if it would otherwise be a taxable distribution. The dollar amount excluded cannot exceed the annual limitation on the individual's HSA contribution for the year (¶ 2197B). The exclusion is lost if the individual ceases to be eligible to contribute to an HSA during the twelve months after the contribution. In such a case, the distribution is subject to tax and a 10-percent penalty is imposed.

Reporting Requirements. Form 8606 is used to report the taxable portion of an IRA distribution if the individual ever made nondeductible contributions to an IRA.

Estate Tax. If the distributee is the beneficiary of the IRA owner and the value of the IRA is included in the owner's estate for federal estate tax purposes, the distributee is entitled to deduct the estate tax allocable to the IRA (¶ 191) (Rev. Rul. 92-47).[163]

Return of Contributions. A distribution from a traditional IRA that represents the return of a contribution made for a particular tax year will not be included in the individual's income if (Code Sec. 408(d)(4)):[164]

- the distribution is made before the due date, including extensions, of the individual's tax return for that year;
- no deduction is allowed with respect to the contribution; and
- the distribution includes any net income earned by the contribution.

The net income earned by the contribution is included in income for the tax year in which the contribution was made even if the distribution is received in the following year.

Recognizing Loss on an IRA. An IRA owner can recognize a loss on traditional IRA investments, but only when all amounts from all of the owner's traditional IRA accounts have been distributed and the total distributions are less than any unrecovered basis in the accounts. The recognized loss is claimed on Schedule A as a miscellaneous itemized deduction, subject to the two-percent floor (IRS Publication 590). If the individual never made nondeductible contributions to any of the traditional IRAs, the realized loss cannot be deducted because the individual has no tax basis in the IRAs.

2153H. Early Distributions - Penalty. Generally, if the individual is under age 59½, a distribution from a traditional IRA is subject to the 10-percent additional tax on early distributions. Exceptions to the early distributions penalty are discussed at ¶ 2153I. If an exception applies, it may be necessary to file Form 5329.

2153I. Early Distributions - Permitted. Many of the exceptions to the tax on early distributions that apply to distributions from qualified plans (¶ 2124C) also apply to early distributions from a traditional IRA with the exception for early retirements which does not apply to distributions from a traditional IRA (Code Sec. 72(t)(3)(A)).[165] In addition, the following exceptions apply to early distributions from an IRA but not to distributions from a qualified plan.

Medical Insurance Premiums of Unemployed Individuals. To the extent that they do not exceed qualifying medical insurance premiums, distributions from an IRA, including a SEP or SIMPLE account, to certain unemployed individuals are *not* subject to the 10-percent additional tax (Code Sec. 72(t)(2)(D)).[166] Eligible unemployed individuals are those who have received federal or state unemployment compensation for 12 consecutive weeks. A self-employed individual will be treated as having received unemployment

References are to Standard Federal Tax Reports; Tax Research Consultant; and Practical Tax Explanations.

[162] ¶ 18,902; COMPEN: 45,064; § 25,450

[163] ¶ 18,922.26; RETIRE: 66,806.05; § 7,110.10

[164] ¶ 18,902; RETIRE: 66,356.05; § 25,430.10

[165] ¶ 6102; RETIRE: 66,506; 25,450.25

[166] ¶ 6102; RETIRE: 42,554.216; 25,450.25

compensation if, under federal or state law, the individual would have received unemployment compensation but for being self-employed. Qualifying premiums are deductible premiums for the medical care of the unemployed individual, spouse and dependents. The distributions must be received in the tax year during which unemployment compensation is received or in the following year. In determining whether the premiums are deductible, the 7.5 percent (10 percent for most taxpayers starting in 2013) medical expense floor (¶ 1015) is ignored. This exception to the 10-percent additional tax ceases to apply after the individual has been reemployed for 60 days (not necessarily consecutive) after initial unemployment.

Education Expenses. The 10-percent additional tax does not apply if the individual uses the IRA distribution to pay for "qualified higher education expenses" for the individual, the individual's spouse or child, or a grandchild of the individual or the individual's spouse. Qualified expenses include tuition at a post-secondary educational institution, books, fees, supplies and equipment (Code Sec. 72(t)(2)(E)).[167]

First-Time Homebuyer Expenses. The 10-percent additional tax does not apply if the individual uses the IRA distribution for certain expenses of a first-time homebuyer. Only $10,000 during the individual's lifetime may be withdrawn without a penalty for this purpose. Qualified expenses include acquisition costs, settlement charges and closing costs. The principal residence may be for the individual or the individual's spouse, child or grandchild, or an ancestor of the individual or the individual's spouse. In order to be considered a "first-time homebuyer," the person buying the residence (and spouse, if married) must not have had an ownership interest in a principal residence during the two-year period ending on the date that the new home is acquired (Code Sec. 72(t)(2)(F)).[168]

Return of Nondeductible Contributions. The 10-percent additional tax does not apply to the portion of the distribution that represents a return of nondeductible IRA contributions (i.e., the individual's cost basis in the IRA) (¶ 2153G).

2154. Roth IRAs. In general, a Roth IRA is subject to the same rules that apply to a traditional IRA (¶ 2153) except that contributions to a Roth IRA are never deductible and the buildup within a Roth IRA (e.g., interest, dividends and/or price appreciation) may be free from federal income tax when the individual withdraws money from the account (Code Sec. 408A).[169]

2154A. Income Limits. The ability of an individual to make a contribution to a Roth IRA depends upon the amount of the individual's modified adjusted gross income (AGI) (Code Sec. 408A(c)). For 2012, the maximum yearly contribution that can be made to a Roth IRA is phased out for a single individual with modified AGI between $110,000 to $125,000, for joint filers with modified AGI between $173,000 to $183,000, and for individuals who are married filing separately with modified AGI between $0 and $10,000. For 2013, the phaseout ranges for single individuals and joint filers is from $112,000 to $127,000 (for singles) and $178,000 to $188,000 (for joint filers), respectively. The phase-out range remains between $0 and $10,000 for individuals who are married filing separately (Notice 2011-90; IRS News Release IR-2012-77).[170] Modified AGI is generally calculated as it is for traditional IRAs (¶ 2153). However, for Roth IRA purposes, modified AGI does not include the income reported from the conversion of a traditional IRA into a Roth IRA.

2154B. Contributions. For 2012, the maximum annual contribution that may generally be made to Roth IRAs and traditional IRAs is $5,000 ($5,500 for 2013) (Notice 2011-90; IRS News Release IR-2012-77). The maximum annual contribution is the amount that may be contributed to *both* types of IRAs combined, not the amount that may be contributed to each type. However, rollover contributions into a Roth IRA are not counted against the annual maximum (Code Sec. 408A(c); Reg. § 1.408A-3).[171] In addi-

References are to Standard Federal Tax Reports; Tax Research Consultant; and Practical Tax Explanations.

[167] ¶ 6102; INDIV: 60,056; 25,450.25

[168] ¶ 6102; RETIRE: 42,554.224; § 25,450.25

[169] ¶ 18,925; RETIRE: 66,750; § 25,501

[170] ¶ 18,925; RETIRE: 66,752; § 25,510

[171] ¶ 18,925, ¶ 18,927; RETIRE: 66,752; § 25,510

tion, unlike traditional IRAs, individuals may make contributions to a Roth IRA after reaching age 70½. An individual who will be at least age 50 by the end of the tax year is permitted to make an additional contribution to a Roth or traditional IRA. The maximum annual amount of the catch-up contribution is $1,000 (Code Sec. 219(b)(5)).

An individual who receives a military death gratuity or payment under the Servicemembers' Group Life Insurance (SGLI) program may contribute an amount up to the sum of the gratuity and SGLI payments received to a Roth IRA, notwithstanding the annual contribution limit and the income phase-out of the contribution limit that otherwise apply to contributions to Roth IRAs. The contribution must be made within one year of the receipt of the payment (Code Sec. 408A(e)). Such contributions are generally treated as though they were a rollover from another Roth IRA. This option is available for amounts paid in connection with deaths from injuries occurring on or after June 17, 2008.

2154C. Qualified Distributions. Qualified distributions from a Roth IRA are not included in the recipient's gross income nor are they subject to the 10-percent additional tax for early withdrawals (¶ 2153A) (Code Sec. 408A(d); Reg. § 1.408A-6).[172] To be treated as a qualified distribution, the Roth IRA distribution, including distributions allocable to rollover contributions, may not be made before the end of the five-year period beginning with the first tax year for which the individual made a contribution to the Roth IRA. The five-year holding period ends on the last day of the individual's fifth consecutive tax year after the holding period started. Generally, each Roth IRA owner has only one five-year period for all of the Roth IRAs that the individual owns.

> **Example:** Jack Martin made his first contribution to a Roth IRA on September 15, 2008, for the 2008 tax year. On December 27, 2009, Jack made another contribution to a Roth IRA, for the 2009 tax year. On December 30, 2010, he made another contribution to a Roth IRA for the 2010 tax year. The five-year holding period for all of Jack's Roth IRAs is considered to have started on January 1, 2008. Distributions made after December 31, 2012, will have satisfied the five-year holding period.

In addition to satisfying the five-year holding period, a distribution will constitute a qualified distribution only if it is (Code Sec. 408A(d)(2)):[173]

- made on or after the date on which the individual attains age 59½,
- made to a beneficiary (or the individual's estate) on or after the individual's death,
- attributable to the individual's being disabled, or
- a distribution to pay for qualified first-time homebuyer expenses (¶ 2153I).

Reporting Roth IRA Distributions. Distributions from Roth IRAs are reported on Form 8606. If the 10-percent additional tax on early distributions applies, it is reported on Form 5329.

Pre-Death Requirements. The *pre-death* required minimum distribution (RMD) requirements (¶ 2124B) that apply to qualified plans and traditional IRAs do *not* apply to Roth IRAs (Code Sec. 408A(c)(5)).[174] Thus, owners of Roth IRAs are not required to take distributions by April 1 of the year following the calendar year in which they attain age 70½. As a general rule, the *post-death* RMD rules do apply to Roth IRAs (Reg. § 1.408A-6, Q&A-14). If the sole beneficiary is the decedent's spouse, the spouse may delay distributions until the decedent would have attained age 70½ or may treat the Roth IRA as his or her own.

2154D. Nonqualified Distributions. When an individual receives a nonqualified distribution from a Roth IRA, a portion of the distribution may be includible in gross income. In order to determine the amount that is includible in gross income, specific ordering rules are applied under which regular Roth contributions are deemed to be withdrawn first, then amounts transferred from traditional IRAs starting with amounts

References are to Standard Federal Tax Reports; Tax Research Consultant; and Practical Tax Explanations.

[172] ¶ 18,925, ¶ 18,928; RETIRE: 66,758; § 25,525.10

[173] ¶ 18,925; RETIRE: 66,758; § 25,525.10

[174] ¶ 18,925; RETIRE: 66,758; § 25,525.10

first transferred (Code Sec. 408A(d)(4)). Withdrawals of transferred amounts are then treated as coming first from amounts that were included in income. Earnings are treated as withdrawn after contributions (Reg. § 1.408A-6, Q&A-8). Thus, no amount is includible in gross income until all the after-tax contributions have been distributed. If an individual receives a nonqualified distribution from a Roth IRA that is includible in gross income, then the 10-percent additional tax for early distributions will generally apply. However, the same exceptions that apply to early distributions from traditional IRAs (¶ 2153I) will also apply to the nonqualified Roth IRA distributions.

2154E. Rollovers and Conversions. Taxpayers can make qualified rollover contributions to a Roth IRA from another Roth IRA, a traditional IRA, and from certain qualified plans.[175] However, unlike rollovers to traditional IRAs (¶ 2125B), qualified rollovers to Roth IRAs may result in the inclusion in income of an amount equal to the amount that would be includible if it were not part of a qualified rollover distribution.

Rollovers from Roth IRAs. In the case of a qualified rollover from another Roth IRA, amounts distributed from the Roth IRA must be contributed either to the same or to another Roth IRA within 60 days of receiving the distribution. However, once a qualified rollover has been made, any other distributions received within the twelve months after the distribution rolled over was received cannot be rolled over. In the case of an individual with more than one Roth IRA, the once-per-12-month restriction applies separately to each Roth IRA.

Conversions of Traditional IRAs. A taxpayer can convert an eligible retirement plan to a Roth IRA as long as the amount contributed to the Roth IRA satisfies the definition of a qualified rollover contribution (Code Sec. 408A(e)). Generally, amounts transferred or converted from a traditional IRA into a Roth IRA must be included in gross income for the tax year in which the amount is distributed or transferred to the extent it does not represent a return of basis. Special treatment was available for conversions in 2010. Taxpayers who made a conversion in 2010 recognize the conversion amount ratably in gross income in 2011 and 2012, unless the taxpayer elected to recognize it all in 2010. If a taxpayer opted to include a 2010 conversion in income ratably in 2011 and 2012, a distribution of conversion amounts before 2012 results in the acceleration of income.[176]

The 10-percent additional tax on early distributions does not apply to the taxable conversion amount. However, if within the five-year period starting with the year in which an individual made a conversion contribution of an amount from a traditional IRA to a Roth IRA, the individual takes a distribution from a Roth IRA of an amount that is attributable to the portion of the conversion contribution that was included in income, then the individual will be liable for the 10-percent additional tax unless one of the exceptions to the tax applies (¶ 2153I) (Reg. § 1.408A-6, Q&A-5(c)). The five-year period is separately determined for each conversion contribution made to a Roth IRA. Individuals can correct a failed Roth conversion by making a proper recharacterization election (¶ 2154F).

Rollovers from Qualified Plans. Distributions from qualified retirement plans (including Code Sec. 403(b) annuities and eligible 457 governmental plans) can be rolled over directly into a Roth IRA. Such rollovers are treated the same as under the conversion rules for traditional IRAs, though rollovers from designated Roth accounts are treated as rollovers from another Roth IRA (Notice 2009-75). In addition, the rollover contribution must meet the rollover requirements applicable to the specific type of retirement plan.

2154F. Recharacterization. An individual who has made contributions to a Roth or traditional IRA may later decide that a contribution to an IRA of the other type is more advantageous. If certain requirements are met, the contribution can be recharacterized and treated as having been originally made to the desired type of IRA (Code Sec. 408A(d)(6)).[177] Recharacterizing an IRA contribution requires transferring amounts previously contributed to a traditional or Roth IRA (plus any resulting net income or minus any resulting net loss) to a new IRA of the opposite type and electing to have the

References are to Standard Federal Tax Reports; Tax Research Consultant; and Practical Tax Explanations.

[175] ¶ 18,925; RETIRE: 66,760; § 25,530

[176] ¶ 18,925; RETIRE: 66,706; § 25,515.20

[177] ¶ 18,925; RETIRE: 66,762; § 25,520.05

amounts treated as having been transferred to the second IRA at the time they actually were contributed to the first IRA (Reg. § 1.408A-5, Q&A-1). The transfer must be from trustee to trustee. Generally, taxpayers have until the due date (including extensions) of the tax return for the year in which the contribution was made to make the recharacterization. A recharacterization must be reported on the taxpayer's tax return. In certain situations, Form 8606 must be filed, along with a statement explaining the nature of the recharacterization (IRS Pub. 590). Once a Roth IRA has been recharacterized back to a (new) traditional IRA, the (new) traditional IRA can be (re)converted back to a Roth IRA, provided the taxpayer meets the eligibility requirements in the reconversion year (¶ 2154G).

2154G. Reconversions. A "reconversion" is a conversion from a traditional IRA to a Roth IRA of an amount that had previously been recharacterized as a contribution to the traditional IRA after having been earlier converted to a Roth IRA (¶ 2154E and ¶ 2154F). An IRA owner who converts an amount from a traditional IRA to a Roth IRA during any tax year and then transfers that amount back to a traditional IRA by means of a recharacterization may not reconvert that amount from the traditional IRA to a Roth IRA before the *later* of: (1) the beginning of the tax year following the tax year in which the amount was converted to a Roth IRA or (2) the end of the 30-day period beginning on the day on which the IRA owner transfers the amount from the Roth IRA back to a traditional IRA by means of a recharacterization (regardless of whether the recharacterization occurs during the tax year in which the amount was converted to a Roth IRA or the following tax year) (Reg. § 1.408A-5, Q&A-9(a)(1)).[178]

2154H. Loss on Roth IRA. Like a traditional IRA (¶ 2153), the owner of a Roth IRA can recognize a loss on investments in the account, but only when all the amounts in all the owner's Roth IRA accounts have been distributed and the total distributions are less than the individual's unrecovered basis in the accounts. The basis is the total amount of the nondeductible contributions in the Roth IRAs. The recognized loss is claimed on Schedule A as a miscellaneous itemized deduction, subject to the two-percent floor (IRS Pub. 590). The loss rule applies separately to each kind of IRA. Thus, to report a loss on a Roth IRA, all the Roth IRAs owned by the individual have to be liquidated, and to report a loss on a traditional IRA, all the traditional IRAs owned by the individual have to be liquidated.

2154I. Deemed Roth IRAs. Qualified plans may allow employees to make voluntary contributions to an account that will be deemed to be a Roth IRA if the account meets all the requirements of a Roth IRA (Code Sec. 408(q)).[179] An employee's contribution to this account counts towards the maximum annual contribution that may be made to a Roth IRA ($5,000 or $6,000 if catch-up contributions are allowable, for 2012; $5,500 or $6,500 for 2013).

2155. SIMPLE Plans. Generally, a SIMPLE IRA must meet the same requirements that apply to traditional IRAs (¶ 2153). However, contributions to an employee's SIMPLE IRA are limited to: (1) employee contributions made under a salary reduction agreement (¶ 2155C) and (2) employer contributions that are made as either "matching contributions" or "nonelective contributions" (¶ 2155D). A SIMPLE IRA may also include an automatic enrollment agreement.

The IRS has issued two model forms that may be used by employers that want to establish a SIMPLE IRA for their employees. Form 5304-SIMPLE is used when the employer permits each employee to choose the financial institution that will receive the SIMPLE IRA contributions. Form 5305-SIMPLE is used when the employer designates the financial institution that will receive the contributions. In that case, an employee must be given a reasonable period of time each year in which to transfer his or her SIMPLE IRA balance without cost or penalty from the designated financial institution to a SIMPLE IRA at another financial institution. Both forms also contain information that can be used to notify employees of the existence of the plan. Although the completed

References are to Standard Federal Tax Reports; Tax Research Consultant; and Practical Tax Explanations.

[178] ¶ 18,927D; RETIRE: 66,764; § 25,520.15

[179] ¶ 18,902; RETIRE: 66,058.10; § 25,405.25

forms do not have to be filed with the IRS, they must be kept in order to show that the plan was adopted by the employer.

Domestic Workers. Compensation paid to certain domestic workers qualifies for SIMPLE plan contributions, even though the compensation may not be subject to income tax withholding.

2155A. Eligible Employers. A SIMPLE 401(k) (¶ 2106G) or SIMPLE IRA (¶ 2155) plan may only be established by any employer that has 100 or fewer employees who received at least $5,000 in compensation during the preceding tax year (Code Sec. 408(p)(2)(C)(i)).[180] As a general rule, the employer may not make contributions to any other qualified plan starting with the year the SIMPLE plan goes into effect. However, employers may adopt a SIMPLE plan for noncollectively bargained employees and at the same time maintain a qualified plan for collectively bargained employees (Code Sec. 408(p)(2)(D)).[181]

2155B. Eligible Employees. If the employer has established a SIMPLE plan, an employee must be eligible to participate in any calendar year if he or she received at least $5,000 of compensation from the employer during each of the *two* preceding calendar years and is reasonably expected to receive at least $5,000 in compensation during the current calendar year (Code Sec. 408(p)(4)).[182] Nonresident alien employees and employees covered by a collective bargaining agreement may be excluded from participation.

If an individual is not self-employed, compensation means the amount described in Code Sec. 6051(a)(3) (wages, tips, and other compensation from the employer subject to income tax withholding under Code Sec. 3401(a)), and amounts described in Code Sec. 6051(a)(8), including elective contributions made under a SIMPLE IRA plan, and compensation deferred under a section 457 plan. Compensation does not include amounts deferred under a cafeteria plan. For purposes of applying the 100-employee limitation, and in determining whether an employee is eligible to participate (i.e., whether the employee had $5,000 in compensation for any 2 preceding years), an employee's compensation also includes the employee's elective deferrals under a 401(k) plan, a salary reduction SEP and a section 403(b) annuity contract.

A self-employed individual is treated as an employee and may participate in a SIMPLE plan if the minimum compensation requirement is met (Code Sec. 408(p)(6)).[183] For this purpose, compensation means compensation for a year is net earnings from self-employment (Schedule SE (Form 1040)) before subtracting any contributions made to a SIMPLE IRA (Code Sec. 408(p)(6)(A)(ii)). Self-employed persons who have elected out of the self-employment tax on religious grounds under Code Sec. 1402(g) may base their retirement plan contributions, including contributions to SIMPLE IRAs, on their self-employment income that is exempt from self-employment tax.

2155C. Employee Salary Reduction Contributions. A SIMPLE IRA plan must permit each eligible employee (¶ 2155B) to elect to have the employer make payments either directly to the employee in cash or as a contribution (expressed as a percentage of compensation) to the employee's SIMPLE account (Code Sec. 408(p)(2)).[184] The plan may be designed so that elective contributions are made only if the employee affirmatively elects to have them made, or as an automatic contribution arrangement, under which employee contributions are made unless the employee affirmatively opts out (Notice 2009-66). Unlike traditional IRAs, the account owner of a SIMPLE IRA may make contributions after age 70½. No contributions other than the employee's salary reduction contributions and employer contributions (¶ 2155D) may be made to a SIMPLE account. However, a rollover from another SIMPLE account may be received (Code Sec. 408(d)(3)(G)).[185] The employer must deposit the employee's elective contri-

References are to Standard Federal Tax Reports; Tax Research Consultant; and Practical Tax Explanations.

[180] ¶ 18,902; RETIRE: 63,552; § 25,110.05

[181] ¶ 18,902; RETIRE: 63,552; § 25,110.15

[182] ¶ 18,902; RETIRE: 63,602; § 25,115.05

[183] ¶ 18,902; RETIRE: 63,602; § 25,115.05

[184] ¶ 18,902; RETIRE: 63,606; § 25,120.10

[185] ¶ 18,902; RETIRE: 63,756; § 25,145.15

butions into the SIMPLE IRA within 30 days after the end of the month in which the amounts would have been paid to the employee. Elective contributions by an employee are fully vested when made (Code Sec. 408(p)(3)).[186]

Dollar Limit on Employee Contributions. An employee's elective contributions to a SIMPLE IRA are limited to $11,500 for 2012 and $12,000 for 2013 (Code Sec. 408(p)(2); Notice 2011-90; IRS News Release IR-2012-77).[187] In addition, employees who will be at least age 50 by the end of the year are allowed to make additional catch-up contributions of $2,500 (Code Sec. 414(v)(2)(B)(ii)). The maximum dollar limit is the only limit on employee contributions. An employer may not place a limit on the percentage of salary an employee may elect to defer in the plan (except in order to comply with the annual dollar limit).

Under a SIMPLE plan, each eligible employee must have the right to elect, during the 60-day period preceding the beginning of any calendar year (and the 60-day period preceding the employee's first day of eligibility), to participate in the plan for that calendar year or to modify the amount of his or her contributions to the plan for that calendar year (Code Sec. 408(p)(5)).[188] In addition, an employee may terminate participation in the SIMPLE plan at any time during a calendar year. However, the plan may prohibit reentry until the beginning of the following calendar year.

2155D. Matching or Nonelective Contributions. An employer is required to make contributions to its employees' SIMPLE IRAs under one of two methods: (1) matching contributions on employee contributions of up to three percent of compensation or (2) nonelective contributions (Code Sec. 408(p)(2)).[189]

Matching Contributions. An employer may elect to limit its matching contribution, for a particular year, to a smaller percentage of compensation but not less than one percent. The election may *not* be made by an employer in more than two out of every five years. If the SIMPLE account did not exist during the full five-year period, the election may still be made in up to two of the years in which it did exist. Employees must be notified of the employer's election to contribute less than three percent a reasonable time before the beginning of the 60-day period at the end of each calendar year during which employees designate the amount of their election contributions for the following calendar year. Matching contributions to SIMPLE IRAs that are made on behalf of self-employed individuals are not treated as elective contributions made by the individuals (Code Sec. 408(p)(9)).

> **Example 1:** Ralph, age 52, participates in his employer's SIMPLE IRA plan and for 2012 his salary will be $50,000. He elects to defer the maximum amount into the plan ($14,000). Under the plan, the employer makes a maximum matching contribution for each participating employee, up to the three percent limit. Therefore, the employer will make a $1,500 ($50,000 × three percent) matching contribution to Ralph's SIMPLE IRA.

Nonelective Contributions. The matching contribution requirement is considered to be satisfied if the employer elects to make nonelective contributions of two percent of the compensation (¶ 2120) for each employee who is eligible to participate in the plan and who has at least $5,000 of compensation from the employer for the calendar year (Code Sec. 408(p)(2)(B)(ii)).[190]

> **Example 2:** Assume the same facts as in Example 1, above, except that Ralph's employer decided to base its contributions on the nonelective contributions option. In this situation, Ralph would still be allowed to contribute $14,000 to his SIMPLE IRA. However, the employer's contribution would be $1,000 ($50,000 × two percent).

References are to Standard Federal Tax Reports; Tax Research Consultant; and Practical Tax Explanations.

[186] ¶ 18,902; RETIRE: 63,612, RETIRE: 63,614; § 25,130.05

[187] ¶ 18,902; RETIRE: 63,650; § 25,120.10

[188] ¶ 18,902; RETIRE: 63,606; § 25,125.05

[189] ¶ 18,902; RETIRE: 63,654.05; § 25,120.05

[190] ¶ 18,902; RETIRE: 63,654.10; § 25,120.20

Vesting. The employee's right to both matching contributions and nonelective contributions of the employer (and the earnings on these contributions) in a SIMPLE IRA must be fully vested at all times (Code Sec. 408(p)(3)).[191]

Employer's Deduction. An employer can deduct SIMPLE IRA contributions in the tax year with or within which the calendar year for which the contributions were made ends. Contributions for a particular tax year may be deducted if they are made for that tax year and are made by the due date, including extensions, of the employer's tax return for that year (Code Sec. 404(m)).[192]

2155E. Distributions. Distributions from a SIMPLE IRA are taxable to the employee (or the beneficiary or estate of the employee) under the rules that govern distributions from traditional IRAs (¶ 2153G) (Code Sec. 408(p)(1)(A)).[193] This includes the 10-percent additional tax that applies to early distributions from an IRA (¶ 2153H) except that the tax is increased to 25 percent when the employee takes an early distribution within two years after the employee's first participation in a SIMPLE arrangement (Code Sec. 72(t)(6)).[194] The two-year period begins on the first day on which contributions made by the individual's employer are deposited in the individual's SIMPLE IRA (Notice 98-4). If the employee has participated in the SIMPLE IRA for at least two years, a distribution may be rolled over into other types of retirement plans (e.g., employer qualified plans, 403(b) plans and 457 plans) (Code Sec. 408(d)(3)(A)). If the employee has not participated in the SIMPLE plan for two years, the distribution may only be rolled over into another SIMPLE plan (Code Sec. 408(d)(3)(G)).

2156. Simplified Employee Pensions (SEPs). A simplified employee pension (SEP) is an IRA-based retirement plan, under which an employer makes contributions to IRAs established on behalf of each of its employees (Code Sec. 408(k)).[195] For 2012, annual contributions by an employer to a SEP are excluded from the employee's gross income to the extent that the contributions do not exceed the *lesser* of: (1) 25 percent of the participant's compensation (¶ 2120) or (2) $50,000 ($51,000 for 2013) (Code Sec. 402(h); Notice 2011-90; IRS News Release IR-2012-77).[196] If the employer exceeds the annual limit on contributions, the employee is generally taxed on the amount of the excess contribution (¶ 2153E). In the case of a SEP established by an unincorporated employer, the compensation of a self-employed participant (partner or proprietor) is earned income. Plans covering self-employed participants are generally discussed at ¶ 2163.

In order to deduct its SEP contributions for a particular year, the employer must make the contributions by the due date (including extensions) of its tax return for that tax year (Code Sec. 404(h)).[197] The contributions are made to the SEP-IRAs that have been established by, or for, each eligible employee.

Although the employer's deduction cannot exceed 25 percent of the employee's compensation (¶ 2144), any excess can be carried over and deducted in later years subject to the percentage limitation. In addition, when an employer maintains another type of defined contribution plan, the contributions to a SEP must be taken into account when determining compliance with the annual limit imposed on deductible contributions to the plans (¶ 2121) (Code Sec. 404(h)(2)).[198]

The employer must decide each year whether and how much to contribute to a SEP plan. If any contribution is made to a plan, nondiscriminatory employer contributions must be made for each employee who: (1) has reached age 21, (2) has performed services for the employer during at least three of the immediately preceding five years, and (3) received at least $550 of compensation for 2012 ($550 for 2013) (Code Sec. 408(k)(2); Notice 2011-90; IRS News Release IR-2012-77). Unlike traditional IRAs, the

References are to Standard Federal Tax Reports; Tax Research Consultant; and Practical Tax Explanations.

[191] ¶ 18,902; RETIRE: 63,612, RETIRE: 63,614; § 25,130.05

[192] ¶ 18,330; RETIRE: 63,700; § 25,145.15

[193] ¶ 18,902; RETIRE: 63,756; § 25,145.10

[194] ¶ 6102; RETIRE: 63,756; § 25,145.10

[195] ¶ 18,902; RETIRE: 63,050; § 25,005

[196] ¶ 18,202; RETIRE: 63,050; § 45,040.20

[197] ¶ 18,330; RETIRE: 63,204; § 25,015.10

[198] ¶ 18,330; RETIRE: 63,202; § 25,015.10

account owner of a SEP-IRA can make contributions after reaching age 70½ (Code Sec. 219(b)(2)).[199]

Employee Contributions. An employee may make contributions to a SEP-IRA that was established by the employer in the name of the employee that are independent of their employer's contributions. However, an employee may not make an elective salary reduction contribution unless the employer established a salary reduction arrangement (SARSEP) as part of the SEP-IRA in a plan year prior to 1997 (¶ 2156A). For 2012, an employee's contribution is subject to the annual limit for traditional IRAs (¶ 2153). Traditional IRA rules regarding the employee's gross income, filing status and employer plan participation determine whether the employee's contributions to the SEP-IRA are deductible (¶ 2153A).

Establishing a SEP-IRA. Most employers are able to establish a SEP plan by completing a Form 5305-SEP. The form is *not* filed with the IRS. Instead, it is retained by the employer as evidence that a SEP plan has been established. All eligible employees must be given a copy of the Form 5305-SEP. Certain employers should not use Form 5305-SEP, e.g., employers that are currently maintaining another qualified plan or use the services of leased employees. An employer may establish a SEP-IRA for a particular year as late as the due date, including extensions, for its income tax return for that year.

Distributions. Distributions from a SEP are taxed under the rules that apply to distributions from an IRA (¶ 2153G) (Code Secs. 402(h)(3) and 408(d)).[200]

Top-Heavy SEP. If a SEP is top heavy (¶ 2118), each participant who is not a key employee must be provided with a contribution that is not less than three percent of his compensation. If the rate for the key employee receiving the largest contribution is less than three percent, the contribution rate for that employee is used to determine the minimum contribution for non-key employees (Code Sec. 408(k)(1)(B)).[201]

2156A. Salary Reduction SEPs (SARSEPs). In plan years beginning before 1997, an employer could establish a salary reduction (cash or deferred arrangement) as part of a SEP.[202] Such an arrangement—commonly known as a SARSEP—may *not* be established in plan years beginning after 1996. However, SARSEPs established before 1997 may continue to operate, subject to the same conditions and requirements that have always applied (Sec. 1421(c) of P.L. 104-188).[203]

Other Plans

2160. Sec. 403(b) Plans (Tax Sheltered Annuities). A public school system or tax-exempt educational, charitable, or religious organization may provide retirement benefits for its employees through the purchase of annuities or by contributing to a custodial account invested in mutual funds (Code Sec. 403(b)(1)(A)). This type of retirement plan is commonly referred to as a "403(b) plan" or "tax-sheltered annuity plan" (TSA). Generally, the employee's rights in the annuity or account must be nonforfeitable (Code Sec. 403(b)(1) and (7)).[204]

Limit on Annual Addition. There is a limit imposed on the total amount of the annual addition that may be made to an employee's 403(b) account. This annual limit is sometimes called the maximum amount contributable (MAC). The annual addition or MAC is made up of the following three types of contributions:

- elective contributions made by the employee,
- nonelective contributions made by the employer, and
- after-tax contributions made by the employee (Code Sec. 403(b)(1)).[205]

Generally, for 2012, the annual addition cannot be more than the *lesser* of $50,000 or 100 percent of the employee's compensation. For 2013, the annual addition cannot be

References are to Standard Federal Tax Reports; Tax Research Consultant; and Practical Tax Explanations.

[199] ¶ 18,902; RETIRE: 63,102; § 25,010.10

[200] ¶ 18,202, ¶ 18,902; RETIRE: 63,256; § 25,015.15

[201] ¶ 18,902; RETIRE: 63,114; § 25,010.30

[202] ¶ 18,902; RETIRE: 63,150; § 25,020

[203] ¶ 18,902; RETIRE: 63,150; § 25,020

[204] ¶ 18,270; RETIRE: 69,056.10, RETIRE: 69,054.15; § 25,205.10, § 25,210.05

[205] ¶ 18,270; RETIRE: 69,058; § 25,215.10

more than the *lesser* of $51,000 or 100 percent of the employee's compensation (¶ 2120) (Code Sec. 415(c)(1); Notice 2011-90; IRS News Release IR-2012-77). There are also limits on the amount of elective deferrals that generally apply to all of an employee's deferrals under any 403(b), SEP, SIMPLE or 401(k) plan (Code Sec. 402(g)(3)). However, employees are not required to coordinate their maximum deferral under a 457 plan with their contributions made to 403(b) plans (Code Sec. 457(c), prior to amendment by the Economic Growth and Tax Relief Reconciliation Act of 2001 (P.L. 107-16). Employees who will be at least age 50 by the end of the year may make "catch-up contributions" to a 403(b) plan. The maximum catch-up contribution to a 403(b) plan is $5,500 for 2012 and 2013 (Code Sec. 414(v); Notice 2011-90; IRS News Release IR-2012-77). Qualified employees of certain organizations, e.g., schools, hospitals, churches, and home health service organizations, who are covered by an annuity contract under a 403(b) plan may defer additional amounts of their compensation (Code Sec. 402(g)(7)(A)). For this purpose, a qualified employee is one who has completed 15 years of service with the organization (Code Sec. 402(g)(7)(C)).

Distributions. Payments to an employee from a 403(b) plan are taxed under the annuity rules explained at ¶ 817. However, any employee contributions that were excluded from wages are not treated as part of the employee's investment in the contract. Distributions may generally be made because of the employee's death, disability, severance from employment, attainment of age 59½, or financial hardship (Code Sec. 403(b)(7)(A)(ii) and (b)(11)). Distributions that do not meet these requirements are subject to the 10-percent additional tax on early distributions (¶ 2124C). The required minimum distribution (RMD) rules also apply (¶ 2124B) (Reg. § 1.403(b)-3).

Rollovers. Distributions from a 403(b) plan may be rolled over into an IRA or another 403(b) plan, as well as to other types of employer plans, e.g., a 401(k) plan or 457 plan (Code Sec. 403(b)(8)(A)). Although the employee has the right to make the rollover, the other plans are not required to accept the rollover. The spousal rollover rules that apply to other types of employer sponsored plans and the written explanation requirements also apply to a beneficiary under a qualified annuity plan (Code Sec. 403(a)(4)(B)). A 403(b) plan that includes a qualified Roth contribution program may now permit a qualified rollover contribution from a participant's non-Roth account to the participant's designated Roth account within the same plan (¶ 2125B; ¶ 2125E) (Code Sec. 402A(c)(4)(B)).

2161. Sec. 457 Plans (Deferred Compensation Plans of Exempt Employers). Special rules apply to certain deferred compensation plans sponsored by state and local governments and private tax-exempt organizations, commonly referred to as Sec. 457 plans. Under a state or local government plan, compensation deferred under the plan is only included in income when it is paid to the employee. However, for plans of tax-exempt organizations, deferred compensation is includible when paid or made available (Code Sec. 457(a)).[206] As with other types of retirement plans, special requirements have to be met by Sec. 457 plans.

Availability of Benefits. Compensation is deferred for any calendar month under a Sec. 457 plan only if an agreement providing for deferral is entered into before the beginning of that month (Code Sec. 457(b)(4)). Benefits are not considered to be made available under the plan if the participant or beneficiary may elect, before any benefits become payable, to defer payment of some or all of them to a fixed or determinable future time. In addition, amounts deferred under an eligible plan are not considered to be made available to the participant solely because the individual may choose among various investment options under the plan, whether before or after benefit payments have commenced (Reg. § 1.457-8(b)(2)).[207] After benefits have become payable but before they have commenced, the participant or beneficiary may elect to defer them to a date later than that originally elected. Only one such election may be made (Code Sec. 457(e)(9)(B)).[208]

References are to Standard Federal Tax Reports; Tax Research Consultant; and Practical Tax Explanations.

206 ¶ 21,531; COMPEN: 15,150; § 25,301

207 ¶ 21,532; COMPEN: 15,156; § 25,310.10

208 ¶ 21,531; COMPEN: 15,156; § 25,310.10

Limitation on Deferral. The maximum amount that can be deferred is the *lesser* of: (1) 100 percent of the participant's includible compensation or (2) $17,000 for 2012 ($17,500 for 2013) (Code Sec. 457(e)(15); Notice 2011-90; IRS News Release IR-2012-77).[209] Participants in a Sec. 457 plan are permitted to make additional deferrals of income for one or more of the last three tax years that end before normal retirement age (Code Sec. 457(b)(3)). The allowable deferral for such participants is increased, up to a limit of twice the standard dollar amount for the year, by the amount of allowable deferrals not made in previous plan years. Alternatively, employees covered by a Code Sec. 457 state or governmental plan who will be at least 50 years of age by the end of the year are able to make special catch-up contributions to the plan (Code Sec. 414(v)). The maximum catch-up contribution is $5,500 for 2012 and 2013 (Notice 2011-90; IRS News Release IR-2012-77). However, during the last three years of employment that end before attaining normal retirement age, a special formula is used to determine the maximum contribution (Code Sec. 457(e)(18)).

Other Requirements. A Sec. 457 plan must satisfy the required minimum distribution (RMD) rules that are generally imposed on qualified plans (¶ 2135) (Code Sec. 457(d)(2)). Distributions of deferred amounts must not be made available before the calendar year in which the participant attains age 70½, is severed from employment, or is faced with an unforeseen emergency (Code Sec. 457(d)(1)).[210] An unforeseeable emergency must be defined in the plan as: (1) a severe financial hardship to the participant that results from a sudden unexpected illness or accident of the participant or a dependent of the participant, or (2) a loss of the participant's property due to casualty or other similar extraordinary and unforeseeable circumstances beyond the control of the participant.

Hardship withdrawals may not be made to the extent that the financial hardship can be relieved by insurance, liquidation of the participant's assets (if liquidation would not cause financial hardship), or by stopping deferrals under the plan. In addition, withdrawals of amounts for unforeseeable emergencies is permitted only to the extent reasonably needed to satisfy the emergency. The need for funds to purchase a new home or to meet the college expenses of the participant's children is *not* an unforeseeable emergency (Reg. § 1.457-6(c)(2)(i)). To the extent allowed under the plan, if the occurrence of an event with regard to the employee's spouse or dependent would be a hardship, the occurrence of the same event with regard to the employee's beneficiary under the plan would also be a hardship (Notice 2007-7, Q&A-5).

Rollovers. An employee participating in a governmental Sec. 457 plan may roll over distributions into a variety of retirement plans (e.g., IRAs, 401(k) plans and 403(b) plans) (Code Sec. 457(e)(16)). Similarly, in some circumstances, assets from these plans may be rolled over into a Sec. 457 plan (¶ 2125A and ¶ 2125B). A Sec. 457 plan that includes a qualified Roth contribution program may permit a qualified rollover contribution from a participant's non-Roth account to the participant's designated Roth account within the same plan (Code Sec. 402A(c)(4)(B)) (¶ 2125E).

Roth 401(k) Plans. Beginning in 2011, Sec. 457 plans may allow participants to designate elective deferrals as Roth contributions. An applicable retirement plan for purposes of offering a qualified Roth contribution program includes eligible deferred compensation plans offered by state and local governments (Code Sec. 402A(e)(1)(C)). Elective deferrals for these purposes include any elective deferral of compensation by an individual under an eligible deferred compensation plan of an eligible employer that is a state or local government (Code Sec. 402A(e)(2)(B)).

Ineligible Plans. Compensation deferred under a nonqualified plan of a state or local government or other tax-exempt organization that is not an eligible Sec. 457 plan is includible in the income of a participant or beneficiary for the first tax year in which there is no substantial risk of forfeiture (Code Sec. 457(f)(1)(A) and (2)(E)).[211]

References are to Standard Federal Tax Reports; Tax Research Consultant; and Practical Tax Explanations.

[209] ¶ 21,531; COMPEN: 15,152.25; § 25,305.20

[210] ¶ 21,531; COMPEN: 15,152.40; § 25,305.30

[211] ¶ 21,531; COMPEN: 15,158; § 22,110.20

2162. Sec. 457A Plans (Tax-Indifferent Parties). In general, any compensation which is deferred under a nonqualified deferred compensation plan of a nonqualified entity, e.g., a foreign entity not subject to a comprehensive income tax, is includible in the service provider's gross income when there is no substantial risk of forfeiture of the rights to the compensation (Code Sec. 457A(a)). If the amount of any compensation is not determinable at the time that it is otherwise includible in gross income, then, in addition to income inclusion when the amount is determinable, the tax imposed for the year in which the compensation is includible in income must be increased by 20 percent of the amount of the compensation, plus an interest charge.

Effective Date. This rule generally applies to amounts deferred which are attributable to services performed after December 31, 2008. In the case of any amount deferred to which the rule does not apply solely by reason of the fact that the amount is attributable to services performed before January 1, 2009, to the extent that amount is not includible in gross income in a tax year beginning before 2018, the amount will be includible in gross income in the later of the last tax year beginning before 2018 or the tax year in which there is no substantial risk of forfeiture of the rights to such compensation.

With respect to a deferred amount attributable to services performed before January 1, 2009, a change in the time and form of payment to conform the date of distribution to the date the amount may be required to be included in income under the Code Sec. 457A special timing rule will not be treated as an impermissible acceleration under the non-qualified deferred compensation rules of Code Sec. 409A, provided that the change was established in writing and was effective on or before December 31, 2011 (Notice 2009-8).

2163. Plans Covering Self-Employed Participants. No distinction is generally made between pension, profit-sharing, and other retirement plans established by corporations and those established by individual proprietors and partnerships. In the past, the terms Keogh Plan or H.R. 10 Plan were used to distinguish a retirement plan established by a self-employed individual from a plan established by a corporation or other entity. However, self-employed retirement plans are now generally referred to by the name that is used for the particular type of plan, e.g., SEP IRA, SIMPLE 401(k), or self-employed 401(k).

Even though there is general parity between retirement plans established by a self-employed individual and plans established by other business entities, special rules have to be considered. For example, the term employee generally includes a participant in a plan of an unincorporated enterprise who is a partner or a sole proprietor (Code Sec. 401(c)).[212] When references are made to the employer, a sole proprietor is treated as his or her own employer. However, a partnership is considered to be the employer of each partner. As a result, sole proprietors may establish their own retirement plans. Only a partnership may establish a retirement plan for its partners.

Contributions and deductions for a self-employed participant covered by a qualified plan are subject to the same basic rules that apply to participants who are common law employees. However, a special computation must be made to figure the maximum deduction for contributions made by a self-employed taxpayer as an employer for themselves. Generally, the deduction limits are based, in part, on the compensation paid to eligible employees participating in the plan. For this purpose, a self-employed individual's compensation is his or her earned income, defined as the net earnings from self-employment (¶ 2670) reduced by: (1) the deduction allowed for contributions made on behalf of the self-employed participant and (2) the deduction from gross income that is allowed for 50 percent of the self-employment tax paid by the self-employed participant (¶ 923) (Code Sec. 401(c)(2)(A)).[213]

References are to Standard Federal Tax Reports; Tax Research Consultant; and Practical Tax Explanations.

[212] ¶ 17,502; RETIRE: 60,052; § 24,135.10

[213] ¶ 17,502; RETIRE: 60,100; § 24,330.05

Since a self-employed taxpayer's deductions for contributions on his or her own behalf and his or her net earnings are dependent on each other, the deduction for the taxpayer's own contributions must be determined indirectly by reducing the contribution rate provided in the plan (referred to as the percentage equivalent adjustment). In IRS Pub. 560, the IRS provides a rate table or rate worksheet to determine the reduced contribution rate for this purpose, depending on whether the plan's contribution rate is a whole percentage or not. For example, under the rate table, if the maximum plan contribution rate is 15 percent, the maximum deduction percentage for contributions to the self-employed individual's own plan is 13.0435 percent, while the 15 percent rate applies to other employees. Similarly, if the plan's maximum contribution rate is 25 percent, a 20 percent rate applies to the self-employed individual, and the 25 percent rate applies to other employees.[214]

401(k) Plan for the Self Employed. In general, the same rules that apply to 401(k) plans established by other types of entities apply to the 401(k) plans of self-employed taxpayers (¶ 2106) (Reg. § 1.401(k)-1(a)(6)(i)). This makes a 401(k) plan more advantageous than other types of self-employment plans because the taxpayer may make both employer contributions and elective employee contributions subject to the general limit for additions to defined contributions plans (¶ 2122A). Self-employed 401(k) plans may also offer the possibility of being able to make loans to participating employees (¶ 2129).

Retirement Contribution for Partner. A partnership's deduction for retirement contributions on behalf of a partner must be allocated solely to that partner (Reg. § 1.404(e)-1A(f)).[215] It cannot be allocated among all of the partners pursuant to the partnership agreement (¶ 428).

Contribution Is Not a Business Expense. A contribution to a qualified plan for the benefit of a self-employed individual is not a business expense of that individual (*D.L. Gale*, 91-2 USTC ¶ 50,356).[216] Thus, it is not deductible on Schedule C of Form 1040 or on Form 1065 and is not deductible in calculating self-employment tax. For a sole proprietorship, the contribution is claimed as an adjustment to gross income on Form 1040. For a partnership, the contribution is shown on Schedule K-1 of Form 1065 and deducted from gross income on the partner's Form 1040 (¶ 431).

SEP-IRA Rules. The rules governing SEP-IRAs are discussed in detail at ¶ 2156.

Plan Terminations

2165. Introduction. A qualified defined benefit plan is terminated for tax purposes when it is voluntarily terminated by the plan administrator or when it is terminated by the Pension Benefit Guaranty Corporation (PBGC). A defined contribution plan is considered terminated on the date when it is voluntarily terminated by the employer or employers who maintain it (Reg. § 1.411(d)-2(c)).

Partial Termination. Whether a partial termination has occurred is determined on a case-by-case basis (Reg. § 1.411(d)-2(b)(1)). A special rule applies where a defined benefit plan ceases or reduces future benefit accruals. In this case, a partial termination occurs if a potential reversion to the employer or employees who maintain the plan is created or increased (Reg. § 1.411(d)-2(b)(2)).

Multiemployer Plans. Multiemployer plans are subject to the vesting, participation, and benefit accrual rules that generally apply to all qualified plans. However, there are special funding and termination rules for multiemployer plans regarding special amortization periods (Code Sec. 412(b)(2)).

2166. Voluntary Terminations. A qualified defined benefit plan may be voluntarily terminated through either a standard termination or a distress termination. The type of termination that the plan administrator uses depends on whether there are, or appear to be, assets sufficient to satisfy Pension Benefit Guaranty Corporation (PBGC) guaranteed benefits.

References are to Standard Federal Tax Reports; Tax Research Consultant; and Practical Tax Explanations.

[214] ¶ 17,933.036; RETIRE: 60,202; § 24,330.05

[215] ¶ 18,359; PART: 21,260; § 24,305.30

[216] ¶ 18,347.17; RETIRE: 60,214; § 24,330.05

Standard Termination. In determining if there are sufficient plan assets to pay benefits, claims are divided into six categories: (1) voluntary employee contributions that are nonforfeitable; (2) mandatory employee contributions, plus interest; (3) annuities provided with employer contributions that have been, or could have been, in pay status at least three years prior to plan termination; (4) the participant's basic-type benefits that do not exceed the guarantee limits; (5) all other nonforfeitable benefits; and (6) all plan benefits not allocated to the above five categories (29 CFR § 4044, Secs. 11-16).

Distress Termination. A distress termination may be initiated by the plan administrator or the PBGC. Initiating a distress termination requires several steps: (1) notice of intent to terminate given to participants, (2) filing forms with PBGC, (3) PBGC review, (4) determination of whether requirements are met, (5) notice of benefit distribution, (6) issuances of notices, (7) distribution of benefits, and (8) filing of post-distribution certificate (ERISA § 4041).

2167. Involuntary Terminations. A qualified defined benefit plan may be involuntarily terminated by the Pension Benefit Guaranty Corporation (PBGC) if it makes a determination that: (1) the plan has not met the minimum funding standard; (2) the plan will be unable to pay benefits when due; (3) there has been a distribution under the plan to a participant who is a substantial owner, the distribution has a value of $10,000 or more, the distribution is not made by reason of the death of the participant, and, immediately after the distribution, the plan has nonforfeitable benefits that are not funded; or (4) the possible long-run loss to the PBGC may be expected to increase unreasonably if the plan is not terminated (ERISA § 4042(a)). When a termination occurs, the termination must not have the effect of discriminating in favor of highly compensated employees, the plan administrator must notify the IRS, all benefits or contributions that are not allocated to employees must be so allocated, benefits must become non-forfeitable, and the plan's assets must be distributed as soon as administratively feasible.

2168. Pension Benefit Guaranty Corporation (PBGC). The Pension Benefit Guarantee Corporation (PBGC) is a corporation operated under the Department of Labor. The primary purpose of the PBGC is to administer the pension plan termination insurance program set forth in Title IV of ERISA. For those plans subject to the termination insurance program, the plan administrator must make certain filings with the PBGC.

Defined benefit multiemployer plans are covered by the plan termination insurance provisions of ERISA and must pay premiums to the PBGC. In return for payment of premiums, employees covered by these plans are paid pension benefits by the PBGC if their particular plans become unable to pay retirement benefits.

Voluntary Compliance

2171. Employee Plan Compliance Resolution System (EPCRS). The Employee Plan Compliance Resolution System (EPCRS) is a comprehensive system of correction programs for sponsors of plans intended to be qualified plans (¶ 2114), SEPs (¶ 2110, ¶ 2156), SIMPLE IRAs (¶ 2109, ¶ 2155), 403(a) plans, or 403(b) annuity plans (¶ 2160) that have not met the qualification requirements for a period of time. EPCRS is discussed in Rev. Proc. 2008-50. The IRS may extend EPCRS to cover other arrangements as well. EPCRS includes the following correction programs: Self-Correction Program (SCP) (¶ 2171A), Voluntary Correction Program (VCP) (¶ 2171B), and Audit Closing Agreement Program (Audit CAP) (¶ 2171C).

2171A. Self-Correction Plans (SCP). The Self-Correction Program (SCP) is available to correct operational failures for qualified plans (¶ 2114) and 403(b) plans (¶ 2160). It is also available to SEPs (¶ 2110, ¶ 2156) or SIMPLE IRA plans (¶ 2109, ¶ 2155), provided the SEP or SIMPLE IRA is established and maintained on a document approved by the IRS. In addition, in the case of a qualified plan that is the subject of a favorable determination letter from the IRS or in the case of a 403(b) plan, the plan sponsor generally may correct significant and insignificant operational failures without payment of any fee or sanction. SEPs and SIMPLE IRAs are eligible for SCP only to correct insignificant operational failures. SCP may also be used to correct significant operational failures for qualified plans or 403(b) plans (Rev. Proc. 2008-50). A plan can self correct an operational failure if given all the facts and circumstances the failure is insignificant. Self correction is available even if the plan or sponsor is under examination and even if the operational failure is discovered on examination.

2171B. Voluntary Correction with Service Approval (VCP). The Voluntary Correction Program (VCP) provides general procedures for correction of operational, plan document, demographic, and employer eligibility qualification failures. VCP is available to qualified plans (¶ 2114), 403(b) plans (¶ 2160), SEPs (¶ 2110, ¶ 2156) or SIMPLE IRA plans (¶ 2109, ¶ 2155). A plan sponsor may, at any time prior to audit, pay a limited fee and receive the IRS's approval for a correction. Under VCP, there are special procedures for anonymous submissions and group submissions. If the plan or plan sponsor is under examination, VCP is not available. However, while the plan or plan sponsor is under examination, insignificant operational failures can be corrected under the Self-Correction Program (SCP) (¶ 2171A) and, if correction has been substantially completed before the plan or plan sponsor is under examination, significant operational failures can be corrected under SCP (Rev. Proc. 2008-50).

VCP is for correction of failures raised by the plan sponsor or failures identified by the IRS in processing the application. Consideration under VCP does not preclude a subsequent examination of the plan or plan sponsor by the IRS with respect to the tax years(s) involved with respect to matters outside the compliance statement. Absent unusual circumstances, a plan that has been properly submitted under VCP will not be examined while the submission is pending. This does not, however, preclude concurrent examination of the plan sponsor's other plan.

2171C. Closing Agreements Programs (Audit CAP). If a failure is identified on audit and has not been corrected through the Self-Correction Program (SCP) (¶ 2171A) or the Voluntary Correction Program (VCP) (¶ 2171B), the plan sponsor may correct the failure and pay a sanction. The sanction imposed will take into account the nature, extent and severity of the failure as well as the extent to which correction occurred before audit. The Audit Closing Agreement Program (Audit CAP) is available for qualified plans (¶ 2114); 403(b) plans (¶ 2160); SEPs (¶ 2110, ¶ 2156) and SIMPLE IRAs (¶ 2109, ¶ 2155) for correction of all failures found on examination that have not been corrected in accordance with SCP or VCP (Rev. Proc. 2008-50). If the IRS and the plan sponsor cannot reach an agreement regarding the correction or the failure(s) or the amount of the sanction, the plan will be disqualified or, in the case of a 403(b) plan, SEP, or SIMPLE IRA, the plan cannot rely on Rev. Proc. 2008-50. The sanction under Audit CAP is a negotiated percentage of the maximum payment amount. For 403(b) plans, SEPs and SIMPLE IRAs, the sanction is a negotiated percentage of the total sanction amount.

Nonqualified Plans

2175. Introduction. An employer may maintain a retirement or other deferred compensation plan that is not a qualified plan (¶ 2114). If a nonqualified plan is *funded,* that is, the employer makes contributions to a trust or purchases an annuity contract or contracts, then the plan participants will realize income (¶ 2177). The employer is entitled to deductions for contributions to a funded nonqualified plan (¶ 2178). *Unfunded* deferred compensation plans are discussed at ¶ 906.

2176. Income of the Plan. In the case of a nonqualified plan funded through a trust, the trust is not exempt, i.e., the plan's earnings are generally taxable to the trust (Code Sec. 641).[217] The grantor trust rules (¶ 571) ordinarily do not apply to a nonqualified plan. Therefore, the participant is not usually treated as the owner of his share of the trust's assets and is not subject to tax on the trust's income. However, if a participant's contributions as of any date exceed the employer's contributions on behalf of the

References are to Standard Federal Tax Reports; Tax Research Consultant; and Practical Tax Explanations.

[217] ¶ 24,260; PLANIND: 15,064; § 25,610.10

participant, the participant is treated as the owner of the portion of the trust attributable to his contributions and is subject to tax on the income from that portion (Reg. § 1.402(b)-1(b)(6)).[218]

2177. Income of a Participant. Contributions of, or premiums paid by, the employer in the case of a nonqualified plan are generally taxable to the participant only when they are actually or constructively received. However, contributions under a plan that does not meet the design and funding requirements of Code Sec. 409A (¶ 2179) are taxable, with an additional penalty imposed, when they are no longer subject to a substantial risk of forfeiture, even if the employee does not have immediate access to them.

Rank-and-file employees are not taxable on amounts contributed to, or earned by, a trust that is not exempt solely because of the plan's failure to satisfy the nondiscriminatory coverage requirements for qualified plans (¶ 2117). However, each highly compensated employee is subject to tax on the value of the vested accrued benefit attributable to employer contributions as of the close of the employer's tax year that ends with or within the tax year in which the trust loses its exemption. If the trust continues to be nonexempt for failure to satisfy the coverage requirements, a highly compensated employee is subject to tax on the excess of the current value of his or her vested accrued benefit attributable to employer contributions over the value of the previously taxed portion of that benefit (Code Sec. 402(b)(4)).[219]

The participant's investment (basis) in a nonqualified plan is increased by any amounts included in his or her income under the above rules. Actual distributions from a nonqualified plan are taxed under the annuity rules described at ¶ 817 and following. However, if the distributions do not take the form of an annuity, they are considered to be derived first from plan earnings and asset appreciation (taxable gain) rather than from the employee's investment (basis) in the plan (Code Secs. 402(b) and 403(c)).[220]

2178. Employer's Deduction. The employer is entitled to a deduction for contributions to, or premiums paid under, a nonqualified plan on behalf of an employee in the tax year of the employer in which an amount attributable to the contribution is includible in the gross income of the employee (¶ 2177) (Code Sec. 404(a)(5)).[221] If more than one employee participates, this rule applies only if separate accounts are maintained for each employee.

2179. Requirements. Unless certain plan design and funding requirements are met, amounts deferred under a nonqualified deferred compensation plan are includible in income of plan participants to the extent they are not subject to a substantial risk of forfeiture, and any tax due is increased by an interest charge, as well as by a penalty equal to 20-percent of the deferred compensation included in income (Code Sec. 409A).[222]

2180. Permissible Payments. To avoid the accelerated recognition regime, a nonqualified deferred compensation plan must allow distributions only if they are "permissible payments" triggered by the employee's separation from service from the employer, the employee's death or disability, a time specified under the plan, or upon a change in the effective ownership or control of the employer, or in the event of an unforeseeable emergency (Code Sec. 409A(a)(2)(A)). Distributions to key employees resulting from a separation from service must not be allowed until six months after the separation, unless the former employee dies in the interim (Code Sec. 409A(a)(2)(B)(i)).[223]

2181. Election Rules. A nonqualified deferred compensation plan must meet certain requirements regarding the participants' elections to defer compensation and to

References are to Standard Federal Tax Reports; Tax Research Consultant; and Practical Tax Explanations.

[218] ¶ 18,208; COMPEN: 15,106; § 25,610.10

[219] ¶ 18,202; RETIRE: 39,700; § 24,105.10

[220] ¶ 18,202, ¶ 18,270; COMPEN: 15,200; § 25,610.10

[221] ¶ 18,330; COMPEN: 15,250; § 25,605

[222] ¶ 18,952; COMPEN: 15,066; § 25,601

[223] ¶ 18,952; COMPEN: 15,056.10; § 25,601

receive distributions (Code Sec. 409A(a)(4)).[224] Compensation for services performed during a tax year generally can be deferred only if the participant's election to defer is made before the close of the preceding tax year.

2182. Funding. Generally, if a nonqualified deferred compensation plan uses an offshore trust, or places assets outside the United States, the plan will *not* defer the compensation (Code Sec. 409A(b)(1)). Also, if the plan provides that its assets will become restricted to the payment of benefits under the plan if there is a change in the employer's financial health, or if the assets actually become so restricted, the plan will not defer compensation (Code Sec. 409A(b)(2)). These rules apply to all deferred compensation, regardless of when it was deferred.

A nonqualified plan will also not defer compensation to the extent of contributions made on behalf of or restricted to benefits for certain employees at a time when the employer or its defined benefit plan are experiencing financial difficulties. This provision applies if the plan is in at-risk status under Code Sec. 430(i), if the plan sponsor is in bankruptcy, and if, during the 12-month period beginning six months before the plan terminates, the plan is underfunded (Code Sec. 409A(b)(3)).[225]

2183. Form W-2 Reporting. The total amount of deferrals under a nonqualified deferred compensation plan are required to be shown on the employee's Form W-2 (Code Sec. 6051(a)(13)). If the individual is not an employee, the amount must be shown on Form 1099-MISC (Code Sec. 6041(g)). These rules apply even if the amount of deferred compensation is not currently taxable. The IRS has the authority to establish minimum amounts that do not have to be shown. If income is recognized because the plan does not satisfy the rules, it is reported with Code Z on Form W-2. For non-employees, the income to be recognized is reported on Form 1099-MISC.

Benefit Administration

2185. Introduction. A key component of the employment relationship between employer and employee is the provision of noncash compensation and other fringe benefits. Most employees have come to expect fringe benefits, such as health insurance, paid vacation leave, and educational assistance as an incident of employment and an obligation of the employer. Employers have also come to realize the importance of attractive fringe benefit packages in recruiting and retaining employees. The value of all fringe benefits must, absent specific exemption, be included in an employee's wages for income tax and employment tax purposes. Employers may deduct the cost of fringe benefits provided to employees, but they are subject to the employer's share of any employment taxes that may be due. Fringe benefits under Code Sec. 132 are discussed beginning at ¶ 2188, welfare benefits beginning at ¶ 2190, work/life benefits at ¶ 2192, cafeteria plans at ¶ 2195, and consumer-driven health plans beginning at ¶ 2197.

Executive Perks. Perks are one of four basic types of benefits currently in use for compensating the executive; the others are: direct compensation, deferred compensation plans, and retirement plans. Perks are those benefits that most employees think of as being fringe benefits. Thus, the perks that an employer may provide its employees consist of such non-cash benefits as company cars, exercise facilities and employee cafeterias.

In the context of executive compensation, however, directors, officers, and managers have come to expect perks "above-and-beyond" those available to the average employee. Therefore, many companies have developed perks that consist of such "extra" benefits as chauffeured limousine services, use of corporate stadium skyboxes, and expenses-paid attendance at trade or professional conventions. Like direct compensation and unlike deferred compensation and retirement benefits, perks provide an immediate economic and financial benefit to recipients. Therefore, unless exempted by Code Sec. 132 (¶ 2188), all perks are taxable as wages.

References are to Standard Federal Tax Reports; Tax Research Consultant; and Practical Tax Explanations.

[224] ¶ 18,952; COMPEN: 15,056.10; § 22,110.20

[225] ¶ 18,952; PLANRET: 3,206.40; § 25,610.20, § 45,040.10

Fringe Benefits Under Section 132

2188. Introduction. For tax purposes, Code Sec. 132 serves as a catchall for several categories of benefits that are not excludable from gross income under other Code sections. Fringe benefits that are qualified under Code Sec. 132 are excluded from the gross income of the employee in whole or in part including: no-additional-cost service (¶ 2188A), qualified employee discount (¶ 2188B), *de minimis* fringe benefit (¶ 2188C), working condition fringe benefit (¶ 2188D), qualified transportation fringe benefit (¶ 2188E), qualified moving expense reimbursement (¶ 2188F), qualified retirement planning services (¶ 2188G), and qualified military base realignment and closure fringe benefits (¶ 2188H) (Code Sec. 132(a)). Also, the value of any on-premises athletic facilities provided and operated by the employer is a nontaxable fringe benefit (Code Sec. 132(j)(4)).[226]

Fringe benefits under Code Sec. 132 that are excluded from an employee's gross income also are excludable from the wage base for purposes of income tax and employment withholding purposes. In the case of taxable noncash fringe benefits in the form of the personal use of an employer-provided vehicle, income tax withholding may be avoided if the employer elects not to withhold and notifies the employee of such election (Social Security and railroad retirement taxes must be withheld). However, the value of the benefit must be included on the employee's Form W-2 (Code Sec. 3402(s)).[227]

2188A. No-Additional-Cost-Services. No-additional-cost-services are free services provided to all employees by an employer where the employer incurs no substantial additional cost in providing the service, and the service is normally offered to the employer's customers in the line of business, such as free travel on a standby basis for airline employees (Code Sec. 132(b); Reg. § 1.132-2).[228] The exclusion is available only if the service is available to employees on a nondiscriminatory basis.

2188B. Qualified Employee Discounts. Discounts provided to employees on their purchase of qualified property or services of their employer are excluded for income and employment tax purposes (Code Sec. 132(c); Reg. § 1.132-3).[229] Qualified employee discounts are discounts provided to all employees on the selling price of certain property or services in the ordinary line of business. In the case of merchandise, the discount cannot exceed the gross profit percentage of the price at which the property is offered to customers. For services, the discount cannot exceed 20 percent of the price at which the service is offered to customers. In order to be excluded, such discounts must be available to employees on a nondiscriminatory basis. Moreover, employees do not receive income if they pay at least fair market value for damaged, distressed, or returned property.

2188C. *De Minimis* Fringe Benefits. If the value of any property or service provided to an employee is so minimal that accounting for the property or service would be unreasonable or administratively impracticable, it is a *de minimis* fringe benefit that is excluded for income and employment tax purposes (Code Sec. 132(e); Reg. § 1.132-6).[230] Such benefits include typing of personal letters by company clerks, limited use of copy machines, occasional parties or picnics, occasional supper money or transit fare due to overtime work, holiday gifts with a small market value, tickets occasionally provided for entertainment events, and employer-furnished coffee and doughnuts. Even a subsidized eating facility can be a *de minimis* fringe if it is located on or near the business premises and the revenue derived from it normally equals or exceeds direct operating costs. In determining whether the *de minimis* exclusion applies, the frequency with which similar fringe benefits (otherwise excludable as *de minimis* fringes) are provided by an employer to its employees is taken into account.

References are to Standard Federal Tax Reports; Tax Research Consultant; and Practical Tax Explanations.

[226] ¶ 7420; COMPEN: 36,050, COMPEN: 36,100, COMPEN: 36,250, COMPEN: 36,300, COMPEN: 36,350, COMPEN: 36,400, COMPEN: 36,450; § 21,101

[227] ¶ 33,542, ¶ 33,591; COMPEN: 33,100; § 22,110.10

[228] ¶ 7420, ¶ 7423; COMPEN: 36,050; § 21,105.05

[229] ¶ 7420, ¶ 7424; COMPEN: 36,100; § 21,110.05

[230] ¶ 7420, ¶ 7427; COMPEN: 36,300; § 21,120.05

Meals that are excludable from an employee's income under Code Sec. 119 are also considered a *de minimis* fringe benefit under Code Sec. 132. If more than one-half of the employees are furnished meals for the convenience of the employer, all meals provided on the premises are treated as furnished for the convenience of the employer. Therefore, the meals are fully deductible by the employer, instead of possibly being subject to the 50-percent limit on business meal deductions, and excludable by the employees.

The value of meals and lodging furnished by an employer to an employee, a spouse, or dependents for the employer's convenience is not includible in the employee's gross income if, in the case of meals, they are furnished on the employer's business premises and if, in the case of lodging, the employee is required to accept the lodging on the employer's business premises as a condition of employment (Code Sec. 119; Reg. § 1.119-1).[231] The fact that the employer imposes a partial charge for meals or that the employee may accept or decline meals does not affect the exclusion if all other conditions are met, but cash reimbursements of the employee's meal expenses are included in gross income (Code Sec. 119(b)).[232] If meals are furnished for the convenience of the employer, they must be furnished for substantial noncompensatory business reasons, e.g., having the employee on call (*Boyd Gaming Inc.*, 99-1 USTC ¶ 50,530),[233] rather than as additional compensation (Reg. § 1.119-1(a)(2)).[234]

The term "business premises of the employer," for this purpose, generally means the place of employment of the employee. It can include a camp located in a foreign country if an employee is furnished lodging.

Faculty Housing. The value of campus lodging furnished to employees by educational or medical research institutions is excludable from the employee's gross income if an adequate rental is charged. A rental is considered inadequate and thus the exclusion will not apply to the extent of the excess of: (a) the lesser of (1) five percent of the appraised value of the lodging or (2) an amount equal to the average of the rentals paid by nonemployees or nonstudents during the year for comparable lodging provided by the institution over (b) the rent paid by the employee for the calendar year (Code Sec. 119(d)).[235] The appraised value under (1), above, will be determined as of the close of the calendar year in which the tax year begins or, in the case of a rental period not greater than one year, at any time during the calendar year in which such period begins.

2188D. Working Condition Fringe Benefits. Working condition fringe benefits consisting of the fair market value of any property or service provided to an employee may be excluded from the employee's gross income provided the cost of the working condition fringe would have been deductible by the employee as a business expense had the employee bought the item on his or her own (Code Sec. 132(d); Reg. § 1.132-5).[236] The general nondiscrimination rules do not apply to working condition fringes; therefore, they can be provided exclusively or on more favorable terms to executives. Example of working condition fringes include use of a company vehicle, airplane transportation, travel expenses including meals and lodging (¶ 873), allowances for business use of cell phones, computers, and internet service, entertainment, and club dues. Denial of a deduction to an employer for its payment of travel expenses of a spouse, dependent, or other individual accompanying an employee on business travel does not preclude those items from qualifying as working condition fringe benefits.

Employer-provided Cell Phones. For tax years after 2009, employer-provided cell phones and similar equipment provided to the employee for non-compensatory business purposes are non-taxable to employees based on a two-prong approach: (1) the use of the phone related to the employer's business is treated as a working condition fringe benefit; and (2) the personal use of the employer-provided cell phone or similar equipment is excludable as a *de minimis* fringe benefit (Notice 2011-72). Under the

References are to Standard Federal Tax Reports; Tax Research Consultant; and Practical Tax Explanations.

[231] ¶ 7220, ¶ 7221; COMPEN: 36,500; § 21,210

[232] ¶ 7220, ¶ 7222.59; COMPEN: 36,510.10; § 21,205

[233] ¶ 7222.29; COMPEN: 36,502, BUSEXP: 24,608; § 21,205

[234] ¶ 7221; COMPEN: 36,510.05; § 21,205

[235] ¶ 7220; COMPEN: 36,506; § 21,230

[236] ¶ 7420, ¶ 7426; COMPEN: 36,250; § 21,115.05

guidance, the business substantiation requirements for the working condition fringe exclusion are automatically satisfied. The IRS also states that employers that require employees to use their personal cell phones primarily for non-compensatory business reasons may treat reimbursements of the employees' expenses for reasonable cell phone coverage as non-taxable. The guidance does not mean, however, that cell phones used for primarily personal reasons are exempt from tax or from the substantiation requirements (IRS News Release 2011-93).

2188E. Qualified Transportation Fringe Benefits. In general, commuting expenses to and from a place of business and home are generally not deductible. However, qualified transportation fringe benefits provided by an employer to an employee may be excluded from the employee's gross income (Code Sec. 132(f); Reg. § 1.132-9).[237] A qualified transportation fringe benefit includes transportation in a commuter highway vehicle if that transportation is in connection with travel between the employee's residence and the place of employment (also referred to as van pooling), a transportation pass, qualified parking, and qualified bicycle commuting reimbursement.

Employees may exclude a maximum of $230 per month from gross income for the value of employer-provided transit passes or van pooling for any month beginning on or after February 17, 2009, and before January 1, 2012 (Code Sec. 132(f); Rev. Proc. 2011-12). However, for 2012, the amount that may be excluded for the value of employer-provided transit passes or van pooling is a maximum of $125 per month (Rev. Proc. 2011-52). For 2012, employees may exclude up to $240 per month for the value of employer-provided parking (Rev. Proc. 2011-52). The exclusion for qualified bicycle commuting reimbursement remains limited to a per employee annual limitation of $20 multiplied by the number of qualified bicycle commuting months during the calendar year.

> **Comment:** Absent further legislation, for 2012, the maximum amount excludable for the value of employer-provided transit passes or van pooling will remain capped at $125 per month.

An employer may simultaneously provide an employee with van pooling, a transportation pass, and qualified parking. However, an employee may not receive a bicycle commuting expense reimbursement for any month in which the employee receives any other qualified transportation fringe benefit. Employers who provide any qualified transportation fringe benefits for their employees may offer employees a choice between cash and one or more qualified transportation benefits without causing the employees to lose the exclusion from income for noncash transportation fringe benefits. However, the amount of cash offered is includible in the employee's income only to the extent that the employee chooses the cash option.

Qualified parking for this purpose is parking provided on or near the business premises of the employer or on or near a location from which the employee commutes to work by mass transit, in a commuter highway vehicle, or by car pool. It does not include parking on or near property used by the employee for residential purposes. A qualifying commuter vehicle for purposes of the van pooling exclusion must seat at least six adults (excluding the driver) and at least 80 percent of its mileage use must be reasonably expected to be for employees' commuting purposes and for trips when the vehicle is at least one-half full (excluding the driver).

2188F. Qualified Moving Expenses Reimbursements. An employee may exclude any qualified moving expenses reimbursement from gross income as a fringe benefit (Code Sec. 132(g)).[238] A qualified moving expenses reimbursement includes any amount received, directly or indirectly, by the employee from the employer as payment or reimbursement of expenses that would be deductible as moving expenses under Code Sec. 217 if directly paid or incurred by the employee. It does not include a payment for (or a reimbursement of) an expense actually deducted by an individual in a prior tax year (¶ 1073). Expenses that would be deductible if paid directly or incurred by the

References are to Standard Federal Tax Reports; Tax Research Consultant; and Practical Tax Explanations.

[237] ¶ 7420, ¶ 7429B; COMPEN: 36,350; § 21,125.05

[238] ¶ 7420; COMPEN: 33,116; § 21,135

employee include the reasonable expenses of moving household goods and personal effects from a former residence to a new residence and traveling, including lodging during the period of travel.

2188G. Qualified Retirement Planning Services. Qualified retirement planning services provided to an employee and his spouse by an employer that maintains a qualified plan are excludable from the employee's income as fringe benefits (Code Sec. 132(m)).[239] Qualified retirement planning services consist of retirement planning advice and information. The exclusion applies to a highly compensated employee only if retirement planning services are available on substantially the same terms to each member of the group of employees that is normally provided with education and information about the employer's qualified plan (Code Sec. 132(m)(2)). In determining the exclusion's application to highly compensated employees, the IRS may allow employers to take into account employee circumstances, i.e., age, other than compensation and position in providing advice to classifications of employees.

2188H. Military Base Realignment and Closure Benefits. A specific exclusion from gross income is provided for payments intended to compensate military personnel and certain civilian employees for a reduction in the fair market value (FMV) of their homes resulting from military or Coast Guard base closure or realignment (Code Sec. 132(n)).[240] The exclusion applies to payments made under the Department of Defense Homeowners Assistance Program (HAP) and in effect February 17, 2009, where: (1) there was a base closure or realignment; (2) the property was purchased before July 1, 2006, and sold between July 1, 2006, and September 30, 2012; (3) the property is the owner's primary residence; and (4) the owner has not previously received benefits under HAP.

Welfare Benefits

2190. Introduction. An employee welfare benefit plan (or welfare plan) is any plan, fund, or program established or maintained by an employer or by an employee organization, or by both, for the purpose of providing any of the following benefits for its participants or their beneficiaries, through the purchase of insurance or otherwise: medical, surgical, or hospital care or benefits; benefits in the event of sickness, accident, disability, death or unemployment; vacation benefits; apprenticeship or other training programs; day care centers; scholarship funds; or prepaid legal services.

Funded Welfare Benefit Plans. Special rules govern deductions for employer contributions to funded welfare benefit plans (Code Sec. 419).[241] The rules also govern contributions to welfare benefit plans on behalf of independent contractors.

Generally, an employer is prohibited from deducting contributions to a welfare benefit plan in excess of the benefits actually paid by the plan during the tax year. However, under some circumstances, for plans providing disability, medical, supplemental unemployment and severance, or life insurance benefits, deductions may also be taken for additions to a reserve (referred to as a "qualified asset account") (Code Sec. 419A(a)).[242] Specifically, the employer may deduct contributions paid or accrued to a welfare benefit fund to the extent that the contributions do not exceed the "qualified cost" of the fund for its tax year ending with or within the tax year of the employer, reduced by the "after-tax income" of the fund for that tax year.

The qualified cost of the fund consists of two elements: the qualified direct cost and the allowable addition, if any, to a qualified asset account (Code Sec. 419(c)(1)).[243] A qualified asset account is one maintained by a welfare benefit fund for the payment of such costs as medical, supplemental unemployment benefits (SUB), severance pay and life insurance benefits including associated administrative costs (Code Sec. 419A(a)).[244] Generally, the allowable addition for a tax year is the amount that will bring the account

References are to Standard Federal Tax Reports; Tax Research Consultant; and Practical Tax Explanations.

239 ¶ 7420; COMPEN: 36,700; § 21,145
240 ¶ 7420; COMPEN: 6,610; § 4,065.25
241 ¶ 19,295; COMPEN: 42,100; § 9,345
242 ¶ 19,298; COMPEN: 42,152; § 9,345
243 ¶ 19,295; COMPEN: 42,106; § 9,345
244 ¶ 19,298; COMPEN: 42,150; § 9,345

to a level (the "account limit") that is reasonably and actuarially necessary to fund the payment of incurred but unpaid benefits and, in the case of post-retirement medical and life insurance benefits, to fund the payment of such benefits on a level basis over the working lives of the covered employees (based on current medical costs). For employers who do not support higher additions to a qualified asset account by actuarial certifications, there are safe harbor additions for the various benefits. Limits are placed on the level of disability and SUB or severance pay benefits that may be considered in establishing the account limit for such benefits.

The after-tax income of a welfare benefit plan is its gross income reduced by the sum of: (1) the deductions allowed by the Code that are directly connected with the production of that income and (2) the federal income tax imposed on the fund (Code Secs. 419).[245] The fund's gross income includes contributions and any other payments by employees. The fund's gross income does not include employer contributions because they already are accounted for in arriving at the qualified direct cost.

VEBAs. Voluntary employees' beneficiary associations (VEBAs), or Sec. 501(c)(9) trusts, are tax-exempt trusts designed primarily, within prescribed guidelines, to provide for: the payment of life benefits, payable on the death of a member or dependent, and sickness and accident benefits (medical benefits, disability income, clinical care by visiting nurses and medical care transportation).[246] VEBAs can also provide other benefits including: vacation benefits, vacation facilities, and reimbursement of vacation expenses; subsidies for recreational activities; child care facilities for preschool and school-age dependents; job readjustment allowances; income maintenance payments in the event of economic dislocation; education or training benefits or courses, including apprentice training programs; legal services through a qualified legal services plan; holiday pay and paid personal days; social, recreational, and cultural benefits for retirees; free membership in recreational organizations; and severance benefits. The advantages of a VEBA include the tax-free accumulation of funds for the provision of VEBA benefits and a deduction for employer contributions that are not taxable to the employee beneficiary at the time of contribution. The tax advantages, however, are predicated on restrictions governing participation, benefits provided, and the administration of the program.

Unfunded Welfare Benefits. Welfare benefits provided directly by an employer to an employee are deductible by the employer only in its tax year that includes the end of the tax year in which the employee includes the benefits in gross income or would include such benefits in gross income if they were taxable to the employee (Code Sec. 404(b)(2)(A)).[247] An employer may not accrue and deduct unpaid welfare benefits. This rule applies to any benefit which—if it were classified as compensation—would be deferred compensation. See ¶ 906 for information regarding the determination of compensation.

2190A. Accident and Health Insurance. Amounts received by employees under employer-financed accident and health plans may qualify for exclusion from gross income (Code Sec. 105; Reg. § 1.105-1).[248] Self-employed individuals are not employees, so exclusions for employer-provided contributions or benefits are not available to them. The exclusion applies to a state government plan (including the District of Columbia) (Code Sec. 105(e)(2); Reg. § 1.105-5),[249] as well as to a plan of a private employer. Amounts received by employees as reimbursement for medical care and payments (computed without regard to the period of absence from work) for permanent injury or loss of bodily function under an employer-financed accident or health plan are excludable. Money, other than reimbursements for medical expenses, received by an employee from accident or health insurance because of personal injuries or sickness generally is includible in income if the amounts (1) are attributable to contributions from the employer to an insurance plan and were not included in the employee's income or (2)

References are to Standard Federal Tax Reports; Tax Research Consultant; and Practical Tax Explanations.

[245] ¶ 19,295; COMPEN: 42,108; § 9,345

[246] ¶ 19,295; COMPEN: 42,204; § 33,005.05

[247] ¶ 18,330; COMPEN: 42,050; § 9,345

[248] ¶ 6700, ¶ 6701; COMPEN: 45,154; § 42,205

[249] ¶ 6700, ¶ 6708; COMPEN: 45,154; § 42,210

are paid directly by the employer (Code Sec. 105(a)).[250] Payments from an accident and health plan are also excludable from an employee's income to the extent that the plan providing the benefits is funded by the employee (Reg. § 1.105-1(c)).[251]

The exclusion also applies to medical care payments that are made to reimburse the taxpayer, not only for the taxpayer's own medical expenses, but also for the medical expenses of a spouse or any dependents. The reimbursement is excludable in full in the year of receipt without limitation as to amount even though the taxpayer does not actually pay the medical expenses until a later year. The exclusion does not apply to amounts deductible as medical expenses in any prior tax year (Reg. § 1.105-2).[252] Reimbursement of nondeductible expenses for cosmetic surgery is not excludable from gross income (¶ 1016).

Payments for permanent injury include payments for permanent loss of use of a member or function of the body, or the permanent disfigurement of the employee, a spouse, or a dependent. The payments must be based on the nature of the injury rather than on the length of time that the employee is absent from work (Code Sec. 105(c); Reg. § 1.105-3).[253]

Excess reimbursements paid to a highly compensated individual under an employer's self-insured medical reimbursement plan that fails to meet certain nondiscrimination requirements are includible in the individual's gross income (Code Sec. 105(h); Reg. § 1.105-11).[254] A highly compensated employee is an employee who is one of the five highest paid officers, who is among the highest paid 25 percent of all employees, or who is a shareholder owning more than 10 percent of the company's stock. The plan must not discriminate in terms of eligibility for coverage or in terms of benefits offered under the plan. For plan years beginning on or after September 23, 2010, similar nondiscrimination requirements apply to group health plans other than self-insured plans. However, the IRS and the other agencies responsible for administering the requirements have determined compliance will not be required until additional guidance is issued (Notice 2011-1).

The entire amount of a reimbursement with respect to a benefit that is available only to highly compensated individuals is treated as an excess reimbursement includible in income. In the case of a plan that discriminates in terms of eligibility, the includible excess reimbursement is equal to all the medical expenses for which the highly compensated individual was reimbursed times a fraction, the numerator of which is the total amount reimbursed to all participants who are highly compensated individuals and the denominator of which is the total amount reimbursed to all employees under the plan for such plan year. If the plan discriminates in terms of eligibility *and* benefits, any amount which is included in income by reason of the benefits not being available to all other participants is not to be taken into account in determining the excess reimbursements that result from the plan being discriminatory in terms of eligibility.

There is no eligibility discrimination if the plan benefits (1) at least 70 percent of all employees or 80 percent of all eligible employees if at least 70 percent of all employees are eligible or (2) a class of employees found by the IRS not to be discriminatory in favor of highly compensated individuals.

Certain employees, such as part-time workers, employees with less than three years of service, employees under age 25, and employees excluded as a result of a collective bargaining agreement, may be excluded from coverage. There is no benefits discrimination if the self-insured medical expense plan provides the same benefits for non-highly compensated employees as it does for highly compensated employees.

Group Health Plan. A group health plan that fails to satisfy continuation coverage requirements or pediatric vaccine health care coverage requirements may be subject to

References are to Standard Federal Tax Reports; Tax Research Consultant; and Practical Tax Explanations.

[250] ¶ 6700; COMPEN: 45,054, COMPEN: 45,058; § 42,225

[251] ¶ 6701; COMPEN: 45,152, COMPEN: 45,154; § 42,225

[252] ¶ 6703; INDIV: 33,408; § 42,225

[253] ¶ 6700, ¶ 6705; COMPEN: 45,302; § 42,225

[254] ¶ 6700, ¶ 6711; COMPEN: 45,100; § 42,230.10

an excise tax (Code Sec. 4980B). Excise taxes generally must be reported on Form 8928.[255]

Improved Coverage Requirements. Group health plans are subject to additional requirements effective September 23, 2010. These plans generally must provide coverage for children until they attain age 26 (Temp. Reg. § 54.9815-2714T). They cannot impose lifetime limits on essential benefits and must gradually eliminate annual limits on essential benefits for plan years prior to January 1, 2014 (Temp. Reg. § 54.9815-2711T). They cannot impose preexisting condition exclusions for children under age 19 and the prohibition extends to all individuals effective January 1, 2014 (Temporary Reg. § 54.9815-2704T). They may not retroactively rescind coverage except for non-payment, fraud, or misrepresentation (Temp. Reg. § 54.9815-2712T). Additional requirements apply to non-grandfathered plans such as coverage for certain preventive services (Temp. Reg. § 54.9815-2713T) and patient protections concerning choice of doctors and access to care (Temp. Reg. § 54.9815-2719AT).[256]

Railroad Unemployment Insurance. Benefits paid to an employee under the Railroad Unemployment Insurance Act for sick days are included in the employee's gross income unless an illness is due to an on-the-job injury (Code Sec. 105(i)).[257]

Government Prescription Drug Plans Subsidy. Employers are allowed to deduct fully all payments for retiree prescription drug plans. To encourage employers to offer retiree prescription drug plans, the federal government, under section 1860D-22 of the Social Security Act, provides an additional subsidy payment. To ensure the continuation of these retiree prescription drug plans during the implementation of improvements to Medicare supplemental insurance for prescription drugs, the subsidy payments received under section 1860D-22 of the Social Security Act are fully excludable from gross income and not taken into account when determining the appropriate deduction for maintaining a retiree prescription drug plan (Code Sec. 139A, prior to amendment by the Patient Protection and Affordable Care Act (P.L. 111-148) and the Health Care and Education Reconciliation Act of 2010 (P.L. 111-52)).

Effective for tax years beginning after December 31, 2012, the rule that allows employers to disregard the value of any subsidy payments received under section 1860D-22 of the Social Security Act in calculating the employer's deduction for retiree prescription drug costs is repealed (Code Sec. 139A, as amended by the P.L. 111-148 and P.L. 111-152). Thus, the amount otherwise allowable as a deduction for retiree prescription drug costs is reduced by the amount of the excludable subsidy payments received.

Medical Benefits for Children Under the Age of 27. Effective on March 30, 2010, children under the age of 27 are considered dependents of a taxpayer for purposes of the general exclusion for reimbursements for medical care expenses of an employee, spouse, and dependents under an employer-provided accident or health plan (Code Sec. 105(b)). A child includes a son, daughter, stepson, or stepdaughter of the taxpayer; a foster child placed with the taxpayer by an authorized placement agency or by judgment, decree, or other order of any court of competent jurisdiction; and a legally adopted child of the taxpayer or a child who has been lawfully placed with the taxpayer for legal adoption (Code Sec. 152(f)(1)).

COBRA Premium Assistance. Certain employers who provide health care benefits for their employees are required to offer certain employees who leave their position with the employer the opportunity to purchase continuing coverage, known as COBRA coverage. Individuals who became eligible to elect such coverage as a result of an involuntary termination of their employment during the period beginning September 1, 2008, and ending May 31, 2010, were required to pay only 35 percent of the premiums for the coverage. Premium assistance for eligible unemployed individuals ended on August 31, 2011. See ¶ 2653 for further discussion of COBRA premium assistance.

Employer Requirement for Providing Minimum Health Coverage. For months beginning after December 31, 2013, large employers who have at least one full-time employee

References are to Standard Federal Tax Reports; Tax Research Consultant; and Practical Tax Explanations.

[255] ¶ 34,600; COMPEN: 45,206; § 42,801

[256] ¶ 44,089K.02; COMPEN: 45,228; § 42,235.05

[257] ¶ 6700; COMPEN: 45,154; § 3,001

enrolled for that month in a qualified health plan for which a premium tax credit or cost-sharing reduction is allowed or paid for the employee, and that fail to offer their full-time employees the opportunity to enroll in minimum essential coverage under an eligible employer-sponsored plan for any month, are subject to an assessable payment (Code Sec. 4980H(a), as added and amended by P.L. 111-148 and amended by P.L. 111-152). The IRS has issued guidance in the form of safe-harbors to assist employers in determining an employee's full-time status, the affordability of coverage based on an employee's W-2 wages, and waiting periods (Notice 2012-58 modifying Notice 2012-17 and Notice 2011-73; Notice 2012-59).

Annual Fee on Health Insurance Providers. For calendar years after 2013, a fee is imposed on providers of insurance for any "United States health risk," which means the health risk of any individual who is a U.S. citizen, a U.S. resident (as defined by Code Sec. 7701(b)(1)(A)), or located in the United States (Act Sec. 9010 of P.L. 111-148).

Reporting. For calendar years beginning after 2013, every person who provides minimum essential health care coverage to an individual during a calendar year is required to file a return reporting such coverage, at such time as the Secretary of the Treasury may prescribe (Code Sec. 6055(a), as added by P.L. 111-148). For periods beginning after December 31, 2013, applicable large employers that are subject to the Code Sec. 4980H rules for shared responsibility regarding health coverage and certain employers that offer minimum essential coverage to their employees through an eligible employer-sponsored plan ("offering employers") are required to file a return reporting on such coverage at such time as the Secretary of the Treasury may prescribe (Code Sec. 6056(a), as added by P.L. 111-148).

Under a separate reporting requirement, the Code requires employers to disclose the aggregate cost of applicable employer-sponsored health care coverage provided to each employee on the employee's Form W-2 (Code Sec. 6051(a)(14)). The requirement is optional for the 2011 tax year, but is mandatory for the 2012 tax year (Notice 2012-9; Notice 2010-69). For certain small employers, the requirement is not mandatory until January 2014 (Notice 2012-9) (¶ 2567).

Disclosure of Return Information. The IRS is permitted to disclose certain return information with respect to program eligibility determinations and verification for the premium assistance tax credit or cost sharing reduction amounts provided to qualified individuals through a Health Insurance Exchange (Code Sec. 6103(l)(21), as amended by P.L. 111-148 and P.L. 111-152).

Indian Health Care Benefits. For benefits and coverage provided after March 23, 2010, the amount of qualified health care benefits provided by Indian tribal governments to a member of an Indian tribe, the member's spouse or dependents are excluded from the beneficiary's gross income (Code Sec. 139D). A qualified health care benefit includes:

- any health service provided or purchased by the Indian Health Service through a grant, contract or compact with an Indian tribe or tribal organization, or through a program funded by the Indian Health Service;
- medical care provided or purchased, or reimbursements for such medical care, by an Indian tribe or tribal organization for a member of an Indian tribe, member's spouse or dependent;
- coverage under an accident or health insurance plan provided by an Indian tribe or tribal organization for medical care to a member of an Indian tribe, member's spouse or dependent; and
- any other medical care provided by an Indian tribe or tribal organization that supplements, replaces or substitutes for medical care programs and services provided by the federal government to Indian tribes or their members.

The exclusion does not apply to Indian health care benefits that are not includible in the beneficiary's gross income under another provision in the Code or to any benefit for which thebeneficiary may claim a deduction.

2190B. Disability Benefits. Disability income plans are employer plans, some mandated by state law, that provide full or partial income replacement for employees who become disabled (Code Sec. 105(c); Reg. § 1.105-4). Employees generally cannot exclude both employer contributions and benefits paid under a disability plan from income. To the extent that the employer pays for the cost of coverage, benefits are generally taxable to employees (Code Sec. 105(a); ¶ 851). For instance, a lump-sum payment received under an employer-employee contributory disability insurance policy and paid with reference to a permanently disabling illness is excludable to the extent that it is attributable to the employee's contributions.[258]

Certain funds can be treated as amounts received through accident or health insurance and may be treated as excludable, such as benefits received under an insurance contract indemnifying an individual against income lost by reason of loss of the use of his body or a portion of his body, or payments under an income replacement policy in the event of illness.[259] Premiums paid to cover certain overhead expenses during a period of disability may be deductible (Rev. Rul. 55-264; Rev. Rul. 58-90). As to excludability of amounts attributable to employer's contributions, see ¶ 2190A.

2190C. Life Insurance Benefits. One of the most common benefits an employer may provide is insurance on the life of the employee. An employer may often provide this coverage for an employee, usually on a group basis (¶ 721), for considerably less than individual coverage because of life insurance rate structures. In some cases, an employer may be able to secure coverage for an employee when age and health precludes the employee from obtaining individual coverage. The employer is generally entitled to deduct amounts spent on premiums, except to the extent that the employer is the beneficiary (¶ 909). Split-dollar insurance is another common funding arrangement for life insurance benefits. Under this arrangement, the employer and the employee join in purchasing an insurance contract on the employee's life. See ¶ 2192C for life insurance benefits provided to domestic partners.

2190D. Vacation Pay. A vacation pay plan is an employer plan that provides compensation to employees for specified periods of vacation, including vacation time that has been earned but not actually taken. Such a plan also generally includes compensation for specified holidays, whether or not those days are actually taken.[260]

Vacation pay plans, like other employee benefit plans, can take a wide variety of forms: the benefits may be vested or unvested; the plan may be funded or unfunded; and the plan may be a single-employer plan or a multiemployer plan. Vacation pay is taxable and is subject to income tax wage withholding (Code Sec. 61; Reg. § 31.3401(a)-1(b)(3)). Vacation pay is also subject to Social Security (FICA) and federal unemployment (FUTA) taxes (Code Sec. 3121(a); Code Sec. 3306(b)).

Vacation pay is generally deductible as reasonable compensation for prior services rendered (Code Sec. 162; Reg. § 1.162-7). An additional discussion of vacation pay deductions can be found at ¶ 1549.

2190E. Leave Sharing. The IRS will not assert that an employee who deposits leave in an employer-sponsored leave bank under a major disaster leave sharing plan realizes income with respect to the deposited leave, provided the plan treats the payments to a leave recipient as wages subject to income tax withholding and payroll taxes and the plan meets specific requirements (Notice 2006-59). However, a contributing employee may not claim an expense, charitable contribution, or loss deduction for the contributed leave.[261] While amounts deposited in a leave bank to be used by employees experiencing medical emergencies are not taxable to contributing employees, they are included in the gross income of the recipients subject to income tax withholding and payroll taxes (Rev. Rul. 90-29). The IRS has not granted favorable tax treatment to other leave-sharing plans. Consequently, the value of leave contributed to such plans remains taxable to contributing employees.

References are to Standard Federal Tax Reports; Tax Research Consultant; and Practical Tax Explanations.

[258] ¶ 6662.26; COMPEN: 45,154.10; § 42,215

[259] ¶ 6662.245; COMPEN: 45,154, COMPEN: 45,304; § 42,205

[260] ¶ 5507.47; COMPEN: 12,212; § 22,210.10

[261] ¶ 11,620.522; COMPEN: 6054; § 3,005.25, § 22,210.10

2190F. Severance Pay. A severance pay plan is a plan that provides payments to employees upon termination of employment. Depending upon the facts and circumstances, severance pay arrangements can qualify as a welfare plan or a retirement plan or may be exempt from certain federal requirements. Generally, the payments are proportionate to length of employment.[262] The plan may be a permanent program or a limited program, e.g., an "open-window" program that offers a group of employees cash payments, increased pension benefits, or both as inducements to voluntarily retire or to separate from employment within a certain time period. The plan may cover voluntary separations, involuntary separations, or both, and may place conditions on payment of benefits, e.g., no benefits are provided if the employee goes to work for a competitor or for a successor employer. In addition, the plan may deny benefits if the employee is terminated for cause.

Golden Parachutes. In a golden parachute agreement, a corporate employer states that it will pay a key employee or a number of key employees an amount over and above other compensation in the event of a change in ownership or control of the corporation or a substantial portion of the corporation's assets (¶ 907). The tax consequences applicable to golden parachute payments are triggered merely by the payment of the requisite amount of compensation, and a termination of employment is not literally required. As a practical matter, however, golden parachute payment provisions in an employment agreement or employer's benefits plan usually are designed to be triggered upon loss of employment within a designated period of time following the acquisition of the employer.

Work/Life Benefits

2192. Introduction. The term "work/life benefits" evolved from the phrase "work/family benefits," or "family-friendly benefits," which described employer-sponsored benefit programs or initiatives designed to help working parents juggle home life and work life. Initially, work/family benefits were geared towards providing parents with dependable and affordable child care and/or flexible work arrangements. Reasons for offering work/life benefits include: employee recruitment and retention; employee morale, performance and productivity; reduced absenteeism; and increased employee commitment. Examples of work/life benefits include: child and dependent care (¶ 2192B); wellness/health/education programs such as employee assistance programs (¶ 2192E) and educational assistance (¶ 2192D); other benefits such as adoption assistance (¶ 2192A); and domestic partner benefits (¶ 2192C).

2192A. Adoption Assistance Programs. Qualified adoption expenses paid to a third party or reimbursed to an employee by an employer under a written adoption assistance program are excludable from the employee's gross income (Code Sec. 137).[263] An adoption assistance program is a written plan that (1) benefits employees who qualify under rules set up by the employer which do not favor highly compensated employees or their dependents; (2) does not pay more than five percent of its payments each year to shareholders or owners of more than five percent of the stock; (3) provides for adequate notice to employees of their eligibility; and (4) requires employees to provide reasonable substantiation of qualified expenses that are to be paid or reimbursed.

In general, the rules for the exclusion parallel the rules for the adoption expenses credit. Thus, qualifying children, special needs children, and qualified adoption expenses are all defined as they are for purposes of the credit (¶ 1307).

For 2012, the aggregate amount of payments that may be excluded from income (for both special needs adoptions and other adoptions) is $12,650 (Rev. Proc. 2011-52). The exclusion is subject to phase out for higher income taxpayers the same as for the adoption credit (¶ 1307). For 2012, the phase-out begins at $189,710 and is complete at $229,710 (Rev. Proc. 2011-52). Both the credit and the exclusion may apply to the same adoption, but not the same expenses (¶ 1307).

References are to Standard Federal Tax Reports; Tax Research Consultant; and Practical Tax Explanations.

[262] ¶ 5507.297; COMPEN: 27,202; § 9,345

[263] ¶ 7600; COMPEN: 36,650; § 4,025

Comment: Absent further legislation, the exclusion will be reduced to a maximum of $6,000 and will only be available for special needs adoptions. It will also be phased out for taxpayers with MAGI between $75,000 and $115,000. The dollar and income limitation amounts for the adoption credit will also no longer be subject to adjustments for inflation beginning after 2012.

2192B. Child and Dependent Care Benefits. Up to $5,000 of child or dependent care assistance services that are paid by an employer and furnished pursuant to a written plan generally are not includible in an employee's gross income (Code Sec. 129).[264] The individual being cared for must be either:

- a dependent of the taxpayer that has not yet attained the age of 13;
- a dependent of the taxpayer who is physically or mentally incapable of caring for themselves and who resides with the taxpayer in their principal place of abode for more than six months of the year; or
- the spouse of the taxpayer who is physically or mentally incapable of caring for themselves and who resides with the taxpayer in their principal place of abode for more than six months of the year (Code Sec. 21(b)(1)).

A dependent care assistance plan generally must not discriminate in favor of employees who are highly compensated. However, if a plan would qualify as a dependent care assistance program except for the fact that it fails to meet discrimination, eligibility, or other requirements of Code Sec. 129(d), then despite the failure the plan may still be treated as a dependent care assistance program in the case of employees who are not highly compensated. The amount excludable from gross income cannot exceed $5,000 ($2,500 in the case of a separate return by a married individual). The amount of any payment exceeding these limits is includible in gross income for the tax year in which the dependent care services were provided, even if payment for the services is received in a subsequent tax year (Code Sec. 129(a)(2)(B)).[265]

The exclusion cannot exceed the earned income of an unmarried employee or the earned income of the lower-earning spouse of married employees. The exclusion does not apply unless the name, address, and taxpayer identification number of the person performing the child or dependent care services are included on the return of the employee benefiting from the exclusion (Code Sec. 129(e)(9)). However, the exclusion may be claimed even though the information is not provided if it can be shown that the taxpayer exercised due diligence in attempting to provide this information. See ¶ 1301 regarding the child and dependent care credit.

2192C. Domestic Partner Benefits. Typical domestic partner benefits offered by employers include health care insurance (medical, dental, vision), access to an employee assistance plan, and dependent life insurance. Employers often require a written affidavit affirming the relationship and may require documents (joint mortgage or lease, proof of registration under a local ordinance, drivers' license, tax returns, bank statements, or joint credit statements).

Health benefits are tax free for spouses and dependents. However, the cost of providing the benefits is included in an employee's income if the domestic partner is not a Code Sec. 152 dependent. Additionally, if a domestic partner is not a Code Sec. 152 dependent, contributions for a partner's coverage must be on an after-tax basis, and the domestic partner is not eligible for reimbursement from health care FSAs. See ¶ 137 for a discussion of who qualifies as a taxpayer's dependent.

2192D. Educational Assistance. An educational assistance program is a tax-favored employer-sponsored plan under which the employer pays for the educational expenses of employees, subject to various limitations. The term "employees" is broadly applied and includes employees who have been voluntarily or involuntarily terminated for any reason (Rev. Rul. 96-41). Payments made to an employee for educational expenses for courses below graduate level are excluded from the gross income of the

References are to Standard Federal Tax Reports; Tax Research Consultant; and Practical Tax Explanations.

[264] ¶ 7380; COMPEN: 36,600; § 20,010

[265] ¶ 7380; COMPEN: 36,600; § 20,010

employee. This exclusion also applies to expenses related to graduate level courses (Code Sec. 127).

Up to $5,250 of payments received by an employee for tuition, fees, books, supplies, etc., under an employer's educational assistance program may be excluded from gross income (Code Sec. 127; Reg. § 1.127-1).[266] Excludable assistance payments may not cover tools or supplies that the employee retains after completion of the course or the cost of meals, lodging, or transportation. Although the courses covered by the plan need not be job related, an exception applies to courses involving sports, games, or hobbies. These courses may only be covered if they involve the employer's business or are required as part of a degree program (Reg. § 1.127-2(c)).[267]

> **Comment:** Absent further legislation, for tax years beginning after December 31, 2012, the exclusion from gross income for income tax purposes under Code Sec. 127 and from wages for employment tax purposes under Code Sec. 3121(a)(18) of up to $5,250 annually will no longer apply. Thus, employer provided educational assistance may be excluded from an employee's gross income and wages beginning in 2013 only if it qualifies as a working condition fringe benefit (¶ 2188D).

Reports and Records. An employer who maintains an educational assistance plan must maintain records and file an information return (Form 5500) for the plan (Code Sec. 6039D). However, the reporting requirement for educational assistance plans has been *suspended* (Notice 2002-24).[268]

2192E. Employee Assistance Programs. Employee assistance programs (EAPs) are generally part of an employer's overall health promotion or wellness programs and may be one of several methods used to reduce health care costs. Although many EAPs are initiated to deal with drug and alcohol abuse, EAPs may also address family problems, stress, job termination, finances, and retirement. Because EAPs commonly provide treatment for drug and alcohol abuse and other similar health and medical problems, they often qualify as employee welfare benefit plans (¶ 2190). However, if an EAP merely provides referrals and does not pay for any services or benefits, the EAP will not be deemed to be an employee welfare benefit plan (PWBA Opinion Letter 91-26A). See ¶ 2192C for employee assistance benefits provided to domestic partners.

Cafeteria Plans and Flexible Spending Arrangements (FSAs)

2195. Cafeteria Plans. Cafeteria plans are employer-sponsored benefit packages that offer employees a choice between taking cash and receiving qualified benefits, such as accident and health coverage, group-term life insurance coverage, or coverage under a dependent care program (Code Sec. 125; Proposed Reg. § 1.125-1).[269] No amount is included in the income of a cafeteria plan participant who chooses among the benefits of the plan; however, if a participant chooses cash, it is includible in gross income as compensation. If qualified benefits are chosen, they are excludable to the extent allowed by law. A cafeteria plan may include: accident and health insurance (¶ 2192A), dependent care assistance program (¶ 2192B), disability coverage (¶ 2190B), group-term life insurance (¶ 2190C), health savings account (HSAs) (¶ 2197B), and 401(k) plans (¶ 2106).

A cafeteria plan cannot offer anything other than cash or qualified benefits. Qualified benefits are benefits that are specifically excludable from gross income. The term qualified benefits includes any group-term life insurance includible in gross income (¶ 721). A qualified benefit does *not* include benefits under Archer medical savings accounts (¶ 2197C), scholarships and fellowship grants (¶ 879), educational assistance benefits provided by an employer (¶ 2192D), and excludable fringe benefits (¶ 2188). Also, qualified benefits do not include products that are advertised, marketed, or offered as long-term care insurance.

References are to Standard Federal Tax Reports; Tax Research Consultant; and Practical Tax Explanations.

[266] ¶ 7350, ¶ 7351; COMPEN: 36,554; § 20,101

[267] ¶ 7352; COMPEN: 36,554.05; § 20,105.15

[268] ¶ 35,660; PENALTY: 3,208.20; § 39,155.25

[269] ¶ 7320, ¶ 7321; COMPEN: 51,000; § 20,801

Highly compensated employees are not entitled to exclude any benefit attributable to a plan year in which the plan discriminates in favor of the highly compensated employees with respect to participation, contributions, and benefits. Key employees are not entitled to exclude any benefit attributable to a plan year in which the statutory qualified benefits provided to key employees exceed 25 percent of the total of such benefits provided to all employees under the plan. In such cases, the benefits must be included in the gross income of the highly compensated employee or key employee for the tax year in which the plan year ends (Code Sec. 125(b)). Reports on cafeteria plans are required (Code Sec. 6039D).[270] However, the reporting requirement for cafeteria plans has been *suspended* (Notice 2002-24).

Generally, a plan that provides deferred compensation is *not* included in the definition of a cafeteria plan. However, elective contributions under a qualified cash or deferred arrangement, profit-sharing plan, stock bonus plan, or contributions by an educational institution for post-retirement group life insurance are permitted.

2195A. Simple Cafeteria Plans. In years beginning after December 31, 2010, certain small employers' cafeteria plans can qualify as simple cafeteria plans, under which the applicable nondiscrimination requirements of a classic cafeteria plan are treated as satisfied (Code Sec. 125(j)).[271] A simple cafeteria plan is a cafeteria plan established and maintained by an eligible employer that meets certain contribution, eligibility and participation requirements. An applicable nondiscrimination requirement that will be deemed as met by an employer establishing a simple cafeteria plan is any nondiscrimination requirement applicable to a classic cafeteria plan (¶ 2195), group-term life insurance (¶ 721), a health plan (¶ 2190A), or a dependent care assistance program (¶ 2192B).

Eligible Employers. To be eligible to establish a simple cafeteria plan, an employer must have employed an average of 100 or fewer employers on business days during either of the two preceding years. An employer that was not in existence throughout the preceding year may be considered as an eligible employer if it reasonably expects to average 100 or fewer employees on business days during the current year. If an employer has 100 or fewer employees for the year and establishes a simple cafeteria plan, then it can be treated as meeting the requirement for any subsequent year even if the employer employs more than 100 employees in the subsequent year. However, this exception does not apply if the employer employs an average of 200 or more employees during the subsequent year (Code Sec. 125(j)(5)(C)(ii)).

For purposes of determining the qualification of a business that has recently changed ownership, the fact that the previous owner had 100 or fewer employees in a preceding year can be used to determine eligibility of the current ownership to establish a simple cafeteria plan. Also, any person treated as a single employer for purposes of the work opportunity credit (¶ 1365G) or for purposes of deferred compensation rules for leased employees under Code Sec. 414(n) or Code Sec. 414(o) shall be treated as one person for purposes of simple cafeteria plans.

Contribution Requirements. The contribution requirements are met if the employer is required by the plan, regardless of whether a qualified employee makes any salary reduction contribution, to make a contribution to provide qualified benefits on behalf of each qualified employee in an amount equal to: (1) a uniform percentage (not less than two percent) of the employee's compensation for the year or (2) an amount not less than the lesser of: (a) six percent of the employee's compensation for the plan year or (b) twice the amount of the salary reduction contributions of each qualified employee (Code Sec. 125(j)(3)). If the employer bases the satisfaction of the contribution requirements on the second option, it will not be treated as met if the rate of contributions with respect to any salary reduction contribution of a highly compensated or key employee is greater than that with respect to any other employee.

Employee Eligibility and Participation Requirements. The minimum eligibility and participation requirements are met if all employees who had at least 1,000 hours of

References are to Standard Federal Tax Reports; Tax Research Consultant; and Practical Tax Explanations.

[270] ¶ 35,660; COMPEN: 51,058; § 39,155.25

[271] ¶ 7320, ¶ 7320; COMPEN: 51,250; § 20,840.05

service for the preceding plan year are eligible to participate and if each employee eligible to participate may elect any benefit under the plan, subject to terms and conditions applicable to all participants (Code Sec. 125(j)(4)). An employer may elect to exclude from the plan, regardless of the satisfaction of the 1,000 hour requirement, employees who have not attained the age of 21 before the close of the plan year, who have less than one year of service with the employer as of any day during the plan year, who are covered under a collective bargaining agreement if there is evidence that the benefits covered under the plan were the subject of good faith bargaining between employee representatives and the employer, or are nonresident aliens working outside the United States whose income did not come from a U.S. source.

2196. Flexible Spending Arrangements (FSAs). A flexible spending arrangement (FSA) is a benefit that provides employees with coverage under which specified, incurred expenses may be reimbursed subject to reimbursement maximums and other reasonable conditions. Flexible spending arrangements are sometimes referred to as flexible spending accounts. These arrangements allow employees to make pre-tax contributions to FSA accounts for reimbursement of health and/or dependent care expenses. However, the employee runs the risk of forfeiture of any unused contributions. Traditionally, any amounts not spent before the end of the year were forfeited; the "use or lose rule" has been eased somewhat in Notice 2005-42; Proposed Reg. § 1.125-1(e)(1). Cafeteria plans may allow the use of a prior year's contributions to a flexible spending account to reimburse expenses incurred during a grace period of not more than two and one-half months. Thus, if a cafeteria plan provides for a grace period, funds contributed during one year can be used to reimburse medical expenses incurred through March 15 of the next year.

For tax years prior to 2011, amounts contributed to a health care FSA could be used to reimburse employees for purchases of over-the-counter medications. However, for tax years beginning after 2010, the cost incurred for a medicine or drug will be treated as a qualified medical expense for purposes of reimbursement through a health care FSA only if the medicine is a prescribed drug determined without regard to whether such drug is available without a prescription or is insulin (Code Sec. 106(f); Rev. Rul. 2010-23, obsoleting Rev. Rul. 2003-102).

In order to qualify as an FSA, a benefit program must provide employees with coverage under which: (1) specified incurred expenses may be reimbursed, subject to reimbursement maximums and any other reasonable conditions; and (2) the maximum amount of reimbursement that is reasonably available to a participant for a period of coverage is not substantially in excess of the total salary reduction and employer flex-credit for such participant's coverage (Prop. Reg. § 1.125-5(a)).

Beginning after December 31, 2012, a health care FSA will not be a qualified benefit under a cafeteria plan unless the plan provides for a $2,500 maximum salary reduction contribution to the FSA (Code Sec. 125(i)). The $2,500 limit applies to the plan year of the cafeteria plan rather than to the employer or employee's tax year (Notice 2012-40). If the plan does allow salary reductions in excess of $2,500, then an employee will be subject to tax on distributions from the health FSA, eliminating any of the tax benefits of health FSA contributions. For tax years beginning after 2013, the $2,500 limitation will be adjusted annually for inflation.

Health Flexible Spending Arrangements for Reservists. Reservists called into active duty may have penalty-free access to unused amounts from health FSAs if allowed by their employer's plan (Code Sec. 125(h)). Health FSA withdrawals by reservists called to active duty are permitted for any purpose, not just for medical or child care expenses.

Family and Medical Leave Act. The Family and Medical Leave Act (P.L. 103-3) (FMLA) imposes certain requirements on employers regarding coverage, including family coverage, under group health plans for employees taking FMLA leave and regarding the restoration of benefits to employees who return from FMLA leave. Reg. § 1.125-3 provides guidance on the effect of the FMLA on the operation of cafeteria plans.

American Health Benefit Exchange Plans. The Patient Protection and Affordable Care Act (P.L. 111-148) requires that each state provide, by January 1, 2014, an

American Health Benefit Exchange and Small Business Health Options Program (SHOP Exchange), under which qualified individuals and qualified small business employers will have access to health plans. In years beginning after December 31, 2013, qualified health plans offered through such an exchange cannot be provided by employers through a cafeteria plan (Code Sec. 125(f)(3), as added by P.L. 111-148).

There are exceptions to this general prohibition. First, Exchange-eligible employers can offer such plans through a cafeteria plan (Code Sec. 125(f)(3)(B), as added by P.L. 111-148). An Exchange-eligible employer is, in tax years beginning after December 31, 2013, a small employer electing to make all of its full-time employees eligible for one or more qualified health plans offered in the small group market through an Exchange (Act Sec. 1312(f)(2)(A) of P.L. 111-148). A small employer is an employer who employed an average of at least one, but not more that 100, employees on business days during the preceding plan year and employs at least one employee on the first day of the current plan year (Act Sec. 1304(b)(2) of P.L. 111-148). The small group market is the health insurance market under which employees obtain health insurance coverage through a group health plan maintained by a small employer (Act Sec. 1304(a)(3) of P.L. 111-148).

Beginning in 2017, the definition of an Exchange-eligible employer is expanded to include large employers in addition to small employers. This will allow all employers to offer an Exchange plan through a cafeteria plan (Act Sec. 1312(f)(2)(B) of P.L. 111-148).

Consumer-Driven Health Plans

2197. Introduction. Consumer-driven health plans (CDHPs) typically link a high deductible health plan with a tax-favored account, such as a health savings account (HSA) (¶ 2197B), an Archer Medical Savings Account (MSA) (¶ 2197C), or a health reimbursement arrangement (HRA) (¶ 2197A). CDHPs are also referred to as consumer-directed health plans and, by some, as a defined contribution health plan. Typically, CDHPs are offered as a choice to employees along side of another medical plan.

2197A. Health Reimbursement Arrangements (HRAs). Under a health reimbursement arrangement (HRA), an employer funds an account for employees from which employees can pay for their medical expenses or health insurance premiums. Under the arrangement, the HRA: (1) is paid for solely by the employer and not provided through a salary reduction arrangement or cafeteria plan; (2) reimburses the employee for medical care expenses incurred by the employee and the employee's spouse and dependents; and (3) provides reimbursements up to a maximum dollar amount for a coverage period with any unused portion of the maximum dollar amount carried forward to increase the maximum reimbursement available in later coverage periods.

Employer-provided contributions and medical care reimbursements made under a reimbursement arrangement that allows unused amounts to be carried forward are excludable from an employee's gross income (¶ 2190) (Rev. Rul. 2006-36, amplifying Rev. Rul. 2002-41). The temptation to convert taxable compensation to tax-favored HRA benefits is negated by a prohibition against cash outs and funding through a salary reduction (Rev. Rul. 2006-36, amplifying Notice 2002-45). An HRA is treated as an employer self-funded accident or health plan in that amounts contributed by the employer and amounts received by the employee qualify for exclusions from employee income (Code Sec. 105(a)).

An HRA can be set up in conjunction with a group health insurance plan with the HRA providing a source for the employee share of the premium as well as medical expenses not covered by the insurance plan. It can be set up in conjunction with a flexible spending account (FSA) so that FSA funds are used first, reducing the risk that FSA funds would be lost. An HRA can be set up as a stand-alone arrangement to pay for health insurance premiums of individually contracted health insurance or for medical expenses not covered by the insurance.

2197B. Health Savings Accounts (HSAs). A health savings account (HSA) is a trust established for the exclusive purpose of paying for qualified medical expenses of the account beneficiary. HSAs can be established by employees through an employer's cafeteria plan (¶ 2195).

Eligibility. To be eligible to establish an HSA in any month, an individual:

(1) must be covered by a high deductible health plan on the first day of the month,

(2) must not be covered by any other plan that is not a high deductible health plan,

(3) must not be enrolled in Medicare, and

(4) cannot be claimed as a dependent on another person's tax return.

However, the individual is still eligible if he or she is covered for any benefit provided by permitted insurance or has permitted coverage by insurance or otherwise. Permitted insurance is generally limited to insurance related to workers compensation liabilities, tort liabilities and liabilities arising from property ownership (i.e., automobile insurance); insurance for a specified disease or illness; or insurance that provides a fixed payment for each period of hospitalization. Permitted coverage is coverage for accidents, disability, dental care, vision care or long-term care. Individual eligibility for an HSA is determined on a monthly basis (Code Sec. 223(c)(1)).[272] Coverage under a health flexible spending arrangement (FSA) (¶ 2196) is disregarded for purposes of determining an individual's HSA eligibility after the end of the FSA plan year if (1) the balance in the individual's FSA at the end of the plan year is zero or (2) the individual is making a qualified HSA distribution equal to the remaining balance (Code Sec. 223(c)(1)(B)(iii)).[273]

A taxpayer who is an eligible individual for an HSA on the first day of the last month of a tax year is treated as eligible during every month of that tax year so the annual limit on deductible contributions for that taxpayer is not reduced. A recapture provision applies if the taxpayer ceases to be eligible during the period beginning with the last month of the tax year and ending on the last day of the 12th month following that month. If recapture applies, the taxpayer must include in gross income an amount equal to the amount actually contributed minus the sum of the monthly contribution limits to which the individual would otherwise have been entitled. An additional 10-percent tax is imposed on this amount. Recapture does not apply if the taxpayer is ineligible due to death or disability (Code Sec. 223(b)(8); Notice 2008-52).[274]

Dependent. For purposes of an HSA, a dependent is as defined in Code Sec. 152 (¶ 137), but without regard to whether the dependent claims dependency exemptions, files a joint return or has gross income in excess of the exemption amount (Code Sec. 223(d)(2)(A)). If certain conditions are met, the IRS will treat the child of divorced or separated parents as a dependent of both parents for HSA purposes, without a declaration by the custodial parent releasing the claim to the dependency exemption (¶ 139A) (Rev. Proc. 2008-48).[275]

Contributions. Contributions to HSAs are deductible in determining adjusted gross income. Workers with high-deductible health insurance coverage can deduct up to $3,100 (for self-only coverage) or $6,250 (for family coverage) for 2012 contributions to their Health Savings Accounts (HSAs) (Code Sec. 223; Rev. Proc. 2011-32). For 2013, the dollar limits are $3,250 and $6,450, respectively (Rev. Proc. 2012-26). Excess contributions are includible in gross income and subject to a six-percent excise tax. Individual eligibility for an HSA is determined on a monthly basis. On the first day of any month an individual must be covered by a high-deductible health plan and not covered under a non-high-deductible health plan.

References are to Standard Federal Tax Reports; Tax Research Consultant; and Practical Tax Explanations.

[272] ¶ 12,776; INDIV: 42,460.05; § 42,510.05

[273] ¶ 12,776; INDIV: 42,454; § 42,510.05

[274] ¶ 12,776, ¶ 12,785.25; COMPEN: 45,064.15, INDIV: 42,452.05; § 42,515.10

[275] ¶ 6702.27; PLANIND: 3,254.05, INDIV: 42,460.05; § 1,215.40

Individuals who reach age 55 by the end of the tax year can increase their annual contributions by $1,000 (Code Sec. 223(b)(3)). Contributions cannot be made after the participant attains age 65, but withdrawals for qualified medical expenses continue to be excludable from gross income. Contributions, including catch-up contributions, cannot be made to a HSA after the participant is enrolled in Medicare (Notice 2008-59, amplifying Notice 2004-2; Notice 2004-50).[276] If a husband and wife are each eligible to make catch-up contributions, each spouse can make such contributions only to his or her own HSA. The maximum annual contribution limit for a married couple is the statutory maximum for family coverage where (1) one spouse has family coverage and the other spouse has self-only coverage, regardless of whether the family coverage includes the spouse with self-only coverage; or (2) both spouses have family coverage, regardless of whether each spouse's family coverage covers the other spouse (Notice 2008-59). A married taxpayer covered under an HDHP can contribute to an HSA for use with qualifying out-of-pocket medical expenses even if his or her spouse's coverage is nonqualifying family coverage, as long as the taxpayer is not covered by the spouse's policy (Rev. Rul. 2005-25).

High-Deductible Health Plan. A high-deductible health plan (HDHP) is defined as a plan with a minimum annual deductible of at least $1,200 for self-only coverage ($2,400 for family coverage) for 2012. For 2013, there must be a minimum annual deductible of at least $1,250 for self-only coverage ($2,500 for family coverage). For 2012, the annual out-of-pocket expenses cannot exceed $6,050 for self-only coverage ($12,100 for family coverage) (Rev. Proc. 2011-32). For 2013, the annual out-of-pocket expenses cannot exceed $6,250 for self-only coverage ($12,500 for family coverage) (Rev. Proc. 2012-26). Out-of-pocket expenses include deductibles, co-payments and other amounts (other than premiums) that must be paid for plan benefits (Code Sec. 223(c)(2)(A); Notice 2008-59, amplifying Notice 2004-2).[277]

Distributions. Amounts are excludable from gross income if paid or distributed from an HSA that is used exclusively to pay the qualified medical expenses of the account beneficiary, his or her spouse or dependents (Notice 2008-59, amplifying Notice 2004-2).[278] In 2011 and in later years, the cost incurred for a medicine or drug will be treated as a qualified medical expense for purposes of a distribution from an HSA only if the medicine is insulin or a prescribed drug. Distributions to pay for over-the-counter medicines may not be excluded from the employee's gross income and will be subject to the additional penalty (Code Sec. 223(d)(2)). Distributions not so used are subject to income tax and a 20-percent additional tax (10 percent before 2011), unless made after the beneficiary reaches age 65, dies or becomes disabled (Code Sec. 223(f)(4)). Similar limitations apply to Archer MSAs (¶ 2197C) as well as health FSAs and HRAs. The additional tax is not treated as a tax liability for purposes of the alternative minimum tax (¶ 1420) (Code Secs. 26(b)(2)(S) and 55(c)(1)). Qualified medical expenses are generally the same expenses that qualify for the medical expenses deduction. Premiums for long-term care and coverage during periods of unemployment, whether through COBRA or not, also qualify.

Married Taxpayers. Generally, for married taxpayers, if either spouse has family coverage under any health plan, then both will be treated as having only family coverage under the plan. If each spouse has family coverage under different plans, then both spouses are treated as having coverage under the plan with the lowest deductible (Code Sec. 223(b)(5)). If only one spouse is an eligible individual, only that spouse may contribute to an HSA (Notice 2004-50). If one or both spouses have family coverage, the contribution limit is the lowest deductible amount, divided equally between the spouses unless they agree on a different division, and further reduced by any contribution to an Archer MSA. Both spouses may make the catch-up contributions for individuals age 55 or over without exceeding the family coverage limit (Notice 2008-59, amplifying Notice 2004-2). If a husband and wife are each eligible to make catch-up contributions, each spouse can make such contributions only to his or her own HSA. The maximum annual

References are to Standard Federal Tax Reports; Tax Research Consultant; and Practical Tax Explanations.

[276] ¶ 12,785.25; INDIV: 42,454.05; § 42,540

[277] ¶ 12,776, ¶ 12,785.25; INDIV: 42,450; § 42,510.10

[278] ¶ 12,785.25; INDIV: 42,460; § 42,515.10, § 42,520.10, § 42,525

contribution limit for a married couple is the statutory maximum for family coverage where:

(1) one spouse has family coverage and the other spouse has self-only coverage, regardless of whether the family coverage includes the spouse with self-only coverage; or

(2) both spouses have family coverage, regardless of whether each spouse's family coverage covers the other spouse (Notice 2008-59).

A married taxpayer covered under an HDHP can contribute to an HSA for use with qualifying out-of-pocket medical expenses even if his or her spouse's coverage is nonqualifying family coverage as long as the taxpayer is not covered by the spouse's policy (Rev. Rul. 2005-25).[279]

Contributions by Partnership or S Corporation. Contributions made by a partnership or S corporation to a partner's or shareholder's HSA are generally treated as payments to the partner or shareholder and are includible in gross income. The individual partner or shareholder may treat the contribution as an above-the-line deduction. However, a contribution to the partner's HSA by the partnership for services rendered is treated as a guaranteed payment, and the partnership may deduct the contribution as a business expense. Similarly, a contribution by the S corporation to a two-percent shareholder's HSA for services rendered is deductible by the S corporation and included in the shareholders income (Notice 2005-8).[280]

Distributions to Fund HSAs. An employer can make a one-time "qualified HSA distribution" from an employee's health flexible spending arrangement (FSA) or health reimbursement account (HRA) to the employee's HSA. Also, an eligible individual can elect a one-time funding distribution directly from his or her individual retirement arrangement (IRA) to his or her HSA (¶ 2153G). The amount that can otherwise be contributed to the HSA for the tax year of the distribution is reduced by the amount contributed from the IRA, and the individual cannot deduct the distribution amount as an HSA contribution (Code Sec. 223(b)(4)(C); Notice 2008-51).[281]

MSAs. Archer MSAs generally cannot be established after 2007, although eligible individuals can still make and receive Archer MSA contributions, and individuals can still receive Archer MSA distributions (¶ 2197C).

The IRS has issued guidance on a broad range of HSAs topics in Notice 2008-52 and Notice 2008-59.[282]

2197C. Archer Medical Savings Accounts (MSAs). An Archer MSA is a tax-exempt trust or custodial account with a financial institution that is used solely to pay the unreimbursed health care expenses of the account holder or the account holder's spouse or dependents (IRS Publication 969). Employees of small businesses and self-employed individuals can take advantage of existing Archer medical savings accounts (MSAs) to pay health care expenses, provided that accounts are used in conjunction with high-deductible health insurance (Code Sec. 220). For purposes of an Archer MSA, a dependent is as defined in Code Sec. 152 (¶ 137), but without regard to whether the dependent claims dependency exemptions, files a joint return or has gross income in excess of the exemption amount (Code Sec. 220(d)(2)(A)). If certain conditions are met, the IRS will treat the child of divorced or separated parents as a dependent of both parents for Archer MSA purposes, without a declaration by the custodial parent releasing the claim to the dependency exemption (¶ 139A) (Rev. Proc. 2008-48).[283]

New Archer MSAs may *not* be established after 2007 (Code Sec. 220(i)(2)). However, all eligible individuals who previously made or received Archer MSA contributions, or who work for employers whose employees previously used Archer MSAs, can make or receive such contributions if they remain eligible individuals. Individuals can also continue to receive distributions from Archer MSAs (Notice 96-53).

References are to Standard Federal Tax Reports; Tax Research Consultant; and Practical Tax Explanations.

[279] ¶ 12,785.25; INDIV: 42,454.10; § 42,515.25

[280] ¶ 12,785.25; INDIV: 42,454.10; § 42,515.05

[281] ¶ 12,776; COMPEN: 45,064.40, COMPEN: 45,212; § 42,515.40

[282] ¶ 12,785.25; COMPEN: 45,064; § 42,501

[283] ¶ 12,675.25; PLANIND: 3,254.05, INDIV: 42,510; § 42,630

Contributions. Within the limits, contributions to an Archer MSA are deductible if made by an eligible individual and excludable from income if made by an employer on behalf of an eligible individual (employer contributions must be reported on the employee's W-2). Annual contributions to an Archer MSA are limited to 75 percent of the deductible of the required health insurance plan (65 percent if a self-only plan). Contributions are also limited by an employee's compensation or the income earned from a self-employed individual's business (Code Sec. 220(b)). Excess contributions are subject to an excise tax.

Deductions. Eligible individuals may claim an above-the-line (or an adjustment to gross income) deduction for contributions they make during the tax year to their Archer medical savings account (Archer MSA). Individuals who are self employed or who work for small employers may be able to maintain Archer MSAs to pay medical expenses, provided that the accounts are used in conjunction with high deductible health inurance (Code Sec. 220; Notice 96-53).[284]

For 2012, the deductibles and limitations are as follows: (1) for individual coverage, the minimum deductible is $2,100, maximum deductible is $3,150 and maximum out-of-pocket limitation is $4,200, and (2) for family coverage, the minimum deductible is $4,200, maximum deductible is $6,300 and maximum out-of-pocket limitation is $7,650 (Rev. Proc. 2011-52). For 2013, the deductibles and limitations are as follows: (1) for individual coverage, the minimum deductible is $2,150, maximum deductible is $3,200 and maximum out-of-pocket limitation is $4,300, and (2) for family coverage, the minimum deductible is $4,300, maximum deductible is $6,450 and maximum out-of-pocket limitation is $7,850 (Rev. Proc. 2012-41).

Distributions. Distributions from an Archer MSA are tax free when used exclusively to pay qualified medical expenses of the account holder, his or her spouse or dependents. In 2011 and in later years, a medicine or drug is considered a qualified medical expense only if the medicine is insulin or a prescribed drug. Distributions not so used are included in income and subject to an additional 20 percent tax (15 percent before 2011) unless made after the participant reaches age 65, dies or becomes disabled (Code Sec. 220(f)(4)). Distributions to pay for over-the-counter medicines may not be excluded from the employee's gross income and are also subject to the additional penalty (Code Sec. 220(d)(2)(A)). The additional tax is not treated as a tax liability for purposes of the alternative minimum tax (¶ 1420) (Code Secs. 26(b)(2)(Q) and 55(c)(1)). Individuals use Form 8853 to calculate their Archer MSA deductions and any taxable distributions.

Medicare Advantage MSAs. Medicare Advantage MSAs are medical savings accounts that must be used in conjunction with a high deductible Medicare Advantage MSA health plan (Code Sec. 138).[285] Individuals eligible for Medicare are permitted to have their Medicare benefits deposited directly into a Medicare Advantage MSA and can make trustee-to-trustee transfers from Archer MSAs to these MSAs. Income earned on the account and withdrawals used to pay health care expenses are not included in the individual's income.

References are to Standard Federal Tax Reports; Tax Research Consultant; and Practical Tax Explanations.

[284] ¶ 12,670, ¶ 12,675.25; INDIV: 42,500; § 5,601, § 42,610.05, § 42,610.15

[285] ¶ 7630; INDIV: 42,466; § 42,615

Chapter 22

CORPORATE ACQUISITIONS REORGANIZATIONS LIQUIDATIONS

Corporate Division

2201. "Spin-Off," "Split-Off," and "Split-Up" Exchanges. Nonrecognition-of-gain benefits apply to receipt of stock in connection with corporate exchanges in distributions known as "spin-offs," "split-offs," or "split-ups."

Spin-Off. A "spin-off" occurs when a corporation distributes pro rata stock or securities in a controlled corporation (at least 80-percent stock ownership). Shareholders do not typically surrender any of their stock in the controlling corporation (Code Sec. 355; Reg. § 1.355-1).[1] A new or existing corporation may be used for the spin-off.

Split-Off. In a "split-off," a parent corporation distributes to some or all of its shareholders stock in a newly formed or pre-existing controlled corporation, under the same conditions as in a "spin-off," except that the shareholders surrender a part of their stock in the parent corporation for the stock in the controlled corporation. The distribution may be pro rata but usually is not.

Split-Up. In a "split-up," the distributing corporation's shareholders surrender all shares held in the distributing corporation and in return receive new shares in two or more controlled subsidiaries the distributing corporation controlled immediately before the distribution. The subsidiaries may be pre-existing or newly formed.

To attain nonrecognition treatment, the distributing and controlled corporation must immediately after the transaction be engaged in the active conduct of a trade or business (Code Sec. 355(b); Reg. § 1.355-3).[2] This requirement does not apply to the distributing corporation if immediately before the distribution, it had no assets other than stock in the controlled corporation. The trade or business must have been actively conducted throughout the five-year period immediately preceding the date of the distribution.

In addition to the active business requirement, the transaction must have a valid corporate business purpose and it cannot be primarily a tax-avoidance device (Reg. § 1.355-2(b)).[3] If, however, a corporate business purpose can be achieved through a nontaxable transaction that does not involve the distribution of stock of a controlled corporation and which is neither impractical nor unduly expensive, then the separation is not carried out for that corporate business purpose. Other limitations relate to continuity of interest on the part of the owners (Reg. § 1.355-2(c)),[4] the amount of

References are to Standard Federal Tax Reports; Tax Research Consultant; and Practical Tax Explanations.

[1] ¶ 16,460, ¶ 16,462; REORG: 30,150

[2] ¶ 16,460, ¶ 16,464; REORG: 30,106

[3] ¶ 16,463; REORG: 30,114

[4] ¶ 16,463; REORG: 30,116

securities distributed, taxable acquisitions within five years, and receipt of other property or "boot" (Code Sec. 355(a)(3)).[5]

Basis Rules. With an exchange of stock and/or securities, the basis of the old stock or securities becomes the basis of the new stock or securities ("substituted basis") (Code Sec. 358).[6] If the exchange is partially taxable, the basis of the old stock or securities is decreased by the sum of the money and fair market value of "other property" received and increased by the amount of gain recognized and the amount treated as a dividend. If any loss is recognized, the basis of the property received is decreased by that amount. If some old stock is retained, allocation is made as though the stock were first surrendered and then received in exchange.

Morris Trust Rules. Restrictions have been imposed on certain spin-offs that follow the fact pattern of *Morris Trust*, SCt, 66-2 USTC ¶ 9718 (Code Sec. 355(e)).[7] If either the controlled or distributing corporation is acquired pursuant to a plan or arrangement in existence on the date of distribution, gain is generally recognized by the distributing corporation as of the date of the distribution. Recognition can be avoided if more than 50 percent of the historical shareholders retain ownership in the distributing and acquiring corporations. Acquisitions occurring within the four-year period beginning two years before the date of distribution are presumed to have occurred pursuant to a plan or arrangement.

Corporate Reorganization

2205. Tax-Free Exchange in Reorganization. A corporation recognizes no gain or loss on the exchange of property solely for stock or securities of another corporation if the corporation is a party to the reorganization (¶ 2221) and the exchange is made pursuant to a plan of reorganization (Code Sec. 361).[8] Both sides of the transaction are eligible for nonrecognition. To achieve such a favorable tax outcome, transactions must satisfy strict statutory and nonstatutory requirements (¶ 2209).

If the corporate transferor receives money or other property ("boot") in the exchange, gain is generally not recognized if the boot is distributed to the shareholders or creditors of the transferor in connection with the reorganization. In the case of distributions to shareholder, however, gain is recognized to the extent of the fair market value of the boot, over the basis of transferred assets, reduced by the amount of any liabilities assumed by the transferee (¶ 2233). Similarly, gain is recognized by the transferor in a divisive "D" reorganization involving a corporate division (¶ 2201) to the extent the amount of boot distributed to creditors is greater than the basis of the transferred assets, reduced by any liabilities assumed by the transferee. For exchanges of depreciable property, see ¶ 1779. See also ¶ 2452 regarding corporate inversion transactions that may be a part of a reorganization.

Basis Rules. Generally, the basis of stock and securities received by a corporation in a reorganization is the same as the basis of the property transferred to the acquiring corporation, adjusted for any gain or loss recognized on the exchange and the value of any money or other property ("boot") received (Code Sec. 358(a)).[9] Boot received from the acquiring corporation generally takes a basis equal to its fair market value at the time of the transaction (Code Sec. 362(b)).[10]

2209. "Reorganization" Defined. A qualified "reorganization" must fall within one of seven categories (each referred to by a letter corresponding to the statutory provisions of Code Sec. 368; Reg. § 1.368-2):[11] In each category, there cannot be a tax-free reorganization unless there is an "exchange" of properties as distinguished from a sale.

References are to Standard Federal Tax Reports; Tax Research Consultant; and Practical Tax Explanations.

[5] ¶ 16,460; REORG: 30,104.05
[6] ¶ 16,550; REORG: 30,104.15
[7] ¶ 16,460, ¶ 16,466.10; REORG: 30,112
[8] ¶ 16,580; CCORP: 39,300
[9] ¶ 16,550; CCORP: 39,302.15
[10] ¶ 16,610; CCORP: 39,302
[11] ¶ 16,750, ¶ 16,752; CCORP: 39,052

Type A reorganization: a statutory merger or consolidation (that is, a merger or consolidation accomplished pursuant to state law or the laws of a foreign jurisdiction, including certain mergers involving disregarded entities (Reg. § 1.368-2(b));[12]

Type B reorganization: the acquisition by one corporation of the stock of another corporation, in exchange solely for all or a part of its own or its parent's voting stock (¶ 2211), if the acquiring corporation has control of the other corporation immediately after the acquisition, whether or not it had control before the acquisition;

Type C reorganization: the acquisition by one corporation of substantially all of the properties of another corporation (¶ 2217), in exchange solely for all or a part of its own or its controlling parent's voting stock (¶ 2211), followed (unless waived by the IRS) by the acquired corporation's distribution of all its property pursuant to the plan of reorganization;

Type D reorganization: a transfer by a corporation of all or a part of its assets to another corporation if, immediately after the transfer, the transferor or one or more of its shareholders is in control of the corporation to which the assets are transferred. The term "shareholders" includes those who were shareholders immediately before the transfer, but only if the stock or securities of the corporation to which the assets are transferred are distributed under the plan of reorganization in a transaction described at ¶ 2201 or ¶ 2205;

Type E reorganization: a recapitalization (¶ 2225);

Type F reorganization: a mere change in the identity, form, or place of organization of one corporation; or

Type G reorganization: a transfer by a corporation in bankruptcy of all or part of its assets to another corporation, but only if stocks or securities of the transferee corporation are distributed to the shareholders tax free or partially tax free.

80-Percent Control Test. For purposes of the corporate reorganization rules, the term "control" means the ownership of stock possessing at least 80 percent of the combined voting power of all classes of stock entitled to vote and at least 80 percent of the total number of shares of all other classes of stock of the corporation (Code Sec. 368(c)).[13] The 80-percent figures are changed to 50 percent in the case of nondivisive D reorganizations (Code Secs. 368(a)(2)(H)(i) and 304(c)).[14]

In order for the control requirement to be satisfied, it is not necessary that the acquiror acquire 80 (or 50) percent of the target's stock in the reorganization, nor that control be attained in the transactions that constitute the reorganization. Rather, it is sufficient that the acquiring corporation is in control of the target corporation immediately after the transaction (Code Sec. 368(a)(1)(B)).[15] Thus, a corporation can acquire stock in one of its subsidiaries in a tax-free reorganization.

S Corporation Reorganization Using QSubs. When an S corporation merges into a newly formed corporation in a transaction qualifying as a Type F reorganization, the newly formed surviving corporation meets the requirements of an S corporation, and the acquiring corporation elects to treat the transferor S corporation as a qualified subchapter S subsidiary (QSub); the reorganization does not terminate the S election (Rev. Ruls. 64-250 and 2008-18).[16] The QSub must retain and use its employer identification number (EIN) when it is treated as a separate corporation for federal tax purposes.

Triangular Reorganizations. Tax-free reorganizations are often structured as triangular reorganizations, which involve use of a subsidiary to acquire the target corporation. There are four types of triangular reorganizations (Reg. § 1.358-6(b)(2)):[17]

(1) triangular B and C reorganizations;

(2) drop-downs (reorganization as a result of successive transfers of assets or stock);

References are to Standard Federal Tax Reports; Tax Research Consultant; and Practical Tax Explanations.

[12] ¶ 16,752; REORG: 6,050
[13] ¶ 16,750; CCORP: 39,052
[14] ¶ 15,375, ¶ 16,750; CCORP: 39,052
[15] ¶ 16,750; CCORP: 39,052
[16] ¶ 32,053.69; REORG: 24,300, SCORP: 304.10; § 28,920
[17] ¶ 16,552F; CCORP: 39,304.10

(3) forward triangular mergers (the acquiring corporation must acquire substantially all the properties of the target corporation); and

(4) reverse triangular mergers (parent stock is used to acquire the target corporation, but an acquisition subsidiary of the parent merges into the target, and the target becomes an 80-percent-owned subsidiary (both by value and for each class of stock) of the parent).

2211. Exchange of Stock or Property Solely for Voting Stock. Under a B reorganization (¶ 2209), the exchange of stock "solely for voting stock" means that the acquiring corporation cannot use cash or nonvoting stock in the exchange or the reorganization becomes taxable (Reg. § 1.368-2(c)).[18]

The "solely" requirement is relaxed for a C reorganization (¶ 2209) in that "substantially all the assets" must be acquired solely for voting stock (¶ 2217). If at least 80 percent of the value of all the property of the transferor corporation is acquired solely for voting stock, the remaining properties may be acquired for money or other property (Code Sec. 368(a)(2)(B)).[19] If the acquiring corporation does transfer money or property in addition to voting stock, then, but only for the purpose of determining whether at least 80 percent of the assets are acquired for voting stock, the amount of any liability assumed by the acquiring corporation or the amount of any liability to which the property acquired is subject will also be treated as money paid for the property.

2217. Substantially All Requirement in C Reorganizations. What constitutes "substantially all" of the properties of a corporation for purposes of a C reorganization (¶ 2209) is not precisely defined in the Code or regulations. However, a special rule provides that a reorganization may still qualify as a C corporation if the acquiring corporation acquires at least 80 percent of all of the target corporation's property solely for voting stock of the acquiring corporation or its parent (Code Secs. 368(a)(1)(C) and (a)(2)(B)).[20] Some courts have held that a transfer of about two-thirds in value of the assets, or 68 percent or even 75 percent of all the corporate property, is not "substantially all." Other courts have held that 85.2 percent or even 90 percent, which included all property except cash, was substantially all. The IRS interprets the substantially all requirement, for the purpose of issuing ruling letters, as requiring a transfer of assets representing at least 90 percent of the fair market value of the net assets and at least 70 percent of the fair market value of the corporation's gross assets held immediately before the transfer (Rev. Proc. 77-37).

2221. Party to a Reorganization—Plan of Reorganization. The reorganization provisions provide for the nonrecognition solely of the gains and losses of the parties to reorganizations and their shareholders and security holders (¶ 2205 and ¶ 2229). The term "party to a reorganization" includes a corporation resulting from a reorganization and both corporations in a reorganization resulting from the acquisition by one corporation of stock or properties of another Code Sec. 368(b); Reg. § 1.368-2(f).[21] In an A, B, C, or G reorganization (¶ 2209), the term "party to a reorganization" includes a controlling corporation if its stock is exchanged and likewise includes a controlled subsidiary that receives any of the assets or stock exchanged.

A plan of reorganization is required in connection with a tax-free exchange (Reg. § 1.368-2(g)).[22] The plan does not need to be a formal written document; however, the safest practice would be to incorporate the plan into the corporate records. The plan may be amended as circumstances change so long as the reorganization remains in compliance with the reorganization requirements (¶ 2209).

References are to Standard Federal Tax Reports; Tax Research Consultant; and Practical Tax Explanations.

[18] ¶ 16,752; REORG: 12,052
[19] ¶ 16,750; REORG: 15,100
[20] ¶ 16,750, ¶ 16,753.53, ¶ 16,753.709; REORG: 15,056
[21] ¶ 16,750, ¶ 16,752; CCORP: 39,054
[22] ¶ 16,752; CCORP: 39,056

2225. Recapitalization. For a transaction to qualify as a recapitalization under an "E" reorganization (¶ 2209), there must be a reshuffling of the capital structure of a corporation (*Southwest Consolidated Corp.*, SCt, 42-1 USTC ¶ 9248)[23] Thus, an E reorganization takes place, for example, when a corporation discharges outstanding bond indebtedness by issuing preferred stock to the shareholders in exchange for the bonds instead of paying them off in cash; when 25 percent of a corporation's preferred stock is surrendered for cancellation and no-par-value common stock is issued; or when previously authorized but unissued preferred stock is issued in exchange for outstanding common stock (Reg. § 1.368-2(e)).[24]

2229. Exchange of Securities or Property for Securities. No gain or loss is generally recognized by a shareholder or securities holder if stock or securities in a corporation that is party to a reorganization (¶ 2221) is exchange solely for stock or securities of another corporation, and the exchange is made pursuant to a plan of reorganization (¶ 2209) or a corporate division (¶ 2201). An exchange of securities in a reorganization is tax free only to the extent that the principal amount received does not exceed the principal amount surrendered (Code Sec. 354).[25] The nonrecognition of gain does not apply if the principal amount of securities received exceeds the principal amount of the securities surrendered. It also does not apply if securities are received and no securities are surrendered. The term "securities" is not defined by the Code or regulations for this purpose. Under case law, however, an instrument with a term of less than five years generally is not a security.[26]

If a shareholder or security holder receives money or other property ("boot") in the exchange, it can result in gain recognition, dividend treatment, or in the case of a corporate division, treatment as a corporate distribution (¶ 2237). Securities received in a Code Sec. 351 exchange are treated as boot for this purpose (¶ 1731). In addition, nonqualified preferred stock is treated as boot (Code Sec. 351(g)).[27] Any liabilities of the shareholder or security holder assumed by a party to the organization are not considered boot (¶ 2233).

If no boot is received in a corporate reorganization or division, the shareholders or security holders retain for the stock or securities they receive the same basis that they had in the stock or securities they surrendered in the exchange (Code Sec. 358).[28] If boot is received, the basis of the nonrecognition property received by a shareholder or security holder is equal to the basis of the stock or securities he has exchanged in the reorganization, adjusted for the boot received. The basis determined for nonrecognition stock and securities must be allocated among all classes of stock or securities involved in the transaction.

2233. Assumption of Liabilities in Reorganizations. A release from liabilities assumed by a transferee or a disposition of property subject to liabilities in a reorganization (¶ 2205 and ¶ 2229), a transfer of property to a controlled corporation (¶ 1731), or certain bankruptcy reorganizations or foreclosures (¶ 2247) is not money or other property ("boot") received by the taxpayer and does not prevent the transaction from being tax free (Code Sec. 357).[29] But if it appears that the principal purpose of the assumption of liabilities is to avoid income tax, or the purpose is not a bona fide business purpose, the liability assumed is treated as boot (unless the taxpayer can prove to the contrary).

If the liabilities assumed, or to which the property is subject, exceed the total basis of all the properties transferred in a Code Sec. 351 exchange or divisive D reorganization involving a corporate division (¶ 2209), the excess is treated as gain from a sale or exchange of a capital asset or a noncapital asset, depending on the nature of the encumbered asset transferred (Code Sec. 357(c)). As to the basis of property after an

References are to Standard Federal Tax Reports; Tax Research Consultant; and Practical Tax Explanations.

[23] ¶ 16,753.476; REORG: 24,050

[24] ¶ 16,752; REORG: 24,052

[25] ¶ 16,431; CCORP: 39,250

[26] ¶ 16,433.61; CCORP: 39,252.05

[27] ¶ 16,402; CCORP: 3,102

[28] ¶ 16,550; CCORP: 39,256

[29] ¶ 16,520; CCORP: 39,252.15, CCORP: 39,302.20; § 26,125.05

assumption of liabilities, see ¶ 1669. A liability is excluded from this exception if it is assumed in a Code Sec. 351 transfer and the payment of the liability by the transferor would give rise to a deduction or would be basically the equivalent of a payment made in liquidation of the interest of a retiring or deceased partner, unless such liability resulted in the creation of, or the increase in, the basis of any property. The liability is now excluded, however, to the extent incurring the liability results in the creation of, or an increase in, the basis of any property.

2237. Dividend Distribution in Reorganization. A distribution of money or other property ("boot") to a stockholder as part of a plan of reorganization (¶ 2229) may be taxed as a dividend if it has the effect of a taxable dividend, even if the money or other property is received in an exchange which is, in part, tax free (Code Sec. 356; Reg. § 1.356-1).[30] The constructive ownership rules discussed at ¶ 743 are applied in determining dividend equivalency. A distribution within this provision is taxable as a dividend, not to exceed the recognized gain, to the extent the distributing company has, on hand, earnings and profits sufficient to cover the distribution.

2241. Liquidation as Part of Reorganization. Under a plan of reorganization (¶ 2209), a corporation often acquires, for all or part of its stock, all of the stock in another corporation from the stockholders of the latter. As the final step in the reorganization, the acquiring corporation may liquidate the latter company, acquiring those assets by surrendering its own stock. This last step in the reorganization may be accomplished tax free under Code Sec. 332, relating to property received by one corporation on complete liquidation of another (¶ 2261).

2247. Reorganizations of Bankrupt or Insolvent Corporations. Corporate restructurings ordered pursuant to certain bankruptcy, foreclosure, and similar proceedings may qualify as corporate reorganizations (Code Sec. 368(a)(1)(G)).[31] To qualify for nonrecognition treatment, a G reorganization must meet six requirements:

(1) The debtor/target corporation must transfer all or part of its assets to an acquiring corporation.

(2) The transfer must take place in a Title 11 or similar case.

(3) The stock or securities of the acquiring corporation must be distributed as part of a plan of reorganization.

(4) There must be continuity of interest.

(5) There must be continuity of business enterprise.

(6) There must be a business purpose for the transaction.

Corporate Liquidation

2253. Gain or Loss to Shareholders in Corporate Liquidations. Amounts distributed in complete liquidation of a corporation are usually treated as full payment in exchange for the stock (Code Sec. 331; Reg. § 1.331-1).[32] The shareholder's gain or loss from a distribution is determined by comparing the amount distributed to the cost or other basis of the stock. Assuming that the stock is a capital asset, the gain or loss to the shareholder is a capital gain or loss.

If property is received in a distribution in a complete liquidation and gain or loss is recognized on receipt of the property, the basis of the property in the hands of the person receiving it is the fair market value of the property at the time of the distribution (Code Sec. 334(a)).[33] When a parent corporation liquidates an 80-percent controlled subsidiary, the parent corporation's basis in the property received is generally the same as the liquidating subsidiary's basis in the property unless the subsidiary recognizes

References are to Standard Federal Tax Reports; Tax Research Consultant; and Practical Tax Explanations.

[30] ¶ 16,490, ¶ 16,491; CCORP: 39,254

[31] ¶ 16,750; REORG: 27,050

[32] ¶ 16,002, ¶ 16,003; CCORP: 27,100; § 26,710

[33] ¶ 16,150; CCORP: 27,122; § 26,710

gain from the transfer (¶ 2261). If property received in a complete liquidation is subject to a liability, the distributee's recognition of gain or loss is adjusted accordingly (¶ 1672).

A distribution that is one of a series of distributions in redemption of all of a corporation's stock pursuant to a plan is treated as a complete liquidation (Code Sec. 346(a)).[34] If a liquidation distribution is made as one of a series of distributions intended eventually to result in complete liquidation of the corporation, no gain is realized by the shareholder until the entire cost of the stock is recovered. If complete liquidation covers two or more consecutive tax years, the distribution first offsets the shareholder's basis for the stock and the excess is gain in the year received. The gain is not allocable to all of the years in which distributions were received (Rev. Rul. 85-48).[35]

Partial Liquidation. A distribution of corporate assets to a *noncorporate* shareholder is treated as being in exchange for stock (whether or not stock is actually surrendered) if the distribution is in partial liquidation of the corporation. Such a distribution must not be essentially equivalent to a dividend (determined by reference to the effect on the corporation rather than the effect on the shareholders) but rather must be made pursuant to a plan and must occur within the tax year in which the plan is adopted or within the succeeding tax year. The Code does not provide a definition of "partial liquidation"—it is generally understood that the phrase refers to a contraction of the business of the corporation—but does provide a "safe harbor". A distribution will qualify as a partial liquidation if it is attributable to the corporation's ceasing to conduct a trade or business that it actively conducted for at least five years ending with the date of the distribution and if the corporation continues to conduct at least one other trade or business immediately after the distribution (Code Sec. 302(b)(4) and (e)).[36]

2257. Recognition of Gain or Loss by Corporation in Complete Liquidation. Generally, property distributed in a complete liquidation of a corporation is deemed to have been sold by the corporation at its fair market value and any gain or loss will be recognized by the liquidating corporation (Code Sec. 336).[37] If the distributed property is subject to a liability or if the distributee assumes a liability upon the distribution, the fair market value of the property is deemed to be no less than the amount of the liability. The following exceptions to this general recognition rule apply:

(1) No gain or loss is recognized upon any distribution of property to shareholders in a tax-free reorganization (¶ 2205 and ¶ 2209) to the extent that the distributee does not recognize gain or loss on the distribution (Code Secs. 336(c) and 361(c)(4)).[38]

(2) No gain or loss is generally recognized in connection with the complete liquidation of a controlled subsidiary into its parent corporation (¶ 2261).

(3) No loss is recognized with respect to a distribution of property to a related person within the meaning of Code Sec. 267 (¶ 905), unless the property (a) is distributed to all shareholders on a pro rata basis and (b) was not acquired by the liquidating corporation in a Code Sec. 351 transaction or as a contribution to capital during the five years preceding the distribution (Code Sec. 336(d)(1)).[39]

(4) Recognition of loss may be limited if the distributed property was initially acquired by the liquidating corporation, either by tax-free transfer to a controlled corporation or as a contribution to capital, as part of a plan whose principal purpose was the recognition of loss on the property in connection with the liquidation. In these circumstances, the basis of the property for purposes of determining loss is reduced, but not below zero, by the excess of the adjusted basis of the property on the date of contribution over its fair market value. There is a presumption of tax-

References are to Standard Federal Tax Reports; Tax Research Consultant; and Practical Tax Explanations.

[34] ¶ 16,351; CCORP: 27,050
[35] ¶ 16,004.163; CCORP: 27,108
[36] ¶ 15,325; CCORP: 21,700; § 26,330.05
[37] ¶ 16,200; CCORP: 27,150; § 26,715
[38] ¶ 16,200, ¶ 16,580; CCORP: 27,156; § 26,720.10
[39] ¶ 16,200; CCORP: 27,160.05; § 26,720.10

avoidance purpose with respect to any such transfer within the two-year period prior to the adoption of the plan of liquidation (Code Sec. 336(d)(2)).[40]

(5) No gain or loss is recognized if a corporation owning 80 percent of the voting power and value of another corporation elects to treat any disposition (sale, exchange or distribution) of the subsidiary's stock as a disposition of all of the subsidiary's assets (Code Sec. 336(e)).[41]

2261. Liquidation of Subsidiary. If distributions in complete liquidation are made by a subsidiary to a parent corporation (owning at least 80 percent by value and voting power of the subsidiary), then no gain or loss on the distributions is recognized by either the parent corporation or the liquidating subsidiary (Code Secs. 332 and 337).[42] For this purpose, the 80-percent control requirement must be met by direct ownership and not by reason of the aggregation rules. In addition, property distributed to a controlling domestic corporation in satisfaction of a debt owed by the liquidating subsidiary will be treated as a distribution in liquidation for these purposes (Code Sec. 337(b)(1)). However, the distribution of earnings by a U.S. holding company to a foreign corporation in a complete liquidation will be treated as a taxable dividend if the U.S. holding company was in existence for less than five years (Code Sec. 332(d)).

If a minority shareholder receives property in such a liquidation, the distribution is treated as a nonliquidating redemption. Thus, gain (but not loss) is recognized by the liquidating corporation (¶ 2257). Gain or loss also is recognized on distributions to 80-percent distributees that are foreign corporations (¶ 2492) and tax-exempt organizations, unless the property is used by that organization in a trade or business unrelated to its tax-exempt purpose (Code Sec. 337(b)(2)).

Basis. After a complete liquidation of a subsidiary, a parent company usually holds the distributed assets with the same basis that the assets formerly had in the hands of the subsidiary. However, the basis of the assets in the hands of the parent corporation will be the fair market value at the time of the distribution if: (1) the subsidiary recognizes gain or loss in the liquidation; or (2) the parent's aggregate adjusted basis in such property exceeds its fair market value immediately after the liquidation (Code Sec. 334(b)).[43]

2265. Acquisition of Stock Treated as Acquisition of Assets. If a parent corporation purchases 80-percent control of a second corporation (the target) within a 12-month period, the parent may irrevocably elect to have the target treated as if it had sold and purchased its own assets (Code Sec. 338; Reg. § 1.338-3).[44] If the election is made, the target corporation is treated as a new corporation after the date of acquisition of 80-percent control. The hypothetical sale is deemed to have occurred on the date of acquisition of control. The target's tax year as the "selling corporation" ends on that date, its carryovers and other tax attributes disappear, and, as the "purchasing corporation," it becomes a member of the affiliated group including the parent on the day following that date. Gain or loss will be recognized by the target as though it had sold all of its assets at fair market value in a single transaction on the acquisition date. Recapture items will typically be taken into account on the final return of the "selling corporation." The election is to be made no later than the 15th day of the 9th month, beginning after the month in which 80-percent control is acquired. The parent is not required to liquidate the target corporation, but, if it does, it will succeed to the basis of the target as increased by the hypothetical purchase.

There are detailed rules to ensure consistency of treatment for acquisitions of stock or assets by and from members of an affiliated group of corporations (Reg. § 1.338-4(h)).[45] A corporate seller may treat a sale of its 80-percent-controlled target as a

References are to Standard Federal Tax Reports; Tax Research Consultant; and Practical Tax Explanations.

[40] ¶ 16,200; CCORP: 27,160.15; § 26,720.15

[41] ¶ 16,200; CCORP: 27,200

[42] ¶ 16,050, ¶ 16,225; CCORP: 27,202, CCORP: 27,210; § 26,730.10, § 26,730.20

[43] ¶ 16,150; CCORP: 27,214.05; § 26,730.10

[44] ¶ 16,275, ¶ 16,278; CCORP: 30,000

[45] ¶ 16,279; CCORP: 30,300

sale of the target corporation's underlying assets. The assets receive a stepped-up basis to fair market value, and the selling consolidated group recognizes gain or loss attributable to the assets, but there is no separate tax on the seller's gain attributable to the stock. This treatment also applies in situations when the selling corporation owns 80 percent of the target's stock by value and voting power but does not file a consolidated return (Code Sec. 338(h)(10)).[46]

Collapsible Corporation

2273. "Collapsible" Corporation. Despite the general rule that amounts distributed to shareholders in complete liquidation of a corporation are treated as payment for the sale of stock (¶ 2253), a shareholder owning more than 5 percent of the stock in a "collapsible" corporation is denied capital gain treatment on the distribution (Code Sec. 341).[47] The collapsible corporation rules, however, are repealed for tax years beginning before December 31, 2012.

> **Comment:** Absent further legislation, the collapsible corporation rules will be effective for tax years beginning after December 31, 2012.

A "collapsible" corporation is formed principally to manufacture, construct, produce, or purchase certain property—or to hold stock in another corporation formed for the same purpose—with a view to distributing the property or selling or exchanging the corporation's stock before the corporation realizes two-thirds of the taxable income to be derived from the property. In this way, the shareholders could realize capital gains for the bulk of the assets rather than ordinary income (Code Sec. 341(b); ¶ 1.341-2).[48] Property held in a collapsible corporation is called "Sec. 341 assets."

The presumption that a corporation is collapsible arises if the fair market value of its Sec. 341 assets is:

(1) 50 percent or more of the fair market value of its total assets (not including cash, stock in other corporations, or bonds, debentures, investment notes, etc., that are capital assets, or any U.S., state or local bonds); and

(2) 120 percent or more of the adjusted basis of its Sec. 341 assets (Code Sec. 341(c); Reg. § 1.341-3).[49]

A stockholder who realizes gain with respect to the stock of a collapsible corporation is not subject to ordinary income treatment if the shareholder owns less than 5 percent of the stock of the corporation, non-collapsible assets account for 30 percent or more of the gain, or to gain realized more than three years after the construction, manufacture, purchase or other acquisition of the collapsible assets (Code Sec. 341(d); § 1.341-4).[50] In addition, the collapsible corporation provisions do not apply if, at the time of the sale or exchange or distribution, the net unrealized appreciation in "subsection (e)" assets of the corporation does not exceed 15 percent of its net worth (Code Sec. 341(e); Reg. § 1.341-6).[51] "Subsection (e)" assets are, in general, property of the corporation that would result in ordinary income if they were sold for a gain. The collapsible corporation provisions also do not apply to a sale of stock in a corporation that consents to recognize gain on the disposition of corporate assets (Code Sec. 341(f); Reg. § 1.341-7).[52]

Carryforwards

2277. Carryovers in Certain Corporate Acquisitions. In a tax-free asset acquisition, certain tax attributes may be transferred or are carried over to the acquiring corporation (Code Sec. 381; Reg. § 1.381(a)-1).[53] This applies to a parent after complete

References are to Standard Federal Tax Reports; Tax Research Consultant; and Practical Tax Explanations.

[46] ¶ 16,275; CCORP: 30,150

[47] ¶ 16,300; CCORP: 33,000; § 27,201

[48] ¶ 16,300, ¶ 16,303; CCORP: 33,100; § 27,210

[49] ¶ 16,300, ¶ 16,305; CCORP: 33,150; § 27,215

[50] ¶ 16,300, ¶ 16,306; CCORP: 33,200; § 27,220.05

[51] ¶ 16,300, ¶ 16,310; CCORP: 33,250

[52] ¶ 16,300, ¶ 16,311; CCORP: 33,300

[53] ¶ 17,002, ¶ 17,003; REORG: 33,150

liquidation of a subsidiary (¶ 2261), as well as a tax-free A, C, D, F, or G reorganization (¶ 2209). In the case of D and G reorganizations, however, the carryover of certain tax attributes only applies to acquisitive reorganizations, where substantially all of the assets are acquired and distributed, not to divisive reorganizations.

The carryover provisions are mandatory, even though in some cases they will work to the disadvantage of the successor. They do not apply after a split-up, split-off, or spin-off type of divisive reorganization (¶ 2201), or a partial liquidation. The tax attribute items covered are listed in Code Sec. 381(c) and include, but are not limited to, net operating losses (NOLs), unused general business credits, capital loss carryovers, method of computing depreciation, and method of accounting. Even if a tax attribute properly carries over to an acquiring corporation, the acquiring corporation's ability to use the attribute may be limited (¶ 2281). If an acquiring corporation makes an election to treat the target corporation as having purchased its own assets (¶ 2265), there is no carryforward of attributes of the subsidiary for the periods prior to the parent's acquisition.

Carrybacks. Carrybacks of net operating losses (¶ 1176) and net capital losses are permitted from one corporate entity to another only in the case of an F reorganization—a mere change in identity, form, or place of organization.

2281. Limitations on Use of Carryforwards in Corporate Acquisitions. After a reorganization or other change in corporate ownership, the use of certain carryforwards may be limited or prohibited (¶ 2277). The carryforwards involved concern:

(1) net operating losses (NOLs);

(2) unused general business credit;

(3) corporate minimum tax credit;

(4) foreign tax credit; and

(5) capital loss carryovers (Code Secs. 382 and 383).[54]

After an ownership change the amount of *income* that a corporation may offset each year by preacquisition NOL carryforwards (¶ 2285) is generally limited to an amount determined by multiplying the value of the equity of the corporation just prior to the ownership change by the federal long-term tax-exempt rate (¶ 85) in effect on the date of the change (Code Sec. 382).[55] Any unused limitation may be carried forward and added to the next year's limitation. In addition, NOL carryforwards are eliminated completely unless the business continuity requirements for reorganizations (¶ 2247) are satisfied for the two-year period following the ownership change. The annual income limitation is reduced by the recognition of any built-in losses (the amount by which a corporation's adjusted basis in its assets exceeds their fair market value on the date of the ownership change) and increased by the recognition of built-in gains. An exception to the limitations on NOL carryforwards is provided in bankruptcy situations, with certain restrictions.

Two kinds of ownership changes can trigger the income limitation: a change involving a 5-percent shareholder, and any tax-free reorganization other than divisive and F reorganizations (¶ 2209). In either case, one or more of the 5-percent shareholders must have increased their percentage of ownership in the corporation by more than 50 percent over their lowest pre-change ownership percentage (generally within three years of the ownership change).

Similar rules apply to the other carryforwards, including those for net capital losses, unused general business credit and foreign taxes (Code Sec. 383; Reg. § 1.383-1).[56]

Pre- and Post-change Allocation. A loss corporation must allocate NOLs or taxable income and net capital loss or gain for the change year between the pre-change period and the post-change period either by:

References are to Standard Federal Tax Reports; Tax Research Consultant; and Practical Tax Explanations.

[54] ¶ 17,101, ¶ 17,200; REORG: 33,000

[55] ¶ 17,101; REORG: 33,200

[56] ¶ 17,200, ¶ 17,204; REORG: 33,250

(1) ratably allocating an equal portion to each day in the change year; or

(2) electing to treat its books as closed on the date of the change (Reg. § 1.382-6).[57]

If a "closing of the books" election is made, the amounts allocated to either period may not exceed the NOL or taxable income and net capital loss or gain for the change year.

Worthless Stock. In order to prevent a double tax benefit, the NOLs of a corporation may not be carried forward after an ownership change if a shareholder with 50-percent-or-more control (prior to the ownership change) claims, within three years, a worthless stock deduction with respect to the stock (Code Sec. 382(g)(4)(D)).[58]

Tax Avoidance Purpose. NOLs and other carryforwards may be disallowed if an acquisition is made with a tax avoidance purpose (¶ 1575).

2285. Limitation on Preacquisition Losses. A corporation (or any member of its affiliated group) may not use its preacquisition losses (NOLs, net built-in losses, net capital losses, and credit carryforwards) against the built-in gains of a company:

(1) whose assets are acquired in an A, C, or D reorganization (¶ 2209); or

(2) that becomes directly or indirectly controlled (80-percent ownership of its stock by vote and value) by the acquiring corporation.

The restriction generally applies to built-in gains recognized within five years of the acquisition date, unless 50 percent or more of the gain company has been owned by the loss corporation (or a member of its group) for five years prior to the acquisition (Code Sec. 384).[59]

The unrealized built-in gains of either the acquired or acquiring corporation are subject to the restriction. It applies to any successor corporation to the same extent as to its predecessor, and all members of the same affiliated group before the acquisition are treated as one corporation.

References are to Standard Federal Tax Reports; Tax Research Consultant; and Practical Tax Explanations.

[57] ¶ 17,111; REORG: 33,208

[58] ¶ 17,101; REORG: 33,200

[59] ¶ 17,300; REORG: 33,300

Chapter 23
SPECIAL CORPORATE STATUS

Mutual Funds

2301. Qualification as a Mutual Fund. Mutual funds (regulated investment companies) are domestic corporations that act as investment agents for their shareholders, typically investing in corporate and government securities and distributing income earned from the investments as dividends. Mutual funds may escape corporate taxation because, unlike ordinary corporations, they are entitled to claim a deduction for dividends paid to shareholders against their ordinary income and net capital gain. A corporation qualifies as a mutual fund if it makes an irrevocable election to be treated as such by filing a tax return on Form 1120-RIC, and it meets all of the following requirements (Code Sec. 851):[1]

- The corporation must be registered under the Investment Company Act of 1940 as a management company, unit investment trust, business development company, or as a type of common trust fund.

- At least 90 percent of its gross income must be derived from dividends, interest, payments with respect to certain securities loans, gains from the sale or disposition of stock or securities, or other income derived from the business of investing, including the net investment income of qualified publicly traded partnerships.

- At the close of each quarter of the tax year, at least 50 percent of its total assets must be invested in cash, government securities, securities of other mutual funds, or the securities of other issuers (so long as the securities of any given issuer do not exceed five percent of the value of the mutual fund's assets or 10 percent of the issuer's outstanding voting securities).

- At the close of each quarter of the tax year, no more than 25 percent of the total value of its assets may be invested in the securities of any one issuer (other than government securities or securities of other mutual funds), the securities of two or more issuers controlled by the mutual fund and engaged in a related trade or business, or the securities of one or more qualified publicly traded partnerships.

- The corporation must distribute at least 90 percent of its annual investment company taxable income (¶ 2303) and its net tax-exempt interest income (¶ 2307) to its shareholders (there is no threshold for net capital gains) (Code Sec. 852(a)).[2]

2303. Taxation of Mutual Funds. A mutual fund (regulated investment company) is subject to taxation at regular corporate income tax rates on its "investment company taxable income" (Code Sec. 852(b); Reg. § 1.852-3).[3] Investment company taxable income is computed on Form 1120-RIC in the same manner as the taxable income of an ordinary corporation (¶ 221) with the following adjustments:

References are to Standard Federal Tax Reports; Tax Research Consultant; and Practical Tax Explanations.

[1] ¶ 26,400; RIC: 3,000, RIC: 3,050; § 19,201, § 45,430.05

[2] ¶ 26,420; RIC: 3,060; § 19,201, § 45,430.05

[3] ¶ 26,420, ¶ 26,424; RIC: 3,200; § 19,201, § 45,430.05

- gross income is the fund's ordinary income (net capital gains are not included);
- a deduction is allowed for any ordinary dividends paid (however, no deduction is allowed for dividends of capital gains or tax-exempt interest);
- no deduction is allowed for dividends received;
- no deduction is allowed for net operating losses (NOLs);
- taxable income of a short tax year is not annualized;
- if the fund so elects, taxable income is computed by disregarding the short-term discount obligation rules of Code Sec. 454(b); and
- a deduction is allowed for the tax imposed on the fund if it fails to meet the asset test or gross income test (¶ 2301).

For purposes of the dividends-paid deduction, dividends declared and payable by a mutual fund in October, November or December in a calendar year are treated as paid on December 31 of that year even if they are actually paid in January of the following calendar year (Code Sec. 852(b)(7)). In addition, a mutual fund may declare and pay "spillover dividends" after the close of a tax year that are considered made out of a mutual fund's earnings and profits for that year. Spillover dividends are also included in the calculation of mutual fund taxable income for that year and are considered in determining whether the mutual fund met its distribution requirements for the year. Spillover dividends in tax years beginning after December 22, 2010, must be declared no later than the fifteenth day of the ninth month following the close of the tax year to which the dividend relates, or the extended due date for the mutual fund's return for the tax year, whichever comes later. The dividend must be paid no later than the date of the first dividend payment *of the same type of dividend* (e.g., capital gains or ordinary) after the declaration, but no later than 12 months after the close of the tax year to which the dividend relates (Code Sec. 855(a)).[4]

23 SPEC. CORP. STATUS

On the other hand, a mutual fund, other than a publicly traded mutual fund, generally may not claim a deduction for dividend distributions if it singles out one class of shareholders, or one or more members of a class of shareholders, for special dividend treatment, unless such treatment was originally intended when the dividend rights were created (Code Sec. 562(c); Rev. Rul. 89-81).[5] However, the IRS has issued guidance describing the conditions under which distributions to mutual fund shareholders may vary and nevertheless be deductible, including the treatment of distributions to shareholders that differ as a result of the allocation and payment of fees and expenses (Rev. Proc. 99-40).[6]

Excise Taxes. A nondeductible excise tax is generally imposed on a mutual fund that does not satisfy minimum distribution requirements (Code Sec. 4982).[7] The tax is four percent of the excess of any "required distribution" for the calendar year over the amount actually distributed for the calendar year. For this purpose, the required distribution is the sum of 98 percent of the fund's ordinary income for the year, plus 98.2 percent of its net capital gain income for the one-year period ending October 31 of the calendar year. (For calendar years before 2011, both amounts were 98 percent.) Special rules apply in how a mutual fund treats post-October 31 capital gains and foreign currency losses. For excise tax purposes, amendments made in 2010 to the capital loss carryover rules (¶ 2305) apply beginning with any net capital loss recognized in the period that determines a mutual fund's required distribution for calendar year 2011 (Rev. Rul. 2012-29).[8]

2305. Capital Gains and Losses of Mutual Funds. A mutual fund (regulated investment company) may avoid corporate level tax on its net capital gains by distribut-

References are to Standard Federal Tax Reports; Tax Research Consultant; and Practical Tax Explanations.

[4] ¶ 26,420, ¶ 26,480; RIC: 3,450; § 19,205.05

[5] ¶ 23,470, ¶ 26,433.50; RIC: 3,204.10; § 26,905.15

[6] ¶ 26,433.28; RIC: 3,204.10; § 26,905.15

[7] ¶ 34,640; RIC: 3,212; § 19,201, § 45,430.05

[8] ¶ 34,642.10; RIC: 3,212; § 19,201, § 45,430.05

ing such gains to shareholders. However, if the mutual fund elects to retain some of its net capital gains, then it is subject to tax at regular capital gains rates on the excess of its net capital gains for the tax year over the amount of any capital gains dividends paid during the year (Code Sec. 852(b)(3)).[9] Form 2438 is used to figure and report the fund's capital gains. Although the fund is taxed on its undistributed net capital gains, it may elect to designate to its shareholders some or all of its undistributed gains and the tax paid on those gains. Form 2439 is used to notify each shareholder of his or her portion of the undistributed capital gains and tax paid for the year (¶ 2309 and ¶ 2311).

Capital Loss Carryovers. For tax years beginning after December 22, 2010, if a mutual fund has a net capital loss for a tax year, any excess of the net short-term capital loss over the net long-term capital gain is treated as a short-term capital loss arising on the first day of the next tax year, and any excess of the net long-term capital loss over the net short-term capital gain is treated as a long-term capital loss arising on the first day of the next tax year (Code Sec. 1212(a)(3)(A)).[10] There is no limit to the number of tax years that a net capital loss of a mutual fund may be carried over. However, for tax years beginning before December 23, 2010, a mutual fund can carry net capital losses forward only for eight years, and losses carried forward are treated as short-term capital losses in the year of use (Code Sec. 1212(a)(1)(C), prior to amendment by the Regulated Investment Company Modernization Act of 2010 (P.L. 111-325)).

If a net capital loss under the general corporate capital loss carryback and carryover rules (¶ 1756) is carried over to a tax year of a mutual fund, amounts treated as a long-term or short-term capital loss arising on the first day of the next tax year under the capital loss carryover rules for mutual funds (discussed above) are determined without regard to amounts treated as a short-term capital loss under the general corporate capital loss carryover rule. Further, in determining the reduction of a carryover by capital gain net income for a prior tax year under the general corporate capital loss carryover rule, any capital loss treated as arising on the first day of the prior tax year under the capital loss carryover rules for mutual funds is taken into account in determining capital gain net income for the prior year (Code Sec. 1212(a)(3)(B)).[11] Capital gain net income is the excess of gains from the sale or exchange of capital assets over losses from such sales or exchanges (Code Sec. 1222(9)).[12]

2307. Tax-Exempt Interest of Mutual Funds. A mutual fund (regulated investment company) may pay tax-exempt interest earned on state or local bonds to its shareholders in the form of exempt-interest dividends, but only if the bonds represent at least 50 percent of the value of the fund's assets at the close of each quarter of its tax year (Code Sec. 852(b)(5)).[13] Form 1099-INT is used to inform shareholders of dividends identified as tax-exempt interest dividends (¶ 2309 and ¶ 2311).

An upper-tier mutual fund that is a qualified fund of funds may pass through exempt-interest dividends and foreign tax credits to its shareholders, without having to meet the 50-percent asset requirement (Code Sec. 852(g)).[14] A qualified fund of funds is a mutual fund if, at the close of each quarter of the tax year, at least 50 percent of the value of its total assets is represented by interests in other mutual funds.

Generally, if a mutual fund shareholder receives an exempt-interest dividend with respect to any share held for six months or less, then any loss on the sale or exchange of such share is disallowed to the extent of the amount of the exempt-interest dividend (Code Sec. 852(b)(4)).[15] However, for losses incurred on shares of stock for which the taxpayer's holding period begins after December 22, 2010, the disallowance of a loss on the sale or exchange of mutual fund shares, on which exempt-interest dividends have been paid, does not apply, except as otherwise provided by regulations, to a regular

References are to Standard Federal Tax Reports; Tax Research Consultant; and Practical Tax Explanations.

[9] ¶ 26,420; RIC: 3,250; § 19,205.05, § 45,430.10

[10] ¶ 30,400; RIC: 3,252; § 16,535

[11] ¶ 30,400, RIC: 3,252; § 16,535

[12] ¶ 30,440; SALES: 15,202.45; § 16,530

[13] ¶ 26,420; RIC: 3,300; § 19,205.05, § 45,430.10

[14] ¶ 26,420; RIC: 3,300; § 19,205.35

[15] ¶ 26,420; RIC: 3,258; § 19,230.15

dividend paid by a mutual fund which declares exempt-interest dividends on a daily basis in an amount not less than 90 percent of its net tax-exempt interest and distributes such dividends on a monthly or more frequent basis.

2309. Designation of Mutual Fund Distributions. A mutual fund (regulated investment company) must report in written statements furnished to its shareholders the portions of distributions made during the tax year which are capital gains dividends (¶ 2305) and exempt-interest dividends (¶ 2307), as well as any foreign tax credits (¶ 2320), tax credit bond credits (¶ 2320), dividends that qualify for the dividends-received deduction (¶ 223), and passed-through ordinary dividends eligible for the reduced tax rate for qualified dividends (¶ 2311) (Code Secs. 852(b)(3)(C) and (5), 853(c), 853A(c), and 854(b)).[16] Capital gain dividends, and dividends received from a tax-exempt corporation, and dividends received from a qualified real estate investment trust (REIT) (¶ 2326) are not eligible for the dividends-received deduction (Code Sec. 854(a) and (b)(2)). The aggregate amount which the mutual fund can report as dividends eligible for the dividends-received deduction is limited to its aggregate dividends received from domestic corporations for the tax year. The aggregate amount which the mutual fund can report as qualified dividend income is limited to its qualified dividend income for the tax year (Code Sec. 854(b)(1)(C)).

Additionally, within 60 days after the close of its tax year, a mutual fund must report and notify its shareholders of the portion of distributions made during the tax year that is designated as undistributed capital gain (Code Sec. 852(b)(3)(D)).

2311. Taxation of Mutual Fund Distributions. The tax treatment of a distribution received from a mutual fund (regulated investment company) depends on how the distribution is designated (¶ 2309). Distributions not designated as capital gain dividends are generally treated by shareholders as ordinary income to the extent of the fund's earnings and profits. However, all or a portion of the distribution may be a qualified dividend eligible to be taxed at capital gains rates (¶ 733), if the aggregate amount of qualified dividends received by the fund during the year is less than 95 percent of its gross income (Code Sec. 854(b)(1)(B)).[17] Distributions reported as tax-exempt interest dividends may generally be excluded from the shareholder's gross income (Code Sec. 852(b)(5)(B)).[18] However, exempt-interest dividends derived from private activity bonds constitute tax preference items for alternative minimum tax (AMT) purposes (¶ 1425).

> **Comment:** Absent further legislation, ordinary income tax rates will apply to qualified dividend income (¶ 733) that is passed through a mutual fund after December 31, 2012.

Distributions received from a mutual fund reported as capital gain dividends may be treated as long-term capital gains by the shareholder for income and AMT purposes, regardless of how long the shareholder held the shares (Code Sec. 852(b)(3)(B)).[19] Similarly, capital gains that the fund elects to pass through to the shareholder are treated as long-term capital gains (¶ 2305). The shareholder is entitled to a credit or refund for its portion of any capital gain taxes paid by the mutual fund on the undistributed capital gains (Code Sec. 852(b)(3)(D)). In addition, the shareholder may increase the basis of its mutual fund shares by the difference between the undistributed capital gains and its deemed portion of taxes paid. The mutual fund must designate distributions as undistributed capital gain dividends, reporting the designation and providing shareholders a written notice within 60 days of the end of its tax year (¶ 2309).

If a shareholder receives a capital gain dividend or has capital gain passed through by the fund with respect to any share or beneficial interest, and holds the share for six months or less, then any loss on the sale of that share is treated as a long-term capital

References are to Standard Federal Tax Reports; Tax Research Consultant; and Practical Tax Explanations.

[16] ¶ 26,420, ¶ 26,440, ¶ 26,448, ¶ 26,460; RIC: 3,400; § 19,205.05, § 45,430.10

[17] ¶ 26,460; RIC: 3,400; § 19,205.10, § 19,205.15

[18] ¶ 26,420; RIC: 3,300; § 19,205.35

[19] ¶ 26,420; RIC: 3,250; § 19,205.20, § 19,205.25

loss to the extent of any long-term capital gain (Code Sec. 852(b)(4)).[20] In addition, the amount of loss that may be claimed must also be reduced by the amount of any exempt-interest dividend received on the shares. These rules do not apply to losses incurred on the disposition of mutual fund shares or beneficial interest pursuant to a plan that provides for the periodic liquidation of such shares or interests. For purposes of determining whether a taxpayer has held mutual fund shares for six months or less, rules similar to those for the dividends-received deduction are applied (¶ 223).

A mutual fund shareholder may also not claim a loss from the sale or exchange of mutual fund shares if the wash sale rules apply (¶ 1935).

A distribution that is not out of a mutual fund's earnings and profits is a return of the shareholder's investment. Return-of-capital distributions are generally not subject to tax, and they reduce the shareholder's basis in the mutual fund shares. On the other hand, mutual fund distributions that are automatically reinvested by the shareholder into more shares of the fund must be taxed as if they had actually been received by shareholder in cash. Thus, reinvested ordinary dividends and reinvested capital gain distributions are generally taxed as income, reinvested exempt-interest dividends are not reported as income, and reinvested return-of-capital distributions are reported as a return of capital (IRS Pub. 550).

2313. Earnings and Profits of Mutual Funds. Dividends from a mutual fund (regulated investment company), just like dividends from most other corporations, must be paid out of earnings and profits (¶ 747—¶ 757) (Code Secs. 301, 312, 316, 561, 562(a), and 852(a)(1)).[21] Thus, a mutual fund must be careful to maintain sufficient current or accumulated earnings and profits to satisfy annual dividend distribution requirements. There should also be enough earnings and profits to avoid the excise tax on the undistributed income of a mutual fund (¶ 2303).

A mutual fund's earnings and profits are generally computed under the rules that apply to ordinary corporations. However, mutual funds do not reduce their current earnings and profits by any amount they are unable to claim as a deduction from taxable income in that year (Code Sec. 852(c)(1)).[22] For tax years beginning after December 22, 2010, net capital loss for a tax year is not taken into account in determining earnings and profits; however, any capital loss treated as arising on the first day of the following tax year is taken into account in determining earnings and profits for that year (subject to the application of the net capital loss rule for that year). Also, in tax years beginning after December 22, 2010, deductions disallowed in computing mutual fund taxable income with respect to tax-exempt interest are allowed in calculating a mutual fund's current earnings and profits (but not accumulated earnings and profits).

Effective for distributions made in tax years beginning after December 22, 2010, if a mutual fund that is not a calendar-year taxpayer makes distributions to its shareholders with respect to any class of stock of the company in excess of the sum of its current and accumulated earnings and profits (i.e., a portion of the distribution constitutes return of capital or capital gain), its current earnings and profits must be allocated first to distributions during the mutual fund's tax year that are made before January 1 (Code Sec. 316(b)(4)).[23] If a mutual fund has more than one class of stock, this rule applies separately to each class of stock, so that distributions made during the corporation's tax year are considered to be made to the shares with higher priority before they are made to shares with lower priority (Rev. Rul. 69-440).[24]

A company that has failed to qualify as a mutual fund because it has not purged itself of non-mutual fund earnings and profits may still qualify if it distributes those earnings and profits with interest to its shareholders (Code Sec. 852(e)).[25] In order to

References are to Standard Federal Tax Reports; Tax Research Consultant; and Practical Tax Explanations.

[20] ¶ 26,420; RIC: 3,258; § 19,210.05

[21] ¶ 15,302, ¶ 15,600, ¶ 15,702, ¶ 23,450, ¶ 23,470, ¶ 26,420; RIC: 3,204.15; § 26,201

[22] ¶ 26,420; RIC: 3,204.15; § 19,201

[23] ¶ 15,702; RIC: 3,204.15; § 26,601

[24] ¶ 15,704.755; CCORP: 12,166, RIC: 3,204.15; § 26,601

[25] ¶ 26,420; RIC: 3,202

qualify, distributions must be specifically designated as non-mutual fund distributions and take place within the 90-day period that begins on the date the corporation is determined not to be a mutual fund (¶ 2317). This option is not available if the corporation was determined not to be a mutual fund because it engaged in fraudulent tax evasion.

2315. Redemption of Mutual Fund Shares. Generally, a redemption of stock by a corporation, including a mutual fund (regulated investment company), is treated as an exchange of stock if the redemption falls within one of four categories of transactions (Code Sec. 302):[26] (1) a redemption that is not essentially equivalent to a dividend; (2) a substantially disproportionate redemption; (3) a redemption that terminates the shareholder's interest in the corporation; or (4) a partial liquidation, in the case of a noncorporate shareholder. Redemptions of corporate stock are discussed in ¶ 742—¶ 745. Because transactions that fall within one of these four categories are treated as exchanges of stock, they normally result in capital gain treatment to the redeemed shareholder. If the redemption does not fall within any of these categories, it is treated as a Code Sec. 301 distribution of property that generally results in dividend treatment.

Special rules apply to redemptions of mutual fund shares. Effective for distributions after December 22, 2010, a distribution in redemption of stock of a publicly offered mutual fund is treated as an exchange for stock if the redemption is upon the demand by the stockholder, and the mutual fund issues only stock that is redeemable upon the demand of the stockholder. A publicly offered mutual fund is a fund whose shares are (1) continuously offered pursuant to a public offering; (2) regularly traded on an established securities market; or (3) held by or for no fewer than 500 persons at all times during the tax year (Code Sec. 67(c)(2)(B)).[27] Additionally, the loss disallowance and deferral rules for transactions between related persons (¶ 1717) do not apply to any redemption of stock of a fund-of-funds mutual fund if the mutual fund issues only stock that is redeemable upon the demand of the stockholder and the redemption is upon the demand of another mutual fund (Code Sec. 267(f)(3)(D)).[28]

2317. Deficiency Dividends of Mutual Funds. If there is a determination that adjustments are needed to certain amounts that a mutual fund (regulated investment company) reports for a tax year, and if the adjustments could cause the entity to lose its mutual fund status, the mutual fund may avoid disqualification by making deficiency dividend distributions, and may claim a deduction for such dividends paid (Code Sec. 860; Reg. §§ 1.860-1—1.860-5).[29] A deficiency dividend is a distribution of property (including money) that would have been includible in calculating the entity's dividends-paid deduction had the property been distributed during the tax year. The distribution must be made within 90 days after the determination date, and before the entity files a deficiency dividend deduction claim, which must be filed on Form 976 within 120 days after the determination date.

For a mutual fund, an adjustment can be (1) an increase in its investment company taxable income, determined without regard to the dividends-paid deduction; (2) an increase in the amount of the excess of its net capital gain over its deduction for capital gain dividends paid; or (3) a decrease in its dividends-paid deduction (determined without regard to capital gains dividends). A determination is a final decision by a court, a closing agreement, an agreement between the IRS and the entity relating to its tax liability, or a statement by the entity attached to its amendment or supplement to a tax return for the relevant tax year. Filing Form 8927 is treated as a "self-determination" by the entity for these purposes (Rev. Proc. 2009-28).[30]

The deficiency dividend deduction is not available if part of the adjustment is due to fraud with intent to evade tax or willful failure to file a timely income tax return.

References are to Standard Federal Tax Reports; Tax Research Consultant; and Practical Tax Explanations.

[26] ¶ 15,325; CCORP: 21,104; § 26,301

[27] ¶ 6060; RIC: 3,204.10; § 19,210.07

[28] ¶ 14,150; CCORP: 21,100, SALES: 39,112.05; § 19,210.07

[29] ¶ 26,580, ¶ 26,581–¶ 26,585; RIC: 3,500

[30] ¶ 42,625.435; RIC: 3,500

2318. Basis in Mutual Fund Shares. A shareholder's basis in the shares of a mutual fund (regulated investment company) is usually the cost to purchase the shares, including any fees or load charges incurred to acquire or redeem them (¶ 1975). However, fees or load charges are not added to the shareholder's original basis if the shareholder acquires a reinvestment right, disposes of the shares within 90 days of being purchased, and acquires new shares in the same (or another) mutual fund for which the fee or load charge is reduced or waived because of the reinvestment right (Code Sec. 852(f)).[31] In such cases, the omission of the load charge from basis applies to the extent the charge does not exceed the reduction in the load charge for the new investment. To the extent that a load charge is not taken into account in determining the purchaser's gain or loss, it is treated as incurred in connection with the acquisition of the second-acquired shares.

For charges incurred in tax years beginning after December 22, 2010, this treatment of load charges applies only if the original mutual fund stock is disposed of within 90 days after the date it was originally acquired. The taxpayer must acquire stock in the same or another mutual fund during the period beginning on the date of the disposition of the original stock, and ending on January 31 of the calendar year following the calendar year that includes the date of such disposition for this rule to apply.

The original basis of mutual fund shares acquired by reinvesting distributions (even exempt-interest dividends) is the amount of the distributions used to buy each full or fractional share (¶ 1975). A shareholder's original basis in shares acquired by gift is generally the donor's adjusted basis (¶ 1630). However, if the fair market value of the shares was more than the donor's adjusted basis, then the shareholder's basis is the donor's adjusted basis at the time of the gift, plus all or part of any gift tax paid. A shareholder's basis in mutual fund shares that are inherited is generally the fair market value of the shares at the decedent's death (or the alternate valuation date if the estate chooses) (¶ 1633). No matter how a shareholder's original basis is determined, it must be adjusted for such post-acquisition occurrences as reinvestment of distributions and return of capital distributions (¶ 2311).

2320. Tax Credit Elections. A mutual fund (regulated investment company) may elect to have its foreign tax credit taken by its shareholders on their tax returns instead of its own. However, the election can only be made if more than 50 percent of the value of the fund's total assets at the close of the tax year consists of stock or securities in foreign corporations and it has distributed at least 90 percent of its investment company taxable income (¶ 2303) and net tax-exempt interest (¶ 2307) for the year (Code Sec. 853).[32]

Effective for tax years beginning after December 22, 2010, an upper-tier mutual fund that is a qualified fund of funds may pass through foreign tax credits to its shareholders without having to meet the 50-percent asset requirement (Code Sec. 852(g)).[33] A "qualified fund of funds" is a mutual fund at least 50 percent of the total value of whose assets (as measured at the close of each quarter of its tax year) is represented by interests in other mutual funds.

A mutual fund may elect to pass through to its shareholders credits attributable to tax credit bonds (¶ 1371) held by the mutual fund (Code Sec. 853A).[34]

Real Estate Investment Trusts

2326. Qualification as a REIT. A corporation, trust or association that acts as an investment agent specializing in real estate and real estate mortgages may choose to be a real estate investment trust (REIT) (Code Sec. 856).[35] REITs may escape corporation taxation because, unlike ordinary corporations, they are entitled to claim a deduction for

References are to Standard Federal Tax Reports; Tax Research Consultant; and Practical Tax Explanations.

[31] ¶ 26,420; SALES: 45,404; § 19,215.05, § 19,215.10

[32] ¶ 26,440; RIC: 3,350; § 19,210.10

[33] ¶ 26,420; RIC: 3,352; § 19,240.10

[34] ¶ 26,448; RIC: 3,364; § 14,505

[35] ¶ 26,500; RIC: 6,050; § 45,440.05

dividends paid to shareholders against their ordinary income and net capital gains. An entity qualifies as a REIT if it makes an election to be treated as such by filing a tax return on Form 1120-REIT and it meets certain requirements as to ownership and organization, source of income, investment of assets, and distribution of income to shareholders. The REIT election may be revoked voluntarily, but the organization will be prohibited from making a new REIT election for the four tax years after revocation. An organization may elect REIT status even if it fails the ownership test in the first year.

Ownership and Organization Requirements. To be eligible for REIT status, an entity must be taxable as a domestic corporation (Code Sec. 856(a)). Foreign corporations, trusts and associations, as well as financial institutions such as banks and insurance companies, are not eligible. An eligible entity must be managed by one or more trustees or directors during the entire tax year. It must also adopt a calendar-year accounting period (Code Sec. 859).[36] An entity making a REIT election may change its accounting period to a calendar year without seeking approval from the IRS.

Beneficial ownership in a REIT must be evidenced by transferable shares or certificates of interest. The REIT must have at least 100 beneficial owners for 335 days of a 12-month tax year (Code Sec. 856(a) and (b)). For this purpose, ownership cannot be closely held as determined under the personal holding company rules (¶ 285) (Code Sec. 856(h)).[37] However, attribution to another partner in a partnership is ignored. In addition, a pension trust generally is not treated as a single owner, but any REIT shares or certificates of interest held by the trust are treated as directly held by its beneficiaries. This look-through rule does not apply if persons disqualified from dealings with the pension trust own five percent or more of the value of the REIT, and the REIT has accumulated earnings and profits attributable to a year it did not qualify as a REIT.

Income Requirements. An entity must satisfy the following income tests each tax year in order to qualify as a REIT (Code Sec. 856(c)(2) and (3)):[38]

- at least 95 percent of the entity's gross income must be from rents from real property, gain from the disposition of real property, dividends, interest, gains from dispositions of stock and securities, abatements and refunds of real property taxes, income and gain from foreclosure property, consideration received or accrued for agreeing to make loans secured by real property mortgages or interests or to purchase or lease real property, and certain mineral royalty income earned from real property owned by a timber REIT; and

- at least 75 percent of the entity's gross income must be from real property sources, which include rents from real property, interest on real property mortgages, gain from the disposition of real property or mortgage interests, dividends and gain from the disposition of shares in other qualifying REITs, abatements and refunds of real property taxes, income and gain from foreclosure property, consideration received or accrued for agreeing to make loans secured by real property mortgages or interests or to purchase or lease real property, and qualified temporary investment income.

For both tests, an entity's gross income does not include the gross income from prohibited transactions (¶ 2329), foreign currency gains in the form of passive foreign exchange gains, or real estate foreign exchange gains (Code Sec. 856(n)),[39] as well as gains from hedging transactions (including foreign currency hedging income) entered into by the entity to reduce its real estate risk (Code Sec. 856(c)(5)(G)).[40] The IRS has the authority to designate income as not constituting gross income for purposes of the REIT income tests and, alternatively, to designate nonqualified income as qualified (Code Sec. 856(c)(5)(J)).[41]

References are to Standard Federal Tax Reports; Tax Research Consultant; and Practical Tax Explanations.

[36] ¶ 26,560; RIC: 6,050; § 38,135.10
[37] ¶ 26,500; RIC: 6,052; § 45,440.05
[38] ¶ 26,500; RIC: 6,054, RIC: 6,056; § 45,440.05
[39] ¶ 26,500; RIC: 6,054.05
[40] ¶ 26,500; RIC: 6,054.15
[41] ¶ 26,500; RIC: 6,054.10, RIC: 6,054.15

Rents from real property generally include: rents from interests in real property; amounts received for customary services (utilities, maintenance), even if separate charges are made for such services; and rent attributable to personal property incidental to rental of real property if the amount allocable to personal property is 15 percent or less of the total rent (Code Sec. 856(d)).[42] Rents from real property do *not* include amounts received from: (1) any noncorporate person in which the REIT owns 10 percent or more in that person's assets or profits; (2) a corporation if the REIT owns 10 percent or more of either the voting stock or the value of all shares issued by the corporation; or (3) amounts received based on income or profits of a tenant or debtor (unless certain conditions are met). Rents from real property also do not include rents that depend on income or profits derived by any person from the property; exceptions exist to this general prohibition.

Amounts paid to a REIT by a taxable REIT subsidiary (¶ 2340) are not excluded from the definition of "rents from real property" if 90 percent of the property at issue is rented to unrelated parties at rents comparable to those paid by other tenants for comparable space. In addition, a taxable REIT subsidiary may lease a "qualified lodging facility" or a "qualified health care property," and the rents paid are treated as rents from real property so long as the facility is operated by an eligible independent contractor for a fee.

An entity that fails to meet either of the income tests for any tax year may still qualify as a REIT if it identifies the failure on a separate schedule prescribed by the IRS and the failure is due to reasonable cause and not willful neglect (Code Sec. 856(c)(6)).[43] The REIT also must pay a tax, equal to the greater of the amount by which the entity fails to meet either the 95-percent or 75-percent income test, multiplied by the fraction of the REIT's taxable income over its gross income for the tax year (Code Sec. 857(b)(5)).[44]

Asset Requirements. A REIT must meet the following requirements regarding its assets at the close of each quarter of the tax year:

- at least 75 percent of the value of its total assets must consist of real estate assets (including interests in a REMIC (¶ 2343)), cash items (including receivables), and government securities;
- no more than 25 percent of the value of its total assets can be invested in securities other than those representing real estate assets or government securities;
- no more than 25 percent of the value of total assets can be invested in securities of taxable REIT subsidiaries (¶ 2340); and
- except for government securities and securities of taxable REIT subsidiaries (¶ 2340), no more than five percent of the value of its total assets can be invested in the securities of any one issuer, and investment in the securities of any one issuer cannot exceed 10 percent of the total value or voting power of that issuer's outstanding securities (Code Sec. 856(c)(4)).[45]

For purposes of the limitation that a REIT may not hold more than 10 percent of the value of the outstanding securities of a single issuer, certain obligations are not treated as securities of an issuer, including "straight debt" securities, loans to an individual or estate, section 467 rental agreements (¶ 1541), or any obligation to pay rents from real property (Code Sec. 856(m)).[46] A straight debt security is debt payable on demand or at a date certain where the interest rate and interest payments are not contingent on profits, the borrower's discretion, or similar factors, and there is no convertibility (directly or indirectly) into stock (Code Sec. 1361(c)(5)(B)).[47] However, special rules permit certain contingencies of straight debt.

References are to Standard Federal Tax Reports; Tax Research Consultant; and Practical Tax Explanations.

[42] ¶ 26,500; RIC: 6,056
[43] ¶ 26,500; RIC: 6,054.20
[44] ¶ 26,520; RIC: 6,054.20; § 45,440.05
[45] ¶ 26,500; RIC: 6,072; § 45,440.05
[46] ¶ 26,500; RIC: 6,072.10
[47] ¶ 32,021; RIC: 6,072.10

An entity that fails to meet any of the asset requirements for a particular tax quarter (other than the 5- or 10-percent asset test) may still qualify as a REIT if:

(1) it identifies the failure on a separate schedule prescribed by the IRS;

(2) failure is due to reasonable cause and not willful neglect;

(3) the assets causing the failure are disposed of within six months of the last day of the quarter in which the failure occurred; and

(4) the REIT pays an excise tax (Code Sec. 856(c)(7)).[48]

The tax is the greater of $50,000 or the tax on the net income generated by the assets during the period of failure at the highest corporate rate. A REIT will not lose its exempt status for a *de minimis* failure to meet the 5- or 10-percent asset requirements if the failure is due to ownership of assets the total value of which does not exceed the lesser of one percent of the total value of the REIT's assets at the end of a tax quarter or $10 million. The REIT must dispose of the assets causing the failure within six months of the last day of the quarter in which the failure occurred.

Distribution of Income. To qualify as a REIT, an entity generally must distribute to its shareholders during the tax year the sum of 90 percent of its ordinary taxable income (determined without the deduction for dividends paid and excluding net capital gain) (¶ 2329) and 90 percent of its net income from foreclosure property (less the tax imposed on that income), minus its excess noncash income (Code Sec. 857(a)).[49] The IRS has the authority to waive this requirement if failure to meet it is due to distributions necessary to avoid imposition of the excise tax on undistributed REIT income (¶ 2329).

Other Failures. If an entity fails to satisfy one or more requirements of REIT qualification other than the income tests or asset requirements, then the entity may still retain REIT qualification if the failure is due to reasonable cause and not willful neglect. However, the REIT must pay a penalty of $50,000 for each failure (Code Sec. 856(g)(5)).[50]

2329. Taxation of REITs. An entity that qualifies as a real estate investment trust (REIT) (¶ 2326) is subject to regular corporate income tax rates on its taxable income (Code Sec. 857(b)).[51] A REIT's taxable income is computed on Form 1120-REIT in the same manner as an ordinary corporation with the following adjustments:

- A deduction is allowed for dividends paid (¶ 259), but is calculated without regard to dividends attributable to the net income from foreclosure property.

- Net income from foreclosure property or a prohibited transaction is disregarded.

- The special deductions available to corporations (¶ 223—¶ 231), including the dividends-received deduction, are not allowed, but the deduction for organizational expenditures (¶ 237) is allowed.

- Any tax imposed on redetermined rents, redetermined deductions, and excess interest under Code Sec. 857(b)(7), and any tax imposed for failures to meet the income, asset, or other REIT qualification requirements (¶ 2326), are deducted.

- Taxable income is not annualized in the case of a change in accounting periods.

For purposes of the dividends-paid deduction, dividends declared and payable in October, November, or December of a calendar year are treated as paid on December 31 of that year even if they are actually paid in January of the following calendar year (Code Sec. 857(b)(9)).[52]

References are to Standard Federal Tax Reports; Tax Research Consultant; and Practical Tax Explanations.

[48] ¶ 26,500; RIC: 6,072.25
[49] ¶ 26,520; RIC: 6,074; § 45,440.05
[50] ¶ 26,500; RIC: 6,078.05
[51] ¶ 26,520; RIC: 6,100; § 45,440.05
[52] ¶ 26,520; RIC: 6,104

Capital Gains. If a REIT has any net capital gains in the tax year, the tax imposed on REIT taxable income is the lesser of: (1) the regular corporate tax on REIT taxable income, or (2) the regular corporate tax on REIT taxable income, determined by excluding net capital gains and by computing the deduction for dividends paid without capital gain dividends, plus 35 percent on the excess of the net capital gain reduced by any capital gain dividends paid (Code Sec. 857(b)(3)).[53]

A REIT may avoid the tax on its net capital gains by distributing such gains to its shareholders (¶ 2331). The REIT must designate any distributions as capital gain dividends in a written notice to the shareholders or beneficiaries with its annual report or within 30 days of the end of the tax year. For purposes of determining the maximum amount of capital gain dividends that a REIT may pay for a tax year, the REIT may not offset its net capital gains with the amount of any net operating losses (NOLs). In addition, the REIT must increase the amount of any NOL carryover to the extent it pays capital gains dividends in excess of its net income.

If the REIT does retain any net capital gains, it may elect to designate to its shareholders some or all of those undistributed amounts and the tax it paid on those gains. The REIT must use Form 2438 to report and determine its tax on undistributed capital gains, and Form 2439 to inform each shareholder of his portion of the undistributed gains and any tax paid. Form 2439 must be provided within 60 days of the close of the REIT's tax year.

Net Operating Losses. NOLs in a tax year that an entity is a REIT may only be carried forward, while NOLs in a tax year an entity is not a REIT may not be carried back to any year the entity was a REIT (¶ 1179) (Code Sec. 172(b)(1)(B)).[54]

Other Taxes. In addition to the tax on its taxable income, a REIT may be subject to the following additional taxes:

- a tax for failure to meet the REIT asset or income requirements for the tax year (¶ 2326);
- a tax at the highest corporate rate on net income from foreclosure property (Code Sec. 857(b)(4));[55]
- a 100-percent tax on the net income derived from a prohibited transaction (e.g., disposition of property, other than foreclosure property, that is held for sale to customers in the ordinary course of business) (Code Sec. 857(b)(6));[56]
- a four-percent excise tax on the amount of any taxable income which is undistributed at the end of the tax year (Code Sec. 4981);[57] and
- a 100-percent tax on the excess portion of rents, deductions, and interest that must be reduced to clearly reflect the income when a REIT and taxable REIT subsidiary (¶ 2340) engage in transactions other than those at arm's length (Code Sec. 857(b)(7)).[58]

2331. Taxation of REIT Distributions. Distributions received from a real estate investment trust (REIT) not designated as capital gain dividends are generally treated by shareholders as ordinary income to the extent of the REIT's earnings and profits. However, all or a portion of the distribution may be a qualified dividend eligible to be taxed at capital gains rates (¶ 733). The amount a REIT can designate as qualified dividend income is limited to the sum of: (1) the REIT's qualified dividend income for the tax year; (2) the excess of the sum of REIT taxable income for the preceding tax year and the income subject to tax under the Code Sec. 337(d) regulations for that preceding tax year, over the taxes payable by the REIT under the REIT rules (¶ 2329) and the Code Sec. 337(d) regulations for that preceding tax year; and (3) the amount of earnings and profits that were distributed by the REIT for the tax year and accumulated in tax years in which the entity was not a REIT. The amount of qualified dividends must

References are to Standard Federal Tax Reports; Tax Research Consultant; and Practical Tax Explanations.

[53] ¶ 26,520; RIC: 6,108
[54] ¶ 12,002; RIC: 6,110; § 17,010.40
[55] ¶ 26,520; RIC: 6,114
[56] ¶ 26,520; RIC: 6,116
[57] ¶ 34,620; RIC: 6,120
[58] ¶ 26,520; RIC: 6,122

be specified by the REIT in a written notice to shareholders no later than 60 days after the close of the tax year (Code Sec. 857(c)(2)).[59]

Comment: Absent further legislation, ordinary income tax rates will apply to qualified dividend income (¶ 733) that is passed through a REIT after December 31, 2012.

Distributions in excess of the REIT's earnings and profits (other than deficiency dividends; ¶ 2337) constitute a return of the shareholder's basis (¶ 754). Dividends received from a REIT do not qualify for the dividends-received deduction for corporations (¶ 223).

Distributions designated as capital gain dividends are treated as long-term capital gains by the shareholders, regardless of how long they held their interests in the REIT (Code Sec. 857(b)(3)).[60] This includes any undistributed capital gains designated by the REIT (¶ 2329). Shareholders are entitled to a credit or refund for their portions of any capital gain taxes paid by the REIT on the undistributed capital gains. In addition, a shareholder must increase the basis of his REIT shares by the difference between his portions of the undistributed capital gains and the deemed taxes paid.

Certain capital gain distributions from REITs to foreign investors are treated as REIT dividends that are not capital gains (Code Sec. 857(b)(3)(F)).

If a shareholder receives a capital gain dividend or the REIT has designated undistributed capital gains with respect to any share or beneficial interest, and the shareholder holds the share for six months or less, then any loss on the sale of that share is treated as a long-term capital loss to the extent of the long-term capital gain dividend (Code Sec. 857(b)(8)).[61] This rule does not apply to losses incurred on the disposition of REIT stock or beneficial interest under a plan that provides for the periodic liquidation of such shares or interests. For purposes of determining whether a taxpayer has held REIT stock or beneficial interest for six months or less, rules similar to those for the dividends-received deduction are applied (¶ 223).

2337. Deficiency Dividends of REITs. If there is a determination that adjustments are needed to certain amounts that a real estate investment trust (REIT) reports for a tax year, and if the adjustments could cause the entity to lose its REIT status, the REIT may avoid disqualification by making deficiency dividend distributions, and may claim a deduction for such dividends paid (Code Sec. 860; Reg. §§1.860-1—1.860-5).[62] For a REIT, an adjustment can be: (1) an increase in the sum of its taxable income (determined without regard to its dividends-paid deduction and excluding any net capital gain), plus the excess of its net income from foreclosure property minus the tax on the foreclosure property net income; (2) an increase in the amount of the excess of its net capital gain over its deduction for capital gain dividends paid; or (3) a decrease in its dividends-paid deduction (determined without regard to capital gains dividends). See ¶ 2317 for further discussion of the deficiency dividend procedure, which is the same as that for mutual funds (regulated investment companies).

2339. REIT Distributions After Tax Year Ends. A real estate investment trust (REIT) that declares a dividend (including a capital gain dividend) before the due date for filing its return (including extensions) for a tax year, but distributes the dividend after the close of the tax year, can treat the dividend as having been paid during the tax year if the entire declared dividend is paid within the 12-month period following the close of the tax year and no later than the date of the first regular dividend payment after the declaration (Code Sec. 858).[63] The shareholder, however, must generally treat the dividend as received in the tax year in which the distribution is made (¶ 2331).

References are to Standard Federal Tax Reports; Tax Research Consultant; and Practical Tax Explanations.

[59] ¶ 26,520; RIC: 6,150, RIC: 6,200; § 19,205.05, § 45,440.10

[60] ¶ 26,520; RIC: 6,108, RIC: 6,200; § 19,205.05, § 45,440.10

[61] ¶ 26,520; RIC: 6,150; § 19,210.05, § 45,440.10

[62] ¶ 26,580, ¶ 26,581–¶ 26,585; RIC: 6,106

[63] ¶ 26,540; RIC: 6,104.05

2340. REIT Subsidiaries. A real estate investment trust (REIT) may own a "qualified REIT subsidiary" and treat all of the subsidiary's assets, liabilities, and items of income, deduction, and credit as its own (Code Sec. 856(i)).[64] A qualified subsidiary is any corporation other than a "taxable REIT subsidiary," all of the stock of which is held by the REIT. A taxable REIT subsidiary is any corporation which is owned, in whole or in part, by the REIT and which both entities elect using Form 8875 to treat as a taxable REIT subsidiary (Code Sec. 856(l)). A taxable REIT subsidiary can be used by the REIT to provide noncustomary services to its tenants or to manage and operate properties without causing the amounts received or accrued to be disqualified as rents from real property (¶ 2326). The election to be treated as a taxable REIT subsidiary can only be revoked with the consent of both the REIT and the subsidiary.

Real Estate Mortgage Investment Conduits

2343. Qualification as a REMIC. A real estate mortgage investment conduit (REMIC) is an entity that holds a fixed pool of mortgages and issues multiple classes of interests to investors (Code Sec. 860D; Reg. § 1.860D-1).[65] A REMIC is treated like a partnership for federal tax purposes with its income passed through to its interest holders (¶ 2344). Thus, a REMIC is not subject to taxation on its income, although it is subject to taxes on prohibited transactions (¶ 2355), income from foreclosure property (¶ 2356), and on certain contributions received after its start-up day (¶ 2357). It also may be required to withhold taxes on amounts paid to foreign holders of regular or residual interests (¶ 2367). An entity qualifies as REMIC if it makes an irrevocable election to be treated as such by filing a tax return on Form 1066 during its first tax year of existence, and if it meets certain requirements as to its investors (¶ 2344) and assets (¶ 2345). If an entity ceases to qualify as a REMIC at any time during the tax year, it will not be treated as a REMIC for that or any later tax year. A REMIC is required to file an information return with the IRS on Form 8811 within 30 days of its start-up day (and 30 days from any change of information provided in a previously-filed Form 8811), identifying its representative for reporting tax information (Reg. § 1.6049-7).[66]

2344. Investors' Interests. In order to qualify as a real estate mortgage investment conduit (REMIC), all of the interests in the entity must be either "regular interests" or "residual interests," and there must be only one class of residual interests (Code Sec. 860D; Reg. § 1.860D-1).[67] However, a *de minimis* interest that is neither a regular nor a residual interest can be created to facilitate the REMIC creation. A regular interest is any interest that is issued on the start-up day of the REMIC with fixed terms and that is designated as a regular interest (Code Sec. 860G(a)(1); Reg. § 1.860G-1).[68] A regular interest may be issued in the form of debt, stock, interest in a partnership or trust, or any other form permitted by state law so long as it unconditionally entitles the holder to receive a specific principal amount and interest based on a fixed rate (or permitted variable rate). An interest-only regular interest may also be issued which entitles the holder to receive interest payments determined by reference to the interest payable on qualified mortgages, rather than a specified principal amount.

An interest does not fail to qualify as a regular interest merely because the timing of principal payments may be contingent on the extent of prepayments on qualified mortgages or the amount of income from permitted investments. In addition, an interest does not fail to be a regular interest solely because the principal amount may be reduced as a result of a nonoccurrence of a contingent payment with respect to a reverse mortgage loan held by the REMIC if the REMIC's sponsor reasonably believes on the start-up day that all principal and interest due under the regular interest will be paid at or prior to the REMIC's liquidation. The REMIC must file information returns on Form

References are to Standard Federal Tax Reports; Tax Research Consultant; and Practical Tax Explanations.

[64] ¶ 26,500; RIC: 6,072.20, RIC: 6,072.30

[65] ¶ 26,660, ¶ 26,661; RIC: 9,050; § 45,445.05

[66] ¶ 36,036; RIC: 9,052

[67] ¶ 26,660, ¶ 26,661; RIC: 9,050; § 45,445.05

[68] ¶ 26,720, ¶ 26,720A; RIC: 9,056; § 45,445.10

1099-INT for each regular interest holder that has been paid $10 or more of interest, including original issue discount (¶ 1952), during the calendar year (Reg. § 1.6049-7).[69]

A residual interest is an interest issued on the REMIC's start-up day that is not a regular interest and that is designated as a residual interest (Code Sec. 860G(a)(2)).[70] There may be only one class of residual interests and any distribution with respect to such interests must be pro rata. Furthermore, a REMIC must have reasonable arrangements to ensure that residual interests are not held by certain disqualified organizations (governments, exempt organizations, cooperatives) (Code Sec. 860D(a)(3) and (6)).[71] For each quarter of its tax year, a REMIC must send a Schedule Q of Form 1066 to residual interest holders reporting their share of the REMIC's income or loss (Reg. § 1.860F-4(e)).[72]

REMIC Interests as Assets in Other Contexts. Regular and residual interests in a REMIC are treated as real estate assets for purposes of determining whether an organization qualifies as a real estate investment trust (REIT) (¶ 2326). However, if for any calendar quarter less than 95 percent of the REMIC's assets are real estate assets, the REIT is treated as holding directly its proportionate share of the assets and income of the REMIC (Code Sec. 856(c)(5)(E); Reg. § 1.856-3(b)).[73] If one REMIC owns interests in a another REMIC, then the character of the second REMIC's assets flow through for purposes of making this determination. Any regular or residual interest in a REMIC can also qualify as an "asset" for purposes of determining whether an organization is a domestic building and loan association (Code Sec. 7701(a)(19); Reg. § 301.7701-13A).[74] If 95 percent or more of REMIC assets qualify as an "asset" for this purpose, then the entire interest in the REMIC can qualify as an asset.

2345. Qualified Mortgages and Permitted Investments of REMICs. In order to qualify as a real estate mortgage investment conduit (REMIC), substantially all of an entity's assets must consist of "qualified mortgages" and "permitted investments" at the close of the third month beginning after the start-up day and all times thereafter (Code Sec. 860D(a)(4)).[75] A qualified mortgage is any obligation that is principally secured by an interest in real property and that:

(1) is transferred to the REMIC on the start-up day in exchange for regular or residual interests;

(2) is purchased by the REMIC within three months after the start-up day pursuant to a fixed price contract in effect on the start-up day; or

(3) represents an increase in the principal under the original terms of the obligation, if the increase (i) is attributable to an advance made to the obligor under the terms of a reverse mortgage or other obligation, (ii) occurs after the start-up day, and (iii) is purchased by the REMIC pursuant to a fixed price contract in effect on the start-up day (Code Sec. 860G(a)(3)).[76]

A qualified mortgage may also include any qualified replacement mortgage, or a regular interest in another REMIC transferred on the start-up day in exchange for a regular or residual interest.

Permitted investments include "cash flow" investments of amounts received under qualified mortgages for a temporary period, intangible property held for payment of expenses as part of a qualified reserve fund, and foreclosure property acquired in connection with the default of a qualified mortgage (Code Sec. 860G(a)(5)).[77]

2349. Transfer of Property to REMICs. No gain or loss is recognized when property is transferred to a real estate mortgage investment conduit (REMIC) in

References are to Standard Federal Tax Reports; Tax Research Consultant; and Practical Tax Explanations.

[69] ¶ 36,036; RIC: 9,052; § 39,110.10

[70] ¶ 26,720; RIC: 9,058, RIC: 9,062

[71] ¶ 26,660; RIC: 9,062

[72] ¶ 26,701; RIC: 9,052

[73] ¶ 26,500, ¶ 26,504; RIC: 6,072.05

[74] ¶ 43,080, ¶ 43,109; RIC: 12,056

[75] ¶ 26,660; RIC: 9,060; § 45,445.05

[76] ¶ 26,720; RIC: 9,060.05; § 45,445.05

[77] ¶ 26,720; RIC: 9,060.10; § 45,445.05

exchange for a regular or residual interest (Code Sec. 860F(b); Reg. § 1.860F-2(b)).[78] The basis of a regular or residual interest received in the exchange is equal to the total adjusted basis of the property transferred, plus any organizational expenses. If the transferor receives more than one interest in the REMIC (both a regular and residual interest), then the basis must be allocated among the interests in accordance with their respective fair market values. The basis of the property received by the REMIC in exchange for a regular or residual interest is its fair market value immediately after the transfer.

The issue price of a regular or residual interest is generally determined under the same rules as for determining the issue price for the original issue discount of debt instruments (¶ 1952) (Code Sec. 860G(a)(10)).[79] If the issue price of a regular interest in a REMIC exceeds its adjusted basis, then the excess is included in the transferor's gross income as if it were a market discount bond (¶ 1958) (Code Sec. 860F(b)(1)(C); Reg. § 1.860F-2(b)(4)). If the issue price of a residual interest exceeds its adjusted basis, then the excess is included in the transferor's gross income ratably over the anticipated weighted average life of the REMIC. If the adjusted basis of a regular interest exceeds the issue price, then the excess is allowable as a deduction to the transferor under the rules similar to those governing amortizable bond premiums (¶ 1967) (Code Sec. 860F(b)(1)(D); Reg. § 1.860F-2(b)(4)). If the adjusted basis of a residual interest exceeds the issue price, then the excess is allowed as a deduction to the transferor over the anticipated weighted average life of the REMIC.

2352. Taxable Income or Loss of REMICs. A real estate mortgage investment conduit (REMIC) is not generally taxed on its income (Code Sec. 860A).[80] However, its taxable income must still be determined for purposes of the taxation of residual interest holders (¶ 2361). REMIC taxable income is determined in the same manner as that of an individual, except that it must use the accrual method of accounting and make the following adjustments:

- Regular interests in the REMIC are treated as debt.
- Market discount on any bond is included in gross income as the discount accrues.
- No item of income, gain, loss, or deduction from a prohibited transaction is taken into account (¶ 2355).
- The deductions for personal exemptions, foreign taxes, charitable contributions, net operating losses (NOLs), itemized deductions for individuals (except those paid or incurred for the production of income), and depletion are not allowed.
- The amount of any net income from foreclosure property is reduced by the amount of tax imposed on that income.
- Gain or loss from the disposition of assets, including qualified mortgages and permitted investments, is treated as ordinary gain or loss rather than gain or loss from a capital asset.
- Interest expenses (other than the portion allocable to tax-exempt interest) may be deducted without regard to the investment interest limitation.
- Debts owed to the REMIC are not treated as nonbusiness debts for purposes of the bad debt deduction.
- The REMIC is not treated as carrying on a trade or business, and ordinary and necessary operating expenses may only be deducted as expenses incurred for the production of income (without regard to the two-percent floor on itemized deductions) (Code Sec. 860C(b); Reg. § 1.860C-2).[81]

References are to Standard Federal Tax Reports; Tax Research Consultant; and Practical Tax Explanations.

[78] ¶ 26,700, ¶ 26,700B; RIC: 9,100

[79] ¶ 26,720; RIC: 9,106

[80] ¶ 26,600; RIC: 9,150; § 45,445.10

[81] ¶ 26,640, ¶ 26,640B; RIC: 9,254; § 45,445.10

A REMIC's net loss is determined by subtracting its gross income from allowable deductions, taking into account the same modifications listed above.

2355. Prohibited Transactions of REMICs. A real estate mortgage investment conduit (REMIC) is required to pay a 100-percent tax on its *net income* from a prohibited transaction (losses are not taken into account for this purpose) (Code Sec. 860F(a)).[82] The disposition of any qualified mortgage is considered a prohibited transaction, but not if the disposition is due to:

(1) the substitution of a qualified replacement mortgage for a qualified mortgage (or the repurchase in lieu of substitution of a defective obligation);

(2) the bankruptcy or insolvency of the REMIC;

(3) a disposition incident to foreclosure or default of a mortgage; or

(4) a qualified liquidation.

A significant modification of a mortgage is considered a disposition (Reg. § 1.860G-2(b)).[83] The IRS has issued procedures (some of them temporary) that set forth conditions under which modifications of certain mortgage loans, as well as subprime mortgage loans, will not be considered a disposition of a qualified mortgage and a prohibited transaction of a REMIC or investment trust that holds the loans (Rev. Proc. 2010-30; Rev. Proc. 2009-45; Rev. Proc. 2009-23).[84]

Prohibited transactions of a REMIC also include: the receipt of any income from an asset that is neither a qualified mortgage or permitted investment (¶ 2345), the receipt of any amount that represents a fee or compensation for services, and the receipt of gain from the disposition of any cash flow investment unless the disposition is made pursuant to a qualified liquidation. A disposition is not treated as a prohibited transaction, however, if it is required to prevent default on a regular interest where the threatened default results from a default on one or more qualified mortgages, or is undertaken to facilitate a clean-up call.

2356. Net Income from Foreclosure Property. A real estate mortgage investment conduit (REMIC) is subject to tax at the highest corporate income tax rate on its *net income* from foreclosure property for the tax year (Code Sec. 860G(c)).[85] For this purpose, net income from foreclosure property is the excess of gain from the sale or other disposition of foreclosure property as described in Code Sec. 1221(a)(1) (i.e., stock in trade or property held by the REMIC for sale to customers in the ordinary course of trade or business), plus the gross income derived from foreclosure property during the tax year, over deductions derived from the production of such income (Code Sec. 857(b)(4)(B)).[86] Foreclosure property is any interest in real property and personal property incident to real property acquired by a REMIC as a result of a default of a lease on the property or a debt securing the property. A REMIC must elect to treat property as foreclosure property by the due date (including extensions) of its annual return for the year in which it acquires the property. Property ceases to be foreclosure property as of the close of the third tax year after the tax year in which it is acquired, unless extensions are granted (Code Sec. 856(e)).[87]

2357. Post-Startup Contributions to REMICs. A real estate mortgage investment conduit (REMIC) that receives contributions of property after its start-up day is subject to a tax equal to the full value of the contribution (Code Sec. 860G(d)).[88] Exceptions to the tax are provided for cash contributions: to facilitate a clean-up call or a qualified liquidation, in the nature of a guarantee, made during the three-month period that begins on the start-up day, made by a holder of a residual interest in the REMIC to a qualified reserve fund, or permitted under regulations.

References are to Standard Federal Tax Reports; Tax Research Consultant; and Practical Tax Explanations.

[82] ¶ 26,700; RIC: 9,152
[83] ¶ 26,720B; RIC: 9,152.10
[84] ¶ 26,721.70; RIC: 9,152.10
[85] ¶ 26,720; RIC: 9,154
[86] ¶ 26,520; RIC: 6,068
[87] ¶ 26,500; RIC: 6,068
[88] ¶ 26,720; RIC: 9,156

2358. Taxation of Regular Interests. Holders of regular interests in a real estate mortgage investment conduit (REMIC) are taxed as if their interests were debt instruments, except that income derived from their interests must be computed under the accrual method of accounting (Code Sec. 860B).[89] Gain on the disposition of a regular interest is treated as ordinary income to the extent of unaccrued original issue discount, computed at 110 percent of the applicable federal rate effective at the time the interest was acquired. The REMIC must report interest payments of $10 or more to regular interest holders and the IRS (¶ 2344).

2361. Taxation of Residual Interests. Holders of residual interests in a real estate mortgage investment conduit (REMIC) must take into account their daily portions of the taxable income or net loss of the REMIC (¶ 2352) for each day during the tax year on which they hold their interests (Code Sec. 860C; Reg. § 1.860C-1).[90] The daily portion is determined on the basis of quarterly computations of the REMIC's taxable income or net loss with such amounts being allocated among all residual interests in proportion to their respective holdings on each day during the quarter (reported on Schedule Q of Form 1066). The holder treats his portion of taxable income and net loss as ordinary income or loss. However, the amount of loss that the holder may take into account in any calendar quarter cannot exceed his adjusted basis in the residual interest (as determined without regard to any required basis decreases for the daily portions of the REMIC's net loss). Any allocated loss which is disallowed may be carried forward to succeeding calendar quarters indefinitely, but it may only be used to offset income from the same REMIC.

Distributions made by the REMIC to a holder of a residual interest are received tax free to the extent that they do not exceed that holder's adjusted basis in his interest. Any excess is treated as gain from the sale or exchange of the interest. The basis of a holder's residual interest is increased by the daily portion of REMIC taxable income allocated to the residual interest holder. The holder's basis is decreased, but not below zero, by the amount of any distribution received and the daily portion of the REMIC net loss allocated to the interest holder. When a residual interest in a REMIC is disposed of, these adjustments are treated as occurring immediately before the disposition.

Income in Excess of Daily Accruals. A holder of a residual interest may not reduce its taxable income (or alternative minimum taxable income) for the tax year below his "excess inclusion" for the year (Code Sec. 860E; Reg. § 1.860E-1).[91] A holder's excess inclusion is equal to the excess of the net income passed through to the holder each calendar quarter over a deemed interest component that is referred to as the "daily accrual." The effect is to prevent a holder from offsetting its excess inclusion by any net operating losses (NOLs) or in calculating alternative minimum tax (AMT). Excess inclusions are also treated as unrelated business taxable income for tax-exempt holders (¶ 655). Where a residual interest is held by a mutual fund, real estate investment trust (REIT), common trust fund, or cooperative, a portion of the dividends paid by such organizations to their shareholders are treated as excess inclusions.

Application of Wash Sale Rules. Except as provided in the regulations, the wash sale rules (¶ 1935) apply to dispositions of residual interests where a seller of the interest acquires any residual interest in any REMIC (or any interest in a taxable mortgage pool (¶ 2368) that is comparable to a residual interest) within a period beginning six months before the date of sale or disposition and ending six months after that date (Code Sec. 860F(d)).[92]

Residual Interests Held by Disqualified Organizations. If a disqualified organization (government, exempt organization, cooperative) holds a residual interest in a REMIC at any time during the tax year, then an excise tax is imposed against the person or entity that has transferred the interest to the organization (Code Sec. 860E(e); Reg.

References are to Standard Federal Tax Reports; Tax Research Consultant; and Practical Tax Explanations.

[89] ¶ 26,620; RIC: 9,202; § 45,445.10

[90] ¶ 26,640, ¶ 26,640A; RIC: 9,252; § 45,445.10

[91] ¶ 26,680, ¶ 26,680A; RIC: 9,256; § 45,445.10

[92] ¶ 26,700; RIC: 9,262; § 45,445.10

§ 1.860E-2).[93] The tax is the highest corporate income tax rate imposed on the present value of the total excess inclusion that is anticipated for the interest after the transfer takes place. If the transfer is through an agent of the disqualified organization, the agent must pay the tax.

Noneconomic Interests. The transfer of a noneconomic residual interest is disregarded for federal tax purposes if a significant purpose of the transfer was to impede the assessment or collection of tax (Reg. § 1.860E-1(c)).[94] A noneconomic residual interest is one for which anticipated distributions are insufficient to meet anticipated tax liabilities.

2367. Foreign Holders of REMIC Interests. If the holder of a residual interest in a real estate mortgage investment conduit (REMIC) is a nonresident alien or a foreign corporation, then for withholding and income tax purposes (¶ 2425): (1) amounts includible in the holder's gross income are taken into account when paid or distributed, or when the interest is disposed of, and (2) no exemption from the 30-percent tax imposed on U.S.-source income not effectively connected with a U.S. business applies to any excess inclusion (¶ 2431) (Code Sec. 860G(b)).[95]

2368. Taxable Mortgage Pools. If a mortgage pool does not elect to be or qualify as a real estate mortgage investment conduit (REMIC) (or as a financial asset securitization investment trust (FASIT) formed prior to January 1, 2005) (¶ 2394), it may qualify as a taxable mortgage pool. An entity is a taxable mortgage pool if:

(1) substantially all the assets of which consist of debt obligations (or interests therein) and more than 50 percent of the obligations (or interests) consist of real estate mortgages;

(2) the entity is the obligor under debt obligations with two or more maturities; and

(3) under the terms of the entity's debt obligations, payments on the obligations referred to in (2) are related to payments on the obligations or interests referred to in (1) (Code Sec. 7701(i)).[96]

A taxable mortgage pool is taxed as a separate corporation and may not join with any other corporation in filing a consolidated return. Any portion of an entity that meets the requirements above is treated as a taxable mortgage pool. However, no domestic savings and loan association can qualify to be a taxable mortgage pool.

Insurance Companies

2370. Taxation of Life Insurance Companies. A life insurance company is generally taxed on its life insurance taxable income at regular corporate tax rates (¶ 219) (Code Sec. 801).[97] If it has net capital gains, however, the company is taxed at the 35-percent corporate capital gain rate (¶ 1738) on its net capital gain, and at regular corporate tax rates on the excess of its life insurance taxable income minus the net capital gain, if this results in a lower tax amount.

Life insurance taxable income for this purpose is the sum of the life insurance company's net premiums, net decreases in reserves, and other items of income, minus deductions for the following: claims, benefits, and losses accrued; net increases in various reserves (¶ 2372); policyholder dividends (¶ 2373); dividends received (subject to limitations); operational losses (¶ 2377); consideration paid for another person's assumption of the company's insurance and annuity liabilities; and dividend reimbursements paid to another insurance company (Code Secs. 803 and 805).[98]

All other deductions allowed to a corporation are also permitted, subject to some modifications (for example, no deduction for net operating losses (NOLs) is allowed). Small life insurance companies (gross assets of less than $500 million at the close of a tax year) may claim an additional deduction based on their tentative taxable income

References are to Standard Federal Tax Reports; Tax Research Consultant; and Practical Tax Explanations.

[93] ¶ 26,680, ¶ 26,680B; RIC: 9,062, RIC: 9,258.05
[94] ¶ 26,680A; RIC: 9,258.10
[95] ¶ 26,720; RIC: 9,252.20, INTL: 33,110.30
[96] ¶ 43,080; RIC: 9,300
[97] ¶ 25,710; CCORP: 12,106.55
[98] ¶ 25,730, ¶ 25,770; CCORP: 100

(Code Sec. 806).[99] A life insurance company uses Form 1120-L to figure and report its taxable income.

A business entity qualifies as a life insurance company if: (1) more than half of its business activities consist of issuing life insurance or annuity contracts or reinsuring risks underwritten by other insurance companies; and (2) more than half of its total reserves for paying off insurance obligations consist of life insurance reserves, plus unearned premiums, and unpaid losses on noncancellable life, accident, or health policies that are not included in life insurance reserves (Code Sec. 816).[100]

2372. Net Change in Reserves. Life insurance companies may deduct the net increase in certain reserves and must include in income the net decrease in such reserves that have occurred during the tax year (Code Sec. 807).[101] In general, the net increase or decrease is computed by comparing the closing balance for reserves to the opening balance of the reserves. The closing balance is reduced by the policyholders' shares of tax-exempt interest and of the increase in cash values of insurance and annuity contracts for the year.

Items that must be taken into account in determining whether reserves have had a net increase or decrease include:

(1) life insurance reserves;

(2) unearned premiums and unpaid losses (Code Sec. 846);[102]

(3) discounted amounts necessary to satisfy obligations arising under contracts that did not involve life, accident, or health contingencies;

(4) dividend accumulations and other amounts held in connection with insurance and annuity contracts;

(5) advanced premiums and liabilities for premium deposit funds; and

(6) reasonable special contingency reserves for group term life insurance or group accident and health contracts.

Insurance companies that are required to discount unpaid losses may claim an additional deduction up to the excess of undiscounted unpaid losses over related discounted unpaid losses (Code Sec. 847).[103]

2373. Policyholder Dividends. Life insurance companies may claim a deduction for dividends or similar distributions paid or accrued to policyholders during the tax year (Code Sec. 808).[104] A policyholder dividend includes excess interest, premium adjustments, experience-rated refunds, and any amount paid or credited to policyholders not based on a fixed amount in the contract but dependent on the experience rate of the company or the discretion of management. However, the policyholder dividends deduction must be reduced by the amount by which such deduction was accelerated due to a change in the life insurance company's business practice.

2377. Operations Loss Deduction. A life insurance company may claim an "operations loss deduction," which is the excess of its life insurance deductions over its life insurance gross income (subject to limitations). An operational loss may be carried back three years and carried forward 15 years (Code Sec. 810).[105] The company, however, may elect to forgo the entire carryback period for an operational loss for any tax year. In addition, if the company qualifies as a new life insurance company, the operational loss for any tax year may be carried forward 18 years.

2378. Taxation of Other Insurance Companies. Insurance companies that do not meet the definition of a "life insurance company" (¶ 2370) (property and casualty companies) are subject to taxation at regular corporate income tax rates on their taxable income (Code Secs. 831(a) and 832).[106] However, such companies are exempt from tax if

References are to Standard Federal Tax Reports; Tax Research Consultant; and Practical Tax Explanations.

[99] ¶ 25,790; FILEBUS: 3,056
[100] ¶ 25,990; CCORP: 36,204
[101] ¶ 25,810
[102] ¶ 26,330
[103] ¶ 26,350
[104] ¶ 25,830
[105] ¶ 25,870; NOL: 9,250
[106] ¶ 26,130, ¶ 26,150; CCORP: 100

gross receipts for the tax year do not exceed $600,000 and more than 50 percent of such receipts consist of premiums ($150,000 and 35 percent, respectively, for mutual insurance companies) (Code Sec. 501(c)(15)).[107] A property and casualty insurance company with net written premiums of no more than $1.2 million for the tax year may elect to be taxed only on its taxable investment income, which is gross investment income less deductions for tax-free interest, investment expenses, real estate expenses, depreciation, paid or accrued interest, capital losses, trade or business deductions and certain corporate deductions (Code Secs. 831(b) and 834).[108]

2380. Foreign Insurance Companies. A foreign company carrying on an insurance business within the United States that would otherwise qualify as an insurance company if it were a domestic company is taxable as an insurance company on its U.S.-source income effectively connected with the conduct of any U.S. trade or business (¶ 2429) (Code Sec. 842).[109]

Other Special Entities

2383. Banks and Other Financial Institutions. Banks and other financial institutions are generally subject to the same tax rules as corporations. However, unlike other taxpayers, banks are not subject to capital loss limitations with respect to the worthlessness of debt securities (¶ 1916). Instead, banks may treat these losses as bad debt losses. In addition, the capital loss limitations generally do apply to a bank with respect to worthless stocks and stock rights in another bank, if it directly owns at least 80 percent of each class of the other bank's stock (Code Sec. 582).[110]

The method that is used to deduct bad debts of a bank depends on the type and size of the institution in question (Code Sec. 585; Reg. §§ 1.585-1—1.585-8).[111] A small bank (average adjusted basis of all assets of $500 million or less) may add to its bad debt reserves an amount based on its actual experience as shown by losses for the current and preceding five tax years. A thrift institution that would be treated as a small bank may utilize this method as well. Large banks, on the other hand, are generally required to use either a specific charge-off method, in which the bank's debt reserves are recaptured over a four-year period, or the cut-off method, in which recoveries and losses are reflected as adjustments to the bank's reserve account.

Definition of a Bank. For this purpose, a bank is defined as a corporation with a substantial part of its business consisting of either receiving deposits and making loans or exercising fiduciary powers similar to those permitted to national banks. This includes commercial banks and trust companies, mutual savings banks, building and loan associations, cooperative banks, and federal savings and loan associations (Code Sec. 581; Reg. § 1.581-2).[112] These latter "banks," however, are allowed a deduction for dividends paid or credited to depositors (Code Sec. 591).[113]

Sale or Exchange of Securities. In the case of certain financial institutions, the sale or exchange of a bond, debenture, note, certificate, or other evidence of indebtedness is not considered a sale or exchange of a capital asset (Code Sec. 582(c)).[114] Instead, net gains and losses from such transactions are treated as ordinary income and losses. A financial institution for this purpose includes commercial banks, mutual savings banks, domestic building and loan associations, cooperative banks, business development corporations, and small business investment companies (¶ 2392).

2389. Common Trust Funds. A common trust fund is an investment vehicle established by a bank in the form of a state-law trust to handle the investment and reinvestment of money contributed to it in its capacity as a trustee, executor, administrator, or guardian, or as a custodian of a Uniform Gifts to Minors account (Code Sec.

References are to Standard Federal Tax Reports; Tax Research Consultant; and Practical Tax Explanations.

[107] ¶ 22,602; EXEMPT: 9,650; § 33,005.05

[108] ¶ 26,130, ¶ 26,190; EXEMPT: 9,650

[109] ¶ 26,250; INTLIN: 3,108

[110] ¶ 23,608; BUSEXP: 30,102.15

[111] ¶ 23,650, ¶ 23,651–¶ 23,661; RIC: 12,202

[112] ¶ 23,602, ¶ 23,604; RIC: 12,050

[113] ¶ 23,690; CCORP: 9,062

[114] ¶ 23,608; RIC: 12,214; § 18,805.05

584).[115] For tax purposes, a common trust fund is treated in a manner similar to that of a partnership. Instead of the trust being subject to tax, each participant that invests in the trust fund must include his proportionate share of the trust fund's income or loss on his own return. This includes a participant's share of dividends received by the fund which are eligible for the reduced tax rate on qualified dividends (¶ 733). The admission and withdrawal of a participant, however, does not result in a gain or loss to the common trust fund.

> **Comment:** Absent further legislation, ordinary income tax rates will apply to qualified dividend income (¶ 733) that is passed through a common trust fund after December 31, 2012.

2392. Small Business Investment Companies. A small business investment company (SBIC) is a private corporation that operates under the Small Business Investment Act of 1958 to provide capital to small business concerns through the purchase of convertible debentures. An SBIC is generally treated as a corporation for federal tax purposes with a few exceptions. First, an SBIC may claim an ordinary loss deduction for any loss on the sale or exchange of stock of a small business concern if the stock was received under the conversion privilege of a debenture acquired on the providing of equity capital to small business concerns (Code Sec. 1243).[116] Second, an SBIC may deduct 100 percent (rather than 70 percent) of the dividends it receives from taxable domestic corporations (Code Sec. 243(a)(2)).[117] See ¶ 1913 for discussion of the treatment of losses on SBIC stock and ¶ 1909 for discussion of the rollover of gain from the sale of publicly traded securities into stock or a partnership interest in an SBIC.

2394. Financial Asset Securitization Investment Trusts. Prior to January 1, 2005, a qualified entity could elect to be treated as a financial asset securitization investment trust (FASIT) (Code Secs. 860H—860L, prior to repeal by the American Jobs Creation Act of 2004 (P.L. 108-357)).[118] A FASIT is a pass-through entity used to securitize debt obligations such as credit card receivables, home equity loans and auto loans. A FASIT must be entirely owned by a taxable C corporation. Any residual income of the FASIT is passed through and taxed to the owner. The advantage offered by a FASIT is that asset-backed securities issued by a FASIT are treated as debt for federal tax purposes. Thus, interest paid to investors is deductible.

The rules regarding FASITs are repealed as of January 1, 2005, but the repeal does not apply to any FASIT in existence on October 22, 2004, to the extent that regular interests already issued by the FASIT remain outstanding in accordance with their original terms.

References are to Standard Federal Tax Reports; Tax Research Consultant; and Practical Tax Explanations.

[115] ¶ 23,630; RIC: 12,300

[116] ¶ 30,770; SALES: 18,304; § 18,245

[117] ¶ 13,051; CCORP: 9,056; § 26,505

[118] ¶ 26,730; RIC: 18,000

Chapter 24

FOREIGN INCOME AND TRANSACTIONS

Overview

2401. Taxation of Worldwide Income. The United States taxes the worldwide income of U.S. citizens, resident aliens, and domestic corporations without regard to whether the income arose from a transaction or activity originating outside its geographic borders (¶ 2402). Nonresident aliens and foreign corporations are generally taxed in the same manner as U.S. citizens and domestic corporations on income that is effectively connected with a U.S. trade or business (¶ 2425). Income not effectively connected with a U.S. trade or business, such as fixed, determinable, annual, or periodical (FDAP) income, is generally taxed at a 30-percent rate. To prevent income from being subject to double taxation—once in the United States and once in a foreign country—U.S. taxpayers may be entitled to a credit or deduction for foreign income taxes paid or accrued during the tax year (¶ 2475). Special rules apply with regard to the taxation of U.S. shareholders of controlled foreign corporations (CFCs) (¶ 2487). U.S. persons are also subject to a number of foreign asset reporting requirements (¶ 2465 and ¶ 2467).

U.S. Citizens and Residents Living Abroad

2402. Foreign Earned Income Exclusion. A qualifying individual (¶ 2404) who lives and works abroad may elect (¶ 2408) to exclude from gross income a certain amount of foreign earned income attributable to his or her residence in a foreign country during the tax year (Code Sec. 911(a)(1) and (b)(2)).[1] The maximum amount of foreign earned income that may be excluded is $95,100 for calendar year 2012 ($97,600 for calendar year 2013) (Rev. Proc. 2011-52; Rev. Proc. 2012-41). The exclusion is computed on a daily basis. Therefore, the maximum limit must be reduced ratably for each day during the calendar year that the taxpayer does not qualify for the exclusion. The exclusion is also limited to the excess of the individual's foreign earned income for the year over his or her foreign housing exclusion (¶ 2403). In the case of married taxpayers, each spouse may compute the limitation separately and without regard to community property laws (if otherwise applicable). Thus, it is possible for a married couple to exclude up to $190,200 for 2012 ($195,200 for calendar year 2013), if each spouse is qualified to claim the exclusion (Reg. § 1.911-5).[2]

Example 1: Andy is a U.S. citizen who qualified as a bona fide resident of Costa Rica for all of 2011 and who received $78,000 in salary for work he did in Costa Rica. Assuming he claimed no foreign housing exclusion, Andy was able to exclude all of the salary from his gross income for 2011. Andy continues to work in Costa Rica until October 31, 2012, when his employer permanently reassigns him to the United States. During this time, Andy received a salary of $90,000 for his

References are to Standard Federal Tax Reports; Tax Research Consultant; and Practical Tax Explanations.

[1] ¶ 28,040; EXPAT: 12,100; § 37,510.05

[2] ¶ 28,045; EXPAT: 12,400; § 37,510.25

work in Costa Rica in 2012. Assuming he claimed no foreign housing exclusion, the maximum amount of foreign earned income he can exclude from his gross income in 2012 is $79,250 ($95,100 multiplied by ratio of the number of days he was a bona fide resident of Costa Rica (305/366).

Foreign Earned Income. Foreign earned income includes wages, salaries, professional fees, and other amounts received as compensation for personal services actually rendered when the taxpayer's tax home was located in a foreign country and the taxpayer meets either the bona fide residence or physical presence test (Code Sec. 911(b)(1) and (d)(2); Reg. § 1.911-3).[3] If the taxpayer engages in a sole proprietorship or partnership where both personal services and capital are material income-producing factors, no more than 30 percent of the taxpayer's share of the net profits can be treated as earned income (30 percent of gross profits if no net profits). Any salary received from a corporation is earned income to the extent it represents reasonable compensation for personal services performed.

Foreign earned income does not include any compensation received after the close of the tax year following the year in which the personal services were performed. It also does not include any reimbursements received under an accountable plan for expenses incurred on an employer's behalf (¶ 952A), the value of meals and lodging that are furnished for the convenience of an employer and excluded from gross income (¶ 2188C and ¶ 2406), employer contributions to a nonqualified retirement plan, or any recaptured moving expenses. Foreign earned income also does not include amounts received as a pension, annuity, or social security payments, amounts paid by the United States or its agencies to its employees, or income earned in a country in which the United States imposes travel restrictions.

A taxpayer that elects to claim the foreign earned income exclusion (or foreign housing exclusion) is prohibited from claiming any deduction, exclusion, or tax credit (including the foreign tax credit) that is properly allocable to the excluded amounts (Code Sec. 911(d)(6); Reg. § 1.911-6(a)).[4] For example, a taxpayer may not deduct unreimbursed employee business expenses against wages that are excluded as foreign earned income.

Determination of Tax Liability. If a taxpayer elects to exclude foreign earned income or foreign housing expenses (or both), then his or her income tax liability and alternative minimum tax (AMT) liability on the nonexcluded amount is determined using the tax rates that would have applied had the exclusion(s) not been claimed (Code Sec. 911(f)).[5] The computation of the tentative minimum tax on the nonexcluded income is made before reduction for the AMT foreign tax credit (¶ 1401). If the taxpayer's net capital gains exceeds his or her taxable income (or alternative minimum taxable income (AMTI)), then the taxpayer is treated as having an adjusted net capital gain equal to the lesser of the excess or the adjusted net capital gain. The excess first reduces the amount of net capital gain without regard to qualified dividend income, and then qualified dividend income. Also, in computing adjusted net capital gain, unrecaptured section 1250 gain, and 28-percent rate gain, the amount of the excess is treated in the same manner as an increase in the long-term capital loss carried to the tax year. The Foreign Earned Income Worksheet in the Form 1040 Instructions or Form 6251 Instructions is used to calculate tax liability for this purpose.

2403. Foreign Housing Exclusion or Deduction. In addition to the election to exclude foreign earned income (¶ 2402), a qualified individual (¶ 2404) may elect (¶ 2408) to exclude from gross income a certain amount of foreign housing expenses paid for with employer-provided amounts included in the taxpayer's foreign earned income (for example, housing allowance or reimbursement) (Code Sec. 911(a)(2)).[6]

References are to Standard Federal Tax Reports; Tax Research Consultant; and Practical Tax Explanations.

[3] ¶ 28,040, ¶ 28,043; EXPAT: 12,200; § 37,510.10

[4] ¶ 28,040, ¶ 28,046; EXPAT: 12,250; § 37,525.05

[5] ¶ 28,040; EXPAT: 12,100; § 37,520

[6] ¶ 28,040; EXPAT: 12,150; § 37,515.05

Caution: The amount of foreign housing expenses (or foreign earned income) excluded from an individual's gross income is used to determine the taxpayer's regular income tax and alternative minimum tax (AMT) liability on his or her nonexcluded income (¶ 2402).

The maximum amount of foreign housing expenses that may be excluded is generally limited to 14 percent of the maximum foreign earned income exclusion for the year (Code Sec. 911(c)). This is the excess of: (1) the taxpayer's reasonable "foreign housing expenses" for the tax year (limited to 30 percent of the maximum foreign earned income exclusion for the year), over (2) a "base housing amount" equal to 16 percent of the maximum foreign earned income exclusion amount for the year. The exclusion is computed on a daily basis and multiplied by the number of days of foreign residence or presence by the taxpayer for the year. Thus, the maximum amount that may be excluded in 2012 is $13,314, or $36.38 per day. The maximum amount that may be excluded in 2013 is $13,664, or $37.44 per day. However, foreign housing expenses may be excluded only to the extent of the lesser of the expenses attributable to employer-provided amounts or the individual's foreign earned income for the tax year.

The reasonable amount of expenses that may be used in calculating the maximum exclusion limit (i.e., the 30 percent of the maximum foreign earned income exclusion) may be adjusted annually by the IRS for specific geographic locations that have higher housing costs relative to the United States (Notice 2012-19).[7] For this purpose, the taxpayer must actually reside within the geographic limits of the high-cost location identified by the IRS to claim the adjusted limit; the taxpayer cannot reside in a suburb of the location.

Housing Expenses. A taxpayer's foreign housing expenses are the reasonable costs paid or incurred during the tax year to provide housing in a foreign country for the taxpayer and for his or her spouse and dependents if they reside with the taxpayer (Reg. § 1.911-4).[8] This may include reasonable expenses related to a second foreign household for the taxpayer's spouse and dependents if they do not reside with the taxpayer due to adverse conditions near the taxpayer's tax home. Eligible expenses include rent or the fair rental value of housing provided in kind by an employer, utilities (other than telephone charges), real or personal property insurance, household repairs, rental of furniture and accessories, and residential parking. They do not include expenses that are otherwise deductible (depreciation, interest, taxes) or that are extravagant. They also do not include the cost of buying property (including mortgage payments), capital improvements to property, purchased furniture or accessories, or the cost of domestic labor. If a husband and wife are both qualified individuals with foreign earned income, special rules apply which may allow them both to claim the foreign housing exclusion or deduction, depending on whether separate households are maintained (Reg. § 1.911-5).[9]

Self-Employment. A self-employed taxpayer is entitled to deduct from gross income a certain amount of foreign housing expenses in lieu of the exclusion (Code Sec. 911(c)(4); Reg. § 1.911-4(e)).[10] The deduction is limited to the amount by which the taxpayer's foreign earned income for the tax year exceeds his or her foreign earned income and housing exclusion. Any amount that exceeds the deduction limit can be carried forward one tax year. If the taxpayer has foreign earned income that consists of both employer-provided amounts and self-employment amounts, then the taxpayer may elect to exclude the part of the housing expenses that are paid for with employer-provided amounts and may claim a deduction for any remaining housing expenses attributed to self-employment income.

2404. Eligibility for Foreign Earned Income and Housing Exclusions. In order to qualify for the foreign earned income exclusion (¶ 2402) or foreign housing exclusion (¶ 2403), an individual's tax home must be in a foreign country and he or she must

References are to Standard Federal Tax Reports; Tax Research Consultant; and Practical Tax Explanations.

[7] ¶ 28,049.225; EXPAT: 12,152; § 37,515.10

[8] ¶ 28,044; EXPAT: 12,154; § 37,515.10

[9] ¶ 28,045; EXPAT: 12,400; § 37,515.25

[10] ¶ 28,040, ¶ 28,044; EXPAT: 12,162; § 37,515.20

satisfy either the bona fide residence test or the physical presence test (Code Sec. 911(d)(1); Reg. §1.911-2).[11] A foreign country is any territory, including airspace and territorial waters, under the sovereignty of a government other than the United States. A foreign country does not include Antarctica or U.S. possessions such as Puerto Rico, Guam, the Commonwealth of the Northern Mariana Islands, the U.S. Virgin Islands, and Johnston Island. A bona fide resident of American Samoa (¶2414) or Puerto Rico (¶2415), however, may be eligible to exclude income from the possession for U.S. tax purposes. The foreign earned income and housing exclusions are denied if the taxpayer is present in a foreign country in which travel is generally restricted (Code Sec. 911(d)(8)).

Tax Home. "Tax home" for this purpose has the same meaning as it does for determining the deductibility of travel expenses away from home (¶950). An individual's tax home is where his or her principal place of business is located, regardless of where he or she maintains a family home (Code Sec. 911(d)(3)). The location of a taxpayer's tax home often depends on whether a work assignment is temporary or indefinite. However, an individual is not considered to have a tax home in a foreign country for any period during which his or her abode is in the United States. Temporary presence or maintenance of a dwelling in the United States does not necessarily mean that an abode is in the United States during that time.

Bona Fide Residence. A U.S. citizen (or resident alien subject to a U.S. income tax treaty) may qualify for the foreign earned income or housing exclusions if he or she is a bona fide resident of a foreign country for an uninterrupted period that includes a full tax year (Code Sec. 911(d)(1)(A) and (d)(5)). This determination is based on all of the facts and circumstances including the taxpayer's intentions regarding the length and nature of their stay. It is not determined by the taxpayer's status under the laws of the foreign country, nor by merely living in a foreign country for a year. However, the taxpayer does not have to be a bona fide resident of the same foreign country for the entire period and the foreign country in which the taxpayer is a bona fide resident does not have to be the primary place of employment. Once the bona fide residence requirement is met, the taxpayer is permitted the exclusions for any tax year in which the period of residence began or ended.

> **Example 1:** Barney is a calendar-year taxpayer whose salary is $100,000 per year. On January 1, 2011, he establishes bona fide residence in Canada. His residence lasts until March 31, 2012. Assuming he claims no foreign housing exclusion, he qualifies in 2011 for the maximum exclusion of $92,900 for his foreign earned income because he established residence for the full year in a foreign country. He also qualifies for the exclusion of $23,645 of his foreign earned income ($95,100 × 91/366) for the portion of the 2012 tax year he was a resident in Canada.

Physical Presence. A U.S. citizen or resident alien may qualify for the foreign income or housing exclusions if he or she is present in a foreign country (or countries) for 330 full days out of any consecutive 12-month period (Code Sec. 911(d)(1)(B)). The taxpayer does not have to be present in the foreign country solely for business purposes and the 330 days do not have to be consecutive. In addition, the taxpayer can select any 12-month period in which he or she meets the physical presence test is met.

> **Example 2:** Betty is a U.S. citizen who leaves New York on February 3, 2012, and arrives in Spain on that same day. During December 2012, Betty vacations in France for ten days. She leaves Spain to move back to the United States on January 10, 2013. Betty will meet the 330-day test during either the 12-month period beginning February 4, 2012, or the 12-month period ending January 10, 2013.

Waiver of Time Requirements. Relief from either the bona fide residence or the physical presence test is provided to an individual if he or she was forced to flee a foreign country because of civil unrest, war, or other adverse conditions (Code Sec.

References are to Standard Federal Tax Reports; Tax Research Consultant; and Practical Tax Explanations.

[11] ¶28,040, ¶28,042; EXPAT: 12,050; §37,505.05

911(d)(4)). To qualify for the relief, the individual must have been a bona fide resident of, or present in, the foreign country on or prior to the date the IRS determines that adverse conditions exist in the foreign country and individuals are required to leave. In addition, the taxpayer must establish that he or she could reasonably be expected to have satisfied the residency requirement had the adverse conditions not arisen. The IRS publishes annually the names of countries for which the waiver is available.[12]

2406. Camps Located in a Foreign Country. In addition to the exclusion of foreign earned income (¶ 2402) and foreign housing expenses (¶ 2403), an individual may be able to exclude from gross income the value of meals and lodging provided by his or her employer in a camp located in a foreign country if three requirements are met (Code Sec. 119(c)).[13] First, the lodging must be provided for the convenience of the employer because the place where the employee's services are performed is in a remote area where satisfactory housing is unavailable. Second, the location of the camp must be as near as practicable to the place where the employee's services are performed. Third, the lodging must be provided in a common area, not open to the public, that normally accommodates 10 or more employees. An employee who works for a U.S. military contractor on a foreign military base cannot exclude from income the value of lodging provided by his or her employer, as the lodging is not considered to be on the employer's business premises (*P.M. Middleton*, TC Memo. 2008-150).[14]

2408. Electing the Foreign Earned Income and Housing Exclusions. A qualified individual (¶ 2404) must make a separate election with respect to the foreign earned income exclusion (¶ 2402) and the foreign housing exclusion (¶ 2403). The elections are made by filing Form 2555 or Form 2555-EZ with the taxpayer's timely-filed income tax return (including extensions), amended return, or a late-filed return if filed within one year after the due date of the return (not including extensions) (Code Sec. 911(e); Reg. § 1.911-7).[15] Once made, the election will remain in effect for the current tax year and all subsequent years unless revoked. A taxpayer that revokes the election, however, will be prohibited from making a new election for at least five tax years without IRS approval. If both a husband and wife qualify for the exclusions, each must file a separate Form 2555 regardless of whether they file a joint return or separate returns. A self-employed taxpayer does not have to make an election in order to claim the foreign housing deduction.

An individual that claims either the foreign earned income or foreign housing exclusion may not claim the foreign tax credit or deduction (¶ 2475) for any income excluded. If a taxpayer attempts to claim the foreign tax credit or deduction, then the election for the foreign earned income and foreign housing exclusions will be considered revoked (IRS Pub. 54). A taxpayer eligible for the earned income tax credit (¶ 1322) may also not claim both the credit and either of the exclusions.

2409. Resident Aliens. A resident alien is generally taxed in the same manner as a U.S. citizen. For this purpose, residency is determined under the lawful permanent residence test ("green card") or the substantial presence test (Code Sec. 7701(b)(1)).[16] An alien who does not qualify under either test is generally treated as a nonresident alien for federal income, employment, and excise tax purposes (but not estate and gift tax purposes). Some individuals may be eligible to elect resident status (¶ 2410). In addition, an individual can be both a resident and nonresident alien during the same tax year (¶ 2411). In the case of an individual who is considered both a U.S. resident and a resident of a foreign country during the year (dual resident taxpayer), a tax treaty may override the normal treatment of the individual as a resident alien for all purposes under the treaty. The green card test and substantial presence test determine whether an alien is a resident of a U.S. possession or territory whose income tax laws mirror those of the

References are to Standard Federal Tax Reports; Tax Research Consultant; and Practical Tax Explanations.

[12] ¶ 28,049.5775; EXPAT: 12,058; § 37,505.15, § 37,505.20

[13] ¶ 7220; EXPAT: 12,302; § 21,235

[14] ¶ 7222.63; EXPAT: 12,302; § 21,235

[15] ¶ 28,040, ¶ 28,047; EXPAT: 12,108, EXPAT: 12,166; § 37,530.05

[16] ¶ 43,080; EXPAT: 3,000; § 37,101

United States. They do not determine whether an individual is a bona fide resident of a U.S. possession or territory (¶ 2414) (Reg. § 301.7701(b)-1(d)).[17]

Green Card Test. An alien who is a lawful permanent resident of the United States under U.S. immigration laws (i.e., receives a “green card”) is considered a resident alien for federal tax purposes (Reg. § 301.7701(b)-1(b)).[18] Resident status begins in the first calendar year in which the alien is a lawful resident and is physically present in the United States for at least one day (¶ 2411). Resident status continues until permanent resident status is terminated or abandoned (¶ 2412).

Substantial Presence Test. An alien is considered a U.S. resident if the individual is physically present in the United States for at least 31 days during the calendar year and 183 days for the current and two preceding calendar years (¶ 2411). For purposes of the 183-day requirement, each day present in the United States during the current calendar year counts as a full day, each day in the first preceding year as ⅓ of a day, and each day in the second preceding year as ⅙ of a day (Code Sec. 7701(b)(3); Reg. § 301.7701(b)-1(c)).[19] There are exceptions as to what days an alien is considered to be physically present in the United States, including days for: (1) regular commuters from Canada or Mexico; (2) days in transit between two places outside the United States; (3) medical conditions preventing departure; (4) exempt individuals including teachers, trainees, and students on temporary visas, and professional athletes competing in a charitable event; (5) crew members of foreign vessels; and (6) foreign government workers. Form 8843 must be completed to exclude days of physical presence in the United States due to a medical condition or as an exempt individual. Presence in U.S. territories or possessions does not count as presence in the United States.

An individual who otherwise meets the substantial presence test may still be treated as a nonresident alien if the individual has a tax home in a foreign country during the tax year, has a closer connection to the foreign country, and was physically present in the United States for less than 183 days during the year. An alien must fully complete Form 8840 and attach it to his or her return for the relevant tax year to prove that he or she satisfies the closer connection exception.

2410. Elective Resident Status. There are two ways alien individuals are permitted to elect resident status if they do not otherwise qualify as a resident alien (¶ 2409). First, an individual who otherwise fails to meet the green card or substantial presence test may elect to be a resident alien for part of the current year (Code Sec. 7701(b)(4); Reg. § 301.7701(b)-4(c)(3)).[20] To qualify for the election, the alien:

- must not be a resident alien in the prior calendar year;
- must meet the substantial presence test in the calendar year following the election year;
- must be present in the United States for at least 31 consecutive days in the election year; and
- must be present in the United States for at least 75 percent of the days during the period from the first day of the 31-day presence period through the end of the election year.

If these requirements are met, the individual's election to be treated as a U.S. resident alien is effective for that portion of the year that begins on the first day of the earliest testing period that the 31-day and 75 percent requirements are met. The election is made by attaching a signed statement to the individual's tax return for the election year that the individual meets the election requirements. The election cannot be made, however, before the individual has met the substantial presence test for the calendar

References are to Standard Federal Tax Reports; Tax Research Consultant; and Practical Tax Explanations.

[17] ¶ 43,117; EXPAT: 3,100; § 37,145

[18] ¶ 43,117; EXPAT: 3,050; § 37,105

[19] ¶ 43,080, ¶ 43,117; EXPAT: 3,100; § 37,110.05

[20] ¶ 43,080, ¶ 43,120; EXPAT: 3,200; § 37,130

year following the election year. Once made, the election can be revoked only with the IRS' consent.

The second way an alien may elect resident status is if the individual is married to a U.S. citizen or resident alien at the end of the tax year—then the election may be made in order to file a joint return (Code Sec. 6013(g) and (h)).[21] The taxpayer may be either a nonresident or resident alien at the end of the tax year for the election to be made. Both spouses must join in the election. It is effective for the entire tax year and all subsequent tax years for federal income tax and withholding purposes unless neither spouse is a U.S. citizen or resident alien at any time during the year. The election may also be jointly revoked by the couple or terminated by reason of death, separation, divorce, or by the IRS for failure of the couple to keep adequate records. Once terminated, the election may not be made again by the couple.

2411. Dual-Status Tax Years. An individual can be both a resident and nonresident alien during the same tax year (¶ 2409). This usually occurs the year of arrival in, or departure from, the United States. An individual who is a dual-status alien has a dual-status tax year. Thus, the individual's income tax liability is computed as a resident alien for the period of residence and as a nonresident alien for the period of nonresidence (¶ 2425) (Reg. § 1.871-13).[22]

If an alien individual is filing a tax return for a dual-status year, then the standard deduction cannot be claimed, the total deduction for exemptions cannot exceed taxable income for the period the individual is a resident alien, and head of household filing status may not be used. A married individual may also not use joint filing status and tax rates for joint filers for the period of residency unless he or she is married to a U.S. citizen or resident alien and the election to be treated as a resident alien for the year is made (¶ 2410) (IRS Pub. 519). The education credits, earned income credit, and the elderly or disabled credit may also not be claimed unless the individual is married and elects to be treated as a resident alien by filing a joint return.

For this purpose, if an alien meets the green card test, residency starts the first day the alien is physically present in the United States while a lawfully admitted resident. If an alien meets the substantial presence test, residency starts the first day the alien is physically present in the United States during the calendar year. However, a *de minimis* exception allows up to ten days to be disregarded in determining the residency starting date under the substantial presence test if the individual has a closer connection to a foreign country. For an alien that satisfies both tests, residency starts on the earlier date when either test is satisfied (Reg. § 301.7701(b)-4).[23] If the individual was a resident alien in the previous tax year, then residency begins on the first day of the current tax year regardless of whether residency status is determined under the green card test or substantial presence test. Residency status may terminate before the end of the tax year under either test, but only if the alien is not a U.S. resident alien at any time during the following tax year.

Departure Requirements. Generally, no alien (whether resident or nonresident) is permitted to depart the United States or any of its possessions without first obtaining a certificate of compliance from the IRS (sailing or departure permit). The certificate is proof that the individual has discharged all of his or her U.S. income tax liability (Code Sec. 6851(d); Reg. § 1.6851-2).[24] The certificate must be obtained at least two weeks before the individual leaves the United States. Resident aliens (whether they have taxable income or not) and nonresident aliens having no taxable income for the tax year must file Form 2063 to obtain the certificate. Nonresident aliens with taxable income for the tax year must file Form 1040-C to obtain the certificate. The forms do not constitute an individual's final tax return and Form 1040 or Form 1040NR must still be filed after the individual's tax year ends. Payment of any tax is not required prior to departure if it

References are to Standard Federal Tax Reports; Tax Research Consultant; and Practical Tax Explanations.

[21] ¶ 35,160; EXPAT: 3,200; § 37,125.05

[22] ¶ 27,341; EXPAT: 3,150; § 37,120.05

[23] ¶ 43,120; EXPAT: 3,150; § 37,120.05

[24] ¶ 40,402, ¶ 40,405; FILEIND: 18,062.10; § 37,010.35

is determined that tax collection will not be jeopardized by the alien's departure. Individuals who abandon U.S. citizenship or long-term residency for tax avoidance purposes are subject to special rules (¶ 2412).

2412. Expatriation to Avoid Tax. Individuals who relinquish their U.S. citizenship or whose long-term residency status is terminated—covered expatriates—are subject to a mark-to-market tax regime under which they are taxed on the unrealized gain in their property to the extent it exceeds $651,000 for 2012 ($668,000 for 2013) (Code Sec. 877A; Notice 2009-85; Rev. Proc. 2012-41; Rev. Proc. 2011-52).[25] For this purpose, a covered expatriate is considered to own any interest in property that would generally be taxable as part of his or her gross estate for federal estate tax purposes if they died on the day before the expatriation date. Special rules apply, however, for deferred compensation items, specified tax deferred accounts, and interests in nongrantor trusts (¶ 566). A U.S. citizen or resident alien is also subject to a special transfer tax upon receipt of property by gift, devise, bequest, or inheritance from a covered expatriate (¶ 2948).

The exclusion amount must be allocated among all built-in gain property that is subject to the mark-to-market regime and is owned by the covered expatriate on the day before the expatriation date. Gain is determined as if a sale of the property for fair market value had taken place on the day before the expatriation date, and that gain is taken into account for the tax year without regard to other Code provisions. Losses from the deemed sale are generally taken into account as otherwise provided in the Code, except that the wash sale rules do not apply (¶ 1935). The taxpayer must make adjustments to the basis of any property by the amount of gain or loss taken into account under these rules.

Covered Expatriate. A covered expatriate is any U.S. citizen who relinquishes citizenship or any long-term U.S. resident who ceases to be a lawful permanent resident of the United States, if the individual has: (1) an average annual net income tax liability for the five preceding years ending before expatriation that exceeds $151,000 for 2012 ($155,000 for 2013), (2) a net worth of $2 million or more on the expatriation date, or (3) fails to certify under penalties of perjury that he or she has complied with all U.S. tax obligations for the preceding five years or fails to submit evidence of compliance required by the IRS on Form 8854 (Code Sec. 877A(g); Notice 2009-85). Dual citizens and minors may be excepted from the tax liability and net worth requirements.

Election to Defer Tax. The covered expatriate may make an irrevocable election to defer payment of the mark-to-market tax that would otherwise be imposed on the deemed sale of property (Code Sec. 877A(b); Notice 2009-85).[26] The election, however, cannot be made without providing adequate security as required by the IRS to ensure payment of the tax. In addition, no election can be made unless the individual makes an irrevocable waiver of any rights under an income tax treaty that would preclude assessment or collection of the tax.

The election is made on an asset-by-asset basis. The tax for a particular property is determined by multiplying the total mark-to-market tax by the ratio of the gain on the deemed sale of the property over the total gain taken into account with respect to all property deemed sold. The election defers payment of the tax until the due date for the return for the tax year in which the property is disposed or until the taxpayer's death. However, payment may not be extended beyond the due date for the return for the tax year in which the covered expatriate dies.

Reporting Requirements. In addition to any other requirements for filing a return, a covered expatriate must also file an information return on Form 8854 in each tax year he or she is subject to the mark-to-market tax (Code Sec. 6039G; Notice 2009-85).[27] The return is also to be used to provide notice that the individual has relinquished his or her U.S. citizenship or long-term residency status.

References are to Standard Federal Tax Reports; Tax Research Consultant; and Practical Tax Explanations.

[25] ¶ 27,430, ¶ 27,438.15; EXPAT: 3,314; § 37,025.05

[26] ¶ 27,430, ¶ 27,438.15; EXPAT: 3,322; § 37,025.10

[27] ¶ 27,438.15, ¶ 35,692; EXPAT: 3,324; § 39,135.25

2414. Resident of U.S. Possessions. Generally, an individual who is a bona fide resident of a U.S. possession during the tax year is subject to U.S. taxation as a U.S. citizen or resident alien, rather than as a nonresident alien (Code Sec. 876).[28] A U.S. possession for this purpose includes American Samoa, Guam, the Northern Mariana Islands, and Puerto Rico. Separate rules apply to a bona fide resident of the U.S. Virgin Islands (¶ 2416). An individual is a bona fide resident of a U.S. possession if the person is physically present in the possession during the tax year, does not have a tax home outside the possession, and does not have a closer connection to the United States or a foreign country than to the possession during the tax year (Code Sec. 937; Reg. § 1.937-1).[29] An individual with worldwide gross income of more than $75,000 must file Form 8898 for the tax year in which the individual becomes or ceases to be a bona fide resident of a U.S. possession. A spouse's income is not included when calculating an individual's worldwide gross income for this purpose. In addition, if married taxpayers are each required to file Form 8898, then a separate Form 8898 must be filed for each spouse regardless of whether a joint return is filed.

A U.S. citizen or resident alien who is a bona fide resident of American Samoa for the entire tax year may exclude from gross income for U.S. tax purposes any income derived from sources within the possession or that is effectively connected with a trade or business by the individual in the possession (Code Sec. 931).[30] The exclusion does not apply to income that is received for services performed as an employee of the United States. The individual may also not claim a tax credit or deduction that is attributable to the amount of excluded income. Form 4563 is used to claim the exclusion and must be attached to a Form 1040 filed with the IRS. A similar rule applies to a bona fide resident of Puerto Rico (¶ 2415).

2415. Resident of Puerto Rico. A U.S. citizen or resident alien who is a bona fide resident of Puerto Rico (¶ 2415) during the entire tax year may exclude from gross income for U.S. tax purposes, any income derived from sources within Puerto Rico (Code Sec. 933).[31] If the taxpayer gives up Puerto Rican residence after having been a bona fide resident for at least two years, then the taxpayer may claim a partial exclusion for the tax year of the residence change. In either case, the exclusion does not apply to income received for services performed as an employee of the United States. The taxpayer may also not claim any tax credit or deduction (except a personal exemption) which is attributable to the amount of excluded income.

A U.S. citizen or resident alien who has income from Puerto Rican sources is liable for the payment of taxes to Puerto Rico and may have to file a tax return with the United States as well. Generally, a U.S. citizen or resident alien who is a bona fide resident of Puerto Rico for the entire tax year must pay taxes to Puerto Rico on income from worldwide sources. However, if U.S. source income is also reported on an individual's Puerto Rican tax return, a credit may be claimed up to the amount allowable for income taxes paid to the United States.

2416. Resident of U.S. Virgin Islands. A U.S. citizen or resident alien (other than a bona fide resident of the U.S. Virgin Islands (¶ 2414)) who has income from sources within the U.S. Virgin Islands or effectively connected with a trade or business in the U.S. Virgin Islands is required to file an income tax return with both the United States and the U.S. Virgin Islands (Code Sec. 932).[32] The tax owed to the U.S. Virgin Islands is determined on Form 8689 by multiplying the total tax owed on the United States return (after certain adjustments) by the ratio of adjusted gross income (AGI) from the U.S. Virgin Islands to worldwide AGI. The U.S. Virgin Islands' tax liability (if paid) is credited against the individual's total U.S. tax liability. An individual who qualifies as a bona fide resident of the U.S. Virgin Islands (or who files a joint U.S. return with a U.S. citizen or resident with U.S. Virgin Islands income) will generally have no U.S. tax liability so long

24 FOREIGN

References are to Standard Federal Tax Reports; Tax Research Consultant; and Practical Tax Explanations.

[28] ¶ 27,400; INTL: 24,300; § 37,145

[29] ¶ 28,395, ¶ 28,396; INTL: 24,300; § 37,145

[30] ¶ 28,240; INTL: 24,300; § 46,005.35

[31] ¶ 28,300; INTL: 24,050

[32] ¶ 28,280; INTL: 24,100; § 37,145

as the taxpayer reports all income from all sources on the return filed with the U.S. Virgin Islands.

2419. Possession Tax Credits. A U.S. domestic corporation with a substantial portion of business in a U.S. possession may elect to claim a tax credit for taxes paid on business income derived from the possession and qualified investment income earned in the possession (¶ 1362) (Code Sec. 936).[33] The credit is generally unavailable to new claimants for tax years beginning after 1995 and is phased out for existing credit claimants for tax years beginning before 2006. An existing claimant with respect to Puerto Rico could figure its credit separately using an economic activity limitation (Code Sec. 30A).[34] A U.S. corporation that is an existing credit claimant with respect to American Samoa may still claim a version of the credit before 2012 (Act Sec. 756(a), of the Tax Relief, Unemployment Insurance Reauthorization, and Job Creation Act of 2010 (P.L. 111-312)). Form 5735 is used to figure the credit.

Nonresident Aliens and Foreign Corporations

2425. Taxation of Nonresident Aliens and Foreign Corporations. A nonresident alien (¶ 2409) and foreign corporation are generally taxed in the same manner as a U.S. citizen or domestic corporation on all income that is effectively connected with the conduct of a trade or business in the United States (¶ 2429). For this purpose, gain or loss from the disposition of a U.S. real property interest is treated as effectively connected income (¶ 2442). If any U.S. source income (¶ 2427) received by a nonresident alien or foreign corporation is not effectively connected with a U.S. trade or business, such as fixed, determinable, annual, or periodical (FDAP) income (¶ 2431) or capital gains (¶ 2435), then it will generally be taxed at a flat 30-percent rate. A nonresident alien and foreign corporation may generally only claim deductions and credits related to effectively connected income (¶ 2446). A flat 30-percent tax rate also applies to the profits (and certain interest amounts) of a U.S. branch of a foreign corporation that are remitted to the foreign corporation during the tax year (¶ 2433).

A nonresident alien or foreign corporation who engages in trade or business in the United States at any time during the tax year or who has taxable income must generally file an income tax return (Code Secs. 6012 and 6072(c)).[35] Form 1040NR is used by a nonresident alien and Form 1120-F is used by a foreign corporation. The returns are due on or before the 15th day of the 6th month following the close of the tax year (June 15 for calendar year taxpayers). Nonresident aliens and foreign corporations who do not engage in a U.S. trade or business at any time during the tax year do not have to file a return for U.S. source income if their tax liability for that year is fully satisfied by withholding of the tax (¶ 2455).

2427. Source of Income Rules. The U.S. taxation of nonresident aliens and foreign corporations (¶ 2425), as well as the application of the foreign tax credit limitations (¶ 2479), is dependent on the determination of the source of a taxpayer's income. Generally, income is either derived from U.S. sources or foreign sources in the following manner (Code Secs. 861, 862, and 865).[36]

- Interest income is generally sourced to the residence or country of incorporation of the obligor. The method and place of payment are irrelevant (see exceptions below). Interest for the guarantee of a debt is analogous to interest paid on a loan and is U.S. source income if paid by a noncorporate U.S. resident, domestic corporation, or any foreign person if effectively connected with a U.S. trade or business.
- Dividend income, scholarships, grants, prizes, and awards are sourced to the residence of the payor (see exceptions below).

References are to Standard Federal Tax Reports; Tax Research Consultant; and Practical Tax Explanations.

[33] ¶ 28,380; INTL: 27,000; § 13,435

[34] ¶ 4058; INTL: 27,000; § 13,435

[35] ¶ 35,142, ¶ 36,720; INTL: 3,750; § 37,010.10, § 37,015.10

[36] ¶ 27,120, ¶ 27,151, ¶ 27,200; INTL: 3,000; § 37,205.05

- Compensation for personal services is sourced to the place where the services are rendered. The location of the payor's residence, where the services are contracted for, and place of payment are irrelevant. If services are performed only partly within the United States, compensation is sourced on the basis of time spent working in each location.
- Rents and royalties are sourced to the location of the property.
- Gain on the sale of real property is sourced to the location of the property (¶ 2442).
- Gain on the sale of inventory is sourced to where the sale occurs (where title to the inventory passes).
- Gain on the sale of personal property that is not inventory is sourced to the residence of the seller (except for depreciable personal property, intangible property, or stock of an affiliate).

Special source rules apply to income that is derived from transportation, space, ocean, and communications activities. Other items of income are allocated or apportioned to sources within or without the United States as provided in regulations or other IRS rulings (for example, mixed-source income) (Code Sec. 863).[37] Where allocation of an item of income is not provided, then it must be construed.

Interest Income Exceptions. Interest paid by a foreign corporation or foreign partnership engaged in a U.S. trade or business is treated as U.S. source income rather than foreign sourced if paid by the U.S. trade or business (Code Secs. 861(a)(1) and 884(f)).[38] Similarly, interest on deposits in foreign branches of U.S. commercial banks is treated as U.S. source income. A qualified fails charge is treated similar to interest but is sourced to the residence of the recipient or the taxpayer's qualified business unit (QBU), unless the income is effectively connected with a U.S. trade or business. Qualified fails charges are amounts paid for the failure to deliver designated securities on the settlement date in a delivery-versus-payment transaction (Reg. § 1.863-10).[39]

Dividend Exceptions. A portion of the dividends paid by a foreign corporation are U.S. source income rather than foreign sourced if: (1) more than 25 percent of the corporation's gross income for a three-year period is effectively connected with a U.S. trade or business, or (2) it is required to figure the dividends received deduction by a U.S. corporation (¶ 223) (Code Sec. 861(a)(2)).[40] Dividends paid by a U.S. corporation electing to be treated as a possession corporation (¶ 2419) are treated as foreign source income.

Allocation of Expenses. U.S. taxpayers are allowed deductions directly related to U.S. source or foreign source income to determine taxable income. Generally, deductions are first allocated to the activity or property from which the class of income is derived. If any expense or loss is not directly related to any specific item of income, then it must be apportioned ratably between certain statutory and residual groupings (Code Secs. 861(b) and 862(b); Reg. § 1.861-8; Temp. Reg. § 1.861-8T).[41] Special apportionment rules, however, are provided for items such as interest expenses, research and development expenses, losses from the disposition of property, net operating losses (NOLs), income taxes, and legal, accounting, and stewardship fees.

Interest expenses are considered related to all income-producing activities and assets of a taxpayer. They are generally allocated to all gross income that the assets of the taxpayer generate (Code Sec. 864(e); Temp. Reg. § 1.861-9T).[42] As a result, allocation and apportionment of interest expenses must be made on the basis of the taxpayer's assets, the various statutory groupings or classes. Taxpayers may choose to value their assets on the basis of fair market value, tax book value, or an alternative tax book value

References are to Standard Federal Tax Reports; Tax Research Consultant; and Practical Tax Explanations.

[37] ¶ 27,160; INTL: 3,000

[38] ¶ 27,120, ¶ 27,540; INTL: 3,100

[39] ¶ 27,173; INTL: 3,325

[40] ¶ 27,120; INTL: 3,150; § 37,205.15

[41] ¶ 27,120, ¶ 27,138, ¶ 27,139, ¶ 27,151; INTL: 6,000; § 37,210.05

[42] ¶ 27,140, ¶ 27,180; INTL: 6,108

24 FOREIGN

method. Exceptions exist for qualified nonrecourse debt, assets acquired in integrated financial transactions, and certain related controlled foreign corporation (CFC) debt. In the case of an affiliated group of corporations, interest expenses must be allocated and apportioned to members based on asset values as if all members were a single taxpayer (the one-taxpayer rule). For tax years beginning after 2020, however, a one-time election may be made to determine foreign source taxable income of an affiliated group, by allocating and apportioning interest expense of the domestic members of the worldwide affiliated group on a worldwide basis, as if all members of the worldwide group were a single corporation (Code Sec. 864(f)).

2429. Income Effectively Connected With U.S. Trade or Business. A nonresident alien (¶ 2409) and foreign corporation are taxed in the same manner as a U.S. citizen or domestic corporation on income that is effectively connected with the conduct of a trade or business in the United States (Code Secs. 871(b) and 882(a)).[43] Generally, all income, gain, or loss from sources within the United States is treated as effectively connected with the conduct of a U.S. trade or business for this purpose, including gain from the disposition of U.S. real property interests (¶ 2442) and any scholarship or fellowship grant of a visiting student, teacher, or trainer (¶ 2448) (Code Sec. 864(c)(3)).[44] There are two exceptions.

First, fixed, determinable, annual, or periodical (FDAP) income (¶ 2431) from U.S. sources, as well as capital gains from U.S. sources (¶ 2435) are treated as income effectively connected with a U.S. trade or business if: (1) the income, gain, or loss is derived from assets used or held for use in the conduct of a U.S. trade or business, or (2) the activities of a U.S. trade or business are a material factor in the realization of the income, gain, or loss. In applying these factors, consideration is given to whether or not the asset or income involved was separately accounted for by the trade or business. In addition, a nonresident alien or foreign corporation who is a member of a partnership or the beneficiary of an estate or trust, which at any time within the tax year is engaged in a trade or business within the United States, is considered to be engaged in a U.S. trade or business (Code Sec. 875).[45] A nonresident alien and foreign corporation may elect to treat investment income from U.S. real property interests as effectively connected income (¶ 2432).

Second, income, gain, or loss from *foreign sources* is treated as effectively connected with the conduct of a U.S. trade or business if the nonresident alien or foreign corporation maintains an office or other fixed place of business in the United States at any time during the tax year to which the income, gain, or loss is attributable (Code Sec. 864(c)(4)).[46] Under these circumstances, the following foreign source income (or the economic equivalent of such income) is treated as effectively connected with a U.S. trade or business:

- rents and royalties derived from the use of intangible property;
- dividends, interest, or amounts received for the guarantees of debt that is either (1) derived from the active conduct of a banking, financial or similar business through securities or debt obligations, or (2) received by a corporation the principal business of which is trading in stocks or securities for its own account; or
- income from the disposition of inventory or personal property held for sale in the normal course of business through a U.S. office.

Trade or Business. Whether a nonresident alien or foreign corporation is conducting a trade or business within the United States is a facts and circumstances test determined on a yearly basis (Reg. § 1.864-2(e)).[47] However, the conduct of a U.S. trade or business denotes a considerable, continuous, and regular course of activity by the taxpayer or

References are to Standard Federal Tax Reports; Tax Research Consultant; and Practical Tax Explanations.

[43] ¶ 27,320, ¶ 27,500; INTLIN: 3,100; § 37,010.20, § 37,015.20

[44] ¶ 27,180; INTLIN: 3,104; § 37,010.20, § 37,015.20

[45] ¶ 27,380; INTLIN: 3,052.10; § 37,010.20, § 37,015.20

[46] ¶ 27,180; INTLIN: 3,106; § 37,010.20, § 37,015.20

[47] ¶ 27,182; INTLIN: 3,052; § 37,010.20, § 37,015.20

through an agent, partnership, estate, or trust. Thus, the taxpayer need not be present in the United States to be engaged in a U.S. trade or business.

For this purpose, a trade or business includes the performance of personal services within the United States at any time during the tax year unless the services are performed by a nonresident alien who is temporarily present in the United States for a period of 90 days or less, compensation received for the services is less than $3,000, and the services are performed for another nonresident alien, foreign corporation, or foreign partnership (Code Sec. 864(b)).[48] A trade or business also does not generally include the trading of stocks, securities, or commodities through a resident broker, commission agent, custodian, or other independent agent unless the individual or foreign corporation is a dealer.

2431. Fixed, Determinable, Annual, or Periodical (FDAP) Income. Fixed, determinable, annual, or periodical (FDAP) income of a nonresident alien or foreign corporation received from U.S. sources is generally taxed at a flat 30-percent rate (or lower rate permitted under a tax treaty) if the income is not effectively connected with the conduct of a U.S. trade or business (¶ 2429). To ensure collection and payment, the tax must be withheld from the payment of FDAP income by a withholding agent (¶ 2455).

FDAP income includes interest, dividends, rents, salaries, wages, premiums, annuities, compensation, remunerations, emoluments, and any other item of annual or periodical gain, profit, or income (Code Secs. 871(a) and 881(a)).[49] It also includes royalties for timber, coal, and iron ore, as well as payments contingent on the productivity, use, or disposition of patents, copyrights, secret processes formulas, and other like property. A nonresident alien and foreign corporation, however, may elect to treat income from U.S. real property interests as effectively connected income (¶ 2432).

A dividend equivalent payment is treated as a dividend from U.S. sources in determining FDAP income (Code Sec. 871(m)). A dividend equivalent payment is any payment (or substantially similar payment) made under a securities lending or sale-repurchase transaction pursuant to a specified notional principal contract determined by, and contingent upon, the payment of U.S. source dividends. With respect to payments made after December 31, 2013, any notional principal contract is a specified notional principal contract unless the IRS determines the contract does not have the potential for tax avoidance (Temp. Reg. § 1.871-16T(b)).

Social Security Benefits. For purposes of computing a nonresident alien's taxable income (as well as for withholding purposes), 85 percent of any Social Security benefits received is considered FDAP income (Code Sec. 871(a)(3)).[50]

Original Issue Discount. For a sale or exchange of an original issue discount (OID) obligation (¶ 1952), the amount of OID accruing while the obligation is held by a nonresident alien or foreign corporation is considered FDAP income. A payment on an OID obligation is also subject to the tax to the extent that the payment reflects OID accruing while the obligation is held by the nonresident alien or foreign corporation (Code Secs. 871(a)(1)(C) and 881(a)(3)).[51] For this purpose, an OID obligation includes any bond or other evidence of indebtedness having OID (Code Sec. 871(g)). It does not include any obligation payable 183 days or less from its date of original issue or any tax-exempt obligation.

Portfolio Interest. U.S. source portfolio interest is generally not considered FDAP income. Exempt portfolio interest includes any interest (including OID) accrued on an obligation issued after March 18, 2012, held by the nonresident alien or foreign corporation that is in registered form (Code Secs. 871(h) and 881(c)).[52] An obligation is considered in registered form if either (1) the beneficial owner has provided the

References are to Standard Federal Tax Reports; Tax Research Consultant; and Practical Tax Explanations.

[48] ¶ 27,180; INTLIN: 3,050; § 37,010.20, § 37,015.20

[49] ¶ 27,320, ¶ 27,480; INTLIN: 3,102, INTL: 3,558; § 37,010.15, § 37,015.15

[50] ¶ 27,320; INTL: 3,556; § 37,010.15

[51] ¶ 27,320, ¶ 27,480; INTL: 3,558.10; § 37,010.15, § 37,015.15

[52] ¶ 27,320, ¶ 27,480; INTL: 3,558.20; § 37,010.15, § 37,015.15

24 FOREIGN

withholding agent with Form W-8 or other statement certifying that the beneficial owner is not a U.S. person, or (2) the IRS has determined that such statement is not required (Notice 2012-20).

For obligations issued on or before March 18, 2012, the portfolio interest exemption applies if the obligation is in bearer or registered form. A bearer obligation is any obligation that is not in registered form: (1) that has arrangements that are reasonably designed to ensure that it will be sold or resold only to non-U.S. persons; (2) where the interest is payable only outside of the United States; and (3) where on the face of the obligation, there is a statement that any U.S. person who holds it will be subject to limitations under U.S. tax law.

Exempt portfolio interest does not include contingent interest or interest received by a nonresident alien or foreign corporation that is a 10-percent shareholder. Interest is generally contingent if it is determined by reference to any receipts, income, or change in value of property of the debtor or a related person (Code Sec. 871(h)(4)). Other types of contingent interest may be identified by the IRS to prevent tax avoidance. A 10-percent shareholder is any person who owns 10 percent or more of the total combined voting power of all classes of stock in a corporation or 10 percent or more of a capital or profits interest in a partnership (Code Sec. 871(h)(3)).

Other Interest and Dividend Income. FDAP does not include a portion of any dividend received by a nonresident alien or foreign corporation paid by a U.S. corporation primarily engaged in an active trade or business in a foreign country (80/20 company), but only if the corporation was an 80/20 company before 2011 (Code Secs. 871(i) and (l), and 881(d)).[53] Payments made by corporations not in existence as of January 1, 2011, are not eligible for the exemption. A grandfathered corporation must meet a modified 80-percent foreign business requirement for each subsequent tax year (rather than over a three year period). The grandfathered corporation must also not have a substantial new line of business after August 10, 2010.

FDAP income of a nonresident alien and foreign corporation does not include other types of interest and dividends, including: (1) interest paid on bank deposits, as long as the interest is not effectively connected with a U.S. trade or business; (2) income derived by a foreign bank of central issue from bankers' acceptances; (3) the portion of a dividend that is paid by a foreign corporation and treated as U.S. source income (¶ 231); and (4) certain interest-related dividends and short-term capital gain dividends received from a regulated investment company if paid with respect to a tax year beginning before January 1, 2012 (Code Secs. 871(i)(2) and (k), and 881(d)).

U.S. Possession Corporations. A corporation created or organized in, or under, the laws of Guam, American Samoa, the Northern Mariana Islands, or the U.S. Virgin Islands is not considered a foreign corporation and thus is not subject to the tax on FDAP income if certain requirements are met. However, U.S. source dividends paid to a Puerto Rico corporation are subject to U.S. taxation and withholding at a 10-percent rate (Code Sec. 881(b)).[54]

2432. Election to Treat Real Property Income as Effectively Connected Income. A nonresident alien and foreign corporation may elect to treat income from U.S. real property interests (¶ 2442) held for investment purposes as effectively connected with the conduct of a U.S. trade or business (Code Secs. 871(d) and 882(d)).[55] The election is available where the income would not otherwise qualify as effectively connected income (¶ 2429), thus allowing the taxpayer to claim deductions associated with the property (¶ 2446). The election applies to all income of the taxpayer from all U.S. real property interests, including rents or royalties from mines, wells, or other natural deposits, as well as certain timber, iron ore, and coal royalties. It does not include mortgage interest, dividends from a real estate investment trust (REIT), income from personal property, and income of a nonresident alien from real property which is not held for the

References are to Standard Federal Tax Reports; Tax Research Consultant; and Practical Tax Explanations.

[53] ¶ 27,320, ¶ 27,480; INTL: 3,558.25; § 37,010.15, § 37,015.15

[54] ¶ 27,480; INTL: 33,158; § 37,010.15, § 37,015.15

[55] ¶ 27,320, ¶ 27,500; INTLIN: 3,114.05; § 37,020

production of income, such as a personal residence (Reg. §§1.871-10 and 1.882-2).[56] The election is made by attaching a statement to the taxpayer's timely filed return or amended return. Once made, the election applies to the current tax year and all subsequent tax years until revoked by filing a timely amended return for all affected years. If the election is revoked, the taxpayer may not make a new election for five years without the IRS' consent.

2433. Branch Profits Tax. A foreign corporation that operates a trade or business in the United States may be required to pay a branch profits tax and a branch-level interest tax in addition to the tax on income effectively connected with the conduct of a U.S. trade or business (¶2429). The branch profits tax is 30 percent (or lower if permitted by a tax treaty) of the foreign corporation's dividend equivalent amount (Code Sec. 884).[57] This is the amount of the foreign corporation's effectively connected after-tax earnings that are not reinvested in a U.S. trade or business by the close of the tax year or disinvested in a later tax year. The branch interest tax is 30 percent (or lower if permitted by a tax treaty) of the amount of interest paid by a U.S. branch of a foreign corporation with respect to a liability and notional excess interest amounts. If there is a conflict between the branch profits tax or branch-level interest tax with any U.S. income tax treaty, special rules are provided to determine the extent to which the treaty takes priority.

2435. Capital Gains of Nonresident Aliens and Foreign Corporations. The net capital gains of a nonresident alien or foreign corporation which are effectively connected with the conduct of a U.S. trade or business (¶2429) are taxed in the same manner as the capital gains of a U.S. citizen, resident alien, or domestic corporation. U.S. sourced capital gains of a nonresident alien or foreign corporation that are not effectively connected income, fixed, determinable, annual, or periodical (FDAP) income (¶2431), or gains from the sale of U.S. real property interests (¶2442) are completely exempt from U.S. taxation (Code Secs. 871(a)(2) and 881(a)).[58] However, in the case of a nonresident alien, the exemption only applies if the individual is not present in the United States for at least 183 days during the tax year. If the 183-day period is met, then the net capital gains of the nonresident alien not effectively connected to conduct of a U.S. trade or business are subject to a flat 30-percent tax on the net gains.

2438. Community Income of Nonresident Aliens. If a nonresident alien is married to a U.S. citizen or resident and does not elect to be treated as a resident (¶2410), then any community income is to be treated as follows:

- earned income (other than from a trade or business or the distributive share of partnership income) is treated as income of the spouse who earned it;
- trade or business income (other than from a partnership) is treated as the separate income of the spouse carrying on the trade or business (unless carried on jointly);
- a distributive share of partnership income is treated as the income of the spouse who is the partner with no portion attributed to the other spouse; and
- all other community income from separate property of one spouse is treated as the income of that spouse (Code Sec. 879).[59]

2442. Sale or Disposition of U.S. Real Property Interest. The gain or loss derived by a nonresident alien or foreign corporation from the sale, exchange, or other disposition of a U.S. real property interest is treated as gain or loss effectively connected with a conduct of a U.S. trade or business (¶2429) (Code Sec. 897).[60] Income from a U.S. real property interest held for investment purposes is not considered income effectively connected with a U.S. trade or business. However, a nonresident alien and foreign

References are to Standard Federal Tax Reports; Tax Research Consultant; and Practical Tax Explanations.

[56] ¶27,338, ¶27,502; INTLIN: 3,114.05; §37,020

[57] ¶27,540; INTLIN: 3,150

[58] ¶27,320, ¶27,480; INTL: 3,560; §37,010.15, §37,015.15

[59] ¶27,460; INDIV: 24,156; §23,210.35, §45,920.10

[60] ¶27,700; INTLIN: 6,050; §37,410.05, §37,425

corporation may elect to treat income from U.S. real property interests held for investment purposes as effectively connected income (¶ 2432). A foreign corporation that holds a U.S. real property interest may elect to be treated as a domestic corporation for this purpose if, under any treaty obligation of the United States, it is entitled to nondiscriminatory treatment of its U.S. real property interests (Code Sec. 897(i)).

Cash or property received by a nonresident alien or foreign corporation in exchange for an interest in a partnership, trust, or estate is considered received from the sale or disposition of U.S. real property interest to the extent attributable to the sale or disposition of a U.S. real property interest (Code Sec. 897(g)). Similarly, special look through rule apply for distributions by qualified investment entities (real estate investment trust or regulated investment company) attributable to dispositions of U.S. real property interests (¶ 2444).

Real Property Interests. A U.S. real property interest is any interest in real property (including a mine, well, or other natural deposit) located in the United States or the U.S. Virgin Islands (Code Sec. 897(c); Reg. § 1.897-1).[61] Real property includes land and improvements, personal property associated with the use of the real property, and unsevered timber, crops, and minerals. The nonresident alien's or foreign corporation's interest can be any interest (other than solely as a creditor), such as a direct ownership, fee-ownership, co-ownership, as well as any leasehold or option to acquire the property.

An interest in U.S. real property also includes any interest (other than solely as a creditor) in a U.S. real property holding corporation (USRPHC), unless the corporation was not a USRPHC during the shorter of the five-year period ending on the date of disposition, or the period the taxpayer held the interest in the corporation. A corporation is a USRPHC if the fair market value of its U.S. real property interests is at least 50 percent of the fair market value of all of its real property interests and any other property used in its business (Reg. § 1.897-2).[62] For this purpose, a corporation is considered to own a proportionate share of the assets held through a partnership, trust or estate, as well as a domestic or foreign corporation in which it holds a controlling interest.

Whether a corporation is a USRPHC is generally determined the last day of the corporation's tax year, the date on which the corporation acquires a U.S. real property interest, *and* the date on which the corporation disposes of a real property interest located outside the United States or disposes of other assets used in a trade or business during the calendar year. The IRS has issued simplified procedures for a taxpayer to establish that a domestic corporation is not a USRPHC (Rev. Proc. 2008-27).[63]

A U.S. real property interest does not include any interest in a corporation if as of the date of disposition, the corporation has already disposed of all of its U.S. real property interests in a transaction in which it recognized gain (the cleansing rule). In addition, if a corporation has a class of stock that is regularly traded on an established securities market, then such stock will be treated as a U.S. real property interest only in the hands of a taxpayer who owns more than five percent of the total fair market value of that class of stock.

Distributions of U.S. Real Property Interests. If a foreign corporation distributes a U.S. real property interest with respect to its stock, then the corporation recognizes gain (but not loss) to the extent the fair market value of the property at the time of distribution exceeds its adjusted basis (Code Sec. 897(d); Temp. Reg. § 1.897-5T(c)).[64] A foreign corporation may avoid recognizing gain, however, if at the time of the distribution, the distributee would be subject to U.S. taxation on a subsequent disposition of the property and if the fair market value of the distributed property in the hands of the distributee is no greater than its carryover basis increased by any amount of gain recognized by the

References are to Standard Federal Tax Reports; Tax Research Consultant; and Practical Tax Explanations.

[61] ¶ 27,700, ¶ 27,701; INTLIN: 6,056; § 37,405

[62] ¶ 27,702; INTLIN: 6,058; § 37,405

[63] ¶ 27,711.60; INTLIN: 6,058.35; § 37,405

[64] ¶ 27,700, ¶ 27,706; INTLIN: 6,060

distributing corporation. The foreign corporation is required to file a U.S. income tax return to report the distribution, even if it has no tax liability.

Nonrecognition Exchanges. Nonrecognition provisions of the Code apply to the exchange of a U.S. real property interest by a nonresident alien or foreign corporation if the property is exchanged for another U.S. real property interest that would be subject to U.S. tax upon its subsequent disposition and the transferor meets certain filing requirements (Code Sec. 897(e); Temp. Reg. § 1.897-6T).[65] Nonrecognition provisions for this purpose include like-kind exchanges (¶ 1721), involuntary conversions (¶ 1713), contributions and distributions related to partnerships (¶ 443 and ¶ 453), and corporate liquidations and reorganizations (¶ 2205 and ¶ 2253). The transfer of a U.S. real property interest in exchange for stock in a foreign corporation may also qualify for nonrecognition treatment. This includes contributions to capital or as paid in surplus (Code Sec. 897(j)).

Withholding. In order to ensure that foreign investors will pay taxes on gain realized on the sale or disposition of a U.S. real property interest, the transferee is generally required to withhold and deduct a tax equal to 10 percent of the amount realized by the foreign person-transferor, unless an exemption applies (Code Sec. 1445; Reg. § 1.1445-1).[66] The withholding rate may be as high as 35 percent in the case of a distribution made by a qualified investment entity. If the transferee fails to withhold the required tax, the transferor may be held liable for the tax. The tax must be reported on Form 8288 or 8288-A and must be transmitted to the IRS within 20 days of the transfer of the property.

2444. Look Through Rules for Disposition of U.S. Real Property Interests. Any distribution by a qualified investment entity to a nonresident alien, foreign corporation, or other qualified investment entity to the extent attributable to gain from the sale or exchange of a U.S. real property interest, must be treated by the recipient as gain from the sale or exchange of a U.S. real property interest (¶ 2442) (Code Sec. 897(h)).[67] A qualified investment entity includes any real estate investment trust (REIT) (¶ 2326) and, effective through December 31, 2011, any regulated investment company or mutual fund (¶ 2301) that is a U.S. real property holding company (USRPHC). However, in determining whether a regulated investment company is a USRPHC, the regularly traded stock exception in defining a USRPHC does not apply. In addition, the regulated investment company must include its interest in any other domestically controlled REIT or regulated investment company that is a USRPHC.

The look-through rule does not apply to any distribution from a qualified investment entity with respect to a class of stock that is regularly traded on an established securities market in the United States if the foreign distributee did not own more than five percent of the class of stock at any time within one year of the distribution. To the extent this exception applies, the distribution from the qualified investment entity is treated as a dividend, and not as income effectively connected with a U.S. trade or business.

An interest in a domestically controlled qualified investment entity (50 percent value of stock) is not treated as a U.S. real property interest and any gain from the sale of the interest does not pass through to a nonresident alien or foreign corporation. However, the gain is passed through if a wash sale transaction is involved. For this purpose, a wash sale transaction is one in which: (1) the interest in a domestically controlled qualified investment entity is disposed of within 30 days prior to a distribution by the qualified entity that would be treated as gain from the sale or exchange of a U.S. real property interest; and (2) a substantially identical interest is reacquired within 61 days of the distribution.

2446. Deductions and Tax Credits of Nonresident Aliens and Foreign Corporations. A nonresident alien and foreign corporation are subject to U.S. income tax on income effectively connected with a U.S. trade or business (¶ 2429) and fixed, determi-

24 FOREIGN

References are to Standard Federal Tax Reports; Tax Research Consultant; and Practical Tax Explanations.

[65] ¶ 27,700, ¶ 27,707; INTLIN: 6,062

[66] ¶ 32,780, ¶ 32,781; INTLIN: 6,100; § 37,415.05

[67] ¶ 27,700; INTLIN: 6,068; § 19,205.30

nable, annual, periodical (FDAP) income from U.S. sources (¶ 2431). Generally, all exclusions from gross income permitted to U.S. citizens and domestic corporations may also be excluded by nonresident aliens and foreign corporations (Code Secs. 872 and 883).[68] In addition, earnings on certain categories of cross-border transactions may also be excluded, such as compensation paid by a foreign employer to an exchange student, teacher, trainee, or specialist (¶ 2448), gambling winnings derived from a legal wager initiated outside the United States, and earnings from the international operation of a ship or aircraft.

A nonresident alien or foreign corporation may only claim deductions and tax credits related to effectively connected income in determining taxable income (Code Secs. 873, 874 and 882(c)).[69] This includes the foreign tax credit subject to the same limitations that apply to U.S. citizens and domestic corporations (¶ 2479) (Code Sec. 906).[70] Deductions and credits are generally not allowed in determining the tax on U.S. sourced FDAP income. However, a charitable contribution deduction can be claimed whether or not related to effectively connected income. Similarly, a nonresident alien may deduct one personal exemption (with certain exceptions) and casualty or theft losses (so long as the property is located in the United States). A nonresident alien and foreign corporation may elect to treat income from U.S. real property interests as effectively connected income in order to claim the deductions associated with the property (¶ 2432).

A nonresident alien or foreign corporation must file an accurate and timely return to claim any allowable deduction or credit. If a return is not filed, then the IRS may prepare one for the taxpayer but no deductions and credits will be allowed other than the credits for withheld taxes, gasoline and special fuels, and for nonresident aliens for taxes paid by a regulated investment company on undistributed capital gains.

2448. Foreign Students, Teachers, or Trainees. A nonresident alien who is not otherwise engaged in a U.S. trade or business but who is temporarily present in the United States under immigration laws on a F, J, M, or Q visa as a visiting student, teacher, trainee, or specialist is considered to be engaged in a U.S. trade or business (Code Sec. 871(c)).[71] This means that any portion of a scholarship or fellowship grant from U.S. sources (including incidental expenses) that is not excludable from gross income (¶ 879) is income effectively connected with the conduct of a U.S. trade or business (¶ 2429). The income is subject to a special withholding rate of 14 percent (¶ 2455) (Code Sec. 1441(b); Reg. § 1.1441-4(c)).[72] Compensation paid by a foreign employer to a person in the United States as a visiting student, teacher, trainee, or specialist is exempt from tax (Code Sec. 872(b)(3)).[73]

2450. Tax Treaties. The United States has negotiated a network of tax treaties with other countries to avoid the double taxation of taxpayers on the same income and to prevent taxpayers from evading taxation. In addition, the United States has enacted strict anti-abuse rules to prevent individual's from treaty shopping and incorporated exchange of information clauses in many tax treaties to facilitate the enforcement of these rules. These anti-abuse rules deny treaty benefits to nonresidents of either the United States or its treaty partner that funnel income through the treaty country only to take advantage of reduced tax rates.

Generally, the Code is to be applied to a taxpayer with "due regard" to treaty obligations of the United States (Code Sec. 894).[74] However, in instances where a U.S. taxpayer takes the position that a treaty overrules or modifies the Code or regulations, disclosure of the position must generally be made with the taxpayer's tax return on

References are to Standard Federal Tax Reports; Tax Research Consultant; and Practical Tax Explanations.

[68] ¶ 27,344, ¶ 27,520; INTL: 3,558.35, INTL: 3,604; § 37,010.25

[69] ¶ 27,360, ¶ 27,363, ¶ 27,500; INTL: 3,554.05; § 37,010.20, § 37,015.20

[70] ¶ 27,920; INTLOUT: 3,152; § 13,405.15

[71] ¶ 27,320; EXPAT: 3,108.25, EXPAT: 3,108.30; § 37,320.20

[72] ¶ 32,702, ¶ 32,708; INTL: 33,110.35; § 37,320.20

[73] ¶ 27,344; INTL: 3,558.35; § 37,010.25

[74] ¶ 27,640; INTL: 18,060; § 37,605

Form 8833 (Code Sec. 6114; Reg. § 301.6114-1).[75] If a return is not otherwise required to be filed, a return must nevertheless be filed for purposes of making the required disclosure. The determination whether a treaty-based return position is required to be reported is made by comparing the taxpayer's tax liability under current law to that same tax liability as it would exist if the relevant treaty positions did not exist. Any difference must be reported. Failure to disclose the difference may result in a penalty (Code Sec. 6712).[76]

Tax treaties between the United States and foreign countries generally reduce the tax rate for income paid. Some countries allow the withholding of tax at the treaty-reduced rate. Other countries, however, withhold tax at their statutory tax rate and refund any difference upon receiving proof of residency. To apply for certification of U.S. residency to receive the benefits under a tax treaty, a taxpayer must file Form 8802 at least 45 days before the certificate is needed. If the application is approved, the IRS will provide the residency certification to the taxpayer on Form 6166. A nonresident alien or foreign corporation is not entitled under any U.S. income tax treaty to any reduced rate of withholding on an item of income derived through an entity treated as a partnership (or other fiscally transparent entity) if: (1) the income is not treated by the treaty partner as an item of income of such foreign person; (2) the foreign country does not impose tax on a distribution of the item by the U.S. entity to the foreign person; and (3) the treaty does not contain a provision addressing its applicability in the case of an item of income derived through a partnership (Code Sec. 894(c)).[77]

2452. Corporate Inversions. Special rules apply for the tax treatment of corporate inversion transactions where a U.S. corporation reincorporates in a foreign jurisdiction and thereby replaces the U.S. parent corporation of a multinational corporate group with a foreign parent corporation. Inversion transactions may take many different forms, including stock inversions, asset inversions, and various combinations. In any case, if former shareholders of a U.S. corporation hold 80 percent or more (by vote or value) of the stock of a foreign corporation after the transaction, the foreign corporation will be treated as a domestic corporation for U.S. tax purposes (Code Sec. 7874).[78] If the former shareholders hold at least 60 percent but less than 80 percent of the stock of the foreign corporation after the transaction, then the inversion transaction is respected but any applicable corporate-level tax imposed as a result of the transaction cannot be offset by tax attributes such as a net operating loss (NOL) or foreign tax credit.

2455. Withholding of Tax on Nonresident Aliens and Foreign Corporations. A foreign person is generally subject to U.S. tax on U.S. source income received during the tax year (¶ 2425). To ensure collection and payment, the tax must be withheld from the payment of the U.S. source income to the foreign person by a withholding agent (Code Secs. 1441 and 1442).[79] Most types of U.S. source income received by a foreign person are subject to a 30-percent withholding rate. Different rates may apply, however, to wages paid to a nonresident alien employee (including pensions paid for personal services), scholarship or fellowship grants of a foreign exchange student (¶ 2448), dispositions of U.S. real property interests (¶ 2442), a foreign partner's distributive share of effectively connected income of a partnership, gross investment income paid to foreign private foundations, and dividends paid to a Puerto Rican corporation. Reduced rates of withholding may also apply, including an exemption, under a tax treaty or convention with the foreign person's country of residence (¶ 2450).

Persons Subject to Withholding. All nonresident aliens and foreign corporations, foreign partnerships, foreign trusts, and foreign estates are subject to withholding on U.S. source income. Withholding also applies to the foreign branch of a U.S. person that furnishes an intermediary withholding certificate on Form W-8 to the withholding agent (Reg. § 1.1441-1(c)).[80] A nonresident alien is any individual who is not a U.S. citizen or

References are to Standard Federal Tax Reports; Tax Research Consultant; and Practical Tax Explanations.

[75] ¶ 37,060, ¶ 37,061; FILEBUS: 12,056; § 37,605

[76] ¶ 40,135; FILEBUS: 12,056; § 37,605

[77] ¶ 27,640; INTL: 18,060; § 37,601

[78] ¶ 43,969; INTL: 30,082.05

[79] ¶ 32,702, ¶ 32,720; INTL: 33,000; § 37,301

[80] ¶ 32,703; INTL: 33,050; § 37,305

resident alien and includes any bona fide resident of Puerto Rico, Guam, the Northern Mariana Islands, the U.S. Virgin Islands, or American Samoa. A nonresident alien who elects resident status for income tax purposes (¶ 2410) is still considered a foreign person for nonresident alien withholding purposes on all income except wages. Withholding may also be required for payments made to certain foreign financial institutions (¶ 2469) and nonfinancial foreign entities (¶ 2473) if certain requirements are not met.

Income Subject to Withholding. Income subject to the withholding requirement includes: (1) fixed, determinable, annual, or periodical (FDAP) income (¶ 2431). If the source of the income cannot be determined at the time of payment (¶ 2427), it is treated as U.S. source income (Code Sec. 1441(b); Reg. § 1.1441-2(a)).[81] In addition, income payable for personal services performed in the United States is treated as from sources within the United States, regardless of where the location of the contract for the services was entered, the place of payment, or residence of payer. Income effectively connected with the conduct of a U.S. trade or business is not subject to the withholding requirements for foreign persons, including income received as wages (¶ 2429). Instead, such income is generally subject to the tax and withholding rules as if the foreign person were a U.S. citizen, resident, or domestic entity. However, special rules apply to the effectively connected income of a partnership (foreign or domestic) that is allocable to its foreign partners (Code Sec. 1446).[82]

Withholding Agent. The withholding agent is the person or entity required to deduct, withhold, and pay any tax on income paid to a foreign person (Reg. § 1.1441-7).[83] This duty is imposed on all persons (acting in whatever capacity) that have control, receipt, custody, disposal, or payment of any items of income which are subject to withholding. Thus, the withholding agent may be any individual, corporation, partnership, trust, or other entity (including a foreign intermediary or partnership). A withholding agent may designate an authorized agent on its behalf.

The withholding agent is personally liable for any tax required to be withheld except in the case of certain conduit financing arrangements (Code Sec. 1461).[84] This liability is independent of the tax liability of the foreign person for whom the tax was withheld from a payment of income. Even if the foreign person pays the tax, the withholding agent may still be liable for any interest, penalty, or addition to tax for failure to withhold (Code Sec. 1463).[85] A refund or credit of any overpayment is made to the withholding agent unless the tax was actually withheld (Code Sec. 1464).[86] The withholding agent is indemnified against any person claiming any tax properly withheld.

A withholding agent is not required to withhold any amount if the payee is a U.S. person or a U.S. person that may be treated as the beneficial owner of the payment. Absent actual knowledge (or reason to know), the withholding agent must obtain valid documentation from the payee that it is either a U.S. payee or beneficial owner. Generally, a U.S. payee is any person required to furnish Form W-9. While such persons are not subject to withholding as a foreign person, they may be subject to Form 1099 reporting and withholding requirements. A U.S. beneficial owner is any person or entity that is required to furnish Form W-8BEN, Form W-8ECI or Form W-8EXP. Payment to an intermediary (whether qualified or not), flow-through entity, or U.S. branch of a foreign entity may be treated as a U.S. payee for these purposes so long as valid documentation is provided on Form W-8IMY. In all cases in which valid documentation cannot be provided, the withholding agent may presume a person to be a U.S. payee or beneficial owner only under specified rules.

Returns. A withholding agent must file an annual information return on Form 1042-S to report income paid to a foreign person during the tax year that is subject to

References are to Standard Federal Tax Reports; Tax Research Consultant; and Practical Tax Explanations.

[81] ¶ 32,702, ¶ 32,704; INTL: 33,100, INTL: 33,150, INTL: 33,200; § 37,320.05

[82] ¶ 32,800; INTL: 33,106; § 37,350.05

[83] ¶ 32,714; INTL: 33,054; § 37,315.05

[84] ¶ 32,820; INTL: 33,056; § 37,315.05

[85] ¶ 32,860; INTL: 33,056; § 37,315.05

[86] ¶ 32,880; INTL: 33,056; § 37,315.05

withholding (unless an exception applies) (Reg. §§1.1461-1 and 1.6302-2).[87] A separate Form 1042-S must be filed for each recipient, as well as for each type of income that is paid to the same recipient. A copy of Form 1042-S must also be provided to the recipient. Form 1042 is used by the withholding agent to report and pay the taxes withheld from the payments of income.

Both forms must be filed by March 15 of the year following the calendar year the income was paid. An automatic six-month extension for filing Form 1042 can be obtained by filing Form 7004. However, the extension of time to file does not extend the time to pay the withheld tax. An automatic 30-day extension for filing Form 1042-S can be obtained by filing Form 8809. A second extension request may be submitted by filing a second Form 8809 before the end of the initial extended due date. The IRS may require that the returns be filed electronically (¶ 2503). Paper Forms 1042-S must be accompanied by Form 1042-T.

The amount of tax required to be withheld will determine whether the withholding agent must deposit the taxes prior to the due date for filing the returns and how frequently such amounts must be deposited. Penalties may be imposed for failure to file, to provide complete and correct information, as well as for failure to pay any taxes.

Reporting Foreign Assets of U.S. Taxpayers

2465. FBAR Reporting (Foreign Financial Assets). A United States person is required to disclose any financial interest in, or signature or other authority over, a foreign bank account, securities account, or other financial account (31 CFR Reg. §1010.350). This information is reported on Form TD F 90-22.1 (commonly referred to as FBAR) if the aggregate value of the foreign financial accounts exceeds $10,000 at any time during the calendar year (¶ 2570).[88]

2467. FATCA Reporting of Specified Foreign Financial Assets (Form 8938). Under the Foreign Account Tax Compliance Act (FATCA), an individual is required to disclose his or her interest in a specified foreign financial asset during the tax year if the aggregate value of all the assets exceeds an applicable threshold amount (¶ 2570) (Code Sec. 6038D).[89] The information is reported on Form 8938 and attached to the individual's tax return for the year.

2469. FATCA Reporting and Withholding Obligations for Foreign Financial Institutions (FFIs). Under the Foreign Account Tax Compliance Act (FATCA), a foreign financial institution (FFI) is required to report to the IRS certain information about financial accounts held by U.S. taxpayers or by foreign entities in which U.S. taxpayers hold substantial ownership interests (Code Sec. 1471(b); Prop. Reg. §1.1471-4).[90] A FFI is a foreign entity that accepts deposits in the ordinary course of a banking business, holds financial assets for the account of others as a substantial part of its business, or is engaged primarily in investing (Code Sec. 1471(d)(4); Prop. Reg. §1.1471-5(e)).[91] A FFI meets the FATCA reporting requirements by entering into an agreement with the IRS (FFI agreement) to:

- identify U.S. accounts it maintains and to comply with certain verification and due diligence procedures;
- report certain information to the IRS regarding the U.S. accounts; and
- deduct and withhold tax on any payment of U.S. source income by the FFI to a non-participating FFI or U.S. account holder who is unwilling to provide the required information.

For a discussion of a participating FFI's obligations under a FFI agreement, including the definition of a U.S. account and information to be reported, see ¶ 2471.

References are to Standard Federal Tax Reports; Tax Research Consultant; and Practical Tax Explanations.

[87] ¶ 32,821, ¶ 38,062; INTL: 33,056; §37,330

[88] ¶ 36,555.33; FILEBUS: 9,104; §37,705

[89] ¶ 35,593; FILEBUS: 9,108; §37,710

[90] ¶ 32,883, ¶ 32,885AP; INTL: 36,050; §37,725.05

[91] ¶ 32,883, ¶ 32,885AS; INTL: 36,054; §37,725.05

24 FOREIGN

If a FFI fails to meet the FATCA reporting requirements, a U.S. withholding agent must deduct and withhold a tax equal to 30 percent on any withholdable payment made to the FFI after December 31, 2013 (Code Sec. 1471(a); Prop. Reg. § 1.1471-2(a)).[92] A withholdable payment includes any payment of U.S.-source fixed, determinable, annual, or periodical (FDAP) income (¶ 2431). It also includes gross proceeds from the sale or other disposition of any property after December 31, 2014, that can produce interest or dividends that are U.S.-source FDAP income (Code Sec. 1473(1); Prop. Reg. § 1.1473-1(a)).[93] Items of income effectively connected with a U.S. trade or business are not withholdable payments (¶ 2429).

Withholding is not required with respect to any payment under a grandfathered obligation or from any gross proceeds from the disposition of a grandfathered obligation (Prop. Reg. § 1.1471-2(b)). A grandfathered obligation is any legal obligation outstanding on January 1, 2013, that produces or could produce a withholdable payment or pass-through payment. It does not include any instrument treated as equity for U.S. tax purposes or any legal agreement that lacks a definitive expiration or term. For example, savings deposits, demand deposits, and other similar accounts are not considered obligations. Similarly, it does not include brokerage accounts, custodial accounts, or similar agreements to hold financial assets in an account for another person. A material modification of a grandfathered obligation will result in the obligation being treated as newly issued and subject to withholding. A payment made under a grandfathered obligation does include a payment made to a flow-through entity such as a partnership or trust. This includes a payment made with respect to the entity's disposition of the obligation.

A U.S. withholding agent for this purpose includes any person in whatever capacity having the control, receipt, custody, disposal, or payment of any withholdable payment (Code Sec. 1473(4)).[94] A U.S. withholding agent that fails to withhold and deposit tax required to be withheld from a withholdable payment made to an FFI is liable for the tax, including penalties (Code Sec. 1474; Prop. Reg. §§ 1.1474-1 and 301.1474-1).[95] Generally, the withholding agent uses Form 1042 to report and pay taxes withheld on payments to FFIs during the tax year. The withholding agent also is required to file an annual information on Form 1042-S to report income paid to an FFI during the tax year subject to withholding. If a financial institution is required to file Form 1042-S, it must file the form electronically.

2471. Participating Foreign Financial Institution (FFI) Agreements. A foreign financial institution (FFI) meets its reporting requirements under the Foreign Account Tax Compliance Act (FATCA) (¶ 2469) by entering into an agreement with the IRS or by being deemed by the IRS to meet the requirements. An FFI that enters into an FFI agreement (a participating FFI) agrees to identify U.S. accounts it maintains and to comply with certain verification and due diligence procedures (Code Sec. 1471(b); Prop. Reg. § 1.1471-4(a) and (b)).[96] The FFI is required to attempt to obtain a waiver in any case where any foreign law would prevent the reporting of the required information of a U.S. account. If a waiver is not obtained within a reasonable period of time, then the account must be closed by the FFI.

An FFI agreement also requires the participating FFI to withhold 30 percent from any withholdable payment (¶ 2469) made after December 31, 2013, passed-through to a recalcitrant account holder or non-participating FFI who is unwilling to provide the required information. A recalcitrant account holder is any account holder that fails to provide the information required to determine whether the account is a U.S. account or the information required to be reported by the FFI, or that fails to provide a waiver of a foreign law that would prevent reporting. A participating FFI may elect not to withhold

References are to Standard Federal Tax Reports; Tax Research Consultant; and Practical Tax Explanations.

[92] ¶ 32,883, ¶ 32,885AJ; INTL: 36,050; § 37,725.05

[93] ¶ 32,893, ¶ 32,895AC; INTL: 36,052; § 37,725.05

[94] ¶ 32,893; INTL: 36,052; § 37,725.05

[95] ¶ 32,898, ¶ 32,899AC, ¶ 32,899AE; INTL: 36,150; § 37,725.05, § 37,730

[96] ¶ 32,883, ¶ 32,885AP; INTL: 36,056; § 37,725.10

on pass-through payments, but instead be subject to withholding on payments it receives which are allocable to a recalcitrant account holder or nonparticipating FFI.

U.S. Accounts. A U.S. account under an FFI agreement is a financial account held by one or more specified U.S. persons or U.S.-owned foreign entity, including any depository or custodial account maintained by the FFI, and any equity or debt interest in the FFI other than an interest regularly traded on an established securities market (Code Sec. 1471(d); Prop. Reg. § 1.1471-5(a)).[97] A specified U.S. person is any U.S. person other than a publicly traded corporation, tax exempt organization, bank, real estate investment trust (REIT), regulated investment company, common trust fund or exempt trust, or State or U.S. possession.

An FFI must use due diligence to identify its U.S. accounts. The due diligence required depends on whether the account is new or preexisting and whether the account is owned by an individual or entity. Generally, accounts with a balance or value of more than $50,000 ($250,000 for a cash value insurance or annuity contract) but less than $1 million are only subject to electronic review of searchable data for indicia of U.S. status. Accounts with a balance that exceeds $1 million are subject to review of electronic and non-electronic files for U.S. indicia, including an inquiry of the actual knowledge of any relationship manager associated with the account (Prop. Reg. § 1.1471-4(c)). A preexisting account of an individual with a balance or value of $50,000 or less, as well as certain cash value insurance contracts with a value of $250,000 or less, are excluded from the due diligence review unless the FFI elects otherwise. Preexisting accounts of an entity with account balances of $250,000 or less are also exempt from review until the account balance exceeds $1 million.

A participating FFI is required to report to the IRS on an annual basis the name, address, and taxpayer identification number (TIN) of each holder of a U.S. account which is a U.S. person. In the case of any account holder which is a U.S.-owned foreign entity, the participating FFI must report the name, address, and TIN of each substantial U.S. owner of such entity (Code Sec. 1471(c); Prop. Reg. § 1.1471-4(d)). The FFI must also report the account number, the year-end account balance or value in U.S. dollars, and the gross amount and character of dividends, interest, or other income paid or credited to the account. This includes the gross proceeds from the sale or redemption of property paid or credited to the account.

Alternatively, the FFI may elect to be subject to the same reporting requirements of U.S. institutions. Thus, the institution must provide a full Form 1099 reporting for every account with a U.S. person or U.S. foreign entity as an account holder. As a result, both U.S. and foreign source amounts (including gross proceeds) are subject to reporting under this election regardless of whether the amounts are paid inside or outside the United States.

2473. FATCA Reporting and Withholding Obligations for Non-Financial Foreign Entities (NFFEs). Under the Foreign Account Tax Compliance Act (FATCA), if a non-financial foreign entity (NFFE) is the beneficial owner of a withholdable payment (¶ 2469) made to the NFFE after December 31, 2013, then the NFFE is required to report certain information to the withholding agent (Code Sec. 1472(b); Prop. Reg. § 1.1472-1(b)).[98] The reporting requirement is satisfied if the NFFE reports the name, address, and taxpayer identification number (TIN) of each substantial U.S. owner or if it certifies that it does not have any substantial U.S. owners. If the NFFE or other payee fails to meet the reporting requirement, then the withholding agent must deduct and withhold a tax of 30 percent from the withholdable payment.

A NFFE for this purpose is any foreign entity that is not a financial institution, meaning the entity does not accept deposits in the ordinary course of a banking business, does not hold financial assets for the account of others as a substantial part of its business, and is not engaged primarily in investing. A substantial U.S. owner is:

References are to Standard Federal Tax Reports; Tax Research Consultant; and Practical Tax Explanations.

[97] ¶ 32,883, ¶ 32,885AS; INTL: 36,056; § 37,725.10

[98] ¶ 32,888; INTL: 36,100; § 37,730

- in the case of a corporation, a U.S. person that owns, directly or indirectly, more than 10 percent of the corporate stock by vote or value;
- in the case of a partnership, a U.S. person that owns directly or indirectly, more than 10 percent of the capital or profits interests of the partnership; and
- in the case of a trust, a U.S. person treated as an owner of any portion of the trust under the grantor trust rules and any U.S. person holding more than 10 percent of the beneficial interests (Code Sec. 1473(2); Prop. Reg. § 1.1473-1(b)).[99]

A withholding agent that receives information about any substantial U.S. owners of an NFFE must report the information to the IRS on or before March 15 of the calendar year following the year in which the withholdable payment is made (Code Sec. 1472(b); Prop. Reg. § 1.1472-1(e)). This includes the name of the NFFE and the name, TIN, and address of each U.S. substantial owner.

So long as the NFFE and the withholding agent satisfy their reporting requirements, withholding is not required unless the withholding agent knows or has reason to know that any information provided about substantial U.S. owners is incorrect. A withholding agent is also not required to withhold taxes if the withholding agent may treat the payment as beneficially owned by an excepted NFFE. An excepted NFFE includes a publicly traded corporation and its related entities, a U.S. possessions entity, the government of a foreign country or U.S. possession, an international organization, or an active NFFE (Code Sec. 1472(c); Prop. Reg. § 1.1472-1(c)).[100] An active NFFE is any NFFE if less than 50 percent of its gross income for the calendar year is passive income, and less than 50 percent of its assets produce or are held for the production of dividends, interest, rents and royalties (other than those derived in the active conduct of a trade or business), annuities, or other passive income. In addition, entities which are by definition not financial institutions are considered excepted NFFEs, including certain holding companies, start-up companies, NFFEs that are liquidating or emerging from reorganization or bankruptcy, and certain hedging entities.

Withholding is not required with respect to any payment under a grandfathered obligation or from any gross proceeds from the disposition of such an obligation. A grandfathered obligation is any legal obligation outstanding on January 1, 2013, that produces or could produce a withholdable payment or pass-through payment. It does not include any instrument treated as equity for U.S. tax purposes or any legal agreement that lacks a definitive expiration or term (Prop. Reg. § 1.1471-2(b)).

Foreign Tax Credit or Deduction

2475. Foreign Tax Credit or Deduction. Subject to certain limitations (¶ 2479), a U.S. taxpayer may elect a credit or deduction against U.S. income and alternative minimum tax (AMT) liability for foreign taxes paid or accrued to a foreign country or U.S. possession during the tax year (Code Sec. 901; Reg. § 1.901-1).[101] The credit and deduction are intended to relieve U.S. taxpayers of double taxation on foreign source income. The election is made on an annual basis (¶ 2476) and is applicable to all creditable foreign taxes paid or incurred during the tax year (¶ 2477).

Taxpayers entitled to claim the foreign tax credit or deduction include U.S. citizens, resident aliens, bona fide residents of Puerto Rico for the entire tax year (¶ 2415), domestic corporations, and nonresident aliens and foreign corporations with respect to foreign taxes paid or accrued on foreign source income effectively connected with the conduct of a U.S. trade or business (¶ 2429). A taxpayer who is a partner in a partnership, shareholder in an S corporation, or beneficiary of an estate or trust may claim the credit or deduction with respect to the taxpayer's proportionate share of creditable foreign taxes paid or accrued by the entity (Code Sec. 901(b) and (c)).[102]

References are to Standard Federal Tax Reports; Tax Research Consultant; and Practical Tax Explanations.

[99] ¶ 32,893; INTL: 36,058.10; § 37,730

[100] ¶ 32,888; INTL: 36,100; § 37,730

[101] ¶ 27,820, ¶ 27,821; INTLOUT: 3,050; § 13,401

[102] ¶ 27,820; INTLOUT: 3,152; § 13,405.05

Similarly, a shareholder of a regulated investment company may be able to claim the credit or deduction based on the shareholder's share of creditable foreign taxes paid by the entity (¶ 2320).

Income Matching. The foreign tax credit or deduction may not be claimed by a taxpayer until the related income is taken into account for U.S. income tax purposes (Code Sec. 909; Temp. Reg. § 1.909-2T).[103] Specifically, the matching rule applies if there is a foreign tax credit splitting event. A splitting event occurs if, in connection with a splitter arrangement, the income related to the foreign taxes is taken into account by a covered person for U.S. income tax purposes. A covered person is a person or entity that has a specified relationship with the taxpayer—at least 10 percent ownership interest, related party, or otherwise specified by the IRS. In the case of a partnership, S corporation, or trust, the matching requirement is applied at the partner, shareholder, or beneficiary level. Special rules apply to a foreign tax credit splitting event involving a Code Sec. 902 corporation, including the application of the matching rule to foreign income taxes paid or accrued in pre-2011 tax years for purposes of applying the deemed paid foreign tax credit (¶ 2485) for periods after 2010 (Temp. Reg. § § 1.909-5T and 1.909-6T).[104]

2476. Election of Foreign Tax Credit or Deduction. The election to claim foreign tax credit or deduction (¶ 2475) is made on an annual basis. It may be made or changed anytime within 10 years from the due date for filing a return for the year in which the taxes were actually paid or accrued, unless the period is extended by agreement with the IRS (Code Sec. 6511(d)(3); Reg. § 1.901-1(d) and (e)).[105] For partnerships and S corporations, the election is made by the individual partners and shareholders, respectively (Code Secs. 702(a)(6), 703(b)(3), and 1366(a)(1)).[106] Corporations in an affiliated group make the election and compute the credit on a consolidated basis for a consolidated return year (Reg. § 1.1502-4).[107]

A taxpayer claims the foreign tax credit by filing Form 1116 (for individuals, estates, and trusts) or Form 1118 (for corporations) with the taxpayer's income tax return. Individuals may elect to claim the foreign tax credit without filing Form 1116 by entering the credit directly on their tax return. An individual is eligible to claim the credit on their return if: (1) all of the individual's foreign source income must be passive income; (2) all of the income and any foreign taxes paid on the income must be reported on a qualified payee statement (Form 1099); and (3) the total creditable foreign taxes must be less than $300 ($600 for joint filers). If a taxpayer makes the election, then the foreign tax credit limitations will not apply (¶ 2479). However, the taxpayer cannot carry over any excess credit to another tax year. The election is not available to estates, trusts, or corporations. An election to take the credit or deduction on a joint return applies to the qualifying foreign taxes paid or accrued by both spouses. If married taxpayers file separate returns, either may take the credit or deduction without regard to the other.

Credit vs. Deduction. Generally, it is more advantageous for a U.S. taxpayer to elect the foreign tax credit rather than the deduction because it is taken against the taxpayer's U.S. liability on a dollar-for-dollar basis. In contrast, a deduction for foreign taxes merely reduces a taxpayer's income subject to tax. In addition, an individual who deducts foreign taxes must claim the taxes as an itemized deduction.

The election to claim the credit or deduction applies to all creditable foreign taxes paid or incurred by the taxpayer during the tax year for which a U.S. return is required (¶ 2477). Thus, a taxpayer cannot claim a credit for some creditable foreign taxes and a deduction for other creditable foreign taxes in the same tax year. Partial credits and partial deductions are not permitted except in limited circumstances (Code Sec. 275(a)(4)).[108] For example, foreign taxes that may otherwise be claimed as an itemized

References are to Standard Federal Tax Reports; Tax Research Consultant; and Practical Tax Explanations.

[103] ¶ 27,971, ¶ 27,973D; INTLOUT: 3,300; § 13,432

[104] ¶ 27,974I, ¶ 27,974N; INTLOUT: 3,304; § 13,432

[105] ¶ 39,060, ¶ 27,821; INTLOUT: 3,054; § 13,413

[106] ¶ 25,080, ¶ 25,100, ¶ 32,080; INTLOUT: 3,054; § 13,405.20

[107] ¶ 33,148; INTLOUT: 3,054

[108] ¶ 14,500; INTLOUT: 3,050; § 13,401

deduction, such as foreign real property taxes, may still be deducted even if the credit is claimed. In addition, a taxpayer on the cash method of accounting may elect to claim a credit for foreign taxes in the year they accrue.

2477. Creditable Foreign Taxes. A U.S. taxpayer is allowed a credit or deduction (¶ 2475) against U.S. income and alternative minimum tax (AMT) liability for any income, war profits, and excess profits taxes imposed on the taxpayer and paid or accrued during the tax year (as well as taxes paid or accrued in lieu of these taxes) to any foreign country or U.S. possession (¶ 2485) (Code Secs. 901 and 903; Reg. § 1.901-2).[109] To be creditable, a foreign tax must be a levy the predominant character of which is that of a compulsory income tax according to U.S. tax principles. Penalties, fines, interest, customs duties, and similar obligations are not creditable foreign taxes, nor is any payment to a foreign government in exchange for a specific economic benefit that is not available on substantially the same terms to all persons subject to income taxes in the foreign country. A foreign tax paid for retirement, unemployment, or disability benefits is generally not a payment for a specific economic benefit. However, no credit or deduction is allowed for social security taxes paid or accrued to a foreign country with which the United States has a social security agreement. In addition, the IRS may disallow foreign tax credits generated in transactions it views as abusive such as structured passive investment arrangements (Reg. § 1.901-2(e)(5)(iv)).

The foreign tax credit or deduction is not available for the withholding of creditable foreign taxes unless certain minimum holding period requirements are met. In order to claim the credit for foreign withholding taxes paid with respect to a dividend or any other item of gain or income (other than a dividend) from property, the taxpayer must hold the underlying stock or property for: (1) 16 days within the 31-day period beginning 15 days before the ex-dividend date, or (2) to the extent that the recipient is under an obligation to make related payments with respect to positions in substantially similar or related property (Code Sec. 901(k) and (l)). In the case of preferred stock with dividends attributable to periods aggregating more than 366 days, the holding period is 46 days within the 91-day period beginning 45 days before the ex-dividend date. The holding period requirements do not apply for any property held in a foreign country in the active conduct of a business of the taxpayer as a securities dealer.

A U.S. taxpayer may not claim the foreign tax credit or deduction for any foreign taxes paid or accrued on income excluded from U.S. gross income. This includes income excluded under the foreign earned income or foreign housing exclusions (¶ 2402 and ¶ 2403), or income from a U.S. possession (¶ 2414). The taxpayer may also not claim a credit or deduction for foreign taxes paid or accrued to the extent that: (1) the taxpayer is certain to receive a refund or credit, or the tax is used as a subsidy; (2) the liability is dependent on the availability of a foreign tax credit in another jurisdiction; (3) the taxes are paid or accrued to a country with which the United States does not conduct diplomatic relations or which is designated as supporting acts of international terrorism; or (4) the taxes are attributable to boycott income (¶ 2496). The amount of foreign taxes a taxpayer may claim will be reduced if the taxpayer controls a foreign corporation (CFC) or partnership that fails to file Form 5471 or Form 8865, respectively (¶ 2487 and ¶ 2494).

Covered Asset Acquisitions. In the case of a covered asset acquisition, a taxpayer may not take into account in determining the foreign tax credit the disqualified portion of any foreign income tax determined with respect to income or gain attributable to the relevant foreign assets (Code Sec. 901(m)).[110] A covered asset acquisition includes: (1) a qualified stock purchase under Code Sec. 338 (¶ 2265); (2) any transaction that is treated as the acquisition of assets for U.S. tax purposes and as the acquisition of stock (or is disregarded) for purposes of the foreign income taxes; (3) any acquisition of an interest in a partnership that has an election in effect under Code Sec. 754 (¶ 459); and

References are to Standard Federal Tax Reports; Tax Research Consultant; and Practical Tax Explanations.

[109] ¶ 27,820, ¶ 27,822, ¶ 27,860; INTLOUT: 3,100; § 13,410.05

[110] ¶ 27,820; INTLOUT: 3,110.30

(4) any other transaction as determined by the IRS. The disqualified portion of any covered asset acquisition for any tax year is the aggregate basis differences allocable to the tax year with respect to all relevant foreign assets, divided by the income on which the foreign income tax is determined.

2479. Foreign Tax Credit Limitations. The foreign tax credit or deduction (¶ 2475) is subject to a two-part limitation that prevents the use of foreign taxes to reduce U.S. income tax liability on U.S. source income. First, an overall limitation provides that the total amount of a taxpayer's foreign tax credit may not exceed the taxpayer's entire U.S. income tax liability (determined without regard to the credit), multiplied by a fraction equal to the taxpayer's foreign source taxable income over worldwide taxable income from all sources (Code Sec. 904(a)).[111] Second, the limitation must be calculated separately for certain categories or baskets of foreign source income (¶ 2481). Special rules also apply if the taxpayer has an overall foreign loss (¶ 2483). The IRS may recharacterize the income of an affiliated group of corporations or modify the consolidated return regulations to the extent necessary to avoid the foreign tax credit limitation rules (Code Sec. 904(j); Reg. § 1.904(i)-1).[112]

For this purpose, foreign source taxable income is the taxpayer's gross income from all geographic sources outside the United States (regardless of the country), less any applicable deductions that properly relate to the income and an allocation of deductions unrelated to any specific item of income (Code Sec. 904(b)). An individual, estate, or trust may not claim deductions for personal and dependency exemptions in calculating taxable income. In the case of a corporation, taxable income does not include any portion of income taken into account for purposes of the possession tax credit (¶ 2419). For all taxpayers, special adjustments are required for capital gains and losses. Specifically, foreign source capital gains and losses are subject to (1) a capital gain net income limitation adjustment (i.e., U.S. capital loss adjustment) and (2) a capital gain rate differential adjustment (Reg. § § 1.904(b)-1 and 1.904(b)-2).[113]

Comment: Absent further legislation, the foreign tax credit is applied against an individual's U.S. tax liability for tax years beginning in 2012 after application of the nonrefundable personal credits (¶ 1315) (Code Sec. 904(i)).

De minimis Exemption. An individual with $300 or less of creditable foreign taxes ($600 if married filing jointly) is exempt from the overall foreign tax credit limitation provided he or she has no foreign source income other than qualified passive income (Code Sec. 904(k)).[114] The exemption is not automatic and an individual must elect to take the exemption for the tax year directly on Form 1040 (¶ 2476).

U.S.-Owned Foreign Corporations. Certain amounts derived from U.S.-owned foreign corporations that would otherwise be treated as foreign source income are treated as U.S. source income for purposes of the foreign tax credit limitations (Code Sec. 904(h); Reg. § 1.904-5(m)).[115] The sourcing rule applies to subpart F income inclusions from a controlled foreign corporation (CFC) (¶ 2488), income from a qualified electing fund (¶ 2490), and interest and dividends paid by a foreign corporation where not less than 10 percent of the corporation's earnings and profits for the tax year are attributable to U.S. sources.

A U.S.-owned foreign corporation is any foreign corporation (including a Code Sec. 902 corporation (¶ 2485)) if 50 percent or more of the total combined voting power of all classes of stock in the corporation entitled to vote, or the total value of the stock of the corporation, is held by U.S. persons. A domestic corporation is also a U.S.-owned foreign corporation for this purpose if it pays (1) a dividend that is treated as foreign sourced because of the election to claim the possession tax credit, or (2) interest before 2011 that

References are to Standard Federal Tax Reports; Tax Research Consultant; and Practical Tax Explanations.

[111] ¶ 27,880; INTLOUT: 6,050; § 13,425.05

[112] ¶ 27,880, ¶ 27,900C; INTLOUT: 6,404

[113] ¶ 27,889, ¶ 27,890; INTLOUT: 6,060; § 13,425.10

[114] ¶ 27,880; INTLOUT: 6,102.05; § 13,425.20

[115] ¶ 27,880, ¶ 27,886; INTLOUT: 6,054.15

24 FOREIGN

is treated as foreign source because the corporation meets the active foreign business test (80/20 corporation) (¶ 2427).

Carryover. When the amount of creditable foreign taxes paid or accrued by a taxpayer during the tax year exceeds the overall limitation for that year (as well as the separate limitation for each separate basket of foreign source income), the unused portion may be carried back one year and then forward ten years (Code Sec. 904(c); Reg. § 1.904-2).[116] The amount that may be carried back and forward is limited to the amount by which the credit limitation in the carryback or forward year exceeds the amount of foreign taxes paid or accrued in that year. In addition, any unused foreign tax must be carried back and forward to its own separate basket of income. A foreign tax credit in one income category can only be carried back and forward to that same category in another tax year. It cannot offset other taxes imposed on income in another basket.

If any unused foreign tax credit is carried back or forward to a tax year in which a foreign tax deduction is claimed (¶ 2476), the taxpayer must compute a foreign tax credit limit as if the credit was elected for that year. Any excess generated in the deduction year cannot be deducted or claimed as a credit for any year, but reduces the amount of unused foreign taxes that can be carried over to another tax year. Alternatively, an amended return may be filed within 10 years from the due date of the return of the deduction year to claim the foreign tax credit rather than the deduction (¶ 2475). For any portion of a foreign tax credit carryback from a tax year attributable to an net operating loss (NOL) carryback or a capital loss carryback from a later tax year, the carryback does stop the running of interest until the filing date for the later tax year (Code Sec. 6601(d)).[117] An individual electing the *de minimis* exemption may not carryback or carryforward any excess foreign taxes to an election year.

2481. Separate Limitations for Various Categories of Income. A taxpayer is generally required to compute the foreign tax credit limitation (¶ 2479) separately for two main categories or baskets of foreign source income: passive category income and general category income (Code Sec. 904(d); Reg. § 1.904-4; Temp. Reg. § 1.904-4T).[118] Passive category income includes investment income such as dividends, interest, rents, royalties, and annuities, as well as income from a qualified electing fund (¶ 2490). It does not include any rents or royalties that are derived in the active conduct of a trade or business, regardless of whether they are received from a related or unrelated person. Passive income also does not include certain export financing interest and highly taxed income. Any foreign source income that is not included in the passive income basket is considered part of the general income basket.

To determine taxable income in each category, a taxpayer must allocate expenses, losses, and other deductions, directly related to the foreign source income allocated to each basket. Similarly, foreign taxes paid or accrued may only include those taxes that are related to income in that basket. If a tax is related to more than one basket, the taxpayer must apportion the tax. However, if creditable foreign taxes were imposed on amounts that do not constitute income under U.S. tax law ("base difference items"), then they will be treated as imposed on general category income.

Look-Through Rules. Foreign source income received by a U.S. shareholder from a controlled foreign corporation (CFC) (¶ 2487) is categorized by applying look-through rules that require identification of underlying income to specific foreign tax credit limitation categories (Code Sec. 904(d)(3) and (4); Reg. § 1.904-5; Temp. Reg. § 1.904-5T).[119] Tracing rules prescribe classification of subpart F income (¶ 2488), interest, rents, royalties, and dividends to various limitation categories. The look-through rules also apply in the case of payments made by Code Sec. 902 corporations (¶ 2485), certain domestic corporations, partnerships, and related look-through entities.

References are to Standard Federal Tax Reports; Tax Research Consultant; and Practical Tax Explanations.

[116] ¶ 27,880, ¶ 27,883; INTLOUT: 6,300; § 13,425.25

[117] ¶ 39,410; INTLOUT: 6,304; § 13,425.25

[118] ¶ 27,880, ¶ 27,885, ¶ 27,885A; INTLOUT: 6,100; § 13,425.15

[119] ¶ 27,880, ¶ 27,886, ¶ 27,886D; INTLOUT: 6,200

In the case of a partner in a partnership, the look-through rule will apply with respect to the partner's distributive share of partnership income unless the partner owns less than 10 percent of the partnership, in which case the income is treated as passive income.

Other Limitations. In addition to the separate foreign tax credit limitations for passive category income and general category income, other provisions in the Code require that the limitation be determined separately for certain other separate categories of income (Reg. § 1.904-4(m)).[120] This includes: (1) any income sourced under a tax treaty as foreign source income including any income derived from foreign sources; (2) income from sanctioned countries; (3) for purposes of the alternative minimum tax (AMT), dividends received from a corporation that qualifies for the possession tax credit if the dividends-received deduction is disallowed under the alternative current earnings (ACE) rules; (4) dividends received from 10-percent owned foreign corporations (¶ 231); (5) gain from the sale of stock in a foreign corporation or intangible property that is treated as foreign source under a tax treaty; (6) lump-sum distributions from retirement plans for which the special averaging treatment is used to figure tax; and (7) combined foreign oil and gas income including foreign oil and gas extraction income (FOGEI) and foreign oil-related income (FORI) (Code Sec. 907).[121]

2483. Recapture of Foreign and U.S. Losses. An overall foreign loss (OFL) is subject to recapture to prevent a double tax benefit from using the OFL to reduce U.S. tax liability on U.S. source income and claiming the foreign tax credit on the same income. If a taxpayer has an OFL in which the foreign tax credit is claimed (¶ 2475), then a portion of the taxpayer's foreign source income earned in a subsequent year is recharacterized as U.S. source income (Code Sec. 904(f)).[122] For this purpose, an OFL is the amount by which gross income from foreign sources is exceeded by the sum of expenses, losses, and other deductions properly allocable to such income, but without taking into account any net operating losses (NOL), foreign expropriation losses, and uncompensated casualty or theft losses. A foreign loss must be determined for each separate foreign tax credit category or basket (¶ 2481), referred to as a separate limitation loss (SLL). Thus, a taxpayer can have an OFL, an SLL for passive income, and a SLL for general income in any given tax year. Foreign losses in one separate foreign tax credit category or basket must be offset against income in other foreign categories before offsetting U.S. income.

Generally, the amount of foreign source income that must be recaptured and recharacterized as U.S. source income is limited to the lesser of the taxpayer's OFL (to the extent not used in prior tax years) or 50 percent of the taxpayer's foreign source taxable income for the tax year. If a taxpayer disposes of assets used in its trade or business predominantly outside the United States in a taxable disposition, or disposes of stock in a controlled foreign corporation (CFC) (¶ 2487) in which it owns more than 50 percent, then 100 percent of the gain must be recaptured. Fifty percent of the recognized gain is recaptured under the general rule above and the remainder recaptured to the extent of the taxpayer's OFL balance. Special recapture rules also apply if the disposition is nontaxable. For these purposes, property is considered used predominantly outside the United States if, during a three-year period ending on the date of disposition, the property was located outside the United States more than 50 percent of the time. Similar recapture rules apply to an overall domestic loss (ODL) requiring U.S. source income earned in a subsequent year to be recharacterized as foreign source income. Special ordering rules are used to allocate NOLs, net capital losses, U.S. source losses and SLLs, and for the recapture of SLLs, OFLs, and overall domestic losses (Temp. Reg. § 1.904(g)-3T).

2485. Deemed Paid Credit. The foreign tax credit is available to a U.S. corporate shareholder that owns 10 percent or more of the voting stock in a foreign corporation from which it receives a dividend (or deemed to receive a dividend through an affiliated

References are to Standard Federal Tax Reports; Tax Research Consultant; and Practical Tax Explanations.

[120] ¶ 27,885; INTLOUT: 6,114; § 13,425.15

[121] ¶ 27,940; INTLOUT: 6,350

[122] ¶ 27,880; INTLOUT: 6,250; § 13,425.30

group or a partnership) (Code Sec. 902).[123] The amount of the "deemed paid" or "indirect credit" is determined by reference to the portion of the foreign corporation's post-1986 foreign income taxes that the dividend received by the domestic corporation bears to the foreign corporation's post-1986 undistributed earnings. However, the deemed paid credit does not include the disqualified portion of any foreign income tax paid by a Code Sec. 902 corporation in a covered asset acquisition and determined with respect to income or gain attributable to the relevant foreign assets (¶ 2477). A corporation electing to take the deemed paid credit must increase ("gross up") its tax base by including not only the dividend but the tax deemed paid by the foreign corporation (Code Sec. 78).[124] Additionally, the deemed paid credit is subject to the foreign tax credit limitation (¶ 2479).

The deemed paid credit is allowed to a domestic shareholder for foreign taxes paid by a lower-tier foreign corporation if the foreign corporation is a member of a qualified group and the foreign corporation owns 10 percent or more of the voting stock of the member of the qualified group from which it receives a dividend (Code Sec. 902(b)). A qualified group includes any foreign corporation in a chain that includes the first-tier corporation and foreign corporations through the sixth-tier. A corporation below the third-tier will not be included in the qualified group unless it is a controlled foreign corporation (CFC) (¶ 2487) and the domestic corporation is a U.S. shareholder. Whether the ownership requirements are met is determined at the time dividends are received. A qualified group cannot aggregate their shares in a foreign corporation to meet the ownership requirements.

U.S. Shareholders of Foreign Corporations

2487. Controlled Foreign Corporations. A U.S. shareholder of a foreign corporation that is a controlled foreign corporation (CFC) for an uninterrupted period of 30 days or more during the tax year must include in gross income its pro rata share of the CFC's subpart F income (¶ 2488) (whether distributed or not) and earnings invested in U.S. property during the year (Code Sec. 951).[125] A foreign corporation is a CFC if more than 50 percent of its total voting power or value is owned by U.S. shareholders (Code Sec. 957).[126] A U.S. shareholder is any U.S. person (U.S. citizen, resident alien, domestic corporation, partnership, estate, or trust) that owns directly, indirectly, or constructively 10 percent or more of the total combined voting power of the foreign corporation (Code Sec. 958).[127]

The U.S. shareholder includes subpart F income and earnings in gross income in its tax year in which the CFC's tax year ends but only if it is a shareholder on the last day of the CFC's tax year. In addition, the shareholder only includes income from that portion of the year that the corporation qualifies as a CFC. The income is treated as a deemed dividend (¶ 733). Actual distributions are excluded from gross income to the extent they have already been accounted for by the shareholder (Code Sec. 959).[128] To prevent double taxation, the basis of the U.S. shareholder's CFC stock and basis in property the shareholder is considered owning through the CFC is increased by the amount of subpart F income required to be included in income and decreased by any distribution that is excluded from income (Code Sec. 961).[129]

A U.S. shareholder of CFC that is a domestic corporation is allowed a foreign tax credit (¶ 2475) for any foreign taxes paid (or deemed paid) by the CFC for income that is attributed or distributed to it as a U.S. shareholder (Code Sec. 960).[130] The credit is limited, however, to the taxes that would have been deemed paid if the foreign corporation had made an actual distribution to the domestic corporation. A deemed-paid credit is also available to any individual U.S. shareholder who elects to be taxed at

References are to Standard Federal Tax Reports; Tax Research Consultant; and Practical Tax Explanations.

[123] ¶ 27,840; INTLOUT: 3,200; § 13,420
[124] ¶ 6350; INTLOUT: 3,200; § 13,420
[125] ¶ 28,470; INTLOUT: 9,000; § 45,520.10
[126] ¶ 28,590; INTLOUT: 9,050
[127] ¶ 28,610; INTLOUT: 9,056
[128] ¶ 28,630; INTLOUT: 9,350
[129] ¶ 28,670; INTLOUT: 9,360
[130] ¶ 28,650; INTLOUT: 9,358

domestic corporate income tax rates on amounts included in gross income (Code Sec. 962).[131]

Investment of Earnings. U.S. shareholders of a CFC are taxed on their pro rata share of the CFC's earnings which are invested in U.S. property during the tax year and which are not distributed or otherwise taxed (Code Sec. 956).[132] Thus, the amount of earnings invested in U.S. property is the economic equivalent of a dividend deemed to have been paid. A CFC acquires a direct interest in U.S. property when it acquires an adjusted basis in the property. U.S. property includes tangible real or personal property located in the United States, stock of domestic corporations, obligations of U.S. persons, and the right to use a patent, copyright, invention, etc., in the United States. Certain properties acquired in normal commercial transactions without the intention of them to remain in the United States indefinitely are not to be treated as U.S. property.

Sale or Exchange of CFC Stock. Any gain recognized by a U.S. shareholder from the sale, exchange, or redemption of stock in a CFC is included in gross income as an ordinary dividend to the extent of the corporation's earnings and profits allocable to the stock (Code Sec. 1248).[133] Any gain exceeding the CFC's earnings and profits is treated as capital gain. The shareholder may claim a foreign tax credit for the taxes paid by the CFC on the income. However, the credit may be less than the indirect credit (¶ 2485) because it will not apply to as many tiers of foreign corporations.

Returns. Every U.S. person (U.S. citizen or resident alien, domestic corporation, domestic partnership, or domestic estate or trust) who is a U.S. shareholder of a CFC must file an information return on Form 5471 about the entity and its subsidiaries (Code Sec. 6038).[134] Failure to timely file the required information may result in penalties and a reduced foreign tax credit. The taxpayer must include information on acquisitions, reorganizations, and dispositions of ownership interests in a CFC during the tax year (Code Sec. 6046).[135] U.S. shareholders of controlled foreign partnerships are subject to similar reporting requirements using Form 8865.

2488. Subpart F Income. Subpart F income of a controlled foreign corporation (CFC) (¶ 2487) is the sum of the corporation's insurance income, foreign base company income, boycott income (¶ 2496), illegal payments (¶ 2497), and income from countries not diplomatically recognized by the U.S. government (Code Sec. 952).[136] It does not include income from sources within the United States that is effectively connected with the conduct of a trade or business by the corporation (¶ 2429) unless that income is exempt from tax or taxed at a reduced rate pursuant to a treaty. Subpart F income for the tax year is also limited to the CFC's total earnings and profits for that year, and may be reduced in certain circumstances to accumulated deficits of earnings and profits.

Subpart F insurance income is generally any income that is attributable to the issuance or reissuance of any insurance or annuity contract if the income would be taxed under the rules that apply to domestic insurance companies, with some modifications. Effective for tax years before January 1, 2012, it generally does not include any insurance income from the insuring or reinsuring risks in the CFC's home country (Code Sec. 953).[137]

The foreign base company income of a CFC is made up of income from foreign personal holding company (FPHC) and foreign base company sales, services, and oil-related income (Code Sec. 954).[138] FPHC income is generally the major component of foreign base income and includes dividends, interest (including otherwise tax-exempt interest), rents, royalties, and annuities. It also includes: amounts received under a contract to furnish personal services; any item of income, gain, deduction, or loss from a notional principal contract; and the excess of gains over losses from the sale or exchange of property (including foreign currency and commodities) unless the CFC is a

References are to Standard Federal Tax Reports; Tax Research Consultant; and Practical Tax Explanations.

[131] ¶ 28,690; INTLOUT: 9,362
[132] ¶ 28,570; INTLOUT: 9,250
[133] ¶ 30,960; INTLOUT: 9,400
[134] ¶ 35,540; INTLOUT: 9,450; § 39,135.05
[135] ¶ 35,940; INTLOUT: 9,456; § 39,135.05
[136] ¶ 28,490; INTLOUT: 9,100
[137] ¶ 28,510; INTLOUT: 9,102
[138] ¶ 28,530; INTLOUT: 9,104

regular dealer. FPHC income does not include rents and royalties from an active trade or business, certain income from related persons, export financing interest and, for tax years beginning before January 1, 2012, certain income derived in the active conduct of a banking, financing or similar business (i.e., active financing income), or in the conduct of an insurance business (i.e., active insurance income).

For purposes of determining FPHC income, the sale of a partnership interest by a CFC is treated as a sale of the proportionate share of partnership assets attributable to that interest, including subpart F income. On the other hand, for tax years beginning before January 1, 2012, no look-through rule applies to dividends, interest, rents and royalties received by a CFC from a related CFC to the extent that it creates or increases a deficit that reduces subpart F income of either the payor or another CFC.

2490. Passive Foreign Investment Company. A U.S. shareholder of a passive foreign investment company (PFIC) who receives an excess distribution with respect to its stock or disposes of its PFIC stock must allocate the income or gain pro rata over the shareholder's holding period for the stock unless the shareholder elects to treat the PFIC as a qualifying electing fund (QEF) or makes a mark-to-market election (Code Sec. 1291).[139] The amount allocated to the shareholder's current tax year, and to the tax years in its holding period before the foreign corporation qualified as a PFIC (pre-PFIC years), are taxed as ordinary income. The amount allocated to any other tax year in the shareholder's holding period is taxed at the highest income tax rate applicable for that year, plus interest from the due date for the taxpayer's return for that year. For this purpose, an excess distribution is any part of a distribution received from the PFIC which is greater than 125 percent of the average distribution received by the shareholder during the three preceding tax years or, if shorter, during the period the shareholder held the stock.

A PFIC is any foreign corporation that derives 75 percent or more of its gross income for the tax year from passive investments or at least 50 percent of its average total assets held for the year produce passive income or are held for the production of passive income (Code Sec. 1297).[140] Passive income generally is the type of income that would be foreign personal holding company income (¶ 2488). Miscellaneous rules apply regarding stock attribution, start-up companies and business changes, the leasing of tangible personal property, intangible assets, and the interaction of the PFIC rules with the taxation of accumulated earnings and subpart F income (Code Sec. 1298).[141] Even if a foreign corporation ceases to qualify as a PFIC, a U.S. shareholder is subject to the PFIC rules for any period stock is held that the corporation was a PFIC. To avoid the PFIC rules, the shareholder can purge PFIC stock by making a deemed sale or deemed dividend election.

Generally, a U.S. person that is a direct or indirect shareholder of a PFIC must file Form 8621 with its tax return for each tax year in which the person receives an excess distribution, disposes of its PFIC stock, or makes an election to purge its PFIC stock, including a QEF or mark-to-market election. The reporting requirement may also meet the FATCA requirements for disclosing information with respect to specified foreign financial assets on Form 8938 (¶ 2570). A separate Form 8621 must be filed for each PFIC in which stock is held.

Qualified electing fund. Instead of paying the additional tax on deferrals (or deemed sale or deemed dividend elections), a U.S. shareholder of a PFIC may elect to treat the corporation as a QEF. If the election is made, the shareholder must include in gross income each year as ordinary income, its pro rata share of earnings of the corporation, and as long-term capital gain, its pro rata share of the net capital gain of the corporation (Code Secs. 1293 and 1295).[142] The inclusions are made for the shareholder's tax year in which or with which the QEF's tax year ends. Once made, the QEF election is revocable

References are to Standard Federal Tax Reports; Tax Research Consultant; and Practical Tax Explanations.

[139] ¶ 31,540; INTLOUT: 18,200

[140] ¶ 31,620; INTLOUT: 18,202

[141] ¶ 31,640; INTLOUT: 18,200

[142] ¶ 31,560, ¶ 31,600; INTLOUT: 18,206

only with the IRS's consent and is effective for the current tax year and all subsequent tax years. Under certain circumstances, the U.S. shareholder can elect to defer payment of the tax on any undistributed earnings of the QEF (Code Sec. 1294).[143]

Mark-to-market election. A U.S. shareholder of a PFIC may also avoid the additional tax on the deferral of income by making a mark-to-market election with respect to its PFIC stock that is marketable (Code Sec. 1296).[144] If the election is made, the shareholder annually includes in gross income as ordinary income an amount equal to the excess of the fair market value of the PFIC stock as of the close of the tax year over its adjusted basis. If the stock has declined in value, an ordinary loss deduction is allowed limited to the net amount of gain previously included in income.

2491. Sale or Exchange of Patent, Etc. to Foreign Corporations. A U.S. person who controls a foreign corporation (at least 50 percent of voting power of all stock) directly or indirectly must recognize gain from the sale or exchange of a patent, invention, model, design, copyright, secret formula or process, or any other similar property right to the foreign corporation as ordinary income rather than capital gain (Code Sec. 1249).[145]

2492. Reorganization Involving Foreign Corporations. Generally, the transfer of appreciated property to a corporation may not be taxable under the organization (¶ 203), reorganization (¶ 2205), and liquidation rules (¶ 2253). However, to prevent a U.S. person from avoiding taxes by transferring property from the United States to a foreign corporation, a taxpayer will be required to recognize gain in what would otherwise be a tax-free transaction (Code Sec. 367).[146] Exceptions exist for assets which are to be used in an active trade or business, qualifying outbound transfers of stock and securities, and tangible assets. Inventory and other noncapital assets denominated in foreign currency do not qualify for the exception. Additionally, a taxpayer who transfers intangible property will be deemed to receive royalty payments for the property. The payments create a super-royalty that is reevaluated on an annual basis.

2493. Transfers to Foreign Trusts. Any U.S. person that transfers property to a foreign trust (other than the trust of an employee benefits plan or tax-exempt organization) with a U.S. beneficiary is treated as the owner of the portion of the trust attributable to the property (Code Sec. 679; Reg. § 1.679-1).[147] If the transferor and another person would be treated as owner of the same portion of the trust, then the U.S. transferor will be treated as the owner. Thus, any income received by the trust with respect to the property is taxable to the transferor under the grantor trust rules (¶ 571). This rule applies without regard to whether the transferor retains any power or interest in the property. It also applies regardless of whether the transfer is direct or indirect. Exceptions exist for foreign trusts established by a will, transfers made by reason of death of the U.S. person (transferor), or transfers of property to the foreign trust in exchange for consideration equal to its fair market value. A U.S. person who is treated as the owner of any portion of a foreign trust under the grantor trust rules is required to ensure that the trust makes a return for the year and provides information to other U.S. persons, or be subject to a penalty (Code Secs. 6048(b) and 6677(a)).[148]

The IRS may presume that when a U.S. person transfers property to a foreign trust the trust has a U.S. beneficiary unless the U.S. person demonstrates otherwise (Code Sec. 679(d)). Thus, an amount will be treated as either paid or accumulated for the benefit of a U.S. person if: (1) the U.S. person's interest in the trust is contingent on a future event; (2) a loan of cash or marketable securities, or the use of any other trust property, is made to any U.S. person; (3) any person has the discretion of making a distribution from the trust to any class of persons that may include a U.S. person; or (4) the U.S. person who transferred property to the trust is involved in any agreement or

References are to Standard Federal Tax Reports; Tax Research Consultant; and Practical Tax Explanations.

[143] ¶ 31,580; INTLOUT: 18,206.15

[144] ¶ 31,610; INTLOUT: 18,202.30

[145] ¶ 30,980; INTLOUT: 9,256.20 § 18,705.05

[146] ¶ 16,640; INTL: 30,000

[147] ¶ 24,820, ¶ 24,820B; INTL: 30,252; § 32,805.10

[148] ¶ 36,000, ¶ 39,815; EST-TRST: 36,258.10; § 39,135.15

understanding that may result in trust income or corpus being paid to or accumulated for the benefit of a U.S. person.

2494. Information Reporting on Foreign Partnerships. A number of reporting requirements apply with respect to foreign partnerships. First, a foreign partnership must file a U.S. partnership return if it has gross income that is either U.S. source income (¶ 2427) or income effectively connected with a U.S. trade or business (¶ 2429) (Code Sec. 6031(e)).[149] A U.S. partner cannot claim distributive shares of any partnership deduction, loss, or credit if a partnership return is not filed (Code Sec. 6231(f)).[150] Second, every U.S. person that controls a foreign partnership (more than 50 percent interest) is required to file an annual information return on Form 8865 (¶ 2487). Additionally, any U.S. person that owns at least 10-percent interest in a foreign partnership must report any changes to his or her ownership in the partnership during the tax year (Code Sec. 6046A).[151] Failure to file an information return will result in a $10,000 penalty per occurrence (Code Sec. 6679).[152] A U.S. person who transfers property to a foreign partnership in a nontaxable transfer must report the transfer if the U.S. person has at least a 10-percent interest in the partnership or if the value of the property transferred exceeds $100,000 (Code Sec. 6038B).[153]

Other Foreign Tax Rules

2495. Foreign Currency Transactions. All federal income tax determinations must be made in the taxpayer's functional currency (Code Sec. 985).[154] Generally, the functional currency of a U.S. taxpayer will be the U.S. dollar. However, in the case of a qualified business unit (QBU), the functional currency is the currency in which the taxpayer conducts a significant part of its activities and which is used in keeping books and records. For this purpose, a QBU is any separate and clearly identified unit of a trade or business of the taxpayer which maintains its own books and records (for example, foreign subsidiary of a U.S. corporation or a foreign corporation) (Code Sec. 989).[155] Special rules apply in determining when foreign earnings and profits and foreign income taxes must be translated into U.S. dollars, as well as the use of a foreign branch of a U.S. taxpayer (Code Secs. 986 and 987).[156]

Foreign currency gain or loss attributable to a nonfunctional currency transaction is treated separately from the underlying transaction. Generally, it is treated as ordinary gain or loss but is not treated as interest income or expenses (Code Sec. 988).[157] However, gain of an individual from the disposition of foreign currency in a personal transaction is not taxable, provided that the gain realized does not exceed $200. A personal transaction is any transaction other than one with respect to which properly allocable expenses are deductible as trade or business expenses or expenses incurred in the production of income. It also refers to an individual's currency exchange transactions that are entered into in connection with business travel but do not affect tax treatment of capital losses (¶ 1754).

2496. International Boycotts. Participation by a taxpayer in, or cooperation with, an international boycott will result in the reduction or denial of the foreign tax credit (¶ 2475), the deferral of tax allowed to foreign subsidiaries (¶ 2485), and the deferral of tax allowed to domestic international sales corporation (DISC) shareholders (¶ 2498) (Code Sec. 999; Temp. Reg. § 7.999-1).[158] The amount of the benefits to be denied is determined from the ratio of the value of the sales or purchases of goods and services

References are to Standard Federal Tax Reports; Tax Research Consultant; and Practical Tax Explanations.

[149] ¶ 35,381; PART: 18,410.05; § 39,155.10

[150] ¶ 37,770; PART: 18,410.05; § 39,155.10

[151] ¶ 35,960; PART: 18,410.15; § 39,135.05

[152] ¶ 39,835; PART: 18,410.15; § 39,135.05

[153] ¶ 35,580; INTL: 30,352.10; § 39,135.10

[154] ¶ 28,840; INTLOUT: 21,050; § 46,015.15

[155] ¶ 28,920; INTLOUT: 21,052; § 46,015.15

[156] ¶ 28,860, ¶ 28,880; INTLOUT: 21,200, INTLOUT: 21,250; § 46,015.15

[157] ¶ 28,900; INTLOUT: 21,100

[158] ¶ 29,080, ¶ 29,081; INTL: 21,000

(or other transactions) arising from the boycott activity to the total value of the foreign sales or purchases of goods and services (or other transactions).

Participation in or cooperation with an international boycott occurs when a person, in order to do business in a certain country, agrees not to do business with a specified second country or with other countries doing business in specified countries. An agreement not to hire employees of, or to do business with, other companies whose employees are of a specified nationality, race or religion is also boycott activity. The following countries may require participation in, or cooperation with, an international boycott: Iraq, Kuwait, Lebanon, Libya, Qatar, Saudi Arabia, Syria, United Arab Emirates, and the Republic of Yemen.[159] The reduction of foreign tax credit extends to the credit that the taxpayer is entitled to as a shareholder as well as to the credit for foreign taxes the taxpayer paid himself or herself (Code Sec. 908).[160] Taxpayers who participate in or cooperate with a boycott and derive income from such activities must report such information to the IRS by filing Form 5713 when their income tax is due (including extensions).

2497. Illegal Payments. If an illegal bribe, kickback, or other payment is made by, or on behalf of, a controlled foreign corporation (CFC) (¶ 2487) or a domestic international sales corporation (DISC) (¶ 2498), either directly or indirectly to an official, employee, or agent-in-fact of a foreign government, the amount of the bribe, kickback or other payment will affect shareholders. In the case of a CFC, the amount is included as subpart F income for the year (¶ 2488) and thus is included in the shareholder's income (Code Sec. 952(a)(4)).[161] In the case of a DISC, the amount is considered a constructive dividend and must be included in the shareholders' income (Code Sec. 995(b)(1)(F)(iii)).[162] However, such payments may be deductible in certain circumstances, despite their possible illegality (¶ 972).

2498. Foreign Trade Income. Prior to 2005, the Code contained a number of rules designed to promote the export of U.S. manufactured products. For example, a percentage of income generated through a domestic international sales corporation (DISC) could be deferred for U.S. tax purposes, while a certain percentage of income from the sale of qualified export property by a foreign sales corporation (FSC) could be completely exempt from U.S. tax. Similarly, any U.S. taxpayer was entitled to exclude from gross income extraterritorial income (ETI) to the extent it was qualifying foreign trade income. These rules have been effectively repealed. However, a DISC geared toward small businesses may still exist if the income deferred by shareholders is limited and an interest charge is paid on such deferred amounts (Code Sec. 995).[163] The election to be treated as an interest-charge DISC is made on Form 4876-A.

2499. Information from Foreign Sources. The IRS may make a formal document request for foreign records if the normal summons procedure fails to produce the requested documentation (Code Sec. 982).[164] The request for formal documentation supplements the administrative summons procedure and does not prevent the use of any other Code provisions to obtain documents.

References are to Standard Federal Tax Reports; Tax Research Consultant; and Practical Tax Explanations.

159 ¶ 29,083.15; INTL: 21,050
160 ¶ 27,964; INTL: 21,306; § 13,410.05
161 ¶ 28,490; INTLOUT: 9,154
162 ¶ 29,020; INTLOUT: 15,510.10
163 ¶ 29,020; INTLOUT: 15,500
164 ¶ 28,820; IRS: 21,260

Chapter 25

RETURNS □ PAYMENT OF TAX

Filing

2501. Income Tax Returns—Types of Returns. Individuals who must file income tax returns use Form 1040, 1040A, or 1040EZ, along with any appropriate schedules; fiduciaries of estates and trusts who must file income tax returns use Form 1041; corporations must file income tax returns on Form 1120; and partnerships must file information returns on Form 1065.

The following specialized income tax return forms for individuals also exist: Form 1040-C for a departing alien; Form 1040NR or Form 1040NR-EZ for a nonresident alien; Form 1040-SS (self-employment) for a resident of the Virgin Islands, Guam, American Samoa or the Northern Mariana Islands; and Form 1040-PR or 1040-SS (self-employment) for a resident of Puerto Rico.

Specialized forms for certain types of corporations also exist:

(1) Schedule PH, attached to Form 1120 for a U.S. personal holding company;

(2) Schedule UTP, attached to the Form 1120 series return for a corporation with at least $100 million in assets that has taken an uncertain tax position;

(3) Form 1120-C for a cooperative association;

(4) Form 1120-F for a foreign corporation;

(5) Form 1120-FSC for a foreign sales corporation;

(6) Form 1120-H for a homeowners association;

(7) Form 1120-IC-DISC for an interest charge domestic international sales corporation;

(8) Form 1120-L for a life insurance company;

(9) Form 1120-ND for a nuclear decommissioning fund;

(10) Form 1120-PC for a property and casualty insurance company;

(11) Form 1120-POL for a political organization;

(12) Form 1120-REIT for a real estate investment trust;

(13) Form 1120-RIC for a regulated investment company;

(14) Form 1120S for an S corporation; and

(15) Form 1120-SF for a settlement fund.

Rules for determining which individuals must file an income tax return are set out at ¶ 101; rules for determining who must pay estimated tax are covered at ¶ 2682. Rules for corporation returns appear at ¶ 211, and rules for S corporations appear at ¶ 351. For rules applicable to partners and partnerships, see ¶ 406. Rules for estates and trusts are found at ¶ 510.

Employers who withhold income tax, social security tax, or both from their employees' wages must file quarterly returns on Form 941 to report the amount of tax withheld and their share of social security tax.[1] Employers with an estimated employment tax liability of $1,000 or less ("small employers") may instead file an annual return on Form 944 (¶ 2650). Employers who pay wages for agricultural labor must file Form 943 annually to report and pay social security taxes and voluntary income tax withholding. In addition, employers must file Form 940 annually to report and pay federal unemployment taxes (Reg. § 31.6011(a)-3).[2]

Individuals who pay annual cash wages of $1,800 or more in 2012 ($1,800 or more in 2013) for domestic services in their private homes must file Schedule H (Form 1040) to report and pay employer and employee social security taxes and any income tax withheld at the employee's request (Notice 2011-102). Individuals also use Schedule H to pay and report federal unemployment taxes if they paid total cash wages of $1,000 or more to household employees in any calendar quarter (Code Sec. 3510; Notice 95-18; IRS Pub. 926).[3]

2503. Electronic Filing. Electronic filing allows qualified filers to transmit tax return information directly to an IRS Service Center, usually over the internet. Taxpayers may e-file their tax returns through a paid preparer (or an electronic return originator), by using a personal computer, access to the internet, and commercial tax preparation software, or by qualifying for and enrolling in the Free File program. Individual taxpayers who e-file their returns can authorize direct debit payment from their checking or savings account on a specified date. Taxpayers may also charge their taxes by credit card or pay their taxes electronically through the Electronic Federal Tax Payment System (EFTPS) (IRS Fact Sheet FS-2011-7).

Free File is a public-private sector initiative with commercial software providers to provide free tax return preparation and electronic filing service for middle- and low-income taxpayers who meet certain adjusted gross income requirements. A Free File Fillable Tax Forms option is also available which allows all taxpayers, regardless of income level, to fill out and file their tax forms electronically (IRS News Release IR-2011-5). Free File is available at the IRS website at www.irs.gov.

Taxpayers who file their tax returns electronically must use electronic signatures (IRS Fact Sheet FS-2011-7). Electronic filers use a Self-Select Personal Identification Number (PIN), or if using a paid preparer, that preparer's Practitioner PIN (IRS Pub. 1345).

Form 8453 is used to transmit certain forms and supporting paper documents that are specifically listed on Form 8453 and are required to be submitted to the IRS with e-filed returns. If paper documentation must be submitted that is not listed on Form 8453, the return cannot be e-filed (Instructions to Form 8453).

Corporations, S corporations, partnerships, and exempt organizations may also elect to electronically file, respectively, Forms 1120, 1120S, 1065, and 990. However, certain organizations are required to submit those returns electronically. Corporations/S corporations with assets of $10 million or more, and that file 250 or more returns during the year, must file Forms 1120/1120S electronically (Reg. § 301.6011-5).[4] A partnership with more than 100 partners must file Form 1065 (and Schedules K-1 and related forms) electronically (Reg. § 301.6011-3).[5] Exempt organizations with assets of $10 million or more, and that file 250 or more returns annually, must file Form 990 electronically. If a private foundation or a Code Sec. 4947(a)(1) trust files 250 or more returns annually, regardless of asset size, it must file Form 990-PF electronically (Reg. § 301.6033-4).[6] Although electronic filing is not required for any corporation, S corporation or exempt organization filing less than 250 returns during the calendar year, the IRS

References are to Standard Federal Tax Reports; Tax Research Consultant; and Practical Tax Explanations.

[1] ¶ 33,662.01; PAYROLL: 6,200; § 22,235.10

[2] ¶ 33,662.01; PAYROLL: 3,352.15; § 22,340.10

[3] ¶ 33,825, ¶ 33,828.30; PAYROLL: 9,158; § 22,125.30, § 22,235.30, § 22,340.20

[4] ¶ 35,125CB; FILEBUS: 3,052.05, FILEBUS: 12,300; § 26,030.10, § 29,010.15, § 39,225.10b

[5] ¶ 35,125C; FILEBUS: 12,302.35, FILEBUS: 12,300; § 30,435

[6] ¶ 35,424C; EXEMPT: 12,252.15, EXEMPT: 12,252.20, FILEBUS: 12,300; § 33,245, § 33,605.05

encourages such organizations to do so. The IRS has updated the procedures that corporations, S corporations, and tax-exempt organizations must use to request a waiver of the electronic filing requirement (Notice 2010-13).

For income tax returns of individuals, estates, or trusts (i.e., individual income tax returns) electronic filing is required if the return is prepared and filed by a specified tax return preparer for the calendar year during which the return is filed. With respect to any calendar year, a "specified tax return preparer" means any tax return preparer (¶ 2517), unless the preparer reasonably expects to file 10 or fewer individual income tax returns during the calendar year (Code Sec. 6011(e)(3)).[7]

An individual income tax return is considered "filed" by a specified return preparer if the preparer submits the return to the IRS on the taxpayer's behalf. A return is not considered filed by a specified return preparer if the preparer obtains a hand-signed and dated statement from the taxpayer that the taxpayer chooses to file the return in paper format and that the taxpayer, and not the preparer, will submit the paper return to the IRS (Reg. § 301.6011-7(a)(4)).[8]

The IRS may grant waivers of the electronic filing requirement for specified return preparers in cases of undue hardship (Reg. § 301.6011-7(c)(1)).[9] Such waivers generally are intended to be granted preparers for undue hardships that can be identified in advance before the preparers would otherwise be required to file individual income tax returns electronically for a particular calendar year and will ordinarily be granted only in rare cases. Requests for a hardship waiver are made by filing Form 8944 (Rev. Proc. 2011-25).

The IRS has provided further administrative exemptions to the electronic filing requirement for certain classes of specified tax return preparers (Notice 2011-26). They include: exempt preparers (preparer members of certain religious groups; foreign preparers without Social Security numbers; and certain preparers ineligible for IRS e-file); exempt individual income tax returns due to preparer's technological difficulties (rejected returns; forms or schedules not supported by the preparer's software package; and other technological difficulties); and exempt individual income tax returns due to IRS e-file limitations (returns currently not accepted and required documentation not accepted electronically). Exemptions are automatic and do not have to be requested, but preparers will be required to show entitlement to exemption upon request by the IRS. Form 8948 was created to explain why an individual tax return that was able to be filed electronically was filed in a paper format.

Foreign Accounts. The IRS is authorized to require a financial institution to electronically file returns with respect to withheld taxes for which the institution is liable as a withholding agent under the nonresident alien and foreign corporation withholding rules (Code Sec. 1461), or under the foreign account withholding rules (Code Sec. 1474), even though the financial institution files less than 250 returns during the tax year (Code Sec. 6011(e)(4)).

2504 Signatures on Returns. Forms 1040, 1040A, and 1040EZ must be signed by the individual taxpayer (Reg. § 1.6061-1).[10] The return contains a declaration that it is made under the penalties of perjury (Code Sec. 6065).[11] In the case of a joint return, both the husband and the wife must sign (Reg. § 1.6013-1(a)(2)).[12] If the taxpayer did not prepare the return, the return must be signed by the taxpayer and the tax return preparer (¶ 2517 and ¶ 2518). If a decedent's return is filed by a representative, the representative should sign the return on the line indicated for the taxpayer and attach a written power of attorney.

For a discussion of signing requirements for electronically filed returns, see ¶ 2503.

References are to Standard Federal Tax Reports; Tax Research Consultant; and Practical Tax Explanations.

[7] ¶ 35,120; FILEBUS: 12,302; § 41,803

[8] ¶ 35,129OC; FILEBUS: 12,302; § 41,803

[9] ¶ 35,129OC; FILEBUS: 12,302; § 41,803

[10] ¶ 36,603; FILEBUS: 12,100, FILEIND: 15,250; § 1,330.05, § 39,010.25, § 41,810.15

[11] ¶ 36,680; FILEBUS: 12,100; § 39,010.25

[12] ¶ 35,161; FILEIND: 15,250; § 1,330.05

2505. Income Tax Returns—When to File. Subject to an exception for deadlines falling on a Saturday, Sunday, or a legal holiday (¶ 2549), the due dates for income tax returns are as follows:

Individual, trust, estate, and partnership income tax returns are due on or before the 15th day of the 4th month following the close of the tax year, typically April 15 in the case of a calendar-year taxpayer (Code Sec. 6072; Reg. § 1.6072-1(a)).[13] For the 2012 calendar tax year, income tax returns must be filed on April 15, 2013. The final income tax return of a decedent for a fractional part of a year is due on the same date as would apply had the taxpayer lived the entire year (i.e., the 15th day of the 4th month following the close of the 12-month period that began on the first day of the fractional year) (Reg. § 1.6072-1(b)).[14]

A domestic corporation or foreign corporation having a U.S. office must file its corporate income tax return on or before the 15th day of the 3rd month after the close of the tax year (March 15 for a calendar-year corporation). A corporation whose foreign sales corporation election is still in effect must file its U.S. income tax return by the 15th day of the 3rd month after the end of its tax year (Instructions for Form 1120-FSC). The return of an interest charge domestic international sales corporation (IC-DISC), an exempt farmers' cooperative, or other cooperative organization is due on or before the 15th day of the 9th month following the close of the tax year (September 15 for a calendar-year taxpayer) (Reg. § 1.6072-2).[15]

The due date for income tax returns of organizations exempt from tax under Code Sec. 501(a) (other than employees' trusts under Code Sec. 401(a)) is the 15th day of the 5th month following the close of the tax year (Reg. § 1.6072-2(c)).[16]

A taxpayer filing as a nonresident alien who is not subject to the wage withholding described at ¶ 2601 and a foreign corporation not having an office or place of business in the U.S. may file a return as late as the 15th day of the 6th month after the close of the tax year (Reg. § § 1.6072-1(c) and 1.6072-2(b)).[17] However, a nonresident alien who has wages subject to withholding is required to file a return on or before the 15th day of the 4th month following the close of the tax year.

A taxpayer may correct an error in a return, without incurring interest or penalties, by filing an amended return (for individuals, Form 1040X) and paying any additional tax due on or before the last day prescribed for filing the original return.[18]

2509. Extension of Time. An individual is granted an automatic extension of six months for filing a return (but *not* for payment of tax) by properly filing Form 4868 on or before the normal due date of the return (Reg. § 1.6081-4).[19] Form 4868 may be filed electronically or by mail. Filing extensions can be obtained without making tax payments, so long as taxpayers properly estimate their tax liability on the form. If the requesting taxpayers do not properly estimate their tax liability, the extension request will be denied, and the IRS will charge interest and a penalty for late payment. If the amount of tax included with the extension request is less than sufficient to cover the taxpayer's liability, the taxpayer will be charged interest on the overdue amount. However, no late-payment penalty will be imposed if the tax paid through withholding, estimated tax payments, or any payment accompanying Form 4868 is at least 90 percent of the total tax due with Form 1040 and if the remaining unpaid balance is paid with the return within the extension period (¶ 2809) (Reg. § 1.6081-4; Reg. § 301.6651-1).[20] An automatic extension should not be requested if the taxpayer has asked the IRS to compute the tax or if the taxpayer is under a court order to file the return by the original due date.

References are to Standard Federal Tax Reports; Tax Research Consultant; and Practical Tax Explanations.

[13] ¶ 36,720, ¶ 36,721; FILEIND: 18,052.20, PART: 18,160.05; § 39,205.10

[14] ¶ 36,721; FILEIND: 18,052.20; § 39,020

[15] ¶ 36,724; FILEBUS: 3,052.05, INTLOUT: 15,058.20, INTLOUT: 15,502.30; § 39,205.05

[16] ¶ 36,724; EXEMPT: 12,252; § 39,205.20

[17] ¶ 36,721, ¶ 36,724; FILEIND: 100, FILEIND: 15,200, CCORP: 36,060; § 39,205

[18] ¶ 35,141.40; FILEBUS: 3,150, FILEIND: 18,150; § 1,315

[19] ¶ 36,793; FILEBUS: 15,100; § 39,215.10

[20] ¶ 36,793, ¶ 39,472; FILEBUS: 15,100; § 39,215.10

Individuals Residing Outside the United States. U.S. citizens or residents living outside the U.S. and Puerto Rico (including military personnel) are granted an automatic extension up to and including the 15th day of the sixth month following the close of their tax year for filing a return and paying the tax if they attach a statement to their return showing that they are entitled to such an extension (Reg. § 1.6081-5).[21] However, interest will be assessed on any unpaid tax from the due date of the return (without regard to the automatic extension) until the tax is paid (IRS Pub. 54). The automatic filing extension runs concurrently with the automatic six-month extension allowed to all individuals. Thus, the maximum automatic extension is only six months from the regular due date. However, the application for the automatic six-month extension is timely if it is filed by the due date established by the two-month extension. If an individual outside the United States needs more than the automatic extension in order to meet either the bona fide residence or the physical presence test for the foreign earned income or housing exclusion, Form 2350 should be filed by the due date for filing the return (June 15 for calendar-year citizens or residents living outside the U.S. and Puerto Rico). Such filing will entitle the individual to additional time for filing the return but not for paying the tax.

Corporations. A corporation or an S corporation is entitled to an automatic extension of six months for filing its return, provided that it timely and properly files Form 7004 and deposits the full amount of the tax due. However, the IRS may terminate this extension at any time by mailing to the corporation (or the parent corporation for an affiliated group filing a consolidated return) notice of such termination at least 10 days prior to the termination date fixed in the notice (Reg. § 1.6081-3).[22]

Other Entities. An automatic extension of time (through the 15th day of the 6th month following the close of the tax year) for filing a return and paying the tax is also granted to a partnership that keeps its books and records outside the U.S. and Puerto Rico, a domestic corporation that transacts its business and keeps its books and records outside the U.S. and Puerto Rico, a foreign corporation that maintains an office or place of business within the U.S., and a domestic corporation whose principal income is from sources within U.S. possessions (Reg. § 1.6081-5(a)).[23] The automatic filing extension runs concurrently with the automatic six-month filing extension allowed for most businesses.

Partnerships filing Form 1065 or Form 8804, and estates and trust filing Form 1041, should use Form 7004 to apply for an automatic *five*-month filing extension (Reg. §§ 1.6081-2 and 1.6081-6).[24]

The following entities must use Form 8868 to apply for extensions of time for filing returns: various trusts filing Forms 1041-A, 5227, and 6069; certain exempt organizations filing Forms 990, 990-PF, 990-EZ, or 990-BL, certain exempt organizations or corporations filing Form 990-T, and Form 4720; and certain charitable organizations filing Form 8870 (Reg. § 1.6081-9).[25] Real estate mortgage investment conduits filing Form 1066 or Form 8831 should use Form 7004 to apply for an automatic six-month filing extension (Reg. § 1.6081-7).[26]

2513. Place for Filing Returns. An individual, estate, or trust must file returns with the Service Center indicated at ¶ 5, except for certain charitable and split-interest trusts and pooled-income funds (see Instructions for Form 1041).

A corporation, S corporation or partnership must file its return with the Service Center indicated in the instructions to the entity's return (Form 1120, Form 1120S or Form 1065).

References are to Standard Federal Tax Reports; Tax Research Consultant; and Practical Tax Explanations.

[21] ¶ 36,795; FILEBUS: 15,100; § 39,215.40

[22] ¶ 36,790; FILEBUS: 15,100; § 39,215.15

[23] ¶ 36,795; FILEBUS: 15,100; § 39,215.20

[24] ¶ 36,788, ¶ 36,797; FILEBUS: 15,104.20; § 30,435, § 32,610.15, § 39,215.20

[25] ¶ 36,798K; FILEBUS: 15,104.35; § 33,245, § 33,605.05, § 33,945

[26] ¶ 36,798; FILEBUS: 15,104.20; § 39,215.05

The place to file certain elections, statements, returns and other documents can be found at the IRS website, at http://www.irs.gov/uac/Where-to-File-Certain-Elections,-Statements,-Returns-and-Other-Documents (Notice 2010-53).

2517. Return Preparers. A person who prepares for compensation (or who employs persons to prepare for compensation) all or a substantial portion of *any* tax returns (or refund claims) is a "tax return preparer" (Code Sec. 7701(a)(36); Reg. § 301.7701-15).[27] In addition to the prohibition against disclosure of return information (¶ 2894), a tax return preparer is subject to the following rules:

(1) The signing tax return preparer must sign a paper return after its completion but before its presentation to the taxpayer for signature (Code Sec. 6695(b); Reg. § 1.6695-1(b)). Paper returns require the preparer to manually sign the return or use any of three alternative methods that include either a facsimile of the preparer's signature or the individual preparer's printed name: (1) rubber stamp, (2) mechanical device, or (3) computer software program (Notice 2004-54). The preparer need not sign an electronically signed return before presenting a completed copy to the taxpayer, but must furnish all information that will be transmitted as the electronically signed return to the taxpayer at the same time that the preparer furnishes Form 8879 or a similar IRS e-file signature form. To e-file a return, the preparer must sign using a Self-Select Personal Identification Number (PIN) or a Practitioner PIN (IRS Pub. 1345).[28]

(2) The signing tax return preparer must include his or her identifying number on the taxpayer's return after its completion but before its presentation to the taxpayer. For returns filed after December 31, 2010, the identifying number is the individual's preparer tax identification number (PTIN) or other number prescribed by the IRS. If the preparer is employed by another person, the employer must furnish the identifying numbers of both the employer and the employee-preparer (Code Sec. 6109(a)(4); Reg. § 1.6109-2; Notice 2011-6).[29]

(3) The signing tax return preparer must provide the taxpayer with a completed copy of the prepared return (in either paper or electronic form) no later than the time the original return is presented for signing. The copy must be in any media acceptable to both the taxpayer and the preparer, and must include all information submitted to the IRS to enable the taxpayer to determine what schedules, forms, electronic files, and other supporting materials have been filed. The copy need not contain the identification number of the paid tax return preparer. The signing tax return preparer must also keep, for three years following the close of the return period, a copy of the return (in either paper or electronic form) or a list of the names, identification numbers, and tax years of taxpayers for whom returns were prepared, and the name of the individual tax return preparer required to sign the return (Code Sec. 6107; Reg. § 1.6107-1).[30] The preparer need not sign the taxpayer's copy of the return.

(4) If a return preparer (or any person) employs any signing tax return preparers to prepare returns for other persons (i.e., not the employer's return), the preparer must keep a record, for three years following the close of the return period to which the record relates, of the name, taxpayer identification number (TIN), and principal place of work of each tax return preparer employed by the preparer at any time during the return period (Code Sec. 6060; Reg. § 1.6060-1).[31] Any individual signing tax return preparer who is not employed by another preparer is treated as his or her own employer. The "return period" is defined as the 12-month period beginning on July 1 of each year.

References are to Standard Federal Tax Reports; Tax Research Consultant; and Practical Tax Explanations.

[27] ¶ 43,080, ¶ 43,113, ¶ 43,114.01; IRS: 6,050; § 41,410.05

[28] ¶ 39,965, ¶ 39,966; IRS: 6,104; § 41,510

[29] ¶ 36,960, ¶ 36,961C; IRS: 6,106; § 41,515

[30] ¶ 36,920, ¶ 36,921; IRS: 6,108, IRS: 6,110.05; § 41,520.05, § 41,520.10

[31] ¶ 36,560, ¶ 36,561; IRS: 6,110.10; § 41,520.20

All tax return preparers must have a PTIN or other prescribed identifying number that was applied for and received at the time and in the manner prescribed by the IRS, including the payment of a user fee. To obtain a PTIN, a tax return preparer must be an attorney, certified public accountant, enrolled agent, or registered tax return preparer authorized to practice before the IRS (Reg. § 1.6109-2(d)). However, the IRS will allow certain individuals who are 18 years old or older, but are not one of these specific types of professionals, to pay the applicable user fee and obtain a PTIN if: (1) the individual is supervised by an attorney, certified public accountant, enrolled agent, enrolled retirement plan agent, or enrolled actuary authorized to practice before the IRS under Circular 230 § 10.3(a)-(e); (2) the supervising attorney, certified public accountant, enrolled agent, enrolled retirement plan agent, or enrolled actuary signs the tax returns or refund claims prepared by the individual; (3) the individual is employed at the law firm, certified public accounting firm, or other recognized firm of the tax return preparer who signs the tax return or refund claim; and (4) the individual passes the requisite tax compliance check and suitability check when available (Notice 2011-6).

A "signing tax return preparer" is the individual preparer with primary responsibility for the overall substantive accuracy of the preparation of tax returns or refund claims. A "nonsigning tax return preparer" is any preparer who is not a signing tax return preparer but who prepares a substantial portion of a return or refund claim regarding events that have occurred at the time advice is rendered (Reg. § 301.7701-15(b)).[32]

The IRS has identified the tax returns and claims for refund that are required to be signed by a tax return preparer, as well as the relevant categories of returns and claims for purposes of the preparer penalty for understatement of tax liability (¶ 2518) (Rev. Proc. 2009-11).

Practice before the IRS is regulated through Circular 230. Effective August 2, 2011, all paid return preparers, regardless of credentials, are subject to Circular 230's rules of practice. Registered tax return preparers are subject to registration, examination, and continuing education requirements.[33]

2518. Return Preparer Penalties. Several penalties may be assessed against tax return preparers.

Failure to Follow Procedures. A tax return preparer who fails to meet the requirements in (1)-(4) as described in ¶ 2517 may be assessed the following penalties, unless the failure is due to reasonable cause and not to willful neglect:

(1) $50 for each failure to sign a return, to furnish an identifying number, or to furnish the taxpayer with a copy of the prepared return;

(2) $50 for each failure to retain and make available a copy of prepared returns or a list of taxpayers for whom returns were prepared, and the name of the individual preparer required to sign the return; and

(3) $50 for each failure to retain and make available a record of preparers employed, plus $50 for each failure to include an item required in such record.

A $500 penalty is assessable against a preparer who endorses or negotiates a taxpayer's refund check (other than a bank preparer who negotiates customers' refund checks for bank account deposits) (Code Sec. 6695; Reg. § 1.6695-1).[34]

Understatement of Taxpayer's Liability. A penalty may be imposed against a return preparer for each tax return or claim for refund that understates the taxpayer's liability due to an unreasonable position that the preparer knew, or reasonably should have known. The penalty is the greater of (a) $1,000 or (b) 50 percent of the income derived (or to be derived) by the preparer with respect to the return or refund claim (Code Sec. 6694(a); Reg. §§ 1.6694-1 and 1.6694-2).[35] The penalty will not be imposed if the preparer

References are to Standard Federal Tax Reports; Tax Research Consultant; and Practical Tax Explanations.

[32] ¶ 43,113; IRS: 6,050; § 41,410

[33] ¶ 43,524; IRS: 3,204.10; § 41,010.20

[34] ¶ 39,965, ¶ 39,966; IRS: 6,104, IRS: 6,106.05, IRS: 6,108, IRS: 6,110.05, IRS: 6,112; § 41,535.05

[35] ¶ 39,955, ¶ 39,956, ¶ 39,957; IRS: 6,150; § 41,610

shows that there was reasonable cause for the understatement and the preparer acted in good faith. Modified rules apply to nonsigning preparers (¶ 2517) (Reg. §§ 1.6694-1(a) and (b), and 1.6694-2(d)(3)(ii)).

A position is treated as unreasonable unless (1) there is or was substantial authority for the position; (2) the position is adequately disclosed and has a reasonable basis; or (3) if the position pertains to a tax shelter (¶ 2858 and ¶ 2870) or a reportable transaction (¶ 2001), it is reasonable to believe that the position would more likely than not be sustained on its merits. Under interim guidance, the term "substantial authority" has the same meaning as it does for the 20-percent accuracy-related penalty for a substantial understatement of income tax (¶ 2858). The guidance also contains penalty compliance rules for tax shelter transactions (Notice 2009-5).[36]

The penalty increases to the greater of (a) $5,000 or (b) 50 percent of the income derived (or to be derived) by the preparer with respect to the return or refund claim if the understatement is willful or reckless (Code Sec. 6694(b); Reg. § 1.6694-3).[37]

Lack of Diligence in Claiming Earned Income Credit. Tax preparers must comply with due diligence requirements for returns or refund claims asserting eligibility for the earned income credit (Code Sec. 6695(g); Reg. § 1.6695-2).[38] Among the due diligence requirements, applicable to returns or refund claims required to be filed on or after December 31, 2011, tax preparers are required to file (or submit to the taxpayer for filing) Form 8867 (or a self-created alternate computation record), with any federal return claiming the earned income credit. Each failure to observe the requirements regarding the amount of, or eligibility for, the credit will result in a penalty of $100 ($500 with respect to returns required to be filed after 2011), in addition to any other penalty imposed.

Aiding or Abetting in Tax Liability Understatement. A penalty of $1,000 may also be imposed on persons for aiding or abetting in an understatement of tax liability on a return, claim or other document ($10,000 for aiding or abetting an understatement of liability on a corporate return) (Code Sec. 6701).[39] Only one penalty may be imposed per taxpayer per period; however, the tax period may not necessarily be a tax year. For instance, understatements on quarterly employment tax returns may give rise to four separate penalties for a calendar year (Code Sec. 6701(b)(3)). According to the Sixth Circuit, no statute of limitations applies to bar the penalty.[40] Generally, this penalty may be imposed in addition to other penalties. However, this penalty will not be imposed if either the return preparer penalty for understatements due to unreasonable positions or the penalty for promoting abusive tax shelters has been applied with respect to the same tax return or refund claim (Code Sec. 6701(f)).[41]

2521. Protest Returns. A civil penalty of $5,000 is imposed upon any person (including an individual, a trust, estate, partnership, association, company, or corporation) who files a purported tax return (income or otherwise) if (1) the purported return fails to contain sufficient information from which the substantial correctness of the amount of tax liability can be judged, or contains information that on its face indicates that the amount of tax shown is substantially incorrect, and (2) such conduct arises from a frivolous position or from a desire to delay or impede administration of the tax laws. This penalty is imposed in addition to any other penalties imposed on the taxpayer (Code Sec. 6702).[42] The penalties may be reduced at the discretion of the Secretary of the Treasury in order to promote compliance with, and administration of, the federal tax laws.

References are to Standard Federal Tax Reports; Tax Research Consultant; and Practical Tax Explanations.

[36] ¶ 39,960.70; IRS: 6,156; § 41,610.10

[37] ¶ 39,955, ¶ 39,957E; IRS: 6,158; § 41,615

[38] ¶ 39,965, ¶ 39,968; IRS: 6,116; § 12,640

[39] ¶ 40,033; PENALTY: 3,258; § 41,620

[40] ¶ 40,035.10; PENALTY: 3,258; § 41,620

[41] ¶ 40,033; PENALTY: 3,258; § 41,620

[42] ¶ 40,040; PENALTY: 3,260; § 40,220

A $5,000 civil penalty may also be imposed on any person who files a "specified frivolous submission." A "specified frivolous submission" is a specified submission that either (1) is based on a position that has been identified as frivolous in a prescribed frivolous positions list; or (2) reflects a desire to delay or impede the administration of federal tax laws. A "specified submission" is a request for a collection due process hearing or an application for an installment agreement, offer in compromise, or taxpayer assistance order. If a person withdraws a submission within 30 days after receiving notice that the return is a specified frivolous submission, the penalty will not be imposed.

The prescribed list of frivolous positions may be found in Notice 2010-33. The list is not conclusive, and will be periodically revised. Returns or submissions that contain positions not prescribed in the Notice, but which on their face have no basis for validity in existing law, or which have been deemed frivolous in a published opinion by the U.S. Tax Court or other court of competent jurisdiction may also be subject to the $5,000 penalty.

Also, up to $25,000 may be assessed by the Tax Court against a taxpayer who institutes or maintains proceedings primarily for delay or on frivolous grounds or who unreasonably fails to pursue available administrative remedies. Other courts may require a taxpayer to pay a penalty of up to $10,000 if the taxpayer's action against the IRS for unauthorized collection activities appears to be a frivolous or groundless proceeding (Code Sec. 6673).[43] The Tax Court has held that a penalty for instituting proceedings primarily for delay is properly assessed against the tax matters person of an S corporation, rather than against the entity or its other shareholders.[44]

2523. Books and Records. Taxpayers are required to keep accurate, permanent books and records so as to be able to determine the various types of income, gains, losses, costs, expenses, and other amounts that affect their income tax liability for the year (Reg. § 1.6001-1(a)).[45] The records must be retained for as long as they may be, or may become, "material" for any federal tax purpose. Generally, records that support an item of income or a deduction on a tax return should be kept at least for the period of limitation for that return. See ¶ 2726, ¶ 2732, ¶ 2734, ¶ 2738, and ¶ 2517 (for return preparers) regarding applicable limitation periods.

Payment of Tax

2525. Place of Payment. The amount of tax shown on a return must be paid to the internal revenue officer with whom the return is filed unless, as in the case of corporations, the tax must be deposited with an authorized depository (Code Sec. 6151(a); Reg. § 1.6302-1).[46] See ¶ 2513.

The IRS requests that individuals use a payment voucher, Form 1040-V, for any balance due on any Forms 1040.

2529. Time of Payment. In general, the tax shown on an income tax return is to be paid, without assessment or notice and demand, at the time fixed for filing the return, determined without regard to any extension of time for filing the return. See ¶ 2505. However, exceptions apply when:

(1) a taxpayer shows that payment on the return due date will result in undue hardship (¶ 2537);

(2) a taxpayer is residing outside the United States on the return due date (¶ 2509); or

References are to Standard Federal Tax Reports; Tax Research Consultant; and Practical Tax Explanations.

[43] ¶ 39,785; LITIG: 6,816; § 40,220.05

[44] ¶ 39,790.47; LITIG: 6,816; § 40,220.05

[45] ¶ 35,102; ACCTNG: 3,052.05; § 39,055

[46] ¶ 37,080, ¶ 38,061; FILEBUS: 6,106.10, FILEIND: 21,152; § 39,305, § 39,320

(3) a taxpayer elects to have the IRS compute the tax (¶ 105), in which case payment is due within 30 days after the IRS mails a notice and demand (Code Sec. 6151(b)(1)).[47]

The IRS also has the authority to enter into a written agreement with the taxpayer, allowing for the full or, in most situations, partial payment of any tax in installments, if such an agreement will facilitate the collection of a tax liability (Code Sec. 6159).[48] The fee for entering into an installment agreement is $105 ($52 for direct debit installment agreements, where the payments are deducted directly from the taxpayer's bank account). For low income taxpayers, the fee is $43, regardless of the method of payment. The fee for reinstating a defaulted agreement, or restructuring an existing agreement, is $45, regardless of income level.[49]

There are three types of installment agreements. The first, referred to as guaranteed installment agreements, must be accepted by the IRS if an individual taxpayer's tax liabilities, without regard to interest, penalties, additions to tax, and any other additional amounts, total $10,000 or less and certain other conditions are met (Code Sec. 6159(c)). The second type of agreement is for individuals who do not qualify for the first type of agreement, and for businesses. The IRS, at the taxpayer's request, enters into a streamlined agreement if the taxpayer owes no more than $50,000, without regard to interest, penalties, additions to tax, or any other additions, and the taxpayer agrees to pay the amount due in full within six years (IRM 5.14.5.2). Prior to March 7, 2012, the maximum tax liability for entering into a streamlined agreement was $25,000 and the maximum amount of time allowed to pay the amount due in full was five years (IRS News Release IR-2012-31). Small business taxpayers are allowed to enter into streamlined agreements if they agree to pay the amount due in full within two years and a direct debit installment agreement is entered into (IRS News Release IR-2011-20). Streamlined agreements do not require a financial analysis and do not involve filing liens. The third type of agreement is for taxpayers owing more than $50,000/$25,000. These agreements are accepted on a case-by-case basis if the IRS determines the taxpayer can eventually pay off the debt, and the agreement will facilitate the collection of the debt.

For taxpayers with $50,000/$25,000 or less in combined tax liability, interest and penalties, an interactive Online Payment Agreement (OPA) application is available at the IRS website. Otherwise, a taxpayer can request an installment agreement by filing Form 9465.

2533. Taxes of Member of Armed Forces upon Death. When a member of the Armed Forces dies while serving in a combat zone (¶ 895) or as a result of wounds, disease, or injury incurred while so serving, the final income tax liability for that individual's year of death and any prior year ending on or after the first day served in a combat zone will not be assessed. Any unpaid taxes of such individual that relate to tax years prior to service in a combat zone may also be abated. A similar tax forgiveness rule applies to U.S. military and civilian employees who die as the result of wounds or injury occurring outside the United States in a terroristic or military action against the United States or any of its allies (Code Sec. 692).[50]

2537. Extension of Time for Payment of Tax. As noted at ¶ 2509, an extension of time for filing the return ordinarily does not postpone the time for payment. The IRS, however, may extend the time of payment of the tax shown on the return for up to six months (or longer if the taxpayer is abroad) upon a showing of undue hardship. A taxpayer applying for an extension of the time to pay tax must file Form 1127 on or before the original due date for payment of the tax. The application must be accompanied by evidence showing the undue hardship that would result if the extension were

References are to Standard Federal Tax Reports; Tax Research Consultant; and Practical Tax Explanations.

[47] ¶ 37,080; FILEBUS: 6,100; § 39,305

[48] ¶ 37,180; FILEBUS: 6,104.40, FILEIND: 21,154.40; § 39,325.05

[49] ¶ 37,180C, ¶ 37,180D; FILEBUS: 6,104.40, FILEIND: 21,154.40; § 39,325.05

[50] ¶ 24,920; COMPEN: 6,604, ESTTRST: 6,300; § 1,005.15

refused, a statement of the assets and liabilities of the taxpayer, and a statement of the receipts and disbursements of the taxpayer for the three months preceding the original due date for payment of tax (Code Sec. 6161(a); Reg. § 1.6161-1).[51]

As a condition to the granting of an extension, the taxpayer may be required to furnish a bond (Code Sec. 6165; Reg. § 1.6165-1).[52] If an extension of time for payment of tax is granted, interest on the tax liability will accrue (¶ 2838) from the original due date until the date on which the balance is fully paid (Reg. § 1.6161-1(d)).[53]

Special Tax Year 2011 Penalty Relief. Special hardship relief has been provided to certain wage earners and self-employed individuals for tax year 2011 (IRS News Release IR-2012-31). For qualifying individuals, the IRS is providing a six-month grace period on failure-to-pay penalties (see ¶ 2805). Penalty relief will be available to two categories of taxpayers: (1) wage earners who have been unemployed at least 30 consecutive days during 2011 or in 2012 up to the April 17 deadline for filing a federal tax return, and (2) self-employed individuals who experienced a 25-percent or greater reduction in business income in 2011 due to the economy. This penalty relief is limited to taxpayers whose income does not exceed $100,000 (single or head of household) or $200,000 (married filing jointly) and whose calendar year 2011 balance due does not exceed $50,000. Eligible taxpayers requesting an extension of time to pay will get relief from the failure-to-pay penalty for tax year 2011 only if the tax, interest, and any other penalties are fully paid by October 15, 2012. Taxpayers meeting the eligibility criteria will need to complete Form 1127-A to request relief. The granting of relief from the failure-to-pay penalty does not extend the time for taxpayers to file their 2011 tax return. Failure-to-file penalties (¶ 2801) applied to unpaid taxes remain in effect and are generally five percent per month, with a 25-percent cap.

Military and Government Personnel. Armed Forces members and civilians serving in support of the Armed Forces who serve in a designated combat zone (¶ 895) or in a contingency operation or are hospitalized outside the United States as a result of an injury received while serving in a combat zone/contingency operation qualify for an extension for filing returns and paying tax for the period of combat/contingency operation service or hospitalization plus 180 days (Code Sec. 7508(a)).[54] This extension is also available to such a taxpayer's spouse who wishes to file a joint return (Code Sec. 7508(c)).[55]

Disaster Areas. The IRS is authorized to postpone deadlines for filing returns and paying taxes for up to one year for taxpayers affected by a federally declared disaster (Code Sec. 7508A).[56] This includes taxpayers affected by terroristic or military actions.

2541. Extension of Time for Payment of Deficiency in Tax. An extension of time for payment of a deficiency of tax may be granted for a period of not more than 18 months where timely payment of the deficiency would result in undue hardship. Such an extension may be applied for according to the procedure for an extension of time for payment of tax outlined in ¶ 2537. An additional period of not more than 12 months may be granted in an exceptional case. A request for an extension will be refused if the deficiency was due to negligence, intentional disregard of income tax rules and regulations, or fraud (Code Sec. 6161(b); Reg. § 1.6161-1(a)(2) and (c)).[57]

2545. Forms of Payment. Payment of taxes must be made by a commercially acceptable means deemed appropriate by the IRS. Such means of payment include personal or cashier's check, money order, credit, debit or charge cards, or electronic funds withdrawal (Code Sec. 6311; Reg. § 301.6311-2).[58] Credit card payments may be

References are to Standard Federal Tax Reports; Tax Research Consultant; and Practical Tax Explanations.

[51] ¶ 37,200, ¶ 37,201; FILEBUS: 6,104, FILEIND: 15,302, FILEIND: 21,154; § 39,310.05

[52] ¶ 37,260, ¶ 37,261; FILEBUS: 6,104; § 39,310.10

[53] ¶ 37,201; FILEBUS: 6,104; § 39,310.10

[54] ¶ 42,686; FILEBUS: 6,104, FILEIND: 15,302, FILEIND: 21,154.30; § 39,215.30

[55] ¶ 42,686; FILEBUS: 6,104; § 39,215.30

[56] ¶ 42,687A; FILEBUS: 6,104, FILEBUS: 15,100; § 39,215.35

[57] ¶ 37,200, ¶ 37,201; FILEBUS: 6,104.15, FILEIND: 21,154.15; § 39,310.05

[58] ¶ 38,085, ¶ 38,088; FILEIND: 21,156; § 39,320.10

charged to VISA, MasterCard, American Express, and Discover cards, although the private companies that process such payments may charge a convenience fee (IRS Fact Sheet FS-2008-6; IRS Pub. 17). Such a convenience fee may be deductible (¶ 1092). Electronic funds withdrawal is free and allows taxpayers to schedule payments to be withdrawn directly from their bank accounts, but is available only to those taxpayers who e-file. Additionally, taxpayers may use the Electronic Federal Tax Payment System (EFTPS), a free tax payment system that allows taxpayers to pay online or via telephone (IRS Pub. 966).

Effective January 1, 2011, electronic funds transfer must be used for all federal tax deposits. For earlier deposits, federal tax deposit coupons could be used for federal deposits of employment taxes, corporate income and corporate estimated taxes, unrelated business income taxes paid by tax-exempt organizations, private foundation excise taxes, taxes withheld on nonresident aliens and foreign corporations, estimated taxes on certain trusts, railroad retirement taxes, nonpayroll taxes, FUTA taxes, and excise taxes reported on Form 720 (Reg. § § 1.6302-1, 1.6302-2, 1.6302-3, and 1.6302-4).

Deadlines

2549. Deadlines Falling on a Weekend or Holiday. If the last day for performing any act (such as filing a return, paying tax, or filing a claim for credit or refund) falls on Saturday, Sunday, or a legal holiday, the act is timely if it is performed on the next day that is not a Saturday, Sunday, or a legal holiday (Reg. § 301.7503-1).[59] The term "legal holiday" means a legal holiday in the District of Columbia (such as Emancipation Day). When a legal holiday in the District of Columbia falls on a Sunday, the next Monday is treated as a legal holiday. When a legal holiday in the District of Columbia, other than Inauguration Day, falls on a Saturday, the preceding Friday is treated as a legal holiday (DC Code Annotated § 28-2701 (2010); Notice 2011-17). In the case of a return, statement, or other document required to be filed with an IRS office, the term "legal holiday" also includes a statewide legal holiday in the state in which the office is located (such as Patriots' Day in Massachusetts) (Code Sec. 7503).[60]

2553. Timely Mailing as Timely Filing and Paying (Mailbox Rule). Any return, claim, statement, or document that must be filed with the IRS or the Tax Court, or any payment required to be made on or before a particular date is regarded as having been timely filed or paid if, on or before the due date (including extensions granted), it is deposited in the mail in the United States in an envelope or other appropriate wrapper, postage prepaid and properly addressed, and the date of the U.S. postmark falls on or before the due date (Code Sec. 7502(a); Reg. § 301.7502-1).[61] The postmark date is deemed the date of delivery or payment. Federal tax returns (including claims, statements, or other documents) mailed from outside the U.S. are timely if they bear the official timely dated postmark of the foreign country (Rev. Rul. 2002-23).

The timely-mailed-is-timely-filed rule applies to designated private delivery services (Code Sec. 7502(f)).[62] See ¶ 5 for a listing of the available delivery services.

Documents or payments properly sent by registered mail are considered to have been filed on time if the registration date falls on or before the due date of the document. Such documents or payments properly sent by certified mail are timely filed if the certified mail sender's receipt is postmarked on or before the due date of the document. Delivery by properly registered or certified mail is presumed to have occurred if the envelope or package was properly addressed to the appropriate agency, officer, or office for filing or payment. Proof of use of a designated private delivery service under criteria established by the IRS is entitled to a similar presumption of delivery (Reg. § 301.7502-1(c)(2), (e)(1), and (e)(2)).[63]

References are to Standard Federal Tax Reports; Tax Research Consultant; and Practical Tax Explanations.

[59] ¶ 42,631; FILEBUS: 15,056; § 39,210.10

[60] ¶ 42,630; FILEBUS: 15,056; § 39,210.10

[61] ¶ 42,620, ¶ 42,621; FILEBUS: 15,052, FILEIND: 15,206; § 39,210.05

[62] ¶ 42,620; FILEBUS: 15,054, FILEIND: 15,206; § 39,210.05

[63] ¶ 42,621; FILEBUS: 15,052, FILEIND: 15,206; § 39,210.05

The timely-mailed-is-timely-filed rule also covers documents filed electronically (Reg. § 301.7502-1(d)). The date of an electronic postmark that is given by an authorized electronic return transmitter and is on or before the filing due date will be deemed to be the filing date.

A tax deposit received by an authorized depository (no longer including Federal Reserve Banks) after the due date for the deposit is timely if it has been properly mailed at least two days before the prescribed due date. However, if any person is required to deposit tax more than once a month and the deposit amounts to $20,000 or more, the deposit must be received on or before the prescribed due date to be timely (Code Sec. 7502(e); Reg. § 301.7502-2).[64]

Information Returns and Payment at Source

2565. Payments Made in Course of Trade or Business. Every person engaged in a trade or business, including a partnership and a nonprofit organization, must file information returns for each calendar year for certain payments made during such year in the course of the payor's trade or business (Code Secs. 6041–6050W).[65] In many cases the information contained on such returns must be reported to the IRS by means of electronic filing through the IRS FIRE (Filing Information Returns Electronically) System. All information returns filed electronically are processed at the IRS Information Returns Branch, Kearneysville, West Virginia (Rev. Proc. 2012-30). Recipients must be furnished a copy of the information return or a comparable statement. While payee statements are generally required to be in written form, persons required to furnish recipients with copies of forms in the Form 1099 series and any other information return issued under Code Secs. 6041–6050W may furnish electronic payee statements (Sec. 401 of the Job Creation and Worker Assistance Act of 2002 (P.L. 107-147)). Payee statements for Form W-2 may also be filed electronically (Reg. § 31.6051-1).[66]

The following information returns are among those currently being filed:

Form 1098. Persons file this form if they receive $600 or more in mortgage interest from an individual in the course of a trade or business. Points paid directly by a borrower (including seller-paid points) for the purchase of a principal residence must be reported on Form 1098.[67] Refunds and reimbursements of overpaid mortgage interest, and mortgage insurance premiums of $600 or more must also be reported on Form 1098 (Reg. § 1.6050H-2).[68]

Form 1098-E. Financial institutions, governmental units, and educational institutions must file this form when, in the course of a trade or business, they receive interest of $600 or more in a calendar year on a student loan that is used solely to pay for qualified higher education expenses.

Form 1098-T. An educational institution must file this form with respect to each individual enrolled for an academic period to report payments received or amounts billed for qualified tuition and related expenses. Also, any person engaged in a trade or business of making payments to any individual under an insurance arrangement as reimbursements or refunds, or similar arrangements, of qualified tuition and related expenses must file this form for each individual for whom reimbursements or refunds are made during the calendar year.

Form 1099-A. Persons who lend money in connection with their trade or business and, in full or partial satisfaction of the debt, acquire an interest in property that is security for the debt must file this form. The form must also be filed if the person has reason to know that the property securing the debt has been abandoned.

Form 1099-B. Brokers are to use this form to report sales (including short sales) of stock, bonds, commodities, regulated futures contracts, foreign currency contracts,

---

References are to Standard Federal Tax Reports; Tax Research Consultant; and Practical Tax Explanations.

[64] ¶ 42,620, ¶ 42,623; PAYROLL: 9,202; § 39,210.05

[65] ¶ 35,820 et seq.; FILEBUS: 9,200; § 39,105

[66] ¶ 36,421; PAYROLL: 3,356.50; § 39,140.10

[67] ¶ 36,186.035; REAL: 6,106; § 39,105.05

[68] ¶ 36,184; REAL: 6,106; § 18,501, § 39,105.05

forward contracts, and debt instruments. A broker that holds shares for a customer in a corporation that the broker knows or has reason to know has engaged in a transaction of acquisition of control or substantial change in capital structure must also file this form. Barter exchanges are to use the form to report exchanges of property or services through the exchange, but are not required to file for transactions involving property or services with a fair market value of less than $1.00 (Notice 2000-6). For 2012 transactions, brokers must furnish Form 1099-B to customers by February 15, 2013 (Code Sec. 6045).[69] Also, trustees and middlemen of widely held fixed investment trusts (WHFITs) must use this form to report the non-*pro rata* partial principal payments, trust sales proceeds, redemption asset proceeds, redemption proceeds, sales asset proceeds and the sales proceeds that are attributable to a trust interest holder (TIH) for the calendar year. Trustees and middlemen of WHFITs must furnish the required statement by March 15, 2013.

Brokers required to file Form 1099-B regarding a covered security must also report the customer's adjusted basis in the security and whether any gain or loss with respect to the security is long-term or short-term (Code Sec. 6045(g)). See ¶ 1980 for further discussion.

Form 1099-C. Financial institutions, credit unions, federal agencies and any organization that lends money on a regular and continuing basis must file this form for each debtor for whom a debt of $600 or more was cancelled. Multiple discharges of debt of less than $600 during a year need not be aggregated unless the separate discharges occurred with the purpose of evading the reporting requirements. The returns must be filed regardless of whether the debtor is subject to tax on the discharged debt. For example, debts discharged in bankruptcy must be reported (Code Sec. 6050P; Reg. § 1.6050P-1).[70]

Form 1099-DIV. Corporate payors file this form for each person:

(1) to whom payments of $10 or more in distributions, such as dividends, capital gains, or nontaxable distributions, were made on stock;

(2) for whom any foreign tax was withheld and paid on dividends and on other distributions on stock if the recipient can claim a credit for the tax;

(3) for whom any federal income tax was withheld under the backup withholding rules; or

(4) to whom payments of $600 or more were made as part of a liquidation.

S corporations use this form only to report distributions made during the calendar year out of accumulated earnings and profits.

Form 1099-G. Government units use this form to report payments of $10 or more for unemployment benefits and state and local tax refunds, credits, or offsets, payments of $600 or more in taxable grants or alternative trade adjustment assistance payments, and agricultural subsidy payments made during the year.

Form 1099-H. Health insurance providers are required to file this return to report any advance payments of the credit for health insurance costs they are entitled to receive on behalf of individuals under Code Sec. 7527 (¶ 1332) (Code Sec. 6050T).

Form 1099-INT. Payors file this form for each person to whom payments of $10 or more in interest were paid, including interest on bearer certificates of deposit and interest on U.S. Savings Bonds, Treasury bills, Treasury notes, and Treasury bonds. Interest of $600 or more is also reportable if paid for a person in the course of a trade or business, such as interest on delayed death benefits paid by a life insurance company, interest received with damages, or interest on a state or federal income tax refund. Form 1099-INT must also be filed to report interest of $10 or more (other than original issue discount) accrued to a real estate mortgage investment conduit (REMIC), a financial asset securitization investment trust (FASIT) regular interest holder, or a holder of a

References are to Standard Federal Tax Reports; Tax Research Consultant; and Practical Tax Explanations.

[69] ¶ 35,920; FILEBUS: 9,250; § 39,120.20

[70] ¶ 36,310, ¶ 36,311B; SALES: 12,450; § 3,401

collateralized debt obligation (CDO). Additionally, trustees and middlemen of WHFITs must report the gross amount of interest exceeding $10 that is attributable to a TIH for the calendar year on this form.

Form 1099-K. Banks and other processors of merchant payment card transactions (e.g., credit and debit cards and internet payment systems) must use this form to report a merchant's annual gross payment card receipts to the IRS and to the merchant (Code Sec. 6050W; Reg. §§1.6050W-1 and 1.6050W-2).[71] Reporting is only required if the aggregate value of third-party network transactions for a merchant is $20,000 or more for the calendar year and if the aggregate number of transactions is 200 or more.

Form 1099-MISC. This form is filed by payors for each person to whom at least $10 in gross royalty payments or broker payments in lieu of dividends or tax-exempt interest, or $600 for rents or services in the course of a trade or business, was paid. Some of the items reported on this form are:

(1) payments for real estate, machine and pasture rentals;

(2) royalties paid to authors;

(3) prizes and awards that were not paid for services rendered;

(4) amounts withheld as backup withholding;

(5) payments by medical and health care insurers to each physician or health care provider under health, accident and sickness insurance programs;

(6) compensation such as fees, commissions and awards, and golden parachute payments paid to a nonemployee for services, including payments to attorneys for legal services (Code Sec. 6045(f));

(7) notification of the occurrence of sales of $5,000 or more of consumer products to a person on a buy-sell or commission basis for resale anywhere other than in a permanent retail establishment;

(8) fishing boat proceeds;

(9) fish purchases of $600 or more paid in cash for resale (Code Sec. 6050R);

(10) crop insurance proceeds of $600 or more; and

(11) any deferrals for the year under a nonqualified deferred compensation plan (Code Sec. 6041(g)).

For 2012 payments, this form must be furnished to recipients by February 15, 2013, if substitute payments in lieu of dividends or tax-exempt interest are being reported in box 8, or gross proceeds paid to an attorney are being reported in box 14.

Form 1099-OID. Issuers of bonds or certificates of deposit, and trustees and middlemen of WHFITs use this form to report original issue discount of $10 or more (Reg. §1.671-5).

Form 1099-PATR. Cooperatives use this form to report patronage dividends and other distributions of $10 or more to patrons.

Form 1099-R. Payors file this form to report any distributions of $10 or more from retirement or profit-sharing plans, individual retirement arrangements (IRAs), simplified employee pensions (SEPs), annuities, or insurance contracts.

Form 1099-S. This form is used to report the sale or exchange of real estate, as well as the real property taxes imposed on the purchaser of a residence. Included are sales or exchanges of residences, land (including air space), commercial buildings, condominium units, stock in cooperative housing corporations, and noncontingent interests in standing timber (i.e., timber that is sold or exchanged for lump-sum payments not based on the amount of timber actually cut).[72] The form must be filed by the person responsible for closing the real estate transaction or, if no such person exists, by the mortgage

References are to Standard Federal Tax Reports; Tax Research Consultant; and Practical Tax Explanations.

[71] ¶36,376, ¶36,378C, ¶36,378G; FILEBUS: 9,320; §39,130

[72] ¶35,929; REAL: 15,458; §39,115

lender, the transferor's broker, the transferee's broker or the transferee, in that order. Payments of timber royalties under a "pay-as-cut" contract are also reported on the form. For 2012 transactions, this form must be furnished to recipients by February 15, 2013.

Forms 3921 and *3922.* These forms must be filed by a corporation to report certain stock transfers to an employee. Form 3921 is used to report a transfer of stock pursuant to an employee's exercise of an incentive stock option. Form 3922 is used to report a transfer of stock pursuant to an employee's exercise of an option granted under an employee stock purchase plan where the exercise price is less than 100 percent of the value of the stock, or is not fixed or determinable, on the date of grant.

Form 5498. This form is filed by the account trustee for each person for whom an IRA (including a deemed IRA) or a simplified employee pension (SEP) was maintained. Contributions made during the year to the IRA (including rollover contributions and contributions under a SEP plan) and the fair market value of the IRA or SEP account on December 31 must be reported here. Form 5498 is due by May 31 of the year following the year of contribution.

Form 8027. Each employer that runs a "large food or beverage establishment" (¶ 2605) must file an annual return of the receipts from food or beverage operations and tips reported by employees. In addition, in certain circumstances, the employer is required to allocate amounts as tips to employees. Establishments filing 250 or more Forms 8027 must file electronically (Rev. Proc. 2012-37).

Form 8300. Each person engaged in a trade or business who, in the course of such trade or business, receives more than $10,000 in cash in one transaction (or two or more related transactions) must file this form. The form is to be filed with the IRS by the 15th day after the transaction, and a similar statement is to be provided to the payor on or before January 31 of the calendar year following the year of receipt.

Form W-2. This form is to be furnished to both the Social Security Administration and the recipient. Employers use the form to report wages, tips, other compensation, and withheld income and FICA taxes. Bonuses, vacation allowances, severance pay, moving expense payments, some kinds of travel allowances and third-party payments of sick pay are included. For Forms W-2 filed for the 2012 tax year (the 2013 tax year for small employers), employers are required to use the form to report the aggregate cost of certain employer-sponsored health coverage provided to employees if the employer was required to file at least 250 Forms W-2 for 2011 (¶ 2567) (Code Sec. 6051(a)(14)).

Due Dates. Unless otherwise specified, the above information returns for 2012 are to be provided to the IRS by February 28, 2013, and to recipients by January 31, 2013. Form W-2 is to be provided to the Social Security Administration by February 28, 2013, and to recipients by January 31, 2013. The due date for electronically filing information returns with the IRS, and for electronically filing Form W-2 with the Social Security Administration, is April 1, 2013 (March 31, 2013, is a Sunday) (Code Sec. 6071(b); Reg. § 31.6071(a)-1(a)(3)(i)). Form 8809 is used to request an automatic 30-day extension of time to file Forms 1098, 1099, W-2G, 1042-S, 5498 and 8027 with the IRS or Form W-2 with the Social Security Administration. One additional 30-day extension may also be obtained by filing Form 8809 before the expiration of the first 30-day extension, but the requester must explain in detail why additional time is needed. Form 8809 cannot be used to request an extension of time to furnish required statements to recipients (Reg. § 1.6081-8).[73]

Other Information Returns. Other information returns are required with respect to:

(1) a U.S. person's acquisition of, or change of interest in, a foreign partnership (Code Sec. 6046A);

(2) cases of liquidation or dissolution of a corporation, including an exempt organization (Code Sec. 6043);

References are to Standard Federal Tax Reports; Tax Research Consultant; and Practical Tax Explanations.

[73] ¶ 36,798F; FILEBUS: 15,106.25; § 39,145.05

(3) corporate recapitalizations (Code Sec. 6043);,

(4) corporate mergers and acquisitions (Code Sec. 6043A);

(5) organizations or reorganizations of foreign corporations (Code Sec. 6046);

(6) creation of or transfers to foreign trusts, or the death of a U.S. citizen or resident who had been treated as the owner of, or whose estate included any portion of, a foreign trust, or any other information required by the IRS to be reported by a U.S. person treated as owner of a foreign trust (Code Sec. 6048);

(7) U.S. persons who own interests in foreign partnerships or corporations (Code Sec. 6038);

(8) U.S. persons who transfer property to foreign partnerships or corporations (Code Sec. 6038B);

(9) payors of long-term care benefits (Code Sec. 6050Q);

(10) U.S. persons (other than tax-exempt organizations) that receive foreign gifts during the tax year totaling more than $10,000 ($14,723 in 2012; $15,102 in 2013) (Code Sec. 6039F);

(11) individuals who lose citizenship, and long-term residents who terminate residency in the United States (Code Sec. 6039G);

(12) Alaska Native Settlement Trusts (Code Sec. 6039H);

(13) dispositions by charitable donees within three years of donated property with a value in excess of $5,000, and, also, charitable donees of intellectual property (Code Sec. 6050L);

(14) employer-owned life insurance contracts issued after August 17, 2006 (Code Sec. 6039I); and

(15) charges or payments made for qualified long-term insurance contracts under combined arrangements (Code Sec. 6050U).

In addition, the head of each federal executive agency generally must file Forms 8596 and 8596-A on a quarterly basis stating the name, address, and taxpayer identification number (TIN) of each person to whom the agency entered into a contract during the calendar year. An agency may also be required to file Form 1099-MISC if in the course of a trade or business it pays remuneration of $600 or more in a calendar year to any person for services provided by that person (Code Secs. 6041A and 6050M; Rev. Rul. 2003-66).[74]

2567. Health Care Coverage Reporting. Employers are required to disclose the aggregate cost of employer-sponsored health insurance coverage provided to their employees on the employee's Form W-2 (Code Sec. 6051(a)(14)).[75] Although the Code requires disclosure on Forms W-2 for the 2011 tax year (filed in 2012), the IRS has deferred the requirement for one year, so that an employer is not treated as failing to meet the reporting requirement, and is not subject to penalties, merely because it does not report the aggregate cost of employer-sponsored coverage on Forms W-2 issued for 2011 (Notice 2010-69). Additionally, in the case of 2012 Forms W-2 and until the issuance of further guidance, an employer is not subject to the reporting requirement if the employer was required to file fewer than 250 Forms W-2 for the preceding year (Notice 2012-9). Therefore, if an employer files fewer than 250 Forms W-2 in 2012, the employer is not subject to the reporting requirements for Forms W-2 for the 2013 calendar year. Contributions to a health savings account (¶ 2197B) or Archer medical savings account (¶ 2197C) of the employee or the employee's spouse, and salary reduction contributions to a flexible spending arrangement under a cafeteria plan (¶ 2196), are not be included in the reporting requirement.

References are to Standard Federal Tax Reports; Tax Research Consultant; and Practical Tax Explanations.

[74] ¶ 35,840, ¶ 36,280; FILEBUS: 9,362; § 39,105.15

[75] ¶ 36,420; COMPEN: 45,236.05; § 42,245.05

Beginning in 2014, any person who provides minimum essential health care coverage (i.e., an insurer) to an individual during a calendar year is required to file an information return reporting such coverage in the form and manner prescribed by the IRS (Code Sec. 6055).[76] Such a person is also required to furnish a written statement to the individual with respect to whom information is reported, detailing the contents of the return.

Also beginning in 2014, certain large employers (generally, employers with an average of at least 50 full-time employees) will be required to report to the IRS whether they offer full time employees and their dependents the opportunity to enroll in minimum essential coverage under an eligible employer sponsored plan, and provide details regarding the coverage offered and other required information (¶ 2190A) (Code Sec. 6056, as amended by the Department of Defense and Full-Year Continuing Appropriations Act, 2011 (P.L. 112-10)).[77] Such employers will also be required to furnish a written statement to each full-time employee with respect to whom information is reported, detailing the contents of the information return.

2570. Interests in Foreign Financial Assets. A U.S. person who has a financial interest in or signature authority over any foreign financial account (e.g., bank, securities, or other financial account) in a foreign country that exceeds $10,000 in aggregate value at any time during the calendar year must report that relationship by filing Form TD F 90-22.1, known as an FBAR, with the Treasury Department before July 1 of the following year. The IRS has extended the due date for filing reports for 2009 and earlier calendar years to November 1, 2011, but only for (1) persons with signature authority over, but no financial interest in, a foreign financial account, and (2) persons with a financial interest in, or signature authority over, a foreign commingled fund (Notice 2011-54).[78] Additional relief has been provided to a small portion of individuals with only signature authority who would otherwise be required to file an FBAR by the June 30, 2011, filing deadline. Under this relief, the June 30, 2011, deadline is extended until June 30, 2013 (after previously being extended until June 30, 2012), for the following individuals: (1) an employee or officer of a covered entity who has signature or other authority over, and no financial interest in, a foreign financial account of another entity more than 50-percent owned, directly or indirectly, by the entity (a controlled person); or (2) an employee or officer of a controlled person of a covered entity who has signature or other authority over, and no financial interest in, a foreign financial account of the entity or another controlled person of the entity (FinCEN Notice 2012-1; IRS News Release IR-2011-57).[79]

Specified Foreign Financial Assets. Under the Foreign Account Tax Compliance Act (FATCA), any individual who holds an interest in a specified foreign financial asset during the tax year must attach Form 8938 to his or her tax return to report certain information for each such asset if the total value of all such assets exceeds an applicable threshold amount (Code Sec. 6038D).[80] A "specified foreign financial asset" includes (1) a depository, custodial, or other financial account maintained by a foreign financial institution, (2) a stock or security issued by a person other than a U.S. person, (3) a financial instrument or contract held for investment that has an issuer or counterparty other than a U.S. person, and (4) an interest in an entity that is not a U.S. person.

The applicable threshold amount that determines whether a taxpayer must file Form 8938 depends on the taxpayer's filing status and whether the individual lives in the United States or abroad. The total value of specified foreign financial assets for this purpose is the asset's fair market value as determined in U.S. dollars using the Treasury's currency exchange rate on the last day of the tax year (Temp. Reg. § 1.6038D-2T; Instructions for Form 8938).[81] The applicable threshold amounts are as follows:

References are to Standard Federal Tax Reports; Tax Research Consultant; and Practical Tax Explanations.

[76] ¶ 36,465E; COMPEN: 45,236.10; § 42,250.15

[77] ¶ 36,467; COMPEN: 45,236.15; § 42,250.10

[78] ¶ 36,555.33; FILEBUS: 9,104; § 37,705

[79] ¶ 36,555.33; FILEBUS: 9,104; § 37,705

[80] ¶ 35,593; FILEBUS: 9,108; § 37,710

[81] ¶ 35,594AI; FILEBUS: 9,108; § 37,710

- Unmarried taxpayers living in the United States must file Form 8938 if the total value of specified foreign financial assets is more than $50,000 on the last day of the tax year or more than $75,000 at any time during the tax year.
- Married taxpayers living in the United States and filing a joint income tax return must file Form 8938 if the value of specified foreign financial assets is more than $100,000 on the last day of the tax year or more than $150,000 at any time during the tax year.
- Married taxpayers living in the United States and filing separate income tax returns must file Form 8938 if the value of specified foreign financial assets is more than $50,000 on the last day of the tax year or more than $75,000 at any time during the tax year.
- Married taxpayers living abroad and filing a joint return must file Form 8938 if the value of specified foreign assets is more than $400,000 on the last day of the tax year or more than $600,000 at any time during the year.
- Other taxpayers living abroad must file Form 8938 if the total value of specified foreign assets is more than $200,000 on the last day of the tax year or more than $300,000 at any time during the year.

The individual must disclose the asset's maximum value during the tax year, and provide specific information based on the asset type. For a financial account, the individual must provide the name and address of the financial institution in which the account is maintained, and the account number. For stock or security, the individual must provide the issuer's name and address, and any other information needed to identify the asset's class or issue. For any other instrument, contract, or interest, the individual must provide any information needed to identify the asset, and the names and addresses of all issuers and counterparties.

An individual who fails to furnish the required information at the time and in the manner prescribed is subject to a $10,000 penalty. If the failure continues for more than 90 days after the IRS mailed notice of the failure to the individual, the individual is subject to an additional $10,000 penalty for each 30-day period (or a fraction thereof) during which the failure continues after the 90-day period; this additional penalty cannot exceed $50,000. For purposes of assessing these penalties, the total value of the individual's foreign financial assets is presumed to exceed $50,000 (or a higher dollar amount prescribed by the IRS) if the individual does not provide sufficient information to demonstrate their total value.

These penalties are not imposed if the failure is due to reasonable cause and not willful neglect. However, the fact that a foreign jurisdiction would impose a civil or criminal penalty for disclosing the required information is not reasonable cause.

To the extent provided by the IRS in regulations or other guidance, these provisions also apply to any domestic entity formed or used to directly or indirectly hold specified foreign financial assets (Code Sec. 6038D(f); Prop. Reg. § 6038D-6).

Additionally, a 40-percent accuracy-related penalty may be imposed for tax underpayment attributable to an undisclosed foreign financial asset understatement (¶ 2864). The statute of limitations for assessments is extended to six years if there is an omission of gross income in excess of $5,000 attributable to a specified foreign financial asset (which may or may not be subject to the reporting requirements discussed above). Also, the three-year limitations period is suspended for failure to timely provide information reporting on specified foreign financial assets.

2579. Taxpayer Identification Number. Persons filing returns and other documents must record on such items a taxpayer identification number (TIN). Individuals use their social security number on Forms 1040, 1040A, and 1040EZ. Executors of individuals' estates who must file Form 706 are to use both their social security number and the decedent's social security number. For corporations, partnerships, estates and trusts, and similar nonindividual taxpayers, the identifying number is the employer identification number.

A prospective adoptive parent can apply for an adoption taxpayer identification number (ATIN) for a child who is in the process of being adopted (Reg. § 301.6109-3). Application for an ATIN must be made on Form W-7A.

Persons who file information returns (¶ 2565) may request the recipient of any payments to furnish his TIN on Form W-9.

Nonresident aliens who cannot obtain a TIN may use an IRS-issued individual number (ITIN) (Notice 2004-1). Form W-7 is used to apply for an ITIN. The Form W-7 must be accompanied by an original, completed income tax return, and documents supporting the information provided on Form W-7. Issuance of ITINs to deceased taxpayers is a business decision to be made by the IRS, and applications for deceased dependents are considered on a case-by-case basis (CCA 200925042).

Effective as of June 22, 2012, the IRS has instituted special interim changes to tighten its procedures for issuing ITINs (IRS News Release IR-2012-62). Through the end of 2012, ITINs are only issued when applications include original documentation, such as passports and birth certificates, or certified copies of these documents from the issuing agency. ITINs are no longer issued based on applications supported by notarized copies of documents. ITINs are also not issued based on applications submitted through certifying acceptance agents, unless they attach original documentation or copies of original documents certified by the issuing agency. Some categories of applicants are not impacted by these interim changes, however. Individuals who should follow the pre-June 22, 2012, procedures include military spouses and dependents without a SSN and non-resident aliens applying for ITINs for the purpose of claiming tax treaty benefits.

A penalty of $50 per failure applies to a taxpayer who omits his own TIN from a required return, statement, or document. Failure to furnish one's TIN to another person when so required or to include another person's TIN in any document for information reporting purposes will also give rise to a $50 penalty. The maximum penalty per calendar year for failure to include TINs is $100,000 (Code Secs. 6723 and 6724(d)(3)).[82]

25 RETURNS

References are to Standard Federal Tax Reports; Tax Research Consultant; and Practical Tax Explanations.

[82] ¶ 40,250, ¶ 40,275; PENALTY: 3,200; § 40,230

Chapter 26

WITHHOLDING ☐ ESTIMATED TAX

Withholding on Wages

2601. Withholding of Income Tax on Wages. Withholding of income tax by an employer is required on each of an employee's wage payments (Code Sec. 3402(a); Reg. § 31.3402(a)-1).[1] Wages generally include all remuneration (other than fees paid to a public official) for services performed by an employee for an employer, including the cash value of all remuneration (including benefits) paid in any medium other than cash (¶ 2604). Thus, salaries, fees, bonuses, commissions on sales or on insurance premiums, taxable fringe benefits, pensions, and retirement pay (unless taxed as an annuity) are, if paid as compensation for services, subject to withholding.

The term "employer" means any person for whom an individual performs or performed any service, of whatever nature, as the employee of such person (Code Sec. 3401(d); Reg. § 31.3401(d)-1).[2] It is not necessary that the services be continuing at the time the wages are paid in order that the status of employer exists. An employer includes not only individuals and organizations engaged in trade or business, but also tax-exempt organizations and federal, state, and local government units (including the District of Columbia and Puerto Rico). An employer also includes any person paying wages on behalf of a nonresident alien individual, foreign partnership, or foreign corporation, not engaged in trade or business within the United States or Puerto Rico.

An individual is an employee if the employer for whom the services are performed has the right to control and direct the individual performing the services not only as to the result to be accomplished by the work, but also as to the details and the means by which that result is accomplished (Code Sec. 3401(c); Reg. § 31.3401(c)-1).[3] An employee also includes any officer, employee, or elected official of federal, state, and local government units. It also includes an officer of a corporation, but not a director. Professionals such as physicians, lawyers, contractors, and others who follow an independent trade, business, or profession in which they offer their services to the public generally are not employees. The designation or description of an employment relationship by the parties is not controlling (¶ 2602).

An employer who fails to withhold income taxes from an employee's wages is liable for the unwithheld amounts (Code Sec. 3403).[4] Any third party who pays wages directly to employees of an employer or to the employee's agent is liable for any required withholding on those wages (Code Sec. 3505).[5]

References are to Standard Federal Tax Reports; Tax Research Consultant; and Practical Tax Explanations.

[1] ¶ 33,542, ¶ 33,543; PAYROLL: 3,052; § 22,105.05

[2] ¶ 33,502, ¶ 33,537; PAYROLL: 3,052; § 22,105.15

[3] ¶ 33,502, ¶ 33,536; COMPEN: 3,000; § 22,005.15

[4] ¶ 33,591; PAYROLL: 6,252; § 22,105.15

[5] ¶ 33,740; PAYROLL: 6,306; § 22,205.25

2602. Employee v. Independent Contractor. An "employee" must be distinguished from an "independent contractor," as an employer does not generally have employment tax obligations with respect to independent contractors. The IRS for many years relied on a 20-factor test to determine whether individuals are employees or independent contractors (Rev. Rul. 87-41).[6] However, it has shifted its analysis to focus on a three-part behavioral analysis—behavioral control, financial control, and relationship of the parties (IRS Pub. 15-A). A worker that may be an independent contractor under this analysis may nevertheless be treated as an employee for FICA and FUTA tax purposes if the worker is classified as a statutory employee (¶ 941B). Either an employer or employee, with or without the other's knowledge or assent, may request that the IRS make a determination as to whether or not a particular worker is an employee. The request is made using Form SS-8.

If an employer erroneously classifies an employee as an independent contractor and has no reasonable basis for doing so, the employer is liable for taxes under the income tax withholding (¶ 2601) and the FICA and FUTA tax provisions (¶ 2648 and ¶ 2649). However, employers may be eligible for reduced rates with respect to income tax withholding (1.5 percent of employee's wages) and the employer's share of FICA tax (20 percent of the amount otherwise due) (Code Sec. 3509).[7] These rates are doubled if the employer failed to file forms consistent with the employer's treatment of the worker as an independent contractor. Reduced rates are not available for statutory employees.

If the employer had a reasonable basis for not treating an individual as an employee, the employer may be entirely relieved of liability for employment taxes with respect to that individual if the employer was consistent in its treatment of the worker as a nonemployee (Section 530 of the Revenue Act of 1978).[8]

The IRS has established a program, known as the Voluntary Classification Settlement Program, that allows an eligible business to voluntarily reclassify some or all of its workers as employees for future tax periods while limiting employment tax liability for past non-employee treatment (Announcement 2011-64).[9] Form 8952 is used for this purpose.

Employees who have been misclassified as independent contractors use Form 8919 to figure and report the employee's share of uncollected social security and Medicare taxes due on their compensation.

2604. Wages Subject to Withholding. Wages subject to income tax withholding (¶ 2601) generally include all remuneration (other than fees paid to a public official) for services performed by an employee for an employer (Code Sec. 3401(a); Reg. § 31.3401(a)-1(a)).[10] It includes salaries, fees, bonuses, and commissions. Withholding is based on *gross* wage payments before deductions such as those under the federal or state unemployment insurance laws, those for pension funds (except deductible contributions to IRAs), insurance, etc., or those for liabilities of the employee paid by the employer. An employer is required to withhold income tax from wages paid for employment regardless of the circumstances under which the employee is employed or the frequency or size of amounts of the individual wage payments.[11] Tax must be withheld from wages paid for *each* payroll period.[12] Some types of compensation, however, are specifically excluded from the definition of wages for income tax withholding purposes (¶ 2609).

If an employee works on two jobs for the same employer, and only a part of the remuneration is wages—for example, for a construction worker who also works on his employer's farm (exempt employment)—all of the remuneration is treated alike. Thus, either (1) all of the wages are subject to withholding if more than half of the time is spent performing services for which wages are received, or (2) all are excluded if more

References are to Standard Federal Tax Reports; Tax Research Consultant; and Practical Tax Explanations.

[6] ¶ 33,538.66; COMPEN: 3,102; § 22,015.05

[7] ¶ 33,820; PAYROLL: 9,306; § 22,020.10

[8] ¶ 33,538.5056; COMPEN: 3,110; § 22,020.15

[9] ¶ 33,538.5057; COMPEN: 3,350; § 22,020.22

[10] ¶ 33,502, ¶ 33,503; PAYROLL: 3,150; § 22,110.05

[11] ¶ 33,593.165; PAYROLL: 6,058; § 22,110.05

[12] ¶ 33,544.20; PAYROLL: 6,056; § 22,110.05

than half of the time spent is in exempt services, provided the payroll period is no longer than 31 consecutive days (Reg. § 31.3402(e)-1).[13]

Compensation. Other forms of compensation besides salaries, fees, bonuses, and commissions are subject to withholding, including tips and other gratuities (¶ 2605), reimbursed employee expenses paid through a nonaccountable plan (¶ 2607) and other supplemental wages (¶ 2606), employee expense amounts in excess of per diem rates (¶ 2608), and payments for the stoppage of work such as severance payments and strike benefits (Reg. § 31.3401(a)-1).[14] Some types of compensation, however, are specifically excluded from the definition of wages for income tax withholding purposes (¶ 2609).

Payments of supplemental unemployment compensation are treated as wages for income tax withholding purposes, but withholding applies only to the extent that such benefits are includible in the employee's gross income (Code Sec. 3402(o)).[15] Guaranteed annual wage payments made during periods of unemployment pursuant to a collective bargaining agreement are wages subject to withholding.[16] However, strike benefits (other than hourly wages received for strike-related duties) paid by a union to its members are not subject to withholding.[17]

Fringe benefits are generally included in wages as supplemental wages (¶ 2606), but some may be partially or wholly exempt (¶ 2609).

Although the value of noncash compensation generally must be included in wages, when a retail commission salesperson is occasionally paid other than in cash, the employer is not required to withhold income tax for the noncash payments (Reg. § 31.3402(j)-1).[18] However, the fair market value of the noncash payments, such as prizes, must be included on the Form W-2 furnished to the employee as part of the total pay earned by the employee during the calendar year.

Withholding is available, if the payee so requests, for wage continuation payments (i.e., sick pay) received from a third party pursuant to a health or accident plan in which the employer participates (Code Sec. 3402(o); Reg. § 31.3402(o)-3).[19] Payments of sick pay made directly by employers to their employees are automatically subject to withholding. Employers who are third-party payors of sick pay are not required to withhold income taxes from payments unless the employee has requested withholding on Form W-4S.

Wages subject to withholding include amounts received under a nonqualified deferred compensation plan that are includible in an employee's gross income under Code Sec. 409A for the year of inclusion (¶ 2175) (Code Sec. 3401(a)).

Differential wage payments. Differential wage payments are included in the definition of wages paid by the employer to the employee for purposes of the federal income tax withholding rules (Code Sec. 3401(h)).[20] A differential wage payment is any payment that: (1) is made by an employer to an individual with respect to any period during which the individual is performing service in the uniformed services while on active duty for a period of more than 30 days and (2) represents all or a portion of the wages the individual would have received from the employer if the individual were performing service for the employer. Differential wage payments are considered supplemental wages and, therefore, are subject to the special rules applicable to such payments (¶ 2606). Differential wage payments, however, are not treated as wages for FICA (¶ 2648) or FUTA (¶ 2649) purposes (Rev. Rul. 2009-11).

2605. Tips and Gratuities Subject to Withholding. Cash tips paid directly to an employee by a customer and charged tips paid over to the employee (¶ 717) must be accounted for by the employee in a written statement furnished to the employer on or before the 10th day of the month following the month when they are received (Code

References are to Standard Federal Tax Reports; Tax Research Consultant; and Practical Tax Explanations.

[13] ¶ 33,551; PAYROLL: 6,058; § 22,105.10

[14] ¶ 33,503; PAYROLL: 3,150; § 22,110.05

[15] ¶ 33,542; PAYROLL: 3,178; § 22,110.40

[16] ¶ 33,506.3683; PAYROLL: 3,150; § 22,110.40

[17] ¶ 33,506.3678; PAYROLL: 3,178; § 22,110.40

[18] ¶ 33,574; PAYROLL: 6,208; § 22,105.10

[19] ¶ 33,542, ¶ 33,584; PAYROLL: 3,206; § 22,125.10

[20] ¶ 33,502; PAYROLL: 6,058; § 22,110.45

Sec. 6053(a)).[21] The employee reports the tips on Form 4070 or on a similar statement. An exception exists if the tips received by the employee in the course of his employment by a single employer amount to less than $20 in a calendar month; these tips are not subject to withholding (Code Secs. 3401(a)(16)).[22] The only tips that an employer must report on Form W-2 are those that are actually reported to him by the employee (Code Sec. 6051(a)).[23]

A large food and beverage establishment (one which normally has more than 10 employees on a typical business day and in which tipping is customary) must file annual information returns using Form 8027 (¶ 2565). These returns must report gross food and beverage sales receipts, employee-reported tip income, total charge receipts, and total charge tips (Code Sec. 6053(c); Reg. § 31.6053-3).[24] Such employers must allocate among their employees who customarily receive tip income an amount equal to the excess of eight percent of gross receipts over reported tips. This allocation is not required if the employees voluntarily report total tips equal to at least eight percent of gross sales. If it can be shown that average tips are less than eight percent of gross sales, the employer or a majority of its employees may apply to the IRS to have the allocation reduced from eight percent but not to below two percent.

2606. Supplemental Wages Subject to Withholding. Special rules apply when the employee is paid supplemental wages (bonus, overtime pay, back pay, commissions, vacation allowance, etc.). If supplemental wages are paid at the same time as regular wages, the two are added together and the withholding tax is computed on the total as a single wage payment. If the supplemental wages are not paid at the same time as the regular wages, the supplemental wages may be added either to the regular wages for the preceding payroll period or for the current payroll period within the same calendar year (Reg. § 31.3402(g)-1).[25]

Under an alternative method, the employer may treat the supplemental wages as wholly separate from regular wages and withhold at a flat rate equal to the third lowest income tax rate (25 percent for tax years beginning in 2012) without any allowance for exemptions and without reference to any regular payment of wages. Once the total of supplemental wage payments made to an employee, within a calendar year, exceeds $1 million, the excess will be subject to withholding at the highest income tax rate (35 percent for tax years beginning in 2012). This rule applies regardless of the method otherwise used to withhold supplemental wages paid to the employee. See IRS Pub. 15 and IRS Pub. 505.

> **Comment:** Absent further legislation, the flat withholding rate for supplemental wages paid after December 31, 2012, under the alternative method will be 28 percent for wages of $1 million or less, and 39.6 percent for supplemental wages exceeding $1 million.

An employer must collect both income tax and employee Social Security or railroad retirement tax on tips reported by an employee from wages due the employee or other funds that the employee makes available. Tips may be treated as if they were supplemental wages subject to the flat withholding rate (25 percent for tax years beginning in 2012) without allowance for exemptions, provided that income tax has been withheld on the employee's regular wages. Otherwise, the tips must be treated as part of the current or preceding wage payment of the same calendar year and are subject to the regular graduated withholding rates (Rev. Rul. 66-190).[26]

2607. Employee Expense Reimbursements Subject to Withholding. An employer's withholding obligations with respect to amounts paid to employees under an expense allowance or reimbursement arrangement depend upon whether the amounts are paid under an accountable or a nonaccountable plan (¶ 943 and ¶ 952A). Amounts paid under an accountable plan, to the extent of an employee's substantiated expenses,

References are to Standard Federal Tax Reports; Tax Research Consultant; and Practical Tax Explanations.

[21] ¶ 36,460; PAYROLL: 3,154; § 21,310
[22] ¶ 33,502; PAYROLL: 3,154; § 21,310
[23] ¶ 36,420; PAYROLL: 3,406, PAYROLL: 9,156; § 21,305.10, § 21,310
[24] ¶ 36,460, ¶ 36,463; PAYROLL: 3,406.05; § 21,305.20
[25] ¶ 33,561; PAYROLL: 6,066; § 22,120.50
[26] ¶ 33,506.3687; PAYROLL: 6,066, PAYROLL: 6,068; § 22,120.50

may be excluded from an employee's gross income, are not required to be reported on the employee's Form W-2, and are exempt from employment tax obligations (income tax withholding, FICA, FUTA, railroad retirement, and railroad unemployment taxes) (Reg. §§1.62-2 and 31.3401(a)-4).[27] Amounts paid under a nonaccountable plan are included in the employee's gross income, reported on Form W-2, and are subject to withholding as supplemental wages (¶2606). If expenses are reimbursed under an accountable plan, but either the expenses are not substantiated within a reasonable period of time or amounts in excess of substantiated expenses are not returned within a reasonable period of time, the excess or unsubstantiated amounts paid are treated as paid under a nonaccountable plan and are subject to withholding no later than the first payroll period following the end of the reasonable period of time.

Expense reimbursements that are subject to withholding may be added to the employee's regular wages for the appropriate payroll period, and withheld taxes may be computed on the total. Alternatively, the employer may withhold at the flat rate applicable to supplemental wages (¶2606) if the expense reimbursement or allowance is paid separately or is separately identified (Reg. §31.3401(a)-4(c); Act Sec. 101(c)(11) of P.L. 107-16).

2608. Per Diem Allowances Subject to Withholding. If the amount of an employee's business expenses are substantiated through the use of an IRS-approved per diem allowance, any amounts paid by the employer to the employee exceeding the amounts deemed substantiated are subject to income tax withholding and other employment taxes (Reg. §§1.62-2(h)(2)(i)(B) and 31.3401(a)-4(b)(1)(ii)).[28] (See ¶947 for standard mileage rate and FAVR allowances for automobile expenses; see ¶954 et seq. for per diem methods relating to meal and lodging expenses.)

For per diem or mileage allowances paid in advance, withholding on any excess must occur no later than the first payroll period following the payroll period in which the expenses for which the advance was paid (i.e., the days or miles of travel) are substantiated by the employee. For a per diem or mileage allowance paid as a reimbursement, the excess amounts reimbursed are subject to withholding when paid.

2609. Compensation Not Subject to Withholding. Some types of compensation are excluded from the definition of wages for income tax withholding purposes (¶2601). This includes amounts paid for or for the services of:

- newspaper carriers under age 18 delivering to customers,
- newspaper and magazine vendors buying at fixed prices and retaining excess from sales to customers,
- agricultural workers who are not subject to FICA withholding,
- household employees,
- cash or noncash tips of less than $20 per month,
- certain employer contributions to IRAs and deferred compensation plans,
- individuals not working in the course of the employer's business (less than $50 paid and less than 24 days worked during the current or preceding quarter),
- employees of foreign governments and international organizations,
- armed forces personnel serving in a combat zone,
- foreign earned income if excludable from gross income, and
- members of a religious order performing services for the order or associated institution (Code Sec. 3401(a)).[29]

Fringe benefits are generally included in wages, but certain qualified employee fringe benefits, such as no-additional-cost services, qualified employee discounts, working condition fringes, *de minimis* fringes, qualified transportation fringes, qualified moving expense reimbursements, and certain employer-provided cell phones, are not

References are to Standard Federal Tax Reports; Tax Research Consultant; and Practical Tax Explanations.

[27] ¶6004, ¶33,508A; PAYROLL: 3,168; §22,110.45, §22,210.45, §22,310.45

[28] ¶6004, ¶33,508A; PAYROLL: 3,168; §10,120.10

[29] ¶33,502; PAYROLL: 3,000; §22,110.05

subject to income tax withholding if it is reasonable to believe the recipient will be able to exclude them from gross income (¶ 863) (Code Sec. 3401(a)(19)).[30]

The employer's cost of group-term life insurance, including any amount in excess of $50,000 coverage that is taxable to the employee as compensation (¶ 721), is exempt from withholding (Code Sec. 3401(a)(14); Reg. § 31.3401(a)(14)-1).[31] However, the employer must report the cost of the insurance coverage includible in the employee's gross income on Form W-2 (Reg. § 1.6052-1).[32] An employer's reimbursement of an employee's moving expenses is also exempt if it is reasonable to believe a moving expense deduction will be allowable to the employee (¶ 1073) (Code Sec. 3401(a)(15)).[33] In addition, the value of any meals or lodging excludable by the employee from gross income (¶ 2188C) is exempt from withholding (Reg. § 31.3401(a)-1(b)(9)).[34] For information concerning amounts paid to employees as advances or reimbursements for traveling, meals, etc., see ¶ 2607 and ¶ 2608.

Benefits provided by an employer to an employee in the form of certain educational assistance (¶ 2192D), dependent care assistance (¶ 2192B), fellowship or scholarship grants (¶ 879), or National Health Service Corps loan repayments (¶ 879) are not subject to withholding if it is reasonable to believe that the employee is entitled to exclude the payment from income (Code Sec. 3401(a)).[35] Benefits provided by the employer in the form of medical care reimbursement made to or for the benefit of an employee under a self-insured medical reimbursement plan are excluded from wages for withholding purposes (Code Sec. 3401(a)(20)). Amounts paid to, or on behalf of, an employee or his beneficiary to an individual retirement plan pursuant to a simplified employee pension are not wages subject to withholding if it is reasonable to believe that the employee will be entitled to an exclusion for such payments (Code Sec. 3401(a)(12)) (see IRS Pub. 15-B).[36]

Death benefit payments to beneficiaries or to the estates of deceased employees and payments to such persons of compensation due but unpaid at the time of the decedent's death are not subject to withholding.[37]

Benefits paid under workers' compensation laws (other than nonoccupational disability benefits) are not taxable compensation for services performed and are not subject to withholding (Code Sec. 104).[38] Nor are amounts received by employees as reimbursements for medical care or as payments for permanent injury or for loss of bodily function (Code Sec. 3401(a)(20)).[39]

Any state and local tax benefits and limited payments provided to volunteer emergency response personnel and excludable from their gross income (¶ 896A) are not subject to withholding for tax years beginning after 2007 and before 2011 (Code Sec. 3401(a)(23)).[40]

Effective for stock acquired pursuant to an option exercised after October 22, 2004, withholding is not required on a disqualifying disposition of stock acquired through exercise of either an incentive stock option (¶ 1925) or through an employee stock purchase plan (ESPP) (¶ 1929) (Code Sec. 421(b)).[41] Neither is withholding required when compensation is recognized in connection with an ESPP discount under Code Sec. 423(c).

Voluntary Withholding. If remuneration is taxable to the employee but is exempt from withholding, the employee may voluntarily request that the employer increase the amount withheld from the employee's other compensation. In many cases, the employee and employer may enter into a mutual agreement for the employer to withhold from the remuneration that would be otherwise exempt from withholding (¶ 2629).

References are to Standard Federal Tax Reports; Tax Research Consultant; and Practical Tax Explanations.

[30] ¶ 33,502; PAYROLL: 3,200; § 22,110.10
[31] ¶ 33,502, ¶ 33,527; PAYROLL: 3,202; § 22,110.10
[32] ¶ 36,441; PAYROLL: 3,356.15; § 21,005.45
[33] ¶ 33,502; PAYROLL: 3,170; § 22,110.10
[34] ¶ 33,503; PAYROLL: 3,208; § 22,110.10
[35] ¶ 33,502; COMPEN: 33,350; § 22,110.10
[36] ¶ 33,502; PAYROLL: 3,300; § 22,110.20
[37] ¶ 33,506.1856; PAYROLL: 3,150; § 22,110.45
[38] ¶ 6660; PAYROLL: 3,206; § 3,705.05
[39] ¶ 33,502, ¶ 33,506.1871; PAYROLL: 3,206; § 22,110.10
[40] ¶ 33,502; INDIV: 33,312; § 22,110.45
[41] ¶ 19,602; COMPEN: 21,058; § 22,110.15

Computation of Withholding on Wages

2612. Calculation of Income Tax Withholding. To calculate an employee's income tax withholding (¶ 2601), an employer should follow a few basic steps:

(1) determine the payroll period, such as weekly, biweekly, or monthly (¶ 2621),

(2) calculate the employee's wages for the applicable payroll period (¶ 2604),

(3) determine the number of the employee's allowances from the filled-out Form W-4 (¶ 2634), and

(4) choose the withholding method (¶ 2614) (Code Sec. 3402(a)).

Other factors to consider in the calculation include whether the employee is a recent hire or only works part-time, whether the employee has more than one employer, and whether the employee receives any supplemental wage payments (¶ 2606).

2614. Methods of Withholding. The law provides two major methods of computing the tax to be withheld from wages: the percentage method (¶ 2616) and the wage bracket method (¶ 2619) (Code Sec. 3402).[42] For other permissible methods of withholding, see ¶ 2627. Regardless of which method is used, the amount of withholding depends upon the amount of wages paid (¶ 2604), the number of exemptions claimed by the employee on the withholding allowance certificate (¶ 2632 and ¶ 2634), the employee's marital status, and the payroll period of the employee (¶ 2621) (see IRS Pub. 15).

2616. Percentage Method. If the employer selects the percentage method of withholding, the employer must:

(1) multiply the amount of one withholding exemption for the payroll period by the number of allowances claimed on the employee's Form W-4 (¶ 2634),

(2) subtract the amount determined in (1) from the employee's wages, and

(3) apply the appropriate percentage rate table to the resulting figure to determine the amount of withholding (Code Sec. 3402(b)).[43]

Each withholding exemption is equal to one personal exemption for the year (¶ 133) prorated to the payroll period (¶ 2621). Thus, in 2012, if the payroll period is monthly and the personal exemption is $3,800, the amount of one withholding exemption is $3,800 divided by 12, or $316.67.

Percentage method withholding tables for both single (including heads of household) and married employees for each of the payroll periods are provided for use in determining the amount of tax to be withheld. See IRS Pub. 15. The IRS has approved and issued alternative formula tables for percentage method withholding that were devised for computing withheld tax under different payroll systems and equipment.

2619. Wage Bracket Method. The wage bracket tables provided by the IRS for graduated withholding cover weekly, biweekly, semimonthly, and monthly payroll periods (Code Sec. 3402(c)).[44] Separate tables for each period are provided for single persons (including heads of household) and married persons. The proper columns to be used by the employer are determined by the total number of allowances claimed on the employee's withholding allowance certificate (¶ 2634). These tables produce about the same result as the percentage method tables and are designed to accommodate different payroll systems and equipment. If the wage bracket method is used, wages in excess of the highest wage bracket in the tables may, at the election of the employer, be rounded off to the nearest dollar. See IRS Pub. 15.

2621. Payroll Period. For purposes of calculating income tax withholding (¶ 2612), the employee's "payroll period" (the period of service for which a payment of wages is ordinarily made to an employee) determines the exemption amount to be used if the employer uses the percentage method (¶ 2616) or the correct table to be used if

References are to Standard Federal Tax Reports; Tax Research Consultant; and Practical Tax Explanations.

[42] ¶ 33,542; PAYROLL: 6,050; § 22,120.05

[43] ¶ 33,542; PAYROLL: 6,054.05; § 22,120.10

[44] ¶ 33,542; PAYROLL: 6,054.10; § 22,120.15

the employer uses the wage bracket method (¶ 2619). Daily, weekly, biweekly, semimonthly, monthly, quarterly, semiannual, and annual payroll periods have separate tables for the percentage computation. Any other payroll period is a miscellaneous payroll period. Wages may also be paid for periods that are not payroll periods (¶ 2624).

2624. Calculation of Withholding Allowance. If an employee has an established payroll period (¶ 2621), the amount of the withholding allowance for the percentage method (¶ 2616) is determined by the payroll period, without regard to the time the employee is actually engaged in performing services during such period. If the payment is for a period that is not a payroll period, such as when wages are paid upon completion of a particular project, the withholding allowance under the percentage method or the amount withheld under the wage bracket method (¶ 2619) is computed based on a miscellaneous payroll period containing a number of days (including Sundays and holidays) equal to those in the period covered by the payment (Code Sec. 3402(b); Reg. § 31.3402(c)-1(c)).[45]

If the wages are paid without regard to any period, the tax to be withheld is the same as for a miscellaneous payroll period containing the number of days equal to the days (including Sundays and holidays) which have elapsed since (1) the date of the last payment of wages by the employer during the calendar year, (2) the date of commencement of employment with the employer during such year, or (3) January 1 of such year, whichever is later.

2627. Alternative Methods of Withholding. An employer may withhold on the basis of average wages by using estimated quarterly wages, annualized wages, cumulative wages, or any method which produces substantially the same amount of withholding as the percentage or wage bracket method (Code Sec. 3402(h)).[46]

2629. Voluntary Withholding. An employee may request on Form W-4 that the employer withhold additional amounts from the employee's wages. An employer must comply with such a request, but only to the extent the additional withholding amount does not reduce the employee's net pay (after other deductions required by law) below zero (Code Sec. 3402(i); Reg. §§ 31.3402(i)-1 and 31.3402(i)-2).[47]

In addition, an employee and employer may enter into an agreement for the employer to withhold from certain types of income that are not subject to mandatory withholding (¶ 2609). Thus, for example, magazine vendors, domestic workers, etc., may enter into an agreement with their employer to have income tax withheld. To effectuate this agreement, the employee must submit Form W-4 to the employer, and the employer must begin withholding (Code Sec. 3402(p); Reg. § 31.3402(p)-1).[48] Taxpayers may use Form W-4V to request voluntary withholding from certain federal payments, including Social Security benefits, crop disaster payments, Commodity Credit Corporation loans, and unemployment compensation.

2632. Claiming Withholding Exemptions and Allowances. Every employee is entitled to his or her own withholding exemption and one for each dependent (¶ 137). A married employee may claim a withholding exemption for his or her spouse if the latter does not claim one. An employee who can be claimed as a dependent on another person's tax return, such as a parent's return, may not claim a withholding exemption for his or her self. No withholding exemption is allowed for unborn children even though the birth is expected to occur within the tax year (Code Sec. 3402(f); Reg. § 31.3402(f)(1)-1).[49] Employees with more than one job may not claim an exemption that is currently in effect with another employer. An employee must file Form W-4 with his employer showing the number of exemptions to which he is entitled (¶ 2634).

In order to avoid excess withholding, a standard deduction allowance equal to one withholding exemption may be claimed by an employee, provided that the employee does not have a spouse who is receiving wages subject to withholding and does not have

References are to Standard Federal Tax Reports; Tax Research Consultant; and Practical Tax Explanations.

[45] ¶ 33,542, ¶ 33,547; PAYROLL: 6,056; § 22,115.05

[46] ¶ 33,542; PAYROLL: 6,054; § 22,120.45

[47] ¶ 33,542, ¶ 33,571, ¶ 33,572; PAYROLL: 6,104; § 22,125.05

[48] ¶ 33,542, ¶ 33,586; PAYROLL: 6,104; § 22,125.25

[49] ¶ 33,542, ¶ 33,553; PAYROLL: 6,060; § 22,115.10, § 22,115.15

withholding certificates in effect with more than one employer. These restrictions do not apply, however, if the wages earned by the spouse or by the employee from another employer are $1,500 or less, combined.

Additional withholding allowances are available to an employee who can show that he or she will have large itemized deductions, deductible alimony payments, moving expenses, employee business expenses, retirement contributions, net losses from Schedules C, D, E, and F of Form 1040, or tax credits (Code Sec. 3402(m); Reg. § 31.3402(m)-1).[50]

2634. Employee's Withholding Allowance Certificate. Before an employee is allowed any withholding exemptions (¶ 2632), he must file a withholding allowance certificate, Form W-4, with his employer showing the number of exemptions to which he is entitled (Code Sec. 3402(f)(2); Reg. § 31.3402(f)(2)-1).[51] Otherwise, withholding must be computed as if the employee were single and claiming no other exemptions. A widow or widower may claim "married" status for purposes of withholding if he qualifies as a surviving spouse (¶ 175) (Code Sec. 3402(l)(3)).

An employee who certifies to his employer that he had no income tax liability for his preceding tax year and anticipates none for the current tax year may be exempt from the withholding provisions (Code Sec. 3402(n); Reg. § 31.3402(n)-1).[52] Form W-4 should be used, and should be renewed annually, by any employee claiming this exemption.

Most Forms W-4 are retained by the employer. Employers need only submit withholding certificates to the IRS if directed to do so by the IRS. Further, the IRS may issue a notice to the employer that specifies the maximum number of withholding exemptions the employee may claim. Generally, the employer is bound by this determination until otherwise advised by the IRS (Reg. § 31.3402(f)(2)-1(g)).[53] A $500 civil penalty may be assessed against any individual who decreases his rate of withholding by claiming excess withholding allowances on Form W-4 (Code Sec. 6682).[54] In addition, a criminal penalty may be imposed against any individual who willfully supplies false withholding information or fails to supply withholding information (Code Sec. 7205).[55]

2637. Changes to Withholding Exemptions and Allowances. An employee may file an amended withholding exemption certificate (¶ 2634), increasing the number of exemptions, at any time that he becomes eligible for an additional dependency exemption or an extra allowance based on one of the deduction or credit items listed at ¶ 2632. An employee must file a new certificate within 10 days if the number of exemptions decreases after the occurrence of any of the following events (Code Sec. 3402(f)(2)(B); Reg. § 31.3402(f)(2)-1(b)):[56]

- the spouse for whom the employee has been claiming an exemption is divorced or legally separated from the employee or claims his or her own exemption on a separate certificate;
- the support of a claimed dependent is taken over by someone else, and the employee no longer expects to claim that person as a dependent;
- the employee discovers that a dependent (other than a qualifying child) for whom an exemption was claimed will receive sufficient income of his own for the calendar year to disqualify him as a dependent (¶ 137); or
- circumstances have changed so that the employee is no longer entitled to claim an exemption based on one of the deduction or credit items listed at ¶ 2632.

An employee who claimed "no liability" must file a new Form W-4 within 10 days from the time he anticipates that he will incur liability for the year or before December 1 if he anticipates liability for the next year (Reg. § 31.3402(f)(2)-1(c)).

References are to Standard Federal Tax Reports; Tax Research Consultant; and Practical Tax Explanations.

[50] ¶ 33,542, ¶ 33,579; PAYROLL: 6,064; § 22,115.15

[51] ¶ 33,542, ¶ 33,554; PAYROLL: 6,062; § 22,115.25

[52] ¶ 33,542, ¶ 33,580; PAYROLL: 6,062; § 22,115.20

[53] ¶ 33,554; PAYROLL: 6,062.10; § 22,115.25

[54] ¶ 39,845; PAYROLL: 6,062.15; § 22,115.25

[55] ¶ 41,325; PAYROLL: 6,358; § 22,115.25

[56] ¶ 33,542, ¶ 33,554; PAYROLL: 6,062; § 22,115.25

The death of a spouse or dependent does not affect the withholding exemption for that year unless the employee's tax year is not a calendar year and the death occurs in that part of the calendar year preceding the employee's tax year (Reg. § 31.3402(f)(2)-1(b)(1)(ii)).[57]

A withholding allowance certificate furnished to the employer that replaces an existing certificate can be effective for the first payment after the certificate is received if so elected by the employer. However, the replacing certificate must be effective for the first payroll period that ends on or after the 30th day after the day on which the new certificate is furnished (Code Sec. 3402(f)(3)(B)).[58]

Withholding on Non-Wage Payments

2642. Withholding on Certain Gambling Winnings. Income tax withholding is required at a flat rate of 25 percent (for 2012) for winnings of more than $5,000 from sweepstakes, wagering pools, and lotteries, and from other types of gambling (including pari-mutual pools with respect to horse races, dog races, and jai alai) if the winnings are also at least 300 times the wager. No withholding is required, however, on winnings from bingo, keno, or slot machines (Code Sec. 3402(q)).[59]

> **Comment:** Absent further legislation, the flat withholding rate on certain gambling winnings paid after December 31, 2012, will be 28 percent.

The payor must report gambling winnings to the taxpayer and the IRS on Form W-2G if the winnings are subject to withholding or if the winner receives $1,200 or more from a bingo game or slot machines, $1,500 from keno, $5,000 from a poker tournament, or, for other gambling winnings, $600 or more and at least 300 times the amount of the wager. If reporting is required, backup withholding must occur if the winner of the reportable amount does not furnish his or her TIN to the payor (¶ 2645). All withheld income reported on Form W-2G must also be reported on Form 945.

2643. Withholding on Pensions, Annuities, and Certain Deferred Income. In the case of taxable payments from an employer-sponsored pension, annuity, profit-sharing, stock bonus, or other deferred compensation plan, income tax withholding is required unless the recipient elects not to have tax withheld (Code Sec. 3405).[60] The same rule applies to an IRA or an annuity, endowment, or life insurance contract issued by a life insurance company. The recipient's election not to have withholding apply remains in effect until revoked. The payor must notify the recipient that an election may be made and of the right to revoke such election. The election is generally not available with respect to payments delivered outside the United States or its possessions to persons subject to U.S. tax on their world-wide income.

The amount withheld depends on whether the distributions are periodic payments or nonperiodic payments. For periodic payments (annuity and similar periodic payments), withholding is made as though the payment was a payment of wages for the appropriate payroll period. If the recipient does not have a withholding exemption certificate (Form W-4P) in effect, he is treated as a married individual claiming three exemptions. However, these exemptions are not available to a payee failing to file a certificate if the payee fails to furnish a taxpayer identification number (TIN) to a payor or if the IRS notifies the payor that the payee's TIN is incorrect.

The withholding rate on nonperiodic distributions is 10 percent. The withholding rate on distributions that were eligible for rollover but not directly transferred from the distributing plan to an eligible transferee plan is 20 percent. The withholding requirement is mandatory and distributees cannot elect to forego withholding on rollover eligible distributions.

References are to Standard Federal Tax Reports; Tax Research Consultant; and Practical Tax Explanations.

[57] ¶ 33,554; PAYROLL: 6,062; § 22,115.10

[58] ¶ 33,542; PAYROLL: 6,062; § 22,115.25

[59] ¶ 33,542; PAYROLL: 3,404.10; § 39,435

[60] ¶ 33,620; RETIRE: 42,700; § 22,140

2645. Backup Withholding. A backup withholding system requires a payor to deduct and withhold income tax at a flat rate of 25 percent (for 2012) from reportable payments, such as interest or dividends, if:

- the payee fails to furnish a correct TIN to the payor in the manner required;
- the IRS notifies the payor that the TIN furnished by the payee is incorrect;
- the IRS notifies the payor that the payee has underreported reportable payments; or
- the payee is required, but fails to certify that he is not subject to withholding (Code Sec. 3406).[61]

Backup withholding is reported on Form 945.

Comment: Absent further legislation, the flat withholding rate for backup withholding on payments made after December 31, 2012, will be 31 percent.

FICA & FUTA Taxes

2648. FICA Tax. Under the Federal Insurance Contributions Act (FICA), an employer is required to withhold Social Security and Medicare taxes from wages paid to each employee during the year, and to pay the employer's own share of these taxes (Code Secs. 3101, 3111, and 3121(a)).[62]

The employee and employer generally each are subject to a tax rate of 7.65 percent of wages paid for FICA purposes, consisting of a 6.2 percent rate for old-age, survivors, and disability insurance (OASDI) (i.e., Social Security) and a 1.45 percent rate for hospital insurance (HI) (i.e., Medicare). However, for wages paid in 2011 and 2012, the employee's Social Security tax rate is reduced to 4.2 percent, limiting the employee's portion of the FICA tax rate to 5.65 percent of wages paid (Act Sec. 601(a) of the Tax Relief, Unemployment Insurance Reauthorization, and Job Creation Act of 2010 (P.L. 111-312), amended by Act Sec. 101 of the Temporary Payroll Tax Cut Continuation Act of 2011 (P.L. 112-78) and Act Sec. 1001 of the Middle Class Tax Relief and Job Creation Act of 2012 (P.L. 112-96)). The Social Security tax rate applies only to wages paid within a Social Security wage base ($110,100 in 2012; $113,700 in 2013). There is no cap on wages subject to the Medicare tax.

Additional 0.9% Medicare Tax. For tax years beginning after 2012, the employee's portion of the Medicare component of FICA taxes is increased by an additional 0.9 percent (to 2.35 percent) for wages in excess of $200,000 ($250,000 in the case of a joint return, $125,000 in the case of a married taxpayer filing separately). In the case of a joint return, the additional tax is imposed on the couple's combined wages (Code Sec. 3101(b)(2)). Although the employer is generally required to withhold the employee's portion from the employee's wages, the employer is not obligated to withhold the additional tax unless the employee receives wages from the employer in excess of $200,000. For this purpose, the employer is permitted to disregard the amount of wages received by the taxpayer's spouse. Thus, because an employee may receive wages from more than one employer, or because the employee's spouse may receive wages, an employee may be subject to the additional tax without the tax being withheld from the employee's wages. The employee is responsible for any portion of the additional 0.9 percent tax that is not withheld. If an employer fails to withhold the additional tax and the employee pays that amount, the employer is not obligated to pay the additional tax but may be subject to penalties and additions to tax for failing to withhold (Code Sec. 3102(f)).

Multiple Employers. If an employee works for more than one employer, each employer must withhold and pay FICA taxes on the wages paid. In such instances, the employee's FICA tax withheld for the year might exceed the maximum employee tax for the year. If this happens, the employee must take the excess as a credit against his income tax or, if he is not required to file an income tax return, he may file a special

References are to Standard Federal Tax Reports; Tax Research Consultant; and Practical Tax Explanations.

[61] ¶ 33,640; FILEBUS: 18,150; §39,401

[62] ¶ 114; PAYROLL: 9,050; §22,201

refund claim (¶ 1321) (Reg. § § 1.31-2 and 31.6413(c)-1). The same rule applies to taxes withheld under the Railroad Retirement Tax Act.

If an individual is concurrently employed by two or more related corporations and all remuneration is disbursed to the individual through a common paymaster for the group, the common paymaster is responsible for the reporting and payment of FICA and FUTA taxes. However, the other related corporations remain jointly and severally liable for their appropriate share of the taxes (Reg. § 31.3121(s)-1).

Domestic Workers. In the case of persons performing domestic services in a private home of the employer and of persons performing agricultural labor, if the employer pays the employee's liability for FICA taxes or state unemployment taxes without deduction from the employee's wages, those payments are not wages for FICA purposes (Code Sec. 3121(a)(6)). Other special rules apply to domestic workers (¶ 2652).

Emergency Responders. Any state and local tax benefits and limited payments provided to volunteer emergency response personnel and excludable from their gross income (¶ 896A) are not subject to FICA taxes for tax years beginning after 2007 and before 2011 (Code Sec. 3121(a)(23)).

Employers' Payroll Tax Holiday (Expired). Employers were provided an exemption from having to pay their share of the 6.2-percent Social Security share of FICA taxes for qualified employees from March 19, 2010, through December 31, 2010 (Code Sec. 3111(d)). The waiver applied automatically if the employer paid the qualified employee for services performed in the employer's trade or business (or in furtherance of its activities if a tax-exempt organization). An employer that did not want to use the payroll tax holiday must have elected out of the waiver.

2649. FUTA Tax. The Federal Unemployment Tax Act (FUTA) imposes a tax on employers (1) who employed one or more persons in covered employment on at least one day in each of 20 weeks during the current or preceding calendar year, or (2) who paid wages (in covered employment) of at least $1,500 ($20,000 for agricultural labor, $1,000 for household employees) in a calendar quarter in the current or preceding calendar year. The tax is based on the first $7,000 of certain wages paid during the calendar year to each employee. The full rate of tax is 6 percent (6.2 percent before July 1, 2011), but the employer is allowed a partial credit against this tax based on its state unemployment insurance tax liability (Code Secs. 3301 and 3302).[63]

In the case of persons performing domestic services in a private home of the employer and persons performing agricultural labor, if the employer pays the employee's liability for FICA taxes or state unemployment taxes without deducting those taxes from the employee's wages, the amounts paid by the employer are not wages for FUTA purposes, but they are wages for income tax withholding purposes (¶ 2601) (Code Sec. 3306(b)(6)).

Any state and local tax benefits and limited payments provided to volunteer emergency response personnel and excludable from their gross income (¶ 896A) are not subject to FUTA taxes for tax years beginning after 2007 and before 2011 (Code Sec. 3306(b)(20)).

Return and Payment by Employer

2650. Employer Returns for Withheld Taxes. An employer subject to either income tax withholding (¶ 2601) or FICA taxes (¶ 2648), or both, must file a quarterly return on Form 941 to report income and FICA taxes withheld from wages, tips, supplemental unemployment compensation benefits, and third-party payments of sick pay (¶ 2604). Small employers with an estimated annual employment tax liability of $1,000 or less may report the taxes annually using Form 944 under the Form 944 Program (see below, *Form 944 Program*). Taxes on wages for agricultural employees, including domestic services on a farm operated for profit, are reported annually on Form 943. Nonpayroll items, such as pension and annuity payments (¶ 2643), are reported

References are to Standard Federal Tax Reports; Tax Research Consultant; and Practical Tax Explanations.

[63] ¶ 114; PAYROLL: 9,100; § 22,301

annually on Form 945. Employers who must pay FUTA tax (¶ 2649) on wages generally must file an annual return using Form 940, to report that amount.

Form 941 is due on or before the last day of the month following the quarter involved. Forms 940, 943, 944, and 945 are all due January 31 of the year following the calendar year for which the return is made. However, for all of these forms, including Form 941, an extension of time for filing is automatically granted to the 10th day of the second month following the close of the calendar quarter if the return is accompanied by receipts showing timely deposits in full payment of taxes due for the period (Reg. § 31.6071(a)-1).[64]

Forms W-2, 1099-R, and W-3 must be filed with the Social Security Administration (SSA) by the last day of February of the year following the year included in the return. The SSA transmits the income tax information on the return to the IRS.

Form 944 Program. The Form 944 Program allows certain small employers to file an annual Form 944 rather than a quarterly Form 941. Generally, Form 944 is due January 31 of the year following the year for which the return is filed (Reg. §§ 31.6011(a)-1(a)(5) and 31.6011(a)-4(a)(4)).[65]

Eligibility for the Form 944 Program is generally limited to employers with an annual estimated employment tax liability of $1,000 or less. An employer that believes it is qualified for the program can contact the IRS to express its desire to file Form 944 instead of Form 941 (Rev. Proc. 2009-51). Only upon a request will the IRS send a notification letter to a qualified employer confirming that it may file Form 944 for that tax year. Employers may opt out of filing Form 944 for any reason by calling or writing the IRS before the applicable due date, stating that they want to opt out of filing Form 944.

Most participating employers can pay their employment taxes annually with their Form 944, rather than making monthly or semi-weekly deposits (¶ 2651). A participating employer, however, may not discover that its actual annual employment tax liability exceeded the $1,000 threshold until it files its Form 944 on the following January 31. These employers can avoid the penalty for failing to make a timely monthly deposit of their January taxes, so long as they fully pay their January employment taxes by March 15 (Reg. § 31.6302-1).[66]

A modified lookback period applies for determining whether a participating employer that eventually discovers that it is not eligible for the Form 944 Program is a monthly or semi-weekly depositor. For those employers, the lookback period is the second calendar year preceding the current calendar year. For instance, the lookback period for 2013 is calendar year 2011.

An employer in the Form 944 Program whose actual total employment tax liability exceeds the $1,000 threshold but whose employment tax liability for a quarter is less than $2,500 is eligible for the *de minimis* rules applicable to quarterly Form 941 filers (¶ 2651). Such an employer is allowed to apply the *de minimis* rules if it deposits the employment taxes that accumulated during a quarter by the last day of the month following the close of the quarter. If an employer's tax liability for a quarter does not qualify for *de minimis* treatment, the employer must make deposits either monthly or semiweekly, whichever is appropriate, in order to avoid the failure-to-deposit penalty (¶ 2658).

2651. Employer Deposit of Withheld Taxes. An employer required to deposit employment taxes (withheld income taxes, FICA, and FUTA) is classified as either a monthly or semiweekly depositor. An employer's status for a given calendar year is determined annually based on the employer's employment tax reporting history during a lookback period. Except for small employers (including employers in the Form 944 Program (¶ 2650)), all employers are required to make deposits electronically (Reg.

References are to Standard Federal Tax Reports; Tax Research Consultant; and Practical Tax Explanations.

[64] ¶ 36,702; PAYROLL: 6,202; § 22,130.05, § 22,235.05, § 22,340.05

[65] ¶ 35,130B, ¶ 35,131; PAYROLL: 3,352.15; § 22,130.15, § 22,235.15

[66] ¶ 38,055B; PAYROLL: 3,352.15; § 22,130.15, § 22,235.15

§ 31.6302-1).[67] Employers that fail to deposit the full amount of taxes in a timely manner will be subject to penalties (¶ 2658).

Deposit Schedule. An employer generally must deposit employment taxes on a monthly basis during 2013 if, during the 12-month lookback period from July 1, 2011, through June 30, 2012, the amount of the aggregate employment taxes reported was $50,000 or less. Monthly depositors are required to deposit each month's taxes on or before the 15th day of the following month. If the 15th day is a Saturday, Sunday, or legal holiday in the District of Columbia, the employer has until the next succeeding business day which is not a Saturday, Sunday, or legal holiday to make the deposit.

An employer that reported more than $50,000 in aggregate employment taxes during the 2011-2012 lookback period will be a semiweekly depositor in 2013. Semiweekly depositors generally are required to deposit their taxes by the Wednesday after payday, if payday falls on a Wednesday, Thursday, or Friday. For all other paydays, the deposit is due by the Friday following payday. Semiweekly depositors always have at least three business days after the payday to make the deposit.

For agricultural employers filing Form 943, the lookback period used to determine monthly or semiweekly depositing status is the second calendar year preceding the current calendar year. For example, the lookback period for calendar year 2013 is calendar year 2011. For new employers, during the first calendar year of business, the tax liability for each quarter of the lookback period is considered to be zero. Therefore, the employer is a monthly depositor for the first calendar year of business.

Notwithstanding these general requirements, under the one-day rule, employers with $100,000 or more of accumulated liability during a monthly or semiweekly period are required to deposit the funds by the next day that is not a Saturday, Sunday, or legal holiday in the District of Columbia. Monthly depositors subject to the one-day rule must switch to making deposits semi-weekly.

As a safe harbor, employers that fail to deposit the full amount of taxes will not be penalized (¶ 2658) if the shortfall does not exceed the greater of $100 or two percent of the amount of employment taxes required to be deposited, provided that the shortfall is deposited on or before a prescribed makeup date. For a monthly depositer, the makeup date is the due date of the return for the period the shortfall occurred. For a semi-weekly depositer, the makeup date is the earlier of the due date of the return for the period of the shortfall, or the first Wednesday or Friday that falls on or after the 15th of the month following the month the shortfall occurred. Penalties may also be abated if an employer shows that a failure to deposit the full amount of the employment taxes was due to reasonable cause.

Amounts withheld under the backup withholding requirements (¶ 2645) are treated as employment taxes subject to these deposit rules. However, employers are permitted to treat the backup withholding amounts separately from other employment taxes for purposes of the deposit rules (Reg. § 31.6302-3).[68] Different monthly and semimonthly deposit requirements apply to taxes withheld from nonresident aliens and foreign corporations (Reg. § 1.6302-2).[69]

De Minimis Exceptions. Two *de minimis* rules allow small employers to make payments with Form 941 (or Form 943, as appropriate) rather than make deposits (Reg. § 31.6302-1(f)(4)).[70] First, deposits are not required if the employer's accumulated employment taxes for the *current* quarter are less than $2,500. Secondly, deposits are not required if the total accumulated employment taxes for the *preceding* quarter were less than $2,500 and the one-day rule does not require a deposit at the close of the next business day. An additional exception to the deposit requirement exists for employers in the Form 944 Program (¶ 2650).

References are to Standard Federal Tax Reports; Tax Research Consultant; and Practical Tax Explanations.

[67] ¶ 38,055B; PAYROLL: 6,106; § 22,135.05, § 22,240.05, § 22,345.05

[68] ¶ 38,055D; PAYROLL: 6,106; § 39,405.15

[69] ¶ 38,062; PAYROLL: 6,106, PAYROLL: 9,200; § 37,335

[70] ¶ 38,055B; PAYROLL: 6,106.05; § 22,240.05

How to Deposit. Employers are required to deposit all employment taxes electronically through the Electronic Federal Tax Payment System (EFTPS) (Reg. § 31.6302-1(h)(2)).[71] A deposit of taxes by electronic funds transfer is deemed made when the amount is withdrawn from the employer's account. Employers are subject to a 10-percent penalty if they are required to make deposits by electronic funds transfer but fail to do so (¶ 2658).

2652. Household Employees (Nanny Tax). Employers must withhold and pay FICA taxes on the wages of their household workers in 2012 if cash wages paid during the calendar year total $1,800 or more (Code Sec. 3121(a)(7)(B) and (x)).[72] The threshold amount for 2013 is also $1,800. An employer must pay FUTA taxes for household employees if it has paid aggregate cash wages of $1,000 or more to household employees in a calendar quarter (Code Sec. 3306(c)(2)).[73]

Employers must report and pay required employment taxes for household employees on Schedule H of their Form 1040 or Form 1040A. While withheld amounts do not have to be deposited on a monthly basis, employers do need an employer identification number (EIN) to include on Form W-2 (¶ 2655) and Schedule H. To obtain an EIN, employers should complete Form SS-4.

Employers must increase either their quarterly estimated tax payments or the income tax withholding on their own wages in order to satisfy employment tax obligations with respect to household employees. Failure to withhold results in liability for the penalty for underpayment of estimated tax (¶ 2682).

2653. COBRA Premium Assistance Reimbursement. Certain individuals who became eligible to elect COBRA continuation health care coverage under their employer's plan as a result of an involuntary termination of their employment during the period beginning September 1, 2008, and ending May 31, 2010, were required to pay only 35 percent of the premiums for the coverage. The 65 percent of the premium not paid by the employee is paid by the employer maintaining the group health plan. The employer is reimbursed for these payments through a credit against the employer's payroll tax liability (Code Sec. 6432).[74] The credit is taken on the employer's employment tax return (¶ 2650). The reimbursement is treated as having paid, on the date that the eligible individual's premium payment is received, payroll taxes in an amount equal to the unpaid portion of the premium. To the extent that the amount treated as paid exceeds the amount of the employer's liability for such taxes, the employer receives a refund or credit in the same manner as if it were an overpayment of taxes. The employer may provide the subsidy, and take the credit on its employment tax return, only after it has received the 35-percent premium payment from the individual. An employer claiming the credit must maintain supporting documentation for the credit claimed. The credit is treated as a deposit made on the first day of the return period. A terminated employee or family member may exclude from gross income the 65-percent premium reduction for COBRA continuation coverage (¶ 896B).

2654. Withholding for Disregarded Entities. A disregarded entity is treated as a separate entity responsible for employment tax liabilities (Reg. § 301.7701-2(c)).[75] The rule applies to such disregarded entities as a qualified subchapter S subsidiary (QSub) and a single-member limited liability company (LLC). The entity continues to be disregarded for other federal tax purposes.

2655. Employee Wage Statements (Form W-2). On or before January 31, every employer is required to furnish every employee with copies of Form W-2 for taxes withheld during the preceding calendar year. Employers may elect, with the consent of the employee, to furnish an electronic, rather than written, payee statement of Form W-2 (Code Sec. 6051(a); Reg. § 31.6051-1).[76] When employment terminates before the end of the calendar year, there is no reasonable expectation of reemployment, and the em-

References are to Standard Federal Tax Reports; Tax Research Consultant; and Practical Tax Explanations.

[71] ¶ 38,055B; PAYROLL: 6,106.45; § 22,240.05

[72] ¶ 114; PAYROLL: 3,358; § 22,235.30

[73] ¶ 114; PAYROLL: 3,106; § 22,340.20

[74] ¶ 38,935; COMPEN: 45,206.45; § 42,845.25

[75] ¶ 43,082; PAYROLL: 9,162

[76] ¶ 36,420, ¶ 36,421; PAYROLL: 6,204; § 22,415.05

ployee submits a written request for the information, Form W-2 must be furnished within 30 days of the written request if the 30-day period ends before January 31.

Form W-2 is a multiple-part wage statement with several copies: Copy A is sent to the Social Security Administration (SSA), Copy 1 is sent to the state where the employee resides, Copy B is kept by the employee and attached to his or her federal tax return, Copy C is retained for the employee's records, Copy 2 is attached to the employee's state, city, or local tax return, and Copy D is kept in the employer's records. Employers must file electronically with the SSA rather than file paper returns if 250 or more Forms W-2 are to be filed. Hardship waivers may be requested (Reg. § 301.6011-2(c)).[77]

If the Social Security tax imposed on tips reported by the employee exceeds the tax that has been collected by the employer, the employer is required to furnish the employee with a statement showing the amount of the excess (Code Sec. 6053(b)).[78]

2658. Employment Tax Penalty for Employers. An employer is primarily liable for deducting and paying employment taxes whether or not the taxes are actually collected from the employee, or if not enough taxes are collected (¶ 2601). Failure to deduct and withhold employment taxes can cause civil and criminal penalties to apply. For example, any responsible person—typically a corporate officer or employee—who willfully fails to withhold, account for, or pay over any tax to the government is subject to a penalty equal to 100 percent of such tax, a $10,000 criminal fine, and up to five years imprisonment (Code Secs. 6672 and 7202).[79] The civil penalty is a collection device, usually assessed only when the tax cannot be collected from the employer, and results in a personal liability not dischargeable by bankruptcy. Civil and criminal penalties can also be imposed if an employer willfully fails to furnish, or furnishes a false or fraudulent, Form W-2 statement (¶ 2655) to an employee (Code Secs. 6674 and 7204).[80]

Failure to Make Timely Deposits. A four-tier graduated penalty applies to failures to make timely deposits of tax, unless the failure is due to reasonable cause and not willful neglect (Code Sec. 6656).[81] The penalty amount varies with the length of time within which the taxpayer corrects the failure to make the required deposit. The penalty is assessed as follows:

- two percent of the amount of the underpayment if the failure is for no more than five days,
- five percent of the amount of the underpayment if the failure is for more than five days but for no more than 15 days, and
- 10 percent of the amount of the underpayment if the failure is for more than 15 days.

The penalty is imposed at the rate of 15 percent of the amount of the underpayment if a required tax deposit is not made on or before the day that is 10 days after the date of the first delinquency notice to the taxpayer, or, if earlier, on or before the day on which notice and demand for immediate payment of tax is given in cases of jeopardy. A failure to deposit includes a failure to make deposits electronically when required to do so, and is penalized at a 10-percent rate.

Deposits generally are applied to the most recent tax liability within the quarter. Any depositor to whom the IRS mails a penalty notice may, within 90 days of the date of the notice, designate how the payment is to be applied in order to minimize the amount of the penalty.

Self-Employment Tax

2664. Self-Employment Tax Rate. The combined rate of tax on self-employment income (¶ 2670) generally is 15.3 percent, consisting of a 12.4 percent component for Social Security (old-age, survivors, and disability insurance (OASDI)) and a 2.9 percent component for Medicare (hospital insurance (HI)) (Code Sec. 1401).[82] In 2011 and 2012,

References are to Standard Federal Tax Reports; Tax Research Consultant; and Practical Tax Explanations.

[77] ¶ 35,125; FILEBUS: 12,302; § 22,405.05

[78] ¶ 36,460; PAYROLL: 3,406.30; § 21,305.15

[79] ¶ 39,775, ¶ 41,310; PAYROLL: 6,300; § 40,315.05

[80] ¶ 39,795, ¶ 41,320; PAYROLL: 6,350; § 40,325.25

[81] ¶ 39,580; PAYROLL: 6,106; § 40,315.15

[82] ¶ 32,541; INDIV: 63,060; § 23,105

however, the combined rate of tax on self-employment income is 13.3 percent, resulting from a two-percent reduction in the Social Security component to 10.4 percent (Act Sec. 601(a) of the Tax Relief, Unemployment Insurance Reauthorization, and Job Creation Act of 2010 (P.L. 111-312), amended by Act Sec. 101 of the Temporary Payroll Tax Cut Continuation Act of 2011 (P.L. 112-78) and Act Sec. 1001 of the Middle Class Tax Relief and Job Creation Act of 2012 (P.L. 112-96)).

If net earnings from self-employment are less than $400, no self-employment tax is payable. The amount of self-employment income subject to the Social Security tax rate in a tax year is limited to the amount of the Social Security wage base for the year ($110,100 in 2012; $113,700 in 2013). If the taxpayer receives wages subject to FICA or railroad retirement tax are received during the year, the Social Security wage base is reduced by the amount of wages on which these taxes were paid (Code Sec. 1402(b)).[83] There is no cap on self-employment income subject to the Medicare tax.

For tax years beginning after 2012, the Medicare portion of the self-employment tax rate is increased by an additional 0.9 percent (to 3.8 percent) for self-employment income in excess of $200,000 ($250,000 in the case of a joint return, $125,000 in the case of a married taxpayer filing separately). In the case of a joint return, the additional tax is imposed on the combined income of the employee and the employee's spouse (Code Sec. 1401(b)(2)). Thus, a taxpayer's self-employment tax rate is 15.3 percent (12.4 percent + 2.9 percent) of the taxpayer's self-employment income up to the wage base in effect for the year, 2.9 percent of self-employment income above that amount not in excess of the threshold amount, and 3.8 percent (2.9 percent + 0.9 percent) of any self-employment income above that threshold amount.

The self-employment tax is computed on Schedule SE of Form 1040 and is treated as part of the taxpayer's income tax liability and must also be taken into account for purposes of the estimated tax (Code Sec. 6654(f)) (¶ 2682). A married couple filing a joint return must file separate Schedules SE where each spouse is self-employed.

2667. Persons Subject to Self-Employment Tax. An individual who is self-employed is subject to a self-employment tax on any self-employment income (¶ 2670). To determine whether an individual is an employee or a self-employed independent contractor, see ¶ 2602. However, certain individuals may be exempt from paying the tax.

Members of religious orders who have taken vows of poverty are not subject to self-employment tax when they perform duties connected with their religious order (Code Sec. 1402(c)).[84] Also, a duly ordained, commissioned, or licensed minister of a church, a member of a religious order (who has not taken a vow of poverty), or a Christian Science practitioner may elect not to be covered by Social Security by filing an exemption certificate on Form 4361 indicating that he is opposed by conscience or religious principle to the acceptance of any public insurance. The statement must include a declaration that he has informed the ordaining, commissioning, or licensing body of the church of his opposition to such insurance. A qualified individual must apply for the exemption on or before the due date of the income tax return for the second tax year for which he had earnings from self-employment of $400 or more from his religious activities (Code Sec. 1402(e)). An individual who has conscientious objections to insurance by reason of an adherence to established tenets or teachings of a religious sect of which he is a member may also be exempt from the self-employment tax (Code Sec. 1402(g)).

Services performed by employees for a church or church-controlled organization may be excluded from Social Security coverage if the church or organization makes a valid election under Code Sec. 3121(w) to be exempt from the employer portion of FICA taxes. However, such employees remain liable for FICA or self-employment tax on remuneration paid for such services unless the remuneration is less than $100 per year (Code Sec. 1402(a)(14) and (j)).[85]

References are to Standard Federal Tax Reports; Tax Research Consultant; and Practical Tax Explanations.

[83] ¶ 32,560; INDIV: 63,050; § 23,110.10

[84] ¶ 32,560; INDIV: 63,400; § 23,501

[85] ¶ 32,560; INDIV: 63,308; § 23,045.10

A U.S. citizen who works for an employer that is exempt from the Social Security tax because it is either a foreign government or instrumentality or an international organization is treated as self-employed (Code Sec. 1402(c)(2)).[86] Nonresident aliens are not subject to self-employment tax, but the tax may apply to a resident of Puerto Rico, the Virgin Islands, Guam or American Samoa who is not a citizen of the United States (Code Sec. 1402(b)).[87]

2670. Self-Employment Income. The self-employment tax (¶ 2664) is imposed on self-employment income, which is generally defined as net earnings from self-employment. "Net earnings from self-employment" consists of: (1) the gross income derived from any trade or business, less allowable deductions attributable to the trade or business, and (2) the taxpayer's distributive share of the ordinary income or loss of a partnership engaged in a trade or business (Code Sec. 1402(b); Reg. § 1.1402(a)-1).[88] The term "trade or business" does not include services performed as an employee other than services relating to certain newspaper and magazine sales, sharing of crops, foreign organizations, and sharing of fishing catches (Code Sec. 1402(c)(2)).[89]

There are special rules for computing net earnings from self-employment (including a special optional method of computing net earnings from nonfarm self-employment; ¶ 2673) (Code Sec. 1402(a)).[90] Rents from real estate and from personal property leased with the real estate, and the attributable deductions, are excluded unless received by the individual in the course of his business as a real estate dealer. Rental real estate income that is otherwise excludable from net earnings from self-employment does not become self-employment income merely because it is held in a qualified joint venture (¶ 402) (CCA 200816030).

Dividends and interest from any bond, debenture, note, certificate or other evidence of indebtedness issued with interest coupons or in registered form by any corporation are excluded from net earnings from self-employment income unless received by a dealer in stocks and securities in the course of his business. Other interest received in the course of any trade or business is not excluded. Gain or loss from the sale or exchange of property that is not stock in trade or held primarily for sale is excluded, as is gain or loss from the sale or exchange of a capital asset.

Termination payments received by former insurance salespersons are excludable from net earnings from self-employment if the amount is received after the termination of the individual's agreement to perform services for the company and the individual performs no services for the company after the termination and before the close of the tax year. In addition, the payment must be conditioned upon the salesperson agreeing not to compete with the company for at least one year following termination. The payment amount must also depend primarily on policies sold by or credited to the individual during the last year of the agreement and/or the extent to which the policies remain in force for some period after the termination and does not depend on the length of service or overall earnings from services performed for the company (Code Sec. 1402(k)).[91]

Even though the rental value of a parsonage (or a parsonage rental allowance) and the value of meals and lodging furnished for the convenience of the employer are not included in a minister's gross income for income tax purposes (¶ 875 and ¶ 2188C), they are taken into account in calculating net earnings from self-employment (Code Sec. 1402(a)(8)).[92] The same is true of amounts excluded from gross income as foreign earned income (¶ 2402). However, self-employment income does not include a minister's retirement benefits received from a church plan or the rental value of a parsonage allowance as long as each was furnished after the date of retirement.

References are to Standard Federal Tax Reports; Tax Research Consultant; and Practical Tax Explanations.

[86] ¶ 32,560; INDIV: 63,154; § 23,045.10

[87] ¶ 32,560; INDIV: 63,302; § 23,110.20

[88] ¶ 32,560, ¶ 32,561; INDIV: 63,100; § 23,205

[89] ¶ 32,560; INDIV: 63,154; § 23,045.10

[90] ¶ 32,560; INDIV: 63,050; § 23,210.05, § 23,215.05

[91] ¶ 32,560; INDIV: 63,100; § 23,210.25

[92] ¶ 32,560; INDIV: 63,402; § 23,505.05

One business deduction that cannot be taken in calculating net earnings from self-employment for the tax year is the deduction allowed for self-employment tax paid during the year (¶ 923). However, the law provides a substitute for that deduction. This is an amount determined by multiplying net earnings from self-employment (calculated without regard to the substitute deduction) by one-half of the self-employment tax rate (Code Sec. 1402(a)(12)).[93] Thus, the deduction equals 7.65 percent of the net earnings from self-employment. The rate of the adjustment remains at 7.65 percent in 2011 and 2012 even though the self-employment tax rate is reduced (¶ 2664) (Act Sec. 601 of the Tax Relief, Unemployment Insurance Reauthorization, and Job Creation Act of 2010 (P.L. 111-312), amended by Act Sec. 1001 of the Middle Class Tax Relief and Job Creation Act of 2012 (P.L. 112-96)). Similarly, for tax years beginning after 2012, taxpayers who reduce self-employment income by an amount equal to one-half of the combined self-employment tax rate do not include the additional 0.9 percent Medicare tax (¶ 2664) in the rate used to make such computation.

Example: Aileen Smith, a self-employed individual, has $40,000 of net earnings from self-employment in 2012 (determined without regard to the substitute deduction). Her self-employment tax for 2012 is computed as follows:

Self-employment net earnings	$40,000
Less: $40,000 × 7.65%	3,060
Reduced self-employment net earnings	$36,940
Tax rate on self-employment income for 2012	× 13.3%
Self-employment tax for 2012	$4,913

2673. Optional Method for Nonfarm Self-Employment. A taxpayer may be able to use an optional method to compute net earnings from self-employment if the net earnings from nonfarm self-employment are, for 2012, less than $4,520 ("lower limit") and less than two-thirds of gross nonfarm income. In addition, this optional method may only be used if the taxpayer had net earnings from self-employment of $400 or more in at least two of the three years immediately preceding the year in which the nonfarm optional method is elected (Code Sec. 1402(a)).[94]

If the taxpayer is eligible to use the optional method, he may report two-thirds of the gross income from his nonfarm business as net earnings from self-employment, provided the gross income from all nonfarm trades or businesses is, for 2012, $6,780 ("upper limit") or less. If, however, the gross income from all nonfarm trades or businesses is more than $4,520, the individual may report $4,520 as net earnings from nonfarm self-employment. The optional nonfarm method may not be used to report an amount less than actual net earnings from self-employment. The purpose of this optional method is to permit taxpayers to pay into the social security system and thus obtain or increase their benefits, even though they are not otherwise eligible because their net self-employment income is under $400. This optional method may not be used more than five times by any individual. Note that the $4,520 amount refers to net earnings after reduction by the 7.65 percent deduction amount (¶ 2670).

2676. Farmer's Self-Employment Income. A special method for determining self-employment net earnings is provided for farm operators whether they own the land they farm, rent on a fixed rental basis, or rent under a share-farming arrangement. Rentals received by the owner or tenant of the land under a share-farming arrangement—the farm is operated by a third party (share-farmer who may be a subtenant)—are treated as self-employment income if the owner or tenant participates materially with the share-farmer working the land in the production or management of the production of an agricultural or horticultural commodity. (There is no material participation if the owner or tenant does not participate in operations and has turned over management of the land to an agent, such as a professional farm management company.) The share-farmer is also considered a self-employed person (Code Sec. 1402).[95]

References are to Standard Federal Tax Reports; Tax Research Consultant; and Practical Tax Explanations.

[93] ¶ 32,560; INDIV: 63,060; § 23,210.30

[94] ¶ 32,560; INDIV: 63,056; § 23,215.10

[95] ¶ 32,560; INDIV: 63,450, INDIV: 63,254; § 23,215.15

Payments made by the U.S. Department of Agriculture under its Conservation Reserve Program (CRP) are considered earnings from a trade or business and are includible in the self-employment income of farmers, regardless of whether the farmer actively engages in farming or ceases all farming activities (Notice 2006-08). However, CRP payments are excluded from an individual's net earnings from self-employment, provided the individual is receiving regular benefits from Social Security or Social Security disability benefits.

A self-employed farmer has to pay the self-employment tax if his net earnings from self-employment are $400 or more (Code Sec. 1402(b)). However, an optional method for reporting income from farming, providing for greater credit toward benefits under Social Security old-age and survivors insurance, is available to a farmer. If his gross income for 2012 is not more than $6,780 ("upper limit"), he can report two-thirds of his gross income as net earnings from self-employment (Code Sec. 1402(a)).

If, for 2012, a farmer has more than $6,780 of gross income from farm operations, he may report either his actual net earnings or, if his net earnings are less than $4,520 ("lower limit"), $4,520 as net earnings (Code Sec. 1402(a)). As in the case of the nonfarm optional method, the $4,520 amount refers to net earnings after reduction by the 7.65 percent deduction (¶ 2670). There is no limit on the number of times a taxpayer may use this optional method.

> **Example:** Breanna Jones owns and operates her own farm. She receives all her income from the operation of the farm. Her gross income (receipts minus cost of goods sold) for 2012 is $6,900, but her net earnings for that year are only $4,000. She cannot simply report $4,600 (⅔ of $6,900) since her gross income is over $6,780, but she can report $4,520 as her net earnings from self-employment even though her actual net earnings are only $4,000. In electing to pay the self-employment tax on $4,520 rather than on $4,000, she will pay a greater tax. The positive effect, however, is that she will theoretically receive a greater credit toward Social Security benefits.

Payment of Estimated Taxes

2682. Estimated Taxes for Individuals. Individuals in some instances may need to pay a portion of their tax liability through estimated tax payments over the course of the tax year rather than when they file their return. Estimated taxes are generally used to pay tax on income that is not subject to withholding such as from self-employment tax, interest, dividends, and gains from the sale of assets. An individual may also have to pay estimated tax if the amount of tax being withheld from wages or other income is not enough. Thus, estimated taxes are used to pay income and self-employment tax for the tax year, as well as other taxes reported on the taxpayer's return, including for tax years beginning after 2012, the 3.8 percent tax on net investment income (¶ 129) and the 0.9 percent additional Medicare tax (¶ 2648 and ¶ 2664) (Code Sec. 6654(f) and (m)), less any estimated credits against tax.

While the law does not directly impose an obligation to pay estimated taxes, it does impose a penalty (or addition to tax) on individuals for failure to pay enough tax either through withholding or estimated taxes (¶ 2875) (Code Sec. 6654).[96] To avoid the penalty, an individual must generally make four required installment payments of estimated taxes based on his or her required annual payment. In general, each installment is 25 percent of the lesser of:

- 90 percent of the tax shown on the individual's tax return for the current year, or
- 100 percent of the tax shown on the prior's year return (110 percent in the case of an individual with adjusted gross income in excess of $150,000; $75,000 for a married individual filing separately), unless the prior year was not a 12-month period (Code Sec. 6654(d)(1)).[97]

References are to Standard Federal Tax Reports; Tax Research Consultant; and Practical Tax Explanations.

[96] ¶ 39,550; FILEIND: 15,350; § 1,401

[97] ¶ 39,550; FILEIND: 15,352; § 1,405.05

A lower required installment payment may be made if the individual annualizes his tax at the end of each payment period bases on a reasonable estimate of income, deductions, and credits (Code Sec. 6654(d)(2)). The annualized installment method may be used if the taxpayer does not receive income evenly throughout the year. Special rules also apply for farmers of fisherman (¶ 2691). Regardless of whether an individual uses the regular or annualized installment method, each required installment must be paid by its due date (¶ 2685), unless the taxpayer files his tax return before January 31 of the following year (¶ 2688).

An individual uses Form 1040-ES to figure his or her required installment of estimated taxes, and payment is made using the appropriate payment voucher attached to the form. In calculating estimated tax payments, any taxes withheld from an individual's wages or other income is deemed a payment of estimated taxes (Code Sec. 6654(g)). Thus, an equal part of withheld taxes is deemed paid on each due date for the tax year, unless the taxpayer establishes the dates when all taxes were actually withheld. For rules on payment of estimated tax by a corporation, or trusts and estates, see ¶ 241 and ¶ 511, respectively.

Exceptions to Penalty. The penalty for failure to pay estimated tax will not apply to an individual whose tax liability for the year is less than $1,000 after credits for withheld taxes and refundable personal credits. Also, a U.S. citizen or resident alien will not be subject to the penalty if he had no tax liability for the preceding tax year, provided such year was a 12-month period. Under certain circumstances or hardship, or following an individual's retirement or disability, the penalty may be waived (Code Sec. 6654(e)).[98]

Married Taxpayers. Individuals who are married may make a joint estimated tax payment, even if they are living separate and apart (Reg. §1.6654-2(e)(5)).[99] Joint estimated payment are not allowed if:

- there is a decree of separate maintenance or divorce;
- the married taxpayers have different tax years; or
- the taxpayer's spouse is a nonresident alien (including a bona fide resident of Puerto Rico or U.S. possession to which Code Sec. 931 applies for the entire tax year (¶ 2414)), unless an election has been made under Code Sec. 6013 to treat the spouse as a resident alien (¶ 2410) or the spouse becomes a resident alien during the tax year.

Joint estimated payments are based on the aggregate taxable income. In the event of married taxpayers filing separately, however, the amount of estimated self-employment tax is based on the separate income of each individual.

Household Employees. Employers of domestic workers who fail to satisfy their obligations for FICA and FUTA withholding, through regular estimated tax payments or increased tax withholding from their own wages, may be liable for estimated tax penalties (¶ 2652).

2685. Estimated Tax Payment Due Dates. For estimated tax purposes of individuals, the year is broken down into four payment periods (Code Sec. 6654(c)(2)).[100] In 2013, a calendar-year individual is required to pay his estimated tax in four installments as follows:

Installment	Due date
First	April 15, 2013
Second	June 17, 2013
Third	September 16, 2013
Fourth	January 15, 2014

For fiscal-year individuals, the due dates for the four estimated tax payments are:

(1) the 15th day of the fourth month of the fiscal year,

(2) the 15th day of the sixth month of the fiscal year,

(3) the 15th day of the ninth month of the fiscal year, and

(4) the 15th day of the first month after the end of the fiscal year.

References are to Standard Federal Tax Reports; Tax Research Consultant; and Practical Tax Explanations.

[98] ¶ 39,550; FILEIND: 15,354; §1,435.05

[99] ¶ 39,553; FILEIND: 15,352; §1,415

[100] ¶ 39,550; FILEIND: 15,352; §1,410

If the due date for making an estimated tax payment falls on a Saturday, Sunday, or legal holiday, the payment will be timely if made on the next day that is not a Saturday, Sunday, or legal holiday (Code Sec. 7503).[101]

If an individual is not liable for estimated tax on March 31, 2013, but his tax situation changes so that he becomes liable for estimated tax at some point after March 31, then he must make estimated tax payments as follows:

- if he becomes required to pay estimated tax after March 31 and before June 1, then he should pay 50 percent of his estimated tax on or before June 17, 2013, 25 percent on September 16, 2013, and 25 percent on January 15, 2014;
- if he becomes required to pay estimated tax after May 31 and before September 1, then he should pay 75 percent of his estimated tax on or before September 16, 2013, and 25 percent on January 15, 2014; or
- if he becomes required to pay estimated tax after August 31, then he should pay 100 percent of his estimated tax by January 15, 2014 (Form 1040-ES; IRS Pub. 505).

Nonresident Alien Individuals. Nonresident alien individuals (except those whose wages are subject to withholding) must pay estimated taxes for 2013 in three installments (June 17, 2013, September 16, 2013, and January 15, 2014). Fifty percent of the annual payment must be made on the first installment due date and 25 percent on each of the remaining two installment due dates (Code Sec. 6654(j)).[102]

2688. Return as Substitute for Last Installment of 2012 Estimated Tax. The fourth (last) tax installment for a tax year need not be made if the taxpayer files a Form 1040 tax return and pays the balance of the tax on or before January 31, 2013, or, for a fiscal year, on or before the last day of the month following the close of the fiscal year. Filing a final 2012 return by January 31, 2013, with payment of any tax due will not avoid an addition to tax for underpayment of any of the first three installments that were due for the year, but it will terminate the period of underpayment (and, therefore, the accrual of further additions) as of January 15, 2013 (Code Sec. 6654(h)).[103]

2691. Farmer or Fisherman. A farmer or fisherman who expects to receive at least two-thirds of his gross income for the tax year from farming or fishing, or who received at least two-thirds of his gross income for the previous tax year from farming or fishing, may pay estimated tax for the year in one installment. Thus, a qualifying farmer or fisherman may wait until January 15, 2013, to make his 2012 estimated tax payment. The entire amount of 2012 estimated tax must be paid at that time. However, the January 15 payment date may be ignored if the farmer or fisherman files his income tax return for 2012 and pays the entire tax due by March 1, 2013. The penalty for underpayment of estimated tax (¶ 2875) does not apply unless a farmer or fisherman underpays his tax by more than one-third (Code Sec. 6654(i)).[104] If a joint return is filed, a farmer or fisherman must consider his or her spouse's gross income in determining whether at least two-thirds of gross income is from farming or fishing.

References are to Standard Federal Tax Reports; Tax Research Consultant; and Practical Tax Explanations.

[101] ¶ 42,630; FILEIND: 21,054.05; § 1,410

[102] ¶ 39,550; FILEIND: 21,052.25; § 1,420

[103] ¶ 39,550; FILEIND: 15,352; § 1,410

[104] ¶ 39,550; FILEIND: 21,052.20; § 1,425.05

Chapter 27

EXAMINATION OF RETURNS

COLLECTION OF TAX

Organization of IRS

2701. IRS Organization and Functions. The Internal Revenue Service (IRS) is the Treasury Department unit that has responsibility for determining, assessing, and collecting internal revenue taxes and enforcing the internal revenue laws. The IRS consists of an Associate Office in Washington, D.C., and a field organization. The Associate Office is the Office of the Commissioner of Internal Revenue, who heads the IRS. Among the principal offices of the IRS are: the Office of the Deputy Commissioner (Operations); the Office of the Associate Commissioner (Policy and Management); the Office of the Associate Commissioner (Computer Services); the Office of the Assistant Commissioner (Taxpayer Service and Returns Processing); and the Office of the Chief Counsel. The Office of Inspector General of the Treasury Department has oversight responsibility for the internal investigations performed by the Office of Assistant Commissioner (Inspection) of the IRS.

The IRS is organized into four operating divisions serving groups of taxpayers with similar needs. These operating divisions are:

(1) Wage and Investment, serving individual taxpayers with wage and investment income,

(2) Small Business/Self-Employed, serving self-employed individuals and small businesses (C corporations, S corporations and partnerships) with assets of $10 million or less,

(3) Large Business and International (formerly, Large and Mid-Size Business), serving corporations, S corporations and partnerships with assets of greater than $10 million, and

(4) Tax-Exempt and Government Entities, serving employee plans, exempt organizations, and government entities.

IRS field offices also include a number of IRS service centers. These service centers currently receive and process tax and information returns, manage accounts, and conduct simple audits. The IRS also maintains a national computer center located near Martinsburg, West Virginia.

In addition, a nine-member IRS Oversight Board has been created to ensure that the IRS is organized and operated to carry out its mission to place a greater emphasis on serving the public and meeting taxpayers' needs (Code Sec. 7802).[1]

References are to Standard Federal Tax Reports; Tax Research Consultant; and Practical Tax Explanations.

[1] ¶ 43,254; IRS: 3,060; § 41,005

2703. Office of Chief Counsel. The legal work of the IRS is performed by the Office of the Chief Counsel (Code Sec. 7803(b)).[2] The Chief Counsel is a member of the Commissioner's executive staff and acts as counsel and legal adviser to the Commissioner in all matters pertaining to the administration and enforcement of the Internal Revenue laws. There are also Division Counsels, subject to the general supervision of the Chief Counsel, in each of the IRS operating divisions (¶ 2701).

2705. Appeals Procedure. If a tax return is examined by the IRS and the taxpayer does not agree with the results of the examination, further appeal within the IRS is permitted (Reg. § 601.106).[3] Once the IRS has issued a preliminary 30-day letter, the taxpayer has the right to appeal to a local Appeals Office by filing a written request for appellate consideration. This is the only level of appeal within the IRS (disregarding the functions of the National Taxpayer Advocate) (¶ 2707). Appeals conferences are conducted in an informal manner. A taxpayer who requests a conference may also need to file a formal written protest. However, if the protested amount is not more than $25,000, a small case request may be made instead of a formal written protest (IRS Pub. 556). Taxpayers who wish to forego the right to submit a protest to the Appeals Office after receiving a 30-day letter can file a petition in the Tax Court within 90 days after the receipt of a statutory notice of deficiency.

The IRS is required to develop certain appeals dispute resolution procedures (Code Sec. 7123).[4] Accordingly, the IRS has established procedures under which any taxpayer may request early referral of issues from the examination or collection division to the Office of Appeals (Rev. Proc. 99-28). Additionally, procedures have been developed under which either a taxpayer or the Office of Appeals may request nonbinding mediation of any unresolved issue at the conclusion of the appeals procedure or an unsuccessful attempt to enter into a closing agreement or an offer in compromise (Rev. Proc. 2009-44). Also, an appeals arbitration process under which the Office of Appeals and the taxpayer may jointly request binding arbitration has been established (Rev. Proc. 2006-44). Effective December 1, 2008, through December 31, 2012, a test period has been established for procedures for arbitration and mediation of offer-in-compromise and trust fund penalty cases being considered in Atlanta, Chicago, Cincinnati, Houston, Indianapolis, Louisville, Phoenix and San Francisco (Announcement 2011-6).

Small business and self-employed taxpayers can resolve their tax disputes through fast-track mediation (Rev. Proc. 2003-41). Disputes will be resolved through this expedited process within 40 days, compared to several months using the regular appeals process.

Large- and mid-size businesses can resolve their tax disputes through a fast-track settlement program (Rev. Proc. 2003-40). The goal for this program is to reach settlement within 120 days. A similar fast-track settlement pilot program exists for small businesses and self-employed taxpayers in Chicago, Houston, Philadelphia, St. Paul and San Diego, as well as Central New Jersey, and Laguna Nigel and Riverside, California. Additional locations may be identified and added by the IRS (Announcement 2011-5). A fast-track settlement program for tax-exempt and government entities has also been established (Announcement 2012-34). The goal for both this program and the small business and self-employed taxpayer program is to reach settlement within 60 days.

2707. Taxpayer Assistance Orders. The National Taxpayer Advocate assists taxpayers in resolving problems with the IRS and has the authority to issue a taxpayer assistance order where the taxpayer is suffering, or is about to suffer, significant hardship as a result of the IRS's actions (Code Secs. 7803(c) and 7811; Reg. § 301.7811-1).[5] "Significant hardship" means any serious privation caused to the taxpayer as the result of the IRS's administration of revenue laws. Mere economic or personal inconvenience to the taxpayer does not constitute significant hardship. The following

References are to Standard Federal Tax Reports; Tax Research Consultant; and Practical Tax Explanations.

[2] ¶ 43,258; IRS: 3,056; § 41,005
[3] ¶ 43,336; IRS: 24,050; § 39,605, § 39,615
[4] ¶ 41,132, ¶ 41,135.10, ¶ 41,135.40; IRS: 24,106; § 39,740.05
[5] ¶ 43,258, ¶ 43,304, ¶ 43,308; IRS: 3,058, IRS: 45,112; § 41,315

four specific factors, among other things, must be considered by the Advocate when determining whether there is a significant hardship:

(1) whether there is an immediate threat of adverse action,

(2) whether there has been a delay of more than 30 days in resolving the taxpayer's account problems,

(3) whether the taxpayer will have to pay significant costs (including fees for professional representation) if relief is not granted, or

(4) whether the taxpayer will suffer irreparable injury, or a long-term adverse impact, if relief is not granted.

An application for a taxpayer assistance order may be filed by the taxpayer or a duly authorized representative who may request remedial action, such as the release of the taxpayer's property from IRS levy or the immediate reissuance of a lost refund check. Form 911 is to be used for this purpose. Any relevant limitations period is suspended from the date on which the application is filed until the Advocate makes a decision on the application, unless the order provides for the continuation of the suspension beyond the date of the order. Such orders are binding on the IRS unless modified or rescinded by the Advocate, IRS Commissioner or Deputy Commissioner. The Advocate can take independent action and issue an assistance order without an application by the taxpayer. The statute of limitations, however, is not suspended when the Advocate issues an order independently.

Examination

2708. Examination of Return. The IRS examines a taxpayer's books and records either at the place of business where the books and records are maintained (a field examination) or at an IRS office (Reg. § 601.105).[6] The type of examination affects the internal appeals procedure (¶ 2705).

The Taxpayer Bill of Rights requires the IRS to provide a written statement detailing the taxpayer's rights and the IRS's obligations during the audit, appeals, refund and collection process. The IRS must also explain the audit and collection (Code Sec. 7521(b)).[7]

The taxpayer has the right to make an audio recording of any in-person interview conducted by the IRS upon 10 days' advance notice (Code Sec. 7521(a); Notice 89-51).[8] Moreover, a taxpayer is guaranteed the right to be represented by any individual currently permitted to practice before the IRS, unless the IRS notifies the taxpayer that the representative is responsible for unreasonable delay or hindrance (Code Sec. 7521(c)).[9] Any interview must be suspended when the taxpayer clearly requests the right to consult with a representative. Further, unless it issues an administrative summons, the IRS cannot require the taxpayer to accompany the representative to the interview.

The IRS may provide administrative relief to taxpayers in hostage situations or in a combat zone, or who are continuously hospitalized as a result of injuries received in a combat zone, or who are affected by a federally declared disaster area, by suspending tax examination and collection actions during their detention (Code Secs. 7508 and 7508A).[10] Examination and collection actions that can be precluded or suspended include tax return audits, mailings of notices and other actions involving the collection of overdue taxes.

2708A. Power of Attorney. A taxpayer generally may choose a person to represent him before the IRS by filing a power of attorney (Reg. § 601.501(a)).[11] A power of attorney is a written authorization for an individual to act on behalf of another individual

References are to Standard Federal Tax Reports; Tax Research Consultant; and Practical Tax Explanations.

[6] ¶ 43,332; IRS: 15,100; § 39,715

[7] ¶ 42,790; IRS: 45,112; § 39,705

[8] ¶ 42,790, ¶ 42,791.30; IRS: 15,110; § 39,715.15

[9] ¶ 42,790; IRS: 18,202; § 39,715.10

[10] ¶ 42,686, ¶ 42,687A; FILEBUS: 15,100; § 39,215.30, § 39,215.35

[11] ¶ 43,408; IRS: 3,208.05; § 41,205.05

or an entity in tax matters. Form 2848, Power of Attorney and Declaration of Representative, can be used to grant a power of attorney, or another equivalent document can be used. If the authorization is not limited, the individual can generally perform all acts that the taxpayer granting the power can perform. The holder of a power of attorney cannot, however, represent the taxpayer before the IRS unless the holder is one of the persons authorized to practice before the IRS (CCA 200321017).

A taxpayer may change his representative by filing a new power of attorney (Reg. § 601.505(a)).[12] The new power revokes any prior power that the taxpayer granted to someone else concerning the same matter unless the new power contains a clause stating that it does not revoke the prior power. A taxpayer may also revoke a power of attorney without authorizing a new representative.

A taxpayer who only wants to have someone answer any questions that may arise regarding his income tax return does not have to file a power of attorney. Instead, the taxpayer can designate anyone to do this, not just a person qualified to practice before the IRS, by checking the appropriate box on his tax return (IRS News Release IR-2000-23).

2709. Third-Party Summonses. The IRS may issue summonses to third-party recordkeepers (attorneys, enrolled agents, banks, brokers, accountants, etc.) and other third parties for the production of records concerning the business transactions or affairs of a taxpayer (Code Sec. 7609).[13] The taxpayer is to be notified of the summons within three days of service of the summons (but in no case later than the 23rd day before the day fixed in the summons for production of records). However, notice is not required with respect to any summons:

(1) served on the person with respect to whose liability the summons is issued, or any officer or employee of the person,

(2) issued to determine whether or not records of the business transactions or affairs of an identified person have been made or kept,

(3) issued solely to determine the identity of any person having a numbered account or similar arrangement with a bank or similar institution,

(4) issued to aid the collection of (a) an assessment or judgment against the person with respect to whose liability the summons is issued, or (b) the liability of that person's transferee or fiduciary, or

(5) issued in certain criminal investigations.

Any taxpayer who is entitled to notice may intervene in any proceeding for the enforcement of the summons in question. The taxpayer also has the right to begin a proceeding to quash the summons if, within 20 days after the day the notice of summons was served on or mailed to him, he files a petition to quash the summons in a district court having jurisdiction and notifies the IRS and the third party by mailing a copy of the petition by certified or registered mail to each one. Although notice is not required for a "John Doe" summons (i.e., issued to determine the identity of a person having a numbered bank account or similar arrangement), such a summons may be issued only after the IRS has shown adequate grounds for serving the summons, and an ex parte court proceeding is held to determine its validity.

If a taxpayer intervenes in a dispute between the IRS and a third party and the dispute is not resolved within six months, the statute of limitations period will be suspended beginning on the date that is six months after the summons is served and continuing until the dispute is resolved. This provision also applies with respect to "John Doe" summonses (Code Sec. 7609(e)).[14]

The IRS is required to provide reasonable notice in advance to a taxpayer before contacting third parties with respect to examination or collection activities regarding the

References are to Standard Federal Tax Reports; Tax Research Consultant; and Practical Tax Explanations.

[12] ¶ 43,424; IRS: 3,208.15; § 41,210

[13] ¶ 42,890; IRS: 21,100, IRS: 21,150; § 39,810

[14] ¶ 42,890; IRS: 21,114; § 39,810

taxpayer (Code Sec. 7602(c); Reg. § 301.7602-2).[15] However, notice is not required: (1) with respect to any contact authorized by the taxpayer, (2) if the IRS determines that the notice would jeopardize collection of any tax, or (3) with respect to any pending criminal investigation.

Assessment and Collection of Tax

2711. Assessment of Deficiency. A "deficiency" is the excess of the correct tax liability over the tax shown on the return (if any), plus amounts previously assessed (or collected without assessment) as a deficiency, and minus any rebates made to the taxpayer (Code Sec. 6211).[16] For this purpose, the tax shown on the return is the amount of tax before credits for estimated tax paid, withheld tax, or amounts collected under a termination assessment (Code Sec. 6211(b)).

The IRS is authorized to assess taxes (Code Sec. 6201; Reg. § 301.6201-1).[17] The collection process begins when a notice of deficiency is sent to the taxpayer's last known address by registered or certified mail (Code Sec. 6212).[18] In each deficiency notice, the IRS must provide a description of the basis for the assessment, an identification of the amount of tax, interest and penalties assessed (Code Sec. 7522),[19] and the date determined to be the last day on which the taxpayer may file a petition with the Tax Court (Code Sec. 6213(a)).[20] However, the failure by the IRS to specify the last day on which to file a petition will not invalidate an otherwise valid deficiency notice if the taxpayer was not prejudiced by the omission.[21]

Within 90 days after notice of the deficiency is mailed (or within 150 days after mailing if the notice is addressed to a person outside the U.S.), the taxpayer may file a petition with the Tax Court for a redetermination of the deficiency (Code Sec. 6213).[22] Payment of the assessed amount after the deficiency notice is mailed does not deprive the Tax Court of jurisdiction over the deficiency (Reg. § 301.6213-1(b)(3)).[23]

If the taxpayer does not file a Tax Court petition within the required time period, the tax may be collected (¶ 2735). A taxpayer's property may be seized to enforce collection if there is a failure to pay an assessed tax within 30 days after notice of levy (Code Sec. 6331).[24] However, the notice and waiting period does not apply if the IRS finds that the collection of tax is in jeopardy (¶ 2713). Notices of levy must provide a description of the levy process in simple and nontechnical terms.

Last Known Address. As noted above, the collection process begins when a notice of deficiency is sent to the taxpayer's last known address by registered or certified mail. A taxpayer's last known address is the address that appears on the taxpayer's most recently filed federal tax return. However, if the taxpayer gives the IRS clear and concise notification of a different address, that address is the taxpayer's last known address (Reg. § 301.6212-2).[25] The IRS uses the National Change of Address database maintained by the U.S. Postal Service to update a taxpayer's last known address. A taxpayer can change his or her last known address with the IRS through any of several means (Rev. Proc. 2010-16).[26] First, the taxpayer can filing a return with new address information. Second, the taxpayer can provide clear and concise written notification to an appropriate IRS address using Form 8822, Form 8822-B for employers, or other written notice satisfying the requirements including returning IRS correspondence with corrections marked (IRS Pub. 15). Next, the taxpayer can provide clear and concise written or oral notification of a change of address to an IRS employee who contacts the client regarding the filing of a return or an adjustment in his account. Finally, the taxpayer can provide

References are to Standard Federal Tax Reports; Tax Research Consultant; and Practical Tax Explanations.

[15] ¶ 42,820, ¶ 42,824; IRS: 21,106; § 39,810

[16] ¶ 37,535; IRS: 27,052; § 39,510.10

[17] ¶ 37,502, ¶ 37,503; IRS: 27,200; § 39,501

[18] ¶ 37,540; IRS: 27,150; § 39,510.15

[19] ¶ 42,800; IRS: 27,154; § 39,510.05

[20] ¶ 37,545; IRS: 27,154; § 39,510.05

[21] ¶ 37,544.25; IRS: 27,154.05; § 39,510.05

[22] ¶ 37,545; IRS: 27,158; § 39,510.05

[23] ¶ 37,546; LITIG: 6,100; § 39,510.05

[24] ¶ 38,185; IRS: 51,054; § 39,945.15

[25] ¶ 37,542; IRS: 27,160; § 39,510.15

[26] ¶ 37,544.28, ¶ 37,549.5023; IRS: 27,160.05; § 39,510.15

the IRS with clear and concise electronic notification through one of the secure applications found on the IRS website.

Mathematical or Clerical Errors. A notice of tax due because of mathematical or clerical errors is not a deficiency notice, and the taxpayer has no right to file a petition with the Tax Court for redetermining the deficiency. A taxpayer who receives notice of additional tax due to mathematical or clerical error has 60 days after the notice is sent in which to file a request for abatement of any part of the assessment. Any reassessment must be made under the regular notice-of-deficiency procedures. During the 60-day period, the IRS cannot proceed to collect upon the summary assessment (Code Sec. 6213(b)(1) and (f)).[27]

Criminal Restitution. Criminal restitution ordered by a court, pursuant to 18 USC § 3556, for a failure to pay tax is assessed and collected as if it were such a tax (Code Sec. 6201(a)(4)(A)).[28] The restitution assessment is excepted from the general restrictions on assessments and filing of Tax Court petitions for deficiency redetermination. The restitution amount may be assessed, or a court proceeding for its collection may be begun without assessment, at any time.

2712. Waiver of Deficiency Restrictions. The taxpayer has the right to waive the restrictions on assessment and collection of all or part of a deficiency at any time, whether or not a notice of deficiency has been issued (Code Sec. 6213(d)).[29] This is done by executing Form 870. Execution of a waiver of the restrictions on assessment and collection of the entire deficiency in advance of the statutory ("90-day") notice relieves the IRS of sending such a notice and precludes appeal to the Tax Court. However, an appeal to the Tax Court is not precluded if the waiver covers only part of the deficiency or is executed after receipt of the 90-day deficiency notice. Payment of an amount as tax before issuance of the statutory notice has the effect of a waiver, and, if the amount paid equals or exceeds the amount of a subsequently determined deficiency, it deprives the Tax Court of jurisdiction (Reg. § 301.6213-1(b)(3)).[30]

2713. Jeopardy and Termination Assessments. The IRS can immediately determine and assess income tax in a termination assessment, if it finds that tax collection is in jeopardy because a taxpayer is leaving the country, or seeking to hide assets, or doing any other act that tends to render collection ineffective (Code Sec. 6851).[31] Similarly, the IRS can immediately assess a deficiency if tax assessment or collection would be jeopardized by delay (Code Sec. 6861).[32] If a jeopardy assessment is made prior to the mailing of the notice of deficiency, the notice must be mailed to the taxpayer within 60 days after the assessment (Code Sec. 6861(b)).[33] If a termination assessment is made, the assessment ends the taxpayer's tax year only for purposes of computing the amount of tax that becomes immediately due and payable. It does not end the tax year for any other purpose. In the case of a termination assessment, the IRS must issue the taxpayer a notice of deficiency within 60 days of the later of (1) the due date (including extensions) of the taxpayer's return for the full tax year or (2) the day on which the taxpayer files the return (Code Sec. 6851(b)).[34]

The IRS may presume that the collection of tax is in jeopardy if an individual in physical possession of more than $10,000 in cash or its equivalent does not claim either ownership of the cash or that it belongs to another person whose identity the IRS can readily ascertain and who acknowledges ownership of the cash. In this case, the IRS may treat the entire amount as gross income taxable at the highest rate specified in Code Sec. 1. The possessor of the cash is entitled to notice of, and the right to challenge, the assessment. However, should the true owner appear, he will be substituted for the possessor and all rights will vest in him (Code Sec. 6867).[35]

References are to Standard Federal Tax Reports; Tax Research Consultant; and Practical Tax Explanations.

[27] ¶ 37,545; IRS: 27,206.15; § 39,515.10

[28] ¶ 37,502; IRS: 27,206.70; § 39,515.10

[29] ¶ 37,545, ¶ 37,549.9612; IRS: 27,208; § 39,540.15

[30] ¶ 37,546; LITIG: 6,110; § 39,540.15

[31] ¶ 40,402; IRS: 54,100; § 39,520, § 39,530

[32] ¶ 40,460; IRS: 54,050; § 39,520, § 39,525

[33] ¶ 40,460; IRS: 54,050; § 39,525.15

[34] ¶ 40,402; IRS: 54,102; § 39,530.20

[35] ¶ 40,580; IRS: 54,152; § 39,525.10

2719. Injunction to Restrain Collection. The Code prohibits a suit to restrain the assessment or collection of any tax or to restrain the enforcement of liability against a transferee or fiduciary (Code Sec. 7421).[36] Nevertheless, injunctive relief may be available in rare cases if irreparable harm will be done to the taxpayer and the taxpayer shows, at the outset of the suit, that the government could not collect the tax under any circumstances.[37] However, injunctive relief may be obtained for assessment or collection actions (other than jeopardy or termination assessments) if a notice of deficiency has not been mailed to the taxpayer, the period for filing a Tax Court petition has not expired, or a Tax Court proceeding with respect to the tax is pending (Code Sec. 6213(a)).[38]

2721. Closing Agreement. The IRS is authorized to enter into a written agreement with a taxpayer in order to determine conclusively the tax liability for a tax period that ended prior to the date of the agreement (Form 866) or to determine one or more separate items affecting the tax liability for any tax period (Form 906). A closing agreement may also be entered for tax periods that end subsequent to the date of the agreement. Closing agreements may be entered into in order to finally resolve questions of tax liability (Code Sec. 7121; Reg. §§301.7121-1 and 601.202).[39] For example, a fiduciary may desire a final determination before an estate is closed or trust assets distributed. Closing agreements are final, conclusive, and binding upon both parties. They cannot be reopened or modified except upon a showing of fraud or malfeasance or the misrepresentation of a material fact.[40] Generally, the IRS is not precluded from later determining additions to tax absent terms in the agreement that specifically address the issue of additions to tax.

2723. Compromise of Tax and Penalty. The IRS may compromise the tax liability in most civil or criminal cases before referral to the Department of Justice for prosecution or defense. The Attorney General or a delegate may compromise any case after the referral. Interest and penalties, as well as tax, may be compromised (Code Sec. 7122; Reg. §301.7122-1).[41] Offers-in-compromise are submitted on Form 656 accompanied by a financial statement on Form 433-A for an individual or Form 433-B for businesses (if based on inability to pay) (Reg. §601.203(b)).[42] A taxpayer who faces severe or unusual economic hardship may also apply for an offer-in-compromise by submitting Form 656. If the IRS accepts an offer-in-compromise, the payment is allocated among tax, penalties, and interest as stated in the collateral agreement with the IRS. If no allocation is specified in the agreement and the amounts paid exceed the total tax and penalties owed, the payments will be applied to tax, penalties, and interest, in that order, beginning with the earliest year. If the IRS agrees to an amount that does not exceed the combined tax and penalties, and there is no agreement regarding allocation of the payment, no amount will be allocated to interest (Rev. Proc. 2002-26).[43]

A $150 user fee is required for many offers-in-compromise (Reg. §300.3).[44] Taxpayers must normally pay the user fee at the time a request to compromise is submitted. No user fee is imposed with respect to offers:

(1) that are based solely on doubt as to liability, or

(2) that are made by low-income taxpayers (i.e., taxpayers whose total monthly income falls at or below income levels based on the U.S. Department of Health and Human Services poverty guidelines).

If an offer is accepted to promote effective tax administration or is accepted based on doubt as to collectibility and a determination that collecting more than the amount offered would create economic hardship, the fee will be applied to the amount of the offer or, upon the taxpayer's request, refunded to the taxpayer. The fee will not be refunded if an offer is withdrawn, rejected or returned as nonprocessible. The IRS treats

References are to Standard Federal Tax Reports; Tax Research Consultant; and Practical Tax Explanations.

[36] ¶41,680; IRS: 45,152; §39,940

[37] ¶41,683.69, ¶41,683.70; IRS: 45,152; §39,940

[38] ¶37,545; IRS: 45,152; §39,940

[39] ¶41,080, ¶41,081, ¶43,364; IRS: 39,050; §40,405.15

[40] ¶41,090.279; IRS: 39,150; §40,405.15

[41] ¶41,110, ¶41,111; IRS: 42,050; §39,920.05

[42] ¶43,372; IRS: 42,100; §39,920.25

[43] ¶9104.63; IRS: 42,150; §39,920.25

[44] ¶41,120; IRS: 42,106; §39,920.25

offers received by taxpayers in bankruptcy as nonprocessible; however, some courts have held that the IRS must consider such offers.[45] The IRS has issued detailed procedures for the submission and processing of offers-in-compromise (Rev. Proc. 2003-71).

Partial Payment Requirement. Taxpayers are required to make nonrefundable partial payments with the submission of any offer-in-compromise (Code Sec. 7122(c)). Taxpayers who submit a lump-sum offer (any offer that will be paid in five or fewer installments) must include a payment of 20 percent of the amount offered. Taxpayers who submit a periodic payment offer must include payment of the first proposed installment with the offer and continue making payments under the terms proposed while the offer is being evaluated. Offers that are submitted to the IRS without the required partial payments will be returned to the taxpayer as nonprocessible. However, the IRS is authorized to issue regulations waiving the payment requirement for offers based solely on doubt as to liability or filed by low-income taxpayers. Pending the issuance of regulations, the IRS has announced that it will waive the partial payment requirement for such offers (Notice 2006-68).

The required partial payments are applied to the taxpayer's unpaid liability and are not refundable. However, taxpayers may specify the liability to which they want their payments applied. Additionally, the user fee (see above) is applied to the taxpayer's outstanding tax liability. Any offer that is not rejected within 24 months of the date it is submitted is deemed to be accepted. However, any period during which the tax liability to be compromised is in dispute in any judicial proceeding is not taken into account in determining the expiration of the 24-month period (Code Sec. 7122(f)).

2724. Partial Payments. Specific written directions from a taxpayer regarding the application of partial payments of assessed federal income taxes, penalties and interest made by the taxpayer will be respected (Rev. Proc. 2002-26).[46] A partial payment on deficiencies received without instructions for its application will be applied to tax, penalties, and interest, in the order of priority that best serves the government's interest.

2726. Statute of Limitations for Assessment and Collection. Generally, all income taxes must be assessed within three years after the original return is filed (the last day prescribed by law for filing if the return was filed before the last day) (Code Sec. 6501; Reg. § 301.6501(a)-1).[47] In the case of pass-through entities, the three-year rule begins to run at the time the pass-through entity's shareholder or other beneficial owner files an individual income tax return. A return filed prior to its due date is deemed to have been filed on the due date. A return executed by an IRS official or employee in which the taxpayer has not filed a return will not start the running of the statute of limitations. A proceeding in court without assessment for collection of the tax must commence within the same period. The period can be extended by a written agreement between the taxpayer and the IRS (Code Sec. 6501(c)(4); Reg. § 301.6501(c)-1(d)).[48] Interest on any tax may be assessed and collected at any time during the period within which the tax itself may be collected (but only up to the date on which payment of the tax is received) (Code Sec. 6601(g); Reg. § 301.6601-1(f)).[49]

If, within the 60-day period ending on the last day of the assessment period, the IRS receives an amended return or written document from the taxpayer showing that additional tax is due for the year in question, the period in which to assess such additional tax is extended for 60 days after the day on which the IRS receives the amended return or written document (Code Sec. 6501(c)(7)).[50]

If unused foreign tax credits have been carried back, the statute of limitations on assessment and collection for the year to which the carryback is made will not close until one year after the expiration of the period within which a deficiency may be assessed for the year from which the carryback was made (Code Sec. 6501(i); Reg.

References are to Standard Federal Tax Reports; Tax Research Consultant; and Practical Tax Explanations.

[45] ¶ 41,130.18; IRS: 42,106

[46] ¶ 39,415.329, ¶ 39,780.14; PENALTY: 9,058.10; § 39,320.35

[47] ¶ 38,960, ¶ 38,961; IRS: 30,050; § 39,505.05

[48] ¶ 38,960, ¶ 38,966; IRS: 30,250; § 39,905

[49] ¶ 39,410, ¶ 39,412; PENALTY: 9,052; § 40,105

[50] ¶ 38,960; IRS: 30,056; § 39,505.05

§ 301.6501(i)-1).[51] Deficiencies attributable to carryback of a net operating loss, a capital loss or the general business credit and research credit may be assessed within the period that applies to the loss or credit year. Deficiencies attributable to the carrying back of one of those credits as a result of the carryback of a net operating loss, capital loss or other credit may be assessed within the period that applies to the loss or other credit year (Code Sec. 6501(h) and (j)).

2728. Request for Prompt Assessment. A corporation that is contemplating dissolution, is in the process of dissolving, or has actually dissolved, or a decedent or an estate of a decedent (for taxes other than the estate tax imposed by chapter 11), may request a prompt assessment (Code Sec. 6501(d); Reg. § 301.6501(d)-1).[52] If such a request is made, an assessment or a proceeding in court without assessment for the collection of any tax must then be begun within 18 months after the receipt of a written request for a prompt assessment. In the case of a corporation, however, the 18-month period will not apply unless the corporation has completed or will eventually complete its dissolution at or before the end of the 18-month period. This provision does not apply in the cases described at ¶ 2732 and ¶ 2734. It also does not apply for personal holding company taxes in certain instances or where a waiver filed by the taxpayer extends the assessment period beyond the 18-month period.

2732. Assessment Period for False Returns or No Return. Tax may be assessed or a court proceeding to collect tax may be commenced at any time if:

(1) the return is false or fraudulent,

(2) there is a willful attempt to evade tax, or

(3) no return is filed (Code Sec. 6501(c); Reg. § 301.6501(c)-1).[53]

In addition, in the case of a fraudulent return, the government may impose additional taxes at any time, without regard to statutes of limitations, although the burden of proof falls on the government to prove fraud by the taxpayer (Code Sec. 7454(a)).[54]

2733. Assessment Period for Listed Transactions. If a taxpayer fails to include with a return any information required relating to a listed transaction (¶ 2001), the statute of limitations with respect to that transaction will not expire before one year after the earlier of: (1) the date on which the information is furnished to the IRS or (2) the date that a material advisor to the listed transaction satisfies certain list maintenance requirements (¶ 2008) with respect to the transaction (Code Sec. 6501(c)(10)).[55]

2734. Assessment Period for Omission of Over 25% of Income. If the taxpayer omits from gross income (total receipts, without reduction for cost) an amount in excess of 25 percent of the amount of gross income stated in the return, a six-year limitation period on assessment and collection of tax applies. An item will not be considered as omitted from gross income if information sufficient to apprise the IRS of the nature and amount of such item is disclosed in the return or in any schedule or statement attached to the return (Code Sec. 6501(e); Reg. § 301.6501(e)-1(a)).[56] The U.S. Supreme Court has held that a taxpayer's overstatement of its basis in an asset that resulted in an understatement of gross income from the asset's sale did not trigger the six-year limitations period because a basis overstatement is not an omission from gross income (*Home Concrete & Supply, LLC*, SCt, 2012-1 USTC ¶ 50,315). The Court's decision invalidated Reg. § 301.6501(e)-1(a)(1)(iii).

2735. Collection After Assessment. After assessment of tax made within the statutory period of limitation (¶ 2726), the tax may be collected by levy or a proceeding in court commenced within 10 years after the assessment or within any period for

References are to Standard Federal Tax Reports; Tax Research Consultant; and Practical Tax Explanations.

[51] ¶ 38,960, ¶ 38,977; IRS: 30,122; § 39,505.30

[52] ¶ 38,960, ¶ 38,968; IRS: 30,118; § 48,225

[53] ¶ 38,960, ¶ 38,966; IRS: 30,102, IRS: 30,104, IRS: 30,106; § 39,505

[54] ¶ 42,081; IRS: 30,104; § 39,505.15

[55] ¶ 38,960; IRS: 30,052, PENALTY: 3,252.10; § 39,015.05

[56] ¶ 38,960, ¶ 38,970; IRS: 30,152; § 39,505.10

collection agreed upon in writing between the IRS and the taxpayer before the expiration of the 10-year period (Code Sec. 6502(a); Reg. § 301.6502-1).[57] The period agreed upon by the parties may be extended by later written agreements, so long as they are made prior to the expiration of the period previously agreed upon. The IRS has to notify taxpayers of their right to refuse an extension each time one is requested (Code Sec. 6501(c)(4)).[58] If a timely court proceeding has commenced for the collection of the tax, then the period during which the tax may be collected is extended until the liability for tax (or a judgment against the taxpayer) is satisfied or becomes unenforceable.

Generally, the 10-year limitations period on collections may not be extended if there has not been a levy on any of the taxpayer's property. If the taxpayer entered into an installment agreement with the IRS, however, the 10-year limitations period may be extended for the period that the limitations period was extended under the original terms of the installment agreement plus 90 days.

Interest accrues on a deficiency from the date the tax was due (determined without regard to extensions) until the date payment is received at the rate specified at ¶ 2838 (Code Sec. 6601(g); Reg. § 301.6601-1(a)(1)).[59] Interest may be assessed and collected during the period in which the related tax may be collected.

Private Debt Collection Agencies. The IRS is authorized to use private debt collection agencies (PDCs) to recover federal debts (Code Sec. 6306).[60] However, in March 2009, the IRS announced that it would not renew its contracts with the two PDCs it had been using (IRS News Release IR-2009-19). Thus, while the IRS is still authorized to use PDCs, it is no longer, in fact, using them.

2736. Suspension of Assessment Period. When an income, estate or gift tax deficiency notice is mailed, the running of the period of limitations on assessment and collection of any deficiency is suspended for 90 days (150 days for a deficiency notice mailed to persons outside the United States) not counting Saturday, Sunday, or a legal holiday in the District of Columbia, plus an additional 60 days thereafter (Code Sec. 6503(a)(1); Reg. § 301.6503(a)-1).[61] If a petition is filed with the Tax Court, the running of the period of limitations is suspended until the Tax Court's decision becomes final and for an additional 60 days thereafter.

The 10-year statute of limitations for collection after assessment is also suspended from the date the IRS wrongfully seizes or receives a third party's property to 30 days after the date the IRS returns the property or the date on which a judgment secured in a wrongful levy action becomes final. Similarly, with respect to wrongful liens, the 10-year limitations period is suspended from the time the third-party owner is entitled to a certificate of discharge of lien until 30 days after the earlier of (1) the date that the IRS no longer holds any amount as a deposit or bond that was used to satisfy the unpaid liability or that was refunded or released or (2) the date that the judgment in a civil action becomes final (¶ 2755) (Code Sec. 6503(f)).[62]

For federal bankruptcy cases, the running of the period of limitations is suspended during the period of the automatic stay on collection of taxes and for an additional period ending 60 days after the day the stay is lifted for assessments and for six months thereafter for collection (Code Sec. 6503(h)).[63] Additionally, in receivership and bankruptcy cases where a fiduciary is required to give written notice to the IRS of an appointment or authorization to act, the assessment period is suspended from the date the proceedings are instituted and ending 30 days after the day of notice to the IRS of such appointment. The extension period cannot exceed two years (Code Sec. 6872).[64]

References are to Standard Federal Tax Reports; Tax Research Consultant; and Practical Tax Explanations.

[57] ¶ 39,010, ¶ 39,011; IRS: 45,200; § 39,910

[58] ¶ 38,960; IRS: 30,254; § 39,905

[59] ¶ 39,410, ¶ 39,412; IRS: 30,114, PENALTY: 9,050; § 40,105

[60] ¶ 38,084B; IRS: 45,250

[61] ¶ 39,030, ¶ 39,031; IRS: 30,202; § 39,910

[62] ¶ 39,030; IRS: 45,204; § 39,910

[63] ¶ 39,030; IRS: 30,208; § 39,550.15

[64] ¶ 40,640; IRS: 30,208; § 39,550.15

If the taxpayer and the IRS agree to the rescission of a deficiency notice, the statute of limitations again begins to run as of the date of the rescission and continues to run for the period of time that remains on the date the notice was issued (Code Sec. 6212(d)).[65]

2738. Suit for Recovery of Erroneous Refund. The government may sue to recover an erroneous refund (including, but not limited to, one made after the applicable refund period described in ¶ 2763) within two years after such refund was paid. However, a suit may be commenced within five years if any part of the refund was induced by fraud or misrepresentation of a material fact (Code Sec. 6532(b); Reg. § 301.6532-2).[66]

2740. Criminal Prosecution. A criminal prosecution must generally be started within three years after the offense is committed (Code Sec. 6531).[67] However, a six-year period applies in a case where there is:

(1) fraud or an attempt to defraud the United States or an agency thereof, by conspiracy or otherwise,

(2) a willful attempt to evade or defeat any tax or payment,

(3) willful aiding or assisting in the preparation of a false return or other document,

(4) willful failure to pay any tax or make any return (except certain information returns) at the time required by law,

(5) a false statement verified under penalties of perjury or a false or fraudulent return, statement or other document,

(6) intimidation of a U.S. officer or employee,

(7) an offense committed by a U.S. officer or employee in connection with a revenue law, or

(8) a conspiracy to defeat tax or payment.

2743. Collection from Transferee of Property. The liability of a transferee of property is generally assessed and collected in the same manner as is any other deficiency imposed by the IRS (Code Sec. 6901; Reg. § 301.6901-1(a)).[68] The term "transferee" includes an heir, legatee, devisee, distributee of an estate of a deceased person, the shareholder of a dissolved corporation, the assignee or donee of an insolvent person, the successor of a corporation, a party to a Code Sec. 368(a) reorganization, and all other classes of distributees. Such term also includes, with respect to the gift tax, a donee (without regard to the solvency of the donor) and, with respect to the estate tax, any person who, under Code Sec. 6324(a)(2), is personally liable for any part of such tax.

2745. Transferee Assessment and Collection Period. Unless a taxpayer has filed a false return with intent to evade tax (¶ 2732), an assessment against a transferee or fiduciary must be made within the following periods:

(1) in the case of an initial transferee, within one year after the expiration of the period of limitation for assessment against the taxpayer,

(2) in the case of a transferee of a transferee, within one year after the expiration of the period of limitation for assessment against the preceding transferee or three years after the expiration of the period of limitation for assessment against the taxpayer, whichever of these two periods expires first,

(3) if a timely court proceeding has been brought against the taxpayer or last preceding transferee, within one year after the return of execution in such proceeding, or

References are to Standard Federal Tax Reports; Tax Research Consultant; and Practical Tax Explanations.

[65] ¶ 37,540; IRS: 30,202; § 39,510.20

[66] ¶ 39,270, ¶ 39,272; IRS: 45,162; § 40,060

[67] ¶ 39,240; IRS: 66,454; § 40,245.05

[68] ¶ 40,700, ¶ 40,701; IRS: 60,250; § 39,545.05

(4) in the case of a fiduciary, within one year after the liability arises or within the limitations period for collection of the tax (¶ 2726), whichever is the later (Code Sec. 6901; Reg. § 301.6901-1(c)).[69]

2747. Collection from Fiduciary. In order to receive advance notice from the IRS with respect to assessments, every fiduciary must give written notice to the IRS of his fiduciary capacity. If this notice (Form 56) is not filed, the IRS may proceed against the property in the hands of the fiduciary after mailing notice of the deficiency or other liability to the taxpayer's last known address, even if the taxpayer is then deceased or is under legal disability. The fiduciary may be relieved of any further liability by filing with the IRS written notice and evidence of the termination (Reg. § 301.6903-1).[70]

2750. Assessment in Bankruptcy or Receiverships. When a taxpayer's assets are taken over by a receiver appointed by the court, the IRS may immediately assess the tax if it has not already been lawfully assessed. The IRS may also assess the tax on (1) the debtor's estate under U.S. Code Title 11 bankruptcy proceedings or (2) the debtor, if the tax liability has become *res judicata* pursuant to a Title 11 bankruptcy determination (Code Sec. 6871).[71] Tax claims may be presented to the court before which the receivership (or a Title 11 bankruptcy) is pending, despite the pendency of proceedings in the Tax Court. However, in the case of a receivership proceeding, no petition may be filed with the Tax Court after the appointment of the receiver. The trustee of the debtor's estate in a Title 11 bankruptcy proceeding may intervene on behalf of the debtor's estate in any Tax Court proceeding to which the debtor is a party (Code Sec. 7464).[72]

Liens and Levies

2751. Property Subject to Liens. If a taxpayer fails to pay an assessed tax for which payment has been demanded, the amount due (including interest and penalties) constitutes a lien in favor of the United States upon all the taxpayer's property (real, personal, tangible, and intangible), including after-acquired property and rights to property (Code Sec. 6321; Reg. § 301.6321-1).[73] Whether the taxpayer owns or has an interest in property is determined under the appropriate state law. Once the taxpayer's rights in the property are established, federal law determines priorities among competing creditors (Code Sec. 6323).[74] Federal law also controls whether specific property is exempt from levy (¶ 2753). Once a tax lien arises, it continues until the tax liability is paid or the lien becomes unenforceable due to a lapse of time (Code Sec. 6322).[75] A lien lapses if 10 years have passed from the date of assessment (or longer, if the taxpayer waives restrictions on collection) during which the IRS has not attempted to collect the tax either by suit or distraint (Code Sec. 6502(a)).[76]

2753. Property Subject to Levy. Although a tax lien attaches to all the debtor's property, some property is exempt from levy. The following are among the items that are exempt from levy to some extent:

(1) wearing apparel and school books;

(2) fuel, provisions, furniture, and personal effects: up to $8,570 for 2012 ($8,790 for 2013);

(3) unemployment benefits;

(4) books and tools of a trade, business, or profession: up to $4,290 for 2012 ($4,400 for 2013);

(5) undelivered mail;

(6) certain annuity and pension payments;

References are to Standard Federal Tax Reports; Tax Research Consultant; and Practical Tax Explanations.

[69] ¶ 40,700; IRS: 60,256; § 39,545

[70] ¶ 40,730, ¶ 40,811; IRS: 60,200; § 39,545

[71] ¶ 40,610; IRS: 57,056; § 39,550

[72] ¶ 42,120; IRS: 57,056; § 39,550

[73] ¶ 38,135, ¶ 38,135A; IRS: 48,050, IRS: 48,100; § 39,925.05

[74] ¶ 38,145; IRS: 48,150; § 39,925.20

[75] ¶ 38,140; IRS: 48,050; § 39,925.10

[76] ¶ 39,010; IRS: 45,202; § 39,925.10

(7) workers' compensation;

(8) judgments for support of minor children;

(9) certain public assistance payments, supplemental security income for the aged, blind, and disabled, state and local welfare payments and Job Training Partnership Act payments;

(10) certain amounts of wages, salary, and other income; and

(11) certain service-connected disability payments (Code Sec. 6334; Rev. Proc. 2011-52).[77]

Certain specified payments are not exempt from levy if the Secretary of the Treasury approves a continuous levy (Code Sec. 6334(f)).[78] The IRS can approve a continuous levy on up to 15 percent (100 percent for payments for goods and services and, after November 21, 2011, sales or leases of real property) of any federal payment other than a payment for which eligibility is not based on the income or assets or both of the payee, unemployment benefits, worker's compensation payments, wages or salary, Social Security disability payments, welfare and public assistance payments, and annuity or pension payments or benefit under the Railroad Retirement Act or Railroad Unemployment Insurance Act.

The IRS may not seize any real property used as a residence by the taxpayer or any real property of the taxpayer (other than rental property) that is used as a residence by another person in order to satisfy a liability of $5,000 or less (including tax, penalties and interest). In the case of the taxpayer's principal residence, the IRS may not seize the residence without written approval of a federal district court judge or magistrate (Code Sec. 6334(a)(13) and (e)).[79] Unless collection of tax is in jeopardy, tangible personal property or real property (other than rented real property) used in the taxpayer's trade or business may not be seized without written approval of an IRS district or assistant director. Such approval may not be given unless it is determined that the taxpayer's other assets subject to collection are not sufficient to pay the amount due and the expenses of the proceedings. Where a levy is made on tangible personal property essential to the taxpayer's trade or business, the IRS must provide an accelerated appeals process to determine whether the property should be released from levy (Code Sec. 6343(a)(2)).[80] See ¶ 2755.

Levies are prohibited if the estimated expenses of the levy and sale exceed the fair market value of the property (Code Sec. 6331(f)).[81] Also, unless the collection of tax is in jeopardy, a levy cannot be made on any day on which the taxpayer is required to respond to an IRS summons (Code Sec. 6331(g)).[82] Further, financial institutions are required to hold amounts garnished by the IRS for 21 days after receiving notice of the levy to provide the taxpayer time to notify the IRS of any errors (Code Sec. 6332(c)).[83]

2754. Recording and Priority of Tax Liens. Until notice of a tax lien has been properly recorded, it is not valid against any bona fide purchaser for value, mechanic's lienor, judgment lien creditor or holder of a security interest (such as a mortgagee or pledgee, for example) (Code Sec. 6323(a)).[84] Also, even a properly recorded tax lien may not be valid against so-called superpriorities, which include purchases of securities and automobiles, retail purchases, casual sales of less than $1,430 for 2012 ($1,470 for 2013), certain possessory liens securing payment for repairs to personal property, real property taxes and special assessment liens, mechanic's liens for repairs and improvements of less than $7,160 for 2012 ($7,350 for 2013) to certain residential property, attorneys' liens, certain insurance contracts and deposit secured loans (previously referred to as passbook loans) (Code Sec. 6323(b)).[85] In addition, security interests arising from

References are to Standard Federal Tax Reports; Tax Research Consultant; and Practical Tax Explanations.

[77] ¶ 38,210; IRS: 51,062; § 39,930.15

[78] ¶ 38,210; IRS: 51,060.35; § 39,930.20

[79] ¶ 38,210; IRS: 51,062.05; § 39,930.15

[80] ¶ 38,270; IRS: 51,154; § 39,930.15

[81] ¶ 38,185; IRS: 51,054; § 39,930.05

[82] ¶ 38,185; IRS: 51,054; § 39,930.05

[83] ¶ 38,185; IRS: 51,064.35; § 39,930.25

[84] ¶ 38,145; IRS: 48,150; § 39,925.20

[85] ¶ 38,145; IRS: 48,160; § 39,925.20

commercial financing agreements may be accorded superpriority status (Code Sec. 6323(c)).[86]

Notice of a federal tax lien must be filed in the one office designated by the state in which the property is situated (Code Sec. 6323(f); Reg. § 301.6323(f)-1).[87] Generally, personal property is situated in the state where the taxpayer resides (rather than where domiciled); for real property, the situs is its physical location. If, in the case of either real or personal property, the state designates more than one office or does not designate an office where notice must be filed, notice of the lien must be filed with the Clerk of the U.S. District Court for the district in which the property is situated. If state law provides that a notice of lien affecting personal property must be filed in the county clerk's office located in the taxpayer's county of residence and also adopts a federal law that requires a notice of lien to be filed in another location in order to attach to a specific type of property, the state is deemed to have designated only one office for the filing of the notice. Thus, to protect its lien, the IRS need only file its notice in the county clerk's office located in the taxpayer's home county (Reg. § 301.6323(f)-1(a)(2)). Notice regarding property located in the District of Columbia is filed with the Recorder of Deeds of the District of Columbia. Special rules apply in a state that requires public indexing for priority liens against realty.

A forfeiture under local law of property seized by any law enforcement agency or other local governmental branch relates back to the time the property was first seized, unless, under local law, a claim holder would have priority over the interest of the government in the property (Code Sec. 6323(i)(3)).[88]

The IRS may not levy against property while a taxpayer has a pending offer in compromise or installment agreement (Code Sec. 6331(k)).[89] If the offer in compromise or installment agreement is ultimately rejected, the levy prohibition remains in effect for 30 days after the rejection and during the pendency of any appeal of the rejection, providing the appeal is filed within 30 days of the rejection. No levy may be made while the installment agreement is in effect. If the installment agreement is terminated by the IRS, no levy may be made for 30 days after the termination and during the pendency of any appeal.

2754A. Notice and Opportunity for Hearing. The IRS must notify any person subject to a lien of the existence of the lien within five days of the lien being filed (Code Sec. 6320; Reg. § 301.6320-1).[90] Among other requirements, the notice must address the person's right to request a hearing during the 30-day period beginning on the sixth day after the lien is filed. Similarly, at least 30 days prior to the IRS filing a notice of levy on any person's property or right to property, the IRS must provide notice of the right to a hearing (Code Sec. 6330; Reg. § 301.6330-1).[91] Whether in connection with the notice of lien or notice of intent to levy, the hearing is to be held by the IRS Office of Appeals. At the hearing, the taxpayer may raise any issue relevant to the appropriateness of the proposed collection activity if such issue was not raised at a previous hearing. The taxpayer has 30 days after the hearing determination to appeal the determination to the Tax Court, which has exclusive jurisdiction over appeals of hearing determinations. A taxpayer subject to a levy for the collection of employment taxes cannot request a hearing if the taxpayer already requested a hearing regarding unpaid employment taxes arising in the two-year period before the beginning of the taxable period at issue.

2755. Release of Tax Liens and Levies. Taxpayers may appeal the filing of a notice of lien in the public record and petition for release (Code Sec. 6326; Reg. § 301.6326-1).[92] If filed in error, the IRS must release the lien and state that the lien was erroneous. The request for relief must be based on one of the following grounds:

References are to Standard Federal Tax Reports; Tax Research Consultant; and Practical Tax Explanations.

[86] ¶ 38,145; IRS: 48,160; § 39,925.20

[87] ¶ 38,145, ¶ 38,153; IRS: 48,056; § 39,925.20

[88] ¶ 38,145; IRS: 48,154; § 39,925.20

[89] ¶ 38,185; IRS: 51,054; § 39,930.05

[90] ¶ 38,132, ¶ 38,133; IRS: 48,058.05; § 39,945.10

[91] ¶ 38,182, ¶ 38,183; IRS: 51,056.05; § 39,945.15

[92] ¶ 38,175, ¶ 38,176; IRS: 48,200; § 39,925.25, § 39,930.30

(1) the tax liability had been satisfied before the lien was filed;

(2) the assessing of the tax liability violated either the notice of deficiency procedures or the Bankruptcy Code; or

(3) the limitations period for collecting the liability had expired prior to the filing of the lien.

Further, the IRS may withdraw a public notice of tax lien before payment in full if:

(1) the filing of the notice was premature or not in accord with administrative procedures;

(2) the taxpayer has entered into an installment agreement to satisfy the tax liability;

(3) withdrawal of the notice would facilitate the collection of the tax liability; or

(4) the withdrawal of the notice would be in the best interest of the taxpayer and the government, as determined by the National Taxpayer Advocate (Code Sec. 6323(j)).[93]

The withdrawal of a notice of tax lien does not affect the underlying tax lien; rather, the withdrawal simply relinquishes any lien priority the IRS had obtained when the notice was filed.

The IRS is required to release a levy if:

(1) the underlying liability is satisfied or becomes unenforceable due to lapse of time;

(2) the IRS determines that the release of the levy will facilitate the collection of tax;

(3) an installment payment agreement has been executed by the taxpayer with respect to the liability;

(4) the IRS determines that the levy is creating a financial hardship; or

(5) the fair market value of the property exceeds the liability, and the partial release of the levy would not hinder the collection of tax (Code Sec. 6343(a)).[94]

In addition, a taxpayer may request that the IRS sell the levied property (Code Sec. 6335(f); Reg. § 301.6335-1(d)).[95]

The IRS has been given authority to return property that has been levied upon if:

(1) the levy was premature or not in accordance with administrative procedure;

(2) the taxpayer has entered into an installment agreement to satisfy the tax liability, unless the agreement provides otherwise;

(3) the return of the property will facilitate collection of the tax liability; or

(4) with the consent of the taxpayer or the Taxpayer Advocate, the return of the property would be in the best interests of the taxpayer and the government (Code Sec. 6343(d)).[96]

Property is returned in the same manner as if the property had been wrongfully levied upon, except that the taxpayer is not entitled to interest.

A taxpayer may bring a suit in federal district court if an IRS employee knowingly or negligently fails to release a tax lien on the taxpayer's property after receiving written notice from the taxpayer of the IRS's failure to release the lien (Code Sec. 7432; Reg. § 301.7432-1).[97] The taxpayer may recover actual economic damages plus the costs of the action. Injuries such as inconvenience, emotional distress, and loss of reputation are

References are to Standard Federal Tax Reports; Tax Research Consultant; and Practical Tax Explanations.

[93] ¶ 38,145; IRS: 48,052.10; § 39,925.25

[94] ¶ 38,270; IRS: 51,154; § 39,930.30

[95] ¶ 38,230, ¶ 38,231; IRS: 51,202; § 39,930.30

[96] ¶ 38,270; IRS: 51,154.05; § 39,930.30

[97] ¶ 41,760, ¶ 41,761; IRS: 48,210; § 39,925.25

not compensable damages unless they result in actual economic harm. Costs of the action that may be recovered are limited generally to certain court costs and do not include administrative costs or attorney's fees, although attorney's fees may be recoverable (¶ 2796). A two-year statute of limitations, measured from the date on which the cause of action accrued, applies.

Third-Party Owners. A third-party owner of property against which a federal tax lien has been filed may obtain a certificate of discharge with respect to the lien on such property (Code Sec. 6325(b)(4); Reg. § 301.6325-1(b)(4)).[98] The certificate is issued if (1) the third-party owner deposits with the IRS an amount of money equal to the value of the government's interest in the property as determined by the IRS or (2) the third-party owner posts a bond covering the government's interest in the property in a form acceptable by the IRS. A third-party owner who is a co-owner of property with the taxpayer against whom the underlying tax was assessed may no longer be automatically barred from obtaining a certificate of discharge with respect to a lien on the property. Third-party owners may request the discharge of a tax lien on property that they own with the person whose tax liability gave rise to the lien.

If the IRS determines that (1) the liability to which the lien relates can be satisfied from other sources or (2) the value of the government's interest in the property is less than the IRS's prior determination of the government's interest in the property, then the IRS will refund (with interest) the amount deposited and release the bond applicable to such property. Within 120 days after a certificate of discharge is issued, the third-party owner may file a civil action against the United States in a federal district court for a determination of whether the government's interest in the property (if any) has less value than that determined by the IRS (Code Sec. 7426(a)(4) and (b)(5)).[99]

Mitigation of Effect of Statute of Limitations

2756. Correction of Errors in Certain Cases. The Code provides relief from some of the inequities caused by the statute of limitations and other provisions that would otherwise prevent equitable adjustment of various income tax hardships (Code Secs. 1311–1314; Reg. § § 1.1311(a)-1–1.1314(c)-1).[100] Adjustments are permitted, even though the limitation period for assessment or refund for the year at issue may have otherwise expired, when a determination under the income tax laws:

(1) requires the inclusion in gross income of an item that was erroneously included in the income of the taxpayer for another tax year or in the gross income of a "related taxpayer" (e.g., spouse, beneficiary, partner, member of affiliated group of corporations, etc.);

(2) allows a deduction or credit that was erroneously allowed to the taxpayer for another tax year or to a related taxpayer;

(3) requires the exclusion from gross income of an item included in a return filed by the taxpayer or with respect to which tax was paid and which was erroneously excluded or omitted from the gross income of the taxpayer for another tax year or from the gross income of a related taxpayer for the same or another tax year;

(4) requires the correction of income or deduction items of estates or trusts or beneficiaries of either as between such related taxpayers;

(5) establishes the basis of property by making adjustments to such basis for items that should have been added to, or deducted from, income of preceding years;

(6) requires the allowance or disallowance of a deduction or credit to a corporation where a correlative deduction or credit should have been allowed (or disallowed) to a related taxpayer that is a member of an affiliated group of corporations (where there is an 80% common ownership);

References are to Standard Federal Tax Reports; Tax Research Consultant; and Practical Tax Explanations.

[98] ¶ 38,165, ¶ 38,166; IRS: 48,204.15; § 39,925.25

[99] ¶ 41,710; IRS: 48,204.15; § 39,925.25

[100] ¶ 31,800–¶ 31,865; IRS: 30,300; § 40,401

(7) requires the exclusion from gross income of an item not included in a return filed by the taxpayer and with respect to which the tax was not paid but which is includible in the gross income of the taxpayer for another tax year or in the gross income of a related taxpayer; or

(8) disallows a deduction or credit that should have been allowed, but was not allowed, to the taxpayer for another tax year or to a related taxpayer for the same or another tax year (Code Sec. 1312).[101]

Refunds and Credits

2759. Claim for Refund or Credit. A claim for refund for an overpayment of income taxes is generally made on the appropriate income tax return. However, once the return has been filed and the taxpayer believes the tax is incorrect, the claim for refund by an individual who filed Form 1040, 1040A, or 1040EZ is made on Form 1040X. The refund claim is made on Form 1120X by a corporation that filed Form 1120. A claim for refund or credit for an overpayment of income taxes for which a form other than Form 1040, 1040A, 1040EZ, 1120, or 990T was filed is made on the appropriate amended tax return (Reg. § 301.6402-3).[102]

2760. Amendment of Refund Claim. A timely claim for refund based upon one or more specific grounds may not be amended to include other and different grounds after the statute of limitations has expired (Reg. § 301.6402-2(b)).[103]

2761. Refund or Credit After Appeal to Tax Court. Where the taxpayer has been mailed a notice of deficiency and has filed a petition with the Tax Court (¶ 2778), no credit or refund is allowable, and the taxpayer may not sue in any other court for any part of the tax for the tax year in question (Code Sec. 6512).[104] A credit or refund may be allowed or a suit may be instituted, however, to recover:

(1) an overpayment determined by a decision of the Tax Court that has become final,

(2) any amount collected in excess of an amount computed in accordance with a final decision of the Tax Court,

(3) any amount collected after the expiration of the period of limitation upon the beginning of levy or a proceeding in court for collection,

(4) overpayments attributable to partnership items,

(5) any amount that was collected within the period following the mailing of a notice of deficiency during which the IRS is prohibited from collecting by levy or through a court proceeding, and

(6) any amount that is not contested on an appeal from a Tax Court decision.

The Tax Court can order the refund of a tax overpayment plus interest if the IRS has not made a refund to the taxpayer within 120 days after the decision fixing the amount of the refund has become final (Code Sec. 6512(b)).[105]

The Tax Court is empowered to resolve disputes regarding the amount of interest to be charged on a tax deficiency redetermined pursuant to a Tax Court order. The action must be brought within one year from the date on which the decision ordering the redetermination of taxes became final. Further, the taxpayer must pay the entire redetermined deficiency, plus the entire amount of interest, before the Tax Court can hear the case (Code Sec. 7481(c)).[106]

2763. Limitations on Credit or Refund. Generally, a taxpayer may file a claim for refund within three years from the time the return was filed or within two years from the time the tax was paid, whichever is later. If no return was filed by the taxpayer, the claim

References are to Standard Federal Tax Reports; Tax Research Consultant; and Practical Tax Explanations.

[101] ¶ 31,820; IRS: 30,300; § 40,405, § 40,410.05

[102] ¶ 38,517; IRS: 33,150; § 40,010.10

[103] ¶ 38,516; IRS: 33,200; § 40,010.25

[104] ¶ 39,090; LITIG: 3,102; § 40,001

[105] ¶ 39,090; LITIG: 6,100; § 40,001

[106] ¶ 42,420; LITIG: 6,114; § 40,001

must be filed within two years from the time the tax was paid (Code Sec. 6511(a)).[107] For this purpose, a return filed before the due date is treated as filed on the due date (Code Sec. 6513(a)).[108] Taxpayers who fail to file a return as of the date the IRS mails a deficiency notice may recover in the Tax Court taxes paid during the three years preceding the IRS mailing date (Code Sec. 6512(b)(3)).[109]

If the claim relates to the deductibility of bad debts or worthless securities, the period is seven years; if it relates to the credit for foreign taxes, the period is 10 years. If the refund claim relates to a net operating loss (NOL) or a capital loss carryback, the period is that period which ends three years after the time prescribed by law for filing the return (including extensions thereof) for the tax year of the NOL or capital loss carryback. To the extent that an overpayment is due to unused credit carrybacks that arise as the result of the carryback of an NOL or capital loss, the claim may be filed during the period that ends three years after the time prescribed by law for filing the return (including extensions) for the tax year of the unused credit that results in the carryback (Code Sec. 6511(d); Reg. § 301.6511(d)-2).[110]

The statute of limitations on refund claims is suspended during any period that an individual is financially disabled—under a medically determinable mental or physical impairment that: (1) can be expected to result in death or that has lasted or can be expected to last for a continuous period of not less than one year and (2) renders the person unable to manage his or her financial affairs (Code Sec. 6511(h)).[111] The suspension of the limitations period does not apply for any period during which the taxpayer's spouse or another person is authorized to act on behalf of the individual in financial matters.

Retired Military Personnel. The time period for retired military personnel to file claims for credits or refunds related to disability determinations by the Department of Veterans Affairs (e.g., determinations after the tax is filed) is extended until one year after the date of the disability determination if that period is later than the normal three-year period of limitation (Code Sec. 6511(d)(8)).[112] This provision does not apply to any tax year that began more than five years before the date of the disability determination.

2764. Refund Reduction for Past-Due, Legally Enforceable Debts. The Treasury Department's Financial Management Service (FMS) will reduce the amount of any tax refund payable to a taxpayer by the amount of any past-due, legally enforceable nontax debt that is owed to any federal agency. Debts that are less than $25 and those that have been delinquent for more than 10 years are exempt. In most cases, the creditor federal agencies must have first attempted to collect the debt by using salary offset and administrative procedures. The federal agency is also required to notify the taxpayer that a debt will be referred to the FMS for refund offset if the debt remains unpaid after 60 days or if there is insufficient evidence that the debt is either not past due or not legally enforceable (31 CFR § 285.2).

The FMS has also promulgated rules governing the offset of tax refunds against past-due child and spousal support (31 CFR § 285.3) and against state income tax debts reduced to judgment (31 CFR § 285.8). Tax refunds may also be offset against past-due debts owed to a state for (1) erroneous payment of unemployment compensation due to fraud or failure to report earnings, or (2) failure to make contributions to a state's unemployment fund for which the state has determined the person to be liable (Code Sec. 6402(f)).[113]

2765. Interest on Refund. When a return has been properly filed in processible form, interest is allowed on a refund from the date of overpayment to a date preceding the date of the refund check by not more than 30 days (Code Sec. 6611(b)(2) and (3)).[114]

References are to Standard Federal Tax Reports; Tax Research Consultant; and Practical Tax Explanations.

[107] ¶ 39,060; IRS: 36,050; § 40,040.05

[108] ¶ 39,120; IRS: 36,050; § 40,040.05

[109] ¶ 39,090; IRS: 36,116; § 40,040.05

[110] ¶ 39,060, ¶ 39,067; IRS: 36,100; § 40,045.05

[111] ¶ 39,060; IRS: 36,052; § 40,040.05

[112] ¶ 39,060; IRS: 36,052; § 40,045.05

[113] ¶ 38,510; IRS: 33,304.20; § 40,015.05

[114] ¶ 39,430; PENALTY: 9,100; § 40,115.05

If a return is filed late, no interest is allowed for any day before the date on which it is filed. No interest is payable on a refund arising from an original tax return if the refund is issued by the 45th day after the later of the due date for the return (determined without regard to any extensions) or the date the return is filed (Code Sec. 6611(e)). Similarly, if a refund claimed on an amended return or claim for refund is issued within 45 days after the date the amended document was filed, interest is not payable for that period, although interest is payable from the due date of the original return to the date the amended document was filed. If a refund is not issued within the 45-day grace period, interest is payable for the period from the due date of the original return to the date the refund is paid.

The interest rate the IRS must pay for overpayment of taxes by noncorporate taxpayers is equal to the federal short-term rate (¶ 83) plus three percentage points (which is equal to the interest rate on underpayments of tax). The interest rate on overpayments by corporate taxpayers is the short-term federal rate plus two percentage points (Code Sec. 6621).[115] For large corporate overpayments (any portion that exceeds $10,000), the rate is reduced to the sum of the short-term federal rate plus one-half of one percentage point. These rates are adjusted quarterly, with each successive rate becoming effective two months after the date of each quarterly adjustment. The rates for the first through fourth quarters of 2012 were 3 percent for noncorporate taxpayers and 2 percent for corporate taxpayers (0.5 percent for large corporate overpayments).[116]

Overlapping Overpayments and Underpayments. The interest rates for overpayments and underpayments have been equalized (sometimes referred to as "global interest netting") for any period of mutual indebtedness between taxpayers and the IRS (Code Sec. 6621(d)).[117] No interest is imposed to the extent that underpayment and overpayment interest run simultaneously on equal amounts. The net zero interest rate applies regardless of whether an underpayment otherwise would be subject to the increased interest rate imposed on large corporate underpayments or an overpayment otherwise would be subject to a reduced interest rate because it was a corporate overpayment in excess of $10,000. Although global interest netting is available to both corporate and noncorporate taxpayers, its effect on noncorporate taxpayers is mitigated due to the equalization of the underpayment and overpayment interest rates for such taxpayers.

2768. Refunds Disregarded for Means-Tested Assistance Programs. Any federal tax refund, or advance payment with respect to a refundable federal tax credit made to any individual cannot be taken into account as income or as resources for a period of 12 months from receipt, for purposes of determining the individual's eligibility (or that of any other individual) for benefits or assistance, or for the amount or extent of benefits or assistance, under (1) any federal program, or (2) any state or local program financed in whole or in part with federal funds (Code Sec. 6409).[118] This treatment will not apply to any amount received after December 31, 2012.

2773. Quick Carryback Refund and Postponement of Tax Payment. A corporation (other than an S corporation) that has an overpayment of tax as a result of a net operating loss (NOL), capital loss, business and research credits, or a claim-of-right adjustment can file an application on Form 1139 for a tentative adjustment or refund of taxes for a year affected by the carryback of such loss or credits or by such adjustment. A noncorporate taxpayer can apply for similar adjustments on Form 1045 (Code Sec. 6411; Temp. Reg. § 5.6411-1).[119] For provisions on the quick refund of a capital loss carryback, see ¶ 1173.

The application itself is not a formal refund claim and its rejection in whole or in part cannot be made the basis of a refund suit. However, the taxpayer can file a regular claim for refund within the limitation period (¶ 2763), and this claim can be made the basis for a suit. For losses and credits, the IRS must allow or disallow the refund or

References are to Standard Federal Tax Reports; Tax Research Consultant; and Practical Tax Explanations.

[115] ¶ 39,450; PENALTY: 9,152; § 40,115.05

[116] ¶ 39,455.51; PENALTY: 9,152

[117] ¶ 39,450; PENALTY: 9,056.05; § 40,120.15

[118] ¶ 38,702; IRS: 33,300; § 40,001

[119] ¶ 38,720, ¶ 38,726; IRS: 33,352; § 40,025

credit within 90 days from the later of (1) the date the application is filed or (2) the last day of the month in which the return for the loss or unused credit year is due (giving effect to extensions of time). For claim-of-right adjustments, the IRS must allow or disallow the refund or credit within 90 days from the later of (1) the date the application is filed or (2) the date of the overpayment.

If a corporation (but no other taxpayer) expects a NOL carryback from the current (unfinished) tax year, it can, subject to certain limitations, extend the time for payment of all or a part of the tax still payable for the immediately preceding year by filing a statement on Form 1138 (Reg. § 1.6164-1).[120]

The Courts

2776. Organization of Tax Court. The primary function of the U.S. Tax Court is to review deficiencies asserted by the IRS for additional income, estate, gift, or self-employment taxes or special excise taxes (Code Secs. 6512 and 7442).[121] The Tax Court is the only judicial body from which relief may be obtained without the payment of tax. The Tax Court also may issue declaratory judgments on the initial or continuing qualification of a retirement plan under Code Sec. 401, a tax-exempt organization under Code Sec. 501(c)(3) or Code Sec. 170(c)(2), a private foundation under Code Sec. 509(a), a private operating foundation under Code Sec. 4942(j)(3), or a tax-exempt farmers' cooperative under Code Sec. 521. However, a revocation of tax-exempt status for failure to file an annual information return or notice is not subject to an action for declaratory judgment relief. The Tax Court also may rule on the tax-exempt interest status of a government bond issue (Code Secs. 7428, 7476 and 7478; Tax Court Rule 210).[122] Declaratory judgment powers are also provided for (1) estate tax installments, (2) gift tax revaluations, and (3) employment status determinations.

The Tax Court's offices and trial rooms are located in Washington, D.C., but trials are also conducted in principal cities throughout the country. At the time of filing a petition, the taxpayer should file a request indicating where he prefers the trial to be held. The court imposes a filing fee of $60 (Code Sec. 7451).[123]

In any Tax Court case, other than small tax cases (¶ 2784), the findings of fact and opinion must generally be reported in writing. However, in appropriate cases, a Tax Court judge may state orally, and record in the transcript of the proceedings, the findings of fact or opinion in the case (Code Sec. 7459).[124] In such cases, the court must provide to all parties in the case either a copy of the transcript pages, which record the findings or opinion, or a written summary of such findings or opinion (Tax Court Rule 152).[125]

2778. Appeal to the Tax Court. Before the IRS can assess a deficiency, it generally must mail a deficiency notice to the taxpayer. The taxpayer then has an opportunity to appeal, within 90 days after the notice is mailed, to the Tax Court, if it has jurisdiction (¶ 2711). A notice based solely upon a mathematical or clerical error is not considered a notice of deficiency (Code Sec. 6213; Reg. § 301.6213-1).[126] If the notice is mailed to a person outside the United States, the period is 150 days instead of 90 days. The period is counted from midnight of the day on which the notice is mailed. Saturday, Sunday, or a legal holiday in the District of Columbia is not counted as the 90th or 150th day.

When a petition to the Tax Court is properly addressed and mailed within the prescribed time for filing, with the postage prepaid, the date of the U.S. postmark stamped on the cover in which the petition is mailed is the date of filing. For a petition that is mailed from a foreign country, this rule applies only if the petition is given to a designated international delivery service (Rev. Rul. 2002-23). If a petition is sent by registered or certified mail, the date of registration or certification is the date of mailing and is prima facie evidence that the petition was delivered to the Tax Court. Similarly,

References are to Standard Federal Tax Reports; Tax Research Consultant; and Practical Tax Explanations.

[120] ¶ 37,241; FILEBUS: 6,104.20; § 40,025

[121] ¶ 39,090, ¶ 42,057; LITIG: 6,100

[122] ¶ 41,720, ¶ 42,134, ¶ 42,154, ¶ 42,370; LITIG: 6,100

[123] ¶ 42,072; LITIG: 6,050

[124] ¶ 42,110; IRS: 27,206

[125] ¶ 42,312; LITIG: 6,802

[126] ¶ 37,545, ¶ 37,546, ¶ 37,549.34; LITIG: 6,202, LITIG: 6,204

the proper use of a private delivery service, under criteria established by the IRS, also constitutes prima facie evidence that the petition was delivered to the Tax Court (Reg. § 301.7502-1).[127]

If a taxpayer has filed a Tax Court petition before a jeopardy assessment or levy is made, the Tax Court is given concurrent jurisdiction with the federal district courts with respect to the taxpayer's challenge of the jeopardy assessment or levy (Code Sec. 7429(b)(2)).[128] Similarly, if there is a premature assessment of tax made while a proceeding with respect to that tax is pending in the Tax Court, the Tax Court has concurrent jurisdiction with the federal district court to restrain the assessment and collection of tax (Code Sec. 6213).[129]

2782. Burden of Proof. The IRS has the burden of proof in the Tax Court with respect to a factual issue that is relevant to determining a taxpayer's tax liability if the taxpayer presents credible evidence with respect to that issue *and* satisfies three applicable conditions discussed below (Code Sec. 7491).[130]

(1) The taxpayer must comply with the substantiation and recordkeeping requirements of the Code and regulations.

(2) The taxpayer must cooperate with reasonable requests by the IRS for witnesses, information, documents, meetings and interviews.

(3) Taxpayers *other than individuals* must meet the net worth limitations that apply for awarding attorneys' fees under Code Sec. 7430. Thus, corporations, trusts, and partnerships whose tax worth exceeds $7 million cannot benefit from this provision.

Further, in any court proceeding where the IRS solely uses statistical information from unrelated taxpayers to reconstruct an item of an *individual* taxpayer's income, such as the average income for taxpayers in the area in which the taxpayer lives, the burden of proof is on the IRS with respect to that item of income. Also with respect to individuals, the IRS must initially come forward with evidence that it is appropriate to apply a penalty, addition to tax, or additional amount before the court can impose the penalty.

In cases in which the burden of proof does not shift to the IRS, the taxpayer generally has the burden of proof in the Tax Court. However, a taxpayer must only establish that the IRS is in error and not whether any tax is owed (Tax Court Rule 142).[131] The IRS bears the burden of proof with respect to any new matter, increase in deficiency, or affirmative defenses raised in its answer. Further, the burden of proving fraud and liability as a transferee is upon the IRS (Code Secs. 6902 and 7454).[132] The IRS also has the burden of proof in proceedings involving a manager of a private foundation where the manager knowingly participated in an act of self-dealing, participated in an investment which jeopardizes the carrying out of an exempt purpose, or agreed to the making of a taxable expenditure.

2784. Small Tax Cases. The Tax Court maintains relatively informal procedures for the filing and handling of cases where neither the tax deficiency in dispute (including additions to tax and penalties) nor the amount of claimed overpayment exceeds $50,000. Usually taxpayers represent themselves, although they may be represented by anyone admitted to practice before the Tax Court. Each decision is final and cannot be appealed by either the taxpayer or the government (Code Sec. 7463).[133] The filing fee is $60 (¶ 2776).

2786. Appeal from Tax Court Decision. A taxpayer who loses in the Tax Court may appeal the case (unless the case was tried as a small tax case, ¶ 2784) to the proper U.S. Court of Appeals by filing a notice of appeal with the clerk of the Tax Court. The notice must be filed within 90 days after the Tax Court decision is entered. However, if

References are to Standard Federal Tax Reports; Tax Research Consultant; and Practical Tax Explanations.

[127] ¶ 42,621; LITIG: 6,214
[128] ¶ 41,725; IRS: 54,204
[129] ¶ 37,545; LITIG: 6,136
[130] ¶ 42,515; LITIG: 3,200
[131] ¶ 42,302, ¶ 42,302.615; LITIG: 6,704
[132] ¶ 40,780, ¶ 42,081; LITIG: 6,708
[133] ¶ 42,118; LITIG: 7,000

one party to the proceeding files a timely notice of appeal, any other party to the proceeding may take an appeal by filing a notice of appeal within 120 days after the decision of the Tax Court is entered (Code Sec. 7483).[134] A taxpayer who wants the assessment postponed pending the outcome of the appeal must file an appeal bond with the Tax Court guaranteeing payment of the deficiency as finally determined (Code Sec. 7485).[135]

2788. Acquiescence and Nonacquiescence by Commissioner. The IRS announces in the Internal Revenue Bulletin if it has decided to acquiesce or not acquiesce in a regular decision of the Tax Court. Any acquiescence or nonacquiescence may be withdrawn, modified or reversed at any time and any such action may be given retrospective, as well as prospective, effect.[136]

An acquiescence or nonacquiescence relates only to the issue or issues decided adversely to the government. Acquiescence means the IRS accepts the conclusion reached and does not necessarily mean acceptance and approval of any or all of the reasons assigned by the court for its conclusions. Acquiescences are to be relied on by IRS officers and others concerned as conclusions of the IRS only with respect to the application of the law to the facts in the particular case.

2790. Suits for Refund of Tax Overpayments. After the IRS rejects a refund claim for an alleged tax overpayment, suit can be maintained in the U.S. Court of Federal Claims or a U.S. District Court. A suit may be brought in the Court of Federal Claims against the United States to recover any overpayment of tax, regardless of amount (Judicial Code Sec. 1491).[137] Final decisions of the Court of Federal Claims are appealable to the U.S. Court of Appeals for the Federal Circuit (Judicial Code Sec. 1295).[138] All civil actions against the United States for the recovery of any internal revenue tax (regardless of amount) alleged to have been erroneously or illegally assessed or collected may be brought against the United States as defendant in a U.S. District Court with right of trial by jury in any action if either party makes a specific request for a jury trial (Judicial Code Secs. 1346 and 2402).[139] Filing a proper claim for refund or credit (¶ 2759) is a condition precedent to a suit for recovery of overpaid taxes (Code Sec. 7422(a)).[140]

If, prior to the hearing on a taxpayer's refund suit in a District Court or the Court of Federal Claims, a notice of deficiency is issued on the subject matter of the taxpayer's suit, then the District Court or Court of Federal Claims proceedings are stayed during the period of time in which the taxpayer can file a petition with the Tax Court (¶ 2778) and for 60 days thereafter. If the taxpayer files a petition with the Tax Court, then the District Court or the Court of Federal Claims loses jurisdiction as to any issues over which the Tax Court acquires jurisdiction. If the taxpayer does not appeal to the Tax Court, the United States may then counterclaim in the taxpayer's suit within the period of the stay of proceedings even though the time for such pleading may otherwise have expired (Code Sec. 7422(e)).[141]

2792. Time to Bring Suit. A suit or proceeding based upon a refund claim must be brought within two years from the date the IRS mails, by registered or certified mail, notice of disallowance of the part of the claim to which such suit or proceeding relates or within two years from the date the taxpayer waives notification of disallowance of his claim (Code Sec. 6532(a)).[142] The two-year period of limitation for filing suit may be extended by written agreement between the taxpayer and the IRS. Unless a bankruptcy proceeding has begun, no action can be brought before the expiration of six months from the date of filing the refund claim unless the IRS renders a decision on the claim before the six months are up. In bankruptcy proceedings, the six-month period is reduced to 120 days.

References are to Standard Federal Tax Reports; Tax Research Consultant; and Practical Tax Explanations.

[134] ¶ 42,477; LITIG: 6,960
[135] ¶ 42,500; LITIG: 6,966
[136] ¶ 43,282.20; IRS: 12,354
[137] ¶ 41,571; LITIG: 9,050
[138] ¶ 41,555; LITIG: 9,210
[139] ¶ 41,560, ¶ 41,589; LITIG: 9,052
[140] ¶ 41,685; LITIG: 9,056
[141] ¶ 41,685; LITIG: 3,102, LITIG: 9,106
[142] ¶ 40,001; LITIG: 9,058; § 40,010.25

2794. Supreme Court. Either party may seek a review of a U.S. Court of Appeals decision by the U.S. Supreme Court through a petition for a writ of certiorari (Code Sec. 7482(a); Judicial Code Sec. 2101)[143]

2796. Attorneys' Fees and Court Costs. A "prevailing party"—any party (other than the United States or a creditor of the taxpayer) who has substantially prevailed with respect to the amount in controversy or the most significant issue or issues—may be awarded reasonable litigation costs in most civil tax litigation, including declaratory judgment proceedings (Code Sec. 7430).[144] In addition, a prevailing party can recover reasonable administrative costs incurred in connection with such administrative proceeding with the IRS.

These awards may be made if the taxpayer meets certain net worth limitations and the IRS fails to prove that its position was substantially justified. When litigation costs are involved, the IRS's position is the government's position taken in the litigation proceeding or administratively by the IRS District Counsel. In the case of administrative costs, the IRS's position is the position taken as of the earlier of (1) the date the taxpayer received a decision notice from the IRS Office of Appeals or (2) the date of the deficiency notice.

Reasonable administrative costs include (1) administrative fees or similar charges imposed by the IRS, and (2) the reasonable expenses incurred with respect to compensating expert witnesses, financing necessary studies and reports, and paying attorneys' fees. The costs can only be awarded if incurred after the earlier of:

(1) the date the taxpayer received the decision notice from the IRS Office of Appeals,

(2) the date of the deficiency notice, or

(3) the date on which the first letter of proposed deficiency is sent that allows the taxpayer an opportunity for administrative review in the IRS Office of Appeals.

Reasonable litigation costs include:

(1) expenses of expert witnesses;

(2) costs of any study, analysis, engineering report, test, or project, which was found by the court to be necessary for the preparation of its case;

(3) fees of an individual authorized to practice before the court or the IRS, whether or not an attorney (generally not in excess of $180 per hour for 2012 and $190 for 2013), unless an affidavit is presented that establishes a special factor for a higher rate, such as the unavailability of qualified representatives at the customary rate; and

(4) court costs.

To be recoverable, litigation costs must generally be paid or incurred by the taxpayer. However, a taxpayer may recover costs paid by a third party if the taxpayer assumes either a noncontingent obligation to repay the advanced fees or a contingent obligation to repay the fees in the event of their eventual recovery (*B.F. Morrison*, CA-9, 2009-1 USTC ¶ 50,387).

For purposes of both reasonable administrative costs and reasonable litigation costs, reasonable attorneys' fees may be awarded to attorneys and specified persons who represent prevailing parties on a pro bono basis or for a nominal fee. Thus, the amount awarded may be more than the amount of fees actually paid or incurred. The award must be paid to the attorney or the attorney's employer.

In order to establish that the taxpayer was a prevailing party, the taxpayer needs to establish that he has substantially prevailed with respect to the amount in controversy or with respect to the most significant issue or set of issues presented (Code Sec.

References are to Standard Federal Tax Reports; Tax Research Consultant; and Practical Tax Explanations.

[143] ¶ 41,583, ¶ 42,440; LITIG: 6,954

[144] ¶ 41,740; LITIG: 3,150; § 41,230.05

7430(c)(4); Reg. §301.7430-5).[145] A taxpayer who meets the timely filing and net worth requirements may be treated as a prevailing party if the taxpayer's liability is determined to be equal to or less than it would have been had the government accepted the taxpayer's last qualified offer to settle the case (including interest). A qualified offer is a written offer made at any time during the time from the issuance of the 30-day letter to a date 30 days before the date the case is first set for trial (Code Sec. 7430(g); Reg. §301.7430-7).[146]

No costs will be awarded where the prevailing party failed to exhaust all of the administrative remedies within the IRS (Code Sec. 7430(b); Reg. §301.7430-1).[147] The tender of a qualified settlement offer (see preceding paragraph) does not satisfy the requirement to exhaust all administrative remedies (*Haas & Associates Accounting Corporation*, 117 TC 48, aff'd CA-9, 2003-1 USTC ¶ 50,253). Further, costs will be denied for any portion of the proceeding where the prevailing party caused unreasonable delay (Code Sec. 7430(b)(4)).[148] A taxpayer who prevails in an IRS proceeding must apply to the IRS for administrative costs before the 91st day after the date the final IRS determination of tax, interest or penalty was mailed to the taxpayer. If the IRS denies the application for costs, the taxpayer must petition the Tax Court within 90 days of the IRS mailing of the denial.

An order granting or denying an award for litigation costs becomes part of the decision or judgment in the case and is subject to appeal in the same manner as the decision or judgment (Code Sec. 7430(f)).[149]

2798. Suit for Damages in Connection with Collection of Tax. A taxpayer may bring a suit in federal district court for damages sustained in connection with the collection of any federal tax because an IRS employee recklessly or intentionally disregarded any provision of the Internal Revenue Code, any IRS regulations or certain provisions of the Bankruptcy Code (Code Sec. 7433; Reg. §301.7433-1).[150] A suit may also be brought for negligent disregard of the Internal Revenue Code or any IRS regulations. Except as provided in Code Sec. 7432 relating to damage awards for failure to release liens (¶ 2755), this action is the taxpayer's exclusive remedy for recovering damages caused by reckless, intentional or negligent disregard of such provisions and regulations by IRS employees. The suit must be brought within two years after the right of action accrues.

The award is limited to the costs of the action plus any actual direct economic damages sustained by the taxpayer, up to a maximum award of $1 million for reckless or intentional actions and $100,000 for acts of negligence. The IRS must comply with certain provisions of the Fair Debt Collection Practices Act so that the treatment of tax debtors by the IRS is at least equal to that required of private sector debt collectors (Code Sec. 6304). Taxpayers may bring a damages action under Code Sec. 7433 against the IRS for violations of these provisions.

References are to Standard Federal Tax Reports; Tax Research Consultant; and Practical Tax Explanations.

[145] ¶ 41,740, ¶ 41,742E, ¶ 41,742H; LITIG: 3,154; §41,230.15

[146] ¶ 41,740, ¶ 41,742H; LITIG: 3,154; §41,230.15

[147] ¶ 41,740, ¶ 41,742; LITIG: 3,150; §41,230.20

[148] ¶ 41,740; LITIG: 3,154; §41,230.30

[149] ¶ 41,740; LITIG: 3,158; §41,230.40

[150] ¶ 41,770, ¶ 41,771; IRS: 45,114; §39,950

Chapter 28

PENALTIES □ INTEREST

Failure to File Returns or Pay Tax

2801. Failure to File Returns. A failure to file any tax return within the time prescribed by the Code may result in an addition to tax. The penalty is 5 percent of the unpaid tax shown on the return, up to 25 percent. If the tax return is not filed within 60 days of the prescribed due date (including extensions), the penalty will not be less than the lesser of $135 or 100 percent of the tax due on the return (Code Sec. 6651(a)).[1] The late-filing addition runs for the period up to the date the IRS actually receives the late return (Rev. Rul. 73-133).[2] The penalty is computed only on the net amount of tax due, if any, on the return after credit has been given for amounts paid through withholding, estimated tax and any other credits claimed on the return (Code Sec. 6651(b); Reg. § 301.6651-1(a), (b) and (d)).[3]

The fraud and accuracy-related penalties (¶ 2854) do not apply in the case of a fraudulent failure to file a return. Instead, the failure-to-file penalty is increased to 15 percent for each month, up to 75 percent (Code Sec. 6651(f)).[4]

The failure-to-file penalty is not imposed when the taxpayer can show that the failure to file was due to reasonable cause and not to willful neglect. Mere absence of willful neglect is not "reasonable cause."[5] "Reasonable cause" did not exist when: (1) the taxpayer relied upon the advice of an agent; (2) the taxpayer relied on the accountant to perform the purely ministerial function of filing;[6] or (3) an officer of the corporate taxpayer misjudged the extension date.[7] However, failure to file a return upon a lawyer's or certified public accountant's advice that there was no income to report, or that the taxpayer was not liable for tax, has been held to be reasonable cause when the taxpayer supplied complete information to the tax professional.[8]

2805. Failure to Pay Tax. A penalty is imposed for failure to pay, when due, those taxes (other than estimated taxes) shown by a taxpayer on his return, unless the failure is due to reasonable cause (Code Sec. 6651(a)(2)).[9] The same penalty is imposed on additional taxes determined to be due on audit for which the IRS has made a demand for payment, but this penalty runs only for the period of nonpayment beginning after the 21st *calendar* day (10th *business* day if the amount demanded is at least $100,000)

References are to Standard Federal Tax Reports; Tax Research Consultant; and Practical Tax Explanations.

[1] ¶ 39,470; PENALTY: 3,050; § 40,205.15

[2] ¶ 39,475.33; PENALTY: 3,050; § 40,205.15

[3] ¶ 39,470, ¶ 39,472; PENALTY: 3,050; § 40,205.15

[4] ¶ 39,470, ¶ 39,475.022; PENALTY: 3,050; § 40,205.15

[5] ¶ 39,475.34; PENALTY: 3,060; § 40,205.15

[6] ¶ 39,475.42, ¶ 39,475.72; PENALTY: 3,060; § 40,205.15

[7] ¶ 39,475.705; PENALTY: 3,060; § 40,205.15

[8] ¶ 39,475.41, ¶ 39,475.68; PENALTY: 3,060; § 40,205.15

[9] ¶ 39,470; PENALTY: 3,062; § 40,205.20

following the demand (Code Sec. 6651(a)(3)). The addition to tax is one-half of one percent of the tax not paid, for each month (or part of a month) it remains unpaid, up to a maximum of 25 percent. The penalty increases to one percent per month beginning with either the 10th day after notice of levy is given or the day on which notice and demand is made in the case of a jeopardy assessment. For taxpayers who enter into installment agreements with the IRS, the penalty for failure to timely pay taxes is reduced to one-quarter of one percent of the tax not paid (Code Sec. 6651(h); Reg. § 301.6651-1(a)(4)). If a taxpayer files a late return that is subject to both the failure-to-file and failure-to-pay penalties, the former may be reduced by the latter. However, if no return is filed or if a late-filed return understates the amount required to be shown on the return, the failure-to-pay penalty attributable to additional tax demanded by the IRS may not be used to offset any portion of the failure-to-file penalty. If the penalty for failure to file beyond 60 days applies, the penalty may not be reduced by a failure-to-pay penalty that is also imposed below the lesser of $135 or 100 percent of the tax due (Code Sec. 6651(a), (c), and (d)).

2809. Automatic Extension of Time for Filing. An automatic extension of time to file a tax return (¶ 2509) is not an extension of time to pay the tax due under the return (Reg. §§ 1.6081-3(c) and 1.6081-4(b)).[10] However, an individual taxpayer can avoid a failure-to-pay penalty by making an estimate of the tax due and paying that estimate (reduced by any amounts already paid through withholding or estimated tax payments over the course of the tax year) with the request for extension of time to file. If the balance of tax due is remitted when the income tax return is filed, no penalty for failure to pay will apply unless the unpaid amount is more than 10 percent of the total tax liability. Similar rules apply for corporations (Reg. § 301.6651-1(c)(3) and (4)).[11]

2811. Frivolous Return Penalty. In addition to other penalties that may be imposed, there is a $5,000 penalty for filing a frivolous return. A frivolous return is one that omits information necessary to determine the taxpayer's tax liability, shows a substantially incorrect tax, is based upon a frivolous position (e.g., that wages are not income), or is based upon the taxpayer's desire to impede the collection of tax. The IRS periodically updates a list of frivolous positions. The most recent list appears in Notice 2010-33. For example, a return based on the taxpayer's altering or striking out the "penalty of perjury" language above the signature line constitutes a frivolous return (Code Sec. 6702).[12]

2813. Abatement of Penalties and/or Interest. The IRS must abate certain penalties that result from reliance on incorrect IRS advice if (1) the advice was furnished in writing in response to a specific written request from the taxpayer and (2) the taxpayer reasonably relied upon the advice (Code Sec. 6404(f)).[13] However, penalties will be abated only if the taxpayer furnished adequate and accurate information in making the request. Taxpayers entitled to abatement should file Form 843 with copies of the relevant written documents attached (Reg. § 301.6404-3(d)).[14]

If the IRS extends the due date for filing income tax returns and for paying any tax due for taxpayers located in a federally declared disaster area, the IRS will abate the interest that would otherwise accrue for the extension period (Code Sec. 6404(h)).[15]

The accrual of interest and penalties will be suspended after 36 months unless the IRS sends the taxpayer a notice within 36 months following the later of: (1) the original due date of the return (without regard to extensions) or (2) the date on which a timely return is filed (Code Sec. 6404(g)).[16] The suspension of interest and penalties is

References are to Standard Federal Tax Reports; Tax Research Consultant; and Practical Tax Explanations.

[10] ¶ 36,790, ¶ 36,793; FILEBUS: 15,102; § 39,215.05

[11] ¶ 39,472; PENALTY: 3,062; § 39,215.10

[12] ¶ 40,040, ¶ 40,043.60, ¶ 40,043.70; PENALTY: 3,250; § 40,220.10

[13] ¶ 38,570; IRS: 33,400; § 40,250.15

[14] ¶ 38,576; IRS: 33,400; § 40,250.15

[15] ¶ 38,570; PENALTY: 9,056; § 39,215.35

[16] ¶ 38,570; PENALTY: 3,350, PENALTY: 9,056; § 40,030.30, § 40,250.10

available only for individuals and only for income taxes. Although the suspension pertains only to tax that is related to timely filed returns (i.e., returns filed by the original due date or by the extended due date), the IRS has expanded this rule to cover additional tax voluntarily reported by a taxpayer, after a timely original return has been filed, on an amended return or in correspondence with the IRS (Rev. Rul. 2005-4). The suspension begins on the day after the end of the 36-month period and ends on the day that is 21 days after the date on which the notice is made. The suspension does not stop the accrual of:

(1) the failure-to-pay and failure-to-file penalties;

(2) any interest, penalty or other addition to tax in a case involving fraud;

(3) any interest, penalty, addition to tax, or additional amount with respect to any tax liability shown on the return;

(4) any interest, penalty or other addition to tax with respect to any gross misstatement;

(5) any interest, penalty or other addition to tax with respect to any reportable avoidance transaction or listed transaction (pertaining to tax shelters); or

(6) any criminal penalty.

Document and Information Return Penalties

2814. Information Reporting Penalties. Three categories of penalties apply to failures to file required information returns and payee statements:

(1) failure to file an information return or to include correct information on an information return (¶ 2816) (Code Sec. 6721);

(2) failure to file a payee statement or to include correct information on a payee statement (¶ 2823) (Code Sec. 6722); and

(3) failure to comply with other information reporting requirements, which includes all reporting failures not covered by the other two categories (¶ 2833) (Code Sec. 6723).

2816. Failure to File Correct Information Returns. A time-sensitive three-tier penalty structure is imposed for (1) any failure (other than a failure due to reasonable cause and not to willful neglect) to file correct information returns (¶ 2565) with the IRS on or before the required filing date, (2) any failure to include all the information required to be shown on a return, or (3) the inclusion of incorrect information (Code Sec. 6721(a)).[17] The penalty applies also to any failure to file electronically, when required, but is imposed only on the number of returns exceeding 250 (Code Sec. 6724(c)).[18] The penalty amounts for each of the prescribed time periods are as follows (Code Sec. 6721):

(1) If a person files a correct information return after the required filing date but on or before the date that is 30 days after the required filing date, the amount of the penalty is $30 per return ("first-tier penalty"), with a maximum penalty of $250,000 per calendar year ($75,000 for "small businesses," i.e., firms with gross receipts of not more than $5 million).

(2) If a person files a correct information return after the date that is 30 days after the prescribed filing date but on or before August 1 of the calendar year in which the required filing date occurs, the amount of the penalty is $60 per return ("second-tier penalty"), with a maximum penalty of $500,000 per calendar year ($200,000 for small businesses).

(3) If a correct information return is not filed on or before August 1 of any year, the amount of the penalty is $100 per return ("third-tier penalty"), with a maximum penalty of $1,500,000 per calendar year ($500,000 for small businesses).

References are to Standard Federal Tax Reports; Tax Research Consultant; and Practical Tax Explanations.

[17] ¶ 40,210; PENALTY: 3,202; § 40,305.10

[18] ¶ 40,275; PENALTY: 3,202; § 40,305.10

A certain *de minimis* number of returns timely filed with incorrect or omitted information that are corrected on or before August 1 of the calendar year in which the returns are due will be treated as having been filed correctly, and no penalty will be imposed on them. This exception is limited to the greater of (1) 10 returns or (2) one-half of one percent of the total number of information returns required to be filed during the calendar year. The *de minimis* exception does not apply to a failure to file an information return (Code Sec. 6721(c)).

If the failure to file an information return or to include all the required correct information is due to intentional disregard of the filing requirements, neither the three-tier penalty nor the *de minimis* exception will apply. Instead, the penalty for each failure is the greater of:

(1) $250; or

(2) 10 percent of the aggregate amount of the items required to be reported correctly in the case of a return other than a return required under Code Sec. 6045(a) (brokers' transactions with customers), Code Sec. 6041A(b) (payments of remuneration for direct sales), Code Sec. 6050H (information on mortgage interest received in a trade or business from individuals), Code Sec. 6050I (information on cash receipts from a trade or business), Code Sec. 6050J (information on foreclosures and abandonments of security), Code Sec. 6050K (information on exchanges of certain partnership interests), or Code Sec. 6050L (information on certain dispositions of donated property).

The penalty equals the greater of $250 or five percent for returns required under Code Sec. 6045(a), Code Sec. 6050K, or Code Sec. 6050L. In the case of a return required under Code Sec. 6050I(a) (cash receipts of more than $10,000 in a trade or business), the penalty equals the greater of $25,000 or the amount of cash received in the transaction, up to a maximum of $100,000. In addition, the intentional disregard penalties are not considered in figuring the yearly maximum penalty of $1,500,000 for failures not attributable to intentional disregard (Code Sec. 6721(e)).

No penalty is imposed for inconsequential omissions and inaccuracies that do not prevent or hinder the IRS from adequately processing the return. Errors and omissions that relate to a taxpayer identification number, to the surname of a person required to receive a copy of the information provided, or to any monetary amounts are never considered inconsequential (Code Sec. 6721(c); Reg. § 301.6721-1(c)).

The information return penalties are to be adjusted for inflation every five years, beginning after 2012 (Code Sec. 6721(f)). Thus, the first inflation adjustments will be due in 2017.

2823. Failure to Furnish Correct Payee Statement. The statutory structure of the penalties for failure to timely furnish a correct payee statement resembles the three-tier Code Sec. 6721 penalties for failure to timely file a correct information return, including reduced maximum penalties for "small businesses" (¶ 2816) (Code Sec. 6722).[19] The penalty regime is as follows:

(1) If a person furnishes a correct payee statement up to 30 days after the required due date, the amount of the first-tier penalty is $30 per statement, with a maximum penalty of $250,000 per calendar year ($75,000 for small businesses).

(2) If a person furnishes a correct payee statement more than 30 days after the prescribed filing date but on or before August 1 of the calendar year in which the required filing date occurs, the amount of the second-tier penalty is $60 per return, with a maximum penalty of $500,000 per calendar year ($200,000 for small businesses).

References are to Standard Federal Tax Reports; Tax Research Consultant; and Practical Tax Explanations.

[19] ¶ 40,230; PENALTY: 3,204; § 40,305.15

(3) If a correct payee statement is not furnished on or before August 1 of any year, the amount of the third-tier penalty is $100 per return, with a maximum penalty of $1,500,000 per calendar year ($500,000 for small businesses).

Payee statements include the following:

(1) information-at-source payments under Code Sec. 6041(d);

(2) payments in connection with services and direct sales under Code Sec. 6041A(e);

(3) taxable mergers and acquisitions under Code Sec. 6043A;

(4) brokers under Code Sec. 6045(b) or (d);

(5) certain stock options under Code Sec. 6039(a);

(6) group-term life insurance under Code Sec. 6052(b);

(7) catch shares of certain fishing boat crews under Code Sec. 6050A(b);

(8) income tax withheld from employees' wages under Code Sec. 6051;

(9) tip income reportable by employers under Code Sec. 6053(b) or (c);

(10) mortgage interest payments under Code Sec. 6050H(d);

(11) cash payments in excess of $10,000 under Code Sec. 6050I(e), (g)(4) or (g)(5);

(12) foreclosures and abandonments under Code Sec. 6050J(e);

(13) exchanges of certain partnership interests under Code Sec. 6050K(b);

(14) certain dispositions of donated property under Code Sec. 6050L(c);

(15) pass-through income, deductions, etc., to partners under Code Sec. 6031(b) or (c), to beneficiaries of estates and trusts under Code Sec. 6034A, and to S corporation shareholders under Code Sec. 6037(b);

(16) payments of royalties under Code Sec. 6050N(b);

(17) statements relating to returns regarding payments of dividends and corporate earnings and profits under Code Sec. 6042(c);

(18) statements regarding payments of patronage dividends under Code Sec. 6044(e);

(19) statements regarding interest payments under Code Sec. 6049(c);

(20) statements relating to the cancellation of indebtedness by certain financial entities under Code Sec. 6050P(d);

(21) payments for certain purchases of fish for resale under Code Sec. 6050R;

(22) distributions from individual retirement accounts under Code Sec. 408(i) and from employee benefit plans under Code Sec. 6047(d);

(23) payments relating to qualified tuition and related expenses under Code Sec. 6050S;

(24) returns relating to certain company-owned life insurance held by a natural person where a trade or business is directly or indirectly the beneficiary under the policy under Code Sec. 264(f)(5)(A)(iv);

(25) charges or payments for qualified long-term insurance contracts under combined arrangements (Code Sec. 6050U);

(26) effective on January 1, 2011, statements to brokers relating to the transfer of covered securities under Code Sec. 6045A (however, see below, regarding transitional relief for 2011); and

(27) effective on January 1, 2011, statements relating to organizational actions affecting basis of specified securities under Code Sec. 6045B.

Note that, regarding (26), above, the IRS has provided transitional relief for certain 2011 transfers (Notice 2010-67). As per that relief, the IRS will not assert penalties for a failure to furnish a transfer statement under Code Sec. 6045A for any transfer of stock in

2011 that is not incidental to the stock's purchase or sale using a cash-on-delivery account or multiple broker arrangement (as described in Reg. § 1.6045A-1(a)(1)(ii)). Further, a receiving broker may treat this stock as a noncovered security.

Note, further, that, regarding (27), above, the IRS has provided transitional relief for corporations that must report any organizational action occurring in 2011 that affects the basis of stock. The IRS will not assert penalties for failure to timely file an issuer return with the IRS before the transitional deadline of January 17, 2012 (Notice 2011-18). An issuer is allowed to report an organizational action by posting either Form 8937 or the required information in a readily accessible format to an issuer's primary public website. Penalties will not be imposed for reporting incorrect information against issuers related to filing and furnishing Form 8937 for 2011 organizational actions, provided that they make a good-faith effort in timely posting the Form 8937 or the required information on the issuers's primary public website or filing accurate Forms 8937 and furnishing the corresponding issuer statements (Notice 2012-11).

In the case of intentional disregard of the requirements with respect to payee statements, the penalty imposed is identical to that for failures to file an information return or to include correct information (¶ 2816). Similarly, the intentional disregard penalty is not considered in applying the yearly maximum penalty of $1,500,000 for failures not attributable to intentional disregard (Code Sec. 6722(e)). In addition, the exception from the imposition of the penalty (Reg. § 301.6721-1(c)) in the case of inconsequential omissions and inaccuracies on a payee statement applies (¶ 2816).

The payee statement penalties are to be adjusted for inflation every five years, beginning after 2012 (Code Sec. 6722(f)). Thus, the first inflation adjustments will be due in 2017.

2833. Failure to Comply with Other Information Reporting Requirements. A penalty of $50, up to a maximum of $100,000 for a calendar year, is imposed for each failure to comply with any specified information reporting requirement on or before the prescribed time (Code Sec. 6723).[20] The penalty will not be imposed if it can be shown that the failure was due to reasonable cause and not to willful neglect.

The specified information reporting requirements that are subject to the penalty include:

(1) the requirement that a transferor of an interest in a partnership promptly give notice to the partnership concerning the transfer;

(2) the requirement that a person include his taxpayer identification number (TIN) on any return, statement, or other document (other than an information return or payee statement), furnish his TIN to another person, or include the TIN of another person on any return, statement, or other document made with respect to that person;

(3) the requirement on returns reporting alimony payments that the TIN of the payee be furnished to the payor or that the payee's TIN be included on the payor's return;

(4) the requirement that a person include the TIN of any dependent on his return; and

(5) the requirement that a person who deducts qualified residence interest under Code Sec. 163 on any seller-provided financing include the name, address, and TIN of the person to whom such interest is paid or accrued (Code Sec. 6724(d)(3)).[21]

Underpayments of Tax—Interest

2838. Interest on Underpayment of Tax. Interest on underpayments of tax is imposed at the federal short-term rate plus three percentage points (Code Sec.

References are to Standard Federal Tax Reports; Tax Research Consultant; and Practical Tax Explanations.

[20] ¶ 40,250; PENALTY: 3,204; § 40,305.20

[21] ¶ 40,275; PENALTY: 3,204; § 40,305.20

6621(a)(2)). The interest rates, which are adjusted quarterly, are determined during the first month of a calendar quarter and become effective for the following quarter.

Interest accrues from the date the payment was due (determined without regard to any extensions of time) until it is received by the IRS, although no underpayment interest accrues for failure to timely pay individual or corporate estimated tax. Interest is compounded daily (Code Sec. 6601).[22] For 2012, the interest rate on underpayments for all four quarters was 3 percent.[23]

If a carryback of a net operating loss, net capital loss, or other credit carryback eliminates or reduces a deficiency otherwise due for such earlier year, the taxpayer remains liable for interest on unpaid income taxes (including deficiencies later assessed by the IRS) for the carryback year. The entire amount of the deficiency will be subject to interest from the last date prescribed for payment of the income tax of the carryback year up to the due date (excluding extensions) for filing the return for the tax year in which the loss or credit occurred (Code Sec. 6601(d); Reg. § 301.6601-1(e)).[24]

Large Corporate Tax Underpayments. Interest on large underpayments of tax by corporations is imposed at the federal short-term rate plus five percentage points (Code Sec. 6621(c)(1); Reg. § 301.6621-3).[25] A large corporate underpayment is any tax underpayment by a C corporation that exceeds $100,000 for any tax period. For purposes of determining the $100,000 threshold, underpayments of different types of taxes (for example, income and employment taxes) as well as underpayments relating to different tax periods are not added together. The tax period is the tax year in the case of income tax or, in the case of any other tax, the period to which the underpayment relates (Code Sec. 6621(c)(3)).

The interest rate applies to time periods after the 30th day after the earlier of (1) the date the IRS sends the first letter of proposed deficiency that allows the taxpayer an opportunity for administrative review in the IRS Office of Appeals (a 30-day letter) or (2) the date the IRS sends a deficiency notice under Code Sec. 6212 (a 90-day letter) (¶ 2778). The 30-day period does not begin unless the underpayment shown in the letter or notice exceeds $100,000 (Code Sec. 6621(c)(2)).[26] An IRS notice that is later withdrawn because it was issued in error will not trigger the higher rate of interest on large corporate underpayments. If the underpayment is not subject to deficiency payments, the 30-day period begins to run following the sending of any letter or notice by the IRS that notifies the taxpayer of the assessment or proposed assessment of the tax. A letter or notice is disregarded if the full amount shown as due is paid during the 30-day period. For 2012, the interest rate on large corporate underpayments for all four quarters was 5 percent.[27]

Overlapping Overpayments and Underpayments. The interest rates for overpayments and underpayments have been equalized (sometimes referred to as "global interest netting") for any period of mutual indebtedness between taxpayers and the IRS (¶ 2765).

Abatement of Interest. The IRS has the authority to abate interest in cases where the additional interest was caused by IRS errors or delays (Code Sec. 6404(e)). However, the IRS may act only if there was an error or delay in performing either a ministerial act or a managerial act (including loss of records by the IRS, transfers of IRS personnel, extended illness, extended personnel training, or extended leave) and only if the abatement relates to a tax of the type for which a notice of deficiency is required. Such taxes would be those relating to income, generation-skipping transfers, estate, gift, and certain excise taxes, but not employment taxes or other excise taxes.

Taxpayers requesting an abatement of interest generally must file a separate Form 843 for each tax period for each type of tax with the IRS Service Center where their tax

References are to Standard Federal Tax Reports; Tax Research Consultant; and Practical Tax Explanations.

[22] ¶ 39,410, ¶ 39,412, ¶ 39,450, ¶ 39,460; PENALTY: 9,050; § 40,105.05

[23] ¶ 175.01; PENALTY: 9,152; § 40,105

[24] ¶ 39,410, ¶ 39,412; PENALTY: 9,056; § 40,105.15

[25] ¶ 39,450, ¶ 39,453; PENALTY: 9,152; § 40,120.05

[26] ¶ 39,450; PENALTY: 9,152; § 40,120.05

[27] ¶ 175.01; PENALTY: 9,152.05; § 40,120

return was filed or, if unknown, with the Service Center where their most recent tax return was filed.

Suspension of Interest. In order to avoid the accrual of underpayment interest, a taxpayer may make a cash deposit with the IRS for future application against an underpayment of income, gift, estate, generation-skipping or certain excise taxes that have not been assessed at the time of the deposit (Code Sec. 6603; Rev. Proc. 2005-18).[28] To the extent that a deposit is used by the IRS to pay a tax liability, the tax is treated as paid when the deposit is made and no interest underpayment is imposed. Furthermore, if the dispute is resolved in favor of the taxpayer or the taxpayer withdraws the deposited money before resolution of the dispute, interest is payable on the deposit at the federal short-term rate.

2845. Interest on Additions and Penalties. Interest on penalties and additions to tax for failure to file, for failure to pay the stamp tax, and for the accuracy-related and fraud penalties (¶ 2854 and ¶ 2866) will be imposed for the period beginning on the due date of the return (including extensions) and ending on the date of payment. However, if payment is made within 21 calendar days after notice and demand is made (10 *business* days if the amount demanded is at least $100,000), then interest will stop running after the date of notice and demand. For all other penalties, interest will be imposed only if the addition to tax or penalty is not paid within the 21- or 10-day period after notice and demand is made and then only for the period from the date of notice and demand to the date of payment (Code Sec. 6601(e)).[29] For rules governing the allocation of interest on tax liabilities paid pursuant to a compromise or partial payment, see ¶ 2723 and ¶ 2724, respectively.

Underpayments of Tax—Penalties

2854. Accuracy-Related Penalty. The two penalties primarily applicable to underpayments of tax are the accuracy-related penalty (Code Sec. 6662)[30] and the fraud penalty (¶ 2866) (Code Sec. 6663).[31]

The accuracy-related penalty consolidates all of the penalties relating to the accuracy of tax returns. It is equal to 20 percent of the portion of the underpayment that is attributable to one or more of the following: (1) negligence or disregard of rules or regulations (¶ 2856), (2) substantial understatement of income tax (¶ 2858), (3) substantial valuation misstatement (¶ 2860), (4) substantial overstatements of pension liabilities (¶ 2862), (5) substantial estate or gift tax valuation understatement (¶ 2862A); and (6) applicable to transactions entered into after March 30, 2010, transactions lacking economic substance (¶ 2863) (Code Sec. 6662(a) and (b)).[32] In addition, a 40-percent accuracy-related penalty is imposed for an underpayment of tax that is attributable to an undisclosed foreign financial asset understatement (¶ 2864) (Code Sec. 6662(b)(7) and (j)).

The accuracy-related penalty is entirely separate from the failure-to-file penalty (¶ 2801) and will not be imposed if no return, other than a return prepared by the IRS when a person fails to make a required return, is filed (Code Sec. 6664(b)).[33] In addition, the accuracy-related penalty will not apply to any portion of a tax underpayment on which the fraud penalty is imposed. Also, with the exception of the penalty for underpayments attributable to transactions lacking economic substance, no penalty is imposed with respect to any portion of any underpayment if the taxpayer shows that there was reasonable cause for the underpayment and that the taxpayer acted in good faith (Code Sec. 6664(c)).[34]

References are to Standard Federal Tax Reports; Tax Research Consultant; and Practical Tax Explanations.

[28] ¶ 39,426, ¶ 39,428.20; IRS: 36,056.25; § 40,110.15

[29] ¶ 39,410; PENALTY: 9,060; § 40,105.05

[30] ¶ 39,651; PENALTY: 3,100; § 40,210.05

[31] ¶ 39,656; PENALTY: 6,100; § 40,215.05

[32] ¶ 39,651; PENALTY: 3,102; § 40,210.05

[33] ¶ 39,660; PENALTY: 3,102; § 40,210.05

[34] ¶ 39,660; PENALTY: 3,102; § 40,210.40

2856. Negligence or Disregard of Rules and Regulations. If any part of an underpayment of tax is due to negligence or careless, reckless, or intentional disregard of rules and regulations, the 20-percent accuracy-related penalty will be imposed on that portion of the underpayment attributable to the negligence or intentional disregard of rules and regulations (Code Sec. 6662(a) and (c)).[35] Negligence includes the failure to reasonably comply with tax laws, to exercise reasonable care in preparing a tax return, to keep adequate books and records, or to substantiate items properly (Reg. § 1.6662-3(b)(1)).[36] Taxpayers may not avoid the negligence penalty merely by adequately disclosing a return position which is "not frivolous" on Form 8275 or Form 8275-R (Conference Committee Report to P.L. 103-66).[37]

2858. Substantial Understatement of Income Tax. The IRS may impose the 20-percent accuracy-related penalty when there is a substantial understatement of income tax. A substantial understatement exists when the understatement for the year exceeds the greater of (1) 10 percent of the tax required to be shown on the return (including self-employment tax) or (2) $5,000. In the case of corporations (other than S corporations or personal holding companies), a substantial understatement exists when the understatement exceeds the lesser of (1) 10 percent of the tax required to be shown on the return (or, if greater, $10,000) or (2) $10,000,000 (Code Sec. 6662(d)).[38]

Taxpayers generally may avoid all or part of the penalty by showing:

(a) that they acted in good faith and there was reasonable cause for the understatement,

(b) that the understatement was based on substantial authority, or

(c) if there was a reasonable basis for the tax treatment of an item, the relevant facts affecting the item's tax treatment were adequately disclosed on Form 8275 (Form 8275-R for return positions contrary to regulations) (Code Secs. 6662(d)(2) and 6664(c); Reg. § 1.6662-4(d), (e), and (f)).[39]

Substantial authority generally means that the likelihood that a taxpayer's position is correct is somewhere between 50 percent and the more lenient reasonable basis standard used in applying the negligence penalty. The disclosure exception does not apply to tax shelter items. Further, a corporation does not have a reasonable basis for its tax treatment of an item attributable to a multi-party financing transaction if the treatment does not clearly reflect the income of the corporation. Some items may be disclosed on the taxpayer's return, instead of on Form 8275 (Rev. Proc. 2012-15).

Only the following are authority for purposes of determining whether a position is supported by substantial authority:

(1) the Internal Revenue Code and other statutory provisions,

(2) proposed, temporary, and final regulations construing the statutes,

(3) revenue rulings and procedures,

(4) tax treaties and the regulations thereunder, and Treasury Department and other official explanations of such treaties,

(5) court cases,

(6) congressional intent as reflected in committee reports, joint explanatory statements of managers included in conference committee reports, and floor statements made prior to enactment by one of a bill's managers,

(7) General Explanations of tax legislation prepared by the Joint Committee on Taxation (the Blue Book),

References are to Standard Federal Tax Reports; Tax Research Consultant; and Practical Tax Explanations.

[35] ¶ 39,651; PENALTY: 3,106; § 40,210.15

[36] ¶ 39,651E; PENALTY: 3,106; § 40,210.15

[37] ¶ 39,651.45; PENALTY: 3,106; § 40,210.15

[38] ¶ 39,651; PENALTY: 3,108; § 40,210.20

[39] ¶ 39,651, ¶ 39,660, ¶ 39,651H; PENALTY: 3,108; § 40,210.20

(8) private letter rulings and technical advice memoranda issued after October 31, 1976,

(9) actions on decisions and general counsel memoranda issued after March 12, 1981 (as well as general counsel memoranda published in pre-1955 volumes of the Cumulative Bulletin),

(10) IRS information and press releases, and

(11) notices, announcements, and other administrative pronouncements published by the IRS in the Internal Revenue Bulletin (Reg. § 1.6662-4(d)(3)(iii)).[40]

2860. Substantial Valuation Misstatement. The 20-percent accuracy-related penalty is imposed on any portion of an underpayment resulting from any substantial income tax valuation misstatement. There is a substantial valuation misstatement if (1) the value of any property, or adjusted basis of any property, claimed on a tax return is 150 percent or more of the amount determined to be the correct amount of the valuation or the adjusted basis, (2) the price for any property, or use of property, or services in connection with any transaction between persons described in Code Sec. 482 is 200 percent or more, or 50 percent or less, of the correct Code Sec. 482 valuation, or (3) the net Code Sec. 482 transfer price adjustment exceeds the lesser of $5 million or 10 percent of the taxpayer's gross receipts (Code Sec. 6662(e)).

The penalty is doubled to 40 percent in cases of "gross valuation misstatements" where claimed value or adjusted basis exceeds the correct value or adjusted basis by 200 percent or more (Code Sec. 6662(h)). A gross valuation misstatement with respect to a controlled taxpayer transaction (Code Sec. 482) occurs if the price claimed exceeds 400 percent or more, or 25 percent or less, of the amount determined to be the correct price, or the net Code Sec. 482 transfer price adjustment for the year exceeds the lesser of $20 million or 20 percent of the taxpayer's gross receipts.

No penalty is imposed unless the portion of the underpayment attributable to the substantial valuation misstatement exceeds $5,000, or $10,000 in the case of corporations other than S corporations or personal holding companies (Code Sec. 6662(e)(2)).[41] The penalty will not be imposed if it is shown that there was reasonable cause for an underpayment and the taxpayer acted in good faith; however, there is no reasonable cause exception for underpayments due to gross valuation misstatements on charitable deduction property, although the exception still exists for substantial valuation misstatements on charitable deduction property and for gross valuation misstatements on property for which a charitable deduction is not being claimed (Code Sec. 6664(c)).[42]

2862. Substantial Overstatement of Pension Liabilities. The 20-percent accuracy-related penalty is imposed on any portion of any underpayment resulting from a substantial overstatement of pension liabilities. A substantial overstatement occurs if the actuarial determination of pension liabilities is 200 percent or more of the amount determined to be correct. The penalty is doubled to 40 percent of the underpayment if a portion of the substantial overstatement to which the penalty applies is attributable to a gross valuation misstatement of 400 percent or more. The penalty applies only if the portion of the underpayment attributable to the overstatement exceeds $1,000 (Code Sec. 6662(a), (f), and (h)).[43] The penalty will not be imposed if it is shown that there was a reasonable cause for an underpayment and the taxpayer acted in good faith (Code Sec. 6664(c)).[44]

2862A. Substantial Estate or Gift Tax Valuation Understatements. The 20-percent accuracy-related penalty applies to the portion of an underpayment that is due to a substantial estate or gift tax valuation understatement (Code Sec. 6662(b)(5), (g), and (h)).[45] There is a substantial estate or gift tax valuation understatement if the value of

References are to Standard Federal Tax Reports; Tax Research Consultant; and Practical Tax Explanations.

[40] ¶ 39,651H; PENALTY: 3,108; § 40,210.20

[41] ¶ 39,651; PENALTY: 3,110; § 40,210.25

[42] ¶ 39,660; PENALTY: 3,110; § 40,210.25

[43] ¶ 39,651; PENALTY: 3,112; § 40,210.30

[44] ¶ 39,660; PENALTY: 3,116; § 40,210.30

[45] ¶ 39,651; PENALTY: 3,114; § 40,210.35

any property claimed on any estate or gift tax return is 65 percent or less of the amount determined to be the correct amount of the valuation. However, the penalty is not imposed unless the portion of the underpayment attributable to the valuation understatements for the taxable period or for the estate of the decedent exceeds $5,000. The penalty is increased from 20 percent to 40 percent if the valuation understatement is a gross valuation misstatement. A valuation understatement is a gross valuation understatement if the value of any property claimed on any estate or gift tax return is 40 percent or less of the amount determined to be the correct amount of the valuation. The penalty will not be imposed if it is shown that there was a reasonable cause for an underpayment and the taxpayer acted in good faith (Code Sec. 6664(c)).[46]

2863. Underpayment Attributable to Transactions Lacking Economic Substance. Applicable to underpayments attributable to transactions entered into after March 30, 2010, a 20-percent accuracy-related penalty is imposed for an underpayment attributable to any disallowance of claimed tax benefits by reason of a transaction lacking economic substance, or failing to meet the requirements of any similar rule of law (Code Sec. 6662(b)(6)).[47] A transaction is treated as having economic substance if (1) apart from the federal income tax effects, it changes in a meaningful way the taxpayer's economic position, and (2) the taxpayer has a substantial purpose for entering into the transaction (Code Sec. 7701(o)).[48] Although the IRS will continue to rely on relevant case law handed down prior to the codification of the economic substance doctrine when applying the two-prong test, taxpayers may not rely on case law that treats a transaction as having economic substance unless the transaction satisfies *both* prongs of the test (Notice 2010-62).

The penalty is increased to 40 percent for an underpayment attributable to a "nondisclosed noneconomic substance transaction" (Code Sec. 6662(i)).[49] A nondisclosed noneconomic substance transaction is any portion of a transaction lacking economic substance with respect to which the relevant facts affecting the tax treatment are not adequately disclosed in the return or in a statement attached to the return. The determination of whether a position is a nondisclosed noneconomic substance transaction will generally be based on the return as originally filed or as amended by the taxpayer prior to being contacted by the IRS.

To satisfy the adequate disclosure requirements, the taxpayer must (1) disclose the relevant facts on a timely filed original return or a qualified amended return, (2) file Form 8275 or Form 8275-R, and (3) if the transaction is a reportable transaction (¶ 2001), satisfy all disclosure requirements under the Code Sec. 6011 regulations (¶ 2004) (Notice 2010-62).

No exceptions, including the reasonable cause exception, are available to the imposition of a penalty for any underpayment or reportable transaction understatement attributable to a transaction lacking economic substance (Code Sec. 6664(c)(2) and (d)(2)).

2864. Underpayment Attributable to Undisclosed Foreign Financial Assets. A 40-percent accuracy-related penalty is imposed for underpayment of tax that is attributable to an undisclosed foreign financial asset understatement (Code Sec. 6662(b)(7) and (j)).[50] For this purpose, an undisclosed foreign financial asset understatement for any tax year is the portion of the understatement for the year that is attributable to any transaction involving undisclosed foreign financial assets. An undisclosed foreign financial asset includes any asset that is subject to the information reporting requirements of Code Secs. 6038 (information reporting with respect to certain foreign corporations and partnerships), 6038B (notice of certain transfers to foreign persons), 6046A (returns as to interests in foreign partnerships), 6048 (information with respect to certain foreign

References are to Standard Federal Tax Reports; Tax Research Consultant; and Practical Tax Explanations.

[46] ¶ 39,660; PENALTY: 3,116; § 40,210.40

[47] ¶ 39,651; PENALTY: 3,122; § 40,210.36

[48] ¶ 43,080; PENALTY: 3,122; § 40,210.36

[49] ¶ 39,651; PENALTY: 3,122; § 40,210.36

[50] ¶ 39,651; PENALTY: 3,120; § 40,210.37

trusts) and 6038D (information with respect to foreign financial assets), but for which the required information was not provided by the taxpayer as required under the applicable reporting provisions.

2866. Fraud. The fraud penalty is imposed at the rate of 75 percent on the portion of any underpayment that is attributable to fraud (Code Sec. 6663).[51] The fraud penalty will not apply, however, if no return is filed other than a return prepared by the IRS when a person fails to make a required return (Code Sec. 6664(b)).[52] Although the failure-to-file penalty is entirely separate from the fraud penalty, in cases of a fraudulent failure to file, the failure-to-file penalty will be imposed at a higher rate (¶ 2801). If any portion is attributable to fraud, it is presumed that the entire underpayment is attributable to fraud, unless the taxpayer establishes otherwise by a preponderance of the evidence with respect to any item. The accuracy-related penalty will not apply to any portion of an underpayment on which the fraud penalty is imposed. The IRS must meet its burden of proof in establishing fraud by clear and convincing evidence (Code Sec. 6663(b)).[53]

2870. Tax Shelters. An accuracy-related penalty is provided for understatements resulting from listed and reportable transactions (Code Sec. 6662A).[54] The penalty applies to understatements attributable to (1) any listed transaction and (2) any reportable transaction with a significant tax avoidance purpose. "Listed transaction" and "reportable transaction" are defined by reference to the return disclosure requirements discussed in ¶ 2001. The accuracy-related penalty on understatements attributable to reportable transactions will not be imposed if the 40-percent penalty is imposed on an underpayment attributable to one or more undisclosed noneconomic substance transactions (¶ 2863).

Underpayments of Estimated Tax

2875. Addition to Tax for Underpayment of Estimated Tax by Individuals. An underpayment of estimated tax by an individual and most trusts and estates will result in imposition of an addition to tax equal to the interest that would accrue on the underpayment for the period of the underpayment (Code Sec. 6654(a)).[55] For the applicable rate of interest, see ¶ 2838. In determining the addition to tax for an underpayment of individual estimated tax, the federal short-term rate that applies during the third month following the tax year of the underpayment will also apply during the first 15 days of the fourth month following such tax year (Code Sec. 6621(b)(2)(B)).[56] Changes in the interest rate apply to amounts of underpayments outstanding on the date of change or arising thereafter (Reg. § 301.6621-1). An individual can avoid any penalty for underpayment of estimated tax by making payments as set forth in ¶ 2682. See ¶ 511 for the rules regarding trusts and estates.

2881. Waiver of Underpayment Penalty. The IRS is authorized to waive the penalty for underpayment of estimated tax if the underpayment is either due to casualty, disaster, or other unusual circumstances and the imposition of the penalty would be against equity and good conscience. The penalty may also be waived for an individual who retired after having attained age 62, or who became disabled, in the tax year for which the estimated payment was due or in the preceding tax year and the underpayment was due to reasonable cause and not to willful neglect (Code Sec. 6654(e)(3)).[57]

2889. "Underpayment" Form 2210. When insufficient estimated tax was paid during the year, the taxpayer should complete and attach Form 2210 (Form 2210-F for farmers and fishermen) to explain which test (¶ 2682) was met to avoid the addition to tax or, if no tests were met, how the amount of the addition to tax due was computed.

References are to Standard Federal Tax Reports; Tax Research Consultant; and Practical Tax Explanations.

[51] ¶ 39,656; PENALTY: 6,100; § 40,215

[52] ¶ 39,660; PENALTY: 6,112; § 40,215

[53] ¶ 39,656; PENALTY: 6,106, PENALTY: 6,158; § 40,215

[54] ¶ 39,665; PENALTY: 3,252

[55] ¶ 39,550; FILEIND: 21,050; § 40,225.10

[56] ¶ 39,450; FILEIND: 21,056; § 40,225.10

[57] ¶ 39,550; FILEIND: 21,056; § 1,435.10

2890. Underpayment of Estimated Tax by Corporations. If estimated taxes are underpaid by a corporation (including an S corporation), a penalty is imposed in the amount of the interest that accrues on the underpayment for the period of the underpayment (Code Sec. 6655).[58] The rate of interest is the rate charged on underpayment of taxes determined under Code Sec. 6621 (¶ 2838). The additions are calculated for quarterly periods ending with the installment due dates. Generally, additions to tax apply to the difference between payments made by the due date of the installment and the lesser of an installment based on (1) 100 percent of the tax shown on the current year's tax return or (2) 100 percent of the tax shown on the preceding year's return (prior-year safe harbor) (for a 12-month tax year). However, use of the prior-year safe harbor is not available to "large" corporations, i.e., corporations that have taxable income of $1 million or more for any of the three immediately preceding tax years. No additions to tax will be assessed if the corporation's tax liability is less than $500 for the tax year.

Erroneous Tax Refund Claims

2891. Erroneous Refund or Credit Claims. Erroneous income tax refund or credit claims made for an "excessive amount" are subject to a penalty equal to 20 percent of the excessive amount (Code Sec. 6676).[59] The penalty does not apply to claims for refunds or credits relating to the earned income credit (¶ 1322), which has a separate set of rules.

An "excessive amount" is the amount by which the refund or credit claim exceeds the amount allowable under the Code for the tax year. However, if it can be shown that the claim for the excessive amount has a reasonable basis, the penalty will not apply. In addition, the penalty does not apply to any portion of the excessive amount of a refund claim or credit that is subject to an accuracy-related penalty (¶ 2854 and ¶ 2870), or the fraud penalty (¶ 2866).

Unauthorized Return Disclosures or Inspections

2892. Confidentiality of Returns. Returns and tax return information are confidential and may not be disclosed to federal or state agencies or employees except as provided in Code Sec. 6103.[60] A return is defined as any tax return, information return, declaration of estimated tax, or claim for refund filed under the Internal Revenue Code. Return information includes the taxpayer's identity, the nature, source or amount of income, payments, receipts, deductions, net worth, tax liability, deficiencies, closing (and similar) agreements, and information regarding the actual or possible investigation of a return. The prohibition on disclosure applies to all officers and employees of the United States, of any state, and of any local child support enforcement agency. It also applies to most other persons who have had access to returns or return information by virtue of permitted disclosures of such returns or information under Code Sec. 6103.

Agreements and information received under a tax convention with a foreign government (including a U.S. possession) are confidential and generally cannot be disclosed (Code Sec. 6105).[61]

2893. Remedies for Unauthorized Disclosures. Taxpayers whose privacy has been invaded by an unlawful disclosure of returns or return information under Code Secs. 6103 or 6104 (pertaining to tax-exempt organizations) may bring a civil suit for damages. Upon a finding of liability, the taxpayer may recover the greater of $1,000 for each unauthorized disclosure or the amount of the actual damages sustained as a result of the disclosure. Punitive damages, as well as litigation costs, may be recovered if the disclosure was willful or grossly negligent (Code Sec. 7431).[62] Felony charges can also be brought against individuals who have made unauthorized and willful disclosures of any return information (Code Sec. 7213).[63]

References are to Standard Federal Tax Reports; Tax Research Consultant; and Practical Tax Explanations.

58 ¶ 39,565; FILEBUS: 6,050; § 40,225.15

59 ¶ 39,801; PENALTY: 3,332; § 40,240

60 ¶ 36,880, ¶ 36,894; IRS: 9,050; § 41,215.15

61 ¶ 36,912; IRS: 9,550

62 ¶ 41,750; IRS: 9,350; § 41,625.05

63 ¶ 41,350; IRS: 66,360

2894. Disclosure of Return Information. A return preparer who uses return information for any purpose other than to prepare a return, or who makes an unauthorized disclosure of return information, is subject to a $250 penalty for each disclosure, up to a maximum of $10,000. If the action is undertaken knowingly or recklessly, the preparer may be subject to criminal penalties or a fine of up to $1,000, or up to a year in jail, or both, together with the cost of prosecution (Code Secs. 6713 and 7216).[64] A taxpayer may bring a civil action for damages against the U.S. government if an IRS employee offers the taxpayer's representative favorable tax treatment in exchange for information about the taxpayer (Code Sec. 7435).[65]

2896. Penalties for Unauthorized Inspections. A taxpayer may bring a civil action against the United States if a government employee knowingly or negligently inspects, without authorization, any return or return information under Code Secs. 6103 or 6104 (pertaining to tax-exempt organizations) of that taxpayer. The same action may also be taken against any other person who browses through returns or return information without proper authorization (Code Sec. 7431).[66] Criminal penalties for willful unauthorized return inspection can also be imposed against any federal employee or IRS contractor. In addition, penalties may be imposed against any state employee or other person who acquires the return or return information under Code Secs. 6103 or 6104 that permits the use of federal return information for other government purposes, such as state tax and child support collection, law enforcement, social welfare program administration, and statistical use (Code Sec. 7213A).[67]

Failure to Notify Health Plan of Ineligibility for COBRA Premium Assistance

2897. Failure to Notify Health Plan. A penalty is imposed on individuals who fail to notify health plans that they cease to be eligible for COBRA premium assistance (Code Sec. 6720C).[68] An individual who paid a reduced premium for COBRA continuation coverage (¶ 2653) was required to provide written notice to the group health plan of eligibility for coverage under another group health plan or Medicare. If the individual failed to provide this notification at the required time and in the required manner, and, as a result, the individual paid reduced COBRA continuation coverage premiums after the termination of the individual's eligibility for the reduction, a penalty is imposed on the individual equal to 110 percent of the premium reduction after termination of eligibility. No penalty is imposed for a failure to notify if it is shown that the failure is due to reasonable cause and not to willful neglect.

Unless it is retroactively extended through legislation, COBRA premium assistance ended on August 31, 2011.

Criminal Penalties

2898. Crimes. Criminal penalties may be incurred when the taxpayer (a) willfully fails to make a return, keep records, supply required information, or pay any tax or estimated tax, (b) willfully attempts in any manner to evade or defeat the tax, or (c) willfully fails to collect and pay over the tax. In addition to the felony charges listed in the preceding sentence, misdemeanor charges can be brought for (1) making fraudulent statements to employees, (2) filing a fraudulent withholding certificate, or (3) failing to obey a summons. The criminal penalties are in addition to the civil penalties (Code Sec. 7201—Code Sec. 7212). A good faith misunderstanding of the law or a good faith belief that one is not violating the law negates the willfulness element of a tax evasion charge.[69]

References are to Standard Federal Tax Reports; Tax Research Consultant; and Practical Tax Explanations.

64 ¶ 40,155, ¶ 41,365; IRS: 6,114; § 41,625.05

65 ¶ 41,785; IRS: 45,116

66 ¶ 41,750; IRS: 9,354; § 41,625.05

67 ¶ 41,354; IRS: 66,360

68 ¶ 40,209G; PENALTY: 3,336; § 42,845.15

69 ¶ 41,318.136; IRS: 66,050; § 40,245.10

Chapter 29

ESTATE, GIFT AND GENERATION-SKIPPING TRANSFER TAX

Transfer Tax System

2901. Estate, Gift, and Generation-Skipping Transfer Tax System. The estate, gift, and generation-skipping transfer (GST) taxes were designed to form a unified transfer tax system on the transfer of property at death (estate tax), during life (gift tax), and on transfers that skip a generation (GST tax). However, the Economic Growth and Tax Relief Reconciliation Act of 2001 (P.L. 107-16) (EGTRRA) prospectively repealed the estate and GST taxes for the estates of decedents dying after December 31, 2009 (Code Sec. 2210(a), as amended by EGTRRA) while retaining the gift tax, although in a modified form.[1] In addition, EGTRRA increased the estate and gift applicable exclusion amount and GST exemption amount to $1 million for 2002 and 2003, but in 2004, the gift tax applicable exclusion amount remained at that level while the estate tax applicable exclusion and GST exemption amounts were gradually increased to $3.5 million in 2009 (¶ 41), thus, effectively "de-unifying" the transfer tax system. Increases in the amount of the applicable exclusion and exemption amounts were accompanied by a gradual decrease in the top marginal tax rates applicable to the estate, gift and GST taxes (¶ 40).

In 2010, the expiration (or "sunset") date of the transfer tax provisions of EGTRRA, which was scheduled to occur after December 31, 2010, was extended through December 31, 2012, by the Tax Relief, Unemployment Insurance Reauthorization, and Job Creation Act of 2010 (P.L. 111-312) (Tax Relief Act of 2010). The Tax Relief Act of 2010 provided that federal estate and GST taxes apply to the estates of decedents dying and GSTs made after December 31, 2009, and before January 1, 2013, but with a higher estate tax applicable exclusion and GST exemption amount of $5 million and lower tax rates (35 percent maximum) than would have applied under the sunset provision. In addition, the modified adjusted carryover basis rules were repealed; the basis of property received from a decedent was again stepped up to its date-of-death value. However, certain estates of decedents who died in 2010 could elect out of the estate tax regime and apply carryover basis (¶ 1633) (Act Sec. 301(c) of P.L. 111-312). The gift tax continues to apply with a maximum tax rate of 35 percent, but with an applicable exclusion amount of $5 million for gifts made after December 31, 2010. Beginning in 2012, the estate and gift tax applicable exclusion amounts and the GST exemption amount are subject to indexing for inflation; accordingly, the applicable exclusion and exemption amounts for 2012 are $5.12 million.

The Tax Relief Act of 2010 also provided an election for estates of decedents dying after December 31, 2010, to allow the unused portion of the applicable exclusion amount of a predeceased spouse to be available to the surviving spouse or his or her estate (this

References are to Federal Estate & Gift Tax Reports; Tax Research Consultant; Practical Tax Explanations.

[1] ¶ 1005; ESTGIFT: 100;
§ 34,001

is known as "portability") (Code Sec. 2010(c)(5)). As a result, the applicable exclusion amount of a surviving spouse for gifts made during 2012, or of the estate of a surviving spouse who died in 2012, would include the predeceased spouse's unused exclusion amount, provided the predeceased spouse's estate made the portability election (¶ 2934, ¶ 2938).

In effect, the Tax Relief Act of 2010 "re-unified" the unified transfer tax with respect to estate, gift, and GSTs made after December 31, 2009. With the exception of a separate tax rate (0%) for GSTs in 2010, and a separate applicable exclusion amount ($1,000,000) for gifts made in 2010, the same tax rates and applicable exclusions/exemption amounts once again apply to the estate, gift, and generation-skipping transfer taxes.

> **Comment:** Absent further legislation, the EGTRRA and Tax Relief Act of 2010 provisions are scheduled to sunset for estates of decedents dying, gifts made, or GSTs made after December 31, 2012. As a result, the Code provisions governing the estate, gift, and GST taxes in effect prior to EGTRRA's 2001 changes will spring back to life in 2013.

Gift Tax

2903. Transfers Subject to Gift Tax. The gift tax applies to the transfer of property by gift, whether the gift is direct or indirect, and whether the transfer is in trust or otherwise. However, transfers to qualifying political organizations are not considered gifts (Code Sec. 2501(a)(4)).[2] The property transferred may be real, personal, tangible, or intangible (Code Sec. 2511; Reg. § 25.2511-1(a)).[3] The donor makes a gift to the extent that the value of the property transferred exceeds the consideration (that is, any property or services received in return for the transfer) (Code Sec. 2512(b)). The transferred property or evidence of it must be delivered to the donee, and the donor must relinquish all control over the property for the gift to be completed (Reg. § 25.2511-2).[4]

Indirect gifts, such as transfers in trust and the cancellation of indebtedness, are subject to the gift tax (Code Sec. 2511). Other examples of indirect gifts include certain assignments of benefits, permission to withdraw funds deposited by a donor from a joint account, and below-market interest rate loans (Reg. § 25.2511-1(c) and (h)). However, a waiver of the right to a joint and survivor annuity in a qualified plan is not a gift (Code Sec. 2503(f)).[5]

A gratuitous transfer of property by a corporation is considered to be a gift by the shareholders to the donee, while a gift to a corporation is considered to be a gift to its shareholders (Reg. § 25.2511-1(h)). In addition, a gift may occur at the creation of a family limited partnership or when transferring control of a closely held company.[6] Transfers of stock or securities are a gift even if the securities are exempt from tax. The transfer of an option is a gift. Also, gratuitous transfers made by guardians or conservators under court orders are gifts. Conversely, a transfer pursuant to a will contest settlement entered into at arm's length is generally not a gift. The treatment of income earned by domestic partners as community property by operation of state law is also not considered a gift.[7]

Valuation. Generally, the value of the property for gift tax purposes is its fair market value on the date of the gift. That is, the price at which the property would change hands between a willing buyer and a willing seller, both knowing all of the relevant facts (Code Sec. 2512; Reg. § 25.2512-1).[8] Special valuation rules apply for determining the amount of a gift if the transferor retains (1) an equity interest in a corporation or partnership

References are to Federal Estate & Gift Tax Reports; Tax Research Consultant; Practical Tax Explanations.

[2] ¶ 9245, ¶ 9340.05; ESTGIFT: 3,150; § 34,805

[3] ¶ 10,514, ¶ 10,528, ¶ 10,555.06; ESTGIFT: 3,050; § 34,805

[4] ¶ 10,568; ESTGIFT: 3,056, ESTGIFT: 3,060; § 34,805.05

[5] ¶ 9649, ¶ 10,181.05; ESTGIFT: 3,100; § 34,805

[6] ¶ 10,514, ¶ 10,555.07; ESTGIFT: 3,154; § 34,801

[7] ¶ 9340.05, ¶ 9340.80; ESTGIFT: 33,000; § 34,601

[8] ¶ 10,622, ¶ 10,649; ESTGIFT: 100; § 34,810.05

transferred to a family member or (2) an interest in a trust to or for the benefit of a family member (Code Secs. 2701, 2702 and 2704).[9]

Qualified Disclaimers. The donee of a gift may make a qualified disclaimer of the entire interest or a portion of it without making a taxable gift. To be a qualified disclaimer, (1) the disclaimer must be in writing; (2) the disclaimer must be received by the transferor (or the transferor's representative) within nine months of the date of the transfer; (3) the beneficiary may not accept any of the benefits from the transferred property; and (4) the property being disclaimed must pass to someone other than, and without direction from, the disclaiming beneficiary (Code Sec. 2518).[10]

Nonresident Alien Donors. A donor who is neither a U.S. citizen nor a U.S. resident (in other words, a nonresident alien) is subject to gift tax on transfers of real and tangible property situated in the United States (Code Sec. 2501(a); Reg. § 25.2501-1).[11] Transfers of intangible property by a nonresident alien generally are not subject to gift tax (Code Sec. 2501(a)(2)). Taxable gifts are taxed at the same rates that apply to U.S. citizens (Code Sec. 2501(a)(1)).[12]

2905. Gift Tax Annual Exclusion. The first $13,000 of gifts of a present interest made by a donor during calendar year 2012 ($14,000 in 2013) to each donee are not included in the total amount of the donor's taxable gifts during that year (Code Sec. 2503(b); Rev. Proc. 2011-52, Rev. Proc. 2012-41). Therefore, these amounts are not taxed and do not use up any of the donor's lifetime gift tax applicable credit amount. Also, spouses who consent to split their gifts may transfer a total of $26,000 per donee in 2012 ($28,000 in 2013), free of gift and generation-skipping transfer (GST) tax (Code Sec. 2513(a)).[13]

If the donor's spouse is not a U.S. citizen, an annual exclusion of $139,000 in 2012 ($143,000 in 2013) is allowed for present interest gifts to the spouse that would qualify for the marital deduction if the spouse were a U.S. citizen (Code Sec. 2523(i)(2); Rev. Proc. 2011-52, Rev. Proc. 2012-41).[14] The annual exclusion is available to all donors, including nonresident citizens.

The annual exclusion is allowed for gifts of present interests but not for gifts of future interests in property. Present interests include any interests, whether vested or contingent, that are available for the donee's immediate use, possession or enjoyment (Reg. § 25.2503-3(b)). A transfer of property for the benefit of a minor pursuant to the Uniform Transfers to Minors Act (UTMA), the Uniform Gifts to Minors Act (UGMA), or the Gifts of Securities to Minors Act (GSMA) is considered to be a completed gift of the full fair market value of the property.[15]

Transfers in Trust. The number of annual exclusions available for a gift in trust is determined by the number of trust beneficiaries who have a present interest in the gifted property. A transfer to a trust that allows a beneficiary the unrestricted right to the immediate use, possession, or enjoyment of the transferred property or the income from the property, such as a life estate or term certain, is a present interest gift that qualifies for the annual exclusion (Reg. § 25.2503-3(b)). However, such unrestricted gifts through a trust are rarely made. Normally, limits are placed on the beneficiary's right to use, possess, or enjoy the trust property. However, a gift of the right to demand a portion of a trust corpus is a gift of a present interest, so long as the donee-beneficiary is aware of his or her right to make the demand. Typically, the beneficiary of such a trust (known as a *Crummey* trust) is given the right to demand an amount of corpus equal to the annual gift tax exclusion for a limited period of time, such as 60 days. If the persons who have a

References are to Federal Estate & Gift Tax Reports; Tax Research Consultant; Practical Tax Explanations.

[9] ¶ 13,551, ¶ 14,001, ¶ 14,651; ESTGIFT: 18,600; § 34,810

[10] ¶ 11,339, ¶ 11,419.03; ESTGIFT: 100; § 34,805.20

[11] ¶ 9245, ¶ 9290; ESTGIFT: 60,050; § 35,010

[12] ¶ 7575.09, ¶ 9245; ESTGIFT: 60,100; § 35,010

[13] ¶ 10,960, ¶ 10,987.06; ESTGIFT: 6,054; § 34,820.10

[14] ¶ 11,662, ¶ 11,850, ¶ 11,884.05; ESTGIFT: 6,050; § 35,010.15

[15] ¶ 9649, ¶ 9950.335, ¶ 10,041.05; ESTGIFT: 6,058, ESTGIFT: 6,060; § 34,820.10

right of withdrawal do not have a present income interest in the trust or a vested remainder interest, however, the IRS may question the claimed annual exclusion.[16]

Gifts to Minors. Gifts to minors may qualify for the annual exclusion if they meet the requirements of Code Sec. 2503(c).[17] The property and income from it must be expended by or for the benefit of the minor, and any income and principal not expended must be paid to the minor at age 21, or to his or her estate if the minor dies before age 21 (Code Sec. 2503(c); Reg. § 25.2503-4(a)).[18] However, if a transfer of property is made under a parent's legal obligation to support a minor, the transfer is not a gift, as is the case with child support.[19]

2907. Exclusion for Educational or Medical Payment. In addition to the annual exclusion (¶ 2905), an unlimited gift tax exclusion is allowed for amounts paid on behalf of a donee *directly* to an educational organization, provided such amounts constitute tuition payments. Amounts paid for books, dormitory fees, or board on behalf of the donee are not eligible for the exclusion. Likewise, amounts paid *directly* to health care providers for medical services on behalf of a donee also qualify for the unlimited gift tax exclusion. Medical expense payments are excludable without regard to the percentage limitations imposed for income tax purposes. Both the medical and tuition exclusions are available without regard to the relationship between the donor and donee (Code Sec. 2503(e)).[20]

2908. Gifts to Spouse. In computing the taxable gifts of a married donor, a marital deduction is allowed for property that passes to the donor's spouse. As a result, an unlimited amount of property (other than certain terminable interests) can be transferred between spouses (Code Sec. 2523). The gift tax marital deduction is not available, however, if the spouse is not a U.S. citizen at the time of the gift. Instead, gifts to a noncitizen spouse are eligible for a gift tax annual exclusion of up to $139,000 in 2012 ($143,000 in 2013) (Code Sec. 2523(i); Rev. Proc. 2011-52, Rev. Proc. 2012-41).[21]

In addition, a gift tax marital deduction is not allowed for transfers of terminable interests in property. A terminable interest in property is an interest that will terminate or fail on the lapse of time or on the occurrence or failure to occur of some contingency. For example, terminable interests include life estates, terms for years, and annuities. However, a gift tax marital deduction will be allowed if the donee spouse is given a life estate with a general power of appointment or qualified terminable interest property (QTIP), or if the donor and spouse are named as the only non-charitable beneficiaries of a qualified charitable remainder trust (¶ 2926).[22]

2909. Gifts to Charity. In determining a donor's taxable gifts, a gift tax charitable deduction is available for transfers to charitable organizations (federal, state and local governmental entities, charitable organizations, fraternal societies (if the property is used for charitable purposes), or veterans' organizations). The charitable deduction is not limited to gifts for use within the United States, unless the donor is a nonresident alien at the time of the gift (Code Sec. 2522).[23] A deduction may also be allowed for the value of the charitable interest in a split-interest transfer (in which there are both charitable and noncharitable beneficiaries) provided the charitable interest is in a qualified form (i.e., charitable remainder annuity trust, charitable remainder unitrust, charitable lead annuity trust, charitable lead unitrust, or a pooled income fund) (¶ 2932).

2910. Computing the Gift Tax Liability. The gift tax is calculated by first determining the total value of the donor's gifts for the current calendar year. The value of a gift is

References are to Federal Estate & Gift Tax Reports; Tax Research Consultant; Practical Tax Explanations.

[16] ¶ 9649, ¶ 9842.055, ¶ 9891, ¶ 9950.07; ESTGIFT: 6,060; § 34,820.10

[17] ¶ 9649, ¶ 9842.05, ¶ 9996; ESTGIFT: 6,060.10; § 34,820.10

[18] ¶ 9996, ¶ 10,041.05; ESTGIFT: 12,056; § 34,820.10

[19] ¶ 11,311, ¶ 11,324.05; ESTGIFT: 12,100; § 34,820.10

[20] ¶ 9649, ¶ 10,095, ¶ 10,139.05; ESTGIFT: 6,100; § 34,820.15

[21] ¶ 11,662, ¶ 11,689.01, ¶ 11,884.05; ESTGIFT: 42,050; § 34,815.10

[22] ¶ 11,662, ¶ 11,702, ¶ 11,709.05; ESTGIFT: 42,058, ESTGIFT: 42,060, ESTGIFT: 42,062; § 34,815.10

[23] ¶ 11,486, ¶ 11,513.01; ESTGIFT: 45,050, ESTGIFT: 45,100, ESTGIFT: 45,350; § 34,815.15

its fair market value on the date of the gift (¶ 2903). That amount is reduced by any exclusions—annual (¶ 2905), and educational and medical (¶ 2907)—and deductions—marital (¶ 2908) and charitable (¶ 2909). The sum of all taxable gifts made by the donor in all prior years is then added to the current year's taxable gifts to arrive at the total taxable gifts. The donor's gift tax liability for 2012 is then determined by (1) calculating a tentative tax on the sum of all taxable gifts made in 2012 and in preceding calendar years, (2) calculating a tentative tax on only the taxable gifts in preceding calendar years, and (3) then subtracting the tentative tax determined in step (2) from the tentative tax determined in step (1) (Code Sec. 2502).[24] For 2010, 2011 and 2012, the Tax Relief, Unemployment Reauthorization, and Job Creation Act of 2010 (P.L. 111-312) requires that any unified credit allocated to the prior periods be redetermined using current gift tax rates, rather than the rates that were effective when the prior gifts were made.

If a gift is adequately disclosed on the gift tax return and the gift tax statute of limitations has expired, the IRS may not revalue the donor's lifetime gifts when computing the estate tax liability upon the donor's death (Code Sec. 2001(f)). There is a three-year statute of limitations for gift tax returns (Code Sec. 2504(c)).[25]

The gift tax applicable credit amount in 2012 is $1,772,800, which effectively shields the first $5.12 million of a donor's lifetime gifts from gift tax (Code Sec. 2010(c); Code Sec. 2505(a)(1); Rev. Proc. 2011-52).[26] (This amount might be higher if the donor is a surviving spouse and the estate of his or her predeceased spouse has elected portability of the deceased spouse's unused exclusion amount (¶ 2934; ¶ 2938).) Note that the 5.12 million and first dollar (that is, the first dollar that becomes taxable) is taxed at the rate that would apply to gifts in the amount of $5,120,001 (35 percent in 2012) rather than the rate that would apply to a gift of $1 (18 percent). The maximum gift tax rate—and the *only* rate that apples in 2012—is 35 percent.

> **Comment:** Absent further legislation, the EGTRRA and Tax Relief Act of 2010 provisions are scheduled to sunset for gifts made after December 31, 2012, and the Code provisions governing the gift tax in effect prior to EGTRRA's 2001 changes will spring back to life in 2013. As a result, the gift tax applicable exclusion will be $1 million and the maximum gift tax rate will be 55 percent.

Filing Requirements. Form 709 must be filed, and any gift tax must be paid, on an annual basis. Generally, the due date for filing the annual gift tax return will be the same as the due date for the income tax return. However, for the calendar year in which the donor dies, the gift tax return will be due on the earlier of the due date (with extensions) for filing the donor's estate tax return, or the "normal" due date with respect to the gifts (Code Sec. 6075(b)).[27] Taxpayers filing gift tax returns for gifts made in 2012 must file by April 15, 2013.

2911. Donor Is Primarily Liable to File Return and Pay Gift Tax. Gift tax returns must be filed by individual donors for gifts of more than $13,000 in 2012 ($14,000 in 2013) that do not qualify for an exclusion. Gift tax returns must be filed on Form 709. The donor is primarily liable for the payment of the gift tax (Code Sec. 6019).[28]

Estate Tax

2912. Gross Estate. The federal estate tax is imposed on the transfer of a person's property at the time of that person's death. The amount of the tax is determined by applying the relevant tax rates to the taxable estate, that is, the gross estate reduced by any deductions. The gross estate of a U.S. citizen or resident decedent includes the value of all property described in Code Sec. 2033 through Code Sec. 2044, whether real or personal, tangible or intangible, wherever situated. Effectively executed disclaimers

References are to Federal Estate & Gift Tax Reports; Tax Research Consultant; Practical Tax Explanations.

[24] ¶ 9385, ¶ 9494.07; ESTGIFT: 100; § 34,830

[25] ¶ 10,235, ¶ 10,368.05; ESTGIFT: 3,300; § 34,835

[26] ¶ 10,403, ¶ 10,448.03; ESTGIFT: 100; § 34,820.20

[27] ¶ 20,301, ¶ 20,330.05; ESTGIFT: 3,300; § 34,830

[28] ¶ 9245, ¶ 20,125, ¶ 20,135.05, ¶ 20,301; ESTGIFT: 3,300; § 34,830

prevent the property subject to the disclaimer from being included in the gross estate (Code Secs. 2046 and 2518).[29]

Qualified terminable interest property (QTIP) for which an election was made to qualify it for the marital deduction in the estate of the first spouse to die (¶ 2926), or on the gift tax return of the donor spouse, is included in the gross estate of the surviving or donee spouse (Code Sec. 2044(a)).[30]

Form 706 includes specific schedules on which the estate must provide details for specific types of property included in the decedent's gross estate. Real estate that the decedent owned or had contracted to purchase is reported on Schedule A. Stocks and bonds included in the gross estate are reported on Schedule B. Mortgages and notes payable to the decedent at the time of death, as well as cash that the decedent possessed on the date of death, are reported on Schedule C. Other Form 706 schedules are specifically designated for other types of property. If an asset in the gross estate is not required to be reported on any other schedule, it must be reported on Schedule F.

2913. Transferred Property in Which Decedent Retained an Interest. When a decedent retains some control over gifts of property made during life, the property may be added back to the decedent's gross estate. The transfers subject to this rule include:

(1) gifts in which the decedent retains a life estate or the right to the income, possession, or enjoyment of the property, or the right to designate who will enjoy the property, including gifts of stock in which voting rights are retained (Code Sec. 2036);[31]

(2) gifts in which the decedent retains a right to a reversionary interest that exceeds five percent of the value of the transferred property and possession or enjoyment of the property can be obtained only by surviving the decedent (Code Sec. 2037(a));[32] and

(3) gifts in which the decedent holds a power to alter, amend, revoke, or terminate the gift (Code Sec. 2038(a)(1); Reg. § 20.2038-1(a)).[33]

If income from transferred property is used to discharge a legal obligation of the decedent, such as the decedent's obligation to support his or her dependents, the decedent is considered to have a right to income from the property and the property is includible in his or her gross estate (Reg. § 20.2036-1(b)(2)).[34]

Such transfers are generally reported on Schedule G of Form 706.

An estate valuation freeze is a technique used to limit the value of closely held business interests owned by an individual by transferring the future appreciation in value of the business to the next generation of the owner's family while retaining certain interests in the business. This technique has been severely limited by the special valuation rules (Code Secs. 2701– 2704), which treat transfers of family business interests unfavorably for gift tax purposes by assigning the value of zero to certain types of interests retained by the donor in such exchanges.[35]

If a lifetime transfer with a retained interest is a sale for adequate and full consideration, the property that is transferred is not included in the transferor's gross estate (Code Sec. 2036(a)). However, if the transfer is not for adequate and full consideration, the amount included in the decedent's estate is the full value of the property subject to the decedent's retained interest. If the interest or right is reserved

References are to Federal Estate & Gift Tax Reports; Tax Research Consultant; Practical Tax Explanations.

[29] ¶ 5980, ¶ 5990.05, ¶ 11,339, ¶ 11,419.03; ESTGIFT: 15,050; § 34,170

[30] ¶ 5901, ¶ 5940.05; ESTGIFT: 15,500; § 34,160

[31] ¶ 4901, ¶ 4955.06, ¶ 4980.05; ESTGIFT: 18,400, ESTGIFT: 18,450, ESTGIFT: 18,600; § 34,135.10

[32] ¶ 5001, ¶ 5075.01; ESTGIFT: 18,500; § 34,135.15

[33] ¶ 5101, ¶ 5135, ¶ 5170.05; ESTGIFT: 18,550; § 34,135.20

[34] ¶ 4925; ESTGIFT: 18,304; § 34,135.10

[35] ¶ 13,551, ¶ 13,670, ¶ 13,690.05, ¶ 14,001, ¶ 14,501, ¶ 14,651; ESTGIFT: 18,600; § 34,810

over only part of the property transferred, only the reserved portion is included in the gross estate (Reg. § 20.2036-1(c)).[36]

2914. Gifts Made Within Three Years of Death. Gifts made within three years of the donor's death ordinarily are not includible in the donor's gross estate. However, gifts made within three years of death are included in the donor's gross estate if the gift consists of interests in property that would otherwise be included in the gross estate because of the donor's retained powers, such as the power to alter, amend, revoke, or terminate the gift (¶ 2913) (Code Sec. 2035(a)). Similarly, a gift of life insurance that would have been includible in the decedent's gross estate because of his retention of incidents of ownership in the policy is includible if the policy was transferred within three years of the decedent's date of death (¶ 2915). Gifts made from a decedent's revocable trust within three years of death, however, are not included in the decedent's gross estate, rather they are treated as if made directly by the decedent (Code Sec. 2035(e); see also Code Sec. 2038). Gift tax paid on all transfers made within three years of death is included in the gross estate (Code Sec. 2035(b)).[37]

Such transfers are generally reported on Schedule G of Form 706.

2915. Life Insurance. Proceeds of insurance on a decedent's life payable to or for the benefit of his or her estate, and insurance payable to other beneficiaries in which the decedent retained incidents of ownership, are included in the decedent's gross estate (Code Sec. 2042(1) and (2); Reg. § 20.2042-1(b)(1)). Insurance that is paid to a named beneficiary but that must be used to satisfy a legal obligation to meet expenses of the decedent's estate, such as debts and taxes, is also included in the decedent's gross estate (Reg. § 20.2042-1(c)(1)).[38]

Incidents of Ownership. If proceeds of insurance on the life of a decedent are payable to a beneficiary other than the decedent's estate, they are included in the decedent's gross estate if the decedent has retained an incident of ownership in the life insurance policy on the date of death (Code Sec. 2042(2); Reg. § 20.2042-1(c)). The term "incidents of ownership" is not limited in its meaning to ownership of the policy in the technical legal sense. The term refers to the right of the insured or his estate to the economic benefits of the policy. Some incidents of ownership include the power to change the beneficiary, the ability to pledge the policy as security for a loan, the ability to borrow against the policy, or a reversionary interest by which the insured or the insured's estate may regain one of the previously stated rights under certain circumstances. If the decedent transfers a life insurance policy or an incident of ownership in the policy within three years of his death, the proceeds are included in his gross estate (Code Sec. 2035(a)).[39] However, generally only one-half of the proceeds of life insurance purchased with community property is included in the estate of the insured spouse, even if the decedent possessed an incident of ownership (Reg. § 20.2042-1(b)(2)).[40]

A person insured under a key-employee insurance arrangement usually has no interest in the insurance. None of its proceeds will be included in the insured's gross estate. However, the arrangement will be accounted for in determining a value for any stock that the insured may have owned in the company.[41]

In the case of split-dollar life insurance, death proceeds from the employee's portion of the policy are included in the employee's estate if:

(1) the proceeds are payable to, or for the benefit of, the employee's estate; or

(2) the employee holds an incident of ownership in the policy at death or transfers an incident of ownership to a third party within three years before death.

References are to Federal Estate & Gift Tax Reports; Tax Research Consultant; Practical Tax Explanations.

36 ¶ 4901, ¶ 4925, ¶ 4955.05; ESTGIFT: 18,100; § 34,135.05

37 ¶ 4801, ¶ 4845.01, ¶ 4845.091; ESTGIFT: 18,200; § 34,150

38 ¶ 5651, ¶ 5715, ¶ 5740.05; ESTGIFT: 21,050; § 34,120

39 ¶ 4801, ¶ 4845.09, ¶ 5651; ESTGIFT: 21,100; § 34,120

40 ¶ 5670, ¶ 5715, ¶ 5740.05; ESTGIFT: 21,200; § 34,120

41 ¶ 5760, ¶ 5780.03; ESTGIFT: 21,150; § 34,105

Gift tax liability for employer-paid premiums may arise if a co-owner of the policy is neither the employer nor the employee.[42]

Life insurance that is included in a decedent's gross estate is generally reported on Schedule D of Form 706. For each policy listed, a separate Form 712 life insurance statement must be completed and attached to Schedule D.

2917. Annuities and Retirement Benefits. In general, the value of an annuity or other payment receivable by any beneficiary by reason of surviving the decedent is included in the decedent's gross estate. The annuity or other payment is not taxable under the rules unless it is payable under a contract by agreement and the following factors exist:

(1) the contract or agreement was entered into after March 31, 1931;

(2) the contract or agreement is not a policy of insurance on the decedent's life;

(3) the decedent possessed the right to receive the payments during his or her lifetime; and

(4) payments under the contract are determined based on the decedent's life or life expectancy (Code Sec. 2039(a)).[43]

The value of an annuity or other payment included in a decedent's gross estate is the portion of its value attributable to the portion of the purchase price contributed by the decedent. Any contribution made by a decedent's employer or former employer by reason of his or her employment is considered to be made by the decedent (Code Sec. 2039(b)).[44]

Annuities that are included in a decedent's gross estate are generally reported on Schedule I of Form 706.

With respect to estate tax valuation of a qualified account, such as an IRA, the value of the account is the fair market value of the assets in the account without any discount for the income tax liability that would be triggered if the estate or beneficiary were to take a distribution of the assets in order to sell them.[45]

2918. Powers of Appointment. Property subject to a general power of appointment is included in the gross estate of the holder of the power if the power exists at the holder's death (Code Sec. 2041(a)(2)). The exercise or release of a general power during the life of the holder is a transfer subject to gift tax (Code Sec. 2514(b)).[46] A power of appointment is a right given to someone other than the donor of property to dispose of the property. The holder of the power of appointment has a general power if the holder may exercise it in favor of himself or herself, the holder's creditors, the holder's estate, or the creditors of the holder's estate (Code Secs. 2041(b), 2514(c)). Powers that expressly cannot be exercised in favor of any of these are special or limited powers (Reg. § 20.2041-1(c)(1)). A power is not general if its exercise is limited by an ascertainable standard (Code Secs. 2041(b)(1)(A), 2514(c)(1)). A power is not general if the creator of the power must join in its exercise or if a co-holder of the power has a substantial adverse interest (Code Secs. 2041(b)(1)(C), 2514(c)(3)(A)). The incompetence or lack of capacity of the holder of the power to exercise the power does not affect whether the power is taxable to the power holder.[47]

Property subject to a power of appointment that is included in a decedent's gross estate is generally reported on Schedule H of Form 706.

2919. Jointly Held Property. The entire value of jointly held property with the right of survivorship, including joint bank accounts and U.S. savings bonds registered in two names, is included in a decedent's gross estate except for the portion of the property

References are to Federal Estate & Gift Tax Reports; Tax Research Consultant; Practical Tax Explanations.

[42] ¶ 5780.045, ¶ 5780.183; COMPEN: 48,150; § 34,105

[43] ¶ 5201, ¶ 5245.05; ESTGIFT: 24,050; § 34,145

[44] ¶ 5201, ¶ 5245.07; ESTGIFT: 24,100; § 34,145

[45] ¶ 3100, ¶ 3220.41; ESTGIFT: 15,202.15; § 34,145

[46] ¶ 5501, ¶ 11,054; ESTGIFT: 27,100; § 34,140, § 34,805.10

[47] ¶ 5630.231; ESTGIFT: 27,050; § 34,805

for which the surviving joint tenant furnished consideration. If the joint property was received by the decedent and the other joint tenants as a gift or bequest, the decedent's fractional share of the property is included in the decedent's gross estate (Code Sec. 2040(a)).[48] If the joint tenants are spouses, it generally does not matter who furnished the consideration for the property; one-half of the value of a "qualified joint interest" is included in the gross estate of the first spouse to die (Code Sec. 2040(b)).[49]

Jointly held property that is included in a decedent's gross estate is generally reported on Schedule E of Form 706.

The creation of a joint interest in property results in a taxable gift by the person supplying the consideration to the noncontributing joint tenant. Creation of a joint bank account or joint brokerage account is not a taxable gift until a joint owner withdraws funds (Reg. § 25.2511-1(h)). If a donor purchased property and conveyed title to himself and another as joint tenants with rights of survivorship, and those rights may be defeated by either owner severing his interest, the donor made a gift to the other joint owner in the amount of one-half of the property's value. A transfer of joint property to a third party is a gift of the value of each joint owner's share.[50]

2921. Community Property. Community property is all property acquired by means other than gift, devise, bequest, and inheritance by spouses domiciled in community property jurisdictions. Separate property is property other than community property.[51] One-half of the value of all community property owned by a married couple is includible in the gross estate of the first of the spouses to die (Code Sec. 2033). This rule of inclusion applies even though the surviving spouse elects to allow his or her share of the community property to pass according to the will of the decedent spouse.[52]

2922. Valuation of Gross Estate. The value of property that is included in the gross estate is its fair market value on the date of the decedent's death (Code Sec. 2031; Reg. § 20.2031-1(b)). The fair market value of property includible in the gross estate is the price at which it would change hands between a willing buyer and a willing seller, both having reasonable knowledge of relevant facts.[53]

Alternate Valuation. Instead of valuing property includible in the gross estate as of the date of death, the executor may elect to value the gross estate at the fair market value of the property on the alternate valuation date, which is the date six months after the date of the decedent's death. To use the alternate valuation election, the value of the gross estate must have decreased and the amount of estate and GST taxes imposed on the property included in the gross estate must also decrease. The alternate valuation election is irrevocable (Code Sec. 2032). The election is made on Form 706. The amount of any marital or charitable deduction is adjusted based on the alternate value of assets passing to charity or a surviving spouse (Code Sec. 2032(b); Reg. § 20.2032-1(g)).[54] When the alternate valuation election is made, all property included in the gross estate is valued as of the alternate valuation date (Reg. § 20.2032-1(d)).[55] However, if property is sold, exchanged, distributed, or otherwise disposed of during the six-month period, it is valued on the date of disposition rather than the alternate valuation date (Code Sec. 2032(a)(1)).[56]

Special Use Valuation. If a farm or real property used in a closely held business is included in the gross estate, the executor may elect to value the property at its "current use" rather than at its "highest and best use." Special use valuation is obtained pursuant to an irrevocable election by an executor to value real property used in a farm, trade or

References are to Federal Estate & Gift Tax Reports; Tax Research Consultant; Practical Tax Explanations.

[48] ¶ 5401, ¶ 5475.05; ESTGIFT: 30,050; § 34,125

[49] ¶ 5401, ¶ 5475.07; ESTGIFT: 30,060; § 34,125

[50] ¶ 10,528, ¶ 10,555.24; ESTGIFT: 30,100; § 34,805.15

[51] ¶ 4620, ¶ 4675.04; ESTGIFT: 33,050; § 34,601

[52] ¶ 4675.11; ESTGIFT: 33,100; § 34,125

[53] ¶ 3011, ¶ 3125.01; ESTGIFT: 100; § 34,101

[54] ¶ 3801, ¶ 3830, ¶ 3870.05; ESTGIFT: 36,050, ESTGIFT: 36,100; § 34,205

[55] ¶ 3830; ESTGIFT: 36,102; § 34,205

[56] ¶ 3801; ESTGIFT: 36,150; § 34,205

business (Code Sec. 2032A).[57] The limitation on the reduction in value resulting from special use valuation is $1,040,000 in 2012 ($1,070,000 in 2013) (Rev. Proc. 2011-52, Rev. Proc. 2012-41).

Special use valuation is elected on the estate tax return (Part 3, line 2 of Form 706) by, among other things, completing the notice of election (Schedule A-1) and submitting a recapture agreement.[58] If the qualified heir ceases to use the farm property for farming or sells the property to a non-family member within 10 years of the decedent's date of death, an additional estate tax, the recapture tax, is due (Code Sec. 2032A(c))[59] and Form 706-A must be filed.

2925. Deductions from Gross Estate—Expenses. A deduction from the gross estate is allowed for funeral expenses, administration expenses, claims against the estate, certain taxes, and unpaid mortgages or other indebtedness allowable under the local law governing the administration of the decedent's estate (Code Sec. 2053(a)). For expenses that are not paid before filing the estate tax return, an estimated amount may be deducted if the amount is ascertainable and there is reasonable certainty that the amount will be paid. Contested and contingent claims and expenses cannot be ascertained with reasonable certainty (Reg. § 20.2053-1(b)(3)).[60] Estate administration expenses may generally be deducted on either the decedent's estate tax return or the estate's income tax return, but not on both (Code Sec. 642(g); Reg. § 1.642(g)-1).[61]

Expenses incurred in connection with the decedent's funeral, including reasonable expenses for a tombstone, mausoleum, or burial lot, are deductible (Code Sec. 2053(a)(1)).[62] Administration expenses are deductible if actually and necessarily incurred in the administration of the estate. Administration expenses include fees paid to surrogates, appraisers, and accountants. Reasonable attorney's fees that meet the requirements of Reg. § 20.2053-1 are deductible (Code Sec. 2053(a)(2); Reg. § 20.2053-3(c)).[63] Fees incurred by beneficiaries incident to litigation with regard to their interests are not deductible, unless the litigation is essential to the proper settlement of the estate. An executor or administrator may deduct the amount of his or her commissions from the decedent's gross estate in an amount actually paid or an amount that is reasonably ascertainable and will be paid (Reg. § 20.2053-3(b)).[64] Miscellaneous expenses necessarily incurred in preserving and distributing estate assets are also deductible as administration expenses (Reg. § 20.2053-3(d)).[65]

Funeral and administrative expenses are generally reported on Schedule J of Form 706.

Claims that are a personal obligation of the decedent are deductible, provided that they are existing and enforceable against him at the time of his death, are allowable under local law, and have actually been paid or meet the requirements of Reg. § 20.2053-1(d)(4). Liabilities imposed by law or arising out of torts committed by the decedent are also deductible. In certain circumstances, an executor may deduct the current value of a claim or claims, which concern the same or similar issue or asset, even if the claim has not yet been paid (Reg. § 20.2053-4).[66] The full value of any unpaid mortgage or other indebtedness charged against property for which the decedent is personally liable, plus interest accrued on the debt to the date of death, is deductible if the property's entire value undiminished by the mortgage or indebtedness is included in the gross estate (Code Sec. 2053(a)(4); Reg. § 20.2053-7).[67]

References are to Federal Estate & Gift Tax Reports; Tax Research Consultant; Practical Tax Explanations.

57 ¶ 4001, ¶ 4240.05; ESTGIFT: 36,200; § 34,210

58 ¶ 4001; ESTGIFT: 36,300; § 34,210

59 ¶ 4001, ¶ 4240.35; ESTGIFT: 36,350; § 34,210

60 ¶ 6050, ¶ 6060.025, ¶ 6060.055; ESTGIFT: 39,050, ESTGIFT: 39,100, ESTGIFT: 39,150; § 34,305

61 ¶ 16,675, ¶ 16,825, ¶ 16,875.05, ¶ 16,875.07; ESTGIFT: 39,050, ESTGIFT: 39,100, ESTGIFT: 39,150; § 34,305

62 ¶ 6040, ¶ 6070, ¶ 6080.03; ESTGIFT: 39,100; § 34,305.10

63 ¶ 6040, ¶ 6090, ¶ 6100.03, ¶ 6130, ¶ 6140.05; ESTGIFT: 39,150, ESTGIFT: 39,158; § 34,305.15

64 ¶ 6110, ¶ 6120; ESTGIFT: 39,154; § 34,305.15

65 ¶ 6150, ¶ 6160.05; ESTGIFT: 39,160; § 34,305.15

66 ¶ 6170, ¶ 6180.01; ESTGIFT: 39,200; § 34,305.20

67 ¶ 6040, ¶ 6230, ¶ 6240.05; ESTGIFT: 39,250; § 34,305.25

Debts, mortgages, and liabilities of the decedent are generally reported on Schedule K of Form 706.

Federal and state estate, succession, legacy, or inheritance taxes are generally not deductible, but unpaid gift taxes on gifts made before death are deductible. Unpaid income taxes are deductible if they are on income properly includible in an income tax return of a decedent for a period before his death (Reg. § 20.2053-6).[68] A deduction is also allowed for losses arising from fires, storms, shipwrecks, or other casualties or thefts that are incurred during estate administration and not compensated for by insurance (Code Sec. 2054).[69]

Such losses and taxes are generally reported on Schedule L of Form 706.

2926. Estate Tax Marital Deduction. In determining a married decedent's taxable estate, an unlimited deduction is allowable for property that passes to the decedent's surviving spouse (Code Sec. 2056). In order to qualify for the deduction, the decedent must be married and survived by his spouse, the spouse must be a U.S. citizen, the property must be included in the decedent's gross estate and pass to the surviving spouse, and the property must not be a nondeductible terminable interest. The estate tax marital deduction is not available if the decedent's surviving spouse is not a U.S. citizen unless the spouse becomes a citizen before the estate tax return is filed or the property passes to a qualified domestic trust (QDOT) (Code Secs. 2056(d) and 2056A).[70]

Passing Requirement. Property must pass from the decedent to a surviving spouse for a transfer to be deductible (Code Sec. 2056(a)). Bequests and inheritances, dower and curtesy interests, joint property, property received under antenuptial agreements, annuities, and life insurance may pass from the decedent to the surviving spouse. Property received by a spouse under a state law right of election against the will satisfies the passing requirement (Code Sec. 2056(c); Reg. § 20.2056(c)-2(c)). Property passing to the spouse as a result of another person's qualified disclaimer is considered to pass from the decedent (Reg. § 20.2056(d)-2(b)).[71]

Terminable Interest Rule. The terminable interest rule bars deduction for any nondeductible terminable interest. A terminable interest in property is an interest that terminates or fails because of the lapse of time or the occurrence of an event (Code Sec. 2056(b)(1)). A nondeductible terminable interest is an interest in which a person, other than the surviving spouse, receives an interest in property from the decedent and, upon the termination of the spouse's interest in the same property, the other person may possess or enjoy the property. Property interests passing to a spouse that are conditioned on the spouse's survival of a period of six months or less, or on the spouse's survival in a common disaster, are not subject to the terminable interest rule (Code Sec. 2056(b)(3)).[72]

Qualified Terminable Interest Property. Qualified terminable interest property (QTIP) is excluded from the terminable interest rule. To qualify as QTIP, the surviving spouse must have the right to all the income from the property for life, payable no less frequently than annually (Code Sec. 2056(b)(7); Reg. § 20.2056(b)-7(a)). A surviving spouse's income interest may be contingent upon the executor's QTIP election and still be considered a "qualifying income interest for life" (Reg. § 20.2056(b)-7).[73] In addition, no person may have a power to appoint any of the property to any person other than the surviving spouse during the surviving spouse's life. An election on Form 706 (Schedule M) is necessary to designate property as QTIP (Code Sec. 2056(b)(7)(B)(v)). Once the QTIP election is made, the surviving spouse must include the property remaining at death in his or her gross estate even though the surviving spouse has no control over its

References are to Federal Estate & Gift Tax Reports; Tax Research Consultant; Practical Tax Explanations.

[68] ¶ 6210, ¶ 6220.05; ESTGIFT: 39,300; § 34,305.20

[69] ¶ 6320, ¶ 6340.03; ESTGIFT: 39,350; § 34,310

[70] ¶ 6501, ¶ 7001, ¶ 7045.05, ¶ 7045.10; ESTGIFT: 42,100, ESTGIFT: 42,150; § 34,320

[71] ¶ 6501, ¶ 6920.03, ¶ 6935, ¶ 6975; ESTGIFT: 42,150; § 34,320

[72] ¶ 6501, ¶ 6701, ¶ 6725.03; ESTGIFT: 42,200; § 34,320.15

[73] ¶ 6825; ESTGIFT: 42,250; § 34,320.20

disposition (Code Sec. 2044). However, the estate tax that is attributable to the QTIP included in the spouse's estate may be recovered from the QTIP (Code Sec. 2207A).[74]

Life Estate with Power of Appointment. A life estate with a power of appointment qualifies for the marital deduction if:

(1) the surviving spouse is entitled to all the income from the entire interest or a specific portion of the interest for life;

(2) the income is payable at least annually;

(3) the spouse has the power to appoint the property (or the specific portion) to himself or to his estate;

(4) the power is exercisable by the spouse alone and in all events; and

(5) no other person has the power to appoint property to anyone but the surviving spouse (Code Sec. 2056(b)(5)).

There is a similar exception to the terminable interest rule for life insurance proceeds held by an insurer in which the spouse has a right to all payments and a power of appointment (Code Sec. 2056(b)(6); Reg. § 20.2056(b)-6(c)).[75]

Amount of the Marital Deduction. The marital deduction is limited to the net value of property passing to the spouse. Death taxes, debts, and administration expenses payable from the marital bequest, mortgages on property passing to the spouse, and insufficient estate assets to fund the marital bequest all reduce the amount of the deduction (Code Sec. 2056(b)(4); Reg. § 20.2056(b)-4).[76] However, administration expenses allocable to an estate's income do not necessarily reduce the amount of the marital deduction (*O. Hubert Est.*, SCt, 97-1 USTC ¶ 60,261).[77]

Transfers for which an estate is taking the estate tax marital deduction are generally reported on Schedule M of Form 706.

2932. Estate Tax Charitable Deduction. An unlimited estate tax charitable deduction is available for transfers to federal, state, and local governmental entities; charitable organizations; fraternal societies (if the property is used for charitable purposes); veterans' organizations; or an employee stock ownership plan if the transfer qualifies as a qualified gratuitous transfer. The bequest must have a public rather than a private purpose (Code Secs. 2055(a)).[78]

Transfers of Partial Interests. If an interest in property passes from a transferor to a charity and an interest in the same property passes to a noncharitable recipient, the transfer must take one of the following forms:

(1) charitable remainder annuity trust, which provides for a fixed-dollar amount to be paid to the noncharitable income beneficiary annually, or charitable remainder unitrust, which provides for a fixed percentage of trust assets, valued annually, to be paid to the noncharitable income beneficiary annually (Code Secs. 2055(e)(2)(A) and 2522(c)(2)(A); Reg. § 20.2055-2(e)(2));[79]

(2) charitable lead trust with guaranteed annuity or unitrust amount paid to charity (Code Secs. 170(f)(2), 2055(e)(2)(B), and 2522(c)(2)(B); Reg. § 20.2055-2(e)(2));[80]

(3) remainder interest in a farm or personal residence (Code Sec. 2055(e)(3)(I); Reg. § 20.2055-2(e)(2));[81]

References are to Federal Estate & Gift Tax Reports; Tax Research Consultant; Practical Tax Explanations.

[74] ¶ 5901, ¶ 6501, ¶ 8800; ESTGIFT: 42,260, ESTGIFT: 42,262; § 34,320.20

[75] ¶ 6501, ¶ 6801, ¶ 6815.05; ESTGIFT: 42,300; § 34,320.20

[76] ¶ 6501, ¶ 6745; ESTGIFT: 42,350; § 34,320.10

[77] ¶ 6755.674; ESTGIFT: 42,356; § 34,320.10

[78] ¶ 6360, ¶ 6370; ESTGIFT: 45,050, ESTGIFT: 45,100, ESTGIFT: 45,350; § 34,315

[79] ¶ 6360, ¶ 6390, ¶ 11,486, ¶ 16,901; ESTGIFT: 45,150, ESTGIFT: 45,200; § 34,315.20

[80] ¶ 6360, ¶ 6390, ¶ 11,486, ¶ 16,901; ESTGIFT: 45,250, ESTGIFT: 45,300; § 34,315.15

[81] ¶ 6360, ¶ 6390; ESTGIFT: 45,158; § 34,315.15

(4) copyrighted work of art separate from its copyright (Code Secs. 2055(e)(4) and 2522(c)(3); Reg. § 20.2055-2(e)(1));[82] or

(5) qualified conservation contribution (Code Sec. 170(f)(3); Reg. § 20.2055-2(e)(2)).[83]

The amount of the estate tax charitable deduction must be reduced by the administration expenses and death taxes paid from the property transferred to charity (Code Sec. 2055(c); Reg. § 20.2055-3(a)).[84] However, administration expenses allocable to an estate's income do not necessarily reduce the amount of the charitable deduction (*O. Hubert Est.*, SCt, 97-1 USTC ¶ 60,261).[85]

Transfers for which an estate is taking the estate tax charitable deduction are generally reported on Schedule O of Form 706.

2933. Family-Owned Business Deduction. (*Repealed 2004 through 2012).* Certain estates of decedents dying after December 31, 1997, and before January 1, 2004, could elect to deduct up to $675,000 of a qualified family-owned business interest (QFOBI) from the decedent's gross estate (Code Sec. 2057).[86] A qualified family-owned business is any interest in a trade or business regardless of form with a principal place of business in the United States, the ownership of which is held at least (1) 50 percent by one family; (2) 70 percent by two families; or (3) 90 percent by three families. If the interest is held by more than one family, the decedent's family must own at least 30 percent of the trade or business. One of the requirements for a decedent's interest to qualify as a QFOBI was that the decedent, or a member of the decedent's family, had to have owned and materially participated in the business for at least five of the eight years preceding the decedent's death. Further, a qualified heir will continue to be subject to a recapture tax after the decedent's death if the heir, or a member of the heir's family, does not materially participate in the business for at least five years of any eight-year period within 10 years following the decedent's death. The principal factors to be considered regarding "material participation" include physical work and participation in management decisions. To report a taxable event for recapture tax purposes, the heir must file Form 706-D. Another requirement for the QFOBI deduction is that the decedent must have been a U.S. citizen or resident at the time of death. In addition, the aggregate value of the decedent's QFOBIs passing to qualified heirs must exceed 50 percent of the decedent's adjusted gross estate.

Recapture Tax After Repeal. Pursuant to the Economic Growth and Tax Relief Reconciliation Act of 2001 (P.L. 107-16) (EGTRRA), the QFOBI deduction is repealed for the estates of decedents dying after December 31, 2003 (Code Sec. 2057(j)).[87]

> **Comment:** Absent further legislation, the EGTRRA and Tax Relief Act of 2010 provisions are scheduled to sunset for estates of decedents dying after December 31, 2012, and the Code provisions governing the estate tax in effect prior to EGTRRA's 2001 changes will spring back to life in 2013. As a result, the QFOBI deduction will be available to the estates of decedents dying after December 31, 2012, if the estate meets the requirements of Code Sec. 2057 and makes the election on the federal estate tax return.

2934. Credits Against the Estate Tax. A number of credits are available to offset a decedent's federal estate tax liability. The most important credit is the applicable credit amount or applicable exclusion amount (formerly, the unified credit) (¶ 2901).[88] The applicable exclusion amount can be used to offset an estate tax liability on a taxable estate of $5,120,000 in 2012, as adjusted for inflation (Rev. Proc. 2011-52).

References are to Federal Estate & Gift Tax Reports; Tax Research Consultant; Practical Tax Explanations.

[82] ¶ 6360, ¶ 6390; ESTGIFT: 45,154; § 34,315.30

[83] ¶ 6390; ESTGIFT: 45,160; § 34,315.15

[84] ¶ 6360, ¶ 6430; ESTGIFT: 45,352, ESTGIFT: 45,354; § 34,315.05

[85] ¶ 6380.18; ESTGIFT: 45,352; § 34,315.05

[86] ¶ 7391, ¶ 7398.01, ¶ 7398.05; ESTGIFT: 15,700; § 34,325.05

[87] ¶ 7391, ¶ 7398.01; ESTGIFT: 15,700; § 34,325.05

[88] ¶ 1401, ¶ 1450.01; ESTGIFT: 51,052.05; § 34,010.40

Comment: Absent further legislation, the EGTRRA and Tax Relief Act of 2010 provisions are scheduled to sunset for estates of decedents dying after December 31, 2012, and the Code provisions governing the estate tax in effect prior to EGTRRA's 2001 changes will spring back to life in 2013. As a result, the estate tax applicable credit amount will be $345,800, resulting in an applicable exclusion amount of $1 million.

Portability of Unused Applicable Exclusion Amount. The applicable exclusion amount for a surviving spouse who dies in 2012 and whose predeceased spouse's estate elected portability is the sum of (1) the basic exclusion amount ($5,120,000 in 2012), plus (2) the aggregate deceased spousal unused exclusion amount (Code Sec. 2010(c)(2) and (4)).[89] The deceased spousal unused exclusion amount is the lesser of (1) the surviving spouse's basic exclusion amount, or (2) the last deceased spouse's applicable exclusion amount minus the amount with respect to which the tentative tax is determined on the last deceased spouse's estate. To take advantage of this special provision, the predeceased spouse must have died after December 31, 2010, and the predeceased spouse's estate must have made an election on Form 706 (¶ 2938).

An executor electing portability must make the election on a timely-filed estate tax return (Form 706), including extensions actually granted, even if there is no estate tax liability. If the executor must otherwise file an estate tax return, but does not wish to make the portability election, the executor should make an affirmative statement to that effect on the return (Temp. Reg. § 20.2010-2T(a)(3)). Not timely filing Form 706 will also effectively prevent the election (Notice 2011-82).

Comment: Absent further legislation, the EGTRRA and Tax Relief Act of 2010 provisions are scheduled to sunset for estates of decedents dying after December 31, 2012, and the Code provisions governing the estate tax in effect prior to EGTRRA's 2001 changes will spring back to life in 2013. As a result, the portability of a predeceased spouse's unused applicable exclusion amount will no longer be available to the estates of decedents dying, or gifts made, after December 31, 2012.

State Death Tax Credit (Repealed through 2012). Prior to 2005, the estate tax was offset by state death taxes actually paid to a state or the District of Columbia. This credit for state death taxes was limited by a graduated rate table that used the adjusted taxable estate as a base (the taxable estate reduced by $60,000 (Code Sec. 2011)[90] (¶ 43). Pursuant to the Economic Growth and Tax Relief Reconciliation Act of 2001 (P.L. 107-16) (EGTRRA), the state death tax credit was reduced annually in 25-percent increments, starting in 2002, until it was completely repealed in 2005. In 2005, the credit was replaced by a state death tax *deduction* (Code Sec. 2058) that will no longer be applicable when the state death tax credit is reinstated beginning in 2013, pursuant to the EGTRRA sunset provision as extended by the Tax Relief, Unemployment Insurance Reauthorization, and Job Creation Act of 2010 (P.L. 111-312). In addition, the state death tax deduction is subject to a limitations period, which generally requires the deduction to be claimed within four years after the estate tax return is filed.[91]

Comment: Absent further legislation, the EGTRRA and Tax Relief Act of 2010 provisions are scheduled to sunset for estates of decedents dying after December 31, 2012, and the Code provisions governing the estate tax in effect prior to EGTRRA's 2001 changes will spring back to life in 2013. As a result, the state death tax credit will again be available, and the state death tax deduction will not apply, to the estates of decedents dying after December 31, 2012.

Federal Estate Tax Paid on Prior Transfers. A credit is available for federal estate tax paid on prior transfers to the decedent from a person who died within 10 years before or two years after the decedent. The credit is limited to the lesser of the estate tax attributable to the transferred property in the transferor's estate or the estate tax attributable to the transferred property in the decedent's estate (Code Sec. 2013). If the transferor predeceased the decedent by more than two years, the allowable credit is

29 ESTATE—GIFT

References are to Federal Estate & Gift Tax Reports; Tax Research Consultant; Practical Tax Explanations.

[89] ¶ 1401, ¶ 1450.08; ESTGIFT: 51,060; § 34,010.45

[90] ¶ 1551; ESTGIFT: 48,050; § 34,505

[91] ¶ 1551, ¶ 1651.03; ESTGIFT: 48,050; § 34,505

reduced by 20 percent for each full two-year period by which the death of the transferor preceded the transferor's death. The credit is claimed on Schedule Q on Form 706.[92]

Foreign Death Taxes. A credit against estate tax is available for foreign death taxes paid on property located in a foreign country but included in the gross estate of a U.S. citizen or resident. The credit is limited to the lesser of the foreign or the U.S. tax attributable to the property. If a treaty exists with the foreign country, the credit provided for under the treaty or Code Sec. 2014 may be used, whichever results in the lower amount of estate tax (Code Sec. 2014).[93] The estate must file Form 706-CE to claim the credit.

Gift Tax Paid on Gifts Included in Gross Estate. For gifts made before 1977, the gift tax paid on gifts included in the gross estate is a credit to the estate tax. The credit is limited to the lesser of the gift tax paid or the estate tax attributable to inclusion of the gift in the gross estate (Code Sec. 2012).[94]

2937. Computing the Estate Tax Liability. The estate tax computation begins with a calculation of the gross estate. The gross estate is valued at the fair market value on the decedent's date of death or, if elected, on the alternate valuation date, which is six months after the date of death (Code Secs. 2031 and 2032). Deductions for charitable and marital bequests, state death taxes (state death tax credit beginning in 2013; ¶ 2934), and estate administration expenses, as well as other allowable deductions are subtracted to determine the taxable estate (Code Sec. 2051). The amount of adjusted taxable gifts made after 1976 is added to the taxable estate. A tentative tax is computed by applying the applicable tax rates from the unified rate schedule (¶ 40) to the sum of the amount of the taxable estate and the adjusted taxable gifts. The tentative tax is then reduced by the amount of gift tax payable on the post-1976 gifts. The resulting amount is the gross estate tax which is reduced by any credits, including the applicable credit amount (Code Sec. 2010(c)), credits for foreign death taxes paid (Code Sec. 2014), the credit for tax on prior transfers (Code Sec. 2013), and the credit for gift tax paid on pre-1977 gifts included in the gross estate (Code Sec. 2012).[95]

For 2010, 2011 and 2012, the Tax Relief, Unemployment Reauthorization, and Job Creation Act of 2010 (P.L. 111-312) (Tax Relief Act of 2010) requires that any unified credit allocated to taxable gifts in prior periods be redetermined using current gift tax rates, rather than the rates that were effective when the prior gifts were made. An estate tax reduction is available for the estates of U.S. citizens or residents who are active members of the Armed Forces and who are killed in action while serving in a combat zone (Code Sec. 2201). This special treatment has been extended to include a "specified terrorist victim," as defined by Code Sec. 692(d)(4) (¶ 2533) and any astronaut whose death occurs in the line of duty.[96]

> **Comment:** Absent further legislation, the EGTRRA and Tax Relief Act of 2010 provisions are scheduled to sunset for gifts made after December 31, 2012, and the Code provisions governing the estate tax in effect prior to EGTRRA's 2001 changes will spring back to life in 2013. As a result, the estate tax applicable exclusion will be $1 million, and the maximum estate tax rate will be 55 percent.

2938. Filing Estate Tax Return and Liability for Payment. Form 706 must be filed for every U.S. citizen or resident decedent whose gross estate exceeds $5,120,000 in 2012. The estate tax table is at ¶ 40.

Filing the Return. The estate tax return must be filed by the executor, administrator, or person in possession of the estate's assets (Code Secs. 2203 and 6018(a)). The return is due within nine months of the decedent's date of death, but a six-month extension of

References are to Federal Estate & Gift Tax Reports; Tax Research Consultant; Practical Tax Explanations.

[92] ¶ 2001, ¶ 2045; ESTGIFT: 48,100; § 34,515

[93] ¶ 2301; ESTGIFT: 48,150; § 34,520

[94] ¶ 1901; ESTGIFT: 48,200; § 34,510

[95] ¶ 1201, ¶ 1401, ¶ 1551, ¶ 1901, ¶ 2001, ¶ 2301, ¶ 3011, ¶ 6010; ESTGIFT: 100; § 34,010

[96] ¶ 8325, ¶ 8375.05, ¶ 8375.10; ESTGIFT: 100; § 34,010.60

time to file is available (Code Sec. 6075(a); Reg. § 20.6075-1).[97] The six-month extension is automatically available if (1) Form 4768 is filed by or before the due date for the estate tax return; (2) the application is filed with the IRS office designated in the application's instructions; and (3) an estimate of the amount of estate and generation-skipping transfer (GST) tax liability is included.

Paying the Tax. The estate tax must be paid within nine months after the decedent's death (Code Secs. 6075(a), 6151(a)) by the executor or person in possession of the estate's property (Code Sec. 2002; Reg. § 20.2002-1).[98] The tax may be paid by check, money order, draft, credit card, or debit card (Code Sec. 6311(a)). The time for payment of the estate tax may be extended, upon reasonable cause, for a period of one year past the due date (Code Sec. 6161(a)(1)).[99] If reasonable cause exists, the time for payment may be extended for up to 10 years (Code Sec. 6161(a)(2)).[100]

Portability Election for Unused Applicable Exclusion Amount. Executors of the estates of decedents dying in 2011 or 2012 can make an election allowing the estate of the decedent's surviving spouse to use the portion of the decedent's applicable exclusion amount that is not used in determining the federal estate tax liability of the decedent's estate (¶ 2934) (Code Sec. 2010(c)(4) and (5)).[101] The executor of the predeceased spouse's estate must file Form 706 within the required filing period (including extensions actually granted) to make the election, even if Form 706 is not otherwise required to be filed (Temp. Reg. § 20.2010-2T(a)). The IRS has issued Temporary Regulations relating to the portability election (Temp. Reg. §§ 20.2010-2T, 20.2010-3T, 20.2505-2T, and 20.2505-3T)).

Comment: Absent further legislation, the EGTRRA and Tax Relief Act of 2010 provisions are scheduled to sunset for estates of decedents dying after December 31, 2012, and the Code provisions governing the estate tax in effect prior to EGTRRA's 2001 changes will spring back to life in 2013. As a result, the portability of a predeceased spouse's unused applicable exclusion amount will no longer be available to the estates of decedents dying, and gifts made, after December 31, 2012.

2939. Election to Pay Estate Tax in Installments. If an estate includes a farm or closely held business whose value exceeds 35 percent of the adjusted gross estate, the executor may elect to pay the estate and generation-skipping transfer taxes in as many as 10 annual installments following a deferral period of as many as five years (Code Sec. 6166(a)(1)). The amount of tax that may be deferred is limited to the tax attributable to the business interest (Code Sec. 6166(a)(2)). A *two-percent* interest rate applies to that portion of the estate tax deferred on the first $1 million in *taxable* value of the closely held business (Code Sec. 6601(j)). The $1 million amount is indexed annually for inflation: $1,390,000 for estates of decedents dying in 2012 ($1,430,000 for decedents dying in 2013) (Rev. Proc. 2011-52, Rev. Proc. 2012-41). A closely held corporation may redeem stock from the estate of a decedent or from the beneficiaries of the estate to pay estate taxes and administrative expenses if the stock comprises 35 percent of the gross estate. This redemption of stock is generally not treated as a disqualifying disposition for purposes of the installment payment of the estate tax (Code Sec. 6166(g)(1)(B)).[102]

The election to pay the estate and GST taxes in installments is made by checking "Yes" on Part 3, line 3 of Form 706 and attaching a statement as described in the instructions to Form 706.

2940. Estate Taxation of Nonresident Aliens. A decedent who is neither a U.S. citizen nor a U.S. resident (in other words, a nonresident alien)[103] is subject to estate tax

References are to Federal Estate & Gift Tax Reports; Tax Research Consultant; Practical Tax Explanations.

[97] ¶ 20,301, ¶ 20,310, ¶ 20,315.05; ESTGIFT: 51,050; § 34,405.10

[98] ¶ 1301, ¶ 1340, ¶ 20,301, ¶ 20,501; ESTGIFT: 51,000; § 34,405

[99] ¶ 20,510, ¶ 20,845; ESTGIFT: 51,108; § 34,410.05

[100] ¶ 20,301, ¶ 20,501, ¶ 20,575, ¶ 20,635; ESTGIFT: 51,110, ESTGIFT: 51,112; § 34,410.05

[101] ¶ 1401, ¶ 1450.08; ESTGIFT: 51,060; § 34,010.45

[102] ¶ 20,650, ¶ 21,620; ESTGIFT: 51,150; § 34,410.20

[103] ¶ 7550; ESTGIFT: 60,050; § 35,005

on real, tangible, and intangible property situated in the United States (Code Sec. 2103). Intangible property situated in the United States includes stock in domestic corporations, bonds, and debt obligations of U.S. obligors, U.S. partnership assets, and U.S. property owned by a trust in which the nonresident alien has an interest. The value of such property in a nonresident alien's gross estate is not reduced by indebtedness secured by the property if the decedent was personally liable for the debt, even though the personal debt deduction allowed a nonresident alien may fall short of the amount actually owed (*H.H. Fung Est.*, CA-9 (unpub. op.), 2003-1 USTC ¶ 60,460, aff'g, 117 TC 247, Dec. 54,560 (2001)).[104]

The estate of a nonresident alien is taxed at the same estate tax rates that apply to U.S. citizens' estates (Code Sec. 2101(b); Reg. § 20.2101-1). Except where provided by treaty, the unified credit is $13,000 (Code Sec. 2102). The estate may claim deductions for a pro rata share of expenses, debts, and losses, a marital deduction if the surviving spouse is a U.S. citizen, and a charitable deduction (Code Sec. 2106(a)(1); Reg. § 20.2106-2(a)(2)). An estate tax return must be filed if a nonresident alien's gross estate situated in the United States exceeds $60,000 (Code Sec. 6018(a)(2)).[105] The estate must file Form 706-NA.

If a former citizen or long-term resident who is subject to the alternative tax regime of Code Sec. 877(b) dies within 10 years of relinquishment of citizenship or residency, an estate tax is imposed on the transfer of U.S.-situs property, including the decedent's pro rata share of the U.S. property held by a foreign corporation. The estate tax is computed on the taxable estate using the same estate tax rate schedule used for the estate of a U.S. citizen or resident (Code Secs. 2107(a), 2501(a)(3)(B); Reg. §§ 20.2107-1(a), 25.2511-1(b)).

Expatriates are also subject to gift tax on transfers of property situated in the United States (Code Sec. 2501(a)(3)).[106] (For the transfer tax imposed on recipients of gifts from "covered expatriates," see ¶ 2948.) An individual is subject to the alternative tax regime if the individual: (1) has average annual net income for the five years preceding the loss of citizenship greater than $151,000 for 2012 ($155,000 for 2013); (2) has net worth on the date of loss of citizenship of $2 million or more; or (3) fails to certify compliance with all federal tax obligations for the five-year period unless he is a dual citizen or minor without substantial contact with the U.S. (Code Secs. 877(a)(2), 2107(a), and 2501(a)(3)(B); Rev. Proc. 2011-52, Rev. Proc. 2012-41).[107]

The estate and gift tax Code provisions may be affected by provisions contained in foreign tax treaties (Code Sec. 7852(d)).[108]

Generation-Skipping Transfer Tax

2942. Transfers Subject to Tax. To ensure that property transfers are subject to transfer tax at least once at each generation, a generation-skipping transfer (GST) tax is imposed on certain transfers (Code Sec. 2601). The GST tax rate is 35 percent for 2012 (¶ 2901).

A GST may take one of three forms: a direct skip, a taxable termination, or a taxable distribution to a skip person. A direct skip is a transfer to a skip person that is also subject to estate or gift tax (Code Sec. 2612(c)). A skip person is defined as (1) a person two generations or more younger than the transferor, or (2) a trust for the benefit of one or more skip persons (Code Sec. 2613(a); Reg. § 26.2612-1). However, if the parent of the skip person predeceases the transferor, a gift to the skip person is not a GST (Code Sec. 2651(e)(1)). A taxable termination occurs when an interest in property held in trust terminates and trust property is held for or distributed to a skip person (Code Sec. 2612(a)). A taxable distribution is any distribution from a trust to a skip person that is

References are to Federal Estate & Gift Tax Reports; Tax Research Consultant; Practical Tax Explanations.

[104] ¶ 7725, ¶ 7825, ¶ 8075.55; ESTGIFT: 60,150; § 35,005.15

[105] ¶ 7525, ¶ 7550, ¶ 7625, ¶ 8025, ¶ 8055, ¶ 20,075; ESTGIFT: 60,200; § 35,005.30

[106] ¶ 8125, ¶ 8150, ¶ 9245, ¶ 10,528; ESTGIFT: 60,250; § 35,015.05

[107] ¶ 8125, ¶ 9245; ESTGIFT: 60,250; § 35,015.05

[108] ¶ 22,870; ESTGIFT: 63,050, ESTGIFT: 63,100; § 35,001

not a taxable termination or a direct skip (Code Sec. 2612(b)). Transfers that are not subject to gift tax because of the unlimited exclusion for direct payment of medical and tuition expenses (¶ 2907), certain transfers to the extent that the property transferred was previously subject to the GST tax, as well as direct skips and certain transfers to trusts that qualify for the annual gift tax exclusion (¶ 2905) or the medical and tuition expense payment exclusion, are not subject to GST tax (Code Secs. 2611(b) and 2642(c)(1)).[109]

2943. Allocation of Lifetime Exemption and Computation of Tax Rate. Individuals are entitled to a lifetime exemption from generation-skipping transfer (GST) tax (Code Sec. 2631). The exemption amount is $5.12 million for GSTs occurring in 2012 (Code Sec. 2631(c); Rev. Proc. 2011-52). The exemption amount is not transferable between spouses, but married couples may elect to "split" a transfer and treat it as being made one-half by each spouse, pursuant to the rules applicable to split gifts (¶ 2905) (Code Sec. 2652(a)(2); Reg. § 26.2652-1(a)(4)).

The GST tax is computed by multiplying the taxable amount of the transfer by the applicable rate (Code Sec. 2602). The applicable rate is a flat rate equal to the product of the maximum estate tax rate (¶ 40) and the "inclusion ratio" with respect to the transfer (Code Sec. 2641(a); Reg. § 26.2641-1).

The inclusion ratio represents the portion of the transfer that is *not* exempted from the GST tax by the transferor's exemption amount. The inclusion ratio for any property transferred in a GST is the excess (if any) of 1 over the "applicable fraction" determined for the trust from which a GST is made or, in the case of a direct skip, the applicable fraction determined for such a skip.

Conversely, the applicable fraction represents the proportion of the transfer, whether in trust or as a direct skip, that is free of tax due to an allocation of the transferor's exemption amount. The numerator of the applicable fraction is the amount of the GST exemption allocated to the trust, or to the property transferred in a direct skip. The denominator is the value of the property transferred to the trust or involved in the direct skip, reduced by the sum of any federal estate or state death tax attributable to the property that was recovered from the trust and any estate or gift tax charitable deductions allowed with respect to the property (Code Sec. 2642; Reg. § 26.2642-1).[110]

The GST tax exemption may be allocated by an individual, or the individual's executor, to any property with respect to which the individual was the transferor (Code Sec. 2632(a)). In the case of property held in trust, the GST tax exemption is allocated to the entire trust rather than to specific assets (Reg. § 26.2632-1). In the case of a lifetime direct skip, any unused GST tax exemption is automatically deemed allocated to the property transferred in an amount necessary to make such property's inclusion ratio equal to zero (Code Sec. 2632(b)(1)). An individual may elect out of this automatic allocation for lifetime direct skips (Code Sec. 2632(b)(3)).

> **Comment:** Absent further legislation, the EGTRRA and Tax Relief Act of 2010 provisions are scheduled to sunset for GSTs made after December 31, 2012, and the Code provisions governing the GST taxes in effect prior to EGTRRA's 2001 changes will spring back to life in 2013. As a result, the applicable exemption amount will be $1 million, as adjusted for inflation as of 2013, and the maximum GST tax rate will be 55 percent.

2944. Filing the Return and Paying the GST Tax. For direct skips occurring at death, the executor must file the return (Form 706, Schedules R and R-1) and pay the tax. The transferor is responsible for filing the return (Form 709) and paying the tax on lifetime direct skips (Code Sec. 2603(a)(3); Reg. § 26.2662-1(c)(1)). The trustee is responsible for filing the return (Form 706-GS(T)) and paying the tax on taxable

References are to Federal Estate & Gift Tax Reports; Tax Research Consultant; Practical Tax Explanations.

[109] ¶ 12,025, ¶ 12,225, ¶ 12,295, ¶ 12,315, ¶ 12,750, ¶ 12,940; ESTGIFT: 57,050; § 34,710

[110] ¶ 12,585, ¶ 12,625, ¶ 12,690, ¶ 12,710, ¶ 12,750, ¶ 12,770, ¶ 12,790, ¶ 12,940, ¶ 12,960; ESTGIFT: 57,100; § 34,725

termination (Code Sec. 2603(a)(2)). The transferee is responsible for filing the return (Form 706-GS(D)) and paying the tax on taxable distributions (Code Sec. 2603(a)(1); Reg. § 26.2662-1(c)(1)).[111]

Although the Economic Growth and Tax Relief Reconciliation Act of 2001 (P.L. 107-16) (EGTRRA) repealed the GST tax for GSTs occurring after 2009, the Tax Relief, Unemployment Insurance Reauthorization, and Job Creation Act of 2010 (P.L. 111-312) (Tax Relief Act of 2010) reinstated the GST tax for the estates of decedents dying, and transfers made, after December 31, 2009. However, the Tax Relief Act of 2010 provided that the applicable rate for GSTs occurring in 2010 was zero.

2945. Effects of EGTRRA Sunset on GST Tax. Under the sunset provision of the Economic Growth and Tax Relief Reconciliation Act of 2001 (P.L. 107-16) (EGTRRA), as amended by the Tax Relief, Unemployment Insurance Reauthorization, and Job Creation Act of 2010 (P.L. 111-312) (Tax Relief Act of 2010), certain amendments made to the Code dealing with the generation-skipping transfer (GST) tax are set to expire. Unless Congress takes further action, these amendments will not apply to GSTs after December 31, 2012. Accordingly, under the sunset assumption, in 2013, the GST lifetime exemption amount would be $1 million, as adjusted for inflation through 2012, and the applicable rate of tax would be based on a maximum estate tax rate of 55 percent.

In addition, certain taxpayer-friendly amendments made by EGTRRA, such as the deemed and retroactive GST allocation provisions (Code Sec. 2632(c) and (d)), would not be operative beginning in 2013. The provision allowing for a qualified severance of a trust for purposes of the GST tax is scheduled to expire for GSTs after December 31, 2012 (Code Sec. 2642(a)(3)). The clarification of the valuation rules with respect to the determination of the inclusion ratio for GST tax purposes is also scheduled to expire for transfers after December 31, 2012 (Code Sec. 2642(b)). Similarly, the provisions providing relief from late GST allocations and elections (Code Sec. 2642(g)(1)), as well as the provision pertaining to substantial compliance (Code Sec. 2642(g)(2)), would not be operative beginning in 2013.

Transfer Tax on Gifts and Bequests from Expatriates

2948. Gifts and Bequests from Expatriates. A U.S. citizen or resident who directly or indirectly receives a "covered gift or bequest"—a gift, devise, bequest, or inheritance from a covered expatriate (¶ 2412)—after the date of expatriation must pay a tax equal to the value of the covered gift or bequest multiplied by the highest rate in effect under Code Sec. 2001(c), or, if greater, the highest rate in effect under Code Sec. 2502(a) (Code Sec. 2801(a) and (b)). The tax rate under both Code Secs. 2001(c) and 2502(a) is 35 percent for 2012. This special transfer tax applies only to the extent that the value of the covered gifts and bequests received by any person during the calendar year exceeds the annual gift tax exclusion amount in effect under Code Sec. 2503(b) ($13,000 for 2012; $14,000 for 2013) (Code Sec. 2801(c)).[112] The tax is reduced by the amount of any gift or estate tax paid to a foreign country with respect to such covered gift or bequest (Code Sec. 2801(d)).

A covered gift or bequest made to a domestic trust is subject to tax in the same manner as for a U.S. citizen or resident, and as the recipient, the trust is required to pay the tax imposed (Code Sec. 2801(e)(4)(A)). A covered gift or bequest made to a foreign trust is also subject to tax, but only at the time a distribution (whether from income or principal) is made to a U.S. citizen or resident from the trust that is attributable to the covered gift or bequest (Code Sec. 2801(e)(4)(B)(i)).[113] The recipient is allowed an income tax deduction under Code Sec. 164 for the amount of tax paid or accrued under Code Sec. 2801 by reason of a distribution from a foreign trust, but only to the extent the tax is imposed on the portion of the distribution included in the recipient's gross income (Code Sec. 2801(e)(4)(B)(ii)). For purposes of Code Sec. 2801 only, a foreign trust may elect to be treated as a domestic trust (Code Sec. 2801(e)(4)(B)(iii)).[114]

References are to Federal Estate & Gift Tax Reports; Tax Research Consultant; Practical Tax Explanations.

[111] ¶ 12,150, ¶ 13,160, ¶ 13,200, ¶ 13,225; ESTGIFT: 57,150; § 34,715.25, § 34,740.05

[112] ¶ 15,501, ¶ 15,525.01, ¶ 15,525.05; ESTGIFT: 60,256; § 35,020

[113] ¶ 15,501, ¶ 15,525.07; ESTGIFT: 60,256; § 35,020

[114] ¶ 15,501, ¶ 15,525.07; ESTGIFT: 60,256; § 35,020

Topical Index

References are to paragraph (¶) numbers

A

C

F

H

O

P

S

T

U

V